Washington
Information Directory
2022–2023

Sara Miller McCune founded SAGE Publishing in 1965 to support the dissemination of usable knowledge and educate a global community. SAGE publishes more than 1000 journals and over 800 new books each year, spanning a wide range of subject areas. Our growing selection of library products includes archives, data, case studies and video. SAGE remains majority owned by our founder and after her lifetime will become owned by a charitable trust that secures the company's continued independence.

Los Angeles | London | New Delhi | Singapore | Washington DC | Melbourne

Washington
Information Directory
2022–2023

SAGE reference | CQPRESS

FOR INFORMATION:

CQ Press
An Imprint of SAGE Publications, Inc.
2455 Teller Road
Thousand Oaks, California 91320
E-mail: order@sagepub.com

SAGE Publications Ltd.
1 Oliver's Yard
55 City Road
London, EC1Y 1SP
United Kingdom

SAGE Publications India Pvt. Ltd.
B 1/I 1 Mohan Cooperative Industrial Area
Mathura Road, New Delhi 110 044
India

SAGE Publications Asia-Pacific Pte. Ltd.
18 Cross Street #10-10/11/12
China Square Central
Singapore 048423

Editor: Laura Notton
Associate Editor: Elizabeth Hernandez
Researchers: Malika Abdoulahi, Amber Armstrong,
    Victoria Heitsch, Mary Hunter, Frances Kerr,
    Heather Kerrigan, Catherine McGee, and
    Ronald Stouffer
Production Editor: Vijayakumar
Typesetter: Hurix Digital
Proofreaders: Benny Willy Stephen
Indexers: TNQ Technologies; Hurix
Cover Designer: Candice Harman

Library of Congress Cataloging-in-Publication Data

The Library of Congress catalogued the first edition of this title as follows:

Washington information directory. 1975/76—
    Washington. Congressional Quarterly Inc.
    1. Washington, D.C.—Directories.
    2. Washington metropolitan area—Directories.
    3. United States—Executive departments—
    Directories. I. Congressional Quarterly Inc.
F192.3.W33   975.3'0025   75-646321

ISBN: 978-1-0718-5344-3

This book is printed on acid-free paper.

22 23 24 25 26 10 9 8 7 6 5 4 3 2 1

Contents

Reference Boxes and Organization Charts

Each chapter also features a box listing the relevant committee and subcommittee resources in Congress.

Preface

Since 1975, the *Washington Information Directory* has been the essential resource for locating information on governmental and nongovernmental organizations in the national capital region. This trusted and user-friendly directory helps researchers find the right contact at the right organization, whether their interest is consumer product and food safety, equal employment opportunities, finance and investments, housing, immigration, terrorism, or a wealth of other timely topics. The directory allows the user to locate accurate, complete, and current information quickly and easily in a way that free Internet searches cannot.

In updating the *Washington Information Directory* every year, we research each existing organization entry to provide current addresses; phone, fax, TTY, and toll-free numbers; email, web addresses, and social media; and key officers and descriptions. In very recent years, federal office contact information has become increasingly difficult for the public to locate on the open web, but the *Washington Information Directory* continues to be the reliable one-stop resource for navigating our government. Our team painstakingly calls each organization and speaks with a member of its Washington office to obtain information. In directory listings, we include contacts' direct lines whenever possible. (Many organizations do not publish these numbers on their websites in an attempt to channel all calls through an operator or answering service.) When a federal department reorganizes, we assess the new divisions and directorates and reorganize the book, along with providing updated organization charts.

Each year brings something new to the directory. Climate change has been discussed widely for years, and the effects are becoming more apparent now more than ever. As such, we've introduced a new compilation of organizations concerned with the increasing impact of climate change. These organizations provide research, resources, contacts, and oversee the provision of targeted sustainability initiatives related to environmental justice. Among the new entries to this edition are the Public Lands Foundation, which is interested in how public lands are used and managed, and the nonpartisan U.S. Term Limits, which advocates for the establishment of term limits for elected offices.

Readers will also find a comprehensive listing of the members of the 117th Congress as well as a handy "Resources in Congress" box at the beginning of each chapter listing relevant committees and subcommittees for that chapter's topic, along with their website and phone number. Readers may also turn to the first appendix, which offers a complete listing of each 117th Congress committee for which information is available and includes full contact information, leadership, membership, and jurisdictions.

The fully updated chapters of the *Washington Information Directory* are supplemented by two appendices comprising a guide to the members and committees of the 117th Congress; a directory of government websites; a list of governors and other state officials; a list of foreign diplomats and embassies, U.S. ambassadors, and State Department country offices; current information on the Freedom of Information Act and legislation; and recent Supreme Court cases and state laws related to privacy. In the congressional delegation section, we have also included Facebook, Twitter, YouTube, and Instagram information in all members' profiles. Print readers can also search and cross-search across the edition in three ways: through the name index, the organization index, or the subject index.

CQ Press seeks to continue the *Washington Information Directory*'s reputation as an invaluable, comprehensive, and authoritative reference of its kind. We welcome feedback related to the book's quality and functionality, as well as suggestions for future editions.

Laura Notton
Editor

How to Use This Directory

The *Washington Information Directory* is designed to make your search for information quick and easy.

Each chapter covers a broad topic, and within the chapters, information is divided into more specific subject areas. This arrangement allows you to find in one place the departments and agencies of the federal government, congressional committees, and nongovernmental organizations that have the information you need.

The directory divides information sources into three main categories: (1) agencies, (2) Congress, and (3) nongovernmental organizations. There is also a small international organizations category. Each entry includes the name, address, and telephone and fax numbers of the organization; the name and title of the director or the best person to contact for information; press, hotline, and TTY numbers, and email, Internet, Twitter, Facebook, YouTube, and blog addresses whenever available; and a description of the work performed by the organization. Congressional committees and subcommittees appear in a box at the beginning of each chapter; a full entry for each committee appears in the first appendix.

HOW INFORMATION IS PRESENTED

The following examples represent the three main categories of entries and the other resources provided in the directory. The examples are drawn from the History and Preservation section in Chapter 4, Culture and Religion. (To read the mailing addresses, check the abbreviations at the end of this guide.)

Agencies

In the first category, government agencies are listed. For example, the National Park Service and its acronym appear in bold type. Next, in parentheses, is the name of its parent organization, the Interior Department. Entries may also include the name of an office within the agency, in this case the Office of Cultural Resources, Partnerships, and Science.

National Park Service (NPS), *(Interior Dept.),* *Cultural Resources, Partnerships, and Science,* 1849 C St. N.W., #3128, 20240-0001; (202) 220-4132. Joy Beasley, Associate Director (Acting). *Web, www.nps.gov/orgs/1345*

Oversees preservation of federal historic sites and administration of buildings programs. Programs include the National Register of Historic Places, National Historic and National Landmark Programs, Historic American Building Survey, Historic American Engineering Record, Archeology and Antiquities Act Program, and Technical Preservation Services. Gives grant and aid assistance and tax benefit information to properties listed in the National Register of Historic Places.

Congress

Congressional committees and subcommittees relevant to each chapter are listed in a box in the beginning of each chapter. Each committee's phone number and website are listed here. For a complete listing of congressional committees, including their full contact information, leadership, memberships, and jurisdictions, please refer to the first appendix. Entries that appear under the "Congress" heading within each chapter are agencies under congressional authority, such as the Government Accountability Office or the Library of Congress. Each entry includes a description of the agency's activities relating to the section in which it appears.

Senate Office of Conservation and Preservation, *S416 CAP, 20510; (202) 224-4550. Leona Faust, Librarian*

Develops and coordinates programs related to the conservation and preservation of Senate records and materials for the secretary of the Senate.

Nongovernmental

Thousands of nongovernmental groups have headquarters or legislative offices in or near Washington. Their staffs are often excellent information sources, and these organizations frequently maintain special libraries or information centers. Here is an example of a group with an interest in the preservation of historic sites:

American Battlefield Trust, *1156 15th St. N.W., #900, 20005; (202) 367-1861. Fax, (202) 367-1865. James Lighthizer, President. General email, info@battlefields.org Web, www.battlefields.org, Twitter, @battlefields,* and *Facebook, www.facebook.com/americanbattlefieldtrust*

Membership: preservation professionals, historians, conservation activists, and citizens. Preserves endangered Civil War battlefields throughout the United States. Conducts preservation conferences and workshops. Advises local preservation groups. Monitors legislation and regulations at the federal, state, and local levels.

How the *Washington Information Directory* Works

The *Washington Information Directory* (WID) directs your search more efficiently and effectively than any other print or online search. This resource does the hard work of pinpointing the information you need. Here is an example of how to use it to find information on the preservation of historic sites and materials:

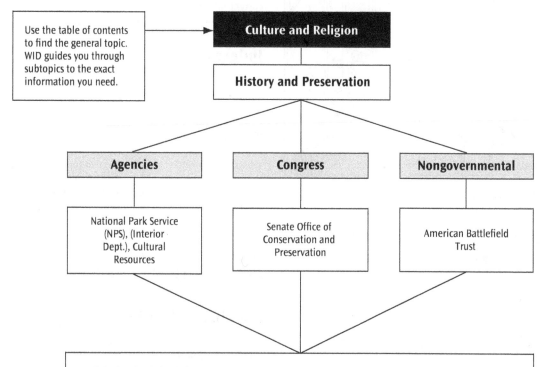

Use the table of contents to find the general topic. WID guides you through subtopics to the exact information you need.

Culture and Religion

History and Preservation

Agencies

Congress

Nongovernmental

National Park Service (NPS), (Interior Dept.), Cultural Resources

Senate Office of Conservation and Preservation

American Battlefield Trust

Each listing includes the name of the director or the best person to contact for information, current address, phone and fax numbers, and, whenever available, email, Internet, Twitter, and Facebook addresses, plus a brief description of the organization's purpose.

Charts and Boxes

This directory includes organization charts to make the hierarchy of federal departments and agencies easy to grasp, as well as reference boxes that provide essential agency contacts and other information. On the topic of historic sites, you can locate the National Park Service within the Interior Department (see chart on p. 306) or consult a list of sites administered by the National Park Service (see box on p. 152). The National Park Service's organization chart appears on page 322. The general organization chart for the federal government appears on page 970.

REFERENCE RESOURCES

Tables of Contents

The table of contents (p. v) lists the directory's chapters and their major subheadings. A list of reference boxes and organization charts within the chapters is provided on page vii. Each chapter opens with a detailed table of contents, including the boxes and charts that appear in the chapter.

Congressional Information

A section on the 117th Congress, beginning on page 839, provides extensive information about members and committees:

State Delegations. Here (p. 840) you can locate senators, representatives, and delegates by state (or territory) and congressional district.

Committees. These sections list the jurisdictions and memberships of committees and subcommittees of the House (p. 845) and Senate (p. 928), as well as the joint committees of Congress (p. 926). Also included are party leaderships and partisan committees of the House (p. 864) and Senate (p. 941).

Members' Offices. For the House (p. 866) and Senate (p. 942), we provide each member's Capitol Hill office

Map of Capitol Hill

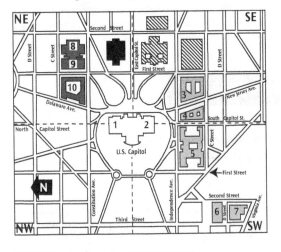

☐ U.S. Capitol, Washington, DC 20510 or 20515*

1. Senate Wing   2. House Wing

▨ House Office Buildings, Washington, DC 20515 or 20024

3. Cannon   4. Longworth
5. Rayburn   6. O'Neill
7. Ford

▨ Senate Office Buildings, Washington, DC 20510

8. Hart   9. Dirksen
10. Russell

■ Supreme Court, Washington, DC 20543

▨ Library of Congress, Washington, DC 20540

* Mail sent to the U.S. Capitol should bear the zip code of the chamber to which it is addressed.

Note: Dashed lines indicate the city's quadrants, which are noted in the corners of the map.

address, telephone and fax numbers, Internet address, social media (if available), key professional aide, committee assignments, and district office contact information.

Ready Reference

A section of reference lists, beginning on page 965, provides information on the following subjects:

Government Information on the Internet. Organized by branch of government, this section (p. 965) lists Web addresses for locating information and social media on the White House, cabinet departments, Congress, and the judiciary.

State Government. The list of state officials (p. 972) provides the name, address, and telephone number for each governor, lieutenant governor, secretary of state, attorney general, and state treasurer. It includes a press contact for the governor and, where applicable, the governor's office representative in Washington, DC.

Diplomats. The foreign embassies section (p. 988) gives the names, official addresses, and telephone numbers of foreign diplomats in Washington; the names of ranking U.S. diplomatic officials abroad; and the phone numbers for State Department country desk offices.

Federal Laws on Information. This section presents current information on the Freedom of Information Act (p. 1007) and privacy legislation (p. 1012).

Indexes

Use the name index (p. 1016) to look up any person listed in the directory. Use the organization index (p. 1054) to find a specific organization or agency. Use the subject index (p. 1103) to locate a particular area of interest. If you need information on a specific topic but do not know a particular source, the index has entries for chapter subsections to help you find where that topic is covered. For example, on the subject of equal employment for women, you can find index entries under Equal Employment Opportunity as well as under Women.

REACHING YOUR INFORMATION SOURCE

Phoning and Faxing

Call information or toll-free numbers first. Often you can get the answer you need without searching any further. If not, an explanation of your query should put you in touch with the person who can answer your question. Rarely will you need to talk to the top administrator.

Offer to fax your query if it is difficult to explain over the phone, but make sure that the person helping you knows to expect your fax. Faxing promptly and limiting your transmission to a single page brings the best results.

Remember that publications and documents are often available from a special office (for federal agencies, see p. 108) and, increasingly, on websites. Ask what is the fastest way to receive the information you need.

Keep in mind the agency or organization, not the name of the director. Personnel changes are common, but for most inquiries you will want to stay within the organization you call, rather than track down a person who may have moved on to a new job.

Concerning congressional questions, first contact one of your members of Congress; representatives have staff assigned to answer questions from constituents. Contact a committee only if you have a technical question that cannot be answered elsewhere.

Writing

Address letters to the director of an office or organization—the contact person listed. Your letter will be directed to the person who can answer your question. Be prepared to follow up by phone.

Using the Internet

Most agencies and governmental organizations have sites on the Internet (for federal departments and agencies, see pp. 116, 965–971) and an email address for general inquiries. Information available from these sources is expanding and is usually free once you are online. However, this approach is not always faster or better than a phone call—Internet connections can be slow, site menus can be complex or confusing, and information can be incomplete or out of date. The office also may be able to alert you to any upcoming changes.

As with faxing, reserve email for inquiries that may be too complex for a phone call, but phone first to establish that someone is ready to help.

ADDRESSES AND AREA CODES

Listings in the directory include full contact information, including telephone area code and, when available, room or suite number and nine-digit zip code. If an office prefers a mailing address that is different from the physical location, we provide both.

Washington, DC, Addresses

For brevity, entries for agencies, organizations, and congressional offices in the District of Columbia (area code 202) do not include the city as part of the address. Here is the beginning of a typical Washington entry:

Equal Employment Opportunity Commission (EEOC), *131 M St. N.E., 20507; (202) 663-4900.*

To complete the mailing address, add "Washington, DC" before the zip code.

Building Addresses

Departments and agencies generally have their own zip codes. Updates to our directory reflect the increasing use of street addresses by the federal government. Federal offices at the following locations are listed by building name or abbreviation:

The White House. Located at 1600 Pennsylvania Ave. N.W., 20500.

Dwight D. Eisenhower Executive Office Building. Located at 17th St. and Pennsylvania Ave. N.W., 20500.

New Executive Office Building. Located at 725 17th St. N.W., 20503.

Main State Department Building. Located at 2201 C St. N.W., 20520.

The Pentagon. Located in Arlington, Virginia, but has a Washington mailing address and different zip codes for each branch of the military.

Navy Annex. Located at Columbia Pike and Southgate Rd., Arlington, VA 20370, but most offices use a Washington mailing address.

U.S. Capitol. Abbreviated as CAP; the letters *H* and *S* before the room number indicate the House or Senate side of the building. Zip codes are 20510 for the Senate, 20515 for the House.

Senate Office Buildings. Mail for delivery to Senate office buildings does not require a street address. The zip code is 20510. Abbreviations, building names, and street locations are as follows:

SDOB	Dirksen Senate Office Bldg., Constitution Ave. between 1st and 2nd Sts. N.E.
SHOB	Hart Senate Office Bldg., 2nd St. and Constitution Ave. N.E.
SROB	Russell Senate Office Bldg., Constitution Ave. between Delaware Ave. and 1st St. N.E.

House Office Buildings. Mail for delivery to House office buildings does not require a street address. The zip code is 20515. Abbreviations, building names, and street locations are as follows:

CHOB	Cannon House Office Bldg., Independence Ave. between New Jersey Ave. and 1st St. S.E.
FHOB	Ford House Office Bldg., 2nd and D Sts. S.W.
LHOB	Longworth House Office Bldg., Independence Ave. between S. Capitol St. and New Jersey Ave. S.E.
OHOB	O'Neill House Office Bldg., 200 C St. S.W. 20024
RHOB	Rayburn House Office Bldg., Independence Ave. between S. Capitol and 1st Sts. S.W.

1

Agriculture, Food, and Nutrition

GENERAL POLICY AND ANALYSIS

Basic Resources

▶AGENCIES

Agricultural Marketing Service (AMS) *(Agriculture Dept.)*, *1400 Independence Ave. S.W., #2055, MS 0201, 20250-0201; (202) 720-4276. Fax, (202) 690-0746. Bruce Summers, Administrator. Public Affairs, (202) 720-8998.*
Web, www.ams.usda.gov, Twitter, @USDA_AMS and Facebook, www.facebook.com/usda

Administers programs that create domestic and international marketing opportunities for U.S. producers of food, fiber, and specialty crops. Also provides marketing, standardization, grading, inspection, and regulatory programs; maintains a market news service to inform producers of price changes; conducts agricultural marketing research and development programs; studies agricultural transportation issues.

Agricultural Marketing Service (AMS) *(Agriculture Dept.), Fair Trade Practices Program, Warehouse and Commodity Management, 1400 Independence Ave. S.W., MS 3601, 20250-0506; (202) 720-2121. Ned Bergman, Director.*
Web, www.ams.usda.gov/services/warehouse

Ensures that agriculture facilities are upholding the rules and regulations set forth by the U.S. Warehouse Act and Commodity Credit Corp. contracts. This office is responsible for issuing license and storage agreements and performing warehouse examinations.

Agriculture Dept. (USDA), *1400 Independence Ave. S.W., #200A, 20250-0002; (202) 720-2791. Thomas J. Vilsack, Secretary. Locator, (202) 720-8732. Press, (202) 720-4623. Toll Free, (833) 663-8732.*
General email, askusda@usda.gov
Web, www.usda.gov, Twitter, @USDA, Facebook, www.facebook.com/usda and Blog, www.usda.gov/media/blog

Serves as principal adviser to the president on agricultural policy; works to increase and maintain farm income and to develop markets abroad for U.S. agricultural products. Provides leadership on food, agriculture, natural resources, rural development, nutrition, and related issues based on public policy, the best available science, and effective management. Also helping to preserve our Nation's natural resources through conservation, restored forests, improved watersheds, and healthy private working lands.

Agriculture Dept. (USDA), *National Appeals Division (NAD), 1320 Braddock Pl., Alexandria, VA 22314; (703) 305-2016. Fax, (703) 535-5161. Frank (Max) M. Wood, Director. Toll-free, (877) 487-3262.*
General email, nadinfo@nad.usda.gov
Web, www.nad.usda.gov

Conducts impartial administrative appeals hearings and reviews of adverse program decisions for participants of programs administered by the Farm Service Agency, Risk Management Agency, Natural Resources Conservation Service, and Rural Development.

Agriculture Dept. (USDA), *Office of the Chief Economist (OCE), 1400 Independence Ave. S.W., #112-A, 20250-3810; (202) 720-4164. Fax, (202) 690-4915. Seth Meyer, Chief Economist. Communications Officer, (202) 527-5130.*
Web, www.usda.gov/oce

Prepares economic and statistical analyses used to plan and evaluate short-range and intermediate-range agricultural policy. Evaluates department policy, proposals, and legislation for their impact on the agricultural economy. Administers department economic agencies, including the Office of Risk Assessment and Cost-Benefit Analysis, Office of Energy and Environmental Policy, Office of Pest Management Policy, and World Agricultural Outlook Board. Publishes the monthly *World Agricultural Supply and Demand Estmates* report.

Agriculture Dept. (USDA), *Office of the Chief Scientist (OCS), 1400 Independence Ave. S.W., #338A, 20250; (202) 720-3444. Shefali V. Mehta, Chief Scientis. (Acting); Dionne F. Toombs, Director.*
Web, www.usda.gov/our-agency/staff-offices/office-chief-scientist-ocs

Informs department policy and regulation decisions with scientific research in the areas of agricultural systems and technology, animal health and production, plant health, renewable energy, natural resources, food safety, nutrition, agricultural economics, and rural communities.

Agriculture Dept. (USDA), *Partnerships and Public Engagement (OPPE), 1400 Independence Ave. S.W., #520-A, MS 0601, 20250-9821; (202) 720-6350. Lisa Ramirez, Director. Toll-free, (800) 880-4183.*
General email, partnerships@usda.gov
Web, www.usda.gov/partnerships

Develops and maintains partnerships which focus on solutions to challenges facing rural and underserved communities; connects communities to the education, tools, and resources available to them through Agriculture Dept. programs and initiatives.

Agriculture Dept. (USDA), *Tribal Relations (OTR), 1400 Independence Ave. S.W., Room 501-A, 20250; (202) 205-2249. Heather Dawn Thompson, Director.*
General email, tribal.relations@osec.usda.gov
Web, www.usda.gov/tribalrelations

Leads the intergovernmental role in its effort to; through consultation, coordination and collaboration, support the preservation of the government to government relationship and enhance access to USDA's various programs and services to tribes, tribal organizations and citizens.

Animal and Plant Health Inspection Service (APHIS)
(Agriculture Dept.), Biotechnology Regulatory Services (BRS), 4700 River Rd., #146, Riverdale, MD 20737; (301)

AGRICULTURE RESOURCES IN CONGRESS

For a complete listing of congressional committees, including their full contact information, leadership, membership, and jurisdictions, please refer to the Appendix on pages 840–963.

HOUSE:

House Agriculture Committee, (202) 225-2171.
Web, https://agriculture.house.gov
   Subcommittee on Biotechnology, Horticulture, and Research, (202) 225-2171.
   Subcommittee on Commodity Exchanges, Energy, and Credit, (202) 225-2171.
   Subcommittee on Conservation and Forestry, (202) 225-2171.
   Subcommittee on General Farm Commodities and Risk Management, (202) 225-2171.
   Subcommittee on Livestock and Foreign Agriculture, (202) 225-2171.
   Subcommittee on Nutrition, Oversight, and Department Operations, (202) 225-2171.
House Appropriations Committee, (202) 225-2771.
Web, https://appropriations.house.gov
   Subcommittee on Agriculture, Rural Development, Food and Drug Administration, and Related Agencies, (202) 225-2638.
House Energy and Commerce Committee, (202) 225-2927.
Web, https://energycommerce.house.gov
   Subcommittee on Health, (202) 225-2927.
House Foreign Affairs Committee, (202) 225-5021.
Web, https://foreignaffairs.house.gov
House Science, Space, and Technology Committee, (202) 225-6375.
Web, https://science.house.gov
   Subcommittee on Research and Technology, (202) 225-6375.
House Small Business Committee, (202) 225-4038.
Web, https://smallbusiness.house.gov
   Subcommittee on Underserved, Agricultural, and Rural Business Development, (202) 225-4038.

SENATE:

Senate Agriculture, Nutrition, and Forestry Committee, (202) 224-2035.
Web, www.agriculture.senate.gov
   Subcommittee on Commodities, Risk Management, and Trade, (202) 224-2035.
   Subcommittee on Conservation, Climate, Forestry, and Natural Resources, (202) 224-2035.
   Subcommittee on Livestock, Dairy, Poultry, Local Food Systems, and Food Safety, (202) 224-2035.
   Subcommittee on Food and Nutrition, Specialty Crop, Organics, and Research, (202) 224-2035.
   Subcommittee on Rural Development and Energy, (202) 224-2035.
Senate Appropriations Committee, (202) 224-7363.
Web, www.appropriations.senate.gov
   Subcommittee on Agriculture, Rural Development, Food and Drug Administration, and Related Agencies, (202) 224-7363.

851-3877. Bernadette R. Juarez, Deputy Administrator. Applications and regulatory requirements, (301) 851-3886. Compliance, (301) 851-3935. Press, (301) 851-4100.
Web, www.aphis.usda.gov/aphis/ourfocus/biotechnology
Email, biotechquery@usda.gov

Administers the Coordinated Framework for Regulation of Biotechnology to regulate genetically engineered organisms that may pose a risk to plant health and other agricultural resources; authorizes permits and notifications for the importation, interstate movement, and environmental release of genetically engineered organisms and performs inspections.

Animal and Plant Health Inspection Service (APHIS)
(Agriculture Dept.), International Services, 4700 River Rd., Riverdale, MD 20737; (202) 799-7132. Cheryle Blakely, Deputy Administrator. Animal Import and Export, (301) 851-8300.
Web, www.aphis.usda.gov/aphis/ourfocus/internationalservices

Collaborates with foreign partners to control pests and diseases that could harm the United States; facilitates safe agricultural trade; ensures effective and efficient management of internationally based programs; invests in international capacity-building with foreign counterparts to prevent the spread of damaging pests and diseases.

Animal and Plant Health Inspection Service (APHIS)
(Agriculture Dept.), Legislative and Public Affairs, South Bldg., 1400 Independence Ave. S.W., #1147, 20250; (301) 955-1203. Bethany Jones, Deputy Administrator, (202) 799-7030. Public Affairs, (301) 851-4100.
Web, www.aphis.usda.gov/aphis/banner/contactus/sa_aphis_contacts/contact_lpa

Manages communications with Congress, industry stakeholders, trading partners, and the media.

Bureau of Economic and Business Affairs (EB) *(State Dept.), Trade Policy and Negotiations (TPN), Agriculture Policy (AGP), 2201 C St. N.W., #4686,*

20520-0002; (202) 647-3090. Fax, (202) 647-1894.
Jeffrey Gianque, Director, (202) 647-0133.
Web, www.state.gov/agricultural-policy

Develops agricultural trade policy; handles questions pertaining to international negotiations on all agricultural products covered by the World Trade Organization (WTO) and bilateral trade agreements. Oversees the distribution of biotechnology outreach funds to promote international acceptance of the technology.

▶ CONGRESS

For a listing of relevant congressional committees and sub-committees, please see page 3 or the Appendix.

Government Accountability Office (GAO), *Natural Resources and Environment (NRE), 441 G St. N.W., 20548; (202) 512-3841. Frank Rusco, Director.*
Web, www.gao.gov/about/careers/our-teams

Audits, analyzes, and evaluates for Congress federal agriculture, food safety, and energy programs; provides guidance on issues including efforts to ensure a reliable and environmentally sound energy supply, land and water resources management, protection of the environment, hazardous and nuclear wastes threat reduction, food safety, and investment in science.

▶ NONGOVERNMENTAL

American Farm Bureau Federation (AFBF), *600 Maryland Ave. S.W., #1000W, 20024-2520; (202) 406-3600. Fax, (202) 406-3606. Zippy Duvall, President.*
General email, webmaster@fb.org
Web, www.fb.org, Twitter, @farmbureau and Facebook, www.facebook.com/AmericanFarmBureau

Federation of state farm bureaus in fifty states and Puerto Rico. Promotes agricultural research. Interests include commodity programs, domestic production, marketing, education, research, financial assistance to the farmer, foreign assistance programs, rural development, the world food shortage, and inspection and certification of food. Monitors legislation and regulations.

Crop Insurance and Reinsurance Bureau, *50 F St. N.W., #450, 20001; (202) 544-0067. Mike Torrey, Executive Vice President.*
Web, http://cropinsurance.org

Membership: approved insurance providers (AIPs), reinsurance companies, and brokerage groups. Involved with writing state policies and providing risk management tools to farmers and ranchers. Represents members before Congress and the federal government.

Environmental Working Group, *1250 Eye St. N.W., #100, 20005; (202) 667-6982. Fax, (202) 232-2592. Kenneth A. Cook, President.*
Web, www.ewg.org, Twitter, @ewg and Facebook, www.facebook.com/ewg

Research and advocacy group that studies and publishes reports on a wide range of agricultural and environmental issues, including farm subsidies and industrial pollution. Monitors legislation and regulations.

Equitable Food Initiative, *200 Massachusetts Ave. N.W., #700, 20001; (202) 730-6672. Peter O'Driscoll, Executive Director.*
General email, info@equitablefood.org
Web, http://equitablefood.org, Twitter, @EquitableFood and Facebook, www.facebook.com/EquitableFoodInitiative

Recognizes the contribution of farmworkers in the produce industry while improving agricultural policy and food safety. Creates a network for workers, growers, retailers, and consumers. Promotes improvement of agriculture working conditions, environmental stewardship, and responsible produce growing.

National Assn. of State Depts. of Agriculture, *4350 N. Fairfax Dr., #810, Arlington, VA 22203; (202) 296-9680. Ted McKinney, Chief Executive Officer.*
General email, nasda@nasda.org
Web, www.nasda.org and Twitter, @NASDAnews

Membership: commissioners, secretaries, and directors of agriculture from the 50 states, Puerto Rico, Guam, American Samoa, and the Virgin Islands. Serves as liaison between federal government, state departments, and stakeholders; coordinates agricultural policies and laws; provides data collection, emergency planning, and training; seeks to protect consumers and the environment. Monitors legislation and regulations.

National Council of Agricultural Employers (NCAE), *525 9th St. N.W., #800, 20004; (202) 629-9320. Michael Marsh, President.*
Web, www.ncaeonline.org and Twitter, @NCAEonline

Membership: employers of agricultural labor. Encourages establishment and maintenance of conditions conducive to an adequate supply of domestic and foreign farm labor.

National Farmers Union, *20 F St. N.W., #300, 20001-1560; (202) 554-1600. Fax, (202) 554-1654. Rob Larew, President.*
General email, info@nfu.org
Web, www.nfu.org, Twitter, @NFUDC and Facebook, www.facebook.com/nationalfarmersunion

Advocates economic and social well-being and quality of life of family farmers, ranchers, fishermen, and consumers and their communities through education, cooperation, and legislation. Encourages sustainable production of food, fiber, feed, and fuel.

National Governors Assn. (NGA), *Natural Resources Committee, 444 N. Capitol St. N.W., #267, 20001-1512; (202) 624-5300. Alex Whitaker, Legislative Director.*
General email, info@nga.org
Web, www.nga.org/advocacy/nga-committees/nrc

Monitors legislation and regulations and makes recommendations on agriculture, energy, environment, and natural resource issues to ensure governors' views and priorities are represented in federal policies and regulations.

Agriculture Department

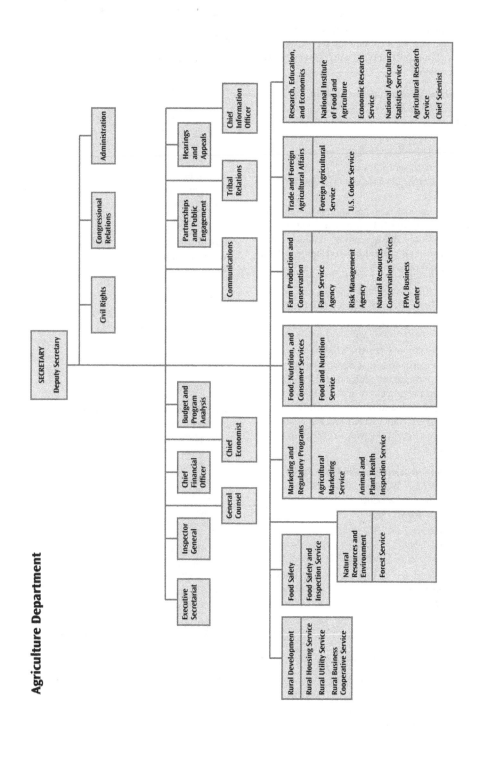

National Grange, *1616 H St. N.W., 10th Floor, 20006-4999; (202) 628-3507. Betsy Huber, President, ext. 112.*
General email, info@nationalgrange.org

Web, www.nationalgrange.org and
Twitter, @NationalGrange

Membership: farmers and others involved in agricultural production and rural community service activities. Coordinates community service programs with state grange organizations.

National Sustainable Agriculture Coalition, *110 Maryland Ave. N.E., #209, 20002-5622; (202) 547-5754. Sarah Hackney, Coalition Director; Eric J. Deeble, Policy Director.*
General email, info@sustainableagriculture.net

Web, www.sustainableagriculture.net,
Twitter, @sustainableag and Facebook, www.facebook.com/sustainableag

National alliance of farm, rural, and conservation organizations. Advocates federal policies that promote environmentally sustainable agriculture, natural resources management, and rural community development. Monitors legislation and regulations.

Rural Coalition, *1029 Vermont Ave. N.W., #601, 20005; (202) 628-7160. Fax, (202) 393-1816. Lorette Picciano, Executive Director.*
General email, ruralco@ruralco.org

Web, www.ruralco.org and Twitter, @RuralCo

Alliance of organizations that develop public policies benefiting rural communities. Collaborates with community-based groups on agriculture and rural development issues, including health and the environment, minority farmers, farmworkers, Native Americans' rights, and rural community development. Provides rural groups with technical assistance.

Union of Concerned Scientists, *Food and Farms Program, 1825 K St. N.W., #800, 20006-1232; (202) 223-6133. Ricardo Salvador, Director.*
General email, ucs@ucsusa.org

Web, www.ucsusa.org/food, Twitter, @ucsusa and Facebook, www.facebook.com/unionofconcernedscientists and YouTube, www.youtube.com/user/ConcernedScientists

Promotes a food system that encourages innovative and environmentally sustainable ways of producing high-quality, safe, and affordable food. Focuses on reducing the unnecessary use of antibiotics and strengthening federal oversight of genetically engineered products for food and agriculture and promoting climate-friendly agricultural practices. (Headquarters in Cambridge, Mass.)

Wallace Genetic Foundation, *4910 Massachusetts Ave. N.W., #221, 20016; (202) 966-2932. Fax, (202) 966-3370. Michaela Oldfield, Executive Director.*
General email, wgfdn@wallacegenetic.org

Web, www.wallacegenetic.org

Supports national and international nonprofits in the areas of sustainable agriculture, agricultural research, preservation of farmland, reduction of environmental toxins, conservation, biodiversity protection, and global climate issues.

Agricultural Research, Education

▶AGENCIES

Agricultural Research Service *(Agriculture Dept.),* *Jamie L. Whitten Bldg., 1400 Independence Ave. S.W., #302A, 20250-0300; (202) 720-3656. Fax, (202) 720-5427. Chavonda Jacobs-Young, Administrator.*
General email, administrator@usda.gov

Web, www.ars.usda.gov, Twitter, @USDA_ARS and Blog, www.usda.gov/media/blog/tag/ars and Facebook, www.facebook.com/AgriculturalResearchService

Conducts research on crops, livestock, poultry, soil and water conservation, agricultural engineering, and control of insects and other pests; develops new uses for farm commodities.

Agricultural Research Service *(Agriculture Dept.),* *National Plant Germplasm System, 5601 Sunnyside Ave., #4-2212, MS 5139, Beltsville, MD 20705-5139; (301) 504-5541. Fax, (301) 504-6191. Peter K. Bretting, National Program Leader.*
Web, https://www.ars-grin.gov/Pages/Collections
Email, peter.bretting@ars.usda.gov

Network of federal and state gene banks that preserve samples of all major field crops and horticultural crops. Collects, preserves, evaluates, and catalogs germplasm and distributes it for specific purposes.

Agriculture Dept. (USDA), *Rural Development, Rural Business–Cooperative Service, 1400 Independence Ave. S.W., #5803-S, MS 3201, 20250-3201; (202) 690-4730. Fax, (202) 690-4737. Karama Neal, Administrator (Acting).*
Web, www.rd.usda.gov/about-rd/agencies/rural-business-cooperative-service

Annually collects financial and other data from farmer, rancher, and fishery cooperatives; publishes marketing, supply, service, fishery, and bargaining cooperatives data.

Agriculture Dept. (USDA), *Small and Disadvantaged Business Utilization (OSDBU), 1400 Independence Ave. S.W., #1085-S, MS 9501, 20250-9501; (202) 720-7117. Michelle Warren, Director (Acting), (202) 720-7835.*
Web, www.dm.usda.gov/smallbus

Provides guidance and technical assistance to Small businesses often owned and run by women, people of diverse ethnic backgrounds and disabled veterans, seeking to do business with the USDA; monitors the development and implementation of contracting policies to prevent barriers to small business participation; works with other federal agencies and public/private partners to increase the number of small businesses participating in the contracting arena.

Agriculture Dept. (USDA), *Under Secretary for Research, Education, and Economics (REE), 1400 Independence Ave. S.W., #214W, MS 0110, 20250-0110; (202) 720-5923.*

Fax, (202) 690-2842. Scott Hutchins, Deputy Under Secretary.

Web, www.ree.usda.gov

Coordinates agricultural research, extension, and teaching programs in the food and agricultural sciences, including human nutrition, home economics, consumer services, agricultural economics, environmental quality, natural and renewable resources, forestry and range management, animal and plant production and protection, aquaculture, and the processing, distribution, marketing, and utilization of food and agricultural products. Oversees the Agricultural Research Service, the National Institute of Food and Agriculture, the Economic Research Service, and the National Agricultural Statistics Service.

Economic Research Service (ERS) *(Agriculture Dept.),*
355 E St. S.W., 20024-3221 (mailing address: 1400 Independence Ave. S.W., MS 1800, Washington, DC 20250-0002); (202) 694-5000. Fax, (202) 245-5467. Spiro Stefanou, Administrator. Public Affairs, (202) 694-5139.

General email, service@ers.usda.gov

Web, www.ers.usda.gov and Twitter, @USDA_ERS

Conducts research on economic and policy issues involving food, natural resources, and rural development.

Economic Research Service *(Agriculture Dept.), Market and Trade Economics,* *355 E St. S.W., 20024-3221 (mailing address: 1400 Independence Ave. S.W., MS 1800, Washington, DC 20250-0002); (202) 694-5540. Utpal Vasavada, Assosicate Director.*

Web, www.ers.usda.gov/about-ers/agency-structure/ market-and-trade-economics-division-mted

Monitors, evaluates, and conducts research on domestic and foreign economic and policy factors affecting agricultural markets and trade, with a focus on policy and program alternatives, domestic and international markets, commodity analysis and forecasts, international food security, and development of analytical tools and data.

Economic Research Service *(Agriculture Dept.), Resource and Rural Economics (RRED),* *1400 Independence Ave. S.W., #214W, MS 1800, 20250-0002; Robert Gibbs, Associate Director, (202) 694-5423.*

Web, www.ers.usda.gov/about-ers/agency-structure/ resource-and-rural-economics-division-rred

Conducts research on the interconnectedness of agricultural, energy, climate, and environmental policies; ecosystem services and land use; research and development of agricultural technologies and agricultural productivity; dynamics of farming; rural development; and the well-being of farm and rural households. Collaborates with the department's National Agricultural Statistics Service to implement the annual national Agricultural Resource Management Survey.

Foreign Agricultural Service (FAS) *(Agriculture Dept.), Global Market Analysis,* *1400 Independence Ave. S.W., #4083S, 20250; (202) 720-6301. Fax, (202) 690-1238. Patrick Packnett Sr., Deputy Administrator.*

Web, www.fas.usda.gov/data

Press, press-fas@usda.gov

Prepares production forecasts, assesses export marketing opportunities, and tracks changes in policies affecting U.S. agricultural trade. Develops and maintains Agriculture Department's data on agricultural production, supply, demand, and trade.

National Agricultural Library *(Agriculture Dept.),* *10301 Baltimore Ave., Beltsville, MD 20705-2351; (301) 504-5755. Fax, (301) 504-7042. Paul Wester, Director, (301) 504-5248. TTY, (301) 504-6856. Toll-Free, (800) 633-7701.*

General email, agref@usda.gov

Web, www.nal.usda.gov

Principal source of agricultural information in the United States. Makes significant information available to researchers, educators, policymakers, and the public; coordinates with state land-grant and Agriculture Dept. field libraries; promotes international cooperation and exchange of information. Deeper interests include food production, food safety, human nutrition, animal welfare, water quality, rural development, and invasive species. Library hours are 8:30 a.m.–4:30 p.m.

National Agricultural Library *(Agriculture Dept.), Alternative Farming Systems Information Center (AFSIC),* *10301 Baltimore Ave., #132, Beltsville, MD 20705-2351; (301) 504-5440. Vanessa S. Gordon, Project Lead. Toll-Free, (800) 633-7701.*

General email, agref@usda.gov

Web, www.nal.usda.gov/afsic

Serves individuals and agencies seeking information on sustainability in agriculture, alternative plants and crops, farm energy options, grazing systems and alternative livestock breeds, alternative marketing and business practices, organic production, ecological pest management, and soil and water management.

National Agricultural Statistics Service *(Agriculture Dept.),* *1400 Independence Ave. S.W., #5041, MS 2001, 20250-2001; (202) 720-2707. Hubert Hamer, Administrator. Library, (202) 690-8127. Public Affairs, (202) 690-8923. Toll-free, (800) 727-9540.*

General email, nass@nass.usda.gov

Web, www.nass.usda.gov and Twitter, @usda_nass

Prepares estimates and reports on production, supply, prices, and other items relating to the U.S. agricultural economy. Reports include statistics on field crops, fruits and vegetables, cattle, hogs, poultry, and related products. Prepares quinquennial national census of agriculture.

National Agricultural Statistics Service *(Agriculture Dept.), Census and Survey,* *1400 Independence Ave. S.W., #6306, MS 2020, 20250-2020; (202) 720-4557. Fax, (202) 720-8738. Barbara Rater, Director.*

General email, nass@nass.usda.gov

Web, www.nass.usda.gov

Conducts a quinquennial agricultural census that provides data on crops, livestock, operator characteristics, land use, farm production expenditures, machinery and equipment, and irrigation for counties, states, regions, and the nation.

National Institute of Food and Agriculture (NIFA)
(Agriculture Dept.), Jaime L. Whitten Bldg., 12th St. S.W. and Jefferson Dr., #305A, 20250 (mailing address: 1400 Independence Ave. S.W., MS 2201, Washington, DC 20250-2201); (202) 720-4423. Fax, (202) 720-8987. Carrie Castille, Director. Information, (202) 720-2791.
General email, nifamediarequests@nifa.usda.gov
Web, https://nifa.usda.gov, Twitter, @USDA_NIFA
Blog, https://nifa.usda.gov/newsroom?f%5B0%5D=type%3Ablog

Supports research, education, and extension of issues pertaining to agricultural production, nutrition, food safety, energy independence, and the sustainability of natural resources. Partners with and funds scientists at academic institutions, particularly the land-grant universities, minority-serving institutions, including black colleges and universities, Hispanic-serving institutions, and tribal colleges, as well as government, private, and nonprofit organizations to address critical issues in agriculture, including global food security and hunger, water resources, climate change, sustainable energy, childhood obesity, and food safety. Partners with agricultural extension offices in all counties, states, and territories.

National Institute of Food and Agriculture (NIFA)
(Agriculture Dept.), Institute of Bioenergy, Climate, and Environment, 800 9th St. S.W., #3231, 20024 (mailing address: 1400 Independence Ave. S.W., MS 2210, Washington, DC 20250-2215); (202) 720-2791. Timothy Conner, Division Director (Acting), (816) 926-1816.
Web, https://nifa.usda.gov/office/institute-bioenergy-climate-and-environment

Administers programs to address national science priorities that advance energy independence and help agricultural, forest, and rangeland production systems adapt to climate change variables. Provides grants to support the development of sustainable bioenergy production systems, agricultural production systems, and natural resource management activities that are adapted to climate variation and activities that otherwise support sustainable natural resource use.

National Institute of Food and Agriculture (NIFA)
(Agriculture Dept.), Institute of Youth, Family, and Community, IYFC, 800 9th St. S.W., #4343, 20024 (mailing address: 1400 Independence Ave. S.W., MS 2250, Washington, DC 20250-2225); Venu (Kal) Kalavacharla, Deputy Director. Hotline, (202) 720-2791.
Web, https://nifa.usda.gov/office/institute-youth-family-and-community

Supports the socio-economic prosperity by strengthening individuals, families, and communities; providing resources for the next generation of food and agricultural scientists; and offering youth leadership experiences. Prepares young people to be responsible citizens and change agents; Develop spragmatic solutions to recurring issues facing individuals, families, and communities; Strengthen the capacity of higher education institutions to develop and implement curricula and teaching programs in the food and agricultural sciences as well as the Science, Technology, Engineering, and Math (STEM) disciplines.

▶**NONGOVERNMENTAL**

National Council of Farmer Cooperatives (NCFC), *50 F St. N.W., #900, 20001-1530; (202) 626-8700. Fax, (202) 626-8722. Charles (Chuck) F. Conner, President.*
General email, info@ncfc.org
Web, www.ncfc.org, Twitter, @FarmerCoop and Facebook, www.facebook.com/FarmerCoop

Membership: cooperative businesses owned and operated by farmers. Conducts educational programs and encourages research on agricultural cooperatives; provides statistics and analyzes trends; presents awards for research papers.

Fertilizer and Pesticides

▶**AGENCIES**

Environmental Protection Agency (EPA), *Chemical Safety and Pollution Prevention (OCSPP), 1200 Pennsylvania Ave. N.W., #4146, MC 7101M, 20460; (202) 564-2910. Fax, (202) 564-0801. Michal Ilana Freedhoff, Assistant Administrator.*
Web, www.epa.gov/aboutepa/about-office-chemical-safety-and-pollution-prevention-ocspp

Registers, controls, and regulates use of pesticides and toxic substances. Manages the Endocrine Disruptor Screening Program, which screens pesticides, chemicals, and environmental contaminants for their potential effect on estrogen, androgen, and thyroid hormone systems.

Environmental Protection Agency (EPA), *Chemical Safety and Pollution Prevention (OCSPP), Pesticide Programs, 1 Potomac Yard, 2777 Crystal Dr., Arlington, VA 22202 (mailing address: 1200 Pennsylvania Ave. N.W., MC 7501P, Washington, DC 20460); (202) 566-1245. Fax, (703) 308-4776. Edward Messina, Director. National Pesticide Information Center, (800) 858-7378.*
General email, pesticidequestions@epa.gov
Web, www.epa.gov/aboutepa/about-office-chemical-safety-and-pollution-prevention-ocspp#opp

Regulates the manufacturing and use of all pesticides, including insecticides, herbicides, rodenticides, disinfectants, and sanitizers, in the United States. Establishes maximum levels for pesticide residues in food. Develops rules that govern labeling and literature accompanying pesticide products. Administers the Integrated Pest Management in Schools and the Pesticide Environmental Stewardship programs. Operates the National Pesticide Information Center (8 a.m.–12 p.m. PST).

Natural Resources Conservation Service *(Agriculture Dept.), Pest Management, 1400 Independence Ave. S.W., #6147, 20250; (202) 253-4376. Eric S. Hesketh, Pest Management Specialist, 413- 253-4374. Information, (202) 720-2791.*

Web, www.nrcs.usda.gov/wps/portal/nrcs/main/national/plantsanimals/invasive/pests

Formulates and recommends agency policy in coordination with the Environmental Protection Agency and other Agriculture Dept. agencies for the establishment of standards, procedures, and management of agronomic, forest, and horticultural use of pesticides. Also to educate farmers in Integrated Pest Management.

►NONGOVERNMENTAL

Beyond Pesticides, *701 E St. S.E., #200, 20003; (202) 543-5450. Fax, (202) 543-4791. Jay Feldman, Executive Director.*
General email, info@beyondpesticides.org
Web, www.beyondpesticides.org,
Twitter, @beyondpesticides and Facebook, www.facebook .com/beyondpesticides

Coalition of family farmers, farmworkers, consumers, home gardeners, physicians, lawyers, and others concerned about pesticide hazards and safety. Issues information to increase public awareness of environmental, public health, and economic problems caused by pesticide abuse; promotes alternatives to pesticide use, such as organic pest management programs.

Croplife America, *4201 Wilson Blvd., #700, Arlington, VA 22203; (202) 296-1585. Christopher (Chris) Novak, President.*
General email, info@croplifeamerica.org
Web, www.croplifeamerica.org, Twitter, @croplifeamerica and Facebook, www.facebook.com/CropLifeAmerica.org

Membership: pesticide manufacturers. Provides information on pesticide safety, development, and use. Monitors legislation and regulations. (Formerly the American Crop Protection Assn.)

Entomological Society of America, *3 Park Pl., #307, Annapolis, MD 21401-3722; (301) 731-4535. Fax, (301) 731-4538. Chris Stelzig, Executive Director, ext. 3012.*
General email, esa@entsoc.org
Web, www.entsoc.org, Twitter, @EntsocAmerica and Facebook, www.facebook.com/entsoc

Advises on crop protection, food chain, and individual and urban health matters dealing with insect pests.

Environmental Working Group, *1250 Eye St. N.W., #100, 20005; (202) 667-6982. Fax, (202) 232-2592. Kenneth A. Cook, President.*
Web, www.ewg.org, Twitter, @ewg and Facebook, www.facebook.com/ewg.org

Research and advocacy organization that studies and reports on the presence of herbicides and pesticides in food and drinking water. Monitors legislation and regulations.

Fertilizer Institute, *4201 Wilson Blvd., #700, Arlington, VA 22203; (202) 962-0490. Fax, (202) 962-0577. Corey Rosenbusch, President, (202) 515-2700.*

General email, info@tfi.org
Web, www.tfi.org, Twitter, @Fertilizer_Inst and Facebook, www.facebook.com/thefertilizerinstitute

Membership: manufacturers, dealers, and distributors of fertilizer, as well as the businesses that support them with goods and services. provides statistical data and other information concerning the effects of fertilizer and its relationship to world food production, food supply, and the environment.

National Agricultural Aviation Assn., *1440 Duke St., Alexandria, VA 22314; (202) 546-5722. Fax, (202) 546-5726. Andrew D. Moore, Chief Executive Officer.*
General email, information@agaviation.org
Web, www.agaviation.org, Twitter, @AgAviationNAAA and Facebook, www.facebook.com/NationalAgricultural AviationAssociation

Membership: agricultural pilots; operating companies that seed, fertilize, and spray land by air; and allied industries. Monitors legislation and regulations. (Affiliated with National Agricultural Aviation Research and Education Foundation.)

National Pest Management Assn., *10460 North St., Fairfax, VA 22030; (703) 352-6762. Fax, (703) 352-3031. Dominique Stumpf, Chief Executive Officer, (571) 224-0376. Toll-free, (800) 678-6722.*
Web, https://npmapestworld.org

Membership: pest control operators. Monitors federal regulations that affect pesticide use; provides members with technical information. Website has a Spanish-language link.

Nutrients for Life Foundation, *4201 Wilson Blvd., #700, Arlington, VA 22203; (800) 962-9065. Harriet Wegmeyer, Executive Director.*
General email, info@nutrientsforlife.org
Web, https://nutrientsforlife.org, Facebook, www.facebook .com/nutrientsforlifefoundation/?ref=ts and Twitter, @Nutrients4Life

Develops and distributes science-based materials to improve plant nutrient literacy, soil health knowledge and promotes fertilizer's role in sustaining a growing population. Utilized by educators across the country.

Horticulture and Gardening

►AGENCIES

National Arboretum *(Agriculture Dept.), 3501 New York Ave. N.E., 20002-1958; (202) 245-4523. Richard T. Olsen, Director, (202) 245-4539.*
Web, www.usna.usda.gov and Twitter, @USDA_ARS

Maintains public display of plants on 446 acres; provides information and makes referrals concerning cultivated plants (exclusive of field crops and fruits); conducts plant breeding and research; maintains herbarium. Effective immediately, the outside grounds of the U.S. National Arboretum (USNA) will be open daily to the public from

8 a.m. to 5 p.m. The National Bonsai & Penjing Museum and Administration Building will continue to be closed to the public. Visitors are still required to follow all posted guidelines designed to maximize the safety and health of all visitors and employees. We will continue to monitor daily visitors and restrict total numbers, as necessary, to ensure everyone's health and safety.

National Arboretum *(Agriculture Dept.)*, *Floral and Nursery Plants Research*, *3501 New York Ave. N.E., #100, 20002; (301) 504-6848. Fax, (301) 504-5096. Margaret Pooler, Research Leader, (301) 504-5218. Web, www.ars.usda.gov/northeast-area/washington-dc/national-arboretum/floral-and-nursery-plants-research and Facebook, www.facebook.com/AgriculturalResearchService*

Supports research and implementation of new technologies in florist and nursery industries. Areas of research include development of new floral, nursery, and turf plants; detection and control of pathogens in ornamental plants; ornamental plant taxonomy; improvement of nursery production systems; and curation of woody landscape plant germplasm as part of the National Plant Germplasm System.

National Arboretum *(Agriculture Dept.)*, *Gardens Research Unit*, *Jamie L. Whitten Bldg., 3501 New York Ave. N.E., 20002; (202) 245-4533. Fax, (202) 245-5973. Scott Aker, Unit Leader, Gardens Unit, (202) 245-4533. Web, www.ars.usda.gov/northeast-area/washington-dc/national-arboretum/gardens-unit and Twitter, @USDA_ARS*

Collects, displays, documents, evaluates, and introduces woody and herbaceous landscape ornamentals; interprets plant collections, display gardens, and Agricultural Research Service and National Arboretum research for the public through signage, exhibits, and programs; and provides educational programs for gardeners and green industry professionals.

Smithsonian Institution, *Botany and Horticulture Library, 10th St. and Constitution Ave. N.W., #W422, 20560-0166 (mailing address: P.O. Box 37012, MS 154, Washington, DC 20013-7012); (202) 633-1685. Robin Everly, Branch Librarian. General email, askalibrarian@si.edu*

Web, https://library.si.edu/libraries/botany, Twitter, @SILibraries and Facebook, www.facebook.com/SmithsonianLibraries and YouTube, www.youtube.com/user/SmithsonianLibraries

Collection includes books, periodicals, and videotapes on horticulture, garden history, and landscape design. Specializes in American gardens and gardening of the late nineteenth and early twentieth centuries. Open to the public by appointment 11:00 a.m.–4:00 p.m. (Housed at the National Museum of Natural History.)

U.S. Botanic Garden, *100 Maryland Ave. S.W., 20001 (mailing address: 245 1st St. S.W., Washington, DC 20024); (202) 225-8333. Saharah Moon Chapotin, Executive Director, (202) 225-1110. Horticulture hotline, (202) 226-4785. Press, (202) 226-4145. Program registration information, (202) 225-1116. Special events, (202) 226-7674. Tour line, (202) 226-2055. General email, usbg@aoc.gov*

Web, www.usbg.gov and Facebook, www.facebook.com/USBotanicGarden

Collects, cultivates, and grows various plants for public display and study; identifies botanic specimens and furnishes information on proper growing methods. Conducts horticultural classes and tours.

▶ **NONGOVERNMENTAL**

American Horticultural Society, *River Farm, 7931 E. Boulevard Dr., Alexandria, VA 22308-1300; (703) 768-5700. Fax, (703) 768-8700. Susan D. Klejst, Vice President of Development. Member Services, ext. 119. General email, webmaster@ahsgardening.org*

Web, http://ahsgardening.org, Twitter, @ahs_gardening and Facebook, www.facebook.com/americanhorticulturalsociety

Promotes the expansion of horticulture in the United States through educational programs for amateur and professional horticulturists. Publishes gardening magazine. Oversees historic house and farm once owned by George Washington, with gardens maintained by staff; house and grounds are rented for special occasions.

American Society for Horticultural Science (ASHS), *1018 Duke St., Alexandria, VA 22314; (703) 836-4606. Michael W. Neff, Executive Director, ext. 106. General email, webmaster@ashs.org*

Web, www.ashs.org, Twitter, @ASHS_Hort and Facebook, www.facebook.com/americansocietyforhorticulturalscience

Membership: educators, government workers, firms, associations, and individuals interested in horticultural science. Promotes scientific research and education in horticulture, including international exchange of information. Publishes the *Journal of the American Society for Horticultural Science.*

AmericanHort, *Washington Office, 525 9th St. N.W., #800, 20004; (202) 789-2900. Fax, (202) 789-1893. Ken Fisher, President, (614) 487-1117. General email, hello@AmericanHort.org*

Web, www.AmericanHort.org and Twitter, @American_Hort

Membership: wholesale growers, garden center retailers, landscape firms, and suppliers to the horticultural community. Monitors legislation and regulations on agricultural, environmental, and small business issues; conducts educational seminars on business management for members. (Headquarters in Columbus, Ohio.)

Society of American Florists, *1001 N. Fairfax St., #201, Alexandria, VA 22314; (703) 836-8700. Fax, (703) 836-8705. Kate Penn, Chief Executive Officer.*

Web, https://safnow.org, Twitter, @SAFdelivers and Facebook, www.facebook.com/SocietyofAmericanFlorists

Membership: growers, wholesalers, and retailers in the floriculture and ornamental horticulture industries. Interests include labor, pesticides, the environment, international trade, and toxicity of plants. Mediates industry problems.

Soil and Watershed Conservation

▶ AGENCIES

Farm Service Agency (FSA) *(Agriculture Dept.),* **Conservation and Environmental Programs (CEPD),** *1400 Independence Ave. S.W., Room 4709-S, MS 0513, 20250-0513; (202) 720-6221. Fax, (202) 720-4619. Vacant, Director (Acting).*
Web, www.fsa.usda.gov

Serves the nations agricultural producers, providing assistance and opportunities for producers to voluntarily invest in safeguarding environmentally sensitive lands, Programs include: biomass crop assistance, conservation reserve, emergency conservations, farmable wetlands, grassland ranch and source water protections,

National Agricultural Library *(Agriculture Dept.),* **Water and Agricultural Information Center (WAIC),** *10301 Baltimore Ave., 1st Floor, Beltsville, MD 20705-2351; (301) 504-6077. Fax, (301) 504-5181. Vacant, Coordinator.*
Web, www.nal.usda.gov/waic
Email, waic@ars.usda.gov

Serves individuals and agencies seeking information on water quality and agriculture. Special subject areas include agricultural environmental management, irrigation, water availability, and water quality.

Natural Resources Conservation Service (NRCS) *(Agriculture Dept.), 1400 Independence Ave. S.W., #6149-S, 20250 (mailing address: P.O. Box 2890, Washington, DC 20013-2890); (202) 720-3210. Terry Cosby, Chief, (202) 720-4613.*
Web, www.nrcs.usda.gov, Twitter, @USDA_NRCS and Facebook, www.facebook.com/USDA

Responsible for soil and water conservation programs, including watershed protection, flood prevention, river basin surveys, resource conservation and development. Provides landowners, operators, state and local units of government, and community groups with technical assistance in carrying out local programs. Inventories and monitors soil, water, and related resource data and resource use trends. Provides information about soil surveys, farmlands, and other natural resources.

▶ NONGOVERNMENTAL

American Farmland Trust (AFT), *1150 Connecticut Ave. N.W., #600, 20036; (202) 331-7300. John Piotti, President, (202) 378-1202. Toll-free, (800) 866-5170.*

General email, info@farmland.org
Web, www.farmland.org, Twitter, @farmland and Facebook, www.facebook.com/AmericanFarmland

Works to protect farmland, promote sound farming practices, and keep farmers on the land through local, regional, and national efforts. Works to help farmers implement practices that protect water quality. Conducts independent analyses of policies that affect farmland and advocates government policies that support farmland conservation and keep farms economically viable.

Irrigation Assn., *8280 Willow Oaks Corporate Dr., #630, Fairfax, VA 22031; (703) 536-7080. Fax, (703) 536-7019. Natasha Rankin, Chief Executive Officer.*
General email, info@irrigation.org
Web, www.irrigation.org and Twitter, @irrigationAssoc

Membership: companies and individuals involved in irrigation, drainage, and erosion control worldwide. Promotes efficient and effective water management through training, education, and certification programs. Interests include economic development and environmental enhancement.

National Assn. of Clean Water Agencies, *1130 Connecticut Ave. N.W., #1050, 20036; (202) 833-2672. Fax, (888) 267-9505. Adam Krantz, Chief Executive Officer, (202) 833-4651.*
General email, info@nacwa.org
Web, www.nacwa.org and Twitter, @NACWA

Represents public wastewater treatment works, public and private organizations, law firms representing public clean water agencies, and nonprofit or academic organizations. Interests include water quality and watershed management. Sponsors conferences. Monitors legislation and regulations.

National Assn. of Conservation Districts (NACD), *509 Capitol Court N.E., 20002-4937; (202) 547-6223. Fax, (202) 547-6450. Jeremy Peters, Chief Executive Officer.*
General email, info@nacdnet.org
Web, www.nacdnet.org, Twitter, @NACDconserve and Facebook, www.facebook.com/NACDconserve

Membership: conservation districts (local subdivisions of state government). Works to promote the conservation of private and public lands, forests, and other natural resources. Interests include erosion and sediment control, water quality, and water and flood plain management.

Winrock International, *Washington Office, 2451 Crystal Dr., #700, Arlington, VA 22202; (703) 302-6500. Fax, (703) 302-6512. Rodney Ferguson, President.*
General email, information@winrock.org
Web, www.winrock.org and Twitter, @WinrockIntl

Addresses international water issues through programs targeting sustainable strategies for use and conservation within communities and watersheds. (Headquarters in Little Rock, Ark.)

COMMODITIES, FARM PRODUCE

General

▶**AGENCIES**

Agricultural Marketing Service (AMS) *(Agriculture Dept.), Fair Trade Practices Program, Country of Origin Labeling (COOL),* 1400 Independence Ave. S.W., #2069-S, MS 0216, 20250-0216; (202) 720-4486. Fax, (202) 260-8369. Michael V. Durando, Deputy Administrator, (202) 720-0219.
General email, cool@ams.usda.gov
Web, www.ams.usda.gov/rules-regulations/cool

Works with businesses to uphold the origin labeling law, which requires retailers to disclose the source of certain foods- including muscle cut and ground meats: lamb, goat, and chicken; wild and farm-raised fish and shellfish; fresh and frozen fruits and vegetables; peanuts, pecans, and macadamia nuts; and ginseng.

Agricultural Marketing Service (AMS) *(Agriculture Dept.), National Organic Program,* 1400 Independence Ave. S.W., #2642-S, MS 0268, 20250; (202) 720-3252. Fax, (202) 260-9151. Jennifer Tucker, Deputy Administrator.
General email, NOP.Guidance@usda.gov
Web, www.ams.usda.gov/about-ams/programs-offices/national-organic-program

Develops national standards and regulations for organically produced agricultural products; accredits certifying agents to certify organic producers and handlers; establishes international organic import and export policies; investigates regulatory violation complaints.

Agricultural Marketing Service (AMS) *(Agriculture Dept.), Transportation and Marketing Program,* 1400 Independence Ave. S.W., #4543, 20250-0264; (202) 690-1300. Tricia Kovacs, Deputy Administrator (Acting).
Web, www.ams.usda.gov/about-ams/programs-offices/transportation-marketing-program

Promotes efficient, cost-effective marketing and transportation for U.S. agricultural products; sets standards for domestic and international marketing of organic products. Provides exporters with market information, educational services, and regulatory representation. Also promotes grant programs benefiting agricultural systems in collaboration with states, municipalities, tribal governments, universities, and agricultural businesses.

Agriculture Dept. (USDA), *Under Secretary for Marketing and Regulatory Programs,* 1400 Independence Ave. S.W., #228W, 20250-0109; (202) 720-4256. Fax, (202) 720-5775. Mae Wu, Deputy Under Secretary.
Web, www.usda.gov/our-agency/about-usda/mission-areas

Administers inspection and grading services and regulatory programs for agricultural commodities through the Agricultural Marketing Service and Animal and Plant Health Inspection Service.

Agriculture Dept. (USDA), *Under Secretary for Trade and Foreign Agricultural Affairs (TFAA),* 1400 Independence Ave. S.W., MS 1001, 20250; (202) 720-3111. Vacant, Under Secretary.
Web, www.fas.usda.gov and Twitter, @USDAForeignAg

Leads on trade policy and international agriculture issues domestically and abroad; facilitates foreign market access and promotes opportunities for U.S. agriculture through trade programs and high-level government negotiations. Oversees the Foreign Agricultural Service and coordinates U.S. participation in the Codex Alimentarius Commission.

Animal and Plant Health Inspection Service (APHIS) *(Agriculture Dept.),* 4700 River Rd., Riverdale, MD 20737; (202) 799-7000. Fax, (202) 720-3982. Kevin A. Shea, Administrator, (202) 799-7017. Animal Import and Export, (301) 851-3300. Customer service, (844) 820-2234. Plants and Plant Products, (877) 770-5990. Press, (202) 799-7030.
General email, customerservicecallcenter@aphis.usda.gov
Web, www.aphis.usda.gov and Twitter, @USDA_APHIS

Administers programs in cooperation with the states to prevent the spread of pests and plant diseases; inspects imported animals, flowers, and plants; licenses the manufacture and marketing of veterinary biologics to ensure purity and effectiveness; certifies that U.S. exports are free of pests and disease.

Bureau of Economic and Business Affairs (EB) *(State Dept.), Trade Policy and Negotiations (TPN), Agriculture Policy (AGP),* 2201 C St. N.W., #4686, 20520-0002; (202) 647-3090. Fax, (202) 647-1894. Jeffrey Gianque, Director, (202) 647-0133.
Web, www.state.gov/agricultural-policy

Negotiates bilateral textile trade agreements with foreign governments concerning cotton, wool, and synthetic textile and apparel products.

Commodity Futures Trading Commission, Three Lafayette Centre, 1155 21st St. N.W., 20581-0001; (202) 418-5000. Fax, (202) 418-5521. Heath P. Tarbert, Chair, (202) 418-5030; Anthony C. Thompson, Executive Director, (202) 418-5697; Ann Wright, Director of Legislative and Government Affairs (Acting). Toll-free, (866) 366-2382. TTY, (202) 418-5428.
General email, questions@cftc.gov
Web, www.cftc.gov, Twitter, @CFTC and Facebook, www.facebook.com/cftcgov

Oversees the Commodity Exchange Act, which regulates all commodity futures and options, including agricultural commodities, such as wheat, corn, and cotton, to prevent fraudulent trade practices.

Farm Service Agency (FSA) *(Agriculture Dept.),* 1400 Independence Ave. S.W., #3086, MS 0506, 20250-0506; (202) 720-3467. Fax, (202) 720-9105. Zach Ducheneaux, Administrator. Press, (202) 720-7807.
Web, www.fsa.usda.gov and Twitter, @usdafsa

Administers farm commodity programs providing crop loans and purchases; provides crop payments when market prices fall below specified levels; sets acreage allotments and marketing quotas; assists farmers in areas affected by natural disasters.

Farm Service Agency (FSA) *(Agriculture Dept.)*, **Commodity Credit Corp. (CCC)**, *1400 Independence Ave. S.W., MS 0599, 20250-0571; (202) 720-0402. Fax, (202) 245-4786. Robert Stephenson, Executive Vice President.* General email, askusda@usda.gov

Web, www.usda.gov/ccc

Finances commodity stabilization programs, domestic and export surplus commodity disposal, foreign assistance, storage activities, and related programs.

Foreign Agricultural Service (FAS) *(Agriculture Dept.)*, *1400 Independence Ave. S.W., #5071S, MS 1001, 20250-1001; (202) 720-3935. Fax, (202) 690-2159. Daniel Whitley, Administrator (Acting). Public Affairs, (202) 720-7115. TTY, (202) 720-1786.* Web, www.fas.usda.gov, Twitter, @USDAForeignAg

Press, press-fas@usda.gov

Promotes exports of U.S. food and agricultural products; represents U.S. agricultural interests in international trade negotiations. Coordinates activities of U.S. representatives in foreign countries who report on crop and market conditions. Provides programs and services that assist U.S. agricultural exporters with promoting their products overseas. Analyzes world demand and production of various commodities. Monitors sales by private exporters.

Foreign Agricultural Service (FAS) *(Agriculture Dept.)*, **Trade Policy and Geographic Affairs**, *1400 Independence Ave. S.W., MS 1020, 20250-1020; (202) 720-9516. Fax, (202) 401-0135. Jeanne Bailey, Deputy Administrator.* Web, www.fas.usda.gov/trade-programs

Press, press-fas@usda.gov

Administers programs and provides services that help U.S. exporters develop and maintain international markets for U.S. farm and food products. Provides credit guarantees to encourage financing of commercial exports of U.S. agricultural products.

▶ **CONGRESS**

For a listing of relevant congressional committees and subcommittees, please see page 3 or the Appendix.

▶ **NONGOVERNMENTAL**

Commodity Markets Council (CMC), *600 Pennsylvania Ave. S.E., #300, 20003; (202) 842-0400. James E. Newsome, President.* Web, www.commoditymkts.org

Federation of commodity futures exchanges, boards of trade, and industry stakeholders, including commodity merchandisers, processors, and refiners; futures commission merchants; food and beverage manufacturers; transportation companies; and financial institutions. Combines members' expertise to formulate positions on market, policy, and contracting issues involving commodities, with an overall goal of facilitating growth in liquidity and transparency in cash and derivative markets. Monitors legislation and regulations. (Formerly the National Grain Trade Council.)

Global Cold Chain Alliance, *241 S. 18th St., #620, Arlington, VA 22202; (703) 373-4300. Fax, (703) 373-4301. Matthew Ott, President, ext. 213.* General email, email@gcca.org

Web, www.gcca.org, Twitter, @gccaorg and Facebook, www.facebook.xom/globalcoldchainalliance

Membership: owners and operators of public refrigerated warehouses. Interests include labor, transportation, taxes, environment, safety, regulatory compliance, and food distribution. Monitors legislation and regulations. (Affiliated with the International Refrigerated Transportation Assn., the International Assn. for Cold Storage Construction, and the International Assn. of Refrigerated Warehouses.)

National Cooperative Business Assn., CLUSA International (NCBA CLUSA), *1775 Eye St. N.W., 8th Floor, 20006; (240) 638-6222. Douglas O'Brien, President.* General email, info@ncba.coop

Web, www.ncbaclusa.coop, Twitter, @NCBACLUSAcoop and Facebook, www.facebook.com/NCBACLUSA and YouTube, www.youtube.com/channel/UC1d9CsZOwqwQJid4uEscEUg

Alliance of cooperatives, businesses, and state cooperative associations. Provides information about starting and managing agricultural cooperatives in the United States and in developing nations. Monitors legislation and regulations.

National Council of Farmer Cooperatives (NCFC), *50 F St. N.W., #900, 20001-1530; (202) 626-8700. Fax, (202) 626-8722. Charles (Chuck) F. Conner, President.* General email, info@ncfc.org

Web, www.ncfc.org, Twitter, @FarmerCoop and Facebook, www.facebook.com/FarmerCoop

Membership: cooperative businesses owned and operated by farmers. Encourages research on agricultural cooperatives; provides statistics and analyzes trends. Monitors legislation and regulations on agricultural trade, transportation, energy, and tax issues.

Organic Trade Assn., *444 N. Capitol St. N.W., #445A, 20001; (202) 403-8520. (202) 403-8630. Laura Batcha, Executive Director, (202) 403-8512.* General email, info@ota.com

Web, www.ota.com, Twitter, @OrganicTrade and Facebook, www.facebook.com/OrganicTrade

Membership: growers, shippers, processors, certifiers, farmers' associations, distributors, importers, exporters, consultants, and retailers of organic foods, beverages, ingredients, and fibers. Promotes organic farming processes. Monitors legislation and regulations.

U.S. Agricultural Export Development Council, *2111 Wilson Blvd., #700, Arlington, VA 22201; (703) 556-9290. Loretta Alfaro, Executive Director; Anita Regmi, Specialist in Agricultural Poliicy.*
General email, lalfaro@usaedc.org
Web, http://usaedc.org

Membership: agricultural growers and processors, commodity trade associations, farmer cooperatives, and state regional trade groups. Works with the Foreign Agricultural Service on projects to create, expand, and maintain agricultural markets abroad. Sponsors seminars and workshops.

Cotton

▶ **INTERNATIONAL ORGANIZATIONS**

International Cotton Advisory Committee, *1629 K St. N.W., #702, 20006-1635; (202) 463-6660. Kai Hughes, Executive Director, ext. 116.*
General email, secretariat@icac.org
Web, https://icac.org

Membership: cotton producing and consuming countries. Provides information on cotton production, trade, consumption, stocks, and prices.

▶ **NONGOVERNMENTAL**

Cotton Council International, *1521 New Hampshire Ave. N.W., 20036-1203; (202) 745-7805. Fax, (202) 483-4040. Bruce Atherley, Executive Director.*
General email, cottonusa@cotton.org
Web, www.cottonusa.org and Facebook, www.facebook .com/cottonusa.global and YouTube, https://www.youtube .com/user/cottonusaglobal

Division of National Cotton Council of America. Promotes U.S. raw cotton and cotton-product exports.

Cotton Warehouse Assn. of America, *316 Pennsylvania Ave. S.E., #401, 20003; (202) 544-5875. Fax, (202) 544-5874. Brett Underwood, President.*
Web, http://cottonwarehouse.org

Membership: Independent, gin, merchant, and transit cotton warehouse operators. Serves as a liaison between members and government agencies; monitors legislation and regulations.

National Cotton Council of America, *Washington Office, 1521 New Hampshire Ave. N.W., 20036-1205; (202) 745-7805. Fax, (202) 483-4040. Reece Langley, Vice President of Washington Operations.*
Web, www.cotton.org, Twitter, @NCottonCouncil and Facebook, www.facebook.com/NationalCottonCouncil

Membership: all segments of the U.S. cotton industry. Provides statistics and information on such topics as cotton history and processing. (Headquarters in Memphis, Tenn.)

Dairy Products and Eggs

▶ **AGENCIES**

Agricultural Marketing Service (AMS) *(Agriculture Dept.), Dairy Program, 1400 Independence Ave. S.W., #2968, MS 0225, 20250-0225; (202) 720-4392. Fax, (202) 690-3410. Dana Coale, Deputy Administrator.*
General email, AskDairy@usda.gov
Web, www.ams.usda.gov/about-ams/programs-offices/ dairy-program and Twitter, @USDA_AMS

Administers dairy product marketing, research, and promotion programs; grades dairy products; maintains a market news service on daily price changes; sets minimum price that farmers receive for milk. Provides export certification. Administers Federal Milk Marketing Orders and provide aggregated Federal Order Statistics.

Agricultural Marketing Service (AMS) *(Agriculture Dept.), Livestock and Poultry Program, 1400 Independence Ave. S.W., MS 0249, 20250-0249; Jennifer Porter, Deputy Administrator, (202) 720-5705. Press, (202) 720-8998.*
General email, AskLP@usda.gov
Web, www.ams.usda.gov/about-ams/programs-offices/ livestock-poultry-program

Sets poultry and egg grading standards. Provides promotion and market news services for domestic and international markets.

Farm Service Agency (FSA) *(Agriculture Dept.), Dairy and Sweeteners Analysis, 1400 Independence Ave. S.W., #3752, MS 0516, 20250-0516; Fax, (202) 690-1480. Barbara Fecso, Branch Chief, (202) 720-4146.*
Web, www.fsa.usda.gov/programs-and-services/economic- and-policy-analysis/dairy-and-sweeteners-analysis

Primary analytical resource for formulating, developing, analyzing, and evaluating national program policies, determinations and program alternatives for dairy, livestock, and sugar (sugarcane, sugar beets, crystalline fructose, and honey), including detailed summaries of impacts on supply, demand, price, income, and CCC outlays.

▶ **NONGOVERNMENTAL**

American Butter Institute (ABI), *2107 Wilson Blvd., #600, Arlington, VA 22201-3062; (703) 243-5630. Tom Balmer, Executive Director, ext. 346.*
General email, info@nmpf.org
Web, www.butterinstitute.org and Twitter, @butterinstitute

Membership: butter manufacturers, processors, marketers, and distributors. Interests include dairy price supports and programs, packaging and labeling, and imports. Monitors legislation and regulations.

Humane Farm Animal Care, *P.O. Box 82, Middleburg, VA 20118; (703) 435-3883. Fax, (703) 435-3981. Adele Douglass Jolley, Chief Executive Officer; Mimi Stein, Executive Director.*

General email, info@certifiedhumane.org

Web, www.certifiedhumane.org,
Twitter, @CertifiedHumane and Facebook, www.facebook
.com/CertifiedHumane

Seeks to improve the welfare of farm animals by providing viable, duly monitored standards for humane food production. Administers the Certified Humane Raised and Handled program for meat, poultry, eggs, and dairy products.

International Dairy Foods Assn., *1250 H St. N.W., #900, 20005-3952; (202) 737-4332. Fax, (202) 331-7820. Michael Dykes, President.*
General email, membership@idfa.org

Web, www.idfa.org and Twitter, @dairyidfa

Membership: processors, manufacturers, marketers, and distributors of dairy foods in the United States and abroad. Provides members with marketing, public relations, training, and management services. Monitors legislation and regulations. (Affiliated with the Milk Industry Foundation, the National Cheese Institute, and the International Ice Cream Assn.)

National Ice Cream Mix Assn., *2107 Wilson Blvd., #600, Arlington, VA 22201; (703) 243-5630. Fax, (703) 841-9328. Tom Balmer, Executive Director.*
Web, www.icecreammix.org

Nonprofit representing the manufacturing industry of ice cream mix, soft serve frozen dessert mix, and shake mix.

National Milk Producers Federation, *2107 Wilson Blvd., #600, Arlington, VA 22201-3062; (703) 243-6111. Fax, (703) 841-9328. Jim Mulhern, Chief Executive Officer.*
General email, info@nmpf.org

Web, www.nmpf.org

Membership: dairy farmer cooperatives. Provides information on development and modification of sanitary regulations, product standards, and marketing procedures for dairy products.

Fruits and Vegetables

▶ AGENCIES

Agricultural Marketing Service (AMS) *(Agriculture Dept.), Fair Trade Practices Program, Perishable Agricultural Commodities Act (PACA), 1400 Independence Ave. S.W., #1510-S, MS 0242, 20250-0242; (202) 720-4180. Fax, (202) 690-4413. Judith W. Rudman, Director. Toll-free, (877) 622-4716.*
Web, www.ams.usda.gov/rules-regulations/paca

Disputes, PACAdispute@usda.gov

Investigations, PACAInvestigations@usda.gov

License, PACALicense@usda.gov

Partners with fresh and frozen fruit and vegetable businesses to enforce fair business practices and resolve disputes involving inspection certificates, contracts, and bankruptcy payments.

Agricultural Marketing Service (AMS) *(Agriculture Dept.), Specialty Crops Program, 1400 Independence Ave. S.W., #1575-S, MS 0235, 20250-0235; (202) 720-4722. Fax, (202) 720-0016. Sonia Jimenez, Deputy Administrator.*
Web, www.ams.usda.gov/about-ams/programs-offices/specialty-crops-program

Administers research, marketing, promotional, and regulatory programs for fruits, vegetables, nuts, ornamental plants, and other specialty crops; focus includes international markets. Sets grading standards for fresh and processed fruits and vegetables; conducts quality inspections; maintains market news service to inform producers of price changes. Partner with State agencies and other industry organizations for the benefit of nationwide growers, shippers, brokers, receivers, processors, retailers and restaurants, direct to consumer sales, and the foodservice industry.

Economic Research Service (ERS) *(Agriculture Dept.), 355 E St. S.W., 20024-3221 (mailing address: 1400 Independence Ave. S.W., MS 1800, Washington, DC 20250-0002); (202) 694-5000. Fax, (202) 245-5467. Spiro Stefanou, Administrator. Public Affairs, (202) 694-5139.*
General email, service@ers.usda.gov

Web, www.ers.usda.gov and Twitter, @USDA_ERS

Conducts market research; studies and forecasts domestic supply-and-demand trends for fruits and vegetables.

▶ NONGOVERNMENTAL

International Fresh Produce Assn., *1901 Pennsylvania Ave. N.W., #1100, 20006; (202) 303-3400. Cathy Burns, President.*
Web, www.freshproduce.com, Twitter, @IntFreshProduce and Facebook, www.facebook.com/InternationalFreshProduceAssociation

Membership: growers, shippers, wholesalers, retailers, food service operators, importers, and exporters involved in producing and marketing fresh fruits and vegetables. Represents the industry before the government and the public sector.

U.S. Apple Assn., *7600 Leesburg Pike, #400 East, Falls Church, VA 22043; (703) 442-8850. James (Jim) Bair, President.*
General email, info@usapple.org

Web, http://usapple.org, Twitter, @usapples and Facebook, www.facebook.com/USApples

Membership: U.S. commercial apple growers and processors, distributors, exporters, importers, and retailers of apples. Promotes nutrition research and marketing; provides information about apples and nutrition to educators. Monitors legislation and regulations.

Wine Institute, *Federal and International Public Policy, 601 13th St. N.W., #330 South, 20005-3866; (202) 408-0870. Fax, (202) 371-0061. Charles Jefferson, Vice President.*

Web, www.wineinstitute.org and
Twitter, @CalifWines_US

Membership: California wineries and affiliated businesses. Seeks international recognition for California wines; conducts promotional campaigns in other countries. Monitors legislation and regulations. (Headquarters in San Francisco, Calif.)

Grains and Oilseeds

▶AGENCIES

Agricultural Marketing Service (AMS) *(Agriculture Dept.), Federal Grain Inspection Service (FGIS), 1400 Independence Ave. S.W., #3614, 20250-3601; (202) 720-9170. Fax, (202) 690-2333. Arthur Neal, Deputy Administrator.*
General email, fgis.oda@usda.gov
Web, www.ams.usda.gov/about-ams/programs-offices/federal-grain-inspection-service

Administers inspection and weighing program for barley, canola, corn, flaxseed, oats, rye, sorghum, soybeans, sunflower seed, triticale, wheat, mixed grain, rice, and pulses; conducts quality inspections based on established standards; supervises the official grain inspection and weighing system. Provides International Services and Outreach Programs.

Agricultural Marketing Service (AMS) *(Agriculture Dept.), Livestock and Poultry Program, 1400 Independence Ave. S.W., MS 0249, 20250-0249; Jennifer Porter, Deputy Administrator, (202) 720-5705. Press, (202) 720-8998.*
General email, AskLP@usda.gov
Web, www.ams.usda.gov/about-ams/programs-offices/livestock-poultry-program

Administers programs for marketing grain, including rice; maintains market news service to inform producers of grain, feedstuffs, wool, bioenergy and their related products, the market situation and daily price changes.

Farm Service Agency (FSA) *(Agriculture Dept.), Feed Grains and Oilseeds Analysis, 1400 Independence Ave. S.W., #3740S, MS 0532, 20250-0532; (202) 720-2791. Joy Harwood, Director, Economic and Policy Analysis; Vacant, Group Director.*
Web, www.fsa.usda.gov/programs-and-services/economic-and-policy-analysis/feed-grains-and-oilseeds-analysis

Develops, analyzes, and implements domestic farm policy focusing on corn, soybeans, and other feed grains and oilseeds. Develops production adjustment and price support programs to balance supply and demand for these commodities.

Farm Service Agency (FSA) *(Agriculture Dept.), Food Grains Analysis, 1400 Independence Ave. S.W., MS 0518, 20250-0532; (202) 720-2891. Fax, (202) 690-2186. Thomas F. Tice, Director.*
Web, www.fsa.usda.gov/programs-and-services/economic-and-policy-analysis/food-grains-analysis

Develops marketing loan and contract crop programs in support of food grain commodities, including wheat, rice, and pulse crops.

▶NONGOVERNMENTAL

American Feed Industry Assn. (AFIA), *2101 Wilson Blvd., #810, Arlington, VA 22201; (703) 524-0810. Fax, (703) 524-1921. Constance Cullman, Chief Executive Officer.*
General email, afia@afia.org
Web, www.afia.org, Twitter, @FeedFolks and Facebook, www.facebook.com/AmericanFeedIndustry Association

Membership: feed manufacturers, including commercial and integrated feed and pet food manufacturers, ingredient suppliers, equipment manufacturers, ingredient suppliers and integrators, and pharmaceutical companies. Conducts seminars on feed grain production, marketing, advertising, and quality control; interests include international trade. Monitors legislation and regulations.

American Seed Trade Assn. (ASTA), *1701 Duke St., #275, Alexandria, VA 22314-2878; (703) 837-8140. Fax, (703) 837-9365. Andrew (Andy) W. LaVigne, President. Toll-free, (888) 890-7333.*
General email, info@betterseed.org
Web, www.betterseed.org, Twitter, @Better_Seed and Facebook, www.facebook.com/BetterSeedBetterLife

Membership: producers and merchandisers of seeds. Conducts seminars on research developments in corn, sorghum, soybean, and other farm and garden seeds; promotes overseas seed market development.

American Soybean Assn., Washington Office, *600 Pennsylvania Ave. S.E., #320, 20003-6300; (202) 969-7040. Steve Censky, Chief Executive Officer; Christy Seyfert, Director, in Washington, DC. Toll-free, (800) 688-7692.*
General email, info@soy.org
Web, https://soygrowers.com and Twitter, @ASA_Soybeans

Membership: soybean farmers. Promotes expanded world markets and research for the benefit of soybean growers; maintains a network of state and international offices. Monitors legislation and regulations. (Headquarters in St. Louis, Mo.)

Bakery, Confectionery, Tobacco Workers, and Grain Millers International Union (BCTGM), *10401 Connecticut Ave., 4th Floor, Kensington, MD 20895-3940; (301) 933-8600. Fax, (301) 946-8452. Anthony Shelton, President.*
General email, bctgmwebmaster@gmail.com
Web, www.bctgm.org, Twitter, @BCTGM and Facebook, www.facebook.com/BCTGM

Membership: approximately 120,000 workers from the bakery, confectionery, grain miller, and tobacco industries in both the USA and Canada. Helps members negotiate pay, benefits, and better working conditions; conducts training programs and workshops. Monitors legislation and regulations. (Affiliated with the AFL-CIO.)

Corn Refiners Assn., *1701 Pennsylvania Ave. N.W., #400, 20006-5805; (202) 331-1634. Fax, (202) 331-2054. John Bode, Chief Executive Officer.*
General email, comments@corn.org

Web, https://corn.org, Twitter, @CornRefiners and Facebook, www.facebook.com/CornRefiners

Promotes research on technical aspects of corn refining and product development; acts as a clearinghouse for members who award research grants to colleges and universities. Monitors legislation and regulations.

National Assn. of Wheat Growers, *25 Massachusetts Ave. N.W., #500B, 20001; (202) 547-7800. Chandler Goule, Chief Executive Officer.*
General email, wheatworld@wheatworld.org

Web, www.wheatworld.org and Twitter, @wheatworld

Federation of state wheat grower associations. Involved with federal farm policy, environmental issues, and the use of biotechnology. Monitors legislation and regulations.

National Corn Growers Assn., *Public Policy, 20 F St. N.W., #900, 20001; (202) 628-7001. Fax, (202) 628-1933. Agus R. Kelly, Director of Public Policy.*
General email, corninfo@ncga.com

Web, www.ncga.com, Twitter, @NationalCorn and Facebook, www.facebook.com/corngrowers

Represents the interests of U.S. corn farmers, including in international trade; promotes the use, marketing, and efficient production of corn; conducts research and educational activities; monitors legislation and regulations. (Headquarters in St. Louis, Mo.)

National Grain and Feed Assn., *1400 Crystal Dr., #260, Arlington, VA 22202; (202) 289-0873. Mike (Randy) Seyfert, President.*
General email, ngfa@ngfa.org

Web, www.ngfa.org, Twitter, @NGFA and Facebook, www.facebook.com/nationalgrainandfeedassociation

Membership: firms that process, handle, and use U.S. grains and oilseeds in domestic and export markets; commodity futures brokers; and others involved with futures markets. Additional panel resolves disputes over trade and commercial regulations.

National Institute of Oilseed Products, *529 14th St. N.W., 20045 (mailing address: P.O. Box 11035 Columbia, SC 29211); (202) 591-2461. Fax, (803) 252-7128. Leigh Wickersham, Executive Director; John C. Dillard, Legal Counsel, Washington Office.*
General email, info@niop.org

Web, www.niop.org

Membership: companies and individuals involved in manufacturing and trading oilseed products. Maintains standards for trading and transport of vegetable oils and oilseeds worldwide. (Headquarters in Columbia, S.C.)

National Oilseed Processors Assn., *1310 L St. N.W., #375, 20005; (202) 842-0463. Fax, (202) 842-9126. Thomas A. Hammer, President.*

General email, jseibert@nopa.org

Web, www.nopa.org

Provides information on oilseed crops, products, processing, and commodity programs; interests include international trade.

North American Export Grain and Oilseed Assn. (NAEGA), *1400 Crystal Dr., #260, Arlington, VA 22202; (202) 682-4030. Fax, (202) 682-4033. Gary C. Martin, President.*
General email, info@naega.org

Web, www.naega.org and Twitter, @GrainExport

Membership: grain and oilseed exporting firms, cooperatives, and others interested in the grain export industry. Provides information on grain export and contracting; sponsors foreign seminars. Monitors domestic and international legislation and regulations.

North American Millers' Assn., *1400 Crystal Dr., #650, Arlington, VA 22202; (202) 484-2200. Jane DeMarchi, President, (202) 484-2209.*
General email, generalinfo@namamillers.org

Web, www.namamillers.org, Twitter, @NAMAmillers and Facebook, www.facebook.com/NAMAmillers

Membership: policymakers, regulators, supply chain partners and consumers. Trade association representing the dry corn, wheat, oats, and rye milling industry. Seeks to inform the public, the industry, and government about issues affecting the domestic milling industry, in 31 states, Puerto Rico and Canada. Monitors legislation and regulations.

U.S. Grains Council, *20 F St. N.W., #900, 20001; (202) 789-0789. Fax, (202) 898-0522. Ryan LeGrand, President; Chad Willis, Chairman.*
General email, grains@grains.org

Web, www.grains.org, Twitter, @USGC and Facebook, www.facebook.com/usgrainscouncil and YouTube, www.youtube.com/USGrainsCouncil

Membership: barley, corn, DDGS, ethanol, and sorghum producers and exporters; and chemical, machinery, malting, and seed companies interested in feed grain exports. Promotes development of U.S. feed grain markets overseas.

U.S. Wheat Associates, *3103 N. 10th St., #300, Arlington, VA 22201; (202) 463-0999. Fax, (703) 524-4399. Vince Peterson, President, (703) 650-0250.*
General email, infoARL@uswheat.org

Web, www.uswheat.org, Twitter, @uswheatassoc and Facebook, www.facebook.com/uswheat

Membership: wheat farmers. Develops export markets for the U.S. wheat industry; provides information on wheat production and marketing. Interests include trade policy, food aid, and biotechnology.

USA Rice Federation, *2101 Wilson Blvd., #610, Arlington, VA 22201; (703) 236-2300. Fax, (703) 236-2301. Betsy Ward, Chief Executive Officer. Toll-free, (800) 888-7423. TTY, (703) 236-2310.*

General email, riceinfo@usarice.com

Web, www.usarice.com, Twitter, @usaricenews and *Facebook, www.facebook.com/usarice*

Membership: rice producers, millers, merchants, and related firms. Provides U.S. and foreign rice trade and industry information; assists in establishing quality standards for rice production and milling. Monitors legislation and regulations.

Sugar

▶ AGENCIES

Economic Research Service (ERS) *(Agriculture Dept.),* *355 E St. S.W., 20024-3221 (mailing address: 1400 Independence Ave. S.W., MS 1800, Washington, DC 20250-0002); (202) 694-5000. Fax, (202) 245-5467. Spiro Stefanou, Administrator. Public Affairs, (202) 694-5139.* *General email, service@ers.usda.gov*

Web, www.ers.usda.gov and *Twitter, @USDA_ERS*

Conducts market research; studies and forecasts domestic supply-and-demand trends for sugar and other sweeteners.

Farm Service Agency (FSA) *(Agriculture Dept.), Dairy and Sweeteners Analysis, 1400 Independence Ave. S.W., #3752, MS 0516, 20250-0516; Fax, (202) 690-1480. Barbara Fecso, Branch Chief, (202) 720-4146.* *Web, www.fsa.usda.gov/programs-and-services/economic-and-policy-analysis/dairy-and-sweeteners-analysis*

Primary analytical resource for formulating, developing, analyzing, and evaluating national program policies, determinations and program alternatives for dairy, livestock, and sugar (sugarcane, sugar beets, crystalline fructose, and honey), including detailed summaries of impacts on supply, demand, price, income, and CCC outlays.

▶ NONGOVERNMENTAL

American Sugar Alliance, *2111 Wilson Blvd., #700, Arlington, VA 22201-3051; (703) 351-5055. Fax, (703) 351-6698. Vickie R. Myers, Executive Director.* *General email, info@sugaralliance.org*

Web, www.sugaralliance.org and *Twitter, @SugarAlliance*

National coalition of sugarcane and sugarbeet farmers, processors, refiners, suppliers, workers, and others dedicated to preserving a strong domestic sweetener industry. Monitors legislation and regulations.

American Sugarbeet Growers Assn., *1155 15th St. N.W., #1100, 20005-1756; (202) 833-2398. Fax, (240) 235-4291. Luther Markwart, Executive Vice President.* *General email, info@americansugarbeet.org*

Web, www.americansugarbeet.org

Membership: sugarbeet growers associations. Serves as liaison to U.S. government agencies, including the Agriculture Dept. and the U.S. Trade Representative; interests include international trade. Monitors legislation and regulations.

Bakery, Confectionery, Tobacco Workers, and Grain Millers International Union (BCTGM), *10401 Connecticut Ave., 4th Floor, Kensington, MD 20895-3940; (301) 933-8600. Fax, (301) 946-8452. Anthony Shelton, President.* *General email, bctgmwebmaster@gmail.com*

Web, www.bctgm.org, Twitter, @BCTGM and *Facebook, www.facebook.com/BCTGM*

Membership: approximately 120,000 workers from the bakery, confectionery, grain miller, and tobacco industries in both the United States and Canada. Helps members negotiate pay, benefits, and better working conditions; conducts training programs and workshops. Monitors legislation and regulations. (Affiliated with the AFL-CIO.)

National Confectioners Assn., *1101 30th St. N.W., #200, 20007; (202) 534-1440. John H. Downs Jr., President.* *General email, info@candyusa.com*

Web, www.candyusa.com, Twitter, @CandyUSA and *Facebook, www.facebook.com/NationalConfectioners Association*

Membership: confectionery manufacturers and suppliers. Provides information on confectionery consumption and nutrition; sponsors educational programs and research on candy technology. Monitors legislation and regulations.

Sugar Assn., *1310 L St. N.W., #400, 20005-4263; (202) 785-1122. Fax, (202) 785-5019. Courtney Gaine, President.* *General email, sugar@sugar.org*

Web, www.sugar.org, Twitter, @MoreToSugar and *Facebook, www.facebook.com/MoreToSugar* and *YouTube, www.youtube.com/channel/UCF2n7ELjTxlN libbzb9VDoQ*

Membership: sugar processors, growers, refiners, and planters. Provides nutritional information, public education, and research on sugar.

U.S. Beet Sugar Assn., *50 F St. N.W., #675, 20001; (202) 296-4820. Fax, (202) 331-2065. Cassie Bladow, President; Carrie Vicenta Meadows, Vice President of Government Affairs.* *General email, USbeet@beetsugar.org*

Web, www.beetsugar.org

Membership: beet sugar processors. Monitors legislation and regulations.

Tobacco and Peanuts

▶ AGENCIES

Economic Research Service (ERS) *(Agriculture Dept.),* *355 E St. S.W., 20024-3221 (mailing address: 1400 Independence Ave. S.W., MS 1800, Washington, DC 20250-0002); (202) 694-5000. Fax, (202) 245-5467. Spiro Stefanou, Administrator. Public Affairs, (202) 694-5139.* *General email, service@ers.usda.gov*

Web, www.ers.usda.gov and *Twitter, @USDA_ERS*

Conducts market research; studies and forecasts domestic supply-and-demand trends for tobacco.

American Peanut Council, *1500 King St., #301, Alexandria, VA 22314-2737; (703) 838-9500. Fax, (703) 838-9508. Richard Owen, President, ext. 106.*
General email, info@peanutsusa.com

Web, www.peanutsusa.com, Twitter, @pnutsusa and Facebook, www.facebook.com/peanutsusa

Membership: peanut growers, shellers, brokers, and manufacturers, as well as allied domestic and international companies. Provides information on economic and nutritional value of peanuts; coordinates research; promotes U.S. peanut exports, domestic production, and market development.

Bakery, Confectionery, Tobacco Workers, and Grain Millers International Union (BCTGM), *10401 Connecticut Ave., 4th Floor, Kensington, MD 20895-3940; (301) 933-8600. Fax, (301) 946-8452. Anthony Shelton, President.*
General email, bctgmwebmaster@gmail.com

Web, www.bctgm.org, Twitter, @BCTGM and Facebook, www.facebook.com/BCTGM

Membership: approximately 120,000 workers from the bakery, confectionery, grain miller, and tobacco industries in both the United States and Canada. Helps members negotiate pay, benefits, and better working conditions; conducts training programs and workshops. Monitors legislation and regulations. (Affiliated with the AFL-CIO.)

Cigar Assn. of America, *1310 G St. N.W., #680, 20005; (202) 223-8204. David M. Ozgo, President.*
General email, dcotter@cigarassociation.org

Web, http://cigarassociation.org, Twitter, @CigarAssoc and Facebook, www.facebook.com/cigarassociation

Membership: growers and suppliers of cigar leaf tobacco; manufacturers, packagers, importers, and distributors of cigars; and suppliers to the cigar industry. Monitors legislation and regulations.

FARM LOANS, INSURANCE, AND SUBSIDIES

General

Agriculture Dept. (USDA), *Rural Development, Civil Rights, 1400 Independence Ave. S.W., #1341-S, MS 0703, 20250-0703; (202) 692-0252. Fax, (844) 496-7792. Sharese C. Paylor, Director, (202) 692-0097. Toll-free, (800) 787-8821.*
General email, ra.rd.mostl.civilrights@usda.gov

Web, www.rd.usda.gov/about-rd/offices/civil-rights

Enforces compliance with laws prohibiting discrimination in credit transactions on the basis of sex, marital status, race, color, religion, age, or disability. Ensures equal opportunity in granting Rural Economic and Community Development housing, farm ownership, and operating loans and a variety of community and business program loans.

Agriculture Dept. (USDA), *Rural Development, Rural Business–Cooperative Service, 1400 Independence Ave. S.W., #5803-S, MS 3201, 20250-3201; (202) 690-4730. Fax, (202) 690-4737. Karama Neal, Administrator (Acting).*
Web, www.rd.usda.gov/about-rd/agencies/rural-business-cooperative-service

Provides financial assistance, including loans, loan guarantees, and grants to individuals, rural businesses, cooperatives, farmers, and ranchers.

Agriculture Dept. (USDA), *Under Secretary for Farm Production and Conservation (FPAC), 1400 Independence Ave. S.W., #227-E, 20250-0501; Gloria Montaño Green, Deputy Under Secretary. Information hotline, (202) 720-2791.*
Web, www.usda.gov/our-agency/about-usda/mission-areas, Twitter, @FarmersGov and Facebook, www.facebook.com/farmersgov

Administers programs to help mitigate the significant risks of farming, using agricultural commodity insurance, farm loans, conservation, crop insurance, emergency assistance, and domestic and international food assistance. Oversees the Farm Service Agency, National Resources Conservation Service, and Risk Management Agency.

Farm Credit Administration, *1501 Farm Credit Dr., McLean, VA 22102-5090; (703) 883-4000. Glen R. Smith, Chief Executive Officer. TTY, (703) 883-4056.*
General email, info-line@fca.gov

Web, www.fca.gov, Twitter, @fcagov and Facebook, www.facebook.com/fcagov

Examines and regulates the cooperative Farm Credit System, which comprises farm credit banks, one agricultural credit bank, agricultural credit associations, and federal land credit associations. Oversees credit programs and related services for farmers, ranchers, producers and harvesters of aquatic products, farm-related service businesses, rural homeowners, agricultural and aquatic cooperatives, and rural utilities.

Farm Credit Administration, *Examination, 1501 Farm Credit Dr., McLean, VA 22102-5090; (703) 883-4265. Mike Duffy, Chief Examiner.*
General email, info-line@fca.gov

Web, www.fca.gov/about/offices/offices.html

Enforces and oversees compliance with the Farm Credit Act. Monitors cooperatively owned member banks' and associations' compliance with laws prohibiting discrimination in credit transactions.

Farm Service Agency (FSA) *(Agriculture Dept.), 1400 Independence Ave. S.W., #3086, MS 0506, 20250-0506; (202) 720-3467. Fax, (202) 720-9105. Zach Ducheneaux, Administrator. Press, (202) 720-7807.*
Web, www.fsa.usda.gov and Twitter, @usdafsa

Oversees farm commodity programs that provide crop loans and purchases. Administers price support programs that provide crop payments when market prices fall below specified levels; conducts programs to help obtain adequate farm and commercial storage and drying equipment for farm products; directs conservation and environmental cost sharing projects and programs to assist farmers during natural disasters and other emergencies.

Farm Service Agency (FSA) *(Agriculture Dept.),* *Commodity Credit Corp. (CCC),* 1400 Independence Ave. S.W., MS 0599, 20250-0571; (202) 720-0402. Fax, (202) 245-4786. Robert Stephenson, Executive Vice President. *General email, askusda@usda.gov*

Web, www.usda.gov/ccc

Administers and finances the commodity stabilization program through loans, purchases, and supplemental payments; sells through domestic and export markets commodities acquired by the government under this program; administers some aspects of foreign food aid through the Food for Peace program; provides storage facilities.

Farm Service Agency (FSA) *(Agriculture Dept.),* *Farm Loan Programs,* 1400 Independence Ave. S.W., #3605-S, MS 0520, 20250-0520; (202) 720-4671. Fax, (202) 690-3573. William (Bill) D. Cobb, Deputy Administrator. *Web, www.fsa.usda.gov/programs-and-services/farm-loan-programs/index*

Provides services and loans to beginning farmers and ranchers and administers emergency farm and ranch loan programs.

Farm Service Agency (FSA) *(Agriculture Dept.),* *Farm Programs,* 1400 Independence Ave. S.W., MS 0510, 20250-0510; (202) 720-3175. Fax, (202) 720-4726. William (Bill) L. Beam, Deputy Administrator. Press, (202) 720-7807. *Web, www.fsa.usda.gov/about-fsa/structure-and-organization/farm-programs/index*

Administers and manages aid programs for farmers and ranchers, including conservation efforts, disaster relief, marketing loans, and safety-net subsidies. Operates through county offices spread throughout the continental United States, Hawaii, and several American territories.

Farm Service Agency (FSA) *(Agriculture Dept.),* *Outreach Program. Minority and Socially Disadvantaged Farmers Assistance,* 1400 Independence Ave. S.W., MS 0503, 20250-0503; (202) 690-1700. Fax, (202) 690-4727. J. Latrice Hill, Director of Outreach. TTY, (202) 720-5132. *General email, oasdfr@osec.usda.gov*

Web, www.fsa.usda.gov

Works with minority and socially disadvantaged farmers who have concerns and questions about loan applications filed with local offices or other Farm Service Agency programs.

Risk Management Agency, *Product Management (Agriculture Dept.),* 1400 Independence Ave. S.W., #6092-S, MS 0801, 20250-0801; (202) 690-2803. Fax, (202) 690-2818. Richard Flournoy, Administrator (Acting).

General email, rma.cco@rma.usda.gov

Web, www.rma.usda.gov and Twitter, @usdaRMA

Operates and manages the Federal Crop Insurance Corp. Provides farmers with insurance against crops lost because of bad weather, insects, disease, and other natural causes.

▶**CONGRESS**

For a listing of relevant congressional committees and subcommittees, please see page 3 or the Appendix.

▶**NONGOVERNMENTAL**

Farm Credit Council, 50 F St. N.W., #900, 20001-1530; (202) 626-8710. Fax, (202) 626-8718. Todd Van Hoose, President, (202) 879-0843; Jeffry W. Shipp, Executive Vice President, Government Affairs, (202) 879-0851. *General email, ask@farmcredit.com*

Web, www.farmcredit.com, Twitter, @thefccouncil and Facebook, www.facebook.com/FarmCredit

Represents the Farm Credit System, a national financial cooperative that makes loans to agricultural producers, rural homebuyers, farmer cooperatives, young, beginning and small farmers, and rural utilities. Finances the export of U.S. agricultural commodities.

Farmer Mac, 1999 K St. N.W., 4th Floor, 20006; (202) 872-7700. Fax, (800) 999-1814. Bradford T. Nordholm, President. Toll-free, (800) 879-3276. *Web, www.farmermac.com, Twitter, @FarmerMacNews and Facebook, www.facebook.com/farmermacnews*

Private corporation chartered by Congress to provide a secondary mortgage market for farm and rural housing loans. Guarantees principal and interest repayment on securities backed by farm and rural housing loans. (Farmer Mac stands for Federal Agricultural Mortgage Corp.)

FOOD AND NUTRITION

General

▶**AGENCIES**

Agricultural Marketing Service (AMS) *(Agriculture Dept.), Science and Technology Program,* 1400 Independence Ave. S.W., MS 0272, 20250-0272 (mailing address: 1400 Independence Ave., South Bldg., Room 2918, Washington, DC 20250); Ruihong Guo, Deputy Administrator, (202) 720-8556. *Web, www.ams.usda.gov/about-ams/programs-offices/science-technology-program*

Provides scientific, certification, and analytical support service to AMS community programs, federal and state agencies, and the private sector food industry; participates in international food safety organizations. Tests commodities traded with specific countries and regions, including butter, honey, eggs, nuts, poultry, and meat; analyzes nutritional value of U.S. military rations.

Agricultural Research Service *(Agriculture Dept.),* Jamie L. Whitten Bldg., 1400 Independence Ave. S.W., #302A, 20250-0300; (202) 720-3656. Fax, (202) 720-5427. Chavonda Jacobs-Young, Administrator.
General email, administrator@usda.gov
Web, www.ars.usda.gov, Twitter, @USDA_ARS and Blog, www.usda.gov/media/blog/tag/ars and Facebook, www.facebook.com/AgriculturalResearchService

Conducts studies on agricultural problems of domestic and international concern through nationwide network of research centers. Studies include research on human nutrition; livestock production and protection; crop production, protection, and processing; postharvest technology; and food distribution and market value.

Agriculture Dept. (USDA), *Under Secretary for Food, Nutrition, and Consumer Services (FNS),* 1400 Independence Ave. S.W., #216E, 20250-0106 (mailing address: Braddock Metro Center II, 1320 Braddock Place, Alexandria, VA 22314); (202) 720-7711. Stacy Dean, Deputy Under Secretary.
Web, www.fns.usda.gov and Twitter, @USDANutrition

Oversees the Food and Nutrition Service. Helps to increase food security and reduce hunger by providing children and low-income people access to food, a healthful diet and nutrition education

Alcohol and Tobacco Tax and Trade Bureau (TTB) *(Treasury Dept.), International Affairs Division,* 1310 G St. N.W., Box 12, 20005; (202) 453-2260. Fax, (202) 453-2970. Karen E. Welch, Director.
General email, iad@ttb.gov
Web, www.ttb.gov/offices/international-affairs-division

Works with the Office of the U.S. Trade Representative and federal executive departments to facilitate the import/export trade in beverage and industrial alcohol. Coordinates briefings and other liaison activities for foreign alcohol and tobacco industry members and foreign government officials.

Alcohol and Tobacco Tax and Trade Bureau (TTB) *(Treasury Dept.), Scientific Services Division (SSD),* 6000 Ammendale Rd., Beltsville, MD 20705-1250; (240) 264-1594. Vacant, Director.
Web, www.ttb.gov/offices/scientific-services-division

Provides technical support to the bureau to aid in revenue collection, consumer protection, unfair and unlawful market activities, minimizing technical trade barriers in international trade of regulated products, and facilitating export of U.S. products. Produces scientific data, maintains state laboratories and a well-trained workforce, and continues in the development of new capabilities. Composed of the Beverage Alcohol Laboratory, the Nonbeverage Alcohol Laboratory, the Compliance Laboratory, and the Tobacco Laboratory.

Center for Nutrition Policy and Promotion (CNPP) *(Agriculture Dept.),* 1320 Braddock Pl., Alexandria, VA 22314; (703) 305-7600. Jackie Haven, Deputy Administrator. USDA National Hunger Hotline, (866) 348-6479. Food and Nutrition, (703) 305-2060.
Web, www.fns.usda.gov/cnpp, Twitter, @USDANutrition and Facebook, www.facebook.com/MyPlate

Defines and coordinates nutrition education policy, promotes food and nutrition guidance, and develops nutrition information materials for consumers, policymakers, and professionals in health, education, industry, and media.

Economic Research Service *(Agriculture Dept.), Food Economics,* 355 E St. S.W., 20024-3221 (mailing address: 1400 Independence Ave. S.W., MS 1800, Washington, DC 20250-0002); (202) 694-5400.
Jayachandran (Jay) Variyam, Director, (816) 929-3024.
Web, www.ers.usda.gov/about-ers/agency-structure/food-economics-division-fed

Conducts economic research and analysis on policy issues related to food safety, food prices, and markets; consumer behavior related to food choices, such as food consumption, diet quality, and nutrition; and food and nutrition assistance programs. Provides data and statistics on food prices, food expenditures, and the food supply chain.

Food and Drug Administration (FDA) *(Health and Human Services Dept.),* White Oak, 10903 New Hampshire Ave., Silver Spring, MD 20993-0002; (888) 463-6332. Fax, (301) 847-3536. Robert M. Califf, Commissioner. Main Library (White Oak in Silver Spring), (301) 796-2039. Press, (301) 796-4540.
Web, www.fda.gov, Twitter, @US_FDA and Facebook, www.facebook.com/FDA
Library email, fdalibrary@fda.hhs.gov

Protects public health by assessing the safety, efficacy, and security of human and veterinary drugs, vaccines, biological products and medical devices. Protects the safety and security of the nation's food supply, cosmetics, diet supplements, and products emitting radiation. Regulates tobacco products. Develops labeling and packaging standards; conducts inspections of manufacturers; issues orders to companies to recall and/or cease selling or producing hazardous products; enforces rulings and recommends action to Justice Dept. when necessary. Libraries open to the public; 24-hour advance appointment required.

Food and Drug Administration (FDA) *(Health and Human Services Dept.), Center for Food Safety and Applied Nutrition (CFSAN),* 5001 Campus Dr., HFS-009, College Park, MD 20740-3835; (240) 402-1600. Fax, (301) 436-2668. Susan T. Mayne, Director. SAFEFOOD Info, (888) 723-3366. TTY, (800) 877-8339.
General email, consumer@fda.gov
Web, www.fda.gov/AboutFDA/CentersOffices/OfficeofFoods/CFSAN and Twitter, @FDAFood

Develops standards of composition and quality of foods (except meat and poultry but including fish); develops safety regulations for food and color additives for foods, cosmetics, and drugs; monitors pesticide residues

Food Safety Resources and Contacts

AGENCIES

Center for Food Safety and Applied Nutrition, Food and Drug Administration (FDA) (Health and Human Services Dept.),
Susan T. Mayne, Director, (888) 723-3366
Office of Food Additive Safety, Dennis M. Keefe, Director, (240) 402-1200
Office of Food Safety, Mark Moorman, Director, (240) 402-1700
Office of Nutrition and Food Labeling, Claudine Kavanaugh, Director, (240) 402-2373

Food Safety and Inspection Service (FSIS), (Agriculture Dept.),
Terri Nintemann, Administrator (Acting), (202) 720-7025

Food Safety Research Information Office, National Agricultural Library, (Agriculture Dept.),
Paul Wester, Director, (301) 504-5248

NOAA Fisheries, National Oceanic and Atmospheric Administration (NOAA),
Paul Doremus, Director (Acting), (301) 427-8000

Office of Ground Water and Drinking Water, Environmental Protection Agency,
Jennifer L. McLain, Director, (202) 564-4029

ORGANIZATIONS

Center for Food Safety,
Andrew Kimbrell, Executive Director, (202) 547-9359
Center for Science in the Public Interest,
Peter Lurie, President, (202) 332-9110 or (866) 293-2774
Food and Water Watch,
Wenonah Hauter, Executive Director, (202) 683-2500
International Food Information Council,
Joseph Clayton, Chief Executive Officer, (202) 296-6540, ext. 701

HOTLINES

FDA Center for Food Safety and Applied Nutrition, (888) SAFEFOOD; (888) 723-3366; www.fda.gov/aboutfda/centersoffices/officeoffoods/cfsan/default.htm
Gateway to Government Food Safety Information, www.foodsafety.gov; www.facebook.com/FoodSafety.gov
Office of Data Integration and Food Protection 24-Hour Emergency Number, (866) 395-9701; www.fsis.usda.gov
Safe Drinking Water Information Hotline, (800) 426-4791; https://water.epa.gov/drink
USDA Meat and Poultry Hotline, (888) 674-6854; Email, mphotline.fsis@usda.gov

---

in foods; conducts food safety and nutrition research; develops analytical methods for measuring food additives, nutrients, pesticides, and chemical and microbiological contaminants; recommends action to Justice Dept.

Food and Drug Administration (FDA) *(Health and Human Services Dept.), Center for Food Safety and Applied Nutrition (CFSAN), Nutrition and Food Labeling (ONFL), CPK-1 Bldg., 5001 Campus Dr., #4C-0965, College Park, MD 20740-3835; (240) 402-2373. Fax, (301) 436-2639. Claudine Kavanaugh, Director. SAFEFOOD Info, (888) 723-3366.*
Web, www.fda.gov/food/food-labeling-nutrition

Scientific and technical component of the Center for Food Safety and Applied Nutrition. Conducts research on nutrients; develops policies, regulations and labeling requirements related to conventional foods and medical foods, as well as infant formulas.

Food and Drug Administration (FDA) *(Health and Human Services Dept.), Regulatory Affairs (ORA), White Oak Bldg. 31, 10903 New Hampshire Ave., #3528, Silver Spring, MD 20993; (301) 796-8800. Fax, (301) 847-7942. Judith A. McMeekin, Associate Commissioner. Web, www.fda.gov/aboutfda/centersoffices/officeofglobalregulatoryoperationsandpolicy/ora and Twitter, @FDA_ORA*

Directs and coordinates the FDA's compliance activities; manages field offices; advises FDA commissioner on domestic and international regulatory policies.

Food and Nutrition Service *(Agriculture Dept.), Braddock Metro Center II, 1320 Braddock Pl., Alexandria, VA 22314; (202) 305-2962. Fax, (703) 305-2908. Cindy Long, Administrator, (703) 305-2060. Snap Toll-Free, (800) 221-5689. Web, www.fns.usda.gov and Twitter, @USDANutrition*

Administers all Agriculture Dept. domestic food assistance, including the distribution of funds and food for school breakfast and lunch programs (preschool through secondary) to public and nonprofit private schools; the Supplemental Nutrition Assistance Program (SNAP, formerly the food stamp program); and a supplemental nutrition program for women, infants, and children (WIC).

Food and Nutrition Service *(Agriculture Dept.), Child Nutrition, 3101 Park Center Dr., #640, Alexandria, VA 22302-1500; (703) 305-2054. Sarah Smith-Holmes, Division Director. Press, (202) 720-4623. General email, cndinternet@fns.usda.gov Web, www.fns.usda.gov/school-meals/child-nutrition-programs*

Administers the transfer of funds to state agencies for the National School Lunch Program, the School Breakfast

Program, the Special Milk Program, the Child and Adult Care Food Program, and the Summer Food Service Program. These programs help fight hunger and obesity by reimbursing organizations such as schools, child care centers, and after-school programs for providing healthy meals to children.

Food and Nutrition Service *(Agriculture Dept.), Child Nutrition Programs, National School Lunch Program,* 3101 Park Center Dr., 6th floor, Alexandria, VA 22302; (703) 305-2590. Kristen Hyatt, Deputy Administrator 9Actung), (703) 305-2054.
Web, https://www.fns.usda.gov/nslp

Administers the federal assistance meal program operating in public and nonprofit private schools and residential child care institutions. Provides daily nutritionally balanced and low-cost or free lunches to children.

Food and Nutrition Service *(Agriculture Dept.), Communications Officer,* 3101 Park Center Dr., #926, Alexandria, VA 22302; (703) 305-2281. Fax, (703) 305-2312. Brooke Hardison, Director (Acting).
Web, www.fns.usda.gov

Provides information concerning the Food and Nutrition Service and its fifteen nutrition assistance programs to the media, program participants, advocates, members of Congress, and the general public. Monitors and analyzes relevant legislation.

Food and Nutrition Service *(Agriculture Dept.), Food Distribution,* 3101 Park Center Dr., #504, Alexandria, VA 22302-1500; (703) 305-2680. Fax, (703) 305-2964. Pam Miller, Administrator.
General email, fdd-pst@fns.usda.gov
Web, www.fns.usda.gov/fdd

Provides food for the National School Lunch Program, the Summer Food Service Program, and the Child and Adult Care Food Program. Administers the Commodity Supplemental Food Program for low-income pregnant and breastfeeding women, new mothers, infants, children, and the elderly. Supplies food to relief organizations for distribution following disasters. Makes commodity food and cash available through the Nutrition Services Incentive Program (formerly the Nutrition Program for the Elderly). Administers the Emergency Food Assistance Program through soup kitchens and food banks and the Food Distribution Program on Indian reservations and to Indian households elsewhere.

Food and Nutrition Service *(Agriculture Dept.), Policy Support,* 3101 Park Center Dr., #1014, Alexandria, VA 22302-1500; (703) 305-2017. Fax, (703) 305-2576. Richard Lucas, Deputy Associate Administrator.
Web, www.fns.usda.gov/ops/research-and-analysis

Evaluates federal nutrition assistance programs; provides results to policymakers and program administrators. Funds demonstration grants for state and local nutrition assistance projects.

Food and Nutrition Service *(Agriculture Dept.), Special Supplemental Nutrition Program for Women, Infants, and Children (WIC),* 3101 Park Center Dr., #520, Alexandria, VA 22302-1594; (703) 305-2746. Fax, (703) 305-2196. Diane Kriviski, Deputy Administrator, (703) 305-2052.
Web, www.fns.usda.gov/wic

Provides health departments and agencies with federal funding for food supplements and administrative expenses to make food, nutrition education, and health services available to infants, young children up to the age of 5, and pregnant, nursing, and postpartum women.

Food and Nutrition Service *(Agriculture Dept.), Supplemental Nutrition Assistance Program (SNAP),* 3101 Park Center Dr., #808, Alexandria, VA 22302-1594; (703) 305-2026. Fax, (703) 305-2454. Jessica Shahin, Associate Administrator, (703) 305-2022.
Web, www.fns.usda.gov/snap

Administers SNAP through state welfare agencies to provide needy persons with Electronic Benefit Transfer cards to increase food purchasing power. Provides matching funds to cover half the cost of EBT card issuance.

Food Safety and Inspection Service *(Agriculture Dept.),* 1400 Independence Ave. S.W., #331E, 20250-3700; (202) 720-7025. Paul Kiecker, Administrator. Consumer inquiries, (800) 535-4555. Press, (202) 720-9113. TTY, (800) 877-8339.
Web, www.fsis.usda.gov and Twitter, @USDAFoodSafety

Inspects meat, poultry, and egg products moving in interstate commerce for use as human food to ensure that they are safe, wholesome, and accurately labeled. Provides safe handling and labeling guidelines.

Health and Human Services Dept. (HHS), *President's Council on Sports, Fitness, and Nutrition (PCSFN),* 1101 Wootton Pkwy., #560, Rockville, MD 20852; (240) 276-9567. Rachel Fisher, Executive Director (Acting).
General email, fitness@hhs.gov
Web, www.fitness.gov and Twitter, @FitnessGov

Promotes programs and initiatives that motivate people of all ages, backgrounds, and abilities to lead active, healthy lives through partnerships with the public, private, and nonprofit sectors; provides online information and resources related to fitness, sports, and nutrition; conducts award programs for children and adults and for schools, clubs, and other institutions.

National Agricultural Library *(Agriculture Dept.), Food and Nutrition Information Center (FNIC),* 10301 Baltimore Ave., #108, Beltsville, MD 20705-2351; (301) 504-5414. Fax, (301) 504-6409. Wendy Shaw, Branch Chief, (301) 504-6369.
General email, fnic@ars.usda.gov
Web, www.nal.usda.gov/fnic

Serves primarily educators, health professionals, and consumers seeking information about nutrition assistance programs and general nutrition. Serves as an online provider of science-based information about food and nutrition and links to such information. Lends books and audiovisual materials for educational purposes through interlibrary loans; provides reference services; develops resource lists of health and nutrition publications. Library open to the public.

National Agricultural Library *(Agriculture Dept.), Food Safety Research Information (FSRIO), 10301 Baltimore Ave., #108-B, Beltsville, MD 20705-2351; (301) 504-5515. Wendy Shaw, Chief, Information, (301) 504-5047. Information Specialist, (301) 504-5022.*
General email, fsrio@ars.usda.gov
Web, www.nal.usda.gov/fsrio

Provides food safety information to educators, industry, researchers, and the general public. Special subject areas include pathogens and contaminants, sanitation and quality standards, food preparation and handling, and food processing and technology. The center includes the Food Safety Research Information Office, which focuses on providing information and reference services to the research community and the general public.

National Institute of Food and Agriculture (NIFA) *(Agriculture Dept.), Jaime L. Whitten Bldg., 12th St. S.W. and Jefferson Dr., #305A, 20250 (mailing address: 1400 Independence Ave. S.W., MS 2201, Washington, DC 20250-2201); (202) 720-4423. Fax, (202) 720-8987. Carrie Castille, Director. Information, (202) 720-2791.*
General email, nifamediarequests@nifa.usda.gov
Web, https://nifa.usda.gov, Twitter, @USDA_NIFA
Blog, https://nifa.usda.gov/newsroom?f%5B0%5D=type%3Ablog

Supports research, education, and extension of issues pertaining to agricultural production, nutrition, food safety, energy independence, and the sustainability of natural resources. Partners with and funds scientists at academic institutions, particularly the land-grant universities, minority-serving institutions, including black colleges and universities, Hispanic-serving institutions, and tribal colleges, as well as government, private, and nonprofit organizations to address critical issues in agriculture, including global food security and hunger, water resources, climate change, sustainable energy, childhood obesity, and food safety. Partners with agricultural extension offices in all counties, states, and territories.

National Institute of Food and Agriculture (NIFA) *(Agriculture Dept.), Institute of Food Production and Sustainability, 800 9th St. S.W., #3305, 20024 (mailing address: 1400 Independence Ave. S.W., MS 2240, Washington, DC 20250-2240); (202) 720-2791. Fax, (202) 401-1782. Deb Hamernik, Deputy Director.*
Web, https://nifa.usda.gov/office/institute-food-production-and-sustainability

Enhances food security through productive and sustainable agricultural systems. Includes divisions of Animal Safety, Plant Systems, Protection, Plant Systems Production, and Agriculture Systems.

National Institute of Food and Agriculture (NIFA) *(Agriculture Dept.), Institute of Food Safety and Nutrition (IFSN), 1400 Independence Ave. S.W., MS 2225, 20250-2225; 305-A Whitten Bldg., 20250; (202) 720-4423.*

Dionne Toombs, Director (Acting). Hotline, (202) 720-2791, ext. 1.
Web, https://nifa.usda.gov/office/institute-food-safety-and-nutrition

Works toward a safer and more sustainable food supply by reducing food-borne illness. Addresses causes of microbial contamination, antimicrobial resistance and emerging fodborne pathogens; educates consumer and food safety professionals; and develops food processing technologies.

National Institute of Food and Agriculture (NIFA) *(Agriculture Dept.), Institute of Youth, Family, and Community, IYFC, 800 9th St. S.W., #4343, 20024 (mailing address: 1400 Independence Ave. S.W., MS 2250, Washington, DC 20250-2225); Venu (Kal) Kalavacharla, Deputy Director. Hotline, (202) 720-2791.*
Web, https://nifa.usda.gov/office/institute-youth-family-and-community

Supports the socio-economic prosperity by strengthening individuals, families, and communities; providing resources for the next generation of food and agricultural scientists; and offering youth leadership experiences. Prepares young people to be responsible citizens and change agents; Develop spragmatic solutions to recurring issues facing individuals, families, and communities; Strengthen the capacity of higher education institutions to develop and implement curricula and teaching programs in the food and agricultural sciences as well as the Science, Technology, Engineering, and Math (STEM) disciplines.

National Oceanic and Atmospheric Administration (NOAA) *(Commerce Dept.), Seafood Inspection Program, 1315 East-West Hwy., Silver Spring, MD 20910; (301) 427-8300. Fax, (301) 713-1081. Alexa Cole, Director. Toll-free, (800) 422-2750.*
General email, nmfs.seafood.services@noaa.gov
Web, www.fisheries.noaa.gov/insight/noaas-seafood-inspection-program

Administers voluntary inspection program for fish products and fish processing plants; certifies fish for wholesomeness, safety, and condition; grades for quality. Conducts training and workshops to help U.S. importers and foreign suppliers comply with food regulations.

►CONGRESS

For a listing of relevant congressional committees and subcommittees, please see page 3 or the Appendix.

►INTERNATIONAL ORGANIZATIONS

Cultivating New Frontiers in Agriculture (CNFA), *1828 L St. N.W., #710, 20036; (202) 296-3920. Fax, (202) 296-1271. Sylvain Roy, President.*
General email, info@cnfa.org
Web, www.cnfa.org, Twitter, @CNFA and Facebook, www.facebook.com/CNFAGlobal

International development organization that has worked in more than 42 countries to provide agricultural solutions to stimulate economic growth and improve livelihoods by cultivating entrepreneurship.

International Food Information Council Foundation, *900 19th St. N.W., #600, 20006; (202) 296-6540. Joseph Clayton, Chief Executive Officer, ext. 701. General email, info@ific.org*

Web, https://ific.org and Twitter, @ific

Membership: food and beverage companies and manufacturers of food ingredients. Provides the media, health professionals, and consumers with science-based information about food safety, health, and nutrition.

U.S. Codex Office, *South Bldg., 1400 Independence Ave. S.W., #4861, 20250-3700; (202) 205-7760. Mary Frances Lowe, U.S. Manager for Codex Alimentarius. Toll-free TTY, (800) 877-8339. General email, uscodex@usda.gov*

Web, www.usda.gov/codex, Twitter, @USDAFoodSafety and Facebook, www.facebook.com/usda and YouTube, www.youtube.com/usda

Acts as national focal point for U.S. Codex Program. Engages stakeholders in developing and advancing science-based food standards to protect the health of consumers and ensure fair practices in the food trade. Manages U.S. involvement in Codex, and develops strategies to accomplish U.S. objectives. (Located in USDA Trade and Foreign Agricultural Affairs.)

▶**NONGOVERNMENTAL**

Academy of Nutrition and Dietetics, *Washington Office, Policy Initiatives and Advocacy, 1120 Connecticut Ave. N.W., #460, 20036-3989; (202) 775-8277. Fax, (202) 775-8284. Jeanne Blankenship, Vice President, (312) 899-0040, ext. 6004. Toll-free, (800) 877-0877. General email, govaffairs@eatright.org*

Web, www.eatright.org, Twitter, @eatright and Facebook, www.facebook.com/EatRightNutrition

Press, media@eatright.org

Membership: dietitians and other nutrition professionals. Works with state and federal legislators and agencies on public policy issues affecting consumers and the practice of dietetics, including Medicare coverage of medical nutrition therapy; licensure of registered dietitians; child nutrition; obesity; food safety. Promotes public health and nutrition; accredits academic programs in clinical nutrition and food service management; sets standards of professional practice. Incorporates research, professional development, technology and practice to foster innovation and discovery. Publishes the *Journal of the Academy of Nutrition and Dietetics.* (Headquarters in Chicago, Ill.)

Center For Food Safety, *518 C St. N.E., #200, 20002; (202) 547-9359. Fax, (202) 547-9429. Andrew Kimbrell, Executive Director.*

General email, office@centerforfoodsafety.org

Web, https://centerforfoodsafety.org, Twitter, @CFSTrueFood and Facebook, www.facebook.com/centerforfoodsafety

Promotes organic foods and ecological and sustainable industrial food alternatives. Educates consumers about organic foods and products.

Center for Science in the Public Interest, *1250 Eye St. N.W., #902, 20005; (202) 332-9110. Fax, (202) 265-4954. Peter Lurie, President. General email, cspi@cspinet.org*

Web, https://cspinet.org, Twitter, @cspi and Facebook, www.facebook.com/CSPInet

Conducts research on food and nutrition. Interests include eating habits, food safety regulations, food additives, organically produced foods, and links between diet and disease. Publishes *Nutrition Action Healthletter.* Monitors U.S. and international policy.

Congressional Hunger Center, *200 Massachusetts Ave. N.W., 7th Floor, 20001; (202) 547-7022. Fax, (202) 547-7575. Shannon Maynard, Executive Director, ext. 11. Web, www.hungercenter.org, Twitter, @HungerCenter and Facebook, www.facebook.com/hungercenter*

Works to increase public awareness of hunger in the United States and abroad. Develops strategies and trains leaders to combat hunger and facilitates collaborative efforts between organizations.

Council for Responsible Nutrition (CRN), *1828 L St. N.W., #810, 20036-5114; (202) 204-7700. Fax, (202) 204-7701. Steven Mister, President, (202) 204-7676. General email, webmaster@crnusa.org*

Web, www.crnusa.org, Twitter, @CRN_Supplements and YouTube, https://www.youtube.com/user/CRNSupplements

Membership: manufacturers, distributors, and ingredient suppliers of dietary supplements. Provides information to members; monitors Food and Drug Administration, Federal Trade Commission, and Consumer Product Safety Commission regulations.

D.C. Central Kitchen, *425 2nd St. N.W., 20001; (202) 234-0707. Michael F. Curtin, Chief Executive Officer, (202) 266-2018. General email, info@dccentralkitchen.org*

Web, www.dccentralkitchen.org, Twitter, @dcck and Facebook, www.facebook.com/dccentralkitchen

Distributes food to D.C.-area homeless shelters, transitional homes, low-income schoolchildren, and corner store "food deserts."

Food Allergy Research and Education (FARE), *7901 Jones Branch Dr., #240, McLean, VA 22102; (703) 691-3179. Fax, (703) 691-2713. Brice Roberts, Chief Executive Officer (Acting). Toll-free, (800) 929-4040. General email, contactfare@foodallergy.org*

Web, www.foodallergy.org, Twitter, @FoodAllergy and Facebook, www.facebook.com/FoodAllergyFARE

Membership: dietitians, nurses, physicians, school staff, government representatives, members of the food and pharmaceutical industries, and food-allergy patients and their families. Provides information and educational resources on food allergies and allergic reactions. Offers research grants.

Food and Water Watch, *1616 P St. N.W., #300, 20036; (202) 683-2500. Fax, (202) 683-2501. Wenonah Hauter, Executive Director. Toll-free, (855) 340-8083.*
General email, info@fwwatch.org
Web, www.foodandwaterwatch.org,
Twitter, @foodandwater and Facebook, www.facebook.com/ FoodandWaterWatch

Consumer organization that advocates stricter water and food safety regulations. Organizes public awareness campaigns and lobbies Congress. Publishes studies of agricultural, food preparation, and drinking water sanitation practices. Chapters in fifteen states and international chapter in Brussels, Belgium.

Food Research and Action Center (FRAC), *1200 18th St. N.W., #400, 20036; (202) 986-2200. Fax, (202) 986-2525. Luis Guardia, President.*
General email, nsmall@frac.org
Web, www.frac.org, Twitter, @fractweets and Facebook, www.facebook.com/foodresearchandaction center

Public interest advocacy center that works to end hunger and undernutrition in the United States. Offers organizational aid, training, and information to groups seeking to improve or expand federal food programs, including food stamp, child nutrition, and WIC (women, infants, and children) programs; conducts studies relating to hunger and poverty; coordinates network of antihunger organizations. Monitors legislation and regulations.

International Life Sciences Institute (ILSI), *North America, 740 15th St. N.W., #600, 20005; (202) 659-0074. Fax, (202) 659-3859. Stéphane Vidry, Global Executive Director.*
General email, info@ilsi.org
Web, https://ilsi.org, Twitter, @ILSI_Global and Facebook, www.facebook.com/InternationalLifesciences Institute

Acts as liaison among scientists from international government agencies, concerned industries, research institutes, and universities regarding the safety of foods and chemical ingredients. Conducts research on caffeine, food coloring, oral health, human nutrition, and other food issues. Promotes international cooperation among scientists.

National Academies of Sciences, Engineering, and Medicine (NASEM), *Agriculture and Natural Resources Board, Keck Center, 500 5th St. N.W., #WS632, 20001; (202) 334-2088. Fax, (202) 334-1978. Robin Schoen, Director.*
General email, skwan@nas.edu
Web, http://dels.nas.edu/banr and Twitter, @NASM_Ag

Promotes and oversees research on the environmental impact of agriculture and food sustainability, including forestry, fisheries, wildlife, and the use of land, water, and other natural resources.

National Center for Food and Agricultural Policy, *1101 Pennsylvania Ave. N.W., #300, 20004; (202) 429-8422. Harry Baumes, Chief Executive Officer.*
General email, info@ncfap.org
Web, www.ncfap.org

Research and educational organization concerned with domestic and international food and agricultural issues. Examines public policy concerning agriculture, food safety and quality, natural resources, and the environment.

Public Citizen, *Health Research Group, 1600 20th St. N.W., 20009-1001; (202) 588-1000. Michael Carome, Director.*
General email, hrg1@citizen.org
Web, www.citizen.org/topic/health-care and Twitter, @CitizenHRG

Citizens' interest group that studies and reports on unsafe foods; monitors and petitions the Food and Drug Administration.

School Nutrition Assn., *2900 S. Quincy St., #700, Arlington, VA 22206; (703) 824-3000. Fax, (703) 824-3015. Patricia Montague, Chief Executive Officer. Toll-free, (800) 877-8822.*
General email, servicecenter@schoolnutrition.org
Web, https://schoolnutrition.org and Twitter, @SchoolLunch

Membership: state and national food service workers and supervisors, school cafeteria managers, nutrition educators, industry members, and others interested in school food programs and child nutrition. Offers credentialing and sponsors National School Lunch Week and National School Breakfast Week. (Formerly the American School Food Service Assn.)

Beverages

▶ **AGENCIES**

Alcohol and Tobacco Tax and Trade Bureau (TTB) *(Treasury Dept.), 1310 G St. N.W., Box 12, 20005; (202) 453-2000. Fax, (202) 453-2912. Mary G. Ryan, Administrator. Public Affairs, (202) 453-2180. TTY, (202) 882-9914.*
General email, TTBInternetQuestions@ttb.gov
Web, www.ttb.gov

Regulates the advertising and labeling of alcohol beverages, including the size of containers; enforces federal taxation of alcohol and tobacco. Authorized to refer violations to Justice Dept. for criminal prosecution.

Alcohol and Tobacco Tax and Trade Bureau (TTB) *(Treasury Dept.), Alcohol Labeling and Formulation Division, 1310 G St. N.W., 4th Floor, Box 12, 20005 (mailing address: UPS, FedEx, etc., 1310 G. St. N.W.,*

#400E, Washington, DC 20005); (202) 453-2250. Fax, (202) 453-2984. Gracie Joy, Director. Toll-free, (866) 927-2533.
General email, alfd@ttb.treas.gov
Web, www.ttb.gov/offices/alcohol-labeling-and-formulation-division

Responsible for tax classification of alcohol beverages, alcohol beverage formula and label compliance with federal laws and regulations, and industry guidance and education on public laws and regulations. Ensures that labels provide consumers with adequate information on the identity and quality of alcohol beverage products.

Alcohol and Tobacco Tax and Trade Bureau (TTB) (Treasury Dept.), Regulations and Rulings Division, 1310 G St. N.W., Box 12, 20005 (mailing address: 1310 G St. N.W., Washington, DC 20005); (202) 453-2265. Amy Greenburg, Director.
General email, regulations@ttb.gov
Web, www.ttb.gov/offices/regulations-and-rulings-division

Develops guidelines for regional offices responsible for issuing permits for producing gasohol and other ethyl alcohol fuels. Writes and interprets regulations for distilleries that produce ethyl alcohol fuels.

▶ **NONGOVERNMENTAL**

American Beverage Assn., 1275 Pennsylvania Ave. N.W., #1100, 20004; (202) 463-6732. Fax, (202) 463-8277. Katherine Lugar, President. Press, (202) 463-6774.
General email, info@americanbeverage.org
Web, www.americanbeverage.org, Twitter, @AmeriBev and Facebook, www.facebook.com/AmeriBev

Membership: companies engaged in producing or distributing nonalcoholic beverages and bottled water. Acts as industry liaison with government and the public.

American Beverage Institute, 1090 Vermont Ave. N.W., 20005; (202) 463-7110. Jackson Shedelbower, Communications Director.
General email, info@abionline.org
Web, https://abionline.org,
Twitter, @AmericanBeverageinstitute and Facebook, www.facebook.com/AmericanBeverageInstitute

Promotes responsible alcohol consumption in restaurants and bars. Opposes restrictions on alcohol use. Monitors legislation and regulations.

American Beverage Licensees (ABL), 5101 River Rd., #108, Bethesda, MD 20816-1560; (301) 656-1494. Fax, (301) 656-7539. John Bodnovich, Executive Director. Toll-free, (888) 656-3241.
General email, info@ablusa.org
Web, www.ablusa.org, Twitter, @ablusa and Facebook, www.facebook.com/ablusa

Membership: state licensed beverage retail associations of on-premise and off-premise beverage alcohol licensees. Monitors legislation and regulations affecting the alcohol beverage industry.

Beer Institute, 440 1st St. N.W., #350, 20001; (202) 737-2337. Fax, (202) 737-7004. James McGreevy III, President. Toll-free, (800) 379-2739.
General email, info@beerinstitute.org
Web, www.beerinstitute.org, Twitter, @beerinstitute and Facebook, www.facebook.com/BeerInstitute and YouTube, www.youtube.com/channel/UCOx5NuR8ZUL0 K9QS2dvJJvQ

Membership: domestic brewers and beer importers and suppliers to the domestic brewing industry. Monitors legislation and regulations.

Distilled Spirits Council of the United States, 1250 Eye St. N.W., #400, 20005-3998; (202) 628-3544. Chris R. Swonger, President.
Web, www.distilledspirits.org, Twitter, @DistilledSpirit and Facebook, www.facebook.com/DistilledSpiritsCouncilUS

Membership: manufacturers and marketers of distilled spirits sold in the United States. Provides consumer information on alcohol-related issues and topics. Monitors legislation and regulations.

International Bottled Water Assn. (IBWA), 1700 Diagonal Rd., #650, Alexandria, VA 22314-2864; (703) 683-5213. Joseph K. Doss, President, (703) 647-4605. Press, (703) 647-4609.
General email, ibwainfo@bottledwater.org
Web, www.bottledwater.org and Twitter, @BottledWaterOrg

Serves as a clearinghouse for industry-related consumer, regulatory, and technical information; interests include international trade. Monitors state and federal legislation and regulations.

National Alcohol Beverage Control Assn. (NABCA), 2900 S. Quincy St., #800, Arlington, VA 22206-2233; (703) 578-4200. Fax, (703) 824-3451. J. Neal Insley, President.
General email, nabca.info@nabca.org
Web, www.nabca.org, Twitter, @NABCA and Facebook, www.facebook.com/alcoholcontrol

Membership: distilleries, importers, brokers, trade associations, and state agencies that control the purchase, distribution, and sale of alcohol beverages. Promotes responsible sale and consumption of these beverages. Serves as an information clearinghouse. Monitors legislation and regulations.

National Beer Wholesalers Assn., 1101 King St., #600, Alexandria, VA 22314-2944; (703) 683-4300. Fax, (703) 683-8965. Craig A. Purser, President. Toll-free, (800) 300-6417.
General email, info@nbwa.org
Web, www.nbwa.org, Twitter, @NBWA and Facebook, www.facebook.com/NBWABeer and YouTube, www.youtube.com/user/NBWABeer

Works to enhance the independent beer wholesale industry. Advocates before government and the public; encourages responsible consumption of beer; sponsors programs and services to benefit members; monitors legislation and regulations.

Wine and Spirits Wholesalers of America (WSWA), *805 15th St. N.W., #1120, 20005-2273; (202) 371-9792. Fax, (202) 789-2405. Michelle L. Korsmo, President.*
General email, info@wswa.org
Web, www.wswa.org and Facebook, www.facebook.com/ wswa

Trade association of wholesale distributors of domestic and imported wine and distilled spirits. Provides information on drinking awareness. Represents members' interests before Congress and federal agencies.

Wine Institute, *Federal and International Public Policy, 601 13th St. N.W., #330 South, 20005-3866; (202) 408-0870. Fax, (202) 371-0061. Charles Jefferson, Vice President.*
Web, www.wineinstitute.org and Twitter, @CalifWines_US

Membership: California wineries and affiliated businesses. Seeks international recognition for California wines; conducts promotional campaigns in other countries. Monitors legislation and regulations. (Headquarters in San Francisco, Calif.)

Food Industries

▶NONGOVERNMENTAL

American Bakers Assn. (ABA), *601 Pennsylvania Ave. N.W., #230, 20004; (202) 789-0300. Fax, (202) 898-1164. Robb MacKie, President.*
General email, info@americanbakers.org
Web, www.americanbakers.org,
Twitter, @AmericanBakers and Facebook, www.facebook .com/AmericanBakersAssoc

Membership: baking industry related companies, from wholesale baking companies, baking industry entrepreneurs, and baking industry suppliers. Develops and implements initiatives; provides networking opportunities; conducts conventions. Monitors legislation and regulations.

American Frozen Food Institute, *1210 S. Glebe Rd., Box 4330, Arlington, VA 22204-9998; (703) 821-0770. Fax, (703) 342-0343. Alison Bodor, President.*
General email, info@affi.com
Web, www.affi.org, Twitter, @affi and Facebook, www .facebook.com/AmericanFrozenFoodInstitute

Membership: frozen food packers, distributors, and suppliers. Testifies before Congress and federal agencies.

American Herbal Products Assn., *8630 Fenton St., #918, Silver Spring, MD 20910; (301) 588-1171. Fax, (301) 588-1174. Michael McGuffin, President, ext. 201.*
General email, ahpa@ahpa.org
Web, www.ahpa.org, Twitter, @AHPAssociation and Facebook, www.facebook.com/AHPAssociation

Membership: domestic and foreign companies that grow, process, manufacture, and market botanicals and herbal products, including foods, beverages, dietary supplements, non-prescription drugs, and cosmetics; associates in education, law, media, and medicine. Supports research; promotes quality standards, consumer access,

and self-regulation in the industry. Monitors legislation and regulations.

Bakery, Confectionery, Tobacco Workers, and Grain Millers International Union (BCTGM), *10401 Connecticut Ave., 4th Floor, Kensington, MD 20895-3940; (301) 933-8600. Fax, (301) 946-8452. Anthony Shelton, President.*
General email, bctgmwebmaster@gmail.com
Web, www.bctgm.org, Twitter, @BCTGM and Facebook, www.facebook.com/BCTGM

Membership: approximately 120,000 workers from the bakery, confectionery, grain miller, and tobacco industries in both the USA and Canada. Helps members negotiate pay, benefits, and better working conditions; conducts training programs and workshops. Monitors legislation and regulations. (Affiliated with the AFL-CIO.)

Consumer Brands Assn., *1001 N. 19th St., Arlington, VA 22209; (571) 378-6760. Geoff Freeman, President.*
General email, info@consumerbrandsassociation.org
Web, www.consumerbrandsassociation.org,
Twitter, @consumerbrands and Facebook, www.facebook .com/ConsumerBrandsAssociation

Membership: manufacturers of food, beverage, and consumer packaged goods sold through the retail grocery trade. Interests include holistic waste management solutions, nutritional labeling, ingredient transparency, and the safety and security of the food supply. Supplies industry information to members. Monitors legislation and regulations. (Formerly the Grocery Manufacturers Assn.)

Food Marketing Institute (FMI), *2345 Crystal Dr., #800, Arlington, VA 22202-4813; (202) 452-8444. Fax, (202) 429-4519. Leslie G. Sarasin, President.*
General email, info@fmi.org
Web, www.fmi.org and Twitter, @FMI_ORG

Trade association of food retailers and wholesalers. Conducts programs in research, education, industry relations, and public affairs; participates in international conferences. Library open to the public by appointment. Advocates in the public service areana.

Food Processing Suppliers Assn. (FPSA), *1451 Dolley Madison Blvd., #101, McLean, VA 22101-3850; (703) 761-2600. Fax, (703) 761-4334. David Seckman, President, (703) 663-1200.*
Web, www.fpsa.org, Twitter, @FPSAorg and Facebook, www.facebook.com/FPSAorg

Membership: equipment and ingredient manufacturers, suppliers, and servicers for the food, dairy, and beverage processing industry. Sponsors food engineering scholarships and the biannual Process Expo. (Merger of the International Assn. of Food Industry Suppliers and the Food Processing Machinery Assn.)

International Foodservice Distributors Assn., *1660 International Dr., #550, McLean, VA 22102; (703) 532-9400. Fax, (703) 880-7117. Mark S. Allen, President, ext. 9933.*
Web, www.ifdaonline.org, Twitter, @IFDA and Facebook, www.facebook.com/IFDAOrg

Trade association of foodservice distribution companies that promotes the interests of members in government and industry affairs through research, education, and communication.

NACS: The Assn. for Convenience and Fuel Retailing,
1600 Duke St., 7th Floor, Alexandria, VA 22314-3421; (703) 684-3600. Fax, (703) 836-4564. Henry Armour, President. Toll-free, (800) 966-6227.
General email, nacs@convenience.org
Web, www.convenience.org, Twitter, @nacsonline and Facebook, www.facebook.com/nasconline

Membership: convenience store and fuel retailers and industry suppliers. Promotes industry position on labor, tax, environment, nccr, alcohol, and food-related issues; conducts research and training programs. Monitors legislation and regulations.

National Automatic Merchandising Assn. (NAMA),
Washington Office, 1777 N. Kent St., #1010, Arlington, VA 22209; (312) 346-0370. Fax, (312) 704-4140.
Carla Balakgie, President.
Web, www.namanow.org, Twitter, @NAMAvending and Facebook, www.facebook.com/NAMANow and YouTube, www.youtube.com/c/NAMANow

Membership: service companies, equipment manufacturers, and product suppliers for the food and refreshment vending, coffee service, and foodservice management industries. Seeks to advance and promote the automatic merchandising and coffee service industries, provide administrative, logistical, and financial assistance to its members. (Headquarters in Chicago, Ill.)

National Council of Chain Restaurants (NCCR), 1101
New York Ave. N.W., #1200, 20005; (202) 783-7971.
Matthew R. Shay, President. Toll-free, (800) 673-4692.
General email, contact@nccr.net
Web, www.nrf.com/who-we-are/retail-communities/chain-restaurants-nccr, Twitter, @NRFnews
Facebook, @NationalRetailFederation

Trade association representing chain restaurant companies. Affiliated with the National Retail Federation. Monitors legislation and regulations.

National Grocers Assn., 601 Pennsylvania Ave. N.W.,
#375, 20004; (202) 938-2570. Fax, (202) 938-2574.
Greg Ferrara, President.
General email, admin@nationalgrocers.org
Web, www.nationalgrocers.org, Twitter, @NationalGrocers
Facebook, www.facebook.com/NationalGrocersAssn and YouTube, www.youtube.com/user/NationalGrocers
Press, communications@nationalgrocers.org

Trade association that represents independent retail and wholesale grocers. Membership also includes affiliated associations, manufacturers, and service suppliers. Provides members with educational materials through a website, publications, and conferences. Monitors legislation and regulations.

National Pasta Assn. (NPA), 1280 National Press Bldg.,
529 14th St. N.W., 20045-1806; (202) 591-2459. Fax, (202) 591-2445. Delia Murphy, Executive Director.
General email, info@ilovepasta.org
Web, https://ilovepasta.org, Twitter, @sharethepasta and Facebook, www.facebook.com/SharethePasta

Membership: U.S. pasta manufacturers, related suppliers, and allied industry representatives. Represents the industry on public policy issues; monitors and addresses technical issues; and organizes events and seminars for the industry.

National Restaurant Assn., 2055 L St. N.W., #700, 20036;
(202) 331-5900. Fax, (202) 331-2429. Martin Irby, Chief Executive Officer (Acting). Toll-free, (800) 424-5156.
General email, askus@restaurant.org
Web, www.restaurant.org and Twitter, @Werrestaurants

Membership: restaurants, cafeterias, clubs, contract feeders, caterers, institutional food services, and other members of the food industry. Supports food service education and research. Monitors legislation and regulations.

North American Meat Institute, 1150 Connecticut Ave.
N.W., 12th Floor, 20036; (202) 587-4200. Fax, (202) 587-4300. Julia Anna Potts, President, (202) 587-4262.
General email, info@meatinstitute.org
Web, www.meatinstitute.org, Twitter, @MeatInstitute and Facebook, www.facebook.com/AmericanMeatInstitute

Membership: national and international meat and poultry packers, suppliers, and processors. Provides statistics on meat production and exports. Funds research projects and consumer education programs. Monitors legislation and regulations. (Formed from merger of the North American Meat Assn. and American Meat Institute.)

Shelf-Stable Food Processors Assn. (SFPA), 1150
Connecticut Ave. N.W., 12th Floor, 20036; (202) 587-4200.
Fax, (202) 587-4300. Julie Anna Potts, President.
General email, info@meatinstitute.org
Web, www.meatinstitute.org and Twitter, @meatinstitute

Membership: shelf-stable food manufacturers and their suppliers. Provides information on the shelf-stable industry, particularly as it pertains to meat products. (Subsidiary of the North American Meat Institute.)

SNAC International, 1560 Wilson Blvd., #550, Arlington,
VA 22209; (703) 836-4500. Fax, (703) 836-8262.
Christine Cochran, Chief Executive Officer, ext. 207.
Toll-free, (800) 628-1334.
Web, www.snacintl.org, Facebook, www.facebook.com/SNACInternational and Twitter, @SNACIntl

Membership: snack food manufacturers and suppliers. Promotes industry sales; compiles statistics; conducts research and surveys; assists members with training and education; provides consumers with industry information. Monitors legislation and regulations.

Tortilla Industry Assn., 1400 N. 14th St., 12th Floor,
Arlington, VA 22209; (800) 944-6099. Fax, (800) 944-6177.
Jim Kabbani, Executive Director, ext. 1.

General email, jkabbaani@tortilla-info.com

Web, www.tortilla-info.com

Membership: tortilla manufacturers, industry suppliers, and distributors. Promotes tortilla consumption. Provides market research and other industry-related information to its members. Sponsors conferences, seminars, and educational events for the industry.

United Food and Commercial Workers International Union (UFCW), *1775 K St. N.W., 20006-1598; (202) 223-3111. Fax, (202) 728-1803. Anthony (Marc) Perrone, President.*
Web, www.ufcw.org, Twitter, @UFCW and Facebook, www.facebook.com/ufcwinternational

Membership: approximately 1.3 million workers primarily in the retail, meatpacking, food processing, and poultry industries. Interests include health care reform, living wages, retirement security, safe working conditions, and the right to unionize. Monitors legislation and regulations.

World Cocoa Foundation, *1025 Connecticut Ave. N.W., #1205, 20036; (202) 737-7870. Fax, (202) 737-7832. Martin Short, President.*
General email, wcf@worldcocoa.org

Web, www.worldcocoafoundation.org, Twitter, @WorldCocoa and Facebook, www.facebook.com/WorldCocoaFoundation

Promotes a sustainable cocoa economy through economic and social development and environmental conservation in cocoa-growing communities. Helps raise funds for cocoa farmers and increases their access to modern farming practices.

Vegetarianism

▶**NONGOVERNMENTAL**

Animal Outlook, *P.O. Box 9773, 20016; (301) 891-2458. Fax, (301) 891-6815. Cheryl Leahy, President.*
General email, info@animaloutlook.org

Web, http://animaloutlook.org and Twitter, @AnimalOutlook

Animal rights organization that focuses primarily on cruelty to animals in agriculture. Promotes vegetarianism.

Farm Animal Rights Movement (FARM), *10101 Ashburton Lane, Bethesda, MD 20817-1729 (mailing address: P.O. Box 4064, Ithaca, NY 14852); (888) 327-6872. Alex Hershaft, President.*
General email, info@farmusa.org

Web, www.farmusa.org, www.livevegan.org, Twitter, @FARMUSA and Facebook, www.facebook.com/farmanimalrights

Works to end use of animals for food. Interests include animal protection, consumer health, agricultural resources, and environmental quality. Conducts national educational campaigns, including World Farm Animals Day, the Live

Vegan program, and the Great American Meatout. Monitors legislation and regulations.

Vegetarian Resource Group, *P.O. Box 1463, Baltimore, MD 21203-1463; (410) 366-8343. Fax, (410) 366-8804. Charles Stahler, Co-Director; Debra Wasserman, Co-Director.*
General email, vrg@vrg.org

Web, www.vrg.org, Twitter, @VegResourceGrp

Press, press@vrg.org

Works to educate the public on vegetarianism and veganism and issues of health, nutrition, ecology, ethics, and world hunger.

World Food Assistance

▶**AGENCIES**

Agency for International Development (USAID), *Bureau for Resilience and Food Security, 1300 Pennsylvania Ave. N.W., 20523; Fax, (202) 216-3380. Jim Barnhart, Assistant to the Administrator.*
Web, www.usaid.gov/who-we-are/organization/bureaus/bureau-resilience-and-food-security

Administers agricultural development programs, including the Feed the Future initiative. Partners with other U.S. government offices, multilateral institutions, NGOs, the public and private sector, and universities to support country-driven agricultural growth strategies.

Agency for International Development (USAID), *Bureau for Resilience and Food Security, Farmer-to-Farmer Program, 1300 Pennsylvania Ave. N.W., #2.10-261, 20523; Evania Robles, Program Analyst; Peggy Carlson, Program Analyst.*
Web, www.usaid.gov/what-we-do/agriculture-and-food-security/supporting-agricultural-capacity-development/john-ogonowski and https://farmer-to-farmer.org and Facebook, www.facebook.com/Farmer2Farmer

Promotes sustainable improvements in food security and agricultural processing, production, and marketing. Provides voluntary assistance to farmers, farm groups, and agribusinesses in developing countries, benefiting approximately one million farmer families in more than 80 countries.

Agriculture Dept. (USDA), *Office of the Chief Economist, Commodity Markets, World Agricultural outlook Board (WAOB), 1400 Independence Ave. S.W., #4419A, MS 3812, 20250; (202) 720-6030. Mark Jekanowski, Chair, (202) 720-5792. Main Phone, (202) 720-9805.*
Web, www.usda.gov/oce/commodity-markets

Coordinates the department's economic intelligence and commodity outlook for the US and world agriculture. which develops the official prognosis of supply, utilization, and prices for commodities worldwide. Works with the National Weather Service to monitor the impact of global weather on agriculture.

Bureau of Economic and Business Affairs (EB) *(State Dept.), Trade Policy and Negotiations (TPN), Agriculture Policy (AGP)*, 2201 C St. N.W., #4686, 20520-0002; (202) 647-3090. Fax, (202) 647-1894. *Jeffrey Gianque, Director, (202) 647-0133. Web, www.state.gov/agricultural-policy*

Makes recommendations on international food policy issues including effects of U.S. food aid on foreign policy; studies and drafts proposals on the U.S. role in Food for Peace and World Food programs.

Foreign Agricultural Service (FAS) *(Agriculture Dept.)*, 1400 Independence Ave. S.W., #5071S, MS 1001, 20250-1001; (202) 720-3935. Fax, (202) 690-2159. *Daniel Whitley, Administrator (Acting). Public Affairs, (202) 720-7115. TTY, (202) 720-1786. Web, www.fas.usda.gov, Twitter, @USDAForeignAg Press, press-fas@usda.gov*

Administers international food programs and provides technical assistance, trade and scientific capacity building support to developing countries.

National Institute of Food and Agriculture (NIFA) *(Agriculture Dept.), Center for International Programs*, 800 9th St. S.W., #2436, 20024 (mailing address: 1400 Independence Ave. S.W., MS 2203, Washington, DC 20250-2203); (202) 720-2791. Fax, (202) 690-2355. *Timothy W. Conner, Director (Acting), (816) 926-1816. Web, https://nifa.usda.gov/office/center-international-programs*

Promotes science education in developing economies and shares research to enhance food production and stabilize economies. Interests include agricultural extension, teaching, and research.

State Dept., *Global Food Security*, 2201 C St. N.W., HST 3822, 20520; (202) 647-3090. Fax, (202) 647-1894. *Ted J. Lyng, Special Representative (Acting). Web, www.state.gov/agricultural-policy/food-security*

Supports country-driven approaches to address the root causes of hunger and poverty, and helps countries transform their own agricultural sectors to grow enough food to sustainably feed their people.

▶ INTERNATIONAL ORGANIZATIONS

CARE, *Washington Office*, 1100 17th St. N.W., #900, 20036; (202) 595-2800. *Ritu Sharma, Vice President, Programs and Policy Advocacy. General email, info@care.org Web, www.care.org, Twitter, @CARE and Facebook, www.facebook.com/carefans*

Works with international governments and communities to ensure sustainable food security and sustainable farming. (U.S. headquarters in Atlanta, Ga.; international headquarters in Geneva, Switzerland.)

Farmer to Farmer, 1424 K St. N.W., #700, 20005; *Anna Snider, Communications Manager; Cathleen McCoy, President. General email, avop@partners.net Web, www.farmer-to-farmer.org, Twitter, @farmertofarmer and Facebook, www.facebook.com/farmer2farmer*

Supports farmers and agribusiness professionals in developing countries to improve their livelihoods and food security. Sends volunteers on need-based assignments to provide hands-on training and mentoring in 36 countries. Is funded by and works with the USAID farmer to farmer program.

Food and Agriculture Organization of the United Nations (FAO), *Washington Office*, Iason Office LOW, 2121 K St. N.W., #800-B, 20037-0001; (202) 653-2400. Fax, (202) 653-5760. *Jocelyn Brown Hall, Director; Thomas Pesek, Senior Liaison Officer. General email, FAOLOW@fao.org Web, www.fao.org/north-america/en, Twitter, @FAONorthAmerica and Facebook, www.facebook.com/UNFAO*

Offers development assistance; collects, analyzes, and disseminates information; provides policy and planning advice to governments regards food and nutrition security; acts as an international forum for debate on food and agricultural issues, including animal health and production, fisheries, and forestry; encourages sustainable agricultural development and a long-term strategy for the conservation and management of natural resources. Coordinates World Food Day. (International headquarters in Rome.)

International Food Policy Research Institute (IFPRI), 1201 Eye St. N.W., 20005-3915; (202) 862-5600. Fax, (202) 862-5606. *Johan Swinnen, Director General. General email, ifpri@cgiar.org Web, www.ifpri.org, Twitter, @IFPRI and Facebook, www.facebook.com/ifpri.org and YouTube, www.youtube.com/user/IFPRI*

Research organization that analyzes the world food situation and suggests ways of making food more available in developing countries. Provides various governments with information on national and international food policy. Sponsors conferences and seminars; publishes research reports. Library open to the public by appointment.

International Fund for Agricultural Development (IFAD), *North American Liaison Office*, 1775 K St. N.W., #500, 20006-1502; (202) 331-9099. *Gilbert F. Houngbo, President; Joanna Veltri, Chief. General email, ifad@ifad.org Web, www.ifad.org*

Financial institution and specialized agency of the United Nations that provides the rural poor of developing nations with cost-effective ways of overcoming hunger, poverty, and malnutrition. Advocates a community-based approach to reducing rural poverty. (International headquarters in Rome.)

ACDI/VOCA, *50 F St. N.W., #1000, 20001-1530; (202) 469-6000. Fax, (202) 469-6257. Charles J. Hall, Chief Executive Officer; Luke Pingel, Chief Legal Officer.*
General email, webmaster@acdivoca.org
Web, www.acdivoca.org, Twitter, @acdivoca and Facebook, www.facebook.com/acdivoca

Promotes agribusiness systems that improve production and link farmers to national, regional, and international markets. Partners with farm supply, processing, and marketing cooperatives; farm credit banks; national farmer organizations; and insurance cooperatives. Provides cooperatives with training and technical, management, and marketing assistance; supports farm credit systems, agribusiness, and government agencies in developing countries.

American Red Cross, *National Headquarters, 431 18th St. N.W., 20006; (202) 303-5000. Gail J. McGovern, President. Headquarters staff directory, (202) 303-5214, ext. 1. Press, (202) 303-5551. Public inquiries, (202) 303-4498. Toll-free, (800) 733-2767.*
Web, www.redcross.org and Twitter, @RedCross

Humanitarian relief and health education organization chartered by Congress. Provides food and supplies to assist in major disaster and refugee situations worldwide. U.S. delegate of the International Federation of Red Cross and Red Crescent Societies in international response efforts.

Bread for the World/Bread for the World Institute, *425 3rd St. S.W., #1200, 20024 (mailing address: P.O. Box 96416, Washington, DC 20090-6416); (202) 639-9400. Fax, (202) 639-9401. Rev. Eugene Cho, President. Toll-free, (800) 822-7323.*
General email, bread@bread.org and institute@bread.org
Web, www.bread.org, Twitter, @bread4theworld and Facebook, www.facebook.com/breadfortheworld

Membership; Christian citizens' movement that works to eradicate world hunger. Organizes and coordinates political action on issues and public policy affecting the causes of hunger.

Center for Strategic and International Studies, *Global Food Security Project, 1616 Rhode Island Ave. N.W., 20036; (202) 775-3235. Caitlin Welsh, Director.*
General email, FoodSecurity@csis.org
Web, www.csis.org/programs/global-food-security-program and Twitter, @CSISFood

Conducts research and provides policy guidance on global food security challenges and agricultural development. Interests include the role of technology in increasing production, the importance of integrating nutrition, and economic growth.

Oxfam America, *Policy and Campaigns, 1101 17th St. N.W., #1300, 20036-4710; (202) 496-1180. Fax, (202) 496-1190. Abby Maxman, President, ext. 2506; Gina Crista Cummings, Vice President of Advocacy,* Alliances and Policy. Press, (202) 496-1169. Toll-free, (800) 776-9326.
General email, info@oxfamamerica.org
Web, www.oxfamamerica.org and Twitter, @OxfamAmerica

Funds disaster relief and long-term development programs internationally. Organizes grassroots support in the United States for issues affecting global poverty and hunger.

RESULTS, *1101 15th St. N.W., #1200, 20005; (202) 783-4800. Fax, (202) 452-9345. Joanne Carter, Executive Director.*
General email, results@results.org
Web, https://results.org, Twitter, @RESULTS_Tweets and Facebook, www.facebook.com/RESULTSEdFund and YouTube, www.youtube.com/user/RESULTSorg

Works to end hunger and poverty nationally and worldwide; encourages grassroots and legislative support of programs and proposals dealing with hunger and hunger-related issues. Monitors legislation and regulations.

Winrock International, *Washington Office, 2451 Crystal Dr., #700, Arlington, VA 22202; (703) 302-6500. Fax, (703) 302-6512. Rodney Ferguson, President.*
General email, information@winrock.org
Web, www.winrock.org and Twitter, @WinrockIntl

Works to increase economic opportunity; sustain natural resources; protect the environment; and increase long-term productivity, equity, and responsible resource management to benefit the world's poor and disadvantaged communities. Matches innovative approaches in agriculture, natural resources management, clean energy, and leadership development with the unique needs of its partners. Links local individuals and communities with new ideas and technology. (Headquarters in Little Rock, Ark.)

LIVESTOCK AND POULTRY

General

Agricultural Marketing Service (AMS) *(Agriculture Dept.), Fair Trade Practices Program, Packers and Stockyards Program (PSD), 1400 Independence Ave. S.W., MS 3601, 20250-3601; (202) 720-7051. Fax, (202) 205-9237. Stuart Frank, Director, (515) 323-2586. Swine Contract Library, (515) 323-2579.*
General email, PSDWashingtonDC@usda.gov
Web, www.ams.usda.gov/services/enforcement/psd
Swine Contract Library email, PSDSwineContractLibrary@usda.gov

Maintains competition in the marketing of livestock, poultry, and meat by prohibiting deceptive and monopolistic marketing practices; tests market scales and conducts check weighings for accuracy. Maintains the Swine Contract Library. Publishes the offical copy of decisions in legal actions taken with USDA.

Agricultural Marketing Service (AMS) *(Agriculture Dept.), Livestock and Poultry Program,* 1400 *Independence Ave. S.W., MS 0249, 20250-0249; Jennifer Porter, Deputy Administrator, (202) 720-5705. Press, (202) 720-8998.*
General email, AskLP@usda.gov

Web, www.ams.usda.gov/about-ams/programs-offices/livestock-poultry-program

Administers meat marketing program; maintains market news service to inform producers of meat market situation and daily price changes; develops, establishes, and revises U.S. standards for classes and grades of livestock and meat; grades, examines, and certifies meat and meat products.

Agriculture Dept. (USDA), *Office for Food Safety (OFS), Under Secretary for Food Safety (FSIS),* 1400 *Independence Ave. S.W., #331E, 20250; (202) 720-0345. Sandra Eskin, Deputy Under Secretary.*
Web, www.fsis.usda.gov/contactus/fsis-offices/office-food-safety-ofs

Develops strategies that ensure the commercial supply of meat, poultry, and egg products is safe, properly labeled, and packaged. Oversees the Food Safety and Inspection Service.

Animal and Plant Health Inspection Service (APHIS) *(Agriculture Dept.), Veterinary Services,* 4700 River Rd., *#39, Riverdale, MD 20737; (301) 851-3300, ext. 2. Rosemary Sifford, Deputy Administrator.*
General email, nvap@aphis.usda.gov

Web, www.aphis.usda.gov/aphis/ourfocus/animalhealth

Works to protect and improve the health, quality, and marketability of our nation's animals and various wildlife and animal products. Creates priorities, objectives, strategies, and field activities for cattle, avian, swine, aquaculture, sheep and goat, equine, and cervid health. Disseminates regulatory information addressing the interstate and importation requirements of genetically engineered animals and insects that may spread animal diseases. Advises on animal health and public issues, including animal welfare, local and commercial livestock, natural resource conservation, and public health; conducts animal health monitoring and surveillance.

Food and Drug Administration (FDA) *(Health and Human Services Dept.), Center for Veterinary Medicine (CVM),* 7500 Standish Pl., HFV-1, Rockville, MD 20855-0001; (240) 402-7002. Fax, (240) 276-9001. *Steven Solomon, Director.*
General email, askcvm@fda.hhs.gov

Web, www.fda.gov/animalveterinary and Twitter, @FDAanimalhealth

Regulates the manufacture and distribution of drugs, food additives, feed, and devices for livestock and pets. Conducts research; works to ensure animal health and the safety of food derived from animals.

Food Safety and Inspection Service *(Agriculture Dept.),* 1400 Independence Ave. S.W., #331E, 20250-3700; (202) 720-7025. Paul Kiecker, Administrator. Consumer inquiries, (800) 535-4555. Press, (202) 720-9113. TTY, (800) 877-8339.
Web, www.fsis.usda.gov and Twitter, @USDAFoodSafety

Inspects meat and poultry products and provides safe handling and labeling guidelines.

►CONGRESS

For a listing of relevant congressional committees and subcommittees, please see page 3 or the Appendix.

►NONGOVERNMENTAL

Animal Health Institute, 1325 G St. N.W., #700, 20005-3104; (202) 637-2440. Fax, (202) 393-1667. *Alexander S. Mathews, President.*
Web, www.ahi.org and Twitter, @AnimalsHealthy

Membership: manufacturers of drugs and other products (including vaccines, pesticides, and vitamins) for pets and food-producing animals. Interests include pet health, livestock health, and disease outbreak prevention. Monitors legislation and regulations.

Animal Outlook, P.O. Box 9773, 20016; (301) 891-2458. Fax, (301) 891-6815. Cheryl Leahy, President.
General email, info@animaloutlook.org

Web, http://animaloutlook.org and Twitter, @AnimalOutlook

Animal rights organization that focuses primarily on cruelty to animals in agriculture. Promotes vegetarianism.

Farm Animal Rights Movement (FARM), 10101 Ashburton Lane, Bethesda, MD 20817-1729 (mailing address: P.O. Box 4064, Ithaca, NY 14852); (888) 327-6872. Alex Hershaft, President.
General email, info@farmusa.org

Web, www.farmusa.org, www.livevegan.org, Twitter, @FARMUSA and Facebook, www.facebook.com/farmanimalrights

Works to end use of animals for food. Interests include animal protection, consumer health, agricultural resources, and environmental quality. Conducts national educational campaigns, including World Farm Animals Day, the Live Vegan program, and the Great American Meatout. Monitors legislation and regulations.

Humane Farm Animal Care, P.O. Box 82, Middleburg, VA 20118; (703) 435-3883. Fax, (703) 435-3981. Adele Douglass Jolley, Chief Executive Officer; Mimi Stein, Executive Director.
General email, info@certifiedhumane.org

Web, www.certifiedhumane.org, Twitter, @CertifiedHumane and Facebook, www.facebook.com/CertifiedHumane

Seeks to improve the welfare of farm animals by providing viable, duly monitored standards for humane food production. Administers the Certified Humane Raised and Handled program for meat, poultry, eggs, and dairy products.

Leader and Hide Council of America, *1150 Connecticut Ave. N.W., 12th Floor, 20036; (202) 587-4250. Stephen Sothmann, President.*
General email, info@USLeather.org
Web, www.usleather.org, Twitter, @_real_leather and Facebook, www.facebook.com/chooserealleather

Membership: producers, brokers, dealers, processors, and exporters of hides and skins. Maintains liaison with allied trade associations and participates in programs on export statistics, hide price reporting, and freight rates; conducts seminars and consumer information programs.

National Cattlemen's Beef Assn., *Washington Office, 1275 Pennsylvania Ave. N.W., #801, 20004; (202) 347-0228. Fax, (202) 638-0607. Colin Woodall, Chief Executive Officer.*
Web, www.beefusa.org

Membership: individual cattlemen, state cattlemen's groups, and breed associations. Provides information on beef research, agricultural labor, beef grading, foreign trade, taxes, marketing, cattle economics, branding, animal health, and environmental management. (Headquarters in Denver, Colo.)

National Chicken Council, *1152 15th St. N.W., #430, 20005; (202) 296-2622. Michael J. Brown, President.*
General email, tsuper@chickenusa.org
Web, www.nationalchickencouncil.org, Twitter, @chickencouncil and Facebook, www.facebook .com/chickenroost

Trade association that represents the vertically integrated producers of 95 percent of the chickens raised and processed for meat in the United States. Monitors domestic and international legislation and regulations.

National Pork Producers Council, *122 C St. N.W., #875, 20001; (202) 347-3600. Fax, (202) 347-5265. Jen Sorenson, President.*
General email, news@nppc.org
Web, http://nppc.org, Twitter, @NPPC and Facebook, www.facebook.com/NationalPorkProducers Council

Membership: pork producers and state pork producer organizations. Interests include pork production, food safety, the environment, trade, and federal regulations.

Monitors legislation and regulations. (Headquarters in Des Moines, Iowa.)

National Renderers Assn., *500 Montgomery St., #310, Alexandria, VA 22314; (703) 686-8174. Fax, (571) 970-2279. Kent Swisher, President.*
General email, info@nara.org
Web, https://nara.org

Membership: manufacturers of meat meal and tallow. Compiles industry statistics; sponsors research; conducts seminars and workshops. Monitors legislation and regulations.

National Turkey Federation, *1225 New York Ave. N.W., #400, 20005-6404; (202) 898-0100. Fax, (202) 898-0203. Joel Brandenberger, President.*
General email, info@turkeyfed.org
Web, www.eatturkey.org, Twitter, @NatlTurkeyFed and Facebook, www.facebook.com/NatlTurkeyFed

Membership: turkey growers, hatcheries, breeders, and processors. Promotes turkey consumption. Monitors legislation and regulations.

North American Meat Institute, *1150 Connecticut Ave. N.W., 12th Floor, 20036; (202) 587-4200. Fax, (202) 587-4300. Julia Anna Potts, President, (202) 587-4262.*
General email, info@meatinstitute.org
Web, www.meatinstitute.org, Twitter, @MeatInstitute and Facebook, www.facebook.com/AmericanMeatInstitute

Membership: national and international meat and poultry packers, suppliers, and processors. Provides statistics on meat production and consumption, livestock, and feed grains. Funds meat research projects and consumer education programs; sponsors conferences and correspondence courses on meat production and processing. Monitors legislation and regulations. (Formed from merger of the North American Meat Assn. and American Meat Institute.)

Shelf-Stable Food Processors Assn. (SFPA), *1150 Connecticut Ave. N.W., 12th Floor, 20036; (202) 587-4200. Fax, (202) 587-4300. Julie Anna Potts, President.*
General email, info@meatinstitute.org
Web, www.meatinstitute.org and Twitter, @meatinstitute

Membership: shelf-stable food manufacturers and their suppliers. Provides information on the shelf-stable industry, particularly as it pertains to meat products. (Subsidiary of the North American Meat Institute.)

2

Business and Economics

GENERAL POLICY AND ANALYSIS

Basic Resources

►AGENCIES

Antitrust Division *(Justice Dept.), Technology and Digital Platforms,* 450 5th St. N.W., #7100, 20530; (202) 307-6200. Fax, (202) 616-8544. Aaron D. Hoag, Chief, (202) 307-6153. General email, antitrust.atr@usdoj.gov
Web, www.justice.gov/atr/about-division/tfs-section

Reviews mergers in the areas of information technology, Internet-related businesses, computer hardware and software, high-technology components, manufacturing, professional associations, financial services, and the securities industry.

Bureau of Economic and Business Affairs (EB) *(State Dept.), Commercial and Business Affairs (CBA),* 2201 C St. N.W., #4480, 20520-5820; (202) 647-0079. Scott B. Ticknor, Special Representative (Acting). General email, cbaweb@state.gov
Web, www.state.gov/bureau-offices/under-secretary-for-economic-growth-enerby-and-the-environment/bureau-of-economic-and-business-affairs

Serves as primary contact in the State Dept. for U.S. businesses. Coordinates efforts to facilitate U.S. business interests abroad, ensures that U.S. business interests are given sufficient consideration in foreign policy, and provides assistance to firms with problems overseas (such as claims and trade complaints). Oversees the Global Entrepreneurship Program.

Commerce Dept., 1401 Constitution Ave. N.W., 20230; (202) 482-2000. Gina Raimondo, Secretary. Library, (202) 482-1154. Press, (202) 482-4883.
Web, www.commerce.gov and Twitter, @CommerceGov

Acts as a principal adviser to the president on federal policy affecting industry and commerce; promotes job creation, national economic growth and development, competitiveness, international trade, and technological development; provides business and government with economic statistics, research, and analysis; encourages minority business; promotes tourism. Library open to the public by appointment.

Commerce Dept., *Business Liaison,* 1401 Constitution Ave. N.W., #5062, 20230; (202) 482-1360. Fax, (202) 482-4054. Laura O'Neil, Director.
General email, businessliaison@doc.gov
Web, www.commerce.gov/bureaus-and-offices/os/business-liaison

Serves as the federal government's central office for business assistance. Handles requests for information and services as well as complaints and suggestions from businesses; provides a forum for businesses to comment on federal regulations; initiates meetings on policy issues with industry groups, business organizations, trade and small business associations, and the corporate community.

Consumer Product Safety Commission (CPSC), *Economic Analysis,* 4330 East-West Hwy., Bethesda, MD 20814;

(301) 504-7782. Alex Moscoso, Associate Executive Director.
Web, www.cpsc.gov

Conducts studies to determine the impact of CPSC's regulations on consumers, the economy, industry, and production. Studies the potential environmental effects of commission actions.

Council of Economic Advisers *(Executive Office of the President),* 1800 G St. N.W., 20502; (202) 395-5084. Cecilia Rouse, Chair.
General email, contact@eoa.eop.gov
Web, www.whitehouse.gov/cea

Advisory body that monitors and analyzes the economy and advises the president on economic developments, trends, and policies and on the economic implications of other policy initiatives. Prepares the annual *Economic Report of the President* for Congress. Assesses economic implications of international policy.

Federal Reserve System, *Board of Governors,* 20th St. and Constitution Ave. N.W., 20551; (202) 452-3000. Jerome H. Powell, Chair; Richard H. Clarida, Vice Chair (Acting). Comments, (202) 974-7008. Congressional Liaison, (202) 452-3456. Information (meetings), (202) 452-3204. Printing and Fulfillment, (202) 452-3245. Public Affairs, (202) 452-2955. TTY, (202) 263-4869.
General email, frboard-publicaffairs@frb.gov
Web, www.federalreserve.gov, Twitter, @federalreserve, Facebook, www.facebook.com/federalreserve and YouTube, www.youtube.com/federalreserve

Sets U.S. monetary policy. Supervises the Federal Reserve System and influences credit conditions through the buying and selling of Treasury securities in the open market by fixing the amount of reserves depository institutions must maintain and by determining discount rates.

National Economic Council (NEC) *(Executive Office of the President),* The White House, 1600 Pennsylvania Ave. N.W., 20502; (202) 456-1111. Brian Deese, Director.
Web, www.whitehouse.gov/nec

Comprises cabinet members and other high-ranking executive branch officials. Coordinates domestic and international economic policymaking, provides economic policy advice to the president, ensures that policy decisions and programs are consistent with the president's economic goals, and monitors the implementation of the president's economic agenda.

National Institute of Standards and Technology (NIST) *(Commerce Dept.), Baldrige Performance Excellence Program,* 100 Bureau Dr., MS 1020, Gaithersburg, MD 20899-1020; (301) 975-2036. Fax, (301) 948-3716. Robert Fangmeyer, Director, (301) 975-4781.
General email, baldrige@nist.gov
Web, www.nist.gov/baldrige and Twitter, @BaldrigeProgram

Public–private partnership that educates business, education, and organization leaders on industry-specific best-practices management. Offers organizational assessment tools and criteria.

National Institute of Standards and Technology (NIST) (Commerce Dept.), Special Programs Office, 100 Bureau Dr., Gaithersburg, MD 20899; General email, spo_inquiries@nist.gov
Web, www.nist.gov/special-programs-office-spo

Fosters collaboration among government, military, academic, professional, and private organizations to respond to critical national needs through science-based standards and technology innovation, including the areas of manufacturing and physical infrastructure.

National Institute of Standards and Technology (NIST) (Commerce Dept.), Standards Services, 100 Bureau Dr., MS 2100, Gaithersburg, MD 20899-1200; (301) 975-4000. Fax, (301) 975-4715. Gordon Gillerman, Director, (301) 975-8406.
General email, sco@nist.gov
Web, www.nist.gov/standardsgov and www.nist.gov/topics/standards

Monitors and participates in industries' development of federal and global standards and standard-enforcement mechanisms. Conducts standards-related research and training and holds workshops for domestic and international audiences. Provides information on industry standards and specifications, conformity assessment, test methods, domestic and international technical regulations, codes, and recommended practices.

National Security Staff (NSS) (Executive Office of the President), International Economic Affairs, The White House, 1600 Pennsylvania Ave. N.W., 20504; (202) 456-1414. Daleep Singh, Deputy National Security Adviser.
Web, www.whitehouse.gov

Advises the president, the National Security Council, and the National Economic Council on all aspects of U.S. foreign policy dealing with U.S. international economic policies.

National Women's Business Council, 409 3rd St. S.W., #210, 20416; (202) 205-3850. Tene Dolphin, Exeuctive Director; Ana Argueta, Program Manager.
General email, info@nwbc.gov
Web, www.nwbc.gov, Twitter, @NWBC and Facebook, www.facebook.com/NWBCgov

Independent, congressionally mandated council established by the Women's Business Ownership Act of 1988. Reviews the status of women-owned businesses nationwide and makes policy recommendations to the president, Congress, and the Small Business Administration. Assesses the role of the federal government in aiding and promoting women-owned businesses. Offers webinars, hosts roundtables, and holds public meetings.

Small Business Administration (SBA), 409 3rd St. S.W., 20416-7000; (202) 205-6605. Fax, (202) 205-6802. Isabella Casillas Guzman, Administrator. ASL

Videophone, (855) 440-4960. Toll-free information (Answer Desk), (800) 827-5722. TTY, (800) 877-8339. General email, answerdesk@sba.gov
Web, www.sba.gov and Twitter, @SBAgov

Maintains and strengthens the nation's economy by aiding, counseling, assisting, and protecting the interests of small businesses and by helping families and businesses recover from natural disasters.

Treasury Dept., 1500 Pennsylvania Ave. N.W., #3330, 20220; (202) 622-2000. Fax, (202) 622-6415. Janet L. Yellen, Secretary. Library, (202) 622-0990. TTY, (800) 877-8339.
General email, treasury.Direct@fiscal.treasury.gov
Web, https://home.treasury.gov, Twitter, @USTreasury and Facebook, www.facebook.com/USTreasuryDept
Library, libraryreference@treasury.gov

Serves as chief financial officer of the government and adviser to the president on economic policy. Formulates and recommends domestic and international financial, economic, tax, and broad fiscal policies; manages the public debt; collects monies owed to the U.S. government; supervises national banks and thrifts. Library open to the public by appointment.

Treasury Dept., Economic Policy, 1500 Pennsylvania Ave. N.W., #3454, 20220; (202) 622-0581. Ben Harris, Assistant Secretary.
Web, https://home.treasury.gov/about/offices/economic-policy

Assists and advises the Treasury secretary in the formulation and execution of domestic and international economic policies and programs; helps prepare economic forecasts for the federal budget.

▶ **CONGRESS**

For a listing of relevant congressional committees and subcommittees, please see pages 38–39 or the Appendix.

▶ **NONGOVERNMENTAL**

American Business Conference, 1828 L St. N.W., #280, 20036; (202) 822-9300. Fax, (202) 467-4070. John Endean, President; Alfred P. West Jr., Chair.
General email, info@americanbusinessconference.org
Web, www.americanbusinessconference.org

Membership: leaders of midsize, high-growth companies. Seeks a public policy role for growth companies. Studies capital formation, tax policy, regulatory reform, and international trade.

American Council for Capital Formation (ACCF), 1001 Connecticut Ave. N.W., #620, 20036; (202) 293-5811. Mark A. Bloomfield, President. Press, (202) 420-9361.
General email, info@accf.org
Web, www.accf.org, Twitter, @ACCFmedia and Facebook, www.facebook.com/ACCFDC

Promotes tax, trade, and environmental policies conducive to saving, investment, and economic growth.

BUSINESS AND ECONOMICS RESOURCES IN CONGRESS

For a complete listing of congressional committees, including their full contact information, leadership, membership, and jurisdictions, please refer to the Appendix on pages 840–963.

HOUSE:

House Agriculture Committee, (202) 225-2171.
Web, agriculture.house.gov
    Subcommittee on Biotechnology, Horticulture, and Research, (202) 225-2171.
House Appropriations Committee, (202) 225-2771.
Web, appropriations.house.gov
    Subcommittee on Commerce, Justice, Science, and Related Agencies, (202) 225-3351.
    Subcommittee on Financial Services and General Government, (202) 225-7245.
    Subcommittee on Transportation, Housing and Urban Development, and Related Agencies, (202) 225-2141.
House Budget Committee, (202) 226-7200.
Web, budget.house.gov
House Energy and Commerce Committee, (202) 225-2927.
Web, energycommerce.house.gov
    Subcommittee on Consumer Protection and Commerce, (202) 225-2927.
    Subcommittee on Energy, (202) 225-2927.
    Subcommittee on Environment and Climate Change, (202) 225-2927.
    Subcommittee on Health, (202) 225-2927.
House Financial Services Committee, (202) 225-4247.
Web, financialservices.house.gov
    Subcommittee on Consumer Protection and Financial Institutions, (202) 225-4247.
    Subcommittee on Housing, Community Development, and Insurance, (202) 225-4247.
    Subcommittee on Investor Protection, Entrepreneurship, and Capitol Markets, (202) 225-4247.
    Subcommittee on National Security, International Development, and Monetary Policy, (202) 225-4247.

House Foreign Affairs Committee, (202) 225-5021.
Web, foreignaffairs.house.gov
    Subcommittee on Western Hemisphere, Civilian Security, Migration and International Economic Policy, (202) 225-3345.
House Judiciary Committee, (202) 225-3951.
Web, judiciary.house.gov
    Subcommittee on Antitrust, Commercial, and Administrative Law, (202) 226-7680.
    Subcommittee on Courts, Intellectual Property, and the Internet, (202) 225-5741.
House Oversight and Reform Committee, (202) 225-5051.
Web, oversight.house.gov
    Subcommittee on Economic and Consumer Policy, (202) 225-5051.
    Subcommittee on Government Operations, (202) 225-5051.
House Science, Space, and Technology Committee, (202) 225-6375.
Web, science.house.gov
    Subcommittee on Research and Technology, (202) 225-6375.
House Select Committee on the Climate Crisis, (202) 225-1106.
Web, climatecrisis.house.gov/
House Small Business Committee, (202) 225-4038.
Web, smallbusiness.house.gov
    Subcommittee on Contracting and Infrastructure, (202) 225-4038.
    Subcommittee on Economic Growth, Tax, and Capital Access, (202) 225-4038.
    Subcommittee on Innovation, Entrepreneurship, and Workforce Development, (202) 225-4038.
    Subcommittee on Oversight, Investigations, and Regulations, (202) 225-4038.
    Subcommittee on Underserved, Agricultural, and Rural Business Development, (202) 225-4038.

Affiliated with the ACCF Center for Policy Research, which conducts and funds research on capital formation topics. Monitors legislation and regulations.

American Enterprise Institute (AEI), *1789 Massachusetts Ave. N.W., 20036; (202) 862-5800. Fax, (202) 862-7177. Robert Doar, President.*
Web, www.aei.org, Twitter, @AEI and Facebook, www.facebook.com/aei

Public policy think tank promoting democracy, free enterprise, and entrepreneurship. Conducts research and sponsors events. Interests include monetary, tax, trade, financial services, and regulatory policy, labor, social security issues, and retirement.

American Society of Assn. Executives (ASAE), *1575 Eye St. N.W., #1100, 20005-1103; (202) 626-2723. Fax, (202) 371-8315. Michelle Mason, President, (202) 626-2780. Toll-free, (888) 950-2723.*
General email, ASAEservice@asaecenter.org
Web, www.asaecenter.org and Twitter, @ASAEcenter

Membership: managers of trade associations, membership societies, and volunteer organizations. Conducts research and provides educational programs on association management, trends, and developments.

Americans for Prosperity Foundation, *1310 N. Courthouse Rd., #700, Arlington, VA 22201;*

House Ways and Means Committee, (202) 225-3625.
Web, waysandmeans.house.gov
    Subcommittee on Trade, (202) 225-6649.

JOINT:
Joint Committee on Taxation, (202) 225-3621.
Web, jct.gov
Joint Economic Committee, (202) 224-5171.
Web, jec.senate.gov

SENATE:
**Senate Agriculture, Nutrition, and Forestry
Committee,** (202) 224-2035.
Web, agriculture.senate.gov
    **Subcommittee on Commodities, Risk
Management, and Trade,** (202) 224-2035.
Senate Appropriations Committee, (202) 224-7363.
Web, appropriations.senate.gov
    **Subcommittee on Commerce, Justice, Science,
and Related Agencies,** (202) 224-7363.
    **Subcommittee on Labor, Health and Human
Services, Education, and Related Agencies,**
(202) 224-7363.
**Senate Banking, Housing, and Urban Affairs
Committee,** (202) 224-7391.
Web, banking.senate.gov
    Subcommittee on Economic Policy,
(202) 224-7391.
    **Subcommittee on Financial Institutions and
Consumer Protection,** (202) 224-7391.
    **Subcommittee on National Security and
International Trade and Finance,**
(202) 224-7391.
    **Subcommittee on Securities, Insurance, and
Investment,** (202) 224-7391.
Senate Budget Committee, (202) 224-0642.
Web, budget.senate.gov

**Senate Commerce, Science, and Transportation
Committee,** (202) 224-0411.
Web, commerce.senate.gov
    **Subcommittee on Consumer Protection,
Product Safety, and Data Security,**
(202) 224-0411.
Senate Finance Committee, (202) 224-4515.
Web, finance.senate.gov
    **Subcommittee on Energy, Natural Resources, and
Infrastructure,** (202) 224-4515.
    **Subcommittee on Fiscal Responsibility and
Economic Growth,** (202) 224-4515.
    Subcommittee on Health Care, (202) 224-4515.
    **Subcommittee on International Trade,
Customs, and Global Competitiveness,**
(202) 224-4515.
    **Subcommittee on Social Security, Pensions and
Family Policy,** (202) 224-4515.
    Subcommittee on Taxation and IRS Oversight,
(202) 224-4515.
**Senate Health, Education, Labor, and Pensions
Committee,** (202) 224-5375.
Web, help.senate.gov
    **Subcommittee on Employment and Workplace
Safety,** (202) 224-5375.
**Senate Homeland Security and Governmental Affairs
Committee,** (202) 224-2627.
Web, hsgac.senate.gov
    Permanent Subcommittee on Investigations,
(202) 224-3721.
Senate Judiciary Committee, (202) 224-7703.
Web, judiciary.senate.gov
    **Subcommittee on Competition Policy, Antitrust,
and Consumer Rights,** (202) 224-3244.
    **Subcommittee on Federal Courts, Oversight,
Agency Action, and Federal Rights,**
(202) 224-2823.

*(703) 224-3200. Fax, (703) 224-3201. Emily Seidel, Chief
Executive Officer. Press, (703) 224-3177.
Web, www.americansforprosperity.org and
Twitter, @AFPhq*

Grassroots organization that seeks to educate citizens
about economic policy and encourage their participation
in the public policy process. Supports limited government
and free markets on the local, state, and federal levels. Specific interests include Social Security, trade, and taxes.
Monitors legislation and regulations.

Aspen Institute, *2300 N St. N.W., #700, 20037; (202) 736-
5800. Fax, (202) 467-0790. Daniel R. Porterfield, President.
Press, (202) 736-3849.*

General email, info@aspeninstitute.org
*Web, www.aspeninstitute.org and
Twitter, @AspenInstitute*

Educational and policy studies organization. Promotes
consideration of the public good in a wide variety of policy
areas, including business management and economic
development. Working with international partners, offers
educational seminars, nonpartisan policy forums, public
conferences and events, and leadership development
initiatives.

Association of Chamber of Commerce Executives, *1330
Braddock Pl., #300, Alexandria, VA 22314; (703) 998-0072.
Sheree Anne Kelly, Chief Executive Officer, (703) 998-3540.*

Commerce Department

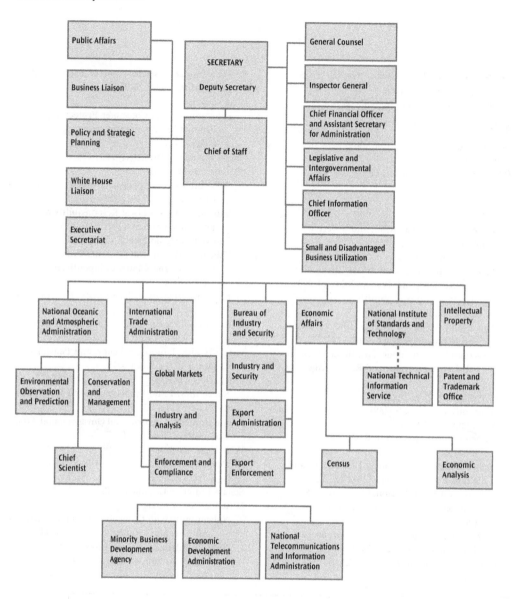

Web, www.acce.org, Twitter, @ACCEHQ and Facebook, www.facebook.com/ACCEHQ

Membership: executives of local, state, and international chambers of commerce, convention and visitors bureaus, and economic development organizations. Conducts educational programs and conferences for members on topics of interest, including professional development, government relations, management symposiums, peer networking, and industry information and data. Assembles special interest committees for members.

Atlas Network, *Two Liberty Center, 4075 Wilson Blvd., #310, Arlington, VA 22203; (202) 449-8449. Fax, (202) 280-1259. Brad Lips, Chief Executive Officer. Press, (202) 449-8441.*

General email, info@atlasnetwork.org

Web, www.atlasnetwork.org, Twitter, @AtlasNetwork and Facebook, www.facebook.com/atlasnetwork

Connects free market–oriented think tanks that seek to reform global economic policy. Distributes grants to new institutes, international student groups, and select partner projects. Administers awards and training programs for free-enterprise organization leaders. Holds forums and events that focus on the advancement of a free-market economic system.

The Brookings Institution, *Center on Regulation and Markets (CRM),* 1775 Massachusetts Ave. N.W., 20036; (202) 797-6105. Sanjay Patnaik, Director.

Federal Trade Commission

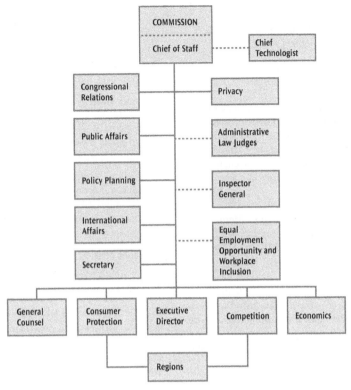

- - - - Denotes independent operation within the agency

General email, regcenter@brookings.edu

Web, www.brookings.edu/center/center-on-regulation-and-markets

Research center promoting rigorous economic scholarship to inform regulatory policymaking, the regulatory process, and the efficient and equitable functioning of economic markets. The Center provides independent, non-partisan research on Artificial intelligence and emerging technologies. Financial markets and fintech,Consumer protection and anti-trust, Climate change and carbon pricing, regulatory policy and efficient and equitable functioning of economic markets; makes regulatory reform recommendations.

The Brookings Institution, *Economic Studies,* 1775 *Massachusetts Ave. N.W., 20036-2188; (202) 797-6414. (202) 540-7721. Stephanie Aaronson, Vice President. General email, escomment@brookings.edu*

Web, www.brookings.edu/economics and Twitter, @BrookingsEcon

Sponsors economic research and publishes studies on domestic and international economics, macroeconomics, worldwide economic growth and stability, public finance, industrial organization and regulation, labor economics, social policy, and the economics of human resources.

The Brookings Institution, *Metropolitan Policy Program,* 1755 Massachusetts Ave. N.W., 20036; (202) 238-3139. Amy Liu, Director.

General email, metro@brookings.edu

Web, www.brookings.edu/metro,

Twitter, @BrookingsMetro

Twitter, Director, @amy_liuw

Provides research and policy analysis to public, private, and nonprofit leaders to drive economic growth and prosperity. Interests include human capital and economic mobility, industrial innovation and productivity, global marketplace engagement, and infrastructure sustainability.

The Business Council, 1901 Pennsylvania Ave. N.W., #307, 20006; (202) 298-7650. Fax, (202) 785-0296. Marlene M. Colucci, Executive Director. Web, https://businesscouncil.com

Membership: current and former chief executive officers of major corporations. Serves as a forum for business and government to exchange views and explore public policy as it affects U.S. business interests.

The Business Roundtable, 1000 Maine Ave. S.W., #500, 20024; (202) 872-1260. Kristen Silverberg, President. General email, info@brt.org

Web, www.businessroundtable.org, Twitter, @BizRoundtable and Facebook, www.facebook.com/BusinessRoundtable

Membership: chief executives of the nation's largest corporations. Examines issues of taxation, antitrust law, corporate governance, international trade, employment policy, and the federal budget. Monitors legislation and regulations.

Business–Higher Education Forum, *1 Dupont Circle, #360, 20036; (202) 853-9052. Janet Chen, Director.*
General email, info@bhef.com
Web, www.bhef.com, Twitter, @BHEF
Press, ursula.gross@bhef.org

Membership: chief executive officers of major corporations, foundations, colleges, and universities. Develops and promotes policy positions to enhance U.S. competitiveness. Interests include improving student achievement and readiness for college and work; and strengthening higher education, particularly in the fields of science, technology, engineering, and math.

Center for Study of Public Choice *(George Mason University), Carow Hall, 4400 University Dr., MS 1D3, Fairfax, VA 22030-4444; (703) 993-2330. Fax, (703) 993-2323. Alexander Tabarrok, Director.*
Web, https://publicchoice.gmu.edu

Promotes research in public choice, an interdisciplinary approach to the study of the relationship between economic and political institutions. Interests include constitutional economics, public finance, federalism and local government, econometrics, and trade protection and regulation. Sponsors conferences and seminars.

Competitive Enterprise Institute, *1310 L St. N.W., 7th Floor, 20005; (202) 331-1010. Kent Lassman, President; Matthew Adams, Government Affairs. Press, (202) 331-2277.*
General email, info@cei.org
Web, https://cei.org, Twitter, @ceidotorg and Facebook, www.facebook.com/CompetitiveEnterprise Institute

Advocates free enterprise and limited government. Produces policy analyses on labor, banking, financial services, infrastructure, transportation, antitrust, biotechnological, and environmental issues. Monitors legislation and litigates against restrictive regulations through its Free Market Legal Program.

Council on Competitiveness, *900 17th St. N.W., #700, 20006; (202) 682-4292. Fax, (202) 682-5150. Deborah L. Wince-Smith, President; William (Bill) C. Bates, Executive Vice President, (202) 969-3395.*
General email, info@compete.org
Web, www.compete.org and Twitter, @CompeteNow

Nonpartisan peer organization. Membership: chief executives from business, education, and labor. Seeks increased public awareness of issues related to economic competitiveness. Works to set a national action agenda for U.S. competitiveness in global markets.

Economic Policy Institute, *1225 Eye St. N.W., #600, 20005; (202) 775-8810. Fax, (202) 775-0819. Heidi Shierholz, President.*
General email, epi@epi.org
Web, www.epi.org, Twitter, @EconomicPolicy and Facebook, www.facebook.com/EconomicPolicy

Nonprofit think tank that researches the impact of economic trends and policies on U.S. workers. Publishes analyses on economics, economic development, competitiveness, income distribution, industrial competitiveness, and investment. Conducts public conferences and seminars.

Economic Strategy Institute, *1730 Rhode Island Ave. N.W., #414, 20036; (202) 213-7051. Fax, (202) 339-0880. Clyde V. Prestowitz Jr., President.*
General email, info@econstrat.org
Web, http://econstrat.org and Twitter, @clydeprestowitz

Works to increase U.S. economic competitiveness through research on domestic and international economic policies, industrial and technological developments, and global security issues. Testifies before Congress and government agencies.

Good Jobs First, *1380 Monroe St. N.W. PMB 405, 20010; (202) 232-1616. Greg LeRoy, Executive Director, (202) 232-4258.*
General email, info@goodjobsfirst.org
Web, www.goodjobsfirst.org, Twitter, @GoodJobsFirst and Facebook, www.facebook.com/GoodJobsFirst

Promotes corporate and government accountability in economic development incentives; primary focus is on state and local job subsidies with emerging work on federal development programs and federal regulatory violations data. Maintains Subsidy Tracker database. Includes Good Jobs New York and the Corporate Research Project.

Greater Washington Board of Trade, *800 Connecticut Ave. N.W., #1001, 20006; (202) 857-5900. Jack McDougle, President.*
General email, info@bot.org
Web, www.bot.org, Twitter, @GWBoardofTrade and Facebook, www.facebook.com/GWBoardofTrade

Promotes and plans economic growth for the capital region. Supports business-government partnerships, technological training, and transportation planning; promotes international trade; works to increase economic viability of the city of Washington. Monitors legislation and regulations at local, state, and federal levels.

Mercatus Center *(George Mason University), 3434 Washington Blvd., 4th Floor, Arlington, VA 22201; (703) 993-4930. Fax, (703) 993-4935. Daniel M. Rothschild, Executive Director. Toll-free, (800) 815-5711.*
General email, mercatus@mercatus.gmu.edu
Web, www.mercatus.org, Twitter, @mercatus, Facebook, www.facebook.com/mercatus and YouTube, www.youtube.com/user/MercatusCenter

Research center that studies sustained prosperity in societies and the conditions that contribute to economic success. Interests include the drivers of social, political, and economic change; international and domestic economic development; entrepreneurship and the institutions that enable it; the benefits and costs of regulatory policy;

government performance and transparency; and good governance practices. Also studies the benefits of market-oriented systems using market process analysis. Seeks to bridge the gap between academic research and public policy problems.

National Assn. of Corporate Directors, *1515 N. Courthouse Rd., #1200, Arlington, VA 22201; (571) 367-3700. Fax, (571) 367-3699. Peter Gleason, President.*
General email, join@nacdonline.org

Web, www.nacdonline.org and Twitter, @NACD

Membership: executives of public, private, and nonprofit companies. Serves as a clearinghouse on corporate governance and current board practices. Sponsors seminars, peer forums, research, publications, and board development programs.

National Assn. of Manufacturers (NAM), *State Affairs, 733 10th St. N.W., #700, 20001; (202) 637-3052. Fax, (202) 637-3182. Amy Rawlings, Executive Director.*
General email, info@nam.org

Web, www.nam.org

Membership: employer associations at the regional, state, and local levels. Works to strengthen the U.S. competitive enterprise system. Represents views of the industry on business and economic issues; sponsors conferences and seminars.

National Assn. of State Budget Officers, *444 N. Capitol St. N.W., #642, 20001-1511; (202) 624-5382. Shelby Kerns, Executive Director, (202) 624-8804.*
General email, nasbo-direct@nasbo.org

Web, www.nasbo.org and Twitter, @NASBO

Membership: state budget and financial officers. Advances state budget practices through research, policy analysis, education, and knowledge sharing. Publishes reports on budget-related issues; shares best practices; provides training and technical assistance. (Affiliate of the National Governors Assn.)

National Economists Club, *P.O. Box 33511, 20033-3511; 7010 Devereux Circle, Alexandria, VA 22315; (703) 493-8824. Fax, (703) 739-9405. Emily Sanchez, President.*
General email, manager@national-economists.org

Web, www.national-economists.org,
Twitter, @NatlEconClub and Facebook, www.facebook .com/NationalEconomistsClub

Provides venues for scholars, policymakers, business leaders, and public figures to present and defend their views on timely economic topics. Offers members employment and networking opportunities.

Partnership for Public Service, *600 14th St. N.W., # 600, 20005; (202) 775-9111. Fax, (202) 775-8885. Max Stier, President. Press, (202) 775-2747.*
Web, www.ourpublicservice.org, Twitter, @RPublicService and Facebook, www.facebook.com/partnershipforpublic service

Membership: large corporations and private businesses, including financial and information technology organizations. Seeks to improve government efficiency,

productivity, and management through a cooperative effort of the public and private sectors.

Prosperity Now, *1200 G St. N.W., #400, 20005; (202) 408-9788. Gary Cunningham, President.*
General email, hello@prosperitynow.org

Web, https://prosperitynow.org, Twitter, @prosperitynow and Facebook, www.facebook.com/ProsperityNow.org

Works to alleviate poverty by expanding economic opportunity and participation, bringing together community practice, public policy, and private markets in new and effective ways. (Formerly Corp. for Enterprise Development.)

U.S. Chamber Litigation Center, *1615 H St. N.W., 20062-2000; (202) 463-5337. Darryl Joseffer, Executive Vice President.*
Web, www.chamberlitigation.com and Twitter, @USCClitigation

Public policy law firm of the U.S. Chamber of Commerce. Advocates businesses' positions in court on such issues as antitrust, bankruptcy, and employment, as well as environmental and constitutional law. Provides businesses with legal assistance and amicus support in legal proceedings before federal courts and agencies.

U.S. Chamber of Commerce, *1615 H St. N.W., 20062-2000; (202) 659-6000. Suzanne Clark, Chief Executive Officer.*
General email, press@uschamber.com

Web, www.uschamber.com, Twitter, @USChamber and Facebook, www.facebook.com/USChamber

Federation of businesses; trade and professional associations; state and local chambers of commerce; and American chambers of commerce abroad. Sponsors programs on management, business confidence, small business, consumer affairs, economic policy, minority business, and tax policy. Monitors legislation and regulations.

U.S. Chamber of Commerce, *Congressional and Public Affairs, 1615 H St. N.W., 20062-2000; (202) 463-5600. Jack Howard, Senior Vice President.*
Web, www.uschamber.com/program/policy/government-affairs

Advocates businesses' position on government and regulatory affairs. Monitors legislation and regulations on antitrust and corporate policy, product liability, and business-consumer relations.

U.S. Chamber of Commerce, *Economic and Tax Policy, 1615 H St. N.W., 20062-2000; (202) 463-5620. Carolyn L. Harris, Chief Tax Policy Counsel. Press, (202) 463-5682.*
Web, www.uschamber.com/taxes, Twitter, @USChamber and Facebook, www.facebook.com/SCC_TaxTeam

Represents the business community's views on economic policy, including government spending, the federal budget, and tax issues. Forecasts the economy of the United States and other industrialized nations and projects the impact of major policy changes. Studies economic trends and analyzes their effect on the business community.

Coins and Currency

▶AGENCIES

Bureau of Engraving and Printing (BEP) *(Treasury Dept.)*, *14th and C Sts. S.W., 20228; (202) 874-3188. Leonard R. Olijar, Director. Toll-free, (877) 874-4114. Tours, (202) 874-2330.*
General email, moneyfactory.info@bep.gov
Web, www.moneyfactory.gov and Facebook, www.facebook/ USMoneyfactory

Designs, engraves, and prints Federal Reserve notes, military certificates, White House invitations, presidential portraits, and special security documents for the federal government.

Bureau of Engraving and Printing (BEP) *(Treasury Dept.)*, *Mutilated Currency Division, 14th and C Sts. S.W., 20228 (mailing address: BEP/MCD, #344A, P.O. Box 37048, Washington, DC 20013); (202) 874-2141. Leonard (Len) R. Olijar, Director, (202) 874-4373. Public tours toll-free, (866) 874-2330. Toll-free, (866) 575-2361.*
General email, moneyfactory.info@bep.gov
Web, www.moneyfactory.gov/bep.gov/services/ currencyredemption.html
Damaged Currency claims information, mcdstatus@ bep.gov

Redeems U.S. currency that has been mutilated.

Bureau of the Fiscal Service *(Treasury Dept.)*, *401 14th St. S.W., #545, 20227 (mailing address: 3201 Pennsy Dr., Bldg. E, Landover, MD 20785); (202) 874-7000. Fax, (202) 622-6415. Timothy (Tim) E. Gribben, Commissioner. Press and Congressional inquiries, (202) 504-3535. Public Affairs, (202) 622-2960. Savings Bonds, (844) 284-2676.*
General email, Treasury.Direct@fiscal.treasury.gov
Web, www.fiscal.treasury.gov, Twitter, @FiscalService, Facebook, www.facebook.com/fiscalservice and YouTube, www.youtube.com/user/TREASURYDIRECT/ featured
Buy and redeem securities online, home.treasury.gov/ services/bonds-and-securities

Prepares and publishes for the president, Congress, and the public monthly, quarterly, and annual statements of government financial transactions, including reports on U.S. currency and coins in circulation.

Federal Reserve System, *Board of Governors, 20th St. and Constitution Ave. N.W., 20551; (202) 452-3000. Jerome H. Powell, Chair; Richard H. Clarida, Vice Chair (Acting). Comments, (202) 974-7008. Congressional Liaison, (202) 452-3456. Information (meetings), (202) 452-3204. Printing and Fulfillment, (202) 452-3245. Public Affairs, (202) 452-2955. TTY, (202) 263-4869.*
General email, frboard-publicaffairs@frb.gov
Web, www.federalreserve.gov, Twitter, @federalreserve, Facebook, www.facebook.com/federalreserve and YouTube, www.youtube.com/federalreserve

Influences the availability of money as part of its responsibility for monetary policy; maintains reading room for inspection of records that are available to the public.

National Museum of American History *(Smithsonian Institution)*, *National Numismatic Collection, 14th St. and Constitution Ave. N.W., 20013 (mailing address: P.O. Box 37012, MS 609, Washington, DC 20013-7012); (202) 633-1000. Ellen Feingold, Curator of National Collection.*
General email, NMAH-NNC@si.edu
Web, http://americanhistory.si.edu/collections/ numismatics

Develops and maintains collections of ancient, medieval, modern, U.S., and world coins; U.S. and world currencies; tokens; medals; orders and decorations; and traditional exchange media. Conducts research and responds to public inquiries. Collection can be viewed online.

Treasury Dept., *1500 Pennsylvania Ave. N.W., #3330, 20220; (202) 622-2000. Fax, (202) 622-6415. Janet L. Yellen, Secretary. Library, (202) 622-0990. TTY, (800) 877-8339.*
General email, treasury.Direct@fiscal.treasury.gov
Web, https://home.treasury.gov
Library, libraryreference@treasury.gov, Twitter, @USTreasury and Facebook, www.facebook.com/ USTreasuryDept

Oversees the manufacture of U.S. coins and currency; submits to Congress final reports on the minting of coins or any changes in currency. Library open to the public by appointment.

Treasury Dept., *Treasurer of the United States, 1500 Pennsylvania Ave. N.W., #2134, 20220; (202) 622-0100. Vacant, Treasurer.*
Web, www.treasury.gov/about/organizational-structure/ offices/Pages/Office-of-the-Treasurer.aspx

Advises the secretary of the Treasury on matters relating to coinage, currency, and the production of other instruments issued by the United States. Has direct oversight over the U.S. Mint, Bureau of Engraving and Printing, and Fort Knox, and is a key liaison with the Federal Reserve. Represents the department in public engagement efforts.

U.S. Mint *(Treasury Dept.)*, *801 9th St. N.W., 8th Floor, 20220; (202) 756-6468. Ventris G. Gibson, Deputy Director. Customer service, (800) 872-6468. Information, (202) 354-7227. Press, (202) 354-7222. Toll-free, 800-USA-MINT. TTY, (888) 321-6468.*
General email, inquiries@usmint.treas.gov
Web, www.usmint.gov, Twitter, @usmint, Facebook, www.facebook.com/UnitedStatesMint and YouTube, www.youtube.com/USMint

Manufactures and distributes all domestic coins; safeguards the government's holdings of precious metals; manufactures and sells commemorative coins and medals of historic interest. Maintains a kiosk at its main building.

Americans for Common Cents, *1401 Eye St. N.W., #800, 20005; (202) 626-8363. Fax, (202) 408-6399. Mark Weller, Executive Director.*
General email, info@pennies.org
Web, www.pennies.org

Educates policymakers and the public about the penny's impact on the economy. Monitors legislation and regulations to advocate keeping the one-cent coin in the U.S. monetary system.

Federal Budget

▶AGENCIES

Bureau of the Fiscal Service *(Treasury Dept.), 401 14th St. S.W., #545, 20227 (mailing address: 3201 Pennsy Dr., Bldg. E, Landover, MD 20785); (202) 874-7000. Fax, (202) 622-6415. Timothy (Tim) E. Gribben, Commissioner. Press and Congressional inquiries, (202) 504-3535. Public Affairs, (202) 622-2960. Savings Bonds, (844) 284-2676. General email, Treasury.Direct@fiscal.treasury.gov, and Web, www.fiscal.treasury.gov, Twitter, @FiscalService, Facebook, www.facebook.com/fiscalservice and YouTube, www.youtube.com/user/TREASURYDIRECT/ featured*
Buy and redeem securities online, home.treasury.gov/ services/bonds-and-securities

Borrows to finance federal government operations by selling public debt securities, Treasury notes, and bonds; maintains all records on series EE and HH savings bonds.

Federal Financing Bank *(Treasury Dept.), 1500 Pennsylvania Ave. N.W., 20220; (202) 622-2470. Christopher Tuttle, Chief Financial Officer.*
General email, FFB@treasury.gov
Web, www.treasury.gov/ffb

Coordinates federal agency borrowing by purchasing securities issued or guaranteed by federal agencies; funds its operations by borrowing from the Treasury.

Office of Management and Budget (OMB) *(Executive Office of the President), 725 17th St. N.W., 20503; (202) 395-3080. Shalanda Young, Director.*
Web, www.whitehouse.gov/omb and Twitter, @OMBPress

Prepares the president's annual budget; works with the Council of Economic Advisers and the Treasury Dept. to develop the federal government's fiscal program; oversees administration of the budget; reviews government regulations; coordinates administration procurement and management policy.

Office of Management and Budget (OMB) *(Executive Office of the President), Energy, Science, and Water, 725*
17th St. N.W., #8002, 20503; (202) 395-3404. John Pasquantino, Deputy Associate Director.
Web, www.whitehouse.gov/omb

Advises in budget preparation for federal energy, pscience, and space programs.

Office of Management and Budget (OMB) *(Executive Office of the President), Transportation, 725 17th St. N.W., #9002, 20503; (202) 395-6138. Fax, (202) 395-4797. David Connolly, Chief.*
Web, www.whitehouse.gov/omb

Assists and advises the OMB director on budget preparation, proposed legislation, and evaluations of Transportation Dept.'s programs, policies, and activities.

Office of Management and Budget (OMB) *(Executive Office of the President), Water and Power, 725 17th St. N.W., #8002, 20503; (202) 395-4590. Fax, (202) 395-4817. Kelly Colyar, Chief.*
Web, www.whitehouse.gov/omb

Reviews all plans and budgets related to federal or federally assisted water power and related land resource projects.

Treasury Dept., *Domestic Finance, Debt Management, 1500 Pennsylvania Ave. N.W., #2417, 20220; (202) 622-1885. Fred Pietrangeli, Director.*
Web, https://home.treasury.gov/about/offices/domestic-finance/financial-markets

Provides financial and economic analysis on government financing and Treasury debt management. Coordinates, analyzes, and reviews government borrowing, lending, and investment activities. Determines interest rates for government borrowing and lending programs.

Treasury Dept., *Domestic Finance, Federal Program Finance, 1500 Pennsylvania Av. N.W., 20220; (202) 622-5447. Jeff Stout, Director.*
Web, https://home.treasury.gov/about/offices/domestic-finance/financial-markets

Analyzes federal credit program principles and standards, legislation, and proposals related to government borrowing, lending, and investment. Furnishes actuarial and mathematical analysis required for Treasury market financing, the Federal Financing Bank, and other government agencies.

Treasury Dept., *Economic Policy, 1500 Pennsylvania Ave. N.W., #3454, 20220; (202) 622-0581. Ben Harris, Assistant Secretary.*
Web, https://home.treasury.gov/about/offices/economic-policy

Assists and advises the Treasury secretary in the formulation and execution of domestic and international economic policies and programs; helps prepare economic forecasts for the federal budget.

▶CONGRESS

For a listing of relevant congressional committees and subcommittees, please see pages 38–39 or the Appendix.

Congressional Budget Office, *FHOB, 2nd and D Sts. S.W., 4th Floor, 20515-6925; (202) 226-2700. Phillip Swagel, Director; Leigh Angres, Director of*

Treasury Department

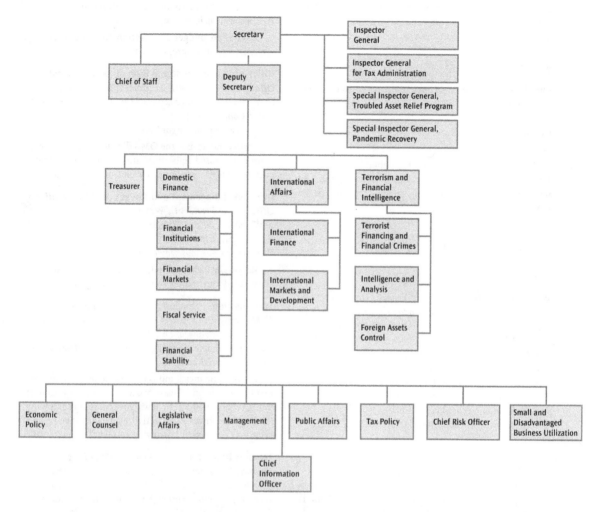

Legislative Affairs, (202) 226-2837. Legislative Affairs, (202) 226-2837. Press, (202) 226-2602.
General email, communications@cbo.gov
Web, www.cbo.gov, Twitter, @USCBO and YouTube, www.youtube.com/uscbo

Nonpartisan office that provides the House and Senate with analyses needed for economic and budget decisions, and with the information and estimates required for the congressional budget process.

Government Accountability Office (GAO), *Contracting and National Security Acquisitions (CNSA), 441 G St. N.W., 20548; (202) 512-4841. John D. Sawyer, Director (Acting).*
Web, www.gao.gov/about/careers/our-teams

Advises Congress and governmental agencies about federal spending and maximizing investments related to acquisitions and procurements.

Government Accountability Office (GAO), *Financial Management and Assurance (FMA), 441 G St. N.W., 20548; (202) 512-9377. Cheryl Clark, Director.*
Web, www.gao.gov/about/careers/our-teams

Audits the federal government's consolidated financial statements and the statements of several other federal agencies; identifies opportunities to improve accountability for federal assets; issues standards for government audits and federal internal controls.

Office of Management and Budget (OMB) *(Executive Office of the President), Housing, 725 17th St. N.W., #9226, 20503; (202) 395-7874. Jessica Lee, Chief, (202) 395-6141.*
Web, www.whitehouse.gov/omb

Assists and advises the OMB director in budget preparation, reorganizations, and evaluations of Housing and Urban Development Dept. programs.

▶ **NONGOVERNMENTAL**

Committee for a Responsible Federal Budget, *1900 M St. N.W., #850, 20036; (202) 596-3597.*
Maya MacGuineas, President.
General email, info@crfb.org
Web, www.crfb.org, Twitter, @BudgetHawks and Facebook, www.facebook.com/BudgetHawks

Bipartisan nonprofit organization that educates the public about issues that have significant fiscal policy impact. Monitors legislation and regulation. (Affiliated with the New America Foundation.)

Concord Coalition, *1530 Wilson Blvd., #550, Arlington, VA 22209; (703) 894-6222. Robert L. Bixby, Executive Director.*
General email, concordcoalition@concordcoalition.org
Web, www.concordcoalition.org and Twitter, @ConcordC

Nonpartisan grassroots organization dedicated to educating the public about responsible fiscal policy and the risks and consequences of federal budget deficits and unsustainable fiscal policies. Interests include the long-term challenges facing America's entitlement programs, how to build a sound foundation for economic growth, and ensuring that Social Security, Medicare, and Medicaid are secure for all generations.

Taxpayers for Common Sense, *651 Pennsylvania Ave. S.E., 20003; (202) 546-8500. Steve Ellis, President. Press, (202) 546-8500, ext. 106.*
General email, info@taxpayer.net
Web, www.taxpayer.net

Nonpartisan budget watchdog organization that promotes transparency with federal spending decisions; oversight, regulation, and independent financial audits of federal programs and agencies; and elimination of earmarks, corporate welfare, and ineffective subsidies.

Statistics, Economic Projections

▶**AGENCIES**

Bureau of Economic Analysis (BEA) *(Commerce Dept.), 4600 Silver Hill Rd., 20233 (mailing address: 4600 Silver Hill Rd., Suitland, MD 20746); (301) 278-9004. Mary Bohman, Director (Acting).*
General email, CustomerService@bea.gov
Web, www.bea.gov, Twitter, @BEA_NEWS and YouTube, www.youtube.com/channel/UCCP9QD1x_z__duUivA6Yb5w

Compiles, analyzes, and publishes data on measures of aggregate U.S. economic activity, including gross domestic product; prices by type of expenditure; personal income and outlays; personal savings; corporate profits; capital stock; U.S. international transactions; and foreign investment. Provides statistics of personal income and employment by industry for regions, states, metropolitan areas, and counties. Refers specific inquiries to economic specialists in the field.

Bureau of Labor Statistics (BLS) *(Labor Dept.), Postal Square Bldg., 2 Massachusetts Ave. N.E., #4040, 20212-0001; (202) 691-5200. Fax, (202) 691-7890. William W. Beach, Commissioner. Press, (202) 691-5902. TTY, (800) 877-8339.*
General email, blsdata_staff@bls.gov
Web, www.bls.gov and Twitter, @BLS_gov

Provides statistical data on the structure and growth of the economy. Publishes reports on these statistical trends, including the *Consumer Price Index, Producer Price Index,* and *Employment and Earnings.*

Bureau of Labor Statistics (BLS) *(Labor Dept.), Prices and Living Conditions (OPLC), 2 Massachusetts Ave. N.E., #3120, 20212-0001; (202) 691-6960. Fax, (202) 691-7080. Jeffrey Hill, Associate Commissioner. Information, (202) 691-7000. Seasonal adjustments, (202) 691-6968.*
Web, www.bls.gov/cpi

Collects, processes, analyzes, and disseminates data relating to prices and consumer expenditures; maintains the Consumer Price Index.

Bureau of Labor Statistics (BLS) *(Labor Dept.), Prices and Living Conditions (OPLC), Industrial Prices and Price Index, 2 Massachusetts Ave. N.E., #3840, 20212-0001; (202) 691-7705. Bonnie Murphy, Assistant Commissioner.*
General email, ppi-info@bls.gov
Web, www.bls.gov/ppi

Compiles statistics on energy, apparel, pharmaceuticals, printing, construction materials, and all U.S. products for the Producer Price Index; analyzes movement of prices for natural gas, petroleum, coal, and electric power in the primary commercial and industrial markets. Records changes over time in the prices domestic producers receive.

Bureau of Labor Statistics (BLS) *(Labor Dept.), Productivity and Technology (OPT), 2 Massachusetts Ave. N.E., #2150, 20212-0001; (202) 691-6598. Fax, (202) 691-5664. Lucy P. Eldridge, Associate Commissioner.*
General email, dipsweb@bls.gov
Web, www.bls.gov/bls/productivity.htm

Develops and analyzes productivity measures for the U.S. business economy and industries, and conducts research on factors affecting productivity.

Census Bureau *(Commerce Dept.), Economic Programs, 4600 Silver Hill Rd., #8H132, Suitland, MD 20746 (mailing address: 4600 Silver Hill Rd., #8H132, Washington, DC 20233-6000); (301) 763-4822. Nick Orsini, Associate Director, (301) 763-6959.*
Web, www.census.gov/topics/business-economy/library/flyers/economic-programs.html

Compiles comprehensive statistics on the level and structure of U.S. economic activity and the characteristics of industrial and business establishments at the national, state, and local levels; collects and publishes foreign trade statistics. Explains proper use of data on county business patterns, classification of industries and commodities, and business statistics. Compiles quarterly reports listing financial data for corporations in certain industrial sectors.

Census Bureau *(Commerce Dept.), Economy-Wide Statistics, 4600 Silver Hill Rd., #8K154, Suitland, MD 20746-2401 (mailing address: 4700 Silver Hill Rd., #8K064,*

Washington, DC 20233-6500); (301) 763-7643.
Kimberly (Kim) P. Moore, Chief.
Web, www.census.gov

Provides data of five-year census programs on retail, wholesale, and service industries. Conducts periodic monthly or annual surveys for specific items within these industries.

Census Bureau ***(Commerce Dept.), International Trade Management,*** *4600 Silver Hill Rd., #6K032, Suitland, MD 20233; Dale Kelly, Division Chief, (301) 763-6937. Trade Outreach Branch Phone, (800) 549-0595, ext. 5.*
General email, eid.international.trade.data@census.gov
Web, www.census.gov/foreign-trade/index.html

Provides detailed statistics on all U.S. imports and exports, including petroleum, advanced technology products, and agricultural products; organizes this information by commodity, country, state, district, and port.

Census Bureau ***(Commerce Dept.), Manufacturing and Construction,*** *4600 Silver Hill Rd., #8K151, Suitland, MD 20746 (mailing address: 4600 Silver Hill Rd., Washington, DC 20233); (301) 763-4673.*
Web, www.census.gov/manufacturing

Collects, tabulates, and publishes statistics for the manufacturing and construction sectors of the Economic Census.

Council of Economic Advisers ***(Executive Office of the President), Statistical Office,*** *725 17th St. N.W., 20502; (202) 395-5062. Cecilia Rouse, Chair.*
Web, www.whitehouse.gov/cea

Compiles and reports aggregate economic data, including national income and expenditures, employment, wages, productivity, production and business activity, prices, money stock, credit, finance, government finance, agriculture, and international statistics.

Economic Research Service (ERS) ***(Agriculture Dept.),*** *355 E St. S.W., 20024-3221 (mailing address: 1400 Independence Ave. S.W., MS 1800, Washington, DC 20250-0002); (202) 694-5000. Fax, (202) 245-5467. Spiro Stefanou, Administrator. Public Affairs, (202) 694-5139.*
General email, service@ers.usda.gov
Web, www.ers.usda.gov and *Twitter, @USDA_ERS*

Conducts market research; studies and forecasts domestic supply-and-demand trends for fruits and vegetables.

Federal Reserve System, ***Research and Statistics,*** *20th and C Sts. N.W., #B3048, 20551; (202) 452-2322. Stacey Tevlin, Director.*
Web, www.federalreserve.gov/econres/rsstaff.htm

Publishes statistical data and analyses on business finance, real estate credit, consumer credit, industrial production, construction, and flow of funds.

Internal Revenue Service (IRS) ***(Treasury Dept.), Statistics of Income,*** *1111 Constitution Ave. N.W., #K-4112, 20224 (mailing address: P.O. Box 2608, Washington, DC 20013-2608); (202) 803-9285. Fax, (202) 803-9393. Tamara Rib, Chief.*
General email, sis@irs.gov
Web, www.irs.gov/statistics/soi-tax-stats-about-soi

Provides the public and the Treasury Dept. with statistical information on tax laws. Prepares statistical information for the Commerce Dept. to use in formulating the gross national product (GNP). Publishes *Statistics of Income*, a series available at cost to the public.

International Trade Administration (ITA) ***(Commerce Dept.), Industry and Analysis (I&A), Trade Policy and Analysis (OTNA),*** *1401 Constitution Ave. N.W., Room 21028, 20230; (202) 482-3177. Fax, (202) 482-4614. Praveen Dixit, Deputy Assistant Secretary.*
Web, https://trade.gov/about-us/trade-policy-analysis

Analyzes international and domestic competitiveness of U.S. industry and component sectors. Assesses impact of regulations on competitive positions. Produces and disseminates U.S. foreign trade and related economic data. Supports U.S. international trade negotiations initiative.

National Agricultural Statistics Service ***(Agriculture Dept.),*** *1400 Independence Ave. S.W., #5041, MS 2001, 20250-2001; (202) 720-2707. Hubert Hamer, Administrator. Library, (202) 690-8127. Public Affairs, (202) 690-8923. Toll-free, (800) 727-9540.*
General email, nass@nass.usda.gov
Web, www.nass.usda.gov and *Twitter, @usda_nass*

Prepares estimates and reports on production, supply, prices, and other items relating to the U.S. agricultural economy. Reports include statistics on field crops, fruits and vegetables, cattle, hogs, poultry, and related products. Prepares quinquennial national census of agriculture.

Securities and Exchange Commission (SEC), ***Economic and Risk Analysis,*** *100 F St. N.E., 20549; (202) 551-6600. Jessica Wachter, Director.*
General email, DERA@sec.gov
Web, www.sec.gov/dera and *Twitter, @SEC_DERA*

Advises the commission and its staff on economic issues as they pertain to the commission's regulatory activities. Publishes data on trading volume of the stock exchanges; compiles statistics on financial reports of brokerage firms; identifies and analyzes issues, trends, and innovations in the marketplace.

Treasury Dept., ***Financial Research,*** *717 14th St. N.W., 20220; (202) 622-3002. Dino Falaschetti, Director.*
Web, www.financialresearch.gov, Twitter, @OFRgov
Congressional inquiries, OFRGovernmentAffairs@ofr.treasury.gov
Press, mediainquiries@ofr.treasury.gov

Conducts research about financial stability and risk management and promotes high-quality financial data, standards, and analysis for the Financial Stability Oversight Council and the public.

Treasury Dept., Risk Management, 1500 Pennsylvania Ave. N.W., 20220; (202) 622-2983. Norman Wyatt, Chief Risk Officer (Acting); Karen Weber, Director.
General email, ORM@Treasury.gov
Web, www.treasury.gov/about/organizational-structure/offices/Pages/chief-risk-management.aspx

Recommends policies and promotes programs to the Treasury Dept. and the federal government relating to the management of credit, market, liquidity, operational, and reputational risks.

U.S. International Trade Commission, Industries, 500 E St. S.W., Washington, DC 20436; (202) 205-3296. Jonathan R. Coleman, Director, (202) 205-3465.
Web, www.usitc.gov/offices/industries and www.usitc.gov/industries

Identifies, analyzes, and develops data on economic and technical matters related to the competitive position of the United States in domestic and world markets in agriculture and forest production, chemicals, textiles, energy, technology, transportation, services and investments, minerals, metals, and machinery.

▶**CONGRESS**

Library of Congress, Science, Technology, and Business Division, John Adams Bldg., 101 Independence Ave. S.E., #LA 500, 20540-4750; (202) 707-0948. Fax, (202) 707-1925. Ronald (Ron) Bluestone, Chief. Business Reference Services, (202) 707-7934. Reading Room, (202) 707-5639. Technical reports, (202) 707-5655.
Web, www.loc.gov/rr/scitech

Offers reference service by telephone, by correspondence, and in person. Maintains a collection of more than 3 million reports on science, technology, business management, and economics. Timed entry pass for visitors required, details at loc.gov/visit. Appointments recommended for researchers.

▶**NONGOVERNMENTAL**

American Statistical Assn., 732 N. Washington St., Alexandria, VA 22314-1943; (703) 684-1221. Fax, (703) 997-7299. Ronald Wasserstein, Executive Director. Toll-free, (888) 231-3473.
General email, asainfo@amstat.org
Web, www.amstat.org, Twitter, @AmstatNews and Facebook, www.facebook.com/AmstatNews

Membership: statistical practitioners in industry, government, and academia. Supports excellence in the development, application, and dissemination of statistical science through meetings, publications, membership services, education, accreditation, and advocacy.

International Monetary Fund (IMF), Statistics, 700 19th St. N.W., 20431; (202) 623-7000. Kristalina Georgieva, Managing Director. Publications, (202) 623-7430.
General email, publicaffairs@imf.org
Web, www.imf.org/en/data

Publications, publications@imf.org and Twitter, @IMFNews

Publishes monthly International Financial Statistics (IFS), which includes comprehensive financial data for most countries, and Direction of Trade Statistics, a quarterly publication, which includes the distribution of exports and imports for many countries. Annual statistical publications include the Balance of Payments Statistics Yearbook, Direction of Trade Statistics Yearbook, Government Finance Statistics Yearbook, and International Financial Statistics Yearbook. Free online and paid print subscriptions available to the public. All four publications are available on the website.

Taxes and Tax Reform

▶**AGENCIES**

Alcohol and Tobacco Tax and Trade Bureau (TTB) (Treasury Dept.), 1310 G St. N.W., Box 12, 20005; (202) 453-2000. Fax, (202) 453-2912. Mary G. Ryan, Administrator. Public Affairs, (202) 453-2180. TTY, (202) 882-9914.
General email, TTBInternetQuestions@ttb.gov
Web, www.ttb.gov

Enforces and administers revenue laws relating to firearms, explosives, alcohol, and tobacco.

Internal Revenue Service (IRS) (Treasury Dept.), 1111 Constitution Ave. N.W., 20224 (mailing address: from outside the United States: IRS International Accounts, Philadelphia, PA 19255-0725); (202) 622-5000. Charles P. Rettig, Commissioner. Identity theft hotline, (800) 908-4490. Information and assistance, (800) 829-1040. Information for businesses, (800) 829-4933. International Taxpayer Service Center, (267) 941-1000. International Taxpayer Service Center fax, (267) 466-1055. National Taxpayer Advocates helpline, (877) 777-4778. International Taxpayer Advocate, (787) 522-8601. Press, (202) 317-4000. TTY, (800) 829-4059.
Web, www.irs.gov, Twitter, @IRSnews, Facebook, www.facebook.com/IRS and YouTube, www.youtube.com/user/IRSvideos

Administers and enforces internal revenue laws and related statutes (except those relating to firearms, explosives, alcohol, and tobacco).

Internal Revenue Service (IRS) (Treasury Dept.), Art Advisory Panel, 1111 Constitution Ave. N.W., #700, C:AP: SO:ART ATTN: AAS, 20224-0002; (305) 982-5364. MariCarmen Cuello, Director, (904) 661-3198.
Web, www.irs.gov/appeals/Art-Appraisal-Services

Panel of twenty-five art professionals that assists the IRS by reviewing and evaluating taxpayers' appraisals on works of art valued at $50,000 or more involved in federal income, estate, and gift taxes.

Internal Revenue Service (IRS) (Treasury Dept.), Passthroughs and Special Industries, Excise Tax Branch, 1111 Constitution Ave. N.W., 20224; (202) 317-3100. Holly Porter, Associate Chief Counsel.
Web, www.irs.gov

Administers excise tax programs, including taxes on diesel, gasoline, and special fuels. Advises district offices, internal IRS offices, and general inquirers on tax policy, rules, and regulations.

Internal Revenue Service (IRS) *(Treasury Dept.),* **Taxpayer Advocate,** *1111 Constitution Ave. N.W., #3031, 20224; (877) 777-4778. Erin M. Collins, National Taxpayer Advocate. Press, (202) 317-6802. TTY, (800) 829-4059.* *Web, https://taxpayeradvocate.irs.gov,* *Twitter, @YourVoiceatIRS and Facebook, www.facebook .com/YourVoiceAtIRS*

Helps taxpayers resolve problems with the IRS and recommends changes to prevent the problems. Represents taxpayers' interests in the formulation of policies and procedures.

Multistate Tax Commission, *444 N. Capitol St. N.W., #425, 20001-1538; (202) 650-0300. Gregory S. Matson, Executive Director.* *General email, mtc@mtc.gov* *Web, www.mtc.gov*

Membership: state governments that have enacted the Multistate Tax Compact. Promotes fair, effective, and efficient state tax systems for interstate and international commerce; works to preserve state tax sovereignty. Encourages uniform state tax laws and regulations for multistate and multinational enterprises. Maintains three regional audit offices that monitor compliance with state tax laws and encourage uniformity in taxpayer treatment. Administers program to identify businesses that do not file tax returns with states.

Treasury Dept., *Tax Policy, 1500 Pennsylvania Ave. N.W., #3120, 20220; (202) 622-0050. Lily Batchelder, Assistant Secretary; Rebecca Kaiser, Deputy Assistant Secretary, (202) 622-0140.* *Web, https://home.treasury.gov/policy-issues/tax-policy*

Formulates and implements domestic and international tax policies and programs; conducts analyses of proposed tax legislation and programs; participates in international tax treaty negotiations; responsible for receipts estimates for the annual budget of the United States.

Treasury Dept., *Tax Policy, International Tax Counsel, 1500 Pennsylvania Ave. N.W., #3058, 20220; (202) 622-1782. Jose Murillo, Deputy Assistant Secretary, International Tax Affairs.* *Web, https://home.treasury.gov/policy-issues/tax-policy/ international-tax*

Analyzes tax policies affecting businesses and international taxation. Negotiates tax treaties with foreign governments and participates in meetings of international organizations. Develops legislative proposals and regulations.

▶JUDICIARY

U.S. Tax Court, *400 2nd St. N.W., 20217; (202) 521-0700. Maurice B. Foley, Chief Judge, (202) 521-0777.* *Web, www.ustaxcourt.gov*

Tries and adjudicates disputes involving income, estate, and gift taxes and personal holding company surtaxes in cases in which deficiencies have been determined by the Internal Revenue Service.

▶NONGOVERNMENTAL

American Enterprise Institute (AEI), *Economic Policy Studies, 1789 Massachusetts Ave. N.W., 20036; (202) 862-5800. Fax, (202) 862-7177. Michael R. Strain, Director, (202) 862-4884.* *Web, www.aei.org/category/economics*

Conducts research on fiscal policy and taxes. Sponsors events.

Americans for Tax Reform, *722 12th St. N.W., #400, 20005; (202) 785-0266. Fax, (202) 785-0261. Grover G. Norquist, President.* *General email, ideas@atr.org* *Web, www.atr.org, Twitter, @taxreformer and Twitter, @GroverNorquist*

Advocates reduction of federal and state taxes; encourages candidates for public office to pledge their opposition to income tax increases through a national pledge campaign.

The Brookings Institution, *Economic Studies, 1775 Massachusetts Ave. N.W., 20036-2188; (202) 797-6414. (202) 540-7721. Stephanie Aaronson, Vice President.* *General email, escomment@brookings.edu* *Web, www.brookings.edu/economics and Twitter, @BrookingsEcon*

Researches and analyzes U.S. tax policy; provides information to policymakers, journalists, and researchers.

Center on Budget and Policy Priorities, *1275 1st St. N.E., #1200, 20002; (202) 408-1080. Fax, (202) 408-1056. Sharon Parrott, President.* *General email, center@cbpp.org* *Web, www.cbpp.org, Twitter, @CenterOnBudget and Facebook, www.facebook.com/CenterOnBudget*

Research group that analyzes changes in federal and state programs, such as tax credits, Medicaid coverage, and food stamps, and their effect on low-income and moderate-income households.

Citizens Against Government Waste, *1100 Connecticut Ave. N.W., #650, 20036; (202) 467-5300. Fax, (202) 467-4253. Thomas A. Schatz, President. Press, (202) 467-5310. Toll-free, 800-USA-DEBT.* *General email, info@cagw.org* *Web, www.cagw.org, Twitter, @GovWaste and Facebook, www.facebook.com/CAGW*

Taxpayer watchdog group that monitors government spending to identify how waste, mismanagement, and inefficiency in government can be eliminated. Has created criteria to identify pork-barrel spending. Publishes the annual *Congressional Pig Book,* which lists the names of politicians and their pet pork-barrel projects. Monitors legislation and regulations.

Citizens for Tax Justice, *1200 18th St. N.W., #675, 20036; (202) 299-1066. Fax, (202) 299-1065. Amy Hanauer, Executive Director.*
General email, info@ctj.org
Web, www.ctj.org, Twitter, @taxjustice and Facebook, www.facebook.com/taxjustice
Press, media@ctj.org

Advocacy organization that works for progressive taxes at the federal, state, and local levels.

Federation of Tax Administrators, *444 N. Capitol St. N.W., #348, 20001; (202) 807-6328. Sheronne R. Bonardi, Executive Director.*
General email, support@taxadmin.org
Web, www.taxadmin.org

Membership: tax agencies in the 50 states, plus New York City, Philadelphia, and the District of Columbia. Provides information upon written request on tax-related issues, including court decisions and legislation. Services include research and information exchange, training, and intergovernmental and interstate coordination. The Federation also represents the interests of state tax administrators before federal policymakers where appropriate. Sponsors workshops and conferences.

FreedomWorks, *111 K St. N.E., #600, 20002; (202) 783-3870. Adam Brandon, President. Toll-free, (888) 564-6273.*
Web, www.freedomworks.org, Twitter, @FreedomWorks and Facebook, www.facebook.com/FreedomWorks

Recruits, educates, trains, and mobilizes citizens to promote lower taxes, less government, and greater economic freedom.

Institute on Taxation and Economic Policy (ITEP), *1200 18th St. N.W, #675, 20036; (202) 299-1066. Fax, (202) 299-1065. Amy Hanauer, Executive Director.*
General email, itep@itep.org
Web, https://itep.org, Twitter, @iteptweets and Facebook, www.facebook.com/instituteontaxation

Research and education organization that promotes tax fairness and sustainability in federal, state, and local tax policy.

National Assn. of Manufacturers (NAM), *Tax and Domestic Economic Policy, 733 10th St. N.W., #700, 20001; (202) 637-3000. Fax, (202) 637-3182. Christopher Netram, Vice President, (202) 637-3077.*
General email, info@nam.org
Web, www.nam.org

Represents and acts as advocate for manufacturers on federal tax and budget policies; acts as a spokesperson for manufacturers on fiscal issues in the media; works with the broader business community to advance pro-growth, pro-competitiveness tax policy; conducts conferences. Monitors legislation and regulations.

National Campaign for a Peace Tax Fund, *2121 Decatur Pl. N.W., 20008-1923; (202) 483-3751. Malachy Killbride, Executive Director. Toll-free, (888) 732-2382.*

General email, info@peacetaxfund.org
Web, www.peacetaxfund.org

Supports legislation permitting taxpayers who are conscientiously opposed to military expenditures to have the military portion of their income tax money placed in a separate, nonmilitary fund.

National Tax Assn., *1100 Vermont Ave. N.W., #650, 20005; (202) 737-3325. Tara Sheehan, Executive Director.*
General email, nta@ntanet.org
Web, www.ntanet.org and Twitter, @NatlTax

Membership: tax lawyers and accountants, academics, legislators, and students. Seeks to advance understanding of tax theory, practice, and policy, as well as other aspects of public finance. Holds conferences and symposiums, including the Annual Conference on Taxation. Publishes the *National Tax Journal*.

National Taxpayers Union, *Communications, 122 C St. N.W., #650, 20001; (703) 683-5700. Peter Sepp, President; Kevin Glass, Vice President Communications.*
General email, ntu@ntu.org
Web, www.ntu.org, Twitter, @NTU and Facebook, www.facebook.com/NationalTaxpayersUnion

Citizens' interest group that promotes tax and spending reduction at all levels of government. Supports constitutional amendments to balance the federal budget and limit taxes.

Tax Analysts, *400 S. Maple Ave., #400, Falls Church, VA 22046; (703) 533-4400. Cara Griffith, President, ext. 4412. Customer Service, (800) 955-2444.*
Web, www.taxnotes.com

Nonpartisan publisher of state, federal, and international tax news and analysis. Advocates tax reforms to develop tax systems that are fair, simple, and efficient. Provides publications to educate tax professionals and the public about tax reform.

The Tax Council, *1200 G St., #300, 20005; (202) 822-8062. Fax, (202) 315-3413. Lynda K. Walker, Executive Director.*
General email, general@thetaxcouncil.org
Web, www.thetaxcouncil.org and Twitter, @TheTaxCouncil

Organization of corporations concerned with tax policy and legislation. Interests include tax rate, capital formation, capital gains, foreign source income, and capital cost recovery. (Affiliated with the Tax Council Policy Institute [TCPI].)

Tax Executives Institute, *1200 G St. N.W., #300, 20005-3814; (202) 638-5601. Fax, (202) 638-5607. Pilar Mata, Director of Operations, (202) 464-8346.*
General email, asktei@tei.org
Web, www.tei.org and Twitter, @TEI_Updates

Membership: accountants, lawyers, and other corporate and business employees dealing with tax issues. Sponsors seminars and conferences on federal, state, local, and international tax issues. Develops and monitors tax legislation, regulations, and administrative procedures.

Consumer Product Safety Commission

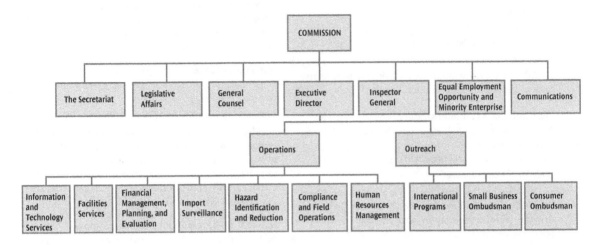

Tax Foundation, *1325 G. St. N.W., #950, 20005; (202) 464-6200. Scott A. Hodge, President.*
General email, tf@taxfoundation.org

Web, https://taxfoundation.org and
Twitter, @taxfoundation

Membership: individuals and businesses interested in federal, state, and local fiscal matters. Conducts research and analysis and prepares reports on taxes and government expenditures. Advocates a simple, transparent, neutral, and stable tax policy.

U.S. Chamber of Commerce, *Economic and Tax Policy, 1615 H St. N.W., 20062-2000; (202) 463-5620. Carolyn L. Harris, Chief Tax Policy Counsel. Press, (202) 463-5682.*
Web, www.uschamber.com/taxes, Twitter, @USChamber and Facebook, www.facebook.com/SCC_TaxTeam

Promotes tax policies that encourage businesses' growth. Opposes tax increases that reduce businesses' ability to grow, invest, and create jobs.

Urban Institute, *Urban-Brookings Tax Policy Center, 500 L'Enfant Plaza S.W., 20024; (202) 833-7200. Nikhita Airi, Director.*
General email, info@taxpolicycenter.org

Web, www.taxpolicycenter.org

Aims to provide independent analyses of current and longer-term tax issues and to communicate its analyses to the public and to policymakers. Combines national experts in tax, expenditure, budget policy, and microsimulation modeling to concentrate on areas of tax policy for use in future debates.

Urban-Brookings Tax Policy Center, *Brookings Institution, 1775 Massachusetts Ave. N.W., 20036, Urban Institute, 500 L'Enfant Plaza S.W., 20024; Fax, (202) 728-0232. Eric Toder, Co-Director; William G. Cole, Co-Director. Brookings Institution Phone, (202) 797-6000. Urban Institute Phone, (202) 833-7200.*

General email, info@taxpolicycenter.org

Web, www.taxpolicycenter.org, Twitter, @TaxPolicyCenter and Facebook, www.facebook.com/taxpolicycenter

Provides analysis of current and pending tax issues to policymakers, journalists, researchers, and citizens. (Joint venture of the Urban Institute and the Brookings Institution.)

CONSUMER PROTECTION AND EDUCATION

General

▶**AGENCIES**

Civil Division *(Justice Dept.), Consumer Protection, 950 Pennsylvania Ave. N.W., 20001; (202) 307-0066. Fax, (202) 514-8742. Gustaw (Gus) W. Eylur, Director.*
Web, www.justice.gov/civil/consumer-protection-branch

Enforces consumer protection statutes to protect health, safety, and economic security and identity integrity of consumers. Handles cases in the areas of pharmaceuticals and medical devices, deceptive trade practices and telemarketing fraud, food and dietary supplements, consumer product safety, odometer fraud, tobacco products, and civil defense litigation.

Consumer Product Safety Commission (CPSC), *Small Business Ombudsman, 4330 East-West Hwy., Bethesda, MD 20814; (301) 504-7945. Will Cusey, Ombudsman.*
General email, sbo@cpsc.gov

Web, www.cpsc.gov

Provides guidance and advice to small businesses and small-batch manufacturers about compliance with CPSC laws and regulations as well as technical assistance in resolving problems.

Federal Communications Commission (FCC), *Consumer and Governmental Affairs Bureau (CGB),* *45 L St. N.E., 20554; (202) 418-1400. Fax, (202) 418-2839. Alejandro Roark, Chief. TTY, (888) 835-5322. General email, cgbweb@fcc.gov*

Web, www.fcc.gov/consumer-governmental-affairs

Develops and implements FCC policies, including disability access. Operates a consumer center that responds to consumer inquiries and complaints. Partners with state, local, and tribal governments in areas of emergency preparedness and implementation of new technologies.

Federal Deposit Insurance Corp. (FDIC), *Consumer Protection and Community Affairs,* *550 17th St. N.W., #F-6012, 20006; (877) 275-3342. (703) 516-1069. Elizabeth Ortiz, Deputy Director. General email, consumer@fdic.gov*

Web, www.fdic.gov/consumers/community/index.html

Coordinates and monitors complaints filed by consumers against federally insured state banks that are not members of the Federal Reserve System; responds to general banking inquiries; answers questions on deposit insurance coverage.

Federal Maritime Commission (FMC), *Consumer Affairs and Dispute Resolution Services,* *800 N. Capitol St. N.W., #1070, 20573; (202) 523-5807. Fax, (202) 275-0059. Zoraya De La Cruz, Director. General email, complaints@fmc.gov*

Web, www.fmc.gov/databases-services/consumer-affairs-dispute-resolution-services

Offers ombuds assistance, mediation, facilitation, and arbitration to resolve challenges and disputes involving cargo shipments, household goods shipments, cruises, and general CADRS resources.

Federal Reserve System, *Consumer and Community Affairs,* *1709 New York Ave. N.W., 20006; (202) 452-2955. Fax, (877) 888-2520. Eric Belsky, Director. Toll-free Consumer Assistance, (888) 851-1920. Web, www.federalreserve.gov/consumerscommunities.htm and www.federalreserveconsumerhelp.gov*

Receives consumer complaints concerning truth-in-lending, fair credit billing, equal credit opportunity, electronic fund transfer, home mortgage disclosure, consumer leasing, and advertising; receives complaints about unregulated practices; refers complaints to district banks. The Federal Reserve monitors enforcement of fair lending laws with regard to state-chartered banks that are members of the Federal Reserve System.

Federal Trade Commission (FTC), *600 Pennsylvania Ave. N.W., 20580; (202) 326-2222. Lina Khan, Chair, (202) 326-0000. Press, (202) 326-2180. Congressional Relations, (202) 326-2195. Identity theft hotline, (877) 438-4338. Library, (202) 326-2395. Web, www.ftc.gov, Twitter, @FTC, Facebook, www.facebook.com/federaltradecommission and YouTube, www.youtube.com/ftcvideos*

Promotes policies designed to maintain strong competitive enterprise and consumer protection within the U.S. economic system. Monitors trade practices and investigates cases involving monopoly, unfair restraints, or deceptive practices. Enforces Truth in Lending and Fair Credit Reporting acts.

Federal Trade Commission (FTC), *Bureau of Consumer Protection,* *600 Pennsylvania Ave. N.W., #470, 20580; (202) 326-3702. Fax, (202) 326-3799. Samuel Levine, Director. Web, www.ftc.gov/about-ftc/bureaus-offices/bureau-consumer-protection*

Stops unfair, deceptive, and fraudulent business practices by collecting complaints and conducting investigations, suing companies and people that break the law, developing rules to maintain a fair marketplace, and educating consumers and businesses about their rights and responsibilities.

Federal Trade Commission (FTC), *Bureau of Consumer Protection, Advertising Practices Division,* *400 7th Ave. S.W., #10418, 20024; (202) 326-3244. Fax, (202) 326-3259. Serena Viswanathan, Associate Director. Web, www.ftc.gov/about-ftc/bureaus-offices/bureau-consumer-protection/our-divisions/division-advertising-practices*

Protects consumers from deceptive and unsubstantiated advertising through law enforcement, public reports, and industry outreach. Focuses on national advertising campaigns for food, dietary supplements and over-the-counter drugs, and medical devices, particularly advertising that makes claims difficult for consumers to evaluate. Monitors alcohol advertising for unfair practices; issues reports on alcohol labeling, advertising, and promotion. Issues reports on the marketing to children of violent movies, video games, and music recordings.

Federal Trade Commission (FTC), *Bureau of Consumer Protection, Consumer and Business Education Division,* *400 7th Ave. S.W., CC-10402, 20024; (202) 326-3650. Fax, (202) 326-3574. Jennifer Leach, Associate Director, (202) 326-3203. Web, www.business.ftc.gov and www.ftc.gov/about-ftc/bureaus-offices/bureau-consumer-protection/our-divisions/division-consumer-business*

Develops educational material about FTC activities in order to inform consumers about their rights and to alert businesses about their compliance responsibilities.

Federal Trade Commission (FTC), *Bureau of Consumer Protection, Consumer Response and Operations Division,* *600 Pennsylvania Ave. N.W., #240, 20580; (202) 326-2830. Maria Mayo, Associate Director (Acting), (202) 326-3438. Consumer Response Center, 877-FTC-HELP. Consumer Sentinel helpline, (877) 701-9595. Do-Not-Call Registry, (888) 382-1222. FTC Complaint, (877) 382-4357. Identity fraud report line, 877-ID-THEFT. TTY, (866) 653-4261.*

General email, crcmessages@ftc.gov

Web, www.ftc.gov/about-ftc/bureaus-offices/bureau-consumer-protection/our-divisions/division-consumer-response and *Consumer Response Center, www.consumer.ftc.gov* and *Consumer Sentinel Network, www.ftc.gov/enforcement/consumer-sentinel-network* and *FTC Complaint Assistant, www.ftccomplaintassistant.gov*

Responds to consumer complaints and inquiries received through the Consumer Response Center. Handles complaints about regulations dealing with unfair or deceptive business practices in advertising, credit, marketing, and service industries; educates consumers and businesses about these regulations.

Federal Trade Commission (FTC), *Bureau of Consumer Protection, Enforcement Division, 400 7th Ave. S.W., CC-9423, 20024; (202) 326-2996. Fax, (202) 326-3197. James A. Kohm, Associate Director, (202) 326-2640. Web, www.ftc.gov/about-ftc/bureaus-offices/bureau-consumer-protection/our-divisions/division-enforcement*

Enforces consumer protection, including advertising and financial practices, data security, high-tech fraud, and telemarketing and other scams. Coordinates FTC actions with criminal law enforcement agencies; litigates civil actions against those who defraud consumers; and develops, reviews, and enforces a variety of consumer protection rules.

Federal Trade Commission (FTC), *Bureau of Consumer Protection, Marketing Practices Division, 600 Pennsylvania Ave. N.W., 20580; (202) 326-3404. Fax, (202) 326-3395. Lois C. Greisman, Associate Director. Web, www.ftc.gov/about-ftc/bureaus-offices/bureau-consumer-protection/our-divisions/division-marketing-practices*

Responds to complaints of consumer fraud in the marketplace, including high-tech Internet and telephone scams, deceptive telemarketing or direct mail marketing schemes, fraudulent business opportunity scams, and violations of the Do Not Call and CAN-SPAM consumer privacy protections.

Federal Trade Commission (FTC), *Bureau of Economics, 600 Pennsylvania Ave. N.W., 20580; (202) 326-3419. Fax, (202) 326-2380. Vacant, Director. Web, www.ftc.gov/about-ftc/bureaus-offices/bureau-economics*

Provides economic analyses for consumer protection and antitrust investigations, cases, and rulemakings; advises the commission on the effect of government regulations on competition and consumers in various industries; develops special reports on competition, consumer protection, and regulatory issues.

Federal Trade Commission (FTC), *International Affairs, 600 Pennsylvania Ave. N.W., #H494, 20580; (202) 326-2600. Fax, (202) 326-2873. Randolph W. Tritell, Director, (202) 326-3051. Web, www.ftc.gov/about-ftc/bureaus-offices/office-international-affairs*

Assists in the enforcement of antitrust laws and consumer protection by arranging appropriate cooperation and coordination with foreign governments in international cases. Negotiates bilateral and multilateral antitrust and consumer protection agreements and represents the United States in international antitrust policy forums. Assists developing countries in moving toward market-based economies.

Food and Drug Administration (FDA) *(Health and Human Services Dept.), Division of Industry and Consumer Education (DICE), White Oak, 10903 New Hampshire Ave., Silver Spring, MD 20993; (301) 796-7100. Fax, (301) 847-8149. Elias Mallis, Director, (301) 796-6216. Toll-free, (800) 638-2041.*
General email, DICE@fda.hhs.gov

Web, www.fda.gov/MedicalDevices/DeviceRegulationandGuidance/ContactDivisionofIndustryandConsumerEducation

Responds to questions from consumers of medical devices and radiation-emitting electronic products.

Food and Drug Administration (FDA) *(Health and Human Services Dept.), External Affairs (OEA), White Oak Bldg. 32, 10903 New Hampshire Ave., #5360, Silver Spring, MD 20993; (301) 796-4540. Erica Jefferson, Associate Commissioner. Consumer inquiries, (888) 463-6332.*
General email, fdaoma@fda.hhs.gov

Web, www.fda.gov/AboutFDA/CentersOffices/OC/OfficeofExternalAffairs

Responds to inquiries on issues related to the FDA. Conducts consumer health education programs for specific groups, including women, older adults, and the educationally and economically disadvantaged. Serves as liaison with national health and consumer organizations.

Food Safety and Inspection Service *(Agriculture Dept.), 1400 Independence Ave. S.W., #331E, 20250-3700; (202) 720-7025. Paul Kiecker, Administrator. Consumer inquiries, (800) 535-4555. Press, (202) 720-9113. TTY, (800) 877-8339.*
Web, www.fsis.usda.gov and *Twitter, @USDAFoodSafety*

Sponsors food safety educational programs to inform the public about measures to prevent foodborne illnesses; sponsors lectures, publications, and public service advertising campaigns. Toll-free hotline answers food safety questions.

General Services Administration (GSA), *USAGov, 1800 F St. N.W., 20405; (844) 872-4681.*
General email, USAContace@gsa.gov
Web, www.gsa.gov

Manages the portal site to U.S. government information, www.usa.gov. Manages kids.gov, a resource that provides government information on education, including primary, secondary, and higher education. Distributes free and low-cost federal publications of consumer interest via the Internet at www.usa.gov and Pueblo.gpo.gov. Assists people with questions about American government agencies, programs, and services via telephone, (800) FED-INFO

Consumer Financial Protection Bureau

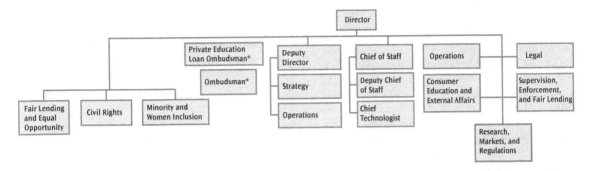

*Position is not part of the Bureau director's office

([800] 333-4636), or website, http://answers.usa.gov. Operates a contact center to provide information in English or Spanish on all federal government agencies, programs, and services via toll-free telephone, email, and chat. Operated under contract by Sykes in Pennsylvania and Florida. Responds to inquiries about federal programs and services. Gives information about or referrals to appropriate offices.

Securities and Exchange Commission (SEC), *Investor Education and Advocacy,* 100 F St. N.E., 20549-0213; (202) 551-6500. Lori Schock, Director. Toll-free, (800) 732-0330.
Web, www.sec.gov/page/oieasectionlanding

Assists individual consumers in investing wisely and avoiding fraud. Provides a variety of services and tools, including publications on mutual funds and annuities, studies and recommendations concerning the evaluation of brokers and advisors, online calculators, and explanations about fees and expenses. Information is also available in Spanish.

Transportation Dept. (DOT), *Aviation Consumer Protection,* 1200 New Jersey Ave. S.E., 20590; (202) 366-2220. Blaine A. Workie, Assistant General Counsel. Air travelers with disabilities hotline, (800) 778-4838. TTY, (202) 366-0511.
Web, www.transportation.gov/airconsumer

Processes consumer complaints; advises the secretary on consumer issues; investigates air travel consumer rule violations; educates the public about air travel via reports and website.

Transportation Security Administration (TSA) *(Homeland Security Dept.),* Contact Center, 601 S. 12th St., 7th Floor, Arlington, VA 20598; (866) 289-9673. Michelle Cartagena, Program Manager.
General email, tsa-contactcenter@tsa.dhs.gov
Web, www.tsa.gov

Answers questions and collects concerns from the public regarding travel security.

▶CONGRESS

For a listing of relevant congressional committees and sub-committees, please see pages 38–39 or the Appendix.

▶NONGOVERNMENTAL

American Assn. of Family and Consumer Sciences, *107 S. West St., #816, Alexandria, VA 22314; (703) 706-4600. Fax, (703) 636-7648. Nancy Bock, Executive Director (Acting), ext. 4613. Toll-free, (800) 424-8080.*
General email, staff@aafcs.org
Web, www.aafcs.org, Twitter, @aafcs and Facebook, www.facebook.com/AAFCSheadquarters
Public Policy, publicpolicy@aafcs.org

Membership: professional home economists. Supports family and consumer sciences education; develops accrediting standards for undergraduate family and consumer science programs; trains and certifies family and consumer science professionals. Monitors legislation and regulations concerning family and consumer issues.

American National Standards Institute (ANSI), *1899 L St. N.W., 11th Floor, 20036; (202) 293-8020. Fax, (202) 293-9287. S. Joe Bhatia, President, (202) 331-3605.*
General email, info@ansi.org
Web, www.ansi.org, Twitter, @ansidotorg and Facebook, www.facebook.com/ansidotorg

Oversees norms and guidelines of many private sectors to strengthen the U.S. market position in a global economy; seeks to protect the health and safety of consumers and the environment.

Better Business Bureau, *International Assn. of Better Business Bureaus (IABBB),* 4250 N. Fairfax Dr., #600, Arlington, VA 22203; (703) 276-0100. Kip Morse, Chief Executive Officer.
General email, info@mybbb.org
Web, www.bbb.org/local-bbb/international-association-of-better-business-bureaus, Twitter, @bbb_us and Facebook, www.facebook.com/BetterBusinessBureau

Membership: Businesses and Better Business Bureaus in the United States, Canada, and Mexico. Promotes ethical business practices and truth in national advertising; mediates disputes between consumers and businesses.

Call for Action, *11820 Parklawn Dr., #340, Rockville, MD 20852; (240) 747-0229. Shirley Rooker, President. Web, https://callforaction.org*

International network of consumer hotlines affiliated with local broadcast partners. Helps consumers resolve problems with businesses, government agencies, and other organizations through mediation. Provides information on privacy concerns.

Center for Auto Safety, *4400 Jenifer St. N.W., #331, 20015-2113; (202) 328-7700. Michael . Brooks, Executive Director (Acting).*

General email, contact@autosafety.org

Web, www.autosafety.org, Twitter, @Ctr4AutoSafety and Facebook, www.facebook.com/CenterForAutoSafety

Public interest organization that receives written consumer complaints against auto manufacturers; monitors federal agencies responsible for regulating and enforcing auto and highway safety rules.

The Center for Consumer Freedom, *1090 Vermont Ave. N.W., #800, 20005 (mailing address: P.O. Box 34557, Washington, DC 20043); (202) 463-7112. Richard Berman, Executive Director.*

General email, info@consumerfreedom.com

Web, www.consumerfreedom.com and Facebook, www.facebook.com/ConsumerFreedom

Membership: restaurants, food companies, and consumers. Seeks to promote personal freedom and protect consumer choices in lifestyle-related and health-related areas such as diet and exercise. Monitors legislation and regulations.

Center for Digital Democracy, *1015 15th St. N.W., #600, 20005; (202) 494-7100. Jeffrey (Jeff) Chester, Executive Director.*

Web, www.democraticmedia.org, Twitter, @DigitalDemoc and Facebook, www.facebook.com/Center-for-Digital-Democracy-Protect-Privacy-Online-281331962264

Tracks and analyzes the online advertising market, including areas affecting public health, news and information, children and adolescents, and financial industries.

Consumer Federation of America, *1620 Eye St. N.W., #200, 20006; (202) 387-6121. Jack Gillis, Executive Director, (202) 939-1018. Press, (202) 939-1018.*

General email, cfa@consumerfed.org

Web, https://consumerfed.org, Twitter, @ConsumerFed and Facebook, www.facebook.com/consumerfederationof america

Federation of national, regional, state, and local proconsumer organizations. Promotes consumer interests in banking, credit, and insurance; telecommunications; housing; food, drugs, and medical care; safety; and energy and natural resources development.

Ethics Research and Compliance Initiative, *2650 Park Tower Dr., #802, Vienna, VA 22180; (703) 647-2185. Fax, (703) 647-2180. Patricia J. Harned, Chief Executive Officer. Toll-free, (800) 777-1285.*

Web, www.ethics.org and Twitter, @ecinitiative

Nonpartisan research organization that fosters ethical practices among individuals and institutions. Interests include research, knowledge building, education, and advocacy.

Household and Commercial Products Assn., *1667 K St. N.W., #300, 20006; (202) 872-8110. Fax, (202) 223-2636. Stephen (Steve) J. Caldeira, President.*

General email, info@thehcpa.org

Web, www.thehcpa.org and Twitter, @TheHCPA

Provides chemical safety information and consumer education programs; sponsors National Inhalants and Poisons Awareness and Aerosol Education Bureau. Monitors legislation and regulations.

International Business Ethics Institute, *1725 Eye St. N.W., #300, 20006; (202) 296-6938. Fax, (202) 296-5897. Lori Tansey Martens, President.*

General email, info@business-ethics.org

Web, https://business-ethics.org

Nonpartisan educational organization that promotes business ethics and corporate responsibility.

Knowledge Ecology International (KEI), *110 Maryland Ave. N.E., #511, 20002; (202) 332-2670. Fax, (202) 332-2673. James Love, Director, (202) 332-2670.*

General email, info@keionline.org

Web, www.keionline.org and Twitter, @jamie_love

Advocates social justice for low-income persons and marginalized groups with consumer access to health care, electronic commerce, competition policy, and information regarding intellectual property rights. Undertakes and publishes research and new ideas; engages in global public interest advocacy; provides technical advice to governments, nongovernmental organizations, and firms.

National Assn. of Consumer Advocates, *1215 17th St. N.W., 5th Floor, 20036; (202) 452-1989. Fax, (202) 452-0099. Ira J. Rheingold, Executive Director, ext. 101.*

General email, info@consumeradvocates.org

Web, www.consumeradvocates.org, Facebook, www.facebook.com/NationalAssociationofConsumerAdvocates and Twitter, @NACAdvocate

Membership: consumer advocate attorneys. Seeks to protect the rights of consumers from fraudulent, abusive, and predatory business practices. Provides consumer law training through conferences and publications. Monitors legislation and regulations on banking, credit, and housing laws.

National Assn. of State Utility Consumer Advocates (NASUCA), *8380 Colesville Rd., #101, Silver Spring, MD 20910-6267; (301) 589-6313. Fax, (301) 589-6380. David Springe, Executive Director, (785) 550-7606.*

General email, nasuca@nasuca.org

Web, www.nasuca.org

Membership: public advocate offices authorized by states to represent ratepayer interests before state and federal utility regulatory commissions. Monitors legislation and regulatory agencies with jurisdiction over electric utilities, telecommunications, natural gas, and water; conducts conferences. Supports privacy protection for telephone customers.

National Consumers League, *1701 K St. N.W., #1200, 20006; (202) 835-3323. Fax, (202) 835-0747.*
Sally Greenberg, Executive Director.
General email, info@nclnet.org
Web, www.nclnet.org and Twitter, @nclnet.org

Advocacy group that engages in research and educational activities related to consumer and worker issues. Interests include fraud, privacy, child labor, product safety, and food and drug safety. Web resources include fakechecks.org, fraud.org, lifesmarts.org, sosrx.org, and stopchildlabor.org.

Public Justice Foundation, *1620 L St. N.W., #630, 20036; (202) 797-8600. Fax, (202) 232-7203. F. Paul Bland Jr., Executive Director, ext. 223.*
Web, www.publicjustice.net, Twitter, @Public_Justice and Facebook, www.facebook.com/publicjustice

Membership: consumer activists, trial lawyers, public interest lawyers, and law professors and students. Litigates to influence corporate and government decisions about products or activities adversely affecting health or safety. Interests include toxic torts, environmental protection, civil rights and civil liberties, workers' safety, consumer protection, and the preservation of the civil justice system. (Formerly Trial Lawyers for Public Justice.)

SAFE KIDS Worldwide, *1255 23rd St. N.W., #400, 20037-1151; (202) 662-0600. Fax, (202) 393-2072. Torine Creppy, President; Kristin Recchiuti, Chair.*
General email, info@safekids.org
Web, https://safekids.org, Twitter, @safekids and Facebook, www.facebook.com/SafeKidsWorldwide

Promotes awareness among adults that unintentional injury is the leading cause of death among children ages nineteen and under. Conducts educational programs on childhood injury prevention. Publishes research reports, safety tip sheets, and monthly newsletter.

U.S. Chamber of Commerce, *Congressional and Public Affairs, 1615 H St. N.W., 20062-2000; (202) 463-5600. Jack Howard, Senior Vice President.*
Web, www.uschamber.com/program/policy/government-affairs

Monitors legislation and regulations regarding business and consumer issues, including legislation and policies affecting the Federal Trade Commission, the Consumer Product Safety Commission, and other agencies.

U.S. Public Interest Research Group (U.S. PIRG), *Federal Advocacy, 600 Pennsylvania Ave. S.E., #400, 20003; (202) 546-9707. Doug Phelps, Chair.*
Web, www.uspirg.org and Twitter, @uspirg

Conducts research and advocacy on consumer issues, including telephone rates, banking practices, insurance, campaign finance reform, product safety, toxic and solid waste, antibiotic overuse, affordable higher education, and modernizing voter registration; monitors private and governmental actions affecting consumers; supports efforts to challenge consumer fraud and illegal business practices. Serves as national office for state groups. (Headquarters in Denver, Colo.)

Credit Practices

▶ **AGENCIES**

Civil Division *(Justice Dept.),* **Consumer Protection,** *950 Pennsylvania Ave. N.W., 20001; (202) 307-0066. Fax, (202) 514-8742. Gustaw (Gus) W. Eylur, Director.*
Web, www.justice.gov/civil/consumer-protection-branch

Files suits to enforce the Truth-in-Lending Act and other federal statutes protecting consumers, generally upon referral by client agencies.

Comptroller of the Currency *(Treasury Dept.),* **Chief Counsel,** *Constitution Center, 400 7th St. S.W., 20219; (202) 649-5400. Benjamin W. McDonough, Chief Counsel.*
Web, www.occ.gov/about/who-we-are/organizations/chief-counsels-office/index-chief-counsels-office.html

Enforces and oversees compliance by nationally chartered banks with laws prohibiting discrimination in credit transactions on the basis of sex or marital status. Enforces regulations concerning bank advertising; may issue cease-and-desist orders.

Comptroller of the Currency *(Treasury Dept.),* **Compliance and Community Affairs,** *Constitution Center, 400 7th St. S.W., MS 7E512, 20219; (202) 649-6420. Grovetta Gardineer, Senior Deputy Comptroller.*
General email, CommunityAffairs@occ.treas.gov
Web, www.occ.gov/topics/consumers-and-communities/community-affairs/index-community-affairs.html

Develops policy for enforcing consumer laws and regulations that affect national banks, including the Bank Secrecy (BSA/AML), Truth-in-Lending, Community Reinvestment, and Equal Credit Opportunity acts.

Comptroller of the Currency *(Treasury Dept.),* **Enterprise Governance and Ombudsman,** *Constitution Center, 400 7th St. S.W., MS 10E-12, 20219; (202) 649-5530. Larry L. Hattix, Ombudsman.*
Web, www.occ.gov and www.occ.gov/about/who-we-are/organizations/office-of-enterprise-governance-and-the-ombudsman/index-office-of-enterprise-governance-and-the-omb

Ensures that bank customers and the banks the agency supervises receive fair and expeditious resolution of their concerns.

Consumer Financial Protection Bureau (CFPB), *1700 G St. N.W., 20552; (855) 411-2372. Rohit Chopra, Director.*

Whistleblower hotline, (855) 695-7974. TTY, (855) 729-2372.
General email, officeofinnovation@consumerfinance.gov
Web, www.consumerfinance.gov, Twitter, @cfpb, Facebook, www.facebook.com/CPFB and YouTube, www.youtube.com/user/cfpbvideo

An independent government agency created per the Dodd-Frank Act of 2010. Functions include implementing and enforcing federal laws pertaining to mortgages, credit cards, and other consumer financial products and services. Supervises bank and nonbank financial institutions for compliance with consumer financial protection regulations. Accepts consumer complaints about financial products and services. Administers regulations including the Truth in Lending Act (TILA), Real Estate Settlement Procedures Act (RESPA), Fair Debt Collection Practices Act (FDCPA), Electronic Fund Transfer Act (EFTA), and Equal Credit Opportunity Act (ECOA).

Federal Deposit Insurance Corp. (FDIC), *Consumer Protection and Community Affairs, 550 17th St. N.W., #F-6012, 20006; (877) 275-3342. (703) 516-1069. Elizabeth Ortiz, Deputy Director.*
General email, consumer@fdic.gov
Web, www.fdic.gov/consumers/community/index.html

Handles complaints concerning truth-in-lending and other fair credit provisions, including charges of discrimination on the basis of sex or marital status.

Federal Deposit Insurance Corp. (FDIC), *Depositor and Consumer Protection, 550 17th St. N.W., #F8000, 20006; (202) 898-7088. Mark Pearce, Director.*
Web, www.fdic.gov/about/contact/directory/#DDCP and www.fdic.gov/consumers/community/index.html

Examines and supervises federally insured state banks that are not members of the Federal Reserve System to ascertain their safety and soundness.

Federal Reserve System, *Consumer and Community Affairs, 1709 New York Ave. N.W., 20006; (202) 452-2955. Fax, (877) 888-2520. Eric Belsky, Director. Toll-free Consumer Assistance, (888) 851-1920.*
Web, www.federalreserve.gov/consumerscommunities.htm and www.federalreserveconsumerhelp.gov

Receives consumer complaints concerning truth-in-lending, fair credit billing, equal credit opportunity, electronic fund transfer, home mortgage disclosure, consumer leasing, and advertising; receives complaints about unregulated practices; refers complaints to district banks. The Federal Reserve monitors enforcement of fair lending laws with regard to state-chartered banks that are members of the Federal Reserve System.

Federal Trade Commission (FTC), *Bureau of Consumer Protection, Financial Practices, 400 7th Ave. S.W., CC-10416, 20024; (202) 326-3224. Fax, (202) 326-3768. Malini Maithal, Associate Director, (202) 326-2972.*
Web, www.ftc.gov/about-ftc/bureaus-offices/bureau-consumer-protection/our-divisions/division-financial-practices

Challenges unfair or deceptive financial practices, including those involving lending, loan servicing, debt negotiation, and debt collection. Enforces specific consumer credit statutes, including the Fair Debt Collection Practices Act, Equal Credit Opportunity Act, Truth-in-Lending Act, Credit Repair Organization Act, Home Ownership and Equity Protection Act, Electronic Fund Transfer Act, Consumer Leasing Act, Holder-In-Due-Course Rule, and Credit Practices Rule. Enforces the Fair Credit Reporting Act, which requires credit bureaus to furnish correct and complete information to businesses evaluating credit, insurance, or job applications.

Federal Trade Commission (FTC), *Bureau of Consumer Protection, Privacy and Identity Protection Division, 600 Pennsylvania Ave. N.W., 20580; (202) 326-2771. Kristin Cohen, Associate Director. Identity theft hotline, (877) 438-4338. TTY identity theft hotline, (866) 653-4261.*
Web, www.ftc.gov/about-ftc/bureaus-offices/bureau-consumer-protection/our-divisions/division-privacy-and-identity and Identity theft assistance, www.identitytheft.gov

Oversees issues related to consumer privacy, credit reporting, identity theft, and information security. Develops policies and enforces the Fair Credit Reporting Act, Gramm-Leach-Bliley Act, and Children's Online Privacy Protection Act.

National Credit Union Administration (NCUA), *Consumer Protection, 1775 Duke St., Alexandria, VA 22314; (703) 518-1140. Fax, (703) 518-6672. Matthew J. Biliouris, Director.*
General email, ocfpmail@ncua.gov
Web, www.NCUA.gov/consumers, Twitter, @TheNCUA and Consumer Assistance Center, www.mycreditunion.gov/consumer-assistance-center

Responsible for consumer financial protection compliance policy and rulemaking, fair lending examinations, and consumer financial literacy efforts. Administers the NCUA's Consumer Assistance Center for consumer inquiries and complaints.

National Credit Union Administration (NCUA), *Examination and Insurance, 1775 Duke St., Alexandria, VA 22314-3428; (703) 518-6360. Fax, (703) 518-6666. Kelly Lay, Director.*
General email, eimail@ncua.gov
Web, www.ncua.gov and Twitter, @TheNCUA

Oversees and enforces compliance by federally chartered credit unions with the Truth-in-Lending Act, the Equal Credit Opportunity Act, and other federal statutes protecting consumers.

Small Business Administration (SBA), *Diversity, Inclusion, and Civil Rights, 409 3rd St. S.W., #6400, 20416; (202) 205-6750. Zina Sutch, Assistant Administrator. Toll-free, (800) 877-8339.*
Web, www.sba.gov/about-sba/sba-locations/headquarters-offices/office-diversity-inclusion-civil-rights

Federal Deposit Insurance Corporation

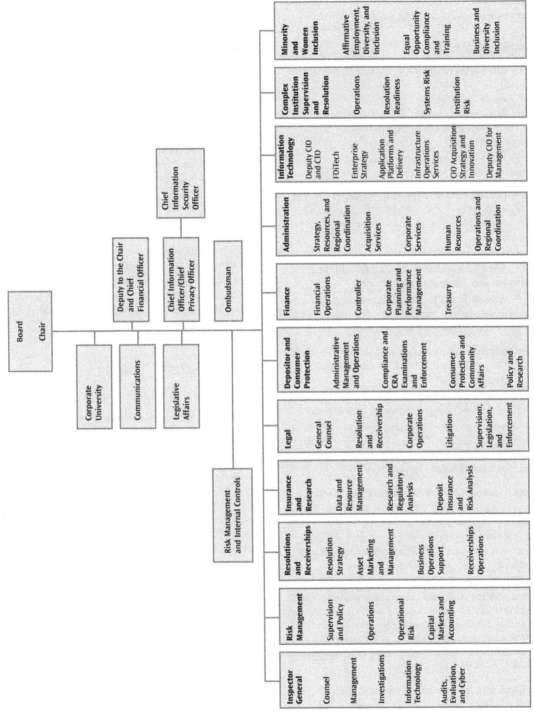

Reviews complaints based on disability against the Small Business Administration by recipients of its assistance in cases of alleged discrimination in credit transactions; monitors recipients for civil rights compliance.

▶NONGOVERNMENTAL

American Bankers Assn. (ABA), *Communications, 1120 Connecticut Ave. N.W., 20036; (800) 226-5377. Rob Nichols, President. Web, www.aba.com, Twitter, @ABABankers and Facebook, www.facebook.com/AmericanBankers Association*

Provides information on a wide range of banking issues and financial management.

American Financial Services Assn. (AFSA), *919 18th St. N.W., #300, 20006-5517; (202) 296-5544. Fax, (202) 223-0321. Bill Himpler, Chief Executive Officer. Press, (202) 466-8613. General email, info@afsamail.org Web, www.afsaonline.org, Twitter, @AFSA_DC and Facebook, www.facebook.com/afsaonline*

Trade association for the consumer credit industry. Focus includes government relations and consumer education. Monitors legislation and regulations.

Consumer Data Industry Assn., *1090 Vermont Ave. N.W., #200, 20005-4905; (202) 371-0910. Francis Creighton, Chief Executive Officer. General email, cdia@cdiaonline.org Web, www.cdiaonline.org and Twitter, @CDIAonline*

Membership: credit reporting, mortgage reporting, background check, and collection service companies. Provides information about credit rights to consumers. Monitors legislation and regulations.

Jump$tart Coalition for Personal Finance Literacy, *1001 Connecticut Ave. N.W., #640, 20036; (202) 846-6780. Laura Levine, President, (202) 846-6791. General email, info@jumpstart.org Web, www.jumpstart.org, Twitter, @NatJumpStart and Facebook, www.facebook.com/natljumpstart*

Coalition of organizations that promote financial literacy for pre-K–12 and college-aged students. Offers teacher training programs and online educational materials. Holds annual conferences for financial education professionals. Produces an annual publication that outlines financial education curriculum and topics.

National Assn. of Consumer Advocates, *1215 17th St. N.W., 5th Floor, 20036; (202) 452-1989. Fax, (202) 452-0099. Ira J. Rheingold, Executive Director, ext. 101. General email, info@consumeradvocates.org Web, www.consumeradvocates.org, Facebook, www .facebook.com/NationalAssociationofConsumerAdvocates and Twitter, @NACAdvocate*

Membership: consumer advocate attorneys. Seeks to protect the rights of consumers from fraudulent, abusive, and predatory business practices. Provides consumer law training through conferences and publications. Monitors legislation and regulations on banking, credit, and housing laws.

National Retail Federation, *1101 New York Ave. N.W., #1200, 20005; (202) 783-7971. Fax, (202) 737-2849. Matthew R. Shay, President; John Furner, Chair. Toll-free, (800) 673-4692. Web, www.nrf.com, Twitter, @NRFnews and Facebook, www.facebook.com/NationalRetailFederation General email, contact@nrf.com*

Membership: national and state associations of retailers and major retail corporations. Provides information on credit, truth-in-lending laws, and other fair credit practices.

U.S. Public Interest Research Group (U.S. PIRG), *Federal Advocacy, 600 Pennsylvania Ave. S.E., #400, 20003; (202) 546-9707. Doug Phelps, Chair. Web, www.uspirg.org and Twitter, @uspirg*

Coordinates grassroots efforts to advance consumer protection laws. Works for the protection of privacy rights, particularly in the area of fair credit reporting. (Headquarters in Denver, Colo.)

Product Safety, Testing

▶AGENCIES

Consumer Product Safety Commission (CPSC), *4330 East West Hwy., #836, Bethesda, MD 20814; (800) 638-2772. Fax, (301) 504-0124. Alexander Hoehn-Saric, Chair; Mary Boyle, Executive Director, (301) 504-7588. National Inquiry Information Clearing House, (301) 504-7921. Press, (301) 504-7908. TTY, (800) 638-8270. General email, info@cpsc.gov Web, www.cpsc.gov, Twitter, @USCPSC, Facebook, www.facebook.com/USCPSC and YouTube, www.youtube .com/uscpsc*

Establishes and enforces product safety standards; collects data; studies the causes and prevention of product-related injuries; identifies hazardous products, including imports, and recalls them from the marketplace.

Consumer Product Safety Commission (CPSC), *Communications, 4330 East-West Hwy., Bethesda, MD 20814-4408; (301) 504-7908. Fax, (301) 504-0862. Jason Levine, Director, (301) 504-7882. General email, info@cpsc.gov Web, www.cpsc.gov*

Provides information concerning consumer product safety; works with local and state governments, school systems, and private groups to develop product safety information and education programs. Toll-free hotline accepts consumer complaints on hazardous products and injuries associated with a product and offers recorded information on product recalls and CPSC safety recommendations.

Consumer Product Safety Commission (CPSC),
Compliance and Field Operations, 4330 East-West Hwy., Bethesda, MD 20814; (301) 504-7912. Robert Kaye, Assistant Executive Director, (301) 504-6960.
Web, www.cpsc.gov

Identifies and acts on defective consumer products; enforces industry compliance with safety standards for domestic and imported products; conducts enforcement litigation. Monitors recall of defective products and issues warnings to consumers.

Consumer Product Safety Commission (CPSC),
Engineering Sciences, 5 Research Pl., Rockville, MD 28050; (301) 987-2234. Fax, (978) 367-9122. Mark Kumagai, Associate Executive Director.
Web, www.cpsc.gov

Develops and evaluates consumer product safety standards, test methods, performance criteria, design specifications, and quality standards; conducts and evaluates engineering tests. Collects scientific and technical data to determine potential hazards of consumer products.

Consumer Product Safety Commission (CPSC),
Epidemiology, 4330 East-West Hwy., Bethesda, MD 20814-4408; (301) 504-7256. Steve Hanway, Associate Executive Director.
Web, www.cpsc.gov

Collects data on consumer product–related hazards and potential hazards; determines the frequency, severity, and distribution of the various types of injuries and investigates their causes; and assesses the effects of product safety standards and programs on consumer injuries. Conducts epidemiological studies and research in the fields of consumer-related injuries.

Consumer Product Safety Commission (CPSC), *Hazard Identification and Reduction,* 4330 East-West Hwy., Bethesda, MD 20814-4408; (301) 504-7622. Fax, (301) 504-0038. Duane Boniface, Associate Executive Director, (301) 504-7671.
Web, www.cpsc.gov

Establishes labeling and packaging regulations. Develops standards in accordance with the Poison Prevention Packaging Act, the Federal Hazardous Substances Act, the Consumer Products Safety Act, and the Consumer Products Safety Improvement Act.

Consumer Product Safety Commission (CPSC), *Health Sciences,* 5 Research Pl., Rockville, MD 20850; (301) 987-2240. Fax, (978) 967-8401. Mary Kelleher, Associate Executive Director.
Web, www.cpsc.gov

Evaluates potential health effects and hazards of consumer products and their foreseeable uses and misuses, and performs exposure and risk assessments for product-related hazards.

Consumer Product Safety Commission (CPSC),
Laboratory Sciences, 5 Research Pl., Rockville, MD 20850;

(301) 987-2037. Fax, (978) 367-1824. Andrew Stadnik, Associate Executive Director.
Web, www.cpsc.gov

Conducts engineering analyses and testing of consumer products, supports the development of voluntary and mandatory standards, and supports the agency's compliance activities through product safety assessments.

National Injury Information Clearinghouse *(Consumer Product Safety Commission),* 4330 East-West Hwy., Bethesda, MD 20814; (301) 504-7921. Fax, (301) 504-0025. James Rolfes, Chief Information Officer. To report consumer product-related accidents or injuries, (800) 638-2772. TTY, (301) 595-7054.
General email, clearinghouse@cpsc.gov

Web, www.cpsc.gov

Disseminates statistics and information relating to the prevention of death and injury associated with consumer products. Provides injury data from electronic data sources and distributes publications, including hazard analyses, special studies, and data summaries.

▶ NONGOVERNMENTAL

American Academy of Pediatrics, *Federal Affairs,* 601 13th St. N.W., #400N, 20005; (202) 347-8600. Fax, (202) 393-6137. Mark Del Monte, Chief Executive Officer.
General email, kids1st@aap.org

Web, www.aap.org, Twitter, @AmerAcadPeds and Facebook, www.facebook.com/AmerAcadPeds

Promotes legislation and regulations concerning child health and safety. Committee on Injury and Poison Prevention drafts policy statements and publishes information on toy safety, poisons, and other issues that affect children and adolescents. (Headquarters in Itasca, Ill.)

Cosmetic Ingredient Review, 1620 L St. N.W., #1200, 20036-4702; (202) 331-0651. Fax, (202) 331-0088. Bart Heldreth, Executive Director.
General email, cirinfo@cir-safety.org

Web, www.cir-safety.org

Voluntary self-regulatory program funded by the Personal Products Council. Reviews and evaluates published and unpublished data to assess the safety of cosmetic ingredients.

Tobacco

▶ AGENCIES

Alcohol and Tobacco Tax and Trade Bureau (TTB) *(Treasury Dept.),* 1310 G St. N.W., Box 12, 20005; (202) 453-2000. Fax, (202) 453-2912. Mary G. Ryan, Administrator. Public Affairs, (202) 453-2180. TTY, (202) 882-9914.
General email, TTBInternetQuestions@ttb.gov

Web, www.ttb.gov

Enforces and administers existing federal laws and tax code provisions relating to the production and taxation of alcohol and tobacco.

Centers for Disease Control and Prevention (CDC) *(Health and Human Services Dept.), Smoking and Health (OSH),* 395 E St. S.W., #9100, 20201; (202) 245-0550. Fax, (202) 245-0554. Letitia Pressley-Cantrell, Director (Acting). Press, (770) 488-5493. Toll-free, (800) 232-4636.

General email, tobaccoinfo@cdc.gov

Web, www.cdc.gov/tobacco/about/osh, Twitter, @CDCTobaccoFree and Facebook, www.facebook .com/cdctobaccofree

Develops, conducts, and supports strategic efforts to protect the public's health in the area of tobacco prevention and control. Funds, trains, and provides technical assistance to states, territories, tribal support centers, and national networks (e.g., National Tobacco Control Program); increases awareness and education about tobacco (e.g., publications, CDC's Smoking & Tobacco Use website, Tips from Former Smokers campaign, earned and digital media); conducts and supports national and international surveillance (e.g., National Youth Tobacco Survey, Global Tobacco Surveillance System).

Food and Drug Administration (FDA) *(Health and Human Services Dept.), Center for Tobacco Products (CTP),* White Oak Bldg. 71, 10903 New Hampshire Ave., Room G335, Silver Spring, MD 20993-002; (877) 287-1373. Mitch Zeller, Director.

General email, askctp@fda.hhs.gov

Web, www.fda.gov/about-fda/fda-organization/center-tobacco-products and Twitter, @FDATobacco

Regulates the manufacture, distribution, and marketing of tobacco products.

Action on Smoking and Health (ASH), 1250 Connecticut Ave. N.W., 7th Floor, 20036; (202) 659-4310. Laurent Huber, Executive Director.

General email, info@ash.org

Web, https://ash.org, Twitter, @ashorg, Facebook, www .facebook.com/ASHglobalAction and Blog, https://ash.org/ blog and YouTube, www.youtube.com/user/AshOrgUSA

Educational and legal organization that works to protect nonsmokers from cigarette smoking; provides information about smoking hazards and nonsmokers' rights.

National Campaign for Tobacco-Free Kids, 1400 Eye St. N.W., #1200, 20005; (202) 296-5469. Fax, (202) 296-5427. Matthew L. Myers, President.

General email, info@tobaccofreekids.org

Web, www.tobaccofreekids.org, Twitter, @TobaccoFreeKids, Facebook, www.facebook.com/ tobaccofreekids and YouTube, www.youtube.com/user/ tobaccofreekids

Seeks to reduce tobacco use by children through public policy change and educational programs. Provides technical assistance to state and local programs.

Truth Initiative, 900 G St. N.W., 4th Floor, 20001; (202) 454-5555. Robin Koval, President. Press, (202) 454-5561.

General email, press@truthinitiative.org

Web, https://truthinitiative.org, Twitter, @Truthinitiative and Facebook, www.facebook.com/Truthinitiative

Develops programs to disseminate information on the health effects of tobacco. Provides prevention and cessation services through grants, technical training and assistance, youth activism, partnerships, and community outreach.

FINANCE AND INVESTMENTS

General

▶**AGENCIES**

Bureau of the Fiscal Service *(Treasury Dept.),* 401 14th St. S.W., #545, 20227 (mailing address: 3201 Pennsy Dr., Bldg. E, Landover, MD 20785); (202) 874-7000. Fax, (202) 622-6415. Timothy (Tim) E. Gribben, Commissioner. Press and Congressional inquiries, (202) 504-3535. Public Affairs, (202) 622-2960. Savings Bonds, (844) 284-2676.

General email, Treasury.Direct@fiscal.treasury.gov

Web, www.fiscal.treasury.gov, Twitter, @FiscalService, Facebook, www.facebook.com/fiscalservice and YouTube, www.youtube.com/user/TREASURYDIRECT/ featured

Buy and redeem securities online, home.treasury.gov/ services/bonds-and-securities

Serves as the government's central financial manager, responsible for cash management and investment of government trust funds, credit administration, and debt collection. Handles central accounting for government fiscal activities; promotes sound financial management practices and increased use of automated payments, collections, accounting, and reporting systems.

Federal Deposit Insurance Corp. (FDIC), *Complex Financial Institutions, Division of Complex Institution Supervision and Resolution (CSIR),* 1776 F St. N.W., #F-3080, 20006; (202) 898-7073. Ricardo (Rick) Delfin, Director; John Kinneally, Administrative Assistant.

Web, www.fdic.gov/about/contact/directory/#OCFI

Reviews and oversees large bank holding companies and nonbank financial companies designated as systemically important by the Financial Stability Oversight Council. Implements orderly liquidations of such companies that fail.

Federal Reserve System, *Financial Stability,* 20th and C Sts. N.W., #B2046, 20551; (202) 452-3000. Andreas Nellie Lehnert, Director, (202) 452-3325. Public Affairs, (202) 779-1664.

Web, www.federalreserve.gov/econres/fsprstaff.htm

Identifies and analyzes potential threats to financial stability; monitors financial markets, institutions, and structures; and assesses and recommends policy alternatives to address these threats. Conducts long-term research in banking, finance, and macroeconomics.

Federal Reserve System

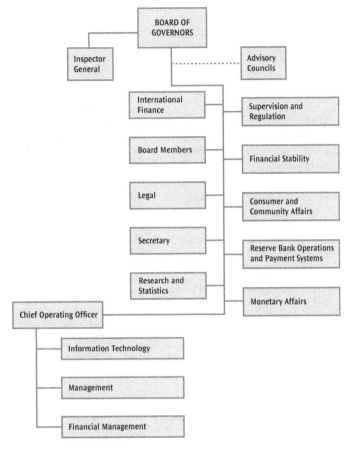

BOARD OF GOVERNORS

Inspector General

Advisory Councils

International Finance

Supervision and Regulation

Board Members

Financial Stability

Legal

Consumer and Community Affairs

Secretary

Reserve Bank Operations and Payment Systems

Research and Statistics

Monetary Affairs

Chief Operating Officer

Information Technology

Management

Financial Management

―― Lines of policy and judicial authority
···· Lines of management and administrative authority

Federal Reserve System, *Monetary Affairs,* 20th and C Sts. N.W., #B3022B, 20551; (202) 785-6001. *Trevor A. Reeve, Director.* Web, www.federalreserve.gov/econres/mastaff.htm

Assists the Federal Reserve Board and the Federal Open Market Committee in the conduct of monetary policy, especially in the areas of finance, money and banking, and monetary policy design and implementation. Provides expertise on open market operations, discount window policy, and reserve markets.

Small Business Administration (SBA), *Investments and Innovation,* 409 3rd St. S.W., #6300, 20416; (202) 205-6510. Fax, (202) 205-6959. *Tom Morris, Associate Administrator (Acting).* Web, www.sba.gov/about-sba/sba-locations/headquarters-offices/office-investment-innovation

Administers and runs the Small Business Investment Companies, Small Business Innovation Research, and Small Business Technology Transfer programs.

Treasury Dept., *Domestic Finance, Financial Markets,* 1500 Pennsylvania Ave. N.W., #5011, 20220; (202) 622-2000. *Josh Frost, Assistant Secretary.*

Web, https://home.treasury.gov/about/offices/domestic-finance/financial-markets

Provides analyses and policy recommendations on financial markets, government financing, and securities, tax implications, and related regulations. Oversees deterrence of U.S. currency counterfeiters.

▶CONGRESS

For a listing of relevant congressional committees and subcommittees, please see pages 38–39 or the Appendix.

Government Accountability Office (GAO), *Financial Markets and Community Investment (FMCI),* 441 G St. N.W., 20548; (202) 512-8678. *Daniel Garcia-Diaz, Managing Director, (202) 512-4802.* Web, www.gao.gov/about/careers/our-teams

Supports congressional efforts to ensure that U.S. financial markets function smoothly and effectively, identifies fraud and abuse, and promotes sound, sustainable community investment by assessing the effectiveness of federal initiatives aimed at small businesses, state and local governments, and communities.

▶NONGOVERNMENTAL

AARP, *601 E St. N.W., 20049; (202) 434-2277.*
Jo Ann C. Jenkins, Chief Executive Officer. Library, (202)
434-6233. Membership, toll-free, (800) 566-0242. Press,
(202) 434-2560. Toll-free, (888) 687-2277. TTY, (877) 434-
7598. Toll-free Spanish, (877) 342-2277. TTY Spanish,
(866) 238-9488.
General email, dcaarp@aarp.org

Web, www.aarp.org, Twitter, @AARP and Facebook,
www.facebook.com/AARP

Membership: people 50 years of age and older. Offers
financial services, including insurance, investment programs, and consumer discounts.

American Institute of Certified Public Accountants,
Washington Office, 1455 Pennsylvania Ave. N.W., #10,
20004-1081; (202) 737-6600. Fax, (202) 638-4512.
Mark Peterson, Executive Vice President of Advocacy.
General email, service@aicpa.org

Web, www.aicpa.org and Twitter, @AICPA

Membership: current and previously licensed CPAs,
students, and professionals working in accounting and
finance. Establishes voluntary professional and ethical regulations for the profession; sponsors conferences and
training workshops. Answers technical auditing and
accounting questions. (Associated with Association of
International Certified Professional Accountants.) (Headquarters in Durham, N.C.)

Americans for Financial Reform, *1615 K St. N.W., 20006;*
(202) 466-1885. Lisa Donner, Executive Director.
General email, info@ourfinancialsecurity.org

Web, www.ourfinancialsecurity.org,
Twitter, @RealBankReform and Facebook, www.facebook
.com/AmericansforFinancialReform

Coalition of groups seeking to increase economic
transparency and financial institution accountability. Analyzes economic public policies. Interests include protecting consumers, reducing large-bank bailouts, improving
the Federal Reserve, regulating Wall Street, and limiting
the influence of financial institutions on policy matters.
Monitors legislation and regulations.

The Brookings Institution, *Hutchins Center on*
Fiscal and Monetary Policy, 1775 Massachusetts
Ave. N.W., 20036; (202) 238-3115. David Wessel,
Director.
Web, www.brookings.edu/center/the-hutchins-center-on-
fiscal-and-monetary-policy, Twitter, @BrookingsEcon and
Twitter, @davidmwessel

Research center promoting improvements in and public understanding of fiscal and monetary policies.

Certified Financial Planner Board of Standards, *1425*
K St. N.W., #800, 20005; (202) 379-2200. Fax, (202)
379-2299. Kevin R. Keller, Chief Executive Officer.
Toll-free, (800) 487-1497.

General email, mail@cfpboard.org

Web, www.cfp.net, Twitter, @CFPBoard, Facebook,
www.facebook.com/CFPLetsMakeAPlan and
YouTube, www.youtube.com/user/CFPBoardofStandards

Grants certification to professional financial planners
through education, examination, and regulation of industry standards. Publishes handbooks and newsletters to
advance financial planning ethics and awareness.

Consumer Data Industry Assn., *1090 Vermont Ave. N.W.,*
#200, 20005-4905; (202) 371-0910. Francis Creighton,
Chief Executive Officer.
General email, cdia@cdiaonline.org

Web, www.cdiaonline.org and Twitter, @CDIAonline

Membership: credit reporting, mortgage reporting,
background check, and collection service companies. Provides information about credit rights to consumers. Monitors legislation and regulations.

Jump$tart Coalition for Personal Finance Literacy, *1001*
Connecticut Ave. N.W., #640, 20036; (202) 846-6780.
Laura Levine, President, (202) 846-6791.
General email, info@jumpstart.org

Web, www.jumpstart.org, Twitter, @NatJumpStart and
Facebook, www.facebook.com/natljumpstart

Coalition of organizations that promote financial literacy for pre-K–12 and college-aged students. Offers teacher
training programs and online educational materials.
Holds annual conferences for financial education professionals. Produces an annual publication that outlines
financial education curriculum and topics.

National Assn. of College and University Business
Officers, *1110 Vermont Ave. N.W., #800, 20005; (202) 861-*
2500. Susan Whealler Johnston, President, (202) 861-2503.
Customer Service, (202) 861-2560.
General email, support@nacubo.org

Web, www.nacubo.org, Twitter, @NACUBO and
Facebook, www.facebook.com/nacubo

Membership: chief business and financial officers at
higher-education institutions. Provides members with
information on financial management, federal regulations,
and other subjects related to the business administration
of universities and colleges; conducts workshops on
issues such as student aid, institutional budgeting, and
accounting.

National Assn. of Investment Companies, *1300*
Pennsylvania Ave. N.W., #700, 20004; (202) 204-3001.
Robert L. Greene, President.
General email, info@naicpe.com

Web, www.naicpe.com

Membership: investment companies that provide
minority-owned businesses with venture capital and management guidance. Provides technical assistance; monitors
legislation and regulations.

National Assn. of State Auditors, Comptrollers, and
Treasurers, *Washington Office, 444 N. Capitol St. N.W.,*
#422, 20001; (202) 624-5451. Fax, (202) 624-5473.

R. Kinney Poynter, Executive Director; Cornelia Chebinou, Washington Director.
Web, www.nasact.org and Twitter, @nasact

Membership: elected and appointed state and territorial officials who deal with the financial management of state government. Provides training and leadership information on financial management, best practices, and research. Monitors legislation and regulations. (Headquarters in Lexington, Ky.)

National Venture Capital Assn., *25 Massachusetts Ave. N.W., #730, 20001; (202) 864-5920. Fax, (202) 864-5930. Bobby Franklin, President, (202) 864-5925.*
General email, info@nvca.org
Web, www.nvca.org, Twitter, @nvca, Facebook, www .facebook.com/nvca.us and YouTube, www.youtube.com/ channel/UCP9Q8zxCi2DcWtNnAq45OjA

Membership: venture capital organizations and individuals and corporate financiers. Promotes understanding of venture capital investment. Facilitates networking opportunities and provides research data on equity investment in emerging growth companies. Monitors legislation.

Banking

▶ **AGENCIES**

Community Development Financial Institutions Fund *(Treasury Dept.), 1801 L St. N.W., 6th Floor, 20036 (mailing address: 1500 Pennsylvania Ave. N.W., Washington, DC 20220); (202) 653-0300. Jodie Harris, Director. Helpline, (202) 653-0421.*
General email, cdfihelp@cdfi.treas.gov
Web, www.cdfifund.gov

Provides funds and tax credits to financial institutions to build private markets, create healthy local tax revenues, and expand the availability of credit, investment capital, affordable housing, and financial services in low-income urban, rural, and Native communities.

Comptroller of the Currency *(Treasury Dept.), Constitution Center, 400 7th St. S.W., 20219; (202) 649-6800. Michael Hsu, Comptroller (Acting). Press, (202) 649-6870.*
General email, publicaffairs3@occ.treas.gov
Web, www.occ.gov, Twitter, @USOCC and YouTube, www.youtube.com/c/OfficeoftheComptrolleroftheCurrency/ videos

Charters and examines operations of national banks, federal savings associations, and U.S. operations of foreign-owned banks; establishes guidelines for bank examinations; handles mergers of national banks with regard to antitrust law. Ensures that national banks and savings associations operate in a safe and sound manner, provide fair access to financial services, treat customers fairly, and comply with applicable laws and regulations.

Comptroller of the Currency *(Treasury Dept.), Chief Counsel, Constitution Center, 400 7th St. S.W., 20219; (202) 649-5400. Benjamin W. McDonough, Chief Counsel.*
Web, www.occ.gov/about/who-we-are/organizations/chief-counsels-office/index-chief-counsels-office.html

Enforces and oversees compliance by nationally chartered banks with laws prohibiting discrimination in credit transactions on the basis of sex or marital status. Enforces regulations concerning bank advertising; may issue cease-and-desist orders.

Comptroller of the Currency *(Treasury Dept.), Enterprise Governance and Ombudsman, Constitution Center, 400 7th St. S.W., MS 10E-12, 20219; (202) 649-5530. Larry L. Hattix, Ombudsman.*
Web, www.occ.gov and www.occ.gov/about/who-we-are/ organizations/office-of-enterprise-governance-and-the-ombudsman/index-office-of-enterprise-governance-and-the-omb

Ensures that bank customers and the banks the agency supervises receive fair and expeditious resolution of their concerns.

Comptroller of the Currency *(Treasury Dept.), Licensing, Constitution Center, 400 7th St. S.W., #3E-218, 20219; (202) 649-6260. Stephen A. Lybarger, Deputy Comptroller.*
Web, www.occ.gov

Advises the comptroller on policy matters and programs related to bank corporate activities and is the primary decision maker on national bank corporate applications, including charters, mergers and acquisitions, conversions, and operating subsidiaries.

Comptroller of the Currency *(Treasury Dept.), Public Affairs, Constitution Center, 400 7th St. S.W., 20219; (202) 649-6870. Fax, (713) 336-4103. Byran Hubbard, Deputy for Public Affairs; Carrie Moore, Congressional Relations. Congressional Relations, (202) 649-6737. Customer Assistance Group, (800) 613-6743.*
General email, publicaffairs3@occ.treas.gov
Web, www.occ.gov/about/who-we-are/organizations/ office-of-public-affairs/index-office-of-public-affairs.html and http://helpwithmybank.gov

Advises the Comptroller on banking industry relations, employee communications, Congressional affairs, disclosure, media relations, minority affairs, and publishing.

Federal Deposit Insurance Corp. (FDIC), *550 17th St. N.W., 20429; (703) 562-2222. Martin J. Gruenberg, Chair. Press, (202) 898-6993. Toll-free, (877) 275-3342. TTY, (800) 877-8339.*
General email, publicinfo@fdic.gov
Web, www.fdic.gov, Twitter, @FCICgov, Facebook, www .facebook.com/FDICgov and YouTube, www.youtube.com/ user/FDICchannel

Insures deposits in national banks and state banks. Conducts examinations of insured state banks that are not members of the Federal Reserve System.

Securities and Exchange Commission

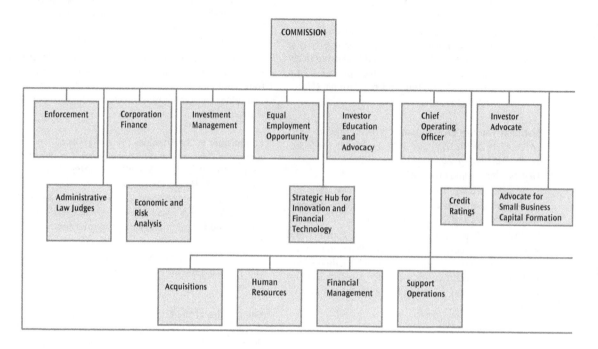

Federal Deposit Insurance Corp. (FDIC), *Ombudsman,*
Virginia Square, L. William Seidman Center, 3501 N.
Fairfax Dr., #E-2022, Arlington, VA 22226; (877) 275-
3342. M. Anthony Lowe, Ombudsman.
General email, ombudsman@fdic.gov

Web, www.fdic.gov/regulations/resources/ombudsman

An independent, neutral, and confidential source of assistance for the public. Provides answers to the public in the areas of depositor concerns, loan questions, asset information, bank closing issues, and any FDIC regulation or policy.

Federal Deposit Insurance Corp. (FDIC), *Resolutions and*
Receiverships, 3701 N. Fairfax Dr., #10072, Arlington, VA
22226; (202) 898-6525. Maureen Sweeny, Director;
Brad Edwards, Administrative Assistant. Toll-free, (888)
206-4662.
Web, www.fdic.gov/about/contact/directory/#HQDRR and
Handbook, www.fdic.gov/bank/historical/reshandbook

Plans, executes, and monitors the orderly and least-cost resolution of failing FDIC-insured institutions. Manages remaining liability of the federal savings and deposit insurance funds.

Federal Deposit Insurance Corp. (FDIC), *Risk*
Management Supervision, 550 17th St. N.W., #5036,
20429; (877) 275-3342. Fax, (202) 898-3638.
Doreen R. Eberley, Director. TTY, (800) 877-8339.

Web, www.fdic.gov/about/contact/directory/#HQDSC and
Policy manual, www.fdic.gov/regulations

Serves as the federal regulator and supervisor of insured state banks that are not members of the Federal Reserve System. Conducts regular examinations and investigations of banks under the jurisdiction of the FDIC; advises bank managers on improving policies and practices. Administers the Bank Insurance Fund, which insures deposits in commercial and savings banks, and the Savings Assn. Insurance Fund, which insures deposits in savings and loan institutions.

Federal Housing Finance Agency (FHFA), *400 7th St. S.W.,*
20219; (202) 649-3800. Sandra L. Thompson, Director.
Ombudsman, (888) 649-5530. Press, (202) 649-3700.
General email, fhfainfo@fhfa.gov

Ombudsman email, CFPBOmbudsman@cfpb.gov,
Web, www.fhfa.gov, Twitter, @FHFA and Facebook,
www.facebook.com/FHFA

Regulates and works to ensure the financial soundness of Fannie Mae (Federal National Mortgage Assn.), Freddie Mac (Federal Home Loan Mortgage Corp.), and the eleven Federal Home Loan banks. FHFA was formed by a legislative merger of the Office of Federal Housing Enterprise Oversight (OFHEO), the Federal Housing Finance Board, and HUD's Government-sponsored Enterprise (GSE) mission team.

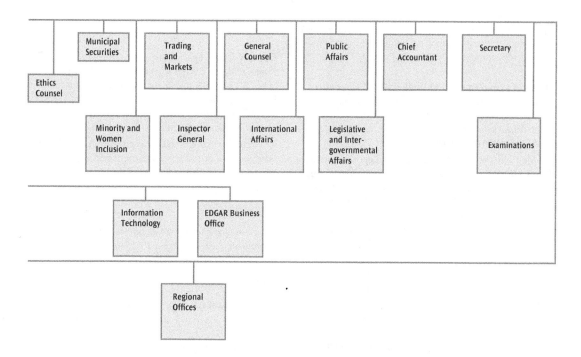

Federal Reserve System, *Board of Governors,* 20th St. and Constitution Ave. N.W., 20551; (202) 452-3000. Jerome H. Powell, Chair; Richard H. Clarida, Vice Chair (Acting). Comments, (202) 974-7008. Congressional Liaison, (202) 452-3456. Information (meetings), (202) 452-3204. Printing and Fulfillment, (202) 452-3245. Public Affairs, (202) 452-2955. TTY, (202) 263-4869.
General email, frboard-publicaffairs@frb.gov

Web, www.federalreserve.gov, Twitter, @federalreserve, Facebook, www.facebook.com/federalreserve and YouTube, www.youtube.com/federalreserve

Serves as the central bank and fiscal agent for the government. Examines Federal Reserve banks and state member banks; supervises bank holding companies. Controls wire system transfer operations and supplies currency for depository institutions.

Federal Reserve System, *Reserve Bank Operations and Payment Systems,* 20th St. and Constitution Ave. N.W., MS 190, 20551; (202) 452-2789. Matthew J. Eichner, Director, (202) 452-2019.
Web, www.federalreserve.gov/econres/rbo

Oversees the Federal Reserve banks' provision of financial services to depository institutions and fiscal agency services to the Treasury Dept. and other federal agencies; provides support, such as information technology and financial cost accounting. Develops policies and regulations to foster the efficiency and integrity of U.S. payment systems; works with other central banks and international organizations to improve payment systems more broadly; and conducts research on payment issues.

Federal Reserve System, *Supervision and Regulation,* 20th St. and Constitution Ave. N.W., 20551; (202) 973-6999. Michael S. Gibson, Director, (202) 452-2495; Christina Kohn, Administrative Assistant.
Web, www.federalreserve.gov/econres/bsrpd-staff.htm

Supervises and regulates state banks that are members of the Federal Reserve System; supervises and inspects all bank holding companies; monitors banking practices; approves bank mergers, consolidations, and other changes in bank structure.

National Credit Union Administration (NCUA), 1775 Duke St., 4th Floor, Alexandria, VA 22314-3428; (703) 518-6300. Todd M. Harper, Chair; Larry Fazio, Executive Director, (703) 518-6320. Press, (703) 518-6336.
General email, EasternMail@ncua.gov

Web, www.ncua.gov, Twitter, @TheNCUA, Facebook, www.facebook.com/NCUAgov and YouTube, www.youtube.com/user/NCUAChannel

Administers the National Credit Union Share Insurance Fund, which, with the backing of the full faith and credit of the U.S. government, operates and manages the

National Credit Union, which insures the deposits of nearly 96 million account holders. Regulates all federally chartered credit unions; charters new credit unions; supervises and examines federal credit unions and insures their member accounts up to $250,000. Insures state-chartered credit unions that apply and are eligible. Manages the Central Liquidity Facility, which supplies emergency short-term loans to members. Conducts research on economic trends and their effect on credit unions and advises the administration's board on economic and financial policy and regulations.

Office of Management and Budget (OMB) *(Executive Office of the President), Housing, Treasury, and Commerce,* 725 17th St. N.W., #9201, 20503; (202) 395-4516. Michelle Enger, Deputy Controller, (202) 395-7874.
Web, www.whitehouse.gov/omb

Monitors the financial condition of deposit insurance funds including the Bank Insurance Fund, the Savings Assn. Insurance Fund, and the Federal Savings and Loan Insurance Corp. (FSLIC) Resolution Fund. Monitors the Securities and Exchange Commission. Has limited oversight over the Federal Housing Finance Board and the Federal Home Loan Bank System.

Securities and Exchange Commission (SEC), *Corporation Finance,* 100 F St. N.E., MS 4613, 20549; (202) 551-3100. Renee Jones, Director.
Web, www.sec.gov/page/corpfin-section-landing

Receives and examines disclosure statements and other information from publicly held companies, including bank holding companies.

Treasury Dept., *Domestic Finance, Financial Institutions,* 1500 Pennsylvania Ave. N.W., #2326, 20220; (202) 622-2610. Michael Barr, Assistant Secretary.
Web, https://home.treasury.gov/about/offices/domestic-finance/financial-institutions

Advises the under secretary for domestic finance and the Treasury secretary on financial institutions, banks, and thrifts. Helps formulate policy on financial institutions and government-sponsored enterprises, critical infrastructure protection and compliance policy, and financial education. Oversees the Terrorism Risk Insurance Program and the Community Development Financial Institutions Fund.

Treasury Dept., *Domestic Finance, Financial Institutions Policy,* 1500 Pennsylvania Ave. N.W., #1310, 20220; (202) 622-2000. John Connolly, Senior Policy Advisor, (202) 622-2813; Jordan Bleicher, Senior Policy Adviser.
General email, OFIP@treasury.gov
Web, https://home.treasury.gov/about/offices/domestic-finance/financial-institutions

Coordinates department efforts on all legislation and regulations affecting financial institutions. Develops department policy on all matters relating to agencies responsible for supervising financial institutions and financial markets.

Treasury Dept., *Domestic Finance, Financial Stability,* 1500 Pennsylvania Ave. N.W., #2428, 20220; (202) 622-2000. Fax, (202) 622-6415. Henry M. Allison Jr., Assistant Secretary (Acting).
Web, www.treasury.gov/initiatives/financial-stability

Seeks to normalize lending. Provides eligible financial institutions with capital assistance; administers mortgage modification programs. Manages the Troubled Asset Relief Program (TARP).

Treasury Dept., *Special Inspector General for the Troubled Asset Relief Program (SIGTARP),* 1801 L St. N.W., 20220; (202) 622-1419. Christy Goldsmith Romero, Special Inspector General. Fraud, waste, and abuse hotline, 877-SIG-2009. Press, (202) 927-8940.
Web, www.sigtarp.gov and Twitter, @SIGTARP

Conducts, supervises, and coordinates audits and investigations of the purchase, management, and sale of assets under the Troubled Asset Relief Program (TARP).

▶**CONGRESS**

For a listing of relevant congressional committees and subcommittees, please see pages 38–39 or the Appendix.

▶**NONGOVERNMENTAL**

American Bankers Assn. (ABA), 1120 Connecticut Ave. N.W., 20036; (202) 663-5000. Rob Nichols, President. Toll-free, (800) 226-5377.
General email, support@aba.com
Web, www.aba.com, Twitter, @ABABankers and Facebook, www.facebook.com/AmericanBankers Association

Membership: commercial banks. Operates schools to train banking personnel; conducts conferences; formulates government relations policies for the banking community.

American Council of State Savings Supervisors, 1129 20th St. N.W., 9th Floor, 20036; (202) 728-5707. Mary Beth Quist, Executive Director.
Web, www.acsss.org

Membership: supervisors and regulators of state-chartered savings associations. Trains state financial regulatory examiners. Monitors legislation and regulations affecting the state-chartered thrift industry.

Assn. for Financial Professionals, 4520 East-West Hwy., #800, Bethesda, MD 20814; (301) 907-2862. Fax, (301) 907-2864. James A. Kaitz, President.
General email, customerservice@afponline.org
Web, www.afponline.org and Twitter, @AFPonline

Membership: more than 16,000 members from a wide range of industries throughout all stages of their careers in various aspects of treasury and financial management. Acts as a resource for continuing education, financial tools and publications, career development, certifications, research, representation to legislators and regulators, and the development of industry standards. (Asia-Pacific Office in Singapore.)

Bank Policy Institute (BPI), *600 13th St. N.W., #400, 20005; (202) 289-4322. Greg Baer, Chief Executive Officer. General email, info@bpi.com*

Web, https://bpi.com, Twitter, @BankPolicy

Twitter CEO, @baerheel

Membership: universal banks, regional banks, and the major foreign banks doing business in the United States. Conducts research and analysis to inform U.S. and global regulators, members of Congress, academics, and media through advocacy, research papers, blog posts, white papers, comment letters, and Congressional testimony. The Business-Innovation-Technology-Security division (BITS) provides a forum for discussing current and emerging technology and innovation, reducing fraud, and improving cybersecurity and risk management practices for the nation's financial sector.

Bankers Association for Foreign Trade (BAFT), *1120 Connecticut Ave. N.W., 5th Floor, 20036-3902; (202) 663-7575. Fax, (202) 663-5538. Tod R. Burwell, Chief Executive Officer, (202) 663-5252.*

General email, info@baft.org

Web, www.baft.org, Twitter, @BAFT_Global and YouTube, www.youtube.com/c/BAFTBankersAssociation forFinanceandTrade

Membership: international financial services providers, including U.S. and non–U.S. commercial banks, financial services companies, and suppliers with major international operations. Provides Advocacy, Thought Leadership, Education and Training, and a global forum for international transaction bankers across the industry. Including iinternational trade, trade finance, payments, compliance, asset servicing, and transaction banking. Monitors and acts as an advocate globally on activities that affect the business of commercial and international banks and nonfinancial companies. (Formerly Bankers' Assn. for Financial Trade.)

Coalition For Integrity, *1100 13th St. N.W., 8th Floor, 20005; (202) 589-1616. Shruti Shah, President. General email, administration@coalitionforintegrity.org*

Web, www.coalitionforintegrity.org, Twitter, @unite4integrity and Facebook, www.facebook .com/unite4integrity

Works to reduce corruption through the promotion of enforcement of international conventions and acts as advocate for global leadership, to increase government transparency and accountability, and to promote private sector integrity. (Formerly Transparency International USA.)

Conference of State Bank Supervisors, *1129 20th St. N.W., 9th Floor, 20036; (202) 296-2840. Fax, (202) 296-1926. John W. Ryan, President, (202) 728-5724. Web, www.csbs.org*

Membership: state officials responsible for supervision of state-chartered banking institutions. Conducts educational programs. Monitors legislation and regulations.

Consumer Bankers Assn., *1225 New York Ave. N.W., #1100, 20005; (202) 552-6380. Richard Hunt, President, (202) 552-6382. Press, (202) 552-6371.*

Web, www.consumerbankers.com, Twitter, @ConsumerBankers and Facebook, www.facebook .com/ComsumerBankersAssociation

Membership: federally insured financial institutions. Provides information on retail banking, including industry trends. Operates the Graduate School of Retail Bank Management to train banking personnel; conducts research and analysis on retail banking trends; sponsors conferences.

Credit Union National Assn., *Washington Office, 99 M St. S.E., #300, 20003; (202) 638-5777. Jim Nussle, President. Toll-free, (800) 356-9655.*

General email, hello@cuna.coop

Web, www.cuna.org

Confederation of credit unions from every state, the District of Columbia, and Puerto Rico. Represents federal and state chartered credit unions. Monitors legislation and regulations. (Headquarters in Madison, Wisc.)

Electronic Funds Transfer Assn., *4000 Legato Rd., #1100, Fairfax, VA 22033; (571) 318-5556. Fax, (571) 318-5557. Kurt Helwig, President, (571) 318-5555.*

Web, https://efta.org and Twitter, @kurtEFTA

Membership: financial institutions, electronic funds transfer hardware and software providers, automatic teller machine networks, and others engaged in electronic commerce. Promotes electronic payments and commerce technologies; sponsors industry analysis. Monitors legislation and regulations.

Employee Benefit Research Institute, *901 D St. S.W., #802, 20024; (202) 659-0670. Fax, (202) 775-6360. Lori Lucas, President.*

General email, info@ebri.org

Web, www.ebri.org

Research institute that focuses on economic security and employee benefit issues. Seeks to raise public awareness about long-term personal financial independence and encourage retirement savings. Does not lobby and does not take public policy positions.

Independent Community Bankers of America, *1615 L St. N.W., #900, 20036; (202) 659-8111. Rebeca Romero Rainey, President. Toll-free, (866) 843-4222.*

General email, info@icba.org

Web, www.icba.org, Twitter, @ICBA and Facebook, www.facebook.com/icbaorg

Membership: approximately 5,700 community banks. Interests include farm credit, deregulation, interstate banking, deposit insurance, and financial industry standards.

NACHA: The Electronic Payments Assn., *2550 Wasser Terrace, #400, Herndon, VA 20171; (703) 561-1100. Fax, (703) 787-0996. Jane Larimer, President. Press, (703) 561-3952.*

General email, info@nacha.org

Web, www.nacha.org, Twitter, @NACHAOnline and Facebook, www.facebook.com/NACHAOnline

Press, media@nacha.org and YouTube, www.youtube.com/c/nacha

Membership: ACH Network participants. Supports ACH Network growth by managing its development, administration, and governance. Facilitates the expansion and diversification of electronic payments, supporting Direct Deposit and Direct Payment via ACH transactions, including credit and debit transactions; recurring and one-time payments; government, consumer, and business-to-business transactions; international payments; and payments plus payment-related information. Develops operating rules and business practices through its collaborative, self-regulatory model. Sponsors workshops and seminars. (Formerly the National Automated Clearing House Assn.)

National Assn. of Federal Credit Unions (NAFCU), 3138 N. 10th St., Arlington, VA 22201-2149; (703) 842-2240. Fax, (703) 522-2734. B. Dan Berger, President, (703) 842-2215. Toll-free, (800) 336-4644. Compliance Helpline, (877) 623-2887.

General email, info@nafcu.org

Web, www.nafcu.org, Twitter, @NAFCU and Facebook, www.facebook.com/nafcu

Membership: federally chartered credit unions. Issues legislative and regulatory alerts for members and consumers. Sponsors briefings on current financial trends, legislation and regulations, and management techniques.

National Assn. of State Credit Union Supervisors, 1655 N. Fort Myer Dr., #650, Arlington, VA 22209-3113; (703) 528-8351. Fax, (703) 528-3248. Brian Knight, Chief Executive Officer.

General email, info@nascus.org

Web, www.nascus.org, Twitter, @NASCUS and Facebook, www.facebook.com/NASCUS

Membership: state credit union supervisors, state-chartered credit unions, and credit union leagues. Interests include state regulatory systems; conducts educational programs for examiners. Represents the interests of state agencies to Congress.

National Bankers Assn., 1513 P St. N.W., 20005; (202) 588-5432. Nicole A. Elam, President.

General email, administration@nationalbankers.org

Web, www.nationalbankers.org and Twitter, @AssocNational

Membership: minority-owned and women-owned financial institutions. Monitors legislation and regulations.

National Society of Accountants, 1330 Braddock Pl., #540, Alexandria, VA 22314; (703) 549-6400. Joshua Caulfield, Chief Executive Officer. Toll-free, (800) 966-6679.

General email, members@nsacct.org

Web, www.nsacct.org, Twitter, @NSAtax and Facebook, www.facebook.com/nsacct

Membership: accountants and tax practioners. Seeks to improve the accounting profession and to enhance the status of individual practitioners. Sponsors seminars and correspondence courses on accounting, auditing, business law, and estate planning; monitors legislation and regulations affecting accountants and their small-business clients.

Stocks, Bonds, and Securities

▶**AGENCIES**

Bureau of the Fiscal Service *(Treasury Dept.),* *Legislative and Public Affairs,* 401 14th St. S.W., 5th Floor, 20227; (202) 504-3502. (202) 622-1900. Fax, (202) 622-0534. Kimberly Smith-Brown, Director, (202) 504-3535.

General email, legaffairs@treasury.gov and CongressionalInquiries@fiscal.treasury.gov

Web, www.fiscal.treasury.gov

Plans, develops, and implements communication regarding Treasury securities.

Federal Reserve System, *Board of Governors,* 20th St. and Constitution Ave. N.W., 20551; (202) 452-3000. Jerome H. Powell, Chair; Richard H. Clarida, Vice Chair (Acting). Comments, (202) 974-7008. Congressional Liaison, (202) 452-3456. Information (meetings), (202) 452-3204. Printing and Fulfillment, (202) 452-3245. Public Affairs, (202) 452-2955. TTY, (202) 263-4869.

General email, frboard-publicaffairs@frb.gov

Web, www.federalreserve.gov, Twitter, @federalreserve, Facebook, www.facebook.com/federalreserve and YouTube, www.youtube.com/federalreserve

Regulates amount of credit that may be extended and maintained on certain securities in order to prevent excessive use of credit for purchase or carrying of securities.

Securities and Exchange Commission (SEC), 100 F St. N.E., 20549; (202) 551-2100. Gary Gensler, Chair, (202) 551-2800; Jen Davitt, Librarian. FOIA, (202) 551-7900. Investor Information and Complaints, (202) 551-6551. Legislative and Intergovernmental Affairs, (202) 551-2010. Personnel locator, (202) 551-6000. Press and Public Affairs, (202) 551-4120. Whistleblower tips, (202) 551-4790. TTY, (800) 877-8339.

Web, www.sec.gov

Requires public disclosure of financial and other information about companies whose securities are offered for public sale, traded on exchanges, or traded over the counter; issues and enforces regulations to prevent fraud in securities markets and investigates securities frauds and violations; supervises operations of stock exchanges and activities of securities dealers, investment advisers, and investment companies; regulates purchase and sale of securities; participates in bankruptcy proceedings involving publicly held companies; has some jurisdiction over municipal securities trading. Public Reference Section makes available corporation reports and statements filed with the SEC. The information is available via the Web (www.sec.gov/edgar.shtml). Library open to the public by appointment.

Securities and Exchange Commission (SEC), *Compliance Inspections and Examinations,* 100 F St. N.E., 20549; (202) 551-6200. Daniel Kahl, Director (Acting).
Web, www.sec.gov/ocie/ocie_org.htm

Analyzes data and conducts examinations in order to ensure compliance with federal security laws, identify and monitor risks, improve industry practices, and prevent fraud.

Securities and Exchange Commission (SEC), *Economic and Risk Analysis,* 100 F St. N.E., 20549; (202) 551-6600. Jessica Wachter, Director.
General email, DERA@sec.gov
Web, www.sec.gov/dera and Twitter, @SEC_DERA

Provides the commission with economic analyses of proposed rule and policy changes and other information to guide the SEC in influencing capital markets. Evaluates the effect of policy and other factors on competition within the securities industry and among competing securities markets; compiles financial statistics on capital formation and the securities industry.

Securities and Exchange Commission (SEC), *Investor Advocate,* 100 F St. N.E., 20549; (202) 551-3302. Rick A. Fleming, Director.
General email, InvestorAdvocate@sec.gov
Web, www.sec.gov/page/investor-advocate-landing-page

Considers investors' interests in policymaking; addresses complaints from retail investors concerning the commission; studies investor behavior.

Securities and Exchange Commission (SEC), *Office of the Whistleblower,* 100 F St. N.E., MS 5631, 20549 (mailing address: SEC/OWB, 14420 Albemarle Point Place, #102, Chantilly, VA 20151-1750); (202) 551-4790. Fax, (703) 813-9322. Nicole Creola Kelly, Chief.
Web, www.sec.gov/whistleblower

Receives information about possible securities law violations and provides information about the whistleblower program.

Securities and Exchange Commission (SEC), *Trading and Markets,* 100 F St. N.E., 20549; (202) 551-5500. Fax, (202) 772-9273. Haoxiang Zhu, Director.
General email, tradingandmarkets@sec.gov
Web, www.sec.gov/divisions/trading-markets

Oversees and regulates the operations of securities exchanges, the Financial Industry Regulatory Authority (FINRA), nationally recognized statistical rating organizations, brokers-dealers, clearing agencies, transfer agents, alternative trading systems, large traders, security-based swap dealers, security futures product exchanges, and securities information processors. Promotes the establishment of a national system for clearing and settling securities transactions. Facilitates the development of a national market system.

Treasury Dept., *Domestic Finance, Financial Markets,* 1500 Pennsylvania Ave. N.W., #5011, 20220; (202) 622-2000. Josh Frost, Assistant Secretary.
Web, https://home.treasury.gov/about/offices/domestic-finance/financial-markets

Provides analyses and policy recommendations on financial markets, government financing, and securities, tax implications, and related regulations. Oversees deterrence of U.S. currency counterfeiters.

▶**NONGOVERNMENTAL**

American Investment Council, 799 9th St. N.W., #200, 20001; (202) 465-7700. Fax, (202) 639-0209. Drew Maloney, President.
General email, info@investmentcouncil.org
Web, www.investmentcouncil.org and Twitter, @AmericaInvests

Advocacy, communications, and research organization and resource center that develops, analyzes, and distributes information about the private equity industry and its contributions to the national and global economy. Monitors legislation and regulations.

Council of Institutional Investors, 1717 Pennsylvania Ave. N.W., #350, 20006; (202) 822-0800. Fax, (202) 822-0801. Amy Borrus, Executive Director, (202) 261-7082.
Web, www.cii.org and Twitter, @CouncilInstInv

Membership: pension funds and other employee benefit funds, foundations, and endowments. Studies investment issues that affect pension plan assets. Focuses on corporate governance and shareholder rights. Monitors legislation and regulations.

Financial Industry Regulatory Authority (FINRA), 1735 K St. N.W., 20006-1506; (202) 728-8000. Fax, (202) 728-8075. Robert W. Cook, Chief Executive Officer. General Inquiries, (301) 590-6500.
Web, www.finra.org, Twitter, @FINRA and Facebook, www.facebook.com/FinancialIndustry RegulatoryAuthority

Membership: investment brokers and dealers authorized to conduct transactions of the investment banking and securities business under federal and state laws. Serves as the self-regulatory mechanism in the over-the-counter securities market. Operates speakers bureau. Has the largest resolution forum in the United States. (Formerly the National Assn. of Securities Dealers.)

Futures Industry Assn. (FIA), North Tower, 2001 K. St. N.W., #725, 20006; (202) 466-5460. Walter (Walt) Lukken, President.
General email, info@fia.org
Web, www.fia.org and Twitter, @FIAAmericas

Membership: futures commission merchants, introducing brokers, exchanges, clearinghouses, and others interested in derivative markets. Serves as a forum for discussion of industry issues; engages in regulatory and legislative advocacy; provides market information and statistical data; offers educational programs; works to establish professional and ethical standards for members.

Intercontinental Exchange, Washington Office, *701 Pennsylvania Ave. N.W., #500, 20004; Robert Eskridge, Director, Government Affairs; Mark Wassersug, Chief Operating Officer.*
General email, everyone-washington@theice.com
Web, www.intercontinentalexchange.com, Twitter, @ICE_Markets and Facebook, www.facebook.com/IntercontinentalExchange

Provides information about risk-management services to market participants around the world. Washington office monitors legislation and regulations. (Headquarters in Atlanta, Ga.)

Investment Company Institute, *1401 H St. N.W., #1200, 20005-2148; (202) 326-5800. Eric J. Pan, President. Press, (202) 371-5413.*
Web, www.ici.org, Twitter, @ici and Facebook, www.facebook.com/ici.org

Membership: mutual funds, exchange-traded funds, and closed-end funds registered under the Investment Company Act of 1940 (including investment advisers to and underwriters of such companies) and the unit investment trust industry. Conducts research and disseminates information on issues affecting mutual funds.

Investor Protection Trust, *750 1st St. N.E., #1140, 20002; (202) 775-2112. Michelle Olympiadis, Executive Director (Acting).*
General email, iptinfo@investorprotection.org
Web, www.investorprotection.org and Twitter, @IPT_info

Provides noncommercial investment information to consumers to help them make informed investment decisions. Serves as an independent source of noncommercial investor education materials. Operates programs under its own auspices and uses grants to underwrite important initiatives carried out by other organizations.

Municipal Securities Rulemaking Board, *1300 Eye St. N.W., #1000, 20005; (202) 838-1500. Fax, (202) 898-1500. Nanette D. Lawson, Chief Operating Officer; Mark T. Kim, Chief Executive Officer.*
General email, MSRBsupport@mrsb.org
Web, www.msrb.org, Twitter, @MSRB_News and Youtube, www.youtube.com/user/MSRBNEWS

Congressionally chartered self-regulatory organization for the municipal securities market. Regulates municipal securities dealers and municipal advisers and seeks to provide market transparency through the Electronic Municipal Market Access website. Conducts education and outreach. Subject to oversight by the Securities and Exchange Commission.

National Assn. of Bond Lawyers, *601 13th St. N.W., #800-S, 20005-3875; (202) 503-3300. Fax, (202) 637-0217. Linda H. Wyman, Chief Operating Officer, ext. 3306; Brian Egan, Director, Government Affairs, ext. 3290.*
General email, nablconnect@nabl.org
Web, www.nabl.org, Twitter, @nabldc and Facebook, www.facebook.com/nabldc

Membership: state and municipal finance lawyers. Educates members and others on the law relating to state and municipal bonds and other obligations. Provides advice and comment at the federal, state, and local levels on legislation, regulations, rulings, and court and administrative proceedings regarding public obligations.

National Assn. of Real Estate Investment Trusts, *1875 Eye St. N.W., #500, 20006-5413; (202) 739-9400. Fax, (202) 739-9401. Steven A. Wechsler, President. Toll-free, (800) 362-7348.*
Web, www.reit.com and Twitter, @REITs_NAREIT

Membership: real estate investment trusts and corporations, partnerships, and individuals interested in real estate securities and the industry. Interests include federal taxation, securities regulation, financial standards and reporting standards and ethics, housing and education, and global investment; compiles industry statistics. Monitors federal and state legislation and regulations.

National Investor Relations Institute, *908 King St., #310, Alexandria, VA 22314; (703) 562-7700. Fax, (703) 562-7701. Gary LaBranche, President, (703) 562-7676.*
General email, niri@niri.org
Web, www.niri.org and Twitter, @NIRI_National

Membership: executives engaged in investor relations and financial communications. Provides publications, educational training sessions, and research on investor relations for members; offers conferences and workshops; maintains job placement and referral services for members.

North American Securities Administrators Assn., *750 1st St. N.E., #1140, 20002; (202) 737-0900. Joseph Brady, Executive Director.*
Web, www.nasaa.org, Twitter, @nasaa and Facebook, www.facebook.com/pages/NASAA/22474512712

Membership: state, provincial, and territorial securities administrators of the United States, Canada, and Mexico. Serves as the national representative of the state agencies responsible for investor protection. Works to prevent fraud in securities markets and provides a national forum to increase the efficiency and uniformity of state regulation of capital markets. Operates the Central Registration Depository, a nationwide computer link for agent registration and transfers, in conjunction with the National Assn. of Securities Dealers. Monitors legislation and regulations.

Public Company Accounting Oversight Board, *1666 K St. N.W., #300, 20006-2803; (202) 207-9100. Fax, (202) 862-8430. Erica Y. Williams, Chair; Holly Greaves, Chief Administrative Officer (Acting). Information, (202) 591-4135.*
Web, https://pcaobus.org and Twitter, @PCAOB_News

Established by Congress to oversee the audits of public companies in order to protect the interests of investors and the public. Also oversees the audits of broker-dealers, including compliance reports filed pursuant to federal securities laws.

Securities Industry and Financial Markets Assn. (SIFMA), Washington Office, 1099 New York Ave. N.W., 6th Floor, 20001; (202) 962-7300. Fax, (202) 962-7305. Kenneth E. Bentsen Jr., Chief Executive Officer. Press, (202) 962-7390.
Web, www.sifma.org, Twitter, @SIFMA
General email, inquiry@sifma.org

Membership: securities firms, banks, and asset managers. Focuses on enhancing the public's trust in markets. Provides educational resources for professionals and investors in the industry. Monitors legislation and regulations. (Headquarters in New York. Merger of the Securities Industry Assn. and the Bond Market Assn.)

Securities Investor Protection Corp. (SIPC), 1667 K St. N.W., #1000, 20006-1620; (202) 371-8300. Fax, (202) 223-1679. William S. Jasien, Chief Executive Officer. General email, asksipc@sipc.org
Web, www.sipc.org, Twitter, @sipc and Facebook, www.facebook.com/sipcorg

Private corporation established by Congress to administer the Securities Investor Protection Act. Acts as a trustee or works with an independent court-appointed trustee to recover funds in brokerage insolvency cases.

Small Business Investor Alliance, 529 14th St. N.W., #400, 20045; (202) 628-5055. Brett Palmer, President. General email, info@sbia.org
Web, www.sbia.org and Twitter, @SmallBusinessPE

Membership: private equity, venture capital, and middle market funds that invest in small businesses. Provides training to fund managers and holds industry networking events. Monitors legislation and regulations.

US SIF: The Forum for Sustainable and Responsible Investment, 1660 L St. N.W., #306, 20036; (202) 872-5361. Fax, (202) 775-8686. Lisa Woll, Chief Executive Officer.
Web, www.ussif.org and Twitter, @US_SIF

Membership association promoting sustainable and socially responsible investing. Conducts research, events, and courses on investments considering environmental, social, and corporate governance criteria. Monitors legislation and regulations. (Formerly Social Investment Forum.)

Tangible Assets

►AGENCIES

Commodity Futures Trading Commission, Three Lafayette Centre, 1155 21st St. N.W., 20581-0001; (202) 418-5000. Fax, (202) 418-5521. Heath P. Tarbert, Chair, (202) 418-5030; Anthony C. Thompson, Executive Director,

(202) 418-5697; Ann Wright, Director of Legislative and Government Affairs (Acting). Toll-free, (866) 366-2382. TTY, (202) 418-5428.
General email, questions@cftc.gov
Web, www.cftc.gov, Twitter, @CFTC and Facebook, www.facebook.com/cftcgov

Enforces federal statutes relating to commodity futures and options, including gold and silver futures and options. Monitors and regulates gold and silver leverage contracts, which provide for deferred delivery of the commodity and the payment of an agreed portion of the purchase price on margin.

U.S. Mint (Treasury Dept.), 801 9th St. N.W., 8th Floor, 20220; (202) 756-6468. Ventris G. Gibson, Deputy Director. Customer service, (800) 872-6468. Information, (202) 354-7227. Press, (202) 354-7222. Toll-free, 800-USA-MINT. TTY, (888) 321-6468.
General email, inquiries@usmint.treas.gov
Web, www.usmint.gov, Twitter, @usmint, Facebook, www.facebook.com/UnitedStatesMint and YouTube, www.youtube.com/USMint

Produces and distributes the national coinage so that the nation can conduct trade and commerce. Produces gold, silver, and platinum coins for sale to investors.

►NONGOVERNMENTAL

Silver Institute, 1400 Eye St. N.W., #550, 20005; (202) 835-0185. Fax, (202) 835-0155. Bradford Cooke, President; Michael (Mike) DiRienzo, Executive Director.
General email, info@silverinstitute.org
Web, www.silverinstitute.org and Twitter, @SilverInstitute

Membership: companies that mine, refine, fabricate, or manufacture silver or silver-containing products. Conducts research on new technological and industrial uses for silver. Compiles statistics on mining; coinage; and the production, distribution, and use of refined silver.

INDUSTRIAL PRODUCTION, MANUFACTURING

General

►AGENCIES

Census Bureau (Commerce Dept.), Manufacturing and Construction, 4600 Silver Hill Rd., #8K151, Suitland, MD 20746 (mailing address: 4600 Silver Hill Rd., Washington, DC 20233); (301) 763-4673. Web, www.census.gov/manufacturing

Collects, tabulates, and publishes statistics for the manufacturing and construction sectors of the Economic Census.

Economic Development Administration (Commerce Dept.), 1401 Constitution Ave. N.W., #71014, 20230; (202)

482-5081. *Alejandra Y. Castillo, Assistant Secretary.*
Public Affairs, (202) 482-4085.
Web, https://eda.gov, Twitter, @US_EDA and
Facebook, www.facebook.com/eda.commerce

Assists U.S. firms in increasing their competitiveness against foreign imports. Certifies eligibility and provides domestic firms and industries adversely affected by increased imports with technical assistance under provisions of the Trade Act of 1974. Administers eleven regional Trade Adjustment Assistance Centers that offer services to eligible U.S. firms.

International Trade Administration (ITA) *(Commerce Dept.), Industry and Analysis (I&A), 1401 Constitution Ave. N.W., Room 2854, 20230; (202) 482-1112. Fax, (202) 482-5697. Anne Driscoll, Assistant Secretary (Acting).*
Web, www.trade.gov/industry-analysis

Conducts industry trade analysis. Shapes U.S. trade policy. Participates in trade negotiations. Organizes trade capacity building programs. Evaluates the impact of domestic and international economic and regulatory policies on U.S. manufacturers and service industries.

International Trade Administration (ITA) *(Commerce Dept.), Industry and Analysis (I&A), Manufacturing, 1401 Constitution Ave. N.W., Room 28004, 20230; (202) 482-1987. Fax, (202) 482-0856. Monica Gorman, Deputy Assistant Secretary.*
Web, www.trade.gov/about-us/manufacturing

Conducts analyses and competitive assessments of high-tech industries, including aerospace, automotive, industrial machinery, medical devices, and the pharmaceutical industry. Develops trade policies for these industries, negotiates market access for U.S. companies, and assists in promoting exports through trade missions, shows, and fairs in major overseas markets.

National Institute of Standards and Technology (NIST) *(Commerce Dept.), Hollings Manufacturing Extension Partnership, 100 Bureau Dr., MS 4800, Gaithersburg, MD 20899-4800; (301) 975-5020. Fax, (301) 963-6556. Pravina Raghavan, Director. Toll-free, (800) 637-4634.*
General email, mfg@nist.gov
Web, www.nist.gov/mep

Collaborates with and advises private manufacturers in the United States on innovation strategies, process improvements, green manufacturing, and market diversification.

National Institute of Standards and Technology (NIST) *(Commerce Dept.), Weights and Measures, 100 Bureau Dr., MS 2600, Gaithersburg, MD 20899-2600; (301) 975-4004. Fax, (301) 975-8091. Katrice Lippa, Chief, (301) 975-2956.*
General email, barbara.cohn@nist.gov
Web, www.nist.gov/pml/weights-and-measures

Promotes uniform standards among the states for packaging and labeling products and for measuring devices, including scales and commercial measurement instruments; advises manufacturers on labeling and packaging laws and on measuring device standards. Partners with the National Conference on Weights and Measures to develop standards.

▶ **NONGOVERNMENTAL**

American Chemistry Council, *700 2nd St. N.E., 20002; (202) 249-7000. Fax, (202) 249-6100. Chris Jahn, President.*
Web, www.americanchemistry.com,
Twitter, @AmChemistry and Facebook, www.facebook .com/AmericanChemistry

Membership: manufacturers of basic industrial chemicals that make or sell chemical products in the United States. Provides members with technical research, communications services, and legal affairs counseling. Sponsors research on chemical risk assessments, biomonitoring, and nanotechnology. Interests include environmental safety and health, transportation, energy, and international trade and security. Monitors legislation and regulations.

American Forest and Paper Assn., *Government and Industry Affairs, 1101 K St. N.W., #700, 20005; (202) 463-2599. Eric J. Steiner, Vice President of Government Affairs; Terry Webber, Vice President of Industry Affairs.*
General email, Government_Industry_Affairs@afandpa.org
Web, http://afandpa.org, Twitter, @ForestandPaper and Facebook, www.facebook.com/ForestandPaper

Membership: pulp, paper, and paper-based product manufacturers and those in related associations. Interests include tax, housing, environmental, international trade, sustainability, and land-use issues that affect the forest products industry.

American Fuel and Petrochemical Manufacturers, *1800 M St. N.W., #900 North, 20036; (202) 457-0480. Fax, (202) 457-0486. Chet Thompson, President.*
General email, info@afpm.org
Web, www.afpm.org, Twitter, @AFPMonline and Facebook, www.facebook.com/AFPMonline

Membership: petroleum, petrochemical, refining companies, and companies that transport hydrocarbon feedstocks. Interests include allocation, imports, refining technology, petrochemicals, and environmental regulations.

American National Standards Institute (ANSI), *1899 L St. N.W., 11th Floor, 20036; (202) 293-8020. Fax, (202) 293-9287. S. Joe Bhatia, President, (202) 331-3605.*
General email, info@ansi.org
Web, www.ansi.org, Twitter, @ansidotorg and Facebook, www.facebook.com/ansidotorg

Administers and coordinates the voluntary U.S. private sector–led consensus standards and conformity assessment system. Serves as the official U.S. representative to the International Organization of Standardization (ISO) and, via the U.S. National Committee, the International Electrotechnical Commission (IEC), and is a U.S. representative to the International Accreditation Forum (IAF).

Assn. for Manufacturing Technology (AMT), *7901 Jones Branch Dr., #900, McLean, VA 22102-4206; (703) 893-2900.*

Fax, (703) 893-1151. Douglas Woods, President, (703) 827-5202. Toll-free, (800) 524-0475.
General email, amt@amtonline.org
Web, www.amtonline.org and Twitter, @amtonline

Supports the U.S. manufacturing industry; sponsors workshops and seminars; fosters safety and technical standards. Monitors legislation and regulations.

Can Manufacturers Institute, 1730 Rhode Island Ave. N.W., #1000, 20036; (202) 232-4677. Fax, (202) 232-5756. Robert Budway, President.
General email, info@cancentral.com
Web, www.cancentral.com, Twitter, @CansRecyclable and Facebook, www.facebook.com/cansrecyclable

Represents can manufacturers and suppliers; promotes the use of the can as a form of food and beverage packaging. Conducts market research. Monitors legislation and regulations.

Chlorine Institute Inc., 1300 Wilson Blvd., #525, Arlington, VA 22209; (703) 894-4140. Frank Reiner, President, (703) 894-4116.
General email, info@cl2.com
Web, www.chlorineinstitute.org, Twitter, @TheChlorineINST, Facebook, www.facebook .com/thechlorineinstitute and YouTube, www.youtube .com/user/TheChlorineInstitute

Safety, health, and environmental protection center of the chlor-alkali (chlorine, caustic soda, caustic potash, and hydrogen chloride) industry. Interests include employee health and safety, resource conservation and pollution abatement, control of chlorine emergencies, product specifications, and public and community relations. Publishes technical pamphlets and drawings.

Envelope Manufacturers Assn., 700 S. Washington St., #260, Alexandria, VA 22314; (703) 739-2200. Fax, (703) 739-2209. Maynard H. Benjamin, President.
General email, tbooks@envelope.org
Web, www.envelope.org and Facebook, www.facebook.com/ 1Envelope

Membership: envelope manufacturers and suppliers. Monitors legislation and regulations.

Flexible Packaging Assn., 185 Admiral Cochrane Dr., #105, Annapolis, MD 21401; (410) 694-0800. Fax, (410) 694-0900. Alison Keane, President.
General email, fpa@flexpack.org
Web, www.flexpack.org, Twitter, @FlexPackOrg and Facebook, www.facebook.com/Perfect-Packaging-346766162622687

Membership: companies that supply or manufacture flexible packaging. Researches packaging trends and technical developments. Compiles industry statistics. Monitors legislation and regulations.

Glass Packaging Institute, 4250 N. Fairfax Dr., #600, Arlington, VA 22203; (703) 684-6359. Scott DeFife, President.

General email, info@gpi.org
Web, www.gpi.org, Twitter, @ChooseGlass and Facebook, www.facebook.com/ChooseGlass

Membership: manufacturers of glass containers and their suppliers. Promotes industry policies to protect the environment, conserve natural resources, and reduce energy consumption; conducts research; monitors legislation affecting the industry. Interests include glass recycling.

Green Seal, 1717 K St. N.W., #900, 20006; (202) 872-6400. Fax, (202) 872-4324. Douglas (Doug) Gatlin, Chief Executive Officer.
General email, greenseal@greenseal.org
Web, www.greenseal.org, Twitter, @GreenSeal and Facebook, www.facebook.com/GreenSeal

Grants certification to environmentally sustainable products, services, hotels, restaurants, and other companies.

Household and Commercial Products Assn., 1667 K St. N.W., #300, 20006; (202) 872-8110. Fax, (202) 223-2636. Stephen (Steve) J. Caldeira, President.
General email, info@thehcpa.org
Web, www.thehcpa.org and Twitter, @TheHCPA

Membership: manufacturers, marketers, packagers, and suppliers in the chemical specialties industry. Focus includes cleaning products and detergents, nonagricultural pesticides, disinfectants, automotive and industrial products, polishes and floor finishes, antimicrobials, air care products and candles, and aerosol products. Monitors scientific developments; conducts surveys and research. Monitors legislation and regulations.

Independent Lubricant Manufacturers Assn., 675 N. Washington St., #275, Alexandria, VA 22314; (703) 684-5574. Fax, (703) 350-4919. Holly Alfano, Chief Executive Officer.
General email, ilma@ilma.org
Web, www.ilma.org and Twitter, @ILMATweets

Membership: U.S. and international companies that manufacture automotive, industrial, and metalworking lubricants; associates include suppliers and related businesses. Conducts two workshops and conferences annually; compiles statistics. Monitors legislation and regulations.

Industrial Designers Society of America (IDSA), 950 Herndon Pkwy, #250, Herndon, VA 20170; (703) 707-6000. Fax, (703) 787-8501. Chris Livaudais, Executive Director, ext. 116.
General email, membership@idsa.org
Web, www.idsa.org, Twitter, @IDSA and Facebook, www.facebook.com/IDSA.org

Membership: designers of products, equipment, instruments, furniture, transportation, packages, exhibits, information services, and related services, and educators of industrial design. Provides the Bureau of Labor Statistics with industry information. Monitors legislation and regulations.

Industrial Energy Consumers of America, *1776 K St. N.W., #720, 20006; (202) 223-1420. Paul N. Cicio, President, (202) 223-1661.*

Web, www.ieca-us.com and Twitter, @IECAUS

National trade association that represents the manufacturing industry and acts as advocate for energy, environmental, and public policy issues. Acts as advocate for greater diversity of and lower costs for energy. Monitors legislation and regulations.

Innovation Research Interchange, *733 10th St. N.W., #700, 20001; (703) 647-2580. Fax, (703) 647-2581. Edward Bernstein, President.*

General email, information@iriweb.org

Web, www.iriweb.org, Twitter, @IRIweb and Facebook, www.facebook.com/iriweb

Membership: companies that maintain laboratories for industrial research. Seeks to improve the process of industrial research by promoting cooperative efforts among companies and federal laboratories, between the academic and research communities, and between industry and the government. Monitors legislation and regulations concerning technology, industry, and national competitiveness. (Formerly Industrial Research Institute, Inc.)

International Brotherhood of Electrical Workers (IBEW), *900 7th St. N.W., 20001; (202) 833-7000. Fax, (202) 728-7676. Lonnie R. Stephenson, International President.*

General email, webmaster@ibew.org

Web, http://ibew.org

Membership: workers in utilities, construction, telecommunications, broadcasting, manufacturing, railroads, and government. Helps members negotiate pay, benefits, and better working conditions; conducts training programs and workshops. Monitors legislation and regulations. (Affiliated with the AFL-CIO.)

International Brotherhood of Teamsters, *25 Louisiana Ave. N.W., 20001; (202) 624-6800. Fax, (202) 624-6918. James P. Hoffa, General President. Press, (202) 624-6911.*

General email, communications@teamster.org

Web, https://teamster.org, Twitter, @Teamsters, Facebook, www.facebook.com/teamsters and YouTube, www.youtube.com/TeamsterPower

Membership: workers in the transportation and construction industries, factories, offices, hospitals, warehouses, and other workplaces. Helps members negotiate pay, benefits, and better working conditions; conducts training programs and workshops. Monitors legislation and regulations.

International Sleep Products Assn., *501 Wythe St., Alexandria, VA 22314-1917; (703) 683-8371. Fax, (703) 683-4503. Ryan Trainer, President.*

General email, info@sleepproducts.org

Web, https://sleepproducts.org

twitter, @ISPAsleep

Membership: manufacturers of bedding and mattresses. Compiles statistics on the industry. (Affiliated

with Sleep Products Safety Council and the Better Sleep Council.)

Laboratory Products Assn., *1114 Fairfax Pl., Box 12, White Post, VA 22663; (703) 836-1360. Fax, (703) 836-6644. Clark Mulligan, President, ext. 101.*

General email, info@lpanet.org

Web, www.lpanet.org and Facebook, www.facebook.com/ LaboratoryProductsAssociation

Membership: manufacturers and distributors and suppliers of laboratory products and optical instruments. (Affiliated with the Optical Imaging Assn.)

Manufacturers Alliance/MAPI, *1600 Wilson Blvd., #1100, Arlington, VA 22209-2594; (703) 841-9000. Stephen Gold, President.*

Web, www.mapi.net, Twitter, @MfrsAlliance and Facebook, www.facebook.com/pages/Manufacturers-AllianceMAPI/117859534199

Membership: companies involved in advanced manufacturing industries, including electronics, telecommunications, precision instruments, computers, and the automotive and aerospace industries. Seeks to increase industrial productivity. Conducts research; organizes discussion councils. Monitors legislation and regulations.

National Assn. of Chemical Distributors (NACD), *4201 Wilson Blvd., #0515, Arlington, VA 22203; (703) 527-6223. Fax, (703) 527-7747. Eric R. Byer, President.*

General email, nacdpublicaffairs@nacd.com

Web, www.nacd.com and Twitter, @NACD_RD

Membership: firms involved in purchasing, processing, blending, storing, transporting, and marketing of chemical products. Provides members with information on such topics as training, safe handling and transport of chemicals, liability insurance, and environmental issues. Manages the NACD Chemical Educational Foundation. Monitors legislation and regulations.

National Assn. of Manufacturers (NAM), *733 10th St. N.W., #700, 20001; (202) 637-3000. Jay Timmons, President, (202) 637-3106. Toll-free, (800) 814-8468.*

General email, info@nam.org

Web, www.nam.org, Twitter, @ShopFloorNAM, Facebook, www.facebook.com/NAMpage and YouTube, www.youtube.com/namvideo

Membership: public and private manufacturing companies. Interests include manufacturing technology, economic growth, international trade, national security, taxation, corporate finance and governance, labor relations, occupational safety, workforce education, health care, energy and natural resources, transportation, and environmental quality. Monitors legislation and regulations.

National Assn. of Manufacturers (NAM), *International Economic Affairs, 733 10th St. N.W., #700, 20001; (202) 637-3144. Fax, (202) 637-3182. Ken Monahan, Vice President.*

General email, info@nam.org

Web, www.nam.org

Represents manufacturing business interests on international economic issues, including trade, international investment, export financing, and export controls.

National Council on Advanced Manufacturing, *2025 M St. N.W., #800, 20036; (202) 367-1247. Robert (Rusty) Patterson, Chief Executive Officer. General email, wentzelf@nacfam.org*

Web, www.nacfam.org

Promotes public policies supportive of advanced manufacturing and industrial modernization conducive to global economic competitiveness. Advocates greater national focus on industrial base modernization, increased investment in plants and equipment, accelerated development and deployment of advanced manufacturing technology, and reform of technical education and training.

Society of Chemical Manufacturers and Affiliates (SOCMA), *1400 Crystal Dr., #630, Arlington, VA 22202; (571) 348-5100. Fax, (571) 348-5138. Jennifer L. Abril, President, (571) 348-5101. General email, info@socma.com*

Web, www.socma.com, Twitter, @socma and Facebook, www.facebook.com/SOCMAsocial

Membership: companies that manufacture, distribute, and market organic chemicals; producers of chemical components; and providers of custom chemical services. Interests include international trade, environmental and occupational safety, chemical security, and health issues; conducts workshops and seminars. Promotes commercial opportunities for members. Monitors legislation and regulations.

Society of the Plastics Industry (SPI), *1425 K St. N.W., #500, 20005; (202) 974-5200. Tony Radoszewski, President. Web, www.plasticsindustry.org, Twitter, @PLASTICS_US and Facebook, www.facebook.com/plasticsindustry association*

Promotes the plastics industry and its processes, raw materials suppliers, and machinery manufacturers. Monitors legislation and regulations.

Clothing and Textiles

▶**AGENCIES**

International Trade Administration (ITA) *(Commerce Dept.), Industry and Analysis (I&A), Textiles and Apparel (OTEXA),* *1401 Constitution Ave. N.W., Room 31008, 20230; (202) 482-5078. Fax, (202) 482-2331. Maria D'Andrea-Yothers, Director, (202) 482-1550. General email, otexa@trade.gov*

Web, http://trade.gov/otexa

Participates in negotiating bilateral textile and apparel import restraint agreements; responsible for export expansion programs and reduction of nontariff barriers for textile and apparel goods; provides data on economic conditions in the domestic textile and apparel markets, including impact of imports.

▶**NONGOVERNMENTAL**

American Apparel and Footwear Assn. (AAFA), *740 6th St. N.W., 3rd and 4th Floors, 20001; (202) 853-9080. Stephanie Lamar, President. Toll-free, (800) 520-2262. Web, www.aafaglobal.org, Twitter, @apparelfootwear and Facebook, www.facebook.com/apparelandfootwear*

Membership: manufacturers of apparel, sewn products, and footwear and their suppliers, importers, and distributors. Provides members with information on the industry, including import and export data. Interests include product flammability and trade promotion. Monitors legislation and regulations.

American Textile Machinery Assn., *201 Park Washington Court, Falls Church, VA 22046-4527; (703) 538-1789. Fax, (703) 241-5603. Clay D. Tyeryar, President. Web, www.atmanet.org*

Membership: U.S.-based manufacturers of textile machinery and related parts and accessories. Interests include competitiveness and expansion of foreign markets. Monitors legislation and regulations.

Dry Cleaning and Laundry Institute, *14700 Sweitzer Lane, Laurel, MD 20707; (301) 622-1900. Fax, (240) 295-4200. Mary Scalco, Chief Executive Officer; Jess Culpepper, President. Toll-free, (800) 638-2627. General email, techline@dlionline.org*

Web, www.dlionline.org and Facebook, www.facebook.com/DryLaunInst

Membership: dry cleaners and launderers. Conducts research and provides information on products and services. Monitors legislation and regulations.

Footwear Distributors and Retailers of America, *1319 F St. N.W., #700, 20004-1179; (202) 737-5660. Fax, (202) 645-0789. Matt Priest, President. General email, info@fdra.org*

Web, www.fdra.org, Twitter, @FDRA and Facebook, www.facebook.com/FDRADC

Membership: companies that operate shoe retail outlets and wholesale footwear companies with U.S. and global brands. It serves the full footwear supply chain and boosts the bottom lines of its members through innovative products, training and consulting on footwear design and development, sourcing and compliance, trade and customs, advocacy, and consumer and sales trend analysis for retailers selling shoes around the world. Interests include intellectual property rights, ocean shipping rates, trade with China, and labeling regulations. Runs a weekly ppodcast.

National Cotton Council of America, *Washington Office, 1521 New Hampshire Ave. N.W., 20036-1205; (202) 745-7805. Fax, (202) 483-4040. Reece Langley, Vice President of Washington Operations.*

Web, www.cotton.org, Twitter, @NCottonCouncil and Facebook, www.facebook.com/NationalCottonCouncil

Membership: all segments of the U.S. cotton industry. Formulates positions on trade policy and negotiations; seeks to improve competitiveness of U.S. exports; sponsors programs to educate the public about flammable fabrics. (Headquarters in Memphis, Tenn.)

National Council of Textile Organizations, *1701 K St. N.W., #625, 20006; (202) 822-8028. Fax, (202) 822-8029. Kimberly Glas, President.*
Web, www.ncto.org, Twitter, @NCTO and Facebook, www .facebook.com/NationalCouncilofTextileOrganizations

Membership: U.S. companies that spin, weave, knit, or finish textiles from natural fibers, and associate members from affiliated industries. Interests include domestic and world markets. Monitors legislation and regulations.

Secondary Materials and Recycled Textiles Assn. (SMART), *3465 Box Hill Corporate Dr., Suite H, Abingdon, MD 21009; (443) 640-1050. Fax, (410) 569-3340. Jackie King, Executive Director, ext. 105. Press, (443) 714-4826.*
General email, smartinfo@kingmgmt.org
Web, www.smartasn.org and Twitter, @SMARTTextile

Membership: organizations and individuals involved in producing, shipping, and distributing recycled textiles and other textile products. Sponsors educational programs; publishes newsletters. Monitors legislation and regulations.

Electronics and Appliances

▶**NONGOVERNMENTAL**

Air-Conditioning, Heating, and Refrigeration Institute (AHRI), *2311 Wilson Blvd., #400, Arlington, VA 22201; (703) 524-8800. Fax, (703) 562-1942. Stephen R. Yurek, President, ext. 306.*
General email, ahricommunications@ahrinet.org
Web, https://ahrinet.org/home, Twitter, @ahriengage OR @AHRIconnect and Facebook, www.facebook.com/ AHRIconnect?ref=sgm

Membership: manufactures residential and commercial air conditioning, space heating, water heating, and commercial refrigeration equipment and components for residential and commercial use and related industries. Develops product performance rating standards and administers programs to verify manufacturers' certified ratings. Advocates product improvement; provides market statistics. Monitors legislation and regulations.

American Boiler Manufacturers Assn., *8221 Old Courthouse Rd., #380, Vienna, VA 22182; (703) 356-7172. Scott Lynch, President.*
General email, info@abma.com
Web, www.abma.com, Twitter, @ABMABoiler and Facebook, www.facebook.com/ABMABoiler

Membership: manufacturers of boiler systems and boiler-related products, including fuel-burning systems. Interests include energy and environmental issues. Monitors legislation and regulations.

Consumer Technology Assn., *1919 S. Eads St., Arlington, VA 22202; (703) 907-7600. Fax, (866) 858-2555. Gary Shapiro, President. Toll-free, (866) 858-1555.*
General email, cta@cta.tech
Web, https://cta.tech, Twitter, @CTATech and Facebook, www.facebook.com/ConsumerTechnology Association

Membership: U.S. consumer electronics companies. Promotes the industry, sponsors seminars and conferences, conducts research, and consults with member companies. Monitors legislation and regulations. (Affiliated with Electronic Industries Alliance. Formerly Consumer Electronics Assn.)

Electronic Components Industry Assn., *13873 Park Center Rd., #315, Herndon, VA 20171; (571) 323-0251. David Loftus, President; Robert Willis, Washington Contact.*
Web, www.ecianow.org

Membership: manufacturers, distributors, and manufacturer representatives of electronic components and semiconductor products. Provides information and data on industry trends; advocates the authorized sale of electronics components to prevent counterfeit product moving through the supply chain. Monitors legislation and regulations.

National Electrical Contractors Assn., *1201 Pennsylvania Ave. N.W., #1200, 20004; (202) 991-6300. Fax, (202) 217-4171. John Grau, Chief Executive Officer.*
General email, necagovaffairs@necanet.org
Web, www.necanet.org, Twitter, @necanet, Facebook, www.facebook.com/NECANET and YouTube, www.youtube.com/user/Necaadmin

Membership: electrical contractors who build and service electrical wiring and equipment, including high-voltage construction and service. Represents members in collective bargaining with union workers; sponsors research and educational programs.

National Electrical Manufacturers Association (NEMA), *1300 N. 17th St., #900, Rosslyn, VA 22209-3801; (703) 841-3200. Fax, (703) 841-5900. Debra Phillips, President. Press, (703) 841-3282.*
General email, press@nema.org
Web, www.nema.org, Twitter, @NEMAupdates and Facebook, www.facebook.com/nemaupdates

Membership: manufacturers of products used in the generation, transmission, distribution, control, and end use of electricity, including manufacturers of medical diagnostic imaging equipment. Develops technical standards; collects, analyzes, and disseminates industry data. Interests include Smart Grid, high-performance building, carbon footprint, energy storage, and an intelligence portal. Monitors legislation, regulations, and international trade activities.

Optica, *Optoelectronics Industrys, 2010 Massachusetts Ave. N.W., 20036; (202) 416-1474. Fax, (202) 416-6130. Ganesh Gopalakrishnan, Executive Technical Director.*

General email, info@osa.org

Web, www.optica.org/industry,

Twitter, @OpticaWorldwide and *Facebook, www.facebook .com/opticaworldwide*

Membership: optoelectronics components and systems providers, businesses, and research institutions, students, scientists, engineers and professionals. In North America, Optica provides the resources, connections and opportunities organizations need to develop and commercialize innovative optics and photonics technologies. (Formerly OSA.)

Steel, Metalworking, Machinery

▶AGENCIES

International Trade Administration (ITA) *(Commerce Dept.), Industry and Analysis (I&A), Manufacturing (OM), Transportation and Machinery (OTM), 1401 Constitution Ave. N.W., Room 22021, 20230-0001; (202) 482-1474. Fax, (202) 482-0674. Scott Kennedy, Director. Web, http://legacy.trade.gov/about-us/office-transportation-and-machinery*

Promotes the export of U.S. aerospace, automotive, and machinery products; compiles and analyzes industry data; seeks to secure a favorable position for the U.S. aerospace, auto, and machinery industries in global markets through policy and trade agreements.

▶NONGOVERNMENTAL

Aluminum Assn., *1400 Crystal Dr., #430, Arlington, VA 22202; (703) 358-2960. Charles Johnson, President, (703) 358-2980; Virgina Gum Hamisevicz, Vice President, Government Relations, (703) 358-2981. Press, (703) 358-2977. Bookstore, (480) 779-6259.*

General email, info@aluminum.org

Web, www.aluminum.org, Twitter, @AluminumNews and *Facebook, www.facebook.com/AluminumAssociation*

Membership; Represents the aluminum industry. Develops voluntary standards and technical data; compiles statistics concerning the industry. There is also a bookstore. Monitors legislation and regulations.

American Gear Manufacturers Assn., *1001 N. Fairfax St., #500, Alexandria, VA 22314-1587; (703) 684-0211. Fax, (703) 684-0242. Matthew (Matt) E. Croson, President. General email, website@agma.org*

Web, www.agma.org, Twitter, @agma and *Facebook, www.facebook.com/AGMAGear*

Membership: gear manufacturers, suppliers, and industry consultants. Conducts workshops, seminars, and conferences; develops industry standards; sponsors research. Tracks emerging technologies, including 3D printing, robots and automation, and new materials. Monitors legislation and regulations.

American Iron and Steel Institute (AISI), *SteelPAC, 25 Massachusetts Ave. N.W., #800, 20001; (202) 452-7114.*

Fax, (202) 452-1039. Adam Shaffer, Director of Trade and Economic Policy.

Web, www.steel.org/public-policy/steelpac,

Twitter, @aisisteel and *Facebook, www.facebook.com/ AISISteel*

Helps elect candidates to the U.S. Congress who support the industry's legislative goals as well as its mission to enhance the competitiveness of the North American steel industry. Acts as advocate to congressional allies and builds new political relationships.

American Iron and Steel Institute (AISI), *Washington Office, 25 Massachusetts Ave. N.W., #800, 20001; (202) 452-7100. Fax, (202) 463-6573. Kevin Dempsey, President. Press, (202) 452-7115.*

Web, www.steel.org, Twitter, @AISISteel, Facebook, www .facebook.com/aisisteel and *YouTube, www.youtube.com/ user/AISIsteel*

Represents the iron and steel industry. Publishes statistics on iron and steel production; promotes the use of steel; conducts research. Monitors legislation and regulations. (Maintains offices in Southfield, Mich., and Pittsburgh, Pa.)

American Metals Supply Chain Institute, *1101 King St., #360, Alexandria, VA 22314; (202) 812-1918. Richard Chriss, President, (571) 225-7105. Web, www.amsci.us*

General email, ajopp@amsci.us

Membership: steel, aluminum, and other metals manufacturers, fabricators, distributors, and users. Conducts market research, provides educational and informational programs, and networking opportunities. Monitors legislation and regulations.

American Wire Producers Assn., *908 King St., #320, Alexandria, VA 22314; (703) 299-4434. Fax, (703) 299-4434. Emily Bardach, Executive Director.*

General email, info@awpa.org

Web, www.awpa.org

Membership: companies that produce carbon, alloy, and stainless steel wire and wire products in the United States, Canada, and Mexico. Interests include imports of rod, wire, and wire products. Publishes survey of the domestic wire industry. Monitors legislation and regulations.

International Assn. of Bridge, Structural, Ornamental, and Reinforcing Iron Workers, *1750 New York Ave. N.W., #400, 20006; (202) 383-4800. Fax, (202) 638-4856. Eric Dean, General President.*

General email, iwmagazine@iwintl.org

Web, www.ironworkers.org, Twitter, @TheIronWorkers, Facebook, www.facebook.com/unionironworkers and *YouTube, www.youtube.com/user/UnionIronWorkers*

Membership: approximately 120,000 iron workers. Helps members negotiate pay, benefits, and better working conditions; conducts training programs and workshops. Monitors legislation and regulations. (Affiliated with the AFL-CIO.)

International Assn. of Machinists and Aerospace Workers, *9000 Machinists Pl., Upper Marlboro, MD 20772-2687; (301) 967-4500. Fax, (301) 967-4587. Robert Martinez Jr., International President. Information, (301) 967-4522.*
General email, info@iamaw.org

Web, www.goiam.org, Twitter, @MachinistsUnion, Facebook, www.facebook.com/MachinistsUnion and YouTube, www.youtube.com/user/FranticHarbor

Membership: machinists in more than 200 industries. Helps members negotiate pay, benefits, and better working conditions; conducts training programs and workshops. Monitors legislation and regulations. (Affiliated with the AFL-CIO, the Canadian Labour Congress, the International Metalworkers Federation, the International Transport Workers' Federation, and the Railway Labor Executives Assn.)

International Brotherhood of Boilermakers, Iron Ship Builders, Blacksmiths, Forgers, and Helpers, Government Affairs, *1750 New York Ave. N.W., #335, 20006; (202) 756-2868. Fax, (202) 756-2869. Cecile Conroy, Director of Government Affairs, ext. 202.*
Web, https://boilermakers.org/structure/departments/government_affairs

Membership: workers in construction, repair, maintenance, manufacturing, shipbuilding and marine repair, mining and quarrying, railroads, cement kilns, and related industries in the United States and Canada. Helps members negotiate pay, benefits, and better working conditions; conducts training programs and workshops. Monitors legislation and regulations. (Headquarters in Kansas City, Kans.; affiliated with the AFL-CIO.)

Machinery Dealers National Assn., *5568 General Washington Dr., # A213D, Alexandria, VA 22312; (703) 836-9300. Fax, (703) 836-9303. Mark Robinson, Executive Vice President, ext. 116.*
General email, office@mdna.org

Web, www.mdna.org, Twitter, @MDNA_Machines and Facebook, www.facebook.com/Machinery-Dealers-National-Association-270644229632807

Membership: machinery dealers, auctioneers, and appraisers of used machinery and used capital equipment. Establishes a code of ethics for members; publishes a buyer's guide that lists members by types of machinery they sell.

Outdoor Power Equipment Institute, *1605 King St., #2726, Alexandria, VA 22314; (703) 549-7600. Fax, (703) 549-7604. Kris Kiser, President.*
General email, info@opei.org

Web, www.opei.org, Twitter, @OPEInstitute and Facebook, www.facebook.com/OPEInstitute

Membership: manufacturers of powered lawn and garden maintenance products, components and attachments, and their suppliers. Promotes safe use of outdoor power equipment; keeps statistics on the industry; fosters exchange of information. Monitors legislation and regulations.

Packaging Machinery Manufacturers Institute, *12930 Worldgate Dr., #200, Herndon, VA 20170; (571) 612-3200. Fax, (703) 243-8556. Jim Pittas, President.*
General email, info@pmmi.org

Web, www.pmmi.org, Twitter, @PMMIorg and Facebook, www.facebook.com/PMMIorg

Membership: manufacturers of packaging, machinery, packaging-related converting machinery, components, processing materials, and containers, as well as providers of related equipment and services to the packaging and processing industry. Provides industry information and statistics; offers educational programs to members.

Sheet Metal, Air, Rail, and Transportation Workers (SMART), *1750 New York Ave. N.W., 6th Floor, 20006; (202) 662-0800. Joseph Sellers Jr., General President. Toll-free, (800) 457-7694.*
General email, info@smart-union.org

Web, https://smart-union.org and Twitter, @smartunionworks

Membership: U.S., Puerto Rican, and Canadian workers in the building and construction trades, manufacturing, and the railroad and shipyard industries. Assists members with contract negotiation and grievances; conducts training programs and workshops. Monitors legislation and regulations. (Affiliated with the Sheet Metal and Air Conditioning Contractors' Assn., the AFL-CIO, and the Canadian Labour Congress.)

Specialty Steel Industry of North America, *3050 K St. N.W., 20007; (202) 342-8630. Fax, (202) 342-8451. Dennis Oates, Chair. Toll-free, (800) 982-0355.*
General email, info@ssina.com

Web, www.ssina.com

Membership: manufacturers of products in stainless and other specialty steels. Establishes manufacturing techniques and issues technical guides; operates a hotline for technical questions.

Steel Manufacturers Assn., *1150 Connecticut Ave. N.W., #1125, 20036; (202) 296-1515. Philip (Phil) K. Bell, President.*
General email, info@steelnet.org

Web, http://steelnet.org, Twitter, @SMA_Steel and Facebook, www.facebook.com/steelmanufacturers

Membership: steel producers and their vendors in North America. Helps members exchange information on technical matters; provides information on the steel industry to the public and government. Monitors legislation and regulations.

United Steelworkers, Legislative, *1155 Connecticut Ave. N.W., #500, 20036; (202) 778-4384. Fax, (202) 293-5308. Roy Houseman, Legislative Director, (202) 778-3312.*
Web, www.usw.org, Twitter, @steelworkers and Facebook, www.facebook.com/steelworkers

Membership: more than one million workers in the steel, paper, rubber, energy, chemical, pharmaceutical, and allied industries. Helps members negotiate pay, benefits, and better working conditions; conducts training programs and workshops. Monitors legislation and regulations. (Affiliated with the AFL-CIO; Headquarters in Pittsburgh, Pa.)

INSURANCE

General

▶ **AGENCIES**

Federal Emergency Management Agency (FEMA) *(Homeland Security Dept.), Resilience, Federal Insurance and Mitigation Administration, 400 C St. S.W., 20472; (202) 646-2781. Nimisha Agorwal, Deputy Associate Administrator (Acting).*
Web, www.fema.gov/about/offices/insurance-mitigation

Administers federal insurance programs, including the National Flood Insurance Program, to reduce future losses from floods, earthquakes, tornadoes, and other natural disasters. Makes low-cost flood insurance available to eligible homeowners.

▶ **CONGRESS**

For a listing of relevant congressional committees and subcommittees, please see pages 38–39 or the Appendix.

Crop Insurance and Reinsurance Bureau, *50 F St. N.W., #450, 20001; (202) 544-0067. Mike Torrey, Executive Vice President.*
Web, http://cropinsurance.org

Membership: approved insurance providers (AIPs), reinsurance companies, and brokerage groups. Involved with writing state policies and providing risk management tools to farmers and ranchers. Represents members before Congress and the federal government.

▶ **NONGOVERNMENTAL**

American Academy of Actuaries, *1850 M St. N.W., #300, 20036; (202) 223-8196. Fax, (202) 872-1948. (202) 974-6007. Mary Downs, Executive Director.*
General email, webmaster@actuary.org
Web, www.actuary.org, Twitter, @Actuary_Dot_Org and Facebook, www.facebook.com/Actuary.Org

Membership: professional actuaries practicing in the areas of life, health, liability, property, and casualty insurance; pensions; government insurance plans; and general consulting. Provides information on actuarial matters, including insurance and pensions; develops professional standards; advises public policymakers.

American Council of Life Insurers, *101 Constitution Ave. N.W., #700, 20001-2133; (202) 624-2000. Susan K. Neely, President.*
General email, contact@acli.com
Web, www.acli.com, Twitter, @ACLINews and Facebook, www.facebook.com/ACLINews

Membership: life insurance companies authorized to do business in the United States. Conducts research and compiles statistics at state and federal levels. Monitors legislation and regulations.

American Property Casualty Insurance Assn. (APCIA), *555 12th St. N.W., #550, 20004; (202) 828-7100. Fax, (202) 293-1219. David A. Sampson, Chief Executive Director.*
Web, www.apci.org, Twitter, @TeamAPCIA and Facebook, www.facebook.com/TeamAPCIA

Membership: companies providing property and casualty insurance. Conducts public relations and educational activities; provides information on issues related to property and casualty insurance. Monitors legislation and regulations. (Headquarters in Chicago, Ill.)

American Society of Pension Professionals and Actuaries, *4401 N. Fairfax Dr., #600, Arlington, VA 22203; (703) 516-9300. Fax, (703) 516-9308. Natalie Wyatt, Chief Executive Officer.*
General email, customercare@asppa-net.org
Web, www.asppa.org and Twitter, @ASPPA

Membership: administrators, actuaries, advisers, lawyers, accountants, and other financial services professionals who provide consulting and administrative services for employee-based retirement plans. Sponsors educational conferences, webcasts, and credentialing programs for retirement professionals. Monitors legislation and regulations.

Council of Insurance Agents and Brokers, *701 Pennsylvania Ave. N.W., #750, 20004; (202) 783-4400. Fax, (202) 783-4410. Ken A. Crerar, President, (202) 662-4420.*
General email, ciab@ciab.com
Web, www.ciab.com and Twitter, @TheCIAB

Represents commercial property and casualty insurance agencies and brokerage firms. Members offer insurance products and risk management services to business, government, and the public.

Finseca, *600 13th St. N.W., #550, 20005; (703) 641-9400. Fax, (703) 641-9885. Marc Cadin, Chief Executive Officer, (703) 641-8149. Toll-free, (888) 275-0092.*
General email, info@finsecafoundation.org
Web, www.finseca.org, Twitter, @Finseca and Facebook, www.facebook.com/WeAreFinseca

Membership: specialized underwriters in the fields of estate analysis, charitable planning, business insurance, pension planning, and employee benefit plans. Monitors legislation and regulations on small-business taxes and capital formation. (Maintains an additional office in Washington, DC.)

GAMA International, *600 13th St. N.W. #500, 20005; (703) 641-9400. Bonnie Godsman, President, (571) 499-4311. Toll-free, (888) 275-0092.*
General email, membership@gammaglobal.com
Web, www.gamaglobal.org, Twitter, @GAMAIntl and Facebook, www.facebook.com/gamaintl

Membership: general agents and managers who provide life insurance and related financial products and services. Provides information, education, and training for members. (Affiliated to Finseca.)

Independent Insurance Agents and Brokers of America, 127 S. Peyton St., Alexandria, VA 22314; (703) 683-4422. Fax, (703) 683-7556. Robert Rusbuldt, President. Toll-free, (800) 221-7917.
General email, info@iiaba.net

Web, www.independentagent.com, Twitter, @IndAgent and Facebook, www.facebook.com/independentagent

Provides educational and advisory services; researches issues pertaining to auto, home, business, life, and health insurance; offers cooperative advertising program to members. Political action committee monitors legislation and regulations.

National Assn. of Independent Life Brokerage Agencies, 10304 Eaton Pl., #100, Fairfax, VA 22030; (703) 884-1525. Fax, (703) 383-6942. Dan LaBert, Chief Executive Officer, (703) 383-3066.
General email, info@nailba.org

Web, www.nailba.org, Twitter, @NAILBA and Facebook, www.facebook.com/NAILBAHQ

Membership: owners of independent life insurance agencies. Fosters the responsible and effective distribution of life and health insurance and related financial services; provides a forum for exchange of information among members. Monitors legislation and regulations.

National Assn. of Insurance and Financial Advisors, 2901 Telestar Court, Falls Church, VA 22042-1205; (703) 770-8102. Fax, (703) 770-8107. Kevin M. Mayeux, Chief Executive Officer, (703) 770-8101. Toll-free, (877) 866-2432.
General email, info@naifa.org

Web, www.naifa.org, Twitter, @NAIFA and Facebook, www.facebook.com/NAIFANational

Federation of state and local life underwriters, agents, and financial advisers. Provides information on life and health insurance and other financial services; sponsors education and training programs.

National Assn. of Insurance Commissioners,
Government Relations, 444 N. Capitol St. N.W., #700, 20001-1509; (202) 471-3990. Fax, (816) 460-7493.
Dean L. Cameron, President; Michael (Mike) F. Consedine, Chief Executive Officer, (202) 471-3390.
Web, www.naic.org and Twitter, @NAIC

Membership: state insurance commissioners, directors, and supervisors. Provides members with information on legal and market conduct, and financial services; publishes research and statistics on the insurance industry. Monitors legislation and regulations. (Affiliated with the Center for Insurance Policy and Research. Headquarters in Kansas City, Mo.)

National Assn. of Professional Insurance Agents, 419 N. Lee St., Alexandria, VA 22314; (703) 836-9340. Fax, (703) 836-1279. Mike Becker, Executive Vice President, (703) 518-1340. Press, (703) 518-1352.

General email, web@pianet.org
Web, www.pianet.com and Twitter, @PIANational

Membership: independent insurance agents and brokers. Provides basic and continuing education for agents through courses, seminars, and educational materials. Monitors legislation and regulations.

Nonprofit Risk Management Center, 204 S. King St., Leesburg, VA 20175; (703) 777-3504.
Melanie Lockwood Herman, Executive Director, ext. 2.
General email, info@nonprofitrisk.org

Web, www.nonprofitrisk.org and Twitter, @nonprofitrisk

Provides information on insurance and risk management issues through conferences, consulting, online tools, and publications for nonprofit organizations.

Reinsurance Assn. of America, 1445 New York Ave. N.W., 7th Floor, 20005; (202) 638-3690. Fax, (202) 638-0936. Franklin W. Nutter, President. Press, (202) 783-8390.
General email, infobox@reinsurance.org

Web, www.reinsurance.org, Twitter, @TheRAA and Facebook, www.facebook.com/ReinsuranceAssociationof America

Membership: companies writing property and casualty reinsurance. Monitors legislation and regulations.

PATENTS, COPYRIGHTS, AND TRADEMARKS

General

▶AGENCIES

Bureau of Economic and Business Affairs (EB) *(State Dept.), Trade Policy and Negotiations (TPN), International Intellectual Property Enforcement (IPE),* 2201 C St. N.W., #4931, 20520-4931; (202) 647-3985. Fax, (202) 647-1537. Tarak Fahmy, Director.
General email, eb-a-ipe-dl@state.gov

Web, www.state.gov/intellectual-property-enforcement

Handles multilateral and bilateral policy formulation involving patents, copyrights, and trademarks, and international industrial property of U.S. nationals.

Civil Division *(Justice Dept.), Commercial Litigation (OCL), Intellectual Property,* 1100 L St. N.W., #8000, 20005; (202) 307-0342. Fax, (202) 307-0345.
Gary Hausken, Director.
Web, www.justice.gov/civil/intellectual-property-section

Represents the United States in patent, copyright, and trademark or trade secret cases. Includes the defense of patent infringement suits; legal proceedings to establish government priority of invention; defense of administrative acts of the Register of Copyrights; and actions on behalf of the government involving the use of trademarks.

Patent and Trademark Office (USPTO) *(Commerce Dept.),* Madison Bldg., 600 Dulany St., #10-D44,

Alexandria, VA 22314 (mailing address: P.O. Box 1450, Alexandria, VA 22313-1450); (571) 272-1000. Fax, (571) 273-8300. Drew Hirshfeld, Under Secretary (Acting). Customer support, (800) 786-9199. Patent search library, (571) 272-3275. Press, (571) 272-8400. TTY, (800) 877-8339. General email, usptoinfo@uspto.gov

Web, www.uspto.gov, Twitter, @USPTO and Facebook, www.facebook.com/uspto.gov

Grants patents, registers trademarks, and provides patent and trademark information. Library and search file of U.S. and foreign patents available for public use.

U.S. Customs and Border Protection (Homeland Security Dept.), Intellectual Property Rights and Restrictions, 1300 Pennsylvania Ave. N.W., Mint Annex, 20229; (202) 325-8000. Charles Stewart, Branch Chief, (202) 325-0093. Public Affairs, (202) 344-1780. General email, hqiprbranch@cbp.dhs.gov

Web, www.cbp.gov/trade/priorityissues/pr/protection?

Responsible for customs recordation of registered trademarks and copyrights. Enforces rules and regulations pertaining to intellectual property rights. Coordinates enforcement of International Trade Commission exclusion orders against unfairly competing goods. Determines admissibility of restricted merchandise and cultural properties. Provides support to and coordinates with international organizations and the Office of the U.S. Trade Representative.

►CONGRESS

For a listing of relevant congressional committees and subcommittees, please see pages 38–39 or the Appendix.

Library of Congress, United States Copyright Office, 101 Independence Ave. S.E., #403, 20559-6000; (202) 707-8350. Shira Perlmutter, Register of Copyrights. Forms and publications hotline, (202) 707-9100. Information, (202) 707-3000. Toll-free, (877) 476-0778. Web, www.copyright.gov, Twitter, @CopyrightOffice Press, press@copyright.gov

Administers the U.S. copyright laws. Provides information to the public on copyright registration procedures and requirements, and on other Copyright Office services. Registers copyright claims and maintains public records of copyright ownership. Conducts copyright records searches on a fee basis. Provides information regarding U.S. and foreign copyright laws but does not give legal advice on copyright matters. Principal advisor to the U.S. Congress on domestic and international copyright issues.

Library of Congress, United States Copyright Office, Licensing Division, James Madison Memorial Bldg., 101 Independence Ave. S.E., Copyright Office LD, 20559-6000; (202) 707-8150. Fax, (202) 707-0905. James (Jim) Enzinna, Chief, (202) 707-6801. Information, (202) 707-3000. General email, licensing@copyright.gov

Web, www.copyright.gov/licensing

Administers statutory licensing for cable television companies and satellite carriers, for making and distributing digital audio recording products, and for use of certain noncommercial broadcasting. Collects and distributes royalty payments under the copyright law. Administers Section 115 licensing for making and distributing phonorecords.

►JUDICIARY

U.S. Court of Appeals for the Federal Circuit, 717 Madison Pl. N.W., 20439; (202) 275-8000. Kimberly A. Moore, Chief Circuit Judge; Peter R. Marksteiner, Clerk of the Court, (202) 272-8020. Mediation, (202) 275-8120. Web, www.cafc.uscourts.gov

Reviews decisions of U.S. Patent and Trademark Office on applications and interferences regarding patents and trademarks; hears appeals on patent infringement cases from district courts.

►NONGOVERNMENTAL

American Intellectual Property Law Assn., 1400 Crystal Dr., #600, Arlington, VA 22202; (703) 415-0780. Fax, (703) 415-0786. Vincent Garlock, Executive Director. General email, aipla@aipla.org

Web, www.aipla.org, Twitter, @aipla and Facebook, www.facebook.com/AIPLA/?ref=tn_tnmn

Membership: lawyers practicing in the field of patents, trademarks, and copyrights (intellectual property law). Advises agencies within the U.S. government and other domestic organizations. Holds continuing legal education conferences.

Assn. of American Publishers, Government Affairs, 455 Massachusetts Ave. N.W., #700, 20001; (202) 347-3375. Fax, (202) 347-3690. Maria A. Pallante, Chief Executive Officer; Mathew Barbian, Vice President of Public Policy. General email, info@publishers.org

Web, www.publishers.org, Twitter, @AmericanPublish and Facebook, www.facebook.com/AmericanPublishers

Represents U.S. book and journal publishing industry priorities on policy, legislation, and regulatory issues regionally, nationally, and worldwide. Interests include intellectual property rights, worldwide copyright enforcement, digital and new-technology issues, tax and trade, and First Amendment rights.

Intellectual Property Owners Assn., 1501 M St. N.W., #1150, 20005; (202) 507-4500. Jessica Landacre, Executive Director. General email, info@ipo.org

Web, https://ipo.org, Twitter, @IPO and Facebook, www.facebook.com/IPOAssociation

Monitors and acts as advocate for intellectual property legislation. Conducts educational programs to protect intellectual property through patents, trademarks, copyrights, and trade secret laws.

International Anticounterfeiting Coalition, *727 15th St. N.W., 9th Floor, 20005; (202) 223-6667.*
Robert C. Barchiesi, President.
General email, iacc@iacc.org

Web, www.iacc.org, Twitter, @IACC_GetReal and Facebook, www.facebook.com/InternationalAntiCounterfeitingCoalition

Works to combat counterfeiting and piracy by promoting laws, regulations, and directives to render theft of intellectual property unprofitable. Oversees anticounterfeiting programs that increase patent, trademark, copyright, service mark, trade dress, and trade-secret protection. Provides information and training to law enforcement officials to help identify counterfeit and pirate products.

International Intellectual Property Alliance, *1000 F St. N.W., 2nd Floor, 20004; (202) 355-7900. Fax, (202) 355-7899. Kevin M. Rosenbaum, Eecutive Director; Linda Quigly, Director of Policy and Legal Affairs.*
General email, info@iipa.org

Web, www.iipa.org

Represents U.S. copyright-based industries in efforts to improve international protection of copyrighted materials. Monitors legislation domestically and abroad; promotes enforcement reform abroad.

International Intellectual Property Institute, *1900 K St. N.W., #725, 20006; (202) 544-6610. Bruce A. Lehman, CEO.*
Web, https://iipi.org, Twitter, @IIPIORG and Facebook, www.facebook.com/IIPI.org

Aims to combat patent infringement and eliminate counterfeit products being imported into the United States. Holds conferences to educate the public on intellectual property rights. Offers training programs and intellectual property guidance for leaders in developing and least developed countries.

National Assn. of Manufacturers (NAM), *Innovation Policy, 733 10th St. N.W., #700, 20001; (202) 637-3000. Fax, (202) 637-3182. Robyn Boerstling, Vice President, (202) 637-3155. Press, (202) 637-3096.*
General email, info@nam.org

Web, www.nam.org

Represents manufacturers in government and the media, advocating pro-manufacturing positions on technology policy issues, including cybersecurity, telecommunication, R&D funding, and intellectual property protection; develops policy and legislation on patents, copyrights, trademarks, and trade secrets; works with the broader business community to advance pro-growth, pro-competitiveness technology policy.

National Music Publishers' Assn., *1900 N St. N.W., #500, 20036; (202) 393-6672. Fax, (202) 393-6673.*
David M. Israelite, President.
General email, pr@nmpa.org

Web, www.nmpa.org and Twitter, @NMPAorg

Works to enforce music copyrights. Sponsors litigation against copyright violators. Monitors and interprets legislation and regulations.

National School Boards Assn., *1680 Duke St., 2nd Floor, Alexandria, VA 22314-3493; (703) 838-6722. Fax, (571) 470-5108. John Heim, Executive Director, (703) 838-6730.*
General email, info@nsba.org

Web, www.nsba.org, Twitter, @NSBAComm and Facebook, www.facebook.com/SchoolBoards

Promotes a broad interpretation of copyright law to permit legitimate scholarly use of published and musical works, videotaped programs, and materials for computer-assisted instruction.

Recording Industry Assn. of America, *1000 F St. N.W., 2nd Floor, 20004; (202) 775-0101. Fax, (202) 775-7253. Mitch Glazier, Chief Executive Officer.*
Web, www.riaa.com, Twitter, @RIAA and Facebook, www.facebook.com/RIAA

Advocates copyright protection for music artists and opposes censorship. Works to prevent recording piracy, counterfeiting, bootlegging, and unauthorized rentals and imports. Monitors legislation and regulations.

SoundExchange, *733 10th St. N.W., 10th Floor, 20001; (202) 640-5858. Fax, (202) 640-5859. Michael Huppe, President.*
General email, info@soundexchange.com

Web, www.soundexchange.com, Twitter, @SoundExchange and Facebook, www.facebook.com/SoundExchange

Artists' rights advocacy group that represents record labels and unsigned artists whose work is broadcast on national and global digital radio. Distributes royalties to musicians, performers, and music copyright owners. Monitors legislation and regulations related to digital music licensing.

U.S. Chamber of Commerce, *Congressional and Public Affairs, 1615 H St. N.W., 20062-2000; (202) 463-5600. Jack Howard, Senior Vice President.*
Web, www.uschamber.com/program/policy/government-affairs

Monitors legislation and regulations on patents, copyrights, and trademarks.

SALES AND SERVICES

General

▶ **AGENCIES**

Census Bureau *(Commerce Dept.), Economy-Wide Statistics, 4600 Silver Hill Rd., #8K154, Suitland, MD 20746-2401 (mailing address: 4700 Silver Hill Rd., #8K064, Washington, DC 20233-6500); (301) 763-7643. Kimberly (Kim) P. Moore, Chief.*
Web, www.census.gov

Provides data of five-year census programs on retail, wholesale, and service industries. Conducts periodic monthly or annual surveys for specific items within these industries.

▶ NONGOVERNMENTAL

American Society of Appraisers (ASA), *2121 Cooperative Way, #210, Herndon, VA 20171; (703) 478-2228. Fax, (703) 742-8471. Johnnie White, Chief Executive Officer, (703) 733-2108. Toll-free, (800) 272-8258.*
General email, asainfo@appraisers.org
Web, www.appraisers.org and Twitter, @ASAappraisers

Membership: accredited appraisers of real property, including land, houses, and commercial buildings; business valuation; machinery and technical specialties; yachts; aircraft; public utilities; personal property, including antiques, fine art, residential contents; and gems and jewelry. Affiliate members include students and professionals interested in appraising. Provides technical information; accredits appraisers; provides consumer information programs.

ASIS International, *1625 Prince St., Alexandria, VA 22314-2882; (703) 519-6200. Fax, (703) 519-6299. Peter J. O'Neil, Chief Executive Officer. Information, (703) 518-1415.*
General email, community@asisonline.org
Web, www.asisonline.org and Twitter, @ASIS_Intl

Membership: security administrators who oversee physical and logistical security for private and public organizations, including law enforcement and the military. Develops security standards; offers educational programs and materials on general and industry-specific practices; and administers certification programs. Monitors legislation and regulations.

Better Business Bureau, *International Assn. of Better Business Bureaus (IABBB), 4250 N. Fairfax Dr., #600, Arlington, VA 22203; (703) 276-0100. Kip Morse, Chief Executive Officer.*
General email, info@mybbb.org
Web, www.bbb.org/local-bbb/international-association-of-better-business-bureaus, Twitter, @bbb_us and Facebook, www.facebook.com/BetterBusinessBureau

Membership: Businesses and Better Business Bureaus in the United States, Canada, and Mexico. Promotes ethical business practices and truth in national advertising; mediates disputes between consumers and businesses.

Consumer Brands Assn., *1001 N. 19th St., Arlington, VA 22209; (571) 378-6760. Geoff Freeman, President.*
General email, info@consumerbrandsassociation.org
Web, www.consumerbrandsassociation.org, Twitter, @consumerbrands and Facebook, www.facebook.com/ConsumerBrandsAssociation

Membership: sales and marketing agents and retail merchandisers of food and consumer products worldwide. Sponsors research, training, and educational programs for members and their trading partners. Monitors legislation and regulations. (Formerly the Grocery Manufacturers Assn.)

Convenience Distribution Assn., *11250 Roger Bacon Dr., #8, Reston, VA 20190; (703) 208-3358. Fax, (703) 573-5738. Kimberly Bolin, President, (703) 208-1650. Toll-free, (800) 482-2962.*
General email, info@cdaweb.net
Web, www.cdaweb.net

Membership: wholesalers, manufacturers, retailers, and brokers who sell or distribute convenience products. Conducts educational programs. Monitors legislation and regulations. (Formerly American Wholesale Marketers Assn.)

DECA Inc., *1908 Association Dr., Reston, VA 20191-1594; (703) 860-5000. Frank Peterson, Executive Director.*
General email, info@deca.org
Web, www.deca.org, Twitter, @DECAInc and Facebook, www.facebook.com/decainc

Educational organization that helps high school and college students develop skills in marketing, management, finance, hospitality, and entrepreneurship. Promotes business and education partnerships.

Equipment Leasing and Finance Assn., *1625 Eye St. N.W., #850, 20006; (202) 238-3400. Fax, (202) 238-3401. Ralph Petta, President.*
General email, rjordan@elfaonline.org
Web, www.elfaonline.org, Twitter, @ELFAOnline and Facebook, www.facebook.com/ELFApage

Membership: independent leasing companies, banks, financial service companies, and independent brokers and suppliers to the leasing industry. Promotes the interests of the equipment leasing and finance industry; assists in the resolution of industry problems; encourages standards. Monitors legislation and regulations.

Green Seal, *1717 K St. N.W., #900, 20006; (202) 872-6400. Fax, (202) 872-4324. Douglas (Doug) Gatlin, Chief Executive Officer.*
General email, greenseal@greenseal.org
Web, www.greenseal.org, Twitter, @GreenSeal and Facebook, www.facebook.com/GreenSeal

Grants certification to environmentally sustainable products, services, hotels, restaurants, and other companies.

International Cemetery, Cremation, and Funeral Assn., *107 Carpenter Dr., #100, Sterling, VA 20164; (703) 391-8400. Fax, (703) 391-8416. Bob Fells, Executive Director, (703) 391-8403. Toll-free, (800) 645-7700.*
General email, hq@iccfa.com
Web, https://iccfa.com and Twitter, @ICCFA

Membership: owners and operators of cemeteries, crematories, funeral homes, mausoleums, and columbaria. Promotes the building and proper maintenance of modern interment places; promotes high ethical standards in the industry; encourages prearrangement of funerals.

International Council of Shopping Centers, *Global Public Policy, 1201 Pnnsylvania Ave. N.W., #210, 20004; (202) 626-1400. Fax, (202) 626-1401. Tom McGee, President; Betsy Laird, Senior Vice President of Global Public Policy. General email, gpp@icsc.com*

Web, www.icsc.com

Membership: shopping center owners, developers, managers, retailers, contractors, and others in the industry worldwide. Provides information, including research data. Monitors legislation and regulations. (Headquarters in New York.)

International Franchise Assn., *1900 K St. N.W., #700, 20006; (202) 628-8000. Robert Cresanti, President. Membership, (202) 662-0767. General email, info@franchise.org*

Web, www.franchise.org, Twitter, @franchising411 and Facebook, www.facebook.com/IFA.DC

Membership: national and international franchisers. Sponsors seminars, workshops, trade shows, and conferences. Monitors legislation and regulations.

NACS: The Assn. for Convenience and Fuel Retailing, *1600 Duke St., 7th Floor, Alexandria, VA 22314-3421; (703) 684-3600. Fax, (703) 836-4564. Henry Armour, President. Toll-free, (800) 966-6227. General email, nacs@convenience.org*

Web, www.convenience.org, Twitter, @nacsonline and Facebook, www.facebook.com/nasconline

Membership: convenience store and fuel retailers and industry suppliers. Promotes industry position on labor, tax, environment, alcohol, and food-related issues; conducts research and training programs. Monitors legislation and regulations.

National Assn. of Wholesaler-Distributors, *1325 G St. N.W., #1000, 20005-3100; (202) 872-0885. Fax, (202) 785-0586. Eric Hoplin, President. General email, naw@naw.org*

Web, www.naw.org, Twitter, @NAWorg, Facebook, www.facebook.com/NAWorganization and YouTube, www.youtube.com/user/NAWInstitute

Membership: wholesale distributors and trade associations, product sellers, manufacturers, and their insurers. Provides members and government policymakers with research, education, and government relations information. Promotes federal product liability tort reform. Monitors legislation and regulations.

National Retail Federation, *1101 New York Ave. N.W., #1200, 20005; (202) 783-7971. Fax, (202) 737-2849. Matthew R. Shay, President; John Furner, Chair. Toll-free, (800) 673-4692. Web, www.nrf.com, Twitter, @NRFnews and Facebook, www.facebook.com/NationalRetailFederation General email, contact@nrf.com*

Membership: international, national, and state associations of retailers and major retail corporations. Concerned with federal regulatory activities and legislation that affect retailers, including tax, employment, trade, and credit issues. Provides information on retailing through seminars, conferences, and publications.

Personal Care Products Council, *1620 L St. N.W., #1200, 20036; (202) 331-1770. Lezlee Westine, President. Web, www.personalcarecouncil.org, Twitter, @PSPC_News and Facebook, www.facebook.com/ThePAAlliance*

Membership: manufacturers and distributors of finished personal care products. Conducts product safety research and advocacy. Represents the industry at the local, state, and national levels. Interests include scientific, legal, international trade, legislation, and regulatory issues. (Formerly Cosmetic, Toiletry, and Fragrance Assn.)

Pool and Hot Tub Alliance *(PHTA), 2111 Eisenhower Ave., #500, Alexandria, VA 22314-4698; (703) 838-0083. Sabeena Hickman, President, (703) 647-2552. General email, phta@phta.org*

Web, www.phta.org, Twitter, @ThePHTA and Facebook, www.facebook.com/PoolHotTubAlliance

Membership: manufacturers, dealers and retailers, service companies, builders, and distributors of pools, spas, and hot tubs. Promotes the industry; provides educational programs for industry professionals; establishes standards for construction and safety. Monitors legislation and regulations.

Retail Industry Leaders Assn., *99 M St. S.E., #700, 20003; (202) 869-0200. Brian Dodge, President. Web, www.rila.org and Twitter, @RILAtweets*

Membership: retailers, consumer product manufacturers, and service suppliers in the United States and abroad. Interests include supply chain, trade, finance, asset protection, workforce issues, and energy. Monitors legislation and regulations.

Security Industry Assn., *8405 Colesville Rd., #500, Silver Spring, MD 20910; (301) 804-4700. Donald (Don) Erickson, Chief Executive Officer, (301) 804-4747. General email, info@securityindustry.org*

Web, www.securityindustry.org and Twitter, @SIAOnline

Membership: manufacturers, service providers, and integrators of electronic security equipment. Sponsors trade shows, develops industry standards, supports educational programs and job training, and publishes statistical research. Monitors legislation and regulations.

Service Station Dealers of America and Allied Trades, *1532 Pointer Ridge Pl., Suite G, Bowie, MD 20716; (301) 390-4405. Pete Kischak, President, (914) 589-9161. General email, rlittlefield2@wmda.net*

Web, www.ssda-at.com

Membership: state associations of gasoline retailers, repair facilities, car washes, and convenience stores. Interests include environmental issues, retail marketing, oil allocation, imports and exports, prices, and taxation. Monitors legislation and regulations.

Society for Imaging Science and Technology, *7003 Kilworth Lane, Springfield, VA 22151; (703) 642-9090.*

Fax, (703) 642-9094. Suzanne E. Grinnan, Executive Director.

General email, info@imaging.org

Web, www.imaging.org and Twitter, @ImagingOrg

Membership: individuals and companies worldwide in fields of imaging science and technology, including digital printing, electronic imaging, color science, image preservation, photo finishing, prepress technology, and hybrid imaging. Gathers and disseminates technical information; fosters professional development.

Society of Independent Gasoline Marketers of America (SIGMA), *1330 Braddock Pl., #501, Alexandria, VA 22314; (703) 709-7000. Ryan McNutt, Chief Executive Officer.*

General email, sigma@sigma.org

Web, www.sigma.org

Membership: marketers and wholesalers of brand and nonbrand gasoline. Seeks to ensure adequate supplies of gasoline at competitive prices. Monitors legislation and regulations affecting gasoline supply and price.

Advertising and Marketing

▶AGENCIES

Federal Highway Administration (FHWA) *(Transportation Dept.), Planning, Environment, and Realty, 1200 New Jersey Ave. S.E., #E76-306, 20590; (202) 366-0116. Fax, (202) 366-3713. Gloria M. Shepherd, Associate Administrator, (202) 366-0581.*

Web, www.fhwa.dot.gov/real_estate

Administers laws concerning outdoor advertising along interstate and federally aided primary highways.

Federal Trade Commission (FTC), *Bureau of Consumer Protection, Advertising Practices Division, 400 7th Ave. S.W., #10418, 20024; (202) 326-3244. Fax, (202) 326-3259. Serena Viswanathan, Associate Director.*

Web, www.ftc.gov/about-ftc/bureaus-offices/bureau-consumer-protection/our-divisions/division-advertising-practices

Protects consumers from deceptive and unsubstantiated advertising through law enforcement, public reports, and industry outreach. Focuses on national advertising campaigns for food, dietary supplements and over-the-counter drugs, and medical devices, particularly advertising that makes claims difficult for consumers to evaluate. Monitors alcohol advertising for unfair practices; issues reports on alcohol labeling, advertising, and promotion. Issues reports on the marketing to children of violent movies, video games, and music recordings.

Federal Trade Commission (FTC), *Bureau of Consumer Protection, Marketing Practices Division, 600 Pennsylvania Ave. N.W., 20580; (202) 326-3404. Fax, (202) 326-3395. Lois C. Greisman, Associate Director.*

Web, www.ftc.gov/about-ftc/bureaus-offices/bureau-consumer-protection/our-divisions/division-marketing-practices

Responds to complaints of consumer fraud in the marketplace, including high-tech Internet and telephone scams, deceptive telemarketing or direct mail marketing schemes, fraudulent business opportunity scams, and violations of the Do Not Call and CAN-SPAM consumer privacy protections.

Food and Drug Administration (FDA) *(Health and Human Services Dept.), Prescription Drug Promotion (OPDP), White Oak Bldg. 51, 10903 New Hampshire Ave., #3314, Silver Spring, MD 20993-0002; (301) 796-1200. Fax, (301) 847-8444 or (301) 847-8445. Catherine Gray, Director.*

Web, www.fda.gov/about-fda/center-drug-evaluation-and-research-cder/office-prescription-drug-promotion-opdp

Monitors prescription drug advertising and labeling; investigates complaints; conducts market research on health care communications and drug issues.

▶NONGOVERNMENTAL

Ad Council, *1707 L St. N.W., #600, 20036; (202) 331-9153. Lisa Sherman, President.*

General email, info@adcouncil.org

Web, www.adcouncil.org, Twitter, @AdCouncil, Facebook, www.facebook.com/adcouncil and YouTube, www.youtube.com/adcouncil

Produces and distributes public service advertisements for nonprofit organizations and federal agencies.

American Advertising Federation, *1101 K St. N.W., #420, 20005; (202) 898-0089. Fax, (202) 898-0159. Steve Pacheco, President. Toll-free, (800) 999-2231.*

General email, aaf@aaf.org

Web, www.aaf.org, Twitter, @AAFNational and Facebook, www.facebook.com/aafnational

Membership: advertising companies (ad agencies, advertisers, media, and services), clubs, associations, and college chapters. A founder of the National Advertising Review Board, a self-regulatory body. Sponsors annual awards for outstanding advertising.

American Assn. of Advertising Agencies, *Government Relations, 1707 L St. N.W., #600, 20036; (202) 331-7345. Fax, (202) 857-3675. Marla Kaplowitz, President; Amanda Anderson, Director of Government Relations.*

General email, wash@aaaadc.org

Web, www.aaaa.org/member-resource-guides/resource-guides-government-advocacy, Twitter, @4As and Facebook, www.facebook.com/aaaaorg

Government relations email, GR@4As.org and YouTube, www.youtube.com/channel/UCrxr1ATwHXcJ6bACXusAqLw

Monitors legislation and regulations at the federal, state, and local level to protect the agency business and the advertising industry as a whole. Advocates on issues affecting agencies, including new taxes on digital advertising and privacy law changes. (Headquarters in New York.)

ANA Nonprofit Federation (ANANF), *2020 K St. N.W., #660, 20006; (202) 861-2427. Xenia (Sonny) Boone, Senior Vice President, (202) 861-2498.*
Web, https://nonprofitfederation.org,
Twitter, @ANANonprofit and Facebook, www.facebook .com/ANANonprofitFederation

Membership: businesses and nonprofit organizations using and supporting direct marketing tools. Advocates standards for marketing, focusing on relevance to consumers. Provides research, education, and networking opportunities to members. Operates a service that removes consumer names from unwanted mailing lists. Monitors legislation and regulations. (Formerly the Direct Marketing Association; headquarters in New York.)

Center for Digital Democracy, *1015 15th St. N.W., #600, 20005; (202) 494-7100. Jeffrey (Jeff) Chester, Executive Director.*
Web, www.democraticmedia.org, Twitter, @DigitalDemoc and Facebook, www.facebook.com/Center-for-Digital-Democracy-Protect-Privacy-Online-281331962264

Tracks and analyzes the online advertising market, including areas affecting public health, news and information, children and adolescents, and financial industries.

Color Marketing Group, *1908 Mount Vernon Ave., Alexandria, VA 22301 (mailing address: P.O. Box 2497, Alexandria, VA 22301); (703) 329-8500. Sharon Griffis, Executive Director.*
Web, https://colormarketing.org, Twitter, @ColorSells and Facebook, www.facebook.com/ColorSells

Provides a forum for the exchange of noncompetitive information by color design professionals; seeks to create color forecast information for design and marketing. Holds meetings; sponsors special events in the United States as well as abroad.

CTAM: Cable and Telecommunications Assn. for Marketing, *120 Waterfront St., #200, National Harbor, MD 20745; (301) 485-8900. Fax, (301) 485-8898. Vicki Lins, President, (301) 485-8920.*
General email, info@ctam.com
Web, www.ctam.com and Twitter, @CTAM

Promotes innovation in the cable and related industries in areas of marketing, research, management, and new product development. Sponsors annual marketing and research conferences; interests include international markets.

Hispanic Marketing Council (HMC), *8280 Willow Oaks Corporate Dr., #600, Fairfax, VA 22031 (mailing address: P.O. Box 3915, Merrifield, VA 22116); (703) 745-5531. Horacio Gavilán, Executive Director.*
General email, info@hispanicmarketingcouncil.org
Web, www.culturemarketingcouncil.org,
Twitter, @hmchispanic and Facebook, www.facebook.com/ CultureMarketingCouncil

Works to grow, strengthen, and protect the Hispanic marketing and advertising industry. Strives to increase Hispanics' awareness of market opportunities and enhance professionalism of the industry. (Formerly the Assn. of Hispanic Advertising Agencies.)

International Sign Assn., *1001 N. Fairfax St., #301, Alexandria, VA 22314; (703) 836-4012. Fax, (703) 836-8353. Lori Anderson, President, ext. 116.*
General email, info@signs.org
Web, www.signs.org, Twitter, @ISAsigns and Facebook, www.facebook.com/ISAsigns

Membership: manufacturers and distributors of signs and other visual communications systems. Promotes the sign industry; conducts workshops and seminars; sponsors annual competition.

Outdoor Advertising Assn. of America (OAAA), *1850 M St. N.W., #1040, 20036; (202) 833-5566. Fax, (202) 833-1522. Anna Bager, President.*
General email, info@oaaa.org
Web, www.oaaa.org, Twitter, @YourOAAA and Facebook, www.facebook.com/YourOAAA

Membership: outdoor advertising companies, operators, suppliers, and affiliates. Serves as a clearinghouse for public service advertising, including digital, campaigns. Monitors legislation and regulations.

Public Utilities

▶**AGENCIES**

Agriculture Dept. (USDA), *Rural Development, Rural Utilities Service, 1400 Independence Ave. S.W., #4121-S, MS 1510, 20250-1510; (202) 720-9540. Christopher (Chris) A. McLean, Administrator (Acting). Web, www.rd.usda.gov/about-rd/agencies/rural-utilities-service*

Makes loans and loan guarantees to provide electricity, telecommunication systems, water and waste disposal services to rural areas.

Federal Energy Regulatory Commission (FERC) *(Energy Dept.), Electric Reliability (OER), 888 1st St. N.E., #9M-01, 20426; (202) 502-8600. Fax, (202) 219-2836. David Ortiz, Director (Acting), (202) 502-6101. Toll-free, (202) 219-2836. Web, www.ferc.gov/about/offices/office-electric-reliability-oer*

Oversees the reliability and security of the nation's bulk power system. Establishes and ensures compliance with reliability and security standards for users, owners, and operators of the bulk power system.

Federal Energy Regulatory Commission (FERC) *(Energy Dept.), Energy Market Regulation (OEMR), 888 1st St. N.E., #8A-01, 20426; (202) 502-6700. Fax, (202) 219-2836. Jette Gebhart, Director. Web, www.ferc.gov/about/offices/office-energy-market-regulation-oemr*

Advises the Commission and processes caseloads related to the economic regulation of the electric utility, natural gas, and oil industries. Concerns include energy markets, tariffs, and pipeline rates relating to electric utility and

Small Business Administration

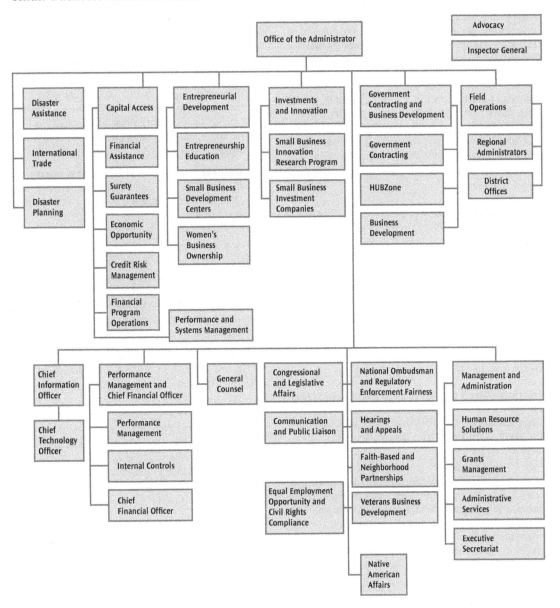

natural gas and oil pipeline facilities and services. Analyzes applications for electric public utility corporate transactions, including public utility mergers, issuance of securities, or the assumption of liabilities, to determine if the proposed transactions are consistent with the public interest.

Federal Energy Regulatory Commission (FERC) *(Energy Dept.), Energy Policy and Innovation (OEPI), 888 1st St. N.E., #7A-01, 20426; (202) 502-8850. Fax, (202) 219-2836. Jignassa Gadani, Director.*
Web, www.ferc.gov/about/offices/office-energy-policy-and-innovation-oepi

Seeks to identify emerging issues affecting wholesale and interstate energy markets. Undertakes outreach to other

regulators and industry, conducts studies, and makes recommendations for Commission action with state and federal agencies and the energy industry, taking into account energy and environmental concerns. Interests include renewable energy, efficiency, smart grid technology, transmission issues, electric vehicles, and carbon and greenhouse gas issues.

▶NONGOVERNMENTAL

American Gas Assn., *400 N. Capitol St. N.W., #450, 20001-1535; (202) 824-7000. Karen A. Harbert, President.*
Web, www.aga.org, Twitter, @aga_naturalgas, Facebook, www.facebook.com/naturalgas and YouTube, www.youtube.com/user/dgibsonagaorg

Membership: natural gas utilities and pipeline companies. Interests include all technical and operational aspects of the gas industry. Publishes comprehensive statistical record of the gas industry; conducts national standard testing for gas appliances. Advocates policies that are favorable to increased supplies and lower prices. Monitors legislation and regulations.

American Gas Assn., *Statistics,* *400 N. Capitol St. N.W., #450, 20001-1535; (202) 824-7133. Paul Pierson, Senior Director.*
Web, www.aga.org/events-community/statistics-survey-system and Facebook, www.facebook.com/naturalgas

Issues statistics on the gas utility industry, including supply and reserves.

American Public Power Assn., *2451 Crystal Dr., #1000, Arlington, VA 22202; (202) 467-2900. Fax, (202) 467-7467. Joy Ditto, President. Press, (202) 467-2927.*
Web, www.publicpower.org, Twitter, @publicpowerorg, Facebook, www.facebook.com/americanpublicpower and YouTube, www.youtube.com/c/AmericanPublicPower AssociationWashington

Membership: local, municipally owned electric utilities nationwide. Represents industry interests before Congress, federal agencies, and the courts; provides educational programs; collects and disseminates information; funds energy research and development projects.

American Water Works Assn., *Government Affairs, 1300 Eye St. N.W., #701W, 20005-3314; (202) 628-8303. Fax, (202) 628-2846. David B. LaFrance, Chief Executive Officer; G. Tracy Mehan III, Executive Director of Government Affairs.*
Web, www.awwa.org

Membership: municipal water utilities, manufacturers of equipment for water industries, water treatment companies, and individuals. Provides information on drinking water treatment and trends and issues affecting water safety; publishes voluntary standards for the water industry; issues policy statements on water supply matters. Monitors legislation and regulations. (Headquarters in Denver, Colo.)

Edison Electric Institute, *701 Pennsylvania Ave. N.W., 20004-2696; (202) 508-5000. Fax, (202) 508-5096. Thomas R. Kuhn, President.*
General email, feedback@eei.org
Web, www.eei.org, Twitter, @Edison_Electric, Facebook, www.facebook.com/edisonelectricinstitute and YouTube, www.youtube.com/user/EEITV

Membership: investor-owned electric power companies. Interests include electric utility operation and concerns, including conservation and energy management, energy analysis, generation and transmission facilities, fuel resources, the environment, cogeneration and renewable energy resources, safety, reliability, taxes, and regulation matters. Provides information and statistics relating to electric energy; aids member companies in generating and selling electric energy; and conducts information forums.

Edison Electric Institute, *Business Information, 701 Pennsylvania Ave. N.W., 20004-2696; (202) 508-5000. Fax, (202) 508-5599. Steve Frauenheim, Senior Manager of Business Analytics. Press, (202) 508-5659.*
General email, sfrauenheim@eei.org
Web, www.eei.org/resourcesandmedia/products

Publishes information and statistics on electric utility operations, including the *Statistical Yearbook of the Electric Power Industry,* which contains data on the capacity, generation, sales, customers, revenue, and finances of the electric utility industry. Also reports on environmental and regulatory concerns.

International Brotherhood of Electrical Workers (IBEW), *900 7th St. N.W., 20001; (202) 833-7000. Fax, (202) 728-7676. Lonnie R. Stephenson, International President.*
General email, webmaster@ibew.org
Web, http://ibew.org

Membership: workers in utilities, construction, telecommunications, broadcasting, manufacturing, railroads, and government. Helps members negotiate pay, benefits, and better working conditions; conducts training programs and workshops. Monitors legislation and regulations. (Affiliated with the AFL-CIO.)

National Assn. of Regulatory Utility Commissioners, *1101 Vermont Ave. N.W., #200, 20005-3521; (202) 898-2200. Fax, (202) 898-2213. Greg R. White, Executive Director, (202) 898-2208.*
General email, jramsay@naruc.org
Web, www.naruc.org and Twitter, @NARUC

Membership: members of federal, state, municipal, and international regulatory commissions that have jurisdiction over utilities and carriers. Interests include water, electricity, natural gas, nuclear power, telecommunications, and transportation.

National Assn. of State Utility Consumer Advocates (NASUCA), *8380 Colesville Rd., #101, Silver Spring, MD 20910-6267; (301) 589-6313. Fax, (301) 589-6380. David Springe, Executive Director, (785) 550-7606.*
General email, nasuca@nasuca.org
Web, www.nasuca.org

Membership: public advocate offices authorized by states to represent ratepayer interests before state and federal utility regulatory commissions. Monitors legislation and regulatory agencies with jurisdiction over electric utilities, telecommunications, natural gas, and water; conducts conferences. Supports privacy protection for telephone customers.

National Hydropower Assn., *601 New Jersey Ave. N.W., #660, 20001; (202) 682-1700. Fax, (202) 682-9478. Malcolm Woolf, President.*
General email, info@hydro.org
Web, www.hydro.org

Membership: investor-owned utilities and municipal and independent companies that generate hydroelectric power and power from new water technologies; consulting, engineering, and law firms; and equipment suppliers and manufacturers. Focus includes regulatory relief, public affairs, and coalition building. Monitors legislation and regulations.

National Rural Electric Cooperative Assn. (NRECA), *4301 Wilson Blvd., Arlington, VA 22203-1860; (703) 907-5500. Fax, (703) 907-5511. Jim Matheson, Chief Executive Officer. Press, (703) 907-5746.*
Web, www.electric.coop, Twitter, @NRECANews and Facebook, www.facebook.com/NRECA.coop

Membership: rural electric cooperative systems and public power and utility districts. Provides members with legislative, legal, and regulatory services. Supports energy and environmental research and offers technical advice and assistance to developing countries.

Utilities Technology Council (UTC), *2550 S. Clark St., #960, Arlington, VA 22202; (202) 872-0030. Fax, (202) 872-1331. Sheryl Osiene Riggs, President.*
General email, marketing@utc.org
Web, www.utc.org and Twitter, @UTCNow

Membership: companies that own, manage, or provide critical telecommunications systems in support of their core business, including energy, gas, and water utility companies, pipeline companies, and radio and international critical infrastructure organizations. Participates in FCC rulemaking proceedings. Interests include fiber security; radio spectrum for fixed and mobile wireless communication; and technological, legislative, and regulatory developments affecting telecommunications operations of energy utilities.

Utility Workers Union of America, *1300 L St. N.W., #1200, 20005; (202) 899-2851. Fax, (202) 899-2852. James Slevin, National President.*
General email, webmaster@uwua.net
Web, www.uwua.net, Twitter, @The_UWUA and Facebook, www.facebook.com/theUWUA

Labor union representing workers in electric, gas, water, and nuclear utility industries. Helps members negotiate pay, benefits, and better working conditions; conducts training programs and workshops. Monitors legislation and regulations. (Affiliated with the AFL-CIO.)

SMALL AND DISADVANTAGED BUSINESS

General

▶**AGENCIES**

Agency for International Development (USAID), *Small and Disadvantaged Business Utilization (OSDBU),* *301 4th St. S.W., #SA-44, Room 848, 20024 (mailing address: 1300 Pennsylvania Ave. N.W., #SA-44, Room 848, Washington, DC 20523); Kimberly Ball, Director. Main, (202) 567-4730.*

General email, osdbu1@usaid.gov
Web, www.usaid.gov/who-we-are/organization/independent-offices/office-small-and-disadvantaged-business-utilization

Counsels small and minority-owned businesses on how to do business with USAID. Identifies opportunities for small businesses in subcontracting with the agency.

Agriculture Dept. (USDA), *Rural Development, Rural Business–Cooperative Service,* *1400 Independence Ave. S.W., #5803-S, MS 3201, 20250-3201; (202) 690-4730. Fax, (202) 690-4737. Karama Neal, Administrator (Acting).*
Web, www.rd.usda.gov/about-rd/agencies/rural-business-cooperative-service

Administers programs that provide the capital, technical support, educational opportunities, and entrepreneurial skills to rural residents to grow businesses or access jobs in agricultural markets. Promotes the use of cooperative businesses. Interests include sustainable renewable energy development; regional food systems development; job creation through recreation and natural resource restoration, conservation, and management; and access to broadband.

Agriculture Dept. (USDA), *Small and Disadvantaged Business Utilization (OSDBU),* *1400 Independence Ave. S.W., #1085-S, MS 9501, 20250-9501; (202) 720-7117. Michelle Warren, Director (Acting), (202) 720-7835.*
Web, www.dm.usda.gov/smallbus

Provides guidance and technical assistance to Small businesses often owned and run by women, people of diverse ethnic backgrounds and disabled veterans, seeking to do business with the USDA; monitors the development and implementation of contracting policies to prevent barriers to small business participation; works with other federal agencies and public/private partners to increase the number of small businesses participating in the contracting arena.

Commerce Dept., *Business Liaison,* *1401 Constitution Ave. N.W., #5062, 20230; (202) 482-1360. Fax, (202) 482-4054. Laura O'Neil, Director.*
General email, businessliaison@doc.gov
Web, www.commerce.gov/bureaus-and-offices/os/business-liaison

Serves as the federal government's central office for business assistance. Handles requests for information and services as well as complaints and suggestions from businesses; provides a forum for businesses to comment on federal regulations; initiates meetings on policy issues with industry groups, business organizations, trade and small business associations, and the corporate community.

Commerce Dept., *Small and Disadvantaged Business Utilization (OSDBU),* *1401 Constitution Ave. N.W., #6411, 20230; (202) 482-1472. Fax, (202) 482-0501. LaJuene Desmukes, Director.*
General email, osdbu@doc.gov
Web, http://osec.doc.gov/osdbu

An advocacy and advisory office that works toward increasing Commerce Dept. contract awards to small, disadvantaged, women-owned, veteran-owned, service disable-owned, and HUBZone small businesses.

Consumer Product Safety Commission (CPSC), *Small Business Ombudsman, 4330 East-West Hwy., Bethesda, MD 20814; (301) 504-7945. Will Cusey, Ombudsman.*
General email, sbo@cpsc.gov

Web, www.cpsc.gov

Provides guidance and advice to small businesses and small-batch manufacturers about compliance with CPSC laws and regulations as well as technical assistance in resolving problems.

Defense Health Agency (DHA) *(Defense Dept.), Small Business Programs, 5109 Leesburg Pike, Falls Church, VA 22041; (703) 882-7111. Cassandra W. Martin, Director.*
Web, https://health.mil/About-MHS/OASDHA/Defense-Health-Agency/Small-Business-Program

Seeks to ensure that small businesses have a fair opportunity to compete and be selected for DHA contracts, at both the prime and subcontract levels. Provides information on agency purchases and the contracting process through forums, mentoring programs, and written materials.

Energy Efficiency and Renewable Energy (EERE) *(Energy Dept.), Advanced Manufacturing (AMO), 1000 Independence Ave. S.W., #5F065, MS EE5A, 20585-0121; (202) 586-9488. Fax, (202) 586-9234. Becca Jones-Albertus, Director (Acting).*
General email, amo_communication@ee.doe.gov

Web, www.energy.gov/eere/amo/advanced-manufacturing-office

Offers financial and technical support to small businesses and individual inventors for establishing technical performance and conducting early development of innovative ideas and inventions that have a significant energy-saving impact and future commercial market potential.

Farm Service Agency (FSA) *(Agriculture Dept.), Outreach Program. Minority and Socially Disadvantaged Farmers Assistance, 1400 Independence Ave. S.W., MS 0503, 20250-0503; (202) 690-1700. Fax, (202) 690-4727. J. Latrice Hill, Director of Outreach. TTY, (202) 720-5132.*
General email, oasdfr@osec.usda.gov

Web, www.fsa.usda.gov

Works with minority and socially disadvantaged farmers who have concerns and questions about loan applications filed with local offices or other Farm Service Agency programs.

Federal Emergency Management Agency (FEMA) *(Homeland Security Dept.), Resilience, Federal Insurance and Mitigation Administration, 400 C St. S.W., 20472; (202) 646-2781. Nimisha Agorwal, Deputy Associate Administrator (Acting).*
Web, www.fema.gov/about/offices/insurance-mitigation

Small and Disadvantaged Business Contacts at Federal Departments and Agencies

DEPARTMENTS

Agriculture, Michelle Warren (Acting), (202) 720-7835

Commerce, LaJuene Desmukes, (202) 482-1472

Defense, Ruby Crenshaw-Lawrence, (571) 372-6191

  Air Force, Scott A. Kiser, (571) 256-8052

  Army, Kimberly D. Buehler, (703) 697-2868

  Marine Corps, Kyle J. Beagle, (703) 432-3946

  Navy, Jimmy D. Smith (202) 685-6485; Email, sdbinfo@navy.mil

Education, Calvin Mitchell (Acting), (202) 245-6300

Energy, Paul Ross (Acting), (202) 586-7377

Health and Human Services, Michelle Street, (202) 690-7300

Homeland Security, Darlene Bullock, (202) 447-5555

  Coast Guard, Rear Adm. Douglas M. Schofield, (202) 475-5795

Housing and Urban Development, Jean Lin Pao (202) 402-5477; TTY, (800) 877-8339

Interior, Megan Olsen (Acting), (202) 208-3493

Justice, Bob Connolly, (202) 616-0521

Labor, Gladys Bailey, (202) 693-7244

State, George L. Price, (703) 875-6822

Transportation, Vacant, (202) 366-1930

Treasury, Donna Ragucci, (202) 622-1071

Veterans Affairs, Sharon G. Ridley, (202) 461-4300

AGENCIES

Agency for International Development, John Watson (Acting), (202) 916-4220

Consumer Product Safety Commission, Shelby Mathis, (301) 504-7865

Environmental Protection Agency, Denise Sirmons, (202) 564-2075 or, (202) 566-2496

General Services Administration, Judith Stackhouse, (202) 708-5804

National Aeronautics and Space Administration, Glenn A. Delgado, (202) 358-2088

Nuclear Regulatory Commission, Vonna Ordaz, (301) 415-7380; TTY, (301) 415-5244

Small Business Administration, Vacant, (202) 205-6766; TTY, (800) 877-8339

Social Security Administration, Leslie Ford, (410) 594-0111

Administers federal flood insurance programs. Makes low-cost flood and crime insurance available to eligible small businesses.

General Services Administration (GSA), *Small Business Utilization,* *1800 F St. N.W., 20405; (202) 501-1021. Exodie Roe III, Associate Administrator. Toll-free, (844) 472-4111. Vendor Support, (866) 727-8363.*
General email, small.business@gsa.gov

Web, www.gsa.gov/small-business

Works to increase small business access to government contract procurement opportunities. Provides policy guidance and direction for GSA Regional Small Business Offices, which offer advice and assistance to businesses interested in government procurement.

Health and Human Services Dept., *White House Initiative on Asian Americans, Native Hawaiians, and Pacific Islanders,* *550 12th St. S.W., 10th Floor, 20202; (202) 482-1375. Krystal Ka'ai, Executive Director.*
General email, whiaanhpi@hhs.gov

Web, www.commerce.gov/whiaapi and Twitter, @whitehouseAAPI

Works to increase Asian American, Native Hawaiian, and Pacific Islander participation in federal business and economic development programs.

Interior Dept. (DOI), *Small and Disadvantaged Business Utilization (OSDBU),* *1849 C St. N.W., Room 4214, 20240; (202) 208-3493. Fax, (202) 208-7444. Colleen Finnegan, Director.*
Web, www.doi.gov/pmb/osdbu

Email, doi_osdbu@ios.doi.gov

Advocates contracting opportunities for small, disadvantaged business communities, including Indian economic enterprises, small disadvantaged, women-owned, veteran-owned, service disabled veteran owned small businesses located in historically underutilized business zones (HUBZone) areas, and the Ability One Program.

Minority Business Development Agency *(Commerce Dept.),* *1401 Constitution Ave. N.W., #5053, 20230; (202) 482-2332. Miguel Estién, National Director (Acting).*
Web, www.mbda.gov, Twitter, @USMBDA and Facebook, www.facebook.com/USMBDA

Assists minority entrepreneurs one-on-one with financial planning, marketing, management, and technical assistance. Focuses on promoting wealth in minority communities.

National Science Foundation (NSF), *Small Business Innovation Research / Small Business Technology Transfer Program,* *2415 Eisenhower Ave., #E14344, Alexandria, VA 22134; (703) 292-8050. Fax, (703) 292-9057. Henry Ahn, Program Director, (703) 292-2174; Peter Atherton, Program Director. TTY, (800) 281-8749.*
General email, sbir@nsf.gov

Web, https://seedfund.nsf.gov and Twitter, @NSFSBIR

Serves as liaison between the small-business community and NSF offices; awards grants and contracts. Administers the Small Business Innovation Research and Small Business Technology Transfer Programs, which fund research proposals from small science/high technology firms and startups. Interests include hard science and technology with high technical risk and potential for significant commercial or societal impact. Offers incentives for commercial development, including NSF-funded research.

National Women's Business Council, *409 3rd St. S.W., #210, 20416; (202) 205-3850. Tene Dolphin, Exeutive Director; Ana Argueta, Program Manager.*
General email, info@nwbc.gov

Web, www.nwbc.gov, Twitter, @NWBC and Facebook, www.facebook.com/NWBCgov

Independent, congressionally mandated council established by the Women's Business Ownership Act of 1988. Reviews the status of women-owned businesses nationwide and makes policy recommendations to the president, Congress, and the Small Business Administration. Assesses the role of the federal government in aiding and promoting women-owned businesses. Offers webinars, hosts roundtables, and holds public meetings.

Small Business Administration (SBA), *409 3rd St. S.W., 20416-7000; (202) 205-6605. Fax, (202) 205-6802. Isabella Casillas Guzman, Administrator. ASL Videophone, (855) 440-4960. Toll-free information (Answer Desk), (800) 827-5722. TTY, (800) 877-8339.*
General email, answerdesk@sba.gov

Web, www.sba.gov and Twitter, @SBAgov

Provides small businesses with financial and management assistance; offers loans to victims of floods, natural disasters, and other catastrophes; licenses, regulates, and guarantees some financing of small-business investment companies; conducts economic and statistical research on small businesses. SBA Answer Desk is an information and referral service. District or regional offices can be contacted for specific loan information.

Small Business Administration (SBA), *Advocacy,* *409 3rd St. S.W., 20416; (202) 205-6533. Fax, (202) 205-6928. Major L. Clark III, Chief Counsel (Acting).*
General email, advocacy@sba.gov

Web, https://advocacy.sba.gov

Acts as an advocate for small business viewpoints in regulatory and legislative proceedings. Economic Research Office analyzes the effects of government policies on small businesses and documents the contributions of small business to the economy.

Small Business Administration (SBA), *Capital Access,* *409 3rd St. S.W., #8200, 20416; Patrick Kelley, Associate Administrator. Toll-free, (800) 877-8339.*
Web, www.sba.gov/about-sba/sba-locations/headquarters-offices/office-capital-access

Provides financial assistance to small business, including microloans, surety bond guarantees, investment, and international trade.

Small Business Administration (SBA), *Credit Risk Management,* *409 3rd St. S.W., #8200, 20416; (202) 205-3049. Fax, (202) 205-6831. Susan E. Streich, Director.*

Web, www.sba.gov/about-sba/sba-locations/headquarters-offices/office-capital-access/office-capital-access-resources

Conducts on-site and off-site analysis and reviews of SBA lending partners' activities; reviews the quality of the SBA loan portfolio through trend analysis and assessment of risk indicators.

Small Business Administration (SBA), *Disaster Assistance, 409 3rd St. S.W., #6050, 20416; (202) 205-6734. Fax, (202) 205-7728. Francisco Sanchez, Associate Administrator. Service Center, (800) 659-2955.*
Web, www.sba.gov/about-sba/sba-locations/headquarters-offices/office-disaster-assistance

General email, disastercustomerassistance@sba.gov

Provides economic injury loans to small businesses for losses to meet necessary operating expenses, provided the business could have paid these expenses prior to the disaster.

Small Business Administration (SBA), *Diversity, Inclusion, and Civil Rights, 409 3rd St. S.W., #6400, 20416; (202) 205-6750. Zina Sutch, Assistant Administrator. Toll free, (800) 877-8339.*
Web, www.sba.gov/about-sba/sba-locations/headquarters-offices/office-diversity-inclusion-civil-rights

Reviews complaints based on disability against the Small Business Administration by recipients of its assistance in cases of alleged discrimination in credit transactions; monitors recipients for civil rights compliance.

Small Business Administration (SBA), *Entrepreneurial Development, 409 3rd St. S.W., #6200, 20416; (202) 205-6239. Mark Madrid, Associate Administrator.*
General email, oed@sba.gov

Web, www.sba.gov/about-sba/sba-locations/headquarters-offices/office-entrepreneurial-development

Responsible for business development programs of the offices of the Small Business Development Centers and the offices of Entrepreneurship Education and Women's Business Ownership.

Small Business Administration (SBA), *Entrepreneurial Development, Entrepreneurship Education, 409 3rd St. S.W., #6200, 20416; (202) 205-6665. Fax, (202) 205-6903. Terry Sutherland, Director.*
Web, www.sba.gov/about-sba/sba-locations/headquarters-offices/office-entrepreneurship-education

Outreach and education arm of SBA. Provides small businesses with instruction and counseling in marketing, accounting, product analysis, production methods, research and development, and management problems. Provides in-person as well as online training and specialized services for underserved markets.

Small Business Administration (SBA), *Entrepreneurial Development, Small Business Development Centers, 409 3rd St. S.W., #6400, 20416; (202) 205-6766. Fax, (202) 205-7727. Andrianna Menchaca-Gendron, Deputy Associate Administrator.*
Web, www.sba.gov/about-sba/sba-locations/headquarters-offices/office-small-business-development-centers

Promotes entrepreneurship, small business growth, and the U.S. economy by providing funding, oversight, and support for the nationwide network of Small Business Development Centers.

Small Business Administration (SBA), *Entrepreneurial Development, Women's Business Ownership, 409 3rd St. S.W., #6600, 20416; (202) 205-6673. Fax, (202) 205-7287. Natalie Colfield, Assistant Administrator.*
General email, womenbusiness@sba.gov

Web, www.sba.gov/about-sba/sba-locations/headquarters-offices/office-womens-business-ownership

Acts as an advocate for current and potential women business owners throughout the federal government and in the private sector. Provides training, counseling, and mentoring through a nationwide network of women's business centers; offers information on national and local resources, including SBA small business programs.

Small Business Administration (SBA), *Government Contracting and Business Development, 409 3rd St. S.W., #8000, 20416; (202) 205-6459. Fax, (202) 205-5206. Bibi Hidalgo, Associate Administrator.*
Web, www.sba.gov/about-sba/sba-locations/headquarters-offices/office-government-contracting-business-development

Oversees the Office of Government Contracting and Office of Business Development. Enhances the effectiveness of small business programs to develop policies, regulations, and statutory changes.

Small Business Administration (SBA), *Government Contracting and Business Development, Business Development, 409 3rd St. S.W., #8800, 20416; (202) 205-5852. Fax, (202) 205-7259. Bibi Hidalgo, Associate Administrator.*
General email, 8abd@sba.gov

Web, www.sba.gov/about-sba/sba-locations/headquarters-offices/office-business-development

Coordinates the services provided by private industry, banks, the SBA, and other government agencies—such as business development and management and technical assistance—to increase the number of small businesses owned by socially and economically disadvantaged Americans.

Small Business Administration (SBA), *International Trade, 409 3rd St. S.W., #2400, 20416; (202) 205-6720. Fax, (202) 205-7272. Gabriel Esparza, Associate Administrator, (202) 205-6750.*
Web, www.sba.gov/about-sba/sba-locations/headquarters-offices/office-international-trade

Ensures interests of small businesses are considered and reflected in trade negotiations; promotes ability of small businesses to export.

Small Business Administration (SBA), *Investments and Innovation, 409 3rd St. S.W., #6300, 20416; (202) 205-6510. Fax, (202) 205-6959. Tom Morris, Associate Administrator (Acting).*
Web, www.sba.gov/about-sba/sba-locations/headquarters-offices/office-investment-innovation

Administers and runs the Small Business Investment Companies, Small Business Innovation Research, and Small Business Technology Transfer programs.

Small Business Administration (SBA), *Native American Affairs, 409 3rd St. S.W., #6700, 20416; (202) 205-6411. Fax, (202) 205-6139. Jackson Brossy, Assistant Administrator.*
Web, www.sba.gov/about-sba/sba-locations/headquarters-offices/office-native-american-affairs

Offers tools and resources to increase Native American, Alaska Native, and Native Hawaiian involvement and opportunities in small business through entrepreneurial development, lending, and procurement programs.

Small Business Administration (SBA), *Veterans Business Development, 409 3rd St. S.W., #5700, 20416; (202) 205-6773. Fax, (202) 205-7292. Larry Stubblefield, Associate Administrator.*
Web, www.sba.gov/about-sba/sba-locations/headquarters-offices/office-veterans-business-development

Helps veterans use SBA loans through counseling, procurement, and training programs in entrepreneurship.

►CONGRESS

For a listing of relevant congressional committees and subcommittees, please see pages 38–39 or the Appendix.

►NONGOVERNMENTAL

Capital Region Minority Supplier Development Council, *10750 Columbia Pike, #200, Silver Spring, MD 20901; (301) 593-5860. Fax, (301) 593-1364. Sharon R. Pinder, President, ext. 102.*
General email, crmsdc@crmsdc.org
Web, www.crmsdc.org, Facebook, www.facebook.com/CRMSDC/same and Twitter, @CRMSDC

Certifies minority (Asian, African American, Hispanic, and Native American) business enterprises. Refers corporate buyers to minority suppliers and supports the development, expansion, and promotion of corporate minority supplier development programs. Offers networking opportunities and gives awards. Disseminates statistics and information. Provides consultation services, educational seminars, technical assistance, and training opportunities. (Regional council of the National Minority Supplier Development Council.)

ECDC Enterprise Development Group (EDG), *901 S. Highland St., Arlington, VA 22204; (703) 685-7230. Fax, (703) 685-4200. Tsehaye Teferra, President.*
General email, info@entdevgroup.org
Web, https://entdevgroup.org, Twitter, @ecdcedg and Facebook, www.facebook.com/ECDCEDG

Provides microloans to clients in the Washington metropolitan area with low-to-moderate income in order to promote new business enterprises and individual self-sufficiency. Offers business training and preloan and postloan technical assistance to entrepreneurs. Operates a matched savings program for low-income refugees and a car loan program for those with inadequate transportation. An independent subsidiary of the Ethiopian Community Development Council.

Institute for Liberty (IFL), *1250 Connecticut Ave. N.W., #200, 20036; (202) 261-6592. Fax, (877) 350-6147. Andrew Langer, President.*
Web, www.instituteforliberty.org

Seeks to protect small businesses from government over-intrusion. Interests include energy and tax policy, health care, property rights, and Internet freedom. Monitors policy and legislation.

MET Community, *1749 Potomac Greens Dr., Alexandria, VA 22314; (202) 792-9338. Yanire Braña, President, (202) 403-7657.*
General email, info@metcommunity.org
Web, http://metcommunity.org, Twitter, @metcommunity_us and Facebook, www.facebook.com/METcommunityUS

International organization that promotes mentoring, entrepreneurship, and training among women; educates companies and international communities on diversity, social responsibility, and innovation. Has a presence in eight countries, including Spain, Colombia, Peru, Brazil and Argentina, and has partnerships with BBVA, World Bank, and BELCORP Foundation.

National Assn. of Investment Companies, *1300 Pennsylvania Ave. N.W., #700, 20004; (202) 204-3001. Robert L. Greene, President.*
General email, info@naicpe.com
Web, www.naicpe.com

Membership: investment companies that provide minority-owned businesses with venture capital and management guidance. Provides technical assistance; monitors legislation and regulations.

National Assn. of Negro Business and Professional Women's Clubs Inc., *1806 New Hampshire Ave. N.W., 20009; (202) 483-4206. Fax, (202) 462-7253. Robin Waley, Executive Director.*
General email, info@nanbpwc.org
Web, www.nanbpwc.org and Twitter, @NANBPWC

Promotes and protects the interests of minority business and professional women, serves as advisors to young people seeking to enter business and the professions, provides scholarship support for secondary education, sponsors workshops, and works to improve the quality of life in local and global communities to foster good fellowship. Monitors legislation and regulations.

National Assn. of Women Business Owners, *South Bldg., 601 Pennsylvania Ave. N.W., #900, 20004; (800) 556-2926. Fax, (202) 403-3788. Jen Earle, Chief Executive Officer.*
General email, national@nawbo.org
Web, www.nawbo.org, Twitter, @NAWBONational, Facebook, www.facebook.com/NAWBO and YouTube, www.youtube.com/user/nawbonat

Promotes the economic, social, and political interests of women business owners through networking, leadership and business development training, and advocacy.

National Black Chamber of Commerce, 601 Pennsylvania Ave. N.W., #900, 20004; (202) 220-3060. Fax, (202) 466-4918. Vacant, President.
General email, info@nationalbcc.org
Web, www.nationalbcc.org, Twitter, @NATIONALBCC and Facebook, www.facebook.com/NationalBCC

Membership: Black-owned businesses. Educates and trains the Black community in entrepreneurship and other economic areas. Monitors legislation and regulations.

National Cooperative Business Assn., CLUSA International (NCBA CLUSA), 1775 Eye St. N.W., 8th Floor, 20006; (240) 638-6222. Douglas O'Brien, President.
General email, info@ncba.coop
Web, www.ncbaclusa.coop, Twitter, @NCBACLUSAcoop, Facebook, www.facebook.com/NCBACLUSA and YouTube, www.youtube.com/channel/UC1d9CsZOwqw QJid4uEscEUg

Alliance of cooperatives, businesses, and state cooperative associations. Supports development of cooperative businesses; promotes and develops trade among domestic and international cooperatives. Monitors legislation and regulations.

National Federation of Independent Business (NFIB), *Washington Office,* 555 N. 12th St., #1001, 20004; (202) 554-9000. Brad Close, President. Toll-free, (800) 634-2669.
Web, www.nfib.com, Twitter, @NFIB, Facebook, www .facebook.com/NFIB and YouTube, www.youtube.com/ user/NFIBSmallBusiness

Membership: independent businesses. Monitors public policy issues and legislation affecting small and independent businesses, including taxation, government regulation, labor-management relations, and liability insurance. (Headquarters in Nashville, Tenn.)

National LGBT Chamber of Commerce, 1032 15th St. N.W., #190, 20005; (202) 234-9181. Fax, (202) 234-9185. Justin G. Nelson, President.
General email, info@nglcc.org
Web, www.nglcc.org, Twitter, @NGLCC and Facebook, www.facebook.com/NGLCC

Communicates ideas and information for and between businesses and organizations. Works with state and local chambers of commerce and business groups on various issues. Acts as an advocate on behalf of lesbian-, gay-, bisexual-, and transgender-owned businesses; professionals; students of business; and corporations.

National Small Business Assn., 1156 15th St. N.W., #502, 20005; (202) 293-8830. Todd McCracken, President, ext. 2906. Toll-free, (800) 345-6728.
General email, info@nsba.biz
Web, www.nsba.biz and Twitter, @NSBAAdvocate

Membership: manufacturing, wholesale, retail, service, exporting, and other small business firms and regional small-business organizations. Represents the interests of small-business before Congress, the administration, and federal agencies. Services to members include a toll-free legislative hotline and group insurance.

SCORE Assn., 1165 Herndon Pkwy., #100, Herndon, VA 20170; (703) 487-3612. Fax, (703) 487-3066. Bridget Weston, Chief Executive Officer. Toll-free, (800) 634-0245.
General email, help@score.org
Web, www.score.org, Twitter, @SCOREMentors and Facebook, www.facebook.com/SCOREMentors

Independent volunteer organization funded by the Small Business Administration through which retired, semiretired, and active business executives use their knowledge and experience to counsel small businesses. (Formerly Service Corps of Retired Executives Assn.)

Small Business and Entrepreneurship Council (SBE Council), 200 Lawyers Rd. N.W., #1506, Vienna, VA 22183; (703) 242-5840. Fax, (703) 242-5841. Karen Kerrigan, President.
General email, info@sbecouncil.org
Web, https://sbecouncil.org, Twitter, @SBECouncil and Facebook, www.facebook.com/sbecouncil

Membership: U.S. entrepreneurs and business owners. Seeks to protect small business and promotes entrepreneurship. Provides networking opportunities, educational resources, and market intelligence for its members. Monitors legislation and regulations.

Small Business Investor Alliance, 529 14th St. N.W., #400, 20045; (202) 628-5055. Brett Palmer, President.
General email, info@sbia.org
Web, www.sbia.org and Twitter, @SmallBusinessPE

Membership: private equity, venture capital, and middle market funds that invest in small businesses. Provides training to fund managers and holds industry networking events. Monitors legislation and regulations.

Small Business Legislative Council, 4800 Hampden Lane, 6th Floor, Bethesda, MD 20814; (301) 652-8302. Paula Calimafde, President; Rob Underwood, Chair. Press, (301) 951-9351.
General email, email@sblc.org
Web, http://sblc.org, Twitter, @SBLC_ORG and Facebook, www.facebook.com/SBLC.ORG

Membership: trade associations that represent small businesses in the manufacturing, retail, professional and technical services, and agricultural, transportation, tourism, and construction sectors. Monitors and proposes legislation and regulations to benefit small businesses.

U.S. Chamber of Commerce, *Small Business Policy,* 1615 H St. N.W., 20062-2000; (202) 659-6000. Thomas M. Sullivan, Vice President.
General email, smallbusiness@uschamber.com
Web, https://uschamber.com/small-business-policy-page and Twitter, @SmallBizNation

Seeks to enhance visibility of small businesses within the national Chamber and the U.S. business community. Provides members with information on national small business programs and legislative issues.

U.S. Hispanic Chamber of Commerce, *1424 K St. N.W., #401, 20015; (202) 842-1212. Ramiro Cavazos, President. General email, info@ushcc.com*

Web, www.ushcc.com, Twitter, @USHCC, Facebook, www.facebook.com/USHCC and YouTube, www.youtube .com/ushcctv

Membership: Hispanic Chambers of Commerce and business organizations. Monitors legislation. Provides technical assistance to Hispanic business associations and owners. Promotes public policies that enhance the economic development of its members, trade between Hispanic businesses in the United States and Latin America, and partnerships with the larger business community.

U.S. Pan Asian American Chamber of Commerce, *1329 18th St. N.W., 20036; (202) 296-5221. Fax, (202) 296-5225. Susan Au Allen, Chief Executive Officer. Toll-free, (800) 696-7818.*

General email, info@uspaacc.com

Web, www.uspaacc.com, Twitter, @USPAACC and Facebook, www.facebook.com/UsPanAsianAmerican ChamberOfCommerce

Helps Asian American–owned businesses gain access to government and corporate contracts.

U.S. Women's Chamber of Commerce, *700 12th St. N.W., #700, 20005; (202) 607-2488. Margot Dorfman, Chief Executive Officer.*

Web, www.uswcc.org, Twitter, @uswcc and Facebook, www.facebook.com/USWomensCC

Provides services and career opportunities to women in business, including networking, leadership training, political advocacy, access to government procurement markets, and technical expertise. Monitors legislation and regulations.

3

Communications and the Media

GENERAL POLICY AND ANALYSIS

Basic Resources

▶ **AGENCIES**

Access Board, *1331 F St. N.W., #1000, 20004-1111; (202) 272-0080. Fax, (202) 272-0081. Sachin Dev Pavithran, Executive Director. Toll-free, (800) 872-2253. Toll-free TTY, (800) 993-2822. TTY, (202) 272-0082.*
General email, info@access-board.gov
Web, www.access-board.gov and Twitter, @accessboard

Develops and maintains accessibility requirements for buildings, transit vehicles, telecommunications equipment, medical diagnostic equipment, and electronic and information technology. Provides technical assistance and training on these guidelines and standards. Enforces access standards for federally funded facilities through the Architectural Barriers Act.

Agriculture Dept. (USDA), *Rural Development, Rural Utilities Service, 1400 Independence Ave. S.W., #4121-S, MS 1510, 20250-1510; (202) 720-9540.*
Christopher (Chris) A. McLean, Administrator (Acting).
Web, www.rd.usda.gov/about-rd/agencies/rural-utilities-service

Administers programs that ensure rural areas have access to affordable, reliable, advanced telecommunications services comparable to those available throughout the rest of the United States.

Federal Communications Commission (FCC), *45 L St. N.E., 20554; (888) 225-5322. Jessica Rosenworcel, Chair, (202) 418-1000. Consumer and Government Affairs, (202) 418-1400. Legislative Affairs, (202) 418-1900. Press, (202) 418-0500. Reference Information Center, (202) 418-1440. Toll-free fax, (866) 418-0232. TTY, (888) 835-5322. Videophone, (844) 432-2275.*
General email, fccinfo@fcc.gov
Web, www.fcc.gov, Twitter, @FCC and Facebook, www.facebook.com/FCC

Regulates interstate and foreign communications by radio, television, wire, cable, microwave, and satellite; consults with other government agencies and departments on national and international matters involving wire and radio telecommunications and with state regulatory commissions on telegraph and telephone matters; reviews applications for construction permits and licenses for such services. Reference Information Center open to the public (except under high-alert status orange and higher).

Federal Communications Commission (FCC), *Economics and Analytics (OEA), 45 L St. N.E., 20554; (202) 418-2030. Giulia McHenry, Chief, (202) 418-2105.*
Web, www.fcc.gov/economics-and-analytics

Responsible for expanding the use of economic analysis into commission policymaking, for enhancing the development and use of auctions, and for implementing consistent and effective agency-wide data practices and policies. Provides economic analysis, including cost-benefit analysis, for rulemakings, transactions, adjudications, and other commission actions; manages FCC auctions in support of and in coordination with FCC bureaus and offices; develops policies and strategies to help manage FCC data resources and establishing best practices for data use throughout the FCC in coordination with FCC bureaus and offices; and conducts long-term research on ways to improve the commission's policies and processes in each of these areas.

Federal Communications Commission (FCC), *Economics and Analytics (OEA), Auctions Division (AD), 45 L St. N.E., 20554; (202) 418-0605. Jonathan Campbell, Division Chief.*
Web, www.fcc.gov/auctions-division

Plans, designs, and conducts all FCC spectrum auctions, including auctions of flexible use licenses in various bands, including the 600 MHz and 700 MHz Bands, Advanced Wireless Services (AWS), and upper microwave bands, and construction permits for over-the-air television and radio services. Implements the commission's incentive auction authority to repurpose spectrum for new uses and conducts reverse auctions to distribute universal service support for fixed and mobile broadband services. Responsible for assuring that all of the commission's auction processes are fair and transparent. In planning for and conducting auctions, the Auctions Division collaborates with the bureaus responsible for regulating and licensing the items to be offered at auction.

Federal Communications Commission (FCC), *Economics and Analytics (OEA), Data Division, 45 L St. N.E., 20554; (202) 418-7991. Chelsea Fallon, Division Chief.*
Web, www.fcc.gov/economics-analytics/data-division

Develops and implements best practices, processes, and standards for data management to meet the needs of commission staff who rely on data to inform policymaking and other core activities of the commission.

Federal Communications Commission (FCC), *Economics and Analytics (OEA), Economic Analysis (EAD), 45 L St. N.E., 20554; (202) 418-2030. Fax, (202) 418-2807. Emily Talaga, Division Chief.*
Web, www.fcc.gov/economics-analytics/economic-analysis-division#block-menu-block-4

Provides analytical and quantitative support as needed to bureaus and offices engaged in rulemakings, transactions, auctions, adjudications, and other matters.

Federal Communications Commission (FCC), *Economics and Analytics (OEA), Industry Analysis Division (IAD), 45 L St. N.E., 20554; (202) 418-7356. Kenneth Lynch, Division Chief.*
Web, www.fcc.gov/economics-analytics/industry-analysis-division

Designs and administers significant, economically relevant data collections used by a variety of FCC bureaus and offices, providing support to bureaus and offices with respect to these data collections as well as support using the data for Continuity of Operations (COOP)/Emergency

COMMUNICATIONS AND MEDIA RESOURCES IN CONGRESS

For a complete listing of congressional committees, including their full contact information, leadership, membership, and jurisdictions, please refer to the Appendix on pages 840–963.

HOUSE:

House Appropriations Committee, (202) 225-2771.
Web, appropriations.house.gov
> **Subcommittee on Labor, Health and Human Services, Education, and Related Agencies,** (202) 225-3508.

House Energy and Commerce Committee, (202) 225-2927.
Web, energycommerce.house.gov
> **Subcommittee on Communications and Technology,** (202) 225-2927.

House Judiciary Committee, (202) 225-3951.
Web, judiciary.house.gov
> **Subcommittee on Courts, Intellectual Property, and the Internet,** (202) 225-5741.
> **Subcommittee on the Constitution, Civil Rights, and Civil Liberties,** (202) 225-3951.

House Science, Space, and Technology Committee, (202) 225-6375.
Web, science.house.gov
> **Subcommittee on Research and Technology,** (202) 225-6375.

JOINT:

Joint Committee on Printing, (202) 225-2061.
Web, cha.house.gov/jointcommittees/joint-committee-on-printing

Joint Committee on the Library, (202) 225-2061.
Web, cha.house.gov/jointcommittees/joint-committee-library

SENATE:

Senate Agriculture, Nutrition, and Forestry Committee, (202) 224-2035.
Web, agriculture.senate.gov
> **Subcommittee on Rural Development and Energy,** (202) 224-2035.

Senate Appropriations Committee, (202) 224-7363.
Web, appropriations.senate.gov
> **Subcommittee on Labor, Health and Human Services, Education, and Related Agencies,** (202) 224-7363.

Senate Commerce, Science, and Transportation Committee, (202) 224-0411.
Web, commerce.senate.gov
> **Subcommittee on Communications, Media, and Broadband,** (202) 224-0411.

Senate Judiciary Committee, (202) 224-7703.
Web, judiciary.senate.gov
> **Subcommittee on Competition Policy, Antitrust, and Consumer Rights,** (202) 224-3244.
> **Subcommittee on Criminal Justice and Counterterrorism,** (202) 224-2921.
> **Subcommittee on Privacy, Technology, and the Law,** (202) 224-7703.
> **Subcommittee on the Constitution,** (202) 224-6361.

Response Group (ERG)/Incident Management Team (IMT), and performing analyses and studies.

Federal Communications Commission (FCC), Engineering and Technology (OET), 45 L St. N.E., 20554; (202) 418-2470. Fax, (202) 418-1944. Ronald Repasi, Chief Engineer (Acting), (202) 418-0768. Lab, (301) 362-3000. General email, oetinfo@fcc.gov

Web, www.fcc.gov/engineering-technology

Advises the FCC on technical and spectrum matters and assists in developing U.S. telecommunications policy. Identifies and reviews developments in telecommunications and related technologies.

National Telecommunications and Information Administration (NTIA) (Commerce Dept.), 1401 Constitution Ave. N.W., #4898, 20230; (202) 482-1840. Alan Davidson, Assistant Secretary. Press, (202) 482-7002. Web, www.ntia.doc.gov, Twitter, @NTIAgov and Facebook, www.facebook.com/ntiagov

Develops domestic and international telecommunications policy for the executive branch; manages federal use of radio spectrum; conducts research on radiowave transmissions and other aspects of telecommunications; serves as information source for federal and state agencies on the efficient use of telecommunications resources.

▶CONGRESS

For a listing of relevant congressional committees and subcommittees, please see page 100 or the Appendix.

Library of Congress, *United States Copyright Office, Licensing Division,* James Madison Memorial Bldg., 101 Independence Ave. S.E., Copyright Office LD, 20559-6000; (202) 707-8150. Fax, (202) 707-0905. James (Jim) Enzinna, Chief, (202) 707-6801. Information, (202) 707-3000. General email, licensing@copyright.gov

Web, www.copyright.gov/licensing

Administers statutory licensing for cable television companies and satellite carriers, for making and distributing digital audio recording products, and for use of certain noncommercial broadcasting. Collects and distributes royalty payments under the copyright law. Administers

Section 115 licensing for making and distributing phono-records.

▶ NONGOVERNMENTAL

Accuracy in Media (AIM), *1717 K. St. N.W., #900, 20006; (202) 670-7729. Fax, (202) 364-4098. Adam Guillete, President; Donald (Don) K. Irvine, Publisher, ext 103.*
General email, info@aim.org
Web, www.aim.org, Twitter, @AccuracyInMedia and Facebook, www.facebook.com/AccuracyinMedia

Analyzes print and electronic news media for bias, omissions, and errors in news; approaches media with complaints. Maintains a speakers bureau and a library on political and media topics.

Alliance for Telecommunications Industry Solutions (ATIS), *1200 G St. N.W., #500, 20005; (202) 628-6380. Susan M. Miller, President, (202) 434-8828.*
General email, atispr@atis.org
Web, www.atis.org, Twitter, @atisupdates and Facebook, www.facaebook.com/atisdotorg

Membership; Develops and promotes the worldwide technical and operations standards for information, entertainment, and communications technologies. Sponsors industry forums; serves as an information clearinghouse. Member of the Inter-American Telecommunication Commission (CITEL). Monitors legislation and regulations.

Center for Media and Public Affairs (CMPA), *2338 S. Queen St., Arlington, VA 22202; (202) 302-5523. S. Robert Lichter, Director.*
Web, https://cmpa.gmu.edu and Twitter, @CMPAatGMU

Nonpartisan research and educational organization that studies media coverage of social and political issues and campaigns, specifically information about health risks, scientific matters, and presidential campaigns. Conducts surveys; publishes materials and reports. (Affiliated with George Mason University.)

Free Press, Washington Office, *1025 Connecticut Ave. N.W., #1110, 20036; (202) 265-1490. Fax, (202) 265-1489. Craig Aaron, Co-Chief Executive Officer; Jessica J. González, Co-Chief Executive Officer.*
Web, www.freepress.net, Twitter, @freepress and Facebook, www.facebook.com/freepress
Twitter Co-CEO, @notaaroncraig and
Twitter Co-CEO, @JGo4Justice
Email, info@freepress.net

Seeks to engage the public in media policymaking. Advocates policies for more competitive and public interest oriented media. Issue involved-free and open internet, media and platform accountability, the future of journalism, media control, privacy and surveillance. Headquarters in Florence, Mass.)

INCOMPAS, *1100 G St. N.W., #800, 20005; (202) 296-6650. Fax, (202) 296-7585. Chip Pickering, Chief Executive Officer.*
Web, www.incompas.org, Twitter, @INCOMPAS and Facebook, www.facebook.com/Incompas-196527610405296

Membership: broadband, cloud, business and enterprise, fiber, international, Internet, tower and backhaul, and wireless providers. Acts as advocate for the competitive telecommunications industry before Congress, the FCC, and state regulatory agencies; sponsors trade shows, conferences, and policy summits. Monitors legislation and regulations. (Formerly COMPTEL.)

Media Institute, *1901 N. Moore St., #804, Arlington, VA 22209; (703) 243-5700. Fax, (703) 243-8808. Richard T. Kapler, President, ext. 102.*
General email, info@mediainstitute.org
Web, www.mediainstitute.org and Twitter, @TheMediaInst

Research foundation that conducts conferences, files court briefs and regulatory comments, and sponsors programs on communications topics. Advocates a competitive media and communications industry and free-speech rights for individuals, media, and corporate speakers.

Media Matters for America, *P.O. Box 44811, 20026; (202) 756-4100. Angelo Carusone, President, ext. 165. Press, (202) 772-8195.*
General email, action@mediamatters.org
Web, www.mediamatters.org, Twitter, @mmfa and Facebook, www.facebook.com/Mediamatters

Web-based research and information center concerned with monitoring and analyzing print, broadcast, cable, radio, and Internet media for inaccurate news and commentary. Seeks to inform journalists and the general public about specific instances of misinformation and provide resources for taking action against false claims.

Media Research Center, *1900 Campus Commons Dr., #600, Reston, VA 20191; (571) 267-3500. Fax, (571) 375-0099. L. Brent Bozell III, President; David Martin, Executive Vice President. Toll-free, (800) 672-1423.*
General email, mrc@mrc.org
Web, www.mrc.org, Twitter, @theMRC and Facebook, www.facebook.com/mediaresearchcenter

Conservative media-watch organization working for balanced and responsible news coverage of political issues. Records and analyzes network news programs; analyzes print media; maintains profiles of media executives and library of recordings.

National Captioning Institute, *14801 Murdock St., #210, Chantilly, VA 20151; Gene Chao, Chief Executive Officer. TTY, (703) 917-7600.*
General email, marketing@ncicap.org
Web, www.ncicap.org, Twitter, @NCICAP and Facebook, www.facebook.com/ncicap

Captions television, cable, webcasting, home video, and DVD programs for the deaf and hard-of-hearing, and produces audio descriptions for the blind on behalf of public and commercial broadcast television networks, cable networks, syndicators, program producers, government agencies, advertisers, and home video distributors. Offers subtitling and language translation services.

Federal Communications Commission

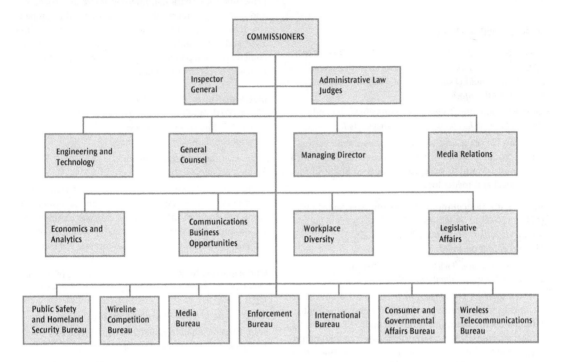

Produces and disseminates information about the national closed-captioning service and audio-description services.

TDI, *940 Thayer Ave., Silver Spring, MD 20910; Eric Kaika, Chief Executive Officer. Phone (voice/video), (301) 563-9112.*
General email, info@TDIforaccess.org
Web, https://tdiforaccess.org, Twitter, @TDIforAccess and Facebook, www.facebook.com/TDIforAccess

Membership: individuals, organizations, and businesses that advocate equal access to telecommunications, media, and information technologies for Americans who are deaf and hard of hearing. Interests include closed captioning for television, movies, DVDs, and online videos; emergency access (911); and TTY and Telecommunications Relay Services. Publishes a quarterly magazine and an annual resource directory. Monitors legislation and regulations.

Telecommunications Industry Assn. (TIA), *1310 N. Courthouse Rd., #890, Arlington, VA 22201; (703) 907-7700. Fax, (703) 907-7727. David Stehlin, Chief Executive Officer.*
General email, tia@tiaonline.org
Web, www.tiaonline.org, Twitter, @TIAonline, Facebook, www.facebook.com/TIAEvents and YouTube, www.youtube.com/user/TheTIANow

Trade association for the information and communications technology industry, including broadband, mobile wireless, information technology, networks, cable, satellite, and unified communications. Develops standards; provides market intelligence; analyzes environmental

regulations; hosts trade shows and facilitates business opportunities for members. Monitors legislation and regulations.

Cable Services

▶AGENCIES

Federal Communications Commission (FCC), *Media Bureau (MB), 45 L St. N.E., 20554; (202) 418-7200. Fax, (202) 418-2376. Holly Saurer, Chief, (202) 418-7283.*
General email, mediarelations@fcc.gov
Web, www.fcc.gov/media

Makes, recommends, and enforces rules governing cable television and other video distribution services; promotes industry growth, competition, and availability to the public; ensures reasonable rates for consumers in areas that do not have competition in cable service.

Federal Communications Commission (FCC), *Media Bureau (MB), Industry Analysis Division, 45 L St. N.E., 20554; (202) 418-2330. Brendan Holland, Chief, (202) 418-2757.*
Web, www.fcc.gov/media/industry/industry-analysis-division

Conducts and participates in proceedings regarding media ownership and the economic aspects of existing and proposed rules and policies; reviews license transfers; collects, compiles, analyzes, and develops reports on industry and market data and information and prepares annual report to Congress; conducts technical reviews of media-related matters and processes MVPD Registration, Cable Television Relay Service (CARS) applications.

Federal Communications Commission (FCC), Media Bureau (MB), Policy Division, 45 L St. N.E., 20554; (202) 418-2120. Fax, (202) 418-1069. Maria Mullarkey, Chief, (202) 418-1067.
Web, www.fcc.gov/media/policy/policy-division

Conducts proceedings concerning broadcast and cable issues. Facilitates competition in the multichannel video programming marketplace by resolving carriage and other complaints involving access to facilities. Administers FCC's programs for political broadcasting and equal opportunity matters. Interests include children's TV, closed captioning, digital broadcasting, leased access, low-power FM and TV, public broadcasting, and V-chip.

▶NONGOVERNMENTAL

CTAM: Cable and Telecommunications Assn. for Marketing, 120 Waterfront St., #200, National Harbor, MD 20745; (301) 485-8900. Fax, (301) 485-8898. Vicki Lins, President, (301) 485-8920.
General email, info@ctam.com
Web, www.ctam.com and Twitter, @CTAM

Promotes innovation in the cable and related industries in areas of marketing, research, management, and new product development. Sponsors annual marketing and research conferences; interests include international markets.

NCTA—The Internet and Television Assn., 25 Massachusetts Ave. N.W., #100, 20001; (202) 222-2300. Michael K. Powell, President. Government Relations, (202) 222-2410. Press, (202) 222-2350.
General email, info@ncta.com
Web, www.ncta.com, Twitter, @NCTAcable and Facebook, www.facebook.com/NCTAitv

Membership: companies that operate cable television systems, cable television programmers, and manufacturers and suppliers of hardware and software for the industry. Represents the industry before federal regulatory agencies, before Congress, and in the courts; provides management and promotional aids and information on legal, legislative, and regulatory matters. (Formerly the National Cable and Telecommunications Assn.)

Enforcement, Judicial, and Legal Actions

▶AGENCIES

Antitrust Division (Justice Dept.), Media, Entertainment, and Communications, 450 5th St. N.W., #7000, 20530; (202) 514-5621. Fax, (202) 514-6381. Yvette Tarlov, Chief (Acting), (202) 514-5808. Press, (202) 514-2007.
Web, www.justice.gov/atr/about-division/mec-section

Investigates and litigates antitrust cases dealing with communications, entertainment, and media. Participates

in agency proceedings and rulemaking concerning communications and media; monitors and analyzes legislation.

Federal Bureau of Investigation (FBI) (Justice Dept.), CALEA Implementation Unit, Engineering Research Facility, Bldg. 27958A, Quantico, VA 22135; (540) 361-4600. Fax, (540) 361-7082. Marybeth Paglino, NDCAC Director, (540) 361-2300. Toll-free, (855) 306-3222.
General email, askNDCAC@fbi.gov
Web, http://ndcac.fbi.gov/calea

Administers enforcement of the Communications Assistance for Law Enforcement Act (CALEA). Sets standards for telecommunications carriers concerning the development and deployment of electronic suveillance technologies. Promotes cooperation between the telecommunications industry, government entities, and law enforcement officials to develop intercept capabilities required by law enforcement.

Federal Communications Commission (FCC), Administrative Law Judges, 45 L St. N.E., 20554; (202) 418-2280. Fax, (202) 418-0195. Jane Hinckley Halprin, Administrative Law Judge.
Web, www.fcc.gov/administrative-law-judges

Presides over hearings and issues initial decisions in disputes concerning FCC adjudication proceedings and applications for licensing.

Federal Communications Commission (FCC), Enforcement Bureau (EB), 45 L St. N.E., 20554; (202) 418-7450. Fax, (202) 418-2810. Loyaan Egal, Chief (Acting). Press, (202) 418-0500. Toll-free, (888) 225-5322.
Web, www.fcc.gov/enforcement

Enforces the provisions of the Communications Act, the FCC's rules and orders, and various licensing terms and conditions. Investigates and responds to potential unlawful conduct to ensure consumer protection, robust competition, efficient and responsible use of the public airwaves, and compliance with public safety-related rules.

▶NONGOVERNMENTAL

Federal Bureau of Prisons (Justice Dept.), Federal Prison Industries, 320 1st St. N.W., 20534; (202) 305-3500. Patrick T. O'Connor, Chief Executive Officer. Customer Service, (800) 827-3168.
Web, www.bop.gov/about/agency/org_fpi.jsp and UNICOR, www.unicor.gov

Administers the inmate-training program operated by the Bureau of Prisons. FPI operates as a wholly owned, self-sustaining government corporation under the trade name UNICOR. FPI employs and provides skills training to federal inmates in diverse factory settings.

Federal Communications Bar Assn., 1020 19th St. N.W., #325, 20036-6101; (202) 293-4000. Fax, (202) 293-4317. Kerry Loughney, Executive Director.
General email, fcba@fcba.org
Web, www.fcba.org

Membership: attorneys, and other professionals, including engineers, consultants, economists, and government officials, involved in the development, interpretation and practice of communications and technology law and policywho practice before the Federal Communications Commission, the courts, and state and local regulatory agencies. Cooperates with the FCC and other members of the bar on legal aspects of communications issues.

Multicultural Media, Telecom, and Internet Council (MMTC), *1250 Connecticut Ave. N.W., 7th Floor, 20036; (202) 261-6543. Robert E. Branson, President.*
General email, info@mmtconline.org
Web, www.mmtconline.org, Twitter, @mmtconline and Facebook, www.facebook.com/mmtconline.com

Membership: lawyers, engineers, broadcasters, cablecasters, telecommunicators, and scholars. Promotes and preserves equal access, representation, and civil rights to minorities in the tech, media, and telecommunication industries. Represents civil rights groups before the FCC on issues concerning equal opportunity and diversity. Promotes equal opportunity and civil rights in the mass media and telecommunications industries. Operates nonprofit media brokerage and offers fellowships for lawyers and law students interested in FCC practice.

The Software Alliance (BSA), *20 F St. N.W., #800, 20001; (202) 872-5500. Fax, (202) 872-5501. Victoria A. Espinel, President.*
General email, info@bsa.org
Web, www.bsa.org, Twitter, @BSAnews and YouTube, www.youtube.com/user/BusinessSftAlliance

Investigates claims of software theft within corporations, financial institutions, academia, state and local governments, and nonprofit organizations. Provides legal counsel and initiates litigation on behalf of members.

Software and Information Industry Assn. (SIIA), *1090 Vermont Ave. N.W., 6th Floor, 20005-4905; (202) 289-7442. Fax, (202) 289-7097. Jeff Joseph, President, (202) 789-4440.*
Web, www.siia.net, Twitter, @SIIA and YouTube, www.youtube.com/channel/UCOggBEPEyAXDIh0U_JlSHyA

Membership: software and digital content companies. Conducts an antipiracy program and other intellectual property initiatives.

International and Satellite Communications

▶AGENCIES

Bureau of Economic and Business Affairs (EB) *(State Dept.), International Communications and Information Policy (CIP), 2201 C St. N.W., #4634, 20520-5820; (202) 647-5212. Fax, (202) 647-5957. Stephen C. Anderson, Deputy Assistant Secretary (Acting), (202) 647-5858.*
Web, www.state.gov/bureaus-offices/under-secretary-for-economic-growth-energy-and-the-environment/bureau-of-economic-and-business-affairs/division-for-inte

Coordinates U.S. government international communication and information policy. Acts as a liaison for other federal agencies and the private sector in international communications issues. Promotes advancement of information and communication technology with expanded access and improved efficiency and security; the creation of business opportunities at home and abroad in this sector; resolution of telecommunications trade issues in conjunction with the Office of the U.S. Trade Representative; and the expansion of access to this technology globally.

Federal Communications Commission (FCC), *International Bureau (IB), 45 L St. N.E., 20554; (202) 418-0437. Fax, (202) 418-2818. Tom Sullivan, Chief, (202) 418-0411.*
General email, contact_ib@fcc.gov
Web, www.fcc.gov/international and Blog, www.fcc.gov/news-events/blog/1621

Coordinates the FCC's international policy activities; represents the FCC in international forums. Licenses international telecommunications carriers, undersea cables, international short wave broadcasters, and satellite facilities. Coordinates the FCC's collection and dissemination of information on communications and telecommunications policy, regulation, and market developments in other countries and the policies and regulations of international organizations.

Federal Communications Commission (FCC), *Media Bureau (MB), Policy Division, 45 L St. N.E., 20554; (202) 418-2120. Fax, (202) 418-1069. Maria Mullarkey, Chief, (202) 418-1067.*
Web, www.fcc.gov/media/policy/policy-division

Conducts proceedings concerning postlicensing Direct Broadcast Satellite issues, including the Satellite Home Viewer Improvement Act.

National Telecommunications and Information Administration (NTIA) *(Commerce Dept.), 1401 Constitution Ave. N.W., #4898, 20230; (202) 482-1840. Alan Davidson, Assistant Secretary. Press, (202) 482-7002.*
Web, www.ntia.doc.gov, Twitter, @NTIAgov and Facebook, www.facebook.com/ntiagov

Represents the U.S. telecommunications sector (along with the State Dept.) in negotiating international agreements, including conferences with the International Telecommunication Union.

▶INTERNATIONAL ORGANIZATIONS

Inter-American Telecommunication Commission (CITEL) *(Organization of American States), 1889 F St. N.W., 6th Floor, 20006; (202) 370-4713. Fax, (202) 458-6854. Oscar Léon, Executive Secretary, (202) 370-0850.*
General email, citel@oas.org
Web, www.citel.oas.org and Twitter, @OEA_CITEL

Membership: OAS member states and associate members from the telecommunications, Internet, electronic, and media industries, and others. Works with the public and private sectors to facilitate the development of universal telecommunications in the Americas.

Satellite Industry Assn. (SIA), *1200 18th St. N.W., #975, 20036; (202) 503-1560. Tom Stroup, President.*
General email, info@sia.org
Web, https://sia.org and Twitter, @sia_satellite

Trade association representing global satellite operators, service providers, manufacturers, launch service providers, and ground equipment suppliers. Promotes the benefits and uses of commercial satellite technology. Monitors legislation and regulations, domestically and abroad.

Radio and Television

▶AGENCIES

Federal Communications Commission (FCC),
Enforcement Bureau (EB), 45 L St. N.E., 20554; (202) 418-7450. Fax, (202) 418-2810. Loyaan Egal, Chief (Acting). Press, (202) 418-0500. Toll-free, (888) 225-5322.
Web, www.fcc.gov/enforcement

Monitors the radio spectrum and inspects broadcast stations; ensures that U.S. radio laws and FCC rules are observed. Develops activities to inform, assist, and educate licensees; provides presentations and information. Manages the Emergency Alert System. Operates the National Call Center in Gettysburg, PA.

Federal Communications Commission (FCC),
Engineering and Technology (OET), 45 L St. N.E., 20554; (202) 418-2470. Fax, (202) 418-1944. Ronald Repasi, Chief Engineer (Acting), (202) 418-0768. Lab, (301) 362-3000.
General email, oetinfo@fcc.gov
Web, www.fcc.gov/engineering-technology

Studies characteristics of radio frequency spectrum. Certifies radios and other electronic equipment to meet FCC standards.

Federal Communications Commission (FCC), *Media Bureau (MB), 45 L St. N.E., 20554; (202) 418-7200. Fax, (202) 418-2376. Holly Saurer, Chief, (202) 418-7283.*
General email, mediarelations@fcc.gov
Web, www.fcc.gov/media

Responsible for the regulation of analog and digital broadcast services. Licenses, regulates, and develops audio and video services in traditional broadcasting and emerging television delivery systems, including digital television (DTV). Processes applications for licensing commercial and noncommercial radio and television broadcast equipment and facilities; handles renewals and changes of ownership; investigates public complaints.

Federal Communications Commission (FCC), *Media Bureau (MB), Policy Division, 45 L St. N.E., 20554; (202) 418-2120. Fax, (202) 418-1069. Maria Mullarkey, Chief, (202) 418-1067.*
Web, www.fcc.gov/media/policy/policy-division

Conducts proceedings concerning broadcast and cable issues. Facilitates competition in the multichannel video programming marketplace by resolving carriage and other complaints involving access to facilities. Administers FCC's programs for political broadcasting and equal opportunity matters. Interests include children's TV, closed captioning, digital broadcasting, leased access, low-power FM and TV, public broadcasting, and V-chip.

National Endowment for the Arts (NEA), *Media Arts, 400 7th St. S.W., 20506; (202) 682-5591. (202) 682-5452. Jax Deluca, Director, (202) 682-5742.*
Web, www.arts.gov

Awards grants to nonprofit organizations for film, video, and radio productions; supports arts programming broadcast nationally on public television and radio.

U.S. Agency for Global Media, *330 Independence Ave. S.W., #3300, 20237; (202) 203-4000. Kelu Chao, Chief Executive Officer (Acting), (202) 920-2342. Press, (202) 203-4400.*
General email, publicaffairs@usagm.gov
Web, www.usagm.gov, Twitter, @USAGMgov and Facebook, www.facebook.com/USAGMgov

Established by Congress to supervise all U.S. government nonmilitary international broadcasting, including Voice of America, Radio and TV Martí, Radio Free Europe/Radio Liberty, Radio Free Asia, and the Middle East Broadcasting Networks (MBN). Assesses the quality and effectiveness of broadcasts with regard to U.S. foreign policy objectives; reports annually to the president and to Congress.

▶NONGOVERNMENTAL

Corp. for Public Broadcasting (CPB), *401 9th St. N.W., 20004-2129; (202) 879-9600. Fax, (202) 879-9700. Patricia de Stacy Harrison, Chief Executive Officer. Comments, (800) 272-2190.*
General email, press@cpb.org
Web, www.cpb.org, Twitter, @CPBmedia and Facebook, www.facebook.com/CorporationForPublic Broadcasting

Private corporation chartered by Congress under the Public Broadcasting Act of 1967 and funded by the federal government. Helps support the operation of more than 1,400 locally owned and locally operated public television and radio stations nationwide; provides general support for national program production and operation, including content for underserved communities; helps fund projects on U.S. and international news, education, arts, culture, history, and natural history; invests in emerging technologies, such as cable and satellite transmission, the Internet, and broadband communication networks, for use by public media.

National Assn. of Broadcasters (NAB), *1 M St. S.E., 20003; (202) 429-5300. Curtis LeGeyt, President. Communications, (202) 429-5350.*

General email, nab@nab.org

Web, www.nab.org, Twitter, @nabtweets and Facebook, www.facebook.com/Broadcasters

Membership: radio and television broadcast stations and broadcast networks holding an FCC license or construction permit; associate members include producers of equipment and programs. Assists members in areas of management, engineering, and research. Monitors legislation and regulations.

National Public Radio, *1111 N. Capitol St. N.E., 20002; (202) 513-2000. Fax, (202) 513-3329. John Lansing, President. Press, (202) 513-2300.*
Web, www.npr.org, Twitter, @NPR and Facebook, www.facebook.com/NPR

Multimedia news organization composed of 849 member stations operated by 269 member organizations nationwide that are locally owned and operated. Produces and distributes news, music, and entertainment programming in all 50 states. Provides program distribution service via satellite. Represents member stations before Congress, the FCC, and other regulatory agencies. Supported by member station programming fees (about 40% of funding); corporate sponsorships; and institutional grants.

Public Broadcasting Service, *1225 S. Clark St., Arlington, VA 22202; (703) 739-5000. Fax, (703) 739-0775. Paula Kerger, President, (703) 739-5015; Ricardo Sandoval-Palos, Public Editor, (703) 739-5290.*
General email, viewer@pbs.org

Web, www.pbs.org, Twitter, @PBS and Facebook, www.facebook.com/pbs

Membership: public television stations nationwide. Selects, schedules, promotes, and distributes national programs; provides public television stations with educational, instructional, and cultural programming; also provides news and public affairs, science and nature, and children's programming. Assists members with technology development and fund-raising.

Telephone and Telegraph

For cellular telephones, see Wireless Telecommunications.

▶AGENCIES

Federal Communications Commission (FCC), *Wireline Competition Bureau (WCB), 45 L St. N.E., 20554; (202) 418-1500. Fax, (202) 418-2825. Trent Harkrader, Chief, (202) 418-2955.*
Web, www.fcc.gov/wireline-competition and Blog, www.fcc.gov/news-events/blog

Creates and recommends policy goals, objectives, programs, and plans for the FCC on matters concerning wireline telecommunications. Objectives include promoting competition in wireline services and markets, deregulation, encouraging economically efficient investment in wireline telecommunications infrastructure, expanding the availability of wireline telecommunications services, and fostering economic growth.

General Services Administration (GSA), *FCC's Telecommunications Relay Service (TRS), Formerly Federal Relay Service (FedRelay), 10304 Eaton Pl., Fairfax, VA 22030; (703) 306-6308.*
Tatyana Mezentseva, Customer Relationship Manager. Customer Service, (844) 472-4111. Speech-to-Speech, (877) 877-8982. TeleBraille, (866) 893-8340. TTY/ASCII, (800) 877-8339. VCO (Voice Carry Over), (877) 877-6280. Voice, (866) 377-8642. Customer Service, (855) 482-4348.
General email, ITCSC@gsa.gov

Web, www.gsa.gov/fedrelay

Provides telecommunications services for conducting official business with and within the federal government to individuals who are deaf or hard of hearing or who have speech disabilities. Federal Relay Service features are Voice, Text Telephone (TTY)/ASCII, HCO, Speech-to-Speech (STS), Spanish, Telebraille, Captioned Telephone Service (CTS), IP Relay, Video Relay Service (VRS), and Relay Conference Captioning (RCC) (including Spanish-to-Spanish captioning). For those with limited English proficiency, contact fas.car@gsa.gov, as services are available in Spanish, Vietnamese, Russian, Portuguese, Polish, Haitian, Creole, and Arabic.

▶NONGOVERNMENTAL

NTCA—The Rural Broadband Assn., *4121 Wilson Blvd., #1000, Arlington, VA 22203-1801; (703) 351-2000. Fax, (703) 351-2001. Shirley Bloomfield, Chief Executive Officer, (703) 351-2030. Government Affairs, (703) 351-2033.*
General email, membership@ntca.org

Web, www.ntca.org, Twitter, @ntcaconnect and Facebook, www.facebook.com/NTCARuralTelecom

Government Affairs, ga@ntca.org

Membership: locally owned and controlled telecommunications cooperatives and companies serving rural and small-town areas. Offers educational seminars, workshops, publications, technical assistance, and various employee benefits programs to members. Monitors legislation and regulations. (Formerly the National Telecommunications Cooperative Assn.)

U.S. Telecom Assn. (USTA), *601 New Jersey Ave. N.W., #600, 20001; (202) 326-7300. Jonathan Spalter, President.*
Web, www.ustelecom.org

Membership: broadband telecommunication service providers and manufacturers and suppliers for these companies. Provides members with information on the industry; conducts webinars; participates in FCC regulatory proceedings.

Wireless Telecommunications

►AGENCIES

Federal Communications Commission (FCC), *Wireless Telecommunications Bureau (WTB),* 45 L St. N.E., 20554; (202) 418-0600. Fax, (202) 418-0787. Joel Taubenblatt, Chief (Acting).
Web, www.fcc.gov/wireless-telecommunications and Blog, www.fcc.gov/news-events/blog/1638

Regulates domestic wireless communications, including cellular telephone, paging, personal communications services, public safety, air and maritime navigation, and other commercial and private radio services. Responsible for implementing the competitive bidding authority for spectrum auctions. Assesses new uses of wireless technologies, including electronic commerce. (Gettysburg office handles all licensing: FCC Wireless Telecommunications Bureau, Spectrum Management Resources and Technologies Division, 1270 Fairfield Rd., Gettysburg, PA 17325; [717] 338-2510.)

►NONGOVERNMENTAL

CTIA—The Wireless Assn., 1400 16th St. N.W., #600, 20036; (202) 736-3200. Meredith Baker, President, ext. 3663. General email, ctiamedrel@ctia.org
Web, www.ctia.org, Twitter, @CTIA and Facebook, www.facebook.com/CTIA.EverythingWireless

Membership: system operators, equipment manufacturers, engineering firms, and others engaged in the cellular telephone and mobile communications industry in domestic and world markets. Monitors legislation and regulations.

Enterprise Wireless Alliance (EWA), 2121 Cooperative Way, #225, Herndon, VA 20171; (703) 528-5115. Fax, (703) 524-1074. Mark Crosby, Chief Strategy Officer, (703) 797-5114. Toll-free, (800) 482-8282. General email, info@enterprisewireless.org
Web, www.enterprisewireless.org

Membership: enterprise wireless companies, dealers, and trade associations. Serves as an information source on radio frequencies, licensing, new products and technology, and market conditions. Monitors legislation and regulations.

Utilities Technology Council (UTC), 2550 S. Clark St., #960, Arlington, VA 22202; (202) 872-0030. Fax, (202) 872-1331. Sheryl Osiene Riggs, President. General email, marketing@utc.org
Web, www.utc.org and Twitter, @UTCNow

Membership: companies that own, manage, or provide critical telecommunications systems in support of their core business, including energy, gas, and water utility companies, pipeline companies, and radio and international critical infrastructure organizations. Participates in FCC rulemaking proceedings. Interests include fiber security; radio spectrum for fixed and mobile wireless communication; and technological, legislative, and regulatory

developments affecting telecommunications operations of energy utilities.

WIA: The Wireless Infrastructure Assn., 2111 Wilson Blvd., #210, Arlington, VA 22201; (703) 739-0300. Fax, (703) 836-1608. Jonathan Adelstein, President. Press, (703) 462-1445. Toll-free, (800) 759-0300. Web, www.wia.org and Twitter, @WIAorg

Represents companies that make up the wireless telecommunications infrastructure industry. Supports wireless communications and information infrastructure.

GOVERNMENT INFORMATION

General

►AGENCIES

General Services Administration (GSA), *Government-wide Policy (OGP), Information, Integrity, and Access,* 1800 F St. N.W., #M1E, 20405; (202) 208-0598. Daniel Pomeroy, Deputy Associate Administrator. Web, www.gsa.gov/governmentwide-initiatives/information-integrity-and-access

Develops, coordinates, and defines ways that electronic and information technology business strategies can assist the Office of Management and Budget and other federal agencies to enhance access to and delivery of information and services to citizens.

General Services Administration (GSA), *Technology Transformation Service,* 1800 F St. N.W., 2nd Floor, 20405; (202) 702-0781. Dave Zvenyach, Commissioner. Main Phone, (844) 872-4681. General email, tts-info@gsa.gov
Web, www.gsa.gov/about-us/organization/federal-acquisition-service/technology-transformation-services

Utilizes current methodologies and technologies to improve the way the federal government provides the public with access to information and services. Works to aid agencies in creating services that are more understandable, attainable, and beneficial to the public.

General Services Administration (GSA), *USAGov,* 1800 F St. N.W., 20405; (844) 872-4681. General email, USAContace@gsa.gov
Web, www.gsa.gov

Manages the portal site to U.S. government information, www.usa.gov. Manages kids.gov, a resource that provides government information on education, including primary, secondary, and higher education. Distributes free and low-cost federal publications of consumer interest via the Internet at www.usa.gov and Pueblo.gpo.gov. Assists people with questions about American government agencies, programs, and services via telephone, (800) FED-INFO ([800] 333-4636), or website, http://answers.usa.gov. Operates a contact center to provide information in English or Spanish on all federal government agencies, programs, and services via toll-free telephone, email, and

Chief Information Officers for Federal Departments and Agencies

DEPARTMENTS

Agriculture, Gary Washington, (202) 720-8833

Commerce, André Mendes, (202) 482-4797

Defense, John Sherman (Acting), (703) 695-0348

　Air Force, Vacant, (703) 697-1361

　Army, Raj Iyer, (703) 695-4366

　Navy, Aaron Weis, (703) 695-1840

Education, Jason Gray, (202) 245-6252

Energy, Rocky Campione, (202) 586-0166

Health and Human Services, Perryn Ashmore (Acting), (202) 690-6162

Homeland Security, Eric Hysen, (202) 282-8000

Housing and Urban Development, Vacant, (202) 708-0306

Interior, William Vajda, (202) 208-6194

Justice, Melinda Rogers, (202) 514-0507

Labor, Gundeep Ahluwalia, (202) 693-4446

State, Keith Jones, (202) 647-2889

Transportation, Vacant, (202) 366-9201

Treasury, Eric Olson, (202) 622-1200

Veterans Affairs, Dominic Cussatt, (202) 461-6910

AGENCIES

Environmental Protection Agency, Vaughn Noga, (202) 566-0307

Federal Communications Commission, Francisco Salguero, (202) 418-0248

Federal Emergency Management Agency, Lytwaive Hutchinson, (202) 646-3006

Federal Trade Commission, Raghav Vajjhala, (202) 326-2667

General Services Administration, David A. Shive, (202) 501-1000

Government Accountability Office, Howard Williams, (202) 512-5589

Government Publishing Office, Layton Clay (Acting), (202) 512-1040

National Aeronautics and Space Administration, Jeffrey Seaton, (202) 358-1824

National Archives and Records Administration, Swarnali Haldar, (301) 837-1583

National Endowment for the Humanities, Brett Bobley, (202) 606-8401

National Science Foundation, Dorothy E. Aronson, (703) 292-4299

Nuclear Regulatory Commission, David Nelson, (301) 415-8700

Office of Management and Budget, Maria Roat (Acting), (202) 395-3080

Office of Personnel Management, Clare Martorana, (202) 418-3093

Office of the Director of National Intelligence, Vacant, (301) 243-1295

Securities and Exchange Commission, David Bottom, (202) 551-8800

Small Business Administration, Keith A. Bluestein, (202) 205-6708

Social Security Administration, Sean Brune, (410) 929-4774

---

chat. Operated under contract by Sykes in Pennsylvania and Florida. Responds to inquiries about federal programs and services. Gives information about or referrals to appropriate offices.

National Archives and Records Administration (NARA),
700 Pennsylvania Ave. N.W., 20408 (mailing address: 8601 Adelphi Rd., College Park, MD 20704-6001); (866) 272-6272. Fax, (202) 357-5901. David S. Ferriero, Archivist of the United States, (202) 357-5900. Public Affairs, (202) 357-5300. Public programs and events, (202) 357-5000. Web, www.archives.gov and Twitter, @USNatArchives

Identifies, preserves, and makes available federal government documents of historic value; administers a network of regional storage centers and archives and operates the presidential library system. Collections include photographs, graphic materials, films, and maps; holdings include records generated by foreign governments (especially in war time) and by international conferences, commissions, and exhibitions.

National Archives and Records Administration (NARA),
Agency Services, 8601 Adelphi Rd., #3600, College Park, MD 20740-6001; (301) 837-3064. Fax, (301) 837-1617. Jay Trainer, Executive.

Web, www.archives.gov and Agency Services, www.archives.gov/foia/directives/nara0101-part07

Manages the federal record centers throughout the country. Works with the record managers to feed records into the National Archives. Oversees the National Declassification Center, the Office of Government Information Services, and the Information Security Oversight Office.

National Archives and Records Administration (NARA),
Electronic Records Division (ERA), 8601 Adelphi Rd., #5320, College Park, MD 20740-6001; (301) 837-0740. Theodore J. Hull, Director, (301) 837-1824. General email, era.program@nara.gov

Web, www.archives.gov/records-mgmt/era/technical.html

Preserves, maintains, and makes available electronic records of the U.S. government. Provides researchers with magnetic tape, CDs, DVDs, and other copies of electronic records on a cost-recovery basis. Offers direct downloads and searches of selected holdings.

National Archives and Records Administration (NARA),
Federal Register (OFR), 7 G St. N.W., #A-734, 20401 (mailing address: NF, 8601 Adelphi Rd., College Park, MD 20740-6001); (202) 741-6000. Fax, (202) 741-6012.

Oliver A. Potts, Director, (202) 741-6100. TTY, (202) 741-6086.
General email, fedreg.info@nara.gov
Web, www.archives.gov/federal-register,
Twitter, @FedRegister
Legal, fedreg.legal@nara.gov

Informs citizens of their rights and obligations by providing access to the official texts of federal laws, presidential documents, administrative regulations and notices, and descriptions of federal organizations, programs, and activities. Provides online and in-person access to documents on file before their publication. Administers the Electoral College and the constitutional amendment process. Publications available from the U.S. Government Printing Office, (301) 317-3953, http://bookstore.gpo.gov.

National Archives and Records Administration (NARA), *Presidential Libraries,* 8601 Adelphi Rd., #2200, College Park, MD 20740-6001; (301) 837-3250. Fax, (301) 837-3199. Susan K. Donius, Director, (202) 357-7451.
Web, www.archives.gov/presidential-libraries and Twitter, @OurPresidents

Administers thirteen presidential libraries. Directs all programs relating to acquisition, preservation, and research use of materials in presidential libraries; conducts oral history projects; publishes finding aids for research sources; provides reference service, including information from and about documentary holdings. Conducts community outreach; oversees museum exhibition programming.

National Archives and Records Administration (NARA), *Reference Services,* 4205 Suitland Rd., Suitland, MD 20746-8001; (301) 778-1600. Channon Harris, Director, (301) 778-1562.
General email, suitland.reference@nara.gov
Web, www.archives.gov/frc/reference-services.html

Provides reference service for unpublished civil and military federal government records. Maintains central catalog of all archival materials. Compiles comprehensive bibliographies of materials related to archival administration and records management. Permits research in American history, archival science, and records management. Maintains collections of the papers of the Continental Congress (1774–1789), U.S. State Dept. diplomatic correspondence (1789–1963), and general records of the U.S. government.

National Archives and Records Administration (NARA), *Research Services,* 8601 Adelphi Rd., #3400, College Park, MD 20740-6001; (301) 837-2000. Fax, (301) 837-3633. Chris C. Naylor, Executive for Research Services, (301) 837-3110. Toll-free, (866) 272-6272.
Web, www.archives.gov/research
Email, Inquires@nara.gov

Preserves and makes available federal records at fifteen National Archives facilities across the country.

National Security Staff (NSS) *(Executive Office of the President), Speechwriting and Strategic Initiatives,* Dwight D. Eisenhower Executive Office Bldg., Pennsylvania Ave. and 17th St. N.W., #302, 20500; (202) 456-1414. Carlyn Reichel, Senior Director. Administrative / Security Office, (202) 456-9301.
Web, www.whitehouse.gov

Advises U.S. government agencies on the direction and theme of the president's message. Assists in the development and coordination of communications programs that disseminate consistent and accurate messages about the U.S. government and policies to the global audience.

National Technical Information Service (NTIS) *(Commerce Dept.),* 5301 Shawnee Rd., Alexandria, VA 22312; (703) 605-6000. Fax, (703) 605-6900. Greg Capella, Director (Acting). Customer support, (703) 605-6060. Toll-free, (800) 363-2068. TTY, (703) 487-4639.
General email, info@ntis.gov
Web, www.ntis.gov, Twitter, @NTISInfo and Facebook, www.facebook.com/NTISCustomerContact Center

Collects and organizes technical, scientific, engineering, and business-related information generated by U.S. and foreign governments and makes it available for commercial use in the private sector. Makes available approximately 3 million works covering research and development, current events, business and management studies, translations of foreign open source reports, foreign and domestic trade, general statistics, environment and energy, health and social sciences, and hundreds of other areas. Provides computer software and computerized data files in a variety of formats, including Internet downloads. Houses the Homeland Security Information Center, a centralized source on major security concerns for health and medicine, food and agriculture, and biochemical war.

Office of Management and Budget (OMB) *(Executive Office of the President), Information and Regulatory Affairs,* 725 17th St. N.W., #10236, 20503; (202) 395-5897. Fax, (202) 395-6102. Dominic J. Mancini, Deputy Administrator.
Web, www.whitehouse.gov/omb/information-regulatory-affairs

Oversees implementation and policy development under the Information Technology Reform Act of 1996 and the Paperwork Reduction Act of 1995; focuses on information technology management and substantive information policy, including records management, privacy, and computer security, and the Freedom of Information Act.

▶ **CONGRESS**

For a listing of relevant congressional committees and subcommittees, please see page 100 or the Appendix.

Government Accountability Office (GAO), *Public Affairs,* 441 G St. N.W., Room 7149, 20548; (202) 512-4800. Charles (Chuck) Young, Managing Director, (202) 512-3823. Publications orders, (202) 512-6000.
General email, contact@gao.gov
Web, www.gao.gov/about/contact-us

Publications Contacts at Federal Departments and Agencies

Many publications for federal departments and agencies may be available through the Government Publishing Office (GPO) and the National Technical Information Service (NTIS). For GPO and NTIS contact information, see below.

GENERAL

Government Publishing Office (GPO), (202) 512-1800 or (866) 512-1800; Fax, (202) 512-2104; www.gpo.gov

House Document Room, (202) 226-5210; https://clerk.house.gov/about/offices_lrc.aspx

Library of Congress, Orders, (202) 707-5093; www.loc.gov/publish

National Technical Information Service (NTIS), (703) 605-6000 or (800) 553-6847; www.ntis.gov

DEPARTMENTS

Agriculture, Information, (301) 504-5755 or (800) 633-7701; TTY, (301) 504-6856; Orders via NTIS; www.nal.usda.gov/main/publications

Commerce, Orders via NTIS; www.commerce.gov/ofm/publications

Defense, Orders via NTIS; www.defense.gov/pubs

Education, Orders, (877) 433-7827; TTY, (877) 576-7734; www2.ed.gov/about/pubs/intro/index.html

Energy, Orders via NTIS and GPO; www.energy.gov/eere/services/publications

Health and Human Services, Information, (877) 696-6775; https://oig.hhs.gov/reports-and-publications/index.asp

Homeland Security, Information, (202) 282-8000; www.dhs.gov/publications

Housing and Urban Development, Orders, (800) 767-7468; Materials related to lead paint, (800) 424-5323; www.hud.gov/program_offices/administration/handbks_forms

Justice, Orders, (800) 851-3420; www.justice.gov/publications or www.justice.gov/archive/index-publications.htm

Labor, Statistics orders, (202) 691-5200; Employee benefits, (866) 444-3272; Audits and other reports, www.oig.dol.gov/auditreports.htm; www.dol.gov/dol/topic/statistics/publications.htm

State, Orders via GPO; www.state.gov/department-reports

Transportation, Orders via NTIS; www.fhwa.dot.gov/publications

Treasury, Orders via NTIS and GPO; www.treasury.gov/tigta/publications.shtml or www.govinfo.gov/collection/treasury-department

Veterans Affairs, www.va.gov/opa/publications

AGENCIES

Census Bureau, Orders, (301) 763-4636 or (800) 923-8282; https://census.gov/library/publications.html

Commission on Civil Rights, Orders, (202) 376-8128; Email, publications@usccr.gov; www.usccr.gov/pubs

Consumer Product Safety Commission, Orders, info@cpsc.gov; Information, (800) 638-2772; www.cpsc.gov/en/Safety-Education/Safety-Guides/General-Information/Publications-Listing

Corp. for National and Community Service (AmeriCorps), Orders, (800) 942-2677; TTY, (800) 833-3722; https://promote.americorps.gov

Energy Information Administration, Orders, (202) 586-8800; www.eia.gov/reports

Environmental Protection Agency, Orders, (800) 490-9198; www.epa.gov/nscep

---

Provides information to the public and media on federal programs, reports, and testimonies; organizes press interviews with GAO officials. GAO publications and information about GAO publications are available upon request in print or online.

Government Publishing Office (GPO), *732 N. Capitol St. N.W., 20401; (202) 512-1800. Hugh N. Halpern, Director. Toll-free, (866) 512-1800.*
General email, contactcenter@gpo.gov
Web, www.gpo.gov, Twitter, @USGPO and Facebook, www.facebook.com/USGPO

The federal government's official digital secure resource for producing, procuring, cataloging, indexing, authenticating, disseminating, and preserving the official information products of the U.S. government. Responsible for the production and distribution of information products and services for all three branches of the federal government, including U.S. passports for the State Dept. as well as the official publications of Congress, the White House, and other federal agencies in digital and print formats. Provides for free permanent public access to federal government information through the Federal Digital System (www.fdsys.gov), partnerships with approximately 1,200 libraries nationwide participating in the Federal Depository Library Program, and a secure online bookstore.

Government Publishing Office (GPO), *Contact Center, 732 N. Capitol St. N.W., MS IDCC, 20401; (202) 512-1800. Fax, (202) 512-2104. Lisa Williams, Director, (202) 512-1065. Toll-free, (866) 512-1800.*
General email, contactcenter@gpo.gov
Web, https://bookstore.gpo.gov/customer-service/contact-us

Provides customer service for the federal government's official digital secure resource for producing, procuring, cataloging, indexing, authenticating, disseminating, and preserving the official information products of the U.S. government.

Government Publishing Office (GPO), *Security and Intelligent Documents Unit (SID), 732 N. Capitol St.*

Equal Employment Opportunity Commission, Orders,
(202) 663-4191; TTY, (202) 663-4494;
www.eeoc.gov/eeoc-publications

Federal Communications Commission, Orders,
(202) 418-7512; www.fcc.gov/reports-research

Federal Election Commission, Orders, (800) 424-9530;
www.fec.gov/about/reports-about-fec

Federal Emergency Management Agency, Orders,
(800) 480-2520; www.ready.gov/publications

Federal Reserve System, Orders, (202) 452-3245;
www.federalreserve.gov/publications.htm

Federal Trade Commission, Orders, (877) 382-4357;
https://bulkorder.ftc.gov or www.consumer.ftc.gov

General Services Administration, Orders, (800) 488-3111;
www.gsa.gov/buying-selling/purchasing-programs/
requisition-programs/gsa-global-supply/easy-ordering-
options

Government Accountability Office, Orders,
(202) 512-6000; Toll-free, (866) 801-7077;
TTY, (202) 512-2537; www.gao.gov/reports-testimonies

**International Bank for Reconstruction and
Development (World Bank),** Orders, (703) 661-1580;
Toll-free, (800) 645-7247; Fax, (703) 661-1501;
www.worldbank.org/en/research

International Trade Administration, Orders via NTIS and
GPO; https://trade.gov/publications

National Aeronautics and Space Administration,
Orders, (202) 358-0168;
www.nasa.gov/centers/hq/library/about

National Archives and Records Administration, Orders,
(202) 357-5332; Toll-free, (866) 272-6272;
www.archives.gov/publications

National Endowment for the Humanities, Orders,
(202) 606-8435; www.neh.gov/content/office-publications

National Park Service, Orders by mail only;
www.nps.gov/aboutus/publications.htm

National Science Foundation, Orders, (703) 292-5111;
TTY, (703) 292-5090 or (800) 281-8749;
Email, warehouse@nsf.gov; www.nsf.gov/publications

National Transportation Safety Board, Information,
(202) 314-6000; www.ntsb.gov/publications/Pages/
default.aspx; postpublication orders via NTIS.

Nuclear Regulatory Commission, Orders, (301) 415-4737
or (800) 397-4209; Orders also from GPO;
www.nrc.gov/reading-rm/pdr.html

Occupational Safety and Health Administration, Orders,
(202) 693-1888; Email, oshapubrequest@dol.gov;
www.osha.gov/publications

Office of Personnel Management, Orders via GPO;
Information, (202) 606-1800;
https://apps.opm.gov/publications

Peace Corps, (855) 855-1961;
www.peacecorps.gov/about/open-government/reports

Securities and Exchange Commission, Orders,
(202) 551-4040; Public documents, (202) 551-8090;
www.sec.gov/reports

Social Security Administration, Orders, (410) 965-2039;
Fax, (410) 965-2037; www.ssa.gov/pubs

U.S. Fish and Wildlife Service, Orders, (703) 358-2196;
Orders via NTIS; www.fws.gov/external-affairs/marketing-
communications/printing-and-publishing

U.S. Geological Survey, Information, (888) 275-8747;
Congressional publishing, (703) 648-4455;
https://store.usgs.gov/books-reports-publications

U.S. Institute of Peace, Orders, (800) 868-8064 or
(703) 661-1590; Fax, (703) 661-1501;
Email, usipmail@presswarehouse.com;
https://bookstore.usip.org/pages/order

N.W., 20401; (202) 512-1000. Stephen (Steve) G. LeBlanc,
Managing Director.
Web, www.gpo.gov

Works with other federal agencies to ensure the safe
and secure design, production, and distribution of security
and intelligence documents such as U.S. passports, travel
documents, immigration forms, and other secure credentials for federal agencies.

Library of Congress, *Federal Library and Information
Network (FEDLINK), John Adams Bldg., 101
Independence Ave. S.E., #LA 217, 20540-4935; (202) 707-
4800. Laurie Neider, Executive Director, (202) 707-4801;
Robin Harvey, Editor-in-Chief, (202) 707-4820;
Melissa Blaschke, Supervising Librarian, (202) 707-2457.
FEDLINK Hotline, (202) 707-4900.
General email, fliccffo@loc.gov*

Web, www.loc.gov/flicc

Organization of federal agencies working together
relating to resources and facilities of federal libraries
and information centers. Promotes common services,

coordinates resources, provides professional education for
federal library and information staff. Serves as a forum for
discussion of federal library and information policies, programs, and procedures; helps inform Congress, federal
agencies, and others concerned with libraries and information centers.

Library of Congress, *Serial and Government
Publications Division, James Madison Memorial Bldg.,
101 Independence Ave. S.E., #LM 133, 20540-4760; (202)
707-5690. Deborah Thomas, Chief.*
Web, www.loc.gov/rr/news

Operates Newspaper and Current Periodical Reading
Room; maintains library's collection of domestic and foreign newspapers, current periodicals, comic books, and
current serially issued publications of federal, state, and
foreign governments; maintains a selective U.S. federal
government publication depository since 1979, a United
Nations document collection, and a Federal Advisory
Committee (FAC) collection. Responds to written or
telephone requests for information on newspapers,

periodicals, or government publications, or online through Ask a Librarian. Lends some microfilm through interlibrary loans. Timed entry pass for visitors required, details at loc.gov/visit. Appointments recommended for researchers.

Senate Historical Office, *201 SHOB, 20510; (202) 224-6900. Betty K. Koed, Historian.*
General email, historian@sec.senate.gov

Web, www.senate.gov/artandhistory/history/common/ generic/Senate_Historical_Office.htm and
Twitter, @SenateHistory

Serves as an information clearinghouse on Senate history, traditions, and members. Collects, organizes, and distributes to the public unpublished Senate documents; collects and preserves photographs and pictures related to Senate history; conducts an oral history program; advises senators and Senate committees on the disposition of their noncurrent papers and records. Produces publications on the history of the Senate.

U.S. House of Representatives, *Legislative Resource Center, B81 CHOB, 20515-6612; (202) 226-5200. Ronald (Dale) Thomas, Chief.*
General email, info.clerkweb@mail.house.gov

Web, http://clerk.house.gov/about/view/LRCDetailss

Provides legislative information, records and registration, historical information, and library services to the House and the public. Reading room contains computer terminals where collections may be viewed or printed out. Print publications include a biographical directory, a guide to research collections of former House members, and books on African Americans and women who have served in Congress. Collections include House and Senate journals (1st Congress to present); *Congressional Record* and its predecessors (1st Congress to present); House reports, documents, bills, resolutions, and hearings; Senate reports and documents; U.S. statutes, treaties, the *Federal Register*, U.S. codes, and numerous other documents. (See website or call for a complete list of collections.)

U.S. House of Representatives, *Office of History, Art, and Archives, B53 CHOB, 20515; (202) 226-1300. Fax, (202) 226-4635. Farar P. Elliott, Chief. Legislative Archives, (202) 357-5350. Toll-free, (866) 272-6272.*
General art email, art@mail.house.gov

General archives email, archives@mail.house.gov

Web, http://history.house.gov, Twitter, @USHouseHistory and YouTube, www.youtube.com/USHouseHistory

Works with the Office of the Historian to provide access to published documents and historical records of the House. Advises members on the disposition of their records and papers; maintains information on manuscript collections of former members; maintains biographical files on former members; houses photographs and artifacts of former members. Produces publications on Congress and its members.

U.S. House of Representatives, *Office of the Historian, B53 CHOB, 20515; (202) 226-1300.*

Matthew A. Wasniewski, House Historian. Legislative Archives, (202) 357-5350.
General email, history@mail.house.gov

Web, http://history.house.gov and
Twitter, @ushousehistory

Works with the Office of Art and Archives to provide access to published documents and historical records of the House. Conducts historical research. Advises members on the disposition of their records and papers; maintains information on manuscript collections of former members; maintains biographical files on former members. Produces publications on Congress and its members.

Freedom of Information

▶**AGENCIES**

Justice Dept. (DOJ), *Information Policy (OIP), GAO Bldg., 441 G St. N.W., 6th Floor, 20530-0001; (202) 514-3642. Fax, (202) 514-1009. Bobak (Bobby) Talebian, Director.*
General email, doj.oip.foia@usdoj.gov

Web, www.justice.gov/oip

Provides federal agencies with advice and policy guidance on matters related to implementing and interpreting the Freedom of Information Act (FOIA). Processes FOIA requests on behalf of the Department's Senior Leadership Offices; adjudicates administrative appeals from Justice Dept. denials of public requests for access to documents; litigates selected FOIA and Privacy Act cases; conducts FOIA training for government agencies.

National Archives and Records Administration (NARA), *Information Security Oversight (ISOO), 700 Pennsylvania Ave. N.W., #100, 20408-0001; (202) 357-5250. Fax, (202) 357-5907. Mark A. Bradley, Director, (202) 357-5205.*
General email, isoo@nara.gov

Web, www.archives.gov/isoo

Receiving guidance from the National Security Council, oversees policy on security classification/declassification on documents and programs for the federal government and industry; develops policies and procedures for sensitive unclassified information.

National Archives and Records Administration (NARA), *National Declassification Center (NDC), 8601 Adelphi Rd., #6350, College Park, MD 20740; (301) 837-0405. Fax, (301) 837-0346. William P. Fischer, Director, (301) 837-0407. Released records requests, (301) 837-3510.*
General email, ndc@nara.gov

Web, www.archives.gov/declassification/ndc

Released records requests, archives2reference@nara.gov

Directs the review and declassification of records and security-classified materials in the National Archives in accordance with Executive Order 13526 and the Freedom of Information Act; assists other federal archival agencies in declassifying security-classified documents in their

Public Affairs Contacts at Federal Departments and Agencies

DEPARTMENTS

Agriculture, Tara Weaver-Missick, (202) 720-1375

Commerce, Brittany Caplin, (202) 482-4883

Defense, John F. Kirby, (703) 697-5131

   Air Force, Brig. Gen. Patrick S. Ryder, (240) 612-6464

   Army, Brig. Gen. Amy E. Hannah, (703) 693-4723

   Marine Corps, Philip J. Kulczewski, (703) 614-4309

   Navy, Rear Adm. Charles M. Brown, (703) 697-5342

Education, Nathan Bailey, (202) 401-2000

Energy, Karla Olsen, (202) 586-4940

Health and Human Services, Mark Weber (Acting), (202) 690-6343

Homeland Security, Marsha Catron Espinosa, (202) 282-8010

   Coast Guard, David French, (202) 372-4630

Housing and Urban Development, Addie Whisenant, (202) 708-0980

Interior, Andrew Wallace, (202) 208-7693

Justice, Anthony Coley, (202) 514-2007

Labor, Elizabeth Alexander, (202) 693-4676

State, Jennifer Hall Godfrey, (202) 647-6088

Transportation, Dani Simons, (202) 366-4570

Treasury, Marti Adams, (202) 622-2960

Veterans Affairs, Kayla M. Williams, (202) 461-7500

AGENCIES

Advisory Council on Historic Preservation, Lynne Richmond, (202) 517-1484

Agency for International Development, Amy Paro, (202) 712-4320

Commission on Civil Rights, Angelia Rorison, (202) 376-8371

Commodity Futures Trading Commission, Mollie Wilken, (202) 418-5080

Consumer Product Safety Commission, Joseph Martyak, (301) 504-7599

Corp. for National and Community Service, Samantha Jo Warfield, (202) 606-6775

Environmental Protection Agency, Lindsay Hamilton, (202) 564-4355

Equal Employment Opportunity Commission, Patricia Crawford, (202) 663-4191

Export-Import Bank, Vacant, (202) 565-3200

Farm Credit Administration, Michael A. Stokke, (703) 883-4056

Federal Communications Commission, Janice Wise, (202) 418-0500

Federal Deposit Insurance Corp., Amy C. Thompson, (202) 898-6993

Federal Election Commission, Vacant, (202) 694-1681

Federal Emergency Management Agency, Justin Knighten, (202) 646-3272

Federal Labor Relations Authority, Aloysius Hogan, (202) 218-7927

Federal Mediation and Conciliation Service, Gregory Goldstein, (202) 606-8081

Federal Reserve System, Eric S. Belsky, (202) 452-2955

Federal Trade Commission, Cathy MacFarlane, (202) 326-2180

General Services Administration, Teressa Wykpisz-Lee, (202) 208-0128

Government Accountability Office, Charles Young, (202) 512-4800

Government Publishing Office, Gary Somerset, (202) 512-1957

Institute of Museum and Library Services, Elizabeth Holtan, (202) 653-4630

National Aeronautics and Space Administration, Jackie McGuinness, (202) 568-2330

National Archives and Records Administration, Megan Phillips, (202) 357-5400

National Capital Planning Commission, Julia Koster, (202) 482-7211

National Credit Union Administration, Ben C. Hardaway, (703) 518-6330

National Endowment for the Arts, Sonia Tower, (202) 682-5606

National Endowment for the Humanities, Paula Wasley, (202) 606-8446

National Institute of Standards and Technology, Jennifer Huergo, (301) 975-6343

National Labor Relations Board, Vacant, (202) 273-1991

National Science Foundation, Amanda Hallberg Greenwell, (703) 292-8070

National Transportation Safety Board, Christopher O'Neil, (202) 314-6100

Nuclear Regulatory Commission, David Castelveter, (301) 415-8200

Occupational Safety and Health Review Commission, Vacant, (202) 606-5370

Office of Personnel Management, Laura Goulding, (202) 606-2402

Office of Special Counsel, Zachary Kurz, (202) 804-7065

Pension Benefit Guaranty Corp., Martha Threatt, (202) 326-4343; TTY, (800) 877-8339

Securities and Exchange Commission, John Nester, (202) 551-4120

Selective Service System, Michael A. Migliara, (703) 605-4017

Small Business Administration, Cynthia Jasso-Rotunno, (202) 205-6919

Social Security Administration, Mark Hinkle, (410) 929-4774

U.S. International Trade Commission, Peg O'Laughlin, (202) 205-1819

U.S. Postal Service, Dave Partenheimer, (202) 268-2155

holdings. Requests to access newly released records can be submitted through Archives II Reference.

Office of Management and Budget (OMB) *(Executive Office of the President), Information and Regulatory Affairs, 725 17th St. N.W., #10236, 20503; (202) 395-5897. Fax, (202) 395-6102. Dominic J. Mancini, Deputy Administrator.*
Web, www.whitehouse.gov/omb/information-regulatory-affairs

Oversees implementation and policy development under the Information Technology Reform Act of 1996 and the Paperwork Reduction Act of 1995; focuses on information technology management and substantive information policy, including records management, privacy, and computer security, and the Freedom of Information Act.

▶ **NONGOVERNMENTAL**

American Civil Liberties Union (ACLU), *Washington Legislative Office, 915 15th St. N.W., 2nd Floor, 20005; (202) 457-0800. David Cole, National Legal Director.*
General email, info@acludc.org
Web, www.aclu.org/legiupdate, Twitter, @ACLU_DC and Facebook, www.facebook.com/aclu.dc

Advocates legislation to guarantee constitutional rights and civil liberties. Monitors agency compliance with the Privacy Act and other access statutes. Produces publications. (Headquarters in New York maintains docket of cases.)

American Library Assn., *Washington Office, 1615 New Hampshire Ave. N.W., 1st Floor, 20009-2520; (202) 628-8410. Fax, (202) 628-8419. Tracie Hall, Executive Director; Alan Inouye, Senior Director for Public Policy and Government Relations. Toll-free, (800) 941-8478.*
General email, alawash@alawash.org
Web, www.ala.org/offices/wo

Advocates public policies that promote public access to government information, open government, and e-Government services. (Headquarters in Chicago, Ill.)

American Society of Access Professionals, *1120 20th St. N.W., #750, 20036; (202) 712-9054. Fax, (202) 216-9646. Ryan Mulvey, President.*
General email, asap@accesspro.org
Web, www.accesspro.org, Facebook, www.facebook.com/ASAPAccessPro and Twitter, @ASAPAccessPro

Membership: federal employees, attorneys, journalists, and others working with or interested in access-to-information laws. Seeks to improve the administration of the Freedom of Information Act, the Privacy Act, and other access statutes. Sponsors training workshops and seminars.

Freedom Forum, *9893 Brewers Court, Laurel, MD 20723; (202) 292-6100. Jan Neuharth, Chief Executive Officer.*

General email, info@freedomforum.org
Web, www.freedomforum.org, Twitter, @1stForAll and Facebook, www.facebook.com/FirstAmendmendment ForAll

Inspired by the five freedoms: Religion. Speech. Press. Assembly. Petition. Raises awareness through education, advocacy and action-training and research that promote free press, free speech, and freedom of information. Interests include the First Amendment and newsroom diversity. Part of the Freedom Forum Institute.

Radio Television Digital News Assn., *529 14th St. N.W., #1240, 20045; (202) 221-4282. Dan Shelley, Executive Director.*
Web, www.rtdna.org, Twitter, @RTDNA and Facebook, www.facebook.com/RTDNA.RTDNF

Membership: electronic journalists in radio, television, and all digital media. Sponsors and promotes education and advocacy concerning First Amendment issues, freedom of information, and government secrecy issues; ethics in reporting; improving coverage; implementing technology; and other news industry issues. Radio and Television News Directors Foundation (RTNDF) is the educational arm of the association.

INTERNET AND RELATED TECHNOLOGIES

General

▶ **AGENCIES**

National Telecommunications and Information Administration (NTIA) *(Commerce Dept.), 1401 Constitution Ave. N.W., #4898, 20230; (202) 482-1840. Alan Davidson, Assistant Secretary. Press, (202) 482-7002.*
Web, www.ntia.doc.gov, Twitter, @NTIAgov and Facebook, www.facebook.com/ntiagov

Responsible for oversight of the technical management of the Internet domain name system (DNS) and the Institute for Telecommunication Science (ITS).

▶ **CONGRESS**

For a listing of relevant congressional committees and subcommittees, please see page 100 or the Appendix.

▶ **NONGOVERNMENTAL**

Accredited Standards Committee (ASC X12), *1405 S. Fern St., #92957, Arlington, VA 22202; (703) 970-4480. Stephanie Fetzer, Chair.*
General email, info@x12.org
Web, https://x12.org and Twitter, @X12standards

Promotes the development and maintenance of cross-industry Electronic Data Interchange (EDI), XML schemas, and Context Inspired Component Architecture (CICA) standards in electronic commerce that help

Freedom of Information Contacts at Federal Departments and Agencies

Visit www.foia.gov to find contact information for federal agencies and departments, and to do research and determine if you need to make an FOIA request.

DEPARTMENTS

Agriculture, Alexis Graves, (202) 690-3318
Commerce, Bobby Parson, (202) 482-3257
Defense, Lisa W. Hershman, (866) 574-4970
  Air Force, Anh Trinh, (703) 614-8500
  Army, Alecia Bolling, (571) 515-0306
  Marine Corps, Sally Hughes, (703) 614-4008
  Navy, Christopher Julka, (703) 697-0031
Education, Tracey St. Pierre, (202) 401-3607
Energy, Alexander Morris, (202) 586-5955
Health and Human Services, Brandon Gaylord, (202) 690-7453
Homeland Security, Lynn Parker Dupree, (202) 343-1743
  Coast Guard, Kathleen Claiffe, (202) 475-3522
Housing and Urban Development, Deborah Snowden, (202) 708-3866
Interior, William Holzerland, (202) 513-0765
Justice, Bobak Talebian, (202) 514-3642
Labor, Thomas G. Hicks Sr., (202) 693-5391
State, Kellie N. Robinson, (202) 261-8484
Transportation, Darlene Wallace, (202) 366-4542
Treasury, Mark Bittner, (202) 622-0930
Veterans Affairs, Lisa Matuszczak, (202) 461-4857

AGENCIES

Agency for International Development, Christopher Colbow, (202) 712-0960
Central Intelligence Agency, E. Riggs Monfort, (703) 613-1287
Commission on Civil Rights, Lenore S. Ostrowsky, (202) 376-8591
Commodity Futures Trading Commission, Jonathan Van Doren, (202) 418-5505
Consumer Product Safety Commission, Robert Dalton or Korinne Super, (800) 638-2772
Council on Environmental Quality, Howard Sun, (202) 456-3621
Drug Enforcement Administration, Deshelia Wallace, (571) 776-2300
Environmental Protection Agency, Timothy R. Epp, (202) 566-1667
Equal Employment Opportunity Commission, Stephanie D. Garner, (202) 663-4634
Export-Import Bank, Lennell C. Jackson, (202) 565-3248
Farm Credit Administration, Autumn R. Agans, (703) 883-4082
Federal Communications Commission, Stephanie Kost, (202) 418-1379
Federal Deposit Insurance Corp., M. Anthony Lowe, (703) 562-6040
Federal Election Commission, Christine McClarin, (202) 694-1485
Federal Emergency Management Agency, Charlene Myrhil, (202) 646-3323

Federal Labor Relations Authority, Brandon Bradley, (202) 218-7766
Federal Maritime Commission, Rachel E. Dickon, (202) 523-5725
Federal Reserve System, Candace Ambrose, (202) 452-3684
Federal Trade Commission, Richard Gold, (202) 326-3355
General Services Administration, Duane Smith, (202) 694-2934 or, (855) 675-3642
Legal Services Corp., Helen Gerostathos Guyton, (202) 295-1633
Merit Systems Protection Board, Karin Kelly, (202) 254-4475
National Aeronautics and Space Administration, Stephen Rowe, (202) 358-0810
National Archives and Records Administration, Gary M. Stern, (301) 837-1750
National Credit Union Administration, Charles Smith, (703) 518-6540
National Endowment for the Humanities, Lisette Voyatzis, (202) 606-8322
National Labor Relations Board, Synta E. Keeling, (202) 273-2995
National Mediation Board, Maria-Kate Dowling, (202) 692-5040
National Science Foundation, Justin Guz, (703) 292-2289
National Transportation Safety Board, Melba D. Moye, (202) 314-6540
Nuclear Regulatory Commission, John Moses, (301) 415-1276
Office of Government Ethics, Jennifer Matis, (202) 482-9216
Office of Management and Budget, Shraddha A. Upadhyaya, (202) 395-3642
Office of National Drug Control Policy, Sandy Slater, (202) 395-6622
Office of Personnel Management, Tiffany Ford, (202) 606-1153
Office of Science and Technology Policy, Nicholas Wittenberg, (202) 456-4444
Office of the U.S. Trade Representative, Monique Ricker, (202) 395-3419
Peace Corps, Virginia Burke, (202) 692-1236
Pension Benefit Guaranty Corp., Robyne Griffin, (202) 326-4040
Securities and Exchange Commission, Ray J. McInerney, (202) 551-7900
Selective Service System, Vacant, (703) 605-4100
Small Business Administration, Delorice P. Ford, (202) 401-8200
Social Security Administration, Mary Ann Zimmerman, (410) 965-1727
U.S. International Trade Commission, Lisa R. Barton, (202) 205-2595
U.S. Postal Service, Jane Eyre, (202) 268-2608

Federal Government Websites

CONGRESS

Government Accountability Office, www.gao.gov

House of Representatives, www.house.gov

Library of Congress, www.loc.gov

Senate, www.senate.gov

WHITE HOUSE

General Information, www.whitehouse.gov

DEPARTMENTS

Agriculture, www.usda.gov

Commerce, www.commerce.gov

Defense, www.defense.gov

  Air Force, www.af.mil

  Army, www.army.mil

  Marine Corps, www.marines.mil

  Navy, www.navy.mil

Education, www.ed.gov

Energy, www.energy.gov

Health and Human Services, www.hhs.gov

Homeland Security, www.dhs.gov

  Coast Guard, www.uscg.mil

Housing and Urban Development, www.hud.gov

Interior, www.doi.gov

Justice, www.justice.gov

Labor, www.dol.gov

State, www.state.gov

Transportation, www.transportation.gov

Treasury, www.treasury.gov

Veterans Affairs, www.va.gov

AGENCIES

Agency of International Development, www.usaid.gov

Consumer Product Safety Commission, www.cpsc.gov

Corp. for Public Broadcasting, www.cpb.org

Drug Enforcement Administration, www.dea.gov

Environmental Protection Agency, www.epa.gov

Export-Import Bank, www.exim.gov

Federal Aviation Administration, www.faa.gov

Federal Bureau of Investigation, www.fbi.gov

Federal Communications Commission, www.fcc.gov

Federal Deposit Insurance Corp., www.fdic.gov

Federal Election Commission, www.fec.gov

Federal Emergency Management Agency, www.fema.gov

Federal Energy Regulatory Commission, www.ferc.gov

Federal Reserve System, www.federalreserve.gov

Federal Trade Commission, www.ftc.gov

Food and Drug Administration, www.fda.gov

General Services Administration, www.gsa.gov

Government Accountability Office, www.gao.gov

Government Publishing Office, www.gpo.gov

Internal Revenue Service, www.irs.gov

National Aeronautics and Space Administration, www.nasa.gov

National Archives and Records Administration, www.archives.gov

National Institute of Standards and Technology, www.nist.gov

National Institutes of Health, www.nih.gov

National Oceanic and Atmospheric Administration, www.noaa.gov or www.climate.gov

National Park Service, www.nps.gov

National Railroad Passenger Corp. (Amtrak), www.amtrak.com

National Science Foundation, www.nsf.gov

National Technical Information Service, www.ntis.gov

National Transportation Safety Board, www.ntsb.gov

Nuclear Regulatory Commission, www.nrc.gov

Occupational Safety and Health Administration, www.osha.gov

Patent and Trademark Office, www.uspto.gov

Peace Corps, www.peacecorps.gov

Pension Benefit Guaranty Corp., www.pbgc.gov

Securities and Exchange Commission, www.sec.gov

Small Business Administration, www.sba.gov

Smithsonian Institution, www.si.edu

Social Security Administration, www.ssa.gov

U.S. Fish and Wildlife Service, www.fws.gov

U.S. Geological Survey, www.usgs.gov

U.S. International Trade Commission, www.usitc.gov

U.S. Postal Service, www.usps.com

organizations improve business methods, lower costs, and increase productivity. Provides administrative and technical support. Chartered by the American National Standards Institute. (Formerly Data Interchange Standards Assn.)

American Library Assn., Washington Office, *1615 New Hampshire Ave. N.W., 1st Floor, 20009-2520; (202) 628-8410. Fax, (202) 628-8419. Tracie Hall, Executive Director; Alan Inouye, Senior Director for Public Policy and Government Relations. Toll-free, (800) 941-8478.*
General email, alawash@alawash.org
Web, www.ala.org/offices/wo

Promotes net neutrality rules that ban blocking, throttling, or degrading of any lawful Internet content. Opposes paid prioritization of content; supports preservation of competitive online markets for content and services. (Headquarters in Chicago, Ill.)

Center for Democracy and Technology, *1401 K St. N.W., #200, 20005; (202) 637-9800. Alexandra Reeve Givens, President. Press, (202) 407-8811.*
General email, info@cdt.org
Web, https://cdt.org, Twitter, @CenDemTech
Press, press@cdt.org and Facebook, www.facebook.com/CenDemTech

Promotes and defends privacy and civil liberties on the Internet. Interests include free expression, social networking and access to the Internet, consumer protection, health information privacy and technology, and government surveillance. Monitors legislation and regulations.

Center for Digital Democracy, *1015 15th St. N.W., #600, 20005; (202) 494-7100. Jeffrey (Jeff) Chester, Executive Director.*
Web, www.democraticmedia.org, Twitter, @DigitalDemoc and Facebook, www.facebook.com/Center-for-Digital-Democracy-Protect-Privacy-Online-281331962264

Seeks to ensure that the public interest is a fundamental part of the digital communications landscape. Conducts public education designed to protect consumer privacy and works to ensure competition in the new media industries, especially at the Federal Trade Commission and the Justice Dept.

Center for Strategic and International Studies, *Strategic Technologies Program, 1616 Rhode Island Ave. N.W., 20036; (202) 887-0200. James Andrew Lewis, Director.*
General email, techpolicy@csis.org
Web, www.csis.org/programs/strategic-technologies-program and Twitter, @CyberCSIS

Conducts and publishes research on emerging technologies, intelligence reform, and space and globalization programs. Interests include cybersecurity, intelligence, privacy and surveillance, technology and innovation, Internet governance, and 5G networks.

Common Cause, *805 15th St. N.W., #800, 20005; (202) 833-1200. Karen Hobert Flynn, President; Aaron Scherb, Director of Legislative Affairs. Press, (202) 736-5712.*
General email, CauseNet@commoncause.org
Web, www.commoncause.org, Twitter, @CommonCause and Facebook, www.facebook.com/CommonCause

Nonpartisan citizens' lobby that works to promote laws and regulations safeguarding the free flow of information online. Supports strong open Internet protections; opposes media consolidation.

Computer and Communications Industry Assn. (CCIA), *25 Massachusetts Ave. N.W., #300C, 20001; (202) 783-0070. Matthew Schruers, President.*
Web, www.ccianet.org, Twitter, @ccianet and Facebook, www.facebook.com/ccianet

Membership: Internet service providers, software providers, and manufacturers and suppliers of computer data processing and communications-related products and services. Interests include Internet freedom, privacy and neutrality, government electronic surveillance, telecommunications policy, tax policy, federal procurement policy, communications and computer industry standards, intellectual property policies, encryption, international trade, and antitrust reform.

Cyber Security Policy and Research Institute *(George Washington University), Tompkins Hall of Engineering, 725 23rd St. N.W., #101B, 20052; (202) 994-5613. Costis Toregas, Director.*
General email, cspriaa@gmail.edu
Web, https://cspri.seas.gwu.edu/about

Promotes education, research, and policy analysis in the areas of computer security and privacy, computer networks, electronic commerce, e-government, and the cultural aspects of cyberspace.

Family Online Safety Institute, *1440 G St. N.W., 20005; (202) 775-0158. Stephen (Steve) Balkam, Chief Executive Officer.*
General email, fosi@fosi.org
Web, www.fosi.org, Twitter, @FOSI, Facebook, www.facebook.com/FamOnlineSafety and YouTube, www.youtube.com/user/fosi
Press, press@fosi.org

Membership: Internet safety advocates in business, government, academia, the media, and the general public. Identifies risks to children on the Internet; develops and promotes solutions for keeping children safe while protecting free speech. Issues reports on online trends among young people; hosts conferences and other educational events; monitors legislation and regulations internationally. (Also has an office in London.)

IDEAlliance, *1800 Diagonal Rd., #320, Alexandria, VA 22314-2862; (703) 837-1070. Fax, (703) 837-1072. Jordan Gorski, Chief Executive Officer.*
General email, membership@idealliance.org
Web, www.idealliance.org, Twitter, @Idealliance and Facebook, www.facebook.com/IdeallianceUS

Membership: firms and customers in the visual communications industry, including content and media creators, print and digital service providers, material suppliers, and technology partners. Helps set industry standards for electronic and Web commerce and conducts studies on new information technologies.

Internet Education Foundation, *1440 G St. N.W., 20005 (mailing address: 655 15th NW, Suite 800, Washington DC 20005); (202) 638-4370. Tim Lordan, Executive Director. Web, www.neted.org and Twitter, @NetEdFound*

Sponsors educational initiatives promoting the Internet as a valuable medium for democratic participation, communications, and commerce. Funds the Congressional Internet Caucus Advisory Committee, which works to inform Congress of important Internet-related policy issues. Monitors legislation and regulations.

Internet Engineering Task Force (IETF), *1000 North West St., #1200, Wilmington, DE, 19801; (703) 439-2120. Fax, (703) 326-9881. Jay Daley, Executive Director. General email, ietf-info@ietf.org*

Web, www.ietf.org

Membership: network designers, operators, vendors, and researchers from around the world who are concerned with the evolution, smooth operation, and continuing development of the Internet. Establishes working groups to address technical concerns. IETF is an organized activity of the Internet Society. (Headquarters in Fremont, Calif.)

Internet Society (ISOC), *11710 Plaza America Dr., St. 400, Reston, VA 20190-5108; (703) 439-2120. Fax, (703) 326-9881. Andrew Sullivan, President. General email, isoc@isoc.org*

Web, www.internetsociety.org, Twitter, @internetsociety and Facebook, www.facebook.com/InternetSociety

Press, media@isoc.org

Membership: individuals, corporations, nonprofit organizations, and government agencies. Focused on ensuring that the Internet continues to evolve as an open platform for innovation, collaboration, and economic development. Engages in a wide spectrum of Internet issues, including policy, governance, technology, and development and availability of the Internet. Conducts research and educational programs; provides information about the Internet.

National Academies of Sciences, Engineering, and Medicine (NASEM), *Computer Science and Telecommunications Board, Keck Center, 500 5th St. N.W., 20001; (202) 334-2689. Fax, (202) 334-2318. Laura M. Hass, Chair; Jon Eisenberg, Director. General email, cstb@nas.edu*

Web, www.nationalacademies.org/cstb/computer-science-and-telecommunications-board

Advises the federal government on technical and public policy issues relating to computing and communications. Research includes computer science, cybersecurity, privacy, the Internet, and electronic voting and voter registration.

Pew Research Center, *Internet, Science, and Technology Project, 1615 L St. N.W., #800, 20036; (202) 419-4300. Fax, (202) 419-8562. Lee Rainie, Director. Web, www.pewinternet.org and Twitter, @PewInternet*

Conducts research, surveys, and analyses to explore the impact of the Internet on families, communities, teens, education, health care, mobile technologies, and civic and political life. Makes its reports available online for public and academic use.

Public Knowledge, *1818 N St. N.W., #410, 20036; (202) 861-0020. Fax, (202) 861-0040. Chris Lewis, President, ext. 116. General email, pk@publicknowledge.org*

Web, www.publicknowledge.org, Twitter, @publicknowledge and Facebook, www.facebook.com/publicknowledge

Coalition of libraries, educators, scientists, artists, musicians, journalists, lawyers, and consumers interested in intellectual property law and technology policy as it pertains to the Internet and electronic information. Encourages openness, access, and competition in the digital age. Supports U.S. laws and policies that provide incentives to innovators as well as ensure a free flow of information and ideas to the public.

StaySafeOnline.org, *National Cyber Security Alliance, 1010 Vermont Ave. N.W., #821, 20005; Jon Check, Chair. General email, info@staysafeonline.org*

Web, www.staysafeonline.org

Public-private partnership that promotes computer safety and responsible online behavior. Designated by the Homeland Security Dept. to provide tools and resources to help home users, small businesses, and schools stay safe online. Online resources include tips, a self-guided cyber security test and checklist, and educational materials.

The Telework Coalition (TelCoa), *204 East St., N.E., 20002; (202) 266-0046. Chuck Wilsker, President. General email, info@telcoa.org*

Web, www.telcoa.org and Twitter, @telcoa

Promotes telework and access to broadband services to increase productivity and provide employment opportunities for disabled, rural, and older workers, while reducing vehicular travel and energy use. Monitors legislation and regulations.

MEDIA PROFESSIONS AND RESOURCES

General

▶ **AGENCIES**

Federal Communications Commission (FCC), *Communications Business Opportunities, 45 L St. N.E., 20554; (202) 418-0716. Fax, (202) 418-0235. Joy Melody Ragsdale, Director.*

General email, ocboinfo@fcc.gov

Web, www.fcc.gov/communications-business-opportunities

Provides technical and legal guidance and assistance to the small, minority, and female business communities in the telecommunications industry. Advises the FCC chair on small, minority, and female business issues. Serves as liaison between federal agencies, state and local governments, and trade associations representing small, minority, and female enterprises concerning FCC policies, procedures, rulemaking activities, and increased ownership and employment opportunities.

Federal Communications Commission (FCC), *Media Bureau (MB), Policy Division, Equal Employment Opportunity (EEO),* 45 L St. N.E., 20554; (202) 418-1450. Fax, (202) 418-1797. Robert Baker, Assistant Chief, (202) 418-1417.

Web, www.fcc.gov/general/equal-employment-opportunity

Responsible for the annual certification of cable television equal employment opportunity compliance. Oversees broadcast employment practices.

National Endowment for the Arts (NEA), *Media Arts,* 400 7th St. S.W., 20506; (202) 682-5591. (202) 682-5452. Jax Deluca, Director, (202) 682-5742; Sarah Burford, Specialist, (202) 682-5591.

Web, www.arts.gov

Awards grants to nonprofit organizations for screen-based projects presented by film, television, video, radio, Internet, mobile technologies, video games, transmedia storytelling, and satellite; supports film and video exhibitions and workshops.

▶**NONGOVERNMENTAL**

Alicia Patterson Foundation, 1100 Vermont Ave. N.W., #900, 20005; (202) 393-5995. Fax, (301) 951-8512. Margaret Engel, Executive Director; Robert Lee Hotz, President.

General email, info@aliciapatterson.org

Web, https://aliciapatterson.org and Facebook, www.facebook.com/AliciaPattersonFoundation

Fosters and promotes the traditions of American journalism. Awards fellowships and grants to professional journalists to pursue independent projects of significant interest or continue projects based on their previous investigative work for *The APF Reporter,* a web magazine published by the Foundation.

American News Women's Club, 1607 22nd St. N.W., 20008; (202) 332-6770. Fax, (202) 265-6092. Mary Catherine Andrews, President.

General email, anwclub@comcast.net

Web, www.anwc.org, Twitter, @NewsWomensClub and Facebook, www.facebook.com/newswomensclub

Membership: women in communications. Promotes the advancement of women in all media. Sponsors professional receptions and lectures.

Audiovisual and Integrated Experience Assn. (AVIXA), 11242 Waples Mill Rd., #200, Fairfax, VA 22030; (703)

273-7200. Fax, (703) 278-8082. David Labuskes, Chief Executive Officer. Toll-free, (800) 659-7469.

General email, membership@avixa.org

Web, www.avixa.org, Twitter, @AVIXA and Facebook, www.facebook.com/TheAVIXA

Membership: video and audiovisual dealers, manufacturers and producers, and individuals. Promotes the professional AV communications industry and seeks to enhance members' ability to conduct business successfully through trade shows, education, certification, standards, market research, and government relations. Monitors legislation and regulations. (Formerly Info Comm International.)

Center for Public Integrity, 910 17th St. N.W., #1030, 20006; (202) 466-1300. Paul Cheung, Chief Executive Officer.

Web, https://publicintegrity.org, Twitter, @PublicIntegrity Press, media@publicintegrity.org

Nonpartisan organization that seeks to produce original investigative journalism on significant issues in the United States and around the world. Organizes and supports investigative journalists committed to transparent and comprehensive reporting. Interests include the environment, public health, public accountability, federal and state lobbying, war profiteering, and financial disclosure.

Communications Workers of America (CWA), 501 3rd St. N.W., 20001; (202) 434-1100. Christopher M. Shelton, President.

Web, https://cwa-union.org and Twitter, @CWAUnion

Membership: approximately 700,000 workers in telecommunications, journalism, publishing, cable television, electronics, and other fields. Interests include workplace democracy and restoring bargaining rights. Represents members in contract negotiations and grievances; conducts training programs and workshops. Monitors legislation and regulations. (Affiliated with the AFL-CIO.)

Freedom Forum, 9893 Brewers Court, Laurel, MD 20723; (202) 292-6100. Jan Neuharth, Chief Executive Officer.

General email, info@freedomforum.org

Web, www.freedomforum.org, Twitter, @1stForAll and Facebook, www.facebook.com/FirstAmendmendment ForAll

Inspired by the five freedoms: Religion. Speech. Press. Assembly. Petition. Raises awareness through education, advocacy and action-training and research that promote free press, free speech, and freedom of information. Interests include the First Amendment and newsroom diversity. Part of the Freedom Forum Institute.

The Fuller Project for International Reporting, 712 H St. N.E., PMB 37, 20002; (202) 964-0854. Xanthe Scharff, Executive Director.

General email, contact@fullerproject.org

Web, http://fullerproject.org, Twitter, @fullerproject and Facebook, www.facebook.com/FullerProject

Promotes the advancement of women in journalism, photography, filmmaking, and other media professions globally. Acts as advocate and delivers independent investigative articles and videos including political, economic, and military-related content. (Headquarters in Istanbul, Turkey.)

Fund for Investigative Journalism, *1110 Vermont Ave. N.W. #800, 20005; (202) 378-0953. Eric Ferrero, Executive Director.*
General email, fij@gmail.com
Web, www.fij.org, Twitter, @fundFIJ and Facebook, www.facebook.com/FundFIJ

Provides investigative reporters working outside the protection and backing of major news organizations with grants to cover the expenses of investigative pieces involving corruption, malfeasance, incompetence, and domestic and international societal ills.

International Center for Journalists (ICFJ), *750 17th St. N.W., #300, 20006; (202) 737-3700. Fax, (202) 737-0530. Sharon Moshavi, President.*
General email, communications@icfj.org
Web, www.icfj.org, Twitter, @ICFJ and Facebook, www .facebook.com/ICFJorg

Fosters international freedom of the press through hands-on training, workshops, seminars, online courses, fellowships, and international exchanges. Offers online mentoring and consulting; publishes media training manuals in various languages.

International Women's Media Foundation (IWMF), *1625 K St. N.W., #1275, 20006; (202) 496-1992. Fax, (202) 496-1977. Elisa Lees Muñoz, Executive Director.*
General email, info@iwmf.org
Web, http://iwmf.org, Twitter, @IWMF and Facebook, www.facebook.com/IWMFpage

Conducts reporting trips and safety training for women journalists, acts as advocate on behalf of women journalists who work under adverse conditions, and makes grants to support women journalists in their projects and endeavors worldwide.

National Assn. of Black Journalists (NABJ), *1100 Knight Hall, #3101, College Park, MD 20742; (301) 405-0248. Drew Berry, Executive Director.*
General email, contact@nabj.org
Web, https://nabjonline.org, Twitter, @NABJOfficial and Facebook, www.facebook.com/NABJOfficial

Membership: African American students and media professionals. Works to increase recognition and career advancement of minority journalists, to expand opportunities for minority students entering the field, and to promote balanced coverage of the African American community. Sponsors scholarships, internship program, and annual convention.

National Assn. of Government Communicators (NAGC), *201 Park Washington Court, Falls Church, VA 22046-4527; (703) 538-1787. Fax, (703) 241-5603. Isaiah Allen, Executive Director, (703) 834-5550, ext. 100.*
General email, info@nagc.com

Web, https://nagc.com, Twitter, @NAGC and Facebook, www.facebook.com/NationalAssociationof GovernmentCommunicators

National network of federal, state, and local government communications employees. Provides professional development through public meetings, exhibitions, workshops, and formal courses of instruction. Promotes high standards for the government communications profession and recognizes noteworthy service.

National Assn. of Hispanic Journalists (NAHJ), *1050 Connecticut Ave. N.W., 5th Floor, 20036; (202) 662-7145. Fax, (202) 772-7144. David Peña Jr., Executive Director.*
General email, nahj@nahj.org
Web, www.nahj.org, Twitter, @NAHJ and Facebook, www.facebook.com/NAHJFan

Membership: professional journalists, educators, students, and others interested in encouraging and supporting the study and practice of journalism and communications by Hispanics. Promotes fair representation and treatment of Hispanics by the media. Provides professional development and computerized job referral service; compiles and updates national directory of Hispanics in the media; sponsors national high school essay contest, journalism awards, and scholarships.

National Federation of Press Women (NFPW), *140B Purcellville Gateway Dr., #120, Purcellville, VA 21032 (mailing address: P.O. Box 5556, Arlington, VA 22205); (571) 295-5900. Karen Rowley, President.*
General email, info@nfpw.org
Web, www.nfpw.org, Twitter, @NFPW and Facebook, www.facebook.com/NFPWomen

Membership: communications professionals, both men and women. Provides professional development opportunities for members, including an annual conference. Advocates freedom of the press. Provides cost-effective libel insurance. Monitors legislation and regulations.

National Hispanic Foundation for the Arts (NHFA), *Washington Square, 1050 Connecticut Ave. N.W., 5th Floor, 20036; (202) 293-8330. Felix Sanchez, Chair.*
General email, info@hispanicarts.org
Web, www.hispanicarts.org, Twitter, @HispanicArts and Facebook, www.facebook.com/hispanicarts

Strives to increase the presence of Hispanics in the media, telecommunications, entertainment industries, and performing arts, and to increase programming for the U.S. Latino community. Provides scholarships for Hispanic students to pursue graduate study in the arts.

National Journalism Center, *11480 Commerce Park Dr., #600, Reston, VA 20191; (703) 318-9608. Fax, (703) 318-9122. Emily Jashinsky, Director. Toll-free, (800) 872-1776.*
General email, njc@yaf.org
Web, www.nationaljournalismcenter.org

Sponsors a comprehensive internship program in journalism composed of a series of training seminars that enhance students' knowledge of policy reporting in the

Media Contacts in Washington, D.C.

MAGAZINES

The Atlantic, 600 New Hampshire Ave. N.W., 20037; (202) 266-6000; www.theatlantic.com

CQ Roll Call Magazine, 1201 Pennsylvania Ave. N.W., 6th Floor, 20004; (202) 650-6500; https://cqrollcall.com

National Journal, 600 New Hampshire Ave. N.W., 20037; (202) 266-7900; www.nationaljournal.com

U.S. News & World Report, 1050 Thomas Jefferson St. N.W., 4th Floor, 20007; (202) 955-2225; www.usnews.com

NEWS SERVICES

Agence France-Presse, 1500 K St. N.W., #600, 20005; (202) 414-0600; www.afp.com

Associated Press, 1100 13th St. N.W., #500, 20005; (202) 641-9541; https://apnews.com

McClatchy, 1025 Connecticut Ave. N.W., #1100, 20036; (202) 383-6001; www.mcclatchydc.com

Reuters, 1333 H St. N.W., #510, 20005; (202) 898-8300; www.reuters.com

United Press International, 1133 19th St. N.W., #800, 20036; (202) 898-8000; www.upi.com

Washington Post News Services & Syndicate, 1301 K St. N.W., 20071; (202) 334-7666; www.washingtonpost.com/syndication

NEWSPAPERS

The New York Times, 1627 Eye St. N.W., #700, 20006; (202) 862-0300; www.nytimes.com

USA Today, 1575 Eye St. N.W., #350, 20005; (703) 854-6000; www.usatoday.com

Wall Street Journal, 1025 Connecticut Ave. N.W., #800, 20036; (202) 862-9200; www.wsj.com

Washington City Paper, 734 15th St. N.W., 20005; (202) 332-2100; https://washingtoncitypaper.com

The Washington Post, 1301 K St. N.W., 20071; (202) 334-6100; www.washingtonpost.com

Washington Times, 3600 New York Ave. N.E., 20002; (202) 636-3000; www.washingtontimes.com

TELEVISION/RADIO NETWORKS

ABC News, 1717 DeSales St. N.W., 20036; (202) 222-7700; https://abcnews.go.com

CBS News, 2020 M St. N.W., 20036; (202) 457-4385; www.cbsnews.com

CNN, 820 1st St. N.E., 20001; (202) 898-7900; www.cnn.com

C-SPAN, 400 N. Capitol St. N.W., #650, 20001; (202) 737-3220; www.c-span.org

Fox News, 400 N. Capitol St. N.W., #550, 20001; (202) 824-6300; www.foxnews.com

National Public Radio, 1111 N. Capitol St. N.E., 20002; (202) 513-2000; www.npr.org

NBC News, 400 N. Capitol St. N.E., #850, 20001; (202) 885-4000; www.nbcnews.com

Public Broadcasting Service, 1225 S. Clark St., Arlington, VA 22202; (703) 739-5000; www.pbs.org

---

areas of economics, education, and business. (Affiliated with Young America's Foundation.)

National Lesbian and Gay Journalists Assn. (NLGJA), *2120 L St. N.W., #850, 20037; (202) 588-9888. Adam Pawlus, Executive Director.*
General email, info@nlgja.org
Web, www.nlgja.org

Membership: journalists, media professionals, educators, and students working in the news industry. Promotes fair and accurate coverage of lesbian, gay, bisexual, and transgender issues; offers professional development resources; hosts a national conference.

National Press Club, *529 14th St. N.W., 13th Floor, 20045; (202) 662-7500. Fax, (202) 662-7537. Jen Judson, President. Library and Research Center, (202) 662-7523.*
General email, info@press.org
Web, www.press.org, Twitter, @pressclubdc and Facebook, www.facebook.com/PressClubDC

Membership: reporters, editors, writers, publishers, cartoonists, producers, librarians, and teachers of journalism at all levels. Interests include advancement of professional standards and skills, and the promotion of free expression. Provides networking opportunities and

manages an online job listing site for members. Library available to members for research.

National Press Foundation (NPF), *1211 Connecticut Ave. N.W., #310, 20036; (202) 663-7280. Fax, (202) 530-2855. Sonni Efron, President.*
General email, npf@nationalpress.org
Web, https://nationalpress.org and Twitter, @natpress

Works to enhance the professional competence of journalists through in-career education projects. Sponsors conferences, seminars, fellowships, and awards; conducts public forums and international exchanges. Supports the National Press Club library.

The Newspaper Guild— Communication Workers of America (CWA), *501 3rd St. N.W., 6th Floor, 20001-2797; (202) 434-7177. Jon Schleuss, President.*
General email, guild@cwa-union.org
Web, www.newsguild.org, Twitter, @newsguild and Facebook, www.facebook.com/NewsGuild

Membership: journalists, sales and media professionals. Advocates higher standards in journalism; equal employment opportunity in the print, broadcast, wire, and Web media industries; and advancement of members' economic interests. (Affiliated with Communications Workers of America, the AFL-CIO, CLC, and IFJ.)

Congressional News Media Galleries

The congressional news media galleries serve as liaisons between members of Congress and their staffs and accredited newspaper, magazine, and broadcasting correspondents. The galleries provide facilities for covering activities of Congress, and gallery staff members ensure that congressional press releases reach appropriate correspondents. Independent committees of correspondents working through the press galleries are responsible for accreditation of correspondents.

House Periodical Press Gallery, H304 CAP, Washington, DC 20515; (202) 225-2941. Robert M. Zatkowski, Director.

House Press Gallery, H315-319 CAP, Washington, DC 20515; (202) 225-3945. Annie Tin, Director.

House Radio and Television Gallery, H320 CAP, Washington, DC 20515; (202) 225-5214. Olga Ramirez Kornacki, Director.

Press Photographers Gallery, S317 CAP, Washington, DC 20510; (202) 224-6548. Jeffrey S. Kent, Director.

Senate Periodical Press Gallery, S320 CAP, Washington, DC 20510; (202) 224-0265. Justin Wilson, Director.

Senate Press Gallery, S316 CAP, Washington, DC 20510; (202) 224-0241. Laura Lytle, Director.

Senate Radio and Television Gallery, S325 CAP, Washington, DC 20510; (202) 224-6421. Mike Mastrian, Director.

Pew Research Center, *News Habits and Media, Journalism and Media Project, 1615 L St. N.W., #800, 20036; (202) 419-4300. Amy Mitchell, Director. Press, (202) 419-3650.*
General email, journalism@pewresearch.org
Web, www.journalism.org and Twitter, @PewJournalism

Evaluates and studies the performance of the press, particularly content analysis using empirical research to quantify what is occurring in the press. Tracks key industry trends. Publishes a daily digest of media news and an annual report on American journalism. (Formerly Project for Excellence in Journalism.)

Society for Technical Communication (STC), *3251 Lee Hwy., #406, Fairfax, VA 22030; (703) 522-4114. Fax, (703) 522-2075. Liz Pohland, Chief Executive Officer, (571) 366-1901.*
General email, stc@stc.org
Web, www.stc.org, Twitter, @stc_org and Facebook, www.facebook.com/stc.org

Membership: writers, publishers, educators, editors, illustrators, and others involved in technical communication. Encourages research and develops training programs; aids educational institutions in devising curricula; awards scholarships.

Washington Press Club Foundation, *National Press Club Bldg., 529 14th St. N.W., #1115, 20045; (202) 393-0613. Fax, (202) 662-7040. Jennifer Bendery, President.*

General email, wpcf@wpcf.org
Web, www.wpcf.org

Seeks to advance professionalism in journalism. Sponsors programs and events to educate students and the public on the role of a free press. Awards paid internships for minorities in D.C.–area newsrooms. Administers an oral history of women in journalism. Sponsors annual Congressional Dinner to welcome Congress back into session.

White House Correspondents' Assn., *600 New Hampshire Ave. N.W., #800, 20037; (202) 499-4187. Fax, (202) 266-7454. Steven Portnoy, President; Steven Thomma, Executive Director.*
General email, director@whca.press
Web, www.whca.press and Twitter, @whca

Membership: reporters with permanent White House press credentials. Acts as a liaison between reporters and White House staff. Sponsors annual WHCA Journalism Awards and Scholarships fund-raising dinner.

Women in Film and Video (WIFV), *1200 18th St. N.W., #300, 20036; (202) 429-9438. Fax, (202) 429-9440. Melissa Houghton, Executive Director.*
General email, membership@wifv.org
Web, www.wifv.org and Twitter, @WIFVDC

Membership organization dedicated to promoting equal employment opportunities and advancing career development and achievement for women working in all areas of screen-based media and related disciplines.

Women's Institute for Freedom of the Press, *1940 Calvert St. N.W., 20009-1502; (202) 656-0893. Martha Leslie Allen, Director.*
General email, ourmediademocracy@gmail.com
Web, www.wifp.org, Twitter, @WIFP and Facebook, www.facebook.com/TheWIFP

Conducts research and publishes in areas of communications and the media that are of particular interest to women. Promotes freedom of the press. Publishes a free online directory of media produced by and for women. Partners with the Global Woman PEACE Foundation.

Accreditation in Washington

▶AGENCIES

Bureau of Global Public Affairs (GPA) *(State Dept.), Foreign Press Centers, 529 14th St. N.W., #898, SA-16, 20045; (202) 504-6300. Fax, (202) 504-6334. Elizabeth (Liz) Detmeister, Director, (202) 504-1317.*
General email, dcfpc@state.gov
Web, www.state.gov/bureaus-offices/under-secretary-for-public-diplomacy-and-public-affairs/bureau-of-global-public-affairs/foreign-press-centers, Twitter, @ForeignPressCtr, Facebook, www.facebook.com/USDoS.FPC and YouTube, www.youtube.com/playlist?=PLNxLozf2cP4tkSJyUbmlxTE1bVXv27-8p

Provides foreign journalists with access to news sources, including wire services and daily briefings from the White

House, State Dept., and Pentagon. Holds live news conferences. Foreign journalists wishing to use the center should check the website for information on what documents to present for admission.

Bureau of Global Public Affairs (GPA) (State Dept.),
Press Operations, 2201 C St. N.W., #2109, 20520-6180; (202) 647-2492. Nick Barnett, Director.
General email, PAPressDuty@state.gov

Web, www.state.gov/bureaus-offices/under-secretary-for-public-diplomacy-and-public-affairs/bureau-of-global-public-affairs/office-of-press-operations

Press, mediarequests@state.gov

Each U.S. journalist seeking a long-term building pass must apply in person with a letter from his or her editor or publisher, two application forms (available from the press office), and proof of citizenship. In addition, foreign correspondents need a letter from the embassy of the country in which their organization is based. Applicants should allow three months for security clearance. Members of the press wishing to attend an individual briefing must present a U.S. government-issued photo ID, a media-issued photo ID, or a letter from their employer and photo ID.

Defense Dept. (DoD), *Public Affairs*, 1400 Defense
Pentagon, #2D961, 20301-1400; (703) 571-3343. Fax, (703) 697-3501. John Kirby, Assistant to the Secretary of Defense for Public Affairs. Press, (703) 697-5131.
Web, www.defense.gov/news

Selects staff of accredited Washington-based media organizations by lottery for rotating assignments with the National Media Pool. Correspondents must be familiar with U.S. military affairs, be available on short notice to deploy to the site of military operations, and adhere to pool ground rules. Issues Pentagon press passes to members of the press regularly covering the Pentagon.

Metropolitan Police Dept., *Office of Communications*,
300 Indiana Ave. N.W., #5126, 20001; (202) 727-4383. Dustin Sternbeck, Director.
General email, mpd.press@dc.gov

Web, https://mpdc.dc.gov/node/138872

Serves as connection between the media and the police department.

National Park Service (NPS) (Interior Dept.), National
Capital Region, 1100 Ohio Dr. S.W., 20242; (202) 619-7020. Kym Hall, Area Director. Permits, (202) 245-4715.
Web, www.nps.gov

Regional office that administers national parks, monuments, historic sites, and recreation areas in the Washington metropolitan area. Issues special permits required for commercial filming on public park lands. News media representatives covering public events that take place on park lands must notify the Office of Public Affairs and Tourism in advance. A White House, Capitol Hill, metropolitan police, or other policy-agency-issued press pass is required in some circumstances. Commercial filming on park lands requires a special-use permit.

White House, *Press Office*, White House, 1600
Pennsylvania Ave. N.W., 20502; Jen Psaki, Press Secretary. White House switchboard, (202) 456-1414. TTY, (202) 456-6213. Comments and information, (202) 456-6213. General email, press@who.eop.gov

Web, www.whitehouse.gov

Briefing Room, press-briefings

Journalists seeking permanent accreditation must meet four criteria. The journalist must be a designated White House correspondent and expected to cover the White House daily; must be accredited by the House and Senate press galleries; must be a resident of the Washington, D.C., area; and must be willing to undergo the required Secret Service background investigation. A journalist's editor, publisher, or employer must write to the press office requesting accreditation. Freelance journalists, camera operators, or technicians wishing temporary accreditation must send letters from at least two news organizations indicating the above criteria.

▶ CONGRESS

House Periodical Press Gallery, H304 CAP, 20515; (202)
225-2941. Robert M. Zatkowski, Director.
General email, periodical.press@mail.house.gov

Web, http://periodical.house.gov

Open by application to periodical correspondents whose chief occupation is gathering and reporting news for periodicals not affiliated with lobbying or membership organizations. Accreditation with the House Gallery covers accreditation with the Senate Gallery. Rotates credentialing duties with the Senate Periodical Press Gallery every four years.

Senate Periodical Press Gallery, S320CAP, 20510; (202)
224-0265. Fax, (202) 228-3480. Justin Wilson, Director.
General email, periodicals@saa.senate.gov

Web, www.periodicalpress.senate.gov/accreditation

Open by application to periodical correspondents whose chief occupation is gathering and reporting news for periodicals not affiliated with lobbying or membership organizations. Accreditation with the House Gallery covers accreditation with the Senate Gallery. Rotates credentialing duties with the House Periodical Press Gallery every four years.

Senate Press Gallery, S316 CAP, 20004; (202) 224-0241.
Fax, (202) 228-1142. Laura Lytle, Director.
General email, Senate_Press_Gallery@SAA.Senate.gov

Web, www.dailypress.senate.gov and
Twitter, @SenatePress

Handles accreditation for daily newspapers, wire services, and online publications that cover Congress. Assists correspondents and maintains their access to Senate proceedings.

Senate Radio-Television Gallery, S325 CAP, 20515; (202)
224-6421. Michael (Mike) Mastrian, Director.
Web, www.radiotv.senate.gov and
Twitter, @SenateRadioTV

Determines eligibility for broadcast media credentials in Congress.

►JUDICIARY

Supreme Court of the United States, *1 1st St. N.E., 20543; (202) 479-3000. John G. Roberts Jr., Chief Justice. Public Information Office, (202) 479-3211. TTY, (202) 479-3472. Visitor information, (202) 479-3030.*
Web, *www.supremecourt.gov* and Contact Form, *www .supremecourt.gov/contact/contact_pio.aspx*

Journalists seeking to cover the Court should be accredited by either the White House or the House or Senate press galleries, but others may apply by submitting a letter from their editors. Contact the public information office to make arrangements.

Broadcasting

►AGENCIES

Federal Communications Commission (FCC), *Media Bureau (MB), Policy Division, 45 L St. N.E., 20554; (202) 418-2120. Fax, (202) 418-1069. Maria Mullarkey, Chief, (202) 418-1067.*
Web, *www.fcc.gov/media/policy/policy-division*

Handles complaints and inquiries concerning the equal time rule, which requires equal broadcast opportunities for all legally qualified candidates for the same office, and other political broadcast, cable, and satellite rules. Interprets and enforces related Communications Act provisions, including the requirement for sponsorship identification of all paid political broadcast, cable, and satellite announcements and the requirement for broadcasters to furnish federal candidates with reasonable access to broadcast time for political advertising. Administers Equal Employment Opportunity (EEO) matters.

U.S. Agency for Global Media, *330 Independence Ave. S.W., #3300, 20237; (202) 203-4000. Kelu Chao, Chief Executive Officer (Acting) FOIA, (202) 920-2342. Press, (202) 203-4400.*
General email, *publicaffairs@usagm.gov*
Web, *www.usagm.gov, Twitter, @USAGMgov* and Facebook, *www.facebook.com/USAGMgov*

Established by Congress to supervise all U.S. government nonmilitary international broadcasting, including Voice of America, Radio and TV Martí, Radio Free Europe/Radio Liberty, Radio Free Asia, and the Middle East Broadcasting Networks (MBN). Assesses the quality and effectiveness of broadcasts with regard to U.S. foreign policy objectives; reports annually to the president and to Congress.

►NONGOVERNMENTAL

Broadcast Education Assn. (BEA), *1 M St. S.E., 20003; (202) 602-0584. Fax, (202) 609-9940. Heather Birks, Executive Director, (202) 602-0584.*

General email, *HELP@BEAweb.org*
Web, *www.beaweb.org, Twitter, @BEAWebTweets* and Facebook, *www.facebook.com/groups/34744282858*

Membership: universities, colleges, and faculty members offering specialized training in the radio, television, and electronic media industries. Promotes improvement of curriculum and teaching methods. Fosters working relationships among academics, students, and professionals in the industry. Interests include documentaries, international business and regulatory practices, gender issues, interactive media and emerging technologies, and electronic media law and policy. Administers scholarships in the field.

National Academy of Television Arts and Sciences (NATAS), *National Capital Chesapeake Bay Chapter Office, 11654 Plaza America Dr., #199, Reston, VA 20190; (703) 234-4055. Carol Wynne, Executive Director.*
General email, *info@capitalemmys.org*
Web, *www.capitalemmys.tv, Twitter, @capitalemmys* and Facebook, *www.facebook.com/capitalemmys*

Membership: professionals in television and related fields and students in communications. Serves the Virginia, Maryland, and Washington, DC, television community. Works to upgrade television programming; awards scholarships to junior, senior, or graduate students in communications. Sponsors annual Emmy Awards. (Headquarters in New York.)

National Assn. of Black Owned Broadcasters (NABOB), *1250 Connecticut Ave. N.W., #700, 20036; (202) 463-8970. James L. Winston, President.*
General email, *nabobinfo@nabob.org*
Web, *www.nabob.org* and Facebook, *www.facebook.com/ NABOBOfficial*

Membership: minority owners and employees of radio and television stations and telecommunications properties. Provides members and the public with information on the broadcast industry and the FCC. Provides members with advocacy resources and information on advertising sales, station acquisition, financing, and federal broadcast regulation. Monitors legislation and regulations.

National Assn. of Broadcast Employees and Technicians (NABET-CWA), *501 3rd St. N.W., 6th Floor, 20001; (202) 434-1254. Fax, (202) 434-1426. Charlie Braico, President.*
General email, *nabet-cwa@cwa-union.org*
Web, *www.nabetcwa.org, Twitter, @NABETCWA*
Facebook, *facebook.com/groups/19196301434*

Membership: commercial broadcast, cable television, and radio personnel. Helps members negotiate pay, benefits, and better working conditions; conducts training programs and workshops. Monitors legislation and regulations. (Broadcast and Cable Television Workers Sector of the Communications Workers of America.)

National Assn. of Broadcasters (NAB), *1 M St. S.E., 20003; (202) 429-5300. Curtis LeGeyt, President. Communications, (202) 429-5350.*

General email, nab@nab.org

Web, www.nab.org, Twitter, @nabtweets and Facebook, www.facebook.com/Broadcasters

Membership: radio and television broadcast stations and broadcast networks holding an FCC license or construction permit; associate members include producers of equipment and programs. Assists members in areas of management, engineering, and research. Monitors legislation and regulations.

Public Broadcasting Service, *1225 S. Clark St., Arlington, VA 22202; (703) 739-5000. Fax, (703) 739-0775. Paula Kerger, President, (703) 739-5015; Ricardo Sandoval-Palos, Public Editor, (703) 739-5290. General email, viewer@pbs.org*

Web, www.pbs.org, Twitter, @PBS and Facebook, www .facebook.com/pbs

Membership: public television stations nationwide. Selects, schedules, promotes, and distributes national programs; provides public television stations with educational, instructional, and cultural programming; also provides news and public affairs, science and nature, and children's programming. Assists members with technology development and fund-raising.

Radio Free Asia, *2025 M St. N.W., #300, 20036; (202) 530-4900. Bay Fang, President. Press, (202) 530-4976. General email, contact@rfa.org*

Web, www.rfa.org and Twitter, @RadioFreeAsia

Independent radio, Internet, and television service funded by federal grants to promote and support democracy where public access to a free press is restricted. Broadcasts programs to East Asian countries, including China, Tibet, North Korea, Vietnam, Cambodia, Laos, and Burma; programming includes news, analysis, and specials on political developments, as well as cultural programs.

Radio Free Europe/Radio Liberty, *Washington Office, 1201 Connecticut Ave. N.W., #400, 20036; (202) 457-6900. Fax, (202) 457-6995. Jamie Fly, President; Daisy Sindelar, Vice President. Press, (202) 457-6948. General email, zvanersm@rferl.org*

Web, www.rferl.org, Twitter, @RFERL and Facebook, www.facebook.com/rferl

Independent radio, Internet, and television service funded by federal grants to promote and support democracy. Broadcasts programs to 23 countries, including Russia, Afghanistan, Pakistan, Iraq, Iran, and the republics of Central Asia; programming includes news, analysis, and specials on political developments, as well as cultural programs. Research materials available to the public by appointment. (Headquarters in Prague, Czech Republic.)

Radio Television Digital News Assn., *529 14th St. N.W., #1240, 20045; (202) 221-4282. Dan Shelley, Executive Director. Web, www.rtdna.org, Twitter, @RTDNA and Facebook, www.facebook.com/RTDNA.RTDNF*

Membership: local and network news executives in broadcasting, cable, and other electronic media in more than 30 countries. Serves as information source for members; provides advice on legislative, political, and judicial problems of electronic journalism; conducts international exchanges.

Senate Radio-Television Gallery, *S325 CAP, 20515; (202) 224-6421. Michael (Mike) Mastrian, Director. Web, www.radiotv.senate.gov and Twitter, @SenateRadioTV*

Membership: broadcast correspondents who cover Congress. Sponsors annual dinner. Acts as a liaison between congressional offices and members of the media, and facilitates broadcast coverage of Senate activities.

Voice of America *(International Broadcasting Bureau), 330 Independence Ave. S.W., 20237; (202) 203-4000. Fax, (202) 203-4960. Yolanda Lopez, Director (Acting). General email, askvoa@voanews.com*

Web, www.voanews.com, Twitter, @VOAnews and Facebook, www.facebook.com/voiceofamerica

A multimedia international broadcasting service funded by the U.S. government through the Broadcasting Board of Governors. Broadcasts news, information, and educational and cultural programming to an estimated worldwide audience of more than 134 million people weekly. Programs are produced in more than forty languages.

Walter Kaitz Foundation, *25 Massachusetts Ave. N.W., #100, 20001; (202) 222-2490. Fax, (202) 222-2496. Michelle A. Ray, Executive Director. Press, (202) 222-2350. General email, info@walterkaitz.org*

Web, www.walterkaitz.org and Twitter, @WalterKaitz

Nonprofit that promotes women, minorities, and veterans working in the media and telecommunications industry. Financially supports and creates programs that provide internships to minority students, educate women on leadership, and advocate diversity in telecommunications. Awards scholarships to professionals in the media and telecommunications industry.

Press Freedom

▶**NONGOVERNMENTAL**

Reporters Committee for Freedom of the Press, *1156 15th St. N.W., #1020, 20005; (202) 795-9300. Fax, (202) 795-9310. Bruce D. Brown, Executive Director, (202) 795-9301. Legal defense hotline, (800) 336-4243. General email, info@rcfp.org*

Web, www.rcfp.org, Twitter, @rcfp and Facebook, www .facebook.com/ReportersCommittee

Legal defense hotline email, hotline@rcpf.org

Committee of reporters and editors that provides journalists and media lawyers with a 24-hour hotline for media law and freedom of information questions. Provides assistance to journalists and media lawyers in media law court cases, and to student journalists. Produces publications on newsgathering legal issues. Interests include freedom of speech abroad, primarily as it affects U.S. citizens in the press.

Reporters Without Borders (Reporters Sans Frontières), Washington Office, Southern Railway Bldg., 1500 K St. N.W., #600, 20005 (mailing address: P.O. Box 34032, Washington, DC 20005); (202) 204-5548. Anna K. Nelson, U.S. Executive Director.
General email, dcdesk@rsf.org

Web, https://rsf.org/en/united-states, https://rsf.org and Twitter, @RSF_inter

Defends journalists who have been imprisoned or persecuted while conducting their work. Works to improve the safety of journalists. Advocates freedom of the press internationally through its offices in eleven countries. Sponsors annual events and awards. (Headquarters in Paris, France.)

Student Press Law Center, 1608 Rhode Island Ave. N.W., #211, 20036; (202) 785-5450. Fax, (202) 822-5045. Hadar Harris, Executive Director; Andrew Benson, Communications and Outreach.
General email, admin@splc.org

Web, https://splc.org, Twitter, @SPLC and Facebook, www.facebook.com/StudentPress

Collects, analyzes, and distributes information on free expression and freedom of information rights of student journalists (print, online, and broadcast) and on violations of those rights in high schools and colleges. Provides free legal advice and referrals to students and faculty advisers experiencing censorship. (Affiliated with the Reporters Committee for Freedom of the Press.)

Women's Institute for Freedom of the Press, 1940 Calvert St. N.W., 20009-1502; (202) 656-0893. Martha Leslie Allen, Director.
General email, ourmediademocracy@gmail.com

Web, www.wifp.org, Twitter, @WIFP and Facebook, www.facebook.com/TheWIFP

Conducts research and publishes in areas of communications and the media that are of particular interest to women. Promotes freedom of the press. Publishes a free online directory of media produced by and for women. Partners with the Global Woman PEACE Foundation.

Print and Online Media

▶ NONGOVERNMENTAL

American Press Institute (API), 4401 N. Fairfax Dr., #300, Arlington, VA 22203; (571) 366-1200. Amy Kovac-Ashley, Executive Director (Acting), (571) 366-1037.
General email, hello@pressinstitute.org

Web, www.americanpressinstitute.org, Twitter, @AmPress and Facebook, www.facebook.com/AmericanPressInstitute

Conducts research and training for journalists. Interests include sustaining a free press, and understanding changing audiences, new revenue models, and best practices for journalism in the digital age.

Assn. Media and Publishing, 1090 Vermont Ave. N.W., 6th Floor, 20005-4905; (202) 289-7442. Jeff Joseph, President.
General email, info@associationmediaandpublishing.com

Web, www.siia.net/amp, Twitter, @siia and Facebook, www.facebook.com/AssociationMediaand Publishing

Membership: association publishers and communications professionals. Works to develop high standards for editorial and advertising content in members' publications. Compiles statistics; bestows editorial and graphics awards; monitors postal regulations. (A division of Connectiv.)

Assn. of American Publishers, Government Affairs, 455 Massachusetts Ave. N.W., #700, 20001; (202) 347-3375. Fax, (202) 347-3690. Maria A. Pallante, Chief Executive Officer; Mathew Barbian, Vice President of Public Policy.
General email, info@publishers.org

Web, www.publishers.org, Twitter, @AmericanPublish and Facebook, www.facebook.com/AmericanPublishers

Membership: U.S. publishers of books, scholarly journals, and multiplatform K–12 and higher education course materials. Represents industry priorities on policy, legislation, and regulatory issues regionally, nationally, and worldwide. Interests include intellectual property rights and copyright protection, tax and trade, new technology, educational and library funding, and First Amendment rights.

Association of Magazine Media (MPA), Government Affairs, 1211 Connecticut Ave. N.W., #610, 20036; (202) 296-7277. Brigitte Schmidt Gwyn, President, (202) 296-2890; Rita Cohen, Senior Vice President, Legislative and Regulatory Policy, (202) 296-1307.
General email, mpa@magazine.org

Web, www.magazine.org, Twitter, @mpamagmedia and Facebook, www.facebook.com/mpamagmedia

Membership: publishers of consumer magazines. Represents members in all aspects of government relations in Washington and state capitals. Interests include intellectual property, the First Amendment, consumer protection, advertising, postal, environmental, and tax policy.

CQ Press, 2600 Virginia Ave. N.W., #600, 20037; (202) 729-1800. Fax, (202) 729-1940. Blaise R. Simqu, Chief Executive Office. Toll-free, (800) 818-7243.
General email, orders@sagepub.com

Web, https://us.sagepub.com/en-us/nam/cqpress, Twitter, @SAGECQPolitics and Facebook, www.facebook.com/SAGEPublishing

Publishes books, directories, periodicals, and online products on U.S. government, history, and politics. Products include CQ Press Encyclopedia of American Government and CQ Researcher. (An imprint of SAGE Publishing; Headquarters in Thousand Oaks, Calif.)

Entertainment Software Assn. (ESA), *601 Massachusetts Ave. N.W., #300, 20001; (202) 223-2400. Stanley Pierre-Louis, President.*
General email, esa@theesa.com

Web, www.theesa.com, Twitter, @theesa and Facebook, www.facebook.com/TheEntertainmentSoftware Association

Membership: publishers of interactive entertainment software. Distributes marketing statistics and information. Administers a worldwide antipiracy program. Established an independent rating system for entertainment software. Monitors legislation and regulations. Interests include First Amendment and intellectual property protection efforts.

Essential Information, *1530 P St. N.W., 20005 (mailing address: P.O. Box 19405, Washington, DC 20036); Fax, (202) 387-8034. John Richard, Executive Director.*
Web, www.essentialinformation.org

Provides writers and the public with information on public policy matters; awards grants to investigative reporters; sponsors conference on investigative journalism. Interests include activities of multinational corporations in developing countries.

Graphic Communications Conference of the International Brotherhood of Teamsters (GCC/IBT), *25 Louisiana Ave. N.W., 20001; (202) 624-6800. Fax, (202) 624-8145. Sean O'Brien, President.*
General email, communications@teamster.org

Web, www.gciu.org, Twitter, @teamsters and Facebook, www.facebook.com/teamsters

Membership: approximately 60,000 members of the print and publishing industries, including lithographers, photoengravers, and bookbinders. Assists members with contract negotiation and grievances; conducts training programs and workshops. Monitors legislation and regulations.

IDEAlliance, *1800 Diagonal Rd., #320, Alexandria, VA 22314-2862; (703) 837-1070. Fax, (703) 837-1072. Jordan Gorski, Chief Executive Officer.*
General email, membership@idealliance.org

Web, www.idealliance.org, Twitter, @Idealliance and Facebook, www.facebook.com/IdeallianceUS

Membership: firms and customers in the visual communication industry, including content and media creators, print and digital service providers, material suppliers, and technology partners. Assists members in production of color graphics and conducts studies on print media management methods.

National Newspaper Publishers Assn. (NNPA), *1816 12th St. N.W., 2nd Floor, 20009; (202) 588-8764. Fax, (202) 588-8960. Karen Carter Richards, Chair; Benjamin Chavis Jr., President.*

General email, info@nnpa.org

Web, www.nnpa.org, Twitter, @NNPA_BlackPress, Facebook, www.facebook.com/BlackPressUSA and YouTube, www.youtube.com/c/blackpressusatv

Membership: newspapers owned by African Americans serving an African American audience. Assists in improving management and quality of the African American press through workshops and merit awards. Sponsors NNPA Media Services, a print and Web advertising-placement and press release distribution service.

News Media Alliance, *4401 Fairfax Dr., #300, Arlington, VA 22203; (571) 366-1000. David Chavern, President, (571) 366-1100.*
General email, info@newsmediaalliance.org

Web, www.newsmediaalliance.org, Twitter, @newsalliance, Facebook, www.facebook.com/NewsMediaAlliance and YouTube, www.youtube.com/c/NewsMediaAlliance

Membership: daily and weekly newspapers, other papers, and online products published in the United States, Canada, other parts of the Western Hemisphere, and Europe. Conducts research and disseminates information on newspaper publishing, including labor relations, legal matters, government relations, technical problems and innovations, telecommunications, economic and statistical data, marketing, and training programs.

Open Markets Institute, *1440 G St. N.W., 20005; (202) 701-1606. Barry C. Lynn, Executive Director.*
General email, info@openmarketsinstitute.org

Web, www.openmarketsinstitute.org, Twitter, @openmarkets and Facebook, www.facebook.com/openmarketsinstitute

Think tank promoting public awareness of political and economic monopolization in the United States; identifies changes in policy and law, and promotes open discussion with citizens and policymakers regarding political economic challenges, including fair pricing and antitrust laws.

Printing United Alliance, *10015 Main St., Fairfax, Va, 22031; (703) 385-1335. Fax, (703) 273-0456. Ford Bowers, Chief Executive Officer; Marci Kinter, Vice President of Government and Regulatory Affairs. Toll-free, (888) 385-3588.*
General email, assist@printing.org

Web, www.printing.org, Twitter, @Printingunited and Facebook, www.facebook.com/printingunited

Membership: printing and graphic design firms and businesses. Represents members before Congress and regulatory agencies. Assists members with labor relations, human resources management, and other business management issues. Sponsors graphic arts competition. Monitors legislation and regulations.

4 📷

Culture and Religion

ARTS AND HUMANITIES

General

▶ **AGENCIES**

General Services Administration (GSA), *Design and Construction, Office of the Chief Architect,* 1800 F St. N.W., #5400, 20405-0001; (202) 501-1888. David Insinga, Chief Architect.
Web, www.gsa.gov/about-us/organization/public-buildings-service

Administers the Art in Architecture Program, which commissions publicly scaled works of art for government buildings and landscapes, and the Fine Arts Program, which manages the GSA's collection of fine artwork that has been commissioned for use in government buildings.

John F. Kennedy Center for the Performing Arts, 2700 F St. N.W., 20566-0001; (202) 416-8000. Deborah F. Rutter, President, (202) 416-8011; David M. Rubenstein, Chair. Performance and ticket information, (202) 467-4600. Toll-free, (800) 444-1324. TTY, (202) 416-8524.
Web, www.kennedy-center.org, Twitter, @Kencen and Facebook, www.facebook.com/KennedyCenter

National cultural center created by Congress that operates independently; funded in part by federal dollars but primarily through private gifts and sales. Sponsors educational programs; presents American and international performances in theater, music, dance, and film; sponsors the John F. Kennedy Center Education Program, which produces the annual American College Theater Festival; and presents and subsidizes events for young people. The Kennedy Center stages free daily performances open to the public 365 days a year on its Millennium Stage in the Grand Foyer.

National Endowment for the Arts (NEA), 400 7th St. S.W., 20506; (202) 682-5400. Maria Rosario Jackson, Chair; Ann Eilers, Deputy Chairman for Management and Budget, (202) 682-5534. TTY, (202) 682-5082.
General email, publicaffairs@arts.gov
Web, www.arts.gov, Twitter, @NEAarts and Facebook, www.facebook.com/NationalEndowmentfortheArts

Independent grant-making agency. Awards grants to support artistic excellence, creativity, and innovation for the benefit of individuals and communities. Works through partnerships with state arts agencies, local leaders, other federal agencies, and the philanthropic sector. Main funding categories include Art Works (replaces Access to Artistic Excellence and Learning in the Arts for Children and Youth); Challenge America Fast-Track (for art projects in underserved communities); and Our Town (for art projects that contribute to the livability of communities).

National Endowment for the Arts (NEA), *Artist Communities,* 400 7th St. S.W., 20506; (202) 682-5428. Brandon Gryde, Director, (202) 682-5697; Jennie Terman, Contact, (202) 682-5566. TTY, (202) 682-5082.
Web, www.arts.gov

Awards grants and provides assistance to artist communities for projects that encourage and nurture the development of individual artists.

National Endowment for the Arts (NEA), *Presenting and Multidisciplinary Arts,* 400 7th St. S.W., 20506; (202) 682-5566. (202) 682-5428. Jennie Terman, Specialist, (202) 628-5566; Katryna Carter, Specialist, (202) 682-5779.
Web, www.arts.gov

Awards grants to traditional presenting programs as well as artistic works and events that present multiple disciplines, combine or integrate art forms, explore boundaries between art disciplines, and seek to create new forms of expression.

National Endowment for the Humanities (NEH), 400 7th St. S.W., 20506; (202) 606-8400. Shelly C. Lowe, Chair; Janice Bell, Librarian, (202) 606-8572. Library, (202) 633-8244. Library, (202) 633-4680. TTY, (800) 877-8399.
General email, questions@neh.gov
Web, www.neh.gov, Twitter, @NEHgov, Facebook, www.facebook.com/nehgov and YouTube, www.youtube.com/channel/UCPQ3xb0ky2WsNM_U1FKjrNQ

Independent federal grant-making agency. Awards grants to individuals and institutions for research, scholarship, and educational and public programs (including broadcasts, museum exhibitions, lectures, and symposia) in the humanities (defined as study of archaeology; history; jurisprudence; language; linguistics; literature; philosophy; comparative religion; ethics; history, criticism, and theory of the arts; and humanistic aspects of the social sciences). Funds preservation of books, newspapers, historical documents, and photographs. Library open by appointment only.

National Foundation on the Arts and the Humanities, *Federal Council on the Arts and the Humanities,* 400 7th St. S.W., 20506; (202) 682-5541. Fax, (202) 682-5721. Patricia Loiko, Chief Indemnity Officer.
General email, fedreg.info@nara.gov
Web, http://federalregister.gov/agencies/federal-council-on-the-arts-and-the-humanities

Membership: leaders of federal agencies sponsoring arts-related activities. Administers the Arts and Artifacts Indemnity Act, which helps museums reduce the costs of commercial insurance for traveling exhibits.

Smithsonian Institution, *International Relations and Global Programs,* 1100 Jefferson Dr. S.W., #3123, 20560 (mailing address: P.O. Box 37012, MS 705, Washington, DC 20013-7012); (202) 633-4795. Aviva Rosenthal, Director.
General email, global@si.edu
Web, https://global.si.edu, Twitter, @GlobalSI, Facebook, www.facebook.com/SmithsonianGlobal and YouTube, www.youtube.com/channel/UCtfCKTPkaoyBFHtE_lEYTyg

Fosters the development and coordinates the international aspects of Smithsonian cultural activities; facilitates basic research in history and art and encourages international collaboration among individuals and institutions.

CULTURE AND RELIGION RESOURCES IN CONGRESS

For a complete listing of congressional committees, including their full contact information, leadership, membership, and jurisdictions, please refer to the Appendix on pages 840–963.

HOUSE:

House Administration Committee, (202) 225-2061.
Web, https://cha.house.gov
House Agriculture Committee, (202) 225-2171.
Web, https://agriculture.house.gov
   Subcommittee on Conservation and Forestry,
      (202) 225-2171.
House Appropriations Committee, (202) 225-2771.
Web, https://appropriations.house.gov
   Subcommittee on Interior, Environment, and
      Related Agencies, (202) 225-3081.
   Subcommittee on Labor, Health and Human
      Services, Education, and Related Agencies,
      (202) 225-3508.
   Subcommittee on Legislative Branch,
      (202) 226-7252.
House Education and Labor Committee,
   (202) 225-3725.
Web, https://edlabor.house.gov
   Subcommittee on Early Childhood, Elementary,
      and Secondary Education, (202) 225-3725.
   Subcommittee on Higher Education and
      Workforce Investment, (202) 225-3725.
House Energy and Commerce Committee,
   (202) 225-2927.
Web, https://energycommerce.house.gov
   Subcommittee on Communications and
      Technology, (202) 225-2927.
   Subcommittee on Consumer Protection and
      Commerce, (202) 225-2927.
House Judiciary Committee, (202) 225-3951.
Web, https://judiciary.house.gov
   Subcommittee on the Constitution, Civil Rights,
      and Civil Liberties, (202) 225-3951.
House Natural Resources Committee, (202) 225-6065.
Web, https://naturalresources.house.gov
   Subcommittee on Indigenous Peoples of the
      United States, (202) 226-9725.
House Science, Space, and Technology Committee,
   (202) 225-6375.
Web, https://science.house.gov
   Subcommittee on Research and Technology,
      (202) 225-6375.
House Ways and Means Committee, (202) 225-3625.
Web, https://waysandmeans.house.gov
   Subcommittee on Select Revenue Measures,
      (202) 225-3625.

JOINT:

Joint Committee on the Library of Congress,
   (202) 225-2061.
Web, https://cha.house.gov/jointcommittees/joint-
   committee-library

SENATE:

Senate Agriculture, Nutrition, and Forestry
   Committee, (202) 224-2035.
Web, agriculture.senate.gov
   Subcommittee on Food and Nutrition,
      Specialty Crop, Organics, and Research,
      (202) 224-2035.
Senate Appropriations Committee, (202) 224-7363.
Web, appropriations.senate.gov
   Subcommittee on Interior, Environment, and
      Related Agencies, (202) 224-7363.
   Subcommittee on Labor, Health and Human
      Services, Education, and Related Agencies,
      (202) 224-7363.
Senate Banking, Housing, and Urban Affairs
   Committee, (202) 224-7391.
Web, banking.senate.gov
   Subcommittee on Housing, Transportation,
      and Community Development,
      (202) 224-7391.
Senate Energy and Natural Resources Committee,
   (202) 224-4971.
Web, energy.senate.gov
   Subcommittee on National Parks,
      (202) 224-4971.
Senate Finance Committee, (202) 224-4515.
Web, finance.senate.gov
   Subcommittee on Energy, Natural Resources, and
      Infrastructure, (202) 224-4515.
Senate Health, Education, Labor, and Pensions
   Committee, (202) 224-5375.
Web, help.senate.gov
   Subcommittee on Children and Families,
      (202) 224-5375.
Senate Indian Affairs Committee, (202) 224-2251.
Web, indian.senate.gov
Senate Judiciary Committee, (202) 224-7703.
Web, judiciary.senate.gov
Senate Rules and Administration Committee,
   (202) 224-6352.
Web, rules.senate.gov

U.S. Commission of Fine Arts, *401 F St. N.W., #312, 20001-2728; (202) 504-2200. Earl A. Powell III, Chair; Thomas Luebke, Secretary.*
General email, cfastaff@cfa.gov
Web, www.cfa.gov, Twitter, @CFA_GOV
Georgetown inquiries, georgetown@cfa.gov

Advises the federal and D.C. governments on matters of art and architecture that affect the appearance of the nation's capital.

▶**CONGRESS**

For a listing of relevant congressional committees and sub-committees, please see page 130 or the Appendix.

▶**NONGOVERNMENTAL**

Americans for the Arts, *1000 Vermont Ave. N.W., 6th Floor, 20005; (202) 371-2830. Fax, (202) 371-0424. Nolen V. Bivens, President.*
Web, www.americansforthearts.org and Twitter, @americans4arts

Membership: groups and individuals promoting advancement of the arts and culture in U.S. communities. Provides information on programs, activities, and administration of local arts agencies; on funding sources and guidelines; and on government policies and programs. Conducts, sponsors, and disseminates research on the social, educational, and economic benefits of arts programs. Monitors legislation and regulations.

Assn. of Performing Arts Presenters *(APAP), 919 18th St. N.W., #650, 20006; (202) 833-2787. Fax, (202) 833-1543. Lisa Richards Toney, President. Toll-free, (888) 820-2787.*
General email, info@apap365.org
Web, www.apap365.org, Twitter, @APAP365 and Facebook, www.facebook.com/APAPNYC

Connects performing artists to audiences and communities around the world. Facilitates the work of presenters, artist managers, and consultants through continuing education, regranting programs, and legislative advocacy.

Center for the Study of Statesmanship (CSS), *313 Caldwell Hall, 620 Michigan Ave. N.E., 20064; (301) 464-4277. Claes G. Ryn, Founding Director Emeritus.*
General email, smithws@cua.edu
Web, https://css.cua.edu/, Twitter, @CSSatCUA and Facebook, www.facebook.com/CSSatCUA

Promotes research, teaching, and public discussion about the meaning of statesmanship and how it can defuse conflict and foster respectful foreign and domestic relations. Explores the sources and prerequisites of sound leadership and how to counter such influences as intemperance and blinding ideology. Affiliated with Catholic University of America.

Federation of State Humanities Councils, *1600 Wilson Blvd., #902, Arlington, VA 22209-2511; (703) 908-9700. Phoebe Stein, President, ext. 213.*

General email, info@statehumanities.org
Web, www.statehumanities.org, Twitter, @HumFed, Facebook, www.facebook.com/HumFed and Youtube, www.youtube.com/channel/UCQ_4hhrCQtxWWkM8PtruqmQ

Membership: humanities councils from U.S. states and territories. Provides members with information; forms partnerships with other organizations and with the private sector to promote the humanities. Monitors legislation and regulations.

National Assembly of State Arts Agencies, *1200 18th St. N.W., #1100, 20036; (202) 347-6352. Fax, (202) 737-0526. Pam Breaux, President. TTY, (202) 296-0567.*
General email, nasaa@nasaa-arts.org
Web, www.nasaa-arts.org, Twitter, @NASAA_Arts and Facebook, www.facebook.com/NASAA.Arts

Membership: state and territorial arts agencies. Provides members with information, resources, and representation. Interests include arts programs for rural and underserved populations and the arts as a catalyst for economic development. Monitors legislation and regulations.

National Humanities Alliance, *21 Dupont Circle N.W., #800, 20036; (202) 296-4994. Fax, (202) 872-0884. Stephen Kidd, Executive Director, ext. 149.*
General email, humanities@nhalliance.org
Web, www.nhalliance.org, Twitter, @HumanitiesAll and Facebook, www.facebook.com/NationalHumanities Alliance

Represents scholarly and professional humanities associations; associations of museums, libraries, and historical societies; higher education institutions; state humanities councils; and independent and university-based research centers. Promotes the interests of individuals engaged in research, writing, and teaching.

National League of American Pen Women, *1300 17th St. N.W., 20036-1901; (202) 785-1997. Fax, (202) 452-6868. Evelyn B. Wofford, National President.*
General email, contact@nlapw.org
Web, www.nlapw.org, Twitter, @NLAPW and Facebook, www.facebook.com/NLAPW

Promotes the development of the creative talents of professional women in the fields of art, letters, and music composition. Conducts and promotes literary, educational, and charitable activities. Offers scholarships, workshops, and discussion groups.

Performing Arts Alliance, *1211 Connecticut Ave. N.W., #200, 20036 (mailing address: P.O. Box 33001, 1800 M St. N.W., Washington, DC 20033); (202) 207-3850. Denise Saunders Thompson, Vice Chair.*
General email, info@thepaalliance.org
Web, www.theperformingartsalliance.org, Twitter, @PAAlliance and Facebook, www.facebook.com/ThePAAlliance

Membership: organizations of the professional, non-profit performing arts and presenting fields. Through legislative and grassroots activities, advocates policies favorable to the performing arts and presenting fields.

Provisions Library Resource Center for Arts and Social Change *(George Mason University), Art and Design Bldg., 4400 University Dr., #L001, MS 1C3, Fairfax, VA 22030; (202) 670-7768. Donald H. Russell, Executive Director.*
General email, provisionslibrary@gmail.com
Web, http://provisionslibrary.com, Twitter, @ProvisionsLib and Facebook, www.facebook.com/provisionslib

Library collection on politics and culture open to the public by appointment. Offers educational and arts programs concerning social change and social justice.

Wolf Trap Foundation for the Performing Arts, *1645 Trap Rd., Vienna, VA 22182-2064; (703) 255-1900. Fax, (703) 255-1905. Arvind Manocha, President. Press, (703) 255-4096. Tickets, (877) 965-3872. TTY, (703) 255-1849.*
General email, wolftrap@wolftrap.org
Web, www.wolftrap.org, Twitter, @wolf_trap and Facebook, www.facebook.com/WolfTrapOfficialPage

Established by Congress; operates as a public–private partnership between the National Park Service, which maintains the grounds, and the Wolf Trap Foundation, which sponsors performances in theater, music, and dance. Conducts educational programs for children, internships for college students, career-entry programs for young singers, and professional training for teachers and performers.

Education

▶ AGENCIES

Elementary and Secondary Education (OESE) *(Education Dept.), Discretionary Grants and Support Services (DGSS), Well-Rounded Education Programs (WREP), Lyndon B. Johnson Bldg., 400 Maryland Ave. S.W., 20202-5950; (202) 453-5501. Jennifer Todd, Director.*
Web, https://oese.ed.gov/offices/office-of-discretionary-grants-support-services/well-rounded-education-programs

Administers discretionary grant programs that support activities designed to advance literacy skills, provide professional learning opportunities to teachers to increase the performance of students in mathematics and science, create leadership pipelines for schools in need of improvement, support arts education, and pay all or a portion of advanced placement fees on behalf of low-income students.

John F. Kennedy Center for the Performing Arts, *Education, 2700 F St. N.W., 20566-0001; (202) 416-8800. Jordan LaSalle, Vice President. Press, (202) 416-8442. TTY, (202) 416-8728.*
General email, kced@kennedy-center.org
Web, www.kennedy-center.org/education

Establishes and supports state committees to encourage arts education in schools; promotes community partnerships between performing arts centers and school systems (Partners in Education); provides teachers, artists, and school and arts administrators with professional development classes; offers in-house and touring performances for students, teachers, families, and the general public; arranges artist and company residencies in schools; sponsors the National Symphony Orchestra education program; presents lectures, demonstrations, and classes in the performing arts for the general public; offers internships in arts management; and produces annually the Kennedy Center American College Theater Festival.

John F. Kennedy Center for the Performing Arts, *School and Community Programs, Networks and Strategic Leadership, 2700 F St. N.W., 20566-0001; (202) 416-8835. Jeanette McCune, Director, (202) 416-8850. Partners in Education, (202) 416-8843. Press, (202) 416-8442. TTY, (202) 416-8728.*
General email, kced@kennedy-center.org
Web, www.kennedy-center.org/education/networks-conferences-and-research/networks-and-strategic-leadership

Supports arts and education institutions throughout the nation by building their capacity to develop and sustain robust arts education programs. Through its two national networks—*Ensuring the Arts for Any Given Child* and *Partners in Education*—it provides professional learning, national peer networking opportunities, and other resources.

National Endowment for the Arts (NEA), *Arts Education, 400 7th St. S.W., 20506; (202) 682-5707. (202) 682-5400. Ayanna N. Hudson, Director, (202) 682-5515. TTY, (202) 682-5082.*
General email, artseducation@arts.gov
Web, www.arts.gov/impact/arts-education, Twitter, @NEAarts and Facebook, www.facebook.com/NationalEndowmentfortheArts

Provides grants for curriculum-based arts education for children and youth (generally between ages 5 and 18) in schools or other community-based settings. Projects must provide participatory learning that engages students with accomplished artists and teachers, align with national or state arts education standards, and include assessments of participant learning. Also provides funding to support professional development opportunities for teachers, teaching artists, and other educators.

National Endowment for the Humanities (NEH), *Division of Public Programs, 400 7th St. S.W., 20506; (202) 606-8269. Jeff Hardwick, Director (Acting), (202) 606-8287.*
General email, publicpgms@neh.gov
Web, www.neh.gov/divisions/public and Twitter, @NEH_PubPrograms

Awards grants to libraries, museums, special projects, and media for projects that enhance public appreciation and understanding of the humanities through books and other resources in American library collections. Projects include conferences, exhibitions, essays, documentaries, radio programs, and lecture series.

National Endowment for the Humanities (NEH), *Division of Research Programs, 400 7th St. S.W., 20506;*

(202) 606-8200. Christopher P. Thornton, Director, (202) 606-8286.
General email, research@neh.gov
Web, www.neh.gov/divisions/research and *Twitter, @NEH_Research*

Sponsors fellowship programs for humanities scholars, including summer stipend programs. Provides support to libraries, museums, and independent centers for advanced study.

National Endowment for the Humanities (NEH), *Education Programs, 400 7th St. S.W., 20506; (202) 606-8500. Carol Peters, Director, (202) 606-8285.*
General email, education@neh.gov
Web, www.neh.gov/divisions/education and *Twitter, @NEH_Education*

Supports the improvement of education in the humanities. Supports classroom resources and faculty training and development.

National Endowment for the Humanities (NEH), *Office of Digital Humanities, 400 7th St. S.W., 20506; (202) 606-8401. Brett Bobley, Director.*
General email, odh@neh.gov
Web, www.neh.gov/divisions/odh and *Twitter, @NEH_ODH*

Encourages and supports projects that utilize or study the impact of digital technology on research, education, preservation, access, and public programming in the humanities.

National Gallery of Art, *Education, 6th St. and Constitution Ave. N.W., 20565 (mailing address: 2000B S. Club Dr., Landover, MD 20785); (202) 842-6269. Damon Reaves, Museum Educator.*
General email, EdResources@nga.gov
Web, www.nga.gov/learn.html

Serves as an educational arm of the gallery by providing free programs for schools, families, and adults. Lends audiovisual educational materials free of charge to schools, colleges, community groups, libraries, and individuals. Provides answers to written and telephone inquiries.

Smithsonian Center for Learning and Digital Access, *600 Maryland Ave. S.W., #1005W, 20024 (mailing address: P.O. Box 37012, MS 508, Washington, DC 20013-7012); (202) 633-5330. Stephanie Norby, Director; Darren Milligan, Director of Educational Technology.*
General email, learning@si.edu
Web, https://learninglab.si.edu/about/ SmithsonianCenterforLearningandDigitalAccess, Twitter, @SmithsonianLab and *Facebook, www.facebook.com/smithsonianeducation*

Serves as the Smithsonian's central education office. Provides elementary and secondary teachers with programs, publications, audiovisual materials, regional workshops, and summer courses on using museums and primary source materials as teaching tools. Publishes books and other educational materials for teachers. (Associated with the Smithsonian Learning Lab.)

Smithsonian Institution, *Fellowships and Internships, 470 L'Enfant Plaza S.W., #7102, 20013-7012 (mailing address: P.O. Box 37012, MS 902, Washington, DC 20013-7012); (202) 633-7070. Vacant, Director.*
General email, siofi@si.edu
Web, si.edu/ofi and *Twitter, @SmithsonianOFI*

Provides fellowships to students and scholars for independent research projects in association with members of the Smithsonian professional research staff. Provides central management for all Smithsonian research fellowship programs. Facilitates the Smithsonian's scholarly interactions with universities, museums, and research institutions around the world.

Smithsonian Institution, *Smithsonian Associates, 1100 Jefferson Dr. S.W., #3077, 20560 (mailing address: P.O. Box 23293, Washington, DC 20026-3293); (202) 633-3030. Fax, (202) 786-2034. Frederica Adelman, Director.*
General email, customerservice@smithsonianassociates.org
Web, https://smithsonianassociates.org/ticketing/, Twitter, @SmithsonianSA, Facebook, www.facebook.com/ SmithsonianAssociates and *YouTube, www.youtube.com/ channel/UC-6oUkyfT3zYqvWIvLPl6gA*

National cultural and educational membership organization that offers courses and lectures for adults and young people. Presents films and offers study tours on subjects related to the arts, humanities, and science; sponsors performances, studio arts workshops, and research.

▶ **NONGOVERNMENTAL**

National Art Education Assn., *901 Prince St., Alexandria, VA 22314; (703) 860-8000. Fax, (703) 860-2960. Mario R. Rossero, Executive Director, (703) 889-1283. Toll-free, (800) 299-8321.*
General email, info@arteducators.org
Web, www.arteducators.org, Twitter, @NAEA and *Facebook, www.facebook.com/arteducators*

Membership: visual art educators (pre-K through university), school administrators, museum staff, and manufacturers and suppliers of art materials. Issues publications on art education theory and practice, research, and current trends; provides technical assistance to art educators. Sponsors awards.

National Assn. for Music Education, *1806 Robert Fulton Dr., Reston, VA 20191-4348; (703) 860-4000. Christopher B. L. Woodside, Executive Director. Toll-free, (800) 336-3768. Toll-free fax, (888) 275-6232.*
General email, memberservices@nafme.org
Web, www.nafme.org, Twitter, @NAfME and *Facebook, www.facebook.com/nafme/*

Membership: music educators (preschool through university). Holds biennial conference and professional development events. Publishes books and teaching aids for music educators. Monitors legislation and regulations.

National Assn. of Schools of Art and Design, *11250 Roger Bacon Dr., #21, Reston, VA 20190-5248; (703) 437-0700.*

Fax, (703) 437-6312. Karen Moynahan, Executive Director, ext. 116.

General email, info@arts-accredit.org

Web, http://nasad.arts-accredit.org

Specialized professional accrediting agency for post-secondary programs in art and design. Conducts and shares research and analysis on topics pertinent to art and design programs and fields of art and design. Offers professional development opportunities for executives of art and design programs.

National Children's Museum, 1300 Pennsylvania Ave. N.W., 20004; (202) 844-2486. Crystal Bowyer, President.

General email, info@nationalchildrensmuseum.org

Web, www.nationalchildrensmuseum.org, Twitter, @NatChildrens and Facebook, www.facebook.com/ NationalChildrensMuseum

A cultural and educational institution serving children and families onsite and through national partners and programs. Exhibits and activities focus on the arts, civic engagement, the environment, global citizenship, health and well-being, and play. Affiliated with the Association of Children's Museums Reciprocal Network.

Wolf Trap Foundation for the Performing Arts, 1645 Trap Rd., Vienna, VA 22182-2064; (703) 255-1900. Fax, (703) 255-1905. Arvind Manocha, President. Press, (703) 255-4096. Tickets, (877) 965-3872. TTY, (703) 255-1849.

General email, wolftrap@wolftrap.org

Web, www.wolftrap.org, Twitter, @wolf_trap and Facebook, www.facebook.com/WolfTrapOfficialPage

Established by Congress; operates as a public–private partnership between the National Park Service, which maintains the grounds, and the Wolf Trap Foundation, which sponsors performances in theater, music, and dance. Conducts educational programs for children, internships for college students, career-entry programs for young singers, and professional training for teachers and performers.

Film, Photography, and Broadcasting

▶**AGENCIES**

National Archives and Records Administration (NARA), Motion Picture, Sound, and Video Branch, 8601 Adelphi Rd.,#3360, College Park, MD 20740-6001; (866) 272-6272). Daniel (Dan) X. Rooney, Chief, Special Media, (301) 837-1995; Ellen L. Mulligan, Chief, Moving Image and Sound, (301) 837-3006; William D. Wade, Chief, Still Pictures, (301) 837-3090.

General email, mopix@nara.gov

Web, www.archives.gov/research/motion-pictures/visit

Selects and preserves audiovisual records produced or acquired by federal agencies; maintains collections from the private sector, including newsreels. Research room open to the public Monday–Saturday, 9:00 a.m.–5:00 p.m.

National Archives and Records Administration (NARA), Still Picture Branch, 8601 Adelphi Rd., NWCS #3360,

College Park, MD 20740-6001; (301) 837-0561. Fax, (301) 837-3621. William D. Wade, Director, (301) 837-3090.

General email, stillpix@nara.gov

Web, www.archives.gov/college-park/photographs

Provides the public with access to and copies of still picture and poster records created or acquired by the federal government; supplies research assistance (both offsite and onsite), finding aids and guides to these materials. Records include still pictures and posters (some in digital format) from more than 200 federal agencies, from the mid-nineteenth century to the present.

National Endowment for the Arts (NEA), Media Arts, 400 7th St. S.W., 20506; (202) 682-5452. Jax Deluca, Director, (202) 682-5742. TTY, (202) 682-5082.

Web, www.arts.gov

Awards grants to nonprofit organizations for screen-based projects presented by film, television, video, radio, Internet, mobile technologies, video games, transmedia storytelling, and satellite; supports film and video exhibitions and workshops.

National Endowment for the Humanities (NEH), Division of Public Programs, 400 7th St. S.W., 20506; (202) 606-8269. Jeff Hardwick, Director (Acting), (202) 606-8287.

General email, publicpgms@neh.gov

Web, www.neh.gov/divisions/public and Twitter, @NEH_ PubPrograms

Promotes public appreciation of the humanities through support of quality public programs of broad significance, reach, and impact. Awards grants for projects that meet NEH goals and standards, including excellence in content and format, broad public appeal, and wide access to diverse audiences.

▶**CONGRESS**

For a listing of relevant congressional committees and subcommittees, please see page 130 or the Appendix.

Library of Congress, Motion Picture, Broadcasting, and Recorded Sound Division, Moving Image Research Center, James Madison Memorial Bldg., 101 Independence Ave. S.E., #LM 336, 20540-4690; (202) 707-8572. Fax, (202) 707-2371. Gregory Lukow, Chief.

General email, mpref@loc.gov

Web, www.loc.gov/rr/mopic

Motion Picture and Broadcasting archives include an extensive range from 1894 to the present of feature films, shorts, animated cartoons, newsreels, television shows, and more. American Film Institute film archives are inter-filed with the division's collections. Use of collections restricted to scholars and researchers; Timed entry pass for visitors required, details at loc.gov/visit. Appointments recommended for researchers.

Library of Congress, National Film Preservation Board, 19053 Mount Pony Rd., Culpeper, VA 22701-7551; (202) 707-5912. Stephen (Steve) Leggett, Staff Coordinator.

Web, www.loc.gov/programs/national-film-preservation-board/about-this-program

Administers the National Film Preservation Plan. Establishes guidelines and receives nominations for the annual selection of twenty-five films of cultural, historical, or aesthetic significance; selections are entered in the National Film Registry to ensure archival preservation in their original form.

Library of Congress, *National Recording Preservation Board,* *101 Independence Ave. S.E., 20540-5698; (202) 707-5912. Fax, (202) 707-2371. Steve Leggett, Staff Coordinator. TTY, (202) 707-6362.*
Web, www.loc.gov/programs/national-recording-preservation-board/about-this-program

Administers the National Recording Preservation Plan aimed at studying the state of and advances in sound recording. Receives nominations for the annual selection of twenty-five recordings demonstrating the range and diversity of American recorded sound heritage. Makes selections for the National Recording Registry.

Library of Congress, *Prints and Photographs Division,* *James Madison Memorial Bldg., 101 Independence Ave. S.E., #LM 337, 20540-4730; (202) 707-6394. Helena Zinkham, Chief, (202) 707-2922.*
Web, www.loc.gov/rr/print

Maintains Library of Congress's collection of pictorial material not in book format, totaling more than 15 million items. U.S. and international collections include artists' prints; historical prints, posters, and drawings; photographs (chiefly documentary); political and social cartoons; and architectural plans, drawings, prints, and photographs. Reference service provided in the Prints and Photographs Reading Room. Reproductions of nonrestricted material available through the Library of Congress's Photoduplication Service; prints and photographs may be borrowed through the Exhibits Office for exhibits by qualified institutions. A portion of the collections and an overview of reference services are available online. Timed entry pass for visitors required, details at loc.gov/visit. Appointments recommended for researchers.

▶NONGOVERNMENTAL

American Film Institute (AFI), *Silver Theatre and Cultural Center,* *8633 Colesville Rd., Silver Spring, MD 20910-3916; (301) 495-6720. Fax, (301) 495-6777. Ray Barry, Director. Recorded information, (301) 495-6700.*
General email, silverinfo@afi.com
Web, https://afisilver.afi.com, Twitter, @AFISilver and Facebook, www.facebook.com/afisilvertheatre

Shows films of historical and artistic importance. AFI theater open to the public.

Motion Picture Assn. of America, *1600 Eye St. N.W., 20006; (202) 293-1966. Fax, (202) 785-3026. Charles H. Rivkin, Chief Executive Officer.*

General email, ContactUs@mpaa.org
Web, www.motionpictures.org, Twitter, @motionpictures and Facebook, www.facebook.com/motionpictures

Membership: motion picture producers and distributors. Advises state and federal governments on copyrights, censorship, cable broadcasting, and other topics; administers volunteer rating system for motion pictures; works to prevent video piracy.

Special Collections in Mass Media and Culture *(University of Maryland),* *Hornbake Library, 4130 Campus Dr., MS32106, College Park, MD 20742-7011; (301) 405-9255. Laura Schnitker, Curator. Reference desk, (301) 405-9212.*
General email, askhornbake@umd.edu
Web, www.lib.umd.edu/special/collections/massmedia/home

Maintains library and archives on the history of radio and television. Houses the National Public Broadcasting Archives. Open to the public. (Formerly Library of American Broadcasting.)

Language and Literature

▶AGENCIES

Administration for Children and Families (ACF) *(Health and Human Services Dept.),* **Administration for Native Americans (ANA),** *Mary E. Switzer Bldg., 330 C St. S.W., Room 4126, 20201; (202) 690-7732. Fax, (202) 690-7441. Hope MacDonald LoneTree, Deputy Commissioner; Michelle Sauve, Executive Director of ICNAA. Toll-free, (877) 922-9262.*
General email, anacomments@acf.hhs.gov
Web, https://acf.hhs.gov/ana and Facebook, www.facebook.com/administrationfornativeamericans

Promotes revitalization and continuation of tribal languages.

National Endowment for the Arts (NEA), *Literary Arts,* *400 7th St. S.W., 20506; (202) 682-5011. Amy Stolls, Director, (202) 682-5771; Jessica Flynn, Specialist, (202) 682-5011. TTY, (202) 682-5082.*
General email, litfellowships@arts.gov
Web, www.arts.gov

Awards grants to published writers, poets, and translators of prose and poetry; awards grants to nonprofit presses, literary magazines, and literature organizations that publish poetry and fiction.

▶CONGRESS

For a listing of relevant congressional committees and subcommittees, please see page 130 or the Appendix.

Library of Congress, *Center for the Book,* *John Adams Bldg., 101 Independence Ave. S.E., #LA 5173, 20540-4920; (202) 707-9217. Fax, (202) 707-0269. Guy Lamolinara, Director.*
General email, cfbook@loc.gov
Web, www.read.gov/cfb

Promotes family and adult literacy, books, reading, and libraries through its programs and events in Washington DC as well as those sponsored by its 56 affiliate Centers for the Book in the United States, Puerto Rico, U.S. Virgin Islands, and the three Pacific island territories.

Library of Congress, *Children's Literature Center,* *Thomas Jefferson Bldg., 101 Independence Ave. S.E., #LJ 129, 20540-4620; (202) 707-5535. Sybille A. Jagusch, Chief, (202) 707-1629.*
General email, childref@loc.gov
Web, www.loc.gov/rr/child

Provides reference and information services by telephone, by correspondence, and in person; maintains reference materials on all aspects of the study of children's literature. Serves children indirectly through assistance given to teachers, librarians, and others who work with youth. Timed entry pass for visitors required, details at loc.gov/visit.

Library of Congress, *Main Reading Room,* *Thomas Jefferson Bldg., 101 Independence Ave. S.E., #LJ 100, 20540-4660; (202) 707-3399. Fax, (202) 707-1957. Melissa Ball, Head.*
Web, www.loc.gov/rr/main

Point of access to the general collection of books and bound periodicals as well as electronic resources, including microform. Offers research orientations. Timed entry pass for visitors required, details at loc.gov/visit. Appointments recommended for researchers.

Library of Congress, *Poetry and Literature Center,* *Thomas Jefferson Bldg., 101 Independence Ave. S.E., #A102, 20540-4861; (202) 707-5394. Robert (Rob) Casper, Head, (202) 707-1308.*
General email, poetry@loc.gov
Web, www.loc.gov/poetry

Advises the library on public literary programs and on the acquisition of literary materials. Sponsors public poetry and fiction readings, lectures, symposia, occasional dramatic performances, and other literary events. Arranges for poets to record readings of their work for the library's tape archive. The poet laureate is appointed annually by the Librarian of Congress on the basis of literary distinction. Timed entry pass for visitors required, details at loc.gov/visit. Appointments recommended for researchers.

Library of Congress, *Rare Book and Special Collections Division,* *Thomas Jefferson Bldg., 101 Independence Ave. S.E., #LJ 239, 20540-4740; (202) 707-2025. Fax, (202) 707-4142. Mark G. Dimunation, Chief. Reading Room, (202) 707-3448. Reference Librarian, (202) 707-1597.*
Web, www.loc.gov/rr/rarebook

Maintains collections of incunabula (books printed before 1501) and other early printed books; early imprints of American history and literature; illustrated books; early Spanish American, Russian, and Bulgarian imprints; Confederate states imprints; libraries of famous personalities (including Thomas Jefferson, Woodrow Wilson, and Oliver Wendell Holmes Jr.); special format collections (miniature books, broadsides, almanacs, and pre-1870

copyright records); special interest collections; and special provenance collections. Reference assistance is provided in the Rare Book and Special Collections Reading Room. Timed entry pass for visitors required, details at loc.gov/visit. Appointments recommended for researchers.

Library of Congress, *Young Readers Center and Programs Lab,* *Thomas Jefferson Bldg., 10 1st St. S.E., #G51, 20540; (202) 707-1950. Fax, (202) 707-0269. Lauren Roszak, Head (Acting).*
General email, learn@loc.gov
Web, www.read.gov/yrc

Promotes books, reading, literacy, libraries, and the scholarly study of books through affiliates and promotional programs. Places special emphasis on young readers through reading and writing contests.

▶ NONGOVERNMENTAL

Alliance Française de Washington, *2142 Wyoming Ave. N.W., 20008-3906; (202) 234-7911. Fax, (202) 234-0125. Sarah Diligenti, Executive Director. Library, (202) 897-3679.*
General email, alliance@francedc.org
Web, www.francedc.org, Twitter, @FranceDC and Facebook, www.facebook.com/AFWDC

Offers courses in French language, culture and literature; presents lectures and cultural events; maintains library of French-language publications for members (restrictions for nonmembers); offers language programs, including on-site corporate language programs.

Applied Research Laboratory for Intelligence and Security (ARLIS) (*University of Maryland*), *7005 52nd Ave., College Park, MD 20742; (301) 226-8900. Fax, (301) 226-8811. William Regli, Executive Director, (301) 405-6738.*
General email, info@arlis.umd.edu
Web, www.arlis.umd.edu

Conducts research in social systems, human-systems integration, and test bed development to support security and intelligence communities; collaborates with government agencies. Joint venture with the Defense Dept.

Center for Applied Linguistics, *4646 40th St. N.W. Washington, DC, 20016-1859; (202) 362-0700. Fax, (202) 362-3740. Joel Gómez, President, Ext. 545.*
General email, info@cal.org
Web, www.cal.org, Facebook, www.facebook.com/CALLinguistics/ and Twitter, @CAL_Linguistics

Research and technical assistance organization that serves as a clearinghouse on application of linguistics to practical language problems. Interests include English as a second language (ESL), teacher training and material development, language education, language proficiency test development, bilingual education, and sociolinguistics.

Folger Shakespeare Library, *201 E. Capitol St. S.E., 20003-1004; (202) 544-4600. Fax, (202) 544-4623. Michael Witmore, Director, (202) 675-0301. Box Office, (202) 544-7077.*

ARTS AND HUMANITIES • 137

General email, info@folger.edu

Web, www.folger.edu, Twitter, @FolgerLibrary and Facebook, www.facebook.com/folgershakespearelibrary

Maintains major Shakespearean and Renaissance materials; awards fellowships for postdoctoral research; presents concerts, theater performances, poetry and fiction readings, exhibits, and other public events. Offers educational programs for elementary, secondary, high school, college, and graduate school students and teachers. Publishes the Folger Shakespeare editions, *Folger Magazine*, and, in association with the George Washington University, *Shakespeare Quarterly.*

The Herb Block Foundation, *1730 M St. N.W., #1020, 20036; (202) 223-8801. Fax, (202) 223-8804. Marcela Brane, Chief Executive Officer; Sarah Armstrong Alex, Executive Director.*
General email, info@herbblock.org

Web, www.herbblockfoundation.org, Twitter, @TheHerbBlockFdn and Facebook, www.facebook.com/herbblockfoundation

Maintains an archive of Herb Block's editorial cartoons through the Library of Congress.

Japan–America Society of Washington DC, *1819 L St. N.W., #410, 20036-3807; (202) 833-2210. Ryan Shaffer, President.*
General email, info@jaswdc.org

Web, www.jaswdc.org, Twitter, @jas_wdc and Facebook, www.facebook.com/jaswdc

Offers lectures and films on Japan; operates a Japanese-language school and an annual nationwide language competition for high school students; partner of the National Cherry Blossom Festival. Maintains library for members.

Joint National Committee for Languages / National Council for Languages and International Studies, *4600 Waverly Ave., Garrett Park, MD 20896 (mailing address: P.O. Box 386, Garrett Park, MD 20896); (202) 580-8684. John Bernstein, Director of Government Relations.*
General email, info@languagepolicy.org

Web, www.languagepolicy.org, Twitter, @JNCLInfo and YouTube, www.youtube.com/channel/UCzJjkf21K26hBOLosqd0Trw

Coalition of professional organizations in teaching, translation, interpreting, testing, and research. Supports a national policy on language study and international education. Provides forum and clearinghouse for professional language and international education associations. National Council for Languages and International Studies is the political arm.

Linguistic Society of America, *522 21st St. N.W., #120, 20006-5012; (202) 835-1714. Fax, (202) 835-1717. Alyson Reed, Executive Director.*
General email, lsa@lsadc.org

Web, www.linguisticsociety.org, Twitter, @LingSocAm and Facebook, www.facebook.com/LingSocAm

Membership: individuals and institutions interested in the scientific analysis of language and its applications. Holds linguistic institutes every other year and an annual meeting.

Malice Domestic Ltd., *P.O. Box 8007, Gaithersburg, MD 20898-8007; (301) 730-1675. Verena Rose, Chair.*
General email, malicedomesticPR@gmail.com

Web, www.malicedomestic.org, Twitter, @Malice_Domestic, Facebook, www.facebook.com/Malice-Domestic and Press, mdregservices@gmail.com

Membership: authors and readers of traditional mysteries. Sponsors annual Agatha Awards and an annual convention. Awards grants to unpublished writers in the genre.

National Foreign Language Center *(University of Maryland),* *5600 Rivertech Ct., Suite K, Riverdale, MD 20737; (301) 405-9828. Fax, (301) 405-9829. Kathy Kilday, Lead Director.*
General email, inquiries@nflc.org

Web, www.nflc.umd.edu and Twitter, @NFLC_UMD

Research and policy organization that develops new strategies for strengthening foreign language competence in the United States. Conducts research on national language needs and assists policymakers in identifying priorities, allocating resources, and designing programs. Interests include the role of foreign language in higher education, national competence in critical languages, ethnic language maintenance, and K–12 and postsecondary language programs.

PEN/Faulkner Foundation, *6218 Georgia Ave. N.W., #1062, 20011; (202) 898-9063. Gwydion Suilebhan, Executive Director.*
General email, info@penfaulkner.org

Web, www.penfaulkner.org, Twitter, @penfaulkner and Facebook, www.facebook.com/penfaulkner

Sponsors an annual juried award for American fiction. Brings authors to visit public schools to discuss their work. The written word plays an essential role in contributing to civil discoursse and in creating empathty within and among communities. Holds readings by noted authors of American fiction.

U.S. English Inc., *5335 Wisconsin Ave. N.W., #930, 20015; (202) 833-0100. Fax, (202) 833-0108. Mauro E. Mujica, Chair. Toll-free, (800) 787-8216.*
General email, info@usenglish.org

Web, www.usenglish.org

Advocates English as the official language of federal and state governments. Affiliate U.S. English Foundation promotes English language education for immigrants.

The Writer's Center, *4508 Walsh St., Bethesda, MD 20815; (301) 654-8664. Margaret Meleney, Executive Director.*
General email, post.master@writer.org

Web, www.writer.org and Twitter, @writerscenter

Museum Education Programs

Alexandria Archaeology, (703) 746-4399;
www.alexandriava.gov/Archaeology

American Alliance of Museums, Museum Assessment Program, (202) 289-9118; www.aam-us.org/programs/accreditation-excellence-programs/museum-assessment-program-map

Arlington Arts Center, (703) 248-6800;
https://arlingtonartscenter.org

Assn. of Science-Technology Centers, (202) 783-7200;
www.astc.org

B'nai B'rith International, (202) 857-6600;
www.bnaibrith.org/museum-and-archives.html

C & O Canal National Historic Park, (301) 739-4200;
www.nps.gov/choh

Corcoran Gallery of Art, (202) 994-1700; www.corcoran.org

Daughters of the American Revolution (DAR) Museum,
(202) 628-1776; www.dar.org/museum

Decatur House, (202) 218-4333; www.nps.gov/places/commodore-stephen-decatur-house.htm

Dumbarton Oaks, (202) 339-6401; www.doaks.org

Folger Shakespeare Library, (202) 544-4600;
www.folger.edu

Gadsby's Tavern Museum, (703) 746-4242;
www.gadsbystavernmuseum.us

Institute of Museum and Library Services,
(202) 653-4657; www.imls.gov

J.F.K. Center for the Performing Arts, (202) 467-4600;
www.kennedy-center.org

The Lyceum: Alexandria's History Museum,
(703) 746-4994; www.alexandriava.gov/Lyceum

Mount Vernon, (703) 780-2000; www.mountvernon.org

National Arboretum, (202) 245-2726 or(202) 245-4523;
www.usna.usda.gov

National Archives, (866) 272-6272; www.archives.gov

National Building Museum, (202) 272-2448; www.nbm.org

National Gallery of Art, (202) 737-4215; www.nga.gov

National Museum of Women in the Arts, (202) 783-5000;
https://nmwa.org

Navy Museum, (202) 685-0589; www.history.navy.mil/content/history/museums/nmusn.html

Octagon Museum, (202) 626-7439;
https://architectsfoundation.org/octagon-museum

Phillips Collection, (202) 387-2151;
www.phillipscollection.org

Smithsonian Institution, (202) 633-1000; www.si.edu

Anacostia Community Museum,
https://anacostia.si.edu/About

Arthur M. Sackler Gallery, (202) 633-0457;
www.si.edu/museums/sackler-gallery

Center for Learning and Digital Access, (202) 633-5330;
https://learninglab.si.edu/about/SmithsonianCenterforLearningandDigitalAccess

Freer Gallery of Art, (202) 633-0457;
www.si.edu/museums/freer-gallery

Hirshhorn Museum and Sculpture Garden,
(202) 633-4674; https://hirshhorn.si.edu

National Air and Space Museum, (202) 633-2214;
https://airandspace.si.edu

National Museum of African Art, (202) 633-4600;
https://africa.si.edu

National Museum of American Art, (202) 633-7970;
https://americanart.si.edu

National Museum of American History, (202) 633-3717;
https://americanhistory.si.edu

National Museum of Natural History, (202) 633-4039;
https://naturalhistory.si.edu

National Museum of the American Indian,
(202) 633-6644 TTY,(202) 633-6751;
https://americanindian.si.edu

National Portrait Gallery, (202) 633-8300;
https://npg.si.edu

Renwick Gallery, (202) 633-7970;
https://americanart.si.edu/visit/renwick

Textile Museum, (202) 994-5200;
https://museum.gwu.edu

Woodrow Wilson House, (202) 387-4062;
www.woodrowwilsonhouse.org

Membership: writers, editors, and interested individuals. Supports the creation, publication, presentation, and dissemination of literary texts. Sponsors workshops in writing. Presents author readings. Maintains a book gallery.

Museums

▶ AGENCIES

American Art Museum *(Smithsonian Institution),*
SAMM Offices, 750 9th St. N.W., #3100, 20001 (mailing address: MS 970, Box 37012, Washington, DC 20013-7012); (202) 633-7970. Fax, (202) 633-8473. Stephanie Stebich, Director.

General email, americanartinfo@si.edu

Web, www.americanart.si.edu, Twitter, @americanart, Facebook, www.facebook.com/americanart and YouTube, www.youtube.com/user/americanartmuseum

Exhibits and interprets American painting, sculpture, photographs, folk art, and graphic art in the permanent collection and temporary exhibition galleries. Maintains a travelling exhibition program and research and scholar center. Library open to the public. (Includes the Renwick Gallery.)

American Art Museum *(Smithsonian Institution),*
Renwick Gallery, 1661 Pennsylvania Ave. N.W., 20006 (mailing address: Renwick Gallery, MRC 510, P.O. Box 37012, Washington, DC 20013-7012); (202) 633-2850.

Robyn Kennedy, Chief Administrator; Stephanie Stebich, Director. Information, (202) 633-7970. Press, (202) 633-8530.

General email, AmericanArtRenwick@si.edu

Web, www.americanart.si.edu/visit/renwick, Twitter, @americanart, Facebook, www.facebook.com/americanart and Blog, https://americanart.si.edu/blog

Curatorial department of the Smithsonian American Art Museum. Exhibits contemporary American crafts and decorative arts.

Anacostia Community Museum (Smithsonian Institution), 1901 Fort Pl. S.E., 20020 (mailing address: P.O. Box 37012, MS 0777, Washington, DC 20013-7012); (202) 633-4820. Fax, (202) 312-1968. Melanie A. Adams, Director. Press, (202) 633-4876. Public programs, (202) 633-4869. Special events, (202) 633-4867.

General email, ACMinfo@si.edu

Web, https://anacostia.si.edu, Twitter, @SmithsonianACM, Facebook, www.facebook.com/SmithsonianAnacostia CommunityMuseum and YouTube, www.youtube.com/user/SmithsonianAnacostia

Explores, documents, and interprets social and cultural issues that impact contemporary urban communities. Presents changing exhibits and programs.

Drug Enforcement Administration Museum and Visitors Center (Justice Dept.), 700 Army Navy Dr., Arlington, VA 22202 (mailing address: 8701 Morrissette Dr., Springfield, VA 22152); (202) 307-3463. Fax, (202) 307-8956. Jan McKay, Director.

General email, staff@deamuseum.org

Web, https://museum.dea.gov and Facebook, www.facebook.com/DEAMuseum

Seeks to educate the public on the role and impact of federal drug law enforcement through state-of-the-art exhibits, displays, interactive stations, and outreach programs. Admission is free; groups of fifteen or more should call ahead for reservations.

Ford's Theatre National Historic Site, 511 10th St. N.W., 20004 (mailing address: 900 Ohio Dr. S.W., Washington, DC 20024); (202) 426-6924. Jeff Jones, Site Manager. Tickets, (888) 616-0270.

General email, NACC_FOTH_Interpretation@nps.gov

Web, www.nps.gov/foth, Twitter, @fordstheatre and Facebook, www.facebook.com/fordstheatrenps

Administered by the National Park Service, which manages Ford's Theatre, Ford's Theatre Museum, and the Petersen House (house where Lincoln died). Presents interpretive talks, exhibits, and tours. Functions as working stage for theatrical productions.

Freer Gallery of Art and Arthur M. Sackler Gallery (Smithsonian Institution), National Museum of Asian Art, 1050 Independence Ave. S.W., 20560 (mailing address: P.O. Box 37012, MS 707, Washington, DC 20013-7012); (202) 633-1000. Fax, (202) 357-4911. Chase F. Robinson, Director. Education Office, (202) 633-0457. Library, (202) 633-0477. TTY, (202) 633-5285.

General email, publicaffairsasia@si.edu

Web, www.asia.si.edu, Twitter, @NatAsianArt and Facebook, www.facebook.com/NatAsianArt

Exhibits ancient and contemporary Asian art from the Mediterranean to Japan and late nineteenth-century and early twentieth-century American art from its permanent collection, including works by James McNeill Whistler. Presents films, lectures, and concerts. Museum open to the public Monday through Friday, 10:00 a.m.–5:30 p.m.

Hirshhorn Museum and Sculpture Garden (Smithsonian Institution), 7th St. and Independence Ave. S.W., 20560 (mailing address: P.O. Box 37012, MS 350, Washington, DC 20013-7012); (202) 633-4674. Fax, (202) 633-8835. Melissa Chiu, Director; Christopher McClesky, Press Officer, (202) 633-2807. Press, (202) 633-2807. TTY, (202) 633-8043. Information, (202) 633-1000.

General email, hmsginquiries@si.edu

Web, www.hirshhorn.si.edu, Twitter, @hirshhorn, Facebook, www.facebook.com/hirshhorn and YouTube, www.youtube.com/hirshhorn

Preserves and exhibits modern and contemporary art. Offers films, lectures, and tours of the collection. Free and open to the public daily 10:00 a.m.–5:30 p.m.

Institute of Museum and Library Services, 955 L'Enfant Plaza North S.W., #4000, 20024-2135; (202) 653-4657. Fax, (202) 653-4600. Crosby Kemper III, Director, (202) 653-4798. Communications and Government Affairs, (202) 653-4757. Grants and policy management, (202) 653-4759. Library services, (202) 653-4700. Museum services, (202) 653-4789. TTY, (202) 653-4614.

General email, imlsinfo@imls.gov

Web, www.imls.gov, Twitter, @US_IMLS and Facebook, www.facebook.com/USIMLS

Independent federal agency established by Congress to assist museums and libraries in increasing and improving their services. Awards grants for the professional development of museum and library staff. Funds research, conferences, and publications.

National Park Service, Frederick Douglass National Historic Site, 1411 W St. S.E., 20020; (202) 426-5961. Fax, (202) 426-0880. Mike Antonioni, Park Curator; Tara D. Morrison, Superintendent. Group Reservations, (877) 559-6777. Reservations, (877) 444-6777.

Web, www.nps.gov/frdo, Twitter, @FredDouglassNPS and Facebook, www.facebook.com/FrederickDouglassNHS

Administered by the National Park Service. Museum of the life and work of abolitionist Frederick Douglass and his family. Offers tours of the home and special programs, such as documentary films, videos, and slide presentations; maintains visitors center and bookstore. Reservations are required for parties of more than ten. Online reservations can be made at www.recreation.gov.

National Air and Space Museum (Smithsonian Institution), 655 Jefferson Dr. S.W., 20560 (mailing address: 6th St. and Independence Ave. S.W., Washington, DC 20560); (202) 633-2214. Chris Browne, Director

(Acting), (202) 633-2350. Archives, (703) 572-4045. Library, (703) 572-4175. Tours, (202) 633-2563. General email, NASMVisitorServices@si.edu

Web, www.airandspace.si.edu, Twitter, @airandspace, Facebook, www.facebook.com/airandspace and YouTube, www.youtube.com/user/airandspace

Maintains the world's largest collection of aviation and space artifacts; exhibits astronautical objects and equipment of historical interest, including the 1903 Wright Flyer, Charles Lindbergh's *Spirit of St. Louis*, the Apollo 11 Command Module *Columbia*, and lunar rock specimens. Planetarium and observatory are available to the public. Library open to the public by appointment.

National Air and Space Museum *(Smithsonian Institution)*, *Steven F. Udvar-Hazy Center*, 14390 Air and Space Museum Pkwy., Chantilly, VA 20151; (703) 572-4118. Chris Browne, Director (Acting), (202) 633-2350. Library, (703) 572-4175. Public Affairs, (202) 633-1000. General email, info@si.edu

Librarian email, AskaLibrarian@si.edu, Web, www.airandspace.si.edu/visit/udvar-hazy-center, Twitter, @airandspace and Facebook, www.facebook.com/ airandspace

Displays and preserves a collection of historical aviation and space artifacts, including the B-29 Superfortress *Enola Gay*, the Lockheed SR-71 Blackbird, the prototype of the Boeing 707, the space shuttle *Discovery*, and a Concorde. Provides a center for research into the history, science, and technology of aviation and space flight. Open to the public daily 10:00 a.m.–5:30 p.m., except December 25.

National Archives and Records Administration (NARA), *National Archives Museum*, 701 Constitution Ave. N.W., 20408; (202) 357-5000. Fax, (202) 357-5926. Patrick Madden, Executive Director. Museum Program Services, (202) 357-5210. Web, https://museum.archives.gov

Plans and directs activities to acquaint the public with the mission and holdings of the National Archives; conducts behind-the-scenes tours; presents hands-on workshops; develops both traditional and interactive exhibits; produces publications.

National Cryptologic Museum *(National Security Agency)*, 8290 Colony Seven Rd., Annapolis Junction, MD 20701 (mailing address: 9800 Savage Rd., #6272, Fort Meade, MD 20755); (301) 688-5849. Vince Houghton, Director Chief. Library, (301) 688-2145. General email, crypto_museum@nsa.gov

Web, www.nsa.gov/about/cryptologic-heritage/museum, Facebook, www.facebook.com/NationalCryptologic Museum and Twitter, @NatCryptoMuseum

Documents the history of the cryptologic profession. Library open to the public. Closed during part of 2022 for renovations.

National Endowment for the Arts (NEA), *Museums*, 400 7th St. S.W., 20506; (202) 682-5529. Toni Lindsay, Contact (Organizations A - N), (202) 682-5529; Tamika Shingler,

Contact (Organizations O - Z), (202) 682-5577. Visual Arts Division, (202) 682-5452. TTY, (202) 682-5496. Web, www.arts.gov

Awards grants to museums for installing and cataloging permanent and special collections; conducts traveling exhibits; trains museum professionals; conserves and preserves museum collections; and develops arts-related educational programs.

National Gallery of Art, 6th St. and Constitution Ave. N.W., 20565 (mailing address: 2000B S. Club Dr., Landover, MD 20785); (202) 737-4215. Kaywin Feldman, Director. Accessibility, (202) 842-6905. Library, (202) 842-6511. Press, (202) 842-6353. Visitor services, (202) 842-6691. General email, visit@nga.gov

Web, www.nga.gov, Twitter, @ngadc and Facebook, www.facebook.com/nationalgalleryofart

Created by a joint resolution of Congress, the museum is a public-private partnership that collects, preserves, and exhibits European and American paintings, sculpture, and decorative and graphic arts. Offers concerts, demonstrations, lectures, symposia, films, tours, and teacher workshops to enhance exhibitions, the permanent collection, and related topics. Lends art to museums in all fifty states and abroad through the National Lending Service. Publishes a bimonthly calendar of events.

National Museum of African Art *(Smithsonian Institution)*, 950 Independence Ave. S.W., 20560 (mailing address: P.O. Box 37012, MS 708, Washington, DC 20013-7012); (202) 633-4600. Fax, (202) 357-4879. Ngaire (Gus) Blankenberg, Director, (202) 663-4604. Press, (202) 633-4649. General email, nmafaweb@si.edu

Web, http://africa.si.edu, Twitter, @si_africanart, Facebook, www.facebook.com/si.africanart and YouTube, www.youtube.com/user/SmithsonianAfricanAr

Collects, studies, and exhibits traditional and contemporary arts of Africa. Exhibits feature objects from the permanent collection and from private and public collections worldwide. Museum is open 10 a.m.–5:30 p.m. daily except December 25. Library and photo archive open to the public by appointment.

National Museum of American History *(Smithsonian Institution)*, 14th St. and Constitution Ave. N.W., #4260, MS 622, 20560-0630 (mailing address: P.O. Box 37012, Washington, DC 20013); (202) 633-3435. Anthea M. Hartig, Director. Library, (202) 633-3865. Press, (202) 633-3129. General email, info@si.edu

Web, http://americanhistory.si.edu, Twitter, @amhistorymuseum, Facebook, www.facebook .com/americanhistory and YouTube, www.youtube.com/ c/nationalmuseumofamericanhistory

Collects and exhibits objects representative of American cultural history, applied arts, industry, national and military history, and science and technology. Library open to the public by appointment.

National Museum of American History *(Smithsonian Institution), Culture and Community Life,* 12th St. and Constitution Ave. N.W., Room 4212, 20560-0616 *(mailing address: P.O. Box 37012, MS 616, Washington, DC 20013-7012); (202) 633-1707. Stacey Kluck, Chair. Press, (202) 633-3129.*
General email, info@si.edu
Web, https://americanhistory.si.edu/about/departments/cultural-and-community-life

Collects and preserves artifacts related to U.S. cultural heritage; supports research, exhibits, performances, and educational programs. Areas of focus include sports, recreation, and leisure; popular culture; music and dance; theater, film, broadcast media, graphic arts, printing, and photographic history.

National Museum of American History *(Smithsonian Institution), National Numismatic Collection,* 14th St. and Constitution Ave. N.W., 20013 *(mailing address: P.O. Box 37012, MS 609, Washington, DC 20013-7012); (202) 633-1000. Ellen Feingold, Curator of National Collection.*
General email, NMAH-NNC@si.edu
Web, http://americanhistory.si.edu/collections/numismatics

Develops and maintains collections of ancient, medieval, modern, U.S., and world coins; U.S. and world currencies; tokens; medals; orders and decorations; and traditional exchange media. Conducts research and responds to public inquiries. Collection can be viewed online.

National Museum of Health and Medicine *(Defense Dept.),* 2500 Linden Lane, Silver Spring, MD 20910 *(mailing address: Bldg. 2500, 2460 Linden Lane, Silver Spring, MD 20910); (301) 319-3300. Fax, (301) 319-3373. Adrianne Noe, Director. Tours, (301) 319-3312.*
General email, usarmy.detrick.medcom-usamrmc.list.medical-museum@mail.mil
Web, www.medicalmuseum.mil and Twitter, @medicalmuseum

Collects and exhibits medical models, tools, and pathological specimens. Maintains exhibits on military medicine and surgery. Open to the public 10:00 a.m.–5:30 p.m., seven days a week. Study collection available to scholars by appointment.

National Museum of Natural History *(Smithsonian Institution),* 10th St. and Constitution Ave. N.W., 20560-0106 *(mailing address: P.O. Box 37012, MS 106, Washington, DC 20013-7012); (202) 633-2664. Kirk Johnson, Director; Katy Roper, Administrative Assistant, (202) 633-2664. Library, (202) 633-1184. Press, (202) 633-2950.*
General email, naturalexperience@si.edu
Web, www.mnh.si.edu, Twitter, @NMNH and Facebook, www.facebook.com/SmithsonianNMNH

Conducts research and maintains exhibitions and collections relating to the natural sciences. Collections are organized into seven research and curatorial departments:

anthropology, botany, entomology, invertebrate zoology, mineral sciences, paleobiology, and vertebrate zoology.

National Museum of Natural History *(Smithsonian Institution), Smithsonian Museum Support Center,* 4210 Silver Hill Rd., MS 534, Suitland, MD 20746-2863; (301) 238-1026. Vacant, Deputy Director. Library, (301) 238-1030.*
General email, libmail@si.edu
Web, https://naturalhistory.si.edu/research/msc

Museum collections management facility dedicated to collections, storage, research, and conservation. Library serves Smithsonian staff, other government agencies, and researchers. Open to the public by appointment.

National Museum of the American Indian *(Smithsonian Institution),* 4th St. and Independence Ave. S.W., 20560; (202) 633-6700. Fax, (202) 633-6920. Cynthia Chavez Lamar, Director, (202) 633-6930; Carol Gardner, Administrative Assistant, (202) 633-6930. General Smithsonian information, (202) 633-1000. Group reservations, (202) 633-6644. TTY, (202) 633-0572. TTY group reservations, (202) 633-6751.*
General email, NMAI-info@si.edu
Web, www.americanindian.si.edu,
Twitter, @SmithsonianNMAI and Facebook, www.facebook.com/NationalMuseumoftheAmericanIndian

Collects, exhibits, preserves, and studies American Indian languages, literature, history, art, and culture. Operates ImagiNations activity center, open to the public. (Affiliated with the George Gustav Heye Center, 1 Bowling Green, New York, NY 10004 and the Cultural Resources Center, 4220 Silver Hill Rd., Suitland, MD 20746.)

National Portrait Gallery *(Smithsonian Institution),* 750 9th St. N.W., #410, 20001 *(mailing address: Victor Bldg., P.O. Box 37012, MS 973, Washington, DC 20013-7012); (202) 633-8300. Fax, (202) 633-8243. Kim Sajet, Director, (202) 663-8276. Library, (202) 633-8230. Press, (202) 255-1843.*
General email, npgaccess@si.edu
Web, https://npg.si.edu, Twitter, @smithsoniannpg and YouTube, www.youtube.com/SmithsonianNPG

Exhibits paintings, photographs, sculpture, drawings, and prints of individuals who have made significant contributions to the history, development, and culture of the United States. Library open to the public.

National Postal Museum *(Smithsonian Institution),* 2 Massachusetts Ave. N.E., 20002 *(mailing address: P.O. Box 37012, MS 570, Washington, DC 20013); (202) 633-5555. Elliot Gruber, Director. Press, (202) 633-5518. Tours and education, (202) 633-5534. TTY, (202) 633-9849.*
Web, http://postalmuseum.si.edu,
Twitter, @PostalMuseum and Facebook, www.facebook.com/SmithsonianNationalPostalMuseum

Exhibits postal history and stamp collections; provides information on world postal and stamp history.

Naval History and Heritage Command *(Navy Dept.),* **Navy Art Collection,** *Washington Navy Yard, Bldg. 67, 822 Sicard St. S.E., 20374 (mailing address: 805 Kidder Breese St. S.E., Washington Navy Yard, DC 20374); (202) 433-3815. Gale Munro, Head Curator.*
General email, NavyArt@navy.mil

Web, www.history.navy.mil/our-collections/art.html

Holdings include more than 20,000 paintings, prints, drawings, and sculptures. Artworks depict naval ships, personnel, and action from all eras of U.S. naval history. Open to the public. Visitors without Defense Dept. or military identification must call in advance. Photo identification required.

Smithsonian Institution, *1000 Jefferson Dr. S.W., 20560 (mailing address: SIB 153, P.O. Box 37012, MS 010, Washington, DC 20013-7012); (202) 633-1000. Lonnie G. Bunch III, Secretary. Library, (202) 633-2240. Group Sales, (866) 868-7774.*
General email, info@si.edu

Web, www.si.edu, Twitter, @Smithsonian, Facebook, www.facebook.com/Smithsonian and YouTube, www.youtube.com/c/Smithsonian

Conducts research; publishes results of studies, explorations, and investigations; presents study and reference collections on science, culture, and history; presents exhibitions in the arts, American history, technology, aeronautics and space exploration, and natural history. Smithsonian Institution sites in Washington, D.C., include the Anacostia Community Museum, Archives of American Art, Arthur M. Sackler Gallery, Arts and Industries Building, Freer Gallery of Art, Hirshhorn Museum and Sculpture Garden, National Air and Space Museum, National Museum of African Art, Renwick Gallery, Smithsonian American Art Museum, National Museum of American History, National Museum of the American Indian, National Museum of Natural History, National Portrait Gallery, National Postal Museum, National Zoological Park, S. Dillon Ripley Center, and Smithsonian Institution Building. Libraries open to the public by appointment; library catalogs are available on the Web. Affiliated with more than 175 organizations in 41 states, Panama, and Puerto Rico. Autonomous organizations affiliated with the Smithsonian Institution include John F. Kennedy Center for the Performing Arts, National Gallery of Art, and Woodrow Wilson International Center for Scholars.

U.S. Botanic Garden, *100 Maryland Ave. S.W., 20001 (mailing address: 245 1st St. S.W., Washington, DC 20024); (202) 225-8333. Saharah Moon Chapotin, Executive Director, (202) 225-1110. Horticulture hotline, (202) 226-4785. Press, (202) 226-4145. Program registration information, (202) 225-1116. Special events, (202) 226-7674. Tour line, (202) 226-2055.*
General email, usbg@aoc.gov

Web, www.usbg.gov and Facebook, www.facebook.com/ USBotanicGarden

Educates the public on the aesthetic, cultural, economic, therapeutic, and ecological importance of plants to the well-being of humankind.

▶**CONGRESS**

For a listing of relevant congressional committees and sub-committees, please see page 130 or the Appendix.

Library of Congress, *Center for Exhibits, John Adams Bldg., 101 Independence Ave. S.E., #LA G25, 20540; (202) 707-5223. Fax, (202) 707-9063. David S. Mandel, Director. Exhibition information, (202) 707-4604.*
Web, www.loc.gov/exhibits

Handles exhibits within the Library of Congress; establishes and coordinates traveling exhibits; handles loans of library material.

▶**NONGOVERNMENTAL**

American Alliance of Museums, *2451 Crystal Dr., #1005, Arlington, VA 22202; (202) 289-1818. Fax, (202) 289-6578. Laura L. Lott, President. Member Services, (866) 226-2150.*
General email, infocenter@aam-us.org

Web, www.aam-us.org, Twitter, @AAMers and Facebook, www.facebook.com/americanmuseums

Membership: individuals, institutions, museums, and museum professionals. Accredits museums; conducts educational programs; promotes international professional exchanges.

Art Services International, *119 Duke St., Alexandria, VA 22314; (703) 548-4554. Fax, (703) 548-3305. Lynn K. Rogerson, Director.*
General email, asi@asiexhibitions.org

Web, www.asiexhibitions.org

Develops, organizes, and circulates fine arts exhibitions throughout the world.

Dumbarton Oaks, *1703 32nd St. N.W., 20007-2961; (202) 339-6400. Fax, (202) 625-0280. Thomas B.F. Cummins, Director. Information, (202) 339-6401.*
General email, museum@doaks.org

Web, www.doaks.org, Twitter, @doaksdc and Facebook, www.facebook.com/doaksDC
Library and Archives, Library@DumbartonOaks

Exhibits Byzantine and pre-Columbian art and artifacts; conducts advanced research and maintains publication programs and library collections in Byzantine and pre-Columbian studies and garden and landscape studies. Offers guided tours of museum and gardens. Gardens open to the public Tuesday through Sunday 2:00–6:00 p.m. in summer, and 2:00–5:00 p.m. in winter (except during inclement weather and on federal holidays; fee charged March 15 through October 31); library open to qualified scholars by advance application. Administered by the trustees for Harvard University.

Hillwood Estate, Museum, and Gardens, *4155 Linnean Ave. N.W., 20008-3806; (202) 686-5807. Fax, (202) 966-7846. Kate Markert, Executive Director, (202) 243-3900. Press, (202) 243-3975.*
General email, info@hillwoodmuseum.org

Web, www.hillwoodmuseum.org and Twitter, @HillwoodMuseum

Former residence of Marjorie Merriweather Post. Maintains and exhibits collection of Russian imperial art, including Fabergé eggs, and eighteenth-century French decorative arts; twelve acres of formal gardens. Gardens and museum open to the public Tuesday through Sunday, 10:00 a.m.–5:00 p.m.; reservations required for large groups.

International Spy Museum, *700 L'Enfant Plaza S.W., 20024; P.O. Box 23137, 20026; (202) 393-7798. Fax, (202) 393-7797. Christopher P. Costa, Executive Director. Press, (202) 654-0946.*
General email, info@spymuseum.org

Web, www.spymuseum.org, Twitter, @IntlSpyMuseum, Facebook, www.facebook.com/IntlSpyMuseum and YouTube, www.youtube.com/user/IntlSpyMuseum

Dedicated to educating the public about the tradecraft, history, and contemporary role of espionage, particularly human intelligence, by examining its role in and effect on current and historical events. Offers a collection of international espionage artifacts. (Affiliated with the Malrite Company.)

National Building Museum, *401 F St. N.W., 20001-2637; (202) 272-2448. Fax, (202) 272-2564. Aileen Fuchs, Executive Director. Press, (202) 849-2495.*
Web, www.nbm.org, Twitter, @BuildingMuseum and Facebook, www.facebook.com/NationalBuildingMuseum
General email, info@nbm.org

Celebrates achievements in building, architecture, urban planning, engineering, and historic preservation through educational programs, exhibitions, tours, lectures, workshops, and publications.

National Children's Museum, *1300 Pennsylvania Ave. N.W., 20004; (202) 844-2486. Crystal Bowyer, President.*
General email, info@nationalchildrensmuseum.org
Web, www.nationalchildrensmuseum.org, Twitter, @NatChildrens and Facebook, www.facebook.com/NationalChildrensMuseum

A cultural and educational institution serving children and families onsite and through national partners and programs. Exhibits and activities focus on the arts, civic engagement, the environment, global citizenship, health and well-being, and play. Affiliated with the Association of Children's Museums Reciprocal Network.

National Geographic Museum, *1145 17th St. N.W., 20036-4688; Kathryn Keane, Executive Director. Tickets and tour information, (202) 857-7700.*
General email, ngtickets@ngs.org
Web, http://nationalgeographic.org/events, Twitter, @InsideNatGeo and Facebook, www.facebook.com/InsideNatGeo

Maintains self-guided exhibits about past and current expeditions, scientific research, and other themes in history and culture. Admission is free; some special exhibitions require ticket purchase.

National Guard Memorial Museum, *1 Massachusetts Ave. N.W., 20001; (202) 789-0031. Fax, (202) 682-9358. Luke Guthrie, Director, (202) 408-5886.*
General email, ngef@ngaus.org

Web, www.ngef.org/national-guard-memorial-museum, Twitter, @NGMuseum and Facebook, www.facebook.com/NationalGuardMemorialMuseum

Features exhibit areas that explore the National Guard from colonial times through the world wars and the cold war to the modern era through timelines, photographs, artifacts, light, and sound. As of publication, the museum is closed until further notice.

National Museum of Civil War Medicine, *48 E. Patrick St., Frederick, MD 21705 (mailing address: P.O. Box 470, Frederick, MD 21705); (301) 695-1864. Fax, (301) 695-6823. David Price, Executive Director.*
General email, info@civilwarmed.org
Web, www.civilwarmed.org and Twitter, @civilwarmed

Maintains artifacts and exhibits pertaining to general and wartime medicine in the 1800s, including dentistry, veterinary medicine, and medical evacuation. Presents information about individual soldiers, surgeons, medics, and nurses. Research department assists with questions about individuals injured in the Civil War.

National Museum of Women in the Arts, *1250 New York Ave. N.W., 20005-3970 (mailing address: 1615 M St. N.W., #200 Washington DC 20036); (202) 783-5000. Susan Fisher Sterling, Director. Library, (202) 266-2835. Press, (202) 783-7373. Toll-free, (800) 222-7270.*
Web, www.nmwa.org, Twitter, @womeninthearts
Library email, lrc@nmwa.org and Facebook, www.facebook.com/womeninthearts and YouTube, www.youtube.com/channel/UCKnelBYlnJyAbjoWNWMz-oQ

Acquires, researches, and presents the works of women artists from the Renaissance to the present. Promotes greater representation and awareness of women in the arts. Library open for research to the public by appointment.

Octagon Museum, *1735 New York Ave. N.W., 20006-5207; (202) 626-7439. Marci B. Reed, Executive Director.*
General email, hello@architectsfoundation.org
Web, www.architectsfoundation.org/octagon-museum, Twitter, @OctagonMuseum and Facebook, www.facebook.com/TheOctagonMuseum

Federal period historic residence open to the public for tours; served as the executive mansion during the War of 1812. Sponsors exhibits, lectures, publications, and educational programs. (Owned by the AIA Foundation [American Institute of Architects].) Guided tours available by appointment. Open for self-guided tours Thursday to Sunday from 1:00 p.m. to 4:00 p.m.

Phillips Collection, *1600 21st St. N.W., 20009; (202) 387-2151. Fax, (202) 387-2436. Dorothy Kosinski, Director. Membership, (202) 387-3036. Press, (202) 387-2151, ext. 220. Shop, (202) 387-2151, ext. 239.*

General email, communications@phillipscollection.org

Web, www.phillipscollection.org, Twitter, @PhillipsMuseum and Facebook, www.facebook.com/ phillipscollection

Maintains permanent collection of European and American paintings, primarily of the nineteenth through twenty-first centuries, and holds special exhibitions from the same periods. Sponsors lectures, gallery talks, and special events, including Sunday concerts (October–May). Library open to researchers and members.

Society of the Cincinnati, *2118 Massachusetts Ave. N.W., 20008; (202) 785-2040. I. Anderson Morse, Executive Director (Acting), ext. 413; Ellen McAllister, Librarian, ext. 426.*

Web, https://societyofthecincinnati.org

Collects and exhibits books, manuscripts, paintings, and other artifacts from the Revolutionary War. Maintains a library for research on the American Revolution. Preserves and operates the Anderson House as a historic landmark and museum. Library open by appointment.

Textile Museum *(George Washington University), 701 21st St. N.W., 20052; (202) 994-5200. John Wetenhall, Director.*

General email, museuminfo@gwu.edu

Web, https://museum.gwu.edu, Twitter, @GWTextileMuseum and Facebook, www.facebook.com/ TextileMuseum

Exhibits historic and handmade textiles and carpets with the goal of expanding appreciation of the artistic and cultural importance of the world's textiles. Exhibitions draw from loans and the permanent collection. Exhibits are open to the public Tuesdays through Saturdays.

Tudor Place, *1644 31st St. N.W., 20007; (202) 965-0400. Mark S. Hudson, Executive Director, (202) 965-1644.*

General email, info@tudorplace.org

Web, www.tudorplace.org, Twitter, @TudorPlace, Facebook, www.facebook.com/tudorplace and YouTube, www.youtube.com/tudorplace1805

Operates a historic property, home of Martha Washington's granddaughter and six generations of Custis-Peter family descendants. Seeks to educate the public about American history and culture, focusing on the capital region from the eighteenth century. Maintains and displays artifacts, maintains a manuscript collection, conducts guided tours, and sponsors educational programs for students and teachers.

U.S. Holocaust Memorial Museum, *100 Raoul Wallenberg Pl. S.W., 20024-2126; (202) 488-0400. Sara J. Bloomfield, Director; Andrew Hollinger, Communications Director, (202) 437-1221. Library, (202) 479-9717. Press, (202) 488-6133. Toll-free, (866) 998-7466. TTY, (202) 488-0406.*

Web, www.ushmm.org, Facebook, www.facebook.com/ HolocaustMuseum, Twitter, @HolocaustMuseum and YouTube, www.youtube.com/ushmm

Preserves documentation about the Holocaust and works to prevent genocide worldwide. Hosts exhibitions and website; conducts public programs, educational outreach, leadership training programs, and Holocaust commemorations; operates the Mandel Center for Advanced Holocaust Studies and the Genocide Prevention Task Force. Library and archives are open to the public.

Woodrow Wilson House *(National Trust for Historic Preservation), 2340 S St. N.W., 20008-4016; (202) 387-4062. Elizabeth A. Karcher, Executive Director, (202) 792-5808.*

General email, wilsonhouse@woodrowwilsonhouse.org

Web, www.woodrowwilsonhouse.org, Twitter, @WWilsonHouse, Events, events@woodrowwilsonhouse .org and Facebook, www.facebook.com/WoodrowWilson House

Georgian Revival home that exhibits state gifts, furnishings, and memorabilia from President Woodrow Wilson's political and postpresidential years.

Music

▶AGENCIES

National Endowment for the Arts (NEA), *Music, 400 7th St. S.W., 20506; (202) 682-5438. Ann Meier Baker, Director, (202) 682-5455; Kirk Burns, Music Specialist, (202) 682-5590. Performing Arts Division, (202) 682-5438. TTY, (202) 682-5496.*

Web, www.arts.gov

Awards grants to support a wide range of music, including classical, opera, contemporary, and jazz. Supports both performing ensembles and music institutions, including chamber music ensembles, opera companies, choruses, early music programs, jazz ensembles, music festivals, and symphony orchestras.

National Museum of American History *(Smithsonian Institution), Culture and Community Life, 12th St. and Constitution Ave. N.W., Room 4212, 20560-0616 (mailing address: P.O. Box 37012, MS 616, Washington, DC 20013-7012); (202) 633-1707. Stacey Kluck, Chair. Press, (202) 633-3129.*

General email, info@si.edu

Web, https://americanhistory.si.edu/about/departments/ cultural-and-community-life

Preserves American culture and heritage through collections, research, exhibitions, publications, teaching and lectures, and broadcasts. Sponsors Jazz Appreciation Month and a chamber music program. Research areas are open by appointment.

National Symphony Orchestra *(John F. Kennedy Center for the Performing Arts), 2700 F St. N.W., 20566-0004 (mailing address: P.O. Box 101510, Arlington, VA 22210); (202) 416-8000. Fax, (202) 416-8105. Gary Ginstling, Executive Director; Gianandrea Noseda, Music Director. Tickets and information, (202) 467-4600. Donations and*

membership, (202) 416-8310. Toll-free, (800) 444-1324. TTY, (202) 416-8524.
Web, www.kennedy-center.org/nso/home,
Twitter, @kencen and Facebook, www.facebook.com/
KennedyCenter

Year-round orchestra that presents a full range of symphonic activities: classical, pops, and educational events; national and international tours; recordings; and special events.

▶CONGRESS

For a listing of relevant congressional committees and subcommittees, please see page 130 or the Appendix.

Library of Congress, Motion Picture, Broadcasting and Recorded Sound Division, Recorded Sound Research Center, James Madison Memorial Bldg., 101 Independence Ave. S.E., #LM 113, 20540-4690; (202) 707-7833. Gregory Lukow, Chief.
General email, rsrc@loc.gov
Web, www.loc.gov/rr/record

Maintains library's collection of musical and vocal recordings. Reflects the entire history of sound technology from the first wax cylinders, through LPs and tape to the latest compact studio discs. Records the library's concert series and other musical events for radio broadcast; produces recordings of music and poetry for sale to the public. Collection also includes sound recordings (1920s–present). Timed entry pass for visitors required, details at loc.gov/visit. Appointments recommended for researchers.

Library of Congress, Music Division, James Madison Memorial Bldg., 101 Independence Ave. S.E., #LM 113, 20540-4710; Susan H. Vita, Chief. Concert information, (202) 707-5502. Performing Arts Reading Room, (202) 707-5507.
Web, www.loc.gov/rr/perform

Maintains and services, through the Performing Arts Reading Room, the library's collection of music scores (printed and manuscript), books and periodicals, instruments, and special collections in music, theater, and dance. Coordinates the library's chamber music concert series; produces radio broadcasts and, for sale to the public, recordings of concerts sponsored by the division; issues publications relating to the field of music and to division collections. Timed entry pass for visitors required, details at loc.gov/visit. Appointments recommended for researchers.

Library of Congress, National Recording Preservation Board, 101 Independence Ave. S.E., 20540-5698; (202) 707-5912. Fax, (202) 707-2371. Steve Leggett, Staff Coordinator. TTY, (202) 707-6362.
Web, www.loc.gov/programs/national-recording-preservation-board/about-this-program

Administers the National Recording Preservation Plan aimed at studying the state of and advances in sound recording. Receives nominations for the annual selection of twenty-five recordings demonstrating the range and diversity of American recorded sound heritage. Makes selections for the National Recording Registry.

▶NONGOVERNMENTAL

American Federation of Musicians, Government Relations, 5335 Wisconsin Ave. N.W., #440, 20015; (202) 274-4756. Fax, (202) 274-4759. Alfonso Pollard, Legislative-Political Director. Toll-free, (800) 762-3444.
Web, www.afm.org

Seeks to improve the working conditions and salary of musicians. Monitors legislation and regulations affecting musicians and the arts. (Headquarters in New York.)

Future of Music Coalition, 2217 14th St. N.W., 2nd Floor, 20009 (mailing address: P.O. Box 73274, Washington DC 20056); (202) 822-2051. Kevin Erickson, Director.
General email, info@futureofmusic.org
Web, www.futureofmusic.org, Twitter, @future_of_music and Facebook, www.facebook.com/Futureofmusiccoalition

Seeks to educate the media, policymakers, and the public on music technology issues. Identifies and promotes innovative business models that will help musicians and citizens benefit from new technologies. Promotes a society where artists are compensated fairly.

League of American Orchestras, Advocacy and Government, 1602 L St. N.W., #611, 20036; (202) 776-0215. Fax, (202) 776-0224. Heather Noonan, Vice President for Advocacy.
Web, www.americanorchestras.org/advocate,
Twitter, @OrchLeague, Facebook, www.facebook.com/orchleague and YouTube, www.youtube.com/user/LeagueAmer

Service and educational organization dedicated to strengthening orchestras. Provides information and analysis on subjects of interest to orchestras through reports, seminars, and other educational forums. Seeks to improve policies that increase public access to orchestral music. Monitors legislation and regulations. (Headquarters in New York.)

National Assn. of Schools of Music, 11250 Roger Bacon Dr., #21, Reston, VA 20190-5248; (703) 437-0700. Fax, (703) 437-6312. Karen Moynahan, Executive Director, ext. 116.
General email, info@arts-accredit.org
Web, http://nasm.arts-accredit.org

Specialized professional accrediting agency for postsecondary programs in music. Conducts and shares research and analysis on topics pertinent to music programs and the field of music. Offers professional development opportunities for executives of music programs.

Recording Industry Assn. of America, 1000 F St. N.W., 2nd Floor, 20004; (202) 775-0101. Fax, (202) 775-7253. Mitch Glazier, Chief Executive Officer.
Web, www.riaa.com, Twitter, @RIAA and Facebook, www.facebook.com/RIAA

Membership: creators, manufacturers, and marketers of sound recordings. Educates members about new technology in the music industry; certifies gold, platinum, and multiplatinum recordings; supports parental advisory labels; publishes statistics on the recording industry. Monitors legislation and regulations.

SoundExchange, *733 10th St. N.W., 10th Floor, 20001; (202) 640-5858. Fax, (202) 640-5859. Michael Huppe, President.*
General email, info@soundexchange.com
Web, www.soundexchange.com, Twitter, @SoundExchange and Facebook, www.facebook.com/SoundExchange

Artists' rights advocacy group that represents record labels and unsigned artists whose work is broadcast on national and global digital radio. Distributes royalties to musicians, performers, and music copyright owners. Monitors legislation and regulations related to digital music licensing.

Theater and Dance

▶AGENCIES

Ford's Theatre National Historic Site, *511 10th St. N.W., 20004 (mailing address: 900 Ohio Dr. S.W., Washington, DC 20024); (202) 426-6924. Jeff Jones, Site Manager. Tickets, (888) 616-0270.*
General email, NACC_FOTH_Interpretation@nps.gov
Web, www.nps.gov/foth, Twitter, @fordstheatre and Facebook, www.facebook.com/fordstheatrenps

Administered by the National Park Service, which manages Ford's Theatre, Ford's Theatre Museum, and the Petersen House (house where Lincoln died). Presents interpretive talks, exhibits, and tours. Functions as working stage for theatrical productions.

National Endowment for the Arts (NEA), *Dance, 400 7th St. S.W., 20506; (202) 682-5764. (202) 682-5438. Sara Nash, Director, (202) 682-5791; Kate Folsom, Dance Manager, (202) 682-5764.*
Web, www.arts.gov

Awards grants to dance companies and presenters for projects in all dance styles, including ballet, modern dance, jazz, folkloric, tap, hip-hop, and other contemporary forms.

National Endowment for the Arts (NEA), *Theater and Musical Theater, 400 7th St. S.W., 20506; (202) 682-5509. Ouida Maedel, Contact (Organizations A - M), (202) 682-5509; Ian-Julian Williams, Contact (Organizations N - Z), (202) 682-5020. Performing Arts Division, (202) 682-5438. TTY, (202) 682-5082.*
Web, www.arts.gov

Awards grants to organizations and artists in all venues of theater, including traditional, musical, classical, new plays, works for young audiences, experimental work, community-based work, circus arts, and puppetry.

Smithsonian Institution, *Discovery Theater, 1100 Jefferson Dr. S.W., 20024 (mailing address: P.O. Box 23293, Washington, DC 20026-3293); (202) 633-8700. Roberta Gasbarre, Director.*
General email, info@discoverytheater.org
Web, https://discoverytheater.org, Facebook, www.facebook.com/SmithsonianDiscoveryTheater and Twitter, @SmithsonianKids

Presents live theatrical performances, including storytelling, dance, music, puppetry, and plays, for young people and their families.

▶NONGOVERNMENTAL

Dance/USA, *1029 Vermont Ave. N.W., #400, 20005; (202) 833-1717. Kellee Edusei, Executive Director.*
General email, danceusa@danceusa.org
Web, www.danceusa.org, Twitter, @DanceUSAorg, Facebook, www.facebook.com/DanceUSAorg and YouTube, www.youtube.com/user/DanceUSAorg

Membership: professional dance companies, artists, artist managers, presenters, service organizations, educators, libraries, businesses, and individuals. Advances the art form by addressing the needs, concerns, and interests of the professional dance community through public communications, research and information services, professional development, advocacy, regranting initiatives, and other projects.

National Assn. of Schools of Dance, *11250 Roger Bacon Dr., #21, Reston, VA 20190-5248; (703) 437-0700. Fax, (703) 437-6312. Karen Moynahan, Executive Director, ext. 116.*
General email, info@arts-accredit.org
Web, http://nasd.arts-accredit.org

Specialized professional accrediting agency for postsecondary programs in dance. Conducts and shares research and analysis on topics pertinent to dance programs and the field of dance. Offers professional development opportunities for executives of dance programs.

National Assn. of Schools of Theatre, *11250 Roger Bacon Dr., #21, Reston, VA 20190-5248; (703) 437-0700. Fax, (703) 437-6312. Karen Moynahan, Executive Director, ext. 116.*
General email, info@arts-accredit.org
Web, http://nast.arts-accredit.org

Specialized professional accrediting agency for postsecondary programs in theatre. Conducts and shares research and analysis on topics pertinent to theatre programs and the field of theatre. Offers professional development opportunities for executives of theatre programs.

National Conservatory of Dramatic Arts, *1556 Wisconsin Ave., 20007; (202) 333-2202. Raymond (Ray) G. Ficca, President; Nan Kyle Ficca, School Director.*
General email, info@theconservatory.org
Web, www.theconservatory.org and Twitter, @MadeNcda

Offers an accredited two-year program in postsecondary professional actor training and a one-year program in advanced professional training. Emphasizes both physical and mental preparedness for acting in the professional entertainment industry.

Shakespeare Theatre Company, *Michael R. Klein Theatre, 450 7th St. N.W., 20004; Sidney Harmon Hall, 610 F St. N.W., 20004; 516 8th St. N.E., 20003-2834; (202) 547-3230. Fax, (202) 608-6350. Chris Jennings, Executive Director; Michael R. Klein, Chair; Simon Godwin, Artistic Director. Box office, (202) 547-1122. Educational programs, (202) 547-5688. Toll-free, (877) 487-8849.*
Web, www.shakespearetheatre.org and Twitter, @ShakespeareinDC

Professional resident theater that presents Shakespearean and other classical plays. Offers actor training program for youths, adults, and professional actors. Produces free outdoor summer Shakespeare plays and free Shakespeare plays for schools.

Visual Arts

►AGENCIES

National Endowment for the Arts (NEA), *Design, 400 7th St. S.W., 20506; (202) 682-5452. Courtney Spearman, Director, (202) 682-5603. TTY, (202) 682-5082.*
Web, www.arts.gov/grants/grants-for-arts-projects/design

Provides grants to nonprofit organizations to fund the role of creative design and visual arts in economic revitalization and creating sustainable communities.

National Endowment for the Arts (NEA), *Visual Arts, 400 7th St. S.W., 20506; (202) 682-5452. Fax, (202) 682-5721. Wendy Clark, Director, (202) 682-5555; Tamika Shingler, Specialist, Museum and Visual Arts, (202) 682-5577. TTY, (202) 682-5082.*
Web, www.arts.gov

Awards grants to nonprofit organizations for creative works and programs in the visual arts, including painting, sculpture, crafts, video, photography, printmaking, drawing, artists' books, and performance art.

Smithsonian Institution, *Archives of American Art, 750 9th St. N.W., #2200, 20001 (mailing address: Victor Bldg., P.O. Box 37012, #2200, MS 937, Washington, DC 20013-7012); (202) 633-7940. Fax, (202) 633-7994. Liza Kirwin, Director (Acting), (202) 633-7992. Reference desk, (202) 633-7950.*
Web, www.aaa.si.edu, Twitter, @ArchivesAmerArt, Facebook, www.facebook.com/archivesofamericanart and YouTube, www.youtube.com/user/SmithsonianAAA

Collects and preserves manuscript items, such as notebooks, sketchbooks, letters, and journals; photos of artists and works of art; tape-recorded interviews with artists, dealers, and collectors; exhibition catalogs; directories; and biographies on the history of visual arts in the United States. Library open to scholars and researchers. Reference centers that maintain microfilm copies of a selection of the Archives' collection include New York; Boston; San Francisco; and San Marino, Calif.

State Dept., *Art in Embassies, 2201 C St. N.W., 20520; (703) 875-4202. Camille Benton, Curator. Toll-free, (800) 877-8339.*

General email, artinembassies@state.gov
Web, http://art.state.gov, Twitter, @ArtinEmbassies and Facebook, www.facebook.com/ArtinembassiesAIE

Exhibits American art in U.S. ambassadorial residences. Borrows artworks from artists, collectors, galleries, and museums.

►CONGRESS

For a listing of relevant congressional committees and subcommittees, please see page 130 or the Appendix.

Library of Congress, *Prints and Photographs Division, James Madison Memorial Bldg., 101 Independence Ave. S.E., #LM 337, 20540-4730; (202) 707-6394. Helena Zinkham, Chief, (202) 707-2922.*
Web, www.loc.gov/rr/print

Maintains Library of Congress's collection of pictorial material not in book format, totaling more than 15 million items. U.S. and international collections include artists' prints; historical prints, posters, and drawings; photographs (chiefly documentary); political and social cartoons; and architectural plans, drawings, prints, and photographs. Reference service provided in the Prints and Photographs Reading Room. Reproductions of nonrestricted material available through the Library of Congress's Photoduplication Service; prints and photographs may be borrowed through the Exhibits Office for exhibits by qualified institutions. A portion of the collections and an overview of reference services are available online. Timed entry pass for visitors required, details at loc.gov/visit. Appointments recommended for researchers.

►NONGOVERNMENTAL

American Institute of Architects, *1735 New York Ave. N.W., 20006-5292; (202) 626-7300. Fax, (202) 626-7547. Lakisha Ann Woods, Chief Executive Officer. Toll-free, (800) 242-3837.*
General email, info@aia.org
Web, www.aia.org, Twitter, @AIANational and Facebook, www.facebook.com/AIANational

Membership: licensed American architects, interns, architecture faculty, engineers, planners, and those in government, manufacturing, or other fields in a capacity related to architecture. Works to advance the standards of architectural education, training, and practice. Promotes the aesthetic, scientific, and practical efficiency of architecture, urban design, and planning; monitors international developments. Offers continuing and professional education programs; sponsors scholarships, internships, and awards. Manages a historical directory archive. Monitors legislation and regulations.

Foundation for Art and Preservation in Embassies (FAPE), *1725 Eye St. N.W., #300, 20006-2423; (202) 349-3724. Fax, (202) 349-3727. Jennifer A. Duncan, Director.*
General email, info@fapeglobal.org
Web, www.fapeglobal.org and Facebook, www.facebook.com/FAPEglobal

Works with the State Dept. to contribute fine art for placement in U.S. embassies worldwide.

International Arts and Artists, *9 Hillyer Court N.W., 20008; (202) 338-0680. Fax, (202) 333-0758. Jeff Freedman, Chief Operating Officer.*
General email, info@artsandartists.org
Web, www.artsandartists.org, Twitter, @IAAHillyer and Facebook, www.facebook.com/artsandartists

Collects multicultural art and plans art exhibits for museums. Offers affordable print and digital services to artists and organizations. Local gallery, the Hillyer Arts Space, exhibits contemporary art.

National Assn. of Schools of Art and Design, *11250 Roger Bacon Dr., #21, Reston, VA 20190-5248; (703) 437-0700. Fax, (703) 437-6312. Karen Moynahan, Executive Director, ext. 116.*
General email, info@arts-accredit.org
Web, http://nasad.arts-accredit.org

Specialized professional accrediting agency for post-secondary programs in art and design. Conducts and shares research and analysis on topics pertinent to art and design programs and fields of art and design. Offers professional development opportunities for executives of art and design programs.

HISTORY AND PRESERVATION

General

▶**AGENCIES**

Advisory Council on Historic Preservation, *401 F St. N.W., #308, 20001-2637; (202) 517-0200. Reid Nelson, Executive Director (Acting).*
General email, achp@achp.gov
Web, www.achp.gov, Twitter, @usachp, Facebook, www.facebook.com/usachp and YouTube, www.youtube.com/channel/UChReeJ63BktsEqSidL396Ng

Advises the president and Congress on historic preservation; reviews and comments on federal projects and programs affecting historic, architectural, archaeological, and cultural resources. Monitors legislation and regulations.

Bureau of Educational and Cultural Affairs (ECA) *(State Dept.), Cultural Heritage Center, 2200 C St. N.W., 5-MO6, 20037 (mailing address: 2200 C St. N.W., SA-5, 5th Fl, U.S. Department of State, Washington, DC, 20522-0505); (202) 632-6197. Alexei Kral, Director.*
General email, culprop@state.gov
Web, http://eca.state.gov/cultural-heritage-center, Twitter, @HeritageAtState and Facebook, www.facebook.com/usafcp

Protects and preserves ancient and historic monuments, objects, and archaeological sites. Reviews country requests for import restrictions on archaeological or ethnological artifacts and makes recommendations on them

to the State Dept. Distributes information to police, customs, museums, dealers, and collectors about cultural heritage objects stolen from archaeological sites, museums, and churches. Administers the Cultural Property Protection program, the U.S. Ambassadors Fund for Cultural Preservation, and the Iraq Cultural Heritage Initiative.

Bureau of Engraving and Printing (BEP) *(Treasury Dept.), 14th and C Sts. S.W., 20228; (202) 874-3188. Leonard R. Olijar, Director. Toll-free, (877) 874-4114. Tours, (202) 874-2330.*
General email, moneyfactory.info@bep.gov
Web, www.moneyfactory.gov and Facebook, www.facebook/USMoneyfactory

Provides information on history, design, and engraving of currency; offers public tours; maintains reading room where materials are brought for special research. (For an appointment, write to the BEP's Historical Resource Center at the email below.)

General Services Administration (GSA), *Design and Construction, Office of the Chief Architect, 1800 F St. N.W., #5400, 20405-0001; (202) 501-1888. David Insinga, Chief Architect.*
Web, www.gsa.gov/about-us/organization/public-buildings-service

Administers the preservation of historic federal buildings.

National Archives and Records Administration (NARA), *Cartographic and Architectural Records, 8601 Adelphi Rd., #3320, College Park, MD 20740-6001; (301) 837-3200. Fax, (301) 837-3622. Peter F. Brauer, Cartographic Supervisor, (301) 837-2036.*
General email, carto@nara.gov
Web, www.archives.gov/publications/general-info-leaflets/26-cartographic.html and Research Room, www.archives.gov/research/cartographic/consultation.carto@nara.gov

Preserves and makes available historical records of federal agencies, including maps, charts, aerial photographs, architectural engineering drawings, patents, lighthouse plans, and ships' plans. Research room open to the public. Records are available for reproduction.

National Archives and Records Administration (NARA), *Preservation Programs, 8601 Adelphi Rd., #1400, College Park, MD 20740-6001; (301) 837-0678. Sarah D. Stauderman, Director, (301) 837-1728.*
General email, preservation@nara.gov
Web, www.archives.gov/preservation and Facebook, www.facebook.com/nationalarchivespreservation

Manages the preservation program for the 44 National Archives facilities across the country. Develops preservation policy, regulations, and planning. Responsible for conserving and reformatting archival holdings. Ensures that the storage environments are designed and maintained to prolong the life of records. Manages records during emergency preparedness and response for the agency; advises other federal agencies in event of need. Conducts research and testing for materials purchased by and used in the archives, as well as deterioration and preservation processes. Monitors and maintains the condition of the Charters of Freedom.

National Archives and Records Administration (NARA), *Research Services,* 8601 Adelphi Rd., #3400, College Park, MD 20740-6001; (301) 837-2000. Fax, (301) 837-3633. Chris C. Naylor, Executive for Research Services, (301) 837-3110. Toll-free, (866) 272-6272.
Web, www.archives.gov/research
Email, Inquires@nara.gov

Preserves and makes available federal records at fifteen National Archives facilities across the country.

National Endowment for the Humanities (NEH), *Division of Preservation and Access,* 400 7th St. S.W., 20506; (202) 606-8570. Briann Greenfield, Director, (202) 606-8442.
General email, preservation@neh.gov
Web, www.neh.gov/divisions/preservation and *Twitter, @NEH_PresAccess*

Sponsors preservation and access projects, the stabilization and documentation of material culture collections, and the National Digital Newspaper program.

National Museum of American History *(Smithsonian Institution), Curatorial Affairs,* 12th St. and Constitution Ave. N.W., 20560 (mailing address: P.O. Box 37012, MS 664, Washington, DC 20013-7012); (202) 633-3497. Fax, (202) 633-4284. Bonnie Campbell Lilienfeld, Assistant Director.
General email, info@si.edu
Web, www.americanhistory.si.edu/about/departments/ curatorial-affairs

Conducts research, develops collections, and creates exhibits on American social and public history, based on collections of folk and popular arts, ethnic and craft objects, textiles, coins, costumes and jewelry, ceramics and glass, graphic arts, musical instruments, photographs, technological innovations, appliances, and machines. Research areas are open by appointment.

National Museum of American History *(Smithsonian Institution), Library,* 14th St. and Constitution Ave. N.W., Room 5016, 20560-0630 (mailing address: Room 5016, P.O. Box 37012, MS 630, Washington, DC 20013-7012); (202) 633-3865. Fax, (202) 633-3427. Trina Brown, Head Librarian, (202) 633-3867.
General email, nmahlibrary@si.edu
Web, https://library.si.edu/libraries/american-history and *Online catalogue, http://siris-libraries.si.edu/ipac20/ipac .jsp?profile=liball*

Supports research on American history, including social, cultural, political, and economic events and development. Maintains collection of trade catalogs and materials about expositions and world fairs. Open to the public by appointment. All library holdings are listed in the online catalog.

National Museum of Health and Medicine *(Defense Dept.),* 2500 Linden Lane, Silver Spring, MD 20910

(mailing address: Bldg. 2500, 2460 Linden Lane, Silver Spring, MD 20910); (301) 319-3300. Fax, (301) 319-3373. Adrianne Noe, Director. Tours, (301) 319-3312.
General email, usarmy.detrick.medcom-usamrmc.list .medical-museum@mail.mil
Web, www.medicalmuseum.mil and *Twitter, @medicalmuseum*

Maintains exhibits related to pathology and the history of medicine, particularly military medicine during the Civil War. Open to the public 10:00 a.m.–5:30 p.m., seven days a week. Study collection available for scholars by appointment.

National Park Service (NPS) *(Interior Dept.), Cultural Resources, Partnerships, and Science,* 1849 C St. N.W., #3128, MIB, 20240-0001; (202) 208-6843. Joy Beasley, Associate Director (Acting).
Web, www.nps.gov/orgs/1345

Oversees preservation of federal historic sites and administration of building programs. Programs include the National Register of Historic Places, National Historic and National Landmark Programs, Historic American Building Survey, Historic American Engineering Record, Archeology and Antiquities Act Program, and Technical Preservation Services. Gives grant and aid assistance and tax benefit information to properties listed in the National Register of Historic Places.

National Park Service (NPS) *(Interior Dept.),* 1849 C St. N.W., #3115, 20240; (202) 208-6843. Fax, (202) 208-7889. Charles (Chuck) F. Sams III, Director.
General email, asknps@nps.gov
Web, www.nps.gov, Twitter, @NatlParkService and *Facebook, www.facebook.com/nationalparkservice*

Administers national parks, monuments, historic sites, and recreation areas.

▶ **CONGRESS**

For a listing of relevant congressional committees and subcommittees, please see page 130 or the Appendix.

Library of Congress, *Serial and Government Publications Division,* James Madison Memorial Bldg., 101 Independence Ave. S.E., #LM 133, 20540-4760; (202) 707-5690. Deborah Thomas, Chief.
Web, www.loc.gov/rr/news

Collects and maintains information on governmental and nongovernmental organizations that are domestically or internationally based, financed, and sponsored. Responds to written or telephone requests to provide information on the history, structure, operation, and activities of these organizations. Collects and maintains domestic and foreign newspapers and periodicals. Some microfilm materials are available for interlibrary loan through the Library of Congress CALM Division. Timed entry pass for visitors required, details at loc.gov/visit. Appointments recommended for researchers.

Senate Office of Conservation and Preservation, B15 SROB, 20510; (202) 224-7106. Leona Faust, Librarian.

Develops and coordinates programs related to the conservation and preservation of Senate records and materials for the secretary of the Senate.

▶NONGOVERNMENTAL

American Battlefield Trust, *1156 15th St. N.W., #900, 20005; (202) 367-1861. Fax, (202) 367-1865. David D. Duncan, President. Toll-free, (800) 298-7878. General email, info@battlefields.org*

Web, www.battlefields.org, Twitter, @battlefields and Facebook, www.facebook.com/americanbattlefieldtrust

Membership: preservation professionals, historians, conservation activists, and citizens. Preserves endangered American Revolution, War of 1812, and Civil War battlefields throughout the United States. Conducts preservation conferences and workshops. Advises local preservation groups. Publishes Hallowed Ground. Monitors legislation and regulations at the federal, state, and local levels.

American Historical Assn., *400 A St. S.E., 20003; (202) 544-2422. Fax, (202) 544-8307. James (Jim) Grossman, Executive Director. General email, info@historians.org*

Web, www.historians.org, Twitter, @AHAHistorians and Facebook, www.facebook.com/AHAHistorians

Membership: university academics, colleges, museums, historical organizations, libraries and archives, independent historians, students, K–12 teachers, government and business professionals, and individuals interested in history. Interests include academic freedom, professional standards, publication, teaching, professional development, networking, and advocacy. Supports public access to government information; publishes original historical research, journals, bibliographies, historical directories, and a job placement bulletin.

American Institute for Conservation, *727 15th St. N.W., #500, 20005-1714; (202) 452-9545. Fax, (202) 452-9328. Tiffani Emig, Director (Acting), (202) 750-3346. General email, info@culturalheritage.org*

Web, www.culturalheritage.org, Twitter, @conservators and Facebook, www.facebook.com/aiconservation

Membership: professional conservators, scientists, students, administrators, cultural institutions, collection care professionals, and others. Promotes the knowledge and practice of the conservation of cultural property; supports research; and disseminates information on conservation. Affiliated with the Foundation for Advancement in Conservation.

American Studies Assn., *1120 19th St. N.W., #301, 20036-3614; (202) 596-1270. John F. Stephens, Executive Director. General email, asastaff@theasa.net*

Web, www.theasa.net, Twitter, @AmeriStudiesAssn and Facebook, www.facebook.com/americanstudiesassoc

Fosters the interdisciplinary exchange of ideas about American culture and history in local and global contexts; awards annual prizes for contributions to American studies; provides curriculum resources.

Daughters of the American Revolution, *National Society, 1776 D St. N.W., 20006-5303; (202) 628-1776. Fax, (202) 879-3227. Denise Doring VanBuren, President General.*

Web, www.dar.org, Twitter, @TodaysDAR and Facebook, www.facebook.com/TodaysDAR

Membership: women descended from American Revolutionary War patriots. Conducts historical, educational, and patriotic activities; maintains a genealogical library, fine arts museum, and documentary collection antedating 1830. Library open to the public.

National Conference of State Historic Preservation Officers, *444 N. Capitol St. N.W., #342, 20001-1512; (202) 624-5465. Fax, (202) 624-5419. Erik Hein, Executive Director.*

Web, https://ncshpo.org, Twitter, @NCSHPO and Facebook, www.facebook.com/NCSHPO

Membership: state and territorial historic preservation officers and deputy officers. Compiles statistics on programs; monitors legislation and regulations.

National Park Trust, *401 E. Jefferson St., #207, Rockville, MD 20850; (301) 279-7275. Fax, (301) 279-7211. Grace K. Lee, Executive Director, ext. 11. General email, info@parktrust.org*

Web, www.parktrust.org and Twitter, @natparktrust

Protects national parks, wildlife refuges, and historic monuments. Uses funds to purchase private land within or adjacent to existing parks and land suitable for new parks; works with preservation organizations to manage acquired resources.

National Preservation Institute, *P.O. Box 1702, Alexandria, VA 22313; (703) 765-0100. Fax, (703) 768-9350. Jere Gibber, Executive Director; Darwina L. Neal, President. General email, info@npi.org*

Web, www.npi.org and Facebook, www.facebook.com/ National-Preservation-Institute-273102762795

Conducts seminars in historic preservation and cultural resource management for those involved in the management, preservation, and stewardship of historic and cultural resources.

National Society of Colonial Dames of America, *Dumbarton House, 2715 Que St. N.W., 20007-3071; (202) 337-2288. Fax, (202) 337-0348. Anna F. Duff, Honorary President; Katherine Conmach, President. Gunston Hall, (703) 350-9220. General email, dames@dumbartonhouse.org*

Web, www.nscda.org, Twitter, @colonialdames and Facebook, www.facebook.com/colonialdames

Membership: descendants of colonists in America before 1750. Conducts historical and educational activities; maintains Dumbarton House, a museum open to the public Tuesday–Sunday; and offers lectures and concerts. Maintains Gunston Hall as a museum open to the public.

National Society of Colonial Dames XVII Century, *1300 New Hampshire Ave. N.W., 20036-1502; (202) 293-1700. Dorothy (Nan) Thompson, President General. General email, cd17th@verizon.net*

Web, www.colonialdames17c.org and *Facebook, www.facebook.com/NSCDXVIIC*

Membership: American women who are lineal descendants of persons who rendered civil or military service and lived in America or one of the British colonies before 1701. Preserves records and shrines; encourages historical research; awards scholarships to undergraduate and graduate students and scholarships in medicine to persons of Native American descent.

National Society of the Children of the American Revolution, *1776 D St. N.W., #224, 20006-5303; (202) 638-3153. Norma L. Griffin, Senior National President. General email, hq@nscar.org*

Web, www.nscar.org and *Twitter, @NSCAR1895*

Membership: descendants, age twenty-two years and under, of American soldiers and patriots of the American Revolution. Conducts historical, educational, and patriotic activities; preserves places of historical interest.

National Trust for Historic Preservation, *2600 Virginia Ave. N.W., #1100, 20037; (202) 588-6000. Fax, (202) 588-6038. Paul Edmondson, President, (202) 588-6101. Toll-free, (800) 944-6847. General email, info@savingplaces.org*

Web, www.savingplaces.org, Twitter, @SavingPlaces, Facebook, www.facebook.com/NationalTrustforHistoricPreservation and *YouTube, www.youtube.com/nationaltrustforhistoricpreservation*

Conducts seminars, workshops, and conferences on topics related to preservation, including neighborhood conservation, main street revitalization, rural conservation, and preservation law; offers financial assistance through loan and grant programs; provides advisory services; operates historic house sites, which are open to the public; and publishes quarterly magazine and e-newsletters.

Preservation Action, *2020 Pennsylvania Ave. N.W., #313, 20006; (202) 463-0970. Fax, (202) 463-1299. Robert Naylor, Associate Director. General email, mail@preservationaction*

Web, www.preservationaction.org, Twitter, @PreservationAct and *Facebook, www.facebook.com/PreservationAction*

Monitors legislation affecting historic preservation and neighborhood conservation. Maintains a nationwide database of activists. Promotes adequate funding for historic preservation programs and policies that support historic resource protection.

Society for American Archaeology, *1990 K St. N.W., #401, 20006; (202) 789-8200. Fax, (202) 789-0284. Deborah L. Nichols, President. General email, info@saa.org*

Web, www.saa.org, Twitter, @SAAorg and *Facebook, www.facebook.com/SAAorgfb*

Promotes greater awareness, understanding, and research of archaeology on the American continents; works to preserve and publish results of scientific data and research; serves as information clearinghouse for members.

Archives and Manuscripts

► **AGENCIES**

National Archives and Records Administration (NARA), *700 Pennsylvania Ave. N.W., 20408 (mailing address: 8601 Adelphi Rd., College Park, MD 20704-6001); (866) 272-6272. Fax, (202) 357-5901. David S. Ferriero, Archivist of the United States, (202) 357-5900. Public Affairs, (202) 357-5300. Public programs and events, (202) 357-5000. Web, www.archives.gov* and *Twitter, @USNatArchives*

Identifies, preserves, and makes available federal government documents of historic value; administers a network of regional storage centers and archives and operates the presidential library system. Collections include photographs, graphic materials, films, and maps; holdings include records generated by foreign governments (especially in war time) and by international conferences, commissions, and exhibitions.

National Archives and Records Administration (NARA), Center for Legislative Archives, *700 Pennsylvania Ave. N.W., #8E, 20408; (202) 357-5350. Fax, (202) 357-5911. Richard H. Hunt, Director, (202) 357-5376. General email, legislative.archives@nara.gov*

Web, www.archives.gov/legislative and *Twitter, @CongressArchive*

Collects and maintains records of congressional committees and legislative files from 1789 to the present. Publishes inventories and guides to these records.

National Archives and Records Administration (NARA), Electronic Records Division (ERA), *8601 Adelphi Rd., #5320, College Park, MD 20740-6001; (301) 837-0740. Theodore J. Hull, Director, (301) 837-1824. General email, era.program@nara.gov*

Web, www.archives.gov/records-mgmt/era/technical.html

Preserves, maintains, and makes available electronic records of the U.S. government. Provides researchers with magnetic tape, CDs, DVDs, and other copies of electronic records on a cost-recovery basis. Offers direct downloads and searches of selected holdings.

National Archives and Records Administration (NARA), Presidential Libraries, *8601 Adelphi Rd., #2200, College Park, MD 20740-6001; (301) 837-3250. Fax, (301) 837-3199. Susan K. Donius, Director, (202) 357-7451. Web, www.archives.gov/presidential-libraries* and *Twitter, @OurPresidents*

Administers thirteen presidential libraries. Directs all programs relating to acquisition, preservation, and research use of materials in presidential libraries; conducts oral history projects; publishes finding aids for research sources; provides reference service, including information from and about documentary holdings.

National Park Service Sites in the Capital Region

The National Park Service administers most parks, circles, and monuments in the District of Columbia, as well as sites in nearby Maryland, Virginia, and West Virginia. For information on facilities not listed here, visit www.nps.gov/findapark/index.htm.

Go to www.recreation.gov for information on visiting and making reservations at federal recreation sites nationwide.

Antietam National Battlefield, (301) 432-5124; www.nps.gov/anti/index.htm

Arlington House, Robert E. Lee Memorial, (703) 235-1530; www.nps.gov/arho/index.htm

C & O Canal National Historical Park, (301) 739-4200; www.nps.gov/choh/index.htm

Great Falls Area (C & O Canal Maryland), (301) 767-3714; www.nps.gov/choh/index.htm

Catoctin Mountain Park, (301) 663-9388; www.nps.gov/cato/index.htm

Clara Barton National Historic Site, (301) 320-1410; www.nps.gov/clba/index.htm

Ford's Theatre National Historic Site, (202) 426-6924; www.nps.gov/foth/index.htm

Fort Washington Park (includes Piscataway Park), (301) 763-4600; www.nps.gov/pisc/index.htm

Frederick Douglass National Historic Site, (202) 426-5961; www.nps.gov/frdo/index.htm

George Washington Memorial Parkway (includes memorials to Theodore Roosevelt, Lyndon Johnson, and U.S. Marine Corps), (703) 289-2500; www.nps.gov/gwmp/index.htm

Glen Echo Park, (301) 634-2222; www.nps.gov/glec/index.htm

Great Falls Park (Virginia), (703) 757-3103; www.nps.gov/grfa/index.htm

Greenbelt Park, (301) 344-3948; www.nps.gov/gree/index.htm

Harpers Ferry National Historical Park, (304) 535-6029; www.nps.gov/hafe/index.htm

Manassas National Battlefield Park, (703) 361-1339; www.nps.gov/mana/index.htm

Mary McLeod Bethune Council House National Historic Site, (202) 673-2402; www.nps.gov/mamc/index.htm

Monocacy National Battlefield, (301) 662-3515; www.nps.gov/mono/index.htm

National Mall (includes presidential and war memorials and Pennsylvania Avenue National Historic Site), (202) 426-6841; www.nps.gov/nama/index.htm

President's Park (White House), (202) 208-1631; www.nps.gov/whho/index.htm

Prince William Forest Park, (703) 221-7181; www.nps.gov/prwi/index.htm

Rock Creek Park, (202) 895-6000; www.nps.gov/rocr/index.htm

Thomas Stone National Historic Site, (301) 392-1776 or (804) 224-1732; www.nps.gov/thst/index.htm

Wolf Trap National Park for the Performing Arts, (703) 255-1800; www.nps.gov/wotr/index.htm

Conducts community outreach; oversees museum exhibition programming.

National Archives and Records Administration (NARA), Reference Services, 4205 Suitland Rd., Suitland, MD 20746-8001; (301) 778-1600. Channon Harris, Director, (301) 778-1562.
General email, suitland.reference@nara.gov
Web, www.archives.gov/frc/reference-services.html

Provides reference service for unpublished civil and military federal government records. Maintains central catalog of all archival materials. Compiles comprehensive bibliographies of materials related to archival administration and records management. Permits research in American history, archival science, and records management. Maintains collections of the papers of the Continental Congress (1774–1789), U.S. State Dept. diplomatic correspondence (1789–1963), and general records of the U.S. government.

National Archives and Records Administration (NARA), Textual Records Division, 8601 Adelphi Rd., #405, College Park, MD 20740-6001; (301) 837-3510. Fax, (301) 837-1752. Trevor K. Plante, Chief, Textual Reference, (202) 357-5287; Dennis M. Edelin, Section Chief, Research Rooms, (202) 357-5266. General Phone, (866) 272-6272.

General email, archives1reference@nara.gov
Web, www.archives.gov/dc/research/textual-records

Provides access to the textual records of the Executive and Judicial Branches of the federal government located in the National Archives in Washington, D.C., and College Park, Md. Makes reproductions for a fee.

National Historical Publications and Records Commission (National Archives and Records Administration), 8601 Adelphi Rd., College Park, MD 20740-6001 (mailing address: 1301 Metzerott Rd., College Park, MD. 20704-6001); (202) 357-5010. Fax, (202) 357-5914. Christopher Eck, Executive Director; Lawrence Brewer, Chief Records Officer; David S. Ferriero, Archivist of the U.S. Toll-free, (866) 272-6272.
General email, nhprc@nara.gov
Web, www.archives.gov/nhprc

Awards grants to nonprofit institutions, educational institutions, and local and state governments to preserve and make accessible historical records, including the papers of nationally significant Americans. Helps preserve electronic records and digitize and publish online collections.

National Museum of American History (Smithsonian Institution), Archives Center, 12th St. and Constitution

Ave. N.W., 20560-0601 (mailing address: P.O. Box 37012, MS 601, Washington, DC 20013-7012); (202) 633-3270. Fax, (202) 312-1990. Robert Horton, Assistant Director. Press, (202) 633-3129. TTY, (202) 357-1729.
General email, archivescenter@si.edu
Web, www.americanhistory.si.edu/archives

Acquires, organizes, preserves, and makes available for research the museum's archival and documentary materials relating to American history and culture. Three-dimensional objects and closely related documents are in the care of curatorial divisions. Research areas are open by appointment.

Smithsonian Institution, *Archives of American Art,* 750 9th St. N.W., #2200, 20001 (mailing address: Victor Bldg., P.O. Box 37012, #2200, MS 937, Washington, DC 20013-7012); (202) 633-7940. Fax, (202) 633-7994. Liza Kirwin, Director (Acting), (202) 633-7992. Reference desk, (202) 633-7950.
Web, www.aaa.si.edu, Twitter, @ArchivesAmerArt, Facebook, www.facebook.com/archivesofamericanart and YouTube, www.youtube.com/user/SmithsonianAAA

Collects and preserves manuscript items, such as notebooks, sketchbooks, letters, and journals; photos of artists and works of art; tape-recorded interviews with artists, dealers, and collectors; exhibition catalogs; directories; and biographies on the history of visual arts in the United States. Library open to scholars and researchers. Reference centers that maintain microfilm copies of a selection of the Archives' collection include New York; Boston; San Francisco; and San Marino, Calif.

▶ CONGRESS

For a listing of relevant congressional committees and sub-committees, please see page 130 or the Appendix.

Library of Congress, *Main Reading Room,* Thomas Jefferson Bldg., 101 Independence Ave. S.E., #LJ 100, 20540-4660; (202) 707-3399. Fax, (202) 707-1957. Melissa Ball, Head.
Web, www.loc.gov/rr/main

Point of access to the general collection of books and bound periodicals as well as electronic resources, including microform. Offers research orientations. Timed entry pass for visitors required, details at loc.gov/visit. Appointments recommended for researchers.

Library of Congress, *Manuscript Division,* James Madison Memorial Bldg., 101 Independence Ave. S.E., #LM 101, 20540-4680; (202) 707-5383. Fax, (202) 707-7791. Janice E. Ruth, Chief. Reading Room, (202) 707-5387.
Web, www.loc.gov/rr/mss

Maintains, describes, and provides reference service on the library's manuscript collections, including the papers of U.S. presidents and other eminent Americans. Manuscript reading room primarily serves serious scholars and researchers; historians and reference librarians are available for consultation. Timed entry pass for visitors required, details at loc.gov/visit. Appointments recommended for researchers.

Library of Congress, *Microform and Electronic Resources Center (MERC),* Thomas Jefferson Bldg., 101 Independence Ave. S.E., #LJ 139, 20540-4660; (202) 707-5471. Maxine Wright, Head.
Web, www.loc.gov/rr/main/ccc.html

Has custody of and services the library's general microform collection. Provides work stations for searching the library's online catalog and accessing the Internet. Timed entry pass for visitors required, details at loc.gov/visit. Appointments recommended for researchers.

Library of Congress, *Preservation Directorate,* 101 Independence Ave. S.E., 20540; Jacob (Jake) Nadal, Director, (202) 707-2068. General Info Phone, (202) 707-5000.
General email, preserve@loc.gov
Web, www.loc.gov/preservation

Responsible for preserving book and paper materials in the library's collections, which is carried out by its five divisions - Preservation Research and Testing, Preservation Reformatting, Conservation, Collections Management, and Binding and Collections Care.

Senate Historical Office, 201 SHOB, 20510; (202) 224-6900. Betty K. Koed, Historian.
General email, historian@sec.senate.gov
Web, www.senate.gov/artandhistory/history/common/generic/Senate_Historical_Office.htm and Twitter, @SenateHistory

Serves as an information clearinghouse on Senate history, traditions, and members. Collects, organizes, and distributes to the public unpublished Senate documents; collects and preserves photographs and pictures related to Senate history; conducts an oral history program; advises senators and Senate committees on the disposition of their noncurrent papers and records. Produces publications on the history of the Senate.

U.S. House of Representatives, *Office of History, Art, and Archives,* B53 CHOB, 20515; (202) 226-1300. Fax, (202) 226-4635. Farar P. Elliott, Chief. Legislative Archives, (202) 357-5350. Toll-free, (866) 272-6272.
General art email, art@mail.house.gov
General archives email, archives@mail.house.gov
Web, http://history.house.gov, Twitter, @USHouseHistory and YouTube, www.youtube.com/USHouseHistory

Works with the Office of the Historian to provide access to published documents and historical records of the House. Advises members on the disposition of their records and papers; maintains information on manuscript collections of former members; maintains biographical files on former members; houses photographs and artifacts of former members. Produces publications on Congress and its members.

U.S. House of Representatives, *Office of the Historian,* B53 CHOB, 20515; (202) 226-1300. Matthew A. Wasniewski, House Historian. Legislative Archives, (202) 357-5350.

General email, history@mail.house.gov

Web, http://history.house.gov and

Twitter, @ushousehistory

Works with the Office of Art and Archives to provide access to published documents and historical records of the House. Conducts historical research. Advises members on the disposition of their records and papers; maintains information on manuscript collections of former members; maintains biographical files on former members. Produces publications on Congress and its members.

▶NONGOVERNMENTAL

Assassination Archives and Research Center, *962 Wayne Ave., #910, Silver Spring, MD 20910; (301) 565-0249. James Lesar, President.*

General email, aarc@aarclibrary.org

Web, www.aarclibrary.org

Acquires, preserves, and disseminates information on political assassinations. Materials and information available on website and by request through mail. On-site access available to the public by appointment only.

Moorland-Spingarn Research Center (MSRC) *(Howard University),* *500 Howard Pl. N.W., #263, 20059; (202) 806-4446. Benjamin Talton, Director. Reading Room, (202) 806-4237. Reference, (202) 806-7252. Library, (202) 806-7250.*

Web, http://library.howard.edu/MSRC,

Twitter, @MoorlandHU and Facebook, www.facebook .com/Howard-University-Libraries-HUL-477400242326423

Comprehensive repository for the documentation of the history and culture of people of African descent in Africa, the Americas, and other parts of the world; collects, preserves, and makes available for research a wide range of resources chronicling the black experience.

National Security Archive *(George Washington University),* *Gelman Library, 2130 H St. N.W., #701, 20037; (202) 994-7000. Fax, (202) 994-7005. Thomas S. Blanton, Director.*

General email, nsarchiv@gwu.edu

Web, www.nsarchive.gwu.edu, Twitter, @NSArchive and Facebook, www.facebook.com/NSArchive

Research institute and library that provides information on U.S. foreign and economic policy and national security affairs. Maintains and publishes collection of declassified and unclassified documents obtained through the Freedom of Information Act. Archive open to the public by appointment. Website has a Russian-language link.

Society of the Cincinnati, *2118 Massachusetts Ave. N.W., 20008; (202) 785-2040. I. Anderson Morse, Executive Director (Acting), ext. 413; Ellen McAllister, Librarian, ext. 426.*

Web, https://societyofthecincinnati.org

Collects and preserves American manuscripts and books from the 1700s. Specializes in documents and artifacts related to the American Revolution. Library open by appointment.

Genealogy

▶AGENCIES

National Archives and Records Administration (NARA), *700 Pennsylvania Ave. N.W., 20408 (mailing address: 8601 Adelphi Rd., College Park, MD 20704-6001); (866) 272-6272. Fax, (202) 357-5901. David S. Ferriero, Archivist of the United States, (202) 357-5900. Public Affairs, (202) 357-5300. Public programs and events, (202) 357-5000.*

Web, www.archives.gov and Twitter, @USNatArchives

Makes available resources for genealogy research, including military, passport, immigration, census, and land records. Holds genealogy consultations at the Microfilm Research desk one Saturday every month. Genealogy lectures and workshops are available nationwide; events may be found on the National Archives calendar www .archives.gov/calendar.

National Archives and Records Administration (NARA), *Textual Records Division, 8601 Adelphi Rd., #405, College Park, MD 20740-6001; (301) 837-3510. Fax, (301) 837-1752. Trevor K. Plante, Chief, Textual Reference, (202) 357-5287; Dennis M. Edelin, Section Chief, Research Rooms, (202) 357-5266. General Phone, (866) 272-6272.*

General email, archives1reference@nara.gov

Web, www.archives.gov/dc/research/textual-records

Assists individuals interested in researching record holdings of the National Archives, including genealogical records; issues research cards to researchers who present photo identification. Users must be at least fourteen years of age.

▶CONGRESS

For a listing of relevant congressional committees and subcommittees, please see page 130 or the Appendix.

Library of Congress, *Local History and Genealogy Reference Services, Thomas Jefferson Bldg., 101 Independence Ave. S.E., #LJ 100, 20540-4660; (202) 707-3399. Fax, (202) 707-1957. Dennis T. Clark, Chief.*

Web, www.loc.gov/rr/genealogy

Provides reference and referral service on topics related to local history, genealogy, and heraldry throughout the United States. Timed entry pass for visitors required, details at loc.gov/visit. Appointments recommended for researchers.

▶NONGOVERNMENTAL

Daughters of the American Revolution, *National Society, 1776 D St. N.W., 20006-5303; (202) 628-1776. Fax, (202) 879-3227. Denise Doring VanBuren, President General.*

Web, www.dar.org, Twitter, @TodaysDAR and Facebook, www.facebook.com/TodaysDAR

Membership: women descended from American Revolutionary War patriots. Maintains a genealogical library and museum, which are open to the public.

National Genealogical Society, *6400 Arlington Blvd., #810, Falls Church, VA 22042-2318; (703) 525-0050. Matt Menashes, Executive Director. Toll-free, (800) 473-0060.*

General email, ngs@ngsgenealogy.org

Web, www.ngsgenealogy.org, Twitter, @ngsgenealogy and Facebook, www.facebook.com/ngsgenealogy

Encourages study of genealogy and publication of all records that are of genealogical interest. Provides online courses and an in-depth home study program; holds an annual conference.

National Museum of Civil War Medicine, *48 E. Patrick St., Frederick, MD 21705 (mailing address: P.O. Box 470, Frederick, MD 21705); (301) 695-1864. Fax, (301) 695-6823. David Price, Executive Director.*

General email, info@civilwarmed.org

Web, www.civilwarmed.org and Twitter, @civilwarmed

Assists individuals with questions about ancestors injured in the Civil War.

National Society Daughters of the American Colonists, *2205 Massachusetts Ave. N.W., 20008-2813; (202) 667-3076. Melanie K. Caroll Platte, President.*

General email, admin@nsdac.org

Web, www.nsdac.org

Membership: women descended from men and women who were resident in or gave civil or military service to the colonies prior to the Revolutionary War. Maintains library of colonial and genealogical records; open to the public by appointment.

Washington D.C. Family History Center, *10000 Stoneybrook Dr., Kensington, MD 20895; (301) 587-0042. Richard (Ben) Mieremet, Director.*

General email, info@wdcfhc.org

Web, www.wdcfhc.org

Maintains genealogical library for research. Collection includes international genealogical index, family group record archives, microfiche registers, and the Family Search Computer Program (www.familysearch.org). Library open to the public. (Sponsored by the Church of Jesus Christ of Latter-day Saints.)

Specific Cultures

▶ AGENCIES

Center for Folklife and Cultural Heritage *(Smithsonian Institution), 600 Maryland Ave. S.W., #2001, 20024 (mailing address: P.O. Box 37012, MS 520, Washington, DC 20013-7012); (202) 633-6440. Fax, (202) 633-6474. Greg Adams, Director (Acting).*

General email, folklife@si.edu

Web, https://folklife.si.edu, Twitter, @SmithsonianFolk, Facebook, www.facebook.com/smithsonianfolklife and YouTube, www.youtube.com/user/SmithsonianFolklife

Promotes and conducts research into traditional U.S. cultures and foreign folklife traditions; produces folkways recordings, films, videos, and educational programs; presents annual Smithsonian Folklife Festival in Washington, D.C.

Interior Dept. (DOI), *Indian Arts and Crafts Board (IACB), 1849 C St. N.W., #2528-MIB, 20240-0001; (202) 208-3773. Meridith Z. Stanton, Director. Toll-free, (888) 278-3253.*

General email, iacb@ios.doi.gov

Web, www.doi.gov/iacb and Facebook, www.facebook.com/IndianArtsandCraftsBoard

Advises Native American artisans and craft guilds; produces a source directory on arts and crafts of Native Americans (including Alaska Natives); maintains museums of native crafts in Montana, South Dakota, and Oklahoma; provides information on the Indian Arts and Crafts Act.

National Museum of the American Indian *(Smithsonian Institution), 4th St. and Independence Ave. S.W., 20560; (202) 633-6700. Fax, (202) 633-6920. Cynthia Chavez Lamar, Director, (202) 633-6930. General Smithsonian information, (202) 633-1000. Group reservations, (202) 633-6644. TTY, (202) 633-0572. TTY group reservations, (202) 633-6751.*

General email, NMAI-info@si.edu

Web, www.americanindian.si.edu, Twitter, @SmithsonianNMAI and Facebook, www.facebook.com/NationalMuseumoftheAmericanIndian

Collects, exhibits, preserves, and studies American Indian languages, literature, history, art, and culture. Operates ImagiNations activity center, open to the public. (Affiliated with the George Gustav Heye Center, 1 Bowling Green, New York, NY 10004 and the Cultural Resources Center, 4220 Silver Hill Rd., Suitland, MD 20746.)

▶ CONGRESS

For a listing of relevant congressional committees and subcommittees, please see page 130 or the Appendix.

Library of Congress, *American Folklife Center, Thomas Jefferson Bldg., 101 Independence Ave. S.E., #LJ-G29, 20540-4610; (202) 707-5510. Fax, (202) 707-2076. Vacant, Director.*

General email, folklife@loc.gov

Web, www.loc.gov/folklife and Facebook, www.facebook.com/americanfolklifecenter

Coordinates national, regional, state and local government, and private folklife activities; contracts with individuals and groups for research and field studies in American folklife and for exhibits and workshops; maintains the National Archive of Folk Culture (an ethnographic collection of American and international folklore, grassroots oral histories, and ethnomusicology) and the Veterans History Project (a collection of oral histories and documentary materials from veterans of World Wars I and II and the Korean, Vietnam, and Persian Gulf wars). Conducts internships at the archive; lectures; sponsors year-round concerts of traditional and ethnic music.

American Folklife Center Reading Room is located in room #LJ G31. Timed entry pass for visitors required, details at loc.gov/visit. Appointments recommended for researchers.

▶NONGOVERNMENTAL

David S. Wyman Institute for Holocaust Studies, *1200 G St. N.W., #800, 20005; (202) 434-8994. Rafael Medoff, Director.*
General email, info@wymaninstitute.org
Web, www.wymaninstitute.org

Educates the public about U.S. response to Nazism and the Holocaust through scholarly research, public events and exhibits, publications, conferences, and educational programs.

National Council for the Traditional Arts, *8757 Georgia Ave., #450, Silver Spring, MD 20910; (301) 565-0654. Fax, (301) 565-0472. Lora Bottinelli, Executive Director.*
General email, info@ncta-usa.org
Web, www.ncta-usa.org, Twitter, @NCTA1933, Facebook, www.facebook.com/NCTA1933 and YouTube, www.youtube.com/user/NatlCouncilTradArts

Seeks to celebrate and honor arts of cultural and ethnic significance, including music, crafts, stories, and dance. Promotes artistic authenticity in festivals, national and international tours, concerts, radio and television programs, CD recordings, and films. Works with national parks and other institutions to create, plan, and present cultural events, exhibits, and other programs. Sponsors the annual National Folk Festival.

National Endowment for the Arts (NEA), *Folk and Traditional Arts, 400 7th St. S.W., 20506; (202) 682-5678. Clifford Murphy, Director, (202) 682-5726; William (Bill) Mansfield, Specialist, (202) 682-5678. TTY, (202) 682-5496.*
Web, www.arts.gov

Awards grants to the folk and traditional arts that are rooted in and reflective of the cultural life of communities.

National Hispanic Foundation for the Arts (NHFA), *Washington Square, 1050 Connecticut Ave. N.W., 5th Floor, 20036; (202) 293-8330. Felix Sanchez, Chair.*
General email, info@hispanicarts.org
Web, www.hispanicarts.org, Twitter, @HispanicArts and Facebook, www.facebook.com/hispanicarts

Strives to increase the presence of Hispanics in the media, telecommunications, entertainment industries, and performing arts, and to increase programming for the U.S. Latino community. Provides scholarships for Hispanic students to pursue graduate study in the arts.

National Italian American Foundation, *1860 19th St. N.W., 20009; (202) 387-0600. Fax, (202) 387-0800. Jerry Jones, Chief Administration Officer, (202) 939-3102; Anthony J. O'Boyle, Director Public Affairs.*
General email, information@niaf.org
Web, www.niaf.org

Membership: U.S. citizens of Italian ancestry. Promotes recognition of Italian American contributions to American society; funds cultural events, educational symposia, antidefamation programs, and grants and scholarships; serves as an umbrella organization for local Italian American clubs throughout the United States.

Pew Research Center, *Hispanic Trends Project, 1615 L St. N.W., #800, 20036; (202) 419-4300. Mark Hugo Lopez, Director, Race and Ethnicity. Press, (202) 419-4372.*
Web, www.pewhispanic.org, Twitter, @PewHispanic Director, Twitter, @mhugolopez

Seeks to improve understanding of the U.S. Hispanic population and its impact on the nation, as well as explore Latino views on a range of social matters and public policy issues, including public opinion, identity, and trends in voting, immigration, work, and education. Conducts public opinion surveys and other studies that are made available to the public.

Washington Area

▶AGENCIES

National Capital Planning Commission, *401 9th St. N.W., #500N, 20004; (202) 482-7200. Fax, (202) 482-7272. Marcel Acosta, Executive Director.*
General email, info@ncpc.gov
Web, www.ncpc.gov, Facebook, www.facebook.com/NCPCgov/ and Twitter, @NCPCgov

Central planning agency for the federal government in the national capital region, which includes the District of Columbia and suburban Maryland and Virginia. Reviews and approves plans for the preservation of certain historic and environmental features in the national capital region, including the annual federal capital improvement plan.

National Park Service (NPS) *(Interior Dept.), National Capital Region, 1100 Ohio Dr. S.W., 20242; (202) 619-7020. Kym Hall, Area Director. Permits, (202) 245-4715.*
Web, www.nps.gov

Provides visitors with information on Washington-area parks, monuments, and Civil War battlefields; offers press services for the media and processes special event applications and permits.

White House Visitor Center *(President's Park), 1849 C St. N.W., #1426, 20240; (202) 208-1631. Fax, (202) 208-1643. Katie Wilmes, Park Manager (Acting); Kathy Langley, Visitor Center Manager; John Stanwich, National Park Service White House Liaison, (202) 619-6344. TTY, (800) 877-8339.*
General email, presidents_park@nps.gov
Web, www.nps.gov/whho, Twitter, @PresParkNPS, Facebook, www.facebook.com/nationalparkservice and YouTube, www.youtube.com/nationalparkservice

Administered by the National Park Service. Educates visitors about the White House through videos, exhibits, and historical artifacts. Public tours of the White House are available to those who submit requests to their member of Congress and are accepted up to six months in advance. (Ellipse Visitor Pavilion Complex located just west of the intersection of 15th and E Sts. N.W.)

►CONGRESS

For a listing of relevant congressional committees and subcommittees, please see page 130 or the Appendix.

Senate Commission on Art, *S411 CAP, 20510; (202) 224-2955. Melinda Smith, Curator of the Senate.*
General email, curator@sec.senate.gov
Web, www.senate.gov/art-artifacts/art-artifacts.htm

Accepts artwork and historical objects for display in Senate office buildings and the Senate wing of the Capitol. Maintains and exhibits Senate collections (paintings, sculptures, furniture, and manuscripts); oversees and maintains old Senate and Supreme Court chambers.

►NONGOVERNMENTAL

Assn. for Preservation of Historic Congressional Cemetery, *1801 E St. S.E., 20003-2499; (202) 543-0539. Fax, (202) 449-8364. Vacant, President.*
General email, staff@congressionalcemetery.org
Web, www.congressionalcemetery.org and
Twitter, @CongCemetery

Administers and maintains the Washington Parish Burial Ground (commonly known as the Congressional Cemetery).

D.C. Preservation League, *1221 Connecticut Ave. N.W., #5A, 20036; (202) 783-5144. Fax, (202) 783-5596. Rebecca A. Miller, Executive Director.*
General email, info@dcpreservation.org
Web, www.dcpreservation.org

Participates in planning and preserving buildings and sites in Washington, D.C. Programs include protection and enhancement of the city's landmarks; educational lectures, tours, and seminars; and technical assistance to neighborhood groups. Monitors legislation and regulations.

Historical Society of Washington, D.C., and the D.C. History Center, *801 K St. N.W., 20001; (202) 516-1363. Laura Brower Hagood, Executive Director, ext.304. Library, ext. 302.*
General email, info@dchistory.org
Web, www.dchistory.org and Twitter, @DCHistory

Maintains research collections on the District of Columbia. Publishes *Washington History* magazine. Research library open to the public by appointment.

Martin Luther King Jr. Memorial Library, D.C. Public Library, Washingtoniana Division, *901 G St. N.W., 20001; (202) 727-1213. Sheryl Katzin, Director of Collections.*
General email, Peoples.archive@dc.gov
Web, www.dclibrary.org/washingtoniana and
Facebook, www.facebook.com/washingtoniana

Maintains reference collections of District of Columbia current laws and regulations, history, and culture. Collections include biographies; travel books; memoirs and diaries; family, church, government, and institutional histories; maps (1612–present); plat books; city, telephone, and real estate directories (1822–present); census schedules; newspapers (1800–present), including the *Washington Evening Star* microfilm (1852–1981) and microfilm of several other historic newspapers dating back to 1800, and a collection of clippings and photographs (1940–1981); periodicals; and oral history materials on local neighborhoods, ethnic groups, and businesses.

National Mall Coalition, *P.O. Box 4709, Rockville, MD 20849; (301) 335-8490. Fax, (301) 340-3947. Judy Scott Feldman, Chair.*
General email, jfeldman@nationalmallcoalition.org
Web, www.nationalmallcoalition.org

Coalition of architects, historians, educators, and citizens promoting the protection and long-range vision planning of the National Mall in Washington, D.C.

Supreme Court Historical Society, *224 E. Capitol St. N.E., 20003; (202) 543-0400. Fax, (202) 547-7730. James Duff, Executive Director.*
Web, http://supremecourthistory.org,
Twitter, @SCHSociety, Facebook, www.facebook.com/SupremeCourtHistory and YouTube, www.youtube.com/channel/UCfYQY9PSM1uBOmtYPr2Rdzg

Acquires, preserves, and displays historic items associated with the Court; conducts and publishes scholarly research. Conducts lecture programs; promotes and supports educational activities about the Court.

Tudor Place, *1644 31st St. N.W., 20007; (202) 965-0400. Mark S. Hudson, Executive Director, (202) 965-1644.*
General email, info@tudorplace.org
Web, www.tudorplace.org, Twitter, @TudorPlace, Facebook, www.facebook.com/tudorplace and YouTube, www.youtube.com/tudorplace1805

Operates a historic property, home of Martha Washington's granddaughter and six generations of Custis-Peter family descendants. Seeks to educate the public about American history and culture, focusing on the capital region from the eighteenth century. Maintains and displays artifacts, maintains a manuscript collection, conducts guided tours, and sponsors educational programs for students and teachers.

U.S. Capitol Historical Society, *200 Maryland Ave. N.E., 20002; (202) 543-8919. Jane L. Campbell, President, ext. 12. Toll-free, (800) 887-9318.*
Web, https://uschs.org, Twitter, @CapitolHistory and Facebook, www.facebook.com/USCapHis/

Membership: members of Congress, individuals, and organizations interested in the preservation of the history and traditions of the U.S. Capitol. Conducts historical research; offers tours, lectures, workshops, and films; holds events involving members of Congress; publishes an annual historical calendar.

White House Historical Assn., *740 Jackson Pl. N.W., 20006 (mailing address: P.O. Box 27624, Washington, DC 20038-7624); (202) 218-4300. Stewart D. McLaurin, President. Toll-free for purchases, (800) 555-2451.*
General email, customerservice@whha.org

Web, www.whitehousehistory.org,
Twitter, @WhiteHouseHstry and
Facebook, www.facebook.com/WhiteHouseHistory

Seeks to enhance the understanding and appreciation of the White House. Publishes books on the White House, its inhabitants, its artworks, its furnishings, and its history. Net proceeds from book sales, videos and DVDs, traveling exhibits, the museum shop, and gift shop go toward the purchase of historic items for the White House permanent collection.

PHILANTHROPY, PUBLIC SERVICE, AND VOLUNTEERISM

General

▶**AGENCIES**

AmeriCorps Seniors *(AmeriCorps), Retired and Senior Volunteer Program, Foster Grandparent Program, and Senior Companion Program, 250 E. St. S.W., 20525; (202) 606-5000. Malcolm Coles, Chief Executive Officer (Acting); Atalaya Sergi, Director, AmeriCorps Seniors. AmeriCorp hotline, (800) 942-2677. Press, (202) 606-6775.*
Web, https://americorps.gov/serve/americorps-seniors, Twitter, @AmeriCorps and Facebook, www.facebook.com/ AmeriCorps

Network of programs that help older Americans find service opportunities in their communities, including the Retired and Senior Volunteer Program, which encourages older citizens to use their talents and experience in community service; the Foster Grandparent Program, which gives older citizens opportunities to work with exceptional children and children with special needs; and the Senior Companion Program, which recruits older citizens to help homebound adults, especially seniors, with special needs.

AmeriCorps *(Corp. for National and Community Service), 250 E St. S.W., 20525; (202) 606-5000. Fax, (202) 606-3475. Malcolm Coles, Chief Executive Officer (Acting). Local TTY, (202) 606-3472. National Service hotline, (800) 942-2677. TTY, (800) 833-3722.*
General email, info@cns.gov

Web, www.nationalservice.gov/programs/americorps, Twitter, @AmeriCorps and Facebook, www.facebook.com/ americorps

Provides Americans age seventeen and older with opportunities to serve their communities on a full-time or part-time basis. Participants work in the areas of education, public safety, human needs, and the environment and earn education awards for college or vocational training.

AmeriCorps *(Corp. for National and Community Service), National Civilian Community Corps, 250 E St.*

S.W., 20024-3208; (202) 606-5000. Fax, (202) 606-3462. Gina Cross, Director (Acting), (202) 606-3233. Local TTY, (202) 565-2799. National Service hotline, (800) 942-2677. TTY, (800) 833-3722.
General email, info@cns.gov

Web, www.nationalservice.gov/programs/americorps/ americorps-nccc, Twitter, @AmeriCorpsNCCC and Facebook, www.facebook.com/AmeriCorpsNCCC

Provides a ten-month residential service and leadership program for men and women ages eighteen to twenty-four of all social, economic, and educational backgrounds. Works to restore and preserve the environment. Working in teams of eight to ten, members provide disaster relief, fight forest fires, restore homes and habitats after natural disasters, and work in a variety of other service projects in every state.

AmeriCorps *(Corp. for National and Community Service), State and National Program, 250 E St. S.W., 20024-3208; (202) 606-5000. Sonali Nijhawan, Director. National Service hotline, (800) 942-2677. TTY, (800) 833-3722.*
General email, help@americorps.gov

Web, www.nationalservice.gov/programs/americorps/ americorps-programs/americorps-state-national, Twitter, @nationalservice and Grants, AmeriCorps Grants@cns.gov

AmeriCorps State administers and oversees AmeriCorps funding distributed to governor-appointed state commissions, which distribute grants to local organizations and to such national organizations as Habitat for Humanity. AmeriCorps National provides grants directly to national public and nonprofit organizations that sponsor service programs, Indian tribes, and consortia formed across two or more states, including faith-based and community organizations, higher education institutions, and public agencies.

AmeriCorps *(Corp. for National and Community Service), Volunteers in Service to America (VISTA), 250 E St. S.W., 20024-3208; (202) 606-5000. Meg Ansara, Director. National Service hotline, (800) 942-2677. TTY, (800) 833-3722.*
Web, www.americorps.gov/programs/americorps/ americorps-vista, Twitter, @AmeriCorpsVISTA and Facebook, www.facebook.com/AmeriCorpsVISTA

Assigns full-time volunteers to public and private nonprofit organizations for one year to alleviate poverty in local communities. Volunteers receive a living allowance, health care, and other benefits and their choice of a post-service stipend or education award.

Corp. for National and Community Service, *250 E St. N.W., 20024; (202) 606-5000. Michael D. Smith, Chief Executive Officer; Samantha Warfield, Press contact, (202) 606-6775. Press, (202) 606-6775. TTY, (800) 833-3722. National Service Hotline, (800) 942-2677.*
General email, help@cns.gov

Web, www.nationalservice.gov, Twitter, @AmeriCorps and Facebook, www.facebook.com/AmeriCorps

Partners people of all ages with national and community-based organizations, schools, faith-based groups, and local agencies to assist with community needs in education, the environment, public safety, homeland security, and other areas. Programs include AmeriCorps-VISTA (Volunteers in Service to America), AmeriCorps-NCCC (National Civilian Community Corps), and the Senior Corps, among others.

Federal Emergency Management Agency (FEMA) (Homeland Security Dept.), Resilience, National Preparedness, Individual and Community Preparedness, 500 C St.Washington, DC, 20472; (800) 621-3362. Alex Amparo, Assistant Administrator. Helpline, (866) 222-3580.
General email, citizencorps@dhs.gov

Web, www.ready.gov/citizen-corps

Conducts research on individual, business, and community preparedness. Administers Citizen Corps, a national network of state, territory, tribal, and local councils that coordinate with local first responders to develop community-specific public education, outreach, training, and volunteer opportunities that address community preparedness and resiliency.

Peace Corps, 1275 1st St. N.E., 20526; (202) 692-1040. Fax, (202) 692-8400. Carol Spahn, Chief Executive Officer. Press, (202) 692-2230. Toll-free, (855) 855-1961.
Web, www.peacecorps.gov, Twitter, @PeaceCorps and Facebook, www.facebook.com/peacecorps

Promotes world peace, friendship, and mutual understanding between the United States and developing nations. Administers volunteer programs to assist developing countries in education, the environment, health, small business development, agriculture, in particular promoting global food security, AIDS relief, eliminating maleria and urban youth development.

▶CONGRESS

For a listing of relevant congressional committees and subcommittees, please see page 130 or the Appendix.

▶NONGOVERNMENTAL

Arca Foundation, 1308 19th St. N.W., 20036; (202) 822-9193. Anna Lefer Kuhn, Executive Director.
General email, proposals@arcafoundation.org

Web, www.arcafoundation.org

Awards grants to nonprofit organizations for philanthropic endeavors in the areas of social equity and justice. Interests include corporate accountability, and civic participation domestically and internationally.

Architects Foundation, 1735 New York Ave. N.W, 20006; (202) 626-7472. Marci B. Reed, Executive Director, (202) 639-7638.
General email, info@ArchitectsFoundation.org

Web, www.ArchitectsFoundation.org and Twitter, @architectsfdn

Philanthropic arm of the American Institute of Architects (AIA). Manages scholarship programs and operates the Octagon as a museum and space for exhibits and events. (Formerly the American Architectual Foundation.)

Assn. of Fundraising Professionals (AFP), 4200 Wilson Blvd., #480, Arlington, VA 22203-4416; (703) 684-0410. Fax, (703) 684-1950. Mike Geiger, President. Toll-free, (800) 666-3863.
General email, afp@afpglobal.org

Web, www.afpglobal.org, Twitter, @AFPIHQ and Facebook, www.facebook.com/AFPFan/

Membership: individuals who serve as fundraising executives for nonprofit institutions or as members of counseling firms engaged in fundraising management. Promotes ethical standards; offers workshops; provides resources for member certification; monitors legislation and regulations. AFP Foundation promotes philanthropy and volunteerism. Library open to the public by appointment.

Best Buddies International, Capitol Region: Virginia and DC, 6231 Leesburg Pike, #310, Falls Church, VA 22044; (703) 533-9420. Fax, (703) 533-9423. Molly Whalen, State Director.
General email, virginia-dc@bestbuddies.org

Web, www.bestbuddies.org/vadc, Twitter, @BestBuddies, Facebook, www.facebook.com/bestbuddies and YouTube, www.youtube.com/bestbuddies

Volunteer organization that provides one-to-one friendships, integrated employment, leadership development and inclusive living for people with Down syndrome, autism, Fragile X, Williams syndrome, cerebral palsy, traumatic brain injury and other undiagnosed disabilities, worldwide. (Headquarters in Miami, Fla.)

Better Business Bureau, Wise Giving Alliance, 3033 Wilson Blvd., #710, Arlington, VA 22201; (703) 247-9321. H. Art Taylor, President.
General email, info@give.org

Web, www.give.org, Twitter, @wisegiving, Facebook, www.facebook.com/BBB-Wise-Giving-Alliance-146493838709799 and YouTube, www.youtube.com/channel/UCxK66eTWA00R9qVk-5SfZyw

Serves as a donor information service on national charities. Evaluates charities in relation to Better Business Bureau standards for charitable solicitation, which address charity finances, solicitations, fund-raising practices, and governance. Produces a guide magaine three times a year that summarizes these findings.

BoardSource, 750 9th St. N.W., #520, 20001; (202) 349-2500. Fax, (202) 349-2599. Anne Wallestad, Chief Executive Officer. Press, (202) 349-2541. Toll-free, (877) 892-6273.
Web, www.boardsource.org, Twitter, @BoardSource and Facebook, www.facebook.com/BoardSource

Email, info@boardsource.org

Membership: works to improve the effectiveness of nonprofit organizations by strengthening their boards of directors. Operates an information clearinghouse;

publishes materials on governing nonprofit organizations; assists organizations in conducting training programs, workshops, and conferences for board members and chief executives.

Capital Research Center, *1513 16th St. N.W., 20036; (202) 483-6900. Fax, (202) 478-1855. Scott Walter, President.*
General email, contact@capitalresearch.org
Web, https://capitalresearch.org, Twitter, @capitalresearch and Facebook, www.facebook.com/capitalresearchcenter

Conservative think tank that researches funding sources, especially foundations, charities, and other non-profits, of public interest and advocacy groups. Analyzes the impact these groups have on public policy. Publishes findings in newsletters and reports.

Caring Institute, *228 7th St. S.E., 20003; (202) 838-8038. Kathleen Halamandaris, President; Christyne K. Brennan, Executive Director.*
General email, info@caring.org
Web, www.caring.org and Twitter, @CaringOrg

Promotes selflessness and public service. Recognizes the achievements of individuals who have demonstrated a commitment to serving others. Operates the Frederick Douglass Museum and Hall of Fame for Caring Americans. Sponsors the National Caring Award and offers scholarhips to high school and college students.

The Congressional Award, *379 FHOB, 20024 (mailing address: P.O. Box 77440, Washington, DC 20013-7440); (202) 226-0130. Erica Wheelan Heyse, National Director.*
General email, information@congressionalaward.org
Web, http://congressionalaward.org, Twitter, @theaward and Facebook, www.facebook.com/thecongressionalaward

Nonpartisan noncompetitive program established by Congress that recognizes the achievements of young people ages thirteen and one-half to twenty-three. Participants are awarded certificates or medals for setting and achieving goals in four areas: volunteer public service, personal development, physical fitness, and expeditions and exploration.

The Corps Network, *1275 K St. N.W., #1050, 20005; (202) 737-6272. Fax, (202) 737-6277. Mary Ellen Sprenkel, President.*
Web, http://corpsnetwork.org, Twitter, @TheCorpsNetwork, Facebook, www.facebook.com/TheCorpsNetwork and YouTube, www.youtube.com/TheCorpsNetwork

Membership: youth corps programs and veterans up to age 35. Produces publications and workshops on starting and operating youth corps and offers technical assistance programs. Holds annual conference. Monitors legislation and regulations.

Council on Foundations, *1255 23rd St. N.W., #200, 20037; (202) 991-2225. Kathleen Enright, President. Toll-free, (800) 673-9036.*
General email, info@cof.org
Web, www.cof.org, Twitter, @COF_ and Facebook, www.facebook.com/CouncilonFoundations

Membership: independent community, family, and public-sponsored and company-sponsored foundations; corporate giving programs; and foundations in other countries. Promotes responsible and effective philanthropy through educational programs, publications, government relations, and promulgation of a set of principles and practices for effective grant making.

Earth Share, *1717 K St. N.W, #900, 20006; (240) 333-0300. Fax, (240) 333-0301. Brad Leibov, Chief Executive Officer. Toll-free, (800) 875-3863.*
General email, info@earthshare.org
Web, www.earthshare.org and Twitter, @EarthShare

Federation of environmental and conservation organizations. Works with government and private payroll contribution programs to solicit contributions to member organizations for environmental research, education, and community programs. Provides information on establishing environmental giving options in the workplace.

Evangelical Council for Financial Accountability, *440 W. Jubal Early Dr., #100, Winchester, VA 22601-6319; (540) 535-0103. Michael Martin, President. Toll-free, (800) 323-9473.*
Web, www.ecfa.org, Twitter, @ecfa and Facebook, www.facebook.com/accountability
Email, information@ecfa.org

Membership: charitable, religious, international relief, and educational nonprofit U.S.-based organizations committed to evangelical Christianity. Assists members in making appropriate public disclosure of their financial practices and accomplishments. Certifies organizations that conform to standards of financial integrity and Christian ethics.

Exponent Philanthropy, *1720 N St. N.W., 20036; (202) 580-6560. Fax, (202) 580-6579. Cynthia Schaal, Chief Executive Officer (Acting).*
General email, info@exponentphilanthropy.org
Web, www.exponentphilanthropy.org, Twitter, @exponentphil and Facebook, www.facebook.com/exponentphilanthropy

Membership: donors, trustees, consultants, and employees of philanthropic foundations that have few or no staff. Offers educational programs and publications, referrals, networking opportunities, and liability insurance to members. (Formerly the Assn. of Small Foundations.)

General Federation of Women's Clubs, *1734 N St. N.W., 20036-2990; (202) 347-3168. Fax, (202) 835-0246. Marian St. Clair, International President; Cheri Meyer, Chief of Operations. Press, (202) 347-8103. Toll-free, (800) 443-4392.*
General email, gfwc@gfwc.org
Web, www.gfwc.org, Twitter, @GFWCHQ and Facebook, www.facebook.com/GFWCMembers

Membership; Nondenominational, nonpartisan international organization of women volunteers. Interests include conservation, education, international and public affairs, domestic violence awareness and prevention, and the arts.

Good360, *675 N. Washington St., #330, Alexandria, VA 22314; (703) 836-2121. Matthew Connelly, Chief Executive Officer.*
General email, press@good360.org
Web, www.good360.org, Twitter, @Good360 and Facebook, www.facebook.com/Good360.org

Online product-donation marketplace that seeks to meet the needs of nonprofit organizations by encouraging corporations to donate new and like-new manufactured products to domestic and international charities. Works with companies to develop in-kind giving programs, coordinates distribution to nonprofit agencies, and provides reporting and impact stories. Cause-neutral, services any vetted, approved nonprofit, church, or school.

Habitat for Humanity International, *Government Relations and Advocacy, 1310 L St. N.W, #350, 20005; (202) 718-4824. Jonathan Reckford, Chief Executive Officer; Chris Vincent, Vice President of Advocacy and Government Relations.*
General email, advocacy@habitat.org
Web, www.habitat.org/about/advocacy

Christian ministry that seeks to eliminate poverty housing. Helps people attain housing through home construction, rehabilitation and repairs, and increased access to improved shelter through programs. Offers housing support services that enable low-income families to make improvements on their homes. Works in more than 70 countries.

Independent Sector, *1602 L St. N.W., #900, 20036; (202) 467-6100. Fax, (202) 467-6101. Dan Cardinali, Chief Executive Officer. Press, (202) 467-6122.*
General email, info@independentsector.org
Web, www.independentsector.org, Twitter, @IndSector and Facebook, www.facebook.com/IndependentSector

Membership: corporations, foundations, and national voluntary, charitable, and philanthropic organizations. Advocates supportive government policies and encourages volunteering, giving, and best practice not-for-profit nonpartisan initiatives by the private sector for public causes.

The Links Inc., *1200 Massachusetts Ave. N.W., 20005-4501; (202) 842-8686. Fax, (202) 842-4020. Kristie Patton Foster, Executive Director, ext. 211; Kimberly Jeffries Leonard, National President.*
General email, info@linksinc.org
Web, www.linksinc.org, Twitter, @linksinc and Facebook, www.facebook.com/thelinksinc

Predominantly African American women's volunteer service organization that works to enrich, sustain, and ensure the culture and economic survival of African Americans and other persons of African ancestry. Areas of focus are services to youth, the arts, national trends and service, international trends and services, and health and human services. Programs are implemented via sharing

---

Faith-Based and Neighborhood Partnerships Contacts at Federal Departments and Agencies

White House Office of Faith-Based and Neighborhood Partnerships.

DEPARTMENTS

Agriculture, Michelle Wert, Director, (202) 720-1176; www.usda.gov/our-agency/staff-offices/office-partnerships-and-public-engagement-oppe/center-faith-based-and

Commerce, Vacant, (202) 482-3235; www.commerce.gov/bureaus-and-offices/os/faith-based-and-neighborhood-partnerships

Education, Vacant; https://sites.ed.gov/cfbnp

Health and Human Services, Heidi Christensen, Director, (202) 260-6501; www.hhs.gov/partnerships

Homeland Security, Jerome Bryant, Director (Acting) (202) 646-3487; www.dhs.gov/dhs-center-faith-based-neighborhood-partnerships

Housing and Urban Development, Vacant, (202) 708-2404; www.hud.gov/offices/fbci

Justice, Vacant, (202) 305-7462; https://ojp.gov/fbnp

Labor, Vacant, (202) 693-6017 or (202) 693-5950; www.dol.gov/general/dol-agencies

State, Daniel Nadel, Amb., (202) 647-1237; www.state.gov/bureaus-offices/under-secretary-for-civilian-security-democracy-and-human-rights/office-of-international-religious-freedom

Veterans Affairs, Vacant, Deputy Director, (202) 461-7689; www.va.gov/cfbnpartnerships

AGENCIES

Agency for International Development, Vacant, (202) 712-4080; www.usaid.gov/faith-and-opportunity-initiatives

Corp. for National and Community Service, Vacant, https://americorps.gov/about/what-we-do

---

of public information and education, economic development, and public policy campaigns.

Lutheran Volunteer Corps, *1226 Vermont Ave. N.W., 20005; (202) 387-3222. Deirdre Bagley, President.*
General email, operations@lutheranvolunteercorps.org
Web, www.lutheranvolunteercorps.org, Twitter, @LVCorps and Facebook, www.facebook.com/LutheranVolunteerCorps

Administers volunteer program in selected U.S. cities; coordinates activities with health and social service agencies, educational institutions, and environmental groups. Places adult volunteers in full-time positions in direct service, community organizing, advocacy, and public policy for 1–2 years.

Mars Foundation, *6885 Elm St., McLean, VA 22101; (703) 821-4900. Anne Vela-Wagner, Executive Officer.*

Web, www.mars.com and Facebook, www.facebook.com/Mars

Twiitter, @Marsglobal

Awards grants in education, arts, health care concerns, animal wildlife environment, and history.

National Committee for Responsive Philanthropy, *1900 L St. N.W., #825, 20036; (202) 387-9177. Aaron Dorfman, President.*

General email, info@ncrp.org

Web, www.ncrp.org, Twitter, @NCRP, Facebook, www.facebook.com/NCRPcommunity and YouTube, www.youtube.com/user/NCRP620

Directs philanthropic giving to benefit the socially, economically, and politically disenfranchised; acts as advocate for groups that represent the poor, minorities, and women. Conducts research; organizes local coalitions. Monitors legislation and regulations.

National Conference on Citizenship (NCOC), *1920 L St. N.W., #450, 20036; (202) 601-7096. Jamie Engel, Program Director.*

General email, ncocadmin@ncoc.net

Web, https://ncoc.org, Twitter, @NCoC and Facebook, www.facebook.com/NCoC1

Congressionally chartered nonpartisan nonprofit that supports the Civic Health Initiative. Encourages citizens to participate in civic services. Holds annual conferences to promote public-service activities in local communities. Produces the *Civic Health Index* to measure civic engagement.

National Peace Corps Assn., *1825 Connecticut Ave. N.W., #800, 20009-5708; (202) 293-7728. Fax, (202) 293-7554. Glenn Blumhorst, President.*

General email, ncpa@peacecorpsconnect.org

Web, www.peacecorpsconnect.org, Twitter, @pcorpsconnect and Facebook, www.facebook.com/PeaceCorpsConnect/

Membership: returned Peace Corps volunteers, staff, and interested individuals. Promotes a global perspective in the United States; seeks to educate the public about the developing world; supports Peace Corps programs; maintains a network of returned volunteers.

The Nonprofit Alliance, *1319 F St. N.W., #800, 20004; (202) 516-5886. Shannon McCracken, Chief Executive Officer.*

General email, membership@msn.com

Web, https://tnpa.org/adrfco/

Membership: businesses in the direct response fundraising industry. Establishes standards of ethical practice in such areas as ownership of direct mail donor lists and mandatory disclosures by fund-raising counsel. Educates nonprofit organizations and the public on direct response fundraising. Represents members' interests before the federal and state governments.

Philanthropy Roundtable, *1120 20th St. N.W., #550 South, 20036; (202) 822-8333. Fax, (202) 822-8325. Elise Westhoff, President.*

General email, main@philanthropyroundtable.org

Web, www.philanthropyroundtable.org, Twitter, @PhilanthropyRnd and Facebook, https://business .facebook.com/PhilanthropyRoundtable

Membership: individual donors, foundation trustees and staff, and corporate giving officers. Helps donors achieve their charitable objectives by offering counsel and peer-to-peer exchange opportunities.

Points of Light Institute, *1400 G St. N.W., 20005; (202) 729-8172. Natalye Paquin.*

General email, info@pointsoflight.org

Web, www.pointsoflight.org, Twitter, @PointsofLight and Facebook, www.facebook.com/beapointoflight/

Promotes mobilization of people for volunteer community service aimed at solving social problems. Through HandsOn Network regional centers, offers technical assistance, training, and information services to nonprofit organizations, public agencies, corporations, and others interested in volunteering. (Headquarters in Atlanta, Ga.)

United Way Worldwide, *701 N. Fairfax St., Alexandria, VA 22314-2045; (703) 836-7112. Fax, (703) 519-0097. Angela F. Williams, President.*

Web, www.unitedway.org and Twitter, @UnitedWay

Membership: independent United Way organizations in 41 countries and territories, including 1,150 in the United States. Provides staff training; fund-raising, planning, and communications assistance; resource management; and national public service advertising. Activities support education, financial stability, and health.

Urban Institute, *Center on Nonprofits and Philanthropy, 500 L'Enfant Plaza S.W., 20024; (202) 833-7200. Shena Ashley, Vice President.*

Web, www.urban.org/research-area/nonprofits-and-philanthropy and Facebook, www.facebook.com/urbaninstitute

Conducts and disseminates research on the role and impact of nonprofit organizations and philanthropy.

Volunteers of America, *1660 Duke St., Alexandria, VA 22314; (703) 341-5000. Fax, (703) 341-7000. Michael King, President. Toll-free, (800) 899-0089.*

General email, info@voa.org

Web, www.voa.org, Twitter, @Vol_of_America and Facebook, www.facebook.com/VolOfAmerica

Faith-based organization that promotes local human services and outreach programs. Facilitates individual and community involvement. Focuses on children at risk, abused and neglected children, older adults, homeless individuals, people with disabilities, veterans, and those formerly incarcerated.

W. O'Neil Foundation, *P.O. Box 15888, Chevy Chase, MD 20825-5588; (301) 656-5848. Helene O'Neil Shere, President.*

General email, woneilfoundation@gmail.com

Awards grants primarily to Roman Catholic organizations providing programs and basic needs of the poor, such as food, clothing, shelter, and basic medical care, both nationally and internationally.

Youth Service America, *1050 Connecticut Ave. N.W., #65525, 20035-5525; (202) 296-2992. Fax, (202) 296-4030. Steven A. Culbertson, President, (202) 296-3008.*
General email, outreach@ysa.org

Web, www.ysa.org and Twitter, @youthservice

Advocates youth service, ages 5–25, at national, state, and local levels. Promotes opportunities for young people to be engaged in community service. Sponsors Global Youth Service Day, 9/11 Day of Service, MLK Day of Service, and Service Vote. Hosts database of U.S. volunteer opportunities.

Washington Area

▶NONGOVERNMENTAL

Boy Scouts of America, *National Capitol Area Council, Marriott Scout Service Center, 9190 Rockville Pike, Bethesda, MD 20814-3897; (301) 530-9360. Fax, (301) 564-9513. Mario Perez, Deputy Scout Executive, (301) 214-9102.*
Web, www.ncacbsa.org, Twitter, @NCACBSA and Facebook, www.facebook.com/NCACBSA

Membership; Educational service organization for youth that supports more than 1,700 local units that provide quality youth programs, including cub scouting, boy scouting, venturing, and exploring. National Capitol Area Council covers the Washington, D.C., metro area, sixteen counties in Maryland and Virginia, and the U.S. Virgin Islands. (Headquarters in Irving, Tex.)

Eugene and Agnes E. Meyer Foundation, *1120 G. St. N.W., #600, 20005; (202) 483-8294. George L. Askew, MD, President.*
Web, www.meyerfoundation.org,
Twitter, @MeyerFoundation and
Facebook, www.facebook.com/meyerfoundation

Seeks to improve the quality of life in Washington, D.C. Awards grants to nonprofit organizations in four program areas: education, employment, asset building, and housing.

Eugene B. Casey Foundation, *16803 Crabbs Branch Way, Rockville, MD 20855; (301) 948-4595. Vacant, Trustee.*

Philanthropic organization that supports the arts, education, and social services in the metropolitan Washington area.

The Herb Block Foundation, *1730 M St. N.W., #1020, 20036; (202) 223-8801. Fax, (202) 223-8804. Marcela Brane, Chief Executive Officer; Sarah Armstrong Alex, Executive Director.*
General email, info@herbblock.org

Web, www.herbblockfoundation.org,
Twitter, @TheHerbBlockFdn and Facebook, www.facebook .com/herbblockfoundation

Awards grants to charitable and educational programs that combat discrimination and poverty and promote citizen involvement in government. Provides scholarships to individuals seeking to attend community colleges in the Washington, D.C., area. Awards prizes for excellence in editorial cartooning to serve as a tool for freedom and to address social issues.

Humane Rescue Alliance, *71 Oglethorpe St. N. W., 20011; P.O. Box 96312, 20090-6312; (202) 576-6664. Fax, (202) 726-2536. Lisa LaFontaine, President. Adoption center, (202) 723-5730. 24-hour animal cruelty and emergency hotline, (202) 723-5730. Spay and neuter center, (202) 608-1356.*
General email, adopt@washhumane.org

Web, www.humanerescuealliance.org,
Twitter, @HumaneRescue and
Press, smiller@humanrescuealliance.org

Congressionally chartered animal welfare agency and open-access animal shelter. Promotes pet adoption; offers low-cost spay and neuter services and trap-and-neuter programs. Operates the D.C. Animal Care and Control.

Junior League of Washington, *3039 M St. N.W., 20007; (202) 337-2001. Amanda Walke, President.*
General email, office@jlw.org

Web, www.jlw.org and Twitter, @JLWDC

Educational and charitable women's organization that promotes volunteerism and works for community improvement through leadership of trained volunteers. Interests include promoting volunteerism and developing the potential of women. Current emphasis is on literacy. (Assn. of Junior Leagues International headquarters in New York.)

Morris and Gwendolyn Cafritz Foundation, *1825 K St. N.W., #1400, 20006; (202) 223-3100. Fax, (202) 296-7567. Calvin Cafritz, President; Mardell Moffett, Executive Director.*
General email, info@cafritzfoundation.org

Web, www.cafritzfoundation.org

Awards grants to educational, arts, and social services institutions in the metropolitan Washington area.

Washington Regional Assn. of Grantmakers, *1100 New Jersey Ave. S.E., #710, 20003; (202) 939-3440. Fax, (202) 939-3442. Ruth LaToison Ifill, President.*
General email, info@washingtongrantmakers.org

Web, www.washingtongrantmakers.org and
Twitter, @WRAGtweets

Network of funders that partners with agencies and nongovernmental organizations in the Washington, D.C., region. Identifies and implements new and innovative forms of philanthropy. Shares best practices. Advocates collective philanthropic community in the region and publishes issue briefs.

RECREATION AND SPORT

General

▶**AGENCIES**

Health and Human Services Dept. (HHS), *President's Council on Sports, Fitness, and Nutrition (PCSFN), 1101 Wootton Pkwy., #560, Rockville, MD 20852; (240) 276-9567. Rachel Fisher, Executive Director (Acting).*
General email, fitness@hhs.gov

Web, www.fitness.gov and Twitter, @FitnessGov

Promotes programs and initiatives that motivate people of all ages, backgrounds, and abilities to lead active, healthy lives through partnerships with the public, private, and nonprofit sectors; provides online information and resources related to fitness, sports, and nutrition; conducts award programs for children and adults and for schools, clubs, and other institutions.

National Park Service (NPS) *(Interior Dept.), 1849 C St. N.W., #3115, 20240; (202) 208-6843. Fax, (202) 208-7889. Charles (Chuck) F. Sams III, Director.*
General email, asknps@nps.gov

Web, www.nps.gov, Twitter, @NatlParkService and Facebook, www.facebook.com/nationalparkservice

Oversees coordination, planning, and financing of public outdoor recreation programs at all levels of government. Conducts recreation research surveys; administers financial assistance program to states for planning and development of outdoor recreation programs. (Some lands designated as national recreation areas are not under NPS jurisdiction.)

▶**NONGOVERNMENTAL**

American Canoe Assn., *2010 College Ave., #100, Fredericksburg, VA 22401 (mailing address: P.O. Box 7996, Fredericksburg, VA 22404); (540) 907-4460. Fax, (888) 229-3792. Beth Spilman, Executive Director (Acting), ext. 103.*
General email, aca@americancanoe.org

Web, www.americancanoe.org, Twitter, @AmericanCanoe and Facebook, www.facebook.com/acapaddlesports

Membership: individuals and organizations interested in the promotion of canoeing, kayaking, and other paddle sports. Works to preserve the nation's recreational waterways. Sponsors programs in safety education, competition, recreation, public awareness, conservation, and public policy. Monitors legislation and regulations.

American Gaming Assn., *799 9th St. N.W., #700, 20001; (202) 552-2675. Fax, (202) 552-2676. Bill Miller, Chief Executive Officer.*
General email, info@americangaming.org

Web, www.americangaming.org, Twitter, @AmerGaming and Facebook, www.facebook.com/americangaming

Membership: commercial and tribal casino operators, U.S. licensed gaming suppliers, and financial institutions. Compiles statistics and serves as an information clearinghouse on the gaming industry. Administers a task force to study gambling addiction, raise public awareness of the condition, and develop assistance programs for it. Monitors legislation and regulations.

American Hiking Society, *8403 Colesville Rd., #1100, Silver Spring, MD 20910; (301) 565-6704. Fax, (301) 565-6714. Kathryn (Kate) Van Waes, Executive Director. Toll-free, (800) 972-8608.*
General email, info@americanhiking.org

Web, https://americanhiking.org, Twitter, @AmericanHiking and Facebook, www.facebook.com/AmericanHiking

Membership: individuals and clubs interested in preserving America's trail system and protecting the interests of hikers and other trail users. Sponsors research on trail construction and a trail maintenance summer program. Provides information on outdoor volunteer opportunities on public lands.

American Sportfishing Assn., *1001 N. Fairfax St., #501, Alexandria, VA 22314; (703) 519-9691. Fax, (703) 519-1872. Glenn Hughes, President, ext. 245.*
General email, info@asafishing.org

Web, www.asafishing.org and Twitter, @ASAfishing

Works to ensure healthy and sustainable fisheries resources and to expand market growth for its members through increased participation in sportfishing. Programs include Keep America Fishing and the Fish America Foundation.

Boat U.S. (Boat Owners Assn. of the United States), *5323 Port Royal Rd., Springfield, VA 22151; (703) 461-2878. Scott Croft, Director of Public Relations, (703) 461-2864.*
General email, govtaffairs@boatus.com

Web, www.boatus.com, Twitter, @BoatUS, Facebook, www.facebook.com/BoatUS and Twitter, @BoatUSFoundation

Membership: owners of recreational boats. Provides insurance, on water towing, provides financing and other resources. Publishes BoatUS magazine. Represents boat owners interests. BoatUS has a Foundation for boating safety and clean water. It aims to reduce accidents and fatalities. The Foundation provides educational outreach directly to boaters and supports partner organizations nationwide.

Club Managers Assn. of America, *1733 King St., Alexandria, VA 22314; (703) 739-9500. Jeffrey (Jeff) Morgan, Chief Executive Officer.*
General email, cmaa@cmaa.org

Web, www.cmaa.org/, Twitter, @CMAA, Facebook, www.facebook.com/MyCMAA and YouTube, www.youtube.com/user/MyCMAA

Membership: managers of membership clubs. Promotes the profession of club management through education and other assistance.

FishAmerica Foundation, *1001 N. Fairfax St., #501, Alexandria, VA 22314; (703) 519-9691. Fax, (703) 519-1872. Walt Sisson, Vice President, ext. 252.*

General email, fafgrants@asafishing.org

Web, www.fishamerica.org, Twitter, @ASAfishing and Facebook, www.facebook.com/ASAfishing

Invests in local communities to restore habitat, improve water quality, and advance fisheries research to increase sportfish populations and sportfishing opportunities. (Affiliated with the American Sportfishing Assn.)

Move United, 451 Hungerford Dr., #608, Rockville, MD 20850; (301) 217-0960. Glenn Merry, Executive Director, (301) 217-9838.

General email, info@moveunitedsport.org

Web, www.moveunitedsport.org, Twitter, @MoveUnitedSport and Facebook, www.facebook.com/MoveUnitedSports

Offers nationwide sports rehabilitation programs in more than forty summer and winter sports; promotes independence, confidence, and fitness through programs for people with permanent disabilities, including wounded service personnel; conducts workshops and competitions through community-based chapters; participates in world championships. (Disabled Sports USA and Adaptive Sports USA merged to become United Sport.)

National Aeronautic Assn., Reagan Washington National Airport, Hangar 7, #226, 20001-6015; (703) 416-4888. Fax, (703) 416-4877. Greg Principato, President.

General email, naa@naa.aero

Web, www.naa.aero, Twitter, @NatlAero and Facebook, www.facebook.com/NationalAeronauticAssociation

Membership: persons interested in development of general and sporting aviation, including skydiving, commercial and military aircraft, and spaceflight. Supervises sporting aviation competitions; administers awards in aviation.

National Club Assn., 1680 Duke St., #420, Alexandria, VA 22314; (202) 822-9822. Fax, (202) 822-9808. Henry Wallmeyer, President.

General email, info@nationalclub.org

Web, www.nationalclub.org and Twitter, @NatlClubAssn

Promotes the interests of private, social, and recreational clubs. Monitors legislation and regulations.

National Collegiate Athletic Assn. (NCAA), Government Relations, 1 Dupont Circle N.W., #310, 20036-1139; (202) 293-3050. Fax, (202) 293-3075. Mark Emmert, President.

Web, www.ncaa.org, Twitter, @NCAA, Facebook, www.facebook.com/ncaa1906 and YouTube, www.youtube.com/user/NCAA

Membership: colleges and universities, conferences, and organizations interested in the administration of intercollegiate athletics. Certifies institutions' athletic programs; compiles records and statistics; produces publications and television programs; administers youth development programs; awards student athletes with postgraduate scholarships and degree-completion grants. (Headquarters in Indianapolis, Ind.)

National Football League Players Assn., 1133 20th St. N.W., #600, 20036; (202) 463-2200. DeMaurice Smith, Executive Director. Toll-free, (800) 372-2000.

Web, www.nflpa.com, Twitter, @NFLPA, Facebook, www.facebook.com/NFLPA and YouTube, www.youtube.com/user/NFLPlayers

Membership: professional football players. Represents members in matters concerning wages, hours, and working conditions. Provides assistance to charitable and community organizations. Sponsors programs and events to promote the image of professional football and its players.

National Indian Gaming Assn. (NIGA), 224 2nd St. S.E., 20003; (202) 546-7711. Jason Giles, Executive Director, (202) 548-3810; Ernest L. Stevens Jr., Chair, (920) 857-3727.

General email, questions@indiangaming.org

Web, www.indiangaming.org and Facebook, www.facebook.com/NIGAIndianGaming

Membership: more than 180 Indian nations as well as other organizations, tribes, and businesses engaged in gaming enterprises. Operates as a clearinghouse for tribes, policymakers, and the public on Indian gaming issues and tribal community development.

National Recreation and Park Assn. NRPA, 22377 Belmont Ridge Rd., Ashburn, VA 20148-4501; (703) 858-0784. Kristine Stratton, Chief Executive Officer. Toll-free, (800) 626-6772.

General email, customerservice@nrpa.org

Web, www.nrpa.org, Twitter, @nrpa_news and Facebook, www.facebook.com/NationalRecreationandParkAssociation

Membership: park and recreation professionals and interested citizens. Promotes to advance parks, recreation and environmental conservation efforts that enhance the quality of life for all people. Facilitates development, expansion, and management of resources; provides technical assistance for park and recreational programs; and provides professional development to members. Monitors legislation and regulations.

Outdoor Recreation Roundtable, 1203 K St. N.W., #350, 20005; Jessica Wahl Turner, Executive Director.

Web, http://recreationroundtable.org, Twitter, @ORRoundtable

Email, orr@recreationroundtable.org

Membership: recreation industry associations, recreation enthusiast groups, and leading corporations in the recreation products and services sectors. Promotes health and well-being by conserving public lands and waterways, enhancing infrastruture and access through outdoor recreation. Seeks to keep public lands open for off-road vehicles. Monitors regulations and legislation.

Road Runners Club of America, 1501 Langston Blvd., #140, Arlington, VA 22209; (703) 525-3890. Fax, (703) 525-3891. Jean Knaack, Executive Director.

General email, office@rrca.org

Web, www.rrca.org, Twitter, @RRCAnational, Facebook, www.facebook.com/Roadrunnersclubofamerica and YouTube, www.youtube.com/channel/ UCjK1GCFO5NZPXEQddA8pJQA

Develops and promotes road races and fitness programs, including the Kids Run the Nation Program and the Women's Distance Festival. Issues guidelines on road races concerning safety, legal issues, and runners with disabilities. Facilitates communication between clubs.

Society of Health and Physical Educators (SHAPE) America, *P.O. Box 225, Annapolis Junction, MD 20701; (703) 476-3400. Fax, (703) 476-9527. Terri Drain, President. Toll-free, (800) 213-7193.*
General email, info@shapeamerica.org

Web, www.shapeamerica.org, Twitter, @SHAPE_America, Facebook, www.facebook.com/SHAPEAmericaFB and YouTube, www.youtube.com/SHAPEAmericaYT

Membership: teachers and others who work with school health, physical education, athletics, recreation, dance, and safety education programs (kindergarten through postsecondary levels). Member associations are National Assn. for Girls and Women in Sport, American Assn. for Health Education, National Dance Assn., National Assn. for Sport and Physical Education, and American Assn. for Physical Activity and Recreation.

Special Olympics International Inc., *1133 19th St. N.W., 20036-3604; (202) 628-3630. Fax, (202) 824-0200. Mary Davis, Chief Executive Officer; Timothy P. Shriver, Chair. Toll-free, (800) 700-8585.*
General email, info@specialolympics.org

Web, www.specialolympics.org, Twitter, @SpecialOlympics and Facebook, www.facebook.com/SpecialOlympics

Offers individuals with intellectual disabilities opportunities for year-round sports training; sponsors athletic competition for 4 million athletes worldwide in twenty-two individual and Olympic-type team sports.

StopPredatoryGambling.org, *100 Maryland Ave. N.E., #310, 20002; (202) 567-6996. Les Bernal, Executive Director, ext. 1.*
General email, mail@stoppredatorygambling.org

Web, www.stoppredatorygambling.org

Seeks to end government support of exploitive forms of gambling. Compiles information on the personal, social, economic, and public health impacts of commercial gambling and disseminates it to citizens and policymakers at the local, state, and national levels. Monitors legislation and regulations.

U.S. Eventing Assn. (USEA), *525 Old Waterford Rd. N.W., Leesburg, VA 20176-2050; (703) 779-0440. Fax, (703) 779-0550. Rob Burk, Chief Executive Officer, ext. 3017.*
General email, info@useventing.com

Web, www.useventing.com, Twitter, @USEventing and Facebook, www.facebook.com/USEventing

Membership: individuals interested in eventing, an Olympic-recognized equestrian sport featuring dressage, cross-country, and show jumping. Registers all national events to ensure that they meet the standards set by the U.S. Equestrian Federation. Sponsors three-day events for members from beginner novice to Olympic levels. Provides educational materials on competition, riding, and care of horses.

U.S. Parachute Assn., *5401 Southpoint Centre Blvd., Fredericksburg, VA 22407-2612; (540) 604-9740. Fax, (540) 604-9741. Albert Berchtold, Executive Director, ext. 325.*
General email, uspa@uspa.org

Web, www.uspa.org and Facebook, www.facebook.com/ SkydiveUSPA and YouTube, www.youtube.com/ SkydiveUSPA

Membership: individuals and organizations interested in skydiving. Develops safety procedures; maintains training programs; issues skydiving licenses and ratings; certifies skydiving instructors; sanctions national competitions; and documents record attempts. Offers liability insurance to members. Monitors legislation and regulations.

RELIGION

General

▶**NONGOVERNMENTAL**

American Friends Service Committee (AFSC), *Public Policy and Advocacy, 1822 R St. N.W., 20009-1604; (202) 483-3341. Fax, (202) 232-3197. Aura Kanegis, Director of Public Policy and Advocacy.*
General email, advocacy@afsc.org

Web, www.afsc.org/national-office-public-policy-and-advocacy-oppa, Twitter, @afsc_org and Facebook, www.facebook.com/AmericanFriendsServiceCommittee

Education, outreach, and advocacy office for the AFSC, an independent organization affiliated with the Religious Society of Friends (Quakers) in America. Sponsors domestic and international service, development, justice, and peace programs. Priorities include Iraq, Israel/Palestine, civil rights and liberties, and economic justice in the United States. Interests include peace education; arms control and disarmament; social and economic justice; gay and lesbian rights, racism, sexism, and civil rights; refugees and immigration policy; crisis response and relief efforts; and international development efforts, especially in Central America, the Middle East, and southern Africa. (Headquarters in Philadelphia, Pa.)

American Humanist Assn., *1821 Jefferson Pl. N.W., 20036; (202) 238-9088. Fax, (202) 238-9003. Sunil Panikkath, President; Nadya Dutchin, Executive Director. Toll-free, (800) 837-3792.*
General email, aha@americanhumanist.org

Web, https://americanhumanist.org, Twitter, @americnhumanist and Facebook, www.facebook.com/ americanhumanist

Seeks to educate the public about Humanism and bring Humanists together for mutual support and action. Defends the civil liberties and constitutional freedoms of Humanists and leads both local and national Humanist organizations toward progressive societal change.

American Islamic Congress, *1030 15th St. N.W., #243, 20005; (202) 595-3160. Zainab Al-Suwaij, Co-Founder. General email, info@aicongress.org*

Web, www.aicongress.org, Twitter, @aicongress and Facebook, www.facebook.com/AmericanIslamicCongress

Independent, nonpartisan initiative of American Muslims challenging negative perceptions of Muslims by advocating interethnic and interfaith understanding. Promotes open multicultural society and civil liberties; advocates women's equality, free expression, and nonviolence. Encourages the denouncement of terrorism, extremism, and hate speech within the Muslim community. Maintains offices in Tunisia and Iraq.

American Jewish Committee, *Government and International Affairs, 1156 15th St. N.W., #1201, 20005; (202) 785-4200. David Harris, Chief Executive Officer; Jason Isaacson, Chief Policy and Political Affairs Officer. General email, washington@ajc.org*

Web, www.ajc.org, Twitter, @AJCGlobal and Facebook, www.facebook.com/AJCGlobal

Human relations agency devoted to protecting civil and religious rights for all people. Interests include church-state issues, research on energy security, Israel and the Middle East, the security and well-being of Jewish diasporic communities worldwide, immigration, social discrimination, civil and women's rights, education, and international cooperation for peace and human rights. (Headquarters in New York.)

Americans United for Separation of Church and State, *1310 L St. N.W., #200, 20005; (202) 466-3234. Fax, (202) 466-3353. Rachel Laser, President. General email, americansunited@au.org*

Web, www.au.org and Twitter, @americansunited

Citizens' interest group. Opposes federal and state aid to parochial schools; works to ensure religious neutrality in public schools; supports free religious exercise; initiates litigation; maintains speakers bureau. Monitors legislation and regulations.

B'nai B'rith International, *1120 20th St. N.W., #300N, 20036; (202) 857-6600. Daniel S. Mariaschin, Chief Executive Officer. Press, (202) 857-6699. Toll-free, (888) 388-4224. General email, info@bnaibrith.org*

Web, www.bnaibrith.org, Twitter, @BnaiBrith and Facebook, www.facebook.com/bnaibrithinternational

International Jewish organization that promotes the security and continuity of the Jewish people and the State of Israel; defends human rights; combats anti-Semitism; and promotes Jewish identity through cultural activities. Interests include strengthening family life and the education and training of youth, providing broad-based services for the benefit of senior citizens, and advocacy on behalf of Jews throughout the world.

Baptist Joint Committee for Religious Liberty, *200 Maryland Ave. N.E., 3rd Floor, 20002; (202) 544-4226. Amanda Tyler, Executive Director. General email, bjc@bjconline.org*

Web, www.bjconline.org, Twitter, @BJContheHill and Facebook, www.facebook.com/ReligiousLiberty

Membership: Baptist conventions and conferences. Interests include religious liberty, separation of church and state, First Amendment religious issues, and government regulation of religious institutions. Files court briefs, leads educational programs, and monitors legislation.

Baptist World Alliance, *405 N. Washington St., Falls Church, VA 22046; (703) 790-8980. Fax, (703) 893-5160. Elijah Brown, General Secretary; Merritt Johnston, Executive Director. General email, info@baptistworld.org*

Web, www.baptistworld.org, Twitter, @BaptistWorld and Facebook, www.facebook.com/BaptistWorld

International Baptist organization. Conducts religious teaching and works to create a better understanding among nations. Organizes development efforts and disaster relief worldwide. Interests include human rights and religious liberty.

Catholic Information Center, *1501 K St. N.W., #175, 20005; (202) 783-2062. Fr. Charles Trullols, Director. General email, info@cicdc.org*

Web, https://cicdc.org, Twitter, @CICDC and Facebook, www.facebook.com/CatholicInformationCenter

Catholic cultural center, hosts lectures and events, offers free counseling services. Includes Catholic bookstore and chapel. Publishes the K Street Catholic Newletter.

Chaplain Alliance for Religious Liberty, *P.O. Box 151353, Alexandria, VA 22315; (571) 293-2427. Capt. Craig Muehler (USN, Ret.), President; Derek LS Jones (USA, Ret.), Executive Director. General email, info@chaplainalliance.org*

Web, http://chaplainalliance.org, Twitter, @CHAP_Alliance and Facebook, www.facebook.com/ChaplainAlliance

Membership: military chaplains and others who support orthodox Christian doctrines. Seeks to ensure that all chaplains and those they serve may exercise their religious liberties without fear of reprisal. Interests include the conflict between official protection for gays in the military and orthodox Christian teachings. Issues press releases; grants media interviews; monitors legislation and regulations.

Christian Science Committee on Publication, *Federal Office, 603 2nd St. N.E., 20002; (202) 296-2190. Tessa E. B. Frost, Director of Federal Government Affairs. General email, federal@christianscience.com*

Web, www.christianscience.com/member-resources/ committee-on-publication and Facebook, www.facebook.com/worldwidechristianscience/

Public service organization that provides information on the religious convictions and practices of Christian Scientists.

Conference of Major Superiors of Men (CMSM), 7300 Hanover Dr., #304, Greenbelt, MD 20770; (301) 588-4030. Fax, (240) 650-3697. Rev. Frank Donio, Executive Director.
General email, postmaster@cmsm.org

Web, https://cmsm.org, Twitter, @cmsmtweets and Facebook, www.facebook.com/CMSMshares

National representative body for more than 17,000 men in 240 religious and apostolic communities in the United States, including foreign missionaries. Collaborates with U.S. bishops and other key groups and organizations that serve church and society.

Council on American–Islamic Relations (CAIR), 453 New Jersey Ave. S.E., 20003-4034; (202) 488-8787. Fax, (202) 488-0833. Nihad Awad, National Executive Director.
General email, info@cair.com

Web, http://cair.com, Twitter, @CAIRNational, Facebook, www.facebook.com/CAIRNational and YouTube, www.youtube.com/user/CAIRtv

Promotes the understanding of Islam to the American public. Seeks to empower the Muslim community in the United States and protect civil liberties through political and social activism.

Episcopal Church, Government Relations, 110 Maryland Ave. N.E., #309, 20002; (202) 547-7300. Fax, (202) 547-4457. Rebecca Linder Blachly, Director. Toll-free, (800) 228-0515.
Web, www.episcopalchurch.org/ministries/office-governmentrelations, Twitter, @TheEPPN
General email, eppn@episcopalchurch.org

Informs Congress, the executive branch, and governmental agencies about the actions and resolutions of the Episcopal Church. Monitors legislation and regulations. (Denominational headquarters in New York.)

Ethics and Public Policy Center, 1730 M St. N.W., #910, 20036; (202) 682-1200. Fax, (202) 408-0632. Ryan T. Anderson, President.
General email, ethics@eppc.org

Web, www.eppc.org, Twitter, @EPPCdc and Facebook, www.facebook.com/EPPC.org

Considers implications of Judeo-Christian moral tradition for domestic and foreign policymaking.

Evangelical Lutheran Church in America, Advocacy, 218 D St. S.E., 20003; Rev. Amy Reumann, Senior Director. Toll-free, (800) 638-3522.
General email, washingtonoffice@elca.org

Web, www.elca.org/advocacy and Twitter, @ELCAadvocacy

Membership: represents the church's ministries, relationships, projects, and relief efforts on behalf of underrepresented people in order to effect policy change.

Monitors and responds to proposed legislation and regulations. (Headquarters in Chicago, Ill.)

Faith in Public Life, P.O. Box 33668, 20033; (202) 499-4095. Rev. Jennifer Butler, Chief Executive Officer.
General email, info@faithinpubliclife.org

Web, www.faithinpubliclife.org,
Twitter, @FaithinPublicLife,
Facebook, www.facebook.com/FaithinPublicLife and
YouTube, www.youtube.com/channel/UCH0jos0W0q7Wrj9iOWYZsEQ

Provides organizing and communications support to diverse faith leaders and organizations working to further justice and the common good in public policy; designs and implements coalitions and initiatives to promote faith as a force for the common good.

General Board of Church and Society of the United Methodist Church, 100 Maryland Ave. N.E., 20002; (202) 488-5600. Rev. Susan Henry-Crowe, General Secretary, (202) 488-5629.
General email, gbcs@umcjustice.org

Web, www.umcjustice.org, Twitter, @UMCjustice and Facebook, www.facebook.com/umcjustice

One of four international general program boards of the United Methodist Church. Provides training and educational resources to member churches on social concerns - poverty, climate, health, peace, civil and human rights. Monitors legislation and regulations. (Has offices at the Church Center for the United Nations.)

General Conference of Seventh-day Adventists, 12501 Old Columbia Pike, Silver Spring, MD 20904-6600; (301) 680-6000. Ted N. C. Wilson, President. Press, (301) 680-6315.
General email, info@contact.adventist.org

Web, www.adventist.org, Twitter, @adventistchurch and Facebook, www.facebook.com/TheAdventistChurch

World headquarters of the Seventh-day Adventist Church. Interests include education, health care, humanitarian relief, and religious liberty. Supplies educational tools for the blind and the hard of hearing. Operates hospitals and schools worldwide. Organizes community service-oriented youth groups.

Institute on Religion and Democracy, 1023 15th St. N.W., #200, 20005-2601; (202) 682-4131. Mark Tooley, President.
General email, info@theird.org

Web, https://theird.org, Twitter, @theIRD and Facebook, www.facebook.com/TheIRD

Interdenominational bipartisan organization that supports democratic and constitutional forms of government consistent with the values of Christianity. Serves as a resource center to promote Christian perspectives on U.S. national and foreign policy questions. Interests include international conflicts, religious liberties, and the promotion of democratic forms of government in the United States and worldwide.

Interfaith Alliance, 2101 L St. N.W., #800, 20037; (202) 466-0567. Fax, (202) 857-3977. Rabbi Jack Moline, President.
General email, info@interfaithalliance.org
Web, www.interfaithalliance.org, Twitter, @intrfthalliance and Facebook, www.facebook.com/interfaithalliance

Membership: 75 faith traditions, including Protestant, Catholic, Jewish, and Muslim clergy, laity, and others who favor a positive, nonpartisan role for religious faith in public life, as well as for those who follow no faith tradition. Advocates mainstream religious values; promotes tolerance and social opportunity; opposes the use of religion to promote political extremism at national, state, and local levels. Monitors legislation and regulations.

International Religious Liberty Assn., 12501 Old Columbia Pike, Silver Spring, MD 20904-6600; (301) 680-6683. Fax, (301) 680-6695. Bettina Krause, Director of Government Affairs.
General email, info@irla.org
Web, http://irla.org, Twitter, @irla-usa and Facebook, www.facebook.com/irla.hq

Seeks to preserve and expand religious liberty and freedom of conscience; advocates separation of church and state; sponsors international and domestic meetings and congresses.

Islamic Society of North America (ISNA), *Office of Interfaith and Community Alliances,* 110 Maryland Ave. N.E., #304, 20002; Basharat Saleem, Executive Director, (317) 839-1808; Christine Warner, Director of Shoulder to Shoulder. Shoulder to Shoulder Phone, (202) 544-5656.
General email, info@isna.net
Web, www.isna.net and Twitter, @ISNAHQ

Conducts outreach to grassroots organizations and engages in joint programs with other religious organizations, including the National Council of Churches, the United States Conference of Catholic Bishops, and the Union for Reform Judaism. Seeks to promote a positive image of Islam and Muslims to national political leaders and strong relationships with U.S. congressional staff and federal government officials. Serves as an outreach resource to the American Muslim community. (Headquarters in Plainfield, Ind. Shoulder to Shoulder is a coalition that ISNA hosts the office, Shouldertoshoulder campaign.org.)

Jesuit Conference, *Social and International Ministries,* 1016 16th St. N.W., 4th Floor, 20036; (202) 462-0400. Fax, (202) 328-9212. Timothy Kesecki, President.
General email, usjc@jesuit.org
Web, www.jesuits.org, Twitter, @jesuitnews and Facebook, www.facebook.com/Jesuits/

Information and advocacy organization of Jesuits and laypersons concerned with peace and social justice issues. Interests include peace and disarmament, domestic poverty, socially responsible investing, and migration and immigration.

Jewish Federations of North America, *Washington Office,* (202) 785-5900. William C. Doroff, Director.
General email, dc@JewishFederations.org
Web, www.jewishfederations.org, Twitter, @jfederations and Facebook, www.facebook.com/jfederations

Acts as advocate for the 148 Jewish federations across the United States on issues of concern, including long-term care, families at risk, and naturally occurring retirement communities. Offers marketing, communications, and public relations support; coordinates a speakers bureau. (Headquarters in New York.)

Jewish Women International, 1129 20th St. N.W., #801, 20036; (202) 857-1300. Fax, (202) 857-1380. Meredith Jacobs, Chief Executive Officer. Toll-free, (800) 343-2823.
General email, jwi@jwi.org
Web, www.jwi.org, Twitter, @JewishWomenIntl and Facebook, www.facebook.com/jewishwomeninternational

Membership: Jewish women, supporters, and partners in the United States and Canada. Interests include empowerment of women and girls, ending domestic and sexual violence, financial literacy and economic security, and highlighting women's leadership at multigenerational intersections.

Leadership Conference of Women Religious, 8737 Colesville Rd., #610, Silver Spring, MD 20910; (301) 588-4955. Fax, (301) 587-4575. Carol Zinn, Executive Director.
General email, asanders@lcwr.org
Web, www.lcwr.org and Facebook, www.facebook.com/lcwr.org

Membership: Roman Catholic women who are the principal administrators of their congregations of Catholic women religious in the United States and around the world. Offers programs and support to members; conducts research; serves as an information clearinghouse.

Loyola Foundation, 10373 Democracy Lane, #B, Fairfax, VA 22030; (571) 435-9401. A. Gregory McCarthy IV, Executive Director.
General email, info@loyolafoundation.org
Web, www.loyolafoundation.org

Assists overseas Catholic mission activities. Awards grants to international missionaries and Catholic dioceses for vehicle and equipment purchase and construction.

Maryknoll Office for Global Concerns *(Catholic Foreign Mission Society of America),* 200 New York Ave. N.W., 20001; (202) 832-1780. Fax, (202) 832-5195. Susan Gunn, Director.
General email, ogc@maryknoll.org
Web, www.maryknollogc.org, Facebook, www.facebook.com/MaryknollOfficeforGlobalConcerns/ and Twitter, @MklGlobalConcer

Conducts education and advocacy for international policies that promote peace, social justice, and ecological integrity. (Headquarters in Maryknoll, N.Y.)

Mennonite Central Committee, *Washington Office, 920 Pennsylvania Ave. S.E., 20003; (202) 544-6564. Tammy Alexander, Director, ext. 62113.*
General email, mccwash@mcc.org

Web, http://mcc.org/get-involved/advocacy/washington, Twitter, @mccwashington, Facebook, www.facebook.com/ MccWashingtonOffice and YouTube, www.youtube.com/ c/mccorg

Christian organization engaged in service and development projects. Monitors legislation and regulations affecting issues of interest to Mennonite and Brethren in Christ churches. Interests include human rights in developing countries, military spending, the environment, world hunger, poverty, and civil and religious liberties. Advocacy work includes analyzing policies from an anabaptist perspective, meeting with legislators and diplomats, petitions, and letter-writing campaigns. (Headquarters in Akron, Pa.)

Muslim Public Affairs Council, *Washington Office, 1020 16th St. N.W., 20036; (202) 547-7701. Fax, (202) 547-7704. Salam Al-Marayati, National President; Mohammad Hurr Ali, Director of Policy and Government Relations.*
General email, hello@mpac.org

Web, www.mpac.org, Twitter, @mpac_national and Facebook, www.facebook.com/mpacnational

Policy advocacy group seeking an accurate portrayal of Islam and Muslims in the media and popular culture. Comments and provides background information to journalists and other media professionals to inform public opinion. (Headquarters in Los Angeles, Calif.)

National Assn. of Evangelicals, *P.O. Box 23269, 20026; (202) 479-0815. Walter Kim, President.*
General email, info@nae.net

Web, www.nae.net, Twitter, @NAEvangelicals and Facebook, www.facebook.com/naevangelicals

Membership: evangelical denominations, nonprofits, churches, schools, and individuals. Works to connect and represent Christian evangelical denominations, nonprofits, churches, schools, and individuals. Interests include church and faith; family; religious liberty; economic policy; church-state relations; immigration and refugee policy; and world relief efforts. Provides networking opportunities and commissions chaplains. Monitors legislation and regulations.

National Clergy Council, *109 2nd St. N.E., 20002; (202) 737-1776. Peggy Nienaber, Vice President.*
General email, faith@faithandlibertyDC.org
Web, www.faithandlibertyDC.org

Informal network of conservative and traditional Christian clergy and heads of religious organizations and societies. Advocates injecting religious morality into public policy debates. Monitors legislation and regulations.

National Council of Catholic Women, *10335-A Democracy Ln., #201, Fairfax, VA 22030; (703) 224-0990. Andrea Cecilli, Executive Director.*
General email, nccw01@nccw.org

Web, www.nccw.org, Twitter, @NCCW1920 and Facebook, www.facebook.com/nationalcouncilofcatholic women

Roman Catholic women's organization. Provides education and information to Catholic women regarding social issues. Interests include women and poverty, employment, family life, abortion, care for older adults, world hunger, global water supplies, genetic engineering research, pornography, capital punishment, immigration, domestic violence, and human trafficking. Special programs include volunteer respite care, leadership training for women, mentoring of mothers, and drug and alcohol abuse education. Monitors legislation and regulations.

National Council of Churches, *110 Maryland Ave. N.E., #108, 20002-5603; (202) 544-2350. Leslie Copeland Tune, Corporate Operations Officer.*
General email, info@nationalcouncilofchurches.us

Web, www.nationalcouncilofchurches.us, Twitter, @ncccusa, Facebook, www.facebook.com/ nationalcouncilofchurches and YouTube, www.youtube .com/channel/UCNdghdVdQi85VP5zV7FM46Q

Membership: thirty-eight Protestant, Anglican, and Orthodox denominations. Interests include interreligious relations, racial and social equality; social welfare, economic justice, environmental justice, peace, and international issues, with a focus on peacemaking and mass incarceration issues; and church-state relations.

National Council of Jewish Women, *2055 L St. N.W., #650, 20036; (202) 296-2588. Dana Gershon, President; Sheila Katz, Corporate Executive Officer; Jody Rabhan, Chief Policy Officer.*
General email, action@ncjwdc.org

Web, www.ncjw.org, Twitter, @NCJW and Facebook, www .facebook.com/NCJWInc

Progressive Jewish women's membership organization. Activities include education, community service, and advocacy. Interests include women's issues, reproductive, civil, and constitutional rights, child care, judicial nominations, religion–state separation, and human needs funding issues.

NCSEJ: National Coalition Supporting Eurasian Jewry, *1120 20th St. N.W, #300N, 20036-3413; (202) 898-2500. Mark B. Levin, Chief Executive Officer, ext. 6201; James Schiller, Chair.*
General email, ncsej@ncsej.org

Web, www.ncsej.org, Twitter, @NCSEJ and Facebook, www.facebook.com/thencsej

Advocacy group promoting political and religious freedom on behalf of Jews in Russia, Ukraine, the Baltic states, and Eurasia. Works with community and government leadership in the United States and in the former Soviet Union addressing issues of anti-Semitism, community relations, and promotion of democracy, tolerance, and U.S. engagement in the region.

Operation Understanding D.C., *4005 Wisconsin Ave. N.W., Box 5705, 20016; (202) 234-6832. Morgan Moeller, Executive Director (Acting).*
General email, info@oudc.org
Web, www.oudc.org and Twitter, @OU_DC

African American and Jewish youth education program promoting leadership and antidiscrimination.

Orthodox Union, *Advocacy Center, 820 1st St. N.E., #730, 20002; (202) 513-6484. Nathan J. Diament, Executive Director, ext. 4.*
General email, ouainfo@ou.org
Web, www.ou.org/public_affairs, Twitter, @OUAdvocacy and Facebook, www.facebook.com/OUAdvocacy

Works to protect Orthodox Jewish interests and freedoms through dissemination of policy briefings to government officials. Encourages Jewish law and a traditional perspective on public policy issues. Coordinates grassroots activities. (Headquarters in New York.)

Pew Research Center, *Religion, Religion and Public Life Project, 1615 L St. N.W., #800, 20036; (202) 419-4300. Alan Cooperman, Director. Press, (202) 419-4564.*
General email, religion@pewresearch.org
Web, www.pewforum.org and Twitter, @PewReligion

Nonpartisan organization that seeks to explore the impact of religion on public affairs, political behavior, the law, domestic policy, and international affairs. Conducts polling and independent research; serves as a clearinghouse and forum on these issues. Delivers findings to journalists, government officials, and other interested groups.

Presbyterian Mission (U.S.A.), *Office of Public Witness, 100 Maryland Ave. N.E., #410, 20002; (202) 543-1126. Fax, (202) 543-7755. Rev. Jimmie Ray Hawkins II, Director, ext. 231.*
General email, ga_washington_office@pcusa.org
Web, www.presbyterianmission.org/ministries/washington, Twitter, @PCUSAWashington and Facebook, www.facebook.com/PCUSAWashington?fref=ts

Provides information on the views of the general assembly of the Presbyterian Church on public policy issues; monitors legislation affecting issues of concern. Interests include budget priorities, foreign policy, arms control, civil rights, religious liberty, church-state relations, economic justice, environmental justice, and public policy issues affecting women. (Headquarters in Louisville, Ky.)

Progressive National Baptist Convention Inc., *601 50th St. N.E., 20019; (202) 396-0558. Fax, (202) 398-4998. Timothy Stewart, President. Toll-free, (800) 876-7622.*
General email, office@pnbc.org
Web, www.pnbc.org, Twitter, @PNBCINC and Facebook, www.facebook.com/pnbcinc

Baptist denomination that supports missionaries, implements education programs, and acts as advocate for civil and human rights.

Public Religion Research Institute, *1023 15th St. N.W., 9th Floor, 20005; (202) 238-9424. Fax, (202) 238-9427. Robert P. Jones, Chief Executive Officer, (202) 238-9426.*
General email, info@prri.org
Web, www.prri.org, Twitter, @PRRIpoll and Facebook, www.facebook.com/PRRIpoll

Nonpartisan nonprofit that conducts surveys and publishes research on the junction of public life and religion. Serves as a resource to help journalists and the public understand the impact of religion on American life and discussions on public policy.

Religious Action Center of Reform Judaism, *Union for Reform Judaism, 2027 Massachusetts Ave. N.W., 20036; (202) 387-2800. Fax, (202) 667-9070. Rabbi Jonah Dov Pesner, Director.*
General email, rac@rac.org
Web, https://rac.org, Twitter, @TheRAC, Facebook, www.facebook.com/TheRAC and YouTube, www.youtube.com/user/racrj

Religious and educational organization that mobilizes the American Jewish community on legislative and social concerns. Interests include economic justice, civil rights, religious liberty, and international peace.

Sojourners, *408 C St. N.E., 20002; (202) 328-8842. Fax, (202) 328-8757. Robert (Rob) Wilson-Black, Chief Executive Officer; Adam R. Taylor, President.*
General email, sojourners@sojo.net
Web, https://sojo.net, Twitter, @Sojourners and Facebook, www.facebook.com/SojournersMagazine

Membership: Catholics, Protestants, Evangelicals, and other interested Christians. Grassroots network that focuses on social injustices and the intersection of faith, politics, and culture. (Merger of Sojourners and Call to Renewal.)

U.S. Conference of Catholic Bishops (USCCB), *3211 4th St. N.E., 20017; (202) 541-3000. Archbishop Jose Gomez, President.*
Web, www.usccb.org, Twitter, @USCCB, Facebook, www.facebook.com/USCCB and YouTube, www.youtube.com/USCCB

Serves as a forum for bishops to exchange ideas, debate concerns of the church, and draft responses to religious and social issues. Provides information on doctrine and policies of the Roman Catholic Church; develops religious education and training programs; formulates policy positions on social issues, including the economy, employment, federal budget priorities, voting rights, energy, health, housing, rural affairs, international military and political matters, human rights, the arms race, global economics, and immigration and refugee policy.

United Church of Christ, *Washington Office, 100 Maryland Ave. N.E., #330, 20002; (202) 543-1517. Fax, (202) 543-5994. Sandra (Sandy) Sorensen, Director.*
Web, www.ucc.org, Twitter, @unitedchurch and Facebook, www.facebook.com/UnitedChurchofChrist

Studies public policy issues and promotes church policy on these issues; organizes legislative advocacy to address church views. Interests include health care, international peace, economic justice, the environment, climate change, civil rights, and immigration. (Headquarters in Cleveland, Ohio.)

Washington Ethical Society, *7750 16th St. N.W., 20012; (202) 882-6650. Lyn Cox, Senior Leader (Acting).*
General email, wes@ethicalsociety.org

Web, www.ethicalsociety.org and Twitter, @EthicalDC

A humanistic religious community that sets standards, distributes ethical culture materials, trains leaders, awards grants, publishes statements on moral issues and public policy, and coordinates national projects such as youth programs. (Affiliated with the American Ethical Union and the Unitarian Universalist Assn.)

Women's Alliance for Theology, Ethics, and Ritual (WATER), *8121 Georgia Ave., #310, Silver Spring, MD 20910; (301) 589-2509. Fax, (301) 589-3150. Diann L. Neu, Co-Director; Mary E. Hunt, Co-Director.*
General email, water@hers.com

Web, www.waterwomensalliance.org and
Twitter, @watervoices

Feminist theological organization that focuses on issues concerning women and religion. Interests include social issues; work skills for women with disabilities; human rights in Latin America; and liturgies, rituals, counseling, and research.

TRAVEL AND TOURISM

General

▶AGENCIES

Bureau of Consular Affairs (CA) *(State Dept.), Passport Services, 600 19th St. N.W., SA-17A, 20006; Rachel Arndt, Deputy Assistant Secretary. Passport Appointments, (877) 487-2778. TTY, (888) 874-7793.*
Web, https://travel.state.gov/content/passports/en/passports.html
National Passport Information Center, NPIC@state.gov

Creates passports and provides information and resources to citizens about how to obtain, replace, and change a U.S. passport.

Bureau of Consular Affairs (CA) *(State Dept.), Special Issuance Agency, 600 19th St. N.W., SA-17A, 20006; (202) 485-8200. (202) 485-8244. Linda M. Blount, Director, (202) 485-8202.*
Web, http://travel.state.gov/content/travel/en/passports.html
National Passport Information Center, NPIC@state.gov

Administers passport laws and issues passports. (Most branches of the U.S. Postal Service and most U.S. district and state courts are authorized to accept applications and payment for passports and to administer the required oath

to U.S. citizens. Completed applications are sent from the post office or court to the nearest State Dept. regional passport office for processing.)

International Trade Administration (ITA) *(Commerce Dept.), Industry and Analysis (I&A), National Travel and Tourism (NTTO), 1401 Constitution Ave. N.W., Room 10003, 20230-0001; (202) 482-4904. Fax, (202) 482-2887. Julie Heizer, Deputy Assistant Secretary (Acting).*
General email, ntto@trade.gov

Web, http://trade.gov/about-us/national-travel-and-tourism-office and Twitter, @nttotradegov

Fosters international tourism trade development, including public-private partnerships; represents the United States in tourism-related meetings with foreign government officials. Assembles, analyzes, and disseminates data and statistics on travel and tourism to and from the United States.

National Park Service (NPS) *(Interior Dept.), National Tourism Program, 1849 C St. N.W., #1357, 20240; (202) 354-6472. Donald Leadbetter, Program Manager.*
General email, donald_leadbetter@nps.gov

Web, www.nps.gov/orgs/1365

Directs and supports the National Park Service's tourism program. Acts as liaison to government departments and agencies on tourism issues. Serves as the primary contact for national and international travel and tourism industry officials and professionals.

▶CONGRESS

For a listing of relevant congressional committees and subcommittees, please see page 130 or the Appendix.

▶NONGOVERNMENTAL

American Hotel and Lodging Assn., *1250 Eye St. N.W., #1100, 20005-3931; (202) 289-3100. Fax, (202) 289-3199. William (Chip) Rogers, Chief Executive Officer.*
General email, info@ahla.com

Web, https://ahla.com, Twitter, @ahla and
Facebook, www.facebook.com/hotelassociation

Membership: U.S. hotel and lodging properties and individuals affiliated with the hotel industry. Provides operations, technical, educational, marketing, and communications services to members. Monitors legislation and regulations.

American Resort Development Assn., *1201 15th St. N.W., #400, 20005-2842; (202) 371-6700. Fax, (202) 289-8544. Jason Gamel, President. Consumer hotline, (855) 939-1515.*
General email, consumer@arda-roc.org

Web, www.arda.org

Membership: U.S. and international developers, builders, financiers, marketing companies, and others involved in resort, recreational, and community development. Serves as an information clearinghouse; monitors federal and state legislation affecting land, time-share, and community development industries.

American Society of Travel Advisors (ASTA), 675
N. Washington St., #490, Alexandria, VA 22314-2963; (703) 739-2782. Fax, (703) 684-8319. Zane Kerby, President, (703) 739-6804. Toll-free, (800) 275-2782. Web, www.asta.org and Twitter, @ASTAAdvisors

Membership: representatives of the travel industry. Works to safeguard the traveling public against fraud, misrepresentation, and other unethical practices. Offers training programs for travel agents. Consumer affairs department offers help for anyone with a travel complaint against a member of the association.

Center for Responsible Travel (CREST), 1225 Eye St.
N.W., #600, 20005; (202) 347-9203. Gregory Miller, Director. Toll-free, (866) 821-6866.
General email, staff@responsibletravel.org
Web, www.responsibletravel.org and Twitter, @CREST_Travel

Designs, monitors, evaluates, and seeks to improve ecotourism and sustainable tourism principles and practices.

Cruise Lines International Assn., 1201 F St. N.W., #250,
20004; (202) 759-9370. Fax, (202) 759-9344. Kelly Craighead, President.
General email, info@cruising.org
Web, www.cruising.org, Twitter, @CLIAGlobal, Facebook, www.facebook.com/CLIAGlobal and YouTube, www.youtube.com/cliaglobal

Advises domestic and international regulatory organizations on shipping policy. Works with U.S. and international agencies to promote safety, public health, security, medical facilities, environmental awareness, and passenger protection. Monitors legislation and regulations.

Destinations International, 2025 M St. N.W., #500,
20036-3309; (202) 296-7888. Fax, (202) 296-7889. Don Welsh II, Chief Executive Officer, (202) 835-4215.
General email, info@destinationinternational.org
Web, https://destinationsinternational.org, Twitter, @destintl, Facebook, www.facebook.com/destintl and YouTube, www.youtube.com/c/DestIntl

Membership: travel- and tourism-related businesses, convention and meeting professionals, and tour operators. Encourages business travelers and tourists to visit local historic, cultural, and recreational areas; assists in meeting preparations. Monitors legislation and regulations.

Global Business Travel Assn., 1101 King St., #500,
Alexandria, VA 22314; (703) 684-0836. Fax, (703) 783-8686. Suzanne Neufang, Executive Director (Acting).
General email, info@gbta.org
Web, www.gbta.org, Twitter, @GlobalBTA and Facebook, www.facebook.com/GBTAonFB

Membership: corporate travel managers and travel service suppliers. Promotes educational advancement of members and provides a forum for exchange of information on U.S. and international travel. Monitors legislation and regulations.

Hostelling International USA—American Youth
Hostels, 8455 Colesville Rd., #1225, Silver Spring, MD 20910; (301) 650-2100. Fax, (240) 650-2094. Russell Hedge, Chief Executive Officer.
General email, members@hiusa.org
Web, www.hiusa.org and Twitter, @HIUSA

Seeks to improve cultural understanding through a nationwide network of hostels and travel-based programs. Provides opportunities for outdoor recreation and inexpensive educational travel and accommodations through hostelling. Member of the International Youth Hostel Federation.

Passenger Vessel Assn., 103 Oronoco St., #200,
Alexandria, VA 22314; (703) 518-5005. Fax, (703) 518-5151. John R. Groundwater, Executive Director, ext. 22; Edmund Welch, Legislative Director, ext. 27.
General email, pvainfo@passengervessel.com
Web, www.passengervessel.com and Facebook, www.facebook.com/PassengerVesselAssociation

Membership: owners, operators, and suppliers for U.S. and Canadian passenger vessels and international vessel companies. Interests include insurance, safety and security, and U.S. congressional impact on dinner and excursion boats, car and passenger ferries, overnight cruise ships, and riverboat casinos. Monitors legislation and regulations.

U.S. Travel Assn., 1100 New York Ave. N.W., #450, 20005-
3934; (202) 408-8422. Roger Dow, President. Press, (202) 408-2183.
Web, www.USTravel.org, Twitter, @USTravel and Facebook, www.facebook.com/U.S.TravelAssociation

Membership: travel-related companies and associations, state tourism offices, convention and visitors bureaus. Advocates increased travel to and within the United States; conducts research, provides marketing, and hosts trade shows. Monitors legislation and regulations.

5

Education

GENERAL POLICY AND ANALYSIS

Basic Resources

▶AGENCIES

Education Dept., *Lyndon B. Johnson Bldg., 400 Maryland Ave. S.W., #7W301, 20202-0001; (202) 401-3000. Fax, (202) 260-7867. Miguel A. Cardona, Secretary. Federal Student Aid Information Center, (800) 433-3243. Fraud, Waste, and Abuse hotline, (800) 647-8733. Press, (202) 401-1576. Publications, (877) 433-7827. Toll-free, (800) 872-5327. TTY, (800) 877-8339.*
Web, www.ed.gov, Twitter, @usedgov and Facebook, www.facebook.com/ED.gov/

Establishes education policy and acts as principal adviser to the president on education matters; administers and coordinates most federal assistance programs on education.

Education Dept., *Educational Technology (OET), Lyndon B. Johnson Bldg., 400 Maryland Ave. S.W., #5W114, 20202; (202) 401-1444. Kristina Ishmael, Deputy Director.*
General email, tech@ed.gov
Web, https://tech.ed.gov and Twitter, @OfficeofEdTech

Develops national educational policy and advocates the transition from print-based to digital learning.

Education Dept., *International Affairs, Lyndon B. Johnson Bldg., 400 Maryland Ave. S.W., #6W108, 20202-0001; (202) 401-0430. Fax, (202) 401-2508. Maureen McLaughlin, Director, (202) 401-8964.*
General email, internationalaffairs@ed.gov
Web, https://sites.ed.gov/international

Responsible for the overall coordination of the Education Dept.'s international presence. Works with department program offices, support units, and senior leadership as well as with external partners, including other federal agencies, state and local agencies, foreign governments, international organizations, and the private sector.

Education Dept., *Legislative and Congressional Affairs (OLCA), Lyndon B. Johnson Bldg., 400 Maryland Ave. S.W., #6W315, 20202-3500; (202) 401-0020. Fax, (202) 401-1438. Gwen Graham, Assistant Secretary.*
General email, olca@ed.gov
Web, www2.ed.gov/about/offices/list/olca

Directs and supervises all legislative activities of the Education Dept. Participates on legislation and regulation development teams within the department and provides legislative history behind the current law.

Educational Resources Information Center (ERIC) *(Education Dept.), 550 12th St. S.W., 7th Floor, 20202-5950 (mailing address: 200 Massachusetts Ave. N.W., #700, Washington, DC, 20001); (202) 245-6909. Mark Schneider, Director.*

General email, ericrequests@ed.gov
Web, https://eric.ed.gov, Twitter, @ERICinfo and Facebook, www.facebook.com/SearchEduResources

Coordinates an online national information system of education literature and resources. Provides a centralized bibliographic and full-text database of journal articles and other published and unpublished materials. Available at no charge to educators worldwide. Managed by the Applied Engineering Management Corp.

National Library of Education *(Education Dept.), 400 Maryland Ave. S.W., 20202-5721; (202) 205-5015. Fax, (202) 401-0547. Karen Tate, Director. Toll-free, (800) 424-1616. TTY, (800) 877-8339.*
General email, askalibrarian@ed.gov
Web, http://ies.ed.gov/ncee/projects/nle

Federal government's main resource center for education information. Provides information, statistical, and referral services to the Education Dept. and other government agencies, the education community, and the public. Library open to the public by appointment only.

▶CONGRESS

For a listing of relevant congressional committees and subcommittees, please see page 176 or the Appendix.

Government Accountability Office (GAO), *Education, Workforce, and Income Security (EWIS), 441 G St. N.W., 20548; (202) 512-7215. Jacqueline Nowicki, Director.*
Web, www.gao.gov/about/careers/our-teams

Assists Congress in analyzing the efficiency and effectiveness of federal agency programs that foster the development, education, and skill attainment of children and adults; provide benefits and protections for workers, families, veterans, and those with disabilities; and ensure an adequate and secure retirement for an aging population.

▶NONGOVERNMENTAL

American Council on Education (ACE), *Division of Government and Public Affairs, 1 Dupont Circle N.W., 20036; (202) 939-9300. Terry Hartle, Senior Vice President.*
General email, HENA@acenet.edu
Web, www.acenet.edu/advocacy/Pages/default.aspx

Coordinates and publicizes higher education to the federal government. Communicates information on educational concerns and ACE policies to the media, college and university officials, and the general public. Monitors legislation and regulations. Supports immigration, labor and employment, and veterans education among others.

Aspen Institute, *2300 N St. N.W., #700, 20037; (202) 736-5800. Fax, (202) 467-0790. Daniel R. Porterfield, President. Press, (202) 736-3849.*
General email, info@aspeninstitute.org
Web, www.aspeninstitute.org and Twitter, @AspenInstitute

Educational and policy studies organization. Promotes consideration of the public good in a wide variety of policy

EDUCATION RESOURCES IN CONGRESS

For a complete listing of congressional committees, including their full contact information, leadership, membership, and jurisdictions, please refer to the Appendix on pages 840–963.

HOUSE:

House Administration Committee, (202) 225-2061.
Web, cha.house.gov
House Agriculture Committee, (202) 225-2171.
Web, agriculture.house.gov
  Subcommittee on Biotechnology, Horticulture, and Research, (202) 225-2171.
House Appropriations Committee, (202) 225-2771.
Web, appropriations.house.gov
  Subcommittee on Interior, Environment, and Related Agencies, (202) 225-3081.
  Subcommittee on Labor, Health and Human Services, Education, and Related Agencies, (202) 225-3508.
  Subcommittee on Legislative Branch, (202) 226-7252.
House Armed Services Committee, (202) 225-4151.
Web, armedservices.house.gov
  Subcommittee on Military Personnel, (202) 225-4151.
House Education and Labor Committee, (202) 225-3725.
Web, edlabor.house.gov
  Subcommittee on Early Childhood, Elementary, and Secondary Education, (202) 225-3725.
  Subcommittee on Higher Education and Workforce Investment, (202) 225-3725.
House Science, Space, and Technology Committee, (202) 225-6375.
Web, science.house.gov
  Subcommittee on Research and Technology, (202) 225-6375.

JOINT:

Joint Committee on the Library of Congress, (202) 225-2061.
Web, cha.house.gov/jointcommittees/joint-committee-library

SENATE:

Senate Agriculture, Nutrition, and Forestry Committee, (202) 224-2035.
Web, agriculture.senate.gov
  Subcommittee on Food and Nutrition, Specialty Crop, Organics, and Research, (202) 224-2035.
Senate Appropriations Committee, (202) 224-7363.
Web, appropriations.senate.gov
  Subcommittee on Interior, Environment, and Related Agencies, (202) 224-7363.
  Subcommittee on Labor, Health and Human Services, Education, and Related Agencies, (202) 224-7363.
  Subcommittee on Legislative Branch, (202) 224-7363.
Senate Armed Services Committee, (202) 224-3871.
Web, armed-services.senate.gov
  Subcommittee on Personnel, (202) 224-3871.
Senate Banking, Housing, and Urban Affairs Committee, (202) 224-7391.
Web, banking.senate.gov
  Subcommittee on Housing, Transportation, and Community Development, (202) 224-7391.
Senate Commerce, Science, and Transportation Committee, (202) 224-0411.
Web, commerce.senate.gov
  Subcommittee on Communications, Media, and Broadband, (202) 224-0411.
  Subcommittee on Oceans, Fisheries, Climate Change, and Manufacturing, (202) 224-0411.
Senate Health, Education, Labor, and Pensions Committee, (202) 224-5375.
Web, help.senate.gov
  Subcommittee on Children and Families, (202) 224-5375.
Senate Indian Affairs Committee, (202) 224-2251.
Web, indian.senate.gov
Senate Rules and Administration Committee, (202) 224-6352.
Web, rules.senate.gov

---

areas, including education. Working with international partners, offers educational seminars, nonpartisan policy forums, public conferences and events, and leadership development initiatives.

The Brookings Institution, *Brown Center on Education Policy, 1775 Massachusetts Ave. N.W., 20036; (202) 797-2472. Jon Valant, Director, (202) 238-3624. Web, www.brookings.edu/center/brown-center-on-education-policy, Twitter, @BrookingsEd and General Email, communications@brookings.edu*

Research center promoting education policymaking. Interests include the impact of curriculum, school accountability, class size, instructional technology, student loans, preschool education, public pensions, teacher evaluation, school district contributions, and the academic achievement of U.S. students on international assessments.

Center for Education Reform, *1455 Pennsylvania Ave. N.W., #462, 20004; (202) 750-0016. Jeanne Allen, Chief Executive Officer. General email, pr@edreform.com*

Education Department

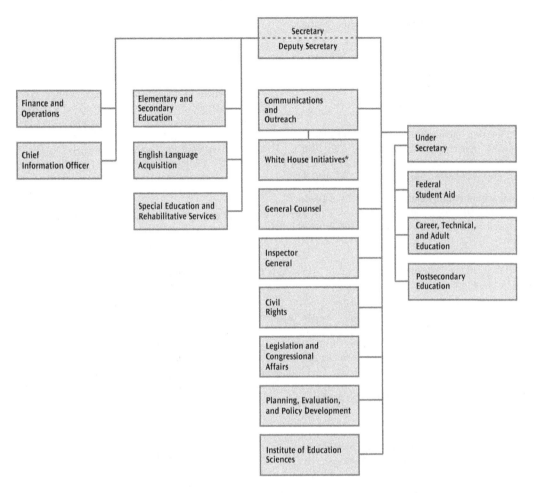

* The White House Initiatives are Office of Faith-Based and Neighborhood Partnerships; White House Initiative on Advancing Educational Equity, Excellence, and Economic Opportunity for Native Americans and Strengthening Tribal Colleges and Universities; White House Initiative on Advancing Educational Equity, Excellence, and Economic Opportunity for Hispanics; White House Initiative on Advancing Educational Equity, Excellence, and Economic Opportunity for Black Americans; and White House Initiative on Advancing Educational Equity, Excellence, and Economic Opportunity through Historically Black Colleges and Universities.

Web, https://edreform.com, Twitter, @edreform, Facebook, www.facebook.com/theCenterforEducation Reform/ and YouTube, www.youtube.com/user/Ctr4EdReform

Research and informational organization that promotes education reform through grassroots advocacy. Interests include charter school laws, school choice programs, teacher qualifications, and educational standards. Website serves as a networking forum for parents, educators, policymakers, and others interested in education reform, providing news reports and information on education seminars throughout the country.

Center for Law and Education, 7011 8th St. N.W., 20012; (202) 986-3000. Paul Weckstein, Co-Director, ext. 101; Kathleen Boundy, Co-Director (in Boston). General email, cle@cleweb.org

Web, www.cleweb.org and Facebook, www.facebook.com/centerforlawandeducation

Works to advance the right of all students nationally, in particular those from low-income families, to a high-quality education. Focuses on assessments, testing, and tracking; rights of students with disabilities (including special education); students with limited English proficiency, including bilingual education; implementation of key parent participation provisions under Title 1; vocational education; excessive/discriminatory discipline; and the education of youth in juvenile justice facilities. (Headquarters in Boston, Mass.)

National Academies of Sciences, Engineering, and Medicine (NASEM), *Office of Testing and Assessment,* Keck Center, 500 5th St. N.W., 11th Floor, 20001; (202) 334-2300. Judy Koenig, Senior Program Officer, (540) 570-1324.

General email, dbasse@nas.edu

Web, http://sites.nationalacademies.org/dbasse/bota

Assists policymakers by providing scientific expertise about critical issues of testing and assessment in education and the workplace.

National Assn. of State Boards of Education, *123 N. Pitt St., #350, Alexandria, VA 22314; (703) 684-4000. Paolo DeMaria, President.*

General email, boards@nasbe.org

Web, www.nasbe.org and Twitter, @nasbe

Membership: members of state boards of education, state board attorneys, and executives of state boards. Works to strengthen state boards as the preeminent educational policymaking bodies for students and citizens.

National School Public Relations Assn., *15948 Derwood Rd., Rockville, MD 20855; (301) 519-0496. Fax, (301) 519-0494. Barbara Hunter, Executive Director; Nicole Kirby, President.*

General email, info@nspra.org

Web, www.nspra.org, Twitter, @nspra and Facebook, www.facebook.com/NSPRAssociation

Membership: educators and individuals interested in improving communications in education. Works to improve communication between educators and the public on the needs of schools. Provides educators with information on public relations and policy developments.

Internships, Fellowships, Grants

▶ **AGENCIES**

Bureau of Educational and Cultural Affairs (ECA) *(State Dept.), Global Educational Programs, 2200 C St. N.W., #4CC17 SA-5, 20520; (202) 632-6345. Anthony D. Koliha, Director.*

Web, http://eca.state.gov/about-bureau/organizational-structure/office-global-educational-programs

Administers the Hubert H. Humphrey Fellowship Program, the Community College Initiative Program, and the Benjamin A. Gilman International Scholarship Program, and programs for the exchange and professional development of secondary school teachers and educators.

Harry S. Truman Scholarship Foundation, *712 Jackson Pl. N.W., 20006-4901; (202) 395-4831. Terry Babcock Lumish, Executive Secretary, (202) 395-3545.*

General email, office@truman.gov

Web, www.truman.gov, Twitter, @TrumanApp and Facebook, www.facebook.com/TrumanScholarship

Memorial to Harry S. Truman established by Congress. Provides students preparing for careers in public service with graduate school scholarship funding. (Candidates are nominated by their respective colleges or universities while in their third year of undergraduate study.)

National Endowment for the Arts (NEA), *400 7th St. S.W., 20506; (202) 682-5400. Maria Rosario Jackson, Chair;*

Ann Eilers, Deputy Chairman for Management and Budget, (202) 682-5534. TTY, (202) 682-5082.

General email, publicaffairs@arts.gov

Web, www.arts.gov, Twitter, @NEAarts and Facebook, www.facebook.com/NationalEndowmentfor theArts

Independent grant-making agency. Awards grants to support artistic excellence, creativity, and innovation for the benefit of individuals and communities. Works through partnerships with state arts agencies, local leaders, other federal agencies, and the philanthropic sector. Main funding categories include Art Works (replaces Access to Artistic Excellence and Learning in the Arts for Children and Youth); Challenge America Fast-Track (for art projects in underserved communities); and Our Town (for art projects that contribute to the livability of communities).

National Endowment for the Humanities (NEH), *400 7th St. S.W., 20506; (202) 606-8400. Shelly C. Lowe, Chair; Janice Bell, Librarian, (202) 606-8572. Library, (202) 633-8244. Library, (202) 633-4680. TTY, (800) 877-8399.*

General email, questions@neh.gov

Web, www.neh.gov, Twitter, @NEHgov, Facebook, www .facebook.com/nehgov and YouTube, www.youtube.com/ channel/UCPQ3xb0ky2WsNM_U1FKjrNQ

Independent federal grant-making agency. Awards grants to individuals and institutions for research, scholarship, and educational and public programs (including broadcasts, museum exhibitions, lectures, and symposia) in the humanities (defined as study of archaeology; history; jurisprudence; language; linguistics; literature; philosophy; comparative religion; ethics; history, criticism, and theory of the arts; and humanistic aspects of the social sciences). Funds preservation of books, newspapers, historical documents, and photographs. Library open by appointment only.

National Endowment for the Humanities (NEH), *Education Programs, 400 7th St. S.W., 20506; (202) 606-8500. Carol Peters, Director, (202) 606-8285.*

General email, education@neh.gov

Web, www.neh.gov/divisions/education and Twitter, @NEH_Education

Supports program development and professional development opportunities for K–12 and higher education faculty.

National Science Foundation (NSF), *Education and Human Resources Directorate (HRD), 2415 Eisenhower Ave., Room C 11000, Alexandria, VA 22314; (703) 292-8600. Fax, (703) 292-9179. Sylvia M. Butterfield, Assistant Director (Acting), (703) 292-5333.*

Web, www.nsf.gov/dir/index.jsp?org=ehr

Provides fellowships and grants for graduate research and teacher education, instructional materials, and studies on the quality of existing science and mathematics programs. Participates in international studies.

National Science Foundation (NSF), *Graduate Education Division, 2415 Eisenhower Ave., Room W*

11200, Alexandria, VA 22314; (703) 292-8630. Fax, (703) 292-9048. Lee L. Zia, Director (Acting), 703- 292-5140. Web, www.nsf.gov/div/index.jsp?div=dge

Supports activities to strengthen the education of research scientists and engineers; promotes career development; offers predoctoral fellowships and traineeships for study and research.

National Security Education Program (NSEP), 4800 Mark Center Dr., #08F09-02, Alexandria, VA 22350-7000 (mailing address: P.O. Box 20010, Arlington, VA 22209); (703) 409-8653. Fax, (703) 692-2615. Michael A. Nugent, Director. Boren Awards information, (800) 618-6737. General email, nsep@nsep.gov Web, https://nsep.gov

Administers Boren Awards and Language Flagship programs; provides scholarships, fellowships, and institutional grants to students and academics with an interest in foreign affairs and national security.

President's Commission on White House Fellowships, 712 Jackson Pl. N.W., 20503; (202) 395-4522. Fax, (202) 395-6179. Elizabeth Pinkerton, Director. General email, whitehousefellows@who.eop.gov Web, www.whitehouse.gov/participate/fellows

Nonpartisan commission that provides professionals from all sectors of national life with the opportunity to observe firsthand the processes of the federal government. Fellows work for one year as special assistants to cabinet members or to principal members of the White House staff. Qualified applicants have demonstrated superior accomplishments early in their careers and have a commitment to leadership and public service.

Smithsonian Institution, Fellowships and Internships, 470 L'Enfant Plaza S.W., #7102, 20013-7012 (mailing address: P.O. Box 37012, MS 902, Washington, DC 20013-7012); (202) 633-7070. Vacant, Director. General email, siofi@si.edu Web, si.edu/ofi and Twitter, @SmithsonianOFI

Administers internships and fellowships in residence for study and research at the Smithsonian Institution in history of science and technology, American and cultural history, history of art, anthropology, evolutionary and systematic biology, environmental sciences, astrophysics and astronomy, earth sciences, and tropical biology.

Woodrow Wilson International Center for Scholars, 1300 Pennsylvania Ave. N.W., 20004-3027; (202) 691-4000. Fax, (202) 691-4001. Mark Green, President. Press, (202) 691-4217. General email, wwics@wilsoncenter.org Web, www.wilsoncenter.org, Twitter, @thewilsoncenter, Fellowship information, fellowships@wilsoncenter.org and Library, library.email@wilsoncenter.org

Supports research in the social studies and humanities. Awards fellowships to individuals from a wide variety of backgrounds, including academia, government, the non-profit sector, and the corporate world. Hosts public policy

and senior scholars who conduct research and write in a variety of disciplines. Offers grant competitions through regional programs, including the Asia Program, the Kennan Institute, East European Studies, and the Canada Institute. Library open for scholars.

▶**NONGOVERNMENTAL**

American Assn. of University Women (AAUW), 1310 L St. N.W., #1000, 20005; (202) 785-7700. Fax, (202) 872-1425. Gloria L. Blackwell, Chief Executive Officer, ext. 7608. Toll-free, (800) 326-2289. TTY, (202) 785-7777. General email, connect@aauw.org Web, www.aauw.org, Twitter, @aauw and Facebook, www.facebook.com/AAUW.National

Awards fellowships and grants to women for various areas of study and educational pursuit. Offers fellowships to women coming to the United States for one year of graduate study. Awards grants to women returning to school for postbaccalaureate education or professional development.

American Political Science Assn. (APSA), Congressional Fellowship Program, 1527 New Hampshire Ave. N.W., 20036-1203; (202) 483-2512. Fax, (202) 483-2657. Meghan McConaughey, Director. General email, cfp@apsanet.org Web, https://apsanet.org/cfp

Places midcareer political scientists, journalists, faculty of medical schools (Robert Wood Johnson Fellowships, Health and Aging Policy Fellowships), and federal executives in congressional offices and committees for nine-month fellowships. Individual government agencies nominate federal executive participants.

Ashoka: Innovators for the Public, 1700 N. Moore St., #2000, Arlington, VA 22209; (703) 527-8300. Fax, (703) 527-8383. Bill Drayton, Chief Executive Officer. General email, info@ashoka.org Web, www.ashoka.org and Twitter, @Ashoka

Supports fellowships for individuals with ideas for social change and entrepreneurship in 70 developing nations. Provides fellows with research support, organizational networking, legal counseling, economic support, and business consulting. Seeks to educate the public about the developing world and the work of its fellows.

Center for the Study of the Presidency and Congress, 601 13th St. N.W., #1050N, 20005; (202) 872-9800. Fax, (202) 872-9811. Glenn C. Nye III, President. General email, center@thepresidency.org Web, www.thepresidency.org, Twitter, @CSPC_DC and YouTube, www.youtube.com/channel/UCYGc48akXXw MgHRtO7v-MWA

Provides fellowships to undergraduate and graduate students studying the U.S. presidency, the public policy-making process, and presidential relations with Congress, allies, the media, and the public.

Congressional Black Caucus Foundation, 1720 Massachusetts Ave. N.W., 20036-1903; (202) 263-2800.

Paul E. Dumars Jr., Co-President (Acting); Donna Fisher-Lewis, Co-President (Acting).
General email, info@cbcfinc.org

Web, www.cbcfinc.org, Twitter, @CBCFInc, Facebook, www.facebook.com/CBCFinc and YouTube, www.youtube.com/user/CBCFINC

Conducts public policy research on issues of concern to African Americans. Sponsors internships and scholarships, as well as fellowship programs in which professionals and academic candidates work on congressional committees and subcommittees.

Council for International Exchange of Scholars, 1400 K St. N.W., #700, 20005; (202) 686-4000. Fax, (202) 686-4029. Allan E. Goodman, President, (212) 984-5321.
General email, scholars@iie.org

Web, www.cies.org, Twitter, @FulbrightPrgrm and Facebook, www.facebook.com/fulbright

Cooperates with the U.S. government in administering Fulbright grants for university teaching and advanced research abroad. (A division of the Institute of International Education.)

Education Trust, 1501 K St. N.W., #200, 20005 (mailing address: 200 Massachusetts Ave. N.W., #700, Washington, DC 20001); (202) 293-1217. Fax, (202) 293-2605.
John B. King Jr., President; Denise Forte, Chief Executive Officer (Acting).
General email, lsingleton@edtrust.org

Web, https://edtrust.org and Twitter, @EdTrust

Researches and disseminates data on student achievement. Provides assistance to school districts, colleges, and other organizations to raise student achievement, especially among poor and minority students. Monitors legislation and regulations.

Eisenhower Institute, 818 Connecticut Ave. N.W., #400, 20006 (mailing address: 200 Massachusetts Ave. N.W., #700, Washington, DC 20001); (202) 628-4444. Fax, (202) 628-4445. Lauren Cole, Program Manager, Washington Office.
General email, ei@gettysburg.edu

Web, www.eisenhowerinstitute.org and Twitter, @eighbc

Provides scholarships, fellowships, internships, and other sponsored opportunities for students to participate in dialogue with prominent figures and to pursue study of public policy and related fields. (Affiliated with Gettysburg College in Gettysburg, Pa.)

The Fund for American Studies (TFAS), 1706 New Hampshire Ave. N.W., 20009; (202) 986-0384. Fax, (202) 986-0390. Roger R. Ream, President.
General email, info@tfas.org

Web, www.tfas.org, Twitter, @TFASorg and Facebook, www.facebook.com/TFASorg

Sponsors internships for college students on comparative political and economic systems, business and government affairs, political journalism, philanthropy, and voluntary service; grants scholarships. Interest include the principles of limited government, free-market economics.

Grantmakers in Health, 1100 Connecticut Ave. N.W., #1100, 20036; (202) 452-8331. Fax, (202) 452-8340. Cara James, President.
General email, info@gih.org

Web, www.gih.org and Twitter, @GIHealth

Seeks to increase the capacity of health foundations and giving programs to enhance public health and health education. Fosters information exchange among grantmakers. Publications include a bulletin on current news in health and human services.

The Herb Block Foundation, 1730 M St. N.W., #1020, 20036; (202) 223-8801. Fax, (202) 223-8804. Marcela Brane, Chief Executive Officer; Sarah Armstrong Alex, Executive Director.
General email, info@herbblock.org

Web, www.herbblockfoundation.org, Twitter, @TheHerbBlockFdn and Facebook, www.facebook.com/herbblockfoundation

Awards grants to charitable and educational programs that combat discrimination and poverty and promote citizen involvement in government. Provides scholarships to individuals seeking to attend community colleges in the Washington, D.C., area. Awards prizes for excellence in editorial cartooning to serve as a tool for freedom and to address social issues.

Institute for Responsible Citizenship, 1227 25th St. N.W., 6th Floor, 20037; (202) 660-2501. William (Bill) A. Keyes IV, President.
Web, www.theinstitute.net and Facebook, www.facebook.com/responsiblecitizenship

Offers grants, internships, and leadership courses for African American men scholars. Academic areas for internships include art, business, finance, philanthropy, education, government, health care, science, technology, law, public relations, and religion.

Institute of Current World Affairs, 1818 N St. N.W., #460, 20036; (202) 364-4068. Gregory Feifer, Executive Director.
General email, icwa@icwa.org

Web, www.icwa.org, Twitter, @ICWAnews and Facebook, www.facebook.com/InstituteOfCurrentWorldAffairs

Offers two-year fellowships to support the independent study of international region-specific issues. Fellows write monthly newsletters to update the institute on their progress and findings. Presents public events on international topics.

Marine Technology Society, One Thomas Circle, # 700, 20005; (202) 717-8705. Fax, (202) 347-4302. Kristina Norman, Executive Director (Acting), (202) 827-7171.
General email, mtsoffice@mtsociety.org

Web, www.mtsociety.org, Twitter, @MTSociety and Facebook, www.facebook.com/MarineTechnologySociety/?ref=hl

Provides scholarships to high school and postsecondary students in marine-related programs with focus in marine technology, marine engineering, and marine science.

National Journalism Center, *11480 Commerce Park Dr., #600, Reston, VA 20191; (703) 318-9608. Fax, (703) 318-9122. Emily Jashinsky, Director. Toll-free, (800) 872-1776. General email, njc@yaf.org*

Web, www.nationaljournalismcenter.org

Sponsors a comprehensive internship program in journalism composed of a series of training seminars that enhance students' knowledge of policy reporting in the areas of economics, education, and business. (Affiliated with Young America's Foundation.)

The Washington Center for Internships and Academic Seminars, *1333 16th St. N.W., 20036-2205; (202) 238-7900. Fax, (202) 238-7700. Kim Churches, President. Toll-free, (800) 486-8921. General email, info@twc.edu*

Web, www.twc.edu, Twitter, @TWCInternships and Facebook, www.facebook.com/TWCInternships

Arranges congressional, agency, and public service internships for college undergraduate students for credit. Sponsors classes and lectures as part of the internship program. Scholarships and stipends available. Fee for internship and housing assistance.

Professional Development, Interests, and Benefits

Elementary and Secondary Education (OESE) *(Education Dept.), Discretionary Grants and Support Services (DGSS), Effective Educator Development Programs (EEDP), Lyndon B. Johnson Bldg., 400 Maryland Ave. S.W., 20202; (202) 453-7740. Venitia Richardson, Director. Web, https://oese.ed.gov/offices/office-of-discretionary-grants-support-services/effective-educator-development-programs and General email, eddmainoffice@ed.gov*

Administers discretionary grants that support the implementation of recruitment, preparation, and professional development programs for teachers and principals.

Elementary and Secondary Education (OESE) *(Education Dept.), Discretionary Grants and Support Services (DGSS), Well-Rounded Education Programs (WREP), Lyndon B. Johnson Bldg., 400 Maryland Ave. S.W., 20202-5950; (202) 453-5501. Jennifer Todd, Director. Web, https://oese.ed.gov/offices/office-of-discretionary-grants-support-services/well-rounded-education-programs*

Administers discretionary grant programs that support activities designed to advance literacy skills, provide professional learning opportunities to teachers to increase the performance of students in mathematics and science, create leadership pipelines for schools in need of improvement, support arts education, and pay all or a portion of advanced placement fees on behalf of low-income students.

American Assn. of Colleges for Teacher Education, *1602 L St. N.W., #601, 20036; (202) 293-2450. Fax, (202) 457-8095. Lynn M. Gangone, President, (202) 478-4505. General email, aacte@aacte.org*

Web, www.aacte.org, Twitter, @aacte and Facebook, www.facebook.com/aacte

Membership: colleges and universities with teacher education programs. Informs members about state and federal policies affecting teacher education and about professional issues such as accreditation, certification, and assessment. Collects and analyzes information on education.

American Assn. of School Administrators (AASA), *1615 Duke St., Alexandria, VA 22314; (703) 528-0700. Fax, (703) 841-1543. Daniel (Dan) A. Domenech, Executive Director, (703) 875-0722. General email, info@aasa.org*

Web, www.aasa.org, Twitter, @aasahq and Facebook, www.facebook.com/AASApage

Membership: more than 13,000 educational leaders, including superintendents, chief executive officers, senior-level school administrators, and professors, as well as aspiring school system leaders. Seeks to support and develop effective school system leaders through publications and professional development workshops.

American Federation of School Administrators, *815 16th St. N.W., #4125, 20006; (202) 986-4209. Fax, (202) 986-4211. Ernest A. Logan, President; Paul Wolotsky, Executive Director. General email, afsa@afsaadmin.org*

Web, www.theschoolleader.org, Twitter, @AFSAUnion and Facebook, www.facebook.com/AFSAUnion

Membership: school administrators, professionals, and supervisors in the United States, Puerto Rico, and U.S. Virgin Islands. Helps members negotiate pay, benefits, and better working conditions; conducts training programs and workshops. Monitors legislation and regulations. (Affiliated with the AFL-CIO.)

American Federation of Teachers (AFT), *555 New Jersey Ave. N.W., 20001-2079; (202) 879-4400. Randi Weingarten, President. Web, www.aft.org, Twitter, @AFTUnion and Facebook, www.facebook.com/AFTUnion*

Membership: over 1.7 million public school teachers and staff, higher education faculty and professional staff, early childhood educators, federal, state, and local government employees, and nurses and health care professionals. Assists members with contract negotiation and grievances; conducts training programs and workshops. Monitors legislation and regulations. (Affiliated with the AFL-CIO.)

American Political Science Assn. (APSA), *1527 New Hampshire Ave. N.W., 20036-1203; (202) 483-2512.*

Fax, (202) 483-2657. Steven Rathgeb Smith, Executive Director.

General email, apsa@apsanet.org

Web, www.apsanet.org, Twitter, @APSAtweets and Facebook, www.facebook.com/likeAPSA

Membership: political scientists, primarily college and university professors. Promotes scholarly inquiry into all aspects of political science, including international affairs and comparative government. Works to increase public understanding of politics; provides services to facilitate and enhance research, teaching, and professional development of its members. Seeks to improve the status of women and minorities in the profession. Offers congressional fellowships, workshops, and awards.

Assn. for Supervision and Curriculum Development (ASCD), 1703 N. Beauregard St., Alexandria, VA 22311-1714; (703) 578-9600. Fax, (703) 575-5400. Ranjit Sidhu, Executive Director. Toll-free, (800) 933-2723.

General email, member@ascd.org

Web, www.ascd.org and Twitter, @ASCD

Membership: professional educators internationally, including superintendents, supervisors, principals, teachers, professors of education, and school board members. Develops professional development programs, products, and services for educators. Holds an annual conference; offers webinars, consulting services, books, and other publications. (Formerly the Assn. for Supervision and Curriculum Development.)

Assn. of School Business Officials International, 44790 Maynard Sq., #200, Ashburn, VA 20147; (703) 478-0405. Fax, (703) 478-0205. David Lewis, Executive Director, (703) 708-7061. Toll-free, (866) 682-2729.

General email, asboreq@asbointl.org

Web, https://asbointl.org, Twitter, @ASBOINTL and Facebook, www.facebook.com/ASBOInternational

Membership: administrators, directors, and others involved in school business management. Provides news and information concerning management best practices and the effective use of educational resources. Hosts conferences; sponsors research; monitors legislation and regulations.

Assn. of Teacher Educators, 11350 Random Hills Rd., #800, PMB 6, Fairfax, VA 22030 (mailing address: P.O. Box 793, Manassas, VA 20113); (703) 659-1708. Alisa Chapman, Executive Director.

General email, info@ate1.org

Web, www.ate1.org, Twitter, @AssocTeacherEd and Facebook, www.facebook.com/assocoftchreducators

Membership: individuals and public and private agencies involved with teacher education. Seeks to promote quality teacher education for school-based and post secondary teacher educators though clinical practise and research; conducts workshops and conferences; produces and disseminates publications.

Center on System Leadership, 2121 K St. N.W., #700, 20037; (202) 449-5060. Fax, (202) 293-1560. Anthony Mackay, Chief Executive Officer.

General email, info@ncee.org

Web, www.ncee.org/what-we-do/center-on-system-leadership and Twitter, @nislorg

Offers research-based professional development programs designed to give principals the knowledge and skills they need to be instructional leaders and improve student achievement in their schools. (Subsidiary of National Center on Education and the Economy [NCEE].)

Council for Advancement and Support of Education, 1201 Eye St. N.W., #530A, 20005-4701; (202) 328-2273. Fax, (202) 387-4973. Sue Cunningham, President, ext. 5677.

General email, membersupportcenter@case.org

Web, www.case.org, Twitter, @CASEAdvance and Facebook, www.facebook.com/caseadvance

Membership: two-year and four-year colleges, universities, and independent schools. Offers professional education, webinars, and training programs to members; advises members on institutional advancement issues, including fundraising, public relations programs, government relations, and management. Library open to professional members by appointment.

Council of Chief State School Officers, 1 Massachusetts Ave. N.W., #800, 20001-1431; (202) 336-7000. Carissa Moffat Miller, Chief Executive Director. Press, (202) 336-7034.

General email, communications@ccsso.org

Web, http://ccsso.org, Twitter, @CCSSO and Facebook, www.facebook.com/ccsso

Membership: the public officials who head departments of elementary and secondary education in the states, the District of Columbia, the Department of Defense Education Activity, and five U.S. extrastate jurisdictions. Provides leadership, advocacy, and technical assistance on major educational issues. Seeks member consensus on major educational issues and acts as advocate on issue positions to civic and professional organizations, federal agencies, Congress, and the public.

Federal Education Assn., 1201 16th St. N.W., #117, 20036; (202) 822-7850. Fax, (202) 822-7867. Brian Chance, President; Richard Tarr, Executive Director (Acting).

General email, fea@feaonline.org

Web, www.feaonline.org, Twitter, @FedEdAssoc and Facebook, www.facebook.com/FedEdAssoc/

Membership: teachers and personnel of Defense Dept. schools for military dependents in the United States and abroad. Provides professional development through workshops and publications. Monitors legislation and regulations.

International Accreditors for Continuing Education and Training (IACET), 21670 Ridgetop Circle, #170, Sterling, VA 20166; (703) 763-0705. Fax, (703) 738-7194. Casandra Blassingame, Chief Executive Officer, ext. 101.

General email, info@iacet.org

Web, www.iacet.org, Twitter, @IACETorg and *Facebook, www.facebook.com/IACETOrg*

Membership: education and training organizations and individuals who use the Continuing Education Unit. (The CEU is defined as ten contact hours of participation in an organized continuing education program that is noncredit.) Authorizes organizations that issue the CEU; develops criteria and guidelines for use of the CEU.

National Assn. of Biology Teachers, *11 Main St., Suite D, Warrenton, VA 20186 (mailing address: P.O. Box 3363, Warrenton, VA 20188); (703) 264-9696. Fax, (202) 962-3939. Jaclyn Reeves-Pepin, Executive Director, ext. 4. Toll-free, (888) 501-6228.*

General email, office@nabt.org

Web, www.nabt.org

Membership: biology teachers and others interested in life sciences education at the elementary, secondary, and collegiate levels. Provides professional development opportunities through its publication program, summer workshops, conventions, and national award programs.

National Assn. of Secondary School Principals, *1904 Association Dr., Reston, VA 20191-1537; (703) 860-0200. Ronn Nozoe, Chief Executive Officer. Toll-free, (800) 253-7746.*

Web, www.nassp.org, Twitter, @nassp, Facebook, www.facebook.com/principals and *YouTube, www.youtube.com/user/NASSPtv*

Membership: principals and assistant principals of middle schools and senior high schools, both public and private, and college-level teachers of secondary education. Conducts training programs for members; serves as clearinghouse for information on secondary school administration. Student activities office provides student councils, student activity advisers, and national and junior honor societies with information on national associations.

National Business Education Assn., *1914 Association Dr., #B, Reston, VA 20191-1596; (703) 860-8300. Fax, (703) 620-4483. Joseph McClary, Executive Director, ext. 101.*

General email, nbea@nbea.org

Web, www.nbea.org and *Twitter, @NBEA*

Membership: business education teachers and others interested in the field. Provides information on business education; offers teaching materials; sponsors conferences. Monitors legislation and regulations affecting business education.

National Council on Teacher Quality, *1032 15th St. N.W., #242, 20005; (202) 393-0020. Kate Walsh, President.*

General email, help@pathtoteach.org

Web, www.nctq.org, Twitter, @NCTQ, Facebook, www.facebook.com/teacherquality and *Path to Teach, www.pathtoteach.org*

Advocacy group for teacher quality and effectiveness. Interests include state and district teacher policy reform. Reviews and reports on national teacher training programs, layoff policies, teacher contracts, and state performance. Analyzes school board policies, teacher performance evaluations, and salary schedules to aid dialogue between school officials and teachers unions.

National Education Assn. (NEA), *1201 16th St. N.W., 20036-3290; (202) 833-4000. Fax, (202) 822-7974. Rebecca (Becky) S. Pringle, President; Kim A. Anderson, Executive Director. Press, (202) 822-7823.*

Web, www.nea.org, Twitter, @NEAToday and *Facebook, www.facebook.com/neatoday*

Membership: more than 3.2 million educators from preschool to university graduate programs. Promotes the interest of the profession of teaching and the cause of public education in the United States. Monitors legislation and regulations at state and national levels.

National Science Teachers Assn., *1840 Wilson Blvd., Arlington, VA 22201-3000; (703) 243-7100. Fax, (703) 243-7177. Erika Shugart, Executive Director.*

General email, pubinfo@nsta.org

Web, www.nsta.org, Twitter, @nsta, Facebook, www.facebook.com/NSTA.FB and *Legislative Affairs, legaffairs@nsta.org*

Membership: science teachers from elementary through college levels, supervisors, administrators, scientists, business and industry representatives, and others involved in and committed to science education. Provides forum for exchange of information. Monitors legislation and regulations.

NEA Foundation, *1201 16th St. N.W., 20036-3207; (202) 822-7840. Fax, (202) 822-7779. Sara A. Sneed, President.*

General email, NEAFoundation@nea.org

Web, www.neafoundation.org, Twitter, @NEAFoundation, Facebook, www.facebook.com/theneafoundation and *YouTube, www.youtube.com/user/neafoundation*

Offers grants and programs to public educators to improve teaching techniques, increase classroom innovations, and otherwise further professional development. Grant areas include science, technology, engineering, mathematics teaching and learning, with a current special emphasis on "green" grants. Program specialties include strategies for improving achievement rates for poor and minority students.

NRTA: AARP's Educator Community, *601 E St. N.W., 20049; (202) 434-2380. Joe Larew, President of AARP Services. AARP, (202) 434-3525. Toll-free, (800) 996-7566.*

General email, gruiz@aarp.org

Web, www.aarp.org/about-aarp/nrta, Twitter, @NRTUSA and *Facebook, www.facebook.com/NRTA.AARP*

Membership: active and retired teachers, other school personnel (elementary through postsecondary), and those interested in education and learning over age 50. Provides members with information on relevant national issues. Holds webinars and Podcasts. Provides state associations of retired school personnel with technical assistance. (Formerly the National Retired Teachers Assn.)

TESOL International Assn., *1925 Ballenger Ave., #550, Alexandria, VA 22314-6820; (703) 518-2500. Amber Crowell Kelleher, Executive Director. Toll-free, (888) 888-4741.*
General email, info@tesol.org
Web, www.tesol.org, Twitter, @TESOL_Assn and Facebook, www.facebook.com/tesol.assn

Provides professional development programs and career services for teachers of English to speakers of other languages. Sponsors professional development programs and provides career management services. Promotes research, standards, and advocacy.

Research

Institute of Education Sciences *(Education Dept.), 550 12th St. S.W., 20202; (202) 245-6940. Fax, (202) 245-6113. Mark Schneider, Director, (202) 245-6909. Library, (202) 205-5015.*
General email, contact.ies@ed.gov
Web, https://ies.ed.gov, Twitter, @IESResearch and Facebook, www.facebook.com/IESResearch

Provides scientific evidence on which to ground education practice and policy through the work of four centers dealing with education research, education statistics, education evaluation and regional assistance, and special education research. Funds studies on ways to improve academic achievement, conducts large-scale evaluations of federal education programs, and reports a wide array of statistics on the condition of education. Library open by appointment.

Institute of Education Sciences *(Education Dept.), National Center for Education Evaluation and Regional Assistance (NCEE), 550 12th St. S.W., #4160, 20202; (202) 245-6940. Matthew (Matt) Soldner, Commissioner, (202) 245-8385.*
Web, https://ies.ed.gov/ncee and Twitter, @IESResearch

Conducts large-scale evaluations and provides research-based technical assistance and information about high-quality research to educators and policymakers. Programs include What Works Clearinghouse, Regional Educational Laboratories Program, and the ERIC library of education research and resources.

Institute of Education Sciences *(Education Dept.), National Center for Education Research (NCER), 550 12th St. S.W., 20202; (202) 245-6940. Fax, (202) 245-6113. Elizabeth (Liz) Albro, Commissioner, (202) 245-8495.*
Web, https://ies.ed.gov/ncer

Supports research to improve student outcomes and education quality; supports training programs to prepare researchers to conduct high-quality scientific education research.

Institute of Education Sciences *(Education Dept.), National Center for Education Statistics (NCES), 550 12th St. S.W., #4061, 20202; (202) 245-6168. Peggy Carr, Commissioner. Press, (202) 245-8419.*
Web, https://nces.ed.gov, Twitter, @EdNCES and Facebook, www.facebook.com/EdNCES

Primary federal entity for collecting and analyzing data related to education. Administers the National Assessment of Educational Progress (NAEP), the "Nation's Report Card."

Institute of Education Sciences *(Education Dept.), National Center for Special Education Research (NCSER), 550 12th St. S.W., #4144, 20202; (202) 245-6940. Fax, (202) 245-6113. Joan McLaughlin, Commissioner, (202) 245-8201.*
Web, http://ies.ed.gov/ncser

Sponsors a comprehensive program of special education research designed to expand the knowledge and understanding of infants, toddlers, and children with disabilities.

National Library of Education *(Education Dept.), 400 Maryland Ave. S.W., 20202-5721; (202) 205-5015. Fax, (202) 401-0547. Karen Tate, Director. Toll-free, (800) 424-1616. TTY, (800) 877-8339.*
General email, askalibrarian@ed.gov
Web, http://ies.ed.gov/ncee/projects/nle

Provides information and answers questions on education statistics and research. Collection focuses on education research but also includes fields such as law, public policy, economics, urban affairs, and sociology. Includes current and historical Education Dept. publications. Library open to the public by appointment only.

American Councils for International Education: ACTR/ ACCELS, *1828 L St. N.W., #1200, 20036; (202) 833-7522. David P. Patton, President, ext. 137.*
General email, info@americancouncils.org
Web, www.americancouncils.org, Twitter, @AC_Global and Facebook, www.facebook.com/AmericanCouncils

Advances education and research worldwide through international programs focused on academic exchange, professional training, distance learning, curriculum and test development, delivery of technical assistance, research, evaluation, and institution building.

American Educational Research Assn., *1430 K St. N.W., #1200, 20005; (202) 238-3200. Fax, (202) 238-3250. Felice J. Levine, Executive Director, ext. 201.*
Web, www.aera.net, Twitter, @AERA_EdResearch and Facebook, www.facebook.com/AERAEdResearch

Membership: educational researchers affiliated with universities and colleges, school systems, think tanks, and federal and state agencies. Publishes original research in education; sponsors publication of reference works in educational research; conducts continuing education programs; studies status of women and minorities in the education field.

American Institutes for Research, *1400 Crystal Dr., 10th Floor, Arlington, VA 22202-3289; (202) 403-5000. Fax, (202) 403-5000. David Myers, Chief Executive Officer. Press, (202) 403-6347.*
General email, inquiry@air.org
Web, www.air.org, Twitter, @AIRInforms and Facebook, www.facebook.com/AmericanInstitutesfor Research/?ref=share

Conducts research on educational evaluation and improvement. Develops and implements assessment and testing services that improve student education as well as meet the requirements set forth by state and federally mandated programs.

The Brookings Institution, *Governance Studies, 1755 Massachusetts Ave. N.W., 20036; (202) 797-6090. (202) 797-6288. Darrell M. West, Director, (202) 797-6481.*
Web, www.brookings.edu/governance, Twitter, @BrookingsGov and Twitter, Director, @DarrWest

Conducts research and provides policy recommendations on topics in education.

Council on Governmental Relations, *1200 New York Ave. N.W., #460, 20005; (202) 289-6655. Fax, (202) 289-6698. Wendy Streitz, President, ext. 111.*
Web, www.cogr.edu

Membership: research universities, institutes, and medical colleges maintaining federally supported programs. Advises members and makes recommendations to government agencies regarding policies and regulations affecting federally funded university research.

Knowledge Alliance, *777 6th St. N.W., #610, 20001; (202) 770-2218. Rachel Dinkes, Chief Executive Officer.*
General email, jball@knowledgeall.net
Web, www.knowledgeall.net and Twitter, @KnowledgeAll

Membership: university-based educational research and development organizations, educational entrepreneurs, and technical assistance providers. Promotes use of scientifically based solutions for improving teaching and learning. (Formerly the National Education Knowledge Industry Assn.)

National Assn. of Independent Colleges and Universities, *1025 Connecticut Ave. N.W., #700, 20036-5405; (202) 785-8866. Fax, (202) 835-0003. Barbara K. Mistick, President.*
General email, geninfo@naicu.edu
Web, www.naicu.edu and Twitter, @NAICUtweets

Membership: liberal arts colleges, research universities, church-related and faith-related institutions, historically black colleges and universities, women's colleges, performing and visual arts institutions, two-year colleges; graduate schools of law, medicine, engineering, business, and other professions. Tracks campus trends, conducts research, analyzes higher-education issues, and helps coordinate state-level activities. Interests include federal policies that affect student aid, taxation, and government regulation. Monitors legislation and regulations.

RAND Corp., *Washington Office, 1200 S. Hayes St., Arlington, VA 22202-5050; (703) 413-1100. Fax, (703) 413-8111. Nicholas Burger, Director.*
Web, www.rand.org

Conducts research on education policy. (Headquarters in Santa Monica, Calif.)

Urban Institute, *Center on Education Data and Policy, 500 L'Enfant Plaza S.W., 20024; (202) 833-7200. Matthew Chingos, Vice President.*
General email, edp@urban.org
Web, www.urban.org/policy-centers/center-education-data-and-policy and Facebook, www.facebook.com/urbaninstitute

Conducts policy research on a wide range of issues from pre-kindergarten through postsecondary education, including research on universal pre-kindergarten programs, school choice, teacher diversity, school segregation, college affordability, and student loan debt. Advances evidence-based analysis through the creation of tools for accessing and analyzing data.

LIBRARIES, TECHNOLOGY, AND EDUCATIONAL MEDIA

General

▶ **AGENCIES**

Dibner Library of the History of Science and Technology *(Smithsonian Institution), National Museum of American History, 10th St. and Constitution Ave. N.W., MS 672, 20560 (mailing address: P.O. Box 37012, MS 154, Washington, DC 20013-7012); (202) 633-3872. Lilla Vekerdy, Head of Special Collections. Press, (202) 633-1522.*
General email, Dibnerlibrary@si.edu
Web, www.library.si.edu/libraries/dibner, Twitter, @SILibraries and Facebook, www.facebook.com/SmithsonianLibraries/

Collection includes major holdings in the history of science and technology dating from the fifteenth century to the nineteenth century. Extensive collections in engineering, transportation, chemistry, mathematics, physics, electricity, and astronomy. Open to the public by appointment.

Education Dept., *Educational Technology (OET), Lyndon B. Johnson Bldg., 400 Maryland Ave. S.W., #5W114, 20202; (202) 401-1444. Kristina Ishmael, Deputy Director.*
General email, tech@ed.gov
Web, https://tech.ed.gov and Twitter, @OfficeofEdTech

Develops national educational policy and advocates the transition from print-based to digital learning.

Institute of Museum and Library Services, *955 L'Enfant Plaza North S.W., #4000, 20024-2135; (202) 653-4657. Fax, (202) 653-4600. Crosby Kemper III, Director, (202) 653-4798. Communications and Government Affairs, (202) 653-4757. Grants and policy management, (202) 653-4759. Library services, (202) 653-4700. Museum services, (202) 653-4789. TTY, (202) 653-4614.*
General email, imlsinfo@imls.gov

Web, www.imls.gov, Twitter, @US_IMLS and Facebook, www.facebook.com/USIMLS

Awards grants to help museums and libraries make their services and resources more accessible for all as well as grants to improve the care of museum collections and the recruitment, training, and development of library and museum staff. All types of libraries and museums are eligible, including African American history and culture museums, and institutions serving Native American, Hawaiian, and Alaskan tribal communities. Collects data, forms strategic partnerships, and advises policymakers and other federal agencies on museum, library, and information services.

National Archives and Records Administration (NARA), *National Archives Museum, 701 Constitution Ave. N.W., 20408; (202) 357-5000. Fax, (202) 357-5926. Patrick Madden, Executive Director. Museum Program Services, (202) 357-5210.*
Web, https://museum.archives.gov

Produces teaching packets that feature National Archives historic documents and online educational tools.

National Archives and Records Administration (NARA), *Presidential Libraries, 8601 Adelphi Rd., #2200, College Park, MD 20740-6001; (301) 837-3250. Fax, (301) 837-3199. Susan K. Donius, Director, (202) 357-7451.*
Web, www.archives.gov/presidential-libraries and Twitter, @OurPresidents

Administers thirteen presidential libraries. Directs all programs relating to acquisition, preservation, and research use of materials in presidential libraries; conducts oral history projects; publishes finding aids for research sources; provides reference service, including information from and about documentary holdings. Conducts community outreach; oversees museum exhibition programming.

National Endowment for the Humanities (NEH), *Division of Public Programs, 400 7th St. S.W., 20506; (202) 606-8269. Jeff Hardwick, Director (Acting), (202) 606-8287. General email, publicpgms@neh.gov*

Web, www.neh.gov/divisions/public and Twitter, @NEH_PubPrograms

Awards grants to libraries, museums, special projects, and media for projects that enhance public appreciation and understanding of the humanities through books and other resources in American library collections. Projects include conferences, exhibitions, essays, documentaries, radio programs, and lecture series.

National Endowment for the Humanities (NEH), *Office of Digital Humanities, 400 7th St. S.W., 20506; (202) 606-8401. Brett Bobley, Director.*

General email, odh@neh.gov

Web, www.neh.gov/divisions/odh and Twitter, @NEH_ODH

Encourages and supports projects that utilize or study the impact of digital technology on research, education, preservation, access, and public programming in the humanities.

Smithsonian Center for Learning and Digital Access, *600 Maryland Ave. S.W., #1005W, 20024 (mailing address: P.O. Box 37012, MS 508, Washington, DC 20013-7012); (202) 633-5330. Stephanie Norby, Director; Darren Milligan, Director of Educational Technology. General email, learning@si.edu*

Web, https://learninglab.si.edu/about/Smithsonian CenterforLearningandDigitalAccess, Twitter, @SmithsonianLab and Facebook, www.facebook.com/smithsonianeducation

Serves as the Smithsonian's central education office. Provides elementary and secondary teachers with programs, publications, audiovisual materials, regional workshops, and summer courses on using museums and primary source materials as teaching tools. Publishes books and other educational materials for teachers. (Associated with the Smithsonian Learning Lab.)

Smithsonian Institution, *Libraries, National Museum of Natural History, 10th St. and Constitution Ave. N.W., Room 29, 20560 (mailing address: P.O. Box 37012, MS 154, Washington, DC 20013-7012); (202) 633-2240. Tamar Evangelestia Dougherty, Director.*
Web, http://library.si.edu, Twitter, @SILibraries and Facebook, www.facebook.com/SmithsonianLibraries

Unites 20 libraries into one system supported by an online catalog of the combined collections. Maintains collection of general reference, biographical, and interdisciplinary materials; serves as an information resource on institution libraries and museum studies. Open to the public by appointment.

► CONGRESS

For a listing of relevant congressional committees and subcommittees, please see page 176 or the Appendix.

Library of Congress, *101 Independence Ave. S.E., 20540; (202) 707-5000. Carla Hayden, Librarian of Congress. Exhibition information, (202) 707-4604. Office of Communications, (202) 707-2905. Visitor information, (202) 707-8000.*
Web, www.loc.gov, Twitter, @librarycongress, Facebook, www.facebook.com/libraryofcongress, Copyright information, https://.copyright.gov, General reference, https://ask.loc.gov, Legislative information, www.congress.gov and YouTube, www.youtube.com/c/loc

The nation's library. Largest library in the world, collections include books, recordings, photographs, newspapers, maps, and manuscripts. Main research arm of congress and home of U.S. Copyright Office and the Law

Libraries at Federal Departments and Agencies

DEPARTMENTS
Agriculture, (301) 504-5755

Commerce, (202) 482-1154

Defense, (703) 695-1992

Education, (202) 205-5015

Energy, (202) 586-4849

Health and Human Services (Law), (202) 619-0190

Homeland Security, (831) 272-2437

Housing and Urban Development, (202) 708-1112; TTY, (202) 708-1455

Interior, (202) 208-5815

Justice, (202) 305-3000

Labor, (202) 693-6600

State, (202) 647-3002

Transportation, (202) 366-3282 or (202) 366-0746

Treasury, (202) 622-2000

Veterans Affairs, (202) 461-7573

AGENCIES
Agency for International Development, (202) 712-0579

Commission on Civil Rights, (202) 376-8110

Commodity Futures Trading Commission, (202) 418-5593 or (202) 418-5105

Consumer Product Safety Commission, (800) 638-2772

Drug Enforcement Administration, (202) 307-8932

Environmental Protection Agency, (202) 566-0556

Equal Employment Opportunity Commission, (202) 663-4630

Export-Import Bank, (202) 565-3984

Federal Communications Commission, (202) 418-0450

Federal Deposit Insurance Corporation, (202) 898-6993 or (703) 562-2200

Federal Election Commission, (202) 694-1120

Federal Labor Relations Authority, (202) 218-7770

Federal Maritime Commission, (202) 523-5762

Federal Reserve Board, Law library, (202) 452-2018; Research library, (202) 452-3333

Federal Trade Commission, (202) 326-3413

Government Accountability Office, (202) 512-5941

International Bank for Reconstruction and Development (World Bank)/International Monetary Fund, (202) 473-2000 or (202) 623-7054

National Aeronautics and Space Administration, (202) 358-0168

National Archives and Records Administration, (301) 837-3415

National Credit Union Administration (Law), (703) 518-6540

National Endowment for the Humanities, (202) 606-8244

National Institutes of Health, (301) 496-1080

National Labor Relations Board, (202) 273-3720

National Library of Medicine, (301) 594-5983

National Science Foundation, (703) 292-7830

Nuclear Regulatory Commission, (301) 415-6239

Occupational Safety and Health Review Commission, (202) 606-5729

Overseas Private Investment Corporation, (202) 336-8488

Postal Regulatory Commission, (202) 789-6800

Securities and Exchange Commission, (202) 551-5450

Small Business Administration Law Library, (202) 205-6533

Smithsonian Institution, (202) 633-2240

American Art and Portrait Gallery, (202) 633-8230

Botany and Horticulture, (202) 633-1685

Cooper Hewitt Library, (212) 849-8330

Dibner Library of the History of Science and Technology, (202) 633-3872

Freer Gallery of Art, (202) 633-0477

Hirshhorn Museum, (202) 633-2773

John Wesley Powell Library of Anthropology, (202) 633-1640

National Air and Space Museum, (703) 572-4175

National Museum of African American History, (202) 633-7498

National Museum of African Art, (202) 633-4680

National Museum of American History, (202) 633-3865

National Museum of Natural History, (202) 633-1680

National Museum of the American Indian, (301) 238-1376

National Postal Museum, (202) 633-5543

National Zoological Park, (202) 633-1030

Social Security Administration, (410) 965-1727

U.S. International Trade Commission, www.usitc.gov/elearning/hts/library/htms/resources1.htm

Law Library, (202) 205-3287

Main Library, (202) 205-3190

Library of Congress Divisions and Programs

African and Middle Eastern Division, (202) 707-7937; www.loc.gov/rr/amed

American Folklife Center, (202) 707-5510; www.loc.gov/folklife

Asian Division, (202) 707-3766; www.loc.gov/rr/asian

Business Reference Services, (202) 707-3156; www.loc.gov/rr/business

Cataloging Distribution Service, (202) 707-6100 or (855) 266-1884; www.loc.gov/cds

Center for the Book, (202) 707-5221; www.read.gov/cfb

Children's Literature Center, (202) 707-5535; www.loc.gov/rr/child

Copyright Office, (877) 476-0778; www.copyright.gov

Electronic Resources Center, (202) 707-3370; www.loc.gov/rr/main/ccc

European Division, (202) 707-4515; www.loc.gov/rr/european

Federal Library and Information Center Committee, (202) 707-4800; www.loc.gov/flicc/aboutfl.html

Geography and Map Division, (202) 707-6277; www.loc.gov/rr/geogmap

Hispanic Division, (202) 707-5397; www.loc.gov/rr/hispanic

Humanities and Social Science Division, (202) 707-3399; https://ask.loc.gov/history-humanities-social-sciences

Interlibrary Loan Division (CALM), (202) 707-5444; www.loc.gov/rr/loan

Interpretive Programs, (202) 707-5223

John W. Kluge Center, (202) 707-3302; www.loc.gov/programs/john-w-kluge-center/about-this-program

Law Library, (202) 707-5079; www.loc.gov/law/index.php

Law Library Reading Room, (202) 707-5080; www.loc.gov/law/visit/readingroom/index.php

Local History and Genealogy Reference Services, (202) 707-3399; www.loc.gov/rr/genealogy

Manuscript Division, Administrative office, (202) 707-5387; Reading room, (202) 707-5387; www.loc.gov/rr/mss

Mary Pickford Theater, (202) 707-5677; www.loc.gov/rr/mopic/pickford/index.html

Microform Reader Services, (202) 707-4773; www.loc.gov/rr/microform

Motion Picture, Broadcasting, and Recorded Sound Division, (202) 707-8572; www.loc.gov/rr/mopic

Music Division, Performing Arts Reading Room, (202) 707-5507; www.loc.gov/programs/john-w-kluge-center/about-this-program

National Library Service for the Blind and Physically Handicapped, (202) 707-5100 or (800) 424-8567; www.loc.gov/nls

Poetry and Literature Center, (202) 707-5394; www.loc.gov/poetry

Preservation Directorate, (202) 707-5000; www.loc.gov/preservation

Prints and Photographs Reading Room, (202) 707-6394; www.loc.gov/pictures

Rare Book and Special Collections Division, (202) 707-3448; www.loc.gov/rr/rarebook

Science, Technology and Business Division, (202) 707-5639; www.loc.gov/rr/scitech/general.html

Serial and Government Publications Division, (202) 707-5690; www.loc.gov/rr/news/brochure.html

---

Library of Congress. Timed entry pass for visitors required, details at loc.gov/visit.

Library of Congress, *Main Reading Room, Thomas Jefferson Bldg., 101 Independence Ave. S.E., #LJ 100, 20540-4660; (202) 707-3399. Fax, (202) 707-1957. Melissa Ball, Head.*
Web, www.loc.gov/rr/main

Point of access to the general collection of books and bound periodicals as well as electronic resources, including microform. Offers research orientations. Timed entry pass for visitors required, details at loc.gov/visit. Appointments recommended for researchers.

▶**NONGOVERNMENTAL**

American Library Assn., *Washington Office, 1615 New Hampshire Ave. N.W., 1st Floor, 20009-2520; (202) 628-8410. Fax, (202) 628-8419. Tracie Hall, Executive Director; Alan Inouye, Senior Director for Public Policy and Government Relations. Toll-free, (800) 941-8478.*

General email, alawash@alawash.org
Web, www.ala.org/offices/wo

Educational organization of librarians, trustees, and educators. Washington office monitors legislation and regulations on libraries and information science. Seeks to maintain and increase federal government funding of libraries and services. (Headquarters in Chicago, Ill.)

Assn. of Research Libraries (ARL), *21 Dupont Circle N.W., #800, 20036-1118; (202) 296-2296. Fax, (202) 872-0884. Mary Lee Kennedy, Executive Director.*
General email, webmgr@arl.org

Web, www.arl.org, Twitter, @ARLnews and Facebook, www.facebook.com/association.of.research. libraries

Membership: libraries and archives in major public and private universities, federal government agencies, and large public institutions in the United States and Canada. Interests include development of library resources in all formats, subjects, and languages; computer information systems and other bibliographic tools; management of research libraries; preservation of library materials; worldwide information policy; public access to federally funded research; and publishing and scholarly communication.

Audiovisual and Integrated Experience Assn. (AVIXA),
11242 Waples Mill Rd., #200, Fairfax, VA 22030; (703) 273-7200. Fax, (703) 278-8082. David Labuskes, Chief Executive Officer. Toll-free, (800) 659-7469.
General email, membership@avixa.org

Web, www.avixa.org, Twitter, @AVIXA and Facebook, www.facebook.com/TheAVIXA

Membership: manufacturers, dealers, and specialists in educational communications products. Provides educators with information on federal funding for audiovisual, video, and computer equipment and materials; monitors trends in educational technology; conducts audiovisual trade shows worldwide. (Formerly Info Comm International.)

The Brookings Institution, *Center for Technology Innovation,* 1775 Massachusetts Ave. N.W., 20036; (202) 797-6090. Nicol E. Turner-Lee, Director, (202) 238-3563.
Web, www.brookings.edu/about/center-for-technology-innovation and Twitter, @drturnerlee

Research center promoting policymaking and public debate about technology innovation, including digital infrastructure, the mobile economy, e-governance, digital media and entertainment, cybersecurity and privacy, digital medicine, and virtual education.

Coalition for Networked Information, *21 Dupont Circle N.W., #800, 20036; (202) 296-5098. Clifford A. Lynch, Executive Director.*
General email, info@cni.org

Web, www.cni.org, Twitter, @cni_org, Facebook, www.facebook.com/cni.org and YouTube, www.youtube.com/user/cnivideo

Membership: higher education institutions, publishing, information technology and telecommunications, information technology, and libraries and library organizations, as well as government agencies and foundations. Promotes networked information technology, scholarly communication, intellectual productivity, and education.

Consortium for School Networking (CoSN), *1325 G St. N.W., #420, 20005; (202) 861-2676. (202) 524-8464. Keith R. Krueger, Chief Executive Officer.*
General email, info@cosn.org

Web, http://cosn.org, Twitter, @CoSN and Facebook, www.facebook.com/mycosn

Membership: teachers and school officials who support educational technology for grades K–12. Grants certification to educators who are fluent in technology and promote the role of technology in teaching. Assists schools in implementing educational technologies. Holds an annual policy summit to support legislation that affects technology education.

Council on Library and Information Resources, *211 N. Union St., #100-PMB1027, Alexandria, VA 22314; Charles Henry, President. Press, (301) 941-7072.*
General email, contact@clir.org

Web, www.clir.org, Twitter, @CLIRnews, Facebook, www.facebook.com/CLIRNews and YouTube, www.youtube.com/user/DLFCLIR

Acts on behalf of the nation's libraries, archives, and universities to develop and encourage collaborative strategies for preserving the nation's intellectual heritage; seeks to strengthen its information systems and learning environments.

Digital Promise, *1001 Connecticut Ave. N.W., #935, 20036; (202) 450-3675. Jean-Claude Brizard, President.*
General email, contact@digitalpromise.org

Web, https://digitalpromise.org, Twitter, @DigitalPromise, Facebook, www.facebook.com/digitalpromise and YouTube, www.youtube.com/digitalpromise

Assists educators, technology developers, and researchers in applying and creating educational technologies that improve student learning. Grants microcredentials to teachers and equips schools with mobile learning technology.

Folger Shakespeare Library, *201 E. Capitol St. S.E., 20003-1004; (202) 544-4600. Fax, (202) 544-4623. Michael Witmore, Director, (202) 675-0301. Box Office, (202) 544-7077.*
General email, info@folger.edu

Web, www.folger.edu, Twitter, @FolgerLibrary and Facebook, www.facebook.com/folgershakespearelibrary

Maintains major Shakespearean and Renaissance materials; awards fellowships for postdoctoral research; presents concerts, theater performances, poetry and fiction readings, exhibits, and other public events. Offers educational programs for elementary, secondary, high school, college, and graduate school students and teachers. Publishes the Folger Shakespeare editions, *Folger Magazine,* and, in association with the George Washington University, *Shakespeare Quarterly.*

Gallaudet University, *Library, 800 Florida Ave. N.E., 20002-3695; Amy Malm, Dean of the University Library, (202) 891-3977. Videophone, (202) 779-9478.*
General email, library.help@gallaudet.edu

Web, www.gallaudet.edu/library and Facebook, www.facebook.com/GallaudetLibrary

Maintains extensive special collection on deafness, including archival materials relating to deaf cultural history and Gallaudet University.

Libraries Without Borders, *Washington Office, 1342 Florida Ave. N.W., 20009; (703) 705-9321. Patrick Weil, Chair; Aaron Greenberg, Executive Director.*
General email, admin@librarieswithoutborders.org

Web, www.librarieswithoutborders.org, Twitter, @BSF_Intl and Facebook, www.facebook.com/LibrariesWithout Borders

Disseminates information globally; provides access to knowledge, education, and training; and promotes libraries and book distribution—Virtual and physical, fixed or mobile. Provides citizens in poor areas access to information with the aim of combating poverty and social inequality.

Lubuto Library Partners, *5614 Connecticut Ave N.W., #368, 20015-2604; (202) 558-5609. Jane Kinney Meyers, President.*
General email, webmail@lubuto.org
Web, www.lubuto.org, Twitter, @LubutoLibrary and Facebook, www.facebook.com/lubutolibrarypartners

International development organization that establishes public libraries for youth in southern African countries, starting in Zambia. Constructs library facilities with support from the U.S. Agency for International Development (USAID), which also supports the purchase of book collections and library technology. Trains local staff to offer services, programs, and outreach from the libraries, which are owned by Zambian nongovernmental organizations, and operates a regional training center in inclusive library services for children and youth.

National Assn. for Music Education, *1806 Robert Fulton Dr., Reston, VA 20191-4348; (703) 860-4000. Christopher B.L. Woodside, Executive Director. Toll-free, (800) 336-3768. Toll-free fax, (888) 275-6232.*
General email, memberservices@nafme.org
Web, www.nafme.org, Twitter, @NAfME and Facebook, www.facebook.com/nafme/

Publishes books and teaching aids for music educators, parents, and administrators.

NewseumEd, *9893 Brewers Court, Laurel, MD 20723; (202) 292-6650. Barbara McCormack, Vice President of Education.*
General email, educationprograms@freedomforum.org
Web, https://newseumed.org

Affiliated with the Freedom Forum as an education and outreach partner. Offers programs and learning platforms for current central debates and political issues within journalism and religion.

Special Libraries Assn., *7918 Jones Branch Dr., #300, McLean, VA 22102; (703) 647-4900. Fax, (703) 506-3266. Monica Evans-Lombe, Managing Director.*
General email, sla@sla.org
Web, www.sla.org, Twitter, @SLAhq and Facebook, www.facebook.com/slahq

Membership: librarians and information managers serving institutions that use or produce information in specialized areas, including business, engineering, law, the arts and sciences, government, museums, and universities. Conducts professional development programs, research projects, and an annual conference. Monitors legislation and regulations.

POSTSECONDARY EDUCATION

General

►**AGENCIES**

National Institutes of Health (NIH) *(Health and Human Services Dept.), Intramural Training and Education (OITE), Bldg. 2, 2 Center Dr., #2E04, MS 0230, Bethesda, MD 20892-0240; (301) 693-1281. Fax, (301) 594-9606. Sharon Milgram, Director, (301) 594-2053.*
General email, trainingwww@mail.nih.gov
Web, www.training.nih.gov

Administers programs and initiatives to recruit and develop individuals who participate in research training activities on the NIH's campuses. Maintains an interactive website for the various research training programs. Supports the training mission of the NIH Intramural Research Program through placement, retention, support, and tracking of trainees at all levels, as well as program delivery and evaluation. Administers the NIH Academy, the Summer Internship Program, the Undergraduate Scholarship Program, the Graduate Partnerships Program, and the Postbac and Technical Intramural Research Training Award programs.

Postsecondary Education (OPE) *(Education Dept.), Lyndon B. Johnson Bldg., 400 Maryland Ave. S.W., 20202; (202) 453-6914. Fax, (202) 502-7677. Michelle Asha Cooper, Assistant Secretary (Acting). TTY, (800) 437-0833.*
Web, www2.ed.gov/about/offices/list/ope/index.html and Twitter, @EDPostsecondary

Formulates federal postsecondary education policy. Administers federal assistance programs for public and private postsecondary institutions; provides financial support for faculty development, construction of facilities, and improvement of graduate, continuing, cooperative, and international education; awards grants and loans for financial assistance to eligible students.

Postsecondary Education (OPE) *(Education Dept.), Fund for the Improvement of Postsecondary Education (FIPSE), Lyndon B. Johnson Bldg., 400 Maryland Ave. S.W., #4W120, 20202; (202) 453-6914. Fax, (202) 502-7877. Vacant, Director.*
General email, fipse@ed.gov
Web, www.ed.gov/ope/fipse/index.html

Works to improve postsecondary education by administering grant competitions.

Postsecondary Education (OPE) *(Education Dept.), Higher Education Programs (HEP), Lyndon B. Johnson Bldg., 400 Maryland Ave. S.W., 20202; (202) 453-6808. Michelle Asha Cooper, Deputy Assistant Secretary.*
Web, www2.ed.gov/about/offices/list/ope/hep.html

Administers programs to increase access to postsecondary education for low-income first-generation students and students with disabilities. Supports higher education facilities and programs through financial support to eligible institutions, and management of programs that recruit and prepare low-income students for successful completion of college. Programs include seven TRIO programs, institutional development programs for minority-serving institutions, and the Fund for the Improvement of Postsecondary Education.

Postsecondary Education (OPE) *(Education Dept.),* *Higher Education Programs (HEP), Institutional Service (IS), Minority Science and Engineering Improvement Program,* Lyndon B. Johnson Bldg., 400 Maryland Ave. S.W., 4th Floor, 20202; (202) 453-7913. Bernadette Hence, Senior Program Manager.
General email, OPE.MSEIP@ed.gov
Web, www2.ed.gov/programs/iduesmsi/index.html

Provides grants to predominantly minority institutions to effect long-range improvement in science and engineering education and to increase the flow of underrepresented ethnic minorities, particularly minority women, into science and engineering careers.

Postsecondary Education (OPE) *(Education Dept.),* *Higher Education Programs (HEP), International and Foreign Language Education (IFLE),* Lyndon B. Johnson Bldg., 400 Maryland Ave. S.W., #3E200, 20202; (202) 453-6950. Fax, (202) 453-5780. Cheryl Gibbs, Senior Director, (202) 453-5690.
Web, www2.ed.gov/about/offices/list/ope/iegps/index.html and Twitter, @GoGlobalED

Advises the Assistant Secretary for Postsecondary Education on matters affecting postsecondary, international, and foreign language education. Responsible for encouraging and promoting the study of foreign languages and cultures of other countries at the elementary, secondary, and postsecondary levels in the United States. Administers programs that increase expertise in foreign languages and area or international studies, and coordinates with related international and foreign language education programs of other federal agencies.

▶ CONGRESS

For a listing of relevant congressional committees and subcommittees, please see page 176 or the Appendix.

▶ NONGOVERNMENTAL

Accuracy in Academia (AIA), 4200 Wisconsin Ave. N.W., 20016 (mailing address: P.O. Box 5647, Derwood, MD. 20855-0647); (240) 686-5964. Malcolm A. Kline, Executive Director.
General email, info@academia.org
Web, www.academia.org, Twitter, @CampusReport, Facebook, www.facebook.com/AccuracyinAcademia and YouTube, www.youtube.com/user/aiacademia

Seeks to eliminate political bias in university education, particularly discrimination against students, faculty, or administrators on the basis of political beliefs. Reports on bias in education. Publishes a monthly newsletter.

ACT Inc. (American College Testing), *Washington Office,* 1 Dupont Circle N.W. #340, 20036-1170; (202) 223-2318. Fax, (202) 293-2223. Janet Godwin, Chief Executive Officer.
Web, www.act.org, Twitter, @ACTStudent and Facebook, www.facebook.com/theacttest

Administers ACT assessment planning and examination for colleges and universities. Provides more than 100 assessment, research, information, and program management services in the areas of education and workforce development to elementary and secondary schools, colleges, professional associations, businesses, and government agencies. (Headquarters in Iowa City, Iowa.)

American Assn. of Colleges of Pharmacy, 1400 Crystal Dr., #300, Arlington, VA 22202; (703) 739-2330. Fax, (703) 836-8982. Lucinda L. Maine, Executive Vice President, ext. 1021.
General email, mail@aacp.org
Web, www.aacp.org, Twitter, @AACPharmacy and Facebook, www.facebook.com/AACPharmacy

Membership: Schools of pharmacy accredited by the Accreditation Council for Pharmaceutical Education and individual members, including administrators, faculty, staff, and students. Sponsors educational programs; conducts research; provides career information; helps administer the Pharmacy College Admissions Test.

American Assn. of Collegiate Registrars and Admissions Officers, 1108 16th St. N.W., #400, 20036; (202) 293-9161. Fax, (202) 872-8857. Melanie Gottlieb, Executive Director (Acting), (202) 355-1055.
General email, info@aacrao.org
Web, www.aacrao.org, Twitter, @aacrao and Facebook, www.facebook.com/AACROA

Membership: degree-granting postsecondary institutions, government agencies, higher education coordinating boards, private education organizations, and education-oriented businesses. Promotes higher education and contributes to the professional development of members working in admissions, enrollment management, financial aid, institutional research, records, and registration. Uses research, technology, and training to maintain compliance standards.

American Assn. of Community Colleges, 1 Dupont Circle N.W., #700, 20036; (202) 728-0200. Fax, (202) 833-2467. Walter G. Bumphus, President, ext. 235.
Web, www.aacc.nche.edu, Twitter, @Comm_College and Facebook, www.facebook.com/CommCollege

Membership: accredited two-year community technical and junior colleges, corporate foundations, international associates, and institutional affiliates. Studies include policies for lifelong education, workforce training programs and partnerships, international curricula, enrollment trends, and cooperative programs with public schools and communities.

American Assn. of State Colleges and Universities, 1717 Rhode Island Ave. N.W., #700, 20036; (202) 293-7070. Fax, (202) 296-5819. Mildred García, President, (202) 478-4647.

Colleges and Universities in the Washington Metropolitan Area

American University, 4400 Massachusetts Ave. N.W., 20016. Switchboard, (202) 885-1000. Sylvia M. Burwell, President, (202) 885-2121

Catholic University of America, 620 Michigan Ave. N.E., 20064. Switchboard, (202) 319-5000. John H. Garvey, President, (202) 319-5100

Corcoran School of the Arts and Design, George Washington University, 500 17th St. N.W., 20006. Switchboard, (202) 994-1700. Kym S. Rice, Director (Acting) (202) 994-1700

Gallaudet University, 800 Florida Ave. N.E., 20002. Switchboard, (202) 651-5000. Roberta J. Cordano, President, (202) 651-5005; Videophone, (202) 250-2837; Fax, (202) 651-5508

George Mason University, 4400 University Dr., Fairfax, VA 22030. Switchboard, (703) 993-1000. Gregory Washington, (703) 993-8700

George Washington University, 1918 F St. N.W., 20052. Switchboard, (202) 994-1000. Thomas J. LeBlanc, President, (202) 994-6500

George Washington University at Mount Vernon Campus, 2100 Foxhall Rd. N.W., 20007. Switchboard, (202) 242-6670. M. Brian Blake, Provost, (202) 994-6510

Georgetown University, 37th and O Sts. N.W., 20057. Switchboard, (202) 687-0100. John J. DeGioia, President, (202) 687-4134

Howard University, 2400 6th St. N.W., 20059. Switchboard, (202) 806-6100. Wayne A.I. Frederick, President, (202) 806-2510

The Institute of World Politics, 1521 16th St. N.W., 20036-1464. Switchboard, (202) 462-2101. John Lenczowski, President, (202) 462-2101

Marymount University, 2807 N. Glebe Rd., Arlington, VA 22207. Switchboard, (703) 522-5600. Irma Becerra, President, (703) 284-1598

Paul H. Nitze School of Advanced International Studies (SAIS), Johns Hopkins University, 1740 Massachusetts Ave. N.W., 20036. Switchboard, (202) 663-5600. Eliot A. Cohen, Dean, (202) 663-5628

Strayer University, 1133 15th St. N.W., #200, 20005. Switchboard, (202) 408-2400. Brian W. Jones, President, (888) 311-0355

Trinity Washington University, 125 Michigan Ave. N.E., 20017. Switchboard, (202) 884-9000. Patricia A. McGuire, President, (202) 884-9050

University of Maryland, College Park, MD 20742. Switchboard, (301) 405-1000. Darryll J. Pines, President, (301) 405-5803

University of the District of Columbia, 4200 Connecticut Ave. N.W., 20008. Switchboard, (202) 274-5000. Ronald Mason Jr., President, (202) 274-6016

University of Virginia (Northern Virginia Center), 7054 Haycock Rd., Falls Church, VA 22043. Switchboard, (703) 536-1100. Alex Hernandez, Dean, (434) 982-5206

Virginia Tech (Northern Virginia Center), 7054 Haycock Rd., Falls Church, VA 22043. Switchboard, (540) 231-6000. Kenneth H. Wong, Director of Northern Virginia Campus, (703) 538-8310

Virginia Theological Seminary, 3737 Seminary Rd., Alexandria, VA 22304. Switchboard, (703) 370-6600 or (800) 941-0083. The Very Rev. Ian S. Markham, Dean, (703) 461-1701

Washington Adventist University, 7600 Flower Ave., Takoma Park, MD 20912. Switchboard, (800) 835-4212 or (301) 891-4000. Weymouth Spence, President, (301) 891-4128

Wesley Theological Seminary, 4500 Massachusetts Ave. N.W., 20016. Switchboard, (202) 885-8600. David McAllister-Wilson, President, (202) 885-8611

General email, info@aascu.org

Web, www.aascu.org, Twitter, @AASCU and Facebook, www.facebook.com/aascu

Membership: state colleges and universities throughout the United States, and in the Bahamas and China. Promotes equity in education and fosters information exchange among members. Interests include student financial aid, international education programs, academic affairs, teacher education, and higher education access and affordability. Monitors legislation and regulations.

American Assn. of University Professors (AAUP), *1133 19th St. N.W., #200, 20036; (202) 737-5900. Fax, (202) 737-5526. Julie Schmid, Executive Director, (202) 594-3644.*

General email, communications@aaup.org

Web, www.aaup.org, Twitter, @AAUP, Facebook, www.facebook.com/AAUPNational and Foundation, info@aaupfoundation.org

Membership: college and other academic professionals. Defends faculties' and professional staffs' academic freedom and tenure; advocates collegial governance; assists in the development of policies ensuring due process. Conducts workshops and education programs. Monitors legislation and regulations.

American Council of Trustees and Alumni, *1730 M St. N.W., #600, 20036-4525; (202) 467-6787. Fax, (202) 467-6784. Michael B. Poliakoff, President.*

General email, info@goacta.org

Web, www.goacta.org, Twitter, @goacta and Facebook, www.facebook.com/GoActa

Membership: college and university alumni and trustees interested in promoting academic freedom, excellence, and accountability. Seeks to help alumni and trustees direct their financial contributions to programs that will raise educational standards at their alma maters. Promotes the role of alumni and trustees in shaping higher-education policies.

American Council on Education (ACE), *1 Dupont Circle N.W., #800, 20036-1193; (202) 939-9300. Ted Mitchell, President. Public Affairs, (202) 939-9365.*
General email, comments@acenet.edu

Web, www.acenet.edu, Twitter, @ACEducation, Facebook, www.facebook.com/AmericanCouncilEducation and YouTube, www.youtube.com/user/ACEducationTV

Membership: presidents of universities and other education institutions. Conducts and publishes research; maintains offices dealing with government relations, women and minorities in higher education, management of higher-education institutions, adult learning and educational credentials (academic credit for nontraditional learning, especially in the armed forces), leadership development, and international education.

Assn. of American Colleges and Universities (AACU), *1818 R St. N.W., 20009; (202) 387-3760. Fax, (202) 265-9532. Lynn Pasquerella, President, (202) 884-0812.*
General email, information@aacu.org

Web, www.aacu.org, Twitter, @aacu and Facebook, www.facebook.com/Association-of-American-Colleges-and-Universities-48308128458

Membership: two-year and four-year public and private colleges, universities, and postsecondary consortia. Works to develop effective academic programs and improve undergraduate curricula and services. Seeks to encourage, enhance, and support student achievement through liberal education for all students, regardless of academic specialization or intended career.

The Assn. of American Law Schools, *1614 20th St. N.W., 20009-1001; (202) 296-8851. Fax, (202) 296-8869. Judith Areen, Executive Director, (202) 296-1526.*
General email, info@aals.org

Web, www.aals.org, Twitter, @TheAALS and Facebook, www.facebook.com/theaals

Membership: law schools, subject to approval. Membership criteria include high-quality academic programs, faculty, scholarship, and students; academic freedom; diversity of people and viewpoints; and emphasis on public service. Hosts meetings and workshops; publishes a directory of law teachers. Acts as advocate on behalf of legal education; monitors legislation and judicial decisions.

Assn. of American Universities, *1200 New York Ave. N.W., #550, 20005; (202) 408-7500. Fax, (202) 408-8184. Barbara R. Synder, President.*
Web, www.aau.edu, Twitter, @AAUniversities and Facebook, www.facebook.com/AAUniversities

Membership: public and private universities in the United States and Canada with emphasis on graduate and professional education and research. Fosters information exchange among presidents of member institutions.

Assn. of Catholic Colleges and Universities, *1 Dupont Circle N.W., #650, 20036; (202) 457-0650. Fax, (202) 728-0977. Dennis Holtschneider, President, ext. 222.*

General email, accu@accunet.org

Web, www.accunet.org, Twitter, @CatholicHighrEd and Facebook, www.facebook.com/Association-of-Catholic-Colleges-and-Universities-111454027995010/

Membership: regionally accredited American Catholic colleges and universities. Offers affiliated status for selected international Catholic universities. Acts as a clearinghouse for information on Catholic institutions of higher education.

Assn. of Collegiate Schools of Architecture, *1735 New York Ave. N.W., 3rd Floor, 20006; (202) 785-2324. Fax, (202) 628-0448. Michael J. Monti, Executive Director.*
General email, info@acsa-arch.org

Web, www.acsa-arch.org, Twitter, @ACSAUpdate and Facebook, www.facebook.com/ACSANational

Membership: U.S. and Canadian institutions that offer at least one accredited architecture degree program. Conducts workshops and seminars for architecture school faculty; presents awards for student and faculty excellence in architecture; publishes a guide to architecture schools in North America.

Assn. of Community College Trustees (ACCT), *1101 17th St. N.W., #300, 20036; (202) 775-4667. Jee Hang Lee, President, (202) 775-4450. Toll-free, (866) 895-2228.*
General email, acctinfo@acct.org

Web, www.acct.org, Twitter, @CCTrustees and Facebook, www.facebook.com/CCTrustees

Provides members of community, technical, and junior college governing boards with training in educational programs and services. Monitors federal education programs and acts as advocate on behalf of community colleges and their trustees.

Assn. of Governing Boards of Universities and Colleges, *1133 20th St. N.W., #300, 20036; (202) 296-8400. Fax, (202) 223-7053. Henry Stoever, President. Toll-free, (800) 356-6317.*
Web, www.agb.org, Twitter, @AGBtweets and Email, membership@agb.org

Membership: presidents, boards of trustees, regents, commissions, and other groups governing colleges, universities, and institutionally related foundations. Interests include the relationship between the president and board of trustees and other subjects relating to governance.

Assn. of Jesuit Colleges and Universities, *1 Dupont Circle N.W., #405, 20036-1140; (202) 862-9893. Fax, (202) 862-8523. Rev. Michael Garonzini, President.*
General email, info@ajcunet.edu

Web, www.ajcunet.edu, Twitter, @jesuitcolleges and Facebook, www.facebook.com/jesuitcolleges

Membership: American Jesuit colleges and universities. Monitors government regulatory and policymaking activities affecting higher education. Publishes the *AJCU Directory* and a monthly newsletter. Promotes national and international cooperation among Jesuit higher-education institutions.

Assn. of Public and Land-Grant Universities, *1220 L St. N.W., #1000, 20005; (202) 478-6040. Fax, (202) 478-6046. Peter McPherson, President, (202) 478-6060.*
General email, info@aplu.org
Web, www.aplu.org, Twitter, @APLU_News and Facebook, www.facebook.com/APLUNews

Membership: land-grant colleges; state and public research universities. Serves as clearinghouse on issues of public higher education.

Business–Higher Education Forum, *1 Dupont Circle, #360, 20036; (202) 853-9052. Janet Chen, Director.*
General email, info@bhef.com
Web, www.bhef.com, Twitter, @BHEF and Press, ursula.gross@bhef.org

Membership: chief executive officers of major corporations, foundations, colleges, and universities. Develops and promotes policy positions to enhance U.S. competitiveness. Interests include improving student achievement and readiness for college and work; and strengthening higher education, particularly in the fields of science, technology, engineering, and math.

Career Education Colleges and Universities (CECU), *1530 Wilson Blvd., #1050, Arlington, VA 22209; (571) 970-3941. Fax, (866) 363-2181. Jason Altmire, President.*
Web, www.career.org, Twitter, @CECUed, Facebook, www.facebook.com/CECUed and Email, communications@career.org

Membership: private postsecondary colleges and career schools in the United States. Works to expand the accessibility of postsecondary career education and to improve the quality of education offered by member institutions. (Formerly Career College Assn.)

College Board, *Advocacy and Policy, 1919 M St. N.W., #300, 20034; (202) 741-4700. David Coleman, Chief Executive Officer; Stephanie Sanford, Chief of Global Policy and External Relations. International, 1-(212) 713-8000.*
Web, www.collegeboard.org, Twitter, @CollegeBoard and Facebook, www.facebook.com/Thecollegeboard

Membership: colleges and universities, secondary schools, school systems, and education associations. Provides direct student support programs and professional development for educators; conducts policy analysis and research; and advocates public policy positions that support educational excellence and promote student access to higher education. (Headquarters in New York.)

Consortium of Universities for Global Health, *1608 Rhode Island Ave. N.W., #240, 20036; (202) 974-6363. Fax, (202) 355-0948. Keith Martin, Executive Director.*
General email, info@cugh.org
Web, www.cugh.org, Twitter, @CUGHnews and Facebook, www.facebook.com/CUGHnews

Assists in regulating curricula and standards for university global health programs. Coordinates academic partnerships between national universities and international educational institutions in developing countries.

Council for Advancement and Support of Education, *1201 Eye St. N.W., #530A, 20005-4701; (202) 328-2273. Fax, (202) 387-4973. Sue Cunningham, President, ext. 5677.*
General email, membersupportcenter@case.org
Web, www.case.org, Twitter, @CASEAdvance and Facebook, www.facebook.com/caseadvance

Membership: two-year and four-year colleges, universities, and independent schools. Offers professional education, webinars, and training programs to members; advises members on institutional advancement issues, including fundraising, public relations programs, government relations, and management. Library open to professional members by appointment.

Council for Christian Colleges & Universities, *321 8th St. N.E., 20002; (202) 546-8713. Fax, (202) 546-8913. Shirley V. Hoogstra, President.*
General email, council@cccu.org
Web, www.cccu.org, Twitter, @cccuorg, Facebook, www.facebook.com/CCCUorg and YouTube, www.youtube.com/user/CCCUvideo

Membership: accredited four-year Christian liberal arts colleges. Offers faculty development conferences on faith and the academic disciplines. Coordinates annual gathering of college administrators. Sponsors internship/seminar programs for students at member colleges. Promotes Christian-affiliated higher education. Interests include religious and educational freedom.

Council of Graduate Schools, *1 Dupont Circle N.W., #230, 20036-1173; (202) 223-3791. Fax, (202) 331-7157. Suzanne T. Ortega, President.*
General email, general_inquiries@cgs.nche.edu
Web, http://cgsnet.org and Twitter, @CGSGradEd

Membership: private and public colleges and universities with significant involvement in graduate education, research, and scholarship. Produces publications and information about graduate education; provides a forum for member schools to exchange information and ideas.

Council of Independent Colleges, *1 Dupont Circle N.W., #320, 20036-1142; (202) 466-7230. Marjorie Hass, President.*
General email, cic@cic.nche.edu
Web, www.cic.edu and Twitter, @CICnotes

Membership: independent liberal arts colleges and universities, and higher education affiliates and organizations. Sponsors development programs for college presidents, deans, and faculty members and communications officers on topics such as leadership, financial management, academic quality, visibility, and other issues crucial to high-quality education and independent liberal arts colleges. Holds workshops and annual meetings, conducts research, and produces publications.

Council on Social Work Education, *333 John Carlyle St., #400, Alexandria, VA 22314; (703) 683-8080. Fax, (703) 683-8099. Darla Spence Coffey, President, (703) 519-2066.*

General email, info@cswe.org

Web, www.cswe.org, Twitter, @CSocialWorkEd and Facebook, www.facebook.com/CSocialWorkEd/

Membership: educational and professional institutions, social welfare agencies, and private citizens. Promotes high-quality education in social work. Accredits social work programs.

DECA Inc., *1908 Association Dr., Reston, VA 20191-1594; (703) 860-5000. Frank Peterson, Executive Director.*
General email, info@deca.org

Web, www.deca.org, Twitter, @DECAInc and Facebook, www.facebook.com/decainc

Educational organization that helps high school and college students develop skills in marketing, management, finance, hospitality, and entrepreneurship. Promotes business and education partnerships.

Educational Testing Service (ETS), *Communications and Public Affairs, 1800 K St. N.W., #900, 20006-2202 (mailing address: 200 Massachusetts Ave. N.W., #700, Washington, DC 20001); (202) 659-0616. Fax, (202) 457-8687. Walt MacDonald, President.*
General email, etsinfo@ets.org

Web, www.ets.org

Administers examinations for admission to educational programs and for graduate and licensing purposes; conducts instructional programs in testing, evaluation, and research in education fields. Washington office handles government and professional relations. Fee for services. (Headquarters in Princeton, NJ.)

NASPA: Student Affairs Administrators in Higher Education, *111 K St. N.E., 10th Floor, 20002; (202) 265-7500. Kevin Kruger, President, ext. 1175.*
General email, office@naspa.org

Web, www.naspa.org, Twitter, @NASPAtweets and Facebook, www.facebook.com/naspaFB

Membership: student affairs administrators, deans, faculty, and graduate and undergraduate students at 2,100 campuses, representing 25 countries. Seeks to develop leadership and improve practices in student affairs administration. Initiates and supports programs and legislation to improve student affairs administration.

National Assn. for College Admission Counseling, *1050 N. Highland St., #400, Arlington, VA 22201; (703) 836-2222. Fax, (703) 243-9375. Angel B. Pérez, Chief Executive Officer, (703) 299-6828. Toll-free, (800) 822-6285.*
General email, info@nacacnet.org

Web, www.nacacnet.org, Twitter, @NACAC and Facebook, www.facebook.com/nacacnet.org/?ref=sgm

Membership: high school guidance counselors, independent counselors, college and university admissions officers, and financial aid officers. Promotes and funds research on admission counseling and on the transition from high school to college. Acts as advocate for student rights in college admissions. Sponsors national college fairs and continuing education for members.

National Assn. of College and University Attorneys, *1 Dupont Circle N.W., #620, 20036-1182; (202) 833-8390. Fax, (202) 296-8379. Ona Alston Dosunmu, President.*
General email, nacua@nacua.org

Web, www.nacua.org and Twitter, @NACUAtweets

Provides information on legal developments affecting postsecondary education. Operates a clearinghouse through which in-house and external legal counselors are able to network with their counterparts on current legal problems.

National Assn. of College and University Business Officers, *1110 Vermont Ave. N.W., #800, 20005; (202) 861-2500. Susan Whealler Johnston, President, (202) 861-2503. Customer Service, (202) 861-2560.*
General email, support@nacubo.org

Web, www.nacubo.org, Twitter, @NACUBO and Facebook, www.facebook.com/nacubo

Membership: chief business and financial officers at higher-education institutions. Provides members with information on financial management, federal regulations, and other subjects related to the business administration of universities and colleges; conducts workshops on issues such as student aid, institutional budgeting, and accounting.

National Assn. of Independent Colleges and Universities, *1025 Connecticut Ave. N.W., #700, 20036-5405; (202) 785-8866. Fax, (202) 835-0003. Barbara K. Mistick, President.*
General email, geninfo@naicu.edu

Web, www.naicu.edu and Twitter, @NAICUtweets

Membership: liberal arts colleges, research universities, church-related and faith-related institutions, historically black colleges and universities, women's colleges, performing and visual arts institutions, two-year colleges; graduate schools of law, medicine, engineering, business, and other professions. Tracks campus trends, conducts research, analyzes higher-education issues, and helps coordinate state-level activities. Interests include federal policies that affect student aid, taxation, and government regulation. Monitors legislation and regulations.

National Council of University Research Administrators, *1015 18th St. N.W., #901, 20036; (202) 466-3894. Fax, (202) 223-5573. Kathleen Larmett, Executive Director.*
General email, info@ncura.edu

Web, www.ncura.edu, Twitter, @NCURA, Facebook, www.facebook.com/ncura1959 and YouTube, www.youtube.com/user/NCURA1959

Membership: individuals involved in grant administration at colleges, universities, and teaching hospitals. Encourages development of effective policies and procedures in the administration of these programs.

National Governors Assn. (NGA), *Center for Best Practices, Post-Secondary Education Division, 444 N. Capitol St. N.W., #267, 2001-1512; (202) 624-5300. Amanda Winters, Director.*

General email, info@nga.org

Web, www.nga.org/bestpractices/post-secondary-education

Provides information, research, policy analysis, and technical assistance to governors and their staff in the areas of post-secondary education. Focus includes efforts to graduate more students from high-quality certificate and degree programs.

Network of Schools of Public Policy, Affairs, and Administration (NASPAA), *1029 Vermont Ave. N.W., #1100, 20005; (202) 628-8965. Fax, (202) 626-4978. Angel Wright-Lanier, Executive Director, (202) 810-7413.*

General email, naspaa@naspaa.org

Web, www.naspaa.org, Twitter, @naspaa and Facebook, www.facebook.com/naspaaglobal

Membership: universities involved in education, research, and training in public management in the United States and internationally.

Washington Higher Education Secretariat, *1 Dupont Circle N.W., #800, 20036-1110; (202) 939-9310. Fax, (202) 833-4760. Ted Mitchell, Chair.*

General email, whs@acenet.edu

Web, www.whes.org

Membership: national higher-education association chief executives representing the different sectors and functions in postsecondary institutions. Provides forum for discussion on national and local education issues. (Coordinated by the president of the American Council on Education.)

College Accreditation

Many college-based or university-based independent post-secondary education programs are accredited by member associations. See specific headings and associations within the chapter.

▶AGENCIES

Education Dept., *Accreditation Group, 400 Maryland Ave. S.W., 20202-0001; (202) 453-7615. Herman Bounds Jr., Director, (202) 453-7615.*

General email, aslrecordsmanager@ed.gov

Web, www.ed.gov/accreditation

Reviews accrediting agencies and state approval agencies that seek initial or renewed recognition by the secretary; provides the National Advisory Committee on Institutional Quality and Integrity with staff support.

▶NONGOVERNMENTAL

Accrediting Commission of Career Schools and Colleges, *2101 Wilson Blvd., #302, Arlington, VA 22201; (703) 247-4212. Fax, (703) 247-4533. Michale S. McComis, Executive Director, (703) 247-4520.*

General email, info@accsc.org

Web, www.accsc.org, Twitter, @ACCSCAccredits and Facebook, www.facebook.com/accsaccreditation

Serves as the national accrediting agency for private postsecondary institutions offering occupational and vocational programs. Sponsors workshops and meetings on academic excellence and ethical practices in career education.

Accrediting Council for Continuing Education and Training (ACCET), *1722 N St. N.W., 20036; (202) 955-1113. Fax, (202) 955-1118. Kate Zulaski, Deputy Director, (202) 984-2282.*

General email, info@accet.org

Web, https://accet.org

Membership for accreditation. Peer-reviewed accrediting agency for noncollegiate continuing education and training institutions. Establishes standards, policies, and procedures to identify best education and training practices.

Accrediting Council for Independent Colleges and Schools (ACICS), *1350 Eye St. N.W., #560, 20005; (202) 336-6780. Fax, (202) 789-1747. Michelle Edwards, President, (202) 336-6845.*

General email, info@acics.org

Web, www.acics.org, Twitter, @ACICSaccredits and Facebook, www.facebook.com/ACICSaccredits

Accredits postsecondary institutions offering programs of study through the master's degree level that are designed to train and educate persons for careers or professions where business applications and concepts constitute or support the career or professional activity. Promotes educational excellence and ethical business practices in its member schools.

American Academy for Liberal Education (AALE), *(202) 389-6550. Mary Ann A. Powers, Executive Director.*

General email, aaleinfo@aale.org

Web, www.aale.org

Accredits colleges, universities, and charter schools whose general education program in the liberal arts meets the academy's accreditation requirements. Provides support for institutions that maintain substantial liberal arts programs and desire to raise requirements to meet AALE standards.

American Academy for Liberal Education (AALE), *(202) 389-6550. Mary Ann A. Powers, Executive Director.*

General email, aaleinfo@aale.org

Web, www.aale.org

Accredits colleges, universities, and charter schools whose general education program in the liberal arts meets the academy's accreditation requirements. Provides support for institutions that maintain substantial liberal arts programs and desire to raise requirements to meet AALE standards.

Council for Higher Education Accreditation, *1 Dupont Circle N.W., #510, 20036; (202) 955-6126. Fax, (202) 915-0818. Cynthia Jackson-Hammond, President.*

General email, chea@chea.org

Web, www.chea.org, Twitter, @CHEAnews and Facebook, www.facebook.com/www.chea.org

Advocates voluntary self-regulation of colleges and universities through accreditation; conducts recognition processes for accrediting organizations; coordinates research, debate, and processes that improve accreditation; mediates disputes and fosters communications among accrediting bodies and the higher education community.

Council for the Accreditation of Educator Preparation (CAEP), 1140 19th St. N.W., #400, 20036; (202) 223-0077. Christopher Koch, President.

General email, caep@caepnet.org

Web, caepnet.org, Twitter, @caepupdates and YouTube, www.youtube.com/channel/UCcoA11nacfh7-JvLBGE9UXA

Evaluates and accredits schools and departments of education at colleges and universities. Publishes list of accredited institutions and standards for accreditation. (Formerly National Council for Accreditation of Teacher Education.)

Council on Education for Public Health (CEPH), 1010 Wayne Ave., #220, Silver Spring, MD 20910; (202) 789-1050. Laura Rasar King, Executive Director.

Web, https://ceph.org and Twitter, @CEPHtweets

Accredits schools of public health and undergraduate and graduate programs in public health.

Distance Education and Accrediting Commission (DEAC), 1101 17th St. N.W., #808, 20036; (202) 234-5100. Leah K. Matthews, Executive Director, ext. 101.

General email, info@deac.org

Web, www.deac.org, Twitter, @DEACaccrediting and Facebook, www.facebook.com/DEACaccrediting

Membership: accredited distance education and online institutions. Accredits distance education and online institutions that offer high school diplomas, postsecondary education programs, and degree programs through to the doctoral level. Recognized by the U.S. Department of Education and the Council for Higher Education Accreditation.

National Architectural Accrediting Board Inc., 107 S. West St. #707, Alexandria, VA 22314; (202) 783-2007. Fax, (202) 783-2822. Rebecca O'Neal, President; Tanya A. Tamarkin, Executive Director.

General email, info@naab.org

Web, www.naab.org, Twitter, @NAABNews and Facebook, www.facebook.com/NationalArchitecturalAccreditingBoard/

Accredits Bachelor, Master, and Doctor of Architecture degree programs in the United States; assists organizations in other countries to develop accreditation standards.

National Assn. of Schools of Dance, 11250 Roger Bacon Dr., #21, Reston, VA 20190-5248; (703) 437-0700.

Fax, (703) 437-6312. Karen Moynahan, Executive Director, ext. 116.

General email, info@arts-accredit.org

Web, http://nasd.arts-accredit.org

Specialized professional accrediting agency for postsecondary programs in dance. Conducts and shares research and analysis on topics pertinent to dance programs and the field of dance. Offers professional development opportunities for executives of dance programs.

National Assn. of Schools of Music, 11250 Roger Bacon Dr., #21, Reston, VA 20190-5248; (703) 437-0700. Fax, (703) 437-6312. Karen Moynahan, Executive Director, ext. 116.

General email, info@arts-accredit.org

Web, http://nasm.arts-accredit.org

Specialized professional accrediting agency for postsecondary programs in music. Conducts and shares research and analysis on topics pertinent to music programs and the field of music. Offers professional development opportunities for executives of music programs.

National Assn. of Schools of Theatre, 11250 Roger Bacon Dr., #21, Reston, VA 20190-5248; (703) 437-0700. Fax, (703) 437-6312. Karen Moynahan, Executive Director, ext. 116.

General email, info@arts-accredit.org

Web, http://nast.arts-accredit.org

Specialized professional accrediting agency for postsecondary programs in theatre. Conducts and shares research and analysis on topics pertinent to theatre programs and the field of theatre. Offers professional development opportunities for executives of theatre programs.

Network of Schools of Public Policy, Affairs, and Administration (NASPAA), 1029 Vermont Ave. N.W., #1100, 20005; (202) 628-8965. Fax, (202) 626-4978. Angel Wright-Lanier, Executive Director, (202) 810-7413.

General email, naspaa@naspaa.org

Web, www.naspaa.org, Twitter, @naspaa and Facebook, www.facebook.com/naspaaglobal

Accredits undergraduate and master's degree programs in public affairs, public policy, and public administration.

Financial Aid to Students

▶**AGENCIES**

Education Dept., Federal Student Aid, 830 1st St. N.E., 20202; (202) 377-3000. Fax, (202) 275-5000. Richard Cordray, Chief Operating Officer. FSA customer service, (800) 433-7327. Student Aid Information Center, (800) 433-3243.

Web, https://studentaid.gov, www2.ed.gov/about/offices/list/fsa/index.html, Twitter, @FAFSA, Facebook, www.facebook.com/FederalStudentAid and YouTube, www.youtube.com/user/FederalStudentAid

Administers federal loan, grant, and work-study programs for postsecondary education to eligible individuals. Administers the Pell Grant Program, the Perkins Loan

Program, the Stafford Student Loan Program (Guaranteed Student Loan)/PLUS Program, the College Work-Study Program, the Supplemental Loans for Students (SLS), and the Supplemental Educational Opportunity Grant Program.

Education Dept., *Health Education Assistance Loan Program (HEAL), 12501 Ardennes Ave., #200, Rockville, MD 20857; (844) 509-8957. Vacant, Supervisor.*
General email, heal@ed.gov
Web, https://ifap.ed.gov/health-education-assistance-loan-information

Insures loans provided by private lenders to students attending eligible health professions schools under the Public Health Service Act. New loans to student borrowers have been discontinued. Refinancing has been terminated.

Postsecondary Education (OPE) *(Education Dept.),* *Higher Education Programs (HEP), Institutional Service (IS), Lyndon B. Johnson Bldg., 400 Maryland Ave. S.W., 2nd Floor, 20202; (202) 453-6914. Fax, (202) 502-7699. Beatriz Ceja, Senior Director.*
General email, OPE_Institutional_Development@ed.gov
Web, www2.ed.gov/about/offices/list/ope/idues/index.html

Provides financial and administrative support for limited resource institutions serving minority and financially disadvantaged students. Administers programs authorized under the Higher Education Act of 1965 and its subsequent amendments. Title III programs include support for Historically Black Colleges and Universities, American Indian Tribally Controlled Colleges and Universities, and Minority Science and Engineering Improvement Program. Title V programs strengthen institutions serving Hispanic and other low-income students. Title VII supports the implementation and evaluation of and shares findings of innovative educational reform ideas.

Postsecondary Education (OPE) *(Education Dept.),* *Higher Education Programs (HEP), Student Service, Lyndon B. Johnson Bldg., 400 Maryland Ave. S.W., 20202; (202) 453-6914. Fax, (202) 502-7857. Gaby Watts, Senior Director.*
General email, OPE_TRIO@ed.gov
Web, www2.ed.gov/about/offices/list/ope/student-service.html

Administers grant programs (TRIO) for low-income, potential first-generation students and individuals with disabilities from middle school to graduate school, in addition to programs focused on college readiness, campus-based child care, and graduate fellowships. TRIO programs include Educational Opportunity Centers, Upward Bound, Upward Bound Math and Science, Talent Search, Student Support Services, Ronald E. McNair Post-baccalaureate Achievement Program, TRIO training program, and Veterans Upward Bound.

▶**NONGOVERNMENTAL**

College Board, *Advocacy and Policy, 1919 M St. N.W., #300, 20034; (202) 741-4700. David Coleman, Chief Executive Officer; Stephanie Sanford, Chief of Global Policy and External Relations. International, 1-(212) 713-8000.*
Web, www.collegeboard.org, Twitter, @CollegeBoard and Facebook, www.facebook.com/Thecollegeboard

Membership: colleges and universities, secondary schools, school systems, and education associations. Provides direct student support programs and professional development for educators; conducts policy analysis and research; and advocates public policy positions that support educational excellence and promote student access to higher education. (Headquarters in New York.)

Education Finance Council, *440 1st St. N.W., #560, 20001 (mailing address: 200 Massachusetts Ave. N.W., #700, Washington, DC 20001); (202) 955-5510. Gail daMata, President.*
General email, info@efc.org
Web, www.efc.org

Membership: Nonprofit and state-based higher-education finance organizations. Participates in the Federal Family Education Loan Program (FFELP). Works to maintain and expand student access to higher education through tax-exempt funding for loans.

National Assn. of Student Financial Aid Administrators, *1801 Pennsylvania Ave. N.W., #850, 20006-3606; (202) 785-0453. Fax, (202) 785-1487. Justin Draeger, President.*
General email, info@nasfaa.org
Web, www.nasfaa.org, Twitter, @nasfaa and Facebook, www.facebook.com/NASFAA

Membership: more than 20,000 financial aid professionals at nearly 3,000 colleges, universities, and career schools. Interests include student aid legislation, regulatory analysis, and training for financial aid administrators.

National Council of Higher Education Resources, *1050 Connecticut Ave. N.W., #65793, 20035; (202) 822-2106. James P. Bergeron, President.*
General email, info@ncher.us
Web, www.ncher.us, Twitter, @ncher_us and Facebook, www.facebook.com/National-Council-of-Higher-Education-Resources-633750116770142

Membership: agencies and organizations involved in servicing and collecting federal student loans and providing debt management, financial literacy, student loan counseling, and other college access and success services. Fosters information exchange among members.

Student Aid Alliance, *1 Dupont Circle N.W., #800, 20036-1193; Barbara K. Mistick, NAICU President. Phone NAICU, (202) 785-8866.*
Web, www.studentaidalliance.org, Twitter, @StuAidAlliance and Facebook, www.facebook.com/studentaidalliance

Membership: coalition of 85 organizations representing students, administrators, and faculty members from all sectors of higher education. Seeks to ensure adequate funding of federal aid programs. Monitors legislation and regulations. (Co-chaired by the National Assn. of Independent Colleges and Universities [NAICU] and the American Council on Education [ACE].)

PRESCHOOL, ELEMENTARY, SECONDARY EDUCATION

General

▶AGENCIES

Administration for Children and Families (ACF) *(Health and Human Services Dept.), Head Start (OHS),* Mary E. Switzer Bldg., 330 C St. S.W., 4th Floor, MS 4301, 20201; (202) 205-8573. Bernadine Futrell, Director. Toll-free, (866) 763-6481.
Web, www.acf.hhs.gov/ohs, Twitter, @HeadStartgov, Facebook, www.facebook.com/HeadStartgov and General email, HeadStart@cclkc.info

Awards grants to nonprofit and for-profit organizations and local governments for operating community Head Start programs (comprehensive development programs for children, ages birth to five, of low-income families); manages parent and child centers, Early Childhood Learning and Knowledge Centers (ECLKC), for families with children up to age five. Programs focus on early learning, health, and family well-being. Conducts research and manages demonstration programs, including those under the Comprehensive Child Care Development Act of 1988; administers the Child Development Associate scholarship program, which trains individuals for careers in child development, often as Head Start teachers.

Defense Dept. (DoD), *Education Activity,* 4800 Mark Center Dr., Alexandria, VA 22350-1400; (571) 372-0590. Fax, (571) 372-5829. Thomas M. Brady, Director.
General email, ER-HD@dodea.edu
Web, www.dodea.edu and Twitter, @DODEA

Civilian office that maintains school system for dependents of all military personnel and eligible civilians in the United States and abroad. Develops uniform curriculum and educational standards; monitors student performance and school accreditation.

Elementary and Secondary Education (OESE) *(Education Dept.),* Lyndon B. Johnson Bldg., 400 Maryland Ave. S.W., #3W315, 20202; (202) 401-0113. Fax, (202) 205-0310. Mark Washington, Deputy Assistant Secretary.
General email, oese@ed.gov
Web, https://oese.ed.gov

Administers federal assistance programs for preschool, elementary, and secondary education (both public and private). Program divisions include Disaster Recovery Unit; State and Grantee Relations and Evidence Based Practices; Discretionary Grants & Support Services; Formula Grants (including Title I aid for disadvantaged children); Indian Education; and Migrant Education.

Elementary and Secondary Education (OESE) *(Education Dept.), Disaster Recovery Unit (DRU),* Lyndon B. Johnson Bldg., 400 Maryland Ave. S.W., 20202-6244; (202) 401-8368. Meredith Miller, Director.
Web, https://oese.ed.gov/offices/disaster-recovery-unit

Leads departmental efforts in disaster recovery work following federally declared natural disasters. Manages the following grant programs: Emergency Impact Aid for Displaced Students, Immediate Aid to Restart School Operations, Assistance for Homeless Children and Youth, and Project School Emergency Response to Violence.

Elementary and Secondary Education (OESE) *(Education Dept.), Discretionary Grants and Support Services (DGSS), Charter School Programs (CSP),* Lyndon B. Johnson Bldg., 400 Maryland Ave. S.W., 20202; (202) 453-5563. Anna Hinton, Director.
General email, sgr@ed.gov
Web, https://oese.ed.gov/offices/office-of-discretionary-grants-support-services/charter-school-programs

Funds the creation of new public charter schools, location of suitable facilities, and national initiatives that support charter schools; disseminates information about effective practices within charter schools.

Elementary and Secondary Education (OESE) *(Education Dept.), Discretionary Grants and Support Services (DGSS), Innovation and Early Learning Programs,* Lyndon B. Johnson Bldg., 400 Maryland Ave. S.W., 20202; (202) 453-5563. Jamila Smith, Director.
Web, https://oese.ed.gov/offices/office-of-discretionary-grants-support-services/innovation-early-learning

Provides funding to create, develop, implement, replicate, or take to scale entrepreneurial, evidence-based, field-initiated innovations to improve student achievement and attainment for high-need students. Promotes school readiness and improved learning outcomes for children from low-income families.

Elementary and Secondary Education (OESE) *(Education Dept.), Discretionary Grants and Support Services (DGSS), School Choice and Improvement Programs (SCIP),* Lyndon B. Johnson Bldg., 400 Maryland Ave. S.W., 20202; (202) 453-5563. Elson Nash, Director.
Web, https://oese.ed.gov/offices/office-of-discretionary-grants-support-services/school-choice-improvement-programs

Administers grant programs and provides technical assistance to promote school choice, improve outcomes, prevent segregation, and educate parents on the various school options available for children, with a specific focus on low-income rural and urban communities.

Elementary and Secondary Education (OESE) *(Education Dept.), Discretionary Grants and Support Services (DGSS), Well-Rounded Education Programs (WREP),* Lyndon B. Johnson Bldg., 400 Maryland Ave. S.W., 20202-5950; (202) 453-5501. Jennifer Todd, Director.
Web, https://oese.ed.gov/offices/office-of-discretionary-grants-support-services/well-rounded-education-programs

Administers discretionary grant programs that support activities designed to advance literacy skills, provide professional learning opportunities to teachers to increase the performance of students in mathematics and science, create leadership pipelines for schools in need of improvement, support arts education, and pay all or a portion of advanced placement fees on behalf of low-income students.

Elementary and Secondary Education (OESE)
(Education Dept.), Formula Grants (OFG), Impact Aid, Lyndon B. Johnson Bldg., 400 Maryland Ave. S.W., #3E105, 20202-6244; (202) 260-3858. Fax, (866) 799-1273. *Faatimah Muhammad, Director.*
General email, impact.aid@ed.gov
Web, https://oese.ed.gov/offices/office-of-formula-grants/impact-aid-program

Provides funds for elementary and secondary educational activities to school districts in federally impacted areas (where federal activities such as military bases enlarge staff and reduce taxable property).

Elementary and Secondary Education (OESE)
(Education Dept.), Formula Grants (OFG), Program and Grantee Support Services (PGSS), Lyndon B. Johnson Bldg., 400 Maryland Ave. S.W., 20202; (202) 453-5563. *Danielle Smith, Director.*
Web, https://oese.ed.gov/offices/office-of-formula-grants/program-and-grantee-support-services

Oversees technical assistance grants and contracts for all U.S. states and territories. Also advises OESE offices on best practices related to technical assistance.

Elementary and Secondary Education (OESE)
(Education Dept.), Formula Grants (OFG), Rural, Insular, and Native Achievement Programs (RINAP), Lyndon B. Johnson Bldg., 400 Maryland Ave. S.W., #3W205, 20202-6400; (202) 401-0039. Fax, (202) 205-5870. *Patrick Carr, Director.*
Web, https://oese.ed.gov/offices/office-of-formula-grants/rural-insular-native-achievement-programs

Provides a coordinated strategy focusing federal resources on supporting improvements in schools; promotes development and implementation of comprehensive improvement plans that direct resources toward improved achievement for all students.

Elementary and Secondary Education (OESE)
(Education Dept.), Formula Grants (OFG), Safe and Supportive Schools (OSSS), Lyndon B. Johnson Bldg., 400 Maryland Ave. S.W., #3E-245, 20202-6135; (202) 453-5563. Fax, (202) 453-6742. *Bryan Williams, Director.*
General email, oese@ed.gov
Web, https://oese.ed.gov/offices/office-of-formula-grants/safe-supportive-schools

Develops policy for the department's drug and violence prevention initiatives for students in elementary and secondary schools and institutions of higher education. Provides financial assistance for drug and violence prevention activities. Coordinates education efforts in drug and violence prevention with those of other federal departments and agencies.

Elementary and Secondary Education (OESE)
(Education Dept.), Formula Grants (OFG), School Support and Accountability (SSA), Lyndon B. Johnson Bldg., 400 Maryland Ave. S.W, Room 3W200, 20202; (202) 453-5563. *Patrick Rooney, Director.*
Web, https://oese.ed.gov/offices/office-of-formula-grants/school-support-and-accountability

Partners with states to support policy development, data analysis, technical assistance, performance management, and reform implementation with a goal of improving student outcomes.

Elementary and Secondary Education (OESE)
(Education Dept.), Formula Grants (OFG), School Support and Accountability (SSA), Education for Homeless Children and Youth Program, Lyndon B. Johnson Bldg., 400 Maryland Ave. S.W., 20202-6132; (202) 453-6777. Fax, (202) 260-7764. *John McLaughlin, Program Officer; Bryan Thurmond, Program Officer.*
General email, HomelessEd@ed.gov
Web, https://oese.ed.gov/offices/office-of-formula-grants/school-support-and-accountability/education-for-homeless-children-and-youths-grants-for-state-and

Provides formula grants to education agencies in the states, Puerto Rico, and through the Bureau of Indian Affairs to Native Americans to educate homeless children and youth and to establish an office of coordinator of education for homeless children and youth in each jurisdiction.

Elementary and Secondary Education (OESE)
(Education Dept.), Indian Education (OIE), Lyndon B. Johnson Bldg., 400 Maryland Ave. S.W., #3E205, 20202-6335; (202) 453-7042. Fax, (202) 260-7779. *Julian Guerrero Jr., Director.*
General email, indian.education@ed.gov
Web, https://oese.ed.gov/offices/office-of-indian-education

Aids local school districts with programs for Native American and Alaska Native students.

Elementary and Secondary Education (OESE)
(Education Dept.), Migrant Education (OME), Lyndon B. Johnson Bldg., 400 Maryland Ave. S.W., #3E317, LBJ, 20202-6135; (202) 453-5563. Fax, (202) 205-0089. *Lisa Gillette, Director.*
Web, https://oese.ed.gov/offices/office-of-migrant-education

Administers grant programs that provide academic and supportive services to the children of families who migrate to find work in the agricultural and fishing industries.

Elementary and Secondary Education (OESE)
(Education Dept.), State and Grantee Relations and Evidence Based Practices, Lyndon B. Johnson Bldg., 400 Maryland Ave. S.W., 20202; (202) 453-5563. *Laura Jimenez, Director, State and Grantee Relations.*
Web, https://oese.ed.gov/offices/office-state-grantee-relations-evidence-based-practices

Identifies best practices to support academic outcomes, improve teaching quality, and ensure educational equity, and provides customer service to states and grantees to help them access necessary resources. Divided into two sub-offices: Evidence-Based Practices and State and Grantee Relations.

English Language Acquisition (OELA) *(Education Dept.)*, *Lyndon B. Johnson Bldg., 400 Maryland Ave. S.W., #5E106, 20202-6510; (202) 401-6781. Fax, (202) 260-1292. Vacant, Assistant Deputy Secretary.*
Web, www2.ed.gov/about/offices/list/oela

Provides grants for the professional development of teachers of English learners and administers the Native American/Alaska-Native Children in School Program and National Professional Development Discretionary Grant Programs.

National Assessment Governing Board, *800 N. Capitol St. N.W., #825, 20002-4233; (202) 357-6938. Lesley Muldoon, Executive Director.*
General email, nagb@ed.gov

Web, www.nagb.org, Twitter, @GovBoard and Facebook, www.facebook.com/TheGoverningBoard

Independent board of local, state, and federal officials, educators, and others appointed by the secretary of education and funded under the National Assessment of Educational Progress (NAEP) program. Sets policy for NAEP, a series of tests measuring achievements of U.S. students since 1969.

United States Presidential Scholars Program
(Education Dept.), 400 Maryland Ave. S.W., #5E228, 20202-8173; (202) 401-0961. Fax, (202) 260-7465. Simone M. Olson, Executive Director. Toll-free, 800-USA-LEARN.
General email, Presidential.Scholars@ed.gov

Web, www2.ed.gov/programs/psp and Twitter, @usedgov

Honorary recognition program that selects 161 graduating high school seniors who demonstrate outstanding achievement in academics, community service, artistic ability, leadership, and career and technical fields.

►CONGRESS

For a listing of relevant congressional committees and subcommittees, please see page 176 or the Appendix.

►NONGOVERNMENTAL

Afterschool Alliance, *1101 14th St. N.W., #700, 20005; (202) 347-2030. Fax, (202) 347-2092. Jodi Grant, Executive Director. Press, (202) 371-1999. Toll-free, (866) 543-7863.*
General email, info@afterschoolalliance.org

Web, www.afterschoolalliance.org, Twitter, @afterschool4all and Facebook, www.facebook .com/afterschoolalliancedc

Advocacy group that campaigns for afterschooland summer programs. Partners include congressional and local government leaders. Trains selected Afterschool Ambassadors to educate policymakers about afterschool programs. Publishes reports supporting afterschool day care.

Alliance for Excellent Education, *1425 K St. N.W., #700, 20005; (202) 828-0828. Fax, (202) 828-0821. Deborah (Deb) Delisle, President, ext. 1.*
Web, www.all4ed.org, Twitter, @all4ed and Facebook, www.facebook.com/All4ed

Policy and advocacy organization committed to expanding equitable educational opportunities for students of color, students from low-income families, and other marginalized groups, graduate from high school and prepared to complete postsecondary education. Works to increase public awareness through webinars, conferences, reports, publications, and press releases. Monitors legislation and regulations.

Assn. for Childhood Education International, *1100 15th St. N.W., 4th Floor, 20005; (202) 372-9986. Fax, (202) 372-9989. Diane Whitehead, Chief Executive Officer. Toll-free, (800) 423-3563.*
General email, headquarters@acei.org

Web, www.acei.org, Twitter, @ChildhoodEdIntl and Facebook, www.facebook.com/ChildhoodEducationIntl/

Membership: educators, parents, and professionals who work with children (infancy to adolescence). Works to promote the rights, education, and well-being of children worldwide. Holds annual conference.

Center for Inspired Teaching, *5614 Connecticut Ave. N.W., #258, 20015; (202) 462-1956. Aleta Margolis, President.*
General email, info@inspiredteaching.org

Web, http://inspiredteaching.org, Twitter, @InspireTeach and Facebook, www.facebook.com/inspiredteaching

Promotes teaching skills that make the most of children's innate desire to learn. Provides professional development through course, mentoring, new teacher certification and residency programs, school partnerships, and a demonstration charter school.

Character.org, *P.O. Box 650307, Sterling, VA 20165; (202) 296-7743. Fax, (202) 296-7779. Arthur Schwartz, President.*
General email, information@character.org

Web, http://character.org, Twitter, @CharacterDotOrg and Facebook, www.facebook.com/characterdotorg

Promotes the integration of character development in schools and education. Trains education professionals to support character development and social-emotional learning skills, and decrease student behavioral problems. Sponsors an annual forum and publication on effective character education practices.

Council for Professional Recognition, *2460 16th St. N.W., 20009-3547; (202) 265-9090. Fax, (202) 265-9161. Calvin Moore Jr., Chief Executive Officer. Toll-free, (800) 424-4310.*
CDA Candidates email, CouncilNetworks@cdacouncil.org, Web, www.cdacouncil.org, Twitter, @cdacouncil, Facebook, www.facebook.com/cdacouncil and YouTube, www.youtube.com/user/theCDACredential

Promotes high standards for early childhood teachers. Awards credentials to family day care, preschool, home visitor, and infant-toddler caregivers. Administers the Child Development Associate National Credentialing Program, designed to assess and credential early childhood education professionals.

Council of Chief State School Officers, *1 Massachusetts Ave. N.W., #800, 20001-1431; (202) 336-7000. Carissa Moffat Miller, Chief Executive Director. Press, (202) 336-7034.*
General email, communications@ccsso.org
Web, http://ccsso.org, Twitter, @CCSSO and Facebook, www.facebook.com/ccsso

Membership: the public officials who head departments of elementary and secondary education in the states, the District of Columbia, the Department of Defense Education Activity, and five U.S. extrastate jurisdictions. Provides leadership, advocacy, and technical assistance on major educational issues. Seeks member consensus on major educational issues and acts as advocate on issue positions to civic and professional organizations, federal agencies, Congress, and the public.

Council of the Great City Schools, *1331 Pennsylvania Ave. N.W., #1100N, 20004-1758; (202) 393-2427. Fax, (202) 393-2400. Raymond (Ray) C. Hart, Executive Director.*
Web, www.cgcs.org and Twitter, @GreatCitySchls

Membership: superintendents and school board members of large urban school districts. Provides research, legislative, and support services for members; interests include elementary and secondary education and school finance.

DECA Inc., *1908 Association Dr., Reston, VA 20191-1594; (703) 860-5000. Frank Peterson, Executive Director.*
General email, info@deca.org
Web, www.deca.org, Twitter, @DECAInc and Facebook, www.facebook.com/decainc

Educational organization that helps high school and college students develop skills in marketing, management, finance, hospitality, and entrepreneurship. Promotes business and education partnerships.

Editorial Projects in Education, Inc., *6935 Arlington Rd., #100, Bethesda, MD 20814-5233; (301) 280-3100. Fax, (301) 280-3200. Michele J. Givens, President. Toll-free, (800) 346-1834.*
Web, www.edweek.org, Twitter, @educationweek and Facebook, www.facebook.com/edweek

Promotes awareness of important issues in K–12 education among professionals and the public. Publishes the journal *Education Week*, books, special reports, and video productions on topics of interest to educators.

Family, Career, and Community Leaders of America, *1910 Association Dr., Reston, VA 20191-1584; (703) 476-4900. Fax, (703) 439-2662. Sandy Spavone, Executive Director.*

General email, national@fcclainc.org
Web, www.fcclainc.org, Twitter, @NationalFCCLA and Facebook, www.facebook.com/nationalfccla

Membership; National vocational student organization that helps students through grade 12 address personal, family, work, and social issues through family and consumer sciences education.

Institute for Educational Leadership (IEL), *4301 Connecticut Ave. N.W., #100, 20008; (202) 822-8405. Fax, (202) 872-4050. Eddie Koen, President.*
General email, iel@iel.org
Web, www.iel.org, Twitter, @IELconnects and Facebook, www.facebook.com/IELconnects

Works with educators, human services personnel, government officials, and association executives to improve educational opportunities for youths; conducts research on education issues.

National Assn. for College Admission Counseling, *1050 N. Highland St., #400, Arlington, VA 22201; (703) 836-2222. Fax, (703) 243-9375. Angel B. Pérez, Chief Executive Officer, (703) 299-6828. Toll-free, (800) 822-6285.*
General email, info@nacacnet.org
Web, www.nacacnet.org, Twitter, @NACAC and Facebook, www.facebook.com/nacacnet.org/?ref=sgm

Membership: high school guidance counselors, independent counselors, college and university admissions officers, and financial aid officers. Promotes and funds research on admission counseling and on the transition from high school to college. Acts as advocate for student rights in college admissions. Sponsors national college fairs and continuing education for members.

National Assn. for the Education of Young Children, *1401 H St. N.W., #600, 20005; (202) 232-8777. Fax, (202) 328-1846. Rhian Evans Allvin, Chief Executive Officer, ext. 8819. Toll-free, (800) 424-2460.*
General email, help@naeyc.org
Web, www.naeyc.org, Twitter, @NAEYC, Facebook, www.facebook.com/NAEYC/ and YouTube, www.youtube.com/channel/UCoqygeWY9InViJE5bGSE_eg

Membership: early childhood teachers, administrators, college faculty, and directors of early childhood programs at the state and local levels. Works to improve the education of and the quality of services to children from birth through age eight. Sponsors professional development opportunities for early childhood educators. Offers an accreditation program and conducts two conferences annually; issues publications.

National Assn. of Elementary School Principals, *1615 Duke St., Alexandria, VA 22314; (703) 684-3345. Fax, (703) 549-5568. L. Earl Franks, Executive Director, ext. 250. Toll-free, (800) 386-2377.*
General email, naesp@naesp.org
Web, www.naesp.org, Twitter, @naesp and Facebook, www.facebook.com/naesp

Membership: elementary school and middle school principals; pre-K through 8. Conducts workshops for members on federal and state policies and programs and on professional development. Offers assistance in contract negotiations.

National Assn. of Secondary School Principals, *1904 Association Dr., Reston, VA 20191-1537; (703) 860-0200. Ronn Nozoe, Chief Executive Officer. Toll-free, (800) 253-7746.*
Web, www.nassp.org, Twitter, @nassp, Facebook, www .facebook.com/principals and YouTube, www.youtube .com/user/NASSPtv

Membership: principals and assistant principals of middle schools and senior high schools, both public and private, and college-level teachers of secondary education. Conducts training programs for members; serves as clearinghouse for information on secondary school administration. Student activities office provides student councils, student activity advisers, and national and junior honor societies with information on national associations.

National Center on Education and the Economy (NCEE), *2121 K St. N.W., #700, 20037; (202) 379-1800. Fax, (202) 293-1560. Vicki Phillips, Chief Executive Officer. General email, info@ncee.org*
Web, www.ncee.org, Twitter, @CtrEdEcon and Facebook, www.facebook.com/TheNCEE

Partnership of states, school districts, corporations, foundations, and nonprofit organizations that provides research, analysis, advocacy, tools, and technical assistance to improve the nation's school systems, student performances, and training for the workplace. (Administers the National Institute for School Leadership.)

National Council for the Social Studies (NCSS), *8555 16th St., #500, Silver Spring, MD 20910; (301) 588-1800. Lawrence Paska, Executive Director, (301) 850-7451. Publications, (800) 683-0812.*
Web, www.socialstudies.org, Twitter, @NCSSNetwork, Facebook, www.facebook.com/socialstudies.org and YouTube, www.youtube.com/channel/ UCNIx1yh7E2FmwXK7yutnNyQ

Membership: curriculum developers, educational administrators, state supervisors, and social studies educators, including K–12 classroom teachers and university professors of history, political science, geography, economics, civics, psychology, sociology, and anthropology. Promotes the teaching of social studies; encourages research; sponsors publications; works with other organizations to advance social studies education.

National Governors Assn. (NGA), *Center for Best Practices, K-12 Education Division, 444 N. Capitol St. N.W., #267, 20001-1512; (202) 624-5300. Seth Gerson, Director.*
General email, info@nga.org
Web, www.nga.org/bestpractices/k-12-education

Provides information, research synthesis, policy analysis, and technical assistance to governors and their staff in the areas of early childhood and K–12 education. Focus areas include whole child; personalized education; human capital; standards, assessments, and accountability; and governance and finance.

National Head Start Assn., *1651 Prince St., Alexandria, VA 22314; (703) 739-0875. Yasmina S. Vinci, Executive Director; Bob Bissen, Director Government Affairs. Toll-free, (866) 677-8724.*
Web, www.nhsa.org, Twitter, @NatlHeadStart, Facebook, www.facebook.com/NatlHeadStart and YouTube, www.youtube.com/channel/UCrsfP8Bs-9MsWFoOxQ2I5hQ

Membership: organizations that represent Head Start children, families, and staff. Recommends strategies on issues affecting Head Start programs; provides training and professional development opportunities. Monitors legislation and regulations.

National PTA, *1250 N. Pitt St., Alexandria, VA 22314; (703) 518-1200. Fax, (703) 836-0942. Nathan R. Monell, Executive Director. Toll-free, (800) 307-4782. General email, info@pta.org*
Web, www.pta.org, Twitter, @NationalPTA and Facebook, www.facebook.com/ParentTeacherAssociation

Membership: parent-teacher associations at the preschool, elementary, and secondary levels. Washington office represents members' interests on education, funding for education, parent involvement, child protection and safety, comprehensive health care for children, AIDS, the environment, children's television and educational technology, child care, and nutrition.

National School Boards Assn., *1680 Duke St., 2nd Floor, Alexandria, VA 22314-3493; (703) 838-6722. Fax, (571) 470-5108. John Heim, Executive Director, (703) 838-6730. General email, info@nsba.org*
Web, www.nsba.org, Twitter, @NSBAComm and Facebook, www.facebook.com/SchoolBoards

Federation of state school board associations. Interests include funding of public education, local governance, and quality of education programs. Sponsors seminars, an annual conference, and an information center. Publishes a monthly journal and various newsletters. Monitors legislation and regulations. Library open to the public by appointment.

Reading Is Fundamental, *750 1st St. N.E., #920, 20002; (202) 536-3400. Fax, (202) 536-3518. Alicia Levi, President. Toll-free, 877-RIF-READ.*
General email, contactus@rif.org
Web, www.rif.org, Twitter, @RIFWEB and Facebook, www.facebook.com/ReadingIsFundamental

Conducts programs and workshops to motivate young people to read. Provides young people in low-income neighborhoods with free books and parents with services to encourage reading at home.

School Nutrition Assn., *2900 S. Quincy St., #700, Arlington, VA 22206; (703) 824-3000. Fax, (703) 824-3015. Patricia Montague, Chief Executive Officer. Toll-free, (800) 877-8822.*

General email, servicecenter@schoolnutrition.org

Web, https://schoolnutrition.org and
Twitter, @SchoolLunch

Membership: state and national food service workers and supervisors, school cafeteria managers, nutrition educators, industry members, and others interested in school food programs and child nutrition. Offers credentialing and sponsors National School Lunch Week and National School Breakfast Week. (Formerly the American School Food Service Assn.)

Teach for America, *Washington Office, 1805 7th St. N.W., 7th Floor, 20001; (202) 552-2400. Ryan Tauriainen, Executive Director. Toll-free, (800) 832-1230.*

General email, admissions@teachforamerica.org

Web, www.teachforamerica.org/where-we-work/dc-region, Twitter, @TFADCRegion and Facebook, www.facebook .com/teachforamerica

A national teacher corps of recent college graduates who teach in underfunded urban and rural public schools. Promotes outstanding teaching methodologies and educational equity. Monitors legislation and regulations. (Headquarters in New York.)

Thomas B. Fordham Institute, *National Office, 1016 16th St. N.W., 8th Floor, 20036; (202) 223-5452. Michael J. Petrilli, President.*

General email, thegadfly@edexcellence.net

Web, https://edexcellence.net, Twitter, @educationgadfly, Facebook, www.facebook.com/educationgadfly and YouTube, www.youtube.com/user/educationgadfly

Advocates education reform to improve the quality of children's school systems. Researches and analyzes education policy issues. Brings scholars to the Capitol to brainstorm solutions to national education issues with education policy experts. Distributes an online course that educates the public about fundamental education policies that affect young students. Publishes the newsletter *The Education Gadfly Weekly.*

Private, Parochial, and Home Schooling

▶NONGOVERNMENTAL

Americans United for Separation of Church and State, *1310 L St. N.W., #200, 20005; (202) 466-3234. Fax, (202) 466-3353. Rachel Laser, President.*

General email, americansunited@au.org

Web, www.au.org and Twitter, @americansunited

Citizens' interest group. Opposes federal and state aid to parochial schools; works to ensure religious neutrality in public schools; supports free religious exercise; initiates litigation; maintains speakers bureau. Monitors legislation and regulations.

Council for American Private Education, *1300 Pennsylvania Ave. N.W., #190-433, 20004; (844) 883-2273. Gary B. Arnold, President.*

General email, cape@capenet.org

Web, http://capenet.org, Twitter, @capenet, Facebook, www.facebook.com/capenet and YouTube, www.youtube.com/user/CapeNet1

Coalition of national private school associations serving private elementary and secondary schools. Acts as a liaison between private education and government, other educational organizations, the media, and the public. Seeks greater access to private schools for all families. Monitors legislation and regulations.

Home School Legal Defense Assn., *P.O. Box 3000, Purcellville, VA 20134-9000; (540) 338-5600. Fax, (540) 338-2733. J. Michael Smith, President.*

General email, info@hslda.org

Web, www.hslda.org and Twitter, @HSLDA

Membership: families who practice home schooling. Provides members with legal consultation and defense. Initiates civil rights litigation on behalf of members. Monitors legislation and regulations.

National Assn. of Independent Schools, *Government Relations, 1129 20th St. N.W., #800, 20036-3425; (202) 973-9700. Fax, (888) 316-3862. Donna Orem, President, (202) 973-9711.*

General email, generalinfo@nais.org

Web, www.nais.org and Twitter, @NAISnetwork

Membership: independent elementary and secondary schools in the United States and abroad. Provides statistical and educational information to members. Monitors legislation and regulations.

National Catholic Educational Assn., *407 Bicksler Sq. S.E., Leesburg, VA 20175-3773; (571) 257-0010. Fax, (703) 243-0025. Lincoln Snyder, President. Toll-free, (800) 711-6232.*

Web, www.ncea.org, Twitter, @NCEATALK and Facebook, www.facebook.com/nceaorg

Membership: Catholic schools (preschool through college and seminary) and school administrators. Provides consultation services to members for administration, curriculum, continuing education, religious education, campus ministry, boards of education, and union and personnel negotiations; conducts workshops and conferences; supports federal aid for private education. (Affiliated with the Assn. of Catholic Colleges and Universities.)

National PTA, *1250 N. Pitt St., Alexandria, VA 22314; (703) 518-1200. Fax, (703) 836-0942. Nathan R. Monell, Executive Director. Toll-free, (800) 307-4782.*

General email, info@pta.org

Web, www.pta.org, Twitter, @NationalPTA and Facebook, www.facebook.com/ParentTeacherAssociation

Membership: parent-teacher associations at the preschool, elementary, and secondary levels. Coordinates the National Coalition for Public Education, which opposes tuition tax credits and vouchers for private education.

U.S. Conference of Catholic Bishops (USCCB), *Secretariat of Catholic Education, 3211 4th St. N.E., 20017-1194; (202) 541-3132. Mary Pat Donoghue, Executive Director.*

Web, www.usccb.org/committees/catholic-education and *Twitter, @USCCBCatholicEd*

Represents Catholic bishops in the United States in public policy educational issues.

SPECIAL GROUPS IN EDUCATION

Gifted and Talented

▶**NONGOVERNMENTAL**

Council for Exceptional Children (CEC), *3100 Clarendon Blvd., #600, Arlington, VA 22201; (703) 620-3660. Chad Rummel, Executive Director, (703) 264-9404. Toll-free, (888) 232-7733.*
General email, service@exceptionalchildren.org
Web, www.exceptionalchildren.org,
Twitter, @CECMembership, Facebook, www.facebook .com/cechq and *YouTube, www.youtube.com/c/Council ExceptionalChildren*

Membership association that acts on behalf of children with exceptionalities through advocacy, standards, and professional development. Sets professional standards for the field; publishes books, journals, newsletters, and other resources; and offers professional development for teachers and administrators, including an annual convention. Sponsors the Yes I Can! Awards for children with disabilities who excel. Monitors legislation and regulations.

National Assn. for Gifted Children, *1300 Eye St. N.W., #400E, 20005; (202) 785-4268. Fax, (202) 785-4248. John Segota, Executive Director.*
General email, nagc@nagc.org
Web, www.nagc.org, Twitter, @NAGCGIFTED and *Facebook, www.facebook.com/nagcgifted/*

Membership: teachers, administrators, state coordinators, and parents. Acts as advocate for increased federal support for intellectually and creatively gifted children in public and private schools. Produces publications and conducts training for educators and parents.

Learning and Physically Disabled

▶**AGENCIES**

Institute of Education Sciences *(Education Dept.), National Center for Special Education Research (NCSER), 550 12th St. S.W., #4144, 20202; (202) 245-6940. Fax, (202) 245-6113. Joan McLaughlin, Commissioner, (202) 245-8201.*
Web, http://ies.ed.gov/ncser

Sponsors a comprehensive program of special education research designed to expand the knowledge and understanding of infants, toddlers, and children with disabilities.

John F. Kennedy Center for the Performing Arts, *VSA and Accessibility, 2700 F St. N.W., 20566 (mailing address: P.O. Box 101510, Arlington, VA 22210); (202) 416-8727. Betty Siegel, JD., Director.*
General email, access@kennedy-center.org
Web, www.kennedy-center.org/education/vsa, Twitter, @accessLEAD and *Facebook, www.facebook.com/ VSAInternational*

Initiates and supports research and program development providing arts training and programming for persons with disabilities to make classrooms and communities more inclusive. Provides technical assistance, webinars, online course and training to VSA Arts state organizations; acts as an information clearinghouse for arts and persons with disabilities. Ensures that performances and facilities accessible to all audiences, and provide resources and opportunities for educators, cultural administrators, emerging and professional artists and performers with disabilities. Programs include VSA playwright discovery, international young soloists, international art and emerging young artists.

Office of Personnel Management (OPM), *Policy, Data, Oversight, Veterans Services, 1900 E St. N.W., #7439, 20415; (202) 606-3602. Fax, (202) 606-6017. Hakeem A. Basheerud-Deen, Director.*
Web, www.opm.gov/policy-data-oversight/veterans-services

Provides outreach to colleges and universities on Schedule A hiring authorities for people with disabilities.

Smithsonian Institution, *Accessibility Program, 14th St. and Constitution Ave. N.W., #1050, 20013-7012 (mailing address: National Museum of American History, P.O. Box 37012, MS 607, Washington, DC 20013-7012); (202) 633-2921. Elizabeth (Beth) Ziebarth, Director.*
General email, access@si.edu
Web, www.si.edu/Accessibility

Coordinates the Smithsonian's efforts to improve accessibility of its programs and facilities to visitors and staff with disabilities. Serves as a resource for museums and individuals nationwide.

Special Education and Rehabilitative Services (OSERS) *(Education Dept.), Lyndon B. Johnson Bldg., 400 Maryland Ave. S.W., 20202-7100; (202) 245-7468. Fax, (202) 245-7638. Katherine Neas, Assistant Secretary (Acting).*
Web, www2.ed.gov/about/offices/list/osers

Administers federal assistance programs for the education and rehabilitation of people with disabilities through the Office of Special Education Programs and the Rehabilitation Services Administration; maintains a national information clearinghouse for people with disabilities. Provides information on federal legislation and programs and national organizations concerning individuals with disabilities.

Special Education and Rehabilitative Services (OSERS) *(Education Dept.), Special Education Programs (OSEP), Lyndon B. Johnson Bldg., 400 Maryland Ave. S.W., 20202-7100; (202) 245-7459. Fax, (202) 245-7323. Valerie C. Williams, Director.*
Web, www2.ed.gov/about/offices/list/osers/osep/index.html

Responsible for special education programs and services designed to meet the needs and develop the full potential of children from infancy through age 21. Programs include support for training of teachers and other professional personnel; grants for research; financial aid to help states initiate and improve their resources; and media services and captioned films for hearing-impaired persons.

▶CONGRESS

For a listing of relevant congressional committees and subcommittees, please see page 176 or the Appendix.

Library of Congress, National Library Service for the Blind and Print Disabled, *1291 Taylor St. N.W., 20542 (mailing address: Library of Congress, Washington, DC 20542); (202) 707-5100. Fax, (202) 707-0712. Jason Broughton, Director. Toll-Free, (800) 424-8567. Toll-free Braille and print, (888) 657-7323. General email, nlsref@loc.gov*

Web, www.loc.gov/nls, Braille email, braille@loc.gov and Facebook, www.facebook.com/thatallmayread

Administers free braille and talking book library service for people with temporary or permanent low vision, blindness, or a physical, perceptual, or reading disability. Coordinates national network of cooperating libraries, circulates books and magazines in braille or audio formats which are downloadable or delivered by mail free of charge. Reference section answers questions relating to blindness and physical disabilities and on library services available to persons with disabilities.

▶NONGOVERNMENTAL

Assn. for Education and Rehabilitation of the Blind and Visually Impaired, *5680 King Centre Dr., #600, Alexandria, VA 22315; (703) 671-4500. Mark Richert, Executive Director (Acting). Toll-free, (877) 492-2708. General email, aer@aerbvi.org*

Web, www.aerbvi.org, Twitter, @AERBVI and Facebook, www.facebook.com/AERBVI

Membership: professionals who work in all phases of education and rehabilitation of children and adults who are blind and visually impaired. Provides support and professional development opportunities through conferences, continuing education, and publications. Issues professional recognition awards and student scholarships. Monitors legislation and regulations.

Assn. of University Centers on Disabilities (AUCD), *1100 Wayne Ave., #1000, Silver Spring, MD 20910; (301) 588-8252. Fax, (301) 588-2842. John Tschida, Executive Director. General email, aucdinfo@aucd.org*

Web, www.aucd.org, Twitter, @AUCDNews and Facebook, www.facebook.com/AUCDnetwork

Network of facilities that diagnose and treat the developmentally disabled. Trains graduate students and professionals in the field; helps state and local agencies develop services. Interests include interdisciplinary training and services, early screening to prevent developmental disabilities, and development of equipment and programs to serve persons with disabilities. Advances policy and practise for families and communities.

Council for Exceptional Children (CEC), *3100 Clarendon Blvd., #600, Arlington, VA 22201; (703) 620-3660. Chad Rummel, Executive Director, (703) 264-9404. Toll-free, (888) 232-7733. General email, service@exceptionalchildren.org*

Web, www.exceptionalchildren.org, Twitter, @CECMembership, Facebook, www.facebook.com/cechq and YouTube, www.youtube.com/c/CouncilExceptionalChildren

Membership association that acts on behalf of children with exceptionalities through advocacy, standards, and professional development. Sets professional standards for the field; publishes books, journals, newsletters, and other resources; and offers professional development for teachers and administrators, including an annual convention. Sponsors the Yes I Can! Awards for children with disabilities who excel. Monitors legislation and regulations.

Council for Opportunity in Education, *1025 Vermont Ave. N.W., #400, 20005-3516; (202) 347-7430. Fax, (202) 347-0786. Maureen Hoyler, President, ext. 321. Web, www.coenet.org, Twitter, @COETalk, Facebook, www.facebook.com/councilforopportunity ineducation and YouTube, www.youtube.com/channel/UCCVcLrUp-XPcyiR-FvHMq-Q/*

Membership: more than 1,000 colleges and agencies. Works in conjunction with colleges and agencies that host the federally funded TRIO programs, designed to help low-income first-generation immigrants, students with disabilities, and veterans enroll in and graduate from college.

Gallaudet University, *800 Florida Ave. N.E., 20002-3695; (202) 651-5000. Roberta (Bobbi) Cordano, President, (202) 250-2837, Videophone. Web, www.gallaudet.edu, Twitter, @GallaudetU, Facebook, www.facebook.com/gallaudetu and Media, public.relations@gallaudet.edu*

Offers undergraduate, graduate, and doctoral degree programs for deaf, hard-of-hearing, and hearing students. Conducts research; maintains the Laurent Clerc National Deaf Education Center and demonstration preschool, elementary (Kendall Demonstration Elementary School), and secondary (Model Secondary School for the Deaf) programs. Sponsors the Center for Global Education, National Deaf Education Network and Clearinghouse, and the Cochlear Implant Education Center. Links to each department's video phone are at www.gallaudet.edu/about_gallaudet/contact_us.html.

National Assn. of Private Special Education Centers, *200 Massachusetts Ave. N.W., #700, 20001; (202) 434-8225. Danielle Damm, Executive Director. General email, napsec@napsec.org*

Web, www.napsec.org

Represents private special education programs, residential therapeutic centers, and early intervention services at the preschool, elementary, and secondary levels and postsecondary levels, as well as adult programs. Acts as advocate for greater education opportunities for children, youth, and adults with disabilities.

National Assn. of State Directors of Special Education, *1800 Diagonal Rd., #600, Alexandria, VA 22314; (703) 519-3800. Fax, (703) 519-3808. John Eisenberg, Executive Director.*
General email, nasdse@nasdse.org
Web, www.nasdse.org, Twitter, @nasdse and Facebook, www.facebook.com/NASDSE

Membership: state directors of special education and others interested in special education policy. Monitors legislation, regulations, policy, and research affecting special education.

Minorities and Women

▶**AGENCIES**

Bureau of Indian Education (BIE) *(Interior Dept.), 1849 C St. N.W., #3609-MIB, 20240; (202) 208-6123. Tony L. Dearman, Director.*
Web, www.bie.edu, Twitter, @BureauIndianEdu and Facebook, www.facebook.com/Bureauofindianeducation

Operates schools and promotes school improvement for Native Americans, including people with disabilities. Provides assistance to Native American pupils in public schools. Aids Native American college students. Sponsors adult education programs designed specifically for Native Americans.

Civil Rights Division *(Justice Dept.), Educational Opportunities (EOS), 150 M St. N.E., #10.202, 20002; (202) 514-4092. Fax, (202) 514-8337. Shaheena Simons, Chief. Toll-free, (877) 292-3804.*
General email, education@usdoj.gov
Web, www.justice.gov/crt/educational-opportunities-section

Initiates litigation to ensure equal opportunities in public education; enforces laws dealing with civil rights in public education. Responsible for enforcing Title IV of the Civil Rights Act of 1964, the Equal Educational Opportunities Act of 1974, and Title II of the Americans with Disabilities Act.

Education Dept., *Civil Rights (OCR), Lyndon B. Johnson Bldg., 400 Maryland Ave. S.W., #4E313, 20202-1100; (202) 453-5900. Fax, (202) 453-6012. Catherine E. Lhamon, Assistant Secretary. Toll-free, (800) 421-3481. TTY, (800) 877-8339.*
General email, ocr@ed.gov
Web, www2.ed.gov/ocr and Twitter, @EDcivilrights

Enforces laws prohibiting use of federal funds for education programs or activities that discriminate on the basis of race, color, sex, national origin, age, or disability; authorized to discontinue funding.

Education Dept., *White House Initiative on Advancing Educational Equity, Excellence, and Economic Opportunity for Hispanics, Lyndon B. Johnson Bldg., 400 Maryland Ave. S.W., #7E324, 20202-3601; (202) 401-1411. Fax, (202) 401-8377. Melody Gonzales, Executive Director.*
General email, whitehousehispanicinitiative@ed.gov
Web, http://sites.ed.gov/hispanic-initiative, Twitter, @WhiteHouseHPI and Facebook, www.facebook.com/WhiteHouseHispanicInitiative

Promotes high-quality education for Hispanic communities and the participation of Hispanics in federal education programs. Disseminates information on educational resources. Promotes parental involvement, engagement of the business community, early learning programs, and enrollment in college. Works directly with communities nationwide in public–private partnerships.

Education Dept., *White House Initiative on Advancing Educational Equity, Excellence, and Economic Opportunity, Historically Black Colleges and Universities, Lyndon B. Johnson Bldg., 400 Maryland Ave. S.W., #7E306, 20202; (202) 453-5634. Fax, (202) 453-5632. Vacant, Executive Director.*
General email, oswhi-hbcu@ed.gov
Web, http://sites.ed.gov/whhbcu

Seeks to expand the participation of the black college community in the programs of the federal government and to engage the private sector to help achieve this objective. Hosts annual conference. Provides information about federal contracts, grants, scholarships, fellowships, and other resources available to historically Black colleges and universities.

Education Dept., *White House Initiative on Advancing Educational Quality, Excellence, and Economic Opportunity for Black Americans, Lyndon B. Johnson Bldg., 400 Maryland Ave. S.W., 20202; Vacant, Executive Director. Press, (202) 401-2000.*
Web, http://sites.ed.gov/whblackeducation, Twitter, @afameducation and Facebook, www.facebook.com/WHBlackEducation

Promotes high-quality education for Black Americans by improving access to learning opportunities for educators and administrators, supporting efforts to increase the number of Black teachers and administrators, enhancing investments in early care and education programs, reinforcing connections to rigorous K–12 courses and increasing access to critical supports, and helping to increase the number of Black students applying to, persisting in, and successfully completing college.

Education Dept., *White House Initiative on Advancing Educational Quality, Excellence, and Economic Opportunity, Native Americans and Strengthening Tribal Colleges and Universities, White House Initiative American Indian and Alaska Native Education, Lyndon B. Johnson Bldg., 400 Maryland Ave. S.W., #4W116, 20002; (202) 453-6600. Fax, (202) 453-5635. Ron Lessard, Program Specialist, (202) 453-5509.*

Web, http://sites.ed.gov/whiaiane and *Twitter, @WhiteHouseAIAN*

Supports activities that expand and improve educational opportunities for American Indians and Alaska Native students. Interests include reducing the student dropout rate, strengthening tribal colleges and universities, and helping students acquire industry-recognized credentials for job attainment and advancement. Supports teaching native languages and histories at all educational levels.

Elementary and Secondary Education (OESE)

(Education Dept.), Indian Education (OIE), Lyndon B. Johnson Bldg., 400 Maryland Ave. S.W., #3E205, 20202-6335; (202) 453-7042. Fax, (202) 260-7779. Julian Guerrero Jr., Director.
General email, indian.education@ed.gov

Web, https://oese.ed.gov/offices/office-of-indian-education

Aids local school districts with programs for Native American and Alaska Native students.

Elementary and Secondary Education (OESE)

(Education Dept.), Migrant Education (OME), Lyndon B. Johnson Bldg., 400 Maryland Ave. S.W., #3E317, LBJ, 20202-6135; (202) 453-5563. Fax, (202) 205-0089. Lisa Gillette, Director.
Web, https://oese.ed.gov/offices/office-of-migrant-education

Administers grant programs that provide academic and supportive services to the children of families who migrate to find work in the agricultural and fishing industries.

Health and Human Services Dept., *White House Initiative on Asian Americans, Native Hawaiians, and Pacific Islanders, 550 12th St. S.W., 10th Floor, 20202; (202) 482-1375. Krystal Ka'ai, Executive Director.*
General email, whiaanhpi@hhs.gov

Web, www.commerce.gov/whiaapi and *Twitter, @whitehouseAAPI*

Works to increase Asian American, Native Hawaiian, and Pacific Islander participation in federal education programs. Supports institutions of higher education through two-year grants to improve academic programs, institutional management, and fiscal stability.

Postsecondary Education (OPE) *(Education Dept.), Higher Education Programs (HEP), Institutional Service (IS), Lyndon B. Johnson Bldg., 400 Maryland Ave. S.W., 2nd Floor, 20202; (202) 453-6914. Fax, (202) 502-7699. Beatriz Ceja, Senior Director.*
General email, OPE_Institutional_Development@ed.gov
Web, www2.ed.gov/about/offices/list/ope/idues/index.html

Provides financial and administrative support for limited resource institutions serving minority and financially disadvantaged students. Administers programs authorized under the Higher Education Act of 1965 and its subsequent amendments. Title III programs include support for Historically Black Colleges and Universities, American Indian Tribally Controlled Colleges and Universities, and Minority Science and Engineering Improvement Program. Title V programs strengthen institutions serving Hispanic and other low-income students. Title VII supports the implementation and evaluation of and shares findings of innovative educational reform ideas.

Postsecondary Education (OPE) *(Education Dept.), Higher Education Programs (HEP), Institutional Service (IS), Minority Science and Engineering Improvement Program, Lyndon B. Johnson Bldg., 400 Maryland Ave. S.W., 4th Floor, 20202; (202) 453-7913. Bernadette Hence, Senior Program Manager.*
General email, OPE.MSEIP@ed.gov

Web, www2.ed.gov/programs/iduesmsi/index.html

Provides grants to predominantly minority institutions to effect long-range improvement in science and engineering education and to increase the flow of underrepresented ethnic minorities, particularly minority women, into science and engineering careers.

U.S. Commission on Civil Rights, *Civil Rights Evaluation, 1331 Pennsylvania Ave. N.W., #1150, 20425; (202) 376-7700. Vacant, Director. Complaints Unit hotline, (202) 376-8513. Toll-free hotline, (800) 552-6843. TTY, (800) 877-8339.*
General email, enforcement@usccr.gov

Web, www.usccr.gov/about/offices

Researches federal policy on education, including desegregation. Library open to the public.

▶ CONGRESS

For a listing of relevant congressional committees and subcommittees, please see page 176 or the Appendix.

▶ NONGOVERNMENTAL

American Assn. of University Women (AAUW), *1310 L St. N.W., #1000, 20005; (202) 785-7700. Fax, (202) 872-1425. Gloria L. Blackwell, Chief Executive Officer, ext. 7608. Toll-free, (800) 326-2289. TTY, (202) 785-7777.*
General email, connect@aauw.org

Web, www.aauw.org, Twitter, @aauw and *Facebook, www.facebook.com/AAUW.National*

Membership: graduates of accredited colleges, universities, and recognized foreign institutions. Interests include advancing gender equity for women and girls through research, education, and advocacy through the workplace, health care, and the family.

American Indian Higher Education Consortium, *121 Oronoco St., Alexandria, VA 22314; (703) 838-0400. Fax, (703) 838-0388. Carrie L. Billy, Chief Executive Officer.*
Web, http://aihec.org, Twitter, @aihec and *Facebook, www.facebook.com/American-Indian-Higher-Education-Consortium-206472546110004/timeline*

Membership: tribal colleges and universities (TCUs). Objectives include increased financial support for TCUs, equitable participation in the land-grant system, expanded technology programs in Indian Country, and development of an accrediting body for postsecondary institutions that serve American Indians.

Assn. of American Colleges and Universities (AACU),
1818 R St. N.W., 20009; (202) 387-3760. Fax, (202) 265-9532. Lynn Pasquerella, President, (202) 884-0812.
General email, information@aacu.org
Web, www.aacu.org, Twitter, @aacu and Facebook, www.facebook.com/Association-of-American-Colleges-and-Universities-48308128458

Serves as clearinghouse for information on women professionals in higher education. Interests include women's studies, women's centers, and women's leadership and professional development.

Assn. of Public and Land-Grant Universities, Office of Access, Success, and Equity, 1220 L St. N.W., #1000, 20005; (202) 478-6040. Fax, (202) 478-6046. Barnard Mair, Vice President (Acting), (202) 478-6083.
General email, info@aplu.org
Web, www.aplu.org and Twitter, @APLU_News

Seeks to improve equity, access, and successful outcomes at all public and land-grant universities with a special focus on underserved students and minority-serving institutions. Conducts research, provides advocacy, implements programs, and provides capacity building for such institutions; acts as a liaison between these institutions, the federal government, and private associations. Monitors legislation and regulations.

Clare Booth Luce Center for Conservative Women, 112 Elden St., Suite P, Herndon, VA 20170; (703) 318-0730. Fax, (703) 318-8867. Michelle Easton, President.
General email, info@cblwomen.org
Web, http://cblpi.org, Twitter, @CBLwomen and Facebook, www.facebook.com/CenterforConservative Women

Seeks to prepare women for effective leadership and to promote conservative values. Offers mentoring, internship, and networking opportunities. (Formerly the Clare Booth Luce Policy Institute.)

Council for Opportunity in Education, 1025 Vermont Ave. N.W., #400, 20005-3516; (202) 347-7430. Fax, (202) 347-0786. Maureen Hoyler, President, ext. 321.
Web, www.coenet.org, Twitter, @COETalk,
Facebook, www.facebook.com/councilforopportunityineducation and YouTube, www.youtube.com/channel/UCCVcLrUp-XPcyiR-FvHMq-Q/

Membership: more than 1,000 colleges and agencies. Works in conjunction with colleges and agencies that host the federally funded TRIO programs, designed to help low-income first-generation immigrants, students with disabilities, and veterans enroll in and graduate from college.

Hispanic Assn. of Colleges and Universities,
Washington Office, 1 Dupont Circle N.W., #430, 20036; (202) 833-8361. Fax, (202) 496-9177. Antonio R. Flores, President.

General email, dcgr@hacu.net
Web, www.hacu.net

Membership: Hispanic-serving institutions (HSIs) and other higher education institutions committed to improving the quality of schools for Hispanics in the United States, Puerto Rico, Latin America, and Spain. Focuses on increased federal funding for HSIs; partnerships with government agencies and industry; faculty development and research; technological assistance; and financial aid and internships for Hispanic students. (Headquarters in San Antonio, Tex.)

Institute for Responsible Citizenship, 1227 25th St. N.W., 6th Floor, 20037; (202) 660-2501.
William (Bill) A. Keyes IV, President.
Web, www.theinstitute.net, Facebook, www.facebook.com/responsiblecitizenship and Email, wkeyes@theinstitute.net

Offers grants, internships, and leadership courses for African American men scholars. Academic areas for internships include art, business, finance, philanthropy, education, government, health care, science, technology, law, public relations, and religion.

League of United Latin American Citizens, 1133 19th St. N.W., #1000, 20036; (202) 833-6130. Fax, (202) 833-6135. Sindy M. Benavides, Chief Executive Officer, ext. 108. Toll-free, (877) 585-2201.
General email, info@lulac.org
Web, https://lulac.org, Twitter, @LULAC and Facebook, www.facebook.com/lulac.national.dc

Seeks to increase the number of minorities, especially Hispanics, attending postsecondary schools; supports legislation to increase educational opportunities for Hispanics and other minorities; provides scholarship funds and educational and career counseling.

NAACP Legal Defense and Educational Fund, Inc.,
Washington Office, 700 14th St. N.W., #600, 20005; (202) 682-1300. Sherrilyn Ifill, President.
Web, www.naacpldf.org, Twitter, @naacp_ldf, Facebook, www.facebook.com/naacpldf and YouTube, www.youtube.com/channel/UCXTfPnpwx-CWVyrzDvkwE1w

Civil rights litigation group that provides legal information about civil rights and advice on educational discrimination against women and minorities; monitors federal enforcement of civil rights laws. Not affiliated with the NAACP. (Headquarters in New York.)

National Assn. for Equal Opportunity in Higher Education (NAFEO), 600 Maryland Ave. S.W. # 800E, 20024; (202) 552-3300. (202) 439-4704. Lezli Baskerville, Esq., President.
Web, www.nafeonation.org, Twitter, @_NAFEO and Facebook, www.facebook.com/NAFEO-461363094210790/

Membership: historically and predominantly black colleges and universities, including public, private, land-grant, two-year, four-year, graduate, and professional schools. Represents and acts as advocate on behalf of its member institutions and the students, faculty, and alumni they serve. Operates a national research and resource center on blacks in higher education.

National Assn. for the Advancement of Colored People (NAACP), Washington Bureau, *1156 15th St. N.W., #915, 20005; (202) 463-2940. Fax, (202) 463-2953. Derrick Johnson, President. General email, washingtonbureau@naacpnet.org*

Web, www.naacp.org, Twitter, @NAACP and Twitter, President, @DerrickNAACP

Membership: persons interested in civil rights for all minorities. Works for equal opportunity for minorities in all areas, including education; seeks to ensure a high-quality desegregated education for all through litigation and legislation. (Headquarters in Baltimore, MD.)

National Assn. of Colored Women's Clubs Inc. (NACWC), *1601 R St. N.W., 20009-6420; (202) 667-4080. Andrea Brooks-Smith, President. General email, nacwcinfo@gmail.com*

Web, www.nacwc.com, Facebook, www.facebook.com/ NACWC and Twitter, @NACWC1896

Seeks to promote education, protect and enforce civil rights, raise the standard of family living, promote interracial understanding, and enhance leadership development. Awards scholarships; conducts programs in education, social service, and philanthropy.

National Hispanic Foundation for the Arts (NHFA), *Washington Square, 1050 Connecticut Ave. N.W., 5th Floor, 20036; (202) 293-8330. Felix Sanchez, Chair. General email, info@hispanicarts.org*

Web, www.hispanicarts.org, Twitter, @HispanicArts and Facebook, www.facebook.com/hispanicarts

Strives to increase the presence of Hispanics in the media, telecommunications, entertainment industries, and performing arts, and to increase programming for the U.S. Latino community. Provides scholarships for Hispanic students to pursue graduate study in the arts.

National Indian Education Assn. (NIEA), *1514 P St. N.W., Suite B, 20005; (202) 544-7290. Diana Cournoyer, Executive Director, (202) 847-0033. General email, niea@niea.org*

Web, www.niea.org, Twitter, @WereNIEA and Facebook, www.facebook.com/NIEAFanPage

Represents American Indian, Alaska Native, and Native Hawaiian educators and students. Seeks to improve educational opportunities and resources for those groups nationwide while preserving their traditional cultures and values. Monitors legislation and regulations.

National Society of Black Engineers, *205 Daingerfield Rd., Alexandria, VA 22314; (703) 549-2207. Fax, (703) 683-5312. Janeen Uzzell, Chief Executive Officer. Web, www.nsbe.org, Twitter, @NSBE and Facebook, www.facebook.com/NSBE1975*

Membership: Black engineers and college students studying engineering. Offers academic excellence programs, scholarships, leadership training, and professional and career development opportunities. Activities include tutorial programs, group study sessions, high school/ junior high outreach programs, technical seminars and workshops, career fairs, and an annual convention.

National Women's Law Center, *11 Dupont Circle N.W., #800, 20036; (202) 588-5180. Fax, (202) 588-5185. Fatima Goss Graves, President. Legal help, (202) 319-3053. General email, info@nwlc.org*

Web, www.nwlc.org, Twitter, @nwlc and Facebook, www .facebook.com/nwlc

Works to protect and advance the rights of women and girls at work, in school, and beyond. Maintains programs that focus on enforcing Title IX's provisions for equal treatment in education and narrowing the gender gap in athletics and the technology-oriented workplace. Other interests include equal pay and benefits, sexual harassment laws, the right to family leave, child care and early learning, poverty and income support, and the preservation of diversity in the workplace.

Operation Understanding D.C., *4005 Wisconsin Ave. N.W., Box 5705, 20016; (202) 234-6832. Morgan Moeller, Executive Director (Acting). General email, info@oudc.org*

Web, www.oudc.org and Twitter, @OU_DC

African American and Jewish youth education program promoting leadership and antidiscrimination.

UnidosUS, *1126 16th St. N.W., #600, 20036-4845; (202) 785-1670. Janet Murguía, President. General email, info@unidos.org*

Web, www.unidosus.org, Twitter, @WeAreUnidosUS, Facebook, www.facebook.com/Weareunidosus and YouTube, www.youtube.com/c/UnidosUS

Provides research, policy analysis, and advocacy on educational status and needs of Hispanics; promotes education reform benefiting Hispanics; develops and tests community-based models for helping Hispanic students succeed in school. Interests include counseling, testing, and bilingual, vocational, preschool through postsecondary, and migrant education.

United Negro College Fund (UNCF), *1805 7th St. N.W., 20001 (mailing address: P.O. Box 10444, Fairfax, VA 22031-0444); (202) 810-0224. Fax, (202) 234-0224. Michael L. Lomax, President. Toll-free, (800) 331-2244. Web, www.uncf.org, Twitter, @UNCF and Facebook, www.facebook.com/UNCF*

Membership: private colleges and universities with historically black enrollment. Raises money for member institutions; monitors legislation and regulations.

Younger Women's Task Force, *1310 L St. N.W., #1000, 20005; (202) 785-7700. Fax, (202) 872-1425. Gloria Blackwell, Chief Executive Officer. Toll-free, (800) 326-2289. TTY, (202) 785-7777. General email, ywtf@aauw.org*

Web, www.aauw.org/membership/ywtf, Twitter, @AAUW and Facebook, www.facebook.com/AAUW.National

Grassroots organization that encourages young women to engage in political activism on issues directly affecting them. Provides leadership training and a local and national network for peer mentoring. (Sponsored by the American Assn. of University Women.)

SPECIAL TOPICS IN EDUCATION

Bilingual and Multicultural

▶**AGENCIES**

Bureau of Educational and Cultural Affairs (ECA) *(State Dept.), English Language Programs, 2200 C St. N.W., #4B16, 20520; (202) 632-9272. Joseph Bookbinder, Director, (202) 632-9281; Zachary Stewart, Administrative Assistant.*
General email, americanenglish@state.gov
Web, http://eca.state.gov/about-bureau/organizational-structure/office-english-language-programs, https://americanenglish.state.gov and YouTube, www.youtube.com/user/StateAmericanEnglish

Promotes the learning and teaching of American English around the world in order to foster mutual understanding between the people of other countries and the people of the United States.

English Language Acquisition (OELA) *(Education Dept.), Lyndon B. Johnson Bldg., 400 Maryland Ave. S.W., #5E106, 20202-6510; (202) 401-6781. Fax, (202) 260-1292. Vacant, Assistant Deputy Secretary.*
Web, www2.ed.gov/about/offices/list/oela

Provides grants for the professional development of teachers of English learners and administers the Native American/Alaska-Native Children in School Program and National Professional Development Discretionary Grant Programs.

Postsecondary Education (OPE) *(Education Dept.), Higher Education Programs (HEP), International and Foreign Language Education (IFLE), Lyndon B. Johnson Bldg., 400 Maryland Ave. S.W., #3E200, 20202; (202) 453-6950. Fax, (202) 453-5780. Cheryl Gibbs, Senior Director, (202) 453-5690.*
Web, www2.ed.gov/about/offices/list/ope/iegps/index.html and Twitter, @GoGlobalED

Advises the Assistant Secretary for Postsecondary Education on matters affecting postsecondary, international, and foreign language education. Responsible for encouraging and promoting the study of foreign languages and cultures of other countries at the elementary, secondary, and postsecondary levels in the United States. Administers programs that increase expertise in foreign languages and area or international studies, and coordinates with related international and foreign language education programs of other federal agencies.

▶**NONGOVERNMENTAL**

National Academies of Sciences, Engineering, and Medicine (NASEM), *Office of Testing and Assessment, Keck Center, 500 5th St. N.W., 11th Floor, 20001; (202)*

334-2300. Judy Koenig, Senior Program Officer, (540) 570-1324.
General email, dbasse@nas.edu
Web, http://sites.nationalacademies.org/dbasse/bota

Seeks to ensure fairness and accuracy in the testing of students with disabilities and English learners.

National Assn. for Bilingual Education, *1775 Eye St. N.W., #1150, 20006; (240) 450-3700. Nilda M. Aguirre, Executive Director (Acting).*
General email, nabe@nabe.org
Web, https://nabe.org, Twitter, @NABEorg and Facebook, www.facebook.com/nabeorg/

Membership: educators, policymakers, paraprofessionals, parents, personnel, students, and researchers. Works to strengthen educational programs for non-English-speaking students and to promote foreign language education among American students. Conducts annual conference and workshops; publishes research.

National Clearinghouse for English Language Acquisition (NCELA), *Language Instruction Educational Programs, 4340 East-West Hwy., #1100, Bethesda, MD 20814; Jennifer Himmell, Project Director.*
General email, askncela@manhattanstrategy.com
Web, https://ncela.ed.gov and Twitter, @askNCELA1

Collects, analyzes, and disseminates information relating to the effective education of linguistically and culturally diverse learners in the United States. Supports the Office of English Language Acquisition, Language Enhancement, and Academic Achievement for Limited English Proficient Students (OELA) in its mission to respond to Title III educational needs, and implement No Child Left Behind (NCLB) as it applies to English language learners. Supports networking among state-level administrators of Title III programs. Serves other stakeholders involved in English learner education, including teachers and other practitioners, parents, university faculty, administrators and federal policymakers. Authorized under Title III of the No Child Left Behind Act of 2001 (NCLB). Since October 2018, NCELA has been operated by Manhattan Strategy Group, under contract from the Education Dept.

National Foreign Language Center *(University of Maryland), 5600 Rivertech Ct., Suite K, Riverdale, MD 20737; (301) 405-9828. Fax, (301) 405-9829. Kathy Kilday, Lead Director; Rebecca Rubin Damari, Director of Research.*
General email, inquiries@nflc.org
Web, www.nflc.umd.edu and Twitter, @NFLC_UMD

Research and policy organization that develops new strategies for strengthening foreign language competence in the United States. Conducts research on national language needs and assists policymakers in identifying priorities, allocating resources, and designing programs. Interests include the role of foreign language in higher education, national competence in critical languages, ethnic language maintenance, and K–12 and postsecondary language programs.

TESOL International Assn., *1925 Ballenger Ave., #550, Alexandria, VA 22314-6820; (703) 518-2500. Amber Crowell Kelleher, Executive Director. Toll-free, (888) 888-4741.*
General email, info@tesol.org
Web, www.tesol.org, Twitter, @TESOL_Assn and Facebook, www.facebook.com/tesol.assn

Provides professional development programs and career services for teachers of English to speakers of other languages. Sponsors professional development programs and provides career management services. Promotes research, standards, and advocacy.

U.S. English Inc., *5335 Wisconsin Ave. N.W., #930, 20015; (202) 833-0100. Fax, (202) 833-0108. Mauro E. Mujica, Chair. Toll-free, (800) 787-8216.*
General email, info@usenglish.org
Web, www.usenglish.org

Advocates English as the official language of federal and state governments. Affiliate U.S. English Foundation promotes English language education for immigrants.

World Learning, *Global Development and Exchange Programs, 1015 15th St. N.W., #950, 20005-2065; (202) 408-5420. Fax, (202) 408-5397. Carol Jenkins, President, (202) 464-6643. Toll-free, (800) 858-0292. TTY, (202) 408-5420, ext. 711.*
General email, info@worldlearning.org
Web, www.worldlearning.org and Twitter, @WorldLearning

Provides training for English language teachers and other education professionals. Increases access to and the quality of basic education. Administered by World Learning's Division of International Development and Exchange Programs. Administers field-based study abroad programs, which offer semester and summer programs for high school, college, and graduate students.

Citizenship Education

▶**NONGOVERNMENTAL**

American Press Institute (API), *4401 N. Fairfax Dr., #300, Arlington, VA 22203; (571) 366-1200. Amy Kovac-Ashley, Executive Director (Acting), (571) 366-1037.*
General email, hello@pressinstitute.org
Web, www.americanpressinstitute.org, Twitter, @AmPress and Facebook, www.facebook.com/AmericanPressInstitute

Supports student programs that focus on newspaper readership and an appreciation of the First Amendment as ways of developing engaged and literate citizens.

Center for the Study of Statesmanship (CSS), *313 Caldwell Hall, 620 Michigan Ave. N.E., 20064; (301) 464-4277. Claes G. Ryn, Founding Director Emeritus.*

General email, smithws@cua.edu
Web, https://css.cua.edu/, Twitter, @CSSatCUA and Facebook, www.facebook.com/CSSatCUA

Promotes research, teaching, and public discussion about the meaning of statesmanship and how it can defuse conflict and foster respectful foreign and domestic relations. Explores the sources and prerequisites of sound leadership and how to counter such influences as intemperance and blinding ideology. Affiliated with Catholic University of America.

Close Up Foundation, *1330 Braddock Pl., #400, Alexandria, VA 22314-1952; (703) 706-3300. Timothy S. Davis, President. Toll-free, (800) 256-7387.*
General email, info@closeup.org
Web, https://closeup.org, Twitter, @CloseUp_DC and Facebook, www.facebook.com/CloseUpWashingtonDC

Sponsors week-long programs on American government in Washington, D.C., for middle and high school students.

Horatio Alger Assn. of Distinguished Americans, *99 Canal Center Plaza, #320, Alexandria, VA 22314; (703) 684-9444. Fax, (703) 684-9445. Terrence J. Giroux, Executive Director.*
General email, association@horatioalger.org
Web, www.horatioalger.org, Twitter, @HoratioAlgerUS and Facebook, www.facebook.com/HoratioAlgerUS

Educates young people about the economic and personal opportunities available in the American free enterprise system. Conducts seminars on careers in public and community service; operates internship program. Presents the Horatio Alger Youth Award to outstanding high school students and the Horatio Alger Award to professionals who have overcome adversity to achieve success in their respective fields. Awards college scholarships to individuals who have overcome adversity.

League of Women Voters (LWV), *1233 20th St. N.W., #5000, 20036-4508; (202) 429-1965. Virginia Kase Solomon, Chief Executive Officer.*
General email, lwv@lwv.org
Web, www.lwv.org, Twitter, @LWV and Facebook, www.facebook.com/leagueofwomenvoters

Promotes citizen knowledge of and involvement in representative government; conducts citizen education on current public policy issues; seeks to increase voter registration and turnout and protect voting rights; sponsors candidate forums and debates.

National 4-H Council, *7100 Connecticut Ave., Chevy Chase, MD 20815-4999; (301) 961-2800. Jennifer Sirangelo, President.*
Web, www.4-h.org, Twitter, @4H and Facebook, www.facebook.com/4-h

4-H membership: young people across America learning leadership, citizenship, life skills, science, healthy living, and food security. National 4-H Council strengthens and complements the 4-H Youth Development Program of the Agricultural Dept.'s cooperative extension system of state land-grant universities. Interests include 4-H afterschool, healthy lifestyle, science engineering and technology, food security, and citizenship in governance. In the United States, 4-H programs are implemented by 109 land-grant universities and more than 3,000 cooperative extension offices. Outside the United States, 4-H programs operate through independent, country-led organizations in more than 50 countries.

Washington Workshops Foundation, *2101 L St. N.W., #400, 20037; (202) 965-3434. Fax, (202) 965-1018. Tom Crossan, President. Toll-free, (800) 368-5688.*
General email, info@workshops.org
Web, www.workshops.org and Twitter, @WorkshopsWire

Educational foundation that provides introductory seminars on American government and politics to junior and senior high school students, including the congressional seminars for high school students.

Continuing, Vocational, and Adult Education

▶AGENCIES

Career, Technical, and Adult Education (OCTAE)
(Education Dept.), 550 12th St. S.W., 11th Floor, 20202-7100 (mailing address: 400 Maryland Ave. S.W., P-OCTAE, Washington, DC 20202-7100); (202) 245-7700. Amy Loyd, Deputy Assistant Secretary. Information, (800) 872-5327.
General email, octae@ed.gov
Web, www2.ed.gov/about/offices/list/ovae and Twitter, @usedgov

Administers programs pertaining to adult education and literacy, career and technical education, and community colleges.

Career, Technical, and Adult Education (OCTAE)
(Education Dept.), Academic and Technical Education, 550 12th St. S.W., #11059, 20202-7100 (mailing address: 400 Maryland Ave. S.W., P-OCTAE, Washington, DC 20202-7100); (202) 245-7700. Fax, (202) 245-7838. Sharon Miller, Director, (202) 245-7846.
General email, octae@ed.gov
Web, www2.ed.gov/about/offices/list/ovae/pi/cte/index .html

Establishes national initiatives that help states implement career and technical education programs. Administers state formula and discretionary grant programs under the Carl D. Perkins Career and Technical Education Act.

Career, Technical, and Adult Education (OCTAE)
(Education Dept.), Adult Education and Literacy, 550 12th St. S.W., 11th Floor, 20202-7100 (mailing address: 400 Maryland Ave. S.W., P-OCTAE, DAEL, Washington, DC 20202); (202) 245-7700. Fax, (202) 245-7838. Cheryl L. Keenan, Director, (202) 245-7810.

General email, octae@ed.gov
Web, www2.ed.gov/about/offices/list/ovae/pi/AdultEd/ index.html and https://aefla.ed.gov

Administers adult education programs for reading, writing, math, English language proficiency, and problem solving. Provides funding to state and local education agencies to implement and improve adult education and literacy activities.

▶NONGOVERNMENTAL

Accrediting Council for Continuing Education and Training (ACCET), *1722 N St. N.W., 20036; (202) 955-1113. Fax, (202) 955-1118. Kate Zulaski, Deputy Executive Director, (202) 984-2282.*
General email, info@accet.org
Web, https://accet.org

Seeks to identify, evaluate, and enhance the delivery of continuing education and training programs. Offers professional development through workshops, conferences, and webinars.

Assn. for Career and Technical Education (ACTE), *1410 King St., Alexandria, VA 22314; (703) 683-3111. Fax, (703) 683-7424. LeAnn Wilson, Executive Director, ext. 347. Toll-free, (800) 826-9972.*
General email, acte@acteonline.org
Web, www.acteonline.org and Twitter, @actecareertech

Membership: teachers, students, supervisors, administrators, and others working or interested in career and technical education (middle school through postgraduate). Interests include the impact of high school graduation requirements on career and technical education; private sector initiatives; and the improvement of the quality and image of career and technical education. Offers an annual convention and other professional development opportunities. Monitors legislation and regulations.

Career Education Colleges and Universities (CECU), *1530 Wilson Blvd., #1050, Arlington, VA 22209; (571) 970-3941. Fax, (866) 363-2181. Jason Altmire, President.*
Web, www.career.org, Twitter, @CECUed, Facebook, www.facebook.com/CECUed and
Email, communications@career.org

Information clearinghouse on trade and technical schools. (Formerly Career College Assn.)

Covenant House, *Washington Office, 2001 Mississippi Ave. S.E., 20020; (202) 610-9600. Angela Jones Hackley, Executive Director.*
Web, http://covenanthousedc.org and
Twitter, @CovenantHouseDC

Protects young people suffering from homelessness, abuse, and neglect. Provides services including GED and adult education and job readiness. (Affiliated with Covenant House International.)

National Assn. of State Directors of Career Technical Education Consortium, *8484 Georgia Ave., #620, Silver*

Spring, MD 20910; (301) 588-9630. Fax, (301) 576-7115. Kimberly A. Green, Executive Director, ext. 12.

General email, info@careertech.org

Web, www.careertech.org

Membership: state career education agency heads, senior staff, and business, labor, and other education officials. Advocates state and national policy to strengthen career technical education and workforce development. Monitors legislation and regulations.

SkillsUSA, 14001 SkillsUSA Way, Leesburg, VA 20176-5494; (703) 777-8810. Fax, (703) 777-8999. Chelle Travis, Executive Director, ext. 601. Educational Resources, (800) 321-8422. Toll-free, (844) 875-4557.

General email, info@skillsusa.org

Web, www.skillsusa.org, Twitter, @SkillsUSA, Facebook, www.facebook.com/SkillsUSA and YouTube, www.youtube.com/c/skillsusa

Membership: students, teachers, and administrators of trade, industrial, technical, and health occupations programs at public high schools, vocational schools, and two-year and four-year colleges. Promotes strong work skills, workplace ethics, understanding of free enterprise, and lifelong education. (Formerly Vocational Industrial Clubs of America.)

University Professional & Continuing Education Assn. (UPCEA), 1 Dupont Circle N.W., #330, 20036; (202) 659-3130. Fax, (202) 785-0374. Robert J. Hansen, Chief Executive Officer.

General email, info@upcea.edu

Web, www.upcea.edu, Twitter, @UPCEA and Facebook, www.facebook.com/upcea

Membership: higher education institutions and nonprofit organizations involved in postsecondary continuing education. Prepares statistical analyses and produces data reports for members; recognizes accomplishments in the field. Monitors legislation and regulations.

Literacy, Basic Skills

▶AGENCIES

AmeriCorps (Corp. for National and Community Service), **Volunteers in Service to America (VISTA),** 250 E St. S.W., 20024-3208; (202) 606-5000. Meg Ansara, Director. National Service hotline, (800) 942-2677. TTY, (800) 833-3722.

Web, www.americorps.gov/programs/americorps/americorps-vista, Twitter, @AmeriCorpsVISTA and Facebook, www.facebook.com/AmeriCorpsVISTA

Assigns volunteers to local and state education departments, to public agencies, and to private nonprofit organizations that have literacy programs. Other activities include tutor recruitment and training and the organization and expansion of local literacy councils, workplace literacy programs, and intergenerational literacy programs.

Career, Technical, and Adult Education (OCTAE) (Education Dept.), **Adult Education and Literacy,** 550 12th St. S.W., 11th Floor, 20202-7100 (mailing address: 400 Maryland Ave. S.W., P-OCTAE, DAEL, Washington, DC 20202); (202) 245-7700. Fax, (202) 245-7838. Cheryl L. Keenan, Director, (202) 245-7810.

General email, octae@ed.gov

Web, www2.ed.gov/about/offices/list/ovae/pi/AdultEd/index.html and https://aefla.ed.gov

Provides state and local education agencies and the general public with information on establishing, expanding, improving, and operating adult education and literacy programs. Emphasizes basic and life skills attainment, English literacy, and high school completion. Awards grants to state education agencies for adult education and literacy programs, including workplace and family literacy.

▶CONGRESS

For a listing of relevant congressional committees and subcommittees, please see page 176 or the Appendix.

Library of Congress, *Center for the Book,* John Adams Bldg., 101 Independence Ave. S.E., #LA 5173, 20540-4920; (202) 707-9217. Fax, (202) 707-0269. Guy Lamolinara, Director.

General email, cfbook@loc.gov

Web, www.read.gov/cfb

Promotes family and adult literacy, books, reading, and libraries through its programs and events in Washington DC as well as those sponsored by its 56 affiliate Centers for the Book in the United States, Puerto Rico, U.S. Virgin Islands, and the three Pacific island territories.

Library of Congress, *Young Readers Center and Programs Lab,* Thomas Jefferson Bldg., 10 1st St. S.E., #G51, 20540; (202) 707-1950. Fax, (202) 707-0269. Lauren Roszak, Head (Acting).

General email, learn@loc.gov

Web, www.read.gov/yrc

Promotes books, reading, literacy, libraries, and the scholarly study of books through affiliates and promotional programs. Places special emphasis on young readers through reading and writing contests.

▶NONGOVERNMENTAL

AFL-CIO Working for America Institute (WAI), 815 16th St. N.W., 20006; (202) 508-3717. Fax, (202) 508-3719. Brad Markell, Executive Director. Press, (202) 637-5018.

General email, info@workingforamerica.org

Web, www.workingforamerica.org

Provides labor unions, employers, education agencies, and community groups with technical assistance for workplace education programs focusing on adult literacy, basic skills, and job training. Interests include new technologies and workplace innovations.

Assn. for Talent Development (ATD), 1640 King St., 3rd Floor, Alexandria, VA 22314; (703) 683-8100. Fax, (703) 683-8723. Tony Bingham, Chief Executive Officer. Toll-free, (800) 628-2783.

General email, customercare@astd.org

Web, www.td.org, Twitter, @atd and Facebook, www.facebook.com/ATD

Membership: trainers and human resource development specialists. Publishes information on workplace literacy.

Center for Applied Linguistics, *4646 40th St. N.W., 20016-1859; (202) 362-0700. Fax, (202) 362-3740. Joel Gómez, President, ext. 545.*
General email, info@cal.org

Web, www.cal.org, Facebook, www.facebook.com/CALLinguistics/ and Twitter, @CAL_Linguistics

Research and technical assistance organization that serves as a clearinghouse on application of linguistics to practical language problems. Interests include English as a second language (ESL), teacher training and material development, language education, language proficiency test development, bilingual education, and sociolinguistics.

First Book, *1319 F St. N.W., #1000, 20004-1155; (202) 393-1222. Fax, (202) 628-1258. Kyle Zimmer, President. Toll-free, (866) 732-3669.*
General email, help@firstbook.org

Web, www.firstbook.org, Twitter, @FirstBook, Facebook, www.facebook.com/FirstBook and YouTube, www.youtube.com/firstbook

A network of educators, schools, and programs serving children in need across the United States and Canada — to bring titles and resources to your classroom or organization. Helps address the needs of the whole child - supporting their education, basic needs and wellness, all essential to educational equality. Organizes fund-raisers to support and promote literacy programs. Supports The First Book:- Network, Marketplace, Research and Insights and accelerator.

General Federation of Women's Clubs, *1734 N St. N.W., 20036-2990; (202) 347-3168. Fax, (202) 835-0246. Marian St. Clair, International President; Cheri Meyer, Chief of Operations. Press, (202) 347-8103. Toll-free, (800) 443-4392.*
General email, gfwc@gfwc.org

Web, www.gfwc.org, Twitter, @GFWCHQ and Facebook, www.facebook.com/GFWCMembers

Membership; Nondenominational, nonpartisan international organization of women volunteers. Develops literacy projects in response to community needs; sponsors tutoring.

National Coalition for Literacy, *P.O. Box 2932, 20013-2932; (202) 364-1964. Deborah Kennedy, Executive Director; Judy Mortrude, President.*
General email, ncl@ncladvocacy.org

Web, www.national-coalition-literacy.org and Twitter, @NCLAdvocacy

Members: national organizations concerned with adult education. Promotes adult education, family literacy, and English language acquisition in the United States.

Reading Is Fundamental, *750 1st St. N.E., #920, 20002; (202) 536-3400. Fax, (202) 536-3518. Alicia Levi, President. Toll-free, 877-RIF-READ.*
General email, contactus@rif.org

Web, www.rif.org, Twitter, @RIFWEB and Facebook, www.facebook.com/ReadingIsFundamental

Conducts programs and workshops to motivate young people to read. Provides young people in low-income neighborhoods with free books and parents with services to encourage reading at home.

Science and Mathematics Education

▶AGENCIES

National Aeronautics and Space Administration (NASA), *STEM Engagement, 300 E St. S.W., 4th Floor, #N, Washington, DC, 20546; (202) 358-0103. Fax, (202) 358-3048. Mike Kincaid, Associate Administrator.*
General email, education@nasa.gov

Web, www.nasa.gov/stem/about.html, Twitter, @NASAStem, Facebook, www.facebook.com/NASASTEMEngagement and YouTube, www.youtube.com/channel/UC9SM7V7J1pAhPabOUST01fw

Coordinates NASA's education programs and activities to meet national educational needs and ensure a sufficient talent pool to preserve U.S. leadership in aeronautical technology and space science.

National Oceanic and Atmospheric Administration (NOAA) *(Commerce Dept.), National Sea Grant College Program, Silver Spring Metro Center 3, 1315 East-West Hwy., #11735, Silver Spring, MD 20910; (301) 734-1066. Fax, (301) 713-0799. Jonathan Pennock, Director, (301) 734-1089.*
General email, SGweb@noaa.gov

Web, www.seagrant.noaa.gov and Twitter, @SeaGrant

Provides grants, primarily to colleges and universities, for marine resource development; sponsors undergraduate and graduate education and the training of technicians at the college level.

National Science Foundation (NSF), *Education and Human Resources Directorate (HRD), 2415 Eisenhower Ave., Room C 11000, Alexandria, VA 22314; (703) 292-8600. Fax, (703) 292-9179. Sylvia M. Butterfield, Assistant Director (Acting), (703) 292-5333.*
Web, www.nsf.gov/dir/index.jsp?org=ehr

Develops and supports programs to strengthen science and mathematics (STEM) education.

National Science Foundation (NSF), *Human Resource Development Division (HRD), 2415 Eisenhower Ave., Room E 11400, Alexandria, VA 22134; (703) 292-8640. Fax, (703) 292-9019. Diana Elder, Director, (703) 292-4437.*
Web, www.nsf.gov/div/index.jsp?div=hrd

Supports and encourages participation in scientific and engineering (STEM) education and research by women, minorities, and people with disabilities. Awards grants and scholarships.

National Science Foundation (NSF), *National Center for Science and Engineering Statistics (NCSES), 2415 Eisenhower Ave., Room W 14200, Alexandria, VA 22134; (703) 292-8780. Fax, (703) 292-9092. Emilda B. Rivers, Director, (703) 292-7773.*
Web, www.nsf.gov/statistics

Supports education and training of researchers in the use of large-scale nationally representative data sets.

National Science Foundation (NSF), *Undergraduate Education Division (DUE), 2415 Eisenhower Ave., Room W 11100, Alexandria, VA 22134; (703) 292-8670. Fax, (703) 292-9015. Rosalyn Hobson Hargraves, Director, (703) 292-7349.*
Web, www.nsf.gov/div/index.jsp?div=DUE

Promotes education in science, technology, engineering, and mathematics (STEM) at two-year and four-year colleges and universities.

Office of Science and Technology Policy (OSTP) *(Executive Office of the President), Science, Eisenhower Executive Office Bldg., 1650 Pennsylvania Ave. N.W., 20504; (202) 456-4444. Francis Collins, Chief Science Advisor.*
General email, info@ostp.gov
Web, www.whitehouse.gov/ostp

Evaluates the effectiveness of science education programs, which include environment, life sciences, physical sciences and engineering, and social, behavioral, and educational sciences.

Postsecondary Education (OPE) *(Education Dept.), Higher Education Programs (HEP), Institutional Service (IS), Minority Science and Engineering Improvement Program, Lyndon B. Johnson Bldg., 400 Maryland Ave. S.W., 4th Floor, 20202; (202) 453-7913. Bernadette Hence, Senior Program Manager.*
General email, OPE.MSEIP@ed.gov
Web, www2.ed.gov/programs/iduesmsi/index.html

Provides grants to predominantly minority institutions to effect long-range improvement in science and engineering education and to increase the flow of underrepresented ethnic minorities, particularly minority women, into science and engineering careers.

▶**NONGOVERNMENTAL**

American Assn. for the Advancement of Science (AAAS), *Education and Human Resources Programs (EHR), 1200 New York Ave. N.W., 6th Floor, 20005; (202) 326-6670 (voice and TTY accessible). Fax, (202) 371-9849. Shirley M. Malcom, Director, (202) 326-6720.*
General email, ehr@aaas.org
Web, www.aaas.org/programs/education-and-human-resources

Membership: scientists, scientific organizations, students, and professionals interested in science, technology, engineering, mathematics, and education. Focuses on expanding science education opportunities for science students and providing opportunities to professionals in the scientific and technology communities.

American Assn. of Physics Teachers, *1 Physics Ellipse, 5th Floor, College Park, MD 20740-3845; (301) 209-3311. Fax, (301) 209-0845. Beth A. Cunningham, Executive Officer.*
General email, eo@aapt.org
Web, www.aapt.org, Twitter, @AAPTHQ and Facebook, www.facebook.com/AAPTHQ

Membership: physics teachers and others interested in physics education. Seeks to advance the institutional and cultural role of physics education. Sponsors seminars and conferences; provides educational information and materials. (Affiliated with the American Institute of Physics.)

American Society for Engineering Education, *1818 N St. N.W., #600, 20036-2479; (202) 331-3500. Fax, (202) 265-8504. Norman L. Fortenberry, Executive Director, (202) 331-3545. Press, (202) 331-5767.*
Web, www.asee.org, Twitter, @ASEE_DC and Facebook, www.facebook.com/ASEEHQ

Membership: engineering faculty and administrators, professional engineers, government agencies, and engineering colleges, corporations, and professional societies. Conducts research, conferences, and workshops on engineering education. Monitors legislation and regulations.

Assn. for Women in Science, *1667 K St. N.W., #300, 20006; (202) 827-9798. Sandra W. Robert, Chief Executive Officer.*
General email, awis@awis.org
Web, www.awis.org and Twitter, @AWISNational

Promotes equal opportunity for women in scientific professions; provides career and funding information. Provides educational scholarships for women in science. Interests include international development.

Assn. of Science and Technology Centers, *818 Connecticut Ave. N.W., 7th Floor, 20006-2734; (202) 783-7200. Fax, (202) 783-7207. Christofer Nelson, President.*
General email, info@astc.org
Web, www.astc.org, Twitter, @ScienceCenters and Facebook, www.facebook.com/ScienceCenters

Membership: more than 600 science centers, science museums, and similar operations in forty-seven countries. Strives to enhance the ability of its members to engage visitors in science activities and explorations of scientific phenomena. Sponsors conferences and informational exchanges on interactive exhibits, hands-on science experiences, and educational programs for children, families, teachers, and older audiences; publishes journal; compiles statistics; provides technical assistance for museums; and speaks for science centers before Congress and federal agencies.

Challenger Center for Space Science Education, *422 1st St. S.E., 3rd Floor, 20003; (202) 827-1580. Fax, (202) 827-0031. Lance Bush, President. Toll-free, (800) 969-5747.*

General email, info@challenger.org

Web, www.challenger.org, Twitter, @ChallengerCtr, Facebook, www.facebook.com/ChallengerCtr and Press, media@challenger.org

Educational organization designed to stimulate interest in science, math, and technology among middle school and elementary school students. Students participate in interactive mission simulations that require training and classroom preparation. Sponsors Challenger Learning Centers across the United States, Canada, the United Kingdom, and Korea.

EarthEcho International, 2101 L St. N.W., #800, 20037; (202) 350-3190. Fax, (202) 857-3977. Philippe Cousteau, President. Press, (202) 870-1818.
General email, info@earthecho.org

Web, www.earthecho.org, Twitter, @EarthEcho and Facebook, www.facebook.com/earthecho

Education resource center that helps students identify environmental issues in their communities and take action to solve them. Holds expeditions to South Florida to investigate the impact of human activity on its natural ecosystems. Provides teachers with learning materials to engage students with real-world data. Specializes in dead zones.

Entomological Society of America, 3 Park Pl., #307, Annapolis, MD 21401-3722; (301) 731-4535. Fax, (301) 731-4538. Chris Stelzig, Executive Director, ext. 3012.
General email, esa@entsoc.org

Web, www.entsoc.org, Twitter, @EntsocAmerica and Facebook, www.facebook.com/entsoc

Membership: entomology researchers, teachers, extension service personnel, administrators, marketing representatives, research technicians, consultants, students, and hobbyists. Sponsors symposia, conferences, journals, and continuing education seminars.

International Technology and Engineering Educators Assn., 1914 Association Dr., #201, Reston, VA 20191-1539; (703) 860-2100. Fax, (703) 860-0353. Kelly Dooley, Executive Director.
General email, iteea@iteea.org

Web, www.iteea.org and Twitter, @iteea

Membership: technology and engineering education teachers, supervisors, teacher educators, and individuals studying to be technology education teachers (elementary school through university level). Technology and engineering education includes the curriculum areas of manufacturing, construction, communications, transportation, robotics, energy, and design.

Marine Technology Society, One Thomas Circle, # 700, 20005; (202) 717-8705. Fax, (202) 347-4302. Kristina Norman, Executive Director (Acting), (202) 827-7171.
General email, mtsoffice@mtsociety.org

Web, www.mtsociety.org, Twitter, @MTSociety and Facebook, www.facebook.com/MarineTechnologySociety/?ref=hl

Provides scholarships to high school and postsecondary students in marine-related programs with focus in marine technology, marine engineering, and marine science.

Mathematical Assn. of America, 1529 18th St. N.W., 20036-1358 (mailing address: P.O. Box 90973, Washington DC. 20077); (202) 387-5200. Fax, (202) 265-2384. Michael Pearson, Executive Director, ext. 470. Toll-free, (800) 741-9415. Service Center, (800) 617-7800.
General email, maahq@maa.org

Web, www.maa.org, Twitter, @maanews and Facebook, www.facebook.com/maanews?ref=nf

Membership: mathematics professors and individuals worldwide with a professional interest in mathematics. Seeks to improve the teaching of collegiate mathematics. Conducts professional development programs.

National Academies of Sciences, Engineering, and Medicine (NASEM), *Life Sciences Board,* Keck Center, 500 5th St. N.W., 6th Floor, 20001; (202) 334-3360. Kavita M. Berger, Director; Barbara A. Schaal, Chair.
General email, bls@nas.edu

Web, www.nationalacademies.org/bls/board-on-life-sciences

Oversees studies on undergraduate-level biology education.

National Academies of Sciences, Engineering, and Medicine (NASEM), *Science Education Board,* Keck Center, 500 5th St. N.W., 20001; (202) 334-1529. Heidi Schweingruber, Director, (202) 334-2009; Susan Rundell Singer, Chair.
General email, bose@nas.edu

Web, www.nationalacademies.org/bose/board-on-science-education

Promotes science education in schools and informal learning environments, such as science museums, aquariums, nature centers, and social networks. Provides guidance in federal legislation, particularly as it relates to STEM education.

National Assn. of Biology Teachers, 11 Main St., Suite D, Warrenton, VA 20186 (mailing address: P.O. Box 3363, Warrenton, VA 20188); (703) 264-9696. Fax, (202) 962-3939. Jaclyn Reeves-Pepin, Executive Director, ext. 4. Toll-free, (888) 501-6228.
General email, office@nabt.org

Web, www.nabt.org

Membership: biology teachers and others interested in life sciences education at the elementary, secondary, and collegiate levels. Interests include teaching standards, science curriculum, and issues affecting biology and life sciences education.

National Council of Teachers of Mathematics, 1906 Association Dr., Reston, VA 20191-1502; (703) 620-9840. Fax, (703) 476-2970. Ken Krehbiel, Executive Director. Toll-free, (800) 235-7566.

General email, nctm@nctm.org

Web, www.nctm.org, Twitter, @NCTM and Facebook, www.facebook.com/TeachersofMathematics

Membership: mathematics educators, researchers, students, and other interested persons. Works for the improvement of classroom instruction at all levels. Serves as forum and information clearinghouse on issues related to mathematics education. Offers educational materials and conferences. Monitors legislation and regulations.

National Geographic Society, *1145 17th St. N.W., 20036-4688; (202) 857-7000. Fax, (202) 828-6679. Jill Tiefenthaler, Chief Executive Officer; Renee Braden, Library Senior Director. Library, (202) 857-7783. Press, (202) 857-7027. Publication information, (800) 647-5463. Web, www.nationalgeographic.org, Library email, library@ngs.org, Twitter, @InsideNatGeo, Facebook, www.facebook.com/InsideNatGeo and YouTube, www.youtube.com/InsideNatGeo*

Educational and scientific organization. Publishes *National Geographic, National Geographic Adventure, National Geographic Traveler, National Geographic Kids,* and *National Geographic Little Kids* magazines; produces maps, books, and films; maintains a museum; offers film-lecture series; produces television specials and the National Geographic Channel. Library open to the public.

National Science Foundation (NSF), *Graduate Education Division, 2415 Eisenhower Ave., Room W 11200, Alexandria, VA 22314; (703) 292-8630. Fax, (703) 292-9048. Lee L. Zia, Director (Acting), 703- 292-5140. Web, www.nsf.gov/div/index.jsp?div=dge*

Supports activities to strengthen the education of research scientists and engineers; promotes career development.

National Science Teachers Assn., *1840 Wilson Blvd., Arlington, VA 22201-3000; (703) 243-7100. Fax, (703) 243-7177. Erika Shugart, Executive Director. General email, pubinfo@nsta.org*

Web, www.nsta.org, Twitter, @nsta, Facebook, www.facebook.com/NSTA.FB and Legislative Affairs, legaffairs@nsta.org

Membership: science teachers from elementary through college levels, supervisors, administrators, scientists, business and industry representatives, and others involved in and committed to science education. Seeks to improve science education. Monitors legislation and regulations.

National Society of Black Engineers, *205 Daingerfield Rd., Alexandria, VA 22314; (703) 549-2207. Fax, (703) 683-5312. Janeen Uzzell, Chief Executive Officer. Web, www.nsbe.org, Twitter, @NSBE and Facebook, www.facebook.com/NSBE1975*

Membership: Black engineers and college students studying engineering. Offers academic excellence programs, scholarships, leadership training, and professional and career development opportunities. Activities include tutorial programs, group study sessions, high school/junior high outreach programs, technical seminars and workshops, career fairs, and an annual convention.

Smithsonian Science Education Center, *901 D St. S.W., #704-B, 20024; P.O. Box 37012, MRC 952, 20013; (202) 633-2972. Fax, (202) 287-2070. Carol L. O'Donnell, Director, odonnellc@si.edu. General email, ScienceEducation@si.edu*

Web, https://ssec.si.edu, Twitter, @SmithsonianScie, Facebook, www.facebook.com/SmithsonianScience EducationCenter and YouTube, www.youtube.com/channel/UC6dyNTnSopdgye2gQBVSNVg/feed

Works to establish effective science programs for all students. Disseminates research information; develops curriculum materials; seeks to increase public support for change of science education through the development of strategic partnerships.

Society for Science and the Public, *1719 N St. N.W., 20036; (202) 785-2255. Fax, (202) 785-3751. Maya Ajmera, Chief Executive Officer. Toll-free, (800) 552-4412. General email, society@societyforscience.org*

Web, www.societyforscience.org, Twitter, @Society4Science, Facebook, www.facebook.com/societyforscience and YouTube, www.youtube.com/user/SocietyforScience

Promotes understanding and appreciation of science and the role it plays in human advancement. Sponsors science competitions and other science education programs in schools; awards scholarships. Publishes *Science News* and *Science News for Students*. Provides funds and training to select U.S. science and math teachers who serve under-resourced students.

6 ⏰

Employment and Labor

GENERAL POLICY AND ANALYSIS

Basic Resources

►AGENCIES

Labor Dept. (DOL), 200 Constitution Ave. N.W., #S-2521, 20210; (202) 693-6000. Fax, (202) 693-6681. Martin Walsh, Secretary. Library, (202) 693-6600. Toll-free, (866) 487-2365. TTY, (877) 889-5627. General email, talktodol@dol.gov

Web, www.dol.gov, Twitter, @USDOL and Facebook, www.facebook.com/departmentoflabor

Promotes and develops the welfare of U.S. wage earners; administers federal labor laws; acts as principal adviser to the president on policies relating to wage earners, working conditions, and employment opportunities. Wirtz Labor Law Library open to the public, 8:15 a.m–4:45 p.m.

Labor Dept. (DOL), *Administrative Law Judges,* 800 K St. N.W., #400N, 20001-8002; (202) 693-7300. Fax, (202) 693-7365. Stephen R. Henley, Chief Administrative Law Judge, (202) 693-7542; Angel Perez, Director Program Operations, ext. 7337. General email, OALJ-Questions@dol.gov

Web, www.oalj.dol.gov

Presides over formal hearings to determine violations of minimum wage requirements, overtime payments, compensation benefits, employee discrimination, grant performance, alien certification, employee protection, the Sarbanes-Oxley Act, and health and safety regulations set forth under numerous statutes, executive orders, and regulations. With few exceptions, hearings are required to be conducted in accordance with the Administrative Procedure Act.

Labor Dept. (DOL), *Administrative Review Board,* 200 Constitution Ave. N.W., #S5220, 20210; (202) 693-6200. Fax, (202) 693-6220. James D. McGinley, Chair and Chief Administrative Appeals Judge. Web, www.dol.gov/arb

Issues final decisions for the secretary of labor on appeals from decisions of the administrator of the Wage and Hour Division and the Office of Administrative Law Judges under a broad range of federal labor laws, including nuclear, environmental, safety and security, financial, and transportation whistleblower protection provisions; contract compliance laws; child labor laws; immigration laws; migrant and seasonal agricultural worker protection laws; the McNamara O'Hara Service Contract Act; and the Davis-Bacon Act.

►CONGRESS

For a listing of relevant congressional committees and subcommittees, please see page 221 or the Appendix.

Government Accountability Office (GAO), *Education, Workforce, and Income Security (EWIS),* 441 G St. N.W., 20548; (202) 512-7215. Jacqueline Nowicki, Director. Web, www.gao.gov/about/careers/our-teams

Assists Congress in analyzing the efficiency and effectiveness of federal agency programs that foster the development, education, and skill attainment of children and adults; provide benefits and protections for workers, families, veterans, and those with disabilities; and ensure an adequate and secure retirement for an aging population.

►NONGOVERNMENTAL

AFL-CIO (American Federation of Labor–Congress of Industrial Organizations), 815 16th St. N.W., 20006; (202) 637-5000. Fax, (202) 637-5058. Elizabeth (Liz) Shuler, President. Press, (202) 637-5018. Toll Free, (866) 832-1560. Web, https://aflcio.org, Twitter, @AFLCIO, Facebook, www.facebook.com/aflcio and Press, pressclips@aflcio.org

Voluntary federation of national and international labor unions in the United States. Represents members before Congress and other branches of government. Each member union conducts its own contract negotiations. Library (located in Silver Spring, Md.) open to the public.

American Enterprise Institute (AEI), 1789 Massachusetts Ave. N.W., 20036; (202) 862-5800. Fax, (202) 862-7177. Robert Doar, President. Web, www.aei.org, Twitter, @AEI and Facebook, www.facebook.com/aei

Research and educational organization that studies trends in employment, earnings, the environment, health care, and income in the United States.

Employment Policies Institute, 1090 Vermont Ave. N.W., #800, 20005-4605; (202) 463-7650. Fax, (202) 463-7107. Michael Saltsman, Managing Director. General email, info@epionline.org

Web, https://epionline.org

Sponsors and conducts research on public policy and employment. Opposes raising the minimum wage. Monitors legislation and regulations.

Good Jobs First, 1380 Monroe St. N.W., PMB 405, 20010; (202) 232-1616. Greg LeRoy, Executive Director, (202) 232-4258. General email, info@goodjobsfirst.org

Web, www.goodjobsfirst.org, Twitter, @GoodJobsFirst and Facebook, www.facebook.com/GoodJobsFirst

Promotes corporate and government accountability in economic development incentives; primary focus is on state and local job subsidies with emerging work on federal development programs and federal regulatory violations data. Maintains Subsidy Tracker database. Includes Good Jobs New York and the Corporate Research Project.

HR Policy Assn., 1001 N. 19th St., #1002, Arlington, VA, 22209; (202) 789-8670. Fax, (202) 789-0064. Timothy Bartl, President. General email, info@hrpolicy.org

Web, www.hrpolicy.org

EMPLOYMENT AND LABOR RESOURCES IN CONGRESS

For a complete listing of congressional committees, including their full contact information, leadership, membership, and jurisdictions, please refer to the Appendix on pages 840–963.

HOUSE:

House Appropriations Committee, (202) 225-2771.
Web, appropriations.house.gov
    Subcommittee on Labor, Health and Human
       Services, Education, and Related Agencies,
       (202) 225-3508.
House Armed Services Committee, (202) 225-4151.
Web, armedservices.house.gov
    Subcommittee on Military Personnel,
       (202) 225-4151.
House Education and Labor Committee,
    (202) 225-3725.
Web, edlabor.house.gov
    Subcommittee on Health, Employment, Labor,
       and Pensions, (202) 225-3725.
    Subcommittee on Higher Education and
       Workforce Investment, (202) 225-3725.
    Subcommittee on Workforce Protections,
       (202) 225-3725.
House Judiciary Committee, (202) 225-3951.
Web, judiciary.house.gov
    Subcommittee on Immigration and Citizenship,
       (202) 225-3926.
House Oversight and Reform Committee,
    (202) 225-5051.
Web, oversight.house.gov
    Subcommittee on Civil Rights and Civil Liberties,
       (202) 225-5051.
    Subcommittee on Government Operations,
       (202) 225-5051.
House Small Business Committee, (202) 225-4038.
Web, smallbusiness.house.gov
    Subcommittee on Contracting and
       Infrastructure, (202) 225-4038.
    Subcommittee on Innovation, Entrepreneurship,
       and Workforce Development,
       (202) 225-4038.
House Veterans' Affairs Committee,
    (202) 225-9756.
Web, veterans.house.gov
    Subcommittee on Economic Opportunity,
       (202) 226-9756.
House Ways and Means Committee,
    (202) 225-3625.
Web, waysandmeans.house.gov
    Subcommittee on Social Security,
       (202) 225-3625.
    Subcommittee on Worker and Family Support,
       (202) 225-3625.

JOINT:

Joint Economic Committee, (202) 224-5171.
Web, jec.senate.gov

SENATE:

Senate Agriculture, Nutrition, and Forestry
    Committee, (202) 224-2035.
Web, agriculture.senate.gov
    Subcommittee on Commodities, Risk
       Management, and Trade, (202) 224-2035.
Senate Appropriations Committee, (202) 224-7363.
Web, appropriations.senate.gov
    Subcommittee on Labor, Health and Human
       Services, Education, and Related Agencies,
       (202) 224-7363.
Senate Armed Services Committee, (202) 224-3871.
Web, armed-services.senate.gov
    Subcommittee on Personnel, (202) 224-3871.
Senate Finance Committee, (202) 224-4515.
Web, finance.senate.gov
    Subcommittee on International Trade, Customs,
       and Global Competitiveness, (202) 224-4515.
    Subcommittee on Social Security, Pensions and
       Family Policy, (202) 224-4515.
    Subcommittee on Taxation and IRS Oversight,
       (202) 224-4515.
Senate Health, Education, Labor, and Pensions
    Committee, (202) 224-5375.
Web, help.senate.gov
    Subcommittee on Employment and Workplace
       Safety, (202) 224-5375.
    Subcommittee on Primary Health and
       Retirement Security, (202) 224-5375.
Senate Homeland Security and Governmental Affairs
    Committee, (202) 224-4751.
Web, hsgac.senate.gov
    Permanent Subcommittee on Investigations,
       (202) 224-3721.
    Subcommittee on Government Operations and
       Border Management, (202) 224-4551.
Senate Judiciary Committee, (202) 224-7703.
Web, judiciary.senate.gov
    Subcommittee on Immigration, Citizenship, and
       Border Safety, (202) 224-6991.
Senate Small Business and Entrepreneurship
    Committee, (202) 224-5175.
Web, sbc.senate.gov
Senate Special Committee on Aging, (202) 224-5364.
Web, aging.senate.gov

Promotes discussion of human resource policy and practice, including strategies and initiatives that promote job growth, employment security, and competitiveness.

National Assn. of Professional Employer Organizations, *707 N. Saint Asaph St., Alexandria, VA 22314; (703) 836-0466. Fax, (703) 836-0976. Pat Cleary, President, (703) 739-8163.*
General email, info@napeo.org
Web, www.napeo.org, Twitter, @NAPEO, Facebook, www.facebook.com/napeo and YouTube, www.youtube.com/channel/UC_Zz2DaAyuocuP3fXq03h9A

Membership: professional employer organizations. Provides code of ethics. Conducts research; sponsors seminars and conferences for members. Monitors legislation and regulations.

National Fund for Workforce Solutions, *1250 Connecticut Ave. N.W., #200, 20036; (202) 223-8994. Amanda Cage, President, ext. 1101; Elicia Wilson, Chief Operating Officer, ext. 1005.*
Web, https://nationalfund.org, Twitter, @National_Fund, Facebook, www.facebook.com/NFWorkforce and YouTube, www.youtube.com/user/nfwsolutions

Partners with employers, individuals, and philanthropic organizations to promote better economic opportunities and prosperous communities. Acts as advocate for policies that help workers, local employers, and economic growth.

People's Action, *1301 Connecticut Ave. N.W., 20036; Sulma Arias, Executive Director.*
Web, https://peoplesaction.org, Twitter, @PplsAction and Facebook, www.facebook.com/pplsaction

Advocates policies to help working people. Supports improved employee benefits, including health care, child care, and paid family leave; promotes lifelong education and training of workers. Seeks full employment, higher wages, and increased productivity. Monitors legislation and regulations. Merger of Campaign for America's Future, Alliance for a Just Society, and Center for Health, Environment, and Justice. (Headquartered in Chicago, Ill.).

Urban Institute, *Center on Labor, Human Services, and Population, 500 L'Enfant Plaza S.W., 20024; (202) 833-7200. Signe-Mary McKernan, Vice President.*
Web, www.urban.org/policy-centers/center-labor-human-services-and-population

Analyzes employment and income trends, studies how the U.S. population is growing, and evaluates programs dealing with homelessness, child welfare, and job training. Other areas of interest include immigration, mortality, sexual and reproductive health, adolescent risk behavior, child care, domestic violence, and youth development.

International Issues

▶**AGENCIES**

Bureau of Democracy, Human Rights, and Labor (DRL) *(State Dept.), 2201 C St. N.W., #7827, 20520-7812;*

(202) 647-1337. Fax, (202) 647-5283. Lisa Peterson, Assistant Secretary (Acting).
Web, www.state.gov/j/drl, Twitter, @StateDRL, Facebook, www.facebook.com/StateDRL and YouTube, www.youtube.com/channel/UCSibCtobezepu_o-bukbglA

Implements U.S. policies relating to human rights, labor, and religious freedom; prepares annual review of human rights worldwide.

Bureau of Democracy, Human Rights, and Labor (DRL) *(State Dept.), Business and Human Rights, 2401 E St. N.W., SA-1, H430, 20037; (202) 663-2895. Lynn Sicade, Director.*
General email, IFBHR@state.gov
Web, www.state.gov/key-topics-bureau-of-democracy-human-rights-and-labor/business-and-human-rights

Fosters implementation of international human rights law and developing commitments in global business and human rights to create space for emerging and critical issues to be debated among relevant stakeholder groups. Seeks to develop and establish tools, training and guidance for U.S. government officials to be more effective envoys on business and human rights.

Bureau of Democracy, Human Rights, and Labor (DRL) *(State Dept.), International Labor Affairs (ILA), 1800 G St. N.W., SA-1, H430, 20006; (202) 663-3569. Stephen Moody, Director, (202) 663-3547.*
General email, DRL-ILA-DL@state.gov
Web, www.state.gov/key-topics-cureau-of-democracy-human-rights-and-labor/international-labor-affairs

Works with organized labor, nongovernmental organizations, international organizations, and corporations to monitor and promote worker rights throughout the world. Contributes to U.S. foreign policy goals related to democracy promotion, trade, development, and human rights.

Bureau of Educational and Cultural Affairs (ECA) *(State Dept.), Private Sector Exchange, 2200 C St. N.W., #05CC14, 20520; (202) 632-9386. (202) 632-2805. Fax, (202) 632-2701. G. Kevin Saba, Deputy Assistant Secretary (Acting), (202) 632-6193.*
General email, jvisas@state.gov
Web, http://eca.state.gov/about-bureau/organizational-structure/office-private-sector-exchange

Administers the Exchange Visitor Program to allow nonimmigrants to participate in work-based and study-based exchange programs in the United States.

Bureau of International Labor Affairs (ILAB) *(Labor Dept.), 200 Constitution Ave. N.W., #S5313, 20210; (202) 693-4770. Fax, (202) 693-4780. Thea Lee, Deputy Under Secretary (Acting). Toll-free, (866) 487-2365.*
General email, Contact-ILAB@dol.gov
Web, www.dol.gov/ilab and Twitter, @USDOL

Assists in formulating international economic and trade policies affecting American workers. Represents the United States in trade negotiations. Helps administer the U.S. labor attaché program. Carries out overseas technical assistance projects. Represents the United States in various international organizations. Houses the Office of Trade

Labor Department

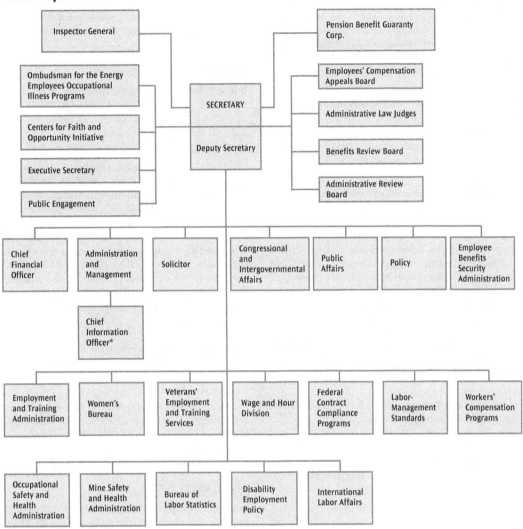

*Indicates direct access to the Secretary

Agreement Implementation, which is responsible for overseeing the implementation of the labor provisions of free trade agreements.

Bureau of International Labor Affairs (ILAB) *(Labor Dept.), Child Labor, Forced Labor, and Human Trafficking (OCFT),* 200 Constitution Ave. N.W., #S5307, 20210; (202) 693-4843. Fax, (202) 693-4830. *Marcia Eugenio, Director.*
General email, globalkids@dol.gov

Web, www.dol.gov/agencies/ilab/our-work/child-forced-labor-trafficking

Conducts research and reporting to inform U.S. foreign policy, trade policy, and cooperation initiatives to combat child labor, forced labor, and human trafficking; works with foreign governments, organizations, and businesses to build capacity and strategies for responding to exploitive labor practices.

Bureau of International Labor Affairs (ILAB) *(Labor Dept.), International Relations (OIR), International Visitors Program,* 200 Constitution Ave. N.W., #S5303, 20210; (202) 693-4793. Patricia Butler, International Program Specialist.
Web, www.dol.gov/agencies/ilab/our-work/diplomacy/ivlp

Works with the State Dept., the Agency for International Development, and other agencies in arranging visits and training programs for foreign officials interested in U.S. labor and trade laws and practices, worker training programs, and employment services.

Bureau of International Labor Affairs (ILAB) *(Labor Dept.), International Relations and Economic Research (OIRER),* 200 Constitution Ave. N.W., #S5317, 20210; (202) 693-4802. Fax, (202) 693-4860. Robert B. Shepard, Director.
General email, Contact-OIRER@dol.gov

Web, www.dol.gov/agencies/ilab/about-us/mission#oirer

Provides administrative support for U.S. participation in the International Labor Organization (ILO) and Asian Pacific Economic Cooperation (APEC) and at the Paris-based Organisation for Economic Co-operation and Development (OECD). Provides research on labor and employment in other countries. Facilitates information sharing between Labor Dept. and other countries.

Bureau of International Labor Affairs (ILAB) *(Labor Dept.), Trade and Labor Affairs (OTLA), 200 Constitution Ave. N.W., #S5317, 20210; (202) 693-4802. Fax, (202) 693-4830. Matthew Levin, Director. General email, Contact-OTLA@dol.gov*

Web, www.dol.gov/ilab

Coordinates international technical cooperation in support of the labor provisions in free trade agreements. Provides services, information, expertise, and technical cooperation programs that support the Labor Dept.'s foreign policy objectives. Administers the U.S. government's responsibilities under the North American Free Trade Agreement on Labor Cooperation and labor chapters of U.S. regional and bilateral free trade agreements. Provides technical assistance for post conflict reconstruction and reintegration activities in countries key to U.S. security. Provides technical assistance globally to help countries observe international labor standards. Supports HIV/AIDS workplace preventive education in countries around the world.

Employment and Training Administration (ETA) *(Labor Dept.), Trade Adjustment Assistance (OTAA), 200 Constitution Ave. N.W., N-5428, 20210 (mailing address: 200 Constitution Ave. N.W., #12-200, Washington, DC 20210); (202) 693-3560. Fax, (202) 693-3584. Norris T. Tyler III, Administrator. Toll-free, (888) 365-6822. General email, taa.petition@dol.gov*

Web, www.dol.gov/agencies/eta/tradeact

Assists American workers who are totally or partially unemployed because of increased imports or a shift in production; offers training, job search and relocation assistance, weekly benefits at state unemployment insurance levels, and other reemployment services.

President's Committee on the International Labor Organization *(Labor Dept.), 900 19th St. N.W., #300, 20006; (202) 617-3952. Kevin Cassidy, Director; Martin Walsh, Chair (Secretary of Labor). General email, washinton@ilo.org*

Web, www.ilo.org/washington

Advisory committee that directs U.S. participation in the International Labor Organization; composed of government, employer, and worker representatives, including secretaries of labor, commerce, and state, the president's national security adviser, the president's national economic adviser, and the presidents of the AFL-CIO and the U.S. Council of International Business. Formulates and coordinates policy on the International Labor Organization (ILO); advises the president and the secretary of labor.

►CONGRESS

For a listing of relevant congressional committees and sub-committees, please see page 221 or the Appendix.

►INTERNATIONAL ORGANIZATIONS

International Labour Organization (ILO), *Washington Office, 900 19th St. N.W., #300, 20006; (202) 617-3952. Fax, (202) 617-3960. Kevin Cassidy, Director. General email, washington@ilo.org*

Web, www.ilo.org/washington and Twitter, @ILO

Works toward advancing social justice through the promotion of international labor standards, employment, social protection, and social dialogue. Carries out research and technical cooperation and advisory services under these four major themes and related subthemes, including labor statistics, wages, occupational safety and health and other working conditions, social security, eradication of child labor and forced labor, equality of treatment in employment and occupation, freedom of association, and bargaining rights. Liaison office for the United States and multilateral organizations in Washington, D.C. (Headquarters in Geneva.)

World Bank, *Human Development Network, 1818 H St. N.W., 20433; (202) 473-1000. Mamta Murthi, Vice President.*

Web, www.worldbank.org

Assists developing countries in delivering effective and affordable health care, education, and social services. Interests include poverty reduction, income protection, nutrition, jobs access, health coverage, and basic education.

►NONGOVERNMENTAL

Fair Labor Assn. (FLA), *2033 K St. N.W., #400, 20006; (202) 898-1000. Fax, (202) 898-9050. Sharon Waxman, Chief Executive Officer.*

Web, www.fairlabor.org, Twitter, @FairLaborAssoc, Facebook, www.facebook.com/fairlaborassociation and Email, info@fairlabor.org

Membership: consumer, human, and labor rights groups; apparel and footwear manufacturers and retailers; colleges and universities. Seeks to protect the rights of workers in the United States and worldwide. Concerns include sweatshop practices, forced labor, child labor, and worker health and benefits. Monitors workplace conditions and reports findings to the public. Develops capacity for sustainable labor compliance.

International Labor Rights Forum, *1634 Eye St. N.W., #1000, 20006; (202) 347-4100. Fax, (202) 347-4885. Jennifer (JJ) Rosenbaum, Executive Director. General email, laborrights@ilrf.org*

Web, https://laborrights.org and Twitter, @ILRF

Promotes the enforcement of international labor rights through policy advocacy; acts as advocate for better protection of workers. Concerns include child labor, sweatshops, and exploited workers. Monitors legislation and regulations on national and international levels.

NumbersUSA, *1400 Crystal Dr., #240, Arlington, VA 22202; 703 816-8820. Roy Beck, President.*
General email, info@numbersusa.com
Web, www.numbersusa.com, Twitter, @NumbersUSA and Facebook, www.facebook.com/numbersusa

Public policy organization that favors immigration reduction as a way of promoting economic justice for American workers. Monitors legislation and regulations.

Solidarity Center, *1130 Connecticut Ave. N.W., #800, 20036; (202) 974-8383. Fax, (202) 974-8384.*
Shawna Bader-Blau, Executive Director. Press, (202) 974-8369.
General email, information@solidaritycenter.org
Web, www.solidaritycenter.org, Twitter, @solidaritycntr, Facebook, www.facebook.com/solidaritycenter and YouTube, www.youtube.com/channel/UCn-GrFX5jg1Fh-1 9povBUpw

Provides assistance to free and democratic trade unions worldwide. Provides trade union leadership courses in collective bargaining, union organization, trade integration, labor–management cooperation, union administration, and political theories. Sponsors social and community development projects; focus includes child labor, human and worker rights, and the role of women in labor unions. (Affiliated with the AFL-CIO.)

Labor Standards and Practices

▶**AGENCIES**

Bureau of Labor Statistics (BLS) *(Labor Dept.),* **Compensation and Working Conditions (OCWC),** *2 Massachusetts Ave. N.E., #4130, 20212; (202) 691-6199. Hilery Z. Simpson, Associate Commissioner.*
General email, NCSinfo@bls.gov
Web, www.bls.gov

Conducts annual survey of occupational requirements, including the physical demands, environmental conditions, training requirements, and cognitive requirements of work.

Housing and Urban Development Dept. (HUD), *Davis Bacon and Labor Standards, 451 7th St. S.W., Room 7122, 20410; (202) 708-0370. Fax, (202) 619-8022. Amanda Herrmann Vasquez, Director, (202) 402-6601.*
Web, www.hud.gov/program_offices/davis_bacon_and_ labor_standards

Seeks to ensure that laborers on HUD-assisted construction projects are paid prevailing wages by contractors. Administers and enforces labor standards provisions within the Davis-Bacon and related acts, the Copeland Act, and Contract Work Hours and Safety Standards Act, and the maintenance wage requirements of the U.S. Housing Act of 1937.

Labor Dept. (DOL), *Wage and Hour Division (WHD), 200 Constitution Ave. N.W., #S3502, 20210; (202) 693-0051. Fax, (202) 693-1406. Jessica Looman, Administrator (Acting). Press, (202) 693-4676. TTY, (877) 889-5627. Toll free, (866) 487-9243.*
Web, www.dol.gov/whd and Twitter, @WHD_DOL

Enforces the minimum-wage, overtime pay, record keeping, and child labor requirements of the Fair Labor Standards Act, the Migrant and Seasonal Agricultural Worker Protection Act, the Employee Polygraph Protection Act, the Family and Medical Leave Act, and a number of employment standards and worker protections as provided in several immigration-related statutes. Also enforces the wage garnishment provisions of the Consumer Credit Protection Act; and the prevailing wage requirements of the Davis-Bacon Act, the Service Contract Act, and other statutes applicable to federal contracts for construction and the provision of goods and services.

Labor Dept. (DOL), *Wage and Hour Division (WHD), Fair Labor Standards Act Enforcement, 200 Constitution Ave. N.W., #S3502, 20210; (202) 693-0067. Fax, (202) 693-1387. Derrick J. Witherspoon, Director.*
Web, www.dol.gov/whd/flsa

Issues interpretations and rulings of the Fair Labor Standards Act of 1938. Interests include minimum wage, overtime pay, hours worked, record keeping, and child labor.

Labor Dept. (DOL), *Wage and Hour Division (WHD), Family and Medical Leave Act, 200 Constitution Ave. N.W., #S3502, 20210; (202) 693-0066. Fax, (202) 693-1387. Helen Applewhaite, Director. Press, (202) 693-4676.*
Web, www.dol.gov/whd/fmla

Oversees implementation of the Family and Medical Leave Act, which entitles eligible employees of covered employers to take unpaid job-protected leave for specified family and medical reasons with continuation of group health insurance coverage.

Labor Dept. (DOL), *Wage and Hour Division (WHD), Government Contracts Enforcement, 200 Constitution Ave. N.W., #S3502, 20210; (202) 693-0574. Fax, (202) 693-1087. Michele King, Director. Toll-free, (866) 487-9243.*
Web, www.dol.gov/agencies/whd/government-contracts

Enforces the Davis-Bacon Act, the Walsh-Healey Public Contracts Act, the Contract Work Hours and Safety Standards Act, the Service Contract Act, and other related government contract labor standards statutes.

Labor Dept. (DOL), *Wage and Hour Division (WHD), Immigration and Farm Labor, 200 Constitution Ave. N.W., #S3502, 20210; (202) 693-0070. Fax, (202) 693-1387. Whitney Ford, Director. Toll-free, (866) 487-9243.*
Web, www.dol.gov/whd

Enforces certain provisions under the Immigration and Nationality Act (INA), including labor standards protections for certain temporary nonimmigrant workers and inspection for compliance with the employment eligibility record-keeping requirements.

Labor Dept. (DOL), *Wage and Hour Division (WHD), Wage Determinations,* 200 Constitution Ave. N.W., #S3502, 20210; (202) 693-0602. Miriam Marte, Branch Chief.
Web, www.dol.gov/whd

Issues prevailing wage determinations under the Service Contract Act of 1965 and other regulations pertaining to wage determination.

▶**CONGRESS**

For a listing of relevant congressional committees and subcommittees, please see page 221 or the Appendix.

▶**NONGOVERNMENTAL**

Fair Labor Assn. (FLA), 2033 K St. N.W., #400, 20006; (202) 898-1000. Fax, (202) 898-9050. Sharon Waxman, Chief Executive Officer.
Web, www.fairlabor.org, Twitter, @FairLaborAssoc, Facebook, www.facebook.com/fairlaborassociation and Email, info@fairlabor.org

Membership: consumer, human, and labor rights groups; apparel and footwear manufacturers and retailers; colleges and universities. Seeks to protect the rights of workers in the United States and worldwide. Concerns include sweatshop practices, forced labor, child labor, and worker health and benefits. Monitors workplace conditions and reports findings to the public. Develops capacity for sustainable labor compliance.

National Whistleblowers Center (NWC), 3238 P. St. N.W., 10th Floor, 20007 (mailing address: P.O. Box 25074, Washington, DC 20027); (202) 342-1903. Siri Nelson, Executive Director.
General email, info@whistleblowers.org
Web, www.whistleblowers.org, Twitter, @STOPFRAUD, Facebook, www.facebook.com/NationalWhistleblowerCenter and YouTube, www.youtube.com/channel/UC_TcOoREYL S2G-V2myhd3cw

Protects employees who legally disclose information about illegal activities of employers. Advocates policy reform for whistleblowers. Educates the public on whistleblower rights and assists whistleblowers in finding attorneys. Coordinates a speakers bureau.

Trabajadores Unidos de Washington D.C.—Workers United of Washington D.C. (TUWDC), 1419 V St. N.W., #305, 20009; (202) 299-0162. Mario Cristaldo, Executive Director.
General email, info.tuwdc@gmail.com
Web, www.tuwdc.org, Twitter, @tu_wdc and Facebook, www.facebook.com/tuwdc.org

Seeks to advance solutions to challenges faced by D.C.–area day laborers, low-wage workers, and migrant workers, including working conditions, discrimination, wage theft, and workplace safety.

Statistics and Information

▶**AGENCIES**

Bureau of International Labor Affairs (ILAB) *(Labor Dept.), International Relations and Economic Research (OIRER),* 200 Constitution Ave. N.W., #S5317, 20210; (202) 693-4802. Fax, (202) 693-4860. Robert B. Shepard, Director.
General email, Contact-OIRER@dol.gov
Web, www.dol.gov/agencies/ilab/about-us/mission#oirer

Conducts research on the effects of international trade and economic policies and developments on earnings, employment, and working conditions of American workers, cross-country comparative and macroeconomic analyses, and methods of ensuring compliance with international workers' rights.

Bureau of Labor Statistics (BLS) *(Labor Dept.),* Postal Square, 2 Massachusetts Ave. N.E., #4040, 20212-0001; (202) 691-5200. Fax, (202) 691-7890. William W. Beach, Commissioner. Press, (202) 691-5902. TTY, (800) 877-8339.
General email, blsdata_staff@bls.gov
Web, www.bls.gov and Twitter, @BLS_gov

Collects, analyzes, and publishes data on labor economics, including employment, unemployment, hours of work, wages, employee compensation, prices, consumer expenditures, labor-management relations, productivity, technological developments, and occupational safety and health. Publishes reports on these statistical trends, including the *Consumer Price Index, Producer Price Index,* and *Employment and Earnings.*

Bureau of Labor Statistics (BLS) *(Labor Dept.), Compensation and Working Conditions (OCWC),* 2 Massachusetts Ave. N.E., #4130, 20212; (202) 691-6199. Hilery Z. Simpson, Associate Commissioner.
General email, NCSinfo@bls.gov
Web, www.bls.gov

Compiles data on occupational safety and health, wages and benefits, and occupational requirements.

Bureau of Labor Statistics (BLS) *(Labor Dept.), Compensation and Working Conditions (OCWC), Compensation Levels and Trends,* 2 Massachusetts Ave. N.E., #4160, 20212-0001; (202) 691-6199. Vacant, Assistant Commissioner.
Web, www.bls.gov/ncs/summary.htm

Compiles data on wages and benefits. Develops the National Compensation Survey. Analyzes, distributes, and disseminates information on occupational earnings, benefits, and compensation trends.

Bureau of Labor Statistics (BLS) *(Labor Dept.), Compensation and Working Conditions (OCWC), Occupational Safety and Health Statistics,* 2 Massachusetts Ave. N.E., #3180, 20212-0001; (202) 691-6170. Fax, (202) 691-6196. Marika Litras, Assistant Commissioner.

General email, iifstaff@bls.gov

Web, www.bls.gov/iif

Compiles and publishes statistics on occupational injuries, illnesses, and fatalities.

Bureau of Labor Statistics (BLS) *(Labor Dept.), Current Employment Statistics (CES), National,* 2 Massachusetts Ave. N.E., #4840, 20212-0001; (202) 691-6555. Fax, (202) 691-6641. Patrick Carey, Assistant Commissioner.
General email, cesinfo@bls.gov

Web, www.bls.gov/ces

Surveys business and government agencies and publishes detailed industry data on employment, hours, and earnings of workers on nonfarm payrolls. Estimates are produced for the nation.

Bureau of Labor Statistics (BLS) *(Labor Dept.), Current Employment Statistics (CES), State and Area Employment,* 2 Massachusetts Ave. N.E., PSB #4860, 20212; (202) 691-6555. Patrick Carey, Assistant Commissioner.
General email, sminfo@bls.gov

Web, www.bls.gov/sae

Surveys business agencies and publishes detailed industry data on employment, hours, and earnings of workers on nonfarm payrolls. Estimates are produced for states and selected metropolitan areas.

Bureau of Labor Statistics (BLS) *(Labor Dept.), Employment and Unemployment Statistics (OEUS),* 2 Massachusetts Ave. N.E., #4945, 20212-0022; (202) 691-6400. Fax, (202) 691-6425. Julie Hatch Maxfield, Associate Commissioner, (202) 691-5473. Press, (202) 691-5902.
General email, cpsinfo@bls.gov

Web, www.bls.gov/bls/employment.htm

Monitors employment and unemployment trends on national and local levels; compiles data on worker and industry employment and earnings.

Bureau of Labor Statistics (BLS) *(Labor Dept.), Employment and Unemployment Statistics (OEUS), Current Employment Analysis,* 2 Massachusetts Ave. N.E., #4675, 20212; Fax, (202) 691-6459. Patrick Carey, Assistant Commissioner, (202) 691-5473. Current Population Survey, (202) 691-6378. Press, (202) 691-5902.
General email, lausinfo@bls.gov

Web, www.bls.gov/lau and Press, *pressoffice@bls.gov*

Issues labor force and unemployment statistics for states, counties, metropolitan statistical areas, cities with populations of 25,000 or more, and the United States as a whole.

Bureau of Labor Statistics (BLS) *(Labor Dept.), Employment and Unemployment Statistics (OEUS), Industry Employment Statistics,* 2 Massachusetts Ave. N.E., #4860, 20212; (202) 691-5440. Fax, (202) 691-6644. Vacant, Assistant Commissioner.
General email, oesinfo@bls.gov

Web, www.bls.gov/emp and *www.bls.gov/bls/industry.htm*

Produces monthly employment statistics, quarterly wage data, business employment dynamics statistics, and job openings and labor turnover statistics.

Bureau of Labor Statistics (BLS) *(Labor Dept.), Productivity and Technology (OPT),* 2 Massachusetts Ave. N.E., #2150, 20212-0001; (202) 691-6598. Fax, (202) 691-5664. Lucy P. Eldridge, Associate Commissioner.
General email, dipsweb@bls.gov

Web, www.bls.gov/bls/productivity.htm

Develops and analyzes productivity measures for the U.S. business economy and industries, and conducts research on factors affecting productivity.

Employment and Training Administration (ETA) *(Labor Dept.), Unemployment Insurance (OUI),* 200 Constitution Ave. N.W., #S4524, 20210; (202) 693-3032. Fax, (202) 693-3229. Jim M. Garner, Administrator.
Web, https://oui.doleta.gov/unemploy

Provides guidance and oversight with respect to federal and state unemployment compensation. Compiles statistics on state unemployment insurance programs. Studies unemployment issues related to benefits.

Occupational Safety and Health Administration (OSHA) *(Labor Dept.), Statistical Analysis,* 200 Constitution Ave. N.W., #N3507, 20210; (202) 693-2300. Elizabeth Grossman, Director.
Web, www.osha.gov/oshstats

Compiles and provides all statistical data for OSHA, such as occupational injury and illness records, which are used in setting standards and making policy.

▶**CONGRESS**

For a listing of relevant congressional committees and sub-committees, please see page 221 or the Appendix.

Unemployment Benefits

▶**AGENCIES**

Employment and Training Administration (ETA) *(Labor Dept.), Trade Adjustment Assistance (OTAA),* 200 Constitution Ave. N.W., N-5428, 20210 (mailing address: 200 Constitution Ave. N.W., #12-200, Washington, DC 20210); (202) 693-3560. Fax, (202) 693-3584. Norris T. Tyler III, Administrator. Toll-free, (888) 365-6822.
General email, taa.petition@dol.gov

Web, www.dol.gov/agencies/eta/tradeact

Assists American workers who are totally or partially unemployed because of increased imports or a shift in production; offers training, job search and relocation assistance, weekly benefits at state unemployment insurance levels, and other reemployment services.

Employment and Training Administration (ETA) *(Labor Dept.), Unemployment Insurance (OUI),* 200 Constitution Ave. N.W., #S4524, 20210; (202) 693-3032. Fax, (202) 693-3229. Jim M. Garner, Administrator.
Web, https://oui.doleta.gov/unemploy

Directs and reviews the state-administered system that provides income support for unemployed workers nationwide; advises state and federal employment security agencies on wage-loss, worker dislocation, and adjustment assistance compensation programs.

►CONGRESS

For a listing of relevant congressional committees and subcommittees, please see page 221 or the Appendix.

►NONGOVERNMENTAL

National Assn. of State Workforce Agencies, *444 N. Capitol St. N.W., #300, 20001; (202) 434-8020. Scott Sanders, Executive Director, (202) 434-8022. General email, naswa@naswa.org*

Web, www.naswa.org, Twitter, @naswaorg and Facebook, www.facebook.com/NASWAorg

Membership: state workforce agency administrators. Informs members of employment training programs, unemployment insurance programs, employment services, labor market information, and legislation. Provides unemployment insurance and workforce development professionals with opportunities for networking and information exchange.

EMPLOYMENT AND TRAINING PROGRAMS

General

►AGENCIES

Employment and Training Administration (ETA) *(Labor Dept.), 200 Constitution Ave. N.W., #S2307, 20210; (202) 693-2772. Angela Hanks, Principal Deputy Assistant Secretary. Press, (215) 861-5100. Toll-free general information, 877-US2-JOBS. TTY, (877) 889-5627. General email, eta.webportal@dol.gov*

Web, www.dol.gov/agencies/eta

Administers federal government job training and worker dislocation programs, federal grants to states for public employment service programs, and unemployment insurance benefits, primarily through state and local workforce development systems.

Employment and Training Administration (ETA) *(Labor Dept.), Workforce Investment (OWI), 200 Constitution Ave. N.W., #C4526, 20210; (202) 693-3980. Fax, (202) 693-3981. Kimberly Vitelli, Administrator.*

Web, www.dol.gov/agencies/eta/workforce-investment

Provides workers with information, job search assistance, and training. Helps employers acquire skilled workers. Provides national leadership, oversight, policy guidance, and technical assistance under the Workforce Innovation and Opportunity Act. Oversees programs administered through the One-Stop delivery system

assisting communities, businesses, and job seekers, including dislocated and transitioning workers, disadvantaged youth, veterans, individuals with disabilities, migrant and seasonal farmworkers, and Native Americans, in a changing global economy.

Employment and Training Administration (ETA) *(Labor Dept.), Workforce Investment (OWI), Division of Strategic Investment, 200 Constitution Ave. N.W., #C4518, 20210; (202) 693-3949. Fax, (202) 693-3890. Jessica Harding, Analyst; Robin Fernkas, Deputy Administrator.*

General email, businessrelations@dol.gov

Web, www.dol.gov/agencies/eta/workforce-investment

Serves as liaison between business and industry and the workforce investment system, a network of state and local resources that connects workers to job opportunities and helps businesses recruit, train, and maintain a skilled workforce. Manages the High Growth Job Training Initiative with the goal of preparing workers for high-growth and high-demand jobs. Targeted industries include advanced manufacturing, aerospace, biotechnology, health care, and information technology, construction, hospitality, transportation, and energy.

Employment and Training Administration (ETA) *(Labor Dept.), Workforce Investment (OWI), National Programs, Tools, and Technical Assistance, 200 Constitution Ave. N.W., #C-4510, 20210-3945; (202) 693-3045. Fax, (202) 693-3015. Steve Rietzke, Chief, 202–693-3913. TTY, (877) 889-5627.*

Web, www.dol.gov/agencies/eta/workforce-investment and WorkforceGPS, www.workforcegps.org

Oversees and provides support for implementation of employment and training services to targeted populations, including National Farmworker Jobs Program; migrant and seasonal farmworker Monitor Advocate activities; and services for individuals with disabilities, including the Disability Employment Initiative, Work Opportunity Tax Credit, and Senior Community Service Employment Program. Provides workers and businesses with labor market information and online career information to help connect skilled workers to businesses. Oversees and provides support for grants to states to produce labor market information; sponsors and oversees the agency's technical assistance platform for use by workforce development professionals, WorkforceGPS.

Employment and Training Administration (ETA) *(Labor Dept.), Workforce Investment (OWI), Workforce Innovation and Opportunity Act (WIOA), 200 Constitution Ave. N.W., #S4209, 20210; (202) 693-3046. Fax, (202) 693-3817. Robert Kight, Chief.*

Web, www.dol.gov/agencies/eta/workforce-investment/adult

Provides targeted job training services for migrant and seasonal farm workers, Native Americans, older workers, veterans, and the disabled. Aims to increase the employment, job retention, earnings, and career advancement of U.S. workers.

Health Resources and Services Administration (HRSA) *(Health and Human Services Dept.)*, *Bureau of Health Workforce (BHW)*, 5600 Fishers Lane, #11 West Wing, Rockville, MD 20857; (301) 443-5794. Luis Padilla, Associate Administrator. Press, (301) 443-3366.
General email, bhwevents@hrsa.gov

Web, www.bhw.hrsa.gov

Supports primary care and public health education and practice. Supports recruitment of health care professionals, including nursing and allied health professionals, for underserved populations. Administers categorical training programs, scholarship and loan programs, and minority and disadvantaged assistance programs. Oversees National Practitioner Data Bank.

Housing and Urban Development Dept. (HUD), *Davis Bacon and Labor Standards*, 451 7th St. S.W., Room 7122, 20410; (202) 708-0370. Fax, (202) 619-8022.
Amanda Herrmann Vasquez, Director, (202) 402-6601.
Web, www.hud.gov/program_offices/davis_bacon_and_labor_standards

Partnership between HUD and the Labor Dept. that assists low-income housing residents in obtaining job training and employment.

▶ **CONGRESS**

For a listing of relevant congressional committees and subcommittees, please see page 221 or the Appendix.

▶ **NONGOVERNMENTAL**

AFL-CIO Working for America Institute (WAI), 815 16th St. N.W., 20006; (202) 508-3717. Fax, (202) 508-3719. Brad Markell, Executive Director. Press, (202) 637-5018.
General email, info@workingforamerica.org

Web, www.workingforamerica.org

Provides technical assistance to labor unions, employers, education agencies, and community groups for workplace programs focusing on dislocated workers, economically disadvantaged workers, and skill upgrading. Interests include new technologies and workplace innovations.

D.C. Central Kitchen, 425 2nd St. N.W., 20001; (202) 234-0707. Michael F. Curtin, Chief Executive Officer, (202) 266-2018.
General email, info@dccentralkitchen.org

Web, www.dccentralkitchen.org, Twitter, @dcck and Facebook, www.facebook.com/dccentralkitchen

Administers the Culinary Jobs Training Program for unemployed, homeless, or formerly incarcerated men and women.

Goodwill Industries International, 15810 Indianola Dr., Rockville, MD 20855; (301) 530-6500. Fax, (301) 530-1516. Steven C. Preston, President. Toll-free, (800) 466-3945.
General email, contactus@goodwill.org

Web, www.goodwill.org, Twitter, @GoodwillIntl and Facebook, www.facebook.com/GoodwillIntl

Serves youth, seniors, veterans, and people with disabilities, criminal records, and other specialized needs by providing education and career services and training, as well as job placement opportunities and postemployment support.

Graduate School USA, *Center for Leadership Management*, 600 Maryland Ave. S.W., 20024-2520; (202) 314-3300. Steve Somers, President. TTY, (888) 744-2717.
General email, customerrelations@graduateschool.edu

Web, www.graduateschool.edu/training/curriculum-offerings/center-leadership-and-management and Twitter, @graduateschool

Trains federal employees with managerial potential for executive positions in the government. Leadership programs serve employees at levels from GS4 through SES.

Institute for Credentialing Excellence, 2001 K St. N.W., 3rd Floor, 20006; (202) 367-1165. Fax, (202) 367-2165. Denise Roosendaal, Executive Director.
General email, info@credentialingexcellence.org

Web, www.credentialingexcellence.org, Twitter, @ICE_Excellence and Facebook, www.facebook.com/credentialingexcellence

Membership: certifying agencies and other groups that issue credentials for professions and occupations. Promotes public understanding of competency assurance certification programs. Oversees commission that establishes certification program standards. Monitors regulations.

National Assn. of State Workforce Agencies, 444 N. Capitol St. N.W., #300, 20001; (202) 434-8020. Scott Sanders, Executive Director, (202) 434-8022.
General email, naswa@naswa.org

Web, www.naswa.org, Twitter, @naswaorg and Facebook, www.facebook.com/NASWAorg

Membership: state employment security administrators. Informs members of federal legislation on job placement, veterans affairs, and employment and training programs. Distributes labor market information; trains new state administrators and executive staff. Provides employment and training professionals with opportunities for networking and information exchange.

National Assn. of Workforce Boards (NAWB), 1155 15th St. N.W., #350, 20005; (202) 857-7900. Fax, (202) 857-7955. Ronald (Ron) Painter, Chief Executive Officer, ext. 101.
General email, nawb@nawb.org

Web, www.nawb.org, Twitter, @Workforceinvest and Facebook, www.facebook.com/NAWB.org

Membership: private industry councils and state job training coordinating councils established under the Job Training Partnership Act of 1982 (renamed Workforce Boards under the Workforce Investment Act). Interests include job training opportunities for youth and unemployed, economically disadvantaged, and dislocated workers; and private sector involvement in federal employment and training policy. Provides members with technical assistance; holds conferences and seminars.

National Governors Assn. (NGA), *Center for Best Practices, Workforce Development and Economic Policy Division, 444 N. Capitol St. N.W., #267, 20001-1512; (202) 624-5300. Rachael Stephens, Director.*
Web, www.nga.org/bestpractices/work-development-economic-policy

Provides information, research, policy analysis, technical assistance, and resource development for governors and their staff across a range of policy issues. Promotes economic development and innovation; workforce development focused on industry-based strategies; pathways to employment and populations with special needs; and human services for children, youth, low-income families, and people with disabilities.

The Telework Coalition (TelCoa), *204 East St. N.E., 20002; (202) 266-0046. Chuck Wilsker, President.*
General email, info@telcoa.org
Web, www.telcoa.org and Twitter, @telcoa

Promotes telework and access to broadband services to increase productivity and provide employment opportunities for disabled, rural, and older workers, while reducing vehicular travel and energy use. Monitors legislation and regulations.

U.S. Chamber of Commerce, *Center for Education and Workforce, 1615 H St. N.W., 20062-2000; (202) 463-5500. Carolyn Cawley, Senior Vice President; Raymond P. Towe, Senior Vice President of Federal Relations.*
General email, foundation@uschamber.com
Web, www.uschamberfoundation.org/center-education-and-workforce, Twitter, @usccfeducation, Facebook, www .facebook.com/usccfeducation and YouTube, www.youtube .com/theuschambericw

Works with U.S. Chamber of Commerce members on workforce development issues, including educational reform, human resources, and job training.

U.S. Conference of Mayors, *Workforce Development Council, 1620 Eye St. N.W., 4th Floor, 20006; (202) 293-7330. Kathleen Amoroso, Assistant Executive Director for Jobs, Education, and the Workforce Development Council, (202) 861-6723.*
Web, www.uscmwdc.org

Offers technical assistance to members participating in federal job training programs; monitors related legislation; acts as an information clearinghouse on employment and training programs.

Worldwide ERC (Employee Relocation Council), *4401 Wilson Blvd., #150, Arlington, VA 2203 (mailing address: P.O. Box 41990, Arlington, VA 22204); (703) 842-3400. Lynn Shotwell, President.*
General email, CustomerSuccess@worldwideerc.org
Web, www.worldwideerc.org, Twitter, @WorldwideERC and Facebook, www.facebook.com/WorldwideERC

Membership: corporations that relocate employees and moving, real estate, and relocation management companies. Researches and recommends policies that provide a smooth transition for relocated employees and their families. Holds conferences and issues publications on employee relocation issues.

Aliens

►**AGENCIES**

Employment and Training Administration (ETA) *(Labor Dept.), Foreign Labor Certification (OFLC), 200 Constitution Ave. N.W., #N-5311, 20210; (202) 693-8200. Brian Pasternak, Administrator.*
Web, www.dol.gov/agencies/eta/foreign-labor

Sets national policies and guidelines for carrying out the responsibilities of the secretary of labor pursuant to the Immigration and Nationality Act regarding the admission of foreign workers to the United States for both temporary and permanent employment; certifies whether U.S. workers are available for positions for which admission of foreign workers is sought and whether employment of foreign nationals will adversely affect the wages and working conditions of similarly employed U.S. workers.

Apprenticeship Programs

►**AGENCIES**

Employment and Training Administration (ETA) *(Labor Dept.), Office of Apprenticeship (OA), 200 Constitution Ave. N.W., #N5311, 20210-0001; (202) 693-2796. Fax, (202) 693-3799. John V. Ladd, Administrator.*
General email, apprenticeship@dol.gov
Web, www.dol.gov/agencies/eta/apprenticeship and www.apprenticeship.gov/?utm_source=dol_gov_agencies_ eta_apprenticeship&utm_medium=text&utm_campaign= apprenticeship_homepage

Advises the secretary of labor on the role of apprenticeship programs in employment training and on safety standards for those programs; encourages sponsors to include these standards in planning apprenticeship programs. Promotes establishment of apprenticeship programs in private industry and the public sector.

Employment and Training Administration (ETA) *(Labor Dept.), Workforce Investment (OWI), Youth Services, 200 Constitution Ave. N.W., #N4508, 20210; (202) 693-3030. Fax, (202) 693-3861. Robin Fernkas, Deputy Administrator.*
General email, youth.services@dol.gov
Web, www.dol.gov/agencies/eta/youth/about

Administers youth grant programs designed to enhance youth education, encourage school completion, and provide career and apprenticeship opportunities. Oversees the Going Home: Serious and Violent Offender Reentry Initiative and YouthBuild.

Dislocated Workers

►**AGENCIES**

Employment and Training Administration (ETA) *(Labor Dept.), Workforce Investment (OWI), 200 Constitution Ave. N.W., #C4526, 20210; (202) 693-3980. Fax, (202) 693-3981. Kimberly Vitelli, Administrator.*
Web, www.dol.gov/agencies/eta/workforce-investment

Provides workers with information, job search assistance, and training. Oversees programs administered through the One-Stop delivery system assisting job seekers, including dislocated and transitioning workers.

Employment and Training Administration (ETA) *(Labor Dept.), Workforce Investment (OWI), Workforce Innovation and Opportunity Act (WIOA),* 200 *Constitution Ave. N.W., #S4209, 20210; (202) 693-3046. Fax, (202) 693-3817. Robert Kight, Chief.*
Web, www.dol.gov/agencies/eta/workforce-investment/ adult

Responsible for adult training and services for dislocated workers funded under the Workforce Investment Act; examines training initiatives.

▶NONGOVERNMENTAL

National Assn. of Workforce Boards (NAWB), *1155 15th St. N.W., #350, 20005; (202) 857-7900. Fax, (202) 857-7955. Ronald (Ron) Painter, Chief Executive Officer, ext. 101.*
General email, nawb@nawb.org
Web, www.nawb.org, Twitter, @Workforceinvest and Facebook, www.facebook.com/NAWB.org

Membership: private industry councils and state job training coordinating councils established under the Job Training Partnership Act of 1982 (renamed Workforce Boards under the Workforce Investment Act). Interests include job training opportunities for youth and unemployed, economically disadvantaged, and dislocated workers; and private sector involvement in federal employment and training policy. Provides members with technical assistance; holds conferences and seminars.

Migrant and Seasonal Farm Workers

▶AGENCIES

Employment and Training Administration (ETA) *(Labor Dept.), Workforce Investment (OWI),* 200 *Constitution Ave. N.W., #C4526, 20210; (202) 693-3980. Fax, (202) 693-3981. Kimberly Vitelli, Administrator.*
Web, www.dol.gov/agencies/eta/workforce-investment

Provides workers with information, job search assistance, and training. Oversees programs administered through the One-Stop delivery system assisting job seekers, including migrant and seasonal farmworkers.

Employment and Training Administration (ETA) *(Labor Dept.), Workforce Investment (OWI), National Farmworker Jobs Program,* 200 *Constitution Ave. N.W., #C-4510, 20210-3945; (202) 693-3045. Fax, (202) 693-3015. Steven Rietzke, Chief.*
General email, NFJP@dol.gov
Web, www.dol.gov/agencies/eta/agriculture

Provides funds for programs that help migrant and seasonal farm workers and their families find better jobs in agriculture and other areas. Services include occupational training, education, and job development and placement. Partners with states to provide services. Provides grants to assist with permanent and temporary housing.

Employment and Training Administration (ETA) *(Labor Dept.), Workforce Investment (OWI), Workforce Innovation and Opportunity Act (WIOA),* 200 *Constitution Ave. N.W., #S4209, 20210; (202) 693-3046. Fax, (202) 693-3817. Robert Kight, Chief.*
Web, www.dol.gov/agencies/eta/workforce-investment/ adult

Provides targeted job training services for migrant and seasonal farm workers.

Labor Dept. (DOL), *Wage and Hour Division (WHD), Immigration and Farm Labor,* 200 *Constitution Ave. N.W., #S3502, 20210; (202) 693-0070. Fax, (202) 693-1387. Whitney Ford, Director. Toll-free, (866) 487-9243.*
Web, www.dol.gov/whd

Administers and enforces the Migrant and Seasonal Agricultural Worker Protection Act, which protects migrant and seasonal agricultural workers from substandard labor practices by farm labor contractors, agricultural employers, and agricultural associations. Also enforces the provisions of the Immigration and Nationality Act that pertain to the employment of H-2A visa workers and U.S. workers in corresponding employment; the temporary labor camp and field sanitation standards of the Occupational Safety and Health Act; and the standards pertaining to employment in agriculture of the Fair Labor Standards Act.

▶NONGOVERNMENTAL

Assn. of Farmworker Opportunity Programs, *1150 Connecticut Ave. N.W., #315, 20036; (202) 963-3200. Daniel Sheehan, Executive Director.*
General email, info@afop.org
Web, www.afop.org, Twitter, @AFOPNational and Facebook, www.facebook.com/AFOPNational

Represents state-level organizations that provide job training and other services and support to migrant and seasonal farm workers. Monitors legislation and conducts research.

Migrant Legal Action Program, *1001 Connecticut Ave. N.W., #915, 20036-5524; (202) 775-7780. Roger C. Rosenthal, Executive Director.*
General email, mlap@mlap.org
Web, www.mlap.org and Facebook, www.facebook.com/ MigrantLegalActionProgram

Supports and assists local legal services, migrant education, migrant health issues, and other organizations and private attorneys with respect to issues involving the living and working conditions of migrant farmworkers. Monitors legislation and regulations.

Internship Coordinators in the Washington Metropolitan Area

For congressional internships, contact members' offices. For opportunities at federal agencies, visit www.usajobs.gov/Help/working-in-government/unique-hiring-paths/students. For information on changes to the federal internship program, see www.opm.gov/policy-data-oversight/hiring-authorities/students-recent-graduates.

American Assn. for the Advancement of Science, (202) 326-6677; www.aaas.org

American Civil Liberties Union, (212) 549-2500; www.aclu.org

American Farm Bureau Federation, (202) 406-3626; www.fb.org

American Federation of Teachers, (202) 879-4439; www.aft.org

American Red Cross, (202) 303-5214; www.redcross.org

Americans for the Arts, (202) 371-2830; www.americansforthearts.org

Amnesty International, (202) 544-0200; www.amnestyusa.org

B'nai B'rith International, (202) 857-6613; www.bnaibrith.org

Carnegie Institution of Washington, (202) 939-1113; www.carnegiescience.edu

Center for Responsive Politics, (202) 857-0044; www.opensecrets.org

Center for Science in the Public Interest, (202) 332-9110; www.cspinet.org

Children's Defense Fund, (202) 662-3507; www.childrensdefense.org

Common Cause, (202) 833-1200; www.commoncause.org

Council on Hemispheric Affairs, www.coha.org

C-SPAN, (202) 737-3220; www.c-span.org

Democratic National Committee, (202) 863-8000; www.democrats.org

Friends of the Earth, (202) 783-7400; www.foe.org

Inter-American Dialogue, (202) 822-9002; www.thedialogue.org

International Assn. of Chiefs of Police, (800) 843-4227; www.theiacp.org

Middle East Institute, (202) 785-1141; www.mei.edu

Motion Picture Assn. of America, (202) 293-1966; www.mpaa.org

National Academy of Sciences, (202) 334-2000; www.nasonline.org

National Assn. for Equal Opportunity in Higher Education, (202) 552-3300 or(202) 487-9125; www.nafeonation.org

National Assn. for the Advancement of Colored People, (202) 463-2940; www.naacpdc.org

National Assn. of Broadcasters, (202) 429-3928 or (202) 429-5300; www.nab.org

National Center for Missing & Exploited Children, (877) 446-2632; www.missingkids.org

National Geographic Society, (202) 857-7000; www.nationalgeographic.com

National Governors Assn., (202) 624-5300; www.nga.org

National Head Start Assn., (703) 739-0875; www.nhsa.org

National Law Center on Homelessness and Poverty, (202) 638-2535; www.nlchp.org

National Organization for Women, (202) 628-8669; www.now.org

National Public Radio, (202) 513-2000; www.npr.org

National Trust for Historic Preservation, (202) 588-6000; www.preservationnation.org

National Wildlife Federation, (703) 438-6265; https://savingplaces.org

The Nature Conservancy, (301) 897-8570; www.nature.org

Points of Light Institute, (404) 979-2900; www.pointsoflight.org

Radio Free Europe/Radio Liberty, (202) 457-6900; www.rferl.org

Republican National Committee, (202) 863-8618; www.gop.com

Special Olympics International, (202) 408-2640; www.specialolympics.org

United Negro College Fund, (202) 810-0258; www.uncf.org

U.S. Chamber of Commerce, (202) 659-6000; www.uschamber.com

Older Workers

▶ AGENCIES

Employment and Training Administration (ETA) *(Labor Dept.), Senior Community Service Employment Program, 200 Constitution Ave. N.W., #C4510, 20210; (202) 693-3045. Fax, (202) 693-3817. Ryan Gilligan, Administrator.*
Web, www.dol.gov/agencies/eta/seniors

Provides funds for part-time community service work-training programs; the programs pay minimum wage and are operated by national sponsoring organizations and state and territorial governments. The program is aimed at unemployed economically disadvantaged persons age 55 and over.

▶ NONGOVERNMENTAL

AARP, *601 E St. N.W., 20049; (202) 434-2277. Jo Ann C. Jenkins, Chief Executive Officer. Library, (202) 434-6233. Membership, toll-free, (800) 566-0242. Press, (202) 434-2560. Toll-free, (888) 687-2277. TTY, (877) 434-7598. Toll-free Spanish, (877) 342-2277. TTY Spanish, (866) 238-9488.*
General email, dcaarp@aarp.org
Web, www.aarp.org, Twitter, @AARP and Facebook, www.facebook.com/AARP

Membership: people 50 years of age and older. Provides members with training, employment information, and volunteer programs.

National Council on Aging, *Senior Community Service Employment Program,* 251 S. 18th St., #500, Arlington, VA 22202; (571) 527-3900. Vacant, Director.
General email, info@ncoa.org
Web, www.ncoa.org/older-adults/money/work-retirement/scsep

Operates a grant through funding from the U.S. Labor Dept. under the authority of the Older Americans Act to provide workers age 55 and over with community service employment and training opportunities in their resident communities.

Workers with Disabilities

▶**AGENCIES**

Employment and Training Administration (ETA) *(Labor Dept.),* **Workforce Investment (OWI),** 200 Constitution Ave. N.W., #C4526, 20210; (202) 693-3980. Fax, (202) 693-3981. Kimberly Vitelli, Administrator.
Web, www.dol.gov/agencies/eta/workforce-investment

Provides workers with information, job search assistance, and training. Oversees programs administered through the One-Stop delivery system assisting job seekers, including individuals with disabilities.

Labor Dept. (DOL), *Disability Employment Policy (ODEP),* 200 Constitution Ave. N.W., #S1303, 20210; (202) 693-7880. Fax, (202) 693-7888. Jennifer Sheehy, Deputy Assistant Secretary. Toll-free, (866) 633-7365. TTY, (877) 889-5627.
General email, odep@dol.gov
Web, www.dol.gov/odep

Influences disability employment policy by developing and promoting the use of evidence-based disability employment policies and practices, building collaborative partnerships, and delivering data on employment of people with disabilities.

Office of Personnel Management (OPM), *Policy, Data, Oversight, Veterans Services,* 1900 E St. N.W., #7439, 20415; (202) 606-3602. Fax, (202) 606-6017. Hakeem A. Basheerud-Deen, Director.
Web, www.opm.gov/policy-data-oversight/veterans-services

Provides federal employees and transitioning military service members and their families, federal human resources professionals, and hiring managers with information on employment opportunities with the federal government. Administers the Disabled Veterans Affirmative Action Program.

Special Education and Rehabilitative Services (OSERS) *(Education Dept.),* **Rehabilitation Services Administration (RSA),** Lyndon B. Johnson Bldg., 400 Maryland Ave. S.W., 20202-7100; (202) 245-7468.
Fax, (202) 245-7591. Carol Dobak, Commissioner (Acting).
Web, https://rsa.ed.gov

Coordinates and directs federal services for eligible persons with physical or mental disabilities, with emphasis on programs that promote employment opportunities. Provides vocational training and job placement; supports projects with private industry; administers grants for the establishment of supported-employment programs.

U.S. AbilityOne Commission, 1401 S. Clark St., #715, Arlington, VA 22202-3259; (703) 603-2100. Fax, (703) 603-0655. Kim Zeich, Deputy Executive Director. Toll-free, (800) 999-5963.
General email, info@abilityone.gov
Web, www.abilityone.gov

Presidentially appointed committee. Determines which products and services are suitable for federal procurement from qualified nonprofit agencies that employ people who are blind or have other significant disabilities; seeks to increase employment opportunities for these individuals. (Formerly Committee for Purchase from People Who Are Blind or Severely Disabled.)

▶**NONGOVERNMENTAL**

Center for Employment and Economic Well-Being (CEEWB), 1300 17th St. North., #340, Arlington, VA 22209; (202) 682-0100. Tracey Wareing Evans, President.
General email, memberservice@aphsa.org
Web, https://aphsa.org/CEEWB/default.aspx and Twitter, @APHSA1

Works to identify the best practices and resources that will help move low-income individuals into sustainable careers. Supports public policies that provide the opportunities for individuals, families, and communities to succeed in the workforce. (Affiliated with the American Public Human Services Association.)

Disability:IN, 3000 Potomac Ave., #101, Alexandria, VA 22305; (800) 706-2710. Fax, (800) 706-1335. Jill Houghton, Chief Executive Officer.
General email, info@disabilityIN.org
Web, https://disabilityin.org, Twitter, @DisabilityIN and Facebook, www.facebook.com/DisabilityIN

Advocates inclusion of people with disabilities in the workplace, supply chain, and marketplaces; provides information on disability inclusion business practices. (Formerly the U.S. Business Leadership Network.)

Youth

▶**AGENCIES**

Employment and Training Administration (ETA) *(Labor Dept.),* **Workforce Investment (OWI), Youth Services,** 200 Constitution Ave. N.W., #N4508, 20210; (202) 693-3030. Fax, (202) 693-3861. Robin Fernkas, Deputy Administrator.
General email, youth.services@dol.gov
Web, www.dol.gov/agencies/eta/youth/about

Administers youth grant programs designed to enhance youth education, encourage school completion, and provide career and apprenticeship opportunities. Oversees the Going Home: Serious and Violent Offender Reentry Initiative and YouthBuild.

Forest Service *(Agriculture Dept.) Recreation, Heritage and Volunteer Resources, Youth Conservation Corps,* *201 14th St. 5-S.W., 20024 (mailing address: 1400 Independence Ave. S.W., MS 1125, Washington, DC 20250-1125); (202) 205-1240. Gordie Blum, Director, (Acting), Recreation, Heritage. Toll-free, (800) 832-1355.* *Web, www.fs.fed.us/working-with-us/opportunities-for-young-people/youth-conservation-corps-opportunities*

Administers, with the National Park Service and the Fish and Wildlife Service, the Youth Conservation Corps, a summer employment and training public works program for youths ages fifteen to eighteen. The program is conducted in national parks, in national forests and grasslands, and on national wildlife refuges.

Labor Dept. (DOL), *Job Corps, 200 Constitution Ave. N.W., #N4463, 20210; (202) 693-3000. Fax, (202) 693-2767. Rachel Torres, Director. Toll-free, (800) 733-5627. TTY, (877) 889-5627.* *General email, nationaloffice@jobcorps.gov* *Web, www.jobcorps.gov and Facebook, www.facebook.com/doljobcorps*

Provides job training for disadvantaged youth at residential centers. Most of the centers are managed and operated by corporations and nonprofit organizations.

Labor Dept. (DOL), *Wage and Hour Division (WHD), Child Labor, 200 Constitution Ave. N.W., #S3502, 20210; (202) 693-0067. Fax, (202) 693-1387.* *Derrick J. Witherspoon, Director. Press, (202) 693-0185. Toll-free, (866) 487-9243.* *Web, www.dol.gov/whd/childlabor.htm*

Administers and enforces child labor, special minimum wage, and other provisions of Section 14 of the Fair Labor Standards Act.

►**NONGOVERNMENTAL**

The Corps Network, *1275 K St. N.W., #1050, 20005; (202) 737-6272. Fax, (202) 737-6277. Mary Ellen Sprenkel, President.* *Web, http://corpsnetwork.org, Twitter, @TheCorpsNetwork, Facebook, www.facebook.com/TheCorpsNetwork and YouTube, www.youtube.com/TheCorpsNetwork*

Membership: youth corps programs and veterans up to age 35. Produces publications and workshops on starting and operating youth corps and offers technical assistance programs. Holds annual conference. Monitors legislation and regulations.

Covenant House, *Washington Office, 2001 Mississippi Ave. S.E., 20020; (202) 610-9600. Angela Jones Hackley, Executive Director.*

Web, http://covenanthousedc.org and Twitter, @CovenantHouseDC

Protects young people suffering from homelessness, abuse, and neglect. Provides services including GED and adult education and job readiness. (Affiliated with Covenant House International.)

EQUAL EMPLOYMENT OPPORTUNITY

General

►**AGENCIES**

Agriculture Dept. (USDA), *Rural Development, Civil Rights, 1400 Independence Ave. S.W., #1341-S, MS 0703, 20250-0703; (202) 692-0252. Fax, (844) 496-7792. Sharese C. Paylor, Director, (202) 692-0097. Toll-free, (800) 787-8821.* *General email, ra.rd.mostl.civilrights@usda.gov* *Web, www.rd.usda.gov/about-rd/offices/civil-rights*

Processes Equal Employment Opportunity complaints for Rural Development employees, former employees, and applicants. Enforces compliance with the Equal Credit Opportunity Act, which prohibits discrimination on the basis of sex, marital status, race, color, religion, disability, or age in rural housing, utilities, and business programs. Provides civil rights training, technical assistance and program suppport to Rural Development's national, state, and field staffs.

Civil Rights Division *(Justice Dept.), Employment Litigation (ELS), 150 M St. N.E., #9.1819, 20002; (202) 514-3831. Fax, (202) 514-1005. Karen Woodward, Chief. TTY, (202) 514-6780.* *Web, www.justice.gov/crt/employment-litigation-section*

Investigates, negotiates, and litigates allegations of employment discrimination by public schools, universities, state and local governments, and federally funded employers; has enforcement power.

Equal Employment Opportunity Commission (EEOC), *131 M St. N.E., 20507; (202) 663-4900. Fax, (202) 663-4110. Charlotte A. Burrows, Chair. Library, (202) 663-4630. Toll-free information, (800) 669-4000. Training Institute, (703) 291-0880. Training Institute toll-free, (866) 446-0940. Training Institute TTY, (800) 828-1120. TTY, (800) 669-6820.* *General email, info@eeoc.gov* *Web, www.eeoc.gov, Twitter, @USEEOC, Facebook, www.facebook.com/USEEOC and Training Institute, eeoc.traininginstitute@eeoc.gov*

Works to end job discrimination by private and government employers based on race, color, religion, sex, national origin, disability, or age. Works to protect employees against reprisal for protest of employment practices alleged to be unlawful in hiring, promotion, firing, wages, and other terms and conditions of employment.

Equal Employment Opportunity Commission

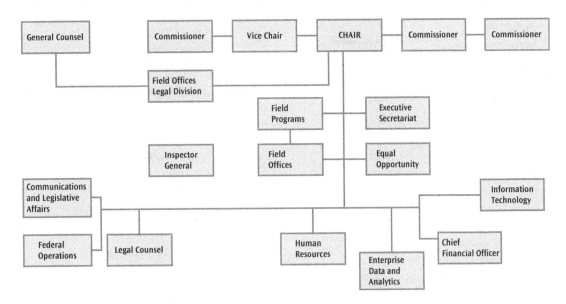

Works for increased employment of persons with disabilities, affirmative action by the federal government, and an equitable work environment for employees with mental and physical disabilities. Enforces Title VII of the Civil Rights Act of 1964, as amended, which includes the Pregnancy Discrimination Act; Americans with Disabilities Act; Age Discrimination in Employment Act; Equal Pay Act; Genetic Information Nondiscrimination Act (GINA); and, in the federal sector, rehabilitation laws. Receives charges of discrimination; attempts conciliation or settlement; can bring court action to force compliance; has review and appeals responsibility in the federal sector. Library open to the public by appointment only.

Equal Employment Opportunity Commission (EEOC), *Field Programs, 131 M St. N.E., 5th Floor, 20507; (202) 663-4801. Fax, (202) 663-7190. Martin (Marty) S. Ebel, Director. Web, www.eeoc.gov/field*

Provides guidance and technical assistance through 15 district offices to employees who suspect discrimination and to employers who are working to comply with equal employment laws.

Federal Communications Commission (FCC), *Media Bureau (MB), Policy Division, Equal Employment Opportunity (EEO), 45 L St. N.E., 20554; (202) 418-1450. Fax, (202) 418-1797. Robert Baker, Assistant Chief, (202) 418-1417. Web, www.fcc.gov/general/equal-employment-opportunity*

Responsible for the annual certification of cable television equal employment opportunity compliance. Oversees broadcast employment practices.

Labor Dept. (DOL), *Civil Rights Center (CRC), 200 Constitution Ave. N.W., #N4123, 20210; (202) 693-6500. Fax, (202) 693-6505. Naomi M. Barry-Perez, Director. TTY, (800) 877-8339.*

General email, civilrightscenter@dol.gov

Web, www.dol.gov/agencies/oasam/centers-offices/civil-rights-center

Resolves complaints of workplace discrimination on the basis of race, color, religion, sex, national origin, age, or disability in programs funded by the department. Library open to the public.

Labor Dept. (DOL), *Federal Contract Compliance Programs (OFCCP), 200 Constitution Ave. N.W., #C3325, 20210; (202) 693-0101. Fax, (202) 693-1304. Jenny R. Yang, Director. Toll-free, (800) 397-6251. TTY, (877) 889-5627. General email, OFCCP-Public@dol.gov*

Web, www.dol.gov/ofccp

Monitors and enforces government contractors' compliance with federal laws and regulations on equal employment opportunities and affirmative action, including employment rights of minorities, women, persons with disabilities, and disabled and Vietnam-era veterans.

Office of Personnel Management (OPM), *Policy, Data, Oversight, Veterans Services, 1900 E St. N.W., #7439, 20415; (202) 606-3602. Fax, (202) 606-6017. Hakeem A. Basheerud-Deen, Director. Web, www.opm.gov/policy-data-oversight/veterans-services*

Administers the Disabled Veterans Affirmative Action Program.

U.S. Commission on Civil Rights, *Civil Rights Evaluation, 1331 Pennsylvania Ave. N.W., #1150, 20425; (202) 376-7700. Vacant, Director. Complaints Unit hotline, (202) 376-8513. Toll-free hotline, (800) 552-6843. TYT, (800) 877-8339. General email, enforcement@usccr.gov Web, www.usccr.gov/about/offices*

Equal Employment Opportunity Contacts at Federal Departments and Agencies

DEPARTMENTS

Agriculture, Winona Lake Scott, (202) 720-3808

Commerce, Susan E. Thomas, (202) 482-8121

Defense, Laura McConnell, (703) 604-9710

Air Force, Audie Sanders, (240) 612-4357

Army, Spurgeon A. Moore, (703) 545-5761

Marine Corps, Penny Thomison, (571) 256-8301

Navy, Celina M. Kline, (901) 874-2507

Education, Michael A. Chew, (202) 401-3560

Energy, Ann Augustyn, (202) 586-5687

Health and Human Services, Cynthia Richardson-Crooks, (202) 690-6555

Homeland Security, Carl Lucas, (202) 357-7700

Coast Guard, Carolyn Hunter, (202) 372-4260

Housing and Urban Development, Jeanine Worden, (202) 402-5188

Interior, Erica White-Dunston, (202) 208-3413

Justice, Richard Toscano, (202) 616-4800

Labor, Samuel Rhames, (202) 693-6500

State, Gregory B. Smith, (202) 647-9295

Transportation, Tami L. Wright, (202) 366-9370

Treasury, Mariam G. Harvey, (202) 622-0316

Veterans Affairs, Perdita Johnson-Abercrombie, (202) 461-6743

AGENCIES

Commission on Civil Rights, Alicia O. McPhie, (202) 606-2460

Commodity Futures Trading Commission, Sarah J. Summerville, (202) 418-5000

Consumer Product Safety Commission, Brittany Woolfolk, (301) 504-7596

Corp. for National and Community Service, Lisa A. Gray (Acting), (202) 606-3221

Environmental Protection Agency, Michael Nieves, (202) 566-1478

Equal Employment Opportunity Commission, Stan Pietrusiak (Acting), (202) 663-7081

Export-Import Bank, Patrease Jones-Brown, (202) 565-3591

Farm Credit Administration, Thais Burlew, (703) 883-4290

Federal Communications Commission, Linda Miller, (202) 418-1799

Federal Deposit Insurance Corp., Michael Moran, (703) 562-6073

Federal Election Commission, Kevin R. Salley, (202) 694-1228

Federal Emergency Management Agency, Jo Linda Johnson, (202) 212-3535

Federal Energy Regulatory Commission (FERC), Madeline H. Lewis, (202) 502-8120

Federal Labor Relations Authority, Emily Sloop, (202) 218-7924

Federal Maritime Commission, Ebony Jarrett, (202) 523-5859

Federal Mediation and Conciliation Service, Denise McKenney, (202) 606-5448

Federal Reserve Board, Sheila Clark, (202) 452-2883

Federal Trade Commission, Kevin D. Williams, (202) 326-2196

General Services Administration, Dewayne Harley, (202) 501-0767

Merit Systems Protection Board, Jessica Lang, (202) 254-4405

National Aeronautics and Space Administration, Richard N. Reback, (202) 358-2180

National Credit Union Administration, Monica Hughes Davy, (703) 518-6325

National Endowment for the Humanities, Julia Nguyen, (202) 606-8213

National Labor Relations Board, Brenda V. Harris, (202) 273-3891

National Science Foundation, Edmund K. Rhynes, (703) 292-2104

National Transportation Safety Board, Sara Guest, (202) 314-6190

Office of Personnel Management, LaShonn M. Woodland, (202) 606-2460

Peace Corps, John W. Burden, (202) 692-2139

Securities and Exchange Commission, Peter Henry, (202) 551-6040

Small Business Administration, Zina Sutch, (202) 205-6750

Smithsonian Institution, Rudy D. Watley, (202) 633-6430

Social Security Administration, Claudia J. Postell, (410) 965-3318

U.S. International Trade Commission, Altivia Jackson, (202) 205-2239

U.S. Postal Service, Eloise Lance, (202) 268-3820

Researches federal policy in areas of equal employment and job discrimination; monitors the economic status of minorities and women, including their employment and earnings. Library open to the public.

▶CONGRESS

For a listing of relevant congressional committees and subcommittees, please see page 221 or the Appendix.

▶NONGOVERNMENTAL

Center for Workplace Compliance (CWC), *1501 M St. N.W., #1000, 20005; (202) 629-5650. Fax, (202) 629-5651. Joseph S. Lakis, President.*
General email, info@cwc.org

Web, www.cwc.org, Twitter, @CWC_alert and Facebook, www.facebook.com/centerforworkplacecompliance

Membership: principal equal employment officers and lawyers. Files amicus curiae (friend of the court) briefs; conducts research and provides information on equal employment law and policy. Monitors legislation and regulations. (Formerly the Equal Employment Advisory Council.)

Minorities

▶AGENCIES

Bureau of Indian Affairs (BIA) *(Interior Dept.), Indian Economic Development (IED), Indian Energy and Economic Development (IEED), 1849 C St. N.W., #4152, 20240; (202) 219-0740. Fax, (202) 208-4564. (202) 208-6764. Jack R. Stevens, Director (Acting). (202) 208-6764.*
Web, www.bia.gov/as-ia/ieed/contact-ieed

Develops policies and programs to promote the achievement of economic goals for members of federally recognized tribes who live on or near reservations. Provides job training; assists those who have completed job training programs in finding employment; provides loan guarantees; and enhances contracting opportunities for individuals and tribes.

Employment and Training Administration (ETA) *(Labor Dept.), Workforce Investment (OWI), Indian and Native American Programs, 200 Constitution Ave. N.W., #S4209, 20210; (202) 693-3046. Fax, (202) 693-3817. Athena R. Brown, Chief, (202) 693-3737.*
Web, www.dol.gov/agencies/eta/dinap

Administers grants for training and employment-related programs to promote employment opportunity; provides unemployed, underemployed, and economically disadvantaged Native Americans and Alaska and Hawaiian Natives with funds for training, job placement, and support services.

Health and Human Services Dept., *White House Initiative on Asian Americans, Native Hawaiians, and Pacific Islanders, 550 12th St. S.W., 10th Floor, 20202; (202) 482-1375. Krystal Ka'ai, Executive Director.*
General email, whiaanhpi@hhs.gov

Web, www.commerce.gov/whiaapi and Twitter, @whitehouseAAPI

Works to expand Asian American, Native Hawaiian, and Pacific Islander federal employment opportunities. Ensures that workers' rights are protected and upheld.

▶NONGOVERNMENTAL

AFL-CIO, *Asian Pacific American Labor Alliance (APALA), 815 16th St. N.W., 2nd Floor, 20006; Alvina Yeh, Executive Director. (202) 800-5811.*
General email, info@apalanet.org

Web, www.apalanet.org, Twitter, @APALAnational and Facebook, www.facebook.com/APALAnational

Membership: Asian American and Pacific Islander (AAPI) union members. Represents regional Asia–Pacific Rim labor activists in a national scope and assists in union member issues. Interests include gender analysis, youth participation, and civil and human rights within the AAPI community.

American Assn. for Access, Equity, and Diversity (AAAED), *1701 Pennsylvania Ave. N.W., #200, 20006; (202) 349-9855. Fax, (202) 355-1399. Shirley J. Wilcher, Executive Director. Toll-free, (866) 562-2233.*
General email, info@aaaed.org

Web, www.aaaed.org, Facebook, www.facebook.com/theaaaed and Twitter, @theaaaed

Membership: professional managers in the areas of affirmative action, equal opportunity, diversity, and human resources. Sponsors education, research, and training programs. Acts as a liaison with government agencies involved in equal opportunity compliance. Maintains ethical standards for the profession. (Formerly the American Assn. for Affirmative Action.)

Blacks in Government, *3005 Georgia Ave. N.W., 20001-3807; (202) 667-3280. Fax, (202) 667-3705. Shirley A. Jones, President.*
General email, bignational@bignet.org

Web, www.bignet.org, Twitter, @BigNational and Facebook, www.facebook.com/BIGNATIONAL

Advocacy organization for public employees. Promotes equal opportunity and career advancement for African American government employees; provides career development information; seeks to eliminate racism in the federal workforce; sponsors programs, business meetings, and social gatherings; represents interests of African American government workers to Congress and the executive branch; promotes voter education and registration.

Center for Equal Opportunity, *7700 Leesburg Pike, #231, Falls Church, VA 22043; (703) 442-0066. Fax, (703) 442-0449. Rudy Gersten, Executive Director.*
General email, comment@ceousa.org

Web, www.ceousa.org

Research organization concerned with issues of race, ethnicity, and assimilation; opposes racial preferences in employment or education, contracting, and other areas. Monitors legislation and regulations.

Coalition of Black Trade Unionists, *1155 Connecticut Ave. N.W., #500, 20036 (mailing address: P.O. Box 66268, Washington, DC 20035); (202) 778-3318. Fax, (202) 419-1486. Terrence (Terry) L. Melvin, President.*
General email, cbtu@cbtu.org
Web, https://cbtu.nationbuilder.com

Monitors legislation affecting African American and other minority trade unionists. Focuses on equal employment opportunity, unemployment, and voter education and registration.

Conference of Minority Transportation Officials, *1330 Braddock Pl., #203, Alexandria, VA 22314; (202) 506-2917. April Rai, President.*
General email, info@comtonational.org
Web, www.comtonational.org, Twitter, @COMTO_National and Facebook, www.facebook.com/COMTO National

Forum for minority professionals working in the transportation sector. Provides opportunities and reinforces networks through advocacy, training, and professional development for minorities in the industry.

Labor Council for Latin American Advancement, *815 16th St. N.W., 3rd Floor, 20006; (202) 508-6919. Fax, (202) 508-6922. Karla Pineda, Deputy Director.*
General email, headquarters@lclaa.org
Web, www.lclaa.org, Twitter, @LCLAA and Facebook, www.facebook.com/LCLAA

Membership: Latino/a trade unionists throughout U.S. and Puerto Rico. Encourages equal employment opportunity, voter registration, and participation in the political process. (Affiliated with the AFL-CIO and the Change to Win Federation.)

NAACP Legal Defense and Educational Fund, Inc., *Washington Office, 700 14th St. N.W., #600, 20005; (202) 682-1300. Sherrilyn Ifill, President.*
Web, www.naacpldf.org, Twitter, @naacp_ldf, Facebook, www.facebook.com/naacpldf and YouTube, www.youtube.com/channel/UCXTfPnpwx-CWVyrzDvkwE1w

Civil rights litigation group that provides legal information about civil rights legislation and advice on employment discrimination against women and minorities; monitors federal enforcement of equal opportunity rights laws. Not affiliated with the NAACP. (Headquarters in New York.)

National Assn. for the Advancement of Colored People (NAACP), *Washington Bureau, 1156 15th St. N.W., #915, 20005; (202) 463-2940. Fax, (202) 463-2953. Derrick Johnson, President.*
General email, washingtonbureau@naacpnet.org
Web, www.naacp.org, Twitter, @NAACP and Twitter, President, @DerrickNAACP

Membership: persons interested in civil rights for all minorities. Advises individuals with employment discrimination complaints. Seeks to eliminate job discrimination

and to bring about full employment for all Americans through legislation and litigation. (Headquarters in Baltimore, Md.)

National Assn. of Hispanic Federal Executives, *1750 Pennsylvania Ave. N.W., #27206, 20038; (202) 315-3942. Al Gallegos, National President; Vacant, DC Chapter President.*
General email, president@nahfe.org
Web, https://nahfe.org

Works to ensure that the needs of the Hispanic American community are addressed in the policymaking levels of the federal government by promoting career and learning opportunities for qualified Hispanics in the federal GS/GM-12/15 grade levels and the Senior Executive Service policymaking positions.

National Assn. of Negro Business and Professional Women's Clubs Inc., *1806 New Hampshire Ave. N.W., 20009; (202) 483-4206. Fax, (202) 462-7253. Robin Waley, Executive Director.*
General email, info@nanbpwc.org
Web, www.nanbpwc.org and Twitter, @NANBPWC

Promotes and protects the interests of minority business and professional women, serves as advisors to young people seeking to enter business and the professions, provides scholarship support for secondary education, sponsors workshops, and works to improve the quality of life in local and global communities to foster good fellowship. Monitors legislation and regulations.

National Lesbian and Gay Journalists Assn. (NLGJA), *2120 L St. N.W., #850, 20037; (202) 588-9888. Adam Pawlus, Executive Director.*
General email, info@nlgja.org
Web, www.nlgja.org

Works within the journalism industry to foster fair and accurate coverage of lesbian, gay, bisexual, and transgender issues. Opposes workplace bias against all minorities and provides professional development for its members.

National Urban League, *Washington Bureau, 1805 7th St. N.W., #520, 20001; (202) 898-1604. Joi O. Cheny, Executive Director, Washington, (202) 629-5755.*
Web, https://nul.org/washington-bureau, Twitter, @NULPolicy and Facebook, www.facebook.com/NULPolicy

Federal advocacy division of social service organization concerned with the social welfare of African Americans and other minorities. Testifies before congressional committees and federal agencies on equal employment; studies and evaluates federal enforcement of equal employment laws and regulations. (Headquarters in New York.)

UnidosUS, *1126 16th St. N.W., #600, 20036-4845; (202) 785-1670. Janet Murguía, President.*
General email, info@unidos.org
Web, www.unidosus.org, Twitter, @WeAreUnidosUS, Facebook, www.facebook.com/Weareunidosus and YouTube, www.youtube.com/c/UnidosUS

Provides research, policy analysis, and advocacy on Hispanic employment status and programs; provides Hispanic community–based groups with technical assistance to help develop effective employment programs with strong educational components. Works to promote understanding of Hispanic employment needs in the private sector. Interests include women in the workplace, affirmative action, equal opportunity employment, and youth employment. Monitors federal employment legislation and regulations.

Washington Government Relations Group, *1325 G St. N.W., #500, 20005; (202) 449-7651. Fax, (202) 449-7701. Danielle McBeth, President.*
General email, info@wgrginc.org
Web, www.wgrginc.org

Works to enrich the careers and leadership abilities of African American government relations professionals working in business, financial institutions, law firms, trade associations, and nonprofit organizations. Increases dialogue between members and senior-level policymakers to produce public policy solutions.

Older Adults

▶NONGOVERNMENTAL

AARP, *601 E St. N.W., 20049; (202) 434-2277. Jo Ann C. Jenkins, Chief Executive Officer. Library, (202) 434-6233. Membership, toll-free, (800) 566-0242. Press, (202) 434-2560. Toll-free, (888) 687-2277. TTY, (877) 434-7598. Toll-free Spanish, (877) 342-2277. TTY Spanish, (866) 238-9488.*
General email, dcaarp@aarp.org
Web, www.aarp.org, Twitter, @AARP and Facebook, www.facebook.com/AARP

Membership: people 50 years of age and older. Promotes a multigenerational workforce and seeks to prevent age discrimination in the workplace.

National Caucus and Center on Black Aging, Inc., *1220 L St. N.W., #800, 20005-2407; (202) 637-8400. Fax, (202) 347-0895. Karyne Jones, President.*
Web, https://ncba-aging.org, Twitter, @NCBA1970 and Facebook, www.facebook.com/ncba.aging.5

Concerned with issues that affect older Black Americans and other minorities. Sponsors employment and housing programs for older adults and education and training for professionals in gerontology. Monitors legislation and regulations.

Women

▶AGENCIES

Women's Bureau *(Labor Dept.),* *200 Constitution Ave. N.W., #S3002, 20210; (202) 693-6710. Fax, (202) 693-6725. Wendy Chun-hoon, Director. Toll-free, (866) 487-2365.*
General email, Womens.Bureau@dol.gov
Web, www.dol.gov/wb

Monitors women's employment issues. Promotes employment opportunities for women; sponsors workshops, job fairs, symposia, demonstrations, and pilot projects. Offers technical assistance; conducts research and provides publications on issues that affect working women; represents working women in international forums.

▶NONGOVERNMENTAL

Assn. for Women in Science, *1667 K St. N.W., #300, 20006; (202) 827-9798. Sandra W. Robert, Chief Executive Officer.*
General email, awis@awis.org
Web, www.awis.org and Twitter, @AWISNational

Promotes equal opportunity for women in scientific professions; provides career and funding information. Provides educational scholarships for women in science. Interests include international development.

Business and Professional Women's Foundation, *1030 15th St. N.W., #B1, Room 148, 20005; (202) 293-1100. Roslyn Ridgeway, Chair.*
General email, foundation@bpwfoundation.org
Web, https://bpwfoundation.org, Twitter, @WomenMisbehavin and Facebook, www.facebook.com/BPWFoundation?ref=hl

Works to eliminate barriers to the full participation of women in the workplace. Interests include pay equity, work-life balance, women veterans, and green jobs for women. Conducts research; provides issue briefs and other publications; monitors legislation and regulations.

Coalition of Labor Union Women, *815 16th St. N.W., 2nd Floor South, 20006-1119; (202) 508-6969. Elise A. Bryant, President, (202) 637-3963; Harriette Scofield, Executive Director (Acting), (202) 508-6951.*
General email, cluw@cluw.org
Web, http://cluw.org, Twitter, @CLUWNational and Facebook, www.facebook.com/CLUWomen

Seeks to make unions more responsive to the needs of women in the workplace; advocates affirmative action and the active participation of women in unions. Monitors legislation and regulations.

Federally Employed Women, *455 Massachusetts Ave. N.W., 20001 (mailing address: P.O. Box 306, Washington, DC 20001); (202) 898-0994. Karen Rainey, President.*
General email, few@few.org
Web, www.few.org, Twitter, @FENNational and Facebook, www.facebook.com/federallyemployedwomen

Membership: women and men who work for the federal government. The four major program areas are Compliance, Diversity, Legislative and Training. Works to eliminate sex discrimination in government employment and to increase job opportunities for women. Monitors legislation and regulations.

Institute for Women's Policy Research (IWPR), *1200 18th St. N.W., #301, 20036; (202) 785-5100. Fax, (202) 833-4362. C. Nicole Mason, President. Press, (202) 684-7534.*

General email, iwpr@iwpr.org

Web, https://iwpr.org, Twitter, @IWPResearch and Facebook, www.facebook.com/iwpresearch

Public policy research organization that focuses on women's issues, including family and work balance and employment and wages.

NAACP Legal Defense and Educational Fund, Inc., Washington Office, *700 14th St. N.W., #600, 20005; (202) 682-1300. Sherrilyn Ifill, President.*

Web, www.naacpldf.org, Twitter, @naacp_ldf, Facebook, www.facebook.com/naacpldf and YouTube, www.youtube .com/channel/UCXTfPnpwx-CWVyrzDvkwE1w

Civil rights litigation group that provides legal information about civil rights legislation and advice on employment discrimination against women and minorities; monitors federal enforcement of equal opportunity rights laws. Not affiliated with the NAACP. (Headquarters in New York.)

National Assn. of Women Business Owners, *South Bldg., 601 Pennsylvania Ave. N.W., #900, 20004; (800) 556-2926. Fax, (202) 403-3788. Jen Earle, Chief Executive Officer.*

General email, national@nawbo.org

Web, www.nawbo.org, Twitter, @NAWBONational, Facebook, www.facebook.com/NAWBO and YouTube, www.youtube.com/user/nawbonat

Promotes the economic, social, and political interests of women business owners through networking, leadership and business development training, and advocacy.

National Partnership for Women and Families, *1875 Connecticut Ave. N.W., #650, 20009-5731; (202) 986-2600. Fax, (202) 986-2539. Jocelyn Frye, President.*

General email, info@nationalpartnership.org

Web, www.nationalpartnership.org

Advocacy organization that promotes fairness in the workplace. Publishes and disseminates information in print and on the Web to heighten awareness of work and family issues. Monitors legislative activity and pending Supreme Court cases and argues on behalf of family issues before Congress and in the courts.

National Women's Law Center, *11 Dupont Circle N.W., #800, 20036; (202) 588-5180. Fax, (202) 588-5185. Fatima Goss Graves, President. Legal help, (202) 319-3053.*

General email, info@nwlc.org

Web, www.nwlc.org, Twitter, @nwlc and Facebook, www .facebook.com/nwlc

Works to protect and advance the rights of women and girls at work, in school, and beyond. Maintains programs that focus on enforcing Title IX's provisions for equal treatment in education and narrowing the gender gap in athletics and the technology-oriented workplace. Other interests include equal pay and benefits, sexual harassment laws, the right to family leave, child care and early learning, poverty and income support, and the preservation of diversity in the workplace.

Women in Film and Video (WIFV), *1200 18th St. N.W., #300, 20036; (202) 429-9438. Fax, (202) 429-9440. Melissa Houghton, Executive Director.*

General email, membership@wifv.org

Web, www.wifv.org and Twitter, @WIFVDC

Membership organization dedicated to promoting equal employment opportunities and advancing career development and achievement for women working in all areas of screen-based media and related disciplines.

Workers with Disabilities

▶**AGENCIES**

Equal Employment Opportunity Commission (EEOC), *131 M St. N.E., 20507; (202) 663-4900. Fax, (202) 663-4110. Charlotte A. Burrows, Chair. Library, (202) 663-4630. Toll-free information, (800) 669-4000. Training Institute, (703) 291-0880. Training Institute toll-free, (866) 446-0940. Training Institute TTY, (800) 828-1120. TTY, (800) 669-6820.*

General email, info@eeoc.gov

Web, www.eeoc.gov, Twitter, @USEEOC, Facebook, www .facebook.com/USEEOC and Training Institute, eeoc. traininginstitute@eeoc.gov

Works for increased employment of persons with disabilities, affirmative action by the federal government, and an equitable work environment for employees with mental and physical disabilities.

Equal Employment Opportunity Commission (EEOC), Legal Counsel, Americans with Disabilities Act Policy Division, *131 M St. N.E., 20507; (202) 663-4665. Fax, (202) 663-6034. Christopher J. Kuczynski, Assistant Legal Counsel. TTY, (202) 663-7026.*

Web, www.eeoc.gov

Provides interpretations, opinions, and technical assistance on the ADA provisions and the provisions of the Genetic Information Nondiscrimination Act (GINA) relating to employment.

Labor Dept. (DOL), *Disability Employment Policy (ODEP), 200 Constitution Ave. N.W., #S1303, 20210; (202) 693-7880. Fax, (202) 693-7888. Jennifer Sheehy, Deputy Assistant Secretary. Toll-free, (866) 633-7365. TTY, (877) 889-5627.*

General email, odep@dol.gov

Web, www.dol.gov/odep

Promotes employment opportunities for people with disabilities.

Assn. of People Supporting Employment First (APSE), *7361 Calhoun Pl., #680, Rockville, MD 20855; (301) 279-0060. Fax, (301) 279-0075. Julie Christensen, Executive Director.*
General email, info@apse.org
CESPC email, cesp@apse.org, Web, www.apse.org, Twitter, @nationalaspse and Facebook, www.facebook.com/nationalapse

Advocates opportunities for equitable employment for those with disabilities. Monitors legislation and regulations.

HUMAN RESOURCES

General

▶ AGENCIES

National Science Foundation (NSF), *Education and Human Resources Directorate (HRD),* 2415 Eisenhower Ave., Room C 11000, Alexandria, VA 22314; (703) 292-8600. Fax, (703) 292-9179. Sylvia M. Butterfield, Assistant Director (Acting), (703) 292-5333.
Web, www.nsf.gov/dir/index.jsp?org=ehr

Supports the development of a diverse and well-prepared STEM workforce through a variety of education and research programs.

National Science Foundation (NSF), *Human Resource Development Division (HRD),* 2415 Eisenhower Ave., Room E11400, Alexandria, VA 22134; (703) 292-8640. Fax, (703) 292-9019. Diana Elder, Director, (703) 292-4437.
Web, www.nsf.gov/div/index.jsp?div=hrd

Supports programs and activities to increase participation of minorities, women, and people with disabilities in the STEM workforce.

Office of Personnel Management (OPM), *Human Resources Solutions,* 1900 E St. N.W., #2469F, 20415-1000; (202) 606-1304. Peter Bonner, Associate Director.
Web, www.opm.gov/about-us/our-people-organization/program-divisions/human-resources-solutions

Manages federal human resources policy, including staffing, compensation, benefits, labor relations, and position classification.

▶ CONGRESS

For a listing of relevant congressional committees and subcommittees, please see page 221 or the Appendix.

▶ NONGOVERNMENTAL

American Assn. for Access, Equity, and Diversity (AAAED), *1701 Pennsylvania Ave. N.W., #200, 20006;* (202) 349-9855. Fax, (202) 355-1399. Shirley J. Wilcher, Executive Director. Toll-free, (866) 562-2233.
General email, info@aaaed.org
Web, www.aaaed.org, Facebook, www.facebook.com/theaaaed and Twitter, @theaaaed

Membership: professional managers in the areas of affirmative action, equal opportunity, diversity, and human resources. Sponsors education, research, and training programs. Acts as a liaison with government agencies involved in equal opportunity compliance. Maintains ethical standards for the profession. (Formerly the American Assn. for Affirmative Action.)

American Assn. for the Advancement of Science (AAAS), *Education and Human Resources Programs (EHR),* 1200 New York Ave. N.W., 6th Floor, 20005; (202) 326-6670 (voice and TTY accessible). Fax, (202) 371-9849. Shirley M. Malcom, Director, (202) 326-6720.
General email, ehr@aaas.org
Web, www.aaas.org/programs/education-and-human-resources

Works to increase and provide information and opportunities to science students and professionals in scientific and technology. Main program areas include schools, libraries, families, higher education research, workforce development, and science for the public.

American Staffing Assn., *277 S. Washington St., #200, Alexandria, VA 22314-3675; (703) 253-2020. Fax, (703) 253-2053. Richard A. Wahlquist, President.*
Web, https://americanstaffing.net, Twitter, @StaffingTweets and Facebook, www.facebook.com/AmericanStaffingAssociation

Membership: companies supplying other companies with workers on a temporary or permanent basis, with outsourcing, with human resources, and with professional employer organizations (PEOs) arrangements. Monitors legislation and regulations. Encourages the maintenance of high ethical standards and provides public relations and educational support to members.

Assn. for Talent Development (ATD), *1640 King St., 3rd Floor, Alexandria, VA 22314; (703) 683-8100. Fax, (703) 683-8723. Tony Bingham, Chief Executive Officer. Toll-free, (800) 628-2783.*
General email, customercare@astd.org
Web, www.td.org, Twitter, @atd and Facebook, www.facebook.com/ATD

Membership: trainers and human resource development specialists. Promotes workplace training programs and human resource development. Interests include productivity, leadership development, and employee retraining and performance improvement. Holds conferences; publishes information about employee learning and development; provides online training. (Formerly American Society for Training and Development.)

Employee Assistance Professionals Assn., *4350 N. Fairfax Dr., #740, Arlington, VA 22203; (703) 387-1000. Fax, (703) 522-4585. Julie Fabsik-Swarts, Chief Executive Officer.*

General email, info@eapassn.org

Web, www.eapassn.org

Membership: professionals in the workplace who assist employees and their family members with personal and behavioral problems, including health, marital, family, financial, alcohol, drug, legal, emotional, stress, or other personal problems that adversely affect employee job performance and productivity.

HR Policy Assn., *1001 N. 19th St., #1002, Arlington, DC, 22209; (202) 789-8670. Fax, (202) 789-0064. Timothy Bartl, President.*
General email, info@hrpolicy.org

Web, www.hrpolicy.org

Membership: chief human resource officers in charge of employee relations. Promotes advancement of the human resource profession; interests include health care, executive compensation, labor law and labor relations, employment rights, immigration, executive compensation, impact of artifical intelligence on work, regulatory reform and enforcement, and retirement security.

Human Resources Research Organization (HumRRO), *66 Canal Center Plaza, #700, Alexandria, VA 22314-1578; (703) 549-3611. Fax, (703) 548-2860. Suzanne Tsacoumis, President.*
Web, www.humrro.org, Twitter, @HumRROorg and Facebook, www.facebook.com/HumRRO

Studies, designs, develops, surveys, and evaluates personnel systems, chiefly in the workplace. Interests include personnel selection and promotion, career progression, performance appraisal, training, program evaluation, leadership assessment, and human capital analytics.

International Public Management Assn. for Human Resources (IPMA-HR), *1617 Duke St., Alexandria, VA 22314; (703) 549-7100. Fax, (703) 684-0948. Cara Woodson Welch, Executive Director.*
General email, ipma@ipma-hr.org

Web, www.ipma-hr.org, Twitter, @IPMAHR and Facebook, www.facebook.com/International-Public-Management-Association-for-Human-Resources-IPMA-HR-38098732966

Provides public sector human resource professionals with industry news, jobs, policies, resources, education, and professional development opportunities.

National Assn. of Manufacturers (NAM), *Infrastructure, Innovation, and Human Resources Policy, 733 10th St. N.W., #700, 20001; (202) 637-3040. Aric Newhouse, SVP, Policy and Government Relations.*
Web, www.nam.org

Interests include health care, Social Security, employee benefits, cost containment, mandated benefits, Medicare, and other federal programs that affect employers. Opposed to government involvement in health care.

Society for Human Resource Management, *1800 Duke St., Alexandria, VA 22314-3499; (703) 548-3440. Fax, (703) 535-6490. Johnny C. Taylor Jr., President. Toll-free, (800) 283-7476.*

General email, shrm@shrm.org

Web, https://shrm.org and Twitter, @SHRM

Membership: human resource management professionals. Provides Human Resource training and certification exams. Monitors legislation and regulations concerning recruitment, training, and employment practices; occupational safety and health; compensation and benefits; employee and labor relations; and equal employment opportunity. Sponsors seminars and conferences.

LABOR-MANAGEMENT OPPORTUNITY

General

▶**AGENCIES**

Defense Dept. (DoD), *National Committee for Employer Support of the Guard and Reserve, 4800 Mark Center Dr., #05E22, Arlington, VA 22350-1200; (703) 882-3747. Capt. Robert Underhill (USN), Executive Director; Ron Bogle, National Chair. Toll-free, (800) 336-4590.*
General email, osd.USERRA@mail.mil

Web, www.esgr.mil and Public Affairs, osd.esgr-pa@mail.mil

Works to gain and maintain employer support for National Guard and Reserve service by recognizing outstanding support and providing service members and employers with information on applicable law. Volunteers provide free education, consultation, and, if necessary, mediation between employers and National Guard and Reserve service members.

Federal Mediation and Conciliation Service (FMCS), *250 E St. S.W., 7th Floor, 20427; (202) 606-8100. Fax, (202) 606-4251. Gregory Goldstein, Director (Acting). Arbitration, (202) 606-5111.*
Web, www.fmcs.gov, Twitter, @FMCS_USA and Facebook, www.facebook.com/fmcs.usa

Independent agency formed under the Labor-Management Relations Act of 1947 (Taft-Hartley Act), which assists labor and management representatives in dispute resolution and conflict management through voluntary mediation and arbitration services; mediates collective bargaining contract negotiation; awards competitive grants to joint labor-management initiatives; trains other federal agencies in mediating administrative disputes and formulating rules and regulations under the Administrative Dispute Resolution Act of 1996 and the Negotiated Rulemaking Act of 1996; provides training to unions and management in cooperative processes; provides international consulting and training to more than 60 countries. Headquartered in Washington, D.C., with offices across the country.

Labor Dept. (DOL), *Labor-Management Standards (OLMS), 200 Constitution Ave. N.W., #N1519, 20210;*

National Labor Relations Board

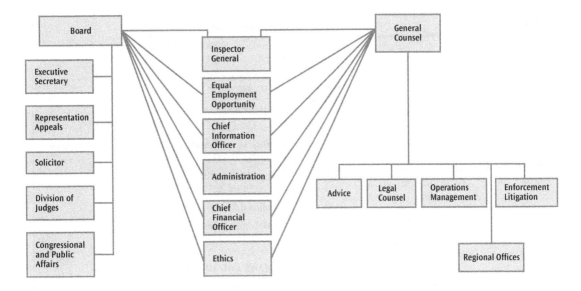

(202) 693-0123. Fax, (202) 693-1340. Jeffrey R. Freund, Director. TTY, (877) 889-5627.
General email, olms-public@dol.gov

Web, www.dol.gov/olms

Administers and enforces the Labor-Management Reporting and Disclosure Act of 1959 (Landrum-Griffin Act), which guarantees union members certain rights; sets rules for electing union officers, handling union funds, and using trusteeships; requires unions, union officers and employees, employers, and labor consultants to file financial and other reports with the Labor Dept. Administers relevant sections of the Civil Service Reform Act of 1978 and the Foreign Service Act of 1980. Administers the employee protection provisions of the Federal Transit law.

National Labor Relations Board (NLRB), 1015 Half St. S.E., 20570-0001; (202) 273-1000. Lauren McFerran, Chair, (202) 273-1770. Library, (202) 273-3734. Toll-free, (844) 762-6572. TTY, (866) 315-6572.
Web, www.nlrb.gov and Twitter, @NLRB

Administers the National Labor Relations Act. Works to prevent and remedy unfair labor practices by employers and labor unions; conducts elections among employees to determine whether they wish to be represented by a labor union for collective bargaining purposes. Complaints may be filed in field offices by calling the toll-free line. Library open to the public.

National Mediation Board, 1301 K St. N.W., #250E, 20005-7011; (202) 692-5000. Fax, (202) 692-5082. Gerald W. Fauth III, Chair. Information, (202) 692-5050. TTY, (202) 692-5001.
General email, infoline@nmb.gov

Web, www.nmb.gov

Mediates labor disputes in the railroad and airline industries; determines and certifies labor representatives for those industries. Library open by appointment.

► **CONGRESS**

For a listing of relevant congressional committees and subcommittees, please see page 221 or the Appendix.

► **NONGOVERNMENTAL**

AFL-CIO (American Federation of Labor–Congress of Industrial Organizations), 815 16th St. N.W., 20006; (202) 637-5000. Fax, (202) 637-5058. Elizabeth (Liz) Shuler, President. Press, (202) 637-5018. Toll Free, (866) 832-1560. Web, https://aflcio.org, Twitter, @AFLCIO, Facebook, www.facebook.com/aflcio and Press, pressclips@aflcio.org

Voluntary federation of national and international labor unions in the United States. Represents members before Congress and other branches of government. Each member union conducts its own contract negotiations. Library (located in Silver Spring, Md.) open to the public.

AFL-CIO Working America, 815 16th St. N.W., 20006; (202) 637-5137. Karen Nussbaum, Founding Director; Matt Morrison, Executive Director.
General email, info@workingamerica.org

Web, https://workingamerica.org, Twitter, @WorkingAmerica and Facebook, www.facebook.com/WorkingAmerica

Acts as advocate on behalf of nonunion workers at the community, state, and national levels. Seeks to secure better jobs, health care, education, and retirement benefits for these workers. Monitors legislation and regulations. (A community affiliate of the AFL-CIO.)

AFL-CIO, *Asian Pacific American Labor Alliance (APALA), 815 16th St. N.W., 2nd Floor, 20006; Alvina Yeh, Executive Director. Main phone, (202) 800-5811.*

General email, info@apalanet.org

Web, www.apalanet.org, Twitter, @APALAnational and Facebook, www.facebook.com/APALAnational

Membership: Asian American and Pacific Islander (AAPI) union members. Represents regional Asia–Pacific Rim labor activists in a national scope and assists in union member issues. Trains union members in areas including organization, development, and political advocacy.

Air Line Pilots Assn., International, *7950 Jones Branch Dr., #400S, McLean, VA 22102; (703) 689-2270. Capt. Joe DePete, President. Press, (703) 481-4440. Toll-free, (888) 359-2572.*

General email, communications@alpa.org

Web, www.alpa.org, Twitter, @wearealpa, Facebook, www.facebook.com/WeAreAlpa and Blog, www.alpa.org/news-and-events/Blog

Membership: airline pilots in the United States and Canada. Promotes air travel safety; assists investigations of aviation accidents. Publishes the *Air Line Pilot Magazine.* Monitors legislation and regulations. (Affiliated with the AFL-CIO and the Canadian Labour Conference.)

American Federation of Musicians, *Government Relations, 5335 Wisconsin Ave. N.W., #440, 20015; (202) 274-4756. Fax, (202) 274-4759. Alfonso Pollard, Legislative-Political Director. Toll-free, (800) 762-3444.*

Web, www.afm.org

Seeks to improve the working conditions and salary of musicians. Monitors legislation and regulations affecting musicians and the arts. (Headquarters in New York.)

Assn. of Flight Attendants–CWA, *501 3rd St. N.W., 20001-2797; (202) 434-1300. Fax, (202) 434-1319. Sara Nelson, President. Press, (202) 550-5520. Toll-free, (844) 232-2228.*

General email, info@afacwa.org

Web, www.afacwa.org, Twitter, @afa_cwa and Facebook, www.facebook.com/afacwa

Membership: approximately 50,000 flight attendants. Helps members negotiate pay, benefits, and better working conditions; conducts training programs and workshops. Monitors legislation and regulations. (Affiliated with the AFL-CIO.)

Bakery, Confectionery, Tobacco Workers, and Grain Millers International Union (BCTGM), *10401 Connecticut Ave., 4th Floor, Kensington, MD 20895-3940; (301) 933-8600. Fax, (301) 946-8452. Anthony Shelton, President.*

General email, bctgmwebmaster@gmail.com

Web, www.bctgm.org, Twitter, @BCTGM and Facebook, www.facebook.com/BCTGM

Membership: approximately 120,000 workers from the bakery, confectionery, grain miller, and tobacco industries in both the United States and Canada. Helps members negotiate pay, benefits, and better working conditions;

AFL-CIO

DEPARTMENTS

Communications, Tim Schlittner, Director, (202) 637-5393

Government Affairs, William Samuel, Director, (202) 637-5320

International, Cathy Feingold, Director, (202) 637-5050

Legal, Craig Becker, General Counsel, (202) 637-5310

Office of the President, Richard L. Trumka, President, (202) 637-5231

Organizing Institute, Lynn Rodenhuis, Director, (202) 639-6225

Political, Vacant(202) 637-5104

Safety and Health, Rebecca L. Reindel, Director, (202) 637-5366

TRADE AND INDUSTRIAL SECTORS

Building and Construction Trades, Sean McGarvey, President, (202) 347-1461

Maritime Trades, Michael Sacco, President, (202) 628-6300

Metal Trades, James V. Hart, President, (202) 508-3705

Professional Employees, Jennifer Dorning, President, (202) 638-0320

Transportation Trades, Greg Regan, President, (202) 628-9262

Union Label and Service Trades, Richard Kline, President, (202) 508-3700

---

conducts training programs and workshops. Monitors legislation and regulations. (Affiliated with the AFL-CIO.)

The Center for Union Facts, *1090 Vermont Ave. N.W., #800, 20005 (mailing address: P.O. Box 34507, Washington, DC 20043); (202) 463-7106. Fax, (202) 463-7107. Richard Berman, Executive Director.*

General email, info@unionfacts.com

Web, www.unionfacts.com

Seeks to educate businesses, union members, and the public about the labor movement's political activities, specifically those of union officials. Interests include management of union dues. Monitors legislation and regulations.

Coalition of Black Trade Unionists, *1155 Connecticut Ave. N.W., #500, 20036 (mailing address: P.O. Box 66268, Washington, DC 20035); (202) 778-3318. Fax, (202) 419-1486. Terrence (Terry) L. Melvin, President.*

General email, cbtu@cbtu.org

Web, https://cbtu.nationbuilder.com

Monitors legislation affecting African American and other minority trade unionists. Focuses on equal employment opportunity, unemployment, and voter education and registration.

Coalition of Labor Union Women, *815 16th St. N.W., 2nd Floor South, 20006-1119; (202) 508-6969. Elise A. Bryant, President, (202) 637-3963; Harriette Scofield, Executive Director (Acting), (202) 508-6951.*
General email, cluw@cluw.org

Web, http://cluw.org, Twitter, @CLUWNational and *Facebook, www.facebook.com/CLUWomen*

Seeks to make unions more responsive to the needs of women in the workplace; advocates affirmative action and the active participation of women in unions. Monitors legislation and regulations.

Communications Workers of America (CWA), *501 3rd St. N.W., 20001; (202) 434-1100. Christopher M. Shelton, President.*
Web, https://cwa-union.org and *Twitter, @CWAUnion*

Membership: approximately 700,000 workers in telecommunications, journalism, publishing, cable television, electronics, and other fields. Interests include workplace democracy and restoring bargaining rights. Represents members in contract negotiations and grievances; conducts training programs and workshops. Monitors legislation and regulations. (Affiliated with the AFL-CIO.)

Federal Education Assn., *1201 16th St. N.W., #117, 20036; (202) 822-7850. Fax, (202) 822-7867. Brian Chance, President; Richard Tarr, Executive Director (Acting).*
General email, fea@feaonline.org

Web, www.feaonline.org, Twitter, @FedEdAssoc and *Facebook, www.facebook.com/FedEdAssoc*

Membership: teachers and personnel of Defense Dept. schools for military dependents in the United States and abroad. Helps members negotiate pay, benefits, and better working conditions.

International Assn. of Bridge, Structural, Ornamental, and Reinforcing Iron Workers, *1750 New York Ave. N.W., #400, 20006; (202) 383-4800. Fax, (202) 638-4856. Eric Dean, General President.*
General email, iwmagazine@iwintl.org

Web, www.ironworkers.org, Twitter, @TheIronWorkers, Facebook, www.facebook.com/unionironworkers and *YouTube, www.youtube.com/user/UnionIronWorkers*

Membership: approximately 120,000 iron workers. Helps members negotiate pay, benefits, and better working conditions; conducts training programs and workshops. Monitors legislation and regulations. (Affiliated with the AFL-CIO.)

International Assn. of Fire Fighters, *1750 New York Ave. N.W., #300, 20006-5395; (202) 737-8484. Fax, (202) 737-8418. Edward A. Kelly, General President.*
General email, tburn@iaff.org

Web, www.iaff.org, Twitter, @IAFFNewsDesk, Facebook, www.facebook.com/IAFFonline and *YouTube, www.youtube.com/user/IAFFTV*

Membership: more than 310,000 professional firefighters and emergency medical personnel. Assists members with contract negotiation and grievances; conducts

training programs and workshops. Monitors legislation and regulations. (Affiliated with the AFL-CIO and the Canadian Labour Congress.)

International Assn. of Heat and Frost Insulators and Allied Workers, *9602 Martin Luther King Hwy., Lanham, MD 20706-1839; (301) 731-9101. Fax, (301) 731-5058. Gregory T. Revard, General President.*
General email, hfi@insulators.org

Web, www.insulators.org, Twitter, @InsulatorsUnion, Facebook, www.facebook.com/InsulatorsUnion and *YouTube, www.youtube.com/user/InsulatorsUnion*

Membership: approximately 30,000 workers in insulation industries. Helps members negotiate pay, benefits, and better working conditions; conducts training programs and workshops. Monitors legislation and regulations. (Affiliated with the AFL-CIO.)

International Assn. of Machinists and Aerospace Workers, *9000 Machinists Pl., Upper Marlboro, MD 20772-2687; (301) 967-4500. Fax, (301) 967-4587. Robert Martinez Jr., International President. Information, (301) 967-4522.*
General email, info@iamaw.org

Web, www.goiam.org, Twitter, @MachinistsUnion, Facebook, www.facebook.com/MachinistsUnion and *YouTube, www.youtube.com/user/FranticHarbor*

Membership: machinists in more than 200 industries. Helps members negotiate pay, benefits, and better working conditions; conducts training programs and workshops. Monitors legislation and regulations. (Affiliated with the AFL-CIO, the Canadian Labour Congress, the International Metalworkers Federation, the International Transport Workers' Federation, and the Railway Labor Executives Assn.)

International Assn. of Machinists and Aerospace Workers, *Transportation Communications Union, 3 Research Pl., Rockville, MD 20850-3279; (301) 948-4910. Arthur P. Maratea, National President.*
Web, www.goiam.org/territories/tcu-union

Membership: approximately 46,000 railway workers. Assists members with contract negotiation and grievances; conducts training programs and workshops. Monitors legislation and regulations. (Affiliated with the AFL-CIO and Canadian Labour Congress.)

International Brotherhood of Boilermakers, Iron Ship Builders, Blacksmiths, Forgers, and Helpers, *Government Affairs, 1750 New York Ave. N.W., #335, 20006; (202) 756-2868. Fax, (202) 756-2869. Cecile Conroy, Director of Government Affairs, ext. 202.*
Web, https://boilermakers.org/structure/departments/government_affairs

Membership: workers in construction, repair, maintenance, manufacturing, shipbuilding and marine repair, mining and quarrying, railroads, cement kilns, and related industries in the United States and Canada. Helps members negotiate pay, benefits, and better working conditions; conducts training programs and workshops. Monitors legislation and regulations. (Headquarters in Kansas City, Kans.; affiliated with the AFL-CIO.)

International Brotherhood of Electrical Workers
(IBEW), *900 7th St. N.W., 20001; (202) 833-7000. Fax, (202) 728-7676. Lonnie R. Stephenson, International President.*
General email, webmaster@ibew.org
Web, http://ibew.org

Membership: workers in utilities, construction, telecommunications, broadcasting, manufacturing, railroads, and government. Helps members negotiate pay, benefits, and better working conditions; conducts training programs and workshops. Monitors legislation and regulations. (Affiliated with the AFL-CIO.)

International Brotherhood of Teamsters, *25 Louisiana Ave. N.W., 20001; (202) 624-6800. Fax, (202) 624-6918. James P. Hoffa, General President. Press, (202) 624-6911.*
General email, communications@teamster.org
Web, https://teamster.org, Twitter, @Teamsters, Facebook, www.facebook.com/teamsters and YouTube, www.youtube .com/TeamsterPower

Membership: workers in the transportation and construction industries, factories, offices, hospitals, warehouses, and other workplaces. Helps members negotiate pay, benefits, and better working conditions; conducts training programs and workshops. Monitors legislation and regulations.

International Longshore and Warehouse Union (ILWU), *Washington Office, 1025 Connecticut Ave. N.W., #507, 20036; (202) 463-6265. Fax, (202) 467-4875. Vacant, Legislative Director.*
General email, washdc@ilwu.org
Web, www.ilwu.org

Membership: longshore and warehouse personnel. Helps members negotiate pay, benefits, and better working conditions; conducts training programs and workshops. Monitors legislation and regulations. (Headquarters in San Francisco, Calif.)

International Longshoremen's Assn., *Washington Office, 1101 17th St. N.W., #400, 20036-4704; (202) 955-6304. Fax, (202) 955-6048. John Bowers Jr., Political Director.*
General email, iladc@aol.com
Web, www.ilaunion.org

Membership: approximately 65,000 longshore personnel. Helps members negotiate pay, benefits, and better working conditions; conducts training programs and workshops. Monitors legislation and regulations. (Headquarters in New Jersey; affiliated with the AFL-CIO.)

International Union of Bricklayers and Allied
Craftworkers, *620 F St. N.W., 20004; (202) 783-3788. Timothy J. Driscoll, President. Toll-free, (888) 880-8222.*
General email, askbac@bacweb.org
Web, www.bacweb.org and Twitter, @IUBAC

Membership: bricklayers, stonemasons, and other skilled craftworkers in the building industry. Helps

members negotiate pay, benefits, and better working conditions; conducts training programs and workshops. Monitors legislation and regulations. (Affiliated with the AFL-CIO and the International Masonry Institute.)

International Union of Operating Engineers, *1125 17th St. N.W., 20036; (202) 429-9100. Fax, (202) 778-2688. James T. Callahan, General President.*
Web, www.iuoe.org

Membership: approximately 400,000 operating engineers, including heavy equipment operators, mechanics, and surveyors in the construction industry, and stationary engineers, including operations and building maintenance staff. Represents members in negotiating pay, benefits, and better working conditions; conducts training programs and workshops. Monitors legislation and regulations in the United States and Canada. (Affiliated with the AFL-CIO.)

International Union of Painters and Allied Trades, *7234 Parkway Dr., Hanover, MD 21076; (410) 564-5900. Fax, (866) 656-4124. James A. Williams Jr., General President.*
General email, mail@iupat.org
Web, www.iupat.org, Twitter, @GoIUPAT and Facebook, www.facebook.com/GoIUPAT

Membership: more than 160,000 industrial and commercial painters, glaziers, floor covering installers, sign makers, convention and show decorators, and workers in allied trades in the United States and Canada. Helps members negotiate pay, benefits, and better working conditions; conducts training programs and workshops. Monitors legislation and regulations. (Affiliated with the AFL-CIO.)

Labor Council for Latin American Advancement, *815 16th St. N.W., 3rd Floor, 20006; (202) 508-6919. Fax, (202) 508-6922. Karla Pineda, Deputy Director.*
General email, headquarters@lclaa.org
Web, www.lclaa.org, Twitter, @LCLAA and Facebook, www.facebook.com/LCLAA

Membership: Latino/a trade unionists throughout U.S. and Puerto Rico. Encourages equal employment opportunity, voter registration, and participation in the political process. (Affiliated with the AFL-CIO and the Change to Win Federation.)

Laborers' International Union of North America
(LIUNA), *905 16th St. N.W., 20006-1765; (202) 737-8320. Terry O'Sullivan, President.*
Web, www.liuna.org, Twitter, @LIUNA, Facebook, www .facebook.com/LaborersInternationalUnionofNorth America and Press, communications@liuna.org

Membership: more than 500,000 workers in construction and energy industries, as well as public employees and the National Postal Handlers Union. Monitors legislation and regulations. (Affiliated with the AFL-CIO.)

National Assn. of Manufacturers (NAM), *Infrastructure, Innovation, and Human Resources Policy, 733 10th St. N.W., #700, 20001; (202) 637-3040. Aric Newhouse, SVP, Policy and Government Relations.*
Web, www.nam.org

Provides information on corporate industrial relations, including collective bargaining, labor standards, international labor relations, productivity, employee benefits, health care, and other current labor issues; monitors legislation and regulations.

National Right to Work Committee, *8001 Braddock Rd., #500, Springfield, VA 22160; (703) 321-9820. Fax, (703) 321-7342. Mark Mix, President. Toll-free, (800) 325-7892. General email, info@nrtwc.org*

Web, https://nrtwc.org, Twitter, @Right2Work and Facebook, www.facebook.com/NationalRightToWork

Citizens' organization opposed to compulsory union membership. Supports right-to-work legislation.

National Right to Work Legal Defense and Education Foundation, *8001 Braddock Rd., #600, Springfield, VA 22160; (703) 321-8510. Fax, (703) 321-9613. Mark Mix, President. Toll-free, (800) 336-3600. General email, info@nrtw.org*

Web, www.nrtw.org

Provides free legal aid for employees in cases of compulsory union membership abuses.

The Newspaper Guild— Communication Workers of America (CWA), *501 3rd St. N.W., 6th Floor, 20001-2797; (202) 434-7177. Jon Schleuss, President. General email, guild@cwa-union.org*

Web, www.newsguild.org, Twitter, @newsguild and Facebook, www.facebook.com/NewsGuild

Membership: journalists, sales and media professionals. Advocates higher standards in journalism; equal employment opportunity in the print, broadcast, wire, and Web media industries; and advancement of members' economic interests. (Affiliated with Communications Workers of America, the AFL-CIO, CLC, and IFJ.)

Operative Plasterers' and Cement Masons' International Assn. of the United States and Canada, *9700 Patuxent Woods Dr., #200, Columbia, MD 21046; (301) 623-1000. Fax, (301) 623-1032. Daniel E. Stepano, General President. General email, opcmiaintl@opcmia.org*

Web, www.opcmia.org, Twitter, @opcmiaint and Facebook, www.facebook.com/OPCMIAIntl

Membership: approximately 58,000 cement masons and plasterers. Helps members negotiate pay, benefits, and better working conditions; conducts training programs and workshops. Publishes a quarterly magazine. Monitors legislation and regulations. (Affiliated with the AFL-CIO.)

Public Service Research Council, *320-D Maple Ave. East, Vienna, VA 22180-4742; (703) 242-3575. Fax, (703) 242-3579. David Y. Denholm, President. General email, info@psrconline.org*

Web, http://psrconline.org

Independent nonprofit research and educational organization. Studies labor unions and labor issues with emphasis on employment in the public sector. Monitors legislation and regulations.

Seafarers International Union of North America, *5201 Capital Gateway Dr., Camp Springs, MD 20746-4275; (301) 899-0675. Fax, (301) 899-7355. Michael Sacco, President.*

Web, www.seafarers.org and Twitter, @SeafarersUnion

Represents professional U.S. merchant mariners sailing aboard U.S.-flag vessels in the deep sea, Great Lakes, and inland trades; works to protect members' job security.

Service Employees International Union, *1800 Massachusetts Ave. N.W., 20036; (202) 730-7000. Mary Kay Henry, President. Press, (202) 730-7162. Toll-free, (800) 424-8592. TTY, (202) 730-7681. General email, media@seiu.org*

Web, www.seiu.org, Twitter, @SEIU and Facebook, www.facebook.com/SEIU

Membership: approximately 2.2 million members in Canada, the United States, and Puerto Rico among health care, public services, and property services employees. Promotes better wages, health care, and job security for workers. Monitors legislation and regulations.

Sheet Metal, Air, Rail, and Transportation Workers (SMART), *1750 New York Ave. N.W., 6th Floor, 20006; (202) 662-0800. Joseph Sellers Jr., General President. Toll-free, (800) 457-7694. General email, info@smart-union.org*

Web, https://smart-union.org and Twitter, @smartunionworks

Membership: U.S., Puerto Rican, and Canadian workers in the building and construction trades, manufacturing, and the railroad and shipyard industries. Assists members with contract negotiation and grievances; conducts training programs and workshops. Monitors legislation and regulations. (Affiliated with the Sheet Metal and Air Conditioning Contractors' Assn., the AFL-CIO, and the Canadian Labour Congress.)

Solidarity Center, *1130 Connecticut Ave. N.W., #800, 20036; (202) 974-8383. Fax, (202) 974-8384. Shawna Bader-Blau, Executive Director. Press, (202) 974-8369. General email, information@solidaritycenter.org*

Web, www.solidaritycenter.org, Twitter, @solidaritycntr, Facebook, www.facebook.com/solidaritycenter and YouTube, www.youtube.com/channel/UCn-GrFX5jg1Fh-19povBUpw

Provides assistance to free and democratic trade unions worldwide. Provides trade union leadership courses in collective bargaining, union organization, trade integration, labor–management cooperation, union administration, and political theories. Sponsors social and community development projects; focus includes child labor, human and worker rights, and the role of women in labor unions. (Affiliated with the AFL-CIO.)

U.S. Chamber of Commerce, *Employment Policy, 1615 H St. N.W., 20062-2000; (202) 463-5522. Fax, (202) 463-3194. Glenn Spencer, Senior Vice President.*
Web, www.uschamber.com/employment-policy, Twitter, @USChamberEPD, ADA information, www.uschamber.com/health-reform and Immigration news, www.uschamber.com/immigration

Formulates and analyzes chamber policy in the areas of labor law, employment nondiscrimination, minimum wage and wage-hour, occupational safety and health, immigration, labor-management relations, work-family issues and leave mandates, and emerging international labor policy issues. Monitors legislation and regulations affecting labor-management relations.

UNITE HERE, *Washington Office, Local 25, 901 K St. N.W., #200, 10001; (202) 737-2225. Fax, (202) 393-3741. John A. Boardman, Executive Secretary-Treasurer.*
Web, www.unitehere.org, Twitter, @unitehere, Twitter, @UNITEHERE23, Facebook, www.facebook.com/UniteHere and YouTube, www.youtube.com/uniteherevideos

Membership: workers in the Washington, D.C., area who work in the hotel industry. Assists members with contract negotiation and grievances; conducts training programs and workshops. Monitors legislation and regulations. (UNITE HERE Headquarters are in New York.)

United Auto Workers (UAW), *Washington Office, 1757 N St. N.W., 20036; (202) 828-8500. Josh Nassar, Legislative Director.*
Web, www.uaw.org, Twitter, @uaw, Facebook, www.facebook.com/uaw.union and YouTube, www.youtube.com/channel/UCtyZlveXsB4K3bLrWjMAv3g

Membership: approximately 400,000 active and 600,000 retired North American workers in aerospace, automotive, defense, manufacturing, steel, technical, and other industries. Assists members with contract negotiations and grievances; conducts training programs and workshops. Monitors legislation and regulations. (Headquarters in Detroit, Mich.)

United Food and Commercial Workers International Union (UFCW), *1775 K St. N.W., 20006-1598; (202) 223-3111. Fax, (202) 728-1803. Anthony (Marc) Perrone, President.*
Web, www.ufcw.org, Twitter, @UFCW and Facebook, www.facebook.com/ufcwinternational

Membership: approximately 1.3 million workers primarily in the retail, meatpacking, food processing, and poultry industries. Interests include health care reform, living wages, retirement security, safe working conditions, and the right to unionize. Monitors legislation and regulations.

United Mine Workers of America, *18354 Quantico Gateway Dr., #200, Triangle, VA 22172-1779; (703) 291-2400. Cecil E. Roberts, President, (703) 291-2420.*
General email, info@umwa.org
Web, www.umwa.org/policy-politics/current-legislation, Twitter, @MineWorkers and Facebook, www.facebook.com/UMWAunion

Membership: coal miners and other mining workers. Represents members in collective bargaining with industry. Conducts educational, housing, and health and safety training programs; monitors federal coal-mining safety programs.

United Steelworkers, Legislative, *1155 Connecticut Ave. N.W., #500, 20036; (202) 778-4384. Fax, (202) 293-5308. Roy Houseman, Legislative Director, (202) 778-3312.*
Web, www.usw.org, Twitter, @steelworkers and Facebook, www.facebook.com/steelworkers

Membership: more than one million workers in the steel, paper, rubber, energy, chemical, pharmaceutical, and allied industries. Helps members negotiate pay, benefits, and better working conditions; conducts training programs and workshops. Monitors legislation and regulations. (Affiliated with the AFL-CIO; Headquarters in Pittsburgh, Pa.)

Utility Workers Union of America, *1300 L St. N.W., #1200, 20005; (202) 899-2851. Fax, (202) 899-2852. James Slevin, National President.*
General email, webmaster@uwua.net
Web, www.uwua.net, Twitter, @The_UWUA and Facebook, www.facebook.com/theUWUA

Labor union representing workers in electric, gas, water, and nuclear utility industries. Helps members negotiate pay, benefits, and better working conditions; conducts training programs and workshops. Monitors legislation and regulations. (Affiliated with the AFL-CIO.)

PENSIONS AND BENEFITS

General

▶**AGENCIES**

Advisory Council on Employee Welfare and Pension Benefit Plans (ERISA Advisory Council) *(Labor Dept.), 200 Constitution Ave. N.W., #N5623, 20210; (202) 693-8337. Fax, (202) 219-8141. Christine Donahue, Executive Secretary, (202) 693-8641. Toll-free, (866) 444-3272.*
Web, www.dol.gov/agencies/ebsa/about-ebsa/about-us/erisa-advisory-council

Advises and makes recommendations to the secretary of labor under the Employee Retirement Income Security Act of 1974 (ERISA).

Bureau of Labor Statistics (BLS) *(Labor Dept.),* **Compensation and Working Conditions (OCWC),** *2 Massachusetts Ave. N.E., #4130, 20212; (202) 691-6199. Hilery Z. Simpson, Associate Commissioner.*
General email, NCSinfo@bls.gov
Web, www.bls.gov

Conducts quarterly surveys of wages and benefits; data used for the quarterly *Employment Cost Index*, the quarterly *Employer Costs for Employee Compensation*, and annual reports on the incidence and provisions of employee benefits.

Employee Benefits Security Administration (EBSA) *(Labor Dept.),* *200 Constitution Ave. N.W., #N5677, 20210; (202) 693-8315. Fax, (202) 219-6531. Ali Khawar, Assistant Secretary (Acting). Toll-free, (866) 444-3272. Press, (202) 693-6588.*
Web, www.dol.gov/ebsa

Administers, regulates, and enforces private employee benefit plan standards established by the Employee Retirement Income Security Act of 1974 (ERISA), with particular emphasis on fiduciary obligations; receives and maintains required reports from employee benefit plan administrators pursuant to ERISA.

Federal Retirement Thrift Investment Board, *77 K St. N.E., #1000, 20002; (202) 942-1600. Fax, (202) 942-1672. Ravindra Deo, Executive Director. TTY, (877) 847-4385.*
Web, www.frtib.gov

Administers the Thrift Savings Plan, a tax-deferred, defined contribution plan that permits federal employees and members of the uniformed services to save for additional retirement security under a program similar to private 401(k) plans.

Internal Revenue Service (IRS) *(Treasury Dept.), Joint Board for the Enrollment of Actuaries, 1111 Constitution Ave. N.W., SE:RPO, Room 3422, 20224; Kevin M. Hacker, Chair; Chet Andrzejewski, Secretary.*
General email, nhqjbea@irs.gov
Web, www.irs.gov/tax-professionals/enrolled-actuaries

Joint board, with members from the departments of Labor and Treasury and the Pension Benefit Guaranty Corp., established under the Employee Retirement Income Security Act of 1974 (ERISA). Promulgates regulations for the enrollment of pension actuaries; examines applicants and grants certificates of enrollment; disciplines enrolled actuaries who have engaged in misconduct in the discharge of duties under ERISA.

Office of Personnel Management (OPM), *Retirement Operations, 1900 E St. N.W., #2H28, 20415; (724) 794-2005. Fax, (724) 794-4323. Kenneth J. Zawodny Jr., Associate Director, (724) 794-7759. Toll-free, (888) 767-6738. TTY, (855) 887-4957.*
General email, retire@opm.gov
Web, www.opm.gov/retire

Provides civil servants with information and assistance on federal retirement payments.

Pension Benefit Guaranty Corp., *1200 K St. N.W., #10277, 20005-4026 (mailing address: P.O. Box 151750, Alexandria, VA 22315-1750); (202) 326-4000. Fax, (202) 326-4047. Gordon Hartogensis, Director. Customer Service, (800) 400-7242. Employers and Practioners, (800) 736-2444. TTY, 711.*
Web, www.pbgc.gov, Twitter, @USPBGC and Facebook, www.facebook.com/uspbgc

Self-financed U.S. government corporation. Insures private-sector defined benefit pension plans; guarantees payment of retirement benefits subject to certain limitations established in the Employee Retirement Income Security Act of 1974 (ERISA). Provides insolvent multi-employer pension plans with financial assistance to enable them to pay guaranteed retirement benefits.

Railroad Retirement Board, *Legislative Affairs, 1310 G St. N.W., #500, 20005-3004; (202) 272-7742. Fax, (202) 272-7728. Beverly Britton-Fraser, Director. Toll-free, (877) 772-5772.*
General email, ola@rrb.gov
Web, https://rrb.gov/OurAgency/OfficeofGeneralCounsel/OfficeofLegislativeAffair

Assists congressional offices with inquiries on retirement, spouse, survivor, unemployment, and sickness benefits for railroad employees and retirees. Assists with legislation. (Headquarters in Chicago, Ill.)

▶**CONGRESS**

For a listing of relevant congressional committees and subcommittees, please see page 221 or the Appendix.

▶**NONGOVERNMENTAL**

AARP, *601 E St. N.W., 20049; (202) 434-2277. Jo Ann C. Jenkins, Chief Executive Officer. Library, (202) 434-6233. Membership, toll-free, (800) 566-0242. Press, (202) 434-2560. Toll-free, (888) 687-2277. Toll-free Spanish, (877) 342-2277. TTY, (877) 434-7598. TTY Spanish, (866) 238-9488.*
General email, dcaarp@aarp.org
Web, www.aarp.org, Twitter, @AARP and Facebook, www.facebook.com/AARP

Researches and testifies on private, federal, and other government employee pension legislation and regulations; conducts seminars; provides information on preretirement preparation.

Alliance for Retired Americans, *815 16th St. N.W., 4th Floor, 20006-4104; (202) 637-5399. Robert Roach Jr., President.*
Web, https://retiredamericans.org, Twitter, @ActiveRetirees, Facebook, www.facebook.com/retiredamericans and email, communications@retiredamericans.org

Membership; Alliance of retired members of unions affiliated with the AFL-CIO, senior citizen clubs, associations, councils, and other groups. Seeks to nationalize health care services and to strengthen benefits to older adults, including improved Social Security payments, secure social and economic justice including civil rights, and education and health programs. (Affiliate of the AFL-CIO.)

American Academy of Actuaries, *1850 M St. N.W., #300, 20036; (202) 223-8196. Fax, (202) 872-1948. (202) 974-6007. Mary Downs, Executive Director.*
General email, webmaster@actuary.org
Web, www.actuary.org, Twitter, @Actuary_Dot_Org and Facebook, www.facebook.com/Actuary.Org

Membership: professional actuaries practicing in the areas of life, health, liability, property, and casualty insurance; pensions; government insurance plans; and general consulting. Provides information on actuarial matters, including insurance and pensions; develops professional standards; advises public policymakers.

American Benefits Council, *1501 M St. N.W., #600, 20005; (202) 289-6700. Fax, (202) 289-4582. James A. Klein, President.*
General email, info@abcstaff.org
Web, www.americanbenefitscouncil.org, Twitter, @benefitscouncil and Facebook, www.facebook.com/benefitscouncil

Membership: Large plan sponsors and service providers who provide retirement, health, compensation, and global benefit programs. Informs members of employee benefits, including private pension benefits, health benefits, and compensation. Monitors legislation and regulations.

American Society of Pension Professionals and Actuaries, *4401 N. Fairfax Dr., #600, Arlington, VA 22203; (703) 516-9300. Fax, (703) 516-9308. Natalie Wyatt, Chief Executive Officer.*
General email, customercare@asppa-net.org
Web, www.asppa.org and Twitter, @ASPPA

Membership: administrators, actuaries, advisers, lawyers, accountants, and other financial services professionals who provide consulting and administrative services for employee-based retirement plans. Sponsors educational conferences, webcasts, and credentialing programs for retirement professionals. Monitors legislation and regulations.

The Brookings Institution, *Economic Studies, 1775 Massachusetts Ave. N.W., 20036-2188; (202) 797-6414. (202) 540-7721. Stephanie Aaronson, Vice President.*
General email, escomment@brookings.edu
Web, www.brookings.edu/economics and Twitter, @BrookingsEcon

Promotes efforts to make retirement saving easier and improve retirement income prospects for American workers.

The Brookings Institution, *Retirement Security Project, 1775 Massachusetts Ave. N.W., 20036; (202) 797-6148. Fax, (202) 797-6181. William G. Gale, Director, (202) 540-7721.*
Web, www.brookings.edu/about/project/retirement-security-project

Promotes policy solutions for improving retirement income and financial security for middle-income and low-income workers who do not have access to employer-sponsored retirement savings plans or traditional pensions.

Council of Institutional Investors, *1717 Pennsylvania Ave. N.W., #350, 20006; (202) 822-0800. Fax, (202) 822-0801. Amy Borrus, Executive Director, (202) 261-7082.*
Web, www.cii.org and Twitter, @CouncilInstInv

Membership: pension funds and other employee benefit funds, foundations, and endowments. Studies investment issues that affect pension plan assets. Focuses on corporate governance and shareholder rights. Monitors legislation and regulations.

Employee Benefit Research Institute, *901 D St. S.W., #802, 20024; (202) 659-0670. Fax, (202) 775-6360. Lori Lucas, President.*
General email, info@ebri.org
Web, www.ebri.org

Research organization serving as an employee benefits information source on health, welfare, and retirement issues. Does not lobby and does not take public policy positions.

Employers Council on Flexible Compensation, *1802 Vernon St. N.W., #1035, 20009; (202) 659-4300. Fax, (202) 618-6060. Christa Day, Executive Director.*
General email, info@ecfc.org
Web, https://ecfc.org and Twitter, @GoECFC

Advocates tax-advantaged, private-employer benefit programs. Supports the preservation and expansion of employee choice in savings and pension plans. Monitors legislation and regulations. Interests include cafeteria plans and 401(k) plans.

ERISA Industry Committee, *701 8th St. N.W., #610, 20001; (202) 789-1400. Fax, (202) 789-1120. Annette Guarisco Fildes, President, (202) 627-1910.*
Web, www.eric.org

Membership: large major U.S. employers. Advocates members' positions on employee retirement, health care coverage, and welfare benefit plans. Monitors legislation and regulations.

National Assn. of Manufacturers (NAM), *Infrastructure, Innovation, and Human Resources Policy, 733 10th St. N.W., #700, 20001; (202) 637-3040. Aric Newhouse, SVP, Policy and Government Relations.*
Web, www.nam.org

Interests include health care, cost containment, mandated benefits, Medicare, and other federal programs that affect employers. Opposed to government involvement in health care and proposed expansion of health care liability.

National Institute on Retirement Security, *1612 K St. N.W., #500, 20006; (202) 457-8190. Dan Doonan, Executive Director.*
General email, info@nirsonline.org
Web, www.nirsonline.org and Twitter, @nirsonline

Researches retirement security policies and educates the public and policymakers about the positive impact of defined benefit pension plans. Advocates broader, more defined retirement plans.

Pension Rights Center, *1050 30th St. N.W., 20007; (202) 296-3776. Karen Friedman, Executive Director. Toll-free, (888) 420-6550.*
General email, kgarrett@pensionrights.org
Web, www.pensionrights.org, Twitter, @PensionRights and Facebook, www.facebook.com/PensionRightsCenter

Works to preserve and expand pension rights; provides information and technical assistance on pension law.

Occupational Safety and Health Administration

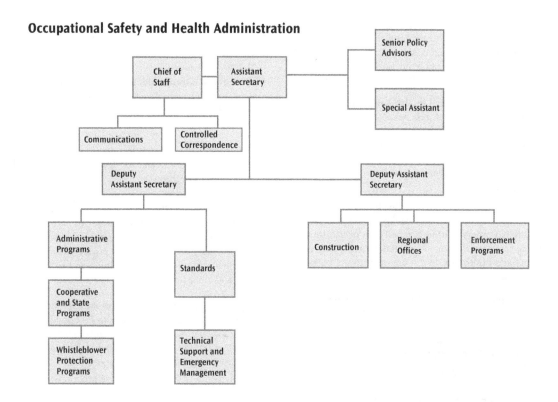

U.S. Chamber of Commerce, *Employment Policy,* 1615 H St. N.W., 20062-2000; (202) 463-5522. Fax, (202) 463-3194. Glenn Spencer, Senior Vice President.
Web, www.uschamber.com/employment-policy, Twitter, @USChamberEPD, ADA information, www.uschamber .com/health-reform and Immigration.news, www .uschamber.com/immigration

Formulates and analyzes chamber policy in the areas of health care, pensions and retirement plans, Social Security, and Medicare. Monitors legislation and regulations affecting employee benefits.

United Mine Workers of America, *Health and Retirement Funds,* 2121 K St. N.W., #350, 20037-1801; (202) 521-2201. Lorraine Lewis, Executive Director. Toll-free, (800) 291-1425.
General email, health1@umwafunds.org
Web, www.umwafunds.org

Labor-management trust fund that provides health and retirement benefits to coal miners. Health benefits are provided to pensioners, their dependents, and, in some cases, their survivors.

Urban Institute, *Income and Benefits Policy Center,* 500 L'Enfant Plaza S.W., 20024; (202) 833-7200. Fax, (202) 833-4388. Gregory Acs, Vice President.
Web, www.urban.org/center/ibp and Retirement policy, http://urban.org/retirement_policy

Studies how public policy influences behavior and the economic well-being of families, particularly the disabled, the elderly, and those with low incomes.

Women's Institute for a Secure Retirement (WISER), 1001 Connecticut Ave. N.W., #730, 20036; (202) 393-5452. Fax, (202) 393-5890. Cindy Hounsell, President.
General email, info@wiserwomen.org
Web, www.wiserwomen.org and Twitter, @WISERWomen

Provides information on women's retirement issues. Monitors legislation and regulations.

WORKPLACE SAFETY AND HEALTH

General

►AGENCIES

Bureau of Labor Statistics (BLS) *(Labor Dept.),* *Compensation and Working Conditions (OCWC),* 2 Massachusetts Ave. N.E., #4130, 20212; (202) 691-6199. Hilery Z. Simpson, Associate Commissioner.
General email, NCSinfo@bls.gov
Web, www.bls.gov

Compiles data on occupational safety and health.

Environment, Health, Safety, and Security (EHSS) *(Energy Dept.), Health and Safety,* 1000 Independence Ave. S.W., AU-10-GTN, 20585; (301) 903-5926. Fax, (301) 903-3445. Brad R. Davy, Director (Acting).
Web, http://energy.gov/ehss/organizational-chart/office-health-and-safety

Establishes hazardous-material worker safety and health requirements and expectations for the Energy Dept.

and assists in their implementation. Conducts and supports domestic and international hazardous material health studies and programs. Supports the Labor Dept. in the implementation of the Energy Employees Occupational Illness Compensation Program Act (EEOICPA).

Federal Mine Safety and Health Review Commission (FMSHRC), *1331 Pennsylvania Ave. N.W., #520N, 20004-1710; (202) 434-9900. Fax, (202) 434-9954. Lisa Boyd, Executive Director, (202) 434-9905; Arthur R. Traynor III, Chair. TTY, (202) 434-4000, ext. 293.*
General email, fmshrc@fmshrc.gov
Web, www.fmshrc.gov

Independent agency established by the Federal Mine Safety and Health Act of 1977. Holds fact-finding hearings and issues orders affirming, modifying, or vacating the labor secretary's enforcement actions regarding mine safety and health. Reading room open to the public by appointment.

Mine Safety and Health Administration (MSHA) *(Labor Dept.), 201 S. 12th St., #401, Arlington, VA 22202-5450; (202) 693-9400. Jeanette J. Galanis, Assistant Secretary (Acting). Emergencies toll-free, (800) 746-1553.*
General email, ASKMSHA@dol.gov
Web, www.msha.gov and Twitter, @MSHA_DOL

Administers and enforces the health and safety provisions of the Federal Mine Safety and Health Act of 1977.

National Institute for Occupational Safety and Health (NIOSH) *(Centers for Disease Control and Prevention), 395 E St. S.W., Patriots Plaza 1, #9200, 20201; (202) 245-0625. Fax, (513) 533-8347. John Howard, Director. Toll-free, (800) 232-4636. TTY, (888) 232-6348.*
General email, cdcinfo@cdc.gov
Web, www.cdc.gov/niosh, Twitter, @NIOSH and Facebook, www.facebook.com/niosh

Entity within the Centers for Disease Control and Prevention in Atlanta. Supports and conducts research on occupational safety and health issues; provides technical assistance and training; develops recommendations for the Labor Dept. Operates an occupational safety and health bibliographic database.

Occupational Safety and Health Administration (OSHA) *(Labor Dept.), 200 Constitution Ave. N.W., #S2315, 20210; (202) 693-2000. Fax, (202) 693-1659. Amanda Edens, Deputy Assistant Secretary; Douglas Parker, Assistant Secretary. Emergency hotline, (800) 321-6742. TTY, (877) 889-5627.*
Web, www.osha.gov, Twitter, @OSHA_DOL, Facebook, www.facebook.com/departmentoflabor and YouTube, www.youtube.com/user/USDepartmentofLabor

Sets and enforces rules and regulations for workplace safety and health. Implements the Occupational Safety and Health Act of 1970. Provides federal agencies and private industries with compliance guidance and assistance. Website has a Spanish-language link.

Occupational Safety and Health Administration (OSHA) *(Labor Dept.), Communications, 200 Constitution Ave.*

N.W., #N3647, 20210; (202) 693-1999. Fax, (202) 693-1635. Francis Meilinger, Director. Emergency hotline, (800) 321-6742.
Web, www.osha.gov/as

Develops strategies, products, and materials to promote public understanding of OSHA standards, regulations, guidelines, policies, and activities to improve the safety and health of employees.

Occupational Safety and Health Administration (OSHA) *(Labor Dept.), Construction, 200 Constitution Ave. N.W., #N3468, 20210; (202) 693-2020. Fax, (202) 693-1689. Scott Ketcham, Director.*
Web, www.osha.gov/construction

Provides technical expertise to OSHA's enforcement personnel; initiates studies to determine causes of construction accidents; works with the private sector to promote construction safety and training and to identify, reduce, and eliminate construction-related hazards.

Occupational Safety and Health Administration (OSHA) *(Labor Dept.), Cooperative and State Programs, 200 Constitution Ave. N.W., #N3700, 20210; (202) 693-2020. Fax, (202) 693-1689. Douglas Kalinowski, Director.*
Web, www.osha.gov/cooperativeprograms

Implements OSHA's cooperative programs; coordinates the agency's compliance assistance and outreach activities; coordinates the agency's relations with state plan states; oversees OSHA international issues; and coordinates small business assistance outreach.

Occupational Safety and Health Administration (OSHA) *(Labor Dept.), Enforcement Programs, 200 Constitution Ave. N.W., #N3119, 20210; (202) 693-2100. Fax, (202) 693-1681. Kim Stille, Director. Emergency, (800) 321-6742. TTY, (877) 889-5627. Whistle-blower hotline, (800) 321-6742. Whistle-blower protection, (202) 693-2199.*
Web, www.osha.gov/dep/enforcement/dep_offices.html

Develops, interprets, and provides guidance for compliance safety standards for agency field personnel, private employees, and employers.

Occupational Safety and Health Administration (OSHA) *(Labor Dept.), Maritime and Agriculture, 200 Constitution Ave. N.W., #N3609, 20210-0001; (202) 693-2222. Fax, (202) 693-1663. Amy Wangdahl, Director, ext. 32066.*
Web, www.osha.gov/dts/maritime/mission.html

Writes occupational safety and health standards and guidance products for the maritime industry and agriculture.

Occupational Safety and Health Administration (OSHA) *(Labor Dept.), Standards and Guidance, 200 Constitution Ave. N.W., #N3718, 20210; (202) 693-1950. Fax, (202) 693-1678. Andrew (Andy) Levinson, Deputy Director.*
Web, www.osha.gov/contactus/byoffice/dsg

Develops new or revised occupational health standards for toxic, hazardous, and carcinogenic substances;

biological and safety hazards; or other harmful physical agents, such as vibration, noise, and radiation.

Occupational Safety and Health Review Commission, *1120 20th St. N.W., 9th Floor, 20036-3457; (202) 606-5100. Fax, (202) 606-5050. Cynthia L. Attwood, Chair, (202) 606-5370; Amanda Wood Laihow, Commissioner, (202) 606-5373. TTY, (877) 889-5627. Library, (202) 606-5729. Web, www.oshrc.gov*

Independent executive branch agency that adjudicates disputes between private employers and the Occupational Safety and Health Administration arising under the Occupational Safety and Health Act of 1970. Library Staff available 7:30 p.m.–2:30 p.m., for reference and reasearch.

▶CONGRESS

For a listing of relevant congressional committees and subcommittees, please see page 221 or the Appendix.

▶NONGOVERNMENTAL

American Industrial Hygiene Assn., *3141 Fairview Park Dr., #777, Falls Church, VA 22042-4507; (703) 849-8888. Fax, (703) 207-3561. Lawrence (Larry) D. Sloan, Chief Executive Officer.*
General email, infonet@aiha.org
Web, www.aiha.org, Twitter, @AIHA and Facebook, www.facebook.com/aihaglobal

Membership: scientists and professionals working with occupational and environmental health and safety in the workplace and community. Promotes industrial hygiene in government, labor, academic institutions, and independent organizations. Conducts research to identify potential dangers; educates workers about job-related risks; monitors safety regulations. Interests include international standards and information exchange.

Fair Labor Assn. (FLA), *2033 K St. N.W., #400, 20006; (202) 898-1000. Fax, (202) 898-9050. Sharon Waxman, Chief Executive Officer.*
Web, www.fairlabor.org, Twitter, @FairLaborAssoc, Facebook, www.facebook.com/fairlaborassociation and Email, info@fairlabor.org

Membership: consumer, human, and labor rights groups; apparel and footwear manufacturers and retailers; colleges and universities. Seeks to protect the rights of workers in the United States and worldwide. Concerns include sweatshop practices, forced labor, child labor, and worker health and benefits. Monitors workplace conditions and reports findings to the public. Develops capacity for sustainable labor compliance.

International Safety Equipment Assn. (ISEA), *1101 Wilson Blve., #1425, Arlington, VA 22209; (703) 525-1695. Fax, (703) 528-2148. Steve Gardner, Chief Executive Officer (Acting).*
Web, https://safetyequipment.org

Trade organization that drafts industry standards for employees' and emergency responders' personal safety and protective equipment; encourages development and use of proper equipment to deal with workplace hazards; participates in international standards activities, especially in North America. Monitors legislation and regulations.

Migrant Legal Action Program, *1001 Connecticut Ave. N.W., #915, 20036-5524; (202) 775-7780. Roger C. Rosenthal, Executive Director.*
General email, mlap@mlap.org
Web, www.mlap.org and Facebook, www.facebook.com/MigrantLegalActionProgram

Monitors legislation, regulations, and enforcement activities of the Environmental Protection Agency and the Occupational Safety and Health Administration in the area of pesticide use as it affects the health of migrant farmworkers. Litigates cases concerning living and working conditions experienced by migrant farmworkers. Works with local groups on implementation of Medicaid block grants.

National Assn. of Manufacturers (NAM), *Infrastructure, Innovation, and Human Resources Policy, 733 10th St. N.W., #700, 20001; (202) 637-3040. Aric Newhouse, SVP, Policy and Government Relations.*
Web, www.nam.org

Conducts research, develops policy, and informs members of toxic injury compensation systems, and occupational safety and health legislation, regulations, and standards internationally. Offers mediation service to business members.

Public Citizen, *Health Research Group, 1600 20th St. N.W., 20009-1001; (202) 588-1000. Michael Carome, Director.*
General email, hrg1@citizen.org
Web, www.citizen.org/topic/health-care and Twitter, @CitizenHRG

Citizens' interest group that studies and reports on occupational diseases; monitors the Occupational Safety and Health Administration and participates in OSHA enforcement proceedings.

Workers' Compensation

▶AGENCIES

Bureau of Labor Statistics (BLS) *(Labor Dept.), Compensation and Working Conditions (OCWC), Occupational Safety and Health Statistics, 2 Massachusetts Ave. N.E., #3180, 20212-0001; (202) 691-6170. Fax, (202) 691-6196. Marika Litras, Assistant Commissioner.*
General email, iifstaff@bls.gov
Web, www.bls.gov/iif

Compiles and publishes statistics on occupational injuries, illnesses, and fatalities.

Labor Dept. (DOL), *Benefits Review Board, 200 Constitution Ave. N.W., #S5220, 20210 (mailing address: 200 Constitution Ave. N.W., #S5220, Washington, DC 20210); (202) 693-6300. Fax, (202) 513-6832.*

Judith S. Boggs, Chair and Chief Administrative Appeals Judge.
Web, www.dol.gov/brb/welcome.html

Reviews appeals of workers seeking benefits under the Longshore and Harbor Workers' Compensation Act and its extensions, including the District of Columbia Workers' Compensation Act, and Title IV (Black Lung Benefits Act) of the Federal Coal Mine Health and Safety Act.

Labor Dept. (DOL), *Employees' Compensation Appeals Board, 200 Constitution Ave. N.W., #S5220, 20210; (202) 693-6420. Fax, (202) 513-6833. Alec J. Koromilas, Chair. Case inquires, (866) 487-2365.*
Web, www.dol.gov/agencies/ecab

Reviews and determines appeals of final determinations of benefit claims made by the Office of Workers' Compensation Programs under the Federal Employees' Compensation Act.

Labor Dept. (DOL), *Workers' Compensation Programs (OWCP), 200 Constitution Ave. N.W., #S3524, 20210; (202) 343-5580. Fax, (202) 693-1378. Christopher Godfrey, Director.*
Web, www.dol.gov/owcp

Administers four federal workers' compensation programs: the Federal Employees' Compensation Program, the Longshore and Harbor Workers' Compensation Program, the Black Lung Benefits Program, and the Energy Employees Occupational Illness Compensation Program.

Workers Compensation (OWCP) *(Labor Dept.), Coal Mine Workers' Compensation, 200 Constitution Ave. N.W., #C3524, 20210 (mailing address: DCMWC,*

P.O. Box 8307, London, KY 40742-8307); (202) 693-0046. Fax, (202) 693-1395. Michael A. Chance, Director. Toll-free Federal Black Lung Program, (800) 347-2502. TTY, (877) 889-5627.
General email, DCMWC-public@dol.gov
Web, www.dol.gov/owcp/dcmwc

Provides direction for administration of the black lung benefits program. Adjudicates all black lung claims; certifies benefit payments and maintains black lung beneficiary rolls.

► **NONGOVERNMENTAL**

American Property Casualty Insurance Assn. (APCIA), *555 12th St. N.W., #550, 20004; (202) 828-7100. Fax, (202) 293-1219. David A. Sampson, Chief Executive Officer.*
Web, www.apci.org, Twitter, @TeamAPCIA and Facebook, www.facebook.com/TeamAPCIA

Membership: companies providing property and casualty insurance. Offers information on workers' compensation legislation and regulations; conducts educational activities. Monitors legislation and regulations. (Headquarters in Chicago, IL.)

National Assn. of Manufacturers (NAM), *Infrastructure, Innovation, and Human Resources Policy, 733 10th St. N.W., #700, 20001; (202) 637-3040. Aric Newhouse, Senior Vice President.*
Web, www.nam.org

Conducts research, develops policy, and informs members of workers' compensation law; provides feedback to government agencies.

7 Energy

GENERAL POLICY AND ANALYSIS

Basic Resources

▶AGENCIES

Energy Dept. (DOE), *1000 Independence Ave. S.W., #7A257, 20585; (202) 586-6210. Fax, (202) 586-4403. Jennifer M. Granholm, Secretary. Locator, (202) 586-5000. Press, (202) 586-4940. TTY, (800) 877-8339. General email, the.secretary@hq.doe.gov*
Web, www.energy.gov

Decides major energy policy issues and acts as principal adviser to the president on energy matters, including strategic reserves and nuclear power; acts as principal spokesperson for the department.

Energy Dept. (DOE), *Advanced Research Projects Agency (ARPA-E), 1000 Independence Ave. S.W., 20585; (202) 287-1005. Fax, (202) 287-5450. Jennifer Gerbi, Principal Deputy Director.*
General email, ARPA-E@hq.doe.gov
Web, www.arpa-e.energy.gov and Twitter, @ARPAE

Seeks to advance energy technologies that are too early for private-sector investment yet have the potential to radically improve U.S. economic prosperity, national security, and environmental well-being. Provides energy researchers with funding, technical assistance, and market readiness through a competitive project selection process and active program management.

Energy Dept. (DOE), *Deputy Secretary, 1000 Independence Ave. S.W., #7B252, 20585; (202) 586-5500. Fax, (202) 586-7210. David Turk, Deputy Secretary. Locator, (202) 586-5000. Press, (202) 586-4940.*
Web, www.energy.gov

Serves as chief operations officer. Manages departmental programs in conservation and renewable energy, fossil energy, energy research, the Energy Information Administration, nuclear energy, civilian radioactive waste management, and the power marketing administrations.

Energy Dept. (DOE), *Economic Impact and Diversity, 1000 Independence Ave. S.W., #5B110, 20585; (202) 586-8383. Fax, (202) 586-3075. Ann Sweeney Augustyn, Director (Acting).*
Web, www.energy.gov/diversity/office-economic-impact-and-diversity

Advises the secretary on the impacts of energy policies, programs, regulations, and other departmental actions on underrepresented communities; minority educational institutions; and minority, small, and women-owned business enterprises.

Energy Dept. (DOE), *Energy Policy and Systems Analysis (EPSA), Energy Security, 1000 Independence Ave. S.W., 20585; (202) 586-4800. Fax, (202) 586-0900. Carla Frisch, Principal Deputy Director.*
Web, www.energy.gov/epsa

Serves as principal adviser to the secretary, deputy secretary, and under secretary in formulating and evaluating departmental policy. Reviews programs, budgets, regulations, and legislative proposals to ensure consistency with departmental policy.

Energy Dept. (DOE), *Strategic Planning and Policy (OSPP), 1000 Independence Ave. S.W., 20585; (202) 586-0133. David Amaral, Director.*
Web, www.energy.gov/ospp/office-strategic-planning-and-policy

Principal energy policy adviser to the secretary and deputy secretary on domestic energy policy development and implementation, as well as Energy Dept. policy analysis and activities. Supports the Energy Dept. Oversees the Laboratory Operations Board.

Energy Dept. (DOE), *Technology Transitions (OTT), 1000 Independence Ave. S.W., 20585; (202) 586-2000. Vanessa Z. Chan, Director.*
General email, OTT@hq.doe.gov
Web, www.energy.gov/technologytransitions/office-technology-transitions

Develops policies and establishes partnerships with the commercial sector to translate agency energy technology research and innovation into products and services for the private sector.

Energy Dept. (DOE), *Under Secretary of Science and Energy, 1000 Independence Ave. S.W., S-4, 20585; (202) 586-0505. Geraldine Richmond, Under Secretary.*
Web, www.energy.gov/person/david-m-turk

Serves as the department's principal adviser on fundamental energy research, energy technologies, and science. Administers programs for nuclear and high energy particle physics, basic energy, advanced computing, fusion, and biological and environmental research. Manages the department's national labs and user facilities.

Environment, Health, Safety, and Security (EHSS) *(Energy Dept.), 1000 Independence Ave. S.W., #4B196, 20585; (202) 586-4399. Fax, (202) 586-5605. Matthew B. Moury, Associate Under Secretary.*
General email, AUUserSupport@hq.doe.gov
Web, https://energy.gov/ehss/environment-health-safety-security

Develops policy and establishes standards to ensure safety and health protection in all department activities. Coordinates and integrates health, safety, environment, and security enforcement at the Energy Dept. Responsible for policy development, technical assistance, safety analysis, education, and training. Addresses federal employee, contractor, and subcontractor concerns related to the environment, safety, health, security, quality, and management.

Environment, Health, Safety, and Security (EHSS) *(Energy Dept.), Environmental Protection and Environmental Safety & Health Reporting, 1000 Independence Ave. S.W., #6B128, 20585; (202) 586-4399. Fax, (202) 586-7330. Michael J. Silverman, Director.*

ENERGY RESOURCES IN CONGRESS

For a complete listing of congressional committees, including their full contact information, leadership, membership, and jurisdictions, please refer to the Appendix on pages 840–963.

HOUSE:

House Agriculture Committee, (202) 225-2171.
Web, agriculture.house.gov
    Subcommittee on Commodity Exchanges,
        Energy, and Credit, (202) 225-2171.
House Appropriations Committee, (202) 225-2771.
Web, appropriations.house.gov
    Subcommittee on Energy and Water
        Development, and Related Agencies,
        (202) 225-3421.
House Energy and Commerce Committee,
    (202) 225-2927.
Web, energycommerce.house.gov
    Subcommittee on Energy, (202) 225-2927.
    Subcommittee on Environment and Climate
        Change, (202) 225-2927.
House Foreign Affairs Committee, (202) 225-5021.
Web, foreignaffairs.house.gov
    Subcommittee on Europe, Energy, the
        Environment, and Cyber, (202) 225-5021.
House Natural Resources Committee,
    (202) 225-6065.
Web, naturalresources.house.gov
    Subcommittee on Energy and Mineral Resources,
        (202) 225-9297.
    Subcommitee on Water, Oceans, and Wildlife,
        (202) 225-8331.
House Oversight and Reform Committee,
    (202) 225-5051.
Web, oversight.house.gov
    Subcommittee on Environment,
        (202) 225-5051.
House Science, Space, and Technology Committee,
    (202) 225-6375.
Web, science.house.gov
    Subcommittee on Energy, (202) 225-6375.
House Select Committee on the Climate Crisis,
    (202) 225-1106.
Web, climatecrisis.house.gov/
House Small Business Committee, (202) 225-4038.
Web, smallbusiness.house.gov
    Subcommittee on Underserved, Agricultural,
        and Rural Business Development,
        (202) 225-4038.
House Transportation and Infrastructure
    Committee, (202) 225-4472.
Web, transportation.house.gov
    Subcommittee on Railroads, Pipelines, and
        Hazardous Materials, (202) 226-0727.
    Subcommittee on Water Resources and
        Environment, (202) 225-4360.

JOINT:

Joint Committee on Taxation, (202) 225-3621.
Web, jct.gov
Joint Economic Committee, (202) 224-5171.
Web, jec.senate.gov

SENATE:

Senate Agriculture, Nutrition, and Forestry
    Committee, (202) 224-2035.
Web, agriculture.senate.gov
    Subcommittee on Rural Development and
        Energy, (202) 224-2035.
Senate Appropriations Committee, (202) 224-7363.
Web, appropriations.senate.gov
    Subcommittee on Energy and Water
        Development, (202) 224-7363.
    Subcommittee on Interior, Environment, and
        Related Agencies, (202) 224-7363.
Senate Commerce, Science, and Transportation
    Committee, (202) 224-0411.
Web, commerce.senate.gov
    Subcommittee on Oceans, Fisheries, Climate
        Change, and Manufacturing, (202) 224-0411.
Senate Energy and Natural Resources Committee,
    (202) 224-4971.
Web, energy.senate.gov
    Subcommittee on Energy, (202) 224-4971.
    Subcommittee on Water and Power,
        (202) 224-4971.
Senate Environment and Public Works Committee,
    (202) 224-8832.
Web, epw.senate.gov
    Subcommittee on Clean Air, Climate, and
        Nuclear Safety, (202) 224-8832.
    Subcommittee on Fisheries, Water, and Wildlife,
        (202) 224-8832.
Senate Finance Committee, (202) 224-4515.
Web, finance.senate.gov
    Subcommittee on Energy, Natural Resources, and
        Infrastructure, (202) 224-4515.
Senate Foreign Relations Committee, (202) 224-4651.
Web, foreign.senate.gov
    Subcommittee on Multilateral International
        Development, Multilateral Institutions, and
        International Economic, Energy, and
        Environmental Policy, (202) 224-4651.
Senate Homeland Security and Governmental Affairs
    Committee, (202) 224-2627.
Web, hsgac.senate.gov
    Subcommittee on Government Operations and
        Border Management, (202) 224-4551.

Web, www.energy.gov/ehss/organizational-chart/office-environmental-protection-sustainability-support-corporate-safety

Establishes policies and guidance for environmental protection and compliance; provides technical assistance to departmental program and field offices in complying with environmental requirements.

Federal Energy Regulatory Commission (FERC) *(Energy Dept.)*, 888 1st St. N.E., 20426; (202) 502-6477. Fax, (202) 502-8612. Richard Glick, Chair, (202) 502-6530. eLibrary, (202) 502-6652. Enforcement hotline, (202) 502-8390. Enforcement toll-free, (888) 889-8030. FOIA, (202) 502-8390. Toll-free, (866) 208-3372. TTY, (202) 502-8659. General email, customer@ferc.gov
Web, www.ferc.gov, Twitter, @FERC and Facebook, www.facebook.com/FERC.gov

Independent agency that regulates the interstate transmission of electricity, natural gas, and oil, including approving rates and charges. Reviews proposals to build liquefied natural gas terminals and interstate natural gas pipelines and approves siting. Licenses and inspects nonfederal hydroelectric projects. Regulates the sale of natural gas for resale in interstate commerce and wholesale interstate sales of electricity. Ensures the reliability of high-voltage interstate transmission systems. Establishes accounting and financial reporting requirements for regulated utilities. Studies and recommends policies and regulations.

Federal Energy Regulatory Commission (FERC) *(Energy Dept.)*, *Energy Market Regulation (OEMR)*, 888 1st St. N.E., #8A-01, 20426; (202) 502-6700. Fax, (202) 219-2836. Jette Gebhart, Director.
Web, www.ferc.gov/about/offices/office-energy-market-regulation-oemr

Advises the Commission and processes caseloads related to the economic regulation of the electric utility, natural gas, and oil industries. Concerns include energy markets, tariffs, and pipeline rates relating to electric utility and natural gas and oil pipeline facilities and services. Analyzes applications for electric public utility corporate transactions, including public utility mergers, issuance of securities, or the assumption of liabilities, to determine if the proposed transactions are consistent with the public interest.

Federal Energy Regulatory Commission (FERC) *(Energy Dept.)*, *Energy Policy and Innovation (OEPI)*, 888 1st St. N.E., #7A-01, 20426; (202) 502-8850. Fax, (202) 219-2836. Jignassa Gadani, Director.
Web, www.ferc.gov/about/offices/office-energy-policy-and-innovation-oepi

Seeks to identify emerging issues affecting wholesale and interstate energy markets. Undertakes outreach to other regulators and industry, conducts studies, and makes recommendations for Commission action with state and federal agencies and the energy industry, taking into account energy and environmental concerns. Interests include renewable energy, efficiency, smart grid technology,

transmission issues, electric vehicles, and carbon and greenhouse gas issues.

National Institute of Standards and Technology (NIST) *(Commerce Dept.)*, *Special Programs Office*, 100 Bureau Dr., Gaithersburg, MD 20899; General email, spo_inquiries@nist.gov
Web, www.nist.gov/special-programs-office-spo

Fosters collaboration among government, military, academic, professional, and private organizations to respond to critical national needs through science-based standards and technology innovation, including energy concerns.

National Nuclear Security Administration (NNSA) *(Energy Dept.)*, *Emergency Operations*, 1000 Independence Ave. S.W., #GH060, 20585; (202) 586-9892. Fax, (202) 586-3904. Hon. Charles L. Hopkins III, Associate Administrator.
Web, www.energy.gov/nnsa/nnsa-offices/emergency-operations

Works to ensure coordinated Energy Dept. responses to energy-related emergencies. Recommends policies to mitigate the effects of energy-supply crises on the United States; recommends government responses to energy emergencies.

Office of Management and Budget (OMB) *(Executive Office of the President)*, *Energy, Science, and Water*, 725 17th St. N.W., #8002, 20503; (202) 395-3404. John Pasquantino, Deputy Associate Director.
Web, www.whitehouse.gov/omb

Advises and assists the president in preparing the budget for energy programs; coordinates OMB energy policy and programs.

Office of Science *(Energy Dept.)*, 1000 Independence Ave. S.W., #7B058, 20585; (202) 586-5430. Fax, (202) 586-4120. V. Stephen Binkley, Director (Acting).
Web, https://science.energy.gov and Twitter, @doescience

Advises the secretary on the department's physical science research and energy research and development programs; the use of multipurpose laboratories (except weapons laboratories); and education and training for basic and applied research activities. Manages the department's high-energy and nuclear physics programs and the fusion energy program. Conducts environmental and health-related research and development programs, including studies of energy-related pollutants and hazardous materials.

► **CONGRESS**

For a listing of relevant congressional committees and subcommittees, please see page 257 or the Appendix.

Government Accountability Office (GAO), *Natural Resources and Environment (NRE)*, 441 G St. N.W., 20548; (202) 512-3841. Frank Rusco, Director.
Web, www.gao.gov/about/careers/our-teams

Audits, analyzes, and evaluates for Congress federal agriculture, food safety, and energy programs; provides guidance on issues including efforts to ensure a reliable and environmentally sound energy supply, land and water resources management, protection of the environment, hazardous and nuclear wastes threat reduction, food safety, and investment in science.

▶NONGOVERNMENTAL

American Assn. of Blacks in Energy (AABE), *1625 K St. N.W., #405, 20006; (202) 371-9530. Ralph Cleveland, President.*
General email, info@aabe.org
Web, www.aabe.org, Twitter, @_AABE and Facebook, www.facebook.com/AABENational

Encourages participation of African Americans and other minorities in energy research and in formulating energy policy. Provides financial aid and scholarships to African American students who pursue careers in energy-related fields. Promotes greater awareness in private and public sectors of the impacts of energy policy on minority communities.

Aspen Institute, *2300 N St. N.W., #700, 20037; (202) 736-5800. Fax, (202) 467-0790. Daniel R. Porterfield, President. Press, (202) 736-3849.*
General email, info@aspeninstitute.org
Web, www.aspeninstitute.org and Twitter, @AspenInstitute

Educational and policy studies organization. Promotes consideration of the public good in a wide variety of policy areas, including energy and the environment. Working with international partners, offers educational seminars, nonpartisan policy forums, public conferences and events, and leadership development initiatives.

Center for Strategic and International Studies, *Energy Security and Climate Change Program, 1616 Rhode Island Ave. N.W., 20036; (202) 775-3115. Joseph Majkut, Director.*
General email, lhyland@csis.org
Web, www.csis.org/programs/energy-security-and-climate-change-program and Twitter, @CSISEnergy

Conducts and publishes research on energy and climate change policy.

Edison Electric Institute, *701 Pennsylvania Ave. N.W., 20004-2696; (202) 508-5000. Fax, (202) 508-5096. Thomas R. Kuhn, President.*
General email, feedback@eei.org
Web, www.eei.org, Twitter, @Edison_Electric, Facebook, www.facebook.com/edisonelectricinstitute and YouTube, www.youtube.com/user/EEITV

Membership: investor-owned electric power companies. Interests include electric utility operation and concerns, including conservation and energy management, energy analysis, resources and environment, cogeneration and renewable energy resources, safety, reliability, taxes, and regulation matters.

Energy Bar Assn., *2000 M St. N.W., #715, 20036; (202) 223-5625. Fax, (202) 833-5596. Lisa A. Levine, Chief Executive Officer.*
General email, admin@eba-net.org
Web, www.eba-net.org and Twitter, @EnergyBarAssoc

Membership: lawyers interested in all areas of energy law. Interests include administration of laws covering production, development, conservation, transmission, and economic regulation of energy.

Environmental and Energy Study Institute (EESI), *1020 19th St. N.W., #650, 20036-6101; (202) 628-1400. Fax, (202) 204-5244. Daniel Bresette, Executive Director, (202) 662-1881.*
General email, info@eesi.org
Web, www.eesi.org, Twitter, @eesionline and Facebook, www.facebook.com/eesionline

Nonpartisan policy education and analysis group established by members of Congress to foster informed debate on environmental and energy issues. Interests include policies for sustainable development, energy, sustainable bioenergy, climate change, agriculture, transportation, and fiscal policy reform.

Industrial Energy Consumers of America, *1776 K St. N.W., #720, 20006; (202) 223-1420. Paul N. Cicio, President, (202) 223-1661.*
Web, www.ieca-us.com and Twitter, @IECAUS

National trade association that represents the manufacturing industry and acts as advocate for energy, environmental, and public policy issues. Acts as advocate for greater diversity of and lower costs for energy. Monitors legislation and regulations.

National Academies of Sciences, Engineering, and Medicine (NASEM), *Energy and Environmental Systems Board, Keck Center, 500 5th St. N.W., #W917, 20001; (202) 334-3344. K. John Holmes, Director; Jared L. Cohen, Chair.*
Web, www.nationalacademies.org/bees/board-on-energy-and-environmental-systems

Conducts studies in order to advise the federal government and the private sector about issues in energy and environmental technology, and related public policy. Focuses on energy supply and demand technologies and systems, including resource extraction through mining and drilling, energy conversion, distribution and delivery, and efficiency of use; environmental consequences of energy-related activities; environmental systems and controls in areas related to fuel production, energy conversion, transmission, and use; and other issues relating to national security and defense. Sponsors studies, workshops, symposia, and a variety of information-dissemination activities.

National Assn. of Energy Service Companies, *1667 K St. N.W., #700, 20006; (202) 822-0950. Timothy D. Unruh, Executive Director, (571) 337-4056.*
General email, info@naesco.org
Web, www.naesco.org and Twitter, @NaescoNews

Energy Department

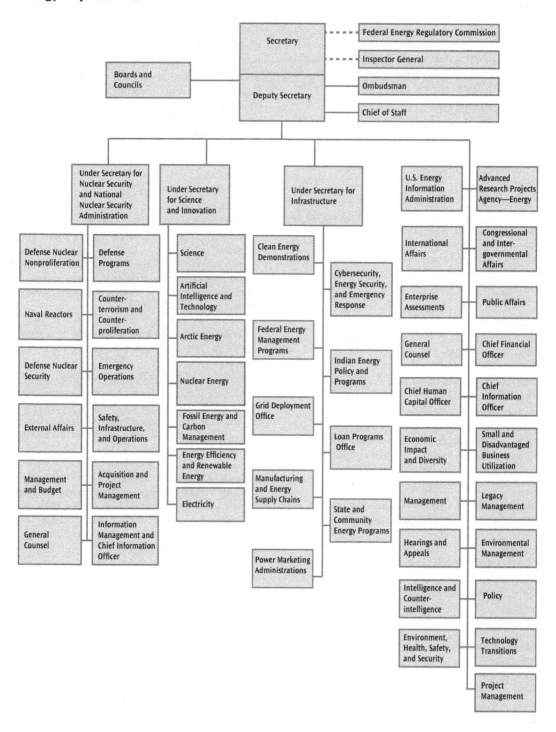

- - - - - - Indicates a support or advisory relationship with the unit

Membership: companies that design, manufacture, finance, and install energy efficiency and renewable energy equipment; energy efficiency and renewable energy services companies; and government officials. Acts as an advocate for and serves as a clearinghouse on energy efficiency strategies. Monitors legislation and regulations.

National Assn. of State Energy Officials (NASEO), *1300 N. 17th St., #1275, Arlington, VA 22209; (703) 299-8800. Fax, (703) 299-6208. David Terry, Executive Director.*
General email, energy@naseo.org
Web, www.naseo.org and Twitter, @NASEO_Energy

Membership: senior officials from each state and territory, plus affiliates from public and private sectors. Seeks to improve energy programs, provide policy analysis, and act as an information clearinghouse. Interests include efficiency, renewables, building codes, emergency preparedness, and fuel production and distribution.

National Governors Assn. (NGA), *Center for Best Practices, Energy Division, 444 N. Capitol St. N.W., #267, 20001-1512; (202) 624-5300. Daniel Lauf, Director.*
General email, info@nga.org
Web, www.nga.org/bestpractices/energy

Identifies best practices for issues regarding energy development and use and shares them with the states.

National Governors Assn. (NGA), *Center for Best Practices, Environment Division, 444 N. Capitol St. N.W., #267, 20001-1512; (202) 624-5300. Jessica Rackley, Director.*
General email, info@nga.org
Web, www.nga.org/bestpractices/environment

Identifies best practices for issues regarding management of state parks and forests, energy production and distribution, wildlife protection, land use, and waste management.

National Governors Assn. (NGA), *Natural Resources Committee, 444 N. Capitol St. N.W., #267, 20001-1512; (202) 624-5300. Alex Whitaker, Legislative Director.*
General email, info@nga.org
Web, www.nga.org/advocacy/nga-committees/nrc

Monitors legislation and regulations and makes recommendations on agriculture, energy, environment, and natural resource issues to ensure governors' views and priorities are represented in federal policies and regulations.

RAND Corp., *Washington Office, 1200 S. Hayes St., Arlington, VA 22202-5050; (703) 413-1100. Fax, (703) 413-8111. Nicholas Burger, Director.*
Web, www.rand.org

Analyzes the effects of existing and proposed energy policies on the environment. (Headquarters in Santa Monica, Calif.)

U.S. Chamber of Commerce, *Environment, Technology, and Regulatory Affairs, 1615 H St. N.W., 20062-2000; (202) 659-6000. Chad S. Whiteman, Vice President of Environment and Regulatory Affairs.*
General email, environment@uschamber.com
Web, www.uschamber.com, Twitter, @Regulations and Facebook, www.facebook.com/uschamber

Develops policy on all issues affecting energy, including alternative energy, emerging technologies, regulatory affairs, energy taxes, telecommunications, and onshore and off-shore mining of energy resources.

Data and Statistics

▶AGENCIES

Census Bureau *(Commerce Dept.), Economic Reimbursable Surveys Branch, 4600 Silver Hill Rd., #6H128, Suitland, MD 20746 (mailing address: 4600 Silver Hill Rd., #6H128, Washington, DC 20233); (301) 763-6033. Kevin E. Deardorff, Chief.*
Web, www.census.gov

Collects and tabulates data for the Manufacturing Energy Consumption Survey for the Energy Dept. concerning combustible and noncombustible energy resources for the U.S. manufacturing sector. Collects data on quarterly plant capacity utilization within the manufacturing and printing sector.

Energy Information Administration (EIA) *(Energy Dept.), 1000 Independence Ave. S.W., #2H027, 20585; (202) 586-6351. Fax, (202) 586-0329. Stephen Nalley, Administrator (Acting). Information, (202) 586-8800.*
General email, infoctr@eia.gov
Web, www.eia.gov, Twitter, @EIA.gov and Facebook, www.facebook.com/eiagov

Collects and publishes data on national and international energy reserves, financial status of energy-producing companies, production, demand, consumption, and other areas; provides long- and short-term analyses of energy trends and data.

Energy Information Administration (EIA) *(Energy Dept.), Electricity, Coal, Nuclear, and Renewable Analysis, 1000 Independence Ave. S.W., #2H073, EI50, 20585; (202) 586-2432. Jim Diefenderfer, Director.*
Web, www.eia.gov

Collects data, compiles statistics, and prepares analyses and forecasts on domestic coal supplies, electric power supplies, uranium supplies and markets, and alternative energy supplies, including biomass, solar, wind, waste, wood, and alcohol. Directs collection of spent fuel data and validation of spent nuclear fuel discharge data for the Civilian Radioactive Waste Management Office. Prepares analyses and forecasts on the availability, production, prices, processing, transportation, and distribution of nuclear energy, both domestically and internationally.

Energy Information Administration (EIA) *(Energy Dept.), Energy Analysis, 1000 Independence Ave. S.W., #2-G022, 20585; (202) 586-6135. Angelina LaRose, Assistant Administrator.*
Web, www.eia.gov/analysis

Analyzes and forecasts alternative energy futures. Develops, applies, and maintains modeling systems for analyzing the interactions of demand, conversion, and supply for all energy sources and their economic and environmental impacts. Concerned with emerging energy markets and U.S. dependence on petroleum imports.

Energy Information Administration (EIA) *(Energy Dept.), Energy Consumption and Efficiency Analysis,* *1000 Independence Ave. S.W., 20585; (202) 586-1762.* *James Turnure, Director.* *Web, www.eia.gov*

Collects and provides data on energy consumption in the residential, commercial, and industrial sectors. Prepares analyses on energy consumption by sector and fuel type, including the impact of conservation measures.

Energy Information Administration (EIA) *(Energy Dept.), Energy Consumption and Efficiency Statistics,* *1000 Independence Ave. S.W., #2F073, 20585; (202) 586-3548. Samson Adeshiyan, Director.* *Web, www.eia.gov*

Conducts national energy consumption surveys and publishes energy consumption data and analysis.

Energy Information Administration (EIA) *(Energy Dept.), Energy Statistics, 1000 Independence Ave. S.W., #2G020, 20585; (202) 586-6012. Fax, (202) 586-9739. Thomas Leckey, Assistant Administrator.* *General email, infoctr@eia.doe.gov* *Web, www.eia.gov*

Conducts survey, statistical methods, and integration activities related to energy consumption and efficiency; electricity; nuclear and renewable energy; oil, gas, and coal supply; and petroleum and biofuels. Manages EIA data collection program and the quality control for statistical reports.

Energy Information Administration (EIA) *(Energy Dept.), Integrated and International Energy Analysis,* *1000 Independence Ave. S.W., MS EI35, 20585; (202) 586-1284. Fax, (202) 586-3045. James Preciado, Director.* *Web, www.eia.gov*

Compiles, interprets, and reports international energy statistics and U.S. energy data for international energy organizations. Analyzes international energy markets; makes projections concerning world prices and trade for energy sources, including oil, natural gas, coal, and electricity; monitors world petroleum market to determine U.S. vulnerability.

Energy Information Administration (EIA) *(Energy Dept.), Petroleum and Biofuel Statistics, 1000 Independence Ave. S.W., #BG041, 20585; (202) 586-4615. Thomas Leckey, Director (Acting).* *General email, infoctr@eia.doe.gov* *Web, www.eia.gov*

Collects, compiles, interprets, and publishes data on domestic production, distribution, and prices of crude oil and refined petroleum products; analyzes and projects availability of petroleum supplies.

Energy Information Administration (EIA) *(Energy Dept.), Stakeholder Outreach and Communications,* *1000 Independence Ave. S.W., 20585; (202) 586-6537. Fax, (202) 586-3045. Lynn Parrish, Director.* *General email, infoctr@eia.doe.gov* *Web, www.eia.gov*

Serves as the information point of contact for federal, state, and local governments; academia, businesses, and industry; foreign governments and international organizations; the news media; and the public. Manages and oversees the Energy Information Administration's public website, printed publications, and a customer contact center.

▶**NONGOVERNMENTAL**

American Gas Assn., Statistics, *400 N. Capitol St. N.W., #450, 20001-1535; (202) 824-7133. Paul Pierson, Senior Director.* *Web, www.aga.org/events-community/statistics-survey-system/ and Facebook, www.facebook.com/naturalgas*

Issues statistics on the gas utility industry, including supply and reserves.

American Petroleum Institute, Statistics, *200 Massachusetts Ave. N.W., #1100, 20001; (202) 682-8000. Fax, (202) 962-4730. Dean Foreman, Chief Economist.* *General email, apidata@api.org* *Web, www.api.org/products-and-services/statistics*

Provides basic statistical information on petroleum industry operations, market conditions, and environmental, health, and safety performance. Includes data on supply and demand of crude oil and petroleum products, exports and imports, refinery operations, drilling activities and costs, environmental expenditures, injuries, illnesses and fatalities, oil spills, and emissions.

National Mining Assn., *101 Constitution Ave. N.W., #500 East, 20001-2133; (202) 463-2600. Fax, (202) 463-2666. Rich Nolan, President. Press, (202) 463-2642.* *General email, webmaster@nma.org* *Web, www.nma.org*

Collects, analyzes, and distributes statistics on the mining industry, including statistics on the production, transportation, and consumption of coal and hard rock minerals.

Energy Conservation

▶**AGENCIES**

Community Planning and Development (CPD) *(Housing and Urban Development Dept.), Environment and Energy, 451 7th St. S.W., #7212, 20410; (202) 402-3988. Liz Zepeda, Director (Acting), (202) 402-3988.* *Web, www.hud.gov/program_offices/comm_planning/library/energy*

Develops policies promoting energy efficiency, conservation, and renewable sources of supply in housing and community development programs.

Energy Efficiency and Renewable Energy (EERE) *(Energy Dept.), 1000 Independence Ave. S.W., #6A013, MS EE1, 20585; (202) 586-9220. Kelly Speakes-Backman, Assistant Secretary (Acting). Press, (202) 586-4940.*
General email, eereic@ee.doe.gov
Web, www.energy.gov/eere/office-energy-efficiency-renewable-energy

Administers financial and technical assistance for state cenergy programs, weatherization for low-income households, and implementation of energy conservation measures by schools, hospitals, local governments, and public care institutions and federal facilities.

Energy Efficiency and Renewable Energy (EERE) *(Energy Dept.), Advanced Manufacturing (AMO), 1000 Independence Ave. S.W., #5F065, MS EE5A, 20585-0121; (202) 586-9488. Fax, (202) 586-9234. Becca Jones-Albertus, Director (Acting).*
General email, amo_communication@ee.doe.gov
Web, www.energy.gov/eere/amo/advanced-manufacturing-office

Conducts research and disseminates information to increase energy end-use efficiency, promote renewable energy use and industrial applications, and reduce the volume of industrial and municipal waste.

Energy Efficiency and Renewable Energy (EERE) *(Energy Dept.), Building Technologies (BTO), 1000 Independence Ave. S.W., MS EE2J, 20585; (202) 586-9127. Fax, (202) 586-4617. David Nemtzow, Director.*
General email, Buildings@ee.doe.gov
Web, www.energy.gov/eere/buildings/building-technologies-office

Funds research to reduce commercial and residential building energy use. Programs include research and development, equipment standards and analysis, and technology validation and market introduction.

Energy Efficiency and Renewable Energy (EERE) *(Energy Dept.), Federal Energy Management Program (FEMP), 1000 Independence Ave. S.W., MS EE5F, 20585; (202) 586-5772. Fax, (202) 586-3000. Leslie Nicholls, Strategic Director.*
Web, www.energy.gov/eere/femp/federal-energy-management-program

Provides federal agencies with information and technology services to implement energy conservation measures. Areas include finance and contract assistance, purchase of energy-efficient products, design and operation of buildings, and vehicle fleet management.

Energy Efficiency and Renewable Energy (EERE) *(Energy Dept.), Vehicle Technologies (VTO), 1000 Independence Ave. S.W., #5G030, 20585; (202) 586-8055. Fax, (202) 586-7409. David Howell, Deputy Director.*
Web, www.energy.gov/eere/vehicles/vehicle-technologies-office

Works with the motor vehicle industry to develop technologies for improved vehicle fuel efficiency and cleaner fuels.

Energy Efficiency and Renewable Energy (EERE) *(Energy Dept.), Weatherization and Intergovernmental Programs (WIP), 1000 Independence Ave. S.W., MS EE5W, 20585; (202) 586-1510. Fax, (202) 586-1233. Anna Maria Garcia, Director.*
General email, monica.areval@nrel.gov
Web, www.energy.gov/eere/wipo/weatherization-and-intergovernmental-programs-office

Supports private and government efforts to improve the energy efficiency of buildings and transportation. Promotes accelerated market penetration of energy efficiency and renewable energy technologies. Provides funding and technical assistance to state and local governments and Indian tribes. Administers weatherization assistance program that assists elderly and low-income persons to make their homes energy efficient. Reviews building codes that promote energy efficiency in buildings.

National Institute of Standards and Technology (NIST) *(Commerce Dept.), Engineering Laboratory, 100 Bureau Dr., MS 8600, Gaithersburg, MD 20899-8600; (301) 975-5900. Fax, (301) 975-4032. Joannie Chin, Director, (301) 975-6815.*
General email, el@nist.gov
Web, www.nist.gov/el

Develops measurement techniques, test methods, and mathematical models to encourage energy conservation in large buildings. Interests include refrigeration, lighting, infiltration and ventilation, heating and air conditioning, indoor air quality, and heat transfer in the building envelope.

▶CONGRESS

For a listing of relevant congressional committees and subcommittees, please see page 257 or the Appendix.

▶NONGOVERNMENTAL

Alliance to Save Energy, *1850 M St. N.W., #610, 20036; (202) 857-0666. Paula R. Glover, President.*
General email, info@ase.org
Web, www.ase.org, Twitter, @ToSaveEnergy and Facebook, www.facebook.com/alliancetosaveenergy

Coalition of business, government, environmental, and consumer leaders who promote the efficient and clean use of energy to benefit consumers, the environment, the economy, and national security. Conducts programs addressing energy efficiency in commercial and residential buildings, utilities, appliances, and equipment, industry, and education. International programs provide technical and financial assistance to national and local partners.

American Council for an Energy-Efficient Economy (ACEEE), *529 14th St. N.W., #600, 20045-1000; (202) 507-4000. Fax, (202) 429-2248. Steven Nadel, Executive Director, (202) 507-4011.*

Web, http://aceee.org, Twitter, @ACEEEdc and Facebook, www.facebook.com/myACEEE

Independent research organization concerned with energy policy, technologies, and conservation. Interests include energy waste, climate change, consumer information, energy efficiency in buildings and appliances, improved transportation efficiency, industrial efficiency, utility issues, and conservation in developing countries.

Building Codes Assistance Project, 1850 M St. N.W., #610, 20036; (202) 530-2211. Maureen Guttman, President.
General email, buildingcodesassistanceproject@gmail.com
Web, http://bcapcodes.org and Twitter, @BCAPOCEAN

Advocacy group that supports and enforces national building energy codes. Assists cities, states, and counties in complying with federal energy efficiency codes, including planning, technical assistance, and training. Provides outreach and coordination activities to provide information about current code data and cost analysis to policymakers. International interests include India, the Asia–Pacific region, Ukraine, and arid regions.

Environmental Defense Fund, Washington Office, 1875 Connecticut Ave. N.W., #600, 20009-5728; (202) 387-3500. Fax, (202) 234-6049. Fred Krupp, President; Carol Andress, Associate Vice President, in Washington, DC.
Information, (800) 684-3322.
Web, www.edf.org/offices/washington-dc,
Twitter, @EnvDefenseFund and Facebook, www.facebook .com/EnvDefenseFund

Citizen interest group staffed by lawyers, economists, and scientists. Provides information on energy issues and advocates energy conservation measures. Interests include China and the Amazon rain forest. Provides utilities and environmental organizations with research and guidance on energy conservation. (Headquarters in New York.)

Friends of the Earth (FOE), 1101 15th St. N.W., 11th Floor, 20005; (202) 783-7400. Fax, (202) 783-0444. Erich Pica, President, (202) 222-0714. Press, (202) 222-0746.
Web, www.foe.org, Twitter, @foe_us, Facebook, www .facebook.com/foe.us, Press, bmiller@foe.org and Youtube, www.youtube.com/c/FriendsoftheEarthInt

Environmental advocacy group. Interests include climate disruption, renewable energy resources, and air and water pollution. Specializes in federal budget and tax issues related to the environment, including the Keystone XL pipeline, World Bank, and U.S. Export-Import Bank.

National Insulation Assn. (NIA), 516 Herndon Parkway, Suite D, Reston, VA 20170; (703) 464-6422. Fax, (703) 464-5896. Michele M. Jones, Chief Executive Officer, ext. 119. Toll-free, (877) 968-7642.
General email, niainfo@insulation.org
Web, www.insulation.org and Twitter, @NIAInfo

Membership: open-shop and union contractors, distributors, laminators, fabricators, and manufacturers that provide thermal insulation, insulation accessories, and components to the commercial, mechanical, and industrial markets. Provides information to members on

industry trends and technologies, and offers service contacts for consumers. Monitors legislation and regulations.

North American Insulation Manufacturers Assn., 11 Canal Center Plaza, #103, Alexandria, VA 22314; (703) 684-0084. Curt Rich, President.
General email, sfitzgerald-redd@naima.org
Web, https://insulationinstitute.org,
Twitter, @knowinsulation and Facebook, www.facebook .com/insulationinstitute

Membership: manufacturers of insulation products for use in homes, commercial buildings, and industrial facilities. Provides information on the use of insulation for thermal efficiency, sound control, and fire safety; monitors research in the industry. Interests include energy efficiency and sustainability. Monitors legislation and regulations.

Power Shift Network, 1875 Connecticut Ave. N.W., 10th Floor, 20009 (mailing address: P.O. Box 73116, Washington DC 20056); Dany Sigwatt, Executive Director.
General email, theteam@powershift.org
Web, https://powershift.org, Twitter, @powershiftnet and Facebook, www.facebook.com/PowerShiftNetwork

Membership: youth-based organizations that support sustainable energy and mitigate climate change. Trains youth leaders to have a larger impact on their local communities. Campaigns for clean energy bills. Holds conferences on climate change and sustainable energy options. Interests include activism on college campuses and environmental justice. (Formerly the Energy Action Coalition.)

Resources for the Future, 1616 P St. N.W., #600, 20036-1400; (202) 328-5000. Fax, (202) 939-3460. Richard G. Newell, President. Press, (202) 328-5114.
General email, info@rff.org
Web, www.rff.org, Twitter, @rff, Facebook, www.facebook .com/ResourcesfortheFuture and Podcast, www.resources mag.org/resources-radio

Research organization that conducts independent studies on economic and policy aspects of energy, environment, conservation, and natural resource management issues worldwide. Interests include climate change, energy, natural resource issues in developing countries, and public health.

Sierra Club, Legislative Office, 50 F St. N.W., 8th Floor, 20001; (202) 547-1141. Fax, (202) 547-6009. Dan Chu, Executive Director (Acting).
General email, information@sierraclub.org
Web, www.sierraclub.org and Twitter, @SierraClub

Citizens' interest group that promotes protection and responsible use of the Earth's ecosystems and its natural resources. Focuses on combating global warming/greenhouse effect through energy conservation, efficient use of renewable energy resources, auto efficiency, and constraints on deforestation. Monitors federal, state, and local legislation relating to the environment and natural resources. (Headquarters in Oakland, Calif.)

International Trade and Cooperation

►AGENCIES

Bureau of Energy Resources (ENR) *(State Dept.), 2201 C St. N.W., #6429, 20520; (202) 647-8543. Harry Kamian, Principal Deputy Assistant; Paul F. Hueper, Director of Energy Programs, (202) 647-8510.*
Web, www.state.gov/e/enr and Twitter, @EnergyAtState

Manages the global energy economy through diplomacy between energy producers and consumers, and stimulates the market forces toward the advancement of sustainable, renewable energy sources.

Bureau of Energy Resources (ENR) *(State Dept.), Policy Analysis and Public Diplomacy, 2201 C St. N.W., #4422, 20520; (202) 647-4535. Fax, (202) 647-7431.*
Matthew McManus, Director (Acting), (202) 647-3423.
Web, www.state.gov/e/enr

Seeks to put energy security interests at the forefront of U.S. foreign policy. Objectives include increasing energy diplomacy with major producers and consumers; stimulating market forces toward energy development and reconstruction, with an emphasis on alternative energies and electricity; and promoting good governance and increased transparency to improve commercially viable and environmentally sustainable access to people without energy services.

Bureau of International Security and Nonproliferation (ISN) *(State Dept.), Nuclear Energy, Safety, and Security Affairs (NESS), 2201 C St. N.W., #3320, 20520; (202) 647-4413. James R. Warden, Director, (202) 647-4431.*
Web, www.state.gov/key-topics-office-of-nuclear-energy-safety-and-security

Coordinates and supervises international nuclear energy policy for the State Dept.; promotes adherence to technical conventions regarding peaceful uses of nuclear energy.

Energy Dept. (DOE), *Energy Policy and Systems Analysis (EPSA), Energy Security, 1000 Independence Ave. S.W., 20585; (202) 586-4800. Fax, (202) 586-0900. Carla Frisch, Principal Deputy Director.*
Web, www.energy.gov/epsa

Advises the assistant secretary and Energy Dept. leadership on energy demand and supply, energy efficiency, energy research and development, and the environment, including air quality and climate. Provides analysis for the development of domestic and international energy policy. Responds to energy market disruptions and emergencies. Recommends science and technology policies.

Energy Dept. (DOE), *International Affairs, 1000 Independence Ave. S.W., #7C016, MS IA1, 20585; (202) 586-5800. Fax, (202) 586-0861. Andrew Light, Assistant Secretary.*
Web, www.energy.gov/ia/office-international-affairs

Advises the Energy Dept. leadership in the development of a national policy concerning domestic and international energy matters. Coordinates the varied interests of the department's divisions and other government organizations. Negotiates and manages international energy agreements. Develops and promotes international partnerships for deployment of greenhouse gas abatement technologies.

Energy Information Administration (EIA) *(Energy Dept.), Integrated and International Energy Analysis, 1000 Independence Ave. S.W., MS EI35, 20585; (202) 586-1284. Fax, (202) 586-3045. James Preciado, Director.*
Web, www.eia.gov

Compiles, interprets, and reports international energy statistics and U.S. energy data for international energy organizations. Analyzes international energy markets; makes projections concerning world prices and trade for energy sources, including oil, natural gas, coal, and electricity; monitors world petroleum market to determine U.S. vulnerability.

International Trade Administration (ITA) *(Commerce Dept.), Industry and Analysis (I&A), Manufacturing (OM), Energy and Environmental Industries (OEEI), 1400 Constitution Ave. N.W., Room 28018, 20230 (mailing address: 1401 Constitution Ave. N.W., MD 4053, Washington, DC 20230); (202) 482-5159. Adam O'Malley, Director.*
Web, www.trade.gov/about-us/office-energy-and-environmental-industries

Promotes global competitiveness of U.S. energy and environmental companies. Conducts analyses of these two sectors and of overseas trade and investment opportunities and trade barriers affecting them. Develops strategies for removing foreign trade barriers and improving investment conditions. Organizes conferences and workshops.

National Nuclear Security Administration (NNSA) *(Energy Dept.), Emergency Operations, 1000 Independence Ave. S.W., #GH060, 20585; (202) 586-9892. Fax, (202) 586-3904. Hon. Charles L. Hopkins III, Associate Administrator.*
Web, www.energy.gov/nnsa/nnsa-offices/emergency-operations

Monitors international energy situations as they affect domestic market conditions; recommends policies on and government responses to energy emergencies; represents the United States in the International Energy Agency's emergency programs and NATO civil emergency preparedness activities.

Nuclear Energy (NE) *(Energy Dept.), International Nuclear Energy Policy and Cooperation, 1000 Independence Ave. S.W., #5A-143, 20585; (202) 586-5253. Aleshia Duncan, Deputy Assistant Secretary.*
Web, www.energy.gov/ne/nuclear-reactor-technologies/international-nuclear-energy-policy-and-cooperation

Responsible for the Energy Dept.'s international civilian nuclear energy activities, including research, development and demonstration cooperation, international framework and partnership development, and international nuclear energy policy.

Nuclear Regulatory Commission, *International Programs (OIP),* 11555 Rockville Pike, MS 04E21, Rockville, MD 20852 (mailing address: Delivery Address. 4934 Boiling Brook Parkway, Rockville, MD 20852); (301) 287-9056. Nader Mamish, Director; David Humerick, Chief, International Operations Branch. Public Affairs, (301) 415-8200.
Web, www.nrc.gov/about-nrc/organization/oipfuncdesc .html

Coordinates application review process for exports and imports of nuclear materials, facilities, and components. Makes recommendations on export-import licensing upon completion of review process. Conducts related policy reviews.

Office of Science *(Energy Dept.),* 1000 Independence Ave. S.W., #7B058, 20585; (202) 586-5430. Fax, (202) 586-4120. V. Stephen Binkley, Director (Acting).
Web, https://science.energy.gov and Twitter, @doescience

Coordinates energy research, science, and technology programs among producing and consuming nations; analyzes existing international research and development activities; pursues international collaboration in research and in the design, development, construction, and operation of new facilities and major scientific experiments; participates in negotiations for international cooperation activities.

U.S. International Trade Commission, *Natural Resources and Metals,* 500 E St. S.W., #511F, 20436; (202) 205-3402. Robert (Bob) Carr, Chief.
Web, www.usitc.gov

Advisory fact-finding agency on tariffs, commercial policy, and foreign trade matters. Analyzes data on oil, crude petroleum, petroleum products, natural gas and its products, and coal and its products (including all forms of coke) traded internationally; investigates effects of tariffs on certain chemical and energy imports.

▶ **CONGRESS**

For a listing of relevant congressional committees and subcommittees, please see page 257 or the Appendix.

▶ **INTERNATIONAL ORGANIZATIONS**

European Union, *Delegation to the United States of America,* 2175 K St. N.W., 20037; (202) 862-9500. Stavros Lambrinidis, Ambassador.
General email, delegation-usa-info@eeas.europa.eu
Web, www.euintheus.org, Twitter, @EUintheUS, Facebook, www.facebook.com/EUintheUS and Twitter, Ambassador, @EUAAmbUS

Information and public affairs office in the United States for the European Union. Advances energy policy cooperation and strategies between the United States and Europe; interests include renewable and clean energy, foreign oil dependence, and green technologies. (Headquarters in Brussels.)

▶ **NONGOVERNMENTAL**

Atlantic Council, *Global Energy Center,* 1030 15th St. N.W., 12th Floor, 20005-5503; (202) 778-4952. Fax, (202) 463-4590. Randolph Bell, Director, (202) 463-7226.
General email, press@program/global.energy.org
Web, www.atlanticcouncil.org/programs/global-energy-center and Twitter, @ACGlobalEnergy

Helps governments, industry, and civil society looking to understand and navigate the energy transition. Seeks to create common understanding of critical energy and environmental issues through nonpartisan policy analysis and recommendations. Studies and makes policy recommendations on the economic, political, and security aspects of energy supply and international environment issues.

U.S. Energy Assn., 1300 Pennsylvania Ave. N.W., #550, Mailbox 142, 20004-3022; (202) 312-1230. Sheila Hollis, Executive Director (Acting).
General email, reply@usea.org
Web, www.usea.org, Twitter, @USEnergyAssn and YouTube, www.youtube.com/USEnergyAssn

Membership: energy-related organizations, including professional, trade, and government groups. Participates in the World Energy Council (headquartered in London). Sponsors seminars and conferences on energy resources, policy management, technology, utilization, and conservation.

Winrock International, *Washington Office,* 2451 Crystal Dr., #700, Arlington, VA 22202; (703) 302-6500. Fax, (703) 302-6512. Rodney Ferguson, President.
General email, information@winrock.org
Web, www.winrock.org and Twitter, @WinrockIntl

Works to sustain natural resources and protect the environment. Matches innovative approaches in agriculture, natural resource management, clean energy, and leadership development with the unique needs of its partners. (Headquarters in Little Rock, Ark.)

ELECTRICITY

General

▶ **AGENCIES**

Energy Dept. (DOE), *Electricity Delivery and Energy Reliability (OE),* 1000 Independence Ave. S.W., #8H033, 20585; (202) 586-1411. Fax, (202) 586-1472. Patricia Hoffman, Assistant Secretary (Acting).
General email, OEwebmaster@hq.doe.gov
Web, www.energy.gov/oe/office-electricity

Develops electricity policies and programs that shape electricity system planning and market operations; develops technologies to improve the grid infrastructure that provides electricity to homes, offices, and factories.

National Institute of Standards and Technology (NIST) *(Commerce Dept.),* **Smart Grid,** 100 Bureau Dr., MS 8200,

Gaithersburg, MD 20899-8200; (301) 975-5987. Fax, (301) 975-4091. Chris Greer, Director, (301) 975-5919.
General email, smartgrid@nist.gov

Web, www.nist.gov/smartgrid

Develops interoperable standards to govern operations and future growth of the national Smart Grid, a planned electricity system that will add digital technology to electricity grids throughout the United States to channel their electric currents at an anticipated lower cost and higher efficiency. Works with manufacturers, consumers, energy providers, and regulators to ensure cohesion throughout the Smart Grid infrastructure.

Tennessee Valley Authority, *Government Affairs, 1 Massachusetts Ave. N.W., #300, 20444; (202) 898-2999. Jeffrey J. (Jeff) Lyash, President.*
General email, tvainfo@tva.gov

Web, www.tva.gov, Twitter, @TVAnews and Facebook, www.facebook.com/TVA

Federal corporation that coordinates resource conservation, development, and land-use programs in the Tennessee River Valley. Uses fossil fuel, nuclear, and hydropower sources to generate and supply wholesale power to municipal and cooperative electric systems, federal installations, and some industries.

►CONGRESS

For a listing of relevant congressional committees and subcommittees, please see page 257 or the Appendix.

►NONGOVERNMENTAL

America's Power, *4601 N. Fairfax Dr., #1050, Arlington, VA 22203; (202) 459-4800. Michelle Bloodworth, President.*
General email, info@americaspower.org

Web, www.americaspower.org, Twitter, @AmericasPower and Facebook, www.facebook.com/AmericasPower

Membership: coal, railroad, and electric utility companies and suppliers. Educates the public, regulators, and policymakers about economic, technological, and scientific research on energy resources employed in generating electricity. Promotes the use of coal in generating electricity and supports development of carbon-sequestration and clean-coal technologies for minimizing coal's environmental impacts. (Formerly American Coalition for Clean Coal Electricity.)

Electric Power Supply Assn., *1401 New York Ave. N.W., #950, 20005-2110; (202) 628-8200. Fax, (202) 628-8260. Todd Snitchler, President.*
Web, https://epsa.org and Twitter, @epsanews

Membership: power generators active in U.S. and global markets, power marketers, and suppliers of goods and services to the industry. Promotes competition in the delivery of electricity to consumers.

Electricity Consumers Resource Council (ELCON), *1101 K St. N.W., #700, 20005; (202) 682-1390. Travis Fisher, President.*

General email, elcon@elcon.org

Web, https://elcon.org

Membership: large industrial users of electricity. Promotes development of coordinated federal, state, and local policies concerning electrical supply for industrial users; studies rate structures and their impact on consumers.

National Electrical Contractors Assn., *1201 Pennsylvania Ave. N.W., #1200, 20004; (202) 991-6300. Fax, (202) 217-4171. John Grau, Chief Executive Officer.*
General email, necagovaffairs@necanet.org

Web, www.necanet.org, Twitter, @necanet, Facebook, www.facebook.com/NECANET and YouTube, www.youtube.com/user/Necaadmin

Membership: electrical contractors who build and service electrical wiring and equipment, including high-voltage construction and service. Represents members in collective bargaining with union workers; sponsors research and educational programs.

National Electrical Manufacturers Association (NEMA), *1300 N. 17th St., #900, Rosslyn, VA 22209-3801; (703) 841-3200. Fax, (703) 841-5900. Debra Phillips, President. Press, (703) 841-3282.*
General email, press@nema.org

Web, www.nema.org, Twitter, @NEMAupdates and Facebook, www.facebook.com/nemaupdates/

Membership: manufacturers of products used in the generation, transmission, distribution, control, and end use of electricity, including manufacturers of medical diagnostic imaging equipment. Develops technical standards; collects, analyzes, and disseminates industry data. Interests include Smart Grid, high-performance building, carbon footprint, energy storage, and an intelligence portal. Monitors legislation, regulations, and international trade activities.

National Hydropower Assn., *601 New Jersey Ave. N.W., #660, 20001; (202) 682-1700. Fax, (202) 682-9478. Malcolm Woolf, President.*
General email, info@hydro.org

Web, www.hydro.org

Membership: investor-owned utilities and municipal and independent companies that generate hydroelectric power and power from new water technologies; consulting, engineering, and law firms; and equipment suppliers and manufacturers. Focus includes regulatory relief, public affairs, and coalition building. Monitors legislation and regulations.

Research and Development

►AGENCIES

National Institute of Standards and Technology (NIST) *(Commerce Dept.), Quantum Measurement Division, 100 Bureau Dr., MS 8420, Gaithersburg, MD 20899-8420; (301) 975-3210. Fax, (301) 990-3038. Gerald J. Fitzpatrick, Chief, (301) 975-8922.*
Web, www.nist.gov/pml/div684

Federal Energy Regulatory Commission

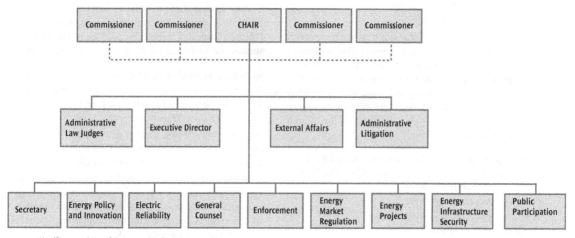

------- Signifies members of the governing body

Conducts research to characterize and define performance parameters of electrical/electronic systems, components, and materials; applies research to advance measurement instrumentation and the efficiency of electric power transmission and distribution; develops and maintains national electrical reference standards, primarily for power, energy, and related measurements, to assist in the development of new products and promote international competitiveness.

Office of Science *(Energy Dept.), Fusion Energy Sciences* *(FES), 19901 Germantown Rd., #SC24, Germantown, MD 20874-1290 (mailing address: Germantown Bldg., 1000 Independence Ave. S.W., #SC24, Washington, DC 20585); (301) 903-4941. Fax, (301) 903-8584. James W. Van Dam, Associate Director.*
Web, www.energy.gov/science/fes/fusion-energy-sciences

Conducts research and development on fusion energy for electric power generation.

►NONGOVERNMENTAL

Electric Power Research Institute (EPRI), *Washington Office, 1325 G St. N.W., #530, 20005; (202) 293-7518. Fax, (202) 296-5436. David Hunter, Senior Advisor of Government and External Relations, (202) 293-7514. Toll-free, (800) 313-3774.*
General email, askepri@epri.com

Web, www.epri.com and Twitter, @EPRINews

Membership: investor-owned and municipally owned electric utilities and rural cooperatives. Conducts research and development in power generation and delivery technologies, including fossil fuel, nuclear, and renewable energy sources used by electric utilities. Studies energy management and utilization, including conservation and environmental issues. (Headquarters in Palo Alto, Calif.)

FOSSIL FUELS

General

►AGENCIES

Fossil Energy and Carbon Management *(Energy Dept.), Forrestal Bldg., 1000 Independence Ave. S.W., #4G084, 20585-1290; (202) 586-6660. Fax, (202) 586-5146. Jennifer Wilcox, Assistant Secretary (Acting).*
Web, www.energy.gov/fe/office-fossil-energy,
Twitter, @fossilenergygov and Facebook, www.facebook .com/FECMgov

Responsible for policy and management of high-risk, long-term research and development in recovering, converting, and using fossil energy, including coal, petroleum, oil shale, and unconventional sources of natural gas. Handles the petroleum reserve and the naval petroleum and oil shale reserve programs; oversees the Clean Coal Program to design and construct environmentally clean coal-burning facilities.

U.S. Geological Survey (USGS) *(Interior Dept.), Energy Resources Program, 12201 Sunrise Valley Dr., MS 913, Reston, VA 20192-0002 (mailing address: 913 National Center, Reston, VA 20192); (703) 648-6470; (703) 648-6471. Walter Scott Guidroz, Program Coordinator, (703) 648-6421.*
General email, Gd-energy-pubs@usgs.gov

Web, www.usgs/gov/energy-and-minerals/energy-resources-program

Conducts research on geologically based energy resources of the United States and the world, including assessments of the quality, quantity, and geographic locations of natural gas, oil, gas hydrates, geothermal, and coal resources. Estimates energy resource availability and recoverability, including hydraulic fracturing ("fracking");

and conducts research on the deleterious environmental impacts of energy resource occurrence and use.

►CONGRESS

For a listing of relevant congressional committees and subcommittees, please see page 257 or the Appendix.

►NONGOVERNMENTAL

Diesel Technology Forum, 5300 Westview Dr., #308, Frederick, MD 21703-2875; (301) 668-7230. Fax, (301) 668-7234. Allen R. Schaeffer, Executive Director. General email, dtf@dieselforum.org

Web, https://dieselforum.org, Twitter, @DieselTechForum and Facebook, www.facebook.com/dieseltechforum

Represents diesel interests, with a focus on environmental protection. Advocates use of diesel engines. Supports energy research and advises policymakers. Monitors legislation and regulations.

Coal

►AGENCIES

Federal Mine Safety and Health Review Commission (FMSHRC), 1331 Pennsylvania Ave. N.W., #520N, 20004-1710; (202) 434-9900. Fax, (202) 434-9954. Lisa Boyd, Executive Director, (202) 434-9905; Arthur R. Traynor III, Chair. TTY, (202) 434-4000, ext. 293. General email, fmshrc@fmshrc.gov

Web, www.fmshrc.gov

Independent agency established by the Federal Mine Safety and Health Act of 1977. Holds fact-finding hearings and issues orders affirming, modifying, or vacating the labor secretary's enforcement actions regarding mine safety and health. Reading room open to the public by appointment.

Mine Safety and Health Administration (MSHA) (Labor Dept.), 201 S. 12th St., #401, Arlington, VA 22202-5450; (202) 693-9400. Jeanette J. Galanis, Assistant Secretary (Acting). Emergencies toll-free, (800) 746-1553. General email, ASKMSHA@dol.gov

Web, www.msha.gov and Twitter, @MSHA_DOL

Administers and enforces the health and safety provisions of the Federal Mine Safety and Health Act of 1977. Monitors underground mining and processing operations of minerals, including minerals used in construction materials; produces educational materials in engineering; and assists with rescue operations following mining accidents.

Surface Mining Reclamation and Enforcement (OSMRE) (Interior Dept.), 1849 C St. N.W., #4512, 20240; (202) 208-4006. Glenda H. Owens, Deputy Director. Press, (202) 208-2565. TTY, (202) 208-2694. General email, getinfo@osmre.gov

Web, www.osmre.gov, Twitter, @OSMRE and Facebook, www.facebook.com/OSMRE

Administers the Surface Mining Control and Reclamation Act of 1977. Establishes and enforces national standards for the regulation and reclamation of surface coal mining and the surface effects of underground coal mining; oversees state implementation of these standards.

►NONGOVERNMENTAL

America's Power, 4601 N. Fairfax Dr., #1050, Arlington, VA 22203; (202) 459-4800. Michelle Bloodworth, President. General email, info@americaspower.org

Web, www.americaspower.org, Twitter, @AmericasPower and Facebook, www.facebook.com/AmericasPower

Membership: coal, railroad, and electric utility companies and suppliers. Educates the public, regulators, and policymakers about economic, technological, and scientific research on energy resources employed in generating electricity. Promotes the use of coal in generating electricity and supports development of carbon-sequestration and clean-coal technologies for minimizing coal's environmental impacts. (Formerly American Coalition for Clean Coal Electricity.)

American Coke and Coal Chemicals Institute, 25 Massachusetts Ave. N.W., #800, 20001; (724) 772-1167. Fax, (866) 422-7794. David C. Ailor, President. General email, information@accci.org

Web, www.accci.org

Membership: producers of metallurgical coke and coal; tar distillers and coal chemical producers; coke and coal brokers; equipment, materials, and service suppliers to the coke industry; builders of coke ovens and coke by-product plants. Maintains committees on coke, coal chemicals, manufacturing, environment, safety and health, human resources, quality, governmental relations, and international affairs.

Assn. of Bituminous Contractors, Inc., 2401 Pennsylvania Ave. N.W., #350, 20037; (202) 522-8700. William Howe, General Counsel.

Membership: independent and general contractors that build coal mines. Represents members before the Federal Mine Safety and Health Review Commission and in collective bargaining with the United Mine Workers of America.

National Coal Council, 1101 Pennsylvania Ave. N.W., #186, 21043; (443) 318-6052. Fax, (443) 906-0673. Janet Gellici, Chief Executive Officer, (602) 717-5112. General email, info@ncc1.org

Web, www.nationalcoalcouncil.org, Twitter, @CoalCouncil and Facebook, www.facebook.com/NationalCoalCouncil

Membership: individuals appointed by the secretary of energy. Represents coal consumers and producers, transporters, engineering firms, equipment and supply vendors, academics, consultants, NGOs, and public officials. Monitors federal policies.

National Mining Assn., 101 Constitution Ave. N.W., #500 East, 20001-2133; (202) 463-2600. Fax, (202) 463-2666. Rich Nolan, President. Press, (202) 463-2642.

General email, webmaster@nma.org

Web, www.nma.org

Membership: coal producers, coal sales and transportation companies, equipment manufacturers, consulting firms, coal resource developers and exporters, coal-burning electric utility companies, and other energy companies. Collects, analyzes, and distributes industry statistics; conducts special studies of competitive fuels, coal markets, production and consumption forecasts, and industry planning. Interests include exports, coal leasing programs, coal transportation, environmental issues, health and safety, national energy policy, slurry pipelines, and research and development, including synthetic fuels. Monitors legislation and regulation. (Merged with Coal Exporters Assn. of the United States.)

United Mine Workers of America, *18354 Quantico Gateway Dr., #200, Triangle, VA 22172-1779; (703) 291-2400. Cecil E. Roberts, President, (703) 291-2420.*

General email, info@umwa.org

Web, www.umwa.org/policy-politics/current-legislation, Twitter, @MineWorkers and Facebook, www.facebook.com/UMWAunion

Membership: coal miners and other mining workers. Represents members in collective bargaining with industry. Conducts educational, housing, and health and safety training programs; monitors federal coal-mining safety programs.

Oil and Natural Gas

▶AGENCIES

Bureau of Ocean Energy Management (BOEM) *(Interior Dept.), Strategic Resources, 1849 C St. N.W., MS DM5238, 20240; (202) 208-6474. Megan Carr, Chief.*

General email, boempublicaffairs@boem.gov

Web, www.boem.gov

Develops and implements the Five-Year Outer Continental Shelf (OCS) Oil and Natural Gas Leasing Program; oversees assessments and inventories of oil, gas, and other mineral resources. Conveys access to marine minerals; maintains official maps and geographic data; conducts economic evaluations that ensure fair market value for OCS leases. Leads efforts to identify and mitigate the financial risks associated with offshore lease activities.

Bureau of Safety and Environmental Enforcement (BSEE) *(Interior Dept.), 1849 C St. N.W., MS 5438, 20240-0001; (202) 208-3985. Scott A. Angelle, Director (Acting). Public Affairs, (202) 208-6184.*

General email, bseepublicaffairs@bsee.gov

Web, www.bsee.gov, Twitter, @BSEEgov, Facebook, www.facebook.com/BSEEgov and YouTube, www.youtube.com/user/bseegov

Responsible for inspections, enforcement, and safety of offshore oil and gas operations. Functions include the development and enforcement of safety and environmental regulations, research, inspections, offshore regulatory and compliance programs, oil spill response, and training of inspectors and industry professionals.

Bureau of Safety and Environmental Enforcement (BSEE) *(Interior Dept.), Offshore Regulatory Programs (OORP), 45600 Woodland Rd., Sterling, VA 20166; (202) 208-3985. (703) 787-1000. Stacey Noem, Chief.*

General email, bseepublicaffairs@bsee.gov

Web, www.bsee.gov/what-we-do/offshore-regulatory-programs

Develops standards, regulations, and compliance programs governing Outer Continental Shelf oil, gas, and minerals exploration and operations. Purview includes safety management programs, safety and pollution prevention research, technology assessments, standards for inspections and enforcement policies, and accident investigation practices.

Fossil Energy (FE) *(Energy Dept.), Carbon Management, Forrestal Bldg., 1000 Independence Ave. S.W., FE-20, 20585; (202) 586-1650. Emily Grubert, Deputy Assistant Secretary.*

Web, www.energy.gov/fe/science-innovation/office-carbon-management

Involved with the policy and management of long-term research and development in transforing fossil energy systems, advancing technologies to cost-effectively capture and securely storing carbon across the economy, and exploring sustainable extraction and processing methods for coal.

Fossil Energy (FE) *(Energy Dept.), Petroleum Reserves, Forrestal Bldg., 1000 Independence Ave. S.W., FE-40, 20585; (202) 586-4410. Doug Macintyre, Deputy Assistant Secretary.*

Web, www.energy.gov/fe/services/petroleum-reserves

Manages programs that provide the United States with strategic and economic protection against disruptions in oil supplies, including the Strategic Petroleum Reserves, the Northeast Home Heating Oil Reserve, and the Naval Petroleum and the Northeast Gasoline Supply Reserve.

Fossil Energy (FE) *(Energy Dept.), Resource Sustainability, Forrestal Bldg., 1000 Independence Ave. S.W., #3E028, 20585; (202) 586-5600. Fax, (202) 586-6221. Ryan Perry, Deputy Assistant Secretary (Acting).*

Web, www.energy.gov/fe/science-innovation/oil-gas-research

Responsible for research and development programs in oil and gas exploration, production, processing, and storage; studies ways to improve efficiency of oil recovery in depleted reservoirs; coordinates and evaluates research and development among government, universities, and industrial research organizations.

▶NONGOVERNMENTAL

American Fuel and Petrochemical Manufacturers, *1800 M St. N.W., #900 North, 20036; (202) 457-0480. Fax, (202) 457-0486. Chet Thompson, President.*

General email, info@afpm.org

Web, www.afpm.org, Twitter, @AFPMonline and Facebook, www.facebook.com/AFPMonline

Membership: petroleum, petrochemical, refining companies, and companies that transport hydrocarbon feedstocks. Interests include allocation, imports, refining technology, petrochemicals, and environmental regulations.

American Petroleum Institute, 200 Massachusetts Ave. N.W., #1100, 20001-5571; (202) 682-8000. Mike Sommers, President. Press, (202) 682-8114.
Web, www.api.org, Twitter, @APIenergy, Facebook, www.facebook.com/TheAmericanPetroleumInstitute and YouTube, www.youtube.com/c/TheAmericanPetroleumInstitute

Membership: producers, refiners, marketers, pipeline operators, and transporters of oil, natural gas, and related products such as gasoline. Provides information on the industry, including data on exports and imports, taxation, transportation, weekly refinery operations and inventories, and drilling activity and costs; conducts research on petroleum and publishes statistical and drilling reports. Develops equipment and operating standards. Certifies compliance of equipment manufacturing and of environmental and occupational safety and health management systems.

American Public Gas Assn. (APGA), 201 Massachusetts Ave. N.E., #C4, 20002-4988; (202) 464-2742. Fax, (202) 464-0246. David Schryver, President.
General email, info@apga.org
Web, www.apga.org, Twitter, @APGA and Facebook, www.facebook.com/publicgas

Membership: municipally owned gas distribution systems. Provides information on federal developments affecting natural gas. Promotes efficiency and works to protect the interests of public gas systems. Sponsors workshops and conferences.

Center for Liquefied Natural Gas, 900 17th St. N.W., #500, 20006; (202) 289-2253. Charlie Riedl, Executive Director.
Web, https://lngfacts.org and Twitter, @LNGfacts

Membership: liquefied natural gas producers, shippers, terminal operators and developers, and energy trade associations. Provides general and technical information on liquefied natural gas. Monitors legislation and regulations.

Compressed Gas Assn. (CGA), 8484 Westpark Dr., #220, McLean, VA 22102; (703) 788-2700. Richard Gottwald, President.
General email, cga@cganet.com
Web, www.cganet.com

Membership: all segments of the compressed gas industry, including producers and distributors of compressed and liquefied gases. Promotes and coordinates technical development and standardization of the industry. Monitors legislation and regulations.

Energy Marketers of America (EMA), 1901 N. Fort Myer Dr., #500, Arlington, VA 22209-1604; (703) 351-8000. Fax, (703) 351-9160. Rob Underwood, President.
General email, info@emamerica.org
Web, www.energymarketersofamerica.org, Twitter, @energy_mkt_USA and Facebook, www.facebook.com/TheEnergyMarketersOfAmerica

Membership: state and regional associations representing independent branded and nonbranded marketers of petroleum products. Provides information on all aspects of petroleum marketing. Hosts meetings and forums, develops service programs. Monitors legislation and regulations. (Formally Petroleum Marketers Assn. of America (PMAA).)

Gas Technology Institute (GTI), *Policy and Regulatory Affairs,* 1250 H St. N.W., #880, 20005; (847) 768-0511. Richard Kaelin, Vice President of Government Affairs.
General email, washingtonops@gti.energy
Web, www.gti.energy and Twitter, @GasTechnology

Membership: all segments of the natural gas industry, including producers, pipelines, and distributors. Conducts research and develops new technology for gas customers and the industry. (Headquarters in Des Plaines, Ill.)

Independent Petroleum Assn. of America, 1201 15th St. N.W., #300, 20005; (202) 857-4722. Fax, (202) 857-4799. Barry Russell, Chief Executive Officer.
Web, www.ipaa.org, Twitter, @IPAAaccess and Facebook, www.facebook.com/IPAAaccess

Membership: independent oil and natural gas producers; service companies; and others with interests in domestic exploration, development, and production of oil and natural gas. Interests include leasing, prices and taxation, foreign trade, environmental restrictions, and improved recovery methods.

International Assn. of Drilling Contractors (IADC), *Government and Regulatory Affairs,* 1901 L St. N.W., #720, 20036; (202) 293-0670. Fax, (713) 292-1946. Jeremy Thigpen, President, (713) 292-1945; Matt Giacona, Director, in Washington, DC.
General email, info@iadc.org
Web, www.iadc.org, Twitter, @DC_Magazine, Facebook, www.facebook.com/iadcorg and YouTube, www.youtube.com/user/DCMagazine/Videos

Membership: oil and gas drilling contractors, oil and gas producers, and others in the industry worldwide. Promotes safe exploration and production of hydrocarbons, advances in drilling technology, and preservation of the environment. Monitors legislation and regulations. (Headquarters in Houston, Tex.)

International Liquid Terminals Assn. (ILTA), 1005 N. Glebe Rd., #600, Arlington, VA 22201; (703) 875-2011. Fax, (703) 875-2018. Kathryn Clay, President.
General email, info@ilta.org
Web, www.ilta.org, Twitter, @ilta_terminals and Facebook, www.facebook.com/ILTATerminals/

Membership: commercial operators of for-hire bulk liquid terminals and tank storage facilities, including those for crude oil and petroleum. Promotes the safe and efficient handling of various types of bulk liquid commodities. Sponsors workshops and seminars and publishes directories. Monitors legislation and regulations.

Interstate Natural Gas Assn. of America, *25 Massachusetts Ave. N.W., #500N, 20001; (202) 216-5800. Amy Andryszak, President. Press, (202) 216-5913. Web, www.ingaa.org, Twitter, @INGAApipelines and Press, media@ingaa.org*

Membership: U.S. interstate, Canadian, and Mexican interprovincial natural gas pipeline companies. Commissions studies and provides legislative and regulatory information on the natural gas pipeline industry.

National Academies of Sciences, Engineering, and Medicine (NASEM), *Gulf Research Program, Keck Center, 500 5th St. N.W., 20001; (202) 334-2138. Lauren Alexander Augustine, Executive Director; David Daniel, Chair. General email, gulfprogram@nas.edu Web, www.nationalacademies.org/gulf and Twitter, @NASEM_Gulf*

Promotes oil system safety and the protection of human health and the environment in the Gulf of Mexico and other U.S. outer continental shelf areas.

National Ocean Industries Assn., *1120 G St. N.W., #900, 20005; (202) 347-6900. Fax, (202) 347-8650. Erik Milito, President. General email, media@noia.org Web, www.noia.org and Twitter, @oceanindustries*

Membership: manufacturers, producers, suppliers, and support and service companies involved in marine, offshore, and ocean work. Interests include offshore oil and gas supply and production, pursuit of offshore renewable-energy opportunities, environmental safeguards, equipment supply, gas transmission, navigation, research and technology, and shipyards.

National Petroleum Council, *1625 K St. N.W., #600, 20006-1656; (202) 393-6100. Fax, (202) 331-8539. Marshall W. Nichols, Executive Director; Darren W. Woods, Chair. General email, info@npc.org Web, www.npc.org*

Federally chartered, privately funded advisory committee to the secretary of energy on matters relating to the petroleum industry, including oil and natural gas. Publishes reports concerning technical aspects of the oil and gas industries.

National Propane Gas Assn., *1140 Conneticut Ave. N.W., #350, 20036; (202) 466-7200. Fax, (202) 466-7205. Stephen Kaminski, President, (202) 355-1338. General email, info@npga.org Web, www.npga.org and Twitter, @NPGApropane*

Membership: retail marketers, producers, wholesale distributors, appliance and equipment manufacturers, equipment fabricators, and distributors and transporters of liquefied petroleum gas. Conducts research, safety, and educational programs; provides statistics on the industry.

Natural Gas Supply Assn., *900 17th St. N.W., #500, 20006; (202) 326-9300. Fax, (202) 326-9308. Dena E. Wiggins, President. Web, www.ngsa.org*

Membership: major and independent producers of domestic natural gas. Interests include the production, consumption, marketing, and regulation of natural gas. Monitors legislation and regulations.

NGVAmerica (Natural Gas Vehicles for America), *400 N. Capitol St. N.W., #450, 20001; (202) 824-7360. Daniel Gage, President. General email, pkerkhoven@ngvamerica.org Web, www.ngvamerica.org, Twitter, @NGVamerican, Facebook, www.facebook.com/NGVAmerica and YouTube, www.youtube.com/user/NGVAmerica*

Membership: natural gas distributors and producers; automobile and engine manufacturers; natural gas vehicle product and service suppliers; research and development organizations; enviromental groups; and state and local government agencies. Advocates installation of natural gas and biomethane fuel stations and development of industry standards. Helps market new products and equipment related to compressed natural gas (CNG), liquefied natural gas (LNG), and biomethane-powered vehicles.

Oil Change International, *714 G St. S.E., #202, 20003; (202) 518-9029. Fax, (202) 330-5952. Elizabeth Bast, Executive Director. Press, (202) 316-3499. General email, info@priceofoil.org Web, www.priceofoil.org and Twitter, @priceofoil*

Advocates national and global clean energy policies with a focus on fossil fuels. Researches the fossil fuel industry and publishes reports aimed to debate the use of oil, gas, and coal. Campaigns against fossil fuel developments.

Society of Independent Gasoline Marketers of America (SIGMA), *1330 Braddock Pl., #501, Alexandria, VA 22314; (703) 709-7000. Ryan McNutt, Chief Executive Officer. General email, sigma@sigma.org Web, www.sigma.org*

Membership: marketers and wholesalers of brand and nonbrand gasoline. Seeks to ensure adequate supplies of gasoline at competitive prices. Monitors legislation and regulations affecting gasoline supply and price.

Pipelines

▶ AGENCIES

Federal Energy Regulatory Commission (FERC) *(Energy Dept.), Energy Market Regulation (OEMR), 888 1st St. N.E., #8A-01, 20426; (202) 502-6700. Fax, (202) 219-2836. Jette Gebhart, Director.*

Web, www.ferc.gov/about/offices/office-energy-market-regulation-oemr

Establishes and enforces maximum rates and charges for oil and natural gas pipelines; establishes oil pipeline operating rules; issues certificates for and regulates construction, sale, and acquisition of natural gas pipeline facilities. Ensures compliance with the Natural Gas Policy Act, the Natural Gas Act, and other statutes.

Federal Energy Regulatory Commission (FERC) *(Energy Dept.), Energy Projects (OEP), 888 1st St. N.E., #6A-01, 20426; (202) 502-8700. Fax, (202) 219-0205. Terry Turpin, Director.*
Web, www.ferc.gov/about/offices/office-energy-projects-oep

Focuses on the engineering and environmental aspects of siting and development of new gas pipeline projects; authorizes and monitors hydroelectric projects for compliance and to safeguard the public.

National Transportation Safety Board (NTSB), *Railroad, Pipeline, and Hazardous Materials Investigations, 490 L'Enfant Plaza East S.W., 20594; (202) 314-6000. Robert Hall, Director.*
Web, www.ntsb.gov/about/organization/RPHM/Pages/office_rph.aspx

Investigates hazardous materials and petroleum pipeline accidents.

Pipeline and Hazardous Materials Safety Administration *(Transportation Dept.), Hazardous Materials Safety, 1200 New Jersey Ave. S.E., #E21-317, 20590; (202) 366-4488. Fax, (202) 366-5713. William S. (Bill) Schoonover, Associate Administrator. Hazardous Materials Information Center, (800) 467-4922.*
General email, phmsa.hmhazmatsafety@dot.gov
Web, www.phmsa.dot.gov/about-phmsa/offices/office-hazardous-materials-safety

Designates fuels, chemicals, and other substances as hazardous materials and regulates their transportation in interstate commerce. Provides technical assistance on hazardous waste materials transportation safety and security to state and local governments. Gathers and analyzes incident data from carriers transporting hazardous materials.

Pipeline and Hazardous Materials Safety Administration *(Transportation Dept.), Pipeline Safety, 1200 New Jersey Ave. S.E., E24-455, 20590; (202) 366-4595. Fax, (202) 366-4566. Alan K. Mayberry, Associate Administrator.*
General email, phmsa.pipelinesafety@dot.gov
Web, www.phmsa.dot.gov/about-phmsa/offices/office-pipeline-safety

Issues and enforces federal regulations for oil, natural gas, and petroleum products pipeline safety. Inspects pipelines and oversees risk management by pipeline operators.

▶NONGOVERNMENTAL

Assn. of Oil Pipe Lines (AOPL), *900 17th St. N.W., #600, 20006; (202) 408-7970. Fax, (202) 280-1949. Andrew J. Black, President. Press, (202) 292-4509.*

General email, aopl@aopl.org
Web, www.aopl.org

Membership: owners and operators of oil pipelines. Analyzes industry statistics. Monitors legislation and regulations.

Interstate Natural Gas Assn. of America, *25 Massachusetts Ave. N.W., #500N, 20001; (202) 216-5800. Amy Andryszak, President. Press, (202) 216-5913.*
Web, www.ingaa.org, Twitter, @INGAApipelines and Press, media@ingaa.org

Membership: U.S. interstate, Canadian, and Mexican interprovincial natural gas pipeline companies. Commissions studies and provides legislative and regulatory information on the natural gas pipeline industry.

NUCLEAR ENERGY

General

▶AGENCIES

Nuclear Regulatory Commission, *11555 Rockville Pike, MS 016G4, Rockville, MD 20852 (mailing address: 4934 Boiling Brook Parkway, Rockville, MD 20852); (301) 415-7000. Christopher T. Hanson, Chair, (301) 415-0566. 24-hour emergency, (301) 816-5100. Fraud, waste, and abuse hotline, (800) 233-3497. Press, (301) 415-8200. Public Affairs, (301) 415-8200. Public Document Room, (301) 397-4209. Safety and Security, (800) 695-7403. Toll-free, (800) 368-5642. TTY, (301) 415-5575.*
General email, opa@nrc.gov
Web, www.nrc.gov, Twitter, @NRCgov, Facebook, www.facebook.com/nrcgov and Public Affairs, opa.resource@nrc.gov

Regulates commercial uses of nuclear energy; responsibilities include licensing, inspection, and enforcement; monitors and regulates the imports and exports of nuclear material and equipment. Also has a library which relaeases numerous documents to the public every day.

Tennessee Valley Authority, *Government Affairs, 1 Massachusetts Ave. N.W., #300, 20444; (202) 898-2999. Jeffrey J. (Jeff) Lyash, President.*
General email, tvainfo@tva.gov
Web, www.tva.gov, Twitter, @TVAnews and Facebook, www.facebook.com/TVA

Coordinates resource conservation, development, and land-use programs in the Tennessee River Valley. Produces and supplies wholesale power to municipal and cooperative electric systems, federal installations, and some industries; interests include nuclear power generation.

▶CONGRESS

For a listing of relevant congressional committees and subcommittees, please see page 257 or the Appendix.

American Physical Society, *Washington Office,* 529 14th St. N.W., #1150, 20045-2001; (202) 662-8700. *Fax,* (202) 662-8711. *Jonathan Bagger, Chief Executive Officer; Francis Slakey, Chief Government Affairs Officer. Press,* (301) 209-3267.
General email, oga@aps.org

Web, www.aps.org, Twitter, @APSphysics and Facebook, www.facebook.com/apsphysics

Scientific and educational society of educators, students, citizens, and scientists, including industrial scientists. Sponsors studies on issues of public concern related to physics, such as reactor safety and energy use. Informs members of national and international developments. (Headquarters in College Park, MD.)

Nuclear Energy Institute, 1201 F St. N.W., #1100, 20004; (202) 739-8000. *Fax,* (202) 785-4019. *Maria G. Korsnick, Chief Executive Officer.*
General email, NEIGA_Nuclearenergy@nei.org

Web, www.nei.org, Twitter, @NEI, Facebook, www .facebook.com/NuclearEnergyInstitute and Press, media@nei.org

Membership: utilities; industries; labor, service, and research organizations; law firms; universities; and government agencies interested in peaceful uses of nuclear energy, including the generation of electricity. Acts as a spokesperson for the nuclear power industry; provides information on licensing and plant siting, research and development, safety and security, waste disposal, and legislative and policy issues.

Nuclear Information and Resource Service, 6930 Carroll Ave., #340, Takoma Park, MD 20912-4446; (301) 270-6477. *Fax,* (301) 270-4291. *Timothy Judson, Executive Director. General email, nirs@nirs.org*

Web, www.nirs.org, Twitter, @nirsnet and Facebook, www.facebook.com/NIRSnet

Information and networking clearinghouse for environmental activists and other individuals concerned about nuclear power plants, radioactive waste, and radiation and sustainable energy issues. Initiates large-scale organizing and public education campaigns and provides technical and strategic expertise to environmental groups. Library open to the public by appointment.

Public Citizen, *Energy Program,* 215 Pennsylvania Ave. S.E., 20003-1155; (202) 546-4996. *Tyson Slocum, Director. General email, energy@citizen.org*

Web, www.citizen.org/topic/climate-energy

Public interest group that promotes energy efficiency and renewable energy technologies; opposes nuclear energy. Interests include nuclear plant safety and energy policy issues.

Union of Concerned Scientists, *Global Security,* 1825 K St. N.W., 20006-1232; (202) 223-6133. *Tara Drozdenko, Director.*
General email, ucs@ucsusa.org

Web, www.ucsusa.org/about/programs/global-security, Twitter, @UCSUSA, Facebook, www.facebook.com/ unionofconcernedscientists and YouTube, www.youtube .com/user/ConcernedScientists

Science advocacy organization with interests in the areas of clean energy, clean transportation, food and agriculture, global warming, nuclear power, and nuclear weapons. Combines technical analysis, education and advocacy, and engagement with the public and scientific communities to promote U.S. energy policy, including nuclear energy economics and power plant safety and security. Monitors the performance of nuclear power plants and their regulators; evaluates the economics of nuclear power relative to other low-carbon energy resources. (Headquarters in Cambridge, Mass.)

Licensing and Plant Siting

Environment, Health, Safety, and Security (EHSS) *(Energy Dept.),* 1000 Independence Ave. S.W., #4B196, 20585; (202) 586-4399. *Fax,* (202) 586-5605. *Matthew B. Moury, Associate Under Secretary. General email, AUUserSupport@hq.doe.gov*

Web, https://energy.gov/ehss/environment-health-safety-security

Develops corporate security policy and standards affecting nuclear weapons facilities, nuclear materials, and classified information and provides security assistance to field elements in planning site protection strategies.

Federal Emergency Management Agency (FEMA) *(Homeland Security Dept.), Resilience, National Preparedness, Technological Hazards,* 400 C St. S.W., MS 3600, 20472-3025; (202) 646-3158. *Fax,* (703) 308-0324. *Michael Casey, Director.*
Web, www.fema.gov/emergency-managers/practitioners/ hazardous-response-capabilities

Reviews offsite preparedness for commercial nuclear power facilities; evaluates emergency plans before plant licensing and submits findings to the Nuclear Regulatory Commission.

Nuclear Regulatory Commission, *Nuclear Material Safety and Safeguards (NMSS),* 11555 Rockville Pike, Rockville, MD 20852-2738; (301) 415-0595. *John W. Lubinski, Director. Public Affairs,* (301) 415-8200. *Web, www.nrc.gov/about-nrc/organization/nmssfuncdesc .html*

Licenses all nuclear facilities and materials except power reactors; directs principal licensing and regulation activities for the management of nuclear waste.

Nuclear Regulatory Commission, *Nuclear Reactor Regulation (NRR),* 11555 Rockville Pike, MS O13H16M, Rockville, MD 20852; (301) 415-1270. *Andrea Veil, (Acting). Public Affairs,* (301) 415-8200.
Web, www.nrc.gov/about-nrc/organization/nrrfuncdesc.html

Responsible for reactor oversight, including operating reactor licensing and new and renewed licenses.

Research and Development

▶AGENCIES

Nuclear Energy (NE) *(Energy Dept.),* 1000 Independence Ave. S.W., #5A143, E-1, 20585; (202) 586-2240. Andrew Griffith, Assistant Secretary (Acting). DOE switchboard, (202) 586-5000.
Web, www.energy.gov/ne/office-nuclear-energy, Facebook, www.facebook.com/NuclearEnergyGov, Blog, www.energy.gov/ne/listings/ne-blog-archive and Twitter, @GovNuclear

Responsible for nuclear technology research and development, management of the Energy Dept.'s nuclear technology infrastructure, uranium activities, and fuel cycle issues. Supports nuclear education, including university reactor instrumentation and equipment upgrades and general support to nuclear engineering programs at U.S. universities. Leads U.S. participation in the Global Nuclear Energy Partnership, which seeks to demonstrate a more proliferation-resistant closed fuel cycle and increase the safety and security of nuclear energy.

Nuclear Energy (NE) *(Energy Dept.), Fuel Cycle Research Technologies,* 1000 Independence Ave. S.W., #5A-107, 20585; (202) 586-2240. Sal Golub, Deputy Assistant Secretary (Acting), (301) 903-7120.
General email, NECommunications@Nuclear.Energy.gov
Web, www.energy.gov/ne/fuel-cycle-technologies/fuel-cycle-research-development

Organizes and conducts research and development through five initiatives: Fuel Cycle Options; Advanced Fuels; Separations and Waste Forms; Used Fuel Disposition; and Material Protection, Control, and Accountability Technologies. Seeks to implement safe strategies for management, storage, and permanent disposal solutions.

Nuclear Energy (NE) *(Energy Dept.), International Nuclear Energy Policy and Cooperation,* 1000 Independence Ave. S.W., #5A-143, 20585; (202) 586-5253. Aleshia Duncan, Deputy Assistant Secretary.
Web, www.energy.gov/ne/nuclear-reactor-technologies/international-nuclear-energy-policy-and-cooperation

Responsible for the Energy Dept.'s international civilian nuclear energy activities, including research, development and demonstration cooperation, international framework and partnership development, and international nuclear energy policy.

Nuclear Regulatory Commission, *Nuclear Regulatory Research (RES),* 11555 Rockville Pike, 2 White Flat, Rockville, MD 20952; (301) 415-1902. Raymond Furstenau, Director.
Web, www.nrc.gov/about-nrc/organization/resfuncdesc.html

Plans, recommends, and implements nuclear regulatory research, standards development, and resolution of safety issues for nuclear power plants and other facilities

regulated by the Nuclear Regulatory Commission; develops and promulgates all technical regulations.

Office of Science *(Energy Dept.), Fusion Energy Sciences (FES),* 19901 Germantown Rd., #SC24, Germantown, MD 20874-1290 (mailing address: Germantown Bldg., 1000 Independence Ave. S.W., #SC24, Washington, DC 20585); (301) 903-4941. Fax, (301) 903-8584. James W. Van Dam, Associate Director.
Web, www.energy.gov/science/fes/fusion-energy-sciences

Conducts research and development on fusion energy for electric power generation.

▶NONGOVERNMENTAL

National Academies of Sciences, Engineering, and Medicine (NASEM), *Nuclear and Radiation Studies Board,* Keck Center, 500 5th St. N.W., 20001; (202) 334-2016. Fax, (202) 334-3077. Charles Ferguson, Director; William H. Tobey, Chair.
General email, nrsb@nas.edu
Web, www.nationalacademies.org/nrsb/nuclear-and-radiation-studies-board

Oversees studies on safety, security, technical efficacy, and other policy and societal issues arising from the application of nuclear and radiation-based technologies, including exposure to radiation, malevolent uses of nuclear and radiation-based technologies, and risks and benefits of nuclear and radiation-based applications.

Safety, Security, and Waste Disposal

▶AGENCIES

Defense Nuclear Facilities Safety Board, 625 Indiana Ave. N.W., #700, 20004-2901; (202) 694-7000. Joyce L. Connery, Chair. Toll-free, (800) 788-4016.
General email, mailbox@dnfsb.gov
Web, www.dnfsb.gov

Independent board created by Congress and appointed by the president to provide external oversight of Energy Dept. defense nuclear weapons production facilities and make recommendations to the secretary of energy regarding public health and safety.

Environment, Health, Safety, and Security (EHSS) *(Energy Dept.),* 1000 Independence Ave. S.W., #4B196, 20585; (202) 586-4399. Fax, (202) 586-5605. Matthew B. Moury, Associate Under Secretary.
General email, AUUserSupport@hq.doe.gov
Web, https://energy.gov/ehss/environment-health-safety-security

Implements nuclear safety management programs, and fire protection and natural phenomena hazard control requirements; ensures protection of workers, the public, and the environment from the hazards associated with nuclear operations; resolves nuclear safety, facility safety, and quality assurance issues.

Nuclear Regulatory Commission

- - - Indicates a support or advisory relationship with the unit rather than a direct reporting relationship

Environmental Management (EM) *(Energy Dept.), 1000 Independence Ave. S.W., #EM-31, 20585; (202) 586-7709. Fax, (301) 903-7236. Todd Shrader, Principal Deputy Assistant Secretary. DOE switchboard, (202) 586-5000. TTY, (800) 877-8339.*
General email, EM.WebContentManager@em.doe.gov

Web, www.energy.gov/em/office-environmental-management and *Facebook, www.facebook.com/DOEEnvironmentalManagement*

Manages Energy Dept. programs that treat, stabilize, and dispose of radioactive waste, including that generated from the decontamination and decommissioning of Energy Dept. facilities and sites. Works to develop a reliable national system for low-level waste management and techniques for treatment and immobilization of waste from former nuclear weapons complex sites. Provides technical assistance to states and Regional Disposal Compacts on the safe and effective management of commercially generated wastes.

Environmental Protection Agency (EPA), *Air and Radiation (OAR), Radiation and Indoor Air, 1200 Pennsylvania Ave. N.W., #5426, MC 6608T, 20460; (202) 343-9320. Fax, (202) 564-1408. Jonathan Edwards, Director. Web, www.epa.gov/aboutepa/about-office-air-and-radiation-oar#oria*

Ensures the safe disposal of radioactive waste. Administers the nationwide Environmental Radiation Ambient Monitoring System (RadNet), which analyzes environmental radioactive contamination. Fields a Radiological Emergency Response Team to respond to radiological incidents.

Federal Emergency Management Agency (FEMA)
(Homeland Security Dept.), 500 C St. S.W., 20472
(mailing address: P.O. Box 10055, Hyattsville, MD 20782-8055); (202) 646-3900. Deanne Criswell, Administrator.
FEMA helpline, (800) 621-3362. Locator, (202) 646-2500.
Press, (202) 646-3272. Toll-free, 800-621-FEMA. TTY,
(800) 462-7585.
General email, askIA@fema.dhs.gov
Web, www.fema.gov, Twitter, @fema, Facebook, www
.facebook.com/FEMA and YouTube, www.youtube.com/
user/FEMA

Assists state and local governments responding to and recovering from natural, technological, and attack-related emergencies, including in communities where accidents at nuclear power facilities have occurred and communities surrounding accidents involving transportation of radioactive materials; operates the National Emergency Training Center. Coordinates emergency preparedness, mitigation, response, and recovery activities, and planning for all federal agencies and departments.

National Transportation Safety Board (NTSB), *Railroad, Pipeline, and Hazardous Materials Investigations,* 490
L'Enfant Plaza East S.W., 20594; (202) 314-6000.
Robert Hall, Director.
Web, www.ntsb.gov/about/organization/RPHM/Pages/
office_rph.aspx

Investigates railroad accidents involving passenger railroads, freight railroads, and commuter rail transit systems -some of these accidents involve the transportation of hazardous materials.

Nuclear Regulatory Commission, *Advisory Committee on Reactor Safeguards (ACRS),* 11545 Rockville Pike,
Rockville, MD 20852 (mailing address: 4934 Boiling Brook Parkway, Rockville, MD 20852); (301) 415-7360.
Joy Rempe, Chair; Scott Moore, Executive Director. Public Affairs, (301) 415-8200.
Web, www.nrc.gov/about-nrc/organization/acrsfuncdesc
.html, Facebook, www.facebook.com/nrcgov and
Twitter, @nrcgov

Advises the commission on the licensing and operation of production and utilization facilities and related safety issues, the adequacy of proposed reactor safety standards, and technical and policy issues related to the licensing of evolutionary and passive plant designs. Reports on the NRC Safety Research Program. Reviews Energy Dept. nuclear activities and facilities and provides technical advice to the Energy Dept.'s Nuclear Safety Board upon request.

Nuclear Regulatory Commission, *Enforcement (OE),*
11555 Rockville Pike, MS O4A 15A, Rockville, MD 20852 (mailing address: 4934 Boiling Brook Parkway, Rockville, MD 20852); (301) 415-2741. Mark Lombard, Director; Juan Peralta, Chief, Enforcement Branch. 24-hour operations, (301) 816-5100. Public Affairs, (301) 415-8200.
General email, allegation@nrc.gov

Web, www.nrc.gov/about-nrc/regulatory/enforcement.html and www.nrc.gov/about-nrc/organization/oefuncdesc .html

Oversees the development and implementation of policies and programs that enforce the commission's procedures concerning public health and safety. Identifies and takes action against violators.

Nuclear Regulatory Commission, *Investigations (OI),*
11555 Rockville Pike, MS O3F1, Rockville, MD 20852; (301) 415-2373. Tracy Higgs, Director. Public Affairs, (301) 415-8200.
Web, www.nrc.gov/about-nrc/organization/oifuncdesc.html

Develops policy, procedures, and standards for investigations of licensees, applicants, and their contractors or vendors concerning wrongdoing. Refers substantiated criminal cases to the Justice Dept. Informs the commission's leadership about investigations concerning public health and safety.

Nuclear Regulatory Commission, *Nuclear Material Safety and Safeguards (NMSS),* 11555 Rockville Pike,
Rockville, MD 20852-2738; (301) 415-0595.
John W. Lubinski, Director. Public Affairs, (301) 415-8200.
Web, www.nrc.gov/about-nrc/organization/nmssfuncdesc .html

Regulates commercial nuclear reactors; storage, transportation and disposal of high-level radioactive waste and spent nuclear fuel; and the transportation of radioactive materials regulated under the Atomic Energy Act. Develops and implements policies for uranium recovery, conversion, and enrichment activities; fuel fabrication and development; and transportation of nuclear materials, including certification of transport containers and reactor spent fuel storage.

Nuclear Regulatory Commission, *Nuclear Reactor Regulation (NRR),* 11555 Rockville Pike, MS O13H16M,
Rockville, MD 20852; (301) 415-1270. Andrea Veil, (Acting). Public Affairs, (301) 415-8200.
Web, www.nrc.gov/about-nrc/organization/nrrfuncdesc .html

Responsible for reactor oversight, including advanced reactors and nonpower production or utilization facilities, risk assessment, engineering and external hazards, and safety systems. Conducts safety inspections of nuclear reactors. Regulates nuclear materials used or produced at nuclear power plants.

Nuclear Regulatory Commission, *Nuclear Regulatory Research (RES),* 11555 Rockville Pike, 2 White Flat,
Rockville, MD 20952; (301) 415-1902. Raymond Furstenau, Director.
Web, www.nrc.gov/about-nrc/organization/resfuncdesc.html

Plans, recommends, and implements resolution of safety issues for nuclear power plants and other facilities regulated by the Nuclear Regulatory Commission.

Nuclear Regulatory Commission, *Nuclear Security and Incident Response,* 11601 Landsdown St., #3WFN09D20,
N. Bethesda, MD 20852; (301) 287-3734. Mirela Gavrilas,

Director. Emergency, (301) 816-5100. Nonemergency, (800) 695-7403.

Web, www.nrc.gov/about-nrc/organization/nsirfuncdesc .html

Evaluates technical issues concerning security at nuclear facilities. Develops and directs the commission's response to incidents. Serves as point of contact with Homeland Security Dept., Energy Dept., Federal Emergency Management Agency, and intelligence and law enforcement offices and other agencies.

Nuclear Waste Technical Review Board, *2300 Clarendon Blvd., #1300, Arlington, VA 22201-3367; (703) 235-4473. Fax, (703) 235-4495. Daniel Ogg, Executive Director (Acting), (703) 235-9139.*
Web, www.nwtrb.gov

Independent federal agency of the executive branch. The board is copmrised of scientists and engineers nominated by the Academy of Sciences and appointed by the president to review, evaluate, and report on Energy Dept. development of waste disposal systems and repositories for spent fuel and high-level radioactive waste. Oversees siting, packaging, and transportation of waste, in accordance with the amendments to the Nuclear Waste Policy Act of 1987.

Pipeline and Hazardous Materials Safety Administration *(Transportation Dept.), Hazardous Materials Safety, 1200 New Jersey Ave. S.E., #E21-317, 20590; (202) 366-4488. Fax, (202) 366-5713. William S. (Bill) Schoonover, Associate Administrator. Hazardous Materials Information Center, (800) 467-4922. General email, phmsa.hmhazmatsafety@dot.gov*
Web, www.phmsa.dot.gov/about-phmsa/offices/office-hazardous-materials-safety

Issues safety regulations and exemptions for the transportation of hazardous materials; works with the International Atomic Energy Agency on standards for international shipments of radioactive materials.

▶**NONGOVERNMENTAL**

Union of Concerned Scientists, *Nuclear Power, 1825 K St. N.W., 20006; (202) 223-6133. Edwin Lyman, Director, Nuclear Power Safety.*
General email, ucs@ucsusa.org

Web, www.ucsusa.org/energy/nuclear-power, Twitter, @ucsusa, Facebook, www.facebook.com/ unionofconcernedscientists and YouTube, www.youtube .com/user/ConcernedScientists

Science advocacy organization with interests in the areas of clean energy, clean transportation, food and agriculture, global warming, nuclear power, and nuclear weapons. Combines technical analysis, education and advocacy, and engagement with the public and scientific communities concerned with U.S. nuclear power policy and ability to respond to nuclear accidents. Interests include nuclear waste storage, storage facility security measures, safe generation of fissure chain reactions, and reactor design.

RENEWABLE ENERGIES, ALTERNATIVE FUELS

General

▶**AGENCIES**

Bureau of Energy Resources (ENR) *(State Dept.), 2201 C St. N.W., #6429, 20520; (202) 647-8543. Harry Kamian, Principal Deputy Assistant; Paul F. Hueper, Director of Energy Programs, (202) 647-8510.*
Web, www.state.gov/e/enr and Twitter, @EnergyAtState

Manages the global energy economy through diplomacy between energy producers and consumers, and stimulates the market forces toward the advancement of sustainable, renewable energy sources.

Bureau of Land Management (BLM) *(Interior Dept.), Energy, Minerals, and Realty Management, 5275 Leesburg Pike, Falls Church, VA 22041; (202) 208-4201. Nicholas Douglas, Assistant Director.*
Web, www.blm.gov/programs/energy-and-minerals

Develops and administers policy, guidance, and performance oversight for the renewable energy program, including wind, solar, and geothermal energy; the fluid minerals program, including oil, gas, and helium; the solid minerals programs, including mining law, coal, oil shale, and salable minerals; the lands and realty programs; and the Public Land Survey System. Provides national leadership and develops national partnerships with organizations interested in energy, minerals, and realty management.

Energy Efficiency and Renewable Energy (EERE) *(Energy Dept.), 1000 Independence Ave. S.W., #6A013, MS EE1, 20585; (202) 586-9220. Kelly Speakes-Backman, Assistant Secretary (Acting). Press, (202) 586-4940.*
General email, eereic@ee.doe.gov

Web, www.energy.gov/eere/office-energy-efficiency-renewable-energy

Develops and manages programs to improve markets for renewable energy sources, including solar, biomass, wind, geothermal, and hydropower, and to increase efficiency of energy use among residential, commercial, transportation, utility, and industrial users.

Energy Efficiency and Renewable Energy (EERE) *(Energy Dept.), Hydrogen and Fuel Cell Technologies (HFTO), 1000 Independence Ave. S.W., #5G082, 20585; (202) 586-3388. Fax, (202) 586-2373. Sunita Satyapal, Director, (202) 586-2336.*
General email, hydrogenfuelcells@ee.doe.gov

Web, www.energy.gov/eere/fuelcells/hydrogen-and-fuel-cell-technologies-office

Works with industry, academia, nonprofit institutions, national labs, government agencies, and other Energy Dept. offices to promote the use of hydrogen, fuel cells, and related technologies.

Office of Science *(Energy Dept.), Basic Energy Sciences (BES), 19901 Germantown Rd., #SC32, Germantown, MD*

20874-1290 (mailing address: Germantown Bldg., 1000 Independence Ave. S.W., #SC22, Washington, DC 20585); (301) 903-3081. Fax, (301) 903-6594. Linda Norton, Director. General email, sc.bes@science.doe.gov

Web, www.energy.gov/science/bes/basic-energy-sciences

Supports research to understand, predict, and control matter and energy at electronic, atomic, and molecular levels to provide foundations for new energy technology.

Office of Science *(Energy Dept.), Biological and Environmental Research (BER), Climate and Environmental Sciences Division (CESD),* 19901 Germantown Rd., #SC23.1, Germantown, MD 20874-1290 (mailing address: Germantown Bldg., 1000 Independence Ave. S.W., #SC23.1, Washington, DC 20585); (301) 903-4775. Fax, (301) 303-8519. Gerald Geernaert, Director. Web, www.energy.gov/science/ber/biological-and-environmental-research

Supports research on atmospheric systems, terrestrial ecosystems, and subsurface biogeochemistry as well as Earth system modeling and regional and global climate change modeling to improve predictive understanding of Earth's climate and environmental systems in order to inform development of sustainable solutions to energy challenges.

►CONGRESS

For a listing of relevant congressional committees and subcommittees, please see page 257 or the Appendix.

►NONGOVERNMENTAL

American Council on Renewable Energy (ACORE), 1150 Connecticut Ave. N.W., #401, 20036 (mailing address: P.O. Box 33518, Washington, DC 20003); (202) 393-0001. Gregory Wetstone, President. Press, (202) 777-7584. General email, info@acore.org

Web, http://acore.org, Twitter, @ACORE and Facebook, www.facebook.com/AmericanCouncilOnRenewableEnergy

Membership: developers, manufacturers, financial institutions, renewable energy buyers, grid technology providers, utilities, professional service firms, and academic institutions across the renewable energy sector. Publishes research to educate the media and the public about renewable electricity, hydrogen, and fuels. Interests include solar power, wind power, biofuels, biomass, geothermal power, marine energy, hydroelectric power, waste-to-energy, and waste heat-to-power.

Electric Power Supply Assn., 1401 New York Ave. N.W., #950, 20005-2110; (202) 628-8200. Fax, (202) 628-8260. Todd Snitchler, President. Web, https://epsa.org and Twitter, @epsanews

Membership: companies that generate electricity, steam, and other forms of energy using a broad spectrum of fossil fuel–fired and renewable technologies.

Fuel Cell and Hydrogen Energy Assn., 1211 Connecticut Ave. N.W., #650, 20036; (202) 261-1331. Frank Wolak, President. General email, info@fchea.org

Web, www.fchea.org, Twitter, @FCHEA_News and Facebook, www.facebook.com/FCHEA

Membership: industry, small businesses, government agencies, and nonprofit organizations. Promotes use of hydrogen as an energy carrier; fosters the development and application of fuel cell and hydrogen technologies. Is an advocacy group, providing a voice in shaping regulations and codes.

Institute for the Analysis of Global Security, 7811 Montrose Rd., #505, Potomac, MD 20854-3363; (866) 713-7527. Gal Luft, Co-Director; Anne Korin, Co-Director. General email, info@iags.org

Web, www.iags.org

Seeks to promote public awareness of the link between energy and security; explores options for strengthening the world's energy security, including approaches to reducing the strategic importance of oil. Conducts and publishes research; hosts conferences; monitors legislation and regulations.

SRI International, *Washington Office,* 1100 Wilson Blvd., #2800, Arlington, VA 22209; (703) 524-2053. David Parekh, Corporate Executive Officer. Web, www.sri.com and Twitter, @SRI_Intl

Conducts energy-related research and development. Interests include power generation, fuel and solar cells, clean energy storage, and advanced batteries. (Headquarters in Menlo Park, Calif.)

Biofuels

►AGENCIES

Energy Efficiency and Renewable Energy (EERE) *(Energy Dept.), Bioenergy Technologies Office (BETO),* 1000 Independence Ave. S.W., MS EE3B, #5H021, 20585; (202) 586-5188. Valerie Sarisky-Reed, Director. General email, eere_bioenergy@ee.doe.gov

Web, https://energy.gov/eere/bioenergy

Partners with public and private stakeholders to develop and demonstrate technologies for producing cost-competitive advanced biofuels from nonfood biomass resources, including cellulosic biomass, algae, and wet waste.

National Institute of Food and Agriculture (NIFA) *(Agriculture Dept.), Institute of Bioenergy, Climate, and Environment,* 800 9th St. S.W., #3231, 20024 (mailing address: 1400 Independence Ave. S.W., MS 2210, Washington, DC 20250-2215); (202) 720-2791. Timothy Conner, Division Director (Acting), (816) 926-1816. Web, https://nifa.usda.gov/office/institute-bioenergy-climate-and-environment

Administers programs to address national science priorities that advance energy independence and help agricultural, forest, and rangeland production systems adapt to climate change variables. Provides grants to support the development of sustainable bioenergy production systems, agricultural production systems, and natural resource management activities that are adapted to climate variation and activities that otherwise support sustainable natural resource use.

Office of Science *(Energy Dept.), Biological and Environmental Research (BER), 19901 Germantown Rd., #SC23, Germantown, MD 20874-1290 (mailing address: Germantown Bldg., 1000 Independence Ave. S.W., #SC23, Washington, DC 20585); (301) 903-3251. Fax, (301) 903-5051. Sharlene Weatherwax, Associate Director.*
General email, sc.ber@science.doe.gov

Web, www.energy.gov/science/ber/biological-and-environmental-research

Advances biological and environmental research and provides scientific user facilities to support innovation in energy security and environmental responsibility.

Office of Science *(Energy Dept.), Biological and Environmental Research (BER), Biological Systems Science Division (BSSD), 19901 Germantown Rd., #SC23.2, Germantown, MD 20874-1290 (mailing address: Germantown Bldg., 1000 Independence Ave. S.W., #SC23.2, Washington, DC 20585); (301) 903-5469. Fax, (301) 903-0567. Todd Anderson, Director.*
Web, www.energy.gov/science/ber/biological-and-environmental-research

Supports research and technology development to achieve predictive systems-level understanding of complex biological systems, including redesign of microbes and plants for sustainable biofuel production, improved carbon storage, and contaminant remediation. Areas of research include genomic science, bioimaging technology, biological systems, and radiological sciences.

Office of Science *(Energy Dept.), Biological and Environmental Research (BER), Biological Systems Science Division (BSSD), Environmental Genomics, 19901 Germantown Rd., #SC72, Germantown, MD 20874-1290; (301) 903-4742. Boris Wawrik, Program Manager.*
Web, http://genomicscience.energy.gov

Supports research using microbial and plant genomic data, high-throughput technologies, and modeling and simulation to develop predictive understanding of biological systems behavior relevant to solving energy and environmental challenges.

▶NONGOVERNMENTAL

Biomass Thermal Energy Council (BTEC), *1211 Connecticut Ave. N.W., #650, 20036-2701; (202) 596-3974. Fax, (202) 223-5537. Emanuel Wagner, Managing Director, ext. 360.*
General email, info@biomassthermal.org

Web, www.biomassthermal.org, Twitter, @BiomassThermal and Facebook, www.facebook.com/BiomassThermal

Membership: biomass fuel producers, appliance manufacturers and distributors, supply chain companies, and nonprofit organizations that seek to advance the use of biomass for heat and other thermal energy applications.

Conducts research, public education, and advocacy for the biomass thermal energy industry. Monitors legislation and regulations.

Hearth, Patio, and Barbecue Assn. (HPBA), *1901 N. Moore St., #600, Arlington, VA 22209-1708; (703) 522-0086. Fax, (703) 522-0548. Jack Goldman, President.*
General email, communications@hpba.org

Web, www.hpba.org, Twitter, @HPBA_ and Facebook, www.facebook.com/HPBAPage

Membership: all sectors of the hearth products industry. Provides industry training programs to its members on the safe and efficient use of alternative fuels and appliances. Works with the Hearth Education Foundation, which certifies gas hearth, fireplace, pellet stove, and wood stove appliances and venting design specialists.

Methanol Institute, *225 Reinekers Lane, #205, Alexandria, VA 22315; (703) 248-3636. Gregory A. Dolan, Chief Executive Officer; Lawrence Navin, Director, Government and Public Affairs.*
General email, sg@methanol.org

Web, www.methanol.org, Twitter, @MethanolToday and Facebook, www.facebook.com/MethanolToday

Membership: global methanol producers and related industries. Encourages use of methanol fuels and development of chemical-derivative markets. Monitors legislation and regulations.

Renewable Fuels Assn., *425 3rd St. S.W., #1150, 20024; (202) 289-3835. Fax, (202) 289-7519. Geoff Cooper, President.*
General email, info@ethanolrfa.org

Web, https://ethanolrfa.org, Twitter, @EthanolRFA and Facebook, www.facebook.com/EthanolRFA

Membership: companies and state governments involved in developing the domestic ethanol industry. Distributes publications on ethanol performance. Monitors legislation and regulations.

Geothermal Energy

▶AGENCIES

Energy Efficiency and Renewable Energy (EERE) *(Energy Dept.), Geothermal Technologies (GTO), 1000 Independence Ave. S.W., MS 5E066, 20585; (202) 287-1818. Susan Hamm, Director.*
General email, geothermal@ee.doe.gov

Web, www.energy.gov/eere/geothermal/geothermal-energy-us-department-energy

Responsible for research and technology development of geothermal energy resources. Conducts outreach to state energy offices and consumers.

U.S. Geological Survey (USGS) *(Interior Dept.), Volcano Hazards Program, 12201 Sunrise Valley Dr., MS 904, Reston, VA 20192-0002; (703) 648-4773. Charles W. Mandeville, Program Coordinator.*

General email, vscweb@usgs.gov

Web, http://volcanoes.usgs.gov

Provides staff support to the U.S. Geological Survey through programs in volcano hazards.

Solar, Ocean, and Wind Energy

►AGENCIES

Bureau of Ocean Energy Management (BOEM) *(Interior Dept.)*, *1849 C St. N.W., #5211, 20240; (202) 208-6300. Amanda Lefton, Director. Public Affairs, (202) 208-6474.*
General email, boempublicaffairs@boem.gov

Web, www.boem.gov, Twitter, @BOEM_DOI and Facebook, www.facebook.com/BureauOfOceanEnergy Management

Manages development of U.S. Outer Continental Shelf energy and mineral resources.

Bureau of Ocean Energy Management (BOEM) *(Interior Dept.)*, *Renewable Energy Programs (OREP)*, *45600 Woodland Rd., VAM-OREP, Sterling, VA 20166; (703) 787-1300. Fax, (703) 787-1708. James (Jim) Bennett, Program Manager.*
General email, boempublicaffairs@boem.gov

Web, www.boem.gov/Renewable-Energy

Grants leases, easements, and rights-of-way for orderly, safe, and environmentally responsible renewable energy development activities on the Outer Continental Shelf, including offshore wind and hydrokinetic projects.

Energy Efficiency and Renewable Energy (EERE) *(Energy Dept.)*, *Solar Energy Technologies (SETO), SunShot Initiative, 950 L'Enfant Plaza, 6th Floor, 20585 (mailing address: 1000 Independence Ave. S.W., Washington, DC 20585); (202) 287-1862. Fax, (202) 586-8148. Garrett Nilson, Director.*
General email, solar@ee.doe.gov

Web, www.energy.gov/eere/solar/sunshot-initiative

Supports research and development of solar technologies of all types through national laboratories and partnerships with industries and universities. Seeks to make solar energy cost-effective through research, manufacturing, and market solutions.

Energy Efficiency and Renewable Energy (EERE) *(Energy Dept.)*, *Water Power Technologies (WPTO), 1000 Independence Ave. S.W., #5H072, MS EE2B, 20585; (202) 586-7595. Jennifer Garson, Director Acting).*
General email, alejandro.moreno@ee.doe.gov

Web, https://energy.gov/eere/water/water-power-technologies-office

Supports research, development, deployment, and commercialization of water power technologies.

Energy Efficiency and Renewable Energy (EERE) *(Energy Dept.)*, *Wind Energy Technologies (WETO), 1000 Independence Ave. S.W., 20585; (202) 586-5348. Bob Marlay, Director.*

Web, www.energy.gov/eere/wind/wind-energy-technologies-office

Supports research, development, deployment, and commercialization of wind energy technologies.

►CONGRESS

For a listing of relevant congressional committees and subcommittees, please see page 257 or the Appendix.

►NONGOVERNMENTAL

American Clean Power Assn., *1501 M St. N.W., #900, 20005-1700; (202) 383-2500. Fax, (202) 293-2505. Heather Zichal, Chief Executive Officer.*
General email, press@cleanpower.org

Web, www.cleanpower.org, Twitter, @USCleanpower and Facebook, www.facebook.com/USCleanpower

Membership: manufacturers, developers, operators, distributors of wind machines and other renewable energy sources; utility companies; and others interested in clean renewable energy. Advocates wind energy and other alternative energy sources; makes industry data available to the public and to federal and state legislators. Promotes export of clean energy technology.

National Ocean Industries Assn., *1120 G St. N.W., #900, 20005; (202) 347-6900. Fax, (202) 347-8650. Erik Milito, President.*
General email, media@noia.org

Web, www.noia.org and Twitter, @oceanindustries

Membership: manufacturers, producers, suppliers, and support and service companies involved in marine, offshore, and ocean work. Interests include ocean thermal energy and new energy sources.

Solar Electric Light Fund, *2021 L St. N.W., #101-344, 20036; (202) 234-7265. Robert A. (Bob) Freling, Executive Director.*
General email, info@self.org

Web, www.self.org, Twitter, @solarfund and Facebook, www.facebook.com/solarelectriclightfund

Promotes and develops solar rural electrification and energy self-sufficiency in developing countries. Assists developing-world communities and governments in acquiring and installing decentralized household and community solar electric systems.

Solar Energy Industries Assn., *1425 K St. N.W., #1000, 20005; (202) 682-0556. Abigail Ross Hopper, Chief Executive Officer. Press, (202) 556-2872.*
General email, info@seia.org

Web, www.seia.org, Twitter, @SEIA, Facebook, www. facebook.com/TheSolarIndusty and YouTube, www. youtube.com/c/SeiaOrg

Membership: industries with interests in the production and use of solar energy. Promotes growth of U.S. and international markets. Interests include photovoltaic, solar thermal power, and concentrating solar power. Conducts conferences. Monitors legislation and regulations.

8

Environment and Natural Resources

GENERAL POLICY AND ANALYSIS

Basic Resources

▶AGENCIES

Agriculture Dept. (USDA), *Under Secretary for Natural Resources and Environment,* 1400 Independence Ave. S.W., #240E, 20250-0108; (202) 720-7173. Fax, (202) 720-0632. Jim Hubbard, Under Secretary.
Web, www.usda.gov/our-agency/about-usda/mission-areas

Formulates and promulgates policy relating to environmental activities and management of natural resources. Oversees the Forest Service.

Council on Environmental Quality *(Executive Office of the President),* 730 Jackson Pl. N.W., 20503; (202) 395-5750. Fax, (202) 456-6546. Brenda Mallory, Chair.
General email, sustainability@ceq.eop.gov
Web, www.whitehouse.gov/ceq and Twitter, @WhiteHouseCSO

Develops environmental priorities; advises and assists the president on national and international environmental policy; evaluates, coordinates, and mediates federal activities on the environment; prepares the president's yearly environmental quality report to Congress.

Environmental Protection Agency (EPA), *Policy,* 1200 Pennsylvania Ave. N.W., #1804A, 20460; (202) 564-4332. Fax, (202) 501-1688. Victoria Arroyo, Associate Administrator.
General email, policyoffice@epa.gov
Web, www.epa.gov/aboutepa/about-office-policy-op

Coordinates agency policy development and standard-setting activities through four divisions: Regulatory Policy and Management, the National Center for Environmental Economics, Strategic Environmental Management, and Sustainable Communities.

Environmental Protection Agency (EPA), *Research and Development (ORD), Center for Public Health and Environmental Assessment (CPHEA),* 1300 Pennsylvania Ave. N.W., #3204R, 20460; (202) 564-6794. Wayne Cascio, Director.
Web, www.epa.gov/aboutepa/about-center-public-health-and-environmental-assessment-cphea

Evaluates animal and human health data to define environmental health hazards and estimate risk to humans. Conducts research and prepares reports and assessments.

Environmental Protection Agency (EPA), *Science Advisory Board,* 1300 Pennsylvania Ave. N.W., #31150, 20004-4164 (mailing address: 1200 Pennsylvania Ave. N.W., MC 1400R, Washington, DC 20460); (202) 564-2221. Fax, (202) 565-2098. Tom Brennan, Director.
General email, sab@epa.gov
Web, www.epa.gov/aboutepa/about-science-advisory-board-sab-and-sab-staff-office

Coordinates nongovernment scientists and engineers who advise the administrator on scientific and technical aspects of environmental problems and issues. Evaluates EPA research projects, the technical basis of regulations and standards, and policy statements.

Federal Highway Administration (FHWA) *(Transportation Dept.), Planning, Environment, and Realty,* 1200 New Jersey Ave. S.E., #E76-306, 20590; (202) 366-0116. Fax, (202) 366-3713. Gloria M. Shepherd, Associate Administrator, (202) 366-0581.
Web, www.fhwa.dot.gov/real_estate

Works with developers and municipalities to ensure conformity with the National Environmental Policy Act (NEPA) project development process.

Interior Dept. (DOI), 1849 C St. N.W., MS 7328, 20240; (202) 208-3100. Debra Anne (Deb) Haaland, Secretary. Library, (202) 208-5815. Press, (202) 208-6416. Toll-Free TTY, (800) 877-8339.
General email, feedback@ios.doi.gov
Web, www.doi.gov, Twitter, @Interior, Facebook, www.facebook.com/USInterior, Blog, www.doi.gov/blog, Library, www.doi.gov/library and Twitter, Secretary, @SecDebHaaland

Principal U.S. conservation agency. Manages most federal land; responsible for conservation and development of mineral and water resources; responsible for conservation, development, and use of fish and wildlife resources; operates recreation programs for federal parks, refuges, and public lands; preserves and administers the nation's scenic and historic areas; reclaims arid lands in the West through irrigation; administers Native American lands and develops relationships with tribal governments. Reference library open to the public 7:45 a.m.–5:00 p.m.

Interior Dept. (DOI), *Communications,* 1849 C St. N.W., #6229, 20240; (202) 208-6416. Melissa Schwartz, Director.
General email, interior_press@ios.doi.gov
Web, http://doi.gov/news

Issues press releases about Interior Dept. events and announcements. Provides information to the general public, tourists, businesses, Native Americans, governments, and others.

Interior Dept. (DOI), *Environmental Policy and Compliance (OEPC),* 1849 C St. N.W., MS 2629, 20240; (202) 208-3891. Stephen G. Tyron, Director.
Web, www.doi.gov/oepc

Provides leadership in conservation stewardship and the sustainable development and use of Department-managed resources for the benefit of the public. We form and foster partnerships to enhance resource use and protection, as well as to expand public access to safe and clean lands under the Department's jurisdiction. Ensures compliance with the National Environmental Policy Act (NEPA), regulations, and reporting requirements; manages funding for long-term cleanup of hazardous materials; oversees Interior Dept.'s protection and recovery activities for natural and cultural resources and historic properties during emergency response efforts.

ENVIRONMENTAL RESOURCES IN CONGRESS

For a complete listing of congressional committees, including their full contact information, leadership, membership, and jurisdictions, please refer to the Appendix on pages 840–963.

HOUSE:

House Agriculture Committee, (202) 225-2171.
Web, agriculture.house.gov
  Subcommittee on Biotechnology, Horticulture, and Research, (202) 225-2171.
  Subcommittee on Conservation and Forestry, (202) 225-2171.
  Subcommittee on Livestock and Foreign Agriculture, (202) 225-2171.
House Appropriations Committee, (202) 225-2771.
Web, appropriations.house.gov
  Subcommittee on Agriculture, Rural Development, Food and Drug Administration, and Related Agencies, (202) 225-2638.
  Subcommittee on Commerce, Justice, Science, and Related Agencies, (202) 225-3351.
  Subcommittee on Energy and Water Development, and Related Agencies, (202) 225-3421.
  Subcommittee on Interior, Environment, and Related Agencies, (202) 225-3081.
House Energy and Commerce Committee, (202) 225-2927.
Web, energycommerce.house.gov
  Subcommittee on Environment and Climate Change, (202) 225-2927.
House Natural Resources Committee, (202) 225-6065.
Web, naturalresources.house.gov
  Subcommittee on Indigenous Peoples of the United States, (202) 226-9725.

Subcommittee on Energy and Mineral Resources, (202) 225-9297.
Subcommittee on National Parks, Forests, and Public Lands, (202) 226-7736.
Subcommittee on Oversight and Investigations, (202) 225-7107.
Subcommittee on Water, Oceans, and Wildlife, (202) 225-8331.
House Oversight and Reform Committee, (202) 225-5051.
Web, oversight.house.gov
  Subcommittee on Environment, (202) 225-5051.
House Science, Space, and Technology Committee, (202) 225-6375.
Web, science.house.gov
  Subcommittee on Environment, (202) 225-6375.
  Subcommittee on Research and Technology, (202) 225-6375.
House Select Committee on the Climate Crisis, (202) 225-1106.
Web, climatecrisis.house.gov
House Small Business Committee, (202) 225-4038.
Web, smallbusiness.house.gov
House Transportation and Infrastructure Committee, (202) 225-4472.
Web, transportation.house.gov
  Subcommittee on Coast Guard and Maritime Transportation, (202) 226-3552.
  Subcommittee on Railroads, Pipelines, and Hazardous Materials, (202) 226-0727.
  Subcommittee on Water Resources and Environment, (202) 225-4360.

Interior Dept. (DOI), *Policy Analysis (PPA), 1849 C St. N.W., MS 3530, 20240; (202) 208-5978. Fax, (202) 208-4867. Jacob Malcom, Director.*
Web, www.doi.gov/ppa

Provides cross-cutting policy planning and analysis to support decision making and policies across the Department; makes recommendations and develops policy options for resolving natural resource problems.

Maritime Administration (MARAD) *(Transportation Dept.), Environment, West Bldg., 1200 New Jersey Ave. S.E., W28-342, 20590; (202) 366-1931. Michael Carter, Associate Administrator.*
Web, www.maritime.dot.gov/ports/office-environment/office-environment

Focuses on environmental stewardship, maritime safety, and maritime security; maritime research and development; and maritime international and domestic rules,

regulations, and standards. Provides environmental support for America's Marine Highway Program and ensures compliance with the National Environmental Policy Act. Advises Maritime Administrator on domestic and international environmental policies that affect maritime transportation.

National Institute of Environmental Health Sciences (NIEHS) *(National Institutes of Health), Washington Office, 31 Center Dr., #B1C02, MS 2256, Bethesda, MD 20892-2256; (301) 496-3511. Fax, (301) 469-0563. Richard (Rick) Waychik, Director; April Bennett, Legislative Liaison.*
General email, webcenter@niehs.nih.gov
Web, www.niehs.nih.gov, Twitter, @NIEHS and Facebook, www.facebook.com/NIH.NIEHS

Conducts and supports research on the human effects of various environmental exposures, expanding the

SENATE:

Senate Agriculture, Nutrition, and Forestry Committee, (202) 224-2035.
Web, agriculture.senate.gov
  Subcommittee on Conservation, Climate, Forestry, and Natural Resources, (202) 224-2035.
  Subcommittee on Livestock, Dairy, Poultry, Local Food Systems, and Food Safety, (202) 224-2035.
  Subcommittee on Rural Development and Energy, (202) 224-2035.

Senate Appropriations Committee, (202) 224-7363.
Web, appropriations.senate.gov
  Subcommittee on Agriculture, Rural Development, Food and Drug Administration, and Related Agencies, (202) 224-7363.
  Subcommittee on Commerce, Justice, Science, and Related Agencies, (202) 224-7363.
  Subcommittee on Energy and Water Development, (202) 224-7363.
  Subcommittee on Interior, Environment, and Related Agencies, (202) 224-7363.

Senate Commerce, Science, and Transportation Committee, (202) 224-0411.
Web, commerce.senate.gov
  Subcommittee on Oceans, Fisheries, Climate Change, and Manufacturing, (202) 224-0411.

Senate Energy and Natural Resources Committee, (202) 224-4971.
Web, energy.senate.gov
  Subcommittee on Energy, (202) 224-4971.
  Subcommittee on National Parks, (202) 224-4971.

  Subcommittee on Public Lands, Forests, and Mining, (202) 224-4971.
  Subcommittee on Water and Power, (202) 224-4971.

Senate Environment and Public Works Committee, (202) 224-8832.
Web, epw.senate.gov
  Subcommittee on Clean Air, Climate, and Nuclear Safety, (202) 224-8832.
  Subcommittee on Fisheries, Water, and Wildlife, (202) 224-8832.
  Subcommittee on Chemical Safety, Waste Management, Environmental Justice, and Regulatory Oversight, (202) 224-8832.
  Subcommittee on Transportation and Infrastructure, (202) 224-8832.

Senate Finance Committee, (202) 224-4515.
Web, finance.senate.gov
  Subcommittee on Energy, Natural Resources, and Infrastructure, (202) 224-4515.

Senate Foreign Relations Committee, (202) 224-4651.
Web, foreign.senate.gov
  Subcommittee on Multilateral International Development, Multilateral Institutions, and International Economic, Energy, and Environmental Policy, (202) 224-4651.

Senate Indian Affairs Committee, (202) 224-2251.
Web, indian.senate.gov

Senate Small Business and Entrepreneurship Committee, (202) 224-5175.
Web, sbc.senate.gov

---

scientific basis for making public health decisions based on the potential toxicity of environmental agents. (Most operations located in Research Triangle, NC.)

National Institute of Standards and Technology (NIST) *(Commerce Dept.), Special Programs Office, 100 Bureau Dr., Gaithersburg, MD 20899;*
General email, spo_inquiries@nist.gov
Web, www.nist.gov/special-programs-office-spo

Fosters collaboration among government, military, academic, professional, and private organizations to respond to critical national needs through science-based standards and technology innovation, including environmental concerns.

National Oceanic and Atmospheric Administration (NOAA) *(Commerce Dept.), Performance, Risk, and Social Science (PRSS), 1315 East-West Hwy., Silver Spring, MD 20910; (301) 713-1632. Fax, (301) 713-0585. Tony Wilhelm, Director, (240) 533-9012.*

General email, PRSS.SocSci@noaa.gov
Web, www.performance.noaa.gov

Oversees NOAA's performance, risk, and social science divisions. Provides business intelligence, quarterly performance updates, risk assessments, social science research, strategic planning, and budget analysis to NOAA leadership.

Office of Management and Budget (OMB) *(Executive Office of the President), Water and Power, 725 17th St. N.W., #8002, 20503; (202) 395-4590. Fax, (202) 395-4817. Kelly Colyar, Chief.*
Web, www.whitehouse.gov/omb

Reviews all plans and budgets related to federal or federally assisted water power and related land resource projects.

►CONGRESS

For a listing of relevant congressional committees and subcommittees, please see pages 284–285 or the Appendix.

Government Accountability Office (GAO), *Natural Resources and Environment (NRE),* 441 G St. N.W., 20548; (202) 512-3841. Frank Rusco, Director. *Web, www.gao.gov/about/careers/our-teams*

Audits, analyzes, and evaluates for Congress federal agriculture, food safety, and energy programs; provides guidance on issues including efforts to ensure a reliable and environmentally sound energy supply, land and water resources management, protection of the environment, hazardous and nuclear wastes threat reduction, food safety, and investment in science.

▶ **NONGOVERNMENTAL**

Aspen Institute, 2300 N St. N.W., #700, 20037; (202) 736-5800. Fax, (202) 467-0790. Daniel R. Porterfield, President. Press, (202) 736-3849. *General email, info@aspeninstitute.org*

Web, www.aspeninstitute.org and Twitter, @AspenInstitute

Educational and policy studies organization. Promotes consideration of the public good in a wide variety of policy areas, including energy and the environment. Working with international partners, offers educational seminars, nonpartisan policy forums, public conferences and events, and leadership development initiatives.

Earth Share, 1717 K St. N.W, #900, 20006; (240) 333-0300. Fax, (240) 333-0301. Brad Leibov, Chief Executive Officer. Toll-free, (800) 875-3863. *General email, info@earthshare.org*

Web, www.earthshare.org and Twitter, @EarthShare

Federation of environmental and conservation organizations. Works with government and private payroll contribution programs to solicit contributions to member organizations for environmental research, education, and community programs. Provides information on establishing environmental giving options in the workplace.

EarthEcho International, 2101 L St. N.W., #800, 20037; (202) 350-3190. Fax, (202) 857-3977. Philippe Cousteau, President. Press, (202) 870-1818. *General email, info@earthecho.org*

Web, www.earthecho.org, Twitter, @EarthEcho and Facebook, www.facebook.com/earthecho

Education resource center that helps students identify environmental issues in their communities and take action to solve them. Holds expeditions to South Florida to investigate the impact of human activity on its natural ecosystems. Provides teachers with learning materials to engage students with real-world data. Specializes in dead zones.

Environment America, *Federal Advocacy Office,* 600 Pennsylvania Ave. S.E., #400, 20003; (202) 683-1250. Fax, (202) 543-6489. Lisa B. Moury, Executive Director. *Web, www.environmentamerica.org and Twitter, @EnvAm*

Coordinates grassroots efforts to advance environmental and consumer protection laws; conducts research on environmental issues, including global warming, clean energy, preservation and conservation, clean water and air, and toxic pollution; compiles reports and disseminates information on such issues; drafts and monitors environmental laws; testifies on behalf of proposed environmental legislation. (Headquarters in Boston, Mass.)

Environmental and Energy Study Institute (EESI), 1020 19th St. N.W., #650, 20036-6101; (202) 628-1400. Fax, (202) 204-5244. Daniel Bresette, Executive Director, (202) 662-1881. *General email, info@eesi.org*

Web, www.eesi.org, Twitter, @eesionline and Facebook, www.facebook.com/eesionline

Nonpartisan policy education and analysis group established by members of Congress to foster informed debate on environmental and energy issues. Interests include policies for sustainable development, energy, sustainable bioenergy, climate change, agriculture, transportation, and fiscal policy reform.

Environmental Council of the States, 1250 H St. N.W., #850, 20005; (202) 266-4920. Fax, (202) 266-4937. Ben Grumbles, President. *General email, ecos@ecos.org*

Web, www.ecos.org, Twitter, @ECOStates and Facebook, www.facebook.com/ECOStates

Works to improve the environment by providing for the exchange of ideas and experiences among states and territories; fosters cooperation and coordination among environmental management professionals.

Environmental Defense Fund, *Washington Office,* 1875 Connecticut Ave. N.W., #600, 20009-5728; (202) 387-3500. Fax, (202) 234-6049. Fred Krupp, President; Carol Andress, Associate Vice President, in Washington, DC. Information, (800) 684-3322. *Web, www.edf.org/offices/washington-dc, Twitter, @EnvDefenseFund and Facebook, www.facebook.com/ EnvDefenseFund*

Citizen interest group staffed by lawyers, economists, and scientists. Takes legal action on environmental issues; provides information on pollution prevention, environmental health, wetlands, toxic substances, acid rain, tropical rain forests, and litigation of water pollution standards. (Headquarters in New York.)

Environmental Law Institute, 1730 M St. N.W., #700, 20036; (202) 939-3800. Fax, (202) 939-3868. Jordan Diamond, President. *Web, www.eli.org, Twitter, @eliorg and Facebook, www .facebook.com/EnvironmentalLawInstitute*

Conducts policy studies on the environment and sustainability. Publishes materials on environmental issues, sponsors education and training courses and conferences on environmental law, issues policy recommendations, and provides technical assistance in the United States and abroad.

Environmental Working Group, 1250 Eye St. N.W., #100, 20005; (202) 667-6982. Fax, (202) 232-2592. Kenneth A. Cook, President.

Environmental Protection Agency

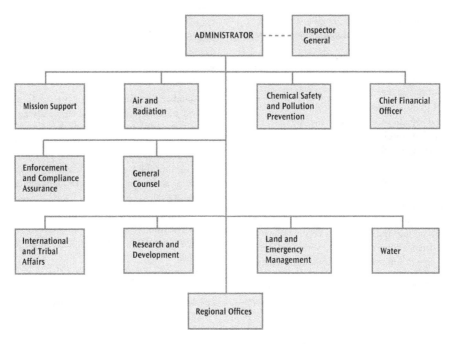

- - - - - Indicates an advisory relationship

Web, www.ewg.org, Twitter, @ewg and Facebook, www .facebook.com/ewg.org

Research and advocacy group that studies and publishes reports on a wide range of agricultural and environmental issues, including farm subsidies and industrial pollution. Monitors legislation and regulations.

Friends of the Earth (FOE), *1101 15th St. N.W., 11th Floor, 20005; (202) 783-7400. Fax, (202) 783-0444. Erich Pica, President, (202) 222-0714. Press, (202) 222-0746.*
Web, www.foe.org, Twitter, @foe_us, Facebook, www .facebook.com/foe.us and YouTube, www.youtube.com/c/ FriendsoftheEarthInt

Environmental advocacy group. Interests include climate and energy, oceans and water, food and emerging technology, and economic drivers of environmental degradation. Specializes in federal budget and tax issues related to the environment, sustainable food systems, corporate power, and natural resources.

Global Council for Science and the Environment, *1776 Eye St. N.W., #750, 20006; (202) 596-3428. Michelle Wyman, Executive Director. General email, gcse@ncseglobal.org*
Web, www.gcseglobal.org, Twitter, @GCSEglobal and Facebook, www.facebook.com/gcseglobal

Membership: coordinates programs that bring together individuals, institutions, and communities to discuss environmental education, research, and public policy decisions affecting the environment.

Green America, *1612 K St. N.W., #1000, 20006; (202) 872-5307. Fax, (202) 331-8166. Alisa Gravitz, President. Press, (202) 872-5310. Toll-free, (800) 584-7336. General email, info@greenamerica.org*
Web, www.greenamerica.org, Twitter, @greenamerica and Facebook, www.facebook.com/greenamerica

Educates consumers and businesses about social and environmental responsibility. Publishes *National Green Pages*, a directory of environmentally and socially responsible businesses, and a financial planning guide for investment.

GreenLatinos, *P.O. Box 60217, 20039; (202) 230-2070. Mark Magaña, President. General email, advocates@greenlatinos.org*
Web, www.greenlatinos.org, Twitter, @GreenLatinos and Facebook, www.facebook.com/GreenLatinos

Provides a platform for Latino leaders to convene and address national, regional, and local environmental, natural resource, and conservation issues affecting Latinos in the United States.

League of Conservation Voters (LCV), *740 15th St. N.W., 7th Floor, 20005; (202) 785-8683. Fax, (202) 835-0491. Gene Karpinski, President.*
Web, www.lcv.org, Twitter, @LCVoters, Facebook, www.facebook.com/LCVoters and General email, feedback@lcv.org

Supports the environmental movement by advocacy for sound environmental policies and helping elect environmentally concerned candidates to public office. Publishes the National Environmental Scorecard and Presidential Report Card.

National Academies of Sciences, Engineering, and Medicine (NASEM), Energy and Environmental Systems Board, Keck Center, 500 5th St. N.W., #W917, 20001; (202) 334-3344. K. John Holmes, Director; Jared L. Cohen, Chair.
Web, www.nationalacademies.org/bees/board-on-energy-and-environmental-systems

Conducts studies in order to advise the federal government and the private sector about issues in energy and environmental technology, and related public policy. Focuses on energy supply and demand technologies and systems, including resource extraction through mining and drilling, energy conversion, distribution and delivery, and efficiency of use; environmental consequences of energy-related activities; environmental systems and controls in areas related to fuel production, energy conversion, transmission, and use; and other issues relating to national security and defense. Sponsors studies, workshops, symposia, and a variety of information-dissemination activities.

National Academies of Sciences, Engineering, and Medicine (NASEM), Environmental Change and Society Board, Keck Center, 500 5th St. N.W., 20001; (202) 334-2121. Fax, (202) 334-3751. Thomas Thorton, Director; Kristie Lee Ebi, Chair.
General email, BECS@nas.edu

Web, www.nationalacademies.org/becs/board-on-environmental-change-and-society

Conducts research on the interactions between human activities and the environment, including climate variation, resource use and decision making, adaptation to change, and risk and resilience.

National Governors Assn. (NGA), Natural Resources Committee, 444 N. Capitol St. N.W., #267, 20001-1512; (202) 624-5300. Alex Whitaker, Legislative Director.
General email, info@nga.org

Web, www.nga.org/advocacy/nga-committees/nrc

Monitors legislation and regulations and makes recommendations on agriculture, energy, environment, and natural resource issues to ensure governors' views and priorities are represented in federal policies and regulations.

Natural Resources Defense Council, Washington Office, 1152 15th St. N.W., #300, 20005; (202) 289-6868. Manish Bapna, President, (202) 513-6242; Ed Yoon, Chief of Policy Advocacy, (202) 289-2387.
General email, nrdcinfo@nrdc.org

Web, www.nrdc.org, Twitter, @NRDC, Facebook, www.facebook.com/nrdc.org and YouTube, www.youtube.com/user/NRDCflix

Environmental organization staffed by lawyers and scientists who conduct litigation and research. Interests include air, water, land use, forests, toxic materials, natural resources management and conservation, preservation of endangered plant species, and ozone pollution. Website has a Spanish-language link. (Headquarters in New York.)

Nature Conservancy, 4245 N. Fairfax Dr., #100, Arlington, VA 22203-1606; (703) 841-5300. Jennifer Morris, Chief Executive Officer; Darci Vetter, Global Head of Policy and Government Relations. Membership Toll-free, (800) 628-6860.
General email, comment@tnc.org

Web, www.nature.org, Twitter, @nature_org and Facebook, www.facebook.com/thenatureconservancy

Membership: maintains an international system of natural sanctuaries; conserves the lands and waters, to protect endangered species and habitats. Collaborates with other conservation organizations, country and local governments, corporations, indigenous peoples and communities, and individuals such as fishermen, ranchers, and farmers to create management plans for natural areas.

Pew Environment Group, 901 E St. N.W., 20004-2008; (202) 552-2000. Fax, (202) 552-2299. Susan K. Urahn, President.
General email, info@pewtrusts.org

Web, www.pewenvironment.org, Twitter, @pewtrusts and Facebook, www.facebook.com/pewcharitabletrusts

Identifies and publicizes environmental issues at the international, national, and local levels, with the goal of strengthening environmental policies and practices. Interests include climate change, clean air, endangered species, global warming, hazardous chemicals, national park pollution, and campaign finance reform. Opposes efforts to weaken environmental laws. Monitors legislation and regulations.

Pinchot Institute for Conservation, 1400 16th St. N.W., #350, 20036; (202) 797-6580. Fax, (202) 797-6583. William C. (Will) Price, President.
Web, www.pinchot.org and Twitter, @pinchotlegacy

Seeks to advance forest conservation and sustainable natural resources management nationally through research and analysis, education and technical assistance, and development of conservation leaders.

Public Employees for Environmental Responsibility (PEER), 962 Wayne Ave., #610, Silver Spring, MD 20910-4453; (202) 265-7337. Fax, (202) 265-4192. Tim Whitehouse, Executive Director.
General email, info@peer.org

Web, www.peer.org, Twitter, @PEERorg and Facebook, www.facebook.com/PEER.org

Service organization for public citizens and employees of federal, state, and local resource management agencies. Defends legal rights of public employees who speak out concerning natural resource management and environmental protection issues. Monitors enforcement of environmental protection laws.

Resources for the Future, 1616 P St. N.W., #600, 20036-1400; (202) 328-5000. Fax, (202) 939-3460. Richard G. Newell, President. Press, (202) 328-5114.

General email, info@rff.org

Web, www.rff.org, Twitter, @rff, Facebook, www.facebook
.com/ResourcesfortheFuture and Podcast, www
.resourcesmag.org/resources-radio

Engages in research and education on environmental
and natural resource issues, including forestry, multiple use
of public lands, costs and benefits of pollution control,
endangered species, environmental risk management,
energy and national security, and climate resources.
Interests include hazardous waste, the Superfund, and
biodiversity. Publishes research findings; offers academic
fellowships. Sponsors a podcast and a blog featuring interviews with experts on important topics.

Sierra Club, Legislative Office, 50 F St. N.W., 8th Floor,
20001; (202) 547-1141. Fax, (202) 547-6009. Dan Chu,
Executive Director (Acting).
General email, information@sierraclub.org

Web, www.sierraclub.org and Twitter, @SierraClub

Citizens' interest group that promotes protection of
natural resources. Interests include the Clean Air Act; the
Arctic National Wildlife Refuge; protection of national forests, parks, and wilderness; toxins; global warming; promotion of responsible international trade; and international
development lending reform. Monitors legislation and
regulations. (Headquarters in Oakland, Calif.)

**U.S. Chamber of Commerce, Environment, Technology,
and Regulatory Affairs,** 1615 H St. N.W., 20062-2000;
(202) 659-6000. Chad S. Whiteman, Vice President of
Environment and Regulatory Affairs.
General email, environment@uschamber.com

Web, www.uschamber.com, Twitter, @Regulations and
Facebook, www.facebook.com/uschamber

Monitors operations of federal departments and agencies responsible for environmental programs, policies, regulatory issues, and food safety. Analyzes and evaluates
legislation and regulations that affect the environment.

Global Warming and Climate Change

▶ **AGENCIES**

**Bureau of Oceans and International Environmental
and Scientific Affairs (OES) (State Dept.), Global Change
(EGC),** 2201 C St. N.W., #2480, 20520; (202) 647-3984.
Trigg Talley, Director.
General email, ClimateComms@State.gov

Web, www.state.gov/e/oes

Addresses climate change challenges through international policy, agreements, and partnerships.

Economic Research Service (ERS) (Agriculture Dept.),
355 E St. S.W., 20024-3221 (mailing address: 1400
Independence Ave. S.W., MS 1800, Washington, DC
20250-0002); (202) 694-5000. Fax, (202) 245-5467.
Spiro Stefanou, Administrator. Public Affairs, (202)
694-5139.

General email, service@ers.usda.gov

Web, www.ers.usda.gov and Twitter, @USDA_ERS

Provides research and economic information to the
USDA. Interests include economic and policy issues
involving food, farm practices and management, natural
resources, and rural development. Website offers a briefing
room on global climate change and other environmental
topics.

**Environmental Protection Agency (EPA), Air and
Radiation (OAR), Atmospheric Programs, Climate
Change Division,** 1200 Pennsylvania Ave. N.W., #5426,
MC 6207A, 20460; (202) 343-9876. Fax, (202) 343-2342.
Paul M. Gunning, Director.
General email, hargrove.anne@epa.gov

Web, www.epa.gov/aboutepa/about-office-air-and-
radiation-oar#oap

Works to address global climate change and the associated risks to human health and the environment. Analyzes
greenhouse gas emissions and reduction options. Educates
the public on climate change and provides climate analysis
and strategies to policymakers, experts, and U.S. climate
negotiators.

**National Oceanic and Atmospheric Administration
(NOAA) (Commerce Dept.), Climate Program Office
(CPO),** Silver Spring Metro Center 3, 1315 East-West
Hwy., #100, Silver Spring, MD 20910; (301) 734-1263.
Fax, (301) 713-0517. R. Wayne Higgins, Director, (301)
734-1263.
General email, cpo.webmaster@noaa.gov

Web, www.cpo.noaa.gov

Manages NOAA-funded research programs that focus
on climate science and assessments on a regional, national,
and international scale.

**National Oceanic and Atmospheric Administration
(NOAA) (Commerce Dept.), Ocean Acidification Program
(OAP),** 1315 East-West Hwy., #10356, Silver Spring, MD
20910; (301) 734-1075. Elizabeth (Libby) Jewett, Director.
General email, noaa.oceanacidification@noaa.gov

Web, https://oceanacidification.noaa.gov and Twitter,
@OA_NOAA

Monitors changes in ocean chemistry due to the continued acidification of the oceans and Great Lakes, and
assesses the socioeconomic impacts. Maintains relationships with scientists, resource managers, stakeholders,
policymakers, and the public to implement adaptation
strategies and monitor the biological responses of ecologically and economically important species. Operates from
NOAA's Office of Oceanic and Atmospheric Research.

**Office of Science (Energy Dept.), Biological and
Environmental Research (BER), Climate and
Environmental Sciences Division (CESD),** 19901
Germantown Rd., #SC23.1, Germantown, MD 20874-1290
(mailing address: Germantown Bldg., 1000 Independence
Ave. S.W., #SC23.1, Washington, DC 20585); (301) 903-
4775. Fax, (301) 303-8519. Gerald Geernaert, Director.

Web, www.energy.gov/science/ber/biological-and-environmental-research

Supports research on atmospheric systems, terrestrial ecosystems, and subsurface biogeochemistry as well as Earth system modeling and regional and global climate change modeling to improve predictive understanding of Earth's climate and environmental systems in order to inform development of sustainable solutions to energy challenges.

U.S. Geological Survey (USGS) *(Interior Dept.), Earth Resources Observation and Science (EROS) Center,* *12201 Sunrise Valley Dr., MS 516, Reston, VA 20192; (703) 648-5320. (605) 594-6151. Christopher Reich, Program Coordinator (Acting), (703) 648-0002; Pete Doucette, Center Director, (605) 594-2586.*
Web, www.usgs.gov/centers/eros

Studies land change and compiles maps and data used by researchers, resource managers and policymakers. Operates the Landsat satellite program with NASA, maintaining the largest civilian collection of Earth images in existence. (Center located in Garretson, S.D.)

▶CONGRESS

For a listing of relevant congressional committees and subcommittees, please see pages 284–285 or the Appendix.

▶NONGOVERNMENTAL

Antarctic and Southern Ocean Coalition, *1320 19th St. N.W., 5th Floor, 20036; (202) 234-2480. Claire Christian, Executive Director.*
General email, info@asoc.org
Web, www.asoc.org and Twitter, @AntarcticaSouth

Promotes research on the impact of climate change on the Antarctic region.

The Brookings Institution, *Climate and Energy Economics Project, 1775 Massachusetts Ave. N.W., 20036; (202) 797-6000. Peter J. Wilcoxen, Senior Fellow.*
Web, www.brookings.edu/project/climate-and-energy-economics-project and Twitter, @BrookingsEcon

Promotes environmentally and economically efficient approaches to mitigating human impacts on climate change, including cap-and-trade.

The Brookings Institution, *Economic Studies, 1775 Massachusetts Ave. N.W., 20036-2188; (202) 797-6414. (202) 540-7721. Stephanie Aaronson, Vice President.*
General email, escomment@brookings.edu
Web, www.brookings.edu/economics and Twitter, @BrookingsEcon

Promotes environmentally sound and economically efficient climate policy, with a focus on the economics of domestic cap-and-trade approaches and global agreement.

Center for Climate and Energy Solutions, *3100 Clarendon Blvd., #800, Arlington, VA 22201; (703) 516-4146. Nat Keohane, President.*

Web, www.c2es.org, Twitter, @C2ES_org, Facebook, www.facebook.com/C2ES.org and Email, press@c2es.org

Independent organization that issues information and promotes discussion by policymakers on the science, economics, and policy of climate change. Library available online.

Climate Institute, *1225 New York Ave. N.W., #800, 20005; (202) 552-0163. Nasir Khattak, Chief Operating Officer.*
General email, info@climate.org
Web, http://climate.org

Educates the public and policymakers on climate change, the greenhouse effect, global warming, and the depletion of the ozone layer. Assesses climate change risks and develops strategies on mitigating climate change in developing countries and in North America.

The Climate Reality Project, *555 11th St. N.W., #601, 20004; (202) 567-6800. Ken Berlin, President.*
General email, info@climatereality.com
Web, www.climaterealityproject.org, Twitter, @ClimateReality, Facebook, www.facebook.com/ClimateReality, YouTube, www.youtube.com/user/ClimateReality and Press, press@climatereality.com

Aims to reduce carbon emissions, supports taxing oil and coal companies that emit large amounts of carbon, and educates the public on climate change and its relation to carbon pollution.

CO2 Coalition, *1621 N. Kent St., #603, Arlington, VA 22209; (571) 970-3180. Gregory Wrightstone, Executive Director.*
General email, info@co2coalition.org
Web, http://co2coalition.org and Twitter, @co2coalition

Educates leaders, policymakers, and the public about climate change and impact of carbon dioxide reduction.

National Academies of Sciences, Engineering, and Medicine (NASEM), *Atmospheric Sciences and Climate Board, Keck Center, 500 5th St. N.W., #602, 20001; (202) 413-2751. Amanda Staudt, Director; Mary Glackin, Chair.*
General email, basc@nas.edu
Web, www.nationalacademies.org/basc/board-on-atmospheric-sciences-and-climate

Supports research on climate change, air pollution, and severe weather in order to address environmental policies, human health, emergency management, energy choices, manufacturing decisions, construction codes, and agricultural methods.

Physicians for Social Responsibility (PSR), *1111 14th St. N.W., #700, 20005 (mailing address: P.O. Box 30159, Bethesda, MD 20824); (202) 667-4260. Fax, (202) 667-4201. Jeff Carter, JD, Executive Director, (202) 587-5240.*
General email, psrnatl@psr.org
Web, www.psr.org, Twitter, @psrenvironment and Facebook, www.facebook.com/psrnational

Membership: doctors, nurses, health scientists, and concerned citizens. Works to slow, stop, and reverse global warming and degradation of the environment. Conducts public education programs, monitors policy, and serves as a liaison with other concerned groups.

Resources for the Future, *1616 P St. N.W., #600, 20036-1400; (202) 328-5000. Fax, (202) 939-3460.*
Richard G. Newell, President. Press, (202) 328-5114.
General email, info@rff.org
Web, www.rff.org, Twitter, @rff, Facebook, www.facebook.com/ResourcesfortheFuture and Podcast, www.resourcesmag.org/resources-radio

Research organization that conducts independent studies on economic and policy aspects of energy, environment, conservation, and natural resource management issues worldwide. Interests include climate change, energy, natural resource issues in developing countries, and public health.

Science and Environmental Policy Project (SEPP), *P.O. Box 1126, Springfield, VA 22151; (703) 978-6025.*
Ken Haapala, President.
General email, info@sepp.org
Web, www.sepp.org

Works to clarify environmental problems and provide effective, economical solutions. Encourages use of scientific knowledge when making health or environmental public policy decisions. Disseminates research and policy papers by skeptics of global warming.

Union of Concerned Scientists, *Climate and Energy Program, 1825 K St. N.W., 20006-1232; (202) 223-6133.*
Julie Ringer, Deputy Director, Climate and Energy Program.
General email, ucs@ucsusa.org
Web, www.ucsusa.org/about/programs/climate-energy, Twitter, @ucsusa, Facebook, www.facebook.com/unionofconcernedscientists and YouTube, www.youtube.com/user/ConcernedScientists

Promotes clean energy and global warming emissions reduction. Advocates international policy responses to the threat of global climate change.

Wallace Genetic Foundation, *4910 Massachusetts Ave. N.W., #221, 20016; (202) 966-2932. Fax, (202) 966-3370.*
Michaela Oldfield, Executive Director.
General email, wgfdn@wallacegenetic.org
Web, www.wallacegenetic.org

Supports national and international nonprofits in the areas of sustainable agriculture, agricultural research, preservation of farmland, reduction of environmental toxins, conservation, biodiversity protection, and global climate issues.

International Issues

▶**AGENCIES**

Bureau of Oceans and International Environmental and Scientific Affairs (OES) *(State Dept.), 2201 C St. N.W., #3880 and #7256, 20520-7818; (202) 647-7575.*
Monica Medina, Assistant Secretary, (202) 647-1554.

Web, www.state.gov/e/oes, Twitter, @SciDiplomacyUSA, Facebook, www.facebook.com/ScienceDiplomacyUSA and YouTube, www.youtube.com/channel/rCumiP05SKp5qlhiZbXBJEiw?view_as=subscriber

Concerned with foreign policy as it affects natural resources and the environment, human health, the global climate, energy production, and oceans and fisheries.

Bureau of Oceans and International Environmental and Scientific Affairs (OES) *(State Dept.), Conservation and Water (ECW), 2201 C St. N.W., #2657, 20520; (202) 647-4683. Christine Dawson, Director.*
Web, www.state.gov/e/oes

Represents the United States in international affairs relating to ecology and conservation issues. Interests include wildlife, tropical forests, coral reefs, and biological diversity.

Bureau of Oceans and International Environmental and Scientific Affairs (OES) *(State Dept.), Environmental Quality and Transboundary Issues (EQT), 2201 C St. N.W., #2726, 20520; (202) 647-2958. Timothy L. Smith, Director, (202) 647-4658.*
Web, www.state.gov/e/oes

Advances U.S. interests internationally regarding multilateral environmental organizations, chemical and hazardous waste and other pollutants, and bilateral and regional environmental policies.

Bureau of Oceans and International Environmental and Scientific Affairs (OES) *(State Dept.), Policy and Public Outreach (PPO), 2201 C St. N.W., #2880, 20520; (202) 647-2958. Timothy L. Smith, Director, (202) 647-4658.*
Web, www.state.gov/about-us-office-of-policy-and-public-outreach

Integrates oceans, environment, polar, science, technology, and health issues into U.S. foreign policy, and works to address these issues in the media, NGOs, the private sector, and Congress.

Environmental Protection Agency (EPA), *International and Tribal Affairs (OITA), 1200 Pennsylvania Ave. N.W., #31106, MC 2610R, 20460; (202) 564-6600. Fax, (202) 565-2407. Jane Nishida, Assistant Administrator.*
General email, oita.contactus@epa.gov
Web, www.epa.gov/aboutepa/about-office-international-and-tribal-affairs-oita

Coordinates the agency's work on international environmental issues and programs, including management of bilateral agreements and participation in multilateral organizations and negotiations. Works to strengthen public health and environmental programs on tribal lands, emphasizing helping tribes administer their own environment programs.

Forest Service *(Agriculture Dept.), International Programs, 1 Thomas Circle N.W., #400, 20005; (202) 644-4600. Fax, (202) 644-4603. Valdis E. Mezainis, Director, (202) 644-4621. Executive Assistant, (202) 644-4550.*
Web, www.fs.fed.us/global

Responsible for the Forest Service's involvement in international forest conservation efforts. Analyzes international resource issues; promotes information exchange; provides planning and technical assistance. Interested in sustainable forest management, covering illegal logging, climate change, and migratory species.

Interior Dept. (DOI), *International Affairs (OIA), 1849 C St. N.W., MS 3559, 20240; Karen Senhadji, Director, (202) 208-5479.*
Web, www.doi.gov/intl

Focuses on international conservation and management of wildlife and natural resources, protection of cultural resources, cooperation on indigenous affairs, and monitoring of natural hazards, including volcanoes and earthquakes.

International Trade Administration (ITA) *(Commerce Dept.), Industry and Analysis (I&A), Manufacturing (OM), Energy and Environmental Industries (OEEI), 1400 Constitution Ave. N.W., Room 28018, 20230 (mailing address: 1401 Constitution Ave. N.W., MD 4053, Washington, DC 20230); (202) 482-5159. Adam O'Malley, Director.*
Web, www.trade.gov/about-us/office-energy-and-environmental-industries

Works to facilitate and increase export of U.S. environmental technologies, including goods and services. Conducts market analysis, business counseling, and trade promotion.

▶**CONGRESS**

For a listing of relevant congressional committees and subcommittees, please see pages 284–285 or the Appendix.

▶**INTERNATIONAL ORGANIZATIONS**

International Conservation Caucus Foundation (ICCF), *25786 Georgetown Station, 20027; (202) 471-4222. John B. Gantt, President.*
General email, hq@iccfoundation.us
Web, www.iccfoundation.us, Twitter, @TheICCFGroup, Facebook, www.facebook.com/theiccfgroup and YouTube, www.youtube.com/user/ICCFoundation

Seeks to improve U.S. efforts in international conservation. Coordinates between policymakers and conservationists to address ecosystem issues. Holds the International Conservation Gala and congressional briefing series. Administers awards to activists. Manages the Ocean Caucus Foundation to protect sea life.

International Joint Commission, *United States and Canada, U.S. Section, 1717 H St. N.W., #835, 20440; (202) 736-9000. Fax, (202) 632-2006. Susan Daniel, Secretary (Acting), (202) 736-9011.*
Web, https://ijc.org/en and Twitter, @IJCSharedWaters

Prevents and resolves disputes between the United States and Canada on transboundary water and air resources. Investigates issues upon request of the governments of the United States and Canada. Reviews applications for water resource projects. (Canadian section in Ottawa; Great Lakes regional office in Windsor, Ontario.)

International Union for the Conservation of Nature, *Washington Office, 1630 Connecticut Ave. N.W., #300, 20009; (202) 387-4826. Fax, (202) 387-4823. Tracy Farrell, Director.*
General email, deborah.good@iucn.org
Web, www.iucn.org/usa

Membership: world governments, their environmental agencies, and nongovernmental organizations. Studies conservation issues from local to global levels. Helps provide links for members and partners around the world to key U.S.-based institutions, such as the U.S. Government and its agencies, the World Bank, the Global Environment Facility, the Inter-American Development Bank, the United Nations, and other organizations. Interests include protected areas, forests, oceans, polar regions, biodiversity, species survival, environmental law, sustainable use of resources, and the impact of trade on the environment. Hosts a number of IUCN staff, programs, and initiatives concerned with global conservation and sustainable development issues. (Headquarters in Gland, Switzerland.)

Organization of American States (OAS), *Executive Secretariat for Integral Development (SEDI), Dept. of Sustainable Development (DSD), 1889 F St. N.W., #710, 20006; (202) 458-3567. Fax, (202) 458-3560. Cletus Springer, Director, ext. 9084.*
General email, sustainable_dev@oas.org
Web, www.oas.org/en/sedi/dsd

Promotes integrated and sustainable development of natural resources in OAS Member States through the design and implementation of policies, programs, and partnerships. Interests include integrated management of shared water resources, hazard risk management, sustainable cities, biodiversity protection, sustainable energy, and environmental law.

▶**NONGOVERNMENTAL**

Conservation International, *2011 Crystal Dr., #600, Arlington, VA 22202; (703) 341-2400. Fax, (703) 553-0654. M. Sanjayan, Chief Executive Officer. Toll-free, (800) 429-5660.*
General email, community@conservation.org
Web, www.conservation.org, Twitter, @ConservationOrg, Facebook, www.facebook.com/conservation.intl and YouTube, www.youtube.com/user/ConservationDotOrg

Works to conserve tropical rain forests through economic development; promotes exchange of debt relief for conservation programs that involve local people and organizations. Interests include fresh water, food, biodiversity, climate, health, and cultural services. Provides private groups and governments with information and technical advice on conservation efforts and collaborates with business and government in these efforts; supports conservation data gathering in the Americas, Europe, Africa, Asia, and the Caribbean, as well as the oceans.

Environmental Investigation Agency (EIA), *P.O. Box 53343, 20009; (202) 483-6621. Fax, (202) 986-8626. Alexander (Sascha) von Bismarck, Executive Director. General email, info@eia-global.org*

Web, www.eia-global.org and Twitter, @EIAEnvironment

Works to expose international environmental crime, including illegal trade of wildlife, illegal logging, and sale of ozone-depleting substances. Monitors legislation and regulations. Also maintains an office in London.

Greenpeace USA, *702 H St. N.W., #300, 20001; (202) 462-1177. Fax, (202) 462-4507. Annie Leonard, Co-Executive Director; Ebony Twilley Martin, Co-Executive Director. Toll-free, (800) 722-6995. General email, connect@greenpeace.org*

Web, www.greenpeace.org, Twitter, @greenpeaceusa and Facebook, www.facebook.com/greenpeaceusa

Seeks to expose global environmental problems and to promote solutions through nonviolent direct action, lobbying, and creative communication. Interests include forests, oceans, toxins, global warming, disarmament, and genetic engineering. (International office in Amsterdam, The Netherlands.)

Institute for Policy Studies, *1301 Connecticut Ave. N.W., #600, 20036; (202) 234-9382. Fax, (202) 387-7915. Tope Folarin, Executive Director. General email, info@ips-dc.org*

Web, https://ips-dc.org, Twitter, @IPS_DC and Facebook, www.facebook.com/InstituteforPolicyStudies

Research and educational think tank focused on social justice and security, especially equality, ecological sustainability, and peace. Interests include environmental protection, sustainable energy solutions, the impact of fossil fuels on climate change, and clean air, land, water, and food.

Species Survival Network (SSN), *2100 L St. N.W., 20037; (301) 548-7769. Fax, (202) 318-0891. Will Travers, President. General email, info@ssn.org*

Web, http://ssn.org

Coalition of organizations seeking to enforce the Convention on International Trade in Endangered Species of Wild Fauna and Flora (CITES). Acts as advocate against exploitation, injury, cruel treatment, and possible extinction of native animals and plants caused by global trade. Researches and analyzes policies to educate the public on their potential impact on the environment.

Winrock International, *Washington Office, 2451 Crystal Dr., #700, Arlington, VA 22202; (703) 302-6500. Fax, (703) 302-6512. Rodney Ferguson, President. General email, information@winrock.org*

Web, www.winrock.org and Twitter, @WinrockIntl

Works to sustain natural resources and protect the environment. Matches innovative approaches in agriculture, natural resource management, clean energy, and leadership development with the unique needs of its partners. (Headquarters in Little Rock, Ark.)

World Resources Institute, *10 G St. N.E., #800, 20002; (202) 729-7600. Fax, (202) 280-1314. Ani Dasgupta, President, (202) 729-7913. Press, (202) 235-2272.*

Web, www.wri.org, Twitter, @worldresources and Facebook, www.facebook.com/worldresources

Conducts research on environmental problems and studies the interrelationships of natural resources, economic growth, and human needs. Interests include forestry and land use, renewable energy, fisheries, and sustainable agriculture. Assesses environmental policies of aid agencies.

World Wildlife Fund (WWF), *1250 24th St. N.W., 20037-1193 (mailing address: P.O. Box 97180, Washington, DC 20090-7180); (202) 293-4800. Fax, (202) 293-9211. Carter S. Roberts, President. Press, (202) 495-4102. Toll-free, (800) 960-0993. General email, membership@wwfus.org*

Web, www.worldwildlife.org, Twitter, @World_Wildlife and Facebook, www.facebook.com/WorldWildlifeFund

Conducts scientific research and analyzes policy on environmental and conservation issues, including pollution reduction, land use, forestry and wetlands management, parks, soil conservation, and sustainable development. Supports projects to promote biological diversity and to save endangered species and their habitats, including tropical forests in Latin America, Asia, and Africa. Awards grants and provides technical assistance to local conservation groups.

ANIMALS AND PLANTS

General

▶**AGENCIES**

Animal and Plant Health Inspection Service (APHIS) *(Agriculture Dept.), Investigative and Enforcement Services (IES), 4700 River Rd., #85, Riverdale, MD 20737-1234; (301) 851-2948. Fax, (301) 734-4328. Robert (Rob) Huttenlocker, Director. Web, www.aphis.usda.gov/aphis/ourfocus/business-services/ies*

Provides investigative and enforcement services and leadership, direction, and support for compliance activities within the service.

Animal and Plant Health Inspection Service (APHIS) *(Agriculture Dept.), Plant Protection and Quarantine (PPQ), 1400 Independence Ave. S.W., #302E, 20250; (202) 799-7163. Fax, (202) 690-0472. Osama El-Lissy, Deputy Administrator. Antismuggling hotline, (800) 877-3835. Permits for plant pests, (301) 734-2357. General email, pest.permits@usda.gov*

Web, www.aphis.usda.gov/plant_health

Encourages compliance with regulations that safeguard agriculture and natural resources from the risks associated with the entry, establishment, or spread of animal and plant pests and noxious weeds. Methods include requirements for the import and export of plants and plant products; partnership agreements with industry groups, community organizations, and government entities; and public education and outreach.

National Zoological Park *(Smithsonian Institution),* *3001 Connecticut Ave. N.W., 20008 (mailing address: DEVS, P.O. Box 37012, MS 5516, Washington, DC 20013-7012); (202) 633-4888 (recorded information line). Steven Monfort, Director. Guest services, (202) 633-2614. Membership office, (202) 633-2922. Press, (202) 633-3055. Web, www.nationalzoo.si.edu, Twitter, @NationalZoo, Facebook, www.facebook.com/nationalzoo and YouTube, www.youtube.com/SmithsonianNZP*

Maintains a public zoo. Conducts research on animal behavior, ecology, nutrition, reproductive physiology, pathology, and veterinary medicine; operates an annex near Front Royal, Va., for the propagation and study of endangered species. Houses a unit of the Smithsonian Institution library open to qualified researchers by appointment. Interlibrary loans available.

U.S. Customs and Border Protection *(Homeland Security Dept.), Agricultural Program and Trade Liaison Office, 1300 Pennsylvania Ave. N.W., 20229; (202) 344-1644. Fax, (202) 344-1442. John P. Leonard, Executive Director. Trade Relations, (202) 344-1440. Public Affairs, (877) 227-5511.* *Web, www.cbp.gov/border-security/protecting-agriculture*

Responsible for safeguarding the nation's animal and natural resources from pests and disease through inspections at ports of entry and beyond.

►**CONGRESS**

For a listing of relevant congressional committees and subcommittees, please see pages 284–285 or the Appendix.

►**NONGOVERNMENTAL**

Animal Health Institute, *1325 G St. N.W., #700, 20005-3104; (202) 637-2440. Fax, (202) 393-1667. Alexander S. Mathews, President.* *Web, www.ahi.org and Twitter, @AnimalsHealthy*

Membership: manufacturers of drugs and other products (including vaccines, pesticides, and vitamins) for pets and food-producing animals. Interests include pet health, livestock health, and disease outbreak prevention. Monitors legislation and regulations.

National Academies of Sciences, Engineering, and Medicine (NASEM), *Agriculture and Natural Resources Board, Keck Center, 500 5th St. N.W., #WS632, 20001; (202) 334-2088. Fax, (202) 334-1978. Robin Schoen, Director.* *General email, skwan@nas.edu* *Web, http://dels.nas.edu/banr and Twitter, @NASM_Ag*

Promotes and oversees research on the environmental impact of agriculture and food sustainability, including forestry, fisheries, wildlife, and the use of land, water, and other natural resources.

Animal Rights and Welfare

►**AGENCIES**

Animal and Plant Health Inspection Service (APHIS) *(Agriculture Dept.), Animal Care, 4700 River Rd., #84, Riverdale, MD 20737-1234; (301) 851-3751. Fax, (301) 734-4978. Betty Goldentyre, Deputy Administrator.* *General email, animalcare@usda.gov* *Web, www.aphis.usda.gov/animal_welfare*

Administers laws for the breeding, exhibition, and care of animals raised for sale and research and transported commercially. Enforces the Animal Welfare Act and Horse Protection Act; accepts animal welfare complaints.

Animal and Plant Health Inspection Service (APHIS) *(Agriculture Dept.), Center for Animal Welfare (CAW), 4700 River Rd., #84, Riverdale, MD 20737; (301) 851-3751. Fax, (301) 734-4978. Betty Goldentyer, Deputy Administrator.* *General email, animalcare@aphis.usda.gov* *Web, www.aphis.usda.gov/aphis/ourfocus/animalwelfare/ CAW*

Provides guidance on policy development and analysis, education and outreach, and scientific research related to animal welfare issues, especially in support of the Animal Welfare Act and the Horse Protection Act. (Headquarters in Kansas City, MO.)

National Agricultural Library *(Agriculture Dept.), Animal Welfare Information Center (AWIC), 10301 Baltimore Ave., #118, Beltsville, MD 20705; (301) 504-6212. Kristina Adams, Coordinator, (301) 504-5486.* *General email, awic@usda.gov* *Web, www.nal.usda.gov/awic*

Provides information for improved animal care and use in research, testing, teaching, and exhibition.

National Institutes of Health (NIH) *(Health and Human Services Dept.), Intramural Research (OIR), Animal Care and Use (OACU), Bldg. 31, 9000 Rockville Pike, #B1C37, MS 2252, Bethesda, MD 20892-2252; (301) 496-5424. Fax, (301) 480-8298. Stephen Denny, Director.* *General email, secoacu@nih.gov* *Web, http://oacu.oir.nih.gov*

Provides guidance for the humane care and use of animals in the intramural research program at NIH.

National Institutes of Health (NIH) *(Health and Human Services Dept.), Laboratory Animal Welfare (OLAW), 6700B Rockledge Dr., #2500, MS 6910, Bethesda, MD 20892-7982; (301) 496-7163. Fax, (301) 480-3394. Patricia A. Brown, Director.* *General email, olaw@mail.nih.gov* *Web, https://olaw.nih.gov/home.htm and Twitter, @NIH_ OLAW*

Develops and monitors policy on the humane care and use of animals in research conducted by any public health service supported research, training, and testing.

►CONGRESS

For a listing of relevant congressional committees and sub-committees, please see pages 284–285 or the Appendix.

►NONGOVERNMENTAL

Alley Cat Allies, *7920 Norfolk Ave., #600, Bethesda, MD 20814-2525; (240) 482-1980. Fax, (240) 482-1990. Becky Robinson, President.*
General email, info@alleycat.org
Web, www.alleycat.org, Twitter, @AlleyCatAllies and Facebook, www.facebook.com/AlleyCatAllies

Clearinghouse for information on feral and stray cats. Advocates the trap–neuter–return method to reduce feral cat populations.

American Humane, *1400 16th St. N.W., #360, 20036; (202) 841-6080. Fax, (202) 450-2335. Robin R. Ganzert, Chief Executive Officer. Toll-free, (800) 227-4645.*
General email, info@americanhumane.org
Web, www.americanhumane.org, Twitter, @AmericanHumane and Facebook, www.facebook.com/americanhumane

Promotes the welfare and safety of animals through disaster response, emergency training, and community events. Provides veterans coping with trauma with free service dogs and reunites retired military dogs from overseas with their former handlers. Sponsors programs such as No Animals Were Harmed, Feed the Hungry, and farm and conservation animal welfare certifications.

American Physiological Society, *6120 Executive Blvd., #600, Rockville, MD 20852-4911; (301) 634-7164. Fax, (301) 634-7241. Scott Steen, Executive Director, (301) 634-7118.*
Web, www.the-aps.org, Twitter, @APSPhysiology and Facebook, www.facebook.com/AmericanPhysiological Society

Works to establish standards for the humane care and use of laboratory animals.

Americans for Medical Progress, *444 N. Capitol St. N.W., #417, 20001; (202) 624-8810. Paula Clifford, Executive Director, (202) 624-8812.*
Web, www.amprogress.org and Twitter, @CureDisease

Promotes and protects animal-based medical research. Serves as a media resource by fact-checking claims of animal rights groups. Conducts public education campaigns on the link between animal research and medical advances.

Animal Outlook, *P.O. Box 9773, 20016; (301) 891-2458. Fax, (301) 891-6815. Cheryl Leahy, President.*
General email, info@animaloutlook.org
Web, http://animaloutlook.org and Twitter, @AnimalOutlook

Animal rights organization that focuses primarily on cruelty to animals in agriculture. Promotes vegetarianism.

Animal Welfare Institute, *900 Pennsylvania Ave. S.E., 20003 (mailing address: P.O. Box 3650, Washington, DC 20027); (202) 337-2332. Fax, (202) 446-2131. Nadia Adawi, Executive Director. Press, (202) 337-2128.*
General email, awi@awionline.org
Web, www.awionline.org and Twitter, @AWIOnline

Works to improve conditions for animals in laboratories, on farms, in commerce, in homes, and in the wild. Promotes efforts to end horse slaughter. Monitors legislation and regulations. (Merged with the Society for Animal Protective Legislation.)

Farm Animal Rights Movement (FARM), *10101 Ashburton Lane, Bethesda, MD 20817-1729 (mailing address: P.O. Box 4064, Ithaca, NY 14852); (888) 327-6872. Alex Hershaft, President.*
General email, info@farmusa.org
Web, www.farmusa.org, www.livevegan.org, Twitter, @FARMUSA and Facebook, www.facebook.com/farmanimalrights

Works to end use of animals for food. Interests include animal protection, consumer health, agricultural resources, and environmental quality. Conducts national educational campaigns, including World Farm Animals Day, the Live Vegan Program, and the Great American Meatout. Monitors legislation and regulations.

Humane Farm Animal Care, *P.O. Box 82, Middleburg, VA 20118; (703) 435-3883. Fax, (703) 435-3981. Adele Douglass Jolley, Chief Executive Officer; Mimi Stein, Executive Director.*
General email, info@certifiedhumane.org
Web, www.certifiedhumane.org, Twitter, @CertifiedHumane and Facebook, www.facebook.com/CertifiedHumane

Seeks to improve the welfare of farm animals by providing viable, duly monitored standards for humane food production. Administers the Certified Humane Raised and Handled Program for meat, poultry, eggs, and dairy products.

Humane Rescue Alliance, *71 Oglethorpe St. N.W., 20011; P.O. Box 96312, 20090-6312; (202) 576-6664. Fax, (202) 726-2536. Lisa LaFontaine, President. 24-hour animal cruelty and emergency hotline, (202) 723-5730. Adoption center, (202) 723-5730. Spay and neuter center, (202) 608-1356.*
General email, adopt@washhumane.org
Web, www.humanerescuealliance.org, Twitter, @HumaneRescue and Press, smiller@humanrescue alliance.org

Congressionally chartered animal welfare agency and open-access animal shelter. Promotes pet adoption; offers low-cost spay and neuter services and trap-and-neuter programs. Operates the D.C. Animal Care and Control.

Humane Society Legislative Fund, *1255 23rd St. N.W., #455, 20037; (202) 676-2314. Fax, (202) 676-2300. Sara Amundson, President. Donations, (800) 876-5170. Press, (301) 548-7778.*

General email, humanesociety@hslf.org

Web, www.hslf.org, Twitter, @HSLegFund and Facebook, www.facebook.com/humanelegislation

Works to pass state and federal laws protecting animals from cruelty and suffering; educates the public about animal protection issues and supports humane candidates for office. (Lobbying arm of the Humane Society of the United States.)

Humane Society of the United States, 1255 23rd St. N.W., #450, 20037; (202) 452-1100. Kitty Block, President. Toll-free, (866) 720-2676.
Web, www.humanesociety.org, Twitter, @HumaneSociety and Facebook, www.facebook.com/humanesociety

Citizens' interest group that sponsors programs in pet and equine protection, disaster preparedness and response, wildlife and habitat protection, animals in research, and farm animal welfare. Interests include legislation to protect pets, provide more humane treatment for farm animals, strengthen penalties for illegal animal fighting, and curb abusive sport hunting practices such as trophy hunting, baiting, and hounding.

National Academies of Sciences, Engineering, and Medicine (NASEM), *Institute for Laboratory Animal Research,* Keck Center, 500 5th St. N.W., #645, 20001; (202) 334-2590. Fax, (202) 334-1687. Teresa Sylvina, Director; Robert C. Ayska, Chair.
General email, ablue@nas.edu

Web, www.nationalacademies.org/ilar/institute-for-laboratory-animal-research

Develops and makes available scientific and technical information on laboratory animals and other biological research resources for the scientific community, institutional animal care and use committees, the federal government, science educators and students, and the public.

National Assn. for Biomedical Research, 1100 Vermont Ave. N.W., #1100, 20005; (202) 857-0540. Matthew R. Bailey, President.
General email, info@nabr.org

Web, www.nabr.org and Twitter, @NABRorg

Membership: scientific and medical professional societies, academic institutions, and research-oriented corporations involved in the use of animals in biomedical research, education and testing. Supports the humane use of animals in medical research, education, and product-safety assessment. Monitors legislation and regulations.

Physicians Committee for Responsible Medicine (PCRM), 5100 Wisconsin Ave. N.W., #400, 20016; (202) 686-2210. Fax, (202) 686-2216. Neal Barnard, President. Press, 202–527-7316.
General email, pcrm@pcrm.org

Web, www.pcrm.org, Twitter, @PCRM, Facebook, www.facebook.com/PCRM.org and President, Twitter, @DrNealBarnard

Investigates alternatives to animal use in medical research experimentation, product testing, and education.

Fish

▶ **AGENCIES**

Atlantic States Marine Fisheries Commission, 1050 N. Highland St., #200 A-N, Arlington, VA 22201; (703) 842-0740. Fax, (703) 842-0741. Robert E. Beal, Executive Director.
General email, info@asmfc.org

Web, www.asmfc.org, Twitter, @ASMFC and Facebook, www.facebook.com/AtlanticStatesMarineFisheries Commission

Interstate compact commission of marine fisheries with representatives from the Atlantic coastal states. Assists states in developing joint fisheries programs; works with other fisheries organizations and the federal government on environmental, natural resource, and conservation issues.

Environment and Natural Resources Division *(Justice Dept.), Wildlife and Marine Resources,* 150 M St. N.E., #3.1102, 20002; (202) 305-0210. Fax, (202) 305-0275. Seth M. Barsky, Section Chief.
Web, www.justice.gov/enrd/wildlife-and-marine-resources-section

Supervises civil cases under federal maritime law and other laws protecting marine fish and mammals.

Environmental Protection Agency (EPA), *Water (OW),* 1200 Pennsylvania Ave. N.W., MC 4101M, 20460; (202) 564-5700. Radhika Fox, Assistant Administrator.
Web, www.epa.gov/aboutepa/about-office-water

Monitors water pollution to promote healthy fish habitats. Issues fish and shellfish advisories and promotes safe eating guidelines.

Forest Service *(Agriculture Dept.), Biological and Physical Resources, Watershed, Fish, Wildlife, Air, and Rare Plants,* 201 14th St. S.W., #35C, 20024 (mailing address: 1400 Independence Ave. S.W., MS 1121, Washington, DC 20250-1121); Fax, (202) 703-1544. Chris Worth, Assistant Director of Wildlife and Air, (202) 205-3199; Michael Eberle, Assistant Director (Acting) of Watershed, (202) 689-5890.
General email, rharper@fs.fed.us

Web, www.fs.fed.us/biology

Provides national policy direction and management for watershed, fish, wildlife, air, and rare plants programs on lands managed by the Forest Service.

Interior Dept. (DOI), *Assistant Secretary for Fish and Wildlife and Parks,* 1849 C St. N.W., #3160, 20240; (202) 208-4416. Fax, (202) 208-4684. Shannon A. Estenoz, Assistant Secretary, (202) 208-4545.
Web, www.doi.gov

Responsible for programs associated with the development, conservation, and use of fish, wildlife, recreational, historical, and national park system resources. Coordinates marine environmental quality and biological resources programs with other federal agencies. Oversees the U.S. Fish and Wildlife Service and National Park Service.

National Oceanic and Atmospheric Administration (NOAA) *(Commerce Dept.),* *1401 Constitution Ave. N.W., #5128, 20230; (202) 482-3436. Fax, (202) 408-9674. Richard W. Spinrad, Under Secretary. Library, (301) 713-2600. Press, (202) 482-6090.*
Web, www.noaa.gov and Twitter, @NOAA

Conducts research in marine and atmospheric sciences; surveys resources of the sea; analyzes economic aspects of fisheries operations; develops and implements policies on international fisheries; provides states with grants to conserve coastal zone areas; protects marine mammals; provides colleges and universities with grants for research, education, and marine advisory services.

National Oceanic and Atmospheric Administration (NOAA) *(Commerce Dept.), National Marine Fisheries Service (NMFS), 1315 East-West Hwy., 14th Floor, Silver Spring, MD 20910; (301) 427-8000. Fax, (301) 713-1940. Janet Coit, Assistant Administrator. Press, (301) 427-8531.*
Web, www.fisheries.noaa.gov and Twitter, @NOAAFisheries

Administers marine fishing regulations, including off-shore fishing rights and international agreements; conducts marine resources research; studies use and management of these resources; administers the Magnuson-Stevens Fishery Conservation and Management Act; manages and protects marine resources, especially endangered species and marine mammals, within the exclusive economic zone.

U.S. Fish and Wildlife Service *(Interior Dept.), 1849 C St. N.W., #3358, 20240; (202) 208-4545. Martha Williams, Principal Deputy Director. Press, (703) 358-2220. Toll-free, (800) 344-9453.*
General email, fisheries@fws.gov
Web, www.fws.gov, Twitter, @USFWS, Facebook, www .facebook.com/USFWS and YouTube, www.youtube.com/ usfws

Works with federal and state agencies and nonprofits to conserve, protect, and enhance fish and wildlife and their habitats for the continuing benefit of the American people.

U.S. Fish and Wildlife Service *(Interior Dept.), Endangered Species and Ecological Services, 5275 Leesburg Pike, Falls Church, VA 22041; (703) 358-2171. Bridget Fahey, Chief, (703) 358-2163.*
Web, www.fws.gov/endangered and Twitter, @USFWSEndsp

Administers federal policy on fish and wildlife under the Endangered Species Act, Marine Mammal Protection Act, Fish and Wildlife Coordination Act, Oil Pollution Act, and other environmental laws. Reviews all federal and federally licensed projects to determine environmental effects on fish and wildlife. Responsible for maintaining the endangered species list and for protecting and restoring species to healthy numbers.

U.S. Fish and Wildlife Service *(Interior Dept.), Fish and Aquatic Conservation, 5275 Leesburg Pike, MS FAC-3C018A, Falls Church, VA 22041-3803; (703) 358-2220. Fax, (703) 358-1792. David Hoskins, Assistant Director, (202) 208-3517.*

General email, fisheries@fws.gov
Web, www.fws.gov/fisheries, Twitter, @USFWSFisheries and Facebook, www.facebook.com/USFWSFisheries

Develops, manages, and protects interstate and international fisheries, including fisheries of the Great Lakes, fisheries on federal lands, aquatic ecosystems, endangered species of fish, and anadromous species. Administers the National Fish Hatchery System and the National Fish and Wildlife Resource Management Offices, as well as the Habitat and Conservation and Environmental Quality Divisions.

U.S. Geological Survey (USGS) *(Interior Dept.), Ecosystems, 12201 Sunrise Valley Dr., MS 300, Reston, VA 20192-0002; (703) 648-4051. Fax, (703) 648-7031. Anne E. Kinsinger, Associate Director.*
Web, www.usgs.gov/ecosystems

Conducts research and monitoring to develop and convey an understanding of ecosystem function and distributions, physical and biological components, and trophic dynamics for freshwater, terrestrial, and marine ecosystems and the human, fish, and wildlife communities they support. Subject areas include invasive species, endangered species and habitats, genetics and genomics, and microbiology.

▶ CONGRESS

For a listing of relevant congressional committees and subcommittees, please see pages 284–285 or the Appendix.

▶ NONGOVERNMENTAL

American Fisheries Society (AFS), *425 Barlow Pl., #110, Bethesda, MD 20814-2144; (301) 897-8616. Fax, (301) 897-8096. Douglas Austen, Executive Director, ext. 208. Bookstore, ext. 227.*
General email, main@fisheries.org
Web, https://fisheries.org, Twitter, @AmFisheriesSoc and Facebook, www.facebook.com/AmericanFisheriesSociety

Membership: biologists and other scientists interested in fisheries. Promotes the fisheries profession, the advancement of fisheries science, and conservation of renewable aquatic resources. Monitors legislation and regulations.

Assn. of Fish and Wildlife Agencies, *1100 1st St. N.E., #825, 20002; (202) 838-3474. Fax, (202) 350-9869. Ron Regan, Executive Director, (202) 838-3465. Press, (202) 838-3461.*
General email, info@fishwildlife.org
Web, www.fishwildlife.org, Twitter, @fishwildlife and Facebook, www.facebook.com/FishWildlifeAgencies

Membership: state, provincial, and territorial fish and wildlife management agencies in the United States, Canada, and Mexico. Encourages balanced, research-based fish and wildlife resource management. Monitors legislation and regulations.

National Fish and Wildlife Foundation, *1133 15th St. N.W., #1000, 20005; (202) 857-0166. Fax, (202) 857-0162. Jeff Trandahl, Executive Director.*
General email, info@nfwf.org

Web, www.nfwf.org, Twitter, @NFWFnews, Facebook, www.facebook.com/FishandWildlife and YouTube, www.youtube.com/user/NFWF

Forges partnerships between the public and private sectors in support of national and international conservation activities that identify and root out causes of environmental problems that affect fish, wildlife, and plants.

National Fisheries Institute, *1544 Spring Hill Rd., #10463, McLean, VA 22102; (703) 752-8890. John Connelly, President; Kedrin Simms Brachman, Director of Government Affairs, (703) 752-8894. Press, (703) 752-8891.*
General email, admin@sirfonline.org

Web, www.aboutseafood.com, Twitter, @NFImedia, Facebook, www.facebook.com/DishonFish and YouTube, www.youtube.com/user/NFImedia

Membership: vessel owners and distributors, processors, wholesalers, importers, traders, and brokers of fish and shellfish. Monitors legislation and regulations on fisheries. Advocates eating seafood for health benefits.

Ocean Conservancy, *1300 19th St. N.W., 8th Floor, 20036; (202) 429-5609. Fax, (202) 872-0619. Janis Searles Jones, Chief Executive Officer. Toll-free, (800) 519-1541.*
General email, membership@oceanconservancy.org

Web, www.oceanconservancy.org, Twitter, @OurOcean, Facebook, www.facebook.com/oceanconservancy and Coastal clean-up, cleanup@oceanconservancy.org

Works to prevent the overexploitation of living marine resources, including fisheries, and to restore depleted marine wildlife populations through research, education, and science-based advocacy.

Trout Unlimited, *1777 N. Kent St., #100, Arlington, VA 22209; (703) 522-0200. Fax, (703) 284-9400. Chris Wood, President, (703) 284-9403. Toll-free, (800) 834-2419.*
Web, www.tu.org, Twitter, @TroutUnlimited, Facebook, www.facebook.com/TroutUnlimited and YouTube, www.youtube.com/user/TroutUnlimitedNatl

Membership: individuals interested in the protection and restoration of cold-water fish and their habitat. Sponsors research projects with federal and state fisheries agencies; administers programs for water-quality surveillance and cleanup of streams and lakes. Monitors legislation and regulations.

Wildlife and Marine Mammals

▶**AGENCIES**

Animal and Plant Health Inspection Service (APHIS) *(Agriculture Dept.), Wildlife Services (WS), 1400 Independence Ave. S.W., #1624 -S, 20250-3402;*
(202) 799-7095. Fax, (202) 690-0053. Janet L. Bucknall, Deputy Administrator. Toll-free, (866) 487-3297.
Web, www.aphis.usda.gov/wildlife_damage

Works to minimize damage caused by wildlife to crops and livestock, natural resources, and human health and safety. Removes or eliminates predators and nuisance birds. Interests include aviation safety and coexistence of people and wildlife in suburban areas. Conducts program delivery, research and other activities through its regional and state offices. Oversees the National Wildlife Research Center in Ft. Collins, CO.

Environment and Natural Resources Division *(Justice Dept.), Wildlife and Marine Resources, 150 M St. N.E., #3.1102, 20002; (202) 305-0210. Fax, (202) 305-0275. Seth M. Barsky, Section Chief.*
Web, www.justice.gov/enrd/wildlife-and-marine-resources-section

Responsible for criminal enforcement and civil litigation under federal fish and wildlife conservation statutes, including protection of wildlife, fish, and plant resources within U.S. jurisdiction, and management and restoration of Florida Everglades. Monitors interstate and foreign commerce of these resources.

Forest Service *(Agriculture Dept.), Biological and Physical Resources, Watershed, Fish, Wildlife, Air, and Rare Plants, 201 14th St. S.W., #35C, 20024 (mailing address: 1400 Independence Ave. S.W., MS 1121, Washington, DC 20250-1121); Fax, (202) 703-1544. Chris Worth, Assistant Director of Wildlife and Air, (202) 205-3199; Michael Eberle, Assistant Director (Acting) of Watershed, (202) 689-5890.*
General email, rharper@fs.fed.us
Web, www.fs.fed.us/biology

Provides national policy direction and management for watershed, fish, wildlife, air, and rare plants programs on lands managed by the Forest Service.

Interior Dept. (DOI), *Assistant Secretary for Fish and Wildlife and Parks, 1849 C St. N.W., #3160, 20240; (202) 208-4416. Fax, (202) 208-4684. Shannon A. Estenoz, Assistant Secretary, (202) 208-4545.*
Web, www.doi.gov

Responsible for programs associated with the development, conservation, and use of fish, wildlife, recreational, historical, and national park system resources. Coordinates marine environmental quality and biological resources programs with other federal agencies. Oversees the U.S. Fish and Wildlife Service and National Park Service.

Marine Mammal Commission, *Bethesda Towers, 4340 East-West Hwy., #700, Bethesda, MD 20814; (301) 504-0087. Fax, (301) 504-0099. Peter O. Thomas, Executive Director.*
General email, mmc@mmc.gov
Web, www.mmc.gov and Twitter, @marinemammalcom

Established by Congress to ensure protection and conservation of marine mammals and the ecosystems of which they are a part. Supports research and makes recommendations to federal agencies to ensure that their activities are consistent with the provisions of the Marine Mammal Protection Act.

National Oceanic and Atmospheric Administration (NOAA) (Commerce Dept.), 1401 Constitution Ave. N.W., #5128, 20230; (202) 482-3436. Fax, (202) 408-9674. Richard W. Spinrad, Under Secretary. Library, (301) 713-2600. Press, (202) 482-6090.
Web, www.noaa.gov and Twitter, @NOAA

Conducts research in marine and atmospheric sciences; surveys resources of the sea; analyzes economic aspects of fisheries operations; develops and implements policies on international fisheries; provides states with grants to conserve coastal zone areas; protects marine mammals; provides colleges and universities with grants for research, education, and marine advisory services.

National Oceanic and Atmospheric Administration (NOAA) (Commerce Dept.), Protected Resources (OPR), 1315 East-West Hwy., 13th Floor, Silver Spring, MD 20910; (301) 427-8400. Fax, (301) 713-0376. Kimberly (Kim) Damon-Randall, Director.
Web, www.fisheries.noaa.gov/about/office-protected-resources and Twitter, @NOAAfisheries

Administers the Endangered Species Act and the Marine Mammal Protection Act. Provides guidance on the conservation and protection of marine mammals, threatened and endangered marine and anadromous species, and their habitat. Develops national guidelines and policies for the implementation of the Acts, including recovery of protected species, review and issuance of permits and authorization under the Acts, and consultations with other agencies on federal actions that may affect protected species or their habitat. Prepares and reviews management and recovery plans and environmental impact analysis.

U.S. Fish and Wildlife Service (Interior Dept.), 1849 C St. N.W., #3358, 20240; (202) 208-4545. Martha Williams, Principal Deputy Director. Press, (703) 358-2220. Toll-free, (800) 344-9453.
General email, fisheries@fws.gov
Web, www.fws.gov, Twitter, @USFWS, Facebook, www.facebook.com/USFWS and YouTube, www.youtube.com/usfws

Works with federal and state agencies and nonprofits to conserve, protect, and enhance fish and wildlife and their habitats for the continuing benefit of the American people.

U.S. Fish and Wildlife Service (Interior Dept.), Bird Habitat Conservation, 5275 Leesburg Pike, MS MB, Falls Church, VA 22041-3803; (703) 358-1784. Fax, (703) 358-2217. Ken Richkus, Division Chief, (703) 358-1780. Migratory bird offices, (703) 358-1714.
Web, www.fws.gov/birds, Twitter, @usfwsBirds and Facebook, www.facebook.com/usfwsmigratorybirds

Coordinates U.S. activities with Canada and Mexico to protect waterfowl habitats, restore waterfowl populations, and set research priorities under the North American Waterfowl Management Plan.

U.S. Fish and Wildlife Service (Interior Dept.), Endangered Species and Ecological Services, 5275 Leesburg Pike, Falls Church, VA 22041; (703) 358-2171. Bridget Fahey, Chief, (703) 358-2163.
Web, www.fws.gov/endangered and Twitter, @USFWSEndsp

Administers federal policy on fish and wildlife under the Endangered Species Act, Marine Mammal Protection Act, Fish and Wildlife Coordination Act, Oil Pollution Act, and other environmental laws. Reviews all federal and federally licensed projects to determine environmental effects on fish and wildlife. Responsible for maintaining the endangered species list and for protecting and restoring species to healthy numbers.

U.S. Fish and Wildlife Service (Interior Dept.), National Wildlife Refuge System, 1849 C St. N.W., #3349, 20240; (202) 208-5333. Cynthia Martinez, Chief. Toll-free, (800) 344-9453.
Web, www.fws.gov/refuges, Twitter, @USFWSRefuges, Facebook, www.facebook.com/USFWSRefuges and YouTube, www.youtube.com/USFWSRefuges

Determines policy for the management of wildlife. Manages the National Wildlife Refuge System and land acquisition for wildlife refuges.

U.S. Fish and Wildlife Service, Division of Realty., Migratory Bird Conservation Commission, 5275 Leesburg Pike, Falls Church, VA 22041-3803 (mailing address: 5275 Leesburg Pike, MS 3N053, Falls Church, VA 22041-3803); (703) 358-1716. Fax, (703) 358-2223. A. Eric Alvarez, Secretary.
General email, realty@fws.gov
Web, www.fws.gov/program/land-acquisition-and-realty/migratory-bird-conservation-commission, Twitter, @USFWSRefuges and Facebook, www.facebook.com/USFWSRefuges

Established by the Migratory Bird Conservation Act of 1929. Decides which areas to purchase for use as migratory bird refuges and the price at which they are acquired.

U.S. Geological Survey (USGS) (Interior Dept.), Ecosystems, 12201 Sunrise Valley Dr., MS 300, Reston, VA 20192-0002; (703) 648-4051. Fax, (703) 648-7031. Anne E. Kinsinger, Associate Director.
Web, www.usgs.gov/ecosystems

Conducts research and monitoring to develop and convey an understanding of ecosystem function and distributions, physical and biological components, and trophic dynamics for freshwater, terrestrial, and marine ecosystems and the human, fish, and wildlife communities they support. Subject areas include invasive species, endangered species and habitats, genetics and genomics, and microbiology.

▶CONGRESS

For a listing of relevant congressional committees and subcommittees, please see pages 284–285 or the Appendix.

▶NONGOVERNMENTAL

Animal Welfare Institute, *900 Pennsylvania Ave. S.E., 20003 (mailing address: P.O. Box 3650, Washington, DC 20027); (202) 337-2332. Fax, (202) 446-2131. Nadia Adawi, Executive Director. Press, (202) 337-2128. General email, awi@awionline.org*

Web, www.awionline.org and Twitter, @AWIOnline

Works to preserve species threatened with extinction and protect wildlife from inhumane means of capture. Promotes efforts to end whaling and shark finning. Programs include preserving American wild horses and promoting nonlethal wildlife management solutions. Monitors legislation and regulations. (Merged with the Society for Animal Protective Legislation.)

Antarctic and Southern Ocean Coalition, *1320 19th St. N.W., 5th Floor, 20036; (202) 234-2480. Claire Christian, Executive Director. General email, info@asoc.org*

Web, www.asoc.org and Twitter, @AntarcticaSouth

Works to protect the fragile environment and biodiversity of the Antarctic continent, including krill conservation, in the Southern Ocean.

Assn. of Fish and Wildlife Agencies, *1100 1st St. N.E., #825, 20002; (202) 838-3474. Fax, (202) 350-9869. Ron Regan, Executive Director, (202) 838-3465. Press, (202) 838-3461. General email, info@fishwildlife.org*

Web, www.fishwildlife.org, Twitter, @fishwildlife and Facebook, www.facebook.com/FishWildlifeAgencies

Membership: state, provincial, and territorial fish and wildlife management agencies in the United States, Canada, and Mexico. Encourages balanced, research-based fish and wildlife resource management. Monitors legislation and regulations.

Defenders of Wildlife, *1130 17th St. N.W., 20036; (202) 682-9400. Jamie Rappaport Clark, President. Press, (202) 772-0269. Toll-free, (800) 385-9712. General email, memberservices@defenders.org*

Web, www.defenders.org, Twitter, @Defenders, Facebook, www.facebook.com/DefendersofWildlife and YouTube, www.youtube.com/defendersofwildlife

Advocacy group that works to protect wild animals, marine life, and plant life in their natural communities. Interests include endangered species and biodiversity. Monitors legislation and regulations.

Ducks Unlimited, *Governmental Affairs, 444 N. Capital St. N.W., #745, 20001; (202) 347-1530. Doug Schoenrock, President; Dan Wrinn, Director. Web, www.ducks.org, Facebook, www.facebook.com/ DucksUnlimited and Twitter, @DucksUnlimited*

Promotes waterfowl and other wildlife conservation through activities aimed at developing and restoring natural nesting and migration habitats. (Headquarters in Memphis, Tenn.)

Humane Society of the United States, *1255 23rd St. N.W., #450, 20037; (202) 452-1100. Kitty Block, President. Toll-free, (866) 720-2676. Web, www.humanesociety.org, Twitter, @HumaneSociety and Facebook, www.facebook.com/humanesociety*

Works for the humane treatment and protection of animals. Interests include protecting endangered wildlife and marine mammals and their habitats and ending inhumane or cruel conditions in zoos.

Jane Goodall Institute, *1120 20th St. N.W., #520, Vienna, VA 22182; (703) 682-9220. Fax, (703) 682-9312. Anna Rathmann, Executive Director. Web, www.janegoodall.org and Twitter, @JaneGoodallInst*

Seeks to increase primate habitat conservation, expand noninvasive primate research, and promote activities that ensure the well-being of primates. (Affiliated with Jane Goodall Institutes in Canada, Europe, Asia, and Africa.)

National Audubon Society, *Public Policy, 1200 18th St. N.W., #500, 20036; (202) 861-2242. (844) 428-3826. Fax, (202) 600-7990. Justin Stokes, Deputy Chief Conservation Officer. General email, audubonaction@audubon.org*

Web, www.audubon.org and Twitter, @audubonsociety

Citizens' interest group that promotes environmental conservation and education, focusing on birds and their habitats. Provides information on bird science, water resources, public lands, rangelands, forests, parks, wildlife conservation, and the National Wildlife Refuge System. Operates state offices, local chapters, and nature centers nationwide. (Headquarters in New York.)

National Fish and Wildlife Foundation, *1133 15th St. N.W., #1000, 20005; (202) 857-0166. Fax, (202) 857-0162. Jeff Trandahl, Executive Director. General email, info@nfwf.org*

Web, www.nfwf.org, Twitter, @NFWFnews, Facebook, www.facebook.com/FishandWildlife and YouTube, www.youtube.com/user/NFWF

Forges partnerships between the public and private sectors in support of national and international conservation activities that identify and root out causes of environmental problems that affect fish, wildlife, and plants.

National Wildlife Federation, *11100 Wildlife Center Dr., Reston, VA 20190-5362 (mailing address: P.O. Box 1583, Merrifield, VA 22116-1583); (703) 438-6000. Collin O'Mara, President. Toll-free, (800) 822-9919. General email, info@nwf.org*

Web, www.nwf.org, Twitter, @NWF, Facebook, www.facebook.com/NationalWildlife, YouTube, www.youtube.com/user/NationalWildlife and Blog, https://blog.nwf.org

Promotes conservation of natural resources; provides information on the environment and resource management; takes legal action on environmental issues. publishes magazines, that are available by subsription.

National Wildlife Refuge Assn., *1001 Connecticut Ave. N.W., #905, 20036; (202) 417-3803. Geoffrey Haskett, President, ext. 40.*

General email, nwra@refugeassociation.org

Web, www.refugeassociation.org, Twitter, @WildRefuge and Facebook, www.facebook.com/RefugeAssociation

Works to improve management and protection of the National Wildlife Refuge System by providing information to administrators, Congress, and the public, via restoration and research. . Advocates adequate funding and improved policy guidance for the Refuge System; assists individual refuges with particular needs.

Ocean Conservancy, *1300 19th St. N.W., 8th Floor, 20036; (202) 429-5609. Fax, (202) 872-0619. Janis Searles Jones, Chief Executive Officer. Toll-free, (800) 519-1541. General email, membership@oceanconservancy.org*

Web, www.oceanconservancy.org, Twitter, @OurOcean, Facebook, www.facebook.com/oceanconservancy and Coastal clean-up, cleanup@oceanconservancy.org

Works to conserve the diversity and abundance of life in the oceans and coastal areas, to prevent the overexploitation of living marine resources and the degradation of marine ecosystems, and to restore depleted marine wildlife populations and their ecosystems.

Wildlife Habitat Council, *8737 Colesville Rd., #800, Silver Spring, MD 20910; (301) 588-8994. Fax, (301) 588-4629. Margaret O'Gorman, President, (301) 588-4219. General email, whc@wildlifehc.org*

Web, www.wildlifehc.org, Twitter, @WildlifeHC, Facebook, www.facebook.com/wildlifehabitatcouncil/?ref=br_rs and YouTube, www.youtube.com/user/WildlifeHC

Membership: corporations, conservation groups, local governments, and academic institutions. Seeks to increase the quality and amount of wildlife habitat on corporate, private, and public lands. Builds partnerships between corporations and conservation groups to find solutions that balance economic growth with a healthy, biodiverse, and sustainable environment. Provides technical assistance and educational programs; fosters collaboration among members.

The Wildlife Society, *425 Barlow Pl., #200, Bethesda, MD 20814-2144; (301) 897-9770. Fax, (301) 530-2471. Ed Arnett, Chief Executive Officer. General email, tws@wildlife.org*

Web, www.wildlife.org, Twitter, @wildlifesociety and Facebook, www.facebook.com/thewildlifesociety

Membership: wildlife biologists and resource management specialists. Provides information on management techniques, sponsors conferences, maintains list of job opportunities for members.

World Wildlife Fund (WWF), *1250 24th St. N.W., 20037-1193 (mailing address: P.O. Box 97180, Washington, DC 20090-7180); (202) 293-4800. Fax, (202) 293-9211. Carter S. Roberts, President. Press, (202) 495-4102. Toll-free, (800) 960-0993. General email, membership@wwfus.org*

Web, www.worldwildlife.org, Twitter, @World_Wildlife and Facebook, www.facebook.com/WorldWildlifeFund

International conservation organization that supports and conducts scientific research and conservation projects to promote biological diversity and to save endangered species and their habitats. Awards grants for habitat protection.

POLLUTION AND TOXINS

General

▶**AGENCIES**

Army Corps of Engineers *(Defense Dept.), 441 G St. N.W., #3K05, 20314-1000; (202) 761-0011. Lt. Gen. Scott A. Spellman (USA), Chief of Engineers. General email, hq-publicaffairs@usace.army.mil*

Web, www.usace.army.mil, Twitter, @USACEHQ and Facebook, www.facebook.com/USACEHQ

Cleans sites contaminated with hazardous, toxic, or radioactive waste and material.

Environment and Natural Resources Division *(Justice Dept.), Environmental Defense (EDS), 150 M St. N.E., #4.1102, 20002 (mailing address: P.O. Box 7611, Washington, DC 20044); (202) 514-2701. Fax, (202) 616-2426. Letitia J. Grishaw, Chief.* Web, www.justice.gov/enrd/environmental-defense-section

Conducts litigation on air, water, noise, pesticides, solid waste, toxic substances, Superfund, and wetlands in cooperation with the Environmental Protection Agency; represents the EPA in suits involving judicial review of EPA actions; represents the U.S. Army Corps of Engineers in cases involving dredge-and-fill activity in navigable waters and adjacent wetlands; represents the Coast Guard in oil and hazardous spill cases; defends all federal agencies in environmental litigation.

Environment and Natural Resources Division *(Justice Dept.), Environmental Enforcement (EES), 150 M St. N.E., #6.202, 20002 (mailing address: P.O. Box 7611, Ben Franklin Station, Washington, DC 20044-7611); (202) 514-2701. Fax, (202) 514-0097. Thomas A. Mariani, Chief.* Web, www.justice.gov/enrd/environmental-enforcement-section

Conducts civil enforcement actions on behalf of the United States for all environmental protection statutes, including air, water, pesticides, hazardous waste, wetland matters investigated by the Environmental Protection Agency, and other civil environmental enforcement.

Environmental Protection Agency (EPA), *Chemical Safety and Pollution Prevention (OCSPP), 1200 Pennsylvania Ave. N.W., #4146, MC 7101M, 20460; (202) 564-2910. Fax, (202) 564-0801. Michal Ilana Freedhoff, Assistant Administrator.* Web, www.epa.gov/aboutepa/about-office-chemical-safety-and-pollution-prevention-ocspp

Studies and makes recommendations for regulating chemical substances under the Toxic Substances Control Act. Compiles list of chemical substances subject to the act.

Environmental Protection Agency (EPA), *Chemical Safety and Pollution Prevention (OCSPP), Pollution Prevention and Toxics,* 1200 Pennsylvania Ave. N.W., #4146, MC 7401M, 20460; (202) 564-3810. Fax, (202) 564-0575. Vacant, Director. Toxic substance hotline, (202) 554-1404.
Web, www.epa.gov/aboutepa/about-office-chemical-safety-and-pollution-prevention-ocspp

Manages programs on pollution prevention and new and existing chemicals in the marketplace, such as asbestos, lead, mercury, formaldehyde, PFOAs, and PCBs. Programs include the High Production Volume Challenge Program, Sustainable Futures, the Green Chemistry Program, Green Suppliers Network, the High Production Volume Challenge Program, Design for the Environment, and the Chemical Right-to-Know Initiative. Selects and implements control measures for new and existing chemicals that present a risk to human health and the environment. Oversees and manages regulatory evaluation and decision-making processes. Evaluates alternative remedial control measures under the Toxic Substances Control Act and makes recommendations concerning the existence of unreasonable risk from exposure to chemicals, including pesticides and fungicides. Develops generic and chemical-specific rules for new chemicals. Operates the toxic substance hotline.

Environmental Protection Agency (EPA), *Children's Health Protection (OCHP),* 1301 Constitution Ave. N.W., #1144, MC 1107T, 20460; (202) 564-4583. Fax, (202) 564-2733. Jeanne Briskin, Director.
Web, www2.epa.gov/aboutepa/about-office-childrens-health-protection-ochp and www.epa.gov/children

Supports and facilitates the EPA's efforts to protect children's health from environmental risks through safe chemicals management. Provides leadership on inter-agency Healthy Homes Work Group and Healthy School Environments Initiative. Offers grants through the Office of Children's Health Protection and Environmental Education (OCHPEE).

Environmental Protection Agency (EPA), *Enforcement and Compliance Assurance (OECA),* 1200 Pennsylvania Ave. N.W., #3204, MC 2201A, 20460; (202) 564-2440. Fax, (202) 501-3842. Lawrence Starfield, Principal Deputy Assistant Administrator.
Web, www.epa.gov/aboutepa/about-office-enforcement-and-compliance-assurance-oeca

Enforces laws that protect public health and the environment from hazardous materials, pesticides, and toxic substances. Implements the Clean Air Act; Clean Water Act; Comprehensive Environmental Response, Compensation, and Liability Act; Emergency Planning and Community Right-to-Know Act; Federal Insecticide, Fungicide, and Rodenticide Act; Marine Protection, Research, and Sanctuaries Act; National Environmental Policy Act; Oil Pollution Act; Resource Conservation and Recovery Act; Safe Drinking Water Act; and Toxic Substances Control Act.

Environmental Protection Agency (EPA), *Land and Emergency Management (OLEM), Federal Facilities Restoration and Reuse,* 1200 Pennsylvania Ave. N.W.,

MC 5106R, 20460; (202) 564-4409. Greg Gervais, Director.
Web, www.epa.gov/fedfac

Works with the Defense Dept., Energy Dept., and other federal offices for more effective and less costly cleanup and reuse of federal facilities.

Environmental Protection Agency (EPA), *Land and Emergency Management (OLEM), Resource Conservation and Recovery,* 1 Potomac Yard, 2777 S. Crystal Dr., Arlington, VA 22202 (mailing address: 1200 Pennsylvania Ave. N.W., #5301P, Washington, DC 20460); (703) 308-8895. Fax, (703) 308-0513. Carolyn Hoskinson, Director, (202) 236-3619.
Web, www.epa.gov/aboutepa/about-office-land-and-emergency-management#orcr

Protects human health and the environment by ensuring responsible national management of hazardous and nonhazardous waste. Administers the Resource Conservation and Recovery Act.

Environmental Protection Agency (EPA), *Policy (OP), Environmental Justice,* 1200 Pennsylvania Ave. N.W., MC 2201A, 20460; (202) 564-2515. Fax, (202) 501-0936. Matthew Tejada, Director, (202) 564-8047. Hotline, (800) 962-6215.
General email, environmental-justice@epa.gov
Web, www.epa.gov/environmentaljustice

Works to protect human health and the environment in communities overburdened with environmental pollution by implementing justice programs, policies, and activities.

Environmental Protection Agency (EPA), *Research and Development (ORD),* 1200 Pennsylvania Ave. N.W., #41222, MC 8101R, 20460; (202) 564-6620. Fax, (202) 565-2430. Maureen Gwinn, Assistant Administrator (Acting).
Web, www2.epa.gov/aboutepa/about-office-research-and-development-ord

Develops scientific data and methods to support EPA standards and regulations. Conducts exposure and risk assessments. Researches applied and long-term technologies to reduce risks from pollution.

▶ **CONGRESS**

For a listing of relevant congressional committees and sub-committees, please see pages 284–285 or the Appendix.

▶ **NONGOVERNMENTAL**

The Brookings Institution, *Climate and Energy Economics Project,* 1775 Massachusetts Ave. N.W., 20036; (202) 797-6000. Peter J. Wilcoxen, Senior Fellow.
Web, www.brookings.edu/project/climate-and-energy-economics-project and Twitter, @BrookingsEcon

Promotes environmentally and economically efficient approaches to mitigating human impacts on climate change, including cap-and-trade.

National Academies of Sciences, Engineering, and Medicine (NASEM), *Environmental Studies and Toxicology Board,* Keck Center, 500 5th St. N.W., 20001; (202) 334-3591. Clifford S. Duke, Director; Frank W. Davis, Chair.
General email, best@nas.edu

Web, www.nationalacademies.org/best/board-on-environmental-studies-and-toxicology

Conducts research on environmental pollution problems affecting human health, human impacts on the environment, and the assessment and management of related risks to human health and the environment. Seeks to improve environmental decision making and public understanding of environmental issues.

Physicians for Social Responsibility (PSR), 1111 14th St. N.W., #700, 20005 (mailing address: P.O. Box 30159, Bethesda, MD 20824); (202) 667-4260. Fax, (202) 667-4201. Jeff Carter, JD, Executive Director, (202) 587-5240.
General email, psrnatl@psr.org

Web, www.psr.org, Twitter, @psrenvironment and Facebook, www.facebook.com/psrnational

Membership: doctors, nurses, health scientists, and concerned citizens. Works to protect the public and environment from toxic chemicals. Conducts public education programs, monitors policy, and serves as a liaison with other concerned groups.

Air Pollution

▶**AGENCIES**

Environmental Protection Agency (EPA), *Air and Radiation (OAR),* 1200 Pennsylvania Ave. N.W., #5426, MC 6101A, 20460; (202) 564-7404. Fax, (202) 564-1408. Joseph Goffman, Principal Deputy Assistant Administrator.
Web, www.epa.gov/aboutepa/about-office-air-and-radiation-oar

Develops national programs, policies, and regulations for controlling air pollution and radiation exposure. Administers air quality standards and planning programs of the Clean Air Act Amendment of 1990. Operates the Air and Radiation Docket and Information Center. Supervises the Office of Air Quality Planning and Standards in Durham, N.C., which develops air quality standards and provides information on air pollution control issues, including industrial air pollution. Administers the Air Pollution Technical Information Center in Research Triangle Park, N.C., which collects and provides technical literature on air pollution.

Environmental Protection Agency (EPA), *Air and Radiation (OAR), Atmospheric Programs,* 1200 Pennsylvania Ave. N.W., #5426, MC 6201A, 20460; (202) 343-9140. Fax, (202) 343-2210. Chris Grundler, Director.
Web, www.epa.gov/aboutepa/about-office-air-and-radiation-oar#oap

Responsible for acid rain, ozone layer protection, climate change, and regional air quality programs. Examines strategies for preventing atmospheric pollution and

mitigating climate change. Administers public-private partnerships, such as ENERGY STAR.

Environmental Protection Agency (EPA), *Air and Radiation (OAR), Atmospheric Programs, Climate Change Division,* 1200 Pennsylvania Ave. N.W., #5426, MC 6207A, 20460; (202) 343-9876. Fax, (202) 343-2342. Paul M. Gunning, Director.
General email, hargrove.anne@epa.gov

Web, www.epa.gov/aboutepa/about-office-air-and-radiation-oar#oap

Implements voluntary programs to reduce non–carbon dioxide emissions.

Environmental Protection Agency (EPA), *Air and Radiation (OAR), Transportation and Air Quality,* 1200 Pennsylvania Ave. N.W., #5426, MC 6401A, 20460; (202) 564-1682. Fax, (202) 564-1408. Sarah Dunham, Director.
General email, otaq@epa.gov

Web, www.epa.gov/aboutepa/about-office-air-and-radiation-oar#otaq and NVFEL, www3.epa.gov/nvfel

Promotes reduction of air pollution and greenhouse gas emissions from automobiles, trucks, buses, farm and construction equipment, lawn and garden equipment, marine engines, aircraft, and locomotives. Establishes national air quality standards for on-road and nonroad mobiles and develops fuel efficiency programs. Supervises the National Vehicle and Fuel Emissions Laboratory (NVFEL) in Ann Arbor, Mich., which provides emissions testing services to aid the development of certifications, enforcement actions, test procedures, and rulemaking.

Federal Aviation Administration (FAA) *(Transportation Dept.), Policy, International Affairs, and Environment (APL), Environment and Energy Research and Development,* 800 Independence Ave. S.W., #900W, 20591; (202) 267-3576. Fax, (202) 267-5594. Julie Marks, Deputy Director; Kevin Welsh, Executive Director.
Web, www.faa.gov/about/office_org/headquarters_offices/apl/research

Develops government standards for aircraft noise and emissions.

▶**CONGRESS**

For a listing of relevant congressional committees and subcommittees, please see pages 284–285 or the Appendix.

▶**NONGOVERNMENTAL**

Alliance for Responsible Atmospheric Policy, 2111 Wilson Blvd., 8th Floor, Arlington, VA 22201; (703) 243-0344. Kevin Fay, Executive Director, (703) 801-3233.
General email, info@alliancepolicy.org

Web, www.alliancepolicy.org and Twitter, @AtmosPolicy

Coalition of users and producers of chlorofluorocarbons (CFCs). Seeks further study of the stratospheric ozone depletion theory. Coordinates industry participation in the development of economically and environmentally beneficial international and domestic atmospheric policies.

Center for Auto Safety, 4400 Jenifer St. N.W., #331, 20015-2113; (202) 328-7700. Michael. Brooks, Executive Director (Acting).
General email, contact@autosafety.org
Web, www.autosafety.org, Twitter, @Ctr4AutoSafety and Facebook, www.facebook.com/CenterForAutoSafety

Public interest organization that conducts research on air pollution caused by auto emissions; monitors fuel economy regulations.

Center for Clean Air Policy, 700 12th St. N.W., #700, 20005; (302) 290-7638. Allison Bender-Corbett, Executive Director.
General email, development@ccap.org
Web, https://ccap.org, Twitter, @CleanAirPolicy and Facebook, www.facebook.com/CleanAirPolicy

Membership: international policymakers, climate negotiators, corporations, environmentalists, and academicians. Analyzes economic and environmental effects of air pollution and related environmental problems. Serves as a liaison among government, corporate, community, and environmental groups.

Climate Institute, 1225 New York Ave. N.W., #800, 20005; (202) 552-0163. Nasir Khattak, Chief Operating Officer.
General email, info@climate.org
Web, http://climate.org

Educates the public and policymakers on climate change, the greenhouse effect, global warming, and the depletion of the ozone layer. Assesses climate change risks and develops strategies on mitigating climate change in developing countries and in North America.

The Climate Reality Project, 555 11th St. N.W., #601, 20004; (202) 567-6800. Ken Berlin, President.
General email, info@climatereality.com
Web, www.climaterealityproject.org, Twitter, @ClimateReality, Facebook, www.facebook.com/ ClimateReality, YouTube, www.youtube.com/user/ ClimateReality and Press, press@climatereality.com

Aims to reduce carbon emissions, supports taxing oil and coal companies that emit large amounts of carbon, and educates the public on climate change and its relation to carbon pollution.

Environmental Defense Fund, Washington Office, 1875 Connecticut Ave. N.W., #600, 20009-5728; (202) 387-3500. Fax, (202) 234-6049. Fred Krupp, President; Carol Andress, Associate Vice President, in Washington, DC.
Information, (800) 684-3322.
Web, www.edf.org/offices/washington-dc, Twitter, @EnvDefenseFund and Facebook, www.facebook.com/ EnvDefenseFund

Citizen interest group staffed by lawyers, economists, and scientists. Conducts research and provides information on pollution prevention, environmental health, and the Clean Air Act. (Headquarters in New York.)

Manufacturers of Emission Controls Assn., 2101 Wilson Blvd., #530, Arlington, VA 22201; (202) 296-4797. Rasto Brezny, Executive Director.

General email, asantos@meca.org
Web, www.meca.org and Twitter, @MECAforCleanAir

Membership: manufacturers of motor vehicle emission control equipment, both mobile and stationary sources. Provides information on emission technology and industry capabilities. Studies the economic and public health impacts of the industry. Monitors regulations and international activities.

National Academies of Sciences, Engineering, and Medicine (NASEM), Atmospheric Sciences and Climate Board, Keck Center, 500 5th St. N.W., #602, 20001; (202) 413-2751. Amanda Staudt, Director; Mary Glackin, Chair.
General email, basc@nas.edu
Web, www.nationalacademies.org/basc/board-on- atmospheric-sciences-and-climate

Supports research on climate change, air pollution, and severe weather in order to address environmental policies, human health, emergency management, energy choices, manufacturing decisions, construction codes, and agricultural methods.

National Assn. of Clean Air Agencies (NACAA), 1530 Wilson Blvd., #320, Arlington, VA 22209; (571) 970-6678. Miles Keogh, Executive Director.
General email, 4cleanair@4cleanair.org
Web, www.4cleanair.org

Membership: air pollution control agencies nationwide. Seeks to improve effective management of air resources by encouraging the exchange of information among air pollution control officials. Monitors federal regulations; publishes reports and analyses; develops model rules for states and localities.

Hazardous Materials

►**AGENCIES**

Agency for Toxic Substances and Disease Registry (ATSDR) (Health and Human Services Dept.), Washington Office, William Jefferson Clinton Bldg., 1200 Pennsylvania Ave. N.W., MC 5202P, 20460; (800) 232-4636. (202) 566-0844. Steve A. Jones, Regional Director, (703) 606-3885.
Web, www.atsdr.cdc.gov/dro/hq.html and Twitter, @CDCEnvironment

Works with state and other federal agencies to prevent exposure to hazardous substances from waste disposal sites. Maintains a registry of persons exposed to hazardous substances and of diseases and illnesses resulting from exposure to hazardous or toxic substances. Conducts public health assessments, health studies, surveillance activities, and health education training in communities around waste sites on the U.S. Environmental Protection Agency National Priorities List. Maintains inventory of hazardous substances and registry of sites closed or restricted because of contamination by hazardous material. (Headquarters in Atlanta, Ga.)

Energy Dept. (DOE), Legacy Management, 1000 Independence Ave. S.W., #6E-041, 20585; (202) 586-7550. Fax, (202) 586-8403. Carmelo Melendez, Director.

General email, LM@hq.doe.gov

Web, www.energy.gov/lm/office-legacy-management

Mitigates community impacts resulting from the cleanup of legacy waste, including radioactive and chemical waste, environmental contamination, and hazardous material. Oversees the legacy waste from the Cold War and World War II; makes legacy records and information accesible to the public.

Environment and Natural Resources Division *(Justice Dept.), Environmental Enforcement (EES), 150 M St. N.E., #6.202, 20002 (mailing address: P.O. Box 7611, Ben Franklin Station, Washington, DC 20044-7611); (202) 514-2701. Fax, (202) 514-0097. Thomas A. Mariani, Chief.*
Web, www.justice.gov/enrd/environmental-enforcement-section

Represents the United States in civil cases under environmental laws that involve the handling, storage, treatment, transportation, and disposal of hazardous waste. Recovers federal money spent to clean up hazardous waste sites or sues defendants to clean up sites under Superfund.

Environmental Protection Agency (EPA), *Chemical Safety and Pollution Prevention (OCSPP), Pollution Prevention and Toxics, 1200 Pennsylvania Ave. N.W., #4146, MC 7401M, 20460; (202) 564-3810. Fax, (202) 564-0575. Vacant, Director. Toxic substance hotline, (202) 554-1404.*
Web, www.epa.gov/aboutepa/about-office-chemical-safety-and-pollution-prevention-ocspp

Assesses the health and environmental hazards of existing chemical substances and mixtures; collects information on chemical use, exposure, and effects; maintains inventory of existing chemical substances; reviews new chemicals and regulates the manufacture, distribution, use, and disposal of harmful chemicals. Implements the Toxic Substances Control Act and the Pollution Prevention Act. Selects and implements control measures for new and existing chemicals that present a risk to human health and the environment. Oversees and manages regulatory evaluation and decision-making processes. Evaluates alternative remedial control measures under the Toxic Substances Control Act and makes recommendations concerning the existence of unreasonable risk from exposure to chemicals, including pesticides and fungicides. Develops generic and chemical-specific rules for new chemicals. Operates the toxic substance hotline.

Environmental Protection Agency (EPA), *Emergency Management, 1200 Pennsylvania Ave. N.W., MC 5104A, 20460; (202) 564-8600. Kathleen Salyer, Director (Acting), (703) 308-8710. Toll-free call center, (800) 424-8802.*
Web, www.epa.gov/emergency-response

Develops and administers chemical emergency preparedness and prevention programs; reviews effectiveness of programs; prepares community right-to-know regulations. Provides guidance materials, technical assistance, and training. Implements the preparedness and community right-to-know provisions of the Superfund Amendments and Reauthorization Act of 1986.

Environmental Protection Agency (EPA), *Enforcement and Compliance Assurance (OECA), Site Remediation Enforcement, 1200 Pennsylvania Ave. N.W., MC 2251A, 20460; (202) 564-5110. Fax, (202) 564-0094. Cyndy Mackey, Director.*
Web, www.epa.gov/aboutepa/about-office-enforcement-and-compliance-assurance-oeca#osre

Requires those responsible for hazardous waste sites to clean up or reimburse the EPA for cleanup. Enforces national hazardous waste cleanup programs, including Superfund programs, Resource Conservation and Recovery Act, Oil Pollution Act, and underground storage tank systems.

Environmental Protection Agency (EPA), *Land and Emergency Management (OLEM), 1200 Pennsylvania Ave. N.W., MC 5101T, 20460; (202) 566-0200. Fax, (202) 566-0207. Barry Breem, Assistant Administrator (Acting). National Response Center, (800) 424-8802. Superfund information hotline, (800) 424-9346. TTY, (202) 272-0165.*
Web, www2.epa.gov/aboutepa/about-office-land-and-emergency-management-olem

Administers and enforces the Superfund act and manages the handling, cleanup, and disposal of hazardous wastes.

Environmental Protection Agency (EPA), *Land and Emergency Management (OLEM), Brownfields and Land Revitalization, 1300 Pennsylvania Ave. N.W., #5105T, 20460; (202) 566-2731. David Lloyd, Director.*
Web, www.epa.gov/land-revitalization and www.epa.gov/brownfields

Provides grants and technical assistance to communities, states, tribes, and other stakeholders needing resources to prevent, assess, safely clean up, and sustainably reuse brownfields and formerly contaminated properties.

Environmental Protection Agency (EPA), *Land and Emergency Management (OLEM), Superfund Remediation and Technology Innovation, 1 Potomac Yard, 2777 Crystal Dr., Arlington, VA 22202 (mailing address: 1200 Pennsylvania Ave. N.W., #5201P, Washington, DC 20460); (703) 603-8722. Larry Douchand, Director.*
Web, www.epa.gov/superfund and www.epa.gov/aboutepa/about-office-land-and-emergency-management#osrt

Responsible for Superfund and contaminated land cleanup; responds to environmental emergencies, oil spills, and natural disasters.

Environmental Protection Agency (EPA), *Land and Emergency Management (OLEM), Underground Storage Tanks, 1300 Pennsylvania Ave N.W., 7th Floor, 20460 (mailing address: 1200 Pennsylvania Ave. N.W., #5401R, Washington, DC 20460); (202) 564-1611. Mark Baralo, Director (Acting).*
Web, www.epa.gov/ust and www.epa.gov/aboutepa/about-office-land-and-emergency-management#oust

Carries out regulations for underground storage tank systems storing petroleum and certain hazardous substances to prevent groundwater contamination.

Interior Department

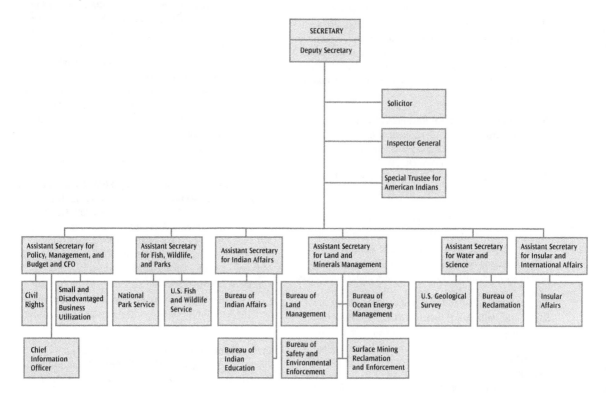

Federal Aviation Administration (FAA) *(Transportation Dept.), Security and Hazardous Materials Safety (ASH),* 800 Independence Ave. S.W., #300E, 20591; (202) 267-7211. Fax, (202) 267-8496. Claudio Manno, Associate Administrator.
Web, www.faa.gov/about/office_org/headquarters_offices/ash

Seeks to ensure air transportation safety by preventing hazardous materials accidents aboard aircraft and protecting FAA employees and facilities from criminal and terrorist acts.

Housing and Urban Development Dept. (HUD), *Lead Hazard Control and Healthy Homes (OLHCHH),* 451 7th St. S.W., #8236, 20410; (202) 708-4337. Fax, (202) 708-0014. Michelle M. Miller, Director, (202) 402-5769.
Web, www.hud.gov/program_offices/healthy_homes and *Twitter, @HUDHealthyHomes*

Advises HUD offices, other agencies, health authorities, and the housing industry on lead poisoning prevention. Develops regulations for lead-based paint; conducts research; makes grants to state and local governments for lead hazard reduction and inspection of housing.

Interior Dept. (DOI), *Natural Resource Damage Assessment and Restoration Program,* 1849 C St. N.W., MS 5538, 20240; (202) 208-4863. Stephen (Steve) Glomb, Director.
Web, www.doi.gov/restoration

Works with the affected state, tribal and federal trustee agencies to restore natural resources that have been compromised as a result of oil spills or hazardous substances released into the environment.

Pipeline and Hazardous Materials Safety Administration *(Transportation Dept.),* 1200 New Jersey Ave. S.E., #E27-300, 20590; (202) 366-4433. Fax, (202) 366-3666. Tristan Brown, Administrator (Acting). Hazardous Materials Information Center, (800) 467-4922. To report an incident, (800) 424-8802.
General email, phmsa.administrator@dot.gov
Web, www.phmsa.dot.gov and *Twitter, @PHMSA_DOT*

Oversees the safe and secure movement of hazardous materials to industry and consumers by all modes of transportation, including pipelines. Works to eliminate transportation-related deaths and injuries. Promotes transportation solutions to protect communities and the environment.

Pipeline and Hazardous Materials Safety Administration *(Transportation Dept.), Hazardous Materials Safety,* 1200 New Jersey Ave. S.E., #E21-317, 20590; (202) 366-4488. Fax, (202) 366-5713. William S. (Bill) Schoonover, Associate Administrator. Hazardous Materials Information Center, (800) 467-4922.
General email, phmsa.hmhazmatsafety@dot.gov
Web, www.phmsa.dot.gov/about-phmsa/offices/office-hazardous-materials-safety

Designates substances as hazardous materials and regulates their transportation in interstate commerce; coordinates international standards regulations.

Pipeline and Hazardous Materials Safety Administration *(Transportation Dept.), Pipeline Safety, 1200 New Jersey Ave. S.E., E24-455, 20590; (202) 366-4595. Fax, (202) 366-4566. Alan K. Mayberry, Associate Administrator.*
General email, phmsa.pipelinesafety@dot.gov
Web, www.phmsa.dot.gov/about-phmsa/offices/office-pipeline-safety

Issues and enforces federal regulations for hazardous liquids pipeline safety.

U.S. Coast Guard (USCG) *(Homeland Security Dept.), National Response Center, 2100 2nd St. S.W., #2111B, 20593-0001; (202) 372-2097. Dana S. Tulis, Director. Hotline, (800) 424-8802. Local, (202) 267-2675.*
General email, NRC@uscg.mil
Web, www.nrc.uscg.mil and www.epa.gov/emergency-response/national-response-center

Maintains 24-hour hotline for reporting oil, biological, radiological, and chemical discharges in the environment. Notifies appropriate federal officials to reduce the effects of accidents. Monitors suspicious activities and security breaches in U.S. waters. Works cooperatively with the Environmental Protection Agency.

▶CONGRESS

For a listing of relevant congressional committees and subcommittees, please see pages 284–285 or the Appendix.

▶NONGOVERNMENTAL

Alliance of Hazardous Materials Professionals, *1300 Piccard Dr. # LL14, Rockville, MD 20850; (301) 329-6850. Fax, (301) 990-9771. Matt Coffindaffer, MBA, Executive Director.*
General email, info@ahmpnet.org
Web, www.ahmpnet.org and Twitter, @AHMPros

Membership: management professionals who work with hazardous materials , environmental issues, health, safety issues and transportation. Offers professional development via trainings and networking opportunities to members. Members must be certified by the Institute of Hazardous Materials Management (IHMM).

Chlorine Institute Inc., *1300 Wilson Blvd., #525, Arlington, VA 22209; (703) 894-4140. Frank Reiner, President, (703) 894-4116.*
General email, info@cl2.com
Web, www.chlorineinstitute.org, Twitter, @TheChlorineINST, Facebook, www.facebook.com/thechlorineinstitute and YouTube, www.youtube.com/user/TheChlorineInstitute

Safety, health, and environmental protection center of the chlor-alkali (chlorine, caustic soda, caustic potash, and hydrogen chloride) industry. Interests include employee health and safety, resource conservation and pollution abatement, control of chlorine emergencies, product specifications, and public and community relations. Publishes technical pamphlets and drawings.

Dangerous Goods Advisory Council, *7501 Greenway Center Dr., #760, Greenbelt, MD 20770; (202) 289-4550. Fax, (202) 289-4074. Vaughn Arthur, President.*
General email, info@dgac.org
Web, www.dgac.org, Twitter, @DGAC_HMAC and Facebook, www.facebook.com/dangerousgoodsadvisory council

Membership: shippers, carriers, container manufacturers and conditioners, emergency response and spill cleanup companies, and trade associations. Promotes safety in the domestic and international transportation of hazardous materials. Provides information and educational services; sponsors conferences, workshops, and seminars. Acts as advocate for uniform hazardous materials regulations. Also known as the Hazardous Materials Advisory Council.

Environmental Technology Council, *1112 16th St. N.W., #420, 20036; (202) 783-0870. Fax, (202) 737-2038. James A. Williams II, Executive Director. Press, ext. 202.*
Web, www.etc.org

Membership: environmental service firms. Interests include the recycling, detoxification, and disposal of hazardous and industrial waste and cleanup of contaminated industrial sites; works to encourage permanent and technology-based solutions to environmental problems. Provides the public with information.

Institute of Hazardous Materials Management (IHMM), *9210 Corporate Blvd., #470, Rockville, MD 20850; (301) 984-8969. Fax, (301) 984-1516. Eugene (Gene) Guilford Jr., Executive Director, ext. 4869.*
General email, info@ihmm.org
Web, www.ihmm.org and Twitter, @TheIHMM

Seeks to educate professionals and the general public about proper handling of hazardous materials; issues certifications. Administers the Certified Hazardous Materials Manager Program, the Certified Hazardous Materials Practitioner program, the Certified Dangerous Goods Professsional (CDGP), and the Certified Dangerous Goods Trainer (CDGT).

Rachel Carson Council Inc., *8600 Irvington Ave., Bethesda, MD 20817; (301) 214-2400. Robert K. (Bob) Musil, President, (301) 493-4571.*
General email, office@rachelcarsoncouncil.org
Web, https://rachelcarsoncouncil.org, Twitter, @RachelCarsonDC and Facebook, www.facebook.com/RachelCarsonCouncil

Acts as a clearinghouse for information on pesticides and alternatives to their use; maintains extensive data on toxicity and the effects of pesticides on humans, domestic animals, and wildlife.

Radiation Protection

▶AGENCIES

Environmental Protection Agency (EPA), *Air and Radiation (OAR),* 1200 Pennsylvania Ave. N.W., #5426, MC 6101A, 20460; (202) 564-7404. Fax, (202) 564-1408. Joseph Goffman, Principal Deputy Assistant Administrator. Web, www.epa.gov/aboutepa/about-office-air-and-radiation-oar

Develops national programs, policies, and regulations for controlling air pollution and radiation exposure. Administers air quality standards and planning programs of the Clean Air Act Amendment of 1990. Operates the Air and Radiation Docket and Information Center. Supervises the Office of Air Quality Planning and Standards in Durham, N.C., which develops air quality standards and provides information on air pollution control issues, including industrial air pollution. Administers the Air Pollution Technical Information Center in Research Triangle Park, N.C., which collects and provides technical literature on air pollution.

Environmental Protection Agency (EPA), *Air and Radiation (OAR), Radiation and Indoor Air,* 1200 Pennsylvania Ave. N.W., #5426, MC 6608T, 20460; (202) 343-9320. Fax, (202) 564-1408. Jonathan Edwards, Director. Web, www.epa.gov/aboutepa/about-office-air-and-radiation-oar#oria

Establishes standards to regulate the amount of radiation discharged into the environment from uranium mining and milling projects and other activities that result in radioactive emissions. Oversees the National Air and Radiation Environmental Laboratory in Montgomery, Ala.

Food and Drug Administration (FDA) *(Health and Human Services Dept.), Division of Industry and Consumer Education, Center for Devices and Radiological Health (CDRH),* White Oak Bldg. 66, 10903 New Hampshire Ave., Silver Spring, MD 20993-0002; (301) 796-7100. Fax, (301) 847-8510. Jeffrey E. Shuren, Director, (301) 796-5900. Toll-free, (800) 638-2041. General email, DICE@fda.hhs.gov and FDADeviceInfo@fda.hhs.gov Web, www.fda.gov/medicaldevices and www.fda.gov/AboutFDA/CentersOffices/OfficeofMedicalProductsandTobacco/CDRH

Administers national programs to control exposure to radiation; establishes standards for emissions from consumer and medical products; conducts factory inspections; provides physicians and consumers with guidelines on radiation-emitting products. Conducts research, training, and educational programs.

▶NONGOVERNMENTAL

National Academies of Sciences, Engineering, and Medicine (NASEM), *Nuclear and Radiation Studies Board,* Keck Center, 500 5th St. N.W., 20001; (202) 334-2016. Fax, (202) 334-3077. Charles Ferguson, Director; William H. Tobey, Chair.

General email, nrsb@nas.edu
Web, www.nationalacademies.org/nrsb/nuclear-and-radiation-studies-board

Oversees studies on safety, security, technical efficacy, and other policy and societal issues arising from the application of nuclear and radiation-based technologies, including generation, use, remediation, and disposition of nuclear materials and radioactive wastes.

National Council on Radiation Protection and Measurements (NCRP), 7910 Woodmont Ave., #400, Bethesda, MD 20814-3095; (301) 657-2652. Fax, (301) 560-8005. Kathryn D. Held, President.
General email, ncrp@ncrponline.org
Web, www.ncrponline.org, Twitter, @NCRP_USA and YouTube, www.youtube.com/channel/UCdDER8FkZYQToU9pmL9MT5Q

Nonprofit organization chartered by Congress that collects and analyzes information and provides recommendations on radiation protection and measurement. Studies radiation emissions from household items and from office and medical equipment. Holds annual conference; publishes reports on radiation protection and measurement.

Recycling and Solid Waste

▶AGENCIES

Environmental Protection Agency (EPA), *Land and Emergency Management (OLEM), Resource Conservation and Recovery,* 1 Potomac Yard, 2777 S. Crystal Dr., Arlington, VA 22202 (mailing address: 1200 Pennsylvania Ave. N.W., #5301P, Washington, DC 20460); (703) 308-8895. Fax, (703) 308-0513. Carolyn Hoskinson, Director, (202) 236-3619. Web, www.epa.gov/aboutepa/about-office-land-and-emergency-management#orcr

Through the Reduce, Reuse, Recycle Program, provides information to communities about conserving energy and the natural environment, reducing waste, and recycling electronics and appliances.

▶CONGRESS

For a listing of relevant congressional committees and subcommittees, please see pages 284–285 or the Appendix.

▶NONGOVERNMENTAL

American Chemistry Council, 700 2nd St. N.E., 20002; (202) 249-7000. Fax, (202) 249-6100. Chris Jahn, President. Web, www.americanchemistry.com, Twitter, @AmChemistry and Facebook, www.facebook.com/AmericanChemistry

Membership: manufacturers of basic industrial chemicals that make or sell chemical products in the United States. Seeks to increase plastics recycling; conducts research on disposal of plastic products; sponsors research on waste-handling methods, incineration, and degradation; supports programs that test alternative waste management technologies. Monitors legislation and regulations.

Assn. of State and Territorial Solid Waste Management Officials (ASTSWMO), *1015 18th St. N.W., #803, 20036; (202) 640-1060. Fax, (202) 331-3254. Dania Rodriguez, Executive Director, (202) 640-1061, ext. 1.*
Web, www.astswmo.org, Twitter, @ASTSWMO and Facebook, www.facebook.com/ASTSWMO

Membership: state, District of Columbia, and territorial solid waste management officials. Works with the Environmental Protection Agency to develop policy affecting waste, materials management, and remediation. Including environmentally sustainable practices and restoration.

Energy Recovery Council, *2200 Wilson Blvd., #310, Arlington, VA 22201; (202) 467-6240.*
Edward (Ted) Michaels, President.
General email, erc@energyrecoverycouncil.org
Web, http://energyrecoverycouncil.org

Membership: companies that design, build, and operate resource recovery facilities. Promotes integrated solutions to municipal solid waste management issues. Encourages the use of waste-to-energy technology.

Environmental Technology Council, *1112 16th St. N.W., #420, 20036; (202) 783-0870. Fax, (202) 737-2038.*
James A. Williams II, Executive Director. Press, ext. 202.
Web, www.etc.org

Membership: environmental service firms. Interests include the recycling, detoxification, and disposal of hazardous and industrial waste and cleanup of contaminated industrial sites; works to encourage permanent and technology-based solutions to environmental problems. Provides the public with information.

EPS Industry Alliance, *1298 Cronson Blvd., #201, Crofton, MD 21114; (410) 451-8340. Fax, (410) 451-8343.*
Betsy Steiner, Executive Director. Toll-free, (800) 607-3772.
Web, www.epsindustry.org and Twitter, @espsrecycle

Membership: companies that recycle foam packaging material (expanded polystyrene). Coordinates national network of collection centers for postconsumer foam packaging products; helps to establish new collection centers.

Foodservice Packaging Institute (FPI), *7700 Leesburg Pike, #143, Falls Church, VA 22043; (703) 592-9889. Fax, (703) 592-9864. Natha Dempsey, President, (571) 255-4212.*
General email, jgoldman@fpi.org
Web, www.fpi.org, Twitter, @FPIHQ and Facebook, www.facebook.com/FoodservicePackagingInstitute

Membership: manufacturers, suppliers, and distributors of disposable products used in food service, packaging, and consumer products. Promotes the use of disposables for commercial and home use.

Glass Packaging Institute, *4250 N. Fairfax Dr., #600, Arlington, VA 22203; (703) 684-6359. Scott DeFife, President.*
General email, info@gpi.org
Web, www.gpi.org, Twitter, @ChooseGlass and Facebook, www.facebook.com/ChooseGlass

Membership: manufacturers of glass containers and their suppliers. Promotes industry policies to protect the environment, conserve natural resources, and reduce energy consumption; conducts research; monitors legislation affecting the industry. Interests include glass recycling.

Institute for Local Self-Reliance, *1200 18th St. N.W., #700, 20036; (202) 898-1610. Fax, (202) 898-1612. Neil N. Seldman, Director of Waste to Wealth Initiative, ext. 5210.*
General email, info@ilsr.org
Web, www.ilsr.org, Twitter, @ilsr and Facebook, www.facebook.com/localselfreliance

Advocates the development of a materials policy at local, state, and regional levels to reduce per capita consumption of raw materials and to shift from dependence on fossil fuels to reliance on renewable resources.

Institute of Scrap Recycling Industries, Inc., *1250 H St. N.W., #400, 20005; (202) 662-8500. Fax, (202) 626-9256. Robin K. Wiener, President, (202) 662-8512.*
General email, info@isri.org
Web, www.isri.org, Twitter, @ISRI and Facebook, www.facebook.com/isri1987

Represents processors, brokers, and consumers of scrap and recyclable paper, glass, plastic, textiles, rubber, ferrous and nonferrous metals, and electronics.

National Waste and Recycling Assn., *1550 Crystal Dr., #804, Arlington, VA 22202; (202) 244-4700. Darrell K. Smith, President, (202) 364-3730. Toll-free, (800) 424-2869.*
General email, info@wasterecycling.org
Web, https://wasterecycling.org, Twitter, @wasterecycling, Facebook, www.facebook.com/waterrecycling and YouTube, www.youtube.com/channel/UCsfdUSRuvAbQW QYfdDG0VCQ

Membership: private sector organizations engaged in refuse collection, processing, and disposal. Provides information on solid and hazardous waste recycling and waste equipment, organics and composting, waste-based energy, and emerging technologies; sponsors workshops. A merger of Environmental Industry Assns. and its sub-associations, the National Solid Waste Management Assn. and the Waste Equipment Technology Assn.

PaintCare Inc., *901 New York Ave. N.W. #300W, 20001; (855) 724-6809. Fax, (855) 358-2020. Marjaneh Zarrehparvar, Executive Director, (202) 719-3683. Press, (202) 719-3707.*
General email, info@paintcare.org
Web, www.paintcare.org, Facebook, www.facebook.com/WeRecyclePaint and Twitter, @WeRecyclePaint

Assists paint manufacturers in planning programs to help recycle or dispose of unneeded paint. Organizes paint drop-off locations. Supports statewide paint stewardship laws.

Secondary Materials and Recycled Textiles Assn. (SMART), *3465 Box Hill Corporate Dr., Suite H, Abingdon, MD 21009; (443) 640-1050. Fax, (410) 569-3340. Jackie King, Executive Director, ext. 105. Press, (443) 714-4826.*
General email, smartinfo@kingmgmt.org
Web, www.smartasn.org and Twitter, @SMARTTextile

Membership: organizations and individuals involved in producing, shipping, and distributing recycled textiles and other textile products. Sponsors educational programs; publishes newsletters. Monitors legislation and regulations.

Solid Waste Assn. of North America (SWANA), *1100 Wayne Ave., #650, Silver Spring, MD 20910-7219; (301) 585-2898. Fax, (301) 589-7068. David Biderman, Executive Director. Toll-free, (800) 467-9262.*
General email, membership@swana.org
Web, https://swana.org, Twitter, @SWANA, Facebook, www.facebook.com/SolidWasteAssociationOfNorth America and YouTube, www.youtube.com/channel/UCV9 SayYDBovqqyg_TTCJRvw

Membership: government and private industry officials who manage municipal solid waste programs. Interests include waste reduction, collection, recycling (including of electronics), combustion, and disposal. Conducts training and certification programs. Operates solid waste information clearinghouse. Monitors legislation and regulations.

U.S. Conference of Mayors, *Municipal Waste Management Assn., 1620 Eye St. N.W., 4th Floor, 20006; (202) 293-7330. Judy Sheahan, Assistant Executive Director for Environmental Policy, (202) 861-6775.*
General email, info@usmayors.org
Web, www.usmayors.org/mwma

Membership: mayors of cities with populations of 30,000 or more, local governments, and private companies involved in planning and developing solid waste management programs, including pollution prevention, waste-to-energy, and recycling. Interests include Superfund, brownfields, air and water quality, and waste-to-energy technologies. Assists communities with financing, environmental assessments, and associated policy implementation.

Water Pollution

▶**AGENCIES**

Bureau of Safety and Environmental Enforcement (BSEE) *(Interior Dept.), 1849 C St. N.W., MS 5438, 20240-0001; (202) 208-3985. Scott A. Angelle, Director (Acting). Public Affairs, (202) 208-6184.*
General email, bseepublicaffairs@bsee.gov
Web, www.bsee.gov, Twitter, @BSEEgov, Facebook, www .facebook.com/BSEEgov and YouTube, www.youtube.com/ user/bseegov

Responsible for inspections, enforcement, and safety of offshore oil and gas operations. Functions include the development and enforcement of safety and environmental regulations, research, inspections, offshore regulatory and compliance programs, oil spill response, and training of inspectors and industry professionals.

Bureau of Safety and Environmental Enforcement (BSEE) *(Interior Dept.), Environmental Compliance Program (ECP), 45600 Woodland Rd., Sterling, VA 20166; (703) 787-1567. David S. Fish (USCG, Ret.), Chief.*
General email, bseepublicaffairs@bsee.gov
Web, www.bsee.gov/what-we-do/environmental-compliance

Responsible for monitoring and improving industry's compliance with environmental standards, by reviewing and enforcing permits, laws, and regulations during the Outer Continental Shelf (OCS) operations.

Bureau of Safety and Environmental Enforcement (BSEE) *(Interior Dept.), Offshore Regulatory Programs (OORP), 45600 Woodland Rd., Sterling, VA 20166; (202) 208-3985. (703) 787-1000. Stacey Noem, Chief.*
General email, bseepublicaffairs@bsee.gov
Web, www.bsee.gov/what-we-do/offshore-regulatory-programs

Develops standards, regulations, and compliance programs governing Outer Continental Shelf oil, gas, and minerals exploration and operations. Purview includes safety management programs, safety and pollution prevention research, technology assessments, standards for inspections and enforcement policies, and accident investigation practices.

Bureau of Safety and Environmental Enforcement (BSEE) *(Interior Dept.), Oil Spill Preparedness Division (OSPD), 45600 Woodland Rd., Sterling, VA 20166; Eric Miller, Chief, (703) 787-1569. Public Affairs, (202) 208-6184.*
General email, bseepublicaffairs@bsee.gov
Web, www.bsee.gov/what-we-do/oil-spill-preparedness

Reviews oil spill response plans and executes team training and exercises; inspects response equipment and resources.

Bureau of Safety and Environmental Enforcement (BSEE) *(Interior Dept.), Safety and Incident Investigations Division (SIID), 1849 C St. N.W., #5438, 20240; Michael Idziorek, Chief, (202) 208-4858. Public Affairs, (202) 208-6184.*
General email, bseepublicaffairs@bsee.gov
Web, www.bsee.gov/what-we-do/incident-investigations

Manages the National Investigations Program, which conducts investigations of major offshore incidents as outlined in the Outer Continental Shelf Lands Act (OCSLA).

Environmental Protection Agency (EPA), *1200 Pennsylvania Ave. N.W., #3000, MC 1101A, 20460; (202) 564-4700. Fax, (202) 501-1450. Michael S. Regan, Administrator. Press, (202) 564-4355. Switchboard, (202) 272-0167. TTY, (800) 877-8339.*
Web, www.epa.gov, Twitter, @EPA, Facebook, www .facebook.com/EPA and YouTube, www.youtube.com/c/ EPAgov

Administers federal environmental policies, research, and regulations; provides information on environmental subjects, including water pollution, pollution prevention, hazardous and solid waste disposal, air and noise pollution, pesticides and toxic substances, and radiation.

Environmental Protection Agency (EPA), *Land and Emergency Management (OLEM), Underground Storage Tanks, 1300 Pennsylvania Ave N.W., 7th Floor, 20460 (mailing address: 1200 Pennsylvania Ave. N.W., #5401R, Washington, DC 20460); (202) 564-1611. Mark Baralo, Director (Acting).*
Web, www.epa.gov/ust and www.epa.gov/aboutepa/about-office-land-and-emergency-management#oust

Carries out regulations for underground storage tank systems storing petroleum and certain hazardous substances to prevent groundwater contamination.

Environmental Protection Agency (EPA), *Water (OW),* *1200 Pennsylvania Ave. N.W., MC 4101M, 20460; (202) 564-5700. Radhika Fox, Assistant Administrator.*
Web, www.epa.gov/aboutepa/about-office-water

Implements the Clean Water Act and portions of the Ocean Dumping Ban Act, Marine Plastics Pollution Research and Control Act, London Dumping Convention, and the International Convention for the Prevention of Pollution from Ships.

Environmental Protection Agency (EPA), *Water (OW),* *Ground Water and Drinking Water, 1200 Pennsylvania Ave. N.W., #2104, MC 4601M, 20460; (202) 564-3750. Fax, (202) 564-3753. Jennifer McLain, Director, (202) 564-4029. Toll-free hotline, (800) 426-4791.*
General email, ogwdw.web@epa.gov
Web, www2.epa.gov/aboutepa/about-office-water#ground

Develops standards for the quality of drinking water supply systems; regulates underground injection of waste and protection of groundwater wellhead areas under the Safe Drinking Water Act; provides information on public water supply systems.

Environmental Protection Agency (EPA), *Water (OW),* *Science and Technology, 1200 Pennsylvania Ave. N.W., #5231, MC 4301M, 20460; (202) 566-0430. Fax, (202) 566-0441. Deborah Nagle, Director.*
General email, ost.comments@epa.gov
Web, www2.epa.gov/aboutepa/about-office-water#science

Develops and coordinates water pollution control programs for the Environmental Protection Agency. Assists state and regional agencies in establishing water quality standards and planning local water resources management. Develops guidelines for industrial and municipal wastewater discharge. Provides grants for water quality monitoring and swimming advisories at recreational coastal and Great Lakes beaches. Formulates shellfish protection policies and issues fish advisories.

Environmental Protection Agency (EPA), *Water (OW),* *Wastewater Management, 1200 Pennsylvania Ave. N.W., #7116A, MC 4201M, 20460; (202) 564-0748. Fax, (202) 501-2238. Andrew Sawyers, Director.*

Web, www2.epa.gov/aboutepa/about-office-water#wastewater

Oversees the issuance of water permits. Responsible for the Pretreatment Program regulating industrial discharges to local sewage treatment. Oversees the State Revolving Funds Program, which provides assistance for the construction of wastewater treatment plants. Implements programs for prevention of water pollution, including the Clean Watersheds Needs Survey, National Pollutant Discharge Elimination System (NPDES), U.S.–Mexico Border Water Infrastructure Grant Program, and WaterSense.

Environmental Protection Agency (EPA), *Water (OW),* *Wastewater Management, Sustainable Water Infrastructure, 1200 Pennsylvania Ave. N.W., #7119A, MC 4204M, 20460; (202) 564-5385. Fax, (202) 501-2346. Raffael Stein, Director.*
Web, www2.epa.gov/aboutepa/about-office-water# wastewater and www.epa.gov/sustainable-water-infrastructure

Directs programs to assist in the design and construction of municipal sewage systems. Develops programs to ensure efficient operation and maintenance of municipal wastewater treatment facilities.

National Drinking Water Advisory Council *(Environmental Protection Agency), 1200 Pennsylvania Ave. N.W., #4100T, MC 4601M, 20460; (202) 564-4029. Jennifer McLain, Director.*
Web, www.epa.gov/ndwac

Membership: members of the general public, state and local agencies, and private groups. Advises the EPA administrator on activities, functions, and policies relating to implementation of the Safe Drinking Water Act.

National Oceanic and Atmospheric Administration (NOAA) *(Commerce Dept.), Response and Restoration (ORR), Bldg. 4, 1305 East-West Hwy., 10th Floor, Silver Spring, MD 20910; (206) 526-6317. Fax, (301) 713-4389. Scott R. Lundgren, Director.*
General email, orr.webmaster@noaa.gov
Web, https://response.restoration.noaa.gov and Twitter, @NOAACleanCoasts

Provides information on damage to marine ecosystems caused by pollution and debris. Offers information on spill trajectory projections and chemical hazard analyses. Researches trends of toxic contamination on U.S. coastal regions.

U.S. Coast Guard (USCG) *(Homeland Security Dept.), Marine Environmental Response Policy (CG-5R), 2703 Martin Luther King Jr. Ave. S.E., MS 7318, 20593-7516; (202) 372-2234. Capt. Ricardo B. Alonso, Chief.*
Web, www.dco.uscg.mil/Our-Organization/Assistant-Commandant-for-Response-Policy-CG-5R/Office-of-Incident-Management-Preparedness-CG-5RI/Marine-Envir

Oversees cleanup operations after spills of oil and other hazardous substances in U.S. waters, on the Outer Continental Shelf, and in international waters. Reviews coastal zone management and enforces international standards for pollution prevention and response.

U.S. Coast Guard (USCG) *(Homeland Security Dept.),* *National Pollution Funds Center, 2703 Martin Luther King Jr. Ave. S.E., MS 7605, 20593-7605; (202) 795-6003. Fax, (202) 795-6900. William R. Grawe, Director, (202) 705-6900. Command duty center, (202) 494-9118. FOIA, (202) 795-6029. National Response Center, (800) 424-8802. Web, www.uscg.mil/npfc*

Certifies pollution liability coverage for vessels and companies involved in oil exploration and transportation in U.S. waters and on the Outer Continental Shelf. Ensures adequacy of funds to respond to oil spills and deters future spills by managing the Oil Spill Liability Trust Fund.

U.S. Coast Guard (USCG) *(Homeland Security Dept.),* *National Response Center, 2100 2nd St. S.W., #2111B, 20593-0001; (202) 372-2097. Dana S. Tulis, Director. Hotline, (800) 424-8802. Local, (202) 267-2675. General email, NRC@uscg.mil*

Web, www.nrc.uscg.mil and www.epa.gov/emergency-response/national-response-center

Maintains 24-hour hotline for reporting oil, biological, radiological, and chemical discharges in the environment. Notifies appropriate federal officials to reduce the effects of accidents. Monitors suspicious activities and security breaches in U.S. waters. Works cooperatively with the Environmental Protection Agency.

►CONGRESS

For a listing of relevant congressional committees and subcommittees, please see pages 284–285 or the Appendix.

►NONGOVERNMENTAL

Assn. of Clean Water Administrators, *1634 Eye St. N.W., #750, 20006; (202) 756-0605. Fax, (202) 793-2600. Julia Anastasio, Executive Director. General email, memberservices@acwa-us.org*

Web, www.acwa-us.org and Twitter, @cleanwaterACWA

Membership: state and interstate water quality regulators. Represents the states' concerns on implementation, funding, and reauthorization of the Clean Water Act. Monitors legislation and regulations.

Clean Water Action, *1444 Eye St. N.W., #400, 20005; (202) 895-0420. Fax, (202) 895-0438. Robert (Bob) Wendelgass, Chief Executive Officer. General email, cwa@cleanwater.org*

Web, https://cleanwateraction.org, Twitter, @cleanh2oaction and Facebook, www.facebook.com/CleanWaterAction

Citizens' organization interested in clean, safe, and affordable water. Works to influence public policy through education, technical assistance, and grassroots organizing. Interests include toxins and pollution, drinking water, water conservation, sewage treatment, pesticides, mass burn incineration, bay and estuary protection, and consumer water issues. Monitors legislation and regulations.

Clean Water Network, *600 Pennsylvania Ave. S.E., #400, 20003; (303) 573-3871, ext. 395. Kristine Oblock, Coordinator.*

Web, www.clean-water-network.org and Twitter, @CleanWaterNet

Advocacy coalition of local and national groups that support clean waterways. Provides resources for organizers to protect waterways against human-caused pollution. (Affiliated with Environment America and Environment Colorado.)

National Assn. of Clean Water Agencies, *1130 Connecticut Ave. N.W., #1050, 20036; (202) 833-2672. Fax, (888) 267-9505. Adam Krantz, Chief Executive Officer, (202) 833-4651; Natham Gardner-Andrews, General Counsel and Advocacy, (202) 833-3692. General email, info@nacwa.org*

Web, www.nacwa.org and Twitter, @NACWA

Represents public wastewater treatment works, public and private organizations, law firms representing public clean water agencies, and nonprofit or academic organizations. Interests include water quality and watershed management. Sponsors conferences. Monitors legislation and regulations.

Ocean Conservancy, *1300 19th St. N.W., 8th Floor, 20036; (202) 429-5609. Fax, (202) 872-0619. Janis Searles Jones, Chief Executive Officer. Toll-free, (800) 519-1541. General email, membership@oceanconservancy.org*

Web, www.oceanconservancy.org, Twitter, @OurOcean, Facebook, www.facebook.com/oceanconservancy and Coastal clean-up, cleanup@oceanconservancy.org

Works to protect the health of oceans and seas. Advocates policies that restrict discharge of pollutants harmful to marine ecosystems.

Water Environment Federation, *601 Wythe St., Alexandria, VA 22314-1304; (703) 684-2400. Fax, (703) 684-2492. Walt Marlowe, Executive Director, (703) 684-2430. Toll-free, (800) 666-0206. General email, csc@wef.org*

Web, www.wef.org and Twitter, @WEForg

Membership: civil and environmental engineers, wastewater treatment plant operators, scientists, government officials, and others concerned with water quality. Works to preserve and improve water quality worldwide. Provides the public with technical information and educational materials. Monitors legislation and regulations.

Water Research Foundation, *1199 N. Fairfax St., #900, Alexandria, VA 22314-1445; (303) 347-6100. Peter Grevatt, Chief Executive Officer, (571) 384-2094. General email, info@WaterRF.org*

Web, www.waterrf.org, Twitter, @WaterResearch and Facebook, www.facebook.com/waterresearchfoundation

Conducts research and promotes technology to treat and recover materials from wastewater, stormwater, and seawater, including water, nutrients, energy, and biosolids. (Headquarters in Denver, Colo.)

RESOURCES MANAGEMENT

General

►AGENCIES

Bureau of Land Management (BLM) *(Interior Dept.)* *Planning and NEPA, Resources and Planning,* 1849 C St. N.W., #5646, 20240; (202) 208-3801. (202) 208-4896. *David Jenkins, Assistant Director.*
Web, www.blm.gov/programs/planning-and-nepa

Manages more than 245 million acres of public land and about 700 million acres of subsurface mineral estate for several uses. Develops and implements natural resource programs for renewable resources use and protection, including management of forested land, rangeland, soil and water quality, recreation, and cultural programs.

Interior Dept. (DOI), 1849 C St. N.W., MS 7328, 20240; (202) 208-3100. *Debra Anne (Deb) Haaland, Secretary.* Library, (202) 208-5815. Press, (202) 208-6416. Toll-Free TTY, (800) 877-8339.
General email, feedback@ios.doi.gov
Web, www.doi.gov, Twitter, @Interior, Facebook, www .facebook.com/USInterior, Blog, www.doi.gov/blog, Library, www.doi.gov/library and Twitter, Secretary, @SecDebHaaland

Manages most federal land through its component agencies. Responsible for conservation and development of mineral, water, and fish and wildlife resources. Operates recreation programs for federal parks, refuges, and public lands. Preserves and administers scenic and historic areas. Administers Native American lands and develops relationships with tribal governments. Reference library open to the public 7:45 a.m.–5:00 p.m.

Interior Dept. (DOI), *Assistant Secretary for Insular and International Affairs (ASIIA),* 1849 C. St. N.W., 20240; (202) 208-6971. *Keone Nakoa, Deputy Assistant Secretary.*
Web, www.doi.gov/asiia

Administers laws and regulations relating to the understanding, conservation, responsible use, and collaborative science-based management of U.S. territories, Guam, American Samoa, the U.S. Virgin Islands, and the Commonwealth of the Northern Mariana Islands, and administers and oversees federal assistance under the Compacts of Free Association (Compact) to the Federated States of Micronesia, the Republic of the Marshall Islands, and the Republic of Palau, freely associated states, international technical engagement, and the oceans, Great Lakes, and coasts. Oversees the Office of Insular Affairs, Office of International Affairs, and the Ocean, Great Lakes and Coastal Program.

Tennessee Valley Authority, *Government Affairs,* 1 Massachusetts Ave. N.W., #300, 20444; (202) 898-2999. *Jeffrey J. (Jeff) Lyash, President.*

General email, tvainfo@tva.gov
Web, www.tva.gov, Twitter, @TVAnews and Facebook, www.facebook.com/TVA

Coordinates resource conservation, development, and land-use programs in the Tennessee River Valley. Activities include forestry and wildlife development.

U.S. Fish and Wildlife Service *(Interior Dept.), Bird Habitat Conservation,* 5275 Leesburg Pike, MS MB, Falls Church, VA 22041-3803; (703) 358-1784. Fax, (703) 358-2217. *Ken Richkus, Division Chief,* (703) 358-1780. Migratory bird offices, (703) 358-1714.
Web, www.fws.gov/birds, Twitter, @usfwsBirds and Facebook, www.facebook.com/usfwsmigratorybirds

Membership: government and private-sector conservation experts. Works to protect, restore, and manage wetlands and other habitats for migratory birds and other animals and to maintain migratory bird and waterfowl populations.

►NONGOVERNMENTAL

The Conservation Fund, 1655 N. Fort Myer Dr., #1300, Arlington, VA 22209-3199; (703) 525-6300. Fax, (703) 525-4610. *Lawrence A. (Larry) Selzer, President.*
General email, webmaster@conservationfund.org
Web, www.conservationfund.org, Twitter, @ConservationFnd, Facebook, www.facebook.com/ theconservationfund and YouTube, www.youtube.com/ user/TheConservationFund

Creates partnerships with the private sector, nonprofit organizations, and public agencies to promote land and water conservation. Operates land trusts, identifies real estate for conservation, and runs loan programs.

Izaak Walton League of America, 707 Conservation Lane, Gaithersburg, MD 20878-2983; (301) 548-0150. Fax, (301) 548-0146. *Scott Kovarovics, Executive Director.* Toll-free, (800) 453-5463.
General email, info@iwla.org
Web, www.iwla.org, Twitter, @IWLA_org and Facebook, www.facebook.com/iwla.org

Grassroots organization that promotes conservation of natural resources and the environment. Interests include air and water pollution, farmland conservation, clean and renewable energy, wildlife habitat protection, and instilling conservation ethics in outdoor recreationists.

National Academies of Sciences, Engineering, and Medicine (NASEM), *Agriculture and Natural Resources Board,* Keck Center, 500 5th St. N.W., #WS632, 20001; (202) 334-2088. Fax, (202) 334-1978. *Robin Schoen, Director.*
General email, skwan@nas.edu
Web, http://dels.nas.edu/banr and Twitter, @NASM_Ag

Promotes and oversees research on the environmental impact of agriculture and food sustainability, including forestry, fisheries, wildlife, and the use of land, water, and other natural resources.

National Audubon Society, Public Policy, 1200 18th St. N.W., #500, 20036; (202) 861-2242. (844) 428-3826. Fax, (202) 600-7990. Justin Stokes, Deputy Chief Conservation Officer.
General email, audubonaction@audubon.org
Web, www.audubon.org and Twitter, @audubonsociety

Citizens' interest group that promotes environmental conservation and education, focusing on birds and their habitats. Provides information on bird science, water resources, public lands, rangelands, forests, parks, wildlife conservation, and the National Wildlife Refuge System. Operates state offices, local chapters, and nature centers nationwide. (Headquarters in New York.)

National Sustainable Agriculture Coalition, 110 Maryland Ave. N.E., #209, 20002-5622; (202) 547-5754. Sarah Hackney, Coalition Director; Eric J. Deeble, Policy Director.
General email, info@sustainableagriculture.net
Web, www.sustainableagriculture.net, Twitter, @sustainableag and Facebook, www.facebook.com/sustainableag

National alliance of farm, rural, and conservation organizations. Advocates federal policies that promote environmentally sustainable agriculture, natural resources management, and rural community development. Monitors legislation and regulations.

National Wildlife Federation, 11100 Wildlife Center Dr., Reston, VA 20190-5362 (mailing address: P.O. Box 1583, Merrifield, VA 22116-1583); (703) 438-6000. Collin O'Mara, President. Toll-free, (800) 822-9919.
General email, info@nwf.org
Web, www.nwf.org, Twitter, @NWF, Facebook, www.facebook.com/NationalWildlife, YouTube, www.youtube.com/user/NationalWildlife and Blog, https://blog.nwf.org

Promotes conservation of natural resources; provides information on the environment and resource management; takes legal action on environmental issues. publishes magazines, that are available by subsription.

Renewable Natural Resources Foundation, 6010 Executive Blvd., #700, N. Bethesda, MD 20852-3827; (301) 770-9101. Fax, (301) 770-9104. Robert D. Day, Executive Director.
General email, info@rnrf.org
Web, https://rnrf.org and Facebook, www.facebook.com/renewablenaturalresourcesfoundation

Consortium of professional, scientific, and education organizations working to advance scientific and public education in renewable natural resources. Encourages the application of sound scientific practices to resource management and conservation. Fosters interdisciplinary cooperation among its member organizations.

U.S. Chamber of Commerce, Environment, Technology, and Regulatory Affairs, 1615 H St. N.W., 20062-2000; (202) 659-6000. Chad S. Whiteman, Vice President of Environment and Regulatory Affairs.
General email, environment@uschamber.com
Web, www.uschamber.com, Twitter, @Regulations and Facebook, www.facebook.com/uschamber

Develops policy on all issues affecting the production, use, and conservation of natural resources, including fuel and nonfuel minerals, timber, water, public lands, onshore and offshore energy, wetlands, and endangered species.

Winrock International, Washington Office, 2451 Crystal Dr., #700, Arlington, VA 22202; (703) 302-6500. Fax, (703) 302-6512. Rodney Ferguson, President.
General email, information@winrock.org
Web, www.winrock.org and Twitter, @WinrockIntl

Works with communities and governments to foster fair resource use, incentives for sustainable land use, and alternative income strategies to reduce pressure on natural resources. (Headquarters in Little Rock, AR.)

Forests and Rangelands

▶ **AGENCIES**

Forest Service (Agriculture Dept.), 201 14th St. S.W., 20024 (mailing address: 1400 Independence Ave. S.W., Washington, DC 20250-1111); (202) 205-1661. Fax, (202) 205-1765. Randy Moore, Chief. Press, (202) 205-1134. Toll-free, (800) 832-1355.
Web, www.fs.fed.us, Twitter, @forestservice and Facebook, www.facebook.com/USForestService

Manages national forests and grasslands for outdoor recreation and sustained yield of renewable natural resources, including timber, water, forage, fish, and wildlife. Cooperates with state and private foresters; conducts forestry research.

Forest Service (Agriculture Dept.) Recreation, Heritage and Volunteer Resources, Youth Conservation Corps, 201 14th St. 5-S.W., 20024 (mailing address: 1400 Independence Ave. S.W., MS 1125, Washington, DC 20250-1125); (202) 205-1240. Gordie Blum, Director, (Acting), Recreation, Heritage. Toll-free, (800) 832-1355.
Web, www.fs.fed.us/working-with-us/opportunities-for-young-people/youth-conservation-corps-opportunities

Administers, with the National Park Service and the Fish and Wildlife Service, the Youth Conservation Corps, a summer employment and training public works program for youths ages fifteen to eighteen. The program is conducted in national parks, in national forests and grasslands, and on national wildlife refuges.

Forest Service (Agriculture Dept.), Fire and Aviation Management, 201 14th St. S.W., 3rd Floor, 3 Central, 20024 (mailing address: 1400 Independence Ave. S.W., MS 1107, Washington, DC 20250-0003); (202) 579-8172. Fax, (703) 605-1401. Jake Nuttall, Director (Acting), (505) 842-3281.
Web, www.fs.fed.us/fire

Responsible for aviation and fire management programs, including fire control planning and prevention, suppression of fires, and the use of prescribed fires. Provides state foresters with financial and technical assistance for fire protection in forests and on rural lands.

Forest Service *(Agriculture Dept.), International Programs,* 1 Thomas Circle N.W., #400, 20005; (202) 644-4600. Fax, (202) 644-4603. Valdis E. Mezainis, Director, (202) 644-4621. Executive Assistant, (202) 644-4550.
Web, www.fs.fed.us/global

Responsible for the Forest Service's involvement in international forest conservation efforts. Analyzes international resource issues; promotes information exchange; provides planning and technical assistance. Interested in sustainable forest management, covering illegal logging, climate change, and migratory species.

Forest Service *(Agriculture Dept.), National Forest System,* 201 14th St. S.W., 4 NW, 20024; (202) 205-1523. Fax, (202) 649-1180. Christopher (Chris) French, Deputy Chief, (202) 205-1689.
Web, www.fs.fed.us

Manages 193 million acres of forests and rangelands. Products and services from these lands include timber, water, forage, wildlife, minerals, and recreation.

Forest Service *(Agriculture Dept.), Research and Development,* 1400 Independence Ave., S.W., 20250-0003 (mailing address: 1400 Independence Ave. S.W., Washington, DC 20250); (202) 205-1665. Fax, (202) 205-1530. Alex Friend, Deputy Chief, (202) 205-1665. Toll-free, (800) 832-1355.
Web, www.fs.fed.us/research

Conducts biological, physical, and economic research related to forestry, including studies on harvesting methods, acid deposition, international forestry, the effects of global climate changes on forests, and forest products. Provides information on the establishment, improvement, and growth of trees, grasses, and other forest vegetation. Works to protect forest resources from fire, insects, diseases, and animal pests. Examines the effect of forest use activities on water quality, soil erosion, and sediment production. Conducts continuous forest survey and analyzes outlook for future supply and demand.

Forest Service *(Agriculture Dept.), State and Private Forestry,* 201 14th St. S.W., #3NW, 20024 (mailing address: 1400 Independence Ave. S.W., MS 1109, Washington, DC 20250-1109); (202) 205-1657. Fax, (202) 205-1174. John Crockett, Associate Deputy Chief (Acting), (703) 517-5211; Jaelith Hall-Rivera, Deputy Chief, (202) 205-1290.
Web, www.fs.usda.gov/about-agency/state-private-forestry

Assists state and private forest owners with the protection and management of 574 million acres of forest and associated watershed lands. Assistance includes fire control, protecting forests from insects and diseases, land-use planning, developing multiple-use management, and improving practices in harvesting, processing, and marketing of forest products.

Smithsonian Tropical Research Institute, *Forest Global Earth Observatory (ForestGEO),* 10th St. and Constitution Ave. N.W., MS 166, 20560; (202) 633-1836. Fax, (202) 786-2563. Stuart J. Davies, Director.
General email, ForestGEO@si.edu
Web, https://forestgeo.si.edu, Twitter, @ForestGEO and Facebook, www.facebook.com/ForestGEO

Conducts long-term forest research and contributes to the scientific community through training, grants, and partnerships with international organizations. Uses research to monitor impacts of climate change and to guide natural resource policy. (Formerly Center for Tropical Forest Science.)

▶**CONGRESS**

For a listing of relevant congressional committees and subcommittees, please see pages 284–285 or the Appendix.

▶**NONGOVERNMENTAL**

American Forests, 1220 L St. N.W., #750, 20005; (202) 737-1944. Fax, (202) 737-2457. Jad Daley, Chief Executive Officer.
General email, info@americanforests.org
Web, www.americanforests.org, Twitter, @AmericanForests and Facebook, www.facebook.com/AmericanForests

Citizens' interest group that promotes protection and responsible management of forests and natural resources. Provides information on conservation, public land policy, and urban forestry. Promotes an international tree-planting campaign to help mitigate climate change. Monitors legislation and regulations.

Forest Resources Assn., 1901 Pennsylvania Ave. N.W., #303, 20006; (202) 296-3937. Deb Hawkinson, President.
General email, info@forestresources.org
Web, www.forestresources.org, Twitter, @forestresources and Facebook, www.facebook.com/ForestResourcesAssociation

Membership: suppliers, brokers, transporters, and consumers of unprocessed wood products, as well as businesses that serve the forest products supply chain. Provides information on the safe, efficient, and sustainable harvest of forest products and their transport from woods to mill; works to ensure continued access to the timberland base. Monitors legislation and regulations. Helps improve skills, elevate technical and operative expertise, identify workforce isses and define proactive solutions, establish leadership development programs.

International Wood Products Assn., 4214 King St., Alexandria, VA 22302; (703) 820-6696. Fax, (703) 820-8550. Bradley McKinney, Executive Director.
General email, info@iwpawood.org
Web, www.iwpawood.org and Twitter, @iwpawood

Membership: companies that handle imported wood products. Encourages environmentally responsible forest management and international trade in wood products.

Sponsors research and environmental education on tropical forestry.

National Assn. of Conservation Districts (NACD), *509 Capitol Court N.E., 20002-4937; (202) 547-6223. Fax, (202) 547-6450. Jeremy Peters, Chief Executive Officer.*
General email, info@nacdnet.org
Web, www.nacdnet.org, Twitter, @NACDconserve and Facebook, www.facebook.com/NACDconserve

Membership: conservation districts (local subdivisions of state government). Works to promote the conservation of private and public lands, forests, and other natural resources. Interests include forestry and wildlife and range management.

National Assn. of State Foresters, *444 N. Capitol St. N.W., #387, 20001; (202) 624-5415. Fax, (202) 624-5407. Jay Farrell, Executive Director.*
General email, nasf@stateforesters.org
Web, www.stateforesters.org, Twitter, @StateForesters, Facebook, www.facebook.com/StateForesters and YouTube, www.youtube.com/channel/UCDuBvUxNVL6C pBumvKBUSlw

Membership: directors of state forestry agencies from all states, the District of Columbia, and U.S. territories. Interests include forest management, employment generated by forestry and forest products, and climate change. Monitors legislation and regulations.

National Lumber and Building Material Dealers Assn., *2001 K St. N.W., 3rd Floor N, 20006; (202) 367-1169. Jonathan M. Paine, President.*
General email, info@dealer.org
Web, www.dealer.org

Membership: federated associations of retailers in the lumber and building material industries. Supports forest conservation programs and environmental safety.

Pinchot Institute for Conservation, *1400 16th St. N.W., #350, 20036; (202) 797-6580. Fax, (202) 797-6583. William C. (Will) Price, President.*
Web, www.pinchot.org and Twitter, @pinchotlegacy

Seeks to advance forest conservation and sustainable natural resources management nationally through research and analysis, education and technical assistance, and development of conservation leaders.

Society of American Foresters, *2121 K St. N.W., #315, 20037; (202) 938-3910. Fax, (202) 938-3911. Terry Baker, Chief Operating Officer. Toll-free, (866) 897-8720.*
General email, membership@safnet.org
Web, www.eforester.org

Association of forestry professionals. Provides technical information on forestry, accredits forestry programs in universities and colleges, and publishes scientific forestry journals.

Sustainable Forestry Initiative, *2121 K St. N.W., #750, 20037; (202) 596-3450. Kathy Abusow, President.*
General email, info@forests.org
Web, www.forests.org, Twitter, @sfiprogram, Facebook, www.facebook.com/SustainableForestryInitiative and YouTube, www.youtube.com/user/SFIProgram

Works to ensure protection of forests while continuing to produce wood and paper products as needed by the economy. Encourages perpetual growing and harvesting of trees and protection of wildlife, plants, soil, water, and air quality. Seeks to mitigate illegal logging. Interests include the economic, environmental, cultural, and legal issues related to forestry.

The Wilderness Society, *1801 Pennsylvania Ave. N.W. #200, 20006; (202) 833-2300. Fax, (202) 429-3958. Jamie Williams, President. Toll-free, (800) 843-9453.*
General email, member@tws.org
Web, www.wilderness.org, Twitter, @wilderness and Faebook, www.facebook.com/TheWildernessSociety

Promotes preservation of wilderness and the responsible management of federal lands, including national parks and forests, wilderness areas, wildlife refuges, and land administered by the Interior Dept.'s Bureau of Land Management.

Land Resources

▶**AGENCIES**

Bureau of Land Management (BLM) *(Interior Dept.), 1849 C St. N.W., #5665, 20240; (202) 208-3801. Fax, (202) 208-5242. Tracy Stone-Manning, Director. Press, (202) 208-6913.*
Web, www.blm.gov, Twitter, @BLMNational, Facebook, www.facebook.com/BLMNational, YouTube, www .youtube.com/user/BLMNational and Email, BLM_ Press@blm.gov

Manages public lands and federally owned mineral resources, including oil, gas, and coal. Resources managed and leased include wildlife habitats, timber, minerals, open space, wilderness areas, forage, and recreational resources. Surveys federal lands and maintains public land records. Sustains the health, diversity and productivity of public lands for present and future generations

Bureau of Land Management (BLM) *(Interior Dept.), Lands, Realty, and Cadastral Survey, 1849 C St. N.W., #2134LM, 20003; (202) 912-7353. Fax, (202) 912-7199. Dominica Van Koten, Chief Cadastral Surveyor, (571) 266-9585.*
Web, www.blm.gov/programs/lands-and-realty and Cadastral Survey, www.blm.gov/programs/lands-and-realty/cadastral-survey

Manages a wide range of public land transactions, such as purchases, acquisitions; sales, exchanges; withdrawals; leases and permits; right-of-way authorizations, cadastral survey services. Energy development, permitting commercial filming, to defining boundaries and maintaining public land records. Facilitate commercial, recreational, and conservation opportunities on public lands.

Bureau of Reclamation *(Interior Dept.), 1849 C St. N.W., MS 7069-MIB, 20240-0001; (202) 513-0501. Fax, (202) 513-0309. M. Camille Camlimlim Touton, Commissioner. Press, (202) 513-0575.*
Web, www.usbr.gov, Twitter, @usbr, Facebook, www .facebook.com/bureauofreclamation and YouTube, www .youtube.com/user/reclamation

Responsible for acquisition, administration, management, and disposal of lands in seventeen western states associated with bureau water resource development projects. Provides overall policy guidance for land use, including agreements with public agencies for outdoor recreation, fish and wildlife enhancement, and land-use authorizations such as leases, licenses, permits, and rights of way. Interests include increasing water-based outdoor recreation facilities and opportunities.

Community Planning and Development (CPD) *(Housing and Urban Development Dept.), Environment and Energy, 451 7th St. S.W., #7212, 20410; (202) 402-3988. Liz Zepeda, Director (Acting), (202) 402-3988.*
Web, www.hud.gov/program_offices/comm_planning/ library/energy

Issues policies and sets standards for environmental and land-use planning and environmental management practices. Oversees HUD implementation of requirements on environment, historic preservation, archaeology, flood plain management, wetlands protection, environmental justice (ensuring that the environment and human health are fairly protected for all people/Executive Order 12898), coastal zone management, sole source aquifers, farmland protection, endangered species, airport clear zones, explosive hazards, and noise.

Environmental Protection Agency (EPA), *Land and Emergency Management (OLEM), 1200 Pennsylvania Ave. N.W., MC 5101T, 20460; (202) 566-0200. Fax, (202) 566-0207. Barry Breem, Assistant Administrator (Acting). National Response Center, (800) 424-8802. Superfund information hotline, (800) 424-9346. TTY, (202) 272-0165.*
Web, www2.epa.gov/aboutepa/about-office-land-and-emergency-management-olem

Administers and enforces the Resource Conservation and Recovery Act and the Brownfields Program and Superfund.

Environmental Protection Agency (EPA), *Land and Emergency Management (OLEM), Brownfields and Land Revitalization, 1300 Pennsylvania Ave. N.W., #5105T, 20460; (202) 566-2731. David Lloyd, Director.*
Web, www.epa.gov/land-revitalization and www.epa.gov/ brownfields

Provides grants and technical assistance to communities, states, tribes, and other stakeholders needing resources to prevent, assess, safely clean up, and sustainably reuse brownfields and formerly contaminated properties.

Environmental Protection Agency (EPA), *Land and Emergency Management (OLEM), Resource Conservation and Recovery, 1 Potomac Yard, 2777 S. Crystal Dr., Arlington, VA 22202 (mailing address:*

1200 Pennsylvania Ave. N.W., #5301P, Washington, DC 20460); (703) 308-8895. Fax, (703) 308-0513. Carolyn Hoskinson, Director, (202) 236-3619.
Web, www.epa.gov/aboutepa/about-office-land-and-emergency-management#orcr

Protects human health and the environment by ensuring responsible national management of hazardous and nonhazardous waste. Administers the Resource Conservation and Recovery Act.

Interior Dept. (DOI), *Assistant Secretary for Land and Minerals Management, 1849 C St. N.W., MS 6628, 20240; (202) 208-6734. Laura Daniel-Davis, Principal Deputy Assistant Secretary.*
Web, www.doi.gov

Directs and supervises the Bureau of Land Management; the Bureau of Ocean Energy Management, Regulation, and Enforcement; Bureau of Safety and Environmental Enforcement; and the Office of Surface Mining. Supervises programs associated with land-use planning, onshore and offshore minerals, surface mining reclamation and enforcement, and Outer Continental Shelf minerals management.

Interior Dept. (DOI), *Office of Hearings and Appeals, Board of Land Appeals (IBLA), 801 N. Quincy St., #300, Arlington, VA 22203; (703) 235-3750. Fax, (703) 235-8349. Steven J. Lechner, Chief Administrative Judge (Acting).*
General email, ibla@oha.doi.gov
Web, www.doi.gov/oha/about-interior-board-land-appeals

Adjunct office of the interior secretary that decides appeals from decisions rendered by the Bureau of Land Management; Bureau of Ocean Energy Management, Regulation, and Enforcement; Office of Surface Mining and Reclamation Enforcement; and Bureau of Indian Affairs concerning the use and disposition of public lands and minerals. (Board is separate and independent from bureaus and offices whose decisions it reviews.)

Interior Dept. (DOI), *Wildland Fire (OWF), 1849 C St. N.W., MS 4447, 20240; (202) 208-2703. Jeff Rupert, Director, (202) 208-2719.*
General email, wildlandfire@ios.doi.gov
Web, www.doi.gov/wildlandfire, Twitter, @DOIWildlandFire and Facebook, www.facebook.com/ DOIWildlandFire

Oversees all wildland fire management programs, policies, budgets, and information technology in order to manage risk to firefighters, communities, and landscapes. Bridges the individual fire programs of the four land management bureaus; supports the wildland fire needs of the bureau.

Natural Resources Conservation Service (NRCS) *(Agriculture Dept.), 1400 Independence Ave. S.W., #6149-S, 20250 (mailing address: P.O. Box 2890, Washington, DC 20013-2890); (202) 720-3210. Terry Cosby, Chief, (202) 720-4613. Information, (202) 720-2791.*
Web, www.nrcs.usda.gov, Twitter, @USDA_NRCS and Facebook, www.facebook.com/USDA

Responsible for soil and water conservation programs, including watershed protection, flood prevention, river basin surveys, resource conservation and development. Provides landowners, operators, state and local units of government, and community groups with technical assistance in carrying out local programs. Website has a Spanish-language link.

Surface Mining Reclamation and Enforcement (OSMRE) *(Interior Dept.),* 1849 C St. N.W., #4512, 20240; (202) 208-4006. Glenda H. Owens, Deputy Director. Press, (202) 208-2565. TTY, (202) 208-2694.
General email, getinfo@osmre.gov
Web, www.osmre.gov, Twitter, @OSMRE and *Facebook, www.facebook.com/OSMRE*

Regulates surface mining of coal and surface effects of underground coal mining. Responsible for reclamation of abandoned coal mine lands.

Tennessee Valley Authority, *Government Affairs,* 1 Massachusetts Ave. N.W., #300, 20444; (202) 898-2999. Jeffrey J. (Jeff) Lyash, President.
General email, tvainfo@tva.gov
Web, www.tva.gov, Twitter, @TVAnews and *Facebook, www.facebook.com/TVA*

Coordinates resource conservation, development, and land-use programs in the Tennessee River Valley. Provides information on land usage in the region.

U.S. Geological Survey (USGS) *(Interior Dept.), Earth Resources Observation and Science (EROS) Center,* 12201 Sunrise Valley Dr., MS 516, Reston, VA 20192; (703) 648-5320. (605) 594-6151. Christopher Reich, Program Coordinator (Acting), (703) 648-0002; Pete Doucette, Center Director, (605) 594-2586.
Web, www.usgs.gov/centers/eros

Studies land change and compiles maps and data used by researchers, resource managers and policymakers. Operates the Landsat satellite program with NASA, maintaining the largest civilian collection of Earth images in existence. (Center located in Garretson, S.D.)

U.S. Geological Survey (USGS) *(Interior Dept.), Land Change Science Program,* 12201 Sunrise Valley Dr., MS 516, Reston, VA 20192-0002; (703) 648-5320. Christopher Reich, Program Coordinator (Acting).
Web, http://usgs.gov/land-resources/land-change-science-program

Conducts research on land cover and documents land change; develops tools to support resource allocation decisions.

►CONGRESS

For a listing of relevant congressional committees and subcommittees, please see pages 284–285 or the Appendix.

►NONGOVERNMENTAL

American Geosciences Institute, 4220 King St., Alexandria, VA 22302-1502; (703) 379-2480. Fax, (703) 379-7563. Jonathan E. Arthur, Executive Director, ext. 202.

General email, agi@americangeosciences.org
Web, www.americangeosciences.org, Twitter, @AGI_ Updates and *Facebook, www.facebook.com/americangeosciences*

Membership: earth science societies and associations. Provides education and outreach. Maintains computerized database of the world's geoscience literature (available to the public for a fee). Monitors legislation and regulations.

American Resort Development Assn., 1201 15th St. N.W., #400, 20005-2842; (202) 371-6700. Fax, (202) 289-8544. Jason Gamel, President. Consumer hotline, (855) 939-1515.
General email, consumer@arda-roc.org
Web, www.arda.org

Membership: U.S. and international developers, builders, financiers, marketing companies, and others involved in resort, recreational, and community development. Serves as an information clearinghouse; monitors federal and state legislation affecting land, time-share, and community development industries.

Land Trust Alliance, 1250 H St. N.W., #600, 20005; (202) 638-4725. Andrew Bowman, Chief Executive Officer, (202) 800-2250.
General email, info@lta.org
Web, www.landtrustalliance.org and *Twitter, @LTalliance*

Membership: organizations and individuals who work to conserve land resources. Serves as a forum for the exchange of information; conducts research and public education programs. Monitors legislation and regulations.

National Assn. of Conservation Districts (NACD), 509 Capitol Court N.E., 20002-4937; (202) 547-6223. Fax, (202) 547-6450. Jeremy Peters, Chief Executive Officer.
General email, info@nacdnet.org
Web, www.nacdnet.org, Twitter, @NACDconserve and *Facebook, www.facebook.com/NACDconserve*

Membership: conservation districts (local subdivisions of state government). Works to promote the conservation of private and public lands , forests, and other natural resources. Interests include forestry, water, flood plain, wildlife, and range management.

Public Lands Council, 1275 Pennsylvania Ave. N.W., #801, 20004; (202) 347-0228. Niels Hansen, President; Kaitlynn Glover, Executive Director, ext. 9128.
Web, http://publiclandscouncil.org, Twitter, @PLCranching and *Facebook, www.facebook.com/PublicLandsCouncil*

Membership: cattle and sheep ranchers who hold permits and leases to graze livestock on public lands. (Affiliated with the National Cattlemen's Beef Association and the American Sheep Industry Association, and the Association of National Grasslands.)

Public Lands Foundation (PLF), P.O. Box 7226, Arlington, VA 22207-0226; (703) 935-0916. Fax, (888) 204-9814. Courtney Lyons-Garcia, Executive Director. Toll-free, (866) 985-9636.

Web, https://publicland.org, Twitter, @PublicLandFdn, Facebook, www.facebook.com/publiclandfdn and YouTube, www.youtube.com/channel/UCN1xue81zjyix7x hR65uSVQ

Membership advocacy organization dedicated to ensuring public lands remain public; interested in public land use and management.

Scenic America, 727 15th St. N.W., #1100, 20005-6029; (202) 792-1300. Mark Falzone, President.
Web, www.scenic.org, Twitter, @ScenicAmerica and Facebook, www.facebook.com/ScenicAmerica

Membership: national, state, and local groups concerned with land-use control, growth management, and landscape protection. Works to enhance the scenic quality of America's communities and countryside. Provides information and technical assistance on scenic byways, tree preservation, economics of aesthetic regulation, billboard and sign control, scenic areas preservation, and growth management.

Wallace Genetic Foundation, 4910 Massachusetts Ave. N.W., #221, 20016; (202) 966-2932. Fax, (202) 966-3370. Michaela Oldfield, Executive Director.
General email, wgfdn@wallacegenetic.org
Web, www.wallacegenetic.org

Supports national and international nonprofits in the areas of sustainable agriculture, agricultural research, preservation of farmland, reduction of environmental toxins, conservation, biodiversity protection, and global climate issues.

The Wilderness Society, 1801 Pennsylvania Ave. N.W. #200, 20006; (202) 833-2300. Fax, (202) 429-3958. Jamie Williams, President. Toll-free, (800) 843-9453.
General email, member@tws.org
Web, www.wilderness.org, Twitter, @wilderness and Faebook, www.facebook.com/TheWildernessSociety

Promotes preservation of wilderness and the responsible management of federal lands, including national parks and forests, wilderness areas, wildlife refuges, and land administered by the Interior Dept.'s Bureau of Land Management.

Metals and Minerals

▶ **AGENCIES**

Bureau of Land Management (BLM) (Interior Dept.), Energy, Minerals, and Realty Management, 5275 Leesburg Pike, Falls Church, VA 22041; (202) 208-4201. Nicholas Douglas, Assistant Director.
Web, www.blm.gov/programs/energy-and-minerals

Develops and administers policy, guidance, and performance oversight for the renewable energy program, including wind, solar, and geothermal energy; the fluid minerals program, including oil, gas, and helium; the solid minerals programs, including mining law, coal, oil shale, and salable minerals; the lands and realty programs; and the Public Land Survey System. Provides national leadership and develops national partnerships with organizations interested in energy, minerals, and realty management.

Bureau of Safety and Environmental Enforcement (BSEE) (Interior Dept.), Offshore Regulatory Programs (OORP), 45600 Woodland Rd., Sterling, VA 20166; (202) 208-3985. (703) 787-1000. Stacey Noem, Chief.
General email, bseepublicaffairs@bsee.gov
Web, www.bsee.gov/what-we-do/offshore-regulatory-programs

Develops standards, regulations, and compliance programs governing Outer Continental Shelf oil, gas, and minerals exploration and operations. Purview includes safety management programs, safety and pollution prevention research, technology assessments, standards for inspections and enforcement policies, and accident investigation practices.

Interior Dept. (DOI), Assistant Secretary for Land and Minerals Management, 1849 C St. N.W., MS 6628, 20240; (202) 208-6734. Laura Daniel-Davis, Principal Deputy Assistant Secretary.
Web, www.doi.gov

Directs and supervises the Bureau of Land Management; the Bureau of Ocean Energy Management, Regulation, and Enforcement; Bureau of Safety and Environmental Enforcement; and the Office of Surface Mining. Supervises programs associated with land-use planning, onshore and offshore minerals, surface mining reclamation and enforcement, and Outer Continental Shelf minerals management.

Interior Dept. (DOI), Natural Resources Revenue (ONRR), Washington Office, 1849 C St. N.W., MS 5134, 20240; (202) 513-0600. Fax, (202) 513-0682. Kimbra Davis, Director.
Web, www.onrr.gov, Twitter, @DOINRR and Facebook, www.facebook.com/DOIONRR

Manages revenues associated with federal offshore and federal and American Indian onshore mineral leases, as well as revenues received through offshore renewable energy efforts. Collects and disburses all natural resources revenues.

Interior Dept. (DOI), Office of Hearings and Appeals, Board of Land Appeals (IBLA), 801 N. Quincy St., #300, Arlington, VA 22203; (703) 235-3750. Fax, (703) 235-8349. Steven J. Lechner, Chief Administrative Judge (Acting).
General email, ibla@oha.doi.gov
Web, www.doi.gov/oha/about-interior-board-land-appeals

Adjunct office of the interior secretary that issues final decisions concerning the Surface Mining Control and Reclamation Act of 1977. (Board is separate and independent from bureaus and offices whose decisions it reviews.)

U.S. Geological Survey (USGS) (Interior Dept.), Mineral Resources Program, 12201 Sunrise Valley Dr., MS 913, Reston, VA 20192-0002; (703) 648-6108.
Thomas C. Crafford, Program Coordinator; Sarah Ryker, Associate Director of Energy and Minerals, (703) 648-5210.

General email, minerals@usgs.gov

Web, www.usgs.gov/energy-and-minerals/mineral-resources-program, Twitter, @USGSMinerals, Facebook, www.facebook.com/USGeologicalSurvey and YouTube, www.youtube.com/usgs

Coordinates mineral resource activities for the Geological Survey, including research and information on U.S. and international mineral resources, baseline information on earth materials, and geochemical and geophysical instrumentation and applications.

U.S. Geological Survey (USGS) *(Interior Dept.), National Minerals Information Center, 12201 Sunrise Valley Dr., MS 991, Reston, VA 20192-0002; (703) 648-4976. Steven D. Textoris, Chief.*
Web, http://usgs.gov/centers/nmic

Collects, analyzes, and disseminates information on ferrous and nonferrous metals, including gold, silver, platinum group metals, iron, iron ore, steel, chromium, and nickel.

► CONGRESS

For a listing of relevant congressional committees and subcommittees, please see pages 284–285 or the Appendix.

► NONGOVERNMENTAL

Mineralogical Society of America, *3635 Concorde Pkwy., #500, Chantilly, VA 20151-1110; (703) 652-9950. Fax, (703) 652-9951. Ann E Benbow, Executive Director.*
General email, business@minsocam.org

Web, www.minsocam.org and Facebook, www.facebook.com/Mineralogical-Society-of-America-146637322076348

Membership: mineralogists, petrologists, crystallographers, geochemists, educators, students, and others interested in mineralogy. Conducts research; sponsors educational programs; promotes industrial application of mineral studies.

National Mining Assn., *101 Constitution Ave. N.W., #500 East, 20001-2133; (202) 463-2600. Fax, (202) 463-2666. Rich Nolan, President. Press, (202) 463-2642.*
General email, webmaster@nma.org

Web, www.nma.org

Membership: domestic producers of coal and industrial-agricultural minerals and metals; manufacturers of mining equipment; engineering and consulting firms; and financial institutions. Interests include mine-leasing programs, mine health and safety, research and development, public lands, and minerals availability. Monitors legislation and regulations.

Native American Trust Resources

► AGENCIES

Administration for Children and Families (ACF) *(Health and Human Services Dept.), Administration for Native Americans (ANA), Mary E. Switzer Bldg., 330 C St. S.W.,* Room 4126, 20201; (202) 690-7732. Fax, (202) 690-7441. Hope MacDonald LoneTree, Deputy Commissioner; Michelle Sauve, Executive Director of ICNAA. Toll-free, (877) 922-9262.
General email, anacomments@acf.hhs.gov

Web, https://acf.hhs.gov/ana and Facebook, www.facebook.com/administrationfornativeamericans

Awards grants to assist tribes with resources to develop legal and organizational capacities to protect their natural environments.

Bureau of Indian Affairs (BIA) *(Interior Dept.), Indian Economic Development (IED), Indian Energy and Economic Development (IEED), 1849 C St. N.W., #4152, 20240; (202) 219-0740. Fax, (202) 208-4564. (202) 208-6764. Jack R. Stevens, Director (Acting). phone, (202) 208-6764.*
Web, www.bia.gov/as-ia/ieed/contact-ieed

Assists tribes with environmentally responsible exploration, development, and management of energy and mineral resources to generate new jobs and sustainable tribal economies.

Bureau of Indian Affairs (BIA) *(Interior Dept.), Indian Services (OIS), 1849 C St. N.W., MS-3645 MIB, 20240; Jeanette Hanna, Deputy Bureau Director. (202) 513-7640.*
Web, www.bia.gov/bia/ois

Assists tribal and Indian landowners with managing natural and energy trust resources. Builds, maintains and moniters housing, transportation, energy, and irrigation infrastructure; and provides law enforcement protection, corrections, and administration of justice services on federal Indian lands.

Bureau of Indian Affairs (BIA) *(Interior Dept.), Trust Services (OTS), 1849 C St. N.W., #4600, 20240; (202) 208-3615. Johnna Blackhair, Deputy Bureau Director.*
Web, www.bia.gov/bia/ots and Email, OTS@bia.gov

Assists in developing and managing bureau programs involving Native American and alaska natives peoples Trust resources (agriculture, forestry, wildlife, water, and power, energy and mineral development, irrigation, real property management probate, and title records).

Bureau of Land Management (BLM) *(Interior Dept.), Energy, Minerals, and Realty Management, 5275 Leesburg Pike, Falls Church, VA 22041; (202) 208-4201. Nicholas Douglas, Assistant Director.*
Web, www.blm.gov/programs/energy-and-minerals

Provides leadership to the Bureau of Land Management's trust management for Indian minerals operations, surveys, and trust patent preparation.

Environment and Natural Resources Division *(Justice Dept.), Indian Resources (IRS), 150 M St. N.E., #3.1142, 20002 (mailing address: P.O. Box 7611, L'Enfant Plaza, Washington, DC 20044); (202) 305-0269. Fax, (202) 305-0275. S. Craig Alexander, Chief.*

Web, www.justice.gov/enrd/Indian-resources-section

Represents the United States in suits, including trust violations, brought on behalf of individual Native Americans and Native American tribes against the government. Also represents the United States as trustee for Native Americans in court actions involving protection of Native American land and resources.

Environmental Protection Agency (EPA), *Water (OW), 1200 Pennsylvania Ave. N.W., MC 4101M, 20460; (202) 564-5700. Radhika Fox, Assistant Administrator.*
Web, www.epa.gov/aboutepa/about-office-water

Works with American Indian tribes to implement the Safe Drinking Water Act and improve access to safe drinking water on tribal lands.

Interior Dept. (DOI), *1849 C St. N.W., MS 7328, 20240; (202) 208-3100. Debra Anne (Deb) Haaland, Secretary. Library, (202) 208-5815. Press, (202) 208-6416. Toll-Free TTY, (800) 877-8339.*
General email, feedback@ios.doi.gov

Web, www.doi.gov, Twitter, @Interior, Facebook, www .facebook.com/USInterior, Blog, www.doi.gov/blog, Library, www.doi.gov/library and Twitter, Secretary, @SecDebHaaland

Principal U.S. conservation agency. Manages most federal land, including Native American lands; develops relationships with tribal governments. Reference library open to the public 7:45 a.m.–5:00 p.m.

Interior Dept. (DOI), *Natural Resources Revenue (ONRR), Washington Office, 1849 C St. N.W., MS 5134, 20240; (202) 513-0600. Fax, (202) 513-0682. Kimbra Davis, Director.*
Web, www.onrr.gov, Twitter, @DOINRR and Facebook, www.facebook.com/DOIONRR

Manages revenues associated with federal offshore and federal and American Indian onshore mineral leases, as well as revenues received through offshore renewable energy efforts. Collects and disburses all natural resources revenues.

Interior Dept. (DOI), *Office of the Solicitor, Indian Affairs, 1849 C St. N.W., MS 6511, 20240; (202) 208-3401. Fax, (202) 219-1791. Ann Marie Bledsoe Downes, Deputy Solicitor (Acting).*
Web, www.doi.gov/solicitor/headquarters

Advises the Bureau of Indian Affairs and the secretary of the interior on all legal matters, including its trust responsibilities toward Native Americans and their natural resources.

► **CONGRESS**

For a listing of relevant congressional committees and subcommittees, please see pages 284–285 or the Appendix.

► **NONGOVERNMENTAL**

Native American Rights Fund, *Washington Office, 1514 P St. N.W. (Rear), Suite D., 20005; (202) 785-4166. Fax, (202) 822-0068. John E. Echohawk, Executive Director.*
General email, info@narf.org

Web, www.narf.org, Facebook, www.facebook.com/Native AmericanRightsFund, Twitter, @NDNrights and YouTube, www.youtube.com/c/NativeAmericanRightsFund

Provides Native Americans and Alaska Natives with legal assistance in land claims, water rights, hunting, and other areas. Practices federal Indian law. (Headquarters in Boulder, Colo.)

Ocean and Coastal Resources

► **AGENCIES**

Bureau of Oceans and International Environmental and Scientific Affairs (OES) *(State Dept.), 2201 C St. N.W., #3880 and #7256, 20520-7818; (202) 647-7575. Monica Medina, Assistant Secretary, (202) 647-1554.*
Web, www.state.gov/e/oes, Twitter, @SciDiplomacyUSA, Facebook, www.facebook.com/ScienceDiplomacyUSA and YouTube, www.youtube.com/channel/rCumiP05SKp5qlhi ZbXBJEiw?view_as=subscriber

Promotes water security, peaceful cooperation on polar issues, and sustainable ocean policy.

Bureau of Oceans and International Environmental and Scientific Affairs (OES) *(State Dept.), Marine Conservation (OMC), 2201 C St. N.W., #2758, 20520; (202) 647-2337. David F. Hogan, Director (Acting).*
Web, www.state.gov/about-us-office-of-marine-conservation

Handles the management, conservation, and restoration of living marine resources. Seeks to maintain a healthy and productive marine environment and ecosystems.

Bureau of Safety and Environmental Enforcement (BSEE) *(Interior Dept.), Safety Enforcement Division (SED), 45600 Woodland Rd., Sterling, VA 20166; Janine Tobias, Chief. Public Affairs, (202) 208-6184.*
General email, bseepublicaffairs@bsee.gov
Web, www.bsee.gov/what-we-do/safety-enforcement

Inspects, monitors, and enforces safety regulations of offshore companies to ensure compliance and conservation of offshore resources.

Environmental Protection Agency (EPA), *Water (OW), 1200 Pennsylvania Ave. N.W., MC 4101M, 20460; (202) 564-5700. Radhika Fox, Assistant Administrator.*
Web, www.epa.gov/aboutepa/about-office-water

Restores and maintains oceans, watersheds, and their aquatic ecosystems. Implements the Clean Water Act and portions of the Coastal Zone Act, Ocean Dumping Ban Act, Marine Protection Act, Shore Protection Act, Marine Plastics Pollution Research and Control Act, and the

National Park Service

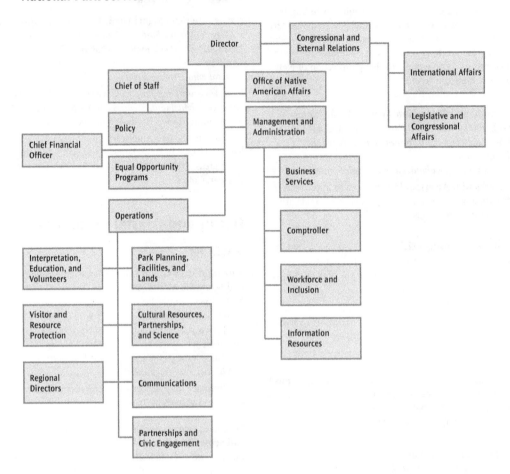

International Convention for the Prevention of Pollution from Ships.

Interior Dept. (DOI), *Ocean, Great Lakes, and Coastal Program,* *1849 C St. N.W., MS 3530, 20240; (202) 208-1378. Liza Johnson, Program Coordinator.*
Web, www.doi.gov/ocean and Facebook, www.facebook.com/USInterioroceancoastsgreatlakes

Works in partnership with federal agencies, tribes, states, and other groups to protect coastal areas along the Pacific and Atlantic Oceans, Gulf of Mexico and, Caribbean, and Great Lakes through habitat conservation and resource management, Conducts diverse scientific and resource monitoring programs, adaptive management strategies and provides data, tools and information. Newswave Newletter, which comes out quarterly.

National Oceanic and Atmospheric Administration (NOAA) *(Commerce Dept.), National Marine Sanctuaries,* *1305 East-West Hwy., 11th Floor, Silver Spring, MD 20910; (301) 713-3125. Fax, (301) 713-0404. Rebecca Holyoke, Deputy Director, (240) 533-0685.*
General email, sanctuaries@noaa.gov
Web, https://sanctuaries.noaa.gov and Twitter, @sanctuaries

Administers the National Marine Sanctuary Program, which seeks to protect the ecology and the recreational and cultural resources of marine and Great Lakes waters.

National Oceanic and Atmospheric Administration (NOAA) *(Commerce Dept.), National Ocean Service (NOS),* *Silver Spring Metro Center 4, 1305 East-West Hwy., #9149, Silver Spring, MD 20910; (301) 713-3074. Fax, (301) 713-4269. Nicole LaBoeuf, Assistant Administrator. Press, (301) 713-3066.*
General email, nos.info@noaa.gov
Web, https://oceanservice.noaa.gov

Manages charting and geodetic services, oceanography and marine services, coastal resource coordination, and marine survey operations; conducts environmental cleanup of coastal pollution.

National Oceanic and Atmospheric Administration (NOAA) *(Commerce Dept.), Ocean Acidification Program (OAP),* *1315 East-West Hwy., #10356, Silver Spring, MD 20910; (301) 734-1075. Elizabeth (Libby) Jewett, Director.*
General email, noaa.oceanacidification@noaa.gov
Web, https://oceanacidification.noaa.gov and Twitter, @OA_NOAA

Monitors changes in ocean chemistry due to the continued acidification of the oceans and Great Lakes, and assesses the socioeconomic impacts. Maintains relationships with scientists, resource managers, stakeholders, policymakers, and the public to implement adaptation strategies and monitor the biological responses of ecologically and economically important species. Operates from NOAA's Office of Oceanic and Atmospheric Research.

National Oceanic and Atmospheric Administration (NOAA) *(Commerce Dept.), Oceanic and Atmospheric Research (OAR), 1315 East-West Hwy., Silver Spring, MD 20910; (301) 713-2458. Craig N. McLean, Assistant Administrator.*
Web, https://research.noaa.gov and Twitter, @NOAAResearch

Works to protect, restore, and manage coastal and ocean resources through ecosystem-based management.

U.S. Geological Survey (USGS) *(Interior Dept.), Coastal and Marine Hazards and Resources, 12201 Sunrise Valley Dr., MS 905, Reston, VA 20192; (703) 648-6422. John W. Haines, Program Coordinator.*
Web, www.usgs.gov/programs/cmhrp

Handles resource assessment, exploration research, and marine geologic and environmental studies on U.S. coastal regions and the Outer Continental Shelf.

►CONGRESS

For a listing of relevant congressional committees and subcommittees, please see pages 284–285 or the Appendix.

►NONGOVERNMENTAL

Blue Frontier Campaign, *1530 P St. N.W., 20005 (mailing address: P.O. Box 19367, Washington, DC 20036); (202) 387-8030. David Helvarg, Executive Director.*
General email, info@bluefront.org
Web, www.bluefront.org, Twitter, @Blue_Frontier, Facebook, www.facebook.com/bluefront.org and YouTube, www.youtube.com/user/seaweedrebel

Promotes ocean conservation. Seeks to strengthen unity among ocean conservationists and encourage public awareness at the local, regional, and national levels. Main office in CA.

Coastal States Organization, *50 F St. N.W., #570, 20001; (202) 800-0580. Derek Brockbank, Executive Director, (202) 800-0633.*
General email, cso@coastalstates.org
Web, www.coastalstates.org, Twitter, @Coastal_States and Facebook, www.facebook.com/CoastalStatesOrganization

Nonpartisan organization that represents governors of 35 U.S. coastal states, territories, and commonwealths on management of ocean, coastal, and Great Lakes resource issues. Interests include ocean dumping, coastal pollution, wetlands preservation and restoration, national oceans policy, and the Outer Continental Shelf. Gathers and analyzes data to assess state coastal needs; sponsors and participates in conferences and workshops.

Joint Ocean Commission Initiative, *c/o Meridian Institute, 1800 M St. N.W., #400N, 20036; (202) 354-6444. Fax, (202) 354-6441. John Ehrmann, Senior Partner.*
General email, joci@merid.org
Web, www.jointoceancommission.org and Twitter, @JointOceanCI

Provides policy information on ocean conservation. Makes recommendations toward the health and productivity of oceans, coasts, and Great Lakes. Promotes public awareness of ocean policy issues. Monitors legislation and regulations.

Marine Technology Society, *One Thomas Circle, # 700, 20005; (202) 717-8705. Fax, (202) 347-4302. Kristina Norman, Executive Director (Acting), (202) 827-7171.*
General email, mtsoffice@mtsociety.org
Web, www.mtsociety.org, Twitter, @MTSociety and Facebook, www.facebook.com/MarineTechnologySociety/?ref=hl

Membership: ocean scientists, engineers,practioners, policymakers, educators and technologists, interested in marine science, technology, and education.

National Academies of Sciences, Engineering, and Medicine (NASEM), *Gulf Research Program, Keck Center, 500 5th St. N.W., 20001; (202) 334-2138. Lauren Alexander Augustine, Executive Director; David Daniel, Chair.*
General email, gulfprogram@nas.edu
Web, www.nationalacademies.org/gulf and Twitter, @NASEM_Gulf

Promotes oil system safety and the protection of human health and the environment in the Gulf of Mexico and other U.S. outer continental shelf areas.

National Academies of Sciences, Engineering, and Medicine (NASEM), *Ocean Studies Board, Keck Center, 500 5th St. N.W., MS 607, 20001; (202) 334-2714. Fax, (202) 334-2885. Claudia Benitez-Nelson, Chair; Susan Roberts, Director.*
General email, osbfeedback@nas.edu
Web, www.nationalacademies.org/osb/ocean-studies-board

Conducts research to understand, manage, and conserve coastal and marine environments. Areas of interest include the ocean's role in the global climate system, technology and infrastructure needs for ocean research, ocean-related aspects of national security, fisheries science and management, and ocean education.

National Ocean Industries Assn., *1120 G St. N.W., #900, 20005; (202) 347-6900. Fax, (202) 347-8650. Erik Milito, President.*
General email, media@noia.org
Web, www.noia.org and Twitter, @oceanindustries

Membership: manufacturers, producers, suppliers, and support and service companies involved in marine, offshore, and ocean work. Interests include offshore oil and gas supply and production, deep-sea mining, ocean thermal energy, and new energy sources.

Oceana, *1025 Connecticut Ave. N.W., #200, 20036; (202) 833-3900. Fax, (202) 833-2070.*
Andrew F. (Andy) Sharpless, Chief Executive Officer.
Toll-Free, (877) 762-3262.
General email, info@oceana.org
Web, www.oceana.org, Twitter, @Oceana, Facebook, www.facebook.com/oceana and Twitter CEO, @Oceana_Andy

Promotes ocean conservation both nationally and internationally; pursues policy changes to reduce pollution and protect fish, marine mammals, and other forms of sea life. Conducts specific scientific, legal, policy, and advocacy campaigns. Monitors legislation and regulations.

Parks and Recreation Areas

►AGENCIES

Bureau of Reclamation *(Interior Dept.), 1849 C St. N.W., MS 7069-MIB, 20240-0001; (202) 513-0501. Fax, (202) 513-0309. M. Camille Camlimlim Touton, Commissioner. Press, (202) 513-0575.*
Web, www.usbr.gov, Twitter, @usbr, Facebook, www.facebook.com/bureauofreclamation and YouTube, www.youtube.com/user/reclamation

Responsible for acquisition, administration, management, and disposal of lands in seventeen western states associated with bureau water resource development projects. Provides overall policy guidance for land use, including agreements with public agencies for outdoor recreation, fish and wildlife enhancement, and land-use authorizations such as leases, licenses, permits, and rights of way. Interests include increasing water-based outdoor recreation facilities and opportunities.

Forest Service *(Agriculture Dept.), Recreation, Heritage, and Volunteer Resources, 400 Independence Ave. S.W., MS 1125, 20003; (202) 205-1240. Fax, (703) 605-5131. Michiko Martin, Director (Acting), (202) 205-1241.*
Web, www.fs.fed.us/recreation

Develops policy and sets guidelines on administering national forests and grasslands for recreational purposes. (The Forest Service administers some of the lands designated as national recreation areas.)

Interior Dept. (DOI), *Assistant Secretary for Fish and Wildlife and Parks, 1849 C St. N.W., #3160, 20240; (202) 208-4416. Fax, (202) 208-4684. Shannon A. Estenoz, Assistant Secretary, (202) 208-4545.*
Web, www.doi.gov

Responsible for programs associated with the development, conservation, and use of fish, wildlife, recreational, historical, and national park system resources. Coordinates marine environmental quality and biological resources programs with other federal agencies. Oversees the U.S. Fish and Wildlife Service and National Park Service.

National Park Service (NPS) *(Interior Dept.), Policy, 1849 C St. N.W., MS 2659-Policy, 20240; (202) 354-3950. Fax, (202) 371-5189. Alma Ripps, Chief, (202) 354-3951.*

Web, www.nps.gov/orgs/1892/index.htm and https://npspolicy.nps.gov

Coordinates the preparation, analysis, review, and communication of NPS policies. Administers the committee management program. Staffs the NPS advisory board; makes recommendations on the historical significance of national trails and landmarks.

National Park Service (NPS), *Interior Dept., 1849 C St. N.W., #3115, 20240; (202) 208-6843. Fax, (202) 208-7889. Charles F. (Chuck) Sams III, Director.*
General email, asknps@nps.gov
Web, www.nps.gov, Twitter, @NatlParkService and Facebook, www.facebook.com/nationalparkservice

Oversees coordination, planning, and financing of public outdoor recreation programs at all levels of government. Conducts recreation research surveys; administers financial assistance program to states for planning and development of outdoor recreation programs. (Some lands designated as national recreation areas are not under NPS jurisdiction.)

Tennessee Valley Authority, *Government Affairs, 1 Massachusetts Ave. N.W., #300, 20444; (202) 898-2999. Jeffrey J. (Jeff) Lyash, President.*
General email, tvainfo@tva.gov
Web, www.tva.gov, Twitter, @TVAnews and Facebook, www.facebook.com/TVA

Operates Land Between the Lakes, a national recreation and environmental education area located in western Kentucky and Tennessee.

U.S. Fish and Wildlife Service *(Interior Dept.), National Wildlife Refuge System, 1849 C St. N.W., #3349, 20240; (202) 208-5333. Cynthia Martinez, Chief. Toll-free, (800) 344-9453.*
Web, www.fws.gov/refuges, Twitter, @USFWSRefuges, Facebook, www.facebook.com/USFWSRefuges and YouTube, www.youtube.com/USFWSRefuges

Manages the National Wildlife Refuge System. Most refuges are open to public use; activities include bird and wildlife watching, fishing, hunting, and environmental education.

►CONGRESS

For a listing of relevant congressional committees and subcommittees, please see pages 284–285 or the Appendix.

►NONGOVERNMENTAL

American Hiking Society, *8403 Colesville Rd., #1100, Silver Spring, MD 20910; (301) 565-6704. Fax, (301) 565-6714. Kathryn (Kate) Van Waes, Executive Director. Toll-free, (800) 972-8608.*
General email, info@americanhiking.org
Web, https://americanhiking.org, Twitter, @AmericanHiking and Facebook, www.facebook.com/AmericanHiking

Membership: individuals and clubs interested in preserving America's trail system and protecting the interests of trail users. Provides information on outdoor volunteer opportunities on public lands.

National Park Foundation, *1500 K St. N.W., #700, 20005; (202) 796-2500. Fax, (202) 796-2509. Will Shafroth, President; Deb Haaland, Ex- Officio Director (Secretary of the Interior). Toll-Free, (888) 467-2757.*
General email, ask-npf@nationalparks.org
Web, www.nationalparks.org, Twitter, @NationalParkFdn, Facebook, www.facebook.com/NationalParkFoundation and YouTube, www.youtube.com/nationalparkfoundation

Encourages private-sector support and builds strategic partnerships to protect and enhance the national park system; provides stewardship, innovation,grants and sponsors educational and cultural acivities. Chartered by Congress and chaired by the Interior secretary.

National Park Trust, *401 E. Jefferson St., #207, Rockville, MD 20850; (301) 279-7275. Fax, (301) 279-7211. Grace K. Lee, Executive Director, ext. 11.*
General email, info@parktrust.org
Web, www.parktrust.org and Twitter, @natparktrust

Protects national parks, wildlife refuges, and historic monuments. Uses funds to purchase private land within or adjacent to existing parks and land suitable for new parks; works with preservation organizations to manage acquired resources.

National Parks Conservation Assn., *777 6th St. N.W., #700, 20001-3723; (202) 223-6722. Fax, (202) 454-3333. Theresa Pierno, President. Toll-free, (800) 628-7275.*
General email, npca@npca.org
Web, www.npca.org, Twitter, @npca and Facebook, www.facebook.com/NationalParks

Citizens interest group that seeks to protect and enhance national parks and other park system areas.

National Recreation and Park Assn. NRPA, *22377 Belmont Ridge Rd., Ashburn, VA 20148-4501; (703) 858-0784. Kristine Stratton, Chief Executive Officer. Toll-free, (800) 626-6772.*
General email, customerservice@nrpa.org
Web, www.nrpa.org, Twitter, @nrpa_news and Facebook, www.facebook.com/NationalRecreationandParkAssociation

Membership: park and recreation professionals and interested citizens. Promotes to advance parks, recreation and environmental conservation efforts that enhance the quality of life for all people. Facilitates development, expansion, and management of resources; provides technical assistance for park and recreational programs; and provides professional development to members. Monitors legislation and regulations.

Outdoor Recreation Roundtable, *1203 K St. N.W., #350, 20005; Jessica Wahl Turner, Executive Director.*
Web, http://recreationroundtable.org, Twitter, @ORRoundtable and Email, orr@recreationroundtable.org

Membership: recreation industry associations, recreation enthusiast groups, and leading corporations in the recreation products and services sectors. Promotes health and well-being by conserving public lands and waterways, enhancing infrastruture and access through outdoor recreation. Seeks to keep public lands open for off-road vehicles. Monitors regulations and legislation.

Rails-to-Trails Conservancy, *2121 Ward Court N.W., 5th Floor, 20037; (202) 331-9696. Fax, (202) 223-9257. Ryan Chao, President. Press, (202) 974-5155.*
Web, www.railstotrails.org, Twitter, @railstotrails and Facebook, www.facebook.com/railstotrails

Promotes the conversion of abandoned railroad corridors into hiking and biking trails for public use. Provides public education programs and technical and legal assistance. Publishes trail guides. Monitors legislation and regulations.

Scenic America, *727 15th St. N.W., #1100, 20005-6029; (202) 792-1300. Mark Falzone, President.*
Web, www.scenic.org, Twitter, @ScenicAmerica and Facebook, www.facebook.com/ScenicAmerica

Membership: national, state, and local groups concerned with land-use control, growth management, and landscape protection. Works to enhance the scenic quality of America's communities and countryside. Provides information and technical assistance on scenic byways, tree preservation, economics of aesthetic regulation, billboard and sign control, scenic areas preservation, and growth management.

Student Conservation Assn., *1310 Courthouse Rd., Arlington, VA 22201; (703) 524-2441. Stephanie Meeks, President.*
General email, webmaster@thesca.org
Web, www.thesca.org

Service organization that provides youth and adults with opportunities for training and work experience in natural resource management and conservation. Volunteers serve in national parks, forests, wildlife refuges, and other public lands.

The Wilderness Society, *1801 Pennsylvania Ave. N.W. #200, 20006; (202) 833-2300. Fax, (202) 429-3958. Jamie Williams, President. Toll-free, (800) 843-9453.*
General email, member@tws.org
Web, www.wilderness.org, Twitter, @wilderness and Faebook, www.facebook.com/TheWildernessSociety

Promotes preservation of wilderness and the responsible management of federal lands, including national parks and forests, wilderness areas, wildlife refuges, and land administered by the Interior Dept.'s Bureau of Land Management.

World Wildlife Fund (WWF), *1250 24th St. N.W., 20037-1193 (mailing address: P.O. Box 97180, Washington, DC 20090-7180); (202) 293-4800. Fax, (202) 293-9211. Carter S. Roberts, President. Press, (202) 495-4102. Toll-free, (800) 960-0993.*

General email, membership@wwfus.org

Web, www.worldwildlife.org, Twitter, @World_Wildlife and Facebook, www.facebook.com/WorldWildlifeFund

International conservation organization that provides funds and technical assistance for establishing and maintaining parks.

Water Resources

▶AGENCIES

Agriculture Dept. (USDA), *Rural Development, Rural Utilities Service,* 1400 Independence Ave. S.W., #4121-S , MS 1510, 20250-1510; (202) 720-9540.
Christopher A. (Chris) McLean, Administrator (Acting).
Web, www.rd.usda.gov/about-rd/agencies/rural-utilities-service

Makes loans and provides technical assistance for development, repair, and replacement of water and waste disposal systems in rural areas.

Army Corps of Engineers *(Defense Dept.),* 441 G St. N.W., #3K05, 20314-1000; (202) 761-0011.
Lt. Gen. Scott A. Spellman (USA), Chief of Engineers.
General email, hq-publicaffairs@usace.army.mil
Web, www.usace.army.mil, Twitter, @USACEHQ and Facebook, www.facebook.com/USACEHQ

Provides local governments with disaster relief, flood control, navigation, and hydroelectric power services.

Bureau of Reclamation *(Interior Dept.),* 1849 C St. N.W., MS 7069-MIB, 20240-0001; (202) 513-0501. Fax, (202) 513-0309. M. Camille Camlimlim Touton, Commissioner. Press, (202) 513-0575.
Web, www.usbr.gov, Twitter, @usbr, Facebook, www .facebook.com/bureauofreclamation and YouTube, www .youtube.com/user/reclamation

Administers federal programs for water and power resource development and management in seventeen western states; oversees municipal and industrial water supplies, hydroelectric power generation, irrigation, flood control, water quality improvement, river regulation, fish and wildlife enhancement, and outdoor recreation. Water resource development projects include dams, power plants, and canals.

Environmental Protection Agency (EPA), *Water (OW),* 1200 Pennsylvania Ave. N.W., MC 4101M, 20460; (202) 564-5700. Radhika Fox, Assistant Administrator.
Web, www.epa.gov/aboutepa/about-office-water

Monitors drinking water safety and restores and maintains oceans, watersheds, and their aquatic ecosystems. Implements the Clean Water Act and Safe Drinking Water Act.

Environmental Protection Agency (EPA), *Water (OW), Wetlands, Oceans, and Watersheds,* 1200 Pennsylvania Ave. N.W., #7301, MC 4501T, 20460; (202) 566-1146. Fax, (202) 566-1147. John Goodin, Director, (202) 566-1373.

General email, ow-owow-internet-comments@epa.gov

Web, www.epa.gov/aboutepa/about-office-water#wetlands

Coordinates federal policies affecting marine and freshwater ecosystems, including watersheds, coastal ecosystems, and wetlands. Regulates and monitors ocean dumping and seeks to minimize polluted runoff and restore impaired waters. Manages dredge-and-fill program under section 404 of the Clean Water Act. Promotes public awareness of resource preservation and management.

Interior Dept. (DOI), *Assistant Secretary for Water and Science,* 1849 C St. N.W., #6641, MS 6340, 20240; (202) 208-3186. Fax, (202) 208-6948. Tanya Trujillo, Assistant Secretary.
Web, www.doi.gov

Administers departmental water, scientific, and research activities. Directs and supervises the Bureau of Reclamation and the U.S. Geological Survey.

Interstate Commission on the Potomac River Basin, 30 W. Gude Dr., #450, Rockville, MD 20850; (301) 984-1908. Mike Nardolilli, Executive Director, ext. 105.
General email, info@icprb.org
Web, www.potomacriver.org and Twitter, @Potomac Commis

Nonregulatory interstate compact commission established by Congress to control and reduce water pollution and to restore and protect living resources in the Potomac River and its tributaries. Monitors water quality; assists metropolitan water utilities; seeks innovative methods for solving water supply and land resource problems. Provides information and educational materials on the Potomac River basin.

National Agricultural Library *(Agriculture Dept.), Water and Agricultural Information Center (WAIC),* 10301 Baltimore Ave., 1st Floor, Beltsville, MD 20705-2351; (301) 504-6077. Fax, (301) 504-5181. Vacant, Coordinator.
Web, www.nal.usda.gov/waic and Email, waic@ars.usda .gov

Serves individuals and agencies seeking information on water quality and agriculture. Special subject areas include agricultural environmental management, irrigation, water availability, and water quality.

Smithsonian Environmental Research Center *(Smithsonian Institution),* 647 Contees Wharf Rd., Edgewater, MD 21037-0028 (mailing address: P.O. Box 28, Edgewater, MD 21037-0028); (443) 482-2200.
Anson (Tuck) Hines, Director, (443) 482-2208. Press, (443) 482-2325. Library, (443) 482-2273.
Web, https://serc.si.edu, Twitter, @SmithsonianEnv, Facebook, www.facebook.com/smithsonian.serc and YouTube, www.youtube.com/channel/UCj6f9cwRLj8VB dwPmYsIxDg

Serves as a research center on water ecosystems in the coastal zone.

Tennessee Valley Authority, *Government Affairs,* 1 Massachusetts Ave. N.W., #300, 20444; (202) 898-2999. Jeffrey J. (Jeff) Lyash, President.

General email, tvainfo@tva.gov

Web, www.tva.gov, Twitter, @TVAnews and Facebook, www.facebook.com/TVA

Coordinates resource conservation, development, and land-use programs in the Tennessee River Valley. Operates the river control system; projects include flood control, navigation development, and multiple-use reservoirs.

U.S. Geological Survey (USGS) (Interior Dept.), Water Resources, 12201 Sunrise Valley Dr., MS 436, Reston, VA 20192-0002; (703) 648-4557. Donald Walter (Don) Cline, Associate Director.
Web, www.usgs.gov/mission-areas/water-resources

Administers the Water Resources Research Act of 1990. Monitors and assesses the quantity and quality of the nation's freshwater resources; collects, analyzes, and disseminates data on water use and the effect of human activity and natural phenomena on hydrologic systems; assesses sources and behavior of contaminants in the water environment, and develops tools to improve management and understanding of water resources. Provides federal agencies, state and local governments, international organizations, and foreign governments with scientific and technical assistance.

►CONGRESS

For a listing of relevant congressional committees and subcommittees, please see pages 284–285 or the Appendix.

►NONGOVERNMENTAL

American Rivers, 1101 14th St. N.W., #1400, 20005; (202) 347-7550. Tom Kiernam, President. Toll-free, (877) 347-7550.
General email, akober@americanrivers.org

Web, www.americanrivers.org, Twitter, @americanrivers and Facebook, www.facebook.com/AmericanRivers

Works to preserve and protect the nation's river systems through public information and advocacy. Collaborates with grassroots river and watershed groups, other conservation groups, sporting and recreation groups, businesses, local citizens, and various federal, state, and tribal agencies. Monitors legislation and regulations.

American Water Works Assn., Government Affairs, 1300 Eye St. N.W., #701W, 20005-3314; (202) 628-8303. Fax, (202) 628-2846. David B. LaFrance, Chief Executive Officer; G. Tracy Mehan III, Executive Director of Government Affairs.
Web, www.awwa.org

Membership: municipal water utilities, manufacturers of equipment for water industries, water treatment companies, and individuals. Provides information on drinking water treatment and trends and issues affecting water safety; publishes voluntary standards for the water industry; issues policy statements on water supply matters. Monitors legislation and regulations. (Headquarters in Denver, Colo.)

Assn. of State Drinking Water Administrators (ASDWA), 1300 Wilson Blvd., #875, Arlington, VA 22209; (703) 812-9505. Fax, (703) 812-9506. Alan Roberson, Executive Director.
General email, info@asdwa.org

Web, www.asdwa.org, Twitter, @ASDWorg and Facebook, www.facebook.com/ASDWAorg

Membership: state officials and administrators responsible for the drinking water supply and enforcement of safety standards. Collects and makes accessible information pertinent to providing safe drinking water. Advises Congress, Us. EPA, and other Federal, STate and local organizations. Monitors legislation and regulations.

Center for Water Security and Cooperation, 1875 Connecticut Ave. N.W., 10th Floor, 20009; (202) 796-8672. Alexandra Campbell-Ferrari, Executive Director.
General email, cwsc@ourwatersecurity.org

Web, www.ourwatersecurity.org, Twitter, @WaterLawyers and Facebook, www.facebook.com/TheCWSC

Nonpartisan organization dedicated to water security and management. Develops and facilitates policy to protect access to water and sewer services. Fosters cooperation and diplomacy in the approach to water security and rights.

Environmental Defense Fund, Washington Office, 1875 Connecticut Ave. N.W., #600, 20009-5728; (202) 387-3500. Fax, (202) 234-6049. Fred Krupp, President; Carol Andress, Associate Vice President, in Washington, DC.
Information, (800) 684-3322.
Web, www.edf.org/offices/washington-dc, Twitter, @EnvDefenseFund and Facebook, www.facebook.com/EnvDefenseFund

Citizen interest group staffed by lawyers, economists, and scientists. Takes legal action on environmental issues; provides information on pollution prevention, environmental health, water resources, water marketing, and sustainable fishing. (Headquarters in New York.)

Irrigation Assn., 8280 Willow Oaks Corporate Dr., #630, Fairfax, VA 22031; (703) 536-7080. Fax, (703) 536-7019. Natasha Rankin, Chief Executive Officer.
General email, info@irrigation.org

Web, www.irrigation.org and Twitter, @irrigationAssoc

Membership: companies and individuals involved in irrigation, drainage, and erosion control worldwide. Promotes efficient and effective water management through training, education, and certification programs. Interests include economic development and environmental enhancement.

Izaak Walton League of America, 707 Conservation Lane, Gaithersburg, MD 20878-2983; (301) 548-0150. Fax, (301) 548-0146. Scott Kovarovics, Executive Director.
Toll-free, (800) 453-5463.
General email, info@iwla.org

Web, www.iwla.org, Twitter, @IWLA_org and Facebook, www.facebook.com/iwla.org

Grassroots organization that promotes conservation of natural resources and the environment. Coordinates a citizen action program to monitor and improve the condition of local streams.

National Academies of Sciences, Engineering, and Medicine (NASEM), *Water Science and Technology Board, Keck Bldg., 500 5th St. N.W., #607, 20001; (202) 334-3422. Fax, (202) 334-1377. Catherine L. Kling, Chair; Deborah Glickson, Director.*
General email, wstb@nas.edu
Web, www.nationalacademies.org/wstb/water-science-and-technology-board

Supports science, engineering, economics, and policy research for the efficient management and use of water resources.

National Assn. of Conservation Districts (NACD), *509 Capitol Court N.E., 20002-4937; (202) 547-6223. Fax, (202) 547-6450. Jeremy Peters, Chief Executive Officer.*
General email, info@nacdnet.org
Web, www.nacdnet.org, Twitter, @NACDconserve and Facebook, www.facebook.com/NACDconserve

Membership: conservation districts (local subdivisions of state government). Develops national policies and works to promote the conservation of water resources. Interests include erosion and sediment control and control of non-point source pollution.

National Assn. of Flood and Stormwater Management Agencies (NAFSMA), *P.O. Box 56764, 20040; (202) 289-8625. Fax, (202) 530-3389. Susan Gilson, Executive Director.*
General email, info@nafsma.org
Web, www.nafsma.org

Membership: state, county, and local governments, and special flood management districts concerned with management of water resources. Interests include stormwater management, disaster assistance, flood insurance, and federal flood management policy. Monitors legislation and regulations.

National Water Resources Assn. (NWRA), *4 E St. S.E., 20003; (202) 698-0693. Kevin Ward, President; Ian Lyle, Executive Vice President.*
Web, http://nwra.org, Twitter, @NWRA_Water and Facebook, www.facebook.com/NWRAWater

Membership: conservation and irrigation districts, municipalities, and others interested in water resources. Works for the development and maintenance of water resources and a sustainable water supply, and public policy. Represents interests of members before Congress and regulatory agencies.

Rural Community Assistance Partnership (RCAP), *1725 Eye St. N.W., #225, 20006; (202) 408-1273. Keith Ashby, Chief Executive Officer (Acting).*
Web, www.rcap.org, Twitter, @RCAPInc, Facebook, www.facebook.com/RCAPInc and General email, info@rcap.org

Provides expertise to rural communities on wastewater disposal, protection of groundwater supply, and access to safe drinking water. Targets communities with predominantly low-income or minority populations. Offers outreach policy analysis, training, and technical assistance to elected officials and other community leaders, utility owners and operators, and residents.

Water Environment Federation, *601 Wythe St., Alexandria, VA 22314-1304; (703) 684-2400. Fax, (703) 684-2492. Walt Marlowe, Executive Director, (703) 684-2430. Toll-free, (800) 666-0206.*
General email, csc@wef.org
Web, www.wef.org and Twitter, @WEForg

Membership: civil and environmental engineers, wastewater treatment plant operators, scientists, government officials, and others concerned with water quality. Works to preserve and improve water quality worldwide. Provides the public with technical information and educational materials. Monitors legislation and regulations.

Water Research Foundation, *1199 N. Fairfax St., #900, Alexandria, VA 22314-1445; (303) 347-6100. Peter Grevatt, Chief Executive Officer, (571) 384-2094.*
General email, info@WaterRF.org
Web, www.waterrf.org, Twitter, @WaterResearch and Facebook, www.facebook.com/waterresearchfoundation

Conducts research and promotes technology to treat and recover materials from wastewater, stormwater, and seawater, including water, nutrients, energy, and biosolids. (Headquarters in Denver, Colo.)

9

Government Operations

GENERAL POLICY AND ANALYSIS

Basic Resources

▶AGENCIES

Administrative Conference of the United States (ACUS),
*1120 20th St. N.W., #706 South, 20036; (202) 480-2080.
Matthew L. Wiener, Executive Director, (202) 480-2104.
Press, (202) 480-2085.
General email, info@acus.gov*

*Web, www.acus.gov, Twitter, @ACUSgov and
Facebook, www.facebook.com/ACUSgov*

Independent federal agency consisting of federal officials and experts from the private sector and academia;
promotes efficiency and fairness in government procedures, regulatory programs, and grant and benefit administration. Conference committees include the Committee
on Adjudication, Committee on Administration and Management, Committee on Judicial Review, Committee on
Regulation, and Committee on Rulemaking.

Domestic Policy Council *(Executive Office of the
President), The White House, 1600 Pennsylvania Ave.
N.W., 20502; Eisenhower Executive Building, Rm. 469,
20502; (202) 456-5594. Fax, (202) 456-3342.
Amb Susan Rice, Director.
Web, www.whitehouse.gov/dpc*

Comprises cabinet officials and staff members. Coordinates the domestic policymaking process to facilitate the
implementation of the president's domestic agenda
throughout federal agencies in such major domestic policy
areas as agriculture, education, energy, environment,
health, housing, labor, and veterans affairs.

Executive Office of the President, *Intergovernmental
Affairs, The White House, 1600 Pennsylvania Ave. N.W.,
20502; (202) 456-1414. Fax, (202) 456-1641.
Julie Chavez Rodriquez, Director.
Web, www.whitehouse.gov/iga*

Seeks to build relationships with constituents and to
connect citizens with their elected officials.

Executive Office of the President, *Public Engagement,
Dwight D. Eisenhower Executive Office Bldg., 1650
Pennsylvania Ave. N.W., #110, 20502; (202) 456-1414.
Fax, (202) 456-1641. Cedric Richmond, Director.
TTY, (202) 456-6213.
Web, www.whitehouse.gov/ope/*

Promotes presidential priorities through outreach to
concerned constituencies and public interest groups.

General Services Administration (GSA), *Administration
(OAS), 1800 F St. N.W., 20405; (202) 527-0095.
Robin Carnahan, Administrator; Bob Stafford, Chief
Administrative Services Officer. FOIA, (855) 675-3642.
General email, GSA.FOIA@gsa.gov*

*Web, www.gsa.gov, Facebook, www.facebook.com/GSA
and Twitter, @USGSA*

Manages all aspects of the Freedom of Information Act
(FOIA) program; responsible for the management of executive correspondence, maintaining the agency's internal
directives, setting travel and charge card policies, and
developing workplace initiatives.

General Services Administration (GSA), *Government-
wide Policy (OGP), Acquisition Policy, 1800 F St. N.W.,
20405; (202) 501-1043. Janet Fry, Director, (703) 774-5274.
General email, FARPolicy@gsa.gov*

*Web, www.gsa.gov/about-us/organization/office-of-
governmentwide-policy/office-of-acquisition-policy*

Develops and implements federal government acquisition policies and procedures; administers Federal Acquisition Regulation (FAR) for civilian agencies. Manages
several GSA-specific and governmentwide acquisition
database systems.

General Services Administration (GSA), *Technology
Transformation Service, 1800 F St. N.W., 2nd Floor,
20405; (202) 702-0781. Dave Zvenyach, Commissioner.
Main Phone, (844) 872-4681.
General email, tts-info@gsa.gov*

*Web, www.gsa.gov/about-us/organization/federal-
acquisition-service/technology-transformation-services*

Utilizes current methodologies and technologies to
improve the way the federal government provides the public with access to information and services. Works to aid
agencies in creating services that are more understandable,
attainable, and beneficial to the public.

General Services Administration (GSA), *USAGov, 1800
F St. N.W., 20405; (844) 872-4681. General
email, USAContace@gsa.gov*

Web, www.gsa.gov

Manages the portal site to U.S. government information, www.usa.gov. Manages kids.gov, a resource that provides government information on education, including
primary, secondary, and higher education. Distributes free
and low-cost federal publications of consumer interest via
the Internet at www.usa.gov and Pueblo.gpo.gov. Assists
people with questions about American government agencies, programs, and services via telephone, (800) FED-
INFO ([800] 333-4636), or website, http://answers.usa.gov.
Operates a contact center to provide information in
English or Spanish on all federal government agencies,
programs, and services via toll-free telephone, email, and
chat. Operated under contract by Sykes in Pennsylvania
and Florida. Responds to inquiries about federal programs
and services. Gives information about or referrals to appropriate offices.

Office of Administration *(Executive Office of the
President), 725 17th St. N.W., #240, 20503; Faisal Amin,
Deputy Director for Management and Administration.
Web, www.whitehouse.gov/administration/executive-
office-of-the-president*

Provides administrative support services to the Executive Office of the President, including financial management
and information technology support, human resources
management, library and research assistance, facilities

management, procurement, printing and graphics support, security, and mail and messenger operations.

Office of Management and Budget (OMB) *(Executive Office of the President),* 725 17th St. N.W., 20503; (202) 395-3080. Shalanda Young, Director.
Web, www.whitehouse.gov/omb and Twitter, @OMBPress

Works with other federal agencies to develop and maintain the website ExpectMore.gov, which uses the Program Assessment Rating Tool (PART) to gauge the effectiveness of federal programs. Holds programs accountable for improving their performance and management.

Office of Management and Budget (OMB) *(Executive Office of the President), Information and Regulatory Affairs,* 725 17th St. N.W., #10236, 20503; (202) 395-5897. Fax, (202) 395-6102. Dominic J. Mancini, Deputy Administrator.
Web, www.whitehouse.gov/omb/information-regulatory-affairs

Oversees development of federal regulatory programs. Supervises agency information management activities in accordance with the Paperwork Reduction Act of 1995, as amended; reviews agency analyses of the effect of government regulatory activities on the U.S. economy.

Office of Management and Budget (OMB) *(Executive Office of the President), Statistical and Science Policy,* 725 17th St. N.W., #10201, 20503; (202) 395-3093. Fax, (202) 395-7245. Margo Schwab, Chief.
Web, www.whitehouse.gov/omb/information-regulatory-affairs/statistical-programs-standards

Carries out the statistical policy and coordination functions under the Paperwork Reduction Act of 1995; develops long-range plans for improving federal statistical programs; develops policy standards and guidelines for statistical data collection, classification, and publication; evaluates statistical programs and agency performance.

Regulatory Information Service Center *(General Services Administration),* 1800 F St. N.W., MR/RISC, 20405; (202) 482-7340. Fax, (202) 482-7360. Robin Carnahan, Administrator (Acting).
General email, risc@gsa.gov
Web, www.gsa.gov/policy-regulations/policy/federal-regulation-policy/regulatory-information-reginfogov, Twitter, @USGSA and Federal regulatory information, www.reginfo.gov/public

Provides the president, Congress, and the public with information on federal regulatory policies and their effects on society; recommends ways to make regulatory information more accessible to government officials and the public. Publishes the Unified Agenda of Federal Regulatory and Deregulatory Actions. See www.reginfo.gov for information about government regulations.

▶ CONGRESS

For a listing of relevant congressional committees and subcommittees, please see pages 332–333 or the Appendix.

Government Accountability Office (GAO), *Strategic Issues (SI),* 441 G St. N.W., 20548; (202) 512-6806. Alissa Czyz, Director (Acting).
Web, www.gao.gov/about/careers/our-teams

Audits, analyzes, and evaluates intergovernmental relations activities, federal grants and regulations, tax issues, census activities, and the nation's overall financial condition.

Library of Congress, *Federal Research Division,* John Adams Bldg., 101 Independence Ave. S.E., #LA 5281, 20540-4840; (202) 707-3900. Fax, (202) 707-3920. Anna (Annie) Rorem, Chief, (202) 707-3920.
General email, frds@loc.gov
Web, www.loc.gov/rr/frd

Provides research, analysis, and translation services to federal agencies, the D.C. government (excluding congress), and authorized federal contractors.

▶ NONGOVERNMENTAL

American Political Science Assn. (APSA), *1527 New Hampshire Ave. N.W., 20036-1203; (202) 483-2512. Fax, (202) 483-2657. Steven Rathgeb Smith, Executive Director. General email, apsa@apsanet.org*
Web, www.apsanet.org, Twitter, @APSAtweets and Facebook, www.facebook.com/likeAPSA

Membership: political scientists, primarily college and university professors. Promotes scholarly inquiry into all aspects of political science, including international affairs and comparative government. Acts as liaison with federal agencies, Congress, and the public. Offers congressional fellowships, workshops, and awards. Provides information on political science issues.

The Brookings Institution, *Governance Studies,* 1755 Massachusetts Ave. N.W., 20036; (202) 797-6090. (202) 797-6288. Darrell M. West, Director, (202) 797-6481.
Web, www.brookings.edu/governance, Twitter, @BrookingsGov and Twitter, Director, @DarrWest

Explores the formal and informal political institutions of democratic governments to assess how they govern, how their practices compare, and how citizens and government servants can advance sound government.

Center for Regulatory Effectiveness (CRE), *1601 Connecticut Ave. N.W., #501, 20009; (202) 265-2383. James J. (Jim) Tozzi, Executive Director. General email, contact@thecre.com*
Web, www.thecre.com

Clearinghouse for methods to improve the federal regulatory process and public access to data and information used to develop federal regulations. Conducts analyses of the activities of the OMB Office of Information and Regulatory Affairs and serves as a regulatory watchdog over executive branch agencies. Acts as advocate on regulatory issues.

Center for the Study of the Presidency and Congress, *601 13th St. N.W., #1050N, 20005; (202) 872-9800. Fax, (202) 872-9811. Glenn C. Nye III, President.*

GOVERNMENT OPERATIONS RESOURCES IN CONGRESS

For a complete listing of congressional committees, including their full contact information, leadership, membership, and jurisdictions, please refer to the Appendix on pages 840–963.

HOUSE:

House Administration Committee, (202) 225-2061.
Web, cha.house.gov

House Appropriations Committee, (202) 225-2771.
Web, appropriations.house.gov

　　Subcommittee on Commerce, Justice, Science, and Related Agencies, (202) 225-3351.

　　Subcommittee on Financial Services and General Government, (202) 225-7245.

　　Subcommittee on Legislative Branch, (202) 226-7252.

House Budget Committee, (202) 226-7200.
Web, budget.house.gov

House Education and Labor, (202) 225-3725.
Web, edlabor.house.gov

　　Subcommittee on Workforce Protections, (202) 225-3725.

House Energy and Commerce Committee, (202) 225-2927.
Web, energycommerce.house.gov

　　Subcommittee on Oversight and Investigations, (202) 225-2927.

House Ethics Committee, (202) 225-7103.
Web, ethics.house.gov

House Financial Services Committee, (202) 225-4247.
Web, financialservices.house.gov

　　Subcommittee on Oversight and Investigations, (202) 225-4247.

House Homeland Security Committee, (202) 226-2616.
Web, homeland.house.gov

　　Subcommittee on Oversight, Management, and Accountability, (202) 226-2616.

House Judiciary Committee, (202) 225-3951.
Web, judiciary.house.gov

　　Subcommittee on the Constitution, Civil Rights, and Civil Liberties, (202) 225-3951.

House Oversight and Reform Committee, (202) 225-5051.
Web, oversight.house.gov

　　Subcommittee on Environment, (202) 225-5051.

　　Subcommittee on Government Operations, (202) 225-5051.

House Rules Committee, (202) 225-9091.
Web, rules.house.gov

Committee on Expedited Procedures, (202) 225-9091.

Committee on Rules and Organization of the House, (202) 225-9091.

House Science, Space, and Technology Committee, (202) 225-6375.
Web, science.house.gov

　　Subcommittee on Investigations and Oversight, (202) 225-6375.

House Select Committee on the Modernization of Congress, (202) 225-1530.
Web, modernizecongress.house.gov

General email, center@thepresidency.org

Web, www.thepresidency.org, Twitter, @CSPC_DC and YouTube, www.youtube.com/channel/UCYGc48akXXw MgHRtO7v-MWA

Membership: college students, government officials, and business leaders interested in the presidency, government, and politics. Conducts conferences, lectures, and symposiums on domestic, economic, and foreign policy issues. Publishes papers, essays, books, and reports on various aspects of the presidency and Congress.

Partnership for Public Service, 600 14th St. N.W., # 600, 20005; (202) 775-9111. Fax, (202) 775-8885. Max Stier, President. Press, (202) 775-2747.

Web, www.ourpublicservice.org, Twitter, @RPublicService and Facebook, www.facebook.com/partnershipforpublic service

Membership: large corporations and private businesses, including financial and information technology organizations. Seeks to improve government efficiency, productivity, and management through a cooperative effort of the public and private sectors.

Buildings and Services

▶**AGENCIES**

General Services Administration (GSA), 1800 F St. N.W., 20405; (202) 501-0800. Robin Carnahan, Administrator. Toll-free, (844) 472-4111.

Web, www.gsa.gov, Twitter, @usgsa, Facebook, www .facebook.com/GSA, Press, press@gsa.gov and Twitter, Administrator, @GSACarnahan

Establishes policies for managing federal government property, including construction and operation of buildings and procurement and distribution of supplies and equipment; manages transportation, telecommunications, and office space for federal employees. Manages disposal of surplus federal property. Responsible for www.USA.gov.

General Services Administration (GSA), Asset and Transportation Management, 1800 F St. N.W., 20405; (202) 501-1777. Fax, (202) 273-4670. Alexander Kurien, Deputy Associate Administrator, (202) 969-4073.

Web, www.gsa.gov/about-us/organization/office-of-governmentwide-policy-overview

House Small Business Committee, (202) 225-4038.
Web, smallbusiness.house.gov
   Subcommittee on Oversight, Investigations, and
      Regulations, (202) 225-4038.
House Veterans' Affairs Committee, (202) 225-9756.
Web, veterans.house.gov
   Subcommittee on Oversight and Investigations,
      (202) 225-9756.
House Ways and Means Committee, (202) 225-3625.
Web, waysandmeans.house.gov
   Subcommittee on Oversight, (202) 225-3625.

SENATE:

Senate Appropriations Committee, (202) 224-7363.
Web, appropriations.senate.gov
   Subcommittee on Commerce, Justice, Science,
      and Related Agencies, (202) 224-7363.
   Subcommittee on Financial Services and General
      Government, (202) 224-7363.
   Subcommittee on Legislative Branch,
      (202) 224-7363.
Senate Budget Committee, (202) 224-0642.
Web, budget.senate.gov
Senate Environment and Public Works Committee,
   (202) 224-8832.
Web, epw.senate.gov
   Subcommittee on Chemical Safety, Waste
      Management, Environmental Justice, and
      Regulatory Oversight, (202) 224-8832.

Subcommittee on Transportation and
   Infrastructure, (202) 224-8832.
Senate Finance Committee, (202) 224-4515.
Web, finance.senate.gov
   Subcommittee on Fiscal Responsibility and
      Economic Growth, (202) 224-4515.
Senate Homeland Security and Governmental Affairs
   Committee, (202) 224-2627.
Web, hsgac.senate.gov
   Permanent Subcommittee on Investigations,
      (202) 224-3721.
   Subcommittee on Emerging Threats and
      Spending Oversight, (202) 224-2254.
   Subcommittee on Government Operations and
      Border Management, (202) 224-4551.
Senate Judiciary Committee, (202) 224-7703.
Web, judiciary.senate.gov
   Subcommittee on Federal Courts, Oversight,
      Agency Action, and Federal Rights,
      (202) 224-2823.
   Subcommittee on the Constitution, (202) 224-6361.
Senate Rules and Administration Committee,
   (202) 224-6352.
Web, rules.senate.gov
Senate Select Committee on Ethics, (202) 224-2981.
Web, ethics.senate.gov
Senate Small Business and Entrepreneurship
   Committee, (202) 224-5175.
Web, sbc.senate.gov

Seeks to improve the management and control of procured transportation services governmentwide, promoting regulatory flexibility and business incentives and tools. Works to direct efficient use of assets through efficient policy formation for travel, employee relocation, personal and real property, motor vehicles, aircraft, transportation, and mail.

General Services Administration (GSA), *Federal Acquisition Service,* 1800 F St. N.W., 20405; (202) 357-5844. Julie Dunne, Commissioner. National Customer Service Center (NCSC), (800) 488-3111.
General email, contactfas@gsa.gov
Web, www.gsa.gov/about-us/organization/federal-acquisition-service and Twitter, @FAS_Outreach

Responsible for providing federal agencies with common-use goods and nonpersonal services and for procurement and online acquisition tools, technology, transportation, travel management, and motor vehicle management.

General Services Administration (GSA), *Government-wide Policy (OGP),* 1800 F St. N.W., 20405; (202) 208-1224. Krystal J Brumfield, Associate Administrator.
Web, www.gsa.gov/ogp

Coordinates GSA policymaking activities, including areas of personal and real property, travel and transportation, acquisition (internal GSA and governmentwide), information technology, regulatory information, and use of federal advisory committees; promotes collaboration between government and the private sector in developing policy and management techniques; works to integrate acquisition, management, and disposal of government property.

General Services Administration (GSA), *National Capital Region (NCR),* 1800 F St. N.W., 20006; (202) 708-9100. Houston Taylor, Regional Commissioner, FAS, (202) 708-6100.
Web, www.gsa.gov/about-us/regions/welcome-to-the-national-capital-region-11

Provides federal agencies with office space and property management services, assisted acquisition services, telecommunication and network services, energy conservation and recycling services, and property management services; has equal status with regional offices.

General Services Administration (GSA), *Portfolio Management and Customer Engagement,* 301 7th St.

White House Offices

OFFICE OF THE PRESIDENT

President, Joseph R. Biden Jr.

 1600 Pennsylvania Ave. N.W., 20500; (202) 456-1414; Comment line, (202) 456-1111; TTY, (202) 456-6213; Web, www.whitehouse.gov; Email, president@whitehouse.gov

Chief of Staff, Ronald A. Klain, (202) 456-1414

Cabinet Affairs, Evan Ryan, Secretary, (202) 456-1414

Communications, Kate Bedingfield, Director, (202) 456-1414

COVID-19 Response Team, Jeffrey Zients, Coordinator, (202) 456-1414

Digital Strategy, Rob Flaherty, Director, (202) 456-1414

Domestic Climate Policy, Gina McCarthy, Advisor, (202) 456-1414

Domestic Policy Council, Susan Rice, Director, (202) 456-1414

Gender Policy Council, Jennifer Klein, Co-Chair; Julissa R. Pantaleón, Co-Chair, (202) 456-1414

Intergovernmental Affairs, Julie Chavez Rodriguez, Director, (202) 456-1414

Legislative Affairs, Louisa Terrell, Director, (202) 456-1414

Management and Administration, Anne Filipic, Director, (202) 456-1414

National Economic Council Brian Deese, Director, (202) 456-1414

National Security Advisor, Jake Sullivan, (202) 456-1414

Oval Office Operations, Annie Tomasini, Director, (202) 456-1414

Political Strategy and Outreach, Emmy Ruiz, Director, (202) 456-1414

Presidential Correspondence, Eva Kemp, Director, (202) 456-1414

Presidential Personnel, Catherine M. Russell, Director, (202) 456-9713

Press Secretary, Jen Psaki, (202) 456-2580 or (202) 456-2673

Public Engagement, Cedric Richmond, Director, (202) 456-1414

Scheduling and Advance, Ryan Montoya, Director, (202) 456-1414

Speechwriting, Vinay Reddy, Director, (202) 456-1414

Staff Secretary, Jessica Hertz, (202) 456-2702

U.S. Secret Service (Homeland Security), James M. Murray, Director, (202) 406-5708; TTY, (202) 406-5370

White House Counsel, Dana A. Remus, Counsel to the President, (202) 456-1414

White House Fellows, Rose Vela, Director, (202) 395-4522

White House Military Office, Keith B. Davids, Director, (202) 456-1414

OFFICE OF THE FIRST LADY

First Lady, Jill T. Biden, 1600 Pennsylvania Ave. N.W., 20500; (202) 456-1414;

 Web, www.whitehouse.gov/administration/dr-jill-biden

Chief of Staff, Julissa R. Pantaleón, (202) 456-1414

Communications, Elizabeth Alexander, Director, (202) 456-1414

OFFICE OF THE VICE PRESIDENT

Vice President, Kamala Harris, 1600 Pennsylvania Ave. N.W., 20500; (202) 456-1414;

 Web, www.whitehouse.gov/administration/vice-president-harris; Email, vice.president@whitehouse.gov

Chief of Staff, Hartina M. Flournoy, (202) 456-1414

Communications, Ashley Etienne, Director, (202) 456-1414

Second Gentleman, Douglas Emhoff, (202) 456-1414

S.W., 20407; (202) 501-0638. James C. (Chris) Wisner, Director, (202) 208-4947.
Web, www.gsa.gov/about-us/organization/public-buildings-service/office-of-portfolio-mgmt-customer-engagement/office-of-portfolio-management and Email, CILP@gsa.gov

 Provides execution, oversight and guidance for governmentwide real property asset management plans and related activities, including the use and disposal of excess real property and the acquisition of leased assets. Promotes and assesses compliance with management policies and regulations for the effective and efficient stewardship of federal real property assets and alternative workplaces.

General Services Administration (GSA), Public Buildings Services, 1800 F St. N.W., #6459, 20405; (202) 501-1100. Nina M. Albert, Commissioner. Toll-free, (844) 472-4111.

Web, www.gsa.gov/about-us/organization/public-buildings-service

 Administers the acquisition, construction, maintenance, and operation of buildings owned or leased by the federal government. Manages and disposes of federal real estate.

General Services Administration (GSA), Urban Development/Good Neighbor Program, 1800 F St. N.W., #3341, 20405-0001; Francis (Frank) Giblin, Program Manager, (202) 494-9236.
Web, www.gsa.gov/real-estate/design-construction/urban-development-good-neighbor-program and Twitter, @GSA_urbdev

 Advises on locations, designs, and renovations of federal facilities in central business areas, historic districts, and local redevelopment areas where they can anchor or promote community development. Collaborates with local

The Cabinet of Joseph R. Biden Jr.

The president's cabinet includes the vice president and the heads of fifteen executive departments. In addition, every president has discretion to elevate any number of other government officials to cabinet-rank status. The cabinet is primarily an advisory group.

VICE PRESIDENT

Kamala Harris, Vice President, (202) 456-1414; Web, www.whitehouse.gov/administration/vice-president-harris; Email, vice.president@whitehouse.gov

EXECUTIVE DEPT. CABINET MEMBERS

Agriculture, Tom Vilsack, Secretary, (202) 720-6630; Web, www.usda.gov

Commerce, Gina M. Raimondo, Secretary, (202) 482-2000; Web, www.commerce.gov

Defense, Lloyd J. Austin III, (703) 571-3343; Web, www.defense.gov

Education, Miguel Cardona, (202) 401-3000; Web, www.ed.gov

Energy, Jennifer M. Granholm, Secretary, (202) 586-6210; Email, The.Secretary@hq.doe.gov; Web, www.energy.gov

Health and Human Services, Xavier Becerra, Secretary, (202) 690-7000; Web, www.hhs.gov

Homeland Security, Alejandro Mayorkas, Secretary, (202) 282-8000; Web, www.dhs.gov

Housing and Urban Development, Marcia Fudge, Secretary, (202) 708-0417; Web, www.hud.gov

Interior, Debra A. Haaland, Secretary, (202) 208-3100; Web, www.doi.gov

Justice, Merrick Garland, Attorney General, (202) 514-2000; Web, www.justice.gov

Labor, Martin Walsh, Secretary, (202) 693-6000; Web, www.dol.gov

State, Anthony Blinken, Secretary, (202) 647-4000; TTY, (800) 877-8339; Web, www.state.gov

Transportation, Pete Buttigieg, Secretary, (202) 366-4000; Web, www.transportation.gov

Treasury, Janet Yellen, Secretary, (202) 622-2000; Web, www.treasury.gov

Veterans Affairs, Denis R. McDonough, Secretary, (202) 461-4800; Web, www.va.gov

OTHER CABINET-RANK OFFICIALS

Council of Economic Advisers, Cecilia Rouse, Chair, (202) 456-1414; Web, www.whitehouse.gov/cea

Environmental Protection Agency, Michael S. Regan, Administrator, (202) 564-4700; Web, www.epa.gov

Office of Management and Budget, Shalanda Young, Director (Acting), (202) 395-3080; Web, www.whitehouse.gov/omb

Office of the White House Chief of Staff, Ronald A. Klain, Chief of Staff, (202) 456-1414; Web, www.whitehouse.gov

Small Business Administration, Isabella Casillas Guzman, Administrator, (202) 205-6708; Web, www.sba.gov

U.S. Mission to the United Nations, Linda Thomas-Greenfield, Amb., (212) 415-4000; Web, https://usun.usmission.gov

U.S. Trade Representative, Katherine Tai, Amb., (202) 395-6890; Web, www.ustr.gov

---

and national civic and other organizations. Serves as clearinghouse for good practices.

System for Award Management, *Asssitance Listings (previously CFDA.gov), 1800 F St. N.W., 20405-0001; Vacant, Product Manager. Web, https://sam.gov/content/assistance-listings*

Disseminates information on federal programs, that provide grants, loans scholarships, insurance and other types of assitant awards available to state and local governments through the CFDA website. Information includes all types of federal aid and explains types of assistance, eligibility requirements, application processes, and suggestions for writing proposals. (Used to be Catalog of Federal Domestic Assistance (CFDA).)

Ethics in Government

▶ AGENCIES

Administrative Conference of the United States (ACUS), *1120 20th St. N.W., #706 South, 20036; (202) 480-2080.*

Matthew L. Wiener, Executive Director, (202) 480-2104. Press, (202) 480-2085. General email, info@acus.gov

Web, www.acus.gov, Twitter, @ACUSgov and Facebook, www.facebook.com/ACUSgov

Independent federal agency consisting of federal officials and experts from the private sector and academia; promotes efficiency and fairness in government procedures, regulatory programs, and grant and benefit administration. Conference committees include the Committee on Adjudication, Committee on Administration and Management, Committee on Judicial Review, Committee on Regulation, and Committee on Rulemaking.

Criminal Division *(Justice Dept.), Public Integrity (PIN), 1301 New York Ave. N.W., 10th Floor, 20005; (202) 514-1412. Fax, (202) 514-3003. Corey R. Amundson, Chief. Web, www.justice.gov/criminal/pin*

Conducts investigations of wrongdoing in selected cases that involve alleged corruption of public office or violations of election law by public officials, including members of Congress.

Government Accountability Office

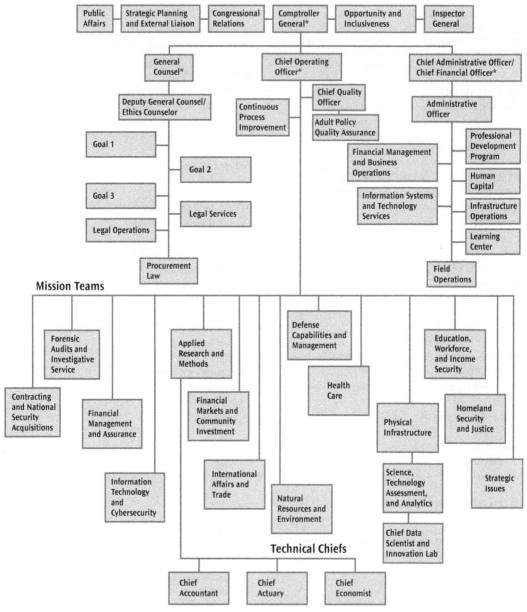

*The Executive Committee

U.S. Office of Government Ethics, *1201 New York Ave. N.W., #500, 20005-3917; (202) 482-9300. Emory A. Rounds III, Director. Press, (202) 482-9206. TTY, (800) 877-8339. General email, contactoge@oge.gov*

Web, www.oge.gov

Ensures that executive branch ethics programs are in compliance with applicable ethics laws and regulations. Administers executive branch policies relating to financial disclosure, employee conduct, and conflict-of-interest laws. Works to prevent conflicts of interest on the part of federal employees and to resolve those that do occur. Provides educational materials and training; conducts outreach to the general public, the private sector, and civil society; shares model practices with and provides technical assistance to state, local, and foreign governments and international organizations; manages email list service to notify federal ethics officials of changes in law and regulations.

U.S. Office of Special Counsel, *1730 M St. N.W., #218, 20036-4505; (202) 804-7000. Fax, (202) 254-3711. Henry Kerner, Special Counsel. Issues relating to the Hatch Act, (202) 804-7002. Toll-free, Hatch Act issues, (800) 854-2824. Fax, Hatch Act issues, (202) 254-3700.*

Press, (202) 804-7065. Prohibited personnel practices, (202) 804-7000. TTY, (800) 872-9855. Whistleblower disclosure hotline, (800) 572-9855.
Web, www.osc.gov, General email, info@osc.gov and Twitter, @US_OSC

Investigates allegations of prohibited personnel practices and prosecutes individuals who violate federal statutes and regulations governing federal employees, military veterans, and reservists. Receives and refers federal employee disclosures of waste, fraud, inefficiency, mismanagement, and other violations in the federal government. Enforces the Hatch Act, which limits political activity by most federal and District of Columbia employees.

► CONGRESS

For a listing of relevant congressional committees and subcommittees, please see pages 332–333 or the Appendix.

Government Accountability Office (GAO), *441 G St. N.W., 20548; (202) 512-5500. Fax, (202) 512-5507. Gene L. Dodaro, Comptroller General. Congressional Relations, (202) 512-4400. Information, (202) 512-3000. Publications and documents, (202) 512-6000.*
General email, contact@gao.gov
Web, www.gao.gov, Twitter, @USGAO and Facebook, www.facebook.com/usgao

Independent, nonpartisan agency in the legislative branch. Serves as the investigating agency for Congress; carries out legal, accounting, auditing, and claims settlement functions; makes recommendations for more effective government operations; makes reports available to Congress and the public.

Government Accountability Office (GAO), *General Counsel (GC), 441 G St. N.W., MS 7182, 20548; (202) 512-5400. Fax, (202) 512-7703. Edda Emmanuelli-Perez, General Counsel.*
Web, www.gao.gov/legal

Adjudicates challenges to the proposed or actual awards of government contracts; renders decisions and opinions on matters of appropriations law; provides legal expertise in support of GAO's functions.

► NONGOVERNMENTAL

Citizens Against Government Waste, *1100 Connecticut Ave. N.W., #650, 20036; (202) 467-5300. Fax, (202) 467-4253. Thomas A. Schatz, President. Press, (202) 467-5310. Toll-free, 800-USA-DEBT.*
General email, info@cagw.org
Web, www.cagw.org, Twitter, @GovWaste and Facebook, www.facebook.com/CAGW

Taxpayer watchdog group that monitors government spending to identify how waste, mismanagement, and inefficiency in government can be eliminated. Has created criteria to identify pork-barrel spending. Publishes the annual *Congressional Pig Book*, which lists the names of politicians and their pet pork-barrel projects. Monitors legislation and regulations.

Citizens for Responsibility and Ethics in Washington (CREW), *1331 F St. N.W., #900, 20004; (202) 408-5565. Noah Bookbinder, Executive Director.*
General email, info@citizensforethics.org
Web, www.citizensforethics.org, Twitter, @CREWcrew and Facebook, www.facebook.org/CitizensforEthics

Promotes ethics and accountability in government and public life. Investigates, reports, and litigates government misconduct. Seeks to enforce government disclosure of information.

Fund for Constitutional Government (FCG), *122 Maryland Ave. N.E., 20002; (202) 546-3799. Fax, (202) 543-3156. Anne B. Zill, President.*
General email, info@fcgonline.org
Web, www.fcgonline.org

Promotes an open and accountable government. Seeks to expose and correct corruption in the federal government and private sector through research and public education. Sponsors the Electronic Privacy Information Center, the Government Accountability Project, the Project on Government Oversight, and OpenTheGovernment.org.

Government Accountability Project (GAP), *1612 K St. N.W., #1100, 20006; (202) 457-0034. Louis Clark, Executive Director.*
General email, info@whistleblower.org
Web, www.whistleblower.org, Twitter, @GovAcctProj and Facebook, www.facebook.com/pg/Government AccountabilityProject

Membership: federal employees, union members, professionals, and interested citizens. Provides legal and strategic counsel to employees in the public and private sectors who seek to expose corporate and government actions that are illegal, wasteful, or repressive; aids such employees in personnel action taken against them; assists grassroots organizations investigating corporate wrongdoing, government inaction, or corruption. Promotes policy and legal reforms of whistleblower laws. (Formerly the National Whistleblower Center.)

Project on Government Oversight, *1100 K. St. N.W., #800, 20005; (202) 347-1122. Fax, (202) 347-1116. Danielle Brian, Executive Director.*
General email, info@pogo.org
Web, www.pogo.org, Twitter, @POGOwatchdog, Facebook, www.facebook.com/pogo.org and Press, cmacneal@pogo.org

Public interest organization that works to expose and investigate,waste, fraud, abuse, and conflicts of interest in all aspects of federal spending.

Executive Reorganization

► AGENCIES

General Services Administration (GSA), *Office of Shared Solutions and Performance Improvement (OSSPI), Government-wide Policy (OGP), President's Management Council (PMC), Dwight D. Eisenhower*

Executive Office Bldg., 1650 Pennsylvania Ave. N.W., #216, 20502; Jeffery (Austin) Price, Council Contact.
General email, pgovsupport@gsa.gov
Web, https://ussm.gsa.gov/about

The PMC advises the President and OMB on government reform initiatives, provides performance and management leadership throughout the Executive Branch, and oversees implementation of government-wide management policies and programs. The PMC comprises the Chief Operating Officers of major agencies, primarily Deputy Secretaries, Deputy Administrators, and agency heads from GSA and OPM.

Office of Management and Budget (OMB) *(Executive Office of the President), Performance and Personnel Management, 725 17th St. N.W., #7236, 20503; (202) 395-5017. Fax, (202) 395-5738. Pam Coleman, Deputy Assistant Director.*
Web, www.whitehouse.gov/omb/management/office-performance-personnel-management

Examines, evaluates, and suggests improvements for agencies and programs within the Office of Personnel Management and the Executive Office of the President.

▶**CONGRESS**

For a listing of relevant congressional committees and subcommittees, please see pages 332–333 or the Appendix.

CENSUS, POPULATION DATA

General

▶**AGENCIES**

Census Bureau *(Commerce Dept.), 4600 Silver Hill Rd., #3J438, Suitland, MD 20746 (mailing address: 4600 Silver Hill Rd., #3J438, Washington, DC 20233-0100); (301) 763-4636. Robert L. Santos, Director. Press, (301) 763-3030. Toll-free, (800) 923-8282. TTY, (800) 877-8339.*
General email, pio@census.gov
Web, www.census.gov, Twitter, @uscensusbureau and Facebook, www.facebook.com/uscensusbureau

Conducts surveys and censuses (including the decennial census of population, the American Community Survey, the economic census, and census of governments); collects and analyzes demographic, social, economic, housing, foreign trade, and data on governmental data; publishes statistics for use by federal, state, and local governments, Congress, businesses, planners, and the public. Provides online resources and data analysis tools. Library open to the public Monday through Friday, 9:30 a.m.–3:30 p.m.

Census Bureau *(Commerce Dept.), Customer Liaison and Marketing Services, 4600 Silver Hill Rd., #8H180, 20233 (mailing address: Customer Service, Bureau of the Census, MS 0801, Washington, DC 20233-0500); (301) 763-0228. Misty L. Reed, Chief. Press, (301) 763-3030.*
Web, www.census.gov

Main contact for information about the Census Bureau's products and services. Census data and maps on counties, municipalities, and other small areas are available on the website and in libraries.

Census Bureau *(Commerce Dept.), Decennial Census, 4600 Silver Hill Rd., #8H122, Suitland, MD 20746 (mailing address: 4600 Silver Hill Rd., #8H122, Washington, DC 20233-7000); (301) 763-9644. (301) 763-2268. Albert E. (Al) Fontenot Jr., Associate Director, (301) 763-4668.*
Web, www.census.gov/programs-surveys/decennial-census/about.html

Provides data from the decennial census (including general plans and procedures); economic, demographic, and population statistics; and information on trends. Conducts preparation for the next census.

Census Bureau *(Commerce Dept.), Families and Living Arrangements, 4600 Silver Hill Rd., 20746; Anthony G. Tersine Jr., Chief. Press, (301) 763-3030.*
Web, www.census.gov/topics/families.html

Provides data and statistics on family composition. Conducts census and survey research on the number of children, young adults, and couples are living in the Untied States. Collects information on child care, households, grandparents and grandchildren, marriage and divorce.

Census Bureau *(Commerce Dept.), Fertility, 4600 Silver Hill Rd., #7H371, Suitland, MD 20746-8500 (mailing address: 4600 Silver Hill Rd., #7H371, Washington, DC 20233); (301) 763-2416. Rose M. Kreider, Chief, (301) 763-6059. Toll-free Census Call Center, (800) 923-8282.*
Web, www.census.gov/topics/health/fertility.html

Provides data and statistics on fertility. Conducts census and survey research on fertility of women in the United States, fertility of men in the United States, and maternity leave.

Census Bureau *(Commerce Dept.), Geography, 4600 Silver Hill Rd., #4H174, Suitland, MD 20746 (mailing address: 4600 Silver Hill Rd., 4th Floor, Washington, DC 20233-7400); (301) 763-1128. Deirdre Dalpiaz Bishop, Chief, (301) 763-1696.*
General email, geo.geography@census.gov
Web, www.census.gov/geo

Manages the MAF TIGER system, a nationwide geographic and address database; prepares maps for use in conducting censuses and surveys and for showing their results geographically; determines names and current boundaries of legal geographic units; defines names and boundaries of selected statistical areas; develops geographic code schemes; maintains computer files of area measurements, geographic boundaries, and map features with address ranges.

Census Bureau *(Commerce Dept.), Population, 4600 Silver Hill Rd., #6H174, Suitland, MD 20746 (mailing address: 4600 Silver Hill Rd., #6H174, Washington, DC 20233-8800); (301) 763-2071. Karen Battle, Chief.*
General email, pop@census.gov
Web, www.census.gov/programs-surveys/popproj.html

Prepares population estimates and projections for national, state, and local areas and congressional districts. Provides data on demographic and social statistics in the following areas: families and households, marital status and living arrangements, farm population, migration and mobility, population distribution, ancestry, fertility, child care, race and ethnicity, language patterns, school enrollment, educational attainment, and voting.

Census Bureau *(Commerce Dept.), Social, Economic, and Housing Statistics, 4600 Silver Hill Rd., #7H174, Suitland, MD 20746 (mailing address: 4600 Silver Hill Rd., #7H174, Washington, DC 20233-8500); (301) 763-9263. David G. Waddington, Chief, (301) 763-3195.*
Web, www.census.gov/topics/housing.html

Develops statistical programs for the decennial census, the American Community Survey, and for other surveys on housing, income, poverty, and the labor force. Collects and explains the proper use of economic, social, and demographic data. Responsible for the technical planning, analysis, and publication of data from current surveys, including the decennial census, the American Community Survey, the American Housing Survey, the Current Population Survey, and the Survey of Income and Program Participation.

▶**CONGRESS**

For a listing of relevant congressional committees and subcommittees, please see pages 332–333 or the Appendix.

▶**NONGOVERNMENTAL**

Population Assn. of America, *1436 Duke St., Alexandria, VA 22314; (301) 565-6710. Fax, (301) 565-7850. Sonalde Desai, President, (301) 405-6312.*
Web, www.populationassociation.org, Twitter, @PopAssocAmerica and Facebook, www.facebook .com/PopAssoc

Membership: university, government, and industry researchers in demography. Publishes newsletters, monitors legislation and related government activities, and supports collaboration of demographers. Holds annual technical sessions to present papers on domestic and international population issues and statistics.

Population Reference Bureau, *1875 Connecticut Ave. N.W., #520, 20009-5728; (202) 483-1100. Fax, (202) 328-3937. Jeffrey Jordan, President. Press, (202) 939-5407. Toll-free, (800) 877-9881.*
General email, communications@prb.org
Web, www.prb.org, Twitter, @PRBdata and Facebook, www.facebook.com/PRBdata

Educational organization engaged in information dissemination, training, and policy analysis on domestic and international population trends and issues. Interests include international development and family planning programs, the environment, and U.S. social and economic policy.

Urban Institute, *Center on Labor, Human Services, and Population, 500 L'Enfant Plaza S.W., 20024; (202) 833-7200. Signe-Mary McKernan, Vice President.*
Web, www.urban.org/policy-centers/center-labor-human-services-and-population

Analyzes employment and income trends, studies how the U.S. population is growing, and evaluates programs dealing with homelessness, child welfare, and job training. Other areas of interest include immigration, mortality, sexual and reproductive health, adolescent risk behavior, child care, domestic violence, and youth development.

CIVIL SERVICE

General

▶**AGENCIES**

National Archives and Records Administration (NARA), *Information Security Oversight (ISOO), 700 Pennsylvania Ave. N.W., #100, 20408-0001; (202) 357-5250. Fax, (202) 357-5907. Mark A. Bradley, Director, (202) 357-5205.*
General email, isoo@nara.gov
Web, www.archives.gov/isoo

Receiving guidance from the National Security Council, oversees policy on security classification on documents for the federal government and industry; monitors performance of all security classification/declassification programs for the federal government and industry; develops policies and procedures for sensitive unclassified information. Evaluates implementation, advises department and agency heads of corrective actions, and prepares an annual report to the president.

Office of Personnel Management (OPM), *1900 E St. N.W., #5A09, 20415-0001; (202) 606-1800. Fax, (202) 606-2573. Kiran Ahuja, Director, (202) 606-1000. Press, (202) 606-2402. TTY, (800) 877-8339.*
Web, www.opm.gov, Twitter, @USOPM and Facebook, www.facebook.com/USOPM

Administers civil service rules and regulations; sets policy for personnel management, labor-management relations, workforce effectiveness, and employment within the executive branch; manages federal personnel activities, including recruitment, pay comparability, and benefit programs.

Office of Personnel Management (OPM), *Data Analysis Group, 1900 E St. N.W., #2449, 20415-0001; (202) 606-1789. Lance Harris, Director (Acting); Kimberly Wells, Director (Acting).*
General email, fedstats@opm.gov
Web, www.opm.gov/policy-data-oversight/data-analysis-documentation/federal-employment-reports

Official government source of statistics on the government workforce. Produces information and analyses for the Office of Personnel Management, Congress, and the

Human Resources for Federal Departments and Agencies

Job seekers interested in additional information can explore federal government career opportunities through the government's official employment information system website, www.usajobs.gov.

DEPARTMENTS

Agriculture, Mary P. Rice, (202) 720-3585

Commerce, John Guenther, (Acting), (202) 482-8247

Defense, William H. Booth, (703) 571-3343

Education, Antonia T. Harris, (202) 401-2000

Energy, Erin Moore, (202) 586-1234

Health and Human Services, Bob Leavitt, (202) 690-6191

Homeland Security, Angela Bailey, (202) 357-8122
    Coast Guard, Rear Adm. Eric Jones, (202) 543-8313

Housing and Urban Development, Lori A. Michalski, (202) 708-0940

Interior, Jennifer Ackerman (Acting), (202) 208-3100; TTY, (800) 877-8339

Justice, Lee J. Lofthus, (202) 514-4350 or (202) 514-3101

Labor, Sydney T. Rose, (202) 693-7600

State, Carol Z. Perez, (202) 647-9898

Transportation, Jennifer Watson, (202) 366-4075

Treasury, J. Trevor Norris, (202) 927-4800

Veterans Affairs, Tracey Therit, (202) 461-7750

AGENCIES

Administrative Office of the U.S. Courts, James R. Baugher, (202) 502-3800

Agency for International Development, Peter Malnak (Acting), (202) 712-1234

Commodity Futures Trading Commission, KerriLaine Prunella, (202) 418-6224

Consumer Product Safety Commission, Donna Simpson, (301) 504-7925

Corp. for National and Community Service, Maelat Mathias, (202) 606-3902

Defense Logistics Agency, Sharyn Saunders, (571) 767-6427

Environmental Protection Agency, Lance McCluney, (202) 564-2944

Equal Employment Opportunity Commission, Sheila Clark, (202) 663-4900; TTY, (202) 663-4494

Export-Import Bank, Maria A. Fleetwood, (202) 565-3300

Farm Credit Administration, Vonda Bell, (703) 883-4200; TTY, (703) 883-4056

Federal Communications Commission, Ellen Standiford, (Acting), (202) 418-0116

Federal Deposit Insurance Corp., Jeff Rosenblum, (877) 275-3342

Federal Election Commission, Kate Higginbothom, (202) 694-1080

Federal Emergency Management Agency, Paige Hinkle-Bowles, (866) 896-8003

Federal Energy Regulatory Commission, Eduardo J. Ribas, (202) 502-8990

Federal Labor Relations Authority, Paula Chandler, (202) 218-7979

Federal Maritime Commission, Karen V. Gregory, (202) 523-5800

Federal Mediation and Conciliation Service, Angie Titcombe, (202) 606-5460

Federal Reserve Board, Tameika Pope, (202) 452-3880

Federal Trade Commission, Vicki A. Barber, (202) 326-2700 or, (202) 326-2021

Food and Drug Administration, Tania Tse, (240) 402-4362

General Services Administration, Traci DiMartini, (202) 501-0398

Government Accountability Office, Renee Caputo, (202) 512-4707

Government Publishing Office, Dan Mielke, (202) 512-1308

Health Resources and Services Administration, Cathy Ganey, (301) 443-0946

National Aeronautics and Space Administration, Jane Datta, (202) 358-0001

National Archives and Records Administration, Valorie Findlater (Acting), (304) 480-8998

National Credit Union Administration, Towanda Brooks, (703) 518-6510

National Endowment for the Arts, Craig McCord, (202) 682-5473

National Endowment for the Humanities, Anthony Mitchell, (202) 606-8415

National Institutes of Health, Sharlis Anthony, (301) 451-4610

National Labor Relations Board, Lawrence Patterson, (202) 273-3900

National Mediation Board, Samantha T. Jones, (202) 692-5081

National Science Foundation, Wonzie L. Gardner Jr., (703) 292-8600 or (703) 292-9457

National Transportation Safety Board, Emily Carroll, (202) 314-6233

Nuclear Regulatory Commission, Mary Lamary, (301) 415-3300

Office of Personnel Management, Tyshawn Thomas, (202) 606-2646

Peace Corps, Vacant, (202) 692-1200; Web, www.peacecorps.gov/volunteer/connect-with-a-recruiter

Securities and Exchange Commission, James P. McNamara, (202) 551-7500

Small Business Administration, Elias Hernandez, (202) 205-6780

Smithsonian Institution, James Douglas, (202) 633-6370

Social Security Administration, Alan S. Frank, (800) 772-1213; TTY, (800) 325-0778

Transportation Security Administration, Patricia Bradshaw, (877) 872-7990; TTY, (877) 872-7992

U.S. International Trade Commission, Eric Mozie, (202) 205-2651

U.S. Postal Service, Simon Storey, (877) 477-3273; TTY, (866) 260-7507

public on statistical aspects of the federal civilian workforce, including trends in composition, grade levels, minority employment, sizes of agencies, and salaries.

Office of Personnel Management (OPM), *Policy, Data, Oversight, Veterans Services,* 1900 E St. N.W., #7439, 20415; (202) 606-3602. Fax, (202) 606-6017. Hakeem A. Basheerud-Deen, Director.
Web, www.opm.gov/policy-data-oversight/veterans-services

Monitors federal agencies' personnel practices and develops policies and programs for veterans.

State Dept., *Bureau of Global Talent Management,* 2201 C St. N.W., #6218, 20520; (202) 647-9898. Fax, (202) 647-5080. Amb. Carol Z. Perez, Director General.
Web, www.state.gov/bureaus-offices/under-secretary-for-management/bureau-of-global-talent-management, Twitter, @StateDG and Facebook, www.facebook.com/StateDeptGTM

Manages human resource policies for the department's Foreign and Civil Service employees in the areas of recruitment, assignment evaluation, promotion, discipline, career development, and retirement.

State Dept., *Bureau of Global Talent Management, Global Community Liaison,* 2201 C St. N.W., HST #2133, 20520-0108; (202) 647-1076. Fax, (202) 647-1670. Gabrielle Hampson, Director, (202) 647-1784.
Toll-free, (800) 440-0397.
General email, GCLO@state.gov

Web, www.state.gov/bureaus-offices/under-secretary-for-management/bureau-of-global-talent-management/global-community-liason-office

Works to improve the quality of life of U.S. government employees and their family members assigned to, or returning from, a U.S. embassy or consulate abroad. Areas of interest are education and youth, family member employment, and support services for personal and past crises, including evacuations. Manages the worldwide Community Liaison Office Program.

U.S. Office of Special Counsel, 1730 M St. N.W., #218, 20036-4505; (202) 804-7000. Fax, (202) 254-3711. Henry Kerner, Special Counsel. Issues relating to the Hatch Act, (202) 804-7002. Toll-free, Hatch Act issues, (800) 854-2824. Fax, Hatch Act issues, (202) 254-3700. Press, (202) 804-7065. Prohibited personnel practices, (202) 804-7000. TTY, (800) 872-9855. Whistleblower disclosure hotline, (800) 572-9855.
Web, www.osc.gov, General email, info@osc.gov and Twitter, @US_OSC

Interprets federal laws, including the Hatch Act, concerning political activities allowed by certain federal employees; investigates allegations of Hatch Act violations and conducts prosecutions. Investigates and prosecutes complaints under the Whistleblower Protection Act.

▶**CONGRESS**

For a listing of relevant congressional committees and subcommittees, please see pages 332–333 or the Appendix.

▶**NONGOVERNMENTAL**

American Federation of Government Employees (AFGE), 80 F St. N.W., 20001; (202) 737-8700. Fax, (202) 639-6490. Everett Kelley, President, (202) 639-6435. Membership, (202) 639-6410. Press, (202) 639-6419.
General email, comments@afge.org
Web, www.afge.org

Membership: approximately 670,000 federal and District of Columbia government employees. Provides legal services to members; assists members with contract negotiations and grievances. Monitors legislation and regulations. (Affiliated with the AFL-CIO.)

Blacks in Government, 3005 Georgia Ave. N.W., 20001-3807; (202) 667-3280. Fax, (202) 667-3705. Shirley A. Jones, President.
General email, bignational@bignet.org
Web, www.bignet.org, Twitter, @BigNational and Facebook, www.facebook.com/BIGNATIONAL

Advocacy organization for public employees. Promotes equal opportunity and career advancement for African American government employees; provides career development information; seeks to eliminate racism in the federal workforce; sponsors programs, business meetings, and social gatherings; represents interests of African American government workers to Congress and the executive branch; promotes voter education and registration.

Federal Managers Assn., 1641 Prince St., Alexandria, VA 22314-2818; (703) 683-8700. Fax, (703) 683-8707. Craig Carter, National President; Todd V. Wells, Executive Director, ext. 102.
General email, info@fedmanagers.org
Web, www.fedmanagers.org, Facebook, www.facebook.com/fedmanagers and Twitter, @FedManagers

Seeks to improve the effectiveness of federal supervisors, managers and executives serving the federal government. Interests include cost-effective government restructuring, competitive civil service pay and benefits, and maintaining the core values of the civil service.

Federally Employed Women, 455 Massachusetts Ave. N.W., 20001 (mailing address: P.O. Box 306, Washington, DC 20001); (202) 898-0994. Karen Rainey, President.
General email, few@few.org
Web, www.few.org, Twitter, @FENNational and Facebook, www.facebook.com/federallyemployedwomen

Membership: women and men who work for the federal government. The four major program areas are Compliance, Diversity, Legislative and Training. Works to eliminate sex discrimination in government employment and to increase job opportunities for women. Monitors legislation and regulations.

Senior Executives Assn., 4829 West Lane, Bethesda, MD 20814; (202) 971-3300. Robert E. Corsi Jr., President.
General email, action@seniorexecs.org
Web, https://seniorexecs.org, Twitter, @seniorexecs and Facebook, www.facebook.com/seniorexecs

Financial Officers for Federal Departments and Agencies

DEPARTMENTS

Agriculture, Scott Soles, (202) 720-0727 or (202) 720-5539

Commerce, Thomas Gilman, (202) 482-4951

Defense, Douglas A. Glenn, (703) 545-6700

    Air Force, Vacant, (703) 697-1974

    Army, Brig. Gen. Mark S. Bennett, (703) 614-4356

    Navy, Alaleh Jenkins, (703) 697-2325

Education, Denise L. Carter, (202) 245-8144

Energy, Vacant, (202) 586-4171

Health and Human Services, Sheila Conley, (202) 690-7084

Homeland Security, Stacy Marcott (Acting), (202) 447-5751

    Coast Guard, Rear Adm. Mark J. Fedor, (202) 475-3704

Housing and Urban Development, Vacant, (202) 402-5911

Interior, Scott Cameron, (202) 208-6115

Justice, Jolene Lauria, (202) 305-9988

Labor, James E. Williams, (202) 693-6800

State, Jeffrey C. Mounts, (202) 261-8620

Transportation, John E. Kramer, (202) 366-9191

Treasury, David Eisner, (202) 649-6800

Veterans Affairs, Jon Rychalski, (202) 461-6600

AGENCIES

Advisory Council on Historic Preservation, Ismail D. Ahmed, (202) 517-0204

Agency for International Development, Reginald Mitchell, (202) 712-0000

Central Intelligence Agency, Vacant, (703) 482-0623

Commission on Civil Rights, John Ratcliffe, (202) 376-8364

Commodity Futures Trading Commission, Joel Mattingley, (202) 418-5310

Consumer Product Safety Commission, James Baker, (301) 574-7575

Corp. for National and Community Service, Malena Brookshire, (202) 606-6652

Corp. for Public Broadcasting, William P. Tayman Jr., (202) 879-9600

Environmental Protection Agency, David Bloom (Acting), (202) 564-1151

Equal Employment Opportunity Commission, Janet Dhillon, (202) 663-4900

Export-Import Bank, Mary Jean Buhler, (202) 565-3946

Farm Credit Administration, Stephen G. Smith, (703) 883-4275; TTY, (703) 883-4056

Federal Bureau of Investigation, David Schlendorf, (202) 324-3000

Federal Communications Commission, Jae Seong, (202) 418-1834

Federal Deposit Insurance Corp., Bret D. Edwards, (202) 898-6130

Federal Election Commission, John Quinlan, (202) 694-1315

Federal Emergency Management Agency, Mary Comans, (202) 646-2500

Federal Energy Regulatory Commission, William Douglas Foster Jr., (202) 502-6118

Federal Home Loan Mortgage Corp. (Freddie Mac), Christian M. Lown, (703) 903-2000 or (800) 424-5401

Federal Maritime Commission, Edward Anthony, (202) 523-5770

Professional association representing Senior Executive Service members and other federal career executives. Sponsors professional education. Interests include management improvement. Monitors legislation and regulations.

Dismissals and Disputes

▶**AGENCIES**

Merit Systems Protection Board, *1615 M St. N.W., 5th Floor, 20419; (202) 653-7200. Fax, (202) 653-7130. Raymond A. Limon, Chair (Acting). Message line, (202) 254-4800. MSPB Inspector General hotline, (800) 424-9121. TTY, (800) 877-8339.*
General email, mspb@mspb.gov
Web, www.mspb.gov

Independent quasi-judicial agency that handles hearings and appeals involving federal employees; protects the integrity of federal merit systems and ensures adequate protection for employees against abuses by agency management. Library open to the public by appointment.

Merit Systems Protection Board, *Appeals Counsel, 1615 M St. N.W., 20419; (202) 653-7200. Fax, (202) 653-6203. Vacant, General Counsel.*
General email, mspb@mspb.gov
Web, www.mspb.gov/appeals/appeals.htm

Analyzes and processes petitions for review of appeals decisions from the regional offices; prepares opinions and orders for board consideration; analyzes and processes cases that are reopened and prepares proposed depositions.

Merit Systems Protection Board, *Policy and Evaluation, 1615 M St. N.W., 20419; (202) 254-4517. Fax, (202) 653-7211. DeeAnn Batten, Director (Acting), (202) 254-4495. Toll-free, (800) 209-8960, ext. 2. TTY, (800) 877-8339.*
General email, studies@mspb.gov
Web, www.mspb.gov/studies/index.htm

Federal Mediation and Conciliation Service, Nicole Wallace, (202) 606-3660

Federal National Mortgage Assn. (Fannie Mae), Celeste Mellet Brown, (800) 232-6643

Federal Trade Commission, David Rebich, (202) 326-2201

General Services Administration, Gerard Badorrek, (202) 501-1721

Government Accountability Office, Karl Maschino, (202) 512-5800

International Bank for Reconstruction and Development (World Bank), Anshula Kant, (202) 473-1000

John F. Kennedy Center for the Performing Arts, Lynne Pratt, (202) 416-8000

Merit Systems Protection Board, Vacant, (202) 653-7200

National Academy of Sciences, Didi Salmon, (202) 334-3990

National Aeronautics and Space Administration, Stephen A. Shinn (Acting), (202) 358-0001

National Archives and Records Administration, Colleen V. Murphy, (301) 837-1723

National Credit Union Administration, Eugene Schied, (703) 518-6570

National Endowment for the Arts, Heidi Ren, (202) 682-5491

National Endowment for the Humanities, Cora Shepherd, (202) 606-8334

National Labor Relations Board, Isabel McConnell, (202) 273-3884

National Mediation Board, Michael Jerger, (202) 695-5000

National Railroad Passenger Corp. (Amtrak), Tracie Winbigler, (202) 906-3000

National Science Foundation, Teresa Grancorvitz, (703) 292-8200

National Transportation Safety Board, Edward Benthall, (202) 314-6000

Nuclear Regulatory Commission, Cherish K. Johnson, (301) 415-7322

Occupational Safety and Health Review Commission, Debra A. Hall, (202) 606-5380

Office of Management and Budget, Shalanda D. Young (Acting), (202) 395-3080

Office of Personnel Management, Dennis D. Coleman, (202) 606-2938

Peace Corps, Vacant, (855) 855-1961

Pension Benefit Guaranty Corp., Patricia Kelly, (202) 229-4170

Postal Regulatory Commission, Erica A. Barker, (202) 789-6800

Securities and Exchange Commission, Caryn Kauffman, (202) 551-7840

Small Business Administration, Tami Perriello, (202) 205-6449

Smithsonian Institution, Janice Lambert, (202) 633-1000

Social Security Administration, Michelle A. King, (410) 965-7748

U.S. International Development Finance Corp., Mildred Callear, (202) 336-8400

U.S. International Trade Commission, John Ascienzo, (202) 205-3175

U.S. Postal Service, Joseph Corbett, (202) 268-5272

Conducts studies on the civil service and other executive branch merit systems; reports to the president and Congress on whether federal employees are adequately protected against political abuses and prohibited personnel practices. Conducts annual oversight review of the Office of Personnel Management.

Merit Systems Protection Board, *Washington Regional Office, 1901 S. Bell St., #950, Arlington, VA 22202; (703) 756-6250. Fax, (703) 756-7112. Hon. Jeremiah Cassidy, Chief Administrative Judge.*
General email, washingtonregionaloffice@mspb.gov
Web, www.mspb.gov

Hears and decides appeals of adverse personnel actions (such as removals, suspensions for more than fourteen days, and reductions in grade or pay), retirement, and performance-related actions for federal civilian employees who work in the Washington, D.C., area, Virginia, North Carolina, or in overseas areas not covered by other regional

board offices. Federal civilian employees who work outside Washington should contact the Merit Systems Protection Board regional office in their area.

Office of Personnel Management (OPM), *Employee Services, Partnership and Labor Relations, Employee Accountability, 1900 E St. N.W., #7H28H, 20415-0001; (202) 606-2930. Debra Buford, Manager.*
General email, er@opm.gov
Web, www.opm.gov/er

Develops, implements, and interprets policy on governmentwide employee relations. Intervenes in or seeks reconsideration of erroneous third-party decisions.

Office of Personnel Management (OPM), *General Counsel, 1900 E St. N.W., #7347, 20415-0001; (202) 606-1700. Fax, (202) 606-2609. Lynn D. Eisenberg, General Counsel.*
Web, www.opm.gov/about-us/our-people-organization/office-of-the-general-counsel

Represents the federal government before the Merit Systems Protection Board, other administrative tribunals, and the courts.

U.S. Office of Special Counsel, *1730 M St. N.W., #218, 20036-4505; (202) 804-7000. Fax, (202) 254-3711. Henry Kerner, Special Counsel. Issues relating to the Hatch Act, (202) 804-7002. Toll-free, Hatch Act issues, (800) 854-2824. Fax, Hatch Act issues, (202) 254-3700. Press, (202) 804-7065. Prohibited personnel practices, (202) 804-7000. TTY, (800) 872-9855. Whistleblower disclosure hotline, (800) 572-9855.*
Web, www.osc.gov, General email, info@osc.gov and Twitter, @US_OSC

Investigates allegations of prohibited personnel practices, including reprisals against whistleblowers (federal employees who disclose waste, fraud, inefficiency, and wrongdoing by supervisors of federal departments and agencies). Initiates necessary corrective or disciplinary action. Enforces the Hatch Act, which limits political activity by most federal and District of Columbia employees.

▶JUDICIARY

U.S. Court of Appeals for the Federal Circuit, *717 Madison Pl. N.W., 20439; (202) 275-8000. Kimberly A. Moore, Chief Circuit Judge; Peter R. Marksteiner, Clerk of the Court, (202) 272-8020. Mediation, (202) 275-8120.*
Web, www.cafc.uscourts.gov

Reviews decisions of the Merit Systems Protection Board.

Hiring, Recruitment, and Training

▶AGENCIES

General Services Administration (GSA), *Federal Acquisition Institute (FAI), OGP/MVB, 1800 F St. N.W., 20405 (mailing address: 9820 Belvoir Rd., Bldg. 270, Ft. Belvoir, VA 22060); Jeffrey Birch, Director. General email, contact@fai.gov*
Web, www.fai.gov and www.gsa.gov/about-us/ organization/office-of-governmentwide-policy/office-of-acquisition-policy/federal-acquisition-institute

Fosters development of a professional acquisition workforce governmentwide; collects and analyzes acquisition workforce data; helps agencies identify and recruit candidates for the acquisitions field; develops instructional materials; evaluates training and career development programs.

Office of Personnel Management (OPM), *Classification and Qualifications Policy, 1900 E St. N.W., #6500, 20415-0001; (202) 606-3600. Fax, (202) 606-4891. April Davis, Manager, (202) 606-1728. General email, fedclass@opm.gov*
Web, www.opm.gov/policy-data-oversight/classification-qualifications

Develops job classification standards for occupations in the general schedule and federal wage system.

Office of Personnel Management (OPM), *Human Resources Solutions, 1900 E St. N.W., #2469F, 20415-1000; (202) 606-1304. Peter Bonner, Associate Director. Web, www.opm.gov/about-us/our-people-organization/program-divisions/human-resources-solutions*

Manages federal human resources policy, including staffing, compensation, benefits, labor relations, and position classification.

Office of Personnel Management (OPM), *Merit System Accountability and Compliance, 1900 E St. N.W., #6484, 20415-5100; (202) 606-2980. Fax, (202) 606-5056. Mark W. Lambert, Associate Director. Web, www.opm.gov/about-us/our-people-organization/program-divisions/merit-system-accountability-and-compliance*

Responsible for training and curriculum development programs for government executives and supervisors.

Office of Personnel Management (OPM), *Policy, Data, Oversight, Veterans Services, 1900 E St. N.W., #7439, 20415; (202) 606-3602. Fax, (202) 606-6017. Hakeem A. Basheerud-Deen, Director. Web, www.opm.gov/policy-data-oversight/veterans-services*

Provides federal employees and transitioning military service members and their families, federal human resources professionals, and hiring managers with information on employment opportunities with the federal government.

Office of Personnel Management (OPM), *Veterans Services, Intergovernmental Personnel Act Mobility Program, 1900 E St. N.W., #7463, 20415-0001; (202) 606-1155. Fax, (202) 606-4430. Hakeem A. Basheerud-Dean, Director, (202) 606-3602. General email, ipa@opm.gov*
Web, www.opm.gov/programs/ipa

Implements temporary personnel exchanges between federal agencies and nonfederal entities, including state and local governments, institutions of higher education, and other organizations.

▶NONGOVERNMENTAL

Society of American Indian Government Employees, *(410) 802-2190. Fredericka Joseph, Chair. General email, info@saige.org*
Web, https://saige.org and Facebook, www.facebook.com/Society-of-American-Indian-Government-Employees-SAIGE-187641439510

Fosters the recruitment, development, and advancement of American Indians and Alaska Natives in the government workforce. Promotes communication among its members. Serves as an information clearinghouse. Coordinates training and conferences for government employees on issues concerning American Indians and Alaska Natives. Monitors legislation and policies. (Headquarters in Skiatook, Okla.)

Labor-Management Relations

▶**AGENCIES**

Federal Labor Relations Authority, *1400 K St. N.W., 20424-0001; (202) 218-7770. Fax, (202) 482-6526. Ernest Dubester, Chair; Michael W. Jeffries, Executive Director. Press, (202) 218-7927.*
General email, EngagetheFLRA@flra.gov
Web, www.flra.gov

Oversees the federal labor-management relations program; administers the law that protects the right of non-postal federal employees to organize, bargain collectively, and participate through labor organizations of their own choosing.

Federal Service Impasses Panel *(Federal Labor Relations Authority), 1400 K St. N.W., #200, 20424-0001; (202) 218-7790. Fax, (202) 482-6674. Kimberly D. Moseley, Executive Director.*
Web, www.flra.gov/components-offices/components/ federal-service-impasses-panel-fsip-or-panel

Assists in resolving contract negotiation impasses over conditions of employment between federal agencies and labor organizations representing federal employees.

Office of Personnel Management (OPM), *Employee Services, Accountability and Workforce Relations (AWR), 1900 E St. N.W., #7H28, 20415-0001; (202) 606-2930. Fax, (202) 606-2613. Timothy F. Curry, Deputy Associate Director.*
Web, www.opm.gov/about-us/our-people-organization/ program-divisions/employee-services

Develops policy for government agencies and unions regarding employee-management and labor-management relations.

Office of Personnel Management (OPM), *General Counsel, 1900 E St. N.W., #7347, 20415-0001; (202) 606-1700. Fax, (202) 606-2609. Lynn D. Eisenberg, General Counsel.*
Web, www.opm.gov/about-us/our-people-organization/ office-of-the-general-counsel

Advises the government on law and legal policy relating to federal labor-management relations; represents the government before the Merit Systems Protection Board.

▶**NONGOVERNMENTAL**

American Foreign Service Assn. (AFSA), *2101 E St. N.W., 20037; (202) 338-4045. Fax, (202) 338-6820. Eric Rubin, President. Press, (202) 944-5508.*
General email, member@afsa.org
Web, www.afsa.org, Twitter, @afsatweets and Facebook, www.facebook.com/afsapage

Membership: active-duty and retired U.S. foreign service employees at Department of State, U.S. Agency for International Development, Foreign Commercial Service, Foreign Agricultural Service, Animal and Plant Health Inspection Service, and U.S. Agency for Global Media. Represents active duty foreign service personnel in labor-management negotiations; seeks to ensure adequate resources for foreign service operations and personnel. Monitors legislation and regulations related to foreign service personnel and retirees.

National Alliance of Postal and Federal Employees (NAPFE), *1640 11th St. N.W., 20001-5008; (202) 939-6325. Fax, (202) 939-6392. Janice F. Robinson, President.*
General email, info@napfe.org
Web, www.napfe.com, Facebook, www.facebook.com/ NAPFE-National-Alliance-of-Postal-and-Federal-Employees-1003292639737381 and Twitter, @NAPFE_DC

Membership: approximately 70,000 postal and federal employees. Helps members negotiate pay, benefits, equal opportunity, and better working conditions; conducts training programs and workshops. Monitors legislation and regulations.

National Assn. of Government Employees (NAGE), *Washington Office, 1020 N. Fairfax St., #200, Alexandria, VA 22314; (703) 519-0300. Fax, (703) 519-0311. David J. Holway, National President. Toll-free, (866) 412-7790.*
Web, www.nage.org, Twitter, @NAGE_National and Facebook, www.facebook.com/NAGEUNION

Membership: federal government employees. Helps members negotiate pay, benefits, and better working conditions; conducts training programs and workshops. Monitors legislation and regulations. (Affiliated with Service Employees International Union. Headquarters in Quincy, Mass.)

National Federation of Federal Employees, *1225 New York Ave. N.W., #450, 20005; (202) 216-4420. Fax, (202) 898-1861. Randy L. Erwin, National President.*
General email, info@nffe.org
Web, www.nffe.org, Twitter, @NFFE_Union and Facebook, www.facebook.com/NFFEUnion

Membership: approximately 100,000 employees throughout various agencies within the federal government. Helps members negotiate pay, benefits, and better working conditions; conducts training programs and workshops. Monitors legislation and regulations. (Affiliated with International Assn. of Machinists & Aerospace Workers, AFL-CIO.)

National Treasury Employees Union (NTEU), *800 K St., #1000, 20001; (202) 572-5500. Fax, (202) 572-56445643. Anthony M. (Tony) Reardon, National President.*
General email, nteu-pr@nteu.org
Web, www.nteu.org, Twitter, @NTEUnews and Facebook, www.facebook.com/nteunational

Membership: approximately 150,000 employees from the Treasury Dept. and thirty other federal agencies and departments. Helps members negotiate pay, benefits, and better working conditions; conducts training programs and workshops. Monitors legislation and regulations.

Public Service Research Council, *320-D Maple Ave. East, Vienna, VA 22180-4742; (703) 242-3575. Fax, (703) 242-3579. David Y. Denholm, President.*

Inspectors General for Federal Departments and Agencies

Departmental and agency inspectors general are responsible for identifying and reporting program fraud and abuse, criminal activity, and unethical conduct in the federal government. In the legislative branch, the Government Accountability Office also has fraud and abuse hotlines: (202) 512-7470. Check www.ignet.gov for additional listings.

DEPARTMENTS

Agriculture,
Hon. Phyllis K. Fong, (202) 720-8001;
Hotline, (800) 424-9121

Commerce,
Hon. Peggy E. Gustafson, (202) 482-4661;
Hotline, (800) 424-5197

Defense,
Hon. Sean O'Donnell (Acting), (703) 604-8300;
Hotline, (800) 424-9098

Education,
Hon. Sandra D. Bruce (Acting), (202) 245-6900;
Hotline, (800) 647-8733

Energy,
Hon. Teri L. Donaldson, (202) 586-1818;
Hotline, (800) 541-1625

Health and Human Services,
Christi Grimm (Acting), (202) 619-3148;
Hotline, (800) 447-8477

Homeland Security and FEMA,
Hon. Joseph Cuffari, (202) 981-6000;
Hotline, (800) 323-8603; Disaster Fraud
Hotline, (866) 720-5721

Housing and Urban Development,
Hon. Rae Oliver Davis, (202) 708-0430;
Hotline, (800) 347-3735

Interior,
Hon. Mark Lee Greenblatt, (202) 208-5745;
Hotline, (800) 424-5081

Justice,
Hon. Michael E. Horowitz, (202) 514-3435;
Hotline, (800) 869-4499

Labor,
Larry D. Turner (Acting), (202) 693-5100;
Hotline, (800) 347-3756

State,
Diana Shaw (Acting), (571) 348-0200;
Hotline, (800) 409-9926

Transportation,
Eric J. Soskin, (202) 366-1959;
Hotline, (800) 424-9071

Treasury,
Richard Delmar, (202) 622-1090;
Hotline, (800) 359-3898

Veterans Affairs,
Hon. Michael J. Missal, (202) 461-4720;
Hotline, (800) 488-8244

AGENCIES

Agency for International Development,
Thomas Ullom (Acting), (202) 712-1150;
Hotline, (800) 230-6539

Appalachian Regional Commission,
Phillip M. Heneghan, (202) 884-7675;
Hotline, (800) 532-4611

Board of Governors of the Federal Reserve System,
Mark Bialek, (202) 973-5000;
Hotline, (800) 827-3340; Fax, (202) 973-5044

Central Intelligence Agency,
Christine Ruppert (Acting), (703) 374-8050;
Hotline, (703) 482-9500

Committee for Purchase From People Who Are Blind or Severely Disabled (AbilityOne Program),
Thomas K. Lehrich, (703) 603-2124;
Hotline, (844) 496-1536

Commodity Futures Trading Commission,
A. Roy Lavik, (202) 418-5110;
Hotline, (202) 418-5510

Consumer Financial Protection Bureau,
Mark Bialek, (202) 973-5000;
Hotline, (800) 827-3340

Consumer Product Safety Commission,
Christoper W. Dentel, (301) 504-7905;
Hotline, (301) 504-7906

Defense Intelligence Agency,
Kristi Waschull, (202) 231-1010;
Hotline, (202) 231-1000

Election Assistance Commission,
Patricia Layfield, (202) 853-2760

Environmental Protection Agency,
Hon. Sean W. O'Donnell, (202) 566-0847;
Hotline, (888) 546-8740

Equal Employment Opportunity Commission,
Milton A. Mayo Jr., (202) 663-4327;
Hotline, (800) 849-4230

Export-Import Bank of the United States,
Jennifer Fain (Acting), (202) 565-3908

Farm Credit Administration,
Wendy R. Laguarda, (703) 883-4030;
Hotline, (800) 437-7322

Federal Communications Commission,
David L. Hunt, (202) 418-0470;
Hotline, (888) 863-2244

Federal Deposit Insurance Corp.,
Hon. Jay N. Lerner, (703) 562-2035;
Hotline, (800) 964-3342

Federal Election Commission,
Christopher Skinner, (202) 694-1015

Federal Housing Finance Agency,
Hon. Laura S. Wertheimer, (202) 730-0881;
Hotline, (800) 793-7724

Federal Labor Relations Authority,
Dana Rooney, (202) 218-7744;
Hotline, (800) 331-3572

Federal Maritime Commission,
Jon Hatfield, (202) 523-5863;
Hotline, (202) 523-5865

Federal Trade Commission,
Andrew Katsaros, (202) 326-3527;
Hotline, (202) 326-2800

General Services Administration,
Hon. Carol Fortine Ochoa, (202) 501-0450;
Hotline, (800) 424-5210

Government Accountability Office,
Adam Trzeciak, (202) 512-5748;
Hotline, (866) 680-7963

Legal Services Corp.,
Jeffrey E. Schanz, (202) 295-1660;
Hotline, (202) 295-1670

National Aeronautics and Space Administration,
Hon. Paul K. Martin, (202) 358-1220;
Hotline, (800) 424-9183

National Credit Union Administration,
James Hagen, (703) 518-6350;
Hotline, (703) 518-6357

National Geospatial-Intelligence Agency,
Cardell Richardson, (800) 380-7729;
Hotline, (571) 557-5400

National Labor Relations Board,
David P. Berry, (202) 273-1960;
Hotline, (800) 736-2983

National Reconnaissance Office,
Hon. Susan S. Gibson, (703) 808-1830;
Hotline, (703) 808-1644

National Science Foundation,
Allison Lerner, (703) 292-7100;
Hotline, (800) 428-2189

National Security Agency,
Hon. Robert P. Storch, (301) 688-6327;
Hotline, (301) 688-6311

Nuclear Regulatory Commission,
Hon. Robert Feitel, (301) 415-5930;
Hotline, (800) 233-3497

Office of Personnel Management,
Norbert Vint, (202) 606-1200;
Hotline, (877) 499-7295

Office of the Inspector General of the Intelligence Community,
Thomas Monheim (Acting), (571) 204-8149;
Hotline, (855) 731-3260

Pension Benefit Guaranty Corp.,
Nick Novak (Acting), (202) 326-4030;
Hotline, (800) 303-9737

Postal Regulatory Commission,
Jack Callender, (202) 789-6817

Securities and Exchange Commission,
Carl W. Hoecker, (202) 551-6061;
Hotline, (833) 732-6441

Small Business Administration,
Hon. Hannibal Ware, (202) 205-6586;
Hotline, (800) 767-0385

Social Security Administration,
Hon. Gail S. Ennis, (410) 965-2905;
Hotline, (800) 269-0271

Special Inspector General for Afghanistan Reconstruction,
John F. Sopko, (703) 545-6000;
Hotline, (866) 329-8893

Special Inspector General for Pandemic Recovery
Hon. Brian D. Miller;
Hotline, (202) 927-7899

Special Inspector General for the Troubled Asset Relief Program,
Hon. Christy Goldsmith Romero, (202) 622-1419;
Hotline, (877) 744-2009

Treasury Inspector General for Tax Administration,
Hon. J. Russell George, (202) 622-6500;
Hotline, (800) 366-4484

U.S. International Development Finance Corporation
Anthony Zakel, (202) 408-6246

U.S. International Trade Commission,
Michael J. Haberstroh (Acting), (202) 205-2000;
Hotline, (202) 205-6542; TTY, (202) 205-1810

U.S. Postal Service,
Tammy L. Whitcomb, (703) 248-2100;
Hotline, (888) 877-7644

OTHER FEDERAL AGENCIES

Amtrak,
Kevin H. Winters, (202) 906-4600;
Hotline, (800) 468-5469

Architect of the Capitol,
J. Brett Blanton, (202) 593-1948;
Hotline, (877) 489-8583

Corp. for National and Community Service,
Deborah J. Jeffrey, (202) 606-9390;
Hotline, (800) 452-8210

Corp. for Public Broadcasting,
Kimberly A. Howell, (202) 879-9604;
Hotline, (800) 599-2170

Government Publishing Office,
Michael P. Leary, (202) 512-0039;
Hotline, (800) 743-7574

Library of Congress,
Kurt W. Hyde, (202) 707-6314

National Archives,
James E. Springs, (301) 837-3000;
Hotline, (301) 837-3500

National Endowment for the Arts,
Ronald Stith, (202) 682-5402;
Hotline, (877) 535-7448

National Endowment for the Humanities,
Laura Davis, (202) 606-8574;
Hotline, (877) 786-7598

Peace Corps,
Kathy A. Buller, (202) 692-2900;
Hotline, (800) 233-5874

Smithsonian Institution,
Cathy L. Helm, (202) 633-7050;
Hotline, (202) 252-0321

U.S. Capitol Police,
Michael A. Bolton, (202) 593-4800;
Hotline, (866) 906-2446

General email, info@psrconline.org

Web, http://psrconline.org

Independent nonprofit research and educational organization. Studies labor unions and labor issues with emphasis on employment in the public sector. Monitors legislation and regulations.

Pay and Employee Benefits

▶ AGENCIES

Labor Dept. (DOL), *Workers' Compensation Programs (OWCP), Federal Employees' Compensation (DFEC),* 200 Constitution Ave. N.W., #S3524, 20210; (202) 693-0040. Antonio Rios, Director, (202) 513-6860. Toll-free, (866) 692-7487 (customers should contact their district office first, www.dol.gov/owcp/dfec/regs/compliance/wc.htm). TTY, (877) 889-5627.

Web, www.dol.gov/owcp/dfec

Administers the Federal Employees Compensation Act, which provides disability compensation for federal employees, including wage replacement benefits, medical treatment, vocational rehabilitation, and other benefits.

Office of Personnel Management (OPM), *Employee Services,* 1900 E St. N.W., #7460 MM, 20415; (202) 606-2520. Vacant, Associate Director.

Web, www.opm.gov/about-us/our-people-organization/program-divisions/employee-services

Develops federal human resource systems for pay and leave, employee development, staffing, recruiting, hiring, Factor Evaluation System (FES) policy, and labor and employee relations, senior executive services, veterans' services, and performance management.

Office of Personnel Management (OPM), *Federal Prevailing Rate Advisory Committee (FPRAC),* 1900 E St. N.W., #5H27-G, 20415; (202) 606-2858. Vacant, Chair; Alexys Stanley, Regulatory Affairs Analyst.

General email, pay-leave-policy@opm.gov

Web, www.opm.gov/about-us/our-people-organization/support-functions/federal-prevailing-rate-advisory-committee

Advises OPM on the governmentwide administration of Federal Wage System employees.

Office of Personnel Management (OPM), *Healthcare and Insurance, Federal Employee Insurance Operations (FEHB),* 1900 E St. N.W., #3425, 20415; (202) 606-4995. Fax, (202) 606-4640. Edward DeHarde, Assistant Director, (202) 606-0522.

Web, www.opm.gov/insure

Administers group life insurance for federal employees and retirees; negotiates rates and benefits with health insurance carriers; settles disputed claims. Administers the Federal Employees' Health Benefits (FEHB), the Federal Employees' Group Life Insurance (FEGLI), the Federal Long Term Care Insurance (FLTCIP), Federal Employee Dental and Vision Benefits (FEDVIP), and the Flexible Spending Accounts (FSA) programs.

Office of Personnel Management (OPM), *Policy, Data, Oversight, Pay and Leave,* 1900 E St. N.W., #7H31, 20415; (202) 606-2507. Fax, (202) 606-4264. Brenda L. Roberts, Deputy Associate Director.

General email, pay-leave-policy@opm.gov

Web, www.opm.gov/policy-data-oversight/pay-leave

Develops and maintains governmentwide agency regulations pertaining to pay and leave. Responsible for the General Schedule and locality pay adjustment process for white-collar federal workers. Supports the Federal Salary Council and the president's "pay agent" (composed of the directors of OPM and the Office of Management and Budget and the secretary of labor). Annual report of the pay agent and General Schedule pay rates are available on OPM's website. Supports the Federal Prevailing Rate Advisory Committee and provides regulations and policies for the administration of the federal wage system for blue-collar federal employees.

Office of Personnel Management (OPM), *Policy, Data, Oversight, Work-Life,* 1900 E St. N.W., #7456, 20415-2000; (202) 606-0846. Kiran Ahuja, Direcotr, OPM. Phone, Front Desk, (202) 606-1800.

General email, worklife@opm.gov

Web, www.opm.gov/policy-data-oversight/worklife

Sets policy and guidelines for federal agencies in establishing and maintaining programs on the federal telework program, employee assistance programs, the Federal Child Care Subsidy Program, and health and wellness.

Office of Personnel Management (OPM), *Retirement Operations,* 1900 E St. N.W., #2H28, 20415; (724) 794-2005. Fax, (724) 794-4323. Kenneth J. Zawodny Jr., Associate Director, (724) 794-7759. Toll-free, (888) 767-6738. TTY, (855) 887-4957.

General email, retire@opm.gov

Web, www.opm.gov/retire

Administers the civil service and federal employees' retirement systems; responsible for monthly annuity payments and other benefits; organizes and maintains retirement records; distributes information on retirement and on insurance programs for annuitants.

State Dept., *Bureau of Administration, Allowances,* 2401 E St. N.W., #L314, SA-1, 20522-0103; (202) 261-8043. Fax, (202) 261-8707. Alexandra S. Aitken, Director, (202) 261-8714.

General email, AllowancesO@state.gov

Web, http://aoprals.state.gov

Develops and coordinates policies, regulations, standards, and procedures to administer the governmentwide allowances and benefits program abroad under the State Dept. Standardized Regulations. Compiles statistics of living costs, hardship differentials, and danger pay allowances to compensate U.S. government civilian employees while on assignments abroad.

State Dept., *Medical Services,* 2401 E St. N.W., #L218, 20522-0102; (202) 663-1649. Fax, (202) 663-1613. Larry Paget, Medical Director.

Office of Personnel Management

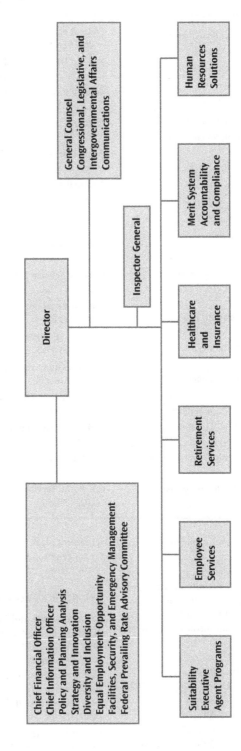

Director

General Counsel
Congressional, Legislative, and Intergovernmental Affairs
Communications

Inspector General

Chief Financial Officer
Chief Information Officer
Policy and Planning Analysis
Strategy and Innovation
Diversity and Inclusion
Equal Employment Opportunity
Facilities, Security, and Emergency Management
Federal Prevailing Rate Advisory Committee

Suitability
Executive
Agent Programs

Employee
Services

Retirement
Services

Healthcare
and
Insurance

Merit System
Accountability
and Compliance

Human
Resources
Solutions

Procurement Officers for Federal Departments and Agencies

DEPARTMENTS

Agriculture, Tiffany J. Taylor, (202) 720-9448

Commerce, Olivia Bradley (Acting), (202) 482-4248

Defense, John M. Tenaglia, (703) 695-4235

Education, Philip Juengst, (202) 401-2000

Energy, Paul Bosco, (202) 586-1784

Health and Human Services, David Dasher, (202) 205-0706

Homeland Security, Soraya Correa, (202) 447-5300

Housing and Urban Development, Ronald Flom, (202) 402-1290

Interior, Megan Olsen, (202) 513-7554

Justice, Michael H. Allen, (202) 514-3101

Labor, Sandra Foster (Acting), (202) 693-4028

State, Corey M. Rindner, (703) 875-6037

Transportation, Vacant, (202) 366-4271

Treasury, Vacant, (202) 622-1039

Veterans Affairs, Angela Billups, (202) 632-4606

AGENCIES

Consumer Product Safety Commission, Eddie Ahmad, (301) 504-7884

Corp. for National and Community Service, Henrietta Young, (202) 606-6988

Environmental Protection Agency, Kimberly Y. Patrick, (202) 564-4310

Export-Import Bank, Richard H. Lee, (202) 565-3338

Farm Credit Administration, Avery D. Becton, (703) 883-4075

Federal Communications Commission, Dawn DiGiorgio (Acting), (202) 418-0314

Federal Deposit Insurance Corp., Thomas D. Harris, (703) 562-2203

Federal Emergency Management Agency, Bobby J. McCane, (202) 646-1895

Federal Maritime Commission, Katona Bryan-Wade, (202) 523-5900

Federal Mediation and Conciliation Service, Cynthia Washington, (202) 606-5477

Federal Reserve System, Kimberly M. Briggs, (202) 452-2527

Federal Trade Commission, Nancy Moreno, (202) 326-3667

General Services Administration, Dannie Crowder, (303) 236-7482

National Aeronautics and Space Administration, Karla Smith Jackson, (202) 358-2090

National Labor Relations Board, Lasharn Hamilton, (202) 273-4210

National Mediation Board, Samantha T. Jones, (202) 692-5010

National Science Foundation, Patrick Breen, (703) 292-8242

Nuclear Regulatory Commission, James C. Corbett, (301) 415-8725

Office of Personnel Management, Todd Anthony, (202) 606-4328

Securities and Exchange Commission, Vance Cathell, (202) 551-8385

Small Business Administration, Amy Kim, (202) 205-6915

Social Security Administration, Dawn Caracci, (410) 965-5499

U.S. International Trade Commission, Debra Bridge, (202) 205-2004

U.S. Postal Service, Jacqueline Krage Strako, (202) 268-3389

Web, www.state.gov/about-us-bureau-of-medical-services

Operates a worldwide primary health care system for U.S. citizen employees, and eligible family members, of participating U.S. government agencies. Conducts physical examinations of Foreign Service officers and candidates; provides clinical services; assists with medical evacuation of patients overseas.

Treasury Dept., *Management, D.C. Pensions, 1500 Pennsylvania Ave. N.W., 20220; (202) 622-0800. Fax, (202) 622-1763. Nancy Ostrowski, Director.*
General email, DCPensions@treasury.gov

Web, https://home.treasury.gov/about/offices/management/human-resources-and-chief-human-capital-officer/dc-pensions

Funds and distributes the D.C. Judges' Retirement Plan and the federal portion of the District of Columbia's retirement plans for teachers, police officers, and firefighters as required by Title XI of the Balanced Budget Act of 1997 law.

▶ **NONGOVERNMENTAL**

National Active and Retired Federal Employees Assn. (NARFE), *606 N. Washington St., Alexandria, VA 22314-1914; (703) 838-7760. Fax, (703) 838-7785. Kenneth J. (Ken) Thomas, President. Toll-free, (800) 456-8410.*
Web, www.narfe.org, Twitter, @NARFEHQ, Facebook, www.facebook.com/NARFEHQ and YouTube, www.youtube.com/channel/UCGZZlpMdu5u-4kNjH1lMJfw

Works to preserve the integrity of the federal employee retirement systems. Provides members with information about benefits for retired federal employees and for survivors of deceased federal employees. Monitors legislation and regulations.

FEDERAL CONTRACTS AND PROCUREMENT

General

▶AGENCIES

Defense Contract Audit Agency *(Defense Dept.)*, 8725 John J. Kingman Rd., #2135, Fort Belvoir, VA 22060-6219; (703) 767-3200. Fax, (703) 767-3267. Anita Bales, Director. Inspector General hotline, (571) 448-3135. Press, (703) 697-5131.
General email, dcaaweb@dcaa.mil
Web, www.dcaa.mil

Performs all contract audits for the Defense Dept. Provides Defense Dept. personnel responsible for procurement and contract administration with accounting and financial advisory services regarding the negotiation, administration, and settlement of contracts and subcontracts.

Defense Contract Management Agency *(Defense Dept.)*, 18th St. South, 100A, Arlington, VA 22202; (804) 734-1488. Fax, (703) 699-2180. Lt. Gen. David G. Bassett (USA), Director. FOIA, (804) 609-4533. Press, (804) 734-1492.
Web, www.dcma.mil and Twitter, @DCMAnews

Ensures the integrity of the contracting process, and provides a broad range of contract-procurement management services, including cost and pricing, quality assurance, contract administration and termination, and small business support.

Defense Dept. (DoD), *Armed Services Board of Contract Appeals,* 5109 Leesburg Pike, Skyline 6, #703, Falls Church, VA 22041-3208; (703) 681-8500. Fax, (703) 681-8535. Judge John J. Thrasher, Chair; Catherine A. Stanton, General Counsel. FOIA, (703) 681-2501.
General email, asbca.recorder@mail.mil
Web, www.asbca.mil

Adjudicates disputes arising under Defense Dept. contracts.

Defense Health Agency (DHA) *(Defense Dept.)*, *Small Business Programs,* 5109 Leesburg Pike, Falls Church, VA 22041; (703) 882-7111. Cassandra W. Martin, Director.
Web, https://health.mil/About-MHS/OASDHA/Defense-Health-Agency/Small-Business-Program

Seeks to ensure that small businesses have a fair opportunity to compete and be selected for DHA contracts, at both the prime and subcontract levels. Provides information on agency purchases and the contracting process through forums, mentoring programs, and written materials.

General Services Administration (GSA), *Civilian Board of Contract Appeals (CBCA),* 1800 M St. N.W., 6th Floor, 20036; (202) 606-8800. Jeri K. Somers, Chair.
General email, CBCAclerk@cbca.gov
Web, www.cbca.gov

Presides over various disputes involving Federal executive branch agencies. Resolves contract disputes between government contractors and agencies under the Contract Dispute Act.

General Services Administration (GSA), *Governmentwide Policy (OGP), Acquisition Policy,* 1800 F St. N.W., 20405; (202) 501-1043. Janet Fry, Director, (703) 774-5274.
General email, FARPolicy@gsa.gov
Web, www.gsa.gov/about-us/organization/office-of-governmentwide-policy/office-of-acquisition-policy

Conducts preaward and postaward contract reviews; suspends and debars contractors for unsatisfactory performance; coordinates and promotes governmentwide career management and training programs for contracting personnel.

General Services Administration (GSA), *Small Business Utilization,* 1800 F St. N.W., 20405; (202) 501-1021. Exodie Roe III, Associate Administrator. Toll-free, (844) 472-4111. Vendor Support, (866) 727-8363.
General email, small.business@gsa.gov
Web, www.gsa.gov/small-business

Works to increase small business access to government contract procurement opportunities. Provides policy guidance and direction for GSA Regional Small Business Offices, which offer advice and assistance to businesses interested in government procurement.

Interior Dept. (DOI), *Small and Disadvantaged Business Utilization (OSDBU),* 1849 C St. N.W., Room 4214, 20240; (202) 208-3493. Fax, (202) 208-7444. Colleen Finnegan, Director.
Web, www.doi.gov/pmb/osdbu and Email, doi_osdbu@ios.doi.gov

Advocates contracting opportunities for small, disadvantaged business communities, including Indian economic enterprises, small disadvantaged, women-owned, veteran-owned, service disabled veteran owned small businesses located in historically underutilized business zones (HUBZone) areas, and the Ability One Program.

Labor Dept. (DOL), *Federal Contract Compliance Programs (OFCCP),* 200 Constitution Ave. N.W., #C3325, 20210; (202) 693-0101. Fax, (202) 693-1304. Jenny R. Yang, Director. Toll-free, (800) 397-6251. TTY, (877) 889-5627.
General email, OFCCP-Public@dol.gov
Web, www.dol.gov/ofccp

Monitors and enforces government contractors' compliance with federal laws and regulations on equal employment opportunities and affirmative action, including employment rights of minorities, women, persons with disabilities, and disabled and Vietnam-era veterans.

Labor Dept. (DOL), *Wage and Hour Division (WHD), Government Contracts Enforcement,* 200 Constitution Ave. N.W., #S3502, 20210; (202) 693-0574. Fax, (202) 693-1087. Michele King, Director. Toll-free, (866) 487-9243.
Web, www.dol.gov/agencies/whd/government-contracts

Enforces the Davis-Bacon Act, the Walsh-Healey Public Contracts Act, the Contract Work Hours and Safety

Standards Act, the Service Contract Act, and other related government contract labor standards statutes.

Minority Business Development Agency *(Commerce Dept.), 1401 Constitution Ave. N.W., #5053, 20230; (202) 482-2332. Miguel Estién, National Director (Acting). Web, www.mbda.gov, Twitter, @USMBDA and Facebook, www.facebook.com/USMBDA*

Assists minority business owners in obtaining federal loans and contract awards; produces an annual report on federal agencies' performance in procuring from minority-owned businesses.

Office of Management and Budget (OMB) *(Executive Office of the President), Federal Procurement Policy, 725 17th St. N.W., #9013, 20503; Vacant, Administrator. Web, www.whitehouse.gov/omb/management/office-federal-procurement-policy*

Oversees and coordinates government procurement policies, regulations, and procedures. Responsible for cost accounting rules governing federal contractors and sub-contractors. Interests include effective use of competition, cost-effective contracting for vehicles, and managing a useful information technology system for federal procurement managers.

Small Business Administration (SBA), *Government Contracting and Business Development, 409 3rd St. S.W., #8000, 20416; (202) 205-6459. Fax, (202) 205-5206. Bibi Hidalgo, Associate Administrator. Web, www.sba.gov/about-sba/sba-locations/headquarters-offices/office-government-contracting-business-development*

Oversees the Office of Government Contracting and Office of Business Development. Enhances the effectiveness of small business programs to develop policies, regulations, and statutory changes.

Small Business Administration (SBA), *Government Contracting and Business Development, Government Contracting, 409 3rd St. S.W., #8000, 20416; (202) 205-6460. Fax, (202) 205-7324. John Klein, Deputy Associate Administrator (Acting). Web, www.sba.gov/about-sba/sba-locations/headquarters-offices/office-government-contracting*

Seeks to maximize participation by small, disadvantaged, and woman-owned businesses in federal government contract awards and large prime subcontract awards. Advocates on behalf of small business in the federal procurement world.

System for Award Management, *Contract Data, (FPDS-NG), 1800 F St. N.W., 20405; (866) 606-8220. Vacant, Director. Help Desk, (800) 488-3111. Web, https://sam.gov/content/contract-data*

Service contracted out by GSA that collects procurement data from all federal government contracts and disseminates these data via the Internet. Reports include agency identification, products or services purchased, dollar obligation, principal place of performance, and contractor identification; also provides socioeconomic indicators

such as business size and business ownership type. Used to be GSA (FPDS-NG).

U.S. AbilityOne Commission, *1401 S. Clark St., #715, Arlington, VA 22202-3259; (703) 603-2100. Fax, (703) 603-0655. Kim Zeich, Deputy Executive Director. Toll-free, (800) 999-5963. General email, info@abilityone.gov Web, www.abilityone.gov*

Presidentially appointed committee. Determines which products and services are suitable for federal procurement from qualified nonprofit agencies that employ people who are blind or have other significant disabilities; seeks to increase employment opportunities for these individuals. (Formerly Committee for Purchase from People Who Are Blind or Severely Disabled.)

▶**CONGRESS**

For a listing of relevant congressional committees and sub-committees, please see pages 332–333 or the Appendix.

Government Accountability Office (GAO), *Contracting and National Security Acquisitions (CNSA), 441 G St. N.W., 20548; (202) 512-4841. John D. Sawyer, Director (Acting). Web, www.gao.gov/about/careers/our-teams*

Advises Congress and governmental agencies about federal spending and maximizing investments related to acquisitions and procurements.

Government Accountability Office (GAO), *General Counsel (GC), 441 G St. N.W., MS 7182, 20548; (202) 512-5400. Fax, (202) 512-7703. Edda Emmanuelli-Perez, General Counsel. Web, www.gao.gov/legal*

Adjudicates challenges to the proposed or actual awards of government contracts; renders decisions and opinions on matters of appropriations law; provides legal expertise in support of GAO's functions.

▶**NONGOVERNMENTAL**

Coalition for Government Procurement, *1990 M St. N.W., #450, 20036; (202) 331-0975. Fax, (202) 521-3533. Roger D. Waldron, President, (202) 315-1051. General email, info@thecgp.org Web, http://thecgp.org and Twitter, @TheCGPOrg*

Alliance of business firms that sell to the federal government. Seeks equal opportunities for businesses to sell to the government; monitors practices of the General Services Administration and government procurement legislation and regulations.

National Contract Management Assn. (NCMA), *21740 Beaumeade Circle, #125, Ashburn, VA 20147; (571) 382-0082. Fax, (703) 448-0939. Kraig Conrad, Chief Executive Officer, (571) 382-1123. Toll-free, (800) 344-8096. General email, ncma@ncmahq.org Web, www.ncmahq.org, Twitter, @NCMA and Facebook, www.facebook.com/NCMAHQ*

Membership: individuals concerned with administering, procuring, negotiating, and managing government and commercial contracts and subcontracts. Sponsors the Certified Professional Contracts Manager Program and various educational and professional programs.

NIGP: The Institute for Public Procurement, *2411 Dulles Corner Park, #350, Herndon, VA 20171; (703) 736-8900. Fax, (703) 736-9644. Rick Grimm, Chief Executive Officer, (703) 429-2590. Toll-free, (800) 367-6447.*
General email, customercare@nigp.org

Web, www.nigp.org, Facebook, www.facebook.com/OfficialNIGP and Twitter, @OfficialNIGP

Membership: governmental purchasing departments, agencies, and organizations at the federal, state, and local levels in the United States, Canada, and internationally. Provides public procurement officers with technical assistance and information, training seminars, and professional certification. (Formerly the National Institute of Governmental Purchasing.)

Professional Services Council (PSC), *4401 Wilson Blvd., #1110, Arlington, VA 22203; (703) 875-8059.*
David J. Berteau, President.
Web, https://pscouncil.org, Twitter, @PSCSpeaks and Facebook, www.facebook.com/PSCspeaks/?ref=sgm

Membership: associations and firms that provide local, state, federal, and international governments with professional, engineering, and technical services. Analyzes the process by which the government awards contracts to private firms. Monitors legislation and regulations.

POSTAL SERVICE

General

►AGENCIES

U.S. Postal Service (USPS), *475 L'Enfant Plaza S.W., 20260-0001; (202) 268-2000. Louis DeJoy, Postmaster General. Library, (202) 268-2906. TTY, (800) 877-8339. Toll-free, (800) 275-8777.*
Web, www.usps.com and Twitter, @USPS

Offers postal service throughout the country as an independent establishment of the executive branch. Library open to the public by appointment.

U.S. Postal Service (USPS), *Inspection Service, 475 L'Enfant Plaza S.W., #3100, 20260-2100; (202) 268-4264. Gary Barksdale, Chief Postal Inspector. Fraud and abuse hotline, (877) 876-2455.*
Web, http://uspis.gov, Twitter, @USPISpressroom and Facebook, www.facebook.com/PostalInspectors

Investigates violations of postal laws, such as theft of mail or posted valuables, assaults on postal employees, organized crime in postal-related matters, and prohibited mailings. Conducts internal audits; investigates postal activities to determine effectiveness of procedures; monitors compliance of individual post offices with postal regulations. (Headquarters in Chicago, Ill.)

►CONGRESS

For a listing of relevant congressional committees and subcommittees, please see pages 332–333 or the Appendix.

Consumer Services

►AGENCIES

Postal Regulatory Commission, *Public Affairs and Government Relations (PAGR), 901 New York Ave. N.W., #200, 20268; (202) 789-6800. Fax, (202) 789-6891. Jennifer Alvarez-Warburton, Director.*
General email, prc-pagr@prc.gov
Web, www.prc.gov/offices/pagr

Supports public outreach and education and media relations; provides information for consumers and responds to their inquiries. Informal complaints regarding individual rate and service inquiries are referred to the Consumer Advocate of the Postal Service.

Employee and Labor Relations

►AGENCIES

U.S. Postal Service (USPS), *Human Resource Management, 475 L'Enfant Plaza S.W., #9840, 20260-4200; (202) 268-3783. Simon Storrey, Vice President, (202) 268-3784.*
Web, www.usps.com

Drafts and implements employment policies and practices and safety and health guidelines.

U.S. Postal Service (USPS), *Labor Relations, 475 L'Enfant Plaza S.W., 20260-4100; (202) 268-7447. Fax, (202) 268-3074. Katherine S. Attridge, Vice President, (202) 268-3613.*
Web, www.usps.com

Handles collective bargaining and contract administration for the U.S. Postal Service.

►NONGOVERNMENTAL

American Postal Workers Union (APWU), *1300 L St. N.W., 20005; (202) 842-4200. Fax, (202) 842-4297. Mark Dimondstein, President, (202) 842-4250.*
Web, www.apwu.org, Twitter, @APWUnational and Facebook, www.facebook.com/APWUnational

Membership: more than 200,000 postal employees and retirees, including clerks, motor vehicle operators, maintenance operators, and retirees. Assists members with contract negotiation and grievances; conducts training programs and workshops. Monitors legislation and regulations. (Affiliated with the Postal, Telegraph, and Telephone International and the AFL-CIO.)

National Alliance of Postal and Federal Employees (NAPFE), *1640 11th St. N.W., 20001-5008; (202) 939-6325. Fax, (202) 939-6392. Janice F. Robinson, President. General email, info@napfe.org*

Web, www.napfe.com, Facebook, www.facebook.com/ NAPFE-National-Alliance-of-Postal-and-Federal-Employees-1003292639737381 and Twitter, @NAPFE_DC

Membership: approximately 70,000 postal and federal employees. Helps members negotiate pay, benefits, equal opportunity, and better working conditions; conducts training programs and workshops. Monitors legislation and regulations.

National Assn. of Letter Carriers, *100 Indiana Ave. N.W., 20001-2144; (202) 393-4695. Fredric V. Rolando, President. Web, www.nalc.org and Twitter, @NALC_National*

Membership: union letter carriers working for, or retired from, the U.S. Postal Service. Assists members with contract negotiation and grievances; conducts training programs and workshops. Monitors legislation and regulations. (Affiliated with the AFL-CIO and the Union Network International.)

National Assn. of Postal Supervisors, *1727 King St., #400, Alexandria, VA 22314-2753; (703) 836-9660. Fax, (703) 836-9665. Ivan Butts, President. General email, napshq@naps.org*

Web, www.naps.org and Twitter, @napshq

Membership: present and retired postal supervisors, managers, and postmasters. Management association that cooperates with other postal management associations, unions, and the U.S. Postal Service to improve the efficiency of the postal service; promotes favorable working conditions and broader career opportunities for all postal employees; provides members with information on current functions and legislative issues of the postal service.

National Rural Letter Carriers' Assn., *1630 Duke St., Alexandria, VA 22314-3467; (703) 684-5545. Ronnie W. Stutts, President. Web, www.nrlca.org*

Membership: more than 100,000 rural letter carriers working for, or retired from, the U.S. Postal Service. Seeks to improve rural mail delivery. Negotiates labor agreements affecting members; conducts training programs and workshops. Monitors legislation and regulations.

National Star Route Mail Contractors Assn., *324 E. Capitol St. N.E., 20003-3897; (202) 543-1661. Fax, (202) 543-8863. Greg Reed, Executive Director. Toll-free, (800) 543-1661. General email, eyoung-scales@nsrmca.net*

Web, www.starroutecontractors.org

Membership: contractors for highway mail transport and selected rural route deliverers. Acts as liaison between contractors and the U.S. Postal Service, Transportation Dept., Labor Dept., and Congress concerning contracts, wages, and other issues. Monitors legislation and regulations.

United Postmasters and Managers of America, *8 Herbert St., Alexandria, VA 22305-2600; (703) 683-9027. Fax, (703) 683-0923. Daniel Heins, President. General email, information@unitedpma.org*

Web, www.unitedpma.org and Twitter, @UPMA15

Membership: present and former postmasters and postal managers of the United States. Promotes the postal service and the welfare of its members. Assists postmasters facing discipline or other adverse actions. Monitors legislation and regulations. (Formerly the National Association of Postmasters of the United States.)

Mail Rates and Classification

▶**AGENCIES**

Postal Regulatory Commission, *901 New York Ave. N.W., #200, 20268-0001; (202) 789-6800. Fax, (202) 789-6891. Michael M. Kubayanda, Chair; Ann C. Fisher, Vice Chair. General email, prc-dockets@prc.gov*

Web, www.prc.gov

Independent agency with regulatory oversight over the U.S. Postal Service. Develops and maintains regulations concerning postal rates; consults with the Postal Service on delivery service standards and performance measures; consults with the State Dept. on international postal policies; prevents anticompetitive postal practices; and adjudicates complaints.

U.S. Postal Service (USPS), *Mail Entry and Payment Technology, 475 L'Enfant Plaza S.W., #2P836, 20260-0911; (202) 268-6406. Randy Workman, Vice President. Web, www.usps.com and Business services, www.usps.com/ business*

Implements policies governing the acceptance and verification of business mail by the U.S. Postal Service.

U.S. Postal Service (USPS), *Mailing Standards, 475 L'Enfant Plaza S.W., #4446, 20260-4446; (202) 268-7281. Lizbeth (Liz) Dobbins, Manager. Web, www.usps.com*

Issues policy statements on domestic mail classification matters. Ensures the accuracy of policies developed by the Postal Regulatory Commission with respect to domestic mail classification schedules.

U.S. Postal Service (USPS), *Pricing and Costing, 475 L'Enfant Plaza S.W., #4100, 20260-5014; (202) 268-8900. Sharon Owens, Vice President. Web, www.usps.com*

Sets prices for U.S. Postal Service product lines using competitive pricing methods.

▶**NONGOVERNMENTAL**

Alliance of Nonprofit Mailers, *1211 Connecticut Ave. N.W., #610, 20036-2705; (202) 360-3776. Stephen (Steve) Kearney, Executive Director, (202) 360-3776.*

General email, alliance@nonprofitmailers.org

Web, www.nonprofitmailers.org,

Twitter, @NonProfitMailer and Facebook, www.facebook
.com/AllianceNM

Works to maintain reasonable mail rates for nonprofit organizations. Represents member organizations before Congress, the U.S. Postal Service, the Postal Regulatory Commission, and federal courts on nonprofit postal rate and mail classification issues, nondiscrimination relative to commercial mailers, and the external discipline of the Consumer Price Index cap.

ANA Nonprofit Federation (ANANF), *2020 K St. N.W.,
#660, 20006; (202) 861-2427. Xenia (Sonny) Boone, Senior
Vice President, (202) 861-2498.*
Web, https://nonprofitfederation.org,

Twitter, @ANANonprofit and Facebook, www.facebook
.com/ANANonprofitFederation

Membership: nonprofit organizations and their suppliers that rely on nonprofit mail and other marketing channels, including digital, email, and telephone, to reach donors. Serves as a liaison between members and the U.S. Postal Service; represents members' interests before regulatory agencies; monitors legislation and regulations. Hosts conferences on fund-raising across marketing channels.

Assn. for Postal Commerce (POSTCOM), *1800 Diagonal
Rd., #600, Alexandria, VA 22314; (703) 524-0096.
Fax, (703) 997-2414. Michael Plunkett, President.*
General email, info@postcom.org

Web, www.postcom.org and Twitter, @PostCom2

Membership: companies and organizations interested in mail as a medium for advertising and product delivery. Provides members with information about postal news worldwide, postal policy, postal rates, and legislation regarding postal regulations. Monitors legislation and regulations.

Package Shippers Assn. (PSA), *1838 Columbia Rd. N.W.,
20009-2002 (mailing address: P.O. Box 7004, Arlington,
VA 22207); (571) 257-7617. Jim Cochrane, Chief Executive
Officer.*
Web, www.packageshippers.org

Voluntary organization of business firms concerned with the shipment of parcels. Works to improve parcel post rates and service; represents members before the Postal Regulatory Commission in matters regarding parcel post rates. Monitors legislation and regulations. (Formally Parcel Shippers).

Stamps, Postal History

▶**AGENCIES**

National Postal Museum *(Smithsonian Institution), 2
Massachusetts Ave. N.E., 20002 (mailing address: P.O. Box
37012, MS 570, Washington, DC 20013); (202) 633-5555.
Elliot Gruber, Director. Press, (202) 633-5518. Tours and
education, (202) 633-5534. TTY, (202) 633-9849.*

Web, http://postalmuseum.si.edu,

Twitter, @PostalMuseum and Facebook, www.facebook
.com/SmithsonianNationalPostalMuseum

Exhibits postal history and stamp collections; provides information on world postal and stamp history.

U.S. Postal Service (USPS), *Citizens' Stamp Advisory
Committee, 475 L'Enfant Plaza S.W., #3300, 20260-3501;
(202) 268-2000. B.J. Bueno, Chair.*
Web, http://about.usps.com/who/csac

Reviews stamp subject nominations, which are open to the public. Develops the annual Stamp Program and makes subject and design recommendations to the Postmaster General.

U.S. Postal Service (USPS), *Stamp Services, 475 L'Enfant
Plaza S.W., #3300, 20260-3501; (202) 268-3326. Fax, (202)
268-4965. William Gicker Jr., Director (Acting).*
Web, www.usps.com

Manages the stamp selection function; develops the basic stamp preproduction design; manages relationship with stamp collecting community.

PUBLIC ADMINISTRATION

General

▶**AGENCIES**

General Services Administration (GSA), *Office of Shared
Solutions and Performance Improvement (OSSPI),
Government-wide Policy (OGP), President's
Management Council (PMC), Dwight D. Eisenhower
Executive Office Bldg., 1650 Pennsylvania Ave. N.W., #216,
20502; Jeffery (Austin) Price, Council Contact.*
General email, pgovsupport@gsa.gov

Web, https://ussm.gsa.gov/about/ and
Email, ussmteam@gsa.gov

The PMC advises the President and OMB on government reform initiatives, provides performance and management leadership throughout the Executive Branch, and oversees implementation of government-wide management policies and programs. The PMC comprises the Chief Operating Officers of major agencies, primarily Deputy Secretaries, Deputy Administrators, and agency heads from GSA and OPM.

President's Commission on White House Fellowships,
*712 Jackson Pl. N.W., 20503; (202) 395-4522. Fax, (202)
395-6179. Elizabeth Pinkerton, Director.*
General email, whitehousefellows@who.eop.gov

Web, www.whitehouse.gov/participate/fellows

Nonpartisan commission that provides professionals from all sectors of national life with the opportunity to observe firsthand the processes of the federal government. Fellows work for one year as special assistants to cabinet members or to principal members of the White House staff. Qualified applicants have demonstrated superior accomplishments early in their careers and have a commitment to leadership and public service.

▶CONGRESS

For a listing of relevant congressional committees and subcommittees, please see pages 332–333 or the Appendix.

▶NONGOVERNMENTAL

American Society for Public Administration, *1730 Rhode Island Ave. N.W., #500, 20036; (202) 393-7878. Fax, (202) 638-4952. William P. Shields Jr., Executive Director, (202) 585-4307.*
General email, info@aspanet.org
Web, www.aspanet.org, Twitter, @ASPANational and Facebook, www.facebook.com/ASPANational

Membership: government administrators, public officials, educators, researchers, and others interested in public administration. Presents awards to distinguished professionals in the field; sponsors workshops and conferences; disseminates information about public administration. Promotes high ethical standards for public service.

Assn. of Government Accountants (AGA), *2208 Mount Vernon Ave., Alexandria, VA 22301; (703) 684-6931. Fax, (703) 519-0039. Ann M. Ebberts, Chief Executive Officer. Toll-free, (800) 242-7211.*
General email, agamembers@agacgfm.org
Web, www.agacgfm.org, Twitter, @AGACGFM and Facebook, www.facebook.com/AGACGFM

Membership: professionals engaged in government accounting, auditing, budgeting, and information systems. Sponsors education, research, and conferences; administers certification program.

Federally Employed Women, *455 Massachusetts Ave. N.W., 20001 (mailing address: P.O. Box 306, Washington, DC 20001); (202) 898-0994. Karen Rainey, President.*
General email, few@few.org
Web, www.few.org, Twitter, @FENNational and Facebook, www.facebook.com/federallyemployedwomen

Membership: women and men who work for the federal government. The four major program areas are Compliance, Diversity, Legislative and Training. Works to eliminate sex discrimination in government employment and to increase job opportunities for women. Monitors legislation and regulations.

International City/County Management Assn. (ICMA), *777 N. Capitol St. N.E., #500, 20002-4201; Fax, (202) 962-3500. (202) 962-3680. Marc A. Ott, Executive Director, (202) 962-3698.*
General email, membership@icma.org
Web, www.icma.org, Twitter, @ICMA, Customer service, customerservices@icma.org and Facebook, www.facebook.com/ICMAORG

Membership: appointed managers and administrators of cities, towns, counties, and other local governments around the world; local government employees; academics; and other individuals with an interest in local government. Provides member support, publications, data and information, peer and results-oriented assistance, and training and professional development to members and others to help build sustainable communities. Sponsors workshops, regional summits, and an annual conference. Publishes resources for local government management professionals.

International Public Management Assn. for Human Resources (IPMA-HR), *1617 Duke St., Alexandria, VA 22314; (703) 549-7100. Fax, (703) 684-0948. Cara Woodson Welch, Executive Director.*
General email, ipma@ipma-hr.org
Web, www.ipma-hr.org, Twitter, @IPMAHR and Facebook, www.facebook.com/International-Public-Management-Association-for-Human-Resources-IPMA-HR-38098732966

Membership: personnel professionals from federal, state, and local governments. Provides information on training procedures, management techniques, and legislative developments on the federal, state, and local levels.

National Academy of Public Administration, *1600 K St. N.W., #400, 20006; (202) 347-3190. Teresa W. (Teri) Gerton, President, (202) 204-3615.*
General email, academy@napawash.org
Web, www.napawash.org, Twitter, @napawash, Facebook, www.facebook.com/napawash and YouTube, www.youtube.com/channel/UCrBcegZJjqMZmhum2oi8RoQ

Membership: scholars and administrators in public management. Chartered by Congress to assist federal, state, and local government agencies, public officials, and foundations with government and management challenges.

National Foundation for Women Legislators, *1727 King St., #300, Alexandria, VA 22314; (703) 518-7931. Jody Thomas, Executive Director.*
General email, nfwl@womenlegislators.org
Web, www.womenlegislators.org, Twitter, @electedwomen and Facebook, www.facebook.com/electedwomen

Provides leadership development and networking resources to elected women leaders at the city, state, and federal levels of government.

National Women's Political Caucus, *1001 Connecticut Ave. N.W., #630, 20036 (mailing address: P.O. Box 65010, Washington, DC 20035); (202) 785-1100. Kate McDonald, Program Director.*
General email, info@nwpc.org
Web, www.nwpc.org, Twitter, @NWPCNational and Facebook, www.facebook.com/NWPC.fb

Seeks to increase the number of women in policymaking positions in federal, state, and local government. Identifies, recruits, trains, and supports prochoice women candidates for public office. Monitors agencies and provides names of qualified women for high-level and mid-level appointments.

Network of Schools of Public Policy, Affairs, and Administration (NASPAA), *1029 Vermont Ave. N.W.,*

#1100, 20005; (202) 628-8965. Fax, (202) 626-4978. Angel Wright-Lanier, Executive Director, (202) 810-7413. General email, naspaa@naspaa.org

Web, www.naspaa.org, Twitter, @naspaa and Facebook, www.facebook.com/naspaaglobal

Serves as a clearinghouse for information on education in public administration, public policy, and public affairs programs in colleges and universities.

Women in Government Relations, *908 King St., #320, Alexandria, VA 22314; (202) 868-6797. Jen Brydges, Executive Director, (202) 868-6797.* General email, info@wgr.org

Web, www.wgr.org and Twitter, @WGRDC

Membership: professionals in business, trade associations, and government whose jobs involve governmental relations at the federal, state, or local level. Serves as a forum for exchange of information among its members.

STATE AND LOCAL GOVERNMENT

General

▶AGENCIES

Multistate Tax Commission, *444 N. Capitol St. N.W., #425, 20001-1538; (202) 650-0300. Gregory S. Matson, Executive Director.* General email, mtc@mtc.gov

Web, www.mtc.gov

Membership: state governments that have enacted the Multistate Tax Compact. Promotes fair, effective, and efficient state tax systems for interstate and international commerce; works to preserve state tax sovereignty. Encourages uniform state tax laws and regulations for multistate and multinational enterprises. Maintains three regional audit offices that monitor compliance with state tax laws and encourage uniformity in taxpayer treatment. Administers program to identify businesses that do not file tax returns with states.

Office of Management and Budget (OMB) *(Executive Office of the President), Federal Financial Management, 725 17th St. N.W., #6025, 20503; Fax, (202) 395-3952. Diedre Harrison, Deputy Controller.* Web, www.whitehouse.gov/omb/management/office-federal-financial-management

Facilitates exchange of information on financial management standards, techniques, and processes among officers of state and local governments.

State Justice Institute, *12700 Fair Lakes Circle, #340, Fairfax, VA 22033; (703) 660-4979. Jonathan D. Mattiello, Executive Director.* General email, contact@sji.gov

Web, www.sji.gov, Twitter, @statejustice and Facebook, www.facebook.com/SJI.gov

Local Government in the Washington Metropolitan Area

DISTRICT OF COLUMBIA

Executive Office of the Mayor,
Muriel Bowser, Mayor,
John A. Wilson Bldg.
1350 Pennsylvania Ave. N.W., # 316, 20004;
(202) 727-2643; TTY, dial 711 then (202) 727-2643;
Email, eom@dc.gov;
Web, www.mayor.dc.gov

MARYLAND

Montgomery County,
Marc Elrich, County Executive,
101 Monroe St., 2nd Floor, Rockville, MD 20850;
(240) 777-0311;
Email, ocemail@montgomerycountymd.gov;
Web, www.montgomerycountymd.gov/exec

Prince George's County,
Angela D. Alsobrooks, County Executive,
1301 McCormick Dr., Upper Marlboro, MD 20774;
(301) 952-4131;
Email, countyexecutive@co.pg.md.us;
Web, www.princegeorgescountymd.gov

VIRGINIA

Arlington County,
Mark Schwartz, County Manager,
2100 Clarendon Blvd. #318, Arlington, VA 22201;
(703) 228-3120; TTY, (703) 228-4611;
Fax, (703) 228-3218;
Email, countymanager@arlingtonva.us;
Web, http://departments.arlingtonva.us/cmo

City of Alexandria,
Justin Wilson, Mayor,
301 King St., Room 2300, Alexandria, VA 22314;
(703) 746-4500;
Web, www.alexandriava.gov/Council

City of Falls Church,
Wyatt Shields, City Manager,
300 Park Ave., #200 E., Falls Church, VA 22046;
(703) 248-5004; TTY, dial 711 then (703) 248-5004;
Fax, (703) 248-5146;
Email, city-manager@fallschurchva.gov;
Web, www.fallschurchva.gov/246/City-Manager

Fairfax County,
Bryan Hill, County Executive,
12000 Government Center Pkwy., #552, Fairfax, VA
22035;(703) 324-2531; TTY, dial 711 then
(703) 324-2531;
Email, 703fairfax@fairfaxcounty.gov;
Web, www.fairfaxcounty.gov/countyexec

Awards grants to state courts and to state agencies for programs that improve state courts' judicial administration. Maintains judicial information clearinghouses and establishes technical resource centers; conducts educational programs; delivers technical assistance.

System for Award Management, *Asssitance Listings (previously CFDA.gov)*, 1800 F St. N.W., 20405-0001; *Vacant, Product Manager.*
Web, https://sam.gov/content/assistance-listings

Disseminates information on federal programs, that provide grants, loans scholarships, insurance and other types of assitant awards available to state and local governments through the CFDA website. Information includes all types of federal aid and explains types of assistance, eligibility requirements, application processes, and suggestions for writing proposals. (Used to be Catalog of Federal Domestic Assistance (CFDA).)

▶ **CONGRESS**

For a listing of relevant congressional committees and subcommittees, please see pages 332–333 or the Appendix.

▶ **NONGOVERNMENTAL**

American Legislative Exchange Council (ALEC), 2900 *Crystal Dr., 6th Floor, Arlington, VA 22202; (703) 373-0933. Fax, (703) 373-0927. Lisa B. Nelson, Chief Executive Officer, ext. 240. Press, (571) 482-5035.*
Web, www.alec.org, Twitter, @ALEC_states, Facebook, www.facebook.com/alec.states and *YouTube, www.youtube.com/user/AmericanLegislative*

Nonpartisan educational and research organization for state legislators. Conducts research and provides information and model state legislation on public policy issues. Supports the development of state policies to limit government, expand free markets, promote economic growth, and preserve individual liberty.

The Brookings Institution, *Metropolitan Policy Program,* 1755 Massachusetts Ave. N.W., 20036; (202) 238-3139. Amy Liu, Director.
General email, metro@brookings.edu
Web, www.brookings.edu/metro and *Twitter, @BrookingsMetro*

Helps U.S. cities and metropolitan areas study and reform their economic, fiscal, and social policies. Conducts research at the national, state, and local levels.

Coalition of Northeastern Governors (CONEG), *Policy Research Center, Inc.,* 400 N. Capitol St. N.W., #370, 20001; (202) 624-8450. Jay Lucey, Executive Director.
General email, info@coneg.org
Web, http://coneg.org and *Twitter, @CONEGgovs*

Membership: governors of seven northeastern states (Connecticut, Maine, Massachusetts, New Hampshire, New York, Rhode Island, and Vermont). Addresses shared interests in regional energy, economic development, transportation, and the environment; serves as an information clearinghouse on regional and federal issues; facilitates joint action among member states. Secretariat to the New England Governors & Eastern Canadian Premiers and to the Northeast Committee on Environment.

Council of State Governments (CSG), *Washington Office,* 444 N. Capitol St. N.W., #401, 20001; (202) 624-5460. Fax, (202) 624-5452. David Adkins, Executive Director; Andy Karellas, Director of Government Affairs. Press, (859) 244-8246.
General email, membership@csg.org
Web, www.csg.org, www.csg.org/federal_affairs.aspx and *Twitter, @CSGovts*

Membership: governing bodies of states, commonwealths, and territories and various affiliated national organizations of state officials. Promotes interstate, federal-state, and state-local cooperation; interests include education, transportation, human services, housing, natural resources, and economic development. Provides services to affiliates and associated organizations, including the National Assn. of State Treasurers, National Assn. of Government Labor Officials, and other state administrative organizations in specific fields. Monitors legislation and executive policy. (Headquarters in Lexington, Ky.)

Government Finance Officers Assn. (GFOA), *Federal Liaison Center,* 660 N. Capitol St. N.W., #410, 20001; (202) 393-8020. Fax, (202) 393-0780. Emily S. Brock, Director, (202) 393-8467.
General email, federalliaison@gfoa.org
Web, www.gfoa.org/flc, Twitter, @GFOA and *Facebook, www.facebook.com/GFOAofUSandCanada*

Membership: state and local government finance managers. Offers training and publications in public financial management. Conducts research in public fiscal management, design and financing of government programs, and formulation and analysis of government fiscal policy. (Headquarters in Chicago, Ill.)

International City/County Management Assn. (ICMA), 777 N. Capitol St. N.E., #500, 20002-4201; Fax, (202) 962-3500. (202) 962-3680. Marc A. Ott, Executive Director, (202) 962-3698.
General email, membership@icma.org
Web, www.icma.org, Twitter, @ICMA, Customer service, customerservices@icma.org and *Facebook, www.facebook.com/ICMAORG*

Membership: appointed managers and administrators of cities, towns, counties, and other local governments around the world; local government employees; academics; and other individuals with an interest in local government. Provides member support, publications, data and information, peer and results-oriented assistance, and training and professional development to members and others to help build sustainable communities. Sponsors workshops, regional summits, and an annual conference. Publishes resources for local government management professionals.

International Municipal Lawyers Assn. (IMLA), 51 *Monroe St., #404, Rockville, MD 20850; (202) 466-5424. Fax, (202) 785-0152. Charles W. (Chuck) Thompson Jr.,*

General Counsel, ext. 7110; Amanda Karras, Executive Director, ext. 7116.
General email, info@imla.org
Web, https://imla.org

Membership: local government attorneys and public law practitioners. Acts as a research service for members in all areas of municipal law; participates in litigation of municipal and constitutional law issues.

National Assn. of Bond Lawyers, *601 13th St. N.W., #800-S, 20005-3875; (202) 503-3300. Fax, (202) 637-0217. Linda H. Wyman, Chief Operating Officer, ext. 3306; Brian Egan, Director, Government Affairs, ext. 3290.*
General email, nablconnect@nabl.org
Web, www.nabl.org, Twitter, @nabldc and Facebook, www.facebook.com/nabldc

Membership: state and municipal finance lawyers. Educates members and others on the law relating to state and municipal bonds and other obligations. Provides advice and comment at the federal, state, and local levels on legislation, regulations, rulings, and court and administrative proceedings regarding public obligations.

National Assn. of Counties (NACo), *660 N. Capitol St. N.W., #400, 20001; (202) 393-6226. Matthew D. Chase, Executive Director. Press, (202) 942-4220. Toll-free, (888) 407-6226.*
General email, dcox@naco.org
Web, www.naco.org and Twitter, @NACoTweets

Membership: county governments and county officials and their staffs through NACo's affiliates. Conducts research, supplies information, and provides technical and public affairs assistance on issues affecting counties. Interests include homeland security, drug abuse, access to health care, and public-private partnerships. Monitors legislation and regulations.

National Assn. of Regional Councils (NARC), *660 N. Capitol St. N.W., #440, 20001; (202) 986-1032. Leslie Wollack, Executive Director, (202) 618-5696.*
General email, info@narc.org
Web, www.narc.org, Twitter, @narcregions, Facebook, www.facebook.com/nationalassociationofregionalcouncils/ and YouTube, www.youtube.com/channel/UCbD0711nQ6EHP DBU6hEU5ZQ

Membership: regional councils of local governments, councils of government, and metropolitan planning organizations. Works to improve local governments' intergovernmental planning and coordination at the regional level. Interests include transportation, economic and community development, workforce development, housing, aging, energy, environment, public safety, and emergency management.

National Assn. of Secretaries of State, *444 N. Capitol St. N.W., #401, 20001; (202) 624-3525. Leslie Reynolds, Executive Director.*
General email, nass@sso.org
Web, www.nass.org and Twitter, @Nassorg

Organization of secretaries of state and lieutenant governors or other comparable state officials from the fifty states, the District of Columbia, Guam, Puerto Rico, and the U.S. Virgin Islands. Interests include budget and finance, elections and voting, state business services and licensing, e-government, and state heritage, including a digital archives initiative.

National Assn. of State Auditors, Comptrollers, and Treasurers, *Washington Office, 444 N. Capitol St. N.W., #422, 20001; (202) 624-5451. Fax, (202) 624-5473. R. Kinney Poynter, Executive Director; Cornelia Chebinou, Washington Director.*
Web, www.nasact.org and Twitter, @nasact

Membership: elected and appointed state and territorial officials who deal with the financial management of state government. Provides training and leadership information on financial management, best practices, and research. Monitors legislation and regulations. (Headquarters in Lexington, Ky.)

National Assn. of State Budget Officers, *444 N. Capitol St. N.W., #642, 20001-1511; (202) 624-5382. Shelby Kerns, Executive Director, (202) 624-8804.*
General email, nasbo-direct@nasbo.org
Web, www.nasbo.org and Twitter, @NASBO

Membership: state budget and financial officers. Advances state budget practices through research, policy analysis, education, and knowledge sharing. Publishes reports on budget-related issues; shares best practices; provides training and technical assistance. (Affiliate of the National Governors Assn.)

National Assn. of Towns and Townships (NATaT), *1901 Pennsylvania Ave. N.W., #700, 20006; (202) 331-8500. Jennifer Imo, Federal Director.*
General email, info@natat.org
Web, www.natat.org

Membership: towns, townships, small communities, and others interested in supporting small-town government. Provides local government officials from small jurisdictions with technical assistance, educational services, and public policy support; conducts research and coordinates training for local government officials nationwide. Interests include tax benefits for local public service volunteers, local economic development, water and wastewater infrastructure, transportation improvements, and allocation of federal resources. (Affiliated with National Center for Small Communities.)

National Black Caucus of Local Elected Officials (NBC/LEO), *National League of Cities, 660 N. Capitol St. N.W., 20001; (202) 626-3000. Leon Andrews, Director for Race, Equity, and Leadership, (202) 626-3039. Toll-free, (877) 827-2385.*
General email, constituencygroups@nlc.org
Web, www.nlc.org/initiative/national-black-caucus-of-local-elected-officials-nbc-leo

Membership: Black elected officials at the local level and other interested individuals. Seeks to increase Black participation on the National League of Cities' steering and policy committees. Informs members on issues, and plans strategies for achieving objectives through legislation and direct action. Interests include cultural diversity, local government and community participation, housing, economics, job training, the family, and human rights. Affiliated with the National League of Cities.

National Black Caucus of State Legislators, *444 N. Capitol St. N.W., #622, 20001; (202) 624-5457. Fax, (202) 508-3826. Paula Hoisington, Executive Director. Web, https://nbcsl.org and Facebook, www.facebook.com/nbcslnews*

Membership: Black state legislators. Promotes effective leadership among Black state legislators through education, research, and training; serves as an information network and clearinghouse for members.

National Conference of State Legislatures, Washington *Office, 444 N. Capitol St. N.W., #515, 20001; (202) 624-5400. Fax, (202) 737-1069. Scott Saiki, President; Molly Ramsdell, Director, DC office. Accessibility Support, (800) 659-2656.*
General email, info@ncsl.org

Web, www.ncsl.org, Twitter, @NCSLorg, Facebook, www .facebook.com/NCSLorg and YouTube, www.youtube.com/user/NCSLorg

Coordinates and represents state legislatures at the federal level; conducts research, produces videos, and publishes reports in areas of interest to state legislatures; conducts an information exchange program on intergovernmental relations; sponsors seminars for state legislators and their staffs. Interests include unfunded federal mandates, state-federal law conflict, and fiscal integrity. Monitors legislation and regulations. (Headquarters in Denver, Colo.)

National Foundation for Women Legislators, *1727 King St., #300, Alexandria, VA 22314; (703) 518-7931. Jody Thomas, Executive Director.*
General email, nfwl@womenlegislators.org

Web, www.womenlegislators.org, Twitter, @electedwomen and Facebook, www.facebook.com/electedwomen

Provides leadership development and networking resources to elected women leaders at the city, state, and federal levels of government.

National Governors Assn. (NGA), *444 N. Capitol St. N.W., #267, 20001-1512; (202) 624-5300. Bill McBride, Executive Director.*
General email, info@nga.org

Web, www.nga.org, Twitter, @NatGovsAssoc, Facebook, www.facebook.com/nationalgovernorsassociation and YouTube, www.youtube .com/channel/UCPk5LFlePYG_NVBOcjZC5Qg

Membership: governors of states, commonwealths, and territories. Provides members with policy and technical assistance. Makes policy recommendations to Congress and the president on community and economic development; education; international trade and foreign relations; energy and the environment; health care and welfare

reform; agriculture; transportation, commerce, and technology; communications; criminal justice; public safety; and workforce development.

National League of Cities, *660 N. Capitol St. N.W., #450, 20001; (202) 626-3000. Fax, (202) 626-3043. Clarence Anthony, Executive Director, (202) 626-3010. Toll-free, (877) 827-2385.*
General email, info@nlc.org

Web, www.nlc.org and Twitter, @leagueofcities

Membership: cities and state municipal leagues. Provides city leaders with training, technical assistance, and publications; investigates needs of local governments in implementing federal programs that affect cities. Holds two annual conferences; conducts research; sponsors awards. Monitors legislation and regulations. (Affiliates include National Black Caucus of Local Elected Officials.)

NIGP: The Institute for Public Procurement, *2411 Dulles Corner Park, #350, Herndon, VA 20171; (703) 736-8900. Fax, (703) 736-9644. Rick Grimm, Chief Executive Officer, (703) 429-2590. Toll-free, (800) 367-6447.*
General email, customercare@nigp.org

Web, www.nigp.org, Facebook, www.facebook.com/OfficialNIGP and Twitter, @OfficialNIGP

Membership: governmental purchasing departments, agencies, and organizations at the federal, state, and local levels in the United States, Canada, and internationally. Provides public procurement officers with technical assistance and information, training seminars, and professional certification. (Formerly the National Institute of Governmental Purchasing.)

Public Risk Management Assn. (PRIMA), *700 S. Washington St., #218, Alexandria, VA 22314; (703) 528-7701. Fax, (703) 739-0200. Jennifer Ackerman, Chief Executive Officer, (703) 253-1267.*
General email, info@primacentral.org

Web, https://primacentral.org

Membership: state and local governments and their risk management practitioners, including benefits and insurance managers, and private sector organizations. Develops and teaches cost-effective management techniques for handling public liability issues; promotes professional development of its members. Gathers and disseminates information about risk management to public and private sectors.

Public Technology Institute (PTI), *322 4th St. N.E., 20002; (202) 626-2400. Alan R. Shark, Executive Director, (202) 626-2445. Press, (202) 626-2432.*
General email, techvoice@comptia.org

Web, www.pti.org, Twitter, @Public_Tech and Facebook, www.facebook.com/Public-Technology-Institute-98024848530

Cooperative research, development, and technology-transfer organization of cities and counties in North America. Assists local governments in increasing efficiency, reducing costs, improving services, and developing public enterprise programs to help local officials create revenues and serve citizens. Participates in international conferences.

Stateline, *901 E St. N.W., 20004-2008; (202) 552-2000. Susan Irahn, Corporate Executive Officer. Press information, (202) 429-4372.*
General email, editor@stateline.org
Web, www.pewtrusts.org/en/research-and-analysis/blogs/ stateline/about, Twitter, @pewtrusts, Facebook, www .facebook.com/pewcharitabletrusts and YouTube, www .youtube.com/pew

Independent online news site and forum. Encourages debate on state-level issues such as health care, tax and budget policy, the environment, and immigration. (Part of the Pew Charitable Trusts.)

U.S. Conference of Mayors, *1620 Eye St. N.W., 4th Floor, 20006; (202) 293-7330. J. Thomas (Tom) Cochran, Executive Director.*
General email, info@usmayors.org
Web, www.usmayors.org, Twitter, @usmayors, YouTube, www.youtube.com/usmayors and Facebook, www.facebook.com/usmayors

Membership: mayors of cities with populations of 30,000 or more. Promotes city-federal cooperation; publishes reports and conducts meetings on federal programs, policies, and initiatives that affect urban and suburban interests. Serves as a clearinghouse for information on urban and suburban problems. (Approximately 1,400 U.S. cities.)

U.S. Term Limits, *1250 Connecticut Ave. N.W., #700, 20036; (202) 261-3532. Fax, (215) 546-0503. Philip Blumel, President.*
Web, www.termlimits.com, Twitter, @USTermLimits, Facebook, www.facebook.com/USTermLimits and YouTube, www.youtube.com/channel/UC6r8rfcE4_- Yv0Z1D2PLlIw

Nonpartisan organization advocating for the establishment and preservation of term limits in all elected offices.

Women In Government, *444 N. Capitol St. N.W., #401, 20001; (202) 434-4850. Meredith Martino, Executive Director, (202) 434-4852.*
Web, www.womeningovernment.org and Twitter, @WomenInGovt

Membership: women state legislators. Seeks to enhance the leadership role of women policymakers by providing issue education and leadership training. Sponsors seminars and conducts educational research.

Washington Area

►CONGRESS

For a listing of relevant congressional committees and subcommittees, please see pages 332–333 or the Appendix.

►NONGOVERNMENTAL

Metropolitan Washington Council of Governments, *777 N. Capitol St. N.E., #300, 20002-4239; (202) 962-3200. Fax, (202) 962-3201. Chuck Bean, Executive Director, (202) 962-3260. Press, (202) 962-3250. TDD, (202) 962-3213.*
General email, ccogdtp@mwcog.org
Web, www.mwcog.org, Twitter, @MWCOG and Facebook, www.facebook.com/MWCOG

Membership: local governments in the Washington area, plus members of the Maryland and Virginia legislatures and the U.S. Congress and the Department of Homeland Security. Analyzes and develops regional responses to issues such as the environment, affordable housing, economic development, health, population growth, human and social services, public safety, and transportation.

Walter E. Washington Convention Center Authority, *801 Mt. Vernon Pl. N.W., 20001; (202) 249-3000. Fax, (202) 249-3397. Gregory A. O'Dell, Chief Executive Officer. Press, (202) 249-3217. Toll-free, (800) 368-9000.*
Web, https://eventsdc.com/venue/walter-e-washington- convention-center, Twitter, @TheEventsDC and Facebook, www.facebook.com/OfficialEventsDC

Promotes national and international conventions, meetings, and trade shows; hosts sports, entertainment, and special events; fosters redevelopment of downtown Washington.

10 Health

GENERAL POLICY AND ANALYSIS

Basic Resources

▶ AGENCIES

Agency for Healthcare Research and Quality (AHRQ) *(Health and Human Services Dept.)*, *5600 Fishers Lane, 7th Floor, Rockville, MD 20857; (301) 427-1104. Robert Otto (Bob) Valdez, Director, (301) 427-1200. Fax, 427-1201. Congressional Affairs, (301) 427-1214. Press, (301) 427-1364. TTY, (888) 586-6340.*
General email, info@ahrq.gov

Web, www.ahrq.gov, Twitter, @AHRQNews and Facebook, www.facebook.com/ahrq.gov

Works to improve the quality, safety, effectiveness, and efficiency of health care in the United States. Promotes improvements in clinical practices and in organizing, financing, and delivering health care services. Conducts and supports comparative effectiveness research, demonstration projects, evaluations, and training; disseminates information on a wide range of activities.

Assistant Secretary for Health (OASH) *(Health and Human Services Dept.)*, *200 Independence Ave. S.W., #716G, 20201; (202) 690-7694. Dr. Rachel L. Levine, Assistant Secretary. Press, (202) 205-0143.*
General email, ASH@hhs.gov

Web, www.hhs.gov/ash and Twitter, @hhsgov

Develops public health policy recommendations across Health and Human Services Dept. offices. Oversees the department's key public health offices and programs, a number of presidential and secretarial advisory committees, ten regional health offices, and the Office of the Surgeon General and the U.S. Public Health Service Commissioned Corps.

Assistant Secretary for Health (OASH) *(Health and Human Services Dept.)*, *Disease Prevention and Health Promotion (ODPHP)*, *1101 Wootton Pkwy., #LL100, Rockville, MD 20852; (240) 453-8280. Fax, (240) 453-8282. Dr. Paul Reed, Director.*
General email, odphpinfo@hhs.gov

Web, https://health.gov, Twitter, @HealthGov and Facebook, www.facebook.com/HHSHealthGov

Develops national policies for disease prevention, clinical preventive services, and health promotion; assists the private sector and agencies with disease prevention, clinical preventive services, and health promotion activities.

Assistant Secretary for Health (OASH) *(Health and Human Services Dept.)*, *National Health Information Center (NHIC)*, *1100 Wootton Pkwy., #LL100, Rockville, MD 20852 (mailing address: P.O. Box 1133, Washington, DC 20013-1133); (240) 453-8280. Fax, (240) 453-8282. Dr. Paul Reed, Director.*
General email, healthfinder@nhic.org and info@nhic.org

Web, www.health.gov/nhic and www.healthfinder.gov

A project of the Office of Disease Prevention and Health Promotion; provides referrals on health topics and resources. Maintains a calendar of National Health Observances.

Assistant Secretary for Health (OASH) *(Health and Human Services Dept.)*, *Surgeon General, Humphrey Bldg., 200 Independence Ave. S.W., #701H, 20201 (mailing address: Tower Bldg., Plaza Level 1, #100, 1101 Wooton Pkwy., Rockville, MD 20852); (240) 401-7529. Vice Adm. (Dr.) Vivek H. Murthy, Surgeon General. Press, (202) 205-0143.*
General email, Surgeongeneral@hhs.gov

Press email, OSGPress@hhs.gov, Web, www.surgeon general.gov, Twitter, @Surgeon_General and Facebook, www.facebook.com/USSurgeonGeneral

Directs activities of the Office of the Assistant Secretary for Health. Serves as the secretary's principal adviser on health concerns; exercises specialized responsibilities in various health areas, including domestic and global health. Advises the public on smoking, AIDS, immunization, diet, nutrition, disease prevention, and other general health issues, including responses to bioterrorism. Oversees the operations of the U.S. Public Health Service Commissioned Corps (USPHS).

Centers for Disease Control and Prevention (CDC) *(Health and Human Services Dept.)*, *Washington Office, 395 E St. S.W., #9100, 20201; (202) 245-0600. Fax, (202) 245-0602. Jeff Reczek, Director, Washington Office. Public inquiries, (800) 232-4636.*
General email, cdcwashington@cdc.gov

Web, www.cdc.gov/washington and Twitter, @CDCgov

Collaborates with state and local health departments to further health promotion; prevention of disease, injury, and disability; and preparedness for new health threats. Monitors the health of individuals, detects and investigates health problems, conducts research to enhance prevention, develops and acts as advocate for public health policies, implements prevention strategies, promotes healthy behaviors, fosters safe and healthful environments, and provides leadership and training. (Headquarters in Atlanta, Ga.)

Health and Human Services Dept. (HHS), *200 Independence Ave. S.W., 20201; (202) 690-7000. Fax, (202) 690-7203. Xavier Becerra, Secretary. Public Affairs, (202) 690-6343. Toll-free, (877) 696-6775. TTY, (800) 877-8339.*
General email, secretary@hhs.gov

Web, www.hhs.gov, Twitter, @HHSGov and Facebook, www.facebook.com/HHS

Acts as principal adviser to the president on health and welfare plans, policies, and programs of the federal government. Encompasses eleven operating divisions, including eight agencies in the U.S. Public Health Service and three human services agencies, including the Centers for Medicare and Medicaid Services, the Administration for Children and Families, the National Institutes of Health, and the Centers for Disease Control and Prevention.

HEALTH RESOURCES IN CONGRESS

For a complete listing of congressional committees, including their full contact information, leadership, membership, and jurisdictions, please refer to the Appendix on pages 840–963.

HOUSE:

House Agriculture Committee, (202) 225-2171.
Web, agriculture.house.gov
    Subcommittee on Nutrition, Oversight, and Department Operations, (202) 225-2171.
House Appropriations Committee, (202) 225-2771.
Web, appropriations.house.gov
    Subcommittee on Agriculture, Rural Development, Food and Drug Administration, and Related Agencies, (202) 225-2638.
    Subcommittee on Labor, Health and Human Services, Education, and Related Agencies, (202) 225-3508.
House Armed Services Committee, (202) 225-4151.
Web, armedservices.house.gov
    Subcommittee on Military Personnel, (202) 225-4151.
House Budget Committee, (202) 226-7200.
Web, budget.house.gov
House Education and Labor Committee, (202) 225-3725.
Web, edlabor.house.gov
    Subcommittee on Health, Employment, Labor, and Pensions, (202) 225-3725.
    Subcommittee on Workforce Protections, (202) 225-3725.
House Energy and Commerce Committee, (202) 225-2927.
Web, energycommerce.house.gov

    Subcommittee on Environment and Climate Change, (202) 225-2927.
    Subcommittee on Health, (202) 225-2927.
House Foreign Affairs Committee, (202) 225-5021.
Web, foreignaffairs.house.gov
    Subcommittee on Africa, Global Health, and Global Human Rights, (202) 225-5021.
House Oversight and Reform Committee, (202) 225-5051.
Web, oversight.house.gov
Select Subcommittee on the Coronavirus Crisis, (202) 225-4400.
House Science, Space, and Technology Committee, (202) 225-6375.
Web, science.house.gov
    Subcommittee on Research and Technology, (202) 225-6375.
House Veterans' Affairs Committee, (202) 225-9756.
Web, veterans.house.gov
    Subcommittee on Health, (202) 225-9756.
House Ways and Means Committee, (202) 225-3625.
Web, waysandmeans.house.gov
    Subcommittee on Health, (202) 225-3625.

SENATE:

Senate Agriculture, Nutrition, and Forestry Committee, (202) 224-2035.
Web, agriculture.senate.gov
    Subcommittee on Food and Nutrition, Specialty Crop, Organics, and Research, (202) 224-2035.
    Subcommittee on Rural Development and Energy, (202) 224-2035.

Health and Human Services Dept. (HHS), *Civil Rights (OCR), Conscience and Religious Freedom Division,* 200 Independence Ave. S.W., 20201; (800) 368-1019. Luis Perez, Deputy Director. TTY, (800) 537-7697.
General email, OCRMail@hhs.gov

Web, www.hhs.gov/conscience/index.html

Works to protect and enforce laws and regulations that protect the conscience and the free exercise of religion and prohibit coercion and religious discrimination in HHS-funded or conducted programs and activities.

Health and Human Services Dept. (HHS), *National Center for Health Statistics, National Committee on Vital and Health Statistics (NCVHS),* 3311 Toledo Rd., Hyattsville, MD 20782; (301) 458-4715. Fax, (301) 458-4022. Rebecca Hines, Executive Secretary; Sharon B. Arnold.
General email, vgh4@cdc.gov

Web, www.ncvhs.hhs.gov

Statutory public advisory body to secretary of health and human services for health data, statistics, privacy, and national health information policy. Serves as forum for interaction between HHS and interested private sector groups on a range of health data issues. Aims to accelerate the evolution of public and private health information systems toward more uniform, shared data standards within the context of privacy and security concerns.

Health and Human Services Dept. (HHS), *National Coordinator for Health Information Technology (ONC),* 330 C St. S.W., Floor 7, 20201; (202) 690-7151. Fax, (202) 690-6079. Micky Tripathi, National Coordinator. Press, (202) 251-1141.
General email, onc.request@hhs.gov

Web, www.healthit.gov and Twitter, @ONC_HealthIT

Coordinates nationwide efforts to implement information technology that allows for electronic use and exchange of health information. Goals include ensuring security for

Senate Appropriations Committee, (202) 224-7363.
Web, appropriations.senate.gov
    Subcommittee on Agriculture, Rural
       Development, Food and Drug
       Administration, and Related Agencies,
       (202) 224-7363.
    Subcommittee on Labor, Health and Human
       Services, Education, and Related Agencies,
       (202) 224-7363.
Senate Armed Services Committee, (202) 224-3871.
Web, armed-services.senate.gov
    Subcommittee on Personnel, (202) 224-3871.
Senate Banking, Housing, and Urban Affairs
    Committee, (202) 224-7391.
Web, banking.senate.gov
    Subcommittee on Securities, Insurance, and
       Investment, (202) 224-7391.
Senate Budget Committee, (202) 224-0642.
Web, budget.senate.gov
Senate Caucus on International Narcotics Control
    (202) 224-9032 .
Web, drugcaucus.senate.gov
Senate Commerce, Science, and Transportation
    Committee, (202) 224-0411.
Web, commerce.senate.gov
    Subcommittee on Consumer Protection,
       Product Safety, and Data Security,
       (202) 224-0411.
Senate Environment and Public Works Committee,
    (202) 224-8832.
Web, epw.senate.gov
    Subcommittee on Clean Air, Climate, and
       Nuclear Safety, (202) 224-8832.

    Subcommittee on Chemical Safety,
       Waste Management, Environmental
       Justice, and Regulatory Oversight,
       (202) 224-8832.
    Subcommittee on Transportation and
       Infrastructure, (202) 224-8832.
    Subcommittee on Health Care, (202) 224-4515.
Senate Finance Committee, (202) 224-4515.
Web, finance.senate.gov
Senate Health, Education, Labor, and Pensions
    Committee, (202) 224-5375.
Web, help.senate.gov
    Subcommittee on Children and Families,
       (202) 224-5375.
    Subcommittee on Employment and Workplace
       Safety, (202) 224-5375.
    Subcommittee on Primary Health and
       Retirement Security, (202) 224-5375.
Senate Indian Affairs Committee, (202) 224-2251.
Web, indian.senate.gov
Senate Judiciary Committee, (202) 224-7703.
Web, judiciary.senate.gov
    Subcommittee on Criminal Justice and
       Counterterrorism, (202) 224-2921.
Senate Small Business and Entrepreneurship
    Committee, (202) 224-5175.
Web, sbc.senate.gov
Senate Special Committee on Aging,
    (202) 224-5364.
Web, aging.senate.gov
Senate Veterans' Affairs Committee,
    (202) 224-9126.
Web, veterans.senate.gov

patient health information, improving health care quality, and reducing health care costs.

Health and Human Services Dept. (HHS), *Office of the Assistant Secretary for Preparedness and Response (ASPR),* 200 Independence Ave. S.W., #638G, 20201; (202) 292-1740. Dawn O'Connell, Assistant Secretary.
Web, www.phe.gov/Preparedness/Pages/default.aspx, Twitter, @PHEgov and Facebook, www.facebook.com/ ASPRgov/

Serves as the secretary's principal adviser on matters relating to bioterrorism and public health emergencies. Directs activities of HHS relating to the protection of the civilian population from acts of bioterrorism and other public health emergencies.

Health and Human Services Dept. (HHS), *Planning and Evaluation (ASPE),* 200 Independence Ave. S.W., #415F, 20201; (202) 690-7858. Fax, (202) 690-7383.

Rececca Haffajee, Assistant Secretary (Acting).
General email, osaspeinfo@hhs.gov

Web, https://aspe.hhs.gov and Twitter, @HHS_ASPE

Advises the secretary on policy development in health, disability, human services, data, and science, and provides advice and analysis on economic policy. Coordinates department's evaluation, research, and demonstration activities. Manages cross-department planning activities such as strategic and legislative planning and regulation review. Conducts research and evaluation studies, develops policy analyses, and estimates the cost and benefits of policy alternatives under consideration by the department or Congress.

Health and Human Services Dept. (HHS), *Planning and Evaluation (ASPE), Health Policy (HP),* 200 Independence Ave. S.W., #415, 20201; (202) 690-6870. Benjamin Sommers, Deputy Assistant Secretary, (202) 260-0413.
Web, https://aspe.hhs.gov/about/offices/hp

Develops, analyzes and coordinates health policy issues for secretary, including assisting in development and review of regulations and budgets and legislation and assisting in survey design efforts.

Health and Human Services Dept. (HHS), *Planning and Evaluation (ASPE), Science and Data Policy (SDP),* 200 *Independence Ave. S.W., #415F, 20201; (202) 690-7100. Laina Bush, Deputy Assistant Secretary. Web, https://aspe.hhs.gov/about/offices/sdp*

Provides analysis on public health science policy and data policy issues and initiatives to the department.

Health Resources and Services Administration (HRSA) *(Health and Human Services Dept.),* 5600 Fishers Lane, *#13N192, Rockville, MD 20857; (301) 443-2216. Carole Johnson, Administrator. Press, (301) 443-3376. TTY, (877) 897-9910. General email, askhrsa.gov*

Web, www.hrsa.gov, Twitter, @HRSAgov and Facebook, www.facebook.com/HRSAgov

Administers federal health service programs related to access, quality, equity, and cost of health care. Supports state and community efforts to deliver care to underserved areas and groups with special health needs. Oversees organ, bone marrow, and cord blood donation; compensates individuals harmed by vaccination; and maintains databases that protect against health care malpractice, waste, fraud, and abuse.

Health Resources and Services Administration (HRSA) *(Health and Human Services Dept.), Federal Office of Rural Health Policy (FORHP),* 5600 Fishers Lane, *#17W45, Rockville, MD 20857; (301) 443-0835. Tom Morris, Associate Administrator. General email, tmorris@hrsa.gov*

Web, www.hrsa.gov/rural-health

Works with federal agencies, states, and the private sector to develop solutions to health care problems in rural communities. Administers grants to rural communities and supports rural health services research. Studies the effects of Medicare and Medicaid programs on rural access to health care.

National Aeronautics and Space Administration (NASA), *Chief Health and Medical Officer,* 300 E St. S.W., 20546; *(202) 358-2390. Dr. James D. Polk, Chief Health and Medical Officer. Web, www.nasa.gov/offices/ochmo/main/index.html*

Ensures the health and safety of NASA employees in space and on the ground. Develops health and medical policy, establishes guidelines for health and medical practices, oversees health care delivery, and monitors human and animal research standards within the agency.

National Center for Health Statistics (NCHS) *(Centers for Disease Control and Prevention),* 3311 Toledo Rd., #7204, *Hyattsville, MD 20782-2064; Fax, (301) 458-4020. Brian C. Moyer, Director. Press, (301) 458-4800. Toll-free, (800) 232-4636.*

General email, cdcinfo@cdc.gov

Web, www.cdc.gov/nchs, Twitter, @NCHStats and Facebook, www.facebook.com/CDCNCHS

Compiles, analyzes, and disseminates national statistics on population health characteristics, health facilities and human resources, health costs and expenditures, and health hazards. Interests include international health statistics.

National Institute for Occupational Safety and Health (NIOSH) *(Centers for Disease Control and Prevention),* 395 E St. S.W., Patriots Plaza 1, #9200, 20201; (202) 245-0625. Fax, (513) 533-8347. Dr. John Howard, Director. Toll-free, (800) 232-4636. TTY, (888) 232-6348. *General email, cdcinfo@cdc.gov*

Web, www.cdc.gov/niosh, Twitter, @NIOSH and Facebook, www.facebook.com/niosh

Supports and conducts research on occupational safety and health issues; provides technical assistance and training; organizes international conferences and symposia; develops recommendations for the Labor Dept. Operates occupational safety and health bibliographic databases; publishes documents on occupational safety and health.

National Institute of Standards and Technology (NIST) *(Commerce Dept.), Special Programs Office,* 100 Bureau Dr., Gaithersburg, MD 20899; General email, spo_inquiries@nist.gov

Web, www.nist.gov/special-programs-office-spo

Fosters collaboration among government, military, academic, professional, and private organizations to respond to critical national needs through science-based standards and technology innovation, including areas of health.

National Institutes of Health (NIH) *(Health and Human Services Dept.),* Bldg. 1, 9000 Rockville Pike, Bethesda, MD 20892-0148; (301) 496-4000. Fax, (301) 496-0017. Dr. Lawrence A. Tabak, Director (Acting). Press, (301) 496-5787. TTY, (301) 402-9612. *Web, www.nih.gov, Twitter, @NIH and Facebook, www.facebook.com/nih.gov*

Comprised of 27 research institutes and centers, including the National Cancer Institute; the National Institute of Allergy and Infectious Diseases; the National Heart, Lung, and Blood Institute; the National Institute on Aging; the National Center for Complementary and Integrative Health; and the National Institute of Diabetes and Digestive and Kidney Diseases. All institutes are located in Bethesda, except the National Institute of Environmental Health Sciences, P.O. Box 12233, Durham, N.C. 27709.

National Institutes of Health (NIH) *(Health and Human Services Dept.), Science Policy (OSP),* 6705 Rockledge Dr., #750, Bethesda, MD 20892-7985; (301) 496-9838. Fax, (301) 496-9839. Lyric Jorgenson, Associate Director (Acting). *General email, sciencepolicy@od.nih.gov*

Web, https://osp.od.nih.gov and Twitter, @NIH_OSP

Advises the NIH director on science policy issues affecting the biomedical research community. Participates in the development of new policy and program initiatives. Monitors and coordinates agency planning and evaluation activities. Plans and implements a comprehensive science education program. Develops and implements NIH policies and procedures for the safe conduct of recombinant DNA and other biotechnology activities.

State Dept., *Medical Services, 2401 E St. N.W., #L218, 20522-0102; (202) 663-1649. Fax, (202) 663-1613. Dr. Larry Paget, Medical Director. Web, www.state.gov/about-us-bureau-of-medical-services*

Operates a worldwide primary health care system for U.S. citizen employees, and eligible family members, of participating U.S. government agencies. Conducts physical examinations of Foreign Service officers and candidates; provides clinical services; assists with medical evacuation of patients overseas.

▶ **CONGRESS**

For a listing of relevant congressional committees and subcommittees, please see pages 362–363 or the Appendix.

Government Accountability Office (GAO), *Health Care (HC), 441 G St. N.W., #5A21, 20548; (202) 512-7114. Alyssa Hundrup, Director. Web, www.gao.gov/about/careers/our-teams*

Provides analyses, recommendations, and policy options to Congress and the executive branch for all federal government health programs, including those administered by the Defense (TRICARE), Health and Human Services, and Veterans Affairs Depts.

▶ **NONGOVERNMENTAL**

Alliance for Health Policy, *1444 Eye St. N.W., #910, 20005-6573; (202) 789-2300. Sarah J. Dash, President. General email, info@allhealthpolicy.org Web, www.allhealthpolicy.org, Twitter, @AllHealthPolicy, Facebook, www.facebook.com/allhealthpolicy.org and President's Twitter, @SarahJDash*

Nonpartisan organization that advocates health care reform, including cost containment and coverage for all. Sponsors conferences, forums, and seminars for journalists, business leaders, policymakers, and the public. Seeks to be a source for unbiased health policy information.

Altarum Institute, *2000 M St. N.W., #400, 20036; (202) 828-5100. Fax, (202) 728-9469. Michael Monson, President. Toll-free, (888) 776-5187. Web, www.altarum.org, Twitter, @Altarum and Facebook, www.facebook.com/altarum*

Nonprofit that helps federal and state health agencies and foundations improve health equity and outcomes through better systems of care. Systems research and consulting organization focusing on health care delivery and financing issues that impact the health of diverse populations. (Headquarters in Ann Arbor, Mich.)

American Public Health Assn., *800 Eye St. N.W., 20001-3710; (202) 777-2742. Fax, (202) 777-2534. Dr. Georges C. Benjamin, Executive Director. TTY, (202) 777-2500. General email, comments@apha.org Web, www.apha.org, Twitter, @PublicHealth and Facebook, www.facebook.com/AmericanPublicHealth Association*

Membership: health providers, educators, environmentalists, policymakers, and health officials at all levels working both within and outside of governmental organizations and educational institutions. Works to protect communities from serious, preventable health threats. Strives to ensure that community-based health promotion and disease prevention activities and preventive health services are universally accessible in the United States. Develops standards for scientific procedures in public health.

American Red Cross, *Government Relations, 431 18th St. N.W., 20006; (202) 303-4371. Cherae Bishop, Senior Vice President of Government Relations. General email, GovtRelations@redcross.org Web, www.redcross.org/about-us/who-we-are/governance/government-relations.html*

Works to create, through legislative and regulatory initiatives, a pubic-policy environment that will forward the mission and objectives of the American Red Cross.

Assn. of State and Territorial Health Officials, *2231 Crystal Dr., #450, Arlington, VA 22202; (202) 371-9090. Fax, (571) 527-3189. Michael Fraser, Executive Director, ext. 4. Web, www.astho.org, www.statepublichealth.org and Twitter, @astho*

Membership: chief health officials of State, Territorial, and District of Columbia public health departments. Serves as legislative review agency and information source for members. Monitors legislation and regulations.

The Brookings Institution, *Economic Studies, 1775 Massachusetts Ave. N.W., 20036-2188; (202) 797-6414. (202) 540-7721. Stephanie Aaronson, Vice President. General email, escomment@brookings.edu Web, www.brookings.edu/economics and Twitter, @BrookingsEcon*

Studies federal health care issues and health programs, including Medicare, Medicaid, and long-term care.

The Brookings Institution, *USC-Brookings Schaeffer Iniative for Health Policy, 1775 Massachusetts Ave. N.W., 20036; (202) 540-7721. Richard G. Frank, Director, (202) 540-7721. General email, paul.ginsburg@usc.edu Web, www.brookings.edu/project/usc-brookings-schaeffer-initiative-for-health-policy/ and Twitter, @BrookingsEcon*

Research center promoting healthcare policy and affordable health care. Interests include Medicare spending and delivery, implementation of the Affordable Healthcare Act and health insurance marketplaces, maximzing the value of innovation in drugs and devices, prescription drug reimbursement, and long-term care.

Grantmakers in Health, *1100 Connecticut Ave. N.W., #1100, 20036; (202) 452-8331. Fax, (202) 452-8340. Cara James, President.*
General email, info@gih.org
Web, www.gih.org and Twitter, @GIHealth

Seeks to increase the capacity of health foundations and giving programs to enhance public health and health education. Fosters information exchange among grantmakers. Publications include a bulletin on current news in health and human services.

Health Policy Institute *(Georgetown University), 3700 O St. N.W., #5000, Box 571444, 20057-1485; (202) 687-0880. Theresa Jordan, Executive Assistant.*
Web, http://hpi.georgetown.edu

Research branch of Georgetown University's McCourt School of Public Policy. Interests include quality of care and outcomes research, health care financing, the uninsured, federal health insurance reforms, and the impact of changes in the health care market on providers and patients.

Healthcare Leadership Council, *750 9th St. N.W., #500, 20001; (202) 452-8700. Fax, (202) 296-9561. Mary R. Grealy, President.*
Web, www.hlc.org, Twitter, @HealthInFocus and Facebook, www.facebook.com/HealthcareLeadership Council

Membership: health care leaders who examine major health issues. Works to implement new public policies and programs for affordable, high-quality health care.

Henry J. Kaiser Family Foundation, *Washington Office, 1330 G St. N.W., 20005; (202) 347-5270. Fax, (202) 347-5274. Drew Altman, President.*
Web, www.kff.org, Twitter, @KFF and Facebook, www .facebook.com/KaiserFamilyFoundation

Offers information on major health care issues. Conducts research and communications programs. Monitors legislation and regulations. (Headquarters in Menlo Park, Calif. Not affiliated with Kaiser Permanente or Kaiser Industries.)

National Academies of Sciences, Engineering, and Medicine (NASEM), *Health and Medicine Division, Keck Center, 500 5th St. N.W., 20001; (202) 334-2352. Fax, 202-334 1412. Monica N. Feit, Executive Director.*
General email, HMD-NASEM@nas.edu
Web, www.nationalacademies.org/hmd/health-and-medicine-division and Twitter, @NASEM_Health

Advises the government and public sector on matters relating to medical research, care, and education; examines policy matters relating to health care and public health.

National Academies of Sciences, Engineering, and Medicine (NASEM), *Health Care Services Board, Keck Center, 500 5th St. N.W., #W712, 20001; (202) 334-2001.*

Fax, (202) 334-2647. Sharyl Nass, Director; Donald M. Berwick, Chair.
General email, bhcs@nas.edu
Web, www.nationalacademies.org/hcs/board-on-health-care-services

Advises policymakers about the healthcare system in general as well as financing, effectiveness, workforce, and delivery of health care.

National Academies of Sciences, Engineering, and Medicine (NASEM), *Health Sciences Policy Board, Keck Center, 500 5th St. N.W., 20001; (202) 334-3232. Fax, (202) 334-1329. Andrew Pope, Director; Sharon Terry, Chair.*
General email, hsp@nas.edu
Web, www.nationalacademies.org/hsp/board-on-health-sciences-policy

Oversees research and activities related to basic biomedical and clinical research, including the role of science in policy and decision making; the education of health and research professionals and the general public, the preparedness, resilience, and sustainability of communities; biomedical ethics.

National Academies of Sciences, Engineering, and Medicine (NASEM), *Human-Systems Integration Board, Keck Center, 500 5th St. N.W., 11th Floor, 20001; (202) 334-2326. Fax, (202) 334-2210. Mary Ellen O'Connell, Director (Acting), (202) 334-2607.*
General email, bohsi@nas.edu
Web, www.nationalacademies.org/bohsi/board-on-human-systems-integration

Conducts studies on human factors and human-systems integration. Areas of research include home health care and disability and rehabilitation research.

National Academies of Sciences, Engineering, and Medicine (NASEM), *Population Health and Public Health Practice Board, Keck Center, 500 5th St. N.W., 20001; (202) 334-2158. Fax, (202) 334-2939. Rose Marie Martinez, Director; Bruce Calonge, Chair.*
General email, bph@nas.edu
Web, www.nationalacademies.org/bph/board-on-population-health-and-public-health-practice

Supports research on public health, including vaccine safety, pandemic preparedness issues, smoking cessation, health disparities, and reducing environmental and occupational hazards.

National Academy of Medicine (NAM), *Keck Center, 500 5th St. N.W., 20001; (202) 334-2000. Dr. Victor J. Dzau, President; Dr. J. Michael McGinnis, Executive Officer. Press, (202) 334-2843.*
General email, NAMedicine@nas.edu
Web, https://nam.edu, Twitter, @theNAMedicine and Facebook, www.facebook.com/NAMedicine

Society whose members are elected in recognition of important contributions to the field of science, technology, and health. Shares responsibility with the National Academy of Sciences for examining questions of science and technology at the request of the federal government;

Health and Human Services Department

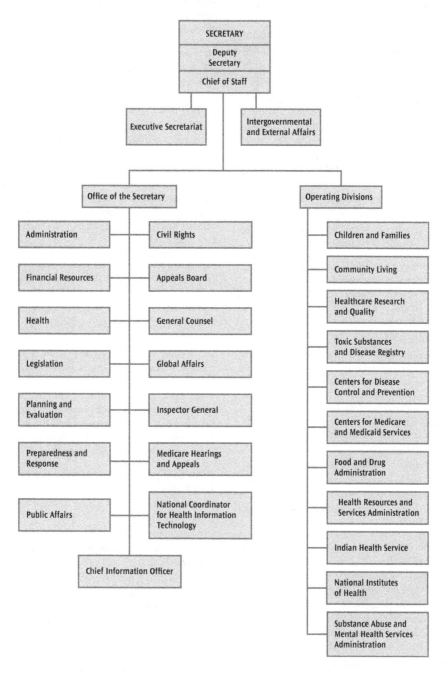

promotes international cooperation. (Affiliated with the National Academies of Sciences, Engineering, and Medicine [NASEM].)

National Assn. of Counties (NACo), *660 N. Capitol St. N.W., #400, 20001; (202) 393-6226. Matthew D. Chase, Executive Director. Press, (202) 942-4220. Toll-free, (888) 407-6226. General email, dcox@naco.org*

Web, www.naco.org and Twitter, @NACoTweets

Promotes federal understanding of county governments' role in providing, funding, and overseeing health services at the local level. Interests include indigent health care, Medicaid and Medicare, prevention of and services for HIV infection and AIDS, long-term care, mental health, maternal and child health, and traditional public health programs conducted by local health departments. Monitors legislation and regulations.

National Assn. of County and City Health Officials, *1201 Eye St. N.W., 4th Floor, 20005; (202) 783-5550. Fax, (202) 783-1583. Lori T. Freeman, Chief Executive Officer, (202) 507-4271.*

General email, info@naccho.org

Web, www.naccho.org, Twitter, @NACCHOalerts and Facebook, www.facebook.com/NACCHOHQ/

Represents the nation's local health departments. Develops resources and programs to support local public health practices and systems. Submits health policy proposals to the federal government.

National Committee for Quality Assurance, *1100 13th St. N.W., 3rd Floor, 20005; (202) 955-3500. Fax, (202) 955-3599. Margaret E. O'Kane, President. Toll-free information on health plans and accreditation, (888) 275-7585.*
Web, www.ncqa.org, Twitter, @NCQA, Facebook, www.facebook.com/NCQA.org and YouTube, www.youtube.com/user/NCQAVideo

Provides information on the quality of health care provided by health care institutions and individual providers. Assesses and reports on managed care plans through accreditation and performance measurement programs.

National Governors Assn. (NGA), *Center for Best Practices, Behavioral Health and Medicaid Division, 444 N. Capitol St. N.W., #267, 20001-1512; (202) 624-5300. Timothy Blute, Director.*
General email, info@nga.org

Web, www.nga.org/bestpractices

Provides technical assistance to states, including cost of care for complex populations, behavioral health and primary care integration, and supportive housing.

National Governors Assn. (NGA), *Center for Best Practices, Health, 444 N. Capitol St. N.W., #267, 20001-1512; (202) 624-5300. Shelby Hockenberry, Director.*
General email, info@nga.org

Web, www.nga.org/bestpractices/health

Focus areas include health care transformation, health workforce, rural health, health equity, data sharing, private health insurance, and maternal and child health. Provides data and analytics.

National Health Council, *1730 M St. N.W., #500, 20036-4561; (202) 785-3910. Fax, (202) 785-5923. Randall L. Rutta, Chief Executive Officer.*
General email, info@nhcouncil.org

Web, www.nationalhealthcouncil.org, Twitter, @NHcouncil, Facebook, www.facebook.com/national healthcouncil and YouTube, www.youtube.com/user/nhcouncil

Membership: voluntary health agencies, associations, and business, insurance, and government groups interested in health. Conducts research on health and health-related issues. Monitors legislation and regulations.

National Quality Forum, *1099 14th St. N.W., #500, 20005; (202) 783-1300. Fax, (202) 783-3434. Danna Gelb Safan, President. Press, (202) 478-9326.*
General email, info@qualityforum.org

Web, www.qualityforum.org

Works to improve the quality of health care in the United States by setting national priorities and goals for performance improvement, endorsing national consensus standards for measuring and publicly reporting on performances, and promoting the attainment of national goals through education and outreach programs.

National Vaccine Information Center, *21525 Ridgetop Circle, #100, Sterling, VA 20166; (703) 938-0342. Fax, (571) 313-1268. Barbara Loe Fisher, President; Theresa Wrangham, Executive Director.*
General email, contactus@gmail.com

Web, www.nvic.org, Twitter, @NVICLoeDown and Facebook, www.facebook.com/national.vaccine.information.center

Educational organization that supports informed vaccination decisions, including the option to forgo vaccination. Provides assistance to parents of children who have experienced vaccine reactions and publishes information on diseases and vaccines. Monitors vaccine research, legislation, and regulations.

Public Citizen, *Health Research Group, 1600 20th St. N.W., 20009-1001; (202) 588-1000. Dr. Michael Carome, Director.*
General email, hrg1@citizen.org

Web, www.citizen.org/topic/health-care and Twitter, @CitizenHRG

Citizens' interest group that conducts policy-oriented research on health care issues. Interests include hospital quality and costs, doctors' fees, physician discipline and malpractice, state administration of Medicare programs, workplace safety and health, unnecessary surgery, comprehensive health planning, dangerous drugs, carcinogens, and medical devices. Favors a single-payer (Canadian-style) comprehensive health program.

RAND Corp., *Health Care Division, Washington Office, 1200 S. Hayes St., Arlington, VA 22202-5050; (703) 413-1100. Fax, (703) 413-8111. Peter S. Hussey, Director. Press, (703) 414-4795.*
General email, RANDHealthCare@rand.org

Web, www.rand.org/health-care/about.html and Twitter, @RANDHealth

Research organization that assesses health issues, including alternative reimbursement schemes for health care. Interests include health care costs and quality, military health, obesity, chronic disease prevention, and public health preparedness. Monitors national and international trends. (Headquarters in Santa Monica, Calif.)

Regulatory Affairs Professionals Society, *5635 Fishers Lane, #400, Rockville, MD 20852; (301) 770-2920, ext. 200. Fax, (301) 841-7956. Bill McMoil, Executive Director (Acting).*
General email, raps@raps.org

Web, www.raps.org, Twitter, @RAPSorg and Facebook, www.facebook.com/RegulatoryAffairsProfessionalsSociety

Membership: regulatory professionals in the medical device, pharmaceutical, and biotechnology product sectors worldwide. Promotes the safety and effectiveness of health care products. Supports the regulatory profession with resources, including education and certification. Monitors legislation and regulations.

Urban Institute, *Health Policy Center, 500 L'Enfant Plaza S.W., 20024; (202) 833-7200. Genevieve M. Kenney, Vice President; Stephen Zuckerman, Vice President. Web, www.urban.org/policy-centers/health-policy-center and Facebook, www.facebook.com/urbaninstitute*

Analyzes trends and underlying causes of changes in health insurance, coverage access to care, and use of health care services by the U.S. population. Researches and analyzes select health issues, including private insurance; the uninsured; Medicaid, Medicare, and the State Children's Health Insurance Program (SCHIP); disability and long-term care; vulnerable populations; and health care reform.

Global Health

▶AGENCIES

Agency for International Development (USAID), *Bureau for Global Health, 1300 Pennsylvania Ave. N.W., #3.64, 20523-3100; (202) 712-4120. Fax, (202) 216-3485. Atul Gawande, Assistant Administrator (Acting). Web, www.usaid.gov/who-we-are/organization/bureaus/bureau-global-health, Twitter, @USAIDGH and Facebook, www.facebook.com/usaidgh*

Participates in global efforts to stabilize world population growth and support women's reproductive rights. Focus includes family planning; reproductive health care; infant, child, and maternal health; and prevention of sexually transmitted diseases, especially AIDS. Conducts demographic and health surveys; educates girls and women.

Agency for International Development (USAID), *Bureau for Global Health, Family Planning and Reproductive Health, 1300 Pennsylvania Ave. N.W., #3.06-011, 20523-3600; (202) 712-4120. Fax, (202) 216-3485. Ellen Starbird, Director. Press, (202) 712-4320. General email, pi@usaid.gov*
Web, www.usaid.gov/global-health/health-areas/family-planning, Twitter, @USAIDGH and Facebook, www.facebook.com/usaidgh

Advances and supports family planning and reproductive health programs in more than 30 countries.

Bureau of Oceans and International Environmental and Scientific Affairs (OES) *(State Dept.), International Health and Biodefense (IHB), 2201 C St. N.W., #2734, 20520; (202) 647-4535. ERic Carlson, Director, (202) 647-1318. Web, www.state.gov/e/oes*

Advances the Global Health Security Agenda and focuses on issues including pandemic preparedness, new outbreaks of disease, new international policy discussions, and the impact of science and technology, medicine, and public health.

Fogarty International Center (FIC) *(National Institutes of Health), 31 Center Dr., B2C02, MS c2220, Bethesda, MD 20892-2220; (301) 496-1415. Fax, (301) 402-2173. Dr. Roger I. Glass, Director. General email, ficinfo@nih.gov*
Web, www.fic.nih.gov, Twitter, @fogarty_NIH and Facebook, www.facebook.com/fogarty.nih

Promotes and supports international scientific research and training to reduce disparities in global health. Leads formulation and implementation of international biomedical research and policy. Supports the conduct of research in high-priority global health areas, including infectious diseases such as HIV/AIDS, and helps build research capacity in the developing world. Supports training the next generation of scientists to address global health needs.

Food and Drug Administration (FDA) *(Health and Human Services Dept.), Global Policy and Strategy, White Oak Bldg. 1, 10903 New Hampshire Ave., Silver Spring, MD 20993; (301) 796-4600. Fax, (301) 595-7937. Mark Abdoo, Associate Commissioner. General email, FDA_Global@fda.hhs.gov*
Web, www.fda.gov/about-fda/office-policy-legislation-and-international-affairs/office-global-policy-and-strategy

Promotes and protects U.S. public health interests by ensuring global considerations are fully integrated into FDA policies and operational activities.

Food and Drug Administration (FDA) *(Health and Human Services Dept.), International Programs (OIP), White Oak Bldg. 32, 10903 New Hampshire Ave., Silver Spring, MD 20993; (301) 796-4600. Fax, (301) 595-7937. Vacant, Associate Commissioner. General email, OIPCommunications@fda.hhs.gov*
Web, www.fda.gov/international-programs

Serves as FDA's liaison with foreign counterpart agencies, international organizations, and the U.S. diplomatic corps. Gathers and assesses information to inform decisions about FDA-regulated product imports. Seeks to advance global public health through distribution of health information, coordination of public health strategies, and promotion of public safety. Seeks to harmonize regulatory standards. Provides technical assistance.

Health and Human Services Dept. (HHS), *Global Affairs (OGA), 200 Independence Ave. S.W., #639H, 20201; (202) 690-6174. (202) 260-0399. Fax, (202) 690-7127. Loyce Pace, Assistant Secretary. General email, globalhealth@hhs.gov*
Web, www.hhs.gov/about/agencies/oga/index.html, Twitter, @HHS_Global and Twitter, @HHS_ASGA

Engages with multilateral organizations, foreign governments, ministries of health, civil society groups, and the private sector to advance policies that protect and promote health nationally and worldwide.

▶INTERNATIONAL ORGANIZATIONS

Pan American Health Organization PAHO, *525 23rd St. N.W., 20037; (202) 974-3000. Fax, (202) 974-3663. Dr. Carissa F. Etienne, Director PAHP/WHO.*

Web, www.paho.org, Twitter, @PAHOWHO and *Facebook, www.facebook.com/PAHOWHO*

Works to extend health services to underserved populations of its member countries and to control or eradicate communicable diseases; promotes technical cooperation between countries and works in partnership with ministries of health and other government agencies, civil society organizations, other international agencies, universities, social security agencies, community groups, and other partners. Serves as Regional Office for the Americas of the World Health Organization. (WHO headquartered in Geneva, Switzerland.)

▶NONGOVERNMENTAL

Consortium of Universities for Global Health, *1608 Rhode Island Ave. N.W., #240, 20036; (202) 974-6363. Fax, (202) 355-0948. Dr. Keith Martin, Executive Director.*
General email, info@cugh.org
Web, www.cugh.org, Twitter, @CUGHnews and *Facebook, www.facebook.com/CUGHnews*

Assists universities in sharing resources and research on global health challenges. Coordinates academic partnerships between national universities and international educational institutions in developing countries. Develops national and global health centers.

Global Health Council, *1199 N. Fairfax St., #300, Alexandria, VA 22314; (703) 659-6480. Fax, (703) 717-5613. Elisha Dunn-Georgiou, President.*
General email, membership@globalhealth.org
Web, www.globalhealth.org, Twitter, @GlobalHealthOrg and *Press, communications@globalhealth.org*

Membership: students, health care professionals, NGOs, foundations, corporations, and academic institutions. Works to secure the information and resources for improved global health.

National Academies of Sciences, Engineering, and Medicine (NASEM), *Global Health Board, Keck Center, 500 5th St. N.W., 20001; (202) 334-2178. Ann Kurth, Chair; Julie Pavlin, Director.*
General email, Cbiffle@nas.edu
Web, www.nationalacademies.org/bgh/board-on-global-health

Carries out activities related to international health policy and health concerns of developing countries; main focus is public health programs for prevention and control of disease and disability.

World Bank, *Human Development Network, 1818 H St. N.W., 20433; (202) 473-1000. Mamta Murthi, Vice President.*
Web, www.worldbank.org

Assists developing countries in delivering effective and affordable health care, education, and social services. Interests include poverty reduction, income protection, nutrition, jobs access, health coverage, and basic education.

Health Insurance, Managed Care

▶AGENCIES

Centers for Medicare and Medicaid Services (CMS) *(Health and Human Services Dept.), Center for Consumer Information and Insurance Oversight (CCIIO), 200 Independence Ave. S.W., #739H, 20001; (301) 492-4304. Dr. Ellen Montz, Deputy Administrator. Affordable Care hotline, (888) 393-2789.*
General email, healthins@hhs.gov
Web, www.cms.gov/cciio and *www.cms.gov/About-CMS/Agency-Information/CMSLeadership/Office_CCIIO*

Assists states in reviewing insurance rates, including oversight of administrative costs as a percentage of expenditures for medical care (medical loss ratio); provides guidance and oversight for state-based insurance exchanges; administers the preexisting condition insurance plan, the temporary high-risk pool program, the early retiree reinsurance program and the consumer operated and oriented plan program; compiles and maintains data for an Internet portal providing information on insurance options.

Centers for Medicare and Medicaid Services (CMS) *(Health and Human Services Dept.), Center for Medicare, 7500 Security Blvd., C5-01-14, Baltimore, MD 21244; (410) 786-0550. Dr. Meena Seshamani, Director, (202) 205-5682. Toll-free, (800) 633-4227. TTY, (877) 486-2048.*
Web, www.cms.gov/medicare/medicare.html, www.cms.gov/About-CMS/Agency-Information/CMSLeadership/Office_CM and *Twitter, @MedicareGov*

Manages the traditional fee-for-service Medicare program, which includes the development of payment policy and management of Medicare fee-for-service contractors.

▶CONGRESS

For a listing of relevant congressional committees and sub-committees, please see pages 362–363 or the Appendix.

▶NONGOVERNMENTAL

Academy Health, *Advocacy and Legislative Action, 1666 K. St. N.W., 20005; (202) 292-6700. Fax, (202) 292-6800. Josh Caplan, Senior Manager.*
Web, https://academyhealth.org/advocacy

Acts as advocate for health services research and and policies that enhance the quality, availability, timeliness, and affordability of data and tools used to produce research.

America's Health Insurance Plans (AHIP), *South Bldg., 601 Pennsylvania Ave. N.W., #500, 20004; (202) 778-3200. Fax, (202) 331-7487. Matt Eyles, President.*

General email, ahip@ahip.org

Web, www.ahip.org, Twitter, @AHIPCoverage and Facebook, www.facebook.com/AHIP/?fref=ts

Membership: companies providing medical expense, long-term care, disability income, dental, supplemental, and stop-loss insurance and reinsurance to consumers, employers, and public purchasers. Acts as advocate for evidence-based medicine, targeted strategies for giving all Americans access to health care, and health care cost savings through regulatory, legal, and other reforms. Provides educational programs and legal counsel. Monitors legislation and regulations. (Merger of the American Assn. of Health Plans and Health Insurance Assn. of America.)

American Medical Assn. (AMA), *Government Relations, 25 Massachusetts Ave. N.W., #600, 20001-7400; (202) 789-7400. Fax, (202) 789-7485. Dr. James L. Madara, Chief Executive Officer. Toll-free, (800) 621-8335.*
Web, www.ama-assn.org, Twitter, @AmeriMedicalAssn and Facebook, www.facebook.com/AmericanMedical Association

Membership: physicians, residents, and medical students. Interests include cost, quality, and access to health care; and physician payment and delivery innovation. Monitors legislation and regulations. (Headquarters in Chicago, Ill.)

Autism Speaks, *Washington Office, 1990 K St. N.W., 2nd Floor, 20006 (mailing address: 1060 State Rd., 2nd Floor, Princeton, NJ 08540); (202) 955-3111. Kisha James, Staff, ext. 1.*
General email, nationalcapitalarea@autismspeaks.org
Web, www.autismspeaks.org/national-capital and Twitter, @autismspeaks

Advocates insurance reform to maximize coverage for evidence-based treatments for autism and autism spectrum disorders.

Blue Cross and Blue Shield Assn., *Washington DC., Office of Policy and Representation, 1310 G St. N.W., 20005; (202) 792-8238. (202) 626-4780. Kim A. Keck, President.*
General email, press@bcbsa.com
Web, www.bcbs.com, Twitter, @BCBSAssociation and Facebook, www.facebook.com/BCBSAssociation

Membership: Owns the Blue Cross and Blue Shield names and marks (brands) and grants several types of licenses to use them; also conducts trade association activities and operates businesses to support its license holders. (Headquarters in Chicago, Ill.)

Council for Affordable Health Coverage (CAHC), *440 1st St. N.W., #430, 20001; (202) 808-8855. Joel White, President.*
Web, www.cahc.net and Twitter, @C4AHC

Membership: insurers, employers, patients, consumers, pharmaceutical manufacturers, and providers. Coalition promoting competitive and transparent market solutions to America's health care problems. Promotes reform measures, including health savings accounts, tax equity,

universal access, medical price disclosure prior to treatment, and caps on malpractice awards. Monitors legislation and regulations at state and federal levels.

Employee Benefit Research Institute, *901 D St. S.W., #802, 20024; (202) 659-0670. Fax, (202) 775-6360. Lori Lucas, President.*
General email, info@ebri.org
Web, www.ebri.org

Research organization serving as an employee benefits information source on health, welfare, and retirement issues. Does not lobby and does not take public policy positions.

Employers Council on Flexible Compensation, *1802 Vernon St. N.W., #1035, 20009; (202) 659-4300. Fax, (202) 618-6060. Christa Day, Executive Director.*
General email, info@ecfc.org
Web, https://ecfc.org and Twitter, @GoECFC

Represents employers who have or are considering flexible compensation plans. Supports the preservation and expansion of employee choice in health insurance coverage. Monitors legislation and regulations.

Families USA, *1225 New York Ave. N.W., #800, 20005; (202) 628-3030. Fax, (202) 347-2417. Frederick Isasi, Executive Director.*
General email, info@familiesusa.org
Web, www.familiesusa.org, Twitter, @FamiliesUSA and Facebook, www.facebook.com/FamiliesUSA

Interests include health care, the Affordable Care Act, Social Security, Medicare, and Medicaid. Offers Enrollment Assister Resource Centers to help consumers and businesses obtain high-quality, affordable health care. Monitors legislation and regulations affecting the elderly. Focuses on communities of color.

Galen Institute, *P.O. Box 130, Paeonian Springs, VA 20129; (703) 687-4665. Fax, (703) 687-4675. Grace-Marie Turner, President.*
General email, galen@galen.org
Web, www.galen.org, Twitter, @galeninstitute and Facebook, www.facebook.com/GalenInstitute

Nonprofit promoting policies that lead to individual responsibility and control over health care and health insurance, lower costs through market competition. Acts as advocate for health savings accounts, competition among private plans in Medicare, and other free-market health reform ideas. Facilitates public debate and education about proposals that support individual freedom, consumer choice, competition, and innovation in the health sector.

National Academy of Social Insurance, *1441 L St. N.W., #530, 20005; (202) 452-8097. Fax, (202) 452-8111. William J. Arnone, Chief Executive Officer.*
General email, info@nasi.org
Web, www.nasi.org, Twitter, @socialinsurance and Facebook, www.facebook.com/NationalAcademyofSocial Insurance

Centers for Medicare and Medicaid Services

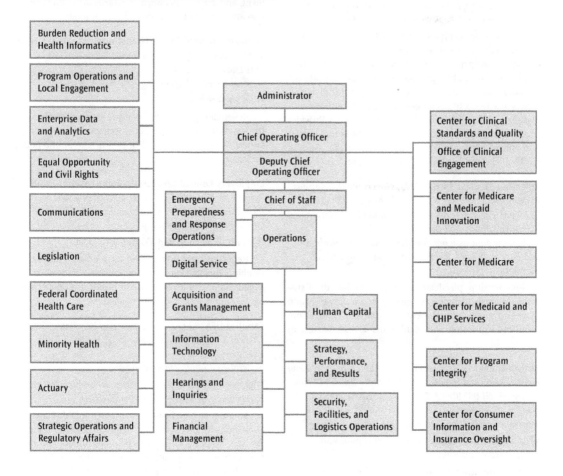

Promotes research and education on Social Security, Medicare, health care financing, and related public and private programs; assesses social insurance programs and their relationship to other programs; supports research and leadership development. Acts as a clearinghouse for social insurance information.

National Assn. of Health Underwriters, *999 E St. N.W., #4000, 20004; (202) 552-5060. Fax, (202) 747-6820. Janet Trautwein, Executive Vice President, (202) 888-0832. Press, (202) 595-3074.*
General email, info@nahu.org
Web, www.nahu.org and Twitter, @nahusocial

Membership: licensed health insurance agents, brokers, consultants, and benefit professionals. Offers continuing education programs as well as business-development tools. Promotes private sector health insurance. Monitors legislation and regulations.

National Business Group on Health, *20 F St. N.W., #200, 20001-6705; (202) 558-3000. Ellen Kelsay, President, (202) 558-3005.*
General email, info@businessgrouphealth.org
Web, www.businessgrouphealth.org and Twitter, @BizGrpHlth

Membership: large corporations with an interest in health care benefits. Interests include reimbursement policies, disease prevention and health promotion, hospital cost containment, health care planning, corporate education, Medicare, and retiree medical costs. Monitors legislation and regulations.

National Coalition on Health Care, *900 16th St. N.W., #400, 20006; (202) 638-7151. John Rother, President.*
General email, contactus@nchc.org
Web, www.nchc.org and Twitter, @NC_HC

Membership: insurers, labor organizations, large and small businesses, consumer groups, and health care providers. Acts as advocate for affordable high quality health care. Monitors legislation and regulations.

National Health Care Anti-Fraud Assn., *1220 L St. N.W., #815, 20005; (202) 659-5955. Fax, (202) 785-6764. Louis Saccoccio, Chief Executive Officer.*
General email, nhcaa@nhcaa.org
Web, www.nhcaa.org

Membership: health insurance companies and regulatory and law enforcement agencies. Members work to identify, investigate, and prosecute individuals and groups defrauding health care reimbursement systems. Offers education and training for fraud investigators, including medical identity theft. Sponsors the Institute for Health Care Fraud Prevention.

Society of Professional Benefit Administrators, *2 Wisconsin Circle, #670, Chevy Chase, MD 20815; (301) 718-7722. Eric Ludwig, Chairman, (919) 877-9933. General email, info@spbatpa.org*
Web, https://spbatpa.org and Twitter, @spbatpa

Membership: third-party administration firms that manage employee benefit plans for client employers. Interests include health care regulations, employee benefits, revision of Medicare programs, and health care cost containment. Monitors industry trends, government compliance requirements, and developments in health care financing.

Hospitals

►AGENCIES

Centers for Medicare and Medicaid Services (CMS) *(Health and Human Services Dept.), Center for Clinical Standards and Quality (CCSQ), Quality and Safety Oversight Group, 7500 Security Blvd., C2-21-16, Baltimore, MD 21244-1850; (410) 786-9493. (410) 786-6841. David Wright, Director.*
Web, www.cms.gov/Medicare/Provider-Enrollment-and-Certification/SurveyCertificationGenInfo/QSOG-Mission-and-Priority-Information

Enforces health care and safety standards for hospitals, nursing homes, health care facilities, and other Medicare and Medicaid certified institutional providers.

►CONGRESS

For a listing of relevant congressional committees and subcommittees, please see pages 362–363 or the Appendix.

►NONGOVERNMENTAL

America's Essential Hospitals, *401 Ninth St. N.W., #900, 20004; (202) 585-0100. Dr. Bruce Siegel, President. Media, (202) 585-0102.*
General email, info@essentialhospitals.org
Web, https://essentialhospitals.org, Twitter, @OurHospitals and Facebook, www.facebook.com/essentialhospitals

Membership: city and county public hospitals and health systems, state universities, and hospital districts and authorities. Interests include Medicaid patients and vulnerable populations, including AIDS patients, the homeless, the mentally ill, and non-English–speaking patients. Holds annual regional meetings. Monitors legislation and regulations. (Formerly National Assn. of Public Hospitals and Health Systems.)

American Hospital Assn., *Washington Office, Two City Center, 800 10th St. N.W., #400, 20001-4956; (202) 638-1100. Richard J. (Rick) Pollack, Chief Executive Officer, (202) 626-2363. Toll-free, (800) 424-4301.*

Web, www.aha.org, Twitter, @AHAhospitals and Facebook, www.facebook.com/ahahospitals

Membership: hospitals, other inpatient care facilities, outpatient centers, Blue Cross plans, areawide planning agencies, regional medical programs, hospital schools of nursing, and individuals. Conducts research and education projects in such areas as provision of comprehensive care, hospital economics, hospital facilities and design, and community relations; participates with other health care associations in establishing hospital care standards. Monitors legislation and regulations. (Headquarters in Chicago, Ill.)

American Medical Rehabilitation Providers Assn. (AMRPA), *529 14th St. N.W., #1280, 20045; (202) 591-2469. Fax, (202) 223-1925. John Ferraro, Executive Director, (202) 207-1121. Toll-free, (888) 346-4624.*
General email, info@amrpa.org
Web, www.amrpa.org, Twitter, @AMRPA and Facebook, www.facebook.com/AmericanMedicalRehabilitation ProvidersAssociation

Association representing a membership of freestanding rehabilitation hospitals and rehabilitation units of general hospitals, outpatient rehabilitation facilities, skilled-nursing facilities, and others. Provides leadership, advocacy, and resources to develop medical rehabilitation services and supports for persons with disabilities and others in need of services. Acts as a clearinghouse for information to members on the nature and availability of services. Monitors legislation and regulations.

Assn. of Academic Health Centers (AAHC), *1400 16th St. N.W., #720, 20036; (202) 265-9600. Fax, (202) 265-7514. Dr. Steven L. Kanter, President.*
Web, www.aahcdc.org, Twitter, @aahcdc, Facebook, www.facebook.com/Association-of-Academic-Health-Centers-AAHC-459070310823248 and General email, support@aahcdc.org

Membership: academic health centers (composed of a medical school, a teaching hospital, and at least one other health professional school or program). Participates in studies and public debates on health professionals' training and education, patient care, and biomedical research.

Children's Hospital Assn., *Washington Office, 600 13th St. N.W., #500, 20005; (202) 753-5500. Fax, (202) 347-5147. Mark Wietecha, Chief Executive Officer.*
General email, mbrsvcs@childrenshospitals.org
Web, www.childrenshospitals.org, Twitter, @hospitals4kids and Facebook, www.facebook.com/childrenshospitals

Membership: more than 220 children's hospitals nationwide. Acts as a resource for pediatric data and analytics for clinical and operational performance. Advocates at the federal level on issues impacting pediatric care, physician training, and research.

Federation of American Hospitals, *750 9th St. N.W., #600, 20001-4524; (202) 624-1500. Fax, (202) 737-6462. Charles N. (Chip) Kahn III, President. Press, (202) 624-1527.*

General email, info@fah.org

Web, www.fah.org, Twitter, @FAHhospitals and *Facebook, www.facebook.com/FedAmHospitals*

Membership: investor-owned or federally owned or managed community hospitals and health systems. Interests include national health care issues, such as cost containment, Medicare and Medicaid, the tax code, and the hospital workforce. Monitors legislation and regulations.

Physician-Led Healthcare For America (PHA), *105 E. St., S.E., 20003 (mailing address: 455 Carriage Lane, Hudson, WI 54016); (202) 367-1113. Fax, (202) 367-2113. Stacie Monroe, Executive Director, (419) 250-5873. phone, (419) 250-5873.*

General email, info@physicianled.us

Web, www.physicianhospitals.org, Twitter, @physicianhosp and *Facebook, www.facebook.com/Physician-Hospitals-of-America-113375608966/?ref=ts*

Membership organization acting as advocate for the physician-owned hospital industry; provides networking and continuing education opportunities.

Medicaid and Medicare

▶ **AGENCIES**

Centers for Medicare and Medicaid Services (CMS) *(Health and Human Services Dept.), 200 Independence Ave. S.W., #314G, 20201; (202) 619-0630. Fax, (202) 690-6262. Chiquita Brooks-LaSure, Administrator, (202) 690-6329. Information, (410) 786-3000. Toll-free, (877) 267-2323. TTY, (410) 786-0727.*

Web, www.cms.gov, www.medicaid.gov, www.medicare.gov, Twitter, @CMSgov and *Facebook, www.facebook.com/medicare*

Administers Medicare (a health insurance program for persons with disabilities or age sixty-five or older who are eligible to participate) and Medicaid (a health insurance program for persons judged unable to pay for health services).

Centers for Medicare and Medicaid Services (CMS) *(Health and Human Services Dept.), Center for Clinical Standards and Quality (CCSQ), 7500 Security Blvd., S3-02-01, Baltimore, MD 21244-1850; (410) 786-6841. Fax, (410) 786-6857. Dr. Lee A. Fleisher, Director, (410) 786-5533.*

Web, www.cms.gov/About-CMS/Agency-Information/CMSLeadership/Office_CCSQ

Develops, establishes, and enforces standards that regulate the quality of care of hospitals and other health care facilities under Medicare and Medicaid programs. Administers operations of survey and peer review organizations that enforce health care standards, primarily for institutional care.

Centers for Medicare and Medicaid Services (CMS) *(Health and Human Services Dept.), Center for Clinical Standards and Quality (CCSQ), Nursing Homes (DNH), 7500 Security Blvd., C2-23-17, Baltimore, MD 21244; (410) 786-8403. Evan Shulman, Director.*

Wweb, www.cms.gov/Medicare/Provider-Enrollment-and-Certification/GuidanceforLawsAndRegulations/Nursing-Homes

Monitors compliance of nursing homes with government standards. Focus includes quality of care, environmental conditions, and participation in Medicaid and Medicare programs.

Centers for Medicare and Medicaid Services (CMS) *(Health and Human Services Dept.), Center for Medicaid and CHIP Services (CMCS), 7500 Security Blvd., C5-21-17, Baltimore, MD 21244; (202) 690-7428. Daniel Tsai, Deputy Administrator, (202) 260-1064.*

Web, www.cms.gov/About-CMS/Agency-Information/CMSLeadership/office_CMCSC and *www.medicaid.gov*

Administers and monitors Medicaid programs to ensure program quality and financial integrity; promotes beneficiary awareness and access to services.

Centers for Medicare and Medicaid Services (CMS) *(Health and Human Services Dept.), Center for Medicaid and CHIP Services (CMCS), Disabled and Elderly Health Programs Group (DEHPG), 7500 Security Blvd., S2-14-26, Baltimore, MD 21244; (410) 786-4699. Alissa Deboy, Director.*

Web, www.medicaid.gov and *www.cms.gov/About-CMS/Agency-Information/CMSLeadership/Office-CMCSC*

Reviews all benefit and pharmacy state plan amendments for all Medicaid populations, Medicaid managed-care delivery systems, home-based and community-based services, and long-term services. Supports transformation grant programs, including Money Follows the Person and the Balancing Incentive Program.

Centers for Medicare and Medicaid Services (CMS) *(Health and Human Services Dept.), Center for Medicare, 7500 Security Blvd., C5-01-14, Baltimore, MD 21244; (410) 786-0550. Dr. Meena Seshamani, Director, (202) 205-5682. Toll-free, (800) 633-4227. TTY, (877) 486-2048.*

Web, www.cms.gov/medicare/medicare.html, www.cms.gov/About-CMS/Agency-Information/CMSLeadership/Office_CM and *Twitter, @MedicareGov*

Manages the contractual framework for the Medicare program; establishes and enforces performance standards for contractors who process and pay Medicare claims. Issues regulations and guidelines for administration of the Medicare program.

Centers for Medicare and Medicaid Services (CMS) *(Health and Human Services Dept.), Center for Medicare and Medicaid Innovation (CMMI), 7500 Security Blvd., WB-06-05, Baltimore, MD 21244; Elizabeth Fowler, Deputy Administrator, (202) 260-7153.*

General email, innovate@cms.hhs.gov

Web, https://innovation.cms.gov and *Twitter, @CMSInnovates*

Established pursuant to the Affordable Care Act of 2010 to explore innovative approaches to Medicare, Medicaid, and CHIP health care delivery and administration, with the goal of improving health outcomes and lowering costs. Solicits input from health care providers, the business community, patients and families, and other interested parties in order to identify best practices. Funds state demonstration projects to evaluate integrated care and payment approaches.

Centers for Medicare and Medicaid Services (CMS)
(Health and Human Services Dept.), Center for Medicare, Chronic Care Management (DCCM), 7500 Security Blvd., C5-05-27, Baltimore, MD 21244; (410) 786-9374. Jana Lindquist, Director.
Web, www.cms.gov/About-CMS/Agency-Information/ OMH/equity-initiatives/chronic-care-management

Administers coverage policy and payment for Medicare patients with two or more chronic conditions expected to last at least twelve months or until the death of the patient.

Centers for Medicare and Medicaid Services (CMS)
(Health and Human Services Dept.), Center for Program Integrity (CPI), 7500 Security Blvd., AR-18-50, Baltimore, MD 21244; (410) 786-1892. Dara Corrigan, Deputy Administrator.
Web, www.cms.gov/About-CMS/Agency-Information/ CMSLeadership/Office_CPI.html

Acts as the central office for all statewide Medicare and Medicaid programs and CHIP integrity fraud and abuse issues. Promotes Medicare and Medicaid program integrity and CHIP by reviewing policies, monitoring programs, and colloborating with other stakeholders, including the Justice Dept. and state law enforcement agencies.

Centers for Medicare and Medicaid Services (CMS)
(Health and Human Services Dept.), Enterprise Data and Analytics (OEDA), 7500 Security Blvd., B2-29-04, Baltimore, MD 21244; (410) 786-6384.
Allison M. Oelschlaeger, Director.
Web, www.cms.gov/About-CMS/Agency-Information/ CMSLeadership/Office-OEDA

Serves as primary federal statistical office for disseminating economic data on Medicare and Medicaid.

Centers for Medicare and Medicaid Services (CMS)
(Health and Human Services Dept.), Strategic Operations and Regulatory Affairs (OSORA), 7500 Security Blvd., C4-26-05, Baltimore, MD 21244; (410) 690-8390. Kathleen Cantwell, Director.
Web, www.cms.gov/About-CMS/Agency-Information/ CMSLeadership/Office_OSORA and www.cms.gov/About-CMS/leadership/office-strategic-operations-regulatory-affairs

Manages CMS decision making and regulatory processes; provides leadership and advocacy in relation to official policy matters. Coordinates the preparation of manuals and other policy instructions of CMS programs.

Centers for Medicare and Medicaid Services (CMS),
Burden Reduction and Health Informatics.
Dr. Mary Greene, Director.
Web, www.cms.gov/About-CMS/OBRHI

Aims to reduce regulatory burdens, set national standards for streamlining working with the medical community, and improve beneficiary experience.

Health Resources and Services Administration (HRSA)
(Health and Human Services Dept.), Federal Office of Rural Health Policy (FORHP), 5600 Fishers Lane, #17W45, Rockville, MD 20857; (301) 443-0835.
Tom Morris, Associate Administrator.
General email, tmorris@hrsa.gov
Web, www.hrsa.gov/rural-health

Studies the effects of Medicare and Medicaid programs on rural access to health care.

▶**NONGOVERNMENTAL**

AARP, 601 E St. N.W., 20049; (202) 434-2277.
Jo Ann C. Jenkins, Chief Executive Officer. Library, (202) 434-6233. Membership, toll-free, (800) 566-0242. Press, (202) 434-2560. Toll-free, (888) 687-2277. TTY, (877) 434-7598. Toll-free Spanish, (877) 342-2277. TTY Spanish, (866) 238-9488.
General email, dcaarp@aarp.org
Web, www.aarp.org, Twitter, @AARP and Facebook, www .facebook.com/AARP

Membership: people fifty years of age and older. Monitors legislation and regulations and disseminates information to members concerning Medicaid and Medicare.

Families USA, 1225 New York Ave. N.W., #800, 20005; (202) 628-3030. Fax, (202) 347-2417. Frederick Isasi, Executive Director.
General email, info@familiesusa.org
Web, www.familiesusa.org, Twitter, @FamiliesUSA and Facebook, www.facebook.com/FamiliesUSA

Interests include health care, the Affordable Care Act, Social Security, Medicare, and Medicaid. Offers Enrollment Assister Resource Centers to help consumers and businesses obtain high-quality, affordable health care. Monitors legislation and regulations affecting the elderly. Focuses on communities of color.

Federation of American Hospitals, 750 9th St. N.W., #600, 20001-4524; (202) 624-1500. Fax, (202) 737-6462. Charles N. (Chip) Kahn III, President. Press, (202) 624-1527.
General email, info@fah.org
Web, www.fah.org, Twitter, @FAHhospitals and Facebook, www.facebook.com/FedAmHospitals

Membership: investor-owned for-profit hospitals and health care systems. Studies Medicaid and Medicare reforms. Maintains speakers bureau; compiles statistics on investor-owned hospitals. Monitors legislation and regulations.

Medicare Rights Center, 1441 Eye St. N.W., #1105, 20005; (202) 637-0961. Fax, (202) 637-0962. Frederic Riccardi, President; Lindsey Copeland, JD, Director, Federal Policy. Helpline, (800) 333-4114.

General email, info@medicarerights.org

Web, www.medicarerights.org, Twitter, @medicarerights and Facebook, www.facebook.com/medicarerights

Advocates affordable health care for seniors and people with disabilities. Educates the public on medicare rights and benefits. Provides free Medicare counseling, as well as courses and training to health care professionals. Monitors legislation and regulations.

National Committee to Preserve Social Security and Medicare, *111 K St. N.E., #700, 20002; (202) 216-0420. Fax, (202) 216-0446. Max Richtman, President. Senior hotline/Legislative updates, (800) 998-0180.*
General email, webmaster@ncpssm.org

Web, www.ncpssm.org, Twitter, @NCPSSM, Facebook, www.facebook.com/NationalCommittee and YouTube, www.youtube.com/user/NationalCommittee

Educational and advocacy organization that focuses on Social Security and Medicare programs and on related income security and health issues. Interests include retirement income protection, health care reform, and the quality of life of seniors. Monitors legislation and regulations.

Medical Devices and Technology

▶ **AGENCIES**

Access Board, *1331 F St. N.W., #1000, 20004-1111; (202) 272-0080. Fax, (202) 272-0081. Sachin Dev Pavithran, Executive Director. Toll-free, (800) 872-2253. Toll-free TTY, (800) 993-2822. TTY, (202) 272-0082.*
General email, info@access-board.gov

Web, www.access-board.gov and Twitter, @accessboard

Develops and maintains accessibility requirements for buildings, transit vehicles, telecommunications equipment, medical diagnostic equipment, and electronic and information technology. Provides technical assistance and training on these guidelines and standards. Enforces access standards for federally funded facilities through the Architectural Barriers Act.

Armed Forces Radiobiology Research Institute *(Defense Dept.), 4301 Jones Bridge Rd., Bethesda, MD 20814; (301) 295-1210. Col. Mohammad Naeem (USA), Director. Public Affairs, (301) 295-1214. Toll-free, (800) 515-5257.*
Web, www.usuhs.edu/afrri

Serves as the principal ionizing radiation radiobiology research laboratory under the jurisdiction of the Uniformed Services University of the Health Sciences. Educates and trains radiation biologists. Participates in international conferences and projects.

Food and Drug Administration (FDA) *(Health and Human Services Dept.), Combination Products (OCP), White Oak Bldg. 32, 10903 New Hampshire Ave., #5142, Silver Spring, MD 20993-0002; (301) 796-8930. Fax, (301) 847-8619. Thinh X. Nguyen, Director, (301) 796-8931.*

General email, combination@fda.gov

Web, www.fda.gov/CombinationProducts

Seeks to streamline the processing of complex drug-device, drug-biologic, and device-biologic combination products. Responsibilities cover the entire regulatory life cycle of combination products, including jurisdiction decisions as well as the timeliness and effectiveness of pre-market review, and the consistency and appropriateness of post market regulation. Responsible for the classification of medical and biological products.

Food and Drug Administration (FDA) *(Health and Human Services Dept.), Division of Industry and Consumer Education (DICE), White Oak, 10903 New Hampshire Ave., Silver Spring, MD 20993; (301) 796-7100. Fax, (301) 847-8149. Elias Mallis, Director, (301) 796-6216. Toll-free, (800) 638-2041.*
General email, DICE@fda.hhs.gov

Web, www.fda.gov/MedicalDevices/DeviceRegulationand Guidance/ContactDivisionofIndustryandConsumer Education

Serves as liaison between small-business manufacturers of medical devices and the FDA. Assists manufacturers in complying with FDA regulatory requirements; sponsors seminars.

Food and Drug Administration (FDA) *(Health and Human Services Dept.), Division of Industry and Consumer Education, Center for Devices and Radiological Health (CDRH), White Oak Bldg. 66, 10903 New Hampshire Ave., Silver Spring, MD 20993-0002; (301) 796-7100. Fax, (301) 847-8510. Dr. Jeffrey E. Shuren, Director, (301) 796-5900. Toll-free, (800) 638-2041.*
General email, DICE@fda.hhs.gov and FDADeviceInfo@fda.hhs.gov

Web, www.fda.gov/medicaldevices and www.fda.gov/ AboutFDA/CentersOffices/OfficeofMedicalProductsand Tobacco/CDRH

Evaluates safety, efficacy, and labeling of medical devices; classifies devices; establishes performance standards; assists in legal actions concerning medical devices; coordinates research and testing; conducts training and educational programs. Accredits and certifies mammography facilities and personnel. Maintains an international reference system to facilitate trade in devices. Library open to the public.

National Institute of Biomedical Imaging and Bioengineering (NIBIB) *(National Institutes of Health), Bldg. 31, 9000 Rockville Pike, #1C14, MS2281, Bethesda, MD 20892; (301) 496-8859. Bruce Tromberg, Director.*
General email, info@nibib.nih.gov

Web, www.nibib.nih.gov, Twitter, @NIBIBgov, Facebook, www.facebook.com/nibibgov and YouTube, www.youtube .com/user/NIBIBTV

Conducts and supports research and development of biomedical imaging and bioengineering techniques and devices to improve the prevention, detection, and treatment of disease.

► NONGOVERNMENTAL

Advanced Medical Technology Assn., *701 Pennsylvania Ave. N.W., #800, 20004-2654; (202) 783-8700. Fax, (202) 783-8750. Scott Whitaker, President, (202) 434-7200. Press, (202) 316-1423.*
General email, info@advamed.org
Web, www.advamed.org, Twitter, @AdvaMedUpdate and Facebook, www.facebook.com/Advamed

Membership: manufacturers of medical devices, diagnostic products, and health care information systems. Interests include safe and effective medical devices; conducts educational seminars. Monitors legislation, regulations, and international issues.

American Assn. for Homecare, *1400 Crystal Dr., #460, Arlington, VA 22202; (202) 372-0107. Fax, (202) 835-8306. Thomas Ryan, President, (202) 372-0753. Toll-free, (866) 289-0492.*
General email, info@aahomecare.org
Web, www.aahomecare.org, Twitter, @aahomecare and Facebook, www.facebook.com/aahomecare?ref=hl

Membership: home medical equipment manufacturers and home health care service providers. Works to serve the medical needs of Americans who require oxygen equipment and therapy, mobility assistive technologies, medical supplies, inhalation drug therapy, home infusion, and other home medical services. Provides members with education, training, and information about industry trends. Monitors legislation and regulations.

American College of Radiology, *Government Relations, 505 9th St. N.W., #910, 20004; (202) 223-1670. Joshua Cooper, Vice President. Toll-free, (800) 227-5463.*
General email, info@acr.org
Web, www.acr.org, Twitter, @RadiologyACR and Facebook, www.facebook.com/AmericanCollegeOfRadiology

Membership: certified radiologists and medical physicists in the United States and Canada. Develops programs in radiation protection, technologist training, practice standards, and health care insurance; maintains a placement service for radiologists; participates in international conferences. (Headquarters in Reston, Va.)

American Institute of Ultrasound in Medicine, *14750 Sweitzer Lane, #100, Laurel, MD 20707-5906; (301) 498-4100. Fax, (301) 498-4450. Glynis V. Harvey, Chief Executive Officer. Toll-free, (800) 638-5352.*
Web, www.aium.org, Twitter, @AIUMUltrasound, Facebook, www.facebook.com/AIUMultrasound and General email, membership@aium.org

Membership: medical professionals who use ultrasound technology in their practices. Promotes multidisciplinary research and education on safe and effective use of diagnostic ultrasound through conventions and educational programs. Develops guidelines for accreditation. Monitors international research.

American Medical Informatics Assn., *143 Rollins Ave., #2248, Rockville, MD 20847; (301) 657-1291. Fax, (301) 657-1296. Tanya Tolpegin, Chief Executive Office, ext. 101.*
Web, www.amia.org, Twitter, @AMIAinformatics, Facebook, www.facebook.com/amiainformatics and YouTube, www.youtube.com/c/AMIAInformatics

Membership: medical professionals and students interested in informatics. Studies and pursues effective uses of biomedical data, information, and knowledge for scientific inquiry, problem solving, and decision making to improve human health. Applications include basic and applied research, clinical services, consumer services, and public health.

American Orthotic and Prosthetic Assn., *330 John Carlyle St., #200, Alexandria, VA 22314-5760 (mailing address: P.O. Box 34711, Alexandria, VA 22334); (571) 431-0876. Fax, (571) 431-0899. Eve Lee, Executive Director, (571) 431-0802.*
General email, info@aopanet.org
Web, www.aopanet.org, Twitter, @AmericanOandP and Facebook, www.facebook.com/AmericanOandP

Membership: companies that manufacture or supply artificial limbs and braces, and patient-care professionals who fit and supervise device use.

American Roentgen Ray Society, *44211 Slatestone Court, Leesburg, VA 20176-5109; (703) 729-3353. Fax, (703) 729-4839. Jonathan Kruskal, President. Toll-free, (866) 940-2777.*
General email, info@arrs.org
Web, www.arrs.org, Twitter, @ARRS_Radiology and Facebook, www.facebook.com/AmericanRoentgenRay Society

Membership: physicians and researchers in radiology and allied sciences. Publishes research; conducts conferences; presents scholarships and awards; monitors international research.

Board of Registered Polysomnographic Technologists, *4201 Wilson Blvd., 3rd Floor, Arlington, VA 22203; Fax, (703) 940-7227. James Magruder, Chief Executive Officer. Toll-free, (800) 935-8115.*
General email, info@brpt.org
Web, www.brpt.org and Facebook, www.facebook.com/ TheBRPT

Provides sleep credentialing, certification, and education for polysomnographic technologists. Offers continuing-education programs and education opportunities.

Health Industry Distributors Assn., *310 Montgomery St., Alexandria, VA 22314-1516; (703) 549-4432. Matthew Rowan, President, (703) 838-6118.*
General email, hida@hida.org
Web, www.hida.org, Twitter, @HIDAorg and Facebook, www.facebook.com/hida.org

Membership: medical products distributors. Sponsors and conducts trade shows and training seminars. Monitors legislation and regulations.

National Academies of Sciences, Engineering, and Medicine (NASEM), *Nuclear and Radiation Studies Board, Keck Center, 500 5th St. N.W., 20001;*

(202) 334-2016. Fax, (202) 334-3077. Charles Ferguson, Director; William H. Tobey, Chair.
General email, nrsb@nas.edu
Web, www.nationalacademies.org/nrsb/nuclear-and-radiation-studies-board

Oversees studies on safety, security, technical efficacy, and other policy and societal issues arising from the application of nuclear and radiation-based technologies, including medical applications.

Program for Appropriate Technology in Health (PATH), *Washington Office, 455 Massachusetts Ave. N.W., #1000, 20001; (202) 822-0033. Fax, (202) 457-1466. Nikolaj Gilbert, President.*
General email, info@path.org
Web, www.path.org

Develops, tests, and implements health technologies and strategies for low-resource countries. Works with community groups, other nongovernmental organizations, governments, companies, and UN agencies to expand the most successful programs. Interests include reproductive health, immunization, maternal-child health, emerging and epidemic diseases, and nutrition. (Headquarters in Seattle, Wash.)

Rehabilitation Engineering and Assistive Technology Society of North America (RESNA), *2001 K St. N.W., 3rd Floor, 20006; (202) 367-1121. Fax, (202) 367-2121. Andrea Van Hook, Executive Director.*
General email, info@resna.org
Web, www.resna.org, Twitter, @RESNAorg and Facebook, www.facebook.com/RESNAorg

Membership: engineers, health professionals, assistive technologists, persons with disabilities, and others. Promotes and supports developments in rehabilitation engineering and technology; acts as an information clearinghouse.

Nursing Homes and Hospices

▶AGENCIES

Centers for Medicare and Medicaid Services (CMS) *(Health and Human Services Dept.), Center for Clinical Standards and Quality (CCSQ), Continuing and Acute Care Providers (DCCP), 7500 Security Blvd., C2-21-16, Baltimore, MD 21244-1850; (410) 786-8021. Vacant, Director.*
Web, www.cms.gov/About-CMS/Agency-Information/CMSLeadership/Office_CCSQ

Monitors compliance with government standards of psychiatric hospitals and long-term and intermediate care facilities, including residential treatment facilities, community mental health centers, intermediate care facilities for mental retardation, outpatient rehabilitation facilities, home health care, hospice care, portable X-ray units, dialysis facilities, and outpatient physical, language, and speech therapy facilities. Focus includes quality of care, environmental conditions, and participation in Medicaid and

Medicare programs. Coordinates health care programs for the mentally challenged.

Centers for Medicare and Medicaid Services (CMS) *(Health and Human Services Dept.), Center for Clinical Standards and Quality (CCSQ), Nursing Homes (DNH), 7500 Security Blvd., C2-23-17, Baltimore, MD 21244; (410) 786-8403. Evan Shulman, Director.*
Wweb, www.cms.gov/Medicare/Provider-Enrollment-and-Certification/GuidanceforLawsAndRegulations/Nursing-Homes

Monitors compliance of nursing homes with government standards. Focus includes quality of care, environmental conditions, and participation in Medicaid and Medicare programs.

Centers for Medicare and Medicaid Services (CMS) *(Health and Human Services Dept.), Center for Clinical Standards and Quality (CCSQ), Quality and Safety Oversight Group, 7500 Security Blvd., C2-21-16, Baltimore, MD 21244-1850; (410) 786-9493. (410) 786-6841. David Wright, Director.*
Web, www.cms.gov/Medicare/Provider-Enrollment-and-Certification/SurveyCertificationGenInfo/QSOG-Mission-and-Priority-Information

Enforces health care and safety standards for nursing homes and other long-term care facilities.

▶NONGOVERNMENTAL

AARP, *Federal Health and Family Advocacy, 601 E St. N.W., 20049; (202) 434-3770. Megan O'Reilly, Director, (202) 434-6987.*
Web, www.aarp.org

Maintains the Legal Counsel for the Elderly, which acts as advocate on behalf of older residents of the District of Columbia who reside in nursing homes and board and care homes. Monitors legislation and regulations.

American College of Health Care Administrators, *1101 Connecticut Ave. N.W., #450, 20036; (202) 536-5120. Bob Lane, President, (800) 561-3148 ext. 702. Toll-free, (800) 561-3148.*
General email, info@achca.org
Web, www.achca.org, Twitter, @ACHCA and Facebook, www.facebook.com/The-American-College-of-Health-Care-Administrators-326597784597

Membership: administrators of long-term health care organizations and facilities, including home health care programs, hospices, day care centers for the elderly, nursing and hospital facilities, retirement communities, assisted-living communities, and mental health care centers. Conducts research on statistical characteristics of nursing home and other medical administrators; conducts seminars and workshops; offers education courses; provides certification for administrators.

American Health Care Assn., *1201 L St. N.W., 20005; (202) 842-4444. Fax, (202) 842-3860. Mark Parkinson, Chief Executive Officer. Press, (202) 898-2814. Publication orders, (800) 321-0343.*

Food and Drug Administration

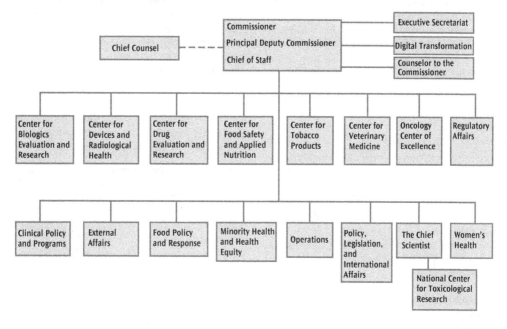

– – – – – Direct report to General Counsel Health and Human Services

General email, help@hctrendtracker.com

Web, www.ahcancal.org, Twitter, @ahcancal and Facebook, www.facebook.com/ahcancal

Association of facility-based long-term and post–acute care providers and affiliates of state health organizations. Advocates high-quality care and services for frail, elderly, and disabled Americans, communicating with government, business leaders, and the general public. Provides information, education, and administrative tools. Monitors legislation and regulations.

Hospice Foundation of America, 1707 L St. N.W., #220, 20036; (202) 457-5811. Fax, (202) 457-5815. Amy Tucci, President. Toll-free, (800) 854-3402.
General email, info@hospicefoundation.org

Web, www.hospicefoundation.org, Facebook, www .facebook.com/hospicefoundation and Twitter, @HFAhospice

Acts as an advocate for the hospice style of health care through ongoing programs of public education and training, information dissemination, and research.

National Assn. for Home Care and Hospice, 228 7th St. S.E., 20003; (202) 547-7424. Fax, (202) 547-3540. William A. Dombi, President, ext. 3203; Calvin McDaniel, Director Government Affairs, ext. 3283.
General email, info@nahc.org

Web, www.nahc.org, Twitter, @OfficialNAHC and Facebook, www.facebook.com/NAHC.org

Membership: hospice, home care, and private-duty providers and other community service organizations assisting those with chronic health problems or life-threatening illness. Works to educate and provide information for the public on hospice and home care. Interests include Medicare, Medicaid, and other insurance for home care and hospice. Monitors legislation and regulations.

National Center for Assisted Living, 1201 L St. N.W., 20005; (202) 842-4444. Fax, (202) 842-3860. LaShaun Bethea, Executive Director.
General email, ahcaleg@ncal.org

Web, www.ahcancal.org/ncal, Twitter, @ahcancal and Facebook, www.facebook.com/ahcancal

Membership: assisted living professionals. Provides networking opportunities and professional development; hosts educational seminars and an annual convention. Provides free resources for consumers looking into assisted living and other long-term care resources. Monitors legislation and regulations. (Affiliated with American Health Care Assn.)

National Consumer Voice for Quality Long-Term Care (NCCNHR), 1025 Connecticut Ave. N.W., #1000, 20036; (202) 332-2275. Fax, (866) 230-9789. Lori O. Smetanka, Executive Director, ext. 206; Robin Grant, Director of Public Policy.
General email, info@theconsumervoice.org

Web, www.theconsumervoice.org, Twitter, @consumervoices and Facebook, www.facebook.com/ theconsumervoice

Advocates high-quality care and quality of life for consumers in all long-term care settings. Promotes citizen participation in all aspects of nursing homes; acts as clearinghouse for nursing home advocacy. Hosts National Long-Term Care Ombudsman Resource Center.

National Hospice and Palliative Care Organization, *1731 King St., Alexandria, VA 22314; (703) 837-1500. Fax, (703) 837-1233. Edo (Don) Banach, President. Toll-free consumer information and referral helpline, (800) 658-8898.*
General email, nhpco_info@nhpco.org
Web, www.nhpco.org, Twitter, @NHPCO_news, Facebook, www.facebook.com/NHPCO and YouTube, www.youtube .com/user/NationalHospice

Membership: institutions and individuals providing hospice and palliative care and other interested organizations and individuals. Promotes supportive care for the terminally ill and their families; sets hospice program standards; provides information on hospices. Monitors legislation and regulations.

National Long-Term Care Ombudsman Resource Center, *1025 Connecticut Ave. N.W. #1000, 20036; (202) 332-2275. Fax, (202) 332-2949. Amity Overall Laib, Director.*
General email, ombudcenter@theconsumervoice.org
Web, www.ltcombudsman.org

Provides technical assistance, management guidance, policy analysis, and program development information on behalf of state and substate ombudsman programs. (Affiliate of the National Consumer Voice for Quality Long-Term Care.)

Pharmaceuticals

▶AGENCIES

Food and Drug Administration (FDA) *(Health and Human Services Dept.), White Oak, 10903 New Hampshire Ave., Silver Spring, MD 20993-0002; (888) 463-6332. Fax, (301) 847-3536. Dr. Robert M. Califf, Commissioner. Main Library, (301) 796-2039. Press, (301) 796-4540.*
Web, www.fda.gov, Twitter, @US_FDA, Facebook, www .facebook.com/FDA and Library email, fdalibrary@fda .hhs.gov

Protects public health by assessing the safety, efficacy, and security of human and veterinary drugs, vaccines, biological products and medical devices. Protects the safety and security of the nation's food supply, cosmetics, diet supplements, and products emitting radiation. Regulates tobacco products. Develops labeling and packaging standards; conducts inspections of manufacturers; issues orders to companies to recall and/or cease selling or producing hazardous products; enforces rulings and recommends action to Justice Dept. when necessary. Libraries open to the public; 24-hour advance appointment required.

Food and Drug Administration (FDA) *(Health and Human Services Dept.), Center for Drug Evaluation and Research (CDER), White Oak Bldg. 51, 10903 New Hampshire Ave., #6133, Silver Spring, MD 20993; (301) 796-5400. Fax, (301) 595-7910. Dr. Patrizia Cavazzoni, Director. Press, (301) 796-3700.*
General email, druginfo@fda.hhs.gov
Web, www.fda.gov/drugs and www.fda.gov/about-fda/fda-organization/center-drug-evaluation-and-research-cder

Reviews and approves applications to investigate and market new drugs; monitors prescription drug advertising; works to harmonize drug approval internationally.

Food and Drug Administration (FDA) *(Health and Human Services Dept.), Center for Drug Evaluation and Research (CDER), Biostatistics (OB), White Oak Bldg. 21, 10903 New Hampshire Ave., #3554, Silver Spring, MD 20993; (301) 796-1700. Fax, (301) 796-9734. Sylva Collins, Director, (301) 348-1932.*
Web, www.fda.gov/aboutfda/centersoffices/officeofmedical productsandtobacco/cder/ucm166250.htm

Conducts research and provides information on statistical methodology for drug regulation and development.

Food and Drug Administration (FDA) *(Health and Human Services Dept.), Center for Drug Evaluation and Research (CDER), Generic Drugs (OGD), White Oak Bldg. 75, 10903 New Hampshire Ave., #1692, Silver Spring, MD 20993; (240) 402-7920. Fax, (301) 595-1147. Sally Choe, Director, (301) 796-7960.*
General email, genericdrugs@fda.hhs.gov
Web, www.fda.gov/about-fda/center-drug-evaluation-and-research-cder/office-generic-drugs

Oversees generic drug review process to ensure the safety and effectiveness of approved drugs.

Food and Drug Administration (FDA) *(Health and Human Services Dept.), Center for Drug Evaluation and Research (CDER), New Drugs (OND), White Oak Bldg. 22, 10903 New Hampshire Ave., #6306, Silver Spring, MD 20993; (301) 796-0700. Fax, (301) 796-9856. Dr. Peter P. Stein, Director, (301) 796-5376.*
General email, ONDCommunications@fda.hhs.gov
Web, www.fda.gov/about-fda/center-drug-evaluation-and-research-cder/office-new-drugs

Provides regulatory oversight for investigational studies during drug development; makes decisions regarding marketing approval for new innovator and nongeneric drugs, including decisions related to changes to already marketed products.

Food and Drug Administration (FDA) *(Health and Human Services Dept.), Center for Drug Evaluation and Research (CDER), Pharmaceutical Quality (OPQ), White Oak Bldg. 51, 10903 New Hampshire Ave., #6133, Silver Spring, MD 20993; (301) 796-2400. Fax, (301) 796-9996. Michael Kopcha, Director, (301) 796-5400.*
General email, CDER-OPQ-Inquiries@fda.hhs.gov
Web, www.fda.gov/AboutFDA/CentersOffices/Officeof MedicalProductsandTobacco/CDER/ucm418347.htm

Reviews the critical quality attributes and manufacturing processes of new drugs, establishes quality standards to ensure safety and efficacy, and facilitates new drug development.

Food and Drug Administration (FDA) *(Health and Human Services Dept.), Orphan Products Development (OOPD), White Oak Bldg. 32, 10903 New Hampshire Ave., #5295, Silver Spring, MD 20993-0002; (301) 796-8660. Fax, (301) 847-8621. Dr. Janet W. Maynard, Director, (301) 796-2978.*
General email, orphan@fda.hhs.gov
Web, www.fda.gov/ForIndustry/developing-products-rare-diseases-conditions

Promotes the development of drugs, devices, and biological and medical food therapies for rare diseases or conditions. Provides incentives for sponsors to develop products for rare diseases. Coordinates activities on the development of orphan drugs among federal agencies, manufacturers, and patient advocacy organizations.

Food and Drug Administration (FDA) *(Health and Human Services Dept.), Prescription Drug Promotion (OPDP), White Oak Bldg. 51, 10903 New Hampshire Ave., #3314, Silver Spring, MD 20993-0002; (301) 796-1200. Fax, (301) 847-8444 or (301) 847-8445. Catherine Gray, Director.*
Web, www.fda.gov/about-fda/center-drug-evaluation-and-research-cder/office-prescription-drug-promotion-opdp

Monitors prescription drug advertising and labeling; investigates complaints; conducts market research on health care communications and drug issues.

Food and Drug Administration (FDA) *(Health and Human Services Dept.), Regulatory Affairs (ORA), White Oak Bldg. 31, 10903 New Hampshire Ave., #3528, Silver Spring, MD 20993; (301) 796-8800. Fax, (301) 847-7942. Judith A. McMeekin, Associate Commissioner.*
Web, www.fda.gov/aboutfda/centersoffices/officeofglobalregulatoryoperationsandpolicy/ora and Twitter, @FDA_ORA

Directs and coordinates the FDA's compliance activities; manages field offices; advises FDA commissioner on domestic and international regulatory policies.

National Institutes of Health (NIH) *(Health and Human Services Dept.), Dietary Supplements (ODS), 6705 Rockledge Dr., #730, MSC 7991, Bethesda, MD 20817; (301) 435-2920. Fax, (301) 480-1845. Joseph Betz, Director (Acting).*
General email, ods@nih.gov
Web, http://ods.od.nih.gov, Twitter, @NIH_ODS and Facebook, www.facebook.com/NIH.ODS

Reviews scientific evidence on the safety and efficacy of dietary supplements. Conducts, promotes, and coordinates scientific research within the NIH relating to dietary supplements. Conducts and supports conferences, workshops, and symposia and publishes research results on scientific topics related to dietary supplements.

▶NONGOVERNMENTAL

American Assn. of Colleges of Pharmacy, *1400 Crystal Dr., #300, Arlington, VA 22202; (703) 739-2330. Fax, (703) 836-8982. Lucinda L. Maine, Executive Vice President, ext. 1021.*
General email, mail@aacp.org
Web, www.aacp.org, Twitter, @AACPharmacy and Facebook, www.facebook.com/AACPharmacy

Represents and acts as advocate for pharmacists in the academic community. Conducts programs and activities in cooperation with other national health and higher education associations.

American Pharmacists Assn., *2215 Constitution Ave. N.W., 20037-2985; (202) 628-4410. Fax, (844) 390-3782. Scott Knoer, Chief Executive Officer, (202) 794-2193. Toll-free, (800) 237-2742. Library, (202) 429-7524.*
General email, infocenter@aphanet.org
Web, www.pharmacist.com, Twitter, @pharmacists and Facebook, www.facebook.com/APhAPharmacists

Membership: practicing pharmacists, pharmaceutical scientists, and pharmacy students. Promotes professional education and training; publishes scientific journals and handbooks on nonprescription drugs; monitors international research. Library open to the public by appointment.

American Society for Pharmacology and Experimental Therapeutics, *1801 Rockville Pike, #210, Rockville, MD 20852-1633; (301) 634-7060. Fax, (301) 634-7061. Vacant, Executive Director.*
General email, info@aspet.org
Web, www.aspet.org, Twitter, @ASPET and Facebook, www.facebook.com/ASPETpage

Membership: researchers and teachers involved in basic and clinical pharmacology primarily in the United States and Canada.

American Society of Consultant Pharmacists (ASCP), *1240 N. Pitt St., #300, Alexandria, VA 22314-3563; (703) 739-1300. Chad Worz, Executive Director. Toll-free, (800) 355-2727.*
General email, info@ascp.com
Web, www.ascp.com, Twitter, @ASCPharm and Facebook, www.facebook.com/ascpharm

Membership: dispensing and clinical pharmacists with expertise in therapeutic medication management for geriatric patients; provides services to long-term care facilities, institutions, and hospices as well as older adults in assisted-living and home-based care. Monitors legislation and regulations.

American Society of Health-System Pharmacists (ASHP), *4500 East-West Hwy., #900, Bethesda, MD 20814; (301) 657-3000. Fax, (301) 657-1251. Paul W. Abramowitz, Chief Executive Officer; Linda S. Taylor, President. Toll-free, (866) 279-0681.*

Web, www.ashp.org, Twitter, @ASHPOfficial, Facebook, www.facebook.com/ASHPofficial/ and Instagram, @ashpofficial

Membership: pharmacists who practice in organized health care settings such as hospitals, health maintenance organizations, and long-term care facilities. Publishes reference materials and provides educational programs and conferences. Accredits pharmacy residency and pharmacy technician training programs. Monitors legislation and regulations.

Assn. for Accessible Medicines, 601 New Jersey Ave. N.W., #850, 20001; (202) 249-7100. Fax, (202) 249-7105. Dan Leonard, President.
General email, info@accessiblemeds.org
Web, http://accessiblemeds.org, Twitter, @AccessibleMeds and Facebook, www.facebook.com/accessiblemeds

Membership: manufacturers and distributors of generic pharmaceuticals and pharmaceutical chemicals and suppliers of goods and services to the generic pharmaceutical industry. Attempts to increase availability and public awareness of safe, effective generic medicines. Monitors legislation and regulations. (Formerly the Generic Pharmaceutical Assn.)

Consumer Healthcare Products Assn., 1625 Eye St. N.W., #600, 20006; (202) 429-9260. Fax, (202) 223-6835. Scott Melville, President.
Web, https://chpa.org, Twitter, @CHPA and Facebook, www.facebook.com/knowyourotcs

Membership: manufacturers and marketers of over-the-counter medicines and dietary supplements; associate members include suppliers, advertising agencies, research and testing laboratories, and others. Promotes the role of self-medication in health care. Monitors legislation and regulations.

Healthcare Distribution Alliance, 901 N. Glebe Rd., #1000, Arlington, VA 22203; (703) 787-0000. Fax, (703) 812-5282. Chester (Chip) Davis, President.
Web, www.hda.org and Twitter, @HDAconnect

Membership: distributors and manufacturers of pharmaceutical and health-related products and information. Serves as a forum on major industry issues. Researches and disseminates information on distribution issues and management practices. Monitors legislation and regulations.

National Assn. of Chain Drug Stores, 1776 Wilson Blvd., #200, Arlington, VA 22209; (703) 549-3001. Fax, (703) 836-4869. Steven Anderson, President, ext. 344.
General email, contactus@nacds.org
Web, www.nacds.org, Twitter, @NACDS and Facebook, www.facebook.com/NACDS.org

Membership: traditional drug stores, supermarkets and mass merchants with pharmacies; associate members include manufacturers, suppliers, publishers, and advertising agencies. Provides information on the pharmacy profession, community pharmacy practice, and retail prescription drug economics. Monitors legislation and regulations.

National Community Pharmacists Assn., 100 Daingerfield Rd., Alexandria, VA 22314; (703) 683-8200. Fax, (703) 683-3619. Michele Belcher, President. Membership, (800) 544-7447.
Web, www.ncpanet.org, Twitter, @Commpharmacy and Facebook, www.facebook.com/commpharmacy

Membership: independent pharmacy owners, including independent pharmacies, independent pharmacy franchises, and independent chains. Promotes the interests of independent community pharmacists to compete in the health care market. Monitors legislation and regulations.

National Pharmaceutical Council, 1717 Pennsylvania Ave. N.W., #800, 20006; (202) 827-2100. Fax, (202) 827-0314. Dr. Robert W. Dubois, Vice President, (202) 827-2079; John M. O'Brien, President.
General email, info@npcnow.org
Web, www.npcnow.org, Twitter, @npcnow and YouTube, www.youtube.com/user/npcnow

Membership: pharmaceutical manufacturers that research and produce trade-name prescription medication and other pharmaceutical products. Sponsors and conducts scientific analyses of the use of pharmaceuticals and the clinical and economic value of innovation.

Parenteral Drug Assn. (PDA), 4350 East-West Hwy., #600, Bethesda, MD 20814; (301) 656-5900. Fax, (301) 986-0296. Richard Johnson, President, ext. 123; Glenn Wright, Vice President, Scientific and Regulatory Affairs, ext. 147.
General email, info@pda.org
Web, www.pda.org, Twitter, @PDAonline and Facebook, www.facebook.com/pdaonline

Membership: scientists involved in the development, manufacture, quality control, and regulation of pharmaceuticals/biopharmaceuticals and related products. Provides science, technology, and regulatory information and education to the pharmaceutical and biopharmaceutical community. Influences FDA regulatory process.

Pharmaceutical Care Management Assn., 325 7th St. N.W. 9th Floor, 20004; (202) 756-5700. Fax, (202) 756-5708. JC Scott, President.
General email, info@pcmanet.org
Web, www.pcmanet.org, Twitter, @pcmanet and Facebook, www.facebook.com/TheOfficialPCM

Membership: companies providing managed care pharmacy and pharmacy benefits management. Promotes legislation, research, education, and practice standards that foster high-quality, affordable pharmaceutical care.

Pharmaceutical Research and Manufacturers of America, 950 F St. N.W., #300, 20004; (202) 835-3400. Stephen J. (Steve) Ubl, President. Press, (202) 835-3460.
Web, www.phrma.org, Twitter, @PhRMA and Facebook, www.facebook.com/PhRMA

Membership: research-based pharmaceutical and biotechnology companies that originate, develop, and manufacture prescription drugs. Advocates public policies that encourage discovery of new medicines. Provides consumer information on drug abuse, the safe and effective use of prescription medicines, and developments in important areas, including the treatment of HIV/AIDS.

U.S. Pharmacopeial Convention, *7135 English Muffin Way, Fredricksburg, VA 21704; (301) 881-0666. Fax, (301) 816-8148. Dr. Ronald Piervincenzi, Chief Executive Officer. Toll-free, (800) 227-8772.*
General email, custsvc@usp.org
Web, www.usp.org and Twitter, @uspharmacopeia

Establishes and revises standards for drug strength, quality, purity, packaging, labeling, and storage of prescription and over-the-counter medications. Publishes drug use information, official drug quality standards, patient education materials, and consumer drug references. Interests include international standards. (Offices in Switzerland, India, China, and Brazil.)

HEALTH PROFESSIONS

General

▶AGENCIES

Centers for Medicare and Medicaid Services (CMS) *(Health and Human Services Dept.), Center for Clinical Standards and Quality (CCSQ), 7500 Security Blvd., S3-02-01, Baltimore, MD 21244-1850; (410) 786-6841. Fax, (410) 786-6857. Dr. Lee A. Fleisher, Director, (410) 786-5533.*
Web, www.cms.gov/About-CMS/Agency-Information/ CMSLeadership/Office_CCSQ

Oversees professional review and other medical review programs; establishes guidelines; prepares issue papers relating to legal aspects of professional review and quality assurance.

Education Dept., *Health Education Assistance Loan Program (HEAL), 12501 Ardennes Ave., #200, Rockville, MD 20857; (844) 509-8957. Vacant, Supervisor.*
General email, heal@ed.gov
Web, https://ifap.ed.gov/health-education-assistance-loan-information

Insures loans provided by private lenders to students attending eligible health professions schools under the Public Health Service Act. New loans to student borrowers have been discontinued. Refinancing has been terminated.

Health Resources and Services Administration (HRSA) *(Health and Human Services Dept.), Bureau of Health Workforce (BHW), 5600 Fishers Lane, #11 West Wing, Rockville, MD 20857; (301) 443-5794. Dr. Luis Padilla, Associate Administrator. Press, (301) 443-3366.*
General email, bhwevents@hrsa.gov
Web, www.bhw.hrsa.gov

Supports primary care and public health education and practice. Supports recruitment of health care professionals, including nursing and allied health professionals, for underserved populations. Administers categorical training programs, scholarship and loan programs, and minority

and disadvantaged assistance programs. Oversees National Practitioner Data Bank.

Health Resources and Services Administration (HRSA) *(Health and Human Services Dept.), Bureau of Health Workforce (BHW), National Practitioner Data Bank (NPDB), 4094 Majestic Lane, PMB 332, Fairfax, VA 22033 (mailing address: P.O. Box 10832, Chantilly, VA 20153–0832); (703) 802-9380. Fax, (703) 803-1964. Dave Loewenstein, Division Director, (301) 443-8263. Toll-free, (800) 767-6732. TTY, (703) 378-3919. Press, (301) 443-3376.*
General email, help@npdb.hrsa.gov
Web, www.npdb.hrsa.gov

Provides information on reports of malpractice payments, adverse state licensure, clinical privileges, and society membership actions (only to eligible entities, including state licensing boards, hospitals, and other health care entities) about physicians, dentists, and other licensed health care practitioners.

Health Resources and Services Administration (HRSA) *(Health and Human Services Dept.), National Health Service Corps (NHSC), 5600 Fishers Lane, #8-05, Rockville, MD 20857; (301) 443-4021. Fax, (301) 443-2080. Israil Ali, Director. Toll-free, (800) 221-9393. TTY, (877) 897-9910.*
Web, www.nhsc.hrsa.gov, Twitter, @NHSCorps and Facebook, www.facebook.com/nationalhealthservicecorps

Supplies communities experiencing a shortage of health care personnel with doctors and other medical professionals.

National Institute of Biomedical Imaging and Bioengineering (NIBIB) *(National Institutes of Health), Bldg. 31, 9000 Rockville Pike, #1C14, MS2281, Bethesda, MD 20892; (301) 496-8859. Bruce Tromberg, Director.*
General email, info@nibib.nih.gov
Web, www.nibib.nih.gov, Twitter, @NIBIBgov, Facebook, www.facebook.com/nibibgov and YouTube, www.youtube .com/user/NIBIBTV

Offers multidisciplinary training programs for scientists and engineers at all stages of their careers in bioimaging and bioengineering.

National Institute of General Medical Sciences (NIGMS) *(National Institutes of Health), Training, Workforce Development, and Diversity, Bldg. 45, 45 Center Dr., #2AS37, MS 6200, Bethesda, MD 20892-6200; (301) 496-7301. Alison Gammie, Director.*
Web, http://nigms.nih.gov/about/overview/Pages/TWD.aspx

Administers research and research training programs aimed at increasing the number of minority biomedical scientists. Funds grants, fellowships, faculty development awards, and development of research facilities.

Uniformed Services University of the Health Sciences *(Defense Dept.), 4301 Jones Bridge Rd., Bethesda, MD 20814-4799; (301) 295-3013. Fax, (301) 295-1960. Rear Adm. William M. Roberts, USN retired, President.*

Registrar, (301) 400-4100. Toll-free information, (800) 515-5257.
General email, registrar@usuhs.edu
Web, www.usuhs.edu and Twitter, @USUhealthsci

An accredited four-year medical and postgraduate dental school under the auspices of the Defense Dept. Awards doctorate and master's degrees in health-related and science-related fields.

► CONGRESS

For a listing of relevant congressional committees and sub-committees, please see pages 362–363 or the Appendix.

► NONGOVERNMENTAL

Aerospace Medical Assn., 320 S. Henry St., Alexandria, VA 22314-3579; (703) 739-2240. Fax, (703) 739-9652. James R. DeVoll, M.D., President; Jeffrey C. Sventek, Executive Director.
General email, inquiries@asma.org
Web, www.asma.org, Twitter, @Aero_Med and Facebook, www.facebook.com/AerospaceMedicalAssociation

Membership: physicians, flight surgeons, aviation medical examiners, flight nurses, scientists, technicians, and specialists in clinical, operational, and research fields of aerospace medicine. It is organized exclusively for charitable, educational, and scientific purposes. Promotes programs to improve aerospace medicine, human performance and to help maintain safety in aviation by examining and monitoring the health of aviation personnel; members may consult in aircraft investigation and cockpit design. Publishes the AMHP journal and several other informational papers.

AFT Healthcare, 555 New Jersey Ave. N.W., 20001; (202) 879-4400. Randi Weingarten, President.
Web, www.aft.org/healthcare, Twitter, @AFTHealthcare and Facebook, www.facebook.com/AFTunion

Membership: teachers, public employees, nurses and other health care workers. Assists members with contract negotiation and grievances; conducts training programs and workshops. Monitors legislation and regulations. (Division of the American Federation of Teachers.)

Alliance for Academic Internal Medicine (AAIM), 330 John Carlyle St., #610, Alexandria, VA 22314; (703) 341-4540. Fax, (703) 519-1893. Vacant, President; Vacant, Executive Vice President.
General email, aaim@im.org
Web, www.im.org, Twitter, @AAIMonline and Facebook, www.facebook.com/AAIMonline

Membership: department and division administrators, division chiefs, and education administrators; residency and fellowship educators, student educators and department chairs and other leaders of internal medicine departments at all U.S. medical schools and several affiliated teaching hospitals. Provides services, training, and educational and research opportunities for leaders in internal

medicine departments to prepare the next generation of physicians etc. Monitors legislation and regulations.

American Assn. of Colleges of Pharmacy, 1400 Crystal Dr., #300, Arlington, VA 22202; (703) 739-2330. Fax, (703) 836-8982. Lucinda L. Maine, Executive Vice President, ext. 1021.
General email, mail@aacp.org
Web, www.aacp.org, Twitter, @AACPharmacy and Facebook, www.facebook.com/AACPharmacy

Represents and acts as advocate for pharmacists in the academic community. Conducts programs and activities in cooperation with other national health and higher education associations.

American College of Health Care Administrators, 1101 Connecticut Ave. N.W., #450, 20036; (202) 536-5120. Bob Lane, President, (800) 561-3148 ext. 702. Toll-free, (800) 561-3148.
General email, info@achca.org
Web, www.achca.org, Twitter, @ACHCA and Facebook, www.facebook.com/The-American-College-of-Health-Care-Administrators-326597784597

Membership: administrators of long-term health care organizations and facilities, including home health care programs, hospices, day care centers for the elderly, nursing and hospital facilities, retirement communities, assisted-living communities, and mental health care centers. Conducts research on statistical characteristics of nursing home and other medical administrators; conducts seminars and workshops; offers education courses; provides certification for administrators.

American College of Radiology, Government Relations, 505 9th St. N.W., #910, 20004; (202) 223-1670. Joshua Cooper, Vice President. Toll-free, (800) 227-5463.
General email, info@acr.org
Web, www.acr.org, Twitter, @RadiologyACR and Facebook, www.facebook.com/AmericanCollegeOfRadiology

Membership: certified radiologists and medical physicists in the United States and Canada. Develops programs in radiation protection, technologist training, practice standards, and health care insurance; maintains a placement service for radiologists; participates in international conferences. (Headquarters in Reston, Va.)

American Health Law Assn., 1099 14th St. N.W., #925, 20005; (202) 833-1100. Fax, (202) 833-1105. David S. Cade, Chief Executive Officer, (202) 833-0777.
Web, www.americanhealthlaw.org, Twitter, @healthlawyers, Facebook, www.facebook.com/ahlafb and Public interest, publicinterest@healthlawyers.org

Membership: corporate, institutional, and government lawyers interested in the health care field; law students; and health professionals. Serves as an information clearinghouse on health law; sponsors health law educational programs and seminars.

American Institute of Ultrasound in Medicine, 14750 Sweitzer Lane, #100, Laurel, MD 20707-5906; (301) 498-4100.

Fax, (301) 498-4450. Glynis V. Harvey, Chief Executive Officer. Toll-free, (800) 638-5352.
Web, www.aium.org, Twitter, @AIUMUltrasound, Facebook, www.facebook.com/AIUMultrasound and General email, membership@aium.org

Membership: medical professionals who use ultrasound technology in their practices. Promotes multidisciplinary research and education on safe and effective use of diagnostic ultrasound through conventions and educational programs. Develops guidelines for accreditation. Monitors international research.

American Medical Group Assn., One Prince St., Alexandria, VA 22314-3318; (703) 838-0033. Fax, (703) 548-1890. Dr. Jerry W. Penso, President, ext. 356.
Web, www.amga.org, Twitter, @theAMGA and Facebook, www.facebook.com/theAMGA

Membership: medical group and health system organizations. Compiles statistics on group practice and clinical best practices. Sponsors a foundation for research and education programs. Advocates the multispecialty group practice model of health care delivery. Provides educational and networking programs and publications, benchmarking data services, and financial and operations assistance. Monitors legislation and regulations.

American Speech-Language-Hearing Assn. (ASHA), 2200 Research Blvd., Rockville, MD 20850-3289; 444 N. Capitol St. N.W., #715, 20001; (202) 624-5951. Fax, (301) 296-8580. Vicki R. Deal, Chief Executive Officer. Press, (301) 296-8732. Toll-free for Action Center, (800) 498-2071 (voice and TTY accessible). Toll-free for nonmembers, (800) 638-8255.
Web, www.asha.org, Twitter, @ASHAWeb and Facebook, www.facebook.com/asha.org

Membership: specialists in speech-language pathology and audiology. Sponsors professional education programs; acts as accrediting agent for graduate programs; certifies audiologists and speech-language pathologists. (National office in Rockville, Md.)

AMSUS—Society of Federal Health Professionals, 12154 Darnstown Rd., #506, Gaithersburg, MD 20878; (301) 897-8800. Brig. Gen. John M. Cho (USA, Ret.), Executive Director.
General email, amsus@amsus.org
Web, www.amsus.org and Twitter, @AMSUS

Membership: health professionals, including nurses, dentists, pharmacists, and physicians, who work or have worked for the U.S. Public Health Service, the VA, or the Army, Navy, Air Force, Guard, and Reserves, and students. Works to improve all phases of federal health services.

Assn. for Healthcare Philanthropy, 2550 S. Clark St., #810, Arlington, VA 22202; (703) 532-6243. Fax, (703) 532-7170. Alice Ayres, President.
General email, ahp@ahp.org
Web, www.ahp.org and Twitter, @AHPIntl

Membership: hospital and health care executives who manage fund-raising activities and organizations and individuals who provide consulting services for such activities.

Acts as a clearinghouse on philanthropy and offers programs, services, and publications and e-communications to members.

Assn. for Prevention Teaching and Research, 1001 Connecticut Ave. N.W., #610, 20036; (202) 463-0550. Fax, (202) 463-0555. Allison L. Lewis, Executive Director. Toll-free, (866) 520-2787.
General email, info@aptrweb.org
Web, www.aptrweb.org and Twitter, @APTRupdate

Membership: faculty, researchers, residents, and students within schools of medicine, schools of public health, schools of nursing, schools of pharmacy, physician assistant programs, graduate programs for public health, and health agencies. Works to advance population-based and public health education, research, and service by linking supporting members from the academic prevention community. Develops curricular resources and professional development programs. (Formerly the Assn. of Teachers of Preventive Medicine.)

Assn. for Professionals in Infection Control and Epidemiology (APIC), 1400 Crystal Dr., #900, Arlington, VA 22202; (202) 789-1890. Fax, (202) 789-1899. Ann Marie Pettis, Chief Executive Officer. Toll-free, (800) 650-9570.
General email, info@apic.org
Web, www.apic.org and Twitter, @apic

Membership: infection prevention health practitioners, including nurses, physicians, public health professionals, epidemiologists, microbiologists, and medical technologists. Monitors legislation and regulations.

Assn. of Schools and Programs of Public Health, 1615 L St., #510, 20036; (202) 296-1099. Fax, (202) 296-1252. Laura Magaña, President, ext. 120.
General email, info@aspph.org
Web, www.aspph.org, Twitter, @ASPPHtweets and Facebook, www.facebook.com/ASPPH

Membership: deans, faculty, and students of accredited graduate schools of public health. Promotes improved education and training of professional public health personnel; interests include disease prevention, health promotion, and international health.

Assn. of Schools of Advancing Health Professions, ASAHP, 122 C St. N.W., #200, 20001; (202) 237-6481. John Colbert, Executive Director.
General email, jacoby@asahp.org
Web, www.asahp.org, Twitter, @ASAHPDC and Facebook, www.facebook.com/ASAHPDC/

Membership: two-year and four-year colleges and academic health science centers with allied health professional training programs; administrators, educators, and practitioners; and professional societies. Serves as information resource; conducts surveys of allied health-education programs. Interests include health promotion and disease prevention, ethics in health care, and the participation of women and persons with disabilities in allied health. Monitors legislation and regulations.

Assn. of University Programs in Health Administration (AUPHA), *1730 Rhode Island Ave., N.W., #820, 20036; (202) 763-7283. Daniel Gentry, President.*
General email, aupha@aupha.org
Web, www.aupha.org/home and Twitter, @AUPHA

Membership: university-based educational programs, faculty, practitioners, and provider organizations. Works to improve the field of health care management and practice by educating entry-level professional managers.

Health Volunteers Overseas, *1900 L St. N.W., #310, 20036; (202) 296-0928. Fax, (202) 296-8018. Nancy A. Kelly, Executive Director.*
General email, info@hvousa.org
Web, www.hvousa.org, Twittter, @HVOUSA and Facebook, www.facebook.com/hvousa

Operates training programs in developing countries for health professionals who wish to teach low-cost health care delivery practices.

Healthcare Financial Management Assn., *Washington Office, 1090 Vermont Ave. N.W., #500, 20005; (202) 296-2920. Fax, (202) 849-3645. Joseph J. Fifer, Chief Executive Officer, (708) 492-3304.*
General email, inquiry@hfma.org
Web, www.hfma.org, Twitter, @hfmaorg and Facebook, www.facebook.com/hfmaorg

Membership: health care financial management specialists. Offers educational programs; provides information on financial management of health care. (Headquarters in Westchester, Ill.)

Hispanic-Serving Health Professions Schools, *11 Main St., Suite D, Warrenton, VA 20186; (202) 808-3480. Fax, (202) 962-3939. Dr. Norma Pérez, President.*
General email, admin@hshps.org
Web, www.hshps.org and Twitter, @HSHPS96

Seeks to increase representation of Hispanics in all health care professions through academic development, initiatives, and training. Monitors legislation and regulations.

National Assn. of County and City Health Officials, *1201 Eye St. N.W., 4th Floor, 20005; (202) 783-5550. Fax, (202) 783-1583. Lori T. Freeman, Chief Executive Officer, (202) 507-4271.*
General email, info@naccho.org
Web, www.naccho.org, Twitter, @NACCHOalerts and Facebook, www.facebook.com/NACCHOHQ/

Membership: city, county, and district health officers. Provides members with information on national, state, and local health developments. Works to develop the technical competence, managerial capacity, and leadership potential of local public health officials.

National Assn. of Healthcare Access Management, *2001 K St. N.W., 3rd Floor North, 20006; (202) 367-1125. Fax, (202) 367-2125. Kirsten Shaffer, Executive Director.*
General email, info@naham.org
Web, www.naham.org and Twitter, @mynaham

Promotes professional growth and recognition of health care patient access managers, who handle hospital patient admissions, registration, finance, and patient relations; provides instructional videotapes; sponsors educational programs.

Physicians for Human Rights, *Washington Office, 1100 13th St., N.W., # 800, 20005; (202) 728-5335. Fax, (202) 728-3053. Jennifer Sime, Executive Director (Acting); Michael Payne, Deputy Director, Advocacy.*
Advocacy Email, advocacy@phr.org, Web, https://phr.org, Twitter, @P4HR and Facebook, www.facebook.com/physiciansforhumanrights

Mobilizes doctors, nurses, health specialists, scientists, and others to promote health and human rights globally. (Headquarters in New York City.)

Society of Health and Physical Educators (SHAPE) America, *P.O. Box 225, Annapolis Junction, MD 20701; (703) 476-3400. Fax, (703) 476-9527. Terri Drain, President. Toll-free, (800) 213-7193.*
General email, info@shapeamerica.org
Web, www.shapeamerica.org, Twitter, @SHAPE_America, Facebook, www.facebook.com/SHAPEAmericaFB and YouTube, www.youtube.com/SHAPEAmericaYT

Membership: health educators and allied health professionals in community and volunteer health agencies, educational institutions, and businesses. Develops health education programs; monitors legislation and regulations.

Chiropractors

▶ **NONGOVERNMENTAL**

American Chiropractic Assn., *1701 Clarendon Blvd., #200, Arlington, VA 22209; (703) 276-8800. Fax, (703) 243-2593. Karen Silberman, Executive Vice President. Press, (703) 812-0226.*
General email, memberinfo@acatoday.org
Web, www.acatoday.org, Twitter, @ACAtoday and Facebook, www.facebook.com/acatoday.org

Association of chiropractic physicians. Promotes standards of care. Interests include health care coverage, sports injuries, physical fitness, internal disorders, and orthopedics. Supports foundation for chiropractic education and research. Maintains a legal action fund to sue on behalf of patients whose insurers deny them coverage of chiropractic services. Monitors legislation and regulations.

International Chiropractors Assn., *6400 Arlington Blvd., #650, Falls Church, VA 22042; (703) 528-5000. Fax, (703) 528-5023. Beth Clay, Executive Director, (571) 765-7560. Toll-free, (800) 423-5023.*
General email, info@chiropractic.org
Web, www.chiropractic.org

Membership: chiropractors, students, educators, and laypersons. Seeks to increase public awareness of chiropractic care. Supports research on health issues; administers scholarship program; monitors legislation and regulations.

International Chiropractors Assn., *Foundation for the Advancement of Chiropractic Tenets and Science (FACTS),* 6400 Arlington Blvd., #650, Falls Church, VA 22042; (703) 528-5000. Fax, (703) 528-5028. Beth Clay, Executive Director (Acting), (571) 765-7560.
General email, info@chiropractic.org

Web, www.chiropractic.org

Offers financial aid for education and research programs in colleges and independent institutions; studies chiropractic services in the United States; provides international relief and development programs. (Affiliate of the International Chiropractors Assn.)

National Assn. of Spine Specialists, Advocacy, *Washington Office,* 20 F St. N.W., #310, 20001; Philip Schneider, Chair. Toll-free, (888) 960-6277.
Web, www.spineadvocacy.org/Advocacy/About-Us and *Twitter, @SpineAdvocacy*

Membership: physicians, nurse practitioners, nurses, physician assistants, chiropractors, physical therapists, researchers, other health care professionals with an interest in the spine. Monitors legislation and regulations. (Headquarters in Burr Ridge, Ill.)

Dentists

▶**AGENCIES**

Veterans Health Administration (VHA) *(Veterans Affairs Dept.), Dentistry,* 810 Vermont Ave. N.W., 10NC7, 20420; Patricia E. Arola, Assistant Under Secretary. Phone, (800) 698-2411.
Web, www.va.gov/dental and *Email, VHA10NC7Action@va.gov*

Administers and coordinates VA oral health care programs; dental care delivered in a VA setting; administration of oral research, education, and training for VA oral health personnel; delivery of care to VA patients in private practice settings.

▶**NONGOVERNMENTAL**

American College of Dentists, 103 N. Adams St., Rockville, MD 20850; (301) 977-3223.
Dr. Theresa S. Gonzales, Executive Director.
General email, office@acd.org

Web, www.acd.org and *Facebook, www.facebook.com/ College1920*

Honorary society of dentists. Fellows are elected based on their contributions to education, research, dentistry, and community and civic organizations. Organizes ethics seminars, award programs, online courses on leadership and dental ethics, and speaker series.

American Dental Education Assn., 655 K St. N.W., #800, 20001; (202) 289-7201. Fax, (202) 289-7204.
Dr. Karen P. West, President.
General email, adea@adea.org

Web, www.adea.org and *Twitter, @adeaweb*

Membership: U.S. and Canadian dental schools; advanced and allied dental education programs; corporations; and faculty and students. Works to influence education, research, and the delivery of oral health care for the improvement of public health. Provides information on dental teaching and research and on admission requirements of U.S. dental schools; publishes a monthly journal and newsletter. Monitors legislation and regulations.

Dental Trade Alliance, 4350 N. Fairfax Dr., #220, Arlington, VA 22203; (703) 379-7755. Fax, (703) 931-9429. Gregory J. Chavez, Chief Executive Officer.
General email, contact@dentaltradealliance.org

Web, https://dentaltradealliance.org, Twitter, @dtanews and *Facebook, www.facebook.com/Dental-Trade-Alliance-160917053994300*

Membership: dental laboratories and distributors and manufacturers of dental equipment and supplies in the United States, Canada, and Mexico. Collects and disseminates statistical and management information; conducts studies, programs, and projects of interest to the industry; acts as liaison with government agencies.

International Assn. for Dental Research, 1619 Duke St., Alexandria, VA 22314-3406; (703) 548-0066. Fax, (703) 548-1883. Dr. Christopher H. Fox, Chief Executive Officer.
General email, memberservice@iadr.org

Web, www.iadr.org, Facebook, www.facebook.com/ DentalResearch and *Twitter, @IADR*

Membership: professionals engaged in dental research worldwide. Conducts annual convention, conferences, and symposia.

National Dental Assn., 3060 Mitchellville Rd., #215, Leesburg, VA 20716; (240) 241-4448. Fax, (240) 297-9181. Pamela Alston, President; Keith Andrew Perry, Executive Director.
General email, info@ndaonline.org

Web, www.ndaonline.org, Twitter, @NDA1913 and *Facebook, www.facebook.com/ndaonline*

Promotes the interests of ethnic minority dentists through recruitment, educational and financial services, and federal legislation and programs.

Medical Researchers

▶**AGENCIES**

National Institutes of Health (NIH) *(Health and Human Services Dept.), Intramural Training and Education (OITE),* Bldg. 2, 2 Center Dr., #2E04, MS 0230, Bethesda, MD 20892-0240; (301) 693-1281. Fax, (301) 594-9606. Sharon Milgram, Director, (301) 594-2053.
General email, trainingwww@mail.nih.gov

Web, www.training.nih.gov

Administers programs and initiatives to recruit and develop individuals who participate in research training activities on the NIH's campuses. Maintains an interactive website for the various research training programs.

Supports the training mission of the NIH Intramural Research Program through placement, retention, support, and tracking of trainees at all levels, as well as program delivery and evaluation. Administers the NIH Academy, the Summer Internship Program, the Undergraduate Scholarship Program, the Graduate Partnerships Program, and the Postbac and Technical Intramural Research Training Award programs.

▶ **NONGOVERNMENTAL**

Alliance for Regenerative Medicine, *1015 18th St. N.W., #1102, 20036; Janet Lynch Lambert, Chief Executive Officer.*
General email, info@alliancerm.org
Web, www.alliancerm.org and Twitter, @alliancerm

Membership: nationally recognized patient advocacy organizations, academic research institutions, companies, health insurers, financial institutions, foundations, and individuals with life-threatening illnesses and disorders. Acts as advocate for research and technologies in regenerative medicine, including stem cell research and somatic cell nuclear transfer; seeks to increase public understanding. (Formerly Coalition for the Advancement of Medical Research.)

American Assn. for Clinical Chemistry, *900 7th St. N.W., #400, 20001; (202) 857-0717. Fax, (202) 887-5093. Mark J. Golden, Chief Executive Officer. Toll-free, (800) 892-1400.*
General email, info@aacc.org
Web, www.aacc.org, Twitter, @_AACC and Facebook, www.facebook.com/AmerAssocforClinChem

International society of chemists, physicians, and other scientists specializing in clinical chemistry, molecular diagnostics, mass spectrometry, translational medicine, lab management, and other areas of progressing laboratory science. Provides educational and professional development services; presents awards for outstanding achievement. Monitors legislation and regulations.

American Assn. of Immunologists, *1451 Rockville Pike, #650, Rockville, MD 20852; (301) 634-7178. Fax, (301) 634-7887. M. Michele Hogan, Chief Executive Officer.*
General email, infoaai@aai.org
Web, www.aai.org, Twitter, @ImmunologyAAI and Facebook, www.facebook.com/ImmunologyAAI

Membership: scientists working in virology, bacteriology, biochemistry, genetics, immunology, and related disciplines. Conducts training courses and workshops; compiles statistics; participates in international conferences; publishes *The Journal of Immunology*. Monitors legislation and regulations.

American Assn. of Pharmaceutical Scientists, *2107 Wilson Blvd., #200, Arlington, VA 22201; (703) 243-2800. Tina Morris, Executive Director, (703) 248-4701. Customer Service, (877) 998-2277. Public Relations, (703) 248-4740.*
General email, aaps@aaps.org
Web, www.aaps.org, Twitter, @AAPSComms and Facebook, www.facebook.com/americanassociationof pharmaceuticalscientists?filter=1

Membership: pharmaceutical scientists from biomedical, biotechnological, and health care fields. Promotes pharmaceutical sciences as an industry. Represents scientific interests within academia and public and private institutions. Provides forums for scientists to engage in dialogue, networking, and career development. Monitors legislation and regulations.

American Medical Writers Assn., *30 W. Gude Dr., #525, Rockville, MD 20850-4347; (240) 238-0940. Fax, (301) 294-9006. Susan Krug, Executive Director, ext. 109.*
General email, amwa@amwa.org
Web, www.amwa.org, Twitter, @AmMedWriters and Facebook, www.facebook.com/amwa.org

Membership: Provides professional education and additional services to writers, editors, and others in the field of biomedical communication, via workshops, conferences, and online. Also facilitates on-site corporate training.

American Society for Clinical Laboratory Science (ASCLS), *1861 International Dr., #200, McLean, VA 22102; (571) 748-3770. Jim Flanigan, Executive Vice President, (571) 748-3796. Press, (571) 748-3771.*
General email, ascls@ascls.org
Web, www.ascls.org, Twitter, @ASCLS and Facebook, www.facebook.com/ASCLS

Membership: clinical laboratory scientists. Conducts continuing education programs for clinical laboratory scientists and laboratory practitioners. Monitors legislation and regulations.

American Society for Clinical Pathology, *Washington Office, 1225 New York Ave. N.W., #350, 20005-6156; (202) 408-1110. Fax, (202) 408-1101. Dr. Blair Holladay, Chief Executive Officer; Jeff Jacobs, Chief Officer for Science, Technology, and Policy. Customer service for members, (800) 267-2727.*
General email, info@ascp.org
Web, www.ascp.org

Membership: pathologists, residents, and other physicians; clinical scientists; registered certified medical technologists; and technicians. Promotes continuing education, educational standards, and research in pathology. Monitors legislation, regulations, and international research. (Headquarters in Chicago, Ill.)

Assn. of Accredited Naturopathic Medical Colleges, *1717 K St. N.W., #900, 20006; (800) 345-7454. JoAnn Yanez, Executive Director.*
General email, info@aanmc.org
Web, www.aanmc.org, Twitter, @AANMC and Facebook, www.facebook.com/TheAANMC

Membership: accredited schools of naturopathic medicine. Provides database of practicing naturopathic physicians and information on how to become a licensed naturopathic doctor.

Assn. of Public Health Laboratories, *8515 Georgia Ave., #700, Silver Spring, MD 20910; (240) 485-2745. Fax, (240) 485-2700. Scott J. Becker, Chief Executive Officer, (240) 485-2747. Press, (240) 485-2793.*
General email, info@aphl.org
Web, www.aphl.org, Twitter, @APHL and Facebook, www .facebook.com/PublicHealthLabs

Membership: state and local public health, environmental health, agricultural, and food safety laboratories. Offers technical assistance to member laboratories; sponsors educational programs for public health and clinical laboratory practitioners; develops systems for electronic exchange of lab data; develops laboratory system in under-resourced countries. Works with the CDC, FDA, EPA, and other federal partners to support disease detection and surveillance, laboratory response to health crises, quality drinking water, and other public health services.

Board of Registered Polysomnographic Technologists, *4201 Wilson Blvd., 3rd Floor, Arlington, VA 22203; Fax, (703) 940-7227. James Magruder, Chief Executive Officer. Toll-free, (800) 935-8115.*
General email, info@brpt.org
Web, www.brpt.org and Facebook, www.facebook.com/ TheBRPT

Provides sleep credentialing, certification, and education for polysomnographic technologists. Offers continuing-education programs and education opportunities.

Society of Research Administrators International (SRA International), *1560 Wilson Blvd., #310, Arlington, VA 22209; (703) 741-0140. Evan Roberts, Executive Director, ext. 215.*
General email, info@srainternational.org
Web, www.srainternational.org, Twitter, @SocietyRAIntl and Facebook, www.facebook.com/SocResAdminINTL

Membership: scientific and medical research administrators in the United States and other countries. Educates the public about the profession; offers professional development services; sponsors mentoring and awards programs.

Society of Toxicology, *11190 Sunrise Valley Dr., #300, Reston, VA 20191; (703) 438-3115. Myrtle Davis, President.*
General email, SOThq@toxicology.org
Web, www.toxicology.org, Twitter, @SOToxicology and Facebook, www.facebook.com/societyoftoxicology

Membership: scientists from academic institutions, government, and industry worldwide who work in toxicology. Promotes professional development, exchange of information, and research to advance toxicological science.

Nurses and Physician Assistants

National Institute of Nursing Research (NINR) *(National Institutes of Health), Bldg. 31, 31 Center Dr., #5B03,* *Bethesda, MD 20892-2178; (301) 496-0207. Fax, (301) 480-4969. Shannon N. Zenk, Director, (301) 496-8230. Press, (301) 496-0235.*
General email, info@ninr.nih.gov
Web, www.ninr.nih.gov and Twitter, @NINR

Provides grants and awards for nursing research and research training. Research focus includes health promotion and disease prevention, quality of life, health disparities, and end-of-life issues.

American Academy of Physician Assistants (AAPA), *2318 Mill Rd., #1300, Alexandria, VA 22314-1552; (703) 836-2272. Fax, (703) 684-1924. Lisa M. Gables, Chief Executive Officer.*
Web, www.aapa.org, Twitter, @aapaorg, Facebook, www .facebook.com/AAPA.org, Advocacy, advocacy@aapa.org and General email, customercare@aapa.org

Membership: physician assistants and physician assistant students. Sponsors continuing medical education programs for recertification of physician assistants; offers malpractice insurance. Interests include health care reform, quality of care, research, and laws and regulations affecting physician assistant practice and patients. Monitors legislation and regulations.

American Assn. of Colleges of Nursing, *655 K. St. N.W., #750, 20001; (202) 463-6930. Fax, (202) 785-8320. Deborah Trautman, Chief Executive Officer, ext. 227.*
General email, web@aacnnursing.org
Web, www.aacnnursing.org, Twitter, @AACNursing and Facebook, www.facebook.com/AACNursing

Promotes high-quality baccalaureate and graduate nursing education; works to secure federal support of nursing education, nursing research, and student financial assistance; operates databank providing information on enrollments, graduations, salaries, and other conditions in nursing higher education. Interests include international practices.

American College of Nurse-Midwives, *8403 Colesville Rd., #1230, Silver Spring, MD 20910-6374; (240) 485-1800. Fax, (240) 485-1818. Katrina Holland, Chief Executive Officer, (240) 485-1821.*
General email, info@acnm.org
Web, www.midwife.org, Twitter, @ACNMmidwives and Facebook, www.facebook.com/ACNMmidwives

Membership: certified nurse-midwives and certified midwives who preside at deliveries and provide postnatal care or primary gynecological care. Establishes clinical practice studies. Interests include preventive health care for women.

American Nurses Assn., *8515 Georgia Ave., #400, Silver Spring, MD 20910; (301) 628-5000. Fax, (301) 628-5001. Loressa Cole, Chief Executive Officer. Toll-free, (800) 284-2378.*

General email, info@ana.org

Web, http://nursingworld.org, Twitter, @RNAction, Twitter, @ANANursingWorld and Facebook, www .facebook.com/AmericanNursesAssociation

Membership: registered nurses. Promotes high standards of nursing practice, the rights of nurses in the workplace, and a positive and realistic view of nursing. Affiliated organizations include the American Nurses Foundation, the American Academy of Nursing, and the American Nurses Credentialing Center. Monitors legislation and regulations.

National Assn. of Nurse Practitioners in Women's Health, P.O. Box 15837, 20003; (202) 543-9693, ext. 81. Heather Maurer, Chief Executive Officer, ext. 83. General email, info@npwh.org

Web, www.npwh.org and Twitter, @NPWH

Develops standards for nurse practitioner training and practices. Sponsors and provides accreditation of women's health nurse practitioner continuing education programs. Provides the public and government with information on nurse practitioner education, practice, and women's health issues.

National Black Nurses Assn., 8630 Fenton St., #910, Silver Spring, MD 20910-3803; (301) 589-3200. Fax, (301) 589-3223. Millicent Gorham, Executive Director. General email, info@nbna.org

Web, www.nbna.org, Twitter, @NbnaInc and Facebook, www.facebook.com/NBNAORG

Membership: Black nurses from the United States, the eastern Caribbean, and Africa. Fosters improvement in the level of care available to minorities, conducts continuing education programs, and builds relationships with public and private agencies and organizations to exert influence on laws and programs. Conducts and publishes research.

Physical and Occupational Therapy

▶NONGOVERNMENTAL

American Occupational Therapy Assn., 6116 Executive Blvd., #200, Bethesda, MD 20852-4929; (301) 652-6611. Fax, (301) 652-7711. Sherry Keramidas, Executive Director. TTY, (800) 377-8555. Web, www.aota.org, Twitter, @AOTAInc and Facebook, www.facebook.com/AmericanOccupationalTherapy AssociationAOTA

Membership: occupational therapists, occupational therapy assistants, and students. Associate members include businesses and organizations supportive of occupational therapy. Accredits educational programs and credentials occupational therapists. Supports research and sponsors scholarships, grants, and fellowships. Monitors legislation and regulations.

American Physical Therapy Assn., 3030 Potomac Ave., #100, Alexandria, VA 22305-3085; (703) 684-2782. Fax, (703) 684-7343. Justin Moore, Chief Executive Officer. Toll-free, (800) 999-2782.

General email, memberservices@apta.org

Web, www.apta.org, Twitter, @APTAtweets and Facebook, www.facebook.com/AmericanPhysicalTherapyAssociation

Membership: physical therapists, assistants, and students. Establishes professional standards and accredits physical therapy programs; seeks to improve physical therapy education, practice, and research.

Physicians

▶NONGOVERNMENTAL

American Academy of Family Physicians (AAFP), Washington Office, 1133 Connecticut Ave. N.W., #1100, 20036-4342; (202) 232-9033. Fax, (202) 232-9044. Stephanie Quinn, Senior Vice President for Advocacy, Practice Advancement, and Policy. Toll-free, (888) 794-7481.

General email, capitol@aafp.org

Web, www.aafp.org, Twitter, @aafp and Facebook, www .facebook.com/familymed

Membership: family physicians, family practice residents, and medical students. Sponsors continuing medical education programs; promotes family practice residency programs. Monitors legislation and regulations. (Headquarters in Leawood, Kans.)

American Academy of Orthopaedic Surgeons, Government Relations, 317 Massachusetts Ave. N.E., #100, 20002; (202) 546-4430. Fax, (202) 546-5051. Graham H. Newson, Vice President of Government Relations.

General email, dc@aaos.org

Web, www.aaos.org/Advocacy and Twitter, @AAOSAdvocacy

Membership: orthopaedic surgeons and musculoskeletal care professionals. Offers continuing education activities; publishes scientific and medical journals and electronic resources. Engages in health policy and acts as advocate on behalf of orthopaedic surgeons and patients.

American Academy of Otolaryngology—Head and Neck Surgery (AAO-HNS), 1650 Diagonal Rd., Alexandria, VA 22314-2857; (703) 836-4444. Dr. Kathleen L. Yaremchuck, President; Dr. James C. Denneny III, Executive Vice President. Press, (703) 535-3762.

General email, memberservices@entnet.org

Web, www.entnet.org, Twitter, @AAOHNS and Facebook, www.facebook.com/AAOHNS

Membership: otolaryngologists—head and neck surgeons. Supports the advancement of scientific medical research. Provides continuing medical education for members. Monitors legislation, regulations, and international research.

American Assn. of Colleges of Osteopathic Medicine, 7700 Old Georgetown Rd.,#250, Bethesda, MD 20814; (301) 968-4100. Fax, (301) 968-4101. Robert A. Cain, President. Government Relations, (202) 844-4217.

General email, webmaster@aacom.org

Web, www.aacom.org, Twitter, @AACOMGR and Facebook, www.facebook.com/AmericanAssociation collegesOsteopathicMedicine

Administers a centralized application service for osteopathic medical colleges; supports an increase in the number of minority and economically disadvantaged students in osteopathic colleges; maintains an information database; sponsors recruitment programs. Monitors legislation and regulations.

American Assn. of Naturopathic Physicians, *300 New Jersey Ave. N.W., #900, 20001; (202) 237-8150. Laura Farr, Executive Director, (202) 849-6306.*
General email, member.services@naturopathic.org

Web, www.naturopathic.org, Twitter, @AANP and Facebook, www.facebook.com/theAANP

Membership: licensed naturopathic physicians, naturopathic medicine students, and other healthcare professionals allied with the naturopathic profession Promotes naturopathic physician education and acceptance of naturopathic medicine in the nation's health care system.

American Assn. of Neurological Surgeons, *Government Affairs, 25 Massachusetts Ave. N.W., #610, 20001; (202) 628-2072. Fax, (202) 628-5264. Katie O. Orrico, Director, Washington Office, ext. 1.*
General email, info@aans.org

Web, www.aans.org/Advocacy/About-the-Washington-Office, Twitter, @neurosurgery and Facebook, www.facebook.com/neurosurgeryblog

Research and education association dedicated to advancing the specialty of neurological surgery; advocates neurosurgeons' interests in public policy. Publishes the *Journal of Neurosurgery* and other publications and resources. (Headquarters in Rolling Meadows, Ill.)

American College of Cardiology, *Heart House, 2400 N St. N.W., 20037; (202) 375-6000, ext. 5603. Fax, (202) 375-7000. Cathleen C. Gates, Chief Executive Officer. Press, (202) 375-6523. Toll-free, (800) 253-4636, ext. 5603.*
General email, membercare@acc.org

Web, www.acc.org, Twitter, @ACCintouch and Facebook, www.facebook.com/AmericanCollegeofCardiology

Membership: physicians, surgeons, and scientists specializing in cardiovascular health care. Sponsors programs in continuing medical education; collaborates with national and international cardiovascular organizations.

American College of Emergency Physicians, *Public Affairs, 901 New York Ave. N.W., #515E, 20001; (202) 728-0610. Fax, (202) 728-0617. Susan Sedory, Executive Director. Toll-free, (800) 320-0610.*
General email, publicaffairs@acep.org

Web, www.acep.org, Twitter, @acepnow and Facebook, www.facebook.com/ACEPFan

Membership: physicians, residents, and interns. Interests include health care reform, Medicare and Medicaid legislation and regulations, medical liability, overcrowding

in emergency departments, access to emergency care, bioterrorism and terrorism preparedness, managed care, and adult and pediatric emergencies. Disseminates public education materials. Monitors legislation and regulations. (Headquarters in Irving, Tex.)

American College of Obstetricians and Gynecologists, *409 12th St. S.W., 20024-2188 (mailing address: P.O. Box 96920, Washington, DC 20024-9998); (202) 638-5577. Dr. Maureen G. Phipps, Chief Executive Officer. Toll-free, (800) 673-8444.*
General email, communications@acog.org

Web, www.acog.org, Twitter, @acog and Facebook, www.facebook.com/ACOGNational

Membership: medical specialists in obstetrics and gynecology. Disseminates standards of clinical practice and promotes patient involvement in medical care. Provides mentorship programs and educational guidelines. Monitors legislation, regulations, and international research on maternal and child health care.

American College of Oral and Maxillofacial Surgeons (ACOMS), *2001 K St. N.W., 3rd Floor North, 20006; (202) 367-1182. Kurt Gallagher, Executive Director.*
General email, info@acoms.org

Web, www.acoms.org, Twitter, @theACOMS and Facebook, www.facebook.com/theACOMS

Professional association serving the specialty of oral and maxillofacial surgery, the surgical arm of dentistry. Provides continuing education courses; holds an annual conference. Publishes the journal *Oral Surgery, Oral Medicine, Oral Pathology, Oral Radiology.* (Headquarters in Rosemont, Ill.)

American College of Osteopathic Surgeons, *1680 Duke St., #500, Alexandria, VA 22314; (703) 684-0416. Fax, (703) 684-3280. Sonjya Johnson, Chief Executive Officer (Acting), (571) 551-2002. General inquiries, (571) 551-2008. Toll-free, (800) 888-1312.*
General email, info@facos.org

Web, www.facos.org, Twitter, @ACOSurgeons and Facebook, www.facebook.com/American-College-of-Osteopathic-Surgeons-ACOS-502454306437329

Membership: osteopathic surgeons in disciplines of neurosurgery, thoracic surgery, cardiovascular surgery, urology, plastic surgery, and general surgery. Offers members continuing surgical education programs and use of the ACOS-sponsored coding and reimbursement online database. Monitors legislation and regulations.

American College of Preventive Medicine, *1200 1st St. N.W., #315, 20002; (202) 466-2044. Donna Grande, Chief Executive Officer, ext. 118.*
General email, info@acpm.org

Web, www.acpm.org, Twitter, @ACPM_HQ and Facebook, www.facebook.com/AmericanCollegeOfPreventive Medicine

Membership: physicians in general preventive medicine, public health, international health, occupational medicine, and aerospace medicine. Provides educational opportunities; advocates public policies consistent with scientific principles of the discipline; supports the investigation and analysis of issues relevant to the field. Monitors legislation and regulations.

American College of Surgeons, *Advocacy and Health Policy,* *20 F St. N.W., #1000, 20001; (202) 337-2701. Fax, (202) 337-4271. Christian Shalgian, Director; Dr. Frank Opelka, Medical Director of Quality and Health Policy; Dr. Patrick Bailey, Medical Director of Advocacy.*
General email, ahp@facs.org

Web, www.facs.org/advocacy

Monitors legislation and regulations concerning surgery; conducts continuing education programs and sponsors scholarships for graduate medical education. Interests include hospital cancer programs, trauma care, hospital accreditation, and international research. (Headquarters in Chicago, Ill.)

American Health Quality Assn., *818 Connecticut Ave. N.W., #1100, 20006; Alison Shafer Teitelbaum, Executive Director.*
General email, info@ahqa.org

Web, www.ahqa.org, Twitter, @AHQA and Facebook, www.facebook.com/AHQA.org

National network of private Quality Improvement Organizations (QIOs) that seek to improve health care provider performance through quality improvement, technical assistance, provider performance measurement feedback, teaching self-assessment techniques, responding to consumer complaints and appeals, and initiating community-based quality improvement programs. Monitors legislation and regulations.

American Medical Assn. (AMA), *Government Relations,* *25 Massachusetts Ave. N.W., #600, 20001-7400; (202) 789-7400. Fax, (202) 789-7485. Dr. James L. Madara, Chief Executive Officer. Toll-free, (800) 621-8335.*
Web, www.ama-assn.org, Twitter, @AmeriMedicalAssn and Facebook, www.facebook.com/AmericanMedical Association

Membership: physicians, residents, and medical students. Provides information on the medical profession and health care; cooperates in setting standards for medical schools and hospital intern and residency training programs; offers physician placement service and counseling on management practices; provides continuing medical education. Interests include international research and peer review. Monitors legislation and regulations. (Headquarters in Chicago, Ill.)

American Osteopathic Assn., *Advocacy Center,* *1090 Vermont Ave. N.W., #500, 20005; (888) 626-9262. Fax, (202) 544-3525. Dr. Joseph A. Giaimo, President; David J. Pugach, Senior Vice President of Public Policy.*
General email, info@osteopathic.org

Web, https://osteopathic.org/about/advocacy, Twitter, @AOAforDOs and Facebook, www.facebook/com/osteopathicphysicians

Membership: osteopathic physicians. Promotes public health, education, and research; accredits osteopathic educational institutions. Monitors legislation and regulations. (Headquarters in Chicago, Ill.)

American Podiatric Medical Assn., *9312 Old Georgetown Rd., Bethesda, MD 20814; (301) 581-9200. Fax, (301) 530-2752. Dr. James R. Christina, Chief Executive Officer; Dr. Jeffrey DeSantis, President.*
Web, www.apma.org, Twitter, @APMA and Facebook, www.facebook.com/theAPMA

Membership: podiatrists in affiliated and related societies. Interests include advocacy in legislative affairs, health policy and practice, scientific meetings, and public education.

American Psychiatric Assn., *800 Maine Ave. S.W., #900, 20024; (202) 559-3900. Dr. Saul Levin, Medical Director. Press, (202) 459-9732. Publishing toll-free, (800) 368-5777. Toll-free, (888) 357-7924.*
General email, apa@psych.org

Web, www.psychiatry.org, Twitter, @APAPsychiatric and Facebook, www.facebook.com/AmericanPsychiatric Association

Membership: psychiatrists. Promotes availability of high-quality psychiatric care; provides the public with information; assists state and local agencies; conducts educational programs for professionals and students in the field; participates in international meetings and research. Library open to members.

American Roentgen Ray Society, *44211 Slatestone Court, Leesburg, VA 20176-5109; (703) 729-3353. Fax, (703) 729-4839. Jonathan Kruskal, President. Toll-free, (866) 940-2777.*
General email, info@arrs.org

Web, www.arrs.org, Twitter, @ARRS_Radiology and Facebook, www.facebook.com/AmericanRoentgenRay Society

Membership: physicians and researchers in radiology and allied sciences. Publishes research; conducts conferences; presents scholarships and awards; monitors international research.

American Society of Addiction Medicine, *11400 Rockville Pike, #200, Rockville, MD 20852; (301) 656-3920. Fax, (301) 656-3815. Julia L. Chang, Executive Vice President.*
General email, email@asam.org

Web, www.asam.org, Twitter, @ASAMorg and Facebook, www.facebook.com/addictionmedicine

Membership: physicians and medical students. Supports the study and provision of effective treatment and care for people with alcohol and drug dependencies; educates physicians. Monitors legislation and regulations.

American Society of Nuclear Cardiology (ASNC), *9302 Lee Hwy., #1210, Fairfax, VA 22031; (703) 459-2555. Fax, (301) 215-7113. Kathleen Flood, Chief Executive Officer.*
General email, info@asnc.org

Web, www.asnc.org and Twitter, @MyASNC

Membership: physicians, scientists, technologists, and other professionals engaged in nuclear cardiology practice or research. Provides professional education programs; establishes standards and guidelines for training and practice; promotes research worldwide. Works with agreement states to monitor user-licensing requirements of the Nuclear Regulatory Commission.

American Society of Transplant Surgeons, *1401 S. Clark St., #1120, Arlington, VA 22202; (703) 414-7870. Fax, (703) 414-7874. Maggie Kebler-Bullock, Executive Director.*
General email, asts@asts.org
Web, www.asts.org, Twitter, @ASTSchimera and Facebook, www.facebook.com/AmericanSocietyof TransplantSurgeons

Promotes education and research on organ and tissue transplantation for patients with end-stage organ failure. Provides information for policy decisions affecting the practice of transplantation. Offers professional development for transplant colleagues.

Assn. of American Medical Colleges (AAMC), *655 K St. N.W., #100, 20001-2399; (202) 828-0400. Fax, (202) 828-1125. Dr. David J. Skorton, President.*
General email, aacas@aamc.org
Web, www.aamc.org, Twitter, @AAMCtoday and Facebook, www.facebook.com/aamctoday

Membership: accredited U.S. and Canadian schools of medicine, teaching hospitals, health systems, academic and scientific societies, medical students and faculty, and residents and resident physicians. Administers Medical College Admission Test.

College of American Pathologists, *Advocacy Division, 1001 G St. N.W., #425 West, 20001; (202) 354-7100. Steven Myers, Chief Executive Officer; John H. Scott, Vice President for Advocacy. Toll-free, (800) 392-9994.*
Web, www.cap.org, Twitter, @Pathologists and Facebook, www.facebook.com/capathologists

Membership: physicians who are board certified in clinical or anatomic pathology. Accredits laboratories and provides them with proficiency testing programs; promotes the practice of pathology and laboratory medicine worldwide. Monitors legislation and regulations. (Headquarters in Northfield, Ill.)

National Medical Assn., *8403 Colesville Rd., #820, Silver Spring, MD 20910; (202) 347-1895. Martin Hamlette, Executive Director.*
Web, www.nmanet.org and Twitter, @NationalMedAssn

Membership: physicians of African descent. Supports increased participation of minorities in the health professions, especially medicine.

Physician-Led Healthcare for America (PHA), *105 E. St., S.E., 20003 (mailing address: 455 Carriage Lane, Hudson, WI 54016); (202) 367-1113. Fax, (202) 367-2113. (419) 250-5873. Stacie Monroe, Executive Director, (419) 250-5873. phone, (419) 250-5873.*

General email, info@physicianled.us
Web, www.physicianhospitals.org, Twitter, @physicianhosp and Facebook, www.facebook.com/Physician-Hospitals-of-America-113375608966/?ref=ts

Membership organization acting as advocate for the physician-owned hospital industry; provides networking and continuing education opportunities.

Physicians Committee for Responsible Medicine (PCRM), *5100 Wisconsin Ave. N.W., #400, 20016; (202) 686-2210. Fax, (202) 686-2216. Dr. Neal Barnard, President. Press, (202) 524-7316.*
General email, pcrm@pcrm.org
Web, www.pcrm.org, Twitter, @PCRM, Facebook, www .facebook.com/PCRM.org and President, Twitter, @DrNealBarnard

Membership: health care professionals, medical students, and laypersons interested in preventive medicine, nutrition, and higher standards in research. Conducts clinical research, educational programs, and public information campaigns; advocates more effective and compassionate health-related policies in government and in public and private institutions.

Society of Thoracic Surgeons, *Advocacy, 20 F St. N.W., #310C, 20001-6702; (202) 787-1230. Fax, (202) 280-1477. John C. Calhoun, President.*
Web, www.sts.org/advocacy, Twitter, @STS_CTsurgery, Facebook, www.facebook.com/societyofthoracicsurgeons and YouTube, www.youtube.com/user/ThoracicSurgeons/ videos

Membership: surgeons, researchers, and allied health care professionals in cardiothoracic surgery. Monitors legislation and regulations. (Headquarters in Chicaco, Ill.)

Veterinarians

▶AGENCIES

Animal and Plant Health Inspection Service (APHIS) *(Agriculture Dept.), Veterinary Services, 4700 River Rd., #39, Riverdale, MD 20737; (301) 851-3300 ext. 2. Rosemary Sifford, Deputy Administrator.*
General email, nvap@aphis.usda.gov
Web, www.aphis.usda.gov/aphis/ourfocus/animalhealth

Regulates veterinary biologics, including vaccines, bacterins, antisera, diagnostic kits, and other products of biological origin, to ensure that the veterinary biologics available for the diagnosis, prevention, and treatment of animal diseases are pure, safe, potent, and effective. Provides veterinary training materials and veterinarian accrediation.

Food and Drug Administration (FDA) *(Health and Human Services Dept.), Center for Veterinary Medicine (CVM), 7500 Standish Pl., HFV-1, Rockville, MD 20855-0001; (240) 402-7002. Fax, (240) 276-9001. Steven Solomon, Director.*

General email, askcvm@fda.hhs.gov

Web, www.fda.gov/animalveterinary and *Twitter, @FDAanimalhealth*

Regulates the manufacture and distribution of drugs, food additives, feed, and devices for livestock and pets. Conducts research; works to ensure animal health and the safety of food derived from animals.

National Zoological Park *(Smithsonian Institution), 3001 Connecticut Ave. N.W., 20008 (mailing address: DEVS, P.O. Box 37012, MS 5516, Washington, DC 20013-7012); (202) 633-4888 (recorded information line). Steven Monfort, Director. Guest services, (202) 633-2614. Membership office, (202) 633-2922. Press, (202) 633-3055.*

Web, www.nationalzoo.si.edu, Twitter, @NationalZoo, Facebook, www.facebook.com/nationalzoo and *YouTube, www.youtube.com/SmithsonianNZP*

Conducts research on animal behavior, ecology, nutrition, reproductive physiology, pathology, and veterinary medicine. Houses a unit of the Smithsonian Institution library open to qualified researchers by appointment. Interlibrary loans available.

▶NONGOVERNMENTAL

American Veterinary Medical Assn., *Governmental Relations, 1910 Sunderland Pl. N.W., 20036-1642; Fax, (202) 223-4877. Dr. Janet D. Donlin, Executive Director. Toll-free, (800) 321-1473.*

Web, www.avma.org and *Twitter, @AVMAvets*

Monitors legislation and regulations that influence animal and human health and advance the veterinary medical profession. (Headquarters in Schaumburg, Ill.)

Assn. of American Veterinary Medical Colleges (AAVMC), *655 K St. N.W., #725, 20005-3536; (202) 371-9195. Fax, (202) 842-0773. Dr. Andrew T. Maccabe, President.*

Web, www.aavmc.org and *Twitter, @AAVMC*

Membership: U.S., Canadian, and international schools and colleges of veterinary medicine, departments of comparative medicine, and departments of veterinary science in agricultural colleges. Produces veterinary reports; provides information about scholarships and continuing education programs and sponsors conferences on veterinary medical issues.

Vision Care

▶AGENCIES

National Eye Institute (NEI) *(National Institutes of Health), 31 Center Dr., #6A32, MS 2510, Bethesda, MD 20892-2510; (301) 496-5248. Dr. Michael F. Chiang, Director.*

General email, 2020@nei.nih.gov

Web, www.nei.nih.gov, Twitter, @NatEyeInstitute, Facebook, www.facebook.com/NationalEyeInsttitute and *YouTube, www.youtube.com/user/neinih*

Conducts and supports research, training, health information dissemination, and other programs with respect to blinding eye diseases, visual disorders, mechanisms of visual function, preservation of sight, and the special health problems and requirements of the blind.

▶NONGOVERNMENTAL

American Academy of Ophthalmology, *Governmental Affairs, 20 F St. N.W., #400, 20001-6701; (202) 737-6662. Fax, (202) 737-7061. Catherine G. (Cathy) Cohen, Vice President for Government Affairs.*

General email, politicalaffairs@aao.org

Web, www.aao.org, Twitter, @AcademyEyeSmart and *Facebook, www.facebook.com/AcademyEyeSmart*

Membership: eye physicians and surgeons. Provides information on eye diseases. Monitors legislation, regulations, and international research. (Headquarters in San Francisco, Calif.)

American Optometric Assn., *Washington Office, 1505 Prince St., #300, Alexandria, VA 22314-2874; (703) 739-9200. Fax, (703) 739-9497. Jon Hymes, Executive Director, (703) 837-1371. Toll-free, (800) 365-2219.*

General email, jfhymes@aoa.org

Web, www.aoa.org, Twitter, @AOAConnect and *Facebook, www.facebook.com/American.Optometric.Association*

Membership: optometrists, optometry students, and paraoptometric assistants and technicians in a federation of state, student, and armed forces optometric associations. Sets professional standards and provides research and information on eye care to the public. Monitors legislation and regulations and acts as liaison with international optometric groups and government optometrists; conducts continuing education programs for optometrists and provides information on eye care. (Headquarters in St. Louis, Mo.)

American Society of Cataract and Refractive Surgery, *12587 Fair Lakes Circle, #348, Fairfax, VA 22033; (703) 591-2220. Fax, (703) 591-0614. Richard S. Hoffman, President.*

Web, www.ascrs.org, Twitter, @ASCRStweets and *Facebook, www.facebook.com/MyASCRS*

Membership: more than 9,000 ophthalmologists who specialize in cataract and refractive surgery. Offers educational programs and services to its members. Monitors regulations affecting ophthalmic practices. Sponsors independent research. Maintains a foundation dedicated to improving public understanding of ophthalmology and providing eye care to underserved parts of the world.

Assn. for Research in Vision and Ophthalmology (ARVO), *5515 Security Lane, #500, Rockville, MD 20852; (240) 221-2900. Fax, (240) 221-0370. Iris M. Rush, Executive Director.*

General email, arvo@arvo.org

Web, www.arvo.org and *Twitter, @ARVOinfo*

Promotes eye and vision research; issues awards for significant research and administers research grant program.

Assn. of Schools and Colleges of Optometry, *6110 Executive Blvd., #420, Rockville, MD 20852-3942; (301) 231-5944. Fax, (301) 770-1828. Dawn Mancuso, Executive Vice President, ext. 3016.*
General email, slau@opted.org

Web, www.optometriceducation.org, Twitter, @OptometricED and Facebook, www.facebook/OptometricEducation

Membership: U.S. and Puerto Rican optometry schools and colleges and foreign affiliates. Provides information about the Optometry College Admission Test to students. Supports the international development of optometric education. Monitors legislation and regulations.

Eye Bank Assn. of America, *1101 17th St. N.W., #400, 20036; (202) 775-4999. Fax, (202) 429-6036. Kevin P. Corcoran, President, ext. 113.*
General email, info@restoresight.org

Web, www.restoresight.org and Twitter, @restoresight

Membership: eye banks in Brazil, Canada, England, Japan, Saudi Arabia, Taiwan, and the United States. Sets and enforces medical standards for processing, storing, evaluating, and distributing ocular and corneal tissue for transplantation; seeks to increase donations to eye, tissue, and organ banks; conducts training and certification programs for eye bank Surgeons and technicians; compiles statistics; accredits eye banks.

International Eye Foundation, *10801 Connecticut Ave., Kensington, MD 20895; (240) 290-0263. Fax, (240) 290-0269. John Barrows, President.*
General email, contact@iefusa.org

Web, www.iefusa.org, Twitter, @iefusa and Facebook, www.facebook.com/iefusa

Operates blindness prevention programs focusing on cataracts, trachoma, "river blindness," and childhood blindness, including vitamin A deficiency. Provides affordable ophthalmic instruments, equipment, and supplies to eye hospitals in developing countries to help lower surgical costs. Works to strengthen management and financial sustainability of eye hospitals and clinics in developing countries. Works with the World Health Organization, ministries of health, and international and indigenous organizations in Africa, Asia, Latin America, and eastern Europe to promote eye care.

The Vision Council, *225 Reinekers Lane, #700, Alexandria, VA 22314; (703) 548-4560. Fax, (703) 548-4580. Ashley Mills, Chief Executive Officer. Toll-free, (866) 826-0290.*
General email, info@thevisioncouncil.org

Web, www.thevisioncouncil.org, Twitter, @opticalindustry and Facebook, www.facebook.com/thevisioncouncil

Sponsors trade shows and public relations programs for the ophthalmic industry. Educates the public on developments in the optical industry. Represents manufacturers and distributors of optical products and equipment.

The Vision Council, *Lab Division, 225 Reinekers Lane, #700, Alexandria, VA 22314; (703) 548-4560. Fax, (703)*
740-2244. Ashley Mills, Chief Executive Officer, (703) 740-1101; Michael Vitale, Lab Division Liaison, (703) 548-2684. Toll-free, (866) 826-0290.
General email, info@thevisioncouncil.org

Web, https://thevisioncouncil.org/divisions

Membership: optical laboratories. Promotes the eyewear industry; collects and disseminates lab performance data; sponsors conferences. Monitors legislation and regulations. (Affiliated with The Vision Council.)

HEALTH SERVICES FOR SPECIAL GROUPS

General

▶**AGENCIES**

Eunice Kennedy Shriver National Institute of Child Health and Human Development (NICHD) *(National Institutes of Health), National Center for Medical Rehabilitation Research (NCMRR), 6710B Rockledge Dr., Room 2107, MS 7002, Bethesda, MD 20817; (301) 496-9233. Theresa Hayes Cruz, Director.*
Web, www.nichd.nih.gov/about/org/ncmrr

Supports research to foster the development of scientific knowledge needed to enhance the health, productivity, independence, and quality of life of persons with disabilities. Supports research and research training on pathophysiology and management of chronically injured nervous and musculoskeletal systems (including stroke, traumatic brain injury, spinal cord injury, and orthopedic conditions); repair and recovery of motor and cognitive function; functional plasticity, adaptation, and windows of opportunity for rehabilitative interventions; rehabilitative strategies; pediatric rehabilitation; secondary conditions associated with chronic disabilities; improved diagnosis, assessment, and outcome measures; and development of orthotics, prosthetics, and other assistive technologies and devices.

Federal Bureau of Prisons *(Justice Dept.), Health Services Division, 320 1st St. N.W., 20534; (202) 307-3055. Rear Adm. Chris Bina, Assistant Director.*
Web, www.bop.gov/about/agency/org_hsd.jsp

Administers health care and treatment programs for prisoners in federal institutions.

Health Resources and Services Administration (HRSA) *(Health and Human Services Dept.), Bureau of Primary Health Care (BPHC), 5600 Fishers Lane, #16W29, Rockville, MD 20857; (301) 594-4110. James Macrae, Associate Administrator. Helpline, (877) 974-2742.*
Web, www.bphc.hrsa.gov

Funds health centers in underserved communities; develops health policies and programs to increase primary and preventive healthcare access and eliminate health disparities.

National Institute on Deafness and Other Communication Disorders (NIDCD) *(National Institutes of Health)*, 31 Center Dr., #3C02, MS 2320, Bethesda, MD 20892-2320; (301) 827-8183. Fax, (301) 402-0018. Debara L. Tucci, Director, (301) 402-0900. Evenings and weekends, (301) 496-3315. Interpreter service, (301) 496-1807. Toll-free, (800) 241-1044. TTY, (800) 241-1055.
General email, nidcdinfo@nidcd.nih.gov
Web, www.nidcd.nih.gov and Twitter, @nidcd

Conducts and supports research and research training and disseminates information on hearing disorders and other communication processes, including diseases that affect hearing, balance, smell, taste, voice, speech, and language. Monitors international research.

National Institute on Minority Health and Health Disparities (NIMHD) *(National Institutes of Health)*, 2 Democracy Plaza, 6707 Democracy Blvd., #800, MS 5465, Bethesda, MD 20892-5465; (301) 402-1366. Fax, (301) 480-4049. Dr. Eliseo J. Perez-Stable, Director.
General email, nimhdinfo@nimhd.nih.gov
Web, www.nimhd.nih.gov, Twitter, @NIMHD, Facebook, www.facebook.com/NIMHD and YouTube, www.youtube.com/channel/UC24wExXe2ynSniF-iKYTQaw

Promotes minority health and leads, coordinates, supports, and assesses the NIH's effort to eliminate health disparities. Conducts and supports basic clinical, social, and behavioral research; promotes research infrastructure and training; fosters emerging programs; disseminates information; and reaches out to minority and other communities suffering from health disparities.

Special Education and Rehabilitative Services (OSERS) *(Education Dept.), Rehabilitation Services Administration (RSA)*, Lyndon B. Johnson Bldg., 400 Maryland Ave. S.W., 20202-7100; (202) 245-7468. Fax, (202) 245-7591. Carol Dobak, Commissioner (Acting).
Web, https://rsa.ed.gov

Allocates funds to state agencies and nonprofit organizations for programs serving eligible physically and mentally disabled persons; services provided by these funds include medical and psychological treatment as well as the establishment of supported-employment programs.

U.S. Immigration and Customs Enforcement (ICE) *(Homeland Security Dept.), ICE Health Service Corps*, 500 12th St. S.W., 2nd Floor, 20536; (202) 732-4600. Dr. Stewart D. Smith, Assistant Director, (202) 732-3047. Web, www.ice.gov/detain/ice-health-service-corps

Consists of U.S. Public Health Service commissioned officers, federal civil servants, and contract support staff. Administers ICE's detainee health care program, providing direct care to detained aliens at designated facilities and overseeing medical care at other detention facilities.

▶CONGRESS

For a listing of relevant congressional committees and subcommittees, please see pages 362–363 or the Appendix.

▶NONGOVERNMENTAL

Assn. of Clinicians for the Underserved (ACU), 1575 Eye St. N.W., #300, 20005; (844) 422-8247. Fax, (703) 562-8801. Amanda Pears Kelly, Executive Director, (202) 834-2592.
General email, acu@clinicians.org
Web, www.clinicians.org, Twitter, @ACUUnderserved and Facebook, www.facebook.com/Cliniciansforthe Underserved/

Membership: clinicians, advocates, and health care organizations. Works to improve the health of underserved populations and eliminate health disparities in the United States. Educates and supports health care clinicians serving these populations. Interests include health care access, transdisciplinary approaches to health care, workforce development and diversity, pharmaceutical access, and health information technology.

Catholic Health Assn. of the United States, 1675 Eye St. N.W., #550, 20006; (202) 296-3993. Fax, (202) 296-3997. Sr. Mary Haddad, RSM, President.
Web, www.chausa.org, Twitter, @TheCHAUSA and Facebook, www.facebook.com/catholichealthassociation

Concerned with the health care needs of the poor and disadvantaged. Promotes health care reform, including universal insurance coverage, and more cost-effective, affordable health care. (Headquarters in St. Louis, Mo.)

National Assn. of Community Health Centers, 7501 Wisconsin Ave., #1100W, Bethesda, MD 20814; (301) 347-0400. Tom Van Coverden, President.
Web, www.nachc.org, Twitter, @NACHC and Facebook, www.facebook.com/nachc

Membership: community, migrant, public housing, and homeless health centers. Represents America's federally qualified health centers. Seeks to ensure the continued development of community health care programs through policy analysis, research, technical assistance, publications, education, and training.

National Health Law Program, *Washington Office,* 1444 Eye St. N.W., #1105, 20005; (202) 289-7661. Elizabeth G. Taylor, Executive Director.
General email, nhelp@healthlaw.org
Web, www.healthlaw.org, Twitter, @NHelp-org and Facebook, www.facebook.com/NHeLProgram

Organization of lawyers representing the economically disadvantaged and minorities. Offers technical assistance, workshops, seminars, and training for health law specialists. Issues include health care reform, medicaid, child and adolescent health, and disability and reproductive rights.

Minority Health

▶AGENCIES

Agency for Healthcare Research and Quality (AHRQ) *(Health and Human Services Dept.)*, 5600 Fishers Lane,

National Institutes of Health

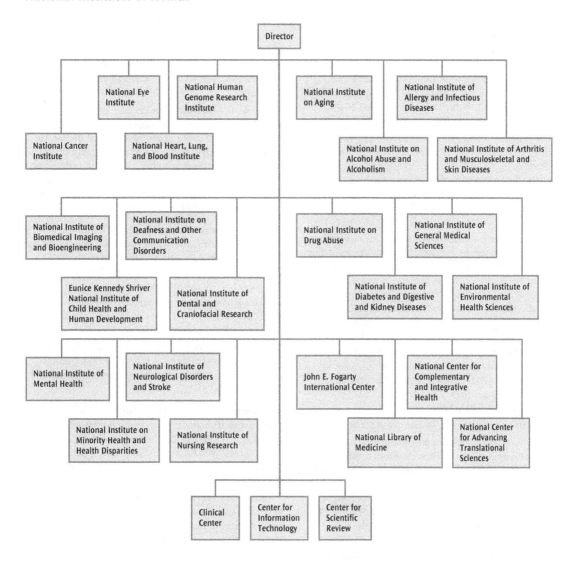

```
                                    Director
```

National Eye Institute

National Human Genome Research Institute

National Institute on Aging

National Institute of Allergy and Infectious Diseases

National Cancer Institute

National Heart, Lung, and Blood Institute

National Institute on Alcohol Abuse and Alcoholism

National Institute of Arthritis and Musculoskeletal and Skin Diseases

National Institute of Biomedical Imaging and Bioengineering

National Institute on Deafness and Other Communication Disorders

National Institute on Drug Abuse

National Institute of General Medical Sciences

Eunice Kennedy Shriver National Institute of Child Health and Human Development

National Institute of Dental and Craniofacial Research

National Institute of Diabetes and Digestive and Kidney Diseases

National Institute of Environmental Health Sciences

National Institute of Mental Health

National Institute of Neurological Disorders and Stroke

John E. Fogarty International Center

National Center for Complementary and Integrative Health

National Institute on Minority Health and Health Disparities

National Institute of Nursing Research

National Library of Medicine

National Center for Advancing Translational Sciences

Clinical Center

Center for Information Technology

Center for Scientific Review

7th Floor, Rockville, MD 20857; (301) 427-1104. Robert Otto (Bob) Valdez, Director, (301) 427-1200. Congressional Affairs, (301) 427-1214. Press, (301) 427-1364. TTY, (888) 586-6340.
General email, info@ahrq.gov

Web, www.ahrq.gov, Twitter, @AHRQNews and Facebook, www.facebook.com/ahrq.gov

Researches health care quality among minorities. Identifies and devises solutions for disparities in access to care, diagnosis, and treatment of illness. Provides health care professionals with research on minority health.

Assistant Secretary for Health (OASH) *(Health and Human Services Dept.), Office of Minority Health (OMH),* *1101 Wootton Pkwy., #100, Rockville, MD 20852; (240) 453-2882. Fax, (240) 453-2883. Dr. Felicia Collins, Director. Toll-free, (800) 444-6472.*

General email, info@minorityhealth.gov

Web, http://minorityhealth.hhs.gov, Twitter, @MinorityHealth and Facebook, www.facebook.com/minorityhealth

Oversees the implementation of the secretary's Task Force on Black and Minority Health and legislative mandates; develops programs to meet the health care needs of minorities; awards grants to coalitions of minority community organizations.

Centers for Medicare and Medicaid Services (CMS) *(Health and Human Services Dept.), Minority Health (OMH),* *7500 Security Blvd., S2-12-17, Baltimore, MD 21244; (410) 786-6842. Dr. LaShawn McIver, Director, (410) 786-6842.*

General email, omh@cms.hhs.gov

Web, www.cms.gov/About-CMS/Agency-Information/CMSLeadership/Office_OMH.html

Seeks to reduce inequalities in health outcomes of minority and disadvantaged populations. Manages disparities data and evaluates impact; coordinates minority health initiatives within the agency; serves as the liaison to other agency offices of minority health.

Food and Drug Administration (FDA) *(Health and Human Services Dept.), Minority Health and Health Equity (OMHHE), White Oak Bldg. 1, 10903 New Hampshire Ave., #4239, Silver Spring, MD 20993-0002; (240) 402-5084. Fax, (301) 847-3536. Rear Adm. Richardae Araojo, Associate Commissioner, (301) 796-1152.*
General email, omh@fda.hhs.gov

Web, www.fda.gov/aboutfda/centersoffices/oc/officeof minorityhealth/default.htm and *Twitter, @FDAHealthEquity*

Serves as the principal adviser to the Commissioner on minority health and health disparities. Provides leadership and direction in identifying agency actions that can help reduce health disparities, including the coordination of efforts across the agency. Promotes effective communication and the dissemination of information to the public, particularly underserved, vulnerable populations.

Health and Human Services Dept. (HHS), *Civil Rights (OCR), 200 Independence Ave. S.W., #509F, 20201; (202) 619-0403. Fax, (202) 619-3437. Lisa J. Pino, Director. Toll-free, (800) 368-1019. TTY, (800) 537-7697.*
General email, OCRMail@hhs.gov

Web, www.hhs.gov/ocr and *Twitter, @HHSOCR*

Administers and enforces laws prohibiting discrimination on the basis of race, color, sex, national origin, religion, age, or disability in programs receiving federal funds from the department; authorized to discontinue funding. Enforces the Health Insurance Portability and Accountability Act (HIPAA); Privacy, Security, and Breach Notification rules; and the Patient Safety Act and Rules.

Health and Human Services Dept. (HHS), *Minority Health (OMH), Tower Oaks Bldg., 1101 Wootton Pkwy., #600, Rockville, MD 20852; (240) 453-2882. Fax, (240) 251-2160. Rear Adm. (Dr.) Felicia Collins, Deputy Assistant Secretary / Director. Press, (202) 690-6343. Toll-free, (800) 444-6472. TTY, (301) 251-1432.*
General email, info@minorityhealth.hhs.gov

Web, www.minorityhealth.hhs.gov, *Twitter, @minorityhealth* and *Facebook, www.facebook.com/ minorityhealth*

Promotes improved health among racial and ethnic minority populations. Advises the Health and Human Services Dept. secretary and the Office of Public Health and Science on public health program activities affecting American Indian and Alaska Native, Black/African American, Asian American, Pacific Islander, Native Hawaiian, and Hispanic populations. Awards grants to programs and projects that address minority health issues, including prevention projects to administer health promotion, education, and disease-prevention programs.

Health and Human Services Dept. (HHS), *Minority Health Resource Center (OMH Resource Center), 1101 Wooton Parkway, #650, Rockville, MD 20852; (301) 251-1797. Fax, (301) 251-2160. Vacant, Program Operations Director. Toll-free, (800) 444-6472. TTY, (301) 251-1432.*
General email, info@minorityhealth.hhs.gov

Web, www.minorityhealth.hhs.gov/omh/browse.aspx?lvl= 1&lvlid=3

Serves as a national resource and referral service on minority health issues. Provides information on health topics such as substance abuse, cancer, heart disease, violence, diabetes, HIV/AIDS, and infant mortality. Provides free services, including online document collections, database and funding searches, customized responses to requests for information, publications, and referrals regarding racial and ethnic minority populations.

Health and Human Services Dept., *White House Initiative on Asian Americans, Native Hawaiians, and Pacific Islanders, 550 12th St. S.W., 10th Floor, 20202; (202) 482-1375. Krystal Ka'ai, Executive Director.*
General email, whiaanhpi@hhs.gov

Web, www.commerce.gov/whiaapi and *Twitter, @whitehouseAAPI*

Works to increase Asian American, Native Hawaiian, and Pacific Islander participation in federal health programs. Interests include reducing health risks, improving access to high-quality health care, and promoting healthful living.

Health Resources and Services Administration (HRSA) *(Health and Human Services Dept.), Bureau of Primary Health Care (BPHC), 5600 Fishers Lane, #16W29, Rockville, MD 20857; (301) 594-4110. James Macrae, Associate Administrator. Helpline, (877) 974-2742.*
Web, www.bphc.hrsa.gov

Advises the associate administrator for primary care on public health activities affecting ethnic, racial, and other minority groups, including migrant and seasonal farmworkers, homeless persons, persons living in public housing, older adults, and women.

Health Resources and Services Administration (HRSA) *(Health and Human Services Dept.), Health Equity (OHE), 5600 Fishers Lane, #1270, Rockville, MD 20857; (301) 443-3238. Fax, (301) 443-7853. Michelle Allender, Director, (301) 443-2042.*
General email, ask@hrsa.gov

Web, www.hrsa.gov/about/organization/bureaus/ohe

Sponsors programs and activities that address the special health needs of socially disadvantaged and underserved populations. Advises the administrator on minority health issues affecting the Health Resources and Services Administration (HRSA) and policy development; collects data on minority health activities within HRSA; represents HRSA programs affecting the health of racial and ethnic minorities to the health community and organizations in the public, private, and international sectors.

Indian Health Service (IHS) *(Health and Human Services Dept.), 5600 Fishers Lane, Rockville, MD 20857;*

(301) 443-3593. Elizabeth A. Fowler, Director (Acting), (301) 443-1083. TTY, (301) 443-6394.
Web, www.ihs.gov, Twitter, @IIHSgov, Facebook, www.facebook.com/IndianHealthService and Public Affairs email, newsroom@ihs.gov

Acts as the health advocate for and operates hospitals and health centers that provide preventive, curative, and community health care for Native Americans and Alaska Natives.

National Institute on Minority Health and Health Disparities (NIMHD) (National Institutes of Health),

2 Democracy Plaza, 6707 Democracy Blvd., #800, MS 5465, Bethesda, MD 20892-5465; (301) 402-1366. Fax, (301) 480-4049. Dr. Eliseo J. Perez-Stable, Director.
General email, nimhdinfo@nimhd.nih.gov
Web, www.nimhd.nih.gov, Twitter, @NIMHD, Facebook, www.facebook.com/NIMHD and YouTube, www.youtube.com/channel/UC24wExXe2ynSniF-iKYTQaw

Promotes minority health and leads, coordinates, supports, and assesses the NIH's effort to eliminate health disparities. Conducts and supports basic clinical, social, and behavioral research; promotes research infrastructure and training; fosters emerging programs; disseminates information; and reaches out to minority and other communities suffering from health disparities.

► NONGOVERNMENTAL

Asian and Pacific Islander American Health Forum,

Government Relations, 1629 K St. N.W., #400, 20006; (202) 466-7772. Fax, (202) 296-0610. Juliet K. Choi, Vice President Policy and Advocacy (Washington DC).
General email, info@apiahf.org
Web, www.apiahf.org and Twitter, @apiahf

Works to improve the health status of and access to care by Asian Americans and Pacific Islanders and to address health disparities, including disability and mental health, HIV/AIDS, smoking, and cancer. Monitors legislation in the areas of health, politics, and social and economic issues that affect Asian Americans, native Hawaiians, and Pacific Islanders. (Headquarters in Oakland, Calif.)

Black Women's Health Imperative, 700 Pennsylvania

Ave. S.E., #2059, 20003; (202) 787-5931.
Linda Goler Blount, President.
General email, imperative@bwhi.org
Web, www.bwhi.org, Twitter, @blkwomenshealth and Facebook, www.facebook.com/BlackWomensHealth Imperative

Provides the tools and information for African American women to prevent health problems, to recognize symptoms and early warning signs, and to understand all of the options available for their specific health situations. Achieves these ends through community outreach, advocacy, resources and research, education, and mobilization. (Formerly the National Black Women's Health Project.)

National Alliance for Hispanic Health, 1501 16th St.

N.W., 20036-1401; (202) 387-5000. Fax, (202) 797-4353.

Jane L. Delgado, President. Toll-free, (866) 783-2645. Toll-free in Spanish, (866) 783-2645.
General email, info@healthyamericas.org
Web, www.healthyamericas.org, Twitter, @Health4Americas and Facebook, www.facebook.com/healthyamericas

Acts as advocate and conducts research to improve the health of Hispanics; promotes research and philanthropy; develops capacity of community-based health and social service organizations. Educates consumers on family and prenatal health, diabetes, depression, ADHD, immunization, HIV/AIDS, women's health, osteoporosis, tobacco control, and environmental health.

National Black Nurses Assn., 8630 Fenton St., #910, Silver

Spring, MD 20910-3803; (301) 589-3200. Fax, (301) 589-3223. Millicent Gorham, Executive Director.
General email, info@nbna.org
Web, www.nbna.org, Twitter, @NbnaInc and Facebook, www.facebook.com/NBNAORG

Membership: Black nurses from the United States, the eastern Caribbean, and Africa. Fosters improvement in the level of care available to minorities.

National Council of Urban Indian Health, 924

Pennsylvania Ave. S.E., 20003; (202) 544-0344.
Francys Crevier, Corporate Executive Officer.
Web, www.ncuih.org, Twitter, @NCUIH_Official, Facebook, www.facebook.com/NCUIH and YouTube, www.youtube.com/channel/UCxaqrokRFUBz_xRof5pjcsw

Membership: Indian health care providers. Supports accessible, high-quality health care programs for American Indians and Alaska Natives living in urban communities. Provides education and training. Monitors legislation and funding.

National Hispanic Medical Assn., 1920 L St. N.W., #725,

20036; (202) 628-5895. Fax, (202) 628-5898.
Dr. Elena V. Rios, President.
General email, nhma@nhmamd.org
Web, www.nhmamd.org, Twitter, @NHMAmd and Facebook, www.facebook.com/NHMAmd.org

Provides policymakers and health care providers with information and support to strengthen the delivery of health care to Hispanic communities in the United States. Areas of interest include high-quality care and increased opportunities in medical education for Latinos. Works with federal officials, other Hispanic advocacy groups, and Congress to eliminate disparities in health care for minorities.

National Minority AIDS Council (NMAC), 1000 Vermont

Ave. N.W., #200, 20005; (202) 815-3129. Paul A. Kawata, Executive Director, (202) 277-2777.
General email, communications@nmac.org
Web, www.nmac.org

Works to build the capacity of small faith- and community-based organizations delivering HIV/AIDS services in communities of color. Holds national conferences; administers treatment and research programs and training; disseminates electronic and printed resource materials; conducts public policy advocacy.

Older Adults

►AGENCIES

Centers for Medicare and Medicaid Services (CMS) *(Health and Human Services Dept.), Center for Clinical Standards and Quality (CCSQ), Nursing Homes (DNH),* 7500 Security Blvd., C2-23-17, Baltimore, MD 21244; (410) 786-8403. Evan Shulman, Director.
Wweb, www.cms.gov/Medicare/Provider-Enrollment-and-Certification/GuidanceforLawsAndRegulations/Nursing-Homes

Monitors compliance of nursing homes with government standards. Focus includes quality of care, environmental conditions, and participation in Medicaid and Medicare programs.

Centers for Medicare and Medicaid Services (CMS) *(Health and Human Services Dept.), Center for Medicaid and CHIP Services (CMCS), Disabled and Elderly Health Programs Group (DEHPG),* 7500 Security Blvd., S2-14-26, Baltimore, MD 21244; (410) 786-4699. Alissa Deboy, Director.
Web, www.medicaid.gov and www.cms.gov/About-CMS/Agency-Information/CMSLeadership/Office-CMCSC

Reviews all benefit and pharmacy state plan amendments for all Medicaid populations, Medicaid managed-care delivery systems, home-based and community-based services, and long-term services. Supports transformation grant programs, including Money Follows the Person and the Balancing Incentive Program.

National Institute on Aging (NIA) *(National Institutes of Health),* Bldg. 31, 31 Center Dr., #5C27, MS 2292, Bethesda, MD 20892-2292; (301) 496-9265. Fax, (301) 496-2525. Dr. Richard J. Hodes, Director. Alzheimer's Disease Education and Referral Center, (800) 438-4380. Information Center, (800) 222-2225. Press, (301) 496-1752. TTY, (800) 222-4225.
General email, niaic@nih.gov
Web, www.nia.nih.gov and Twitter, @nihaging

Conducts and supports biomedical, social, and behavioral research and training related to the aging process and the diseases and special problems of the aged. Manages the Alzheimer's Disease Education and Referral Center (www.alzheimers.nia.nih.gov).

Veterans Health Administration (VHA) *(Veterans Affairs Dept.), Geriatrics and Extended Care,* 810 Vermont Ave. N.W., #10P4G, 20420; (202) 461-6750. Fax, (202) 495-5167. Dr. Catherine McVearry Kelso, Deputy Executive Director; Scotte R. Hartronft, Executive Director.
Web, www.va.gov/geriatrics

Administers research, educational, and clinical health care programs in geriatrics at VA and community nursing homes, in personal care homes, in VA domiciliaries, in state veterans' homes, and in home-based and other non-institutional care.

►NONGOVERNMENTAL

AARP, 601 E St. N.W., 20049; (202) 434-2277. Jo Ann C. Jenkins, Chief Executive Officer. Library, (202) 434-6233. Membership, toll-free, (800) 566-0242. Press, (202) 434-2560. Toll-free, (888) 687-2277. TTY, (877) 434-7598. Toll-free Spanish, (877) 342-2277. TTY Spanish, (866) 238-9488.
General email, dcaarp@aarp.org
Web, www.aarp.org, Twitter, @AARP and Facebook, www.facebook.com/AARP

Membership: people 50 years of age and older. Promotes healthy living for older adults and disseminates information about the Affordable Care Act and health care laws, health products, health and life insurance, and brain and mental health. Offers member discounts on health care needs, including prescriptions and glasses.

AARP, *Federal Health and Family Advocacy,* 601 E St. N.W., 20049; (202) 434-3770. Megan O'Reilly, Director, (202) 434-6987.
Web, www.aarp.org

Maintains the Legal Counsel for the Elderly, which acts as advocate on behalf of older residents of the District of Columbia who reside in nursing homes and board and care homes. Monitors legislation and regulations.

Alliance for Aging Research, 1700 K St. N.W., #740, 20006; (202) 293-2856. Sue Peschin, President.
General email, info@agingresearch.org
Web, www.agingresearch.org, Twitter, @Aging_Research and Facebook, www.facebook.com/AllianceforAging Research

Membership: senior corporate and foundation executives, science leaders, and congressional representatives. Citizen advocacy organization that seeks to improve the health and independence of older Americans through public and private research. Monitors legislatioon and research.

Alliance for Retired Americans, 815 16th St. N.W., 4th Floor, 20006-4104; (202) 637-5399. Robert Roach Jr., President.
Web, https://retiredamericans.org, Twitter, @ActiveRetirees, Facebook, www.facebook.com/retiredamericans and email, communications@retiredamericans.org

Membership; Supports expansion of Medicare, improved health programs, national health care, and reduced cost of drugs. Nursing Home Information Service provides information on nursing home standards and regulations. Monitors legislation and regulations. (Affiliate of the AFL-CIO.)

Alzheimer's Assn., *Public Policy Office,* 1212 New York Ave. N.W., #800, 20005-6105; (202) 393-7737. Joanne Pike, President; Robert J. Egge, Chief of Public Policy, ext. 8660.
General email, advocateinfo@alz.org
Web, www.alz.org, Twitter, @alzassociation, Facebook, www.facebook.com/actionalz and Virtual library, www.alz.org/library

Works with lawmakers to advance policies and improve the lives of those affected by dementia, including the Comphensive Care for Alzheimers Act. Offers family support services and educates the public about Alzheimer's disease, a neurological disorder mainly affecting the brain tissue in older adults. Promotes research and long-term care protection and coverage; maintains liaison with Alzheimer's associations abroad. Monitors legislation and regulations. (Headquarters in Chicago, Ill.)

American Assn. for Geriatric Psychiatry, *6728 Old McLean Village Dr., McLean, VA 22101; (703) 556-9222. Fax, (703) 556-8729. Rebecca Morgan, Executive Director. General email, main@aagponline.org*

Web, www.aagponline.org, Twitter, @GeriPsyc and Facebook, www.facebook.com/GeriPsyc

Works to improve the practice of geriatric psychiatry and mental health through professional education, public advocacy, and support for career development for clinicians, educators, and researchers. Monitors legislation and regulations. Publishes the *American Journal of Geriatric Psychiatry.*

American Society of Consultant Pharmacists (ASCP), *1240 N. Pitt St., #300, Alexandria, VA 22314-3563; (703) 739-1300. Chad Worz, Executive Director. Toll-free, (800) 355-2727. General email, info@ascp.com*

Web, www.ascp.com, Twitter, @ASCPharm and Facebook, www.facebook.com/ascpharm

Membership: dispensing and clinical pharmacists with expertise in therapeutic medication management for geriatric patients; provides services to long-term care facilities, institutions, and hospices as well as older adults in assisted-living and home-based care. Monitors legislation and regulations.

Gerontological Society of America, *1220 L St. N.W., #901, 20005-4018; (202) 842-1275. James Appleby, Chief Executive Officer, (202) 587-2821. General email, geron@geron.org*

Web, www.geron.org, Twitter, @geronsociety and Facebook, www.facebook.com/geronsociety

Membership; Scientific organization of researchers, educators, and professionals in the field of aging. Promotes the study of aging and the application of research to public policy. Interests include health and civic engagement.

Leading Age, *2519 Connecticut Ave. N.W., 20008-1520; (202) 783-2242. Katie Smith Sloan, Chief Executive Officer. Press, (202) 508-9407. General email, info@leadingage.org*

Web, www.leadingage.org, Twitter, @LeadingAge and Facebook, www.facebook.com/LeadingAge

Membership: nonprofit nursing homes, housing, and health-related facilities for the elderly sponsored by religious, fraternal, labor, private, and governmental organizations. Conducts research on long-term care for the elderly; sponsors institutes and workshops on accreditation, financing, and institutional life. Monitors legislation and regulations.

National Assn. for Home Care and Hospice, *228 7th St. S.E., 20003; (202) 547-7424. Fax, (202) 547-3540. William A. Dombi, President, ext. 3203; Calvin McDaniel, Director Government Affairs, ext. 3283. General email, info@nahc.org*

Web, www.nahc.org, Twitter, @OfficialNAHC and Facebook, www.facebook.com/NAHC.org

Membership: hospice, home care, and private-duty providers. Advocates the rights of the aged, disabled, and ill to remain independent in their own homes as long as possible. Monitors legislation and regulations.

National Caucus and Center on Black Aging, Inc., *1220 L St. N.W., #800, 20005-2407; (202) 637-8400. Fax, (202) 347-0895. Karyne Jones, President.*

Web, https://ncba-aging.org, Twitter, @NCBA1970 and Facebook, www.facebook.com/ncba.aging.5

Concerned with issues that affect older Black Americans and other minorities. Sponsors employment and housing programs for older adults and education and training for professionals in gerontology. Monitors legislation and regulations.

National Council on Aging, *251 S. 18th St., #500, Arlington, VA 22202; (571) 527-3900. Ramsey Alwin, President, ext. 1. Eldercare locator, (800) 677-1116. General email, kathleen.zuke@ncoa.org*

Web, www.ncoa.org, Twitter, @NCOAging, Facebook, www.facebook.com/NCOAging and YouTube, www.youtube.com/user/ncoaging

Promotes the physical, mental, and emotional health of older persons and studies adult day care and community-based long-term care. Monitors legislation and regulations.

National Hispanic Council on Aging, *2201 12th St. N.W., #101, 20009; (202) 347-9733. Fax, (202) 853-3803. Yanira Cruz, President. General email, nhcoa@nhcoa.org*

Web, www.nhcoa.org, Twitter, @NHCOA, Facebook, www.facebook.com/NHCOA and YouTube, www.youtube.com/user/NHCOA

Membership: senior citizens, health care workers, professionals in the field of aging, and others in the United States and Puerto Rico who are interested in topics related to Hispanics and aging. Provides research training, policy analysis, consulting, and technical assistance; sponsors seminars, workshops, and management internships.

National Long-Term Care Ombudsman Resource Center, *1025 Connecticut Ave. N.W. #1000, 20036; (202) 332-2275. Fax, (202) 332-2949. Amity Overall Laib, Director. General email, ombudcenter@theconsumervoice.org*

Web, www.ltcombudsman.org

Provides technical assistance, management guidance, policy analysis, and program development information on behalf of state and substate ombudsman programs.

(Affiliate of the National Consumer Voice for Quality Long-Term Care.)

Prenatal, Maternal, and Child Health Care

▶ AGENCIES

Assistant Secretary for Health (OASH) *(Health and Human Services Dept.), Population Affairs (OPA)*, 200 Independence Ave. S.W., 20201; (240) 453-2800. (240) 453-2846. Fax, (240) 453-2801. Jessica Swafford Marcella, Deputy Assistant Secretary.
General email, opa@hhs.gov
Web, www.hhs.gov/opa and Twitter, @hhspopaffairs

Supports and evaluates teen pregnancy prevention programs; coordinates HHS efforts related to adolescent health promotion and disease prevention.

Centers for Medicare and Medicaid Services (CMS) *(Health and Human Services Dept.), Center for Medicaid and CHIP Services (CMCS)*, 7500 Security Blvd., C5-21-17, Baltimore, MD 21244; (202) 690-7428. Daniel Tsai, Deputy Administrator, (202) 260-1064.
Web, www.cms.gov/About-CMS/Agency-Information/CMSLeadership/office_CMCSC and www.medicaid.gov

Develops health care policies and programs for needy children under Medicaid; works with the Public Health Service and other related agencies to coordinate the department's child health resources. (Known as the Children's Health Insurance Program.)

Environmental Protection Agency (EPA), *Children's Health Protection (OCHP)*, 1301 Constitution Ave. N.W., #1144, MC 1107T, 20460; (202) 564-4583. Fax, (202) 564-2733. Jeanne Briskin, Director.
Web, www2.epa.gov/aboutepa/about-office-childrens-health-protection-ochp and www.epa.gov/children

Supports and facilitates the EPA's efforts to protect children's health from environmental risks through safe chemicals management. Provides leadership on interagency Healthy Homes Work Group and Healthy School Environments Initiative. Offers grants through the Office of Children's Health Protection and Environmental Education (OCHPEE).

Eunice Kennedy Shriver National Institute of Child Health and Human Development (NICHD) *(National Institutes of Health)*, Bldg. 31, 31 Center Dr., #2A03, MS 2425, Bethesda, MD 20892-2425 (mailing address: NICHD Information Resource Center, P.O. Box 3006, Rockville, MD 20847); Dr. Diana W. Bianchi, Director. Press, (301) 496-5133. Toll-free, (800) 370-2943. Toll-free fax, (866) 760-5947.
General email, nichdinformationresourcecenter@mail.nih.gov
Web, www.nichd.nih.gov, Twitter, @NICHD_NIH, Facebook, www.facebook.com/nichdgov and Press email, nichdpress@mail.nih.gov

Supports and conducts research in biomedical, behavioral, and social sciences related to child, fetal, and maternal health, medical rehabilitation, and reproductive sciences. Interests include demography, social sciences, and population dynamics; male/female fertility and infertility; developing and evaluating contraceptive methods; safety and efficacy of pharmaceuticals for pregnant women, infants, and children; maternal/pediatric HIV/AIDS infections (including HIV/AIDS and Zika), transmission, and treatment-associated infections; pediatric growth and endocrine research; child development and behavior; developmental biology, typical and atypical development; intellectual and developmental disabilities; gynecologic health conditions, including pelvic floor disorders; pregnancy, labor, and delivery; fetal and infant health; sudden infant death syndrome (SIDS); childhood injury and critical illness; genetics, genomics, and rare diseases; epidemiology and biostatistics; health behavior; medical rehabilitation, including brain injury, stroke, and spinal cord injury, cerebral palsy, and spina bifida.

Eunice Kennedy Shriver National Institute of Child Health and Human Development (NICHD) *(National Institutes of Health), Division of Extramural Research (DER), Child Development and Behavior Branch (CDBB)*, 6710B Rockledge Dr., Room 2113, MS 7002, Bethesda, MD 20817; (301) 435-2307. James Griffin, Chief.
Web, www.nichd.nih.gov/about/org/der/branches/cdbb

Develops scientific initiatives and supports research and research training relevant to the psychological, neurocognitive, physical, social-emotional, and behavioral development and health of children. Major research areas include effects of technology and digital media use on children and adolescent development; neurodevelopment, neuroplasticity, and sensitive periods; use of neurocognitive sensitive periods and rick/protective factors to inform targeted prevention and treatment strategies; understanding social determinants of health and developmentally informed strategies to mitigate health disparities.

Eunice Kennedy Shriver National Institute of Child Health and Human Development (NICHD) *(National Institutes of Health), Division of Extramural Research (DER), Developmental Biology and Structural Variation Branch (DBSVB)*, 6710B Rockledge Dr., Room 2442, MS 7002, Bethesda, MD 20817; (301) 451-1390. Fax, (301) 480-0303. James Coulombe, Chief.
Web, www.nichd.nih.gov/about/org/der/branches/dbsvb

Supports research and training focused on understanding the biological processes that control normal embryonic development, as well as the mechanisms that underlie molecular susceptibility and etiology of structural birth defects. Major program areas for the branch include developmental genetics, systems developmental biology, early embryonic development, biophysics/biomechanics of development, developmental neurobiology and neural, organogenesis, regenerative biology, stem cells biology, and structural birth defects.

Eunice Kennedy Shriver National Institute of Child Health and Human Development (NICHD) *(National Institutes of Health), Division of Extramural Research (DER), Maternal and Pediatric Infectious Disease Branch (MPIDB),* 6710B Rockledge Dr., Room 2146, MS 7002, Bethesda, MD 20817; (301) 594-4783. Fax, (301) 480-3882. Dr. Sonia S. Lee, Chief (Acting).
Web, www.nichd.nih.gov/about/org/der/branches/mpidb

Supports and conducts research into the epidemiology, natural history, pathogenesis, transmission, diagnosis, treatment, and prevention of infections, including congenital infections such as Zika and cytomegalovirus; emerging infectious diseases; and vaccine-preventable disease in infants, children, adolescents, and women.

Eunice Kennedy Shriver National Institute of Child Health and Human Development (NICHD) *(National Institutes of Health), Division of Extramural Research (DER), Obstetric and Pediatric Pharmacology and Therapeutics Branch (OPPTB),* 6710B Rockledge Dr., Room 2334, MS 7002, Bethesda, MD 20817; (301) 451-7299. Aaron Pawlyk, Chief.
Web, www.nichd.nih.gov/about/org/der/branches/opptb

Promotes basic, translational, and clinical research to improve the safety and efficacy of therapeutics, such as pharmaceuticals, drugs, biologics, medical devices, and regenerative tissue constructs. Develops and supports an understanding of how to appropriately treat disease during pregnancy, the post-partum period, infancy, childhood, adolescence, and the transition from adolescence to adulthood, using therapeutic approaches, to assure that medications are appropriately tested for dosing, safety, and effectiveness within their target populations.

Eunice Kennedy Shriver National Institute of Child Health and Human Development (NICHD) *(National Institutes of Health), Division of Extramural Research (DER), Pediatric Growth and Nutrition Branch (PGNB),* 6710B Rockledge Dr., Room 2444, MS 7002, Bethesda, MD 20817; (301) 402-7886. Dr. Andrew Bremer, Chief.
Web, www.nichd.nih.gov/about/org/der/branches/pgnb

Supports research on understanding basic and clinical aspects of growth and development, including the biological processes that underlie normal growth and development, as well as research on how these biological processes go awry. Major research programs include how nutrition promotes healthy growth and development; lactation and breastfeeding; the causes of obesity in childhood and sequelae of childhood obesity in adulthood; the genetic, nutritional, and hormonal antecedents of bone health and the origins of osteoporosis; the neuroendocrine basis of growth and the onset of puberty; and the development of the hypothalamo-pituitary adrenal, gonadal, and thyroid axes.

Eunice Kennedy Shriver National Institute of Child Health and Human Development (NICHD) *(National Institutes of Health), Division of Extramural Research (DER), Pediatric Trauma and Critical Illness Branch (PTCIB),* 6710B Rockledge Dr., Room 2336, MS 7002, Bethesda, MD 20817; (301) 496-1514. Valerie Maholmes, Chief.
Web, www.nichd.nih.gov/about/org/der/branches/ptcib

Supports research and research training focused on preventing, treating, and reducing all forms of childhood trauma, injury, and critical illness across the continuum of care. Topics of interest include respiratory failure, multiple organ dysfunction syndrome, traumatic brain injury, sepsis, end-of-life issues in pediatric intensive care unit populations, child maltreatment, violence, and other causes of severe traumatic injury.

Eunice Kennedy Shriver National Institute of Child Health and Human Development (NICHD) *(National Institutes of Health), Division of Extramural Research (DER), Pregnancy and Perinatology Branch (PPB),* 6710B Rockledge Dr., Room 2444, MS 7002, Bethesda, MD 20817; (301) 402-7886. Dr. Andrew Bremer, Chief (Acting).
Web, www.nichd.nih.gov/about/org/der/branches/ppb

Supports research to improve the health of women before, during, and after pregnancy; reduce the number of preterm births and other birth complications; increase infant survival free from disease and disability; and ensure the long-term health of mothers and their children. Supports training grants for medical researchers in maternal-fetal medicine, neonatology, and related fields.

Food and Drug Administration (FDA) *(Health and Human Services Dept.), Clinical Policy and Programs (OCPP), Pediatric Therapeutics (OPT),* White Oak Bldg. 32, 10903 New Hampshire Ave., #5150, Silver Spring, MD 20993-0002; (301) 796-8659. Fax, (301) 847-8640. Dr. Dionna Green, Director, (301) 796-1543.
General email, opt@fda.hhs.gov
Web, www.fda.gov/about-fda/office-clinical-policy-and-programs/office-pediatric-therapeutics

Works to provide timely access to medical products proven to be safe and effective for children. Designs clinical studies that expand the knowledge of pediatrics.

Health Resources and Services Administration (HRSA) *(Health and Human Services Dept.), Maternal and Child Health Bureau (MCHB),* 5600 Fishers Lane, #18W, Rockville, MD 20857; (301) 443-2170. Dr. Michael Warren, Associate Administrator.
Web, www.mchb.hrsa.gov

Administers programs for prenatal, maternal, and child health care. Funds block grants to states for mothers and children and for children with special health needs; awards funding for research training, genetic disease testing, counseling and information dissemination, hemophilia diagnostic and treatment centers, and demonstration projects to improve the health of mothers and children. Interests also include emergency medical services for children, universal newborn hearing screening, and traumatic brain injury.

Health Resources and Services Administration (HRSA) *(Health and Human Services Dept.), National Vaccine Injury Compensation Program (VICP),* Parklawn Bldg., 5600 Fishers Lane, #08N146B, Rockville, MD 20857; (301) 443-6593. (800) 338-2382. Tamara Overby, Director (Acting).
General email, vaccinecompensation@hrsa.gov
Web, www.hrsa.gov/vaccine-compensation/index.html

Provides a no-fault alternative to the traditional legal system for resolving vaccine injury petitions for individuals thought to be injured by certain childhood vaccines; including rotavirus vaccine; diphtheria and tetanus toxoids and pertussis vaccine; measles, mumps, and rubella vaccine; varicella, hepatitis A and B, HiB vaccine; oral polio and inactivated polio vaccines; and influenza, pneumococcal conjugate, meningococcal, and human papillomavirus vaccines.

▶NONGOVERNMENTAL

American Academy of Child and Adolescent Psychiatry (AACAP), *3615 Wisconsin Ave. N.W., 20016-3007; (202) 966-7300. Fax, (202) 464-0131. Heidi B. Fordi, Executive Director. Government Affairs, govaffairs@aacap.org*
Web, www.aacap.org, Twitter, @aacap and Facebook, www.facebook.com/American-Academy-of-Child-Adolescent-Psychiatry-145459865751

Membership: child and adolescent psychiatrists trained to promote healthy development and to evaluate, diagnose, and treat children, adolescents, and families affected by mental illness. Sponsors annual meeting and review for medical board examinations. Provides information, advocacy, education, and research on child and adolescent development and mental illnesses. Monitors international research and U.S. legislation concerning children with mental illness.

American Academy of Pediatrics, *Federal Affairs, 601 13th St. N.W., #400N, 20005; (202) 347-8600. Fax, (202) 393-6137. Mark Del Monte, Chief Executive Officer. General email, kids1st@aap.org*
Web, www.aap.org, Twitter, @AmerAcadPeds and Facebook, www.facebook.com/AmerAcadPeds

Advocates maternal and child health legislation and regulations. Interests include increased access and coverage for persons under age twenty-one, immunizations, injury prevention, environmental hazards, child abuse, emergency medical services, biomedical research, Medicaid, disabilities, pediatric AIDS, substance abuse, and nutrition. (Headquarters in Itasca, IL.)

American College of Nurse-Midwives, *8403 Colesville Rd., #1230, Silver Spring, MD 20910-6374; (240) 485-1800. Fax, (240) 485-1818. Katrina Holland, Chief Executive Officer, (240) 485-1821. General email, info@acnm.org*
Web, www.midwife.org, Twitter, @ACNMmidwives and Facebook, www.facebook.com/ACNMmidwives

Membership: certified nurse-midwives and certified midwives who preside at deliveries and provide postnatal care or primary gynecological care. Establishes clinical practice studies. Interests include preventive health care for women.

American College of Obstetricians and Gynecologists, *409 12th St. S.W., 20024-2188 (mailing address: P.O. Box 96920, Washington, DC 20024-9998); (202) 638-5577. Dr. Maureen G. Phipps, Chief Executive Officer. Toll-free, (800) 673-8444.*

General email, communications@acog.org
Web, www.acog.org, Twitter, @acog and Facebook, www.facebook.com/ACOGNational

Membership: medical specialists in obstetrics and gynecology. Disseminates standards of clinical practice and promotes patient involvement in medical care. Provides mentorship programs and educational guidelines. Monitors legislation, regulations, and international research on maternal and child health care.

Assn. of Maternal and Child Health Programs (AMCHP), *1825 K St. N.W., #250, 20006; (202) 775-0436. Fax, (202) 478-5120. Terrance E. Moore, Chief Executive Officer, (202) 486-5991. General email, info@amchp.org*
Web, www.amchp.org, Twitter, @DC_AMCHP and Facebook, www.facebook.com/AMCHPofficlal/

Membership: state public health leaders and others. Works to improve the health and well-being of women, children, and youth, including those with special health care needs and their families.

Assn. of Women's Health, Obstetric, and Neonatal Nurses (AWHONN), *1800 M St. N.W.,#7405, 20036; (202) 261-2400. Fax, (202) 728-0575. Jonathan Webb, Chief Executive Officer. Customer Service, (800) 354-2268. Toll-free, (800) 673-8499. General email, customerservice@awhonn*
Web, www.awhonn.org, Twitter, @AWHONN and Facebook, www.facebook.com/AWHONN

Membership: Promotes the health of women and newborns. Provides nurses with information and support. Produces educational materials and legislative programs.

Children's Defense Fund, *840 1st St. N.E., #300, 20002; (202) 628-8787. Rev. Dr. Starsky Wilson, President. Press, (202) 662-3554. General email, cdfinfo@childrensdefense.org*
Web, www.childrensdefense.org, Twitter, @ChildDefender and Facebook, www.facebook.com/ChildrensDefenseFund

Advocacy group concerned with programs for children and youth. Assesses adequacy of the Early and Periodic Screening, Diagnosis, and Treatment Program for Medicaid-eligible children. Promotes adequate prenatal care for adolescent and lower-income women; works to prevent adolescent pregnancy.

Children's Hospital Assn., *Washington Office, 600 13th St. N.W., #500, 20005; (202) 753-5500. Fax, (202) 347-5147. Mark Wietecha, Chief Executive Officer. General email, mbrsvcs@childrenshospitals.org*
Web, www.childrenshospitals.org, Twitter, @hospitals4kids and Facebook, www.facebook.com/childrenshospitals

Promotes education and research on child health care related to more than 220 children's hospitals in the United States and internationally; compiles statistics and provides information on pediatric hospitalizations.

Guttmacher Institute, *Public Policy, 1301 Connecticut Ave. N.W., #700, 20036-3902; (202) 296-4012.*

Information Sources on Women's Health

ABCD After Breast Cancer Diagnosis, (800) 977-4121;
www.abcdbreastcancersupport.org

HIVinfo (NIH), (800) 448-0440; www.hivinfo.nih.gov

American College of Obstetricians and Gynecologists,
(202) 638-5577; (800) 673-8444; www.acog.org

American Society for Reproductive Medicine,
(205) 978-5000; (202) 863-4985 www.asrm.org

Guttmacher Institute, www.guttmacher.org

**Health Resources and Services Administration (HRSA),
Maternal and Child Health (HHS),** (301) 443-2170;
www.mchb.hrsa.gov

Healthfinder (HHS), www.healthfinder.gov

Lamaze International, (202) 367-1128; www.lamaze.org

MedlinePlus (NIH), www.medlineplus.gov/women.html

National Breast Cancer Coalition, (202) 296-7477;
(800) 622-2838; www.stopbreastcancer.org

National Cancer Institute (NIH), (800) 422-6237;
www.cancer.gov

National Center for Health Research (202) 223-4000;
www.center4research.org

National Institute of Mental Health (866) 615-6464;
www.nimh.nih.gov/health/topics/women-and-mental-
health/index.shtml

National Institute on Aging (NIH), Information Center,
(800) 222-2225; www.nia.nih.gov

Bone Health and Osteoporosis Foundation,
(202) 223-2226 or (800) 231-4222;
www.bonehealthandosteoporosis.org

National Women's Health Network, (202) 682-2640;
www.nwhn.org

Office on Women's Health (HHS), (202) 690-7650;
(800) 994-9662; www.womenshealth.gov

Planned Parenthood Federation of America,
(202) 347-8500; www.plannedparenthood.org

U.S. National Library of Medicine (NIH), (301) 594-5983;
www.nlm.nih.gov

Fax, (202) 223-5756. Herminia Palacio, President; Heather D. Boonstra, Vice President for Public Policy. Toll-free, (877) 823-0262.
General email, info@guttmacher.org
Web, www.guttmacher.org, Twitter, @Guttmacher and Facebook, www.facebook.com/Guttmacher

Conducts research, policy analysis, and public education in reproductive health issues, including maternal and child health. (Headquarters in New York.)

Healthy Teen Network, *P.O. Box 741, Churchville, MD 21028; (410) 685-0410. Janet Max, President.*
General email, info@healthyteennetwork.org
Web, www.healthyteennetwork.org, Twitter, @healthyteen and Facebook, www.facebook.com/healthyteennetwork

Membership: health and social work professionals, community and state leaders, and individuals. Promotes services to prevent and resolve problems associated with adolescent sexuality, pregnancy, and parenting. Helps to develop stable and supportive family relationships through program support and evaluation. Monitors legislation and regulations.

Lamaze International, *2001 K St. N.W., 3rd Floor, 20006; (202) 367-1128. Fax, (202) 367-2128. Sarah Chilton, Operation Manager, (202) 367-2413.*
General email, info@lamaze.org
Web, www.lamaze.org, Twitter, @LamazeOnline and Facebook, www.facebook.com/LamazeChildbirth

Membership: supporters of the Lamaze philosophy of childbirth, including parents, physicians, childbirth educators, and other health professionals. Trains and certifies Lamaze educators. Provides referral service for parents seeking Lamaze classes.

March of Dimes, *Government Affairs, 1550 Crystal Dr., #1300, Arlington, VA 22202; (202) 659-1800. Adrian P. Mollo, General Counsel. Toll-free, (888) 663-4637.*
Web, www.marchofdimes.org/advocacy-and-government-affairs-issues-and-advocacy-priorities.aspx, Twitter, @MarchofDimes and Email, askus@marchofdimes.org

Works to prevent birth defects, low birth weight, and infant mortality. Awards grants for research and provides funds for treatment of birth defects. Medical services grantees provide prenatal counseling. Monitors legislation and regulations. (Headquarters in White Plains, N.Y.)

The National Alliance to Advance Adolescent Health, *5335 Wisconsin Ave., N.W. # 440, 20015; (202) 769-0486. Margaret A. McManus, President.*
General email, jshorr@thenationalalliance.org
Web, www.thenationalalliance.org, Twitter, @TheNatlAlliance and Facebook, www.facebook.com/The.National.Alliance/

Seeks to increase adolescents' access to integrated physical, behavioral, and sexual health care and insurance coverage - to reduce health risk behaviors, identify health problems earlier, and equip adolescents to manage their health conditions. Promotes expanded comprehensive clinical and community prevention health strategies for adolescents. Helps with transition to adult care.

National Assn. of School Psychologists, *4340 East-West Hwy., #402, Bethesda, MD 20814; (301) 657-0270. Fax, (301) 657-0275. Kathleen Minke, Executive Director. Toll-free, (866) 331-6277.*
Web, www.nasponline.org and Twitter, @nasponline

Membership: graduate education students and professors, school psychologists, supervisors of school psychological services, and others who provide mental health services for children in school settings. Provides professional education and development to members. Provides school safety and crisis response direct services. Fosters information exchange; advises local, state, and federal policymakers and agencies that develop children's mental health educational services. Develops professional ethics and standards.

National Center for Education in Maternal and Child Health, *3300 Whitehaven St. N.W., 2007-2292 (mailing address: Georgetown University, Box 571272, Washington, DC 20057-1272); (202) 784-9552. Rochelle Mayer, Director; Olivia Pickett, Director of Library Services.*
General email, mchnavigator@ncemch.org

Web, www.ncemch.org, Twitter, @NCEMCH and Facebook, www.facebook.com/NCEMCH

Collects and disseminates information about maternal and child health to health professionals and the general public. Carries out special projects for the U.S. Maternal and Child Health Bureau. Library open to the public by appointment. (Affiliated with McCourt School of Public Policy, Georgetown University.)

National Organization on Fetal Alcohol Syndrome, *1200 Eton Court N.W., 3rd Floor, 2007; (202) 785-4585. Fax, (202) 466-6456. Tom Donaldson, President. Toll-free, (800) 666-6327.*
General email, information@nofas.org

Web, www.nofas.org and Twitter, @nofas_usa

Works to eradicate fetal alcohol syndrome and alcohol-related birth defects through public education, conferences, medical school curricula, and partnerships with federal programs interested in fetal alcohol syndrome.

Zero to Three: National Center for Infants, Toddlers, and Families, *2445 M St. N.W., #600, 20037; (202) 638-1144. Fax, (202) 638-0851. Matthew Melmed, Executive Director. Toll-free, (800) 899-4301.*
General email, 0to3@presswarehouse.com

Web, www.zerotothree.org, Twitter, @zerotothree and Facebook, www.facebook.com/ZEROTOTHREE

Works to improve infant and toddler health, mental health, and development. Sponsors training programs for professionals, offers fellowships, and publishes books, curricula, assessment tools, videos, and practical guidebooks. Supports parents with practical resources and provides private and government organizations with information on early childhood development issues.

Women's Health

▶**AGENCIES**

Assistant Secretary for Health (OASH) *(Health and Human Services Dept.), Women's Health (OWH),* *200 Independence Ave. S.W., #712E, 20201; (202) 690-7650. Fax, (202) 205-2631. Dr. Dorothy Fink, Director. Information, (800) 994-9662. TTY, (888) 220-5446.*

General email, womenshealth@hhs.gov

Web, www.womenshealth.gov, www.girlshealth.gov, Twitter, @womenshealth and Facebook, www.facebook.com/HHSOWH/

Promotes better health for girls and women as well as health equity through sex/gender-specific approaches. Methods include educating health professionals and motivating behavior change in consumers through the dissemination of health information.

Eunice Kennedy Shriver National Institute of Child Health and Human Development (NICHD) *(National Institutes of Health), Division of Extramural Research (DER), Gynecologic Health and Disease Branch (GHDB),* *6710B Rockledge Dr., MS 7002, Bethesda, MD 20817; (301) 827-4663. Fax, (301) 480-3668. Dr. Daniel S. Johnston, Chief (Acting).*
Web, www.nichd.nih.gov/about/org/der/branches/ghdb

Supports basic, translational, and clinical programs and research training programs related to gynecologic health throughout the reproductive life span, beginning at puberty and extending through early menopause. Areas of interest include healthy functionary endometrium and menstruation, fibroids, endometriosis, ovarian cysts and polycystic ovary syndrome, pelvic floor dysfunction. Obstetric fistula and female genital cutting are also of interest as they apply to both international and immigrant communities.

Eunice Kennedy Shriver National Institute of Child Health and Human Development (NICHD) *(National Institutes of Health), Division of Extramural Research (DER), Pediatric Growth and Nutrition Branch (PGNB),* *6710B Rockledge Dr., Room 2444, MS 7002, Bethesda, MD 20817; (301) 402-7886. Dr. Andrew Bremer, Chief.*
Web, www.nichd.nih.gov/about/org/der/branches/pgnb

Supports research on understanding basic and clinical aspects of growth and development, including the biological processes that underlie normal growth and development, as well as research on how these biological processes go awry. Major research programs include how nutrition promotes healthy growth and development; lactation and breastfeeding; the causes of obesity in childhood and sequelae of childhood obesity in adulthood; the genetic, nutritional, and hormonal antecedents of bone health and the origins of osteoporosis; the neuroendocrine basis of growth and the onset of puberty; and the development of the hypothalamo-pituitary adrenal, gonadal, and thyroid axes.

Food and Drug Administration (FDA) *(Health and Human Services Dept.), Women's Health (OWH),* *White Oak Bldg. 32, 10903 New Hampshire Ave., #2333, Silver Spring, MD 20993; (301) 796-9440. Fax, (301) 847-8604. Dr. Kaveeta P. Vasisht, Associate Commissioner.*
General email, owh@fda.gov

Web, www.fda.gov/AboutFDA/CentersOffices/OC/OfficeofWomensHealth and Twitter, @FDAWomen

Supports scientific research on women's health and collaborates with other government agencies and national organizations to sponsor scientific and consumer outreach on women's health issues. Interests include breast cancer, cardiovascular disease, diabetes, pregnancy, menopause, and the safe use of medications.

Health Resources and Services Administration (HRSA) (Health and Human Services Dept.), Women's Health (OWH), 5600 Fishers Lane, Rockville, MD 20857; (301) 945-5146. Nancy Mautone-Smith, Director.
Web, www.hrsa.gov/about/organization/bureaus/owh

Works to improve health care by reducing sex- and gender-based disparities. Supports dissemination of information on topics related to women's health, including health insurance and violence prevention.

National Institutes of Health (NIH) (Health and Human Services Dept.), Research on Women's Health (ORWH), 6707 Democracy Blvd., #400, MS 5484, Bethesda, MD 20892-5484; (301) 402-1770. Fax, (301) 402-1798. Dr. Janine Austin Clayton, Director. Toll-free, (888) 346-3656.
General email, ORWHinfo@mail.nih.gov

Web, http://orwh.od.nih.gov, Twitter, @NIH_ORWH and Facebook, www.facebook.com/NIHORWH/

Collaborates with NIH institutes and centers to establish NIH goals and policies for research related to women's health and sex-based or gender-based studies of the differences between women and men. Supports expansion of research on diseases, conditions, and disorders that affect women; monitors inclusion of women and minorities in clinical research; develops opportunities and support for recruitment and advancement of women in biomedical careers.

Women's Health Initiative (WHI), 2 Rockledge Center, 6701 Rockledge Dr., #9192, MS 7913, Bethesda, MD 20892-7935; (301) 435-6667. Fax, (301) 480-5158. Jared Reis, WHI Contact. Information, (301) 592-8573. Press, (301) 496-4236. Toll free, (800) 218-8145.
General email, helpdesk@whi.org

Web, www.whi.org

Supports clinical trials and observational studies to improve understanding of the causes and prevention of major diseases affecting the health of women. Interests include cardiovascular disease, cancer, fractures, and hormone therapy. Sponsored by the National Heart, Lung, and Blood Institute (NHLBI).

▶NONGOVERNMENTAL

Assn. of Women's Health, Obstetric, and Neonatal Nurses (AWHONN), 1800 M St. N.W.,#7405, 20036; (202) 261-2400. Fax, (202) 728-0575. Jonathan Webb, Chief Executive Officer. Customer Service, (800) 354-2268. Toll-free, (800) 673-8499.
General email, customerservice@awhonn

Web, www.awhonn.org, Twitter, @AWHONN and Facebook, www.facebook.com/AWHONN

Membership: promotes the health of women and newborns. Provides nurses with information and support. Produces educational materials and legislative programs.

Black Women's Health Imperative, 700 Pennsylvania Ave. S.E., #2059, 20003; (202) 787-5931. Linda Goler Blount, President.
General email, imperative@bwhi.org

Web, www.bwhi.org, Twitter, @blkwomenshealth and Facebook, www.facebook.com/BlackWomensHealth Imperative

Provides the tools and information for African American women to prevent health problems, to recognize symptoms and early warning signs, and to understand all of the options available for their specific health situations. Achieves these ends through community outreach, advocacy, resources and research, education, and mobilization. (Formerly the National Black Women's Health Project.)

Institute for Women's Policy Research (IWPR), 1200 18th St. N.W., #301, 20036; (202) 785-5100. Fax, (202) 833-4362. C. Nicole Mason, President. Media, (202) 684-7534.
General email, iwpr@iwpr.org

Web, https://iwpr.org, Twitter, @IWPResearch and Facebook, www.facebook.com/iwpresearch

Public policy research organization that focuses on women's issues, including health care and comprehensive family and medical leave programs.

National Center for Health Research, 1001 Connecticut Ave. N.W., #1100, 20036; (202) 223-4000. Diana Zuckerman, President.
General email, info@center4research.org

Web, www.center4research.org, Twitter, @NC4HR and Facebook, www.facebook.com/nationalresearchcenter

Utilizes scientific and medical research to improve the quality of women's lives and the lives of family members. Seeks to educate policymakers about medical and scientific research through hearings, meetings, and publications. Affiliated with the Cancer Prevention and Treatment Fund.

National Women's Health Network, 1413 K St. N.W., 4th Floor, 20005; (202) 682-2640. Fax, (202) 682-2648. Denys Symonette Mitchell, Director Public Policy.
General email, nwhn@nwhn.org

Web, www.nwhn.org, Twitter, @TheNWHN, Facebook, www.facebook.com/TheNWHN and Health questions, healthquestions@nwhn.org

Acts as an information clearinghouse on women's health issues; monitors federal health policies and legislation. Interests include older women's health issues, sexual and reproductive health, contraception, menopause, abortion, unsafe drugs, AIDS, breast cancer, and universal health.

Society for Women's Health Research, 1025 Connecticut Ave. N.W., #1104, 20036; (202) 223-8224. Fax, (202) 833-3472. Kathryn G. Schubert, President.
General email, info@swhr.org

Web, https://swhr.org, Twitter, @SWHR and Facebook, www.facebook.com/SocietyForWomensHealthResearch

Promotes public and private funding for women's health research and changes in public policies affecting women's health. Seeks to advance women as leaders in the health professions and to inform policymakers, educators, and the public of research outcomes. Sponsors meetings; produces reports; conducts educational campaigns.

WomenHeart: National Coalition for Women with Heart Disease, *1100 17th St. N.W., #500, 20036; (202) 728-7199. Fax, (202) 688-2861. Celina Gorre, Chief Executive Officer. Spanish hotline, (800) 676-6002.*
General email, mail@womenheart.org

Web, www.womenheart.org, Twitter, @WomenHeartOrg and Facebook, www.facebook.com/WomenHeartNational/

Patient-centered organization that seeks to advance women's heart health through advocacy, community education, and patient support.

HEALTH TOPICS: RESEARCH AND ADVOCACY

General

▶**AGENCIES**

Assistant Secretary for Health (OASH) *(Health and Human Services Dept.), Human Research Protections (OHRP),* Tower Bldg., 1101 Wootton Pkwy., #200, Rockville, MD 20852; (240) 453-6900. Fax, (240) 453-6909. Dr. Jerry Menikoff, Director.*
General email, ohrp@hhs.gov

Web, www.hhs.gov/ohrp

Promotes the rights, welfare, and well-being of subjects involved in research conducted or supported by the Health and Human Services Dept.; helps ensure that research is carried out in accordance with federal regulations by providing clarification and guidance, developing educational programs and materials, and maintaining regulatory oversight.

Eunice Kennedy Shriver National Institute of Child Health and Human Development (NICHD) *(National Institutes of Health), Division of Extramural Research (DER),* 6710B Rockledge Dr., Room 2314, MS 7002, Bethesda, MD 20817; (301) 435-6868. Dr. Rohan Hazra, M.D., Director.*
Web, www.nichd.nih.gov/about/org/der

Develops, implements, and coordinates cross-cutting, multidisciplinary research activities within NICHD's broad research portfolio, which includes biological, behavioral, and clinical research related to conception and pregnancy; normal and abnormal development in childhood; reproductive health; and population dynamics across the life span. Coordinates and funds research and training programs across the United States and many other countries through grants and contracts.

Food and Drug Administration (FDA) *(Health and Human Services Dept.), Center for Biologics Evaluation and Research (CBER),* White Oak Bldg. 71, 10903 New Hampshire Ave., Silver Spring, MD 20993-0002;

(240) 402-8010. Fax, (301) 595-1310. Dr. Peter Marks, Director, (240) 402-8000. Toll-free, (800) 835-4709. Press and publications, (240) 402-7800.
General email, ocod@fda.hhs.gov

Web, www.fda.gov/about-fda/center-biologics-evaluation-and-research-cber/contacts-center-biologics-evaluation-research-cber and Twitter, @FDACBER

Regulates biological and related products for human use under applicable federal laws, including the Public Health Service Act and Federal Food Drug and Cosmetic Act. Interests include blood and blood products, vaccines, allergenics, cellular and gene therapies, and tissues.

Health Resources and Services Administration (HRSA) *(Health and Human Services Dept.), Healthcare Systems Bureau (HSB), Transplantation (DoT),* 5600 Fishers Lane, #8W, Rockville, MD 20857; (301) 945-3118. Frank Hollomon, Director.*
General email, donation@hrsa.gov

Web, www.organdonor.gov, www.hrsa.gov/about/organization/bureaus/hsb and Press, press@hrsa.gov

Implements organ donation and transplantation programs, including Organ Procurement and Transplantation Network (OPTN) and Scientific Registry of Transplant Recipients (SRTR). Provides information on federal programs involved in transplantation; supports the national network for deceased donor organ procurement and matching; maintains information on transplant recipients; awards grants to increase organ donation and transplantation.

Health Resources and Services Administration (HRSA), Healthcare Systems Bureau (HSB), 5600 Fishers Lane, Rockville, MD 20857; (301) 443-3300. Cheryl R. Dammons, Associate Administrator.*
Web, www.hrsa.gov/about/organization/bureaus/hsb/index.html

Administers programs in areas of public health, including organ donation and transplantation, poison control, bone marrow and cord blood transplantation, drug pricing, injury compensation, and Hansen's Disease (leprosy).

Mark O. Hatfield Clinical Research Center *(National Institutes of Health),* 10 Center Dr., Bethesda, MD 20892; (301) 496-4000. Dr. James K. Gilman, Chief Executive Officer, (301) 496-4114. Admissions, (301) 496-3141. Patient recruitment, (800) 411-1222.*
Web, http://clinicalcenter.nih.gov, Twitter, @NIHClinicalCntr, Facebook, www.facebook.com/NIHClinicalCenter and YouTube, www.youtube.com/c/NIHClinicalCenter

Provides inpatient and outpatient care and conducts clinical research. Promotes the application of scientific laboratory research to benefit patient health and medical care. With the Warren Grant Magnuson Clinical Center, forms the NIH Clinical Center.

National Heart, Lung, and Blood Institute (NHLBI) *(National Institutes of Health),* Bldg. 31, 31 Center Dr., #5A52, MS 2486, Bethesda, MD 20892-2486 (mailing address: P.O. Box 30105, Bethesda, MD 20824);

(301) 592-8573. Fax, (240) 629-3246. Dr. Gary H. Gibbons, Director, (301) 496-5166. Toll-free, (877) 645-2448. TTY, (240) 629-3255.

General email, nhlbiinfo@nhlbi.nih.gov

Web, www.nhlbi.nih.gov, Twitter, @nih_nhlbi, Facebook, www.facebook.com/NHLBI and YouTube, www.youtube.com/user/NHLBI

Collects and disseminates information on diseases of the heart, lungs, and blood, with an emphasis on disease prevention. Works with patients, families, health care professionals, scientists, community organizations, and the media to promote the application of research results to address public health needs. Promotes international collaboration in its educational programs for scientists and clinicians.

National Institute of General Medical Sciences (NIGMS) *(National Institutes of Health)*, 45 Center Dr., #3AN44E, MS 6200, Bethesda, MD 20892-6200; (301) 496-7301. Jon R. Lorsch, Director.

General email, info@nigms.nih.gov

Web, www.nigms.nih.gov, Twitter, @NIGMS and Facebook, www.facebook.com/nigms.nih.gov

Primarily supports basic biomedical research and training that lay the foundation for advances in disease diagnosis, treatment, and prevention. Areas of special interest include bioinformatics, cell biology, developmental biology, physiology, biological chemistry genetics, and computational biology.

National Institute of General Medical Sciences (NIGMS) *(National Institutes of Health), Training, Workforce Development, and Diversity,* Bldg. 45, 45 Center Dr., #2AS37, MS 6200, Bethesda, MD 20892-6200; (301) 496-7301. Alison Gammie, Director.

Web, http://nigms.nih.gov/about/overview/Pages/TWD.aspx

Administers research and research training programs aimed at increasing the number of minority biomedical scientists. Funds grants, fellowships, faculty development awards, and development of research facilities.

National Institutes of Health (NIH) *(Health and Human Services Dept.),* Bldg. 1, 9000 Rockville Pike, Bethesda, MD 20892-0148; (301) 496-4000. Fax, (301) 496-0017. Dr. Lawrence A. Tabak, Director (Acting). Press, (301) 496-5787. TTY, (301) 402-9612.

Web, www.nih.gov, Twitter, @NIH and Facebook, www.facebook.com/nih.gov

Provides leadership and direction to programs designed to improve the health of the nation by conducting and supporting research relating to the causes, diagnosis, prevention, and cure of human diseases; processes of human growth and development; biological effects of environmental contaminants; understanding of mental, addictive, and physical disorders; and directing programs for collection, dissemination, and exchange of information in medicine and health.

National Institutes of Health (NIH) *(Health and Human Services Dept.), Center for Information Technology (CIT),* 6555 Rock Spring Dr., #3G04, Bethesda, MD 20817;

(301) 496-4357. Fax, (301) 402-1754. Andrea T. Norris, Director. Toll Free, (866) 319-4357. TTY, (800) 877-8339. Web, https://cit.nih.gov

Collaborates with NIH intramural communities in areas of computational bioscience, engineering, infomatics, and statistics.

National Institutes of Health (NIH) *(Health and Human Services Dept.), Center for Scientific Review (CSR),* 6701 Rockledge Dr., #3030, MS 7768, Bethesda, MD 20892-7768; (301) 435-1111. Fax, (301) 480-3965. Noni Byrnes, Director, (301) 435-1023.

General email, csrdrr@mail.nih.gov

Web, www.csr.nih.gov and Twitter, @CSRpeerreview

Conducts scientific merit review of research grant and fellowship applications submitted to the NIH. Participates in formulating grant and award policies.

National Institutes of Health (NIH) *(Health and Human Services Dept.), National Center for Advancing Translational Sciences (NCATS),* 1 Democracy Plaza, 6701 Democracy Blvd., 9th Floor, #900, MS 4874, Bethesda, MD 20892-4874 (mailing address: Use zip code 20817 for express mail); (301) 594-8966. Joni L. Rutter, Director (Acting). Press, (301) 435-0888.

General email, info@ncats.nih.gov

Web, www.ncats.nih.gov, Twitter, @ncats.nih.gov and Facebook, www.facebook.com/ncats.nih.gov

Works in partnership with regulatory, academic, nonprofit, and private sectors to identify and overcome hurdles that slow the development of effective treatments and cures.

National Institutes of Health (NIH) *(Health and Human Services Dept.), National Center for Complementary and Integrative Health (NICCIH),* 9000 Rockville Pike, MS 282, Bethesda, MD 20892; (301) 435-6826. Fax, (301) 402-4741. Dr. Helene Langevin, Director. Toll-free, (888) 644-6226. TTY, (866) 464-3615.

General email, info@nccih.nih.gov

Web, www.nccih.nih.gov, Twitter, @NIH_NCCIH and Facebook, www.facebook.com/nih.nccih

Conducts and supports research on complementary and health products and practices; trains researchers and disseminates information to practitioners and the public.

National Institutes of Health (NIH) *(Health and Human Services Dept.), Stem Cell Research,* Bldg. 31, 9000 Rockville Pike, 31 Center Dr., #8A52, MS 2540, Bethesda, MD 20892-2540; (301) 496-3765. Timothy J. LaVaute, Director.

General email, stemcell@mail.nih.gov

Web, https://stemcells.nih.gov

The federal government's primary source for stem cell research, policy, and funding. Enables and speeds the pace of stem cell research by identifying resources and developing measures to enhance such resources.

National Library of Medicine *(National Institutes of Health),* Bldg. 38, 8600 Rockville Pike, #2E17, MS 3808, Bethesda, MD 20894; (301) 594-5983. Fax, (301) 402-1384.

Dr. Patricia Flatley Brennan, Director, (301) 496-6221. TTY, (888) 346-3656.

General email, custserv@nlm.nih.gov

Web, www.nlm.nih.gov, Twitter, @nlm_nih and PubMed Central, www.ncbi.nlm.nih.gov/pmc

Offers medical library services and computer-based reference service to the public, health professionals, libraries in medical schools and hospitals, and research institutions. Operates a toxicology information service for the scientific community, industry, and federal agencies. Assists medical libraries through the National Network of Libraries of Medicine. Assists in the improvement of basic library resources. Reading room open to the public Monday through Friday, 8:30 a.m.–5:00 p.m.

National Library of Medicine *(National Institutes of Health), Health Information Programs Development, Office of Strategic Initiatives,* Bldg. 38, 8600 Rockville Pike, #2S20, MS 12, Bethesda, MD 20894; (301) 496-2311. Fax, (301) 496-4450. Michael F. (Mike) Huerta, Director, (301) 496-8834.

General email, custserv@nlm.nih.gov

Web, www.nlm.nih.gov/od/osi/osi_home.html

Facilitates worldwide use of the library's medical databases through agreements with individual nations, international organizations, and commercial vendors. Helps the library acquire and share international biomedical literature.

National Library of Medicine *(National Institutes of Health), Lister Hill National Center for Biomedical Communications,* Bldg. 38A, 8600 Rockville Pike, #07N707, Bethesda, MD 20894; (301) 496-4441. Fax, (301) 435-3146. Dr. Oliver Bodenreider, Director (Acting), (301) 827-4982. Visitor Center, (301) 496-7771.

Web, http://lhncbc.nlm.nih.gov

A research and development division of the National Library of Medicine. Conducts and supports research and development in the dissemination of high-quality imagery, medical language processing, high-speed access to biomedical information, intelligent database systems development, multimedia visualization, knowledge management, data mining, machine-assisted indexing, terminology, and data structure and standards for exchanging clinical data.

National Library of Medicine *(National Institutes of Health), National Center for Biotechnology Information,* Bldg. 38A, 8600 Rockville Pike, 8th Floor, Bethesda, MD 20892; (301) 435-5978. Fax, (301) 480-4559. Stephen Sherry, Director (Acting).

General email, info@ncbi.nlm.nih.gov

Web, www.ncbi.nlm.nih.gov

Creates automated systems for storing and analyzing knowledge of molecular biology and genetics. Develops new information technologies to aid in understanding the molecular processes that control human health and disease. Conducts basic research in computational molecular biology. Sponsors PubMed Central, a publicly accessible digital archive of life sciences journal literature.

Naval Medical Research Center *(Defense Dept.),* 503 Robert Grant Ave., #1W28, Silver Spring, MD 20910-7500; (301) 319-7403. (301) 319-9378. Fax, (301) 319-7424. Capt. William M. Deniston (USN), Commanding Officer; Steven S. Legette, Executive Director, (301) 319-3381.

General email, svc.pao.nmrc@med.navy.mil

Web, www.med.navy.mil/Naval-Medical-Research-Center/ and Facebook, www.facebook.com/NavalMedicalRC

Performs basic and applied biomedical research in areas of military importance, including infectious diseases, hyperbaric medicine, wound repair enhancement, environmental stress, and immunobiology. Provides support to field laboratories and naval hospitals; monitors research internationally.

NIH Clinical Center *(National Institutes of Health),* 10 Center Dr., #6-2551, Bethesda, MD 20892-1504; (301) 496-4000. Dr. James K. Gilman, Chief Executive Officer, (301) 496-4114. Communications, (301) 496-2563.

Web, www.cc.nih.gov, Twitter, @NIHClinicalCntr, Facebook, www.facebook.com/NIHClinicalCenter and Press, molly.friemuth@nih.gov

Serves as a clinical research center for the NIH; patients are referred by physicians and self-referred throughout the United States and overseas.

Walter Reed Army Institute of Research *(Defense Dept.),* 503 Robert Grant Ave., Silver Spring, MD 20910-7500; (301) 319-9000. Fax, (301) 319-9549. Col. Chad Koenig, Commander. Public Affairs, (301) 319-9471. Reference Library, (301) 319-9555.

General email, usarmy.detrick.medcom-wrair.mbx.public-affairs@mail.mil

Web, www.wrair.army.mil and Twitter, @wrair

Provides research, education, and training in support of the Defense Dept.'s health care system. Develops vaccines and drugs to prevent and treat infectious diseases. Other research efforts include surveillance of naturally occurring infectious diseases of military importance and study of combat casualty care (blood loss, resuscitation, and brain and other organ system trauma), battle casualties, operational stress, sleep deprivation, and medical countermeasures against biological and chemical agents.

►CONGRESS

For a listing of relevant congressional committees and subcommittees, please see pages 362–363 or the Appendix.

►NONGOVERNMENTAL

Academy Health, 1666 K St. N.W., #1100, 20006; (202) 292-6700. Fax, (202) 292-6800. Dr. Lisa A. Simpson, M.B, President; Megan Collado, M.P.H., Director; Lauren Gerlach, M.P.P., Director.

Web, https://academyhealth.org, Twitter, @AcademyHealth, Facebook, www.facebook.com/Academy Health and Email, communications@academyhealth.org

Membership: individuals and organizations with an interest in health services research, including health policymakers, universities, private research organizations, professional associations, consulting firms, advocacy organizations, insurers, managed care companies, health care systems, and pharmaceutical companies. Serves as an information clearinghouse on health services research and policy; communicates with policymakers concerning state and federal health policies; works to increase public and private funding for health services research, including comparative effectiveness and public health systems and services research. Offers professional development and training programs for health services researchers and policymakers. Maintains a repository of articels from industry journals. Monitors legislation and regulations. (Formerly Academy for Health Services Research and Health Policy.)

American Clinical Laboratory Assn., *1201 Pennsylvania Ave. N.W., #810, 20004; (202) 637-9466. Andrew Young, Senior Coordinator.*
General email, info@acla.com
Web, www.acla.com, Twitter, @ACLAlabs and Facebook, www.facebook.com/ACLAlabs

Membership: clinical laboratories and laboratory service companies. Advocates laws and regulations that recognize the role of laboratory services in cost-effective health care. Works to ensure the confidentiality of patient test results. Provides education, information, and research materials to members. Monitors legislation and regulations.

American Physiological Society, *6120 Executive Blvd., #600, Rockville, MD 20852-4911; (301) 634-7164. Fax, (301) 634-7241. Scott Steen, Executive Director, (301) 634-7118.*
Web, www.the-aps.org, Twitter, @APSPhysiology and Facebook, www.facebook.com/AmericanPhysiological Society

Membership: physiologists, students, and laypersons interested in physiology. Researches how the body and its organ systems function. Promotes scientific research, education, and dissemination of information through publication of peer-reviewed journals; monitors international research. Works to establish standards for the humane care and use of laboratory animals. Offers travel fellowships for scientific meetings; encourages minority participation in physiological research. Publishes seven scientific journals and a newsletter.

American Trauma Society, *201 Park Washington Court, Falls Church, VA 22046; (703) 538-3544. Fax, (703) 241-5603. Suzanne M. Prentiss, Executive Director.*
Toll-free, (800) 556-7890.
General email, info@amtrauma.org
Web, www.amtrauma.org and Twitter, @ATSTrauma

Seeks to prevent trauma and improve its treatment. Coordinates programs aimed at reducing the incidence and severity of trauma; sponsors research; provides training to nurses and others involved in the trauma field. Provides support to trauma survivors. Monitors legislation and regulations.

Center for Applied Proteomics and Molecular Medicine (CAPMM) *(George Mason University), 10920 George Mason Circle, Room 2008, MS 1A9, Manassas, VA 20110 (mailing address: 10900 University Blvd., #325, MS 1A9, Manassas, VA 20110); (703) 993-9526. Fax, (703) 993-8606. Dr. Lance A. Liotta, Co-Director; Emanuel Petricoin III, Co-Director.*
Web, http://capmm.gmu.edu

Conducts translational medical research in order to tailor treatment to individual patients. Participates in clinical trials.

Council on Education for Public Health (CEPH), *1010 Wayne Ave., #220, Silver Spring, MD 20910; (202) 789-1050. Laura Rasar King, Executive Director.*
Web, https://ceph.org and Twitter, @CEPHtweets

Works to strengthen public health programs through research and other means.

Foundation for the National Institutes of Health (FNIH), *11400 Rockville Pike, #600, North Bethesda, MD 20852; (301) 402-5311. Fax, (301) 480-2752. David Wholley, President (Acting), (301) 443-1811.*
General email, foundation@fnih.org
Web, https://fnih.org, Twitter, @FNIH_Org and Facebook, www.facebook.com/FNIHorg

Established by Congress to support the NIH's mission of developing new knowledge through biomedical research. Works to foster collaborative relationships in education, research, and related activities between the NIH, industry, academia, and nonprofit organizations; supports basic and clinical research to advance medical knowledge; supports training and advanced education programs for future researchers; and invests in educational programs related to medical research.

Howard Hughes Medical Institute, *4000 Jones Bridge Rd., Chevy Chase, MD 20815-6789; (301) 215-8500. Fax, (301) 215-8863. Erin O'Shea, President.*
Web, www.hhmi.org, Twitter, @HHMINEWS, Facebook, www.facebook.com/HowardHughesMed and YouTube, www.youtube.com/c/hhmi

Conducts biomedical research programs in major academic medical centers, hospitals, and universities. Areas of research include cell biology, computational biology, genetics, immunology, neuroscience, and structural biology. Maintains a grants program in science education, including precollege, undergraduate, graduate, and postgraduate levels. Supports selected biomedical researchers in foreign countries.

International Epidemiology Institute, *1455 Research Blvd., #550, Rockville, MD 20850; (301) 424-1054. Fax, (301) 424-1053. William J. (Bill) Blot, Chief Executive Officer.*
General email, info@iei.us
Web, www.iei.us

Investigates biomedical problems and environmental health issues for the public and private sectors, universities, and other institutions. Conducts studies and clinical trials. Helps identify potential risks and benefits associated with new medicines and new medical devices, including implants. (Affiliated with Vanderbilt University in Nashville, Tenn.)

Johns Hopkins University Applied Physics Laboratory, *Research and Exploratory Development, 11100 Johns Hopkins Rd., Laurel, MD 20723-6099; (240) 228-5000. Jim Schatz, Mission Area Executive. Press, (240) 228-5020. Web, www.jhuapl.edu/OurWork/ResearchandExploratory Development*

Research and development laboratory that seeks to improve warfighter survivability, sustainment, and performance through battlefield trauma prevention and mitigation, along with medical device evaluation and development. Programs include improvement of soldier protection equipment, the development of a neurally integrated upper extremity prosthetic, and blast-related traumatic brain injury research.

National Center for Healthy Housing, *10320 Little Patuxent Pkwy., #200, Columbia, MD 21044; (410) 992-0712. Amanda Reddy, Executive Director, (443) 539-4152. General email, info@nchh.org*

Web, www.nchh.org, Twitter, @NCHH and Facebook, www.facebook.com/HealthyHousing

Collects, analyzes, and distributes information on creating and maintaining safe and healthful housing. Provides technical assistance and training to public health, housing, and environmental professionals. Interests include aging in place for older adults, radon, allergens, pest management, and lead poisoning.

National Institute of Environmental Health Sciences (NIEHS) *(National Institutes of Health), Washington Office, 31 Center Dr., #B1C02, MS 2256, Bethesda, MD 20892-2256; (301) 496-3511. Fax, (301) 469-0563. Richard (Rick) Waychik, Director. General email, webcenter@niehs.nih.gov*

Web, www.niehs.nih.gov, Twitter, @NIEHS and Facebook, www.facebook.com/NIH.NIEHS

Conducts and supports research on the human effects of various environmental exposures, expanding the scientific basis for making public health decisions based on the potential toxicity of environmental agents. (Most operations located in Research Triangle, N.C.)

Research!America, *241 S. 18th St., #501, Arlington, VA 22202; (703) 739-2577. Fax, (703) 739-2372. Mary Woolley, President. Web, www.researchamerica.org, Twitter, @ResearchAmerica and Facebook, www.facebook.com/ ResearchAmerica.org*

Membership: academic institutions, professional societies, voluntary health organizations, corporations, and individuals interested in promoting medical research. Provides information on the benefits of medical and health research and seeks to increase funding for research. Monitors legislation and regulations.

Science Communication Network, *6511 Winnepeg Rd., Bethesda, MD 20817; Amy Kostant, Executive Director. General email, info@sciencecom.org*

Web, http://sciencecommunicationnetwork.org

Conducts educational workshops to give environmental health scientists the media tools to enable their work to be accurately reported to the public and journalists. Focuses on issues including environmental health and reproductive health connections; effects of energy exploration on health, including fracking; population health disparities; environmental contaminant links to autoimmune diseases, such as allergies; diseases of aging such as Parkinson's disease and dementia; and health effects associated with climate change.

SRI International, *Washington Office, 1100 Wilson Blvd., #2800, Arlington, VA 22209; (703) 524-2053. David Parekh, Corporate Executive Officer. Web, www.sri.com and Twitter, @SRI_Intl*

Research and consulting organization. Conducts studies on biotechnology, genetic engineering, drug metabolism, cancer, toxicology, disease control systems, and other areas of basic and applied research; monitors international research. (Headquarters in Menlo Park, Calif.)

Alternative Medicine

▶**AGENCIES**

Food and Drug Administration (FDA) *(Health and Human Services Dept.), Center for Food Safety and Applied Nutrition (CFSAN), 5001 Campus Dr., HFS-009, College Park, MD 20740-3835; (240) 402-1600. Fax, (301) 436-2668. Susan T. Mayne, Director. SAFEFOOD Info, (888) 723-3366. TTY, (800) 877-8339. General email, consumer@fda.gov*

Web, www.fda.gov/AboutFDA/CentersOffices/ OfficeofFoods/CFSAN and Twitter, @FDAFood

Develops standards for dietary supplements taken as part of alternative medicine treatments.

National Cancer Institute (NCI) *(National Institutes of Health), Cancer Treatment and Diagnosis (DCTD), Cancer Complementary and Alternative Medicine (OCCAM), 9609 Medical Center Dr., Room 5W136, Rockville, MD 20892-9702; (240) 276-6595. Fax, (240) 276-7893. Dr. Jeffrey D. White, Director. TTY, (800) 332-8615. General email, ncioccam1-r@mail.nih.gov*

Web, https://cam.cancer.gov

Investigates approaches to cancer therapy using complementary and alternative medicine. Conducts research on lifestyle modifications, including diet, exercise, and mind–body approaches, for their impact on cancer outcomes.

National Institutes of Health (NIH) *(Health and Human Services Dept.), National Center for Complementary and Integrative Health (NICCIH), 9000 Rockville Pike, MS 282, Bethesda, MD 20892; (301) 435-6826. Fax, (301) 402-4741. Dr. Helene Langevin, Director. Toll-free, (888) 644-6226. TTY, (866) 464-3615. General email, info@nccih.nih.gov*

Web, www.nccih.nih.gov, Twitter, @NIH_NCCIH and Facebook, www.facebook.com/nih.nccih

Works with the Food and Drug Administration (FDA) to develop regulations for the research and use of alternative medicine.

American Assn. of Naturopathic Physicians, *300 New Jersey Ave. N.W., #900, 20001; (202) 237-8150. Laura Farr, Executive Director, (202) 849-6306. General email, member.services@naturopathic.org*

Web, www.naturopathic.org, Twitter, @AANP and Facebook, www.facebook.com/theAANP

Membership: licensed naturopathic physicians, naturopathic medicine students, and other healthcare professionals allied with the naturopathic profession. Promotes the combination of modern medicine and natural and traditional therapies, including therapeutic nutrition, botanical medicine, homeopathy, and natural childbirth.

American Assn. of Pharmaceutical Scientists, *2107 Wilson Blvd., #200, Arlington, VA 22201; (703) 243-2800. Tina Morris, Executive Director, (703) 248-4701. Customer Service, (877) 998-2277. Public Relations, (703) 248-4740. General email, aaps@aaps.org*

Web, www.aaps.org, Twitter, @AAPSComms and Facebook, www.facebook.com/americanassociationof pharmaceuticalscientists?filter=1

Through its philanthropic arm, the American Association of Pharmaceutical Scientists Foundation, provides funding to advance research, education, and training for therapies, drug development, and manufacturing.

American Music Therapy Assn., *8455 Colesville Rd., #1000, Silver Spring, MD 20910; (301) 589-3300. Fax, (301) 589-5175. Adonia Calhoun Coates, CEO. General email, info@musictherapy.org*

Web, www.musictherapy.org, Twitter, @AMTAInc and Facebook, www.facebook.com/AMTAinc

Promotes the therapeutic use of music by approving degree programs and clinical training sites, establishing professional competencies and clinical practice standards for music therapists, and conducting research in the music therapy field.

Assn. of Accredited Naturopathic Medical Colleges, *1717 K St. N.W., #900, 20006; (800) 345-7454. JoAnn Yanez, Executive Director. General email, info@aanmc.org*

Web, www.aanmc.org, Twitter, @AANMC and Facebook, www.facebook.com/TheAANMC

Promotes naturopathic and medical education, research, and teaching.

Arthritis, Bone Diseases

National Institute of Arthritis and Musculoskeletal and Skin Diseases (NIAMS) *(National Institutes of Health), Bldg. 31, 31 Center Dr., #4C32, MS 2350, Bethesda, MD 20892-2350; (301) 495-4484. Dr. Lindsey A. Criswell, Director, (301) 496-3651. Health information, (877) 226-4267. General email, niamsinfo@mail.nih.gov*

Web, www.niams.nih.gov, Twitter, @NIH_NIAMS, Facebook, www.facebook.com/NIH_NIAMS and YouTube, www.youtube.com/user/NIAMSNIH

Conducts and funds research on arthritis, rheumatic, skin, muscle, and bone diseases and musculoskeletal disorders. Funds national arthritis centers.

National Institute of Arthritis and Musculoskeletal and Skin Diseases (NIAMS) *(National Institutes of Health), Information Clearinghouse, 1 AMS Circle, Rm 4C32, MS 2350, Bethesda, MD 20892-3675; (301) 495-4484. Fax, (301) 402-3607. Dr. Lindsey A. Criswell, Director, (301) 496-4353. Toll-free, (877) 226-4267. TTY, (301) 565-2966. General email, niamsinfo@mail.nih.gov*

Web, www.niams.nih.gov

Supports medical research into the causes, treatment, and prevention of diseases of the bones, muscles, joints, and skin. Provides general information on health conditions and referrals to organizations.

National Institutes of Health (NIH) *(Health and Human Services Dept.), Osteoporosis and Related Bone Diseases - National Resource Center (ORBD-NRC), 2 AMS Circle, Bethesda, MD 20892; (202) 223-0344. Fax, (202) 293-2356. Dr. Lindsey A. Criswell, Director. Toll-free, (800) 624-2663. TTY, (202) 466-4315. General email, NIHBoneInfo@mail.nih.gov*

Web, www.bones.nih.gov

Provides patients, health professionals, and the public with resources and information on metabolic bone diseases, including osteoporosis, Paget's disease of bone, and osteogenesis imperfecta. Seeks to increase the awareness, knowledge, and understanding of the prevention, early detection, and treatment of osteoporosis and related bone diseases.

American Society for Bone and Mineral Research (ASBMR), *2001 K St. N.W., 3rd Floor, 20006; (202) 367-1161. Fax, (202) 367-2161. Douglas Fesler, Executive Director. General email, asbmr@asbmr.org*

Web, www.asbmr.org, Twitter, @ASBMR and Facebook, www.facebook.com/ASBMR

Membership: scientists and physicians who study bone and mineral metabolism and related fields. Promotes public awareness of bone diseases. Publishes the *Journal of Bone and Mineral Research* and the *Primer on the Metabolic Bone Diseases and Disorders of Mineral Metabolism*. Awards grants for member research.

Bone Health and Osteoporosis Foundation (BHOF), *251 18th St., #630, Arlington, VA 22202; (703) 647-3000. Fax, (703) 414-3742. Claire Gill, Chief Executive Officer. Toll-free, (800) 231-4222.*

General email, info@bonehealthandosteoporosis.org

Web, www.bonehealthandosteoporosis.org/, Twitter, @bonehealthBHOF and Facebook, www.facebook.com/bonehealthandosteoporosisfoundation

Volunteer health organization that seeks to prevent osteoporosis and related bone fractures, to promote life-long bone health, to improve the lives of those affected by osteoporosis and Paget's Disease and to find a cure through programs of awareness, advocacy, and public health education and research. Monitors legislation and international research.

Osteogenesis Imperfecta Foundation, 656 Quince Orchard Rd., #650, Gaithersburg, MD 20878; (301) 947-0083. Fax, (301) 947-0456. Tracy Smith Hart, Chief Executive Officer. Toll-free, (844) 889-7579.
General email, bonelink@oif.org

Web, www.oif.org and Twitter, @OIFoundation

Provides health care professionals and patients with information about osteogenesis imperfecta (OI), also known as brittle bone disease; offers research grants; promotes public policy that supports people living with OI. Additional resources include the OI clinic directory, newsletters and support networkd. Holds conferences and events.

Blood, Bone Marrow

▶AGENCIES

National Heart, Lung, and Blood Institute (NHLBI)
(National Institutes of Health), Blood Diseases and Resources Division (DBDR), 6701 Rockledge Dr., #9030, MS 7950, Bethesda, MD 20892-7950; (301) 435-0080. Fax, (301) 480-0867. Dr. W. Keith Hoots, Director.
General email, NHLBI-Blood-training@nhlbi.nih.gov

Web, www.nhlbi.nih.gov/about/divisions/division-blood-diseases-and-resources

Supports research and training on the causes, diagnosis, treatment, and prevention of nonmalignant blood diseases and research in transfusion medicine and blood banking, stem cell biology, and blood supply adequacy and safety. Provides biospecimens and cellular resources to the scientific community.

National Heart, Lung, and Blood Institute (NHLBI)
(National Institutes of Health), Blood Diseases and Resources Division (DBDR), Blood Epidemiology and Clinical Therapeutics Branch, 6701 Rockledge Dr., #9142, MS 7950, Bethesda, MD 20892-7950; (301) 435-0065. Dr. Simone Glynn, Branch Chief.
Web, www.nhlbi.nih.gov/about/divisions/division-blood-diseases-and-resources

Responsible for oversight, support, and stimulation of epidemiologic, clinical, and implementation research throughout the spectrum of blood science. Branch responsibilities include oversight, support, and stimulation of epidemiologic health services and observational clinical research; oversight, support, and stimulation of therapeutic and interventional clinical trials (T2 Research); acquisition and maintenance of expertise in clinical study and trial design and administration on behalf of the Division; oversight, support, and stimulation of implementation science and research (T3 Research); training of blood science workforce; and scientific liaison for epidemiologic, clinical, and implementation research across the Division, NHLBI, NIH, and partner federal agencies.

National Heart, Lung, and Blood Institute (NHLBI)
(National Institutes of Health), Blood Diseases and Resources Division (DBDR), Molecular, Cellular, and Systems Blood Science Branch, 6701 Rockledge Dr., #9168, Bethesda, MD 20892-7950; (301) 435-0070.
Yu-Chang Yang, Branch Chief.
Web, www.nhlbi.nih.gov/about/divisions/division-blood-diseases-and-resources

Provides oversight, support, and stimulation of fundamental basic research and early stage laboratory translation of the biology of blood, the blood-forming elements, and the interface between each of the latter with other cellular and organ systems. Branch responsibilities include oversight, support, and stimulation of discovery science focused on the explication of the physiology and pathophysiology of blood, bone marrow, and blood vessels; oversight support and stimulation of systems of biological approaches to understanding the critical role of blood/bone marrow/vascular endothelium in animal and human organs and organisms; oversight, support, and stimulation of the application of fundamental genetics, proteomic and metabolomic tools to understanding hematologic physiology and pathophysiology; administration of and liaison to the HNLBI/NIH resources related to basic research in nonneoplastic hematology; and fostering scientific communication across the Division, NHLBI, NIH, and partner federal agencies.

National Heart, Lung, and Blood Institute (NHLBI)
(National Institutes of Health), Blood Diseases and Resources Division (DBDR), Translational Blood Science and Resource Branch, 6701 Rockledge Dr., #90930, Bethesda, MD 20892-7950; (301) 435-0050.
Traci Heath Mondoro, Branch Chief.
Web, www.nhlbi.nih.gov/about/divisions/division-blood-diseases-and-resources

Provides oversight, support, and stimulation of translational research throughout the spectrum of blood science, as well as the resources required to support heart, lung, blood, and sleep research. Branch responsibilities include oversight, support, and stimulation of post discovery science, preclinical research, and early phase clinical studies and trials (TI, T2 Research); oversight, support, and stimulation of SBIR/STTR initiatives in the blood sciences; administration of and liaison to NHLBI resources related to translational research; training of the blood science workforce; and scientific liaison for translation research across the Division, NHLBI, NIH, and partner federal agencies.

National Heart, Lung, and Blood Institute (NHLBI)
(National Institutes of Health), Health Information Center, Bldg. 31, 31 Center Dr., Bethesda, MD 20892-2480 (mailing address: P.O. Box 30105, Bethesda, MD

20824-0105); (301) 592-8573. Lenora Johnson, Director, (301) 496-4236. Communications, (202) 496-4236. Toll-free, (877) 645-2448.
General email, nhlbilnfo@nhlbi.nih.gov
Web, www.nhlbi.nih.gov/about/contact/health-information-and-clinical-trials

Provides public and patient education materials on the prevention and treatment of heart, lung, and blood diseases.

National Institute of Diabetes and Digestive and Kidney Diseases (NIDDK) *(National Institutes of Health), Kidney, Urologic, and Hematologic Diseases (KUH),* 2 Democracy Plaza, 6707 Democracy Blvd., #625, MS 5458, Bethesda, MD 20892; (301) 496-6325. Fax, (301) 480-3510.
Dr. Robert A. Star, Director. Press, (301) 496-3583. Toll-free, (800) 891-5390.
Web, www.niddk.nih.gov/about-niddk/offices-divisions/division-kidney-urologic-hematologic-diseases

Supports basic research on and clinical studies of the states of blood cell formation, mobilization, and release. Interests include anemia associated with chronic diseases, iron and white blood cell metabolism, and genetic control of hemoglobin.

Warren Grant Magnuson Clinical Center *(National Institutes of Health), Transfusion Medicine,* Bldg. 10, 10 Center Dr., #1C711, MS 1184, Bethesda, MD 20892-1184; (301) 496-4506. Fax, (301) 402-1360.
Dr. Barbara Jean Bryant, Chief, (301) 594-8382. Press, (301) 496-2563.
Web, http://clinicalcenter.nih.gov/dtm and Twitter, @NIHClinicalCntr

Supplies blood and blood components for research and patient care. Provides training programs and conducts research in the preparation and transfusion of blood and blood products. Research topics include hepatitis, automated cell separation, immunohematology, and AIDS transmittal through transfusions.

▶ **NONGOVERNMENTAL**

American Red Cross, *National Headquarters,* 431 18th St. N.W., 20006; (202) 303-5000. Gail J. McGovern, President. Headquarters staff directory, (202) 303-5214, ext. 1. Press, (202) 303-5551. Public inquiries, (202) 303-4498. Toll-free, (800) 733-2767.
Web, www.redcross.org and Twitter, @RedCross

Humanitarian relief and health education organization chartered by Congress; provides services in the United States and internationally, when requested. Collects blood and maintains blood centers; conducts research; operates the national bone marrow registry and a rare-donor registry. Serves as U.S. member of the International Federation of Red Cross and Red Crescent Societies.

Assn. for the Advancement of Blood and Biotheopies (AABB), 4550 Montgomery Ave., #700, North Tower, Bethesda, MD 20814; (301) 907-6977. Fax, (301) 907-6895. Debra BenAvram, Chief Executive Officer. Press, (301) 215-6526.

General email, aabb@aabb.org
Web, www.aabb.org, Twitter, @aabb and Facebook, www.facebook.com/AABBupdates

Membership: Physicians, nurses, scientists, researchers, administrators, medical technologists, and other health care providers; hospital and community blood centers, transfusion and transplantation services, and individuals involved in transfusion medicine and related biotherapies. Develops and implements standards, accreditation and educational programs, and services that optimize patient and donor care and safety. Encourages the voluntary donation of blood and other tissues and organs through education and public information. (Formerly the American Assn. of Blood Banks.)

Cancer

▶ **AGENCIES**

National Cancer Institute (NCI) *(National Institutes of Health),* 9609 Medical Center Dr., MS 9760, Bethesda, MD 20850; (800) 422-6237. Dr. Norman (Ned) Sharpless, Director.
General email, NCIinfo@nih.gov
Web, www.cancer.gov, Twitter, @theNCI, Facebook, www.facebook.com/cancer.gov and YouTube, www.youtube.com/NCIgov

Conducts and funds research on the causes, diagnosis, treatment, prevention, control, and biology of cancer and the rehabilitation of cancer patients; administers the National Cancer Program; coordinates international research activities. Sponsors regional and national cancer information services.

National Cancer Institute (NCI) *(National Institutes of Health), Cancer Biology (DCB),* 9609 Medical Center Dr., MS 9747, Bethesda, MD 20892; (240) 276-6180. Fax, (240) 276-7861. Daniel Gallahan, Director.
Web, www.cancer.gov/about-nci/organization/dcb and Twitter, @NCICancerBio

Supports and provides funding for basic research in cancer biology at academic institutions and research foundations. Interests include immunology, hematology, DNA, tumor biology, and structural biology.

National Cancer Institute (NCI) *(National Institutes of Health), Cancer Control and Population Sciences (DCCPS),* 9609 Medical Center Dr., Rm 4E442, Rockville, MD 20850; (240) 276-6990. Katrina Goddard, Director.
Web, https://cancercontrol.cancer.gov and Twitter, @NCICancerCtrl

Researches the causes and distribution of cancer in populations, supports the development and delivery of effective interventions, and monitors and analyzes cancer trends in all segments of the population.

National Cancer Institute (NCI) *(National Institutes of Health), Cancer Epidemiology and Genetics (DCEG),* 9609 Medical Center Dr., MS 9776, Bethesda, MD 20892; (240) 276-7150. Dr. Stephen J. Chanock, Director.

General email, ncicontactdceg@mail.nih.gov

Web, https://dceg.cancer.gov and *Twitter, @NCIEpiTraining*

Researches the causes of cancer and pathways to prevention through epidemiologic, clinical, and laboratory observations.

National Cancer Institute (NCI) *(National Institutes of Health), Cancer Prevention (DCP), 9609 Medical Center Dr., Bethesda, MD 20892; (240) 276-7120. Philip Castle, Director.*

Web, http://prevention.cancer.gov and *Twitter, @NCIprevention*

Seeks to plan, direct, implement, and monitor cancer research focused on early detection, cancer risk, chemoprevention, and supportive care. Focuses on intervention in the process of carcinogenesis to prevent development into invasive cancer. Supports various approaches, from preclinical discovery and development of biomarkers and chemoprevention agents, including pharmaceuticals and micronutrients, to Phase III clinical testing. Programs are carried out with other National Cancer Institute divisions, NIH institutes, and federal and state agencies.

National Cancer Institute (NCI) *(National Institutes of Health), Cancer Treatment and Diagnosis (DCTD), Bldg. 31, 31 Center Dr., Room 3A-44, Bethesda, MD 20892; (240) 781-3320. Fax, (240) 541-4515. Dr. James H. Doroshow, Director.*

General email, ncidctdinfo@mail.nih.gov

Web, https://dctd.cancer.gov

Seeks to take prospective detection and treatment leads, facilitate their paths to clinical application, and expedite the initial and subsequent large-scale testing of new agents, biomarkers, imaging tests, and other therapeutic interventions, including radiation, surgery, and immunotherapy.

National Cancer Institute (NCI) *(National Institutes of Health), Cancer Treatment and Diagnosis (DCTD), Biometric Research Program, 9609 Medical Center Dr., #5W130, Rockville, MD 20850; (240) 276-6041. Fax, (240) 276-7888. Dr. Lisa Meier McShane, Associate Director, (240) 276-6037.*

General email, brb@brb.nci.nih.gov

Web, https://brb.nci.nih.gov

Supports cancer research on carcinogenesis and systems pharmacology, and identifies molecular targets, resistance mechanisms and effective new drugs, drug combinations, and biomarker mechanisms.

National Cancer Institute (NCI) *(National Institutes of Health), Cancer Treatment and Diagnosis (DCTD), Cancer Complementary and Alternative Medicine (OCCAM), 9609 Medical Center Dr., Room 5W136, Rockville, MD 20892-9702; (240) 276-6595. Fax, (240) 276-7893. Dr. Jeffrey D. White, Director. TTY, (800) 332-8615.*

General email, ncioccam1-r@mail.nih.gov

Web, https://cam.cancer.gov

Investigates approaches to cancer therapy using complementary and alternative medicine. Conducts research on lifestyle modifications, including diet, exercise, and mind–body approaches, for their impact on cancer outcomes.

National Cancer institute (NCI) *(National Institutes of Health), Cancer Treatment and Diagnosis (DCTD), Cancer Diagnosis Program, 9609 Medical Center Dr., MS 7420, 4th Floor, Rockville, MD 20890; (240) 276-6012. (240) 276-6817. Fax, (240) 276-7889. Dr. Lyndsay Harris, Associate Director (Acting), (240) 276-6327.*

General email, NCICDPNews@mail.nih.gov

Web, https://cdp.cancer.gov

Funds cancer resources and research for the development of innovative in vitro diagnostics and novel diagnostic technologies in order to improve cancer detection, evaluation, and treatment.

National Cancer Institute (NCI) *(National Institutes of Health), Cancer Treatment and Diagnosis (DCTD), Cancer Therapy Evaluation Program, 9609 Medical Center Dr., Rm W536, Bethesda, MD 20892; (240) 276-6515. Fax, (240) 276-7892. Dr. Meg Mooney, Associate Director, (240) 276-5904.*

General email, NCINCTNRFA.mail.nih.gov

Web, https://ctep.cancer.gov and *Twitter, @NCICTEP_ClinRes*

Supports cancer research by funding and sponsoring clinical trials to evaluate new anticancer agents, with an emphasis on translational research on molecular targets and mechanisms of drug effects.

National Cancer Institute (NCI) *(National Institutes of Health), Cancer Treatment and Diagnosis (DCTD), Developmental Therapeutics Program, 9609 Medical Center Dr., Bethesda, MD 20892-9735; (240) 276-5949. Rosemarie Aurigemma, Associate Director.*

General email, ncidtpinfo@mail.nih.gov

Web, https://dtp.cancer.gov

Provides resources about new cancer therapeutic agents and services to public and private research communities; makes grants to fund drug discovery and biochemical pharmacology research.

National Cancer Institute (NCI) *(National Institutes of Health), Cancer Treatment and Diagnosis (DCTD), Translational Research Program, 9609 Medical Center Dr., #3W110, MS 9726, Bethesda, MD 20892; (240) 276-5730. Fax, (240) 276-7881. Toby T. Hecht, Associate Director, ext. 1.*

General email, ncitrp-r@mail.nih.gov

Web, https://trp.cancer.gov

Administers SPORE grants (the Specialized Programs of Research Excellence). Encourages the study of organ-specific cancers, blood malignancies, and other cancers. Promotes and funds interdisciplinary research and information exchange between basic and clinical science to move basic research findings from the laboratory to applied settings involving patients and populations. Encourages laboratory and clinical scientists to work collaboratively to plan, design, and implement research programs on cancer prevention, detection, diagnosis, treatment, and control.

National Cancer Institute (NCI) *(National Institutes of Health), Center for Cancer Research (CCR),* Bldg. 31, 31 Center Dr., Room 3A11, Bethesda, MD 20892; (240) 760-6400. Dr. Tom Misteli, Director, (240) 760-6669.
Web, https://ccr.cancer.gov and Twitter, @NCIResearchCtr

Supports clinical cancer research, with a focus on individual genes and proteins, drug discovery, biomedical devices and technology, and advances in treatment.

National Cancer Institute (NCI) *(National Institutes of Health), Communications and Public Liaison,* 9609 Medical Center Dr., MS 9760, Bethesda, MD 20892-9760; (240) 276-6600. Peter Garrett, Director.
General email, nciocpl@mail.nih.gov

Web, www.cancer.gov/about-nci/organization/ocpl and Twitter, @theNCI

Collects and disseminates scientific information on cancer biology, etiology, screening, prevention, treatment, and supportive care for patients, caregivers, health professionals, researchers, advocates, and media. Provides core communications for cancer information.

President's Cancer Panel, *c/o National Cancer Institute,* Bldg. 31, 9000 Rockville Pike, #B2B37, MS 2590, Bethesda, MD 20892; Maureen R. Johnson, Executive Secretary.
General email, prescancerpanel@mail.nih.gov

Web, https://prescancerpanel.cancer.gov and Twitter, @PresCancerPanel

Presidentially appointed committee that monitors and evaluates the National Cancer Program; reports to the president and Congress.

▶ **NONGOVERNMENTAL**

American Cancer Society, *Cancer Action Network,* 655 15th St. N.W., 20005; (202) 661-5700. Lisa Lacasse, President; Karen E. Knudsen, Chief Executive Officer.
Web, www.fightcancer.org, Twitter, @ACSCAN and Facebook, www.facebook.com/ACSCAN

Supports evidence-based policy and legislation designed to eliminate cancer as a major health problem; works to encourage elected officials and candidates to make cancer a top national priority. Monitors legislation and regulations. (Headquarters in Atlanta, Ga.)

American Childhood Cancer Organization, 6868 Distribution Dr., Beltsville, MD 20705 (mailing address: P.O. Box 498, Kensington, MD 20895-0498); (855) 858-2226. Ruth I. Hoffman, Chief Executive Officer, (202) 262-9949.
General email, staff@acco.org

Web, www.acco.org, Twitter, @aacorg and Facebook, www.facebook.com/americanchildhoodcancer

Membership: families of children with cancer, survivors of childhood cancer, and health and education professionals. Serves as an information and educational network; sponsors self-help groups for parents of children and adolescents with cancer. Monitors legislation and regulations.

American Institute for Cancer Research, 1560 Wilson Blvd., #1000, Arlington, VA 22209 (mailing address: P.O. Box 97167, Washington, DC 20090-7167); (202) 328-7744. Fax, (202) 328-7226. Marilyn Gentry, President. Toll-free, (800) 843-8114.
General email, aicrweb@aicr.org

Web, www.aicr.org, Twitter, @aicrtweets and Facebook, www.facebook.com/AmericanInstituteforCancerResearch

Funds research and fellowship programs on the relationship of nutrition, physical activity, and weight management to cancer risk. Interprets scientific literature; sponsors education programs on cancer prevention.

American Society for Radiation Oncology (ASTRO), 251 S. 18th St., 8th Floor, Arlington, VA 22202; (703) 502-1550. Fax, (703) 502-7852. Laura Thevenot, Chief Executive Officer, (703) 839-7302.
General email, information@astro.org

Web, www.astro.org, Twitter, @ASTRO_org and Facebook, www.facebook.com/AmericanSocietyforRadiationOncology

Radiation oncology, biology, and physics organization that seeks to improve patient care through education, clinical practice, the advancement of science, and advocacy.

American Society of Clinical Oncology (ASCO), 2318 Mill Rd., #800, Alexandria, VA 22314; (703) 229-0158. Fax, (703) 299-0255. Clifford A. Hudis, Chief Executive Officer. Toll-free, (888) 282-2552.
General email, info@conquer.org

Web, www.asco.org, Twitter, @ASCO and Facebook, www.facebook.com/ASCOCancer

Membership: physicians and scientists specializing in cancer prevention, treatment, education, and research. Promotes exchange of information in clinical research and patient care relating to all stages of cancer; monitors international research.

Assn. of Community Cancer Centers, 1801 Research Blvd., #400, Rockville, MD 20850; (301) 984-9496. Fax, (301) 770-1949. Christian G. Downs, Executive Director.
Web, www.accc-cancer.org, Twitter, @ACCCBuzz and Facebook, www.facebook.com/accccancer/

Membership: individuals from community hospitals involved in multidisciplinary cancer programs, including physicians, administrators, nurses, medical directors, pharmacists, and other members of the cancer care team. Supports comprehensive cancer care for all. Monitors legislation and regulations.

Cancer Support Community, 5614 Connecticut Ave., N.W. #280, 20015; (202) 659-9709. Heather Badt, Executive Officer; Elizabeth Franklin, President. Hotline, (888) 793-9355.
General email, help@cancersupportcommunity.org

Web, www.cancersupportcommunity.org, Twitter, @CancerSupportHQ and Facebook, www.facebook.com/CancerSupportCommunity

Membership; Research and advocacy organization providing support services to those facing cancer. Research and Training Institute supports cancer-related psychosocial, behavioral, and surviorship research.

Go2 Foundation for Lung Cancer, *2033 K. St., N.W. #500, 20006 (mailing address: P.O. Box 65860, Washington, D.C. 20006); (202) 463-2080. Laurie Fenton Ambrose, President. Toll-free helpline, (800) 298-2436.*
General email, info@go2foundation.org

Web, www.go2foundation.org, Twitter, @Go2Foundation and Facebook, www.facebook.com/GO2Foundation/

Advocates lung cancer research and access to screenings, treatments, diagnostics, and testing. Provides information about lung cancer risks and early detection. (Formerly Lung Cancer Alliance.)

Leukemia and Lymphoma Society, *National Capital Area Chapter, 3601 Eisenhower Ave., #450, Alexandria, VA 22304; (703) 399-2900. Fax, (703) 399-2901. Ria Freydberg, Executive Director, (703) 399-2905. Toll-free, (888) 557-7177.*
Web, www.lls.org/national-capital-area, Twitter, @LLSusa and Facebook, www.facebook.com/LLSUSA

Voluntary health organization that funds blood cancer research, education, and patient services. Seeks to find cures for leukemia, lymphoma, Hodgkin's disease, and myeloma, and to improve the quality of life of patients and their families. Local chapters provide blood cancer patients with disease and treatment information, financial assistance, counseling, and referrals. (Headquarters in White Plains, NY.)

National Breast Cancer Coalition, *2001 L St. N.W., #500, PMB #5001, 20036; (202) 296-7477. Fax, (202) 314-3458. Frances M. (Fran) Visco, President. Toll-free, (800) 622-2838.*
General email, info@stopbreastcancer.org

Web, www.stopbreastcancer.org and Twitter, @NBCCSTOPBC

Membership: organizations, local coalitions, and individuals. Supports increasing funding for breast cancer research; monitors how funds are spent; seeks to expand access to quality health care for all; and ensures that trained advocates influence all decision making that impacts breast cancer.

National Coalition for Cancer Survivorship, *8455 Colesville Rd., #930, Silver Spring, MD 20910; (301) 650-9127. Shelley Fuld Nasso, Chief Executive Officer. Toll-free, (877) 622-7937.*
General email, info@canceradvocacy.org

Web, www.canceradvocacy.org, Twitter, @CancerAdvocacy, Facebook, www.facebook.com/cancersurvivorship and YouTube, www.youtube.com/user/CancerSurvivorship

Membership: survivors of cancer (newly diagnosed, in treatment, and living beyond cancer), their families and friends, health care providers, and support organizations. Distributes information, including the Cancer Survival Toolbox, about living with cancer diagnosis and treatment; offers free publications and resources that help enable individuals to take charge of their own care or the care of others.

Ovarian Cancer Research Alliance, *1101 14th St. N.W., #850, 20005; (202) 331-1332. Fax, (202) 331-2292. Audra Moran, President. Toll-free, (866) 399-6262.*
General email, info@ocrahope.org

Web, www.ocrahope.org, Facebook, www.facebook.com/ocrahope/ and Twitter, @ocrahope

Acts as an advocate at the federal and state levels for adequate and sustained funding for ovarian cancer research and awareness programs. Promotes legislation that would improve the quality of life and access to care for all cancer patients. Provides information and resources for survivors, women at risk, and health providers.

Dental Care

▶ AGENCIES

National Institute of Dental and Craniofacial Research (NIDCR) *(National Institutes of Health), Bldg. 31, 31 Center Dr., #2C39, MS 2290, Bethesda, MD 20892-2190; (301) 496-4261. Dr. Rena D'Souza, Director, (301) 496-3571. Toll-free, (866) 232-4528.*
General email, nidcrinfo@mail.nih.gov

Web, www.nidcr.nih.gov, Twitter, @NIDCR and YouTube, www.youtube.com/channel/UCl9SindJU9lU22duP1e19cg

Conducts and funds clinical research and promotes training and career development in oral, dental, and craniofacial health. Monitors international research and evaluates its implications for public policy.

▶ NONGOVERNMENTAL

American Dental Assn. (ADA), *Government Relations, 1111 14th St. N.W., #1100, 20005; (202) 898-2400. Michael (Mike) Graham, Senior Vice President Government and Public Affairs.*
General email, govtpol@ada.org

Web, www.ada.org/en/advocacy and Twitter, @AmerDentalAssn

Conducts research, provides dental education materials, compiles statistics on dentistry and dental care. Monitors legislation and regulations. (Headquarters in Chicago, Ill.)

International Assn. for Dental Research, *1619 Duke St., Alexandria, VA 22314-3406; (703) 548-0066. Fax, (703) 548-1883. Dr. Christopher H. Fox, Chief Executive Officer.*
General email, memberservice@iadr.org

Web, www.iadr.org, Facebook, www.facebook.com/DentalResearch and Twitter, @IADR

Membership: professionals engaged in dental research worldwide. Conducts annual convention, conferences, and symposia.

Dermatology, Skin Disorders

▶**AGENCIES**

National Institute of Arthritis and Musculoskeletal and Skin Diseases (NIAMS) *(National Institutes of Health),* Bldg. 31, 31 Center Dr., #4C32, MS 2350, Bethesda, MD 20892-2350; (301) 495-4484. Dr. Lindsey A. Criswell, Director, (301) 496-3651. Health information, (877) 226-4267.
General email, niamsinfo@mail.nih.gov
Web, www.niams.nih.gov, Twitter, @NIH_NIAMS, Facebook, www.facebook.com/NIH_NIAMS and YouTube, www.youtube.com/user/NIAMSNIH

Supports research on the causes and treatment of skin diseases, including psoriasis, eczema, and acne.

▶**NONGOVERNMENTAL**

American Academy of Dermatology, *Government Affairs,* 1201 Pennsylvania Ave. N.W., 20004; (202) 842-3555. Fax, (202) 842-4355. Barbara Greenan, Senior Vice President.
General email, govtaffairs@aad.org
Web, www.aad.org, Twitter, @AADskin and Facebook, www.facebook.com/AADskin

Membership: practicing dermatologists. Promotes the science and art of medicine and surgery related to the skin, hair, and nails. Advocates high-quality dermatologic care and higher standards of care. Monitors legislation and regulations. (Headquarters in Rosemont, Ill.)

American Academy of Facial Plastic and Reconstructive Surgery (AAFPRS), 310 S. Henry St., Alexandria, VA 22314; (703) 299-9291. Fax, (703) 299-8898. Steven J. Jurich, Executive Vice President, ext. 231.
General email, info@aafprs.org
Web, www.aafprs.org, Twitter, @AAFPRS and Facebook, www.facebook.com/AAFPRS

Membership: facial plastic and reconstructive surgeons and other board-certified surgeons whose focus is surgery of the face, head, and neck. Promotes research and study in the field. Helps train residents in facial plastic and reconstructive surgery; offers continuing medical education. Sponsors scientific and medical meetings, international symposia, fellowship training program, seminars, and workshops. Provides videotapes on facial plastic and reconstructive surgery.

Melanoma Research Foundation, 1420 K St. N.W., #7th Floor, 20005; (202) 347-9675. Fax, (202) 347-9678. Kyleigh LiPira, Chief Executive Officer. Toll-free, (800) 673-1290.
Web, www.melanoma.org, Twitter, @curemelanoma, Facebook, www.facebook.com/Melanoma.Research. Foundation and YouTube, www.youtube.com/user/Cure Melanoma

Educates patients, caregivers, and physicians about the diagnosis, prevention, and treatment of melanoma; advocates medical research for effective treatments.

Diabetes, Digestive Diseases

▶**AGENCIES**

National Institute of Diabetes and Digestive and Kidney Diseases (NIDDK) *(National Institutes of Health),* Bldg. 31, 31 Center Dr., #9A52, MS 2560, Bethesda, MD 20892-2560; (301) 496-5741. Fax, (301) 402-2125. Dr. Griffin P. Rodgers, Director. Press, (301) 496-3583. TTY, (866) 569-1162. Toll-free, (800) 860-8747.
General email, healthinfo@niddk.nih.gov
Web, www.niddk.nih.gov, Twitter, @NIDDKgov, Facebook, www.facebook.com/NIDDKgov and YouTube, www.youtube.com/user/NIDDKgov

Conducts and supports basic and clinical research and research training on diabetes and other endocrine and metabolic diseases, digestive diseases, nutrition, obesity, and kidney, urologic, and hematologic diseases. Website provides evidence-based health information.

National Institute of Diabetes and Digestive and Kidney Diseases (NIDDK) *(National Institutes of Health), Diabetes, Endocrinology, and Metabolic Diseases (DEM),* 2 Democracy Plaza, 6707 Democracy Blvd., #683, MS 2560, Bethesda, MD 20892; (301) 496-7349. Fax, (301) 480-3503. Dr. William T. Cefalu, Director, (301) 435-1011. Press, (301) 496-3583.
Web, www.niddk.nih.gov/about-niddk/offices-divisions/ division-diabetes-endocrinology-metabolic-diseases

Provides research funding and support for basic and clinical research in the areas of type 1 and type 2 diabetes and other metabolic disorders, including cystic fibrosis; endocrinology and endocrine disorders; obesity, neuro-endocrinology, and energy balance; and development, metabolism, and basic biology of liver, fat, and endocrine tissues.

National Institute of Diabetes and Digestive and Kidney Diseases (NIDDK) *(National Institutes of Health), Digestive Diseases and Nutrition (DDN),* 2 Democracy Plaza, 6707 Democracy Blvd., #677, MS 5450, Bethesda, MD 20892-5450; (301) 594-7680. Fax, (301) 480-8300. Dr. Stephen P. James, Director. Press, (301) 496-3583.
Web, www.niddk.nih.gov/about-niddk/offices-divisions/ division-digestive-diseases-nutrition

Awards grants and contracts to support basic and clinical research related to digestive diseases and nutrition, as well as training and career development. Conducts and supports research concerning liver and biliary diseases; pancreatic diseases; gastrointestinal disease, including neuroendocrinology, motility, immunology, absorption, and transport in the gastrointestinal tract; nutrient metabolism; obesity; and eating disorders.

National Institute of Diabetes and Digestive and Kidney Diseases Health Information Center (NIDDK) *(National Institutes of Health),* 1 Information Way, Bethesda, MD 20892-3560; (800) 860-8747. Dr. Griffin P. Rodgers, Director. TTY, (866) 569-1162.

General email, healthinfo@niddk.nih.gov

Web, www.niddk.nih.gov/health-information, Twitter, @NIDDKgov and Facebook, www.facebook.com/ NIDDKgov

Provides central information on the prevention and management of diabetes, digestive diseases, kidney disease, weight management, liver disease, urologic diseases, endocrine diseases, diet and nutrition, and blood diseases. Responds to written and telephone inquiries, develops and distributes publications, and provides referrals to disease organizations. Maintains database of patient and professional education materials and provides results of literature searches.

▶NONGOVERNMENTAL

American Diabetes Assn. (ADA), *2451 Crystal Dr., #900, Arlington, VA 22202; (703) 549-1500. Vacant, Chief Executive Officer. Toll-free, (800) 342-2383.*
General email, askada@diabetes.org

Web, www.diabetes.org, Twitter, @AmDiabetesAssn and Facebook, www.facebook.com/AmericanDiabetes Association

Works to improve access to quality care and to eliminate discrimination against people because of their diabetes. Provides local affiliates with education, information, and referral services. Conducts and funds research on diabetes. Monitors international research. Monitors legislation and regulations.

American Gastroenterological Assn., *4930 Del Ray Ave., Bethesda, MD 20814; (301) 654-2055. Fax, (301) 654-5920. Tom Serena, Chief Executive Officer. Press, (301) 272-1603.*
General email, member@gastro.org

Web, www.gastro.org, Twitter, @amergastroassn and Facebook, www.facebook.com/AmerGastroAssn

Membership: 16,000 gastroenterology clinicians, scientists, health care professionals, and educators. Sponsors scientific research on digestive diseases; disseminates information on new methods of prevention and treatment. Publishes the Clinician's Companion, among other scientific journals. Monitors legislation and regulations. (Affiliated with the Foundation of Digestive Health and Nutrition.)

Endocrine Society, *2055 L St. N.W., #600, 20036; (202) 971-3636. Fax, (202) 736-9705. Kate Fryer, Chief Executive Officer. Toll-free, (888) 363-6274.*
General email, info@endocrine.org

Web, www.endocrine.org and Twitter, @TheEndoSociety

Membership: scientists, doctors, health care educators, clinicians, nurses, and others interested in endocrine glands and their disorders. Promotes endocrinology research and clinical practice; sponsors seminars and conferences; gives awards and travel grants.

JDRF, *Advocacy, 1400 K St. N.W., #1212, 20005; (202) 371-9746. Cynthia Rice, Chief Mission Strategy Officer. Toll-free, (800) 533-1868.*
General email, advocacy@jdrf.org

Web, www.jdrf.org

Conducts research, education, and public awareness programs aimed at improving the lives of people with type 1 (juvenile) diabetes and finding a cure for diabetes and its related complications. Monitors legislation and regulations. (Formerly the Juvenile Diabetes Research Foundation.) (Headquarters in New York.)

Family Planning and Population

▶AGENCIES

Agency for International Development (USAID), *Bureau for Global Health, Family Planning and Reproductive Health, 1300 Pennsylvania Ave. N.W., #3.06-011, 20523-3600; (202) 712-4120. Fax, (202) 216-3485. Ellen Starbird, Director. Press, (202) 712-4320.*
General email, pi@usaid.gov

Web, www.usaid.gov/global-health/health-areas/family-planning, Twitter, @USAIDGH and Facebook, www .facebook.com/usaidgh

Advances and supports family planning and reproductive health programs in more than 30 countries.

Assistant Secretary for Health (OASH) *(Health and Human Services Dept.), Population Affairs (OPA), 200 Independence Ave. S.W., 20201; (240) 453-2800. (240) 453-2846. Fax, (240) 453-2801. Jessica Swafford Marcella, Deputy Assistant Secretary.*
General email, opa@hhs.gov

Web, www.hhs.gov/opa and Twitter, @hhspopaffairs

Responsible for Title X Family Planning Program, which provides family planning services, health screening services, and screening for STDs (including HIV) to all who want and need them, with priority given to low-income persons; the Embryo Adoption Awareness program; the Teen Pregnancy Prevention Program.

Census Bureau *(Commerce Dept.), Families and Living Arrangements, 4600 Silver Hill Rd., 20746; Anthony G. Tersine Jr., Chief. Toll free, (800) 923-8282. Press, (301) 763-3030.*
Web, www.census.gov/topics/families.html

Provides data and statistics on family composition. Conducts census and survey research on the number of children, young adults, and couples are living in the Untied States. Collects information on child care, households, grandparents and grandchildren, marriage and divorce.

Census Bureau *(Commerce Dept.), Fertility, 4600 Silver Hill Rd., #7H371, Suitland, MD 20746-8500 (mailing address: 4600 Silver Hill Rd., #7H371, Washington, DC 20233); (301) 763-2416. Rose M. Kreider, Chief, (301) 763-6059. Census Call Center (toll free), (800) 923-8282.*
Web, www.census.gov/topics/health/fertility.html

Provides data and statistics on fertility. Conducts census and survey research on fertility of women in the United States, fertility of men in the United States, and maternity leave.

Eunice Kennedy Shriver National Institute of Child Health and Human Development (NICHD) *(National Institutes of Health), Division of Extramural Research (DER), Contraceptive Research Branch (CRB), 6710B Rockledge Dr., Room 2432, MS 7002, Bethesda, MD 20817; (301) 827-4663. Fax, (301) 480-1972. Daniel S. Johnston, Chief.*
Web, www.nichd.nih.gov/about/org/der/branches/crb

Develops and supports research and research training programs in effects of contraceptive use on human health; development of new and improved methods of contraception; and targeted studies to improve the development of new and improved methods of contraception. Major research areas include contraceptive research and development and prevention of HIV transmission/acquisition through better understanding of reproductive health.

Eunice Kennedy Shriver National Institute of Child Health and Human Development (NICHD) *(National Institutes of Health), Division of Extramural Research (DER), Fertility and Infertility Branch (FI), 6710B Rockledge Dr., Room 2347, MS 7002, Bethesda, MD 20817; (301) 496-6517. Fax, (301) 480-3885. Susan Taymans, Chief.*
Web, www.nichd.nih.gov/about/org/der/branches/fib

Encourages, enables, and supports scientific research aimed at alleviating human infertility, discovering new ways to control fertility, and expanding knowledge of processes that underlie human reproduction. Funds basic, clinical, and translational studies that enhance understanding of normal reproduction and reproductive pathophysiology, as well as enable the development of more effective strategies for the diagnosis, management, and prevention of conditions that compromise fertility.

Eunice Kennedy Shriver National Institute of Child Health and Human Development (NICHD) *(National Institutes of Health), Division of Extramural Research (DER), Population Dynamics Branch (PDB), 6710B Rockledge Dr., Room 2206, MS 7002, Bethesda, MD 20817; (301) 496-1175. Fax, (301) 480-3863. Rebecca L. Clark, Chief.*
Web, www.nichd.nih.gov/about/org/der/branches/pdb

Conducts research and research training in demography, which includes the study of human populations, including fertility, mortality and morbidity, migration, population distribution, nuptiality, family demography, population growth and decline, and the causes and consequences of demographic change; reproductive health, including behavioral and social science research on sexually transmitted diseases, HIV/AIDS, family planning, and infertility; and in population health, which focuses on human health, productivity, behavior, and development at the population level using methods including inferential statistics, natural experiments, policy experiments, statistical modeling, and gene/environment interaction studies.

▶**NONGOVERNMENTAL**

Advocates for Youth, *1325 G. St. N.W., #980, 20005; (202) 419-3420. Fax, (202) 419-1448. Debra Hauser, President; Jennifer Augustine, Executive Vice President.*
General email, information@advocatesforyouth.org
Web, www.advocatesforyouth.org, Twitter, @AdvocatesTweets and Facebook, www.facebook.com/Advocates4Youth

Seeks to reduce the incidence of unintended teenage pregnancy, sexually transmitted infections, and HIV through public education, training and technical assistance, research, and media programs.

American Society for Reproductive Medicine, *J. Benjamin Younger Office of Public Affairs, 726 7th St. S.E., 20003; (202) 863-4985. Sean B. Tipton, Chief Advocacy, Policy, and Development Officer.*
General email, asrm@asrm.dc.org
Web, www.asrm.org, Twitter, @reprodmed and Facebook, www.facebook.com/ASRMFB

Membership: obstetrician/gynecologists, urologists, reproductive endocrinologists, embryologists, mental health professionals, internists, nurses, practice administrators, laboratory technicians, pediatricians, research scientists, and veterinarians. Seeks to educate health care professionals, policymakers, and the public on the science and practice of reproductive medicine and associated legal and ethical issues. Monitors legislation and regulations. (Headquarters in Birmingham, Ala.)

Guttmacher Institute, *Public Policy, 1301 Connecticut Ave. N.W., #700, 20036-3902; (202) 296-4012. Fax, (202) 223-5756. Herminia Palacio, President; Heather D. Boonstra, Vice President for Public Policy. Toll-free, (877) 823-0262.*
General email, info@guttmacher.org
Web, www.guttmacher.org, Twitter, @Guttmacher and Facebook, www.facebook.com/Guttmacher

Conducts research, policy analysis, and public education in reproductive health, fertility regulation, population, and related areas of U.S. and international health. (Headquarters in New York.)

National Abortion Federation (NAF), *1090 Vermont Ave. N.W., #1000, 20005; (202) 667-5881. Fax, (202) 667-5890. Katherine Hancock Ragsdale, President. Hotline, (800) 772-9100.*
General email, naf@prochoice.org
Web, www.prochoice.org, Twitter, @NatAbortionFed and Facebook, www.facebook.com/nationalabortionfederation

Professional association of abortion providers in the United States, Canada, and Mexico City. Offers information on medical, legal, and social aspects of abortion; sets quality standards for abortion care. Conducts training and accredited continuing medical education. Runs a toll-free hotline for women seeking information or referrals. Monitors legislation and regulations.

National Family Planning and Reproductive Health Assn., *1025 Vermont Ave. N.W., #800, 20005; (202) 293-3114. Clare Coleman, President.*
General email, info@nfprha.org
Web, www.nfprha.org, Twitter, @NFPRHA and Facebook, www.facebook.com/NFPRHA

Represents family planning providers, including nurses, nurse practitioners, administrators, and other health care professionals nationwide. Provides advocacy, education, and training for those in the family planning and reproductive health care field. Interests include family planning for the low-income and uninsured, and reducing rates of unintended pregnancy.

Planned Parenthood Federation of America, *Public Policy, 1110 Vermont Ave. N.W., #300, 20005; (202) 973-4800. Fax, (202) 296-3242. Jacqueline Ayers, Vice President, Government Affairs and Public Policy. Toll-free, (800) 230-7526.*
Web, www.plannedparenthood.org, Twitter, @PPFA and Vice President, Twitter, @JacqAyers

Educational, research, and medical services organization. Washington office conducts research and monitors legislation on health care topics, including reproductive health, women's health, contraception, family planning, abortion, and global health. (Headquarters in New York accredits affiliated local centers, which offer medical services, birth control, and family planning information.)

Population Action International, *1300 19th St. N.W., #200, 20036; (202) 557-3400. Nabeeha Kazi Hutchins, President. Press, (202) 728-3426.*
General email, info@pai.org
Web, www.pai.org, Twitter, @pai.org and Facebook, www.facebook.com/paiwdc

Promotes population stabilization through public education and universal access to voluntary family planning. Library open to the public by appointment.

Population Connection, *2120 L St. N.W., #500, 20037 (mailing address: Population Connection, P.O.Box 97129, Washington , DC. @0090); (202) 332-2200. Fax, (202) 332-2302. John Seager, President, (202) 974-7700. Toll-free, (800) 767-1956.*
General email, info@populationconnection.org
Web, www.populationconnection.org, Twitter, @popconnect and Facebook, www.facebook.com/PopulationConnection

Membership: persons interested in sustainable world populations. Promotes the expansion of domestic and international family planning programs; supports a voluntary population stabilization policy and women's access to abortion and family planning services; works to protect the earth's resources and environment. Publishes a quarterly magazine. (Formerly Zero Population Growth.)

Population Institute, *105 2nd St. N.E., 20002; (202) 544-3300. Fax, (202) 544-0068. Kathleen Mogelgaard, President.*
General email, info@populationinstitute.org
Web, www.populationinstitute.org and Twitter, @PopInstitute

Promtes and advocates for gender equality and universal access to sexual and reproductive health services, voluntary family planning. Seeks to increase public awareness of social, economic, and environmental consequences of rapid population growth. Advocates a balance between global population and natural resources to policymakers in developing and industrialized nations. Recruits and trains population activists.

Population Reference Bureau, *1875 Connecticut Ave. N.W., #520, 20009-5728; (202) 483-1100. Fax, (202) 328-3937. Jeffrey Jordan, President. Press, (202) 939-5407. Toll-free, (800) 877-9881.*
General email, communications@prb.org
Web, www.prb.org, Twitter, @PRBdata and Facebook, www.facebook.com/PRBdata

Educational organization engaged in information dissemination, training, and policy analysis on domestic and international population trends and issues. Interests include international development and family planning programs, the environment, and U.S. social and economic policy.

Power to Decide, *1776 Massachusetts Ave. N.W., #200, 20036; (202) 478-8500. Fax, (202) 478-8588. Raegan McDonald-Mosley, Chief Executive Officer.*
General email, info@powertodecide.org
Web, www.powertodecide.org, Twitter, @powertodecide and Facebook, www.facebook.com/powertodecide

Nonpartisan initiative that seeks to reduce the U.S. teen and unplanned pregnancy rates. Provides education and information regarding contraception. (Formerly the National Campaign to Prevent Teen and Unplanned Pregnancy.)

Genetics, Genetic Disorders

▶**AGENCIES**

Eunice Kennedy Shriver National Institute of Child Health and Human Development (NICHD) *(National Institutes of Health), Division of Extramural Research (DER), Intellectual and Developmental Disabilities Branch (IDDB), 6710B Rockledge Dr., Room 2328, MS 7002, Bethesda, MD 20817; (301) 496-1383. Fax, (301) 480-5665. Dr. Melissa Ann Parisi, Chief. Web, www.nichd.nih.gov/about/org/der/branches/iddb*

Supports research projects, training programs, and research centers dedicated to understanding, preventing, and ameliorating intellectual and related developmental disabilities. Major research areas include common and rare neuromuscular and neurodevelopmental disorders, such as Down, Fragile X, and Rett syndromes; inborn errors of metabolism; autism spectrum disorders; and conditions currently and soon-to-be detectable through newborn screening.

Health Resources and Services Administration (HRSA) *(Health and Human Services Dept.), Maternal and Child Health Bureau (MCHB), 5600 Fishers Lane, #18W, Rockville, MD 20857; (301) 443-2170. Dr. Michael Warren, Associate Administrator.*
Web, www.mchb.hrsa.gov

Awards funds, including demonstration grants, to develop or enhance regional, local, and state genetic screening, diagnostic, counseling, and follow-up programs; assists states in their newborn screening programs; provides funding for regional hemophilia treatment centers; and supports comprehensive care for individuals and families with Cooley's anemia, and those with sickle cell anemia identified through newborn screening.

National Human Genome Research Institute (NHGRI) *(National Institutes of Health),* Bldg. 31, 31 Center Dr., #4B09, MS 2152, Bethesda, MD 20892-2152; (301) 402-0911. Fax, (301) 402-2218. Dr. Eric D. Green, Director, (310) 496-0844. Information, (301) 496-0844.
Web, www.genome.gov and *Twitter, @genome_gov*

Conducts and funds a broad range of studies aimed at understanding the structure and function of the human genome and its role in health and disease. Supports the development of resources and technology that will accelerate genome research and its application to human health. Studies the ethical, legal, and social implications of genome research, and supports the training of investigators, as well as the dissemination of genome information to the public and to health professionals.

National Institute of Allergy and Infectious Diseases (NIAID) *(National Institutes of Health), Allergy, Immunology, and Transplantation (DAIT),* 5601 Fishers Lane, #7C13, MS 9828, Rockville, MD 20852; (301) 496-1886. Fax, (301) 402-0175. Dr. Daniel Rotrosen, Director.
Web, www.niaid.nih.gov/about/dait

Supports extramural basic and clinical research to increase understanding of the causes and mechanisms that lead to the development of immunologic diseases and to expand knowledge that can be applied to developing improved techniques of diagnosis, treatment, and prevention. Interests include lupus; allergic diseases, such as asthma, hay fever, and contact dermatitis; and acute and chronic inflammatory disorders.

National Institute of General Medical Sciences (NIGMS) *(National Institutes of Health), Genetics and Molecular, Cellular, and Developmental Biology,* 45 Center Dr., #2AS25K, MS 6200, Bethesda, MD 20892-6200; (301) 496-7301. Fax, (301) 480-2228. Dorit Zuk, Director.
General email, info@nigms.nih.gov
Web, www.nigms.nih.gov/about/overview/Pages/GDB.aspx

Supports research and research training in genetics. Maintains Human Genetic Cell Repository; distributes cell lines and DNA samples to research scientists.

▶**NONGOVERNMENTAL**

Center for Sickle Cell Disease *(Howard University),* 2041 Georgia Ave., 20060; (202) 865-8424. Fax, (202) 232-6719. James G. Taylor VI, Director, (202) 865-8287.
General email, sicklecell@howard.edu
Web, http://huhealthcare.com/healthcare/hospital/specialty-services/sickle-cell-disease-center

Screens and tests for sickle cell disease; conducts research; promotes public education and community involvement; provides counseling, patient care, and transition support from pediatric to adult care services.

Cystic Fibrosis Foundation, 4550 Montgomery Ave., #1100N, Bethesda, MD 20814; (301) 951-4422. Dr. Michael P. Boyle, President. Toll-free, (800) 344-4823.
General email, info@cff.org
Web, www.cff.org, Twitter, @CF_Foundation and *Facebook, www.facebook.com/cysticfibrosisfoundation*

Conducts research on cystic fibrosis, a genetic disease affecting the respiratory and digestive systems. Focuses on medical research to identify a cure and to improve quality of life for those living with cystic fibrosis.

Genetic Alliance, 26400 Woodfield Rd., #189, Damascus, MD 20872; (202) 966-5557. Fax, (202) 966-8563. Sharon Terry, Chief Executive Officer.
General email, info@geneticalliance.org
Web, www.geneticalliance.org, Twitter, @GeneticAlliance and *Facebook, www.facebook.com/GeneticAlliance*

Coalition of government, industry, advocacy organizations, and private groups that seeks to advance genetic research and its applications. Promotes increased funding for research, improved access to services, and greater support for emerging technologies, tests, and treatments. Acts as an advocate on behalf of individuals and families living with genetic conditions to help transform health systems to recognize genetic issues.

Genetics Society of America, 6120 Executive Blvd., #550, Rockville, MD 20852; (240) 880-2000. Tracey A. DePellegrin, Executive Director.
General email, society@genetics-gsa.org
Web, www.genetics-gsa.org, Twitter, @GeneticsGSA and *Facebook, www.facebook.com/GeneticsGSA/*

Membership; Facilitates professional cooperation among persons conducting research in and teaching genetics. Advocates research funding; sponsors meetings; holds conferences and publishes scholarly research journals.

Kennedy Institute of Ethics *(Georgetown University),* Healy Hall, 3700 O St. N.W., 4th Floor, 20057; (202) 687-8099. Dr. David Sulmasy, Director. Library, (202) 687-3885.
General email, kennedyinstitute@georgetown.edu
Web, https://kennedyinstitute.georgetown.edu, Twitter, @kieatgu and *Facebook, www.facebook.com/KennedyInstituteofEthics*

Carries out teaching and research on bioethics, including legal and ethical definitions of death, allocation of health resources, and recombinant DNA and human gene therapy. Sponsors the annual Intensive Bioethics Course. Conducts international programs. Serves as the home of the Bioethics Research Library at Georgetown University (http://bioethics.georgetown.edu). Provides free reference assistance and bibliographic databases covering all ethical issues in health care, genetics, and biomedical research. Publishes the *Kennedy Institute of Ethics Journal.* Library open to scholars, students, and educators. Open to the public by appointment.

March of Dimes, *Government Affairs, 1550 Crystal Dr., #1300, Arlington, VA 22202; (202) 659-1800. Adrian P. Mollo, General Counsel. Toll-free, (888) 663-4637. Web, www.marchofdimes.org/advocacy-and-government-affairs-issues-and-advocacy-priorities.aspx, Twitter, @MarchofDimes and Email, askus@marchofdimes.org*

Works to prevent and treat birth defects. Awards grants for research and provides funds for treatment of birth defects. Monitors legislation and regulations. (Headquarters in White Plains, NY.)

Osteogenesis Imperfecta Foundation, *656 Quince Orchard Rd., #650, Gaithersburg, MD 20878; (301) 947-0083. Fax, (301) 947-0456. Tracy Smith Hart, Chief Executive Officer. Toll-free, (844) 889-7579. General email, bonelink@oif.org*

Web, www.oif.org and Twitter, @OIFoundation

Provides health care professionals and patients with information about osteogenesis imperfecta (OI), also known as brittle bone disease; offers research grants; promotes public policy that supports people living with OI. Additional resources include the OI clinic directory, newsletters and support networkd. Holds conferences and events.

Heart Disease, Strokes

▶AGENCIES

National Heart, Lung, and Blood Institute (NHLBI) *(National Institutes of Health), Cardiovascular Sciences Division (DCVS), 6701 Rockledge Dr., #8128, Bethesda, MD 20892; (301) 435-0422. Dr. David C. Goff Jr., Director. General email, lauerm@nhlbi.nih.gov*

Web, www.nhlbi.nih.gov/about/divisions/division-cardiovascular-sciences

Supports basic, clinical, population, and health services research on the causes, prevention, and treatment of cardiovascular disease and technology development. Interests include disease and risk factor patterns in populations; clinical trials of interventions; and genetic, behavioral, sociocultural, environmental, and health-systems factors of disease risk and outcomes.

National Heart, Lung, and Blood Institute (NHLBI) *(National Institutes of Health), Health Information Center, Bldg. 31, 31 Center Dr., Bethesda, MD 20892-2480 (mailing address: P.O. Box 30105, Bethesda, MD 20824-0105); (301) 592-8573. Lenora Johnson, Director, (301) 496-4236. Communications, (202) 496-4236. Toll-free, (877) 645-2448. General email, nhlbilnfo@nhlbi.nih.gov*

Web, www.nhlbi.nih.gov/about/contact/health-information-and-clinical-trials

Acquires, maintains, and disseminates information on cholesterol, high blood pressure, heart attack awareness, and asthma to the public and health professionals.

National Institute of Neurological Disorders and Stroke (NINDS) *(National Institutes of Health), Bldg. 31, 31 Center Dr., #8A52, MS 2540, Bethesda, MD 20824 (mailing address: P.O. Box 5801, Bethesda, MD 20824); (301) 496-3167. Fax, (301) 402-2186. Dr. Walter J. Koroshetz, Director. Information, (301) 496-5751. Toll-free, (800) 352-9424. Web, www.ninds.nih.gov, Twitter, @NINDSnews and Facebook, www.facebook.com/NINDSandPartners*

Conducts research and disseminates information on the causes, prevention, diagnosis, and treatment of neurological disorders and stroke; supports basic and clinical research in related scientific areas. Provides research grants to public and private institutions and individuals. Operates a program of contracts for the funding of research and research-support efforts.

▶NONGOVERNMENTAL

American Heart Assn., *Federal Advocacy, 1150 Connecticut Ave. N.W., #300, 20036; (202) 785-7900. Fax, (202) 785-7955. Nancy Brown, Chief Executive Officer; Emily J. Holubowich, Vice President of Federal Advocacy, (202) 785-7912. Web, www.heart.org/en/get-involved/advocate/federal-priorities, Twitter, @Americanheart and Facebook, www.facebook.com/AmericanHeart*

Membership: physicians, scientists, and other interested individuals. Supports research, patient advocacy, treatment, and community service programs that provide information about heart disease and stroke; participates in international conferences and research. Monitors legislation and regulations. (Headquarters in Dallas, Tex.)

WomenHeart: National Coalition for Women with Heart Disease, *1100 17th St. N.W., #500, 20036; (202) 728-7199. Fax, (202) 688-2861. Celina Gorre, Chief Executive Officer. Spanish hotline, (800) 676-6002. General email, mail@womenheart.org*

Web, www.womenheart.org, Twitter, @WomenHeartOrg and Facebook, www.facebook.com/WomenHeartNational/

Patient-centered organization that seeks to advance women's heart health through advocacy, community education, and patient support.

HIV and AIDS

▶AGENCIES

Assistant Secretary for Health (OASH) *(Health and Human Services Dept.), Infectious Disease and HIV Policy (OIDP), 330 C St. S.W., #L001, 20024; (202) 795-7697. Fax, (202) 691-2102. B. Kaye Hayes, Director (Acting). General email, oidp@hhs.gov*

Web, www.hhs.gov/ash/ohaidp, HIV/AIDS information, www.hiv.gov, Twitter, @HIVgov and Facebook, www.facebook.com/HIVgov/

Advises the assistant secretary for health and senior Health and Human Services officials on the implementation and development of policies, programs, and activities related to HIV/AIDS, viral hepatitis, other infectious diseases of public health significance, and blood safety and availability.

Assistant Secretary for Health (OASH) *(Health and Human Services Dept.), Office of Minority Health (OMH),* 1101 Wootton Pkwy., #100, Rockville, MD 20852; (240) 453-2882. Fax, (240) 453-2883. Dr. Felicia Collins, Director. Toll-free, (800) 444-6472.
General email, info@minorityhealth.gov

Web, http://minorityhealth.hhs.gov, Twitter, @MinorityHealth and Facebook, www.facebook.com/minorityhealth

Awards grants to minority AIDS education and prevention projects.

Centers for Disease Control and Prevention (CDC) *(Health and Human Services Dept.), Washington Office,* 395 E St. S.W., #9100, 20201; (202) 245-0600. Fax, (202) 245-0602. Jeff Reczek, Director, Washington Office. Public inquiries, (800) 232-4636.
General email, cdcwashington@cdc.gov

Web, www.cdc.gov/washington and Twitter, @CDCgov

Conducts research to prevent and control acquired immune deficiency syndrome (AIDS); promotes public awareness through guidelines for health care workers, educational packets for schools, and monthly reports on incidences of AIDS. (Headquarters in Atlanta, Ga.)

Eunice Kennedy Shriver National Institute of Child Health and Human Development (NICHD) *(National Institutes of Health), Division of Extramural Research (DER), Maternal and Pediatric Infectious Disease Branch (MPIDB),* 6710B Rockledge Dr., Room 2146, MS 7002, Bethesda, MD 20817; (301) 594-4783. Fax, (301) 480-3882. Dr. Sonia S. Lee, Chief (Acting).
Web, www.nichd.nih.gov/about/org/der/branches/mpidb

Supports and conducts domestic and international research related to the epidemiology, diagnosis, clinical manifestations, pathogenesis, transmission, diagnosis, treatment, and prevention of HIV infection and its complications in infants, children, adolescents, and pregnant and non-pregnant women. Investigates the effects of HIV and other infectious agents and their therapies on pregnant women, pregnancy outcomes, fetuses, and children, and the impact of pregnancy on the course of HIV disease and other infectious diseases.

Food and Drug Administration (FDA) *(Health and Human Services Dept.), Center for Drug Evaluation and Research (CDER),* White Oak Bldg. 51, 10903 New Hampshire Ave., #6133, Silver Spring, MD 20993; (301) 796-5400. Fax, (301) 595-7910. Dr. Patrizia Cavazzoni, Director. Press, (301) 796-3700.
General email, druginfo@fda.hhs.gov

Web, www.fda.gov/drugs and www.fda.gov/about-fda/fda-organization/center-drug-evaluation-and-research-cder

Approves new drugs for AIDS and AIDS-related diseases. Reviews and approves applications to investigate and market new drugs; works to harmonize drug approval internationally.

Health Resources and Services Administration (HRSA) *(Health and Human Services Dept.), HIV/AIDS Bureau (HAB),* 5600 Fishers Lane, #09W37, Rockville, MD 20857; (301) 443-1993. Dr. Laura Cheever, Associate Administrator.
Web, www.hrsa.gov/about/organization/bureaus/hab and https://ryanwhite.hrsa.gov/

Administers Ryan White HIV/AIDS Program, provides system of HIV primary medical care, medications, and essential support services for low-income people with HIV. Administers grants to organizations to provide care and treatment services. Conducts AIDS/HIV education and training activities for health professionals.

National Institute of Allergy and Infectious Diseases (NIAID) *(National Institutes of Health), AIDS,* 5601 Fishers Lane, #8D33, MS 9831, Rockville, MD 20852; (301) 496-9112. Fax, (301) 402-1505. Carl W. Dieffenbach, Director.
Web, www.niaid.nih.gov/about/daids

Supports extramural basic and clinical research to better understand HIV/AIDS and how it causes disease; finds new tools to prevent HIV infection, including a preventative vaccine; develops new and more effective treatments for people infected with HIV; and works toward a cure.

National Institute of Mental Health (NIMH) *(National Institutes of Health), AIDS Research Division (DAR),* 5601 Fishers Lane, Room 8D20, Rockville, MD 20852; (240) 627-3874. Dianne M. Rausch, Director.
General email, drausch@mail.nih.gov

Web, www.nimh.nih.gov/about/organization/dar

Supports research programs that reduce the incidence of HIV/AIDS worldwide and decrease the burden of living with HIV/AIDS.

National Institutes of Health (NIH) *(Health and Human Services Dept.), AIDS Research (OAR),* 5601 Fishers Lane, #2F40, MS 9310, Rockville, MD 20852; (301) 496-0357. Fax, (301) 496-2119. Maureen M. Goodenow, Director.
General email, oarinfo@nih.gov

Web, www.oar.nih.gov and Twitter, @NIH_OAR

Responsible for the scientific, budgetary, legislative, and policy elements of the NIH AIDS research program. Plans, coordinates, evaluates, and funds all NIH AIDS research.

State Dept., U.S. Global AIDS Coordinator and Global Health Diplomacy, 1800 G St. N.W., SA-22, #10300, 20037; (202) 663-2579. Fax, (202) 663-2979. Angeli L. Achrekar, Coordinator and Special Representative, (202) 663-2802.
General email, SGACPublicAffairs@state.gov

Web, www.state.gov/pepfar, Twitter, @PEPFAR, Facebook, www.facebook.com/PEPFAR and YouTube, www.youtube.com/user/USPEPFAR

Oversees and coordinates all U.S. international HIV/AIDS activities, including implementation of the President's Emergency Plan for AIDS Relief.

Walter Reed Army Institute of Research *(Defense Dept.), U.S. Military HIV Research Program,* 6720A Rockledge Dr., #400, Bethesda, MD 20817; (301) 500-3600. Fax, (301) 500-3666. Col. Julie Ake, USA, Director.

General email, communications@hivresearch.org

Web, www.hivresearch.org, Twitter, @MHRPinfo and Facebook, www.facebook.com/hivresearch

Conducts HIV research, encompassing vaccine development, prevention, disease surveillance, and care and treatment options.

Warren Grant Magnuson Clinical Center *(National Institutes of Health), Transfusion Medicine, Bldg. 10, 10 Center Dr., #1C711, MS 1184, Bethesda, MD 20892-1184; (301) 496-4506. Fax, (301) 402-1360. Dr. Barbara Jean Bryant, Chief, (301) 594-8382. Press, (301) 496-2563.*

Web, http://clinicalcenter.nih.gov/dtm and Twitter, @NIHClinicalCntr

Supplies blood and blood components for patient care and research. Conducts research on diseases transmissible by blood, primarily AIDS and hepatitis.

▶ **NONGOVERNMENTAL**

The AIDS Institute, *1705 Desales St. N.W. #700, 20036; (202) 835-8373. Rachel Klein, Deputy Executive Director, ext. 201.*

General email, info@taimail.org

Web, www.theaidsinstitute.org, Twitter, @AIDSadvocacy and Facebook, www.facebook.com/TheAIDSInstitute/

Conducts research and disseminates information on health care and HIV issues. Develops and promotes policy aimed at improving the health and welfare of children, youth, and families affected by HIV. Provides training and technical assistance to health care providers and consumers. Monitors legislation and regulations. Program office is in Tampa, Florida.

AIDS United, *1634 Eye St., #1100, 20006; (202) 408-4848. Fax, (202) 408-1818. Jesse Milan Jr., President, (202) 876-2817.*

General email, aidsaction@aidsaction.org

Web, www.aidsunited.org, Twitter, @AIDS_United, Facebook, www.facebook.com/AIDSUnited and Blog, www.aidsunited.org/blog

Channels resources to community-based organizations to fight HIV/AIDS at the local level. Provides grants, capacity building, policy and advocacy, plus technical assistance and research to nearly 400 organizations, principally for prevention efforts.

American Red Cross, *National Headquarters, 431 18th St. N.W., 20006; (202) 303-5000. Gail J. McGovern, President. Headquarters staff directory, (202) 303-5214, ext. 1. Press, (202) 303-5551. Public inquiries, (202) 303-4498. Toll-free, (800) 733-2767.*

Web, www.redcross.org and Twitter, @RedCross

Humanitarian relief and health education organization chartered by Congress. Conducts public education campaigns on HIV/AIDS. Operates worldwide vaccination program. Serves as U.S. member of the International Federation of Red Cross and Red Crescent Societies.

Children's AIDS Fund International, *P.O. Box 16433, 20041; (703) 433-1560. Fax, (703) 433-1561. Anita M. Smith, President, ext. 106.*

General email, info@childrensaidsfund.org

Web, http://childrensaidsfund.org

Provides care, services, resources, referrals, and education to children and their families affected by HIV disease. Focuses on children from birth through age 24 who are infected with HIV, have been orphaned by HIV, or will potentially be orphaned by HIV.

DKT International, *1001 Connecticut Ave. N.W., #800, 20036; (202) 223-8780. Christopher H. Purdy, President, ext. 1.*

General email, info@dktinternational.org

Web, www.dktinternational.org, Twitter, @dktchangeslives and YouTube, www.youtube.com/user/DKTHQ

Supports HIV/AIDS prevention by managing international social marketing campaigns for contraceptives. Assists in family planning and providing safe abortions. Interests include high-risk populations in developing countries.

The Foundation for AIDS Research (amfAR), *Public Policy, 1100 Vermont Ave. N.W., #600, 20005; (202) 331-8600. Fax, (202) 331-8606. Greg Millett, Director.*

General email, info@amfar.org

Web, www.amfar.org, Twitter, @amfAR and Facebook, www.facebook.com/amfarthefoundationforaidsresearch

Supports funding for basic biomedical and clinical AIDS research; promotes AIDS prevention education worldwide; advocates effective AIDS-related public policy. Monitors legislation, regulations, and international research. (Headquarters in New York.)

Human Rights Campaign (HRC), *1640 Rhode Island Ave. N.W., 20036-3278; (202) 628-4160. Fax, (202) 347-5323. Joni Madison, President (Acting). Toll-free, (800) 777-4723. TTY, (202) 216-1572.*

General email, hrc@hrc.org

Web, www.hrc.org, Twitter, @HRC and Facebook, www.facebook.com/humanrightscampaign

Promotes legislation to fund HIV/AIDS research and educates the LGBT community and our allies about the realities of HIV prevention, treatment, and care.

National Minority AIDS Council (NMAC), *1000 Vermont Ave. N.W., #200, 20005; (202) 815-3129. Paul A. Kawata, Executive Director, (202) 277-2777.*

General email, communications@nmac.org

Web, www.nmac.org

Works to build the capacity of small faith- and community-based organizations delivering HIV/AIDS services in communities of color. Holds national conferences; administers treatment and research programs and training; disseminates electronic and printed resource materials; conducts public policy advocacy.

Infectious Diseases, Allergies

▶AGENCIES

Assistant Secretary for Health (OASH) *(Health and Human Services Dept.), Infectious Disease and HIV Policy (OIDP),* 330 C St. S.W., #L001, 20024; (202) 795-7697. Fax, (202) 691-2102. B. Kaye Hayes, Director (Acting). General email, oidp@hhs.gov

Web, www.hhs.gov/ash/ohaidp, HIV/AIDS information, www.hiv.gov, Twitter, @HIVgov and Facebook, www.facebook.com/HIVgov/

Advises the assistant secretary for health and senior Health and Human Services officials on the implementation and development of policies, programs, and activities related to HIV/AIDS, viral hepatitis, other infectious diseases of public health significance, and blood safety and availability.

Eunice Kennedy Shriver National Institute of Child Health and Human Development (NICHD) *(National Institutes of Health), Division of Extramural Research (DER), Maternal and Pediatric Infectious Disease Branch (MPIDB),* 6710B Rockledge Dr., Room 2146, MS 7002, Bethesda, MD 20817; (301) 594-4783. Fax, (301) 480-3882. Dr. Sonia S. Lee, Chief (Acting).
Web, www.nichd.nih.gov/about/org/der/branches/mpidb

Supports and conducts research into the epidemiology, natural history, pathogenesis, transmission, diagnosis, treatment, and prevention of infections, including congenital infections such as Zika and cytomegalovirus; emerging infectious diseases; and vaccine-preventable disease in infants, children, adolescents, and women.

Health and Human Services Dept. (HHS), *Office of Infectious Diseases and HIV/AIDS Policy (OIDP), National Vaccine Program (NVPO),* 330 C St. S.W., #L001, 20024; (202) 795-7697. Fax, (202) 691-2102. Kaye Hayes, Director (Acting). Vaccine finder, (800) 232-0233.
General email, nvpo@hhs.gov

Web, www.hhs.gov/nvpo, www.vaccines.gov, Twitter, @HHSvaccines and General email, oidp@hhs.gov

Coordinates with federal offices about vaccine and immunization activities. Carries out National Vaccine Plan goals to prevent infectious diseases.

National Institute of Allergy and Infectious Diseases (NIAID) *(National Institutes of Health),* 5601 Fishers Lane, MS 2520, Bethesda, MD 20892-9806; (301) 496-2263. Fax, (301) 496-4409. Dr. Anthony S. Fauci, Director. Press, (301) 402-1663. Toll-free health and research information, (866) 284-4107. TTY health and research information, (800) 877-8339.
General email, ocpostoffice@niaid.nih.gov

Web, www.niaid.nih.gov, Twitter, @NIAIDNews, Facebook, www.facebook.com/niaid.nih and YouTube, www.youtube.com/user/niaid

Conducts research and supports research worldwide on the causes of infectious and immune-mediated diseases

to develop better means of prevention, diagnosis, and treatment.

National Institute of Allergy and Infectious Diseases (NIAID) *(National Institutes of Health), Allergy, Immunology, and Transplantation (DAIT),* 5601 Fishers Lane, #7C13, MS 9828, Rockville, MD 20852; (301) 496-1886. Fax, (301) 402-0175. Dr. Daniel Rotrosen, Director. Web, www.niaid.nih.gov/about/dait

Supports extramural basic and clinical research to increase understanding of the causes and mechanisms that lead to the development of immunologic diseases and to expand knowledge that can be applied to developing improved techniques of diagnosis, treatment, and prevention. Interests include lupus; allergic diseases, such as asthma, hay fever, and contact dermatitis; and acute and chronic inflammatory disorders.

National Institute of Allergy and Infectious Diseases (NIAID) *(National Institutes of Health), Microbiology and Infectious Diseases (DMID),* 5601 Fishers Lane, #7G51, MS 9826, Rockville, MD 20892; (301) 435-3384. Emily Erbelding, Director.
Web, www.niaid.nih.gov/about/dmid

Supports extramural basic and clinical research to control and prevent diseases caused by virtually all human infectious agents except HIV by providing funding and resources for researchers.

▶NONGOVERNMENTAL

Allergy and Asthma Network, 8229 Boone Blvd., #260, Vienna, VA 22182-2661; (703) 641-9595. Fax, (703) 288-5271. Tonya Winders, President. Toll-free, (800) 878-4403. General email, info@allergyasthmanetwork.org

Web, https://allergyasthmanetwork.org, Twitter, @AllergyAsthmaHQ and Facebook, www.facebook.com/AllergyAsthmaHQ

Membership: families dealing with asthma and allergies. Works to eliminate suffering and death due to asthma, allergies, and related conditions through education, advocacy, research, and community outreach.

Asthma and Allergy Foundation of America (AAFA), 1235 S. Clark St., #305, Arlington, VA 22202; (202) 466-7643. Kenneth Mendez, President.
General email, info@aafa.org

Web, www.aafa.org, Twitter, @AAFANational and Facebook, www.facebook.com/AAFANational

Membership: provides information on asthma and allergies; awards research grants to asthma and allergic disease professionals; offers in-service training to allied health professionals, child care providers, and others.

Food Allergy Research and Education (FARE), 7901 Jones Branch Dr., #240, McLean, VA 22102; (703) 691-3179. Fax, (703) 691-2713. Brice Roberts, Chief Executive Officer (Acting). Toll-free, (800) 929-4040.
General email, contactfare@foodallergy.org

Web, www.foodallergy.org, Twitter, @FoodAllergy and Facebook, www.facebook.com/FoodAllergyFARE

Membership: dietitians, nurses, physicians, school staff, government representatives, members of the food and pharmaceutical industries, and food-allergy patients and their families. Provides information and educational resources on food allergies and allergic reactions. Offers research grants.

National Center for Biodefense and Infectious Diseases *(George Mason University), 10650 Pyramid Pl., MS 1J5, Manassas, VA 20110; (703) 993-9610. Fax, (703) 993-4280. Ali Andalibi, Chief Scientific Officer.*
General email, aandalibi@gmu.edu

Web, http://ncbid.gmu.edu and http://cos.gmu.edu

Researches and develops diagnostics and treatments for emerging infectious diseases as well as those pathogens that could be used as terrorist weapons that require special containment. Manages a graduate education program.

National Foundation for Infectious Diseases, *7201 Wisconsin Ave., #750, Bethesda, MD 20814; 1629 K St. N.W., #300, 20006; (301) 656-0003. Marla Dalton, Executive Director.*
General email, info@nfid.org

Web, www.nfid.org, Twitter, @NFIDvaccines, Facebook, www.facebook.com/nfidvaccines and YouTube, www .youtube.com/nfidvideos

Works to educate the public and health care professionals about the causes, treatment, and prevention of infectious diseases.

Kidney Disease

▶**AGENCIES**

National Institute of Diabetes and Digestive and Kidney Diseases (NIDDK) *(National Institutes of Health), Bldg. 31, 31 Center Dr., #9A52, MS 2560, Bethesda, MD 20892-2560; (301) 496-5741. Fax, (301) 402-2125. Dr. Griffin P. Rodgers, Director. Press, (301) 496-3583. TTY, (866) 569-1162. Toll-free, (800) 860-8747.*
General email, healthinfo@niddk.nih.gov

Web, www.niddk.nih.gov, Twitter, @NIDDKgov, Facebook, www.facebook.com/NIDDKgov and YouTube, www .youtube.com/user/NIDDKgov

Conducts and supports basic and clinical research and research training on diabetes and other endocrine and metabolic diseases, digestive diseases, nutrition, obesity, and kidney, urologic, and hematologic diseases. Website provides evidence-based health information.

National Institute of Diabetes and Digestive and Kidney Diseases (NIDDK) *(National Institutes of Health), Kidney, Urologic, and Hematologic Diseases (KUH), 2 Democracy Plaza, 6707 Democracy Blvd., #625, MS 5458, Bethesda, MD 20892; (301) 496-6325. Fax, (301) 480-3510. Dr. Robert A. Star, Director. Press, (301) 496-3583. Toll-free, (800) 891-5390.*
Web, www.niddk.nih.gov/about-niddk/offices-divisions/ division-kidney-urologic-hematologic-diseases

Funds research on the prevention, diagnosis, and treatment of renal disorders. Conducts research and reviews grant proposals concerning maintenance therapy for persons with chronic kidney, urologic, and renal diseases.

▶**NONGOVERNMENTAL**

American Kidney Fund, *11921 Rockville Pike, #300, Rockville, MD 20852; LaVarne A. Burton, Chief Executive Officer. Helpline, (866) 300-2900. Toll-free, (800) 638-8299. General email, helpline@kidneyfund.org*

Web, http://kidneyfund.org, Twitter, @KidneyFund, Facebook, www.facebook.com/AmericanKidneyFund and YouTube, www.youtube.com/user/kidneyfund

Provides direct financial support to dialysis and kidney transplant patients in need; supports health education and kidney disease prevention efforts. Monitors legislation and regulations.

American Society of Nephrology (ASN), *1401 H St. N.W., #900, 20005; (202) 640-4660. Fax, (202) 637-9793. Dr. Susan E. Quaggin, President.*
General email, email@asn-online.org

Web, www.asn-online.org, Twitter, @ASNKidney and Facebook, www.facebook.com/AmericanSocietyof Nephrology

Membership: health professionals who specialize in kidney disease. Holds the annual Kidney Week meeting for members to share research. Advocates awareness of kidney disease. Publishes the *Journal of the American Society of Nephrology* and the *Clinical Journal of the American Society of Nephrology.* Offers online courses and information on training programs for nephrologists. Awards grants and fellowships to members who conduct research on kidney disease treatment and prevention.

National Kidney Foundation, *Government Relations, 1600 Tysons Blvd., #3300, McLean, VA 22102; (202) 244-7900. Fax, (202) 244-7405. Michele Anthony, Executive Director. Toll-free, (800) 622-9010.*
General email, infowdc@kidney.org

Web, www.kidney.org and Twitter, @nkf

Supports funding for kidney dialysis and other forms of treatment for kidney disease; provides information on detection and screening of kidney diseases; supports organ transplantation programs. Monitors legislation, regulations, and international research. (Headquarters in New York.)

Lung Disease

▶**AGENCIES**

National Heart, Lung, and Blood Institute (NHLBI) *(National Institutes of Health), Health Information Center, Bldg. 31, 31 Center Dr., Bethesda, MD 20892-2480 (mailing address: P.O. Box 30105, Bethesda, MD 20824-0105); (301) 592-8573. Lenora Johnson, Director, (301) 496-4236. Communications, (202) 496-4236. Toll-free, (877) 645-2448.*

General email, nhlbilnfo@nhlbi.nih.gov

Web, www.nhlbi.nih.gov/about/contact/health-information-and-clinical-trials

Acquires, maintains, and disseminates information on asthma and other lung ailments.

National Heart, Lung, and Blood Institute (NHLBI) *(National Institutes of Health), Lung Diseases Division (DLD), 2 Rockledge Center, 6701 Rockledge Dr., #10042, MS 7952, Bethesda, MD 20892; (301) 435-0233. James P. Kiley, Director.*

Web, www.nhlbi.nih.gov/science/lung-diseases and Twitter, @NHLBI_LUNGDir

Plans, implements, and monitors research and training programs in lung diseases and sleep disorders, including research on causes, diagnosis, treatments, prevention, and health education. Interests include COPD, genetics, cystic fibrosis, asthma, bronchopulmonary dysplasia, immunology, respiratory neurobiology, sleep-disordered breathing, critical care and acute lung injury, developmental biology and pediatric pulmonary diseases, immunologic and fibrotic pulmonary disease, rare lung disorders, pulmonary vascular disease, and pulmonary complications of AIDS and tuberculosis.

▶**NONGOVERNMENTAL**

American Lung Assn., *1331 Pennsylvania Ave. N.E., #1425N, 20004; (202) 785-3355. Harold P. Wimmer, President. Toll-free, (800) 586-4872.*

General email, info@lung.org

Web, www.lung.org, Twitter, @LungAssociation and Facebook, www.facebook.com/lungusa

Promotes improved lung health and the prevention of lung disease through research, education, and advocacy. Interests include antismoking campaigns; lung-related biomedical research; air pollution; and all lung diseases, including asthma, COPD, and lung cancer. (Headquarters in Chicago, Ill.)

Cystic Fibrosis Foundation, *4550 Montgomery Ave., #1100N, Bethesda, MD 20814; (301) 951-4422. Dr. Michael P. Boyle, President. Toll-free, (800) 344-4823.*

General email, info@cff.org

Web, www.cff.org, Twitter, @CF_Foundation and Facebook, www.facebook.com/cysticfibrosisfoundation

Conducts research on cystic fibrosis, a genetic disease affecting the respiratory and digestive systems. Focuses on medical research to identify a cure and to improve quality of life for those living with cystic fibrosis.

Go2 Foundation for Lung Cancer, *2033 K. St., N.W. #500, 20006 (mailing address: P.O. Box 65860, Washington, D.C. 20006); (202) 463-2080. Laurie Fenton Ambrose, President. Toll-free helpline, (800) 298-2436.*

General email, info@go2foundation.org

Web, www.go2foundation.org, Twitter, @Go2Foundation and Facebook, www.facebook.com/GO2Foundation/

Advocates lung cancer research and access to screenings, treatments, diagnostics, and testing. Provides information

about lung cancer risks and early detection. (Formerly Lung Cancer Alliance.)

Neurological and Muscular Disorders

▶**AGENCIES**

Eunice Kennedy Shriver National Institute of Child Health and Human Development (NICHD) *(National Institutes of Health), Division of Extramural Research (DER), Intellectual and Developmental Disabilities Branch (IDDB), 6710B Rockledge Dr., Room 2328, MS 7002, Bethesda, MD 20817; (301) 496-1383. Fax, (301) 480-5665. Dr. Melissa Ann Parisi, Chief.*

Web, www.nichd.nih.gov/about/org/der/branches/iddb

Supports research projects, training programs, and research centers dedicated to understanding, preventing, and ameliorating intellectual and related developmental disabilities. Major research areas include common and rare neuromuscular and neurodevelopmental disorders, such as Down, Fragile X, and Rett syndromes; inborn errors of metabolism; autism spectrum disorders; and conditions currently and soon-to-be detectable through newborn screening.

National Institute of Mental Health (NIMH) *(National Institutes of Health), Neuroscience and Basic Behavioral Science Division (DNBBS), 6001 Executive Blvd., #7204, MS 9645, Rockville, MD 20892; (301) 443-3563. Fax, (301) 443-1731. Linda S. Brady, Director.*

Web, www.nimh.nih.gov/about/organization/dnbbs

Supports research programs in the areas of basic neuroscience, genetics, basic behavioral science, research training, resource development, drug discovery, and research dissemination. Responsible for ensuring that relevant basic science knowledge is generated to create improved diagnosis, treatment, and prevention of mental and behavioral disorders.

National Institute of Neurological Disorders and Stroke (NINDS) *(National Institutes of Health), Bldg. 31, 31 Center Dr., #8A52, MS 2540, Bethesda, MD 20824 (mailing address: P.O. Box 5801, Bethesda, MD 20824); (301) 496-3167. Fax, (301) 402-2186. Dr. Walter J. Koroshetz, Director. Information, (301) 496-5751. Toll-free, (800) 352-9424.*

Web, www.ninds.nih.gov, Twitter, @NINDSnews and Facebook, www.facebook.com/NINDSandPartners

Conducts research and disseminates information on the causes, prevention, diagnosis, and treatment of neurological disorders and stroke; supports basic and clinical research in related scientific areas. Provides research grants to public and private institutions and individuals. Operates a program of contracts for the funding of research and research-support efforts.

▶**NONGOVERNMENTAL**

Alzheimer's Assn., *Public Policy Office, 1212 New York Ave. N.W., #800, 20005-6105; (202) 393-7737. Joanne Pike, President; Robert J. Egge, Chief of Public Policy, ext. 8660.*

General email, advocateinfo@alz.org

Web, www.alz.org, Twitter, @alzassociation, Facebook, www.facebook.com/actionalz and Virtual library, www.alz.org/library

Works with lawmakers to advance policies and improve the lives of those affected by dementia, including the Comprehensive Care for Alzheimers Act. Offers family support services and educates the public about Alzheimer's disease, a neurological disorder mainly affecting the brain tissue in older adults. Promotes research and long-term care protection and coverage; maintains liaison with Alzheimer's associations abroad. Monitors legislation and regulations. (Headquarters in Chicago, Ill.)

American Academy of Orthopaedic Surgeons, *Government Relations, 317 Massachusetts Ave. N.E., #100, 20002; (202) 546-4430. Fax, (202) 546-5051. Graham H. Newson, Vice President of Government Relations.*
General email, dc@aaos.org

Web, www.aaos.org/Advocacy and Twitter, @AAOSAdvocacy

Membership: orthopaedic surgeons and musculoskeletal care professionals. Offers continuing education activities; publishes scientific and medical journals and electronic resources. Engages in health policy and acts as advocate on behalf of orthopaedic surgeons and patients.

Autism Speaks, *Washington Office, 1990 K St. N.W., 2nd Floor, 20006 (mailing address: 1060 State Rd., 2nd Floor, Princeton, N.J. 08540); (202) 955-3111. Kisha James, Staff, ext. 1.*
General email, nationalcapitalarea@autismspeaks.org

Web, www.autismspeaks.org/national-capital and Twitter, @autismspeaks

Science and advocacy organization that funds biomedical research to determine the causes, prevention, treatments, and cure for autism. Using advocacy and support.

Brain Injury Assn. of America, *3057 Nutley St., #805, Fairfax, VA 22031-1931; (703) 761-0750. Fax, (703) 761-0755. Susan H. Connors, President. Toll-free, (800) 444-6443.*
General email, braininjuryinfo@biausa.org

Web, www.biausa.org, Twitter, @biaamerica and Facebook, www.facebook.com/BrainInjuryAssociationof America

Works to improve the quality of life for persons with traumatic brain injuries and for their families. Promotes the prevention of head injuries through public awareness and education programs. Offers state-level support services for individuals and their families. Monitors legislation and regulations.

CHADD: The National Resource on ADHD, *4221 Forbes Blvd., #270, Lanham, MD 20706; (301) 306-7070. Fax, (301) 306-7090. Rhonda Buckley, Chief Executive Officer (Acting). En Español, (866) 200-8098.*
Web, www.chadd.org, Twitter, @CHADD_ADHD, Facebook, www.facebook.com/CHADD.org and YouTube, www.youtube.com/HelpforADHD

Membership: health care and mental health professionals, educators, and individuals with ADHD or ADHD-related symptoms. Conducts advocacy and outreach to policymakers at the state and federal levels in areas including health care reform, bullying in schools, and mental health parity. The affiliated National Research Center is a CDC-funded clearinghouse for evidence-based information about ADHD.

Epilepsy Foundation, *3540 Crain Hiway, #675, Bowie, MD 20716; (301) 459-3700. Fax, (301) 577-2684. Laura Thrall, Chief Executive Officer. Spanish language, (866) 748-8008. Toll-free, (800) 332-1000.*
General email, contactus@efa.org

Web, www.epilepsy.com, Twitter, @EpilepsyFdn and Facebook, www.facebook.com/EpilepsyFoundationof America

Promotes research and treatment of epilepsy; makes research grants; disseminates information and educational materials. Affiliates provide direct services for people with epilepsy and make referrals when necessary.

National Assn. of Spine Specialists, Advocacy, *Washington Office, 20 F St. N.W., #310, 20001; Philip Schneider, Chair. Toll-free, (888) 960-6277.*
Web, www.spineadvocacy.org/Advocacy/About-Us and Twitter, @SpineAdvocacy

Supports research and advocacy for quality, ethical, evidence-based spine care for patients. (Headquarters in Burr Ridge, Ill.)

National Multiple Sclerosis Society, *Washington Chapter, 1800 M St. N.W., #B50 North, 20036; (202) 296-5363. Fax, (202) 296-3425. Chartese Berry, Chapter President, (202) 375-5616. Toll-free, (800) 344-4867.*
General email, info-dcmd@nmss.org

Web, www.msandyou.org

Seeks to advance medical knowledge of multiple sclerosis, a disease of the central nervous system; disseminates information worldwide. (Headquarters in New York.)

Society for Neuroscience, *1121 14th St. N.W., #1010, 20005; (202) 962-4000. Marty Saggese, Executive Director.*
General email, info@sfn.org

Web, www.sfn.org, Twitter, @SfNtweets and Facebook, www.facebook.com/societyforneuroscience

Membership: scientists and physicians worldwide who research the brain, spinal cord, and nervous system. Interests include the molecular and cellular levels of the nervous system; systems within the brain, such as vision and hearing; and behavior produced by the brain. Promotes education in the neurosciences and the application of research to treat nervous system disorders.

Spina Bifida Assn., *1600 Wilson Blvd., #600, Arlington, VA 22209; (202) 944-3285. Fax, (202) 944-3295. Sara Struwe, Chief Executive Officer, ext. 12. Toll-free, (800) 621-3141.*

General email, sbaa@sbaa.org

Web, http://spinabifidaassociation.org, Twitter, @SpinaBifidaAssn and Facebook, www.facebook.com/spina.bifida.learn

Membership: individuals with spina bifida, their supporters, and concerned professionals. Offers educational programs, scholarships, and support services; acts as a clearinghouse; provides referrals and information about treatment and prevention. Serves as U.S. member of the International Federation for Hydrocephalus and Spina Bifida, which is headquartered in Geneva, Switzerland. Monitors legislation and regulations.

United Cerebral Palsy (UCP), 1825 K St. N.W., #600, 20006; (202) 776-0406. Armando Contreras, President. Toll-free, (800) 872-5827.
General email, info@ucp.org

Web, www.ucp.org, Twitter, @UCPnational, Facebook, www.facebook.com/unitedcerebralpalsy and YouTube, www.youtube.com/user/UnitedCerebralPalsy

National network of state and local affiliates that assists individuals with cerebral palsy and other developmental disabilities and their families. Provides parent education, early intervention, employment services, family support and respite programs, therapy, assistive technology, and vocational training.

Nutrition

Center for Nutrition Policy and Promotion (CNPP) (Agriculture Dept.), 1320 Braddock Pl., Alexandria, VA 22314; (703) 305-7600. Jackie Haven, Deputy Administrator. USDA National Hunger Hotline, (866) 348-6479. Food and Nutrition check #, (703) 305-2060.
Web, www.fns.usda.gov/cnpp, Twitter, @USDANutrition and Facebook, www.facebook.com/MyPlate

Defines and coordinates nutrition education policy, promotes food and nutrition guidance, and develops nutrition information materials for consumers, policymakers, and professionals in health, education, industry, and media.

Eunice Kennedy Shriver National Institute of Child Health and Human Development (NICHD) (National Institutes of Health), Division of Extramural Research (DER), Pediatric Growth and Nutrition Branch (PGNB), 6710B Rockledge Dr., Room 2444, MS 7002, Bethesda, MD 20817; (301) 402-7886. Dr. Andrew Bremer, Chief.
Web, www.nichd.nih.gov/about/org/der/branches/pgnb

Supports research on understanding basic and clinical aspects of growth and development, including the biological processes that underlie normal growth and development, as well as research on how these biological processes go awry. Major research programs include how nutrition promotes healthy growth and development; lactation and breastfeeding; the causes of obesity in childhood and sequelae of childhood obesity in adulthood; the

genetic, nutritional, and hormonal antecedents of bone health and the origins of osteoporosis; the neuroendocrine basis of growth and the onset of puberty; and the development of the hypothalamo-pituitary adrenal, gonadal, and thyroid axes.

Food and Drug Administration (FDA) (Health and Human Services Dept.), Center for Food Safety and Applied Nutrition (CFSAN), 5001 Campus Dr., HFS-009, College Park, MD 20740-3835; (240) 402-1600. Fax, (301) 436-2668. Susan T. Mayne, Director. SAFEFOOD Info, (888) 723-3366. TTY, (800) 877-8339.
General email, consumer@fda.gov

Web, www.fda.gov/AboutFDA/CentersOffices/OfficeofFoods/CFSAN and Twitter, @FDAFood

Conducts research about dietary supplements and nutrition in general.

National Agricultural Library (Agriculture Dept.), Food and Nutrition Information Center (FNIC), 10301 Baltimore Ave., #108, Beltsville, MD 20705-2351; (301) 504-5414. Fax, (301) 504-6409. Wendy Shaw, Branch Chief, (301) 504-6369.
General email, fnic@ars.usda.gov

Web, www.nal.usda.gov/fnic

Serves primarily educators, health professionals, and consumers seeking information about nutrition assistance programs and general nutrition. Serves as an online provider of science-based information about food and nutrition and links to such information. Lends books and audiovisual materials for educational purposes through interlibrary loans; provides reference services; develops resource lists of health and nutrition publications. Library open to the public.

National Institute of Diabetes and Digestive and Kidney Diseases (NIDDK) (National Institutes of Health), Digestive Diseases and Nutrition (DDN), 2 Democracy Plaza, 6707 Democracy Blvd., #677, MS 5450, Bethesda, MD 20892-5450; (301) 594-7680. Fax, (301) 480-8300. Dr. Stephen P. James, Director. Press, (301) 496-3583.
Web, www.niddk.nih.gov/about-niddk/offices-divisions/division-digestive-diseases-nutrition

Awards grants and contracts to support basic and clinical research related to digestive diseases and nutrition, as well as training and career development. Conducts and supports research concerning liver and biliary diseases; pancreatic diseases; gastrointestinal disease, including neuroendocrinology, motility, immunology, absorption, and transport in the gastrointestinal tract; nutrient metabolism; obesity; and eating disorders.

National Institute of Food and Agriculture (NIFA) (Agriculture Dept.), Institute of Food Safety and Nutrition (IFSN), 1400 Independence Ave. S.W., MS 2225, 20250-2225; 305-A Whitten Building, 20250; (202) 720-4423. Carrie Castille, Director (NIFA); Suzanne Stluka, Deputy Director IFSN, (816) 908-3305; Shoushan (Steve) Zeng, Division Director. Hotline, (202) 720-2791 ext. 1.

Web, https://nifa.usda.gov/office/institute-food-safety-and-nutrition

Promotes programs to improve Americans' health through better nutrition, reducing childhood obesity, and malnutrition, improving food safety and quality.

National Institutes of Health (NIH) *(Health and Human Services Dept.), Dietary Supplements (ODS), 6705 Rockledge Dr., #730, MSC 7991, Bethesda, MD 20817; (301) 435-2920. Fax, (301) 480-1845. Joseph Betz, Director (Acting).*
General email, ods@nih.gov

Web, http://ods.od.nih.gov, Twitter, @NIH_ODS and Facebook, www.facebook.com/NIH.ODS

Reviews scientific evidence on the safety and efficacy of dietary supplements. Conducts, promotes, and coordinates scientific research within the NIH relating to dietary supplements. Conducts and supports conferences, workshops, and symposia and publishes research results on scientific topics related to dietary supplements.

National Institutes of Health (NIH) *(Health and Human Services Dept.), Nutrition Research (ONR), 2 Democracy Plaza, 6707 Democracy Blvd., #677, MS 5450, Bethesda, MD 20892; (301) 827-3356. Fax, (301) 480-3768. Dr. Christopher J. Lynch, Director (Acting).*
General email, nutritionresearch@mail.nih.gov

Web, https://dpcpsi.nih.gov/onr

Supports research on nutritional requirements, dietary fiber, obesity, eating disorders, energy regulation, clinical nutrition, trace minerals, and basic nutrient functions.

▶**NONGOVERNMENTAL**

Academy of Nutrition and Dietetics, *Washington Office, Policy Initiatives and Advocacy, 1120 Connecticut Ave. N.W., #460, 20036-3989; (202) 775-8277. Fax, (202) 775-8284. Jeanne Blankenship, Vice President, (312) 899-0040, ext. 6004. Toll-free, (800) 877-0877.*
General email, govaffairs@eatright.org

Web, www.eatright.org, Twitter, @eatright, Facebook, www.facebook.com/EatRightNutrition and Press, media@eatright.org

Membership: dietitians and other nutrition professionals. Works with state and federal legislators and agencies on public policy issues affecting consumers and the practice of dietetics, including Medicare coverage of medical nutrition therapy; licensure of registered dietitians; child nutrition; obesity; food safety. Promotes public health and nutrition; accredits academic programs in clinical nutrition and food service management; sets standards of professional practice. Incorporates research, professional development, technology and practice to foster innovation and discovery. Publishes the *Journal of the Academy of Nutrition and Dietetics.* (Headquarters in Chicago, Ill.)

American Society for Nutrition, *9211 Corporate Blvd., #300, Rockville, MD 20850; (240) 428-3650. Fax, (240) 404-6797. John E. Courtney, Executive Officer.*

General email, info@nutrition.org

Web, www.nutrition.org, Twitter, @nutritionorg and Facebook, www.facebook.com/AmerSocNutr

Membership: nutritional research scientists and practitioners, including clinical nutritionists. Supports and advocates research on the role of human nutrition in health and disease; encourages undergraduate and graduate nutrition education; supports minority affairs; offers awards for research. (Merger of the American Society for Clinical Nutrition and the American Society for Nutritional Sciences.)

American Society for Parenteral and Enteral Nutrition (ASPEN), *8401 Colesville Rd., #510, Silver Spring, MD 20910-3805; (301) 587-6315. Fax, (301) 587-2365. Wanda Johnson, Chief Executive Officer, ext. 126.*
General email, aspen@nutr.org

Web, www.nutritioncare.org, Twitter, @ASPEN_nutrition and Facebook, www.facebook.com/nutritioncare.org

Membership: health care professionals who provide patients with intravenous nutritional support during hospitalization and rehabilitation at home. Develops nutrition guidelines; provides educational materials; conducts annual meetings.

Eating Disorders Coalition for Research, Policy, and Action, *P.O. Box 96503-98807, 20090; (202) 543-9570. David Jaffe, Executive Director.*
General email, manager@eatingdisorderscoalition.org

Web, http://eatingdisorderscoalition.org, Twitter, @EDCoalition and Facebook, www.facebook.com/EatingDisordersCoalition

Seeks greater national and federal recognition of eating disorders. Promotes recognition of eating disorders as a public health priority and the implementation of more accessible treatment and more effective prevention programs. Monitors legislation and regulations.

Obesity Society, *1110 Bonifant St., #500, Silver Spring, MD 20910; (301) 563-6526. Anthony Comuzzie, Chief Executive Director.*
General email, contact@obesity.org

Web, www.obesity.org, Twitter, @ObesitySociety and Facebook, www.facebook.com/TheObesitySociety

Membership: scientists and health professionals dedicated to understanding obesity. Promotes research, education, and advocacy to better understand, prevent, and treat obesity. Informs the medical community and the public of new advances.

Sleep Disorders

▶**AGENCIES**

National Heart, Lung, and Blood Institute (NHLBI) *(National Institutes of Health), Lung Diseases Division (DLD), National Center on Sleep Disorders Research (NCSDR), 6701 Rockledge Dr., #10170, MS 7952, Bethesda, MD 20892; (301) 435-0199. Marishka K. Brown, Director.*

General email, ncsdr@nih.gov

Web, www.nhlbi.nih.gov/about/divisions/division-lung-diseases/national-center-sleep-disorders-research and www.nhlbi.nih.gov/science/sleep-science-and-sleep-disorders

Supports research and training related to sleep and cir-cadian rhythm risks contributing to heart, lung, and blood disorders. Serves as a point of contact and coordination for sleep research and education across NIH, several federal agencies, and outside organizations.

▶ NONGOVERNMENTAL

American Sleep Apnea Assn., 1250 Connecticut Ave. N.W., #700, 20036; (888) 293-3650. Fax, (888) 293-3650. Gilles Frydman, Executive Director.
General email, asaa@sleepapnea.org

Web, www.sleepapnea.org, Twitter, @sleepapneaorg and Facebook, www.facebook.com/sleepapneaorg

Promotes continuing improvements in treatments for sleep apnea and acts as advocate on behalf of sleep apnea patients. Monitors legislation and regulations.

Circadian Sleep Disorders Network, 4619 Woodfield Rd., Bethesda, MD 20814; Peter Mansbach, President.
General email, csd-n@csd-n.org

Web, www.circadiansleepdisorders.org and Twitter, @CSD_N

Seeks to increase awareness of circadian sleep disorders among the medical community and general public. Acts as advocate for accommodation of patients in education and employment.

National Sleep Foundation, 1010 N. Glebe Rd., #420, Arlington, VA 22201; (703) 243-1697. John Lupos, Chief Executive Officer.
General email, nsf@sleepfoundation.org

Web, www.sleepfoundation.org, Twitter, @sleepfoundation and Facebook, www.facebook.com/nationalsleep foundation

Supports sleep-related public education and research to understand sleep problems and sleep disorders, including insomnia, sleep apnea, and narcolepsy. Works to prevent sleep-related accidents, especially those that involve driv-ing. Monitors legislation and regulations related to sleep, alertness, and safety, such as hours-of-service rules for commercial drivers. (Headquarters in Seattle, Wash.)

National Sleep Foundation, Sleep for Kids, 1010 N. Glebe Rd., #310, Arlington, VA 22201; John Lupos, Chief Executive Officer.
General email, nsf@sleepfoundation.org

Web, www.sleepforkids.org

Provides information about the importance of sleep for children and sleep disorders, and tips for parents and teachers to help school-age children develop good sleep habits.

Substance Abuse

▶ AGENCIES

Elementary and Secondary Education (OESE) (Education Dept.), Formula Grants (OFG), Safe and Supportive Schools (OSSS), Lyndon B. Johnson Bldg., 400 Maryland Ave. S.W., #3E-245, 20202-6135; (202) 453-5563. Fax, (202) 453-6742. Bryan Williams, Director.
General email, oese@ed.gov

Web, https://oese.ed.gov/offices/office-of-formula-grants/safe-supportive-schools

Develops policy for the department's drug and violence prevention initiatives for students in elementary and secondary schools and institutions of higher education. Provides financial assistance for drug and violence pre-vention activities. Coordinates education efforts in drug and violence prevention with those of other federal departments and agencies.

National Drug Control Policy (ONDCP) (Executive Office of the President), President's Commission on Combating Drug Addiction and the Opioid Crisis, The White House, 1600 Pennsylvania Ave. N.W., 20500; (202) 456-1111. (202) 395-6700. Dr. Roland Gupta, Director.
General email, commission@ondcp.eop.gov

Web, www.whitehouse.gov/ondcp/presidents-commission

Conducts research and studies around ways to combat and treat drug abuse, addiction, and the opioid crisis that affects communities across the United States.

National Institute on Alcohol Abuse and Alcoholism (NIAAA) (National Institutes of Health), 6700 Rockledge Dr., Bethesda, MD 20817; (301) 443-3860. Fax, (301) 443-7043. Dr. George F. Koob, Director. Press, (301) 443-2857.
General email, niaaaweb-r@exchange.nih.gov

Web, www.niaaa.nih.gov

Supports basic and applied research on preventing and treating alcoholism and alcohol-related problems; con-ducts research and disseminates findings on alcohol abuse and alcoholism. Participates in U.S. and international research.

National Institute on Drug Abuse (NIDA) (National Institutes of Health), 301 N. Stonestreet Ave., #3WFN, MS C6024, Bethesda, MD 20892; (301) 443-1124. Fax, (301) 480-2485. Dr. Nora D. Volkow, Director. Press, (301) 443-6245. Hotline, (800) 662-4357.
Web, www.nida.nih.gov, Twitter, @NIDAnews, Facebook, www.facebook.com/NIDANIH and YouTube, www .youtube.com/user/NIDANIH

Conducts and sponsors research on the prevention, effects, and treatment of drug abuse. Monitors inter-national policy and research.

Substance Abuse and Mental Health Services Administration (SAMHSA) (Health and Human Services Dept.), 5600 Fishers Lane, Rockville, MD 20857; (240) 276-2000. Fax, (240) 489-1450. Miriam E. Delphin-Rittmon, Assistant Secretary. Helpline, (800) 662-4357. Information,

(877) 726-4727. Press, (240) 276-2130 (press 4). TTY, (800) 487-4889. Workplace helpline, (800) 967-5752.
General email, samhsainfo@samhsa.hhs.gov

Web, www.samhsa.gov, Twitter, @samhsagov and Facebook, www.facebook.com/samhsa

Provides and manages block grants and special programmatic funding aimed at reducing the impact of substance abuse and mental illness on communities. Provides states, providers, communities, and the public with information about behavioral health issues and prevention/treatment approaches. Administers substance abuse and mental health treatment referral service: (800) 662-4357 or www.samhsa.gov/treatment. Offers behavioral health publications and other resources: http://store.samhsa.gov.

Substance Abuse and Mental Health Services Administration (SAMHSA) *(Health and Human Services Dept.), Center for Substance Abuse Prevention (CSAP), 5600 Fishers Lane, Rockville, MD 20857; (240) 276-2420. Fax, (301) 480-8480. Capt. Jeffrey Coady, Director (Acting).*
Web, www.samhsa.gov/about-us/who-we-are/offices-centers/csap

Demonstrates, evaluates, and disseminates strategies for preventing alcohol and drug abuse.

Substance Abuse and Mental Health Services Administration (SAMHSA) *(Health and Human Services Dept.), Center for Substance Abuse Treatment (CSAT), 5600 Fishers Lane, Rockville, MD 20857; (240) 276-1660. Fax, (301) 480-6596. Dr. Yngvild K. Olsen, Director (Acting).*
General email, csat@samhsa.hhs.gov

Web, www.samhsa.gov/about-us/who-we-are/offices-centers/csat

Develops and supports policies and programs that improve and expand treatment services for alcoholism, substance abuse, and addiction. Administers grants that support private and public addiction prevention and treatment services. Evaluates alcohol treatment programs and other drug treatment programs and delivery systems.

▶INTERNATIONAL ORGANIZATIONS

International Commission for the Prevention of Alcoholism and Drug Dependency, *12501 Old Columbia Pike, Silver Spring, MD 20904 (mailing address: 9705 Patuxent Woods Drive, Columbia, MD 21046); (301) 680-6719. Fax, (301) 680-6707. Dr. Peter N. Landless, Executive Director; Angeline Brauer, North American Region Office, (443) 391-7238.*
Web, http://icpaworld.org

Membership: health officials, physicians, educators, clergy, and judges worldwide. Promotes scientific research on prevention of alcohol and drug dependencies; provides information about medical effects of alcohol and drugs; conducts world congresses. (Health Ministries Dept. of the General Conference of Seventh-Day Adventists.)

▶NONGOVERNMENTAL

American Society of Addiction Medicine, *11400 Rockville Pike, #200, Rockville, MD 20852; (301) 656-3920. Fax, (301) 656-3815. Julia L. Chang, Executive Vice President.*
General email, email@asam.org

Web, www.asam.org, Twitter, @ASAMorg and Facebook, www.facebook.com/addictionmedicine

Membership: physicians and medical students. Supports the study and provision of effective treatment and care for people with alcohol and drug dependencies; educates physicians. Monitors legislation and regulations.

Assn. for Addiction Professionals (AAP), *44 Canal Center Plaza, #301, Alexandria, VA 22314; (703) 741-7686. Fax, (703) 741-7698. Cynthia Moreno Tuohy, Executive Director. Toll-free, (800) 548-0497.*
General email, naadac2@naadac.org

Web, www.naadac.org, Twitter, @NAADACorg and Facebook, www.facebook.com/NAADAC/

Membership: professionals in the addiction field. Supports professional development by providing educational resources, certification programs, workshops, and conferences for treatment professionals. (Formerly National Assn. of Alcoholism and Drug Abuse Counselors.)

Drug Policy Alliance, *National Affairs, 1620 Eye St. N.W., #925, 20006; (202) 683-2030. Fax, (202) 216-0803. Maritza Perez, Director of National Affairs.*
General email, dc@drugpolicy.org

Web, www.drugpolicy.org, Twitter, @DrugPolicyOrg and Facebook, www.facebook.com/drugpolicy

Supports reform of current drug control policy; seeks to broaden debate on drug policy to include considering alternatives to incarceration, expanding lawful maintenance therapies, and restoring constitutional protections; advocates medical treatment to control drug abuse; opposes random drug testing; studies drug policy in other countries. Sponsors the biennial International Conference on Drug Policy Reform. Monitors legislation and regulations. (Headquarters in New York.)

Drug Strategies, *2101 L St. N.W., #800, 20037; Mathea Falco, President.*
General email, drugstrategies@gmail.com

Web, www.drugstrategies.com

Researches effectiveness of drug abuse prevention, treatment, and education. Supports effective practices and educates the public on treating substance abuse. Special interests include teenagers and prescription pill abuse.

Mothers Against Drunk Driving (MADD), *Government Affairs, 1200 18th St. N.W., #700, 20036; (202) 688-1193. Stephanie Manning, Chief Government Affairs Officer; Ellen Willmott, Executive Officer (Acting). 24-hour helpline, 877-MADD-HELP. Toll-free, (877) 275-6233.*
General email, policy@madd.org

Web, www.madd.org, Facebook, www.facebook.com/MADD.Official and Twitter, @MADDOnline

Advocacy group that seeks to stop drunk driving and prevent underage drinking. Monitors legislation and regulations. (Headquarters in Irving, Tex.)

National Assn. of State Alcohol and Drug Abuse Directors (NASADAD), *1919 Pennsylvania Ave. N.W., #M250, 20006; (202) 293-0090. Fax, (202) 293-1250. Robert (Rob) Morrison, Executive Director, ext. 4862. General email, dcoffice@nasadad.org*

Web, http://nasadad.org

Provides information on drug abuse treatment and prevention; contracts with federal and state agencies for design of programs to fight and prevent drug abuse.

Treatment Communities of America (TCA), *2200 Pennsylvania Ave. N.W., #4075E, 20037; (202) 296-3503. Patricia Clay, Executive Director. General email, pat@treatmentcommunities.com*

Web, www.treatmentcommunitiesofamerica.org and Facebook, www.facebook.com/TreatmentCommunities America

Membership: nonprofit organizations that provide substance abuse and mental health treatment and rehabilitation. Provides policy analysis and educates the public on substance abuse and treatment issues. Promotes the interests of therapeutic communities, their clients, and staffs. Monitors legislation and regulations.

MENTAL HEALTH

General

▶AGENCIES

National Institute of Mental Health (NIMH) *(National Institutes of Health), 6001 Executive Blvd., #6200, MS 9663, Bethesda, MD 20892-9663; (301) 443-4513. Fax, (301) 443-4279. Dr. Joshua A. Gordon, Director, (301) 443-3673. Toll-free, (866) 615-6464. Toll-free TTY, (866) 415-8051. TTY, (301) 443-8431. General email, nimhinfo@nih.gov*

Web, www.nimh.nih.gov, Twitter, @NIMHgov and Facebook, www.facebook.com/nimhgov

Conducts research on the cause, diagnosis, treatment, and prevention of mental disorders; provides information on mental health problems and programs. Participates in international research.

National Institute of Mental Health (NIMH) *(National Institutes of Health), Disparities Research and Workforce Diversity (ODWD), 6001 Executive Blvd., #7155, MS 9629, Bethesda, MD 20892-9629; 301443-2638. Lauren Hill, Director (Acting). Press email, nimhpress@nih.gov and Web, www.nimh.nih .gov/about/organization/od/odwd/index.shtml*

Works to reduce mental health disparities, promote equity both within and outside of the United States; coordinates efforts to diversify mental health research workforce.

National Institute of Mental Health (NIMH) *(National Institutes of Health), Neuroscience and Basic Behavioral Science Division (DNBBS), 6001 Executive Blvd., #7204, MS 9645, Rockville, MD 20892; (301) 443-3563. Fax, (301) 443-1731. Linda S. Brady, Director. Web, www.nimh.nih.gov/about/organization/dnbbs*

Supports research programs in the areas of basic neuroscience, genetics, basic behavioral science, research training, resource development, drug discovery, and research dissemination. Responsible for ensuring that relevant basic science knowledge is generated to create improved diagnosis, treatment, and prevention of mental and behavioral disorders.

National Institute of Mental Health (NIMH) *(National Institutes of Health), Services and Intervention Research Division (DSIR), 6001 Executive Blvd., Room 7141, MS 9629, Rockville, MD 20852; (301) 435-0371. Robert K. Heinssen, Director. Web, www.nimh.nih.gov/about/organization/dsir*

Supports research programs to evaluate the effectiveness of pharmacologic, psychosocial, somatic, rehabilitative, and combination interventions on mental and behavior disorders; conducts mental health services research.

National Institute of Mental Health (NIMH) *(National Institutes of Health), Translational Research Division (DTR), 6001 Executive Blvd., #7121, MS 9032, Bethesda, MD 20892; (301) 451-3029. Fax, (301) 480-4415. Dr. Sarah H. Lisanby, Director. Web, www.nimh.nih.gov/about/organization/dtr*

Directs, plans, and supports programs of research and research training that translate knowledge from basic science to discover the etiology, pathophysiology, and trajectory of mental disorders and develops effective interventions for children and adults. Supports integrative, multidisciplinary research on the following areas: the phenotype characterization and risk factors for psychiatric disorders; neurobehavioral mechanisms of psychopathology; trajectories of risk and resilience based on the interactive influences of genetics, brain development, environment, and experience; and design and testing of innovative psychosocial, psychopharmacologic, and somatic treatment interventions.

National Institutes of Health (NIH) *(Health and Human Services Dept.), Behavioral and Social Sciences Research (OBSSR), Bldg. 31, 31 Center Dr., #B1C19, Bethesda, MD 20892-0183; (301) 402-1146. Fax, (301) 402-1150. Christine Hunter, Associate Director (Acting). General email, obssrnews@mail.nih.gov*

Web, http://obssr.od.nih.gov, Twitter, @NIHOBSSR and Facebook, www.facebook.com/OBSSR.NIH/

Works to advance behavioral and social sciences training, to integrate a biobehavioral perspective across the NIH, and to improve communication among stakeholders within and outside of the federal government, including scientists and with the public. Develops funding initiatives for research and training. Sets priorities for research. Provides training and career development opportunities for behavioral and social scientists. Links minority students with mentors. Organizes cultural workshops and lectures.

Substance Abuse and Mental Health Services Administration (SAMHSA) *(Health and Human Services Dept.)*, *5600 Fishers Lane, Rockville, MD 20857; (240) 276-2000. Fax, (240) 489-1450. Miriam E. Delphin-Rittmon, Assistant Secretary. Helpline, (800) 662-4357. Information, (877) 726-4727. Press, (240) 276-2130 (press 4). TTY, (800) 487-4889. Workplace helpline, (800) 967-5752.*
General email, samhsainfo@samhsa.hhs.gov

Web, www.samhsa.gov, Twitter, @samhsagov and Facebook, www.facebook.com/samhsa

Provides and manages block grants and special programmatic funding aimed at reducing the impact of substance abuse and mental illness on communities. Provides states, providers, communities, and the public with information about behavioral health issues and prevention/treatment approaches. Administers substance abuse and mental health treatment referral service: (800) 662-4357 or www.samhsa.gov/treatment. Offers behavioral health publications and other resources: http://store.samhsa.gov.

Substance Abuse and Mental Health Services Administration (SAMHSA) *(Health and Human Services Dept.)*, *Center for Mental Health Services (CMHS), 5600 Fishers Lane, Rockville, MD 20857; (240) 276-1310. Fax, (240) 276-1320. Dr. Anita Everett, Director.*
Web, www.samhsa.gov/about-us/who-we-are/offices-centers/cmhs

Works with federal agencies, tribal entities and territories, and state and local governments to demonstrate, evaluate, and disseminate service delivery models to treat mental illness, promote mental health, and prevent the developing or worsening of mental illness.

Veterans Health Administration (VHA) *(Veterans Affairs Dept.)*, *Mental Health Services, 810 Vermont Ave. N.W., MS 10P4M, 20420; (202) 461-4170. Fax, (202) 495-5933. Marsden McGuire, Deputy Chief Consultant. Crisis Hotline, (800) 273-8255, ext. 1. Homeless Veterans, hotline, (877) 424-3838. WomenVeterans Hotline, (855) 829-6636.*
Web, www.mentalhealth.va.gov/index.asp and Coaching-into-Care Web, www.mirecc.va.gov/coaching

Develops ambulatory and inpatient psychiatry and psychology programs for the mentally ill and for drug and alcohol abusers; programs are offered in VA facilities and 21 Veterans Integrated Services Networks. Incorporates special programs for veterans suffering from posttraumatic stress disorders, serious mental illness, addictive disorders, and homelessness.

▶CONGRESS

For a listing of relevant congressional committees and subcommittees, please see pages 362–363 or the Appendix.

▶NONGOVERNMENTAL

Active Minds, *2001 S St. N.W., #630, 20009; (202) 332-9595. Fax, (202) 332-9599. Alison Malmon, Executive Director, ext. 101.*
General email, info@activeminds.org

Web, www.activeminds.org, Twitter, @active_minds and Facebook, www.facebook.com/activemindsinc

Supports student-run chapters nationwide to help promote youth mental health awareness on college campuses. Offers mental health and mental illness information and resources.

American Academy of Child and Adolescent Psychiatry (AACAP), *3615 Wisconsin Ave. N.W., 20016-3007; (202) 966-7300. Fax, (202) 464-0131. Heidi B. Fordi, Executive Director.*
Web, www.aacap.org, Twitter, @aacap, Facebook, www.facebook.com/American-Academy-of-Child-Adolescent-Psychiatry-145459865751 and Government Affairs, govaffairs@aacap.org

Membership: child and adolescent psychiatrists trained to promote healthy development and to evaluate, diagnose, and treat children, adolescents, and families affected by mental illness. Sponsors annual meeting and review for medical board examinations. Provides information, advocacy, education, and research on child and adolescent development and mental illnesses. Monitors international research and U.S. legislation concerning children with mental illness.

American Assn. for Geriatric Psychiatry, *6728 Old McLean Village Dr., McLean, VA 22101; (703) 556-9222. Fax, (703) 556-8729. Rebecca Morgan, Executive Director.*
General email, main@aagponline.org

Web, www.aagponline.org, Twitter, @GeriPsyc and Facebook, www.facebook.com/GeriPsyc

Works to improve the practice of geriatric psychiatry and mental health through professional education, public advocacy, and support for career development for clinicians, educators, and researchers. Monitors legislation and regulations. Publishes the *American Journal of Geriatric Psychiatry.*

American Assn. of Suicidology, *1321 Upland Dr., PMB 1600, Houston, TX, 77043 (mailing address: 1321 Upland Dr., PMB 1600, Houston, TX 77043); (202) 237-2280. Fax, (202) 237-2282. Chris Maxwell, Deputy Director (Acting). Suicide prevention lifeline, (800) 273-8255.*
General email, info@suicidology.org

Web, www.suicidology.org, Twitter, @AAsuicidolgy and Facebook, www.facebook.com/AASuicidology

Membership: educators, researchers, suicide prevention centers, school districts, volunteers, and survivors affected by suicide. Works to understand and prevent suicide; provides suicide prevention training; serves as an information clearinghouse.

American Foundation for Suicide Prevention, *Public Policy, 440 1st St. N.W., #300, 20001; (202) 449-3600. Fax, (202) 449-3601. Robert Gebbia, Chief Executive Officer; Laurel Stine, Senior Vice President of Public Policy, ext. 1103. National Suicide Prevention Lifeline, (800) 273-8255. Text, TALK to 741741.*

General email, info@afsp.org

Web, https://afsp.org

Seeks to understand and prevent suicide through research, education, and advocacy. Provides programs and resources for survivors of suicide loss and people at risk, funds scientific research, offers educational programs for professionals, educates the public about mood disorders and suicide prevention, and promotes policies that impact suicide and prevention. Monitors legislation and regulations. (Headquarters in New York.)

American Mental Health Counselors Assn., *107 S. West St., #779, Alexandria, VA 22314; (703) 548-6002. Melissa McShepard, Director of Operations, Finance, and Membership. Toll-free, (800) 326-2642.*

Web, www.amhca.org, Twitter, @AMHCA1 and Facebook, www.facebook.com/amhca

Membership: professional counselors and graduate students in the mental health field. Sponsors leadership training and continuing-education programs for professionals in the field of mental health counseling; holds annual conference. Monitors legislation and regulations.

American Psychiatric Assn., *800 Maine Ave. S.W., #900, 20024; (202) 559-3900. Dr. Saul Levin, Medical Director. Press, (202) 459-9732. Publishing toll-free, (800) 368-5777. Toll-free, (888) 357-7924.*

General email, apa@psych.org

Web, www.psychiatry.org, Twitter, @APAPsychiatric and Facebook, www.facebook.com/AmericanPsychiatric Association

Membership: psychiatrists. Promotes availability of high-quality psychiatric care; provides the public with information; assists state and local agencies; conducts educational programs for professionals and students in the field; participates in international meetings and research. Library open to members.

American Psychological Assn., *750 1st St. N.E., 20002-4242; (202) 336-5500. Fax, (202) 336-5502. Arthur C. Evans Jr., Chief Executive Officer. Library, (202) 336-5640. Toll-free, (800) 374-2721.*

General email, apaservice@apa.org

Web, www.apa.org, Twitter, @APA and Facebook, www .facebook.com/AmericanPsychologicalAssociation

Membership: professional psychologists, educators, and behavioral research scientists. Supports research, training, and professional services; works toward improving the qualifications, competence, and training programs of psychologists. Monitors international research and U.S. legislation on mental health. Library open to the public by appointment.

American Psychosomatic Society, *6728 Old McLean Village Dr., McLean, VA 22101-3906; (703) 718-6038. Fax, (703) 556-8729. Laura E. Degnon, Executive Director. General email, info@psychosomatic.org*

Web, www.psychosomatic.org, Twitter, @connectAPS and Facebook, www.facebook.com/AmericanPsychosomatic Society

Advances and disseminates scientific understanding of relationships among biological, psychological, social, and behavioral factors in medicine through publications, annual meetings, conferences, and interest groups. Offers educational resources and sponsors awards and scholarships.

Anxiety and Depression Assn. of America, *8701 Georgia Ave., #412, Silver Spring, MD 20910; (240) 485-1001. Fax, (240) 485-1035. Susan K. Gurley, Executive Director. Press, (240) 485-1016.*

General email, information@adaa.org

Web, www.adaa.org and Twitter, @Got_Anxiety

Membership: clinicians and researchers who treat and study anxiety and depression disorders; individuals with these disorders and their families; and other interested individuals. Promotes prevention, treatment, and cure of anxiety and depression disorders by disseminating information, linking individuals to treatment, and encouraging research and advancement of scientific knowledge.

Assn. of Black Psychologists, *7119 Allentown Rd., #203, Ft. Washington, MD 20744; (301) 449-3082. Fax, (301) 449-3084. Donell Barnett, President.*

General email, abpsi@abpsi.org

Web, www.abpsi.org, Twitter, @ABPsiSC and Facebook, www.facebook.com/TheABPsi/?fref=ts

Membership: psychologists, psychology students, and others in the mental health field. Develops policies and resources to foster mental health in the African American community; holds annual convention.

Bazelon Center for Mental Health Law, *1090 Vermont Ave. N.W., #220, 20005; (202) 467-5730. Holly O'Donnell, Chief Executive Officer.*

General email, communications@bazelon.org

Web, www.bazelon.org, Twitter, @BazelonCenter and Facebook, www.facebook.com/bazeloncenter

Public interest law firm. Works to establish and advance the legal rights of children and adults with mental disabilities and ensure their equal access to services and resources needed for full participation in community life. Provides technical support to lawyers and other advocates. Conducts test case litigation to defend rights of persons with mental disabilities. Conducts policy analysis, builds coalitions, issues advocacy alerts, publishes handbooks, and maintains advocacy resources online. Monitors legislation and regulations.

Eating Disorders Coalition for Research, Policy, and Action, *P.O. Box 96503-98807, 20090; (202) 543-9570. David Jaffe, Executive Director.*

General email, manager@eatingdisorderscoalition.org

Web, http://eatingdisorderscoalition.org, Twitter, @EDCoalition and Facebook, www.facebook.com/ EatingDisordersCoalition

Seeks greater national and federal recognition of eating disorders. Promotes recognition of eating disorders as a public health priority and the implementation of more accessible treatment and more effective prevention programs. Monitors legislation and regulations.

Mental Health America, *500 Montgomery St., #820, Alexandria, VA 22314; (703) 684-7722. Fax, (703) 684-5968. Schroeder Stribling, President. Toll-free, (800) 969-6642. General email, info@mentalhealthamerica.net*

Web, www.mentalhealthamerica.net, Twitter, @mentalhealtham and Facebook, www.facebook.com/ mentalhealthamerica

Works to increase accessible and appropriate care for adults and children with mental disorders. Informs and educates public about mental illnesses and available treatment, part of their focus is on early identification and intervention, with the ultimate goal of Recovery. Supports research on illnesses and services.

National Action Alliance for Suicide Prevention, *1025 Thomas Jefferson St. N.W., #700W, 20007; (202) 572-3737. Colleen Carr, Director. Hotline, (800) 273-8255. General email, info@theactionalliance.org*

Web, www.theactionalliance.org, Twitter, @Action_ Alliance, Facebook, www.facebook.com/ActionAlliance and YouTube, www.youtube.com/TheActionAlliance

Seeks to advance the National Strategy for Suicide Prevention (NSSP) and reduce the rate of suicide. Advocates that health care reform include suicide prevention methods and improve data on suicide.

National Alliance on Mental Illness (NAMI), *4301 Wilson Blvd., #300, Arlington, VA 22203; (703) 524-7600. Fax, (703) 524-9094. Daniel H. Gillison Jr., Chief Executive Officer (Acting). Toll-free, (800) 950-6264. General email, info@nami.org*

Web, www.nami.org, Twitter, @NAMICommunicate and Facebook, www.facebook.com/NAMI

Membership: mentally ill individuals and their families and caregivers. Works to eradicate mental illness and improve the lives of those affected by brain disorders; sponsors public education and advocacy. Monitors legislation and regulations.

National Assn. for Behavioral Healthcare, *900 17th St. N.W., #420, 20006-2507; (202) 393-6700. Fax, (202) 783-6041. Shawn Coughlin, President. General email, nabh@nabh.org*

Web, www.nabh.org, Twitter, @GovBoard and Facebook, www.facebook.com/TheGoverningBoard

Membership: behavioral health care systems that provide inpatient, residential, and outpatient treatment and prevention and care programs for children, adolescents, adults, and older adults with mental and substance use disorders.

National Assn. of School Psychologists, *4340 East-West Hwy., #402, Bethesda, MD 20814; (301) 657-0270. Fax, (301) 657-0275. Kathleen Minke, Executive Director. Toll-free, (866) 331-6277.*

Web, www.nasponline.org and Twitter, @nasponline

Membership: graduate education students and professors, school psychologists, supervisors of school psychological services, and others who provide mental health services for children in school settings. Provides professional education and development to members. Provides school safety and crisis response direct services. Fosters information exchange; advises local, state, and federal policymakers and agencies that develop children's mental health educational services. Develops professional ethics and standards.

National Assn. of State Mental Health Program Directors, *66 Canal Center Plaza, #302, Alexandria, VA 22314-1591; (703) 739-9333. Brian Hepburn, Executive Director.*

Web, www.nasmhpd.org, Twitter, @nasmhpd and Facebook, www.facebook.com/National-Association-of-State-Mental-Health-Program-Directors-2306988989556540

Membership: officials in charge of state mental health agencies. Compiles data on state mental health programs. Fosters collaboration among members; provides technical assistance and consultation. Maintains research institute. Operates under a cooperative agreement with the National Governors Association. (Affiliated with NASMHPD Research Institute, Inc., Falls Church, VA.)

National Council for Mental Wellbeing, *1400 K St. N.W., #400, 20005; (202) 684-7457. Charles Ingoglia, President. General email, communications@thenationalcouncil.org*

Web, www.TheNationalCouncil.org, Twitter, @nationalcouncil, Facebook, www.facebook.com/ TheNationalCouncil and YouTube, www.youtube.com/ user/NationalCouncil

Membership: community mental health agencies and state community mental health associations. Conducts research on community mental health activities; provides information, technical assistance, and referrals. Operates a job bank; publishes newsletters and a membership directory. Monitors legislation and regulations affecting community mental health facilities. (Formerly National Council for Community Behavioral Healthcare.)

National Register of Health Service Psychologists, *1200 New York Ave. N.W., #800, 20005; (202) 783-7663. Fax, (202) 347-0550. Morgan T. Sammons, Chief Officer. Web, www.nationalregister.org*

Credentials and promotes health service psychologists that meet the National Register's requirements. Conducts biannual investigations of ethical behavior of health service psychologists. Maintains a database of licensed and accredited health service psychologists. Sponsors free continuing-education programs. Monitors legislation and regulations related to health care reform.

Psychiatric Rehabilitation Assn., Virginia Psychiatric Rehabilitation Assn. (VAPRA), *7918 Jones Branch Dr., #300, McLean, VA 22102; (703) 442-2078. Fax, (703) 506-3266. Lee K. Lowery, Managing Director. General email, info@psychrehabassociation.org*

Web, www.psychrehabassociation.org, Twitter, @PsychRehab, Facebook, www.facebook.com/ PsychRehabAssociation and Web, www.vapra.org/#!

Membership: agencies, mental health practitioners, researchers, policymakers, family groups, and consumer organizations. Supports the community adjustment of persons with psychiatric disabilities. Promotes the role of rehabilitation in mental health systems; opposes discrimination based on mental disability. Certifies psychosocial rehabilitation practitioners. (Headquarters in South Bend, Ind.)

The Treatment Advocacy Center, *200 N. Glebe Rd., #801, Arlington, VA 22203; (703) 294-6001. Fax, (703) 294-6010. Lisa Dailey, Executive Director. Press, (703) 294-6003.*
General email, info@treatmentadvocacycenter.org
Web, www.treatmentadvocacycenter.org, Twitter, @TreatmentAdvCtr and Facebook, www.facebook.com/ TreatmentAdvocacyCtr/

Works to eliminate legal and other barriers to treatment of severe mental illness.

Treatment Communities of America (TCA), *2200 Pennsylvania Ave. N.W., #4075E, 20037; (202) 296-3503. Patricia Clay, Executive Director.*
General email, pat@treatmentcommunities.com
Web, www.treatmentcommunitiesofamerica.org and Facebook, www.facebook.com/TreatmentCommunities America

Membership: nonprofit organizations that provide substance abuse and mental health treatment and rehabilitation. Provides policy analysis and educates the public on substance abuse and treatment issues. Promotes the interests of therapeutic communities, their clients, and staffs. Monitors legislation and regulations.

11 Housing and Development

GENERAL POLICY AND ANALYSIS

Basic Resources

▶AGENCIES

Agriculture Dept. (USDA), *Rural Development, External Affairs (OEA)*, *1400 Independence Ave. S.W., MS 0705, 20250-0705; Marie Wheat, Director. Congressional inquiries, (202) 720-9928.*
Web, www.rd.usda.gov/about-rd/offices/office-of-external-affairs and Press Email, RD.Press@usda.gov

Disseminates information to the media and general public about policy matters related to housing and rural development.

Economic Development Administration *(Commerce Dept.)*, *1401 Constitution Ave. N.W., #71014, 20230; (202) 482-5081. Alejandra Y. Castillo, Assistant Secretary. Public Affairs, (202) 482-4085.*
Web, https://eda.gov, Twitter, @US_EDA and Facebook, www.facebook.com/eda.commerce

Advises the commerce secretary on domestic economic development. Administers development assistance programs that provide financial and technical aid to economically distressed areas to stimulate economic growth and create jobs. Awards public works and technical assistance grants to public institutions, nonprofit organizations, and Native American tribes; assists state and local governments with economic adjustment problems caused by long-term or sudden economic dislocation.

Housing and Urban Development Dept. (HUD), *451 7th St. S.W., #10000, 20410; (202) 708-1112. Marcia Fudge, Secretary. Congressional and Intergovernmental Relations, (202) 708-0005.*
Web, www.hud.gov, Twitter, @HUDGOV and Facebook, www.facebook.com/HUD

Responsible for federal programs concerned with housing needs, fair housing opportunities, and improving and developing the nation's urban and rural communities. Administers mortgage insurance, rent subsidy, preservation, rehabilitation, and antidiscrimination in housing programs. Advises the president on federal policy and makes legislative recommendations on housing and community development issues.

Housing and Urban Development Dept. (HUD), *Policy Development and Research (PD&R)*, *451 7th St. S.W., #8100, 20410-6000; P.O. Box 23268, 20026-3268; (202) 708-1600. Ben Winter, Deputy Assistant Secretary, (202) 402-5706. Toll-free, (800) 245-2691. Toll-free TTY, (800) 245-2691.*
General email, helpdesk@huduser.gov
Web, www.huduser.gov/portal/home

Studies ways to improve the effectiveness and equity of HUD programs; analyzes housing and urban issues, including national housing goals, the operation of housing financial markets, the management of housing assistance programs, and statistics on federal and housing insurance programs; conducts the American Housing Survey; develops policy recommendations to improve federal housing programs. Works to increase the affordability of rehabilitated and newly constructed housing through technological and regulatory improvements.

Office of Management and Budget (OMB) *(Executive Office of the President), Housing,* *725 17th St. N.W., #9226, 20503; (202) 395-7874. Jessica Lee, Chief, (202) 395-6141.*
Web, www.whitehouse.gov/omb

Assists and advises the OMB director in budget preparation, reorganizations, and evaluations of Housing and Urban Development Dept. programs.

▶CONGRESS

For a listing of relevant congressional committees and subcommittees, please see page 444 or the Appendix.

▶NONGOVERNMENTAL

Housing and Development Law Institute, *630 Eye St. N.W., 20001-3736; (202) 289-3400. Fax, (202) 289-3401. Lisa L. Walker, Chief Executive Officer.*
General email, hdli@hdli.org
Web, www.hdli.org

Membership organization that assists agencies and developers in public and affordable housing and community development in addressing common legal concerns and problems; publishes a quarterly compilation of nationwide case law affecting housing agencies; conducts seminars on legal issues and practices in the housing and community development field.

National Assn. of Housing and Redevelopment Officials, *630 Eye St. N.W., 20001-3736; (202) 289-3500. Fax, (202) 289-8181. Mike Gerber, Chief Executive Officer (Acting). Toll-free, (877) 866-2476.*
General email, nahro@nahro.org
Web, www.nahro.org and Twitter, @NAHROnational

Membership: housing, community, and urban development practitioners and organizations, and state and local government agencies and personnel. Works with federal government agencies to improve community development and affordable and public housing programs; conducts training programs.

National Center for Healthy Housing, *10320 Little Patuxent Pkwy., #200, Columbia, MD 21044; (410) 992-0712. Amanda Reddy, Executive Director, (443) 539-4152.*
General email, info@nchh.org
Web, www.nchh.org, Twitter, @NCHH and Facebook, www.facebook.com/HealthyHousing

Collects, analyzes, and distributes information on creating and maintaining safe and healthful housing. Provides technical assistance and training to public health, housing, and environmental professionals. Interests include aging in place for older adults, radon, allergens, pest management, and lead poisoning.

HOUSING AND DEVELOPMENT RESOURCES IN CONGRESS

For a complete listing of congressional committees, including their full contact information, leadership, membership, and jurisdictions, please refer to the Appendix on pages 840–963.

HOUSE:

House Agriculture Committee, (202) 225-2171.
Web, agriculture.house.gov
   Subcommittee on Commodity Exchanges,
      Energy, and Credit, (202) 225-2171.
   Subcommittee on Conservation and Forestry,
      (202) 225-2171.
House Appropriations Committee, (202) 225-2771.
Web, appropriations.house.gov
   Subcommittee on Agriculture, Rural
      Development, Food and Drug
      Administration, and Related Agencies,
      (202) 225-2638.
   Subcommittee on Financial Services and General
      Government, (202) 225-7245.
   Subcommittee on Transportation, Housing and
      Urban Development, and Related Agencies,
      (202) 225-2141.
House Budget Committee, (202) 226-7200.
Web, budget.house.gov
House Financial Services Committee, (202) 225-4247.
Web, financialservices.house.gov
   Subcommittee on Diversity and Inclusion,
      (202) 225-4247.
   Subcommittee on Housing, Community
      Development, and Insurance, (202) 225-4247.
   Subcommittee on Investor Protection,
      Entrepreneurship, and Capital Markets,
      (202) 225-4247.
   Subcommittee on National Security,
      International Development, and Monetary
      Policy, (202) 225-4247.
   Subcommittee on Oversight and Investigations,
      (202) 225-4247.
House Small Business Committee, (202) 225-4038.
Web, smallbusiness.house.gov
   Subcommittee on Underserved, Agricultural,
      and Rural Business Development,
      (202) 225-4038.
House Transportation and Infrastructure
   Committee, (202) 225-4472.
Web, transportation.house.gov
   Subcommittee on Economic Development,
      Public Buildings, and Emergency
      Management, (202) 225-3014.
House Ways and Means Committee, (202) 225-3625.
Web, waysandmeans.house.gov
   Subcommittee on Oversight, (202) 225-3625.

SENATE:

Senate Agriculture, Nutrition, and Forestry
   Committee, (202) 224-2035.
Web, agriculture.senate.gov
   Subcommittee on Rural Development and
      Energy, (202) 224-2035.
Senate Appropriations Committee, (202) 224-7363.
Web, appropriations.senate.gov
   Subcommittee on Agriculture, Rural
      Development, Food and Drug
      Administration, and Related Agencies,
      (202) 224-7363.
   Subcommittee on Financial Services and General
      Government, (202) 224-7363.
   Subcommittee on Transportation, Housing and
      Urban Development, and Related Agencies,
      (202) 224-7363.
Senate Banking, Housing, and Urban Affairs
   Committee, (202) 224-7391.
Web, banking.senate.gov
   Subcommittee on Economic Policy,
      (202) 224-7391.
   Subcommittee on Financial Institutions and
      Consumer Protection, (202) 224-7391.
   Subcommittee on Housing, Transportation,
      and Community Development,
      (202) 224-7391.
   Subcommittee on Securities, Insurance, and
      Investment, (202) 224-7391.
Senate Budget Committee, (202) 224-0642.
Web, budget.senate.gov
Senate Finance Committee, (202) 224-4515.
Web, finance.senate.gov
   Subcommittee on Fiscal Responsibility and
      Economic Growth, (202) 224-4515.
   Subcommittee on Social Security, Pensions, and
      Family Policy, (202) 224-4515.
Senate Indian Affairs Committee, (202) 224-2251.
Web, indian.senate.gov
Senate Judiciary Committee, (202) 224-7703.
Web, judiciary.senate.gov
   Subcommittee on the Constitution,
      (202) 224-6361.
Senate Small Business and Entrepreneurship
   Committee, (202) 224-5175.
Web, sbc.senate.gov
Senate Special Committee on Aging, (202) 224-5364.
Web, aging.senate.gov

Housing and Urban Development Department

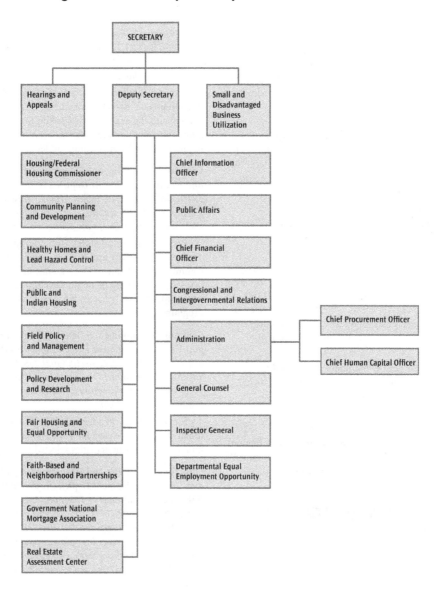

Research and Statistics

Census Bureau *(Commerce Dept.), Social, Economic, and Housing Statistics,* 4600 Silver Hill Rd., #7H174, Suitland, MD 20746 (mailing address: 4600 Silver Hill Rd., #7H174, Washington, DC 20233-8500); (301) 763-9263. David G. Waddington, Chief, (301) 763-3195. Web, www.census.gov/topics/housing.html

Publishes decennial census of housing and the American Housing Survey, which describe housing inventory characteristics. Also publishes a quarterly survey of market absorption. Survey on housing vacancy is available on the website.

Housing and Urban Development Dept. (HUD), *Economic Development,* 451 7th St. S.W., #8204, 20410-6000; (202) 402-5899. Fax, (202) 708-1159. Robin Keegan, Deputy Assistant Secretary, (202) 402-3921. Web, www.hud.gov

Assembles data on housing markets and subsidized housing programs; conducts housing statistical surveys, analyzes housing finance markets; analyzes economic effects of HUD regulations; gathers local housing market intelligence; and conducts other economic research.

Housing and Urban Development Dept. (HUD), *Policy Development and Research (PD&R),* 451 7th St. S.W., #8100, 20410-6000; P.O. Box 23268, 20026-3268; (202) 708-1600. Ben Winter, Deputy Assistant Secretary,

(202) 402-5706. Toll-free, (800) 245-2691. Toll-free TTY, (800) 245-2691.
General email, helpdesk@huduser.gov

Web, www.huduser.gov/portal/home

Assesses and maintains information on housing needs, market conditions, and programs; conducts research on housing and community development issues such as building technology, economic development, and urban planning.

Housing and Urban Development Dept. (HUD), *Policy Development and Research (PD&R), HUD USER, 451 7th St. S.W., #8110, 20026-3268; (800) 245-2691. Fax, (703) 742-7889. Todd M. Richardson, General Deputy Assistant Secretary. TTY, (800) 927-7589.*
General email, helpdesk@huduser.gov

Web, www.huduser.org, Twitter, @HUDUSERnews and Facebook, www.facebook.com/HUD-User-183685747712

Research information service and clearinghouse for HUD research reports. Provides information on past and current HUD research; maintains HUD USER, an in-house database. Extensive collection of publications and documents available online. Clearinghouse help desk opens Monday through Friday, 8:30 a.m.–5:00 p.m.

Housing and Urban Development Dept. (HUD), *Program Evaluation Division, 451 7th St. S.W., #8120, 20410; (202) 402-6139. Carol S. Star, Director.*
General email, carol.s.star@hud.gov

Web, www.hud.gov

Conducts research, program evaluations, and demonstrations for all HUD housing, community development, and fair housing and equal opportunity programs.

COMMUNITY AND REGIONAL DEVELOPMENT

General

►AGENCIES

Bureau of Indian Affairs (BIA) *(Interior Dept.), Indian Services (OIS), 1849 C St. N.W., MS-3645 MIB, 20240; Jeanette Hanna, Deputy Bureau Director. General Phone, (202) 513-7640. Phone, Human Services, (202) 513-7642. Phone, Self Determination, (202) 513-0781. Phone, Transportation, (202) 513-7714. Phone, Tribal Govt., (202) 513-7641. Phone, Workforce, (202) 219-3938.*
Web, www.bia.gov/bia/ois

Assists tribal and Indian landowners with managing natural and energy trust resources. Builds, maintains and moniters housing, transportation, energy, and irrigation infrastructure; and provides law enforcement protection, corrections, and administration of justice services on federal Indian lands.

Community Development Financial Institutions Fund *(Treasury Dept.), 1801 L St. N.W., 6th Floor, 20036 (mailing address: 1500 Pennsylvania Ave. N.W., Washington, DC 20220); (202) 653-0300. Jodie Harris, Director. Helpline, (202) 653-0421.*
General email, cdfihelp@cdfi.treas.gov

Web, www.cdfifund.gov

Provides funds and tax credits to financial institutions to build private markets, create healthy local tax revenues, and expand the availability of credit, investment capital, affordable housing, and financial services in low-income urban, rural, and Native communities.

Community Planning and Development (CPD) *(Housing and Urban Development Dept.), 451 7th St. S.W., #7100, 20410; (202) 402-3921. James Arthur Jemison, Principal Deputy Assistant Secretary. TTY, (202) 708-1455.*
Web, www.hud.gov/program_offices/comm_planning

Provides cities and states with community and economic development and housing assistance, including community development block grants. Encourages public-private partnerships in urban development and private sector initiatives. Oversees enterprise zone development program.

Community Planning and Development (CPD) *(Housing and Urban Development Dept.), Block Grant Assistance, 451 7th St. S.W., #7286, 20410; (202) 708-3587. Fax, (202) 401-2044. Jessie Kome, Director, (202) 402-5539.*
Web, www.hud.gov/program_offices/comm_planning/communitydevelopment

Provides grants on a formula basis to states, cities, and urban counties to be used for a wide range of eligible community development activities selected by the grantee.

Community Planning and Development (CPD) *(Housing and Urban Development Dept.), Block Grant Assistance, Entitlement Communities Division, 451 7th St. S.W., #7282, 20410; (202) 708-1577. Fax, (202) 401-2044. James Hoemann, Director, (202) 402-5716.*
Web, www.hudexchange.info/programs/cdbg-entitlement, Twitter, @HUDExchangeInfo, Facebook, www.facebook .com/HUD and YouTube, www.youtube.com/user/HUDexchange

Provides entitled cities and counties with block grants to provide housing, community, revitalization, and economic opportunity for low-income and moderate-income people.

Community Planning and Development (CPD) *(Housing and Urban Development Dept.), Block Grant Assistance, States and Small Cities Division, 451 7th St. S.W., #7184, 20410; (202) 708-3587. Fax, (202) 401-2044. Robert Peterson, Director.*
Web, www.hud.gov/program_offices/comm_planning/communitydevelopment

Provides states with grants for distribution to small cities (fewer than 50,000 persons) and small counties (fewer than 200,000 persons) that do not receive funding through the Entitlement Community Development Block Grant Program. Funds benefit low-income and moderate-income persons, eliminate slums and blighted conditions, or meet other urgent community development needs. All states (except Hawaii), plus Puerto Rico, receive State Community Development Block Grant (CDBG) program funding. In Hawaii, HUD provides funding directly to the local governments. A separate program also provides funding to the Insular Areas.

Community Planning and Development (CPD) *(Housing and Urban Development Dept.), Economic Development, 451 7th St. S.W., #7136, 20410; (202) 708-4091. Larry B. Jackson II, Deputy Assistant Secretary (Acting). General email, economicdevelopment@hud.gov*

Web, www.hud/topics/economicdevelopment

Manages economic development programs, including Empowerment Zones/Renewal Communities, Rural Housing and Economic Development, and Brownfields Economic Development Initiatives. Encourages private–public partnerships for development through neighborhood development corporations. Formulates policies and legislative proposals on economic development.

Community Planning and Development (CPD) *(Housing and Urban Development Dept.), Environment and Energy, 451 7th St. S.W., #7212, 20410; (202) 402-3988. Liz Zepeda, Director (Acting), (202) 402-3988. Web, www.hud.gov/program_offices/comm_planning/library/energy*

Issues policies and sets standards for environmental and land-use planning and for environmental management practices. Develops policies promoting energy efficiency, conservation, and renewable sources of supply in housing and community development programs.

Community Planning and Development (CPD) *(Housing and Urban Development Dept.), Technical Assistance and Management, 451 7th St. S.W., #7228, 20410; (202) 708-3176. Fax, (202) 708-4275. Edward Turner, Director, Management Division, (202) 402-4440; Stephanie Stone, Director, Technical Assistance Division, (202) 402-7418. Web, www.hud.gov/program_offices/comm_planing/about/cpdta*

Develops program policies and designs and implements technical assistance plans for state and local governments for use in community planning and development programs.

Defense Dept. (DoD), *Local Defense Community Cooperation, 2231 Crystal Dr., #520, Arlington, VA 22202-4704; (703) 697-2130. Fax, (703) 607-0170. Patrick J. O'Brien, Director, (703) 697-2123. Web, www.oea.gov*

Assists communities where defense activities are being expanded. Serves as the staff for the Economic Adjustment Committee, an interagency group that coordinates federal technical and financial transition assistance to localities.

Health and Human Services Dept., *White House Initiative on Asian Americans, Native Hawaiians, and Pacific Islanders, 550 12th St. S.W., 10th Floor, 20202; (202) 482-1375. Krystal Ka'ai, Executive Director.*

General email, whiaanhpi@hhs.gov

Web, www.commerce.gov/whiaapi and Twitter, @whitehouseAAPI

Works to increase Asian American, Native Hawaiian, and Pacific Islander participation in federal housing and community development programs. Interests include creating sustainable communities by connecting housing to jobs and helping to build clean-energy communities.

Housing and Urban Development Dept. (HUD), *Field Policy and Management, 451 7th St. S.W., #7108, 20410; (202) 708-2426. Fax, (202) 708-1558. Vacant, Assistant Deputy Secretary. Web, www.hud.gov/program_offices/field_policy_mgt*

Acts as liaison and coordinates all activities between the Office of Community Planning and Development and regional and field offices; evaluates the performance of regional and field offices. Conducts policy analyses and evaluations of community planning and development programs, including the Community Development Block Grant Program, the Empowerment Zones/Enterprise Communities Program, and the McKinney Act programs.

▶**CONGRESS**

For a listing of relevant congressional committees and subcommittees, please see page 444 or the Appendix.

▶**NONGOVERNMENTAL**

American Planning Assn., *1030 15th St. N.W., #750W, 20005; (202) 872-0611. Fax, (202) 872-0643. Joel Albizo, Chief Executive Officer. Web, www.planning.org, Twitter, @APA_Planning and Facebook, www.facebook.com/AmericanPlanning Association*

Membership: professional planners and others interested in urban, suburban, and rural planning. Serves as a clearinghouse for planners. Sponsors professional development workshops conducted by the American Institute of Certified Planners. Prepares studies and technical reports; conducts seminars and conferences. (Headquarters in Chicago, Ill.)

American Resort Development Assn., *1201 15th St. N.W., #400, 20005-2842; (202) 371-6700. Fax, (202) 289-8544. Jason Gamel, President. Consumer hotline, (855) 939-1515. General email, consumer@arda-roc.org Web, www.arda.org*

Membership: U.S. and international developers, builders, financiers, marketing companies, and others involved in resort, recreational, and community development. Serves as an information clearinghouse; monitors federal and state legislation affecting land, time-share, and community development industries.

APPA: Leadership in Educational Facilities, *1643 Prince St., Alexandria, VA 22314-2818; (703) 684-1446. Fax, (703) 549-2772. E. Lander Medlin, Executive Vice President, (703) 542-3829.*

General email, webmaster@appa.org

Web, www.appa.org and Twitter, @APPA_facilities

Membership: professionals involved in the administration, maintenance, planning, and development of buildings and facilities used by colleges and universities, K–12 private and public schools, museums, libraries, and other educational institutions. Interests include maintenance and=upkeep of housing facilities. Provides information on campus energy management programs and campus accessibility for people with disabilities. (Formerly the Assn. of Higher Education Facilities Officers.)

Center for Community Change, *1536 U St. N.W., 20009; (202) 339-9300. Fax, (202) 387-4892. Dorian Warren, Co-President; Lorella Praeli, Co-President.*

General email, info@communitychange.org

Web, https://communitychange.org, Twitter, @communitychange and Facebook, www.facebook.com/communitychange

Works to strengthen grassroots organizations that help low-income people, working-class people, and minorities develop skills and resources to improve their communities and change the policies and institutions that affect their lives. Monitors legislation and regulations.

Council of State Community Development Agencies (COSCDA), *630 Eye St. N.W., 20001; (202) 293-5820. Dianne E. Taylor, Executive Director.*

General email, coscda@coscda.org

Web, http://coscda.org and Twitter, @COSCDA

Membership: directors and staff of state community development agencies. Promotes common interests among the states, including community and economic development, housing, homelessness, infrastructure, and state and local planning.

Institute for Local Self-Reliance, *1200 18th St. N.W., #700, 20036; (202) 898-1610. Fax, (202) 898-1612. Neil N. Seldman, Director of Waste to Wealth Initiative, ext. 5210.*

General email, info@ilsr.org

Web, www.ilsr.org, Twitter, @ilsr and Facebook, www.facebook.com/localselfreliance

Conducts research and provides technical assistance on environmentally sound economic development for government, small businesses, and community organizations. Advocates policies that enable communities to invest in and support locally owned telecommunications infrastructure, small, independent businesses, diverting organic waste from the waste stream, and local ownership and deployment of renewable energy resources, including economic analyses of solar and wind at a variety of scalable levels.

International Institute of Site Planning, *715 G St. S.E., 20003; (202) 546-2322. Fax, (202) 546-2722. Beatriz de Winthuysen Coffin, Director.*

General email, iisitep@aol.com

Web, www.iisp-insitu.com

Directs research and provides information on site planning development and design of sites and buildings; conducts study and travel programs.

KaBOOM!, *4301 Connecticut Ave. N.W., #ML-1, 20008; (202) 659-0215. Fax, (202) 659-0210. Lysa Ratliff, Chief Executive Officer. Press, (202) 464-6167.*

General email, webmaster@kaboom.org

Web, www.kaboom.org, Twitter, @kaboom, Facebook, www.facebook.com/kaboom and YouTube, www.youtube.com/user/kaboomplay

Offers grants to develop and manage playgrounds in low-income communities. Publishes research on public policy and the impact of play areas in neighborhoods.

Local Initiatives Support Corp., Washington Office, *1825 K St. N.W., #1100, 20006; (202) 739-9284. Ramon Jacobson, Executive Director, (202) 739-9273.*

General email, washingtondc@lisc.org

Web, www.liscdc.org, Twitter, @LISC_DC and Facebook, www.facebook.com/DCLISC

Provides Washington DC. community development corporations and nonprofit organizations with financial and technical assistance to build affordable, inclusive and equitable housing and revitalize distressed neighborhoods. (Headquarters in New York.)

National Assn. of Conservation Districts (NACD), *509 Capitol Court N.E., 20002-4937; (202) 547-6223. Fax, (202) 547-6450. Jeremy Peters, Chief Executive Officer.*

General email, info@nacdnet.org

Web, www.nacdnet.org, Twitter, @NACDconserve and Facebook, www.facebook.com/NACDconserve

Membership: conservation districts (local subdivisions of state government). Works to promote the conservation of private and public lands, forests, and other natural resources. Interests include rural development and urban and community conservation.

National Assn. of Counties (NACo), Community and Economic Development (CED), *660 N. Capitol St. N.W., #400, 20001; (202) 393-6226. (202) 942-4236; Matthew D. Chase, Executive Director,. Toll-Free, (888) 407-6226.*

General email, pguequierre@naco.org

Web, www.naco.org/topics/community-economic-development, Facebook, www.facebook.com/NACoDC and Twitter, @NACoTweets

Membership: county governments. Conducts research and provides information on community development block grants, assisted low-income housing, and other housing and economic development programs. Monitors legislation and regulations.

National Assn. of Development Organizations, *122 C St. N.W., #830, 20001; (202) 921-4440. Fax, (202) 921-4455. Joe McKinney, Executive Director, (202) 921-4441.*

General email, info@nado.org

Web, www.nado.org

Membership: organizations interested in regional, local, and rural economic development. Provides information on federal, state, and local development programs and revolving loan funds; sponsors conferences and training.

National Assn. of Housing and Redevelopment Officials, 630 Eye St. N.W., 20001-3736; (202) 289-3500. Fax, (202) 289-8181. Mike Gerber, Chief Executive Officer (Acting). Toll-free, (877) 866-2476.
General email, nahro@nahro.org
Web, www.nahro.org and Twitter, @NAHROnational

Membership: housing, community, and urban development practitioners and organizations, and state and local government agencies and personnel.

National Assn. of Regional Councils (NARC), 660 N. Capitol St. N.W., #440, 20001; (202) 986-1032. Leslie Wollack, Executive Director, (202) 618-5696.
General email, info@narc.org
Web, www.narc.org, Twitter, @narcregions, Facebook, www.facebook.com/nationalassociationofregionalcouncils/ and YouTube, www.youtube.com/channel/UCbD0711n Q6EHPDBU6hEU5ZQ

Membership: regional councils of local governments and metropolitan planning organizations. Works with member local governments to encourage areawide economic growth and cooperation between public and private sectors, with emphasis on community development.

National Community Development Assn., 1775 Eye St. N.W., #1150, 20006; (202) 587-2772. Vicki Watson, Executive Director.
Web, www.ncdaonline.org, Twitter, @NCDAonline and Facebook, www.facebook.com/NCDAonline

Membership: local governments that administer federally supported community and economic development, housing, and human service programs.

National Trust for Historic Preservation, 2600 Virginia Ave. N.W., #1100, 20037; (202) 588-6000. Fax, (202) 588-6038. Paul Edmondson, President, (202) 588-6101. Toll-free, (800) 944-6847.
General email, info@savingplaces.org
Web, www.savingplaces.org, Twitter, @SavingPlaces, Facebook, www.facebook.com/NationalTrustforHistoric Preservation and YouTube, www.youtube.com/national trustforhistoricpreservation

Conducts seminars, workshops, and conferences on topics related to preservation, including neighborhood conservation, main street revitalization, rural conservation, and preservation law; offers financial assistance through loan and grant programs; provides advisory services; operates historic house sites, which are open to the public; and publishes quarterly magazine and e-newsletters.

Partners for Livable Communities, 740 15th St. N.W., #339, 20005; (202) 531-6813. Robert H. (Bob) McNulty, President; Melanie Bourne, Communications Director.
General email, mbourne@livable.org
Web, www.livable.org

Promotes working partnerships among public, private, and governmental sectors to improve the quality of life and economic development at local and regional levels.

Conducts conferences and workshops; maintains referral clearinghouse; provides technical assistance.

Scenic America, 727 15th St. N.W., #1100, 20005-6029; (202) 792-1300. Mark Falzone, President.
Web, www.scenic.org, Twitter, @ScenicAmerica and Facebook, www.facebook.com/ScenicAmerica

Membership: national, state, and local groups concerned with land-use control, growth management, and landscape protection. Works to enhance the scenic quality of America's communities and countryside. Provides information and technical assistance on scenic byways, tree preservation, economics of aesthetic regulation, billboard and sign control, scenic areas preservation, and growth management.

Smart Growth America, 1152 15th St. N.W., #450, 20005; (202) 207-3355. Fax, (202) 207-3349. Calvin Gladney, President.
General email, info@smartgrowthamerica.org
Web, https://smartgrowthamerica.org, Twitter, @SmartGrowthUSA and Facebook, www.facebook.com/ smartgrowthamerica

Coalition of advocacy groups that supports citizen-driven planning that coordinates development, transportation, revitalization of older areas, and preservation of open space and the environment.

The Woodson Center, 1625 K St. N.W., #410, 20006; (202) 518-6500. Fax, (202) 588-0314. Robert L. Woodson Sr., President.
General email, info@woodsoncenter.org
Web, http://woodsoncenter.org, Twitter, @woodsoncenter, Facebook, www.facebook.com/woodsoncenter and YouTube, www.youtube.com/channel/UCOYHupe99uil GCQl5E7abAw

Seeks to empower community-based leaders to promote solutions that reduce crime and violence, restore families, revitalize underserved communities, and assist in the creation of economic enterprise.

Urban Institute, Housing Finance Policy Center, 500 L'Enfant Plaza S.W., 20024; (202) 833-7200. Janneke Ratcliffe, Vice President.
General email, hfpcpress@urban.org
Web, www.urban.org/policy-centers/housing-finance-policy-center

Provides data and analysis on housing finance; shows how the housing finance system affects households, communities, and the broader economy; and contributes to public policy, efficient markets, and economic opportunity.

Rural Areas

▶**AGENCIES**

Agriculture Dept. (USDA), Rural Development (RD), 1400 Independence Ave. S.W., #205W, 20250-0107; (202) 720-4581. Xochitl Torres Small, Under Secretary.
Web, www.rd.usda.gov and Twitter, @usdaRD

Acts as chief adviser to the secretary on agricultural credit and related matters; coordinates rural development policies and programs throughout the federal government; supervises the Rural Utilities Service, Rural Housing Service, and Rural Business-Cooperative Service.

Agriculture Dept. (USDA), *Rural Development, Rural Business–Cooperative Service,* *1400 Independence Ave. S.W., #5803-S, MS 3201, 20250-3201; (202) 690-4730. Fax, (202) 690-4737. Karama Neal, Administrator (Acting).*
Web, www.rd.usda.gov/about-rd/agencies/rural-business-cooperative-service

Administers community development programs that provide technical assistance and help communities and regions to establish strategic, long-term economic development goals.

Agriculture Dept. (USDA), *Rural Development, Rural Housing Service,* *1400 Independence Ave. S.W., #5014, MS 0701, 20250-0701; (202) 692-0268. Joaquin Altoro, Administrator (Acting). Toll-free, (800) 414-1226.*
Web, www.rd.usda.gov/about-rd/agencies/rural-housing-service

Offers financial assistance to apartment dwellers and homeowners in rural areas; provides funds to construct or improve single-family and multifamily housing and community facilities.

Agriculture Dept. (USDA), *Rural Development, Rural Utilities Service,* *1400 Independence Ave. S.W., #4121-S , MS 1510, 20250-1510; (202) 720-9540.*
Christopher A. (Chris) McLean, Administrator (Acting).
Web, www.rd.usda.gov/about-rd/agencies/rural-utilities-service

Makes loans and loan guarantees to rural electric and telephone companies providing service in rural areas. Administers the Rural Telephone Bank, which provides supplemental financing from federal sources. Makes loans for economic development and creation of jobs in rural areas, for water and waste disposal, and for distance learning and telemedicine.

Farm Service Agency (FSA) *(Agriculture Dept.),* *Farm Loan Programs, 1400 Independence Ave. S.W., #3605- S, MS 0520, 20250-0520; (202) 720-4671. Fax, (202) 690-3573. William D. (Bill) Cobb, Deputy Administrator.*
Web, www.fsa.usda.gov/programs-and-services/farm-loan-programs/index

Supports rural development through farm program loans, including real estate, farm production, and emergency loans.

National Agricultural Library *(Agriculture Dept.),* *Rural Information Center (RIC), 10301 Baltimore Ave., #123, Beltsville, MD 20705-2351; Phone, (301) 504-5755; Vanessa S. Gordon, Program Lead, (301) 504-5440. Toll-Free, (800) 633-7701.*
General email, ric@ars.usda.gov
Web, www.nal.usda.gov/ric

Provides services for rural communities, local officials, organizations, businesses, and rural citizens in the interest of maintaining rural areas. Interests include community development, tourism promotion, water quality, recycling, and technology transfer.

▶**CONGRESS**

For a listing of relevant congressional committees and subcommittees, please see page 444 or the Appendix.

▶**NONGOVERNMENTAL**

Farm Credit Council, *50 F St. N.W., #900, 20001-1530; (202) 626-8710. Fax, (202) 626-8718. Todd Van Hoose, President, (202) 879-0843; Jeffry W. Shipp, Executive Vice President, Government Affairs, (202) 879-0851.*
General email, ask@farmcredit.com
Web, www.farmcredit.com, Twitter, @thefccouncil and Facebook, www.facebook.com/FarmCredit

Represents the Farm Credit System, a national financial cooperative that makes loans to agricultural producers, rural homebuyers, farmer cooperatives, young, beginning and small farmers, and rural utilities. Finances the export of U.S. agricultural commodities.

Irrigation Assn., *8280 Willow Oaks Corporate Dr., #630, Fairfax, VA 22031; (703) 536-7080. Fax, (703) 536-7019. Natasha Rankin, Chief Executive Officer.*
General email, info@irrigation.org
Web, www.irrigation.org and Twitter, @irrigationAssoc

Membership: companies and individuals involved in irrigation, drainage, and erosion control worldwide. Promotes efficient and effective water management through training, education, and certification programs. Interests include economic development and environmental enhancement.

National Cooperative Business Assn., CLUSA International (NCBA CLUSA), *1775 Eye St. N.W., 8th Floor, 20006; (240) 638-6222. Douglas O'Brien, President.*
General email, info@ncba.coop
Web, www.ncbaclusa.coop, Twitter, @NCBACLUSAcoop, Facebook, www.facebook.com/NCBACLUSA and YouTube, www.youtube.com/channel/UC1d9CsZOwqwQJid4uEscEUg

Alliance of cooperatives, businesses, and state cooperative associations. Provides information about starting and managing agricultural cooperatives in the United States and in developing nations. Monitors legislation and regulations.

National Council of Farmer Cooperatives (NCFC), *50 F St. N.W., #900, 20001-1530; (202) 626-8700. Fax, (202) 626-8722. Charles F. (Chuck) Conner, President.*
General email, info@ncfc.org
Web, www.ncfc.org, Twitter, @FarmerCoop and Facebook, www.facebook.com/FarmerCoop

Membership: cooperative businesses owned and operated by farmers. Encourages research on agricultural cooperatives; provides statistics and analyzes trends. Monitors legislation and regulations on agricultural trade, transportation, energy, and tax issues.

National Rural Electric Cooperative Assn. (NRECA), *4301 Wilson Blvd., Arlington, VA 22203-1860; (703) 907-5500. Fax, (703) 907-5511. Jim Matheson, Chief Executive Officer. Press, (703) 907-5746.*
Web, www.electric.coop, Twitter, @NRECANews and Facebook, www.facebook.com/NRECA.coop

Membership: rural electric cooperative systems and public power and utility districts. Provides members with legislative, legal, and regulatory services. Supports energy and environmental research and offers technical advice and assistance to developing countries.

National Rural Housing Coalition, *1155 15th St. N.W., #400, 20005; (202) 393-5225. Fax, (202) 393-3034. Sam Rapoza, Director of Legislative Policy.*
General email, nrhc@ruralhousingcoalition.org
Web, https://ruralhousingcoalition.org and Twitter, @RuralCoalition

Acts as advocate for improved housing for low-income rural families; works to increase public awareness of rural housing problems; administers the Self-Help Housing Fund, Farm Worker Housing Fund, Rural Community Assistance Fund, and HUD Task Force. Monitors legislation and regulations.

National Sustainable Agriculture Coalition, *110 Maryland Ave. N.E., #209, 20002-5622; (202) 547-5754. Sarah Hackney, Coalition Director; Eric J. Deeble, Policy Director.*
General email, info@sustainableagriculture.net
Web, www.sustainableagriculture.net, Twitter, @sustainableag and Facebook, www.facebook.com/sustainableag

National alliance of farm, rural, and conservation organizations. Advocates federal policies that promote environmentally sustainable agriculture, natural resources management, and rural community development. Monitors legislation and regulations.

NTCA—The Rural Broadband Assn., *4121 Wilson Blvd., #1000, Arlington, VA 22203-1801; (703) 351-2000. Fax, (703) 351-2001. Shirley Bloomfield, Chief Executive Officer, (703) 351-2030. Government Affairs, (703) 351-2033.*
General email, membership@ntca.org
Web, www.ntca.org, Twitter, @ntcaconnect, Facebook, www.facebook.com/NTCARuralTelecom and Government Affairs, ga@ntca.org

Membership: locally owned and controlled telecommunications cooperatives and companies serving rural and small-town areas. Offers educational seminars, workshops, publications, technical assistance, and various employee benefits programs to members. Monitors legislation and regulations. (Formerly the National Telecommunications Cooperative Assn.)

Rural Coalition, *1029 Vermont Ave. N.W., #601, 20005; (202) 628-7160. Fax, (202) 393-1816. Lorette Picciano, Executive Director.*
General email, ruralco@ruralco.org
Web, www.ruralco.org and Twitter, @RuralCo

Alliance of organizations that develop public policies benefiting rural communities. Collaborates with community-based groups on agriculture and rural development issues, including health and the environment, minority farmers, farmworkers, Native Americans' rights, and rural community development. Provides rural groups with technical assistance.

Rural Community Assistance Partnership (RCAP), *1725 Eye St. N.W., #225, 20006; (202) 408-1273. Keith Ashby, Chief Executive Officer (Acting).*
Web, www.rcap.org, Twitter, @RCAPInc, Facebook, www.facebook.com/RCAPInc and General email, info@rcap.org

Provides expertise to rural communities on wastewater disposal, protection of groundwater supply, and access to safe drinking water. Targets communities with predominantly low-income or minority populations. Offers outreach policy analysis, training, and technical assistance to elected officials and other community leaders, utility owners and operators, and residents.

Specific Regions

▶ **AGENCIES**

Appalachian Regional Commission, *1666 Connecticut Ave. N.W., #700, 20009-1068; (202) 884-7700. Fax, (202) 884-7691. Brandon McBride, Executive Director. Press, (202) 884-7771.*
General email, info@arc.gov
Web, www.arc.gov

Federal–state–local partnership for economic development of the region, including West Virginia and parts of Alabama, Georgia, Kentucky, Maryland, Mississippi, New York, North Carolina, Ohio, Pennsylvania, South Carolina, Tennessee, and Virginia. Plans and provides technical and financial assistance and coordinates federal and state efforts for economic development of Appalachia.

Interstate Commission on the Potomac River Basin, *30 W. Gude Dr., #450, Rockville, MD 20850; (301) 984-1908. Mike Nardolilli, Executive Director, ext. 105.*
General email, info@icprb.org
Web, www.potomacriver.org and Twitter, @PotomacCommis

Nonregulatory interstate compact commission established by Congress to control and reduce water pollution and to restore and protect living resources in the Potomac River and its tributaries. Monitors water quality; assists metropolitan water utilities; seeks innovative methods for solving water supply and land resource problems. Provides information and educational materials on the Potomac River basin.

National Capital Planning Commission, *401 9th St. N.W., #500N, 20004; (202) 482-7200. Fax, (202) 482-7272. Marcel Acosta, Executive Director.*
General email, info@ncpc.gov
Web, www.ncpc.gov, Facebook, www.facebook.com/ NCPCgov and Twitter, @NCPCgov

Central planning agency for the federal government in the national capital region, which includes the District of Columbia and suburban Maryland and Virginia. Reviews and approves plans for the physical growth and development of the national capital area, using environmental, historic, and land-use criteria.

Tennessee Valley Authority, *Government Affairs, 1 Massachusetts Ave. N.W., #300, 20444; (202) 898-2999. Jeffrey J. (Jeff) Lyash, President.*
General email, tvainfo@tva.gov
Web, www.tva.gov, Twitter, @TVAnews and Facebook, www.facebook.com/TVA

Federal corporation that coordinates resource conservation, development, and land-use programs in the Tennessee River Valley. Uses fossil fuel, nuclear, and hydropower sources to generate and supply wholesale power to municipal and cooperative electric systems, federal installations, and some industries.

▶**NONGOVERNMENTAL**

Greater Washington Board of Trade, *800 Connecticut Ave. N.W., #1001, 20006; (202) 857-5900. Jack McDougle, President.*
General email, info@bot.org
Web, www.bot.org, Twitter, @GWBoardofTrade and Facebook, www.facebook.com/GWBoardofTrade

Promotes and plans economic growth for the capital region. Supports business-government partnerships, technological training, and transportation planning; promotes international trade; works to increase economic viability of the city of Washington. Monitors legislation and regulations at local, state, and federal levels.

New England Council, *Washington Office, 1411 K. St. N.W. #700, 20005; (202) 547-0048. Fax, (202) 547-9149. James T. Brett, President; Griffin Doherty, Director of Federal Affairs.*
General email, necouncil@newenglandcouncil.com
Web, https://newenglandcouncil.com

Provides information on business and economic issues concerning New England; serves as liaison between the New England congressional delegations and business community. (Headquarters in Boston, Mass.)

Northeast–Midwest Institute, *Universal North Bldg., 1875 K St., 4th Floor #411, 20006; (410) 615-4951. Michael Goff, President, (410) 615-4951.*
General email, info@nemw.org
Web, www.nemw.org and Facebook, www.facebook.com/ NEMWinstituteMississippiRiverPolicy

Public policy research organization that promotes the economic vitality and environmental sustainability of the northeast and midwest regions. Interests include distribution of federal funding to regions, economic development, human resources, energy, and natural resources.

Urban Areas

▶**AGENCIES**

Community Planning and Development (CPD) *(Housing and Urban Development Dept.), Affordable Housing Programs, 451 7th St. S.W., #7164, 20410; (202) 708-2684. Virginia Sardone, Director, (202) 549-7212.*
Web, www.hud.gov/program_offices/comm_planning/ affordablehousing

Coordinates with cities to convey publicly owned, abandoned property to low-income families in exchange for their commitment to repair, occupy, and maintain the property.

General Services Administration (GSA), *Urban Development/Good Neighbor Program, 1800 F St. N.W., #3341, 20405-0001; Phone, (202) 501-1866. Francis (Frank) Giblin, Program Manager, (202) 494-9236.*
Web, www.gsa.gov/real-estate/design-construction/urban-development-good-neighbor-program and Twitter, @GSA_urbdev

Advises on locations, designs, and renovations of federal facilities in central business areas, historic districts, and local redevelopment areas where they can anchor or promote community development. Collaborates with local and national civic and other organizations. Serves as clearinghouse for good practices.

▶**NONGOVERNMENTAL**

Assn. of Metropolitan Planning Organizations, *444 N. Capitol St. N.W., #532, 20001; (202) 624-3680. Fax, (202) 624-3685. Bill Keyrouze, Executive Director.*
General email, ampo@ampo.org
Web, www.ampo.org, Twitter, @ASSOC_MPOS and Facebook, www.facebook.com/AssocMPOs/

Membership: more than 385 metropolitan councils of elected officials and transportation professionals responsible for planning local transportation systems. Provides a forum for professional and organizational development; sponsors conferences and training programs.

International Downtown Assn., *1275 K St. N.W., #1000, 20005; (202) 393-6801. David T. Downey, President, (202) 798-5922.*
General email, customerservice@downtown.org
Web, https://downtown.org

Membership: organizations, corporations, public agencies, and individuals interested in the development and management of city downtown areas. Supports cooperative efforts between the public and private sectors to revitalize downtowns and adjacent neighborhoods; provides members with information, technical assistance, and advice.

Milton S. Eisenhower Foundation, *1875 Connecticut Ave. N.W., #410, 20009; (202) 234-8104. Fax, (202) 234-8484. Alan Curtis, President.*
General email, tfelder@eisenhowerfoundation.org

Web, www.eisenhowerfoundation.org

Strives to help urban communities combat violence by supporting programs with proven records of success. Provides funding, technical assistance, evaluation, and supervision to communities wishing to replicate successful programs.

National Assn. for the Advancement of Colored People (NAACP), *Washington Bureau, 1156 15th St. N.W., #915, 20005; (202) 463-2940. Fax, (202) 463-2953. Derrick Johnson, President.*
General email, washingtonbureau@naacpnet.org

Web, www.naacp.org, Twitter, @NAACP and Twitter, President, @DerrickNAACP

Membership: persons interested in civil rights for all minorities. Works to eliminate discrimination in housing and urban affairs. Interests include programs for urban redevelopment, urban homesteading, and low-income housing. Supports programs that make affordable rental housing available to minorities and that maintain African American ownership of urban and rural land. (Headquarters in Baltimore, Md.)

National Assn. of Neighborhoods, *1300 Pennsylvania Ave. N.W., #700, 20004; (202) 332-7766. Ricardo C. Byrd, Executive Director.*
General email, info@nanworld.org

Web, www.nanworld.org

Federation of neighborhood groups that provides technical assistance to local governments, neighborhood groups, and businesses. Seeks to increase influence of grassroots groups on decisions affecting neighborhoods; sponsors training workshops promoting neighborhood awareness.

National League of Cities, *660 N. Capitol St. N.W., #450, 20001; (202) 626-3000. Fax, (202) 626-3043. Clarence Anthony, Executive Director, (202) 626-3010. Toll-free, (877) 827-2385.*
General email, info@nlc.org

Web, www.nlc.org and Twitter, @leagueofcities

Membership: cities and state municipal leagues. Aids city leaders in developing programs; investigates needs of local governments in implementing federal community development programs.

National Urban League, *Washington Bureau, 1805 7th St. N.W., #520, 20001; (202) 898-1604. Joi O. Cheny, Executive Director, Washington, (202) 629-5755.*
Web, https://nul.org/washington-bureau, Twitter, @NULPolicy and Facebook, www.facebook.com/NULPolicy

Federal advocacy division of social service organization concerned with the social welfare of African Americans and other minorities. Conducts legislative and policy analysis on housing and urban affairs. Operates a job network. (Headquarters in New York.)

NeighborWorks America, *999 N. Capitol St. N.E., #900, 20002; (202) 760-4000. Fax, (202) 376-2600. Marietta Rodriguez, President.*
General email, editor@nw.org

Web, www.neighborworks.org, Twitter, @neighborworks and Facebook, www.facebook.com/NeighborWorks America

Chartered by Congress to assist localities in developing and operating local neighborhood-based programs designed to reverse decline in urban residential neighborhoods and rural communities. Oversees the National NeighborWorks Network, an association of local non-profit organizations concerned with urban and rural development.

Urban Institute, *Metropolitan Housing and Communities Policy Center, 500 L'Enfant Plaza S.W., 20024; (202) 833-7200. Mary K. Cunningham, Vice President.*
Web, www.urban.org/policy-centers/metropolitan-housing-and-communities-policy-center

Research center that deals with urban problems. Researches federal, state, and local policies; focus includes community development block grants, neighborhood rehabilitation programs, and housing issues.

Urban Land Institute, *2001 L St. N.W., #200, 20036; (202) 624-7000. Fax, (202) 403-3849. W. Edward (Ed) Walter, Global Chief Executive Officer. Customer Service, (800) 321-5011.*
General email, Customerservice@uli.org

Web, www.uli.org, Twitter, @UrbanLandInst and Facebook, www.facebook.com/ULIGlobal

Membership: land developers, planners, state and federal agencies, financial institutions, home builders, consultants, and Realtors. Provides responsible leadership in the use of land to enhance the total environment; monitors trends in new community development.

CONSTRUCTION

General

▶ **NONGOVERNMENTAL**

American Public Works Assn., *Washington Office, 25 Massachusetts Ave. N.W., #500A, 20001; (202) 408-9541. Andrea Eales, Director of Government Affairs, (202) 218-6730. Toll-free, (800) 848-2792.*
General email, apwa.washington@gmail.com

Web, www.apwa.net, Twitter, @APWATweets and Facebook, www.facebook.com/AmericanPublicWorks Association

Membership: engineers, architects, and others who maintain and manage public works facilities and services. Conducts research and education and promotes exchange of information on transportation and infrastructure-related issues. (Headquarters in Kansas City, Mo.)

American Subcontractors Assn., *1004 Duke St., Alexandria, VA 22314-3588; (703) 684-3450. Richard Bright, Chief Operating Officer, (410) 869-3253. General email, asaoffice@asa-hq.com*

Web, www.asaonline.com, Twitter, @ASAupdate and *Facebook, www.facebook.com/Subcontractors*

Membership: construction subcontractors, specialty contractors, and their suppliers. Addresses business, contract, and payment issues affecting all subcontractors. Interests include procurement laws, payment practices, and lien laws. Monitors legislation and regulations.

Associated Builders and Contractors, *440 1st St. N.W., #200, 20001; (202) 595-1505. Michael Bellaman, President. General email, gotquestion@abc.org*

Web, www.abc.org, Twitter, @ABCNational and *Facebook, www.facebook.com/ABCNational*

Membership: construction contractors engaged primarily in nonresidential construction, subcontractors, and suppliers. Sponsors apprenticeship, safety, and training programs. Provides labor relations information; compiles statistics. Monitors legislation and regulations.

Associated General Contractors of America, *2300 Wilson Blvd., #300, Arlington, VA 22201; (703) 548-3118. Fax, (703) 548-3119. Stephen E. Sandherr, Chief Executive Officer. General email, info@agc.org*

Web, www.agc.org, Twitter, @AGCofA and *Facebook, www.facebook.com/AGCofA*

Membership: general contractors engaged primarily in nonresidential construction; subcontractors; suppliers; accounting; insurance and bonding; and law firms. Conducts training programs, conferences, seminars, and market development activities for members. Members are served by four occupational divisions—Building, Federal and Heavy Construction, Highway and Transportation, and Utility Infrastructure. Produces position papers on construction issues. Monitors legislation and regulations.

Construction Management Assn. of America (CMAA), *7926 Jones Branch Dr., #800, McLean, VA 22102-3303; (703) 356-2622. Andrea S. Rutledge, President. General email, communications@cmaanet.org*

Web, https://cmaanet.org, Twitter, @CMAA_HQ, Facebook, www.facebook.com/CMAAHQ and *YouTube, www.youtube.com/user/jjmckeown/videos*

Promotes the development of construction management as a profession through publications, education, a certification program, and an information network. Serves as an advocate for construction management in the legislative, executive, and judicial branches of government.

Construction Specifications Institute (CSI), *123 N. Pitt St., #450, Alexandria, VA 22314; (800) 689-2900. Mark Dorsey, Chief Executive Officer, (703) 706-4760.*

General email, csi@csinet.org

Web, http://csiresources.org, Twitter, @CSIConstruction, Facebook, www.facebook.com/CSIConstruction and *YouTube, www.youtube.com/user/CSIConstruction*

Membership: architects, engineers, contractors, and others in the construction industry. Promotes construction technology; publishes reference materials to help individuals prepare construction documents; sponsors certification programs for construction specifiers and manufacturing representatives. Bookstore available for both members and nonmembers.

Mechanical Contractors Assn. of America, *1385 Piccard Dr., Rockville, MD 20850; (301) 869-5800. Timothy (Tim) Brink, Chief Executive Officer. Toll-free, (800) 556-3653. General email, help@mcaa.org*

Web, www.mcaa.org, Twitter, @mcaanews and *Facebook, www.facebook.com/mcaaeducation/?fref=ts*

Membership: mechanical contractors and members of related professions. Seeks to improve building standards and codes. Provides information, publications, and training programs; conducts seminars and annual convention. Monitors legislation and regulations.

National Academies of Sciences, Engineering, and Medicine (NASEM), *Infrastructure and the Constructed Environment Board, Keck Center, 500 5th St. N.W., #WS938, 20001; (202) 334-3505. Fax, (202) 334-3718. Cameron Oskvig, Director; Thomas Bostick, Chair. General email, bice@nas.edu*

Web, www.nationalacademies.org/bice/board-on-infrastructure-and-the-constructed-environment

Advises the government, the private sector, and the public on technology, science, and public policy related to the design, construction, operations, maintenance, security, and evaluation of buildings, facilities, and infrastructure systems; the relationship between the constructed and natural environments and their interaction with human activities; the effects of natural and man-made hazards on constructed facilities and infrastructure; and the interdependencies of infrastructure systems, including power, water, transportation, telecommunications, wastewater, and buildings.

National Assn. of Home Builders (NAHB), *1201 15th St. N.W., 20005-2800; (202) 266-8200. Fax, (202) 266-8400. Gerald (Jerry) Howard, Executive Officer, (800) 368-5242, ext. 8257. Press, (202) 266-8254. Toll-free, (800) 368-5242. General email, info@nahb.org*

Web, www.nahb.org and *Twitter, @NAHBhome*

Membership: contractors, builders, architects, engineers, mortgage lenders, and others interested in home building and residential real estate construction. Participates in updating and developing building codes and standards; offers technical information. Interests include environmental and land-use policies. Monitors legislation and regulations.

National Assn. of Minority Contractors, *1050 Connecticut Ave. N.W., #500, 20036; (202) 296-1600. Fax, (202) 296-1644. Dan Moncrief III, President.*
General email, info@namcnational.org

Web, www.namcnational.org and Twitter, @NAMCNational

Membership: minority businesses and related firms, women contractors, strategic alliances, and individuals serving those businesses in the construction industry. Advises members on commercial and government contracts; provides technical assistance and industry-specific training; provides bid information on government contracts. Monitors legislation and regulations. Acts as advocate for legislative changes.

National Assn. of Plumbing-Heating-Cooling Contractors, *180 S. Washington St., #100, Falls Church, VA 22046; (703) 237-8100. Fax, (703) 237-7442. Mark S. Ingaro, Chief Executive Officer. Toll-free, (800) 533-7694.*
General email, naphcc@naphcc.org

Web, www.phccweb.org and Twitter, @phccnatl

Provides education and training for the plumbing and HVACR industry. Offers career information, internships, and scholarship programs for business and engineering students to encourage careers in the plumbing and mechanical contracting field. Promotes health, safety, and protection of the environment.

National Electrical Contractors Assn., *1201 Pennsylvania Ave. N.W., #1200, 20004; (202) 991-6300. Fax, (202) 217-4171. John Grau, Chief Executive Officer.*
General email, necagovaffairs@necanet.org

Web, www.necanet.org, Twitter, @necanet, Facebook, www.facebook.com/NECANET and YouTube, www.youtube.com/user/Necaadmin

Membership: electrical contractors who build and service electrical wiring and equipment, including high-voltage construction and service. Represents members in collective bargaining with union workers; sponsors research and educational programs.

National Utility Contractors Assn. (NUCA), *3925 Chain Bridge Rd., #300, Fairfax, VA 22030; (703) 358-9300. Doug Carlson, Chief Executive Officer.*
General email, nuca@nuca.com

Web, www.nuca.com, Twitter, @NUCA_National and Facebook, www.facebook.com/nuca1964

Membership: contractors who perform water, sewer, and other underground utility construction. Sponsors NUCA University, webinars, scholarships, conferences, and other trainings; conducts surveys. Publishes a quarterly business journal. Monitors public works legislation and regulations.

Sheet Metal and Air Conditioning Contractors' National Assn., *4201 Lafayette Center Dr., Chantilly, VA 20151-1219; Capitol Hill Office, 305 4th St. N.E., 20002-5815; (703) 803-2980. Fax, (703) 803-3732. Aaron Hilger, Chief Executive Officer; Stanley E. Kolbe Jr., Director of Legislative and Political Affairs. Capitol Hill, (202) 547-8202. Capitol Hill fax, (202) 547-8810.*
General email, info@smacna.org

Web, www.smacna.org

Membership: unionized sheet metal and air conditioning contractors. Provides information on standards and installation and fabrication methods. Interests include energy efficiency and sustainability.

U.S. Green Building Council, *2101 L St. N.W., #500, 20037; (202) 742-3792. Vacant, Chief Executive Officer. Toll-free, (800) 795-1747.*
General email, info@usgbc.org

Web, www.usgbc.org, Twitter, @USGBC, Facebook, www.facebook.com/USGBC and YouTube, www.youtube.com/USGBC

Promotes buildings that are environmentally responsible, profitable, and healthy. Rates green buildings in order to accelerate implementation of environmentally friendly design practices.

Architecture and Design

▶ AGENCIES

General Services Administration (GSA), *Design and Construction, Office of the Chief Architect, 1800 F St. N.W., #5400, 20405-0001; (202) 501-1888. David Insinga, Chief Architect.*
Web, www.gsa.gov/about-us/organization/public-buildings-service

Administers the Design Excellence Program, which reviews designs of federal buildings and courthouses.

▶ NONGOVERNMENTAL

American Institute of Architects, *1735 New York Ave. N.W., 20006-5292; (202) 626-7300. Fax, (202) 626-7547. Lakisha Ann Woods, Chief Executive Officer. Toll-free, (800) 242-3837.*
General email, info@aia.org

Web, www.aia.org, Twitter, @AIANational and Facebook, www.facebook.com/AIANational

Membership: licensed American architects, interns, architecture faculty, engineers, planners, and those in government, manufacturing, or other fields in a capacity related to architecture. Works to advance the standards of architectural education, training, and practice. Promotes the aesthetic, scientific, and practical efficiency of architecture, urban design, and planning; monitors international developments. Offers continuing and professional education programs; sponsors scholarships, internships, and awards. Manages a historical directory archive. Monitors legislation and regulations.

American Society of Interior Designers, *1152 15th St. N.W., #910, 20005; (202) 546-3480. Fax, (202) 546-3240. Gary Wheeler, Chief Executive Officer.*

General email, membership@asid.org

Web, www.asid.org

Offers certified professional development courses addressing the technical, professional, and business needs of designers; bestows annual scholarships, fellowships, and awards; supports licensing efforts at the state level.

American Society of Landscape Architects, *636 Eye St. N.W., 20001-3736; (202) 898-2444. Fax, (202) 898-1185. Torey Carter-Conneen, Chief Executive Officer. Toll-free, (888) 999-2752.*

General email, info@asla.org

Web, www.asla.org, Twitter, @NationalASLA and Facebook, www.facebook.com/AmericanSocietyof LandscapeArchitects

Membership: professional landscape architects. Advises government agencies on land-use policy and environmental matters. Accredits university-level programs in landscape architecture; conducts professional education seminars for members.

AmericanHort, *Washington Office, 525 9th St. N.W., #800, 20004; (202) 789-2900. Fax, (202) 789-1893. Ken Fisher, President, (614) 487-1117.*

General email, hello@AmericanHort.org

Web, www.AmericanHort.org and Twitter, @American_ Hort

Serves as an information clearinghouse on the technical aspects of nursery and landscape business and design. (Headquarters in Columbus, Ohio.)

Assn. of Collegiate Schools of Architecture, *1735 New York Ave. N.W., 3rd Floor, 20006; (202) 785-2324. Fax, (202) 628-0448. Michael J. Monti, Executive Director.*

General email, info@acsa-arch.org

Web, www.acsa-arch.org, Twitter, @ACSAUpdate and Facebook, www.facebook.com/ACSANational

Membership: U.S. and Canadian institutions that offer at least one accredited architecture degree program. Conducts workshops and seminars for architecture school faculty; presents awards for student and faculty excellence in architecture; publishes a guide to architecture schools in North America.

Industrial Designers Society of America (IDSA), *950 Herndon Pkwy, #250, Herndon, VA 20170; (703) 707-6000. Fax, (703) 787-8501. Chris Livaudais, Executive Director, ext. 116.*

General email, membership@idsa.org

Web, www.idsa.org, Twitter, @IDSA and Facebook, www .facebook.com/IDSA.org

Membership: designers of products, equipment, instruments, furniture, transportation, packages, exhibits, information services, and related services, and educators of industrial design. Provides the Bureau of Labor Statistics with industry information. Monitors legislation and regulations.

Landscape Architecture Foundation, *1200 17th St. N.W., #210, 20036; (202) 331-7070. Fax, (202) 331-7079. Barbara Deutsch, Chief Executive Officer, ext. 12.*

General email, rbooher@lafoundation.org

Web, www.lafoundation.org, Twitter, @lafoundation and Facebook, www.facebook.com/lafoundation.org

Conducts research and provides educational and scientific information on sustainable landscape architecture and development and related fields. Awards scholarships and fellowships.

National Architectural Accrediting Board Inc., *107 S. West St. #707, Alexandria, VA 22314; (202) 783-2007. Fax, (202) 783-2822. Rebecca O'Neal, President; Tanya A. Tamarkin, Executive Director.*

General email, info@naab.org

Web, www.naab.org, Twitter, @NAABNews and Facebook, www.facebook.com/NationalArchitecturalAccrediting Board/

Accredits Bachelor, Master, and Doctor of Architecture degree programs in the United States; assists organizations in other countries to develop accreditation standards.

National Assn. of Landscape Professionals, *12500 Fair Lakes Circle, #200, Fairfax, VA 22033; (703) 736-9666. Fax, (703) 322-2066. Britt Wood, Chief Executive Officer, (703) 456-4208. Toll-free, (800) 395-2522.*

General email, info@landscapeprofessionals.org

Web, www.landscapeprofessionals.org and Twitter, @the_ nalp

Membership: lawn care professionals, exterior maintenance contractors, installation/design/building professionals, and interiorscapers. Provides members with education, business management and marketing tools, and networking opportunities. Offers certification program. Focus is the green industry. Monitors legislation.

National Assn. of Schools of Art and Design, *11250 Roger Bacon Dr., #21, Reston, VA 20190-5248; (703) 437-0700. Fax, (703) 437-6312. Karen Moynahan, Executive Director, ext. 116.*

General email, info@arts-accredit.org

Web, http://nasad.arts-accredit.org

Specialized professional accrediting agency for postsecondary programs in art and design. Conducts and shares research and analysis on topics pertinent to art and design programs and fields of art and design. Offers professional development opportunities for executives of art and design programs.

National Council of Architectural Registration Boards (NCARB), *1401 H St. N.W., #500, 20005; (202) 879-0520. Michael J. Armstrong, Chief Executive Officer.*

General email, customerservice@ncarb.org

Web, www.ncarb.org, Twitter, @NCARB, Facebook, www .facebook.com/NCARB and YouTube, www.youtube.com/ user/NCARBorg

Membership: state architectural registration boards. Develops examinations used in the United States and its territories for licensing architects; certifies architects.

Society for Marketing Professional Services, *625 N. Washington St., #302, Alexandria, VA 22314-1936; (703) 549-6117. Fax, (703) 549-2498. Michael V. Geary, Chief Executive Officer. Toll-free, (800) 292-7677.*
General email, info@smps.org

Web, www.smps.org, Twitter, @SMPSHQ and Facebook, www.facebook.com/SMPSHQ

Membership: individuals who provide professional services to the building industry. Assists individuals who market design services in the areas of architecture, engineering, planning, interior design, landscape architecture, and construction management. Provides seminars, workshops, and publications for members. Maintains job banks.

Codes, Standards, and Research

►AGENCIES

Access Board, *1331 F St. N.W., #1000, 20004-1111; (202) 272-0080. Fax, (202) 272-0081. Sachin Dev Pavithran, Executive Director. Toll-free, (800) 872-2253. Toll-free TTY, (800) 993-2822. TTY, (202) 272-0082.*
General email, info@access-board.gov

Web, www.access-board.gov and Twitter, @accessboard

Develops and maintains accessibility requirements for buildings, transit vehicles, telecommunications equipment, medical diagnostic equipment, and electronic and information technology. Provides technical assistance and training on these guidelines and standards. Enforces access standards for federally funded facilities through the Architectural Barriers Act.

Energy Efficiency and Renewable Energy (EERE) *(Energy Dept.),* **Building Technologies (BTO),** *1000 Independence Ave. S.W., MS EE2J, 20585; (202) 586-9127. Fax, (202) 586-4617. David Nemtzow, Director.*
General email, Buildings@ee.doe.gov

Web, www.energy.gov/eere/buildings/building-technologies-office

Funds research to reduce commercial and residential building energy use. Programs include research and development, equipment standards and analysis, and technology validation and market introduction.

Environmental Protection Agency (EPA), *Air and Radiation (OAR), Radiation and Indoor Air, 1200 Pennsylvania Ave. N.W., #5426, MC 6608T, 20460; (202) 343-9320. Fax, (202) 564-1408. Jonathan Edwards, Director.*
Web, www.epa.gov/aboutepa/about-office-air-and-radiation-oar#oria

Establishes standards for measuring radon. Develops model building codes for state and local governments. Provides states and building contractors with technical assistance and training on radon detection and mitigation. Oversees the Radiation and Indoor Environments Laboratory in Las Vegas, Nev. Administers the Clean Air Act.

Federal Housing Administration (FHA) *(Housing and Urban Development Dept.),* **Manufactured Housing Programs,** *451 7th St. S.W., #9164, 20410-8000;*

(202) 402-5365. Fax, (202) 402-2480. Teresa Payne, Administrator, (202) 402-5365. Consumer complaints, (800) 927-2891.
General email, mhs@hud.gov

Web, www.hud.gov/program_offices/housing/rmra/mhs/mhshome

Establishes and maintains standards for selection of new materials and methods of construction; evaluates technical suitability of products and materials; develops uniform, preemptive, and mandatory national standards for manufactured housing; enforces standards through design review and quality control inspection of factories; administers a national consumer protection program. Handles dispute resolution.

Housing and Urban Development Dept. (HUD), *Lead Hazard Control and Healthy Homes (OLHCHH), 451 7th St. S.W., #8236, 20410; (202) 708-4337. Fax, (202) 708-0014. Michelle M. Miller, Director, (202) 402-5769.*
Web, www.hud.gov/program_offices/healthy_homes and Twitter, @HUDHealthyHomes

Advises HUD offices, other agencies, health authorities, and the housing industry on lead poisoning prevention. Develops regulations for lead-based paint; conducts research; makes grants to state and local governments for lead hazard reduction and inspection of housing.

National Institute of Standards and Technology (NIST) *(Commerce Dept.), Bldg. 101, 100 Bureau Dr., #A1134, Gaithersburg, MD 20899-1000 (mailing address: 100 Bureau Dr., MS 1000, Gaithersburg, MD 20899); (301) 975-2000. Fax, (301) 869-8972. James Olthoff, Under Secretary. Information, (301) 975-6478. TTY, (800) 877-8339.*
General email, director@nist.gov

Web, www.nist.gov

Provides services to support National Safety Construction Team Act investigations to assess building performance, emergency response, and evacuation procedures.

National Institute of Standards and Technology (NIST) *(Commerce Dept.), Engineering Laboratory, 100 Bureau Dr., MS 8600, Gaithersburg, MD 20899-8600; (301) 975-5900. Fax, (301) 975-4032. Joannie Chin, Director, (301) 975-6815.*
General email, el@nist.gov

Web, www.nist.gov/el

Performs analytical, laboratory, and field research in the area of building technology and its applications for building usefulness, safety, and economy; produces performance criteria and evaluation, test, and measurement methods for building owners, occupants, designers, manufacturers, builders, and federal, state, and local regulatory authorities. Researches architecture, materials construction, energy production and distribution, and manufacturing to develop recommendations for constructing buildings that maximize safety, withstand earthquakes and other natural disasters, and are energy efficient. Contributes standards and codes development; provides performance metrics, measurement and testing methods, and protocols; and evaluates systems and practices.

U.S. Fire Administration *(Federal Emergency Management Agency), 16825 S. Seton Ave., Emmitsburg, MD 21727-8998; (301) 447-1000. Lori Moore-Merrell, Administrator. Press, (301) 447-1853. Toll-free, (800) 238-3358. Toll-free National Fire Incident Reporting System Help Desk (NFIRS), (888) 382-3827. Toll-free publications, (800) 561-3356.*
Web, www.usfa.fema.gov, Twitter, @usfire and Facebook, www.facebook.com/usfire

Conducts research and collects, analyzes, and disseminates data on combustion, fire prevention, firefighter safety, and the management of fire prevention organizations; studies and develops arson-prevention programs and fire-prevention codes; maintains the National Fire Incident Reporting System.

▶NONGOVERNMENTAL

American Society of Civil Engineers (ASCE), *1801 Alexander Bell Dr., Reston, VA 20191-4400; Washington Office, 25 Massachusetts Ave. N.W., #500, 20001; (202) 789-7850. Thomas W. Smith III, Executive Director. International inquiries, (703) 295-6300. Press, (202) 789-7853. Toll-free, (800) 548-2723.*
Web, www.asce.org and Twitter, @ascetweets

Membership: professionals and students in civil engineering. Develops standards by consensus for construction documents and building codes, and standards for civil engineering education, licensure, and ethics. Organizes international conferences; maintains technical and professional reference materials; hosts e-learning sites. Advocates improvements in public infrastructure; monitors legislation and regulations.

American Society of Heating, Refrigerating, and Air Conditioning Engineers (ASHRAE), *Government Affairs, 1255 23rd St. N.W., #825, 20037; (202) 833-1830. Fax, (202) 833-0118. Mick Schwedler, Executive Vice President; Alice Yates, Director of Government Affairs.*
General email, GovAffairs@ASHRAE.org
Web, www.ashrae.org, Twitter, @ashraenews, Facebook, www.facebook.com/ASHRAEupdates and YouTube, www.youtube.com/ASHRAEvideo

Membership: engineers and others involved with the heating, ventilation, air conditioning, and refrigeration industry in the United States and abroad, including students. Sponsors research, meetings, and educational activities. Develops industry standards; publishes technical data. Monitors legislation and regulations. (Headquarters in Atlanta, Ga.)

Asphalt Roofing Manufacturers Assn., *2331 Rock Spring Rd., Forest Hill, MD 21050; (443) 640-1075. Fax, (443) 640-1031. Reed Hitchcock, Executive Vice President. Press, (443) 640-1075, ext. 1144.*
General email, info@asphaltroofing.org
Web, www.asphaltroofing.org and Facebook, www.facebook.com/AsphaltRoofingManufacturersAssociation/

Membership: manufacturers of bitumen-based roofing products. Assists in developing local building codes and standards for asphalt roofing products. Provides technical information; supports research. Monitors legislation and regulations.

Building Codes Assistance Project, *1850 M St. N.W., #610, 20036; (202) 530-2211. Maureen Guttman, President.*
General email, buildingcodesassistanceproject@gmail.com
Web, http://bcapcodes.org and Twitter, @BCAPOCEAN

Advocacy group that supports and enforces national building energy codes. Assists cities, states, and counties in complying with federal energy efficiency codes, including planning, technical assistance, and training. Provides outreach and coordination activities to provide information about current code data and cost analysis to policymakers. International interests include India, the Asia–Pacific region, Ukraine, and arid regions.

Center for Auto Safety, *4400 Jenifer St. N.W., #331, 20015-2113; (202) 328-7700. Michael Brooks, Executive Director (Acting).*
General email, contact@autosafety.org
Web, www.autosafety.org, Twitter, @Ctr4AutoSafety and Facebook, www.facebook.com/CenterForAutoSafety/

Monitors Federal Trade Commission warranty regulations and HUD implementation of federal safety and construction standards for manufactured mobile homes.

Home Innovation Research Labs, *400 Prince George's Blvd., Upper Marlboro, MD 20774; (301) 249-4000. Fax, (301) 430-6180. J. Michael Luzier, President. Toll-free, (800) 638-8556.*
Web, www.homeinnovation.com and Twitter, @HomeResearchLab

Conducts contract research and product labeling and certification for U.S. industry, government, and trade associations related to home building and light commercial industrial building. Interests include energy conservation, new technologies, international research, public health issues, affordable housing, special needs housing for the elderly and persons with disabilities, building codes and standards, land development, and environmental issues. (Independent subsidiary of the National Assn. of Home Builders [NAHB].)

International Code Council, *500 New Jersey Ave. N.W., 6th Floor, 20001-2070; (202) 370-1800. Fax, (202) 783-2348. Dominic Sims, Chief Executive Officer. Toll-free, (888) 422-7233.*
General email, customersuccess@iccsafe.org
Web, www.iccsafe.org, Twitter, @IntlCodeCouncil and Facebook, www.facebook.com/InternationalCodeCouncil

Membership association dedicated to building safety and sustainability. Develops codes used to construct residential and commercial buildings, including homes and schools. Offers "green" standards accreditation for businesses providing energy-efficient and sustainable infrastructure.

National Fire Protection Assn., *Government Affairs,* 50 F St. N.W., #625, 20001; (202) 898-0222. Fax, (202) 898-0044. Jim Pauley, Chief Executive Officer, (617) 984-7275; Seth Statler, Government Affairs Director.
General email, wdc@nfpa.org

Web, www.nfpa.org/About-NFPA/Offices/Government-Affairs, Twitter, @NFPA and Facebook, www.facebook.com/theNFPA

Membership: individuals and organizations interested in fire protection. Develops and updates fire protection codes and standards; sponsors technical assistance programs; collects fire data statistics. Monitors legislation and regulations. (Headquarters in Quincy, Mass.)

National Institute of Building Sciences, 1090 Vermont Ave. N.W., #700, 20005-4950; (202) 289-7800. Stephen T. Ayers, Corporate Executive Officer (Acting).
General email, nibs@nibs.org

Web, www.nibs.org, Twitter, @bldgsciences and Facebook, www.facebook.com/bldgsciences

Public-private partnership authorized by Congress to improve the regulation of building construction, facilitate the safe introduction of innovative building technology, and disseminate performance criteria and other technical information.

Pool and Hot Tub Alliance *(PHTA),* 2111 Eisenhower Ave., #500, Alexandria, VA 22314-4698; (703) 838-0083. Sabeena Hickman, President, (703) 647-2552.
General email, phta@phta.org

Web, www.phta.org, Twitter, @ThePHTA and Facebook, www.facebook.com/PoolHotTubAlliance

Membership: manufacturers, dealers and retailers, service companies, builders, and distributors of pools, spas, and hot tubs. Promotes the industry; provides educational programs for industry professionals; establishes standards for construction and safety. Monitors legislation and regulations.

Materials and Labor

▶NONGOVERNMENTAL

American Coatings Assn., 901 New York Ave. N.W., #300 West, 20001; (202) 462-6272. Fax, (202) 462-8549. J. Andrew (Andy) Doyle, President.
General email, aca@paint.org

Web, www.paint.org and Facebook, www.facebook.com/AmericanCoatingsAssociation

Membership: paint and coatings manufacturers, raw materials suppliers, distributors, and other industry professionals. Provides educational and public outreach programs for the industry; interests include health, safety, and the environment. Monitors legislation and regulations.

American Concrete Pavement Assn. (ACPA), *Washington Office,* 660 N. Capitol St. N.W., #850, 20001; (202) 638-2272. Fax, (202) 638-2688. Leif Wathne, Executive Vice President; Laura O'Neill Kaumo, Chief Executive Officer.

General email, acpa@acpa.org

Web, www.acpa.org, Twitter, @PaveConcrete and Facebook, www.facebook.com/paveconcrete63

Represents the concrete pavement industry. Promotes use of concrete for airport, highway, street, and local road pavements. Provides members with project assistance, educational workshops, and training programs. Supports research of concrete pavement design, construction, and rehabilitation. (Headquarters in Rosemont, IL.)

American Forest and Paper Assn., *Government and Industry Affairs,* 1101 K St. N.W., #700, 20005; (202) 463-2599. Heidi Brock, Chief Executive Officer; Eric J. Steiner, Vice President of Government Affairs; Terry Webber, Vice President of Industry Affairs.
General email, Government_Industry_Affairs@afandpa.org

Web, http://afandpa.org, Twitter, @ForestandPaper and Facebook, www.facebook.com/ForestandPaper/

Membership: wood and specialty products manufacturers and those in related associations. Interests include tax, housing, environmental, international trade, natural resources, and land-use issues that affect the wood and paper products industry.

Architectural Woodwork Institute, 46179 Westlake Dr., #120, Potomac Falls, VA 20165-5874; (571) 323-3636. Fax, (571) 323-3630. Doug Hague, Executive Vice President, (571) 762-4890.
General email, info@awinet.org

Web, www.awinet.org and Twitter, @AWInational

Membership: architectural woodworkers, suppliers, design professionals, and students. Promotes the use of architectural woodworking and networking among members; establishes industry standards; conducts seminars and workshops.

Asphalt Roofing Manufacturers Assn., 2331 Rock Spring Rd., Forest Hill, MD 21050; (443) 640-1075. Fax, (443) 640-1031. Reed Hitchcock, Executive Vice President. Press, (443) 640-1075 ext. 1144.
General email, info@asphaltroofing.org

Web, www.asphaltroofing.org and Facebook, www.facebook.com/AsphaltRoofingManufacturersAssociation/

Membership: manufacturers of bitumen-based roofing products. Assists in developing local building codes and standards for asphalt roofing products. Provides technical information; supports research. Monitors legislation and regulations.

Assn. of the Wall and Ceiling Industries, 513 W. Broad St., #210, Falls Church, VA 22046-3257; (703) 538-1600. Fax, (703) 534-8307. Michael F. Stark, Chief Executive Officer, (703) 538-1618.
General email, awci@awci.org

Web, www.awci.org, Twitter, @AWCI_INFO, Facebook, www.facebook.com/AWCIwall and YouTube, www.youtube.com/user/AWCImedia

Membership: contractors and suppliers working in the wall and ceiling industries. Sponsors conferences and seminars. Monitors legislation and regulations.

The Brick Industry Assn., *12007 Sunrise Valley Dr., #430, Reston, VA 20191; (703) 620-0010. Fax, (703) 620-3928. Raymond W. (Ray) Leonhard, President, (703) 674-1533; Joseph Casper, Sr. Vice President, Government and Regulatory Affairs, (703) 674-0741.*
General email, brickinfo@bia.org

Web, www.gobrick.com, Twitter, @BrickIndustry and Facebook, www.facebook.com/brickindustry

Membership: manufacturers and distributors of clay brick. Provides technical expertise and assistance; promotes bricklaying vocational education programs; maintains collection of technical publications on brick masonry construction. Monitors legislation and regulations.

Building Systems Councils of the National Assn. of Home Builders, *1201 15th St. N.W., 7th Floor, 20005-2800; (800) 368-5242. Devin Perry, Executive Director, (202) 266-8577.*
General email, info@nahb.org

Web, www.nahb.org/nahb-community/councils/building-systems-councils, Twitter, @NAHBhome and Facebook, www.facebook.com/NAHBhome/

Membership: manufacturers and suppliers of off site home building products and services, includes concrete, log, timber, modular, and panelized homes; Represents all segments of the industry. Assists in developing National Assn. of Home Builders policies regarding building codes, legislation, and government regulations affecting manufacturers of model-code-compliant, factory-built housing. Sponsors educational programs; conducts plant tours of member operations.

Composite Panel Assn., *19465 Deerfield Ave., #306, Leesburg, VA 20176; (703) 724-1128. Fax, (703) 724-1588. Andy O'Hare, President, ext. 243.*
General email, admin@decorativesurfaces.org

Web, www.CompositePanel.org, Twitter, @theDecorSurface and Facebook, www.facebook.com/Composite_Panel_Association

Membership: manufacturers of particleboard, medium-density fiberboard, and hardboard engineered woodsiding/trim, and decorative surfaces in North America. Promotes use of these materials; conducts industry education; offers a certification program for recycled and low-emitting products (Eco-Certified Composite [ECC] Sustainability and Certification Program). Monitors legislation and regulations.

Decorative Hardwoods Assn., *42777 Trade West Dr., Sterling, VA 20166; (703) 435-2900. Fax, (703) 435-2537. Keith (Kip) Christman, President, ext. 103.*
General email, Resources@decorativehardwoods.org

Web, www.decorativehardwoods.org, Twitter, @DecHardwoods and Facebook, www.facebook.com/DecorativeHardwoods

Membership: manufacturers, distributors, wholesalers, suppliers, and sales agents of hardwood, plywood, veneer, and engineered wood flooring. Disseminates business information; sponsors workshops and seminars; issues certifications; conducts research.

Door and Hardware Institute, *2001 K St. N.W., 3rd Floor, 20006; (202) 367-1134. Fax, (202) 367-2134. Cedric Calhoun, Chief Executive Officer.*
General email, info@dhi.org

Web, www.dhi.org, Twitter, @DHIorg and Facebook, www.facebook.com/DHIorg

Membership: companies and individuals that manufacture or distribute doors and related fittings. Promotes the industry. Interests include building security, life safety and exit devices, and compliance with the Americans with Disabilities Act. Publishes *Door Security and Safety Magazine.* Monitors legislation and regulations.

Gypsum Assn., *962 Wayne Ave., #620, Silver Spring, MD 20910; (301) 277-8686. Fax, (301) 277-8747. Stephen H. Meima, Executive Director, (301) 277-8743.*
General email, info@gypsum.org

Web, www.gypsum.org

Membership: manufacturers of gypsum wallboard and other gypsum panel products. Assists members, code officials, builders, designers, and others with technical problems and building code questions; publishes *Fire Resistance and Sound Control Design Manual* referenced by major building codes; conducts safety programs for member companies. Monitors legislation and regulations.

International Assn. of Bridge, Structural, Ornamental, and Reinforcing Iron Workers, *1750 New York Ave. N.W., #400, 20006; (202) 383-4800. Fax, (202) 638-4856. Eric Dean, General President.*
General email, iwmagazine@iwintl.org

Web, www.ironworkers.org, Twitter, @TheIronWorkers, Facebook, www.facebook.com/unionironworkers and YouTube, www.youtube.com/user/UnionIronWorkers

Membership: approximately 120,000 iron workers. Helps members negotiate pay, benefits, and better working conditions; conducts training programs and workshops. Monitors legislation and regulations. (Affiliated with the AFL-CIO.)

International Assn. of Heat and Frost Insulators and Allied Workers, *9602 Martin Luther King Hwy., Lanham, MD 20706-1839; (301) 731-9101. Fax, (301) 731-5058. Gregory T. Revard, General President.*
General email, hfi@insulators.org

Web, www.insulators.org, Twitter, @InsulatorsUnion, Facebook, www.facebook.com/InsulatorsUnion and YouTube, www.youtube.com/user/InsulatorsUnion

Membership: approximately 30,000 workers in insulation industries. Helps members negotiate pay, benefits, and better working conditions; conducts training programs and workshops. Monitors legislation and regulations. (Affiliated with the AFL-CIO.)

International Brotherhood of Boilermakers, Iron Ship Builders, Blacksmiths, Forgers, and Helpers, *Government Affairs, 1750 New York Ave. N.W., #335, 20006; (202) 756-2868. Fax, (202) 756-2869. Cecile Conroy, Director of Government Affairs, ext. 202.*
Web, https://boilermakers.org/structure/departments/government_affairs

Membership: workers in construction, repair, maintenance, manufacturing, shipbuilding and marine repair, mining and quarrying, railroads, cement kilns, and related industries in the United States and Canada. Helps members negotiate pay, benefits, and better working conditions; conducts training programs and workshops. Monitors legislation and regulations. (Headquarters in Kansas City, Kans.; affiliated with the AFL-CIO.)

International Brotherhood of Electrical Workers (IBEW), *900 7th St. N.W., 20001; (202) 833-7000. Fax, (202) 728-7676. Lonnie R. Stephenson, International President. General email, webmaster@ibew.org*

Web, http://ibew.org

Membership: workers in utilities, construction, telecommunications, broadcasting, manufacturing, railroads, and government. Helps members negotiate pay, benefits, and better working conditions; conducts training programs and workshops. Monitors legislation and regulations. (Affiliated with the AFL-CIO.)

International Brotherhood of Teamsters, *25 Louisiana Ave. N.W., 20001; (202) 624-6800. Fax, (202) 624-6918. James P. Hoffa, General President. Press, (202) 624-6911. General email, communications@teamster.org*

Web, https://teamster.org, Twitter, @Teamsters, Facebook, www.facebook.com/teamsters and YouTube, www.youtube .com/TeamsterPower

Membership: workers in the transportation and construction industries, factories, offices, hospitals, warehouses, and other workplaces. Helps members negotiate pay, benefits, and better working conditions; conducts training programs and workshops. Monitors legislation and regulations.

International Union of Bricklayers and Allied Craftworkers, *620 F St. N.W., 20004; (202) 783-3788. Timothy J. Driscoll, President. Toll-free, (888) 880-8222. General email, askbac@bacweb.org*

Web, www.bacweb.org and Twitter, @IUBAC

Membership: bricklayers, stonemasons, and other skilled craftworkers in the building industry. Helps members negotiate pay, benefits, and better working conditions; conducts training programs and workshops. Monitors legislation and regulations. (Affiliated with the AFL-CIO and the International Masonry Institute.)

International Union of Operating Engineers, *1125 17th St. N.W., 20036; (202) 429-9100. Fax, (202) 778-2688. James T. Callahan, General President. Web, www.iuoe.org*

Membership: approximately 400,000 operating engineers, including heavy equipment operators, mechanics, and surveyors in the construction industry, and stationary engineers, including operations and building maintenance staff. Represents members in negotiating pay, benefits, and better working conditions; conducts training programs and workshops. Monitors legislation and regulations in the United States and Canada. (Affiliated with the AFL-CIO.)

International Union of Painters and Allied Trades, *7234 Parkway Dr., Hanover, MD 21076; (410) 564-5900.*

Fax, (866) 656-4124. James A. Williams Jr., General President. General email, mail@iupat.org

Web, www.iupat.org, Twitter, @GoIUPAT and Facebook, www.facebook.com/GoIUPAT

Membership: more than 160,000 industrial and commercial painters, glaziers, floor covering installers, sign makers, convention and show decorators, and workers in allied trades in the United States and Canada. Helps members negotiate pay, benefits, and better working conditions; conducts training programs and workshops. Monitors legislation and regulations. (Affiliated with the AFL-CIO.)

Kitchen Cabinet Manufacturers Assn., *1768 Business Center Dr., #390, Reston, VA 20190; (703) 264-1690. Fax, (703) 620-6530. Betsy Natz, Chief Executive Officer. General email, info@kcma.org*

Web, www.kcma.org and Twitter, @KCMA.org

Represents cabinet manufacturers and suppliers to the industry. Provides government relations, management statistics, marketing information, and plant tours. Administers cabinet testing and certification programs.

National Concrete Masonry Assn., *13750 Sunrise Valley Dr., Herndon, VA 20171-4662; (703) 713-1900. Fax, (703) 713-1910. Robert D. Thomas, President. General email, info@ncma.org*

Web, www.ncma.org, Twitter, @ConcreteMasonry, Facebook, www.facebook.com/ NationalConcreteMasonryAssociation and YouTube, www.youtube.com/channel/UCU9BEyXp6di6jvpaR7IpmiA

Membership: producers and suppliers of concrete, masonry, and related goods and services. Conducts research; provides members with technical, marketing, government relations, and communications assistance.

National Glass Assn. (NGA), *344 Maple Ave. West, Unit 272, Vienna, VA 22180; (703) 442-4890. Guy Selinske, Chair. Toll-free, (866) 342-5642.*

Web, www.glass.org, Twitter, @glassnation and Facebook, www.facebook.com/glassnation

Membership: companies in all aspects of glazing and glass building products industry. Provides education and training programs to promote quality workmanship, ethics, and safety standards in the architectural, automotive, and window and door glass industries. Acts as a clearinghouse for information and links professionals with job listings, suppliers, and technical support. Monitors legislation and regulations.

National Insulation Assn. (NIA), *516 Herndon Parkway, Suite D, Reston, VA 20170; (703) 464-6422. Fax, (703) 464-5896. Michele M. Jones, Chief Executive Officer, ext. 119. Toll-free, (877) 968-7642.*

General email, niainfo@insulation.org

Web, www.insulation.org and Twitter, @NIAInfo

Membership: open-shop and union contractors, distributors, laminators, fabricators, and manufacturers that provide thermal insulation, insulation accessories, and components to the commercial, mechanical, and industrial markets. Provides information to members on industry trends and technologies, and offers service contacts for consumers. Monitors legislation and regulations.

National Lumber and Building Material Dealers Assn., *2001 K St. N.W., 3rd Floor N, 20006; (202) 367-1169. Jonathan M. Paine, President.*
General email, info@dealer.org
Web, www.dealer.org

Membership: federated associations of retailers in the lumber and building material industries. Provides statistics training and networking opportunities to members. Monitors legislation and regulations.

North American Insulation Manufacturers Assn., *11 Canal Center Plaza, #103, Alexandria, VA 22314; (703) 684-0084. Curt Rich, President.*
General email, sfitzgerald-redd@naima.org
Web, https://insulationinstitute.org, Twitter, @knowinsulation and Facebook, www.facebook.com/ insulationinstitute

Membership: manufacturers of insulation products for use in homes, commercial buildings, and industrial facilities. Provides information on the use of insulation for thermal efficiency, sound control, and fire safety; monitors research in the industry. Interests include energy efficiency and sustainability. Monitors legislation and regulations.

Operative Plasterers' and Cement Masons' International Assn. of the United States and Canada, *9700 Patuxent Woods Dr., #200, Columbia, MD 21046; (301) 623-1000. Fax, (301) 623-1032. Daniel E. Stepano, General President.*
General email, opcmiaintl@opcmia.org
Web, www.opcmia.org, Twitter, @opcmiaint and Facebook, www.facebook.com/OPCMIAIntl/

Membership: approximately 58,000 cement masons and plasterers. Helps members negotiate pay, benefits, and better working conditions; conducts training programs and workshops. Publishes a quarterly magazine. Monitors legislation and regulations. (Affiliated with the AFL-CIO.)

Portland Cement Assn., *Washington Office, 200 Massachusetts Ave. N.W., #200, 20001; (202) 408-9494. Fax, (202) 408-0877. Sean O'Neill, Senior Vice President of Government Affairs, (202) 719-1974.*
Web, www.cement.org, Twitter, @PCA_Daily and Facebook, www.facebook.com/PCACement

Membership: producers of portland cement. Monitors legislation and regulations. (Headquarters in Skokie, Ill.)

Roof Coatings Manufacturers Assn., *529 14th St. N.W., #1280, 20045; (202) 591-2452. Fax, (202) 591-2445. Will Lorenz, President.*
General email, questions@roofcoatings.org
Web, www.roofcoatings.org

Membership: firms, partnerships, and corporations that manufacture or supply cold-applied protective roof coatings. Provides guidance on building codes and standards and technical developments. Affiliated with the Reflective Roof Coatings Institute.

Sheet Metal, Air, Rail, and Transportation Workers (SMART), *1750 New York Ave. N.W., 6th Floor, 20006; (202) 662-0800. Joseph Sellers Jr., General President. Toll-free, (800) 457-7694.*
General email, info@smart-union.org
Web, https://smart-union.org and Twitter, @smartunionworks

Membership: U.S., Puerto Rican, and Canadian workers in the building and construction trades, manufacturing, and the railroad and shipyard industries. Assists members with contract negotiation and grievances; conducts training programs and workshops. Monitors legislation and regulations. (Affiliated with the Sheet Metal and Air Conditioning Contractors' Assn., the AFL-CIO, and the Canadian Labour Congress.)

FIRE PREVENTION AND CONTROL

General

▶**AGENCIES**

Forest Service *(Agriculture Dept.), Fire and Aviation Management, 201 14th St. S.W., 3rd Floor, 3 Central, 20024 (mailing address: 1400 Independence Ave. S.W., MS 1107, Washington, DC 20250-0003); (202) 579-8172. Fax, (703) 605-1401. Jake Nuttall, Director (Acting), (505) 842-3281.*
Web, www.fs.fed.us/fire

Responsible for aviation and fire management programs, including fire control planning and prevention, suppression of fires, and the use of prescribed fires. Provides state foresters with financial and technical assistance for fire protection in forests and on rural lands.

Interior Dept. (DOI), *Wildland Fire (OWF), 1849 C St. N.W., MS 4447, 20240; (202) 208-2703. Jeff Rupert, Director, (202) 208-2719.*
General email, wildlandfire@ios.doi.gov
Web, www.doi.gov/wildlandfire, Twitter, @DOIWildlandFire and Facebook, www.facebook.com/DOIWildlandFire/

Oversees all wildland fire management programs, policies, budgets, and information technology in order to manage risk to firefighters, communities, and landscapes. Bridges the individual fire programs of the four land management bureaus; supports the wildland fire needs of the bureau.

National Institute of Standards and Technology (NIST) *(Commerce Dept.), Engineering Laboratory, 100 Bureau Dr., MS 8600, Gaithersburg, MD 20899-8600; (301) 975-5900. Fax, (301) 975-4032. Joannie Chin, Director, (301) 975-6815.*
General email, el@nist.gov
Web, www.nist.gov/el

Conducts basic and applied research on fire and fire resistance of construction materials; develops testing methods, standards, design concepts, and technologies for fire protection and prevention.

U.S. Fire Administration *(Federal Emergency Management Agency)*, 16825 S. Seton Ave., Emmitsburg, MD 21727-8998; (301) 447-1000. Lori Moore-Merrell, Administrator. Press, (301) 447-1853. Toll-free, (800) 238-3358. Toll-free National Fire Incident Reporting System Help Desk (NFIRS), (888) 382-3827. Toll-free publications, (800) 561-3356.
Web, www.usfa.fema.gov, Twitter, @usfire and Facebook, www.facebook.com/usfire

Conducts research and collects, analyzes, and disseminates data on combustion, fire prevention, firefighter safety, and the management of fire prevention organizations; studies and develops arson-prevention programs and fire-prevention codes; maintains the National Fire Incident Reporting System.

U.S. Fire Administration *(Federal Emergency Management Agency)*, National Fire Academy, 16825 S. Seton Ave., Emmitsburg, MD 21727-8998; (301) 447-1117. Eriks Gabliks, Superintendent, (301) 447-1117.
General email, netcadmissions@fema.dhs.gov
Web, www.usfa.dhs.gov/training/nfa

Trains fire officials and related professionals in fire-prevention and management, current firefighting technologies, and the administration of fire prevention organizations.

▶**NONGOVERNMENTAL**

International Assn. of Fire Chiefs, 4795 Meadow Wood Lane, #100, Chantilly, VA 20151; (703) 273-0911. Fax, (703) 273-9363. James Robert (Rob) Brown Jr., Chief Executive Officer, (703) 896-4829.
Web, www.iafc.org, Twitter, @IAFC and Facebook, www.facebook.com/firechiefs

Membership: fire service chiefs and chief officers. Conducts research on fire control; testifies before congressional committees. Monitors legislation and regulations affecting fire safety codes.

International Assn. of Fire Fighters, 1750 New York Ave. N.W., #300, 20006-5395; (202) 737-8484. Fax, (202) 737-8418. Edward A. Kelly, General President.
General email, tburn@iaff.org
Web, www.iaff.org, Twitter, @IAFFNewsDesk, Facebook, www.facebook.com/IAFFonline and YouTube, www.youtube.com/user/IAFFTV

Membership: more than 310,000 professional firefighters and emergency medical personnel. Assists members with contract negotiation and grievances; conducts training programs and workshops. Monitors legislation and regulations. (Affiliated with the AFL-CIO and the Canadian Labour Congress.)

National Fire Protection Assn., *Government Affairs,* 50 F St. N.W., #625, 20001; (202) 898-0222. Fax, (202) 898-0044. Jim Pauley, Chief Executive Officer, (617) 984-7275; Seth Statler, Government Affairs Director.

General email, wdc@nfpa.org
Web, www.nfpa.org/About-NFPA/Offices/Government-Affairs, Twitter, @NFPA and Facebook, www.facebook.com/theNFPA

Membership: individuals and organizations interested in fire protection. Develops and updates fire protection codes and standards; sponsors technical assistance programs; collects fire data statistics. Monitors legislation and regulations. (Headquarters in Quincy, Mass.)

HOUSING

General

▶**AGENCIES**

Housing and Urban Development Dept. (HUD), *Housing Office,* 451 7th St. S.W., #9100, 20410; (202) 708-2601. Janet Golnick, Assistant Secretary. TTY, (202) 708-1455.
Web, www.hud.gov/program_offices/housing

Administers housing programs, including the production, financing, and management of housing; directs preservation and rehabilitation of the housing stock; manages regulatory programs.

▶**CONGRESS**

For a listing of relevant congressional committees and subcommittees, please see page 444 or the Appendix.

▶**NONGOVERNMENTAL**

Habitat for Humanity International, *Government Relations and Advocacy,* 1310 L St. N.W., #350, 20005; (202) 718-4824. Jonathan Reckford, Chief Executive Officer; Chris Vincent, Vice President of Advocacy and Government Relations.
General email, advocacy@habitat.org
Web, www.habitat.org/about/advocacy

Christian ministry that seeks to eliminate poverty housing. Helps people attain housing through home construction, rehabilitation and repairs, and increased access to improved shelter through programs. Offers housing support services that enable low-income families to make improvements on their homes. Works in more than 70 countries.

National Community Stabilization Trust (NCST), 910 17th St. N.W., #810, 20006; (202) 223-3237. Julia Gordon, President.
Web, www.stabilizationtrust.org, Twitter, @_NCST and Facebook, www.facebook.com/stabilzationtrust

Assists local housing providers in acquiring vacant, abandoned, and foreclosed properties from financial institutions to build new affordable living properties. Manages funds for community stabilization programs from public and private investors. Coordinates management and rehabilitation of foreclosed properties. Works with housing organizations to solve policy issues.

National Housing and Rehabilitation Assn., *1400 16th St. N.W., #420, 20036; (202) 939-1750. Fax, (202) 265-4435. Peter H. Bell, Chief Executive Officer, (202) 939-1741; Thom Amdur, President, (202) 939-1753.*
General email, info@housingonline.com
Web, www.housingonline.com, Twitter, @HousingOnline and YouTube, www.youtube.com/user/HousingOnline

Membership: historic rehabilitation businesses, development firms and organizations, and city, state, and local agencies concerned with affordable multifamily housing. Monitors government policies affecting multifamily development and rehabilitation.

National Housing Conference (NHC), *1900 M St. N.W., #550, 20036; (202) 466-2121. David M. Dworkin, President.*
General email, info@nhc.org
Web, www.nhc.org, Twitter, @natlhousingconf, Facebook, www.facebook.com/natlhousingconf and YouTube, www .youtube.com/user/affordablehomestoday

Membership: state and local housing officials, community development specialists, builders, bankers, lawyers, civic leaders, tenants, architects and planners, labor and religious groups, and national housing and housing-related organizations. Mobilizes public support for community development and affordable housing programs; conducts educational sessions. Supports the Center for Housing Policy, NHC's research affiliate.

National Leased Housing Assn., *1900 L St. N.W., #300, 20036; (202) 785-8888. Fax, (202) 785-2008.*
Denise B. Muha, Executive Director.
General email, info@hudnlha.com
Web, www.hudnlha.com and Twitter, @leasedhousing

Membership: public and private organizations and individuals concerned with multifamily low and moderate income and government-assisted housing programs. Conducts training seminars. Monitors legislation and regulations.

National Low Income Housing Coalition, *1000 Vermont Ave. N.W., #500, 20005; (202) 662-1530. Fax, (202) 393-1973. Diane Yentel, President, ext. 225.*
General email, outreach@nlihc.org
Web, www.nlihc.org and Twitter, @NLIHC

Membership: organizations and individuals that support low-income housing. Works to end the affordable housing crisis in America. Interests include the needs of the lowest-income people and those who are homeless. Monitors legislation and regulations.

Fair Housing, Special Groups

▶AGENCIES

Community Planning and Development (CPD) *(Housing and Urban Development Dept.), HIV/AIDS Housing, 451 7th St. S.W., #7248, 20410; (202) 402-5374. Rita Harcrow, Director, (202) 402-5374.*

General email, HOPWA@hud.gov
Web, www.hud.gov/program_offices/comm_planning/ aidshousing, Twitter, @HUD_HOPWA and HOPWA information, www.hudexchange.info/programs/hopwa

Makes grants to local communities, states, and non-profit organizations for projects that benefit low-income persons living with HIV/AIDS and their families. Manages the Housing Opportunities for Persons With AIDS (HOPWA) program.

Fair Housing and Equal Opportunity (FHEO) *(Housing and Urban Development Dept.), 451 7th St. S.W., #5100, 20410-2000; (202) 402-5188. Jeanine Worden, Assistant Secretary (Acting) and Associate General Counsel. Housing discrimination hotline, (800) 669-9777.*
Web, www.hud.gov/fairhousing

Monitors compliance with legislation requiring equal opportunities in housing for minorities, persons with disabilities, and families with children. Monitors compliance with construction codes to accommodate people with disabilities in multifamily dwellings. Hotline answers inquiries about housing discrimination.

Fair Housing and Equal Opportunity (FHEO) *(Housing and Urban Development Dept.), Fair Housing Initiatives Programs, 451 7th St. S.W., #5230, 20410; (202) 402-7095. Fax, (202) 708-4445. Myron P. Newry, Director, (202) 708-2288.*
General email, AllAboutFHIP@hud.gov
Web, www.hud.gov/program_offices/fair_housing_equal_ opp/partners

Awards grants to public and private organizations and to state and local agencies. Funds projects that educate the public about fair housing rights; investigates housing discrimination complaints. Programs are designed to prevent or eliminate discriminatory housing practices.

Public and Indian Housing *(Housing and Urban Development Dept.), Native American Programs, 451 7th St. S.W., #4126, 20410-5000; (202) 401-7914. Fax, (202) 401-7909. Heidi J. Frechette, Deputy Assistant Secretary.*
General email, codetalk@hud.gov
Web, www.hud.gov/program_offices/public_indian_ housing/ih

Administers federal assistance for Native American tribes. Assistance programs focus on housing and community and economic development through competitive and formula grants. Funds for approved activities are provided directly to tribes or Alaska Native villages or to a tribally designated housing authority.

▶NONGOVERNMENTAL

National American Indian Housing Council, *122 C St. N.W., #505, 20001; (202) 789-1754. Fax, (202) 789-1758. Tony Walters, Executive Director, (202) 454-0928. Toll-free, (800) 284-9165.*
General email, info@naihc.net
Web, www.naihc.net, Twitter, @naihc_national and Facebook, www.facebook.com/NationalAmericanIndian HousingCouncil

Membership: Native American housing authorities. Clearinghouse for information on Native American housing issues; works for safe and sanitary dwellings for Native American and Alaska Native communities; monitors policies of the Housing and Urban Development Dept. and housing legislation; provides members with training and technical assistance in managing housing assistance programs.

National Assn. for the Advancement of Colored People (NAACP), *Washington Bureau, 1156 15th St. N.W., #915, 20005; (202) 463-2940. Fax, (202) 463-2953. Derrick Johnson, President.*
General email, washingtonbureau@naacpnet.org
Web, www.naacp.org, Twitter, @NAACP and *Twitter, President, @DerrickNAACP*

Membership: persons interested in civil rights for all minorities. Works to eliminate discrimination in housing and urban affairs. Supports programs that make affordable rental housing available to minorities and that maintain African American ownership of land. (Headquarters in Baltimore, Md.)

National Assn. of Real Estate Brokers, *9831 Greenbelt Rd., #309, Lanham, MD 20706; (301) 552-9340. Fax, (301) 552-9216. C. Renee Wilson, Executive Director.*
General email, nareb@nareb.com
Web, www.nareb.com

Membership: minority real estate brokers, appraisers, contractors, property managers, and salespersons. Works to prevent discrimination in housing policies and practices; conducts seminars on contracting and federal policy.

National Multifamily Housing Council, *1775 Eye St. N.W., #1100, 20006; (202) 974-2300. Fax, (202) 775-0112. Douglas Bibby, President, (202) 974-2323.*
General email, info@nmhc.org
Web, www.nmhc.org

Membership: owners, financiers, managers, and developers of multifamily housing. Serves as a clearinghouse on rent control, condominium conversion, taxes, fair housing, and environmental issues.

National Rural Housing Coalition, *1155 15th St. N.W., #400, 20005; (202) 393-5225. Fax, (202) 393-3034. Sam Rapoza, Director of Legislative Policy.*
General email, nrhc@ruralhousingcoalition.org
Web, https://ruralhousingcoalition.org and *Twitter, @RuralCoalition*

Acts as advocate for improved housing for low-income rural families; works to increase public awareness of rural housing problems; administers the Self-Help Housing Fund, Farm Worker Housing Fund, Rural Community Assistance Fund, and HUD Task Force. Monitors legislation and regulations.

UnidosUS, *1126 16th St. N.W., #600, 20036-4845; (202) 785-1670. Janet Murguía, President.*
General email, info@unidos.org
Web, www.unidos.org, Twitter, @WeAreUnidosUS, Facebook, www.facebook.com/Weareunidosus and *YouTube, www.youtube.com/c/UnidosUS*

Helps Hispanic community–based groups obtain funds, develop and build low-income housing and community facilities, and develop and finance community economic development projects; conducts research and provides policy analysis on the housing status and needs of Hispanics; monitors legislation on fair housing and government funding for low-income housing.

Public and Subsidized Housing

▶AGENCIES

Community Planning and Development (CPD) *(Housing and Urban Development Dept.), Affordable Housing Programs, 451 7th St. S.W., #7164, 20410; (202) 708-2684. Virginia Sardone, Director, (202) 549-7212.*
Web, www.hud.gov/program_offices/comm_planning/affordablehousing

HOME program helps to expand the supply of decent, affordable housing for low-income and very-low-income families by providing grants to states and local governments to help renters, new home buyers, or existing homeowners. SHOP program provides funds for nonprofit organizations to purchase home sites and develop or improve the infrastructure needed to facilitate sweat equity and volunteer-based homeownership programs for low-income families.

Community Planning and Development (CPD) *(Housing and Urban Development Dept.), Rural Housing and Economic Development (RHED), 451 7th St. S.W., #7240, 20410; (202) 708-2290. Jackie Williams, Director, (202) 402-4611. TTY, (202) 708-1455.*
General email, rhed@hud.gov
Web, www.hudexchange.info/programs/rhed

Promotes decent housing and economic opportunities for low-income and middle-income individuals; offers rental, homebuyer, and homeowner assistance and resources for homeless persons, youth, and veterans.

Federal Housing Administration (FHA) *(Housing and Urban Development Dept.), Assisted Housing Oversight, 451 7th St. S.W., #6158, 20410-8000; (202) 441-1644. Belinda Koros, Director, (202) 441-1644.*
Web, www.hud.gov/program_offices/housing/mfh/hsgmfbus/aboutam and *www.hud.gov/program_offices/housing/dirhousi*

Administers Section 8 contracts and other rental subsidy programs. Ensures that Section 8 subsidized properties meet the department's goal of providing decent, safe, and sanitary housing to low-income families.

Federal Housing Administration (FHA) *(Housing and Urban Development Dept.), Policy and Grant Administration, 451 7th St. S.W., #9224, 20410-8000; (202) 402-5415. Fax, (202) 708-3537. Brian Siebenlist, Director.*
Web, www.hud.gov/program_offices/spm/gmomgmt/grantsinfo

Directs and oversees the housing assistance and grant programs, including project-based Section 8 housing assistance, Section 202/811 capital advance and project rental assistance programs, the Assisted-Living Conversion Program (ALCP), rent supplements, service coordinator, and congregate housing services grant programs.

Public and Indian Housing (*Housing and Urban Development Dept.*), *451 7th St. S.W., #4100, 20410-0800; (202) 708-0950. Fax, (202) 619-8478. Dominique Blom, General Deputy Assistant Secretary. TTY, (202) 708-1455. Web, www.hud.gov/program_offices/public_indian_housing*

Seeks to ensure that safe, decent, and affordable housing is available to low-income and Native American families, the elderly, and persons with disabilities.

Public and Indian Housing (*Housing and Urban Development Dept.*), *Housing Voucher Management and Operations, 451 7th St. S.W., #4210, 20410; (202) 402-6050. Fax, (202) 708-0690. Rebecca Primeaux, Director. Web, www.hud.gov/program_offices/public_indian_housing/programs/hcv*

Administers certificate and housing voucher programs and moderate rehabilitation authorized by Section 8 of the Housing Act of 1937, as amended. Provides rental subsidies to lower-income families.

Public and Indian Housing (*Housing and Urban Development Dept.*), *Public Housing and Voucher Programs, 451 7th St. S.W., #4130, 20410-5000; (202) 708-2815. Fax, (202) 708-0690. Danielle Bastarache, Deputy Assistant Secretary, (202) 402-5264. Section 8, (202) 708-0477. Web, www.hud.gov/program_offices/public_indian_housing/programs/ph*

Establishes policies and procedures for low-income public housing and rental assistance programs, including special needs for the elderly and disabled, standards for rental and occupancy, utilities and maintenance engineering, and financial management.

Public and Indian Housing (*Housing and Urban Development Dept.*), *Public Housing Investments, 451 7th St. S.W., #4130, 20410-0050; (202) 402-4780. Fax, (202) 401-2370. Robert Mulderig, Deputy Assistant Secretary. Web, www.hud.gov/program_offices/public_indian_housing*

Establishes development policies and procedures for low-income housing programs, including criteria for site approval and construction standards; oversees administration of the Capital Fund for modernizing existing public housing, the Choice Neighborhood Program, and the Moving to Work demonstration program for public housing authorities. Administers the HOPE VI Program and manages the Special Applications Center.

Real Estate Assessment Center (REAC) (*Housing and Urban Development Dept.*), *451 7th St. S.W., 20410; (202) 475-7949. David Vargas, Deputy Assistant Secretary. HUD Switchboard, (202) 708-1112. Toll-free, (888) 245-4860. TTY, (202) 708-1455.*

General email, reac_tac@hud.gov

Web, www.hud.gov/reac

Conducts physical inspections and surveys of resident satisfaction in publicly owned, insured, or subsidized housing. Assesses financial condition and management operations of public housing agencies.

▶NONGOVERNMENTAL

Council of Large Public Housing Authorities, *455 Massachusetts Ave. N.W., #425, 20001; (202) 638-1300. Sunia Zaterman, Executive Director.*

General email, clpha@clpha.org

Web, http://clpha.org, Twitter, @CLPHA and Facebook, www.facebook.com/clpha

Works to preserve and improve public housing through advocacy, research, policy analysis, and public education.

Enterprise Community Partners, *10 G St. N.E., #580, 20002; (202) 842-9190. Fax, (410) 964-1376. Priscilla Almodovar, President; Marion Mollegen McFadden, Vice President, Public Policy, (302) 649-3920. Toll-free, (800) 624-4298.*

Web, www.enterprisecommunity.org, Twitter, @EnterpriseNow and Facebook, www.facebook.com/ EnterpriseCommunityPartners

Works with local groups to help provide decent, affordable housing for low-income individuals and families, including green affordable housing. Works to link public transit to affordable housing.

Housing Assistance Council, *1025 Vermont Ave. N.W., #606, 20005-3516; (202) 842-8600. Fax, (202) 347-3441. David Lipsetz, Chief Executive Officer.*

General email, hac@ruralhome.org

Web, www.ruralhome.org, Twitter, @RuralHome and Facebook, www.facebook.com/HousingAssistanceCouncil

Operates in rural areas and in cities of fewer than 25,000 citizens. Advises low-income and minority groups seeking federal assistance for improving rural housing and community facilities; studies and makes recommendations for federal, state, and local housing policies; makes low-interest loans for housing programs for low-income and minority groups living in rural areas, including Native Americans and farm workers; publishes technical guides and reports on rural housing issues.

Public Housing Authorities Directors Assn., *511 Capitol Court N.E., 20002-4937; (202) 546-5445. Fax, (202) 546-4381. Timothy G. Kaiser, Executive Director. Web, www.phada.org, Twitter, @PHADA_USA and Facebook, www.facebook.com/PHADAUSA*

Membership: executive directors of public housing authorities. Serves as liaison between members and the Housing and Urban Development Dept. and Congress; conducts educational seminars and conferences. Monitors legislation and regulations.

Urban Institute, *Metropolitan Housing and Communities Policy Center, 500 L'Enfant Plaza S.W., 20024; (202) 833-7200. Mary K. Cunningham, Vice President.*

Web, www.urban.org/policy-centers/metropolitan-housing-and-communities-policy-center

Research center that deals with urban problems. Researches housing policy problems, including housing management, public housing programs, finance, and rent control.

Senior Living

►NONGOVERNMENTAL

AARP, *601 E St. N.W., 20049; (202) 434-2277. Jo Ann C. Jenkins, Chief Executive Officer. Library, (202) 434-6233. Membership, toll-free, (800) 566-0242. Press, (202) 434-2560. Toll-free, (888) 687-2277. TTY, (877) 434-7598. Toll-free Spanish, (877) 342-2277. TTY Spanish, (866) 238-9488. General email, dcaarp@aarp.org*

Web, www.aarp.org, Twitter, @AARP and Facebook, www.facebook.com/AARP

Promotes safe and affordable housing for older adults, including safe communities, physical disability accomodation, adequate transportation options, and access to grocery stores, doctors, and community activities.

American Seniors Housing Assn., *5225 Wisconsin Ave. N.W., #502, 20015; (202) 237-0900. Fax, (202) 237-1616. David Schless, President, (202) 885-5560. General email, info@seniorshousing.org*

Web, www.ashaliving.org

Membership: development, finance, and operation professionals working in seniors apartments, independent and assisted living communities, and retirement communities. Promotes the advancement of quality seniors housing and health care through research, education, and monitoring legislation and regulations.

Argentum, *1650 King St., #602, Alexandria, VA 22314; (703) 894-1805. Fax, (703) 894-1831. James Balda, President. Press, (703) 562-1184. General email, info@argentum.org*

Web, www.argentum.org and Twitter, @argentum

Represents operators of communities for seniors, including independent-living, assisted-living, and Alzheimer's care facilities, but not including nursing homes or hospices. Promotes the development of standards and increased awareness for the senior living industry. Provides members with information on policy, funding access, and quality of care. Interests include informed choice, safe environments, caring and competent staff, and funding alternatives to increase accessibility to senior communities. Monitors legislation and regulations. (Formerly Assisted Living Federation of America.)

B'nai B'rith International, *Center for Senior Services, 1120 20th St. N.W., #300N, 20036; Fax, (202) 857-6600. Mark D. Olshan, Associate Executive Vice President, ext. 1. Toll-free, (866) 999-6596. General email, seniors@bnaibrith.org*

Web, www.bnaibrith.org/seniors

Acts as an advocate on behalf of the aging population in America. Works with local groups to sponsor federally assisted housing for independent low-income senior citizens and persons with disabilities, regardless of race or religion.

Leading Age, *2519 Connecticut Ave. N.W., 20008-1520; (202) 783-2242. Katie Smith Sloan, Chief Executive Officer. Press, (202) 508-9407. General email, info@leadingage.org*

Web, www.leadingage.org, Twitter, @LeadingAge and Facebook, www.facebook.com/LeadingAge

Membership: nonprofit nursing homes, housing, and health-related facilities for the elderly. Provides research and technical assistance for providers of long-term care for the elderly. Monitors legislation and regulations.

National Caucus and Center on Black Aging, Inc., *1220 L St. N.W., #800, 20005-2407; (202) 637-8400. Fax, (202) 347-0895. Karyne Jones, President. Web, https://ncba-aging.org, Twitter, @NCBA1970 and Facebook, www.facebook.com/ncba.aging.5*

Concerned with issues that affect older Black Americans and other minorities. Sponsors employment and housing programs for older adults and education and training for professionals in gerontology. Monitors legislation and regulations.

National Council on Aging, *251 S. 18th St., #500, Arlington, VA 22202; (571) 527-3900. Ramsey Alwin, President, ext. 1. Eldercare locator, (800) 677-1116. General email, kathleen.zuke@ncoa.org*

Web, www.ncoa.org, Twitter, @NCOAging, Facebook, www.facebook.com/NCOAging and YouTube, www.youtube.com/user/ncoaging

Serves as an information clearinghouse on aging. Works to ensure quality housing for older persons. Monitors legislation and regulations.

REAL ESTATE

General

►AGENCIES

Bureau of Land Management (BLM) *(Interior Dept.), Lands, Realty, and Cadastral Survey, 1849 C St. N.W., #2134LM, 20003; (202) 912-7353. Fax, (202) 912-7199. Dominica Van Koten, Chief Cadastral Surveyor, (571) 266-9585. Web, www.blm.gov/programs/lands-and-realty and Cadastral Survey, www.blm.gov/programs/lands-and-realty/cadastral-survey*

Manages a wide range of public land transactions, such as purchases, acquisitions; sales, exchanges; withdrawals; leases and permits; right-of-way authorizations, cadastral survey services. Energy development, permitting commercial filming, to defining boundaries and maintaining public land records. Facilitate commercial, recreational, and conservation opportunities on public lands.

Federal Highway Administration (FHWA)
(Transportation Dept.), Planning, Environment, and Realty, 1200 New Jersey Ave. S.E., #E76-306, 20590; (202) 366-0116. Fax, (202) 366-3713. Gloria M. Shepherd, Associate Administrator, (202) 366-0581.
Web, www.fhwa.dot.gov/real_estate

Works with developers and municipalities to ensure conformity with the National Environmental Policy Act (NEPA) project development process.

►CONGRESS

For a listing of relevant congressional committees and subcommittees, please see page 444 or the Appendix.

►NONGOVERNMENTAL

American Land Title Assn., *1800 M St. N.W., #300S, 20036; (202) 296-3671. Fax, (202) 223-5843. Diane Tomb, Chief Executive Officer, ext. 218. Toll-free, (800) 787-2582. Toll-free fax, (800) 329-2582.*
General email, service@alta.org
Web, www.alta.org, Twitter, @ALTAonline, Facebook, www.facebook.com/altaonline and YouTube, www.youtube.com/user/altavideos

Membership: land title insurance underwriting companies, abstracters, lawyers, and title insurance agents. Searches, reviews, and insures land titles to protect real estate investors, including home buyers and mortgage lenders; provides industry information. Monitors legislation and regulations.

American Land Trust Assn., *Title Industry Political Action Committee (TIPAC), 1800 M St. N.W., #300S, 20036; (202) 296-3671. Leah Shimp Vass, Director of Political Affairs, ext. 233.*
Web, www.alta.org/advocacy/tipac.cfm

PAC representing the land title industry. Raises money to elect and reelect candidates who support and understand the issues affecting the land title industry.

American Resort Development Assn., *1201 15th St. N.W., #400, 20005-2842; (202) 371-6700. Fax, (202) 289-8544. Jason Gamel, President. Consumer hotline, (855) 939-1515.*
General email, consumer@arda-roc.org
Web, www.arda.org

Membership: U.S. and international developers, builders, financiers, marketing companies, and others involved in resort, recreational, and community development. Serves as an information clearinghouse; monitors federal and state legislation.

American Society of Appraisers (ASA), *2121 Cooperative Way, #210, Herndon, VA 20171; (703) 478-2228. Fax, (703) 742-8471. Johnnie White, Chief Executive Officer, (703) 733-2108. Toll-free, (800) 272-8258.*

General email, asainfo@appraisers.org
Web, www.appraisers.org and Twitter, @ASAappraisers

Membership: accredited appraisers of real property, including land, houses, and commercial buildings; business valuation; machinery and technical specialties; yachts; aircraft; public utilities; personal property, including antiques, fine art, residential contents; and gems and jewelry. Affiliate members include students and professionals interested in appraising. Provides technical information; accredits appraisers; provides consumer information programs.

Appraisal Foundation, *1155 15th St. N.W., #1111, 20005; (202) 347-7722. David S. Bunton, President.*
General email, info@appraisalfoundation.org
Web, www.appraisalfoundation.org and Twitter, @theappraisalfdn

Ensures that real estate appraisers are qualified to offer their services by promoting uniform appraisal standards and establishing education, experience, and examination requirements.

Appraisal Institute, *Government Relations, 440 1st St. N.W., #880, 20001; (202) 298-6449. Fax, (202) 298-5547. William (Bill) Garber, Director of Government and External Relations, (202) 298-5597.*
General email, insidethebeltway@appraisalinstitute.org
Web, www.appraisalinstitute.org

Provides Congress, regulatory agencies, and the executive branch with information on real estate appraisal matters. (Headquarters in Chicago, Ill.)

Assn. of Foreign Investors in Real Estate, *1300 Pennsylvania Ave. N.W., 20004-3020; (202) 312-1400. Gunnar Branson, Chief Executive Officer, (202) 312-1401.*
General email, info@afire.org
Web, www.afire.org and Twitter, @AFIREglobal

Represents foreign institutions that are interested in the laws, regulations, and economic trends affecting the U.S. commercial real estate market. Informs the public and the government of the contributions foreign investment makes to the U.S. economy. Examines current issues and organizes seminars for members.

Manufactured Housing Institute, *1655 Ft. Myer Dr., #104, Arlington, VA 22209; (703) 558-0400. Fax, (703) 558-0401. Lesli Gooch, Chief Executive Officer; Mark Bowersox, President.*
General email, info@mfghome.org
Web, www.manufacturedhousing.org, Twitter, @ManufacturedHousingInstitute and Facebook, www.facebook.com/ManufacturedHousingInstitute

Represents community owners and developers, financial lenders, and builders, suppliers, and retailers of manufactured and modular homes and affiliated state organizations. Provides information on manufactured and modular home construction standards, finance, site development, property management, and marketing.

National Assn. of Home Builders (NAHB), *1201 15th St. N.W., 20005-2800; (202) 266-8200. Fax, (202) 266-8400.*

Federal Housing Finance Agency

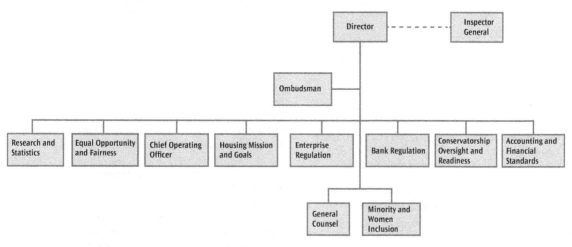

- - - - Indicates a support or advisory relationship with the unit rather than a direct reporting relationship

Gerald (Jerry) Howard, Executive Officer, (800) 368-5242, ext. 8257. Press, (202) 266-8254. Toll-free, (800) 368-5242. General email, info@nahb.org

Web, www.nahb.org and Twitter, @NAHBhome

Membership: contractors, builders, architects, engineers, mortgage lenders, and others interested in home building and residential real estate construction. Offers educational programs and information on housing policy in the United States. Monitors legislation and regulations.

National Assn. of Real Estate Brokers, 9831 Greenbelt Rd., #309, Lanham, MD 20706; (301) 552-9340. Fax, (301) 552-9216. C. Renee Wilson, Executive Director. General email, nareb@nareb.com

Web, www.nareb.com

Membership: minority real estate brokers, appraisers, contractors, property managers, and salespersons. Works to prevent discrimination in housing policies and practices; conducts seminars on contracting and federal policy.

National Assn. of Real Estate Investment Trusts, 1875 Eye St. N.W., #500, 20006-5413; (202) 739-9400. Fax, (202) 739-9401. Steven A. Wechsler, President. Toll-free, (800) 362-7348.

Web, www.reit.com and Twitter, @REITs_NAREIT

Membership: real estate investment trusts and corporations, partnerships, and individuals interested in real estate securities and the industry. Interests include federal taxation, securities regulation, financial standards and reporting standards and ethics, housing and education, and global investment; compiles industry statistics. Monitors federal and state legislation and regulations.

National Assn. of Realtors, Government Affairs, 500 New Jersey Ave. N.W., 11th Floor, 20001-2020; (202) 383-1000. Vijay Yadlapati, Director, (202) 383-1090. Toll-free, (800) 874-6500.

Web, www.nar.realtor/political-advocacy, Twitter, @nardorealtor and Facebook, www.facebook.com/NARdotRealtor/

Sets professional standards, trademark regulations, and code of ethics for the real estate business; promotes education, research, and exchange of information. Interests include housing markets, property rights, and federal housing finance and insurance programs and agencies. Monitors legislation and regulations. (Headquarters in Chicago, Ill.)

The Real Estate Roundtable, 801 Pennsylvania Ave. N.W., #720, 20004; (202) 639-8400. Fax, (202) 639-8442. Jeffrey D. DeBoer, President. General email, info@rer.org

Web, www.rer.org

Membership: real estate owners, advisers, builders, investors, lenders, and managers. Serves as forum for public policy issues, including taxes, energy, homeland security, the environment, capital, credit, and investments.

Society of Industrial and Office Realtors, 1201 New York Ave. N.W., #350, 20005-6126; (202) 449-8200. Robert Thornburgh, Chief Executive Officer, (202) 449-8202. General email, admin@sior.com

Web, www.sior.com

Membership: commercial and industrial real estate brokers worldwide. Certifies brokers; sponsors seminars and conferences; mediates and arbitrates business disputes for members; sponsors a speakers bureau. (Affiliated with the National Assn. of Realtors.)

Mortgages and Finance

▶**AGENCIES**

Agriculture Dept. (USDA), Rural Development, Rural Housing Service, 1400 Independence Ave. S.W., #5014,

MS 0701, 20250-0701; (202) 692-0268. Joaquin Altoro, Administrator (Acting). Toll-free, (800) 414-1226.
Web, www.rd.usda.gov/about-rd/agencies/rural-housing-service

Makes loans and grants in rural communities (population under 20,000) to low-income borrowers, including the elderly and persons with disabilities, for buying, building, or improving single-family and multifamily houses. Makes grants for rehabilitating homes and making health and safety improvements.

Comptroller of the Currency *(Treasury Dept.), Chief Counsel,* Constitution Center, 400 7th St. S.W., 20219; (202) 649-5400. Benjamin W. McDonough, Chief Counsel.
Web, www.occ.gov/about/who-we-are/organizations/chief-counsels-office/index-chief-counsels-office.html

Enforces and oversees compliance by nationally chartered banks with laws prohibiting discrimination in credit transactions on the basis of sex or marital status. Enforces regulations concerning bank advertising; may issue cease-and-desist orders.

Consumer Financial Protection Bureau (CFPB), *1700 G St. N.W.,* 20552; (855) 411-2372. Rohit Chopra, Director. Whistleblower hotline, (855) 695-7974. TTY, (855) 729-2372.
General email, officeofinnovation@consumerfinance.gov
Web, www.consumerfinance.gov, Twitter, @cfpb, Facebook, www.facebook.com/CPFB and YouTube, www.youtube .com/user/cfpbvideo

Responsible for helping home buyers become better shoppers for settlement services and eliminating kickbacks and referral fees that unnecessarily increase the costs of certain settlement services. Administers mortgage regulations including the Ability-to-Repay/Qualified Mortgage rule, which prohibits certain predatory lending practices and requires mortgage creditors to make a reasonable and good-faith effort to verify a borrower's ability to repay a loan.

Fannie Mae *(Federal Housing Finance Agency),* 400 7th St. S.W., 20219; (202) 752-1234. Sandra L. Thompson, Director (Acting). Consumer information, (800) 232-6643.
Web, www.fanniemae.com, www.fhfa.gov, Twitter, @FHFA, Facebook, www.facebook.com/FHFA and YouTube, www.youtube.com/channel/YCokP70mbas RkEav9yInFekn

Congressionally chartered, shareholder-owned corporation under conservatorship of the Federal Housing Finance Agency. Makes mortgage funds available by buying conventional and government-insured mortgages in the secondary mortgage market; raises capital through sale of short-term and long-term obligations, mortgages, and stock; issues and guarantees mortgage-backed securities; administers the mortgage fraud program. (Fannie Mae stands for Federal National Mortgage Assn.)

Federal Housing Administration (FHA) *(Housing and Urban Development Dept.),* 451 7th St. S.W., #9100,

20410; (202) 708-2601. Janet Golrick, Assistant Secretary (Acting). FHA Resource Center, (800) 225-5342. FHA Resource Center TTY, (800) 877-8339.
General email, answers@hud.gov
Web, www.hud.gov/federal_housing_administration, Twitter, @FHAgov and Facebook, www.facebook.com/HUD

Provides mortage insurance on loans made by approved lenders for single and multifamily homes and hospitals.

Federal Housing Administration (FHA) *(Housing and Urban Development Dept.), Multifamily Housing,* 451 7th St. S.W., #6106, 20410; (202) 402-7220. Fax, (202) 708-2583. Ethan D. Handelman, Deputy Assistant Secretary.
Web, www.hud.gov/program_offices/housing/mfh

Determines risk and administers programs associated with government-insured mortgage programs, architectural procedures, and land development programs for multifamily housing. Administers the Rural Rental Housing Program and the development of congregate housing facilities that provide affordable housing, adequate space for meals, and supportive services.

Federal Housing Administration (FHA) *(Housing and Urban Development Dept.), Multifamily Housing Production,* 451 7th St. S.W., #6134, 20410-8000; (202) 708-1142. Fax, (202) 708-3104. Thomas Bernaciak, Director (Acting), (202) 402-3242.
Web, www.hud.gov/program_offices/housing/mfh/ hsgmfbus/aboutmfd

Establishes procedures for the origination of FHA-insured mortgages for multifamily housing. Administers the mortgage insurance programs for rental, cooperative, and condominium housing, nursing homes, and assisted living systems.

Federal Housing Administration (FHA) *(Housing and Urban Development Dept.), Single Family Housing,* 451 7th St. S.W., #9282, 20410; (202) 708-2601. Fax, (202) 708-2582. Julienne Joseph, Deputy Assistant Secretary, (202) 402-5945.
Web, www.hud.gov/program_offices/housing/sfh

Determines risk and administers programs associated with government-insured mortgage programs for single family housing. Administers requirements to obtain and maintain federal government approval of mortgages.

Federal Housing Administration (FHA) *(Housing and Urban Development Dept.), Single Family Program Development,* 451 7th St. S.W., #9278, 20410-8000; (202) 708-2121. Fax, (202) 708-4308. Elissa Saunders, Director, (202) 402-2278.
Web, www.hud.gov/program_offices/housing/sfh and www .hud.gov/hudprograms/offhmi

Establishes procedures for mortgage insurance programs related to the purchase or rehabilitation of single family homes.

Resources for Mortgage Financing and Other Housing Assistance

The following agencies and organizations offer consumer information pertaining to mortgages and other housing issues.

Center for Responsible Lending, (202) 349-1850; www.responsiblelending.org

Center on Budget and Policy Priorities, (202) 408-1080; www.cbpp.org

Consumer Federation of America, (202) 387-6121; www.consumerfed.org

Council for Affordable and Rural Housing, (703) 837-9001; www.carh.org

Fannie Mae, (202) 752-1234; www.fanniemae.com

Freddie Mac, (703) 903-2000; www.freddiemac.com

Housing and Urban Development Dept., (202) 708-1112; www.hud.gov

Housing Assistance Council, (202) 842-8600; www.ruralhome.org

Mortgage Bankers Assn., (202) 557-2700; www.mbaa.org

National Assn. of Development Companies, (202) 349-0070; www.nadco.org

National Assn. of Home Builders, (800) 368-5242; www.nahb.org

National Assn. of Local Housing Finance Agencies, (202) 367-1197; www.nalhfa.org

National Assn. of Realtors, (800) 874-6500; www.nar.realtor

National Council of State Housing Agencies, (202) 624-7710; www.ncsha.org

National Housing Conference, (202) 466-2121; www.nhc.org

National Housing Trust, (202) 333-8931; www.nhtinc.org

National Leased Housing Assn., (202) 785-8888; www.hudnlha.com

National Low Income Housing Coalition, (202) 662-1530; www.nlihc.org

National Reverse Mortgage Lenders Assn., (202) 939-1760; www.reversemortgage.org or www.nrmlaonline.org

NeighborWorks America, (202) 760-4000; www.neighborworks.org/home

Smart Growth America, (202) 207-3355; www.smartgrowthamerica.org

Urban Institute, (202) 833-7200; www.urban.org

Federal Housing Administration (FHA) *(Housing and Urban Development Dept.), Title I Insurance, 451 7th St. S.W., #9266, 20410; (202) 708-2121. Fax, (202) 401-8951. Kevin Stevens, Director, (202) 402-4317. Web, www.hud.gov/program_offices/housing/sfh/title*

Sets policy for Title I loans on manufactured home and property improvement loans. Provides information to borrowers and lenders on policy issues.

Federal Housing Finance Agency (FHFA), *400 7th St. S.W., 20219; (202) 649-3800. Sandra L. Thompson, Director. Ombudsman, (888) 649-5530. Press, (202) 649-3700. General email, fhfainfo@fhfa.gov*

Ombudsman email, CFPBOmbudsman@cfpb.gov, Web, www.fhfa.gov, Twitter, @FHFA and Facebook, www.facebook.com/FHFA

Regulates and works to ensure the financial soundness of Fannie Mae (Federal National Mortgage Assn.), Freddie Mac (Federal Home Loan Mortgage Corp.), and the eleven Federal Home Loan banks. FHFA was formed by a legislative merger of the Office of Federal Housing Enterprise Oversight (OFHEO), the Federal Housing Finance Board, and HUD's Government-sponsored Enterprise (GSE) mission team.

Federal Housing Finance Agency (FHFA), *Enterprise Regulation, 400 7th St. S.W., 20219; (202) 649-3809. Andre D. Galeano, Deputy Director. General email, DeputyDirector-Enterprises@FHFA.gov Web, www.fhfa.gov/supervisionregulation*

Responsible for ensuring that Fannie Mae and Freddie Mac are adequately capitalized and operate in a safe and sound manner. Supervision includes programs for accounting and disclosure, capital adequacy, examination, financial analysis, and supervision infrastructure.

Federal Housing Finance Agency (FHFA), *Federal Home Loan Bank Regulation (FHLBank Regulation), 400 7th St. S.W., 20219; (202) 649-3800. Louis Scalza, Deputy Director (Acting). General email, DeputyDirector-FHLBanks@FHFA.gov Web, www.fhfa.gov/supervisionregulation/Federal HomeLoanBanks*

Responsible for ensuring that the Federal Home Loan Banks operate in a fiscally sound manner, have adequate capital, and are able to raise funds in capital markets. Conducts safety and soundness examinations, Affordable Housing Program examinations, examination and supervisory policy and program development, FHLBank analysis, risk modeling, risk monitoring and information management, and risk analysis and research.

Freddie Mac *(Federal Housing Finance Agency), 400 7th St. S.W., 20219; (202) 649-3800. Sandra Thompson, Director (Acting). Homeowners hotline, (800) 373-3343. Press, (703) 903-3933. Toll-free, (800) 424-5401. General email, CongressionalAffairs@FHFA.gov Web, www.fhfa.gov, Twitter, @FHFA and Facebook, www.facebook.com/FHFA*

Chartered by Congress to support homeownership and rental housing by increasing the flow of funds for residential mortgages and mortgage-related securities. Purchases loans from lenders to replenish their supply of funds so that they may make more mortgage loans to borrowers. (Freddie Mac stands for Federal Home Loan Mortgage Corp.)

Ginnie Mae *(Housing and Urban Development Dept.),* *425 3rd St. S.W., #500, 20024 (mailing address: 451 7th St. S.W., #B-133, Washington, DC 20410); (202) 475-4930. Alanna McCargo, Executive Vice President, (202) 708-0926.*
General email, ginniemaecommunications@hud.gov
Web, www.ginniemae.gov, Twitter, @GinnieMaeGov, Facebook, www.facebook.com/ginniemae.gov and YouTube, www.youtube.com/channel/UCgSyjdqxuqg VWOhikmjHvgg

Supports government housing objectives by expanding affordable housing finance via secondary markets for multifamily and single-family residential, hospital, and nursing home mortgages. The wholly owned government corporation serves as a vehicle for channeling funds from domestic and global capital markets into the U.S. mortgage market through mortgage-backed securities programs and helps to increase the supply of credit available for housing. Guarantees privately issued securities backed by Federal Housing Administration, Veterans Affairs Dept., USDA Rural Development, and HUD's Office of Public and Indian Housing mortgages. (Ginnie Mae stands for Government National Mortgage Assn.)

Housing and Urban Development Dept. (HUD), *Housing Office, 451 7th St. S.W., #9100, 20410; (202) 708-2601. Janet Golnick, Assistant Secretary. TTY, (202) 708-1455.*
Web, www.hud.gov/program_offices/housing

Administers all Federal Housing Administration (FHA) mortgage insurance programs; approves and monitors all lending institutions that conduct business with HUD.

Small Business Administration (SBA), *Disaster Assistance, 409 3rd St. S.W., #6050, 20416; (202) 205-6734. Fax, (202) 205-7728. Francisco Sanchez, Associate Administrator. Service Center, (800) 659-2955.*
General email, disastercustomerassistance@sba.gov
Web, www.sba.gov/about-sba/sba-locations/headquarters-offices/office-disaster-assistance

Provides low-interest disaster loans to homeowners and renters to repair or replace real estate, personal property, machinery and equipment, inventory, and business assets that have been damaged or destroyed in a declared disaster.

Veterans Benefits Administration (VBA) *(Veterans Affairs Dept.), Loan Guaranty Service, 1800 G St. N.W., #851, 20006 (mailing address: 810 Vermont Ave. N.W., Washington, DC 20420); (202) 632-8862. Fax, (202) 495-5798. Vacant, Director. Toll-free, (877) 827-3702.*
Web, www.benefits.va.gov/homeloans

Guarantees private institutional financing of home loans (including manufactured-home loans) for veterans; provides disabled veterans with direct loans and grants for specially adapted housing; administers a direct loan program for Native American veterans living on trust land.

▶**CONGRESS**

For a listing of relevant congressional committees and subcommittees, please see page 444 or the Appendix.

▶**NONGOVERNMENTAL**

American Bankers Assn. (ABA), *1120 Connecticut Ave. N.W., 20036; (202) 663-5000. Rob Nichols, President. Toll-free, (800) 226-5377.*
General email, support@aba.com
Web, www.aba.com, Twitter, @ABABankers and Facebook, www.facebook.com/AmericanBankers Association

Membership: insured depository institutions involved in finance, including community banking. Provides information on issues that affect the industry. Monitors economic issues affecting savings institutions; publishes real estate lending survey. Monitors legislation and regulations. (America's Community Bankers merged with the American Banking Assn.)

Center for Responsible Lending, *Washington Office, 910 17th St. N.W., #800, 20006; (202) 349-1850. Michael Calhoun, President.*
Web, www.responsiblelending.org and Twitter, @CRLONLINE

Seeks to protect homeownership and family wealth by working to eliminate abusive financial practices. Conducts studies on lending practices, assists consumer attorneys, and provides information to policymakers. Provides a Web-based archive of information for public use. Monitors legislation and regulations at state and federal levels.

Consumer Data Industry Assn., *1090 Vermont Ave. N.W., #200, 20005-4905; (202) 371-0910. Francis Creighton, Chief Executive Officer.*
General email, cdia@cdiaonline.org
Web, www.cdiaonline.org and Twitter, @CDIAonline

Membership: credit reporting, mortgage reporting, background check, and collection service companies. Provides information about credit rights to consumers. Monitors legislation and regulations.

Farmer Mac, *1999 K St. N.W., 4th Floor, 20006; (202) 872-7700. Fax, (800) 999-1814. Bradford T. Nordholm, President. Toll-free, (800) 879-3276.*
Web, www.farmermac.com, Twitter, @FarmerMacNews and Facebook, www.facebook.com/farmermacnews

Private corporation chartered by Congress to provide a secondary mortgage market for farm and rural housing loans. Guarantees principal and interest repayment on securities backed by farm and rural housing loans. (Farmer Mac stands for Federal Agricultural Mortgage Corp.)

Mortgage Bankers Assn., *1919 M St. N.W., 5th Floor, 20036; (202) 557-2700. Robert D. Broeksmit, President. Toll-free, (800) 793-6222.*
Web, www.mba.org, Twitter, @MBAMortgage, Facebook, www.facebook.com/mbamortgage and Research, mbaresearch@mba.org

Membership: institutions involved in real estate finance. Maintains School of Mortgage Banking; collects statistics on the industry. Conducts seminars and workshops in specialized areas of mortgage finance. Monitors legislation and regulations.

National Assn. of Affordable Housing Lenders, *1025 Connecticut Ave. N.W., #710, 20036; (202) 293-9850. Benson (Buzz) Roberts, President.*
General email, naahl@naahl.org
Web, www.naahl.org and Twitter, @NAAHCDC

Membership: lenders who specialize in providing private capital for affordable housing and community development in low- and moderate-income areas.

National Assn. of Consumer Advocates, *1215 17th St. N.W., 5th Floor, 20036; (202) 452-1989. Fax, (202) 452-0099. Ira J. Rheingold, Executive Director, ext. 101.*
General email, info@consumeradvocates.org
Web, www.consumeradvocates.org, Facebook, www .facebook.com/NationalAssociationofConsumerAdvocates/ and Twitter, @NACAdvocate

Membership: consumer advocate attorneys. Seeks to protect the rights of consumers from fraudulent, abusive, and predatory business practices. Provides consumer law training through conferences and publications. Monitors legislation and regulations on banking, credit, and housing laws.

National Assn. of Home Builders (NAHB), *1201 15th St. N.W., 20005-2800; (202) 266-8200. Fax, (202) 266-8400. Gerald (Jerry) Howard, Executive Officer, (800) 368-5242, ext. 8257. Press, (202) 266-8254. Toll-free, (800) 368-5242. General email, info@nahb.org*
Web, www.nahb.org and Twitter, @NAHBhome

Membership: contractors, builders, architects, engineers, mortgage lenders, and others interested in home building and residential real estate construction. Interests include policies to stimulate the housing market, taxation, and mortgage financing. Monitors legislation and regulations.

National Assn. of Local Housing Finance Agencies, *2001 K St., 3rd Floor North, 20036; (202) 367-1197. Fax, (202) 367-2197. Jonathan Paine, Executive Director, (202) 367-2496.*
General email, info@nalhfa.org
Web, www.nalhfa.org and Twitter, @NALHFAnews

Membership: professionals of city and county governments, nonprofits, and private firms that finance affordable housing. Provides professional development programs in new housing finance and other areas. Monitors legislation and regulations.

National Council of State Housing Agencies, *444 N. Capitol St. N.W., #438, 20001; (202) 624-7710. Fax, (202) 624-5899. Stockton Williams, Executive Director. General email, info@ncsha.org*
Web, www.ncsha.org, Twitter, @NCSHAhome, Facebook, www.facebook.com/NCSHA1 and YouTube, www.youtube .com/user/NCSHAvideos

Membership: state housing finance agencies. Promotes greater opportunities for lower-income people to rent or buy affordable housing.

National Reverse Mortgage Lenders Assn., *1400 16th St. N.W., #420, 20036; (202) 939-1760. Fax, (202) 265-4435. Peter H. Bell, Chief Executive Officer, (202) 939-1741; Steve Irwin, President, (202) 939-1776.*
General email, info@nrmlaonline.org
Web, www.nrmlaonline.org

National trade association for firms that originate, service, and invest in reverse mortgages. Monitors legislation and regulations.

Property Management

►AGENCIES

Federal Housing Administration (FHA) *(Housing and Urban Development Dept.), Multifamily Asset Management and Portfolio Oversight, 451 7th St. S.W., #6162, 20410; (202) 402-2059. Fax, (202) 708-3104. Toby J. Halliday, Director, (202) 402-2059.*
Web, www.hud.gov/program_offices/housing/mfh/ hsgmfbus/aboutam

Oversees HUD management, ownership, and sale of properties, which HUD owns by virtue of default and foreclosure or for which HUD is mortgagee-in-possession.

Federal Housing Administration (FHA) *(Housing and Urban Development Dept.), Procurement Management, 451 7th St. S.W., #2222, 20410; (202) 402-7127. Fax, (202) 708-3698. Amelia McCormick, Director.*
Web, www.hud.gov/program_offices/cpo

Develops and implements policies and procedures and conducts contract administration for the Office of Housing and the Federal Housing Administration headquarters' procurement actions.

►NONGOVERNMENTAL

Building Owners and Managers Assn. International, *1101 15th St. N.W., #800, 20005; (202) 326-6300. Fax, (202) 326-6377. Henry Chamberlain, President, (202) 326-6325.*
General email, info@boma.org
Web, www.boma.org and Twitter, @BOMAIntl

Membership: represents owners and managers, service providers and other property professionals of all commercial building types, including office, industrial, medical, corporate and mixed-use. Reviews changes in model codes and building standards; conducts seminars and workshops on building operation and maintenance issues; sponsors educational and training programs. Monitors legislation and regulations.

Community Associations Institute, *6402 Arlington Blvd., #500, Falls Church, VA 22042; (703) 970-9220. Fax, (703) 970-9558. Thomas (Tom) Skiba, Chief Executive Officer. Press, (703) 970-9558. Toll-free, (888) 224-4321. General email, cai-info@CAIonline.org*

Web, www.caionline.org, Twitter, @CAIsocial, Facebook, www.facebook.com/CAIsocial and YouTube, www .youtube.com/c/CommunityAssociationsInstituteHQ/ featured

Membership: homeowner associations, builders, lenders, owners, managers, Realtors, insurance companies, and public officials. Provides members with information on creating, financing, and maintaining common facilities and services in condominiums and other planned developments.

NAIOP Commercial Real Estate Development Assn., *2355 Dulles Corner Blvd., #750, Herndon, VA 20171; (703) 904-7100. Fax, (703) 904-7942.*
Thomas J. (Tom) Bisacquino, President, ext. 104.
Web, www.naiop.org, Twitter, @NAIOP and Facebook, www.facebook.com/NAIOPCorporate

Membership: developers, planners, designers, builders, financiers, and managers of industrial and office properties. Provides research and continuing education programs. Monitors legislation and regulations on capital gains, real estate taxes, impact fees, growth management, environmental issues, and hazardous waste liability.

National Apartment Assn., *4300 Wilson Blvd., #800, Arlington, VA 22203; (703) 518-6141. Fax, (703) 248-9440. Robert (Bob) Pinnegar, President, (703) 797-0686. General email, webmaster@naahq.org*

Web, www.naahq.org, Twitter, @NAAhq and Facebook, www.facebook.com/NAAhq

Membership: state and local associations of owners, managers, investors, developers, and builders of apartment houses or other rental properties. Conducts educational and professional certification programs. Monitors legislation and regulations.

National Assn. of Housing and Redevelopment Officials, *630 Eye St. N.W., 20001-3736; (202) 289-3500. Fax, (202) 289-8181. Mike Gerber, Chief Executive Officer (Acting). Toll-free, (877) 866-2476. General email, nahro@nahro.org*

Web, www.nahro.org and Twitter, @NAHROnational

Conducts studies and provides training and certification in the operation and management of rental housing.

National Assn. of Housing Cooperatives, *1120 20th St. N.W., #750, 20036-3441; (202) 737-0797. Fax, (202) 216-9646. Mik Bauer, Executive Director. General email, info@nahc.coop*

Web, www.coophousing.org and Twitter, @NAHC1960

Membership: housing cooperative professionals and organizations that provide services to housing cooperatives. Promotes housing cooperatives; provides technical assistance in all phases of cooperative housing; sponsors educational programs and on-site training; provides legal service referrals; monitors legislation; maintains an information clearinghouse on housing cooperatives. Online resources include a directory of financial, legal, and management services experts in the housing cooperative community.

National Cooperative Business Assn., CLUSA International (NCBA CLUSA), *1775 Eye St. N.W., 8th Floor, 20006; (240) 638-6222. Douglas O'Brien, President. General email, info@ncba.coop*

Web, www.ncbaclusa.coop, Twitter, @NCBACLUSAcoop, Facebook, www.facebook.com/NCBACLUSA and YouTube, www.youtube.com/channel/UC1d9CsZOwqw QJid4uEscEUg

Alliance of cooperatives, businesses, and state cooperative associations. Provides information about starting and managing housing cooperatives. Monitors legislation and regulations.

National Multifamily Housing Council, *1775 Eye St. N.W., #1100, 20006; (202) 974-2300. Fax, (202) 775-0112. Douglas Bibby, President, (202) 974-2323. General email, info@nmhc.org*

Web, www.nmhc.org

Membership: owners, financiers, managers, and developers of multifamily housing. Advocates policies and programs at the federal, state, and local levels to increase the supply and quality of multifamily units in the United States; serves as a clearinghouse on rent control, condominium conversion, taxes, fair housing, and environmental issues.

Property Management Assn., *7508 Wisconsin Ave., 4th Floor, Bethesda, MD 20814; (301) 657-9200. Tom Cohn, Executive Vice President. General email, info@pma-dc.org*

Web, www.pma-dc.org, Twitter, @PMAAssociation and Facebook, www.facebook.com/PropertyManagement Association

Membership: property managers and firms that offer products and services needed in the property management field. Promotes information exchange on property management practices.

12 International Affairs

GENERAL POLICY AND ANALYSIS

Basic Resources

▶AGENCIES

Bureau of Intelligence and Research (INR) *(State Dept.),* *2201 C St. N.W., #6468, 20520-6531; (202) 647-9177. Brett M. Holmgren, Assistant Secretary. Web, www.state.gov/s/inr*

Coordinates foreign policy–related research, analysis, and intelligence programs for the State Dept. and other federal agencies.

Bureau of International Organization Affairs (IO) *(State Dept.), 2201 C St. N.W., #6323, 20520-6319; (202) 647-9600. Amb. Erica Barks-Ruggles, Senior Bureau Official; Michele Sison, Assistant Secretary. Press, (202) 647-6899. General email, IOmailbox@state.gov*

Web, www.state.gov/p/io and Twitter, @State_IO

Coordinates and develops policy guidelines for U.S. participation in the United Nations and in other international organizations and conferences.

Bureau of International Organization Affairs (IO) *(State Dept.), International Conferences, 2401 E St. N.W., #SA-1, H436, 20522; (202) 663-1024. Sammie Shirey, Director. Web, www.state.gov/p/io*

Coordinates U.S. participation in multilateral conferences and accredits delegations.

Bureau of International Organization Affairs (IO) *(State Dept.), United Nations Political Affairs (UNP), 2201 C St. N.W., #1828, 20520-6319; (202) 647-2393. Fax, (202) 647-0039. Alejandro Baez, Director. Web, www.state.gov/p/io*

Deals with UN political and institutional matters and international security affairs.

Bureau of Oceans and International Environmental and Scientific Affairs (OES) *(State Dept.), Policy and Public Outreach (PPO), 2201 C St. N.W., #2880, 20520; (202) 647-2958. Timothy L. Smith, Director, (202) 647-4658. Web, www.state.gov/about-us-office-of-policy-and-public-outreach/*

Integrates oceans, environment, polar, science, technology, and health issues into U.S. foreign policy, and works to address these issues in the media, NGOs, the private sector, and Congress.

Defense Dept. (DoD), *International Security Affairs, 2000 Defense Pentagon, 20301-2000; (703) 697-2788. Fax, (703) 697-3279. Ilan Goldenberg, Assistant Secretary (Acting). Web, http://policy.defense.gov/OUSDPOffices/ASDfor InternationalSecurityAffairs*

Advises the secretary of defense and recommends policies on regional security issues in the Middle East, Africa, Russia/Eurasia, and Europe/NATO.

National Security Staff (NSS) *(Executive Office of the President), International Economic Affairs, The White House, 1600 Pennsylvania Ave. N.W., 20504; (202) 456-1414. Daleep Singh, Deputy National Security Adviser. Web, www.whitehouse.gov*

Advises the president, the National Security Council, and the National Economic Council on all aspects of U.S. foreign policy dealing with U.S. international economic policies.

State Dept., *2201 C St. N.W., HST 226, 20520; (202) 647-4000. Fax, (202) 647-3340. Antony J. Blinken, Secretary. Press, (202) 647-2492. Web, www.state.gov, Twitter, @StateDept, Facebook, www .facebook.com/statedept, YouTube, www.youtube.com/ user/statevideo and Blog, https://blogs.state.gov*

Directs and coordinates U.S. foreign relations and interdepartmental activities of the U.S. government overseas.

State Dept., *Policy Planning Staff, 2201 C St. N.W., #7311, 20520; (202) 647-2972. Fax, (202) 647-0844. Salman Ahmed, Director. General email, policyplanning@state.gov Web, www.state.gov/about-us-policy-planning-staff*

Advises the secretary and other State Dept. officials on foreign policy matters.

State Dept., *Under Secretary for Civilian Security, Democracy, and Human Rights, 2201 C St. N.W., #7261, 20520; (202) 647-1189. Fax, (202) 647-0753. Yzra Zeya, Under Secretary. Web, www.state.gov/bureaus-offices/under-secretary-for-civilian-security-democracy-and-human-rights*

Advises the secretary on transnational issues. Oversees the Bureau of Conflict and Stabilization Operations; Bureau of Counterterrorism; Bureau of Democracy, Human Rights, and Labor; Bureau of International Narcotics and Law Enforcement; Bureau of Population, Refugees, and Migration; Office of Global Criminal Justice; Office of International Religious Freedom; and Office of Monitor and Combat Trafficking in Persons.

State Dept., *Under Secretary for Management, 2201 C St. N.W., #7207, 20520; (202) 647-1500. Fax, (202) 647-0168. John R. Bass, Under Secretary. Web, www.state.gov/bureaus-offices/under-secretary-for-management*

Serves as principal adviser to the secretary on management matters, including budgetary, administrative, and personnel policies of the department and the Foreign Service. Oversees the Bureau of Administration; Bureau of Budget and Planning; Bureau of the Comptroller and Global Financial Services; Bureau of Consular Affairs; Bureau of Diplomatic Security; Bureau of Human Resources; Bureau of Information Resource Management; Bureau of Overseas Buildings Operations; Director of Diplomatic Reception Rooms; Foreign Service Institute; Office of Management Policy, Rightsizing, and Innovation; Office of Medical Services; and Office of White House Liaison.

State Dept., *Under Secretary for Political Affairs,* 2201 C St. N.W., #7250, 20520; (202) 647-0995. Fax, (202) 647-4780. Amb. Victoria Nuland, Under Secretary, (202) 647-2471.
Web, www.state.gov/bureaus-offices/under-secretary-for-political-affairs

Manages regional and bilateral policy issues and assists in the overall direction of the department. Oversees the Africa, East Asia and the Pacific, Europe and Eurasia, Near East, South and Central Asia, Western Hemisphere, and International Organizations bureaus.

State Dept., *Under Secretary for Public Diplomacy and Public Affairs,* 2201 C St. N.W., #7531, 20520; (202) 647-9199. Fax, (202) 647-9140. Jennifer Hall Godfrey, Senior Official.
Web, www.state.gov/bureaus-offices/under-secretary-for-public-diplomacy-and-public-affairs and Twitter, @UnderSecPD

Seeks to broaden public affairs discussion on foreign policy with U.S. citizens, media, and institutions. Oversees the Bureau of Education and Cultural Affairs; Bureau of Global Public Affairs; Global Engagement Center; and Office of Policy, Planning, and Resources.

► **CONGRESS**

For a listing of relevant congressional committees and sub-committees, please see pages 478–479 or the Appendix.

Government Accountability Office (GAO), *International Affairs and Trade (IAT),* 441 G St. N.W., 20548; (202) 512-2964. Chelsa L. Kenney, Director.
Web, www.gao.gov/about/careers/our-teams

Audits, analyzes, and evaluates international programs and trade; evaluates economic, political, and security problems worldwide. In addition to federal departments, oversight work includes U.S. Agency for International Development, Office of the U.S. Trade Representative, Broadcasting Board of Governors, North Atlantic Treaty Organization, World Bank, International Monetary Fund, and United Nations.

House Democracy Partnership, 169 CHOB, 20515; (202) 225-1784. Fax, (202) 225-2014. Rep. David Price, Chair; Derek Luyten, Executive Director.
General email, house_democracy_partnership@mail.house.gov
Web, https://hdp.house.gov and Twitter, @house_democracy

Provides advice to members and staff of parliaments of select countries that have established or are developing democratic governments.

► **INTERNATIONAL ORGANIZATIONS**

International Monetary Fund (IMF), 700 19th St. N.W., 20431; 1900 Pennsylvania Ave. N.W., 20431; (202) 623-7000. Fax, (202) 623-4661. Elizabeth Shortino, U.S. Executive Director; Kristalina Georgieva, Managing Director. Legislative Affairs, (202) 623-6220. Press, (202) 623-7100.

General email, publicaffairs@imf.org
Web, www.imf.org

International organization of 188 member countries that promotes policies for financial stability and economic growth, works to prevent financial crises, and helps members solve balance-of-payment problems through loans funded by member contributions.

Organisation for Economic Co-operation and Development (OECD), *Washington Center,* 1776 Eye St. N.W., #450, 20006; (202) 785-6323. Will Davis, Head of Center, (202) 822-3869.
General email, washington.contact@oecd.org
Web, www.oecd.org/washington, Twitter, @oced_washington and Facebook, www.facebook.com/OECDWashington/

Membership: 34 nations, including Australia, Canada, Japan, Mexico, New Zealand, the United States, and western European nations. Serves as a forum for government officials to exchange information on their countries' policies. (Headquarters in Paris.)

Organization of American States (OAS), 17th St. and Constitution Ave. N.W., 20006; Administration Bldg., 19th St. and Constitution Ave. N.W., 20006; General Secretariat Bldg., 1889 F St. N.W., 20006; (202) 370-5000. Fax, (202) 458-3967. Luis Almagro Lemes, Secretary General. Library, (202) 458-6041.
General email, ai@oas.org
Web, www.oas.org and Twitter, @oas_official

Membership: the United States, Canada, and all independent Latin American and Caribbean countries. Funded by quotas paid by member states and by contributions to special multilateral funds. Works to promote democracy, eliminate poverty, and resolve disputes among member nations. Provides member states with technical and advisory services in cultural, educational, scientific, social, and economic areas. Library open to the public (at 19th and Constitution).

United Nations Information Center, 1775 K St. N.W., #500, 20006; (202) 331-8670. Fax, (202) 331-9191. Stefania Piftanelli, Director.
General email, unicdc@unic.org
Web, www.unicwash.org and Twitter, @unicdc

Lead United Nations (UN) office in Washington. Serves as a resource for information and materials about the United Nations.

► **NONGOVERNMENTAL**

American Enterprise Institute (AEI), *Foreign and Defense Policy Studies,* 1789 Massachusetts Ave. N.W., 20036; (202) 862-5800. Fax, (202) 862-7177. Kori N. Schake, Director.
Web, www.aei.org/category/foreign-and-defense-policy

Research and educational organization that conducts conferences, seminars, and debates and sponsors research on international affairs.

INTERNATIONAL AFFAIRS RESOURCES IN CONGRESS

For a complete listing of congressional committees, including their full contact information, leadership, membership, and jurisdictions, please refer to the Appendix on pages 840–963.

HOUSE:

House Appropriations Committee, (202) 225-2771.
Web, appropriations.house.gov
>   Subcommittee on Commerce, Justice, Science, and Related Agencies, (202) 225-3351.
>   Subcommittee on Interior, Environment, and Related Agencies, (202) 225-3081.
>   Subcommittee on State, Foreign Operations, and Related Programs, (202) 225-2041.

House Armed Services Committee, (202) 225-4151.
Web, armedservices.house.gov
>   Subcommittee on Strategic Forces, (202) 225-4151.

House Energy and Commerce Committee, (202) 225-2927.
Web, energycommerce.house.gov
>   Subcommittee on Consumer Protection and Commerce, (202) 225-2927.

House Financial Services Committee, (202) 225-4247.
Web, financialservices.house.gov
>   Subcommittee on National Security, Inernational Development, and Monetary Policy, (202) 225-4247.

House Foreign Affairs Committee, (202) 225-5021.
Web, foreignaffairs.house.gov
>   Subcommittee on Africa, Global Health, and Global Human Rights, (202) 225-5021.
>   Subcommittee on Asia, the Pacific, Central Asia, and Nonproliferation, (202) 226-6434.
>   Subcommittee on Europe, Energy, the Environment, and Cyber, (202) 225-5021.
>   Subcommittee on Middle East, North Africa, and Global Counterterrorism, (202) 226-7812.
>   Subcommittee on International Development, International Organizations, and Global Corporate Social Impact, (202) 225-5021.
>   Subcommittee on the Western Hemisphere, Civilian Security, Migration, and International Economic Policy, (202) 225-3345.

House Homeland Security Committee, (202) 226-2616.
Web, homeland.house.gov
>   Subcommittee on Border Security, Facilitation, and Operations, (202) 226-2616.

House Judiciary Committee, (202) 225-3951.
Web, judiciary.house.gov
>   Subcommittee on Crime, Terrorism, and Homeland Security, (202) 225-5727.
>   Subcommittee on Immigration and Citizenship, (202) 225-3926.

House Natural Resources Committee, (202) 225-6065.
Web, naturalresources.house.gov
>   Subcommittee on Water, Oceans, and Wildlife, (202) 225-8331.

House Oversight and Reform Committee, (202) 225-5051.
Web, oversight.house.gov
>   Subcommittee on National Security, (202) 225-5051.

House Permanent Select Committee on Intelligence, (202) 225-7690.
Web, intelligence.house.gov

House Science, Space, and Technology Committee, (202) 225-6375.
Web, science.house.gov
>   Subcommittee on Research and Technology, (202) 225-6375.
>   Subcommittee on Space and Aeronautics, (202) 225-6375.

House Small Business Committee, (202) 225-4038.
Web, smallbusiness.house.gov
>   Subcommittee on Economic Growth, Tax, and Capital Access, (202) 225-4038.
>   Subcommittee on Underserved, Agricultural, and Rural Business Development, (202) 225-4038.

American Foreign Policy Council, *509 C St. N.E., 20002; (202) 543-1006. Fax, (202) 543-1007. Herman Pirchner Jr., President.*
General email, afpc@afpc.org
Web, http://afpc.org, Twitter, @afpc and Facebook, www.facebook.com/americanforeignpolicy council

Provides policymakers with information on foreign policy issues and options. Assists international leaders in establishing democracies. Holds meetings between Congressional officials and officials in other countries. Publishes articles on current foreign affairs. Interests include terrorism in Europe and Asia, the Russia–China alliance, and nuclear weapons.

Applied Research Laboratory for Intelligence and Security (ARLIS) *(University of Maryland), 7005 52nd Ave., College Park, MD 20742; (301) 226-8900. Fax, (301) 226-8811. William Regli, Executive Director, (301) 405-6738.*
General email, info@arlis.umd.edu
Web, www.arlis.umd.edu

Conducts research in social systems, human-systems integration, and test bed development to support security

House Transportation and Infrastructure Committee, (202) 225-4472.
Web, transportation.house.gov
Subcommittee on Coast Guard and Maritime Transportation, (202) 226-3552.
House Ways and Means Committee, (202) 225-3625.
Web, waysandmeans.house.gov
Subcommittee on Trade, (202) 225-6649.

JOINT:

Joint Economic Committee, (202) 224-5171.
Web, jec.senate.gov

SENATE:

Senate Appropriations Committee, (202) 224-7363.
Web, appropriations.senate.gov
Subcommittee on State, Foreign Operations, and Related Programs, (202) 224-7363.
Senate Armed Services Committee, (202) 224-3871.
Web, armed-services.senate.gov
Subcommittee on Airland, (202) 224-3871.
Subcommittee on Emerging Threats and Capabilities, (202) 224-3871.
Subcommittee on Seapower, (202) 224-3871.
Subcommittee on Strategic Forces, (202) 224-3871.
Senate Banking, Housing, and Urban Affairs Committee, (202) 224-7391.
Web, banking.senate.gov
Subcommittee on National Security and International Trade and Finance, (202) 224-7391.
Senate Commerce, Science, and Transportation Committee, (202) 224-0411.
Web, commerce.senate.gov
Subcommittee on Oceans, Fisheries, Climate Change, and Manufacturing, (202) 224-0411.
Senate Energy and Natural Resources Committee, (202) 224-4971.
Web, energy.senate.gov
Subcommittee on Energy, (202) 224-4971.

Senate Finance Committee, (202) 224-4515.
Web, finance.senate.gov
Subcommittee on International Trade, Customs, and Global Competitiveness, (202) 224-4515.
Subcommittee on Africa and Global Health Policy, (202) 224-4651.
Subcommittee on East Asia, the Pacific, and International Cybersecurity Policy, (202) 224-4651.
Subcommittee on Europe and Regional Security Cooperation, (202) 224-4651.
Subcommittee on Multilateral International Development, Multilateral Institutions, and International Economic, Energy, and Environmental Policy, (202) 224-4651.
Subcommittee on Near East, South Asia, Central Asia, and Counterterrorism, (202) 224-4651.
Subcommittee on State Department and USAID Management, International Operations, and Bilateral International Development, (202) 224-4651.
Subcommittee on Western Hemisphere, Transnational Crime, Civilian Security, Democracy, Human Rights, and Global Women's Issues, (202) 224-4651.
Senate Foreign Relations Committee, (202) 224-4651.
Web, foreign.senate.gov
Senate Homeland Security and Governmental Affairs Committee, (202) 224-2627.
Web, hsgac.senate.gov
Subcommittee on Government Operations and Border Management, (202) 224-4551.
Senate Judiciary Committee, (202) 224-7703.
Web, judiciary.senate.gov
Subcommittee on Immigration, Citizenship, and Border Safety, (202) 224-6991.
Subcommittee on Criminal Justice and Counterterrorism, (202) 224-2921.

and intelligence communities; collaborates with government agencies. Joint venture with the Defense Dept.

Aspen Institute, *2300 N St. N.W., #700, 20037; (202) 736-5800. Fax, (202) 467-0790. Daniel R. Porterfield, President. Press, (202) 736-3849.*
General email, info@aspeninstitute.org
Web, www.aspeninstitute.org and Twitter, @AspenInstitute

Educational and policy studies organization. Promotes consideration of the public good in a wide variety of policy areas, including international relations and homeland security. Working with international partners, offers educational seminars, nonpartisan policy forums, public conferences and events, and leadership development initiatives.

Atlantic Council, *1030 15th St. N.W., 12th Floor, 20005; (202) 778-4952. Fax, (202) 463-7241. Frederick Kempe, President, (202) 463-7226. Press, (202) 778-4967. Toll-free, (800) 380-6004.*
General email, info@atlanticcouncil.org
Web, www.atlanticcouncil.org, Twitter, @ATLANTICCOUNCIL and Facebook, www.facebook .com/AtlanticCouncil

State Department

- - - - Denotes independent agencies that receive guidance from the secretary of state

Promotes constructive leadership and engagement in international affairs based on the Atlantic Community's central role in meeting global challenges. The Council provides an essential forum for navigating the dramatic economic and political changes defining the twenty-first century by informing and galvanizing its uniquely influential network of global leaders. Conducts studies and makes policy recommendations on U.S. foreign security and international economic and political policies in the Atlantic and Pacific communities; sponsors conferences and educational exchanges.

The Brookings Institution, *Foreign Policy Studies,* 1775 *Massachusetts Ave. N.W., 20036; (202) 797-6103. Suzanne Maloney, Director. Web, www.brookings.edu/foreign-policy, Twitter, @BrookingsFP and Twitter, @MaloneySuzanne*

Conducts studies on foreign policy, national security, regional and global affairs, and economic policies. Includes five policy centers: Center for Middle East Policy, the Center for East Asia Policy Studies, the Center on the United States and Europe, Center for 21st Century Security and Intelligence, and the John L. Thornton China Center.

The Brookings Institution, *Project on International Order and Strategy,* *1775 Massachusetts Ave. N.W., 20036; (202) 757-6103. Bruce Jones, Director, (202) 797-6072.*

Web, www.brookings.edu/about/projects/international-order-strategy and Twitter, Director, @Brucebookings

Fosters research, policy engagement, and debate on international order and strategy. Interests include the rise of new powers on the international stage, the diffusion of political and military power, Western economic difficulties, challenges in the Middle East, and territorial disputes in Asia.

Center for International Policy, *1050 Connecticut Ave. N.W., 20036; (202) 232-3317. Nancy Okail, President.*

Web, www.internationalpolicy.org and Twitter, @CIPolicy

Research and educational organization concerned with peace and security worldwide. Special interests include military spending, U.S. intelligence policy, and U.S. policy. Promotes cooperation, transparency, and accountability in international relations. Through research and advocacy, offers solutions to address global threats, including war, corruption, inequality, and climate change. Publishes the *International Policy Report.*

Center for Strategic and International Studies, *1616 Rhode Island Ave. N.W., 20036; (202) 887-0200. Fax, (202) 775-3199. John J. Hamre, Chief Executive Officer. Press, (202) 775-3242.*

General email, webmaster@csis.org

Web, www.csis.org, Twitter, @CSIS, Facebook, www .facebook.com/CSIS.org and YouTube, www.youtube.com/ CSISDC

A bipartisan organization that seeks to advance global security and prosperity by providing strategic insights and practical policy solutions to decision makers. Expertise includes defense and international security, emerging global issues, cybersecurity, global health, human rights, and regional transformation.

Center for the National Interest, *1025 Connecticut Ave. N.W., #1200, 20036-5651; (202) 887-1000. Fax, (202) 887-5222. Dimitri K. Simes, President.*

General email, info@cftni.org

Web, https://cftni.org and Twitter, @CFTNI

Works to develop new principles for U.S. global engagement and security; energy security and climate change; immigration and national security; and U.S. relations with China, Japan, the Middle East, Russia, and America's European allies. Publishes topical reports and a bimonthly magazine, *The National Interest.*

Citizens for Global Solutions, *5 Thomas Circle, 20005; (202) 546-3950. Bob Flax, Executive Director.*

General email, info@globalsolutions.org

Web, www.globalsolutions.org, Twitter, @GlobalSolutions and Facebook, www.facebook.com/citizensforglobal solutions

Encourages U.S. global engagement on a broad range of foreign policy issues, including UN reform, international law and justice, health and the environment, international institutions, and peace and security.

The Conservative Caucus (TCC), *332 W. Lee Hwy., #221, Warrenton, VA 20816 (mailing address: P.O. Box 1890, Merrifield, VA 22116); (540) 219-4536. Peter J. Thomas, Chair.*

General email, info@conservativeusa.org

Web, www.conservativeusa.org, Twitter, @Conserv.Caucus and Facebook, www.facebook.com/ConservativeCaucus

Legislative interest organization that promotes grassroots activity on national defense and foreign policy.

Council on Foreign Relations, *Washington Office, 1777 F St. N.W., 20006; (202) 509-8400. Fax, (202) 509-8490. Richard N. Haass, President; James M. Lindsay, Senior Vice President.*

General email, communications@cfr.org

Web, www.cfr.org/, Twitter, @CFR_org and Facebook, www.facebook.com/councilonforeignrelations

Promotes understanding of U.S. foreign policy and international affairs. Awards research grants through its International Affairs Fellowship Program. Publishes *Foreign Affairs* bimonthly. (Headquarters in New York.)

Ethics and Public Policy Center, *1730 M St. N.W., #910, 20036; (202) 682-1200. Fax, (202) 408-0632. Ryan T. Anderson, President.*

General email, ethics@eppc.org

Web, www.eppc.org, Twitter, @EPPCdc and Facebook, www.facebook.com/EPPC.org

Considers implications of Judeo-Christian moral tradition for domestic and foreign policymaking. Conducts research and holds conferences on foreign policy, including the role of the U.S. military abroad.

Freedom House, *1850 M St. N.W., 11th Floor, 20036; (202) 296-5101. Michael J. Abramowitz, President.*

General email, info@freedomhouse.org

Web, www.freedomhouse.org, Twitter, @FreedomHouse, Facebook, www.facebook.com/FreedomHouseDC and Twitter, President, @abramowitz

Independent watchdog organization working to defend human rights and promote democratic change, with a focus on political rights and civil liberties; women's rights; LGBTI rights; elections; intergovernmental bodies; free markets; the rule of law; independent media, including Internet freedom; and U.S. engagement in international affairs through education, advocacy, and training initiatives. Collects and analyzes data on political rights and civil liberties worldwide; publishes comparative surveys and reports; sponsors conferences and training programs.

Friends Committee on National Legislation (FCNL), *245 2nd St. N.E., 20002-5795; (202) 547-6000. Fax, (202) 547-6019. Bridget Moix, General Secretary. Toll-free, (800) 630-1330.*

General email, fcnl@fcnl.org

Web, www.fcnl.org, Twitter, @FCNL and Facebook, www .facebook.com/quakerlobby

Seeks to broaden public interest and affect legislation and policy concerning regional and global institutions, peace processes, international development, and the work of the United Nations. (Affiliated with the Religious Society of Friends [Quakers].)

Institute for Policy Studies, *1301 Connecticut Ave. N.W., #600, 20036; (202) 234-9382. Fax, (202) 387-7915. Tope Folarin, Executive Director.*
General email, info@ips-dc.org

Web, https://ips-dc.org, Twitter, @IPS_DC and Facebook, www.facebook.com/InstituteforPolicyStudies

Research and educational think tank focused on social justice and security, especially equality, ecological sustainability, and peace. Interests include foreign policy, income inequality, and human rights.

Institute for Policy Studies, *Foreign Policy in Focus, 1301 Connecticut Ave. N.W., #600, 20036; (202) 234-9382. Fax, (202) 387-7915. Peter Certo, Editorial Manager.*
General email, info@ips-dc.org

Web, https://fpif.org, Twitter, @FPIF and Facebook, www.facebook.com/ForeignPolicyInFocus

Think tank that provides analysis of U.S. foreign policy and international affairs and recommends progressive policy alternatives. Publishes reports; organizes briefings for the public, media, and policymakers. Interests include climate change, global poverty, nuclear weapons, terrorism, and military conflict.

Institute of Current World Affairs, *1818 N St. N.W., #460, 20036; (202) 364-4068. Gregory Feifer, Executive Director.*
General email, icwa@icwa.org

Web, www.icwa.org, Twitter, @ICWAnews and Facebook, www.facebook.com/InstituteOfCurrentWorldAffairs

Offers two-year fellowships to support the independent study of international region-specific issues. Fellows write monthly newsletters to update the institute on their progress and findings. Presents public events on international topics.

Institute of World Politics, *1521 16th St. N.W., 20036-1464; (202) 462-2101. Fax, (202) 464-0335. John Lenczowski, Chancellor; Amb. Aldona Wos, President (Acting). Toll-free, (888) 566-9497.*
General email, info@iwp.edu

Web, www.iwp.edu, Twitter, @theIWP and Facebook, www.facebook.com/theiwp

Offers master's degree and professional education in national security, statecraft, and international affairs.

International Center, *700 Pennsylvania Ave. S.E., #2050, 20003 (mailing address: P.O. Box 41720, Arlington, VA 22204); (202) 285-4328. Virginia Foote, President.*
General email, theinternationalcenter@theintlcenter.org

Web, http://theintlcenter.org and Email, lhouse@theintlcenter.org

Research, advocacy, and aid organization concerned with U.S. foreign policy in developing countries. Project arms include trade and investment between the United States and Vietnam, reforestation and agroforestry training in Central America and the Caribbean, rehabilitation services and equipment for Cambodians with disabilities, land-mine clearance and school upgrades in Vietnam, and youth sports exchange programs.

International Foundation for Electoral Systems (IFES), *2011 Crystal Dr., 10th Floor, Arlington, VA 22202; (202) 350-6700. Fax, (202) 350-6701. Anthony Banbury, President.*
General email, info@ifes.org

Web, www.ifes.org, Twitter, @IFES1987 and Facebook, www.facebook.com/IFES1987

Nonpartisan organization providing professional support to electoral democracies, both emerging and mature. Through fieldwork and applied research and advocacy, strives to promote citizen participation, transparency, and accountability in political life and civil society.

International Republican Institute (IRI), *1225 Eye St. N.W., #800, 20005; (202) 408-9450. Daniel (Dan) Twining, President.*
General email, info@iri.org

Web, www.iri.org, Twitter, @IRIGlobal and Facebook, www.facebook.com/InternationalRepublicanInstitute

Created under the National Endowment for Democracy Act. Fosters democratic self-rule through closer ties and cooperative programs with political parties and other nongovernmental institutions overseas.

Just Foreign Policy, *4410 Massachusetts Ave. N.W., #290, 20016; (202) 448-2898. Erik Sperling, Executive Director.*
General email, info@justforeignpolicy.org

Web, www.justforeignpolicy.org, Twitter, @justfp and Facebook, www.facebook.com/justforeignpolicy

Nonpartisan membership organization that seeks to influence U.S. foreign policy through education, organization, and mobilization of citizens. Advocates cooperation, international law, and diplomacy as means to achieve a just foreign policy.

National Democratic Institute for International Affairs (NDI), *455 Massachusetts Ave. N.W., 8th Floor, 20001-2621; (202) 728-5500. Derek Mitchell, President. Toll-free fax, (888) 875-2887.*
General email, contactndi@ndi.org

Web, www.ndi.org, Twitter, @NDI and Facebook, www.facebook.com/National.Democratic.Institute

Conducts nonpartisan international programs to help maintain and strengthen democratic institutions worldwide. Focuses on party building, governance, and electoral systems.

National Endowment for Democracy, *1201 Pennsylvania Ave. N.W., #1100, 20004; (202) 378-9700. Fax, (202) 378-9407. Damon Wilson, President.*
General email, info@ned.org

Web, www.ned.org, Twitter, @NEDemocracy, Facebook, www.facebook.com/National.Endowment.for.Democracy and YouTube, www.youtube.com/nationalendowmentfordemocracy

Grant-making organization that receives funding from Congress. Awards grants to private organizations involved in democratic development abroad, including the areas of democratic political processes; pluralism; and education, culture, and communications.

National Security Archive *(George Washington University),* *Gelman Library, 2130 H St. N.W., #701, 20037; (202) 994-7000. Fax, (202) 994-7005. Thomas S. Blanton, Director.*
General email, nsarchiv@gwu.edu

Web, www.nsarchive.gwu.edu, Twitter, @NSArchive and Facebook, www.facebook.com/NSArchive

Research institute and library that provides information on U.S. foreign and economic policy and national security affairs. Maintains and publishes collection of declassified and unclassified documents obtained through the Freedom of Information Act. Archive open to the public by appointment. Website has a Russian-language link.

Partnership for a Secure America (PSA), *1990 M. St. N.W., #250, 20036; (202) 293-8580. Curtis M. Silvers, Executive Director.*
General email, psa@psaonline.org

Web, www.psaonline.org, Twitter, @PSAonline and Facebook, www.facebook.com/psaonline

Supports a bipartisan approach to foreign policy issues. Researches and publishes reports on international policies and their impact on foreign relations. Organizes conferences for political parties to debate and develop consensus on issues.

Paul H. Nitze School of Advanced International Studies, John Hopkins, *1740 Massachusetts Ave. N.W., 20036; (202) 663-5600. Eliot A. Cohen, Dean.*
General email, saiswebsite@jhu.edu

Web, www.sais-jhu.edu, Twitter, @SAISHopkins and Facebook, www.facebook.com/SAISHopkins

Offers graduate and nondegree programs in international relations, economics, public policy, regional and functional studies, and foreign languages. Sponsors the Johns Hopkins Foreign Policy Institute and several other research centers. (Affiliated with Johns Hopkins University.)

Pew Research Center, *International Affairs, Global Attitudes and Trends Project,* *1615 L St. N.W., #800, 20036; (202) 419-4300. Fax, (202) 419-8562. Richard Wike, Director; James Bell, Vice President, Global Strategy. Press, (202) 419-4372.*
General email, info@pewglobal.org

Web, www.pewglobal.org and Twitter, @PewGlobal

Conducts public opinion surveys about world affairs and makes results available to journalists, academics, policymakers, and the public. Attempts to gauge attitudes in every region of the world toward globalization, democracy, trade, terrorism, and other key issues.

The Truman Center for National Policy, *1250 Eye St. N.W., #500, 20005; (202) 216-9723. Fax, (202) 682-1818. Jenna Ben-Yehuda, President.*

General email, info@Trumancnp.org

Web, http://trumancenter.org, Twitter, @TrumanCenter, Facebook, www.facebook.com/trumancenter and YouTube, www.youtube.com/TrumanProjectTrumanCenter

Public policy research and educational organization that serves as a forum for development of national policy alternatives. Leads discussion and advances policies aimed at promoting U.S. global engagement and leadership in the twenty-first century. Focus on issues such as cybersecurity and defense energy. (Partner of the Truman National Security Project.)

Truman National Security Project, *1250 Eye St. N.W., #500, 20005; (202) 216-9723. Fax, (202) 682-1818. Jenna Ben-Yehuda, President.*
General email, info@trumanproject.org

Web, http://trumanproject.org and Twitter, @TrumanProject

Membership: veterans and policy and political leaders. Forum for development of national policy alternatives. Promotes national security policy coordination, strengthening the U.S. military and intelligence, foreign affairs and diplomacy, democracy, and open trade. (Partner of the Truman Center for National Policy.)

U.S. Global Leadership Coalition (USGLC), *1120 20th St. N.W., #300, 20036; (202) 689-8911. Liz Schrayer, President.*
General email, info@usglc.org

Web, www.usglc.org, Twitter, @UGLC, Facebook, www.facebook.com/usglc and YouTube, www.youtube.com/usglc

Advocates strengthening the International Affairs Budget. Seeks to combat global terrorism, diseases, and poverty. Interests include emerging world markets, developing countries, and humanitarian aid. Holds summits and publishes annual reports on global policy issues and proposals.

Women's Foreign Policy Group, *1801 F St. N.W., 3rd Floor, 20006; (202) 429-2692. Patricia Ellis, President Emeritus; Shaz Akram, Executive Director.*
General email, programs@wfpg.org

Web, www.wfpg.org, Twitter, @wfpg, Facebook, www.facebook.com/WomenForeignPolicyGroup/ and YouTube, www.youtube.com/channel/UCV2Q25TkC4QDHk87mxJjnFw

Promotes women's leadership and women's interests in international affairs professions. Conducts policy programs, mentoring, and research.

World Affairs Councils of America, *1010 Vermont Ave. N.W., #516, 20005; (202) 833-4557. Fax, (202) 833-4555. Bill Clifford, President.*
General email, waca@worldaffairscouncils.org

Web, www.worldaffairscouncils.org, Twitter, @WACAmerica and Facebook, www.facebook.com/WACAmerica

Nonpartisan network that supports and represents local councils dedicated to educating the public on international issues at a grassroots level. Holds a national annual conference for member councils of each state. Coordinates expert speaker arrangements for small communities and provides fellowships for international business leaders. Supports programs that educate high school students on global affairs.

Diplomats and Foreign Agents

▶AGENCIES

Bureau of Diplomatic Security (DS) *(State Dept.), 2201 C St. N.W., #6316, 20520; (202) 647-1479. Fax, (571) 345-2527. Gentry Smith, Assistant Secretary, (202) 647-6290. General email, DSPAStaff@state.gov*

Web, www.state.gov/m/ds, Twitter, @StateDeptDSS and Facebook, www.facebook.com/StateDeptDSS

Federal law enforcement and security arm of U.S. State Department. Provides a secure environment for conducting U.S. diplomacy abroad and in the United States.

Bureau of Diplomatic Security (DS) *(State Dept.), Countermeasures Directorate, 1801 N. Lynn St., #23J04, Rosslyn, VA 22209; (571) 345-3834. (202) 647-4000. Ronald W. Stuart, Deputy Assistant Secretary.*

Web, www.state.gov/bureaus-offices/under-secretary-for-management/bureau-of-diplomatic-security

Manages the development and implementation of all physical and technical countermeasure security standards and policies that apply to State Dept. facilities domestically and overseas; securely transports classified diplomatic materials across international borders; provides defensive equipment to protect the lives of U.S. government personnel, classified information, and property.

Bureau of Diplomatic Security (DS) *(State Dept.), Diplomatic Security Service (DSS), 1801 N. Lynn St., 23rd Floor, Rosslyn, VA 22209; (571) 345-3816. Fax, (202) 647-0122. Carlos F. Matus, Director. Diplomatic Service Command Center, (571) 345-3146. Public Affairs, (571) 345-2502.*

Web, www.state.gov/bureaus-offices/under-secretary-for-management/bureau-of-diplomatic-security

Oversees the day-to-day law enforcement and security operations within the bureau. Responsible for the safety and security of U.S. diplomats, property and information at U.S. embassies and consulates worldwide; conducts and oversees visa fraud investigations, threat analysis, cybersecurity, antiterrorism training, and security technology for the State Dept. Provides protection for the secretary of state and foreign dignitaries who are visiting the United States.

Foreign Service Institute *(State Dept.), 4000 Arlington Blvd., F-2101, SA-42, Arlington, VA 22204-1500 (mailing address: U.S. Dept. of State, Washington, DC 20522-4201); (703) 302-6708. Fax, (703) 302-7227. Joan A. Polaschik, Director (Acting), (703) 302-6703. Student messages and course information, (703) 302-7144. General email, FSIPublicAffairs@state.gov*

Web, www.state.gov/bureaus-offices/under-secretary-for-management/foreign-service-institute and Twitter, @FSIatState

Provides training for U.S. government personnel involved in foreign affairs agencies, including employees of the State Dept., USAID, and the Defense Dept. Includes the Schools of Applied Information Technology, Language Studies, Leadership and Management, and Professional and Area Studies as well as the Transition Center and the Assn. for Diplomatic Studies and Training.

National Security Division *(Justice Dept.), Foreign Agents Registration Unit (FARA), Constitution Square Bldg. 3, 175 N St. N.E., #1.204, 20002; (202) 233-0777. Fax, (202) 233-2147. Matthew Olsen, Assistant Attorney General for National Security. General email, fara.public@usdoj.gov*

Web, www.justice.gov/nsd-fara

Receives and maintains the registration of agents representing foreign countries, companies, organizations, and individuals. Compiles semiannual report on foreign agent registrations. Foreign agent registration files are open for public inspection.

State Dept., Bureau of Administration, Overseas Schools, *2401 E St. N.W., #H328, SA-1, 20522-0103; (202) 261-8200. Fax, (202) 261-8224. Mark E. Ulfers, Director, (202) 261-8201. General email, OverseasSchools@state.gov*

Web, www.state.gov/bureaus-offices/under-secretary-for-management/bureau-of-administration/office-of-overseas-schools

Promotes high-quality educational opportunities at the elementary and secondary school levels for dependents of American citizens carrying out the programs and interests of the U.S. government abroad.

State Dept., Bureau of Global Talent Management, Global Community Liaison, *2201 C St. N.W., HST #2133, 20520-0108; (202) 647-1076. Fax, (202) 647-1670. Gabrielle Hampson, Director, (202) 647-1784. Toll-free, (800) 440-0397. General email, GCLO@state.gov*

Web, www.state.gov/bureaus-offices/under-secretary-for-management/bureau-of-global-talent-management/global-community-liason-office

Works to improve the quality of life of U.S. government employees and their family members assigned to, or returning from, a U.S. embassy or consulate abroad. Areas of interest are education and youth, family member employment, and support services for personal and past crises, including evacuations. Manages the worldwide Community Liaison Office Program.

State Dept., Chief of Protocol, *2201 C St. N.W., #1238, 20520; (202) 647-2663. Fax, (202) 647-3980. Amb. Rufus Gifford, Chief of Protocol. General email, ProtocolHelp@state.gov*

Web, www.state.gov/bureaus-offices/secretary-of-state/office-of-the-chief-of-protocol and Twitter, @US_Protocol

Serves as principal adviser to the president, vice president, secretary, and other high-ranking government officials on matters of diplomatic procedure governed by law or international customs and practice.

State Dept., *Foreign Missions, 2201 C St. N.W., #2236, 20520; (202) 647-3417. Fax, (202) 736-4145. Cliff Seagroves, Director (Acting).*
General email, ofm-info@state.gov
Web, www.state.gov/ofm and Facebook, www.facebook .com/ofmdc/?notif_t=page_fan

Regulates the benefits, privileges, and immunities granted to foreign missions and their personnel in the United States on the basis of the treatment accorded U.S. missions abroad and considerations of national security and public safety.

►CONGRESS

For a listing of relevant congressional committees and subcommittees, please see pages 478–479 or the Appendix.

►NONGOVERNMENTAL

American Foreign Service Assn. (AFSA), *2101 E St. N.W., 20037; (202) 338-4045. Fax, (202) 338-6820. Eric Rubin, President. Press, (202) 944-5508.*
General email, member@afsa.org
Web, www.afsa.org, Twitter, @afsatweets and Facebook, www.facebook.com/afsapage

Membership: active-duty and retired U.S. foreign service employees at Department of State, U.S. Agency for International Development, Foreign Commercial Service, Foreign Agricultural Service, Animal and Plant Health Inspection Service, and U.S. Agency for Global Media. Offers scholarship programs; maintains club for members; represents active duty foreign service personnel in labor-management negotiations. Seeks to ensure adequate resources for foreign service operations and personnel. Conducts outreach programs to educate the public on diplomacy. Interests include business-government collaboration and international trade. Monitors legislation and regulations related to foreign service personnel and retirees.

Council of American Ambassadors, *888 17th St. N.W., #306, 20006-3312; (202) 296-3757. Fax, (202) 296-0926. Timothy A. Chorba, President; Kathleen Sheehan, Executive Director.*
General email, council@americanambassadors.org
Web, https://americanambassadors.org, Twitter, @AmerAmbassadors and Facebook, www.facebook.com/ AmericanAmbassadors

Membership: noncareer U.S. ambassadors. Seeks to educate the public on foreign policy issues affecting the national interest. Hosts discussions, lectures, and conferences. Offers fellowships for students and foreign service personnel.

Executive Council on Diplomacy, *655 15th St. N.W., #570, 20005; (202) 466-5199. Melissa A. San Miguel, Executive Director.*
General email, ecd@ibgc.com
Web, www.diplomacycouncil.org

Brings foreign diplomats from international organizations such as the United Nations and World Bank into

contact with their U.S. counterparts. Provides a forum for discussion on issues such as agriculture, international trade, education, and the arts.

Institute for the Study of Diplomacy *(Georgetown University), 1316 36th St. N.W., 20007; (202) 687-0120. Fax, (202) 965-5811. Amb. Barbara K. Bodine, Director. Toll-free, (877) 703-4660.*
General email, diplomacy@georgetown.edu
Web, http://isd.georgetown.edu, Twitter, @GUDiplomacy and Facebook, www.facebook.com/GUdiplomacy

Part of the Edmund A. Walsh School of Foreign Service. Focuses on the practical implementation of foreign policy objectives; draws on academic research and the concrete experience of diplomats and other members of the policy community.

Humanitarian Aid

►AGENCIES

Administration for Children and Families (ACF) *(Health and Human Services Dept.), Refugee Resettlement (ORR), Mary E. Switzer Bldg., 330 C St. S.W., Room 5123, 20201; (202) 401-9246. Fax, (202) 401-4678. Cindy Huang, Director. Parent Hotline, (800) 203-7001.*
Web, https://acf.hhs.gov/orr

Directs a domestic resettlement program for refugees; reimburses states for costs incurred in giving refugees monetary and medical assistance; awards funds to voluntary resettlement agencies for providing refugees with monetary assistance and case management.

Agency for International Development (USAID), *Bureau for Conflict Prevention and Stabilization (CPS), Office of Transition Initiatives (OTI), 1300 Pennsylvania Ave. N.W., #B3.06-124, 20523-8602; (202) 712-0284. Brittany Brown, Director, (202) 712-1409. Public Affairs, (202) 712-4320.*
General email, DCHA.OTIOutreachMailList@usaid.gov
Web, www.usaid.gov/who-we-are/organization/bureaus/ bureau-conflict-prevention-and-stabilization/office-transition-initiatives, Twitter, @USAIDOTI and Facebook, www.facebook.com/USAIDOTI

Provides efficient short-term assistance to countries in crisis in order to stabilize their governments.

Bureau of Population, Refugees, and Migration (PRM) *(State Dept.), 2201 C St. N.W., #HST 7817, 20520-5824; (202) 647-7360. Fax, (202) 647-8162. Nancy Izzo Jackson, Senior Bureau Official.*
Web, www.state.gov/bureaus-offices/under-secretary-for-civilian-security-democracy-and-human-rights/bureau-of-population-refugees-and-migration, Twitter, @StatePRM, Facebook, www.facebook.com/State.PRM and Press, PRMPress@state.gov

Develops and implements policies and programs on matters relating to international refugees, internally displaced persons, and victims of conflict, including repatriation and resettlement programs; funds and monitors overseas relief, assistance, and repatriation programs; manages refugee admission to the United States.

Health and Human Services Dept. (HHS), *Global Affairs (OGA), 200 Independence Ave. S.W., #639H, 20201; (202) 690-6174. (202) 260-0399. Fax, (202) 690-7127. Loyce Pace, Assistant Secretary.*
General email, globalhealth@hhs.gov
Web, www.hhs.gov/about/agencies/oga/index.html, Twitter, @HHS_Global and Twitter, @HHS_ASGA

Represents the Health and Human Services Dept. before other governments, U.S. government agencies, international organizations, and the private sector on international and refugee health issues. Promotes international cooperation; provides health-related humanitarian and developmental assistance. Serves as the primary liaison to the World Health Organization.

State Dept., *U.S. Foreign Assistance, 2201 C St. N.W., #5923, 20520; (202) 647-2608. Fax, (202) 647-2529. Dafna Rand, Director.*
Web, www.state.gov/bureaus-offices/secretary-of-state/office-of-foreign-assistance

Works to ensure the strategic and effective allocation, management, and use of foreign assistance resources.

State Dept., *U.S. Global AIDS Coordinator and Global Health Diplomacy, 1800 G St. N.W., SA-22, #10300, 20037; (202) 663-2579. Fax, (202) 663-2979. Angeli L. Achrekar, Coordinator and Special Representative, (202) 663-2802.*
General email, SGACPublicAffairs@state.gov
Web, www.state.gov/pepfar, Twitter, @PEPFAR, Facebook, www.facebook.com/PEPFAR and YouTube, www.youtube.com/user/USPEPFAR

Oversees and coordinates all U.S. international HIV/AIDS activities, including implementation of the President's Emergency Plan for AIDS Relief.

►CONGRESS

For a listing of relevant congressional committees and subcommittees, please see pages 478–479 or the Appendix.

►INTERNATIONAL ORGANIZATIONS

The Global Fund for Children, *1411 K St. N.W., #1200, 20005; (202) 331-9003. John Hecklinger, Chief Executive Officer.*
General email, info@globalfundforchildren.org
Web, www.globalfundforchildren.org, Twitter, @Global4Children and Facebook, www.facebook.com/GlobalFundforChildren

Funds grassroots organizations that help impoverished, abused, and refugee children in foreign countries. Assists in management, planning, and networking between other organizations. Holds workshops for grantees to share knowledge, experience, and practices aimed at helping vulnerable children.

International Assn. for Human Values, *Washington Office, 2401 15th St. N.W., 20009; (202) 250-3405. Fax, (202) 747-6543. Filiz Odabas-Geldiay, Executive Director.*
General email, info@iahv.org
Web, https://us.iahv.org and Facebook, www.facebook.com/iahv

Humanitarian organization offering programs to promote nonviolence and service projects. Interests include youth empowerment, leadership, disaster relief and rehabilitation, sustainable rural and community development, women's empowerment, veterans' trauma relief, and prisoner reform programs.

International Committee of the Red Cross (ICRC), *Washington Office, 1100 Connecticut Ave. N.W., #500, 20036; (202) 587-4600. Hamilton Patrick, Head of Delegation; Alexandra Boivin, Head of U.S. Delegation. Press, (202) 361-1566.*
General email, washington.was@icrc.org
Web, www.icrc.org

Serves as the ICRC's main point of contact with U.S. authorities on issues concerning operations and international humanitarian law in over 90 countries. Supports efforts internationally to help people affected by armed conflict. (Headquarters in Geneva, Switzerland.)

International Organization for Migration (IOM), *Washington Office, 1752 N St. N.W., #600, 20036; (202) 862-1826. Fax, (202) 862-1879. Luca Dall'Oglio, Chief of Mission, ext. 229; António Vitorino, Director General.*
General email, iomwashington@iom.int
Web, www.iom.int/countries/united-states-america and Twitter, @UNmigration

Nonpartisan organization that plans and operates resource mobilization functions (RMF), including refugee resettlement, national migration, and humanitarian assistance to displaced populations at the request of its member governments. Advises governments on migration policies, supports victims of human trafficking, assists returning migrants, and raises awareness about the benefits of migration. Recruits skilled professionals for developing countries. (Headquarters in Geneva, Switzerland.)

Jesuit Refugee Service / USA, *1627 K St. N.W., #1100, 20006; (202) 462-5200. Fax, (202) 328-9212. Joan Rosenhauer, Executive Director.*
General email, jrsusa@jesuit.org
Web, www.jrsusa.org and Twitter, @jrsusa

U.S. Jesuit organization that aids refugees and other forcibly displaced persons worldwide, through accompaniment, advocacy, and service. Mobilizes the U.S. Jesuit response to forced displacement; provides advocacy and funding support to programs throughout the world. Monitors refugee and immigration legislation. (International headquarters in Rome.)

U.S. Fund for the United Nations Children's Fund (UNICEF), *Public Policy and Advocacy, 1775 K St. N.W.,*

International Disaster Relief Organizations

Action Against Hunger, (212) 967-7800; www.actionagainsthunger.org

American Jewish Joint Distribution Committee, (212) 687-6200; www.jdc.org

American Red Cross, (800) 733-2767 or (202) 303-5214; www.redcross.org/about-us/our-work/disaster-relief.html

AmeriCares, (203) 658-9500; www.americares.org

CARE, (202) 595-2800; www.care.org

Catholic Relief Services, Donor Services Line (888) 277-7575 or (877) 435-7277; www.crs.org

Child Fund International, (800) 776-6767; www.childfund.org

Church World Service, (800) 297-1516; www.cwsglobal.org

Direct Relief International, (805) 964-4767 or (800) 676-1638; www.directrelief.org

Episcopal Relief and Development, (855) 312-4325; www.episcopalrelief.org

Health Right International, (212) 226-9890; www.healthright.org

InterAction, www.interaction.org

International Federation of Red Cross and Red Crescent Societies (UN), (212) 338-0161; www.ifrc.org

International Medical Corps, (202) 828-5155; (424) 252-6008; www.internationalmedicalcorps.org

International Rescue Committee, (212) 551-3000; www.rescue.org

Islamic Relief USA, (855) 447-1001; www.irusa.org

Lutheran World Relief, (800) 597-5972; www.lwr.org

Mercy Corps, (202) 463 7383;(800) 292-3355; www.mercycorps.org

Operation USA, (323) 413-2353; www.opusa.org

Oxfam America, (800) 776-9326; www.oxfamamerica.org

Pan American Health Organization, (202) 974-3000; www.paho.org/disasters

Save the Children, (800) 728-3843 or (203) 221-4000 or (202) 794-1500; www.savethechildren.org

UNICEF, (202) 296-4242 or (800) 367-5437; www.unicefusa.org

World Food Programme (UN), (202) 627-3737; www.wfp.org

World Vision, (888) 511-6548; www.worldvision.org

#360, 20006; (202) 296-4242. Mark Engman, Vice President for Policy and Advocacy, (202) 802-9102. Toll-free, (800) 367-5437.
General email, washington@unicefusa.org
Web, www.unicefusa.org/mission/help/advocate and Twitter, @UNICEFUSA

Serves as the information reference service on UNICEF; advocates policies to advance the well-being of the world's children. Interests include international humanitarian assistance, U.S. volunteerism, child survival, and international health. (Headquarters in New York.)

United Nations High Commissioner for Refugees (UNHCR), Washington Office, 1800 Massachusetts Ave. N.W., #500, 20036; (202) 296-5191. Fax, (202) 296-5660. Matthew Reynolds, USA Regional Representative; Flippo Grandi, High Commissioner.
General email, usawa@unhcr.org
Web, www.unhcr.org, Twitter, @UNHCRUSA and Facebook, www.facebook.com/UNHCR

Works with governments and voluntary organizations to protect and assist refugees worldwide. Promotes long-term alternatives to refugee camps, including voluntary repatriation, local integration, and resettlement overseas. (Headquarters in Geneva, Switzerland.)

▶ **NONGOVERNMENTAL**

American Red Cross, National Headquarters, 431 18th St. N.W., 20006; (202) 303-5000. Gail J. McGovern, President. Headquarters staff directory, (202) 303-5214,

ext. 1. Press, (202) 303-5551. Public inquiries, (202) 303-4498. Toll-free, (800) 733-2767.
Web, www.redcross.org and Twitter, @RedCross

Humanitarian organization chartered by Congress to provide domestic and international disaster relief and to act as a medium of communication between the U.S. armed forces and their families in time of war and personnel emergencies. Provides shelter, food, emotional support, supplies, funds, and technical assistance for relief in domestic and major international disasters through the International Federation of Red Cross and Red Crescent Societies.

Center for Civilians in Conflict, 1828 L St. N.W., #1050, 20036; (202) 558-6958. Federico Borello, Executive Director.
General email, comms@civiliansinconflict.org
Web, https://civiliansinconflict.org, Twitter, @CivCenter and Facebook, www.facebook.com/CiviliansInConflict

Acts as advocate to national governments and militaries for recognition, compensation, and other assistance to civilians they have harmed in armed conflicts.

Christian Relief Services, 8301 Richmond Hwy., #900, Alexandria, VA 22309; (703) 317-9086. Paul Krizek, Executive Director. Toll-free, 800-33-RELIEF. TTY, (800) 828-1140.
General email, info@christianrelief.org
Web, www.christianrelief.org/, Twitter, @CRSvcs and Facebook, www.facebook.com/ChristianReliefServices/

Promotes economic development and the alleviation of poverty in urban areas of the United States, Appalachia, Native American reservations, Haiti, Mexico, Honduras, Lithuania, the Czech Republic, and Africa. Donates medical supplies and food; administers housing, hospital, and school construction programs; provides affordable housing for low-income individuals and families.

Evangelical Lutheran Church in America, *Advocacy,* 218 D St. S.E., 20003; Rev. Amy Reumann, Senior Director. Toll-free, (800) 638-3522.
General email, washingtonoffice@elca.org
Web, www.elca.org/advocacy and Twitter,
@ELCAadvocacy

Membership: Lutheran Immigration and Refugee Service responds to people caught in conflict and facing persecution, acts as advocate for their needs and interests, helps people access resources for basic human needs, works with foster care programs for minors, offers legal assistance, and develops new and innovative service programs and partnerships. (Headquarters in Chicago, Ill.)

Health Volunteers Overseas, 1900 L St. N.W., #310, 20036; (202) 296-0928. Fax, (202) 296-8018. Nancy A. Kelly, Executive Director.
General email, info@hvousa.org
Web, www.hvousa.org, Twittter, @HVOUSA and Facebook, www.facebook.com/hvousa

Operates training programs in developing countries for health professionals who wish to teach low-cost health care delivery practices.

International Rescue Committee, *Public Policy and Advocacy,* 1730 M St. N.W., #505, 20036; (202) 822-0166. Fax, (202) 822-0089. David Miliband, President. Central office (NYC), (212) 551-3000. Press, (646) 761-0307.
General email, advocacy@theIRC.org
Web, www.rescue.org, Twitter, @RESCUEorg, Facebook, www.facebook.com/InternationalRescueCommittee and YouTube, www.youtube.com/RESCUEorg

Provides worldwide emergency aid, protection, resettlement services, educational support, and advocacy for refugees, displaced persons, and victims of oppression and violent conflict; recruits volunteers. (Headquarters in New York.)

National Council of Churches, 110 Maryland Ave. N.E., #108, 20002-5603; (202) 544-2350. Leslie Copeland Tune, Corporate Operations Officer.
General email, info@nationalcouncilofchurches.us
Web, www.nationalcouncilofchurches.us, Twitter, @ncccusa, Facebook, www.facebook.com/nationalcouncil ofchurches and YouTube, www.youtube.com/channel/ UCNdghdVdQi85VP5zV7FM46Q

Works to foster cooperation among Christian congregations across the nation in programs concerning poverty, racism, family, environment, and international humanitarian objectives.

Oxfam America, *Policy and Campaigns,* 1101 17th St. N.W., #1300, 20036-4710; (202) 496-1180. Fax, (202) 496-1190. Abby Maxman, President, ext. 2506; Gina Crista Cummings, Vice President of Advocacy, Alliances and Policy. Press, (202) 496-1169. Toll-free, (800) 776-9326.

General email, info@oxfamamerica.org
Web, www.oxfamamerica.org and Twitter,
@OxfamAmerica

Funds disaster relief and long-term development programs internationally. Organizes grassroots support in the United States for issues affecting global poverty, including climate change, aid reform, and corporate transparency. (Headquarters in Boston, Mass.)

Program for Appropriate Technology in Health (PATH), *Washington Office,* 455 Massachusetts Ave. N.W., #1000, 20001; (202) 822-0033. Fax, (202) 457-1466. Nikolaj Gilbert, President.
General email, info@path.org
Web, www.path.org

Develops, tests, and implements health technologies and strategies for low-resource countries. Works with community groups, other nongovernmental organizations, governments, companies, and UN agencies to expand the most successful programs. Interests include reproductive health, immunization, maternal-child health, emerging and epidemic diseases, and nutrition. (Headquarters in Seattle, Wash.)

Refugees International, 1800 M St. N.W., #405N, 20036 (mailing address: P.O. Box 33036, Washington, DC 20033); (202) 828-0110. Fax, (202) 828-0819. Eric Schwartz, President. Press, (202) 540-7026. Toll-free, (800) 733-8433.
General email, ri@refugeesinternational.org
Web, www.refugeesinternational.org, Twitter, @RefugeesIntl and Facebook, www.facebook.com/ RefugeesInternational

Advocates assistance and protection for displaced people worldwide. Conducts field studies to identify basic needs and makes recommendations to policymakers and aid agencies.

Salvation Army Disaster Service, 615 Slaters Lane, Alexandria, VA 22314; (703) 684-5500. Kenneth G. Hodder, National Commander.
Web, https://disaster.salvationarmyusa.org, Twitter, @salarmyeds and Facebook, www.facebook.com/ SalArmyEDS

Provides U.S. and international disaster victims and rescuers with emergency support, including food, clothing, and counseling services.

U.S. Committee for Refugees and Immigrants, 2231 Crystal Dr., #350, Arlington, VA 22202-3794; (703) 310-1130. Eskinder Negash, Chief Executive Officer.
General email, uscri@uscridc.org
Web, www.refugees.org, Facebook, www.facebook.com/ USCRI and Twitter, @uscridc

Defends rights of refugees in the United States and abroad. Helps immigrants and refugees adjust to American society; assists in resettling recently arrived immigrants and refugees; offers information, counseling services, and temporary living accommodations through its member agencies nationwide; issues publications on refugees and refugee resettlement; collects and disseminates information on refugee issues. Monitors legislation and regulations.

U.S. Conference of Catholic Bishops (USCCB), *Migration and Refugee Services,* 3211 4th St. N.E., 20017-1194; (202) 541-3169. Bill Canny, Executive Director, (202) 541-3169; Rachel Pollock, Director of Resettlement Services, (202) 541-3345.
General email, mrs@usccb.org

Web, www.usccb.org/mrs and Twitter, @mrsserves

Acts as advocate for immigrants, refugees, migrants, and victims of human trafficking. Works with legislative and executive branches of the U.S. government and with national and international organizations such as the UN High Commissioner for Refugees to promote fair and responsive immigration and refugee policy.

Women for Women International, 2000 M St. N.W., #200, 20036; (202) 737-7705. Fax, (202) 737-7709. Laurie Adams, Chief Executive Officer.
General email, general@womenforwomen.org

Web, www.womenforwomen.org, Twitter, @WomenforWomen, Facebook, www.facebook.com/ womenforwomen and YouTube, www.youtube.com/user/ WomenforWomenIntl

Helps women in war-torn regions rebuild their lives through financial and emotional support, job skills training, rights education, access to capital, and assistance for small-business development.

World Vision, *Advocacy,* 300 Eye St. N.E., 20002; (202) 635-7600. Margaret Schuler, Senior Vice President of International Programs. Press, (202) 679-1620. Toll-free, (888) 511-6548.
General email, mworsley@worldvision.org

Web, www.worldvision.org and Twitter, @WorldVisionUSA

Christian humanitarian and development organization that works with children, their families, and their communities worldwide. Interests include social injustice and the causes of poverty. Provides emergency disaster relief and long-term development programs domestically and abroad. (Headquarters in Seattle, Wash.)

Information and Exchange Programs

▶AGENCIES

Bureau of Educational and Cultural Affairs (ECA) *(State Dept.),* 2200 C St. N.W., #5BB17/SA-5, 20522-0500; (202) 632-6459. Fax, (202) 632-6116. Lee A. Satterfield, Assistant Secretary, (202) 647-5763. Press, (202) 632-6445.
General email, eca-press@state.gov

Web, www.eca.state.gov, Twitter, @ECAatState, Facebook, www.facebook.com/ExchangeProgramsAtState and YouTube, www.youtube.com/user/exchangesvideo

Seeks to promote mutual understanding between the people of the United States and other countries through international educational and training programs. Promotes personal, professional, and institutional ties between private citizens and organizations in the United States and abroad; presents U.S. history, society, art, and culture to overseas audiences.

Bureau of Educational and Cultural Affairs (ECA) *(State Dept.), Academic Programs,* 2200 C St. N.W., #4B06, SA5, 20520; (202) 632-3234. Ethan Rosenzweig, Deputy Assistant Secretary; Mary Kirk, Director. Fulbright Program, (202) 632-3238.
General email, DeputyAssistantSecforAcademic@state.gov

Fulbright email, fulbright@state.gov and Web, http://eca .state.gov/programs-and-initiatives

Provides opportunities for international study and research from the undergraduate through postdoctoral and professional levels. Works with the Fulbright Program, Global Undergraduate Exchange Program, Edmund S. Muskie Graduate Fellowship Program, and Study of the United States Institutes.

Bureau of Educational and Cultural Affairs (ECA) *(State Dept.), Citizen Exchanges,* 2200 C St. N.W., #3B16 SA-5, 20520; (202) 615-3712. Robert Ogburn, Director.
General email, professionalexchange@state.gov

Web, https://eca.state.gov/about-bureau/organizational-structure/office-citizen-exchanges

Provides professional, youth, cultural, and sports exchange opportunities for U.S. and foreign participants.

Bureau of Educational and Cultural Affairs (ECA) *(State Dept.), English Language Programs,* 2200 C St. N.W., #4B16, 20520; (202) 632-9272. Joseph Bookbinder, Director, (202) 632-9281.
General email, americanenglish@state.gov

Web, http://eca.state.gov/about-bureau/organizational-structure/office-english-language-programs, https:// americanenglish.state.gov and YouTube, www.youtube .com/user/StateAmericanEnglish

Promotes the learning and teaching of American English around the world in order to foster mutual understanding between the people of other countries and the people of the United States.

Bureau of Educational and Cultural Affairs (ECA) *(State Dept.), Global Educational Programs,* 2200 C St. N.W., #4CC17 SA-5, 20520; (202) 632-6345. Anthony D. Koliha, Director.
Web, http://eca.state.gov/about-bureau/organizational-structure/office-global-educational-programs

Monitors the flow of international students to the United States and of U.S. students to other countries. Administers the Hubert H. Humphrey Fellowship Program, the Community College Initiative Program, and the Benjamin A. Gilman International Scholarship Program.

Bureau of Educational and Cultural Affairs (ECA) *(State Dept.), International Visitors,* 2200 C St. N.W., #3B06 SA-5, 20520; (202) 632-6383. Anne Grimes, Director.

General email, eca-press@state.gov

Web, http://eca.state.gov/about-bureau/organizational-structure/office-international-visitors, Twitter, @StateIVLP and Facebook, www.facebook.com/StateIVLP

Seeks to build mutual understanding between the United States and other nations through short-term visits to the United States for current and emerging foreign leaders.

Bureau of Educational and Cultural Affairs (ECA) *(State Dept.), Policy and Evaluation, 2200 C St. N.W., #5E02, 20520; (202) 632-2742. Nini Forino, Deputy Secretary for Policy (Acting), (202) 632-6311; Natalie Donahue, Division Chief, Office of Monitoring, Evaluation, Learning and Innovation (MELT), (202) 632-6193.*

General email, ecaevaluation@state.gov

Web, https://eca.state.gov/about-bureau/organizational-structure/office-policy-and-evaluation

Evaluates Bureau programs and measures performance to ensure quality and consistency. Houses the Cultural Heritage Center.

Bureau of Educational and Cultural Affairs (ECA) *(State Dept.), Private Sector Exchange, 2200 C St. N.W., #05CC14, 20520; (202) 632-9386. (202) 632-2805. Fax, (202) 632-2701. G. Kevin Saba, Deputy Assistant Secretary (Acting), (202) 632-6193.*

General email, jvisas@state.gov

Web, http://eca.state.gov/about-bureau/organizational-structure/office-private-sector-exchange

Administers the Exchange Visitor Program to allow nonimmigrants to participate in work-based and study-based exchange programs in the United States.

Bureau of Global Public Affairs (GPA) *(State Dept.), 2201 C St. N.W., #6634, SA-5, 20520; (202) 632-2848. Elizabeth Allen, Assistant Secretary, (202) 647-6088.*

Web, www.state.gov/bureaus-offices/under-secretary-for-public-diplomacy-and-public-affairs/bureau-of-global-public-affairs, Twitter, @GPS_AS, Facebook, www.facebook.com/usdos and YouTube, www.youtube.com/user/StateVideo

Implements strategic communications programs—including Internet and print publications, traveling and electronically transmitted speaker programs, and information resource services—that reach key international audiences and support department initiatives. Explains U.S. foreign policy. Develops governmentwide technology policies that help disseminate this information.

National Institute of Standards and Technology (NIST) *(Commerce Dept.), International and Academic Affairs, 100 Bureau Dr., MS 1090, Gaithersburg, MD 20899-1090; (301) 975-3069. Fax, (301) 975-3530. Claire M. Saundry, Director, (301) 975-2386. TTY, (301) 975-8295.*

General email, oiaa@nist.gov

Web, www.nist.gov/iaao

Represents the institute in international functions involving science and technology; coordinates programs with foreign institutions; assists scientists from foreign countries who visit the institute for consultation. Administers a postdoctoral research associates program and oversees NIST's cooperation with academic institutions and researchers.

U.S. Agency for Global Media, *330 Independence Ave. S.W., #3300, 20237; (202) 203-4000. Kelu Chao, Chief Executive Officer (Acting); Daniel Rosenholtz, FOIA Officer, (202) 920-2342.*

General email, publicaffairs@usagm.gov

Web, www.usagm.gov, Twitter, @USAGMgov and Facebook, www.facebook.com/USAGMgov/

Established by Congress to supervise all U.S. government nonmilitary international broadcasting, including Voice of America, Radio and TV Martí, Radio Free Europe/Radio Liberty, Radio Free Asia, and the Middle East Broadcasting Networks (MBN). Assesses the quality and effectiveness of broadcasts with regard to U.S. foreign policy objectives; reports annually to the president and to Congress.

Voice of America *(International Broadcasting Bureau), 330 Independence Ave. S.W., 20237; (202) 203-4000. Fax, (202) 203-4960. Yolanda Lopez, Director (Acting).*

General email, askvoa@voanews.com

Web, www.voanews.com, Twitter, @VOAnews and Facebook, www.facebook.com/voiceofamerica

A multimedia international broadcasting service funded by the U.S. government through the Broadcasting Board of Governors. Broadcasts news, information, and educational and cultural programming to an estimated worldwide audience of more than 134 million people weekly. Programs are produced in more than forty languages.

▶ **NONGOVERNMENTAL**

Alliance for International Exchange, *1828 L St. N.W., #1150, 20036; (202) 293-6141. Fax, (202) 293-6144. Ilir Zherka, Executive Director.*

General email, info@alliance-exchange.org

Web, www.alliance-exchange.org, Twitter, @AllianceExchnge and Facebook, www.facebook.com/AllianceIntlExchange

Membership: U.S. organizations and companies comprising the educational and cultural exchange community. Promotes public policies that support the growth of international exchange between the United States and other countries. Provides professional representation, resource materials, publications, and public policy research for those involved in international exchanges.

American Bar Assn. (ABA), *International Legal Exchange Program (ILEX), 1050 Connecticut Ave. N.W., #400, 20036; (202) 662-1660. Fax, (202) 662-1669. Jinny Choi, Associate Director, (202) 662-1675.*

General email, intilex@americanbar.org

Web, www.americanbar.org/groups/international_law/international-projects/international-legal-exchange/

Facilitates entry into the United States for foreign lawyers offered training in U.S. law firms. Serves as designated U.S. government overseer for the J-1 visa and accepts applications from foreign lawyers. Houses the International Legal Resource Center.

American Council of Young Political Leaders, *1030 15th St. N.W., #580 West, 20005; (202) 857-0999. Libby Rosenbaum, Chief Executive Officer, (202) 448-9331. Web, www.acypl.org, Twitter, @ACYPL and Facebook, www.facebook.com/ACYPL*

Bipartisan political education organization that promotes understanding among young elected leaders and political professionals around the world. Designs and manages international educational exchanges.

American Councils for International Education: ACTR/ ACCELS, *1828 L St. N.W., #1200, 20036; (202) 833-7522. David P. Patton, President, ext. 137. General email, info@americancouncils.org*

Web, www.americancouncils.org, Twitter, @AC_Global and Facebook, www.facebook.com/AmericanCouncils

Conducts educational exchanges for high school, university, and graduate school students as well as scholars with the countries of Africa, Europe, Eurasia, South and Central Asia, East Asia and the Pacific, and the Middle East.

Atlas Corps, *99 M St. S.E., 4th Floor, 20003; (202) 391-0694. Bidjan Nashat, Chief Executive Officer. General email, info@atlascorps.org*

Web, www.atlascorps.org, Twitter, @atlascorps, Facebook, www.facebook.com/atlascorps and Twitter CEO, @bnashat

Provides U.S. fellowships to international leaders in public service and leaders of social issues in order to globally promote innovation in the nonprofit sector. Provides training programs and a global alumni community.

Business–Higher Education Forum, *1 Dupont Circle, #360, 20036; (202) 853-9052. Janet Chen, Director. General email, info@bhef.com*

Web, www.bhef.com, Twitter, @BHEF and Press, ursula .gross@bhef.org

Membership: chief executive officers of major corporations, museums, colleges, and universities. Promotes the development of industry–university alliances around the world. Provides countries in central and eastern Europe with technical assistance in enterprise development, management training, market economics, education, and infrastructure development.

Center for Intercultural Education and Development *(Georgetown University), 2115 Wisconsin Ave. N.W., 4th Floor, 20007 (mailing address: P.O. Box 579400, Washington, DC 20007); (202) 687-1400. Chantal Santelices, Executive Director, (202) 687-1918. General email, cied@georgetown.edu*

Web, http://cied.georgetown.edu

Designs and administers programs aimed at improving the quality of lives of economically disadvantaged people; provides technical education, job training, leadership skills

development, and business management training; runs programs in Central America, the Caribbean, Central Europe, the Middle East, and Southeast Asia.

Council for International Exchange of Scholars, *1400 K St. N.W., #700, 20005; (202) 686-4000. Fax, (202) 686-4029. Allan E. Goodman, President, (212) 984-5321. General email, scholars@iie.org*

Web, www.cies.org, Twitter, @FulbrightPrgrm and Facebook, www.facebook.com/fulbright

Cooperates with the U.S. government in administering Fulbright grants for university teaching and advanced research abroad. (A division of the Institute of International Education.)

English-Speaking Union, *Washington Office, 700 New Hampshire Ave. N.W., 20037; (202) 244-6140. Fax, (202) 333-8258. Heather B. McCabe, President. General email, washingtondc@esuus.org*

Web, www.esuus.org/washingtondc

Member organization for individuals interested in international educational and cultural exchange programs with countries in which English is a major language. Presents programs on the culture and history of the English-speaking world; sponsors annual Shakespeare competition among Washington metropolitan area schools. (National headquarters in New York.)

Global Ties U.S., *1250 H St. N.W., #305, 20005; (202) 842-1414. Katherine Brown, President. General email, info@globaltiesus.org*

Web, www.globaltiesus.org, Facebook, www.facebook.com/ GlobalTiesUS and Twitter, @globaltiesus

Members coordinate international exchange programs and bring international visitors to communities throughout the United States. Provides its members, from all 50 states and more than 20 countries, with connections, leadership development, and professional resources. (Formerly National Council for International Visitors.)

Graduate School USA, *International Institute, 600 Maryland Ave. S.W., #320, 20024-2520; (888) 744-4723. Fax, (866) 221-6761. Nina Bankova, Director. General email, intlinst@graduateschool.edu*

Web, www.graduateschool.edu, Email, CustomerRelations@graduateschool.edu, Twitter, @thegradschool and Facebook, www.facebook.com/ GraduateSchoolUSA

Offers professional development training and educational services to foreign and domestic audiences, including federally funded exchange program participants, foreign governments, international organizations, nongovernmental agencies, academia, and employees of U.S. agencies engaged in international activities. Provides tailored programs in the areas of capacity building, professional and educational exchanges, and governance.

Institute of International Education, *Washington Office, 1400 K St. N.W., #700, 20005-2403; (202) 898-0600. Fax, (202) 326-7754. Allan E. Goodman, Chief Executive*

Officer; *Edith Cecil, Senior Vice President, Program Management, Government.*

Web, www.iie.org/Why-IIE/Offices/Washington-DC and Facebook, www.facebook.com/IIEglobal

Educational exchange, scholarship, and training organization that arranges professional programs for international visitors; conducts training courses in energy, environment, journalism, human resource development, educational policy and administration, and business-related fields; provides developing countries with short-term and long-term technical assistance in human resource development; arranges professional training and support for staff of human rights organizations; sponsors fellowships and applied internships for midcareer professionals from developing countries; manages programs sending U.S. teachers, undergraduate and graduate students, and professionals abroad; implements contracts and cooperative agreements for the State Dept., the U.S. Agency for International Development, foreign governments, philanthropic foundations, multilateral banks, and other organizations. (Headquarters in New York.)

International Arts and Artists, *9 Hillyer Court N.W., 20008; (202) 338-0680. Fax, (202) 333-0758. Jeff Freedman, Chief Operating Officer.*

General email, info@artsandartists.org

Web, www.artsandartists.org, Twitter, @IAAHillyer and Facebook, www.facebook.com/artsandartists

Assists international artists and institutions in obtaining visas. Provides international internships and training programs. Offers an exchange program for artists to travel and complete international art-related internships.

International Research and Exchanges Board (IREX), *1275 K St. N.W., #600, 20005; (202) 628-8188. Fax, (202) 628-8189. Kristin M. Lord, President.*

General email, communications@irex.org

Web, www.irex.org, Twitter, @IREXintl and Facebook, www.facebook.com/irexinternational

Provides programs, grants, and consulting expertise in more than 100 countries to improve the quality of education, strengthen independent media, and foster pluralistic civil society development.

Libraries Without Borders, *Washington Office, 1342 Florida Ave. N.W., 20009; (703) 705-9321. Patrick Weil, Chair; Aaron Greenberg, Executive Director.*

General email, admin@librarieswithoutborders.org

Web, www.librarieswithoutborders.org, Twitter, @BSF_Intl and Facebook, www.facebook.com/LibrariesWithout Borders

Disseminates information globally; provides access to knowledge, education, and training; and promotes libraries and book distribution—Virtual and physical, fixed or mobile. Provides citizens in poor areas access to information with the aim of combating poverty and social inequality.

Meridian International Center, *1630 Crescent Pl. N.W., 20009; (202) 667-6800. Fax, (202) 667-1475.*

Hon. Stuart W. Holliday, Chief Executive Officer. Toll-free, (800) 424-2974.

General email, info@meridian.org

Web, www.meridian.org, Twitter, @MeridianIntl, Facebook, www.facebook.com/MeridianInternational Center and YouTube, www.youtube.com/c/Meridian Community

Conducts international educational and cultural programs; provides foreign visitors and diplomats in the United States with services, including cultural orientation, seminars, and language assistance. Offers international exhibitions for Americans.

NAFSA: Assn. of International Educators, *1425 K. St.,. N.W., #1200, 20005; (202) 737-3699. Esther D. Brimmer, Executive Director.*

General email, inbox@nafsa.org

Web, www.nafsa.org, Twitter, @NAFSA and Facebook, www.facebook.com/nafsa

Membership: individuals engaged in the field of international education and exchange at the postsecondary level. Promotes educational opportunities across national boundaries. Sets and upholds standards of good practice and provides professional education and training.

Radio Free Asia, *2025 M St. N.W., #300, 20036; (202) 530-4900. Bay Fang, President. Press, (202) 530-4976.*

General email, contact@rfa.org

Web, www.rfa.org and Twitter, @RadioFreeAsia

Independent radio, Internet, and television service funded by federal grants to promote and support democracy where public access to a free press is restricted. Broadcasts programs to East Asian countries, including China, Tibet, North Korea, Vietnam, Cambodia, Laos, and Burma; programming includes news, analysis, and specials on political developments, as well as cultural programs.

Radio Free Europe/Radio Liberty, *Washington Office, 1201 Connecticut Ave. N.W., #400, 20036; (202) 457-6900. Fax, (202) 457-6995. Jamie Fly, President; Daisy Sindelar, Vice President. Press, (202) 457-6948.*

General email, zvanersm@rferl.org

Web, www.rferl.org, Twitter, @RFERL and Facebook, www.facebook.com/rferl

Independent radio, Internet, and television service funded by federal grants to promote and support democracy. Broadcasts programs to 23 countries, including Russia, Afghanistan, Pakistan, Iraq, Iran, and the republics of Central Asia; programming includes news, analysis, and specials on political developments, as well as cultural programs. Research materials available to the public by appointment. (Headquarters in Prague, Czech Republic.)

Sister Cities International, *1012 14th St. N.W., #1400, 20005; (202) 347-8630. Fax, (202) 393-6524. Leroy R. Allala, President.*

General email, info@sistercities.org

Web, https://sistercities.org, Twitter, @SisterCitiesInt and Facebook, www.facebook.com/SisterCitiesInternational

A network of more than 2,300 partnerships between U.S. and foreign cities. Promotes global cooperation at the municipal level, cultural understanding, and economic stimulation through exchanges of citizens, ideas, and materials. Serves as information clearinghouse for economic and sustainability issues and as program coordinator for trade missions. Sponsors youth programs.

World Learning, *Global Development and Exchange Programs, 1015 15th St. N.W., #950, 20005-2065; (202) 408-5420. Fax, (202) 408-5397. Carol Jenkins, President, (202) 464-6643. Toll-free, (800) 858-0292. TTY, (202) 408-5420, ext. 711.*
General email, info@worldlearning.org
Web, www.worldlearning.org and Twitter, @WorldLearning

Assists public and private organizations engaged in international cooperation and business. Works with governments and private counterparts to support foreign professional exchanges. Develops tailored technical training programs for midcareer professionals. Provides technical expertise, management support, travel, and business development services. Administers programs that place international exchange students in U.S. colleges and universities. Implements youth exchanges focused on leadership, current issues, and peacebuilding. Administered by World Learning's Division of International Development and Exchange Programs. Administers field-based study abroad programs, which offer semester and summer programs for high school, college, and graduate students.

Youth for Understanding USA, *6856 Eastern Ave. N.W., #310, 20012; (202) 774-5200. Fax, (202) 588-7571. Sean Nelson, Chief Executive Officer. Teen information, (800) 833-6243.*
General email, info@yfu.org
Web, www.yfuusa.org, Twitter, @yfu_usa and Facebook, www.facebook.com/YFU.USA.Fan

Educational organization that administers international exchange programs, primarily for high school students. Administers scholarship programs that sponsor student exchanges.

War, Conflict, and Peacekeeping

▶**AGENCIES**

Agency for International Development (USAID), *Bureau for Conflict Prevention and Stabilization (CPS), 1300 Pennsylvania Ave. N.W., 20523; (202) 712-0100. Robert Jenkins, Assistant to the Administrator.*
General email, conflict@usaid.gov
Web, www.usaid.gov/who-we-are/organization/bureaus/bureau-conflict-prevention-and-stabilization

Supports USAID's works to contribute to peace and stability through programs, funding, and technical services focusing on social, communal, and political aspects of crises, and political transition; acts as a technical and analytical expertise on peacebuilding, conflict, and violence prevention.

Agency for International Development (USAID), *Bureau for Humanitarian Assistance (BHA), 1300 Pennsylvania Ave. N.W., 20523-8601; Sarah Charles, Assistant to the Administrator.*
General email, AskBHA@usaid.gov
Web, www.usaid.gov/who-we-are/organization/bureaus/bureau-humanitarian-assistance

Manages U.S. foreign disaster assistance, emergency and developmental food aid, and programs to assist countries transitioning out of crises and natural disasters.

Bureau of Conflict and Stabilization Operations (CSO) *(State Dept.), 2201 C St. N.W., #HSA-9, 20522; (202) 647-7391. Anne A. Witkowsky, Assistant Secretary.*
General email, csopublic@state.gov
Web, www.state.gov/j/cso, Twitter, @StateCSO and Facebook, www.facebook.com/stateCSO

Advances U.S. national security by working with partners in select countries to mitigate and prevent violent conflict. Conducts conflict analysis to identify factors contributing to mass violence or instability; develops prioritized strategies to address these factors; provides experienced leadership and technical experts to operationalize U.S. government and host-nation plans. Provides funding and training.

Bureau of International Organization Affairs (IO) *(State Dept.), Peace Support Operations, Sanctions, and Counterterrorism (PSC), 2201 C St. N.W., #HST1827, 20520; (202) 736-7733. William E. Moeller, Director, Peacekeeping; Erin C. Flaherty, Director, Sanctions and Counterterrorism, (202) 736-4815.*
Web, www.state.gov/p/io

Works with the United Nations to implement peacekeeping operations; manages State Dept. coordination of counterterrorism issues in the UN system.

Bureau of Political-Military Affairs (PM) *(State Dept.), 2201 C St. N.W., #6212, 20520; (202) 647-9022. Jessica Lewis, Assistant Secretary.*
Web, www.state.gov/t/pm

Liaison between the State Dept. and Defense Dept. Provides policy direction in the areas of international security, security assistance, military operations, defense strategy and policy, military use of space, and defense trade.

Bureau of Political-Military Affairs (PM) *(State Dept.), Global Programs and Initiatives (GPI), 2025 E St. N.W., #SA-9, 20520; (202) 453-8380. Michael L. Smith, Director, (202) 453-8425.*
Web, www.state.gov/t/pm

Facilitates training and equipping of international peacekeepers; supports programs that enable international cooperation on security issues, including UN and regional peacekeeping operation capabilities, aircraft policy and diplomatic clearance for foreign state aircraft and naval vessels seeking to enter U.S. territory, port security and sea access, and foreign partners assistance for addressing emergent challenges to their security.

State Dept., *Policy Planning Staff*, *2201 C St. N.W., #7311, 20520; (202) 647-2972. Fax, (202) 647-0844. Salman Ahmed, Director.*
General email, policyplanning@state.gov
Web, www.state.gov/about-us-policy-planning-staff

Advises the secretary and other State Dept. officials on foreign policy matters, including international peacekeeping and peace enforcement operations.

▶CONGRESS

For a listing of relevant congressional committees and subcommittees, please see pages 478–479 or the Appendix.

▶NONGOVERNMENTAL

Act Now to Stop War and End Racism (ANSWER) Coalition, *617 Florida Ave. N.W., Lower Level, 20001; (202) 265-1948. Sarah Sloan, National Staff Director.*
General email, info@answercoalition.org
Web, www.answercoalition.org and Facebook, www .facebook.com/AnswerCoalition

Works to end war and conflict, with an emphasis on the Middle East and Somalia. Conducts demonstrations with other peace and antiwar groups, especially ethnic and cultural identity groups concerned with ending racism.

Carnegie Endowment for International Peace, *1779 Massachusetts Ave. N.W., 20036-2103; (202) 483-7600. Fax, (202) 483-1840. Mariano-Florentino (Tino) Cueller, President.*
General email, info@carnegieendowment.org
Web, https://carnegieendowment.org and Twitter, @CarnegieEndow

Global network of policy research centers in Russia, China, Europe, the Middle East, India, and the United States. Conducts research on international affairs and U.S. foreign policy in order to promote peace. Program activities cover a broad range of military, political, and economic issues; sponsors panel discussions.

Center for Advanced Defense Studies, *1201 Eye St. N.W., #200, 20005; (202) 289-3332. Lt. Col. David E. A. Johnson (USA, Ret.), Executive Director.*
General email, info@c4ads.org
Web, https://c4ads.org, Twitter, @C4ADS and Press, communications@c4ads.org

Analyzes global data and publishes reports on transnational conflict and security concerns. Conducts field research in conflict areas.

Conflict Solutions International, *1629 K St. N.W., #300, 20006; (202) 349-3972. Vacant, President.*
General email, info@csiorg.org
Web, www.csiorg.org, Facebook, www.facebook.com/ ConflictSolutionsInternational and YouTube, www .youtube.com/channel

All-volunteer nonpartisan organization that reviews and analyzes global issues to support ending violent conflict. Holds forums to educate the public and increase awareness of religious movements, civil conflict, and independence groups. Interests include relations between the United States and Cuba, including negotiations to release political prisoners.

Enough Project, *1420 K St. N.W., #200, 20005; (202) 580-7690. John Prendergast, Director. Press, (310) 717-0606.*
General email, info@enoughproject.org
Web, https://enoughproject.org, Twitter, @enoughproject and Facebook, www.facebook.com/enoughproj

Research and policy organization aimed at protecting peace and human rights in African conflict zones; countering armed groups and violent kleptocratic regimes; preventing transnational crime and terror; and ending the trafficking of ivory, gold, diamonds, conflict minerals, and other natural resources. Conducts field research in conflict zones, develops and advocates for policy recommendations, supports social movements in affected countries, and mobilizes public campaigns.

Friends Committee on National Legislation (FCNL), *245 2nd St. N.E., 20002-5795; (202) 547-6000. Fax, (202) 547-6019. Bridget Moix, General Secretary. Toll-free, (800) 630-1330.*
General email, fcnl@fcnl.org
Web, www.fcnl.org, Twitter, @FCNL and Facebook, www .facebook.com/quakerlobby

Supports world disarmament; international cooperation; domestic, economic, peace, and social justice issues; and improvement in relations between the United States and the former Soviet Union. Opposes conscription. (Affiliated with the Religious Society of Friends [Quakers].)

Fund for Peace, *1101 14th St. N.W., #1020, 20005; (202) 223-7940. Paul Turner, Executive Director.*
Web, www.fundforpeace.org, Twitter, @fundforpeace and Facebook, www.facebook.com/fund4peace

Promotes international sustainable security. Produces the Failed States Index and the Conflict Assessment System Tool (CAST) that gathers information for determining conflict risk. Works with policymakers, government agencies, nonprofits, journalists, and private organizations to advocate nonviolent conflict resolution. Interests include early warning, election violence, and preventing violence against women, fragile states index

Global Center on Cooperative Security, *Washington Office, 1201 14th St. N.W., #915, 20005; Jason Ipe, Chief of Operations.*
General email, info@globalcenter.org
Web, www.globalcenter.org, Facebook, www.facebook.com/ GlobalCtr and Twitter, @GlobalCtr

Conducts research and training to advance global cooperation by advancing human rights-based policies, partnerships and practises, to address transnational threats, including terrorism, nuclear proliferation, and drug trafficking. Works with government, civil society and private sector partners to deliver programming that is globally informed and locally grounded. Has a extensive selection of articles, books, reports, publications and interviews relating to sanctions and incentives, violent extremism and terrorism.

International Center on Nonviolent Conflict (ICNC), *600 New Hampshire Ave. N.W., #700, 20037; (202) 416-4720. Fax, (202) 466-5918. Hardy Merriman, Senior Advisor; Perter Ackerman, Chair.*
General email, icnc@nonviolent-conflict.org
Web, www.nonviolent-conflict.org, Twitter, @civilresistance and Facebook, www.facebook.com/CivilResistance

Advocates nonviolent methods to protect international human rights and democracy. Supports research and education to broaden these methods. Holds seminars on successful nonviolent conflict practices.

International Crisis Group, *Washington Office, 1629 K St. N.W., #1000, 20006; (202) 785-1601. Comfort Ero, President; Michael Wahid Hamna, US Program Director.*
General email, washington@crisisgroup.org
Web, www.crisisgroup.org, Twitter, @CrisisGroup, Facebook, www.facebook.com/crisisgroup and YouTube, www.youtube.com/user/crisisgroup

Private, multinational organization that seeks to prevent international conflict. Writes and distributes reports and raises funds. (Headquarters in Brussels.)

International Peace and Security Institute (IPSI), *5225 Wisconsin Ave. N.W., #104, 20015; (202) 966-9501. Cameron M. Chishom, Executive Director.*
General email, info@creativelearning.org
Web, https://ipsinstitute.org, Twitter, @IPSInstitute and Facebook, www.facebook.com/IPSInstituteDC

Researches and analyzes global conflict. Holds educational symposiums and offers training programs to promote peacebuilding skills. Publishes weekly reports on international conflict management and current affairs.

International Stability Operations Assn. (ISOA), *1725 Eye St. N.W., #300, 20006; (703) 336-3940. Howard R. (Howie) Lind, President.*
General email, isoa@stability-operations.org
Web, www.stability-operations.org and Twitter, @StabilityOps

Membership: private-sector service companies involved in all sectors of peace and stability operations around the world, including mine clearance, logistics, security, training, and emergency humanitarian aid. Works to institute standards and codes of conduct. Monitors legislation.

Refugees International, *1800 M St. N.W., #405N, 20036 (mailing address: P.O. Box 33036, Washington, DC 20033); (202) 828-0110. Fax, (202) 828-0819. Eric Schwartz, President. Press, (202) 540-7026. Toll-free, (800) 733-8433.*

General email, ri@refugeesinternational.org
Web, www.refugeesinternational.org, Twitter, @RefugeesIntl and Facebook, www.facebook.com/RefugeesInternational

Advocates assistance and protection for displaced people worldwide. Conducts field studies to identify basic needs and makes recommendations to policymakers and aid agencies.

Search for Common Ground (SFCG), *1730 Rhode Island Ave. N.W., #1101, 20036; (202) 265-4300. Fax, (202) 232-6718. Shamil Idriss, Chief Executive Officer.*
General email, webinfo@sfcg.org
Web, www.sfcg.org, Twitter, @SFCG_ and Facebook, www.facebook.com/sfcg.org

International nonprofit that seeks to end global violent conflict at a grassroots level. Provides mediation services and training for youth and women activists. Produces print and video media to encourage discussions on how to solve issues nonviolently. Supports theater and sports programs for youth in politically disadvantaged areas.

U.S. Conference of Catholic Bishops (USCCB), *International Justice and Peace, 3211 4th St. N.E., 20017-1194; (202) 541-3160. Lucas Koach, Executive Director, (202) 541-3181.*
General email, sgross@usccb.org
Web, www.usccb.org/committees/international-justice-and-peace and Twitter, @wearesaltlight

Works with the U.S. State Dept., foreign government offices, and international organizations on issues of peace, justice, and human rights.

U.S. Institute of Peace, *2301 Constitution Ave. N.W., 20037; (202) 457-1700. George E. Moose, Chair; Lise Grande, President. Press, (202) 429-3869. Congressional inquiries, (202) 429-4175.*
Web, www.usip.org, Twitter, @USIP, Facebook, www.facebook.com/usinstituteofpeace and YouTube, www.youtube.com/usinstituteofpeace

Independent, nonpartisan institution established by Congress. Aims to prevent and resolve violent international conflicts, promote postconflict stability, and increase peace-building capacity, tools, and intellectual capital worldwide. Provides training, analysis, and other resources to people, organizations, and governments working to build world peace.

Win Without War, *1 Thomas Circle N.W., #700Washington, DC, 20005; (202) 656-4999. Stephen Miles, President.*
General email, info@winwithoutwar.org
Web, www.winwithoutwar.org and Twitter, @winwithoutwar

Network of activists and national organizations promoting international cooperation and agreements as the best means for securing peace. Encourages U.S. foreign policies of counterterrorism and weapons nonproliferation, but opposes unilateral military preemption.

IMMIGRATION AND NATURALIZATION

General

▶AGENCIES

Administration for Children and Families (ACF) *(Health and Human Services Dept.), Refugee Resettlement (ORR),* Mary E. Switzer Bldg., 330 C St. S.W., Room 5123, 20201; (202) 401-9246. Fax, (202) 401-4678. Cindy Huang, Director. Parent Hotline, (800) 203-7001.
Web, https://acf.hhs.gov/orr

Directs a domestic resettlement program for refugees; reimburses states for costs incurred in giving refugees monetary and medical assistance; awards funds to voluntary resettlement agencies for providing refugees with monetary assistance and case management.

Bureau of Consular Affairs (CA) *(State Dept.), Visa Services,* 2401 E St. N.W., 12.204 SA-17, 20522-0106; (202) 485-7561. Julie Stufft, Deputy Assistant Secretary. National Visa Center (immigrant inquiries), (603) 334-0700. National Visa Center (nonimmigrant inquiries), (603) 334-0888.
Web, http://travel.state.gov/content/travel/en/us-visas.html

Supervises visa issuance system, which is administered by U.S. consular offices abroad.

Civil Division *(Justice Dept.), Immigration Litigation (OIL),* 450 5th St. N.W., 20001 (mailing address: P.O. Box 878, Ben Franklin Station, Washington, DC 20044); Fax, (202) 305-7000. David McConnell, Director (Appellate Section); William Peachey, Director (District Court Section). Phone (Appellate Section), (202) 616-4900. Phone (District Court Section), (202) 307-8700.
Web, www.justice.gov/civil/office-immigration-litigation

Oversees all civil litigation arising under immigration and nationality laws.

Executive Office for Immigration Review *(Justice Dept.),* 5107 Leesburg Pike, 8th Floor, #2600, Falls Church, VA 22041; (304) 625-2050. Fax, (703) 605-0365. David L. Neal, Director. Case Information System, (800) 898-7180. Employer Sanctions and Antidiscrimination Cases, (703) 305-0864. Legislative and Public Affairs, (703) 305-0289. TTY, (800) 828-1120.
General email, PAO.EOIR@usdoj.gov
Web, www.justice.gov/eoir, Twitter, @DOJ_EOIR and Facebook, www.facebook.com/doj.eoir

Quasi-judicial body that includes the Board of Immigration Appeals and offices of the chief immigration judge and the chief administration hearing officer. Interprets immigration laws; conducts hearings and hears appeals on immigration issues.

U.S. Citizenship and Immigration Services (USCIS) *(Homeland Security Dept.),* 20 Massachusetts Ave. N.W., 20529; (800) 375-5283. Tracy Renaud, Director (Acting).

Customer Service Center, (800) 375-5283. TTY, (800) 767-1833.
Web, www.uscis.gov, Twitter, @USCIS and Facebook, www.facebook.com/USCIS

Responsible for the administration of immigration and naturalization adjudication functions and establishing immigration services policies and priorities.

U.S. Coast Guard (USCG) *(Homeland Security Dept.), Law Enforcement, Maritime Security and Defense Operations Policy,* 2703 Martin Luther King Jr. Ave. S.E., MS 7516, 20593-7516; (202) 372-2161. Capt. John Paul (Paul) Gregg, Director. Press, (202) 372-4630.
General email, mediarelations@uscg.mil
Web, www.dco.uscg.mil/Our-Organization/Assistant-Commandant-for-Response-Policy-CG-5R

Interdicts illegal migrants at sea and assists in repatriation.

▶CONGRESS

For a listing of relevant congressional committees and subcommittees, please see pages 478–479 or the Appendix.

▶INTERNATIONAL ORGANIZATIONS

International Catholic Migration Commission (ICMC), *Washington Office,* 3211 4th St. N.E., #141, 20017-1194; (202) 541-3389. Giorgio Bertin, President; Limnyuy Konglim, Head of U.S. Liaison Office.
General email, info@icmc.net
Web, www.icmc.net

Supports ICMC's worldwide programs by liaising with the U.S. government, nongovernmental organizations, and the American public. Works with refugees, internally displaced persons, migrants, asylum seekers, and trafficking victims. Responds to refugees' immediate needs while working for return to and reintegration in their home country, local integration, or resettlement in a third country. (Headquarters in Geneva, Switzerland.)

International Organization for Migration (IOM), *Washington Office,* 1752 N St. N.W., #600, 20036; (202) 862-1826. Fax, (202) 862-1879. Luca Dall'Oglio, Chief of Mission, ext. 229; António Vitorino, Director General.
General email, iomwashington@iom.int
Web, www.iom.int/countries/united-states-america and Twitter, @UNmigration

Nonpartisan organization that plans and operates resource mobilization functions (RMF), including refugee resettlement, national migration, and humanitarian assistance to displaced populations at the request of its member governments. Advises governments on migration policies, supports victims of human trafficking, assists returning migrants, and raises awareness about the benefits of migration. Recruits skilled professionals for developing countries. (Headquarters in Geneva, Switzerland.)

▶ NONGOVERNMENTAL

American Immigration Lawyers Assn., *1331 G St. N.W., #300, 20005-3142; (202) 507-7600. Fax, (202) 783-7853. Benjamin Johnson, Executive Director.*
General email, membership@aila.org
Web, http://aila.org, Twitter, @ailanational and Facebook, www.facebook.com/AILANational

Association for lawyers interested in immigration law. Provides information and continuing education programs on immigration law and policy; offers workshops and conferences. Acts as advocate for a fair and just immigration law policy. Monitors legislation and regulations.

Center for Immigration Studies, *1629 K St. N.W., #600, 20006; (202) 466-8185. Fax, (202) 466-8076. Mark Krikorian, Executive Director.*
General email, center@cis.org
Web, https://cis.org, Twitter, @CIS_org and Facebook, www.facebook.com/CenterforImmigrationStudies

Nonpartisan organization that conducts research and policy analysis of the economic, social, demographic, and environmental impact of immigration on the United States. Sponsors symposiums.

Ethiopian Community Development Council, Inc., *901 S. Highland St., Arlington, VA 22204; (703) 685-0510. Fax, (703) 685-0529. Tsehaye Teferra, President.*
General email, info@ecdcus.org
Web, www.ecdcus.org, Twitter, @ECDCUS and Facebook, www.facebook.com/ECDCUS.org

A National Resettlement Agency, serves refugees from around the world. Seeks to improve quality of life for immigrants and refugees, with focus on the African newcomer community, in the United States through local and national programs. Interests include the resettlement and acculturation of refugees, health education, and cultural outreach for communities. Also provides business loans and management training for minority-owned and women-owned businesses in the Washington metropolitan area.

Federation for American Immigration Reform (FAIR), *25 Massachusetts Ave. N.W., #330, 20001; (202) 328-7004. Fax, (202) 387-3447. Daniel A. Stein, President.*
General email, fair@fairus.org
Web, www.fairus.org, Twitter, @FAIRImmigration and Press, mtragesser@fairus.org

Organization of individuals interested in immigration reform. Monitors immigration laws and policies.

Institute for the Study of International Migration *(Georgetown University), 3300 Whitehaven St. N.W., 3rd Floor, 20007; (202) 687-2350. Fax, (202) 687-2541. Katharine M. Donato, Director.*
General email, isim@georgetown.edu
Web, https://isim.georgetown.edu, Twitter, @GUMigration and Facebook, www.facebook.com/ISIM.Georgetown

Researches international migration policy, cause, and conflict through the study of social, economic, environmental, and political dimensions of international migration. Administers academic certificates to students in subjects such as Refugee and Humanitarian Emergencies and Human Rights Law. Offers scholarship programs for international researchers and students to study independent topics. (Part of the School of Foreign Service.)

Lutheran Immigration and Refugee Service, *Advocacy, 110 Maryland Ave., N.E., 20002; (202) 381-1030. Jill Marie Bussey, Director of Public Policy. Press, (443) 257-6310.*
General email, dc@lirs.org
Web, https://lirsconnect.org/advocacy, Twitter, @LIRSorg, Facebook, www.facebook.com/LIRSorg and Press, tyoung@lirs.org

Resettles refugees and provides them with case management, job training, English language, and legal assistance. Provides specialized foster care services for unaccompanied refugee youth and facilitates the reunification of unaccompanied immigrant children in federal custody with their parents or relatives. Funds and provides technical assistance to local projects that offer social and legal services to immigrants and refugees, particularly those in immigration detention. (Headquarters in Baltimore, Md.)

Migration Policy Institute, *1275 K. St. N.W., #800, 20005; (202) 266-1940. Fax, (202) 266-1900. Andrew Selee, President, (202) 266-1933. Press, (202) 266-1910.*
General email, info@migrationpolicy.org
Web, www.migrationpolicy.org, Twitter, @MigrationPolicy and Facebook, www.facebook.com/MigrationPolicy Institute

Nonpartisan think tank that studies the movement of people within the United States and worldwide. Provides analysis, development, and evaluation of migration, integration, and refugee policies at local, national, and international levels.

National Immigration Forum, *10 G St., #500, 20002; (202) 347-0040. Ali Noorani, Executive Director.*
General email, media@immigrationforum.org
Web, www.immigrationforum.org, Twitter, @NatImmForum, Facebook, www.facebook.com/ NationalImmigrationForum and YouTube, www.youtube .com/channel/UCvxciqcn-jlX0Ht6AihN5EA

Pro-immigration advocacy organization that provides policy analysis, research, and updates on immigration policy developments to members and allies across the country. Monitors legislation and regulations related to immigrants and immigration. Works with broad cross-section of immigrant-advocacy, immigrant-serving, religious, business, and labor organizations to advance policies welcoming to immigrants.

NumbersUSA, *1400 Crystal Dr., #240, Arlington, VA 22202; 703 816-8820. Roy Beck, President.*
General email, info@numbersusa.com
Web, www.numbersusa.com, Twitter, @NumbersUSA and Facebook, www.facebook.com/numbersusa

Public policy organization that favors immigration reduction as a way of promoting economic justice for American workers. Monitors legislation and regulations.

Pew Research Center, *Hispanic Trends Project,* 1615 L St. N.W., #800, 20036; (202) 419-4300. *Mark Hugo Lopez, Director, Race and Ethnicity. Press, (202) 419-4372.* *Web, www.pewhispanic.org, Twitter, @PewHispanic and Director, Twitter, @mhugolopez*

Seeks to improve understanding of the U.S. Hispanic population and its impact on the nation, as well as explore Latino views on a range of social matters and public policy issues, including public opinion, identity, and trends in voting, immigration, work, and education. Conducts public opinion surveys and other studies that are made available to the public.

U.S. Committee for Refugees and Immigrants, 2231 Crystal Dr., #350, Arlington, VA 22202-3794; (703) 310-1130. *Eskinder Negash, Chief Executive Officer.* *General email, uscri@uscridc.org* *Web, www.refugees.org, Facebook, www.facebook.com/ USCRI and Twitter, @uscridc*

Defends rights of refugees in the United States and abroad. Helps immigrants and refugees adjust to American society; assists in resettling recently arrived immigrants and refugees; offers information, counseling services, and temporary living accommodations through its member agencies nationwide; issues publications on refugees and refugee resettlement; collects and disseminates information on refugee issues. Monitors legislation and regulations.

U.S. Conference of Catholic Bishops (USCCB), *Migration and Refugee Services,* 3211 4th St. N.E., 20017-1194; (202) 541-3169. *Bill Canny, Executive Director, (202) 541-3169; Rachel Pollock, Director of Resettlement Services, (202) 541-3345.* *General email, mrs@usccb.org* *Web, www.usccb.org/mrs and Twitter, @mrsserves*

Acts as advocate for immigrants, refugees, migrants, and victims of human trafficking. Works with legislative and executive branches of the U.S. government and with national and international organizations such as the UN High Commissioner for Refugees to promote fair and responsive immigration and refugee policy.

UnidosUS, 1126 16th St. N.W., #600, 20036-4845; (202) 785-1670. *Janet Murguía, President.* *General email, info@unidos.org* *Web, www.unidosus.org, Twitter, @WeAreUnidosUS, Facebook, www.facebook.com/Weareunidosus and YouTube, www.youtube.com/c/UnidosUS*

Provides research, policy analysis, and advocacy relating to immigration policy and programs. Monitors federal legislation on immigration, legalization, employer sanctions, employment discrimination, and eligibility of immigrants for federal benefit programs. Assists community-based groups involved in immigration and education services and educates employers about immigration laws.

INTERNATIONAL LAW AND AGREEMENTS

General

▶**AGENCIES**

Bureau of Economic and Business Affairs (EB) *(State Dept.), Trade Policy and Negotiations (TPN), Bilateral Trade Affairs (BTA),* 2201 C St. N.W., #4452, 20520; (202) 647-3784. Fax, (202) 647-6540. *Robert D. Manogue, Director, (202) 647-4017.* *Web, www.state.gov/bilateral-trade-affairs*

Develops, negotiates, and implements free trade agreements, trade and investment framework agreements, and trade preference programs.

Bureau of Economic and Business Affairs (EB) *(State Dept.), Transportation Affairs (TRA), Aviation Negotiations (AN),* 2201 C St. N.W., #3425, 20520-3425; (202) 647-5865. Fax, (202) 647-9143. *Aaron P. Forsberg, Director, (202) 647-9797.* *General email, EEB-A-TRA-AN-DL@state.gov* *Web, www.state.gov/about-us-division-for-transportation-affairs/*

Manages bilateral aviation relationships; works with the Transporation Dept. and private sector to negotiate bilateral agreements to support and improve commercial aviation.

Bureau of International Narcotics and Law Enforcement Affairs (INL) *(State Dept.), Anti-Crime Office,* 2401 E St. N.W., #SA-1, L600, 20037; (202) 663-1860. *Susan Snyder, Director.* *Web, https://2009-2017.state.gov/j/inl/c/index.htm*

Works with international governments to combat international organized crime, high-level corruption, money laundering, terrorist financing, cyber and intellectual property crimes, threats to border security, narcotics trafficking, and other smuggling and trafficking crimes.

Bureau of International Organization Affairs (IO) *(State Dept.), Peace Support Operations, Sanctions, and Counterterrorism (PSC),* 2201 C St. N.W., #HST1827, 20520; (202) 736-7733. *William E. Moeller, Director, Peacekeeping; Erin C. Flaherty, Director, Sanctions and Counterterrorism, (202) 736-4815.* *Web, www.state.gov/p/io*

Structures and enforces United Nations sanctions so that they be effective and humane, and builds support for peacekeeping and sanctions from Congress and private organizations.

Bureau of Political-Military Affairs (PM) *(State Dept.), Security Negotiations and Agreements (SNA),* 2201 C St. N.W., HST #3242, 20520; (202) 647-0622. *Donna A. Welton, Senior Advisor, (202) 617-8325.* *Web, www.state.gov/t/pm*

Negotiates and oversees implementation of international security agreements, including defense cooperation agreements, burden-sharing and facilities access agreements, transit and overflight arrangements, and state flights agreements, in order to facilitate the deployment and movement of U.S. forces and materiel abroad and provide protections for U.S. service members operating overseas.

Federal Bureau of Investigation (FBI) *(Justice Dept.)*, *International Operations Division,* 935 Pennsylvania Ave. N.W., #7825, 20535; (202) 324-5904. Fax, (202) 324-5292. Brian Boetig, Assistant Director (Acting).
Web, www.fbi.gov/about/leadership-and-structure/international-operations

Supports FBI involvement in international investigations; oversees liaison offices in U.S. embassies abroad. Maintains contacts with other federal agencies, Interpol, foreign police and security officers based in Washington, DC, and national law enforcement associations.

Internal Revenue Service (IRS) *(Treasury Dept.)*, *Criminal Investigation,* 1111 Constitution Ave. N.W., 20224; (202) 317-3200. James Lee, Chief. Tax fraud hotline, (800) 366-4184. TTY/ TDD, (800) 877-8339.
Web, www.irs.gov/compliance/criminal-investigation and Twitter, @IRSnews

Manages the Offshore Voluntary Disclosure Program to allow taxpayers to disclose previously undisclosed offshore accounts and assets.

National Telecommunications and Information Administration (NTIA) *(Commerce Dept.)*, 1401 Constitution Ave. N.W., #4898, 20230; (202) 482-1840. Alan Davidson, Assistant Secretary. Press, (202) 482-7002.
Web, www.ntia.doc.gov, Twitter, @NTIAgov and Facebook, www.facebook.com/ntiagov

Represents the U.S. telecommunications sector (along with the State Dept.) in negotiating international agreements, including conferences with the International Telecommunication Union.

State Dept., *Global Criminal Justice,* 2201 C St. N.W., #7806, 20520; (202) 647-8177. Fax, (202) 736-4465. Michael G. Kozak, Senior Official.
Web, www.state.gov/bureaus-offices/under-secretary-for-civilian-security-democracy-and-human-rights/office-of-global-criminal-justice and Twitter, @StateDept_GCJ

Oversees U.S. stance on the creation of courts and other judicial mechanisms to bring perpetrators of crimes under international law to justice. Engages in diplomacy with foreign governments whose nationals have been captured in the war on terrorism. Has primary responsibility for policy on Iraqi war crimes.

State Dept., *Office of the Legal Adviser,* 2201 C St. N.W., #6421 HST, 20520-6310; (202) 647-5036. Richard C. Visek, Deputy Legal Adviser.
Web, www.state.gov/bureaus-offices/secretary-of-state/office-of-the-legal-adviser

Provides the secretary and the department with legal advice on domestic and international problems;

participates in international negotiations; represents the U.S. government in international litigation and in international conferences related to legal issues.

State Dept., *Office of the Legal Adviser, International Claims and Investment Disputes,* 2430 E St. N.W., SA-O4A #207, 20520; (202) 776-8325. Fax, (202) 776-8389. Lisa J. Grosh, Assistant Legal Adviser.
Web, www.state.gov/bureaus-offices/secretary-of-state/office-of-the-legal-adviser/international-claims-and-investment-disputes

Handles claims by foreign governments and their nationals against the U.S. government, as well as claims against the State Dept. for negligence under the Federal Tort Claims Act. Administers the Iranian claims program and negotiates agreements with other foreign governments on claims settlements.

State Dept., *Office of the Legal Adviser, Law Enforcement and Intelligence,* 2201 C St. N.W., HST 4331, 20520; (202) 647-5654. Fax, (202) 647-4802. Karen Johnson, Assistant Legal Adviser.
Web, www.state.gov/bureaus-offices/secretary-of-state/office-of-the-legal-adviser/office-of-the-legal-adviser-for-law-enforcement-and-intelligence

Negotiates extradition treaties, legal assistance treaties in criminal matters, and other agreements relating to international criminal matters.

State Dept., *Office of the Legal Adviser, Treaty Affairs,* 2201 C St. N.W., #5420, 20520; (202) 647-1092. Fax, (202) 647-9844. Robert Dalton, Senior Legal Adviser for Treaty Practice, 202–776-8446; Mike Matler, Administrative Assistant, (202) 647-1092.
General email, treatyoffice@state.gov
Web, www.state.gov/bureaus-offices/treaty-affairs

Provides legal advice on treaties and other international agreements, including constitutional questions, drafting, negotiation, and interpretation of treaties; maintains records of treaties and executive agreements.

Transportation Dept. (DOT), *International Aviation,* 1200 New Jersey Ave. S.E., #W86-316, 20590; (202) 366-2423. Fax, (202) 366-3694. Benjamin (Ben) Taylor, Director, (202) 366-1213.
Web, www.transportation.gov/policy/aviation-policy/office-international-aviation

Responsible for international aviation regulation and negotiations, including fares, tariffs, and foreign licenses; represents the United States at international aviation meetings.

U.S. Coast Guard (USCG) *(Homeland Security Dept.), Law Enforcement, Maritime Security and Defense Operations Policy,* 2703 Martin Luther King Jr. Ave. S.E., MS 7516, 20593-7516; (202) 372-2161. Capt. John Paul (Paul) Gregg, Director. Press, (202) 372-4630.
General email, mediarelations@uscg.mil
Web, www.dco.uscg.mil/Our-Organization/Assistant-Commandant-for-Response-Policy-CG-5R

U.S. Customs and Border Protection

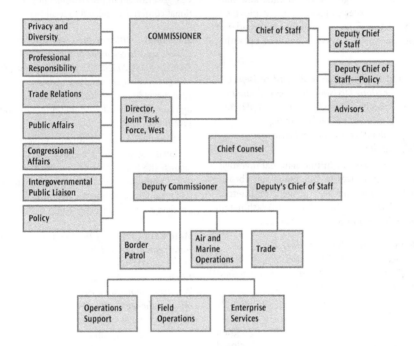

Oversees enforcement of federal laws and treaties and other international agreements to which the United States is party on, over, and under the high seas and waters subject to the jurisdiction of the United States.

►CONGRESS

For a listing of relevant congressional committees and sub-committees, please see pages 478–479 or the Appendix.

►INTERNATIONAL ORGANIZATIONS

INTERPOL Washington *(Justice Dept.)*, *950 Pennsylvania Ave. N.W., 20530-0001; (202) 616-9000. Fax, (202) 616-8400. Michael A. Hughes, Director.*
Web, www.justice.gov/interpol-washington and *Twitter, @INTERPOL_USA*

U.S. representative to INTERPOL; participates in international investigations on behalf of U.S. police; coordinates the exchange of investigative information on crimes, including drug trafficking, counterfeiting, missing persons, and terrorism. Coordinates law enforcement requests for investigative assistance in the United States and abroad. Assists with extradition processes. Serves as liaison between foreign and U.S. law enforcement agencies at federal, state, and local levels. (Headquarters in Lyons, France.)

►NONGOVERNMENTAL

American Arbitration Assn., *Government Relations,*
1120 Connecticut Ave. N.W., #490, 20036; (202) 223-7093. Jean Baker, Vice President. Toll-free, (800) 778-7879.

Web, www.adr.org, Twitter, @adrorg and *YouTube, www.youtube.com/c/AmericanArbitrationAssociation/videos*

Provides dispute resolution services and information. Administers international arbitration and mediation systems. (Headquarters in New York.)

American Bar Assn. (ABA), *International Law, 1050 Connecticut Ave. N.W., 20036; (202) 662-1660. Fax, (202) 662-1669. Christina Heid, Section Director, (202) 662-1034. General email, intlaw@americanbar.org*

Web, www.americanbar.org/groups/international_law, Twitter, @ABInternatl and *Facebook, www.facebook.com/ABAInternational*

Monitors and makes recommendations concerning developments in the practice of international law that affect ABA members and the public. Conducts programs, including International Legal Exchange, and produces publications covering the practice of international law.

American Bar Assn. (ABA), *Rule of Law Initiative, 1050 Connecticut Ave. N.W., #450, 20036; (202) 662-1950. Fax, (202) 662-1597. Alberto J. Mora, Executive Director. General email, rol@americanbar.org*

Web, www.americanbar.org/advocacy/rule_of_law, Twitter, @ABARuleofLaw and *Facebook, www.facebook.com/ABA.Rule.of.Law.Initiative*

Promotes the rule of law and specific legal reforms in developing countries throughout the world; recruits volunteer legal professionals from the United States and western Europe. Interests include human rights, anticorruption initiatives, criminal law, efforts against human trafficking, judicial reform, legal education reform, civic education, reforming the legal profession, and women's rights.

American Society of International Law, *2223 Massachusetts Ave. N.W., 20008-2864; (202) 939-6001. Fax, (202) 797-7133. Mark D. Agrast, Executive Director. Web, www.asil.org, Twitter, @asilorg, Facebook, www .facebook.com/AmericanSocietyofInternationalLaw and YouTube, www.youtube.com/asl1966*

Membership: lawyers, academics, corporate counsel, judges, representatives of government and nongovernmental organizations, international civil servants, students, and others interested in international law. Conducts research and study programs on international law. Publishes articles, notes and editorials by scholars and practitioners on issues and developments in international law, economics, trade and foreign affairs. Holds an annual meeting on current issues in international law. Library open to the public 9:00 a.m.–4:00 p.m.

Antarctic and Southern Ocean Coalition, *1320 19th St. N.W., 5th Floor, 20036; (202) 234-2480. Claire Christian, Executive Director. General email, info@asoc.org Web, www.asoc.org and Twitter, @AntarcticaSouth*

Promotes effective implementation of the Antarctic Treaty System aimed at peaceful and free scientific research in the region.

Inter-American Bar Assn., *1889 F St. N.W., #355, 20006; (202) 466-5944. Fax, (202) 466-5946. Lourdes Escaffi-Venes, Secretary General. General email, iaba@iaba.org Web, www.iaba.org and Twitter, @IABA_FIA*

Membership: lawyers and bar associations in the Western Hemisphere with associate members in Europe. Works to promote uniformity of national and international laws; holds conferences; makes recommendations to national governments and organizations. Library open to the public by appointment only.

International Law Institute, *1055 Thomas Jefferson St. N.W., #M-100, 20007; (202) 247-6006. Fax, (202) 247-6010. Kim Phan, Executive Director. General email, info@ili.org Web, www.ili.org*

Performs scholarly research, offers training programs, and provides technical assistance in the areas of international law and economic development. Sponsors international conferences.

U.S. Codex Office, *South Bldg., 1400 Independence Ave. S.W., #4861, 20250-3700; (202) 205-7760. Mary Frances Lowe, U.S. Manager for Codex Alimentarius. Toll-free TTY, (800) 877-8339. General email, uscodex@usda.gov Web, www.usda.gov/codex, Twitter, @USDAFoodSafety, Facebook, www.facebook.com/usda and YouTube, www .youtube.com/usda*

Acts as national focal point for U.S. Codex Program. Engages stakeholders in developing and advancing science-based food standards to protect the health of consumers and ensure fair practices in the food trade. Manages U.S.

involvement in Codex, and develops strategies to accomplish U.S. objectives. (Located in USDA Trade and Foreign Agricultural Affairs.)

World Justice Project (WJP), *1025 Vermont Ave. N.W., #1200, 20005; (202) 407-9330. Fax, (202) 747-5816. Elizabeth Andersen, Executive Director. General email, wjp@worldjusticeproject.org Web, www.worldjusticeproject.org, Twitter, @TheWJP and Facebook, www.facebook.com/thewjp*

Supports the international rule of law in order to enforce civil and criminal justice, open government, and absence of corruption. Publishes journals and researches the rule of law and its influence on international economies and politics. Produces the annual Rule of Law Index, which measures countries' effectiveness at practicing the rule of law. Holds conferences and other outreach activities to advance practical solutions to strengthen the rule of law.

Americans Abroad

▶**AGENCIES**

Bureau of Consular Affairs (CA) (State Dept.), *2201 C St. N.W., SA-17, 20520-4818; (202) 485-6409. Rena Bitter, Assistant Secretary. Assistance to U.S citizens overseas, (888) 407-4747 in United States and Canada or (202) 501-4444 if overseas during business hours or (202) 647-4000 after hours. National Passport Information Center, (877) 487-2778 with credit card (fees are charged for calls to this number). Press, (202) 485-6150. Web, https://travel.state.gov, Twitter, @TravelGov, Facebook, www.facebook.com/travelgov, Blog, https://state .gov/blogs and YouTube, www.youtube.com/user/statevideo*

Issues passports to U.S. citizens and visas to immigrants and nonimmigrants seeking to enter the United States. Provides protection, assistance, and documentation for U.S. citizens abroad.

Bureau of Consular Affairs (CA) (State Dept.), Children's Issues, *2201 C. St. N.W., 9th Floor, #SA17, 20522-1709; Allison Dillworth, Director, (202) 485-6262. Phone (U.S. and Canada), (888) 407-4747. Outside U.S., (202) 501-4444. Abduction fax, (202) 485-6221. Prevention fax, (202) 485-6222. General email, AbductionQuestions@state.gov Web, http://travel.state.gov/content/travel/en/ Internacountry-Adoption/html and Abduction email, PreventAbduction1@state.gov*

Assists with consular aspects of children's services and fulfills U.S. treaty obligations relating to the abduction of children. Advises foreign service posts on international parental child abduction and intercountry adoption.

Bureau of Consular Affairs (CA) (State Dept.), Fraud Prevention Programs, *600 19th St. N.W., #8-204, 20522; (202) 485-6753. Stephen Ashby, Deputy Director, (202) 485-6754. Web, https://state.gov/passport-and-visa-fraud*

Provides resources, tools, and information to consular officials in order to identify and prevent passport and visa fraud.

Bureau of Consular Affairs (CA) (State Dept.), Overseas Citizens Services (OCS), 600 19th St. N.W., 10th Floor, #SA17, 20006; (202) 485-6234. Nousher Ali, Director. Phone (U.S. and Canada), (888) 407-4747.
Web, http://travel.state.gov/content/travel/en/international-travel/emergencies.html

Handles matters involving protective services for Americans abroad, including arrests, assistance in death cases, loans, medical emergencies, welfare and whereabouts inquiries, travel warnings and consular information, nationality and citizenship determination, document issuance, judicial and notarial services, estates, property claims, third-country representation, and disaster assistance.

Bureau of Consular Affairs (CA) (State Dept.), Overseas Citizens Services (OCS), Legal Affairs, 600 19th St. N.W., 12#SA17402, 20037; (202) 485-7583. Fax, (202) 485-8033. David Newman, Deputy Assistant Legal Advisor. 24-hour traveler's hotline, (202) 647-5225. Toll-free for emergencies abroad, (888) 407-4747.
General email, ask-ocs-l-attyreplies@state.gov
Web, http://travel.state.gov/content/travel/en/legal.html

Offers guidance concerning the administration and enforcement of laws on citizenship and on the appropriate documentation of Americans traveling and residing abroad; gives advice on legislative matters, including implementation of new laws, and on treaties and agreements; reconsiders the acquisition and loss of U.S. citizenship in complex cases; and administers the overseas federal benefits program.

Bureau of Consular Affairs (CA) (State Dept.), Passport Services, 600 19th St. N.W., SA-17A, 20006; Rachel Arndt, Deputy Assistant Secretary. Passport Appointments, (877) 487-2778. TDD/TDY, (888) 874-7793.
Web, https://travel.state.gov/content/passports/en/passports.html and National Passport Information Center, NPIC@state.gov

Creates passports and provides information and resources to citizens about how to obtain, replace, and change a U.S. passport.

Bureau of Consular Affairs (CA) (State Dept.), Special Issuance Agency, 600 19th St. N.W., SA-17A, 20006; (202) 485-8200. (202) 485-8244. Linda M. Blount, Director, (202) 485-8202.
Web, http://travel.state.gov/content/travel/en/passports.html and National Passport Information Center, NPIC@state.gov

Maintains a variety of records received from the Overseas Citizens Services, including consular certificates of witness to marriage and reports of birth and death. (Individuals wishing to apply for a U.S. passport may seek additional information via the phone number or web address listed above.)

Foreign Claims Settlement Commission of the United States (Justice Dept.), 441 G St. N.W., Room 6330, 20579 (mailing address: 601 D St. N.W., #10300, Washington, DC 20579); (202) 616-6975. Fax, (202) 616-6993. Patrick Hovakimian, Commissioner; Sylvia Becker, Commissioner.
General email, info.fcsc@usdoj.gov
Web, www.justice.gov/fcsc

Processes claims by U.S. nationals against foreign governments for property losses sustained.

National Security Division (Justice Dept.), Justice for Victims of Overseas Terrorism, 950 Pennsylvania Ave. N.W., 20530; (202) 233-0701. Fax, (202) 233-0770. Andria Kerney, Director. Toll-free, (877) 738-0153.
General email, nsd.ovt@usdoj.gov
Web, www.justice.gov/nsd-ovt

Monitors the investigation and prosecution of terrorist attacks against U.S. citizens abroad; works with other Justice Dept. offices to ensure that the rights of victims are respected.

State Dept., Office of the Legal Adviser, International Claims and Investment Disputes, 2430 E St. N.W., SA-O4A #207, 20520; (202) 776-8325. Fax, (202) 776-8389. Lisa J. Grosh, Assistant Legal Adviser.
Web, www.state.gov/bureaus-offices/secretary-of-state/office-of-the-legal-adviser/international-claims-and-investment-disputes

Handles claims by U.S. government and citizens against foreign governments; handles claims by owners of U.S. flag vessels for reimbursements of fines, fees, licenses, and other direct payments for illegal seizures by foreign governments in international waters under the Fishermen's Protective Act.

Boundaries

▶**AGENCIES**

Bureau of Western Hemisphere Affairs (State Dept.), Canadian Affairs, 2201 C St. N.W., #3918, 20520; (202) 647-2170. Laura Lochman, Director, (202) 647-2273. Public Affairs, (202) 647-7137.
Web, www.state.gov/p/wha

Advises the secretary on Canadian affairs. Acts as liaison between the United States and Canada in international boundary and water matters as defined by binational treaties and agreements. Also involved with border health and environmental issues, political and defense cooperation, and economics and trade.

Bureau of Western Hemisphere Affairs (State Dept.), Mexican Affairs, 2201 C St. N.W., #3924, 20520-6258; (202) 647-8766. Jennifer Brown, Director (Acting), (202) 647-8113.
Web, www.state.gov/p/wha

Advises the secretary on Mexican affairs. Acts as liaison between the United States and Mexico in international boundary and water matters as defined by binational treaties and agreements. Also involved with border health and environmental issues, new border crossings, and significant modifications to existing crossings.

Saint Lawrence Seaway Development Corp.

(Transportation Dept.), 1200 New Jersey Ave. S.E., #E311, 20590; (202) 366-0091. Fax, (202) 366-7147. Craig H. Middlebrook, Deputy Administrator. Toll-free, (800) 785-2779. General email, gls@dot.gov

Web, www.seaway.dot.gov and Twitter, @seawayusdot

Operates and maintains the Saint Lawrence Seaway within U.S. territorial limits; conducts development programs and coordinates activities with its Canadian counterpart.

▶ INTERNATIONAL ORGANIZATIONS

International Boundary Commission, *United States and Canada, U.S. Section, 1717 H St. N.W., #845, 20006; (202) 736-9100. Fax, (202) 254-0008. Kyle K. Hipsley, Commissioner for the U.S., (202) 736-9102. Web, www.internationalboundarycommission.org and Email, moorej@ibcusca.org*

Defines and maintains the international boundary line between the United States and Canada. Rules on applications for approval of projects affecting boundary or transboundary waters. Assists the United States and Canada in protecting the transboundary environment. Alerts the governments to emerging issues that may give rise to bilateral disputes. Jointly reports to the U.S. and Canadian governments on an annual basis. (Canadian section in Ottawa.)

International Joint Commission, *United States and Canada, U.S. Section, 1717 H St. N.W., #835, 20440; (202) 736-9000. Fax, (202) 632-2006. Susan Daniel, Secretary (Acting), (202) 736-9011. Web, https://ijc.org/en and Twitter, @IJCSharedWaters*

Handles disputes concerning the use of boundary waters; negotiates questions dealing with the rights, obligations, and interests of the United States and Canada along the border; establishes procedures for the adjustment and settlement of questions. (Canadian section in Ottawa; Great Lakes regional office in Windsor, Ontario.)

Extradition and Prisoner Transfer

▶ AGENCIES

Criminal Division *(Justice Dept.), International Affairs (OIA), 1301 New York Ave. N.W., #300, 20530; (202) 514-0000. Vaughn A. Ary, Director. General email, criminal.division@usdoj.gov*

Web, www.justice.gov/criminal-oia

Performs investigations necessary for extradition of fugitives from the United States and other nations. Handles U.S. and foreign government requests for mutual legal assistance, including documentary evidence.

Criminal Division *(Justice Dept.), International Affairs (OIA), International Prisoner Transfer Program, John C. Keeney Bldg., 1301 New York Ave. N.W., 10th Floor, 20005; (202) 514-3173. Fax, (202) 514-9003. Vaughn A. Ary, Director; Paula A. Wolff, Associate Director. Web, www.justice.gov/criminal-oeo/international-prisoner-transfer-program*

Implements prisoner transfer treaties with foreign countries.

State Dept., *Office of the Legal Adviser, Law Enforcement and Intelligence, 2201 C St. N.W., HST 4331, 20520; (202) 647-5654. Fax, (202) 647-4802. Karen Johnson, Assistant Legal Adviser. Web, www.state.gov/bureaus-offices/secretary-of-state/office-of-the-legal-adviser/office-of-the-legal-adviser-for-law-enforcement-and-intelligence*

Negotiates and approves extradition of fugitives between the United States and other nations.

Fishing, Law of the Sea

▶ AGENCIES

Bureau of Oceans and International Environmental and Scientific Affairs (OES) *(State Dept.), Marine Conservation (OMC), 2201 C St. N.W., #2758, 20520; (202) 647-2337. David F. Hogan, Director (Acting). Web, www.state.gov/about-us-office-of-marine-conservation/*

Promotes food security through sustainable fisheries.

Bureau of Oceans and International Environmental and Scientific Affairs (OES) *(State Dept.), Oceans and Polar Affairs (OPA), 2201 C St. N.W., #2665, 20520; (202) 647-3925. John Griffith, Director (Acting). Web, www.state.gov/about-us-office-of-ocean-and-polar-affairs/*

Promotes U.S. interests in ocean and polar affairs through implementation of the Law of the Sea Convention, participation in international conferences, and negotiation of formal agreements.

National Oceanic and Atmospheric Administration (NOAA) *(Commerce Dept.), National Marine Fisheries Service (NMFS), 1315 East-West Hwy., 14th Floor, Silver Spring, MD 20910; (301) 427-8000. Fax, (301) 713-1940. Janet Coit, Assistant Administrator. Press, (301) 427-8531. Web, www.fisheries.noaa.gov and Twitter, @NOAAFisheries*

Administers marine fishing regulations, including offshore fishing rights and international agreements.

U.S. Coast Guard (USCG) *(Homeland Security Dept.), Law Enforcement, Maritime Security and Defense Operations Policy, 2703 Martin Luther King Jr. Ave. S.E., MS 7516, 20593-7516; (202) 372-2161. Capt. John Paul (Paul) Gregg, Director. Press, (202) 372-4630.*

General email, mediarelations@uscg.mil

Web, www.dco.uscg.mil/Our-Organization/Assistant-Commandant-for-Response-Policy-CG-5R

Enforces domestic fisheries laws and international fisheries agreements.

▶**CONGRESS**

For a listing of relevant congressional committees and subcommittees, please see pages 478–479 or the Appendix.

Human Rights

▶**AGENCIES**

Bureau of Democracy, Human Rights, and Labor (DRL) *(State Dept.), 2201 C St. N.W., #7827, 20520-7812; (202) 647-1337. Fax, (202) 647-5283. Lisa Peterson, Assistant Secretary (Acting).*
Web, www.state.gov/j/drl, Twitter, @StateDRL, Facebook, www.facebook.com/StateDRL and YouTube, www.youtube.com/channel/UCSibCtobezepu_o-bukbglA

Implements U.S. policies relating to human rights, labor, and religious freedom; prepares annual review of human rights worldwide.

Bureau of Democracy, Human Rights, and Labor (DRL) *(State Dept.), Business and Human Rights, 2401 E St. N.W., SA-1, H430, 20037; (202) 663-2895. Lynn Sicade, Director.*
General email, IFBHR@state.gov
Web, www.state.gov/key-topics-bureau-of-democracy-human-rights-and-labor/business-and-human-rights

Fosters implementation of international human rights law and developing commitments in global business and human rights to create space for emerging and critical issues to be debated among relevant stakeholder groups. Seeks to develop and establish tools, training and guidance for U.S. government officials to be more effective envoys on business and human rights.

Bureau of Democracy, Human Rights, and Labor (DRL) *(State Dept.), International Labor Affairs (ILA), 1800 G St. N.W., SA-1, H430, 20006; (202) 663-3569. Stephen Moody, Director, (202) 663-3547.*
General email, DRL-ILA-DL@state.gov
Web, www.state.gov/key-topics-cureau-of-democracy-human-rights-and-labor/international-labor-affairs

Works with organized labor, nongovernmental organizations, international organizations, and corporations to monitor and promote worker rights throughout the world. Contributes to U.S. foreign policy goals related to democracy promotion, trade, development, and human rights.

Bureau of International Organization Affairs (IO) *(State Dept.), Human Rights and Humanitarian Affairs (HRH), 2401 E St. N.W., #SA-1, #L409, 20037; (202) 663-1176. Khaghayar Ghashghai, Director.*
Web, www.state.gov/p/io

Works with UN bodies to advance U.S. policy relating to human rights, democracy promotion, humanitarian assistance, women's issues, indigenous issues, and social affairs.

Criminal Division *(Justice Dept.), Human Rights and Special Prosecutions (HRSP), John C. Keeney Bldg., 1301 New York Ave. N.W., #215, 20530; (202) 616-2492. Fax, (202) 616-2491. Teresa McHenry, Chief.*
Web, www.justice.gov/criminal-hrsp

Tracks war criminals within the United States with connections to world genocidal conflicts; investigates and prosecutes human rights violators for torture, war crimes, recruitment or use of child soldiers, female genital mutilation, international antiquities trafficking, and immigration and naturalization fraud. Handles legal action to ensure denaturalization and/or deportation.

State Dept., *Global Women's Issues, 2201 C St. N.W., #7532, 20520; (202) 647-7285. Fax, (202) 647-7288. Katrina Fotovat, Senior Official.*
Web, www.state.gov/bureaus-offices/secretary-of-state/office-of-global-womens-issues, Twitter, @StateGWI and Facebook, www.facebook.com/StateGWI

Works to promote the human rights of women within U.S. foreign policy. Participates in international organizations and conferences; advises other U.S. agencies; disseminates information.

State Dept., *International Religious Freedom (IRF), 2201 C St. N.W., #5822, 20520; (202) 647-1237. Rashad Hussein, Ambassador-at-large.*
Web, www.state.gov/j/drl/irf and Twitter, @IRF-Ambassador

Monitors religious persecution and discrimination worldwide, recommends and implements regional policies, and develops programs to promote religious freedom.

State Dept., *Monitor and Combat Trafficking in Persons, 2025 E St. N.W., SA-9, 20520; (202) 453-8478. Fax, (202) 312-9637. Kari Johnstone, Deputy Senior Official.*
General email, tipoutreach@state.gov
Web, www.state.gov/bureaus-offices/under-secretary-for-civilian-security-democracy-and-human-rights/office-to-monitor-and-combat-trafficking-in-persons and Twitter, @JTIP_State

Combats trafficking in persons domestically and internationally. Publishes annual *Trafficking in Persons Report*, which assesses the progress of other governments, analyzes best practices and new data, and summarizes U.S. efforts to combat human trafficking at home. Funds programs that provide related law enforcement training, offer comprehensive victim services, and raise public awareness.

U.S. Commission on International Religious Freedom, *732 N. Capitol St. N.W., #A714, 20401; (202) 523-3240. Erin P. Singshinsuk, Executive Director.*
General email, media@uscirf.gov
Web, www.uscirf.gov, Twitter, @USCIRF, Facebook, www.facebook.com/uscirf and YouTube, www.youtube.com/USCIRF09

Agency created by the International Religious Freedom Act of 1998 to monitor religious freedom worldwide and to advise the president, the secretary of state, and Congress on how best to promote it.

►CONGRESS

For a listing of relevant congressional committees and sub-committees, please see pages 478–479 or the Appendix.

►NONGOVERNMENTAL

American Bar Assn. (ABA), *Rule of Law Initiative,* 1050 Connecticut Ave. N.W., #450, 20036; (202) 662-1950. Fax, (202) 662-1597. *Alberto J. Mora, Executive Director.* General email, rol@americanbar.org

Web, www.americanbar.org/advocacy/rule_of_law, Twitter, @ABARuleofLaw and Facebook, www.facebook .com/ABA.Rule.of.Law.Initiative

Promotes the rule of law and specific legal reforms in developing countries throughout the world; recruits volunteer legal professionals from the United States and western Europe. Interests include human rights, anticorruption initiatives, criminal law, efforts against human trafficking, judicial reform, legal education reform, civic education, reforming the legal profession, and women's rights.

Amnesty International USA, *Washington National Office,* 600 Pennsylvania Ave. S.E., 5th Floor, 20003; (202) 544-0200. Fax, (202) 546-7142. *Paul O'Brian, Executive Director; Joanne Lin, National Director for Advocacy and Government.* Toll-free, 800-AMNESTY. General email, aimember@aiusa.org

Web, www.amnestyusa.org and Twitter, @amnesty

International organization that investigates, exposes, and responds to human rights abuses. Works for the release of men and women imprisoned anywhere in the world for their beliefs, political affiliation, color, ethnic origin, sex, language, or religion, provided they have neither used nor advocated violence. Opposes torture and the death penalty; urges fair and prompt trials for all political prisoners. (U.S. headquarters in New York.)

Center for Human Rights and Humanitarian Law *(American University),* 4300 Nebraska Ave. N.W., 20016; (202) 274-4158. *Melissa C. del Aguila, Director (Acting).* General email, humlaw@wcl.american.edu

Web, www.wcl.american.edu/impact/initiatives-programs/ center, Twitter, @humanrts and Facebook, www.facebook .com/WCLCenterForHumanRights

Seeks to promote human rights and humanitarian law. Establishes training programs for judges, lawyers, and law schools; assists emerging democracies and other nations in developing laws and institutions that protect human rights; organizes conferences with public and private institutions. (Affiliated with the Washington College of Law at American University.)

ChildFund International, *Washington Office,* 1200 18th St. N.W., #718, 20036; (804) 756-2700. *Anne Lynam Goddard, President.* Toll-free, (800) 776-6767.

General email, questions@childfund.org

Web, www.childfund.org and Twitter, @ChildFund

Works internationally to ensure the survival, protection, and development of children. Promotes the improvement in quality of life of children within the context of family, community, and culture. Helps children in unstable situations brought on by war, natural disasters, and other high-risk circumstances. (Headquarters in Richmond, Va.)

FAIR Girls, 2021 L St. N.W., # 101-254, 20036; (202) 520-9777. *Dawanna Kennedy, Executive Director (Acting).* Crisis Hotline, (855) 900-3247. National Trafficking Hotline, (888) 373-7888. General email, info@fairgirls.org

Web, www.fairgirls.org, Twitter, @fair_girls and Facebook, www.facebook.com/fairgirls.org

Provides interventionist holistic care for survivors of trafficking who identify as girls or young women through prevention education and policy advocacy. Works to eradicate human trafficking and create improved outcomes for survivors.

Free the Slaves, 1320 19th St. N.W., #600, 20036; (202) 775-7480. Fax, (202) 775-7485. *Bukeni Waruzi, Executive Director.* General email, info@freetheslaves.net

Web, http://freetheslaves.net, Twitter, @FreeTheSlaves, Facebook, www.facebook.com/FreetheSlaves and Press, lily.bivins@freetheslaves.net

Conducts field operations in India, Nepal, Haiti, Ghana, Congo, and Senegal to liberate slaves and help them rebuild their lives and advocacy initiatives in the United States and overseas to change the economic, legal, and social conditions that allow modern slavery to exist. Partners with governments, international institutions, faith communities, and the business community to engage their assistance in creating an enabling environment for anti-slavery projects. Develops new monitoring and evaluation methods to establish slavery prevalence and programmatic impact.

Genocide Watch *(George Mason University),* School of Conflict Analysis, 3351 N. Fairfax Dr., MS 4D3, Arlington, VA 22201; *Gregory H. Stanton, Founding President,* (202) 643-1405. General email, communications@genocidewatch.org

Web, www.genocidewatch.com, Twitter, @genocide_watch and Facebook, www.facebook.com/GenocideWatch

Educates the public and policymakers about the causes, processes, and warning signs of genocide; seeks to create the institutions and the political will to prevent and stop genocide and to bring perpetrators of genocide to justice. (Coordinator of the Alliance Against Genocide.)

GoodWeave USA, 1111 14th St. N.W., #820, 20005; (202) 234-9050. Fax, (202) 234-9056. *Nina Smith, Chief Executive Officer.* General email, info@goodweave.org

Web, www.goodweave.org, Twitter, @GoodWeave and Facebook, www.facebook.com/GoodWeave

International human rights organization working to end child labor around the Globe. Especially the Indian, Nepalese, and Afghanistani global supply chains. Inspects and certifies workplace conditions. Runs schools and rehabilitation centers for former child workers.

Human Rights First, Washington Office, *805 15th St. N.W., #900, 20005-2207; (202) 547-5692. Fax, (202) 543-5999. Michael Breen, President. Press, (202) 370-3319. General email, press@humanrightsfirst.org*

Web, www.humanrightsfirst.org, Twitter, @humanrights1st and Facebook, www.facebook.com/humanrightsfirst

Promotes human rights as guaranteed by the International Bill of Human Rights. Mobilizes activists and the legal community to pressure the U.S. government and private companies to respect human rights and rule of the law. Advocates American leadership to secure core freedoms worldwide.

Human Rights Watch, Washington Office, *1275 K St. N.W., #1100, 20005; (202) 612-4321. Fax, (202) 612-4333. Sarah Yager, Washington Director. General email, hrwdc@hrw.org*

Web, www.hrw.org, Twitter, @hrw and Facebook, www .facebook.com/HumanRightsWatch

International, nonpartisan human rights organization that monitors human rights violations worldwide, subdivided into five regional concentrations—Africa, the Americas, Asia, Europe and Central Asia, and the Middle East and North Africa. Coordinates thematic projects on women's rights, LGBT rights, arms, children's rights, health and disability rights, business and human rights, counterterrorism, and international justice. Conducts fact-finding missions in more than 90 countries around the world; publicizes violations and encourages international protests; maintains file on human rights violations. (Headquarters in New York.)

International Assn. of Official Human Rights Agencies (IAOHRA), *444 N. Capitol St. N.W., #237, 20001; (202) 624-5410. Robin S. Toma, President. General email, iaohra@sso.org*

Web, www.iaohra.org

Works with government and human rights agencies worldwide to promote civil and human rights, including elimination of unlawful discrimination in employment, housing, education, and public accommodations. Offers management training for human rights executives and civil rights workshops for criminal justice agencies; develops training programs in investigative techniques, settlement and conciliation, and legal theory. Serves as an information clearinghouse on human rights laws and enforcement.

International Justice Mission, *P.O. Box 2202, Arlington, VA 22202; (703) 465-5495. Fax, (703) 774-3921. Philip Langford, President United States. General email, contact@ijm.org*

Web, www.ijm.org

Seeks to help people suffering injustice and oppression who cannot rely on local authorities for relief. Documents and monitors conditions of abuse and oppression, educates churches and the public about abuses, and mobilizes intervention on behalf of victims.

Jubilee Campaign USA, *9689-C Main St., Fairfax, VA 22031; (703) 503-2260. Fax, (703) 503-0792. Ann Buwalda, Executive Director. Toll-free, (877) 654-4331. General email, jubilee@jubileecampaign.org*

Web, www.jubileecampaign.org, Twitter, @JubileeC and Facebook, www.facebook.com/JubileeCampaignUSA/

Promotes human rights and religious liberty for ethnic and religious minorities in countries that oppress them. Advocates the release of prisoners of conscience and revising laws to achieve this. Especially interested in ending the exploitation of children.

Physicians for Human Rights, Washington Office, *1100 13th St. N.W., # 800, 20005; (202) 728-5335. Fax, (202) 728-3053. Jennifer Sime, Executive Director (Acting); Michael Payne, Deputy Director, Advocacy. Email, advocacy@phr.org,*

Web, https://phr.org, Twitter, @P4HR and Facebook, www.facebook.com/physiciansforhumanrights

Investigates and seeks to end human rights abuses, including, mass atrocities, sexual violence, weapons, asylum and persecution and when doctors harm. Advocates for justice around the world. Issues reports and press releases; conducts training programs on health and human rights issues; acts as advocate before policymakers. (Headquarters in New York City.)

Polaris Project, *P.O. Box 65323, 20035; (202) 790-6300. Fax, (202) 745-1119. Catherine Chen, Chief Executive Officer. 24-hour hotline, (888) 373-7888. Text, 233733. General email, info@polarisproject.org*

Web, www.polarisproject.org, Twitter, @Polaris_Project, Facebook, www.facebook.com/polarisproject and Legislative email, policy@polarisproject.org

Fights human trafficking at the local, national, and international levels with an emphasis on policy advocacy and survivor support. Operates the 24-hour National Human Trafficking Resource Center Hotline for victims, law enforcement agencies, and others.

Robert F. Kennedy Human Rights, *1300 19th St. N.W., #750, 20036-1651; (202) 463-7575. Kerry Kennedy, President. General email, communications@rfkhumanrights.org*

Web, https://rfkhumanrights.org, Twitter, @RFKHumanRights and Facebook, www.facebook.com/RFKHumanRights/

Presents annual book, journalism, and human rights awards and carries out programs that support the work of the human rights award laureates in their countries. Investigates and reports on human rights; campaigns to heighten awareness of these issues, stop abuses, and encourage governments, international organizations, and corporations to adopt policies that ensure respect for human rights. Provides training for human rights advocates.

International Trade Administration

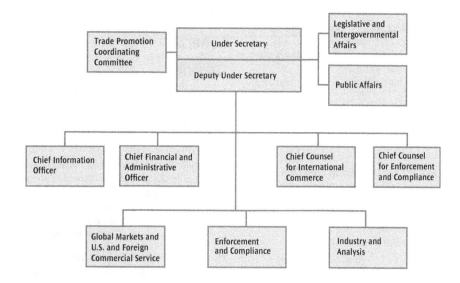

Torture Abolition and Survivors Support Coalition International (TASSC), *4121 Harewood Rd. N.E., Suite B, 20017-1597; (202) 529-2991. Léonce Byimana, Executive Director.*
General email, info@tassc.org

Web, www.tassc.org, Twitter, @TASSCintl and Facebook, www.facebook.com/tasscinternational

Coalition of torture survivors seeking to end torture through public education and political advocacy. Provides resources and information to survivors of torture and their families.

U.S. Conference of Catholic Bishops (USCCB),
International Justice and Peace, 3211 4th St. N.E., 20017-1194; (202) 541-3160. Lucas Koach, Executive Director, (202) 541-3181.
General email, sgross@usccb.org

Web, www.usccb.org/committees/international-justice-and-peace and Twitter, @wearesaltlight

Works with the U.S. State Dept., foreign government offices, and international organizations on issues of peace, justice, and human rights.

Narcotics Trafficking

▶AGENCIES

Bureau of International Narcotics and Law Enforcement Affairs (INL) *(State Dept.), 2201 C St. N.W., #HST7826, 20520-7512; (202) 647-8464.*
Todd D. Robinson, Assistant Secretary.
General email, INL-PAPD@state.gov

Web, www.state.gov/j/inl, Facebook, www.facebook.com/StateINL, Twitter, @StateINL and Blog, www.state.gov/blogs

Coordinates efforts to establish and facilitate stable criminal justice systems in order to strengthen international law enforcement and judicial effectiveness, bolster cooperation in legal affairs, and support the rule of law, while respecting human rights. Seeks to disrupt the overseas production and trafficking of illicit drugs by means of counterdrug and anticrime assistance and coordination with foreign nations and international organizations.

Defense Dept. (DoD), *Counternarcotics and Global Threats, 2500 Defense Pentagon, #5C653, 20301-2500; (703) 697-7202. Fax, (703) 692-6947.*
Joseph J. McMenamin, Deputy Assistant Secretary (Acting).
Web, https://policy.defense.gov/OUSDP-Offices/Under-Secretary-of-Defense-for-Policy/Counternarcotics-and-Global-Threats

Coordinates and monitors Defense Dept. support of civilian drug law enforcement agencies and interagency efforts to detect and monitor the maritime and aerial transit of illegal drugs into the United States. Represents the secretary on drug control matters outside the department.

Drug Enforcement Administration (DEA) *(Justice Dept.), 700 Army Navy Dr., Arlington, VA 22202 (mailing address: 8701 Morrissette Dr., MS AES, Springfield, VA 22152); (202) 307-1000. Fax, (202) 307-4540. Anne Milgram, Administrator. D.C. Division office, (202) 305-8500. Public Affairs, (202) 307-7977. Phone (Command Center), (202) 307-4228.*
Web, www.dea.gov

Assists foreign narcotics agents; cooperates with the State Dept., embassies, the Agency for International Development, and international organizations to strengthen narcotics law enforcement and to reduce supply and demand in developing countries; trains and advises narcotics enforcement officers in developing nations.

Internal Revenue Service (IRS) *(Treasury Dept.),* *Criminal Investigation,* *1111 Constitution Ave. N.W., 20224; (202) 317-3200. James Lee, Chief. Tax fraud hotline, (800) 366-4184. TTY, (800) 877-8339.*
Web, www.irs.gov/compliance/criminal-investigation and *Twitter, @IRSnews*

Lends support in counterterrorism and narcotics investigations conducted in conjunction with other law enforcement agencies, both foreign and domestic.

U.S. Coast Guard (USCG) *(Homeland Security Dept.), Law Enforcement, Maritime Security and Defense Operations Policy, 2703 Martin Luther King Jr. Ave. S.E., MS 7516, 20593-7516; (202) 372-2161. Capt. John Paul (Paul) Gregg, Director. Press, (202) 372-4630.*
General email, mediarelations@uscg.mil
Web, www.dco.uscg.mil/Our-Organization/Assistant-Commandant-for-Response-Policy-CG-5R

Combats smuggling of narcotics and other drugs into the United States via the Atlantic and Pacific Oceans and the Gulf of Mexico. Works with U.S. Customs and Border Protection on drug law enforcement.

U.S. Customs and Border Protection *(Homeland Security Dept.), Border Patrol, 1300 Pennsylvania Ave. N.W., #6.5E, 20229; (877) 227-5511. Raul L. Ortiz, Chief. TTY, (800) 877-8339.*
Web, www.cbp.gov/border-security/along-us-borders/overview

Mobile uniformed law enforcement arm of the Homeland Security Dept. Primary mission is to detect and prevent the illegal trafficking of people and contraband across U.S. borders.

U.S. Customs and Border Protection *(Homeland Security Dept.), Field Operations, 1300 Pennsylvania Ave. N.W., 20229; (202) 344-1620. Pete Flores, Executive Assistant Commissioner.*
Web, www.cbp.gov/border-security/ports-entry

Interdicts and seizes contraband, including narcotics and other drugs, at the U.S. border.

U.S. Immigration and Customs Enforcement (ICE) *(Homeland Security Dept.), 500 12th St. S.W., 20536; (202) 732-3000. Tae D. Johnson, Director (Acting). Press, (202) 732-4646. Hotline, (866) 347-2423. TTY, (802) 872-6196.*
General email, ICEmedia@ice.dhs.gov
Web, www.ice.gov, Twitter, @ICEgov, Facebook, www.facebook.com/wwwicegov and *YouTube, www.youtube.com/wwwicegov*

Investigates narcotics smuggling, including money laundering, document and identity fraud, and immigration enforcement; interdicts flow of narcotics into the United States.

INTERNATIONAL TRADE AND DEVELOPMENT

General

▶**AGENCIES**

Agriculture Dept. (USDA), *Under Secretary for Trade and Foreign Agricultural Affairs (TFAA), 1400 Independence Ave. S.W., MS 1001, 20250; (202) 720-3111. Vacant, Under Secretary.*
Web, www.fas.usda.gov and *Twitter, @USDAForeignAg*

Leads on trade policy and international agriculture issues domestically and abroad; facilitates foreign market access and promotes opportunities for U.S. agriculture through trade programs and high-level government negotiations. Oversees the Foreign Agricultural Service and coordinates U.S. participation in the Codex Alimentarius Commission.

Alcohol and Tobacco Tax and Trade Bureau (TTB) *(Treasury Dept.), International Affairs Division, 1310 G St. N.W., Box 12, 20005; (202) 453-2260. Fax, (202) 453-2970. Karen E. Welch, Director.*
General email, iad@ttb.gov
Web, www.ttb.gov/offices/international-affairs-division

Works with the Office of the U.S. Trade Representative and federal executive departments to facilitate the import/export trade in beverage and industrial alcohol. Coordinates briefings and other liaison activities for foreign alcohol and tobacco industry members and foreign government officials.

Antitrust Division *(Justice Dept.), International, 450 5th St. N.W., #11000, 20530; (202) 514-5816. Fax, (202) 514-4508. Lynda K. Marshall, Chief, (202) 598-2264.*
General email, ATR.International@usdoj.gov
Web, www.justice.gov/atr/international-program-4

Acts as the division's liaison with foreign governments and international organizations, including the European Union, regarding antitrust enforcement and competition issues. Works with the State Dept. to exchange information with foreign governments concerning investigations involving foreign corporations and nationals.

Bureau of Economic and Business Affairs (EB) *(State Dept.), 2201 C St. N.W., #4932, 20520-5820; (202) 647-7971. Fax, (202) 647-5713. Ramin Toloui, Assistant Secretary.*
Web, www.state.gov/e/eb, Twitter, @EconAtState, Facebook, www.facebook.com/EconAtState and *Blog, https://blogs.state.gov/issues/economic-and-business-issues*

Formulates and implements policies related to U.S. economic relations with foreign countries, including international business practices, communications and information, trade, finance, investment, development, natural resources, energy, and transportation.

Bureau of Economic and Business Affairs (EB) *(State Dept.), Commercial and Business Affairs (CBA), 2201 C St. N.W., #4480, 20520-5820; (202) 647-0079. Scott B. Ticknor, Special Representative (Acting).*

General email, cbaweb@state.gov

Web, www.state.gov/bureau-offices/under-secretary-for-economic-growth-enerby-and-the-environment/bureau-of-economic-and-business-affairs

Serves as primary contact in the State Dept. for U.S. businesses. Coordinates efforts to facilitate U.S. business interests abroad, ensures that U.S. business interests are given sufficient consideration in foreign policy, and provides assistance to firms with problems overseas (such as claims and trade complaints). Oversees the Global Entrepreneurship Program.

Bureau of Economic and Business Affairs (EB) *(State Dept.), Counter Threat Finance and Sanctions (TFS),* 2201 C St. N.W., #3425, 20520; (202) 647-2586. Erik Woodhouse, Deputy Assistant Secretary.
Web, www.state.gov/bureaus-offices/under-secretary-for-economic-growth-energy-and-the-environment/bureau-of-economic-and-business-affairs/division-for-coun

Coordinates efforts to create, modify, or terminate unilateral sanctions on regimes in countries such as such as Iran, Syria, and Cuba as appropriate to the changing international situation; builds international support for combating terrorist finance; provides foreign policy guidance to the Treasury and Commerce Depts. on specific commercial business, export, import, and general licensing issues.

Bureau of Economic and Business Affairs (EB) *(State Dept.), Counter Threat Finance and Sanctions (TFS), Economic Sanctions Policy and Implementation (SPI),* 2201 C St. N.W., #4657, 20520; (202) 647-7489. Fax, (202) 647-4064. Jim Mullinax, Director, (202) 647-7677.
Web, www.state.gov/economic-sanctions-policy-and-implementation

Develops and implements U.S. economic sanctions policy to maximize sanctions' economic impact and minimize the damage to U.S. economic interests, builds international support for implementation of economic sanctions. Cooperates with the Commerce, the Treasury Dept., and Congress regarding export controls.

Bureau of Economic and Business Affairs (EB) *(State Dept.), Trade Policy and Negotiations (TPN),* 2201 C St. N.W., #4652, 20520-5820; (202) 647-5911. Fax, (202) 647-1825. Tony Fernandez, Deputy Assistant Secretary.
General email, ebtpn@state.gov

Web, www.state.gov/bureaus-offices/under-secretary-for-economic-growth-energy-and-the-environment/bureau-of-economic-and-business-affairs/division-for-trad, Twitter, @EconAtState and Facebook, www.facebook.com/EconAtState

Develops and administers policies and programs on international trade, including trade negotiations and agreements, import relief, unfair trade practices, trade relations with developing countries, export development, and export controls (including controls imposed for national security or foreign policy purposes).

Bureau of Economic and Business Affairs (EB) *(State Dept.), Trade Policy and Negotiations (TPN), Agriculture Policy (AGP),* 2201 C St. N.W., #4686,

20520-0002; (202) 647-3090. Fax, (202) 647-1894. Jeffrey Gianque, Director, (202) 647-0133.
Web, www.state.gov/agricultural-policy

Develops agricultural trade policy; handles questions pertaining to international negotiations on all agricultural products covered by the World Trade Organization (WTO) and bilateral trade agreements. Oversees the distribution of biotechnology outreach funds to promote international acceptance of the technology.

Bureau of Economic and Business Affairs (EB) *(State Dept.), Trade Policy and Negotiations (TPN), Bilateral Trade Affairs (BTA),* 2201 C St. N.W., #4452, 20520; (202) 647-3784. Fax, (202) 647-6540. Robert D. Manogue, Director, (202) 647-4017.
Web, www.state.gov/bilateral-trade-affairs

Develops, negotiates, and implements free trade agreements, trade and investment framework agreements, and trade preference programs.

Bureau of Economic and Business Affairs (EB) *(State Dept.), Trade Policy and Negotiations (TPN), Intellectual Property Enforcement (IPE),* 2201 C St. N.W., #4931, 20520; (202) 647-3985. Fax, (202) 647-1825. Tarek Fahmy, Director.
Web, www.state.gov/intellectual-property-enforcement/

Leads the State Dept. innovation and intellectual property related initiatives in the G7 and the U.S.–China Strategic Economic Dialogue (SED); engages in IPR negotiations in the world's international organizations; oversees the distribution of training and technical assistance funds to help developing countries build IPR law enforcement capacity; undertakes public diplomacy programs. Participates in Strategy Targeting Organized Piracy (STOP!).

Bureau of Economic and Business Affairs (EB) *(State Dept.), Trade Policy and Negotiations (TPN), Multilateral Trade Affairs (MTA),* 2201 C St. N.W., #4725, 20520; (202) 647-6324. (202) 647-6956. Fax, (202) 647-0892. Amy E. Holman, Director.
Web, www.state.gov/multilateral-trade-affairs

Leads the State Dept. trade policy activities in multilateral institutions, including the World Trade Organization, World Customs Organization, and Organisation for Economic Co-operation and Development. Provides technical expertise in regional and bilateral trade negotiations, including labor, environment, services, government procurement, customs, trade remedies and enforcement, textiles, standards, regulatory cooperation, and trade capacity building.

Bureau of Economic and Business Affairs (EB) *(State Dept.), Transportation Affairs (TRA),* 2201 C St. N.W., #3817, 20520-3425; (202) 647-4045. Fax, (202) 647-4324. Richard Yoneoka, Deputy Assistant Secretary (Acting).
General email, EEB-A-TRA-DL@state.gov

Web, www.state.gov/bureaus-offices/under-secretary-for-economic-growth-energy-and-the-environment/bureau-of-economic-and-business-affairs/division-for-tran, Twitter, @EconAtState and Facebook, www.facebook.com/EconAtState

Supports the U.S. global transportation industry; negotiates international air services agreements; works with other departments on safe transportation infrastructure policies. Oversees the offices of Aviation Negotiations and Transportation Policy.

Bureau of Industry and Security (BIS) *(Commerce Dept.), 14th St. and Constitution Ave. N.W., #3898, 20230; (202) 482-4811. Jeremy Pelter, Under Secretary (Acting). Export licensing information, (202) 482-4811. Press, (202) 482-2721.*
Web, www.bis.doc.gov and Twitter, @BISgov

Administers the Export Administration Act; coordinates export administration programs of federal departments and agencies; maintains control lists and performs export licensing for the purposes of national security, foreign policy, and short supply. Monitors impact of foreign boycotts on the United States; ensures availability of goods and services essential to industrial performance on contracts for national defense. Assesses availability of foreign products and technology to maintain control lists and licensing.

Census Bureau *(Commerce Dept.), International Trade Management, 4600 Silver Hill Rd., #6K032, Suitland, MD 20233; Dale Kelly, Division Chief, (301) 763-6937. Trade Outreach Branch Phone, (800) 549-0595, ext. 5. General email, eid.international.trade.data@census.gov*
Web, www.census.gov/foreign-trade/index.html

Provides data on all aspects of foreign trade in commodities. Compiles information for 240 trading partners, including China, Japan, and Mexico, through all U.S. states and ports. Publishes the monthly economic indicator, U.S. International Trade in Goods and Services, in conjunction with the U.S. Bureau of Economic Analysis.

Federal Maritime Commission (FMC), *800 N. Capitol St. N.W., 20573-0001; (202) 523-5725. Daniel B. Maffei, Chair, (202) 523-5911; Lucille L. Marvin, Managing Director. TTY, (800) 877-8339. General email, inquiries@fmc.gov*
Web, www.fmc.gov, Twitter, @FMC_gov and Library, Libraryinquiries@fmc.gov

Regulates the foreign ocean shipping of the United States; reviews agreements (on rates, services, and other matters) filed by ocean common carriers for compliance with shipping statutes and grants limited antitrust immunity. Monitors the laws and practices of foreign governments that could have a discriminatory or otherwise adverse impact on shipping conditions in the United States. Enforces special regulatory requirements applicable to ocean common carriers owned or controlled by foreign governments (controlled carriers). Adjudicates claims filed by regulated entities and the shipping public. Library open to the public (Monday–Friday, 8:00 a.m.–4:30 p.m.).

Federal Trade Commission (FTC), *International Affairs, 600 Pennsylvania Ave. N.W., #H494, 20580; (202) 326-2600. Fax, (202) 326-2873. Randolph W. Tritell, Director, (202) 326-3051.*
Web, www.ftc.gov/about-ftc/bureaus-offices/office-international-affairs

Assists in the enforcement of antitrust laws and consumer protection by arranging appropriate cooperation and coordination with foreign governments in international cases. Negotiates bilateral and multilateral antitrust and consumer protection agreements and represents the United States in international antitrust policy forums. Assists developing countries in moving toward market-based economies.

Foreign Agricultural Service (FAS) *(Agriculture Dept.), 1400 Independence Ave. S.W., #5071S, MS 1001, 20250-1001; (202) 720-3935. Fax, (202) 690-2159. Daniel Whitley, Administrator (Acting). Public Affairs, (202) 720-7115. TTY, (202) 720-1786.*
Web, www.fas.usda.gov, Twitter, @USDAForeignAg and Press, press-fas@usda.gov

Expands and maintains access to foreign markets for U.S. agricultural products by removing trade barriers and enforcing U.S. rights under existing trade agreements. Works with foreign governments, international organizations, and the Office of the U.S. Trade Representative to establish international standards and rules to improve accountability and predictability for agricultural trade.

International Trade Administration (ITA) *(Commerce Dept.), 1401 Constitution Ave. N.W., Room 3850, 20230; (202) 482-2867. Marisa Lago, Under Secretary. Toll-free, (800) 872-8723.*
Web, www.trade.gov and Twitter, @TradeGov

Seeks to strengthen the competitiveness of U.S. industry, promote trade and investment, and ensure fair trade and compliance with trade law and agreements.

International Trade Administration (ITA) *(Commerce Dept.), Enforcement and Compliance (E&C), 1401 Constitution Ave. N.W., Room 3099B, 20230; (202) 482-1780. Fax, (202) 482-0947. Lisa Wang, Assistant Secretary. Communications, (202) 482-0063.*
Web, http://trade.gov/resolve-trade-problem

Safeguards and enhances the competitive strength of U.S. industries against unfair trade through the enforcement of U.S. antidumping duty (AD) and countervailing duty (CVD) trade laws and ensures compliance with trade agreements negotiated on behalf of U.S. industries. Promotes the creation and maintenance of U.S. jobs and economic growth by supporting the negotiation of international trade agreements to open foreign markets. Administers the Foreign Trade Zones Program and certain sector-specific agreements and programs, such as the Steel Import Monitoring and Analysis licensing program.

International Trade Administration (ITA) *(Commerce Dept.), Global Markets, 1401 Constitution Ave. N.W., Room 38006, 20230 (mailing address: 1401 Constitution Ave. N.W., MD 3868A, Washington, DC 20230); (202) 482-5777. Fax, (202) 482-5444. Dale Tasharski, Assistant Secretary (Acting).*
Web, www.trade.gov/global-markets

Develops and implements trade and investment policies affecting countries, regions, or international organizations to improve U.S. market access abroad. Provides information and analyses of foreign market barriers and economic conditions to the U.S. private sector; monitors foreign compliance with trade agreements signed with the United States.

International Trade Administration (ITA) *(Commerce Dept.), Global Markets, North and Central America, 1401 Constitution Ave. N.W., Room 30020, #3826, 20230 (mailing address: 1401 Constitution Ave. N.W., MD 30019, Washington, DC 20230); (202) 482-1545. Fax, (202) 482-5013. Geri Word, Director.*
Web, www.trade.gov

Coordinates Commerce Dept. activities and assists U.S. business regarding export to Mexico, Canada, Central America, and the Caribbean. Helps negotiate and ensures compliance with U.S. free trade agreements, including USMCA (United States–Mexico–Canada Agreement) and the Dominican Republic–Central American Free Trade Agreement (CAFTA-DR).

International Trade Administration (ITA) *(Commerce Dept.), Global Markets, SelectUSA, 1401 Constitution Ave. N.W., Room 30033, 20230-0001 (mailing address: 1401 Constitution Ave. N.W., MD 30031, Washington, DC 20230); (202) 482-5244. Fax, (202) 482-3643. William Burwell, Executive Director (Acting). Call Center, (202) 482-6800.*
General email, SelectUSA@trade.gov

Web, http://selectusa.gov and Twitter, @SelectUSA

Manages foreign direct investment promotion and encourages U.S. companies to expand, add new facilities, and bring back jobs from abroad. Facilitates investor inquiries, conducts outreach to foreign investors, provides support for state and local governments' investment promotion efforts, and serves as an ombudsman in Washington, DC, for the international investment community. Website available in eight languages.

International Trade Administration (ITA) *(Commerce Dept.), Global Markets, U.S. and Foreign Commercial Service, 1401 Constitution Ave. N.W., Room 38006, 20230 (mailing address: 1401 Constitution Ave. N.W., MD 3868A, Washington, DC 20230); (202) 482-5777. Dale N. Tasharski, Deputy Director General.*
Web, www.trade.gov/

Promotes the export of U.S. goods and services; protects and advocates U.S. business interests abroad; provides counseling and information on overseas markets, international contacts, and trade promotion.

International Trade Administration (ITA) *(Commerce Dept.), Industry and Analysis (I&A), 1401 Constitution Ave. N.W., Room 2854, 20230; (202) 482-1112. Fax, (202) 482-5697. Anne Driscoll, Assistant Secretary (Acting).*
Web, www.trade.gov/industry-analysis

Seeks to strengthen the international competitiveness of U.S. businesses; coordinates export promotion programs and trade missions; compiles and analyzes trade data.

Divisions focus on basic industries, service industries and finance, technology and aerospace, consumer goods, tourism, and environmental technologies exports.

International Trade Administration (ITA) *(Commerce Dept.), Industry and Analysis (I&A), Industry Engagement, Strategic Partnership Program, 1401 Constitution Ave. N.W., Room 2065, 20230; (202) 482-1124. Jamie Merriman, Director of Strategic Partnership Program.*
General email, partners@trade.gov
Web, www.trade.gov/strategic-partnership-program

Works in conjunction with trade associations, private corporations, chambers of commerce, government entities, and other organizations to leverage combined resources to further U.S. exports.

International Trade Administration (ITA) *(Commerce Dept.), Industry and Analysis (I&A), National Travel and Tourism (NTTO), 1401 Constitution Ave. N.W., Room 10003, 20230-0001; (202) 482-4904. Fax, (202) 482-2887. Julie Heizer, Deputy Assistant Secretary (Acting).*
General email, ntto@trade.gov
Web, http://trade.gov/about-us/national-travel-and-tourism-office and Twitter, @nttotradegov

Fosters international tourism trade development, including public-private partnerships; represents the United States in tourism-related meetings with foreign government officials. Assembles, analyzes, and disseminates data and statistics on travel and tourism to and from the United States.

International Trade Administration (ITA) *(Commerce Dept.), Industry and Analysis (I&A), Trade Policy and Analysis (OTNA), 1401 Constitution Ave. N.W., Room 21028, 20230; (202) 482-3177. Fax, (202) 482-4614. Praveen Dixit, Deputy Assistant Secretary.*
Web, https://trade.gov/about-us/trade-policy-analysis

Monitors and analyzes U.S. international trade and competitive performance, foreign direct investment in the United States, and international economic factors affecting U.S. trade; identifies future trends and problems.

National Institute of Food and Agriculture (NIFA) *(Agriculture Dept.), Center for International Programs, 800 9th St. S.W., #2436, 20024 (mailing address: 1400 Independence Ave. S.W., MS 2203, Washington, DC 20250-2203); (202) 720-2791. Fax, (202) 690-2355. Timothy W. Conner, Director (Acting), (816) 926-1816. Web, https://nifa.usda.gov/office/center-international-programs*

Promotes science education in developing economies and shares research to enhance food production and stabilize economies. Interests include agricultural extension, teaching, and research.

National Institute of Standards and Technology (NIST) *(Commerce Dept.), Standards Services, 100 Bureau Dr., MS 2100, Gaithersburg, MD 20899-1200; (301) 975-4000. Fax, (301) 975-4715. Gordon Gillerman, Director, (301) 975-8406.*

General email, sco@nist.gov

*Web, www.nist.gov/standardsgov and www.nist.gov/topics/
standards*

Monitors and participates in industries' development
of federal and global standards and standard-enforcement
mechanisms. Conducts standards-related research and
training and holds workshops for domestic and international audiences. Provides information on industry
standards and specifications, conformity assessment, test
methods, domestic and international technical regulations,
codes, and recommended practices.

President's Export Council *(Commerce Dept.), 1401
Constitution Ave. N.W., #4043, 20230; (202) 482-5876.
Fax, (202) 482-4452. Diane Farrell, Under Secretary.
Web, www.trade.gov/pec*

Advises the president on all aspects of export trade,
including export controls, promotion, and expansion.
Composed of up to 28 private-sector leaders in business,
agriculture, and federal, state, and local government.

Small Business Administration (SBA), *International
Trade, 409 3rd St. S.W., #2400, 20416; (202) 205-6720.
Fax, (202) 205-7272. Gabriel Esparza, Associate
Administrator, (202) 205-6750.
Web, www.sba.gov/about-sba/sba-locations/headquarters-
offices/office-international-trade*

Offers instruction, assistance, and information on
exporting through counseling and conferences. Helps businesses gain access to export financing through loan guarantee programs.

State Dept., *Under Secretary for Economic Growth,
Energy, and the Environment, 2201 C St. N.W., #7256,
20520-7512; (202) 647-7575. Fax, (202) 647-0675.
Jose W. Fernandez, Under Secretary.
Web, www.state.gov/bureaus-offices/under-secretary-for-
economic-growth-energy-and-the-environment, Twitter,
@State_E and Facebook, www.facebook.com/StateDeptE*

Advises the secretary on formulation and implementa-
tion of international economic policies and programs,
including international monetary and financial affairs,
trade, telecommunications, energy, agriculture, commodi-
ties, investments, and international transportation issues.
Coordinates economic summit meetings. Oversees the
Bureau of Economic and Business Affairs, Bureau of
Energy Resources, Bureau of Oceans and International
Environmental and Scientific Affairs, Office of the Chief
Economist, and Office of the Science and Technology
Adviser.

Trade Promotion Coordinating Committee, *14th St.
and Constitution Ave. N.W., #31027, 20230; (202)
482-5455. Fax, (202) 482-4137. Gina M. Raimondo,
Secretary of Commerce; Tricia Van Orden, Deputy
Director.
Web, www.trade.gov/tpcc, Twitter, @TradeGov, Facebook,
www.facebook.com/TradeGov and YouTube, www
.youtube.com/TradeGov*

Coordinates all export promotion and export financing activities of the U.S. government. Composed of heads

of the departments of Commerce, State, Treasury, Defense,
Homeland Security, Interior, Agriculture, Labor, Transpor-
tation, and Energy, OMB, U.S. Trade Representative,
National Security Council/National Economic Council,
EPA, Small Business Administration, AID, Export-Import
Bank, Overseas Private Investment Corp., and the U.S.
Trade and Development Agency. Secretary of Commerce
is the chair.

Treasury Dept., *International Affairs, International
Trade, 1500 Pennsylvania Ave. N.W., #5204, 20220; (202)
622-2000. Fax, (202) 622-1731. Lailee Moghtader, Director,
(202) 622-1819.
Web, https://home.treasury.gov/about/offices/
international-affairs*

Formulates Treasury Dept. foreign trade policies and
coordinates them with other agencies through the U.S.
Trade Representative.

Treasury Dept., *Terrorism and Financial Intelligence,
Foreign Assets Control (OFAC), 1500 Pennsylvania Ave.
N.W., Treasury Annex, 20220; (202) 622-2490.
Andrea G. Gacki, Director. Licensing Division, (202) 622-
2480. Toll-free, (800) 540-6322.
General email, ofac_feedback@treasury.gov
Web, www.treasury.gov/about/organizational-structure/
offices/Pages/Office-of-Foreign-Assets-Control.aspx*

Administers and enforces economic and trade sanctions against targeted foreign countries and regimes, terrorists, international narcotics traffickers, transnational
criminal organizations, and those engaged in activities
related to the proliferation of weapons of mass destruction.
Acts under presidential wartime and national emergency
powers, as well as under authority granted by specific legislation, to impose controls on transactions and freeze foreign assets under U.S. jurisdiction.

U.S. Customs and Border Protection *(Homeland
Security Dept.), 1300 Pennsylvania Ave. N.W., #4.4A,
20229; (202) 325-8000. Chris Magnus, Commissioner.
Toll-free, (877) 227-5511. Hotline, (800) 232-5378. Public
Affairs, (202) 344-1780. TTY, (800) 877-8339.
Web, www.cbp.gov, Twitter, @cbp and Facebook, www
.facebook.com/CBPgov*

Collects import and export data for international trade
statistics. Library open to the public by appointment.

U.S. Customs and Border Protection *(Homeland
Security Dept.), Commercial Targeting and Analysis
Center, 1300 Pennsylvania Ave. N.W., 20229; (571)
468-2600. Pinky S. Khan, Branch Chief.
General email, ctac@cdp.dhs.gov
Web, www.cbp.gov/trade/priority-issues/import-safety/ctac*

Facilitates information sharing among participating
government agencies to prevent, deter, interdict, and investigate violations of U.S. import and export laws.

U.S. Foreign Trade Zones Board *(Commerce Dept.),
1401 Constitution Ave. N.W., #21013, 20230; (202) 482-
2862. Andrew McGilvray, Executive Secretary;
Diane Farrell, Under Secretary for International Trade.*

Web, www.trade.gov/ftz, Twitter, @TradeGov, Facebook, www.facebook.com/TradeGov and General email, ftz@trade.gov

Authorizes public and private corporations to establish foreign trade zones to which foreign and domestic goods can be brought without being subject to customs duties.

U.S. International Trade Commission, *500 E St. S.W., 20436; (202) 205-2000. Jason E. Kearns, Chair; Rashmi Bartlett, Inspector General. Press, (202) 205-1819. TDD, (202) 205-1810.*
Web, www.usitc.gov

Provides Congress, the president, and the U.S. trade representative with technical information and advice on trade and tariff matters. Determines the impact of imports on U.S. industries in antidumping and countervailing duty investigations. Directs actions against certain unfair trade practices, such as intellectual property infringement. Investigates and reports on U.S. industries and the global trends that affect them. Publishes the Harmonized Tariff Schedule of the United States. Library open to the public.

U.S. International Trade Commission, *Industries,* *500 E St. S.W. 500 E St. S.W., 20436, 20436; (202) 205-3296. Jonathan R. Coleman, Director, (202) 205-3465.*
Web, www.usitc.gov/offices/industries and www.usitc.gov/industries

Identifies, analyzes, and develops data on economic and technical matters related to the competitive position of the United States in domestic and world markets in agriculture and forest production, chemicals, textiles, energy, technology, transportation, services and investments, minerals, metals, and machinery.

U.S. Trade and Development Agency, *1101 Wilson Blvd., #1100, Arlington, VA 22209-3901; (703) 875-4357. Vinai Thummlapally, Director (Acting).*
Web, www.ustda.gov, Twitter, @USTDA and YouTube, www.youtube.com/USTDA

Independent federal government agency assisting U.S. companies exporting to developing and middle-income countries. Provides grants for feasibility studies. Offers technical assistance and identifies commercial opportunities in these countries.

U.S. Trade Representative *(Executive Office of the President),* *600 17th St. N.W., 20508; 202-395-2870. Amb. Katherine Tai, U.S. Trade Representative. Congressional affairs, (202) 395-3406. Hotline, (202) 395-5725.*
General email, media@ustr.eop.gov
Web, www.ustr.gov and Twitter, @USTradeRep

Serves as principal adviser to the president and primary trade negotiator on international trade policy. Develops and coordinates U.S. trade policy, including commodity and direct investment matters, import remedies, East-West trade policy, U.S. export expansion policy, and the implementation of MTN (Multilateral Trade Negotiations) agreements. Conducts international trade negotiations and represents the United States in World Trade Organization (WTO) matters.

U.S. Trade Representative *(Executive Office of the President), Intergovernmental Affairs and Public Engagement (IAPE),* *600 17th St. N.W., #107, 20508; (202) 395-2870. Juan A. Millan, Assistant U.S. Trade Representative for Monitoring and Enforcement.*
Web, www.ustr.gov/about-us/policy-offices/intergovernmental-affairs

Leads the U.S. Trade Representative's public outreach efforts to state and local governments; business and agricultural communities; and labor, environmental, and consumer groups. Oversees the U.S. Trade Advisory Committee system.

► **CONGRESS**

For a listing of relevant congressional committees and subcommittees, please see pages 478–479 or the Appendix.

Government Accountability Office (GAO), *International Affairs and Trade (IAT),* *441 G St. N.W., 20548; (202) 512-2964. Chelsa L. Kenney, Director.*
Web, www.gao.gov/about/careers/our-teams

Audits, analyzes, and evaluates international programs and trade; evaluates economic, political, and security problems worldwide. In addition to federal departments, oversight work includes U.S. Agency for International Development, Office of the U.S. Trade Representative, Broadcasting Board of Governors, North Atlantic Treaty Organization, World Bank, International Monetary Fund, and United Nations.

► **JUDICIARY**

U.S. Court of Appeals for the Federal Circuit, *717 Madison Pl. N.W., 20439; (202) 275-8000. Kimberly A. Moore, Chief Circuit Judge; Peter R. Marksteiner, Clerk of the Court, (202) 272-8020. Mediation, (202) 275-8120.*
Web, www.cafc.uscourts.gov

Reviews decisions concerning the International Trade Commission.

► **INTERNATIONAL ORGANIZATIONS**

European Union, *Delegation to the United States of America,* *2175 K St. N.W., 20037; (202) 862-9500. Stavros Lambrinidis, Ambassador.*
General email, delegation-usa-info@eeas.europa.eu
Web, www.euintheus.org, Twitter, @EUintheUS, Facebook, www.facebook.com/EUintheUS and Twitter, Ambassador, @EUAAmbUS

Information and public affairs office in the United States for the European Union. Advances transatlantic trade policies and direct foreign investment; negotiates the Transatlantic Trade and Investment Partnership (TTIP). (Headquarters in Brussels.)

Food and Agriculture Organization of the United Nations (FAO), *Washington Office,* *Iason Office LOW, 2121 K St. N.W., #800-B, 20037-0001; (202) 653-2400.*

Fax, (202) 653-5760. Jocelyn Brown Hall, Director; Thomas Pesek, Senior Liaison Officer.

General email, FAOLOW@fao.org

Web, www.fao.org/north-america/en, Twitter, @FAONorthAmerica and Facebook, www.facebook.com/ UNFAO

Offers development assistance; collects, analyzes, and disseminates information; provides policy and planning advice to governments regards food and nutition security; acts as an international forum for debate on food and agricultural issues, including animal health and production, fisheries, and forestry; encourages sustainable agricultural development and a long-term strategy for the conservation and management of natural resources. Coordinates World Food Day. (International headquarters in Rome.)

International Economic Development Council, *1275 K St. N.W., #300, 20005; (202) 223-7800. Fax, (202) 223-4745. Jeffrey (Jeff) Finkle, President.*

General email, mail@iedconline.org

Web, www.iedconline.org, Twitter, @IEDCtweets and Facebook, www.facebook.com/iedcONLINE

Membership: public economic development directors, chamber of commerce staff, utility executives, academicians, and others who design and implement development programs. Provides information to members on job creation, attraction, and retention.

Organisation for Economic Co-operation and Development (OECD), *Washington Center, 1776 Eye St. N.W., #450, 20006; (202) 785-6323. Will Davis, Head of Center, (202) 822-3869.*

General email, washington.contact@oecd.org

Web, www.oecd.org/washington, Twitter, @oced_ washington and Facebook, www.facebook.com/ OECDWashington/

Membership: 34 nations, including Australia, Canada, Japan, Mexico, New Zealand, the United States, and western European nations. Funded by membership contributions. Serves as a forum for members to exchange information and coordinate their economic policies; compiles statistics. Washington Center sells OECD publications and software; maintains a reference library that is open to the public. (Headquarters in Paris.)

Organization of American States (OAS), *Executive Secretariat for Integral Development (SEDI), Dept. of Economic Development (DED), 1889 F St. N.W., #750, 20024; (202) 370-9953. Fax, (202) 458-3561. Maryse Robert, Director, ext. 9953.*

General email, mrobert@oas.org

Web, www.oas.org/en/sedi/desd

Responsible for matters related to economic development in the hemisphere, with a focus on micro, small, and medium-sized enterprises. Works to promote economic growth, social inclusion, competition, and innovation.

The SEEP Network (The Small Enterprise Education and Promotion Network), *1621 N. Kent St., #900, Arlington,*

VA 22209; (202) 534-1400. Fax, (703) 276-1433. Alex Sander, Executive Director.

General email, seep@seepnetwork.org

Web, https://seepnetwork.org/Our-Story and Twitter, @TheSEEPNetwork

Membership: international organizations seeking to end poverty. Promotes inclusive markets and financial systems to improve impoverished areas. Conducts research on industry trends, opinions, and practices in developing countries. Interests include financial services and business development.

Trans-Atlantic Business Council, *1601 K St. N.W., 20001; (202) 778-9073. Fax, (202) 778-9100. Bart Gordon, U.S. Director.*

Web, http://transatlanticbusiness.org and Twitter, @TABC_Council

Membership: a consortium of more than 70 multinational corporations with operations in Europe and the United States. Promotes a barrier-free transatlantic market that contributes to economic growth, innovation, and security.

World Bank, *1818 H St. N.W., 20433; (202) 473-1000. Fax, (202) 477-6391. David Malpass, President; DJ Nordquist, U.S. Executive Director. Anticorruption hotline, (202) 458-7677. Press, (202) 473-7660. Publications, (800) 645-7247 or (703) 661-1580.*

General email, info_us@worldbank.org

Web, www.worldbank.org/en/country/unitedstates and Twitter, @worldbank

International development institution funded by government membership subscriptions and borrowings on private capital markets. Aims to end extreme poverty and advance education, health, and economies. Finances economic development projects in agriculture, environmental protection, education, public utilities, telecommunications, water supply, sewerage, public health, and other areas.

▶**NONGOVERNMENTAL**

Ashoka: Innovators for the Public, *1700 N. Moore St., #2000, Arlington, VA 22209; (703) 527-8300. Fax, (703) 527-8383. Bill Drayton, Chief Executive Officer.*

General email, info@ashoka.org

Web, www.ashoka.org and Twitter, @Ashoka

Supports fellowships for individuals with ideas for social change and entrepreneurship in seventy developing nations. Provides fellows with research support, organizational networking, legal counseling, economic support, and business consulting. Seeks to educate the public about the developing world and the work of its fellows.

Assn. of Foreign Investors in Real Estate, *1300 Pennsylvania Ave. N.W., 20004-3020; (202) 312-1400. Gunnar Branson, Chief Executive Officer, (202) 312-1401.*

General email, info@afire.org

Web, www.afire.org and Twitter, @AFIREglobal

Represents foreign institutions that are interested in the laws, regulations, and economic trends affecting the U.S.

commercial real estate market. Informs the public and the government of the contributions foreign investment makes to the U.S. economy. Examines current issues and organizes seminars for members.

Assn. of Women in International Trade, *100 M St. S.E., #600, 20003 (mailing address: P.O. Box 76825, Washington, DC 20013); (202) 869-3775. Emily Beline, President.*
General email, info@wiit.org
Web, www.wiit.org, Twitter, @wiit_dc and Facebook, www .facebook.com/WIIT.org

Membership: women and men from all sectors concerned with international trade, including import-export firms, government, corporations, and nonprofit organizations. Provides members with opportunities for professional development. Maintains job bank and sponsors mentoring program.

British–American Business Assn. BABA, *Washington D.C., P.O. Box 16482, 20041; (202) 293-0010. Fax, (202) 296-3332. LeeAnn Petersen, Executive Director.*
General email, info@babawashington.org
Web, www.babawashington.org, Twitter, @BABADC and Facebook, www.facebook.com/British-American-Business-Association-285855604285

Organization dedicated to the development of business relations between the United Kingdom and the United States. Including policy and market developments.

The Brookings Institution, *Global Economy and Development Studies, 1775 Massachusetts Ave. N.W., 20036; (202) 238-3552. Brahima Sangafowa Coulibaly, Director, (202) 540-7753.*
General email, globalmedia@brookings.edu
Web, www.brookings.edu/global and Twitter, @BrookingsGlobal

Facilitates international policy debate on globalization, poverty reduction, global economy, and public goods.

Center for Global Development, *2055 L St. N.W., #500, 20036; (202) 416-4000. Fax, (202) 416-4050. Masood Ahmed, President. Press, (202) 416-4040.*
General email, info@cgdev.org
Web, www.cgdev.org, Twitter, @CGDev and Facebook, www.facebook.com/CGDEV

Works to reduce global poverty and inequality through policy-oriented research and active engagement on development issues with policymakers and the public. Conducts independent research to develop practical ideas for global prosperity.

Center for International Private Enterprise, *1211 Connecticut Ave. N.W., #700, 20036; (202) 721-9200. Fax, (202) 280-1000. Andrew Wilson, Executive Director.*
General email, info@cipe.org
Web, www.cipe.org, Twitter, @CIPEglobal and Facebook, www.facebook.com/CIPEDC

Promotes global democratic development through private enterprise and market-oriented reform. Supported by the National Endowment for Democracy, works with business leaders, policymakers, and journalists to build civic institutions. Key program areas include anticorruption, access to information, the informal sector and property rights, and women and youth.

Cultivating New Frontiers in Agriculture (CNFA), *1828 L St. N.W., #710, 20036; (202) 296-3920. Fax, (202) 296-1271. Sylvain Roy, President.*
General email, info@cnfa.org
Web, www.cnfa.org, Twitter, @CNFA and Facebook, www .facebook.com/CNFAGlobal

International development organization that has worked in more than 42 countries to provide agricultural solutions to stimulate economic growth and improve livelihoods by cultivating entrepreneurship.

Economic Strategy Institute, *1730 Rhode Island Ave. N.W., #414, 20036; (202) 213-7051. Fax, (202) 339-0880. Clyde V. Prestowitz Jr., President.*
General email, info@econstrat.org
Web, http://econstrat.org and Twitter, @clydeprestowitz

Works to increase U.S. economic competitiveness through research on domestic and international economic policies, industrial and technological developments, and global security issues. Testifies before Congress and government agencies.

Global Business Dialogue Inc., *1140 Connecticut Ave. N.W., #950, 20036; R. K. (Judge) Morris, President.*
General email, comments@gbdinc.org
Web, www.gbdinc.org

Promotes discussion of trade and investment policies within the global business community.

Institute for Sustainable Communities, *Washington Office, 888 17th St. N.W., #610, 20006; (802) 255-2946. Deeohn Ferris, President, Washington Office. Toll-free, (802) 225-2900.*
General email, isc@sustain.org
Web, https://sustain.org, Twitter, @SustainableComm and Facebook, www.facebook.com/SustainableComm

Provides training and technical assistance to communities around the world to engage citizens in developing and implementing plans for a sustainable future. Interests include civil and human rights, public health, arms control, and environmental and consumer affairs. Aids groups in making better use of resources, such as access to the media and coalition building. (Headquarters in Montpelier, Vt.)

International Business Ethics Institute, *1725 Eye St. N.W., #300, 20006; (202) 296-6938. Fax, (202) 296-5897. Lori Tansey Martens, President.*
General email, info@business-ethics.org
Web, https://business-ethics.org

Works to increase public awareness and dialogue about international business ethics issues through various educational resources and activities. Works with companies to assist them in establishing effective international ethics programs.

International Executive Service Corps (IESC), *2000 M St. N.W., #250, 20036; (202) 589-2600. David Hartingh, President.*
General email, iesc@iesc.org
Web, https://iesc.org and Twitter, @IESCorps

Promotes self-sustainable economic growth in developing countries. Implements financial and management programs to improve trade, technology, and tourism. Includes the Geekcorps division to assist in managing technical programs.

National Assn. of Manufacturers (NAM), *International Economic Affairs, 733 10th St. N.W., #700, 20001; (202) 637-3144. Fax, (202) 637-3182. Ken Monahan, Vice President.*
General email, info@nam.org
Web, www.nam.org

Represents manufacturing business interests on international economic issues, including trade, international investment, export financing, and export controls.

National Customs Brokers and Forwarders Assn. of America, *8601 Georgia Ave., Suite 612, Silver Spring, MD 20910; (202) 466-0222. Jan Fields, President; Federico (Kiko) Zuniga, Executive Director.*
General email, membership@ncbfaa.org
Web, www.ncbfaa.org

Membership: customs brokers and freight forwarders in the United States. Fosters information exchange within the industry. Monitors legislation and regulations.

National Foreign Trade Council, *1225 New York Ave. N.W., #650B, 20005; (202) 887-0278. Fax, (202) 452-8160. Jake Colvin, President.*
General email, nftcinformation@nftc.org
Web, www.nftc.org, Twitter, @NFTC and Facebook, www.facebook.com/National-Foreign-Trade-Council

Membership: U.S. companies engaged in international trade and investment. Advocates open international trading, export expansion, and policies to assist U.S. companies competing in international markets. Provides members with information on international trade topics. Sponsors seminars and conferences.

U.S. Chamber of Commerce, *International Affairs Division, 1615 H St. N.W., 20062-2000; (202) 463-5460. Myron Brilliant, Executive Vice President.*
Web, www.uschamber.com/international-affairs-division and Twitter, @ChamberGlobal

Provides liaison with network of U.S. chambers of commerce abroad; administers bilateral business councils; responsible for international economic policy development; informs members of developments in international affairs, business economics, and trade; sponsors seminars and conferences. Monitors legislation and regulations.

United States Council for International Business, *Policy and Government Affairs, 1400 K St. N.W., #525, 20005; (202) 371-1316. Fax, (202) 371-8249. Declan Daly, Senior Vice President.*
General email, info@uscib.org
Web, www.uscib.org/policy-advocacy and Twitter, @USCIB

Membership: multinational corporations, service companies, law firms, and business associations. Represents U.S. business positions before intergovernmental bodies, foreign governments, and business communities. Promotes an open system of world trade, finance, and investment. (Headquarters in New York.)

Urban Institute, *Center on International Development and Governance, 500 L'Enfant Plaza S.W., 20024; (202) 833-7200. Charles Cadwell, Past President and Institute Fellow. Press, (202) 261-5709.*
General email, idginfo@urban.org
Web, www.urban.org/research-area/international-development and Facebook, www.facebook.com/urbaninstitute

Promotes economic and democratic development in developing and transition countries. Conducts research and works with government officials, international development agencies, and international financial institutions to provide technical assistance toward local governance, service delivery, and public finance.

Washington International Trade Assn., *1300 Pennsylvania Ave. N.W., #G-329, 20004-3014; (202) 312-1600. Fax, (202) 312-1601. Kenneth I. (Ken) Levinson, Executive Director.*
General email, wita@wita.org
Web, https://wita.org, Twitter, @WITA_DC and Facebook, www.facebook.com/WITA.org

Membership: trade professionals. Conducts programs and provides neutral forums to discuss international trade issues. Monitors legislation and regulations.

Development Assistance

▶AGENCIES

Agency for International Development (USAID), *Bureau for Development, Democracy and Innovation (DDI), Center for Education, 1300 Pennsylvania Ave. N.W., #3.08-095, 20523-3901; (202) 712-0000, ext. 63427. Leanna Marr, Deputy Assistant Administrator (Acting).*
General email, education@usaid.gov
Web, www.usaid.gov/education, Twitter, @USAIDEducation and Facebook, www.facebook.com/USAIDEducation/

Provides field support, technical leadership, and research to help foreign missions and countries manage and develop their human resources. Improves the means of basic and higher education as well as training. Administers the USAID Participant Training Program, which provides students and midcareer professionals from developing countries with academic and technical training, and the Entrepreneur International Initiative, a short-term training/trade program that matches developing-country entrepreneurs with their American counterparts to familiarize them with American goods, services, and technology.

Agency for International Development (USAID), *Bureau for Development, Democracy, and Innovation (DDI),* *1300 Pennsylvania Ave. N.W., #3.9, 20523-3900; (202) 712-0670. Fax, (202) 216-3239. Karl Fickenscher, Assistant Administrator (Acting).*
Web, www.usaid.gov/who-we-are/organization/bureaus/bureau-development-democracy-innovation

Assists with the economic growth of developing countries by providing policy, technical, and financial assistance for cost-effective, reliable energy programs and other infrastructure. Works to foster increased capability of foreign missions to collaborate with governments, entrepreneurs, and other local institutions and individuals to encourage country-based assistance programs. Divisions focus on economic growth, including business, microenterprise development, and institutional reform; the environment and energy use; human capacity development, including education and training; and women in development.

Agency for International Development (USAID), *Bureau for Global Health, 1300 Pennsylvania Ave. N.W., #3.64, 20523-3100; (202) 712-4120. Fax, (202) 216-3485. Atul Gawande, Assistant Administrator (Acting).*
Web, www.usaid.gov/who-we-are/organization/bureaus/bureau-global-health, Twitter, @USAIDGH and Facebook, www.facebook.com/usaidgh

Participates in global efforts to stabilize world population growth and support women's reproductive rights. Focus includes family planning; reproductive health care; infant, child, and maternal health; and prevention of sexually transmitted diseases, especially AIDS. Conducts demographic and health surveys; educates girls and women.

Agency for International Development (USAID), *Bureau for Humanitarian Assistance (BHA), 1300 Pennsylvania Ave. N.W., 20523-8601; Sarah Charles, Assistant to the Administrator.*
General email, AskBHA@usaid.gov
Web, www.usaid.gov/who-we-are/organization/bureaus/bureau-humanitarian-assistance

Manages U.S. foreign disaster assistance, emergency and developmental food aid, and programs to assist countries transitioning out of crises and natural disasters.

Agency for International Development (USAID), *Bureau for Resilience and Food Security, 1300 Pennsylvania Ave. N.W., 20523; Fax, (202) 216-3380. Jim Barnhart, Assistant to the Administrator.*
Web, www.usaid.gov/who-we-are/organization/bureaus/bureau-resilience-and-food-security

Administers agricultural development programs, including the Feed the Future initiative. Partners with other U.S. government offices, multilateral institutions, NGOs, the public and private sector, and universities to support country-driven agricultural growth strategies.

Agency for International Development (USAID), *Bureau for Resilience and Food Security, Farmer-to-Farmer Program, 1300 Pennsylvania Ave. N.W., #2.10-261, 20523; Evania Robles, Program Analyst; Peggy Carlson, Program Analyst.*
Web, www.usaid.gov/what-we-do/agriculture-and-food-security/supporting-agricultural-capacity-development/john-ogonowski, https://farmer-to-farmer.org and Facebook, www.facebook.com/Farmer2Farmer

Promotes sustainable improvements in food security and agricultural processing, production, and marketing. Provides voluntary assistance to farmers, farm groups, and agribusinesses in developing countries, benefiting approximately one million farmer families in more than 80 countries.

Bureau of International Organization Affairs (IO) *(State Dept.), Economic and Development Affairs (EDA), 2201 C St. N.W., #2830, 20520; (202) 647-1269. Kristen L. Pisani, Director, (202) 647-1545.*
Web, www.state.gov/p/io

Works with the United Nations Food and Agricultural Organization, World Food Program, and World Health Organization to implement U.S. policy initiatives on human security, with particular focus on economic growth and sustainable development, global food security, and global health issues.

Criminal Division *(Justice Dept.), International Criminal Investigative Training Assistance Program (ICITAP), 1331 F St. N.W., #500, 20530; (202) 305-8190. Gregory Ducot, Director.*
Web, www.justice.gov/criminal-icitap

Works with foreign governments to develop professional and transparent law enforcement institutions that protect human rights, combat corruption, and reduce the threat of transnational crime and terrorism. Provides international development assistance that supports both national security and foreign policy objectives.

Millennium Challenge Corp., *1099 14th St. N.W., #700, 20005-3550; (202) 521-3600. Alice Albright, Chief Executive Officer. Legislative Affairs, (202) 521-3880.*
General email, press@mcc.gov
Web, www.mcc.gov, Twitter, @MCCgov and Facebook, www.facebook.com/MCCgov

Government corporation that provides financial assistance to developing nations that encourage economic freedom. Funds are used for agricultural development, education, enterprise and private-sector development, governance, health, and building trade capacity. Monitors legislation and regulations.

Peace Corps, *1275 1st St. N.E., 20526; (202) 692-1040. Fax, (202) 692-8400. Carol Spahn, Chief Executive Officer. Press, (202) 692-2230. Toll-free, (855) 855-1961.*
Web, www.peacecorps.gov, Twitter, @PeaceCorps and Facebook, www.facebook.com/peacecorps

Promotes world peace, friendship, and mutual understanding between the United States and developing nations. Administers volunteer programs to assist developing countries in education, the environment, health, small business development, agriculture, in particular promoting global food security, AIDS relief, eliminating maleria and urban youth development.

State Dept., *Global Food Security, 2201 C St. N.W., HST 3822, 20520; (202) 647-3090. Fax, (202) 647-1894. Ted J. Lyng, Special Representative (Acting). Web, www.state.gov/agricultural-policy/food-security*

Supports country-driven approaches to address the root causes of hunger and poverty, and helps countries transform their own agricultural sectors to grow enough food to sustainably feed their people.

▶ INTERNATIONAL ORGANIZATIONS

CARE, *Washington Office, 1100 17th St. N.W., #900, 20036; (202) 595-2800. Ritu Sharma, Vice President, Programs and Policy Advocacy. General email, info@care.org*

Web, www.care.org, Twitter, @CARE and Facebook, www.facebook.com/carefans

Assists the developing world's poor through emergency assistance and community self-help programs that focus on sustainable development, agriculture, agroforestry, water and sanitation, health, family planning, and income generation. Community-based efforts are centered on providing resources to poor women. (U.S. headquarters in Atlanta, Ga.; international headquarters in Geneva, Switzerland.)

Grameen Foundation, *1400 K St. N.W., #1255, 20005; (202) 628-3560. Fax, (202) 628-2341. Brent Chism, President (Acting). Web, www.grameenfoundation.org, Twitter, @GrameenFdn, Facebook, www.facebook.com/StopPovertyNow/ and YouTube, www.youtube.com/user/grameen*

Seeks to eliminate poverty by providing microfinance and technology products and services in sub-Saharan Africa, Asia, the Middle East and North Africa (MENA) region, Latin America, and the Caribbean. Develops mobile phone–based solutions that address "information poverty" among the poor, providing tools, information, and services in the fields of health, agriculture, financial services, and livelihood creation. Focuses on assistance to women seeking to start or expand their own businesses.

International Development Assn., *1818 H St. N.W., MSN MCG5-501, 20433; (202) 473-1000. Alex van Trotsenburg, Managing Director of Operations. Web, http://ida.worldbank.org*

Affiliate of the World Bank funded by membership contributions and transfers of funds from the World Bank. Provides long-term, low-interest, and interest-free loans and grants to the poorest countries.

TechnoServe, *1777 N. Kent St., #1100, Arlington, VA 22209; (202) 785-4515. Fax, (202) 785-4544. Will Warshauer, President. Donor Support, (800) 999-6757. Press, (202) 650-5713. General email, info@technoserve.org*

Web, www.technoserve.org, Twitter, @TechnoServe, Facebook, www.facebook.com/TechnoServe and YouTube, www.youtube.com/user/technoserveglobal

International nonprofit that assists entrepreneurs in poor and developing countries. Provides access to technology, information, and resources that connect business owners to suppliers and industry networks to increase their revenue. Specializes in farming and agricultural enterprises.

United Nations Development Programme (UNDP), *Washington Office, 1775 K St. N.W., #500, 20006; (202) 331-9130. Fax, (202) 331-9363. Achim Steiner, Administrator (New York); Don Gressett, Director. General email, undp.washington@undp.org*

Web, www.us.undp.org and Twitter, @UNDPDC

Funded by voluntary contributions from national governments. Administers United Nations support for economic and social development in developing countries, democratic governance, poverty reduction, crisis prevention and recovery, energy and the environment, and HIV/AIDS. (Headquarters in New York.)

United Way Worldwide, *701 N. Fairfax St., Alexandria, VA 22314-2045; (703) 836-7112. Fax, (703) 519-0097. Angela F. Willliams, President. Web, www.unitedway.org and Twitter, @UnitedWay*

Membership: independent United Way organizations in 41 countries and territories, including 1,150 in the United States. Provides staff training; fund-raising, planning, and communications assistance; resource management; and national public service advertising. Activities support education, financial stability, and health.

Women for Women International, *2000 M St. N.W., #200, 20036; (202) 737-7705. Fax, (202) 737-7709. Laurie Adams, Chief Executive Officer. General email, general@womenforwomen.org*

Web, www.womenforwomen.org, Twitter, @WomenforWomen, Facebook, www.facebook.com/womenforwomen and YouTube, www.youtube.com/user/WomenforWomenIntl

Helps women in war-torn regions rebuild their lives through financial and emotional support, job skills training, rights education, access to capital, and assistance for small-business development.

World Bank, *Human Development Network, 1818 H St. N.W., 20433; (202) 473-1000. Mamta Murthi, Vice President. Web, www.worldbank.org*

Assists developing countries in delivering effective and affordable health care, education, and social services. Interests include poverty reduction, income protection, nutrition, jobs access, health coverage, and basic education.

▶ NONGOVERNMENTAL

ACDI/VOCA, *50 F St. N.W., #1000, 20001-1530; (202) 469-6000. Fax, (202) 469-6257. Charles J. Hall, Chief Executive Officer; Luke Pingel, Chief Legal Officer. General email, webmaster@acdivoca.org*

Web, www.acdivoca.org, Twitter, @acdivoca and Facebook, www.facebook.com/acdivoca

Recruits professionals for voluntary, short-term technical assistance to cooperatives, environmental groups, and agricultural enterprises in developing countries and emerging democracies. Interests include poverty reduction, community stabilization, and market integration. Promotes rural finance for micro-sized to medium-sized enterprises.

Adventist Development and Relief Agency (ADRA), *12501 Old Columbia Pike, Silver Spring, MD 20904; (301) 680-6380. Fax, (301) 680-6370. Michael Kruger, President. Toll-free, (800) 424-2372.*
General email, info@adra.org

Web, https://adra.org, Twitter, @ADRAIntl and Facebook, www.facebook.com/joinADRA

Worldwide humanitarian agency of the Seventh-day Adventist Church. Works to alleviate poverty in developing countries and responds to disasters. Sponsors activities that improve health, foster economic and social well-being, and build self-reliance.

American Jewish World Service, *Government Affairs, 1001 Connecticut Ave. N.W., #1200, 20036-3405; (202) 379-4300. Robert Bank, President; Rori Kramer, Director of U.S. Advocacy, (202) 379-4270. Toll-free, (800) 889-7146. Web, www.ajws.org/get-involved/ajws-in-your-community/washington-dc/, Twitter, @ajws, General email, ajws@ajws.org and Facebook, www.facebook.com/americanjewishworldservice*

International development organization that works to alleviate poverty and promote human rights around the world. Provides grants to grassroots organizations; offers volunteer services, advocacy, and education for society building, sustainable development, and protection of human rights. Promotes global citizenship within the Jewish community. (Headquarters in New York.)

Bikes for the World, *11720 Parklawn Dr., Rockville, MD 20852; (703) 740-7856. Taylor Jones, Executive Director.*
General email, office@bikesfortheworld.org

Web, www.bikesfortheworld.org, Twitter, @bikeftworld and Facebook, www.facebook.com/Bikesftworld

Collects unwanted bicycles and related paraphernalia in the United States and delivers them to low-cost community development programs assisting the poor in developing countries.

Center for Intercultural Education and Development *(Georgetown University), 2115 Wisconsin Ave. N.W., 4th Floor, 20007 (mailing address: P.O. Box 579400, Washington, DC 20007); (202) 687-1400. Chantal Santelices, Executive Director, (202) 687-1918.*
General email, cied@georgetown.edu

Web, http://cied.georgetown.edu

Designs and administers programs aimed at improving the quality of lives of economically disadvantaged people; provides technical education, job training, leadership skills development, and business management training; runs programs in Central America, the Caribbean, Central Europe, the Middle East, and Southeast Asia.

Development Gateway, *1110 13 St. N.W., #800, 20005; (202) 572-9200. Josh Powell, Chief Executive Officer.*
General email, info@developmentgateway.org

Web, https://developmentgateway.org, Twitter, @dgateway and Facebook, www.facebook.com/Development-Gateway-104900753640/

Provides international and grassroots development organizations with visual translations of data and analysis. Assists in applying data-based solutions to policies. Seeks to improve evaluation, decision making, and management of international development efforts.

Foundation for International Community Assistance (FINCA), *1201 15th St. N.W., 8th Floor, 20005; (202) 682-1510. Fax, (202) 318-3090. Rupert Scofield, President.*
General email, info@finca.org

Web, www.finca.org, Twitter, @FINCA and Facebook, www.facebook.com/FINCA.International

Provides financial services to low-income entrepreneurs outside the United States in order to create jobs, build assets, and improve standards of living. Delivers microfinance products and services through a network of wholly owned programs in Africa, Eurasia, the Middle East, and Latin America, operating on commercial principles of performance and sustainability. Focuses efforts on those living on less than $2.50/day, with a loan portfolio of approximately $1 billion estimated to reach about 2 million people worldwide.

Global Communities, *8601 Georgia Ave., #300, Silver Spring, MD 20910-3440; (301) 587-4700. David A. Weiss, Chief Executive Officer.*
General email, contact@globalcommunities.org

Web, www.globalcommunities.org

Works under contract with the Agency for International Development, United Nations, and World Bank to strengthen local government housing departments abroad.

Institute for State Effectiveness, *1050 30th St. N.W., 20007; (202) 298-5959. Fax, (202) 298-5564. Clare Lockhart, Director.*
General email, info@effectivestates.org

Web, https://effectivestates.org

Aims to improve international government accountability by creating policies and educating local leaders and citizens on successful accountability practices. Studies how nations build accountable governments and creates similar tools for developing countries and leaders.

InterAction, *1400 16th St. N.W., #210, 20036; (202) 667-8227. Samuel A. Worthington, Chief Executive Officer.*
General email, ia@interaction.org

Web, www.interaction.org, Twitter, @InterActionOrg, Facebook, www.facebook.com/InterActionOrg/ and YouTube, www.youtube.com/user/interaction

Alliance of nearly 200 U.S.-based international development and humanitarian nongovernmental organizations. Provides a forum for exchange of information on development assistance issues, including food aid and other relief services, migration, and refugee affairs. Monitors legislation and regulations.

International Center for Research on Women, *1120 20th St. N.W., #500N, 20036; (202) 797-0007. Fax, (202) 797-0020. Peggy Clark, President.*
General email, info@icrw.org
Web, www.icrw.org, Twitter, @ICRW and Facebook, www.facebook.com/ICRWDC

Advances gender equality and human rights, fights poverty, and promotes sustainable economic and social development through research, program implementation, information gathering, publications, and strategic media outreach. Conducts empirical research and promotes practical, evidence-based solutions that enable women to control their own lives and fully participate in their societies.

Leadership Initiatives, *Youth Development Programs, 4410 Massachusetts Ave. N.W., #236, 20016; (202) 738-1115. Marshall Bailly, Executive Director.*
General email, info@lichange.org
Web, https://bethechangenow.org, Facebook, www.facebook.com/LIchange18 and YouTube, www.youtube.com/channel/UCCIo0EOWuJQE8XaDBVzkfHA

Offers entrepreneurship training and leadership courses to individuals in developing countries. Connects high school students to international leaders to solve local business issues. Interests include mentoring orphans and youth. Focuses on communities in Nigeria, Namibia, and the Philippines.

Millennium Institute, *2200 Pennsylvania Ave. N.W., 4th Floor East Tower, 20037; (202) 507-5820. Hans R. Herren, President.*
General email, info@millennium-institute.org
Web, www.millennium-institute.org, Twitter, @millenniuminst, Facebook, www.facebook.com/millenniuminstituteDC and YouTube, www.youtube.com/channel/UCqw4q7NcFM1y0axE5t1uT_w

Research and international development organization that provides computer modeling services for planning and building a sustainable economic and ecological future.

National Peace Corps Assn., *1825 Connecticut Ave. N.W., #800, 20009-5708; (202) 293-7728. Fax, (202) 293-7554. Glenn Blumhorst, President.*
General email, ncpa@peacecorpsconnect.org
Web, www.peacecorpsconnect.org, Twitter, @pcorpsconnect and Facebook, www.facebook.com/PeaceCorpsConnect/

Membership: returned Peace Corps volunteers, staff, and interested individuals. Promotes a global perspective in the United States; seeks to educate the public about the developing world; supports Peace Corps programs; maintains a network of returned volunteers.

Oxfam America, *Policy and Campaigns, 1101 17th St. N.W., #1300, 20036-4710; (202) 496-1180. Fax, (202) 496-1190. Abby Maxman, President, ext. 2506; Gina Crista Cummings, Vice President of Advocacy, Alliances and Policy. Press, (202) 496-1169. Toll-free, (800) 776-9326.*
General email, info@oxfamamerica.org
Web, www.oxfamamerica.org and Twitter, @OxfamAmerica

Funds disaster relief and long-term development programs internationally. Organizes grassroots support in the United States for issues affecting global poverty, including climate change, aid reform, and corporate transparency. (Headquarters in Boston, Mass.)

PYXERA Global, *99 M St. S.E., #400, 20003; (202) 872-0933. Fax, (202) 872-0923. Deirdre White, Chief Executive Officer.*
General email, info@pyxeraglobal.org
Web, www.pyxeraglobal.org, Twitter, @PYXERAGlobal and Facebook, www.facebook.com/PYXERAGlobal

Recruits and coordinates public, private, and volunteer resources to strengthen small and medium-sized businesses and the institutions, governments, and industries that drive economic growth in emerging markets through five practice areas: global citizenship and volunteerism, supply chain development, tourism development, security and economic recovery, and access to finance for development. (Formerly CDC Development Solutions.)

Salvation Army World Service Office, *615 Slaters Lane, Alexandria, VA 22314 (mailing address: P.O. Box 1428, Alexandria, VA 22313); (703) 684-5500. Fax, (703) 684-5536. Maj. George L. Baker (USN), National Secretary; Bramwell Bailey, Assistant National Secretary. Press, (703) 647-4796.*
General email, SAWSO.Communications@usn.salvationarmy.org
Web, www.sawso.org, Twitter, @saworldservice and Facebook, www.facebook.com/saworldservice/

Works in Eastern Europe, Latin America, the Caribbean, Africa, Asia, and the South Pacific to provide technical assistance to local Salvation Army programs of health services, vocational and business training, literacy, microenterprise, and relief and reconstruction assistance. (International headquarters in London.)

Vital Voices Global Partnership, *1509 16th St. N.W., 20039; (202) 861-2625. Alyse Nelson, Chief Executive Officer.*
General email, info@vitalvoices.org
Web, www.vitalvoices.org, Twitter, @VitalVoices and Facebook, www.facebook.com/vitalvoices

Worldwide organization of volunteers with governmental, corporate, or other leadership expertise that trains and mentors emerging women leaders in Asia, Africa, Eurasia, Latin America and the Caribbean, and the Middle East. Seeks to expand women's political participation and representation, increase women's entrepreneurship and business leadership, and combat human rights violations affecting women.

World Cocoa Foundation, *1025 Connecticut Ave. N.W., #1205, 20036; (202) 737-7870. Fax, (202) 737-7832. Martin Short, President.*

General email, wcf@worldcocoa.org

Web, www.worldcocoafoundation.org, Twitter, @WorldCocoa and Facebook, www.facebook.com/WorldCocoaFoundation

Promotes a sustainable cocoa economy through economic and social development and environmental conservation in cocoa-growing communities. Helps raise funds for cocoa farmers and increases their access to modern farming practices.

World Learning, *Global Development and Exchange Programs,* 1015 15th St. N.W., #950, 20005-2065; (202) 408-5420. Fax, (202) 408-5397. Carol Jenkins, President, (202) 464-6643. Toll-free, (800) 858-0292. TTY, (202) 408-5420, ext. 711.
General email, info@worldlearning.org

Web, www.worldlearning.org and Twitter, @WorldLearning

Partners with nongovernmental organizations, government institutions, schools, universities, and others to strengthen local capacity and performance. Develops training programs that prepare local organizations to lead development initiatives. Provides technical assistance, mentoring, and small-grant funding. Administered by World Learning's Division of International Development and Exchange Programs.

Finance, Investment, and Monetary Affairs

► **AGENCIES**

Bureau of Economic Analysis (BEA) *(Commerce Dept.),* 4600 Silver Hill Rd., 20233 (mailing address: 4600 Silver Hill Rd., Suitland, MD 20746); (301) 278-9004. Mary Bohman, Director (Acting).
General email, CustomerService@bea.gov

Web, www.bea.gov, Twitter, @BEA_NEWS and YouTube, www.youtube.com/channel/UCCP9QD1x_z__duUivA6Yb5w

Compiles, analyzes, and publishes data on measures of aggregate U.S. economic activity, including gross domestic product; prices by type of expenditure; personal income and outlays; personal savings; corporate profits; capital stock; U.S. international transactions; and foreign investment. Provides statistics of personal income and employment by industry for regions, states, metropolitan areas, and counties. Refers specific inquiries to economic specialists in the field.

Bureau of Economic Analysis (BEA) *(Commerce Dept.),* *Direct Investment Division,* 4600 Silver Hill Rd., 20233 (mailing address: 4600 Silver Hill Rd., Suitland, MD 20746); (301) 278-9004. Jessica Hanson, Chief.
General email, internationalaccounts@bea.gov

Web, www.bea.gov/data/intl-trade-investment/direct-investment-country-and-industry

Compiles statistics on foreign direct investment in the United States and U.S. direct investment abroad.

Bureau of Economic Analysis (BEA) *(Commerce Dept.),* *International Economics, Balance of Payments Division,* 4600 Silver Hill Rd., 20233 (mailing address: 4600 Silver Hill Rd., Suitland, MD 20746); (301) 278-9004. Patricia Abaroa, Chief.
General email, internationalaccounts@bea.gov

Web, www.bea.gov

Compiles, analyzes, and publishes quarterly and annual statistics on the U.S. international transactions accounts and the U.S. international investment position accounts. Publishes a monthly release with U.S. Census Bureau on U.S. trade in goods and services. Conducts research and analysis on the international economic accounts.

Bureau of Economic and Business Affairs (EB) *(State Dept.),* *International Finance and Development (IFD),* 2201 C St. N.W., #4871, 20520; (202) 647-9426. Roland F. de Marcellus, Deputy Assistant Secretary (Acting).
Web, www.state.gov/bureaus-offices/under-secretary-for-economic-growth-energy-and-the-environment/bureau-of-economic-and-business-affairs/division-for-inte

Formulates and implements policies related to multinational investment and insurance; activities of the World Bank and regional banks in the financial development of various countries; bilateral aid; international monetary reform; international antitrust cases; and international debt, banking, and taxation.

Bureau of Economic and Business Affairs (EB) *(State Dept.),* *International Finance and Development (IFD),* *Development Finance (ODF),* 2201 C St. N.W., #4871, 20520; (202) 647-5585. Karen Enstrom, Director, (202) 647-1689.
General email, ODF-OMS@state.gov

Web, www.state.gov/development-finance

Fosters development of new markets overseas, supports export opportunities, and seeks to strengthen U.S. international economic ties. Works with international bank organizations, including the World Bank, to promote U.S. economic policies.

Bureau of Economic and Business Affairs (EB) *(State Dept.),* *International Finance and Development (IFD),* *Investment Affairs (OIA),* 2201 C St. N.W., #4669, 20520-5820; (202) 736-4907. Fax, (202) 647-0320. Michael K. Tracton, Director, (202) 736-4188.
General email, eb-a-oia-dl@state.gov

Web, www.state.gov/investment-affairs

Develops U.S. investment policy. Makes policy recommendations regarding multinational enterprises and the expropriation of and compensation for U.S. property overseas. Negotiates bilateral and multilateral investment agreements. Coordinates the State Dept.'s position with respect to the Committee for Foreign Investments in the United States.

Bureau of Economic and Business Affairs (EB) *(State Dept.),* *International Finance and Development (IFD),* *Monetary Affairs (OMA),* 2201 C St. N.W., #4880, 20520; (202) 647-9497. Gregory Schiffer, Director, (202) 647-5935.

General email, eb-a-oma-dl@state.gov

Web, www.state.gov/monetary-affairs

Monitors global macroeconomic developments and identifies financial trends and potential crises in countries affecting U.S. interests. Formulates debt relief policies and negotiates debt relief agreements.

Committee on Foreign Investment in the United States *(Treasury Dept.),* 1500 Pennsylvania Ave. N.W., #5221, 20220; (202) 622-1860. Laura Black, Director, Investment Security Policy and International Relations, (202) 622-3425.

General email, cfius@treasury.gov

Web, www.treasury.gov/cfius

Reviews foreign acquisition of U.S. companies and determines whether they pose national security threats. Conducts investigations into such acquisitions.

Export-Import Bank of the United States, 811 Vermont Ave. N.W., 20571; (202) 565-3946. James G. Burrows, Chair (Acting); hazeen Ashby, Chief of Staff, White House Liaison. Toll-Free Hotline, (800) 565-3946.

General email, info@exim.gov

Web, www.exim.gov, Facebook, www.facebook.com/ eximbankus/ and Twitter, @eximbankus

Membership; Independent agency of the U.S. government with 12 regional offices. Aids in financing exports of U.S. goods and services; guarantees export loans made by commercial lenders, working capital guarantees, and export credit insurance; conducts an intermediary loan program. finance Lease Guarantee, Direct Loans. National Contact Center advises businesses in using U.S. government export programs.

Federal Reserve System, *International Finance,* 20th and C Sts. N.W., #B1242C, 20551-0001; (202) 452-3770. Beth Anne Wilson, Director. Press, (202) 452-3799.

Web, www.federalreserve.gov/econres/ifstaff.htm

Provides the Federal Reserve's board of governors with economic analyses of international developments. Compiles data on exchange rates.

Securities and Exchange Commission (SEC), *International Affairs,* 100 F St. N.E., 20549; (202) 551-6690. Y.T. Fischer, Director).

Web, www.sec.gov/oia

Promotes investor protection, cross-border securities transactions, and fair, efficient, and transparent markets by advancing international regulatory and enforcement cooperation, promoting the adoption of high regulatory standards worldwide, and formulating technical assistance programs to strengthen the regulatory structure in global finance markets. Works with a global network of securities regulators and law enforcement authorities to facilitate cross-border regulatory compliance and help ensure that international borders are not used to escape detection and prosecution of fraudulent securities activities. Provides the commission and SEC staff with advice and assistance in international enforcement and regulatory efforts.

Treasury Dept., *International Affairs,* 1500 Pennsylvania Ave. N.W., #3432, 20220; (202) 622-1270. Brett McIntosh, Under Secretary. Press, (202) 622-2960.

Web, https://home.treasury.gov/about/offices/ international-affairs

Coordinates and implements U.S. international economic and financial policy in cooperation with other government agencies. Works to improve the international monetary and investment system; monitors international gold and foreign exchange operations; coordinates development lending; coordinates Treasury Dept. participation in foreign investment in the United States; studies international monetary, economic, and financial issues; analyzes data on international transactions.

Treasury Dept., *International Affairs, Asia,* 1500 Pennsylvania Ave. N.W., #3217, 20220; (202) 622-2000. Robert Kaproth, Deputy Assistant Secretary, (202) 622-0132.

Web, https://home.treasury.gov/about/offices/ international-affairs

Provides economic analysis of countries in East Asia, including Australia, China, Hong Kong, Japan, the Koreas, Mongolia, New Zealand, the Pacific Islands, and Taiwan. Plays a role in managing the U.S.–China Strategic and Economic Dialogue and U.S. engagement with Asian regional initiatives.

Treasury Dept., *International Affairs, Europe and Eurasia,* 1500 Pennsylvania Ave N.W., #4138, 20220; (202) 622-2137. Andy Baukol, Deputy Assistant Secretary (Acting), (202) 622-2159; Evangelia (Lea) Bouzis, Director, (202) 622-9190.

Web, https://home.treasury.gov/about/offices/ international-affairs

Guides and develops economic policies toward more than 50 economies in Europe and Eurasia.

Treasury Dept., *International Affairs, International Monetary Policy,* 1500 Pennsylvania Ave. N.W., #3034, 20220; (202) 622-2129. Andy Baukol, Deputy Assistant Secretary, (202) 622-6407.

Web, https://home.treasury.gov/about/offices/ international-affairs

Provides policy analysis and recommendations with respect to U.S. participation in the International Monetary Fund, an international organization made up of 189 countries working toward global fiscal unity.

Treasury Dept., *International Affairs, Investment Security,* 1500 Pennsylvania Ave. N.W., #5221, 20220; (202) 622-1860. Thomas Feddo, Deputy Assistant Secretary, (202) 622-7222.

General email, cifius@do.treas.gov

Web, https://home.treasury.gov/about/offices/ international-affairs

Oversees U.S. open investment initiatives. Responsible for the implementation of the Treasury Dept.'s responsibilities as chair of the Committee on Foreign Investment in the United States.

Treasury Dept., *International Affairs, Middle East and North Africa,* 1500 Pennsylvania Ave. N.W., 20220; (202) 622-2156. Eric Meyer, Deputy Assistant Secretary.
Web, https://home.treasury.gov/about/offices/international-affairs

Develops and guides economic policy and loan and development programs toward 49 sub-Saharan African economies.

Treasury Dept., *International Affairs, Technical Assistance,* 1750 Pennsylvania Ave. N.W., 8th Floor, 20006; (202) 622-7610. William Larry McDonald, Deputy Assistant Secretary, (202) 622-5504; Jason Orlando, Director, (202) 622-5792.
General email, info@ota.treas.gov
Web, https://home.treasury.gov/about/offices/international-affairs/technical-assistance

Works with finance ministries and central banks of developing and transition countries to improve their ability to manage public finances and safeguard their financial sectors by promoting effective revenue policies, strengthening ministries of finance, providing assistance with domestic government securities, and combating economic crimes, including tax evasion, money laundering, terrorism financing, and supporting the development of strong financial sectors.

Treasury Dept., *International Affairs, Western Hemisphere,* 1500 Pennsylvania Ave. N.W., #3037, 20220; (202) 622-4262. Michael Kaplan, Deputy Assistant Secretary.
Web, https://home.treasury.gov/about/offices/international-affairs

Responsible for economic analysis, financial diplomacy, and U.S. policy initiatives in 35 countries in Latin America, the Caribbean, and Canada.

U.S. International Development Finance Corp., 1100 New York Ave. N.W., 20527; (202) 336-8400. Dev Jagadesan, Chief Executive Officer (Acting). Anticorruption hotline, (202) 712-1023. Press, (202) 312-2188. Toll-free, (800) 230-6539.
General email, info@dfc.gov
Web, www.dfc.gov and Press, press@dfc.gov

Provides assistance through political risk insurance, direct loans, and loan guarantees to qualified U.S. private investors to support their investments in emerging markets. Offers preinvestment information and counseling. Provides insurance against the risks of expropriation, political violence, and inconvertibility of local currency.

▶**CONGRESS**

For a listing of relevant congressional committees and subcommittees, please see pages 478–479 or the Appendix.

▶**INTERNATIONAL ORGANIZATIONS**

Coalition for Integrity, 1100 13th St. N.W., 8th Floor, 20005; (202) 589-1616. Shruti Shah, President.

General email, administration@coalitionforintegrity.org
Web, www.coalitionforintegrity.org, Twitter, @unite4integrity and Facebook, www.facebook.com/unite4integrity

Seeks to curb corruption in international transactions. Promotes reform of government, business, and development assistance transactions through effective anticorruption laws and policies. (Formerly Transparency International USA.)

Institute of International Finance, 1333 H St. N.W., #800 East, 20005-4770; (202) 857-3600. Fax, (202) 775-1430. Timothy D. (Tim) Adams, President.
General email, info@iif.com
Web, www.iif.com and Twitter, @IIF

Global association of financial institutions. Provides analysis and research on emerging markets. Identifies and analyzes regulatory, financial, and economic policy issues. Promotes the development of sound financial systems with particular emphasis on emerging markets.

Inter-American Development Bank, 1300 New York Ave. N.W., 20577; (202) 623-1000. Fax, (202) 623-3096. Mauricio Claver-Carone, President; James Andrew Catto, U.S. Executive Director. Library, (202) 623-3211. Press, (202) 623-1555.
Web, www.iadb.org, Twitter, @the_IDB and Facebook, www.facebook.com/IADB.org

Promotes, through loans and technical assistance, the investment of public and private capital in member countries of Latin America and the Caribbean for social and economic development purposes. Facilitates economic integration of the Latin American region, operating the Inter-American Investment Corp. and the Multilateral Investment Fund. Library open to the public by appointment.

Intercontinental Exchange, *Washington Office,* 701 Pennsylvania Ave. N.W., #500, 20004; Robert Eskridge, Director, Government Affairs; Mark Wassersug, Chief Operating Officer.
General email, everyone-washington@theice.com
Web, www.intercontinentalexchange.com, Twitter, @ICE_Markets and Facebook, www.facebook.com/IntercontinentalExchange

Provides information about risk-management services to market participants around the world. Washington office monitors legislation and regulations. (Headquarters in Atlanta, Ga.)

International Centre for Settlement of Investment Disputes (ICSID), 1818 H St. N.W., MS C3-300, 20433; (202) 458-1534. Fax, (202) 522-2615. Meg Kinnear, Secretary General, (202) 473-5531.
General email, ICSIDsecretariat@worldbank.org
Web, https://icsid.worldbank.org and Twitter, @icsid

Handles the conciliation and arbitration of investment disputes between contracting states and foreign investors. Has more than 140 member states and is affiliated with the World Bank.

International Finance Corp., *2121 Pennsylvania Ave. N.W., 20433; (202) 473-1000. Makhtar Diop, Managing Director. Press, (202) 458-2278.*
Web, www.ifc.org and Twitter, @ifc_org

A member of the World Bank Group that lends to private-sector companies and financial institutions. Works with the private sector to encourage entrepreneurship and build sustainable businesses: advising them on a wide range of issues, including environmental, social, and governance standards, energy and efficiency, and supply chains. Helps expand access to critical finance for individuals and micro, small, and medium enterprises through its work with financial intermediary clients.

International Monetary Fund (IMF), *700 19th St. N,W., 20431; 1900 Pennsylvania Ave. N.W., 20431; (202) 623-7000. Fax, (202) 623-4661. Elizabeth Shortino, U.S. Executive Director; Kristalina Georgieva, Managing Director. Legislative Affairs, (202) 623-6220. Press, (202) 623-7100.*
General email, publicaffairs@imf.org
Web, www.imf.org

International organization of 188 member countries that promotes policies for financial stability and economic growth, works to prevent financial crises, and helps members solve balance-of-payment problems through loans funded by member contributions.

International Monetary Fund (IMF), *Statistics,* *700 19th St. N.W., 20431; (202) 623-7000. Kristalina Georgieva, Managing Director. Publications, (202) 623-7430.*
General email, publicaffairs@imf.org
Web, www.imf.org/en/data, Publications, publications@imf.org and Twitter, @IMFNews

Publishes monthly *International Financial Statistics (IFS)*, which includes comprehensive financial data for most countries, and *Direction of Trade Statistics*, a quarterly publication, which includes the distribution of exports and imports for many countries. Annual statistical publications include the *Balance of Payments Statistics Yearbook, Direction of Trade Statistics Yearbook, Government Finance Statistics Yearbook*, and *International Financial Statistics Yearbook*. Free online and paid print subscriptions available to the public. All four publications are available on the website.

Multilateral Investment Guarantee Agency, *1818 H St. N.W., 20433; (202) 458-2538. Fax, (202) 522-0316. Hiroshi Matano, Executive Vice President. Press, (202) 458-9771.*
General email, migainquiry@worldbank.org
Web, www.miga.org and Twitter, @MIGA

World Bank affiliate that encourages foreign investment in developing countries. Provides guarantees against losses due to currency transfer, expropriation, war, civil disturbance, breach of contract, and the nonhonoring of a sovereign financial obligation. Provides dispute resolution services for guaranteed investments to prevent disruptions to developmentally beneficial projects. Membership open to World Bank member countries.

World Bank, *1818 H St. N.W., 20433; (202) 473-1000. Fax, (202) 477-6391. David Malpass, President; DJ Nordquist, U.S. Executive Director. Anticorruption hotline, (202) 458-7677. Press, (202) 473-7660. Publications, (800) 645-7247 or (703) 661-1580.*
General email, info_us@worldbank.org
Web, www.worldbank.org/en/country/unitedstates and Twitter, @worldbank

International organization encouraging the flow of public and private foreign investment into developing countries through low-interest loans, credits, and grants; collects data on selected economic indicators, world trade, and external public debt. Consists of the International Bank for Reconstruction and Development, the International Development Assn., the International Finance Corp., the Multilateral Investment Guarantee Agency, and the International Centre for Settlement of Investment Dispute.

▶**NONGOVERNMENTAL**

Bankers Association for Foreign Trade (BAFT), *1120 Connecticut Ave. N.W., 5th Floor, 20036-3902; (202) 663-7575. Fax, (202) 663-5538. Tod R. Burwell, Chief Executive Officer, (202) 663-5252.*
General email, info@baft.org
Web, www.baft.org, Twitter, @BAFT_Global and YouTube, www.youtube.com/c/BAFTBankersAssociation forFinanceandTrade

Membership: international financial services providers, including U.S. and non–U.S. commercial banks, financial services companies, and suppliers with major international operations. Provides Advocacy, Thought Leadership, Education and Training, and a global forum for international transaction bankers across the industry. Including iinternational trade, trade finance, payments, compliance, asset servicing, and transaction banking. Monitors and acts as an advocate globally on activities that affect the business of commercial and international banks and nonfinancial companies. (Formerly Bankers' Assn. for Financial Trade.)

Bretton Woods Committee, *1701 K St. N.W., #950, 20006; (202) 331-1616. Emily Slater, Executive Director.*
General email, info@brettonwoods.org
Web, www.brettonwoods.org and Twitter, @BrettonWoodsCom

Works to increase public understanding of the World Bank, the regional development institutions, the International Monetary Fund, and the World Trade Organization.

Financial Transparency Coalition, *2000 M St. N.W., #720, 20036; (202) 232-3317. Fax, (202) 232-3440. Matti Kohonen, Director.*
General email, info@financialtransparency.org
Web, https://financialtransparency.org, Twitter, @FinTrCo and Facebook, www.facebook.com/Financial TransparencyCoalition

Research and educational organization concerned with improving international financial transparency in order to decrease illicit financial flows. Encourages multinational corporations to report their profits and taxes, create open information sources on beneficial ownership, and automate tax information exchange. Works to curtail illicit financial flows. (The FTC's Secretariat is hosted by TSNE MissionWorks in Boston, MA.).

Global Business Alliance (GBA), *99 M St. S.E., #200, 20003; (202) 659-1903. Fax, (202) 659-2293. Nancy McLernon, President. General email, nmclernon@globalbiz.org Web, www.globalbusiness.org and Twitter, @GlobalBiz*

Membership: U.S. subsidiaries of international companies. Provides data on international investment in the United States, including reports on exports, tax revenue, and job creation. Monitors legislation and regulations concerning the business operations of U.S. subsidiaries.

Global Financial Integrity (GFI), *1100 17th St. N.W., #505, 20036; (202) 293-0740. Fax, (202) 293-1720. Raymond Baker, President, ext. 226; Tom Cardamone, President. General email, gfi@gfintegrity.org Web, www.gfintegrity.org, Twitter, @IllicitFlows, Twitter, President, @TCardamoneJrGFI and Facebook, www .facebook.com/GlobalFinancialIntegrity*

Nonprofit that researches and acts as advocate against illicit financial flows between foreign countries. Publishes reports that analyze illegal monetary transfers around the world. Assists developing countries in applying policies to prevent illicit transactions due to drug trafficking, political corruption, money laundering, and terrorist funding.

Peterson Institute for International Economics (PIIE), *1750 Massachusetts Ave. N.W., 20036-1903; (202) 328-9000. Adam S. Posen, President. Press, (202) 454-1334. General email, comments@piie.com Web, www.piie.com, Twitter, @PIIE, Facebook, www.facebook.com/PIIEonline and Bookstore Orders, piiepress@piie.com*

Conducts studies and makes policy recommendations on international economic issues, including monetary affairs, trade, investment, energy, exchange rates, commodities, and North–South and East–West economic relations. Has a bookstore.

REGIONAL AFFAIRS

See also Foreign Embassies, U.S. Ambassadors, and Country Desk Offices (Appendix).

Africa

For North Africa, see Near East and South Asia.

► **AGENCIES**

Agency for International Development (USAID), *Bureau for Africa, 1300 Pennsylvania Ave. N.W., 20523-4801;* (202) 712-0500. *Diana Putman, Senior Deputy Assistant Administrator. Web, www.usaid.gov/who-we-are/organization/bureaus/ bureau-africa*

Advises the USAID administrator on U.S. policy toward developing countries in Africa.

Bureau of African Affairs *(State Dept.), 2201 C St. N.W., #6234A, 20520-3430; (202) 647-2530. Fax, (202) 647-6301. Molly Phee, Assistant Secretary. Web, www.state.gov/p/af*

Advises the secretary on U.S. policy toward sub-Saharan Africa. Directors, assigned to different regions in Africa, aid the assistant secretary.

Bureau of African Affairs *(State Dept.), Central African Affairs, 2201 C St. N.W., #4244, 20520-2902; (202) 663-6491. Fax, (202) 647-1726. Margaret Bond, Director. Web, www.state.gov/p/af*

Includes Burundi, Cameroon, Central African Republic, Chad, the Democratic Republic of Congo, the Republic of Congo, Equatorial Guinea, Gabon, Rwanda, and São Tomé and Príncipe.

Bureau of African Affairs *(State Dept.), East African Affairs, 2201 C St. N.W., #4248, 20520; (202) 647-5242. Fax, (202) 647-0810. Peter Lord Amadeo, Deputy Assistant Secretary. Web, www.state.gov/p/af*

Includes Comoros, Djibouti, Eritrea, Ethiopia, Kenya, Madagascar, Mauritius, Seychelles, Somalia, Tanzania, Sudan and South Sudan, and Uganda.

Bureau of African Affairs *(State Dept.), Southern African Affairs, 2201 C St. N.W., #4236, 20520; (202) 647-2447. (202) 647-8434. Fax, (202) 647-5007. Akunna Cook, Deputy Assistant Secretary; Jasmine Holland, Administrative Assistant. Web, www.state.gov/p/af*

Includes Angola, Botswana, Lesotho, Malawi, Mozambique, Namibia, South Africa, Swaziland, Zambia, and Zimbabwe.

Bureau of African Affairs *(State Dept.), West African Affairs and Sahel Region, 2201 C St. N.W., #6234, 20520-3430; (202) 647-3395. (571) 482-0646. Fax, (202) 647-4855. Michael C. Gonzales, Deputy Assistant Secretary; Sheila Shea Palmer, Administrative Assistant. Web, www.state.gov/p/af*

Includes Benin, Burkina Faso, Cape Verde, Côte d'Ivoire, the Gambia, Ghana, Guinea, Guinea-Bissau, Liberia, Mali, Mauritania, Niger, Nigeria, Senegal, Sierra Leone, and Togo.

Defense Dept. (DoD), *International Security Affairs, 2000 Defense Pentagon, 20301-2000; (703) 697-2788. Fax, (703) 697-3279. Ilan Goldenberg, Assistant Secretary (Acting). Web, http://policy.defense.gov/OUSDPOffices/ ASDforInternationalSecurityAffairs*

Advises the secretary of defense and recommends policies on regional security issues in the Middle East, Africa, Russia/Eurasia, and Europe/NATO.

Defense Dept. (DoD), *International Security Affairs, Africa,* 2000 Defense Pentagon, 20301-2000; (703) 697-2788. Cindi Blyden, Deputy Assistant Secretary. Web, https://policy.defense.gov/OUSDP-Offices/ASD-for-International-Security-Affairs/African-Affairs

Advises the assistant secretary for international security affairs on matters dealing with Africa.

United States African Development Foundation (USADF), 1400 Eye St. N.W., 20005-2248; (202) 233-8800. Fax, (202) 673-3810. Travis Atkins, President. Press, (202) 673-3916, ext. 8811.
General email, info@usadf.gov

Web, www.usadf.gov, Twitter, @USADF and Facebook, www.facebook.com/USADF

Established by Congress to work with and fund organizations and individuals involved in community-based development projects in Africa. Gives preference to projects involving extensive participation by local Africans. Work focuses on conflict and postconflict areas.

► **CONGRESS**

For a listing of relevant congressional committees and subcommittees, please see pages 478–479 or the Appendix.

Library of Congress, *African and Middle Eastern Division,* Thomas Jefferson Bldg., 101 Independence Ave. S.E., #LJ 229, 20540-4660; (202) 707-7937. Lanisa Kitchiner, Chief. Reading Room, (202) 707-4188. General email, amed@loc.gov

Web, www.loc.gov/rr/amed

Maintains collections of African, Near Eastern, and Hebraic material. Prepares bibliographies and special studies relating to Africa and the Middle East. Reference service and reading rooms available to the public. (Need reader's card to use.) Timed entry pass for visitors required, details at loc.gov/visit. Appointments recommended for researchers.

► **INTERNATIONAL ORGANIZATIONS**

World Bank, *Africa Region,* 1818 H St. N.W., 20433; (202) 473-1000. Ousmane Diagana, Vice President, (202) 473-8302.
General email, africateam@worldbank.org

Web, www.worldbank.org/en/region/afr, Twitter, @WorldBankAfrica and Facebook, www.facebook.com/WorldBankAfrica

Aims to reduce poverty in middle-income countries and creditworthy poorer countries by promoting sustainable development through low-interest loans, zero to low-interest credits, grants, guarantees, risk management products, and analytical and advisory services. Priorities in Africa include education, health, public administration, infrastructure, financial and private sector development, agriculture, and environmental and natural resource management.

► **NONGOVERNMENTAL**

Africa Faith and Justice Network (AFJN), 3025 4th St. N.E., 2nd Floor, 20017 (mailing address: 3025 4th St. N.E., #122, Washington, DC 20017); (202) 817-3670. Vacant, Executive Director; Ntama Bahati, Policy analyst.
General email, afjn@afjn.org

Web, https://afjn.org, Twitter, @AFJN_DC and Facebook, www.facebook.com/AfricaFaithandJusticeNetwork

Acts as an advocate with Catholic missionary congregations and Africa-focused coalitions for U.S. economic and political policies that benefit Africa. Promotes the Catholic view of peace building, human rights, and social justice. Interests include ending armed conflict, equitable trade with and investment in Africa, and sustainable development. Monitors legislation and regulations.

The Brookings Institution, *Global Economy and Development Studies, Africa Growth Initiative,* 1775 Massachusetts Ave. N.W., 20036; (202) 238-3552. Fax, (202) 797-6004. Aloysius Uche Ordu, Director. General email, AGI@Brookings.edu

Web, www.brookings.edu/about/projects/africa-growth

Conducts policy research and analysis focusing on sustainable economic growth in Africa. Interests include financial development, risks to growth including, macroeconmic shocks, climate change and epidemics, trade and regional integration, governance transparency, reduction of gender barriers, and youth employment.

Corporate Council on Africa, 1100 17th St. N.W., #1200, 20036; (202) 835-1115. Florizelle (Florie) Liser, President.
General email, cca@corporatecouncilonafrica.com

Web, www.corporatecouncilonafrica.com, Twitter, @CorpCnclAfrica, Facebook, www.facebook.com/CorporateCouncilonAfrica and YouTube, www.youtube.com/UCSPD/hIexTKLArSvOF1r-DW/

Membership: American corporations working with African agriculture, energy, finance, health, trade, communication technology, and security industries. Promotes business relations between the United States and Africa. Facilitates government and business advancements in Africa's trade industry. Monitors legislation and regulations that impact African commercial relations.

Lubuto Library Partners, 5614 Connecticut Ave N.W., #368, 20015-2604; (202) 558-5609. Jane Kinney Meyers, President.
General email, webmail@lubuto.org

Web, www.lubuto.org, Twitter, @LubutoLibrary and Facebook, www.facebook.com/lubutolibrarypartners

International development organization that establishes public libraries for youth in southern African countries, starting in Zambia. Constructs library facilities with support from the U.S. Agency for International Development (USAID), which also supports the purchase of book collections and library technology. Trains local staff to offer services, programs, and outreach from the libraries, which are owned by Zambian nongovernmental organizations, and operates a regional training center in inclusive library services for children and youth.

Sudan Sunrise, *10508 James Wren Way, Fairfax, VA 22030; (202) 499-6984. Tom Prichard, Executive Director. General email, info@sudansunrise.org*

Web, http://sudansunrise.org, Twitter, @SudanSunrise, Facebook, www.facebook.com/SudanSunrise and YouTube, www.youtube.com/user/SudanSunrise

Supports schools and education programs for children of various religions, tribes, and communities in Sudan and South Sudan.

East Asia and Pacific

▶AGENCIES

Agency for International Development (USAID), *Bureau for Asia, 1300 Pennsylvania Ave. N.W., 20523-4900; (202) 712-0200. Fax, (202) 216-3386. Änjali Kaur, Deputy Assistant Administrator.*
Web, www.usaid.gov/who-we-are/organization/bureaus/bureau-asia

Advises the USAID administrator on U.S. economic development policy in Asia.

Bureau of East Asian and Pacific Affairs *(State Dept.), 2201 C St. N.W., #6205, 20520-6205; (202) 647-9596. Daniel Kritenbrink, Assistant Secretary. Press, (202) 647-2538.*
Web, www.state.gov/p/eap and Twitter, @USAsiaPacific

Advises the secretary on U.S. policy toward East Asian and Pacific countries. Directors assigned to specific countries within the bureau aid the assistant secretary.

Bureau of East Asian and Pacific Affairs *(State Dept.), Australia, New Zealand, and Pacific Island Affairs, 2201 C St. N.W., #4318, 20520; (202) 736-4659. Fax, (202) 647-0118. Taylor V. Ruggles, Director.*
Web, www.state.gov/p/eap

Bureau of East Asian and Pacific Affairs *(State Dept.), Chinese and Mongolian Affairs, 2201 C St. N.W., #4318, 20520; (202) 647-6796. Fax, (202) 736-7809. Henry Hand, Director, (202) 647-6787.*
Web, www.state.gov/p/eap

Bureau of East Asian and Pacific Affairs *(State Dept.), Japanese Affairs, 2201 C St. N.W., #4206, 20520; (202) 647-2913. Katherine Monahan, Director, (202) 647-1311.*
Web, www.state.gov/p/eap

Bureau of East Asian and Pacific Affairs *(State Dept.), Korean Affairs, 2201 C St. N.W., #4206, 20520; (202) 647-7719. Scott Walker, Director.*
Web, www.state.gov/p/eap

Bureau of East Asian and Pacific Affairs *(State Dept.), Mainland Southeast Asia Affairs, 2201 C St. N.W., #5206, 20520-6310; (202) 647-4495. Fax, (202) 647-3069. Robert Ogburn, Director.*
Web, www.state.gov/p/eap

Includes Burma, Cambodia, Laos, Thailand, and Vietnam.

Bureau of East Asian and Pacific Affairs *(State Dept.), Maritime Southeast Asia Affairs, 2201 C St. N.W., #5210, 20520; (202) 647-2143. Fax, (202) 736-4559. Amy Archibald, Director.*
Web, www.state.gov/p/eap

Includes the Philippines, Malaysia, Brunei, Indonesia, East Timor, and Singapore.

Bureau of East Asian and Pacific Affairs *(State Dept.), North Korea Affairs, 2201 C St. N.W., #7321, 20520-5209; (202) 647-0704. Amy Reid, Office Management Specialist.*
Web, www.state.gov/p/eap

Bureau of East Asian and Pacific Affairs *(State Dept.), Taiwan Coordination, 2201 C St. N.W., #4312, 20520; (202) 647-7711. Daniel Biers, Director, (202) 647-7112.*
Web, www.state.gov/p/eap

Defense Dept. (DoD), *East Asia Security Affairs, 2700 Defense Pentagon, #5D688, 20301-2700; (703) 695-4175. Siddharth Mohandas, Principal Deputy Assistant Secretary.*
Web, https://policy.defense.gov/OUSDP-Offices/ASD-for-Indo-Pacific-Security-Affairs/East-Asia/

Advises the under secretary of defense on matters dealing with China, Japan, Mongolia, North and South Korea, and Taiwan.

Defense Dept. (DoD), *Indo-Pacific Security Affairs, 2700 Defense Pentagon, #5D688, 20301-2400; (703) 695-4175. Ely Ratner, Assistant Secretary. Press, (703) 697-5131.*
Web, https://policy.defense.gov/OUSDP-Offices/ASD-for-Indo-Pacific-Security-Affairs

Advises the under secretary of defense on matters dealing with Asia and the Pacific.

Japan–United States Friendship Commission, *1201 15th St. N.W., #330, 20005-2842; (202) 653-9800. Fax, (202) 653-9802. Paige Cottingham-Streater, Executive Director.*
General email, jusfc@jusfc.gov
Web, www.jusfc.gov

Independent agency established by Congress that makes grants and administers funds and programs promoting educational and cultural exchanges between Japan and the United States.

▶CONGRESS

For a listing of relevant congressional committees and subcommittees, please see pages 478–479 or the Appendix.

Congressional–Executive Commission on China, *243 FHOB, 20515; (202) 226-3766. Fax, (202) 226-3804.*

Rep. Jim McGovern, Co-Chair; Sen. Jeff Merkley, Co-Chair; Matt Squeri, Staff Director, (202) 841-1017.
General email, infocecc@mail.house.gov
Web, www.cecc.gov, Twitter, @CECCgov, Facebook, www.facebook.com/ChinaCommission and YouTube, www.youtube.com/channel/CongressionalExecutive Commissionchina/videos

Independent agency created by Congress. Membership includes individuals from the executive and legislative branches. Monitors human rights and the development of the rule of law in the People's Republic of China. Submits an annual report to the president and Congress.

Library of Congress, International Collections, Asian Division, Thomas Jefferson Bldg., 10 1st St. S.E., #LJ 150, 20540-4810; (202) 707-3766. Fax, (202) 707-1724. Dongfang Shao, Chief, (202) 707-5919. Reading Room, (202) 707-5426.
Web, www.loc.gov/rr/asian

Maintains collections from across Asia, including Asian-American Pacific, Chinese, Korean, Japanese, Southeast Asian, South Asian, and Tibetan and Mongolian material. Reference service is provided in the Asian Reading Room, room #150. Timed entry pass for visitors required, details at loc.gov/visit. Appointments recommended for researchers.

U.S.–China Economic and Security Review Commission, 444 N. Capitol St. N.W., #602, 20001; (202) 624-1407. Daniel Peck, Executive Director, (202) 624-1407.
General email, contact@uscc.gov
Web, www.uscc.gov and Twitter, @USCC_GOV

Investigates the national security implications of the bilateral trade and economic relationship between China and the United States. Makes recommendations to Congress based on its findings.

▶**INTERNATIONAL ORGANIZATIONS**

World Bank, East Asia and Pacific Region, 1818 H St. N.W., 9th Floor, 20433; (202) 473-1000. Manula Ferro, Vice President.
General email, mmontemayor@worldbank.org
Web, www.worldbank.org/en/region/eap and Twitter, @WB_AsiaPacific

Works to fight poverty and improve the living standards of low- and middle-income people in the countries of East Asia and the Pacific by providing loans, policy advice, technical assistance, and knowledge-sharing services. Areas of interest include finance, economic development, education, water supply, agriculture, public health, and environmental protection.

▶**NONGOVERNMENTAL**

American Institute in Taiwan, 1300 17th St. N., #750, Arlington, VA 22209; (703) 525-8474. Fax, (703) 841-1385. Amb. James F. (Jim) Moriarty, Chair; Ingrid D. Larson, Managing Director.

Web, www.ait.org.tw/en, Twitter, @AIT.Social.Media and Facebook, www.facebook.com/AIT.Social.Media

Chartered by Congress to coordinate commercial, cultural, and other activities between the people of the United States and Taiwan. Represents U.S. interests and maintains offices in Taiwan.

Asia Foundation, Washington Office, 1779 Massachusetts Ave. N.W., #815, 20036; (202) 588-9420. Fax, (202) 588-9409. Nancy Yuan, Director, Washington Office.
General email, dc.general@asiafoundation.org
Web, www.asiafoundation.org and Twitter, @Asia_Foundation

Provides grants and technical assistance in Asia and the Pacific Islands (excluding the Middle East). Seeks to strengthen legislatures, legal and judicial systems, market economies, the media, and nongovernmental organizations. (Headquarters in San Francisco, Calif.)

Asia Policy Point (APP), 1730 Rhode Island Ave. N.W., #414, 20036; (202) 822-6040. Fax, (202) 822-6044. Mindy Kotler, Director.
General email, asiapolicyhq@gmail.com
Web, www.jiaponline.org and Blog, http://newasiapolicy point.blogspot.com

Studies Japanese and Northeast Asian security and public policies as they relate to the United States. Researches and analyzes issues affecting Japan's relationship with the West. (Formerly the Japan Information Access Project.)

Asia Society Policy Institute, Washington Office, 1779 Massachusetts Ave. N.W., #805, 20036; (202) 833-2742. Fax, (202) 833-0189. Wendy Cutler, Managing Director, Washington Office.
General email, asiadc@asiasociety.org
Web, www.asiasociety.org, Twitter, @AsiaSociety and Facebook, www.facebook.com/asiasociety

Membership: individuals, organizations, and corporations interested in Asia and the Pacific (excluding the Middle East). Focuses on U.S. and Asian foreign policy issues. Sponsors seminars and lectures on political, economic, and cultural issues. (Headquarters in New York.)

The Brookings Institution, Center for East Asia Policy Studies, 1775 Massachusetts Ave. N.W., 20036; (202) 238-3118. (202) 797-6103. Mireya Solis, Director.
Web, www.brookings.edu/center/center-for-east-asia-policy-studies

Conducts research, analysis, and exchange to enhance policy development on political, security, and economic issues in East Asia. Administers a visiting fellowship program annually. Interests include Taiwan relations; U.S.–ROK relations; Japanese politics and foreign policies; U.S.–China strategic relations; and Southeast Asia's growing strategic, economic, and diplomatic importance.

The Brookings Institution, John L. Thornton China Center, 1775 Massachusetts Ave. N.W., 20036; (202) 797-6103. Cheng Li, Director.

Web, www.brookings.edu/center/john-l-thornton-china-center and Twitter, @brookingschina

Research center promoting policies concerning China and its increasingly greater role in foreign affairs. Interests include secure energy sources, economic reforms, social and economic inequality, and citizen participation in government.

East–West Center, Washington Office, 1819 L St. N.W., #600, 20036; (202) 293-3995. Fax, (202) 293-1402. Satu P. Limaye, Director, (202) 327-9759. General email, washington@eastwestcenter.org

Web, www.eastwestcenter.org/ewc-in-washington, Twitter, @EWCinWashington and Facebook, www.facebook.com/ewcinwashington

Promotes strengthening of relations and understanding among countries and peoples of Asia, the Pacific, and the United States. Plans to undertake substantive programming activities, including collaborative research, training, seminars, and outreach; publications; and congressional study groups. (Headquarters in Honolulu, Hawaii.)

Eurasia Foundation, 1990 K St. N.W., #615, 20006; (202) 234-7370. Fax, (202) 234-7377. Lisa Coll, President. General email, info@eurasia.org

Web, www.eurasia.org, Twitter, @EFNetwork and Facebook, www.facebook.com/eurasiafoundation

Operates in Eurasia and Europe, the Middle East and North Africa, Asia and North America. Provides capacity building, entrepreneurship training, advocacy education, social entrepreneurship training, and fellowship exchanges to support small business growth, local institutional performance, the responsiveness of local governments, and the leadership of young people.

Formosan Assn. for Public Affairs, 552 7th St. S.E., 20003; (202) 547-3686. Fax, (202) 543-7891. Minze V. Chien, National President. General email, home@fapa.org

Web, www.fapa.org, Twitter, @FAPA_HQ and Facebook, www.facebook.com/FormosanAssociationforPublicAffairs

Political group that advocates the independence of Taiwan and promotes democracy. Seeks to improve relations between the United States and Taiwan. Educates the public, policymakers, and the media about current issues in Taiwan. Monitors legislation and regulations related to Taiwan's relationship with the United States.

Heritage Foundation, Asian Studies Center, 214 Massachusetts Ave. N.E., 20002-4999; (202) 546-4400. Walter Lohman, Director. Press, (202) 675-1761. General email, info@heritage.org

Web, www.heritage.org/asia

Conducts research and provides information on U.S. policies in Asia and the Pacific. Interests include economic and security issues in the Asia Pacific region. Hosts speakers and visiting foreign policy delegations; sponsors conferences.

International Campaign for the Rohingya, P.O. Box 48698, 20002-0698; (617) 596-6158. Simon Billenness, Executive Director. General email, info@rohingyacampaign.org

Web, www.rohingyacampaign.org and Twitter, @Rohingya_ICR

Acts as advocate for the Rohingya people with international organizations, governments, corporations, and civil society through education. Works to reduce genocide through the "No Business With Genocide" campaign by building a global movement to hold corporations accountable and put pressure on corporations in key sectors to stop supporting regimes complicit in genocide and crimes against humanity.

Jamestown Foundation, 1310 L St. N.W., #810, 20005; (202) 483-8888. Fax, (202) 483-8337. Glen E. Howard, President. General email, pubs@jamestown.org

Web, www.jamestown.org, Twitter, @JamestownTweets and Facebook, www.facebook.com/JamestownFoundation

Provides policymakers with information about events and trends in societies that are strategically or tactically important to the United States and that frequently restrict access to such information. Serves as an alternative source to official or intelligence channels, especially with regard to Eurasia, China, and terrorism. Publishes the Militant Leadership Monitor, covering leaders of major insurgencies and militant movements.

Japan–America Society of Washington DC, 1819 L St. N.W., #410, 20036-3807; (202) 833-2210. Ryan Shaffer, President. General email, info@jaswdc.org

Web, www.jaswdc.org, Twitter, @jas_wdc and Facebook, www.facebook.com/jaswdc

Conducts programs on U.S.–Japan political, security, and economic issues. Cultural programs include lectures, a Japanese-language school, and assistance to Japanese performing artists. Maintains library for members. Participates in National Cherry Blossom Festival.

Taipei Economic and Cultural Representative Office (TECRO), 4201 Wisconsin Ave. N.W., 20016; (202) 895-1800. Bi-khim Hsiao, Representative. General email, usa@mofa.gov.tw

Web, www.taiwanembassy.org and Twitter, @TECRO_USA

Represents political, economic, and cultural interests of the government of the Republic of China (Taiwan) in the United States.

U.S.–Asia Institute, 232 E. Capitol St. N.E., 20003; (202) 544-3181. Fax, (202) 747-5889. Mary Sue Bissell, President. General email, usai@usasiainstitute.org

Web, www.usasiainstitute.org, Twitter, @usasiainstitute and Facebook, www.facebook.com/USAI1979

Organization of individuals interested in Asia. Encourages dialogue among political and business leaders in the United States and Asia. Interests include foreign policy, international trade, Asian and American cultures, education, and employment. Conducts research and sponsors conferences and workshops in cooperation with the State Dept. to promote greater understanding between the United States and Asian nations.

U.S.–China Business Council, *1818 N St. N.W., #200, 20036-2470; (202) 429-0340. Fax, (202) 775-2476. Craig Allen, President. General email, info@uschina.org*

Web, www.uschina.org and Twitter, @USChinaBusiness

Member-supported organization that represents U.S. companies engaged in business relations with the People's Republic of China. Participates in U.S. policy issues relating to China and other international trade. Publishes research reports. (Maintains offices in Beijing and Shanghai.)

United States–Indonesia Society, *1625 Massachusetts Ave. N.W., #550, 20036-2260; (202) 232-1400. Fax, (202) 232-7300. David (Dave) Merrill, President. General email, usindo@usindo.org*

Web, www.usindo.org, Twitter, @USINDO and Facebook, www.facebook.com/USINDO

Seeks to strengthen relations between the United States and Indonesia. Educates and holds forums on economic and political trends in Indonesia. Grants scholarships and fellowships to students and professionals to travel from or to the United States and Indonesia.

Europe

(Includes the Baltic states)

▶ **AGENCIES**

Agency for International Development (USAID), *Bureau for Europe and Eurasia, 301 4th St. S.W., #247, 20523 (mailing address: 1300 Pennsylvania Ave. N.W., Washington, DC 20521); (202) 567-4020. Fax, (202) 567-4256. Margot Ellis, Assistant Administrator (Acting). Web, www.usaid.gov/who-we-are/organization/bureaus/bureau-europe-and-eurasia*

Advises the USAID administrator on U.S. economic development policy in Europe and Eurasia.

Bureau of European and Eurasian Affairs (EUR) *(State Dept.), 2201 C St. N.W., HST #6226, 20520; (202) 647-6285. Karen E. Donfried, Assistant Secretary (Acting), (202) 647-9626. Press, (202) 647-5116. Web, www.state.gov/p/eur, Twitter, @StateEUR and Press, EUR-Press-DL@state.gov*

Advises the secretary on U.S. policy toward European and Eurasian countries. Directors assigned to specific countries within the bureau aid the assistant secretary.

Bureau of European and Eurasian Affairs *(State Dept.), Central European Affairs, 2201 C St. N.W., #4230, 20520; (202) 647-1484. Alan Meltzer, Deputy Director, (202) 647-2307. Web, www.state.gov/p/eur*

Includes Austria, Bulgaria, Czech Republic, Hungary, Liechtenstein, Poland, Romania, Slovak Republic, Slovenia, and Switzerland.

Bureau of European and Eurasian Affairs *(State Dept.), European Security and Political Affairs, 2201 C St. N.W., #6511, 20520; (202) 647-1626. Kami Witmer, Director, (202) 647-2188. Web, www.state.gov/p/eur*

Coordinates and advises, with the Defense Dept. and other agencies, the U.S. mission to NATO and the U.S. delegation to the Organization for Security and Cooperation in Europe regarding political, military, and arms control matters.

Bureau of European and Eurasian Affairs *(State Dept.), European Union and Regional Affairs, 2201 C St. N.W., #3332, 20520; (202) 647-3474. Daniela Ballard, Deputy Director, (202) 647-3206. Web, www.state.gov/p/eur*

Handles all matters concerning the European Union, with emphasis on trade issues. Monitors export controls and economic activities for the North Atlantic Treaty Organization and the Organization for Security and Co-operation in Europe.

Bureau of European and Eurasian Affairs *(State Dept.), Nordic and Baltic Affairs, 2201 C St. N.W., #3331, 20520; (202) 647-5669. Stacie C. Bishop, Director, (202) 647-8908. Web, www.state.gov/p/eur*

Includes Denmark, Estonia, Finland, Iceland, Latvia, Lithuania, Norway, and Sweden.

Bureau of European and Eurasian Affairs *(State Dept.), South Central European Affairs, 2201 C St. N.W., #5219, 20520; (202) 647-0608. Henry M. McDonnell, Director, (202) 647-3024. Web, www.state.gov/p/eur*

Includes Albania, Bosnia-Herzegovina, Croatia, Kosovo, Macedonia, Serbia, and Montenegro.

Bureau of European and Eurasian Affairs *(State Dept.), Southern European Affairs, 2201 C St. N.W., #5511, 20520; (202) 647-6112. Maria Olsen, Director, (202) 647-6994. Web, www.state.gov/p/eur*

Includes Cyprus, Greece, and Turkey.

Bureau of European and Eurasian Affairs *(State Dept.), Special Envoy for Holocaust Issues, 2201 C St. N.W., #6219, 20520-6219; (202) 647-4753. Ellen J. Germain, Special Envoy. Web, www.state.gov/about-us-office-of-the-special-envoy-for-holocaust-issues and Twitter, @StateSEHI*

Bureau of European and Eurasian Affairs *(State Dept.), Western European Affairs, 2201 C St. N.W., #5218, 20520; (202) 647-3072. Howard Soloman, Director, (202) 647-1469. Web, www.state.gov/p/eur*

Includes Andorra, Belgium, Bermuda, France, Ireland, Italy, Luxembourg, Malta, Monaco, the Netherlands,

Portugal, San Marino, Spain, the United Kingdom, and the Vatican.

Defense Dept. (DoD), *International Security Affairs,* 2000 Defense Pentagon, 20301-2000; (703) 697-2788. Fax, (703) 697-3279. Ilan Goldenberg, Assistant Secretary (Acting).
Web, http://policy.defense.gov/OUSDPOffices/ ASDforInternationalSecurityAffairs

Advises the secretary of defense and recommends policies on regional security issues in the Middle East, Africa, Russia/Eurasia, and Europe/NATO.

Defense Dept. (DoD), *International Security Affairs, European and NATO Policy,* 2000 Defense Pentagon, #5B652, 20301-2000; (703) 695-5553. Spencer P. Boyer, Deputy Assistant Secretary.
Web, https://policy.defense.gov/OUSDP-Offices/ASD-for-International-Security-Affairs/Europe-and-NATO

Advises the assistant secretary for international security affairs on matters dealing with Europe and NATO.

►**CONGRESS**

For a listing of relevant congressional committees and sub-committees, please see pages 478–479 or the Appendix.

Library of Congress, *Latin American, Caribbean, and European Division (LAC&E), European Reading Room,* Thomas Jefferson Bldg., 101 Independence Ave. S.E., #LJ 249, 20540-4830; (202) 707-4515. Fax, (202) 707-8482. Suzanne Schadl, Division Chief; Michael Neubert, Head. General email, eurref@loc.gov
Web, www.loc.gov/rr/european

Provides reference service on the library's European collections (except collections on Spain, Portugal, and the British Isles). Prepares bibliographies and special studies relating to European countries, including Russia and the other states of the former Soviet Union and eastern bloc. Maintains current unbound Slavic language periodicals and newspapers, which are available at the European Reference Desk. Recommends materials for acquisition. Timed entry pass for visitors required, details at loc.gov/ visit. Appointments recommended for researchers.

►**INTERNATIONAL ORGANIZATIONS**

European Parliament Liaison Office, 2175 K St. N.W., #600, 20037; (202) 862-4734. Joseph Dunne, Director, (202) 862-4731.
General email, epwashington@ep.europa.eu
Web, www.europarl.europa.eu/us and Twitter, @EPWashingtonDC

Acts as the contact point between the European Parliament and the U.S. Congress. Seeks to intensify working relations between the European Parliament and the U.S. Congress at all levels, particularly between corresponding committees of jurisdiction, and between European Parliament lawmakers and U.S. regulators. Represents the Parliament's viewpoint to the U.S. administration and Congress. Principal issues addressed are human rights, the

threat of terrorism, economic growth, and environmental protection.

European Union, *Delegation to the United States of America,* 2175 K St. N.W., 20037; (202) 862-9500. Stavros Lambrinidis, Ambassador.
General email, delegation-usa-info@eeas.europa.eu
Web, www.euintheus.org, Twitter, @EUintheUS, Facebook, www.facebook.com/EUintheUS and Twitter, Ambassador, @EUAAmbUS

Information and public affairs office in the United States for the European Union. Provides social policy data on the European Union and provides statistics and information on member countries, including those related to energy, economics, development and cooperation, commerce, agriculture, industry, and technology. (Headquarters in Brussels.)

World Bank, *Europe and Central Asia Region,* 1818 H St. N.W., 20433; (202) 473-1000. Anna Bjerde, Vice President. General email, eca@worldbank.org
Web, www.worldbank.org/en/region/eca, Twitter, @WorldBankECA and Facebook, www.facebook.com/ WorldBankEuropeCentralAsia

Works to fight poverty and improve the living standards of low- and middle-income people in the countries of eastern Europe by providing loans, policy advice, technical assistance, and knowledge-sharing services. Areas of interest include finance, economic development, education, water supply, agriculture, public health, and environmental protection.

►**NONGOVERNMENTAL**

American Hellenic Institute, 1220 16th St. N.W., 20036-3202; (202) 785-8430. Fax, (202) 785-5178. Nick Larigakis, President.
General email, info@ahiworld.org
Web, http://ahiworld.org, Twitter, @TheAHIinDC, Facebook, www.facebook.com/AmericanHellenicInstitute and Library Portal, www.ahiworld.org/ahif-library

Works to strengthen relations between Greece, Cyprus, Turkey, southeastern Europe, and the United States and within the American Hellenic community.

The Brookings Institution, *Center on the United States and Europe (CUSE),* 1775 Massachusetts Ave. N.W., 20036; (202) 797-6103. (202) 797-6072. Thomas Wright, Director.
Web, www.brookings.edu/center/center-on-the-united-states-and-europe and Twitter, @thomaswright08

Research center promoting U.S.–Europe policy. Interests include transformation of the European Union, engagement strategies for the Balkans, Caucasus, Russia, Turkey, and Ukraine, and NATO and European security. Holds seminars and public forums on policy-relevant issues.

Center for European Policy Analysis, 1275 Pennsylvania Ave. N.W., #400, 20004; (202) 551-9200. Alina Polyakova, President. Press, (202) 664-6506.

General email, info@cepa.org

Web, www.cepa.org and Twitter, @cepa

Researches public policy in Central and Eastern European countries and seeks to improve their relations with the United States. Holds conferences on issues affecting transnational business, economy, security, and energy resources.

German American Business Council, *910 M St. N.W., #807, 20001; Ulrich Gamerdinger, President.*
General email, gabc@gabcwashington.com

Web, http://gabcwashington.com

Promotes transatlantic business dialogue between Germany and the United States through improved communication between embassies, industry, governments, and academia.

German Marshall Fund of the United States, *1744 R St. N.W., 20009; (202) 683-2650. Fax, (202) 265-1662. Heather A. Conley, President.*
General email, info@gmfus.org

Web, www.gmfus.org/our-offices/washington-dc and Twitter, @gmfus

American institution created by a gift from Germany as a permanent memorial to Marshall Plan aid. Seeks to stimulate exchange of dialogue, debate, policy analysis and ideas promoting transatlantic cooperation. Awards grants to promote the study of international and domestic policies; supports comparative research and debate on key issues.

Irish National Caucus, *P.O. Box 15128, 20003-0849; (202) 544-0568. Fax, (202) 488-7537. Fr. Sean McManus, President.*
General email, support@irishnationalcaucus.org

Web, www.irishnationalcaucus.org and Twitter, @FrSeanMcManus1

Educational organization concerned with protecting human rights in Northern Ireland. Seeks to end anti-Catholic discrimination in Northern Ireland through implementation of the McBride Principles, initiated in 1984. Advocates nonviolence and supports the peace process in Northern Ireland. Monitors legislation and regulations.

Joint Baltic American National Committee (JBANC), *400 Hurley Ave., Rockville, MD 20850-3121; (301) 340-1954. Karl Altau, Managing Director.*
General email, jbanc@jbanc.org

Web, www.jbanc.org, Twitter, @JBANCchatter and Facebook, www.facebook.com/JointBalticAmericanNationalCommittee

Washington representative of the Estonian, Latvian, and Lithuanian American communities in the United States; acts as a representative on issues affecting the Baltic states.

Trans-Atlantic Business Council, *1601 K St. N.W., 20001; (202) 778-9073. Fax, (202) 778-9100. Bart Gordon, U.S. Director.*
Web, http://transatlanticbusiness.org and Twitter, @TABC_Council

Membership: A consortium of more than 70 multinational corporations with operations in Europe and the United States. Promotes a barrier-free transatlantic market that contributes to economic growth, innovation, and security.

Latin America, Canada, and the Caribbean

▶AGENCIES

Agency for International Development (USAID), *Bureau for Latin America and the Caribbean, 1300 Pennsylvania Ave. N.W., #5.09, 20523-5900; (202) 712-4760. Fax, (202) 216-3012. Marcela Escobari, Assistant Administrator (Acting). Press, (202) 712-5952.*
Web, www.usaid.gov/who-we-are/organization/bureaus/bureau-latin-america-and-caribbean

Advises the USAID administrator on U.S. policy toward developing Latin American and Caribbean countries. Designs and implements assistance programs for developing nations.

Bureau of Western Hemisphere Affairs *(State Dept.), 2201 C St. N.W., #6262, 20520; (202) 647-5780. Brian A. Nichols, Assistant Secretary. Press, (202) 647-6575.*
Web, www.state.gov/p/wha, Twitter, @WHAAsstSecty and YouTube, www.youtube.com/user/whabureau

Advises the secretary on U.S. policy toward North, Central, and South America. Directors assigned to specific regions within the bureau aid the assistant secretary.

Bureau of Western Hemisphere Affairs *(State Dept.), Andean Affairs, 2201 C St. N.W., #4915, 20520; (202) 647-1715. Joaquin Monserrate, Director, (202) 647-3143.*
Web, www.state.gov/p/wha

Includes Bolivia, Colombia, Ecuador, Peru, and Venezuela.

Bureau of Western Hemisphere Affairs *(State Dept.), Brazilian and Southern Cone Affairs, 2201 C St. N.W., #4258, 20520; (202) 647-1715. Robin D. Meyer, Director, (202) 647-3403.*
Web, www.state.gov/p/wha

Includes Argentina, Brazil, Chile, Paraguay, and Uruguay.

Bureau of Western Hemisphere Affairs *(State Dept.), Canadian Affairs, 2201 C St. N.W., #3918, 20520; (202) 647-2170. Laura Lochman, Director, (202) 647-2273. Public Affairs, (202) 647-7137.*
Web, www.state.gov/p/wha

Bureau of Western Hemisphere Affairs *(State Dept.), Caribbean Affairs, 2201 C St. N.W., #4262, 20520-6258; (202) 736-2308. Nan Fife, Director, (202) 736-1675.*
Web, www.state.gov/p/wha

Includes Antigua and Barbuda, Aruba, Bahamas, Barbados, Dominica, Dominican Republic, Grenada, Guyana, Jamaica, Netherlands Antilles, St. Kitts and Nevis, St. Lucia, St. Vincent and the Grenadines, Suriname, and Trinidad and Tobago.

Bureau of Western Hemisphere Affairs *(State Dept.),* *Central American Affairs, 2201 C St. N.W., #5906, 20520; (202) 647-6754. Patrick Ventrell, Director, (202) 647-0087.* *Web, www.state.gov/p/wha*

Includes Belize, Costa Rica, El Salvador, Guatemala, Honduras, Nicaragua, and Panama.

Bureau of Western Hemisphere Affairs *(State Dept.),* *Cuban Affairs, 2201 C St. N.W., #SA-09 4174, 20520; (202) 453-8464. Rebecca L. Landis, Deputy Director, (202) 453-8465.* *Web, www.state.gov/p/wha*

Bureau of Western Hemisphere Affairs *(State Dept.),* *Haitian Affairs, 2201 C St. N.W., #4908, 20520-6258; (202) 647-4736. Stacy D. Williams, Deputy Director (Acting), (202) 453-9909. Public Affairs, (202) 647-9468.* *General email, HaitiSpecialCoordinator@state.gov* *Web, www.state.gov/p/wha*

Coordinates assistance to Haiti. Oversees U.S. government engagement with Haiti, including implementation of a reconstruction strategy in partnership with the Haitian government.

Bureau of Western Hemisphere Affairs *(State Dept.),* *Mexican Affairs, 2201 C St. N.W., #3924, 20520-6258; (202) 647-8766. Jennifer Brown, Director (Acting), (202) 647-8113.* *Web, www.state.gov/p/wha*

Bureau of Western Hemisphere Affairs *(State Dept.),* *U.S. Mission to the Organization of American States, 2201 C St. N.W., #5914, 20520-6258; (202) 647-9376. (202) 647-9377. Fax, (202) 647-0911. Bradley Freden, U.S. Permanent Representative, (202) 647-9422.* *Web, https://usoas.usmission.gov/mission/oas, Twitter, @USAmbOAS and Facebook, www.facebook.com/ OASofficial*

Formulates U.S. policy and represents U.S. interests at the Organization of American States (OAS).

Defense Dept. (DoD), *International Security Affairs, Western Hemisphere, 2000 Defense Pentagon, #3E806, 20301-2000; (703) 697-7200. Fax, (703) 697-6602. Daniel Erikson, Deputy Assistant Secretary.* *Web, https://policy.defense.gov/OUSDP-Offices/ASD-for-International-Security-Affairs/Western-Hemisphere*

Advises the assistant secretary for international security affairs on inter-American matters; aids in the development of U.S. policy toward Latin America.

Inter-American Foundation, *1331 Pennsylvania Ave. N.W., #1200 North, 20004; (202) 360-4530. Lesley Duncan, President (Acting).*

General email, inquiries@iaf.gov *Web, www.iaf.gov, Twitter, @IAFgrassroots and Facebook, www.facebook.com/iafgrassroots*

Supports small-scale Latin American and Caribbean social and economic development efforts through grassroots development programs, grants, and fellowships.

International Trade Administration (ITA) *(Commerce Dept.), Global Markets, North and Central America, 1401 Constitution Ave. N.W., Room 30020, #3826, 20230 (mailing address: 1401 Constitution Ave. N.W., MD 30019, Washington, DC 20230); (202) 482-1545. Fax, (202) 482-5013. Geri Word, Director.* *Web, www.trade.gov/*

Coordinates Commerce Dept. activities and assists U.S. business regarding export to Mexico, Canada, Central America, and the Caribbean. Helps negotiate and ensures compliance with U.S. free trade agreements, including USMCA (United States–Mexico–Canada Agreement) and the Dominican Republic–Central American Free Trade Agreement (CAFTA-DR).

▶CONGRESS

For a listing of relevant congressional committees and sub-committees, please see pages 478–479 or the Appendix.

Library of Congress, *Latin American, Caribbean, and European Division, Hispanic Reading Room, Thomas Jefferson Bldg., 101 Independence Ave. S.E., #LJ 240, 20540-4850; (202) 707-5400. Fax, (202) 707-2005. Suzanne M. Schadl, Division Chief; Carlos Olave, Head. Reading Room, (202) 707-5397.* *Web, www.loc.gov/rr/hispanic*

Orients researchers and scholars in the area of Iberian, Latin American, Caribbean, and U.S. Latino studies. All major subject areas are represented with emphasis on history, literature, and the social sciences. Primary and secondary source materials are available in the library's general collections for the study of all periods, from pre-Columbian to the present. The collection includes the "Archive of Hispanic Literature on Tape" with recordings of nearly 700 authors reading their own material, available in the reading room and with a select number of recordings available for streaming online as the collection is being digitized. Timed entry pass for visitors required, details at loc.gov/visit. Appointments recommended for researchers.

▶INTERNATIONAL ORGANIZATIONS

Inter-American Development Bank, *1300 New York Ave. N.W., 20577; (202) 623-1000. Fax, (202) 623-3096. Mauricio Claver-Carone, President; James Andrew Catto, U.S. Executive Director. Library, (202) 623-3211. Press, (202) 623-1555.* *Web, www.iadb.org, Twitter, @the_IDB and Facebook, www.facebook.com/IADB.org*

Promotes, through loans and technical assistance, the investment of public and private capital in member countries of Latin America and the Caribbean for social and economic development purposes. Facilitates economic integration of the Latin American region, operating the Inter-American Investment Corp. and the Multilateral Investment Fund. Library open to the public by appointment.

Inter-American Telecommunication Commission (CITEL) *(Organization of American States)*, *1889 F St. N.W., 6th Floor, 20006; (202) 370-4713. Fax, (202) 458-6854. Oscar Léon, Executive Secretary, (202) 370-0850.*
General email, citel@oas.org
Web, www.citel.oas.org and Twitter, @OEA_CITEL

Membership: OAS member states and associate members from the telecommunications, Internet, electronic, and media industries, and others. Works with the public and private sectors to facilitate the development of universal telecommunications in the Americas.

Organization of American States (OAS), *17th St. and Constitution Ave. N.W., 20006; Administration Bldg., 19th St. and Constitution Ave. N.W., 20006; General Secretariat Bldg., 1889 F St. N.W., 20006; (202) 370-5000. Fax, (202) 458-3967. Luis Almagro Lemes, Secretary General. Library, (202) 458-6041.*
General email, ai@oas.org
Web, www.oas.org and Twitter, @oas_official

Membership: the United States, Canada, and all independent Latin American and Caribbean countries. Funded by quotas paid by member states and by contributions to special multilateral funds. Works to promote democracy, eliminate poverty, and resolve disputes among member nations. Provides member states with technical and advisory services in cultural, educational, scientific, social, and economic areas. Library open to the public (at 19th and Constitution).

United Nations Economic Commission for Latin America and the Caribbean (CEPAL), *Washington Office, 1825 K St. N.W., #1120, 20006-1210; (202) 596-3713. Inés Bustillo, Director; Raquel Artecona, Officer In Charge.*
General email, eclacwash@eclac.org
Web, www.cepal.org/en/headquarters-and-offices/eclac-washington-dc and Twitter, @eclac_un

Membership: Latin American, Caribbean, and some industrially developed Western nations. Seeks to strengthen economic relations between countries both within and outside Latin America through research and analysis of socioeconomic problems, training programs, and advisory services to member governments. (Headquarters in Santiago, Chile.)

World Bank, *Latin America and the Caribbean Region, 1818 H St. N.W., 20433; (202) 473-1000. Carlos Felipe Jaramillo, Vice President.*
Web, www.worldbank.org/lac, Twitter, @WorldBank and Facebook, www.facebook.com/worldbank

Works to fight poverty and improve the living standards of poor and middle-income people in the countries of Latin America and the Caribbean by providing loans, policy advice, technical assistance, and knowledge-sharing services. Areas of interest include finance, economic development, education, water supply, agriculture, and infrastructure, public health, and environmental protection.

▶**NONGOVERNMENTAL**

Americas Society / Council of the Americas, *Washington Office, 1615 L St. N.W., #250, 20036; (202) 659-8989. Fax, (202) 659-7755. Susan Segal, President; Eric Farnsworth, Vice President, Washington Office.*
Web, www.as-coa.org and Twitter, @ASCOA

Membership: businesses with interests and investments in Latin America. Seeks to expand the role of private enterprise in development of the region. (Headquarters in New York.)

Council on Hemispheric Affairs, *2501 Calvert St. N.W., #401, 20008 (mailing address: PO Box 34646, Washington DC, 20043); (202) 223-4975. Fax, (202) 248-0745. Frederick B. Mills, Co-Director (English); Patricio Zamorano, Co-Director (Spanish).*
General email, coha@coha.org
Web, www.coha.org, Twitter, @COHAofficial and Facebook, www.facebook.com/council.on.hemispheric.affairs

Seeks to expand interest in inter-American relations and increase press coverage of Latin America and Canada. Monitors U.S., Latin American, and Canadian relations, with emphasis on human rights, trade, growth of democratic institutions, freedom of the press, and hemispheric economic and political developments; provides educational materials and analyzes issues. Issues annual survey on human rights and freedom of the press. Publishes a biweekly newsletter.

Group of Fifty (Grupo de los Cincuenta), *1875 Connecticut Ave. N.W., 20009; (202) 808-3360. Marianella Morales, Executive Director. Toll-free, (888) 798-2366.*
General email, Contact@G50.org
Web, www.g-50.org

Membership: business leaders who own Latin American enterprises. Holds an annual forum to improve networking between business executives and to promote economic growth in Latin America.

Guatemala Human Rights Commission/USA, *3321 12th St. N.E., 20017-4008; (202) 998-2191. Isabel Solis, Director.*
General email, ghrc-usa@ghrc-usa.org
Web, www.ghrc-usa.org and Twitter, @GHRCUSA

Provides information and collects and makes available reports on human rights violations in Guatemala; publishes a quarterly report of documented cases of specific abuses. Takes on special projects and leads delegations to further sensitize the public and the international community to human rights abuses in Guatemala.

Inter-American Dialogue, *1155 15th St. N.W., #800, 20005; (202) 822-9002. Fax, (202) 822-9553. Michael Shifter, President, (202) 204-5556.*

General email, iad@thedialogue.org

Web, www.thedialogue.org, Twitter, @The_Dialogue and Facebook, www.facebook.com/InterAmericanDialogue

Serves as a forum for communication and exchange among leaders of the Americas. Provides analyses and policy recommendations on issues of hemispheric concern. Interests include economic integration, trade, and the strengthening of democracy in Latin America. Hosts private and public exchanges; sponsors conferences and seminars; publishes daily newsletter, *Latin America Advisor*.

Latin America Working Group, *2029 P St. N.W., #301, 20036; (202) 546-7010. Lisa Haugaard, Co-Director, ext. 6811; Daniella Burgi-Palomino, Co-Director, ext. 6812.*
General email, lawg@lawg.org

Web, www.lawg.org, Twitter, @lawgaction and Facebook, www.facebook.com/lawgaction

Represents organizations concerned with advancing human rights, and social, environmental, and economic justice in Latin America and the Caribbean. Encourages U.S. policies toward Latin America that promote human rights, justice, peace, and sustainable development.

Pan American Development Foundation, *1889 F St. N.W., 2nd Floor, 20006; (202) 458-3969. Fax, (202) 458-6316. Katie Taylor, Executive Director.*
Donations, (877) 572-4484.
Web, www.padf.org, Twitter, @PADForg, Email, connect@padf.org and Facebook, www.facebook.com/PADForg

Works to address the needs of vulnerable populations across Latin America and the Caribbean, promote sustainable livelihoods, and advance rights and justice. Associated with the Organization of American States (OAS).

Partners of the Americas, *1424 K St. N.W., #700, 20005-2410; (202) 628-3300. Fax, (202) 628-3306. John McPhail, President.*
General email, info@partners.net

Web, www.partners.net, Twitter, @PartnersAmericas and Facebook, www.facebook.com/partnersamericas

Membership: chapters, individuals, and organizations in the United States, Latin America, Brazil, and the Caribbean. Sponsors technical assistance projects and cultural exchanges between the United States, Latin America, Brazil, and the Caribbean; supports self-help projects in food security and agricultural development, sport for development, youth and children, climate change and environmental protection, professional leadership exchanges, civil society and governance, and women and gender equality.

U.S.–Mexico Chamber of Commerce, *P.O. Box 14414, 20044; (469) 567-0923. Albert C. Zapanta, President.*
General email, info@usmcoc.org

Web, www.usmcoc.org and Twitter, @USMCOC

Promotes trade and investment between the United States and Mexico. Provides members with information and expertise on conducting business between the two countries as pertains to NAFTA. Serves as a clearinghouse for information. (Headquarters in Irving, Tex.)

Washington Office on Latin America, *1666 Connecticut Ave. N.W., #400, 20009; (202) 797-2171. Carolina Jimenez Sandoval, President.*
General email, wola@wola.org

Web, www.wola.org, Twitter, @WOLA_org, Press, press@wola.org and Facebook, www.facebook.com/WOLA.org

Acts as a liaison between government policymakers and groups and individuals concerned with human rights and U.S. policy in Latin America and the Caribbean. Serves as an information resource center; monitors legislation.

Near East and South Asia

(Includes North Africa)

▶**AGENCIES**

Agency for International Development (USAID), *Afghanistan and Pakistan Affairs, 1300 Pennsylvania Ave. N.W., #5.6-027, 20523; (202) 712-5002. Karen L. Freeman, Assistant Administrator (Acting); Peter Duffy, Mission Director. Main Switchboard, (202) 712-0000.*
General email, infoafghanistan@usaid.gov

Web, www.usaid.gov/who-we-are/organization/bureaus/bureau-asia

Advises the USAID administrator on U.S. economic development policy in Afghanistan and Pakistan.

Agency for International Development (USAID), *Bureau for Asia, 1300 Pennsylvania Ave. N.W., 20523-4900; (202) 712-0200. Fax, (202) 216-3386. Änjali Kaur, Deputy Assistant Administrator.*
Web, www.usaid.gov/who-we-are/organization/bureaus/bureau-asia

Advises the USAID administrator on U.S. economic development policy in Asia.

Agency for International Development (USAID), *Bureau for Middle East, 1300 Pennsylvania Ave. N.W., #4.09-006, 20523-4900; (202) 712-0300. Andrew Plitt, Assistant Administrator (Acting).*
Web, www.usaid.gov/who-we-are/organization/bureaus/bureau-middle-east

Advises the USAID administrator on U.S. economic development policy in the Middle East.

Bureau of Near Eastern Affairs *(State Dept.), 2201 C St. N.W., #6242, 20520-6243; (202) 647-7207. Yael Lempert, Assistant Secretary (Acting). Communications, (202) 647-6575.*
General email, NEA-PublicInquiries@state.gov

Web, www.state.gov/p/nea and Twitter, @StateDept_NEA

Advises the secretary on U.S. policy toward countries of the Near East and North Africa. Directors assigned to specific countries within the bureau aid the assistant secretary.

Bureau of Near Eastern Affairs *(State Dept.), Arabian Peninsula Affairs,* 2201 C St. N.W., #1251, 20520-6243; (202) 647-6184. *Evyenia M. Sidereas, Director.*
General email, nea-arp-dl@state.gov
Web, www.state.gov/p/nea

Includes Bahrain, Kuwait, Oman, Qatar, Saudi Arabia, United Arab Emirates, and Yemen.

Bureau of Near Eastern Affairs *(State Dept.), Assistance Coordination,* 2201 C St. N.W., #SA-4 Central, 20520; (202) 776-8383. *Danika Walters, Director, (202) 776-8681.*
Web, www.state.gov/p/nea

Oversees U.S. foreign assistance and aid to the Middle East and North Africa and establishes programs that advance U.S. policy priorities.

Bureau of Near Eastern Affairs *(State Dept.), Egypt Affairs,* 2201 C St. N.W., #HST 4440, 20520; (202) 647-8078. *Ramsey Alqaisi, Desk Officer, (202) 647-2261.*
Web, www.state.gov/countries-areas/egypt

Bureau of Near Eastern Affairs *(State Dept.), Iranian Affairs,* 2201 C St. N.W., #4827, 20520; (202) 647-6351. *Ian Harper, Director (Acting), (202) 647-9405.*
Web, www.state.gov/p/nea

Bureau of Near Eastern Affairs *(State Dept.), Iraq Affairs,* 2201 C St. N.W., #4827, 20520; (202) 647-6351. *Ian Hoppwe, Director (Acting), (202) 647-9405.*
Web, www.state.gov/p/nea

Bureau of Near Eastern Affairs *(State Dept.), Israel and Palestinian Affairs,* 2201 C St. N.W., #6251, 20520; (202) 647-3672. *Emily Katkar, Director, (202) 647-3644.*
Web, www.state.gov/p/nea

Bureau of Near Eastern Affairs *(State Dept.), Levant Affairs,* 2201 C St. N.W., #4241, 20520-6243; (202) 647-1091. *Steven Butler, Director, (202) 647-9539.*
Web, www.state.gov/p/nea

Includes Jordan, Lebanon, and Syria.

Bureau of Near Eastern Affairs *(State Dept.), Maghreb Affairs,* 2201 C St. N.W., #4440, 20520-6243; (202) 647-8078. *Katie Kaiser, Director (Acting), (202) 647-8070; David Green, Team Lead.*
Web, www.state.gov/p/nea

Includes Algeria, Libya, Morocco, Tunisia, and Mauritania.

Bureau of South and Central Asian Affairs *(State Dept.),* 2201 C St. N.W., #6254, 20520-6258; (202) 736-4324. *Donald Lu, Assistant Secretary, (202) 736-4022.*
Web, www.state.gov/p/sca and Twitter, @State_SCA

Advises the secretary on U.S. policy toward South and Central Asian countries. Directors assigned to specific countries within the bureau aid the assistant secretary.

Bureau of South and Central Asian Affairs *(State Dept.), Afghanistan Affairs,* 2201 C St. N.W., #1334, 20520-6258; (202) 647-0343. *Mark R. Evans, Director, (202) 647-6708.*
Web, www.state.gov/p/sca

Bureau of South and Central Asian Affairs *(State Dept.), India Affairs,* 2201 C St. N.W., #5251, 20520-6243; (202) 647-1450. *Laura Stone, Director, (202) 647-4033.*
Web, www.state.gov/p/sca

Bureau of South and Central Asian Affairs *(State Dept.), Nepal, Sri Lanka, Bangladesh, Bhutan, and Maldives Affairs,* 2201 C St. N.W., #5250, 20520-6243; (202) 647-1613. *Kelly Kiederling, Director.*
Web, www.state.gov/p/sca

Bureau of South and Central Asian Affairs *(State Dept.), Pakistan Affairs,* 2201 C St. N.W., #1808, 20520-6258; (202) 647-9434. *Lesslie C. Viguerie, Deputy Assistant Secretary. Press, (202) 647-6575.*
Web, www.state.gov/p/sca

Defense Dept. (DoD), *Afghanistan, Pakistan, and Central Asia Security Affairs,* 2700 Defense Pentagon, #5D688, 20301; (703) 695-4175. Fax, (703) 614-9721. *Kelly E. Magsamen, Principal Deputy Assistant Secretary.*
Web, https://policy.defense.gov/OUSDP-Offices/ASD-for-Indo-Pacific-Security-Affairs/Afghanistan-Pakistan-and-Central-Asia

Advises the under secretary of defense on matters dealing with Afghanistan, Pakistan, and Central Asia.

Defense Dept. (DoD), *International Security Affairs,* 2000 Defense Pentagon, 20301-2000; (703) 697-2788. Fax, (703) 697-3279. *Ilan Goldenberg, Assistant Secretary (Acting).*
Web, http://policy.defense.gov/OUSDPOffices/ASDforInternationalSecurityAffairs

Advises the secretary of defense and recommends policies on regional security issues in the Middle East, Africa, Russia/Eurasia, and Europe/NATO.

Defense Dept. (DoD), *International Security Affairs, Middle East,* 2000 Defense Pentagon, #5B712, 20301-2000; (703) 697-1335. Fax, (703) 693-6795. *Dana Stroul, Deputy Assistant Secretary.*
Web, https://policy.defense.gov/OUSDP-Offices/ASD-for-International-Security-Affairs/Middle-East

Advises the assistant secretary for international security affairs on matters dealing with the Middle East and South Asia.

Defense Dept. (DoD), *South and Southeast Asia Security Affairs,* 2700 Defense Pentagon, #5D688, 20301-2700; (703) 695-4175. *Lindsey W. Ford, Deputy Assistant Secretary.*
General email, osd.pentagon.ousd-policy.list.all-south-south-east-asia@mail.mil

Web, http://policy.defense.gov/OUSDP-Offices/ASD-for-Indo-Pacific-Security-Affairs/South-and-Southeast-Asia

Advises the under secretary of defense on all policy matters pertaining to development and implementation of defense strategies and plans for the region, and bilateral security relations with India and all other South Asian countries.

►CONGRESS

For a listing of relevant congressional committees and sub-committees, please see pages 478–479 or the Appendix.

Library of Congress, *African and Middle Eastern Division,* *Thomas Jefferson Bldg., 101 Independence Ave. S.E., #LJ 229, 20540-4660; (202) 707-7937. Lanisa Kitchiner, Chief. Reading Room, (202) 707-4188. General email, amed@loc.gov*

Web, www.loc.gov/rr/amed

Maintains collections of African, Near Eastern, and Hebraic material. Prepares bibliographies and special studies relating to Africa and the Middle East. Reference service and reading rooms available to the public. (Need reader's card to use.) Timed entry pass for visitors required, details at loc.gov/visit. Appointments recommended for researchers.

Library of Congress, *International Collections, Asian Division,* *Thomas Jefferson Bldg., 10 1st St. S.E., #LJ 150, 20540-4810; (202) 707-3766. Fax, (202) 707-1724. Dongfang Shao, Chief, (202) 707-5919. Reading Room, (202) 707-5426.*

Web, www.loc.gov/rr/asian

Maintains collections from across Asia, including Asian-American Pacific, Chinese, Korean, Japanese, Southeast Asian, South Asian, and Tibetan and Mongolian material. Reference service is provided in the Asian Reading Room, room #150. Timed entry pass for visitors required, details at loc.gov/visit. Appointments recommended for researchers.

►INTERNATIONAL ORGANIZATIONS

League of Arab States, *Washington Office,* *1100 17th St. N.W., #602, 20036; (202) 265-3210. Fax, (202) 331-1525. Amb. Salah A. Sarhan, Chief Representative. General email, arableague@aol.com*

Web, www.arableague-us.org

Membership: Arab countries in the Near East, North Africa, and the Indian Ocean. Coordinates members' policies in political, cultural, economic, and social affairs; mediates disputes among members and between members and third parties. Washington office maintains the Arab Information Center. (Headquarters in Cairo.)

Southeast Asia Resource Action Center (SEARAC), *1628 16th St. N.W., 3rd Floor, 20009; (202) 601-2960. Quyen Dinh, Executive Director. General email, searac@searac.org*

Web, www.searac.org, Twitter, @SEARAC, Facebook, www.facebook.com/searac and YouTube, www.youtube.com/channel/UCu24IlraDLG8FMeZglaYeNQ/featured

Works to advance Cambodian, Hmong, Laotian, and Vietnamese refugee rights through leadership and advocacy training. Collects and analyzes data on Southeast Asian Americans; publishes reports.

World Bank, *Middle East and North Africa Region,* *1818 H St. N.W., 20433; (202) 473-1000. Ferid Belhaj, Vice President. General email, mnateam@worldbank.org*

Web, www.worldbank.org/en/region/mena and Twitter, @WorldBankMENA

Works to fight poverty and improve the living standards of low- and middle-income people in the countries of the Middle East and North Africa by providing loans, policy advice, technical assistance, and knowledge-sharing services. Areas of interest include finance, economic development, education, water supply, agriculture, public health, and environmental protection.

World Bank, *South Asia Region,* *1818 H St. N.W., 20433; (202) 473-1000. Hartwig Schafer, Vice President. Web, www.worldbank.org/en/region/sar and Twitter, @WorldBankSAsia*

Works to fight poverty and improve the living standards of low- and middle-income people in the countries of South Asia by providing loans, policy advice, technical assistance, and knowledge-sharing services. Areas of interest include finance, economic development, education, water supply, agriculture, public health, and environmental protection.

►NONGOVERNMENTAL

American Israel Public Affairs Committee, *251 H St. N.W., 20001-2017; (202) 639-5200. Howard Kohr, Chief Executive Officer. General email, information@aipac.org*

Web, www.aipac.org, Twitter, @AIPAC, Facebook, www.facebook.com/aipac and YouTube, www.youtube.com/user/AIPACPC

Works to maintain and improve relations between the United States and Israel. Holds educational seminars.

American Jewish Committee, *Project Interchange,* *1156 15th St. N.W., 20005; (202) 833-0025. Fax, (202) 331-7702. Robin S. Levenston, Executive Director. Web, www.projectinterchange.org, Twitter, @projinterchange and Facebook, www.facebook.com/projectinterchange*

Sponsors policymakers, industry leaders, journalists, and scholars to travel to Israel to meet and take part in seminars with Israeli government officials, business leaders, and academics to learn about current developments and issues affecting education, immigration, human rights, and the economy in Israel.

American Kurdish Information Network (AKIN), *4412 Sedgwick St. N.W., 20016; (202) 483-6444. Kani Xulam, Director. General email, akin@kurdistan.org*

Web, http://kurdistan.org, Twitter, @AKINinfo and Facebook, www.facebook.com/FreeKurdistan

Membership: Americans of Kurdish origin, recent Kurdish immigrants and refugees, and others. Collects and disseminates information about the Kurds, an ethnic group living in parts of Turkey, Iran, Iraq, and Syria. Monitors human rights abuses against Kurds; promotes self-determination in Kurdish homelands; fosters Kurdish American friendship and understanding.

American Near East Refugee Aid (ANERA), *1111 14th St. N.W., #400, 20005; (202) 266-9700. Fax, (202) 266-9701. Sean Carroll, President.*
General email, anera@anera-jwg.org
Web, www.anera.org, Twitter, @ANERAorg, Facebook, www.facebook.com/ANERAorg and YouTube, www .youtube.com/user/ANERAorg

Works with local institutions and partner organizations to provide sustainable development, health, education, and employment programs to Palestinian and Lebanese communities and impoverished families throughout the Middle East. Delivers humanitarian aid during emergencies. (Field offices in the West Bank, Gaza, and Lebanon.)

AMIDEAST, *2025 M St. N.W., #600, 20036-3363; (202) 776-9600. Fax, (202) 776-7000. Amb. Theodore H. Kattouf, President.*
General email, inquiries@amideast.org
Web, www.amideast.org and Twitter, @AMIDEASThq

Promotes understanding and cooperation between Americans and the people of the Middle East and North Africa through education, information, and development programs in the region. Produces educational material to help improve teaching about the Middle East and North Africa in American schools and colleges.

Asia Society Policy Institute, *Washington Office, 1779 Massachusetts Ave. N.W., #805, 20036; (202) 833-2742. Fax, (202) 833-0189. Wendy Cutler, Managing Director, Washington Office.*
General email, asiadc@asiasociety.org
Web, www.asiasociety.org, Twitter, @AsiaSociety and Facebook, www.facebook.com/asiasociety/

Membership: individuals, organizations, and corporations interested in Asia and the Pacific (excluding the Middle East). Focuses on U.S. and Asian foreign policy issues. Sponsors seminars and lectures on political, economic, and cultural issues. (Headquarters in New York.)

B'nai B'rith International, *1120 20th St. N.W., #300N, 20036; (202) 857-6600. Daniel S. Mariaschin, Chief Executive Officer. Press, (202) 857-6699. Toll-free, (888) 388-4224.*
General email, info@bnaibrith.org
Web, www.bnaibrith.org, Twitter, @BnaiBrith and Facebook, www.facebook.com/bnaibrithinternational

International Jewish organization that promotes the security and continuity of the Jewish people and the State of Israel; defends human rights; combats anti-Semitism; and promotes Jewish identity through cultural activities. Interests include strengthening family life and the education and training of youth, providing broad-based services for the benefit of senior citizens, and advocacy on behalf of Jews throughout the world.

The Brookings Institution, *Center for Middle East Policy, 1775 Massachusetts Ave. N.W., 20036; (202) 797-6103. Natan Sachs, Director, (202) 797-6411.*
Web, www.brookings.edu/center/center-for-middle-east-policy and Twitter, @natansachs

Research center promoting policymaking on the Middle East. Interests include the Israeli–Palestinian conflict; the Iran nuclear deal; civil war in Syria, Libya, and Yemen; refugees and reconstruction; trends in political Islam; combatting extremism and terrorism; and U.S. strategies in the Middle East.

Center for Contemporary Arab Studies *(Georgetown University), 241 Intercultural Center, 37th and O Sts. N.W., 20057-1020; (202) 687-5793. Fax, (202) 687-7001. Joseph Sassoon, Director.*
General email, ccasinfo@georgetown.edu
Web, https://ccas.georgetown.edu, Twitter, @ccasGU and Facebook, www.facebook.com/ccasGU

The master's program at Georgetown University; sponsors lecture series, seminars, and conferences. Conducts a community outreach program that assists secondary school teachers in the development of instructional materials on the Middle East; promotes the study of the Arabic language in area schools.

Center for Democracy and Human Rights in Saudi Arabia, *1629 K St. N.W., #300, 20006; (202) 558-5552. Ali Alyami, Executive Director, (202) 413-0084.*
General email, cdhr@cdhr.info
Web, http://cdhr.info and Facebook, www.facebook.com/ The-Center-for-Democracy-and-Human-Rights-in-Saudi-Arabia-24834356502

Monitors relations between the United States and Saudi Arabia. Promotes democratic reform of Saudi policies and studies the global impact of current events in Saudi Arabia. Interests include women's rights, religious and press freedom, secular judiciary systems, and government accountability. Holds conferences to analyze Saudi policies, international relations, current events, and strict interpretations of Islam. Educates the public, policymakers, and the media on related issues.

Center for Strategic and International Studies, *Middle East Program, 1616 Rhode Island Ave. N.W., 20036; (202) 775-3179. Jon B. Alterman, Director.*
General email, middleeastprogram@csis.org
Web, www.csis.org/programs/middle-east-program, Twitter, @CSISMidEast and Facebook, www.facebook .com/CSISMidEast

Conducts research and publishes on regional trends in the Middle East. Interests include political, social, and economic change in North Africa, Asian strategies toward the Middle East, shifting dynamics in the Gulf, and radicalism and insurgencies. Publishes the monthly newsletter *Middle East Notes and Comment,* and holds conferences and online discussions, including a weekly podcast, *Babel.*

Eurasia Foundation, *1990 K St. N.W., #615, 20006; (202) 234-7370. Fax, (202) 234-7377. Lisa Coll, President.*
General email, info@eurasia.org

Web, www.eurasia.org, Twitter, @EFNetwork and Facebook, www.facebook.com/eurasiafoundation

Operates in Eurasia and Europe, the Middle East and North Africa, Asia and North America. Provides capacity building, entrepreneurship training, advocacy education, social entrepreneurship training, and fellowship exchanges to support small business growth, local institutional performance, the responsiveness of local governments, and the leadership of young people.

Foundation for Middle East Peace, *2025 M St. N.W., #600, 20036; (202) 835-3650. Fax, (202) 835-3651. Lara Friedman, President.*
General email, info@fmep.org

Web, www.fmep.org, Twitter, @FMEP and Facebook, www.facebook.com/Foundation-for-Middle-East-Peace-82038934261

Educational organization that seeks to promote understanding and resolution of the Israeli-Palestinian conflict. Provides media with information; promotes research, awards grants to organizations and activities that contribute to the solution of the conflict.

Hollings Center for International Dialogue, *2101 L St. N.W., #800, 20037; (202) 833-5090. Michael Carroll, Executive Director.*
General email, info@hollingscenter.org

Web, www.hollingscenter.org and Twitter, @HollingsCenter

Holds conferences to encourage mutual understanding and policy debate between the United States and Muslim-oriented regions in North Africa, the Middle East, and South Asia. Participants include younger generation leaders, academics, government officials, and business leaders. Awards grants for independent study of issues that arise between the United States and Muslim-dominated territories.

Institute for Palestine Studies, *Washington Office, 3501 M St. N.W., 20007-2624; (202) 599-4836. Fax, (202) 342-3927. Stephen Bennett, Director (Acting).*
General email, ipsdc@palestine-studies.org

Web, www.palestine-studies.org, Twitter, @PalStudies and Facebook, www.facebook.com/palstudies

Scholarly research institute that specializes in the history and development of the Palestine problem, the Arab–Israeli conflict, and their peaceful resolution. Conducts educational outreach, holds panels and lectures for the public, and produces a quarterly journal. (Maintains offices in Beirut and Jerusalem.)

Middle East Institute, *1763 N. St. N.W., 20036; (202) 785-1141. Paul Salem, President, ext. 212. Press, (202) 785-1141, ext. 241.*
General email, info@mei.edu

Web, www.mei.edu, Twitter, @middleeastinstitute, Facebook, www.facebook.com/middleeastinstitute and

YouTube, www.youtube.com/channel/UCclgK8IW7x Kzd6z9DLk8slg

Membership: individuals interested in the Middle East. Seeks to broaden knowledge of the Middle East through research, conferences and seminars, language classes, lectures, and exhibits. Library open to members and the press Monday through Friday, 10:00 a.m.–5:00 p.m.

Middle East Media Research Institute (MEMRI), *P.O. Box 27837, 20038-7837; (202) 955-9070. Steven Stalinsky, Executive Director.*
General email, memri@memri.org

Web, www.memri.org, Twitter, @MEMRIReports, Facebook, www.facebook.com/memri.org, Press, media@memri.org and YouTube, www.youtube.com/channel/UC59Cpk70K2TwdmApJOTuW9g

Explores the Middle East through the region's media. Seeks to inform the debate over U.S. policy in the Middle East.

Middle East Policy Council, *1730 M St. N.W., #512, 20036-4505; (202) 296-6767. Fax, (202) 296-5791. Hon. Richard J. Schmierer, President; Bassima Alghussein, Executive Director.*
General email, info@mepc.org

Web, www.mepc.org, Twitter, @MidEastPolicy and Facebook, www.facebook.com/mideastpolicy

Encourages public discussion and understanding of issues affecting U.S. policy in the Middle East. Sponsors conferences for the policy community; conducts educational outreach program; publishes journal and an e-newsletter.

National Council on U.S.–Arab Relations, *1730 M St. N.W., #503, 20036; (202) 293-6466. Fax, (202) 293-7770. John Duke Anthony, President.*
General email, info@ncusar.org

Web, http://ncusar.org, Twitter, @NCUSAR, Facebook, www.facebook.com/NCUSAR and YouTube, www .youtube.com/c/ncusarorg

Educational organization that works to improve mutual understanding between the United States and the Middle East and North Africa (MENA) region. Serves as a clearinghouse on Arab issues and maintains speakers bureau. Coordinates trips for U.S. professionals and congressional delegations to the MENA region.

National U.S.–Arab Chamber of Commerce, *1201 15th St. N.W., #200, 20005; (202) 289-5920. David Hamod, President.*
General email, info@nusacc.org

Web, www.nusacc.org, Twitter, @nusacc and Facebook, www.facebook.com/nusacc.dc

Promotes trade between the United States and the Middle East and North Africa (MENA) region. Offers members informational publications, research and certification services, and opportunities to meet with international delegations. Operates four regional offices.

New Israel Fund, *Washington Office, 1320 19th St. N.W., #400, 20036; (202) 842-0900. Fax, (202) 842-0991.*

Tali Herskowitz, Director, Washington Office, (202) 513-7870.

General email, dc@nif.org

Web, www.nif.org, Twitter, @NewIsraelFund and Facebook, www.facebook.com/newisraelfund

International philanthropic partnership of North Americans, Israelis, and Europeans. Supports activities that defend civil and human rights, promote Jewish–Arab equality and coexistence, advance the status of women, nurture tolerance, bridge social and economic gaps, encourage government accountability, and assist citizen efforts to protect the environment. Makes grants and provides capacity-building assistance to Israeli public interest groups; trains civil rights lawyers. (Headquarters in New York City.)

Project on Middle East Democracy (POMED), 1730 Rhode Island Ave. N.W., #617, 20036; (202) 828-9660. Fax, (202) 828-9661. Stephen McInerney, Executive Director.

Web, https://pomed.org and Twitter, @POMED

Researches and publishes reports to educate policymakers on methods the United States can use to build democracies in the Middle East. Holds conferences to address U.S.–Middle East policy issues. Advocates democracy in the Middle East and supports prodemocracy foreign policies.

S. Daniel Abraham Center for Middle East Peace, 1725 Eye St. N.W., #300, 20006; (202) 624-0850. Robert Wexler, President; S. Daniel Abraham, Chair.

General email, info@centerpeace.org

Web, https://centerpeace.org and Twitter, @AbrahamCenter

Membership: Middle Eastern policymakers, U.S. government officials, and international business leaders. Serves as a mediator to encourage a peaceful resolution to the Arab–Israeli conflict; sponsors travel to the region, diplomatic exchanges, and conferences for Middle Eastern and U.S. leaders interested in the peace process.

United Palestinian Appeal (UPA), 1330 New Hampshire Ave. N.W., #104, 20036-6350; (202) 659-5007. Fax, (202) 296-0224. Saleem F. Zaru, Executive Director. Toll-free, (855) 659-5007.

General email, contact@helpupa.org

Web, http://upaconnect.org, Twitter, @UPAConnect and Facebook, www.facebook.com/upaconnect

An American charitable organization dedicated to improving the quality of life for Palestinians in the Middle East, particularly those in the West Bank, the Gaza Strip, and refugee camps. Provides funding for community development projects, health care, education, children's services, and emergency relief. Funded by private donations from individuals and foundations in the United States and the Middle East and North Africa (MENA) region.

Washington Institute for Near East Policy, 1111 19th St. N.W., #500, 20036; (202) 452-0650. Fax, (202) 223-5364. Robert Satloff, Executive Director.

Web, www.washingtoninstitute.org, Twitter, @washinstitute and General email, press@washingtoninstitute

Research and educational organization that seeks to improve the effectiveness of U.S. policy in the Middle East by promoting debate among policymakers, journalists, and scholars.

Russia and New Independent States

For the Baltic states, see Europe.

▶AGENCIES

Agency for International Development (USAID), Bureau for Europe and Eurasia, 301 4th St. S.W., #247, 20523 (mailing address: 1300 Pennsylvania Ave. N.W., Washington, DC 20521); (202) 567-4020. Fax, (202) 567-4256. Margot Ellis, Assistant Administrator (Acting).

Web, www.usaid.gov/who-we-are/organization/bureaus/bureau-europe-and-eurasia

Advises the USAID administrator on U.S. economic development policy in Europe and Eurasia.

Bureau of European and Eurasian Affairs (EUR) (State Dept.), 2201 C St. N.W., HST #6226, 20520; (202) 647-6285. Karen E. Donfried, Assistant Secretary (Acting), (202) 647-9626. Press, (202) 647-5116.

Web, www.state.gov/p/eur, Twitter, @StateEUR and Press, EUR-Press-DL@state.gov

Advises the secretary on U.S. policy toward European and Eurasian countries. Directors assigned to specific countries within the bureau aid the assistant secretary.

Bureau of European and Eurasian Affairs (State Dept.), Caucasus Affairs and Regional Conflicts, 2201 C St. N.W., #4220, 20520-7512; (202) 647-8741. Jamie Gusack, Director (Acting), (202) 647-9116.

Web, www.state.gov/p/eur

Includes Armenia, Azerbaijan, Georgia, and conflict regions.

Bureau of European and Eurasian Affairs (State Dept.), Russian Affairs, 2201 C St. N.W., #3806, 20520-7512; (202) 647-6150. John J. Sullivan, Ambassador; Marcus Mitchell, Director, (202) 647-6735.

Web, www.state.gov/countries-areas/russia

Bureau of European and Eurasian Affairs (State Dept.), Ukraine, Moldova, and Belarus Affairs, 2201 C St. N.W., #3806, 20520-7512; (202) 647-8303. John L. Armstrong, Director, (202) 647-6750.

Web, www.state.gov/p/eur

Bureau of South and Central Asian Affairs (State Dept.), Central Asian Affairs, 2201 C St. N.W., #1822, 20520; (202) 647-9370. Brian Stimmler, Director.

Web, www.state.gov/p/sca

Includes Kazakhstan, Kyrgyzstan, Tajikistan, Turkmenistan, and Uzbekistan.

Defense Dept. (DoD), *International Security Affairs,* *2000 Defense Pentagon, 20301-2000; (703) 697-2788. Fax, (703) 697-3279. Ilan Goldenberg, Assistant Secretary (Acting).* Web, http://policy.defense.gov/OUSDPOffices/ ASDforInternationalSecurityAffairs

Advises the secretary of defense and recommends policies on regional security issues in the Middle East, Africa, Russia/Eurasia, and Europe/NATO.

Defense Dept. (DoD), *International Security Affairs, Russia, Ukraine, and Eurasia, 2000 Defense Pentagon, 20301-2000; (703) 571-0231. Laura K. Cooper, Deputy Assistant Secretary.* Web, https://policy.defense.gov/OUSDP-Offices/ASD-for-International-Security-Affairs/Russia-Ukraine-and-Eurasia

Advises the assistant secretary for international security affairs on matters dealing with Russia, Ukraine, and Eurasia.

►CONGRESS

For a listing of relevant congressional committees and subcommittees, please see pages 478–479 or the Appendix.

Library of Congress, *Latin American, Caribbean, and European Division (LAC&E), European Reading Room,* *Thomas Jefferson Bldg., 101 Independence Ave. S.E., #LJ 249, 20540-4830; (202) 707-4515. Fax, (202) 707-8482. Suzanne Schadl, Division Chief; Michael Neubert, Head.* General email, eurref@loc.gov

Web, www.loc.gov/rr/european

Provides reference service on the library's European collections (except collections on Spain, Portugal, and the British Isles). Prepares bibliographies and special studies relating to European countries, including Russia and the other states of the former Soviet Union and eastern bloc. Maintains current unbound Slavic language periodicals and newspapers, which are available at the European Reference Desk. Recommends materials for acquisition. Timed entry pass for visitors required, details at loc.gov/visit. Appointments recommended for researchers.

►INTERNATIONAL ORGANIZATIONS

World Bank, *Europe and Central Asia Region, 1818 H St. N.W., 20433; (202) 473-1000. Anna Bjerde, Vice President.* General email, eca@worldbank.org

Web, www.worldbank.org/en/region/eca, Twitter, @WorldBankECA and Facebook, www.facebook.com/WorldBankEuropeCentralAsia

Works to fight poverty and improve the living standards of low- and middle-income people in the countries of eastern Europe and central Asia, including states of the former Soviet Union, by providing loans, policy advice, technical assistance, and knowledge-sharing services. Interests include finance, economic development, education,

water supply, agriculture, public health, and environmental protection.

►NONGOVERNMENTAL

Armenian Assembly of America, *1032 15th St. N.W., #416, 20005; (202) 393-3434. Fax, (202) 638-4904. Bryan Ardouny, Executive Director.* General email, info@aaainc.org

Web, www.armenian-assembly.org and Twitter, @aramac.dc

Promotes public understanding and awareness of Armenian issues; advances research and data collection and disseminates information on the Armenian people; advocates greater Armenian American participation in the American democratic process; works to alleviate human suffering of Armenians. (Regional office located in Gendale, Calif.)

Armenian National Committee of America, *1711 N St. N.W., 20036; (202) 775-1918. Fax, (202) 223-7964. Aram Hamparian, Executive Director.* General email, anca@anca.org

Web, www.anca.org and Twitter, @ANCA_DC

Armenian American grassroots political organization. Works to advance concerns of the Armenian American community. Interests include strengthening U.S.–Armenian relations.

Center for Strategic and International Studies, *Europe, Russia, and Eurasia Program, 1616 Rhode Island Ave. N.W., 20036; (202) 457-8750. Roksana Gabidullina, Program Manager.* Web, www.csis.org/programs/europe-russia-and-eurasia-program and Twitter, @CSISerep

Seeks to develop a deeper understanding of Europe's political, security, and economic evolution and its future role in the world; geopolitical developments in the circumpolar Arctic; the implications of Russia's foreign and defense policies for transatlantic security; and political and economic developments in Russia and Eurasia.

Eurasia Foundation, *1990 K St. N.W., #615, 20006; (202) 234-7370. Fax, (202) 234-7377. Lisa Coll, President.* General email, info@eurasia.org

Web, www.eurasia.org, Twitter, @EFNetwork and Facebook, www.facebook.com/eurasiafoundation

Operates in Eurasia and Europe, the Middle East and North Africa, Asia and North America. Provides capacity building, entrepreneurship training, advocacy education, social entrepreneurship training, and fellowship exchanges to support small business growth, local institutional performance, the responsiveness of local governments, and the leadership of young people.

Institute for European, Russian, and Eurasian Studies *(The George Washington University), 1957 E St. N.W., 20052-0001; (202) 994-6340. Marlene Laruelle, Director, (202) 994-3368.* General email, ieresgwu@gwu.edu

Web, https://ieres.elliott.gwu.edu, Twitter, @IERES_GWU and Facebook, www.facebook.com/ieresgwu

Studies and researches European, Russian, and Eurasian affairs. Sponsors a master's program in European and Eurasian studies. (Affiliated with The George Washington University Elliott School of International Affairs.)

Jamestown Foundation, *1310 L St. N.W., #810, 20005; (202) 483-8888. Fax, (202) 483-8337. Glen E. Howard, President.*
General email, pubs@jamestown.org
Web, www.jamestown.org, Twitter, @JamestownTweets and Facebook, www.facebook.com/JamestownFoundation

Provides policymakers with information about events and trends in societies that are strategically or tactically important to the United States and that frequently restrict access to such information. Serves as an alternative source to official or intelligence channels, especially with regard to Eurasia, China, and terrorism. Publishes the *Militant Leadership Monitor,* covering leaders of major insurgencies and militant movements.

Kennan Institute, *1 Woodrow Wilson Plaza, 1300 Pennsylvania Ave. N.W., 20004-3027; (202) 691-4100. Fax, (202) 691-4247. William E. Pomeranz, Director (Acting).*
General email, kennan@wilsoncenter.org
Web, www.wilsoncenter.org/program/kennan-institute, Twitter, @kennaninstitute and Facebook, www.facebook .com/Kennan.Institute

Offers residential research scholarships to academic scholars and to specialists from government, media, and the private sector for studies to improve American knowledge about Russia, Ukraine, Belarus, Central Asia, and the Caucasus. Sponsors lectures; publishes reports; promotes dialogue between academic specialists and policymakers. (Affiliated with the Woodrow Wilson International Center for Scholars.)

NCSEJ: National Coalition Supporting Eurasian Jewry, *1120 20th St. N.W, #300N, 20036-3413; (202) 898-2500. Mark B. Levin, Chief Executive Officer, ext. 6201; James Schiller, Chair.*
General email, ncsej@ncsej.org
Web, www.ncsej.org, Twitter, @NCSEJ and Facebook, www.facebook.com/thencsej

Membership: national Jewish organizations and local federations. Coordinates efforts by members to aid Jews in the former Soviet Union.

U.S.–Russia Business Council, *1101 17th St. N.W., #600, 20036; (202) 739-9180. Daniel A. Russell, President, (202) 739-9180; Wesley Fox, Research Director, (202) 739-9187.*
General email, info@usrbc.org
Web, www.usrbc.org

Membership: U.S. companies involved in trade and investment in Russia. Promotes commercial ties between the United States and Russia; provides business services. Monitors legislation and regulations. (Maintains office in Moscow.)

U.S.–Ukraine Foundation, *Washington Office, 6312 Seven Corners Center, #361, Falls Church, VA 22044; (202) 789-4467. Rusty Brooks, Chair.*
General email, info@usukraine.org
Web, www.usukraine.org, Twitter, @usukraine and Facebook, www.facebook.com/usukraine

Encourages and facilitates democratic and human rights development and free market reform in the Ukraine. Creates and sustains communications channels between the United States and Ukraine. Manages the U.S.–Ukraine Community Partnerships Project. (Maintains office in Kiev, Ukraine.)

Ukrainian National Information Service, *Washington Office, 311 Massachusetts Ave. N.E., 20002; (202) 547-0018. Andriy Futey Jr., President.*
General email, unis@ucca.org
Web, www.ucca.org, Twitter, @UkrCongComAm, Facebook, www.facebook.com/UCCA.org and YouTube, www.youtube.com/channel/UCjtndw7Ssh–TTshAF_ 0pxg

Information bureau of the Ukrainian Congress Committee of America in New York. Monitors U.S. policy and foreign assistance to Ukraine. Supports educational, cultural, and humanitarian activities in the Ukranian-American community. (Headquarters in New York.)

U.S. Territories and Associated States

▶ AGENCIES

Interior Dept. (DOI), *Insular Affairs (OIA), 1849 C St. N.W., MS 2429, 20240; (202) 208-4736. Nikolao Pula, Director.*
Web, www.doi.gov/oia, Twitter, @InsularAffairs, Facebook, www.facebook.com/InsularAffairs and Email, OIAPress@ios.doi.gov

Promotes economic, social, and political development of U.S. territories (Guam, American Samoa, the U.S. Virgin Islands, and the Commonwealth of the Northern Mariana Islands). Administers and oversees federal assistance under the Compacts of Free Association to the Federated States of Micronesia, the Republic of the Marshall Islands, and the Republic of Palau. Supervises federal programs for the Freely Associated States (Federated States of Micronesia, Republic of the Marshall Islands, and Republic of Palau).

National Conference of Puerto Rican Women, *1220 L St. N.W., #100-177, 20005; Vilma Colom, National President; Milagros V. McGuire, President of the Washington, DC, Chapter.*
General email, v_colom@yahoo.com
Web, www.nacoprw.org

Nonprofit, nonpartisan organization promoting the participation of Puerto Rican and other Hispanic women in their economic, social, and political life. Provides training, mentorship, and leadership development at local and national levels through workshops and institutes; provides scholarships to Hispanic individuals.

►CONGRESS

For a listing of relevant congressional committees and subcommittees, please see pages 478–479 or the Appendix.

American Samoa's Delegate to Congress, *1339 LHOB, 20515; (202) 225-8577. Fax, (202) 225-8757. Rep. Aumua Amata C. Radewagen, Delegate.*
Web, http://radewagen.house.gov, Twitter, @repamata and Facebook, www.facebook.com/aumnaamata

Represents American Samoa in Congress.

Guam's Delegate to Congress, *1632 LHOB, 20515; (202) 225-1188. Rep. Michael F.Q. San Nicolas, Delegate. Toll-free, (844) 482-6671.*
Web, https://sannicolas.house.gov, Twitter, @GuamCongressman, Facebook, www.facebook.com/ CongressmanMichaelF.Q.SanNicolas and YouTube, www .youtube.com/channel/UCVroMJWH3jsh4shPSlp24sw

Represents Guam in Congress.

Northern Mariana Islands' Delegate to Congress, *2267 RHOB, 20515; (202) 225-2646. Fax, (202) 226-4249. Rep. Gregorio Kilili Camacho Sablan, Delegate. Toll-free, (877) 446-3465.*
Web, https://sablan.house.gov

Represents the Northern Mariana Islands in Congress.

Puerto Rican Resident Commissioner, *2338 RHOB, 20515; (202) 225-2615. Fax, (202) 225-2154. Rep. Jenniffer González-Colón, Resident Commissioner. Web, https://gonzalez-colon.house.gov, Twitter, @repjenniffer and Facebook, www.facebook.com/ RepJenniffer*

Represents the Commonwealth of Puerto Rico in Congress.

Virgin Islands' Delegate to Congress, *2404 RHOB, 20515; (202) 225-1790. Fax, (202) 225-5517. Rep. Stacey Plaskett, Delegate.*
General email, samantha.roberts@mail.house.gov
Web, http://plaskett.house.gov, Twitter, @StaceyPlaskett and Facebook, www.facebook.com/repstaceyplaskett

Represents the Virgin Islands in Congress.

►NONGOVERNMENTAL

Commonwealth of Puerto Rico Federal Affairs Administration, *1100 17th St. N.W., #701, 20036; (202) 778-0710. Carmen Feliciano, Executive Director.*
General email, info@prfaa.pr.gov
Web, http://prfaa.pr.gov and Twitter, @PRFAA

Represents the governor and the government of the Commonwealth of Puerto Rico before Congress and the executive branch; conducts research; serves as official press information center for the Commonwealth of Puerto Rico. Monitors legislation and regulations.

13 ⚖

Law and Justice

GENERAL POLICY AND ANALYSIS

Basic Resources

►AGENCIES

Justice Dept. (DOJ), *950 Pennsylvania Ave. N.W., 20530-0001; (202) 514-2000. Fax, (202) 307-6777. Merrick Garland, Attorney General. Public Affairs, (202) 514-2007. Public comments, (202) 353-1555. TTY, (800) 877-8339.*
General email, askdoj@usdoj.gov
Web, www.justice.gov and Twitter, @TheJusticeDept

Serves as counsel for the U.S. government. Represents the government in enforcing the law in the public interest. Plays key role in protecting against criminals and subversion, in ensuring healthy competition of business in U.S. free enterprise system, in safeguarding the consumer, and in enforcing drug, immigration, and naturalization laws. Plays a significant role in protecting citizens through effective law enforcement, crime prevention, crime detection, and prosecution and rehabilitation of offenders. Conducts all suits in the Supreme Court in which the United States is concerned. Represents the government in legal matters generally, furnishing legal advice and opinions to the president, the cabinet, and the heads of executive departments, as provided by law. Justice Dept. organization includes divisions on antitrust, civil law, civil rights, criminal law, environment and natural resources, and taxes, as well as the Bureau of Alcohol, Tobacco, Firearms, and Explosives; Drug Enforcement Administration; Executive Office for Immigration Review; Federal Bureau of Investigation; Federal Bureau of Prisons; Foreign Claims Settlement Commission; Office of Justice Programs; U.S. Attorneys; U.S. Marshals Service; U.S. Parole Commission; and U.S. Trustees.

Justice Dept. (DOJ), *Office of Legal Policy (OLP), 950 Pennsylvania Ave. N.W., #4234, 20530-0001; (202) 514-4601. Fax, (202) 514-2424. Hampton Dellinger, Assistant Attorney General.*
Web, www.justice.gov/olp

Develops and implements the Justice Dept.'s major policy initiatives, often with the cooperation of other offices within the department and among other agencies. Works with the Office of Legislative Affairs to promote the department's policies in Congress.

Justice Dept. (DOJ), *Solicitor General, 950 Pennsylvania Ave. N.W., #5143, 20530-0001; (202) 514-2203. Fax, (202) 514-9769. Elizabeth Prelogar, Solicitor General. Information on pending cases, (202) 514-2217/18.*
Web, www.justice.gov/osg

Represents the federal government before the Supreme Court of the United States.

National Security Division *(Justice Dept.), 950 Pennsylvania Ave. N.W., #7339, 20530; (202) 514-2007. Fax, (202) 514-5331. Matthew G. Olsen, Assistant Attorney General. Comment line, (202) 353-1555.*
General email, nsd.public@usdoj.gov
Web, www.justice.gov/nsd

Provides legal assistance and advice, in coordination with the Office of Legal Counsel as appropriate, to all branches of government on matters of national security law and policy.

Office of Justice Programs (OJP) *(Justice Dept.), 810 7th St. N.W., 20531; (202) 514-2000. Fax, (202) 514-7805. Amy Solomon, Principal Deputy Assistant Attorney General. Press, (202) 532-0703.*
General email, askojp@usdoj.gov
Web, https://ojp.gov, Twitter, @OJPgov and Facebook, www.facebook.com/DOJOJP

Provides federal leadership, coordination, and assistance in developing the nation's capacity to prevent and control crime, administer justice, and assist crime victims. Includes the Bureau of Justice Assistance, which supports state and local criminal justice strategies; the Bureau of Justice Statistics, which collects, analyzes, and disseminates criminal justice data; the National Institute of Justice, which is the primary research and development agency of the Justice Dept.; the Office of Juvenile Justice and Delinquency Prevention, which supports state and local efforts to combat juvenile crime and victimization; the Office of Victims of Crime, which provides support for crime victims and leadership to promote justice and healing for all crime victims; and the Community Capacity Development Office, which provides resources to support community-based anti-crime efforts.

State Justice Institute, *12700 Fair Lakes Circle, #340, Fairfax, VA 22033; (703) 660-4979. Jonathan D. Mattiello, Executive Director.*
General email, contact@sji.gov
Web, www.sji.gov, Twitter, @statejustice and Facebook, www.facebook.com/SJI.gov

Awards grants to state courts and to state agencies for programs that improve state courts' judicial administration. Maintains judicial information clearinghouses and establishes technical resource centers; conducts educational programs; delivers technical assistance.

►CONGRESS

For a listing of relevant congressional committees and subcommittees, please see pages 546–547 or the Appendix.

►JUDICIARY

Administrative Office of the U.S. Courts, *1 Columbus Circle N.E., 20544-0001; (202) 502-2600. Hon. Roslynn R. Mauskopf, Director.*
Web, www.uscourts.gov and Twitter, @uscourts

Provides administrative support to the federal courts, including the procurement of supplies and equipment; the administration of personnel, budget, and financial control services; and the compilation and publication of statistical data and reports on court business. Implements the

LAW AND JUSTICE RESOURCES IN CONGRESS

For a complete listing of congressional committees, including their full contact information, leadership, membership, and jurisdictions, please refer to the Appendix on pages 840–963.

HOUSE:

House Administration Committee, (202) 225-2061.
Web, cha.house.gov
House Appropriations Committee, (202) 225-2771.
Web, appropriations.house.gov
    Subcommittee on Commerce, Justice, Science, and Related Agencies, (202) 225-3351.
    Subcommittee on Homeland Security, (202) 225-5834.
House Education and Labor Committee, (202) 225-3725.
Web, edlabor.house.gov
    Subcommittee on Workforce Protections, (202) 225-3725.
House Energy and Commerce Committee, (202) 225-2927.
Web, energycommerce.house.gov
    Subcommittee on Consumer Protection and Commerce, (202) 225-2927.
    Subcommittee on Energy, (202) 225-2927.
    Subcommittee on Health, (202) 225-2927.
House Ethics Committee, (202) 225-7103.
Web, ethics.house.gov
House Financial Services Committee, (202) 225-4247.
Web, financialservices.house.gov
    Subcommittee on Investor Protection, Entrepreneurship, and Capital Markets, (202) 225-4247.
House Homeland Security Committee, (202) 226-2616.
Web, homeland.house.gov
    Subcommittee on Border Security, Facilitation, and Operations, (202) 226-2616.

House Judiciary Committee, (202) 225-3951.
Web, judiciary.house.gov
    Subcommittee on Antitrust, Commercial, and Administrative Law, (202) 226-7680.
    Subcommittee on Courts, Intellectual Property, and the Internet, (202) 225-5741.
    Subcommittee on Crime, Terrorism, and Homeland Security, (202) 225-5727.
    Subcommittee on Immigration and Citizenship, (202) 225-3926.
    Subcommittee on the Constitution, Civil Rights, and Civil Liberties, (202) 225-3951.
House Natural Resources Committee, (202) 225-6065.
Web, naturalresources.house.gov
    Subcommittee on Energy and Mineral Resources, (202) 225-9297.
House Oversight and Reform Committee, (202) 225-5051.
Web, oversight.house.gov
    Subcommittee on Government Operations, (202) 225-5051.
House Small Business Committee, (202) 225-4038.
Web, smallbusiness.house.gov
    Subcommittee on Oversight, Investigations, and Regulations, (202) 225-4038.

SENATE:

Senate Agriculture, Nutrition, and Forestry Committee, (202) 224-2035.
Web, agriculture.senate.gov
    Subcommittee on Livestock, Dairy, Poultry, Local Food Systems, and Food Safety, (202) 224-2035.

policies of the Judicial Conference of the United States and supports its committees. Recommends plans and strategies to manage court business. Procures needed resources, legislation, and other assistance for the judiciary from Congress and the executive branch.

Administrative Office of the U.S. Courts, *Court Services Division, 1 Columbus Circle N.E., 20544-0001; (202) 502-1500. Mary Louise Mitterhoff, Associate Director. Public Affairs, (202) 502-2600.*
Web, www.uscourts.gov/about-federal-courts/judicial-administration and *Twitter, @uscourts*

Provides staff, policy, legal, operational, and program support for the appeals, district, and U.S. bankruptcy courts.

Federal Judicial Center, *Thurgood Marshall Federal Judiciary Bldg., 1 Columbus Circle N.E., 20002-8003; (202) 502-4160. Fax, (202) 502-4099. (202) 502-4000. John S. Cooke, Director. Editorial and Information*

Services, (202) 502-4250. International Judicial relations, (202) 502-4191. phone, (202) 502-4000.
Web, www.fjc.gov

Conducts research and education on the operations of the federal court system; develops and conducts continuing education and training programs for judges and judicial personnel; and makes recommendations to improve the administration of the courts. Provides International Judicial Relations and houses a publications catalog.

Judicial Conference of the United States, *1 Columbus Circle N.E., #7430, 20544; (202) 502-2600. Fax, (202) 502-3019. John G. Roberts Jr., Chief Justice of the United States; Roslynn R. Mauskopf, Director.*
Web, www.uscourts.gov and *Twitter, @uscourts*

Serves as the policymaking and governing body for the administration of the federal judicial system; advises

Senate Appropriations Committee, (202) 224-7363.
Web, appropriations.senate.gov
  Subcommittee on Commerce, Justice, Science,
    and Related Agencies, (202) 224-7363.
  Subcommittee on Homeland Security,
    (202) 224-7363.
Senate Commerce, Science, and Transportation
  Committee, (202) 224-0411.
Web, commerce.senate.gov
  Subcommittee on Consumer Protection,
    Product Safety, and Data Security,
    (202) 224-0411.
  Subcommittee on Oceans, Fisheries,
    Climate Change, and Manufacturing,
    (202) 224-0411.
Senate Finance Committee, (202) 224-4515.
Web, finance.senate.gov
  Subcommittee on Taxation and IRS Oversight,
    (202) 224-4515.
Senate Foreign Relations Committee, (202) 224-4651.
Web, foreign.senate.gov
  Subcommittee on Western Hemisphere,
    Transnational Crime, Civilian Security,
    Democracy, Human Rights, and Global
    Women's Issues, (202) 224-4651.
Senate Health, Education, Labor, and Pensions
  Committee, (202) 224-5375.
Web, help.senate.gov
  Subcommittee on Children and Families,
    (202) 224-5375.
  Subcommittee on Employment and Workplace
    Safety, (202) 224-5375.
Senate Homeland Security and Governmental Affairs
  Committee, (202) 224-2627.
Web, hsgac.senate.gov

Permanent Subcommittee on Investigations,
  (202) 224-3721.
Senate Indian Affairs Committee, (202) 224-2251.
Web, indian.senate.gov
Senate Judiciary Committee, (202) 224-7703.
Web, judiciary.senate.gov
  Subcommittee on Competition Policy,
    Antitrust, and Consumer Rights,
    (202) 224-3244.
  Subcommittee on Immigration, Citizenship, and
    Border Safety, (202) 224-6991.
  Subcommittee on Criminal Justice and
    Counterterrorism, (202) 224-2921.
  Subcommittee on Federal Courts, Oversight,
    Agency Action, and Federal Rights,
    (202) 224-2823.
  Subcommittee on Intellectual Property,
    (202) 224-5042.
  Subcommittee on Human Rights and the Law,
    (202) 224-7703.
  Subcommittee on Privacy, Technology, and the
    Law, (202) 224-7703.
  Subcommittee on the Constitution,
    (202) 224-6361.
Senate Rules and Administration Committee,
  (202) 224-6352.
Web, rules.senate.gov
Senate Select Committee on Ethics, (202) 224-2981.
Web, ethics.senate.gov
Senate Small Business and Entrepreneurship
  Committee, (202) 224-5175.
Web, sbc.senate.gov
Senate Special Committee on Aging,
  (202) 224-5364.
Web, aging.senate.gov

Congress on the creation of new federal judgeships. Interests include international judicial relations.

Supreme Court of the United States, *1 1st St. N.E., 20543; (202) 479-3000. John G. Roberts Jr., Chief Justice. Public Information Office, (202) 479-3211. TTY, (202) 479-3472. Visitor information, (202) 479-3030.*
Web, www.supremecourt.gov and Contact Form, www.supremecourt.gov/contact/contact_pio.aspx

Highest appellate court in the federal judicial system. Interprets the U.S. Constitution, federal legislation, and treaties. Provides information on new cases filed, the status of pending cases, and admissions to the Supreme Court Bar. Library open to Supreme Court Bar members only.

▶ **NONGOVERNMENTAL**

American Bar Assn. (ABA), *Governmental Affairs, 1050 Connecticut Ave. N.W., #400, 20036; (202) 662-1760.*

Fax, (202) 662-1762. Holly Cook, Director, (202) 662-1860.
Web, www.americanbar.org/advocacy/governmental_legislative_work and Twitter, @ABAGrassroots

Acts as advocate before Congress, the executive branch, and other governmental entities on issues of importance to the legal profession. Publishes the *ABA Washington Letter,* a monthly online legislative analysis; and *ABA Washington Summary,* a daily online publication.

American Tort Reform Assn., *1101 Connecticut Ave. N.W., #400, 20036-4351; (202) 682-1163. Fax, (202) 682-1022. Sherman Joyce, President.*
Web, www.atra.org, Twitter, @AMTortReform and Facebook, www.facebook.com/AmTortReform

Membership: businesses, associations, trade groups, professional societies, and individuals interested in reforming the civil justice system in the United States.

Develops model state legislation and position papers on tort liability and reform. Monitors legislation, regulations, and legal rulings.

Aspen Institute, *2300 N St. N.W., #700, 20037; (202) 736-5800. Fax, (202) 467-0790. Daniel R. Porterfield, President. Press, (202) 736-3849.*
General email, info@aspeninstitute.org
Web, www.aspeninstitute.org and Twitter, @AspenInstitute

Educational and policy studies organization. Brings together individuals from diverse backgrounds to discuss how to deal with longstanding philosophical disputes and contemporary social challenges in law and justice.

The Federalist Society, *1776 Eye St. N.W., #300, 20006; (202) 822-8138. Fax, (202) 296-8061. Eugene B. Meyer, President.*
General email, info@fedsoc.org
Web, www.fedsoc.org, Twitter, @FedSoc and Facebook, www.facebook.com/Federalist.Society

Promotes conservative and libertarian principles among lawyers, judges, law professors, law students, and the general public. Sponsors lectures, debates, seminars, fellowships, and awards programs.

Government Accountability Project (GAP), *1612 K St. N.W., #1100, 20006; (202) 457-0034. Louis Clark, Executive Director.*
General email, info@whistleblower.org
Web, www.whistleblower.org, Twitter, @GovAcctProj and Facebook, www.facebook.com/pg/Government AccountabilityProject

Membership: federal employees, union members, professionals, and interested citizens. Supports and represents employee whistleblowers. Works to ensure that whistleblower disclosures about improper government and industry actions that are harmful to the environment, public health, national security, food safety, the financial sector, and several other areas are defended and heard. Represents whistleblower clients in legal actions and operates attorney referral service through National Whistleblower Legal Defense and Education Fund. (Formerly the National Whistleblower Center.)

Justice Policy Institute, *1012 14th St. N.W., #600, 20005; (202) 558-7974. Fax, (202) 558-7978. Marc Schindler, Executive Director, (202) 568-6569. Press, (202) 888-6748.*
General email, info@justicepolicy.org
Web, www.justicepolicy.org, Twitter, @JusticePolicy and Facebook, www.facebook.com/JusticePolicy

Research, advocacy, and policy development organization. Analyzes current and emerging adult and juvenile criminal justice problems; educates the public about criminal justice issues; provides technical assistance to communities seeking to reform incarceration policies. Interests include new prison construction, alternatives to incarceration, antigang legislation, and curfew laws.

National Center for State Courts, *Government Relations, 111 2nd St. N.E., 20002; (202) 684-2622. Mary McQueen, President; Michael Buenger, Executive Vice President, (757)*
259-1831; Philip Bye, Director of Government Relations. Toll-free, (800) 616-6164.
General email, govrel@ncsc.org
Web, www.ncsc.org

Works to improve state court systems through research, technical assistance, and training programs. Monitors legislation affecting court systems; interests include state-federal jurisdiction, family law, criminal justice, court administration, international agreements, and automated information systems. Serves as secretariat for eleven state court organizations, including the Conference of Chief Justices, Conference of State Court Administrators, American Judges Assn., and National Assn. for Court Management. (Headquarters in Williamsburg, Va.)

RAND Corp., Washington Office, *1200 S. Hayes St., Arlington, VA 22202-5050; (703) 413-1100. Fax, (703) 413-8111. Nicholas Burger, Director.*
Web, www.rand.org

Analyzes current problems of the American civil and criminal justice systems and evaluates recent and pending changes and reforms. (Headquarters in Santa Monica, Calif.)

U.S. Chamber of Commerce, Congressional and Public Affairs, *1615 H St. N.W., 20062-2000; (202) 463-5600. Jack Howard, Senior Vice President.*
Web, www.uschamber.com/program/policy/government-affairs

Federation of individuals, firms, corporations, trade and professional associations, and local, state, and regional chambers of commerce. Monitors legislation and regulations in administrative law, antitrust policy, civil justice reform, and product liability reform.

U.S. Chamber of Commerce, Institute for Legal Reform, *1615 H St. N.W., 20062-2000; (202) 463-5724. Harold Kim, President.*
General email, ilr@uschamber.com
Web, https://instituteforlegalreform.com, Twitter, @LegalReform and Facebook, www.facebook.com/instituteforlegalreform

Works to reform state and federal civil justice systems. Strives to reduce excessive litigation. Hosts public forums on legal and tort reform.

Urban Institute, Justice Policy Center, *500 L'Enfant Plaza S.W., 20024; (202) 833-7200. Fax, (202) 659-8985. Preeti Chauhan, Vice President.*
Web, www.urban.org/policy-centers/justice-policy-center

Conducts research and evaluation designed to improve justice and public safety policies and practices at the national, state, and local levels. Works with practitioners, public officials, and community groups to generate evidence on effectiveness of existing programs and to provide guidance on improvements.

Justice Department

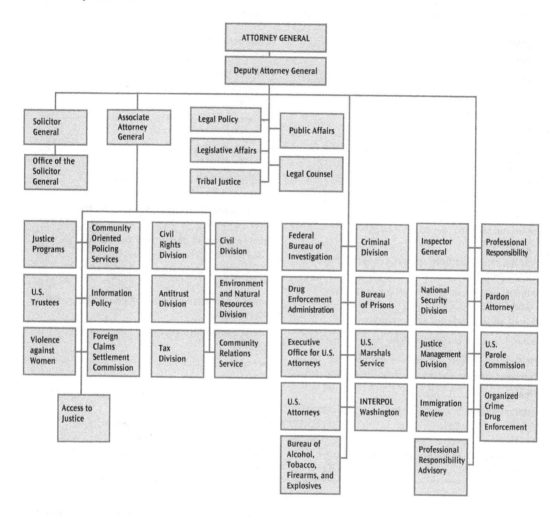

Dispute Resolution

Justice Dept. (DOJ), *Community Relations Service (CRS),* 145 N St. N.E., #5E.300, 20530; (202) 305-2935. *Gerri Ratliff, Deputy Director.* General email, askcrs@usdoj.gov

Web, www.justice.gov/crs and Twitter, @DOJ_CRS

Works with state and local governments, private and public organizations, civil rights groups, and local community leaders to promote conflict resolution for community challenges arising from differences of race, color, national origin, gender, gender identity, sexual orientation, religion, and disability. Assists communities in developing local mechanisms and community capacity to prevent tension and violent hate crimes from occurring in the future.

Occupational Safety and Health Review Commission, 1120 20th St. N.W., 9th Floor, 20036-3457; (202) 606-5100. Fax, (202) 606-5050. Cynthia L. Attwood,

Chair, (202) 606-5370; Amanda Wood Laihow, Commissioner, (202) 606-5373. TTY, (877) 889-5627. Library, (202) 606-5729. Web, www.oshrc.gov

Independent executive branch agency that adjudicates disputes between private employers and the Occupational Safety and Health Administration arising under the Occupational Safety and Health Act of 1970. Library Staff available 7:30 p.m.–2:30 p.m. for reference and reasearch.

►NONGOVERNMENTAL

American Arbitration Assn., *Government Relations,* 1120 Connecticut Ave. N.W., #490, 20036; (202) 223-7093. Jean Baker, Vice President. Toll-free, (800) 778-7879. Web, www.adr.org, Twitter, @adrorg and YouTube, www .youtube.com/c/AmericanArbitrationAssociation/ videos

General Counsels for Federal Departments and Agencies

DEPARTMENTS

Agriculture, Janie S. Hipp, (202) 720-3351

Commerce, Quentin Palfrey (Acting), (202) 482-4772

Defense, Caroline D. Krass, (703) 695-3341

Air Force, Craig A. Smith, (703) 697-0941

Army, Carrie F. Ricci, (703) 697-9235

Navy, Garrett L. Ressing (Acting), (703) 614-1994

Education, Emma Leheny (Acting), (202) 401-6000

Energy, Samuel T. Walsh, (202) 586-5281

Health and Human Services, Daniel J. Barry (Acting), (202) 690-7741

Homeland Security, Jonathan E. Meyer, (202) 282-9822

Housing and Urban Development, Damon Y. Smith, (202) 708-2244

Interior, Robert T. Anderson, (202) 208-4423; TTY, (800) 877-8339

Justice, Elizabeth Prelogar, (202) 514-2203

Labor, Seema Nanda, (202) 693-5260

State, Richard C. Visek (Acting), (202) 647-8460

Transportation, John E. Putnam (Acting), (202) 366-4702

Treasury, Vacant, (202) 622-2000

Veterans Affairs, Richard J. Hipolit (Acting), (800) 698-2411

AGENCIES

Advisory Council on Historic Preservation, Javier Marques, (202) 517-0192; Email, jmarques@achp.gov

Agency for International Development, Margaret L. Taylor, (202) 712-0900

Central Intelligence Agency, Vacant, (703) 482-0623

Commission on Civil Rights, J. Christian Adams, (202) 376-7622

Commodity Futures Trading Commission, Robert Schwartz, (202) 418-5958

Consumer Product Safety Commission, Austin Schlick, (240) 429-6069 or (301) 504-7479

Corp. for National and Community Service, Fernando Laguarda, (202) 606-6985

Environmental Protection Agency, Jeffrey Prieto (202) 564-8040

Equal Employment Opportunity Commission, Vacant, (202) 663-4900; TTY, (202) 663-4494

Farm Credit Administration, Clark Olgilvie, (703) 883-4020; TTY, (703) 883-4056

Federal Communications Commission, P. Michele Ellison, (202) 418-1700

Federal Deposit Insurance Corp., Harrel M. Pettway, (703) 562-2035

Federal Election Commission, Lisa J. Stevenson (Acting), (202) 694-1650

Federal Emergency Management Agency, Adrian Sevier, (202) 212-5875

Federal Energy Regulatory Commission, Matthew Christiansen, (202) 502-6599

Federal Labor Relations Authority, Charlotte A. Dye (Acting), (202) 218-7770

Provides alternative dispute resolution services to governments and the private sector. (Headquarters in New York.)

American Bar Assn. (ABA), *Dispute Resolution,* 1050 Connecticut Ave. N.W., #400, 20036; (202) 662-1680. Fax, (202) 662-1683. Jennifer Michel, Director, (312) 833-5006.
Web, www.americanbar.org/groups/dispute_resolution, Twitter, @ABA_DR, Facebook, www.facebook.com/ABADisputeResolution1 and General email, ashley.jackson@americanbar.org

Provides training and resources to lawyers, law students, mediators, and arbitrators on dispute resolution.

Better Business Bureau, *Dispute Handling and Resolution,* 1411 K St. N.W., 10th Floor, 20005; Lisa Clay, Dispute Resolution, 410-347-9761; Jerica Johnson, Dispute Resolution, (410) 735-1586.
General email, contactdr@iabbb.org
Web, www.bbb.org/all/bbb-dispute-handling-and-resolution

Administers mediation and arbitration programs through Better Business Bureau complaints departments nationwide to assist in resolving disputes between businesses and consumers. Assists with unresolved disputes between car owners and automobile manufacturers, and disputes between customers and telecommunication providers, moving and storage industies, and small local firms and individuals. Maintains pools of certified arbitrators nationwide. Provides mediation training.

Call for Action, 11820 Parklawn Dr., #340, Rockville, MD 20852; (240) 747-0229. Shirley Rooker, President. Web, https://callforaction.org

International network of consumer hotlines affiliated with local broadcast partners. Helps consumers resolve problems with businesses, government agencies, and other organizations through mediation. Provides information on privacy concerns.

Judicial Appointments

▶AGENCIES

Justice Dept. (DOJ), *Office of Legal Policy (OLP),* 950 Pennsylvania Ave. N.W., #4234, 20530-0001; (202) 514-4601.

Federal Maritime Commission, Steven J. Andersen, (202) 523-5740

Federal Mediation and Conciliation Service, Sarah Cudahy, (202) 606-5444

Federal Reserve System, Mark E. Van Der Weide, (202) 452-3000

Federal Trade Commission, Reilly Dolan (Acting), (202) 326-2424

General Services Administration, Nitin Shah, (202) 501-2200

International Bank for Reconstruction and Development (World Bank), Sandie Okoro, (202) 473-1000

Merit Systems Protection Board, Tristan Leavitt, (202) 653-7171

National Aeronautics and Space Administration, Sumara M. Thompson-King, (202) 358-2450

National Credit Union Administration, Frank Kressman, (703) 518-6540

National Endowment for the Arts, India Pinkney, (202) 682-5418

National Endowment for the Humanities, Michael McDonald, (202) 606-8322

National Labor Relations Board, Jennifer Abruzzo, (202) 273-3700

National Mediation Board, Maria-Kate Dowling, (202) 692-5040

National Railroad Passenger Corp. (Amtrak), Eleanor D. Acheson, (202) 906-3000

National Science Foundation, Peggy A. Hoyle, (703) 292-8060

National Transportation Safety Board, Kathleen Silbaugh, (202) 314-6080

Nuclear Regulatory Commission, Marian Zobler, (301) 415-1743

Occupational Safety and Health Review Commission, Nadine N. Mancini, (202) 606-5410

Office of Personnel Management, Lynn D. Eisenberg, (202) 606-1700

Peace Corps, Robert Shanks, (855) 855-1961

Pension Benefit Guaranty Corp., Russell Dempsey, (202) 229-4000

Postal Regulatory Commission, David A. Trissell, (202) 789-6820

Securities and Exchange Commission, Dan M. Berkovitz, (202) 551-5100

Small Business Administration, Peggy D. Hamilton, (202) 205-6642; TTY, (800) 877-8339

Smithsonian Institution, Judith E. Leonard, (202) 633-5115

Social Security Administration, Royce B. Min, (410) 965-0600

U.S. International Development Finance Corp., Sarah E. Fandell, (202) 336-8400

U.S. International Trade Commission, Dominic L. Bianchi, (202) 205-3408

U.S. Postal Service, Thomas J. Marshall, (202) 268-2950

Fax, (202) 514-2424. Hampton Dellinger, Assistant Attorney General.
Web, www.justice.gov/olp

Investigates and processes prospective candidates for presidential appointment (subject to Senate confirmation) to the federal judiciary.

►CONGRESS

For a listing of relevant congressional committees and sub-committees, please see pages 546–547 or the Appendix.

►JUDICIARY

Administrative Office of the U.S. Courts, *1 Columbus Circle N.E., 20544-0001; (202) 502-2600.*
Hon. Roslynn R. Mauskopf, Director.
Web, www.uscourts.gov and Twitter, @uscourts

Supervises all administrative matters of the federal court system, except the Supreme Court. Transmits to Congress the recommendations of the Judicial Conference of the United States concerning creation of federal judgeships and other legislative proposals.

Judicial Conference of the United States, *1 Columbus Circle N.E., #7430, 20544; (202) 502-2600. Fax, (202) 502-3019. John G. Roberts Jr., Chief Justice of the United States; Roslynn R. Mauskopf, Director.*
Web, www.uscourts.gov and Twitter, @uscourts

Serves as the policymaking and governing body for the administration of the federal judicial system; advises Congress on the creation of new federal judgeships. Interests include international judicial relations.

►NONGOVERNMENTAL

Alliance for Justice (AFJ), *11 Dupont Circle N.W., #500, 20036; (202) 822-6070. Rakim Brooks, President.*
General email, alliance@afj.org
Web, www.afj.org, Twitter, @AFJustice, Facebook, www .facebook.com/AllianceforJustice and YouTube, www.youtube.com/user/alliance4justice

Monitors candidates for vacancies in the federal judiciary via The Bolder Advocacy Program; independently reviews nominees' records; maintains statistics on the judiciary.

BUSINESS AND TAX LAW

Antitrust

▶**AGENCIES**

Antitrust Division *(Justice Dept.)*, 950 Pennsylvania Ave. N.W., #3322, 20530-0001; (202) 514-2401. Fax, (202) 616-2645. Jonathan Kanter, Assistant Attorney General. Press, (202) 514-2007.
General email, antitrust.atr@usdoj.gov
Web, www.usdoj.gov/atr and Twitter, @JusticeATR

Enforces antitrust laws to prevent monopolies and unlawful restraint of trade; has civil and criminal jurisdiction; coordinates activities with the Bureau of Competition of the Federal Trade Commission.

Antitrust Division *(Justice Dept.)*, **Antitrust Documents Group,** 450 5th St. N.W., #1000, 20530; (202) 514-2692. Fax, (202) 616-4529. Kenneth Hendricks, Chief.
General email, antitrust.foia@usdoj.gov
Web, www.justice.gov/atr/antitrust-foia

Maintains files and handles requests for information on federal civil and criminal antitrust cases; provides the president and Congress with copies of statutory reports prepared by the division on a variety of competition-related issues; issues opinion letters on whether certain business activity violates antitrust laws.

Antitrust Division *(Justice Dept.)*, **Defense, Industrials, and Aerospace,** 450 5th St. N.W., #8700, 20530; (202) 307-0924. Fax, (202) 514-9033. Katrina Rouse, Chief.
Web, www.justice.gov/atr/about/lit2.html

Investigates and litigates cases involving defense, waste industries, avionics and aeronautics, road and highway construction, metals and mining, industrial equipment, and banking.

Antitrust Division *(Justice Dept.)*, **Healthcare and Consumer Products,** 450 5th St. N.W., #4100, 20530-0001; (202) 307-0001. Fax, (202) 307-5802. Eric Welsh, Chief.
General email, Antitrust.ATR@usdoj.gov
Web, www.justice.gov/atr/about-division/hcp-section and Twitter, @JusticeATR

Investigates and litigates cases involving health care, paper, pulp, timber, food products, cosmetics and hair care, bread, beer, appliances, and insurance.

Antitrust Division *(Justice Dept.)*, **Media, Entertainment, and Communications,** 450 5th St. N.W., #7000, 20530; (202) 514-5621. Fax, (202) 514-6381. Yvette Tarlov, Chief (Acting), (202) 514-5808. Press, (202) 514-2007.
Web, www.justice.gov/atr/about-division/mec-section

Investigates and litigates antitrust cases dealing with communications, entertainment, and media, including mobile wireless services, broadband Internet, satellite communications services, voice communication services, video programming distribution, gambling, television production, and business telecommunications services.

Antitrust Division *(Justice Dept.)*, **Media, Entertainment, and Professional Services,** 450 5th St. N.W., #4000, 20530-0001; (202) 305-8376. Fax, (202) 514-7308. Owen M. Kendler, Chief.
General email, ATR.MEP.Information@usdoj.gov
Web, www.justice.gov/atr/about-division/mep-section

Investigates and litigates certain antitrust cases involving such commodities as movies, radio, TV, newspapers, performing arts, sports, and credit and debit cards. Handles certain violations of antitrust laws that involve patents, copyrights, and trademarks. Deals with mergers and acquisitions.

Antitrust Division *(Justice Dept.)*, **Technology and Digital Platforms,** 450 5th St. N.W., #7100, 20530; (202) 307-6200. Fax, (202) 616-8544. Aaron D. Hoag, Chief, (202) 307-6153.
General email, antitrust.atr@usdoj.gov
Web, www.justice.gov/atr/about-division/tfs-section

Investigates and litigates certain antitrust cases involving financial institutions, including securities, commodity futures, computer hardware and software, professional associations, and high-technology component manufacturing; participates in agency proceedings and rulemaking in these areas; monitors and analyzes legislation.

Antitrust Division *(Justice Dept.)*, **Transportation, Energy, and Agriculture (TEA),** 450 5th St. N.W., #8000, 20530; (202) 307-6349. Fax, (202) 616-2441. Robert Lepore, Chief, (202) 532-4928.
General email, ATR.TEA@usdoj.gov
Web, www.justice.gov/atr/about-division/transportation-energy-and-agriculture-section

Responsible for civil antitrust enforcement, competition advocacy, and competition policy in the area of domestic and international aviation, bus and leisure travel, railroads, trucking, and ocean shipping, hotels, restaurants, and travel services, electricity, oil-field services, food products, crops, seeds, fish and livestock, and agricultural biotech. Participates in proceedings before the Federal Energy Regulatory Commission, Environmental Protection Agency, Agriculture Dept., Energy Dept., State Dept., Commerce Dept., Transportation Dept., and the Federal Maritime Commission.

Comptroller of the Currency *(Treasury Dept.)*, Constitution Center, 400 7th St. S.W., 20219; (202) 649-6800. Michael Hsu, Comptroller (Acting). Press, (202) 649-6870.
General email, publicaffairs3@occ.treas.gov
Web, www.occ.gov, Twitter, @USOCC and YouTube, www.youtube.com/c/OfficeoftheComptrolleroftheCurrency/videos

Charters and examines operations of national banks, federal savings associations, and U.S. operations of foreign-owned banks; establishes guidelines for bank examinations; handles mergers of national banks with regard to antitrust law. Ensures that national banks and savings associations operate in a safe and sound manner, provide fair access to financial services, treat customers fairly, and comply with applicable laws and regulations.

Federal Communications Commission (FCC), Wireline Competition Bureau (WCB), 45 L St. N.E., 20554; (202) 418-1500. Fax, (202) 418-2825. Trent Harkrader, Chief, (202) 418-2955.

Web, www.fcc.gov/wireline-competition and Blog, www.fcc .gov/news-events/blog

Regulates mergers involving common carriers (wireline facilities that furnish interstate communications services).

Federal Deposit Insurance Corp. (FDIC), Risk Management Supervision, 550 17th St. N.W., #5036, 20429; (877) 275-3342. Fax, (202) 898-3638. Doreen R. Eberley, Director. TTY, (800) 877-8339.

Web, www.fdic.gov/about/contact/directory/#HQDSC and Policy manual, www.fdic.gov/regulations

Studies and analyzes applications for mergers, consolidations, acquisitions, and assumption transactions between insured banks.

Federal Energy Regulatory Commission (FERC) (Energy Dept.), 888 1st St. N.E., 20426; (202) 502-6477. Fax, (202) 502-8612. Richard Glick, Chair, (202) 502-6530. eLibrary, (202) 502-6652. Enforcement hotline, (202) 502-8390. Enforcement toll-free, (888) 889-8030. FOIA, (202) 502-8390. Toll-free, (866) 208-3372. TTY, (202) 502-8659. General email, customer@ferc.gov

Web, www.ferc.gov, Twitter, @FERC and Facebook, www .facebook.com/FERC.gov

Regulates mergers, consolidations, and acquisitions of electric utilities; regulates the acquisition of interstate natural gas pipeline facilities.

Federal Reserve System, Supervision and Regulation, 20th St. and Constitution Ave. N.W., 20551; (202) 973-6999. Michael S. Gibson, Director, (202) 452-2495; Christina Kohn, Administrative Assistant.

Web, www.federalreserve.gov/econres/bsrpd-staff.htm

Approves bank mergers, consolidations, and other alterations in bank structure.

Federal Trade Commission (FTC), 600 Pennsylvania Ave. N.W., 20580; (202) 326-2222. Lina Khan, Chair, (202) 326-0000. Press, (202) 326-2180. Congressional Relations, (202) 326-2195. Identity theft hotline, (877) 438-4338. Library, (202) 326-2395.

Web, www.ftc.gov, Twitter, @FTC, Facebook, www .facebook.com/federaltradecommission and YouTube, www.youtube.com/ftcvideos

Promotes policies designed to maintain strong competitive enterprise and consumer protection within the U.S. economic system. Monitors trade practices and investigates cases involving monopoly, unfair restraints, or deceptive practices. Enforces Truth in Lending and Fair Credit Reporting acts.

Federal Trade Commission (FTC), Bureau of Competition, 600 Pennsylvania Ave. N.W., #CC-5422, 20580; (202) 326-3300. Fax, (202) 326-2884. Holly Vedova, Director. General email, antitrust@ftc.gov

Web, www.ftc.gov/about-ftc/bureaus-offices/bureau-competition

Enforces antitrust laws and investigates possible violations, mergers and acquisitions, and anticompetitive practices; seeks voluntary compliance and pursues civil judicial remedies; reviews premerger filings; coordinates activities with the Antitrust Division of the Justice Dept.

Federal Trade Commission (FTC), Bureau of Competition, Anticompetitive Practices Division (ACP), 600 Pennsylvania Ave. N.W., #CC-5422, 20024; (202) 326-2641. Fax, (202) 326-3496. Geoffrey Green, Assistant Director. Toll-free, (877) 382-4357. General email, antitrust@ftc.gov

Web, www.ftc.gov/about-ftc/bureaus-offices/bureau-competition

Investigates nonmerger anticompetitive practices in real estate and a variety of other industries. Interests include intellectual property and professional and regulatory boards.

Federal Trade Commission (FTC), Bureau of Competition, Compliance Division, 600 Pennsylvania Ave. N.W., #CC-5422, 20024; (202) 326-2681. Fax, (202) 326-3396. Maribeth Petrizzi, Assistant Director, (202) 326-2564. General email, bccompliance@ftc.gov

Web, www.ftc.gov/about-ftc/bureaus-offices/bureau-competition/inside-bureau-competition

Monitors and enforces competition orders and oversees required remediations in company conduct. Investigates possible violations of the Hart-Scott-Rodino Act and recommends enforcement actions.

Federal Trade Commission (FTC), Bureau of Competition, Health Care Division, 600 Pennsylvania Ave. N.W., #CC-5422, 20024; (202) 326-3300. Fax, (202) 326-3384. Markus H. Meier, Assistant Director, (202) 326-3759.

Web, www.ftc.gov/advice-guidance/competition-guidance/industry-guidance/competition-health-care-marketplace

Investigates and litigates nonmerger anticompetitive practices among physicians, hospitals, and health insurers in the health care industry, including the pharmaceutical industry. Works against pay-for-delay agreements among pharmaceutical companies that insulate brand-name drugs from competition with lower cost generic drugs.

Federal Trade Commission (FTC), Bureau of Competition, Honors Paralegal Program, 600 Pennsylvania Ave. N.W., #CC-5422, 20024; (202) 326-2750. Fax, (202) 326-3496. Kimberly Burris, Coordinator.

Web, www.ftc.gov/about-ftc/careers-ftc/work-ftc/honors-paralegal-program

Federal Maritime Commission

```
                    ┌──────────────────────────────────────────────┐
         Commissioner      Commissioner      CHAIR      Commissioner      Commissioner
                    └──────────────────────────────────────────────┘
                                                │
         ┌──────────────────────────┬──────────┴──────────┬──────────────────────────┐
    Secretary   General    Administrative   Managing    Equal            Inspector General
                Counsel    Law Judges       Director    Employment
                                                         Opportunity
                                                │
    ┌────────────┬─────────────┬──────────┬────┴──────┬───────────┬──────────┬─────────────┐
  Consumer    Enforcement  Certification  Trade     Area        Human     Budget     Management   Information
  Affairs                  and            Analysis  Representatives Resources and        Resources    Technology
  and Dispute              Licensing                              Finance
  Resolution
  Services
```

Administers paralegal program for individuals considering a career in law, economics, business, or public service. Honors paralegals are given significant responsibility and hands-on experience while assisting attorneys and economists in the investigation and litigation of antitrust matters. Applicants are appointed for fourteen-month to four-year terms.

Federal Trade Commission (FTC), *Bureau of Competition, Mergers I,* 600 Pennsylvania Ave. N.W., #CC-5422, 20024; (202) 326-2682. Fax, (202) 326-2655. Stephen Mohr, Assistant Director (Acting).
General email, antitrust@ftc.gov

Web, www.ftc.gov/about-ftc/bureaus-offices/bureau-competition/inside-bureau-competition

Investigates and litigates antitrust violations in mergers and acquisitions, primarily in the health care–related industries, including pharmaceutical manufacturing and distribution and medical devices. Also handles scientific, industrial, defense, and technology industries.

Federal Trade Commission (FTC), *Bureau of Competition, Mergers II,* 600 Pennsylvania Ave. N.W., #CC-5422, 20024; (202) 326-3505. Fax, (202) 326-2071. Peggy Bayer Femenella, Assistant Director (Acting).
General email, antitrust@ftc.gov

Web, www.ftc.gov/about-ftc/bureaus-offices/bureau-competition/inside-bureau-competition

Investigates and litigates antitrust violations in mergers and acquisitions in the chemicals, coal mining, technology, entertainment, and computer hardware and software industries.

Federal Trade Commission (FTC), *Bureau of Competition, Mergers III,* 600 Pennsylvania Ave. N.W., #CC-5422, 20024; (202) 326-2563. Fax, (202) 326-3383. Peter Richman, Assistant Director.
General email, antitrust@ftc.gov

Web, www.ftc.gov/about-ftc/bureaus-offices/bureau-competition/inside-bureau-competition

Investigates and litigates antitrust violations in mergers and acquisitions concerning the oil and gas, ethanol, industrial spray equipment, and energy industries.

Federal Trade Commission (FTC), *Bureau of Competition, Mergers IV,* 600 Pennsylvania Ave. N.W., #CC-5422, 20024; (202) 326-2769. Fax, (202) 326-2286. Mark Seidman, Assistant Director.
General email, antitrust@ftc.gov

Web, www.ftc.gov/about-ftc/bureaus-offices/bureau-competition/inside-bureau-competition

Investigates and litigates antitrust violations in mergers and acquisitions concerning hospitals, the grocery food product industry, the media, funeral homes, and consumer goods.

Federal Trade Commission (FTC), *Bureau of Competition, Premerger Notification (PNO),* 400 7th Ave. S.W., #5301, 20024; (202) 326-3100. Fax, (202) 326-2624. Robert L. Jones, Assistant Director, (202) 326-2740.

General email, HSRHelp@ftc.gov

Web, www.ftc.gov/enforcement/premerger-notification-program

Reviews premerger filings under the Hart-Scott-Rodino Act for the FTC and Justice Dept. Coordinates investigative work with federal and state agencies; participates in international projects.

Federal Trade Commission (FTC), *Bureau of Economics,* 600 Pennsylvania Ave. N.W., 20580; (202) 326-3419. Fax, (202) 326-2380. Vacant, Director.
Web, www.ftc.gov/about-ftc/bureaus-offices/bureau-economics

Provides economic analyses for consumer protection and antitrust investigations, cases, and rulemakings; advises the commission on the effect of government regulations on competition and consumers in various industries; develops special reports on competition, consumer protection, and regulatory issues.

Federal Trade Commission (FTC), *International Affairs,* 600 Pennsylvania Ave. N.W., #H494, 20580; (202) 326-2600. Fax, (202) 326-2873. Randolph W. Tritell, Director, (202) 326-3051.
Web, www.ftc.gov/about-ftc/bureaus-offices/office-international-affairs

Assists in the enforcement of antitrust laws and consumer protection by arranging appropriate cooperation and coordination with foreign governments in international cases. Negotiates bilateral and multilateral antitrust and consumer protection agreements and represents the United States in international antitrust policy forums. Assists developing countries in moving toward market-based economies.

Surface Transportation Board (STB), 395 E St. S.W., #1220, 20423-0001; (202) 245-0245. Martin J. Oberman, Chair. Library, (202) 245-0288. Press, (202) 245-0238/1760. TTY, (800) 877-8339.
Web, www.stb.gov and Email, rcpa@stb.gov

Has jurisdiction over railroad rate, practice, and service issues and rail restructuring transactions, including mergers, line sales, line construction, and line abandonments. The STB also has jurisdiction over certain passenger rail matters, the intercity bus industry, non-energy pipelines, household goods carriers' tariffs, and rate regulation of non-contiguous domestic water transportation (marine freight shipping involving the mainland United States, Hawaii, Alaska, Puerto Rico, and other U.S. territories and possessions). Library open to the public.

▶ CONGRESS

For a listing of relevant congressional committees and subcommittees, please see pages 546–547 or the Appendix.

▶ NONGOVERNMENTAL

American Antitrust Institute (AAI), 1025 Connecticut Ave. N.W., #1000, 20036; (202) 828-1226. Diana L. Moss, President.

Web, www.antitrustinstitute.org and *Twitter,*
@AntitrustInst

Pro-antitrust organization that provides research and policy analysis to journalists, academic researchers, lawyers, economists, businesspeople, government officials, courts, and the general public. Seeks to educate the public on the importance of fair competition. Monitors legislation and regulations on competition-oriented policies.

The Business Roundtable, *1000 Maine Ave. S.W., #500, 20024; (202) 872-1260. Kristen Silverberg, President. General email, info@brt.org*

Web, www.businessroundtable.org, Twitter, @BizRoundtable and *Facebook, www.facebook.com/ BusinessRoundtable*

Membership: chief executives of the nation's largest corporations. Examines issues of concern to business, including antitrust law.

U.S. Chamber Litigation Center, *1615 H St. N.W., 20062-2000; (202) 463-5337. Darryl Joseffer, Executive Vice President. Web, www.chamberlitigation.com* and *Twitter, @USCClitigation*

Public policy law firm of the U.S. Chamber of Commerce. Advocates businesses' positions in court on such issues as antitrust, bankruptcy, and employment, as well as environmental and constitutional law. Provides businesses with legal assistance and amicus support in legal proceedings before federal courts and agencies.

Bankruptcy

▶**AGENCIES**

Executive Office for U.S. Trustees *(Justice Dept.), 441 G St. N.W., #6150, 20530; (202) 307-1399. Fax, (202) 307-0672. Clifford J. White III, Director, (202) 307-1391. Employee Hotline, (800) 801-0166. General email, ustrustee.program@usdoj.gov*

Web, www.justice.gov/ust

Handles the administration and oversight of bankruptcy and liquidation cases filed under the Bankruptcy Reform Act, including detecting and combating bankruptcy fraud. Provides individual U.S. trustee offices with administrative and management support.

▶**CONGRESS**

For a listing of relevant congressional committees and subcommittees, please see pages 546–547 or the Appendix.

▶**NONGOVERNMENTAL**

American Bankruptcy Institute, *66 Canal Center Plaza, #600, Alexandria, VA 22314-1592; (703) 739-0800. Fax, (703) 739-1060. Amy A. Quackenboss, Executive Director. Toll-free, (866) 921-1027. General email, support@abiworld.org*

Web, www.abi.org, Twitter, @abiworld and *Facebook, www.facebook.com/TheAmericanBankruptcyInstitute*

Membership: lawyers, federal and state legislators, and representatives of accounting and financial services firms, lending institutions, credit organizations, and consumer groups. Provides information and educational services on insolvency, reorganization, and bankruptcy issues; sponsors conferences, seminars, and workshops.

National Assn. of Consumer Bankruptcy Attorneys, *2200 Pennsylvania Ave. N.W., 4th Floor, 20037; (800) 499-9040. Fax, (866) 408-9515. Krista D'Amelio, Director of Government Affairs. General email, admin@nacba.org*

Web, www.nacba.org and *Twitter, @NACBAorg*

Acts as advocate on behalf of consumer debtors and their attorneys. Files amicus briefs on behalf of parties in the U.S. courts of appeal and Supreme Court, and provides educational programs and workshops for attorneys. Monitors legislation and regulations.

U.S. Chamber Litigation Center, *1615 H St. N.W., 20062-2000; (202) 463-5337. Darryl Joseffer, Executive Vice President. Web, www.chamberlitigation.com* and *Twitter, @USCClitigation*

Public policy law firm of the U.S. Chamber of Commerce. Advocates businesses' positions in court on such issues as antitrust, bankruptcy, and employment, as well as environmental and constitutional law. Provides businesses with legal assistance and amicus support in legal proceedings before federal courts and agencies.

Tax Violations

▶**AGENCIES**

Internal Revenue Service (IRS) *(Treasury Dept.), Criminal Investigation, 1111 Constitution Ave. N.W., 20224; (202) 317-3200. James Lee, Chief. Tax fraud hotline, (800) 366-4184. TTY, (800) 877-8339. Web, www.irs.gov/compliance/criminal-investigation* and *Twitter, @IRSnews*

Investigates money laundering, criminal violations of the tax law, and related financial crimes.

Internal Revenue Service (IRS) *(Treasury Dept.), Procedures and Administration (P&A), 1111 Constitution Ave. N.W., #5503, 20224; (202) 317-3400. Katherine (Kathy) Zuba, Associate Chief Counsel. e-Fax, (855) 591-7870. Press, (202) 317-4000. Coronavirus information, (202) 317-5436. Web, www.irs.gov*

Oversees field office litigation of civil cases that involve underpayment of taxes when the taxpayer chooses to challenge the determinations of the IRS in the U.S. Tax Court, or when the taxpayer chooses to pay the amount in question and sue the IRS for a refund. Reviews briefs and defense letters prepared by field offices for tax cases; drafts legal advice memos; prepares tax litigation advice memoranda; coordinates litigation strategy. Makes recommendations concerning appeal and certiorari. Prepares tax regulations, rulings, and other published guidance regarding the Internal Revenue Code, as enacted.

Tax Division *(Justice Dept.), 950 Pennsylvania Ave. N.W., #4141, 20530-0001; (202) 514-2901. Fax, (202) 514-5479. David A. Hubbert, Deputy Assistant Attorney General.*
Web, *www.justice.gov/tax*

Authorizes prosecution of all criminal cases involving tax violations investigated and developed by the Internal Revenue Service (IRS); represents the IRS in civil litigation except in U.S. Tax Court proceedings; represents other agencies, including the Defense and Interior Depts., in cases with state or local tax authorities.

▶ **CONGRESS**

For a listing of relevant congressional committees and subcommittees, please see pages 546–547 or the Appendix.

▶ **JUDICIARY**

U.S. Tax Court, *400 2nd St. N.W., 20217; (202) 521-0700. Maurice B. Foley, Chief Judge, (202) 521-0777.*
Web, *www.ustaxcourt.gov*

Tries and adjudicates disputes involving income, estate, and gift taxes and personal holding company surtaxes in cases in which deficiencies have been determined by the Internal Revenue Service.

▶ **NONGOVERNMENTAL**

American Bar Assn. (ABA), *Taxation, 1050 Connecticut Ave. N.W., #400, 20036; (202) 662-8670. Fax, (202) 662-8682. Haydee Moore, Director, (202) 662-8679.*
General email, *tax@americanbar.org*

Web, *www.americanbar.org/groups/taxation, Twitter, @ABATAXSECTION and Facebook, www.facebook.com/ABATaxSection*

Studies and recommends policies on taxation; provides information on tax issues; sponsors continuing legal education programs; monitors tax laws and legislation.

CIVIL RIGHTS

General

▶ **AGENCIES**

Civil Rights Division *(Justice Dept.), 950 Pennsylvania Ave. N.W., #5643, 20530-0001; (202) 514-3847. Kristen Clarke, Assistant Attorney General. Complaint line, (855) 856-1247. Press, (202) 514-2007. TTY, (202) 514-0716.*
General email, *civilrightsdivision@usdoj.gov*

Web, *www.justice.gov/crt, Twitter, @TheJusticeDept and Facebook, www.facebook.com/DOJ*

Enforces federal civil rights laws prohibiting discrimination on the basis of race, color, religion, sex, disability, familial status, military status, or national origin in voting, education, employment, credit, housing, public accommodations and facilities, credit, and federally assisted programs.

Civil Rights Division *(Justice Dept.), Disability Rights (DRS), 950 Pennsylvania Ave. N.W., 20530; (202) 307-0663. Fax, (202) 307-1197. Rebecca Bond, Chief. Information and ADA specialist, (800) 514-0301. TTY, (800) 514-0383.*
Web, *www.justice.gov/crt/disability-rights-section*

Litigates cases under Titles I, II, and III of the Americans with Disabilities Act, which prohibits discrimination on the basis of disability in places of public accommodation and in all activities of state and local government. Provides technical assistance to businesses and individuals affected by the law.

Civil Rights Division *(Justice Dept.), Educational Opportunities (EOS), 150 M St. N.E., #10.202, 20002; (202) 514-4092. Fax, (202) 514-8337. Shaheena Simons, Chief. Toll-free, (877) 292-3804.*
General email, *education@usdoj.gov*

Web, *www.justice.gov/crt/educational-opportunities-section*

Initiates litigation to ensure equal opportunities in public education; enforces laws dealing with civil rights in public education. Responsible for enforcing Title IV of the Civil Rights Act of 1964, the Equal Educational Opportunities Act of 1974, and Title II of the Americans with Disabilities Act.

Education Dept., *Civil Rights (OCR), Lyndon B. Johnson Bldg., 400 Maryland Ave. S.W., #4E313, 20202-1100; (202) 453-5900. Fax, (202) 453-6012. Catherine E. Lhamon, Assistant Secretary. Toll-free, (800) 421-3481. TTY, (800) 877-8339.*
General email, *ocr@ed.gov*

Web, *www2.ed.gov/ocr and Twitter, @EDcivilrights*

Enforces laws prohibiting use of federal funds for education programs or activities that discriminate on the basis of race, color, sex, national origin, age, or disability; authorized to discontinue funding.

Health and Human Services Dept. (HHS), *Civil Rights (OCR), 200 Independence Ave. S.W., #509F, 20201; (202) 619-0403. Fax, (202) 619-3437. Lisa J. Pino, Director. Toll-free, (800) 368-1019. TTY, (800) 537-7697.*
General email, *OCRMail@hhs.gov*

Web, *www.hhs.gov/ocr and Twitter, @HHSOCR*

Administers and enforces laws prohibiting discrimination on the basis of race, color, sex, national origin, religion, age, or disability in programs receiving federal funds from the department; authorized to discontinue funding. Enforces the Health Insurance Portability and Accountability Act (HIPAA); Privacy, Security, and Breach Notification rules; and the Patient Safety Act and Rules.

U.S. Commission on Civil Rights, *1331 Pennsylvania Ave. N.W., #1150, 20425; (202) 376-7700. Norma V. Cantu, Chair. Press, (202) 376-8359. TTY, (202) 376-8116.*

Selected Minorities-Related Resources

ADVOCACY AND ANTI-DISCRIMINATION

American-Arab Anti-Discrimination Committee,
(202) 244-2990; www.adc.org

Anti-Defamation League, (212) 885-7700;
www.adl.org

Arab American Institute, (202) 429-9210;
www.aaiusa.org

Human Rights Campaign, (202) 628-4160;
www.hrc.org

Japanese American Citizens League, (202) 223-1240;
www.jacl.org

Mexican American Legal Defense and Education Fund,
(213) 629-2512; www.maldef.org

NAACP (National Assn. for the Advancement of Colored People), (202) 463-2940; www.naacp.org

National Council of La Raza, (202) 785-1670;
www.nclr.org

National Gay and Lesbian Task Force, (202) 393-5177;
www.thetaskforce.org

National Organization for Women, (202) 628-8669;
www.now.org

Organization of Asian Pacific Americans, (202) 223-5500;
www.ocanational.org

The Rainbow PUSH Coalition,
https://rainbowpushwallstreetproject.org

BUSINESS AND LABOR

Business and Professional Women USA, (202) 293-1100;
www.bpwfoundation.org

Council of Federal EEO and Civil Rights Executives,
(800) 669-4000; www.eeoc.gov

Minority Business Development Agency, (202) 482-2332;
www.mbda.gov

National Assn. of Hispanic Federal Executives Inc.,
(202) 315-3942; www.nahfe.org

National Assn. of Minority Contractors, (202) 296-1600;
www.namcnational.org

National Assn. of Women Business Owners,
(800) 556-2926; www.nawbo.org

National Black Chamber of Commerce, (202) 220-3060;
www.nationalbcc.org

National U.S.-Arab Chamber of Commerce,
(202) 289-5920; www.nusacc.org

U.S. Hispanic Chamber of Commerce, (202) 842-1212;
www.ushcc.com

U.S. Pan Asian American Chamber of Commerce,
(202) 296-5221; www.uspaacc.com

EDUCATION

American Assn. for Access, Equity and Diversity
(202) 349-9855 or(866) 562-2233; www.aaaed.org

American Indian Higher Education Consortium,
(703) 838-0400; www.aihec.org

Assn. of American Colleges and Universities,
(202) 387-3760; www.aacu.org

Assn. of Research Libraries, (202) 296-2296;
www.arl.org/category/our-priorities/diversity-equity-inclusion

---

General email, *publicaffairs@usccr.gov*

Web, www.usccr.gov, Twitter, @USCCRgov, Facebook, www.facebook.com/USCCRgov and Civil rights complaints, referrals@usccr.gov

Assesses federal laws, policies, and legal developments to determine the nature and extent of denial of equal protection under the law on the basis of race, color, religion, sex, national origin, age, or disability in employment, voting rights, education, administration of justice, and housing. Issues reports and makes recommendations to the president and Congress; serves as national clearinghouse for civil rights information; receives civil rights complaints and refers them to the appropriate federal agency for action. Library open to the public.

U.S. Commission on Civil Rights, *Civil Rights Evaluation, 1331 Pennsylvania Ave. N.W., #1150, 20425; (202) 376-7700. Vacant, Director. Complaints Unit hotline, (202) 376-8513. Toll-free hotline, (800) 552-6843. TYT, (800) 877-8339. General email, enforcement@usccr.gov*

Web, www.usccr.gov/about/offices

Develops national civil rights policy and enforcement of federal civil rights laws; studies alleged deprivations of

voting rights and alleged discrimination based on race, color, religion, sex, age, disability, or national origin, or in the administration of justice.

▶CONGRESS

For a listing of relevant congressional committees and subcommittees, please see pages 546–547 or the Appendix.

▶NONGOVERNMENTAL

American Assn. for Access, Equity, and Diversity (AAAED), *1701 Pennsylvania Ave. N.W., #200, 20006; (202) 349-9855. Fax, (202) 355-1399. Shirley J. Wilcher, Executive Director. Toll-free, (866) 562-2233. General email, info@aaaed.org*

Web, www.aaaed.org, Facebook, www.facebook.com/theaaaed and Twitter, @theaaaed

Membership: professional managers in the areas of affirmative action, equal opportunity, diversity, and human resources. Sponsors education, research, and training programs. Acts as a liaison with government agencies involved in equal opportunity compliance. Maintains ethical

National Assn. for Equal Opportunity in Higher Education, (202) 552-3300; www.nafeonation.org

GOVERNMENT, LAW, AND PUBLIC POLICY

Asian American Justice Center, (202) 296-2300; www.advancingjustice-aajc.org

Blacks in Government, (202) 667-3280; www.bignet.org

Congressional Black Caucus Foundation, Inc., (202) 263-2800; www.cbcfinc.org

Congressional Hispanic Caucus Institute, (202) 543-1771; www.chci.org

Council on American-Islamic Relations, (202) 488-8787; www.cair.com

Institute for Women's Policy Research, (202) 785-5100; www.iwpr.org

Joint Center for Political and Economic Studies, (202) 789-3500; www.jointcenter.org

Leadership Conference on Civil Rights, (202) 466-3311; www.civilrights.org

National Congress on American Indians, (202) 466-7767; www.ncai.org

National Women's Law Center, (202) 588-5180; www.nwlc.org

National Women's Political Caucus, (202) 785-1100; www.nwpc.org

Society of American Indian Government Employees, info@saige.org; www.saige.org

HEALTH

Asian and Pacific Islander American Health Forum, (202) 466-7772; www.apiahf.org

National Alliance for Hispanic Health, (202) 387-5000; www.healthyamericas.org

National Black Nurses Assn., (301) 589-3200; www.nbna.org

National Council of Urban Indian Health, (202) 544-0344; www.ncuih.org

National Hispanic Medical Assn., (202) 628-5895; www.nhmamd.org

National Minority AIDS Council, (202) 815-3129; www.nmac.org

MEDIA

Center for Digital Democracy, (202) 494-7100; www.democraticmedia.org

International Women's Media Foundation, (202) 496-1992; www.iwmf.org

Multicultural Media, Telecom and Internet Council, (202) 261-6543; www.mmtconline.org

National Assn. of Black Owned Broadcasters, (202) 463-8970; www.nabob.org

National Assn. of Hispanic Journalists, contact@nahj.org; www.nahj.org

National Lesbian and Gay Journalists Assn., (202) 588-9888; www.nlgja.org

standards for the profession. (Formerly the American Assn. for Affirmative Action.)

Lawyers' Committee for Civil Rights Under Law, *1500 K St. N.W., #900, 20005-2124; (202) 662-8600. Fax, (202) 783-0857. Damon Hewitt, Executive Director. Toll-free, (888) 299-5227.*
General email, info@lawyerscommittee.org
Web, www.lawyerscommittee.org, Twitter, @LawyersComm and Facebook, www.facebook.com/lawyerscommittee

Provides minority groups and the poor with legal assistance in such areas as voting rights, employment discrimination, education, environment, and equal access to government services and benefits.

Leadership Conference on Civil and Human Rights, *1620 L St. N.W., #1100, 20036; (202) 466-3311. Fax, (202) 466-3435. Maya Wiley, President. Press, (202) 869-0398.*
General email, info@civilrights.org
Web, www.civilrights.org, Twitter, @civilrightsorg, Facebook, www.facebook.com/civilandhumanrights and YouTube, www.youtube.com/user/LCCREF

Coalition of national organizations representing minorities, women, labor, older Americans, people with disabilities, and religious groups. Works for enactment and enforcement of civil rights, human rights, and social welfare legislation; acts as clearinghouse for information on civil rights legislation and regulations.

NAACP Legal Defense and Educational Fund, Inc., *Washington Office, 700 14th St. N.W., #600, 20005; (202) 682-1300. Sherrilyn Ifill, President.*
Web, www.naacpldf.org, Twitter, @naacp_ldf, Facebook, www.facebook.com/naacpldf and YouTube, www.youtube.com/channel/UCXTfPnpwx-CWVyrzDvkwE1w

Civil rights litigation group that provides legal information on civil rights issues, including employment, housing, and educational discrimination; monitors federal enforcement of civil rights laws. Not affiliated with the NAACP. (Headquarters in New York.)

National Coalition Building Institute, *Metro Plaza Bldg., 8403 Colesville Rd., #1100, Silver Spring, MD 20910; (240) 638-2813. Cherie Brown, Chief Executive Officer.*

General email, info@ncbi.org

Web, www.ncbi.org, Twitter, @NCBIworld and Facebook, www.facebook.com/ncbiinternational

Offers national and global leadership workshops and programs that combat racism and prejudice. Publishes reports on effective practices in reducing racism in education and the workplace.

Poverty and Race Research Action Council, *740 15th St. N.W., #300, 20005; (202) 866-0802. Fax, (202) 842-2885. Philip Tegeler, President.*

General email, info@prrac.org

Web, www.prrac.org and Twitter, @PRRAC_DC

Civil rights law and policy orgnization. Facilitates cooperative links between researchers and activists who work on race and poverty issues. Publishes bimonthly *Poverty & Race* newsletter and a civil rights history curriculum guide. Policy research areas include housing, education, and health disparities.

Rainbow PUSH Coalition, *Public Policy Institute, Government Relations and Telecommunications Project, 727 15th St. N.W., #1200, 20005; (301) 256-8587. Fax, (202) 393-1495. Stephen L. Smith Sr., President. Press, (773) 373-3366.*

General email, info@rainbowpush.org

Web, www.rainbowpush.org, Twitter, @RPCoalition and Facebook, www.facebook.com/Rainbow.PUSH

Independent civil rights organization concerned with public policy toward political, economic, and social justice for women, workers, and minorities. (Headquarters in Chicago, Ill.)

African Americans

▶ **NONGOVERNMENTAL**

Joint Center for Political and Economic Studies, *633 Pennsylvania Ave. N.W., 20004; (202) 789-3500. Fax, (202) 789-6390. Spencer Overton, President.*

General email, info@jointcenter.org

Web, www.jointcenter.org, Twitter, @JointCenter, Facebook, www.facebook.com/JointCenter1970 and YouTube, www.youtube.com/channel/UCp9whNSjWmlq W8v4K1-tyvA

Documents and analyzes the political and economic status of African Americans, focusing on political participation, economic advancement, and health policy. Disseminates information through forums and conferences.

National Assn. for the Advancement of Colored People (NAACP), *Washington Bureau, 1156 15th St. N.W., #915, 20005; (202) 463-2940. Fax, (202) 463-2953. Derrick Johnson, President.*

General email, washingtonbureau@naacpnet.org

Web, www.naacp.org, Twitter, @NAACP and Twitter, President, @DerrickNAACP

Membership: persons interested in civil rights for all minorities. Seeks, through legal, legislative, and direct action, to end discrimination in all areas, including discriminatory practices in the administration of justice. Studies and recommends policy on court administration and jury selection. Maintains branch offices in many state and federal prisons. (Headquarters in Baltimore, Md.)

National Assn. of Colored Women's Clubs Inc. (NACWC), *1601 R St. N.W., 20009-6420; (202) 667-4080. Andrea Brooks-Smith, President.*

General email, nacwcinfo@gmail.com

Web, www.nacwc.com, Facebook, www.facebook.com/ NACWC and Twitter, @NACWC1896

Seeks to promote education, protect and enforce civil rights, raise the standard of family living, promote interracial understanding, and enhance leadership development. Awards scholarships; conducts programs in education, social service, and philanthropy.

National Black Caucus of Local Elected Officials (NBC/LEO), *National League of Cities, 660 N. Capitol St. N.W., 20001; (202) 626-3000. Leon Andrews, Director for Race, Equity, and Leadership, (202) 626-3039. Toll-free, (877) 827-2385.*

General email, constituencygroups@nlc.org

Web, www.nlc.org/initiative/national-black-caucus-of-local-elected-officials-nbc-leo

Membership: Black elected officials at the local level and other interested individuals. Seeks to increase Black participation on the National League of Cities' steering and policy committees. Informs members on issues, and plans strategies for achieving objectives through legislation and direct action. Interests include cultural diversity, local government and community participation, housing, economics, job training, the family, and human rights. Affiliated with the National League of Cities.

National Black Caucus of State Legislators, *444 N. Capitol St. N.W., #622, 20001; (202) 624-5457. Fax, (202) 508-3826. Paula Hoisington, Executive Director. Web, https://nbcsl.org and Facebook, www.facebook.com/ nbcslnews*

Membership: Black state legislators. Interests include legislation and public policies that impact the general welfare of African American consituents within respective jurisdictions.

National Black Justice Coalition, *P.O. Box 71395, 20024; (202) 319-1552. Fax, (202) 478-2194. David J. Johns, Executive Director.*

General email, info@nbjc.org

Web, www.nbjc.org, Twitter, @NBJContheMove and Facebook, www.facebook.com/NationalBlackJustice Coalition

Seeks equality for Black lesbian, gay, bisexual, and transgender people by fighting racism and homophobia through education initiatives.

National Council of Negro Women, *633 Pennsylvania Ave. N.W., 20004-2605; (202) 737-0120. Johnnetta Betsch Cole, President; Janice Mathis, Executive Director.*

General email, info@ncnw.org

Web, www.ncnw.org, Twitter, @NCNWHQ, Facebook, www.facebook.com/NCNW633?fref=ts and YouTube, www.youtube.com/channel/UCWlKKLWtESSdadido6geT_w

Seeks to advance opportunities for African American women, their families, and communities through research, advocacy, and national and community-based programs in the United States and Africa.

National Urban League, *Washington Bureau, 1805 7th St. N.W., #520, 20001; (202) 898-1604. Joi O. Cheny, Executive Director, Washington, (202) 629-5755.* Web, https://nul.org/washington-bureau, Twitter, @NULPolicy and Facebook, www.facebook.com/NULPolicy

Federal advocacy division of social service organization concerned with the social welfare of African Americans and other minorities. Seeks elimination of racial segregation and discrimination; monitors legislation, policies, and regulations to determine impact on minorities; interests include employment, health, welfare, education, housing, and community development. (Headquarters in New York.)

Hispanics

▶**NONGOVERNMENTAL**

League of United Latin American Citizens, *1133 19th St. N.W., #1000, 20036; (202) 833-6130. Fax, (202) 833-6135. Sindy M. Benavides, Chief Executive Officer, ext. 108. Toll-free, (877) 585-2201.* General email, info@lulac.org

Web, https://lulac.org, Twitter, @LULAC and Facebook, www.facebook.com/lulac.national.dc

Seeks full social, political, economic, and educational rights for Hispanics in the United States. Programs include housing projects for the poor, employment and training for youth and women, and political advocacy on issues affecting Hispanics, including immigration. Affiliated with National Educational Service Centers (LNESCs), which award scholarships. Holds exposition open to the public.

Mexican American Legal Defense and Educational Fund (MALDEF), *National Public Policy, 1016 16th St. N.W., #100, 20036; (202) 293-2828. Andrea Senteno, Regional Counsel for Legislative and Regulatory Affairs.* General email, info@maldef.org

Web, www.maldef.org/public-policy, Twitter, @MALDEF, Facebook, www.facebook.com/MALDEF and YouTube, www.youtube.com/user/maldef

Works with Congress and the White House to promote legislative advocacy for minority groups. Interests include equal employment, voting rights, bilingual education, immigration, and discrimination. Monitors legislation and regulations. (Headquarters in Los Angeles, Calif.)

U.S. Conference of Catholic Bishops (USCCB), *Cultural Diversity in the Church, 3211 4th St. N.E., 20017-1194; (202) 541-3350. Mar Musoz-Visoso, Executive Director.*

General email, diversity@usccb.org

Web, www.usccb.org/committees/cultural-diversity-church and Twitter, @USCulturalDiver

Acts as an information clearinghouse on communications and pastoral and liturgical activities; serves as liaison for other church institutions and government and private agencies; provides information on legislation; acts as advocate for their five intercultural competencies (African-Americans, Asian/Pacific Islanders, Hispanic/Latino, Native Americans, and Pastoral Care of Migrants, Refugees and Travelers) within the National Conference of Catholic Bishops.

UnidosUS, *1126 16th St. N.W., #600, 20036-4845; (202) 785-1670. Janet Murguía, President.* General email, info@unidos.org

Web, www.unidosus.org, Twitter, @WeAreUnidosUS, Facebook, www.facebook.com/Weareunidosus and YouTube, www.youtube.com/c/UnidosUS

Seeks to reduce poverty of and discrimination against Hispanic Americans. Offers assistance to Hispanic community-based organizations. Conducts research and policy analysis. Interests include education, employment and training, asset development, immigration, language access issues, civil rights, and housing and community development. Monitors legislation and regulations.

Lesbian, Gay, Bisexual, and Transgender People

▶**NONGOVERNMENTAL**

Dignity USA, *Washington Office, 1601 18th St. N.W., #1, 20009; (202) 546-2235. Fax, (202) 521-3954. Thomas Yates, President, ext. 4. Toll-free, (800) 877-8797.* General email, dignity@dignitywashington.org

Web, https://dignitywashington.org, Twitter, @DignityDC, Facebook, www.faceboook.com/DignityWashington and YouTube, www.youtube.com/channel/UCDFCzr8E2Hc-TQ2qreLMGBQ

Membership: gay, lesbian, bisexual, and transgender Catholics, their families, and friends. Works to promote spiritual development, social interaction, educational outreach, and acceptance within the Catholic community. Sponsors a Spanish language affiliate group, Grupo Latino. (Headquarters in Medford, MA.)

Gay & Lesbian Victory Leadership Institute, *Victory Fund, 1225 Eye St. N.W., #525, 20005; (202) 842-8679. Fax, (202) 289-3863. Josh Roth, Victory Cabinet Manager; Ruben J. Gonzales, Executive Director.* Web, www.victoryinstitute.org/about, www.victoryfund .org, Facebook, www.facebook.com/victoryfund and Twitter, @VictoryFund

Supports the candidacy of openly LGBTQ individuals in federal, state, and local elections.

Gay and Lesbian Activists Alliance of Washington (GLAA), *P.O. Box 75265, 20013; (202) 797-4421. Bobbi Strang, President.*

General email, equal@glaa.org

Web, www.glaa.org and Twitter, @glaadc

Advances the rights of gays, lesbians, and transgender people within the Washington community.

Human Rights Campaign (HRC), *1640 Rhode Island Ave. N.W., 20036-3278; (202) 628-4160. Fax, (202) 347-5323. Joni Madison, President (Acting). Toll-free, (800) 777-4723. TTY, (202) 216-1572.*
General email, hrc@hrc.org

Web, www.hrc.org, Twitter, @HRC and Facebook, www .facebook.com/humanrightscampaign

Provides campaign support and educates the public to ensure the rights of lesbian, gay, bisexual, and transgender people at home, work, school, and in the community. Works to prohibit workplace discrimination based on sexual orientation and gender identity, combat hate crimes, and fund AIDS research, care, and prevention.

National Black Justice Coalition, *P.O. Box 71395, 20024; (202) 319-1552. Fax, (202) 478-2194. David J. Johns, Executive Director.*
General email, info@nbjc.org

Web, www.nbjc.org, Twitter, @NBJContheMove and Facebook, www.facebook.com/NationalBlackJustice Coalition

Seeks equality for Black lesbian, gay, bisexual, and transgender people by fighting racism and homophobia through education initiatives.

National Center for Transgender Equality (NCTE), *1032 15th St. N.W., #199, 20005; (202) 642-4542. Mara Keisling, Executive Director.*
General email, ncte@transequality.org

Web, www.transequality.org, Twitter, @TransEquality and Facebook, www.facebook.com/TransEqualityNow

Works to advance the equality of transgender people through advocacy, collaboration, and empowerment, and to make them safe from discrimination and violence. Provides resources to local efforts nationwide.

National Lesbian and Gay Journalists Assn. (NLGJA), *2120 L St. N.W., #850, 20037; (202) 588-9888. Adam Pawlus, Executive Director.*
General email, info@nlgja.org

Web, www.nlgja.org

Works within the journalism industry to foster fair and accurate coverage of lesbian, gay, bisexual, and transgender issues. Opposes workplace bias against all minorities and provides professional development for its members.

National LGBTQ Task Force, *1050 Connecticut Ave. N.W., #65500, 20035; (202) 393-5177. Kierra Johnson, Executive Director.*
General email, thetaskforce@thetaskforce.org

Web, www.thetaskforce.org, Twitter, @TheTaskForce and Facebook, www.facebook.com/thetaskforce

Works toward equal rights for the lesbian, gay, bisexual, and transgender community. Trains activists working at the state and local levels. Conducts research and public policy analysis. Monitors legislation. (Formerly National Gay and Lesbian Task Force [NGLTF].)

National Organization for Women (NOW), *1100 H St. N.W., #300, 20005; (202) 628-8669. Christian F. Nunes, President.*
General email, info@now.org

Web, https://now.org and Twitter, @NationalNOW

Membership: women and men interested in feminist civil rights. Promotes the development and enforcement of legislation prohibiting discrimination on the basis of sexual orientation.

Parents, Families, and Friends of Lesbians and Gays (PFLAG), *1625 K St. N.W., #700, 20006; (202) 467-8180. Fax, (202) 467-8194. Brian Bond, Executive Director.*
General email, info@pflag.org

Web, www.pflag.org, Twitter, @PFLAG, Facebook, www .facebook.com/PFLAG and YouTube, www.youtube.com/ pflag

Promotes the health and well-being of gay, lesbian, transgender, and bisexual persons, their families, and their friends through support, education, and advocacy. Works to change public policies and attitudes toward lesbian,gay, bisexual, transgender, and queer persons (LGBTQ+). Monitors legislation and regulations.

Supporting and Mentoring Youth Advocates and Leaders (SMYAL), *410 7th St. S.E., 20003-2707; (202) 546-5940. David Penchina, Executive Director (Acting).*
General email, supporterinfo@smyal.org

Web, https://smyal.org, Twitter, @SMYALDMV, Facebook, www.facebook.com/SMYAL and YouTube, www.youtube .com/channel/UCg6X7FyGtqmbTVcTVWOTM7w

Provides support to youth who are lesbian, gay, bisexual, transgender, intersex, or who may be questioning their sexuality. Facilitates youth center and support groups; promotes HIV/AIDS awareness; coordinates public education programs about homophobia. (Formerly Sexual Minority Youth Assistance League [SMYAL].)

Woodhull Freedom Foundation, *3302 Gleneagles Dr., Silver Spring, MD 20906; (888) 960-3332. Fax, (202) 330-5282. Ricci Joy Levy, President.*
General email, info@woodhullfoundation.org

Web, www.woodhullfoundation.org

Advocacy group for sexual and gender identity. Interests include reducing discrimination based on family structure. Presents awards to activists who advance sexual freedom as a human right. Holds annual summits to share experiences and solutions to current human rights issues related to sex, gender, and family. Monitors legislation and regulation on sexual freedom.

Native Americans

▶ **AGENCIES**

Administration for Children and Families (ACF) (*Health and Human Services Dept.*), *Administration for Native*

Americans (ANA), Mary E. Switzer Bldg., 330 C St. S.W., Room 4126, 20201; (202) 690-7732. Fax, (202) 690-7441. Hope MacDonald LoneTree, Deputy Commissioner; Michelle Sauve, Executive Director of ICNAA. Toll-free, (877) 922-9262. fax, (202) 690-7441.
General email, anacomments@acf.hhs.gov

Web, https://acf.hhs.gov/ana and Facebook, www.facebook .com/administrationfornativeamericans

Serves all Native Americans, including federally recognized tribes, American Indian and Alaska Native organizations, Native Hawaiian organizations and Native populations troughout the Pacific Basin (including American Samoa, Guam, and the Commonwealth of the Northern Mariana Islands). Awards grants for locally determined social and economic development strategies; promotes Native American economic and social self-sufficiency; provides grant funding for community development projects. Executive Director chairs the Intradepartmental Council on Indian Affairs (ICNAA), which coordinates Native American–related programs.

Bureau of Indian Affairs (BIA) *(Interior Dept.), 1849 C St. N.W., MS-4606, 20240; (202) 208-5116. Fax, (202) 208-6334. Darryl Lacounte, Director. Press, (202) 208-3710.*
General email, as-ia_opa@bia.gov

Web, www.bia.gov, Facebook, www.facebook.com/ USIndianAffairs and Twitter, @USIndianAffairs

Works with federally recognized Indian tribal governments and Alaska Native communities in a government-to-government relationship. Encourages and supports tribes' efforts to govern themselves and to provide needed programs and services on the reservations. Manages land held in trust for Indian tribes and individuals. Funds educational benefits, road construction and maintenance, social services, police protection, economic development efforts, and special assistance to develop governmental and administrative skills.

Interior Dept. (DOI), *Assistant Secretary for Indian Affairs, 4660 C St. N.W., MS 4160-MIB, 20240; (202) 208-7163. Bryan Newland, Assistant Secretary (Acting).*
Web, www.doi.gov

Administers laws and regulations relating to Indian tribes, individual Indian tribal members, and Indian affairs. Oversees the Bureau of Indian Affairs and Bureau of Indian Education.

Justice Dept. (DOJ), *Tribal Justice (OTJ), 950 Pennsylvania Ave. N.W., 20530-0001; (202) 514-8812. Tracy Toulou, Director.*
Web, www.justice.gov/otj

Serves as the Justice Dept.'s point of contact for communication with Native American tribes and their concerns. Collaborates with federal and other government agencies to promote consistent, informed government-wide policies, operations, and initiatives related to Native American tribes.

Tribal Justice and Safety *(Justice Dept.), 950 Pennsylvania Ave. N.W., 20530; (202) 514-8812.*

Tracy Toulou, Director. Grants management hotline, (888) 549-9901, option 3.
General email, tribalgrants@usdoj.gov
Web, www.justice.gov/tribal

Represents tribal community interests, including law enforcement policy, communications, detention facilities, federal prosecution in Indian country, tribal court development, domestic violence, drug courts and substance abuse, federal litigation involving tribes, and civil rights. Coordinates assistance grant funding from across various Justice Dept. offices and agencies.

►CONGRESS

For a listing of relevant congressional committees and subcommittees, please see pages 546–547 or the Appendix.

►JUDICIARY

U.S. Court of Federal Claims, *717 Madison Pl. N.W., 20439; (202) 357-6400. Elaine D. Kaplan, Chief Judge; Lisa Reyes, Clerk of the Court.*
Web, www.uscfc.uscourts.gov

Deals with Native American tribal claims against the government that are founded on the Constitution, congressional acts, government regulations, and contracts. Examples include congressional reference cases; patent cases; claims for land, water, and mineral rights; and the accounting of funds held for Native Americans under various treaties.

►NONGOVERNMENTAL

National Congress of American Indians, *Embassy of Tribal Nations, 1516 P St. N.W., 20005; (202) 466-7767. Fax, (202) 466-7797. Fawn Sharp, President.*
Web, www.ncai.org, Twitter, @NCAI1944 and Facebook, www.facebook.com/NCAI1944

Membership: American Indian and Alaska Native tribal governments and individuals. Provides information and serves as general advocate for tribes. Monitors legislative and regulatory activities affecting Native American affairs.

Native American Rights Fund, *Washington Office, 1514 P St. N.W. (Rear), Suite D 20005; (202) 785-4166. Fax, (202) 822-0068. John E. Echohawk, Executive Director.*
General email, info@narf.org

Web, www.narf.org, Facebook, www.facebook.com/ NativeAmericanRightsFund, Twitter, @NDNrights and YouTube, www.youtube.com/c/NativeAmericanRights Fund

Provides Native Americans and Alaska Natives with legal assistance in land claims, water rights, hunting, and other areas. Practices federal Indian law. (Headquarters in Boulder, Colo.)

Navajo Nation, *Washington Office, 750 1st St. N.E., #940, 20002; (202) 682-7390. Santee Lewis, Executive Director.*

General email, info@nnwo.org

Web, www.nnwo.org, Twitter, @nnwodc and Facebook, www.facebook.com/nnwodc

Monitors legislation and regulations affecting the Navajo people; serves as an information clearinghouse on the Navajo Nation. (Headquarters in Window Rock, Ariz.)

Older Adults

▶AGENCIES

Administration for Community Living (ACL) *(Health and Human Services Dept.), Administration on Aging (AOA),* Mary E. Switzer Bldg., 330 C St. S.W., 20201; (202) 401-4634, ext. 3. Edwin L. Walker, Deputy Assistant Secretary. Eldercare locator, (800) 677-1116.
Web, www.acl.gov/about-acl/administration-aging

Advocacy agency for older Americans and their concerns. Collaborates with tribal organizations, community and national organizations, and state and area agencies to implement grant programs and services designed to improve the quality of life for older Americans, such as information and referral, adult day care, elder abuse prevention, home-delivered meals, in-home care, transportation, and services for caregivers.

▶CONGRESS

For a listing of relevant congressional committees and subcommittees, please see pages 546–547 or the Appendix.

▶NONGOVERNMENTAL

60 Plus, *American Assn. of Senior Citizens,* 2121 Eisenhower Ave., #229, Alexandria, VA 22314; (703) 807-2070. Fax, (703) 807-2073. James (Jim) L. Martin, Chair.
General email, info@60plus.org

Web, www.60plus.org, Twitter, @60plusAssoc and Facebook, www.facebook.com/60Plus.org

Acts as advocate for the rights of senior citizens. Interests include free enterprise, less government regulation, and tax reform. Works to eliminate estate taxes. Monitors legislation and regulations.

AARP Foundation, *Legal Advocacy,* 601 E St. N.W., 20049; (202) 434-2060. William (Bill) Alvarado Rivera, Senior Vice President of Litigation.
General email, litigation@aarp.org

Web, www.aarp.org/aarp-foundation/our-work/legal-advocacy, Twitter, @AARPFoundation and Facebook, www.facebook.com/AARPFoundation

Acts as advocate for the legal rights of citizens age fifty years and older. Where Aging and Socail justice intersects. Addresses the age discrimination in the workplace; consumer and financial fraud and utilities issues; employee benefits, including pensions; investor protection; health, including long-term services and supports, Medicaid, Medicare, and prescription drug affordability; housing, including predatory mortgage lending and livable communities; low-income benefits, including the Supplemental Nutrition Assistance Program; and voting rights.

Justice in Aging, 1444 Eye St. N.W., #1100, 20005; (202) 289-6976. Fax, (202) 289-7224. Kevin Prindiville, Executive Director.
Web, www.justiceinaging.org, Twitter, @justiceinaging and Facebook, www.facebook.com/JusticeinAging

Provides training, technical assistance, and litigation for attorneys representing the elderly poor and persons with disabilities. Does not provide direct legal representation to individuals. Represents clients before Congress and federal departments and agencies. Focus includes Social Security, Medicare, Medicaid, long-term care residents' rights, home health care, pensions, and protective services. Funded by the Administration on Aging and various charitable foundations. Formerly National Senior Citizens Law Center.

National Hispanic Council on Aging, 2201 12th St. N.W., #101, 20009; (202) 347-9733. Fax, (202) 853-3803. Yanira Cruz, President.
General email, nhcoa@nhcoa.org

Web, www.nhcoa.org, Twitter, @NHCOA, Facebook, www.facebook.com/NHCOA and YouTube, www.youtube.com/user/NHCOA

Membership: senior citizens, health care workers, professionals in the field of aging, and others in the United States and Puerto Rico who are interested in topics related to Hispanics and aging. Provides research training, policy analysis, consulting, and technical assistance; sponsors seminars, workshops, and management internships.

Seniors Coalition, 1250 Connecticut Ave. N.W., #700, 20036-2643; (202) 261-3594. Fax, (866) 728-5450. Joseph L. Bridges, Chief Executive Officer.
General email, tsc@senior.org

Web, http://senior.org

Seeks to protect the quality of life and economic well-being of older Americans. Interests include health care, Social Security, taxes, pharmaceutical issues, and Medicare. Conducts seminars and monitors legislation and regulations.

Other Minority Groups

▶AGENCIES

Health and Human Services Dept., *White House Initiative on Asian Americans, Native Hawaiians, and Pacific Islanders,* 550 12th St. S.W., 10th Floor, 20202; (202) 482-1375. Krystal Ka'ai, Executive Director.
General email, whiaanhpi@hhs.gov

Web, www.commerce.gov/whiaapi and Twitter, @whitehouseAAPI

Ensures that Asian Americans, Native Hawaiians, and Pacific Islanders have equal access to federal programs and services. Methods include expanding language access and increasing enforcement efforts to combat discrimination.

►NONGOVERNMENTAL

American–Arab Anti-Discrimination Committee (ADC), *1705 DeSales St. N.W., #500, 20036; (202) 244-2990. Fax, (202) 333-6470. Samer E. Khalaf, President. Web, www.adc.org and Twitter, @adctweets*

Nonpartisan and nonsectarian organization that promotes and seeks to protect the human rights and cultural heritage of Americans of Arab descent. Works to combat discrimination against Arab Americans in employment, education, and political life and to prevent stereotyping of Arabs in the media. Monitors legislation and regulations.

Anti-Defamation League, *Washington Office, 1100 Connecticut Ave. N.W., #1020, 20036; (202) 452-8310. Fax, (202) 296-2371. Jonathan Greenblatt, Chief Executive Officer; Max Sevillia, Director of Government Relations. General email, washington-dc@adl.org Web, www.adl.org and Twitter, @ADL_WashDC*

Seeks to combat anti-Semitism and other forms of bigotry. Interests include discrimination in employment, housing, voting, and education; U.S. foreign policy in the Middle East; and the treatment of Jews worldwide. Monitors legislation and regulations affecting Jewish interests and the civil rights of all Americans. (Headquarters in New York.)

Asian Americans Advancing Justice (AAJC), *1620 L St. N.W., #1050, 20036; (202) 296-2300. Fax, (202) 296-2318. Michelle Boykins, Senior Director of Strategic Communications, ext. 0144. General email, information@advancingequality.org Web, www.advancingjustice-aajc.org and Twitter, @AAAJ_AAJC*

Works to advance the human and civil rights of Asian Americans and other minority groups through advocacy, public policy, public education, and litigation. Promotes civic engagement at the local, regional, and national levels. Interests include affirmative action, hate crimes, media diversity, census, broadband and telecommunications, youth advocacy, immigrant rights, language access, and voting rights.

Japanese American Citizens League, *Washington Office, 1629 K St. N.W., #400, 20006; (202) 223-1240. David Inoue, Executive Director. General email, dc@jacl.org Web, www.jacl.org and Twitter, @JACL_National*

Monitors legislative and regulatory activities affecting the rights of Japanese Americans. Supports civil rights of all Americans, with a focus on Asian and Asian Pacific Americans. (Headquarters in San Francisco, Calif.)

Muslim Public Affairs Council, *Washington Office, 1020 16th St. N.W., 20036; (202) 547-7701. Fax, (202) 547-7704. Salam Al-Marayati, National President; Mohammad Hurr Ali, Director of Policy and Government Relations.*

General email, hello@mpac.org Web, www.mpac.org, Twitter, @mpac_national and Facebook, www.facebook.com/mpacnational

Promotes the civil rights of American Muslims and the integration of Islam into American pluralism; assists victims of hate crimes; advises government agencies on national security and civil rights issues. (Headquarters in Los Angeles, Calif.)

OCA: Asian Pacific American Advocates, *900 19th St. N.W., 6th Floor, 20006; (202) 223-5500. Fax, (202) 296-0540. Thu Nguyen, Executive Director, ext. 5. General email, oca@ocanational.org Web, www.ocanational.org, Twitter, @OCANational and Facebook, www.facebook.com/ocanational*

Advocacy group seeking to advance the social, political, and economic well-being of Asian Pacific Americans in the United States through education, racial equity and inclusion, civic engagement and census, and workforce development.

Organization of Chinese American Women, *P.O. Box 3443, Oakton, VA 22124; (301) 907-3898. Donna Byler, Executive Director. General email, info@ocawwomen.org Web, www.ocawwomen.org*

Promotes equal rights and opportunities for Chinese and other Asian Pacific American women in professional and nonprofessional fields. Provides members with leadership and skills training and newly arrived immigrants with career development.

Women

►NONGOVERNMENTAL

Independent Women's Forum (IWF), *4 Weems Lane #312, Winchester, VA 22601; (202) 807-9986. Carrie Lukas, President. General email, info@iwf.org Web, www.iwf.org, Twitter, @IWF and Facebook, www .facebook.com/independentwomensforum*

Membership: women and men interested in advancing limited government, equality under the law, property rights, free markets, strong families, and a powerful and effective national defense and foreign policy. Publishes policy papers; makes appearances on radio and television broadcasts; maintains speakers bureau. Interests include school choice, Social Security, health care reform, and democracy promotion and women's human rights in the Middle East.

Institute for Women's Policy Research (IWPR), *1200 18th St. N.W., #301, 20036; (202) 785-5100. Fax, (202) 833-4362. C. Nicole Mason, President. Media, (202) 684-7534. General email, iwpr@iwpr.org Web, https://iwpr.org, Twitter, @IWPResearch and Facebook, www.facebook.com/iwpresearch*

Public policy research organization that focuses on women's issues, including the status of women in the United States and discrimination based on gender, race, or ethnicity.

International Center for Research on Women, *1120 20th St. N.W., #500N, 20036; (202) 797-0007. Fax, (202) 797-0020. Peggy Clark, President.*
General email, info@icrw.org

Web, www.icrw.org, Twitter, @ICRW and Facebook, www .facebook.com/ICRWDC

Advances gender equality and human rights, fights poverty, and promotes sustainable economic and social development through research, program implementation, information gathering, publications, and strategic media outreach. Conducts empirical research and promotes practical, evidence-based solutions that enable women to control their own lives and fully participate in their societies.

Jewish Women International, *1129 20th St. N.W., #801, 20036; (202) 857-1300. Fax, (202) 857-1380. Meredith Jacobs, Chief Executive Officer. Toll-free, (800) 343-2823.*
General email, jwi@jwi.org

Web, www.jwi.org, Twitter, @JewishWomenIntl and Facebook, www.facebook.com/jewishwomeninternational

Membership: Jewish women, supporters, and partners in the United States and Canada. Interests include empowerment of women and girls, ending domestic and sexual violence, financial literacy and economic security, and highlighting women's leadership at multigenerational intersections.

National Organization for Women (NOW), *1100 H St. N.W., #300, 20005; (202) 628-8669. Christian F. Nunes, President.*
General email, info@now.org

Web, https://now.org and Twitter, @NationalNOW

Membership: women and men interested in feminist civil rights. Uses traditional and nontraditional forms of political activism, including nonviolent civil disobedience, to improve the status of all women regardless of age, income, sexual orientation, or race. Maintains liaisons with counterpart organizations worldwide.

National Partnership for Women and Families, *1875 Connecticut Ave. N.W., #650, 20009-5731; (202) 986-2600. Fax, (202) 986-2539. Jocelyn Frye, President.*
General email, info@nationalpartnership.org

Web, www.nationalpartnership.org

Advocacy organization that promotes reproductive health and rights, access to affordable health care, and policies that create equal opportunities for women and families. Publishes and disseminates information in print and on the Web to heighten awareness of work and family issues. Monitors legislative activity and pending Supreme Court cases and argues on behalf of family issues before Congress and in the courts.

National Women's Law Center, *11 Dupont Circle N.W., #800, 20036; (202) 588-5180. Fax, (202) 588-5185. Fatima Goss Graves, President. Legal help, (202) 319-3053. General email, info@nwlc.org*

Web, www.nwlc.org, Twitter, @nwlc and Facebook, www .facebook.com/nwlc

Works to expand and protect women's legal rights through advocacy and public education. Interests include reproductive rights, health, education, employment, income security, and family support.

YWCA USA, *1400 Eye St. 19th St., #325, 20036; (202) 467-0801. Fax, (202) 467-0802. Margaret Mitchell, Chief Executive Officer.*
General email, info@ywca.org

Web, www.ywca.org, Twitter, @ywcausa and Facebook, www.facebook.com/ywca.org

Strives to empower women and girls and to eliminate racism. Provides services and programs concerning child care and youth development, economic empowerment, global awareness, health and fitness, housing and shelter, leadership development, racial justice and human rights, and violence prevention. (YWCA stands for Young Women's Christian Association.)

CONSTITUTIONAL LAW AND CIVIL LIBERTIES

General

▶**AGENCIES**

Justice Dept. (DOJ), *Legal Counsel (OLC), 950 Pennsylvania Ave. N.W., #5218, 20530-0001; (202) 514-2051. Fax, (202) 514-0539. Christopher H. Schroeder, Assistant Attorney General.*
Web, www.justice.gov/olc

Advises the attorney general, the president, and executive agencies on questions regarding constitutional law.

U.S. Commission on Civil Rights, *1331 Pennsylvania Ave. N.W., #1150, 20425; (202) 376-7700. Norma V. Cantu, Chair. Press, (202) 376-8359. TTY, (202) 376-8116. General email, publicaffairs@usccr.gov*

Web, www.usccr.gov, Twitter, @USCCRgov, Facebook, www.facebook.com/USCCRgov and Civil rights complaints, referrals@usccr.gov

Assesses federal laws, policies, and legal developments to determine the nature and extent of denial of equal protection under the law on the basis of race, color, religion, sex, national origin, age, or disability in employment, voting rights, education, administration of justice, and housing. Issues reports and makes recommendations to the president and Congress; serves as national clearinghouse for civil rights information; receives civil rights complaints and refers them to the appropriate federal agency for action. Library open to the public.

►CONGRESS

For a listing of relevant congressional committees and sub-committees, please see pages 546–547 or the Appendix.

►JUDICIARY

Supreme Court of the United States, *1 1st St. N.E., 20543; (202) 479-3000. John G. Roberts Jr., Chief Justice. Public Information Office, (202) 479-3211. TTY, (202) 479-3472. Visitor information, (202) 479-3030.*
Web, www.supremecourt.gov and Contact Form, www.supremecourt.gov/contact/contact_pio.aspx

Highest appellate court in the federal judicial system. Interprets the U.S. Constitution, federal legislation, and treaties. Provides information on new cases filed, the status of pending cases, and admissions to the Supreme Court Bar. Library open to Supreme Court Bar members only.

►NONGOVERNMENTAL

American Civil Liberties Union (ACLU), *Washington Legislative Office, 915 15th St. N.W., 2nd Floor, 20005; (202) 457-0800. David Cole, National Legal Director.*
General email, info@acludc.org
Web, www.aclu.org/legiupdate, Twitter, @ACLU_DC and Facebook, www.facebook.com/aclu.dc

Seeks to protect constitutional rights and civil liberties of citizens, including federal employees of the District of Columbia. Focuses on minority and women's rights, gay and lesbian rights, and privacy; supports legalized abortion, opposes government-sponsored school prayer and legislative restrictions on television content. Interests include First Amendment rights, privacy, and due process. Washington office monitors legislative and regulatory activities and public policy. (Headquarters in New York maintains docket of cases.)

American Constitution Society, *1899 L St. N.W., #200, 20036; (202) 393-6181. Fax, (202) 393-6189. Russ Feingold, President.*
General email, info@acslaw.org
Web, www.acslaw.org, Twitter, @acslaw, Facebook, www.facebook.com/acslaw and YouTube, www.youtube.com/c/AcslawOrg

National association of lawyers, law students, judges, legal scholars, and policymakers that promotes a progressive vision of constitutional law and public policy. Produces issue briefs and publications. Organizes lectures, conferences, seminars, and two annual student competitions.

Center for Democracy and Technology, *1401 K St. N.W., #200, 20005; (202) 637-9800. Alexandra Reeve Givens, President. Press, (202) 407-8811.*
General email, info@cdt.org
Web, https://cdt.org, Twitter, @CenDemTech, Press, press@cdt.org and Facebook, www.facebook.com/CenDemTech

Promotes civil liberties and democratic values in computer and communications media, both in the United States and abroad. Interests include free speech, privacy, and open access to the Internet. Monitors legislation and regulations.

Center for Individual Rights, *1100 Connecticut Ave. N.W., #625, 20036; (202) 833-8400. Fax, (202) 833-8410. Terence (Terry) J. Pell, President.*
General email, cir@cir-usa.org
Web, www.cir-usa.org and Twitter, @CIRights

Public interest law firm that provides free representation to individuals who cannot afford adequate legal counsel in cases raising constitutional questions of individual rights. Interests include freedom of speech and religious expression, civil rights, and Congress's enumerated powers.

The Constitution Project (POGO), *1100 13th St. N.W., #800, 20005; (202) 347-1122. Fax, (202) 347-1116. Danielle Brian, Executive Director.*
General email, info@pogo.org
Web, https://pogo.org/the-constitution-project

Think tank, affiliated with the Project on Government Oversight, that brings together policy experts and legal practitioners from across the political and ideological spectrum to address current constitutional challenges. Interests include checks and balances, counterterrorism policies and practices, criminal discovery, data collection and privacy, the death penalty, DNA collection, government surveillance and searches, immigration, right to counsel, sentencing, and transparency and accountability. Hosts discussions and online forums; issues written reports and press releases.

Constitutional Accountability Center, *1200 18th St. N.W., #501, 20036; (202) 296-6889. Elizabeth B. Wydra, President. Information, ext. 302.*
General email, kco@theusconstitution.org
Web, https://theusconstitution.org, Twitter, @MyConstitution and Facebook, www.facebook.com/ConstitutionAccountability

Nonprofit think tank, law firm, and advocacy group that supports Constitutional rights and freedoms by working with courts, the government, and academic professionals. Publishes books and reports on Constitutional issues. Manages cases related to Constitutional law. Interests include civil rights, citizenship, corporations, and the environment.

Electronic Privacy Information Center (EPIC), *1519 New Hampshire Ave. N.W., 20036; (202) 483-1140. Fax, (202) 483-1248. Alan Butler, Executive Director.*
General email, info@epic.org
Web, https://epic.org and Twitter, @EPICprivacy

Public interest research center. Conducts research and conferences on domestic and international civil liberties issues, including privacy, free speech, information access, computer security, and encryption; litigates cases. Monitors legislation and regulations. Operates an online bookstore.

Ethics and Public Policy Center, *1730 M St. N.W., #910, 20036; (202) 682-1200. Fax, (202) 408-0632. Ryan T. Anderson, President.*
General email, ethics@eppc.org
Web, www.eppc.org, Twitter, @EPPCdc and Facebook, www.facebook.com/EPPC.org

Examines current issues of jurisprudence, especially those relating to constitutional interpretation.

Freedom Forum Institute, *First Amendment Center, 9893 Brewers Court, Laurel, MD 20001; Lata Nott, Executive Director. Press, (202) 292-6200.*
General email, firstamendmentcenter@newseum.org
Web, www.firstamendmentcenter.org and Facebook, www.facebook.com/firstamendmentcenter

Provides educational resources about First Amendment freedoms. Serves as a nonpartisan forum for the study and exploration of free-expression issues, including freedom of speech, the press, religion, and the rights to assemble and to petition the government. Co-sponsors the Religious Freedom Education Project. The center is an operating program of the Freedom Forum and is associated with the Diversity Institute and has offices in the John Seigenthaler Center at Vanderbilt University in Nashville, Tenn.

Institute for Justice, *901 N. Glebe Rd., #900, Arlington, VA 22203; (703) 682-9320. Fax, (703) 682-9321. Scott G. Bullock, President.*
General email, general@ij.org
Web, www.ij.org, Twitter, @IJ and Facebook, www.facebook.com/instituteforjustice

Sponsors seminars to train law students, grassroots activists, and practicing lawyers in applying advocacy strategies in public-interest litigation. Seeks to protect individuals from arbitrary government interference in free speech, private property rights, parental school choice, and economic liberty. Litigates cases.

National Organization for Women (NOW), *1100 H St. N.W., #300, 20005; (202) 628-8669. Christian F. Nunes, President.*
General email, info@now.org
Web, https://now.org and Twitter, @NationalNOW

Membership: women and men interested in civil rights for women. Works to end discrimination based on gender, to preserve abortion rights, and to pass an equal rights amendment to the Constitution.

Open Society Foundations (OSF), *Washington Office, 1730 Pennsylvania Ave. N.W., 7th Floor, 20006; (202) 721-5600. Fax, (202) 530-0128. Thomas Perriello, Executive Director.*
Web, www.opensocietyfoundations.org, Twitter, @OpenSociety, Facebook, www.facebook.com/OpenSocietyFoundations and Press, media@opensocietyfoundations.org

Addresses violations of civil liberties in the United States and around the world. Interests include criminal and civil justice reform educatiuon, global economic policies, and human and women's rights, information and digital rights and democratic practices. (Headquarters in New York. Affiliated with the Soros Foundation Network.)

Abortion and Reproductive Issues

▶**NONGOVERNMENTAL**

Catholics for Choice, *1436 U St. N.W., #301, 20009-3997; (202) 986-6093. Jamie L. Manson, President.*
General email, cfc@catholicsforchoice.org
Web, www.catholicsforchoice.org, Twitter, @Catholic4Choice and Facebook, www.facebook.com/CatholicsforChoice

Works to change church positions and public policies that limit individual freedom, particularly those related to sexuality and reproduction. Provides the public, policymakers, and groups working for change with information and analysis.

Center for Law and Religious Freedom, *8001 Braddock Rd., #302, Springfield, VA 22151; (703) 642-1070. Kimberlee Wood Colby, Director, ext. 401.*
General email, clshq@clsnet.org
Web, www.clsreligiousfreedom.org

Provides legal assistance and advocacy on antiabortion and religious-freedom issues. Monitors legislation and regulations. (Affiliated with the Christian Legal Society.)

Feminists for Life of America, *P.O. Box 151567, Alexandria, VA 22315; Serrin M. Foster, President.*
General email, info@feministsforlife.org
Web, www.feministsforlife.org, Facebook, www.facebook.com/FeministsForLife and Twitter, @Feminists4Life

Membership: women and men who are against abortion and in favor of feminism. Opposes abortion, euthanasia, and capital punishment; seeks to redress economic and social conditions that cause women to choose abortion.

March for Life Education and Defense Fund, *1012 14th St. N.W., #300, 20005; Jeanne F. Mancini, President. Phone, Defense Fund, (202) 234-3300.*
General email, info@marchforlife.org
Web, www.marchforlife.org, Twitter, @March_for_Life and Facebook, www.facebook.com/marchforlife

Membership: individuals and organizations that support government action prohibiting abortion. Sponsors annual march in Washington each January 22. Monitors legislation and regulations.

U.S. Courts

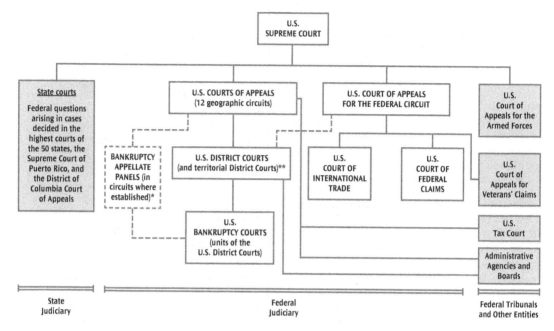

* Authorized to hear appeals from bankruptcy courts that would have otherwise been heard by the U.S. Court of Appeals

** Some U.S. District Court decisions can be appealed to the Federal Circuit

NARAL Pro-Choice America, *1725 Eye St. N.W., #900, 20006; (202) 973-3000. Fax, (202) 973-3096. Mini Timmaraju, President. Press, ext. 2. Web, www.prochoiceamerica.org, Twitter, @NARAL and Facebook, www.facebook.com/naralprochoiceamerica*

Membership: persons who support using the political process to guarantee women a range of reproductive choices, including preventing unintended pregnancy, bearing healthy children, and choosing legal abortion; promotes paid parental leave. (Formerly National Abortion and Reproductive Rights Action League.)

National Abortion Federation (NAF), *1090 Vermont Ave. N.W., #1000, 20005; (202) 667-5881. Fax, (202) 667-5890. Katherine Hancock Ragsdale, President. Hotline, (800) 772-9100. General email, naf@prochoice.org Web, www.prochoice.org, Twitter, @NatAbortionFed and Facebook, www.facebook.com/nationalabortionfederation*

Membership: abortion providers. Seeks to ensure that abortion is safe, legal, and accessible.

National Committee for a Human Life Amendment, *P.O. Box 34116, 20043; (240) 478-0794. Brian Duggan, Executive Director. General email, info@nchla.org Web, www.humanlifeaction.org, Twitter, @HumanLifeAction, Facebook, www.facebook.com/ HumanLifeAction and YouTube, www.youtube.com/ channel/UC6O48FsOPH8quhpMGBtQb7A*

Supports legislation and a constitutional amendment prohibiting abortion.

National Organization for Women (NOW), *1100 H St. N.W., #300, 20005; (202) 628-8669. Christian F. Nunes, President. General email, info@now.org Web, https://now.org and Twitter, @NationalNOW*

Membership: women and men interested in civil rights for women. Works to preserve abortion rights.

National Right to Life Committee, *1446 Duke St., Alexandria, VA 22314; (202) 626-8800. Fax, (202) 737-9189. Carol Tobias, President. Press, (202) 626-8825. General email, nrlc@nrlc.org Web, www.nrlc.org, Press, mediarelations@nrlc.org and Twitter, @nrlc*

Association of fifty state right-to-life organizations. Opposes abortion, infanticide, and euthanasia; supports legislation prohibiting abortion except when the life of the mother is endangered. Operates an information clearinghouse and speakers bureau. Monitors legislation and regulations.

National Women's Health Network, *1413 K St. N.W., 4th Floor, 20005; (202) 682-2640. Fax, (202) 682-2648. Denys Symonette Mitchell, Director Public Policy. General email, nwhn@nwhn.org Web, www.nwhn.org, Twitter, @TheNWHN, Facebook, www.facebook.com/TheNWHN and Health questions, healthquestions@nwhn.org*

Advocacy organization interested in women's health. Seeks to preserve legalized abortion; monitors legislation and regulations; testifies before Congress.

Religious Coalition for Reproductive Choice, *1413 K St. N.W., 14th Floor, 20005; (202) 628-7700. Fax, (202) 628-7716. Rev. Katey Zeh, Chief Executive Officer.*
General email, info@rcrc.org
Web, https://rcrc.org, Twitter, @RCRChoice and Facebook, www.facebook.com/RCRChoice

Coalition of religious groups favoring birth control, sexuality education, and access to legal abortion. Opposes constitutional amendments and federal and state legislation restricting access to abortion services in most cases. Monitors legislation and regulations.

U.S. Conference of Catholic Bishops (USCCB), *Secretariat of Pro-Life Activities, 3211 4th St. N.E., 20017-1194; (202) 541-3070. Tom Grenchik, Executive Director.*
General email, prolife@usccb.org
Web, www.usccb.org/prolife

Provides information on the position of the Roman Catholic Church on abortion. Monitors legislation on abortion, embryonic stem-cell research, human cloning, and related issues. Promotes alternatives to abortion.

Claims Against the Government

▶**AGENCIES**

Civil Division *(Justice Dept.),* **Commercial Litigation (OCL),** *National Courts, 1100 L St. N.W., #10000, 20530; (202) 514-7300. Fax, (202) 307-0972. Robert E. Kirschman Jr., Director.*
Web, www.justice.gov/civil/national-courts-section-0

Represents the United States before the U.S. Court of Federal Claims, U.S. Court of Appeals for the Federal Circuit, and the U.S. Court of International Trade. Practice areas include government contracts, constitutional claims, government pay and personnel appeals, veterans benefits appeals, and international trade matters.

Civil Division *(Justice Dept.),* **Torts Branch, Aviation, Space, and Admiralty Litigation,** *175 N St N.E., 8th Floor, 20002 (mailing address: P.O. Box 14271, Washington, DC 20044-4271); (202) 616-4100. Fax, (202) 616-4002. Barry Benson, Director.*
Web, www.justice.gov/aviation-space-admirality-litigation-section

Represents the federal government in civil suits concerning the maritime industry and aviation and admiralty incidents and accidents.

Environment and Natural Resources Division *(Justice Dept.), 950 Pennsylvania Ave. N.W., #2143, 20530-0001; (202) 514-2701. Fax, (202) 514-5331. Todd Kim, Assistant Attorney General. Press, (202) 514-2007.*
General email, webcontentmgr.enrd@usdoj.gov
Web, www.justice.gov/enrd

Supreme Court Justices

CHIEF JUSTICE
John G. Roberts Jr.
Appointed chief justice by President George W. Bush, sworn in Sept. 29, 2005.

ASSOCIATE JUSTICES
In order of appointment

Clarence Thomas
Appointed by President George H. W. Bush, sworn in Oct. 23, 1991.

Stephen G. Breyer
Appointed by President Bill Clinton, sworn in Aug. 3, 1994.

Samuel A. Alito Jr.
Appointed by President George W. Bush, sworn in Jan. 31, 2006.

Sonia Sotomayor
Appointed by President Barack Obama, sworn in Aug. 8, 2009.

Elena Kagan
Appointed by President Barack Obama, sworn in Aug. 7, 2010.

Neil M. Gorsuch
Appointed by President Donald J. Trump, sworn in Apr. 10, 2017.

Brett M. Kavanaugh
Appointed by President Donald J. Trump, sworn in Oct. 6, 2018.

Amy Coney Barrett
Appointed by President Donald J. Trump, sworn in Oct. 27, 2020.

Represents the United States in the U.S. Court of Federal Claims in cases arising from acquisition of property, Indian rights and claims, and environmental challenges to federal programs and activities.

Environment and Natural Resources Division *(Justice Dept.),* **Indian Resources (IRS),** *150 M St. N.E., #3.1142, 20002 (mailing address: P.O. Box 7611, L'Enfant Plaza, Washington, DC 20044); (202) 305-0269. Fax, (202) 305-0275. S. Craig Alexander, Chief.*
Web, www.justice.gov/enrd/Indian-resources-section

Represents the United States in suits, including trust violations, brought on behalf of individual Native Americans and Native American tribes against the government.

State Dept., *Office of the Legal Adviser, International Claims and Investment Disputes, 2430 E St. N.W., SA-O4A #207, 20520; (202) 776-8325. Fax, (202) 776-8389. Lisa J. Grosh, Assistant Legal Adviser.*
Web, www.state.gov/bureaus-offices/secretary-of-state/office-of-the-legal-adviser/international-claims-and-investment-disputes

Handles claims by U.S. government and citizens against foreign governments, as well as claims by foreign governments and their nationals against the U.S. government; negotiates international claims agreements. Handles claims against the State Dept. for negligence (under the Federal Tort Claims Act) and claims by owners of U.S. flag vessels due to illegal seizures by foreign governments in international waters (under the Fishermen's Protective Act).

Tax Division *(Justice Dept.), 950 Pennsylvania Ave. N.W., #4141, 20530-0001; (202) 514-2901. Fax, (202) 514-5479. David A. Hubbert, Deputy Assistant Attorney General.*
Web, www.justice.gov/tax

Represents the United States and its officers in all civil and criminal litigation arising under the internal revenue laws, other than proceedings in the U.S. Tax Court.

► **CONGRESS**

For a listing of relevant congressional committees and subcommittees, please see pages 546–547 or the Appendix.

► **JUDICIARY**

U.S. Court of Federal Claims, *717 Madison Pl. N.W., 20439; (202) 357-6400. Elaine D. Kaplan, Chief Judge; Lisa Reyes, Clerk of the Court.*
Web, www.uscfc.uscourts.gov

Renders judgment on any nontort claims for monetary damages against the United States founded on the Constitution, statutes, government regulations, and government contracts. Examples include compensation for taking of property, claims arising under construction and supply contracts, certain patent cases, cases involving the refund of federal taxes, and statutory claims made by foreign governments against the United States. Hears cases involving Native American claims.

Privacy

► **AGENCIES**

Office of Management and Budget (OMB) *(Executive Office of the President), Information and Regulatory Affairs, 725 17th St. N.W., #10236, 20503; (202) 395-5897. Fax, (202) 395-6102. Dominic J. Mancini, Deputy Administrator; Sharon Block, Associate Administrator.*
Web, www.whitehouse.gov/omb/information-regulatory-affairs

Oversees implementation of the Privacy Act of 1974 and other privacy-related and security-related statutes. Issues guidelines and regulations.

► **CONGRESS**

For a listing of relevant congressional committees and subcommittees, please see pages 546–547 or the Appendix.

► **NONGOVERNMENTAL**

American Library Assn., *Washington Office, 1615 New Hampshire Ave. N.W., 1st Floor, 20009-2520; (202) 628-8410. Fax, (202) 628-8419. Tracie Hall, Executive Director; Alan Inouye, Senior Director for Public Policy and Government Relations. Toll-free, (800) 941-8478.*
General email, alawash@alawash.org
Web, www.ala.org/offices/wo

Works with public interest groups, think tanks, and the private sector to promote privacy rights; opposes government warrantless searches of browser histories. (Headquarters in Chicago, Ill.)

Center for Democracy and Technology, *1401 K St. N.W., #200, 20005; (202) 637-9800. Alexandra Reeve Givens, President. Press, (202) 407-8811.*
General email, info@cdt.org
Web, https://cdt.org, Twitter, @CenDemTech, Press, press@cdt.org and Facebook, www.facebook.com/CenDemTech

Promotes and defends privacy and civil liberties on the Internet. Interests include free expression, social networking and access to the Internet, consumer protection, health information privacy and technology, and government surveillance. Monitors legislation and regulations.

Communications Workers of America (CWA), *501 3rd St. N.W., 20001; (202) 434-1100. Christopher M. Shelton, President.*
Web, https://cwa-union.org and Twitter, @CWAUnion

Membership: telecommunications, broadcast, and printing and publishing workers. Opposes electronic monitoring of productivity, eavesdropping by employers, and misuse of drug and polygraph tests.

Future of Privacy Forum, *1350 Eye St. N.W., #350, 20005; (202) 643-9853. Jules Polonetsky, Chief Executive Officer.*
General email, info@fpf.org
Web, www.fpf.org, Twitter, @futureofprivacy and Facebook, www.facebook.com/FutureofPrivacy

Think tank focusing on privacy leadership and scholarship, advancing principled data practices in support of emerging technologies.; encourages consensus on ethical norms, policies, and practices regarding information and technology privacy.

National Consumers League, *1701 K St. N.W., #1200, 20006; (202) 835-3323. Fax, (202) 835-0747. Sally Greenberg, Executive Director.*
General email, info@nclnet.org
Web, www.nclnet.org and Twitter, @nclnet

Advocacy group concerned with privacy rights of consumers. Interests include credit and financial records, medical records, direct marketing, telecommunications, and workplace privacy.

Privacy Resources

For general information and additional privacy contacts, visit www.identitytheft.gov. See government agencies' individual websites for their privacy policies and freedom of information procedures.

AGENCIES AND CONGRESS

Federal Trade Commission, Identity Theft hotline, (877) 438-4338; www.ftc.gov/idtheft; Privacy Initiatives, www.ftc.gov/privacy-policy

House Judiciary Committee, Subcommittee on the Constitution and Civil Justice, (202) 225-3951; https://judiciary.house.gov

Office of Management and Budget (concerning the Privacy Act), (202) 395-3647; www.fpc.gov/resources/omb

Senate Judiciary Committee, (202) 224-5225 (Majority), (202) 224-7703 (Minority); www.judiciary.senate.gov

Stop Unwanted Robocalls and Texts (888) 382-1222; www.fcc.gov/consumers/guides/stop-unwanted-robocalls-and-texts

U.S. Postal Service, (800) 275-8777; http://about.usps.com/who-we-are/privacy-policy/privacy-policy-highlights.htm

NONGOVERNMENTAL

American Bar Assn., (202) 662-1000; www.americanbar.org/groups/legal_services/flh-home

American Civil Liberties Union, (202) 457-0800; www.aclu.org/issues/privacy-technology

Call for Action, (240) 747-0229; www.callforaction.org

Center for Democracy and Technology, (202) 637-9800; www.cdt.org

Center for Study of Responsive Law, (202) 387-8030; www.csrl.org

Consumer Data Industry Assn., (202) 371-0910; www.cdiaonline.org

Consumer Reports, (202) 462-6262; www.consumerreports.org/cro/index.htm

Direct Marketing Assn., (212) 768-7277; www.thedma.org

Electronic Privacy Information Center, (202) 483-1140; www.epic.org

Health Privacy Project, (202) 637-9800; www.cdt.org/health-privacy

National Consumers League, (202) 835-3323; www.nclnet.org

U.S. Postal Inspection Service, (877) 876-2455; www.uspis.gov

U.S. Public Interest Research Group, (202) 546-9707; www.uspirg.org

Religious Freedom

▶ **AGENCIES**

Health and Human Services Dept. (HHS), *Civil Rights (OCR), Conscience and Religious Freedom Division, 200 Independence Ave. S.W., 20201; (800) 368-1019. Luis Perez, Deputy Director. TTY, (800) 537-7697. General email, OCRMail@hhs.gov*

Web, www.hhs.gov/conscience/index.html

Works to protect and enforce laws and regulations that protect the conscience and the free exercise of religion and prohibit coercion and religious discrimination in HHS-funded or conducted programs and activities.

▶ **NONGOVERNMENTAL**

Americans United for Separation of Church and State, *1310 L St. N.W., #200, 20005; (202) 466-3234. Fax, (202) 466-3353. Rachel Laser, President. General email, americansunited@au.org*

Web, www.au.org and Twitter, @americansunited

Citizens' interest group that opposes government-sponsored prayer in public schools and tax aid for parochial schools.

Becket Fund for Religious Liberty, *1919 Pennsylvania Ave., #400, 20006; (202) 955-0095.*

Fax, (202) 955-0090. Mark Rienzi, President. Press, (202) 349-7226.

Web, www.becketlaw.org, Twitter, @BECKETlaw, Facebook, www.facebook.com/becketlaw and YouTube, www.youtube.com/user/BecketFundVideo

Public interest law firm that promotes freedom of expression for people of all faiths. Works to ensure that people and institutions of all faiths, domestically and abroad, are entitled to a voice in public affairs.

Center for Law and Religious Freedom, *8001 Braddock Rd., #302, Springfield, VA 22151; (703) 642-1070. Kimberlee Wood Colby, Director, ext. 401. General email, clshq@clsnet.org*

Web, www.clsreligiousfreedom.org

Provides legal assistance and advocacy on antiabortion and religious-freedom issues. Monitors legislation and regulations. (Affiliated with the Christian Legal Society.)

Christian Legal Society, *8001 Braddock Rd., #302, Springfield, VA 22151 (mailing address: P.O. Box 7712, McLean, VA 22106-7712); (703) 642-1070. David Nammo, Chief Executive Officer, ext. 501. General email, clshq@clsnet.org*

Web, www.christianlegalsociety.org

Membership: Christian lawyers, judges, paralegals, law professors, law students, and others. Interests include the defense of religious freedom and the provision of legal aid to the poor.

Freedom Forum Institute, *Religious Freedom Center,* *9893 Brewers Court, Laurel, MD, 20723; (202) 292-6293. Charles C. Haynes, Founder.*
General email, religion@freedomforum.org
Web, www.religiousfreedomcenter.org and Twitter, @RelFreedomCenter

Nonpartisan national initiative focused on educating the public about the religious liberty principles of the First Amendment.

International Religious Liberty Assn., *12501 Old Columbia Pike, Silver Spring, MD 20904-6600; (301) 680-6683. Fax, (301) 680-6695. Bettina Krause, Director of Government Affairs.*
General email, info@irla.org
Web, http://irla.org, Twitter, @irla-usa and Facebook, www.facebook.com/irla.hq

Seeks to preserve and expand religious liberty and freedom of conscience; advocates separation of church and state; sponsors international and domestic meetings and congresses.

National Assn. of Evangelicals, *P.O. Box 23269, 20026; (202) 479-0815. Walter Kim, President.*
General email, info@nae.net
Web, www.nae.net, Twitter, @NAEvangelicals and Facebook, www.facebook.com/naevangelicals

Membership: evangelical churches, organizations (including schools), and individuals. Supports religious freedom. Monitors legislation and regulations.

Separation of Powers

▶**NONGOVERNMENTAL**

Public Citizen, *Litigation Group, 1600 20th St. N.W., 20009-1001; (202) 588-1000. Allison Zieve, Director of Litigation.*
General email, litigation@citizen.org
Web, www.citizen.org/topic/justice-the-courts

Conducts litigation for Public Citizen, a citizens' interest group, in cases involving separation of powers; represents individuals and groups with similar interests.

CRIMINAL LAW

General

▶**AGENCIES**

Bureau of International Narcotics and Law Enforcement Affairs (INL) *(State Dept.), Anti-Crime Office, 2401 E St. N.W., #SA-1, L600, 20037; (202) 663-1860. Susan Snyder, Director.*
Web, https://2009-2017.state.gov/j/inl/c/index.htm

Works with international governments to combat international organized crime, high-level corruption, money laundering, terrorist financing, cyber and intellectual property crimes, threats to border security, narcotics trafficking, and other smuggling and trafficking crimes.

Criminal Division *(Justice Dept.), 950 Pennsylvania Ave. N.W., 20530-0001; (202) 353-4641. Kenneth Polite Jr., Assistant Attorney General.*
General email, Criminal.Division@usdoj.gov
Web, www.justice.gov/criminal

Enforces all federal criminal laws except those specifically assigned to the antitrust, civil rights, environment and natural resources, and tax divisions of the Justice Dept. Supervises and directs U.S. attorneys in the field on criminal matters and litigation; supervises international extradition proceedings. Coordinates federal enforcement efforts against white-collar crime, fraud, and child pornography; handles civil actions under customs, liquor, narcotics, gambling, and firearms laws; coordinates enforcement activities against organized crime. Directs the National Asset Forfeiture Program for seizing the proceeds of criminal activity. Investigates and prosecutes criminal offenses involving public integrity and subversive activities, including treason, espionage, and sedition; Nazi war crimes; and related criminal offenses. Handles all civil cases relating to internal security and counsels federal departments and agencies regarding internal security matters. Drafts responses on proposed and pending criminal law legislation.

Criminal Division *(Justice Dept.), Capital Case Section (CCS), 950 Pennsylvania Ave. N.W., 20530; Rich Burns, Chief. Switchboard, (202) 514-2000.*
Web, www.justice.gov/criminal/capital-case-section

Promotes consistency and fairness in the application of the death penalty throughout the United States; provides expertise and resources for federal prosecutors involved with capital cases.

Federal Bureau of Investigation (FBI) *(Justice Dept.), 935 Pennsylvania Ave. N.W., #7176, 20535-0001; (202) 324-3000. Christopher Wray, Director. Press, (202) 324-3691. Toll-free, (800) 225-5324.*
Web, www.fbi.gov, Twitter, @FBI and Facebook, www.facebook.com/FBI

Investigates all violations of federal criminal laws except those assigned specifically to other federal agencies. Exceptions include alcohol, counterfeiting, and tobacco violations (Justice Dept. and Commerce Dept.); customs violations and illegal entry of aliens (Homeland Security Dept.); and postal violations (U.S. Postal Service). Priorities include protecting the United States against terror attacks; protecting civil rights; combating public corruption at all levels, transnational/national criminal organizations and enterprises, white-collar crime, and significant violent crime; and supporting federal, state, local, and international partners. Services to other law enforcement agencies include fingerprint identifications, laboratory services, police training, and access to the National Crime

Information Center (a communications network among federal, state, and local police agencies).

Federal Bureau of Investigation (FBI) *(Justice Dept.)*, *Criminal Investigative Division (CID)*, *935 Pennsylvania Ave. N.W., 20535; (202) 324-4260. Fax, (202) 324-0027. Jay Greenberg, Assistant Director (Acting).*
Web, www.fbi.gov/investigate/violent-crime

Investigates mass killings, sniper murders, serial killings, criminal street gangs, crimes against children, child prostitution, bank robberies and other violent robberies, carjackings, kidnappings, fugitives and missing persons, jewelry and gem theft, crimes on Native American reservations, active shooters, and assaults and threats of assault on the president and other federal officials.

Federal Bureau of Investigation (FBI) *(Justice Dept.)*, *Critical Incident Response Group (CIRG), Strategic Information and Operations Center (SIOC), 935 Pennsylvania Ave. N.W., 20535; (703) 632-4100. Fax, (202) 323-2212. Paul H. Haertel, Assistant Director. Press, (202) 324-3691. Toll-free, (877) 324-6324.*
General email, sioc@ic.fbi.gov

Web, www.fbi.gov.services/cirg/sioc

Serves as a twenty-four-hour crisis management and information processing center. Coordinates initial and crisis response investigations of violations of federal law relating to terrorism, sabotage, espionage, treason, sedition, and other matters affecting national security.

Office of Justice Programs (OJP) *(Justice Dept.)*, *National Institute of Justice (NIJ), 810 7th St. N.W., 7th Floor, 20531; (202) 307-2942. Fax, (202) 307-6394. Jennifer Scherer, Director (Acting). Press, (202) 307-0703.*
General email, ojp.ocom@usdoj.gov

Web, www.nij.gov and Facebook, www.facebook.com/OJPNIJ

Conducts research on all aspects of criminal justice, including crime prevention, enforcement, adjudication, and corrections; evaluates programs; develops model programs using new techniques. Serves as an affiliated institute of the United Nations Crime Prevention and Criminal Justice Program (UNCPCJ); studies transnational issues, especially within the Western Hemisphere. Maintains the National Criminal Justice Reference Service, which provides information on criminal justice research topics, including community policing, faith-based initiatives, self-protection, gang crime, hate crime, property crime, terrorism, human trafficking, and violent crime: (800) 851-3420; international callers, (202) 836-6998; Web, www.ncjrs.gov. Sponsors the National Missing and Unidentified Persons System, a clearinghouse for missing persons and unidentified decedent records: http://NamUs.gov.

►CONGRESS

For a listing of relevant congressional committees and sub-committees, please see pages 546–547 or the Appendix.

►INTERNATIONAL ORGANIZATIONS

INTERPOL Washington *(Justice Dept.)*, *950 Pennsylvania Ave. N.W., 20530-0001; (202) 616-9000. Fax, (202) 616-8400. Michael A. Hughes, Director.*
Web, www.justice.gov/interpol-washington and Twitter, @INTERPOL_USA

U.S. representative to INTERPOL; participates in international investigations on behalf of U.S. police; coordinates the exchange of investigative information on crimes, including drug trafficking, counterfeiting, missing persons, and terrorism. Coordinates law enforcement requests for investigative assistance in the United States and abroad. Assists with extradition processes. Serves as liaison between foreign and U.S. law enforcement agencies at federal, state, and local levels. (Headquarters in Lyons, France.)

►NONGOVERNMENTAL

American Bar Assn. (ABA), *Criminal Justice, 1050 Connecticut Ave. N.W., #400, 20036; (202) 662-1500. Fax, (202) 662-1501. Kevin Scruggs, Director, (202) 662-1503.*
General email, crimjustice@americanbar.org

Web, www.americanbar.org/groups/criminal_justice, Twitter, @ABACJS and Facebook, www.facebook.com/ABACJS

Responsible for all matters pertaining to criminal law and procedure for the association. Studies and makes recommendations on all facets of the criminal and juvenile justice systems, including sentencing, juries, pretrial procedures, grand juries, and white-collar crime. Publishes *Criminal Justice Magazine*. (Headquarters in Chicago, Ill.)

Justice Research and Statistics Assn., *1000 Vermont Ave. N.W., #450, 20005; (202) 842-9330. Fax, (202) 304-1417. Jeffrey Sedgwick, Executive Director.*
General email, cjinfo@jrsa.org

Web, www.jrsa.org and Twitter, @JRSAinfo

Promotes nonpartisan research and analysis to inform criminal and juvenile justice policy and decisionmaking. Disseminates policy- and justice-related research and information to the justice community, and convenes informational seminars on new research, programs, and technologies.

National Crime Prevention Council, *1100 15th St. N.W., 4th Floor, 20005; (202) 919-4222. Paul DelPonte, Executive Director.*
Web, www.ncpc.org, Twitter, @McGruffatNCPC and Facebook, www.facebook.com/McGruff

Educates public on crime prevention through media campaigns, supporting materials, and training workshops; sponsors McGruff public service campaign; runs demonstration programs in schools.

National Criminal Justice Assn., *720 7th St. N.W., 3rd Floor, 20001; (202) 628-8550. Chris Asplen, Executive Director, (202) 448-1712.*

General email, info@ncja.org

Web, www.ncja.org, Twitter, @thencja and Facebook, www.facebook.com/thencja

Membership: criminal and juvenile justice organizations and professionals. Provides federal, state, local, and tribal justice agencies with technical assistance and information, including crime prevention and crime control issues. Assists criminal justice agencies in development and implementation of criminal justice policy.

Child Abuse, Domestic Violence, and Sexual Assault

▶**AGENCIES**

Air Force Dept. *(Defense Dept.), Sexual Assault Prevention and Response (SAPR) (AF/CVS),* 220 Brookley Ave., Bldg 4. JBAB, 20032; Amy Nowak, Coordinator. 24/7 AF SAPR Capitol-region hotline, (202) 767-7272. DoD safe helpline, (877) 995-5247. General Email, 11wg.cvs.sarc_sapr@us.af.mil and Web, www.resilience.af.mil/SAPR

Works to eliminate the occurrence of sexual assault in the Air Force, and acts as advocate for recovery and prevention.

Criminal Division *(Justice Dept.), Child Exploitation and Obscenity Section (CEOS),* 1400 New York Ave. N.W., 6th Floor, 20005; (202) 514-5780. Steven J. Grocki, Chief. Web, www.justice.gov/criminal-ceos

Enforces federal child exploitation, obscenity, and pornography laws; prosecutes cases involving violations of these laws, including international trafficking and kidnapping. Maintains collection of briefs, pleadings, and other material for use by federal, state, and local prosecutors. Assists the U.S. Attorney's Office with investigations, trials, and appeals pertaining to these offenses. Advises and trains law enforcement personnel, federal prosecutors, and Justice Dept. officials.

Criminal Division *(Justice Dept.), Child Exploitation and Obscenity Section (CEOS), Project Safe Childhood,* 810 7th St. N.W., 20531; (202) 514-5780. Steven J. Grocki. General email, AskDOJ@usdoj.gov

Web, www.justice.gov/criminal-ceos and Project Safe Childhood, www.justice.gov/psc

Combines law enforcement efforts, community action, and public awareness to combat child exploitation, particularly in regard to child pornography, online enticement, child sex tourism, commercial sexual exploitation, and sexual exploitation in Indian Country. Offers resources and publications.

Criminal Division *(Justice Dept.), Organized Crime and Gang Section (OCGS),* 1301 New York Ave. N.W., #700, 20005; (202) 514-3594. David L. Jaffe, Chief. Labor Unit, (202) 514-3954. Litigation Unit, (202) 514-8405. RICO Review Unit, (202) 514-1214 or (202) 514-1215. Web, www.justice.gov/criminal-ocgs

Maintains responsibility over all domestic violent crime–related statutes within the U.S. code.

Defense Dept. (DoD), *Sexual Assault Prevention and Response,* 4800 Mark Center Dr., #07G21, Alexandria, VA 22350; (571) 372-2657. Maj. Gen. Clement S. Coward (USA), Director. Hotline, (877) 995-5247. General email, whs.mc-alex.wso.mbx.SAPRO@mail.mil Web, www.sapr.mil

Serves as the single point of accountability for the Defense Dept.'s sexual assault policy. Responsible for improving prevention, enhancing reporting and response, and holding perpetrators appropriately accountable.

Justice Dept. (DOJ), *Elder Justice Initiative (EJI),* 950 Pennsylvania Ave. N.W., 20530; Andy Mao, Coordinator, (202) 616-0539. Eldercare locator helpline, (800) 677-1116. General email, elder.justice@usdoj.gov

Web, www.justice.gov/elderjustice and Rural and tribal resources, www.justice.gov/elderjustice/rural-and-tribal-resources

Coordinates the department's elder justice efforts, including law enforcement actions against nursing homes that provide substandard services to Medicare and Medicaid beneficiaries; develops resources and information to enhance federal, state, and local efforts to prevent and combat elder abuse, neglect, and financial exploitation.

Justice Dept. (DOJ), *Violence Against Women (OVW),* 145 N St. N.E., #10W.121, 20530; (202) 307-6026. Fax, (202) 305-2589. Nadine M. Neufville, Director (Acting). National Domestic Violence Hotline, 800-799-SAFE. National Sexual Assault Hotline, 800-656-HOPE. National Teen Dating Abuse Hotline, (800) 331-9474. National Victims of Crime Hotline, 855-4-VICTIM. TTY, (202) 307-2277. General email, ovw.info@usdoj.gov

Web, www.justice.gov/ovw and Twitter, @OVWJustice

Seeks more effective policies and services to combat domestic violence, sexual assault, stalking, and other crimes against women. Helps administer grants to states to fund shelters, crisis centers, and hotlines, and to hire law enforcement officers, prosecutors, and counselors specializing in cases of sexual violence and other violent crimes against women.

Office of Justice Programs (OJP) *(Justice Dept.), National Institute of Justice (NIJ),* 810 7th St. N.W., 7th Floor, 20531; (202) 307-2942. Fax, (202) 307-6394. Jennifer Scherer, Director (Acting). Press, (202) 307-0703. General email, ojp.ocom@usdoj.gov

Web, www.nij.gov and Facebook, www.facebook.com/OJPNIJ

Conducts research on all aspects of criminal justice, including AIDS issues for law enforcement officials. Studies on rape and domestic violence available from the National Criminal Justice Reference Service: (800) 851-3420; in Maryland, (301) 519-5500; Web, www.ncjrs.gov.

Office of Justice Programs (OJP) *(Justice Dept.), Sex Offender Sentencing, Monitoring, Apprehending, Registering, and Tracking (SMART),* 810 7th St. N.W.,

20531; (202) 514-4689. Fax, (202) 616-2906. Dawn Doran, Director (Acting).

General email, AskSMART@usdoj.gov

Web, www.smart.gov, Twitter, @DOJSMART and Facebook, www.facebook.com/DOJSMART

Administers the standards for the Sex Offender Registration and Notification Program. Administers grant programs, including those relating to sex offender registration and notification. Works with and provides technical assistance to states, principal U.S. territories, local governments, tribal governments, and other public and private entities involved in activities related to sex offender registration or notification or to other measures for the protection of children or other members of the public from sexual abuse or exploitation.

▶NONGOVERNMENTAL

American Bar Assn. (ABA), Center on Children and the Law, 1050 Connecticut Ave. N.W., #400, 20036; (202) 662-1720. Prudence Beidler Carr, Director.

General email, ctrchildlaw@americanbar.org

Web, www.americanbar.org/groups/public_interest/child_law, Twitter, @ABACCL and Facebook, www.facebook.com/abaCCL

Provides state and private child welfare organizations with training and technical assistance. Interests include child abuse and neglect, adoption, foster care, and medical neglect.

Maryland Network Against Domestic Violence (MNADV), 4601 Presidents Dr., #300, Lanham, MD 20706; (301) 429-3601. Jennifer (Jenn) Pollitt Hill, Executive Director (Acting). 24-hour hotline, (800) 799-7233.

General email, info@mnadv.org

Web, www.mnadv.org, Twitter, @MNADV and Facebook, www.facebook.com/marylandnetwork

Maryland's state domestic violence coalition that encourages collaboration between victim service providers, allied professionals, and interested individuals to reduce intimate partner and family violence. Provides information and written and oral testimony to legislators, and monitors bills related to domestic violence.

National Alliance to End Sexual Violence (NAESV), 655 15th St., N.W. #800, 20005; (202) 869-8520. Terri Poore, Policy Director.

General email, info@endsexualviolence.org

Web, www.endsexualviolence.org, Twitter, @endsxlviolence and Facebook, www.facebook.com/endsxlviolence

Coalition of allied national level antiviolence organizations. Acts as an advocate for sexual abuse and sexual violence victims; educates policymakers about federal laws and legislation impacting the efforts to end sexual violence; publishes analysis, tracks legislation, and advises the federal government on matters of sexual violence.

National Center for Missing and Exploited Children, 333 John Carlyle St., #125, Alexandria, VA 22314-5950; (703) 224-2150. Fax, (703) 224-2122. John F. Clark, Chief Executive Officer. Toll-free hotline, (800) 843-5678.

General email, media@ncmec.org

Web, www.missingkids.com, Twitter, @MissingKids, Facebook, www.facebook.com/MissingKids and YouTube, www.youtube.com/missingkids

Private organization that assists parents and citizens' groups in locating and safely returning missing children; offers technical assistance to law enforcement agencies; coordinates public and private missing children programs; maintains database that coordinates information on missing children.

National Coalition Against Domestic Violence, Public Policy, 1130 3rd St. N.E., 2nd Floor, 20002; (202) 714-7662. Rachel Graber, Director of Public Policy. National Domestic Violence Hotline, (800) 799-7233. TTY, (800) 787-3224.

General email, publicpolicy@ncadv.org

Web, www.ncadv.org, Twitter, @NCADV and Facebook, www.facebook.com/NationalCoalitionAgainst DomesticViolence

Monitors legislation and public policy initiatives concerning victims and survivors of domestic violence. Work includes empowering victims, promoting and coordinating direct services, and educating the public about domestic violence. Offers the Cosmetic & Reconstructive Support Program to survivors. (Headquarters in Denver, Colo.)

National Network to End Domestic Violence (NNEDV), 1325 Massachusetts Ave. N.W., 7th Floor, 20005; (202) 543-5566. Fax, (202) 543-5626. Deborah J. Vagins, President. National Domestic Violence Hotline, (800) 799-7233. TTY, (800) 787-3224.

Web, www.nnedv.org and Twitter, @nnedv

Represents state domestic violence coalitions at the federal level. Acts as advocate for stronger legislation against domestic violence.

Rape, Abuse, and Incest National Network (RAINN), 1220 L St. N.W., #505, 20005; (202) 544-1034. Fax, (202) 544-3556. Scott Berkowitz, President. National Sexual Assault hotline, (800) 656-4673. Press, (202) 544-5537.

Web, www.rainn.org, Twitter, @RAINN and Facebook, www.facebook.com/RAINN01

Links sexual assault victims to confidential local services through national sexual assault hotline. Operates the Defense Dept.'s sexual assault helpline. Provides extensive public outreach and education programs nationwide on sexual assault prevention, prosecution, and recovery. Promotes national policy efforts to improve services to victims.

Stop Child Predators, 5185 MacArthur Blvd., #575, 20016; (202) 248-7052. Fax, (202) 248-4427. Stacie D. Rumenap, President.

General email, info@stopchildpredators.org

Web, www.stopchildpredators.org, Twitter, @StopPredators and Facebook, www.facebook.com/StopChildPred/?ref=bookmark

Advocacy organization that seeks to protect children from crime and hold their victimizers accountable. Works with victims' families, law enforcement, and decision makers to develop effective policies and solutions. Goals include establishing penalty enhancements for those who commit sexual offenses against children and creating an integrated nationwide sex offender registry.

Virginia Sexual And Domestic Violence Action Alliance (VSDVA), *1118 W. Main St., Richmond, VA 23220; (804) 377-0335. Kristi VanAudenhove, Executive Director. Hotline, (800) 838-8238.*
General email, info@vsdvalliance.org
Web, vsdvalliance.org, Twitter, @VActionAlliance and Facebook, www.facebook.com/VActionAlliance

Coalition of rape crisis center and professionals and service providers working with sexual assault survivors. Involved with policy advocacy and technical assistance, and provides training outreach and prevention for attorneys, rape crisis staff, volunteers, and other professionals working with survivors. Acts as advocate for accessible and compassionate care, and works to hold offenders accountable.

Cyber Crime

▶**AGENCIES**

Criminal Division *(Justice Dept.),* **Computer Crime and Intellectual Property Section (CCIPS),** *John C. Keeney Bldg., 10th and Constitution Ave. N.W., #600, 20530; (202) 514-1026. Fax, (202) 514-6113. John Lynch, Chief.*
Web, www.justice.gov/criminal-ccips

Investigates and litigates criminal cases involving computers, intellectual property, and the Internet. Administers the Computer Crime Initiative, a program designed to combat electronic penetrations, data theft, and cyberattacks on critical information systems. Provides specialized technical and legal assistance to other Justice Dept. divisions; coordinates international efforts; formulates policies and proposes legislation on computer crime and intellectual property issues.

Federal Bureau of Investigation (FBI) *(Justice Dept.),* **Cyber Division,** *935 Pennsylvania Ave. N.W., 20535; (202) 324-7770. Fax, (202) 324-2840. Bryan A. Vorndran, Assistant Director.*
Web, www.fbi.gov/investigate/cyber

Coordinates the investigations of federal violations in which the Internet or computer networks are exploited for terrorist, foreign government–sponsored intelligence, or criminal activities, including copyright violations, fraud, pornography, child exploitation, and malicious computer intrusions.

U.S. Immigration and Customs Enforcement (ICE) *(Homeland Security Dept.),* **Cyber Crimes Center (C3),** *500 12th St. S.W., 20536; (703) 293-8005. Peter Buchan, Program Manager. Press, (202) 732-4646.*
Web, www.ice.gov/cyber-crimes

Focuses on the investigation of international Internet crimes, such as money laundering, financing of terrorist activities, child sexual exploitation, human smuggling and trafficking, intellectual property rights violations, identity and document fraud, illegal arms trafficking, and drug trafficking.

U.S. Secret Service *(Homeland Security Dept.),* **Criminal Investigative Division,** *950 H St. N.W., 20001; (202) 406-5708. Jeremy C. Sheridan, Assistant Director.*
Web, www.secretservice.gov/investigation

Plans, reviews, and coordinates criminal investigations involving reports of telecommunications and computer crimes.

Drug Control

▶**AGENCIES**

Criminal Division *(Justice Dept.),* **Narcotic and Dangerous Drug Section (NDDS),** *145 N St. N.E., 20002; (202) 514-2000. Arthur G. Wyatt, Chief.*
Web, www.justice.gov/criminal/ndds

Investigates and prosecutes participants in criminal syndicates involved in the large-scale importation, manufacture, shipment, or distribution of illegal narcotics and other dangerous drugs. Trains agents and prosecutors in the techniques of major drug litigation.

Defense Dept. (DoD), **Counternarcotics and Global Threats,** *2500 Defense Pentagon, #5C653, 20301-2500; (703) 697-7202. Fax, (703) 692-6947.*
Joseph J. McMenamin, Deputy Assistant Secretary (Acting).
Web, https://policy.defense.gov/OUSDP-Offices/Under-Secretary-of-Defense-for-Policy/Counternarcotics-and-Global-Threats

Advises the secretary on Defense Dept. policies and programs in support of federal counternarcotics operations and the implementation of the president's national drug control policy.

Drug Enforcement Administration (DEA) *(Justice Dept.),* *700 Army Navy Dr., Arlington, VA 22202 (mailing address: 8701 Morrissette Dr., MS AES, Springfield, VA 22152); (202) 307-1000. Fax, (202) 307-4540. Anne Milgram, Administrator. D.C. Division office, (202) 305-8500. Public Affairs, (202) 307-7977.*
Web, www.dea.gov

Enforces federal laws and statutes relating to narcotics and other dangerous drugs, including addictive drugs, depressants, stimulants, and hallucinogens; manages the National Narcotics Intelligence System in cooperation with federal, state, and local officials; investigates violations and regulates legal trade in narcotics and dangerous drugs. Provides school and community officials with drug abuse policy guidelines. Provides information on drugs and drug abuse.

Federal Bureau of Investigation (FBI) *(Justice Dept.),* *935 Pennsylvania Ave. N.W., #7176, 20535-0001; (202)*

324-3000. *Christopher Wray, Director. Press, (202) 324-3691. Toll-free, (800) 225-5324.*
Web, www.fbi.gov, Twitter, @FBI and Facebook, www.facebook.com/FBI

Shares responsibility with the Drug Enforcement Administration for investigating violations of federal criminal drug laws; investigates organized crime involvement with illegal narcotics trafficking.

Food and Drug Administration (FDA) *(Health and Human Services Dept.), Center for Drug Evaluation and Research (CDER), White Oak Bldg. 51, 10903 New Hampshire Ave., #6133, Silver Spring, MD 20993; (301) 796-5400. Fax, (301) 595-7910. Patrizia Cavazzoni, Director. Press, (301) 796-3700.*
General email, druginfo@fda.hhs.gov
Web, www.fda.gov/drugs and www.fda.gov/about-fda/fda-organization/center-drug-evaluation-and-research-cder

Makes recommendations to the Justice Dept.'s Drug Enforcement Administration on narcotics and dangerous drugs to be controlled.

Internal Revenue Service (IRS) *(Treasury Dept.), Criminal Investigation, 1111 Constitution Ave. N.W., 20224; (202) 317-3200. James Lee, Chief. Tax fraud hotline, (800) 366-4184. TTY, (800) 877-8339.*
Web, www.irs.gov/compliance/criminal-investigation and Twitter, @IRSnews

Lends support in counterterrorism and narcotics investigations conducted in conjunction with other law enforcement agencies, both foreign and domestic.

National Drug Control Policy (ONDCP) *(Executive Office of the President), 1800 G St. N.W., 20006; (202) 395-6700. Fax, (202) 395-6708. Dr. Rahul Gupta, Director.*
General email, executive_secretariat@ondcp.eop.gov
Web, www.whitehouse.gov/ondcp and Twitter, @ONDCP

Establishes policies and oversees the implementation of a national drug control strategy with the goal of reducing illicit drug use, manufacturing, trafficking, and drug-related crimes, violence, and health consequences. Coordinates the international and domestic antidrug efforts of executive branch agencies and ensures that such efforts sustain and complement state and local antidrug activities. Oversees the National Drug Control Strategy and Budget. Advises the president and the National Security Council on drug control policy. (Clearinghouse address: P.O. Box 6000, Rockville, MD 20849-6000.)

Office of Justice Programs (OJP) *(Justice Dept.), Bureau of Justice Assistance (BJA), 810 7th St. N.W., 4th Floor, 20531; (202) 616-6500. Fax, (202) 305-1367. Kristen Mahoney, Director (Acting). Press, (202) 307-0703.*
General email, askbja@usdoj.gov
Web, www.bja.gov, Facebook, www.facebook.com/DOJBJA and Twitter, @DOJBJA

Awards grants and provides eligible state, local, and tribal governments with training and technical assistance to enforce laws relating to narcotics and other dangerous drugs.

▶**NONGOVERNMENTAL**

Drug Policy Alliance, *National Affairs, 1620 Eye St. N.W., #925, 20006; (202) 683-2030. Fax, (202) 216-0803. Maritza Perez, Director of National Affairs.*
General email, dc@drugpolicy.org
Web, www.drugpolicy.org, Twitter, @DrugPolicyOrg and Facebook, www.facebook.com/drugpolicy

Supports reform of current drug control policy; seeks to broaden debate on drug policy to include considering alternatives to incarceration, expanding lawful maintenance therapies, and restoring constitutional protections; advocates medical treatment to control drug abuse; opposes random drug testing; studies drug policy in other countries. Sponsors the biennial International Conference on Drug Policy Reform. Monitors legislation and regulations. (Headquarters in New York.)

Marijuana Policy Project, *P.O. Box 21824, 20009; (202) 462-5747. Tol Hutchison, President. Press, (202) 462-5747, ext. 8301.*
General email, info@mpp.org
Web, www.mpp.org, Twitter, @MarijuanaPolicy and Facebook, www.facebook.com/MarijuanaPolicyProject

Promotes reform of marijuana policies and regulations. Opposes the prohibition of responsible growing and use of marijuana by adults. Interests include allowing doctors to recommend marijuana to seriously ill patients and eliminating criminal penalties for marijuana use.

National Assn. of State Alcohol and Drug Abuse Directors (NASADAD), *1919 Pennsylvania Ave. N.W., #M250, 20006; (202) 293-0090. Fax, (202) 293-1250. Robert (Rob) Morrison, Executive Director, ext. 4862.*
General email, dcoffice@nasadad.org
Web, http://nasadad.org

Provides information on drug abuse treatment and prevention; contracts with federal and state agencies for design of programs to fight and prevent drug abuse.

National Organization for the Reform of Marijuana Laws (NORML), *1420 K St. N.W., #350, 20005; (202) 483-5500. Erik Altieri, Executive Director; Rick Steves, Chair.*
General email, norml@norml.org
Web, https://norml.org

Works to reform federal, state, and local marijuana laws and policies. Educates the public and conducts litigation on behalf of marijuana consumers. Monitors legislation and regulations.

RAND Corp., *Drug Policy Research Center, Washington Office, 1200 S. Hayes St., Arlington, VA 22202-5050; (703) 413-1100. Fax, (703) 413-8111. Beau Kilmer, Director.*
General email, dprc@rand.org
Web, www.rand.org/well-being/justice-policy/centers/dprc.html

Studies and analyzes the nation's drug problems and policies. Emphasis on empirical research and policy recommendations; interests include international and local policy, trafficking, interdiction, modeling and forecasting, prevention, and treatment. Provides policy-makers with information. (Headquarters in Santa Monica, Calif.)

Environmental Crime

▶ AGENCIES

Environment and Natural Resources Division *(Justice Dept.),* 950 Pennsylvania Ave. N.W., #2143, 20530-0001; (202) 514-2701. Fax, (202) 514-5331. Todd Kim, Assistant Attorney General. Press, (202) 514-2007.
General email, webcontentmgr.enrd@usdoj.gov
Web, www.justice.gov/enrd

Handles civil suits involving the federal government in all areas of the environment and natural resources; handles some criminal suits involving pollution control, wildlife protection, stewardship of public lands, and natural resources.

Environment and Natural Resources Division *(Justice Dept.),* **Environmental Crimes (ECS),** 150 M St. N.E., #4.202, 20002 (mailing address: P.O. Box 7611, Washington, DC 20044); (202) 514-2701.
Deborah L. Harris, Chief.
Web, www.justice.gov/enrd/environmental-crimes-section

Conducts criminal enforcement actions on behalf of the United States for all environmental protection statutes, including air, water, pesticides, hazardous waste, wetland matters investigated by the Environmental Protection Agency, and other criminal environmental enforcement. Supervises criminal cases under federal maritime law and other laws protecting marine fish and mammals. Focuses on smugglers and black market dealers of protected wildlife.

Environment and Natural Resources Division *(Justice Dept.),* **Environmental Defense (EDS),** 150 M St. N.E., #4.1102, 20002 (mailing address: P.O. Box 7611, Washington, DC 20044); (202) 514-2701. Fax, (202) 616-2426. Letitia J. Grishaw, Chief.
Web, www.justice.gov/enrd/environmental-defense-section

Conducts litigation on air, water, noise, pesticides, solid waste, toxic substances, Superfund, and wetlands in cooperation with the Environmental Protection Agency; represents the EPA in suits involving judicial review of EPA actions; represents the U.S. Army Corps of Engineers in cases involving dredge-and-fill activity in navigable waters and adjacent wetlands; represents the Coast Guard in oil and hazardous spill cases; defends all federal agencies in environmental litigation.

Environment and Natural Resources Division *(Justice Dept.),* **Environmental Enforcement (EES),** 150 M St. N.E., #6.202, 20002 (mailing address: P.O. Box 7611, Ben Franklin Station, Washington, DC 20044-7611); (202) 514-2701. Fax, (202) 514-0097. Thomas A. Mariani, Chief.
Web, www.justice.gov/enrd/environmental-enforcement-section

Conducts civil enforcement actions on behalf of the United States for all environmental protection statutes, including air, water, pesticides, hazardous waste, wetland matters investigated by the Environmental Protection Agency, and other civil environmental enforcement.

Environment and Natural Resources Division *(Justice Dept.),* **Indian Resources (IRS),** 150 M St. N.E., #3.1142, 20002 (mailing address: P.O. Box 7611, L'Enfant Plaza, Washington, DC 20044); (202) 305-0269. Fax, (202) 305-0275. S. Craig Alexander, Chief.
Web, www.justice.gov/enrd/Indian-resources-section

Represents the United States in suits, including trust violations, brought on behalf of individual Native Americans and Native American tribes against the government. Also represents the United States as trustee for Native Americans in court actions involving protection of Native American land and resources.

Environment and Natural Resources Division *(Justice Dept.),* **Wildlife and Marine Resources,** 150 M St. N.E., #3.1102, 20002; (202) 305-0210. Fax, (202) 305-0275. Seth M. Barsky, Section Chief.
Web, www.justice.gov/enrd/wildlife-and-marine-resources-section

Responsible for criminal enforcement and civil litigation under federal fish and wildlife conservation statutes, including protection of wildlife, fish, and plant resources within U.S. jurisdiction, and management and restoration of Florida Everglades. Monitors interstate and foreign commerce of these resources.

Environmental Protection Agency (EPA), *Enforcement and Compliance Assurance (OECA), Criminal Enforcement, Forensics, and Training,* 1200 Pennsylvania Ave. N.W., MS 2201A, 20460; (202) 564-2480.
Henry Barnet, Director.
Web, www.epa.gov/aboutepa/about-office-enforcement-and-compliance-assurance-oeca and Twitter, @EPAJustice

Investigates violations of environmental laws and provides technical and forensic services for civil and criminal investigations and council for legal and policy matters. Enforcement activities target the most serious water, air, and chemical hazards.

▶ NONGOVERNMENTAL

Environmental Defense Fund, *Washington Office,* 1875 Connecticut Ave. N.W., #600, 20009-5728; (202) 387-3500. Fax, (202) 234-6049. Fred Krupp, President; Carol Andress, Associate Vice President (in Washington, D.C.).
Information, (800) 684-3322.
Web, www.edf.org/offices/washington-dc, Twitter, @EnvDefenseFund and Facebook, www.facebook.com/EnvDefenseFund

Citizen interest group staffed by lawyers, economists, and scientists. Takes legal action on environmental issues; provides information on pollution prevention, environmental health, wetlands, toxic substances, acid rain, tropical rain forests, sustainable fishing, clean energy, and litigation of water pollution standards. (Headquarters in New York.)

Gun Control

▶**AGENCIES**

Bureau of Alcohol, Tobacco, Firearms, and Explosives (ATF) *(Justice Dept.)*, *99 New York Ave. N.E., 20226; (202) 648-7080. Marvin Richardson, Director (Acting). Firearm theft hotline, (888) 930-9275. Illegal firearm activity hotline, (800) 283-4867. Public and Governmental Affairs, (202) 648-8520.*
General email, ATFTips@atf.gov
Web, www.atf.gov, Twitter, @ATFHQ and Facebook, www .facebook.com/HQATF

Enforces and administers laws to eliminate illegal possession and use of firearms. Investigates criminal violations and regulates legal trade, including imports and exports. Receives reports of illegal firearms activity and firearm theft.

▶**NONGOVERNMENTAL**

Brady Center to Prevent Gun Violence, *840 1st St. N.E., #400, 20002; (202) 370-8100. Fax, (202) 370-8102. Kris Brown, President. Press, (202) 370-8128.*
General email, media@bradyunited.org
Web, www.bradyunited.org, Twitter, @Bradybuzz and Facebook, www.facebook.com/bradycampaign

Educational, research, and legal action organization that seeks to allay gun violence, especially among children. Library open to the public.

Coalition to Stop Gun Violence, *805 15th St. N.W., 20005; (202) 408-0061. Joshua (Josh) Horwitz, Executive Director.*
General email, csgv@csgv.org
Web, www.csgv.org, Twitter, @CSGV and Facebook, www .facebook.com/CoalitiontoStopGunViolence

Membership: Works to reduce gun violence by fostering effective community and national action.

Educational Fund to Stop Gun Violence, *805 15th St. N.W., #502, 20005 (mailing address: 200 Massachusetts Ave. N.W., #700, Washington, DC, 20001); (202) 408-7560. Josh Horwitz, Executive Director.*
General email, efsgv@efsgv.org
Web, https://efsgv.org, Twitter, @EFSGV and Facebook, www.facebook.com/EFSGV

Group of national organizations, including faith-based groups, child welfare advocates, public health professionals, and social justice organizations, that seeks to reduce gun violence through research and education. Monitors legislation and regulations. (Affiliated with the Coalition to Stop Gun Violence.)

Gun Owners of America, *8001 Forbes Pl., #202, Springfield, VA 22151; (703) 321-8585. Erich Pratt, Senior Vice President.*
Web, www.gunowners.org, Twitter, @GunOwners and Facebook, www.facebook.com/GunOwners

Seeks to preserve the right to bear arms and to protect the rights of law-abiding gun owners. Administers

foundation that provides gun owners with legal assistance in suits against the federal government. Monitors legislation, regulations, and international agreements.

National Rifle Assn. of America (NRA), *11250 Waples Mill Rd., Fairfax, VA 22030; (703) 267-3820. Fax, (703) 267-3976. Wayne LaPierre, Chief Executive Officer; Carolyn D. Meadows, President. Toll-free, (800) 672-3888. Web, https://home.nra.org and Twitter, @NRA*

Membership: target shooters, hunters, gun collectors, gunsmiths, police officers, and others interested in firearms. Promotes shooting sports and recreational shooting and safety; studies and makes recommendations on firearms laws. Opposes gun control legislation. (Affiliated with the Institute for Legislative Action, the NRA's lobbying arm.)

Juvenile Justice

▶**AGENCIES**

Office of Justice Programs (OJP) *(Justice Dept.)*, *Juvenile Justice and Delinquency Prevention (OJJDP), 810 7th St. N.W., 20531; (202) 307-5911. Fax, (301) 240-5830. Chyrl Jones, Administrator (Acting), (202) 353-0798. Clearinghouse, (800) 851-3420.*
Web, www.ojjdp.gov, Twitter, @OJPOJJDP and Facebook, www.facebook.com/OJPOJJDP

Administers federal programs related to prevention and treatment of juvenile delinquency; missing and exploited children; child victimization; and training, technical assistance, and research and evaluation in these areas. Operates the Juvenile Justice Clearinghouse. Sponsors the National Criminal Justice Reference Service ((800) 851-3420).

Office of Justice Programs (OJP) *(Justice Dept.)*, **National Institute of Justice (NIJ),** *810 7th St. N.W., 7th Floor, 20531; (202) 307-2942. Fax, (202) 307-6394. Jennifer Scherer, Director (Acting). Press, (202) 307-0703. General email, ojp.ocom@usdoj.gov*
Web, www.nij.gov and Facebook, www.facebook.com/ OJPNIJ

Maintains the National Criminal Justice Reference Service, which provides data and information on juvenile justice research topics, including child protection, juvenile courts, missing children, gangs, bullying, school safety, and mentoring: (800) 851-3420; international callers, (202) 836-6998; Web, www.ncjrs.gov.

▶**NONGOVERNMENTAL**

Coalition for Juvenile Justice, *1629 K St. N.W., #300, 20006-1631; (202) 827-9751. Naomi Smoot Evans, Executive Director, ext. 113.*
General email, info@juvjustice.org
Web, http://juvjustice.org, Twitter, @4juvjustice and Facebook, www.facebook.com/juvjustice

Nationwide coalition of governor-appointed advisory groups, practitioners, and volunteers. Seeks to improve juvenile justice and to prevent children and youth from becoming involved in the courts. Issues include the removal of youth from adult jails and lockups and attention to the disproportionate number of youth of color in the juvenile justice system.

Justice Research and Statistics Assn., *1000 Vermont Ave. N.W., #450, 20005; (202) 842-9330. Fax, (202) 304-1417. Jeffrey Sedgwick, Executive Director.*
General email, cjinfo@jrsa.org
Web, www.jrsa.org and Twitter, @JRSAinfo

Promotes nonpartisan research and analysis to inform criminal and juvenile justice policy and decisionmaking. Disseminates policy- and justice-related research and information to the justice community, and convenes informational seminars on new research, programs, and technologies.

Organized Crime

▶**AGENCIES**

Criminal Division *(Justice Dept.), Narcotic and Dangerous Drug Section (NDDS), 145 N St. N.E., 20002; (202) 514-2000. Arthur G. Wyatt, Chief.*
Web, www.justice.gov/criminal/ndds

Investigates and prosecutes participants in criminal syndicates involved in the large-scale importation, manufacture, shipment, or distribution of illegal narcotics and other dangerous drugs. Trains agents and prosecutors in the techniques of major drug litigation.

Criminal Division *(Justice Dept.), Organized Crime and Gang Section (OCGS), 1301 New York Ave. N.W., #700, 20005; (202) 514-3594. David L. Jaffe, Chief. Labor Unit, (202) 514-3954. Litigation Unit, (202) 514-8405. RICO Review Unit, (202) 514-1214 or (202) 514-1215.*
Web, www.justice.gov/criminal-ocgs

Enforces federal criminal laws when subjects under investigation are alleged racketeers or part of syndicated criminal operations or gangs; coordinates efforts of federal, state, and local law enforcement agencies against organized crime, including emerging international groups; formulates violent crime and gang prosecution policy; maintains responsibility over all firearms-related statutes within the U.S. code. Cases include extortion, murder, bribery, fraud, money laundering, narcotics, labor racketeering, and violence that disrupts the criminal justice process.

Federal Bureau of Investigation (FBI) *(Justice Dept.), Criminal Investigative Division (CID), Transnational Organized Crime (TOC), 935 Pennsylvania Ave. N.W., #3352, 20535-0001; (202) 324-5625. Fax, (202) 324-0880. Calvin Shivers, Assistant Director.*
Web, www.fbi.gov/investigate/organized-crime

Coordinates all FBI organized-crime investigations. Determines budget, training, and resource needs for investigations, including those related to international organized crime. Conducts undercover operations, surveillance, and multiagency investigations, and works with international partners.

Other Violations

▶**AGENCIES**

Bureau of Alcohol, Tobacco, Firearms, and Explosives (ATF) *(Justice Dept.), 99 New York Ave. N.E., 20226; (202) 648-7080. Marvin Richardson, Director (Acting). Firearm theft hotline, (888) 930-9275. Illegal firearm activity hotline, (800) 283-4867. Public and Governmental Affairs, (202) 648-8520.*
General email, ATFTips@atf.gov
Web, www.atf.gov, Twitter, @ATFHQ and Facebook, www.facebook.com/HQATF

Performs law enforcement functions relating to alcohol (beer, wine, distilled spirits), tobacco, arson, explosives, and destructive devices; investigates criminal violations and regulates legal trade.

Criminal Division *(Justice Dept.), Fraud Section (FRD), 950 Constitution Ave. N.W., 20530; (202) 514-2000. Fax, (202) 514-3708. Joseph Beemsterboer, Chief (Acting).*
Web, www.justice.gov/criminal-fraud

Administers federal enforcement activities related to fraud and white-collar crime. Focuses on frauds against government programs, transnational and multidistrict fraud, and cases involving the security and commodity exchanges, banking practices, and consumer victimization.

Criminal Division *(Justice Dept.), Money Laundering and Asset Recovery Section (MLARS), 1400 New York Ave. N.W., #10100, 20005; (202) 514-1263. Deborah Connor, Chief.*
Web, www.justice.gov/criminal-mlars

Investigates and prosecutes money laundering and criminal and civil forfeiture offenses involving illegal transfer of funds within the United States and from the United States to other countries. Oversees and coordinates legislative policy proposals. Advises U.S. attorneys' offices in multidistrict money laundering and criminal and civil forfeiture prosecutions. Represents Justice Dept. in international antimoney laundering and criminal and civil forfeiture initiatives.

Criminal Division *(Justice Dept.), Organized Crime and Gang Section (OCGS), 1301 New York Ave. N.W., #700, 20005; (202) 514-3594. David L. Jaffe, Chief. Labor Unit, (202) 514-3954. Litigation Unit, (202) 514-8405. RICO Review Unit, (202) 514-1214 or (202) 514-1215.*
Web, www.justice.gov/criminal-ocgs

Reviews and advises on prosecutions of criminal violations concerning the operation of employee benefit plans in the private sector, labor-management relations, the operation of employee pension and health care plans, and internal affairs of labor unions.

Criminal Division *(Justice Dept.), Public Integrity (PIN), 1301 New York Ave. N.W., 10th Floor, 20005; (202) 514-1412. Fax, (202) 514-3003. Corey R. Amundson, Chief.*
Web, www.justice.gov/criminal/pin

Supervises enforcement of federal criminal laws related to campaigns and elections. Oversees investigation of deprivation of voting rights; intimidation and coercion of voters; denial or promise of federal employment or other benefits; illegal political contributions, expenditures, and solicitations; and all other election violations referred to the division.

National Security Division *(Justice Dept.),* **Counterintelligence and Export Control (CES),** *950 Pennsylvania Ave. N.W., 20530; (202) 514-1057. (202) 514-5000. Jay Bratt, Chief.*
General email, nsd.public@usdoj.gov
Web, www.justice.gov/nsd/sections-offices#intelexport

Supervises the investigation and prosecution of cases affecting national security, foreign relations, and the export of military and strategic commodities and technology. Has executive responsibility for authorizing the prosecution of cases under criminal statutes relating to espionage, sabotage, neutrality, and atomic energy. Provides legal advice to U.S. Attorneys' offices and investigates agencies on federal statutes concerning national security. Coordinates criminal cases involving the application of the Classified Information Procedures Act. Administers and enforces the Foreign Agents Registration Act of 1938 and related disclosure statutes.

National Security Division *(Justice Dept.),* **Counterterrorism (CTS),** *950 Pennsylvania Ave. N.W., 20530; (202) 514-0849. (202) 514-5000. Matthew Olsen, Assistant Attorney General for National Security.*
General email, nsd.public@usdoj.gov
Web, www.justice.gov/nsd/counterterrorism-section

Seeks to assist, through investigation and prosecution, in preventing and disrupting acts of terrorism anywhere in the world that impact significant U.S. interests and persons.

National Security Division *(Justice Dept.),* **Law and Policy,** *950 Pennsylvania Ave. N.W., 20530; (202) 616-0903. Brad Wiegmann, Deputy Assistant Attorney General.*
General email, nsd.justice@usdoj.gov
Web, www.justice.gov/nsd/sections-offices#law

Provides legal assistance, advice, and overall support on matters of national security law.

Securities and Exchange Commission (SEC), *Office of the Whistleblower, 100 F St. N.E., MS 5631, 20549 (mailing address: SEC/OWB, 14420 Albemarle Point Place, #102, Chantilly, VA 20151-1750); (202) 551-4790. Fax, (703) 813-9322. Nicole Creola Kelly, Chief.*
Web, www.sec.gov/whistleblower

Receives information about possible securities law violations and provides information about the whistleblower program.

U.S. Customs and Border Protection *(Homeland Security Dept.),* **Field Operations,** *1300 Pennsylvania Ave. N.W., 20229; (202) 344-1620. Pete Flores, Executive Assistant Commissioner.*
Web, www.cbp.gov/border-security/ports-entry

Combats smuggling of funds; enforces statutes relating to the processing and regulation of people, carriers, cargo, and mail into and out of the United States. Investigates counterfeiting, child pornography, commercial fraud, and Internet crimes.

U.S. Postal Service (USPS), *Inspection Service, 475 L'Enfant Plaza S.W., #3100, 20260-2100; (202) 268-4264. Gary Barksdale, Chief Postal Inspector. Fraud and abuse hotline, (877) 876-2455.*
Web, http://uspis.gov, Twitter, @USPISpressroom and Facebook, www.facebook.com/PostalInspectors

Protects mail, postal funds, and property from criminal violations of postal laws, such as mail fraud or distribution of obscene materials. (Headquarters in Chicago, Ill.)

U.S. Secret Service *(Homeland Security Dept.), 245 Murray Ln. S.W., Bldg. T-5, 20223; (202) 406-5800. James M. Murray, Director. Information, (202) 406-5708.*
Web, www.secretservice.gov and Twitter, @SecretService

Investigates violations of laws relating to counterfeiting of U.S. currency; financial crimes, including access device fraud, financial institution fraud, identity theft, and computer fraud; and computer-based attacks on the financial, banking, and telecommunications infrastructure.

U.S. Secret Service *(Homeland Security Dept.), Criminal Investigative Division, 950 H St. N.W., 20001; (202) 406-5708. Jeremy C. Sheridan, Assistant Director.*
Web, www.secretservice.gov/investigation

Investigates crimes associated with financial institutions. Jurisdiction includes bank fraud, access device fraud involving credit and debit cards, telecommunications and computer crimes, fraudulent identification, fraudulent government and commercial securities, and electronic funds transfer fraud.

▶ **NONGOVERNMENTAL**

International Anticounterfeiting Coalition, *727 15th St. N.W., 9th Floor, 20005; (202) 223-6667. Robert C. Barchiesi, President.*
General email, iacc@iacc.org
Web, www.iacc.org, Twitter, @IACC_GetReal and Facebook, www.facebook.com/InternationalAntiCounterfeitingCoalition

Works to combat counterfeiting and piracy by promoting laws, regulations, and directives to render theft of intellectual property unprofitable. Oversees anticounterfeiting programs that increase patent, trademark, copyright, service mark, trade dress, and trade-secret protection. Provides information and training to law enforcement officials to help identify counterfeit and pirate products.

Stalking Resource Center, *National Center for Victims of Crime, 2000 M St. N.W., #480, 20036; (202) 467-8700. Renee Williams, Executive Director. Referrals, (855) 484-2846. DC Victim Hotline, 844-4HELPDC.*
General email, info@victimsofcrime.org
Web, www.victimsofcrime.org/our-programs/stalking-resource-center, Twitter, @CrimeVictimsOrg,

Facebook, www.facebook.com/ncvcfan and YouTube, www.youtube.com/channel/UCiWV-ZxE5rHdC7d7_PIb-nQ

Acts as an information clearinghouse on stalking. Works to raise public awareness of the dangers of stalking. Encourages the development and implementation of multidisciplinary responses to stalking in local communities, and policy and protocol enhancements for the criminal justice system. Offers practitioner training and technical assistance. (Affiliated with the National Center for Victims of Crime.)

Sentencing and Corrections

▶ AGENCIES

Federal Bureau of Prisons *(Justice Dept.),* 320 1st St. N.W., 20534; (202) 307-3198. Michael Carvajal, Director, (202) 307-3250. Inmate locator service, (202) 307-3126. Press, (202) 514-6551.
Web, www.bop.gov, Twitter, @OfficialFBOP and Facebook, www.facebook.com/bureauofprisons

Supervises operations of federal correctional institutions, community treatment facilities, and commitment and management of federal inmates; oversees contracts with local institutions for confinement and support of federal prisoners. Regional offices are responsible for administration; central office in Washington coordinates operations and issues standards and policy guidelines. Central office includes Federal Prison Industries, a government corporation providing prison-manufactured goods and services for sale to federal agencies, and the National Institute of Corrections, an information and technical assistance center on state and local corrections programs.

Federal Bureau of Prisons *(Justice Dept.), Health Services Division,* 320 1st St. N.W., 20534; (202) 307-3055. Rear Adm. Chris Bina, Assistant Director.
Web, www.bop.gov/about/agency/org_hsd.jsp

Administers health care and treatment programs for prisoners in federal institutions.

Federal Bureau of Prisons *(Justice Dept.), National Institute of Corrections,* 320 1st St. N.W., #901D, 20534; (202) 307-3106. Shaina Vanek, Director (Acting). Toll-free, (800) 995-6423.
General email, support@nicic.gov
Web, https://nicic.gov and www.bop.gov/about/agency/org_nic.jsp

Provides training, technical assistance, information clearinghouse services, and policy/program development assistance to federal, state, and local corrections agencies.

Justice Dept. (DOJ), *Pardon Attorney,* RFK Bldg., 950 Pennsylvania Ave. N.W., 20530 (mailing address: 145 N St. N.E., #5E508, Washington, DC 20530); (202) 616-6070. Fax, (202) 616-6069. Rosalind Sargent-Burns, Pardon Attorney (Acting).

General email, USpardon.attorney@usdoj.gov
Web, www.justice.gov/pardon

Advises the president on the exercise of executive clemency power, including pardons, commutations of sentence, remissions of fine or restitution, and reprieves. Receives and reviews petitions to the president for all forms of executive clemency, including pardons and sentence reductions; initiates investigations and prepares the deputy attorney general's recommendations to the president on petitions.

Office of Justice Programs (OJP) *(Justice Dept.), Bureau of Justice Assistance (BJA),* 810 7th St. N.W., 4th Floor, 20531; (202) 616-6500. Fax, (202) 305-1367. Kristen Mahoney, Director (Acting). Press, (202) 307-0703.
General email, askbja@usdoj.gov
Web, www.bja.gov, Facebook, www.facebook.com/DOJBJA and Twitter, @DOJBJA

Provides states and communities with funds and technical assistance for corrections demonstration projects.

Office of Justice Programs (OJP) *(Justice Dept.), National Institute of Justice (NIJ),* 810 7th St. N.W., 7th Floor, 20531; (202) 307-2942. Fax, (202) 307-6394. Jennifer Scherer, Director (Acting). Press, (202) 307-0703.
General email, ojp.ocom@usdoj.gov
Web, www.nij.gov and Facebook, www.facebook.com/OJPNIJ

Conducts research on all aspects of criminal justice, including crime prevention, enforcement, adjudication, and corrections; seeks to reduce incarceration and probation while maintaining public safety and holding offenders accountable. Maintains the National Criminal Justice Reference Service, which provides information on corrections research topics, including jails and prisons, inmate assistance, parole and probations, recidivism, and reentry: (800) 851-3420; international callers, (202) 836-6998; Web, www.ncjrs.gov.

U.S. Parole Commission *(Justice Dept.),* 90 Pennsylvania Ave. N.W., 20530-0001; (202) 346-7000. Anthony Coley, Director. Comment line, (202) 353-1555. Press, (202) 514-2007. TTY, (800) 877-8339.
General email, public.inquiries@usdoj.gov
Web, www.justice.gov/uspc and Press, uspc.media@usdoj.gov

Makes release and revocation decisions for all federal prisoners serving sentences of more than one year for offenses committed before November 1, 1987, and for D.C. Code offenders serving parolable offenses or subject to a term of supervised release.

U.S. Sentencing Commission, 1 Columbus Circle N.E., #2-500 South Lobby, 20002-8002; (202) 502-4500. Kenneth P. Cohen, Staff Director. Helpline, (202) 502-4545.
General email, pubaffairs@ussc.gov
Web, www.ussc.gov and Twitter, @TheUSSCgov

Establishes sentencing guidelines and policy for all federal courts, including guidelines prescribing the appropriate form and severity of punishment for those convicted of federal crimes. Provides training and research on sentencing-related issues. Serves as an information resource.

Administrative Office of the U.S. Courts, *1 Columbus Circle N.E., 20544-0001; (202) 502-2600.*
Hon. Roslynn R. Mauskopf, Director.
Web, www.uscourts.gov and Twitter, @uscourts

Supervises all administrative matters of the federal court system, except the Supreme Court; collects statistical data on business of the courts.

Administrative Office of the U.S. Courts, *Probation and Pretrial Services, 1 Columbus Circle N.E., #4-300, 20544-0001; (202) 502-2600. Fax, (202) 502-1677.*
Charles Robinson, Deputy Assistant Director.
Web, www.uscourts.gov/services-forms/probation-and-pretrial-services

Determines the resource and program requirements of the federal and pretrial services system. Provides policy guidance, program evaluation services, management and technical assistance, and training to probation and pretrial services officers.

American Bar Assn. (ABA), *Criminal Justice, 1050 Connecticut Ave. N.W., #400, 20036; (202) 662-1500. Fax, (202) 662-1501. Kevin Scruggs, Director, (202) 662-1503.*
General email, crimjustice@americanbar.org
Web, www.americanbar.org/groups/criminal_justice, Twitter, @ABACJS and Facebook, www.facebook.com/ABACJS

Studies and makes recommendations on all aspects of the correctional system, including overcrowding in prisons and the privatization of prisons and correctional institutions. (Headquarters in Chicago, Ill.)

American Civil Liberties Union Foundation, *National Prison Project, 915 15th St. N.W., 7th Floor, 20005; (202) 393-4930. Fax, (202) 393-4931. David C. Fathi, Director, (202) 548-6603.*
Web, www.aclu.org/issues/prisoners-rights

Litigates on behalf of prisoners through class action suits. Seeks to improve prison conditions and the penal system by ensuring that prisons, jails, and detention centers comply with the Constitution, domestic law, and human rights principles; serves as resource center for prisoners' rights.

American Correctional Assn. (ACA), *206 N. Washington St., #200, Alexandria, VA 22314; (703) 224-0000. Fax, (703) 224-0179. James Gondles, Executive Director. Information, (800) 222-5646.*
General email, membership@aca.org
Web, www.aca.org, Twitter, @ACAinfo, Facebook, www .facebook.com/AmericanCorrectionalAssociation and

YouTube, www.youtube.com/user/AmericanCorrectional/ featured

Membership: corrections professionals in all aspects of corrections, including juvenile and adult facilities, community facilities, and academia; affiliates include state and regional corrections associations in the United States and Canada. Conducts and publishes research; provides state and local governments with technical assistance; certifies corrections professionals. Offers professional development courses and accreditation programs. Monitors legislation and regulation. Interests include criminal justice issues, correctional standards, and accreditation programs. Library open to the public.

Amnesty International USA, *Washington National Office, 600 Pennsylvania Ave. S.E., 5th Floor, 20003; (202) 544-0200. Fax, (202) 546-7142. Paul O'Brian, Executive Director; Joanne Lin, National Director for Advocacy and Government. Toll-free, 800-AMNESTY.*
General email, aimember@aiusa.org
Web, www.amnestyusa.org and Twitter, @amnesty

International organization that opposes retention or reinstitution of the death penalty; advocates humane treatment of all prisoners. (U.S. headquarters in New York.)

Death Penalty Information Center, *1701 K St. N.W., #205, 20006; (202) 289-2275. Robert Dunham, Executive Director.*
General email, dpic@deathpenaltyinfo.org
Web, www.deathpenaltyinfo.org, Twitter, @DPinfoCtr and Facebook, www.facebook.com/deathpenaltyinfo

Provides the media and public with analysis and information on issues concerning capital punishment. Conducts briefings for journalists; prepares reports; issues press releases.

Families Against Mandatory Minimums, *1100 H St. N.W., #1000, 20005; (202) 822-6700. Kevin Ring, President.*
Web, www.famm.org, Twitter, @FAMMFoundation, Twitter, President, @KevinARing, Facebook, www .facebook.com/FAMMFoundation and Email, famm@famm.org

Seeks to repeal statutory mandatory minimum prison sentences. Works to increase public awareness of inequity of mandatory minimum sentences through grassroots efforts and media outreach programs.

NAACP Legal Defense and Educational Fund, Inc., *Washington Office, 700 14th St. N.W., #600, 20005; (202) 682-1300. Sherrilyn Ifill, President.*
Web, www.naacpldf.org, Twitter, @naacp_ldf, Facebook, www.facebook.com/naacpldf and YouTube, www.youtube. com/channel/UCXTfPnpwx-CWVyrzDvkwE1w

Civil rights litigation group that supports abolition of capital punishment; assists attorneys representing prisoners on death row; focuses public attention on race discrimination in the application of the death penalty. Not affiliated with the NAACP. (Headquarters in New York.)

National Center on Institutions and Alternatives, *7130 Rutherford Rd., Baltimore, MD 21244; (443) 780-1300. Herbert J. Hoelter, Chief Executive Officer. General email, info@ncianet.org*

Web, www.ncianet.org and Twitter, @NCIA_Baltimore

Seeks to reduce incarceration as primary form of punishment imposed by criminal justice system; advocates use of extended community service, work-release, and halfway house programs; operates youth and adult residential programs; provides defense attorneys and courts with specific recommendations for sentencing and parole. (Affiliated with the Augustus Institute. Headquarters in Baltimore, Md.)

National Coalition to Abolish the Death Penalty, *1629 K St., #300, 20006; (703) 957-8198. Diann Rust-Tierney, Executive Director. 90 Million Strong, (646) 346-4289. General email, admin-info@ncadp.org*

Web, www.ncadp.org, Twitter, @ncadp and Facebook, www.facebook.com/ncadp

Membership: organizations and individuals opposed to the death penalty. Maintains collection of death penalty research. Provides training, resources, and conferences. Works with families of murder victims; tracks execution dates. Launched the 90 Million Strong campaign to form a coalition of partners who oppose the death penalty. Monitors legislation and regulations.

Prison Fellowship Ministries, *44180 Riverside Pkwy., Lansdowne, VA 20176; (703) 478-0100. James J. Ackerman, Chief Executive Officer. Toll-free, (800) 206-9764. Angle Tree, (800) 552-6435. General email, info@pfm.org*

Web, www.prisonfellowship.org, Twitter, @prisonfellowship and Facebook, www.facebook.com/PFMinistries

Religious organization that ministers to prisoners and ex-prisoners, victims, and the families involved. Offers counseling, seminars, and support for readjustment after release; works to increase the fairness and effectiveness of the criminal justice system. Runs the Prison fellowship Angel Tree program.

The Sentencing Project, *1705 DeSales St. N.W., 8th Floor, 20036; (202) 628-0871. Fax, (202) 628-1091. Amy Fettig, Executive Director. General email, staff@sentencingproject.org*

Web, www.sentencingproject.org, Twitter, @SentencingProj, Facebook, www.facebook.com/Thesentencingproject and YouTube, www.youtube.com/user/thesentencingproject

Engages in research and advocacy on criminal justice policy issues, including sentencing, incarceration, juvenile justice, racial disparity, alternatives to incarceration, and felony disenfranchisement. Publishes research.

Victim Assistance

▶**AGENCIES**

Federal Bureau of Investigation (FBI) *(Justice Dept.),* **Victim Services Division (VSD),** *935 Pennsylvania Ave. N.W., #3329, 20535; (202) 324-1339. Fax, (202) 324-2113. Regina Thompson, Assistant Director. Victim Notification System Call Center, (866) 365-4968. General email, nk-victim-assistance@fbi.gov*

Web, www.fbi.gov/resources/victim-services

Ensures that victims of crimes investigated by the FBI are identified, offered assistance, and given information about case events. Manages the Victim Assistance Program in the fifty-six FBI field offices as well as the FBI's international offices. Trains agents and personnel to work with victims. Coordinates resources and services to victims in cases of terrorism and crimes against citizens that occur outside the United States. Coordinates with other federal agencies on behalf of victims.

Justice Dept. (DOJ), *Elder Justice Initiative (EJI), 950 Pennsylvania Ave. N.W., 20530; Andy Mao, Coordinator, (202) 616-0539. Eldercare locator helpline, (800) 677-1116. General email, elder.justice@usdoj.gov*

Web, www.justice.gov/elderjustice and Rural and tribal resources, www.justice.gov/elderjustice/rural-and-tribal-resources

Makes available training and resources for elder abuse victim specialists; maintains a victim resource locator to help victims and their families identify support and other resources.

Justice Dept. (DOJ), *Violence Against Women (OVW), 145 N St. N.E., #10W.121, 20530; (202) 307-6026. Fax, (202) 305-2589. Nadine M. Neufville, Director (Acting). National Domestic Violence Hotline, 800-799-SAFE. National Sexual Assault Hotline, 800-656-HOPE. National Teen Dating Abuse Hotline, (800) 331-9474. National Victims of Crime Hotline, 855-4-VICTIM. TTY, (202) 307-2277. General email, ovw.info@usdoj.gov*

Web, www.justice.gov/ovw and Twitter, @OVWJustice

Seeks more effective policies and services to combat domestic violence, sexual assault, stalking, and other crimes against women. Helps administer grants to states to fund shelters, crisis centers, and hotlines, and to hire law enforcement officers, prosecutors, and counselors specializing in cases of sexual violence and other violent crimes against women.

National Security Division *(Justice Dept.),* **Justice for Victims of Overseas Terrorism,** *950 Pennsylvania Ave. N.W., 20530; (202) 233-0701. Fax, (202) 233-0770. Andria Kerney, Director. Toll-free, (877) 738-0153. fax, (202) 233-0770. General email, nsd.ovt@usdoj.gov*

Web, www.justice.gov/nsd-ovt

Monitors the investigation and prosecution of terrorist attacks against U.S. citizens abroad; works with other

Justice Dept. offices to ensure that the rights of victims are respected.

Office of Justice Programs (OJP) *(Justice Dept.), National Institute of Justice (NIJ), 810 7th St. N.W., 7th Floor, 20531; (202) 307-2942. Fax, (202) 307-6394. Jennifer Scherer, Director (Acting). Press, (202) 307-0703.*
General email, ojp.ocom@usdoj.gov

Web, www.nij.gov and Facebook, www.facebook.com/OJPNIJ

Researches victimization trends and evaluates victim advocacy programs. Maintains the National Criminal Justice Reference Service, which provides data and information on victim research topics, including intervention, restorative justice, and victimization of special populations: (800) 851-3420; international callers, (202) 836-6998; Web, www.ncjrs.gov.

Office of Justice Programs (OJP) *(Justice Dept.), Victims of Crime (OVC), 810 7th St. N.W., 2nd Floor, 20531; (202) 307-5983. Fax, (202) 514-6383. Kristina Rose, Director. Resource Center, (800) 851-3420 or TTY, (301) 240-6310. Victim hotline, (800) 331-0075 or TTY, (800) 553-2508.*
General email, askovc@ncjrs.gov

Web, www.ovc.gov, Twitter, @OJPOVC and Facebook, www.facebook.com/OJPOVC

Works to advance the rights of and improve services to the nation's crime victims. Supports programs and initiatives to assist other federal agencies, state and local governments, tribal governments, private nonprofit organizations, and the international community in their efforts to aid victims of violent and nonviolent crime. Provides emergency funding and services for victims of terrorism and mass violence and victims of human trafficking. Funds the development of training and technical assistance for victim service providers and other professionals through the Training and Technical Assistance Center, (866) 682-8822 or TTY (866) 682-8880. Funds demonstration projects and coordinates annual observances of National Crime Victims' Rights Week. Website has a Spanish-language link.

▶**NONGOVERNMENTAL**

FAIR Girls, *2021 L St. N.W., # 101-254, 20036; (202) 520-9777. Dawanna Kennedy, Executive Director (Acting). Crisis Hotline, (855) 900-3247. National Trafficking Hotline, (888) 373-7888.*
General email, info@fairgirls.org

Web, www.fairgirls.org, Twitter, @fair_girls and Facebook, www.facebook.com/fairgirls

Provides interventionist holistic care for survivors of trafficking who identify as girls or young women through prevention education and policy advocacy. Works to eradicate human trafficking and create improved outcomes for survivors.

Maryland Coalition Against Sexual Assault (MCASA), *P.O. Box 8782, Silver Spring, MD 20907; (301) 328-7023. Fax, (301) 328-7168. Lisae C. Jordan, Executive*

Director. Legal services, (301) 565-2277. Toll-free, (800) 983-7273.
General email, info@mcasa.org

Web, www.mcasa.org, Twitter, @mcasaorg and Facebook, www.facebook.com/mcasaorg

Coalition of seventeen rape crisis centers, professionals, and service providers working with sexual assult survivors. Involved with policy advocacy and technical assistance, and provides training, outreach and prevention for attorneys, rape crisis staff, volunteers, and other professionals working with survivors. Acts as advocate for accessible and compassionate care, and works to hold offenders accountable.

National Assn. of Crime Victim Compensation Boards, *P.O. Box 16003, Alexandria, VA 22302; (703) 780-3200. Dan Eddy, Executive Director.*
General email, dan.eddy@nacvcb.org

Web, www.nacvcb.org

Provides state compensation agencies with training and technical assistance. Provides public information on victim compensation.

National Center for Missing and Exploited Children, *333 John Carlyle St., #125, Alexandria, VA 22314-5950; (703) 224-2150. Fax, (703) 224-2122. John F. Clark, Chief Executive Officer. Toll-free hotline, (800) 843-5678.*
General email, media@ncmec.org

Web, www.missingkids.com, Twitter, @MissingKids, Facebook, www.facebook.com/MissingKids and YouTube, www.youtube.com/missingkids

Works with law enforcement, social service agencies, and mental health agencies to provide support networks for child victims and their families; offers legal resources for attorneys and families.

National Center for Victims of Crime, *2000 M St. N.W., #480, 20036; (202) 467-8700. Renee Williams, Executive Director.*
General email, info@vicitimsofcrime.org

Web, www.victimsofcrime.org, Twitter, @CrimeVictimsOrg and Facebook, www.facebook.com/ncvcfan

Works with victims' groups and criminal justice agencies to protect the rights of crime victims through state and federal statutes and policies. Promotes greater responsiveness to crime victims through training and education; provides research and technical assistance in the development of victim-related legislation.

National Children's Alliance, *516 C St. N.E., 20002; (202) 548-0090. Teresa Huizar, Executive Director.*
Web, www.nationalchildrensalliance.org, Facebook, www.facebook.com/NationalChildrensAlliance and Twitter, @NCAforCACs

Accrediting body for Children's Advocacy Centers (CACs). Provides support, technical assistance, and quality assurance for CACs; helps promote and support communities in providing a coordinated investigation and comprehensive response to child victims of abuse.

National Coalition Against Domestic Violence, *Public Policy, 1130 3rd St. N.E., 2nd Floor, 20002; (202) 714-7662. Rachel Graber, Director of Public Policy. National Domestic Violence Hotline, (800) 799-7233. TTY, (800) 787-3224.*
General email, publicpolicy@ncadv.org
Web, www.ncadv.org, Twitter, @NCADV and Facebook, www.facebook.com/NationalCoalitionAgainst DomesticViolence

Monitors legislation and public policy initiatives concerning victims and survivors of domestic violence. Work includes empowering victims, promoting and coordinating direct services, and educating the public about domestic violence. Offers the Cosmetic & Reconstructive Support Program to survivors. (Headquarters in Denver, Colo.)

National Organization for Victim Assistance, *510 King St., #424, Alexandria, VA 22314; (703) 535-6682. Fax, (703) 535-5500. Claire Ponder Selib, Executive Director. Toll-free and referral line, (800) 879-6682.*
Web, www.trynova.org and Twitter, @NOVAVictims

Membership: persons involved with victim and witness assistance programs, criminal justice professionals, researchers, crime victims, and others interested in victims' rights. Monitors legislation; provides victims and victim support programs with technical assistance, referrals, and program support; provides information on victims' rights.

Rape, Abuse, and Incest National Network (RAINN), *1220 L St. N.W., #505, 20005; (202) 544-1034. Fax, (202) 544-3556. Scott Berkowitz, President. National Sexual Assault hotline, (800) 656-4673. Press, (202) 544-5537.*
Web, www.rainn.org, Twitter, @RAINN and Facebook, www.facebook.com/RAINN01

Links sexual assault victims to confidential local services through national sexual assault hotline. Operates the Defense Dept.'s sexual assault helpline. Provides extensive public outreach and education programs nationwide on sexual assault prevention, prosecution, and recovery. Promotes national policy efforts to improve services to victims.

Stalking Resource Center, *National Center for Victims of Crime, 2000 M St. N.W., #480, 20036; (202) 467-8700. Renee Williams, Executive Director. Referrals, (855) 484-2846. DC Victim Hotline, 844-4HELPDC.*
General email, info@victimsofcrime.org
Web, www.victimsofcrime.org/our-programs/stalking-resource-center, Twitter, @CrimeVictimsOrg, Facebook, www.facebook.com/ncvcfan and YouTube, www.youtube .com/channel/UCiWV-ZxE5rHdC7d7_PIb-nQ

Acts as an information clearinghouse on stalking. Works with professionals and organizations to provide victim-centered responses to stalking; develops and enhances services for victims of stalking. Offers confidential referrals for crime victims. Provides training events on topics including intimate partner violence, sexual assault, technology use and stalking, investigating and prosecuting stalking, safety planning, and coordinated community

response. (Affiliated with the National Center for Victims of Crime.)

LAW ENFORCEMENT

General

▶AGENCIES

Bureau of International Narcotics and Law Enforcement Affairs (INL) *(State Dept.), Anti-Crime Office, 2401 E St. N.W., #SA-1, L600, 20037; (202) 663-1860. Susan Snyder, Director.*
Web, https://2009-2017.state.gov/j/inl/c/index.htm

Supports a global network of International Law Enforcement Academies to combat international drug trafficking, criminality, and terrorism.

Community Oriented Policing Services (COPS) *(Justice Dept.), 145 N St. N.E., 20530; (202) 616-2888. Robert Chapman, Director (Acting). FOIA, (202) 514-1873. Press, (202) 514-9079. Response Center, (800) 421-6770.*
General email, askCopsRC@usdoj.gov
Web, https://cops.usdoj.gov, Twitter, @COPSOffice and Facebook, www.facebook.com/DOJCOPS

Awards grants to tribal, state, and local law enforcement agencies to hire and train community policing professionals, acquire and deploy crime-fighting technologies, and develop and test policing strategies. Community policing emphasizes crime prevention through partnerships between law enforcement and citizens.

Criminal Division *(Justice Dept.), International Criminal Investigative Training Assistance Program (ICITAP), 1331 F St. N.W., #500, 20530; (202) 305-8190. Gregory Ducot, Director.*
Web, www.justice.gov/criminal-icitap

Works with foreign governments to develop professional and transparent law enforcement institutions that protect human rights, combat corruption, and reduce the threat of transnational crime and terrorism. Provides international development assistance that supports both national security and foreign policy objectives.

Federal Bureau of Investigation (FBI) *(Justice Dept.), Partner Engagement (OPE), 935 Pennsylvania Ave. N.W., #7128, 20535; (202) 324-7126. George P. Beach II, Assistant Director.*
General email, olec@leo.gov
Web, www.fbi.gov/about/partnerships/office-of-partner-engagement

Advises FBI executives on the use of state and local law enforcement and resources in criminal, cyber, and counterterrorism investigations. Coordinates the bureau's intelligence-sharing and technological efforts with state and local law enforcement. Serves as a liaison with the Homeland Security Dept. and other federal entities.

Federal Law Enforcement Training Centers (FLETC)

(Homeland Security Dept.), *National Capital Region (NCR)*, *1717 H St. N.W., 7th Floor, #16, 20006; (202) 233-0260. Fax, (202) 233-0258. Thomas J. Walters, Director, (912) 267-2070.*
General email, FLETC-WashingtonOffice@dhs.gov
Web, www.fletc.gov/washington-operations-wo, Twitter, @FLETC, Facebook, www.facebook.com/fletc and YouTube, www.youtube.com/c/FederalLawEnforcementTrainingCenters

Trains federal law enforcement personnel. Provides services to state, local, tribal, and international law enforcement agencies. (Headquarters in Glynco, Ga.)

Federal Trade Commission (FTC), *Bureau of Consumer Protection, Consumer Response and Operations Division*, 600 Pennsylvania Ave. N.W., #240, 20580; (202) 326-2830. Maria Mayo, Associate Director (Acting), (202) 326-3438. Consumer Response Center, 877-FTC-HELP. Consumer Sentinel helpline, (877) 701-9595. Do-Not-Call Registry, (888) 382-1222. FTC Complaint, (877) 382-4357. Identity fraud report line, 877-ID-THEFT. TTY, (866) 653-4261.

General email, crcmessages@ftc.gov
Web, www.ftc.gov/about-ftc/bureaus-offices/bureau-consumer-protection/our-divisions/division-consumer-response, Consumer Response Center, www.consumer.ftc.gov, Consumer Sentinel Network, www.ftc.gov/enforcement/consumer-sentinel-network and FTC Complaint Assistant, www.ftccomplaintassistant.gov

Collects and analyzes data in the Consumer Sentinel Network, which provides law enforcement members with access to FTC consumer complaints.

Financial Crimes Enforcement Network *(Treasury Dept.)*, P.O. Box 39, Vienna, VA 22183-0039; (703) 905-3591. Himamauli Das, Director. Press, (703) 905-3770. Toll-free, (800) 767-2825.

General email, frc@fincen.gov
Web, www.fincen.gov

Administers an information network in support of federal, state, and local law enforcement agencies in the prevention and detection of terrorist financing, money-laundering operations, and other financial crimes. Administers the Bank Secrecy Act.

Interior Dept. (DOI), *Law Enforcement and Security (OLES)*, 1849 C St. N.W., MS 3428-MIB, 20240; (202) 208-6319. Fax, (202) 219-1185. Robert D. MacLean, Director.

Web, www.doi.gov/pmb/oles

Develops law enforcement staffing models; establishes departmental training requirements and monitors their implementation; oversees the hiring of key law enforcement and security personnel; and reviews law enforcement and security budgets.

Office of Justice Programs (OJP) *(Justice Dept.)*, *Bureau of Justice Assistance (BJA)*, 810 7th St. N.W., 4th Floor, 20531; (202) 616-6500. Fax, (202) 305-1367. Kristen Mahoney, Director (Acting). Press, (202) 307-0703.

General email, askbja@usdoj.gov
Web, www.bja.gov, Facebook, www.facebook.com/DOJBJA and Twitter, @DOJBJA

Provides funds to eligible state and local governments and to nonprofit organizations for criminal justice programs, primarily those that combat drug trafficking and other drug-related crime.

Office of Justice Programs (OJP) *(Justice Dept.)*, *National Institute of Justice (NIJ)*, 810 7th St. N.W., 7th Floor, 20531; (202) 307-2942. Fax, (202) 307-6394. Jennifer Scherer, Director (Acting). Press, (202) 307-0703.

General email, ojp.ocom@usdoj.gov
Web, www.nij.gov and Facebook, www.facebook.com/OJPNIJ

Develops practices and policies that improve performance in law enforcement personnel and criminal justice agencies; evaluates ways to limit deaths and injuries of law enforcement and suspects; seeks to expand the use of DNA evidence and forensic science. Maintains the National Criminal Justice Reference Service, which provides information on various law enforcement topics, including crime mapping, crime scene investigation, profiling, community policing, training, and stress management: (800) 851-3420; international callers, (202) 836-6998; Web, www.ncjrs.gov.

Transportation Security Administration (TSA) *(Homeland Security Dept.)*, *Office of Law Enforcement, Federal Air Marshal Service*, TSA-18, 601 S. 12th St., Arlington, VA 20598-6018; (703) 487-3400. Fax, (703) 487-3405. Michael A. Ondocin, Executive Assistant Administrator.

Web, www.tsa.gov

Protects air security in the United States. Promotes public confidence in the U.S. civil aviation system. Deploys marshals on flights around the world to detect and deter hostile acts targeting U.S. air carriers, airports, passengers, and crews.

U.S. Marshals Service *(Justice Dept.)*, 2604 Jefferson Davis Hwy., CS-3, #1200, Alexandria, VA 22301; (202) 307-9100. Ronald L. Davis, Director, (202) 307-9100.

General email, us.marshals@usdoj.gov
Web, www.usmarshals.gov

Acts as the enforcement arm of the federal courts and U.S. attorney general. Responsibilities include court and witness security, prisoner custody and transportation, prisoner support, maintenance and disposal of seized and forfeited property, and special operations. Administers the Federal Witness Security Program. Apprehends fugitives, including those wanted by foreign nations and believed to be in the United States; oversees the return of fugitives apprehended abroad and wanted by U.S. law enforcement. Carries out the provisions of the Adam Walsh Child Protection and Safety Act.

▶ **CONGRESS**

For a listing of relevant congressional committees and subcommittees, please see pages 546–547 or the Appendix.

Feminist Majority Foundation, *1600 Wilson Blvd., #801, Arlington, VA 22209; (703) 522-2214. Fax, (703) 522-2219. Katherine Spillar, Executive Director.*
General email, media@feminist.org
Web, https://feminist.org and General Email, feedback@feminist.org

Research and public policy development, public education programs, grassroots organizing projects, leadership training and development programs, and participates in and organizes forums on issues of women's equality and empowerment.

International Assn. of Chiefs of Police, *44 Canal Center Plaza, #200, Alexandria, VA 22314; (703) 836-6767. Fax, (703) 836-4543. Vincent (Vince) Talucci, Executive Director. Toll-free, (800) 843-4227.*
General email, information@theiacp.org
Web, www.theiacp.org, Twitter, @TheIACP, Facebook, www.facebook.com/TheIACP and YouTube, www .youtube.com/user/TheIACP

Membership: foreign and U.S. police executives and administrators at federal, state, and local levels. Consults and conducts research on all aspects of police activity; conducts training programs and develops educational aids; conducts public education programs.

International Assn. of Chiefs of Police, *Advisory Committee for Patrol and Tactical Operations, 44 Canal Center Plaza, #200, Alexandria, VA 22314; (703) 836-6767. Sabrina Rhodes Fernandez, Program Manager. Toll-free, (800) 843-4227.*
General email, committees@theiacp.org
Web, www.theiacp.org/workinggroup/Committee/patrol-and-tactical-operations-committee

Membership: foreign and U.S. police executives and administrators. Maintains liaison with civil defense and emergency service agencies in the United States and other nations; prepares guidelines for police cooperation with emergency and disaster relief agencies during emergencies.

National Organization of Black Law Enforcement Executives, *4609-F Pinecrest Office Park Dr., Alexandria, VA 22312-1442; (703) 658-1529. Fax, (703) 658-9479. Capt. Frederick L. Thomas, President.*
Web, https://noblenational.org, Twitter, @noblenatl, Facebook, www.facebook.com/NOBLEOrganization and YouTube, www.youtube.com/channel/UCYhwqpBNkns YV-rNVJg7A4Q

Membership: African American police chiefs and senior law enforcement executives. Works to increase community involvement in the criminal justice system and to enhance the role of African Americans in law enforcement. Provides urban police departments with assistance in police operations, community relations, and devising strategies to sensitize the criminal justice system to the problems of the African American community.

National Policing Institute, *2550 S. Clark St.# 1130, Arlington, VA 22202; (202) 833-1460. Fax, (202) 659-9149. Jim Burch, President.*
General email, info@policinginstitute.org
Web, www.policinginstitute.org, Twitter, @Policinginst, Facebook, www.facebook.com/policinginstitute and YouTube, www.youtube.com/channel/ UC6BcbT3k4lmM4t3igpvCO8A

Scientific research, innovation and education foundation that conducts studies to improve police procedures; provides training and technical assistance for law enforcement strategies, including community-oriented policing. provides assessments and after action reviews. (Formerly National Police Foundation)

National Sheriffs' Assn. (NSA), *1450 Duke St., Alexandria, VA 22314-3490; (703) 838-5341. Fax, (703) 838-5349. Vernon Stanforth, President. Toll-free, (800) 424-7827.*
Web, www.sheriffs.org, Twitter, @NationalSheriff and Facebook, www.facebook.com/Nationalsheriffsassociation

Membership: sheriffs and other municipal, state, and federal law enforcement officers. Conducts research and training programs for members in law enforcement, court procedures, and corrections. Publishes *Sheriff* magazine and an e-newsletter.

Police Executive Research Forum, *1120 Connecticut Ave. N.W., #930, 20036; (202) 466-7820. Fax, (202) 466-7826. Chuck Wexler, Executive Director, (202) 454-8326.*
General email, perf@policeforum.org
Web, www.policeforum.org

Membership: law enforcement executives. Conducts research on law enforcement issues and disseminates criminal justice and law enforcement information. A provider of management services, technical assistance, and executive-level education to support law enforcement agencies.

LEGAL PROFESSIONS AND RESOURCES

General

Executive Office for U.S. Attorneys *(Justice Dept.), 950 Pennsylvania Ave. N.W., #2242, 20530-0001; Fax, (202) 252-1415. onty Wilkinson, Director. Switchboard, (202) 514-2000.*
Web, www.justice.gov/usao/eousa, Twitter, @USAttorneys and YouTube, www.youtube.com/c/ UnitedStatesAttorneysOffices

Provides the offices of U.S. attorneys with technical assistance and supervision in areas of legal counsel, personnel, and training. Publishes the *U.S. Attorneys' Manual* and *United States Attorneys' Bulletin.* Administers the Attorney General's Office of Legal Education, which conducts workshops and seminars to develop the litigation skills of the department's attorneys in criminal and civil trials. Develops and implements Justice Dept. procedures for collecting criminal fines.

Justice Dept. (DOJ), *Office of Legal Policy (OLP),* 950 *Pennsylvania Ave. N.W., #4234, 20530-0001; (202) 514-4601. Fax, (202) 514-2424. Hampton Dellinger, Assistant Attorney General.*
Web, www.justice.gov/olp

Works to improve the availability and quality of legal defense for vulnerable populations; seeks fair and just outcomes for those facing financial and other disadvantages effectively and efficiently. Works collaboratively with local, state, tribal, and federal participants to implement solutions.

Justice Dept. (DOJ), *Professional Responsibility (OPR),* 950 *Pennsylvania Ave. N.W., #3266, 20530-0001; (202) 514-3365. Fax, (202) 514-5050. Jeffrey R. Ragsdale, Counsel.*
General email, opr.complaints@usdoj.gov
Web, www.justice.gov/opr

Receives and reviews allegations of misconduct by Justice Dept. attorneys; refers cases that warrant further review to appropriate investigative agency or unit; makes recommendations to the attorney general for action on certain misconduct cases.

Legal Services Corp., 3333 *K St. N.W., 3rd Floor, 20007-3522; (202) 295-1500. Ronald S. Flagg, President.*
General email, info@lsc.gov
Web, www.lsc.gov, Twitter, @lsctweets and Facebook, www .facebook.com/LegalServicesCorporation

Independent nonprofit established by Congress. Awards grants to local agencies that provide the poor with legal services. Library open to the public by appointment only.

▶NONGOVERNMENTAL

American Assn. for Justice, 777 *6th St. N.W., #200, 20001; (202) 965-3500. Linda Lipsen, Chief Executive Officer, ext. 8300. Press, (202) 684-9588. Toll-free, (800) 424-2725. Web, www.justice.org, Twitter, @JusticeDotOrg, Facebook, www.facebook.com/JusticeDotOrg and General email, membership@justice.org*

Membership: attorneys, judges, law professors, and law students. Interests include aspects of legal and legislative activity relating to the adversary system and trial by jury, victims' rights, property and casualty insurance, revisions of federal rules of evidence, criminal code, jurisdictions of courts, juries, and consumer law. (Formerly the Assn. of Trial Lawyers of America.)

American Bar Assn. (ABA), *Commission on Disability Rights,* 1050 *Connecticut Ave. N.W., #400, 20036; (202) 662-1570. Fax, (202) 442-3439. Amy L. Allbright, Director.*
General email, cdr@americanbar.org
Web, www.americanbar.org/groups/diversity/ disabilityrights, Twitter, @ABADisability and Facebook, www.facebook.com/ABA.CDR

Promotes the rule of law for persons with mental, physical, and sensory disabilities and their full and equal participation in the legal profession. Offers online resources, publications, and continuing-education opportunities on disability law topics and engages in national initiatives to remove barriers to the education, employment, and advancement of lawyers with disabilities.

American Bar Assn. (ABA), *International Law,* 1050 *Connecticut Ave. N.W., 20036; (202) 662-1660. Fax, (202) 662-1669. Christina Heid, Section Director, (202) 662-1034. General email, intlaw@americanbar.org*
Web, www.americanbar.org/groups/international_law, Twitter, @ABInternatl and Facebook, www.facebook.com/ ABAInternational

Monitors and makes recommendations concerning developments in the practice of international law that affect ABA members and the public. Conducts programs, including International Legal Exchange, and produces publications covering the practice of international law.

American Bar Assn. (ABA), *International Legal Exchange Program (ILEX),* 1050 *Connecticut Ave. N.W., #400, 20036; (202) 662-1660. Fax, (202) 662-1669. Jinny Choi, Associate Director, (202) 662-1675. General email, intilex@americanbar.org*
Web, www.americanbar.org/groups/international_law/ international-projects/international-legal-exchange

Facilitates entry into the United States for foreign lawyers offered training in U.S. law firms. Serves as designated U.S. government overseer for the J-1 visa and accepts applications from foreign lawyers. Houses the International Legal Resource Center.

American Bar Assn. (ABA), *Washington Office,* 1050 *Connecticut Ave. N.W., #400, 20036; (202) 662-1000. Fax, (202) 662-1762. Jack L. Rives, Executive Director. Toll-free, (800) 285-2221.*
Web, www.americanbar.org, Twitter, @abaesq and Facebook, www.facebook.com/AmericanBarAssociation

Membership: lawyers, law students, and individuals interested in law. Provides resources to law professionals, accredits law schools, and establishes ethical codes. Composed of the Governmental Affairs Office, Public Services Division, Government and Public Sector Lawyers Division, International Law and Practice Section, Criminal Justice Section, Taxation Section, Individual Rights and Responsibilities Section, Dispute Resolution Section, Administrative Law and Regulatory Practice Section, Rule of Law Initiative, and others. Publishes the *ABA Journal.* (Headquarters in Chicago, Ill.)

American Health Law Assn., 1099 *14th St. N.W., #925, 20005; (202) 833-1100. Fax, (202) 833-1105. David S. Cade, Chief Executive Officer, (202) 833-0777.*
Web, www.americanhealthlaw.org, Twitter, @healthlawyers, Facebook, www.facebook.com/ahlafb and Public interest, publicinterest@healthlawyers.org

Membership: corporate, institutional, and government lawyers interested in the health care field; law students; and health professionals. Serves as an information clearinghouse on health law; sponsors health law educational programs and seminars.

American Immigration Lawyers Assn., *1331 G St. N.W., #300, 20005-3142; (202) 507-7600. Fax, (202) 783-7853. Benjamin Johnson, Executive Director.*
General email, membership@aila.org
Web, http://aila.org, Twitter, @ailanational and Facebook, www.facebook.com/AILANational

Association for lawyers interested in immigration law. Provides information and continuing education programs on immigration law and policy; offers workshops and conferences. Acts as advocate for a fair and just immigration law policy. Monitors legislation and regulations.

American Inns of Court Foundation, *225 Reinekers Lane, #770, Alexandria, VA 22314; (703) 684-3590. Brig. Gen. Malinda E. Dunn (USA, Ret.), Executive Director, ext. 102. Toll-free, (800) 233-3590.*
General email, info@innsofcourt.org
Web, http://home.innsofcourt.org, Twitter, @innsofcourt and Facebook, www.facebook.com/AmericanInnsofCourt

Promotes professionalism, ethics, civility, and legal skills of judges, lawyers, academicians, and law students in order to improve the quality and efficiency of the legal profession.

The Assn. of American Law Schools, *1614 20th St. N.W., 20009-1001; (202) 296-8851. Fax, (202) 296-8869. Judith Areen, Executive Director, (202) 296-1526.*
General email, info@aals.org
Web, www.aals.org, Twitter, @TheAALS and Facebook, www.facebook.com/theaals

Membership: law schools, subject to approval. Membership criteria include high-quality academic programs, faculty, scholarship, and students; academic freedom; diversity of people and viewpoints; and emphasis on public service. Hosts meetings and workshops; publishes a directory of law teachers. Acts as advocate on behalf of legal education; monitors legislation and judicial decisions.

Assn. of Corporate Counsel, *1001 G St. N.W., #300W, 20001; (202) 293-4103. Fax, (202) 293-4701. Veta T. Richardson, President. Toll-free, (866) 868-9092.*
Web, www.acc.com, Twitter, @ACCinhouse, Membership email, membership@acc.com and Facebook, www.facebook.com/AssnCorpCnsl

Membership: practicing lawyers in corporate law departments, associations, and legal departments of other private-sector organizations. Provides information on corporate law issues, including securities, health and safety, the environment, intellectual property, litigation, international legal affairs, pro bono work, and labor benefits. Monitors legislation and regulations, with primary focus on issues affecting in-house attorneys' ability to practice law. (Formerly American Corporate Counsel Assn.)

Assn. of Transportation Law Professionals, *P.O. Box 5407, Annapolis, MD 21403; (410) 268-1311. Fax, (410) 268-1322. Lauren Michalski, Executive Director.*
General email, info@atlp.org
Web, www.atlp.org

Membership: transportation of all modes, attorneys and company counsel, government officials, and industry practitioners. Provides members with continuing educational development in transportation law and practice.

Center for Workplace Compliance (CWC), *1501 M St. N.W., #1000, 20005; (202) 629-5650. Fax, (202) 629-5651. Joseph S. Lakis, President.*
General email, info@cwc.org
Web, www.cwc.org, Twitter, @CWC_alert and Facebook, www.facebook.com/centerforworkplacecompliance

Membership: principal equal employment officers and lawyers. Files amicus curiae (friend of the court) briefs; conducts research and provides information on equal employment law and policy. Monitors legislation and regulations. (Formerly the Equal Employment Advisory Council.)

Energy Bar Assn., *2000 M St. N.W., #715, 20036; (202) 223-5625. Fax, (202) 833-5596. Lisa A. Levine, Chief Executive Officer.*
General email, admin@eba-net.org
Web, www.eba-net.org and Twitter, @EnergyBarAssoc

Membership: lawyers interested in all areas of energy law. Interests include administration of laws covering production, development, conservation, transmission, and economic regulation of energy.

Federal Bar Assn., *1220 N. Fillmore St., #444, Arlington, VA 22201; (571) 481-9100. Fax, (571) 481-9090. Stacy King, Executive Director.*
General email, fba@fedbar.org
Web, www.fedbar.org, Twitter, @federalbar and Facebook, www.facebook.com/FederalBar

Membership: attorneys employed by the federal government or practicing before federal courts or agencies. Concerns include professional ethics, legal education (primarily continuing education), and legal services.

Federal Circuit Bar Assn., *1620 Eye St. N.W., #801, 20006; (202) 466-3923. Fax, (202) 833-1061. Deborah M. Miron, Executive Director, (202) 558-2421.*
General email, miron@@fedcirbar.org
Web, www.fedcirbar.org

Represents practitioners before the Court of Appeals for the Federal Circuit. Fosters discussion between different groups within the legal community; sponsors regional seminars; publishes a scholarly journal.

Hispanic National Bar Assn. (HNBA), *2020 Pennsylvania Ave. N.W., #279, 20006; (202) 223-4777. Fax, (202) 503-3403. Alba Cruz-Hacker, Executive Director, (504) 568-1990.*
General email, nationaloffice@hnba.com
Web, www.hnba.com, Twitter, @HNBANews and Facebook, www.facebook.com/HNBANational

Membership: Hispanic American attorneys, judges, law professors, paralegals, and law students. Seeks to increase professional opportunities in law for Hispanic Americans and to increase Hispanic American representation in law schools. (Affiliated with National Hispanic Leadership Agenda and the American Bar Assn.)

Inter-American Bar Assn., *1889 F St. N.W., #355, 20006; (202) 466-5944. Fax, (202) 466-5946. Lourdes Escaffi-Venes, Secretary General.*
General email, iaba@iaba.org
Web, www.iaba.org and Twitter, @IABA_FIA

Membership: lawyers and bar associations in the Western Hemisphere with associate members in Europe. Works to promote uniformity of national and international laws; holds conferences; makes recommendations to national governments and organizations. Library open to the public by appointment only.

International Law Institute, *1055 Thomas Jefferson St. N.W., #M-100, 20007; (202) 247-6006. Fax, (202) 247-6010. Kim Phan, Executive Director.*
General email, info@ili.org
Web, www.ili.org

Performs scholarly research, offers training programs, and provides technical assistance in the areas of international law and economic development. Sponsors international conferences.

Lawyers for Civil Justice, *1530 Wilson Blvd., #1030, Arlington, VA 22209; (202) 429-0045. Dan Steen, Executive Director, ext. 1.*
Web, www.lfcj.com, Twitter, @LCJReform and Facebook, www.facebook.com/Lawyers-for-Civil-Justice-337086056853133

Membership: defense lawyers and corporate counsel. Interests include tort reform, litigation cost containment, and tort and product liability. Monitors legislation and regulations affecting civil justice reform.

National Assn. of Attorneys General, *1850 M St. N.W., 12th Floor, 20036; (202) 326-6000. Chris Toth, Executive Director. Press, (202) 326-6047.*
General email, support@naag.org
Web, www.naag.org, Twitter, @NatlAssnAttysGn and Facebook, www.facebook.com/NAGTRI

Membership: attorneys general of the states, territories, and commonwealths. Fosters interstate cooperation on legal and law enforcement issues, conducts policy research and analysis, and facilitates communication between members and all levels of government.

National Assn. of Bond Lawyers, *601 13th St. N.W., #800-S, 20005-3875; (202) 503-3300. Fax, (202) 637-0217. Linda H. Wyman, Chief Operating Officer, ext. 3306; Brian Egan, Director, Government Affairs, ext. 3290.*
General email, nablconnect@nabl.org
Web, www.nabl.org, Twitter, @nabldc and Facebook, www.facebook.com/nabldc

Membership: state and municipal finance lawyers. Educates members and others on the law relating to state and municipal bonds and other obligations. Provides advice and comment at the federal, state, and local levels on legislation, regulations, rulings, and court and administrative proceedings regarding public obligations.

National Assn. of College and University Attorneys, *1 Dupont Circle N.W., #620, 20036-1182; (202) 833-8390. Fax, (202) 296-8379. Ona Alston Dosunmu, President.*
General email, nacua@nacua.org
Web, www.nacua.org and Twitter, @NACUAtweets

Provides information on legal developments affecting postsecondary education. Operates a clearinghouse through which in-house and external legal counselors are able to network with their counterparts on current legal problems.

National Assn. of Consumer Bankruptcy Attorneys, *2200 Pennsylvania Ave. N.W., 4th Floor, 20037; (800) 499-9040. Fax, (866) 408-9515. Krista D'Amelio, Director of Government Affairs.*
General email, admin@nacba.org
Web, www.nacba.org and Twitter, @NACBAorg

Acts as advocate on behalf of consumer debtors and their attorneys. Files amicus briefs on behalf of parties in the U.S. courts of appeal and Supreme Court, and provides educational programs and workshops for attorneys. Monitors legislation and regulations.

National Assn. of Criminal Defense Lawyers, *1660 L St. N.W., 12th Floor, 20036; (202) 872-8600. Fax, (202) 872-8690. Lisa Monet Wayne, Executive Director.*
General email, memberservices@nacdl.org
Web, www.nacdl.org, Twitter, @NACDL and Facebook, www.facebook.com/NACDL

Volunteer bar association of criminal defense attorneys and their local, state, and international affiliates. Provides members with continuing education, a brief bank, an ethics hotline, and specialized assistance in such areas as forensic science. Offers free legal assistance to members threatened with sanctions. Interests include eliminating mandatory minimum sentencing, forensic lab reform, death penalty reform, protection of privacy rights, indigent defense reform, overcriminalization, and civil liberties. Monitors legislation and regulations.

National Bar Assn., *1816 12th St. N.W., 4th Floor, 20009 (mailing address: P.O. Box 90500, Washington, DC 20090); (202) 842-3900. Fax, (202) 842-3901. Carlos Moore, President.*
General email, communications@nationalbar.org
Web, www.nationalbar.org, Twitter, @nationalbar and Facebook, www.facebook.com/NationalBar

Membership: primarily Black attorneys, legal professionals, judges, and law students. Interests include legal education and improvement of the judicial process. Sponsors legal education seminars in all states that require continuing legal education for lawyers.

National Court Reporters Assn., *12030 Sunrise Valley Dr., #400, Reston, VA 20191; (703) 556-6272. Fax, (703) 391-0629. Dave Wenhold, Executive Director, (703) 584-9035. Toll-free, (800) 272-6272.*

General email, membership@ncra.org

Web, www.ncra.org, Twitter, @NCRA, Facebook, www .facebook.com/NCRAfb and YouTube, www.youtube.com/ user/NCRAOnline

Membership organization that offers certification and continuing education for court reporting and captioning. Acts as a clearinghouse on technology and information for and about court reporters; certifies legal video specialists. Monitors legislation and regulations.

National District Attorneys Assn. (NDAA), 1400 Crystal Dr., #330, Arlington, VA 22202; (703) 549-9222. Fax, (703) 836-3195. Nelson O. Bunn, Executive Director, (703) 519-1666.

Web, www.ndaa.org, Twitter, @ndaajustice, Facebook, www.facebook.com/ndaajustice and YouTube, www .youtube.com/channel/UCw5FuTGifAzMIM8TlQayX-w

Membership: prosecutors. Sponsors conferences and workshops on such topics as criminal justice, district attorneys, the courts, child abuse, national traffic laws, community prosecution, violence against women, gun violence, and others; conducts research; provides information, training, and technical assistance to prosecutors; and analyzes policies related to improvements in criminal prosecution.

National Legal Aid and Defender Assn., 1901 Pennsylvania Ave. N.W., #500, 20006; (202) 452-0620. Fax, (202) 872-1031. Jo-Ann Wallace, President, ext. 206. Web, www.nlada.org and Twitter, @NLADA

Membership: national organizations and individuals providing indigent clients, including prisoners, with legal aid and defender services. Serves as a clearinghouse for member organizations; provides training and support services.

Women's Bar Assn., 2800 Eisenhower Ave. #210, Alexandria, VA 22314; (202) 639-8880. Fax, (202) 639-8889. Carol Montoya, Executive Director. General email, admin@wbadc.org

Web, www.wbadc.org, Twitter, @WBADC and Facebook, www.facebook.com/WBADC

Membership: women and men who are judges, attorneys in the public and private sectors, law students, and lawyers at home who remain professionally active. Promotes appointment of members to positions in the judiciary and legislative policies that foster the advancement of women.

Data and Research

▶**AGENCIES**

Community Oriented Policing Services (COPS) (Justice Dept.), 145 N St. N.E., 20530; (202) 616-2888. Robert Chapman, Director (Acting). FOIA, (202) 514-1873. Press, (202) 514-9079. Response Center, (800) 421-6770. General email, askCopsRC@usdoj.gov

Web, https://cops.usdoj.gov, Twitter, @COPSOffice and Facebook, www.facebook.com/DOJCOPS

Provides publications and other educational materials on a wide range of law enforcement concerns and community policing topics.

Justice Dept. (DOJ), Elder Justice Initiative (EJI), 950 Pennsylvania Ave. N.W., 20530; Andy Mao, Coordinator, (202) 616-0539. Eldercare locator helpline, (800) 677-1116. General email, elder.justice@usdoj.gov

Web, www.justice.gov/elderjustice and Rural and tribal resources, www.justice.gov/elderjustice/rural-and-tribal-resources

Provides access to a database containing bibliographic information for thousands of scientific, legal, and general elder abuse and financial exploitation articles and reviews.

Justice Dept. (DOJ), Justice Programs, National Criminal Justice Reference Service (NCJRS), P.O. Box 6000, Rockville, MD 20849-6000; (800) 851-3420. Fax, (301) 240-5830. General email, responsecenter@ncjrs.gov

Web, www.ojp.gov/ncjrs

Offers justice and drug-related information and resources to support research, policy, and program development. Curates the NCJRS Virtual Library.

Office of Justice Programs (OJP) (Justice Dept.), Bureau of Justice Statistics (BJS), 810 7th St. N.W., 2nd Floor, 20531; (202) 307-0765. Fax, (202) 307-5846. Doris James, Director (Acting).
General email, askbjs@usdoj.gov

Web, www.bjs.gov, Twitter, @BJSgov and Facebook, www .facebook.com/BJSgov

Collects, evaluates, publishes, and provides statistics on criminal justice. Data available from the National Criminal Justice Reference Service: P.O. Box 6000, Rockville, Md., 20849-6000; toll-free, (800) 851-3420; international callers, (301) 519-5500; TTY (877) 712-9279; and from the National Archive of Criminal Justice Data in Ann Arbor, Mich., (800) 999-0960.

Office of Justice Programs (OJP) (Justice Dept.), National Institute of Justice (NIJ), 810 7th St. N.W., 7th Floor, 20531; (202) 307-2942. Fax, (202) 307-6394. Jennifer Scherer, Director (Acting). Press, (202) 307-0703. General email, ojp.ocom@usdoj.gov

Web, www.nij.gov and Facebook, www.facebook.com/OJPNIJ

Conducts research on all aspects of criminal justice, including crime prevention, enforcement, adjudication, and corrections; evaluates programs; develops model programs using new techniques. Serves as an affiliated institute of the United Nations Crime Prevention and Criminal Justice Programme (UNCPCJ); studies transnational issues. Maintains the National Criminal Justice Reference Service, which provides information on criminal justice, including activities of the Office of National Drug Control Policy and law enforcement in Latin America: (800) 851-3420 or (202) 836-6998; Web, www.ncjrs.gov.

▶**CONGRESS**

For a listing of relevant congressional committees and subcommittees, please see pages 546–547 or the Appendix.

Library of Congress, *Law Library, James Madison Memorial Bldg., 101 Independence Ave. S.E., #LM 242, 20540-3129; (202) 707-5079/80. Fax, (202) 707-1820. Aslihan Bulut, Law Librarian.*
Web, www.loc.gov/law, Twitter, @LawLibCongress and Facebook, www.facebook.com/lawlibraryofcongress

Maintains collections of foreign, international, and comparative law texts organized jurisdictionally by country. Covers all legal systems, including common, civil, Roman, canon, religious, and ancient and medieval law. Services include a public reading room; a microtext facility, with readers and printers for microfilm and microfiche; and foreign law/rare book reading areas. Staff of legal specialists is competent in approximately forty languages; does not provide advice on legal matters. Timed entry pass for visitors required, details at loc.gov/visit. Appointments recommended for researchers.

▶ JUDICIARY

Administrative Office of the U.S. Courts, *1 Columbus Circle N.E., 20544-0001; (202) 502-2600. Hon. Roslynn R. Mauskopf, Director.*
Web, www.uscourts.gov and Twitter, @uscourts

Supervises all administrative matters of the federal court system, except the Supreme Court; prepares statistical data and reports on the business of the courts, including reports on juror utilization; caseloads of federal, public, and community defenders; and types of cases adjudicated.

Administrative Office of the U.S. Courts, *Data and Analysis, 1 Columbus Circle N.E., #2-250, 20544; (202) 502-3900. Erin Short, Chief. Public Affairs, (202) 502-2600.*
Web, www.uscourts.gov/statistics-reports

Compiles information and statistics from civil, criminal, appeals, and bankruptcy cases. Publishes statistical reports on court management; juror utilization; federal offenders; equal access to justice; the Financial Privacy Act; caseloads of federal, public, and community defenders; and types of cases adjudicated.

Supreme Court of the United States, *Library, 1 1st St. N.E., 20543; (202) 479-3177. Linda Maslow, Librarian.*
Web, www.supremecourt.gov

Maintains collection of Supreme Court documents dating from the mid-1800s. Records, briefs, and depository documents available for public use.

▶ NONGOVERNMENTAL

Federal Bar Assn., *1220 N. Fillmore St., #444, Arlington, VA 22201; (571) 481-9100. Fax, (571) 481-9090. Stacy King, Executive Director.*
General email, fba@fedbar.org
Web, www.fedbar.org, Twitter, @federalbar and Facebook, www.facebook.com/FederalBar

Conducts research and programs in fields that include tax, environment, veterans health, intellectual property, Social Security, transportation, Native American, antitrust, immigration, and international law.

Justice Research and Statistics Assn., *1000 Vermont Ave. N.W., #450, 20005; (202) 842-9330. Fax, (202) 304-1417. Jeffrey Sedgwick, Executive Director.*
General email, cjinfo@jrsa.org
Web, www.jrsa.org and Twitter, @JRSAinfo

Provides information on the collection, analysis, dissemination, and use of data concerning crime and criminal justice at the state level; serves as liaison between the Justice Dept. Bureau of Justice Statistics and the states; develops standards for states on the collection, analysis, and use of statistics. Offers courses in criminal justice and in research and evaluation methodologies in conjunction with its annual conference.

National Consumer Law Center, *Washington Office, 1001 Connecticut Ave. N.W., #510, 20036-5528; (202) 452-6252. Fax, (202) 296-4062. Richard DuBois, Executive Director; Lauren Sanders, Associate Director, Washington Office, ext. 105.*
General email, consumerlaw@nclc.org
Web, www.nclc.org, Twitter, @NCLC4consumers and Facebook, www.facebook.com/nationalconsumerlawcenter

Provides lawyers funded by the Legal Services Corp. with research and assistance; provides lawyers with training in consumer and energy law. (Headquarters in Boston, Mass.)

PUBLIC INTEREST LAW

General

▶ AGENCIES

Justice Dept. (DOJ), *950 Pennsylvania Ave. N.W., 20530-0001; (202) 514-2000. Fax, (202) 307-6777. Merrick Garland, Attorney General. Public Affairs, (202) 514-2007. Public comments, (202) 353-1555. TTY, (800) 877-8339.*
General email, askdoj@usdoj.gov
Web, www.justice.gov and Twitter, @TheJusticeDept

Serves as counsel for the U.S. government. Represents the government in enforcing the law in the public interest. Plays key role in protecting against criminals and subversion, in ensuring healthy competition of business in U.S. free enterprise system, in safeguarding the consumer, and in enforcing drug, immigration, and naturalization laws. Plays a significant role in protecting citizens through effective law enforcement, crime prevention, crime detection, and prosecution and rehabilitation of offenders. Conducts all suits in the Supreme Court in which the United States is concerned. Represents the government in legal matters generally, furnishing legal advice and opinions to the president, the cabinet, and the heads of executive departments, as provided by law. Justice Dept. organization includes divisions on antitrust, civil law, civil rights, criminal law, environment and natural resources, and taxes, as well as the Bureau of Alcohol, Tobacco, Firearms, and Explosives; Drug Enforcement Administration; Executive Office for

Immigration Review; Federal Bureau of Investigation; Federal Bureau of Prisons; Foreign Claims Settlement Commission; Office of Justice Programs; U.S. Attorneys; U.S. Marshals Service; U.S. Parole Commission; and U.S. Trustees.

Legal Services Corp., *3333 K St. N.W., 3rd Floor, 20007-3522; (202) 295-1500. Ronald S. Flagg, President.*
General email, info@lsc.gov

Web, www.lsc.gov, Twitter, @lsctweets and Facebook, www.facebook.com/LegalServicesCorporation

Independent nonprofit established by Congress. Awards grants to local agencies that provide the poor with legal services. Library open to the public by appointment only.

► CONGRESS

For a listing of relevant congressional committees and subcommittees, please see pages 546–547 or the Appendix.

► NONGOVERNMENTAL

Alliance for Justice (AFJ), *11 Dupont Circle N.W., #500, 20036; (202) 822-6070. Rakim Brooks, President.*
General email, alliance@afj.org

Web, www.afj.org, Twitter, @AFJustice, Facebook, www.facebook.com/AllianceforJustice and YouTube, www.youtube.com/user/alliance4justice

Membership: public interest lawyers and advocacy, environmental, civil rights, and consumer organizations. Promotes reform of the legal system, via The justice Program; to ensure access to the courts; monitors selection of federal judges; works to preserve the rights of nonprofit organizations to advocate on behalf of their constituents.

Appleseed, *700 12th St. N.W. #700, 20015; (202) 905-2788. Brett Magnuson, Executive Director.*
General email, appleseed@appleseednetwork.org

Web, www.appleseednetwork.org and Twitter, @appleseednetwork

Network of seventeen public interest justice centers in the United States and Mexico advocating reforms designed to provide greater access to economic opportunity, fair courts, criminal justice, housing, education, food, and accountable government.

Bazelon Center for Mental Health Law, *1090 Vermont Ave. N.W., #220, 20005; (202) 467-5730. Holly O'Donnell, Chief Executive Officer.*
General email, communications@bazelon.org

Web, www.bazelon.org, Twitter, @BazelonCenter and Facebook, www.facebook.com/bazeloncenter

Public interest law firm. Works to establish and advance the legal rights of children and adults with mental disabilities and ensure their equal access to services and resources needed for full participation in community life. Provides technical support to lawyers and other advocates. Conducts test case litigation to defend rights of persons with mental disabilities. Conducts policy analysis, builds coalitions, issues advocacy alerts, publishes handbooks, and maintains advocacy resources online. Monitors legislation and regulations.

Becket Fund for Religious Liberty, *1919 Pennsylvania Ave., #400, 20006; (202) 955-0095. Fax, (202) 955-0090. Mark Rienzi, President. Press, (202) 349-7226.*
Web, www.becketlaw.org, Twitter, @BECKETlaw, Facebook, www.facebook.com/becketlaw and YouTube, www.youtube.com/user/BecketFundVideo

Public interest law firm that promotes freedom of expression for people of all faiths. Works to ensure that people and institutions of all faiths, domestically and abroad, are entitled to a voice in public affairs.

Brady Center to Prevent Gun Violence, *840 1st St. N.E., #400, 20002; (202) 370-8100. Fax, (202) 370-8102. Kris Brown, President. Press, (202) 370-8128.*
General email, media@bradyunited.org

Web, www.bradyunited.org, Twitter, @Bradybuzz and Facebook, www.facebook.com/bradycampaign

Public interest organization that works for gun control legislation and serves as an information clearinghouse. Monitors legislation and regulations.

Center for Individual Rights, *1100 Connecticut Ave. N.W., #625, 20036; (202) 833-8400. Fax, (202) 833-8410. Terence (Terry) J. Pell, President.*
General email, cir@cir-usa.org

Web, www.cir-usa.org and Twitter, @CIRights

Public interest law firm that provides free representation to individuals who cannot afford adequate legal counsel in cases raising constitutional questions of individual rights. Interests include freedom of speech and religious expression, civil rights, and Congress's enumerated powers.

Center for Law and Education, *7011 8th St. N.W., 20012; (202) 986-3000. Paul Weckstein, Co-Director, ext. 101; Kathleen Boundy, Co-Director (in Boston).*
General email, cle@cleweb.org

Web, www.cleweb.org and Facebook, www.facebook.com/centerforlawandeducation

National advocacy organization committed to improving education of low-income students. Works with students, parents, their advocates, and members of the school community to implement and effectuate school and district level changes. Focuses on school and district reform and civil rights; uses multiforum advocacy (legislative, administrative advocacy, and litigation, as needed) on behalf of low-income individuals. (Headquarters in Boston, Mass.)

Center for Law and Social Policy (CLASP), *1310 L St. N.W., #900, 20005; (202) 906-8000. Olivia Golden, Executive Director.*
Web, www.clasp.org and Twitter, @CLASP_DC

Public policy organization with expertise in national, state, and local policy affecting low-income Americans. Seeks to improve the economic security and educational and workforce prospects of low-income children, youth, adults, and families. Works to develop, promote, and implement federal, state, and local policies in legislation, regulation, and on the ground.

Center for Study of Responsive Law, *1530 P St. N.W., 20005 (mailing address: P.O. Box 19367, Washington, DC 20036); (202) 387-8030. John Richard, Administrator.*
General email, info@csrl.org
Web, http://csrl.org

Consumer-interest clearinghouse that conducts research and holds conferences on public interest issues. Interests include white-collar crime, the environment, occupational health and safety, the postal system, banking deregulation, insurance, freedom of information policy, and broadcasting.

Christian Legal Society, *8001 Braddock Rd., #302, Springfield, VA 22151 (mailing address: P.O. Box 7712, McLean, VA 22106-7712); (703) 642-1070. David Nammo, Chief Executive Officer, ext. 501.*
General email, clshq@clsnet.org
Web, www.christianlegalsociety.org

Membership: Christian lawyers, judges, paralegals, law professors, law students, and others. Interests include the defense of religious freedom and the provision of legal aid to the poor.

Civil Rights Clinic *(Georgetown University), 600 New Jersey Ave. N.W., #352, 20001; (202) 661-6739. Aderson Francois, Director.*
General email, civilrightsclinic@georgetown.edu
Web, www.law.georgetown.edu/experiential-learning/ clinics/our-clinics/civil-rights-clinic

Public-interest law firm funded by Georgetown University Law Center. Studies federal administrative law and federal court litigation. Gives graduate fellows an opportunity to work on unique, large-scale projects. Interests include civil rights and voting rights.

Electronic Privacy Information Center (EPIC), *1519 New Hampshire Ave. N.W., 20036; (202) 483-1140. Fax, (202) 483-1248. Alan Butler, Executive Director.*
General email, info@epic.org
Web, https://epic.org and Twitter, @EPICprivacy

Public interest research center. Conducts research and conferences on domestic and international civil liberties issues, including privacy, free speech, information access, computer security, and encryption; litigates cases. Monitors legislation and regulations. Operates an online bookstore.

Foundation for Advancing Alcohol Responsiblity, *2345 Crystal Dr., #710, Arlington, VA 22202; (202) 637-0077. Chris Swonger, President.*
Web, www.responsibility.org, Twitter, @GoFARR, Facebook, www.facebook.com/GoFAAR and YouTube, www.youtube.com/user/GoFAAR

Works with state and federal government to craft and promote policies and legislation to combat impaired driving. Leading efforts to elimate underage drinking.

Institute for Justice, *901 N. Glebe Rd., #900, Arlington, VA 22203; (703) 682-9320. Fax, (703) 682-9321. Scott G. Bullock, President.*
General email, general@ij.org
Web, www.ij.org, Twitter, @IJ and Facebook, www .facebook.com/instituteforjustice

Sponsors seminars to train law students, grassroots activists, and practicing lawyers in applying advocacy strategies in public-interest litigation. Seeks to protect individuals from arbitrary government interference in free speech, private property rights, parental school choice, and economic liberty. Litigates cases.

Institute for Public Representation, *600 New Jersey Ave. N.W., #312, 20001; (202) 662-9535. Fax, (202) 662-9634. Hope Babcock, Co-Director, (202) 662-9481; Laura Moy, Co-Director.*
General email, gulcipr@law.georgetown.edu
Web, www.law.georgetown.edu/experiential-learning/ clinics/our-clinics/communications-technology-law-clinic- ipr/our-history and Blog, instituteforpublicrepresentation .org

Public interest law firm funded by Georgetown University Law Center that studies federal administrative law and federal court litigation. Gives graduate fellows an opportunity to work on unique, large-scale projects. Interests include first amendment and media law, environmental law, and general public interest matters.

Mexican American Legal Defense and Educational Fund (MALDEF), *National Public Policy, 1016 16th St. N.W., #100, 20036; (202) 293-2828. Andrea Senteno, Regional Counsel for Legislative and Regulatory Affairs.*
General email, info@maldef.org
Web, www.maldef.org/public-policy, Twitter, @MALDEF, Facebook, www.facebook.com/MALDEF and YouTube, www.youtube.com/user/maldef

Provides Mexican Americans and other Hispanics with high-impact litigation in the areas of employment, education, immigration rights, and voting rights. Monitors legislation and regulations. (Headquarters in Los Angeles, Calif.)

Migrant Legal Action Program, *1001 Connecticut Ave. N.W., #915, 20036-5524; (202) 775-7780. Roger C. Rosenthal, Executive Director.*
General email, mlap@mlap.org
Web, www.mlap.org and Facebook, www.facebook.com/ MigrantLegalActionProgram

Provides both direct representation to farmworkers and technical assistance and support to health, education, and legal services programs for migrants. Monitors legislation and regulations.

National Consumer Law Center, *Washington Office, 1001 Connecticut Ave. N.W., #510, 20036-5528; (202) 452-6252. Fax, (202) 296-4062. Richard DuBois, Executive Director; Lauren Sanders, Associate Director, Washington Office, ext. 105.*

General email, consumerlaw@nclc.org

Web, www.nclc.org, Twitter, @NCLC4consumers and Facebook, www.facebook.com/nationalconsumerlawcenter

Provides lawyers funded by the Legal Services Corp. with research and assistance; researches problems of low-income consumers and develops alternative solutions. (Headquarters in Boston, Mass.)

National Health Law Program, Washington Office, 1444 Eye St. N.W., #1105, 20005; (202) 289-7661. Elizabeth G. Taylor, Executive Director.

General email, nhelp@healthlaw.org

Web, www.healthlaw.org, Twitter, @NHelp-org and Facebook, www.facebook.com/NHeLProgram

Organization of lawyers representing the economically disadvantaged and minorities. Offers technical assistance, workshops, seminars, and training for health law specialists. Issues include health care reform, medicaid, child and adolescent health, and disability and reproductive rights.

National Homeless Law Center, 2000 M St. N.W., #750-E, 20036; (202) 638-2535. Fax, (202) 628-2737. Antonia Fasanelli, Executive Director.

General email, email@nlchp.org

Web, www.nlchp.org and Twitter, @homeless_law

Legal advocacy group that works to prevent and end homelessness through impact litigation, legislation, and education. Conducts research on homelessness issues. Acts as a clearinghouse for legal information and technical assistance. Monitors legislation and regulations.

National Legal Aid and Defender Assn., 1901 Pennsylvania Ave. N.W., #500, 20006; (202) 452-0620. Fax, (202) 872-1031. Jo-Ann Wallace, President, ext. 206. Web, www.nlada.org and Twitter, @NLADA

Membership: national organizations and individuals providing indigent clients, including prisoners, with legal aid and defender services. Serves as a clearinghouse for member organizations; provides training and support services.

Public Citizen, Litigation Group, 1600 20th St. N.W., 20009-1001; (202) 588-1000. Allison Zieve, Director of Litigation.

General email, litigation@citizen.org

Web, www.citizen.org/topic/justice-the-courts

Conducts litigation for Public Citizen, a consumer advocacy group, in the areas of consumer rights, access to courts, health and safety, government and corporate accountability, and separation of powers; represents other individuals and nonprofit groups with similar interests.

Public Justice Foundation, 1620 L St. N.W., #630, 20036; (202) 797-8600. Fax, (202) 232-7203. F. Paul Bland Jr., Executive Director, ext. 223.

Web, www.publicjustice.net, Twitter, @Public_Justice and Facebook, www.facebook.com/publicjustice

Membership: consumer activists, trial lawyers, public interest lawyers, and law professors and students. Litigates to influence corporate and government decisions about products or activities adversely affecting health or safety. Interests include toxic torts, environmental protection, civil rights and civil liberties, workers' safety, consumer protection, and the preservation of the civil justice system. (Formerly Trial Lawyers for Public Justice.)

Street Law, Inc., 1010 Wayne Ave., #870, Silver Spring, MD 20910; (301) 589-1130. Fax, (301) 589-1131. Ashok Regmi, Executive Director.

General email, learnmore@streetlaw.org

Web, www.streetlaw.org, Twitter, @StreetLawInc and Facebook, www.facebook.com/StreetLawInc

International educational organization that promotes public understanding of law, the legal system, democracy, and human rights. Provides curriculum materials, training, and technical assistance to secondary school systems, law schools, departments of corrections, juvenile justice systems, bar associations, community groups, and state, local, and foreign governments.

Washington Legal Foundation, 2009 Massachusetts Ave. N.W., 20036; (202) 588-0302. Constance Claffey Larcher, Chief Executive Officer.

General email, info@wlf.org

Web, www.wlf.org and Twitter, @WLF

Public interest law and policy center. Seeks a legal and regulatory environment supportive of free enterprise through litigation, education, and advocacy. Interests include free-market principles, limited government, and civil liberties.

14

Military Personnel and Veterans

GENERAL POLICY AND ANALYSIS

Basic Resources

▶**AGENCIES**

Air Force Dept. *(Defense Dept.), Manpower, Personnel, and Services,* 1040 Air Force Pentagon, #4E168, 20330-1040; (703) 697-6088. Lt. Gen. Brian T. Kelly, Deputy Chief of Staff.
Web, www.af.mil

Military office that coordinates military and civilian personnel policies of the Air Force Dept.

Air Force Dept. *(Defense Dept.), Manpower, Personnel, and Services, Military Force Management Policy,* 1400 W. Perimeter Rd., #4770, Joint Base Andrews, MD 20762; (703) 695-6770. Brig. Gen. Troy E. Dunn, Director.
Web, www.afpc.af.mil

Establishes department management policies regarding the accession, assignment, evaluation, skills analysis and management, promotion, readiness, retraining, separation, and retirement of Air Force military and civilian personnel. Oversees total force contingency, mobilization, training management, and rated force policy. (Headquarters in Tex.)

Army Dept. *(Defense Dept.), G-1,* 300 Army Pentagon, #2E446, 20310-0300; (703) 697-8060.
Lt. Gen. Gary M. Brito (USA), Deputy Chief of Staff, G-1.
Web, www.army.mil/G-1, Twitter, @MRA_G1_PAO and Facebook, www.facebook.com/HQDAMRAG1

Military office that coordinates military and civilian personnel policies of the Army Dept.

Defense Dept. (DoD), *Community and Public Outreach,* 1400 Defense Pentagon, 2E984, 20301-1400; (703) 693-2337. Fax, (703) 697-2577. Patricia Montes Barron, Deputy Assistant Secretary. Press, (703) 697-5131. Public Affairs, (703) 571-3343. Toll-free (Military OneSource), (800) 342-9647.
Web, www.defense.gov

Administers Pentagon tours; hosts Joint Civilian Orientation Conference (JCOC), enabling senior American business, education, and community leaders to engage with military personnel; replies to inquiries from the general public; serves as primary liaison to national veterans and military organizations.

Defense Dept. (DoD), *Military Personnel Policy,* 4000 Defense Pentagon, #5A678, 20301-4000; (703) 571-0116. Fax, (703) 571-0120. Lernes Hebert (USNAF, Ret.), Deputy Assistant Secretary.
General email, osd.pentagon.ousd-p-r.mbx.osd-military-personnel–policy@mail.mil
Web, https://prhome.defense.gov/M-RA/Inside-M-RA/MPP

Military office that coordinates military personnel policies of the Defense Dept. and reviews military personnel policies of the individual services.

Defense Dept. (DoD), *Personnel and Readiness,* 4000 Defense Pentagon, #3E986, 20301-4000; (703) 697-2121. Fax, (703) 571-5363. Gilbert R. Cisneros, Under Secretary; Julie Blanks, Executive Director. Military OneSource International, (800) 342-9647. Military OneSource International Collect, (703) 253-7599. Military OneSource Toll-free, (800) 342-9647.
Web, https://prhome.defense.gov/ and Military OneSource, www.militaryonesource.mil

Coordinates civilian and military personnel policies of the Defense Dept. and reviews personnel policies of the individual services. Handles equal opportunity policies; serves as focal point for all readiness issues. Administers Military OneSource, a 24/7 toll-free information and referral telephone service for matters relating to education, financial aid, relocation, housing, child care, counseling, and other employee concerns. Military OneSource is available worldwide to military personnel and their families.

Defense Dept. (DoD), *Public Affairs,* 1400 Defense Pentagon, #2D961, 20301-1400; (703) 571-3343. Fax, (703) 697-3501. John Kirby, Assistant to the Secretary of Defense for Public Affairs. Press, (703) 697-5131.
Web, www.defense.gov/news

Responds to public inquiries concerning Defense Dept. mission, activities, policies, and personnel.

Navy Dept. *(Defense Dept.), Military Personnel, Plans, and Policy,* 701 S. Courthouse Rd., Arlington, VA 22204; (703) 604-5562. Rear Admiral James Waters III (USN), Director.
Web, www.navy.mil

Military office that coordinates naval personnel policies, including promotions, professional development, and compensation, for officers and enlisted personnel.

Navy Dept. *(Defense Dept.), Naval Personnel,* 701 S. Courthouse Rd., Arlington, VA 22204; (703) 604-2863. Vice Adm. John B. Nowell Jr. (USN), Chief. MyNavy Career Center, (833) 330-6622.
General email, mynavyhr@navy.mil
Web, www.mynavyhr.navy.mil, Twitter, @MyNAVYHR and Facebook, www.facebook.com/MyNAVYHR

Responsible for planning and programming of manpower and personnel resources, budgeting for Navy personnel, developing systems to manage total force manpower and personnel resources, and assignment of Navy personnel. (Office based in Millington, Tenn.)

▶**CONGRESS**

For a listing of relevant congressional committees and subcommittees, please see page 600 or the Appendix.

▶**NONGOVERNMENTAL**

Air Force Assn. (AFA), 1501 Lee Hwy., #400, Arlington, VA 22209-1198; (703) 247-5800. Fax, (703) 247-5853. Lt. Gen. Bruce (Orville) Wright (USAF, Ret.), President. Press, (703) 247-5818. Toll-free, (800) 727-3337.

MILITARY PERSONNEL AND VETERANS RESOURCES IN CONGRESS

For a complete listing of congressional committees, including their full contact information, leadership, membership, and jurisdictions, please refer to the Appendix on pages 840–963.

HOUSE:

House Appropriations Committee, (202) 225-2771.
Web, appropriations.house.gov
  Subcommittee on Defense, (202) 225-2847.
  Subcommittee on Military Construction,
    Veterans Affairs, and Related Agencies,
    (202) 225-3047.
House Armed Services Committee, (202) 225-4151.
Web, armedservices.house.gov
  Subcommittee on Cyber, Innovative
    Technologies, and Information Systems,
    (202) 225-4151.
  Subcommittee on Intelligence and Special
    Operations, (202) 225-4151.
  Subcommittee on Military Personnel,
    (202) 225-4151.
  Subcommittee on Readiness, (202) 225-4151.
  Subcommittee on Seapower and Protection
    Forces, (202) 225-4151.
  Subcommittee on Strategic Forces,
    (202) 225-4151.
  Subcommittee on Tactical Air and Land Forces,
    (202) 225-4151.
House Financial Services Committee, (202) 225-4247.
Web, financialservices.house.gov
  Subcommittee on Financial Institutions and
    Consumer Credit, (202) 225-4247.
  Subcommittee on Housing, Community
    Development, and Insurance, (202) 225-4247.
  Subcommittee on Oversight and Investigations,
    (202) 225-4247.
House Oversight and Reform Committee,
    (202) 225-5051.
Web, oversight.house.gov
  Subcommittee on National Security,
    (202) 225-5051.
House Permanent Select Committee on Intelligence,
    (202) 225-7690.
Web, intelligence.house.gov
House Transportation and Infrastructure
    Committee, (202) 225-4472.
Web, transportation.house.gov
  Subcommittee on Coast Guard and Maritime
    Transportation, (202) 226-3552.
House Veterans' Affairs Committee, (202) 225-9756.
Web, veterans.house.gov

  Subcommittee on Disability Assistance and
    Memorial Affairs, (202) 225-9756.
  Subcommittee on Economic Opportunity,
    (202) 225-9756.
  Subcommittee on Health, (202) 225-9756.
  Subcommittee on Oversight and Investigations,
    (202) 225-9756.
  Subcommittee on Technology Modernization,
    (202) 224-9756.

SENATE:

Senate Appropriations Committee, (202) 224-7363.
Web, appropriations.senate.gov
  Subcommittee on Defense, (202) 224-7363.
  Subcommittee on Military Construction,
    Veterans Affairs, and Related Agencies,
    (202) 224-7363.
Senate Armed Services Committee, (202) 224-3871.
Web, armed-services.senate.gov
  Subcommittee on Airland, (202) 224-3871.
  Subcommittee on Cybersecurity, (202) 224-3871.
  Subcommittee on Emerging Threats and
    Capabilities, (202) 224-3871.
  Subcommittee on Personnel, (202) 224-3871.
  Subcommittee on Readiness and Management
    Support, (202) 224-3871.
  Subcommittee on Seapower, (202) 224-3871.
  Subcommittee on Strategic Forces, (202) 224-3871.
Senate Banking, Housing, and Urban Affairs
    Committee, (202) 224-7391.
Web, banking.senate.gov
  Subcommittee on Financial Institutions and
    Consumer Protection, (202) 224-7391.
Senate Foreign Relations Committee, (202) 224-4651.
Web, foreign.senate.gov
  Subcommittee on State Department and USAID
    Management, International Operations, and
    Bilateral International Development,
    (202) 224-4651.
Senate Homeland Security and Governmental Affairs
    Committee, (202) 224-2627.
Web, hsgac.senate.gov
  Subcommittee on Government Operations and
    Border Management, (202) 224-4551.
Senate Veterans' Affairs Committee, (202) 224-9126.
Web, veterans.senate.gov

General email, membership@afa.org
Web, www.afa.org, Twitter, @AirForceAssoc and
Facebook, www.facebook.com/AirForceAssociation

Membership: civilians and active duty, reserve, retired, and cadet personnel of the Air Force and Space Force. Informs members and the public of developments in the

aerospace field. Monitors legislation and Defense Dept. policies. Library on aviation history open to the public by appointment.

Air Force Sergeants Assn. (AFSA), *5211 Auth Rd., Suitland, MD 20746; (301) 899-3500. Fax, (301) 899-8136. Keith A. Reed, Executive Director. Toll-free, (800) 638-0594.*

General email, afsacomm@hqafsa.org

Web, www.hqafsa.org, Twitter, @afsahq and Facebook, www.facebook.com/AFSAHQ

Membership: active duty, reserve, National Guard, retired, and veteran enlisted Air Force personnel; Public Health Services and National Oceanic Atmospheric Administration personnel; and family members of uniformed service members. Monitors and advocates legislation, education, and policies that promote quality of life and economic fairness benefits for its members. Offers scholarships to dependent children of enlisted Air Force members. Provides insurance, banking, and transitional support.

U.S. Army Warrant Officers Assn., 462 Herndon Pkwy., #207, Herndon, VA 20170-5235; (703) 742-7727. CWO John (Jack) DuTeil (USA, Ret.), Executive Director. Toll-free, (800) 587-2962.

General email, HQ@usawoa.org

Web, https://usawoa.org

Membership: active duty, guard, reserve, and retired and former warrant officers. Monitors and makes recommendations to Defense Dept., Army Dept., and Congress on policies and programs affecting Army warrant officers and their families. Provides professional development programs for members.

United Service Organizations (USO), 2111 Wilson Blvd., #1200, Arlington, VA 22201-7677 (mailing address: P.O. Box 96860, Washington, DC 20077); (703) 908-6400. Fax, (703) 908-6402. J. D. Crouch II, President. Toll-free, (888) 484-3876.

Web, www.uso.org, Twitter, @the_USO, Facebook, www .facebook.com/theUSO and YouTube, www.youtube.com/ theuso

Voluntary civilian organization chartered by Congress. Provides military personnel and their families in the United States and overseas with social, educational, and recreational programs.

DEFENSE PERSONNEL

Chaplains

▶AGENCIES

Air Force Dept. *(Defense Dept.), Chief of Chaplains,* 229 Brookley Ave. S.W., Bldg.520, #112, Bolling Air Force Base, 20032; (202) 404-1637. Maj. Gen. Randall E. Kitchens, Chief of Chaplains.

General email, af.hc.workflow@us.af.mil

Web, www.resilience.af.mil/chaplain-corps, Facebook, www.facebook.com/AirForceChaplainCorps and Twitter, @DafResilience

Oversees chaplains and religious services within the Air Force; maintains liaison with religious denominations.

Army Dept. *(Defense Dept.), Chief of Chaplains,* 2700 Army Pentagon, #3E524, 20310-2700; (703) 695-1133.

Fax, (703) 695-9834. Maj. Gen. Thomas L. Solhjem, Chief of Chaplains.

Web, www.army.mil/chaplaincorps, Twitter, @ArmyChaplains, Facebook, www.facebook.com/ ArmyChaplainCorps and Email, usarmy.pentagon.hqda- occh.mbx.occh-dach-communications@army.mil

Oversees chaplains and religious services within the Army; maintains liaison with religious denominations.

Defense Dept. (DOD), *Armed Forces Chaplains Board,* OUSD (P&R) MPP-AFCB, 4000 Defense Pentagon, #2D580, 20301-4000; (703) 697-9015. Lt. Col. Dale Marlowe (USN), Executive Director.

General email, osd.afcb5120@mail.mil

Web, https://prhome.defense.gov/M-RA/Inside-M-RA/ MPP/AFCB

Membership: chiefs and deputy chiefs of chaplains of the armed services; works to coordinate religious policies and services among the military branches.

Marine Corps *(Defense Dept.), Chaplain,* Bldg. 29, 3000 Navy Pentagon, Henderson Hall, 1st. Fl., 20350; (703) 614-9280. Rear Adm. Gregory N. Todd (USN), Chaplain.

Web, www.hqmc.marines.mil/Agencies/Headquarters andServiceBattalion/chaplainoffice.aspx and Facebook, www.facebook.com/ChapsUSMC

Oversees chaplains and religious services within the Marine Corps; maintains liaison with religious denominations.

National Guard Bureau *(Defense Dept.), Chaplain Services,* 111 S. George Mason Dr., Arlington, VA 22204; (703) 607-8657. Fax, (703) 607-5295. Brig. Gen. Thomas G. Behling (ARNG), Director.

General email, ng.ncr.arng.mbx.office-of-the- chaplain@mail.mil

Web, www.nationalguard.mil/Leadership/Joint-Staff/ Special-Staff/Chaplain

Represents the Chief National Guard Bureau on all aspects of the chaplains' mission. Directs and oversees the activities and policies of the National Guard Chaplain Services. Oversees chaplains and religious services within the National Guard; maintains liaison with religious denominations.

Navy Dept. *(Defense Dept.), Chief of Chaplains,* 2000 Navy Pentagon, #5E270, 20350-1000; (703) 614-4043. Rear Adm. Brent W. Scott (USN), Chief.

Web, www.navy.mil

Oversees chaplains and religious services within the Navy; maintains liaison with religious denominations.

U.S. Coast Guard (USCG) *(Homeland Security Dept.), Chaplain,* 2703 Martin Luther King Jr. Ave. S.E., MS 7000, 20593-7000; (202) 372-4434. Fax, (202) 372-8305. Capt. Thomas J. Walcott, Chaplain.

General email, HQS-SMB-CG-00A-ChaplainOffice@uscg .mil

Web, www.uscg.mil/Leadership/Senior-Leadership/ Chaplain-of-the-Coast-Guard

Oversees chaplains and religious services within the Coast Guard; maintains liaison with religious denominations.

▶NONGOVERNMENTAL

Chaplain Alliance for Religious Liberty, *P.O. Box 151353, Alexandria, VA 22315; (571) 293-2427. Capt. Craig Muehler (USN, Ret.), President; Derek LS Jones (USA, Ret.), Executive Director.*
General email, info@chaplainalliance.org
Web, http://chaplainalliance.org, Twitter, @CHAP_ Alliance and Facebook, www.facebook.com/Chaplain Alliance

Membership: military chaplains and others who support orthodox Christian doctrines. Seeks to ensure that all chaplains and those they serve may exercise their religious liberties without fear of reprisal. Interests include the conflict between official protection for gays in the military and orthodox Christian teachings. Issues press releases; grants media interviews; monitors legislation and regulations.

Military Chaplains Assn. of the United States of America, *5541 Lee Hwy., Arlington, VA 22207-7056 (mailing address: P.O. Box 7056, Arlington, VA 22207-7056); (703) 533-5890. Maj. Gen. Razz Waff (USA, Ret.), Executive Director.*
General email, chaplains@mca-usa.org
Web, www.mca-usa.org, Twitter, @usamilitarychaplains and Facebook, www.facebook.com/usamilitarychaplain

Membership: chaplains of all faiths in all branches of the armed services and chaplains of veterans affairs and civil air patrol. Provides training opportunities for chaplains and a referral service concerning chaplains and chaplaincy. Publishes *The Military Chaplain.* Sponsors awards and scholarships. Also shares information and referral services for those within and outside the federal government arena.

National Conference on Ministry to the Armed Forces, *P.O. Box 7572, Arlington, VA 22207-9998; (703) 608-2100. Capt. John (Jack) H. Lea III (CHC USN, Ret.), Executive Director.*
General email, info@ncmaf.com
Web, www.ncmaf.net, Twitter, @NCMAForg and Facebook, www.facebook.com/NCMAF

Connects member faith groups and religious diversity with the armed forces and Veterans Affairs Dept. chaplaincies.

National Conference on Ministry to the Armed Forces, *Endorsers Conference for Veterans Affairs Chaplaincy, P.O. Box 7572, Arlington, VA 22207-9998; (703) 608-2100. Jack Lea, Executive Director; Klon kitchen, Chair.*
General email, info@ncmaf.com
Web, www.ncmaf.net, Twitter, @NCMAForg and Facebook, www.facebook.com/NCMAF

Endorses and connects clergypersons and faith based groups with militaty and VA chaplaincies, and celebrates religious diversity. they are the point of contact between the DOD and over 150 religions and faiths.

Civilian Employees

▶AGENCIES

Army Dept. *(Defense Dept.), Civilian Personnel,* 300 *Army Pentagon, #2E485, 20310-0300; (703) 614-8143. Paula Patrick, Director.*
Web, www.asamra.army.mil/org_cslmo.html and Email, usarmy.pentagon.hqda-dcs-g-1.mbx.icomplaints-helpdesk@mail.mil

Develops and reviews Army civilian personnel policies and advises the Army leadership on civilian personnel matters.

Army Dept. *(Defense Dept.), Equity and Inclusion,* 111 *Army Pentagon, #2A332, 20310-0111; (703) 545-5781. Fax, (703) 614-5279. Anselm A. Beach, Deputy Assistant Secretary.*
Web, www.army.mil/armyequityandinclusion

Civilian office that administers equal employment opportunity and civil rights programs and policies for civilian employees of the Army.

Defense Dept. (DoD), *Employment and Compensation, 4800 Mark Center Dr., #06F15, SCTP Division, Alexandria, VA 22350-1100; (703) 882-5196. Kelly Cruz, Director.*
Web, www.dcpas.osd.mil/EC

Manages workforce restructuring programs for Defense Dept. civilians, including downsizing, placement, voluntary early retirement, and transition assistance programs.

Marine Corps *(Defense Dept.), Human Resources and Organizational Management, Code ARH, 3000 Marine Corps Pentagon, #2C253, 20350-3000; Mann Hall, 2004 Barnett Ave., Quantico, VA 22134; (703) 614-8371. Nadia Patterson, Director. Phone (Quantico), (703) 784-2049.*
General email, SMBHQMCHROMDIR@usmc.mil
Web, www.hqmc.marines.mil/hrom/unit-home/ HRONSFArlingtonOffice and Facebook, www.facebook .com/USMC.HROM

Develops and implements personnel and equal employment opportunity programs for civilian employees of the Marine Corps headquarters.

Navy Dept. *(Defense Dept.), Civilian Human Resources, 614 Sicard St. S.E., #100, 20374-5072; (703) 695-4356. Garry R. Newton, Deputy Assistant Secretary. Employment Information Center, (800) 378-4559.*
General email, donhrfaq@navy.mil
Web, www.secnav.navy.mil/donhr/Pages/default.aspx

Civilian office that develops and reviews Navy and Marine Corps civilian personnel and equal opportunity programs and policies.

U.S. Coast Guard (USCG) *(Homeland Security Dept.), Human Resources Directorate, 2703 Martin Luther King Jr. Ave. S.E., MS 7907, 20593-7907; (202) 475-5002. Rear Adm. Eric Jones, Assistant Commandant.*
Web, www.uscg.mil/hr

Responsible for hiring, recruiting, and training all military and nonmilitary Coast Guard personnel. Administers employee benefits.

Equal Opportunity

▶AGENCIES

Air Force Dept. *(Defense Dept.), Equal Opportunity (EO), 1602 California Ave., #217, Joint Base Andrews, MD 20762; (703) 767-4451. Maritza M. Sayle-Walker, Director. Affirmative employment program, (240) 612-1365. Disability and reasonable accommodation, (240) 612-4006. Discrimination and sexual harassment hotline, (888) 231-4058.*
General email, usaf.pentagon.af-a1.mbx.a1q–workflow@mail.mil
Web, www.af.mil/Equal-Opportunity

Office that develops and administers Air Force equal opportunity programs and policies for civilians and military personnel.

Army Dept. *(Defense Dept.), Equity and Inclusion, 111 Army Pentagon, #2A332, 20310-0111; (703) 545-5781. Fax, (703) 614-5279. Anselm A. Beach, Deputy Assistant Secretary.*
Web, www.army.mil/armyequityandinclusion

Develops policy and conducts program reviews for the Dept. of Army Civilian Equal Employment Opportunity and Affirmative Employment Programs.

Civil Rights Division *(Justice Dept.), Employment Litigation (ELS), 150 M St. N.E., #9.1819, 20002; (202) 514-3831. Fax, (202) 514-1005. Karen Woodward, Chief. TTY, (202) 514-6780.*
Web, www.justice.gov/crt/employment-litigation-section

Enforces the Uniform Services Employment and Reemployment Rights Act, which prohibits employers from discriminating or retaliating against an employee due to past, current, or future military obligation.

Defense Dept. (DoD), *Defense Advisory Committee on Women in the Services, 4800 Mark Center Dr., #04J25-01, Alexandria, VA 22350-9000; (703) 697-2122. Fax, (703) 614-6233. Col. Seana M. Jaidin (USA), Military Director.*
General email, osd.pentagon.ousd-p-r.mbx.dacowits@mail.mil
Web, http://dacowits.defense.gov

Provides the DoD with advice and recommendations on matters and policies relating to the recruitment and retention, treatment, employment, integration, and well-being of highly qualified professional women in the armed forces.

Defense Dept. (DoD), *Diversity Management and Equal Opportunity, 4800 Mark Center Dr., Alexandria, VA 22350; (571) 372-0964. Jason S. Osborne, Chief.*
Web, www.dodea.edu/Offices/DMEO

Formulates equal opportunity policy for the Defense Dept.

Marine Corps *(Defense Dept.), Opportunity, Diversity, and Inclusion Branch, MRA (MPE), 3280 Russell Rd., 4th Floor, Quantico, VA 22134-5103; (703) 784-9371/2/3/4. Fax, (703) 784-9812. Alfrita Jones, Deputy.*
Web, www.manpower.usmc.mil and General email, mpe@usmc.mil

Military office that develops, monitors, and administers Marine Corps equal opportunity and diversity programs.

Navy Dept. *(Defense Dept.), Civilian Human Resources, 614 Sicard St. S.E., #100, 20374-5072; (703) 695-4356. Garry R. Newton, Deputy Assistant Secretary. Employment Information Center, (800) 378-4559.*
General email, donhrfaq@navy.mil
Web, www.secnav.navy.mil/donhr/Pages/default.aspx

Civilian office that develops and reviews Navy and Marine Corps civilian personnel and equal opportunity programs and policies.

Navy Dept. *(Defense Dept.), Diversity and Equity, 701 S. Courthouse Rd., #3R180, Arlington, VA 22204; (703) 604-5480. Jessica Milam, Advisor.*
Web, www.navy.com/who-we-are/diversity

Military office that develops and administers Navy diversity programs and policies.

U.S. Coast Guard (USCG) *(Homeland Security Dept.), Civil Rights Directorate, 2703 Martin Luther King Jr. Ave. S.E., MS 7000, 20593-7000; (202) 372-4500. Terri A. Dickerson, Director. Toll-free, (888) 992-7387.*
General email, OCR@uscg.mil
Web, www.uscg.mil/Resources/Civil-Rights

Administers equal opportunity regulations and programs for Coast Guard military and civilian personnel.

▶NONGOVERNMENTAL

Human Rights Campaign (HRC), *1640 Rhode Island Ave. N.W., 20036-3278; (202) 628-4160. Fax, (202) 347-5323. Joni Madison, President (Acting). Toll-free, (800) 777-4723. TTY, (202) 216-1572.*
General email, hrc@hrc.org
Web, www.hrc.org, Twitter, @HRC and Facebook, www.facebook.com/humanrightscampaign

Promotes legislation affirming the rights of lesbian, gay, bisexual, and transgender people. Focus includes discrimination in the military.

Family Services

▶AGENCIES

Air Force Dept. *(Defense Dept.), Military and Family Support Center, 1191 Menoher Dr., Joint Base Andrews, MD 20762; (301) 981-7087. Fax, (301) 981-9215. Jason Gunnarson, Flight Chief. Public Affairs, (240) 612-6464.*

General email, 316.FSS.MFSC@us.af.mil

Web, www.andrewsfss.com/mfsc, Facebook, www.facebook
.com/jbamfsc and Twitter, @Andrewsfss

Military policy office that monitors and reviews services provided to Air Force families and civilian employees with family concerns at Joint Base Andrews; oversees Airman and Family Readiness Centers.

Defense Dept. (DoD), *Education Activity,* 4800 Mark Center Dr., Alexandria, VA 22350-1400; (571) 372-0590. Fax, (571) 372-5829. Thomas M. Brady, Director. Web, www.dodea.edu, General email, ER-HD@dodea.edu and Twitter, @DODEA

Civilian office that maintains school system for dependents of all military personnel and eligible civilians in the United States and abroad. Develops uniform curriculum and educational standards; monitors student performance and school accreditation.

Defense Dept. (DoD), *Resources and Oversight,* 4000 Defense Pentagon, #2E319, 20301-4000; (703) 571-2373. Carolee Van Horn, Director. Web, www.defense.gov

Coordinates policies related to quality of life of military personnel and their families.

Marine Corps *(Defense Dept.),* **Marine and Family Programs,** M and RA (MF), 3280 Russell Rd., Quantico, VA 22134-5103; (703) 784-9501. Fax, (703) 432-9269. Marie C. Balocki, Director. Web, www.marines.mil/Family

Sponsors family service centers located on major Marine Corps installations. Oversees the administration of policies affecting the quality of life of Marine Corps military families. Administers relocation assistance programs.

Navy Dept. *(Defense Dept.),* **Personnel Readiness and Community Support,** 701 S. Courthouse Rd., Arlington, VA 22204; (703) 604-5045. Gilbert Cisneros, Under Secretary. Web, https://prhome.defense.gov

Acts as liaison between DC area and Navy quality of life programs located in Tennessee, which provide naval personnel and families being sent overseas with information and support; addresses problems of abuse and sexual assault within families; helps Navy spouses find employment; facilitates communication between Navy families and Navy officials; and assists in relocating Navy families during transition from military to civilian life.

U.S. Coast Guard (USCG) *(Homeland Security Dept.),* **Health, Safety, and Work-Life,** 2703 Martin Luther King Jr. Ave. S.E., 20593; (202) 475-5130. (202) 372-1595. Fax, (202) 475-5906. Rear Adm. Dana Thomas, Director. General email, germaine.y.jefferson@uscg.mil

Web, www.dcms.uscg.mil/Our-Organization/Assistant-Commandant-for-Human-Resources-CG-1/Health-Safety-and-Work-Life-CG-11

Oversees all health, safety, and work-life aspects of the Coast Guard, including individual and family support programs.

▶**CONGRESS**

For a listing of relevant congressional committees and subcommittees, please see page 600 or the Appendix.

▶**NONGOVERNMENTAL**

Air Force Aid Society, 1550 Crystal Dr., #809, Arlington, VA 22202 (mailing address: P.O. Box 2208, Arlington, VA 22202); (703) 972-2650. Kaleth O. Wright (USAF, Ret.), Chief Executive Officer. General email, afas@afas-hq.org

Web, https://afas.org, Twitter, @AFASHQ, Emergency assistance, ea@afas-hq.org and Facebook, www.facebook .com/AirForceAidSociety

Membership: Air Force and Space Force active duty, reserve, and retired military personnel and their dependents. Provides active duty and retired Air Force and Space Force military personnel with personal emergency loans for basic needs, travel, or dependents' health expenses; assists families of active duty, deceased, or retired Air Force personnel with postsecondary education grants.

American Red Cross, *Service to the Armed Forces,* **Military Families,** 431 18th St. N.W., 20006; (202) 303-5000, ext. 2. Fax, (202) 303-0216. Koby L. Langley, Senior Vice President. Emergency communication services, (877) 272-7337. Web, www.redcross.org/about-us/our-work/military-families.html

Provides emergency services for active duty armed forces personnel and their families, including verified communications, financial assistance, information and referral, and counseling. Mandated by Congress to contact military personnel in family emergencies; provides military personnel with verification of family situations for emergency leave applications.

Armed Forces Hostess Assn., 1155 Defense Pentagon, Room 1E541, 20310-1155; (703) 614-0350. Elaine Freeman, President. General email, whs.pentagon.fsd.mbx.afha@mail.mil

Web, https://home.army.mil/jbmhh/index.php/my-fort/all-services/armed-forces-hostess-association

Volunteer office staffed by retirees and spouses of military personnel of all armed services. Serves as an information clearinghouse for military and civilian Defense Dept. families; maintains information on military bases in the United States and abroad; issues information handbook for families in the Washington area.

Army Distaff Foundation (Knollwood), 6200 Oregon Ave. N.W., 20015-1543; (202) 541-0492. Fax, (202) 541-0129. (202) 541-0400. Maj. Gen. Timothy P. McHale (USA, Ret.), Chief Executive Officer. Admission, (202) 541-0149.

General email, info@armydistaff.org

Web, www.armydistaff.org

Nonprofit continuing care retirement community for career military officers and their families. Provides retirement housing and health care services.

Army Emergency Relief, 2530 Crystal Dr., #13161, Alexandria, VA 22202; (703) 428-0000. Fax, (571) 389-8522. Lt. Gen. Raymond V. Mason (USA, Ret.), Director. Toll-free, (866) 878-6378.

General email, aer@aerhq.org

Web, www.armyemergencyrelief.org, Twitter, @aerhq and Facebook, www.facebook.com/AERHQ

Provides emergency financial assistance to retirees and to soldiers and family members of the U.S. Army, Army Reserves, and National Guard who are on extended active duty; provides scholarships to further the education of service members' spouses and dependents.

EX-POSE: Ex-Partners of Servicemembers for Equality, P.O. Box 11191, Alexandria, VA 22312-0191; (703) 941-5844. Sue Arroyo, Office Staff; Janice Stucki, Office Staff.

General email, expose1980@gmail.com

Web, www.ex-pose.org

Membership: military members, retirees, current/former spouses and their children. Educates military couples going through divorce. Provides explanation of possible legal interests and legal entitlements depending on the length of marriage. Open Tuesday and Wednesday, 10:00 a.m–3:00 p.m.

Fisher House Foundation, 12300 Twinbrook Pkwy., #410, Rockville, MD 20852; (301) 294-8560. Fax, (301) 294-8562. David A. Coker, President. Toll-free, (888) 294-8560.

General email, info@fisherhouse.org

Web, www.fisherhouse.org, Twitter, @FisherHouseFdtn, Facebook, www.facebook.com/FisherHouse and YouTube, www.youtube.com/user/FisherHouseFoundatio

Builds new houses on the grounds of major military and VA hospitals to enable families of hospitalized service members to stay within walking distance. Donates the Fisher Houses to the U.S. government. Administers the Hero Miles Program, which uses donated frequent flier miles to purchase airline tickets for hospitalized service members and their families. Provides scholarships for military children.

Freedom Alliance, 22570 Markey Court, #240, Dulles, VA 20166; (703) 444-7940. Fax, (703) 444-9893. Thomas (Tom) P. Kilgannon, President. Toll-free, (800) 475-6620.

General email, info@freedomalliance.org

Web, https://freedomalliance.org, Twitter, @FreedomAlliance and Facebook, www.facebook.com/FreedomAlliance

Promotes strong national defense and honors military service. Awards monetary grants to wounded troops; assists soldiers and their families with housing and travel expenses; provides active duty troops with meals, clothing, entertainment, and other comforts. Provides college scholarships to children of those killed or permanently disabled in an operations mission or training accident.

Marine Corps League, 3619 Jefferson Davis Hwy., #115, Stafford, VA 22554 (mailing address: P.O. Box 1990, Stafford, VA 22555-1990); (703) 207-9588. Johnny Baker, Chief Operating Officer.

General email, info@mclnational.org

Web, www.mclnational.org, Twitter, @MCL_HQ and Facebook, www.facebook.com/mclnational

Membership: active duty, retired, and reserve Marine Corps groups. Promotes the interests of the Marine Corps and works to preserve its traditions. Administers programs related to veteran homelessness, injured veterans, and youth programs; founded and runs Toys For Tots. Publishes quarterly Semper Fi magazine. Monitors legislation and regulations.

National Military Family Assn., 2800 Eisenhower Ave., #250, Alexandria, VA 22314; (703) 931-6632. Fax, (703) 931-4600. Tina W. Jonas, Chair; Besa Pinchotti, Executive Director.

General email, info@militaryfamily.org

Web, www.militaryfamily.org

Membership: active duty and retired military, National Guard, and reserve personnel of all U.S. uniformed services, civilian personnel, families, and other interested individuals. Works to improve the quality of life for military families.

Naval Services FamilyLine, Bldg. 154, 1043 Harwood St. S.E., #100, Washington Navy Yard, DC 20374-5067; (202) 433-2333. Fax, (202) 433-4622. Beth Weber, Chair. Toll-free, (877) 673-7773.

General email, info@nsfamilyline.org

Web, www.nsfamilyline.org, Facebook, www.facebook.com/ nsfamilyline and Twitter, @nsfamilyline

Offers support services to spouses of Navy, Marine Corps, and Coast Guard families. Disseminates information on all aspects of military life; fosters sense of community among sea service personnel and their families.

Navy–Marine Corps Relief Society, 875 N. Randolph St., #225, Arlington, VA 22203-1977; (703) 696-4904. Lt. Gen. Jack W. Klimp (USMC, Ret.), President. Toll-free, (800) 654-8364.

Web, www.nmcrs.org, Facebook, www.facebook.com/ NMCRS and General email, communications@nmcrs.org

Assists active duty and retired Navy and Marine Corps personnel (those with a military ID) and their families in times of need. Disburses interest-free loans and grants. Provides educational scholarships and loans; visiting nurse services; and other services, including thrift shops, budget counseling, and volunteer training.

Our Military Kids, Inc., 2911 Hunter Mill Rd., #203, Oakton, VA 22124; (703) 734-6654. Kara Dallman, Executive Director. Toll-free, (866) 691-6654.

General email, omkinquiry@ourmilitarykids.org

Web, www.ourmilitarykids.org, Facebook, www.facebook. com/OurMilitaryKids?fref=ts and

Twitter, @OurMilitaryKids

Provides grants for extracurricular activities for school-aged children of deployed and severely injured soldiers, including Reserve and National Guard military personnel.

Financial Services

▶AGENCIES

Air Force Dept. *(Defense Dept.), Financial Management and Comptroller (SAF/FM), 1130 Air Force Pentagon, #4E978, 20330-1130; (703) 697-1974. Stephen Herrera, Assistant Secretary (Acting).*
General email, usaf.pentagon.saf-fm.mbx.saf-fm-workflow@mail.mil

Web, www.saffm.hq.af.mil and Facebook, www.facebook .com/USAFComptroller

Provides financial management and analysis to the secretary of the Air Force; directs program and budget development; oversees acquisition and operational cost analysis. Provides resources, financial services, and decision support to deliver air, space, and cyber capabilities to the nation.

Defense Dept. (DoD), *Accounting and Finance Policy Analysis, 1100 Defense Pentagon, #3D150, 20301-1100; (703) 571-1396. Kim Laurance, Deputy Chief Financial Officer (Acting).*
Web, www.defense.gov

Develops accounting policy for the Defense Dept. federal management regulation.

▶CONGRESS

For a listing of relevant congressional committees and sub-committees, please see page 600 or the Appendix.

▶NONGOVERNMENTAL

Armed Forces Benefit Assn., *909 N. Washington St., Alexandria, VA 22314; (703) 549-4455. Fax, (703) 706-5961. Larry O. Spencer (USAF, Ret.), President. Toll-free, (800) 776-2322.*
Web, www.afba.com and Twitter, @AFBAbenefits

Membership: active duty and retired personnel of the uniformed services, federal civilian employees, government contractors, first responders, and family members. Offers low-cost life, health, and long-term care insurance and financial, banking, and investment services worldwide.

Army and Air Force Mutual Aid Assn., *102 Sheridan Ave., Fort Myer, VA 22211-1110; (703) 707-4600. Fax, (888) 210-4882. Brig. Gen. Michael Meese (USA, Ret.), President. Toll-free, (888) 973-8490.*
General email, info@aafmaa.com

Web, www.aafmaa.com

Private organization that offers member and family life insurance, financial, and survivor assistance services to all ranks of Army, Air Force, Coast Guard, Marine Corps, and Navy who are active duty or veterans; Guard, Reserve, USAFA, USCGA, USMA, USMMA, and USNA cadets or midshipmen; ROTC contract/scholarship cadets; and retirees.

Army Emergency Relief, *2530 Crystal Dr., #13161, Alexandria, VA 22202; (703) 428-0000. Fax, (571) 389-8522. Lt. Gen. Raymond V. Mason (USA, Ret.), Director. Toll-free, (866) 878-6378.*
General email, aer@aerhq.org

Web, www.armyemergencyrelief.org, Twitter, @aerhq and Facebook, www.facebook.com/AERHQ

Provides emergency financial assistance to retirees and to soldiers and family members of the U.S. Army, Army Reserves, and National Guard who are on extended active duty; provides scholarships to further the education of service members' spouses and dependents.

Defense Credit Union Council, *1627 Eye St. N.W., #935, 20006; (202) 734-5007. Fax, (202) 821-1329. Delbert Lee Morgan, Chief Executive Officer.*
General email, admin@dcuc.org

Web, www.dcuc.org, Twitter, @DCUC_HQ and Facebook, www.facebook.com/DCUCWashington

Trade association of credit unions serving the Defense Dept.'s military and civilian personnel. Works with the National Credit Union Administration to solve problems concerning the operation of credit unions for the military community; maintains liaison with the Defense Dept.

The Enlisted Assn., *Washington Office, 1001 Fairfax St., #102, Alexandria, VA 22314; (703) 684-1981. Fax, (703) 548-4876. William (Bill) McCabe, Director, Legislative Affairs. Toll-free, (800) 554-8732. VA caregiver support, (855) 260-3274.*
General email, info@treadc.org

Web, www.trea.org and Twitter, @trea_dc

Membership: enlisted personnel of the armed forces, including active duty, reserve, guard, and retirees. Runs scholarship, legislative, and veterans service programs, including food assistance, disaster relief, disability assistance, vocational education training, and prostheses and canine dogs for wounded veterans. (Also known as Retired Enlisted Assn.; headquarters in Aurora, Colo.)

Health Care

▶AGENCIES

Air Force Dept. *(Defense Dept.), Sexual Assault Prevention and Response (SAPR) (AF/CVS), 220 Brookley Ave., Bldg 4. JBAB, 20032; Amy Nowak, Coordinator. 24/7 AF SAPR Capitol-region hotline, (202) 767-7272. DoD safe helpline, (877) 995-5247.*
General Email, 11wg.cvs.sarc_sapr@us.af.mil and Web, www.resilience.af.mil/SAPR

Works to eliminate the occurrence of sexual assault in the Air Force, and acts as advocate for recovery and prevention.

Air Force Dept. *(Defense Dept.), Surgeon General (AF/SG),* 1780 Air Force Pentagon, #4E268, 20330-1780; (703) 692-6800. Lt. Gen. Robert I. Miller, Surgeon General. Congressional and Public Affairs, (703) 681-7921.
General email, usaf.pentagon.af-sg.mbx.af-sg-public-affairs@mail.mil

Web, www.airforcemedicine.af.mil,
Twitter, @USAFMedicine, Facebook, www.facebook.com/USAFMedicine and YouTube, www.youtube.com/c/AirForceMedicalService

Directs the provision of medical and dental services for Air Force personnel and their beneficiaries.

Army Dept. *(Defense Dept.), Command Policy and Programs,* 300 Army Pentagon, 20310-0300; (703) 695-7370. Lt. Col. Brandy M. Culp (USA), Chief, (703) 679-0957.
Web, www.army.mil/asamra

Develops policies and initiatives to enhance soldiers' health, fitness, and morale, with the goal of improving personnel readiness and institutional strength of the army. Interests include weight control and suicide prevention.

Army Dept. *(Defense Dept.), Recovery Care Program, (ARCP),* 2530 Crystal Dr., 10th Floor, Arlington, VA 22202; Col. Myron B. McDaniels, Deputy Chief of Staff. Wounded soldier and family hotline, (800) 984-8523. Hotline, (877) 393-9058.
Web, www.arcp.army.mil, General email, hq-publicaffairs@usace.army.mil, Twitter, @armyARCP and Facebook, www.facebook.com/usarmyarcp

Provides leadership, command, and control for wounded soldiers' health and welfare, military administrative requirements, and readiness. Collaborates with medical providers in order to facilitate quality care, disposition, and transition. Manages recovery for wounded, ill, and injured soldiers across all Army components. Supports the needs of wounded warriors and their families; supports the professional growth of all personnel. (Formerly Warrior Care and Transition which also now incorporates the Wounded Warrior Program).

Army Dept. *(Defense Dept.), Surgeon General,* 7700 Arlington Blvd., #4SW112, Falls Church, VA 22042-5140; (703) 681-3000. Fax, (703) 681-3167.
Lt. Gen. R. Scott Dingle (USA), Surgeon General.
General email, OTSGWebPublisher@amedd.army.mil

Web, www.armymedicine.health.mil,
Twitter, @ArmyMedicine and Facebook, www.facebook.com/OfficialArmyMedicine

Directs the provision of medical and dental services for Army personnel and their dependents.

Assistant Secretary for Health (OASH) *(Health and Human Services Dept.), Surgeon General, Commissioned Corps of the U.S. Public Health Service (PHS),* 1101 Wootton Pkwy., Plaza Level, #100, Rockville, MD 20852; (240) 453-6000. Fax, (240) 453-6109. Rear Adm. Denise Hinton, Director (Acting). Recruitment, (888) 225-3302.
General email, CCHelpDesk@hhs.gov

Web, www.usphs.gov, Twitter, @usphscc, Recruitment, usphs.gov/apply-now and Facebook, www.facebook.com/USPHS

Responsible for the overall force management, operations, and deployment readiness and response of the Commissioned Corps of the U.S. Public Health Service. Manages officer medical records and evaluations, recruitment, and calls to active duty.

Defense Dept. (DoD), *Force Health Protection and Readiness,* 7700 Arlington Blvd., #5101, Falls Church, VA 22042; (703) 681-8456. David J. Smith, Assistant Secretary of Defense and Health Affairs (Acting).
General email, FHPR.communications@tma.osd.mil

Web, http://health.mil

Advises the secretary of defense on measures to improve the health of deployed forces. Maintains communication between the Defense Dept., service members, veterans, and their families.

Defense Dept. (DoD), *Health Affairs, Clinical Program Policy,* 1200 Defense Pentagon, #3E1082, 20301-1200; (703) 681-1708. Fax, (703) 681-3655. Darrell Landreaux, Director.
Web, www.health.mil

Develops policies for the medical benefits programs for active duty and retired military personnel and dependents in the Defense Dept.

Defense Dept. (DoD), *National Intrepid Center of Excellence,* 4860 S. Palmer Rd., Bethesda, MD 20889; (301) 295-1719. Capt. Carlos Williams (USN), Director. 24-hour helpline, (301) 319-3600.
General email, dha.bethesda.ncr-medical.list.wrnm-nicoe-referral@mail.mil

Web, https://walterreed.tricare.mil/NICoE

Provides evaluation, treatment planning, research, and education for service members and their families dealing with the interactions of mild traumatic brain injury and psychological health conditions. Primary patient population is active duty service members who are not responding to current therapy; provider-referral required.

Defense Health Agency (DHA) *(Defense Dept.),* 7700 Arlington Blvd., #5101, Falls Church, VA 22042-5101; (703) 681-1730. Lt. Gen. Ronald J. Place (USA), Director.
Web, https://health.mil/About-MHS/OASDHA/Defense-Health-Agency

Combat support agency directing medical services for the Army, Navy, Air Force, and Marine Corps. Administers the TRICARE health plan providing medical, dental, and pharmacy programs worldwide to service members, retirees, and their families. Manages inpatient facilities and associated clinics in the national capital region.

Marine Corps *(Defense Dept.), Marine and Family Programs,* M and RA (MF), 3280 Russell Rd., Quantico, VA 22134-5103; (703) 784-9501. Fax, (703) 432-9269. Marie C. Balocki, Director.
Web, www.marines.mil/Family

Military office that directs Marine Corps health care, family violence, and drug and alcohol abuse policies and programs.

Naval Medical Research Center *(Defense Dept.),* 503 Robert Grant Ave., #1W28, Silver Spring, MD 20910-7500; (301) 319-7403. Fax, (301) 319-7424. (301) 319-9378. Capt. William M. Deniston (USN), Commanding Officer; Steven S. Legette, Executive Director, (301) 319-3381. phone, (301) 319-9378.
General email, svc.pao.nmrc@med.navy.mil
Web, www.med.navy.mil/Naval-Medical-Research-Center and *Facebook, www.facebook.com/NavalMedicalRC*

Performs basic and applied biomedical research in areas of military importance, including infectious diseases, hyperbaric medicine, wound repair enhancement, environmental stress, and immunobiology. Provides support to field laboratories and naval hospitals; monitors research internationally.

Navy Dept. *(Defense Dept.), Bureau of Medicine and Surgery,* (BUMED), 7700 Arlington Blvd., #5113, Falls Church, VA 22042; (703) 681-5200. Rear Adm. Bruce L. Gillingham, Chief of CMS/ Surgeon General. Public Affairs, (703) 681-9038.
Web, www.med.navy.mil, Twitter, @NavyMedicine, Facebook, www.facebook.com/USNavyMedicine and *General email, usn.ncr.bumedfchva.mbx.bumed-general-inquiries@mail.mil*

Military office that interprets and oversees the implementation of Navy health care policy. Assists in the development of eligibility policy for medical benefits programs for Navy and Marine Corps military personnel.

Navy Dept. *(Defense Dept.), Bureau of Medicine and Surgery, Navy Tricare Representative,* 7700 Arlington Blvd. #2NW221, Falls Church, VA 22042; (703) 681-9134. Sharon Beamer, Navy Tricare Representative. Inspector General, (301) 295-9009. Public Affairs, (202) 445-0781. *General email, usn.ncr.bumedfchva.mbx.bumed-general-inquiries@mail.mil*
Web, www.med.navy.mil

Military office that interprets and oversees the implementation of Navy health care policy. Assists in the development of eligibility policy for Tricare health benefits programs for Navy and Marine Corps military personnel.

Navy Dept. *(Defense Dept.), Manpower and Reserve Affairs, Health Affairs,* 1000 Navy Pentagon, #4D548, 20350-1000; (703) 693-0238. Capt. Matthew Holcomb (USN), Division Director.
Web, www.secnav.navy.mil/mra/Pages/default.aspx

Reviews medical programs for Navy and Marine Corps military personnel and develops and reviews policies relating to these programs.

U.S. Coast Guard (USCG) *(Homeland Security Dept.), Health, Safety, and Work-Life,* 2703 Martin Luther King Jr. Ave. S.E., 20593; (202) 475-5130. (202) 372-1595. Fax, (202) 475-5906. Rear Adm. Dana Thomas, Director. *General email, germaine.y.jefferson@uscg.mil*
Web, www.dcms.uscg.mil/Our-Organization/Assistant-Commandant-for-Human-Resources-CG-1/Health-Safety-and-Work-Life-CG-11

Oversees all health, safety, and work-life aspects of the Coast Guard, including the operation of medical and dental clinics and sick bays on ships. Investigates Coast Guard accidents, such as the grounding of ships and downing of aircraft. Oversees all work-life–related programs, including health promotion, mess halls and galleys, and individual and family support programs.

Walter Reed Army Institute of Research *(Defense Dept.),* 503 Robert Grant Ave., Silver Spring, MD 20910-7500; (301) 319-9000. Fax, (301) 319-9549. Col. Chad Koenig, Commander. Public Affairs, (301) 319-9471. Reference Library, (301) 319-9555. *General email, usarmy.detrick.medcom-wrair.mbx.public-affairs@mail.mil*
Web, www.wrair.army.mil and *Twitter, @wrair*

Provides research, education, and training in support of the Defense Dept.'s health care system. Develops vaccines and drugs to prevent and treat infectious diseases. Other research efforts include surveillance of naturally occurring infectious diseases of military importance and study of combat casualty care (blood loss, resuscitation, and brain and other organ system trauma), battle casualties, operational stress, sleep deprivation, and medical countermeasures against biological and chemical agents.

▶**NONGOVERNMENTAL**

AMSUS—Society of Federal Health Professionals, 12154 Darnstown Rd., #506, Gaithersburg, MD 20878; (301) 897-8800. Brig. Gen. John M. Cho (USA, Ret.), Executive Director.
General email, amsus@amsus.org
Web, www.amsus.org and *Twitter, @AMSUS*

Membership: health professionals, including nurses, dentists, pharmacists, and physicians, who work or have worked for the U.S. Public Health Service, the VA, or the Army, Navy, Air Force, Guard, and Reserves, and students. Works to improve all phases of federal health services.

CAUSE (Comfort for America's Uniformed Services), 1100 N. Glebe Rd., #373, Arlington, VA 22201 (mailing address: 4201 Wilson Blvd., #110-284, Arlington, VA 22203); (703) 591-4965. Fax, (703) 591-0066. Kelly Kreis, Executive Director.
General email, info@cause-usa.org
Web, https://cause-usa.org, Twitter, @ComfortforamericasUniformedServices and *Facebook, www.facebook.com/ComfortforAmericasUniformedServices*

Provides comfort items and organizes recreational programs for U.S. Armed Service personnel and those supporting them, who are undergoing medical treatment or recuperating in government hospitals or rehabilitation facilities.

Commissioned Officers Assn. of the U.S. Public Health Service, *8201 Corporate Dr., #615, Landover, MD 20785; (301) 731-9080. Fax, (301) 731-9084.*
Jacqueline Rychnovsky, Executive Director.
Web, http://coausphs.org, Twitter, @COAUSPHS and Facebook, www.facebook.com/coausphs

Membership: commissioned officers of the U.S. Public Health Service. Supports improvements to public health, especially through the work of the PHS Commissioned Corps. Sponsors conferences and training workshops. Monitors legislation and regulations.

Injured Marine Semper Fi Fund/Semper Fi Fund, *715 Broadway St., Quantico, VA 22134 (mailing address: Wounded Warrior Center Bldg., H49, Box 555193, Camp Pendleton, CA 92055-5193); (760) 725-3860. Fax, (760) 725-3685. Karen Guenther, President.*
General email, info@thefund.org
Web, https://thefund.org, Twitter, @SemperFiFund, Facebook, www.facebook.com/semperfifund, YouTube, www.youtube.com/user/SemperFiFund and Press email, media@thefund.org

With its program America's First, provides financial assistance and lifetime support to post-9/11 combat-wounded, critically ill, and catastrophically injured members of all branches of the U.S. Armed Forces and their families, ensuring that they have the resources needed during recovery and transition back to their communities. West coast office is in Camp Pendleton, California.

Missing in Action, Prisoners of War

▶AGENCIES

Air Force Dept. *(Defense Dept.), Manpower, Personnel, and Services, 1040 Air Force Pentagon, #4E168, 20330-1040; (703) 697-6088. Lt. Gen. Brian T. Kelly, Deputy Chief of Staff.*
Web, www.af.mil

Military office that responds to inquiries about missing in action (MIA) personnel for the Air Force; refers inquiries to the Military Personnel Center at Randolph Air Force Base in San Antonio, Tex.

Bureau of East Asian and Pacific Affairs *(State Dept.), Mainland Southeast Asia Affairs, 2201 C St. N.W., #5206, 20520-6310; (202) 647-4495. Fax, (202) 647-3069. Robert Ogburn, Director.*
Web, www.state.gov/p/eap

Handles issues related to Americans missing in action in Indochina; serves as liaison with Congress, international organizations, and foreign governments on developments in these countries.

Defense Dept. (DoD), *Defense POW/MIA Accounting, 241 S. 18th St., #800, Arlington, VA 22202; (703) 699-1102.*
Fax, (703) 602-1890. Kelly K. McKeague, Director. Press, (703) 699-1420.
Web, www.dpaa.mil

Civilian office responsible for policy matters relating to prisoners of war and missing personnel issues. Represents the Defense Dept. before Congress, the media, veterans organizations, and prisoner of war and missing personnel families.

Defense Dept. (DoD), *Public Affairs, 1400 Defense Pentagon, #2D961, 20301-1400; (703) 571-3343. Fax, (703) 697-3501. John Kirby, Assistant to the Secretary of Defense for Public Affairs. Press, (703) 697-5131.*
Web, www.defense.gov/news

Responds to public inquiries concerning Defense Dept. personnel.

Marine Corps *(Defense Dept.), Casualty Assistance Section, 2008 Elliott Rd., Quantico, VA 22134-5102; (703) 784-9512. Fax, (703) 784-4134. Gerald Castle, Head. Toll-free, (800) 847-1597.*
General email, casualty.section@usmc.mil
Web, http://usmc-mccs.org/services/benefits/casualty-assistance, www.manpower.usmc.mil/webcenter/portal/MF_MPS_CA/pages_casualtyassistancecommandrepresentative, www.manpower.usmc.mil/webcenter/portal/MF_MPS_CA/pages_casualtyassistancecallsofficercaco and Facebook, www.facebook.com/MCCSHQ

Military office that acts as liaison for inquiries about missing in action (MIA) personnel for the Marine Corps and distributes information about Marine Corps MIAs to the next of kin.

Navy Dept. *(Defense Dept.), Naval Personnel, 701 S. Courthouse Rd., Arlington, VA 22204; (703) 604-2863. Vice Adm. John B. Nowell Jr. (USN), Chief. MyNavy Career Center, (833) 330-6622.*
General email, mynavyhr@navy.mil
Web, www.mynavyhr.navy.mil, Twitter, @MyNAVYHR and Facebook, www.facebook.com/MyNAVYHR

Military office that responds to inquiries about missing in action (MIA) personnel for the Navy and distributes information about Navy MIAs. (Office based in Millington, Tenn.)

▶CONGRESS

For a listing of relevant congressional committees and subcommittees, please see page 600 or the Appendix.

▶NONGOVERNMENTAL

National League of Families of American Prisoners and Missing in Southeast Asia, *5673 Columbia Pike, #100, Falls Church, VA 22041; (703) 465-7432. Fax, (703) 465-7433. Ann Mills-Griffith, Chair.*
General email, admin@pow-miafamilies.org

Web, www.pow-miafamilies.org,
Twitter, @POWMIAFamilies1 and Facebook, www
.facebook.com/powmiafamilies

Membership: family members of MIAs and POWs and returned POWs of the Vietnam War are voting members; nonvoting associate members include veterans and other interested people. Works for the release of all prisoners of war, an accounting of the missing, and repatriation of the remains of those who have died serving their country in Southeast Asia. Works to raise public awareness of these issues; maintains regional and state coordinators.

Pay and Compensation

▶**AGENCIES**

Air Force Dept. *(Defense Dept.), Manpower, Personnel, and Services, Military Compensation Policy Division,* *1500 Perimeter Rd., #4790, Joint Base Andrews, MD 20762; (240) 612-4351. Col. Nekita Little, Chief.* *Web, www.afpc.af.mil*

Military office that develops and administers Air Force policy regarding personnel travel, entitlements, housing allowances, uniforms, leave and absence, and compensation.

Army Dept. *(Defense Dept.), MyArmyBenefits, 2530 Crystal Dr., #6000, Arlington, VA 22202; (703) 286-2560. Chelsea Ortiz, Program Manager. Toll-free, (888) 721-2769.* *General email, usarmy.myarmybenefits@mail.mil* *Web, http://myarmybenefits.us.army.mil*

Military office that provides Army benefits information.

Defense Dept. (DoD), *Military Compensation, 4000 Defense Pentagon, #3D1067, 20301-4000; (703) 693-1058. Jerilyn (Jeri) B. Busch, Director. Customer Service, (888) 332-7411.* *Web, http://militarypay.defense.gov*

Promulgates military pay and compensation policies to the uniformed services and advises the secretary of defense on military compensation policy.

Marine Corps *(Defense Dept.), Military Manpower Policy, 3280 Russell Rd., Quantico, VA 22134-5105; (703) 784-9352. Fax, (703) 784-9812.* *Brig. Gen. Ahmed Williamson, Director.* *General email, manpower@usmc.mil* *Web, www.quantico.marines.mil/Offices-Staff/G-1-Manpower*

Military office that develops and administers Marine Corps personnel pay and compensation policies.

Navy Dept. *(Defense Dept.), Military Pay and Compensation Policy, 701 S. Courthouse Rd., Arlington, VA 22204; (703) 604-4718. Jeff Krusling, Branch Head.* *General email, nxag_n130@navy.mil* *Web, www.navy.com/what-to-expect/navy-benefits-compensation-and-pay*

Military office that develops and administers Navy military pay, compensation, and personnel policies.

Fleet Reserve Assn. (FRA), *125 N. West St., Alexandria, VA 22314-2754; (703) 683-1400. Fax, (703) 549-6610. Christopher J. Slawinski, National Executive Director, ext. 101. Membership/Customer Service, (800) 372-1924.* *General email, fra@fra.org*

Web, www.fra.org, Twitter, @FRAHQ and Facebook, www *.facebook.com/FRA.org*

Membership: current and former enlisted members of the Navy, Marine Corps, and Coast Guard. Interests include health care, pay, benefits, and quality-of-life programs for sea services personnel. Monitors legislation and regulations.

Recruitment

▶**AGENCIES**

Army Dept. *(Defense Dept.), Manpower and Reserve Affairs, 111 Army Pentagon, #2E460, 20310-0111; (703) 697-9253. Fax, (703) 692-9000. Mark R. Lewis, Assistant Secretary (Acting); Jeffrey P. Angers, Director (Acting).* *Web, www.army.mil/asamra, Twitter, @MRA_G1_PAO and Facebook, www.facebook.com/HQDAMRAG1*

Civilian office that reviews policies and programs for Army personnel and reserves; makes recommendations to the secretary of the Army. Oversees training, military preparedness, and mobilization for all civilians and active and reserve members of the Army.

Defense Dept. (DoD), *Accession Policy, 4000 Defense Pentagon, #3D1066, 20301-4000; (703) 695-5525. Stephanie P. Miller, Director.* *Web, https://prhome.defense.gov/M-RA/Inside-M-RA/ MPP/Accession-Policy*

Military office that monitors Defense Dept. recruiting programs and policies, including advertising, market research, and enlistment standards. Coordinates with the individual services on recruitment of military personnel.

Defense Dept. (DoD), *Manpower and Reserve Affairs, 1500 Defense Pentagon, #2E556, 20301-1500; (703) 697-6631. Fax, (703) 697-1682. Virginia Penrod, Assistant Secretary (Acting).* *Web, www.people.mil*

Civilian office that addresses all policy matters pertaining to the six reserve components of the military services. Develops and delivers civilian and military personnel policy and implements human resource solutions that support the Total Force and mission readiness.

Marine Corps *(Defense Dept.), Human Resources and Organizational Management, Code ARH, 3000 Marine Corps Pentagon, #2C253, 20350-3000; Mann Hall, 2004 Barnett Ave., Quantico, VA 22134; (703) 614-8371. Nadia Patterson, Director. Phone (Quantico), (703) 784-2049.* *General email, SMBHQMCHROMDIR@usmc.mil*

Web, www.hqmc.marines.mil/hrom/unit-home/ HRONSFArlingtonOffice and Facebook, www.facebook .com/USMC.HROM

Develops and implements personnel and equal employment opportunity programs to recruit, develop, and maintain the workforce at Marine Corps headquarters.

Marine Corps *(Defense Dept.), Manpower and Reserve Affairs, James Wesley Marsh Center, Bldg. 3280, 3280 Russell Rd., Quantico, VA 22134; (703) 784-9012. (703) 784-9864. Lt. Gen. David A. Ottignon, Deputy Commandant.*
Web, www.manpower.usmc.mil/webcenter/portal/ MRAHome and General email, SMB_HQMC_ HROMDIR@usmc.mil

Oversees planning, directing, coordinating, and supervising of both active, reserve, veteran, and civilian Marine Corps forces.

Marine Corps *(Defense Dept.), Recruiting Command, 3280 Russell Rd., Quantico, VA 22134-5105; (703) 784-9400. (800) 627-4637. Maj. Gen. Jason Q. Bohm (USMC), Commanding General.*
General email, mcrcpa@marines.usmc.mil
Web, www.mcrc.marines.mil and Facebook, www.facebook .com/marinecorps

Military office that administers and executes policies for Marine Corps officer and enlisted recruitment programs.

Navy Dept. *(Defense Dept.), Manpower and Reserve Affairs, 1000 Navy Pentagon, #4E590, 20350-1000; (703) 695-4333. Robert D. Hogue, Assistant Secretary (Acting).*
Web, www.secnav.navy.mil/mra/Pages/default.aspx and General email, m&ra_webmailbox.fct@navy.mil

Civilian office that oversees the recruitment of active and reserve Navy personnel, government civilians, contractors, and volunteers. Provides programs and policy related to military personnel (active, reserve, and retired), family members, and government civilian workforce.

Selective Service System, *1515 Wilson Blvd., #400, Arlington, VA 22209-2425; (703) 605-4100. Fax, (703) 605-4106. Craig T. Brown, Director (Acting). Locator, (703) 605-4000. Toll-free, (888) 655-1825. TTY, (800) 877-8339. TTY Español, (800) 845-6136.*
General email, information@sss.gov
Web, www.sss.gov, Twitter, @sss_gov and Facebook, www .facebook.com/SSSregistration

Supplies the armed forces with manpower when authorized; registers male citizens of the United States ages 18 to 25. In an emergency, would institute a draft and would provide alternative service assignments to men classified as conscientious objectors.

U.S. Coast Guard (USCG) *(Homeland Security Dept.), Human Resources Directorate, 2703 Martin Luther King Jr. Ave. S.E., MS 7907, 20593-7907; (202) 475-5002. Rear Adm. Eric Jones, Assistant Commandant.*
Web, www.uscg.mil/hr

Responsible for hiring, recruiting, and training all military and nonmilitary Coast Guard personnel. Administers employee benefits.

Retirement, Separation

▶**AGENCIES**

Armed Forces Retirement Home—Washington, *140 Rock Creek Church Rd. N.W., 20011-8400 (mailing address: 3700 N. Capitol St. N.W., Washington, DC 20011-8400); (800) 422-9988. (202) 541-7501. Fax, (202) 541-7519. Maj. Gen. Stephen T. Rippe (USA, Ret.), Chief Executive Officer.*
General email, public.affairs@afrh.gov
Web, www.afrh.gov

Gives domiciliary and medical care to retired members of the armed services or career service personnel unable to earn a livelihood. Formerly known as U.S. Soldiers' and Airmen's Home. (Armed Forces Retirement Home in Gulfport, Miss., reopened in 2010.)

Army Dept. *(Defense Dept.), Retirement Services, 251 S. 18th St., #210, Arlington, VA 22202-3531; (703) 571-7232. Mark E. Overberg (USA, Ret.), Director, (571) 482-0872. Alternate phone, (703) 545-2637. Help desk, (888) 721-2769.*
Web, https://soldierforlife.army.mil/Retirement

Military office that makes retirement policy and oversees retirement programs for Army military personnel.

Defense Dept. (DoD), *Military Compensation, 4000 Defense Pentagon, #3D1067, 20301-4000; (703) 693-1058. Jerilyn (Jeri) B. Busch, Director. Customer Service, (888) 332-7411.*
Web, http://militarypay.defense.gov

Develops retirement policies and reviews administration of retirement programs for all Defense Dept. military personnel.

Marine Corps *(Defense Dept.), Manpower, Retired Services and Pay, 3280 Russell Rd., Quantico, VA 22134-5103; (703) 784-9310/1/2. Fax, (703) 784-9834. Vincent Tate, Section Head. Toll-free, (800) 336-4649.*
General email, smb.manpower.mmsr6@usmc.mil
Web, www.hqmc.marines.mil/Agencies/Manpower-Reserve-Affairs-MMSR-6

Military office that administers retirement programs and benefits for Marine Corps retirees and the Marine Corps retirement community survivor benefit plan.

▶**NONGOVERNMENTAL**

Army Distaff Foundation (Knollwood), *6200 Oregon Ave. N.W., 20015-1543; (202) 541-0492. Fax, (202) 541-0129. (202) 541-0400. Maj. Gen. Timothy P. McHale (USA, Ret.), Chief Executive Officer. Admission, (202) 541-0149.*
General email, info@armydistaff.org
Web, www.armydistaff.org

Nonprofit continuing care retirement community for career military officers and their families. Provides retirement housing and health care services.

MILITARY EDUCATION AND TRAINING

General

▶AGENCIES

Air Force Dept. *(Defense Dept.), Force Management Integration,* 1660 Air Force Pentagon, #5E1083, 20330-1660; (703) 614-4751. Mark R. Engelbaum, Deputy Assistant Secretary.
General email, SAF.MRM.Workflow@us.af.mil
Web, www.af.mil/About-Us/Biographies/Display/Article/622067/mark-r-engelbaum

Civilian office that monitors and reviews military and civilian personnel matters to include recruitment; accession; education, training and development; assignment; utilization; promotion; sustainment; compensation, entitlements, retirement and separation. This includes oversight of education policies of the US Air Force Academy at Colorado Springs and officer candidates' training and Reserve Officers Training Corps (ROTC) programs for the Air Force. Advises the Secretary of the Air Force on education matters, including graduate education, voluntary education programs, and flight, specialized, and recruit training.

Army Dept. *(Defense Dept.), Military Personnel Management,* 300 Army Pentagon, #2E446, 20310-0300; (703) 695-5871. Fax, (703) 695-6012. Maj. Gen. Jeffrey P. Angers (USA), Director.
Web, www.army.mil

Military office that supervises operations and policies of the U.S. Military Academy and officer candidates' training and Reserve Officers Training Corps (ROTC) programs. Advises the chief of staff of the Army on academy and education matters.

Army Dept. *(Defense Dept.), Training Development Directorate,* Bldg. 5020, 2221 Adams Ave., Fort Lee, VA 23801-2102; (804) 765-1885. Lt. Col. Seneta Burns (USA), Deputy Director.
General email, usarmy.lee.tradoc.mbx.leee-scoe-g3-mailbox@army.mil
Web, www.cascom.army.mil/g_staff/g3/tdd.htm

Military office that plans and monitors program resources for active duty and reserve unit training readiness programs.

Civil Air Patrol National Capital Wing, 200 McChord St. S.W., #111, Joint Base Anacostia-Bolling, 20032; (202) 767-4405. Col. David E. Sterling, Wing Commander.
General email, cc@natcapwing.org
Web, www.natcapwg.cap.gov

Official auxiliary of the U.S. Air Force. Sponsors a cadet training and education program for junior and senior high school age students. Conducts emergency services, homeland security missions, and an aerospace education program. (Headquarters at Maxwell Air Force Base, Ala.)

Defense Acquisition University *(Defense Dept.),* 9820 Belvoir Rd., Fort Belvoir, VA 22060-5565; (703) 805-3459. Fax, (703) 805-2639. James P. Woolsey, President. Toll-free, (866) 568-6924.
General email, DAUhelp@dau.edu
Web, www.dau.edu and Twitter, @DAUNow

Academic institution that offers courses to military and civilian personnel who specialize in acquisition and procurement. Conducts research to support and improve management of defense systems acquisition programs.

Defense Dept. (DoD), *Accession Policy,* 4000 Defense Pentagon, #3D1066, 20301-4000; (703) 695-5525. Stephanie P. Miller, Director.
Web, https://prhome.defense.gov/M-RA/Inside-M-RA/MPP/Accession-Policy

Reviews and develops education policies of the service academies, service schools, graduate and voluntary education programs, education programs for active duty personnel, tuition assistance programs, and officer candidates' training and Reserve Officers Training Corps (ROTC) programs for the Defense Dept. Advises the secretary of defense on education matters.

Defense Dept. (DoD), *Force Education and Training,* 4000 Defense Pentagon, #1E537, 20301-4000; (703) 695-2618. Fax, (703) 692-2855. Caroline Baxter, Deputy Assistant Secretary.
Web, http://prhome.defense.gov

Develops, reviews, and analyzes legislation, policies, plans, programs, resource levels, and budgets for the training of military personnel and military units. Develops the substantive-based framework, working collaboratively across the defense, federal, academic, and private sectors, for the global digital knowledge environment. Manages with other government agencies the sustainability and modernization of DoD training ranges.

Dwight D. Eisenhower School for National Security and Resource Strategy *(Defense Dept.),* 260 5th Ave. S.W., #2308, 20319 (mailing address: Fort Lesley J. McNair, 408 4th Ave. S.W., Bldg. 59, Washington DC, 20319-5062); (202) 685-4278. Brig. Gen. Joy L. Curriera (USA), Commandant. Administration, (202) 685-4333.
General email, university-registrar@ndu.edu
Web, http://es.ndu.edu

Division of National Defense University. Offers professional level courses for senior military officers and senior civilian government officials. Academic program focuses on management of national resources, mobilization, and industrial preparedness. (Formerly known as the Industrial College of the Armed Forces.)

Marine Corps *(Defense Dept.), Alfred M. Gray Research Center,* 2040 Broadway St., Quantico, VA 22134;

Greg Cina, Deputy Director, (703) 432-5058. Conference Center, (703) 784-2240. Archives, (703) 784-4685. Library, (703) 784-4409.
Conference Center email, grc_conference@usmcu.edu, Web, http://grc-usmcu.libguides.com/gray-research-center and Library email, mcu_grc_reference@usmcu.edu

Supports academic research, study, instruction, and collaboration for Marine Corps University educational programs as well as professional research throughout the Marine Corps. Houses the Library of the Marine Corps; Brute Krulak Center for Innovation and Future Warfare; Leadership Communication Skills Center; and GRC Conference Center.

Marine Corps *(Defense Dept.),* **Training and Education Command,** *1019 Elliot Rd., Quantico, VA 22134-5010; (703) 432-1837. (703) 432-0817. (703) 784-3730. Lt. Gen. Kevin M. Liams, Commanding General. Web, www.tecom.marines.mil*

Military office that develops and implements training and education programs for regular and reserve personnel and units.

National Defense University *(Defense Dept.), Fort Lesley J. McNair, Bldg. 62, 300 5th Ave. S.W., #305A, 20319-5066; (202) 685-4700. Fax, (202) 685-3935. Lt. Gen. Michael T. Plehn (USAF), President. Press, (202) 685-3140. General email, NDUWebmaster@ndu.edu*
Web, www.ndu.edu, Twitter, @NDU_EDU and Facebook, www.facebook.com/ndu.edu

Specialized university sponsored by the Joint Chiefs of Staff to prepare individuals for senior executive duties in the national security establishment. Offers master of science degrees in national resource strategy, national security strategy, joint campaign planning and strategy, and government information leadership; a master of arts degree in strategic security studies; and nondegree and certificate programs and courses.

National War College *(Defense Dept.), Fort Lesley J. McNair, Bldg. 61, 300 D St. S.W., 20319-5078; (202) 685-3674. Brig. Gen. Jeff Hurlbert (USAF), Commandant. Web, https://nwc.ndu.edu*

Division of National Defense University. Offers professional level courses for senior military officers, senior civilian government officials, and foreign officers. Academic program focuses on the formulation and implementation of national security policy and military strategy.

Navy Dept. *(Defense Dept.),* **Manpower and Reserve Affairs,** *1000 Navy Pentagon, #4E590, 20350-1000; (703) 695-4333. Robert D. Hogue, Assistant Secretary (Acting). Web, www.secnav.navy.mil/mra/Pages/default.aspx and General email, me&ra_webmailbox.fct@navy.mil*

Civilian office that reviews policies of the U.S. Naval Academy, Navy and Marine Corps service schools, and officer candidates' training and Reserve Officer Training Corps (ROTC) programs. Advises the secretary of the Navy on education matters, including voluntary education programs.

U.S. Naval Academy *(Defense Dept.), 121 Blake Rd., Annapolis, MD 21402-5000; (410) 293-1000. Vice Adm. Sean Buck (USN), Superintendent; Andrew Phillips, Dean of Admissions. Admissions/Candidate guidance, (410) 293-1858. Public Affairs, (410) 293-1520. Visitor information, (410) 293-8687.*
Web, www.usna.edu, Twitter, @NavalAcademy, Admissions, www.usna.edu/Admissions and Facebook, www.facebook.com/USNavalAcademy

Provides undergraduate education for young men and women who have been nominated by members of their state's congressional delegation or, in some cases, the president or vice president of the United States. Graduates receive bachelor of science degrees and are commissioned as either an ensign in the U.S. Navy or a second lieutenant in the U.S. Marine Corps.

Uniformed Services University of the Health Sciences *(Defense Dept.), 4301 Jones Bridge Rd., Bethesda, MD 20814-4799; (301) 295-3013. Fax, (301) 295-1960. Rear Adm. William M. Roberts (USN, Ret.), President. Registrar, (301) 400-4100. Toll-free information, (800) 515-5257. General email, registrar@usuhs.edu*
Web, www.usuhs.edu and Twitter, @USUhealthsci

An accredited four-year medical and postgraduate dental school under the auspices of the Defense Dept. Awards doctorate and master's degrees in health-related and science-related fields.

▶**CONGRESS**

For a listing of relevant congressional committees and subcommittees, please see page 600 or the Appendix.

▶**NONGOVERNMENTAL**

Assn. of Military Colleges and Schools of the U.S., *210 Doncaster Rd., Arnold, MD 21012; (703) 272-8406. Col. Ray Rottman (USAF, Ret.), Executive Director. General email, amcsus1@gmail.com*
Web, www.amcsus.org, Twitter, @CharacterisKey and Facebook, www.facebook.com/amcsus

Membership: nonfederal military colleges and universities, junior colleges, and preparatory secondary schools that emphasize character development, leadership, and knowledge. Interests include Reserve Officers Training Corps (ROTC). Publishes a newsletter; sponsors an annual meeting and outreach activities. Represents member schools before the Defense Dept., Education Dept., and the general public.

George and Carol Olmsted Foundation, *80 East Jefferson St., #300B, Falls Church, VA 22046; (703) 536-3500. Maj. Gen. Bruce K. Scott (USA, Ret.), President, ext. 10. Toll-free, (877) 656-7833. General email, scholars@olmstedfoundation.org*
Web, www.olmstedfoundation.org, Twitter, @OlmstedScholars and Facebook, www.facebook.com/OlmstedFoundation

Administers grants, for selected officers of the armed forces, for two years of graduate study overseas, including foreign language study,.

Military Order of the World Wars, *435 N. Lee St., Alexandria, VA 22314-2301; (703) 683-4911. Fax, (703) 683-4501. Col. Mike Farrell (USMC, Ret.), Chief of Staff, ext. 4.*
Web, www.moww.org, Facebook, www.facebook.com/militaryorder and Twitter, @militaryorder

Membership: retired and active duty commissioned officers, warrant officers, and flight officers. Supports a strong national defense; supports patriotic education in schools; presents awards to outstanding Junior and Senior Reserve Officers Training Corps (ROTC) cadets, Boy Scouts, and Girl Scouts.

National Academies of Sciences, Engineering, and Medicine (NASEM), *Air Force Studies Board, Keck Center, 500 5th St. N.W., 9th Floor, 20001; (202) 334-3111. Gen. Ellen M. Pawlikowski (USAF, Ret.), Chair; Ellen Chou, Director.*
General email, afsb@nas.edu
Web, www.nationalacademies.org/afsb/air-force-studies-board

Supports activities related to the development of science and technology within the Air Force. Interests of study include fuel efficiency, acquisition processes, and assuring the future scientific and technical qualification of Air Force personnel.

Navy League of the United States, *2300 Wilson Blvd., #200, Arlington, VA 22201-5424; (703) 528-1775. Fax, (703) 528-2333. David J. Reilly, President. Toll-free, (800) 356-5760.*
Web, www.navyleague.org, Twitter, @NavyLeagueUS, Facebook, www.facebook.com/NavyLeagueUS and General email, communications@navyleague.org

Membership: retired and reserve military personnel and civilians interested in the U.S. Navy, Marine Corps, Coast Guard, and Merchant Marine. Distributes literature, provides speakers, and conducts seminars to promote interests of the sea services. Sponsors Naval Sea Cadet Corps and Navy League Sea Cadet Corps for young people ages ten through eighteen. Graduates are eligible to enter the Navy at advanced pay grades. Monitors legislation.

MILITARY GRIEVANCES AND DISCIPLINE

General

▶**AGENCIES**

Air Force Dept. *(Defense Dept.), Inspector General (SAF/IG), 1140 Air Force Pentagon, 20330-1140; (210) 565-3200. Lt. Gen. Sami D. Said, Inspector General. Hotline, (202) 404-5354. Hotline toll-free, (800) 538-8429.*

General email, daf.ighotline@us.af.mil
Web, www.afinspectorgeneral.af.mil and Hotline, usaf.ighotline@mail.mil

Military office that handles intelligence oversight; criminal investigations; counterintelligence operations; complaints; and fraud, waste, and abuse programs. Oversees the Air Force Inspection Agency and Air Force Office of Special Investigations.

Air Force Dept. *(Defense Dept.), Manpower and Reserve Affairs (SAF/MR), Air Force Review Boards Agency (AFRBA), 1500 W. Perimeter Rd., #3700, Joint Base Andrews, MD 20762-7002; (240) 612-5400. Fax, (240) 612-6016. Gerald Curry, Director.*
Web, www.af.mil/About-Us/Fact-Sheets/Display/Article/104511/air-force-review-boards-agency and General email, staff.mrb.workflow@us.af.mil

Civilian office that responds to complaints from Air Force military and civilian personnel and assists in seeking corrective action.

Army Dept. *(Defense Dept.), Army Review Boards Agency, 251 18th St. South, #385, Arlington, VA 22202-3531; (703) 545-6900. Alexander Conyers, Deputy Assistant Secretary.*
General email, army.arbainquiry@mail.mil
Web, http://arba.army.pentagon.mil

Civilian office that administers boards reviewing appeals cases. Administers 15 boards, including the Army Grade Determination Review Board, Army Board for Correction of Military Records, and the Army Discharge Review Board.

Defense Dept. (DoD), *Diversity Management and Equal Opportunity, 4800 Mark Center Dr., Alexandria, VA 22350; (571) 372-0964. Jason S. Osborne, Chief.*
Web, www.dodea.edu/Offices/DMEO

Evaluates civil rights complaints from military personnel, including issues of sexual harassment and recruitment.

Defense Dept. (DoD), *Legal Policy, 4000 Defense Pentagon, #2C548A, 20301-4000; (703) 697-3387. Vacant, Director.*
Web, www.defense.gov

Coordinates policy in a variety of personnel-related areas, including the Members Civil Relief Act, legal assistance, political activities, and corrections.

Defense Dept. (DoD), *Sexual Assault Prevention and Response, 4800 Mark Center Dr., #07G21, Alexandria, VA 22350; (571) 372-2657. Maj. Gen. Clement S. Coward (USA), Director. Hotline, (877) 995-5247.*
General email, whs.mc-alex.wso.mbx.SAPRO@mail.mil
Web, www.sapr.mil

Serves as the single point of accountability for the Defense Dept.'s sexual assault policy. Responsible for improving prevention, enhancing reporting and response, and holding perpetrators appropriately accountable.

Defense Legal Services Agency *(Defense Dept.), General Counsel, 1600 Defense Pentagon, #3E788, 20301-1600;*

(703) 695-3341. *Caroline Kasz, Principal Deputy General Counsel.*
Web, https://ogc.osd.mil

Provides legal guidance to the Air Force, Army, Navy, and other Defense Dept. agencies. Administers programs governing military standards and conduct.

Marine Corps *(Defense Dept.), Inspector General of the Marine Corps, Bldg. 12, 701 S. Courthouse Rd., #1J165, Arlington, VA 22204; (703) 604-4626. Fax, (703) 604-1006. (703) 604-4681. SES Carl E. Shelton Jr., Inspector General (Acting). Complaint hotline, (866) 243-3887. phone, (703) 604-4681.*
General email, ORGMB_IGMC_ADMIN@usmc.mil
Web, www.hqmc.marines.mil/igmc

Military office that investigates complaints from Marine Corps personnel and assists in seeking corrective action.

Navy Dept. *(Defense Dept.), Manpower and Reserve Affairs, 1000 Navy Pentagon, #4E590, 20350-1000; (703) 695-4333. Robert D. Hogue, Assistant Secretary (Acting).*
Web, www.secnav.navy.mil/mra/Pages/default.aspx and General email, m&ra_webmailbox.fct@navy.mil

Civilian office that receives complaints from Navy and Marine Corps military personnel and assists in seeking corrective action.

►CONGRESS

For a listing of relevant congressional committees and sub-committees, please see page 600 or the Appendix.

Correction of Military Records

►AGENCIES

Air Force Dept. *(Defense Dept.), Board for the Correction of Military Records (AFBCMR), 3351 Celmers Ln., Joint Base Andrews, MD 20762; (240) 612-5400. Fax, (240) 612-5619. Nicole Jackson, Executive Director, (240) 612-5392. AFPC Service Center, (800) 525-0102.*
General email, SAF.MRBC.Workflow@us.af.mil
Web, https://afrba-portal.cce.af.mil/#board-info/bcmr/navbar

Civilian board that reviews appeals for corrections to Air Force personnel records and makes recommendations to the secretary of the Air Force.

Army Dept. *(Defense Dept.), Board for the Correction of Military Records, 251 18th St. South, #385, Arlington, VA 22202-3523; (703) 545-6900. Fax, (703) 601-0703. Dennis Dingle, Director.*
Web, http://arba.army.pentagon.mil

Civilian board that reviews appeals for corrections to Army personnel records and makes recommendations to the secretary of the Army under Section 1552 of Title 10 of the U.S. Code.

Defense Dept. *(DoD), Legal Policy, 4000 Defense Pentagon, #2C548A, 20301-4000; (703) 697-3387. Vacant, Director.*
Web, www.defense.gov

Coordinates policy for armed services boards charged with correcting military records.

Navy Dept. *(Defense Dept.), Board for Correction of Naval Records, Bldg. 12, 701 S. Courthouse Rd., #1001, Arlington, VA 22204-2490; (703) 604-6884. Fax, (703) 604-3437. Elizabeth (Beth) Hill, Executive Director.*
General email, BCNR_Correspondence.fct@navy.mil
Web, www.secnav.navy.mil/mra/bcnr/Pages/default.aspx and Applications, BCNR_Application@navy.mil

Civilian board that reviews appeals for corrections to Navy and Marine Corps personnel records and makes recommendations to the secretary of the Navy.

U.S. Coast Guard (USCG) *(Homeland Security Dept.), Board for Correction of Military Records, 2707 Martin Luther King Jr. Ave. S.E., MS 0485, 20528-485; (202) 447-4099. Julia Andrews, Chair.*
General email, cgbcmr@dhs.gov
Web, www.uscg.mil/Resources/legal/BCMR

Civilian board (an adjunct to the U.S. Coast Guard) that reviews appeals for corrections to Coast Guard personnel records and makes recommendations to the general counsel of the Homeland Security Dept.

Legal Proceedings

►AGENCIES

Air Force Dept. *(Defense Dept.), Judge Advocate General (JAG), 1420 Air Force Pentagon, #4E252, 20330-1420; (703) 614-5732. Lt. Gen. Jeffrey A. Rockwell, Judge Advocate General.*
General email, usaf.pentagon.af-ja.mbx.workflow@mail.mil
Web, www.afjag.af.mil

Military office that prosecutes and defends Air Force personnel during military legal proceedings. Gives legal advice and assistance to Air Force personnel.

Army Dept. *(Defense Dept.), Army Clemency and Parole Board, Crystal Square 5, 251 18th St. South, #385, Arlington, VA 22202-3531; (703) 571-0532. Fax, (703) 601-0493. Christopher Glover, Chair.*
General email, army.arbainquiry@mail.mil
Web, http://arba.army.pentagon.mil/clemency-parole.html

Conducts clemency, parole, and mandatory supervised release hearings for eligible Army prisoners and supervisees.

Army Dept. *(Defense Dept.), Judge Advocate General, 2200 Army Pentagon, #3E542, 20310-2200; (703) 697-5151. Fax, (703) 697-1059. Lt. Gen. Stuart W. Risch (USA), Judge Advocate General. Support desk, (703) 693-0000.*
Web, www.jagcnet.army.mil/sites/JAGC.nsf

Military policy office for the field offices that prosecute and defend Army personnel during military legal proceedings. Serves as an administrative office for military appeals court, which hears legal proceedings involving Army personnel.

Defense Dept. (DoD), *Court of Appeals for the Armed Forces,* *450 E St. N.W., 20442-0001; (202) 761-1448. Fax, (202) 761-4672. Joseph Perlak, Clerk of the Court. Web, www.armfor.uscourts.gov*

Serves as the appellate court for cases involving dishonorable or bad conduct discharges, confinement of a year or more, and the death penalty, and for cases certified to the court by the judge advocate general of an armed service. Less serious cases are reviewed by the individual armed services.

Marine Corps *(Defense Dept.),* **Judge Advocate,** *3000 Marine Corps Pentagon, #4D558, 20350-3000; (703) 614-8661. Maj. Gen. David J. Bligh (USMC), Staff Judge Advocate; Col. Christopher Tolar, Deputy Director. Legal assistance, (703) 692-7442. Victims Legal Counsel, (703) 693-9526. Safe helpline, (877) 995-5247. Web, www.hqmc.marines.mil/sja*

Military office that administers legal proceedings involving Marine Corps personnel.

Navy Dept. *(Defense Dept.),* **Judge Advocate General,** *1322 Patterson Ave. S.E., #3000, Washington Navy Yard, DC 20374-5066; (703) 614-7420. Vice Adm. Darse (Del) E. Crandall (USN), Judge Advocate General. Press, (202) 685-5275. Web, www.jag.navy.mil, Facebook, www.facebook.com/ navyjag, Twitter, @Navy_JAG and Public Affairs email, patricia.babb5.civ@us.navy.mil*

Military office that administers the Judge Advocate General's Corps, which conducts legal proceedings involving Navy and Marine Corps personnel.

Military Police and Corrections

▶**AGENCIES**

Army Dept. *(Defense Dept.),* **Provost Marshal General,** *2800 Army Pentagon, #1E596, 20310-2800; (703) 692-6966. Fax, (703) 614-5628. Maj. Gen. Duane R. Miller (USA), Provost Marshal General. Web, www.army.mil/opmg, Twitter, @ArmyOPMG and Facebook, www.facebook.com/armyopmg*

Develops policies and supports military police and corrections programs in all branches of the U.S. Army. Operates the Military Police Management Information System (MPMIS), which automates incident reporting and tracks information on facilities, staff, and inmates, including enemy prisoners of war.

Defense Dept. (DoD), *Legal Policy, 4000 Defense Pentagon, #2C548A, 20301-4000; (703) 697-3387. Vacant, Director. Web, www.defense.gov*

Coordinates and reviews Defense Dept. policies and programs relating to deserters.

MILITARY HISTORY AND HONORS

General

▶**AGENCIES**

Air Force Dept. *(Defense Dept.),* **Air Force History and Museums Program,** *1190 Air Force Pentagon, #4E1062, 20330-1190 (mailing address: 3 Brookley Ave. S.W., Box 94 Joint Base Anacostia-Bolling, Washington, DC 20032); (703) 697-5600. Vacant, Director. Historian, (202) 404-2264. General email, usaf.pentagon.af-ho.mbx.afhso-research@mail.mil Web, www.afhistoryandmuseums.af.mil*

Publishes histories, studies, monographs, and reference works; directs worldwide Air Force History and Museums Program and provides guidance to the Air Force Historical Research Agency at Maxwell Air Force Base in Alabama, Air Force Historical Support Division in Washington, D.C., and National Museum of the USAF in Ohio; supports Air Force Air Staff agencies and responds to inquiries from the public and the U.S. government.

Air Force Dept. *(Defense Dept.),* **Historical Support Division,** *Joint Base Anacostia-Bolling, 2822 Doherty Dr. S.W., #404, 20373 (mailing address: 3 Brookley Ave., Box 94, JBAB, Washington, DC 20032); (334) 953-5697. Vacant, Director of Air Force History and Museums. General email, usaf.pentagon.af-ho.mbx.af-hoh-workflow@mail.mil Web, www.afhistory.af.mil*

Supports the Director of Air Force History and Museums and conducts research and analysis of the service's major operational activities. Publishes books, monographs, studies, and reports covering the history of the Air Force. (Connected with the Air Force Historical Research Agency located at Maxwell Air Force Base, Ala.)

Army Dept. *(Defense Dept.),* **Institute of Heraldry,** *9325 Gunston Rd., #S113, Fort Belvoir, VA 22060-5579; (571) 515-0346. Charles Mugno, Director. General email, usarmy.belvoir.hqda.mbx.tioh-webmaster@army.mil Web, https://tioh.army.mil*

Furnishes heraldic services to the armed forces and other U.S. government agencies, including the Executive Office of the President. Responsible for research, design, development, and standardization of official symbolic items, including seals, decorations, medals, insigne, badges, flags, and other items awarded to or authorized for official wear or display by government personnel and agencies. Limited research and information services on these items are provided to the general public.

Army Dept. *(Defense Dept.),* **U.S. Army Center of Military History,** *Fort Lesley J. McNair, Bldg. 35, Collins Hall, 102 4th Ave., 20319-5060; (202) 685-2706. Fax, (202) 685-4570. Charles Bowrey, Executive Director. General email, usarmy.mcnair.cmh.mbx.answers@mail.mil*

Web, www.history.army.mil and Facebook, www.facebook. com/armyhistory

Publishes the official history of the Army. Provides information on Army history; coordinates Army museum system and art program. Works with Army school system to ensure that history is included in curriculum. Provides Heraldic products and services in support of federal government. Sponsors professional appointments, fellowships, and awards.

Defense Dept. (DoD), *Center of Military History, 1777 N. Kent St., #5000, Arlington, VA 22209; Erin R. Mahan, Chief Historian.*
Web, http://history.defense.gov and Facebook, www .facebook.com/OSDHO

Researches and writes historical accounts of the office of the secretary of defense; coordinates historical activities of the Defense Dept. and prepares special studies at the request of the secretary.

Defense Dept. (DoD), *Joint History Office, 9999 Defense Pentagon, #1A466, 20318-9999; (703) 695-2137. Fax, (703) 614-6243. John F. Shortal, Director.*
Web, www.jcs.mil/About/Joint-Staff-History

Provides historical support services to the chair of the Joint Chiefs of Staff and the Joint Staff, including research; writes the official history of the Joint Chiefs. Supervises field programs encompassing nine Unified Commands.

Marine Corps *(Defense Dept.),* **History Division,** *Simmons Center, 2044 Broadway St., Quantico, VA 22134; (703) 432-4877. Edward T. Negloski, Director. Archives, (703) 784-4685. Press, (703) 432-4880.*
General email, history.division@usmcu.edu
Web, www.usmcu.edu/Research/History-Division, Twitter, @CorpsHistory and Facebook, www.facebook.com/ MarineCorpsU

Writes official histories of the corps for government agencies and the public; answers inquiries about Marine Corps history.

National Archives and Records Administration (NARA), *Reference Services, 4205 Suitland Rd., Suitland, MD 20746-8001; (301) 778-1600. Channon Harris, Director, (301) 778-1562.*
General email, suitland.reference@nara.gov
Web, www.archives.gov/frc/reference-services.html

Contains Army records from the Revolutionary War to the Vietnam War, Navy records from the Revolutionary War to the Korean War, and Air Force records from 1947 to 1954. Handles records captured from enemy powers at the end of World War II and a small collection of records captured from the Vietnamese. Conducts research in response to specific inquiries; makes records available for reproduction or examination in research room.

National Museum of American History *(Smithsonian Institution),* **Armed Forces History,** *14th St. and Constitution Ave. N.W., #4032, MS 620, 20560-0620; (202) 633-3950. Jennifer Locke Jones, Chair.*

Web, https://americanhistory.si.edu/about/departments/ armed-forces-history/collections

Maintains collections relating to the history of the U.S. armed forces, U.S. military technology, and the American flag; includes manuscripts, documents, correspondence, uniforms, small arms and weapons, and other personal memorabilia of armed forces personnel of all ranks. Research areas are open by appointment.

National Museum of Health and Medicine *(Defense Dept.), 2500 Linden Lane, Silver Spring, MD 20910 (mailing address: Bldg. 2500, 2460 Linden Lane, Silver Spring, MD 20910); (301) 319-3300. Fax, (301) 319-3373. Adrianne Noe, Director. Tours, (301) 319-3312.*
General email, usarmy.detrick.medcom-usamrmc.list. medical-museum@mail.mil
Web, www.medicalmuseum.mil and Twitter, @medicalmuseum

Maintains exhibits related to pathology and the history of medicine, particularly military medicine during the Civil War. Open to the public 10:00 a.m.–5:30 p.m., seven days a week. Study collection available for scholars by appointment.

Naval History and Heritage Command *(Navy Dept.), 805 Kidder Breese St. S.E., Washington Navy Yard, DC 20374-5060; 1022 O St. S.E., 20003; (202) 433-7880. Fax, (202) 781-0021. Rear Adm. Samuel Cox (USN, Ret.), Director. Archives, (202) 433-3224. Art Gallery, (202) 433-3815. Library, (202) 433-4132. Museum, (202) 433-4882. Press, (202) 433-7880.*
General email, NHHCPublicAffairs@navy.mil
Web, www.history.navy.mil, Twitter, @USNHistory and Facebook, www.facebook.com/USNHistory

Produces publications on naval history. Maintains historical files on Navy ships, operations, shore installations, and aviation. Collects Navy art, artifacts, and photographs. Library, archives, museum, and gallery are open to the public by appointment.

Naval History and Heritage Command *(Navy Dept.),* **Navy Art Collection,** *Washington Navy Yard, Bldg. 67, 822 Sicard St. S.E., 20374 (mailing address: 805 Kidder Breese St. S.E., Washington Navy Yard, DC 20374); (202) 433-3815. Gale Munro, Head Curator.*
General email, NavyArt@navy.mil
Web, www.history.navy.mil/our-collections/art.html

Holdings include more than 20,000 paintings, prints, drawings, and sculptures. Artworks depict naval ships, personnel, and action from all eras of U.S. naval history. Open to the public. Visitors without Defense Dept. or military identification must call in advance. Photo identification required.

U.S. Coast Guard (USCG) *(Homeland Security Dept.),* **Historian,** *2703 Martin Luther King Jr. Ave. S.E., MS 7031, 20593-7031; (202) 372-4651. Scott Price, Chief Historian.*
General email, History@uscg.mil
Web, www.history.uscg.mil

Collects and maintains Coast Guard historical artifacts and documents. Archives are available to the public by appointment only.

Air Force Historical Foundation, *602 California Ave., #F162, Joint Base Andrews, MD 20762 (mailing address: P.O. Box 790, Clinton, MD 20735-0790); (301) 736-1959. Lt. Col. James (Jim) A. Vertenten (USAF, Ret.), Executive Director, (703) 395-7261.*
General email, ed@afhistory.org
Web, www.afhistory.org, Twitter, @AFHF and Facebook, www.facebook.com/AFHISTFOUND

Membership: individuals interested in the history of the U.S. Air Force and U.S. air power. Bestows awards on Air Force Academy and Air War College students and to other active duty personnel. Funds research and publishes books on aviation and Air Force history.

American Battlefield Trust, *1156 15th St. N.W., #900, 20005; (202) 367-1861. Fax, (202) 367-1865. David D. Duncan, President. Toll-free, (800) 298-7878.*
General email, info@battlefields.org
Web, www.battlefields.org, Twitter, @battlefields and Facebook, www.facebook.com/americanbattlefieldtrust

Membership: preservation professionals, historians, conservation activists, and citizens. Preserves endangered American Revolution, War of 1812, and Civil War battlefields throughout the United States. Conducts preservation conferences and workshops. Advises local preservation groups. Publishes Hallowed Ground. Monitors legislation and regulations at the federal, state, and local levels.

Marine Corps Heritage Foundation, *18900 Jefferson Davis Hwy., Triangle, VA 22172; (703) 640-7965. Maj. Gen. James W. Lukeman (USMC, Ret.), President. Toll-free, (800) 397-7585.*
General email, info@marineheritage.org
Web, www.marineheritage.org, Twitter, @MarineCorpsHeritageFdn and Facebook, www.facebook.com/MarineCorpsHeritageFdn

Preserves and promotes Marine Corps history through education, awards, and publications. Offers funding for the study of Marine Corps history. Funds the ongoing expansion of the National Museum of the Marine Corps.

Military Order of the World Wars, *435 N. Lee St., Alexandria, VA 22314-2301; (703) 683-4911. Fax, (703) 683-4501. Col. Mike Farrell (USMC, Ret.), Chief of Staff, ext. 4. Web, www.moww.org, Facebook, www.facebook.com/militaryorder and Twitter, @militaryorder*

Membership: retired and active duty commissioned officers, warrant officers, and flight officers. Presents awards to outstanding Reserve Officers Training Corps (ROTC) cadets; gives awards to Boy Scouts and Girl Scouts; conducts youth leadership conferences.

National Guard Educational Foundation, *1 Massachusetts Ave. N.W., 20001; (202) 789-0031. Fax, (202) 682-9358. Luke Guthrie, Director; Keith Brown,*

Archivist, (202) 408-5887. Library, (202) 408-5890. Toll-free, (800) 464-8273.
General email, ngef@ngef.org
Web, www.ngef.org and Twitter, @NGMusseum

Promotes public awareness of the National Guard by providing information about its history and traditions. Museum and library open to the public.

National Guard Memorial Museum, *1 Massachusetts Ave. N.W., 20001; (202) 789-0031. Fax, (202) 682-9358. Luke Guthrie, Director, (202) 408-5886.*
General email, ngef@ngaus.org
Web, www.ngef.org/national-guard-memorial-museum, Twitter, @NGMuseum and Facebook, www.facebook.com/NationalGuardMemorialMuseum

Features exhibit areas that explore the National Guard from colonial times through the world wars and the cold war to the modern era through timelines, photographs, artifacts, light, and sound. As of publication, the museum is closed until further notice.

National Museum of American Jewish Military History, *1811 R St. N.W., 20009; (202) 265-6280. Fax, (202) 462-3192. Michael B. Berman, President. Tours, (202) 265-6280.*
General email, nmajmh@nmajmh.org
Web, www.nmajmh.org and Twitter, @NMAJMH

Collects, preserves, and displays memorabilia of Jewish men and women in the military; conducts research; sponsors seminars; provides information on the history of Jewish participation in the U.S. armed forces.

Naval Historical Foundation, *1306 Dahlgren Ave. S.E., Washington Navy Yard, DC 20374-5055 (mailing address: P.O. Box 15304, Washington, DC 20003); (202) 678-4333. Rear Adm. Edward (Sonny) Masso (USN, Ret.), Executive Director.*
General email, info@navyhistory.org
Web, www.navyhistory.org, Twitter, @USNavyHistory and Facebook, www.facebook.com/navalhistoricalfoundation

Collects private documents and artifacts relating to naval history; maintains collection on deposit with the Library of Congress for public reference; conducts oral history and heritage speakers programs; raises funds to support the Navy Museum and historical programs.

Cemeteries and Memorials

Air Force Memorial Foundation, *1 Air Force Memorial Dr., Arlington, VA 22204; (703) 462-4093. Zachary Steele, Events and Outreach Coordinator. Alternate Phone, (240) 612-0478.*
General email, afmemorial@mail.mil
Web, www.afdw.af.mil/afmemorial and Facebook, www.facebook.com/AirForceMemorial

Oversees daily management of and directs event planning and fund-raising in support of the Air Force Memorial. Open daily 8 a.m.–8 p.m.

American Battle Monuments Commission, *Courthouse Plaza 2, 2300 Clarendon Blvd., #500, Arlington, VA 22201-3367; (703) 584-1501. Robert J. Dalessandro, Secretary (Acting).*
General email, info@abmc.gov
Web, www.abmc.gov, Twitter, @usabmc and Facebook, www.facebook.com/usabmc

Manages military cemeteries overseas and certain memorials in the United States; provides next of kin with grave site and related information.

Army Dept. *(Defense Dept.), Arlington National Cemetery, Interment Services, 1 Memorial Ave., Arlington, VA 22211; (877) 907-8585. Karen Durham-Aguilera, Executive Director. Fax (for documents), (571) 256-3334.*
Email (for documents), arlingtoncemetery.isb@mail.mil and Web, www.arlingtoncemetery.mil/Funerals/Scheduling-a-Funeral

Arranges interment services and provides eligibility information for burials at Arlington National Cemetery.

National Cemetery Administration *(Veterans Affairs Dept.), 810 Vermont Ave. N.W., #400, 20420; (202) 461-6112. Ronald Walters, Deputy Under Secretary for Memorial Affairs. Toll-free, (800) 698-2411.*
Web, www.cem.va.gov and https://gravelocator.cem.va.gov

Administers VA national cemeteries; furnishes markers and headstones for deceased veterans; administers state grants to establish, expand, and improve veterans' cemeteries. Provides presidential memorial certificates to next of kin.

▶**CONGRESS**

For a listing of relevant congressional committees and subcommittees, please see page 600 or the Appendix.

▶**NONGOVERNMENTAL**

U.S. Navy Memorial Foundation, *701 Pennsylvania Ave. N.W., #123, 20004-2608; (202) 380-0710. (202) 737-2300. Rear Adm. Frank Thorp IV (USN, Ret.), President, (202) 380-0739.*
Web, www.navymemorial.org, Twitter, @Navymemorial and Facebook, www.facebook.com/Navymemorial

Educational foundation authorized by Congress. Focuses on U.S. naval history; built and supports the national Navy memorial to honor those who serve or have served in the sea services.

Women in Military Service for America Memorial Foundation, *200 N. Glebe Rd., #400, Arlington, VA 22203; (703) 533-1155. Fax, (703) 931-4208. CW5 Phyllis Wilson (USA, Ret.), President. The Women's Memorial, (703) 892-2606. Toll-free, (800) 222-2294.*
General email, hq@womensmemorial.org
Web, www.womensmemorial.org and YouTube, www.youtube.com/channel/UC_wOUyMQYwIESrm_jux-6Ng?view_as=subscriber

Authorized by Congress to create, build, and operate the national memorial to honor women who serve or have served in the U.S. armed forces from the Revolutionary War to the present. Mailing address is for donations. Memorial is located at the Gateway at Arlington National Cemetery.

Ceremonies, Military Bands

▶**AGENCIES**

Air Force Dept. *(Defense Dept.), Air Force Bands, 1690 Air Force Pentagon, Room 1D887, 20330-1690; (202) 767-4310. Col. Don Schofield, Chief Manager. Band at nonmilitary functions, (202) 685-4990.*
Web, www.music.af.mil, Facebook, www.facebook.com/AirForceBands and Twitter, @AFBands1

Disseminates information to the public regarding various Air Force bands, including their schedules and performances. Oversees policy, training, and personnel assignments for Air Force bands.

Army Dept. *(Defense Dept.), Army Field Band, 4214 Field Band Dr., #5330, Fort Meade, MD 20755-7055; (301) 677-6586. Col. Jim R. Keene (USA), Commander.*
General email, usarmyfieldband@mail.mil
Web, www.armyfieldband.com, Twitter, @armyfieldband and Facebook, www.facebook.com/ArmyFieldBand

Supports the Army by providing musical services for official military ceremonies and community events. Sponsors vocal and instrumental clinics for high school and college students.

Army Dept. *(Defense Dept.), Ceremonies and Outreach Directorate, Fort Lesley J. McNair, 103 3rd Ave., 20319-5058; (202) 685-4921. Fax, (202) 685-3379. Gary C. Hardy, Chief of Ceremonies, (202) 909-3623.*
General email, usarmy.mcnair.mdw.mbx.jfhqncr-special-events-request@mail.mil
Web, www.mdwhome.mdw.army.mil/ceremonial-support/requesting-ceremonial-support and Twitter, @MDW_USARMY

Coordinates and schedules public ceremonies and special events, including appearances of all armed forces bands and honor guards.

Army Dept. *(Defense Dept.), The U.S. Army Band, Attn: TUSAB, 400 McNair Rd., Fort Myer, VA 22211-1306; (571) 867-4040. Fax, (703) 696-0279. Col. Andrew J. Esch (USA), Commander. Music Library, (703) 696-3648.*
Web, www.usarmyband.com, Twitter, @theusarmyband and Facebook, www.facebook.com/usarmyband

Supports the Army by providing musical services for official military ceremonies and community events.

Defense Dept. *(DoD), Community and Public Outreach, 1400 Defense Pentagon, 2E984, 20301-1400; (703) 693-2337. Fax, (703) 697-2577. Patricia Montes Barron, Deputy Assistant Secretary. Press, (703) 697-5131. Public Affairs,*

(703) 571-3343. Toll-free (Military OneSource), (800) 342-9647.
Web, www.defense.gov

Administers requests for ceremonial bands and other military assets for public events.

Marine Corps *(Defense Dept.), Marine Band, Marine Barracks Annex, 7th St. and K St. S.E., 20003 (mailing address: Marine Barracks Washington, 8th St. and Eye St. S.E., Washington, DC 20390); (202) 433-5809. Col. Jason K. Fettig, Director. Concert information, (202) 433-4011. National tours, (703) 614-1405. Library, (202) 433-4298.*
General email, marineband.communication@usmc.mil
Web, www.marineband.marines.mil and Facebook, www.facebook.com/marineband

Provides music for the U.S. President and the Commandant of the Marine Corps. Supports the Marine Corps by providing musical services for official military ceremonies and community events.

Navy Dept. *(Defense Dept.), Navy Band, 617 Warrington Ave. S.E., Washington Navy Yard, DC 20374-5054; (202) 433-3676. Capt. Kenneth Collins (USN), Commanding Officer. Auditions, (202) 433-2840. Information, (202) 433-3366. Public Affairs, (202) 433-4777.*
General email, usnavyband@navy.mil
Web, www.navyband.navy.mil, Twitter, @usnavyband and Facebook, www.facebook.com/usnavyband

Supports the Navy by providing musical services for official military ceremonies and community events.

U.S. Naval Academy *(Defense Dept.), Band, 101 Buchanan Rd., Annapolis, MD 21402-1258; (410) 293-3282. Fax, (410) 293-2116. Cmdr. Diane Nichols, Director. Concert information, (410) 293-1257. Press, (410) 293-1262.*
General email, bandops@usna.edu
Web, www.usna.edu/USNABand and Facebook, www.facebook.com/USNAband

The Navy's oldest continuing musical organization. Supports the Navy by providing musical services for official military ceremonies and community events.

U.S. Naval Academy *(Defense Dept.), Drum and Bugle Corps, U.S. Naval Academy, Alumni Hall, 675 Decatur Rd., Annapolis, MD 21402-5086; (410) 293-3602. (410) 293-2439. Fax, 41–293-3218. Matthew Halligan, Corps Director.*
General email, weir@usna.edu
Web, www.usna.edu/USNADB

One of the oldest drum and bugle corps in the United States. The all-midshipmen drum and bugle corps plays for Brigade of Midshipmen at sporting events, pep rallies, parades, and noon formations. Supports the Navy by providing musical services for official military ceremonies and community events.

RESERVES AND NATIONAL GUARD

General

▶**AGENCIES**

Air Force Dept. *(Defense Dept.), Air Force Reserve (AFR), 1150 Air Force Pentagon, #4E138, 20330-1150; (703) 695-9225. Lt. Gen. Richard W. Scobee, Chief of Air Force Reserve. Public Affairs, (478) 327-1748.*
Web, www.afrc.af.mil, Twitter, @USAFReserve, Facebook, www.facebook.com/usairforcereserve and Public Affairs, afrc.paworkflow@us.af.mil

Units of commissioned officers and enlisted airmen who are ready for active duty and are performing specialized missions and operations for the Air Force.

Air Force Dept. *(Defense Dept.), Manpower and Reserve Affairs (SAF/MR), 1660 Air Force Pentagon, #5D742, 20330-1660; (703) 697-2302. Fax, (703) 695-2701. John A. Fedrigo, Assistant Secretary (Acting). Public Affairs, (703) 695-0640.*
Web, www.af.mil

Civilian-led office responsible for overseeing the Air Force Reserve and developing policies concerning manpower, military and civilian personnel issues, Reserve component affairs, and readiness support for the Air Force. (Headquarters in Ga.)

Army Dept. *(Defense Dept.), Army Reserve, 6075 Goethals Rd., Fort Belvoir, VA 22060; (703) 695-0031. Lt. Gen. Jody J. Daniels (USA), Chief.*
Web, www.usar.army.mil, Twitter, @USArmyReserve and Facebook, www.facebook.com/usarmyreserve

Military office that monitors legislative affairs as well as coordinates and directs Army Reserve matters (excluding the Army National Guard).

Army Dept. *(Defense Dept.), Manpower and Reserve Affairs, 111 Army Pentagon, #2E460, 20310-0111; (703) 697-9253. Fax, (703) 692-9000. Mark R. Lewis, Assistant Secretary (Acting); Jeffrey P. Angers, Director (Acting).*
Web, www.army.mil/asamra, Twitter, @MRA_G1_PAO and Facebook, www.facebook.com/HQDAMRAG1

Civilian office that reviews policies and programs for Army personnel and reserves; makes recommendations to the secretary of the Army. Oversees training, military preparedness, and mobilization for all civilians and active and reserve members of the Army.

Defense Dept. (DoD), *Manpower and Reserve Affairs, 1500 Defense Pentagon, #2E556, 20301-1500; (703) 697-6631. Fax, (703) 697-1682. Virginia Penrod, Assistant Secretary (Acting).*
Web, www.people.mil

Civilian office that addresses all policy matters pertaining to the six reserve components of the military services. Develops and delivers civilian and military personnel policy and implements human resource solutions that support the Total Force and mission readiness.

Defense Dept. (DoD), *National Committee for Employer Support of the Guard and Reserve,* 4800 Mark Center Dr., #05E22, Arlington, VA 22350-1200; (703) 882-3747. Capt. Robert Underhill (USN), Executive Director; Ron Bogle, National Chair. Toll-free, (800) 336-4590. General email, osd.USERRA@mail.mil

Web, www.esgr.mil and Public Affairs, osd.esgr-pa@mail.mil

Works to gain and maintain employer support for National Guard and Reserve service by recognizing outstanding support and providing service members and employers with information on applicable law. Volunteers provide free education, consultation, and, if necessary, mediation between employers and National Guard and Reserve service members.

Marine Corps *(Defense Dept.),* *Manpower and Reserve Affairs,* James Wesley Marsh Center, Bldg. 3280, 3280 Russell Rd., Quantico, VA 22134; (703) 784-9012. (703) 784-9864. Lt. Gen. David A. Ottignon, Deputy Commandant.
Web, www.manpower.usmc.mil/webcenter/portal/MRAHome and General email, SMB_HQMC_HROMDIR@usmc.mil

Oversees planning, directing, coordinating, and supervising of both active, reserve, veteran, and civilian Marine Corps forces.

National Guard Bureau *(Defense Dept.),* 111 S. George Mason Dr., Arlington, Va, 22204; (703) 607-3643. Fax, (703) 607-1313. Gen. Daniel R. Hokanson (USAF), Chief. Press, (703) 607-6767.
General email, ng.NCR.mbx.gomailbox@mail.mil

Web, www.nationalguard.mil, Twitter, @USnationalguard and Facebook, www.facebook.com/TheNationalGuard

Military office that oversees and coordinates activities of the Air National Guard and Army National Guard.

National Guard Bureau *(Defense Dept.),* *Air National Guard,* 1000 Airforce Pentagon, #4E126, 20330; (703) 614-8033. Lt. Gen. Michael A. Loh (ANG), Director. Press, (703) 601-6767.
Web, www.ang.af.mil, Facebook, www.facebook.com/AirNationalGuard and Twitter, @AirNatlGuard

Military office that coordinates and directs Air National Guard matters.

National Guard Bureau *(Defense Dept.),* *Army National Guard,* 111 S. George Mason Dr., Arlington, VA 22204; (703) 607-7017. Fax, (703) 607-7088. Lt. Gen. Jon Jensen (ARNG), Director, (703) 607-7000. Public Affairs, (703) 601-6767. Toll-free, (800) 464-8273.
Web, www.nationalguard.com and Facebook, www.facebook.com/nationalguard

Military office that coordinates and directs Army National Guard matters.

National Guard Bureau *(Defense Dept.),* *Chaplain Services,* 111 S. George Mason Dr., Arlington, VA 22204; (703) 607-8657. Fax, (703) 607-5295. Brig. Gen. Thomas G. Behling (ARNG), Director.

General email, ng.ncr.arng.mbx.office-of-the-chaplain@mail.mil

Web, www.nationalguard.mil/Leadership/Joint-Staff/Special-Staff/Chaplain

Represents the Chief National Guard Bureau on all aspects of the chaplains' mission. Directs and oversees the activities and policies of the National Guard Chaplain Services. Oversees chaplains and religious services within the National Guard; maintains liaison with religious denominations.

Navy Dept. *(Defense Dept.),* *Manpower and Reserve Affairs,* 1000 Navy Pentagon, #4E590, 20350-1000; (703) 695-4333. Robert D. Hogue, Assistant Secretary (Acting). Web, www.secnav.navy.mil/mra/Pages/default.aspx and General email, m&ra_webmailbox.fct@navy.mil

Civilian office that oversees the recruitment of active and reserve Navy personnel, government civilians, contractors, and volunteers. Provides programs and policy related to military personnel (active, reserve, and retired), family members, and government civilian workforce.

Navy Dept. *(Defense Dept.),* *Navy Reserve,* 2000 Navy Pentagon, CNO-N095, #4E426, 20350-2000; (703) 693-5757. Vice Adm. John B. Mustin (USN), Chief. Duty office, (757) 445-8506.
Web, www.navy.com/forward and Twitter, @navy_reserve

Military office that coordinates and directs Navy Reserve matters. (Headquarters in Norfolk, Va.)

U.S. Coast Guard (USCG) *(Homeland Security Dept.),* *Reserve Affairs,* 2703 Martin Luther King Jr. Ave. S.E., MS 7907, 20593-7097; (202) 475-5420. Vice Admiral Scott Buschman, Deputy Commandant for Operations; George M. Williamson, Master Chief. General email, cgreserve@uscg.mil

Web, www.reserve.uscg.mil and Facebook, www.facebook.com/uscoastguardreserve

Develops and oversees military personnel policy programs to recruit, train, and support all U.S. Coast Guard reserve and active duty forces. Publishes *The Reservist* magazine.

► NONGOVERNMENTAL

Assn. of Civilian Technicians (ACT), 12620 Lake Ridge Dr., Woodbridge, VA 22192-2354; (703) 494-4845. Fax, (703) 494-0961. Tom Mahoney, National President.
Web, www.chooseact.com and General email, actnational@actnat.com

Membership: federal civil service employees of the National Guard and Title 5 federal employees. Represents members before federal agencies and Congress.

Assn. of the U.S. Navy, 5904 Richmond Hwy., #530, Alexandria, VA 22303; (703) 548-5800. Fax, (703) 683-3647. Jason Beardsley, Executive Director. Toll-free, (877) 628-9411. Veteran's Crisis Hotline, (800) 273-8255. General email, info@ausn.org

Web, www.ausn.org, Twitter, @AUSNTweets and Facebook, www.facebook.com/AUSN1

Membership: active duty and retired Navy and Navy Reserve officers and their families and persons interested in the U.S. Navy. Supports and promotes U.S. military and naval policies, particularly the interests of Navy personnel and Navy veterans. Offers education programs, reviews of officer and enlisted records, and scholarships for the education of family members. Provides the public with information on national security issues. Assists members with Navy careers, military retirement, and veterans' benefits.

Assn. of the United States Army, *2425 Wilson Blvd., Arlington, VA 22201; (703) 841-4300. Fax, (703) 525-9039. Gen. Robert B. Brown (USA, Ret.), President, (703) 907-2664. Toll-free, (800) 336-4570.*
General email, membersupport@ausa.org
Web, www.ausa.org, Twitter, @AUSAorg and Facebook, www.facebook.com/AUSA.org

Membership: civilians and active duty and retired members of the armed forces. Conducts symposia on defense issues and researches topics that affect the military.

Enlisted Assn. of the National Guard of the United States, *1 Massachusetts Ave. N.W., #880, 20001; (703) 519-3846. Fax, (703) 519-3849. Matt Krenz, Executive Director; Kevin Hollinger, Legislative Director. Toll-free, (800) 234-3264.*
General email, eangus@eangus.org
Web, https://eangus.org

Membership: active duty and retired enlisted members and veterans of the National Guard. Promotes a strong national defense and National Guard. Sponsors scholarships, conducts seminars, and provides information concerning members and their families.

National Guard Assn. of the United States, *1 Massachusetts Ave. N.W., 20001-1431; (202) 789-0031. Fax, (202) 682-9358. Brig. Gen. Roy Robinson (ARNG, Ret.), President, (202) 408-5894.*
General email, ngaus@ngaus.org
Web, www.ngaus.org, Twitter, @NGAUS1878, Facebook, www.facebook.com/NGAUS1878 and YouTube, www.youtube.com/user/NGAUS1878

Membership: active duty and retired officers of the National Guard. Works to promote a strong national defense and to maintain a strong, ready National Guard.

Reserve Organization of America, *1 Constitution Ave. N.E., 20002-5618; (202) 479-2200. Fax, (202) 547-1641. Jeff Philips, Executive Director, (202) 646-7701. Toll-free, (800) 809-9448.*
General email, roainfo@roa.org
Web, www.roa.org, Twitter, @ReserveOrg, Facebook, www.facebook.com/ReserveOrganization and YouTube, www.youtube.com/channel/UCWrnkYsC1z0xJ37nxQOKTRg

Membership: active duty and inactive commissioned and noncommissioned officers of all uniformed services. Supports continuation of a reserve force to enhance national security. Monitors legislation and regulations.

VETERANS

General

▶**AGENCIES**

Armed Forces Retirement Home—Washington, *140 Rock Creek Church Rd. N.W., 20011-8400 (mailing address: 3700 N. Capitol St. N.W., Washington, DC 20011-8400); (800) 422-9988. (202) 541-7501. Fax, (202) 541-7519. Maj. Gen. Stephen T. Rippe (USA, Ret.), Chief Executive Officer.*
General email, public.affairs@afrh.gov
Web, www.afrh.gov

Gives domiciliary and medical care to retired members of the armed services or career service personnel unable to earn a livelihood. Formerly known as U.S. Soldiers' and Airmen's Home. (Armed Forces Retirement Home in Gulfport, Miss., reopened in 2010.)

Center for Minority Veterans *(Veterans Affairs Dept.),* *810 Vermont Ave. N.W., #436, MC 00M, 20420; (202) 461-6191. James Albino, Executive Director.*
Web, www.va.gov/centerforminorityveterans and Email, vacocenterforminorit@va.gov

Advises the secretary on adoption and implementation of policies and programs affecting minority veterans, specifically Pacific Islander, Asian American, African American, Hispanic/Latino, and Native American, including American Indian, Alaska Native, and Native Hawaiian veterans.

Center for Women Veterans *(Veterans Affairs Dept.),* *810 Vermont Ave. N.W., #435, MC 00W, 20420; (202) 461-6193. Lourdes Tiglao, Director.*
General email, 00w@va.gov
Web, www.va.gov/womenvet and Twitter, @VAWomenVets

Advises the secretary on policy on matters related to women veterans; monitors and coordinates VA administration of health care and benefits services and programs for women veterans; recognizes the service and contributions of women veterans and women in the military.

Navy Dept. *(Defense Dept.), Council of Review Boards,* *Bldg. 36, 720 Kennon St. S.E., #309, 20374-5023; (202) 685-6408. Fax, (202) 685-6610. Jeffrey Riehl (USMC, Ret.), Director.*
General email, crsc@navy.mil
Web, www.secnav.navy.mil/mra/CORB/Pages/default.aspx

Includes the Naval Clemency and Parole Board, which reviews cases of Navy and Marine Corps prisoners; the Naval Discharge Review Board, which considers former service members' less-than-honorable discharge for potential upgrade; the Physical Evaluation Board, which makes determinations about physical fitness for continuation of military service; and the Combat-Related Special Compensation Board, which makes determinations about combat-related conditions and appropriate compensation. All boards make recommendations to the secretary of the Navy.

Veterans Affairs Department

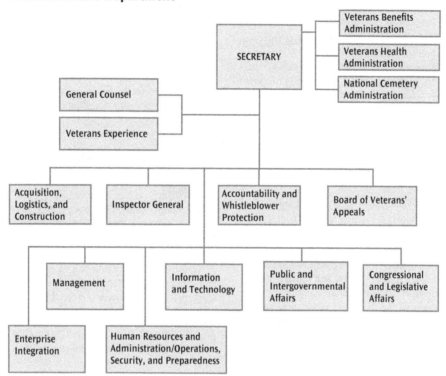

Veterans Affairs Dept. (VA), *810 Vermont Ave. N.W., MC 00, 20420; (202) 461-4800. Fax, (202) 495-5463. Denis McDonough, Secretary. Toll-free, (800) 698-2411. Health Benefits, (877) 222-8387. VA benefits, (800) 827-1000.*
Web, www.va.gov, Twitter, @DeptVetAffairs and Information System (IRIS), https://iris.va.gov

Administers programs benefiting veterans, including disability compensation, pensions, education, home loans, insurance, vocational rehabilitation, medical care at veterans' hospitals and outpatient facilities, and burial benefits.

Veterans Affairs Dept. (VA), *Office of Enterprise Integration (OEI), 810 Vermont Ave. N.W., #300, MS 008, 20420; (202) 461-5800. Fax, (202) 273-5993. Guy T. Kiyokawa, Assistant Secretary (Acting). General email, vacontactopp@va.gov*
Web, www.va.gov/oei

Serves as the single departmentwide repository, clearinghouse, and publication source for veterans' demographic and statistical information. Provides advice and support to the secretary in the areas of strategic planning, policy development, program analysis and management, and data governance.

►CONGRESS

For a listing of relevant congressional committees and subcommittees, please see page 600 or the Appendix.

►NONGOVERNMENTAL

American Legion, *Legislative Affairs, 1608 K St. N.W., 20006; (202) 263-5752. Fax, (202) 861-2786. (202) 861-2700. Lawrence Montreuil, Legislative Director, (202) 753-2207. Press, (202) 263-2991.*
Web, www.legion.org/legislative and Twitter, @AmericanLegion

Membership: honorably discharged veterans who served on active duty during periods of declared military conflict. Chartered by Congress to assist veterans with claims for benefits; offers a large array of programs and services for veterans and their families. (National headquarters in Indianapolis, Ind.)

AMVETS (American Veterans), *4647 Forbes Blvd., Lanham, MD 20706; (301) 459-9600. Fax, (301) 459-7924. Joseph R. Chenelly, Executive Director. Toll-free, (877) 726-8387. General email, amvets@amvets.org*
Web, www.amvets.org and Twitter, @AMVETSHQ

Membership: those who are serving or have served honorably in any branch of the military from WWII to the present. Helps members obtain benefits and services; participates in community programs; operates a volunteer service that donates time to hospitalized veterans and warrior transition programs. Monitors legislation and regulations.

Military Officers Assn. of America, *201 N. Washington St., Alexandria, VA 22314-2539; (703) 549-2311. Lt. Gen. Dana T. Atkins (USAF, Ret.), President. Toll-free, (800) 234-6622.*

General email, msc@moaa.org

Web, www.moaa.org, Twitter, @MilitaryOfficer and Facebook, www.facebook.com/moaa

Membership: officers, former officers, and surviving spouses of officers of the uniformed services. Assists members, their dependents, and survivors with military personnel matters, including service status and retirement problems; provides employment assistance. Monitors legislation affecting active duty officers, retirees, and veterans' affairs, health, and military compensation issues.

Military Order of the Purple Heart of the U.S.A., 5413 Backlick Rd., Suites B and C, Springfield, VA 22151-3960; (703) 642-5360. James McCormick, National Commander. Toll-free, (888) 668-1656.
General email, communications@purpleheart.org

Web, www.purpleheart.org, Twitter, @MOPHUSUA and Facebook, www.facebook.com/MOPHUSA

Membership: veterans awarded the Purple Heart for combat wounds. Chartered by Congress to assist veterans and their families. Conducts service and welfare work on behalf of disabled and needy veterans and their families, especially those requiring claims assistance, those who are homeless, and those requiring employment assistance. Organizes volunteers to provide assistance to hospitalized veterans at VA medical facilities and State Veterans Homes.

National Coalition for Homeless Veterans, 1001 Connecticut Ave. N.W., #840, 20036; (202) 546-1969. Fax, (202) 546-2063. Kathryn Monet, Chief Executive Officer. Toll-free Crisis Line, (877) 424-3838. Toll-free Referral, (800) 838-4357.
General email, info@nchv.org

Web, www.nchv.org, Twitter, @NCHVorg and Facebook, www.facebook.com/NCHV.org

Community-based organization providing resources and technical assistance to service providers and local, state and federal agencies that provide emergency and supportive housing, food, health services, job training and placement assistance, legal aid and case management support for homeless veterans. It is also the primary liaison between the nation's care providers, Congress and the Executive Branch agencies.

National Veterans Legal Services Program, 1600 K St. N.W., #500, 20006 (mailing address: P.O. Box 65762, Washington, DC 20035); (202) 265-8305. Paul Wright, Executive Director.
General email, info@nvlsp.org

Web, www.nvlsp.org, Twitter, @Lawyer4Warriors, Facebook, www.facebook.com/LawyersServingWarriors and YouTube, www.youtube.com/user/LawyersServing

Represents the interests of veterans and active-duty personnel through educational programs, advocacy, public policy programming, and litigation.

Vietnam Veterans of America, 8719 Colesville Rd., #100, Silver Spring, MD 20910-3710; (301) 585-4000. Fax, (301) 585-0519. Jack McCanus, President. Toll-free, (800) 882-1316.
General email, communications@vva.org

Web, www.vva.org, Twitter, @VVAmerica and Facebook, www.facebook.com/VietnamVeteransofAmerica

Congressionally chartered membership organization that provides information on legislation that affects Vietnam-era veterans and their families. Engages in legislative and judicial advocacy in areas relevant to Vietnam-era veterans. Provides information concerning benefits and initiates programs that ensure access to education and employment opportunities. Promotes full accounting of POWs and MIAs.

Appeals of VA Decisions

▶**AGENCIES**

Defense Dept. (DoD), *Legal Policy,* 4000 Defense Pentagon, #2C548A, 20301-4000; (703) 697-3387. Vacant, Director.
Web, www.defense.gov

Coordinates policy in a variety of personnel-related areas, including the Members Civil Relief Act, legal assistance, political activities, and corrections.

Navy Dept. *(Defense Dept.),* **Council of Review Boards,** Bldg. 36, 720 Kennon St. S.E., #309, 20374-5023; (202) 685-6408. Fax, (202) 685-6610. Jeffrey Riehl (USMC, Ret.), Director.
General email, crsc@navy.mil

Web, www.secnav.navy.mil/mra/CORB/Pages/default.aspx

Military office that administers boards that review appeal cases for the Navy and the Marine Corps. Composed of the Physical Evaluation Board, the Naval Discharge Review Board, the Naval Clemency and Parole Board, the Combat-Related Special Compensation (CRSC) Branch, and the Board for Decorations and Medals.

Veterans Affairs Dept. (VA), *Board of Veterans Appeals,* 810 Vermont Ave. N.W., 20420 (mailing address: P.O. Box 27063, Washington, DC 20038); (800) 923-8387. Fax, (844) 678-8979. Cheryl L. Mason, Chair. Claims status, (202) 565-5436.
Web, www.bva.va.gov

Final appellate body within the department; reviews claims for veterans benefits on appeal from agencies of original jurisdiction. Decisions of the board are subject to review by the U.S. Court of Appeals for Veterans Claims.

▶**JUDICIARY**

U.S. Court of Appeals for the Federal Circuit, 717 Madison Pl. N.W., 20439; (202) 275-8000. Kimberly A. Moore, Chief Circuit Judge; Peter R. Marksteiner, Clerk of the Court, (202) 272-8020. Mediation, (202) 275-8120.
Web, www.cafc.uscourts.gov

Reviews decisions concerning the Veterans' Judicial Review Provisions.

U.S. Court of Appeals for Veterans Claims, 625 Indiana Ave. N.W., #900, 20004-2950; (202) 501-5970.

Fax, (202) 501-5848. Margaret Bartley, Chief Judge; Gregory O. Block, Clerk of the Court.
General email, efiling@uscourts.cavc.gov
Web, www.uscourts.cavc.gov and Twitter, @UscavcL

Independent court that reviews decisions of the VA's Board of Veterans Appeals concerning benefits. Focuses primarily on disability benefits claims.

► **NONGOVERNMENTAL**

American Legion, *Discharge Review and Correction Boards Unit,* 1608 K St. N.W., 20006-2847; (202) 861-2700. Fax, (202) 833-4452. Ralph P. Bozella, Chair, Veterans Affairs and Rehabilitation.
Web, www.legion.org

Membership: honorably discharged veterans who served during declared military conflicts. Represents before the Defense Dept. former military personnel seeking to upgrade less-than-honorable discharges and to correct alleged errors in military records.

American Legion, *Legislative, Claims Services, Affairs, and Rehabilitation Division,* 1608 K St. N.W., 20006; (202) 861-2700. Fax, (202) 833-4452. Chanin Nuntavong, Executive Director.
Web, www.legion.org, Twitter, @AmericanLegion and Facebook, www.facebook.com/americanlegionhq

Membership: honorably discharged veterans who served during declared military conflicts. Provides advocates programs, services to help all veterans. Assists veterans with appeals before the Veterans Affairs Dept. for compensation and benefits claims. (National headquarters in Indianapolis IN.)

Disabled American Veterans (DAV), *National Service and Legislative Headquarters,* 807 Maine Ave. S.W., 20024-2410; (202) 554-3501. Edward (Randy) R. Reese, Executive Director.
Web, www.dav.org, Twitter, @davhq and Facebook, www.facebook.com/DAV

Membership: Oversees regional offices in assisting disabled veterans with claims, benefits, and appeals, including upgrading less-than-honorable discharges. Monitors legislation. (Headquarters in Cold Spring, KY.)

National Veterans Legal Services Program, 1600 K St. N.W., #500, 20006 (mailing address: P.O. Box 65762, Washington, DC 20035); (202) 265-8305. Paul Wright, Executive Director.
General email, info@nvlsp.org
Web, www.nvlsp.org, Twitter, @Lawyer4Warriors, Facebook, www.facebook.com/LawyersServingWarriors and YouTube, www.youtube.com/user/LawyersServing

Represents the interests of veterans and active-duty personnel through educational programs, advocacy, public policy programming, and litigation.

Veterans of Foreign Wars of the United States, 200 Maryland Ave. N.E., 20002-5724; (202) 543-2239. Fax, (202) 543-6719. Matthew (Fritz) M. Mihelcic, Commander-in-Chief; Robert (Bob) E. Wallace, Executive

Director. Helpline, (800) 839-1899. Member Service Center, (833) 839-8387.
General email, vfw@vfw.org
Web, www.vfw.org, Twitter, @VFWHQ and Facebook, www.facebook.com/VFWFans

Assists veterans and their dependents and survivors with appeals before the Veterans Affairs Dept. for benefits claims. Assists with cases in the U.S. Court of Appeals for Veterans Claims. (Headquarters in Kansas City, Mo.)

Benefits

► **AGENCIES**

Center for Women Veterans *(Veterans Affairs Dept.),* 810 Vermont Ave. N.W., #435, MC 00W, 20420; (202) 461-6193. Lourdes Tiglao, Director.
General email, 00w@va.gov
Web, www.va.gov/womenvet and Twitter, @VAWomenVets

Seeks to ensure that women veterans receive benefits and services on par with those of male veterans.

Veterans Affairs Dept. (VA), *Office of Public and Ingovernmental Affairs, Office of Intergovernmental Affairs (IGA),* 810 Vermont Ave. N.W., #915, 20420; (202) 461-7402. Fax, (202) 273-5716. Kayla M. Williams, Assistant Secretary.
Web, www.va.gov/iga

Acts as the conduit between the White House and the VA, federal, state, local, American Indian, and Native Alaskan Government officials on projects affecting VA initiatives. Responds to veterans' complaints concerning VA benefits and services.

Veterans Benefits Administration (VBA) *(Veterans Affairs Dept.),* 1800 G St. N.W., #520, 20223 (mailing address: 810 Vermont Ave. N.W., #520, Washington, DC 20420); (202) 461-9300. Fax, (202) 275-3591. Thomas J. Murphy, Under Secretary (Acting). Toll-free insurance hotline, (800) 669-8477. VBA Support, (800) 827-1000.
Web, www.vba.va.gov, Twitter, @VaVetBenefits, Facebook, www.facebook.com/VeteransBenefits and YouTube, www.youtube.com/user/vavetbenefits

Administers nonmedical benefits programs for veterans, their dependents and survivors. Benefits include veterans' compensation (including disability compensation) and pensions, survivors' benefits, education and rehabilitation assistance, home loan benefits, insurance coverage, and burials.

Veterans Benefits Administration (VBA) *(Veterans Affairs Dept.), Compensation Service,* 810 Vermont Ave. N.W., #645, MS 21, 20420; (202) 461-9700. Fax, (202) 530-9094. Beth Murphy, Executive Director. Toll-free, (800) 827-1000.
Web, www.benefits.va.gov/compensation

Administers disability payments; handles claims for burial and plot allowances by veterans' survivors. Provides information on and assistance with benefits legislated by Congress for veterans of active military, naval, or air service.

►**CONGRESS**

For a listing of relevant congressional committees and sub-committees, please see page 600 or the Appendix.

►**NONGOVERNMENTAL**

American Red Cross, *Service to the Armed Forces, Military Families,* 431 18th St. N.W., 20006; (202) 303-5000, ext. 2. Fax, (202) 303-0216. (202) 303-4498. *Koby L. Langley, Senior Vice President. Emergency communication services, (877) 272-7337. Web, www.redcross.org/about-us/our-work/military-families.html*

Assists veterans and their dependents with claims for benefits on a limited basis; supports medical care and rehabilitation services at military and veterans hospitals.

Blinded Veterans Assn., *1101 King St., #300, Alexandria, VA 22314 (mailing address: P.O. Box 90770, Washington, DC 20090); (202) 371-8880. Fax, (202) 371-8258. Donald D. Overton Jr., Executive Director, ext. 305. Toll-free, (800) 669-7079. General email, bva@bva.org*

Web, www.bva.org, Twitter, @BlindedVeterans, Facebook, www.facebook.com/blindedveteransassociation and YouTube, www.youtube.com/user/BlindedVeterans

Chartered by Congress to assist veterans with claims for benefits. Seeks out blinded veterans to make them aware of benefits and services available to them.

Fleet Reserve Assn. (FRA), *125 N. West St., Alexandria, VA 22314-2754; (703) 683-1400. Fax, (703) 549-6610. Christopher J. Slawinski, National Executive Director, ext. 101. Membership/Customer Service, (800) 372-1924. General email, fra@fra.org*

Web, www.fra.org, Twitter, @FRAHQ and Facebook, www.facebook.com/FRA.org

Recognized by the Veterans Affairs Dept. to assist veterans and widows and widowers of veterans with benefit claims. Monitors legislation and regulations.

Jewish War Veterans of the U.S.A., *1811 R St. N.W., 20009; (202) 265-6280. Fax, (202) 234-5662. Kenneth Greenberg, National Executive Director. General email, jwv@jwv.org*

Web, www.jwv.org, Twitter, @JewishWarVets and Facebook, www.facebook.com/JewishWarVeterans

Membership: recognized by the Veterans Affairs Dept. to assist veterans with claims for benefits. Offers programs in community relations and services, foreign affairs, national defense, and veterans affairs. Monitors legislation and regulations that affect veterans.

Paralyzed Veterans of America, *801 18th St. N.W., 20006-3517; (202) 872-1300. Heather Ansley, Associate Executive Director of Government Relations. Toll-free, (800) 424-8200. TTY, (800) 795-4327. General email, info@pva.org*

Web, www.pva.org, Twitter, @PVA1946 and Facebook, www.facebook.com/ParalyzedVeterans

Membership: Congressionally chartered veterans service organization that assists veterans with claims for benefits. Distributes information on special education for paralyzed veterans; acts as advocate for high-quality care, and supports and raises funds for medical research.

Veterans for Common Sense, *1140 3rd St. N.E., #2138, 20002; Anthony Hardie, Director. General email, info@veteransforcommonsense.org*

Web, www.veteransforcommonsense.org and Twitter, @Vets4CommonSens

Grassroots policy advocacy nonprofit that aims to protect veterans benefits and rights, including toxic exposure issues. Monitors legislation and regulations.

Veterans of Foreign Wars of the United States, *200 Maryland Ave. N.E., 20002-5724; (202) 543-2239. Fax, (202) 543-6719. Matthew (Fritz) M. Mihelcic, Commander-in-Chief; Robert (Bob) E. Wallace, Executive Director. Helpline, (800) 839-1899. Member Service Center, (833) 839-8387. General email, vfw@vfw.org*

Web, www.vfw.org, Twitter, @VFWHQ and Facebook, www.facebook.com/VFWFans

Chartered by Congress to assist veterans with claims for benefits, including disability compensation, education, and pensions. Inspects VA health care facilities and cemeteries. Monitors medical updates and employment practices regarding veterans. (Headquarters in Kansas City, Mo.)

Veterans of Modern Warfare, *P.O. Box 96503, 20090; Joseph F. Morgan, President. Suicide hotline, (800) 273-8255. General email, info@vmwusa.org and Twitter, @VMWUSA*

Chapter-based membership organization. Provides information and assistance in obtaining benefits to all veterans, including active duty and National Guard and Reserve components, as well as any veteran who has served in the U.S. Armed Forces since August 2, 1990. Acts as advocate for veterans.

Education, Economic Opportunity

►**AGENCIES**

Office of Personnel Management (OPM), *Policy, Data, Oversight, Veterans Services,* 1900 E St. N.W., #7439, 20415; (202) 606-3602. Fax, (202) 606-6017. *Hakeem A. Basheerud-Deen, Director. Web, www.opm.gov/policy-data-oversight/veterans-services*

Provides federal employees and transitioning military service members and their families, federal human resources professionals, and hiring managers with information on employment opportunities with the federal government. Administers the Disabled Veterans Affirmative Action Program.

Small Business Administration (SBA), *Veterans Business Development,* 409 3rd St. S.W., #5700, 20416; (202) 205-6773. Fax, (202) 205-7292. *Larry Stubblefield, Associate Administrator.*

Web, www.sba.gov/about-sba/sba-locations/headquarters-offices/office-veterans-business-development

Helps veterans use SBA loans through counseling, procurement, and training programs in entrepreneurship.

Veterans Benefits Administration (VBA) *(Veterans Affairs Dept.), Education Service, 1800 G St. N.W., #601, 20006 (mailing address: 810 Vermont Ave. N.W., #520, Washington, DC 20420); Charmain Bogue, Executive Director. Bill information, (888) 442-4551.*
Web, www.benefits.va.gov/gibill, Facebook, www.facebook .com/gibillEducation and YouTube, www.youtube.com/ channel/UCBvOzPLmbzjtpX-Htstp2vw

Administers VA's education program, including financial support for veterans' education and for spouses and dependent children of deceased and disabled veterans; provides eligible veterans and dependents with educational assistance under the G.I. Bill and Veterans Educational Assistance Program. Provides postsecondary institutions with funds, based on their enrollment of eligible veterans.

Veterans Benefits Administration (VBA) *(Veterans Affairs Dept.), Loan Guaranty Service, 1800 G St. N.W., #851, 20006 (mailing address: 810 Vermont Ave. N.W., Washington, DC 20420); (202) 632-8862. Fax, (202) 495-5798. Vacant, Director. Toll-free, (877) 827-3702.*
Web, www.benefits.va.gov/homeloans

Guarantees private institutional financing of home loans (including manufactured-home loans) for veterans; provides disabled veterans with direct loans and grants for specially adapted housing; administers a direct loan program for Native American veterans living on trust land.

Veterans Benefits Administration (VBA) *(Veterans Affairs Dept.), Veteran Readiness and Employment Service (VR&E), 1800 G St. N.W., 20006 (mailing address: 810 Vermont Ave. N.W., #520, Washington, DC 20420); (800) 698-2411. EsterJohnson-Ellis, Assistant Director. Main Phone, (800) 827-1000.*
Web, www.benefits.va.gov/vocrehab/index.asp

Administers VA's vocational rehabilitation and employment program, which provides service-disabled veterans with services and assistance; helps veterans to become employable and to obtain and maintain suitable employment. (Formerly known as Vocational Rehabilitation and Employment.)

Veterans' Employment and Training Service (VETS) *(Labor Dept.), 200 Constitution Ave. N.W., #S1325, 20210; (202) 693-4700. Fax, (202) 693-4755. James Rodriguez, Principal Deputy Assistant Secretary. Toll-free, (800) 487-2365.*
Web, www.dol.gov/agencies/vets and Twitter, @VETS_DOL

Works with and monitors state employment offices to see that preference is given to veterans seeking jobs; advises the secretary on veterans' issues.

► **CONGRESS**

For a listing of relevant congressional committees and subcommittees, please see page 600 or the Appendix.

► **NONGOVERNMENTAL**

Blinded Veterans Assn., *1101 King St., #300, Alexandria, VA 22314 (mailing address: P.O. Box 90770, Washington, DC 20090); (202) 371-8880. Fax, (202) 371-8258. Donald D. Overton Jr., Executive Director, ext. 305. Toll-free, (800) 669-7079.*
General email, bva@bva.org
Web, www.bva.org, Twitter, @BlindedVeterans, Facebook, www.facebook.com/blindedveteransassociation and YouTube, www.youtube.com/user/BlindedVeterans

Provides blind and disabled veterans with vocational rehabilitation.

Council for Opportunity in Education, *1025 Vermont Ave. N.W., #400, 20005-3516; (202) 347-7430. Fax, (202) 347-0786. Maureen Hoyler, President, ext. 321.*
Web, www.coenet.org, Twitter, @COETalk, Facebook, www.facebook.com/ councilforopportunityineducation and YouTube, www .youtube.com/channel/UCCVcLrUp-XPcyiR-FvHMq-Q

Membership: more than 1,000 colleges and agencies. Works in conjunction with colleges and agencies that host the federally funded TRIO programs, designed to help low-income first-generation immigrants, students with disabilities, and veterans enroll in and graduate from college.

National Assn. of State Workforce Agencies, *444 N. Capitol St. N.W., #300, 20001; (202) 434-8020. Scott Sanders, Executive Director, (202) 434-8022.*
General email, naswa@naswa.org
Web, www.naswa.org, Twitter, @naswaorg and Facebook, www.facebook.com/NASWAorg

Membership: state employment security administrators. Provides veterans employment and training professionals with opportunities for networking and information exchange. Monitors legislation and regulations that affect veterans employment and training programs involving state employment security agencies.

Paralyzed Veterans of America, *801 18th St. N.W., 20006-3517; (202) 872-1300. Heather Ansley, Associate Executive Director of Government Relations. Toll-free, (800) 424-8200. TTY, (800) 795-4327.*
General email, info@pva.org
Web, www.pva.org, Twitter, @PVA1946 and Facebook, www.facebook.com/ParalyzedVeterans

Membership: Congressionally chartered veterans service organization that assists veterans with claims for benefits. Promotes access to educational and public facilities and to public transportation for people with disabilities; seeks modification of workplaces.

Health Care, VA Hospitals

Veterans Health Administration (VHA) *(Veterans Affairs Dept.),* 810 Vermont Ave. N.W., #800, 20420 (mailing address: 810 Vermont Ave. N.W., #520, Washington, DC 20420); (202) 461-7000. Steven L. Lieberman, Under Secretary (Acting), (202) 461-7008. Toll-free, (877) 222-8387. Web, www.va.gov/health, Twitter, @VeteransHealth and Facebook, www.facebook.com/VeteransHealth

Oversees all health care policies for all eligible veterans. Recommends policy and administers medical and hospital services for eligible veterans. Publishes guidelines on treatment of veterans exposed to Agent Orange.

Veterans Health Administration (VHA) *(Veterans Affairs Dept.),* **Academic Affiliations,** 810 Vermont Ave. N.W., #4, 20420 (mailing address: 810 Vermont Ave. N.W., #520, Washington, DC 20420); (202) 461-9490. Fax, (202) 461-9855. Marjorie A. Bowman, Chief Academic Affiliations Officer.
Web, www.va.gov/oaa and Email, oaahelp@va.gov

Administers education and training programs for health professionals, students, and residents through partnerships with affiliated academic institutions. Offers training programs.

Veterans Health Administration (VHA) *(Veterans Affairs Dept.),* **Center for Development and Civic Engagement CDCE,** 810 Vermont Ave. N.W., 10B2A, 20420; (202) 461-7300. Fax, (202) 495-6208. Sabrina Clark, Director.
General email, VHA10BCOM1VAVSStaff@va.gov
Web, www.volunteer.va.gov and www.volunteer.va.gov/AboutVAVS.asp

Supervises volunteer programs in VA medical centers. (Previously volunteer Services.)

Veterans Health Administration (VHA) *(Veterans Affairs Dept.),* **Chief Strategy Office,** 810 Vermont Ave. N.W., 10P1, 20420; (202) 461-7100. Fax, (202) 273-9030. Valerie Mattison, Assistant Deputy Under Secretary.
General email, vha108csoactions@va.gov
Web, www.va.gov/healthpolicyplanning

Advises on the development, implementation, and impact of various aspects of VHA national policy development, analysis and planning initiatives. anddata management. Develops policy, programs, and funds initiatives within the Veterans Affairs Dept. that advance the health of veterans in rural America. (Formerly Health Policy and Planning.)

Veterans Health Administration (VHA) *(Veterans Affairs Dept.),* **Dentistry,** 810 Vermont Ave. N.W., 10NC7, 20420; Patricia E. Arola, Assistant Under Secretary f. Main PHone, (800) 698-2411.
Web, www.va.gov/dental and
Email, VHA10NC7Action@va.gov

Administers and coordinates VA oral health care programs; dental care delivered in a VA setting; administration of oral research, education, and training for VA oral health personnel; delivery of care to VA patients in private practice settings.

Veterans Health Administration (VHA) *(Veterans Affairs Dept.),* **Geriatrics and Extended Care,** 810 Vermont Ave. N.W., #10P4G, 20420; (202) 461-6750. Fax, (202) 495-5167. Catherine McVearry Kelso, Deputy Executive Director; Scotte R. Hartronft, Executive Director.
Web, www.va.gov/geriatrics

Administers research, educational, and clinical health care programs in geriatrics at VA and community nursing homes, in personal care homes, in VA domiciliaries, in state veterans' homes, and in home-based and other non-institutional care.

Veterans Health Administration (VHA) *(Veterans Affairs Dept.),* **Mental Health Services,** 810 Vermont Ave. N.W., MS 10P4M, 20420; (202) 461-4170. Fax, (202) 495-5933. Marsden McGuire, Deputy Chief Consultant. Crisis Hotline, (800) 273-8255, ext. 1. Homeless Veterans, hotline, 877424-3838. WomenVeterans Hotline, (855) 829-6636.
Web, www.mentalhealth.va.gov/index.asp and Coaching-into-Care Web, www.mirecc.va.gov/coaching

Develops ambulatory and inpatient psychiatry and psychology programs for the mentally ill and for drug and alcohol abusers; programs are offered in VA facilities and twenty-one Veterans Integrated Services Networks. Incorporates special programs for veterans suffering from posttraumatic stress disorders, serious mental illness, addictive disorders, and homelessness.

Veterans Health Administration (VHA) *(Veterans Affairs Dept.),* **Patient Care Services,** 810 Vermont Ave. N.W., 20420; (202) 461-7800. Fax, (202) 495-5243. Beth Taylor, Assitant Under Secretary, (202) 461-6988.
Web, www.patientcare.va.gov/index.asp

Provides a full continuum of health services: health promotion and disease prevention, screening and diagnosis, treatment of common medical and surgical conditions, management and occupational and deployment-related environmental exposures, rehabilitation, palliative care and continually monitoring the health of our patient and employee populations for opportunities to improve our services. Through policy and program development we aim to deliver those services with dignity and respect, utilizing innovative approaches and interdisciplinary collaboration among VHA and external partners.

Veterans Health Administration (VHA) *(Veterans Affairs Dept.),* **Readjustment Counseling Service,** 1717 H St. N.W., #444, 20006; (202) 461-6525. Fax, (202) 495-6206. Michael W. Fisher, Chief Officer. Toll-free, (877) 927-8387. Web, www.va.gov and VA Center, www.vetcenter.va.gov

Responsible for community-based centers for veterans, service members, and military families nationwide. Provides outreach and counseling services for readjustment counseling, military sexual trauma causes, and bereavement counseling services. Offers Mobile Vet Centers that focus on services that help veterans make the transition between military and civilian life.

Veterans Health Administration (VHA) *(Veterans Affairs Dept.), Research and Development, RAD,* 810 Vermont Ave. N.W., (10P9), MS 10P9, 20420; (202) 443-5600. Fax, (202) 495-6196. Rachel B. Ramoni, Chief Research and Development Officer, (202) 443-5707.
General email, vha10P9ordops@va.gov

Web, www.research.va.gov

Formulates and implements policy for the research and development program of the Veterans Health Administration; advises the under secretary for health on research-related matters and on management of the VA's health care system; represents the VA in interactions with external organizations in matters related to biomedical and health services research.

▶CONGRESS

For a listing of relevant congressional committees and sub-committees, please see page 600 or the Appendix.

▶NONGOVERNMENTAL

American Red Cross, *Service to the Armed Forces, Military Families,* 431 18th St. N.W., 20006; (202) 303-5000, ext. 2. Fax, (202) 303-0216. (202) 303-4498. Koby L. Langley, Senior Vice President. Emergency communication services, (877) 272-7337.
Web, www.redcross.org/about-us/our-work/military-families.html

Assists veterans and their dependents with claims for benefits on a limited basis; supports medical care and rehabilitation services at military and veterans hospitals.

Army Distaff Foundation (Knollwood), 6200 Oregon Ave. N.W., 20015-1543; (202) 541-0492. Fax, (202) 541-0129. Maj. Gen. Timothy P. McHale (USA, Ret.), Chief Executive Officer. Admission, (202) 541-0149.
General email, info@armydistaff.org

Web, www.armydistaff.org

Nonprofit continuing care retirement community for career military officers and their families. Provides retirement housing and health care services.

Disabled American Veterans (DAV), *National Service and Legislative Headquarters,* 807 Maine Ave. S.W., 20024-2410; (202) 554-3501. Edward (Randy) R. Reese, Executive Director.
Web, www.dav.org, Twitter, @davhq and Facebook, www.facebook.com/DAV

Membership: Chartered by Congress to assist veterans with claims for benefits; represents veterans seeking to correct alleged errors in military records. Assists families of veterans with disabilities. (Headquarters in Cold Spring, KY.)

Marine Corps League, 3619 Jefferson Davis Hwy., #115, Stafford, VA 22554 (mailing address: P.O. Box 1990, Stafford, VA 22555-1990); (703) 207-9588. Johnny Baker, Chief Operating Officer.
General email, info@mclnational.org

Web, www.mclnational.org, Twitter, @MCL_HQ and Facebook, www.facebook.com/mclnational

Membership: active duty, retired, and reserve Marine Corps groups. Chartered by Congress to assist veterans with claims for benefits. Operates a volunteer service program in VA hospitals. assists veterans and their survivors. Monitors legislation and regulations.

National Assn. of Veterans Affairs Physicians and Dentists, P.O. Box 15418, Arlington, VA 22215-0418; (866) 836-3520. Fax, (540) 972-1728. Joseph Abate, President.
General email, opscoord@navapd.org

Web, www.navapd.org

Seeks to improve the quality of care and conditions at VA hospitals. Monitors legislation and regulations on veterans' health care.

National Conference on Ministry to the Armed Forces, *Endorsers Conference for Veterans Affairs Chaplaincy,* P.O. Box 7572, Arlington, VA 22207-9998; (703) 608-2100. Jack Lea, Executive Director; Klon kitchen, Chair.
General email, info@ncmaf.com

Web, www.ncmaf.net, Twitter, @NCMAForg and Facebook, www.facebook.com/NCMAF

Endorses and connects clergypersons and faith based groups with militaty and VA chaplaincies, and celebrates religious diversity. they are the point of contact between the DOD and over 150 religions and faiths.

Paralyzed Veterans of America, 801 18th St. N.W., 20006-3517; (202) 872-1300. Heather Ansley, Associate Executive Director of Government Relations. Toll-free, (800) 424-8200. TTY, (800) 795-4327.
General email, info@pva.org

Web, www.pva.org, Twitter, @PVA1946 and Facebook, www.facebook.com/ParalyzedVeterans

Membership: Congressionally chartered veterans service organization. Consults with the Veterans Affairs Dept. on the establishment and operation of spinal cord injury treatment centers.

Veterans of Foreign Wars of the United States, 200 Maryland Ave. N.E., 20002-5724; (202) 543-2239. Fax, (202) 543-6719. Matthew (Fritz) M. Mihelcic, Commander-in-Chief; Robert (Bob) E. Wallace, Executive Director. Helpline, (800) 839-1899. Member Service Center, (833) 839-8387.
General email, vfw@vfw.org

Web, www.vfw.org, Twitter, @VFWHQ and Facebook, www.facebook.com/VFWFans

Chartered by Congress to assist veterans with claims for benefits, including disability compensation, education, and pensions. Inspects VA health care facilities and cemeteries. Monitors medical updates and employment practices regarding veterans. (Headquarters in Kansas City, Mo.)

Vietnam Veterans of America, *Veterans Health Council,* 8719 Colesville Rd., #100, Silver Spring, MD 20910-3710; (301) 585-4000. Fax, (301) 585-3180. Vacant, Deputy Director. Toll-free, (800) 882-1316.

General email, vhc@vva.org

Web, www.vva.org/?s=veterans+health+council

Health education and information network for veterans and their families.

Spouses, Dependents, Survivors

►**AGENCIES**

Air Force Dept. *(Defense Dept.), Manpower, Personnel, and Services,* 1040 Air Force Pentagon, #4E168, 20330-1040; (703) 697-6088. Lt. Gen. Brian T. Kelly, Deputy Chief of Staff.
Web, www.af.mil

Military office that responds to inquiries concerning deceased Air Force personnel and their beneficiaries; refers inquiries to the Military Personnel Center at Randolph Air Force Base in San Antonio, Tex.

Marine Corps *(Defense Dept.), Casualty Assistance Section,* 2008 Elliott Rd., Quantico, VA 22134-5102; (703) 784-9512. Fax, (703) 784-4134. Gerald Castle, Head. Toll-free, (800) 847-1597.
General email, casualty.section@usmc.mil

Web, http://usmc-mccs.org/services/benefits/casualty-assistance, www.manpower.usmc.mil/webcenter/portal/MF_MPS_CA/pages_casualtyassistancecommand representative, www.manpower.usmc.mil/webcenter/portal/MF_MPS_CA/pages_casualtyassistancecalls officercaco and Facebook, www.facebook.com/MCCSHQ

Confirms beneficiaries of deceased Marine Corps personnel for benefits distribution.

Veterans Health Administration (VHA) *(Veterans Affairs Dept.), Readjustment Counseling Service,* 1717 H St. N.W., #444, 20006; (202) 461-6525. Fax, (202) 495-6206. Michael W. Fisher, Chief Officer. Toll-free, (877) 927-8387.
Web, www.va.gov and VA Center, www.vetcenter.va.gov

Offers bereavement counseling to parents, spouses, siblings, and children of armed forces personnel who died in service to their country and to family members of reservists and those in the National Guard who died while federally activated. Services include outreach, counseling, and referrals. Counseling provided without cost at community-based Vet Centers. Offers Mobile Vet Centers that focus on services that help veterans make the transition between military and civilian life.

►**NONGOVERNMENTAL**

American Gold Star Mothers Inc., 2128 Leroy Pl. N.W., 20008-1893; (202) 265-0991. Jo Ann Maitland, President.
General email, nso@goldstarmoms.com

Web, http://goldstarmoms.com, Twitter, @AGSM_National and Facebook, www.facebook.com/American-Gold-Star-Mothers-National-Official-108308072594520

Membership: mothers who have lost sons or daughters in military service. Members serve as volunteers in VA hospitals and around the country.

Army and Air Force Mutual Aid Assn., 102 Sheridan Ave., Fort Myer, VA 22211-1110; (703) 707-4600. Fax, (888) 210-4882. Brig. Gen. Michael Meese (USA, Ret.), President. Toll-free, (888) 973-8490.
General email, info@aafmaa.com

Web, www.aafmaa.com

Private service organization that offers member and family insurance services to U.S. armed forces personnel. Recognized by the Veterans Affairs Dept. as assisting veterans and their survivors with claims for benefits.

EX-POSE: Ex-Partners of Servicemembers for Equality, P.O. Box 11191, Alexandria, VA 22312-0191; (703) 941-5844. Sue Arroyo, Office Staff; Janice Stucki, Office Staff.
General email, expose1980@gmail.com

Web, www.ex-pose.org

Membership: military members, retirees, current/former spouses and their children. Educates military couples going through divorce. Provides explanation of possible legal interests and legal entitlements depending on the length of marriage. Open Tuesday and Wednesday, 10:00 a.m.–3:00 p.m.

Marine Corps League, 3619 Jefferson Davis Hwy., #115, Stafford, VA 22554 (mailing address: P.O. Box 1990, Stafford, VA 22555-1990); (703) 207-9588. Johnny Baker, Chief Operating Officer.
General email, info@mclnational.org

Web, www.mclnational.org, Twitter, @MCL_HQ and Facebook, www.facebook.com/mclnational

Membership: active duty, retired, and reserve Marine Corps groups. Chartered by Congress to assist veterans with claims for benefits. Operates a volunteer service program in VA hospitals. assists veterans and their survivors. Monitors legislation and regulations.

Tragedy Assistance Program for Survivors, Inc. (TAPS), 3033 Wilson Blvd., 3rd Floor, Arlington, VA 22201; (202) 588-8277. Fax, (571) 385-2524. Bonnie Carroll, President. Toll-free 24-hour crisis intervention hotline, (800) 959-8277.
General email, info@taps.org

Web, www.taps.org, Twitter, @TAPSorg, Facebook, www.facebook.com/TAPSorg and YouTube, www.youtube.com/c/tapsorg

Offers emotional support to those who have lost a loved one in military service. Has caseworkers who act as liaisons to military and veterans agencies. Provides 24/7 resource and information help line. Hosts Good Grief camps for children, seminars for adults, and online and in-person support groups. Publishes a quarterly magazine on grief and loss.

15

National and Homeland Security

GENERAL POLICY AND ANALYSIS

Basic Resources

▶ **AGENCIES**

Air Force Dept. *(Defense Dept.),* *1670 Air Force Pentagon, #4E878, 20330-1670; (703) 697-7376. Fax, (703) 695-8809. Frank Kendall, Secretary. Press, (703) 695-0640. fax, (703) 695-8809. Public Inquiries, (703) 697-3039. Toll-free, (800) 423-8723.*
General email, saf_os.workflow@us.af.mil

Web, www.af.mil, Twitter, @usairforce and Facebook, www.facebook.com/USairforce

Civilian office that develops and reviews Air Force national security policies in conjunction with the chief of staff of the Air Force and the secretary of defense.

Air Force Dept. *(Defense Dept.),* **Chief of Staff (CSAF),** *1670 Air Force Pentagon, 20330-1670; (703) 697-9225. Fax, (703) 693-9297. Gen. Charles Q. Brown Jr., Chief of Staff. Public Affairs, (703) 695-0640.*
Web, www.af.mil/AboutUs/AirForceSeniorLeaders/CSAF, Twitter, @GenCQBrownJr and Facebook, www.facebook.com/CSAFOfficial

Military office that develops and directs Air Force national security policies in conjunction with the Secretary of the Air Force, Secretary of Defense, National Security Council, and the president.

Air Force Dept. *(Defense Dept.),* **Information Dominance and Chief Information Officer,** *1800 Air Force Pentagon, #4E226, 20330-1800; (703) 695-6829. Lauren Barrett Knausenberger, Chief Information Officer. Press, (703) 695-0640.*
General email, DAF.Cybersecurity.awareness@us.af.mil

Web, www.safcn.af.mil

Responsible for cyberspace policymaking, planning, programming, and evaluating performance of the Air Force's command, control, communications, and computer (C-4) system; advises on information technology, cyberspace, and national security systems.

Army Dept. *(Defense Dept.),* *101 Army Pentagon, #3E700, 20310-0101; (703) 695-1717. Fax, (703) 697-8036. Hon. Christine E. Wormuth, Secretary.*
General email, usarmy.pentagon.hqda_secarmy.mbx .secarmy@army.mil

Web, www.army.mil, Twitter, @USArmy, Facebook, www.facebook.com/USarmy and YouTube, www.youtube .com/USarmy

Civilian office that develops and reviews Army national security policies in conjunction with the chief of staff of the Army and the secretary of defense.

Army Dept. *(Defense Dept.),* **Chief of Staff,** *200 Army Pentagon, #3E672, 20310-0200; (703) 697-0900. Fax, (703) 614-5268. Gen. James C. McConville, Chief of Staff.*

Web, www.army.mil/leaders/csa, Twitter, @ArmyChiefStaff and Facebook, www.facebook.com/ USArmyChiefofStaff

Military office that develops and administers Army national security policies in conjunction with the secretary of the Army and the secretary of defense.

Defense Dept. (DoD), *1000 Defense Pentagon, 20301-1000; (703) 692-7100. Fax, (703) 571-8951. Lloyd J. Austin III, Secretary. Information, (703) 571-3343. Pentagon operator, (703) 545-6700. Press, (703) 697-5131. Tours, (703) 697-1776.*
Web, www.defense.gov, Twitter, @DeptofDefense and Facebook, www.facebook.com/DeptofDefense

Civilian office that develops national security policies and has overall responsibility for administering national defense; responds to public and congressional inquiries about national defense matters.

Defense Dept. (DoD), *Chief Information Officer,* *6000 Defense Pentagon, #3E1030, 20301-6000; (703) 695-0348. John Sherman, Chief Information Officer (Acting).*
Web, http://dodcio.defense.gov and Twitter, @DOD_cio

Civilian office with policy oversight for all command, control, and communications matters.

Defense Dept. (DoD), *Command, Control, Communications, and Computers/Cyber,* *9999 Joint Staff Pentagon, #2D932, 20318-9999; (703) 695-3562. Lt. Gen. Dennis A. Crall (USAF), Director.*
Web, www.jcs.mil/Directorates/J6-C4-Cyber

Advises the secretary of defense on policy for command, control, communications, and computer/cyber matters throughout the Defense Dept.

Defense Dept. (DoD), *Homeland Defense and Global Security,* *2600 Defense Pentagon, #3C852A, 20301-2600; (703) 697-7728. Jennifer Walsh, Assistant Secretary (Acting).*
Web, http://policy.defense.gov/OUSDP-Offices/ASD-for-Homeland-Defense-and-Global-Security

Develops and coordinates national security and defense strategies and advises on the resources, forces, and contingency plans necessary to implement those strategies. Ensures the integration of defense strategy into the department's resource allocation and force structure development. Evaluates the capability of forces to accomplish defense strategy. Also serves as primary liaison between the Defense Dept. and the Homeland Security Dept. Supervises all Defense Dept. homeland defense activities.

Defense Dept. (DoD), *Joint Chiefs of Staff,* *9999 Defense Pentagon, #2D932, 20318-9999; (703) 697-9121. Fax, (703) 697-6002. Gen. Mark Milley (USA), Chair. Press, (703) 697-4272.*
Web, www.jcs.mil, Twitter, @thejointstaff and Facebook, www.facebook.com/TheJointStaff

Joint military staff office that assists the president, the National Security Council, and the secretary of defense in developing national security policy and in coordinating operations of the individual armed services.

Defense Dept. (DoD), *Policy,* 2000 Defense Pentagon, #3E806, 20301; (703) 697-7200. Fax, (703) 697-6602. *Colin Kahl, Under Secretary.*
Web, http://policy.defense.gov

Civilian office responsible for policy matters relating to international security issues and political-military affairs. Oversees such areas as arms control, foreign military sales, intelligence collection and analysis, and NATO and regional security affairs.

Defense Dept. (DoD), *Special Operations and Low-Intensity Conflict,* 2500 Defense Pentagon, #3C852A, 20301-2500; (703) 695-9667. Fax, (703) 693-6335. *Christopher Maier, Assistant Secretary.*
General email, osd.pentagon.ousd-policy.list.solic-front-office@mail.mil

Web, https://policy.defense.gov/OUSDP-Offices/ASD-for-Special-Operations-Low-Intensity-Conflict/Stability-and-Humanitarian-Affairs/bcsi-ac-cde40c890bd19f3d

Serves as special staff assistant and civilian adviser to the secretary of defense on matters related to special operations and international terrorism. Oversees and serves as advocate for Special Operations and Irregular Warfare throughout the Defense Dept. to ensure these capabilities are resourced, ready, and properly employed in accordance with the National Defense Strategy.

Homeland Security Dept. (DHS), 3801 Nebraska Ave. N.W., 20528; 301 7th St. S.W., MS 0501, 20528; Fax, (202) 447-5437. *Alejandro Mayorkas, Secretary.*
Switchboard, (202) 282-8000. Comments, (202) 282-8495. Legislative Affairs, (202) 447-5890. Press, (202) 282-8010. *General email, DHSExecSec@hq.dhs.gov*

Web, www.dhs.gov, Twitter, @DHSgov and Facebook, www.facebook.com/homelandsecurity

Responsible for the development and coordination of a comprehensive national strategy to protect the United States against terrorist attacks and other threats and hazards.

Marine Corps *(Defense Dept.),* **Commandant, (CMC),** *Marine Corps Headquarters,* 3000 Marine Corps Pentagon, #2C253, 20350-3000; (703) 614-2500. Fax, (703) 697-7246. *Gen. David H. Berger (USMC), Commandant.*
Information, (703) 614-2500.
Web, www.hqmc.marines.mil/cmc, Twitter, @USMC and Facebook, www.facebook.com/marines

Member of the Joint Chief of Staff, military office that develops and directs Marine Corps national security policies, plans, and programs. Reports directly to the secretary of Navy. Advises the President, the secretary of defense, the national security council, the homeland security council, and the secretary of Navy on matters involving the Marine Corps.in conjunction with the secretary of defense and the secretary of the Navy.

National Institute of Standards and Technology (NIST) *(Commerce Dept.),* **Special Programs Office,** 100 Bureau Dr., Gaithersburg, MD 20899;
General email, spo_inquiries@nist.gov

Web, www.nist.gov/special-programs-office-spo

Fosters collaboration among government, military, academic, professional, and private organizations to respond to critical national needs through science-based standards and technology innovation, including areas of homeland security and cybersecurity.

National Security Council (NSC) *(Executive Office of the President),* The White House, 1650 Pennsylvania Ave. N.W., 20504; (202) 456-1414. *Jake Sullivan, National Security Advisor.*
Web, www.whitehouse.gov/nsc

Advises the president on domestic, foreign, and military policies relating to national security.

National Security Education Program (NSEP), 4800 Mark Center Dr., #08F09-02, Alexandria, VA 22350-7000 (mailing address: P.O. Box 20010, Arlington, VA 22209); (703) 409-8653. Fax, (703) 692-2615. *Michael A. Nugent, Director. Boren Awards information, (800) 618-6737.*
General email, nsep@nsep.gov
Web, https://nsep.gov

Administers Boren Awards and Language Flagship programs; provides scholarships, fellowships, and institutional grants to students and academics with an interest in foreign affairs and national security.

National Security Staff (NSS) *(Executive Office of the President),* **Defense Policy and Strategy,** The White House, 1600 Pennsylvania Ave. N.W., 20504; (202) 456-9191. (202) 456-1414. *Jonathan Finer, Deputy National Security Adviser.*
Web, www.whitehouse.gov

Advises the assistant to the president for national security affairs on matters concerning defense policy.

Navy Dept. *(Defense Dept.),* 1200 Navy Pentagon, #4D652, 20350-1200; (703) 697-7391. *Carlo Del Toro, Secretary.*
General email, secnavypa.fct@navy.mil

Web, www.navy.mil, Twitter, @USNavy and Facebook, www.facebook.com/USNavy

Civilian office that develops and reviews Navy and Marine Corps national security policies in conjunction with the chief of naval operations, the commandant of the Marine Corps, and the secretary of defense.

Navy Dept. *(Defense Dept.),* **Chief of Naval Operations,** 2000 Navy Pentagon, #4E658, 20350-2000; (703) 695-5664. *Adm. Michael M. Gilday (USN), Chief.*
Web, www.navy.mil/cno, Twitter, @USNavyCNO and Facebook, www.facebook.com/USNavyCNO

Military office that develops Navy national security policies in conjunction with the secretary of defense and the secretary of the Navy and in cooperation with the commandant of the Marine Corps.

State Dept., *Foreign Missions,* 2201 C St. N.W., #2236, 20520; (202) 647-3417. Fax, (202) 736-4145. *Cliff Seagroves, Director (Acting).*
General email, ofm-info@state.gov

Web, www.state.gov/ofm and Facebook, www.facebook.com/ofmdc/?notif_t=page_fan

NATIONAL AND HOMELAND SECURITY RESOURCES IN CONGRESS

For a complete listing of congressional committees, including their full contact information, leadership, membership, and jurisdictions, please refer to the Appendix on pages 840–963.

HOUSE:

House Appropriations Committee, (202) 225-2771.
Web, appropriations.house.gov
  Subcommittee on Defense, (202) 225-2847.
  Subcommittee on Energy and Water
    Development, and Related Agencies,
    (202) 225-3421.
  Subcommittee on Financial Services and General
    Government, (202) 225-7245.
  Subcommittee on Homeland Security,
    (202) 225-5834.
  Subcommittee on Interior, Environment, and
    Related Agencies, (202) 225-3081.
  Subcommittee on Military Construction,
    Veterans Affairs, and Related Agencies,
    (202) 225-3047.
  Subcommittee on State, Foreign Operations, and
    Related Programs, (202) 225-2041.
House Armed Services Committee, (202) 225-4151.
Web, armedservices.house.gov
  Subcommittee on Cyber, Innovative
    Technologies, and Information Systems,
    (202) 225-4151.
  Subcommittee on Intelligence and Special
    Operations, (202) 225-4151.
  Subcommittee on Military Personnel,
    (202) 225-4151.
  Subcommittee on Readiness, (202) 225-4151.
  Subcommittee on Seapower and Projection
    Forces, (202) 225-4151.
  Subcommittee on Strategic Forces,
    (202) 225-4151.
  Subcommittee on Tactical Air and Land Forces,
    (202) 225-4151.
House Energy and Commerce Committee,
  (202) 225-2927.
Web, energycommerce.house.gov
  Subcommittee on Health, (202) 225-2927.
House Financial Services Committee, (202) 225-4247.
Web, financialservices.house.gov
  Subcommittee on Housing, Community
    Development, and Insurance, (202) 225-4247.
  Subcommittee on National Security,
    International Development, and Monetary
    Policy, (202) 225-4247.

House Foreign Affairs Committee, (202) 225-5021.
Web, foreignaffairs.house.gov
  Subcommittee on Asia, the Pacific, Central Asia,
    and Nonproliferation, (202) 226-6434.
  Subcommittee on Middle East, North Africa,
    and Global Counterterrorism,
    (202) 226-7812.
  Subcommittee on Western Hemisphere, Civilian
    Security, Migration, and International
    Economic Policy, (202) 225-3345.
House Homeland Security Committee,
  (202) 226-2616.
Web, homeland.house.gov
  Subcommittee on Border Security, Facilitation,
    and Operations, (202) 226-2616.
  Subcommittee on Cybersecurity,
    Infrastructure Protection, and Innovation,
    (202) 226-2616.
  Subcommittee on Emergency Preparedness,
    Response, and Recovery, (202) 226-2616.
  Subcommittee on Intelligence and
    Counterterrorism, (202) 226-2616.
  Subcommittee on Oversight, Management, and
    Accountability, (202) 226-2616.
  Subcommittee on Transportation and Maritime
    Security, (202) 226-2616.
House Judiciary Committee, (202) 225-3951.
Web, judiciary.house.gov
  Subcommittee on the Constitution, Civil Rights,
    and Civil Liberties, (202) 225-3951.
  Subcommittee on Crime, Terrorism, and
    Homeland Security, (202) 225-5727.
  Subcommittee on Immigration and Citizenship,
    (202) 225-3926.
House Oversight and Reform Committee,
  (202) 225-5051.
Web, oversight.house.gov
  Subcommittee on National Security,
    (202) 225-5051.
House Permanent Select Committee on Intelligence,
  (202) 225-7690.
Web, intelligence.house.gov
  Subcommittee on Counterterrorism,
    Counterintelligence, and
    Counterproliferation, (202) 225-7690.

Authorized to control the numbers, locations, and travel privileges of foreign diplomats and diplomatic staff in the United States.

Transportation Security Administration (TSA) *(Homeland Security Dept.), Policy, Plans, and Engagement, TSA-28, 601 S. 12th St., Arlington, VA 20598-6028; (571) 227-1417.*

Eddie Mayenschein, Assistant Administrator; Wanda Shotner, Executive Assistant.
Web, www.tsa.gov and Twitter, @TSA

Formulates policy and shares information related to security in various segments of the transportation industry, including commercial airports, commercial airlines, general aviation, mass transit and passenger rail, freight

Subcommittee on Defense Intelligence and
Warfighter Support, (202) 225-7690.
Subcommittee on Intelligence Modernization
and Readiness, (202) 225-7690.
Subcommittee on Strategic Technologies and
Advanced Research, (202) 225-7690.
House Select Committee to Investigate the January
6th Attack on the U.S. Capitol, (202) 225-7800.
Web, january6th.house.gov
House Science, Space, and Technology Committee,
(202) 225-6375.
Web, science.house.gov
Subcommittee on Research and Technology,
(202) 225-6375.
House Transportation and Infrastructure
Committee, (202) 225-4472.
Web, transportation.house.gov
Subcommittee on Economic Development,
Public Buildings, and Emergency
Management, (202) 225-3014.

SENATE:

Senate Appropriations Committee,
(202) 224-7363.
Web, appropriations.senate.gov
Subcommittee on Defense, (202) 224-7363.
Subcommittee on Energy and Water
Development, (202) 224-7363.
Subcommittee on Financial Services and General
Government, (202) 224-7363.
Subcommittee on Homeland Security,
(202) 224-7363.
Subcommittee on Interior, Environment, and
Related Agencies, (202) 224-7363.
Subcommittee on Military Construction,
Veterans Affairs, and Related Agencies,
(202) 224-7363.
Subcommittee on State, Foreign Operations, and
Related Programs, (202) 224-7363.
Senate Armed Services Committee, (202) 224-3871.
Web, armed-services.senate.gov
Subcommittee on Airland, (202) 224-3871.
Subcommittee on Cybersecurity, (202) 224-3871.
Subcommittee on Emerging Threats and
Capabilities, (202) 224-3871.
Subcommittee on Personnel, (202) 224-3871.

Subcommittee on Readiness and Management
Support, (202) 224-3871.
Subcommittee on Seapower, (202) 224-3871.
Subcommittee on Strategic Forces,
(202) 224-3871.
Senate Banking, Housing, and Urban Affairs
Committee, (202) 224-7391.
Web, banking.senate.gov
Subcommittee on National Security and
International Trade and Finance,
(202) 224-7391.
Senate Environment and Public Works Committee,
(202) 224-8832.
Web, epw.senate.gov
Subcommittee on Clean Air, Climate, and
Nuclear Safety, (202) 224-8832.
Subcommittee on Transportation and
Infrastructure, (202) 224-8832.
Senate Foreign Relations Committee,
(202) 224-4651.
Web, foreign.senate.gov
Subcommittee on Western Hemisphere,
Transnational Crime, Civilian Security,
Democracy, Human Rights, and Global
Women's Issues, (202) 224-4651.
Senate Homeland Security and Governmental Affairs
Committee, (202) 224-2627.
Web, hsgac.senate.gov
Subcommittee on Emerging Threats and
Spending Oversight,
(202) 224-2254.
Permanent Subcommittee on Investigations,
(202) 224-3721.
Subcommittee on Government Operations and
Border Management, (202) 224-4551.
Senate Judiciary Committee, (202) 224-7703.
Web, judiciary.senate.gov
Subcommittee on Immigration, Citizenship, and
Border Safety, (202) 224-6991.
Subcommittee on Criminal Justice and
Counterterrorism, (202) 224-2921.
Subcommittee on the Constitution,
(202) 224-6361.
Senate Select Committee on Intelligence,
(202) 224-1700.
Web, intelligence.senate.gov

rail, maritime, highway and motor carrier, pipeline, and air cargo. Coordinates with the U.S. Coast Guard.

U.S. Coast Guard (USCG) *(Homeland Security Dept.), 2703 Martin Luther King Jr. Ave. S.E., MS 7000, 20593-7000; (202) 372-4000. Fax, (202) 372-8302. Adm. Karl L. Schultz, Commandant. Public Affairs, (202) 372-4600.*

Web, www.uscg.mil, Twitter, @USCG, Facebook, www.facebook.com/UScoastguard and YouTube, www.youtube.com/USCGImagery

Provides homeland security for U.S. harbors, ports, and coastlines. Implements heightened security measures for commercial, tanker, passenger, and merchant vessels. Enforces federal laws on the high seas and navigable waters of the United States and its possessions; maintains a state of military readiness to assist the Navy in time of war or when directed by the president.

U.S. Coast Guard (USCG) *(Homeland Security Dept.)*, *Response Policy (CG-5R)*, 2703 Martin Luther Jr. Ave. S.W., MS 7318, 20593-7318; (202) 372-2011. (202) 372-2014. Rear Adm. Douglas Fears, Assistant Commandant. Web, www.dco.uscg.mil/Our-Organization/Assistant-Commandant-for-Response-Policy-CG-5R

Operates the Coast Guard National Response Center; participates in defense operations and homeland security; assists with law enforcement/drug interdictions.

► CONGRESS

For a listing of relevant congressional committees and subcommittees, please see pages 634–635 or the Appendix.

Government Accountability Office (GAO), *Defense Capabilities and Management (DCM)*, 441 G St. N.W., 20548; (202) 512-2775. Elizabeth Field, Director. Web, www.gao.gov/about/careers/our-teams

Provides analyses, recommendations, and policy options to Congress in areas of defense, including planning and force structure, readiness and training, war-fighter support, emerging threats, irregular warfare, homeland defense, strategic human-capital management, logistics, infrastructure, business operations, and budgeting.

Government Accountability Office (GAO), *Homeland Security and Justice (HSJ)*, 441 G St. N.W., #6H19, 20548; (202) 512-8777. Gretta L. Goodwin, Director. Web, www.gao.gov/about/careers/our-teams

Audits, analyzes, and evaluates for Congress federal administration of homeland security and justice areas and national preparedness programs and activities.

► NONGOVERNMENTAL

Air Force Assn. (AFA), 1501 Lee Hwy., #400, Arlington, VA 22209-1198; (703) 247-5800. Fax, (703) 247-5853. Lt. Gen. Bruce (Orville) Wright (USAF, Ret.), President. Press, (703) 247-5818. Toll-free, (800) 727-3337. General email, membership@afa.org

Web, www.afa.org, Twitter, @AirForceAssoc and Facebook, www.facebook.com/AirForceAssociation

Membership: civilians and active duty, reserve, retired, and cadet personnel of the Air Force and Space Force. Informs members and the public of developments in the aerospace field. Monitors legislation and Defense Dept. policies. Library on aviation history open to the public by appointment.

American Conservative Union (ACU), 1199 N. Fairfax St., #500, Alexandria, VA 22314; (202) 347-9388. Fax, (202) 347-9389. Matt Schlapp, Chairman. General email, contact@conservative.org

Web, http://conservative.org, Twitter, @ACUConservative and Facebook, www.facebook.com/ACUConservative

Legislative interest organization concerned with national defense policy, legislation related to nuclear weapons, U.S. strategic position vis-à-vis the former Soviet Union, missile defense programs, U.S. troops under UN command, and U.S. strategic alliance commitments.

American Enterprise Institute (AEI), *Foreign and Defense Policy Studies*, 1789 Massachusetts Ave. N.W., 20036; (202) 862-5800. Fax, (202) 862-7177. Kori N. Schake, Director. Web, www.aei.org/category/foreign-and-defense-policy

Research and educational organization that conducts conferences, seminars, and debates and sponsors research on national security, defense policy, and arms control.

American Security Council Foundation, 1300 Pennsylvania Ave. N.W., #700, 20004; (772) 388-2490. Laurence Sanford, Director of Operations. General email, info@ascf.us

Web, https://ascf.us, Twitter, @ASCFUS, Facebook, www.facebook.com/ascfusa and Press, press@ascfusa.org

Nonpartisan organization that promotes developing and maintaining military, economic, and diplomatic strength to preserve national security. Monitors legislation and conducts educational activities.

American Security Project, 1201 Pennsylvania Ave. N.W., #520, 20004; Patrick Costello, Chief Executive Officer; Matthew Wallin, Chief Operations Officer. Phone, (202) 347-4267. General email, press@americansecurityproject.org

Web, www.americansecurityproject.org, Twitter, @AmSecProject and Facebook, www.facebook.com/AmSecProject

Nonprofit, nonpartisan organization that educates the public on the advancement of national security. Distributes analyses on security issues to the media, publications, and events. Promotes action and holds meetings to discuss new national security strategies.

ASIS International, 1625 Prince St., Alexandria, VA 22314-2882; (703) 519-6200. Fax, (703) 519-6299. Peter J. O'Neil, Chief Executive Officer. Information, (703) 518-1415. General email, community@asisonline.org

Web, www.asisonline.org and Twitter, @ASIS_Intl

Membership: security administrators who oversee physical and logistical security for private and public organizations, including law enforcement and the military. Develops security standards; offers educational programs and materials on general and industry-specific practices; and administers certification programs. Monitors legislation and regulations.

Aspen Institute, 2300 N St. N.W., #700, 20037; (202) 736-5800. Fax, (202) 467-0790. Daniel R. Porterfield, President. Press, (202) 736-3849. General email, info@aspeninstitute.org

Web, www.aspeninstitute.org and Twitter, @AspenInstitute

Educational and policy studies organization. Promotes consideration of the public good in a wide variety of policy

Defense Department

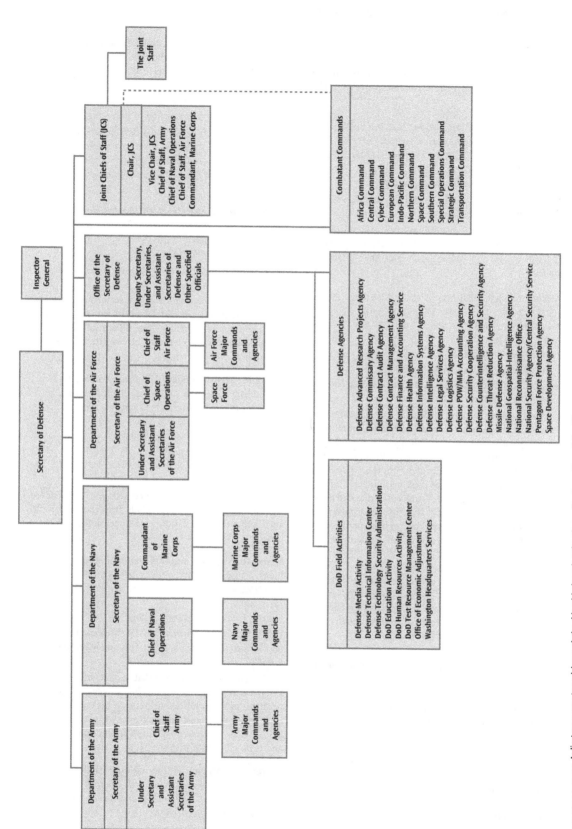

Secretary of Defense

Inspector General

Department of the Army
Secretary of the Army

Under Secretary and Assistant Secretaries of the Army

Chief of Staff Army

Army Major Commands and Agencies

Department of the Navy
Secretary of the Navy

Chief of Naval Operations

Commandant of Marine Corps

Navy Major Commands and Agencies

Marine Corps Major Commands and Agencies

Department of the Air Force
Secretary of the Air Force

Under Secretary and Assistant Secretaries of the Air Force

Chief of Space Operations

Chief of Staff Air Force

Space Force

Air Force Major Commands and Agencies

Office of the Secretary of Defense
Deputy Secretary, Under Secretaries, and Assistant Secretaries of Defense and Other Specified Officials

Joint Chiefs of Staff (JCS)
Chair, JCS

Vice Chair, JCS
Chief of Staff, Army
Chief of Naval Operations
Chief of Staff, Air Force
Commandant, Marine Corps

The Joint Staff

Combatant Commands
Africa Command
Central Command
Cyber Command
European Command
Indo-Pacific Command
Northern Command
Space Command
Southern Command
Special Operations Command
Strategic Command
Transportation Command

DoD Field Activities
Defense Media Activity
Defense Technical Information Center
Defense Technology Security Administration
DoD Education Activity
DoD Human Resources Activity
DoD Test Resource Management Center
Office of Economic Adjustment
Washington Headquarters Services

Defense Agencies
Defense Advanced Research Projects Agency
Defense Commissary Agency
Defense Contract Audit Agency
Defense Contract Management Agency
Defense Finance and Accounting Service
Defense Health Agency
Defense Information Systems Agency
Defense Intelligence Agency
Defense Legal Services Agency
Defense Logistics Agency
Defense POW/MIA Accounting Agency
Defense Security Cooperation Agency
Defense Counterintelligence and Security Agency
Defense Threat Reduction Agency
Missile Defense Agency
National Geospatial-Intelligence Agency
National Reconnaissance Office
National Security Agency/Central Security Service
Pentagon Force Protection Agency
Space Development Agency

- - - - - - - - -   Indicates a support or advisory relationship with the unit rather than a direct reporting relationship

areas, including international relations and homeland security. Working with international partners, offers educational seminars, nonpartisan policy forums, public conferences and events, and leadership development initiatives.

Assn. of the United States Army, *2425 Wilson Blvd., Arlington, VA 22201; (703) 841-4300. Fax, (703) 525-9039. Gen. Robert B. Brown (USA, Ret.), President, (703) 907-2664. Toll-free, (800) 336-4570.*
General email, membersupport@ausa.org
Web, www.ausa.org, Twitter, @AUSAorg and Facebook, www.facebook.com/AUSA.org

Membership: civilians and active duty and retired members of the armed forces. Conducts symposia on defense issues and researches topics that affect the military.

Atlantic Council, *1030 15th St. N.W., 12th Floor, 20005; (202) 778-4952. Fax, (202) 463-7241. Frederick Kempe, President, (202) 463-7226. Press, (202) 778-4967. Toll-free, (800) 380-6004.*
General email, info@atlanticcouncil.org
Web, www.atlanticcouncil.org, Twitter, @ATLANTICCOUNCIL and Facebook, www.facebook.com/AtlanticCouncil

Promotes constructive leadership and engagement in international affairs based on the Atlantic Community's central role in meeting global challenges. The Council provides an essential forum for navigating the dramatic economic and political changes defining the twenty-first century by informing and galvanizing its uniquely influential network of global leaders. Conducts studies and makes policy recommendations on U.S. foreign security and international economic and political policies in the Atlantic and Pacific communities; sponsors conferences and educational exchanges.

The Brookings Institution, *Center for Security, Strategy, and Technology (CSST), 1775 Massachusetts Ave. N.W., 20036; (202) 797-6103. Michael E. O'Hanlon, Co-Director.*
Web, www.brookings.edu/center/center-for-security-strategy-and-technology and Twitter, @MichaelEOHanlon

Research center with focus on American leadership: U.S. grand strategy, US military affairs, American alliances, and the multilateral order; national security: U.S. defense policy, strategic weapons and technology; and transnational threats: non-state actors and sub-state challenges.

The Brookings Institution, *Foreign Policy Studies, 1775 Massachusetts Ave. N.W., 20036; (202) 797-6103. Suzanne Maloney, Director.*
Web, www.brookings.edu/foreign-policy, Twitter, @BrookingsFP and Twitter, @MaloneySuzanne

Research and educational organization that focuses on major national security topics, including U.S. armed forces, weapons decisions, terrorism threats, employment policies, and the security aspects of U.S. foreign relations.

Business Executives for National Security (BENS), *1030 15th St. N.W., #200 East, 20005; (202) 296-2125. Fax, (202) 296-2490. Gen. Joseph L. Votel (USA, Ret.), Chief Executive Officer.*
General email, bens@bens.org
Web, www.bens.org and Twitter, @BENS_org

Membership; monitors legislation on national security issues from a business perspective; holds conferences, congressional forums, and other meetings on national security issues; works with other organizations on defense policy issues.

Center for Naval Analyses (CNA), *3003 Washington Blvd., Arlington, VA 22201-2117; (703) 824-2000. Katherine A. W. McGrady, President.*
General email, inquiries@cna.org
Web, www.cna.org, Twitter, @CNA_org and Facebook, www.facebook.com/CNA.org

Conducts research on homeland security and defense, weapons acquisitions, tactical problems, naval operations, and air traffic management. Parent organization is CNA, which also operates CNA Institute for Public Research.

Center for Security Policy, *2020 Pennsylvania Ave. N.W., #189, 20006; (202) 835-9077. Fax, (202) 835-9066. Frank J. Gaffney Jr., Executive Chair, ext. 1006; Don Woodsmall, President (Acting).*
General email, info@securefreedom.org
Web, www.centerforsecuritypolicy.org, Twitter, @securefreedom and Facebook, www.facebook.com/SecureFreedom

Educational institution concerned with U.S. defense and foreign policy. Interests include arms control compliance and verification policy and technology transfer policy.

Center for Strategic and International Studies, *1616 Rhode Island Ave. N.W., 20036; (202) 887-0200. Fax, (202) 775-3199. John J. Hamre, Chief Executive Officer. Press, (202) 775-3242.*
General email, webmaster@csis.org
Web, www.csis.org, Twitter, @CSIS, Facebook, www.facebook.com/CSIS.org and YouTube, www.youtube.com/CSISDC

A bipartisan organization that seeks to advance global security and prosperity by providing strategic insights and practical policy solutions to decision makers. Expertise includes defense and international security, emerging global issues, cybersecurity, global health, human rights, and regional transformation.

Center for Strategic and International Studies, *Strategic Technologies Program, 1616 Rhode Island Ave. N.W., 20036; (202) 887-0200. James Andrew Lewis, Director.*
General email, techpolicy@csis.org
Web, www.csis.org/programs/strategic-technologies-program and Twitter, @CyberCSIS

Conducts and publishes research on emerging technologies, intelligence reform, and space and globalization

Homeland Security Department

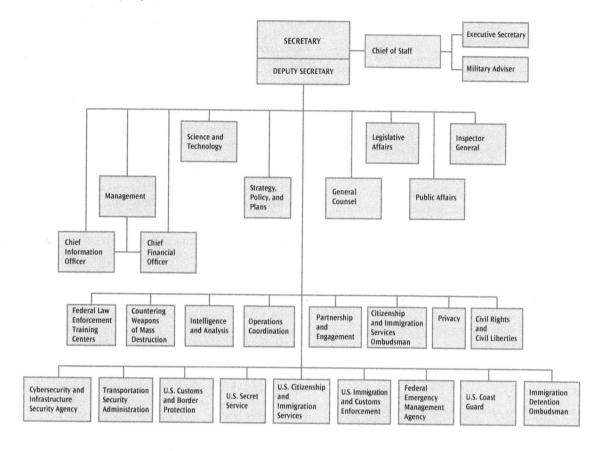

programs. Interests include cybersecurity, intelligence, privacy and surveillance, technology and innovation, Internet governance, and 5G networks.

The Conservative Caucus (TCC), *332 W. Lee Hwy., #221, Warrenton, VA 20816 (mailing address: P.O. Box 1890, Merrifield, VA 22116); (540) 219-4536. Peter J. Thomas, Chair.*
General email, info@conservativeusa.org
Web, www.conservativeusa.org, Twitter, @Conserv.Caucus and Facebook, www.facebook.com/ConservativeCaucus

Legislative interest organization that promotes grassroots activity on national defense and foreign policy.

Defense Orientation Conference Assn. (DOCA), *9245 Old Keene Mill Rd., #100, Burke, VA 22015-4202 (mailing address: P.O. Box 1294, Centreville, VA 20122); (703) 451-1200. Gary J.D. Hubert, President.*
General email, doca@doca.org
Web, https://doca.org

Membership: citizens interested in national defense. Under the auspices of the Defense Dept., promotes continuing education of members on national security issues through visits to embassies and tours of defense installations in the United States and abroad.

Henry L. Stimson Center, *1211 Connecticut Ave. N.W., 8th Floor, 20036; (202) 223-5956. Fax, (202) 238-9604. Brian Finlay, President.*
General email, communications@stimson.org
Web, www.stimson.org, Twitter, @StimsonCenter and Facebook, www.facebook.com/StimsonCenter

Research organization that studies arms control and international security, focusing on policy, technology, and politics.

Hudson Institute, *National Security Studies, 1201 Pennsylvania Ave. N.W., 4th Floor, 20004; (202) 974-2400. Fax, (202) 974-2410. John P. Walters, Chief Executive Officer. Press, (202) 974-2417.*
General email, info@hudson.org
Web, www.hudson.org, Twitter, @HudsonInstitute and Facebook, www.facebook.com/HudsonInstitute

Public policy research organization that conducts studies on U.S. overseas bases, U.S.–NATO relations, and missile defense programs. Focuses on long-range implications for U.S. national security.

Institute for Science and International Security, *440 1st St. N.W., #800, 20001; (202) 547-3633. David Albright, President.*

General email, isis@isis-online.org

Web, https://isis-online.org and Facebook, www.facebook
.com/Institute-for-Science-and-International-Security-
351457957011

Analyzes scientific and policy issues affecting national
and international security, including the spread of nuclear
weapons, the problems of war, regional and global arms
races, and the environmental, health, and safety hazards
of nuclear weapons production.

**Jewish Institute for National Security of America
(JINSA)**, 1101 14th St. N.W., #1030, 20005; (202) 667-3900.
Michael Makovsky, Chief Executive Officer.

General email, info@jinsa.org

Web, www.jinsa.org and Twitter, @jinsadc

Seeks to educate the public about the importance of
effective U.S. defense capability and inform the U.S. defense
and foreign affairs community about Israel's role in Mediterranean and Middle Eastern affairs. Sponsors lectures and
conferences; facilitates dialogue between security policymakers, military officials, diplomats, and the general public.

National Institute for Public Policy, 9302 Lee Hwy.,
#750, Fairfax, VA 22031-1214; (703) 293-9181. Fax, (703)
293-9198. Keith B. Payne, President.

Web, www.nipp.org

Studies public policy and its relation to national security. Interests include arms control, strategic weapons systems and planning, and foreign policy.

**National Security Archive (George Washington
University),** Gelman Library, 2130 H St. N.W., #701,
20037; (202) 994-7000. Fax, (202) 994-7005.
Thomas S. Blanton, Director.

General email, nsarchiv@gwu.edu

Web, www.nsarchive.gwu.edu, Twitter, @NSArchive and
Facebook, www.facebook.com/NSArchive

Research institute and library that provides information on U.S. foreign and economic policy and national
security affairs. Maintains and publishes collection of
declassified and unclassified documents obtained through
the Freedom of Information Act. Archive open to the public by appointment. Website has a Russian-language link.

Partnership for a Secure America (PSA), 1990 M St.
N.W., #250, 20036; (202) 293-8580. Curtis M. Silvers,
Executive Director.

General email, psa@psaonline.org

Web, www.psaonline.org, Twitter, @PSAonline and
Facebook, www.facebook.com/psaonline

Supports a bipartisan approach to national security
policies and issues. Researches and publishes reports on
national security threats such as terrorism. Organizes conferences for political parties to debate and develop consensus on issues.

**RAND Corp., Homeland Security Operational Analysis
Center (HSOAC),** 1200 S. Hayes St., Arlington, VA 22202;
(703) 413-1100. Fax, (703) 413-8111. K. Jack Riley,
Director. Press, (703) 414-4795.
Web, www.rand.org/hsrd/hsoac.html

Federally funded research development center (FFRDC)
chartered to provide independent analysis of homeland
security issues. Conducts research, works to promote
dialogue, and provides executive education through workshops, conferences, publications and reports, and outreach
programs.

RAND Corp., Washington Office, 1200 S. Hayes St.,
Arlington, VA 22202-5050; (703) 413-1100. Fax, (703) 413-
8111. Nicholas Burger, Director; Anita Chandra, Director
for Social and Economic Well-Being, ext. 5323.
Web, www.rand.org

Conducts research on national security issues, including political/military affairs of the former Soviet Union
and U.S. strategic policy. Research focuses on citizen preparedness, defense strategy, and military force planning.
(Headquarters in Santa Monica, Calif.)

The Truman Center for National Policy, 1250 Eye St.
N.W., #500, 20005; (202) 216-9723. Fax, (202) 682-1818.
Jenna Ben-Yehuda, President.

General email, info@Trumancnp.org

Web, http://trumancenter.org, Twitter, @TrumanCenter,
Facebook, www.facebook.com/trumancenter and YouTube,
www.youtube.com/TrumanProjectTrumanCenter

Public policy research and educational organization
that serves as a forum for development of national policy
alternatives. Leads discussion and advances policies aimed
at promoting U.S. global engagement and leadership in
the 21st century. Focus on issues such as cybersecurity and
defense energy. (Partner of the Truman National Security
Project.)

Truman National Security Project, 1250 Eye St. N.W.,
#500, 20005; (202) 216-9723. Fax, (202) 682-1818.
Jenna Ben-Yehuda, President.

General email, info@trumanproject.org

Web, http://trumanproject.org and Twitter,
@TrumanProject

Membership: veterans and policy and political leaders.
Forum for development of national policy alternatives.
Promotes national security policy coordination, strength-
ening the U.S. military and intelligence, foreign affairs and
diplomacy, democracy, and open trade. (Partner of the
Truman Center for National Policy.)

Women in International Security (WIIS), 1250
Connecticut Ave. N.W., #700, 20036; (202) 684-6010.
Ann Blatter, President.

General email, info@wiisglobal.org

Web, http://wiisglobal.org, Twitter, @WIIS_Global and
Facebook, www.facebook.com/wiisnetwork

Seeks to advance the leadership and professional
development of women in the field of international peace
and security decision and policymaking. Maintains a database of women foreign and defense policy specialists
worldwide; organizes conferences in the United States and
elsewhere; disseminates information on jobs, internships,
and fellowships. Has chapters in the United States and international affiliates. (Affiliated with SIPRI North America.)

Civil Rights and Liberties

Homeland Security Dept. (DHS), *Civil Rights and Civil Liberties (CRCL),* 2702 MLK Jr. Ave. S.E., 20528-0190; (202) 401-1474. Fax, (202) 401-4708. Katherine Culliton-Gonzales, Officer. Toll-free, (866) 644-8360. Toll-free TTY, (866) 644-8361. TTY, (202) 401-0470.
General email, crcl@dhs.gov
Web, www.dhs.gov/office-civil-rights-and-civil-liberties and Facebook, CivilRightsAndCivilLiberties

Provides legal and policy advice to the secretary and senior officers of the department on civil rights and civil liberties issues; maintains dialogue with minority communities; investigates and resolves complaints filed by members of the public.

Homeland Security Dept. (DHS), *Privacy Office,* Bldg. 110, 245 Murray Lane, 20528-0655; (202) 343-1717. Sarah Knight, Chief Privacy Officer.
General email, privacy@dhs.gov
Web, www.dhs.gov/privacy-office

Responsible for ensuring that department policies and use of technology sustain individual privacy. Makes annual report to Congress and enforces the provisions of the 1974 Privacy Act and evaluates legislative and regulatory proposals involving collection, use, and disclosure of personal information by the federal government.

National Security Agency (NSA) *(Defense Dept.),* *Civil Liberties and Privacy,* 9800 Savage Rd., #6272, Fort Meade, MD 20755-6000; (301) 688-6311. Rebecca (Becky) Richards, Civil Liberties and Privacy Director.
Web, www.nsa.gov/culture/Civil-Liberties-and-Privacy

Advises the director of the NSA to ensure that privacy and civil liberties protections are inherent in strategic decisions, particularly in the areas of technology and processes. Seeks to increase transparency.

Office of Management and Budget (OMB) *(Executive Office of the President), Information and Regulatory Affairs,* 725 17th St. N.W., #10236, 20503; (202) 395-5897. Fax, (202) 395-6102. Dominic J. Mancini, Deputy Administrator; Sharon Block, Associate Administrator.
Web, www.whitehouse.gov/omb/information-regulatory-affairs

Oversees implementation of the Privacy Act of 1974 and other privacy-related and security-related statutes. Issues guidelines and regulations.

For a listing of relevant congressional committees and subcommittees, please see pages 634–635 or the Appendix.

American Civil Liberties Union (ACLU), *Washington Legislative Office,* 915 15th St. N.W., 2nd Floor, 20005; (202) 457-0800. Caroline Fredrickson, Executive Director; David Cole, National Legal Director; Ronald Newman, National Political Director.
General email, info@acludc.org
Web, www.aclu.org/legiupdate, Twitter, @ACLU_DC and Facebook, www.facebook.com/aclu.dc

Advocates legislation to guarantee constitutional rights and civil liberties. Monitors agency compliance with the Privacy Act and other access statutes. Produces publications. (Headquarters in New York maintains docket of cases.)

Foundation for Defense of Democracies (FDD), P.O. Box 33249, 20033-0249; (202) 207-0190. Fax, (202) 207-0191. Clifford D. May, President; Mark Dubowitz, Chief Executive Officer.
General email, info@fdd.org
Web, www.fdd.org, Twitter, @FDD and Facebook, www.facebook.com/followFDD

Research institute focusing on national security and foreign policy. Conducts actionable research, prepared by experts and scholars from a variety of backgrounds – including government, intelligence, military, private sector, academia, and journalism. It brings proficiency in foreign languages, law, finance, technology, and other skills to its work.

Reporters Committee for Freedom of the Press, 1156 15th St. N.W., #1020, 20005; (202) 795-9300. Fax, (202) 795-9310. Bruce D. Brown, Executive Director, (202) 795-9301. Legal defense hotline, (800) 336-4243.
General email, info@rcfp.org
Web, www.rcfp.org, Twitter, @rcfp, Facebook, www.facebook.com/ReportersCommittee and Legal defense hotline email, hotline@rcpf.org

Committee of reporters, news editors, publishers, and lawyers from the print and broadcast media. Maintains a legal defense and research fund for members of the news media involved in freedom of the press court cases; interests include access to information and privacy issues faced by journalists covering antiterrorism initiatives and military actions abroad.

Defense and Homeland Security Budgets

Army Dept. *(Defense Dept.), Chief Information Officer / G-6,* 107 Army Pentagon, #3E608, 20310-0107; (210) 466-0166. Fax, (703) 695-3091. Raj Iyer, Chief Information Officer.
Web, www.army.mil/ciog6, Twitter, @ArmyCIOG6 and Facebook, www.facebook.com/ArmyCIO

Oversees policy and budget for the Army's information systems and programs.

Defense Contract Audit Agency *(Defense Dept.),* 8725 John J. Kingman Rd., #2135, Fort Belvoir, VA 22060-6219;

(703) 767-3200. Fax, (703) 767-3267. Anita Bales, Director. Inspector General hotline, (571) 448-3135. Press, (703) 697-5131.
General email, dcaaweb@dcaa.mil
Web, www.dcaa.mil

Performs all contract audits for the Defense Dept. Provides Defense Dept. personnel responsible for procurement and contract administration with accounting and financial advisory services regarding the negotiation, administration, and settlement of contracts and subcontracts.

Defense Contract Management Agency *(Defense Dept.), 18th St. South, 100A, Arlington, VA 22202; (804) 734-1488. Fax, (703) 699-2180. Lt. Gen. David G. Bassett (USA), Director. FOIA, (804) 609-4533. Press, (804) 734-1492.*
Web, www.dcma.mil and Twitter, @DCMAnews

Ensures the integrity of the contracting process, and provides a broad range of contract-procurement management services, including cost and pricing, quality assurance, contract administration and termination, and small business support.

Defense Dept. (DoD), *Comptroller, 1100 Defense Pentagon, #3E770, 20301-1100; (703) 695-3237. Michael J. McCord, Comptroller (Acting).*
Web, http://comptroller.defense.gov

Supervises and reviews the preparation and implementation of the defense budget. Advises the secretary of defense on fiscal matters. Collects and distributes information on the department's management of resources.

Homeland Security Dept. (DHS), *Management Directorate, 3801 Nebraska Ave. N.W., 20528 (mailing address: 245 Murray Lane, MS 04401, Washington, DC 20528); (202) 447-3400. (202) 447-3106. Randolph (Tex) D. Alles, Under Secretary (Acting); Miranda Morton, Administrative Assistant, (202) 447-3106.*
Web, www.dhs.gov/directorate-management

Responsible for department budget, appropriations, expenditure of funds, accounting and finance, procurement, human resources and personnel, information technology systems, facilities, property, equipment and other material resources, and performance measurement.

Office of Management and Budget (OMB) *(Executive Office of the President), Homeland Security, 725 17th St. N.W., #9208, 20503; (202) 395-3080. Fax, (202) 395-3888. Kimberly Newman, Chief.*
Web, www.whitehouse.gov/omb

Assists and advises the OMB director on budget preparation, proposed legislation, and evaluations of Homeland Security Dept. programs, policies, and activities.

Office of Management and Budget (OMB) *(Executive Office of the President), National Security, 725 17th St. N.W., #10001, 20503; (202) 395-3884. Fax, (202) 395-3307. Ed Meier, Associate Director.*
Web, www.whitehouse.gov/omb

Supervises preparation of the Defense Dept., intelligence community, and veterans affairs portions of the federal budget.

▶**CONGRESS**

For a listing of relevant congressional committees and subcommittees, please see pages 634–635 or the Appendix.

Government Accountability Office (GAO), *Defense Capabilities and Management (DCM), 441 G St. N.W., 20548; (202) 512-2775. Elizabeth Field, Director.*
Web, www.gao.gov/about/careers/our-teams

Audits, analyzes, and evaluates Defense Dept. acquisition, spending, and international programs.

▶**NONGOVERNMENTAL**

Center for Strategic and Budgetary Assessments (CSBA), *1667 K St. N.W., #900, 20006-1659; (202) 331-7990. Fax, (202) 331-8019. Thomas G. Mahnken, President. Press, (202) 719-1358.*
General email, info@csbaonline.org
Web, https://csbaonline.org, Twitter, @CSBA_ and Facebook, www.facebook.com/CSBAonline

Think tank that promotes deliberation of national security strategy, the future of the U.S. military, and defense investment options. Conducts analyses of defense budget and programmatic analysis. Compares the relative strengths and weaknesses of the United States and potential military competitors. Conducts seminar-style wargames to analyze the operational and strategic levels of conflict, as well as strategy and investment alternatives. Anticipates future military trends, based on analysis of historical trends.

National Campaign for a Peace Tax Fund, *2121 Decatur Pl. N.W., 20008-1923; (202) 483-3751. Malachy Killbride, Executive Director. Toll-free, (888) 732-2382.*
General email, info@peacetaxfund.org
Web, www.peacetaxfund.org

Supports legislation permitting taxpayers who are conscientiously opposed to military expenditures to have the military portion of their income tax money placed in a separate, nonmilitary fund.

Women's Action for New Directions (WAND), *Washington Office, 810 7th St. N.E., 20002; (202) 459-4769. Fax, (202) 544-7612. Nancy Parrish, Executive Director.*
General email, peace@wand.org
Web, www.wand.org and Twitter, @WomensAction

Seeks to redirect federal spending priorities from military spending toward domestic needs; works to develop citizen expertise through education and political involvement; provides educational programs and material about nuclear and conventional weapons; monitors defense legislation, budget policy legislation, and legislation affecting women. (Headquarters in Arlington, Mass.)

Military Aid and Peacekeeping

▶AGENCIES

Bureau of European and Eurasian Affairs *(State Dept.),* **European Security and Political Affairs,** *2201 C St. N.W., #6511, 20520; (202) 647-1626. Kami Witmer, Director, (202) 647-2188.*
Web, www.state.gov/p/eur

Coordinates and advises, with the Defense Dept. and other agencies, the U.S. mission to NATO and the U.S. delegation to the Organization for Security and Cooperation in Europe regarding political, military, and arms control matters.

Bureau of Political-Military Affairs (PM) *(State Dept.),* **Security Assistance,** *2401 E St. N.W., SA-1, 20037; (202) 663-3040. Kevin O'Keefe, Director, (202) 663-3450.*
Web, www.state.gov/t/pm

Administers funding for security assistance and capacity-building programs in foreign countries.

Defense Dept. (DoD), *International Security Affairs,* **European and NATO Policy,** *2000 Defense Pentagon, #5B652, 20301-2000; (703) 695-5553. Spencer P. Boyer, Deputy Assistant Secretary.*
Web, https://policy.defense.gov/OUSDP-Offices/ASD-for-International-Security-Affairs/Europe-and-NATO

Advises the assistant secretary for international security affairs on matters dealing with Europe and NATO.

Defense Security Cooperation Agency *(Defense Dept.),* *2800 Defense Pentagon, 20301-2800; (703) 697-9709. Jed Royal, Director (Acting). Public Affairs, (703) 604-6617. General email, dsca.ncr.lmo.mbx.info@mail.mil*
Web, www.dsca.mil

Administers programs providing defense articles and services, military training and education, humanitarian assistance, and landmine removal to international partners in furtherance of U.S. policies and strategic objectives.

▶CONGRESS

For a listing of relevant congressional committees and subcommittees, please see pages 634–635 or the Appendix.

▶INTERNATIONAL ORGANIZATIONS

Inter-American Defense Board, *2600 16th St. N.W., 20441-0002; (202) 939-6041. Fax, (202) 319-2847. Vice Adm. Alexandre Rabello de Faria, Chair (in Brazil); Brig. Gen. Porfirio Fuentes Vélez, Director General (in Mexico); Maj. Gen. James E. Taylor, Inter-American Defense College Director. Inter-American Defense College, (202) 646-1337. General email, jid@jid.org*
Web, www.jid.org/en

Membership: military officers from 28 countries of the Western Hemisphere. Plans for the collective self-defense of the American continents. Develops procedures for standardizing military organization and operations; operates the Inter-American Defense Board and Inter-American Defense College. Advises the Organization of American States on military and defense matters.

▶NONGOVERNMENTAL

International Stability Operations Assn. (ISOA), *1725 Eye St. N.W., #300, 20006; (703) 336-3940. Howard (Howie) R. Lind, President. General email, isoa@stability-operations.org*
Web, www.stability-operations.org and Twitter, @StabilityOps

Membership: private-sector service companies involved in all sectors of peace and stability operations around the world, including mine clearance, logistics, security, training, and emergency humanitarian aid. Works to institute standards and codes of conduct. Monitors legislation.

ARMS CONTROL, DISARMAMENT, AND THREAT REDUCTION

General

▶AGENCIES

Bureau of Arms Control, Verification, and Compliance (AVC) *(State Dept.), 2201 C St. N.W., #5950, 20520; (202) 647-6830. Alexandra Bell, Senior Bureau Official, (202) 647-7693.*
Web, www.state.gov/bureaus-offices/under-secretary-for-arms-control-and-international-security-affairs/bureau-of-arms-control-verification-and-compliance and Twitter, @StateAVC

Leads development of U.S. arms control, missile defense, and space policies, including negotiation and implementation of international nonproliferation and disarmament agreements.

Bureau of Arms Control, Verification, and Compliance (AVC) *(State Dept.),* **Emerging Security Challenges (ESC),** *2201 C St. N.W., #5751, 20520; (202) 647-7620. Eric E. Desautels, Director.*
Web, www.state.gov/bureaus-offices/under-secretary-for-arms-control-and-international-security-affairs/bureau-of-arms-control-verification-and-compliance/o

Provides research and recommendations on all policy and threat issues related to missile defense systems and cooperation, outer space security issues and transparency, cyberstability, and Arctic and Antarctic security issues.

Bureau of Arms Control, Verification, and Compliance (AVC) *(State Dept.),* **Euro-Atlantic Security Affairs (ESA),** *2201 C St. N.W., #5724, 20520; (202) 647-5628. David Weekman, Director.*
Web, www.state.gov/bureaus-offices/under-secretary-for-arms-control-and-international-security-affairs/bureau-of-arms-control-verification-and-compliance/o

Handles matters relating to existing and prospective European and Euro-Atlantic arms control, nonproliferation, disarmament agreements, and security arrangements concerning conventional and non-strategic nuclear weapons and forces.

Bureau of Arms Control, Verification, and Compliance (AVC) *(State Dept.), Strategic Stability and Deterrence Affairs (SSD), 2201 C St. N.W., #5871, 20520; (202) 736-4467. Katharine C. Crittenberger, Director, (202) 647-3760.*
Web, www.state.gov/bureaus-offices/under-secretary-for-arms-control-and-international-security-affairs/bureau-of-arms-control-verification-and-compliance/o

Promotes stability and reduces nuclear threats through policy development, negotiation, and implementation of arms control to ensure U.S. security.

Bureau of Arms Control, Verification, and Compliance (AVC) *(State Dept.), Verification, Planning, and Outreach (VPO), 2201 C St. N.W., #5669, 20520; (202) 647-0902. Neil Couch, Director.*
Web, www.state.gov/bureaus-offices/under-secretary-for-arms-control-and-international-security-affairs/bureau-of-arms-control-verification-and-compliance/o

Identifies and prioritizes emerging verification and compliance issues, and recommends the appropriate use of the Bureau's resources for both current and future arms control challenges, including the application of technological and analytical solutions.

Bureau of Economic and Business Affairs (EB) *(State Dept.), Counter Threat Finance and Sanctions (TFS), Threat Finance Countermeasures (TFC), 2201 C St. N.W., #3843, 20520; (202) 647-5763. Fax, (202) 647-7407. Andrew (Drew) J. Weinschenk, Director.*
Web, www.state.gov/threat-finance-countermeasures

Seeks to minimize the funding available to groups and individuals that prove a threat to domestic, international, and regional security.

Bureau of Industry and Security (BIS) *(Commerce Dept.), 14th St. and Constitution Ave. N.W., #3898, 20230; (202) 482-4811. Jeremy Pelter, Under Secretary (Acting). Export licensing information, (202) 482-4811. Press, (202) 482-2721.*
Web, www.bis.doc.gov and Twitter, @BISgov

Administers the Export Administration Act; maintains control lists and performs export licensing for the purposes of national security, foreign policy, and prevention of short supply. Seeks to prevent proliferation of dual-use exports, especially weapons of mass destruction.

Bureau of International Security and Nonproliferation (ISN) *(State Dept.), 2201 C St. N.W., #3932, 20520; (202) 647-9612. C. S. Eliot Kang, Assistant Secretary (Acting), (202) 647-5999; Ann Ganzer, Deputy Assistant Secretary.*
Web, www.state.gov/t/isn, Twitter, @StateISN and Facebook, www.facebook.com/StateDepartment.ISNBureau

Leads U.S. efforts to prevent the spread of weapons of mass destruction (WMD, including nuclear, chemical, and biological weapons) and their delivery systems; spearheads efforts to promote international consensus on WMD

proliferation; supports efforts of foreign partners to prevent, protect against, and respond to the threat or use of WMD by terrorists.

Bureau of International Security and Nonproliferation (ISN) *(State Dept.), Biological Policy Staff (BPS), 2201 C St. N.W., #3651, 20520; (202) 647-8768. Christopher Park, Director, (202) 647-7903.*
Web, www.state.gov/about-us-office-of-the-biological-policy-staff

Oversees implementation of the Biological Weapons convention with the aim to prevent or regress the threat of acquisition or use of biological weapons by state and nonstate actors; supports policies and strategies for countering biological threats, misuse of advances in the life sciences, and use of nonproliferation tools.

Bureau of International Security and Nonproliferation (ISN) *(State Dept.), Conventional Arms Threat Reduction (CATR), 2201 C St. N.W., #5528, 20520; (202) 647-2371. Renee Sondermann, Director, (202) 647-7515.*
Web, www.state.gov/key-topics-office-of-conventional-arms-threat-reduction

Works to combat the proliferation of advanced conventional weapons and related dual-use goods and technologies, including tanks, aircraft, missiles, sensor and lasers, man-portable air defense systems, and precision-guided munitions; leads policy on commercial remote-sensing.

Bureau of International Security and Nonproliferation (ISN) *(State Dept.), Cooperative Threat Reduction (CTR), 2201 C St. N.W., #3326/3327, 20520; (202) 647-3046. Ryan Taugher, Director, (202) 736-1362.*
Web, www.state.gov/t/isn/offices/ctr/index.htm

Oversees the diplomatic aspects of programs aimed at reducing the threat posed by terrorist organizations or states seeking to acquire weapons of mass destruction expertise, materials, and equipment.

Bureau of International Security and Nonproliferation (ISN) *(State Dept.), Counterproliferation Initiatives (CPI), 2201 C St. N.W., #3452, 20520; (202) 647-5193. Tom (Tony) Zarkecki, Director, (202) 647-7594.*
Web, www.state.gov/key-topics-office-of-counterproliferation-initiatives

Leads efforts to develop, implement, and improve counterproliferation policies to impede the proliferation of weapons of mass destruction; implements nuclear sanctions; ensures U.S. policy is in accordance with the UN Security Council Resolution 1540.

Bureau of International Security and Nonproliferation (ISN) *(State Dept.), Export Control Cooperation (ECC), 2201 C St. N.W., #3317, 20520; (202) 647-0224. Kathryn Insley, Director, (202) 647-1966.*
Web, www.state.gov/about-us-office-of-export-control-cooperation

Provides assistance to foreign governments to ensure strategic trade control systems meet international standards and establish independent capabilities to regulate transfers of weapons of mass destruction, WMD-related items, conventional arms, and related dual-use items, and to detect, interdict, investigate, and prosecute illicit transfers of such items.

Bureau of International Security and Nonproliferation (ISN) (State Dept.), Nonproliferation and Disarmament Fund (NDF), 2201 C St. N.W., #3208, 20520; (202) 647-0094. Matt Brechwald, Director.
Web, www.state.gov/about-us-office-of-the-nonproliferation-and-disarmament-fund

Responds to high-priority and unanticipated nonproliferation and disarmament issues, frequently in areas where other programs do not have authority.

Bureau of International Security and Nonproliferation (ISN) (State Dept.), Weapons of Mass Destruction Terrorism (WMDT), 2201 C St. N.W., #3733, 20520; (202) 647-8699. Josh Archibald, Director (Acting), (202) 647-3391.
Web, www.state.gov/key-topics-office-of-weapons-of-mass-destruction-terrorism

Works to reduce the threat of weapons of mass destruction terrorism by establishing, strengthening, and maintaining the capabilities of international partners to prevent, detect, and respond to terrorist attempts to acquire radiological or nuclear materials; helps build capacity to respond to chemical, biological, radiological, and nuclear incidents.

Bureau of Political-Military Affairs (PM) (State Dept.), Weapons Removal and Abatement (WRA), 2025 E St. N.W., #NE2025, SA9, 20520; (202) 453-8301. Stan Brown, Director, (202) 453-8304.
Web, www.state.gov/t/pm

Manages programs aimed at reducing and destroying stockpiled, poorly-secured, at-risk, illicitly proliferated, and indiscriminately used conventional weapons of war.

Defense Dept. (DoD), Homeland Defense and Global Security, 2600 Defense Pentagon, #3C852A, 20301-2600; (703) 697-7728. Jennifer Walsh, Assistant Secretary (Acting).
Web, http://policy.defense.gov/OUSDP-Offices/ASD-for-Homeland-Defense-and-Global-Security

Advises the secretary on reducing and countering nuclear, biological, chemical, and missile threats to the United States and its forces and allies; arms control negotiations, implementation, and verification policy; nuclear weapons policy, denuclearization, threat reduction, and nuclear safety and security; and technology transfer and cyber security.

Defense Dept. (DoD), Plans and Posture, 2400 Defense Pentagon, #5E384, 20301; (703) 614-0462. Fax, (703) 695-7230. Samuel Brannen, Deputy Assistant Secretary.
Web, www.defense.gov

Formulates national policies to prevent and counter the proliferation of nuclear, chemical, and biological weapons; missiles; and conventional technologies. Devises arms control agreements, export controls, technology transfer policies, and military planning policies.

Defense Threat Reduction Agency (Defense Dept.), 8725 John Jay Kingman Rd., MS 6201, Fort Belvoir, VA 22060-6201; (703) 767-4883. Rhys M. Williams, Director (Acting). Press, (703) 767-5870.
General email, dtra.belvoir.JO.mbx.dtra-publicaffairs@mail.mil

Web, www.dtra.mil and Twitter, @doddtra

Seeks to reduce, eliminate, and counter the threat to the United States and its allies from weapons of mass destruction; conducts technology security activities, cooperative threat reduction programs, arms control treaty monitoring, and on-site inspection; provides technical support on weapons of mass destruction matters to the Defense Dept. components.

Homeland Security Dept. (DHS), Countering Weapons of Mass Destruction (CWMD), 1125 15th St. N.W., 20221; (202) 254-7799. Gary Rasicot, Assistant Secretary (Acting).
Web, www.dhs.gov/countering-weapons-mass-destruction-office#

Responsible for countering attempts by terrorists or other threat actors to carry out an attack against the United States or its interests using a weapon of mass destruction.

Joint Improvised-Threat Defeat Organization (Defense Dept.), 8725 John J. Kingman Rd., MS 6201, Fort Belvoir, VA 22060-6201; (703) 995-6900. Maj. Gen. Chris Bentley, Director. Operational support, (703) 995-5553.
General email, jida.ncr.j3.mbx.operational-support@mail.mil

Web, https://dtra.mil/mission/JIDO

Combat support agency handling actions to counter improvised threats, especially improvised explosive devices (IEDs). It is a subordinate to the Defense Threat Reduction Agency (DTRA).

State Dept., National and Nuclear Risk Reduction Center (NRRC), 2201 C St. N.W., #5635, 20520; (202) 647-3645. Jody Daniel, Director.
Web, www.state.gov/bureaus-offices/under-secretary-for-arms-control-and-international-security-affairs/bureau-of-arms-control-verification-and-compliance

Supports implementation of arms control and security agreements with foreign governments by operating government-to-government communications systems.

State Dept., Under Secretary for Arms Control and International Security, 2201 C St. N.W., #7208, 20520-7512; (202) 647-1522. Amb Bonnie Denise Jenkins, Under Secretary.
Web, www.state.gov/bureaus-offices/under-secretary-for-arms-control-and-international-security-affairs and Twitter, @UnderSecT

Works with the secretary of state to develop policy on nonproliferation, arms control, regional security and defense relations, and arms transfers and security assistance. Oversees the Bureau of Arms Control, Verification and Compliance, Bureau of International Security and Nonproliferation, and Bureau of Political-Military Affairs.

▶CONGRESS

For a listing of relevant congressional committees and sub-committees, please see pages 634–635 or the Appendix.

▶NONGOVERNMENTAL

Arms Control Assn., *1200 18th St. N.W., #1175, 20005; (202) 463-8270. Fax, (202) 463-8273. Daryl G. Kimball, Executive Director, ext. 107.*
Web, www.armscontrol.org and Twitter, @ArmsControlNow

Nonpartisan organization that seeks to broaden public understanding and support for effective arms control and disarmament in national security policy through education and media programs. Publishes *Arms Control Today.*

Council for a Livable World, *820 1st St. N.E., #LL-180, 20002; (202) 543-4100. John Tierney, Executive Director, ext. 2108.*
General email, advocacy@clw.org
Web, https://livableworld.org, Twitter, @Livableworld and YouTube, www.youtube.com/channel/UC2zgzMV7CjH_4ZV9/Uyj-yhA/featured

Citizens' interest group that supports nuclear arms control treaties, strengthened biological and chemical weapons conventions, reduced military spending, peace-keeping, and tight restrictions on international arms sales.

Federation of American Scientists (FAS), *1112 16th St. N.W., #400, 20036; (202) 454-4660. Daniel (Dan) Correa, Chief Executive Officer.*
General email, fas@fas.org
Web, www.fas.org, Twitter, @FAScientists and Facebook, www.facebook.com/fascientists

Opposes the global arms race and supports nuclear disarmament and limits on government secrecy. Promotes national security, science, technology and innovation; conducts studies and monitors legislation on U.S. weapons policy; provides the public with information on arms control and related issues.

GlobalSecurity.org, *300 N. Washington St., #B-100, Alexandria, VA 22314-2540; (703) 548-2700. Fax, (703) 548-2424. John E. Pike, Director.*
General email, info@globalsecurity.org
Web, www.globalsecurity.org, Twitter, @Globesec and Twitter, @pri_security

Provides background information and covers developing news stories on the military, weapons proliferation, space, homeland security, and intelligence. Offers profiles of agencies, systems, facilities, and current operations as well as a library of primary documentation.

High Frontier, *500 N. Washington St., Alexandria, VA 22314; (703) 535-8774. Amb. Henry (Hank) F. Cooper, Chair.*
General email, info@highfrontier.org
Web, www.highfrontier.org and Facebook, www.facebook .com/highfrontier.org

Educational organization that provides information on missile defense programs and proliferation. Advocates development of a single-stage-to-orbit space vehicle, a moon base program, and a layered missile defense system. Operates speakers bureau; monitors defense legislation.

Nonproliferation Policy Education Center (NPEC), *1600 Wilson Blvd., #640, Arlington, VA 22209 (mailing address: P.O. Box 17678, Arlington VA. 22216); (571) 970-3187. Henry D. Sokolski, Executive Director.*
General email, info@npolicy.org
Web, www.npolicy.org and Twitter, @NuclearPolicy

Conducts and publishes research on strategic weapons proliferation issues and makes it available to the press, congressional and executive branch staff, foreign officials, and international organizations.

Nuclear Threat Initiative (NTI), *1776 Eye St. N.W., #600, 20006; (202) 296-4810. Fax, (202) 296-4811. Joan Rohlfing, President; Ernest J. Moniz, Chief Executive Officer.*
General email, contact@nti.org
Web, www.nti.org, Twitter, @NTI_WMD and Facebook, www.facebook.com/nti.org

Works to reduce threats from nuclear, biological, and chemical weapons; publishes monthly and quarterly e-newsletters.

Peace Action, *8630 Fenton St., #934, Silver Spring, MD 20910-5642 (mailing address: P.O.Box 8637, Silver Springs, MD. 20907); (301) 565-4050. Fax, (301) 562-7305. Kevin Martin, President, ext. 307; Paul Kawika Martin, Senior Director, Policy and Political Affairs, ext. 316.*
Web, www.peace-action.org, Twitter, @PeaceAction and Facebook, www.facebook.com/peaceaction

Grassroots organization that supports a negotiated comprehensive test ban treaty. Seeks a reduction in the military budget and a transfer of those funds to nonmilitary programs. Works for an end to international arms trade.

Physicians for Social Responsibility (PSR), *1111 14th St. N.W., #700, 20005 (mailing address: P.O.Box 30159, Bethesda, MD. 20824); (202) 667-4260. Fax, (202) 667-4201. Jeff Carter, Executive Director, (202) 587-5240.*
General email, psrnatl@psr.org
Web, www.psr.org, Twitter, @psrenvironment and Facebook, www.facebook.com/psrnational

Membership: doctors, nurses, health scientists, and concerned citizens. Works toward the elimination of nuclear weapons and use of nuclear power. Conducts public education programs, monitors policy, and serves as a liaison with other concerned groups.

Union of Concerned Scientists, *Global Security, 1825 K St. N.W., 20006-1232; (202) 223-6133. Tara Drozdenko, Director.*
General email, ucs@ucsusa.org
Web, www.ucsusa.org/about/programs/global-security, Twitter, @UCSUSA, Facebook, www.facebook.com/ unionofconcernedscientists and YouTube, www.youtube .com/user/ConcernedScientists

Combines technical analysis, education and advocacy, and engagement with the public and scientific community to promote policies that enhance national and international security. Focuses on technical issues, including verified reductions of nuclear arsenals, fissile material controls, missile defense, and space security. Plays a role in increasing the number of independent scientists and technical analysts working professionally on security issues worldwide. (Headquarters in Cambridge, Mass.)

Nuclear Weapons and Power

►AGENCIES

Bureau of Arms Control, Verification, and Compliance (AVC) *(State Dept.), Multilateral and Nuclear Affairs (MNA)*, 2201 C St. N.W., #5751, 20520; (202) 647-3760. *Katharine Crittenberger, Director (Acting).*
Web, www.state.gov/bureaus-offices/under-secretary-for-arms-control-and-international-security-affairs/bureau-of-arms-control-verification-and-compliance/o

Coordinates U.S. policy on bilateral and multilateral nuclear arms control and disarmament agreements and commitments, verification, and compliance issues.

Bureau of International Security and Nonproliferation (ISN) *(State Dept.), Multilateral Nuclear and Security Affairs (MNSA)*, 2201 C St. N.W., #5821, 20520; (202) 647-8136. *Kurt G. Kessler, Director.*
Web, www.state.gov/about-us-office-of-multilateral-nuclear-and-security-affairs

Leads development and implementation of U.S. policies related to global nuclear nonproliferation, including international treaties, protocols, and nuclear-related security assurances. Coordinates U.S. policy regarding International Atomic Energy Agency safeguards.

Bureau of International Security and Nonproliferation (ISN) *(State Dept.), Nuclear Energy, Safety, and Security Affairs (NESS)*, 2201 C St. N.W., #3320, 20520; (202) 647-4413. *James R. Warden, Director, (202) 647-4431.*
Web, www.state.gov/key-topics-office-of-nuclear-energy-safety-and-security

Advises the secretary on policy matters relating to nonproliferation and export controls, nuclear technology and safeguards, and nuclear safety. Negotiates bilateral and multilateral agreements pertaining to nuclear trade, safety, and physical protection.

Defense Nuclear Facilities Safety Board, *625 Indiana Ave. N.W., #700, 20004-2901; (202) 694-7000. Joyce L. Connery, Chair. Toll-free, (800) 788-4016. General email, mailbox@dnfsb.gov*
Web, www.dnfsb.gov

Independent board created by Congress and appointed by the president to provide external oversight of Energy Dept. defense nuclear weapons production facilities and make recommendations to the secretary of energy regarding public health and safety.

Energy Dept. (DOE), *Under Secretary for Nuclear Security, 1000 Independence Ave. S.W., #7A049, 20585; (202) 586-5555. Fax, (202) 586-4892. Jill Hruby, Under Secretary. Press, (202) 586-7371.*
Web, www.energy.gov/nnsa

Maintains the safety, security, and effectiveness of the U.S. nuclear weapons stockpile without nuclear testing; provides the U.S. Navy with safe and effective nuclear propulsion; provides the nation with nuclear counterterrorism and incident response capability.

Homeland Security Dept. (DHS), *Countering Weapons of Mass Destruction (CWMD), Domestic Nuclear Detection (DNDO), 3801 Nebraska Ave. N.W., 20528; (202) 254-7280. James F. McDonnell, Director.*
Web, www.dhs.gov/domestic-nuclear-detection-office

Seeks to improve the nation's capability to detect and report unauthorized attempts to import, possess, store, develop, or transport nuclear or radiological material for use against the nation, as well as integration of federal nuclear forensics programs. Oversees the development of an integrated global and domestic nuclear detection program with partners from federal, state, local, and international governments and the private sector, and the deployment of a nuclear detection system.

National Nuclear Security Administration (NNSA) *(Energy Dept.), Counterterrorism and Counterproliferation, 1000 Independence Ave. S.W., #7B048, 20585; (202) 586-1734. Jay Tilden, Associate Administrator.*
Web, www.energy.gov/nnsa/missions/counterterrorism

Responds and counters nuclear threats through innovative science, technology, and policies. Seeks to reduce danger posed by proliferant nations pursuing a nuclear weapons capability.

National Nuclear Security Administration (NNSA) *(Energy Dept.), Defense Nuclear Nonproliferation, 1000 Independence Ave. S.W., #7F075, 20585; (202) 586-5000. Fax, (202) 586-1348. Corey Hindenstein, Deputy Administrator.*
Web, www.energy.gov/nnsa/missions/nonproliferation

Works globally to prevent state and nonstate actors from developing nuclear weapons or acquiring nuclear or radiological materials, equipment, technology, and expertise. Researches and develops new technology to monitor overseas nuclear activity.

National Nuclear Security Administration (NNSA) *(Energy Dept.), Defense Programs, 1000 Independence Ave. S.W., #4A019, 20585; (202) 586-5000. Fax, (202) 586-5670. Charles Verdon, Deputy Administrator. Press, (202) 586-7371.*
Web, www.energy.gov/nnsa/missions/maintaining-stockpile

Responsible for maintaining and modernizing the nuclear stockpile through the Stockpile Stewardship and Management Program.

National Nuclear Security Administration *(Energy Dept.), Naval Nuclear Propulsion Program, 1240 Isaac*

Hull Ave. S.E., MS 8037, Washington Navy Yard, DC 20376-8037; (202) 781-6172. Adm. James F. Caldwell Jr. (USN), Director.
Web, www.energy.gov/nnsa/missions/powering-navy

Responsible for militarily effective nuclear propulsion plants.

State Dept., *National and Nuclear Risk Reduction Center (NRRC),* 2201 C St. N.W., #5635, 20520; (202) 647-3645. Jody Daniel, Director.
Web, www.state.gov/bureaus-offices/under-secretary-for-arms-control-and-international-security-affairs/bureau-of-arms-control-verification-and-compliance

Handles notification regimes for conventional, nuclear, chemical, and cyber arms, including inspection notices, strategic offensive arms data exchanges, major exercises or unit restructuring, and any other treaty-required communications.

▶**CONGRESS**

For a listing of relevant congressional committees and sub-committees, please see pages 634–635 or the Appendix.

▶**NONGOVERNMENTAL**

Center for Arms Control and Nonproliferation, 820 1st St. N.E., #LL-180, 20002; (202) 546-0795. John Tierney, Executive Director, ext. 2108.
General email, info@armscontrolcenter.org
Web, https://armscontrolcenter.org, Twitter, @nukes_of_hazzard and Facebook, www.facebook.com/armscontrolcenter

Advocates reducing nuclear weapon arsenals, preventing the spread of nuclear weapons, and minimizing the risk of nuclear war by educating the public and policymakers about arms control through policy analysis and research.

Center for Strategic and International Studies, *Project on Nuclear Issues,* 1616 Rhode Island Ave. N.W., 20036; (202) 775-3132. Rebecca Hersman, Director.
Web, www.csis.org/programs/international-security-program/project-nuclear-issues, Twitter, @CSISponi and Facebook, www.facebook.com/CSISPONI

Conducts and publishes research on proliferation reduction, nuclear arms control, and peaceful nuclear energy fuel cycles.

Global Center on Cooperative Security, *Washington Office,* 1201 14th St. N.W., #915, 20005; Jason Ipe, Chief of Operations.
General email, info@globalcenter.org
Web, www.globalcenter.org, Facebook, www.facebook.com/GlobalCtr and Twitter, @GlobalCtr

Conducts research and training to advance global cooperation by advancing human rights-based policies, partnerships and practices, to address transnational threats, including terrorism, nuclear proliferation, and drug trafficking. Works with government, civil society and private sector partners to deliver programming that is globally informed and locally grounded. Has an extensive selection of articles, books, reports, publications and interviews relating to sanctions and incentives, violent extremism and terrorism.

Institute for Science and International Security, 440 1st St. N.W., #800, 20001; (202) 547-3633. David Albright, President.
General email, isis@isis-online.org
Web, https://isis-online.org and Facebook, www.facebook.com/Institute-for-Science-and-International-Security-351457957011

Conducts research and analysis on nuclear weapons production and nonproliferation issues.

Other Weapons

▶**AGENCIES**

Bureau of Arms Control, Verification, and Compliance (AVC) *(State Dept.),* **Chemical and Biological Weapons Affairs (CBW),** 2201 C St. N.W., #3828, 20520; (202) 647-6693. Laura Gross, Director.
Web, www.state.gov/bureaus-offices/under-secretary-for-arms-control-and-international-security-affairs/bureau-of-arms-control-verification-and-compliance/o

Responsible for U.S. implementation of the Chemical Weapons Convention, which promotes a global ban on chemical weapons; leads compliance assessment of the CWC and the Biological and Toxins Weapons Convention.

Bureau of International Security and Nonproliferation (ISN) *(State Dept.),* **Missile, Biological, and Chemical Nonproliferation (MBC),** 2201 C St. N.W., #3758, 20520; (202) 647-4930. Pamela Durham, Director, (202) 647-4931.
Web, www.state.gov/t/isn

Leads efforts to impede, roll back, and eliminate the proliferation of chemical and biological weapons, missile delivery systems for weapons of mass destruction, and related equipment, materials, and technology; implements missile sanctions; leads U.S. participation in the Australia Group CBW nonproliferation regime, the Hague Code of Conduct Against Ballistic Missile Proliferation, and the Missile Technology Control Regime.

Defense Dept. (DoD), *Nuclear, Chemical, and Biological Defense Programs,* 3050 Defense Pentagon, #5B1064, 20301-3050; (703) 693-9410. Fax, (703) 695-0476. Deborah G. Rosenblum, Assistant Secretary.
Web, www.acq.osd.mil/ncbdp/index.html

Provides capabilities to deter, prevent, protect, mitigate, respond, and recover from chemical, biological, radiological, and nuclear threats. Coordinates, integrates, and provides oversight for the Joint Services Chemical and Biological Defense Program.

▶**NONGOVERNMENTAL**

Center for Arms Control and Nonproliferation, 820 1st St. N.E., #LL-180, 20002; (202) 546-0795. John Tierney, Executive Director, ext. 2108.

Immigration Reform and Advocacy Resources

The following agencies, organizations, blogs, and hotlines offer information pertaining to immigrant and refugee advocacy and immigration reform.

ADVOCACY

American Immigration Lawyers Assn., (202) 507-7600; www.aila.org

Amnesty International, (202) 544-0200; www.amnestyusa.org

Ayuda, (202) 387-4848; www.ayuda.com

Capital Area Immigrants' Rights (CAIR) Coalition, (202) 331-3320; www.caircoalition.org

Catholic Legal Immigration Network, Inc., (301) 565-4800; www.cliniclegal.org

Center for Community Change, (202) 339-9300; www.communitychange.org

Commission on Immigration at the American Bar Assn., (202) 662-1005;(800) 285-2221; www.americanbar.org/groups/public_services/immigration.html

Detention Watch Network, www.detentionwatchnetwork.org

Institute for Policy Studies, (202) 234-9382; www.ips-dc.org

United Nations Refugee Agency, (202) 461-2356; www.unrefugees.org

U.S. Committee for Refugees and Immigrants, (703) 310-1130; www.refugees.org

U.S. Conference of Catholic Bishops, Migration and Refugee Services, (202) 541-3064;(202) 541-3352; www.usccb.org/about/migration-and-refugee-services/index.cfm

REFORM

American Immigration Council, (202) 507-7500; www.americanimmigrationcouncil.org

America's Voice, www.americasvoice.org

Center for Immigration Studies, (202) 466-8185; Fax,(202) 466-8076; www.cis.org

Federation for American Immigration Reform (FAIR), (202) 328-7004; Fax,(202) 387-3447; www.fairus.org

Immigration Equality, (212) 714-2904; If you are in detention,(917) 654-9696; Fax, (315) 825-4058; www.immigrationequality.org

Immigration Reform Law Institute, (202) 232-5590; www.irli.org

ImmigrationWorks USA, (202) 506-4541; Fax, (202) 595-8962; www.opportunityamericaonline.org

Migration Policy Institute, (202) 266-1940; www.migrationpolicy.org

National Immigration Forum, (202) 347-0040; www.immigrationforum.org

UnidosUS, (202) 785-1670; www.unidosus.org

SOCIAL MEDIA AND BLOGS

Center for Immigration Studies Blog, www.cis.org/ImmigrationBlog

Progressives for Immigration Reform Blog, (202) 543-5325; www.progressivesforimmigrationreform.org/posts

HOTLINES

Office of Special Counsel for Immigration-Related Unfair Employment Practices, U.S. Dept. of Justice, Civil Rights Division, Worker hotline (800) 255-7688; Employer hotline, (800) 255-8155; www.justice.gov/crt/immigrant-and-employee-rights-section

U.S. Citizenship and Immigration Services National Customer Service Center, (800) 375-5283; TTY, (800) 767-1833; www.uscis.gov/contactcenter

---

General email, info@armscontrolcenter.org

Web, https://armscontrolcenter.org, Twitter, @nukes_of_hazzard and Facebook, www.facebook.com/armscontrolcenter

Promotes research and education on all misuse of biology; supports the Biological and Chemical Weapons Conventions. Interests include preventing the development of biochemical disabling agents as weapons, promoting international measures to monitor biological weapons-capable activities, promoting global cooperative measures for combating infectious diseases, ethical education of bioscientists, monitoring U.S. biodefense and anti-bioterrorism activities, and opposing risky or dangerous biological research.

Nuclear Threat Initiative (NTI), *1776 Eye St. N.W., #600, 20006; (202) 296-4810. Fax, (202) 296-4811. Joan Rohlfing, President; Ernest J. Moniz, Chief Executive Officer.*

General email, contact@nti.org

Web, www.nti.org, Twitter, @NTI_WMD and Facebook, www.facebook.com/nti.org

Works to reduce threats from nuclear, biological, and chemical weapons; publishes monthly and quarterly e-newsletters.

BORDERS, CUSTOMS, AND IMMIGRATION

General

▶AGENCIES

Homeland Security Dept. (DHS), *Citizenship and Immigration Services Ombudsman, MS 0180, 20528-0180;*

Air Force Department

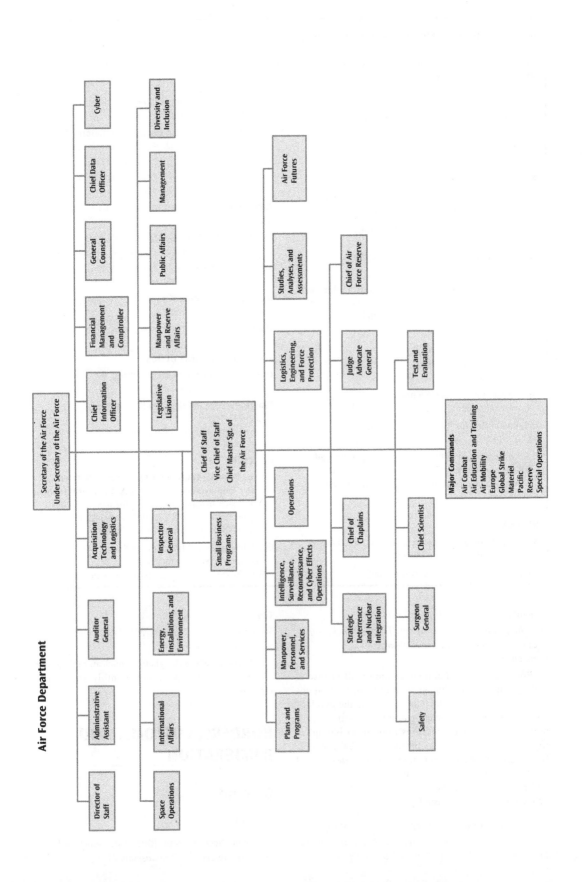

---

(202) 357-8100. Phyllis Coven, Ombudsman. Toll-free, (855) 882-8100.
General email, cisombudsman@hq.dhs.gov
Web, www.dhs.gov/cisombudsman

Assists individuals and employers in resolving problems with the U.S. Citizenship and Immigration Services (USCIS); proposes changes in the administrative practices of USCIS in an effort to mitigate identified problems.

U.S. Citizenship and Immigration Services (USCIS)
(Homeland Security Dept.), 20 Massachusetts Ave. N.W., 20529; (800) 375-5283. Tracy Renaud, Director (Acting). Customer Service Center, (800) 375-5283. TTY, (800) 767-1833.
Web, www.uscis.gov, Twitter, @USCIS and Facebook, www.facebook.com/USCIS

Responsible for the delivery of immigration and citizenship services. Priorities include the promotion of national security and the implementation of measures to improve service delivery.

U.S. Customs and Border Protection *(Homeland Security Dept.), 1300 Pennsylvania Ave. N.W., #4.4A, 20229; (202) 325-8000. Chris Magnus, Commissioner. Toll-free, (877) 227-5511. Hotline, (800) 232-5378. Public Affairs, (202) 344-1780. TTY, (800) 877-8339.*
Web, www.cbp.gov, Twitter, @cbp and Facebook, www.facebook.com/CBPgov

Assesses and collects duties and taxes on imported merchandise; processes persons and baggage entering the United States; controls export carriers and goods to prevent fraud and smuggling. Library open to the public by appointment.

U.S. Customs and Border Protection *(Homeland Security Dept.), Agricultural Program and Trade Liaison Office, 1300 Pennsylvania Ave. N.W., 20229; (202) 344-1644. Fax, (202) 344-1442. John P. Leonard, Executive Director. Trade Relations, (202) 344-1440. Public Affairs, (877) 227-5511.*
Web, www.cbp.gov/border-security/protecting-agriculture

Responsible for safeguarding the nation's animal and natural resources from pests and disease through inspections at ports of entry and beyond.

U.S. Customs and Border Protection *(Homeland Security Dept.), Border Patrol, 1300 Pennsylvania Ave. N.W., #6.5E, 20229; (877) 227-5511. Raul L. Ortiz, Chief. TTY, (800) 877-8339.*
Web, www.cbp.gov/border-security/along-us-borders/overview

Mobile uniformed law enforcement arm of the Homeland Security Dept. Primary mission is to detect and prevent the illegal trafficking of people and contraband across U.S. borders.

U.S. Immigration and Customs Enforcement (ICE)
(Homeland Security Dept.), 500 12th St. S.W., 20536; (202) 732-3000. Tae D. Johnson, Director (Acting). Press, (202) 732-4646. Hotline, (866) 347-2423. TTY, (802) 872-6196.
General email, ICEmedia@ice.dhs.gov
Web, www.ice.gov, Twitter, @ICEgov, Facebook, www.facebook.com/wwwicegov and YouTube, www.youtube.com/wwwicegov

Enforces immigration and customs laws within the United States. Focuses on the protection of specified federal buildings and on air and marine enforcement. Undertakes investigations and conducts interdictions.

► **CONGRESS**

For a listing of relevant congressional committees and subcommittees, please see pages 634–635 or the Appendix.

DEFENSE TRADE AND TECHNOLOGY

General

► **AGENCIES**

Air Force Dept. *(Defense Dept.), Air Combat Command (ACC), Langley-Eustis Air Force Base, 115 Thompson St., #211, Hampton, VA 23665-1987; (757) 764-5471. Gen. Mark D. Kelly, Commander. Public Affairs, (757) 764-5007.*
General email, acc.pai@langley.af.mil
Web, www.acc.af.mil, Twitter, @USAF_ACC and Facebook, www.facebook/ACConFB

Primary provider of air combat forces to U.S. warfighting commanders; provides command, control, communications and intelligence systems; conducts global information operations.

Air Force Dept. *(Defense Dept.), Space Force (USSF), 1670 Air Force Pentagon, 4E858, 20330-1640; (703) 695-8773. (703) 695-9387. Gen. John (Jay) W. Raymond, Chief of Space Operations. Press, (703) 695-0640.*
Web, www.spaceforce.mil, Twitter, @SpaceForceDoD, Facebook, www.facebook.com/USSpaceForceDoD and General email, hqsf.ussf.cso_workflow@us.af.mil

Manages the planning, programming, and training of joint U.S. space forces, as well as the acquisition of space and cyberspace systems.

Bureau of Industry and Security (BIS) *(Commerce Dept.), 14th St. and Constitution Ave. N.W., #3898, 20230; (202) 482-4811. Jeremy Pelter, Under Secretary (Acting). Export licensing information, (202) 482-4811. Press, (202) 482-2721.*
Web, www.bis.doc.gov and Twitter, @BISgov

Assists in providing for an adequate supply of strategic and critical materials for defense activities and civilian needs, including military requirements, and other domestic energy supplies; develops plans for industry to meet national emergencies. Studies the effect of imports on national security and recommends actions. Manages the nation's dual-use export control laws and regulations.

Bureau of Industry and Security (BIS) *(Commerce Dept.), Export Administration (OEA), Strategic Industries and Economic Security*, 1401 Constitution Ave. N.W., #3876, 20230; (202) 482-4506. Fax, (202) 482-5650. Eric Longnecker, Director.
Web, www.bis.doc.gov/index.php/other-areas/strategic-industries-and-economic-security-sies

Administers the Defense Production Act and provides industry with information on the allocation of resources falling under the jurisdiction of the act.

Bureau of Industry and Security (BIS) *(Commerce Dept.), Export Enforcement (OEE)*, 14th St. and Constitution Ave. N.W., #4508, 20230; (202) 482-5079. Fax, (202) 482-5889. John Sonderman, Director.
Web, www.bis.doc.gov/index.php/oee

Enforces dual-use export controls on exports of U.S. goods and technology for purposes of national security, nonproliferation, counterterrorism, foreign policy, and short supply. Enforces the antiboycott provisions of the Export Administration Regulations.

Bureau of Political-Military Affairs (PM) *(State Dept.)*, 2201 C St. N.W., #6212, 20520; (202) 647-9022. Jessica Lewis, Assistant Secretary.
Web, www.state.gov/t/pm

Liaison between the State Dept. and Defense Dept. Provides policy direction in the areas of international security, security assistance, military operations, defense strategy and policy, military use of space, and defense trade.

Bureau of Political-Military Affairs (PM) *(State Dept.), Defense Trade Controls (DDTC)*, 2401 E St. N.W., SA-1, RMH #1205D, 20037; (202) 663-3704. Michael (Mike) F. Miller, Deputy Assistant Secretary (Acting), (202) 663-2861.
Web, www.pmddtc.state.gov/ddtc_public

Controls the commercial export of defense articles, services, and related technical data; authorizes the permanent export and temporary import of such items.

Bureau of Political-Military Affairs (PM) *(State Dept.), Regional Security and Arms Transfers (RSAT)*, 2401 E St. N.W., #H1012, 20037; (202) 663-3056. Laura Cressey, Office Director, (202) 663-3441.
Web, www.state.gov/t/pm

Manages bilateral and multilateral political-military and regional security relations and the sale and transfer of U.S.-origin defense articles and services to foreign governments.

Defense Dept. (DoD), *Defense Technology Security Administration*, 4800 Mark Center Dr., #03D08, Alexandria, VA 22350-1600; (571) 372-2301. Michael Laychak, Director. Press, (703) 697-5131.
Web, www.dtsa.mil and Twitter, @dtsamil

Develops and implements technology security policy for international transfers of defense-related goods, services, and technologies. Participates in interagency and international activities and regimes that monitor, control,

and prevent transfers that could threaten U.S. national security interests.

Homeland Security Dept. (DHS), *Science and Technology Directorate (S&T)*, 245 Murray Lane, 20528; (202) 254-6006. Karen Coulter Mitchell, Under Secretary (Acting). Press, (202) 282-8010.
Web, www.dhs.gov/st-directorate, Twitter, @dhsscitech and Facebook, www.facebook.com/dhsscitech

Responsible for oversight and coordination of the development and augmentation of homeland security technology.

▶CONGRESS

For a listing of relevant congressional committees and subcommittees, please see pages 634–635 or the Appendix.

Research and Development

▶AGENCIES

Air Force Dept. *(Defense Dept.), Air Force Acquisition, Technology, and Logistics (SAF/AQ)*, 1060 Air Force Pentagon, #4E962, 20330-1060; (703) 697-6361. Fax, (703) 693-6400. Darlene Costello, Assistant Secretary (Acting). Public inquiries, (703) 697-3039.
Web, ww3.safaq.hq.af.mil

Air Force office that directs and reviews Air Force research, development, and acquisition of weapons systems and program sustainment activities.

Air Force Dept. *(Defense Dept.), Office of Scientific Research (AF/OSR)*, 875 N. Randolph St., #325, Arlington, VA 22203-1768; (703) 696-7797. Fax, (703) 696-9556. Shery L. Welsh, Director.
General email, info@us.af.mil
Web, www.afrl.af.mil/AFOSR and Facebook, www.facebook.com/afosr

Sponsors and sustains basic research; assists in the transfer of research results to the war-fighter; supports Air Force goals of control and maximum utilization of air, space, and cyberspace.

Army Corps of Engineers *(Defense Dept.), Research and Development*, 441 G St. N.W., #3417, 20314-1000; (202) 761-1839. Fax, (202) 761-0907. David W. Pittman, SES, Director.
Web, www.usace.army.mil/Missions/Research-and-Development and General email, hq-publicaffairs@usace.army.mil

Supports the research and development efforts of the corps by providing strategic planning and strategic direction and oversight, developing policy and doctrine, developing national program integration, and advising the chief of engineers on science and technology issues.

Army Dept. *(Defense Dept.), Acquisition, Logistics, and Technology*, 103 Army Pentagon, #2E532, 20310-0103; (703) 695-6154. Fax, (703) 693-9728. Douglas R. Bush, Assistant Secretary.

Army Department

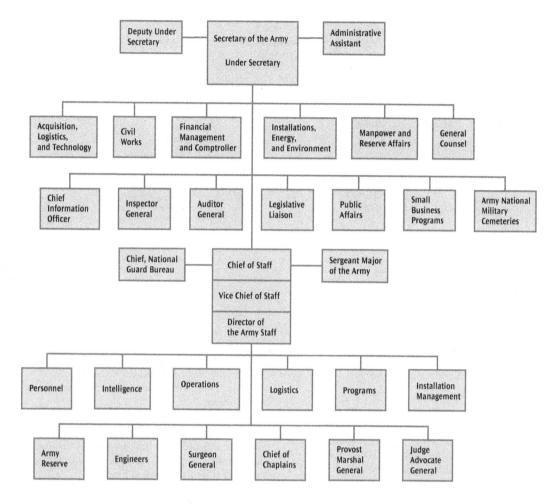

Civilian office that directs Army acquisition research and development of weapons systems and missiles.

Army Dept. *(Defense Dept.), DEVCOM Army Research Laboratory, 2800 Powder Mill Rd., Adelphi, MD 20783-1138; (301) 394-2515. Patrick Baker, Director.*
Web, www.army.mil/arl, Twitter, @ArmyResearchLab, Facebook, www.facebook.com/ArmyResearchLaboratory and YouTube, www.youtube.com/ARLTVNews

The U.S. Army Combat Capabilities Development Command (DEVCOM) Army Research Laboratory is the Army's research laboratory focused on scientific discovery, technological innovation, and transition of knowledge products.

Defense Advanced Research Projects Agency *(Defense Dept.), 675 N. Randolph St., Arlington, VA 22203-2114; (703) 526-6630. Stephanie Tompkins, Director.*
Web, www.darpa.mil

Sponsors basic and applied research to maintain U.S. technological superiority and prevent strategic surprise by adversaries. Develops technologically advanced research ideas, assesses technical feasibility, and develops prototypes.

Defense Dept. (DoD), *International Cooperation, 3070 Defense Pentagon, #5A1062B, 20301-3070; (703) 697-4431. Fax, (703) 693-2026. Michael J. Vaccaro, Executive Director. General email, osd.pentagon.ousd-atl.mbx.icwebmaster@ mail.mil*

Web, www.acq.osd.mil/ic

Advises the under secretary of defense for Acquisitions, Technology, and Logistics on cooperative research and development, production, procurement, and follow-up support programs with foreign nations; monitors the transfer of secure technologies to foreign nations.

Defense Dept. (DoD), *Research and Engineering, 3030 Defense Pentagon, #3E272, 20301-3030; (703) 695-9604. Heidi Shyce, Under Secretary. General email, osd.pentagon.ousd-re.mbx. communications@mail.mil*

Web, www.cto.mil

Civilian office responsible for policy, guidance, and oversight for the Defense Dept.'s Science and Technology

Navy Department

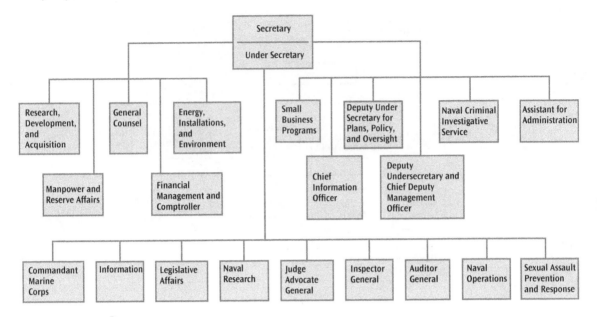

Program. Serves as focal point for in-house laboratories, university research, and other science and technology matters.

Defense Technical Information Center *(Defense Dept.),* 8725 John Jay Kingman Rd., Fort Belvoir, VA 22060-6218; (703) 767-9100. Christopher E. Thomas, Administrator; Thomas Gillespie, Director. Toll-free, (800) 225-3842. General email, dtic.belvoir.us.mbx.reference@mail.mil

Web, https://discover.dtic.mil and Twitter, @DoDDTIC

Acts as a central repository for the Defense Dept.'s collection of current and completed research and development efforts in all fields of science and technology. Disseminates research analysis and development information to contractors, grantees, and registered organizations working on government research and development projects, particularly for the Defense Dept. Users must register with the center.

Marine Corps *(Defense Dept.), Systems Command,* 2200 Lester St., Quantico, VA 22134-6050; (703) 432-3958. Brig. Gen. Arthur T. Pasagian (USMC), Commander; William S. Williford III, Executive Director. General email, MCSCPAO@usmc.mil

Web, www.marcorsyscom.marines.mil, Facebook, www .facebook.com/MARCORSYSCOM and Twitter, @MCSC_ Quantico

Military office that directs Marine Corps acquisition. Contracting and technical authority for marine corps ground weapon and information technology programs.

Marine Corps. *(Defense Dept.), Systems Command, Contracts Directorate,* 2201A Willis St., Quantico, VA 22134-6050 (mailing address: Attn: Contracts Directorate,

2200 Lester St., Quantico, VA 22134-6050); (703) 432-3949. Johany M. Deal, Director, (703) 432-3919. Web, www.marcorsyscom.marines.mil/Staff/Professional-Staff/Contracts

Manages contracting technical functions. Awards and administers contracts for marine corps ground weapons programs, assigned IT systems programs or components, and relevant professional, research, and engineering services, except for naval aviation programs.

Missile Defense Agency *(Defense Dept.),* Bldg. 245, 5700 18th St., Fort Belvoir, VA 22060-5573; Vice Adm. Jon A. Hill (USAF), Director. Fraud, waste, and abuse hotline, (800) 424-9098. General email, mda.info@mda.mil

Web, www.mda.mil

Manages and directs the ballistic missile defense acquisition and research and development programs. Seeks to deploy improved theater missile defense systems and to develop options for effective national missile defenses while increasing the contribution of defensive systems to U.S. and allied security.

Naval Research Laboratory *(Defense Dept.),* 4555 Overlook Ave. S.W., 20375-5320; (202) 767-2996. Capt. Gregory T. Petrovic (USN), Commanding Officer; Bruce G. Danly, Director of Research. Press, (202) 480-3746. Library, (202) 767-2134. FOIA, (202) 404-8317. General email, nrlpao@nrl.navy.mil

Web, www.nrl.navy.mil, Twitter, @USNRL and Facebook, www.facebook.com/USNRL

Conducts scientific research and develops advanced technology for the Navy and Marine Corps. Research,

U.S. Coast Guard

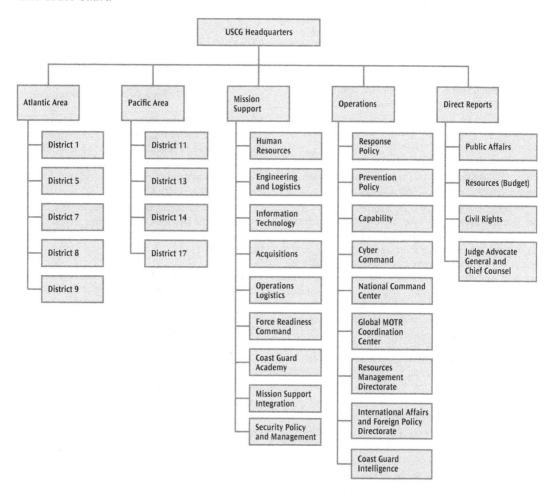

both basic and applied, covers scientific disciplines for both immediate and long-range national defense needs.

Navy Dept. *(Defense Dept.), Naval Research,* 875 N. Randolph St., #1425, Arlington, VA 22203-1995; (703) 696-5031. Fax, (703) 696-5940. Rear Adm. Lorin C. Selby (USN), Chief.
General email, onrpublicaffairs@navy.mil

Web, www.onr.navy.mil, Twitter, @USNavyResearch and Facebook, www.facebook.com/OfficeofNavalResearch

Oversees the offices of Naval Research, Naval Technology, and Advanced Technology; works to ensure transition of research and technology to the fleet; sponsors and supports basic research at Navy laboratories, universities, and other public and private organizations.

Navy Dept. *(Defense Dept.), Research, Development, and Acquisition,* 1000 Navy Pentagon, #4E665, 20350-1000; (703) 695-6315. Frederick J. Stefany (USN), Assistant Secretary (Acting).
Web, www.secnav.navy.mil/rda/Pages/default.aspx

Civilian office that directs and reviews Navy and Marine Corps research and development of weapons systems.

Office of Science and Technology Policy (OSTP) *(Executive Office of the President),* Eisenhower Executive Office Bldg., 1650 Pennsylvania Ave. N.W., 20504; (202) 456-4444. Alondria Nelson, Director. Press, (202) 456-6124.
General email, engagement@ostp.gov

Web, www.whitehouse.gov/ostp and Twitter, @WHOSTP

Advises the president on science and technology matters as they affect national security; coordinates science and technology initiatives at the interagency level. Interests include nuclear materials, security, nuclear arms reduction, and counterterrorism.

U.S. Coast Guard (USCG) *(Homeland Security Dept.), Design and Engineering Standards (CG-ENG),* 2703 Martin Luther King Jr. Ave. S.E., MS 7509, 20593-7509; (202) 372-1352. Capt. Benjamin Hawkins, Chief.
Web, www.dco.uscg.mil/CG-ENG

Develops and maintains engineering standards for the building of ships, aircraft, shore infrastructure, and Coast Guard facilities. Supports maritime safety, security, mobility, national defense, and protection of natural resources.

▶**CONGRESS**

For a listing of relevant congressional committees and sub-committees, please see pages 634–635 or the Appendix.

▶**NONGOVERNMENTAL**

AFCEA (Armed Forces Communications and Electronics Assn.), *4114 Legato Rd., #1000, Fairfax, VA 22033; (703) 631-6100. Fax, (703) 631-6169. Lt. Gen. Susan Lawrence (USA, Ret.), President. Customer Service Center, (703) 631-6158. Toll-free, (800) 336-4583.*
General email, service@afcea.org
Web, www.afcea.org/site, Twitter, @AFCEA and Facebook, www.facebook.com/AFCEA.International

Membership: industrial organizations, scientists, military and government personnel. Develops networking and educational opportunities and providing them in an ethical forum. This enables military, government, industry and academia to align technology and strategy to meet the needs of those who serve. Consults with the Defense Dept. and other federal agencies on design and maintenance of command, control, communications, computer, and intelligence systems; holds events displaying latest communications products.

American Society of Naval Engineers (ASNE), *1423 Powhatan St., #1, Alexandria, VA 22314; (703) 836-6727. Fax, (703) 836-7491. D. (Ike) Kid Lumme (USN, Ret.), Executive Director.*
General email, asnehq@navalengineers.org
Web, www.navalengineers.org, Twitter, @NavalEngineers and Facebook, www.facebook.com/navalengineers

Membership: civilian, active duty, and retired naval engineers. Provides forum for an exchange of information between industry and government involving all phases of naval engineering.

Analytic Services Inc. (ANSER), *5275 Leesburg Pike, #N5000, Falls Church, VA 22041; (703) 416-2000. Steve Hopkins, Chief Executive Officer. Toll-free, (877) 339-4389.*
Web, www.anser.org and Twitter, @ANSERCorp

Systems analysis organization funded by government contracts. Conducts weapons systems analysis.

Center for Advanced Defense Studies, *1201 Eye St. N.W., #200, 20005; (202) 289-3332. Lt. Col. David E. A. Johnson (USA, Ret.), Executive Director.*
General email, info@c4ads.org
Web, https://c4ads.org, Twitter, @C4ADS and Press, communications@c4ads.org

Conducts field research in conflict areas. Awards annual fellowships to experts in weapons trafficking, conflict prevention, terrorism, and global crime.

Institute for Defense Analyses (IDA), *730 E. Glebe Rd., Alexandria, VA 22305-3086; (703) 845-2000. Fax, (703) 845-2588. Norton Schwartz, President. Library, (703) 845-2087.*

General email, Communications@ida.org
Web, www.ida.org and Twitter, @IDA_org

Operates three federally funded research and development centers that focus on national security and defense: Systems and Analysis Center, Science and Technology Policy Institute, and Center for Communication and Computing. Conducts research, systems evaluation, and policy analysis for Defense Dept. and other agencies.

Johns Hopkins University Applied Physics Laboratory, *11100 Johns Hopkins Rd., Laurel, MD 20723-6099; (240) 228-5000. Ralph D. Semmel, Director. Public Affairs, (240) 228-5020.*
Web, www.jhuapl.edu, Twitter, @JHUAPL and Facebook, www.facebook.com/JHUAPL

Research and development organization that conducts research for the Defense Dept. and other federal agencies. Interests include defense, national security, and space technologies.

Johns Hopkins University Applied Physics Laboratory, *Research and Exploratory Development, 11100 Johns Hopkins Rd., Laurel, MD 20723-6099; (240) 228-5000. Jim Schatz, Mission Area Executive. Press, (240) 228-5020.*
Web, www.jhuapl.edu/OurWork/ResearchandExploratoryDevelopment

Research and development laboratory that seeks to improve warfighter survivability, sustainment, and performance through battlefield trauma prevention and mitigation, along with medical device evaluation and development. Programs include improvement of soldier protection equipment, the development of a neurally integrated upper extremity prosthetic, and blast-related traumatic brain injury research.

LMI, *7940 Jones Branch Dr., Tysons, VA 22102; (703) 917-9800. Doug Wagoner, President. Toll-free, (800) 213-4817.*
Web, www.lmi.org, Twitter, @LMI_org and Facebook, www.facebook.com/LMI.org

Conducts research for federal civilian and defense agencies; including transportation, logistics, supply and maintenance, force management, acquisition, health systems, international programs, energy and environment, mathematical modeling, weapons support, installations, operations, and information systems. (Formerly Logistics Management Institute.)

Military Operations Research Society (MORS), *2111 Wilson Blvd., #700, Alexandria, VA 22201; (703) 933-9070. Fax, (703) 933-9066. Jennifer Ferat, Chief Executive Officer, (703) 933-9074.*
General email, morsoffice@mors.org
Web, www.mors.org, Twitter, @MORS_News and Facebook, www.facebook.com/groups/114364660845

Membership: Defense analysts, operators and managers from government, industry and academia. Fosters information exchange; promotes professional development and high ethical standards; educates members on emerging issues, analytical techniques, and applications of research. Publishes *Phalanx* and the *MOR Journal*.

National Academies of Sciences, Engineering, and Medicine (NASEM), *Air Force Studies Board,* Keck Center, 500 5th St. N.W., 9th Floor, 20001; (202) 334-3111. Gen. Ellen M. Pawlikowski (USAF, Ret.), Chair; Ellen Chou, Director.
General email, afsb@nas.edu

Web, www.nationalacademies.org/afsb/air-force-studies-board

Supports activities related to the development of science and technology within the Air Force. Interests of study include fuel efficiency, acquisition processes, and assuring the future scientific and technical qualification of Air Force personnel.

National Academies of Sciences, Engineering, and Medicine (NASEM), *Army Research and Development Board,* Keck Center, 500 5th St. N.W., 9th Floor, 20001; (202) 334-3218. Katharina McFarland, Chair; William (Bruno) Millonig, Director, (202) 334-3952.
General email, theboard@nas.edu

Web, www.nationalacademies.org/board/board-on-army-research-and-development

Provides classified and unclassified forums for leading technical and intelligence experts to evaluate scientific and technology approaches to facilitate threat-informed acquisition decisions.

National Academies of Sciences, Engineering, and Medicine (NASEM), *Human-Systems Integration Board,* Keck Center, 500 5th St. N.W., 11th Floor, 20001; (202) 334-2326. Fax, (202) 334-2210. Mary Ellen O'Connell, Director (Acting), (202) 334-2607.
General email, bohsi@nas.edu

Web, www.nationalacademies.org/bohsi/board-on-human-systems-integration

Conducts studies on human factors and human-systems integration. Areas of research include nuclear safety and military simulation.

National Academies of Sciences, Engineering, and Medicine (NASEM), *Naval Studies Board,* Keck Center, 500 5th St. N.W., 9th Floor, 20001; (202) 334-3523. Fax, (202) 334-3695. Gary Roughead, Chair; Ellen Y. Chou, Director.
General email, nsb@nas.edu

Web, www.nationalacademies.org/nsb/naval-studies-board

Conducts research and supports activities that help provide scientific and technical planning advice to the Navy.

Society of American Military Engineers, 1420 King St., #100, Alexandria, VA 22314; (703) 549-3800. Brig. Gen. Joseph Schroedel (USA, Ret.), Executive Director, ext. 110.
General email, conference@same.org

Web, www.same.org and Twitter, @same_national

Membership: military and civilian engineers, architects, and construction professionals. Conducts workshops and conferences on subjects related to military engineering.

SRI International, *Washington Office,* 1100 Wilson Blvd., #2800, Arlington, VA 22209; (703) 524-2053. David Parekh, Corporate Executive Officer.
Web, www.sri.com and Twitter, @SRI_Intl

Research organization supported by government and private contracts. Conducts research on military technology, including lasers and computers. Other interests include strategic planning and armed forces interdisciplinary research. (Headquarters in Menlo Park, Calif.)

EMERGENCY PREPAREDNESS AND RESPONSE

General

▶AGENCIES

Army Corps of Engineers *(Defense Dept.),* *Contingency Operations and Office of Homeland Security,* 441 G St. N.W., 20314-1000; (202) 761-4601. Fax, (202) 761-5096. Stephen L. Hill, Director of Contingency Operations.
General email, hq-publicaffairs@usace.army.mil

Web, www.usace.army.mil

Assists military combatant commands, as well as federal, state, and local emergency management and emergency response organizations, with mitigation, planning, training, and exercises to build and sustain capabilities to protect from and respond to any emergency or disaster, including natural disasters and terrorist attacks involving weapons of mass destruction.

Civil Air Patrol National Capital Wing, 200 McChord St. S.W., #111, Joint Base Anacostia-Bolling, 20032; (202) 767-4405. Col. David E. Sterling, Wing Commander.
General email, cc@natcapwing.org

Web, www.natcapwg.cap.gov

Official auxiliary of the U.S. Air Force. Conducts search-and-rescue missions for the Air Force; participates in emergency airlift and disaster relief missions. (Headquarters at Maxwell Air Force Base, Ala.)

Elementary and Secondary Education (OESE) *(Education Dept.),* *Disaster Recovery Unit (DRU),* Lyndon B. Johnson Bldg., 400 Maryland Ave. S.W., 20202-6244; (202) 401-8368. Meredith Miller, Director.
Web, https://oese.ed.gov/offices/disaster-recovery-unit

Leads departmental efforts in disaster recovery work following federally declared natural disasters. Manages the following grant programs: Emergency Impact Aid for Displaced Students, Immediate Aid to Restart School Operations, Assistance for Homeless Children and Youth, and Project School Emergency Response to Violence.

Federal Emergency Management Agency (FEMA) *(Homeland Security Dept.),* 500 C St. S.W., 20472 (mailing address: P.O. Box 10055, Hyattsville, MD 20782-8055); (202) 646-3900. Deanne Criswell, Administrator. FEMA helpline,

(800) 621-3362. Locator, (202) 646-2500. Press, (202) 646-3272. Toll-free, 800-621-FEMA. TTY, (800) 462-7585. General email, askIA@fema.dhs.gov

Web, www.fema.gov, Twitter, @fema, Facebook, www.facebook.com/FEMA and YouTube, www.youtube.com/user/FEMA

Manages federal response and recovery efforts following natural disasters, terrorist attacks, and all other kinds of national emergencies. Initiates mitigation activities; works with state and local emergency managers; manages the National Flood Insurance Program.

Federal Emergency Management Agency (FEMA) *(Homeland Security Dept.), Resilience, Federal Insurance and Mitigation Administration, 400 C St. S.W., 20472; (202) 646-2781. Nimisha Agorwal, Deputy Associate Administrator (Acting).*
Web, www.fema.gov/about/offices/insurance-mitigation

Administers federal insurance programs, including the National Flood Insurance Program, to reduce future losses from floods, earthquakes, tornadoes, and other natural disasters. Makes low-cost flood insurance available to eligible homeowners.

Federal Emergency Management Agency (FEMA) *(Homeland Security Dept.), Resilience, Grant Programs, 400 C St. S.W, #3NW, 20472-3645; (800) 368-6498. Christopher Logan, Assistant Administrator (Acting). General email, askcsid@fema.gov*
Web, www.fema.gov/grants

Administers and manages nondisaster grants to states, local communities, regional authorities, and tribal jurisdictions to mitigate hazards and to prevent, deter, respond to, and recover from terrorism and other threats to national security.

Federal Emergency Management Agency (FEMA) *(Homeland Security Dept.), Resilience, National Preparedness, Technological Hazards, 400 C St. S.W., MS 3600, 20472-3025; (202) 646-3158. Fax, (703) 308-0324. Michael Casey, Director.*
Web, www.fema.gov/emergency-managers/practitioners/hazardous-response-capabilities

Oversees the Radiological Emergency Preparedness Program to ensure that the health and safety of citizens living around commercial nuclear power plants would be adequately protected in the event of a nuclear power plant accident; the Chemical Stockpile Emergency Preparedness Program (CSEPP), a partnership between the FEMA and the U.S. Dept. of the Army that provides emergency preparedness assistance and resources to communities surrounding the Army's chemical warfare agent stockpiles; and the Federal Radiological Preparedness Coordinating Committee, a national-level forum for the development and coordination of radiological prevention and preparedness policies and procedures.

Federal Emergency Management Agency (FEMA) *(Homeland Security Dept.), Response and Recovery (ORR), 500 C St. S.W., 20472; (202) 212-1946. David Bibo, Associate Administrator (Acting).*
Web, www.fema.gov/office-response-and-recovery

Responsible for coordination of the president's disaster relief program. Comprises the Doctrine and Policy Office, Business Management Office, Response Directorate, Recovery Directorate, Logistics Management Directorate, and Field Operations Directorate.

Health and Human Services Dept. (HHS), *National Disaster Medical System (NDMS), 200 Independence Ave. S.W, #415I, 20201; (202) 475-2479. Vacant, Branch Chief. Public Affairs, (202) 205-8114. General email, NDMSsupprt@hhs.gov*
Web, http://phe.gov/ndms

Provides local, state, and tribal governments with medical response, patient movement, and the definitive care of victims of major emergencies and presidentially declared disasters, including those resulting from natural, technological, and human-caused hazards, such as transportation accidents and acts of terrorism involving chemical, biological, radiological, nuclear, and explosive weapons. Maintains a national capability to provide medical, veterinary, and mortuary teams, supplies, and equipment at the sites of disasters, and in transit from the impacted area into participating definitive care facilities.

National Nuclear Security Administration (NNSA) *(Energy Dept.), Emergency Operations, 1000 Independence Ave. S.W., #GH060, 20585; (202) 586-9892. Fax, (202) 586-3904. Hon. Charles L. Hopkins III, Associate Administrator.*
Web, www.energy.gov/nnsa/nnsa-offices/emergency-operations

Works to ensure coordinated Energy Dept. responses to energy-related emergencies. Recommends policies to mitigate the effects of energy-supply crises on the United States; recommends government responses to energy emergencies.

Small Business Administration (SBA), *Disaster Assistance, 409 3rd St. S.W., #6050, 20416; (202) 205-6734. Fax, (202) 205-7728. Francisco Sanchez, Associate Administrator. Service Center, (800) 659-2955.*
Web, www.sba.gov/about-sba/sba-locations/headquarters-offices/office-disaster-assistance and General email, disastercustomerassistance@sba.gov

Provides victims of physical disasters with disaster and economic injury loans for homes, businesses, and personal property. Lends funds for uncompensated losses incurred from any disaster declared by the president of the United States or the administrator of the SBA.

U.S. Coast Guard (USCG) *(Homeland Security Dept.), Counterterrorism and Defense Policy, 2703 Martin Luther King Jr. Ave. S.E., MS 7516, 20593-7516; (202) 372-2101. Fax, (202) 372-8361. RADM Scott w. Clendenin, Assistant Commandant for Response Policy.*
Web, www.dco.uscg.mil/Our-Organization/Assistant-Commandant-for-Response-Policy-CG-5R/Office-of-Counterterrorism-Defense-Operations-Policy-CG-ODO/CG

Ensures that the Coast Guard can mobilize effectively during national emergencies, including those resulting from enemy military attack.

Federal Emergency Management Agency

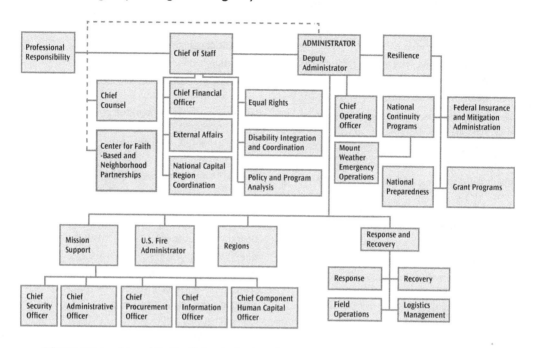

- - - Indicates a support or advisory relationship with the unit rather than a direct reporting relationship

U.S. Coast Guard (USCG) *(Homeland Security Dept.),* *National Response Center,* 2100 2nd St. S.W., #2111B, 20593-0001; (202) 372-2097. Dana S. Tulis, Director. Hotline, (800) 424-8802. Local, (202) 267-2675. *General email, NRC@uscg.mil*

Web, www.nrc.uscg.mil and www.epa.gov/emergency-response/national-response-center

Maintains 24-hour hotline for reporting oil, biological, radiological, and chemical discharges in the environment. Notifies appropriate federal officials to reduce the effects of accidents. Monitors suspicious activities and security breaches in U.S. waters. Works cooperatively with the Environmental Protection Agency.

U.S. Coast Guard (USCG) *(Homeland Security Dept.),* *Response Policy (CG-5R),* 2703 Martin Luther Jr. Ave. S.W., MS 7318, 20593-7318; (202) 372-2011. (202) 372-2014. Rear Adm. Douglas Fears, Assistant Commandant. *Web, www.dco.uscg.mil/Our-Organization/Assistant-Commandant-for-Response-Policy-CG-5R*

Conducts search-and-rescue and polar and domestic ice-breaking operations.

U.S. Fire Administration *(Federal Emergency Management Agency),* 16825 S. Seton Ave., Emmitsburg, MD 21727-8998; (301) 447-1000. Lori Moore-Merrell, Administrator. Press, (301) 447-1853. Toll-free, (800) 238-3358. Toll-free National Fire Incident Reporting System Help Desk (NFIRS), (888) 382-3827. Toll-free publications, (800) 561-3356. *Web, www.usfa.fema.gov, Twitter, @usfire and Facebook, www.facebook.com/usfire*

Provides public education, first responder training, technology, and data initiatives in an effort to prevent losses due to fire and related emergencies. Administers the Emergency Management Institute and the National Fire Academy for firefighters and emergency management personnel.

▶**CONGRESS**

For a listing of relevant congressional committees and sub-committees, please see pages 634–635 or the Appendix.

▶**INTERNATIONAL ORGANIZATIONS**

European Union, *Delegation to the United States of America,* 2175 K St. N.W., 20037; (202) 862-9500. Stavros Lambrinidis, Ambassador. *General email, delegation-usa-info@eeas.europa.eu*

Web, www.euintheus.org, Twitter, @EUintheUS, Facebook, www.facebook.com/EUintheUS and Twitter, Ambassador, @EUAAmbUS

Information and public affairs office in the United States for the European Union. Advances collaboration on civilian and military crisis management and conflict prevention initiatives to ensure global security. (Headquarters in Brussels.)

▶**NONGOVERNMENTAL**

American Red Cross, *Disaster Preparedness and Response,* 431 18th St. N.W., 20006; (202) 303-5214, ext. 1. Gail J. McGovern, President. Press and public

Domestic Disaster Relief Organizations

Adventist Development & Relief Agency International, (800) 424-2372; www.adra.org

American Red Cross, (800) 733-2767 or (202) 303-5214; www.redcross.org

AmeriCares, (203) 658-9500; www.americares.org

Ananda Marga Universal Relief Team, Inc., (301) 738-7122; www.amurt.net

Catholic Charities USA, (703) 549-1390; www.catholiccharitiesusa.org

Catholic Relief Services, (877) 435-7277 or (888) 277-7575; www.crs.org

Children's Miracle Network (Osmond Foundation for the Children of the World), (801) 214-7400; www.cmn.org

Church World Service, (800) 297-1516 or (574) 264-3102; www.cwsglobal.org

Direct Relief International, (805) 964-4767 or (800) 676-1638; www.directrelief.org

Episcopal Relief & Development, (855) 312-4325; www.episcopalrelief.org

Federal Employee Education and Assistance Fund (FEEA), (202) 554-0007; www.feea.org

Feed the Children, (800) 627-4556; www.feedthechildren.org

Feeding America, (800) 771-2303; www.feedingamerica.org

Habitat for Humanity International, (800) 422-4828; www.habitat.org

HealthRight International, (212) 226-9890; www.healthright.org

Help the Children, (888) 818-4483; www.helpthechildren.org

InterAction, www.interaction.org

International Federation of Red Cross/Red Crescent, (212) 338-0161; www.ifrc.org

International Rescue Committee, (212) 551-3000; www.rescue.org

Islamic Relief USA, (855) 447-1001; www.irusa.org

Medical Teams International, (800) 959-4325; www.medicalteams.org

Mercy Corps, (202) 463-7383; www.mercycorps.org

Operation Blessing, (800) 730-2537; www.ob.org

Operation USA, (323) 413-2353; www.opusa.org

Oxfam America, (800) 776-9326 or (202) 496-1180; www.oxfamamerica.org

Rebuilding Together, (800) 473-4229; www.rebuildingtogether.org

Save the Children, (800) 728-3843 or (203) 221-4000; www.savethechildren.org

United Methodist Committee on Relief, (800) 554-8583; www.umcor.org

United Way Worldwide, (703) 836-7112; www.unitedway.org

World Health Organization (Pan American Health Organization), (202) 974-3000; www.who.int or www.paho.org

World Vision, (888) 511-6548; www.worldvision.org

---

inquiries, *(202) 303-5551. Toll-free, (800) 733-2767. Training/Certification, 800-RED-CROSS. Public Inquiry, (202) 303-4498.*

Web, www.redcross.org, Twitter, @redcross, Facebook, www.facebook.com/redcross and Disaster preparedness, www.redcross.org/about-us/our-work/distaster-relief .html

Chartered by Congress to administer disaster relief. Provides disaster victims with food, shelter, first aid, medical care, and access to other available resources. Feeds emergency workers; handles inquiries from concerned family members outside the disaster area; helps promote disaster preparedness and prevention through training. Recruits blood donors and maintains blood stocks in the United States.

National Assn. of State EMS Officials (NASEMSO), *201 Park Washington Ct., Falls Church, VA 22046-4527; (703) 538-1799. Fax, (703) 241-5603. Dia Gainor, Executive Director.*
General email, info@nasemso.org

Web, www.nasemso.org, Twitter, @NASEMSO and Facebook, www.facebook.com/NASEMSO1

Supports development of effective emergency medical services (EMS) systems at the local, state, and regional levels. Works to formulate national EMS policy and foster communication and sharing among state EMS officials.

National Emergency Management Assn., *Washington Office, 444 N. Capitol St. N.W., #401, 20001-1557; (202) 624-5460. Fax, (202) 624-5875. Matt Cowles, Deputy Director, (202) 624-5459; Erica Bournemann, President. General email, mcowles@csg.org*

Web, www.nemaweb.org and Twitter, @NEMA_WEB

Professional association of state emergency managers. Promotes improvement of emergency management through strategic partnerships and innovative programs. (Member of the Council of State Governments; headquarters in Lexington, Ky.)

Salvation Army Disaster Service, *615 Slaters Lane, Alexandria, VA 22314; (703) 684-5500. Kenneth G. Hodder, National Commander. Web, https://disaster.salvationarmyusa.org, Twitter, @salarmyeds and Facebook, www.facebook.com/ SalArmyEDS*

Provides U.S. and international disaster victims and rescuers with emergency support, including food, clothing, and counseling services.

Union of Concerned Scientists, *Nuclear Power, 1825 K St. N.W., 20006; (202) 223-6133. Edwin Lyman, Director, Nuclear Power Safety.*
General email, ucs@ucsusa.org

Web, www.ucsusa.org/energy/nuclear-power, Twitter, @ucsusa, Facebook, www.facebook.com/ unionofconcernedscientists and YouTube, www.youtube .com/user/ConcernedScientists

Science advocacy organization with interests in the areas of clean energy, clean transportation, food and agriculture, global warming, nuclear power, and nuclear weapons. Combines technical analysis, education and advocacy, and engagement with the public and scientific communities concerned with U.S. nuclear power policy and ability to respond to nuclear accidents. Interests include nuclear waste storage, storage facility security measures, safe generation of fissure chain reactions, and reactor design.

Coordination and Partnerships

▶**AGENCIES**

Bureau of Political-Military Affairs (PM) *(State Dept.), State-Defense Integration (SDI), 2201 C St. N.W., #1805, 20520; (202) 647-7508. Debby Robinson, Director, (202) 647-4081.*
Web, www.state.gov/bureau-of-political-military-affairs- office-of-state-defense-integration-pm-sdi

Military exercise liaison between State Dept. and Defense Dept. Manages the Foreign Policy Advisor (POLAD) program to advise U.S. military combatant and component commanders about military operations, planning, and exercises. Supports the Military Advisor (MILAD) program to assign U.S. military personnel to State Dept. offices to advise on military operations and exercises, postconflict reconstruction, counterterrorism, and Pentagon approval processes.

Federal Bureau of Investigation (FBI) *(Justice Dept.), National Joint Terrorism Task Force, 935 Pennsylvania Ave. N.W., 20535-0001; (571) 280-5688. Fax, (571) 280-6922. Vacant, Chief; Jill Sanborn, Assistant Director Counterterrorism Division. Public Affairs, (202) 324-0201.*
Web, www.fbi.gov/investigate/terrorism/joint-terrorism- task-forces

Group of more than 50 agencies from the fields of intelligence, public safety, and federal, state, and local law enforcement that collects terrorism information and intelligence and funnels it to the more than five hundred JTTFs (teams of local, state, and federal agents based at FBI field offices), various terrorism units within the FBI, and partner agencies. Helps the FBI with terrorism investigations.

Federal Bureau of Investigation (FBI) *(Justice Dept.), National Security Branch (NSB), Counterterrorism Division, 935 Pennsylvania Ave. N.W., #4204, 20535;*

(202) 324-2770. Fax, (202) 324-7050. Timothy Langan, Assistant Director. National security hotline, (202) 324-3000. Press, (202) 324-3691.
Web, www.fbi.gov/investigate/terrorism#related-webpages

Collects, analyzes, and shares information and intelligence with authorities to combat international terrorism operations within the United States and in support of extraterritorial investigations, domestic terrorism operations, and counterterrorism. Maintains the Joint Terrorism Task Force, which includes representatives from the Defense Dept., Energy Dept., Federal Emergency Management Agency, CIA, U.S. Customs and Border Protection, U.S. Secret Service, and Immigration and Customs Enforcement.

Federal Bureau of Investigation (FBI) *(Justice Dept.), National Security Branch (NSB), Terrorist Screening Center (TSC), 935 Pennsylvania Ave. N.W., 20535; (571) 350-5678. Charles H. Kable, Director. Press, (571) 350-6397. Toll-free, (866) 872-5678.*
General email, tsc@tsc.gov

Web, www.fbi.gov/about/leadership-and-structure/ national-security-branch/tsc and Press, media@tsc.gov

Coordinates access to terrorist watch lists from multiple agencies. Provides operational support to federal screeners and state and local law enforcement officials.

Federal Bureau of Investigation (FBI) *(Justice Dept.), Partner Engagement (OPE), 935 Pennsylvania Ave. N.W., #7128, 20535; (202) 324-7126. George P. Beach II, Assistant Director.*
General email, olec@leo.gov

Web, www.fbi.gov/about/partnerships/office-of-partner- engagement

Advises FBI executives on the use of state and local law enforcement and resources in criminal, cyber, and counterterrorism investigations. Coordinates the bureau's intelligence-sharing and technological efforts with state and local law enforcement. Serves as a liaison with the Homeland Security Dept. and other federal entities.

Federal Emergency Management Agency (FEMA) *(Homeland Security Dept.), Emergency Management Institute, 16825 S. Seton Ave., Emmitsburg, MD 21727; (301) 447-1000. Fax, (301) 447-1658. Jeffrey Stern, Superintendent, (301) 447-1286.*
Web, www.training.fema.gov/EMI

Provides federal, state, tribal, and local government personnel and some private organizations engaged in emergency management with technical, professional, and vocational training. Educational programs include hazard mitigation, emergency preparedness, and disaster response.

Federal Emergency Management Agency (FEMA) *(Homeland Security Dept.), Resilience, 500 C St. S.W., 20472; (202) 646-3100. Fax, (202) 786-0851. Victoria Salinas, Deputy Administrator (Acting). Disaster Assistance, 800-621-FEMA. TTY, (800) 462-7585.*
Web, www.fema.gov/about/offices/resilience, National Incident Management System (NIMS), www.fema.gov/ national-incident-management-system and Regional

NIMS Coordinators, www.fema.gov/fema-regional-nims-contacts

Coordination of preparedness and protection-related activities throughout FEMA, including grants, planning, training, exercises, individual and community preparedness, assessments, lessons learned, continuity of government, and national capital region coordination. Includes the following offices and components: Federal Insurance and Mitigation Administration, Grant Programs Directorate, National Continuity Programs, and National Preparedness Directorate. Oversees the National Incident Management System (NIMS). Integrates federal, state, local, and tribal emergency response and preparedness practices into a national framework. Promotes standardized structures and procedures and interoperable communications systems. Operates ten regional offices.

Federal Emergency Management Agency (FEMA) *(Homeland Security Dept.), Resilience, National Continuity Programs, 500 C St. S.W., 20472; (202) 646-4145. Fax, (202) 646-3921. Michael George, Assistant Administrator (Acting).*
Web, www.fema.gov/about/offices/continuity

Responsible for the coordination of all Federal Emergency Management Agency national security programs. Manages Integrated Public Alert Warning System (IPAWS).

Federal Emergency Management Agency (FEMA) *(Homeland Security Dept.), Resilience, National Preparedness, Individual and Community Preparedness, 500 C St. S.W., 20472; (800) 621-3362. Alex Amparo, Assistant Administrator. Helpline, (866) 222-3580.*
General email, citizencorps@dhs.gov
Web, www.ready.gov/citizen-corps

Conducts research on individual, business, and community preparedness. Administers Citizen Corps, a national network of state, territory, tribal, and local councils that coordinate with local first responders to develop community-specific public education, outreach, training, and volunteer opportunities that address community preparedness and resiliency.

Financial Crimes Enforcement Network *(Treasury Dept.), P.O. Box 39, Vienna, VA 22183-0039; (703) 905-3591. Himamauli Das, Director. Press, (703) 905-3770. Toll-free, (800) 767-2825.*
General email, frc@fincen.gov
Web, www.fincen.gov

Administers an information network in support of federal, state, and local law enforcement agencies in the prevention and detection of terrorist financing, money-laundering operations, and other financial crimes. Administers the Bank Secrecy Act.

Homeland Security Dept. (DHS), *Bombing Prevention (OBP), 3801 Nebraska Ave. N.W., 20528; (703) 235-8147. Sean Haglund, Associate Director. CISA, (888) 282-0870.*
General email, OBP@cisa.dhs.gov
Web, www.cisa.gov/office-bombing-prevention-obp

Coordinates national efforts to detect, prevent, and respond to terrorist improvised explosive device (IED) threats and leads the Homeland Security Dept. efforts to implement the National Counter-IED policy. Works with federal agencies, state and local governments, and the private sector to promote information sharing and IED awareness. Maintains database on equipment, training, and assets required for effective response to IED threats. Sponsors Technical Resource for Incident Prevention (TRIPwire), an online information-sharing network for bomb technicians and other law enforcement officials.

Homeland Security Dept. (DHS), *Office of Strategy, Policy, and Plans, Bldg. 81, 3801 Nebraska Ave. N.W., #17, 20528; (202) 282-8484. Robert Silvers, Under Secretary. Press, (202) 282-8010.*
General email, private.sector@dhs.gov
Web, www.dhs.gov/office-policy

Works to facilitate outreach to industry and flow of information between industry and the department on security topics ranging from protecting critical infrastructure from sabotage to securing computer networks from hackers. Administers the Loaned Executive Program to partner with executive-level experts on a volunteer basis for specific needs.

Homeland Security Dept. (DHS), *Operations Coordination, Bldg. 3, 3801 Nebraska Ave. N.W., #01107, 20528; (202) 282-9580. Rear Adm. Christopher Tomney (USGC, Ret.), Director.*
Web, www.dhs.gov/office-operations-coordination

Collects and fuses intelligence and enforcement activities information that may have a terrorist nexus from a variety of federal, state, territorial, tribal, local, and private sector partners to continually monitor the nation's threat environment. Coordinates incident management activities within the department and with state governors, homeland security advisors, law enforcement partners, and critical infrastructure operators in all states and major urban areas nationwide.

Homeland Security Dept. (DHS), *Partnership and Engagement (OPE), 245 Murray Lane S.W., 20528-0075; Eve Millona, Assistant Secretary. State and Local Law Enforcement, (202) 282-9545.*
Web, www.dhs.gov/partnership-engagement

Coordinates agency outreach efforts with critical stakeholders nationwide, including state, local, tribal, territorial governments, elected officials, law enforcement, the private sector, and colleges and universities to ensure a unified approach to external engagement.

Transportation Dept. (DOT), *Intelligence, Security, and Emergency Response, 1200 New Jersey Ave. S.E., #56125, 20590; (202) 366-6525. Fax, (202) 366-7261. Richard Chávez, Director.*
Web, www.transportation.gov/mission/administrations/intelligence-security-emergency-response

Advises the secretary on transportation intelligence and security policy. Develops, coordinates, and reviews transportation emergency preparedness programs for use in emergencies affecting national defense and in emergencies caused by natural and man-made disasters and crisis situations.

Transportation Security Administration (TSA)
(Homeland Security Dept.), Freedom Center, 13555 EDS Dr., Herndon, VA 20171 (mailing address: TSOC Annex, 601 S. 12th St., Arlington, VA 22202); (866) 655-7023. Vacant, Deputy Administrator.
Web, www.tsa.gov

Operations center that provides continual federal, state, and local coordination, communications, and domain awareness for all of the Homeland Security Dept.'s transportation-related security activities worldwide. Transportation domains include highway, rail, shipping, and aviation.

▶CONGRESS

For a listing of relevant congressional committees and subcommittees, please see pages 634–635 or the Appendix.

▶INFORMATION SHARING AND ANALYSIS CENTERS

A 1998 decision directive issued by President Bill Clinton defined various infrastructure industries critical to the national economy and public well-being. The directive proposed the creation of Information Sharing and Analysis Centers (ISACs), which would be established by each critical infrastructure industry to communicate with its members, its government partners, and other ISACs about threat indications, vulnerabilities, and protection strategies. Each ISAC is led by a government agency or private entity. ISACs led by Washington-area agencies or companies are listed below.

Communications ISAC *(Homeland Security Dept.), c/o CISA (Cybersecurity Infrastructure Security Agency) Operational Center, 110 N. Glebe Rd., Arlington, VA 20528-0380 (mailing address: 245 Murray Lane, CISA Stop 0380, Washington, DC 20520); (888) 282-0870. Jen Easterly, Director. Press, (703) 235-2010.*
General email, info@us-cert.gov and central@cisa.dhs.gov
Web, www.us-cert.cisa.gov

Communications network that links federal civilian, military, diplomatic, and intelligence agencies with private sector cyber and telecommunications providers to protect the nation's telecommunications infrastructure and restore it from disruptions caused by attacks or natural disasters. Includes CISA, a 24/7 center for protection of computer and communications across federal, state, and local governments; intelligence and law enforcement agencies; and the private sector.

Financial Services ISAC (FS-ISAC), *12020 Sunrise Valley Dr., #230, Reston, VA 20191; (571) 252-8517. Steven Silberstein, Chief Executive Officer. Toll-free, (877) 612-2622.*
General email, admin@fsisac.com
Web, www.fsisac.com and Twitter, @FSISAC

Membership; Provides a confidential venue for sharing security vulnerabilities and solutions, including data obtained from such sources as other ISACs, law enforcement agencies, technology providers, and security associations. Works to facilitate trust, cooperation, and information sharing among its participants and assesses proactive means of mitigating cybersecurity risks. Provides exercises and training, holds regional Summits and briefings plus webinars.

Surface Transportation Information Sharing and Analysis Center (ISAC), *c/o EWA Information and Infrastructure Technologies, Inc., 13873 Park Center Rd., #200, Herndon, VA 20171-5406; (703) 478-7600. Todd Steinmetz, Program Director. Toll-free, (866) 784-7221.*
General email, st-isac@surfacetransportationisac.org
Web, www.surfacetransportationisac.org

Protects physical and electronic infrastructure of surface transportation and public transit carriers. Collects, analyzes, and distributes critical security and threat information from worldwide resources; shares best security practices and provides 24/7 immediate physical and cyberthreat warnings.

U.S. Fire Administration *(Federal Emergency Management Agency), Critical Infrastructure Protection, 16825 S. Seton Ave., Emmitsburg, MD 21727-8920; (301) 447-1325. Greg Williams, Branch Chief. National Emergency training switchboard, (301) 447-1000. Toll-free, (800) 238-3358.*
General email, emr-isac@fema.dhs.gov
Web, www.usfa.fema.gov/operations/ops_cip.html, Twitter, @usfire, Facebook, www.facebook.com/usfire and YouTube, www.youtube.co/USFireAdministration

Collects, analyzes, and disseminates information to support the critical infrastructure protection and resilience efforts of the nation's emergency services sector. Researches current physical and cyber protection issues, operates an information center, issues alerts and messages, and prepares instructional materials relevant to the emergency services community.

WaterISAC, *1620 Eye St. N.W., #500, 20006-4027; (202) 331-0479. Diane VanDe Hei, Executive Director. Toll-free, (866) 426-4722.*
General email, info@waterisac.org
Web, www.waterisac.org and Twitter, @WaterISAC

Gathers, analyzes, and disseminates threat information concerning the water community from utilities' security incident reports and agencies of the federal government. Provides the water community with access to sensitive information and resources about cyber, physical, and contamination threats.

▶NONGOVERNMENTAL

International Assn. of Chiefs of Police, *Advisory Committee for Patrol and Tactical Operations, 44 Canal Center Plaza, #200, Alexandria, VA 22314; (703) 836-6767.*

Sabrina Rhodes Fernandez, Program Manager. Toll-free, (800) 843-4227.
General email, committees@theiacp.org
Web, www.theiacp.org/workinggroup/Committee/patrol-and-tactical-operations-committee

Membership: foreign and U.S. police executives and administrators. Maintains liaison with civil defense and emergency service agencies in the United States and other nations; prepares guidelines for police cooperation with emergency and disaster relief agencies during emergencies.

National Governors Assn. (NGA), *Center for Best Practices, Homeland Security Division,* 444 N. Capitol St. N.W., #267, 20001-1512; (202) 624-5300. Timothy Blute, Director.
General email, info@nga.org
Web, www.nga.org/bestpractices/homeland-security

Provides support to governors in responding to the challenges of homeland security through technical assistance. Current national policy issues include violence prevention, energy assurance, public health emergency preparedness, and emergency management.

National Governors Assn. (NGA), *Center for Best Practices, Public Safety and Legal Counsels,* 444 N. Capitol St. N.W., #267, 20001-1512; (202) 624-5300. Ken Hardy, Director.
General email, info@nga.org
Web, www.nga.org/bestpractices/public-safety-legal-counsels

Develops solutions to states' public safety challenges. Focus includes adult criminal justice reform, opioids and stimulants addiction, corrections, school safety, human trafficking, traffic safety, and juvenile justice.

National Voluntary Organizations Active in Disaster (NVOAD), 1727 King St, Alexandria, VA 22314 (mailing address: P.O. Box 26125, Alexandria, VA 22314); (703) 778-5088. April Wood, President; Katherine Boatwright, Director of Operations.
General email, info@nvoad.org
Web, www.nvoad.org, Twitter, @NationalVOAD and Facebook, www.facebook.com/NVOAD

Membership. Seeks to promote communication, cooperation, coordination, and collaboration among voluntary agencies that participate in disaster response, relief, and recovery nationally.

Emergency Communications

▶ AGENCIES

D.C. Homeland Security and Emergency Management Agency, 2720 Martin Luther King Ave. S.E., 20032; (202) 727-2985. Fax, (202) 715-7289.
Christopher (Chris) Rodriguez, Director. TTY, (202) 730-0488.
Web, http://hsema.dc.gov, Twitter, @DC_HSEMA and Facebook, www.facebook.com/HSEMADC

Leads planning and coordination of homeland security and emergency management efforts to ensure that the District of Columbia is prepared to prevent, protect against, respond to, mitigate, and recover from all threats and hazards. Provides emergency planning services, training, and seminars. Remains updated on potential threats and hazards, and keeps the community informed of hazards and safety planning.

Defense Dept. (DoD), *White House Communications Agency,* U.S. Naval Station, Anacostia Annex, 2743 Defense Blvd. S.W., #399, 20373-5815; (202) 757-6706. (202) 757-5150. Col. Joy M. Kaczor Jr. (USAF), Vice Commacdor.
Web, www.whitehousecommsagency.mil

Responsible for presidential communications.

Federal Communications Commission (FCC), *Emergency Alert System,* 45 L St. N.E., 20554; (202) 418-1300. Debra Jordan, Public Safety Bureau Chief, (202) 418-7849. FCC 24/7 Operations Center, (202) 418-1122.
General email, eas@fcc.gov
Web, www.fcc.gov/general/emergency-alert-system-eas-0#block-menu-block4 and FCC 24/7 Operations Center, FCCOPCenter@fcc.gov

Develops rules and regulations for the Emergency Alert System, which is the national warning system the president would use to communicate with the public during a national emergency in the event that access to normal media outlets becomes unavailable. It is also used by state and local officials for weather-related and man-made emergencies.

Federal Communications Commission (FCC), *Public Safety and Homeland Security Bureau (PSHSB),* 45 L St. N.E., 20554; (888) 225-5322. Fax, (866) 418-0232. Lisa M. Fowlkes, Chief, (202) 418-7452. 24-Hour Operations Center, (202) 418-1122. Press, (202) 418-0500.
General email, fccopcenter@fcc.gov
Web, www.fcc.gov/public-safety-homeland-security

Develops, recommends, and administers the FCC's policies pertaining to public safety communications issues, including 911 and E911. Responsible for the operability and interoperability of public safety communications, communications infrastructure protection and disaster response, and network security and reliability. Administers the Emergency Response Interoperability Network (ERIC), establishing and maintaining a broadband public safety wireless network, including authentication and encryption.

Homeland Security Dept. (DHS), *Cybersecurity and Infrastructure Security Agency (CISA), Emergency Communications Division (ECD),* 245 Murray Lane, MS 0615, Arlington, VA 20528-0615; Billie Bob Brown Jr., Executive Assistant Director. CISA Service Desk, (888) 282-0870.
General email, ECD@cisa.dhs.gov
Web, www.cisa.gov/emergency-communications-division

Ensures that the federal government has the necessary communications capabilities to permit its continued operation during a national emergency; provides emergency responders and government officials with communications support as it directs the nation's recovery from a major disaster; provides training, coordination, tools, and guidance to help federal, state, local, tribal, territorial, and industry partners develop their emergency communications capabilities.

National Communications System *(Homeland Security Dept.), President's National Security Telecommunications Advisory Committee,* 245 Murray Ln., 20528-0380; John Donovan, Chair. CISA central, (888) 282-0870. DHS switchboard, (202) 282-8000.
General email, central@cisa.gov
Web, www.cisa.gov/nstac, Twitter, @CISAgov and Facebook, www.facebook.com/CISA

Advises the president, the National Security Council, the Office of Science and Technology Policy, and the Office of Management and Budget on specific measures to improve telecommunications for the federal government. Areas of major focus include strengthening national security, enhancing cybersecurity, maintaining the global communications infrastructure, assuring communications for disaster response, and addressing infrastructure interdependencies and dependencies.

U.S. Coast Guard (USCG) *(Homeland Security Dept.), National Response Center,* 2100 2nd St. S.W., #2111B, 20593-0001; (202) 372-2097. Dana S. Tulis, Director. Hotline, (800) 424-8802. Local, (202) 267-2675.
General email, NRC@uscg.mil
Web, www.nrc.uscg.mil and www.epa.gov/emergency-response/national-response-center

Maintains 24-hour hotline for reporting oil, biological, radiological, and chemical discharges in the environment. Notifies appropriate federal officials to reduce the effects of accidents. Monitors suspicious activities and security breaches in U.S. waters. Works cooperatively with the Environmental Protection Agency.

Industrial and Military Planning and Mobilization

▶ **AGENCIES**

Bureau of Political-Military Affairs (PM) *(State Dept.), State-Defense Integration (SDI),* 2201 C St. N.W., #1805, 20520; (202) 647-7508. Debby Robinson, Director, (202) 647-4081.
Web, www.state.gov/bureau-of-political-military-affairs-office-of-state-defense-integration-pm-sdi

Military exercise liaison between State Dept. and Defense Dept. Manages the Foreign Policy Advisor (POLAD) program to advise U.S. military combatant and component commanders about military operations, planning, and exercises. Supports the Military Advisor (MILAD) program to assign U.S. military personnel to State Dept. offices to advise on military operations and exercises, post-conflict reconstruction, counterterrorism, and Pentagon approval processes.

Defense Logistics Agency *(Defense Dept.), Logistics Operations,* 8725 John Jay Kingman Rd., Fort Belvoir, VA 22060-6221; (703) 767-1600. Fax, (703) 767-1588. R. Adm. Joseph Noble (USN), Director. Press, (703) 767-6200.
Web, www.dla.mil/HQ/LogisticsOperations

Oversees management, storage, and distribution of items used to support logistics for the military services and federal agencies. Synchronizes the Defense Logistics Agency's capabilities with the combatant commands, military services, the joint staff, other combat support defense agencies, and designated federal agencies. Provides logistics policy, with an emphasis on modernizing business systems and maximizing readiness and combat logistics support.

Maritime Administration (MARAD) *(Transportation Dept.), Sealift Operations and Emergency Preparedness,* West Bldg., 1200 New Jersey Ave. S.E., W23-302, 20590; (202) 366-1031. Fax, (202) 366-8215.
Capt. Douglas M. Harrington, Deputy Associate Administrator for Federal Sealift. Federal Sealift, (202) 366-1875.
Web, www.maritime.dot.gov/ports/strong-ports/emergency-and-preparedness-response

Plans for the transition of merchant shipping from peacetime to wartime operations under the direction of the National Shipping Authority. Participates in interagency planning and policy development for maritime security-related directives. Coordinates port personnel and the military for deployments through the commercial strategic seaports. Represents the United States at the NATO Planning Board for Ocean Shipping. (The National Shipping Authority is a stand-by organization that is activated upon the declaration of a war or other national emergency.)

Maritime Administration (MARAD) *(Transportation Dept.), Ship Operations,* West Bldg., 1200 New Jersey Ave. S.E., MAR-610, MS 2, W25-336, 20590; (202) 366-1875. Kevin M. Tokarski, Associate Administrator for Strategic Sealift.
Web, www.maritime.dot.gov/strategic-sealift/office-ship-operations/office-ship-operations

Maintains the National Defense Reserve Fleet, a fleet of older vessels traded in by U.S. flag operators that are called into operation during emergencies; manages and administers the National Defense Reserve Fleet, a fleet of ships available for operation within 4 to 20 days, to meet the nation's sealift readiness requirements.

Maritime Administration (MARAD) *(Transportation Dept.), Strategic Sealift,* West Bldg., 1200 New Jersey Ave. S.E., Mar-600, MS 1, W25-330, 20590; (202) 366-5400. (202) 366-1875. Fax, (202) 366-5904. Kevin M. Tokarski, Associate Administrator; Capt. Douglas M. Harrington, Deputy Associate Administrator for Federal Sealift.
Web, www.maritime.dot.gov/national-security/strategic-sealift/strategic-sealift

Administers strategic sealift programs for the Maritime Administration and ensures that merchant shipping is available in times of war or national emergency.

►CONGRESS

For a listing of relevant congressional committees and sub-committees, please see pages 634–635 or the Appendix.

►NONGOVERNMENTAL

National Defense Industrial Assn. (NDIA), *2101 Wilson Blvd., #700, Arlington, VA 22201-3061; (703) 522-1820. Fax, (703) 522-1885. Gen. Herbert (Hawk) J. Carlisle (USAF, Ret.), Chief Executive Officer, (703) 247-2550. General email, nriveiro@NDIA.org*

Web, www.ndia.org, Twitter, @NDIAToday, Facebook, www.facebook.com/NDIAMembership and YouTube, www.youtube.com/user/NDIAToday

Membership: U.S. citizens and businesses interested in national security. Also open to individuals and businesses in nations that have defense agreements with the United States. Provides information and expertise on defense preparedness issues; works to increase public awareness of national defense preparedness through education programs; serves as a forum for dialogue between the defense industry and the government.

National Defense Transportation Assn. (NDTA), *50 S. Pickett St., #220, Alexandria, VA 22304; (703) 751-5011. Fax, (703) 823-8761. Vice Adm. William A. Brown (USN, Ret.), President. Toll-free, (844) 620-2715. Web, www.ndtahq.com, Twitter, @NDTAHQ and Facebook, www.facebook.com/ NationalDefenseTransportatoinAssociation*

Membership: transportation service companies. Maintains liaison with the Defense Dept., the Transportation Dept., and the Transportation Security Administration to prepare emergency transportation plans.

Infrastructure Protection

►AGENCIES

Army Corps of Engineers *(Defense Dept.), 441 G St. N.W., #3K05, 20314-1000; (202) 761-0011. Lt. Gen. Scott A. Spellman (USA), Chief of Engineers. General email, hq-publicaffairs@usace.army.mil*

Web, www.usace.army.mil, Twitter, @USACEHQ and Facebook, www.facebook.com/USACEHQ

Devises hurricane and storm damage reduction infrastructure.

Cybersecurity and Infrastructure Security Agency *(Homeland Security Dept.), Bldg. 410, 245 Murray Lane S.W., MS 0635, 20598; (888) 282-0870. Brandon Wales, Executive Director. Press, (703) 235-2010. General email, central@cisa.gov*

Web, www.cisa.gov, Twitter, @CISAgov and Facebook, www.facebook.com/CISA

Leads and coordinates efforts to improve the nation's cybersecurity capabilities; promotes cyber information sharing; and manages cyber risks to the nation through detection, analysis, communication, coordination, and response activities.

Energy Dept. (DOE), *Electricity Delivery and Energy Reliability (OE), 1000 Independence Ave. S.W., #8H033, 20585; (202) 586-1411. Fax, (202) 586-1472. Patricia Hoffman, Assistant Secretary (Acting). General email, OEwebmaster@hq.doe.gov*

Web, www.energy.gov/oe/office-electricity

Leads the federal response to energy emergencies, guides technology research and development on the security and reliability of the nation's energy systems, provides training and support for stakeholders, and works to assess and mitigate energy system vulnerabilities. Works in conjunction with the Homeland Security Dept. and other DOE programs, federal groups, state and local governments, and private industry.

Federal Bureau of Investigation (FBI) *(Justice Dept.), Cyber Division, 935 Pennsylvania Ave. N.W., 20535; (202) 324-7770. Fax, (202) 324-2840. Bryan A. Vorndran, Assistant Director.*

Web, www.fbi.gov/investigate/cyber

Coordinates the investigations of federal violations in which the Internet or computer networks are exploited for terrorist, foreign government–sponsored intelligence, or criminal activities, including copyright violations, fraud, pornography, child exploitation, and malicious computer intrusions.

Federal Energy Regulatory Commission (FERC) *(Energy Dept.), Energy Infrastructure Security (OEIS), 888 1st St. N.E., #9M-13, 20426; (202) 502-8867. Fax, (202) 219-2836. Joseph H. McClelland, Director, (302) 502-8867.*

Web, www.ferc.gov/about/offices/office-energy-infrastructure-security-oeis

Seeks to identify risk and vulnerability to potential physical and cyber attacks and to coordinate collaborative mitigation actions. Formulates and makes recommendations for Commission action with state and federal agencies and the energy industry.

Federal Protective Service (FPS) *(Homeland Security Dept.), 800 N. Capitol St. N.W., 5th Floor, 20002; L. Eric Patterson, Director. DHS Switchboard, (202) 282-8000.*

Web, www.dhs.gov/about-federal-protective-service

Works to ensure that appropriate levels of security are in place in General Services Administration–managed facilities throughout the United States. Conducts assessments on all GSA-controlled facilities to evaluate threats and tailor appropriate security countermeasures. Has enforcement capability to detain and arrest people, seize goods or conveyances, obtain arrest and search warrants, respond to incidents and emergency situations, provide protection during demonstrations or civil unrest, and be deputized for law enforcement response in special situations.

Homeland Security Dept. (DHS), *Cybersecurity and Infrastructure Security, Bldg. 410, 245 Murray Lane S.W.,*

MS 8570, 20528-8570; (888) 282-0870. Jen Easterly, Director. Press, (703) 235-2010. TTY, (202) 282-8000.
General email, centrak@cisa.gov

Web, www.dhs.gov/office-cybersecurity-divisiona

Works with the public and private sectors as well as international partners to enhance the security of the nation's cyber and communications infrastructure. Works with other federal agencies in developing comprehensive plans to prevent and mitigate cyber-based attacks. Identifies security vulnerabilities and coordinates warning and response procedures.

Homeland Security Dept. (DHS), *Cybersecurity and Infrastructure Security Agency (CISA),* Bldg. 5, 3801 Nebraska Ave. N.W., 20528 (mailing address: 245 Murray Lane, Washington, DC 20528-0380); Brandon Wales, Director (Acting). Press, (703) 235-2010. Service Desk, (888) 282-0870. General email, CISARegion3@hq.dhs.gov and central@cisa.gov

Web, www.cisa.gov

Identifies and assesses threats to the nation's physical and cyber infrastructure; issues warnings to prevent damage.

Interior Dept. (DOI), *Law Enforcement and Security (OLES),* 1849 C St. N.W., MS 3428-MIB, 20240; (202) 208-6319. Fax, (202) 219-1185. Robert D. MacLean, Director.
Web, www.doi.gov/pmb/oles

Provides direction, policy guidance, and oversight and coordination to the Interior Dept.'s law enforcement, intelligence, counter intelligence/insider threat, information sharing and security programs. Works to protect critical infrastructure facilities, national icons, and monuments.

Interior Dept. (DOI), *Office of Emergency Management,* 1849 C St. N.W., MS 3428, 20240; (202) 208-4679. Fax, (202) 219-3421. Tom Balint, Director. Watch Office (24/7), (202) 208-4108.
General email, DOI_Watch_Office@ios.doi.gov

Web, www.doi.gov/emergency

Establishes and disseminates policy and coordinates the development of Interior Dept. programs for emergency prevention, planning, response, and recovery that affects federal and tribal lands, facilities, infrastructure, and resources. Provides assistance to other units of government under federal laws, executive orders, interagency emergency response plans such as the National Response Framework, and other agreements.

National Aeronautics and Space Administration (NASA), *Protective Services,* 300 E St. S.W., #6T39, 20546; Joseph S. Mahaley, Assistant Administrator.
Web, www.nasa.gov/nojmo-pso

Serves as the focal point for policy formulation, oversight, coordination, and management of NASA's security, counterintelligence, counterterrorism, emergency preparedness and response, and continuity of operations programs.

National Institute of Standards and Technology (NIST) *(Commerce Dept.), Computer Security Division,* 100 Bureau Dr., MS 8930, Gaithersburg, MD 20899-8930;

(301) 975-6442. Suzanne Lightman, Senior Security Advisor.
General email, itl_inquiries@nist.gov

Web, www.nist.gov/itl/csd

Develops cybersecurity standards, guidelines, tests, and metrics to protect federal information systems. Works to improve information systems security by raising awareness of information technology risks, vulnerabilities, and protection requirements; researches and advises government agencies of risks; devises measures for cost-effective security and privacy of sensitive federal systems.

Pentagon Force Protection Agency, 9000 Defense Pentagon, 20301; (703) 697-1001. Fax, (703) 695-0681. Daniel P. Walsh, Director. Emergency line, (703) 697-5555.
General email, pfpa.pentagon.cco.mbx.general@mail.mil

Web, www.pfpa.mil, Twitter, @PFPAofficial and Facebook, www.facebook.com/PFPAOfficial

Civilian agency providing protection for the Pentagon Reservation and in DoD-occupied facilities in the National Capitol Region, for the occupants, visitors, and infrastructure, including law enforcement, security, surveillance, and crisis prevention.

Transportation Security Administration (TSA) *(Homeland Security Dept.),* TSA-1, 601 S. 12th St., 7th Floor, Arlington, VA 20598-6001; (571) 227-1398. David P. Pekoske, Administrator. Press, (571) 227-2829. TSA Contact Center, (866) 289-9673.
General email, TSA-ContactCenter@tsa.dhs.gov

Web, www.tsa.gov and Twitter, @TSA

Responsible for aviation, rail, land, and maritime transportation security. Programs and interests include the stationing of federal security directors and federal passenger screeners at airports, the Federal Air Marshal Program, improved detection of explosives, and enhanced port security.

Transportation Security Administration (TSA) *(Homeland Security Dept.), Intelligence and Analysis,* TSA-10, 601 S. 12th St., 6th Floor, Arlington, VA 22202-4220; (703) 601-3100. Nancy Nykamp, Assistant Administrator.
Web, www.tsa.gov

Conducts a range of programs designed to ensure that known or suspected terrorists do not gain access to sensitive areas of the nation's transportation system, including the Alien Flight, Registered Traveler, Secure Flight, and Transportation Worker Identification Credential programs and Hazmat Materials Truck Drivers Background Checks.

Treasury Dept., *Domestic Finance, Cybersecurity and Critical Infrastructure Protection,* 1500 Pennsylvania Ave. N.W., 20220; (202) 622-2000. Sarah Nur, Deputy Chief.
Web, https://home.treasury.gov/about/offices/management/chief-information-officer/cybersecurity

Works with the private sector to protect the nation's financial infrastructure. Maintains privacy protections for personal financial information. Develops regulations against money laundering and terrorism financing. Serves as the department's principal liaison with the Homeland Security Dept. on infrastructure protection issues.

U.S. Coast Guard (USCG) *(Homeland Security Dept.), Deputy for Operations Policy and Capabilities, 2703 Martin Luther King Jr. Ave. S.E., MS 7318, 20593-7318; (202) 372-2000. Rear Adm. Pat DeQuattro, Deputy. Web, www.dco.uscg.mil/Our-Organization/Deputy-for-Operations-Policy-and-Capabilities-DCO-D*

Establishes and enforces regulations for port safety; environmental protection; vessel safety, inspection, design, documentation, and investigation; licensing of merchant vessel personnel; and shipment of hazardous materials.

U.S. Secret Service *(Homeland Security Dept.), 245 Murray Ln. S.W., Bldg T-5, 20223; (202) 406-5800. James M. Murray, Director. Information, (202) 406-5708. Web, www.secretservice.gov and Twitter, @SecretService*

Protects the president and vice president of the United States and their immediate family members, foreign heads of state and their spouses, and other individuals as designated by the president. Investigates threats against these protectees; protects the White House, vice president's residence, and foreign missions; and plans and implements security designs for national special security events.

▶ **CONGRESS**

For a listing of relevant congressional committees and subcommittees, please see pages 634–635 or the Appendix.

Government Accountability Office (GAO), *Physical Infrastructure (PI), 441 G St. N.W., #2063, 20548 (mailing address: 441 G St. N.W., #2T23B, Washington, DC 20548); (202) 512-2834. Andrew Von Ah, Director. Web, www.gao.gov/about/careers/our-teams*

Provides guidance to Congress on the efficiency, safety, and security of the nation's infrastructure, including transportation systems, telecommunications networks, oil and gas pipelines, and federal facilities owned, funded, and operated by both the public and private sectors.

▶ **NONGOVERNMENTAL**

SANS Institute, *11200 Rockville Pike, #200, North Bethesda, MD 20852; (301) 654-7267. Fax, (301) 951-0140. Vacant, President. General email, info@sans.org*

Web, www.sans.org, Twitter, @SANSInstitute, Facebook, www.facebook.com/sansinstitute and YouTube, www.youtube.com/user/TheSANSInstitute

Develops, maintains, and makes available at no cost the largest collection of research documents about information security. Operates Internet Storm Center, the Internet's early warning system. (Also known as SysAdmin, Audit, Network, Security Institute.)

Public Health and Environment

▶ **AGENCIES**

Agency for Toxic Substances and Disease Registry (ATSDR) *(Health and Human Services Dept.), Washington Office, William Jefferson Clinton Bldg., 1200 Pennsylvania Ave. N.W., MC 5202P, 20460; (800) 232-4636. (202) 566-0844. Steve A. Jones, Regional Director, (703) 606-3885. Web, www.atsdr.cdc.gov/dro/hq.html and Twitter, @CDCEnvironment*

Works with state and other federal agencies to prevent exposure to hazardous substances from waste disposal sites. Maintains a registry of persons exposed to hazardous substances and of diseases and illnesses resulting from exposure to hazardous or toxic substances. Conducts public health assessments, health studies, surveillance activities, and health education training in communities around waste sites on the U.S. Environmental Protection Agency National Priorities List. Maintains inventory of hazardous substances and registry of sites closed or restricted because of contamination by hazardous material. (Headquarters in Atlanta, Ga.)

Assistant Secretary for Health (OASH) *(Health and Human Services Dept.), Surgeon General, Commissioned Corps of the U.S. Public Health Service (PHS), 1101 Wootton Pkwy., Plaza Level, #100, Rockville, MD 20852; (240) 453-6000. Fax, (240) 453-6109. Rear Adm. Denise Hinton, Director (Acting). Recruitment, (888) 225-3302. General email, CCHelpDesk@hhs.gov*

Web, www.usphs.gov, Twitter, @usphscc, Recruitment, usphs.gov/apply-now and Facebook, www.facebook.com/USPHS

Responsible for the overall force management, operations, and deployment readiness and response of the Commissioned Corps of the U.S. Public Health Service, uniformed service health professionals with a wide range of specialties who respond to emergencies, conduct research, and care for patients in underserved communities through federal agencies such as the National Institutes of Health, the Centers for Disease Control and Prevention, the Indian Health Service, and the Bureau of Prisons.

Bureau of Oceans and International Environmental and Scientific Affairs (OES) *(State Dept.), International Health and Biodefense (IHB), 2201 C St. N.W., #2734, 20520; (202) 647-4535. Eric Carlson, Director, (202) 647-1318. Web, www.state.gov/e/oes*

Advances the Global Health Security Agenda and focuses on issues including pandemic preparedness, new outbreaks of disease, new international policy discussions, and the impact of science and technology, medicine, and public health.

Centers for Disease Control and Prevention (CDC) *(Health and Human Services Dept.), Washington Office, 395 E St. S.W., #9100, 20201; (202) 245-0600. Fax, (202)*

245-0602. *Jeff Reczek, Director, Washington Office. Public inquiries, (800) 232-4636.*
General email, cdcwashington@cdc.gov
Web, www.cdc.gov/washington and Twitter, @CDCgov

Supports the CDC's Bioterrorism and Preparedness and Response Program, which develops federal, state, and local capacity to respond to bioterrorism. (Headquarters in Atlanta, Ga.)

Environmental Protection Agency (EPA), *Emergency Management, 1200 Pennsylvania Ave. N.W., MC 5104A, 20460; (202) 564-8600. Kathleen Salyer, Director (Acting), (703) 308-8710. Toll-free call center, (800) 424-8802.*
Web, www.epa.gov/emergency-response

Responsible for planning for and responding to the harmful effects of the release or dissemination of toxic chemicals. Areas of responsibility include helping state and local responders plan for emergencies, coordinating with key federal partners, training first responders, and providing resources in the event of a terrorist incident. Carries out preparedness and response activities for intentional and accidental CBRN (Chemical, Biological, Radiation, and Nuclear) events.

Health and Human Services Dept. (HHS), *Global Affairs (OGA), 200 Independence Ave. S.W., #639H, 20201; (202) 690-6174. (202) 260-0399. Fax, (202) 690-7127. Loyce Pace, Assistant Secretary.*
General email, globalhealth@hhs.gov
Web, www.hhs.gov/about/agencies/oga/index.html, Twitter, @HHS_Global and Twitter, @HHS_ASGA

Oversees the Office of Pandemics and Emerging Threats (PET). Works with other U.S. government agencies, foreign governments, and multilateral organizations to prevent, detect, and respond to health threats.

Health and Human Services Dept. (HHS), *National Disaster Medical System (NDMS), 200 Independence Ave. S.W, #415I, 20201; (202) 475-2479. Vacant, Branch Chief. Public Affairs, (202) 205-8114.*
General email, NDMSsupprt@hhs.gov
Web, http://phe.gov/ndms

Federally coordinated program that collaborates with other federal agencies; tribal, state, and local governments; private businesses; and civilian volunteers to ensure the delivery of medical resources following a disaster.

Health and Human Services Dept. (HHS), *Office of the Assistant Secretary for Preparedness and Response (ASPR), 200 Independence Ave. S.W., #638G, 20201; (202) 292-1740. Dawn O'Connell, Assistant Secretary.*
Web, www.phe.gov/Preparedness/Pages/default.aspx, Twitter, @PHEgov and Facebook, www.facebook.com/ASPRgov

Responsible for coordinating U.S. medical and public health preparedness and response to emergencies, including natural disasters, pandemic and emerging infectious disease, and acts of biological, chemical, and nuclear terrorism. Manages advanced research and development of medical countermeasures. Oversees the

hospital preparedness grant program, which provides funding to state governments.

Homeland Security Dept. (DHS), *Countering Weapons of Mass Destruction (CWMD), Health Affairs (OHA), 650 Massachusetts Ave. N.W., MS 0020, 20528; (202) 254-6479. Dr. Pritesh Gandhi, Chief Medical Officer.*
General email, healthaffairs@dhs.gov
Web, www.dhs.gov/office-health-affairs

Guides DHS leaders on medical and public health issues related to national security; analyzes data and monitors biological and chemical threats and responses to pandemics.

National Institute of Allergy and Infectious Diseases (NIAID) *(National Institutes of Health), 5601 Fishers Lane, MS 2520, Bethesda, MD 20892-9806; (301) 496-2263. Fax, (301) 496-4409. Dr. Anthony S. Fauci, Director. Press, (301) 402-1663. Toll-free health and research information, (866) 284-4107. TTY health and research information, (800) 877-8339.*
General email, ocpostoffice@niaid.nih.gov
Web, www.niaid.nih.gov, Twitter, @NIAIDNews, Facebook, www.facebook.com/niaid.nih and YouTube, www.youtube.com/user/niaid

Responsible for coordinating and administering a medical program to counter radiological and nuclear threats. Works with the National Cancer Institute and other federal agencies, academia, and industry to develop medical measures to assess, diagnose, and care for civilians exposed to radiation.

▶ CONGRESS

For a listing of relevant congressional committees and subcommittees, please see pages 634–635 or the Appendix.

▶ NONGOVERNMENTAL

American Public Health Assn., *800 Eye St. N.W., 20001-3710; (202) 777-2742. Fax, (202) 777-2534. Georges C. Benjamin, Executive Director. TTY, (202) 777-2500.*
General email, comments@apha.org
Web, www.apha.org, Twitter, @PublicHealth and Facebook, www.facebook.com/AmericanPublicHealthAssociation

Membership: health providers, educators, environmentalists, policymakers, and health officials at all levels working both within and outside of governmental organizations and educational institutions. Works to protect communities from serious, preventable health threats. Strives to ensure that community-based health promotion and disease prevention activities and preventive health services are universally accessible in the United States. Develops standards for scientific procedures in public health.

American Red Cross, *Disaster Preparedness and Response, 431 18th St. N.W., 20006; (202) 303-5214, ext. 1. Gail J. McGovern, President. Press, (202) 303-5551.*

Toll-free, (800) 733-2767. Training/Certification, 800-RED-CROSS. Public Inquiry, (202) 303-4498.
Web, www.redcross.org, Twitter, @redcross, Facebook, www.facebook.com/redcross and Disaster preparedness, www.redcross.org/about-us/our-work/distaster-relief.html

Chartered by Congress to administer disaster relief. Provides disaster victims with food, shelter, first aid, medical care, and access to other available resources. Feeds emergency workers; handles inquiries from concerned family members outside the disaster area; helps promote disaster preparedness and prevention through training. Recruits blood donors and maintains blood stocks in the United States.

Assn. of Public Health Laboratories, 8515 Georgia Ave., #700, Silver Spring, MD 20910; (240) 485-2745. Fax, (240) 485-2700. Scott J. Becker, Chief Executive Officer, (240) 485-2747. Press, (240) 485-2793.
General email, info@aphl.org
Web, www.aphl.org, Twitter, @APHL and Facebook, www.facebook.com/PublicHealthLabs

Membership: state and local public health, environmental health, agricultural, and food safety laboratories. Offers technical assistance to member laboratories; sponsors educational programs for public health and clinical laboratory practitioners; develops systems for electronic exchange of lab data; develops laboratory system in underresourced countries. Works with the CDC, FDA, EPA, and other federal partners to support disease detection and surveillance, laboratory response to health crises, quality drinking water, and other public health services.

Assn. of Schools and Programs of Public Health, 1615 L St., #510, 20036; (202) 296-1099. Fax, (202) 296-1252. Laura Magaña, President, ext. 120.
General email, info@aspph.org
Web, www.aspph.org, Twitter, @ASPPHtweets and Facebook, www.facebook.com/ASPPH

Membership: deans, faculty, and students of accredited graduate schools of public health. Promotes improved education and training of professional public health personnel; interests include disease prevention, health promotion, and international health.

Assn. of State and Territorial Health Officials, 2231 Crystal Dr., #450, Arlington, VA 22202; (202) 371-9090. Fax, (571) 527-3189. Michael Fraser, Executive Director, ext. 4.
Web, www.astho.org, www.statepublichealth.org and Twitter, @astho

Membership: chief health officials of State, Territorial, and District of Columbia public health departments. Serves as legislative review agency and information source for members. Monitors legislation and regulations.

National Academies of Sciences, Engineering, and Medicine (NASEM), *Global Health Board,* Keck Center, 500 5th St. N.W., 20001; (202) 334-2178. Ann Kurth, Chair; Julie Pavlin, Director.

General email, Cbiffle@nas.edu
Web, www.nationalacademies.org/bgh/board-on-global-health

Carries out activities related to international health policy and health concerns of developing countries; main focus is public health programs for prevention and control of disease and disability.

National Academies of Sciences, Engineering, and Medicine (NASEM), *Population Health and Public Health Practice Board,* Keck Center, 500 5th St. N.W., 20001; (202) 334-2158. Fax, (202) 334-2939. Rose Marie Martinez, Director; Bruce Calonge, Chair.
General email, bph@nas.edu
Web, www.nationalacademies.org/bph/board-on-population-health-and-public-health-practice

Supports research on public health, including vaccine safety, pandemic preparedness issues, smoking cessation, health disparities, and reducing environmental and occupational hazards.

National Academies of Sciences, Engineering, and Medicine (NASEM), *Resilient America Roundtable, Roundtable on Risk and Resilience of Extreme Events,* Keck Center, 500 5th St. N.W., 20001; (202) 334-2000. Sarah Slaughter Sr., Co-Chair; Negin Sobhani, Senior Program Officer.
General email, Resilience@nas.edu
Web, nationalacademies.org/our-work/resilient-america-roundtable

Facilitates the exchange of ideas among scientists, practitioners, and policymakers to help communities and the country build resilience to extreme events, save lives and reduce costs of disasters.

National Assn. of State EMS Officials (NASEMSO), 201 Park Washington Ct., Falls Church, VA 22046-4527; (703) 538-1799. Fax, (703) 241-5603. Dia Gainor, Executive Director.
General email, info@nasemso.org
Web, www.nasemso.org, Twitter, @NASEMSO and Facebook, www.facebook.com/NASEMSO1

Supports development of effective emergency medical services (EMS) systems at the local, state, and regional levels. Works to formulate national EMS policy and foster communication and sharing among state EMS officials.

National Center for Biodefense and Infectious Diseases *(George Mason University),* 10650 Pyramid Pl., MS 1J5, Manassas, VA 20110; (703) 993-9610. Fax, (703) 993-4280. Ali Andalibi, Chief Scientific Officer.
General email, aandalibi@gmu.edu
Web, http://ncbid.gmu.edu and http://cos.gmu.edu

Researches and develops diagnostics and treatments for emerging infectious diseases as well as those pathogens that could be used as terrorist weapons that require special containment. Manages a graduate education program.

Counterterrorism Resources and Contacts

The following agencies, organizations, and hotlines offer information pertaining to terrorism and counterterrorism issues.

AGENCIES

Bureau of Counterterrorism, John T. Godfrey, Coordinator (Acting), (202) 647-9892 (State Dept.)

Bureau of Industry and Security, Jeremy Pelter, Under Secretary, (800) 424-2980 (Commerce Dept.)

Central Intelligence Agency, David S. Cohen, Director, (703) 482-0623 (Justice Dept.)

Counter-Terrorism and Emergency Coordination Staff (FDA), Rosemary Roberts, Director, (301) 796-2210 (Health and Human Services Dept.)

Defense Intelligence Agency, Lt. Gen. Scott D. Berrier, Director, (202) 231-5554 (Defense Dept.)

FBI Counterterrorism Division, Jill Sanborn, Assistant Director, (202) 324-3000 (Justice Dept.)

Homeland Security Advisory Council, Mike Miron, Director (Acting), (202) 447-3135 (Homeland Security Dept.)

Homeland Security Dept., Alejandro Mayorkas, Secretary, (202) 282-8000

INTERPOL, Michael A. Hughes, Director (Acting), (202) 514-9000 (Justice Dept.)

National Counterterrorism Center, Steve Vanech, Director (Acting), (703) 275-3700 or, (703) 733-8600

National Nuclear Security Administration, Charles P. Verdon, Administrator (Acting) (202) 586-5000; TTY, (800) 877-8339 (Energy Dept.)

National Security Agency/Central Security Service, Paul M. Nakasone, Director, (301) 688-6311 (Defense Dept.)

National Security Council, Jake Sullivan, National Security Advisor, (202) 456-1414 (Executive Office of the President)

National Security Division, John C. Demers, Assistant Attorney General, (202) 514-2007 (Justice Dept.)

Office of Foreign Assets Control, Andrea Gacki, Director, (800) 540-6322 or, (202) 622-2490 (Treasury Dept.)

Office of Nuclear Security and Incident Response, Mirela Gavrilas, Director, (301) 415-7000 or, (301) 415-1270

Office of Terrorism and Financial Intelligence, Vacant, Under Secretary, (202) 622-8260 (Treasury Dept.)

Office of the Director of National Intelligence, Avril Haines, Director, (703) 733-8600

Transportation Security Administration, David P. Pekoske, Administrator, (866) 289-9673 (Homeland Security Dept.)

U.S. Immigration and Customs Enforcement, Tae D. Johnson, Director (Acting), (202) 732-5000 (Homeland Security Dept.)

U.S. Secret Service, James M. Murray, Director, (202) 406-5708 (Homeland Security Dept.)

ORGANIZATIONS

Foundation for Defense of Democracies, Clifford D. May, President, (202) 207-0190; Web, www.fdd.org

International Center for Terrorism Studies, Michael S. Swetnam, Chief Executive Officer, (703) 525-0770; Web, https://potomacinstitute.org

RAND Corp., Michael D. Rich, President, (703) 414-4795 (310) 451-6913; Web, www.rand.org

HOTLINES

Federal Bureau of Investigation, (202) 324-3000

Office of Foreign Assets Control, (800) 540-6322

Transportation Security Administration, (866) 289-9673

U.S. Immigration and Customs Enforcement, (855) 488-6423

National Governors Assn. (NGA), *Center for Best Practices, Public Health,* 444 N. Capitol St. N.W., #267, 20001-1512; (202) 624-5300. Brittney Roy, Director. *General email,* info@nga.org

Web, www.nga.org/bestpractices/Health/#public

Supports governors on public health topics including maternal and child health and prescription drug abuse.

National Vaccine Information Center, *21525 Ridgetop Circle, #100, Sterling, VA 20166; (703) 938-0342. Fax, (571) 313-1268. Barbara Loe Fisher, President; Theresa Wrangham, Executive Director. General email,* contactus@gmail.com

Web, www.nvic.org, *Twitter,* @NVICLoeDown and *Facebook,* www.facebook.com/national.vaccine .information.center

Educates the public and provides research on vaccination safety procedures and effectiveness; supports reform of the vaccination system; publishes information on diseases and vaccines; and monitors legislation and regulations.

Pan American Health Organization PAHO, *525 23rd St. N.W., 20037; (202) 974-3000. Fax, (202) 974-3663. Carissa F. Etienne, Director PAHP/WHO. Web,* www.paho.org, *Twitter,* @PAHOWHO and *Facebook,* www.facebook.com/PAHOWHO

Works to extend health services to underserved populations of its member countries and to control or eradicate communicable diseases; promotes technical cooperation between countries and works in partnership with ministries of health and other government agencies, civil society organizations, other international agencies, universities, social security agencies, community groups, and other partners. Serves as Regional Office for the Americas of the World Health Organization. (WHO headquartered in Geneva, Switzerland.)

Selective Service

▶AGENCIES

Selective Service System, *1515 Wilson Blvd., #400, Arlington, VA 22209-2425; (703) 605-4100. Fax, (703) 605-4106. Craig T. Brown, Director (Acting). Locator, (703) 605-4000. Toll-free, (888) 655-1825. TTY, (800) 877-8339. TTY Español, (800) 845-6136.*
General email, information@sss.gov

Web, www.sss.gov, Twitter, @sss_gov and Facebook, www.facebook.com/SSSregistration

Supplies the armed forces with manpower when authorized; registers male citizens of the United States ages 18 to 25. In an emergency, would institute a draft and would provide alternative service assignments to men classified as conscientious objectors.

▶CONGRESS

For a listing of relevant congressional committees and subcommittees, please see pages 634–635 or the Appendix.

Strategic Stockpiles

▶AGENCIES

Defense Dept. (DoD), *Industrial Policy, 1400 Defense Pentagon, #3B854, 20301-3300; (703) 697-0051. Fax, (703) 695-4885. Jesse Salazar, Deputy Assistant Secretary.*
General email, osd.mibp.inquiries@mail.mil

Web, www.businessdefense.gov

Develops and oversees policy, assessment and analysis, and investment programs for maintaining the U.S. defense industrial base.

Defense Logistics Agency *(Defense Dept.),* **Strategic Materials,** *8725 John Jay Kingman Rd., #3229, Fort Belvoir, VA 22060-6223; (703) 767-5500. Fax, (703) 767-3316. Ronnie Favors, Administrator. Press, (703) 767-6479.*
Web, www.dla.mil/HQ/Acquisition/Strategicmaterials and Twitter, @DLAmil

Manages the national defense stockpile of strategic and critical materials. Purchases strategic materials, including beryllium and newly developed high-tech alloys. Disposes of excess materials, including tin, silver, industrial diamond stones, tungsten, and vegetable tannin.

Fossil Energy (FE) *(Energy Dept.),* **Petroleum Reserves,** *Forrestal Bldg., 1000 Independence Ave. S.W., FE-40, 20585; (202) 586-4410. Doug Macintyre, Deputy Assistant Secretary.*
Web, www.energy.gov/fe/services/petroleum-reserves

Manages programs that provide the United States with strategic and economic protection against disruptions in oil supplies, including the Strategic Petroleum Reserves, the Northeast Home Heating Oil Reserve, and the Naval Petroleum and the Northeast Gasoline Supply Reserve.

▶CONGRESS

For a listing of relevant congressional committees and subcommittees, please see pages 634–635 or the Appendix.

INTELLIGENCE AND COUNTERTERRORISM

General

▶AGENCIES

Air Force Dept. *(Defense Dept.),* **Intelligence, Surveillance, Reconnaissance, and Cyber Effects Operations (ISR),** *A26, 1070 Air Force Pentagon, 20330-1060; (703) 695-5613. Lt. Gen. Mary F. O'Brien, Deputy Chief of Staff.*
Web, www.af.mil/ISR.aspx

Collects and analyzes crucial information and data about enemy targets and distributes intelligence to other Air Force departments.

Army Dept. *(Defense Dept.),* **Intelligence and Security Command,** *8825 Beulah St., Fort Belvoir, VA 22060-5246; (703) 428-4965. Maj. Gen. Michele H. Bredenkamp (USA), Commanding General.*
General email, army.inscom.pao@mail.mil

Web, www.inscom.army.mil

Military office that executes mission command of operational intelligence and security forces; conducts, synchronizes, and integrates worldwide multi-discipline and all-source intelligence and security operations; and delivers linguist support and intelligence related advanced skills training, acquisition support, logistics, communications, and other specialized capabilities in support of Army, Joint, and Coalition commands and the U.S. intelligence community.

Bureau of Counterterrorism (CT) *(State Dept.),* *2201 C St. N.W., #2509, 20520; (202) 647-9892. Fax, (202) 647-9256. John Godfrey, Coordinator (Acting). Press, (202) 647-1515.*
Web, www.state.gov/j/ct and Twitter, @StateDeptCT

Implements U.S. counterterrorism policy and coordinates activities with foreign governments; responds to terrorist acts; works to promote a stronger counterterrorism stance worldwide through diplomatic engagement, regional capacity building, designations, and information sharing to target specific terrorist networks and branches.

Bureau of Intelligence and Research (INR) *(State Dept.), 2201 C St. N.W., #6468, 20520-6531; (202) 647-9177. Brett M. Holmgren, Assistant Secretary.*
Web, www.state.gov/s/inr

Coordinates foreign policy–related research, analysis, and intelligence programs for the State Dept. and other federal agencies.

Central Intelligence Agency (CIA), *CIA Headquarters, 930 Dolley Madison Blvd., McLean, VA 20505 (mailing* address: CIA Headquarters, Washington, DC 20505); (703) 482-0623. William (Bill) Burns, Director. FOIA Hotline, (703) 613-1287.

Web, www.cia.gov and Twitter, @CIA

Gathers and evaluates foreign intelligence to assist the president and senior U.S. government policymakers in making foreign policy and national security decisions. Reports directly to the Office of National Intelligence, which coordinates intelligence functions of all government agencies involved with homeland security.

Defense Dept. (DoD), Intelligence and Security, 5000 Defense Pentagon, #3E834, 20301-5000; (703) 695-0971. Fax, (703) 693-5706. Ronald S. Moultrie, Under Secretary. Web, www.ousdi.defense.gov

Responsible for ensuring the secretary of defense's access to intelligence information.

Defense Dept. (DoD), Intelligence Oversight, 9010 Defense Pentagon, 20301-7200; (571) 372-6363. Mark D. Dupont, Assistant to the Secretary. Web, https://dodsioo.defense.gov

Responsible for the independent oversight of all Defense Dept. intelligence, counterintelligence, and related activities, and for the formulation of intelligence oversight policy; reviews intelligence operations and investigates and reports on possible violations of federal law or regulations.

Defense Dept. (DoD), Special Operations and Low-Intensity Conflict, 2500 Defense Pentagon, #3C852A, 20301-2500; (703) 695-9667. Fax, (703) 693-6335. Christopher Maier, Assistant Secretary. General email, osd.pentagon.ousd-policy.list.solic-front-office@mail.mil

Web, https://policy.defense.gov/OUSDP-Offices/ASD-for-Special-Operations-Low-Intensity-Conflict/Stability-and-Humanitarian-Affairs/bcsi-ac-cde40c890bd19f3d

Serves as special staff assistant and civilian adviser to the secretary of defense on matters related to special operations and international terrorism. Oversees and serves as advocate for Special Operations and Irregular Warfare throughout the Defense Dept. to ensure these capabilities are resourced, ready, and properly employed in accordance with the National Defense Strategy.

Defense Information Systems Agency (Defense Dept.), 6910 Cooper Ave., Fort Meade, MD 20755; (703) 607-6001. Lt. Gen. Robert J. Skinner (USAF), Director. Service Desk, (844) 347-2457. General email, disa.mpeo@mail.mil Web, www.disa.mil

The Defense Dept. agency responsible for information technology and the central manager for major portions of the defense information infrastructure. Units include the White House Communications Agency.

Defense Intelligence Agency (Defense Dept.), 200 MacDill Blvd., 20340; (202) 231-5554. Fax, (202) 231-0851. Lt. Gen. Scott D. Berrier (USA), Director. General email, DIA-PAO@dodiis.mil Web, www.dia.mil and Twitter, @DefenseIntel

Collects and evaluates foreign military–related intelligence information to satisfy the requirements of the secretary of defense, Joint Chiefs of Staff, selected components of the Defense Dept., Office of National Intelligence, and other authorized agencies.

Federal Bureau of Investigation (FBI) (Justice Dept.), National Joint Terrorism Task Force, 935 Pennsylvania Ave. N.W., 20535-0001; (571) 280-5688. Fax, (571) 280-6922. Vacant, Chief; Jill Sanborn, Assistant Director Counterterrorism Division. Public Affairs, (202) 324-0201. Web, www.fbi.gov/investigate/terrorism/joint-terrorism-task-forces

Group of more than 50 agencies from the fields of intelligence, public safety, and federal, state, and local law enforcement that collects terrorism information and intelligence and funnels it to the more than five hundred JTTFs (teams of local, state, and federal agents based at FBI field offices), various terrorism units within the FBI, and partner agencies. Helps the FBI with terrorism investigations.

Federal Bureau of Investigation (FBI) (Justice Dept.), National Security Branch (NSB), Counterintelligence Division, 935 Pennsylvania Ave. N.W., 20535; (202) 324-4614. Allan E. Kohler Jr., Assistant Director. National security hotline, (202) 324-3000. Web, www.fbi.gov/investigate/counterintelligence

Provides centralized management and oversight of all foreign counterintelligence investigations. Integrates law enforcement with intelligence efforts to investigate violations of federal laws against espionage, including economic espionage. Seeks to prevent foreign acquisition of weapons of mass destruction, penetration of the U.S. intelligence community and government agencies and contractors, and compromise of U.S. critical national assets.

Federal Bureau of Investigation (FBI) (Justice Dept.), National Security Branch (NSB), Counterterrorism Division, 935 Pennsylvania Ave. N.W., #4204, 20535; (202) 324-2770. Fax, (202) 324-7050. Timothy Langan, Assistant Director. National security hotline, (202) 324-3000. Press, (202) 324-3691. Web, www.fbi.gov/investigate/terrorism#related-webpages

Collects, analyzes, and shares information and intelligence with authorities to combat international terrorism operations within the United States and in support of extraterritorial investigations, domestic terrorism operations, and counterterrorism. Maintains the Joint Terrorism Task Force, which includes representatives from the Defense Dept., Energy Dept., Federal Emergency Management Agency, CIA, U.S. Customs and Border Protection, U.S. Secret Service, and Immigration and Customs Enforcement.

Federal Bureau of Investigation (FBI) (Justice Dept.), National Security Branch (NSB), Terrorist Screening Center (TSC), 935 Pennsylvania Ave. N.W., 20535; (571) 350-5678. Charles H. Kable, Director. Press, (571) 350-6397. Toll-free, (866) 872-5678. General email, tsc@tsc.gov

Web, www.fbi.gov/about/leadership-and-structure/national-security-branch/tsc and Press, media@tsc.gov

Coordinates access to terrorist watch lists from multiple agencies. Provides operational support to federal screeners and state and local law enforcement officials.

Homeland Security Council *(Executive Office of the President)*, 2707 MLK Jr. Ave. S.E., MS0385, 20502; (202) 447-3135. Jason Mayer, Executive Director; Mike Miron, Deputy Executive Director.
General email, hsac@hq.dhs.gov

Web, dhs.gov/homeland-security-advisory-council

Advises the president on combating global terrorism and homeland security policy.

Homeland Security Dept. (DHS), 3801 Nebraska Ave. N.W., 20528; 301 7th St. S.W., MS 0501, 20528; Fax, (202) 447-5437. Alejandro Mayorkas, Secretary.
Switchboard, (202) 282-8000. Comments, (202) 282-8495. Legislative Affairs, (202) 447-5890. Press, (202) 282-8010.
General email, DHSExecSec@hq.dhs.gov

Web, www.dhs.gov, Twitter, @DHSgov and Facebook, www.facebook.com/homelandsecurity

Coordinates the strategy of the executive branch with those of state and local governments and private entities to detect, prepare for, protect against, respond to, and recover from terrorist attacks and other emergencies in the United States. Administers the National Terrorism Advisory System to communicate information about terrorist threats to the public.

Homeland Security Dept. (DHS), *Countering Weapons of Mass Destruction (CWMD)*, 1125 15th St. N.W., 20221; (202) 254-7799. Gary Rasicot, Assistant Secretary (Acting).
Web, www.dhs.gov/countering-weapons-mass-destruction-office#

Responsible for countering attempts by terrorists or other threat actors to carry out an attack against the United States or its interests using a weapon of mass destruction.

Homeland Security Dept. (DHS), *Intelligence and Analysis (I&A)*, Bldg. 19, 3801 Nebraska Ave. N.W., 20528; (202) 447-4154. John Cohen, Under Secretary (Acting).
Web, www.dhs.gov/office-intelligence-and-analysis

Uses intelligence from multiple sources to identify and assess current and future threats to the United States; provides guidance to the secretary on homeland security issues.

Marine Corps *(Defense Dept.)*, *Intelligence*, 3000 Marine Corps Pentagon, #1A262B, 20350-3000; (703) 614-2522. Fax, (703) 614-5888. Brig. Gen. Melvin G. Carter (USMC), Director.
Web, www.hqmc.marines.mil/intelligence

Military office that directs Marine Corps intelligence policy and coordinates activities with other intelligence agencies.

National Aeronautics and Space Administration (NASA), *Protective Services*, 300 E St. S.W., #6T39, 20546; Joseph S. Mahaley, Assistant Administrator.
Web, www.nasa.gov/nojmo-pso

Serves as the focal point for policy formulation, oversight, coordination, and management of NASA's security, counterintelligence, counterterrorism, emergency preparedness and response, and continuity of operations programs.

National Geospatial-Intelligence Agency *(Defense Dept.)*, 7500 Geoint Dr., MS N73, Springfield, VA 22150-7500; (571) 557-5400. Fax, (571) 558-3169. Vice Adm. Robert D. Sharp (USN), Director. Maps and imagery products, (571) 557-5400.
General email, publicaffairs@nga.mil

Web, www.nga.mil, Twitter, @NGA_GEOINT and Facebook, www.facebook.com/NatlGEOINTAgency

Combat support agency that develops imagery and map-based intelligence in support of national defense objectives.

National Reconnaissance Office (NRO) *(Defense Dept.)*, 14675 Lee Rd., Chantilly, VA 20151-1715; (703) 808-5050. Fax, (703) 808-1171. Christopher Scolese, Director.
General email, publicaffairs@nro.mil

Web, www.nro.gov, Twitter, @NatReconOfc and Facebook, www.facebook.com/NationalReconnaissanceOffice

Researches, develops, and operates intelligence satellites. Gathers intelligence for various purposes, including indications and warnings, monitoring of arms control agreements, military operations and exercises, and monitoring of natural disasters and other environmental issues.

National Security Agency (NSA) *(Defense Dept.)*, 9800 Savage Rd., #6272, Fort Meade, MD 20755-6000; (301) 688-6311. Fax, (301) 688-6198. Gen. Paul M. Nakasone (USA), Director. FOIA, (301) 688-6527. Applicants, (844) 424-4737.
General email, nsapao@nsa.gov

Web, www.nsa.gov, Twitter, @NSAGov and Facebook, www.facebook.com/NSAUSGov

Provides technology, products, and services to secure information and information infrastructure critical to U.S. national security interests. Organizes and controls all foreign signals collection and processing activities of the United States in accordance with requirements established by the Defense Dept., the Office of the Director of National Intelligence, and by national policies with the advice of the National Foreign Intelligence Board.

National Security Division *(Justice Dept.)*, 950 Pennsylvania Ave. N.W., #7339, 20530; (202) 514-2007. Fax, (202) 514-5331. Matthew G. Olsen, Assistant Attorney General. Comment line, (202) 353-1555.
General email, nsd.public@usdoj.gov

Web, www.justice.gov/nsd

Coordinates the Justice Dept.'s intelligence, counterterrorism, counterespionage, and other national security activities.

National Security Division *(Justice Dept.)*, *Counterintelligence and Export Control (CES)*, 950 Pennsylvania Ave. N.W., 20530; (202) 514-1057. (202) 514-5000. Jay Bratt, Chief.

Office of the Director of National Intelligence

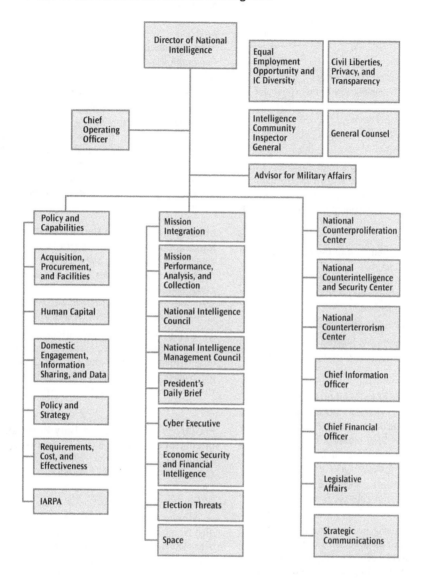

General email, nsd.public@usdoj.gov

Web, www.justice.gov/nsd/sections-offices#intelexport

Supervises the investigation and prosecution of cases affecting national security, foreign relations, and the export of military and strategic commodities and technology. Has executive responsibility for authorizing the prosecution of cases under criminal statutes relating to espionage, sabotage, neutrality, and atomic energy. Provides legal advice to U.S. Attorneys' offices and investigates agencies on federal statutes concerning national security. Coordinates criminal cases involving the application of the Classified Information Procedures Act. Administers and enforces the Foreign Agents Registration Act of 1938 and related disclosure statutes.

National Security Division *(Justice Dept.),*
Counterterrorism (CTS), *950 Pennsylvania Ave. N.W.,*
20530; (202) 514-0849. (202) 514-5000. Matthew Olsen,
Assistant Attorney General for National Security.
General email, nsd.public@usdoj.gov

Web, www.justice.gov/nsd/counterterrorism-section

Responsible for the design, implementation, and support of law enforcement efforts, legislative initiatives, policies, and strategies related to combating international and domestic terrorism.

National Security Division *(Justice Dept.), Intelligence,*
950 Pennsylvania Ave. N.W., 20530; (202) 514-5600.
Matthew Olsen, Assistant Attorney General for National
Security.
General email, nsd.public@usdoj.gov

Web, www.justice.gov/nsd/office-intelligence

Seeks to ensure that Intelligence Community agencies have the legal authorities necessary to conduct intelligence operations, oversight, and litigation, particularly operations involving the Foreign Intelligence Surveillance Act (FISA). Oversees various national security activities of Intelligence Community agencies; participates in FISA-related litigation.

National Security Division *(Justice Dept.), Justice for Victims of Overseas Terrorism*, 950 Pennsylvania Ave. N.W., 20530; (202) 233-0701. Fax, (202) 233-0770. Andria Kerney, Director. Toll-free, (877) 738-0153.
General email, nsd.ovt@usdoj.gov

Web, www.justice.gov/nsd-ovt

Responsible for establishing a Joint Task Force with the State Dept. in the event of a terrorist incident against U.S. citizens overseas. Responds to congressional and citizens' inquiries on the department's response to such attacks.

National Security Division *(Justice Dept.), Law and Policy*, 950 Pennsylvania Ave. N.W., 20530; (202) 616-0903. Brad Wiegmann, Deputy Assistant Attorney General; Wyn Hornbuckle, Spokesperson for NSD, (202) 616-0903.
General email, nsd.justice@usdoj.gov

Web, www.justice.gov/nsd/sections-offices#law

Develops and implements Justice Dept. policies with regard to intelligence, counterterrorism, and other national security matters.

Office of the Director of National Intelligence (DNI), *Intelligence Campus*, 1500 Tysons McClean Dr., McLean, VA 22102; (703) 733-8600. Fax, (703) 275-1225. Avril Haines, Director; Tyler Schwartz, Communications, (571) 280-6160. Press and Public Affairs, (703) 275-3637.
General email, DNI-Media@dni.gov

Web, www.dni.gov, Twitter, @ODNIgov, Facebook, www .facebook.com/dni.gov and YouTube, www.youtube.com/ ODNIgov

Leads a unified intelligence community and serves as the principal adviser to the president on intelligence matters. Orders the collection of new intelligence to ensure the sharing of information among agencies and to establish common standards for the intelligence community's personnel. Responsible for determining the annual budgets for all national intelligence agencies and for directing how these funds are spent.

Office of the Director of National Intelligence (DNI), *National Counterintelligence and Security Center*, Liberty Crossing, ICC-B, 1500 Tysons McLean Dr., McLean, VA 22102; (571) 280-6160. Michael Orlando, National Counterintelligence Executive; , (571) 280-6160.
Web, www.dni.gov/index.php/ncsc-home

Conducts foreign intelligence threat assessments; promotes collaboration and information sharing throughout the U.S. counterintelligence community through conferences and other outreach and training activities; makes recommendations to decision makers concerning national counterintelligence strategy.

Office of the Director of National Intelligence (DNI), *National Counterterrorism Center*, Liberty Crossing, 1500 Tysons McLean Dr., McLean Dr., VA 22102; (571) 280-6160. Fax, (703) 275-1225. Christine Abizaid, Director; Abby Johnson, Executive Director; Tyler Schwartz, Communications, (571) 280-6160.
General email, nctcpao@nctc.gov

Web, www.dni.gov/index.php/nctc-home

Serves as a hub for terrorism threat–related information collected domestically and abroad. Responsible for assessing, integrating, and disseminating terrorist threat information and all-source analysis; maintains U.S. government's central database on known and suspected terrorists; and identifies collection requirements related to the terrorist threat. Participates in strategic planning for counterterrorism activities.

Office of the Director of National Intelligence (DNI), *National Intelligence Council*, CIA Headquarters, Langley, VA 20505; (703) 482-6724. Fax, (703) 482-8652. Avril Haines, Chair; Taylor Schwartz, Communications, (571) 280-6160.
Web, www.dni.gov/index.php/who-we-are/organizations/ nic/nic-who-we-are and Twitter, @ODNI_NIC

Supports the director of national intelligence and serves as the intelligence community's center for mid- and long-term strategic thinking. Provides a focal point for policymakers' inquiries and needs. Establishes contacts with private sector and academic experts in the intelligence field.

President's Intelligence Advisory Board and Intelligence Oversight Board *(Executive Office of the President)*, New Executive Office Bldg., 725 17th St. N.W., #5020, 20502; (202) 395-9915. Carol Bales, Chair.
Web, www.whitehouse.gov

Members appointed by the president. Assesses the quality, quantity, and adequacy of foreign intelligence collection and of counterintelligence activities by all government agencies; advises the president on matters concerning intelligence and national security.

State Dept., *Global Engagement Center*, 2201 C St. N.W., #2429, 20520; (202) 736-7531. Leah Bray, Coordinator (Acting).
Web, www.state.gov/bureaus-offices/under-secretary-for-public-diplomacy-and-public-affairs/global-engagement-center

Works to recognize, understand, expose and counter foreign state and non-state propaganda and disinformation efforts aimed at undermining or influencing security and stability of the United States.

Transportation Dept. (DOT), *Intelligence, Security, and Emergency Response*, 1200 New Jersey Ave. S.E., #56125, 20590; (202) 366-6525. Fax, (202) 366-7261. Richard Chávez, Director.
Web, www.transportation.gov/mission/administrations/ intelligence-security-emergency-response

Advises the secretary on transportation intelligence and security policy. Acts as liaison with the intelligence community, federal agencies, corporations, and interest groups; administers counterterrorism strategic planning processes.

Transportation Security Administration (TSA) *(Homeland Security Dept.), Intelligence and Analysis,* TSA-10, 601 S. 12th St., 6th Floor, Arlington, VA 22202-4220; (703) 601-3100. Nancy Nykamp, Assistant Administrator.
Web, www.tsa.gov

Conducts a range of programs designed to ensure that known or suspected terrorists do not gain access to sensitive areas of the nation's transportation system, including the Alien Flight, Registered Traveler, Secure Flight, and Transportation Worker Identification Credential programs and Hazmat Materials Truck Drivers Background Checks.

Treasury Dept., *Terrorism and Financial Intelligence, Foreign Assets Control (OFAC),* 1500 Pennsylvania Ave. N.W., Treasury Annex, 20220; (202) 622-2490. Andrea G. Gacki, Director. Licensing Division, (202) 622-2480. Toll-free, (800) 540-6322.
General email, ofac_feedback@treasury.gov
Web, www.treasury.gov/about/organizational-structure/offices/Pages/Office-of-Foreign-Assets-Control.aspx

Authorized under the Enemy Act, the International Emergency Economic Powers Act, and United Nations Participation Act, and other relevant statutory authorities to control financial and commercial dealings with certain countries and their foreign nationals in times of war or emergencies. Administers regulations involving foreign assets control, narcotics, nonproliferation, and commercial transactions currently apply in varying degrees to its listed geographical areas of concern, as well as terrorists wherever located and transnational criminal organizations.

Treasury Dept., *Terrorism and Financial Intelligence, Terrorist Financing and Financial Crime,* 1500 Pennsylvania Ave. N.W., 20220; (202) 622-2960. Fax, (202) 622-3915. Andrew Koch, Deputy Assistant Secretary, (202) 622-1634.
Web, https://home.treasury.gov/about/offices/terrorism-and-financial-intelligence/terrorist-financing-and-financial-crimes

Sets strategy and policy for combating the financing of terrorism both domestically and abroad.

Treasury Dept., *Terrorism and Illicit Finance,* 1500 Pennsylvania Ave. N.W., #4316, 20220; (202) 622-8260. Vacant, Under Secretary. Press, (202) 622-2960.
Web, https://home.treasury.gov/policy-issues/terrorism-and-illicit-finance

Develops and maintains the Treasury Dept.'s strategies to combat terrorist financing domestically and internationally; develops and implements the National Money Laundering strategy as well as other policies and programs to fight financial crimes.

U.S. Coast Guard (USCG) *(Homeland Security Dept.), Counterterrorism and Defense Policy,* 2703 Martin Luther King Jr. Ave. S.E., MS 7516, 20593-7516; (202) 372-2101. Fax, (202) 372-8361. Rear Adm. Scott W. Clendenin, Assistant Commandant for Response Policy.
Web, www.dco.uscg.mil/Our-Organization/Assistant-Commandant-for-Response-Policy-CG-5R/Office-of-Counterterrorism-Defense-Operations-Policy-CG-ODO/CG

Provides advanced tactical skills to aid in response to terrorist incidents or to incidents involving weapons of mass destruction.

U.S. Coast Guard (USCG) *(Homeland Security Dept.), Intelligence,* 2703 Martin Luther King Jr. Ave. S.E., MS 7301, 20593-7301; (202) 372-2700. Fax, (202) 372-2956. Rear Adm. Andrew Sugimoto, Assistant Commandant. Response Center, (800) 424-8802.
Web, www.dco.uscg.mil/Our-Organization/Intelligence-CG-2

Manages all Coast Guard intelligence activities and programs.

U.S. Customs and Border Protection *(Homeland Security Dept.), Office of Intelligence,* 1300 Pennsylvania Ave. N.W., #7.3D, 20229; (202) 344-1150. James Collins, Assistant Commissioner. Information, (877) 227-5511. TTY, (800) 877-8339.
Web, www.cbp.gov/about/leadership-organization/executive-assistant-commissioners-offices/operations-support-assistant-commissioners-offices

Coordinates the effort to prevent the introduction of weapons of mass destruction into the United States and to prevent international terrorists from obtaining weapons of mass destruction materials, technologies, arms, funds, and other support.

►CONGRESS

For a listing of relevant congressional committees and subcommittees, please see pages 634–635 or the Appendix.

►NONGOVERNMENTAL

Assn. of Former Intelligence Officers (AFIO), 7700 Leesburg Pike, #324, Falls Church, VA 22043; (703) 790-0320. Fax, (703) 991-1278. James R. Hughes, President.
General email, afio@afio.com
Web, www.afio.com and Twitter, @AFIO

Membership: current and former military and civilian intelligence officers. Encourages public support for intelligence agencies; supports increased intelligence education in colleges and universities; and provides guidance to students seeking careers in intelligence.

The Brookings Institution, *Center for Security, Strategy, and Technology (CSST),* 1775 Massachusetts Ave. N.W., 20036; (202) 797-6103. Michael E. O'Hanlon, Director.
Web, www.brookings.edu/center/center-for-security-strategy-and-technology and Twitter, @MichaelEOHanlon

Research center with focus on American leadership: U.S. grand strategy, US military affairs, American alliances, and the multilateral order; national security: U.S. defense policy, strategic weapons and technology; and transnational threats: non-state actors and sub-state challenges.

Global Center on Cooperative Security, *Washington Office, 1201 14th St. N.W., #915, 20005; Jason Ipe, Chief of Operations.*
General email, info@globalcenter.org

Web, www.globalcenter.org, Facebook, www.facebook.com/GlobalCtr and Twitter, @GlobalCtr

Conducts research and training to advance global cooperation by advancing human rights-based policies, partnerships and practices, to address transnational threats, including terrorism, nuclear proliferation, and drug trafficking. Works with government, civil society and private sector partners to deliver programming that is globally informed and locally grounded. Has an extensive selection of articles, books, reports, publications and interviews relating to sanctions and incentives, violent extremism and terrorism.

Potomac Institute for Policy Studies, *International Center for Terrorism Studies (ICTS), 901 N. Stuart St., #1200, Arlington, VA 22203-1821; (703) 525-0770. Fax, (703) 525-0299. Yonah Alexander, Director; Jennifer Buss, Chief Executive Director.*
General email, webmaster@potomacinstitute.org

Web, https://potomacinstitute.org/academic-centers/international-center-for-terrorism-studies-icts, Twitter, @PotomacInst and Facebook, www.facebook.com/potomacinstitute

Public policy research institute that conducts studies on key science and technology issues. The ICTS focuses on all forms of terrorism and the potential for terrorism, including biological, chemical, or nuclear violence, as well as information warfare and cyberterrorism.

Internal (Agency) Security

▶**AGENCIES**

Air Force Dept. *(Defense Dept.), Special Investigations (AF/OSI), 27130 Telegraph Rd., #W1642, Quantico, VA 22134; (571) 305-8028. Brig. Gen. Terry L. Bullard, Commander; Jude R. Sunderbruch, Executive Director. Toll Free Crimebusters, (877) 246-1453.*
General email, hqafosi.watch@us.af.mil

Web, www.osi.af.mil, Twitter, @AirForceOSI and Facebook, www.facebook.com/AirForceOSI

Develops and implements policy on investigations of foreign intelligence, terrorism, and other crimes as they relate to Air Force security.

Bureau of Diplomatic Security (DS) *(State Dept.), 2201 C St. N.W., #6316, 20520; (202) 647-1479. Fax, (571) 345-2527. Gentry Smith, Assistant Secretary, (202) 647-6290.*

Web, www.state.gov/m/ds, Twitter, @StateDeptDSS, Facebook, www.facebook.com/StateDeptDSS and General email, DSPAStaff@state.gov

Federal law enforcement and security arm of U.S. State Department. Provides a secure environment for conducting U.S. diplomacy abroad and in the United States.

Bureau of Diplomatic Security (DS) *(State Dept.), Cyber and Technology Security, 1801 N. Lynn St., SA-20, Rosslyn, VA 22209; (202) 258-2636. Gharun Lacy, Assistant Director.*
Web, www.state.gov/bureaus-offices/under-secretary-for-management/bureau-of-diplomatic-security

Oversees planning, policy development, coordination, and implementation of the technology countermeasures and cybersecurity programs.

Bureau of Diplomatic Security (DS) *(State Dept.), Domestic Operations, 1801 N. Lynn St., 23rd Floor, Rosslyn, VA 22209; (571) 345-3785. Mark Sullo, Deputy Assistant Secretary.*
Web, www.state.gov/bureaus-offices/under-secretary-for-management/bureau-of-diplomatic-security and www.state.gov/leadership-bureau-of-diplomatic-security

Manages and directs bureau activities within the continental United States, including all field offices, criminal investigations, counterintelligence, and protective operations.

Bureau of Diplomatic Security (DS) *(State Dept.), High Threat Programs (HTP), 1801 N. Lynn St., 23B12, SA-20, Rosslyn, VA 22209; (571) 345-3492. Greg Sherman, Deputy Assistant Secretary.*
Web, www.state.gov/bureaus-offices/under-secretary-for-management/bureau-of-diplomatic-security

Protects and promotes U.S. interests abroad by leading policy, planning, and operational initiatives; managing risk and fosters interagency partnerships.

Bureau of Diplomatic Security (DS) *(State Dept.), International Programs (IP), 1801 N. Lynn St., 22nd Floor, #SA20, 23L09, Rosslyn, VA 22209; (571) 345-3841. (202) 647-4000. Cornell Chasten Jr., Deputy Assistant Secretary.*
Web, www.state.gov/m/ds

Oversees security and law enforcement policy and programs for over 270 U.S. diplomatic posts overseas, including local embassy guards, marine security guards, chief of mission and principal officer bodyguards, emergency planning, and surveillance detection.

Bureau of Diplomatic Security (DS) *(State Dept.), Security Infrastructure (SI), 1801 N. Lynn St., D08, #SA20, Rosslyn, VA 22209; (571) 345-3791. Donald Blersch, Senior Coordinator, (571) 345-3788.*
Web, www.state.gov/bureaus-offices/under-secretary-for-management/bureau-of-diplomatic-security

Manages matters relating to security infrastructure in the functional areas of information security, computer security, and personnel security and suitability.

Bureau of Diplomatic Security (DS) *(State Dept.),*
Threat Investigations and Analysis (TIA), *1801 N. Lynn
St., 23rd Floor, SA20, Rosslyn, VA 22209; (571) 345-3809.
(202) 647-4000. Andrew Wroblewski, Assistant Director
(Acting).*
*Web, www.state.gov/bureaus-offices/under-secretary-for-
management/bureau-of-diplomatic-security*

Oversees all threat management programs within the
Bureau of Diplomatic Security that gather, analyze, investigate, and disseminate information on threats directed
against diplomatic missions, interagency partners, and the
U.S. private sector.

Bureau of Diplomatic Security (DS) *(State Dept.),*
*Training, 1801 N. Lynn St., #SA11B, Rosslyn, VA 22209;
(571) 226-9761. (202) 647-4000. Julie S. Cabus, Deputy
Assistant Director.*
*Web, www.state.gov/bureaus-offices/under-secretary-for-
management/bureau-of-diplomatic-security*

Formulates and implements all security and law
enforcement training programs and policies with the
bureau.

Defense Counterintelligence and Security *(Defense
Dept.), 27130 Telegraph Rd., Quantico, VA 22134; (571)
305-6562. Fax, (571) 305-6869. William (Bill) K. Lietzau,
Director. Public Affairs, (571) 305-6562.*
Web, www.dcsa.mil and Twitter, @DCSAgov

Administers programs to protect classified government information and resources, including the National
Industrial Security Program (NISP). Serves the Defense
Dept. and other executive departments and agencies
through vetting personnel and protecting critical technology. Operates the Center for Development and Security
Excellence to educate, train, and enhance awareness of
security matters.

Energy Dept. (DOE), *Intelligence and
Counterintelligence, 1000 Independence Ave. S.W.,
#2610, 20585; (202) 586-2610. Fax, (202) 287-5999.
Steven K. Black, Director.*
*Web, www.energy.gov/office-intelligence-and-
counterintelligence*

Identifies and deters intelligence threats directed at
Energy Dept. facilities, personnel, information, and technology. Protects nuclear weapons secrets and other sensitive scientific projects.

INTERPOL Washington *(Justice Dept.), 950 Pennsylvania
Ave. N.W., 20530-0001; (202) 616-9000. Fax, (202) 616-
8400. Michael A. Hughes, Director.*
*Web, www.justice.gov/interpol-washington and Twitter,
@INTERPOL_USA*

U.S. representative to INTERPOL; interacts in international investigations of terrorism on behalf of U.S. police.
Serves as liaison between foreign and U.S. law enforcement agencies. Headquarters office sponsors forums
enabling foreign governments to discuss counterterrorism
policy. (Headquarters in Lyons, France.)

National Archives and Records Administration (NARA),
*Information Security Oversight (ISOO), 700
Pennsylvania Ave. N.W., #100, 20408-0001; (202) 357-
5250. Fax, (202) 357-5907. Mark A. Bradley, Director,
(202) 357-5205.*
General email, isoo@nara.gov
Web, www.archives.gov/isoo

Receiving guidance from the National Security Council, administers governmentwide security classification
program under which information is classified, declassified, and safeguarded for national security purposes.
Develops policies and procedures for sensitive unclassified
information.

National Nuclear Security Administration (NNSA)
*(Energy Dept.), Defense Nuclear Security (DNS), 1000
Independence Ave. S.W., #GF261, 20585; (202) 586-8900.
Jeffrey R. Johnson, Associate Administrator.*
*Web, www.energy.gov/nnsa/nnsa-offices/defense-nuclear-
security*

Ensures the protective force, physical security, information security, material control and accountability, personnel security, and security program operations and
planning measures in agency offices and facilities are
effectively being carried out.

National Security Agency (NSA) *(Defense Dept.), 9800
Savage Rd., #6272, Fort Meade, MD 20755-6000; (301)
688-6311. Fax, (301) 688-6198. Gen. Paul M. Nakasone
(USA), Director. FOIA, (301) 688-6527. Applicants, (844)
424-4737.*
General email, nsapao@nsa.gov
*Web, www.nsa.gov, Twitter, @NSAGov and Facebook,
www.facebook.com/NSAUSGov*

Maintains and operates the Defense Dept.'s Computer
Security Center; ensures communications and computer
security within the government.

Navy Dept. *(Defense Dept.), Naval Criminal
Investigative Service, 27130 Telegraph Rd., Quantico,
VA 22134; (571) 305-9000. Omar Lopez, Director. Hotline,
(877) 579-3648.*
General email, ncispublicaffairs@ncis.navy.mil
*Web, www.ncis.navy.mil, Twitter, @RealNCIS and
Facebook, www.facebook.com/NCIS.Official*

Handles felony criminal investigations, counterintelligence, counterterrorism, and security for the Navy Dept.,
working with federal, state, local, and foreign agencies to
investigate crimes; processes security clearances for the
Navy Dept.

MILITARY INSTALLATIONS

General

▶AGENCIES

Air Force Dept. *(Defense Dept.), Energy, Installations,
and Environment(SAF/EIE), Operational Energy, 1665*

Air Force Pentagon, #4B941, 20330-1665; (571) 256-4711. Roberto Guerrero, Deputy Assistant Secretary. Public Affairs, (703) 697-4936.
Web, www.safie.hq.af.mil/OpEnergy

Provides policy, governance, and oversight of energy optimization programs, including waste elimination, uninterrupted access to fuel, and improved resiliency.

Air Force Dept. *(Defense Dept.), Energy, Installations, and Environment, (SAF/EIE), Environment, Safety and Infrastructure, 1665 Air Force Pentagon, #4B941, 20330-1665; (703) 697-9297. Fax, (703) 693-7568.*
James A. Sample, Deputy Assistant Secretary (Acting). Public Affairs, (703) 697-4936.
General email, safie.workflow@pentagon.af.mil
Web, www.safie.hq.af.mil/environment

Responsible for policy, governance, and oversight of Air Force environmental compliance, natural and cultural resource management, installation energy, facilities and utilities, and occupational health and safety. Interests include radioactive materials management and safety.

Air Force Dept. *(Defense Dept.), Energy, Installations, and Environment, (SAF/EIE), Installations, 1665 Air Force Pentagon, #4B941, 20330-1665; (703) 695-3592. Robert E. Moriarty, Deputy Assistant Secretary. Public Affairs, (703) 697-4936.*
Web, www.safie.hq.af.mil/Programs/Installations

Military office that provides management oversight for Air Force installations, including asset management, base closures, military construction, family housing, community and congressional interface, joint use of airfields, ranges, and disposal of real property.

Army Dept. *(Defense Dept.), Installations, Energy, and Environment, 110 Army Pentagon, #3E464, 20310-0110; (703) 692-9800. Fax, (703) 692-9808.*
Hon. Paul (Jack) W. Farnan, Assistant Secretary (Acting). Web, www.army.mil/asaiee, Twitter, @ASArmyIEE and Facebook, www.facebook.com/ASAIEE

Civilian office that establishes policy, provides strategic direction, and supervises all matters pertaining to infrastructure, Army installations and contingency bases, energy, and environmental programs to enable global Army operations.

National Nuclear Security Administration (NNSA) *(Energy Dept.), Naval Nuclear Propulsion, Bldg. 197, 1333 Isaac Hull Ave. S.E., MS 1070, 20376; (202) 781-4195. Fax, (202) 781-4588. Adm. James Frank Caldwell Jr. (USN), Deputy Administrator.*
Web, www.energy.gov/nnsa/missions/powering-navy

Designs, develops, and operates the militarily effective nuclear propulsion plants and ships. Responsible for maintaining and improving related facilities, radiological controls, and environmental safety.

National Nuclear Security Administration (NNSA) *(Energy Dept.), Safety, Infrastructure, and Operations, 1000 Independence Ave. S.W., #6G092, 20585; (202) 586-4379. James McConnell, Associate Administrator.*

Web, www.energy.gov/nnsa/nnsa-offices/safety-infrastructure-operations

Implements programs, policies, procedures, and new technology to ensure existing facilities are safely operated, managed, and that new facilities are up to safety and quality standards.

▶CONGRESS

For a listing of relevant congressional committees and subcommittees, please see pages 634–635 or the Appendix.

Base Closings, Economic Impact

▶AGENCIES

Air Force Dept. *(Defense Dept.), Energy, Installations, and Environment, (SAF/EIE), 1665 Air Force Pentagon, #4B996, SAF/IE, 20330-1665; (703) 695-5023. Fax, (703) 693-7568. Jeniffer L. Miller, Principal Deputy Assistant Secretary. Public Affairs, (703) 697-4936.*
General email, safie.workflow@pentagon.af.mil
Web, www.safie.hq.af.mil, Twitter, @AFEnergy and Facebook, www.facebook.com/AirForceEnergy

Civilian office that plans and reviews the building, repairing, renovating, and closing of Air Force bases.

Air Force Dept. *(Defense Dept.), Energy, Installations, and Environment, (SAF/EIE), Installations, 1665 Air Force Pentagon, #4B941, 20330-1665; (703) 695-3592. Robert E. Moriarty, Deputy Assistant Secretary. Public Affairs, (703) 697-4936.*
Web, www.safie.hq.af.mil/Programs/Installations

Military office that provides management oversight for implementing base closings and base realignment under the Base Realignment Act (BRAC).

Defense Dept. (DoD), *Employment and Compensation, 4800 Mark Center Dr., #06F15, SCTP Division, Alexandria, VA 22350-1100; (703) 882-5196. Kelly Cruz, Director. Web, www.dcpas.osd.mil/EC*

Manages workforce restructuring programs for Defense Dept. civilians, including downsizing, placement, voluntary early retirement, and transition assistance programs.

Defense Dept. (DoD), *Local Defense Community Cooperation, 2231 Crystal Dr., #520, Arlington, VA 22202-4704; (703) 697-2130. Fax, (703) 607-0170. Patrick J. O'Brien, Director, (703) 697-2123. Web, www.oea.gov*

Civilian office that helps community officials develop strategies and coordinate plans to alleviate the economic effect of major defense program changes, including base closings (BRAC) and contract cutbacks.

Marine Corps *(Defense Dept.), Installation Command, Installation and Logistics, 3000 Marine Corps Pentagon, #2D153A, 20350-3000; (703) 695-8570. Fax, (703) 697-7543. Brig. Gen. Daniel B. Conley (USMC), Assistant Deputy Commandant.*

Web, www.mcicom.marines.mil, www.iandl.marines.mil, Press, mcicomcommstrat@usmc.mil and Facebook, www.facebook.com/InstallationsandLogistics

Military office that reviews studies on base closings under the Base Realignment Act (BRAC).

Commissaries, PXs, and Service Clubs

► AGENCIES

Defense Commissary Agency *(Defense Dept.),* 1300 E Ave., Fort Lee, VA 23801-1800; (804) 734-8253. William F. Moore, Director.
Web, https://commissaries.com, Twitter, @YourCommissary and Facebook, www.facebook.com/YourCommissary

Serves as a representative for the Defense Commissary Agency in the Pentagon and the Washington, DC, area. Monitors legislation and regulations.

Defense Dept. (DoD), *Army and Air Force Exchange, Washington Office,* 2530 Crystal Dr., #4158, Arlington, VA 22202; (703) 602-8975. Thomas C. Shull, Director. Toll-free, (800) 527-2345. Toll-free store locator, (800) 527-6790.
Web, www.shopmyexchange.com

Delivers goods and services to the military community at competitively low prices. Returns earnings to Army and Air Force to support morale, welfare, and recreation programs. (Headquarters in Dallas, Tex.)

Navy Dept. *(Defense Dept.),* *Manpower and Reserve Affairs,* 1000 Navy Pentagon, #4E590, 20350-1000; (703) 695-4333. Robert D. Hogue, Assistant Secretary (Acting).
Web, www.secnav.navy.mil/mra/Pages/default.aspx and General email, m&ra_webmailbox.fct@navy.mil

Civilian office that develops policies for Navy and Marine Corps commissaries, exchanges, and service clubs and reviews their operations.

Navy Dept. *(Defense Dept.),* *Navy Exchange Service Command, (NEXCOM),* 701 S. Courthouse Rd., Arlington, VA 22204; (757) 631-4170. Andy Howell, Vice President of Policy and Washington Affairs. Online store, (877) 810-9030.
Web, www.mynavyexchange.com and Facebook, www.facebook.com/NavyExchange

Civilian office that serves as a liaison among the Navy Exchange Service Command, the Navy Supply Systems Command, Congress, and the Defense Dept. (Headquarters in Virginia Beach, Va.)

► CONGRESS

For a listing of relevant congressional committees and subcommittees, please see pages 634–635 or the Appendix.

► NONGOVERNMENTAL

American Logistics Assn., 1101 Vermont Ave. N.W., #1002, 20005 (mailing address: 1200 18th St. N.W., #700, Washington DC 20036); (202) 466-2520. Fax, (240) 823-9181. Steve Rosetti, President, ext. 4162.
General email, membership@ala-national.org
Web, www.ala-national.org and Twitter, @ALA_National

Membership: suppliers of military commissaries and exchanges. Acts as liaison between the Defense Dept. and service contractors; monitors legislation and testifies on issues of interest to members. Monitors legislation.

United Service Organizations (USO), 2111 Wilson Blvd., #1200, Arlington, VA 22201-7677 (mailing address: P.O. Box 96860, Washington, DC 20077); (703) 908-6400. Fax, (703) 908-6402. J. D. Crouch II, President. Toll-free, (888) 484-3876.
Web, www.uso.org, Twitter, @the_USO, Facebook, www.facebook.com/theUSO and YouTube, www.youtube.com/theuso

Voluntary civilian organization chartered by Congress. Provides military personnel and their families in the United States and overseas with social, educational, and recreational programs.

Construction, Housing, and Real Estate

► AGENCIES

Air Force Dept. *(Defense Dept.),* *Civil Engineer Center (AFCEC),* 1260 Air Force Pentagon, 20330; (703) 695-0640. Fax, (703) 693-4893. Brig. Gen Patrick Ryder III, Director.
General email, afimsc.pa.workflow@us.af.mil
Web, www.afcec.af.mil and Facebook, www.facebook.com/TheAFCEC

Military office that plans and directs construction of Air Force facilities in the United States and overseas. Oversees the Civil Engineer Center in San Antonio, Texas.

Air Force Dept. *(Defense Dept.),* *Energy, Installations, and Environment, (SAF/EIE),* 1665 Air Force Pentagon, #4B996, SAF/IE, 20330-1665; (703) 695-5023. Fax, (703) 693-7568. Jeniffer L. Miller, Principal Deputy Assistant Secretary. Public Affairs, (703) 697-4936.
General email, safie.workflow@pentagon.af.mil
Web, www.safie.hq.af.mil, Twitter, @AFEnergy and Facebook, www.facebook.com/AirForceEnergy

Civilian office that plans and reviews construction policies and programs of Air Force military facilities (including the Military Construction Program), basing of major weapons systems and units, housing programs, and real estate buying, selling, and leasing in the United States.

Air Force Dept. *(Defense Dept.),* *Energy, Installations, and Environment, (SAF/EIE), Installations,* 1665 Air Force Pentagon, #4B941, 20330-1665; (703) 695-3592. Robert E. Moriarty, Deputy Assistant Secretary. Public Affairs, (703) 697-4936.
Web, www.safie.hq.af.mil/Programs/Installations

Military office that provides management oversight for Air Force installations, including asset management, military construction, family housing, and disposal of real property.

Air Force Dept. *(Defense Dept.)*, *Housing,* 1260 Air Force Pentagon, #4C1057, 20330-1260; (703) 692-2644. *Alvin Boone, Branch Chief.*
Web, www.housing.af.mil

Military office responsible for Air Force Family and Unaccompanied Housing programs at military installations in the United States and overseas.

Army Corps of Engineers *(Defense Dept.)*, 441 G St. N.W., #3K05, 20314-1000; (202) 761-0011. *Lt. Gen. Scott A. Spellman (USA), Chief of Engineers.* General email, hq-publicaffairs@usace.army.mil
Web, www.usace.army.mil, Twitter, @USACEHQ and Facebook, www.facebook.com/USACEHQ

Military office that establishes policy and designs, directs, and manages civil works and military construction projects of the Army Corps of Engineers; directs the Army's real estate leasing and buying for military installations and civil works projects.

Defense Dept. (DoD), *Construction,* 3400 Defense Pentagon, #5C646, 20301-3400; (703) 697-6195. *Michael McAndrew, Deputy Assistant Secretary.*
Web, www.acq.osd.mil/eie/FIM/FIM_index.html

Responsible for military construction and facility-related legislative proposals and policies to manage worldwide defense installations and to acquire, construct, maintain, modernize, and dispose of defense facilities. Prepares the department's annual military construction budget; manages military construction, real property maintenance, and base operations; oversees host nation programs for facilities; and develops procedures for measuring the effect of defense facilities on military readiness.

Marine Corps *(Defense Dept.)*, *Installation Command, Installation and Logistics,* 3000 Marine Corps Pentagon, #2D153A, 20350-3000; (703) 695-8570. Fax, (703) 697-7543. *Brig. Gen. Daniel B. Conley (USMC), Assistant Deputy Commandant.*
Web, www.mcicom.marines.mil, www.iandl.marines.mil, Press, mcicomcommstrat@usmc.mil and Facebook, www.facebook.com/InstallationsandLogistics

Military office responsible for military construction and the acquisition, management, and disposal of Marine Corps real property.

Marine Corps *(Defense Dept.)*, *Installations Command,* 3000 Marine Corps Pentagon, #2E208, 20350-3000; (703) 695-6824. *Todd Calhoun, Executive Director; Brig. Gen. Daniel B. Conley, Commander.*
Web, www.mcicom.marines.mil, Twitter, @MCICOM_HQ and Facebook, www.facebook.com/MCICOM.HQ

Control point for the Marine Corps divisions of public works, family housing, and natural resources and environmental affairs.

Navy Dept. *(Defense Dept.)*, *Energy, Installations, and Environment,* 1000 Navy Pentagon, #4E739, 20350-1000; (703) 693-4530. Fax, (703) 693-1165. *Meredith A. Berger, Assistant Secretary.*
Web, www.secnav.navy.mil/eie, Twitter, @ASNavyEIE and Facebook, www.facebook.com/ASNEIE

Civilian office that monitors and reviews construction of Navy military facilities and housing and the buying and leasing of real estate in the United States and overseas. Interests include environmental planning, protection, and restoration; conservation of natural resources.

Navy Dept. *(Defense Dept.)*, *Naval Facilities Engineering Systems Command,* 1322 Patterson Ave. S.E., #1000, Washington Navy Yard, DC 20374-5065; (202) 685-9000. (202) 685-9499. *Rear Adm. John Korka (USN), Commander; Jennifer LaTorre, Executive Director.*
Web, www.navfac.navy.mil, Twitter, @NAVFAC and Facebook, www.facebook.com/navfac

Military command that plans, designs, and constructs facilities for Navy and other Defense Dept. activities around the world and manages Navy public works, utilities, environmental programs, and real estate.

Navy Dept. *(Defense Dept.)*, *Real Estate,* 1322 Patterson Ave. S.E. #1000, Washington Navy Yard, DC 20374-5065; (703) 614-5848. *Traci Hennessy, Director,* (703) 614-5848; *Nikki Hunt, Director Oversight and Governance,* (202) 685-9204.
Web, www.navfac.navy.mil/products_and_services/am/products_and services/real_estate.html, Twitter, @NAVFAC and Facebook, www.facebook.com/navfac

Military office that directs the Navy's real estate leasing, buying, and disposition for military installations.

U.S. Coast Guard (USCG) *(Homeland Security Dept.)*, *Housing Policy Division,* 2703 Martin Luther King Jr. Ave. S.E., MS 7907, 20593-7907; (202) 475-5407. *Melissa Fredrickson, Chief.*
General email, HQS-SMB-CG-HOUSING@uscg.mil
Web, www.dcms.uscg.mil

Provides housing and management for uniformed Coast Guard personnel.

Veterans Affairs Dept. (VA), *Construction and Facilities Management (CFM),* 425 Eye St. N.W., 6th Floor, 20001 (mailing address: 810 Vermont Ave. N.W., MS 003C, Washington, DC 20420); (202) 632-4607. *Michael D. Brennan, Executive Director (Acting).*
General email, cfm@va.gov
Web, www.cfm.va.gov

Principal construction and real estate arm of the Veterans Administration. Manages all major VA construction and leasing projects.

▶ **CONGRESS**

For a listing of relevant congressional committees and subcommittees, please see pages 634–635 or the Appendix.

PROCUREMENT, ACQUISITION, AND LOGISTICS

General

▶**AGENCIES**

Air Force Dept. *(Defense Dept.), Air Force Acquisition (SAF/AQ), Logistics and Product Support (SAF/AQD),* 1060 Air Force Pentagon, #4D138, 20330-1060; (703) 693-2185. Angela (Angie) L. Tymofichuk, Deputy Assistant Secretary.
Web, ww3.safaq.hq.af.mil/Organizations

Facilitates the supply chain process to provide secure and sustainable resources for the Air Force.

Air Force Dept. *(Defense Dept.), Air Force Acquisition (SAF/AQ), Program Executive Office for Combat and Mission Support (PEO-CM),* Joint Base Anacostia-Bolling, 112 Luke Ave. S.W., #330, 20032; (202) 404-3207. Fax, (202) 404-6351. Nancy K. Andrews, Executive Officer. General email, afpeocm-shared@pentagon.af.mil
Web, ww3.safaq.hq.af.mil/Organizations/AFPEO-CM

Regulates the acquisition and delivery of the Air Force's operational and mission support services.

Air Force Dept. *(Defense Dept.), Air Force Acquisition, Contracting (SAF/AQC),* 1060 Air Force Pentagon, 20330-1060; (571) 256-2397. Fax, (571) 256-2431. Maj. Gen. Cameron G. Holt, Deputy Assistant Secretary.
Web, ww3.safaq.hq.af.mil/contracting

Develops, implements, and enforces contracting policies on Air Force acquisitions worldwide, including research and development services, weapons systems, logistics services, and operational contracts.

Air Force Dept. *(Defense Dept.), Air Force Acquisition, Global Power Programs (SAF/AQP),* 1060 Air Force Pentagon, #4A122, 20330; (571) 256-0191. Fax, (571) 256-0280. Maj. Gen. John J. Nichols, Director. Public inquiries, (703) 697-3039.
Web, ww3.safaq.hq.af.mil/Organizations

Military office that directs Air Force acquisition and development programs within the tactical arena.

Air Force Dept. *(Defense Dept.), Air Force Acquisition, Technology, and Logistics (SAF/AQ),* 1060 Air Force Pentagon, #4E962, 20330-1060; (703) 697-6361. Fax, (703) 693-6400. Darlene Costello, Assistant Secretary (Acting). Public inquiries, (703) 697-3039.
Web, ww3.safaq.hq.af.mil

Air Force office that directs and reviews Air Force procurement policies and programs.

Army Dept. *(Defense Dept.), Procurement,* 103 Army Pentagon, #2D528, 20310-0103; (703) 695-2488. Megan Dake, Deputy Assistant Secretary.
Web, www.army.mil

Directs and reviews Army procurement policies.

Defense Acquisition University *(Defense Dept.),* 9820 Belvoir Rd., Fort Belvoir, VA 22060-5565; (703) 805-3459. Fax, (703) 805-2639. James P. Woolsey, President. Toll-free, (866) 568-6924.
General email, DAUhelp@dau.edu
Web, www.dau.edu and Twitter, @DAUNow

Academic institution that offers courses to military and civilian personnel who specialize in acquisition and procurement. Conducts research to support and improve management of defense systems acquisition programs.

Defense Dept. *(DoD), Acquisition and Sustainment,* 3010 Defense Pentagon, #3E1010, 20301-3010; (703) 697-7021. Gregory M. Kausner, Under Secretary (Acting).
Web, www.acq.osd.mil

Supervises Dept.'s acquisitions; establishes policies for acquisition, including procurement of goods and services, research and development, developmental testing, and contract administration, as well as policies for logistics, maintenance, and sustainment support.

Defense Dept. *(DoD), Defense Acquisition Regulations System (DARS) Directorate and DARS Council,* 3060 Defense Pentagon, #3B938, 20301-3060; (571) 372-6176. Linda Neilson, Director.
Web, www.acq.osd.mil/dpap/dars

Develops procurement regulations and manages changes to procurement regulations for the Defense Dept.

Defense Dept. *(DoD), Defense Pricing and Contracting,* 3060 Defense Pentagon, #3B938, 20301-3060; (703) 695-7145. Fax, (571) 256-7004. John M. Tenaglia, Principal Director.
Web, www.acq.osd.mil/asda/dpc/index.html

Responsible for all acquisition and procurement policy matters for the Defense Dept. Serves as principal adviser to the under secretary of defense for acquisition, technology, and logistics on strategies relating to all major weapon systems programs, major automated information systems programs, and services acquisitions.

Defense Dept. *(DoD), Operational Test and Evaluation,* 1700 Defense Pentagon, #3E1088, 20301-1700; (703) 697-3655. Fax, (703) 614-9103. Nikolas H. Guerttin Jr., Director.
Web, www.dote.osd.mil

Ensures that major acquisitions, including weapons systems, are operationally effective and suitable prior to full-scale investment. Provides the secretary of defense and Congress with independent assessment of these programs.

Defense Dept. *(DoD), Sustainment,* 3500 Defense Pentagon, #1E518, 20301-3500; (703) 697-1369. Fax, (703) 693-0555. Steven J. Morani, Assistant Secretary.
General email, osd.pentagon.ousd-atl.mbx@mail.mil
Web, www.acq.osd.mil/log

Formulates and implements department policies and programs for the conduct of logistics, maintenance, materiel readiness, strategic mobility, and sustainable support.

Defense Logistics Agency *(Defense Dept.)*, *8725 John Jay Kingman Rd., #2533, Fort Belvoir, VA 22060-6221; (703) 767-5200. Fax, (703) 767-5207. Vice Adm. Michelle C. Skubic (USN), Director. Press, (703) 767-6200.*

Web, www.dla.mil and Twitter, @DLAmil

Administers defense contracts; acquires, stores, and distributes food, clothing, medical, and other supplies used by the military services and other federal agencies; administers programs related to logistical support for the military services; and assists military services with developing, acquiring, and using technical information and defense materiel and disposing of materiel no longer needed.

Defense Logistics Agency *(Defense Dept.)*, *Energy, 8725 John Jay Kingman Rd., #4950, Fort Belvoir, VA 22060-6222; (703) 767-5042. Fax, (703) 767-9690. Brig. Gen. Jimmy R. Canlas (USAF), Commander, (571) 767-9706. Public Affairs, (703) 767-4108. Toll-free, (877) 352-2255. DLA Energy Operations Center, (571) 767-8240.*

General email, dlaenergypublicaffairs@dla.mil

Web, www.dla.mil/Energy

Provides the Defense Dept. and other federal agencies with products and services to meet energy-related needs; facilitates the cycle of storage and deployment of fuels and other energy sources, including petroleum, electricity, water, and natural gas, as well as space and missile propellants. Provides information on alternative fuels and renewable energy and serves as the executive agent for the Defense Dept.'s bulk petroleum supply chain.

Defense Logistics Agency *(Defense Dept.)*, *Logistics Operations, 8725 John Jay Kingman Rd., Fort Belvoir, VA 22060-6221; (703) 767-1600. Fax, (703) 767-1588. R. Adm. Joseph Noble (USN), Director. Press, (703) 767-6200.*

Web, www.dla.mil/HQ/LogisticsOperations

Oversees management, storage, and distribution of items used to support logistics for the military services and federal agencies. Synchronizes the Defense Logistics Agency's capabilities with the combatant commands, military services, the joint staff, other combat support defense agencies, and designated federal agencies. Provides logistics policy, with an emphasis on modernizing business systems and maximizing readiness and combat logistics support.

Defense Logistics Agency *(Defense Dept.)*, *Strategic Materials, 8725 John Jay Kingman Rd., #3229, Fort Belvoir, VA 22060-6223; (703) 767-5500. Fax, (703) 767-3316. Ronnie Favors, Administrator. Press, (703) 767-6479.*

Web, www.dla.mil/HQ/Acquisition/Strategicmaterials and Twitter, @DLAmil

Manages the national defense stockpile of strategic and critical materials. Purchases strategic materials, including beryllium and newly developed high-tech alloys. Disposes of excess materials, including tin, silver, industrial diamond stones, tungsten, and vegetable tannin.

Marine Corps *(Defense Dept.)*, *Contracts Division (LB), Contracting System (HQMC I-L HCA), 701 S. Courthouse Rd., #2000, Arlington, VA 22204; (703) 604-3580. Fax, (703) 604-6675. Jamie Thompson, Asst. Deputy Commander, (703) 604-3583.*

Web, www.iandl.marines.mil/divisions/contracts(LB) .aspx

Military office responsible for award and administration of contracts for supplies and services to support installation and logistics requirements of the Marine Corps Operating Forces and supporting establishments. directs Marine Corps procurement programs.

National Nuclear Security Administration (NNSA) *(Energy Dept.)*, *Acquisition and Project Management, 1000 Independence Ave. S.W., #IJ009, 20585; (202) 586-5627. Fax, (202) 586-6002. Robert B. Raines, Associate Administrator.*

Web, www.energy.gov/nnsa/nnsa-offices/acquisition-and-project-management

Monitors necessary federal acquisition and project management policies and regulations. Seeks to improve agency's program cost and scheduling performance.

Navy Dept. *(Defense Dept.)*, *Procurement, 1000 Navy Pentagon, #BF992A, 20350-1000; (703) 614-9595. Cindy R. Shaver, Deputy Assistant Secretary; Steven A. Nickle, Executive Director.*

Web, www.secnav.navy.mil/rda/Pages/DASN_P.aspx

Directs and reviews Navy acquisition and logistics issues.

U.S. Coast Guard (USCG) *(Homeland Security Dept.)*, *Acquisition Directorate, 2703 Martin Luther King Jr. Ave. S.E., MS 7816, 20593-7816; (202) 475-3000. Rear Adm. Douglas Schofield, Assistant Commandant.*

General email, acquisition@uscg.mil

Web, www.dcms.uscg.mil/Our-Organization/Assistant-Commandant-for-Acquisitions-CG-9

Administers all procurement made through the Acquisition Contract Support Division.

▶CONGRESS

For a listing of relevant congressional committees and subcommittees, please see pages 634–635 or the Appendix.

▶NONGOVERNMENTAL

CompTIA, *Public Advocacy, 322 4th St. N.E., 20002-5824; Fax, (630) 678-8384. Todd Thibodeaux, President. Press, (202) 682-4458. Toll-free, (866) 835-8020.*

General email, techvoice@comptia.org

Web, www.comptia.org, Twitter, @CompTIA and YouTube, www.youtube.com/c/comptia

Membership: companies providing information technology and electronics products and services to government organizations at the federal, state, and local levels. Provides information on governmental affairs, business intelligence, industry trends, and forecasts. Monitors legislation and regulation on federal procurement of technology products and services. (Headquarters in Downers Grove, Ill.)

National Defense Transportation Assn. (NDTA), *50 S. Pickett St., #220, Alexandria, VA 22304; (703) 751-5011. Fax, (703) 823-8761. Vice Adm. William A. Brown (USN, Ret.), President. Toll-free, (844) 620-2715.*

Web, www.ndtahq.com, Twitter, @NDTAHQ and Facebook, www.facebook.com/NationalDefense TransportationAssociation

Membership: transportation users, manufacturers, and mode carriers; information technology firms; and related military, government, and civil interests worldwide. Promotes a strong U.S. transportation capability through coordination of private industry, government, and the military.

16

Science and Technology

GENERAL POLICY AND ANALYSIS

Basic Resources

▶ AGENCIES

National Institute of Standards and Technology (NIST) *(Commerce Dept.), Special Programs Office,* 100 Bureau Dr., Gaithersburg, MD 20899;
General email, spo_inquiries@nist.gov

Web, www.nist.gov/special-programs-office-spo

Fosters collaboration among government, military, academic, professional, and private organizations to respond to critical national needs through science-based standards and technology innovation, including areas of forensic science and information technology.

National Institutes of Health (NIH) *(Health and Human Services Dept.), Science Policy (OSP),* 6705 Rockledge Dr., #750, Bethesda, MD 20892-7985; (301) 496-9838. Fax, (301) 496-9839. Lyric Jorgenson, Associate Director (Acting).
General email, sciencepolicy@od.nih.gov

Web, https://osp.od.nih.gov and Twitter, @NIH_OSP

Advises the NIH director on science policy issues affecting the biomedical research community. Participates in the development of new policy and program initiatives. Monitors and coordinates agency planning and evaluation activities. Plans and implements a comprehensive science education program. Develops and implements NIH policies and procedures for the safe conduct of recombinant DNA and other biotechnology activities.

National Science Foundation (NSF), 2415 Eisenhower Ave., Alexandria, VA 22314; (703) 292-5111. Fax, (703) 292-9232. Sethuramen Panchanathan, Director, (703) 292-8000. Legislative and Public Affairs, (703) 292-8010. Library, (703) 292-7830. TTY, (800) 281-8749.
General email, info@nsf.gov

Web, www.nsf.gov, Twitter, @NSF, Facebook, www .facebook.com/US.NSF and YouTube, www.youtube.com/ user/VideosatNSF

Sponsors scientific and engineering research; develops and helps implement science and engineering education programs; fosters dissemination of scientific information; promotes international cooperation within the scientific community; and assists with national science policy planning.

National Science Foundation (NSF), *National Science Board,* 2415 Eisenhower Ave., Room W 19200, Alexandria, VA 22134; (703) 292-7000. Fax, (703) 292-9008. John Veysey, Executive Officer, (703) 292-4527.
Web, www.nsf.gov/nsb and Facebook, www.facebook.com/ NationalScienceBoard

Formulates policy for the National Science Foundation; advises the president on national science policy.

Office of Management and Budget (OMB) *(Executive Office of the President), Energy, Science, and Water,* 725 17th St. N.W., #8002, 20503; (202) 395-3404. John Pasquantino, Deputy Associate Director.
Web, www.whitehouse.gov/omb

Assists and advises the OMB director in budget preparation; analyzes and evaluates programs in space and science, including the activities of the National Science Foundation and the National Aeronautics and Space Administration; coordinates OMB science, energy, and space policies and programs.

Office of Science and Technology Policy (OSTP) *(Executive Office of the President),* Eisenhower Executive Office Bldg., 1650 Pennsylvania Ave. N.W., 20504; (202) 456-4444. Alondria Nelson, Director. Press, (202) 456-6124.
General email, engagement@ostp.gov

Web, www.whitehouse.gov/ostp and Twitter, @WHOSTP

Advises the president and Executive Branch on the scientific, engineering, and technological aspects of the economy, national security, homeland security, health, foreign relations, the environment, and the technological recovery and use of resources, among other topics. Leads interagency science and technology policy coordination efforts.

Office of Science and Technology Policy (OSTP) *(Executive Office of the President), National Science and Technology Advisory Council,* Eisenhower Executive Office Bldg., 1650 Pennsylvania Ave. N.W., 20504; (202) 456-4444. Maria Zuber, Co-chair; Frances Arnold, Co-chair.
General email, nstc@ostp.op.gov

Web, www.whitehouse.gov/ostp/nstc and Twitter, @WHOSTP45

Coordinates science and technology research, development activities, policies, and programs that involve more than one federal agency. Activities concern earth sciences, materials, forestry research, and radiation policy.

Office of Science and Technology Policy (OSTP) *(Executive Office of the President), Science,* Eisenhower Executive Office Bldg., 1650 Pennsylvania Ave. N.W., 20504; (202) 456-4444. Francis Collins, Chief Science Advisor.
General email, info@ostp.gov

Web, www.whitehouse.gov/ostp

Advises the president and others within the executive office on the impact of science and technology on domestic and international affairs; coordinates executive office and federal agency actions related to these issues. Analyzes policies on biological, physical, social, and behavioral sciences and engineering; coordinates executive office and federal agency actions related to these issues. Evaluates the effectiveness of government science programs. Provides technical support to Homeland Security Dept.

Office of Science and Technology Policy (OSTP) *(Executive Office of the President), Technology and Innovation,* Eisenhower Executive Office Bldg., 1650 Pennsylvania Ave. N.W., 20504; (202) 456-4444. Fax, (202) 395-1224. Alondra Nelson, Deputy Director.
Press, engagement@ostp.eop.gov.

SCIENCE AND TECHNOLOGY RESOURCES IN CONGRESS

For a complete listing of congressional committees, including their full contact information, leadership, membership, and jurisdictions, please refer to the Appendix on pages 840–963.

HOUSE:

House Administration Committee, (202) 225-2061.
Web, cha.house.gov

House Agriculture Committee, (202) 225-2171.
Web, agriculture.house.gov

Subcommittee on Biotechnology, Horticulture, and Research, (202) 225-2171.

Subcommittee on Conservation and Forestry, (202) 225-2171.

House Appropriations Committee, (202) 225-2771.
Web, appropriations.house.gov

Subcommittee on Commerce, Justice, Science, and Related Agencies, (202) 225-3351.

Subcommittee on Interior, Environment, and Related Agencies, (202) 225-3081.

Subcommittee on Labor, Health and Human Services, Education, and Related Agencies, (202) 225-3508.

House Armed Services Committee, (202) 225-4151.
Web, armedservices.house.gov

Subcommittee on Cyber, Innovative Technologies, and Information Systems, (202) 225-4151.

House Education and Labor Committee, (202) 225-3725.
Web, edlabor.house.gov

Subcommittee on Early Childhood, Elementary, and Secondary Education, (202) 225-3725.

Subcommittee on Higher Education and Workforce Investment, (202) 225-3725.

House Energy and Commerce Committee, (202) 225-2927.
Web, energycommerce.house.gov

Subcommittee on Communications and Technology, (202) 225-2927.

House Homeland Security Committee, (202) 226-2616.
Web, homeland.house.gov

Subcommittee on Cybersecurity, Infrastructure Protection, and Innovation, (202) 226-2616.

House Judiciary Committee, (202) 225-3951.
Web, judiciary.house.gov

Subcommittee on Courts, Intellectual Property, and the Internet, (202) 225-5741.

House Natural Resources Committee, (202) 225-6065.
Web, naturalresources.house.gov

Subcommittee on Energy and Mineral Resources, (202) 225-9297.

Subcommittee on National Parks, Forests, and Public Lands, (202) 226-7736.

Subcommittee on Oversight and Investigations, (202) 225-7107.

Subcommittee on Water, Oceans, and Wildlife, (202) 225-8331.

House Oversight and Reform Committee, (202) 225-5051.
Web, oversight.house.gov

Subcommittee on Environment, (202) 225-5051.

House Science, Space, and Technology Committee, (202) 225-6375.
Web, science.house.gov

Subcommittee on Energy, (202) 225-6375.

Subcommittee on Environment, (202) 225-6375.

Subcommittee on Investigations and Oversight, (202) 225-6375.

General email, info@ostp.gov

Web, www.whitehouse.gov/ostp

Analyzes policies and advises the president on technology and related issues of physical, computational, and space sciences; coordinates executive office and federal agency actions related to these issues. Issues include national broadband access; advancing health IT; modernizing public safety communications; and clean manufacturing.

Office of Science (*Energy Dept.*), *1000 Independence Ave. S.W., #7B058, 20585; (202) 586-5430. Fax, (202) 586-4120. V. Stephen Binkley, Director (Acting).*
Web, https://science.energy.gov and Twitter, @doescience

Advises the secretary on the department's physical science and energy research and development programs; the management of the nonweapons multipurpose laboratories; and education and training activities required for basic and applied research. Manages the department's

high-energy physics, nuclear physics, fusion energy sciences, basic energy sciences, health and environmental research, and computational and technology research. Provides and operates the large-scale facilities required for research in the physical and life sciences.

▶**CONGRESS**

For a listing of relevant congressional committees and subcommittees, please see pages 688–689 or the Appendix.

Government Accountability Office (GAO), *Natural Resources and Environment (NRE), 441 G St. N.W., 20548; (202) 512-3841. Frank Rusco, Director.*
Web, www.gao.gov/about/careers/our-teams

Audits, analyzes, and evaluates for Congress federal agriculture, food safety, and energy programs; provides guidance on issues including efforts to ensure a reliable and environmentally sound energy supply, land and water

Subcommittee on Research and Technology, (202) 225-6375.

Subcommittee on Space and Aeronautics, (202) 225-6375.

House Small Business Committee, (202) 225-4038.
Web, smallbusiness.house.gov

Subcommittee on Innovation, Entrepreneurship, and Workforce Development, (202) 225-4038.

SENATE:

Senate Agriculture, Nutrition, and Forestry Committee, (202) 224-2035.
Web, agriculture.senate.gov

Subcommittee on Conservation, Climate, Forestry, and Natural Resources, (202) 224-2035.

Subcommittee on Food and Nutrition, Specialty Crop, Organics, and Research, (202) 224-2035.

Senate Appropriations Committee, (202) 224-7363.
Web, appropriations.senate.gov

Subcommittee on Commerce, Justice, Science, and Related Agencies, (202) 224-7363.

Subcommittee on Interior, Environment, and Related Agencies, (202) 224-7363.

Subcommittee on Labor, Health and Human Services, Education, and Related Agencies, (202) 224-7363.

Senate Armed Services Committee, (202) 224-3871.
Web, armed-services.senate.gov

Subcommittee on Cybersecurity, (202) 224-3871.

Subcommittee on Emerging Threats and Capabilities, (202) 224-3871.

Subcommittee on Strategic Forces, (202) 224-3871.

Senate Commerce, Science, and Transportation Committee, (202) 224-0411.
Web, commerce.senate.gov

Subcommittee on Aviation Safety, Operations, and Innovation, (202) 224-0411.

Subcommittee on Communications, Media, and Broadband, (202) 224-0411.

Subcommittee on Consumer Protection, Product Safety, and Data Security, (202) 224-0411.

Subcommittee on Oceans, Fisheries, Climate Change, and Manufacturing, (202) 224-0411.

Subcommittee on Space and Science, (202) 224-0411.

Subcommittee on Surface Transportation, Maritime, Freight, and Ports, (202) 224-0411.

Senate Energy and Natural Resources Committee, (202) 224-4971.
Web, energy.senate.gov

Subcommittee on Energy, (202) 224-4971.

Subcommittee on Public Lands, Forests, and Mining, (202) 224-4971.

Subcommittee on Water and Power, (202) 224-4971.

Senate Environment and Public Works Committee, (202) 224-8832.
Web, epw.senate.gov

Subcommittee on Clean Air, Climate, and Nuclear Safety, (202) 224-8832.

Subcommittee on Fisheries, Water, and Wildlife, (202) 224-8832.

resources management, protection of the environment, hazardous and nuclear wastes threat reduction, food safety, and investment in science.

▶ **NONGOVERNMENTAL**

American Assn. for the Advancement of Science (AAAS), *1200 New York Ave. N.W., 12th Floor, 20005; (202) 326-6400. Sudip Parikh, Chief Executive Officer. Press, (202) 326-6440.*
Web, www.aaas.org, Twitter, @AAAS and Facebook, www .facebook.com/AAAS.Science

Membership: scientists, affiliated scientific organizations, and individuals interested in science. Promotes science education; the increased participation of women, minorities, and the disabled in the science and technology workforce; the responsible use of science in public policy; international cooperation in science; and the increased public engagement with science and technology. Sponsors

national and international symposia, workshops, and meetings; publishes *Science* magazine.

American Assn. for the Advancement of Science (AAAS), *Office of Government Relations, 1200 New York Ave. N.W., 20005; (202) 326-6600. Fax, (202) 289-4950. Joanne Padron Carney, Chief. General email, govrelations@aaas.org*
Web, www.aaas.org/programs/office-government-relations and Twitter, @AAAS_GR

Serves as bridge between the science and engineering and the policymaking communities, and as a resource on science policy and research budgets. Advocates for the importance of scientific research and research enterprise, the use of science in policymaking, and education and engagement.

Center for Strategic and International Studies, *Strategic Technologies Program, 1616 Rhode Island Ave. N.W., 20036; (202) 887-0200. James Andrew Lewis, Director.*

General email, techpolicy@csis.org

Web, www.csis.org/programs/strategic-technologies-program and Twitter, @CyberCSIS

Conducts and publishes research on emerging technologies, intelligence reform, and space and globalization programs. Interests include cybersecurity, intelligence, privacy and surveillance, technology and innovation, Internet governance, and 5G networks.

Council of Scientific Society Presidents, 1155 16th St. N.W., 20005; (202) 872-6023. Cindy Reed Paska, Executive Director. Membership, (254) 776-3550.

General email, cpaska@sciencepresidents.org

Web, www.sciencepresidents.org

Membership: presidents, presidents-elect, and immediate past presidents of professional scientific societies and federations. Supports professional science education. Serves as a forum for discussion of emerging scientific issues, formulates national science policy, and develops the nation's scientific leadership.

Federation of American Scientists (FAS), 1112 16th St. N.W., #400, 20036; (202) 454-4660. Daniel (Dan) Correa, Chief Executive Officer.

General email, fas@fas.org

Web, www.fas.org, Twitter, @FAScientists and Facebook, www.facebook.com/fascientists

The policy and advocacy organization was founded to meet national security challenges with evidence-based, scientifically-driven, and nonpartisan policy, analysis, and research. Conducts studies and monitors legislation on issues and problems related to science and technology, especially U.S. nuclear arms policy, energy, arms transfer, and civil aerospace issues.

Information Technology and Innovation Foundation, 700 K St. N.W., #600, 20001; (202) 449-1351. Fax, (202) 638-4922. Robert D. Atkinson, President. Press, (202) 626-5744.

General email, mail@itif.org

Web, www.itif.org, Twitter, @ITIFdc and Facebook, www.facebook.com/innovationpolicy

Nonprofit think tank that supports the advancement of science and technology. Studies and publishes reports on policy. Holds forums for policymakers to discuss issues affecting technological innovation.

National Academies of Sciences, Engineering, and Medicine (NASEM), Keck Center, 500 5th St. N.W., 20001; (202) 334-2000. Fax, (202) 334-2419. Marcia McNutt, President; Ken Fulton, Executive Officer. Library, (202) 334-2125. Press, (202) 334-2138. Publications, (800) 624-6242.

General email, contact@nas.edu

Web, www.nationalacademies.org, Twitter, @theNASEM and Facebook, www.facebook.com/NationalAcademies

Serves as the principal operating agency of the National Academy of Sciences, National Academy of Engineering, and the National Academy of Medicine. Program units focus on physical, social, and life sciences; applications

of science, including medicine, transportation, and education; international affairs; and U.S. government policy. Library open to the public by appointment.

National Academies of Sciences, Engineering, and Medicine (NASEM), *Government-University-Industry Research Roundtable (GUIRR),* Keck Center, 500 5th St. N.W., #WS516, 20001; (202) 334-3486. Fax, (202) 334-1369. Susan Sauer Sloan, Director.

General email, guirr@nas.edu

Web, www.nationalacademies.org/guirr/government-university-industry-research-roundtable

Forum sponsored by the National Academy of Sciences, National Academy of Engineering, and Institute of Medicine. Provides scientists, engineers, and members of government, academia, and industry with an opportunity to discuss ways to catalyze productive cross-sector collaboration, take action on scientific matters of national importance, and improve the infrastructure for science and technology research.

National Academy of Science (NAS), Keck Center, 500 5th St. N.W., 20001; (202) 334-2000. Marcia McNutt, President; Ken Fulton, Executive Director. Press, (202) 334-2138.

General email, worldwidewebfeedback@nas.edu

Web, www.nasonline.org, Twitter, @theNASciences, Facebook, www.facebook.com/theNASciences, Press, news@nas.edu and YouTube, www.youtube.com/user/theNASciences

Society whose members are elected in recognition of important contributions to the field of engineering and technology. Examines questions of science and technology at the request of the federal government; promotes international cooperation. (Affiliated with the National Academies of Sciences, Engineering, and Medicine [NASEM].)

Society for Science and the Public, 1719 N St. N.W., 20036; (202) 785-2255. Fax, (202) 785-3751. Maya Ajmera, Chief Executive Officer. Toll-free, (800) 552-4412.

General email, society@societyforscience.org

Web, www.societyforscience.org, Twitter, @Society4Science, Facebook, www.facebook.com/societyforscience and YouTube, www.youtube.com/user/SocietyforScience

Promotes understanding and appreciation of science and the role it plays in human advancement. Sponsors science competitions and other science education programs in schools; awards scholarships. Publishes *Science News* and *Science News for Students*. Provides funds and training to select U.S. science and math teachers who serve under-resourced students.

Data, Statistics, and References

▶ **AGENCIES**

Dibner Library of the History of Science and Technology (*Smithsonian Institution*), National Museum of American History, 10th St. and Constitution Ave. N.W., MS 672, 20560 (mailing address: P.O. Box 37012, MS 154,

Washington, DC 20013-7012); (202) 633-3872.
Lilla Vekerdy, Head of Special Collections. Press, (202)
633-1522.
General email, Dibnerlibrary@si.edu

Web, www.library.si.edu/libraries/dibner, Twitter,
@SILibraries and Facebook, www.facebook.com/
SmithsonianLibraries

Collection includes major holdings in the history of
science and technology dating from the fifteenth century to the nineteenth century. Extensive collections
in engineering, transportation, chemistry, mathematics,
physics, electricity, and astronomy. Open to the public
by appointment.

Goddard Space Flight Center *(National Aeronautics and*
Space Administration), Science Proposal Support Office
(SPSO), 8800 Greenbelt Rd., Ms 605, Greenbelt, MD 20771;
(301) 286-0807. David T. Leisawitz, Chief.
General email, spso@gsfc.nasa.gov

Web, http://science.gsfc.nasa.gov/spso

Supports the writing of proposals for NASA, within
the Goddard Space Flight Center.

Goddard Space Flight Center *(National Aeronautics and*
Space Administration), Solar System Exploration Data
Services (SSEDSO), 8800 Greenbelt Rd., MS 690.1,
Greenbelt, MD 20771; (301) 286-1743. Stephanie A. Getty,
Director (Acting), (301) 614-5442.
General email, request@nssdc.gsfc.nasa.gov

Web, http://science.gsfc.nasa.gov/solarsystem

Coordinates data management and archiving plans
within NASA's Science Mission. Operates the National
Space Science Data Center (NSSDC) as a permanent
archive for data associated with NASA's missions, the
Crustal Dynamics Data Information System (CDDIS),
and the Planetary Data System (PDS).

National Institute of Standards and Technology (NIST)
(Commerce Dept.), Bldg. 101, 100 Bureau Dr., #A1134,
Gaithersburg, MD 20899-1000 (mailing address: 100
Bureau Dr., MS 1000, Gaithersburg, MD 20899); (301)
975-2000. Fax, (301) 869-8972. James Olthoff, Under
Secretary. Information, (301) 975-6478. TTY, (800)
877-8339.
General email, director@nist.gov

Web, www.nist.gov

Nonregulatory agency that serves as national reference
and measurement laboratory for the physical and engineering sciences.

National Institute of Standards and Technology (NIST)
(Commerce Dept.), Information Services (ISO), Research
Library, 100 Bureau Dr., MS 2500, Gaithersburg, MD
20899-2500; (301) 975-3052. Fax, (301) 869-8071.
Susan Makar, Librarian, (301) 975-3054.
General email, library@nist.gov

Web, www.nist.gov/nvl

Creates and maintains a virtual knowledge base that
supports research and administrative needs for the institute. Includes material on engineering, chemistry, physics,

mathematics, materials science, and computer science.
Home to NIST museum and history program. Publication
and information services available to the public.

National Institute of Standards and Technology (NIST)
(Commerce Dept.), Information Technology Lab,
Statistical Engineering, Bldg. 222, 100 Bureau Dr.,
#A-247, MS 8980, Gaithersburg, MD 20899-8980; (301)
975-2839. Fax, (301) 975-3144. William F. Guthrie,
Division Chief, (301) 975-2854.
Web, www.nist.gov/itl/sed

Promotes the use of effective statistical techniques for
planning analysis of experiments in the physical sciences
within industry and government; interprets experiments
and data collection programs. Offers training courses and
workshops in methods and techniques.

National Institute of Standards and Technology (NIST)
(Commerce Dept.), Material Measurement Laboratory,
Bldg. 227, 100 Bureau Dr., #A311, MS 8300, Gaithersburg,
MD 20899-8300; (301) 975-8300. Fax, (301) 975-3845.
Stephanie Hooker, Director (Acting).
General email, mmlinfo@nist.gov

Web, www.nist.gov/mml

Serves as the national reference laboratory for measurements in the chemical, biological, and material sciences.
Researches industrial, biological, and environmental
materials and processes to support development in
manufacturing, nanotechnology, electronics, energy, health
care, law enforcement, food safety, and other areas. Disseminates reference measurement procedures, certified
reference materials, and best-practice guides.

National Institute of Standards and Technology (NIST)
(Commerce Dept.), Physical Measurement Laboratory,
Bldg. 221, 100 Bureau Dr., #B160, MS 8400, Gaithersburg,
MD 20899-8400; (301) 975-4200. Fax, (301) 975-3038.
James G. Kushmerick, Director.
Web, www.nist.gov/pml

Develops and disseminates national standards of
measurement for length, mass, force, acceleration, time,
wavelength, frequency, humidity, and radiation. Collaborates with industries, universities, and professional and
standards-setting organizations.

National Institute of Standards and Technology (NIST)
(Commerce Dept.), Reference Materials, 100 Bureau Dr.,
MS 2300, Gaithersburg, MD 20899-2300; (301) 975-2200.
Steven Choquette, Chief.
General email, srminfo@nist.gov

Web, www.nist.gov/srm

Supports accurate and compatible measurements by
certifying and providing over 1,200 Standard Reference
Materials.

National Institute of Standards and Technology (NIST)
(Commerce Dept.), Standard Reference Data, 100 Bureau
Dr., MS 6410, Gaithersburg, MD 20899-8500; Fax, (301)
975-4553. Adam Morey, Chief, (301) 975-3173. Toll-free,
(844) 374-0183.

General email, data@nist.gov

Web, www.nist.gov/srd

Collects and disseminates critically evaluated physical, chemical, and materials properties data in the physical sciences and engineering for use by industry, government, and academic laboratories. Develops databases in a variety of formats, including disk, CD-ROM, and online.

National Museum of American History (*Smithsonian Institution*), *Library, 14th St. and Constitution Ave. N.W., Room 5016, 20560-0630 (mailing address: Room 5016, P.O. Box 37012, MS 630, Washington, DC 20013-7012); (202) 633-3865. Fax, (202) 633-3427. Trina Brown, Head Librarian, (202) 633-3867.*

General email, nmahlibrary@si.edu

Web, https://library.si.edu/libraries/american-history and Online catalogue, http://siris-libraries.si.edu/ipac20/ipac.jsp?profile=liball

Collection includes materials on the history of medicine, science, and technology, with concentrations in engineering, transportation, and applied science. Open to the public by appointment. All library holdings are listed in the online catalog.

National Oceanic and Atmospheric Administration (NOAA) (*Commerce Dept.*), *Central Library, Silver Spring Metro Center 3, 1315 East-West Hwy., 2nd Floor, Silver Spring, MD 20910; (301) 713-2600. Fax, (301) 713-4598. Deirdre (Dee) Clarkin, Director, (301) 713-2606. Reference service, (301) 713-2600, ext. 157. TTY, (301) 713-2779.*

General email, library.reference@noaa.gov

Web, https://library.noaa.gov

Collection includes electronic NOAA documents, reports, and videos; electronic and print journals; the NOAA Photo Library; bibliographic database of other NOAA libraries; and climate data. Makes interlibrary loans; library open to the public, with two forms of photo ID, Monday through Friday, 9:00 a.m.–4:00 p.m.

National Oceanic and Atmospheric Administration (NOAA) (*Commerce Dept.*), *National Centers for Environmental Information (NCEI), Silver Spring Metro Center 3, 1315 East-West Hwy., 4th Floor, Silver Spring, MD 20910-3282; (301) 713-3277. Fax, (301) 713-3300. Joe Pica, Director (Acting).*

General email, ncei.info@noaa.gov

Web, www.ncei.noaa.gov

Responsible for hosting and providing access to comprehensive oceanic, atmospheric, and geophysical data. Provides world's largest collection of freely available oceanographic data, including water temperatures dating back to the late 1700s and measuring thousands of meters deep, scientific journals, rare books, historical photo collections, and maps through the NOAA Central Library, and data management expertise and training. Merger of NOAA's three data centers: National Climatic Data Center, National Geophysical Data Center, and National Oceanographic Data Center, which includes the National Coastal Data Development Center.

National Oceanic and Atmospheric Administration (NOAA) (*Commerce Dept.*), *National Environmental Satellite, Data, and Information Service (NESDIS), Silver Spring Metro Center 1, 1335 East-West Hwy., 8th Floor, Silver Spring, MD 20910; (301) 713-3578. Fax, (301) 713-1249. Stephen Volz, Assistant Administrator. Press, (301) 713-0214.*

Web, www.nesdis.noaa.gov and Twitter, @NOAASatellites

Acquires and disseminates global environmental (marine, atmospheric, solid earth, and solar-terrestrial) satellite data. Maintains comprehensive data and information referral service.

National Science Foundation (NSF), *National Center for Science and Engineering Statistics (NCSES), 2415 Eisenhower Ave., Room W 14200, Alexandria, VA 22134; (703) 292-8780. Fax, (703) 292-9092. Emilda B. Rivers, Director, (703) 292-7773.*

Web, www.nsf.gov/statistics

Compiles, analyzes, and disseminates quantitative information about domestic and international resources devoted to science, engineering, and technology. Provides information to other federal agencies for policy formulation.

National Technical Information Service (NTIS) (*Commerce Dept.*), *5301 Shawnee Rd., Alexandria, VA 22312; (703) 605-6000. Fax, (703) 605-6900. Greg Capella, Director (Acting). Customer support, (703) 605-6060. Toll-free, (800) 363-2068. TTY, (703) 487-4639.*

General email, info@ntis.gov

Web, www.ntis.gov, Twitter, @NTISInfo and Facebook, www.facebook.com/NTISCustomerContactCenter

Collects and organizes technical, scientific, engineering, and business-related information generated by U.S. and foreign governments and makes it available for commercial use in the private sector. Makes available approximately 3 million works covering research and development, current events, business and management studies, translations of foreign open source reports, foreign and domestic trade, general statistics, environment and energy, health and social sciences, and hundreds of other areas. Provides computer software and computerized data files in a variety of formats, including Internet downloads. Houses the Homeland Security Information Center, a centralized source on major security concerns for health and medicine, food and agriculture, and biochemical war.

Smithsonian Institution, *Libraries, National Museum of Natural History, 10th St. and Constitution Ave. N.W., Room 29, 20560 (mailing address: P.O. Box 37012, MS 154, Washington, DC 20013-7012); (202) 633-2240. Tamar Evangelestia Dougherty, Director.*

Web, http://library.si.edu, Twitter, @SILibraries and Facebook, www.facebook.com/SmithsonianLibraries

Maintains collection of general reference, biographical, and interdisciplinary materials; serves as an information resource on institution libraries, a number of which have collections in scientific subjects, including horticulture, botany, science and technology, and anthropology.

U.S. Geological Survey (USGS) *(Interior Dept.), Library,* 950 National Center, #1D100, Reston, VA 20192 *(mailing address: 12201 Sunrise Valley Dr., #1D100, MS 950, Reston, VA 20192); (703) 648-4301. Catharine (Cate) Canevari, Library Director, (703) 648-7182.*
General email, library@usgs.gov

Web, www.usgs.gov/core-science-systems/usgs-library

Maintains collection of books, periodicals, serials, maps, and technical reports on geology, mineral and water resources, mineralogy, paleontology, petrology, soil and environmental sciences, biology, and physics and chemistry as they relate to natural sciences. Open to the public Monday–Friday; makes interlibrary loans.

▶**CONGRESS**

For a listing of relevant congressional committees and sub-committees, please see pages 688–689 or the Appendix.

Library of Congress, *Science, Technology, and Business Division,* John Adams Bldg., 101 Independence Ave. S.E., #LA 500, 20540-4750; (202) 707-0948. Fax, (202) 707-1925. *Ronald (Ron) Bluestone, Chief. Business Reference Services, (202) 707-7934. Reading Room, (202) 707-5639. Technical reports, (202) 707-5655.*
Web, www.loc.gov/rr/scitech

Offers reference service by telephone, by correspondence, and in person. Maintains a collection of more than 3 million reports on science, technology, business management, and economics. Timed entry pass for visitors required, details at loc.gov/visit. Appointments recommended for researchers.

▶**NONGOVERNMENTAL**

American Statistical Assn., 732 N. Washington St., Alexandria, VA 22314-1943; (703) 684-1221. Fax, (703) 997-7299. *Ronald Wasserstein, Executive Director. Toll-free, (888) 231-3473.*
General email, asainfo@amstat.org

Web, www.amstat.org, Twitter, @AmstatNews and Facebook, www.facebook.com/AmstatNews

Membership: statistical practitioners in industry, government, and academia. Supports excellence in the development, application, and dissemination of statistical science through meetings, publications, membership services, education, accreditation, and advocacy.

International Programs

▶**AGENCIES**

Bureau of International Organization Affairs (IO) *(State Dept.), Specialized and Technical Agencies (STA),* 2401 E St. N.W., #SA-1, L409, 20037; (202) 663-3121. *David E. Brown, Director.*
Web, www.state.gov/p/io

Oversees U.S. participation in international specialized and technical organizations, including the International Atomic Energy Agency, the United Nations Environment Programme, and the Commission on Sustainable Development. Works to ensure that United Nations agencies follow United Nations Conference on Environment and Development recommendations on sustainable growth.

Bureau of Oceans and International Environmental and Scientific Affairs (OES) *(State Dept.),* 2201 C St. N.W., #3880 and #7256, 20520-7818; (202) 647-7575. *Monica Medina, Assistant Secretary, (202) 647-1554.*
Web, www.state.gov/e/oes, Twitter, @SciDiplomacyUSA, Facebook, www.facebook.com/ScienceDiplomacyUSA and YouTube, www.youtube.com/channel/rCumiP05SKp5qlhi ZbXBJEiw?view_as=subscriber

Formulates and implements policies and proposals for U.S. international scientific, technological, environmental, oceanic and marine, Arctic and Antarctic, and space programs; coordinates international science and technology policy with other federal agencies.

Bureau of Oceans and International Environmental and Scientific Affairs (OES) *(State Dept.), Policy and Public Outreach (PPO),* 2201 C St. N.W., #2880, 20520; (202) 647-2958. *Timothy L. Smith, Director, (202) 647-4658.*
Web, www.state.gov/about-us-office-of-policy-and-public-outreach

Integrates oceans, environment, polar, science, technology, and health issues into U.S. foreign policy, and works to address these issues in the media, NGOs, the private sector, and Congress.

Bureau of Oceans and International Environmental and Scientific Affairs (OES) *(State Dept.), Science and Technology Cooperation (STC),* 1800 G St. N.W., #10100, SA-22, 20006; (202) 663-2623. *Reece Smith, Director.*
Web, www.state.gov/about-us-office-of-science-and-technology-cooperation, Twitter, @SciDiplomacyUSA and Facebook, www.facebook.com/ScienceDiplomacyUSA

Advances U.S. foreign policy through science and technology, and fosters a global environment that supports innovation and transparency in government.

National Institute of Standards and Technology (NIST) *(Commerce Dept.), International and Academic Affairs,* 100 Bureau Dr., MS 1090, Gaithersburg, MD 20899-1090; (301) 975-3069. Fax, (301) 975-3530. *Claire M. Saundry, Director, (301) 975-2386. TTY, (301) 975-8295.*
General email, oiaa@nist.gov

Web, www.nist.gov/iaao

Represents the institute in international functions involving science and technology; coordinates programs with foreign institutions; assists scientists from foreign countries who visit the institute for consultation. Administers a postdoctoral research associates program and oversees NIST's cooperation with academic institutions and researchers.

National Oceanic and Atmospheric Administration (NOAA) *(Commerce Dept.), National Environmental Satellite, Data, and Information Service (NESDIS),* Silver

Spring Metro Center 1, 1335 East-West Hwy., 8th Floor, Silver Spring, MD 20910; (301) 713-3578. Fax, (301) 713-1249. Stephen Volz, Assistant Administrator. Press, (301) 713-0214.
Web, www.nesdis.noaa.gov and Twitter, @NOAASatellites

Acquires and disseminates global environmental satellite data: marine, atmospheric, solid earth, and solar-terrestrial. Participates, with the National Meteorological Center, in the United Nations World Weather Watch Programme developed by the World Meteorological Organization. Manages U.S. civil earth-observing satellite systems and atmospheric, oceanographic, geophysical, and solar data centers. Provides the public, businesses, and government agencies with environmental data and information products and services.

National Oceanic and Atmospheric Administration (NOAA) *(Commerce Dept.), National Weather Service (NWS), National Centers for Environmental Prediction (NCEP), 5830 University Research Court, College Park, MD 20740; (301) 683-1314. Fax, (301) 683-1325. Mike Farrar, Director, (301) 683-1315.*
Web, www.ncep.noaa.gov

The National Center for Environmental Prediction and the National Environmental Satellite, Data, and Information Service are part of the World Weather Watch Programme developed by the United Nations World Meteorological Organization. Collects and exchanges data with other nations; provides other national weather service offices, private meteorologists, and government agencies with products, including forecast guidance products.

National Science Foundation (NSF), *International Science and Engineering (OISE), 2415 Eisenhower Ave., Room W17220, Alexandria, VA 22134; (703) 292-8710. Fax, (703) 292-9481. Kendra Sharp, Head.*
Web, www.nsf.gov/dir/index.jsp?org=OISE

Serves as the foundation's focal point for international scientific and engineering activities; promotes new partnerships between U.S. scientists and engineers and their foreign colleagues; provides support for U.S. participation in international scientific organizations from three overseas offices (Paris, Tokyo, and Beijing).

Smithsonian Institution, *International Relations and Global Programs, 1100 Jefferson Dr. S.W., #3123, 20560 (mailing address: P.O. Box 37012, MS 705, Washington, DC 20013-7012); (202) 633-4795. Aviva Rosenthal, Director.*
General email, global@si.edu
Web, https://global.si.edu, Twitter, @GlobalSI, Facebook, www.facebook.com/SmithsonianGlobal and YouTube, www.youtube.com/channel/UCtfCKTPkaoyBFHtE_lEYTyg

Fosters the development and coordinates the international aspects of Smithsonian scientific activities; facilitates basic research in the natural sciences and encourages international collaboration among individuals and institutions.

▶ **INTERNATIONAL ORGANIZATIONS**

InterAcademy Partnership, *Washington Office, 500 5th St. N.W., #K505, 20001; Teresa de la Puente, Executive Director.*
General email, iap@twas.org
Web, www.interacademies.org/33326/IAP-R and Twitter, @IAPartnership

Global network of science, engineering, and medical academies in countries worldwide. Promotes communication among leading authorities in the natural and social sciences; establishes regional networks of academies to identify critical issues, thereby building capacity for advice to governments and international organizations. Interests include science education, the engagement of women in science, and sustainable management of water, energy, and other resources. (Hosted by National Academies of Science, Engineering, and Medicine.)

▶ **NONGOVERNMENTAL**

American Assn. for the Advancement of Science (AAAS), *Office of International and Security Affairs (OISA), 1200 New York Ave. N.W., 20005; (202) 326-6650. Fax, (202) 289-4958. Kimberly (Kim) Montgomery, Director, (202) 326-7047.*
Web, www.aaas.org/programs/office-international-and-security-affairs

Promotes international cooperation among scientists. Helps build scientific infrastructure in developing countries. Works to improve the quality of scientific input in international discourse.

National Academies of Sciences, Engineering, and Medicine (NASEM), *Policy and Global Affairs, Keck Center, 500 5th St. N.W., #528, 20001; (202) 334-2425. Anne Petersen, Chair; Vaughan Turekian, Executive Director.*
General email, pga@nas.edu
Web, www.nationalacademies.org/pga/policy-and-global-affairs

Serves the international interests of the National Research Council, National Academy of Sciences, National Academy of Engineering, and Institute of Medicine. Promotes effective application of science and technology to the economic and social problems of industrialized and developing countries, and advises U.S. government agencies.

Research Applications

▶ **AGENCIES**

Defense Technical Information Center *(Defense Dept.), 8725 John Jay Kingman Rd., Fort Belvoir, VA 22060-6218; (703) 767-9100. Christopher E. Thomas, Administrator; Thomas Gillespie, Director. Toll-free, (800) 225-3842.*
Web, https://discover.dtic.mil, General email, dtic.belvoir.us.mbx.reference@mail.mil and Twitter, @DoDDTIC

Acts as a central repository for the Defense Dept.'s collection of current and completed research and development efforts in all fields of science and technology. Disseminates research analysis and development information to contractors, grantees, and registered organizations working on government research and development projects, particularly for the Defense Dept. Users must register with the center.

Energy Dept. (DOE), *Technology Transitions (OTT), 1000 Independence Ave. S.W., 20585; (202) 586-2000. Vanessa Z. Chan, Director.*
General email, OTT@hq.doe.gov

Web, www.energy.gov/technologytransitions/office-technology-transitions

Develops policies and establishes partnerships with the commercial sector to translate agency energy technology research and innovation into products and services for the private sector.

National Aeronautics and Space Administration (NASA), *Science Mission Directorate (SMD), 300 E St. S.W., 20546; (202) 358-3889. Thomas Zurbuchen, Associate Administrator.*
General email, science@hq.nasa.gov

Web, http://science.nasa.gov and Twitter, @NASAScienceCast

Sponsors scientific research and analysis. Exchanges information with the international science community. Primary areas of study are astronomy and astrophysics, earth sciences, heliophysics, and planetary science.

National Institutes of Health (NIH) *(Health and Human Services Dept.), Intramural Research (OIR), Technology Transfer (OTT), 6011 Executive Blvd., #325, MS 7660, Rockville, MD 20852-3804; (301) 496-7057. Fax, (301) 402-0220. Tara Kirby, Director, (301) 827-6515.*
General email, nihott@mail.nih.gov

Web, www.ott.nih.gov and Twitter, @NIH_OTT

Evaluates, protects, monitors, and manages the NIH invention portfolio. Oversees patent prosecution, negotiates, monitors and enforces patent rights and licensing agreements, and provides oversight and central policy review of cooperative research and development agreements. Responsible for the central development and implementation of technology transfer policies for two research components of the Public Health Service—the NIH and the Centers for Disease Control and Prevention.

National Science Foundation (NSF), *National Nanotechnology Initiative (NNI), 2415 Eisenhower Ave., Room C14016, Alexandria, VA 22134; (703) 292-7032. Fax, (703) 292-9467. Mihail C. Roco, Senior Adviser.*
Web, www.nsf.gov/crssprgm/nano

Coordinates multiagency efforts in understanding nanoscale phenomena and furthering nanotechnology research and development.

▶ **NONGOVERNMENTAL**

American Assn. for the Advancement of Science (AAAS), *Center for Science Diplomacy, 1200 New York Ave. N.W., 20005; (202) 326-6400. Kimberly (Kim) Montgomery, Director, (202) 326-7047.*

General email, diplomacy@aaas.org

Web, aaas.org/programs/center-science-diplomacy, Twitter, @SciDip and Facebook, www.facebook.com/sciencediplomacy

Works to elevate the role of science and diplomacy in foreign policy. Promotes science diplomacy with stakeholders in science, technology, policy, and international relations who contribute to and benefit from science diplomacy. Helps develop educational tools, training, and resources for scientists and international affairs professional in the United States and internationally. Publishes Science & Diplomacy.

American Assn. for the Advancement of Science (AAAS), *Science, Policy, and Society Programs (OSPSP), 1200 New York Ave. N.W., 20005; (202) 326-6788. Julia MacKenzie, Chief Program Officer. Press, (202) 326-6440.*
Web, www.aaas.org/programs/office-science-policy-and-society

Promotes conduct of and advise on investment in scientific research and applications. Supports dialogue between scientists and communities, including STEM education, government, workforce capacity, religion, and law.

American Assn. for the Advancement of Science (AAAS), *Scientific Responsibility, Human Rights, and Law Program (SRHRL), 1200 New York Ave. N.W., 8th Floor, 20005; (202) 326-6604. Theresa Harris, Director (Acting).*
General email, srhrl@aaas.org

Web, www.aaas.org/programs/scientific-responsibility-human-rights-law, Twitter, @AAAS-SRHRL and Facebook, www.facebook.com/SRHRL

Engages policymakers and the general public on the ethical, legal, and human-rights issues related to the conduct and application of science and technology. Defends the freedom to engage in scientific inquiry; promotes responsible research practices; advances the application of science and technology to document human rights violations.

American National Standards Institute (ANSI), *1899 L St. N.W., 11th Floor, 20036; (202) 293-8020. Fax, (202) 293-9287. S. Joe Bhatia, President, (202) 331-3605.*
General email, info@ansi.org

Web, www.ansi.org, Twitter, @ansidotorg and Facebook, www.facebook.com/ansidotorg

Administers and coordinates the voluntary U.S. private sector–led consensus standards and conformity assessment system. Serves as the official U.S. representative to the International Organization of Standardization (ISO) and, via the U.S. National Committee, the International Electrotechnical Commission (IEC), and is a U.S. representative to the International Accreditation Forum (IAF).

The Brookings Institution, *Center for Technology Innovation, 1775 Massachusetts Ave. N.W., 20036; (202) 797-6090. Nicol E. Turner-Lee, Director, (202) 238-3563.*

Web, www.brookings.edu/about/center-for-technology-innovation and Twitter, @drturnerlee

Research center promoting policymaking and public debate about technology innovation, including digital infrastructure, the mobile economy, e-governance, digital media and entertainment, cybersecurity and privacy, digital medicine, and virtual education.

The Brookings Institution, *Governance Studies, 1755 Massachusetts Ave. N.W., 20036; (202) 797-6090. (202) 797-6288. Darrell M. West, Director, (202) 797-6481. Web, www.brookings.edu/governance, Twitter, @BrookingsGov and Twitter, Director, @DarrWest*

Promotes public debate on technology innovation and develops data-driven scholarship to understand the legal, economic, social, and governance impact of technology.

National Academies of Sciences, Engineering, and Medicine (NASEM), *Behavioral, Cognitive, and Sensory Sciences Board, Keck Center, 500 5th St. N.W., 11th Floor, 20001; (202) 334-2678. Fax, (202) 334-2210. Terrie E Moffitt, Chair; Alix Beatty, Senior Program Officer. General email, BBCSS@nas.edu Web, www.nationalacademies.org/bbcss/board-on-behavioral-cognitive-and-sensory-sciences*

Advises government agencies on policies relating to the behavioral, cognitive, and sensory sciences.

Public Technology Institute (PTI), *322 4th St. N.E., 20002; (202) 626-2400. Alan R. Shark, Executive Director, (202) 626-2445. Press, (202) 626-2432. General email, techvoice@comptia.org Web, www.pti.org, Twitter, @Public_Tech and Facebook, www.facebook.com/Public-Technology-Institute-98024848530*

Cooperative research, development, and technology-transfer organization of cities and counties in North America. Applies available technological innovations and develops other methods to improve public services.

RAND Corp., *Washington Office, 1200 S. Hayes St., Arlington, VA 22202-5050; (703) 413-1100. Fax, (703) 413-8111. Nicholas Burger, Director; Anita Chandra, Director for Social and Economic Well-Being, ext. 5323. Web, www.rand.org*

Conducts research on energy, emerging technologies and critical systems, space and transportation, technology policies, international cooperative research, water resources, ocean and atmospheric sciences, and other technologies in defense and nondefense areas. (Headquarters in Santa Monica, Calif.)

SRI International, *Washington Office, 1100 Wilson Blvd., #2800, Arlington, VA 22209; (703) 524-2053. David Parekh, Corporate Executive Officer. Web, www.sri.com and Twitter, @SRI_Intl*

Research and consulting organization that conducts basic and applied research for government, industry, and business. Interests include engineering, physical and life sciences, and international research. (Headquarters in Menlo Park, Calif.)

Union of Concerned Scientists, *Washington Office, 1825 K St. N.W., #800, 20006; (202) 223-6133. Annette Williams, Director, DC Operations; Lisa Nurnberger, Press, (202) 331-6959. Press, (202) 331-6959. General email, ucs@ucsusa.org Web, www.ucsusa.org, Twitter, @UCSUSA, Facebook, www.facebook.com/unionofconcernedscientists and YouTube, www.youtube.com/user/ConcernedScientists*

Science advocacy organization with interests in the areas of clean energy, clean transportation, food and agriculture, global warming, nuclear power, and nuclear weapons. Combines technical analysis, education and advocacy, and engagement with the public and scientific communities to advocate for science-based policies and programs. (Headquarters in Cambridge, Mass.)

Scientific Research Practices

▶ **AGENCIES**

Assistant Secretary for Health (OASH) *(Health and Human Services Dept.),* **Human Research Protections (OHRP),** *Tower Bldg., 1101 Wootton Pkwy., #200, Rockville, MD 20852; (240) 453-6900. Fax, (240) 453-6909. Jerry Menikoff, Director. General email, ohrp@hhs.gov Web, www.hhs.gov/ohrp*

Promotes the rights, welfare, and well-being of subjects involved in research conducted or supported by the Health and Human Services Dept.; helps ensure that research is carried out in accordance with federal regulations by providing clarification and guidance, developing educational programs and materials, and maintaining regulatory oversight.

Assistant Secretary for Health (OASH) *(Health and Human Services Dept.),* **Research Integrity (ORI),** *Tower Bldg., 1101 Wootton Pkwy., #240, Rockville, MD 20852; (240) 453-8200. Fax, (301) 443-5351. Wanda Jones, Director (Acting). General email, askori@hhs.gov Web, https://ori.hhs.gov and Twitter, @HHS_ORI*

Seeks to promote the quality of Public Health Service extramural and intramural research programs. (Extramural programs provide funding to research institutions that are not part of the federal government. Intramural programs provide funding for research conducted within federal government facilities.) Provides oversight of institutional inquiries and investigations of research misconduct and technical assistance to institutions during these proceedings; reviews institutional findings and process and proposes administrative actions to the Health and Human Services Dept. when the Office of Research Integrity makes a finding of research misconduct; sponsors educational programs and activities for professionals interested in research integrity; sponsors grants for conferences and basic research on research integrity; administers institutional assurance program; and coordinates with institutions to protect from retaliation individuals involved in research misconduct matters.

Education Dept., *Chief Financial Officer (CFO), Finance and Operations (OFO),* 400 Maryland Ave. S.W., #214-32, 20202; Fax, (202) 205-0765. Denise Carter, Assistant Secretary (Acting).
General email, jim.clemmens@ed.gov
Web, www2.ed.gov/about/offices/list/ofo/index.html?src=oc

Advises grantees and applicants for department-supported research on regulations for protecting human subjects. Provides guidance to the Education Dept. on the requirements for complying with the regulations. Serves as the primary Education Dept. contact for matters concerning the protection of human subjects in research.

Food and Drug Administration (FDA) *(Health and Human Services Dept.), Good Clinical Practice (OGCP),* White Oak Bldg. 32, 10903 New Hampshire Ave., #5103, Silver Spring, MD 20993; (301) 796-8340. Fax, (301) 847-8640. Joanne Less, Director.
General email, gcp.questions@fda.hhs.gov
Web, www.fda.gov/science-research/clinical-trials-and-human-subject-protection/regulations-good-clinical-practice-and-clinical-trials

Provides information to the FDA Commissioner about clinical human research trials and impacts on policy.

National Aeronautics and Space Administration (NASA), *Chief Health and Medical Officer,* 300 E St. S.W., 20546; (202) 358-2390. James D. Polk, Chief Health and Medical Officer.
Web, www.nasa.gov/offices/ochmo/main/index.html

Monitors human and animal research and clinical practice to ensure that NASA adheres to appropriate medical and ethical standards and satisfies all regulatory and statutory requirements.

National Institutes of Health (NIH) *(Health and Human Services Dept.), Human Subjects Research Protections (OHSRP),* Clinic Center, Bldg. 10, 6700B Rockledge Dr., #4300, Bethesda, MD 20817; (301) 402-3713. Fax, (301) 402-3443. Jonathan M. Green, Director.
General email, IRB@od.nih.gov
Web, https://irbo.nih.gov/confluence

Helps NIH investigators understand and comply with ethical principles and regulatory requirements involved in human subjects research. Assists NIH components in administering and regulating human subjects research activities.

National Institutes of Health (NIH) *(Health and Human Services Dept.), Intramural Research (OIR), Animal Care and Use (OACU),* Bldg. 31, 9000 Rockville Pike, #B1C37, MS 2252, Bethesda, MD 20892-2252; (301) 496-5424. Fax, (301) 480-8298. Stephen Denny, Director.
General email, secoacu@nih.gov
Web, http://oacu.oir.nih.gov

Provides guidance for the humane care and use of animals in the intramural research program at NIH.

National Institutes of Health (NIH) *(Health and Human Services Dept.), Laboratory Animal Welfare (OLAW),* 6700B Rockledge Dr., #2500, MS 6910, Bethesda, MD 20892-7982; (301) 496-7163. Fax, (301) 480-3394. Patricia A. Brown, Director.
General email, olaw@mail.nih.gov
Web, https://olaw.nih.gov/home.htm and Twitter, @NIH_OLAW

Develops and monitors policy on the humane care and use of animals in research conducted by any public health service supported research, training, and testing.

National Institutes of Health (NIH) *(Health and Human Services Dept.), Stem Cell Research,* Bldg. 31, 9000 Rockville Pike, 31 Center Dr., #8A52, MS 2540, Bethesda, MD 20892-2540; (301) 496-3765. Timothy J. LaVaute, Director.
General email, stemcell@mail.nih.gov
Web, https://stemcells.nih.gov

Seeks the advice of scientific leaders in stem cell research about the challenges to advancing the stem cell research agenda and strategies for overcoming them.

Office of Science *(Energy Dept.), Biological and Environmental Research (BER), Biological Systems Science Division (BSSD), Human Subjects Protection Program,* 19901 Germantown Rd., #SC23.2, Germantown, MD 20874-1290 (mailing address: Germantown Bldg., 1000 Independence Ave. S.W., #SC23.2, Washington, DC 20585); (301) 903-7693. Fax, (301) 903-0567. Elizabeth (Libby) White, Program Manager.
General email, humansubjects@science.doe.gov
Web, https://science.osti.gov/ber/human-subjects

Works to protect the rights and welfare of human subject research volunteers by establishing guidelines and enforcing regulations on scientific research that uses human subjects, including research that involves identifiable or high-risk data, worker populations or subgroups; human testing devices, products, or materials; and bodily materials. Acts as an educational and technical resource to investigators, administrators, and institutional research boards.

▶ **NONGOVERNMENTAL**

American Assn. for Laboratory Accreditation (A2LA), 5202 Presidents Court, #220, Frederick, MD 21703; (301) 644-3248. Fax, (240) 454-9449. Lonnie Spires, President.
General email, info@a2la.org
Web, www.a2la.org, Twitter, @A2LA_ and Facebook, www.facebook.com/a2laaccreditation

Monitors and supports formal recognition of competent testing and calibration laboratories (including medical laboratories), biobanking facilities, inspection bodies, product certification bodies, proficiency testing providers, and reference material producers. Offers education, networking, and advertising benefits.

American Assn. for the Advancement of Science (AAAS), *Scientific Responsibility, Human Rights, and Law Program (SRHRL),* *1200 New York Ave. N.W., 8th Floor, 20005; (202) 326-6604. Theresa Harris, Director (Acting).*
General email, srhrl@aaas.org

Web, www.aaas.org/programs/scientific-responsibility-human-rights-law, Twitter, @AAAS-SRHRL and Facebook, www.facebook.com/SRHRL

Engages policymakers and the general public on the ethical, legal, and human-rights issues related to the conduct and application of science and technology. Defends the freedom to engage in scientific inquiry; promotes responsible research practices; advances the application of science and technology to document human rights violations.

American Council of Independent Laboratories (ACIL), *1300 Eye St. N.W., #400E, 20005; (202) 887-5872. Fax, (202) 887-0021. Richard Bright, Chief Operating Officer, ext. 103.*
General email, info@acil.org

Web, www.acil.org, Twitter, @acilnews and Facebook, www.facebook.com/acil.info

Membership: independent commercial scientific and engineering firms and testing laboratories. Promotes professional and ethical business practices in providing analysis, testing, product certification, and research and consulting services in engineering, food sciences, analytical chemistry, and environmental geosciences.

AOAC International, *2275 Research Blvd., #300, Rockville, MD 20850-3250; (301) 924-7077. Fax, (301) 924-7089. David B. Schmidt, Executive Director, ext. 102. Toll-free, (800) 379-2622.*
General email, customerservice@aoac.org

Web, www.aoac.org and Twitter, @AOACNews

International association of analytical science professionals, companies, government agencies, nongovernmental organizations, and institutions. Supports the standards and method development, evaluation, and publication of reliable chemical and biological methods of analysis for foods, drugs, feed, fertilizers, pesticides, water, and other substances. Promotes voluntary consensus standards development for analytical methodology, fit-for-purpose methods, and quality measurements in the analytical sciences.

Humane Society of the United States, *Animal Research Issues,* *1255 23rd St. N.W., #450, 20037; (202) 452-1100. Kathleen (Katy) Conlee, Vice President.*
General email, ari@humanesociety.org

Web, www.humanesociety.org/about/departments/animals_research.html

Seeks to end the suffering of animals in research. Promotes the use of alternatives that replace, refine, or reduce the use of animals in scientific research, education, and consumer product testing. Conducts outreach programs aimed toward the public and the scientific community.

National Academies of Sciences, Engineering, and Medicine (NASEM), *Laboratory Assessments Board,* *Keck Center, 500 5th St. N.W., #W900, 20001; (202) 334-3311. Fax, (202) 334-2791. James P. McGee, Director; Jennie S. Hwang, Chair.*
General email, lab@nas.edu

Web, www.nationalacademies.org/lab/laboratory-assessments-board

Reviews and assesses the quality of internal research conducted at NRC laboratories, including those established by federal agencies at national laboratories and at government-owned, contractor-operated facilities.

National Assn. for Biomedical Research, *1100 Vermont Ave. N.W., #1100, 20005; (202) 857-0540. Matthew R. Bailey, President.*
General email, info@nabr.org

Web, www.nabr.org and Twitter, @NABRorg

Membership: scientific and medical professional societies, academic institutions, and research-oriented corporations involved in the use of animals in biomedical research, education and testing. Supports the humane use of animals in medical research, education, and product-safety assessment. Monitors legislation and regulations.

Society of Research Administrators International (SRA International), *1560 Wilson Blvd., #310, Arlington, VA 22209; (703) 741-0140. Evan Roberts, Executive Director, ext. 215.*
General email, info@srainternational.org

Web, www.srainternational.org, Twitter, @SocietyRAIntl and Facebook, www.facebook.com/SocResAdminINTL

Membership: scientific and medical research administrators in the United States and other countries. Educates the public about the profession; offers professional development services; sponsors mentoring and awards programs.

BIOLOGY AND LIFE SCIENCES

General

▶ **AGENCIES**

National Institute of General Medical Sciences (NIGMS) *(National Institutes of Health),* *45 Center Dr., #3AN44E, MS 6200, Bethesda, MD 20892-6200; (301) 496-7301. Jon R. Lorsch, Director.*
General email, info@nigms.nih.gov

Web, www.nigms.nih.gov, Twitter, @NIGMS and Facebook, www.facebook.com/nigms.nih.gov

Primarily supports basic biomedical research and training that lay the foundation for advances in disease diagnosis, treatment, and prevention. Areas of special interest include bioinformatics, cell biology, developmental biology, physiology, biological chemistry genetics, and computational biology.

National Museum of Natural History (*Smithsonian Institution*), 10th St. and Constitution Ave. N.W., 20560-0106 (mailing address: P.O. Box 37012, MS 106, Washington, DC 20013-7012); (202) 633-2664. *Kirk Johnson, Director; Katy Roper, Administrative Assistant, (202) 633-2664. Library, (202) 633-1184. Press, (202) 633-2950.*
General email, naturalexperience@si.edu

Web, www.mnh.si.edu, Twitter, @NMNH and Facebook, www.facebook.com/SmithsonianNMNH

Conducts research and maintains exhibitions and collections relating to the natural sciences. Collections are organized into seven research and curatorial departments: anthropology, botany, entomology, invertebrate zoology, mineral sciences, paleobiology, and vertebrate zoology.

National Museum of Natural History (*Smithsonian Institution*), **Library**, 10th St. and Constitution Ave. N.W., East Court, 1st Floor, 20560-0154 (mailing address: P.O. Box 37012, MS 154, Washington, DC 20013-7012); (202) 633-1680. *Barbara P. Ferry, Manager (Acting), (202) 633-1785.*
General email, askalibrarian@si.edu

Web, www.library.si.edu/libraries/national-museum-natural-history-library

Maintains reference collections covering anthropology, biodiversity, biology, botany, ecology, entomology, ethnology, mineral sciences, paleobiology, and zoology; permits on-site use of the collections. Open to the public by appointment; makes interlibrary loans.

National Oceanic and Atmospheric Administration (NOAA) (*Commerce Dept.*), **National Marine Fisheries Service (NMFS)**, 1315 East-West Hwy., 14th Floor, Silver Spring, MD 20910; (301) 427-8000. Fax, (301) 713-1940. *Janet Coit, Assistant Administrator. Press, (301) 427-8531.*
Web, www.fisheries.noaa.gov and Twitter, @NOAAFisheries

Conducts research and collects data on marine ecology and biology; collects, analyzes, and provides information through the Marine Resources Monitoring, Assessment, and Prediction Program. Administers the Magnuson-Stevens Fishery Conservation and Management Act and marine mammals and endangered species protection programs. Works with the Army Corps of Engineers on research into habitat restoration and conservation.

National Science Foundation (NSF), *Biological Sciences Directorate*, 2415 Eisenhower Ave., Room C 12000, Alexandria, VA 22314; (703) 292-8400. Fax, (703) 292-9154. *Joanne Tornow, Assistant Director.*
Web, www.nsf.gov/dir/index.jsp?org=bio

Serves as a forum for addressing biology research issues, sharing information, identifying gaps in scientific knowledge, and developing consensus among concerned federal agencies. Facilitates continuing cooperation among federal agencies on topical issues.

National Science Foundation (NSF), *Environmental Biology Division (DEB)*, 2415 Eisenhower Ave., Room W

12100, Alexandria, VA 22134; (703) 292-8480. Fax, (703) 292-9064. *Stephanie Hampton, Director.*
Web, www.nsf.gov/bio/deb/about.jsp

Supports research on populations, species, communities, and ecosystems, including biodiversity, phylogenetic systematics, molecular evolution, life history evolution, natural selection, ecology, biogeography, ecosystem services, conservation biology, global change, and biogeochemical cycles.

National Science Foundation (NSF), *Molecular and Cellular Biosciences Division (MCB)*, 2415 Eisenhower Ave., Room E 12400, Alexandria, VA 22134; (703) 292-8440. Fax, (703) 292-9061. *Theresa A. Good, Director, (703) 292-2450.*
Web, www.nsf.gov/div/index.jsp?div=MCB

Supports research and understanding of complex living systems at molecular, subcellular, and cellular levels.

Office of Science (*Energy Dept.*), *Biological and Environmental Research (BER)*, 19901 Germantown Rd., #SC23, Germantown, MD 20874-1290 (mailing address: Germantown Bldg., 1000 Independence Ave. S.W., #SC23, Washington, DC 20585); (301) 903-3251. Fax, (301) 903-5051. *Sharlene Weatherwax, Associate Director.*
General email, sc.ber@science.doe.gov

Web, www.energy.gov/science/ber/biological-and-environmental-research

Advances biological and environmental research and provides scientific user facilities to support innovation in energy security and environmental responsibility.

U.S. Geological Survey (USGS) (*Interior Dept.*), *Ecosystems*, 12201 Sunrise Valley Dr., MS 300, Reston, VA 20192-0002; (703) 648-4051. Fax, (703) 648-7031. *Anne E. Kinsinger, Associate Director.*
Web, www.usgs.gov/ecosystems

Conducts research and monitoring to develop and convey an understanding of ecosystem function and distributions, physical and biological components, and trophic dynamics for freshwater, terrestrial, and marine ecosystems and the human, fish, and wildlife communities they support. Subject areas include invasive species, endangered species and habitats, genetics and genomics, and microbiology.

▶ NONGOVERNMENTAL

American Institute of Biological Sciences, 950 Herndon Parkway, #450, Herndon, VA 20170; (703) 674-2500. Fax, (703) 674-2509. *Scott Glisson, Chief Executive Officer, ext. 202.*
Web, www.aibs.org and Twitter, @AIBSbiology

Membership: biologists, biology educators, academic institutions and departments, museums and science collections, and professional associations. Promotes interdisciplinary cooperation among members engaged in biological research and education; conducts educational programs for members; reviews projects supported by government grants. Publishes BioScience journal. Monitors legislation and regulations.

American Society for Biochemistry and Molecular Biology (ASBMB), 6120 Executive Blvd., #400, Bethesda, MD 20852-3110; (240) 283-6600. Fax, (301) 881-2080. Stephen Miller, Executive Director.

General email, asbmbtoday@asbmb.org

Web, www.asbmb.org, Twitter, @ASBMB and Facebook, www.facebook.com/asbmb

Membership: professional biological chemists. Participates in the International Union of Biochemistry and Molecular Biology. Publishes several journals; holds workshops and webinars. Offers scholarships and awards to minority members. Monitors legislation and regulations.

American Society for Cell Biology, 6120 Executive Blvd., #750, Rockville, MD 20852; (301) 347-9300. Fax, (301) 347-9310. Rebecca Alvania, Chief Executive Officer, (301) 347-9311.

General email, ascbinfo@ascb.org

Web, www.ascb.org, Twitter, @ASCBiology and Facebook, www.facebook.com/ASCBiology

Membership: scientists who have education or research experience in cell biology or an allied field. Promotes scientific exchange worldwide; organizes courses, workshops, and symposia. Monitors legislation and regulations.

American Society for Microbiology, 1752 N St. N.W., 20036-2904; (202) 737-3600. Stefano Bertuzzi, Chief Executive Officer, (202) 942-9303. Press, (202) 942-9365.

General email, service@asmusa.org

Web, www.asm.org, Twitter, @ASMicrobiology and Facebook, www.facebook.com/asmfan

Membership: microbiologists. Encourages education, training, scientific investigation, and application of research results in microbiology and related subjects; participates in international research.

American Type Culture Collection, 10801 University Blvd., Manassas, VA 20110-2209 (mailing address: P.O. Box 1549, Manassas, VA 20108); (703) 365-2700. Fax, (703) 365-2701. Raymond H. Cypress, Chief Executive Officer. Toll-free, (800) 638-6597.

Web, www.atcc.org, Twitter, @officialatcc and Facebook, www.facebook.com/officialatcc

Provides research and development tools, reagents, and related biological material management services to government agencies, academic institutions, and private industry worldwide. Serves as a bioresource center of live cultures and genetic material.

Carnegie Institute for Science, 5251 Broad Branch Rd. N.W., 20015; (202) 387-6400. Fax, (202) 387-8092. Eric D. Isaacs, President.

Web, https://carnegiescience.edu and Twitter, @carnegiescience

Conducts research in plant science biology, genetic and developmental biology, earth and planetary sciences, astronomy, and global ecology and matter at extreme states at the Carnegie Institution's six research departments:

Dept. of Embryology (Baltimore, Md.); Geophysical Laboratory (Washington, DC); Dept. of Global Ecology (Stanford, Calif.); Dept. of Plant Biology (Stanford, Calif.); Dept. of Terrestrial Magnetism (Washington, DC); and The Observatories (Pasadena, Calif., and Las Campanas, Chile).

Ecological Society of America, 1990 M St. N.W., #700, 20036; (202) 833-8773. Fax, (202) 833-8775. Catherine O'Riordan, Executive Director, ext. 206.

General email, esahq@esa.org

Web, www.esa.org, Twitter, @esa_org, Facebook, www.facebook.com/esa.org and YouTube, www.youtube.com/user/ESAVideos

Membership: scientists, researchers, decision makers, policy managers, and educators dedicated to understanding life on earth. Promotes research in ecology and the scientific study of the relationship between organisms and their past, present, and future environments. Interests include biotechnology; management of natural resources, habitats, and ecosystems to protect biological diversity; and ecologically sound public policies.

Federation of American Societies for Experimental Biology (FASEB), 9650 Rockville Pike, Bethesda, MD 20814-3998 (mailing address: P.O. Box 2288, Rockville, MD. 20847); (301) 634-7000. Fax, (301) 634-7001. Frank J. Krause Jr., Chief Executive Officer, (301) 634-7290.

General email, info@faseb.org

Web, www.faseb.org, Twitter, @FASEBorg and Facebook, www.facebook.com/FASEB.org

Membership; Advances biological science through collaborative advocacy for research policies that promote scientific progress and education and lead to improvements in human health. Provides educational meetings and publications to disseminate biological research results. Represents 27 scientific societies and more than 120,000 biomedical researchers around the world. Sponsors awards and fellowships.

National Academies of Sciences, Engineering, and Medicine (NASEM), *Life Sciences Board,* Keck Center, 500 5th St. N.W., 6th Floor, 20001; (202) 334-3360. Kavita M. Berger, Director; Barbara A. Schaal, Chair.

General email, bls@nas.edu

Web, www.nationalacademies.org/bls/board-on-life-sciences

Supports technical and policy research in the life sciences, including bioterrorism, genomics, biodiversity conservation, and basic biomedical research, such as stem cells.

Biotechnology

▶ AGENCIES

Animal and Plant Health Inspection Service (APHIS) (Agriculture Dept.), Biotechnology Regulatory Services (BRS), 4700 River Rd., #146, Riverdale, MD 20737; (301) 851-3877. Fax, (301) 734-8910. Bernadette R. Juarez,

Deputy Administrator. Applications and regulatory requirements, (301) 851-3886. Compliance, (301) 851-3935. Press, (301) 851-4100. fax, (301) 734-8910.
Web, www.aphis.usda.gov/aphis/ourfocus/biotechnology and Email, biotechquery@usda.gov

Regulates genetically engineered organisms as part of the Coordinated Framework for Regulation of Biotechnology to ensure that genetically engineered products are used in a manner that is safe for plant and animal health, human health, and the environment.

National Institutes of Health (NIH) *(Health and Human Services Dept.), Office of Science Policy (OSP), Biosafety, Biosecurity, and Emerging Biotechnology Division,* 6705 Rockledge Dr., #750, MS 7985, Bethesda, MD 20892; (301) 496-9838. Fax, (301) 496-9839. Cari Young, Director (Acting), (301) 451-4431.
General email, oba-osp@od.nih.gov
Web, https://osp.od.nih.gov/biosafety-biosecurity-and-emerging-biotechnology

Development and implementation of policies to conduct and oversee life sciences research.

National Library of Medicine *(National Institutes of Health), National Center for Biotechnology Information,* Bldg. 38A, 8600 Rockville Pike, 8th Floor, Bethesda, MD 20892; (301) 435-5978. Fax, (301) 480-4559.
Stephen Sherry, Director (Acting).
General email, info@ncbi.nlm.nih.gov
Web, www.ncbi.nlm.nih.gov

Creates automated systems for storing and analyzing knowledge of molecular biology and genetics. Develops new information technologies to aid in understanding the molecular processes that control human health and disease. Conducts basic research in computational molecular biology. Sponsors PubMed Central, a publicly accessible digital archive of life sciences journal literature.

Office of Science *(Energy Dept.), Biological and Environmental Research (BER), Biological Systems Science Division (BSSD),* 19901 Germantown Rd., #SC23.2, Germantown, MD 20874-1290 (mailing address: Germantown Bldg., 1000 Independence Ave. S.W., #SC23.2, Washington, DC 20585); (301) 903-5469. Fax, (301) 903-0567. Todd Anderson, Director.
Web, www.energy.gov/science/ber/biological-and-environmental-research

Supports research and technology development to achieve predictive systems-level understanding of complex biological systems, including redesign of microbes and plants for sustainable biofuel production, improved carbon storage, and contaminant remediation. Areas of research include genomic science, bioimaging technology, biological systems, and radiological sciences.

Office of Science *(Energy Dept.), Biological and Environmental Research (BER), Biological Systems Science Division (BSSD), Environmental Genomics,* 19901 Germantown Rd., #SC72, Germantown, MD 20874-1290; (301) 903-4742. Boris Wawrik, Program Manager.
Web, http://genomicscience.energy.gov

Supports research using microbial and plant genomic data, high-throughput technologies, and modeling and simulation to develop predictive understanding of biological systems behavior relevant to solving energy and environmental challenges.

▶**NONGOVERNMENTAL**

Biotechnology Innovation Organization, 1201 Maryland Ave. S.W., #900, 20024; (202) 962-9200.
Michelle McMurry-Heath, President. Press, (202) 962-9505.
General email, info@bio.org
Web, www.bio.org, Twitter, @IAmBiotech and Faceboook, www.facebook.com/IAmBiotech

Membership: U.S. and international companies engaged in biotechnology. Monitors government activities at all levels; promotes educational activities; conducts workshops.

Friends of the Earth (FOE), 1101 15th St. N.W., 11th Floor, 20005; (202) 783-7400. Fax, (202) 783-0444. Erich Pica, President, (202) 222-0714. Press, (202) 222-0746.
Web, www.foe.org, Twitter, @foe_us, Facebook, www.facebook.com/foe.us and YouTube, www.youtube.com/c/FriendsoftheEarthInt

Monitors legislation and regulations on issues related to seed industry consolidation and patenting laws and on business developments in genetic engineering and synthetic biology and their effect on farming, food production, genetic resources, and the environment.

Genetic Alliance, 26400 Woodfield Rd., #189, Damascus, MD 20872; (202) 966-5557. Fax, (202) 966-8563.
Sharon Terry, Chief Executive Officer.
General email, info@geneticalliance.org
Web, www.geneticalliance.org, Twitter, @GeneticAlliance and Facebook, www.facebook.com/GeneticAlliance

Coalition of government, industry, advocacy organizations, and private groups that seeks to advance genetic research and its applications. Promotes increased funding for research, improved access to services, and greater support for emerging technologies, tests, and treatments. Acts as an advocate on behalf of individuals and families living with genetic conditions to help transform health systems to recognize genetic issues.

J. Craig Venter Institute, 9605 Medical Center Dr., #150, Rockville, MD 20850; (301) 795-7000. J. Craig Venter, Chief Executive Officer.
Web, www.jcvi.org and Twitter, @JCVenterInst

Research institute that analyzes genomes and gene products for medical, nutritional, and agricultural uses; studies genomic sciences and their ethical, legal, and economic implications for society. Produces reports; offers courses, workshops, and internships.

Kennedy Institute of Ethics *(Georgetown University),* Healy Hall, 3700 O St. N.W., 4th Floor, 20057; (202) 687-8099. David Sulmasy, Director. Library, (202) 687-3885.

General email, kennedyinstitute@georgetown.edu

Web, https://kennedyinstitute.georgetown.edu, Twitter, @kieatgu and Facebook, www.facebook.com/ KennedyInstituteofEthics

Carries out teaching and research on bioethics, including legal and ethical definitions of death, allocation of health resources, and recombinant DNA and human gene therapy. Sponsors the annual Intensive Bioethics Course. Conducts international programs. Serves as the home of the Bioethics Research Library at Georgetown University (http://bioethics.georgetown.edu). Provides free reference assistance and bibliographic databases covering all ethical issues in health care, genetics, and biomedical research. Publishes the *Kennedy Institute of Ethics Journal*. Library open to scholars, students, and educators. Open to the public by appointment.

Botany

National Arboretum *(Agriculture Dept.)*, 3501 New York Ave. N.E., 20002-1958; (202) 245-4523. Richard T. Olsen, Director, (202) 245-4539.
Web, www.usna.usda.gov and Twitter, @USDA_ARS

Maintains public display of plants on 446 acres; provides information and makes referrals concerning cultivated plants (exclusive of field crops and fruits); conducts plant breeding and research; maintains herbarium.

National Arboretum *(Agriculture Dept.)*, *Floral and Nursery Plants Research*, 3501 New York Ave. N.E., #100, 20002; (301) 504-6848. Fax, (301) 504-5096.
Margaret Pooler, Research Leader, (301) 504-5218.
Web, www.ars.usda.gov/northeast-area/washington-dc/ national-arboretum/floral-and-nursery-plants-research and Facebook, www.facebook.com/AgriculturalResearchService

Supports research and implementation of new technologies in florist and nursery industries. Areas of research include development of new floral, nursery, and turf plants; detection and control of pathogens in ornamental plants; ornamental plant taxonomy; improvement of nursery production systems; and curation of woody landscape plant germplasm as part of the National Plant Germplasm System.

National Museum of Natural History *(Smithsonian Institution)*, *Botany*, 10th St. and Constitution Ave. N.W., 20560-0166 (mailing address: P.O. Box 37012, MS 166, Washington, DC 20013-7012); (202) 633-0920. Fax, (202) 786-2563. Eric Schuettpelz, Chair.
Library, (202) 633-1680.
Web, www.botany.si.edu

Seeks to discover and describe the diversity of plant life in terrestrial and marine environments, interpret the origins of diversity, and explain the processes responsible for diversity. Research includes systematics, phylogenetics,

anatomy, morphology, biogeography, and ecology. Studies how humans are affected by, and have altered, plant diversity. Works to manage, grow, and conserve the collection in the United States National Herbarium (more than 5 million specimens) as a global plant resource. Library open to the public Monday through Friday, 10:00 a.m.–4:00 p.m., by appointment only.

Smithsonian Institution, *Botany and Horticulture Library*, 10th St. and Constitution Ave. N.W., #W422, 20560-0166 (mailing address: P.O. Box 37012, MS 154, Washington, DC 20013-7012); (202) 633-1685.
Robin Everly, Branch Librarian.
General email, askalibrarian@si.edu

Web, https://library.si.edu/libraries/botany, Twitter, @SILibraries, Facebook, www.facebook.com/ SmithsonianLibraries and YouTube, www.youtube.com/ user/SmithsonianLibraries

Collections include taxonomic botany, plant morphology, general botany, history of botany, grasses, and algae. Permits on-site use of collections (11:00 a.m.–4:00 p.m.; appointment necessary); makes interlibrary loans. (Housed at the National Museum of Natural History.)

Smithsonian Tropical Research Institute, *Forest Global Earth Observatory (ForestGEO)*, 10th St. and Constitution Ave. N.W., MS 166, 20560; (202) 633-1836. Fax, (202) 786-2563. Stuart J. Davies, Director.
General email, ForestGEO@si.edu

Web, https://forestgeo.si.edu, Twitter, @ForestGEO and Facebook, www.facebook.com/ForestGEO

Conducts long-term forest research and contributes to the scientific community through training, grants, and partnerships with international organizations. Uses research to monitor impacts of climate change and to guide natural resource policy. (Formerly Center for Tropical Forest Science.)

For a listing of relevant congressional committees and subcommittees, please see pages 688–689 or the Appendix.

U.S. Botanic Garden, 100 Maryland Ave. S.W., 20001 (mailing address: 245 1st St. S.W., Washington, DC 20024); (202) 225-8333. Saharah Moon Chapotin, Executive Director, (202) 225-1110. Horticulture hotline, (202) 226-4785. Press, (202) 226-4145. Program registration information, (202) 225-1116. Special events, (202) 226-7674. Tour line, (202) 226-2055.
General email, usbg@aoc.gov

Web, www.usbg.gov and Facebook, www.facebook.com/ USBotanicGarden

Collects, cultivates, and grows various plants for public display and study.

American Society for Horticultural Science (ASHS), *1018 Duke St., Alexandria, VA 22314; (703) 836-4606. Michael W. Neff, Executive Director, ext. 106. General email, webmaster@ashs.org*

Web, www.ashs.org, Twitter, @ASHS_Hort and Facebook, www.facebook.com/americansocietyforhorticulturalscience

Membership: educators, government workers, firms, associations, and individuals interested in horticultural science. Promotes scientific research and education in horticulture, including international exchange of information. Publishes the *Journal of the American Society for Horticultural Science.*

American Society of Plant Biologists, *15501 Monona Dr., Rockville, MD 20855-2768; (301) 251-0560. Fax, (301) 279-2996. Crispin Taylor, Chief Executive Officer, (301) 296-0900. General email, info@aspb.org*

Web, www.aspb.org and Twitter, @ASPB

Membership: plant physiologists, plant biochemists, and molecular biologists. Seeks to educate and promote public interest in the plant sciences. Publishes journals; provides job listings for members; sponsors awards, annual conference, meetings, courses, and seminars.

Zoology

Animal and Plant Health Inspection Service (APHIS) *(Agriculture Dept.), Veterinary Services, 4700 River Rd., #39, Riverdale, MD 20737; (301) 851-3300 ext. 2. Rosemary Sifford, Deputy Administrator. General email, nvap@aphis.usda.gov*

Web, www.aphis.usda.gov/aphis/ourfocus/animalhealth

Works to protect and improve the health, quality, and marketability of our nation's animals and various wildlife and animal products. Creates priorities, objectives, strategies, and field activities for cattle, avian, swine, aquaculture, sheep and goat, equine, and cervid health. Disseminates regulatory information addressing the interstate and importation requirements of genetically engineered animals and insects that may spread animal diseases. Advises on animal health and public issues, including animal welfare, local and commercial livestock, natural resource conservation, and public health; conducts animal health monitoring and surveillance.

National Agricultural Library *(Agriculture Dept.),* **National Invasive Species Information Center (NISIC),** *10301 Baltimore Ave., Room 109-HH, Beltsville, MD 20705; Joyce Bolton, Coordinator, (301) 504-6454. Toll-Free, (800) 633-7701. General email, invasive@ars.usda.gov*

Web, www.invasivespeciesinfo.gov and Twitter, @InvasiveInfo

Serves as a reference gateway to information, organizations, and services about invasive species - plants, animals or pathogens.

National Museum of Natural History *(Smithsonian Institution), Entomology, 10th St. and Constitution Ave. N.W., 20560-0105 (mailing address: P.O. Box 37012, MS 188, #CE-723, Washington, DC 20013-7012); (202) 633-1016. Fax, (202) 786-2894. Sean G. Brady, Curator, (202) 633-0997; Gary Hamill, Specialist, (202) 633-1016. Library, (202) 633-1680.*

Web, http://entomology.si.edu

Conducts worldwide research in entomology. Maintains the national collection of insects; lends insect specimens to specialists for research and classification; conducts scholarly training and lectures; publishes research; and maintains databases. Library open to the public by appointment.

National Museum of Natural History *(Smithsonian Institution), Invertebrate Zoology, 10th St. and Constitution Ave. N.W., 20560-0163 (mailing address: P.O. Box 37012, MS 163, Washington, DC 20013-7012); (202) 633-1740. Ellen Strong, Chair. Library, (202) 633-1680.*

Web, http://invertebrates.si.edu

Conducts research on the identity, morphology, histology, life history, distribution, classification, and ecology of marine, terrestrial, and freshwater invertebrate animals (except insects); maintains the national collection of invertebrate animals; aids exhibit and educational programs; conducts predoctoral and postdoctoral fellowship programs; provides facilities for visiting scientists in the profession.

National Museum of Natural History *(Smithsonian Institution), Paleobiology, 10th St. and Constitution Ave. N.W., 20560-0121 (mailing address: P.O. Box 37012, MS 121, Washington, DC 20013-7012); (202) 633-1328. Fax, (202) 786-2832. Gene Hunt, Chair. General email, paleodept@si.edu*

Web, http://paleobiology.si.edu and Loans and visiting the collections, paleovisits@si.edu

Conducts research worldwide on invertebrate paleontology, paleobotany, sedimentology, and vertebrate paleontology; provides information on paleontology, paleoclimatology, paleoceanography, ecosystem dynamics, and processes of evolution and extinction. Maintains national collection of fossil organisms and sediment samples.

National Museum of Natural History *(Smithsonian Institution), Vertebrate Zoology, 10th St. and Constitution Ave. N.W., 20560-0159 (mailing address: P.O. Box 37012, MS 163, Washington, DC 20013-7012); (202) 633-0790. Fax, (202) 633-0182. Carole Baldwin, Chair. Library, (202) 633-1680.*

Web, http://vertebrates.si.edu

Conducts research worldwide on the systematics, ecology, evolution, zoogeography, and behavior of mammals, birds, reptiles, amphibians, and fish; maintains the national collection of specimens. Processes, sorts, and distributes to scientists specimens of marine vertebrates; engages in taxonomic sorting, community analysis, and specimen and sample data management.

▶**NONGOVERNMENTAL**

Assn. of Zoos and Aquariums, *8403 Colesville Rd., #710, Silver Spring, MD 20910-3314; (301) 562-0777. Fax, (301) 562-0888. Dan Ashe, President.*
General email, generalinquiry@aza.org
Web, www.aza.org, Twitter, @zoos_aquariums, Facebook, www.facebook.com/ZoosAquariums and YouTube, www .youtube.com/user/zooaquariumnetwork

Membership: interested individuals and professionally run zoos and aquariums in North America. Administers professional accreditation program; participates in worldwide conservation, education, and research activities.

Entomological Society of America, *3 Park Pl., #307, Annapolis, MD 21401-3722; (301) 731-4535. Fax, (301) 731-4538. Chris Stelzig, Executive Director, ext. 3012.*
General email, esa@entsoc.org
Web, www.entsoc.org, Twitter, @EntsocAmerica and Facebook, www.facebook.com/entsoc

Scientific association that promotes the science of entomology and the interests of professionals in the field, with branches throughout the United States.

Jane Goodall Institute, *1120 20th St. N.W., #520, Vienna, VA 22182; (703) 682-9220. Fax, (703) 682-9312. Anna Rathmann, Executive Director.*
Web, www.janegoodall.org and Twitter, @JaneGoodallInst

Seeks to increase primate habitat conservation, expand noninvasive primate research, and promote activities that ensure the well-being of primates. (Affiliated with Jane Goodall Institutes in Canada, Europe, Asia, and Africa.)

ENGINEERING

General

▶**AGENCIES**

National Institute of Standards and Technology (NIST) *(Commerce Dept.), Engineering Laboratory, 100 Bureau Dr., MS 8600, Gaithersburg, MD 20899-8600; (301) 975-5900. Fax, (301) 975-4032. Joannie Chin, Director, (301) 975-6815.*
General email, el@nist.gov
Web, www.nist.gov/el

Performs analytical, laboratory, and field research in the area of building technology and its applications for building usefulness, safety, and economy; produces performance criteria and evaluation, test, and measurement methods for building owners, occupants, designers, manufacturers, builders, and federal, state, and local regulatory authorities.

National Science Foundation (NSF), *Engineering Directorate (ENG/OAD), 2415 Eisenhower Ave., Room C 14000, Alexandria, VA 22314; (703) 292-8300. Fax, (703) 292-9467. Stacey Standridge, Director, (202) 517-1035.*
Web, www.nsf.gov/dir/index.jsp?org=eng

Supports fundamental research and education in engineering through grants and special equipment awards. Programs are designed to enhance international competitiveness and to improve the quality of engineering in the United States.

▶**NONGOVERNMENTAL**

American Council of Engineering Companies, *1015 15th St. N.W., 8th Floor, 20005-2605; (202) 347-7474. Fax, (202) 898-0068. Linda Bauer Darr, President.*
General email, acec@acec.org
Web, www.acec.org, Twitter, @acec_national and Facebook, www.facebook.com/acecnational

Membership: state and regional councils representing practicing engineering firms, architects, land surveyors and other specialists. Serves as an information clearinghouse for member companies in such areas as legislation, legal cases, marketing, management, professional liability, business practices, and insurance. Monitors legislation and regulations.

American Society for Engineering Education, *1818 N St. N.W., #600, 20036-2479; (202) 331-3500. Fax, (202) 265-8504. Norman L. Fortenberry, Executive Director, (202) 331-3545. Press, (202) 331-5767.*
Web, www.asee.org, Twitter, @ASEE_DC and Facebook, www.facebook.com/ASEEHQ

Membership: engineering faculty and administrators, professional engineers, government agencies, and engineering colleges, corporations, and professional societies. Conducts research, conferences, and workshops on engineering education. Monitors legislation and regulations.

American Society of Civil Engineers (ASCE), *1801 Alexander Bell Dr., Reston, VA 20191-4400; Washington Office, 25 Massachusetts Ave. N.W., #500, 20001; (202) 789-7850. Thomas W. Smith III, Executive Director. International inquiries, (703) 295-6300. Press, (202) 789-7853. Toll-free, (800) 548-2723.*
Web, www.asce.org and Twitter, @ascetweets

Membership: professionals and students in civil engineering. Organizes international conferences; maintains technical and professional reference materials; hosts e-learning sites.

American Society of Heating, Refrigerating, and Air Conditioning Engineers (ASHRAE), *Government Affairs, 1255 23rd St. N.W., #825, 20037; (202) 833-1830.*

Fax, (202) 833-0118. Mick Schwedler, Executive Vice President; Alice Yates, Director of Government Affairs.
General email, GovAffairs@ASHRAE.org

Web, www.ashrae.org, Twitter, @ashraenews, Facebook, www.facebook.com/ASHRAEupdates and YouTube, www.youtube.com/ASHRAEvideo

Membership: engineers and others involved with the heating, ventilation, air conditioning, and refrigeration industry in the United States and abroad, including students. Sponsors research, meetings, and educational activities. Monitors legislation and regulations. (Headquarters in Atlanta, Ga.)

American Society of Mechanical Engineers (ASME), Government Relations, 1828 L St. N.W., #510, 20036-5104; (202) 785-7390. Fax, (202) 429-9417.
Thomas Costabile, Executive Director; Kathryn Holmes, Director of Government Relations, (202) 785-7390.
Toll-free, (800) 843-2763.
General email, GRdept@asme.org

Web, www.asme.org, Twitter, @ASMEdotorg and Facebook, www.facebook.com/ASME.org

Serves as a clearinghouse for sharing of information between the federal government and the engineering profession. Monitors legislation and regulations. (Headquarters in New York.)

American Society of Naval Engineers (ASNE), 1423 Powhatan St., #1, Alexandria, VA 22314; (703) 836-6727. Fax, (703) 836-7491. D. (Ike) Kid Lumme (USN, Ret.), Executive Director.
General email, asnehq@navalengineers.org

Web, www.navalengineers.org, Twitter, @NavalEngineers and Facebook, www.facebook.com/navalengineers

Membership: civilian, active duty, and retired naval engineers. Provides forum for an exchange of information between industry and government involving all phases of naval engineering.

Geoprofessional Business Assn., 15800 Crabbs Branch Way, #300, Rockville, MD 20855; (301) 565-2733. (240) 669-9380. Joel G. Carson, Executive Director.
General email, info@geoprofessional.org

Web, www.geoprofessional.org, Twitter, @GBAssn and Facebook, www.facebook.com/GBAssn

Membership: geoprofessional service firms, including firms that perform geotechnical and infrastructure engineering, environmental services, and construction materials engineering and testing. Conducts conferences and a peer review program on quality control policies and procedures in geoprofessional service firms.

Institute of Electrical and Electronics Engineers–USA (IEEE-USA), Washington Office, 2001 L St. N.W., #700, 20036; (202) 785-0017. Fax, (202) 785-0835.
Chris Brantley, Managing Director, (202) 530-8349.
General email, ieeeusa@ieee.org

Web, https://ieeeusa.org, Twitter, @IEEEUSA and Facebook, www.facebook.com/ieeeusa

U.S. arm of an international technological and professional organization concerned with all areas of electrotechnology policy, including aerospace, computers, communications, biomedicine, electric power, and consumer electronics. (Headquarters in New York.)

Institute of Transportation Engineers (ITE), 1627 Eye St. N.W., #550, 20006; (202) 785-0060. Fax, (202) 785-0609. Jeffrey F. Paniati, Executive Director, ext. 131.
General email, ite_staff@ite.org

Web, www.ite.org and Twitter, @ITEhq

Membership: international professional transportation engineers. Conducts research, seminars, and training sessions; provides professional and scientific information on transportation standards and recommended practices.

International Test and Evaluation Assn., 11350 Random Hills Rd., #800, Fairfax, VA 22030; (703) 631-6220. Fax, (703) 631-6221. Carl Peterson, Vice President.
General email, info@itea.org

Web, www.itea.org

Membership: engineers, scientists, managers, and other industry, government, and academic professionals interested in testing and evaluating products and complex systems. Provides a forum for information exchange; monitors international research.

National Academies of Sciences, Engineering, and Medicine (NASEM), Infrastructure and the Constructed Environment Board, Keck Center, 500 5th St. N.W., #WS938, 20001; (202) 334-3505. Fax, (202) 334-3718. Cameron Oskvig, Director; Thomas Bostick, Chair.
General email, bice@nas.edu

Web, www.nationalacademies.org/bice/board-on-infrastructure-and-the-constructed-environment

Advises the government, the private sector, and the public on technology, science, and public policy related to the design, construction, operations, maintenance, security, and evaluation of buildings, facilities, and infrastructure systems; the relationship between the constructed and natural environments and their interaction with human activities; the effects of natural and manmade hazards on constructed facilities and infrastructure; and the interdependencies of infrastructure systems, including power, water, transportation, telecommunications, wastewater, and buildings.

National Academies of Sciences, Engineering, and Medicine (NASEM), National Material and Manufacturing Board, Keck Center, 500 5th St. N.W., #WS921, 20001; (202) 334-3505. Fax, (202) 334-3575. James Lancaster, Director; Theresa Kotanchek, Chair.
General email, nmmb@nas.edu

Web, www.nationalacademies.org/nmmb/national-materials-and-manufacturing-board

Conducts research on materials and manufacturing, including at the atomic, molecular, and nano scales, and innovative applications of new and existing materials, including pilot-scale and large-scale manufacturing, the design of new devices, and disposal.

National Academy of Engineering (NAE), *Keck Center, 500 5th St. N.W., 20001; (202) 334-3200. Fax, (202) 334-2290. John L. Anderson, President, (202) 334-3201; Alton D. Romig Jr., Executive Officer, (202) 334-3677. Press, (202) 334-2138.*
Web, www.nae.edu and Twitter, @theNAEng

Society whose members are elected in recognition of important contributions to the field of science and technology. Shares responsibility with the National Academy of Sciences for examining questions of science and technology at the request of the federal government; promotes international cooperation. (Affiliated with the National Academies of Sciences, Engineering, and Medicine [NASEM].)

National Society of Black Engineers, *205 Daingerfield Rd., Alexandria, VA 22314; (703) 549-2207. Fax, (703) 683-5312. Janeen Uzzell, Chief Executive Officer.*
Web, www.nsbe.org, Twitter, @NSBE and Facebook, www .facebook.com/NSBE1975

Membership: Black engineers and college students studying engineering. Offers leadership training, professional and career development opportunities, technical seminars and workshops, and career fairs. Holds an annual convention.

National Society of Professional Engineers (NSPE), *1420 King St., Alexandria, VA 22314-2794; (703) 684-2800. Fax, (703) 684-2821. Monica Schulz, Executive Director. Member services, (888) 285-6773.*
Web, www.nspe.org

Membership: U.S.-licensed professional engineers from all disciplines. Holds engineering seminars; operates an information center.

The Optical Society, *2010 Massachusetts Ave. N.W., 20036; (202) 223-8130. Fax, (202) 223-1096. Elizabeth (Liz) A. Rogan, Chief Executive Officer, (202) 416-1467. Press, (202) 416-1443.*
General email, info@osa.org
Web, www.osa.org and Twitter, @OpticalSociety

Membership: global optics and photonic scientists, engineers, educators, students, technicians, business professionals, and others interested in optics and photonics worldwide. Promotes research and information exchange; conducts conferences; publishes a scientific journal; sponsors technical groups and programming as well as outreach and educational activities.

ENVIRONMENTAL AND EARTH SCIENCES

General

▶ **AGENCIES**

National Aeronautics and Space Administration (NASA), *Science Mission Directorate (SMD), 300 E St. S.W., 20546;*

(202) 358-3889. Thomas Zurbuchen, Associate Administrator.
General email, science@hq.nasa.gov
Web, http://science.nasa.gov and Twitter, @NASAScienceCast

Seeks to understand the integrated functioning of the earth and the sun. Administers space mission programs and mission-enabling programs, including sub-orbital missions. Sponsors scientific research and analysis. Exchanges information with the international science community. Interests include earth climate and environmental change.

National Oceanic and Atmospheric Administration (NOAA) (Commerce Dept.), National Centers for Environmental Information (NCEI), *Silver Spring Metro Center 3, 1315 East-West Hwy., 4th Floor, Silver Spring, MD 20910-3282; (301) 713-3277. Fax, (301) 713-3300. Joe Pica, Director (Acting).*
General email, ncei.info@noaa.gov
Web, www.ncei.noaa.gov

Responsible for hosting and providing access to comprehensive oceanic, atmospheric, and geophysical data. Provides world's largest collection of freely available oceanographic data, including water temperatures dating back to the late 1700s and measuring thousands of meters deep, scientific journals, rare books, historical photo collections, and maps through the NOAA Central Library, and data management expertise and training. Merger of NOAA's three data centers: National Climatic Data Center, National Geophysical Data Center, and National Oceanographic Data Center, which includes the National Coastal Data Development Center.

National Oceanic and Atmospheric Administration (NOAA) (Commerce Dept.), National Environmental Satellite, Data, and Information Service (NESDIS), *Silver Spring Metro Center 1, 1335 East-West Hwy., 8th Floor, Silver Spring, MD 20910; (301) 713-3578. Fax, (301) 713-1249. Stephen Volz, Assistant Administrator. Press, (301) 713-0214.*
Web, www.nesdis.noaa.gov and Twitter, @NOAASatellites

Provides satellite observations of the environment by operating polar orbiting and geostationary satellites; develops satellite techniques; increases the utilization of satellite data in environmental services.

National Science Foundation (NSF), *Geosciences Directorate, 2415 Eisenhower Ave., Room C 8000, Alexandria, VA 22314; (703) 292-8500. Fax, (703) 292-9448. Alexandra R. Isern, Assistant Director.*
Web, www.nsf.gov/div/index.jsp?org=geo

Directorate that supports research about the earth, including its atmosphere, continents, oceans, and interior. Works to improve the education and human resource base for the geosciences; participates in international and multidisciplinary activities, especially to study changes in the global climate.

National Science Foundation (NSF), *Polar Programs (OPP), 2415 Eisenhower Ave., Room W 7100, Alexandria,*

VA 22134; (703) 292-8030. Fax, (703) 292-9081. Roberta Marinelli, Director.

Web, www.nsf.gov/div/index.jsp?div=OPP and Facebook, www.facebook.com/NSFOPP

Funds and manages U.S. activity in Antarctica and the Arctic; provides grants for arctic programs in polar biology and medicine, earth sciences, atmospheric sciences, meteorology, ocean sciences, and glaciology. The Polar Information Program serves as a clearinghouse for polar data and makes referrals on specific questions.

Smithsonian Environmental Research Center
(*Smithsonian Institution*), 647 Contees Wharf Rd., Edgewater, MD 21037-0028 (mailing address: P.O. Box 28, Edgewater, MD 21037-0028); (443) 482-2200. Anson (Tuck) H. Hines, Director, (443) 482-2208. Press, (443) 482-2325. Library, (443) 482-2273.

Web, https://serc.si.edu, Twitter, @SmithsonianEnv, Facebook, www.facebook.com/smithsonian.serc and YouTube, www.youtube.com/channel/UCj6f9cwRLj8VB dwPmYsIxDg

Performs laboratory and field research that measures physical, chemical, and biological interactions to determine the mechanisms of environmental responses to humans' use of air, land, and water. Evaluates properties of the environment that affect the functions of living organisms. Maintains research laboratories, public education program, facilities for controlled environments, and estuarine and terrestrial lands. Wildlife sanctuary open to the public Monday through Saturday, 9:00 a.m.–4:30 p.m., except federal holidays.

U.S. Arctic Research Commission, 4350 N. Fairfax Dr., #510, Arlington, VA 22203; (703) 525-0111. John W. Farrell, Executive Director, (703) 525-0113. General email, info@arctic.gov

Web, www.arctic.gov, Twitter, @US_ARC and Facebook, www.facebook.com/arcticresearchcommission

Presidential advisory commission that develops policy for arctic research; assists the interagency Arctic Research Policy Committee in implementing a national plan of arctic research; recommends improvements in logistics, data management, and dissemination of arctic information.

U.S. Geological Survey (USGS) (*Interior Dept.*), 12201 Sunrise Valley Dr., MS 100, Reston, VA 20192-0002; (703) 648-5953. Dave Applegate, Exercising the Authority of Director, (703) 648-6600; Melanie A. Ruiz, FOIA Officer, (571) 512-8459. Library, (703) 648-4301. Press, (703) 648-4460. Switchboard, (703) 648-4000. Toll-free, 888-ASK-USGS. FOIA, (571) 512-8459.
General email, ask@usgs.gov

Web, www.usgs.gov, Twitter, @USGS, Facebook, www .facebook.com/USGeologicalSurvey and YouTube, www .youtube.com/usgs

Provides reports, maps, and databases that describe and analyze water, energy, biological, and mineral resources; the land surface; and the underlying geological structure and dynamic processes of the Earth.

U.S. Geological Survey (USGS) (*Interior Dept.*), **Library,** 950 National Center, #1D100, Reston, VA 20192 (mailing address: 12201 Sunrise Valley Dr., #1D100, MS 950, Reston, VA 20192); (703) 648-4301. Catharine (Cate) Canevari, Library Director, (703) 648-7182.
General email, library@usgs.gov

Web, www.usgs.gov/core-science-systems/usgs-library

Maintains collection of books, periodicals, serials, maps, and technical reports on geology, mineral and water resources, mineralogy, paleontology, petrology, soil and environmental sciences, biology, and physics and chemistry as they relate to natural sciences. Open to the public Monday–Friday; makes interlibrary loans.

►CONGRESS

For a listing of relevant congressional committees and subcommittees, please see pages 688–689 or the Appendix.

►NONGOVERNMENTAL

American Academy of Environmental Engineers and Scientists, 147 Old Solomons Island Rd., #303, Annapolis, MD 21401; (410) 266-3311. Fax, (410) 266-7653. Ilyse Shapiro, Executive Director (Acting).
General email, info@aaees.org

Web, www.aaees.org, Twitter, @AAEESdotORG and Facebook, www.facebook.com/AAEESdotORG

Membership: state-licensed environmental engineers and scientists who have passed examinations in environmental engineering and/or science specialties, including general environment, air pollution control, solid waste management, hazardous waste management, industrial hygiene, radiation protection, water supply, environmental sustainability, and wastewater.

American Geophysical Union, 2000 Florida Ave. N.W., 20009-1277; (202) 462-6900. Fax, (202) 328-0566. Susan Lozier, President; Randy W. Fiser, Executive Director. Toll-free, (800) 966-2481.
General email, service@agu.org

Web, http://sites.agu.org, Twitter, @theagu and Facebook, www.facebook.com/AmericanGeophysicalUnion

Membership: scientists and technologists who study the environments and components of the earth, sun, and solar system. Promotes international cooperation; disseminates information.

National Academies of Sciences, Engineering, and Medicine (NASEM), *Polar Research Board,* Keck Center, 500 5th St. N.W., #602, 20001; (202) 334-1518. Diana Wall, Chair; Amanda Staudt, Director, (202) 334-3512.
General email, prb@nas.edu

Web, www.nationalacademies.org/prb/polar-research-board

Promotes polar science and provides scientific guidance to federal agencies and the nation on issues in the Arctic, the Antarctic, and cold regions in general.

Atmospheric Sciences

►AGENCIES

National Oceanic and Atmospheric Administration (NOAA) *(Commerce Dept.), 1401 Constitution Ave. N.W., #5128, 20230; (202) 482-3436. Fax, (202) 408-9674. Richard W. Spinrad, Under Secretary. Library, (301) 713-2600. Press, (202) 482-6090.*
Web, www.noaa.gov and Twitter, @NOAA

Conducts research in marine and atmospheric sciences; issues weather forecasts and warnings vital to public safety and the national economy; maintains a national environmental center with data from satellite observations and other sources, including meteorological, oceanic, geodetic, and seismological data centers; provides colleges and universities with grants for research, education, and marine advisory services; prepares and provides nautical and aeronautical charts and maps.

National Oceanic and Atmospheric Administration (NOAA) *(Commerce Dept.), Climate Program Office (CPO), Silver Spring Metro Center 3, 1315 East-West Hwy., #100, Silver Spring, MD 20910; (301) 734-1263. Fax, (301) 713-0517. R. Wayne Higgins, Director, (301) 734-1263.*
General email, cpo.webmaster@noaa.gov

Web, www.cpo.noaa.gov

Manages NOAA-funded research programs that focus on climate science and assessments on a regional, national, and international scale.

National Oceanic and Atmospheric Administration (NOAA) *(Commerce Dept.), Marine and Aviation Operations (OMAO), 8403 Colesville Rd., #500, Silver Spring, MD 20910-3282; (301) 713-1045. Fax, (301) 713-1541. Rear Adm. Michael J. Silah, Director, (301) 713-7600. Press, (301) 713-7671.*
Web, www.omao.noaa.gov

Uniformed service of the Commerce Dept. that operates and manages NOAA's fleet of atmospheric, hydrographic, oceanographic, and fisheries research ships and aircraft. Supports NOAA's scientific programs.

National Oceanic and Atmospheric Administration (NOAA) *(Commerce Dept.), National Weather Service (NWS), 1325 East-West Hwy., #18150, Silver Spring, MD 20910; (301) 713-9095. Fax, (301) 713-0610. Mary C. Erickson, Director (Acting). Library, (301) 683-1307. National Weather Service forecast office, (703) 996-2200.*
Web, www.weather.gov and Twitter, @nws

Issues warnings of hurricanes, severe storms, and floods; provides weather forecasts and services for the general public and for aviation and marine interests.

National Oceanic and Atmospheric Administration (NOAA) *(Commerce Dept.), National Weather Service (NWS), Climate Prediction Center (CPC), 5830 University Research Court, College Park, MD 20740; (301) 683-3428. David DeWitt, Director. Press, (301) 427-9000.*
Web, www.cpc.ncep.noaa.gov

Provides climate forecasts, assesses the impact of short-term climate variability, and warns of potentially extreme climate-related events.

National Oceanic and Atmospheric Administration (NOAA) *(Commerce Dept.), National Weather Service (NWS), National Centers for Environmental Prediction (NCEP), 5830 University Research Court, College Park, MD 20740; (301) 683-1314. Fax, (301) 683-1325. Mike Farrar, Director, (301) 683-1315.*
Web, www.ncep.noaa.gov

The National Center for Environmental Prediction and the National Environmental Satellite, Data, and Information Service are part of the World Weather Watch Programme developed by the United Nations World Meteorological Organization. Collects and exchanges data with other nations; provides other national weather service offices, private meteorologists, and government agencies with products, including forecast guidance products.

National Oceanic and Atmospheric Administration (NOAA) *(Commerce Dept.), Oceanic and Atmospheric Research (OAR), 1315 East-West Hwy., Silver Spring, MD 20910; (301) 713-2458. Craig N. McLean, Assistant Administrator.*
Web, https://research.noaa.gov and Twitter, @NOAAResearch

Researches weather and water information in order to provide better forecasts and earlier warnings for natural disasters. Promotes the understanding of climate change and variability.

National Science Foundation (NSF), *Atmospheric and Geospace Sciences Division, 2415 Eisenhower Ave., Room W 8200, Alexandria, VA 22314; (703) 292-8520. Fax, (703) 292-9022. Candace O. Major, Director, (703) 292-7597.*
General email, geowebmaster@nsf.gov
Web, www.nsf.gov/div/index.jsp?div=ags

Supports research on the earth's atmosphere and the sun's effect on it, including studies of the physics, chemistry, and dynamics of the earth's upper and lower atmospheres and its space environment; climate processes including climate and air quality variations; and the natural global cycles of gases and particles in the earth's atmosphere.

Office of Science *(Energy Dept.), Biological and Environmental Research (BER), Climate and Environmental Sciences Division (CESD), 19901 Germantown Rd., #SC23.1, Germantown, MD 20874-1290 (mailing address: Germantown Bldg., 1000 Independence Ave. S.W., #SC23.1, Washington, DC 20585); (301) 903-4775. Fax, (301) 303-8519. Gerald Geernaert, Director.*
Web, www.energy.gov/science/ber/biological-and-environmental-research

Supports research on atmospheric systems, terrestrial ecosystems, and subsurface biogeochemistry as well as Earth system modeling and regional and global climate change modeling to improve predictive understanding of

Earth's climate and environmental systems in order to inform development of sustainable solutions to energy challenges.

Alliance for Responsible Atmospheric Policy, *2111 Wilson Blvd., 8th Floor, Arlington, VA 22201; (703) 243-0344. Kevin Fay, Executive Director, (703) 801-3233.*
General email, info@alliancepolicy.org
Web, www.alliancepolicy.org and Twitter, @AtmosPolicy

Coalition of users and producers of chlorofluorocarbons (CFCs). Seeks further study of the stratospheric ozone depletion theory. Coordinates industry participation in the development of economically and environmentally beneficial international and domestic atmospheric policies.

Climate Institute, *1225 New York Ave. N.W., #800, 20005; (202) 552-0163. Nasir Khattak, Chief Operating Officer.*
General email, info@climate.org
Web, http://climate.org

Educates the public and policymakers on climate change, the greenhouse effect, global warming, and the depletion of the ozone layer. Assesses climate change risks and develops strategies on mitigating climate change in developing countries and in North America.

National Academies of Sciences, Engineering, and Medicine (NASEM), *Atmospheric Sciences and Climate Board, Keck Center, 500 5th St. N.W., #602, 20001; (202) 413-2751. Amanda Staudt, Director; Mary Glackin, Chair.*
General email, basc@nas.edu
Web, www.nationalacademies.org/basc/board-on-atmospheric-sciences-and-climate

Supports research on climate change, air pollution, and severe weather in order to address environmental policies, human health, emergency management, energy choices, manufacturing decisions, construction codes, and agricultural methods.

Geology and Earth Sciences

Interior Dept. (DOI), *Assistant Secretary for Water and Science, 1849 C St. N.W., #6641, MS 6340, 20240; (202) 208-3186. Fax, (202) 208-6948. Tanya Trujillo, Assistant Secretary.*
Web, www.doi.gov

Administers departmental water, scientific, and research activities. Directs and supervises the Bureau of Reclamation and the U.S. Geological Survey.

National Museum of Natural History *(Smithsonian Institution), Mineral Sciences, 10th St. and Constitution Ave. N.W., 4th Floor, East Wing, 20560 (mailing address: P.O. Box 37012, MS 119, Washington, DC 20013-7012); (202) 633-1860. Fax, (202) 357-2476. Tim McCoy, Curator-In-Charge; Phyllis McKenzie, Specialist, (202) 633-1860. Library, (202) 633-1680.*

General email, NMMH-MineralSciences@si.edu
Web, www.mineralsciences.si.edu

Conducts research on gems, minerals, meteorites, rocks, and ores. Interests include mineralogy, petrology, volcanology, and geochemistry. Maintains the Global Volcanism Network, which reports worldwide volcanic and seismic activity. Library open to the public by appointment.

National Museum of Natural History *(Smithsonian Institution), Paleobiology, 10th St. and Constitution Ave. N.W., 20560-0121 (mailing address: P.O. Box 37012, MS 121, Washington, DC 20013-7012); (202) 633-1328. Fax, (202) 786-2832. Gene Hunt, Chair; Brian Huber, Specialist, (202) 633-1328.*
General email, paleodept@si.edu
Web, http://paleobiology.si.edu and Loans and visiting the collections, paleovisits@si.edu

Conducts research worldwide on invertebrate paleontology, paleobotany, sedimentology, and vertebrate paleontology; provides information on paleontology, paleoclimatology, paleoceanography, ecosystem dynamics, and processes of evolution and extinction. Maintains national collection of fossil organisms and sediment samples.

National Science Foundation (NSF), *Earth Sciences Division (EAR), 2415 Eisenhower Ave., Room E 8300, Alexandria, VA 22314; (703) 292-8550. Fax, (703) 292-9447. Steven Goldstein, Director, (703) 292-8246.*
Web, www.nsf.gov/div/index.jsp?div=ear

Provides grants for research in geology, geophysics, geochemistry, and related fields, including tectonics, hydrologic sciences, and continental dynamics.

Office of Science *(Energy Dept.), Biological and Environmental Research (BER), Climate and Environmental Sciences Division (CESD), 19901 Germantown Rd., #SC23.1, Germantown, MD 20874-1290 (mailing address: Germantown Bldg., 1000 Independence Ave. S.W., #SC23.1, Washington, DC 20585); (301) 903-4775. Fax, (301) 303-8519. Gerald Geernaert, Director.*
Web, www.energy.gov/science/ber/biological-and-environmental-research

Supports research on atmospheric systems, terrestrial ecosystems, and subsurface biogeochemistry as well as Earth system modeling and regional and global climate change modeling to improve predictive understanding of Earth's climate and environmental systems in order to inform development of sustainable solutions to energy challenges.

U.S. Geological Survey (USGS) *(Interior Dept.), Coastal and Marine Hazards and Resources, 12201 Sunrise Valley Dr., MS 905, Reston, VA 20192; (703) 648-6422. John W. Haines, Program Coordinator.*
Web, www.usgs.gov/programs/cmhrp

Handles resource assessment, exploration research, and marine geologic and environmental studies on U.S. coastal regions and the Outer Continental Shelf.

U.S. Geological Survey (USGS) *(Interior Dept.),* *Earthquake and Geologic Hazards,* 12201 Sunrise Valley Dr., MS 905, Reston, VA 20192-0002; (703) 648-6786. Gavin Hayes, Senior Science Advisor, (303) 374-4449. National Earthquake Information Center, (303) 273-8500.
Web, http://earthquake.usgs.gov

Manages geologic, geophysical, and engineering investigations, including assessments of hazards from earthquakes; conducts research on the mechanisms and occurrences of earthquakes worldwide and their relationship to the behavior of the crust and upper mantle; develops methods for predicting the time, place, and magnitude of earthquakes; conducts engineering and geologic studies on ground failures.

U.S. Geological Survey (USGS) *(Interior Dept.),* *Earthquake Hazards,* 12201 Sunrise Valley Dr., MS 905, Reston, VA 20192-0002; (703) 648-6714. Cecily J. Wolfe, Associate Program Coordinator, (703) 648-6714.
Web, www.usgs.gov/programs/earthquake-hazards

Monitors and researches seismic activity globally through a network of seismological and geophysical sensors.

U.S. Geological Survey (USGS) *(Interior Dept.),* *Land Change Science Program,* 12201 Sunrise Valley Dr., MS 516, Reston, VA 20192-0002; (703) 648-5320. Christopher Reich, Program Coordinator (Acting).
Web, http://usgs.gov/land-resources/land-change-science-program

Collects, analyzes, and disseminates information about natural and human-induced changes to the Earth's surface to better understand the rates, causes, and consequences of climate and land use change. Develops methods and processes for the use of land-surface science in public policy.

U.S. Geological Survey (USGS) *(Interior Dept.),* *National Cooperative Geologic Mapping Program,* 12201 Sunrise Valley Dr., MS 908, Reston, VA 20192; (703) 648-6053. John C. Brock, Program Coordinator.
Web, www.usgs.gov/core-science-systems/national-cooperative-geologic-mapping-program and *Twitter, @USGSNgmdb*

Funds the production of geologic maps in the United States. Provides geologic mapping data from across North America to public and private organizations.

U.S. Geological Survey (USGS) *(Interior Dept.),* *Volcano Hazards Program,* 12201 Sunrise Valley Dr., MS 904, Reston, VA 20192-0002; (703) 648-4773. Charles W. Mandeville, Program Coordinator.
General email, vscweb@usgs.gov
Web, http://volcanoes.usgs.gov

Manages geologic, geophysical, and engineering investigations, including assessments of hazards from volcanoes; conducts research worldwide on the mechanisms of volcanoes and on igneous and geothermal systems. Issues warnings of potential volcanic hazards.

▶**NONGOVERNMENTAL**

American Geosciences Institute, 4220 King St., Alexandria, VA 22302-1502; (703) 379-2480. Fax, (703) 379-7563. Jonathan E. Arthur, Executive Director, ext. 202.
General email, agi@americangeosciences.org
Web, www.americangeosciences.org, Twitter, @AGI_Updates and *Facebook, www.facebook.com/americangeosciences*

Membership: earth science societies and associations. Maintains a computerized database with worldwide information on geology, engineering and environmental geology, oceanography, and other geological fields (available to the public for a fee). Monitors legislation and regulations.

Carnegie Institute for Science, 5251 Broad Branch Rd. N.W., 20015; (202) 387-6400. Fax, (202) 387-8092. Eric D. Isaacs, President.
Web, https://carnegiescience.edu and *Twitter, @carnegiescience*

Conducts research in plant science biology, genetic and developmental biology, earth and planetary sciences, astronomy, and global ecology and matter at extreme states at the Carnegie Institution's six research departments: Dept. of Embryology (Baltimore, Md.); Geophysical Laboratory (Washington, DC); Dept. of Global Ecology (Stanford, Calif.); Dept. of Plant Biology (Stanford, Calif.); Dept. of Terrestrial Magnetism (Washington, DC); and The Observatories (Pasadena, Calif., and Las Campanas, Chile).

National Academies of Sciences, Engineering, and Medicine (NASEM), *Earth Sciences and Resources Board,* Keck Center, 500 5th St. N.W., #616, 20001; (202) 334-2744. Fax, (202) 334-1377. Deborah Glickson, Director; Isabel P. Montañez, Chair.
General email, besr@nas.edu
Web, www.nationalacademies.org/besr/board-on-earth-sciences-and-resources

Coordinates activities, oversees research, and advises policymakers on solid-earth sciences issues. Interests include geography, geological and geotechnical engineering, mapping, and seismology and geodynamics.

Oceanography

▶**AGENCIES**

National Museum of Natural History *(Smithsonian Institution), Botany,* 10th St. and Constitution Ave. N.W., 20560-0166 (mailing address: P.O. Box 37012, MS 166, Washington, DC 20013-7012); (202) 633-0920. Fax, (202) 786-2563. Eric Schuettpelz, Chair. Library, (202) 633-1680.
Web, www.botany.si.edu

Investigates the biology, evolution, and classification of tropical and subtropical marine algae and sea grasses. Acts as curator of the national collection in this field. Develops and participates in scholarly programs. Library open to the public Monday through Friday, 10:00 a.m.–4:00 p.m., by appointment only.

National Oceanic and Atmospheric Administration (NOAA) *(Commerce Dept.), 1401 Constitution Ave. N.W., #5128, 20230; (202) 482-3436. Fax, (202) 408-9674. Richard W. Spinrad, Under Secretary. Library, (301) 713-2600. Press, (202) 482-6090.*
Web, www.noaa.gov and Twitter, @NOAA

Conducts research in marine and atmospheric sciences; issues weather forecasts and warnings vital to public safety and the national economy; maintains a national environmental center with data from satellite observations and other sources, including meteorological, oceanic, geodetic, and seismological data centers; provides colleges and universities with grants for research, education, and marine advisory services; prepares and provides nautical and aeronautical charts and maps.

National Oceanic and Atmospheric Administration (NOAA) *(Commerce Dept.), Marine and Aviation Operations (OMAO), 8403 Colesville Rd., #500, Silver Spring, MD 20910-3282; (301) 713-1045. Fax, (301) 713-1541. Rear Adm. Michael J. Silah, Director, (301) 713-7600. Press, (301) 713-7671.*
Web, www.omao.noaa.gov

Uniformed service of the Commerce Dept. that operates and manages NOAA's fleet of atmospheric, hydrographic, oceanographic, and fisheries research ships and aircraft. Supports NOAA's scientific programs.

National Oceanic and Atmospheric Administration (NOAA) *(Commerce Dept.), National Ocean Service (NOS), Silver Spring Metro Center 4, 1305 East-West Hwy., #9149, Silver Spring, MD 20910; (301) 713-3074. Fax, (301) 713-4269. Nicole LaBoeuf, Assistant Administrator. Press, (301) 713-3066.*
General email, nos.info@noaa.gov
Web, https://oceanservice.noaa.gov

Manages charting and geodetic services, oceanography and marine services, coastal resource coordination, and marine survey operations; conducts environmental cleanup of coastal pollution.

National Oceanic and Atmospheric Administration (NOAA) *(Commerce Dept.), National Sea Grant College Program, Silver Spring Metro Center 3, 1315 East-West Hwy., #11735, Silver Spring, MD 20910; (301) 734-1066. Fax, (301) 713-0799. Jonathan Pennock, Director, (301) 734-1089.*
General email, SGweb@noaa.gov
Web, www.seagrant.noaa.gov and Twitter, @SeaGrant

Provides institutions with grants for marine research, education, and advisory services; provides marine environmental information.

National Science Foundation (NSF), *Ocean Sciences Division (OSE), 2415 Eisenhower Ave., Room W 8100, Alexandria, VA 22134; (703) 292-8580. Fax, (703) 292-9449. Terence M. Quinn, Director, (703) 292-7240.*
Web, www.nsf.gov/div/index.jsp?div=OCE

Conducts research and provides educational resources about all aspects of global oceans and their interactions with the earth and atmosphere. Awards grants and contracts for acquiring, upgrading, and operating oceanographic research facilities that lend themselves to shared usage. Facilities supported include ships, submersibles, and shipboard and shorebased data logging and processing equipment. Supports development of new drilling techniques and systems.

U.S. Geological Survey (USGS) *(Interior Dept.), Coastal and Marine Hazards and Resources, 12201 Sunrise Valley Dr., MS 905, Reston, VA 20192; (703) 648-6422. John W. Haines, Program Coordinator.*
Web, www.usgs.gov/programs/cmhrp

Surveys the continental margins and the ocean floor to provide information on the mineral resources potential of submerged lands.

▶NONGOVERNMENTAL

Marine Technology Society, *One Thomas Circle, # 700, 20005; (202) 717-8705. Fax, (202) 347-4302. Kristina Norman, Executive Director (Acting), (202) 827-7171.*
General email, mtsoffice@mtsociety.org
Web, www.mtsociety.org, Twitter, @MTSociety and Facebook, www.facebook.com/MarineTechnologySociety/?ref=hl

Membership: ocean scientists, engineers, practitioners, policymakers, educators and technologists, interested in marine science, technology, and education.

National Academies of Sciences, Engineering, and Medicine (NASEM), *Ocean Studies Board, Keck Center, 500 5th St. N.W., MS 607, 20001; (202) 334-2714. Fax, (202) 334-2885. Claudia Benitez-Nelson, Chair; Susan Roberts, Director.*
General email, osbfeedback@nas.edu
Web, www.nationalacademies.org/osb/ocean-studies-board

Conducts research to understand, manage, and conserve coastal and marine environments. Areas of interest include the ocean's role in the global climate system, technology and infrastructure needs for ocean research, ocean-related aspects of national security, fisheries science and management, and ocean education.

INFORMATION SCIENCE AND TECHNOLOGY

General

▶AGENCIES

Defense Information Systems Agency *(Defense Dept.), 6910 Cooper Ave., Fort Meade, MD 20755; (703) 607-6001. Lt. Gen. Robert J. Skinner (USAF), Director. Service Desk, (844) 347-2457.*

Web, www.disa.mil and *General email, disa.mpeo@ mail.mil*

The Defense Dept. agency responsible for information technology and the central manager for major portions of the defense information infrastructure. Units include the White House Communications Agency.

Health and Human Services Dept. (HHS), *National Coordinator for Health Information Technology (ONC),* *330 C St. S.W., Floor 7, 20201; (202) 690-7151. Fax, (202) 690-6079. Micky Tripathi, National Coordinator.* *Press, (202) 251-1141.* *General email, onc.request@hhs.gov* *Web, www.healthit.gov* and *Twitter, @ONC_HealthIT*

Coordinates nationwide efforts to implement information technology that allows for electronic use and exchange of health information. Goals include ensuring security for patient health information, improving health care quality, and reducing health care costs.

National Institute of Standards and Technology (NIST) *(Commerce Dept.), Information Technology Lab, Bldg.* *225, 100 Bureau Dr., #B264, MS 8900, Gaithersburg,* *MD 20899-8900; (301) 975-2900. Fax, (301) 975-2378.* *Charles (Chuck) H. Romine, Director.* *General email, itl_inquiries@nist.gov* *Web, www.nist.gov/itl* and *Twitter, @nistcyber*

Collaborates with other institute laboratories, other federal agencies, the U.S. private sector, standards development organizations, and other national and international stakeholders in the development and application of new information technologies to help meet national priorities; develops and deploys standards, tests, and metrics to assure secure, reliable, and interoperable information systems; collaborates to develop cybersecurity standards, guidelines, and techniques for federal agencies and U.S. industry; conducts research in computer science and technology.

National Science Foundation (NSF), *Information and Intelligent Systems Division (IIS), 2415 Eisenhower Ave.,* *Room W10100, Alexandria, VA 22134; (703) 292-8930.* *Fax, (703) 292-9073. Henry A. Kautz, Director, (703) 292-2606.* *Web, www.nsf.gov/div/index.jsp?div=iis*

Supports research and education that develop new knowledge about the role people play in the design and use of information technology; advances the ability to represent, collect, store, organize, and visualize, and communicate about data and information; and advances knowledge about how computational systems can perform tasks autonomously, robustly, and with flexibility. Awards grants.

Networking and Information Technology Research and Development (NITRD), *National Coordination Office,* *490 L'Enfant Plaza S.W., #8001, 20024 (mailing address:* *2415 Eisenhower Ave., Alexandria, VA 22314); (292)* *459-9674. Fax, (202) 459-9673. Kamie Roberts, Director.* *General email, nco@nitrd.gov* *Web, www.nitrd.gov* and *Twitter, @NITRDgov*

Coordinates multiagency research and development projects that involve computing, networking, and software. Reports to the National Science and Technology Council; provides information to Congress, U.S. and foreign organizations, and the public.

►CONGRESS

For a listing of relevant congressional committees and subcommittees, please see pages 688–689 or the Appendix.

Government Accountability Office (GAO), *Information Technology and Cybersecurity (ITC), 441 G St. N.W.,* *#4T21, 20548; (202) 512-4456. Carol C. Harris, Director.* *Web, www.gao.gov/about/careers/our-teams*

Audits, analyzes, and evaluates for Congress federal information management and information security programs to improve performance and reduce costs.

►NONGOVERNMENTAL

Accredited Standards Committee (ASC X12), *1405 S. Fern St., #92957, Arlington, VA 22202; (703) 970-4480.* *Stephanie Fetzer, Chair.* *General email, info@x12.org* *Web, https://x12.org* and *Twitter, @X12standards*

Promotes the development and maintenance of cross-industry Electronic Data Interchange (EDI), XML schemas, and Context Inspired Component Architecture (CICA) standards in electronic commerce that help organizations improve business methods, lower costs, and increase productivity. Provides administrative and technical support. Chartered by the American National Standards Institute. (Formerly Data Interchange Standards Assn.)

American Council for Technology and Industry Advisory Council (ACT/IAC), *3040 Williams Dr., #500, Fairfax, VA 22031; (703) 208-4800. Fax, (703) 208-4805.* *David M. Wennergren, Chief Executive Officer.* *General email, ACT-IAC@actiac.org* *Web, www.actiac.org, Twitter, @ACTIAC* and *Facebook, www.facebook.com/act.iac*

Brings government and industry IT executives together to enhance government's ability to use information technologies, artificial intelligence, and intelligent automation technologies. Activities include conferences, white papers, professional development programs, and other events to foster education, the exchange of information, and collaboration.

Assn. for Competitive Technology (ACT), *1401 K St. N.W., #501, 20005; (202) 331-2130. Fax, (202) 331-2139.* *Morgan Reed, President.* *General email, ACTPress@actonline.org* *Web, www.actonline.org* and *Twitter, @actonline*

Membership: businesses that engage in or support the information technology industry. International education and advocacy organization for information technology companies worldwide. Interests include intellectual property, international trade, e-commerce, privacy, tax policy, antitrust, and commercial piracy issues. Focuses predominantly on the interests of small and midsized entrepreneurial technology companies. Monitors legislation and regulations. (Office in Brussels, Belgium.)

Assn. for Information and Image Management (AIIM), 8403 Colesville Rd., #1100, Silver Spring, MD 20910; (301) 587-8202. Fax, (301) 587-2711. Peggy Winton, President. Toll-free, (800) 477-2446.
General email, hello@aiim.org

Web, www.aiim.org and Twitter, @AIIMinfo

Membership: manufacturers and users of image-based information systems. Works to advance the profession of information management; develops training standards on information management and document formats.

Assn. for Information Science and Technology (ASIS&T), 673 Potomac Station Dr., #155, Leesberg, VA 20176; (301) 495-0900. Fax, (301) 495-0810. Lydia Middleton, Executive Director, ext. 1200.
General email, asist@asist.org

Web, www.asist.org and Twitter, @assist_org

Membership: information specialists from such fields as computer science, linguistics, management, librarianship, engineering, law, medicine, chemistry, and education. Advocates research and development in basic and applied information science. Offers continuing-education programs.

Coalition for Networked Information, 21 Dupont Circle N.W., #800, 20036; (202) 296-5098. Clifford A. Lynch, Executive Director.
General email, info@cni.org

Web, www.cni.org, Twitter, @cni_org, Facebook, www .facebook.com/cni.org and YouTube, www.youtube.com/ user/cnivideo

Membership: higher education institutions, publishing, information technology and telecommunications, information technology, and libraries and library organizations, as well as government agencies and foundations. Promotes networked information technology, scholarly communication, intellectual productivity, and education.

Future of Privacy Forum, 1350 Eye St. N.W., #350, 20005; (202) 643-9853. Jules Polonetsky, Chief Executive Officer. General email, info@fpf.org

Web, www.fpf.org, Twitter, @futureofprivacy and Facebook, www.facebook.com/FutureofPrivacy

Think tank focusing on privacy leadership and scholarship, advancing principled data practices in support of emerging technologies.; encourages consensus on ethical norms, policies, and practices regarding information and technology privacy.

Information Sciences Institute, *Washington Office,* 3811 N. Fairfax Dr., #200, Arlington, VA 22203; (703) 812-3700. Fax, (703) 812-3712. Craig Knoblock, Executive Director. General email, info@isi.edu

Web, www.isi.edu, Twitter, @USC_ISI and Facebook, www.facebook.com/USCISI

Conducts basic and applied research in advanced computer, communications, and information processing technologies. Works with public- and private-sector customers to develop diverse information technologies for civilian and military uses, often bridging multiple technology disciplines. Projects include advanced communications and network research; distributed databases and pattern recognition with applications in law enforcement, inspection systems, and threat detection; and computing architectures and devices. (Headquarters in Marina del Rey, Calif.; part of the University of Southern California.)

Information Technology Industry Council (ITI), 700 K St. N.W., #600, 20001; (202) 737-8888. Fax, (202) 638-4922. Jason Oxman, President, (202) 626-5753. Press, (202) 626-5753.
General email, info@itic.org

Web, www.itic.org, Twitter, @ITI_TechTweets and Facebook, www.facebook.com/ITI.dc

Membership: providers of information and communications technology products and services. Acts as advocate for member companies in the areas of privacy, immigration reform, cybersecurity, intellectual property, tax reform, telecommunications, STEM education, trade, accessibility, voluntary standards, sustainability, and Internet governance.

Institute of Electrical and Electronics Engineers–USA (IEEE-USA), *Washington Office,* 2001 L St. N.W., #700, 20036; (202) 785-0017. Fax, (202) 785-0835. Chris Brantley, Managing Director, (202) 530-8349. General email, ieeeusa@ieee.org

Web, https://ieeeusa.org, Twitter, @IEEEUSA and Facebook, www.facebook.com/ieeeusa

U.S. arm of an international technological and professional organization. Interests include computing and information technology and promoting career and technology policy interests of members. (Headquarters in New York.)

Technology CEO Council, 1341 G St. N.W., #1100, 20005; (202) 585-0258. Bruce Mehlman, Executive Director. General email, info@techceocouncil.org

Web, www.techceocouncil.org

Membership: chief executive officers from U.S. information technology companies. Monitors legislation and regulations on technology and trade issues. Interests include health care information technology, telecommunications, international trade, innovation, digital rights management, export and knowledge controls, privacy, and competitiveness.

Computer Science

▶AGENCIES

National Institute of Standards and Technology (NIST) *(Commerce Dept.), Information Technology Lab,* Bldg. 225, 100 Bureau Dr., #B264, MS 8900, Gaithersburg, MD 20899-8900; (301) 975-2900. Fax, (301) 975-2378. Charles (Chuck) H. Romine, Director.

General email, itl_inquiries@nist.gov

Web, www.nist.gov/itl and Twitter, @nistcyber

Collaborates in mathematical, statistical, and computer sciences with other institute laboratories, other federal agencies, the U.S. private sector, standards development organizations, and other national and international stakeholders; provides consultations, methods, and research supporting the institute's scientific and engineering projects.

National Science Foundation (NSF), *Advanced Cyberinfrastructure Division, 2415 Eisenhower Ave., Room E 10400, Alexandria, VA 22314; (703) 292-8970. Fax, (703) 292-9060. Manish Parashar, Director, (703) 292-2274.*

Web, www.nsf.gov/div/index.jsp?div=OAC

Supports and coordinates the development, acquisition, and provision of state-of-the-art cyberinfrastructure resources, tools, and services for the advancement and transformation of science and engineering. Supports research and education to expand the future capabilities of cyberinfrastructure specific to science and engineering, including the development of computing and information infrastructure that is made accessible to scientists and engineers nationwide. Interests include computing and communication, network systems, cyberinfrastructure, and information and intelligent systems.

National Science Foundation (NSF), *Computer and Information Science and Engineering Directorate, 2415 Eisenhower Ave., Room C 10000, Alexandria, VA 22314; (703) 292-8900. Fax, (703) 292-9074. Margaret Martonosi, Assistant Director, (703) 292-5312.*

Web, www.nsf.gov/dir/index.jsp?org=cise

Supports investigator-initiated research in computer science and engineering. Promotes the use of advanced computing, communications, and information systems. Provides grants for research and education.

National Science Foundation (NSF), *Computer and Network Systems Division, 2415 Eisenhower Ave., Room E 10300, Alexandria, VA 22314; (703) 292-8950. Fax, (703) 292-9010. Gurdup Singh, Deputy Director, (703) 292-7826.*

Web, www.nsf.gov/div/index.jsp?div=CNS

Supports research and education activities that strive to create new computing and networking technologies and that explore new ways to utilize existing technologies. Seeks to foster the creation of better abstractions and tools for designing, building, analyzing, and measuring future systems. Supports the computing infrastructure that is required for experimental computer science and coordinates cross-divisional activities that foster integration of research and education and broadening of participation in the computer, information science, and engineering (CISE) workforce. Awards grants.

National Science Foundation (NSF), *Computing and Communication Foundations Division (CCF), 2415 Eisenhower Ave., Room W 10200, Alexandria, VA 22314; (703) 292-8910. Fax, (703) 292-9059. Walter (Rance) Cleaveland II, Director.*

Web, www.nsf.gov/div/index.jsp?div=ccf

Supports research and educational activities exploring the foundations of computing and communication devices and their usage. Seeks advances in computing and communication theory, algorithms for computer and computational sciences, and architecture and design of computers and software. Awards grants.

Office of Science *(Energy Dept.), Advanced Scientific Computing Research (ASCR), 19901 Germantown Rd., #SC31, Germantown, MD 20874-1290 (mailing address: Germantown Bldg., 1000 Independence Ave. S.W., #SC21, Washington, DC 20585); (301) 903-7486. Fax, (301) 903-4846. Barbara Helland, Associate Director.*

General email, sc.ascr@science.doe.gov

Web, www.energy.gov/science/ascr/advanced-scientific-computing-research

Supports mathematical, computational, and computer science research on behalf of the Energy Dept.

▶**NONGOVERNMENTAL**

CompTIA, *Public Advocacy, 322 4th St. N.E., 20002-5824; Fax, (630) 678-8384. Todd Thibodeaux, President. Toll-free, (866) 835-8020.*

General email, techvoice@comptia.org

Web, www.comptia.org, Twitter, @CompTIA and YouTube, www.youtube.com/c/comptia

Trade association for technology companies offering hardware, software, electronics, telecommunications, and information technology products and services. Offers business services and networking programs to members. Monitors legislation and regulations. (Headquarters in Downers Grove, Ill.)

Computer and Communications Industry Assn. (CCIA), *25 Massachusetts Ave. N.W., #300C, 20001; (202) 783-0070. Matthew Schruers, President.*

Web, www.ccianet.org, Twitter, @ccianet and Facebook, www.facebook.com/ccianet

Membership: Internet service providers, software providers, and manufacturers and suppliers of computer data processing and communications-related products and services. Interests include Internet freedom, privacy and neutrality, government electronic surveillance, telecommunications policy, tax policy, federal procurement policy, communications and computer industry standards, intellectual property policies, encryption, international trade, and antitrust reform.

National Academies of Sciences, Engineering, and Medicine (NASEM), *Computer Science and Telecommunications Board, Keck Center, 500 5th St. N.W., 20001; (202) 334-2689. Fax, (202) 334-2318. Laura M. Hass, Chair; Jon Eisenberg, Director.*

General email, cstb@nas.edu

Web, www.nationalacademies.org/cstb/computer-science-and-telecommunications-board

Advises the federal government on technical and public policy issues relating to computing and communications.

Research includes computer science, cybersecurity, privacy, the Internet, and electronic voting and voter registration.

National Academies of Sciences, Engineering, and Medicine (NASEM), *Human-Systems Integration Board, Keck Center, 500 5th St. N.W., 11th Floor, 20001; (202) 334-2326. Fax, (202) 334-2210. Mary Ellen O'Connell, Director (Acting), (202) 334-2607.*
General email, bohsi@nas.edu

Web, www.nationalacademies.org/bohsi/board-on-human-systems-integration

Conducts studies on human factors and human-systems integration. Areas of research include virtual reality, human–computer interaction, and modeling social networks.

The Software Alliance (BSA), *20 F St. N.W., #800, 20001; (202) 872-5500. Fax, (202) 872-5501. Victoria A. Espinel, President.*
General email, info@bsa.org

Web, www.bsa.org, Twitter, @BSAnews and YouTube, www.youtube.com/user/BusinessSftAlliance

Membership: personal and business computer software publishing companies. Promotes growth of the software industry worldwide; helps develop electronic commerce.

Software and Information Industry Assn. (SIIA), *1090 Vermont Ave. N.W., 6th Floor, 20005-4905; (202) 289-7442. Fax, (202) 289-7097. Jeff (Ken) Joseph, President, (202) 789-4440.*
Web, www.siia.net, Twitter, @SIIA and YouTube, www.youtube.com/channel/UCOggBEPEyAXDIh0U_JlSHyA

Membership: software and digital content companies. Promotes the industry worldwide; sponsors conferences, seminars, and other events. Monitors legislation and regulations.

MATHEMATICAL AND PHYSICAL SCIENCES

General

▶ **AGENCIES**

National Institute of Standards and Technology (NIST) *(Commerce Dept.), Bldg. 101, 100 Bureau Dr., #A1134, Gaithersburg, MD 20899-1000 (mailing address: 100 Bureau Dr., MS 1000, Gaithersburg, MD 20899); (301) 975-2000. Fax, (301) 869-8972. James Olthoff, Under Secretary. Information, (301) 975-6478. TTY, (800) 877-8339.*
General email, director@nist.gov

Web, www.nist.gov

Nonregulatory agency that serves as national reference and measurement laboratory for the physical and engineering sciences. Works with industry, government

agencies, and academia; promotes U.S. innovation and industrial competitiveness. Research interests include advanced manufacturing, information technology and cybersecurity, energy, health care, environment and consumer safety, and physical infrastructure.

National Institute of Standards and Technology (NIST) *(Commerce Dept.), Information Technology Lab, Bldg. 225, 100 Bureau Dr., #B264, MS 8900, Gaithersburg, MD 20899-8900; (301) 975-2900. Fax, (301) 975-2378. Charles (Chuck) H. Romine, Director.*
General email, itl_inquiries@nist.gov

Web, www.nist.gov/itl and Twitter, @nistcyber

Collaborates in mathematical, statistical, and computer sciences with other institute laboratories, other federal agencies, the U.S. private sector, standards development organizations, and other national and international stakeholders; provides consultations, methods, and research supporting the institute's scientific and engineering projects.

National Institutes of Health (NIH) *(Health and Human Services Dept.), Center for Information Technology (CIT), 6555 Rock Spring Dr., #3G04, Bethesda, MD 20817; (301) 496-4357. Fax, (301) 402-1754. Andrea T. Norris, Director. Toll Free, (866) 319-4357. TTY, (800) 877-8339.*
Web, https://cit.nih.gov

Serves as the primary scientific and technological resource for the NIH in the areas of high-performance computing, database applications, mathematics, statistics, laboratory automation, engineering, computer science and technology, telecommunications, and information resources management.

National Science Foundation (NSF), *Mathematical and Physical Sciences Directorate (MPS), 2415 Eisenhower Ave., Room C 9000, Alexandria, VA 22134; (703) 292-8800. Fax, (703) 292-9151. Sean L. Jones, Assistant Director, (703) 292-2986.*
Web, www.nsf.gov/dir/index.jsp?org=mps

Directorate that supports research in the mathematical and physical sciences; divisions focus on physics, chemistry, materials research, mathematical sciences, and astronomical sciences. Works to improve the education and human resource base for these fields; participates in international and multidisciplinary activities.

Office of Science *(Energy Dept.), Basic Energy Sciences (BES), 19901 Germantown Rd., #SC32, Germantown, MD 20874-1290 (mailing address: Germantown Bldg., 1000 Independence Ave. S.W., #SC22, Washington, DC 20585); (301) 903-3081. Fax, (301) 903-6594. Linda Norton, Director.*
General email, sc.bes@science.doe.gov

Web, www.energy.gov/science/bes/basic-energy-sciences

Supports research to understand, predict, and control matter and energy at electronic, atomic, and molecular levels to provide foundations for new energy technology.

Chemistry

▶AGENCIES

National Institute of Standards and Technology (NIST) *(Commerce Dept.), Center for Nanoscale Science and Technology, 100 Bureau Dr., MS 6200, Gaithersburg, MD 20899-6200; (301) 975-3712. Fax, (301) 975-8026. B. Robert Ilic, NanoFas Manager.*
General email, cnst@nist.gov

Web, www.nist.gov/cnst

Provides nanoscale measurement and fabrication methods and access to nanoscale construction technologies to NIST labs, universities, and industries. Offers researchers training and use of in-house nanotechnology tools. Researches nanoscale measurement instruments and methods, and promotes collaboration and shared use.

National Institute of Standards and Technology (NIST) *(Commerce Dept.), Center for Neutron Research, Bldg. 235, 100 Bureau Dr., MS 6100, Gaithersburg, MD 20899-8100; (301) 975-6210. Fax, (301) 869-4770. Robert Dimeo, Director.*
General email, ncnr@nist.gov

Web, www.nist.gov/ncnr

Provides neutron measurement capabilities to the U.S. research community, universities, and industry.

National Institute of Standards and Technology (NIST) *(Commerce Dept.), Physical Measurement Laboratory, Bldg. 221, 100 Bureau Dr., #B160, MS 8400, Gaithersburg, MD 20899-8400; (301) 975-4200. Fax, (301) 975-3038. James G. Kushmerick, Director.*
Web, www.nist.gov/pml

Conducts molecular and atomic research and research on physics, electromagnetics, and the properties of solids, liquids, and radio waves.

National Science Foundation (NSF), *Chemistry Division, 2415 Eisenhower Ave., Room E 9300, Alexandria, VA 22314; (703) 292-8840. Fax, (703) 292-9450. David Berkowitz, Director.*
Web, www.nsf.gov/div/index.jsp?div=che and Press email, medrel@nsf.gov

Awards grants to research programs in organic and macromolecular chemistry, experimental and theoretical physical chemistry, analytical and surface chemistry, and inorganic, bioinorganic, and organometallic chemistry; provides funds for instruments needed in chemistry research; coordinates interdisciplinary programs. Monitors international research.

National Science Foundation (NSF), *Materials Research Division (DMR), 2415 Eisenhower Ave., Room E 9400, Alexandria, VA 22134; (703) 292-8810. Fax, (703) 292-9035. Linda S. Sapochak, Director, (703) 292-4932.*
Web, www.nsf.gov/div/index.jsp?div=dmr

Provides grants for research in condensed matter physics, solid-state and materials, chemistry, polymers, metallic materials and nanostructures, ceramics, electronic and photonic materials, and condensed matter and materials theory. Supports multidisciplinary research in these areas through Materials Research Science and Engineering Centers (MRSEC) and national facilities, such as the National High Magnetic Field Laboratory (NHMFL) and Synchrotron Radiation Center (SRC); funds major instrumentation projects as well as the acquisition and development of instrumentation for research to create new or advance current capabilities; and encourages international collaboration to positively impact the global advancement of materials research.

▶NONGOVERNMENTAL

American Assn. for Clinical Chemistry, *900 7th St. N.W., #400, 20001; (202) 857-0717. Fax, (202) 887-5093. Mark J. Golden, Chief Executive Officer. Toll-free, (800) 892-1400.*
General email, info@aacc.org

Web, www.aacc.org, Twitter, @_AACC and Facebook, www.facebook.com/AmerAssocforClinChem

International society of chemists, physicians, and other scientists specializing in clinical chemistry, molecular diagnostics, mass spectrometry, translational medicine, lab management, and other areas of progressing laboratory science. Provides educational and professional development services; presents awards for outstanding achievement. Monitors legislation and regulations.

American Chemical Society, *1155 16th St. N.W., 20036; (202) 872-4600. Fax, (202) 872-4615. Thomas M. Connelly Jr., Executive Director. Information, (800) 227-5558. Press, (202) 872-6042.*
General email, help@acs.org

Web, www.acs.org, Twitter, @AmerChemSociety and Facebook, www.facebook.com/AmericanChemicalSociety

Membership: professional chemists and chemical engineers. Maintains educational programs, including those that evaluate college chemistry departments and high school chemistry curricula. Administers grants and fellowships for basic research; sponsors international exchanges; presents achievement awards.

American Chemical Society, *Petroleum Research Fund, 1155 16th St. N.W., 20036; (202) 872-4481. Fax, (202) 872-6319. Nancy Jensen, Assistant Director for Research Grants, (202) 872-6186.*
General email, prfinfo@acs.org

Web, www.acs.org/content/acs/en/funding-and-awards/grants/prf.html and Facebook, www.facebook.com/AmericanChemicalSociety

Makes grants to nonprofit institutions for advanced scientific education and fundamental research related to the petroleum industry in chemistry, geology, and engineering.

American Chemistry Council, *700 2nd St. N.E., 20002; (202) 249-7000. Fax, (202) 249-6100. Chris Jahn, President. Web, www.americanchemistry.com, Twitter, @AmChemistry and Facebook, www.facebook.com/AmericanChemistry*

Membership: manufacturers of basic industrial chemicals that make or sell chemical products in the U.S. Provides members with technical research, communications services, and legal affairs counseling. Sponsors research on chemical risk assessments, biomonitoring, and nanotechnology. Interests include environmental safety and health, transportation, energy, and international trade and security. Monitors legislation and regulations.

National Academies of Sciences, Engineering, and Medicine (NASEM), *Chemical Sciences and Technology Board,* Keck Center, 500 5th St. N.W., 20001; (202) 334-3536. Fax, (202) 334-1393. Maggie Wasler, Director (Acting). General email, bcst@nas.edu

Web, www.nationalacademies.org/bcst/board-on-chemical-sciences-and-technology

Advises policymakers and decisionmakers about matters related to chemistry and chemical engineering.

National Academies of Sciences, Engineering, and Medicine (NASEM), *National Material and Manufacturing Board,* Keck Center, 500 5th St. N.W., #WS921, 20001; (202) 334-3505. Fax, (202) 334-3575. James Lancaster, Director; Theresa Kotanchek, Chair. General email, nmmb@nas.edu

Web, www.nationalacademies.org/nmmb/national-materials-and-manufacturing-board

Conducts research on materials and manufacturing, including at the atomic, molecular, and nano scales, and innovative applications of new and existing materials, including pilot-scale and large-scale manufacturing, the design of new devices, and disposal.

Society of Chemical Manufacturers and Affiliates (SOCMA), 1400 Crystal Dr., #630, Arlington, VA 22202; (571) 348-5100. Fax, (571) 348-5138. Jennifer L. Abril, President, (571) 348-5101. General email, info@socma.com

Web, www.socma.com, Twitter, @socma and Facebook, www.facebook.com/SOCMAsocial

Membership: companies that manufacture, distribute, and market organic chemicals; producers of chemical components; and providers of custom chemical services. Interests include international trade, environmental and occupational safety, chemical security, and health issues; conducts workshops and seminars. Promotes commercial opportunities for members. Monitors legislation and regulations.

Mathematics

▶AGENCIES

National Institute of Standards and Technology (NIST) *(Commerce Dept.), Information Technology Lab,* Bldg. 225, 100 Bureau Dr., #B264, MS 8900, Gaithersburg, MD 20899-8900; (301) 975-2900. Fax, (301) 975-2378. Charles (Chuck) H. Romine, Director. General email, itl_inquiries@nist.gov

Web, www.nist.gov/itl and Twitter, @nistcyber

Seeks to develop applied and computational mathematics to solve problems arising in measurement science and engineering applications; collaborates with NIST and external scientists; disseminates related reference data and software; develops and applies statistical and probabilistic methods and techniques supporting research in measurement science, technology, and the production of standard reference materials.

National Science Foundation (NSF), *Mathematical and Physical Sciences Directorate (MPS),* 2415 Eisenhower Ave., Room C 9000, Alexandria, VA 22134; (703) 292-8800. Fax, (703) 292-9151. Sean L. Jones, Assistant Director, (703) 292-2986.

Web, www.nsf.gov/dir/index.jsp?org=mps

Provides grants for research in the mathematical sciences in the following areas: classical and modern analysis, geometric analysis, topology and foundations, algebra and number theory, applied and computational mathematics, and statistics and probability. Maintains special projects program, which supports scientific computing equipment for mathematics research and several research institutes. Sponsors conferences, workshops, and postdoctoral research fellowships. Monitors international research.

National Science Foundation (NSF), *Mathematical Sciences Division (MPS/DMS),* 2415 Eisenhower Ave., Room E 9400, Alexandria, VA 22134; (703) 292-8870. Fax, (703) 292-9450. David Manderscheid, Director, (703) 292-2899.

Web, www.nsf.gov/div/index.jsp?org=DMS

Supports research on the properties and applications of mathematics and statistics.

Office of Science *(Energy Dept.), Advanced Scientific Computing Research (ASCR),* 19901 Germantown Rd., #SC31, Germantown, MD 20874-1290 (mailing address: Germantown Bldg., 1000 Independence Ave. S.W., #SC21, Washington, DC 20585); (301) 903-7486. Fax, (301) 903-4846. Barbara Helland, Associate Director. General email, sc.ascr@science.doe.gov

Web, www.energy.gov/science/ascr/advanced-scientific-computing-research

Supports mathematical, computational, and computer science research on behalf of the Energy Dept.

▶NONGOVERNMENTAL

Mathematical Assn. of America, 1529 18th St. N.W., 20036-1358 (mailing address: P.O.Box 90973, Washington DC. 20077); (202) 387-5200. Fax, (202) 265-2384. Michael Pearson, Executive Director, ext. 470. Toll-free, (800) 741-9415. Service Center, (800) 617-7800. General email, maahq@maa.org

Web, www.maa.org, Twitter, @maanews and Facebook, www.facebook.com/maanews?ref=nf

Membership: mathematics professors and individuals worldwide with a professional interest in mathematics. Seeks to improve the teaching of collegiate mathematics. Conducts professional development programs.

National Academies of Sciences, Engineering, and Medicine (NASEM), *Mathematical Sciences and Analytics Board,* Keck Center, 500 5th St. N.W., #K960, 20001; (202) 334-1682. Fax, (202) 334-2422. Michelle K. Schwalbe, Director; Mark L. Green, Chair.
Web, www.nationalacademies.org/bmsa/board-on-mathematical-sciences-and-their-applications

Leads NRC mathematical sciences activities. Main interests include core mathematics, applied mathematics, statistics, operations research, scientific computing, and financial and risk analysis.

Physics

▶**AGENCIES**

Goddard Space Flight Center *(National Aeronautics and Space Administration),* **Heliophysics Science Division (HSD),** 8800 Greenbelt Rd., MS 670, Greenbelt, MD 20771; (301) 286-0084. Antti Alexsi Pulkkinen, Director (Acting), (301) 286-0652.
Web, http://hsd.gsfc.nasa.gov

Provides scientific expertise necessary to achieve NASA's strategic science goals in solar physics, heliospheric physics, geospace physics, and space weather. Houses the Solar Physics Laboratory, the Heliospheric Physics Laboratory, the Geospace Physics Laboratory, and the Space Weather Laboratory.

National Institute of Standards and Technology (NIST) *(Commerce Dept.),* **Physical Measurement Laboratory,** Bldg. 221, 100 Bureau Dr., #B160, MS 8400, Gaithersburg, MD 20899-8400; (301) 975-4200. Fax, (301) 975-3038. James G. Kushmerick, Director.
Web, www.nist.gov/pml

Conducts molecular and atomic research and research on physics, electromagnetics, and the properties of solids, liquids, and radio waves.

National Science Foundation (NSF), *Materials Research Division (DMR),* 2415 Eisenhower Ave., Room E 9400, Alexandria, VA 22134; (703) 292-8810. Fax, (703) 292-9035. Linda S. Sapochak, Director, (703) 292-4932.
Web, www.nsf.gov/div/index.jsp?div=dmr

Provides grants for research in condensed matter physics, solid-state and materials, chemistry, polymers, metallic materials and nanostructures, ceramics, electronic and photonic materials, and condensed matter and materials theory. Supports multidisciplinary research in these areas through Materials Research Science and Engineering Centers (MRSEC) and national facilities, such as the National High Magnetic Field Laboratory (NHMFL) and Synchrotron Radiation Center (SRC); funds major instrumentation projects as well as the acquisition and development of instrumentation for research to create new or advance current capabilities; and encourages international collaboration to positively impact the global advancement of materials research.

National Science Foundation (NSF), *Physics Division (PHY),* 2415 Eisenhower Ave., Room W 9200, Alexandria, VA 22134; (703) 292-8890. Fax, (703) 292-9078. C. Denise Caldwell, Director, (703) 292-7371.
Web, www.nsf.gov/div/index.jsp?div=phy

Awards grants for research and special programs in atomic, molecular, and optical physics; elementary particle physics; and nuclear, theoretical, and gravitational physics.

Office of Science *(Energy Dept.),* **High Energy Physics (HEP),** Germantown Bldg., 1000 Independence Ave. S.W., #SC25, 20585; (301) 903-3624. Fax, (301) 903-2597. James L. Siegrist, Associate Director.
General email, sc.hep@science.doe.gov
Web, www.energy.gov/science/hep/high-energy-physics

Provides grants and facilities for research in high energy (or particle) physics. Constructs, operates, and maintains particle accelerators used in high energy research.

Office of Science *(Energy Dept.),* **Nuclear Physics (NP),** 19901 Germantown Rd., #SC36, Germantown, MD 20874-1290 (mailing address: Germantown Bldg., 1000 Independence Ave. S.W., #SC26, Washington, DC 20585); (301) 903-3613. Fax, (301) 903-3833. Timothy J. Hallman, Associate Director.
General email, sc.np@science.doe.gov
Web, www.energy.gov/science/np/nuclear-physics

Provides grants and facilities for research in nuclear physics. Manages the nuclear data program. Develops, constructs, and operates accelerator facilities and detectors used in nuclear physics research.

▶**NONGOVERNMENTAL**

American Institute of Physics, 1 Physics Ellipse, College Park, MD 20740-3843; (301) 209-3100. Michael H. Moloney, Chief Executive Director, (301) 209-3131.
Web, www.aip.org and Twitter, @AIP_HQ

Fosters cooperation within the physics community; improves public understanding of science; disseminates information on scientific research.

American Institute of Physics, *Center for History of Physics,* 1 Physics Ellipse, College Park, MD 20740-3843; (301) 209-3165. Vacant, Director. Library, (301) 209-3177. Library Fax, (301) 209-0882.
General email, chp@aip.org
Library email, nbl@aip.org, Web, www.aip.org/history-programs/physics-history, Twitter, @AIP_history and Facebook, www.facebook.com/AIPhistory

Records and preserves the history of modern physics and allied fields, including astronomy, meteorology, acoustics, and optics. Maintains a documentation program containing interviews, unpublished data, and historical records and photographs. Manages the Niels Bohr Library, which is open to the public.

American Physical Society, *Washington Office,* 529 14th St. N.W., #1150, 20045-2001; (202) 662-8700. Fax, (202) 662-8711. Jonathan Bagger, Chief Executive

Officer; Francis Slakey, Chief Government Affairs Officer. Press, (301) 209-3267.

General email, oga@aps.org

Web, www.aps.org, Twitter, @APSphysics and Facebook, www.facebook.com/apsphysics

Scientific and educational society of educators, students, citizens, and scientists, including industrial scientists. Sponsors studies on issues of public concern related to physics, such as reactor safety and energy use. Informs members of national and international developments. (Headquarters in College Park, Md.)

Biophysical Society, 5515 Security Ln., #1110, Rockville, MD 20852; (240) 290-5600. Fax, (240) 290-5555. Jennifer Pesanelli, Executive Director.

General email, society@biophysics.org

Web, www.biophysics.org, Twitter, @BiophysicalSoc and Facebook, www.facebook.com/biophysicalsociety

Membership: scientists, professors, and researchers engaged in biophysics or related fields. Encourages development and dissemination of knowledge in biophysics through meetings, publications, and outreach activities.

National Academies of Sciences, Engineering, and Medicine (NASEM), Physics and Astronomy Board, Keck Center, 500 5th St. N.W., 20001; (202) 334-1311. Fax, (202) 334-3575. Andrew (Avi) Lankford, Chair; Colleen Hartman, Director.

General email, bpa@nas.edu

Web, www.nationalacademies.org/bpa/board-on-physics-and-astronomy

Provides information to the government and public on scientific matters relating to physics and astronomy, including atomic, molecular, and optical sciences, astronomy and astrophysics, plasma science, radio frequencies, and condensed matter and materials.

The Optical Society, 2010 Massachusetts Ave. N.W., 20036; (202) 223-8130. Fax, (202) 223-1096. Elizabeth (Liz) A. Rogan, Chief Executive Officer, (202) 416-1467. Press, (202) 416-1443.

General email, info@osa.org

Web, www.osa.org and Twitter, @OpticalSociety

Membership: global optics and photonic scientists, engineers, educators, students, technicians, business professionals, and others interested in optics and photonics worldwide. Promotes research and information exchange; conducts conferences; publishes a scientific journal; sponsors technical groups and programming as well as outreach and educational activities.

Weights and Measures, Metric System

▶ **AGENCIES**

National Institute of Standards and Technology (NIST) (Commerce Dept.), Material Measurement Laboratory, Bldg. 227, 100 Bureau Dr., #A311, MS 8300, Gaithersburg, MD 20899-8300; (301) 975-8300. Fax, (301) 975-3845. Stephanie Hooker, Director (Acting).

General email, mmlinfo@nist.gov

Web, www.nist.gov/mml

Serves as the national reference laboratory for measurements in the chemical, biological, and material sciences. Researches industrial, biological, and environmental materials and processes to support development in manufacturing, nanotechnology, electronics, energy, health care, law enforcement, food safety, and other areas. Disseminates reference measurement procedures, certified reference materials, and best-practice guides.

National Institute of Standards and Technology (NIST) (Commerce Dept.), Physical Measurement Laboratory, Bldg. 221, 100 Bureau Dr., #B160, MS 8400, Gaithersburg, MD 20899-8400; (301) 975-4200. Fax, (301) 975-3038. James G. Kushmerick, Director.

Web, www.nist.gov/pml

Develops and disseminates national standards of measurement for length, mass, force, acceleration, time, wavelength, frequency, humidity, and radiation.

National Institute of Standards and Technology (NIST) (Commerce Dept.), Quantum Measurement Division, 100 Bureau Dr., MS 8420, Gaithersburg, MD 20899-8420; (301) 975-3210. Fax, (301) 990-3038. Gerald J. Fitzpatrick, Chief, (301) 975-8922.

Web, www.nist.gov/pml/div684

Applies research to advance measurement instrumentation and the efficiency of electric power transmission and distribution; develops and maintains national electrical reference standards, primarily for power, energy, and related measurements.

National Institute of Standards and Technology (NIST) (Commerce Dept.), Weights and Measures, 100 Bureau Dr., MS 2600, Gaithersburg, MD 20899-2600; (301) 975-4004. Fax, (301) 975-8091. Katrice Lippa, Chief, (301) 975-2956.

General email, barbara.cohn@nist.gov

Web, www.nist.gov/pml/weights-and-measures

Promotes uniformity in weights and measures law and enforcement. Provides weights and measures agencies with training and technical assistance; assists state and local agencies in adapting their weights and measures to meet national standards; conducts research; sets uniform standards and regulations. As the U.S. representative to the International Organization of Legal Metrology, works to harmonize international standards and regulatory practices.

National Institute of Standards and Technology (NIST) (Commerce Dept.), Weights and Measures, Laws and Regulations Group, 100 Bureau Dr., MS 2600, Gaithersburg, MD 20899-2600; (301) 975-3690. Fax, (301) 975-8091. Elizabeth Benham, Metric Coordinator.

General email, owm@nist.gov

Web, www.nist.gov/pml/weights-and-measures/laws-and-regulations

Coordinates federal metric conversion transition to ensure consistency in the interpretation and enforcement of packaging, labeling, net content, and other laws; provides the public with technical and general information about the metric system; assists state and local governments, businesses, and educators with metric conversion activities.

▶CONGRESS

For a listing of relevant congressional committees and subcommittees, please see pages 688–689 or the Appendix.

SOCIAL SCIENCES

General

▶AGENCIES

National Institutes of Health (NIH) *(Health and Human Services Dept.), Behavioral and Social Sciences Research (OBSSR), Bldg. 31, 31 Center Dr., #B1C19, Bethesda, MD 20892-0183; (301) 402-1146. Fax, (301) 402-1150. Christine Hunter, Associate Director (Acting).*
General email, obssrnews@mail.nih.gov

Web, http://obssr.od.nih.gov, Twitter, @NIHOBSSR and Facebook, www.facebook.com/OBSSR.NIH

Works to advance behavioral and social sciences training, to integrate a biobehavioral perspective across the NIH, and to improve communication among stakeholders within and outside of the federal government, including scientists and with the public. Develops funding initiatives for research and training. Sets priorities for research. Provides training and career development opportunities for behavioral and social scientists. Links minority students with mentors. Organizes cultural workshops and lectures.

National Museum of Natural History *(Smithsonian Institution), Library, 10th St. and Constitution Ave. N.W., East Court, 1st Floor, 20560-0154 (mailing address: P.O. Box 37012, MS 154, Washington, DC 20013-7012); (202) 633-1680. Barbara P. Ferry, Manager (Acting), (202) 633-1785.*
General email, askalibrarian@si.edu

Web, www.library.si.edu/libraries/national-museum-natural-history-library

Maintains reference collections covering anthropology, biodiversity, biology, botany, ecology, entomology, ethnology, mineral sciences, paleobiology, and zoology; permits on-site use of the collections. Open to the public by appointment; makes interlibrary loans.

National Science Foundation (NSF), *Social, Behavioral, and Economic Sciences Directorate (SBE/ OAD), 2415 Eisenhower Ave., Room C 13000, Alexandria, VA 22134; (703) 292-8700. Fax, (703) 292-9083. Kellina M. Craig-Henderson, Assistant Director (Acting).*
Web, www.nsf.gov/dir/index.jsp?org=SBE

Directorate that awards grants for research in behavioral and cognitive sciences, social and economic sciences, science resources studies, and international programs. Provides support for workshops, symposia, and conferences.

▶NONGOVERNMENTAL

American Institutes for Research, *1400 Crystal Dr., 10th Floor, Arlington, VA 22202-3289; (202) 403-5000. Fax, (202) 403-5000. David Myers, Chief Executive Officer. Press, (202) 403-6347.*
General email, inquiry@air.org

Web, www.air.org, Twitter, @AIRInforms and Facebook, www.facebook.com/AmericanInstitutesforResearch/?ref=share

Conducts behavioral and social science research and provides technical assistance both domestically and internationally in the areas of education, health, and workforce productivity.

American Psychological Assn., *750 1st St. N.E., 20002-4242; (202) 336-5500. Fax, (202) 336-5502. Arthur C. Evans Jr., Chief Executive Officer. Library, (202) 336-5640. Toll-free, (800) 374-2721.*
General email, apaservice@apa.org

Web, www.apa.org, Twitter, @APA and Facebook, www.facebook.com/AmericanPsychologicalAssociation

Membership: professional psychologists, educators, and behavioral research scientists. Supports research, training, and professional services; works toward improving the qualifications, competence, and training programs of psychologists. Monitors international research and U.S. legislation on mental health. Library open to the public by appointment.

American Psychosomatic Society, *6728 Old McLean Village Dr., McLean, VA 22101-3906; (703) 718-6038. Fax, (703) 556-8729. Laura E. Degnon, Executive Director.*
General email, info@psychosomatic.org

Web, www.psychosomatic.org, Twitter, @connectAPS and Facebook, www.facebook.com/AmericanPsychosomaticSociety

Advances and disseminates scientific understanding of relationships among biological, psychological, social, and behavioral factors in medicine through publications, annual meetings, conferences, and interest groups. Offers educational resources and sponsors awards and scholarships.

American Sociological Assn., *1430 K St. N.W., #600, 20005; (202) 383-9005. Fax, (202) 638-0882. Nancy Kidd, Executive Officer, (202) 247-9855.*
General email, asa@asanet.org

Web, www.asanet.org and Twitter, @ASAnews

Membership: sociologists, social scientists, and others interested in research, teaching, and application of sociology in the United States and internationally. Sponsors professional development program, teaching resources center, and education programs; offers congressional fellowships for sociologists with a PhD or substantial work experience, and predoctoral sociology fellowships for minorities.

Consortium of Social Science Assns., *1430 K St. N.W., #550, 20005; (202) 842-3525. Wendy A. Naus, Executive Director.*
General email, jmilton@cossa.org
Web, www.cossa.org, Twitter, @COSSADC and Facebook, www.facebook.com/SocialScienceAssociations

Consortium of more than 100 associations, scientific societies, universities, research centers, and institutions in the fields of criminology, economics, history, political science, psychology, sociology, statistics, geography, linguistics, law, and social science. Advocates support for research and monitors federal funding in the social and behavioral sciences; conducts seminars; publishes a biweekly electronic newsletter.

Linguistic Society of America, *522 21st St. N.W., #120, 20006-5012; (202) 835-1714. Fax, (202) 835-1717. Alyson Reed, Executive Director.*
General email, lsa@lsadc.org
Web, www.linguisticsociety.org, Twitter, @LingSocAm and Facebook, www.facebook.com/LingSocAm

Membership: individuals and institutions interested in the scientific analysis of language and its applications. Holds linguistic institutes every other year and an annual meeting.

National Academies of Sciences, Engineering, and Medicine (NASEM), *Behavioral, Cognitive, and Sensory Sciences Board, Keck Center, 500 5th St. N.W., 11th Floor, 20001; (202) 334-2678. Fax, (202) 334-2210. Terrie E Moffitt, Chair; Alix Beatty, Senior Program Officer.*
General email, BBCSS@nas.edu
Web, www.nationalacademies.org/bbcss/board-on-behavioral-cognitive-and-sensory-sciences

Membership: experts in the fields of cognition, human development, sensory sciences, social psychology, cognitive neuroscience, behavioral neuroscience, social neuroscience, medical ethics, evolutionary and economic anthropology, and health psychology.

National Academies of Sciences, Engineering, and Medicine (NASEM), *Children, Youth, and Families Board, Keck Center, 500 5th St. N.W., 7th Floor, 20001; (202) 334-1996. Fax, (202) 334-2201. Natacha Blain, Director; David Britt, Chair.*
General email, bcyf@nas.edu
Web, www.nationalacademies.org/bcyf/board-on-children-youth-and-families

Interdisciplinary scientific body seeking to analyze the challenges and critical issues facing children, youth, and families. Interests include the intersection of poverty, education, and life expectancy.

Pew Research Center, *1615 L St. N.W., #800, 20036; (202) 419-4300. Fax, (202) 419-8562. Michael Dimock, President. Press, (202) 419-4372.*
General email, info@pewresearch.org
Web, www.pewresearch.org, Twitter, @PewResearch and Facebook, www.facebook.com/pewresearch

Nonpartisan research organization that studies issues of public interest in America and around the world. Conducts public opinion polling and social science research; reports news; analyzes news coverage, the internet and technology; religion; race and ethnicity; international affairs; social, demographic and economic trends; science; research methodology and data science; immigration and migration.; holds forums and briefings.

Pew Research Center, *Publications, Social and Demographic Trends Project, 1615 L St. N.W., #800, 20036; (202) 419-4300. Kim Parker, Director. Press, (202) 419-4372.*
Web, www.pewsocialtrends.org, Twitter, @allthingscensus and Director, Twitter, @kim_c_parker

Studies behaviors and attitudes of Americans in key realms of their daily lives, using original survey research and analysis of government data. Topics of study include the racial wealth gap, the millennial generation, population geography, demographics, immigration, and marriage and family needs.

Urban Institute, *Research to Action Lab, 500 L'Enfant Plaza S.W., 20024; (202) 833-7200. Justin Milner, Associate Vice President.*
General email, externalaffairs@urban.org
Web, www.urban.org/policy-centers/research-action-lab

Innovation lab serving decision-makers and thinkers interested in social change. Draws on the Urban Institute's research to test new strategies, develop tools, programs, and trainings, and provide strategic and philanthropic advice to public, nonprofit, and private-sector leaders in localities throughout the United States.

Anthropology

▶**AGENCIES**

Anacostia Community Museum *(Smithsonian Institution), 1901 Fort Pl. S.E., 20020 (mailing address: P.O. Box 37012, MS 0777, Washington, DC 20013-7012); (202) 633-4820. Fax, (202) 312-1968. Melanie A. Adams, Director. Press, (202) 633-4876. Public programs, (202) 633-4869. Special events, (202) 633-4867.*
General email, ACMinfo@si.edu
Web, https://anacostia.si.edu, Twitter, @SmithsonianACM, Facebook, www.facebook.com/SmithsonianAnacostiaCommunityMuseum and YouTube, www.youtube.com/user/SmithsonianAnacostia

Explores, documents, and interprets social and cultural issues that impact contemporary urban communities. Presents changing exhibits and programs.

National Museum of Natural History *(Smithsonian Institution), Anthropology, 10th St. and Constitution Ave. N.W., 20560-0112 (mailing address: P.O. Box 37012, MS 112, Washington, DC 20013-7012); (202) 633-1920. Igor Krupnik, Curator. Library, (202) 633-1680.*
General email, anthroPublicInquiry@si.edu
Web, http://anthropology.si.edu

Studies humanity, past and present. Research tools include human-environmental interactions, population migrations, origins of domestication and agriculture, endangered languages and knowledge, and physical and forensic anthropology. Maintains archaeological, ethnographic, and skeletal biology collections; the National Anthropological Archive; the Human Studies Film Archives; and public exhibitions of human cultures.

National Park Service (NPS) *(Interior Dept.), Cultural Anthropology Program, 1849 C St. N.W., 20240-0001; (202) 354-2090. Jennifer Talken-Spaulding, Program Manager.*
Web, www.nps.gov/orgs/1209

Supports cultural anthropological research through funding provided to parks, and by supporting partners in educational institutions. includes the following programs; Tribal Relations and American Cultures, Tribal Historic Preservation, Native American Graves Protection and Repatriation Act and the Cultural Resources Office of Interpretation and Education.

▶**NONGOVERNMENTAL**

American Anthropological Assn., *2300 Claredon Blvd., #1301, Arlington, VA 22201; (703) 528-1902. Fax, (703) 528-3546. Edward (Ed) Liebow, Executive Director, ext. 1168.*
Web, www.americananthro.org, Twitter, @AmericanAnthro and Facebook, www.facebook.com/AmericanAnthropologicalAssociation

Membership: anthropologists, educators, students, and others interested in anthropological studies. Publishes research studies of member organizations, sponsors workshops, a paid summer internship program, and disseminates to members information concerning developments in anthropology worldwide. Publishes more than 20 journals, including *Anthropology News.*

Pre-Columbian Society of Washington, D.C., *1701 17th St. N.W., 20009; Kevin Kelly, President.*
Web, www.pcswdc.org and Facebook, www.facebook.com/The-Pre-Columbian-Society-of-Washington-DC-212117688825149

Membership. General public with interests in pre-Columbian society. Educational organization dedicated to understanding pre-Columbian peoples and cultures of the Americas. Hosts monthly lectures.

Society for American Archaeology, *1990 K St. N.W., #401, 20006; (202) 789-8200. Fax, (202) 789-0284. Deborah L. Nichols, President.*
General email, info@saa.org
Web, www.saa.org, Twitter, @SAAorg and Facebook, www.facebook.com/SAAorgfb

Promotes greater awareness, understanding, and research of archaeology on the American continents; works to preserve and publish results of scientific data and research; serves as information clearinghouse for members.

Washington Assn. of Professional Anthropologists, *P.O. Box 34684, 20043-4684; Suzanne Heurtin-Roberts, President.*
General email, admin@wapadc.org
Web, http://wapadc.org, Twitter, @WAPADC and Facebook, www.facebook.com/WAPAdc

Membership: professional anthropologists, students, and individuals interested in the field. Promotes research and the application of anthropological perspectives; provides practical and educational services, including a mentoring program to provide career advice.

Geography and Mapping

▶**AGENCIES**

Bureau of Intelligence and Research (INR) *(State Dept.), Office of the Geographer and Global Issues (GGI), 2201 C St. N.W., #6722, 20520; (202) 647-1988. Lee R. Schwartz, Director.*
Web, www.state.gov/about-us-bureau-of-intelligence-and-research

Advises the State Dept. and other federal agencies on geographic and cartographic matters. Furnishes technical and analytical research and advice in the field of geography.

Census Bureau *(Commerce Dept.), Geography, 4600 Silver Hill Rd., #4H174, Suitland, MD 20746 (mailing address: 4600 Silver Hill Rd., 4th Floor, Washington, DC 20233-7400); (301) 763-1128. Deirdre Dalpiaz Bishop, Chief, (301) 763-1696.*
General email, geo.geography@census.gov
Web, www.census.gov/geo

Manages the MAF TIGER system, a nationwide geographic and address database; prepares maps for use in conducting censuses and surveys and for showing their results geographically; determines names and current boundaries of legal geographic units; defines names and boundaries of selected statistical areas; develops geographic code schemes; maintains computer files of area measurements, geographic boundaries, and map features with address ranges.

National Archives and Records Administration (NARA), *Cartographic and Architectural Records, 8601 Adelphi Rd., #3320, College Park, MD 20740-6001; (301) 837-3200. Fax, (301) 837-3622. Peter F. Brauer, Cartographic Supervisor, (301) 837-2036.*
General email, carto@nara.gov
Web, www.archives.gov/publications/general-info-leaflets/26-cartographic.html and Research Room, www.archives.gov/research/cartographic/consultation.carto@nara.gov

Makes information available on federal government cartographic records, architectural drawings, and aerial mapping films; prepares descriptive guides and inventories of records. Research room open to the public. Records may be reproduced for a fee.

National Geospatial-Intelligence Agency *(Defense Dept.), 7500 Geoint Dr., MS N73, Springfield, VA 22150-7500;*

(571) 557-5400. Fax, (571) 558-3169. Vice Adm. Robert D. Sharp (USN), Director. Maps and imagery products, (571) 557-5400.
General email, publicaffairs@nga.mil
Web, www.nga.mil, Twitter, @NGA_GEOINT and Facebook, www.facebook.com/NatlGEOINTAgency

Combat support agency that develops imagery and map-based intelligence in support of national defense objectives.

National Oceanic and Atmospheric Administration (NOAA) *(Commerce Dept.), National Geodetic Survey (NGS), Silver Spring Metro Center 3, 1315 East-West Hwy., #8716, Silver Spring, MD 20910-3282; (301) 713-3242. Fax, (301) 713-4172. Juliana Blackwell, Director.*
General email, ngs.infocenter@noaa.gov
Web, www.ngs.noaa.gov

Develops and maintains the National Spatial Reference System, a national geodetic reference system that serves as a common reference for latitude, longitude, height, scale, orientation, and gravity measurements. Maps the nation's coastal zone and waterways; conducts research and development programs to improve the collection, distribution, and use of spatial data; coordinates the development and application of new surveying instrumentation and procedures.

National Oceanic and Atmospheric Administration (NOAA) *(Commerce Dept.), National Ocean Service (NOS), Coast Survey, Silver Spring Metro Center 3, 1315 East-West Hwy., #6147, Silver Spring, MD 20910-3282; (301) 713-2770. Fax, (301) 713-4019. Rear Adm. Ben Evans, Director. Toll-free, (888) 990-6622.*
Web, www.nauticalcharts.noaa.gov and Twitter, @NOAAcharts

Directs programs and conducts research to support fundamental scientific and engineering activities and resource development for safe navigation of the nation's waterways and territorial seas. Prints on demand and distributes nautical charts.

U.S. Board on Geographic Names, *12201 Sunrise Valley Dr., MS 523, Reston, VA 20192-0523 (mailing address: 523 National Center, Reston, VA 20192); (703) 648-4552. David Applegate, Director, (703) 648-6600. Toll-free, 888-ASK-USGS.*
General email, ask@usgs.gov
Web, http://geonames.usgs.gov

Interagency organization established by Congress to standardize geographic names used by the U.S. government. Board members are representatives from the departments of Agriculture, Commerce, Defense, Homeland Security, Interior, and State; the Central Intelligence Agency; the Government Printing Office; the Library of Congress; and the U.S. Postal Service. Sets policy governing the use of both domestic and foreign geographic names as well as undersees feature names and Antarctic feature names. (Affiliated with the U.S. Geological Survey.)

U.S. Geological Survey (USGS) *(Interior Dept.), 12201 Sunrise Valley Dr., MS 100, Reston, VA 20192-0002;*

(703) 648-5953. Dave Applegate, Exercising the Authority of Director, (703) 648-6600; Melanie A. Ruiz, FOIA Officer, (571) 512-8459. Library, (703) 648-4301. Press, (703) 648-4460. Switchboard, (703) 648-4000. Toll-free, 888-ASK-USGS. FOIA, (571) 512-8459.
General email, ask@usgs.gov
Web, www.usgs.gov, Twitter, @USGS, Facebook, www.facebook.com/USGeologicalSurvey and YouTube, www.youtube.com/usgs

Provides reports, maps, and databases that describe and analyze water, energy, biological, and mineral resources; the land surface; and the underlying geological structure and dynamic processes of the Earth.

U.S. Geological Survey (USGS) *(Interior Dept.), National Cooperative Geologic Mapping Program, 12201 Sunrise Valley Dr., MS 908, Reston, VA 20192; (703) 648-6053. John C. Brock, Program Coordinator.*
Web, www.usgs.gov/core-science-systems/national-cooperative-geologic-mapping-program and Twitter, @USGSNgmdb

Funds the production of geologic maps in the United States. Provides geologic mapping data from across North America to public and private organizations.

U.S. Geological Survey (USGS) *(Interior Dept.), National Geospatial Program, 12201 Sunrise Valley Dr., MS 511, Reston, VA 20192 (mailing address: 511 National Center, Reston, VA 20192); (703) 648-4725. Michael Allan Tischler, Director.*
Web, www.usgs.gov/core-science-systems/national-geospatial-program and National Map, www.usgs.gov/core-science-systems/national-geospatial-program/national-map

Provides a foundation of digital geospatial data representing the topography, natural landscape, and built environment of the United States. Provides data downloads at The National Map, an interactive map-based application.

▶ CONGRESS

For a listing of relevant congressional committees and subcommittees, please see pages 688–689 or the Appendix.

Library of Congress, *Geography and Map Division, James Madison Memorial Bldg., 101 Independence Ave. S.E., #LM B01, 20540-4650; (202) 707-8530. Fax, (202) 707-8531. Paulette Hasier, Chief, (202) 707-3400. Reading Room, (202) 707-6277.*
Web, www.loc.gov/rr/geogmap

Maintains cartographic collection of maps, atlases, globes, and reference books. Reference service provided; reading room open to the public. Interlibrary loans available through the library's loan division. Restricted copying privileges. Free copies may be made for personal use only (self-service). Timed entry pass for visitors required, details at loc.gov/visit. Appointments recommended for researchers.

National Aeronautics and Space Administration

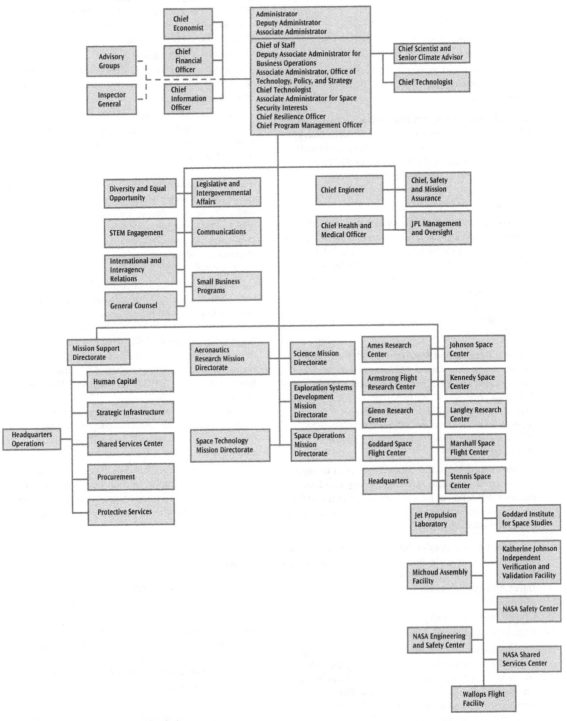

- - - Operate Independently

American Assn. of Geographers, *1710 16th St. N.W., 20009-3198; (202) 234-1450. Fax, (202) 234-2744. Gary Langham, Executive Director.*
General email, gaia@aag.org

Web, www.aag.org, Twitter, @theAAG and Facebook, www.facebook.com/geographers

Membership: educators, students, business executives, government employees, and scientists in the field of geography and related professionals. Seeks to advance professional studies in geography and encourages the application of geographic research in education, government, and business. Publishes scholarly journals and an online newsletter.

Institute of Navigation, *8551 Rixlew Lane, #360, Manassas, VA 20109; (703) 366-2723. Fax, (703) 366-2724. Lisa Beaty, Executive Director.*
General email, membership@ion.org

Web, www.ion.org, Twitter, @ionavigation and Facebook, www.facebook.com/InstituteOfNavigation

Membership: individuals and organizations interested in navigation and position-determining systems. Encourages research in navigation and establishment of uniform practices in navigation operations and education; conducts symposia on air, space, marine, and land navigation, as well as position determination. Sponsors awards celebrating developments in satellite navigation.

National Society of Professional Surveyors, *5119 Pegasus Ct., Suite Q, Frederick, MD 21704; (240) 439-4615. Fax, (240) 439-4952. Timothy Burch, Executive Director, ext. 114.*
General email, info@nsps.org

Web, www.nsps.us.com, Twitter, @NSPSINC and Facebook, www.facebook.com/nspsinc

Membership: professionals working worldwide in surveying, cartography, geodesy, and geographic/land information systems (computerized mapping systems used in urban, regional, and environmental planning). Sponsors workshops and seminars for surveyors and mapping professionals; participates in accreditation of college and university surveying and related degree programs; grants scholarships; develops and administers certification programs for hydrographers and survey technicians. Monitors legislation and regulations.

SPACE SCIENCES

General

Bureau of Oceans and International Environmental and Scientific Affairs (OES) *(State Dept.), Space Affairs, 1800 G St. N.W., #10100, SA22, 20006; (202) 663-2398. Kenneth (Ken) D. Hodgkins, Director.*
Web, www.state.gov/about-us-office-of-space-affairs

Works with U.S. space policies and multilateral science activities to support U.S. foreign policy objectives in order to enhance U.S. space and technological competitiveness.

Goddard Space Flight Center *(National Aeronautics and Space Administration), 8800 Greenbelt Rd., MS 130, Greenbelt, MD 20771; (301) 286-2000. Fax, (301) 286-1707. Dennis Andrucyk, Director. Press, (301) 286-8955. Tours, (301) 286-3978. Visitors Center, (301) 286-8981. General email, karen.m.smale@nasa.gov*

Web, www.nasa.gov/centers/goddard, Twitter, @NASAGoddard and Facebook, www.facebook.com/NASAGoddard

Conducts space and earth science research; develops and operates flight missions; maintains spaceflight tracking and data acquisition networks; develops technology and instruments; develops and maintains advanced information systems for the display, analysis, archiving, and distribution of space and earth science data; and develops National Oceanic and Atmospheric Administration (NOAA) satellite systems that provide environmental data for forecasting and research.

Goddard Space Flight Center *(National Aeronautics and Space Administration), Heliophysics Science Division (HSD), 8800 Greenbelt Rd., MS 670, Greenbelt, MD 20771; (301) 286-0084. Antti Alexsi Pulkkinen, Director (Acting), (301) 286-0652.*
Web, http://hsd.gsfc.nasa.gov

Provides scientific expertise necessary to achieve NASA's strategic science goals in solar physics, heliospheric physics, geospace physics, and space weather. Houses the Solar Physics Laboratory, the Heliospheric Physics Laboratory, the Geospace Physics Laboratory, and the Space Weather Laboratory.

Goddard Space Flight Center *(National Aeronautics and Space Administration), National Space Science Data Coordinated Archive (NSSDCA), 8800 Greenbelt Rd., MS 690.1, Greenbelt, MD 20771; (301) 286-1258. Fax, (301) 286-1683. David R. Williams, Head (Acting). General email, gsfc-d/-nssdca-request@mail.nasa.gov*
Web, http://nssdc.gsfc.nasa.gov

Permanent archive for NASA space science mission data. Acquires, catalogs, and distributes NASA mission data to the international space science community, including research organizations and scientists, universities, and other interested organizations worldwide. Teams with NASA's discipline-specific space science "active archives," which provide researchers and, in some cases, the general public with access to data. Provides software tools and network access, including online information databases about NASA and non-NASA data, to promote collaborative data analysis. (Mail data requests to Coordinated Request User Support Office, Code 690.1, NASA Space Science Data Coordinated Archive, NASA Goddard Space Flight Center, Greenbelt, MD 20771.)

Goddard Space Flight Center *(National Aeronautics and Space Administration), Sciences and Exploration Directorate (SED), 8800 Greenbelt Rd., MS 600, Greenbelt,*

MD 20771; (301) 286-4828. Marc Clampin, Director, (301) 286-6066.
Web, http://science.gsfc.nasa.gov/sci

Plans, organizes, implements, and evaluates a broad system of theoretical and experimental scientific research in the study of the earth-sun system, the solar system and the origins of life, and the birth and evolution of the universe. Develops technology for space-based research. Activities include modeling and basic research, flight experiment development, and data analysis.

Goddard Space Flight Center *(National Aeronautics and Space Administration), Solar System Exploration Data Services (SSEDSO), 8800 Greenbelt Rd., MS 690.1, Greenbelt, MD 20771; (301) 286-1743. Stephanie A. Getty, Director (Acting), (301) 614-5442.*
General email, request@nssdc.gsfc.nasa.gov
Web, http://science.gsfc.nasa.gov/solarsystem

Coordinates data management and archiving plans within NASA's Science Mission. Operates the National Space Science Data Center (NSSDC) as a permanent archive for data associated with NASA's missions, the Crustal Dynamics Data Information System (CDDIS), and the Planetary Data System (PDS).

National Aeronautics and Space Administration (NASA),
300 E St. S.W., 20546 (mailing address: 300 E St. S.W., Washington, DC 20546-0001); (202) 358-0001. Fax, (202) 358-4338. Bill Nelson, Administrator. Library, (202) 358-0168. TTY, (800) 877-0996.
General email, public-inquiries@hq.nasa.gov
Web, www.nasa.gov, Twitter, @NASA, Facebook, www.facebook.com/NASA and Library, www.hq.nasa.gov/office/hqlibrary

Develops, manages, and has oversight of the agency's programs and missions. Interacts with Congress and state officials and responds to national and international inquiries. Serves as the administrative office for the agency. Library open to the public.

National Aeronautics and Space Administration (NASA),
Aeronautics Research Mission Directorate (ARMD), 300 E St. S.W., 20546; (202) 358-2587. Robert (Bob) A. Pearce, Associate Administrator.
Web, www.nasa.gov/aeroresearch and Twitter, @NASAAero

Conducts research in aerodynamics, materials, structures, avionics, propulsion, high-performance computing, human factors, aviation safety, and space transportation in support of national space and aeronautical research and technology goals. Manages the following NASA research centers: Ames (Moffett Field, Calif.), Dryden (Edwards, Calif.), Langley (Hampton, Va.), and Glenn (Cleveland, Ohio).

National Aeronautics and Space Administration (NASA),
Chief Engineer, 300 E St. S.W., 20546; (202) 358-1823. Ralph R. Roe Jr., Chief Engineer, (757) 864-2400.
Web, www.nasa.gov/oce

Serves as the agency's principal adviser on matters pertaining to the technical readiness and execution of programs and projects.

National Aeronautics and Space Administration (NASA),
Chief Health and Medical Officer, 300 E St. S.W., 20546; (202) 358-2390. Dr. James D. Polk, Chief Health and Medical Officer.
Web, www.nasa.gov/offices/ochmo/main/index.html

Ensures the health and safety of NASA employees in space and on the ground. Develops health and medical policy, establishes guidelines for health and medical practices, oversees health care delivery, and monitors human and animal research standards within the agency.

National Aeronautics and Space Administration (NASA),
Exploration Systems Development Mission Directorate (ESDMD), 300 E St. S.W., 20546; (202) 358-2015. Jim Free, Associate Administrator.
Web, www.nasa.gov/directorates/exploration-systems-development

Defines and manages systems development for Artemis and is in charge of planning an integrated Moon to Mars exploration strategy. Manages the human exploration system development for lunar orbital, lunar surface, and Mars exploration; leads the human aspects of the Artemis activities as well as the integration of science into the human system elements. Is responsible for development of the lunar and Mars architectures. Programs in the mission directorate include Orion, Space Launch System, Exploration Ground Systems, Gateway, Human Landing System, and Extravehicular Activity (xEVA) and Human Surface Mobility.

National Aeronautics and Space Administration (NASA),
NASA Advisory Council, 300 E St. S.W., 20546; (202) 358-4510. Lester L. Lyles (USAF, Ret.), Chair; Diane Rausch, Executive Director.
Web, www.nasa.gov/offices/nac/home/index.html

Advises the administrator on programs and issues of importance to NASA. The council consists of nine committees: Aeronautics; Audit, Finance, and Analysis; Commercial Space; Education and Public Outreach; Exploration; Information Technology Infrastructure; Science; Space Operations; and Technology and Innovation.

National Aeronautics and Space Administration (NASA),
National Space Council, Users' Advisory Group, 300 E St. S.W., #5R30, 20546; Adm. James O. Ellis Jr. (USN, Ret.), Chair.
General email, contact@mail.nasa.gov
Web, www.nasa.gov/content/national-space-council-users-advisory-group

Advises the President regarding national space policy and strategy. Focuses on space policy, including long-range goals, developing strategies and recommendations on space-related issues, and fostering close coordination, cooperation, and technology and information exchange among the civil, national security, and commercial space sectors.

National Aeronautics and Space Administration (NASA),
Protective Services, 300 E St. S.W., #6T39, 20546; Joseph S. Mahaley, Assistant Administrator.
Web, www.nasa.gov/nojmo-pso

Serves as the focal point for policy formulation, oversight, coordination, and management of NASA's security, counterintelligence, counterterrorism, emergency preparedness and response, and continuity of operations programs.

National Aeronautics and Space Administration (NASA), Safety and Mission Assurance (OSMA), 300 E St. S.W., #5A42, 20546; (202) 358-2406. W. Russ DeLoach, Chief. General email, nasa-sma@mail.nasa.gov

Web, https://sma.nasa.gov

Evaluates the safety and reliability of NASA systems and programs. Alerts officials to technical execution and physical readiness of NASA projects. Oversees the Mission Support Division, Safety and Assurance Requirements Division, NASA Safety Center, and Independent Verification and Validation Facility.

National Aeronautics and Space Administration (NASA), STEM Engagement, 300 E St. S.W., 4th Floor, Washington, DC 20546; (202) 358-0103. Fax, (202) 358-3048. Mike Kincaid, Associate Administrator. General email, education@nasa.gov

Web, www.nasa.gov/stem/about.html, Twitter, @NASAStem, Facebook, www.facebook.com/ NASASTEMEngagement and YouTube, www.youtube .com/channel/UC9SM7V7J1pAhPabOUST01fw

Coordinates NASA's education programs and activities to meet national educational needs and ensure a sufficient talent pool to preserve U.S. leadership in aeronautical technology and space science.

National Air and Space Museum (Smithsonian Institution), 655 Jefferson Dr. S.W., 20560 (mailing address: 6th St. and Independence Ave. S.W., Washington, DC 20560); (202) 633-2214. Chris Browne, Director (Acting), (202) 633-2350. Archives, (703) 572-4045. Library, (703) 572-4175. Tours, (202) 633-2563. General email, NASMVisitorServices@si.edu

Web, www.airandspace.si.edu, Twitter, @airandspace, Facebook, www.facebook.com/airandspace and YouTube, www.youtube.com/user/airandspace

Collects, preserves, and exhibits astronautical objects and equipment of historical interest, including aircraft, spacecraft, and communications and weather satellites. Library open to the public by appointment.

National Air and Space Museum (Smithsonian Institution), Steven F. Udvar-Hazy Center, 14390 Air and Space Museum Pkwy., Chantilly, VA 20151; (703) 572-4118. Chris Browne, Director (Acting), (202) 633-2350. Library, (703) 572-4175. Public Affairs, (202) 633-1000. General email, info@si.edu

Librarian email, AskaLibrarian@si.edu, Web, www. airandspace.si.edu/visit/udvar-hazy-center, Twitter, @airandspace and Facebook, www.facebook.com/ airandspace

Displays and preserves a collection of historical aviation and space artifacts, including the B-29 Superfortress Enola Gay, the Lockheed SR-71 Blackbird, the prototype of the Boeing 707, the space shuttle Discovery, and a Concorde. Provides a center for research into the history, science, and technology of aviation and space flight. Open to the public daily 10:00 a.m.–5:30 p.m., except December 25.

National Oceanic and Atmospheric Administration (NOAA) (Commerce Dept.), Space Commercialization, 1401 Constitution Ave. N.W., #2518, 20230; (202) 482-6125. Fax, (202) 482-4429. Mark Paese, Director (Acting). General email, space.commerce@noaa.gov

Web, www.space.commerce.gov

The principal unit for space commerce within NOAA and the Commerce Dept. Promotes economic growth and technological advancement of U.S. commercial space industry focusing on sectors including satellite navigation, satellite imagery, space transportation, and entrepreneurial space business. Participates in discussions of national space policy.

►CONGRESS

For a listing of relevant congressional committees and subcommittees, please see pages 688–689 or the Appendix.

►INTERNATIONAL ORGANIZATIONS

European Space Agency (ESA), Washington Office, 1201 F St. N.W., #470, 20004; (202) 488-4158. Josef Aschbacher, Director General (in Paris); Sylvie Espinasse, Head of ESA, DC. Web, www.esa.int/ESA

Intergovernmental agency that promotes international collaboration in space research and development and the use of space technology for peaceful purposes. Members include Austria, Belgium, Czech Republic, Denmark, Estonia, Finland, France, Germany, Greece, Hungary, Ireland, Italy, Luxembourg, the Netherlands, Norway, Poland, Portugal, Romania, Spain, Sweden, Switzerland, and the United Kingdom. Canada participates in some programs, and Slovenia is a member state. (Headquarters in Paris.)

►NONGOVERNMENTAL

American Astronautical Society, 6352 Rolling Mill Pl., #102, Springfield, VA 22152-2370; (703) 866-0020. Fax, (703) 866-3526. Jim Way, Executive Director, (703) 866-0021. General email, aas@astronautical.org

Web, www.astronautical.org, Twitter, @astrosociety and Facebook, www.facebook.com/AmericanAstronautical Society

Scientific and technological society of researchers, scientists, astronauts, and other professionals in the field of astronautics and spaceflight engineering. Organizes national and local meetings and symposia; promotes international cooperation.

American Institute of Aeronautics and Astronautics (AIAA), 12700 Sunrise Valley Dr., #200, Reston, VA 20191-5807; (703) 264-7500. Daniel (Dan) L. Dumbacher, Executive Director. Toll-free, (800) 639-2422.

General email, custserv@aiaa.org

*Web, www.aiaa.org, Twitter, @aiaa and Facebook, www
.facebook.com/AIAAFan*

Membership: engineers, scientists, students, and corporations in the aerospace field. Holds workshops on aerospace technical issues for congressional subcommittees; sponsors international conferences. Offers computerized database through its Technical Information Service.

National Academies of Sciences, Engineering, and Medicine (NASEM), *Aeronautics and Space Engineering Board, Keck Center, 500 5th St. N.W., #W932, 9th Floor, 20001; (202) 334-3477. Fax, (202) 334-3701.
Colleen Hartman, Director.*
General email, aseb@nas.edu

Web, www.nationalacademies.org/aseb

Membership: aeronautics and space experts. Advises government agencies on aeronautics and space engineering research, technology, experiments, international programs, and policy. Library open to the public by appointment.

National Academies of Sciences, Engineering, and Medicine (NASEM), *Space Studies Board, Keck Center, 500 5th St. N.W., 9th Floor, 20001; (202) 334-3477. Fax, (202) 334-3701. Margaret G. Kivelson, Chair;
Colleen Hartman, Director.*
General email, ssb@nas.edu

*Web, www.nationalacademies.org/ssb/space-studies-board
and Twitter, @SSB_ASEB_News*

Provides advice to the government on space policy issues and issues concerning space science activities, including space-based astrophysics, heliophysics, solar system exploration, earth science, and microgravity life and physical sciences. Produces discipline-based "Decadal Surveys," which set priorities for government investments over ten-year time periods.

National Space Society, *1300 I St. N.W., #400E, 20005; (202) 424-2899. Fax, (703) 234-4147. Anita Gale, Chief Executive Officer; Michelle Hanlon, President. Support Center, (703) 234-4135.*
General email, nsshq@nss.org

*Web, www.space.nss.org, Twitter, @nss and Facebook,
www.facebook.com/NSS*

Membership: individuals interested in space programs and applications of space technology. Provides information on NASA, commercial space activities, and international cooperation; promotes public education on space exploration and development; conducts conferences and workshops; publishes quarterly magazine. Monitors legislation and regulations.

Resources for the Future, *1616 P St. N.W., #600, 20036-1400; (202) 328-5000. Fax, (202) 939-3460.
Richard G. Newell, President. Press, (202) 328-5114.*
General email, info@rff.org

*Web, www.rff.org, Twitter, @rff, Facebook, www.facebook
.com/ResourcesfortheFuture and Podcast, www
.resourcesmag.org/resources-radio*

Examines the economic aspects of U.S. space policy, including policy on communications satellites and space debris. Focuses on the role of private business versus that of government.

Space Policy Institute *(George Washington University), 1957 E St. N.W., #403, 20052; (202) 994-1592. Scott Pace, Director, (202) 994-7292.*
General email, spi@gwu.edu

Web, https://spi.elliott.gwu.edu

Conducts research on space policy issues; organizes seminars, symposia, and conferences. Focuses on civilian space activities, including competitive and cooperative interactions on space between the United States and other countries.

Astronomy

▶**AGENCIES**

National Aeronautics and Space Administration (NASA), *Science Mission Directorate (SMD), 300 E St. S.W., 20546; (202) 358-3889. Thomas Zurbuchen, Associate Administrator.*
General email, science@hq.nasa.gov

*Web, http://science.nasa.gov and Twitter,
@NASAScienceCast*

Seeks to understand the origins, evolution, and structure of the solar system and the universe; to understand the integrated functioning of the earth and the sun; and to ascertain the potential for life elsewhere. Administers space mission programs and mission-enabling programs, including suborbital missions. Sponsors scientific research and analysis.

National Aeronautics and Space Administration (NASA), *Space Operations Mission Directorate (SOMD), 300 E St. S.W., 20546; (202) 358-2015. Kathy Lueders, Associate Administrator.*
Web, www.nasa.gov/directorates/space-operations-mission-directorate

Manages NASA's current and future space operations in and beyond low-Earth orbit (LEO), including commercial launch services to the International Space Station. Operates and maintains exploration systems, develops and operates space transportation systems, and performs broad scientific research on orbit. Is responsible for managing the space transportation services for NASA and NASA-sponsored payloads that require orbital launch, and the agency's space communications and navigation services supporting all NASA's space systems currently in orbit.

National Science Foundation (NSF), *Astronomical Sciences Division, 2415 Eisenhower Ave., Room W 9100, Alexandria, VA 22314; (703) 292-8820. Fax, (703) 292-9034. Debra Ann Fischer, Director, (703) 292-2639.*
Web, www.nsf.gov/div/index.jsp?div=ast

Provides grants for ground-based astronomy and astronomical research on planetary astronomy, stellar astronomy and astrophysics, galactic astronomy, extragalactic astronomy and cosmology, and advanced technologies and instrumentation. Maintains astronomical facilities; participates in international projects.

U.S. Naval Observatory *(Defense Dept.), 3450 Massachusetts Ave. N.W., 20392-5420; (202) 762-1438. Capt. Hartwell (Rip) Coke (USN), Superintendent. Library, (202) 762-1463.*
General email, USNO_PAO@navy.mil

Library email, NOBS_LIBRARY@navy.mil and Web, www.usno.navy.mil/USNO

Determines the precise positions and motions of celestial bodies. Operates the U.S. master clock. Provides the U.S. Navy and Defense Dept. with astronomical and timing data for navigation, precise positioning, and command, control, and communications. Maintains a library, with the catalog available on the website. Library open to outside researchers by appointment only.

▶ **NONGOVERNMENTAL**

American Astronomical Society, *1667 K St. N.W., #800, 20006; (202) 328-2010. Fax, (202) 234-2560. Kevin B. Marvel, Executive Officer, ext. 114.*
General email, aas@aas.org

Web, www.aas.org, Twitter, @AAS_Office and Facebook, www.facebook.com/AmericanAstronomicalSociety

Membership: astronomers and other professionals interested in the advancement of astronomy in North America and worldwide. Publishes technical journals; holds scientific meetings; participates in international organizations; awards prizes for outstanding scientific achievements.

American Geophysical Union, *2000 Florida Ave. N.W., 20009-1277; (202) 462-6900. Fax, (202) 328-0566. Susan Lozier, President; Randy W. Fiser, Executive Director. Toll-free, (800) 966-2481.*
General email, service@agu.org

Web, http://sites.agu.org, Twitter, @theagu and Facebook, www.facebook.com/AmericanGeophysicalUnion

Membership: scientists and technologists who study the environments and components of the earth, sun, and solar system. Promotes international cooperation; disseminates information.

Assn. of Universities for Research in Astronomy (AURA), *1331 Pennsylvania Ave. N.W., 20004; (202) 483-2101. Fax, (202) 483-2106. Matt Mountain, President.*
Web, www.aura-astronomy.org, Twitter, @AURADC, Facebook, www.facebook.com/AURAastronomy and YouTube, www.youtube.com/channel/UCmOQVtia5yfPT2jT8iKWW9A

Membership: Consortium of US institutions and international affiliates that operate astronomical observatories for the National Science Foundation and NASA. Establishes, nurtures, and promotes public observatories and facilities that advance innovative astronomical research. Manages and operates three centers: NSF's National Optical-Infrared Astronomy Research Laboratory (NOIRLab), the National Solar Observatory (NSO), and the Space Telescope Science Institute (STScI).

Carnegie Institute for Science, *5251 Broad Branch Rd. N.W., 20015; (202) 387-6400. Fax, (202) 387-8092. Eric D. Isaacs, President.*
Web, https://carnegiescience.edu and Twitter, @carnegiescience

Conducts research in plant science biology, genetic and developmental biology, earth and planetary sciences, astronomy, and global ecology and matter at extreme states at the Carnegie Institution's six research departments: Dept. of Embryology (Baltimore, Md.); Geophysical Laboratory (Washington, DC); Dept. of Global Ecology (Stanford, Calif.); Dept. of Plant Biology (Stanford, Calif.); Dept. of Terrestrial Magnetism (Washington, DC); and The Observatories (Pasadena, Calif., and Las Campanas, Chile).

National Academies of Sciences, Engineering, and Medicine (NASEM), *Physics and Astronomy Board, Keck Center, 500 5th St. N.W., 20001; (202) 334-1311. Fax, (202) 334-3575. Andrew (Avi) Lankford, Chair; Colleen Hartman, Director.*
General email, bpa@nas.edu

Web, www.nationalacademies.org/bpa/board-on-physics-and-astronomy

Provides information to the government and public on scientific matters relating to physics and astronomy, including atomic, molecular, and optical sciences, astronomy and astrophysics, plasma science, radio frequencies, and condensed matter and materials.

17 ⚖

Social Services and Disabilities

GENERAL POLICY AND ANALYSIS

Basic Resources

▶AGENCIES

Administration for Children and Families (ACF) *(Health and Human Services Dept.), Administration for Native Americans (ANA),* Mary E. Switzer Bldg., 330 C St. S.W., Room 4126, 20201; (202) 690-7732. Fax, (202) 690-7441. Hope MacDonald LoneTree, Deputy Commissioner; Michelle Sauve, Executive Director of ICNAA.
Toll-free, (877) 922-9262.
General email, anacomments@acf.hhs.gov
Web, https://acf.hhs.gov/ana and Facebook, www.facebook .com/administrationfornativeamericans

Serves all Native Americans, including federally recognized tribes, American Indian and Alaska Native organizations, Native Hawaiian organizations and Native populations throughout the Pacific Basin (including American Samoa, Guam, and the Commonwealth of the Northern Mariana Islands). Awards grants for locally determined social and economic development strategies; promotes Native American economic and social self-sufficiency; provides grant funding for community development projects. Executive Director chairs the Intradepartmental Council on Indian Affairs (ICNAA), which coordinates Native American–related programs.

Corp. for National and Community Service, 250 E St. N.W., 20024; (202) 606-5000. Michael D. Smith, Chief Executive Officer. Press, (202) 606-6775. TTY, (800) 833-3722. National Service Hotline, (800) 942-2677.
General email, help@cns.gov
Web, www.nationalservice.gov, Twitter, @AmeriCorps and Facebook, www.facebook.com/AmeriCorps

Independent corporation that administers federally sponsored domestic volunteer programs that provide disadvantaged citizens with services, including AmeriCorps, AmeriCorps-VISTA (Volunteers in Service to America), AmeriCorps-NCCC (National Civilian Community Corps), and the Senior Corps.

Food and Nutrition Service *(Agriculture Dept.),* **Supplemental Nutrition Assistance Program (SNAP),** 3101 Park Center Dr., #808, Alexandria, VA 22302-1594; (703) 305-2026. Fax, (703) 305-2454. Jessica Shahin, Associate Administrator, (703) 305-2022.
Web, www.fns.usda.gov/snap

Administers SNAP through state welfare agencies to provide needy persons with Electronic Benefit Transfer cards to increase food purchasing power. Provides matching funds to cover half the cost of EBT card issuance.

Health and Human Services Dept. (HHS), 200 Independence Ave. S.W., 20201; (202) 690-7000. Fax, (202) 690-7203. Xavier Becerra, Secretary, (202) 690-7000. Public Affairs, (202) 690-6343. Toll-free, (877) 696-6775. TTY, (800) 877-8339.
General email, secretary@hhs.gov
Web, www.hhs.gov, Twitter, @HHSGov and Facebook, www.facebook.com/HHS

Acts as principal adviser to the president on health and welfare plans, policies, and programs of the federal government. Encompasses eleven operating divisions, including eight agencies in the U.S. Public Health Service and three human services agencies, including the Centers for Medicare and Medicaid Services, the Administration for Children and Families, the National Institutes of Health, and the Centers for Disease Control and Prevention.

Health and Human Services Dept. (HHS), *Planning and Evaluation (ASPE),* 200 Independence Ave. S.W., #415F, 20201; (202) 690-7858. Fax, (202) 690-7383. Rececca Haffajee, Assistant Secretary (Acting).
General email, osaspeinfo@hhs.gov
Web, https://aspe.hhs.gov and Twitter, @HHS_ASPE

Advises the secretary on policy development in health, disability, human services, data, and science, and provides advice and analysis on economic policy. Coordinates department's evaluation, research, and demonstration activities. Manages cross-department planning activities such as strategic and legislative planning and regulation review. Conducts research and evaluation studies, develops policy analyses, and estimates the cost and benefits of policy alternatives under consideration by the department or Congress.

Health and Human Services Dept. (HHS), *Planning and Evaluation (ASPE), Behavioral Health, Disability, and Aging Policy (BHDAP),* 200 Independence Ave. S.W., #424E, 20201; (202) 690-6443. Fax, (202) 401-7733. Tisamarie Sherry, Deputy Assistant Secretary, (202) 839-0176.
Web, http://aspe.hhs.gov/about/offices/bhdap

Responsible for developing, evaluating, and coordinating department policies and programs that support the independence, productivity, health, and long-term care needs of people with disabilities, older adults, and people with mental and substance use disorders.

Health and Human Services Dept. (HHS), *Planning and Evaluation (ASPE), Human Services Policy (HSP), Division of Data and Technical Analysis,* 200 Independence Ave. S.W., #415E, 20201; (202) 690-7409. Robin Ghertner, Director.
Web, https://aspe.hhs.gov/about/offices/office-human-services-policy-hsp/ddta

Develops policies and programs concerning low-income and disadvantaged populations. Conducts data collection activities, secondary data analysis, modeling, and cost analyses. Issues annual updates to the poverty guidelines and reports to Congress on welfare dependence indicators.

Health and Human Services Dept. (HHS), *Planning and Evaluation (ASPE), Human Services Policy (HSP), Division of Family and Community Policy,* 200 Independence Ave. S.W., #415F, 20201; (202) 730-3904. Kelly Kinnison, Director, (202) 730-3904.
Web, www.aspe.hhs.gov/about/offices/hsp

SOCIAL SERVICES AND DISABILITIES RESOURCES IN CONGRESS

For a complete listing of congressional committees, including their full contact information, leadership, membership, and jurisdictions, please refer to the Appendix on pages 840–963.

HOUSE:

House Agriculture Committee, (202) 225-2171.
Web, agriculture.house.gov
　Subcommittee on Nutrition, Oversight, and
　　Department Operations, (202) 225-2171.
House Appropriations Committee, (202) 225-2771.
Web, appropriations.house.gov
　Subcommittee on Agriculture, Rural
　　Development, Food and Drug
　　Administration, and Related Agencies,
　　(202) 225-2638.
　Subcommittee on Financial Services and General
　　Government, (202) 225-7245.
　Subcommittee on Labor, Health and Human
　　Services, Education, and Related Agencies,
　　(202) 225-3508.
　Subcommittee on Military Construction,
　　Veterans Affairs, and Related Agencies,
　　(202) 225-3047.
　Subcommittee on Transportation, Housing and
　　Urban Development, and Related Agencies,
　　(202) 225-2141.
House Education and Labor Committee,
　(202) 225-3725.
Web, edlabor.house.gov
　Subcommittee on Early Childhood, Elementary,
　　and Secondary Education, (202) 225-3725.
　Subcommittee on Health, Employment, Labor,
　　and Pensions, (202) 225-3725.
　Subcommittee on Higher Education and
　　Workforce Investment, (202) 225-3725.
House Energy and Commerce Committee,
　(202) 225-2927.
Web, energycommerce.house.gov
　Subcommittee on Health, (202) 225-2927.
House Financial Services Committee, (202) 225-4247.
Web, financialservices.house.gov
　Subcommittee on Housing, Community
　　Development, and Insurance, (202) 225-4247.
House Veterans' Affairs Committee, (202) 225-9756.
Web, veterans.house.gov
　Subcommittee on Disability Assistance and
　　Memorial Affairs, (202) 225-9756.

House Ways and Means Committee, (202) 225-3625.
Web, waysandmeans.house.gov
　Subcommittee on Health, (202) 225-3625.
　Subcommittee on Social Security, (202) 225-3625.

SENATE:

**Senate Agriculture, Nutrition, and Forestry
　Committee,** (202) 224-2035.
Web, agriculture.senate.gov
　Subcommittee on Food and Nutrition,
　　Specialty Crop, Organics, and Research,
　　(202) 224-2035.
Senate Appropriations Committee, (202) 224-7363.
Web, appropriations.senate.gov
　Subcommittee on Agriculture, Rural
　　Development, Food and Drug
　　Administration, and Related Agencies,
　　(202) 224-7363.
　Subcommittee on Labor, Health and Human
　　Services, Education, and Related Agencies,
　　(202) 224-7363.
　Subcommittee on Military Construction,
　　Veterans Affairs, and Related Agencies,
　　(202) 224-7363.
　Subcommittee on Transportation, Housing and
　　Urban Development, and Related Agencies,
　　(202) 224-7363.
Senate Finance Committee, (202) 224-4515.
Web, finance.senate.gov
　Subcommittee on Health Care, (202) 224-4515.
　Subcommittee on Social Security, Pensions, and
　　Family Policy, (202) 224-4515.
**Senate Health, Education, Labor, and Pensions
　Committee,** (202) 224-5375.
Web, help.senate.gov
　Subcommittee on Children and Families,
　　(202) 224-5375.
　Subcommittee on Primary Health and
　　Retirement Security, (202) 224-5375.
Senate Special Committee on Aging, (202) 224-5364.
Web, aging.senate.gov
Senate Veterans' Affairs Committee, (202) 224-9126.
Web, veterans.senate.gov

Develops policies and procedures affecting low-income populations, including homelessness and reentry, welfare-to-work issues, child support and enforcement, and domestic violence.

► **CONGRESS**

For a listing of relevant congressional committees and subcommittees, please see page 732 or the Appendix.

► **NONGOVERNMENTAL**

American Public Human Services Assn., *1300 17th St. N., #340, Arlington, VA 22209-3801; (202) 682-0100. Fax, (202) 289-6555. Tracy Wareing Evans, President, ext. 231. General email, memberservice@aphsa.org*
Web, www.aphsa.org and Twitter, @APHSA1

　Membership: state and local human services administrators. Works toward an integrated human services system to improve the health and well-being of individuals and communities. Exchanges knowledge and best practices through conferences and publications; implements policies in partnership with government, businesses, and community organizations; monitors legislation and regulations.

Catholic Charities USA, 2050 Ballenger Ave., #400, Alexandria, VA 22314; (703) 549-1390. Fax, (703) 549-1656. Sister Donna Markham, President.
General email, info@catholiccharitiesusa.org
Web, www.catholiccharitiesusa.org, Twitter, @CCharitiesUSA and Facebook, www.facebook.com/catholiccharitiesusa

Member agencies and institutions provide assistance to persons of all backgrounds; community-based services include day care, counseling, food, and housing. Immigration Advocacy and Refugee Services. National office provides members with advocacy and professional support, including networking, training and consulting, program development, and financial benefits. Represents the Catholic community in times of domestic disaster.

Center for Community Change, 1536 U St. N.W., 20009; (202) 339-9300. Fax, (202) 387-4892. Dorian Warren, Co-President; Lorella Praeli, Co-President.
General email, info@communitychange.org
Web, https://communitychange.org, Twitter, @communitychange and Facebook, www.facebook.com/communitychange

Works to strengthen grassroots organizations that help low-income people, working-class people, and minorities develop skills and resources to improve their communities and change the policies and institutions that affect their lives. Monitors legislation and regulations.

Center for Law and Social Policy (CLASP), 1310 L St. N.W., #900, 20005; (202) 906-8000. Olivia Golden, Executive Director.
Web, www.clasp.org and Twitter, @CLASP_DC

Public policy organization with expertise in national, state, and local policy affecting low-income Americans. Seeks to improve the economic security and educational and workforce prospects of low-income children, youth, adults, and families. Works to develop, promote, and implement federal, state, and local policies in legislation, regulation, and on the ground.

Center for the Study of Social Policy, 1575 Eye St. N.W., #500, 20005-3922; (202) 371-1565. Fax, (202) 371-1472. Judith Meltzer, President. Press, (202) 866-6572.
General email, info@cssp.org
Web, www.cssp.org, Twitter, @CtrSocialPolicy, Facebook, www.facebook.com/CtrSocialPolicy and Press, communications@cssp.org

Assists states and communities in organizing, financing, and delivering human services, with a focus on children and families. Helps build capacity for local decision making; helps communities use informal supports in the protection of children; promotes nonadversarial approach to class action litigation on behalf of dependent children.

Center on Budget and Policy Priorities, 1275 1st St. N.E., #1200, 20002; (202) 408-1080. Fax, (202) 408-1056. Sharon Parrott, President.
General email, center@cbpp.org
Web, www.cbpp.org, Twitter, @CenterOnBudget and Facebook, www.facebook.com/CenterOnBudget

Research group that analyzes changes in federal and state programs, such as tax credits, Medicaid coverage, and food stamps, and their effect on low-income and moderate-income households.

Central American Resource Center (CARECEN), 1460 Columbia Rd. N.W., #C-1, 20009; (202) 328-9799. Fax, (202) 328-7894. Abel Nuñez, Executive Director.
General email, info@carecendc.org
Web, http://carecendc.org, Twitter, @CarecenDC and Facebook, www.facebook.com/CARECEN.DC

Helps Central American and Latino immigrants obtain and maintain legal status. Seeks to address the legal and social service needs of Latinos in the Washington area; to facilitate Latinos' transition to life in the United States; and to provide Latinos with the resources and leadership skills necessary to promote the community's development. Works closely with other community-based agencies.

Christian Relief Services, 8301 Richmond Hwy., #900, Alexandria, VA 22309; (703) 317-9086. Paul Krizek, Executive Director. Toll-free, 800-33-RELIEF. TTY, (800) 828-1140.
General email, info@christianrelief.org
Web, www.christianrelief.org, Twitter, @CRSvcs and Facebook, www.facebook.com/ChristianReliefServices

Promotes economic development and the alleviation of poverty in urban areas of the United States, Appalachia, Native American reservations, Haiti, Mexico, Honduras, Lithuania, the Czech Republic, and Africa. Donates medical supplies and food; administers housing, hospital, and school construction programs; provides affordable housing for low-income individuals and families.

Coalition on Human Needs, 1825 K St. N.W., #411, 20006; (202) 223-2532. Fax, (202) 223-2538. Deborah Weinstein, Executive Director, ext. 111.
General email, info@chn.org
Web, www.chn.org, Twitter, @Voice4HumanNeed and Facebook, www.facebook.com/voice4humanneed

Promotes public policies that address the needs of low-income and other vulnerable populations. Members include civil rights, religious, labor, and professional organizations and service providers concerned with the well-being of children, women, the elderly, and people with disabilities.

Community Action Partnership, 1020 19th St. N.W., #700, 20036; (202) 265-7546. Denise Harlow, Chief Executive Officer, (202) 860-1020.
General email, info@communityactionpartnership.com
Web, https://communityactionpartnership.com, Twitter, @CAPartnership and Facebook, www.facebook.com/CommunityActionPartnershipNationallOffice

Provides community action agencies with information, training, and technical assistance; acts as advocate, at all levels of government, for low-income people. Interests include Head Start, job training, housing, food banks, energy assistance, and financial education.

Council on Social Work Education, *333 John Carlyle St., #400, Alexandria, VA 22314; (703) 683-8080. Fax, (703) 683-8099. Darla Spence Coffey, President, (703) 519-2066.*
General email, info@cswe.org
Web, www.cswe.org, Twitter, @CSocialWorkEd and Facebook, www.facebook.com/CSocialWorkEd

Membership: educational and professional institutions, social welfare agencies, and private citizens. Promotes high-quality education in social work. Accredits social work programs.

Food Research and Action Center (FRAC), *1200 18th St. N.W., #400, 20036; (202) 986-2200. Fax, (202) 986-2525. Luis Guardia, President.*
General email, nsmall@frac.org
Web, www.frac.org, Twitter, @fractweets and Facebook, www.facebook.com/foodresearchandactioncenter

Public interest advocacy center that works to end hunger and undernutrition in the United States. Offers organizational aid, training, and information to groups seeking to improve or expand federal food programs, including food stamp, child nutrition, and WIC (women, infants, and children) programs; conducts studies relating to hunger and poverty; coordinates network of antihunger organizations. Monitors legislation and regulations.

Jewish Federations of North America, *Washington Office, (202) 785-5900. William C. Doroff, Director.*
General email, dc@JewishFederations.org
Web, www.jewishfederations.org, Twitter, @jfederations and Facebook, www.facebook.com/jfederations

Acts as advocate for the 148 Jewish federations across the United States on issues of concern, including long-term care, families at risk, and naturally occurring retirement communities. Offers marketing, communications, and public relations support; coordinates a speakers' bureau. (Headquarters in New York.)

National Assn. for the Advancement of Colored People (NAACP), *Washington Bureau, 1156 15th St. N.W., #915, 20005; (202) 463-2940. Fax, (202) 463-2953. Derrick Johnson, President.*
General email, washingtonbureau@naacpnet.org
Web, www.naacp.org, Twitter, @NAACP and Twitter, President, @DerrickNAACP

Membership: persons interested in civil rights for all minorities. Interests include welfare reform and related social welfare matters. Administers programs that create employment and affordable housing opportunities and that improve health care. Monitors legislation and regulations. (Headquarters in Baltimore, MD.)

National Assn. of Social Workers, *750 1st St. N.E., #800, 20002-4241; (202) 408-8600. Angelo McClain, Chief*

Executive Officer. Member Services, (800) 742-4089. Press, (202) 336-8324.
General email, membership@socialworkers.org
Web, www.socialworkers.org and Twitter, @nasw

Membership: graduates of accredited social work education programs and students in accredited programs. Promotes the interests of social workers and their clients; promotes professional standards; offers professional development opportunities; certifies members of the Academy of Certified Social Workers; conducts research. Monitors legislation and regulations.

National Community Action Foundation (NCAF), *400 N. Capitol St. N.W., #780, 20001 (mailing address: P.O. Box 78214, Washington, DC 20013); (202) 842-2092. Fax, (202) 842-2095. David Bradley, Chief Executive Officer.*
General email, info@ncaf.org
Web, www.ncaf.org, Twitter, @NCAFNews and Facebook, www.facebook.com/NCAFNews

Organization for community action agencies concerned with issues that affect the poor. Provides information on Community Services Block Grants, low-income energy assistance, employment and training, weatherization of low-income housing, nutrition, and the Head Start Program.

National Human Services Assembly, *700 12th St. N.W., #700, PMB 97571, 20005; (202) 347-2080. Victor Valentine, Executive Director.*
General email, info@nassembly.org
Web, www.nassembly.org and Twitter, @NatlAssembly

Membership: national nonprofit health and human service organizations. Provides collective leadership in the areas of health and human service. Provides members' professional staff and volunteers with a forum to share information. Supports public policies, programs, and resources that advance the effectiveness of health and human service organizations and their service delivery.

National Urban League, *Washington Bureau, 1805 7th St. N.W., #520, 20001; (202) 898-1604. Joi O. Cheny, Executive Director, Washington, (202) 629-5755.*
Web, https://nul.org/washington-bureau, Twitter, @NULPolicy and Facebook, www.facebook.com/NULPolicy

Federal advocacy division of social service organization concerned with the social welfare of African Americans and other minorities. (Headquarters in New York.)

Poverty and Race Research Action Council, *740 15th St. N.W., #300, 20005; (202) 866-0802. Fax, (202) 842-2885. (202) 360-3906. Philip Tegeler, President.*
General email, info@prrac.org
Web, www.prrac.org and Twitter, @PRRAC_DC

Civil rights law and policy organization. Facilitates cooperative links between researchers and activists who work on race and poverty issues. Publishes bimonthly *Poverty & Race* newsletter and a civil rights history curriculum guide. Policy research areas include housing, education, and health disparities.

Public Welfare Foundation, *1200 U St. N.W., 20009-4443; (202) 965-1800. Fax, (202) 265-8851. Candice C. Jones, President. Press, ext. 242. General email, info@publicwelfare.org*

Web, www.publicwelfare.org, Twitter, @PublicWelfare and Facebook, www.facebook.com/publicwelfarefdn

Seeks to assist disadvantaged populations in overcoming barriers to full participation in society. Works to end overincarceration. Awards grants to nonprofits in the following areas: criminal and juvenile justice and workers' rights.

Salvation Army, *615 Slaters Lane, Alexandria, VA 22314 (mailing address: P.O. Box 269, Alexandria, VA 22313-0269); (703) 684-5500. Kenneth G. Hodder, National Commander. Donating Goods, (800) 728-7825. Toll-free, (800) 725-2769.*

Web, www.salvationarmyusa.org and Twitter, @SalvationArmyUS

International Christian social welfare organization that provides food, clothing, shelter, and social services to the homeless, the elderly, children, and persons with illness or disabilities. (International headquarters in London.)

U.S. Conference of Mayors, *Children, Health and Human Services, 1620 Eye St. N.W., 4th Floor, 20006; (202) 293-7330. Vacant, Assistant Executive Director. General email, info@usmayors.org*

Web, www.usmayors.org/the-conference/committees-and-task-forces

Promotes improved social services for specific urban populations through meetings, technical assistance, and training programs for members; fosters information exchange among federal, state, and local governments, human services experts, and other groups concerned with human services issues.

Urban Institute, *500 L'Enfant Plaza S.W., 20024; (202) 833-7200. Sarah Rosen Wartell, President. Public Affairs, (202) 261-5709. General email, media@urban.org; externalaffairs@urban .org*

Web, www.urban.org, Twitter, @urbaninstitute and Facebook, www.facebook.com/urbaninstitute

Nonpartisan public policy research and education organization. Interests include states' use of federal funds; delivery of social services to specific groups, including children of mothers in welfare reform programs; retirement policy, income, and community-based services for the elderly; job placement and training programs for welfare recipients; health care cost reform; food stamps; child nutrition; the homeless; housing; immigration; justice policy and prisoner reentry; federal, state, and local tax policy; and education policy.

Urban Institute, *Center on Labor, Human Services, and Population, 500 L'Enfant Plaza S.W., 20024; (202) 833-7200. Signe-Mary McKernan, Vice President.*

Web, www.urban.org/policy-centers/center-labor-human-services-and-population

Analyzes employment and income trends, studies how the U.S. population is growing, and evaluates programs dealing with homelessness, child welfare, and job training. Other areas of interest include immigration, mortality, sexual and reproductive health, adolescent risk behavior, child care, domestic violence, and youth development.

Urban Institute, *Income and Benefits Policy Center, 500 L'Enfant Plaza S.W., 20024; (202) 833-7200. Fax, (202) 833-4388. Gregory Acs, Vice President.*

Web, www.urban.org/center/ibp and Retirement policy, http://urban.org/retirement_policy

Studies how public policy influences behavior and the economic well-being of families, particularly the disabled, the elderly, and those with low incomes.

CHILDREN AND FAMILIES

General

▶**AGENCIES**

Administration for Children and Families (ACF) *(Health and Human Services Dept.), Mary E. Switzer Bldg., 330 C St. S.W., 20201; (202) 401-9200. Jennifer Cannistra, Assistant Secretary (Acting). Domestic violence hotline, (800) 799-7233; TTY, (800) 787-3244. Human trafficking tip hotline, (888) 373-7888. National child abuse hotline, (800) 422-4453. National runaway safeline, (800) 786-2929. Public Affairs, (202) 401-9215.*

Web, https://acf.hhs.gov, Twitter, @ACFHHS, Facebook, www.facebook.com/ChildrenAndFamilies and YouTube, www.youtube.com/usgovacf

Administers and funds national assistance programs for Native Americans, children, youth, low-income families, and those with intellectual and developmental disabilities to promote stability, economic security, responsibility, and self-support for families; supervises programs and the use of funds to provide the most needy with aid and to increase alternatives to public assistance. Responsible for Social Services Block Grants to the states; coordinates Health and Human Services Dept. policy and regulations on child protection, day care, foster care, adoption services, child abuse and neglect, and special services for those with disabilities. Programs include Temporary Assistance for Needy Families, Head Start, child welfare, child support enforcement, human trafficking, and refugee resettlement.

Administration for Children and Families (ACF) *(Health and Human Services Dept.), Child Support Enforcement (OCSE), Mary E. Switzer Bldg., 330 C St. S.W., 5th Floor, MS 5602, 20201 (mailing address: 370 L'Enfant Promenade S.W., Washington, DC 20447); (202) 401-9373. Fax, (202) 401-5428. Tanguler Gray, Commissioner.*

Web, https://acf.hhs.gov/css

Partners with federal, state, tribal, and local governments. Helps states and tribes develop, manage, and operate child support programs. Maintains the Federal Parent Locator Service and the National Directory of New Hires, which provide state and local child support agencies with information for locating absent parents. State enforcement agencies locate absent parents, establish paternity, establish and enforce support orders, and collect child support payments.

Administration for Children and Families (ACF) *(Health and Human Services Dept.), Children's Bureau (CB),* Mary E. Switzer Bldg., 330 C St. S.W., 3rd Floor, 20201; (202) 205-8618. Fax, (202) 205-9721. Aysha E. Schomburg, Associate Commissioner.
General email, info@childwelfare.gov
Web, https://acf.hhs.gov/cb and Facebook, www.facebook.com/thechildrensbureau

Works with state and local agencies to develop programs that focus on preventing the abuse of children in troubled families, protecting children from further abuse, and finding permanent placements for those who cannot safely return to their homes. Administers grants.

Administration for Children and Families (ACF) *(Health and Human Services Dept.), Community Services (OCS),* Mary E. Switzer Bldg., 330 C St. S.W., 5th Floor, 20201; (202) 401-9333. Fax, (202) 401-4694. Lanikque Howard, Director.
Web, https://acf.hhs.gov/ocs

Partners with states, communities, and agencies to reduce the causes of poverty, increase opportunity and economic security of individuals and families, and revitalize communities. Administers the Social Services Block Grant, Community Services Block Grant, Community Economic Development, Rural Community Development, Low Income Home Energy Assistance, Low Income Household Water Assistance, and the Assets for Independence programs.

Administration for Children and Families (ACF) *(Health and Human Services Dept.), Family and Youth Services Bureau (FYSB),* Mary E. Switzer Bldg., 330 C St. S.W., 20201; (202) 205-8102. Fax, (202) 260-9333.
Kimberly A. Waller, Associate Commissioner. Domestic violence hotline, (800) 799-7233. Runaway safeline, (800) 786-2929.
Web, https://acf.hhs.gov/fysb, Twitter, @FYSBgov and Facebook, www.facebook.com/FYSBgov

Supports organizations and communities that work with ending youth homelessness, adolescent pregnancy, and domestic violence. Administers federal discretionary grant programs for projects serving runaway and homeless youth and for projects that deter youth involvement in gangs. Provides youth service agencies with training and technical assistance. Monitors federal policies, programs, and legislation. Supports research on youth development issues, including gangs, runaways, and homeless youth. Operates national clearinghouse on families and

youth. Issues grants and monitors abstinence education programs.

Administration for Children and Families (ACF) *(Health and Human Services Dept.), Family Assistance (OFA),* Mary E. Switzer Bldg., 330 C St. S.W., 20201; (202) 401-9275. Fax, (202) 205-5887. Susan Golonka, Director (Acting).
General email, info.OFA@acf.hhs.gov
Web, https://acf.hhs.gov/ofa and Twitter, @OFA_ACF

Provides leadership, direction, and technical guidance to the states, tribes, and territories on administration of the Temporary Assistance for Needy Families (TANF), Tribal Temporary Assistance for Needy Families (Tribal TANF), and Native Employment Works programs, and the Healthy Marriage and Responsible Fatherhood and the Health Professional Opportunity grants. Focuses efforts to increase economic independence and productivity for families. Provides direction and guidance in collection and dissemination of performance and other data for these programs.

Administration for Children and Families (ACF) *(Health and Human Services Dept.), Head Start (OHS),* Mary E. Switzer Bldg., 330 C St. S.W., 4th Floor, MS 4301, 20201; (202) 205-8573. Bernadine Futrell, Director. Toll-free, (866) 763-6481.
Web, www.acf.hhs.gov/ohs, Twitter, @HeadStartgov, Facebook, www.facebook.com/HeadStartgov and General email, HeadStart@cclkc.info

Awards grants to nonprofit and for-profit organizations and local governments for operating community Head Start programs (comprehensive development programs for children, ages birth to five, of low-income families); manages parent and child centers, Early Childhood Learning and Knowledge Centers (ECLKC), for families with children up to age five. Programs focus on early learning, health, and family well-being. Conducts research and manages demonstration programs, including those under the Comprehensive Child Care Development Act of 1988; administers the Child Development Associate scholarship program, which trains individuals for careers in child development, often as Head Start teachers.

Administration for Children and Families (ACF) *(Health and Human Services Dept.), Human Services, Emergency Preparedness, and Response (OHSEPR),* Mary E. Switzer Bldg., 330 C St. S.W., #4006, 20201; (202) 401-4966. (202) 401-9200. Fax, (202) 205-8446. Natalie Grant, Director.
General email, ohsepr@acf.hhs.gov
Web, https://acf.hhs.gov/ohsepr, Twitter, @ACF_OHSEPR and Facebook, www.facebook.com/profile.php?id=100066204115008

Oversees human services, such as child care, child welfare, and energy assistance, in preparedness, response, and recovery from disasters and public health emergencies. Creates emergency plans and provides technical assistance and preparedness training to families and communities.

Manages the Disaster Human Services Case Management Program.

Administration for Children and Families (ACF) *(Health and Human Services Dept.), Office of Child Care (OCC),* Mary E. Switzer Bldg., 330 C St. S.W., 4th Floor, 20201; 202- 690-6782. Fax, (202) 690-5600. Ruth Friedman, Director.
Web, www.acf.hhs.gov/occ and Press, media@acf.hhs.gov

Supports low-income working families by providing access to affordable, high-quality early care and after-school programs. Partners with state, territory, and tribal governments to administer the Child Care and Development Fund Program. Oversees policy implementation to improve and support child care licensing and child care worker training and education.

Administration for Children and Families (ACF) *(Health and Human Services Dept.), Refugee Resettlement (ORR),* Mary E. Switzer Bldg., 330 C St. S.W., Room 5123, 20201; (202) 401-9246. Fax, (202) 401-4678. Cindy Huang, Director. Parent Hotline, (800) 203-7001.
Web, https://acf.hhs.gov/orr

Provides critical resources to assist refugees, Cuban and Haitian entrants, asylees, trafficking and torture victims, special immigrant visa holders, Amerasians, and unaccompanied alien children. Seeks to help individuals achieve economic self-sufficiency and social adjustment to help them integrate fully into American society. Provides states and nonprofit agencies with grants for refugee social services such as English language and employment training.

Administration for Children and Families (ACF) *(Health and Human Services Dept.), Trafficking in Persons (OTIP),* Mary E. Switzer Bldg., 330 C St. S.W., 4th Floor, 20201; (202) 401-9372. Fax, (202) 401-4678.
Katherine Chon, Director. Foreign national adults with certification helpline, (866) 401-5510. Foreign national minors with eligibility assistance helpline, (202) 205-4582. Human trafficking tip hotline, (888) 373-7888.
General email, endtrafficking@acf.hhs.gov
Web, https://acf.hhs.gov/otip and Human trafficking tip email, help@humantraffickinghotline.org

Develops antitrafficking strategies, policies, and programs to prevent human trafficking; promotes increased health and human service capacity to respond to human trafficking and access to services for survivors.

Administration for Children and Families (ACF) *(Health and Human Services), Legislative Affairs and Budget,* Mary E. Switzer Bldg., 330 C St., MS 4002, 20201; (202) 401-9223. Fax, (202) 401-4562. Amanda Barlow, Director.
General email, media@acf.hhs.gov
Web, www.acf.hhs.gov/olab

Advises the assistant secretary for children and families on all policy and program matters. Serves as the primary contact for the department, the executive branch and the congress on all legislative, budget development and execution, and regulatory activities.

Bureau of Indian Affairs (BIA) *(Interior Dept.), Indian Services (OIS),* 1849 C St. N.W., MS-3645 MIB, 20240; General (202) 513-7640. Jeanette Hanna, Deputy Bureau Director.
Web, www.bia.gov/bia/ois

Gives assistance, in accordance with state payment standards, to American Indians and Alaska Natives of federally recognized tribes living on or near reservations and in tribal service areas, and provides family and individual counseling and child welfare services. The Workforce division administers job training and placement. and programs relating to education, childcare, welfare and economic development.

Food and Nutrition Service *(Agriculture Dept.),* Braddock Metro Center II, 1320 Braddock Pl., Alexandria, VA 22314; (202) 305-2962. Fax, (703) 305-2908. Cindy Long, Administrator, (703) 305-2060. Snap Toll-Free, (800) 221-5689.
Web, www.fns.usda.gov and Twitter, @USDANutrition

Administers all Agriculture Dept. domestic food assistance, including the distribution of funds and food for school breakfast and lunch programs (preschool through secondary) to public and nonprofit private schools; the Supplemental Nutrition Assistance Program (SNAP, formerly the food stamp program); and a supplemental nutrition program for women, infants, and children (WIC).

Food and Nutrition Service *(Agriculture Dept.), Child Nutrition,* 3101 Park Center Dr., #640, Alexandria, VA 22302-1500; (703) 305-2054. Sarah Smith-Holmes, Division Director. Press, (202) 720-4623.
General email, cndinternet@fns.usda.gov
Web, www.fns.usda.gov/school-meals/child-nutrition-programs

Administers the transfer of funds to state agencies for the National School Lunch Program, the School Breakfast Program, the Special Milk Program, the Child and Adult Care Food Program, and the Summer Food Service Program. These programs help fight hunger and obesity by reimbursing organizations such as schools, child care centers, and after-school programs for providing healthy meals to children.

Food and Nutrition Service *(Agriculture Dept.), Child Nutrition Programs, National School Lunch Program,* 3101 Park Center Dr., 6th Floor, Alexandria, VA 22302; (703) 305-2590. Kristen Hyatt, Deputy Administrator (Acting), (703) 305-2054.
Web, www.fns.usda.gov/nslp

Administers the federal assistance meal program operating in public and nonprofit private schools and residential child care institutions. Provides daily nutritionally balanced and low-cost or free lunches to children.

Food and Nutrition Service *(Agriculture Dept.), Communications Officer,* 3101 Park Center Dr., #926, Alexandria, VA 22302; (703) 305-2281. Fax, (703) 305-2312. Brooke Hardison, Director (Acting).
Web, www.fns.usda.gov

Provides information concerning the Food and Nutrition Service and its fifteen nutrition assistance programs to the media, program participants, advocates, members of Congress, and the general public. Monitors and analyzes relevant legislation.

Food and Nutrition Service *(Agriculture Dept.), Food Distribution, 3101 Park Center Dr., #504, Alexandria, VA 22302-1500; (703) 305-2680. Fax, (703) 305-2964. Pam Miller, Administrator.*
General email, fdd-pst@fns.usda.gov
Web, www.fns.usda.gov/fdd

Administers the purchasing and distribution of food to state agencies for child care centers, public and private schools, public and nonprofit charitable institutions, and summer camps. Coordinates the distribution of special commodities, including surplus cheese and butter. Administers the National Commodity Processing Program, which facilitates distribution, at reduced prices, of processed foods to state agencies.

Food and Nutrition Service *(Agriculture Dept.), Policy Support, 3101 Park Center Dr., #1014, Alexandria, VA 22302-1500; (703) 305-2017. Fax, (703) 305-2576. Richard Lucas, Deputy Associate Administrator.*
Web, www.fns.usda.gov/ops/research-and-analysis

Evaluates federal nutrition assistance programs; provides results to policymakers and program administrators. Funds demonstration grants for state and local nutrition assistance projects.

Food and Nutrition Service *(Agriculture Dept.), Special Supplemental Nutrition Program for Women, Infants, and Children (WIC), 3101 Park Center Dr., #520, Alexandria, VA 22302-1594; (703) 305-2746. Fax, (703) 305-2196. Diane Kriviski, Deputy Administrator, (703) 305-2052.*
Web, www.fns.usda.gov/wic

Provides health departments and agencies with federal funding for food supplements and administrative expenses to make food, nutrition education, and health services available to infants, young children up to the age of 5, and pregnant, nursing, and postpartum women.

Health and Human Services Dept. (HHS), *Planning and Evaluation (ASPE), Human Services Policy (HSP), 200 Independence Ave. S.W., #415E, 20201; (202) 690-7409. Miranda Lynch-Smith, Deputy Assistant Secretary, (202) 260-6821.*
Web, https://aspe.hhs.gov/about/offices/hsp

Conducts policy research, analysis, evaluation, and coordination on issues across the department, including poverty and measurement, vulnerable populations, early childhood education and child welfare, economic support for families, and youth development.

Health and Human Services Dept. (HHS), *Planning and Evaluation (ASPE), Human Services Policy (HSP), Division of Children and Youth Policy, 200 Independence Ave. S.W., #415F, 20201; (202) 690-6806.*

Fax, (202) 690-6562. Sarah Oberlander, Director (Acting), (202) 205-1002.
Web, www.aspe.hhs.gov/office-human-services-policy

Develops policies and procedures for programs that benefit children, youth, and families. Interests include early care and education, home visiting, youth development and risky behaviors, parenting and family support, child welfare and foster care, and linkages with physical and mental health. (Located within the Office of Human Services Policy.)

Office of Justice Programs (OJP) *(Justice Dept.), Juvenile Justice and Delinquency Prevention (OJJDP), 810 7th St. N.W., 20531; (202) 307-5911. Fax, (301) 240-5830. Chyrl Jones, Administrator (Acting), (202) 353-0798. Clearinghouse, (800) 851-3420.*
Web, www.ojjdp.gov, Twitter, @OJPOJJDP and Facebook, www.facebook.com/OJPOJJDP

Coordinates with youth programs of the Agriculture, Education, Housing and Urban Development, Interior, Labor, and Health and Human Services Depts., including the Center for Studies of Crime and Delinquency.

▶**CONGRESS**

For a listing of relevant congressional committees and subcommittees, please see page 732 or the Appendix.

▶**NONGOVERNMENTAL**

Active Minds, *2001 S St. N.W., #630, 20009; (202) 332-9595. Fax, (202) 332-9599. Alison Malmon, Executive Director, ext. 101.*
General email, info@activeminds.org
Web, www.activeminds.org, Twitter, @active_minds and Facebook, www.facebook.com/activemindsinc

Supports student-run chapters nationwide to help promote youth mental health awareness on college campuses. Offers mental health and mental illness information and resources.

America's Promise Alliance, *1110 Vermont Ave. N.W., #900, 20005; (202) 657-0600. Fax, (202) 657-0601. Mike O'Brien, Chief Executive Officer.*
General email, info@americaspromise.org
Web, www.americaspromise.org, Twitter, @AmericasPromise and Facebook, www.facebook.com/americaspromise

Works with national and local organizations to support America's youth. Interests include adult mentoring, safe environments, physical and psychological health, effective education, and opportunities to help others. Seeks to reduce the high school dropout rate.

American Assn. for Marriage and Family Therapy, *112 S. Alfred St., #300, Alexandria, VA 22314-3061; (703) 838-9808. Fax, (703) 838-9805. Tracy A. Todd, Chief Executive Officer.*

General email, central@aamft.org

Web, www.aamft.org, Twitter, @TheAAMFT and Facebook, www.facebook.com/TheAAMFT

Membership: professional marriage and family therapists. Promotes professional standards in marriage and family therapy through training programs; provides the public with educational material and online referral service for marriage and family therapy.

American Bar Assn. (ABA), *Center on Children and the Law,* 1050 Connecticut Ave. N.W., #400, 20036; (202) 662-1720. Prudence Beidler Carr, Director.
General email, ctrchildlaw@americanbar.org

Web, www.americanbar.org/groups/public_interest/child_law, Twitter, @ABACCL and Facebook, www.facebook.com/abaCCL

Works to increase lawyer representation of children; sponsors speakers and conferences; monitors legislation. Interests include child sexual abuse and exploitation, missing and runaway children, parental kidnapping, child support, foster care, and adoption of children with special needs.

American Humane, 1400 16th St. N.W., #360, 20036; (202) 841-6080. Fax, (202) 450-2335. Robin R. Ganzert, Chief Executive Officer. Toll-free, (800) 227-4645.
General email, info@americanhumane.org

Web, www.americanhumane.org, Twitter, @AmericanHumane and Facebook, www.facebook.com/americanhumane

Promotes the welfare and safety of animals through disaster response, emergency training, and community events. Provides veterans coping with trauma with free service dogs and reunites retired military dogs from overseas with their former handlers. Sponsors programs such as No Animals Were Harmed, Feed the Hungry, and farm and conservation animal welfare certifications.

Boys and Girls Clubs of America, *Government Relations,* 440 1st St. N.W., #1020, 20001; (202) 507-6670. Jim Clark, President; Missy Dugan, Senior Vice President, Government Relations.
General email, info@bgca.org

Web, www.bgca.org

National network of neighborhood-based facilities that provide programs for underserved children six to eighteen years old, conducted by professional staff. Programs emphasize leadership development, education and career exploration, financial literacy, health and life skills, the arts, sports, fitness and recreation, and family outreach. (Headquarters in Atlanta, Ga.)

The Brookings Institution, *Center on Children and Families,* 1775 Massachusetts Ave. N.W., 20036; (202) 797-6496. Kristin F. Butcher, Director, (202) 540-7721. Main Phone, (202) 797-6000.
Web, www.brookings.edu/center/center-on-children-and-families and Twitter, @BrookingsCCF

Research center promoting policies that affect the well-being of America's children, especially children in less advantaged families, and combat issues of poverty, inequality, and lack of opportunity. Interests include education and economic mobility, opportunities for low-income families; single-parent families; and growing elderly population economic challenges. Houses the Future of the Middle Class Initiative.

The Brookings Institution, *Economic Studies,* 1775 Massachusetts Ave. N.W., 20036-2188; (202) 797-6414. (202) 540-7721. Stephanie Aaronson, Vice President.
General email, escomment@brookings.edu

Web, www.brookings.edu/economics and Twitter, @BrookingsEcon

Studies policies for the well-being of children and families to address poverty, inequality, and lack of opportunity.

Caregiver Action Network, 1150 Connecticut Ave. N.W., #501, 20036-3904; (202) 454-3970. John A. Schall, Chief Executive Officer, ext. 102.
General email, info@caregiveraction.org

Web, https://caregiveraction.org, Twitter, @CaregiverAction and Facebook, www.facebook.com/CaregiverActionNetwork

Seeks to increase the quality of life of family caregivers by providing practical help, support and information; works to raise public awareness of caregiving through educational activities. (Formerly National Family Caregivers Assn.)

Child Welfare League of America *(CWLA),* 727 15th St. N.W., #1200, 20005; (202) 688-4200. Christine L. James-Brown, President.
General email, cwla@cwla.org

Web, www.cwla.org, Twitter, @CWLAofficial and Facebook, www.facebook.com/CWLAUpdates

Membership: public and private child welfare agencies. Develops standards for the field; provides information on adoption, early childhood education, foster care, group home services, child protection, residential care for children and youth, services to pregnant adolescents and young parents, and other child welfare issues. Monitors and acts as advocate on federal children and family legislation.

ChildFund International, *Washington Office,* 1200 18th St. N.W., #718, 20036; (804) 756-2700. Anne Lynam Goddard, President. Toll-free, (800) 776-6767.
General email, questions@childfund.org

Web, www.childfund.org and Twitter, @ChildFund

Nonsectarian international humanitarian organization that promotes improved child welfare standards and services worldwide by supporting long-term sustainable development. Provides children in emergency situations brought on by war, natural disaster, and other circumstances with education, medical care, food, clothing, and shelter. Provides aid and promotes the development potential of children of all backgrounds. (Headquarters in Richmond, Va.)

Children's Defense Fund, 840 1st St. N.E., #300, 20002; (202) 628-8787. Rev. Starsky Wilson, President. Press, (202) 662-3554.
General email, cdfinfo@childrensdefense.org
Web, www.childrensdefense.org, Twitter, @ChildDefender and Facebook, www.facebook.com/ChildrensDefenseFund

Advocacy group concerned with programs and policies for children and youth, particularly poor and minority children. Interests include health care, child welfare and mental health, early childhood development, education and youth development, child care, job training and employment, and family support. Works to ensure educational and job opportunities for youth.

Children's Home Society of Minnesota, *Washington Office,* 15800 Crabbs Branch Way, #300, Rockville, MD 20855; (301) 562-6500. Patrick Thueson, Chief Executive Officer.
General email, inquire@chlss.org
Web, https://chlss.org and Facebook, www.facebook.com/chlssadoption

Provides information on international adoption; sponsors seminars and workshops for adoptive and prospective adoptive parents. Affiliated with Lutheran Social Services of Minnesota. (Headquarters in St. Paul, Minn.)

Children's Rights Council (CRC), 1296 Cronson Blvd., #3086, Crofton, MD 21114; (301) 459-1220. Lesa D. Britt, Chief Executive Officer.
General email, info@crckids.org
Web, www.crckids.org

Membership: parents and professionals. Works to strengthen families through education and advocacy. Supports family formation and preservation. Conducts conferences and serves as an information clearinghouse. Interests include children whose parents are separated, unwed, or divorced.

Congressional Coalition on Adoption Institute (CCAI), 655 New York Ave. N.W., 20001 (mailing address: P.O. Box 75157, Washington, DC 20013); (202) 544-8500. Kate McLean, Executive Director.
General email, info@ccainstitute.org
Web, http://ccainstitute.org, Twitter, @CCAInstitute, Facebook, www.facebook.com/theccai/?v=info and YouTube, www.youtube.com/user/CCAInstitute

Promotes awareness of children without families. Educates policymakers about foster care and adoption issues.

Council for Professional Recognition, 2460 16th St. N.W., 20009-3547; (202) 265-9090. Fax, (202) 265-9161. Calvin Moore Jr., Chief Executive Officer. Toll-free, (800) 424-4310.
CDA Candidates email, CouncilNetworks@cdacouncil.org, Web, www.cdacouncil.org, Twitter, @cdacouncil, Facebook, www.facebook.com/cdacouncil and YouTube, www.youtube.com/user/theCDACredential

Promotes high standards for early childhood teachers. Awards credentials to family day care, preschool, home visitor, and infant-toddler caregivers. Administers the Child Development Associate National Credentialing Program, designed to assess and credential early childhood education professionals.

Covenant House, *Washington Office,* 2001 Mississippi Ave. S.E., 20020; (202) 610-9600. Angela Jones Hackley, Executive Director.
Web, http://covenanthousedc.org and Twitter, @CovenantHouseDC

Protects young people suffering from homelessness, abuse, and neglect. Provides services including transitional housing, GED and adult education, and job readiness. (Affiliated with Covenant House International.)

Cradle of Hope, 8630 Fenton St., #310, Silver Spring, MD 20910; (301) 587-4400. Fax, (301) 588-3091. Linda Perilstein, Executive Director. 24-hour helpline, (301) 905-9999.
General email, info@cradlehope.org
Web, www.cradlehope.org and Facebook, www.facebook.com/cradlehope

International adoption center specializing in the placement of children from China. Offers preadoption and postadoption support services. Sponsors the Bridge of Hope program, a summer camp where older Chinese children meet and spend time with potential host families, in several U.S. locations, including the Washington, DC, metro region.

FAIR Girls, 2021 L St. N.W., #101-254, 20036; (202) 520-9777. Dawanna Kennedy, Executive Director (Acting). Crisis Hotline, (855) 900-3247. National Trafficking Hotline, (888) 373-7888.
General email, info@fairgirls.org
Web, www.fairgirls.org, Twitter, @fair_girls and Facebook, www.facebook.com/fairgirls.org

Provides interventionist holistic care for survivors of trafficking who identify as girls or young women through prevention education and policy advocacy. Works to eradicate human trafficking and create improved outcomes for survivors.

Generations United, 80 F St. N.W., 20001; (202) 289-3979. Donna M. Butts, Executive Director.
General email, gu@gu.org
Web, www.gu.org, Twitter, @GensUnited and Facebook, www.facebook.com/generationsunited

Membership organization that promotes intergenerational programs and public policies. Focuses on the economic, social, and personal benefits of intergenerational cooperation. Encourages collaboration between organizations that represent different age groups.

Girl Scouts of the U.S.A., *Public Policy and Advocacy,* 816 Connecticut Ave. N.W., 3rd Floor, 20006; (202) 659-3780. Sofia Chang, Chief Executive Officer.
General email, advocacy@girlscouts.org
Web, www.girlscouts.org/en/about-girl-scouts/advocacy.html

Educational service organization for girls grades K–12 that promotes personal development through development of life skills, the outdoors, leadership, entrepreneurship, and other projects. Areas of advocacy include girls' healthy living, increasing girls' participation in STEM (science, technology, engineering, and math) fields, financial literacy, career education, and supporting girls in underserved communities. (Headquarters in New York.)

Hispanic Access Foundation, *1030 15th St. N.W., Suite B/1, #150, 20005; (202) 640-4342. Fax, (202) 640-4343. Maite Arce, President, (202) 640-4344.*
General email, info@hispanicaccess.org
Web, https://hispanicaccess.org, Twitter, @HispanicAccess and Facebook, www.facebook.com/HispanicAccess Foundation

Nonprofit that partners with faith, community, and grassroots organizations to provide resources and information to Latinos about economics, health, education, and the environment, and connect them to bilingual service providers. Promotes civil engagement and improving the lives of Hispanics.

Kidsave, *DC (mailing address: P.O. Box 5441, Washington, DC 20016-1041); (202) 503-3100. Fax, (202) 503-3131. Randi E. Thompson, Chief Executive Officer; Bonnie Williams, Director of Development.*
General email, info@kidsave.org
Web, www.kidsave.org, Twitter, @Kidsave_Intl, Facebook, www.facebook.com/KidsaveInternational and YouTube, www.youtube.com/channel/UCvWeJfXIgO5jjiq7KGP 2HwQ

Maintains programs that provide children age eight and older in orphanages and foster care the opportunity for weekend visits and short stays with families in the community with the goal of permanent adoption or long-term mentoring. Monitors child welfare legislation and regulations worldwide. (Headquarters in Los Angeles, CA.)

National Assn. for the Education of Young Children, *1401 H St. N.W., #600, 20005; (202) 232-8777. Fax, (202) 328-1846. Rhian Evans Allvin, Chief Executive Officer, ext. 8819. Toll-free, (800) 424-2460.*
General email, help@naeyc.org
Web, www.naeyc.org, Twitter, @NAEYC, Facebook, www.facebook.com/NAEYC and YouTube, www.youtube.com/channel/UCoqygeWY9InViJE5bGSE_eg

Membership: early childhood teachers, administrators, college faculty, and directors of early childhood programs at the state and local levels. Works to improve the quality of early childhood care and education. Administers national accreditation system for early childhood programs. Maintains information service.

National Black Child Development Institute, *8455 Colesville Rd., #910, Silver Spring, MD 20910; (202) 833-2220. Fax, (202) 833-8222. Lea Austin, President. Toll-free, (800) 556-2234.*
General email, moreinfo@nbcdi.org
Web, www.nbcdi.org, Twitter, @NBCDI and Facebook, www.facebook.com/nbcdi

Advocacy group for Black children, youth, and families. Interests include child care, adoption, and health, and early childhood education. Provides information on government policies that affect Black children, youth, and families.

National Child Support Enforcement Assn., *7918 Jones Branch Dr., #300, McLean, VA 22102; (703) 506-2880. Fax, (703) 506-3266. Ann Marie Ruskin, Executive Director, ext. 4359.*
General email, customerservice@ncsea.org
Web, www.ncsea.org, Twitter, @NCSEA1 and Facebook, www.facebook.com/ncsea1

Promotes enforcement of child support obligations and educates social workers, attorneys, judges, and other professionals on child support issues. Fosters exchange of ideas among child support professionals. Monitors legislation and regulations.

National Children's Alliance, *516 C St. N.E., 20002; (202) 548-0090. Teresa Huizar, Executive Director.*
Web, www.nationalchildrensalliance.org, Facebook, www.facebook.com/NationalChildrensAlliance and Twitter, @NCAforCACs

Accrediting body for Children's Advocacy Centers (CACs). Provides support, technical assistance, and quality assurance for CACs; helps promote and support communities in providing a coordinated investigation and comprehensive response to child victims of abuse.

National Collaboration for Youth, *700 12th St., #700, PMB9571, 20005; (202) 347-2080. Victor Valentine, Executive Director.*
General email, policy@nassembly.org
Web, www.nationalassembly.org/collaboration/national-collaboration-for-youth, Twitter, @NatlAssembly and Facebook, www.facebook.com/NationalHumanServices Assembly

Membership: national youth-serving organizations. Works to improve members' youth development programs through information exchange and other support. Raises public awareness of youth issues. Monitors legislation and regulations. (Affiliate of the National Human Services Assembly.)

National Council for Adoption, *431 North Lee St., Alexandria, VA 22314-2561; (703) 299-6633. Fax, (703) 299-6004. Ryan Hanlon, Chief Executive Officer (Acting).*
General email, ncfa@adoptioncouncil.org
Web, www.adoptioncouncil.org, Twitter, @AdoptionCouncil and Facebook, www.facebook.com/AdoptionCouncil

Organization of individuals, national and international agencies, and corporations interested in adoption. Supports adoption through legal, ethical agencies; advocates the right to confidentiality in adoption. Conducts research and holds conferences; provides information; supports pregnancy counseling, maternity services, and

Resources for Older Adults

ADVOCACY

AARP, (888) 687-2277; Toll-free Spanish,(877) 342-2277; TTY, dial 711 then (877) 434-7598; TTY Spanish, dial 711 then (866) 238-9488; www.aarp.org

Alliance for Retired Americans, (202) 637-5399; www.retiredamericans.org

National Caucus and Center on Black Aging, Inc., (202) 637-8400; www.ncba-aging.org

National Committee to Preserve Social Security and Medicare, (800) 966-1935 or (202) 216-0420; www.ncpssm.org

National Consumers League, (202) 835-3323; www.nclnet.org

National Council of Gray Panthers Networks (248) 549-5170; www.facebook.com/NationalCouncilof GrayPanthersNetworks

National Hispanic Council on Aging, (202) 347-9733; www.nhcoa.org

Seniors Coalition, (202) 261-3594; www.senior.org

60 Plus, (703) 807-2070; www.60plus.org

AGENCIES

Administration for Community Living, (202) 401-4634; www.acl.gov

Centers for Medicare and Medicaid Services (CMS), (410) 786-3000; TTY,(410) 786-0727; www.cms.gov

Employment and Training Administration, Senior Community Service Employment Program, (877) 872-5627; www.doleta.gov/seniors

National Assn. of Area Agencies on Aging, Eldercare Locator, (202) 872-0888; www.n4a.org

National Institute on Aging (NIA), (800) 222-2225; www.nia.nih.gov

Social Security Administration (SSA), (800) 772-1213; www.ssa.gov

Veterans Affairs Dept., (800) 827-1000; www.va.gov

HEALTH

Alliance for Aging Research, (202) 293-2856; www.agingresearch.org

Alzheimer's Assn., (800) 272-3900; www.alz.org

American Assn. for Geriatric Psychiatry (AAGP), (703) 556-9222; www.gmhfonline.org

Families USA, (202) 628-3030; www.familiesusa.org

National Osteoporosis Foundation, (800) 231-4222; www.nof.org

HOUSING, NURSING HOMES, ASSISTED LIVING

Armed Forces Retirement Home, (202) 541-7500; www.afrh.gov

Army Distaff Foundation, (202) 541-0492; www.armydistaff.org

B'nai B'rith International, Center for Senior Services, (866) 999-6596; www.bnaibrith.org/seniors.html

Consumer Consortium on Assisted Living, www.ccal.org

National Consumer Voice for Quality Long-term Care, (202) 332-2275; www.theconsumervoice.org

SERVICES, COMMUNITY SERVICE

American Veterans (AMVETS), (877) 726-8387; www.amvets.org

Jewish Council for the Aging of Greater Washington, (301) 255-4200 or (703) 425-0999; www.accessjca.org

National Council on Aging, (571) 527-3900; www.ncoa.org

Senior Community Service Employment Program, (877) 872-5627; www.doleta.gov/seniors

Senior Corps, www.nationalservice.gov/programs/ senior-corps

---

counseling for infertile couples. Monitors legislation and regulations.

National Fatherhood Initiative, *12410 Milestone Center Dr., #600, Germantown, MD 20876 (mailing address: P.O. Box 37635, PMB84123, Philadelphia, PA 19101-0635); (301) 948-0599. Fax, (301) 948-6776. Christopher (Chris) Brown, President. General email, info@fatherhood.org*

Web, www.fatherhood.org, Twitter, @thefatherfactor and Facebook, www.facebook.com/nationalfatherhoodinitiative

Works to improve the well-being of children by increasing the proportion of children growing up with involved, responsible, and committed fathers. Provides curricula, training, and assistance to state and community fatherhood initiatives. Conducts public awareness campaigns and research. Monitors legislation.

National Head Start Assn., *1651 Prince St., Alexandria, VA 22314; (703) 739-0875. Yasmina S. Vinci, Executive Director; Bob Bissen, Director of Government Affairs. Toll-free, (866) 677-8724.*
Web, www.nhsa.org, Twitter, @NatlHeadStart, Facebook, www.facebook.com/NatlHeadStart and YouTube, www.youtube.com/channel/UCrsfP8Bs-9MsWFoOxQ2I5hQ

Membership: organizations that represent Head Start children, families, and staff. Recommends strategies on issues affecting Head Start programs; provides training and professional development opportunities. Monitors legislation and regulations.

National Network for Youth (NN4Y), *781 8th St. S.E., 20003; (202) 783-7949. Darla Bardine, Executive Director. National Runaway Safeline, (800) 786-2929.*

General email, info@nn4youth.org

Web, www.nn4youth.org

Membership: providers of services related to runaway and homeless youth. Offers technical assistance to new and existing youth projects. Monitors legislation and regulations.

National PTA, *1250 N. Pitt St., Alexandria, VA 22314; (703) 518-1200. Fax, (703) 836-0942. Nathan R. Monell, Executive Director. Toll-free, (800) 307-4782.*
General email, info@pta.org

Web, www.pta.org, Twitter, @NationalPTA and Facebook, www.facebook.com/ParentTeacherAssociation

Membership: parent-teacher associations at the preschool, elementary, and secondary levels. Supports school breakfast and lunch programs; works as an active member of the Child Nutrition Forum, which supports federally funded nutrition programs for children.

National Urban League, *Washington Bureau, 1805 7th St. N.W., #520, 20001; (202) 898-1604. Joi O. Cheny, Executive Director, Washington, (202) 629-5755.*
Web, https://nul.org/washington-bureau, Twitter, @NULPolicy and Facebook, www.facebook.com/NULPolicy

Federal advocacy division of social service organization concerned with the social welfare of African Americans and other minorities. Youth Development division provides local leagues with technical assistance for youth programs and seeks training opportunities for youth within Urban League programs. (Headquarters in New York.)

Power to Decide, *1776 Massachusetts Ave. N.W., #200, 20036; (202) 478-8500. Fax, (202) 478-8588. Raegan McDonald-Mosley, Chief Executive Officer.*
General email, info@powertodecide.org

Web, www.powertodecide.org, Twitter, @powertodecide and Facebook, www.facebook.com/powertodecide

Nonpartisan initiative that seeks to reduce the U.S. teen and unplanned pregnancy rates. Provides education and information regarding contraception. (Formerly the National Campaign to Prevent Teen and Unplanned Pregnancy.)

Share Our Strength, *No Kid Hungry Campaign, 1030 15th St. N.W., #1100W, 20005; (202) 393-2925. Fax, (202) 289-9003. Bill (Billy) Shore, Executive Chair. Toll-free, (800) 969-4767. fax, (202) 289-9003.*
General email, info@strength.org

Web, www.nokidhungry.org, Twitter, @nokidhungry and Facebook, www.facebook.com/nokidhungry

Works to alleviate and prevent hunger and poverty for children in the United States. Provides food assistance; treats malnutrition; seeks long-term solutions to hunger and poverty through fund-raising, partnerships with corporations and nonprofit organizations, grants, and educational programs.

Social Current, *Public Policy and Mobilization, Alliance for Strong Families and Communities and The Council on Accreditation, 1825 K St. N.W., #600, 20006; (800) 221-3726. Jody Levinson-Johnson, President.*
Web, www.social-current.org, Twitter, @SoCurrentNews and Facebook, www.facebook.com/SocialCurrentNews

Provides resources and leadership to nonprofit child-serving and family-serving organizations in the United States and Canada. Works to strengthen community-based programs and services to families, children, and communities. Monitors legislation and regulations.

U.S. Conference of Mayors, *Task Force on Hunger and Homelessness, 1620 Eye St. N.W., 4th Floor, 20006; (202) 293-7330. Eugene T. Lowe, Assistant Executive Director for Community Development and Housing, (202) 861-6710.*
Web, www.usmayors.org/the-conference/committees-and-task-forces

Tracks trends in hunger, homelessness, and community programs that address homelessness and hunger in U.S. cities; issues reports. Monitors legislation and regulations.

Urban Institute, *Low-Income Working Families Initiative, 500 L'Enfant Plaza S.W., 20024; (202) 833-7200. Fax, (202) 833-4388. Gregory Arcs, Vice President of Income and Benefits Policy; Genevieve M. Kenney, Vice President of Health Policy.*
Web, www.urban.org/tags/families-low-incomes

Studies low-income families, identifies factors that contribute to poor outcomes, and develops public policy solutions. Interests include economic security, the public programs safety net, better life chances for children, and racial and ethnic disparities.

Older Adults

▶**AGENCIES**

Administration for Community Living (ACL) *(Health and Human Services Dept.), Mary E. Switzer Bldg., 330 C St. S.W., 20201; (202) 401-4634. Alison Barkoff, Principal Deputy Administrator. Eldercare locator, (800) 677-1116. Press, (202) 357-3507. TTY, (800) 877-8339.*
General email, aclinfo@acl.hhs.gov

Web, https://acl.gov, Twitter, @aclgov and Facebook, www.facebook.com/aclgov

Oversees programs that provide assistance to older adults, persons with disabilities, and family caregivers. Represents and acts as advocate for individuals with disabilities and older adults throughout the federal government, seeking to ensure that these individuals are as involved as appropriate in the development and implementation of policies, programs, and regulations related to community living.

Administration for Community Living (ACL) *(Health and Human Services Dept.), Administration on Aging (AOA), Mary E. Switzer Bldg., 330 C St. S.W., 20201; (202)*

401-4634, ext. 3. Edwin L. Walker, Deputy Assistant Secretary. Eldercare locator, (800) 677-1116.
Web, www.acl.gov/about-acl/administration-aging

Advocacy agency for older Americans and their concerns. Collaborates with tribal organizations, community and national organizations, and state and area agencies to implement grant programs and services designed to improve the quality of life for older Americans, such as information and referral, adult day care, elder abuse prevention, home-delivered meals, in-home care, transportation, and services for caregivers.

AmeriCorps Seniors (AmeriCorps), Retired and Senior Volunteer Program, Foster Grandparent Program, and Senior Companion Program, 250 E. St. S.W., 20525; (202) 606-5000. Malcolm Coles, Chief Executive Officer (Acting); Atalaya Sergi, Director, AmeriCorps Seniors. AmeriCorp hotline, (800) 942-2677. Press, (202) 606-6775.
Web, https://americorps.gov/serve/americorps-seniors, Twitter, @AmeriCorps and Facebook, www.facebook.com/AmeriCorps

Network of programs that help older Americans find service opportunities in their communities, including the Retired and Senior Volunteer Program, which encourages older citizens to use their talents and experience in community service; the Foster Grandparent Program, which gives older citizens opportunities to work with exceptional children and children with special needs; and the Senior Companion Program, which recruits older citizens to help homebound adults, especially seniors, with special needs.

►CONGRESS

For a listing of relevant congressional committees and subcommittees, please see page 732 or the Appendix.

►NONGOVERNMENTAL

AARP, 601 E St. N.W., 20049; (202) 434-2277. Jo Ann C. Jenkins, Chief Executive Officer. Library, (202) 434-6233. Membership, toll-free, (800) 566-0242. Press, (202) 434-2560. Toll-free, (888) 687-2277. TTY, (877) 434-7598. Toll-free Spanish, (877) 342-2277. TTY Spanish, (866) 238-9488.
General email, dcaarp@aarp.org
Web, www.aarp.org, Twitter, @AARP and Facebook, www.facebook.com/AARP

Membership: people 50 years of age and older. Conducts educational and counseling programs in areas concerning older adults, such as widowed persons services, health promotion, housing, consumer protection, and food insecurity.

AARP Foundation, 601 E St. N.W., 20049; Fax, (202) 434-6593. Lisa Marsh Ryerson, President. Foundation, (202) 434-6200. Press, (202) 434-2560. Toll-free Foundation, (800) 775-6776. Toll-free TTY, (877) 434-7598.

General email, info@aarpfoundation.org
Web, www.aarp.org/aarp-foundation, Twitter, @AARPFoundation, Facebook, www.facebook.com/AARPFoundation and Foundation email, giving@aarp.org

Seeks to educate the public on aging issues; sponsors conferences and produces publications on age-related concerns. Interests include aging and living environments for older persons. Funds age-related research, educational grants, legal hotlines, senior employment programs, and reverse mortgage projects. (Affiliated with AARP.)

Advancing States, 241 S. 18th St., #403, Arlington, VA 22202; (202) 898-2578. Fax, (202) 898-2583. Martha Roherty, Executive Director.
General email, info@advancingstates.org
Web, www.advancingstates.org and Twitter, @ADvancingStates

Membership: state and territorial governmental units that work with older adults, people with disabilities, and their caregivers. Provides members with information, technical assistance, and professional training. Monitors legislation and regulations. (Formerly the National Assn. of States United for Aging and Disabilities.)

Alliance for Retired Americans, 815 16th St. N.W., 4th Floor, 20006-4104; (202) 637-5399. Robert Roach Jr., President.
Web, https://retiredamericans.org, Twitter, @ActiveRetirees, Facebook, www.facebook.com/retiredamericans and email, communications@retiredamericans.org

Membership; Seeks to strengthen benefits to the elderly, including improved Social Security payments, increased employment, and education and health programs. (Affiliate of the AFL-CIO.)

American Seniors Housing Assn., 5225 Wisconsin Ave. N.W., #502, 20015; (202) 237-0900. Fax, (202) 237-1616. David Schless, President, (202) 885-5560.
General email, info@seniorshousing.org
Web, www.ashaliving.org

Membership: development, finance, and operation professionals working in seniors apartments, independent and assisted living communities, and retirement communities. Promotes the advancement of quality seniors housing and health care through research, education, and monitoring legislation and regulations.

Jewish Council for the Aging of Greater Washington, 12320 Parklawn Dr., Rockville, MD 20852-1726; (301) 255-4200. (703) 425-0999. Fax, (301) 231-9360. Shane Rock, Chief Executive Officer.
General email, seniorhelpline@accessjca.org
Web, www.accessjca.org, Twitter, @AccessJCA and Facebook, www.facebook.com/AccessJCA

Nonsectarian organization that provides programs and services throughout the metropolitan D.C. area to help older people continue living independent lives. Offers employment services, computer training, adult day care, social day care, transportation, information services and referrals for transportation and in-home services, and volunteer opportunities.

National Caucus and Center on Black Aging, Inc., *1220 L St. N.W., #800, 20005-2407; (202) 637-8400. Fax, (202) 347-0895. Karyne Jones, President.*
Web, https://ncba-aging.org, Twitter, @NCBA1970 and Facebook, www.facebook.com/ncba.aging.5

Concerned with issues that affect older Black Americans and other minorities. Sponsors employment and housing programs for older adults and education and training for professionals in gerontology. Monitors legislation and regulations.

National Council on Aging, *251 S. 18th St., #500, Arlington, VA 22202; (571) 527-3900. Ramsey Alwin, President, ext. 1. Eldercare locator, (800) 677-1116. General email, kathleen.zuke@ncoa.org*
Web, www.ncoa.org, Twitter, @NCOAging, Facebook, www.facebook.com/NCOAging and YouTube, www.youtube.com/user/ncoaging

Serves as an information clearinghouse on training, technical assistance, advocacy, and research on every aspect of aging. Provides information on social services for older persons. Monitors legislation and regulations.

National Hispanic Council on Aging, *2201 12th St. N.W., #101, 20009; (202) 347-9733. Fax, (202) 853-3803. Yanira Cruz, President.*
General email, nhcoa@nhcoa.org
Web, www.nhcoa.org, Twitter, @NHCOA, Facebook, www.facebook.com/NHCOA and YouTube, www.youtube.com/user/NHCOA

Membership: senior citizens, health care workers, professionals in the field of aging, and others in the United States and Puerto Rico who are interested in topics related to Hispanics and aging. Provides research training, policy analysis, consulting, and technical assistance; sponsors seminars, workshops, and management internships.

US Aging, *1100 New Jersey Ave. S.E., #350, 20003; (202) 872-0888. Fax, (202) 872-0057. Sandy Markwood, Chief Executive Officer.*
General email, info@usaging.org
Web, www.usaging.org and Twitter, @theUSAging

Membership: network of area agencies on aging and the Native American aging programs. Works to establish an effective national policy on aging; provides local agencies on aging and Native American aging programs with training and technical assistance; disseminates information to these agencies and the public. Monitors legislation and regulations. (Formally National Assn. of Area Agencies on Aging.)

US Aging, *Eldercare Locator, 1100 New Jersey Ave. S.E., #350, 20003; (202) 872-0888, ext. 1. Fax, (202) 872-0057. Sara Tribe-Clark, Director. Toll-free, (800) 677-1116. General email, info@usaging.org*
Web, www.usaging.org/eldercareloc and Facebook, www.facebook.com/eldercarelocator

National toll-free directory assistance service that connects older people and caregivers with local support

resources, including meal services, home care, transportation, housing alternatives, home repair, recreation, social activities, and legal services. Language interpretation service for 150 languages available 9:00 a.m.–8:00 p.m. at the toll-free number. (Provided by the U.S. Administration on Aging) Formally National Assn. of Area Agencies on Aging.

DISABILITIES

General

▶**AGENCIES**

Access Board, *1331 F St. N.W., #1000, 20004-1111; (202) 272-0080. Fax, (202) 272-0081. Sachin Dev Pavithran, Executive Director. Toll-free, (800) 872-2253. Toll-free TTY, (800) 993-2822. TTY, (202) 272-0082.*
General email, info@access-board.gov
Web, www.access-board.gov and Twitter, @accessboard

Develops and maintains accessibility requirements for buildings, transit vehicles, telecommunications equipment, medical diagnostic equipment, and electronic and information technology. Provides technical assistance and training on these guidelines and standards. Enforces access standards for federally funded facilities through the Architectural Barriers Act.

Administration for Community Living (ACL) *(Health and Human Services Dept.), Mary E. Switzer Bldg., 330 C St. S.W., 20201; (202) 401-4634. Alison Barkoff, Principal Deputy Administrator. Eldercare locator, (800) 677-1116. Press, (202) 357-3507. TTY, (800) 877-8339.*
General email, aclinfo@acl.hhs.gov
Web, https://acl.gov, Twitter, @aclgov and Facebook, www.facebook.com/aclgov

Oversees programs that provide assistance to older adults, persons with disabilities, and family caregivers. Represents and acts as advocate for individuals with disabilities and older adults throughout the federal government, seeking to ensure that these individuals are as involved as appropriate in the development and implementation of policies, programs, and regulations related to community living.

Administration for Community Living (ACL) *(Health and Human Services Dept.), National Institute on Disability, Independent Living, and Rehabilitation Research (NIDILRR), Mary E. Switzer Bldg., 330 C St. S.W., Room 1304, 20201; (202) 401-4634, ext. 5. Fax, (202) 205-0392. Anjali J. Forber-Pratt, Director.*
General email, nidilrr-mailbox@acl.hhs.gov
Web, www.acl.gov/about-acl/about-national-institute-disability-independent-living-and-rehabilitation-research

Supports applied research, training, and development to improve the lives of individuals with disabilities from birth to adulthood. Generates new knowledge and promotes its effective use to improve the abilities of people with disabilities to perform activities of their choice in the community, and also to expand society's capacity to provide full opportunities and accommodations for its citizens with disabilities. Awards grants for rehabilitation research programs and scientific, technical, and methodological research; coordinates federal rehabilitation research programs; offers field research fellowships.

Civil Rights Division *(Justice Dept.)*, **Disability Rights (DRS)**, *950 Pennsylvania Ave. N.W., 20530; (202) 307-0663. Fax, (202) 307-1197. Rebecca Bond, Chief. Information and ADA specialist, (800) 514-0301. TTY, (800) 514-0383.*
Web, www.justice.gov/crt/disability-rights-section

Litigates cases under Titles I, II, and III of the Americans with Disabilities Act, which prohibits discrimination on the basis of disability in places of public accommodation and in all activities of state and local government. Provides technical assistance to businesses and individuals affected by the law.

Eunice Kennedy Shriver National Institute of Child Health and Human Development (NICHD) *(National Institutes of Health)*, **National Center for Medical Rehabilitation Research (NCMRR)**, *6710B Rockledge Dr., Room 2107, MS 7002, Bethesda, MD 20817; (301) 496-9233. Theresa Hayes Cruz, Director.*
Web, www.nichd.nih.gov/about/org/ncmrr

Supports research to foster the development of scientific knowledge needed to enhance the health, productivity, independence, and quality of life of persons with disabilities. Supports research and research training on pathophysiology and management of chronically injured nervous and musculoskeletal systems (including stroke, traumatic brain injury, spinal cord injury, and orthopedic conditions); repair and recovery of motor and cognitive function; functional plasticity, adaptation, and windows of opportunity for rehabilitative interventions; rehabilitative strategies; pediatric rehabilitation; secondary conditions associated with chronic disabilities; improved diagnosis, assessment, and outcome measures; and development of orthotics, prosthetics, and other assistive technologies and devices.

John F. Kennedy Center for the Performing Arts, **VSA and Accessibility**, *2700 F St. N.W., 20566 (mailing address: P.O. Box 101510, Arlington, VA 22210); (202) 416-8727. Betty Siegel, JD., Director.*
General email, access@kennedy-center.org
Web, www.kennedy-center.org/education/vsa, Twitter, @accessLEAD and Facebook, www.facebook.com/VSAInternational

Initiates and supports research and program development providing arts training and programming for persons with disabilities to make classrooms and communities more inclusive. Provides technical assistance, webinars, online course and training to VSA Arts state organizations; acts as an information clearinghouse for arts and persons with disabilities. Ensures that performances and facilities accessible to all audiences, and provide resources and opportunities for educators, cultural administrators, emerging and professional artists and performers with disabilities. Programs include VSA playwright discovery, international young soloists, international art and emerging young artists.

Labor Dept. (DOL), **Disability Employment Policy (ODEP)**, *200 Constitution Ave. N.W., #S1303, 20210; (202) 693-7880. Fax, (202) 693-7888. Jennifer Sheehy, Deputy Assistant Secretary. Toll-free, (866) 633-7365. TTY, (877) 889-5627.*
General email, odep@dol.gov
Web, www.dol.gov/odep

Seeks to eliminate physical and psychological barriers to the disabled through education and information programs; promotes education, training, rehabilitation, and employment opportunities for people with disabilities.

National Council on Disability, *1331 F St. N.W., #850, 20004-1107; (202) 272-2004. Fax, (202) 272-2022. Anne C. Sommers McIntosh, Executive Director.*
General email, ncd@ncd.gov
Web, www.ncd.gov, Twitter, @NatCounDis and Facebook, www.facebook.com/NCDgov

Independent federal agency providing advice to the president, Congress, and executive branch agencies to promote policies and programs that ensure equal opportunity for individuals with disabilities and enable individuals with disabilities to achieve self-sufficiency and full integration into society.

Smithsonian Institution, **Accessibility Program**, *14th St. and Constitution Ave. N.W., #1050, 20013-7012 (mailing address: National Museum of American History, P.O. Box 37012, MS 607, Washington, DC 20013-7012); (202) 633-2921. Elizabeth (Beth) Ziebarth, Director.*
General email, access@si.edu
Web, www.si.edu/Accessibility

Coordinates the Smithsonian's efforts to improve accessibility of its programs and facilities to visitors and staff with disabilities. Serves as a resource for museums and individuals nationwide.

Social Security Administration (SSA), **Disability Determinations**, *3570 Annex Bldg., 6401 Security Blvd., Baltimore, MD 21235; (410) 966-7241. Fax, (410) 965-6503. John E. Owen, Associate Commissioner; Gina P. Clemons, Associate Commissioner for Disability Policy. Toll-free, (800) 772-1213. TTY, (800) 325-0778.*
Web, www.ssa.gov/disability

Administers and regulates the disability insurance program and disability provisions of the Supplemental Security Income (SSI) program.

Special Education and Rehabilitative Services (OSERS) *(Education Dept.)*, *Lyndon B. Johnson Bldg., 400 Maryland Ave. S.W., 20202-7100; (202) 245-7468 (main phone is voice and TTY accessible). Fax, (202) 245-7638. Katherine Neas, Assistant Secretary (Acting).*
Web, www2.ed.gov/about/offices/list/osers

Provides information on federal legislation and programs and national organizations concerning individuals with disabilities.

Special Education and Rehabilitative Services (OSERS) *(Education Dept.), Rehabilitation Services Administration (RSA)*, Lyndon B. Johnson Bldg., 400 Maryland Ave. S.W., 20202-7100; (202) 245-7468. Fax, (202) 245-7591. Carol Dobak, Commissioner (Acting). Web, https://rsa.ed.gov

Coordinates and directs major federal programs for eligible physically and mentally disabled persons. Administers distribution of grants for training and employment programs and for establishing supported-employment and independent-living programs. Provides vocational training and job placement.

Workers Compensation (OWCP) *(Labor Dept.), Coal Mine Workers' Compensation*, 200 Constitution Ave. N.W., #C3524, 20210 (mailing address: DCMWC, P.O. Box 8307, London, KY 40742-8307); (202) 693-0046. Fax, (202) 693-1395. Michael A. Chance, Director. Toll-free Federal Black Lung Program, (800) 347-2502. TTY, (877) 889-5627.
General email, DCMWC-public@dol.gov
Web, www.dol.gov/owcp/dcmwc

Provides direction for administration of the black lung benefits program. Adjudicates all black lung claims; certifies benefit payments and maintains black lung beneficiary rolls.

▶**CONGRESS**

For a listing of relevant congressional committees and sub-committees, please see page 732 or the Appendix.

Library of Congress, *National Library Service for the Blind and Print Disabled*, 1291 Taylor St. N.W., 20542 (mailing address: Library of Congress, Washington, DC 20542); (202) 707-5100. Fax, (202) 707-0712. Jason Broughton, Director. Toll-Free, (800) 424-8567. Toll-free Braille and print, (888) 657-7323.
General email, nlsref@loc.gov
Web, www.loc.gov/nls, Braille email, braille@loc.gov and Facebook, www.facebook.com/thatallmayread

Administers free braille and talking book library service for people with temporary or permanent low vision, blindness, or a physical, perceptual, or reading disability. Coordinates national network of cooperating libraries, circulates books and magazines in braille or audio formats which are downloadable or delivered by mail free of charge. Reference section answers questions relating to blindness and physical disabilities and on library services available to persons with disabilities.

▶**NONGOVERNMENTAL**

Advancing States, 241 S. 18th St., #403, Arlington, VA 22202; (202) 898-2578. Fax, (202) 898-2583. Martha Roherty, Executive Director.
General email, info@advancingstates.org
Web, www.advancingstates.org and Twitter, @ADvancingStates

Membership: state and territorial governmental units that work with older adults, people with disabilities, and their caregivers. Provides members with information, technical assistance, and professional training. Monitors legislation and regulations. (Formerly the National Assn. of States United for Aging and Disabilities.)

American Assn. of People with Disabilities (AAPD), 2013 H St. N.W., 5th Floor, 20006; (202) 521-4316. Maria Town, President. Toll-free, (800) 840-8844.
General email, communications@aapd.com
Web, www.aapd.com, Twitter, @AAPD and Facebook, www.facebook.com/DisabilityPowered

Works to organize the disability community to effect political, economic, and social change through programs on employment, independent living, and assistive technology. Seeks to educate the public and policymakers on issues affecting persons with disabilities. Works in coalition with other organizations toward full enforcement of disability and antidiscrimination laws.

American Bar Assn. (ABA), *Commission on Disability Rights*, 1050 Connecticut Ave. N.W., #400, 20036; (202) 662-1570. Fax, (202) 442-3439. Amy L. Allbright, Director.
General email, cdr@americanbar.org
Web, www.americanbar.org/groups/diversity/disabilityrights, Twitter, @ABADisability and Facebook, www.facebook.com/ABA.CDR

Promotes the rule of law for persons with mental, physical, and sensory disabilities and their full and equal participation in the legal profession. Offers online resources, publications, and continuing-education opportunities on disability law topics and engages in national initiatives to remove barriers to the education, employment, and advancement of lawyers with disabilities.

American Counseling Assn., 6101 Stevenson Ave., #600, Alexandria, VA 22304-3300; (703) 823-9800. Richard Yep, Chief Executive Officer, ext. 231. Toll-free, (800) 347-6647. Toll-free fax, (800) 473-2329.
General email, membership@counseling.org
Web, www.counseling.org, Twitter, @CounselingViews and Facebook, www.facebook.com/American.Counseling.Association

Membership: counselor educators, agency, clinical professional, school, and career counselors, and other mental health professionals. Establishes counseling and research standards; encourages establishment of rehabilitation facilities; conducts leadership training and continuing education programs. Monitors legislation and regulations.

American Medical Rehabilitation Providers Assn. (AMRPA), 529 14th St. N.W., #1280, 20045; (202) 591-2469. Fax, (202) 223-1925. John Ferraro, Executive Director, (202) 207-1121. Toll-free, (888) 346-4624.
General email, info@amrpa.org
Web, www.amrpa.org, Twitter, @AMRPA and Facebook, www.facebook.com/AmericanMedicalRehabilitationProvidersAssociation

Association representing a membership of freestanding rehabilitation hospitals and rehabilitation units of general hospitals, outpatient rehabilitation facilities, skilled-nursing facilities, and others. Provides leadership, advocacy, and resources to develop medical rehabilitation services and supports for persons with disabilities and others in need of services. Acts as a clearinghouse for information to members on the nature and availability of services. Monitors legislation and regulations.

American Network of Community Options and Resources (ANCOR), *1101 King St., #380, Alexandria, VA 22314; (703) 535-7850. Fax, (703) 535-7860. Barbara Merrill, Chief Executive Officer. General email, ancor@ancor.org*

Web, www.ancor.org, Twitter, @TheRealANCOR and Facebook, www.facebook.com/TheRealANCOR

Membership: privately operated agencies and corporations that provide support and services to people with disabilities. Advises and works with regulatory and consumer agencies that serve people with disabilities; provides information and sponsors seminars and workshops. Monitors legislation and regulations.

American Occupational Therapy Assn., *6116 Executive Blvd., #200, Bethesda, MD 20852-4929; (301) 652-6611. Fax, (301) 652-7711. Sherry Keramidas, Executive Director. TTY, (800) 377-8555. Web, www.aota.org, Twitter, @AOTAInc and Facebook, www.facebook.com/ AmericanOccupationalTherapyAssociationAOTA*

Provides evidence-based practice resources for disability rehabilitation, including practice guidelines, a critically appraised papers repository and exchange, and podcast series. Publishes the *American Journal of Occupational Therapy.*

American Orthotic and Prosthetic Assn., *330 John Carlyle St., #200, Alexandria, VA 22314-5760 (mailing address: P.O. Box 34711, Alexandria, VA 22334); (571) 431-0876. Fax, (571) 431-0899. Eve Lee, Executive Director, (571) 431-0802. General email, info@aopanet.org*

Web, www.aopanet.org, Twitter, @AmericanOandP and Facebook, www.facebook.com/AmericanOandP

Membership: companies that manufacture or supply artificial limbs and braces, and patient-care professionals who fit and supervise device use.

American Physical Therapy Assn., *3030 Potomac Ave., #100, Alexandria, VA 22305-3085; (703) 684-2782. Fax, (703) 684-7343. Justin Moore, Chief Executive Officer. Toll-free, (800) 999-2782. General email, memberservices@apta.org*

Web, www.apta.org, Twitter, @APTAtweets and Facebook, www.facebook.com/AmericanPhysicalTherapyAssociation

Membership: physical therapists, assistants, and students. Establishes professional standards and accredits physical therapy programs; seeks to improve physical therapy education, practice, and research.

American Speech-Language-Hearing Assn. (ASHA), *2200 Research Blvd., Rockville, MD 20850-3289; 444 N. Capitol St. N.W., #715, 20001; (202) 624-5951. Fax, (301) 296-8580. Vicki R. Deal, Chief Executive Officer. Press, (301) 296-8732. Toll-free for Action Center, (800) 498-2071 (voice and TTY accessible). Toll-free for nonmembers, (800) 638-8255.*

Web, www.asha.org, Twitter, @ASHAWeb and Facebook, www.facebook.com/asha.org

Advocates the rights of the communicatively disabled; provides information on speech, hearing, and language problems. Provides referrals to speech-language pathologists and audiologists. Interests include national and international standards for bioacoustics and noise. (National office in Rockville, Md.)

Assn. of University Centers on Disabilities (AUCD), *1100 Wayne Ave., #1000, Silver Spring, MD 20910; (301) 588-8252. Fax, (301) 588-2842. John Tschida, Executive Director. General email, aucdinfo@aucd.org*

Web, www.aucd.org, Twitter, @AUCDNews and Facebook, www.facebook.com/AUCDnetwork

Network of facilities that diagnose and treat the developmentally disabled. Trains graduate students and professionals in the field; helps state and local agencies develop services. Interests include interdisciplinary training and services, early screening to prevent developmental disabilities, and development of equipment and programs to serve persons with disabilities. Advances policy and practice for families and communities.

Brain Injury Assn. of America, *3057 Nutley St., #805, Fairfax, VA 22031-1931; (703) 761-0750. Fax, (703) 761-0755. Susan H. Connors, President. Toll-free, (800) 444-6443. General email, braininjuryinfo@biausa.org*

Web, www.biausa.org, Twitter, @biaamerica and Facebook, www.facebook.com/BrainInjuryAssociationof America

Works to improve the quality of life for persons with traumatic brain injuries and for their families. Promotes the prevention of head injuries through public awareness and education programs. Offers state-level support services for individuals and their families. Monitors legislation and regulations.

Center for Employment and Economic Well-Being (CEEWB), *1300 17th. St. N., #340, Arlington, VA 22209; (202) 682-0100. Tracey Wareing Evans, President. General email, memberservice@aphsa.org*

Web, https://aphsa.org/CEEWB/default.aspx and Twitter, @APHSA1

Works to identify the best practices and resources that will help move low-income individuals into sustainable careers. Supports public policies that provide the opportunities for individuals, families, and communities to succeed in the workforce. (Affiliated with the American Public Human Services Assn.)

Consortium for Citizens with Disabilities (CCD), *820 1st St. N.E., #740, 20002; (202) 567-3516. Fax, (202) 408-9520. Laura Weidner, Chair, (310) 918-3766.*
General email, info@c-c-d.org
Web, www.c-c-d.org, Twitter, @ccd4pwd and Facebook, www.facebook.com/ConsortiumforCitizenswithDisabilities

Coalition of national disability organizations. Advocates for a national public policy that ensures the self-determination, independence, empowerment, and integration in all aspects of society for children and adults with disabilities.

Disability Rights International, *1825 K. St. N.W., #600, 20006; (202) 296-0800. Fax, (202) 697-5422. Laurie Ahern, President, ext. 651; Eric Rosenthal, Executive Director, ext. 650.*
General email, info@driadvocacy.org
Web, www.driadvocacy.org, Twitter, @DRI_advocacy and Facebook, www.facebook.com/DisabilityRights International

Challenges discrimination of and abuse faced by people with disabilities worldwide, with special attention to protecting the rights of children living in orphanages or other institutions. Documents conditions, publishes reports, and trains grassroots advocates.

Disabled American Veterans (DAV), *National Service and Legislative Headquarters, 807 Maine Ave. S.W., 20024-2410; (202) 554-3501. Edward R. (Randy) Reese, Executive Director.*
Web, www.dav.org, Twitter, @davhq and Facebook, www.facebook.com/DAV

Membership: Chartered by Congress to assist veterans with claims for benefits; represents veterans seeking to correct alleged errors in military records. Assists families of veterans with disabilities. (Headquarters in Cold Spring, KY.)

Easterseals, *Washington Region Office, 1420 Spring St., Silver Spring, MD 20910; (301) 588-8700. Jonathan (Jon) Horowitch, President. Toll-free, (800) 886-3771.*
Web, www.easterseals.com/DCMDVA, Twitter, @ESealsDCMDVA and Facebook, www.facebook.com/ESealsDCMDVA

Promotes equal opportunity for people with autism, disabilities, and other special needs. Interests include child development, early childhood education, adult medical daycare services, and services aimed to aid military veterans and their families as they reenter their communities. (Headquarters in Chicago, Ill.)

Epilepsy Foundation, *3540 Crain Hwy. #675, Bowie, MD 20716; (301) 459-3700. Fax, (301) 577-2684. Laura Thrall, Chief Executive Officer. Spanish language, (866) 748-8008. Toll-free, (800) 332-1000.*
General email, contactus@efa.org
Web, www.epilepsy.com, Twitter, @EpilepsyFdn and Facebook, www.facebook.com/EpilepsyFoundationof America

Promotes research and treatment of epilepsy; makes research grants; disseminates information and educational materials. Affiliates provide direct services for people with epilepsy and make referrals when necessary.

Girl Scouts of the U.S.A., *Public Policy and Advocacy, 816 Connecticut Ave. N.W., 3rd Floor, 20006; (202) 659-3780. Sofia Chang, Chief Executive Officer.*
General email, advocacy@girlscouts.org
Web, www.girlscouts.org/en/about-girl-scouts/advocacy.html

Educational service organization for girls grades K–12. Promotes personal development through development of life skills, the outdoors, leadership, entrepreneurship, and such programs as Girl Scouting for Handicapped Girls. (Headquarters in New York.)

Helen A. Kellar Institute for Human Disabilities *(George Mason University), 4400 University Dr., MS 1F2, Fairfax, VA 22030; (703) 993-3670. Fax, (703) 993-3681. Linda Mason, Director, (703) 993-5080.*
Web, http://kihd.gmu.edu

Combines resources from local, state, national, public, and private affiliations to develop products, services, and programs for persons with disabilities.

International Code Council, *500 New Jersey Ave. N.W., 6th Floor, 20001-2070; (202) 370-1800. Fax, (202) 783-2348. Dominic Sims, Chief Executive Officer. Toll-free, (888) 422-7233.*
General email, customersuccess@iccsafe.org
Web, www.iccsafe.org, Twitter, @IntlCodeCouncil and Facebook, www.facebook.com/InternationalCodeCouncil

Provides review board for the American National Standards Institute accessibility standards, which ensure that buildings are accessible to persons with physical disabilities.

Move United, *451 Hungerford Dr., #608, Rockville, MD 20850; (301) 217-0960. Glenn Merry, Executive Director, (301) 217-9838.*
General email, info@moveunitedsport.org
Web, www.moveunitedsport.org, Twitter, @MoveUnitedSport and Facebook, www.facebook.com/MoveUnitedSports

Offers nationwide sports rehabilitation programs in more than 40 summer and winter sports; promotes independence, confidence, and fitness through programs for people with permanent disabilities, including wounded service personnel; conducts workshops and competitions through community-based chapters; participates in world championships. (Disabled Sports USA and Adaptive Sports USA merged to become United Sport.)

National Assn. of Councils on Developmental Disabilities, *1825 K St. N.W., #600, 20006; (202) 506-5813. Fax, (202) 506-5846. Donna A. Meltzer, Chief Executive Officer, ext. 103.*
General email, info@nacdd.org
Web, www.nacdd.org, Twitter, @NACDD and Facebook, www.facebook.com/NACDD

Membership: state and territorial councils authorized by the Developmental Disabilities Act. Promotes the interests of people with developmental disabilities. Interests include services, supports, and equal opportunity. Monitors legislation and regulations.

National Council on Independent Living, *2013 H St. N.W., 6th Floor, 20006 (mailing address: P.O. Box 31260, Washington, DC 20030); (202) 207-0334. Fax, (202) 207-0341. Darrell Lynn Jones, Executive Director (Acting); Lindsay Baran, Policy Director. Toll-free, (844) 778-7961. TTY, (202) 207-0340.*
General email, ncil@ncil.org

Web, www.ncil.org

Membership: independent living centers, individuals with disabilities, and organizations that acts as advocate for the human and civil rights of people with disabilities. Assists member centers in building their capacity to promote social change, eliminate disability-based discrimination, and create opportunities for people with disabilities to participate in the legislative process. Offers members training programs, conducts an annual conference, and disseminates related news and research. Monitors legislation and regulations.

National Disability Institute, *1667 K St. N.W., #480, 20006; (202) 296-2040. Thomas Foley, Executive Director.*
General email, info@ndi-inc.org

Web, www.nationaldisabilityinstitute.org, Twitter, @Natdisability, Facebook, www.facebook.com/ NationalDisability and YouTube, www.youtube.com/user/ RealEconomicImpact

Advocates public policies that address the economic interests of those with disabilities and their families. Interests include tax education and preparation, asset development, financial education, and employment programs.

National Disability Rights Network, *820 1st St. N.E., #740, 20002; (202) 408-9514. Fax, (202) 408-9520. Curtis L. (Curt) Decker, Executive Director. TTY, (202) 408-9521.*
General email, info@ndrn.org

Web, http://ndrn.org, Twitter, @NDRNadvocates and Facebook, www.facebook.com/NDRNadvocates

Membership: agencies working for people with disabilities. Provides state agencies with training and technical assistance; maintains an electronic mail network. Monitors legislation and regulations. (Formerly the National Assn. of Protection and Advocacy Systems and Client Assistance Programs [P&A/CAP].)

National Multiple Sclerosis Society, *Washington* **Chapter,** *1800 M St. N.W., #B50 North, 20036; (202) 296-5363. Fax, (202) 296-3425. Chartese Berry, Chapter President, (202) 375-5616. Toll-free, (800) 344-4867.*
General email, info-dcmd@nmss.org

Web, www.msandyou.org

Provides multiple sclerosis patient services, including individual and family counseling, exercise programs, equipment loans, medical and social service referrals, transportation assistance, back-to-work training programs, and inservice training seminars for nurses, homemakers, and physical and occupational therapists. (Headquarters in New York.)

National Rehabilitation Assn., *1602 Belle View Blvd., #5142, Alexandria, VA 22307; (703) 836-0850. Fax, (703) 836-0848. Lou Adams, President. Toll-free, (888) 258-4295.*
General email, info@nationalrehab.org

Web, www.nationalrehab.org

Membership: administrators, counselors, therapists, disability examiners, vocational evaluators, instructors, job placement specialists, disability managers in the corporate sector, and others interested in rehabilitation of the physically and mentally disabled. Sponsors conferences and workshops. Monitors legislation and regulations.

National Rehabilitation Information Center (NARIC), *8400 Corporate Dr., #500, Landover, MD 20785; (301) 459-5900. Fax, (301) 459-4263. Mark X. Odum, Director. Toll-free, (800) 346-2742. TTY, (301) 459-5984.*
General email, naricinfo@heitechservices.com

Web, https://naric.com

Provides information on disability and rehabilitation research. Acts as referral agency for disability and rehabilitation facilities and programs. Website has a Spanish-language link.

Paralyzed Veterans of America, *801 18th St. N.W., 20006-3517; (202) 872-1300. Heather Ansley, Associate Executive Director of Government Relations. Toll-free, (800) 424-8200. TTY, (800) 795-4327.*
General email, info@pva.org

Web, www.pva.org, Twitter, @PVA1946 and Facebook, www.facebook.com/ParalyzedVeterans

Membership: Congressionally chartered veterans service organization that assists veterans with claims for benefits. Distributes information on special education for paralyzed veterans; acts as advocate for high-quality care, and supports and raises funds for medical research.

Rehabilitation Engineering and Assistive Technology Society of North America (RESNA), *2001 K St. N.W., 3rd Floor, 20006; (202) 367-1121. Fax, (202) 367-2121. Andrea Van Hook, Executive Director.*
General email, info@resna.org

Web, www.resna.org, Twitter, @RESNAorg and Facebook, www.facebook.com/RESNAorg

Membership: engineers, health professionals, assistive technologists, persons with disabilities, and others. Promotes and supports developments in rehabilitation engineering and technology; acts as an information clearinghouse.

Special Olympics International Inc., *1133 19th St. N.W., 20036-3604; (202) 628-3630. Fax, (202) 824-0200. Mary Davis, Chief Executive Officer; Timothy P. Shriver, Chair. Toll-free, (800) 700-8585.*
General email, info@specialolympics.org

Web, www.specialolympics.org, Twitter, @SpecialOlympics and Facebook, www.facebook.com/SpecialOlympics

Offers individuals with intellectual disabilities opportunities for year-round sports training; sponsors athletic competition for 4 million athletes worldwide in 22 individual and Olympic-type team sports.

Spina Bifida Assn., *1600 Wilson Blvd., #600, Arlington, VA 22209; (202) 944-3285. Fax, (202) 944-3295. Sara Struwe, Chief Executive Officer, ext. 12. Toll-free, (800) 621-3141. General email, sbaa@sbaa.org*

Web, http://spinabifidaassociation.org, Twitter, @SpinaBifidaAssn and Facebook, www.facebook.com/spina.bifida.learn

Membership: individuals with spina bifida, their supporters, and concerned professionals. Offers educational programs, scholarships, and support services; acts as a clearinghouse; provides referrals and information about treatment and prevention. Serves as U.S. member of the International Federation for Hydrocephalus and Spina Bifida, which is headquartered in Geneva, Switzerland. Monitors legislation and regulations.

TASH, *The Association for the Severely Handicapped,* *1101 15th St. N.W., #206, 20005; (202) 817-3264. Fax, (202) 999-4722. Michael Brogioli, Executive Director, (202) 891-7126. General email, info@tash.org*

Web, www.tash.org, Twitter, @TASHtweet, Facebook, www.facebook.com/TASHorg and YouTube, www.youtube.com/user/TASHvideo

International human rights advocacy group for people with disabilities. Educates the public and policymakers on issues such as equal education, employment, and community living for people with disabilities. Publishes journals and conducts research to improve living practices for severely disabled people. Monitors legislation and regulations on antidiscrimination measures.

United Cerebral Palsy (UCP), *1825 K St. N.W., #600, 20006; (202) 776-0406. Armando Contreras, President. Toll-free, (800) 872-5827. General email, info@ucp.org*

Web, www.ucp.org, Twitter, @UCPnational, Facebook, www.facebook.com/unitedcerebralpalsy and YouTube, www.youtube.com/user/UnitedCerebralPalsy

National network of state and local affiliates that assists individuals with cerebral palsy and other developmental disabilities and their families. Provides parent education, early intervention, employment services, family support and respite programs, therapy, assistive technology, and vocational training. Promotes research on cerebral palsy; supports the use of assistive technology and community-based living arrangements for persons with cerebral palsy and other developmental disabilities.

Blind and Visually Impaired

▶**CONGRESS**

For a listing of relevant congressional committees and subcommittees, please see page 732 or the Appendix.

Library of Congress, *National Library Service for the Blind and Print Disabled,* *1291 Taylor St. N.W., 20542 (mailing address: Library of Congress, Washington, DC 20542); (202) 707-5100. Fax, (202) 707-0712.* *Jason Broughton, Director. Toll-Free, (800) 424-8567. Toll-free Braille and print, (888) 657-7323. General email, nlsref@loc.gov*

Web, www.loc.gov/nls, Braille email, braille@loc.gov and Facebook, www.facebook.com/thatallmayread

Administers free braille and talking book library service for people with temporary or permanent low vision, blindness, or a physical, perceptual, or reading disability. Coordinates national network of cooperating libraries, circulates books and magazines in braille or audio formats which are downloadable or delivered by mail free of charge. Reference section answers questions relating to blindness and physical disabilities and on library services available to persons with disabilities.

▶**NONGOVERNMENTAL**

American Council of the Blind (ACB), *1703 N. Beauregard St., #420, Alexandria, VA 22311; (202) 467-5081. Fax, (703) 465-5085. Eric Bridges, Executive Director, ext. 12040. Toll-free, (800) 424-8666. General email, info@acb.org*

Web, www.acb.org, Twitter, @acbnational, Facebook, www.facebook.com/AmericanCounciloftheBlindOfficial and Advocacy, advocacy@acb.org

Membership organization serving blind and visually impaired individuals. Interests include telecommunications, rehabilitation services, and transportation. Provides blind individuals with information and referral services; advises state organizations and agencies serving the blind; sponsors scholarships for the blind and visually impaired. Provides information to the public.

American Foundation for the Blind, *Public Policy Center,* *1401 S. Clark St., #730, Arlington, VA 22202; (212) 502-7600. Stephanie Enyart, Chief Public Policy and Research Officer. Toll-free, (800) 232-5463. Public Policy, (202) 469-6831. General email, communications@afb.org*

Web, www.afb.org/info/programs-and-services/public-policy-center/12, Twitter, @AFB1921, Facebook, www.facebook.com/americanfoundationfortheblind and YouTube, www.youtube.com/c/AfbOrg

Advocates equality of access and opportunity for the blind and visually impaired. Conducts research and provides consulting; develops and implements public policy and legislation. Maintains the Helen Keller Archives. (Headquarters in New York.)

Assn. for Education and Rehabilitation of the Blind and Visually Impaired, *5680 King Centre Dr., #600, Alexandria, VA 22315; (703) 671-4500. Mark Richert, Executive Director (Acting). Toll-free, (877) 492-2708. General email, aer@aerbvi.org*

Web, www.aerbvi.org, Twitter, @AERBVI and Facebook, www.facebook.com/AERBVI

Membership: professionals who work in all phases of education and rehabilitation of children and adults who are blind and visually impaired. Provides support and professional development opportunities through conferences, continuing education, and publications. Issues professional recognition awards and student scholarships. Monitors legislation and regulations.

Blinded Veterans Assn., *1101 King St., #300, Alexandria, VA 22314 (mailing address: P.O. Box 90770, Washington, DC 20090); (202) 371-8880. Fax, (202) 371-8258. Donald D. Overton Jr., Executive Director, ext. 305. Toll-free, (800) 669-7079.*
General email, bva@bva.org

Web, www.bva.org, Twitter, @BlindedVeterans, Facebook, www.facebook.com/blindedveteransassociation and YouTube, www.youtube.com/user/BlindedVeterans

Chartered by Congress to assist veterans with claims for benefits. Seeks out blinded veterans to make them aware of benefits and services available to them.

National Federation of the Blind, *200 E. Wells St., Baltimore, MD 21230; (410) 659-9314. Fax, (410) 685-5653. Mark A. Riccobono, President.*
General email, nfb@nfb.org

Web, www.nfb.org, Twitter, @nfb_voice and Facebook, www.facebook.com/NationalFederationoftheBlind

Membership organization providing support networks for the blind and information about blindness and vision loss, assistive technologies, education, and employment services.

National Industries for the Blind (NIB), *3000 Potomac Ave., Alexandria, VA 22305; (703) 310-0500. Kevin A. Lynch, Chief Executive Officer.*
General email, communications@nib.org

Web, www.nib.org, Twitter, @NatIndBlind, Facebook, www.facebook.com/NatIndBlind and YouTube, www .youtube.com/user/NatIndBlind1938

Works to develop and improve opportunities for evaluating, training, employing, and advancing people who are blind and visually disabled. Develops business opportunities in the federal, state, and commercial marketplaces for organizations employing people who are blind or visually impaired.

Prevention of Blindness Society of Metropolitan Washington, *415 2nd St. N.E., #200, 20002; (202) 234-1010. Fax, (202) 234-1020. Caren Forsten, Chief Executive Officer.*
General email, communications@youreyes.org

Web, www.youreyes.org, Twitter, @youreyesdc and Facebook, www.facebook.com/youreyesdc

Conducts preschool and elementary school screening program and glaucoma screening; provides information and referral service on eye health care; assists low-income persons in obtaining eye care and provides eyeglasses for a nominal fee to persons experiencing financial stress; conducts macular degeneration support group.

Deaf and Hard of Hearing

►AGENCIES

General Services Administration (GSA), *FCC's Telecommunications Relay Service (TRS), Formerly Federal Relay Service (FedRelay)., 10304 Eaton Pl., Fairfax, VA 22030; (703) 306-6308. Tatyana Mezentseva, Customer Relationship Manager. Customer Service, (844) 472-4111. Speech-to-Speech, (877) 877-8982. TeleBraille, (866) 893-8340. TTY/ASCII, (800) 877-8339. VCO (Voice Carry Over), (877) 877-6280. Voice, (866) 377-8642. Customer Service, (855) 482-4348.*
General email, ITCSC@gsa.gov

Web, www.gsa.gov/fedrelay

Provides telecommunications services for conducting official business with and within the federal government to individuals who are deaf or hard of hearing or who have speech disabilities. Federal Relay Service features are Voice, Text Telephone (TTY)/ASCII, HCO, Speech-to-Speech (STS), Spanish, Telebraille, Captioned Telephone Service (CTS), IP Relay, Video Relay Service (VRS), and Relay Conference Captioning (RCC) (including Spanish-to-Spanish captioning). For those with limited English proficiency, contact fas.car@gsa.gov, as services are available in Spanish, Vietnamese, Russian, Portuguese, Polish, Haitian, Creole, and Arabic.

National Institute on Deafness and Other Communication Disorders (NIDCD) *(National Institutes of Health), 31 Center Dr., #3C02, MS 2320, Bethesda, MD 20892-2320; (301) 827-8183. Fax, (301) 402-0018. Debara L. Tucci, Director, (301) 402-0900. Evenings and weekends, (301) 496-3315. Interpreter service, (301) 496-1807. Toll-free, (800) 241-1044. TTY, (800) 241-1055.*
General email, nidcdinfo@nidcd.nih.gov

Web, www.nidcd.nih.gov and Twitter, @nidcd

Conducts and supports research and research training and disseminates information on hearing disorders and other communication processes, including diseases that affect hearing, balance, smell, taste, voice, speech, and language. Monitors international research.

►NONGOVERNMENTAL

Alexander Graham Bell Assn. for the Deaf and Hard of Hearing, *3417 Volta Pl. N.W., 20007-2778; (202) 337-5220. Fax, (202) 337-8314. Emilio Alonso-Mendoza, Chief Executive Officer, ext. 129. TTY, (202) 337-5221.*
General email, info@agbell.org

Web, www.agbell.org, Twitter, @AGBellAssoc and Facebook, www.facebook.com/AGBellAssociation

Membership; provides hearing-impaired children in the United States and abroad with information and special education programs; works to improve employment opportunities for deaf persons; acts as a support group for parents of deaf persons.

American Academy of Audiology, *11480 Commerce Park Dr., #220, Reston, VA 20191; (703) 790-8466. Fax, (703)*

790-8631. Patrick E. Gallagher, Executive Director, ext. 1050. Toll-free, (800) 222-2336.

General email, infoaud@audiology.org

Web, www.audiology.org, Twitter, @AcademyofAuD and Facebook, www.facebook.com/theamericanacademyof audiology

Membership: more than 12,000 audiologists. Provides consumer information on testing and treatment for hearing loss and balance care; sponsors research and continuing education for audiologists. Monitors legislation and regulations.

American Speech-Language-Hearing Assn. (ASHA), 2200 Research Blvd., Rockville, MD 20850-3289; 444 N. Capitol St. N.W., #715, 20001; (202) 624-5951. Fax, (301) 296-8580. Vicki R. Deal, Chief Executive Officer. Press, (301) 296-8732. Toll-free for Action Center, (800) 498-2071 (voice and TTY accessible). Toll-free for nonmembers, (800) 638-8255.

Web, www.asha.org, Twitter, @ASHAWeb and Facebook, www.facebook.com/asha.org

Advocates the rights of the communicatively disabled; provides information on speech, hearing, and language problems. Provides referrals to speech-language pathologists and audiologists. Interests include national and international standards for bioacoustics and noise. (National office in Rockville, MD.)

Gallaudet University, 800 Florida Ave. N.E., 20002-3695; (202) 651-5000. Roberta (Bobbi) Cordano, President, (202) 250-2837.

Web, www.gallaudet.edu, Twitter, @GallaudetU, Facebook, www.facebook.com/gallaudetu and Press, public .relations@gallaudet.edu

Offers undergraduate, graduate, and doctoral degree programs for deaf, hard-of-hearing, and hearing students. Conducts research; maintains the Laurent Clerc National Deaf Education Center and demonstration preschool, elementary (Kendall Demonstration Elementary School), and secondary (Model Secondary School for the Deaf) programs. Sponsors the Center for Global Education, National Deaf Education Network and Clearinghouse, and the Cochlear Implant Education Center. Links to each department's video phone are at www.gallaudet.edu/ about_gallaudet/contact_us.html.

Hearing Industries Assn., 655 New York Ave. N.W., 6th Floor, 20001; (202) 975-0905. Kate Carr, President.

General email, info@betterhearing.org

Web, https://betterhearing.org, Twitter, @better_hearing and Facebook, www.facebook.com/betterhearingHIA

Membership: hearing aid manufacturers and companies that supply hearing aid components. Conducts national public information programs on hearing loss, hearing aids, and other treatments.

Hearing Loss Assn. of America, 6116 Executive Blvd., #320, Rockville, MD 20852; (301) 657-2248. Fax, (301) 913-9413. Barbara Kelley, Executive Director.

Web, www.hearingloss.org, Twitter, @HLAA and Facebook, www.facebook.com/HearingLossAssociation

Promotes understanding of the nature, causes, and remedies of hearing loss. Provides hearing-impaired people with support and information. Seeks to educate the public about hearing loss and the problems of the hard of hearing. Provides travelers with information on assistive listening devices in museums, theaters, and places of worship. Holds annual convention for people with hearing loss and professionals.

Laurent Clerc National Deaf Education Center, Planning, Development, and Dissemination, 800 Florida Ave. N.E., 20002-3695; Elizabeth (Betsy) Meynardie, Executive Director. Phone, TTY/Voice, (202) 651-5855. Laurent Clerc, (202) 651-5346.

General email, clerc.center@gallaudet.edu

Web, wwwclerccenter.gallaudet.edu, Twitter, @InsideClercCenter and Facebook, www.facebook.com/ InsideClercCenter

Provides information on topics dealing with hearing loss and deafness for children and young adults up to age 21, and operates elementary and secondary demonstration schools. Houses the Cochlear Implant Education Center and serves as a clearinghouse for information on questions related to deafness. (Affiliated with Gallaudet University.)

National Assn. of the Deaf, 8630 Fenton St., #820, Silver Spring, MD 20910-3819; (301) 587-1788. Fax, (301) 587-1791. Howard A. Rosenblum, Chief Executive Officer. TTY, (301) 587-1789. Videophone, (301) 587-1788.

General email, nad.info@nad.org

Web, www.nad.org and Twitter, @NAD1880

Membership: state associations, affiliate organizations, and individuals that promote, protect, and preserve the civil, human, and linguistic rights of deaf and hard of hearing individuals in the United States. Provides advocacy and legal expertise in the areas of early intervention, education, employment, health care, technology and telecommunications. Provides youth leadership training. Represents the United States to the World Federation of the Deaf (WFD).

National Captioning Institute, 14801 Murdock St., #210, Chantilly, VA 20151; Gene Chao, Chief Executive Officer. Phone/TTY, (703) 917-7600.

General email, marketing@ncicap.org

Web, www.ncicap.org, Twitter, @NCICAP and Facebook, www.facebook.com/ncicap

Captions television, cable, webcasting, home video, and DVD programs for the deaf and hard-of-hearing, and produces audio descriptions for the blind on behalf of public and commercial broadcast television networks, cable networks, syndicators, program producers, government agencies, advertisers, and home video distributors. Offers subtitling and language translation services. Produces and disseminates information about the national closed-captioning service and audio-description services.

Registry of Interpreters for the Deaf, 333 Commerce St., Alexandria, VA 22314; (703) 838-0030. Fax, (703) 838-0454. Elijah Sow, Chief Operating Officer. Video phone, (571) 257-3957.

Social Security Administration

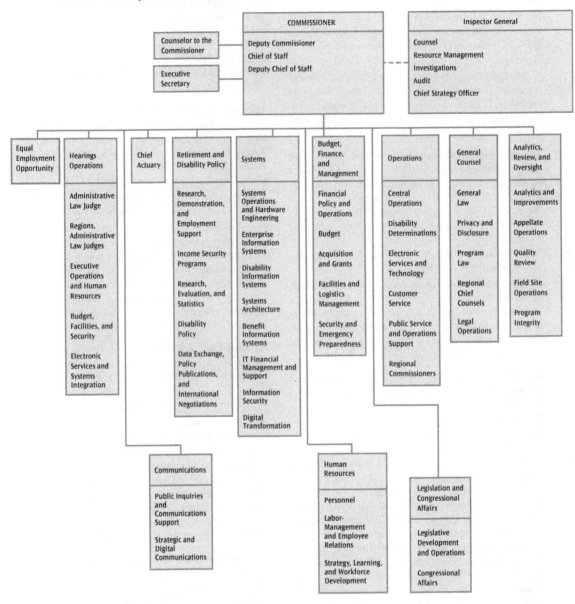

- - - - The Inspector General is directly responsible to the Commissioner

General email, RIDinfo@rid.org

Web, https://rid.org and Facebook, www.facebook.com/ RIDInc

Membership: professional interpreters, transliterators, interpretation students, and educators. Trains, tests, and certifies interpreters; maintains registry of certified interpreters; establishes certification standards. Sponsors training workshops and conferences; publishes professional development literature.

TDI, 940 Thayer Ave., Silver Spring, MD 20910; Eric Kaika, Chief Executive Officer. Phone (voice/video), (301) 563-9112.

General email, info@TDIforaccess.org

Web, https://tdiforaccess.org, Twitter, @TDIforAccess and Facebook, www.facebook.com/TDIforAccess

Membership: individuals, organizations, and businesses that advocate equal access to telecommunications, media, and information technologies for Americans who are deaf and hard of hearing. Interests include closed captioning for television, movies, DVDs, and online videos; emergency access (911); and TTY and Telecommunications Relay Services. Publishes a quarterly magazine and an annual resource directory. Monitors legislation and regulations.

Intellectual and Developmental Disabilities

▶AGENCIES

Administration for Community Living (ACL) *(Health and Human Services Dept.), Administration on Disabilities (AoD), Mary E. Switzer Bldg., 330 C St. S.W., 20201; (202) 401-4634, ext. 4. Jill Jacobs, Commissioner.*
General email, aclinfo@acl.hhs.gov
Web, https://acl.gov/about-acl/administration-disabilities-0

Works with states, communities, and partners in disability networks to increase the independence, productivity, and community integration of individuals with disabilities; helps improve opportunities for people with disabilities to access quality services and supports, achieve economic self-sufficiency, and experience equality and inclusion in all facets of community life. Acts as advocate for state protection, offers grants to university centers for research. Supports the President's Committee on Intellectual Disabilities. Administers two federally funded programs, the State Councils on Developmental Disabilities and the University Centers for Excellence in Development Disability.

Eunice Kennedy Shriver National Institute of Child Health and Human Development (NICHD) *(National Institutes of Health), Division of Extramural Research (DER), Intellectual and Developmental Disabilities Branch (IDDB), 6710B Rockledge Dr., Room 2328, MS 7002, Bethesda, MD 20817; (301) 496-1383. Fax, (301) 480-5665. Melissa Ann Parisi, Chief.*
Web, www.nichd.nih.gov/about/org/der/branches/iddb

Supports research projects, training programs, and research centers dedicated to understanding, preventing, and ameliorating intellectual and related developmental disabilities. Major research areas include common and rare neuromuscular and neurodevelopmental disorders, such as Down, Fragile X, and Rett syndromes; inborn errors of metabolism; autism spectrum disorders; and conditions currently and soon-to-be detectable through newborn screening.

▶NONGOVERNMENTAL

American Assn. on Intellectual and Developmental Disabilities (AAIDD), *8403 Colesville Rd., #900, Silver Spring, MD 20910; (202) 387-1968. Fax, (202) 387-2193. Margaret A. (Maggie) Nygren, Executive Director. Bookstore, ext. 216.*
Web, www.aaidd.org, Twitter, @_AAIDD and Facebook, www.facebook.com/TheAAIDD

Association for professionals who work in the field of intellectual and developmental disabilities. Promotes progressive policy, sound research, effective practices, and human rights for people with intellectual and developmental disabilities. Sponsors conferences and training workshops. Monitors legislation and regulations.

The Arc, *1825 K St. N.W., #1200, 20006; (202) 534-3700. Fax, (202) 534-3731. Peter V. Berns, Chief Executive Officer. Toll-free, (800) 433-5255.*
Web, www.thearc.org, Twitter, @TheArcUS, Facebook, www.facebook.com/thearcus and Public Policy, www.thearc.org/policy-advocacy

Membership: people with intellectual and developmental disabilities and their service providers. Provides oversight and technical assistance for local groups that provide services and support for individuals with disabilities and their families. Monitors federal legislation, regulations, and legal decisions.

Autism Society of America, *6110 Executive Blvd., #305, Rockville, MD 20852; (301) 657-0881. Christopher Banks, President. Toll-free, (800) 328-8476.*
General email, info@autism-society.org
Web, www.autism-society.org, Twitter, @AutismSociety and Facebook, www.facebook.com/AutismSociety

Monitors legislation and regulations affecting support, education, training, research, and other services for individuals with autism. Offers referral service and information to the public.

Best Buddies International, *Capitol Region: Virginia and DC, 6231 Leesburg Pike, #310, Falls Church, VA 22044; (703) 533-9420. Fax, (703) 533-9423. Molly Whalen, State Director.*
General email, virginia-dc@bestbuddies.org
Web, www.bestbuddies.org/vadc, Twitter, @BestBuddies, Facebook, www.facebook.com/bestbuddies and YouTube, www.youtube.com/bestbuddies

Volunteer organization that provides one-to-one friendships, integrated employment, leadership development and inclusive living for people with Down syndrome, autism, Fragile X, Williams syndrome, cerebral palsy, traumatic brain injury and other undiagnosed disabilities, worldwide. (Headquarters in Miami, FL.)

Joseph P. Kennedy Jr. Foundation, *1133 19th St. N.W., 12th Floor, 20036-3604; (202) 393-1250. Steve Eidelman, Executive Director.*
General email, jpkjrfdn@gmail.com
Web, www.jpkf.org

Seeks to enhance the quality of life of persons with intellectual disabilities and their families through public policy advocacy. Provides information and training on the policymaking process.

National Assn. of State Directors of Developmental Disabilities Services (NASDDDS), *301 N. Fairfax St., #101, Alexandria, VA 22314-2633; (703) 683-4202. Mary P. Sowers, Executive Director, (703) 414-9953.*
Web, www.nasddds.org and Email, CMCGRAW@NASDDDS.ORG

Membership: chief administrators of state intellectual and developmental disability programs. Coordinates exchange of information on intellectual and developmental disability programs among the states; provides technical assistance to members and information on state programs.

National Children's Center, *8757 Georgia Ave., Silver Spring, MD 20910; (202) 722-2300. Patricia A. Browne, President.*

Web, www.nccinc.org, Twitter, @ncc_inc and Facebook, www.facebook.com/NationalChildrensCenter

Provides educational, social, and clinical services to infants, children, and adults with intellectual and other developmental disabilities. Services provided through a 24-hour intensive treatment program, group homes and independent living programs, educational services, adult treatment programs, and early intervention programs for infants with disabilities or infants at high risk. Operates a child development center for children with and without disabilities.

Psychiatric Rehabilitation Assn., *Virginia Psychiatric Rehabilitation Assn. (VAPRA), 7918 Jones Branch Dr., #300, McLean, VA 22102; (703) 442-2078. Fax, (703) 506-3266. Lee K. Lowery, Managing Director.*
General email, info@psychrehabassociation.org

Web, www.psychrehabassociation.org, Twitter, @PsychRehab, Facebook, www.facebook.com/ PsychRehabAssociation and Web, www.vapra.org/#!

Membership: agencies, mental health practitioners, researchers, policymakers, family groups, and consumer organizations. Supports the community adjustment of persons with psychiatric disabilities. Promotes the role of rehabilitation in mental health systems; opposes discrimination based on mental disability. Certifies psychosocial rehabilitation practitioners. (Headquarters in South Bend, Ind.)

HOMELESSNESS

General

▶**AGENCIES**

Career, Technical, and Adult Education (OCTAE)
(Education Dept.), Adult Education and Literacy, 550 12th St. S.W., 11th Floor, 20202-7100 (mailing address: 400 Maryland Ave. S.W., P-OCTAE, DAEL, Washington, DC 20202); (202) 245-7700. Fax, (202) 245-7838. Cheryl L. Keenan, Director, (202) 245-7810.
General email, octae@ed.gov

Web, www2.ed.gov/about/offices/list/ovae/pi/AdultEd/ index.html and https://aefla.ed.gov

Provides state and local agencies and community-based organizations with assistance in establishing education programs for homeless adults.

Community Planning and Development (CPD)
(Housing and Urban Development Dept.), 451 7th St. S.W., #7100, 20410; (202) 402-3921.
James Arthur Jemison, Principal Deputy Assistant Secretary. TTY, (202) 708-1455.
Web, www.hud.gov/program_offices/comm_planning

Gives supplemental assistance to facilities that aid the homeless; awards grants for innovative programs that address the needs of homeless families with children.

Community Planning and Development (CPD) *(Housing and Urban Development Dept.), Special Needs Assistance Programs, Community Assistance Division, 451 7th St. S.W., #7266, 20410; (202) 402-5697. Tonya Park, Director (Acting).*
Web, www.hud.gov

Advises and represents the secretary on homelessness matters; promotes cooperation among federal agencies on homelessness issues; coordinates assistance programs for the homeless under the McKinney Act. Trains HUD field staff in administering homelessness programs. Distributes funds to eligible nonprofit organizations, cities, counties, tribes, and territories for shelter, care, transitional housing, and permanent housing for the disabled homeless. Programs provide for acquisition and rehabilitation of buildings, prevention of homelessness, counseling, and medical care. Administers the Federal Surplus Property Program and spearheads the initiative to lease HUD-held homes to the homeless.

Elementary and Secondary Education (OESE)
(Education Dept.), Formula Grants (OFG), School Support and Accountability (SSA), Education for Homeless Children and Youth Program, Lyndon B. Johnson Bldg., 400 Maryland Ave. S.W., 20202-6132; (202) 453-6777. Fax, (202) 260-7764. John McLaughlin, Program Officer; Bryan Thurmond, Program Officer.
General email, HomelessEd@ed.gov

Web, www.ed.gov/programs/homeless/index.html

Provides formula grants to education agencies in the states, Puerto Rico, and through the Bureau of Indian Affairs to Native Americans to educate homeless children and youth and to establish an office of coordinator of education for homeless children and youth in each jurisdiction.

Emergency Food and Shelter National Board Program,
701 N. Fairfax St., #310, Alexandria, VA 22314-2064; (703) 706-9660. Fax, (703) 706-9677. James Yu, Director.
General email, efsp@uww.unitedway.org

Web, www.efsp.unitedway.org

Public/private partnership created by Congress to help meet the needs of hungry and homeless by allocating federal funds for the provision of food and shelter. Administers the Emergency Food and Shelter Program under the McKinney-Vento Act; gives supplemental assistance to more than 14,000 human service agencies. Does not provide direct assistance to the public.

Health and Human Services Dept. (HHS), *Planning and Evaluation (ASPE), Human Services Policy (HSP), Division of Family and Community Policy, 200 Independence Ave. S.W., #415F, 20201; (202) 730-3904. Kelly Kinnison, Director, (202) 730-3904.*
Web, www.aspe.hhs.gov/about/offices/hsp

Develops policies around homelessness and reentry. (Located within the Office of Human Services Policy.)

►NONGOVERNMENTAL

Covenant House, Washington Office, 2001 Mississippi Ave. S.E., 20020; (202) 610-9600. Angela Jones Hackley, Executive Director.
Web, http://covenanthousedc.org and Twitter, @CovenantHouseDC

Protects young people suffering from homelessness, abuse, and neglect. Provides services including transitional housing, GED and adult education, and job readiness. (Affiliated with Covenant House International.)

D.C. Central Kitchen, 425 2nd St. N.W., 20001; (202) 234-0707. Michael F. Curtin, Chief Executive Officer, (202) 266-2018.
General email, info@dccentralkitchen.org
Web, www.dccentralkitchen.org, Twitter, @dcck and Facebook, www.facebook.com/dccentralkitchen

Distributes food to D.C.-area homeless shelters, transitional homes, low-income schoolchildren, and corner store "food deserts."

National Alliance to End Homelessness, 1518 K St. N.W., 2nd Floor, 20005; (202) 638-1526. Fax, (202) 638-4664. Nan Roman, President.
General email, info@naeh.org
Web, www.naeh.org, Twitter, @naehomelessness and Facebook, www.facebook.com/naehomelessness

Policy, research, and capacity-building organization that works to prevent, alleviate, and end problems of the homeless. Provides data and research to policymakers and the public; encourages public-private collaboration for stronger programs to reduce the homeless population, and works with communities to improve assistance programs for the homeless.

National Coalition for Homeless Veterans, 1001 Connecticut Ave. N.W., #840, 20036; (202) 546-1969. Fax, (202) 546-2063. Kathryn Monet, Chief Executive Officer. Toll-free Crisis Line, (877) 424-3838. Toll-free Referral, (800) 838-4357.
General email, info@nchv.org
Web, www.nchv.org, Twitter, @NCHVorg and Facebook, www.facebook.com/NCHV.org

Community based organization providing resources and technical assistance to service providers and local, state and federal agencies that provide emergency and supportive housing, food, health services, job training and placement assistance, legal aid and case management support for homeless veterans. It is also the primary liaison between the nation's care providers, Congress and the Executive Branch agencies

National Coalition for the Homeless, 2201 P St. N.W., 20037-1033; (202) 462-4822. Donald Whitehead, Executive Director.
General email, info@nationalhomeless.org
Web, www.nationalhomeless.org, Twitter, @Ntl_Homeless, Facebook, www.facebook.com/

NationalCoalitionfortheHomeless and YouTube, www.youtube.com/user/nationalhomelesscoal

Advocacy network of persons who are or have been homeless, state and local coalitions, other activists, service providers, housing developers, and others. Seeks to create the systemic and attitudinal changes necessary to end homelessness. Works to meet the needs of persons who are homeless or at risk of becoming homeless.

National Homeless Law Center, 2000 M St. N.W., #750-E, 20036; (202) 638-2535. Fax, (202) 628-2737. Antonia Fasanelli, Executive Director.
General email, email@nlchp.org
Web, www.nlchp.org and Twitter, @homeless_law

Legal advocacy group that works to prevent and end homelessness through impact litigation, legislation, and education. Conducts research on homelessness issues. Acts as a clearinghouse for legal information and technical assistance. Monitors legislation and regulations.

Salvation Army, 615 Slaters Lane, Alexandria, VA 22314 (mailing address: P.O. Box 269, Alexandria, VA 22313-0269); (703) 684-5500. Kenneth G. Hodder, National Commander. Donating Goods, (800) 728-7825. Toll-free, (800) 725-2769.
Web, www.salvationarmyusa.org and Twitter, @SalvationArmyUS

International religious social welfare organization that provides the homeless with residences and social services, including counseling, emergency help, and employment services. (International headquarters in London.)

U.S. Conference of Mayors, Task Force on Hunger and Homelessness, 1620 Eye St. N.W., 4th Floor, 20006; (202) 293-7330. Eugene T. Lowe, Assistant Executive Director for Community Development and Housing, (202) 861-6710.
Web, www.usmayors.org/the-conference/committees-and-task-forces

Tracks trends in hunger, homelessness, and community programs that address homelessness and hunger in U.S. cities; issues reports. Monitors legislation and regulations.

SOCIAL SECURITY

General

►AGENCIES

Social Security Administration (SSA), 6401 Security Blvd., Baltimore, MD 21235; (410) 965-3120. Kilolo Kijakazi, Commissioner (Acting). Press, (410) 929-4774. Toll-free, (800) 772-1213. TTY, (800) 325-0778.
Web, www.ssa.gov, Twitter, @SocialSecurity and Facebook, www.facebook.com/socialsecurity

Administers national Social Security programs and the Supplemental Security Income Program.

Social Security Administration (SSA), *Disability Determinations,* *3570 Annex Bldg., 6401 Security Blvd., Baltimore, MD 21235; (410) 966-7241. Fax, (410) 965-6503. John E. Owen, Associate Commissioner; Gina P. Clemons, Associate Commissioner for Disability Policy. Toll-free, (800) 772-1213. TTY, (800) 325-0778.*
Web, www.ssa.gov/disability

Provides direction for administration of the disability insurance program, which is paid out of the Social Security Trust Fund. Administers disability and blindness provisions of the Supplemental Security Income (SSI) program. Responsible for claims filed under black lung benefits program before July 1, 1973.

Social Security Administration (SSA), *Hearings Operations,* *5107 Leesburg Pike, #1600, Falls Church, VA 22041-3255; Theresa L. Gruber, Deputy Commissioner. Toll-free, (800) 772-1213. TTY, (800) 325-0778.*
Web, www.ssa.gov/appeals/about_us.html

Administers a nationwide system of administrative law judges who conduct hearings and decide appealed cases concerning benefits provisions. Reviews decisions for appeals council action, if necessary, and renders the secretary's final decision. Reviews benefits cases on disability, retirement and survivors' benefits, and supplemental security income.

Social Security Administration (SSA), *Operations,* *6401 Security Blvd., West High Rise, #1204, Baltimore, MD 21235; Grace M. Kim, Deputy Commissioner. Toll-free, (800) 772-1213. TTY, (800) 325-0778.*
Web, www.ssa.gov

Issues Social Security numbers; maintains earnings and beneficiary records; reviews and authorizes claims, including claims for benefits under the disability insurance program and all claims for beneficiaries living abroad; certifies benefits; maintains beneficiary rolls; and makes post adjudicative changes in beneficiary records for retirement, survivors and disability insurance, and black lung claims. Maintains toll-free number for workers who want information on future Social Security benefits.

Social Security Administration (SSA), *Quality Review,* *Altmeyer Bldg., 6401 Security Blvd., #252, Baltimore, MD 21235; (410) 966-0607. Fax, (420) 965-8582. Vera Bostic-Borden, Associate Commissioner.*
Web, www.ssa.gov

Reviews, evaluates, and reports on the integrity and quality of the administration of Social Security programs; conducts broad-based reviews, studies, and analyses of agency operations with emphasis on compliance with laws, regulations, and policies.

Social Security Administration (SSA), *Research, Evaluation, and Statistics,* *250 E St. S.W., 8th Floor,* *20254; (202) 358-6020. Katherine N. Bent, Associate Commissioner. Publications, (202) 358-6405.*
General email, research@ssa.gov
Web, www.ssa.gov/policy/about/ORES.html

Compiles statistics on beneficiaries; conducts research on the economic status of beneficiaries and the relationship between Social Security, the American people, and the economy; analyzes the effects of proposed Social Security legislation, especially on lower-income and middle-income individuals and families; disseminates results of research and statistical programs through publications.

Workers Compensation (OWCP) *(Labor Dept.),* *Coal Mine Workers' Compensation,* *200 Constitution Ave. N.W., #C3524, 20210 (mailing address: DCMWC, P.O. Box 8307, London, KY 40742-8307); (202) 693-0046. Fax, (202) 693-1395. Michael A. Chance, Director. Toll-free Federal Black Lung Program, (800) 347-2502. TTY, (877) 889-5627.*
General email, DCMWC-public@dol.gov
Web, www.dol.gov/owcp/dcmwc

Provides direction for administration of the black lung benefits program. Adjudicates all black lung claims; certifies benefit payments and maintains black lung beneficiary rolls.

▶ CONGRESS

For a listing of relevant congressional committees and subcommittees, please see page 732 or the Appendix.

▶ NONGOVERNMENTAL

AARP, *601 E St. N.W., 20049; (202) 434-2277. Jo Ann C. Jenkins, Chief Executive Officer. Library, (202) 434-6233. Membership, toll-free, (800) 566-0242. Press, (202) 434-2560. Toll-free, (888) 687-2277. TTY, (877) 434-7598. Toll-free Spanish, (877) 342-2277. TTY Spanish, (866) 238-9488.*
General email, dcaarp@aarp.org
Web, www.aarp.org, Twitter, @AARP and Facebook, www.facebook.com/AARP

Membership: people 50 years of age and older. Works to address members' needs and interests through education, advocacy, and service. Monitors legislation and regulations and disseminates information on issues affecting older Americans, including issues related to Social Security.

National Academy of Social Insurance, *1441 L St. N.W., #530, 20005; (202) 452-8097. Fax, (202) 452-8111. William J. Arnone, Chief Executive Officer.*
General email, info@nasi.org
Web, www.nasi.org, Twitter, @socialinsurance and Facebook, www.facebook.com/NationalAcademyof SocialInsurance

Promotes research and education on Social Security, Medicare, health care financing, and related public and private programs; assesses social insurance programs and their relationship to other programs; supports research and leadership development. Acts as a clearinghouse for social insurance information.

National Committee to Preserve Social Security and Medicare, *111 K St. N.E., #700, 20002; (202) 216-0420. Fax, (202) 216-0446. Max Richtman, President. Senior hotline/Legislative updates, (800) 998-0180.*

General email, webmaster@ncpssm.org

Web, www.ncpssm.org, Twitter, @NCPSSM, Facebook, www.facebook.com/NationalCommittee and YouTube, www.youtube.com/user/NationalCommittee

Educational and advocacy organization that focuses on Social Security and Medicare programs and on related income security and health issues. Interests include retirement income protection, health care reform, and the quality of life of seniors. Monitors legislation and regulations.

18 Transportation

GENERAL POLICY AND ANALYSIS

Basic Resources

▶AGENCIES

Access Board, *1331 F St. N.W., #1000, 20004-1111; (202) 272-0080. Fax, (202) 272-0081. Sachin Dev Pavithran, Executive Director. Toll-free, (800) 872-2253. Toll-free TTY, (800) 993-2822. TTY, (202) 272-0082.*
General email, info@access-board.gov
Web, www.access-board.gov and Twitter, @accessboard

Develops and maintains accessibility requirements for buildings, transit vehicles, telecommunications equipment, medical diagnostic equipment, and electronic and information technology. Provides technical assistance and training on these guidelines and standards. Enforces access standards for federally funded facilities through the Architectural Barriers Act.

Bureau of Economic and Business Affairs (EB) *(State Dept.), Transportation Affairs (TRA), 2201 C St. N.W., #3817, 20520-3425; (202) 647-4045. Fax, (202) 647-4324. Richard Yoneoka, Deputy Assistant Secretary (Acting).*
General email, EEB-A-TRA-DL@state.gov
Web, www.state.gov/bureaus-offices/under-secretary-for-economic-growth-energy-and-the-environment/bureau-of-economic-and-business-affairs/division-for-tran, Twitter, @EconAtState and Facebook, www.facebook.com/EconAtState

Supports the U.S. global transportation industry; negotiates international air services agreements; works with other departments on safe transportation infrastructure policies. Oversees the offices of Aviation Negotiations and Transportation Policy.

Bureau of Economic and Business Affairs (EB) *(State Dept.), Transportation Affairs (TRA), Transportation Policy (OTP), 2201 C St. N.W., #3817, 20520; (202) 647-8001. Fax, (202) 647-8628. Megan Walklet-Tighe, Director, (202) 647-9341.*
General email, EEB-A-TRA-OTP-DL@state.gov
Web, www.state.gov/about-us-division-for-transportation-affairs

Develops and coordinates policy on international civil aviation, maritime, and land transport, including policy research, safety and security, discriminatory and unfair practices, commercial and operational problems encountered abroad, overflight and landing authorizations, port access, environmental protection, and accident investigations.

National Transportation Safety Board (NTSB), *490 L'Enfant Plaza East S.W., 20594-2000; (202) 314-6000. Hon. Jennifer Homendy, Chair; Dana Schulze, Managing Director. Press, (202) 314-6100. 24-Hour Accident Response, (844) 373-9922.*
Web, www.ntsb.gov, Twitter, @NTSB, Facebook, www.facebook.com/NTSBgov and YouTube, www.youtube.com/user/NTSBgov

Promotes transportation safety through independent investigations of accidents and other safety problems. Makes recommendations for safety improvement. Operates three regional offices.

National Transportation Safety Board (NTSB), *Research and Engineering, 490 L'Enfant Plaza East S.W., 20594-2000; (202) 314-6000. Jim Ritter, Director.*
Web, www.ntsb.gov/about/organization/RE/Pages/office_re.aspx

Evaluates effectiveness of federal, state, and local safety programs. Identifies transportation safety issues not being addressed by government or industry. Conducts studies on specific safety problems. Provides technical support to accident investigations. Operates in four divisions: Safety Research and Statistical Analysis; Vehicle Performance; Vehicle Recorder; and Materials Laboratory.

National Transportation Safety Board (NTSB), *Safety Recommendations and Communications, 490 L'Enfant Plaza East S.W., 20594-2000; (202) 314-6000. Kathryn Catania, Director (Acting).*
Web, www.ntsb.gov/about/organization/OC

Makes transportation safety recommendations to federal and state agencies on all modes of transportation. Produces the annual "Most Wanted" list of critical transportation safety projects.

Office of Management and Budget (OMB) *(Executive Office of the President), Transportation, 725 17th St. N.W., #9002, 20503; (202) 395-6138. Fax, (202) 395-4797. David Connolly, Chief.*
Web, www.whitehouse.gov/omb

Assists and advises the OMB director on budget preparation, proposed legislation, and evaluations of Transportation Dept. programs, policies, and activities.

Office of the Assistant Secretary of Research and Technology *(Transportation Dept.), 1200 New Jersey Ave. S.E., 20590; (202) 366-3282. Fax, (202) 366-3759. Robert C. Hampshire, Assistant Secretary (Acting). DOT library, (800) 853-1351. Toll-free, (800) 853-1351.*
General email, ritainfo@dot.gov
Web, www.transportation.gov/administrations/research-and-technology

Coordinates and manages the department's research portfolio and expedites implementation of innovative technologies. Oversees the Bureau of Transportation Statistics, Volpe National Transportation Systems Center (in Cambridge, Mass.), and the Transportation Safety Institute (in Oklahoma City).

Office of the Assistant Secretary of Research and Technology *(Transportation Dept.), Bureau of Transportation Statistics, 1200 New Jersey Ave. S.E., #E34-314, 20590; (202) 366-1270. Patricia S. Hu, Director. Press, (202) 366-5568. Toll-free, (800) 853-1351.*
General email, btsinfo@dot.gov
Web, www.bts.gov

Works to improve public awareness of the nation's transportation systems. Collects, analyzes, and publishes

TRANSPORTATION RESOURCES IN CONGRESS

For a complete listing of congressional committees, including their full contact information, leadership, membership, and jurisdictions, please refer to the Appendix on pages 840–963.

HOUSE:

House Appropriations Committee, (202) 225-2771.
Web, appropriations.house.gov
  **Subcommittee on Energy and Water
    Development, and Related Agencies,**
    (202) 225-3421.
  Subcommittee on Homeland Security,
    (202) 225-5834.
  **Subcommittee on Transportation, Housing and
    Urban Development, and Related Agencies,**
    (202) 225-2141.
House Energy and Commerce Committee,
    (202) 225-2927.
Web, energycommerce.house.gov
  **Subcommittee on Consumer Protection and
    Commerce,** (202) 225-2927.
House Homeland Security Committee,
    (202) 226-2616.
Web, homeland.house.gov
  **Subcommittee on Border Security,
    Facilitation, and Operations,**
    (202) 226-2616.
  **Subcommittee on Transportation and Maritime
    Security,** (202) 226-2616.
House Natural Resources Committee,
    (202) 225-6065.
Web, naturalresources.house.gov
  Subcommittee on Water, Oceans, and Wildlife,
    (202) 225-8331.
House Science, Space, and Technology Committee,
    (202) 225-6375.
Web, science.house.gov
  Subcommittee on Research and Technology,
    (202) 225-6375.
  Subcommittee on Space and Aeronautics,
    (202) 225-6375.
**House Transportation and Infrastructure
  Committee,** (202) 225-4472.
Web, transportation.house.gov

  Subcommittee on Aviation, (202) 226-3220.
  **Subcommittee on Coast Guard and Maritime
    Transportation,** (202) 226-3552.
  Subcommittee on Highways and Transit,
    (202) 225-6715.
  **Subcommittee on Railroads, Pipelines, and
    Hazardous Materials,** (202) 226-0727.
  **Subcommittee on Water Resources and
    Environment,** (202) 225-4360.

SENATE:

Senate Appropriations Committee, (202) 224-7363.
Web, appropriations.senate.gov
  **Subcommittee on Transportation, Housing and
    Urban Development, and Related Agencies,**
    (202) 224-7363.
**Senate Banking, Housing, and Urban Affairs
  Committee,** (202) 224-7391.
Web, banking.senate.gov
  **Subcommittee on Housing, Transportation,
    and Community Development,**
    (202) 224-7391.
**Senate Commerce, Science, and Transportation
  Committee,** (202) 224-0411.
Web, commerce.senate.gov
  **Subcommittee on Aviation Safety, Operations,
    and Innovation,** (202) 224-0411.
  **Subcommittee on Surface Transportation,
    Maritime, Freight, and Ports,**
    (202) 224-0411.
Senate Environment and Public Works Committee,
    (202) 224-8832.
Web, epw.senate.gov
  **Subcommittee on Transportation and
    Infrastructure,** (202) 224-8832.
Senate Finance Committee, (202) 224-4515.
Web, finance.senate.gov
  **Subcommittee on Energy, Natural Resources, and
    Infrastructure,** (202) 224-4515.

a comprehensive, cross-modal set of transportation statistics.

Office of the Assistant Secretary of Research and Technology *(Transportation Dept.), Research, Development, and Technology, 1200 New Jersey Ave. S.E., #E33-304, 20590-0001; (202) 366-1351. Fax, (202) 366-3759. Firas Ibrahim, Director. Toll-free, (800) 853-1351.*
Web, www.transportation.gov/new-and-emerging-technologies

Supports transportation innovation research, engineering, education, and safety training. Focus includes intermodal transportation; partnerships among government, universities, and industry; and economic growth

and competitiveness through use of new technologies. Monitors international research.

Pipeline and Hazardous Materials Safety Administration *(Transportation Dept.), 1200 New Jersey Ave. S.E., #E27-300, 20590; (202) 366-4433. Fax, (202) 366-3666. Tristan Brown, Administrator (Acting). Hazardous Materials Information Center, (800) 467-4922. To report an incident, (800) 424-8802.*
General email, phmsa.administrator@dot.gov
Web, www.phmsa.dot.gov and Twitter, @PHMSA_DOT

Oversees the safe and secure movement of hazardous materials to industry and consumers by all modes of

Transportation Department

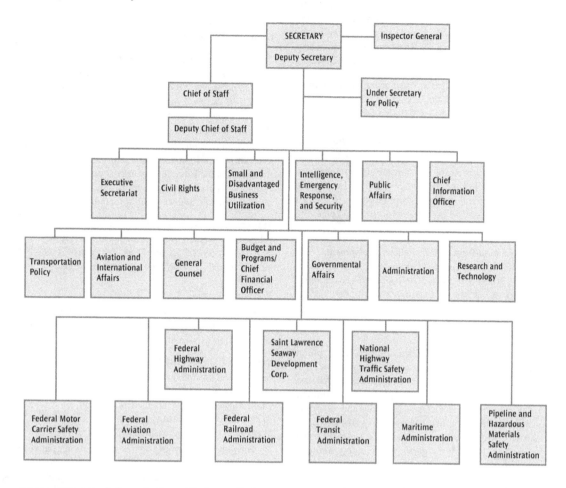

transportation, including pipelines. Works to eliminate transportation-related deaths and injuries. Promotes transportation solutions to protect communities and the environment.

Pipeline and Hazardous Materials Safety Administration *(Transportation Dept.), Hazardous Materials Safety, 1200 New Jersey Ave. S.E., #E21-317, 20590; (202) 366-4488. Fax, (202) 366-5713.*
William S. (Bill) Schoonover, Associate Administrator. Hazardous Materials Information Center, (800) 467-4922.
General email, phmsa.hmhazmatsafety@dot.gov

Web, www.phmsa.dot.gov/about-phmsa/offices/office-hazardous-materials-safety

Federal safety authority for the transportation of hazardous materials by air, rail, highway, and water. Works to reduce dangers of hazardous materials transportation. Issues regulations for classifications, communications, shipper and carrier operations, training and security requirements, and packaging and container specifications.

Surface Transportation Board (STB), *Public Assistance, Governmental Affairs, and Compliance, 395 E St. S.W., #1202, 20423-0001; (202) 245-0238. Michael Higgins,*

Director (Acting). Toll-free, (866) 254-1792. TTY, (800) 877-8339.
General email, rcpa@stb.gov
Web, www.stb.gov/about-stb/offices/opagac

Informs members of Congress, executive agencies, state and local governments, news media, stakeholders, and other interested persons to provide information and informal guidance as to the STB's procedures, regulations, and actions Prepares testimony for hearings; comments on proposed legislation; assists the public in matters involving transportation regulations.

Transportation Dept. (DOT), *1200 New Jersey Ave. S.E., 20590; (202) 366-4000. Pete Buttigieg, Secretary. Press, (202) 366-4570. Toll-free, (855) 368-4200. TTY, (800) 877-8339.*
General email, pressoffice@dot.gov

Web, www.transportation.gov, Twitter, @USDOT and Facebook, www.facebook.com/USDOT

Responsible for shaping and administering policies and programs to protect and enhance the transportation system and services. Includes the Federal Aviation Administration, Federal Highway Administration, Federal Motor Carrier Safety Administration, Federal Railroad

Administration, Maritime Administration, National Highway Traffic Safety Administration, Pipeline and Hazardous Materials Safety Administration, Federal Transit Administration, and the Saint Lawrence Seaway Development Corp. The Surface Transportation Board is also administratively affiliated but decisionally independent.

Transportation Dept. (DOT), *Intelligence, Security, and Emergency Response,* 1200 New Jersey Ave. S.E., #56125, 20590; (202) 366-6525. Fax, (202) 366-7261. *Richard Chávez, Director.*
Web, www.transportation.gov/mission/administrations/ intelligence-security-emergency-response

Advises the secretary on transportation intelligence and security policy. Acts as liaison with the intelligence community, federal agencies, corporations, and interest groups; administers counterterrorism strategic planning processes.

Transportation Dept. (DOT), *Policy Development, Strategic Planning, and Performance,* 1200 New Jersey Ave. S.E., #W84-310, 20590; (202) 366-4416. Fax, (202) 366-0263. *Maria Lafevre, Executive Director, Office of Planning.* TTY, (800) 877-8339.
Web, www.transportation.gov/policy/office-policy-planning-performance

Develops, coordinates, and evaluates public policy with respect to safety, environmental, energy, and accessibility issues affecting all aspects of transportation. Assesses the economic and institutional implications of domestic transportation matters. Oversees legislative and regulatory proposals affecting transportation. Provides advice on research and development requirements. Develops policy proposals to improve the performance, safety, and efficiency of the transportation system.

Transportation Security Administration (TSA) *(Homeland Security Dept.),* TSA-1, 601 S. 12th St., 7th Floor, Arlington, VA 20598-6001; (571) 227-1398. *David P. Pekoske, Administrator.* Press, (571) 227-2829. *TSA Contact Center, (866) 289-9673.*
General email, TSA-ContactCenter@tsa.dhs.gov
Web, www.tsa.gov and Twitter, @TSA

Protects the nation's transportation systems to ensure freedom of movement for people and commerce.

Transportation Security Administration (TSA) *(Homeland Security Dept.),* **Acquisition Program,** TSA-25, 601 S. 12th St., Arlington, VA 20598-6025; (571) 227-2161. Fax, (571) 227-2911. *Mario Wilson, Assistant Administrator.*
Web, www.tsa.gov

Administers contract grants, cooperative agreements, and other transactions in support of TSA's mission. Develops acquisitions strategies, policies, programs, and processes.

Transportation Security Administration (TSA) *(Homeland Security Dept.),* **Contact Center,** 601 S. 12th St., 7th Floor, Arlington, VA 20598; (866) 289-9673. *Michelle Cartagena, Program Manager.*

General email, tsa-contactcenter@tsa.dhs.gov
Web, www.tsa.gov

Answers questions and collects concerns from the public regarding travel security.

Transportation Security Administration (TSA) *(Homeland Security Dept.),* **Freedom Center,** 13555 EDS Dr., Herndon, VA 20171 (mailing address: TSOC Annex, 601 S. 12th St., Arlington, VA 22202); (866) 655-7023. *Vacant, Deputy Administrator.*
Web, www.tsa.gov

Operations center that provides continual federal, state, and local coordination, communications, and domain awareness for all of the Homeland Security Dept.'s transportation-related security activities worldwide. Transportation domains include highway, rail, shipping, and aviation.

Transportation Security Administration (TSA) *(Homeland Security Dept.),* **Intelligence and Analysis,** TSA-10, 601 S. 12th St., 6th Floor, Arlington, VA 22202-4220; (703) 601-3100. *Nancy Nykamp, Assistant Administrator.*
Web, www.tsa.gov

Oversees TSA's intelligence gathering and information sharing as they pertain to national security and the safety of the nation's transportation systems.

Transportation Security Administration (TSA) *(Homeland Security Dept.),* **Policy, Plans, and Engagement,** TSA-28, 601 S. 12th St., Arlington, VA 20598-6028; (571) 227-1417. *Eddie Mayenschein, Assistant Administrator; Wanda Shotner, Executive Assistant.*
Web, www.tsa.gov and Twitter, @TSA

Formulates policy and shares information related to security in various segments of the transportation industry, including commercial airports, commercial airlines, general aviation, mass transit and passenger rail, freight rail, maritime, highway and motor carrier, pipeline, and air cargo. Coordinates with the U.S. Coast Guard.

Transportation Security Administration (TSA) *(Homeland Security Dept.),* **Strategic Communications and Public Affairs,** TSA-4, 601 S. 12th St., Arlington, VA 20598-6028; (571) 227-2829. Fax, (571) 227-2552. *Alexa Lopez, Assistant Administrator (Acting).*
General email, tsamedia@tsa.dhs.gov
Web, www.tsa.gov/press

Responsible for TSA's communications and public information outreach, both externally and internally.

▶CONGRESS

For a listing of relevant congressional committees and subcommittees, please see page 762 or the Appendix.

▶NONGOVERNMENTAL

American Public Works Assn., Washington Office, 25 Massachusetts Ave. N.W., #500A, 20001; (202) 408-9541. *Andrea Eales, Director of Government Affairs,* (202) 218-6730. Toll-free, (800) 848-2792.

Transportation Security Administration

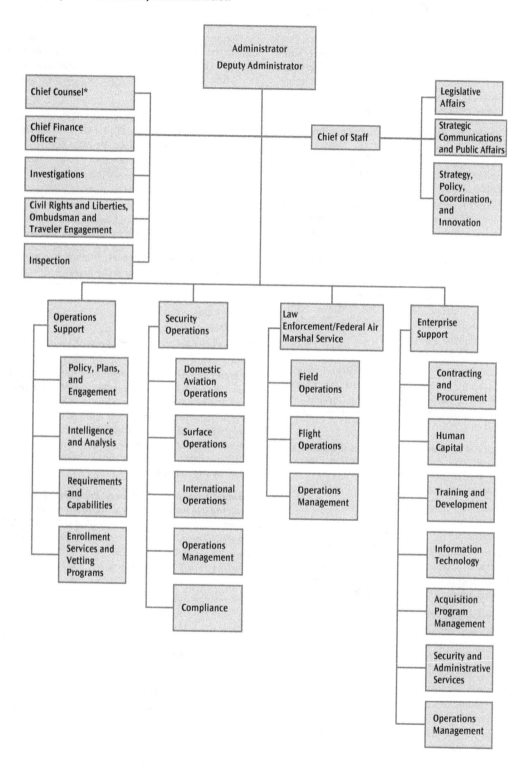

* The Office of the Chief Counsel reports to the Department of Homeland
  Security Office of the General Counsel

General email, *apwa.washington@gmail.com*

Web, www.apwa.net, Twitter, @APWATweets and *Facebook, www.facebook.com/AmericanPublicWorks Association*

Membership: engineers, architects, and others who maintain and manage public works facilities and services. Conducts research and education and promotes exchange of information on transportation and infrastructure-related issues. (Headquarters in Kansas City, Mo.)

Americans for Transportation Mobility Coalition, *U.S. Chamber of Commerce, 1615 H St. N.W., 20062; (202) 463-5842. Janet Kavinoky, Executive Director.*
Web, www.fasterbettersafer.org and *Twitter, @ATMCoalition*

Advocates increased dedicated federal and private sector funding for roads, bridges, and public transportation systems. Members include associations involved in designing, building, or maintaining transportation infrastructure. Monitors legislation. (Affiliated with the U.S. Chamber of Commerce.)

Assn. of Transportation Law Professionals, *P.O. Box 5407, Annapolis, MD 21403; (410) 268-1311. Fax, (410) 268-1322. Lauren Michalski, Executive Director.*
General email, info@atlp.org
Web, www.atlp.org

Membership: transportation attorneys and company counsel, government officials, and industry practitioners. Interests include railroad, motor, energy, pipeline, antitrust, labor, logistics, safety, environmental, air, and maritime matters.

Conference of Minority Transportation Officials, *1330 Braddock Pl., #203, Alexandria, VA 22314; (202) 506-2917. April Rai, President.*
General email, info@comtonational.org
Web, www.comtonational.org, Twitter, @COMTO_National and *Facebook, www.facebook.com/COMTONational*

Forum for minority professionals working in the transportation sector. Provides opportunities and reinforces networks through advocacy, training, and professional development for minorities in the industry.

Diesel Technology Forum, *5300 Westview Dr., #308, Frederick, MD 21703-2875; (301) 668-7230. Fax, (301) 668-7234. Allen R. Schaeffer, Executive Director.*
General email, dtf@dieselforum.org
Web, https://dieselforum.org, Twitter, @DieselTechForum and *Facebook, www.facebook.com/dieseltechforum*

Membership: vehicle and engine manufacturers, component suppliers, petroleum refineries, and emissions control device makers. Advocates use of diesel engines. Provides information on diesel power technology use and efforts to improve fuel efficiency and emissions control. Monitors legislation and regulations.

Eno Center for Transportation, *1629 K St. N.W., #200, 20006; (202) 879-4700. Robert Puentes, President, (202) 879-4711.*

General email, *publicaffairs@enotrans.org*
Web, www.enotrans.org, Twitter, @enotrans and *Facebook, www.facebook.com/enocenterfortransportation*

Nonpartisan think tank that seeks continuous improvement in transportation and its public and private leadership in order to increase the system's mobility, safety, and sustainability. Offers professional development programs, policy forums, and publications.

Institute of Transportation Engineers (ITE), *1627 Eye St. N.W., #550, 20006; (202) 785-0060. Fax, (202) 785-0609. Jeffrey F. Paniati, Executive Director, ext. 131.*
General email, ite_staff@ite.org
Web, www.ite.org and *Twitter, @ITEhq*

Membership: international professional transportation engineers. Conducts research, seminars, and training sessions; provides professional and scientific information on transportation standards and recommended practices.

National Academies of Sciences, Engineering, and Medicine (NASEM), *Transportation Research Board, Keck Center, 500 5th St. N.W., 7th Floor, 20001; (202) 334-2934. Fax, (202) 334-2003. Neil J. Pedersen Jr., Executive Director, (202) 334-2942.*
General email, mytrb@nas.edu
Web, www.nationalacademies.org/trb/transportation-research-board

Promotes research in transportation systems planning and administration and in the design, construction, maintenance, and operation of transportation facilities. Provides information to state and national highway and transportation departments; operates research information services; conducts studies, conferences, and workshops; publishes technical reports. Library open to the public by appointment.

National Academies of Sciences, Engineering, and Medicine (NASEM), *Transportation Research Board Library, Keck Center, 500 5th St. N.W., #439, 20001; (202) 334-2947. Fax, (202) 334-2527. Alexandra Briseno, Senior Librarian. Press, (202) 334-3252.*
General email, TRBlibrary@nas.edu
Web, www.trb.org/library

Primary archive for the Transportation Research Board, Highway Research Board, Strategic Highway Research Program, and Marine Board. Subject areas include transportation, aviation, engineering, rail, roads, and transit. Provides information to transportation-related federal agencies. Library open to the public by appointment.

National Defense Transportation Assn. (NDTA), *50 S. Pickett St., #220, Alexandria, VA 22304; (703) 751-5011. Fax, (703) 823-8761. Vice Adm. William A. Brown (USN, Ret.), President. Toll-free, (844) 620-2715.*
Web, www.ndtahq.com, Twitter, @NDTAHQ and *Facebook, www.facebook.com/NationalDefense TransportatoinAssociation*

Membership: transportation users, manufacturers, and mode carriers; information technology firms; and related military, government, and civil interests worldwide.

Promotes a strong U.S. transportation capability through coordination of private industry, government, and the military.

National Governors Assn. (NGA), *Center for Best Practices, Infrastructure Division, 444 N. Capitol St. N.W., #267, 20001-1512; (202) 624-5300. Thomas Curtin, Director.*
General email, info@nga.org

Web, www.nga.org/bestpractices/infrastructure

Identifies best practices for issues regarding enhancement of infrastructure, including funding streams, public-private partnerships, regulatory delays, transparency, and innovation.

Surface Transportation Information Sharing and Analysis Center (ISAC), *c/o EWA Information and Infrastructure Technologies, Inc., 13873 Park Center Rd., #200, Herndon, VA 20171-5406; (703) 478-7600. Todd Steinmetz, Program Director. Toll-free, (866) 784-7221.*
General email, st-isac@surfacetransportationisac.org

Web, www.surfacetransportationisac.org

Protects physical and electronic infrastructure of surface transportation and public transit carriers. Collects, analyzes, and distributes critical security and threat information from worldwide resources; shares best security practices and provides 24/7 immediate physical and cyberthreat warnings.

Freight and Intermodalism

▶**AGENCIES**

Maritime Administration (MARAD) *(Transportation Dept.), Port Infrastructure Development, West Bldg., 1200 New Jersey Ave. S.E., MAR-510, W21-308, 20590; (202) 366-5076. Fax, (202) 366-6988. Robert Bouchard, Director.*
Web, www.maritime.dot.gov/ports/office-port-infrastructure-development/office-port-infrastructure-development

Provides coordination and management of port infrastructure projects; provides leadership in national congestion mitigation efforts that involve waterway and port issues; promotes the development and improved utilization of ports and port facilities, including intermodal connections, terminals, and distribution networks; and provides technical information and advice to other agencies and organizations concerned with intermodal development. Information and advice include the analysis of intermodal economics, the development of applicable information systems, investigation of institutional and regulatory impediments, and the application of appropriate transportation management systems.

Surface Transportation Board (STB), *395 E St. S.W., #1220, 20423-0001; (202) 245-0245. Martin J. Oberman, Chair. Library, (202) 245-0288. Press, (202) 245-0238/1760. TTY, (800) 877-8339.*
Web, www.stb.gov and Email, rcpa@stb.gov

Regulates rates for water transportation and intermodal connections in noncontiguous domestic trade (between the mainland and Alaska, Hawaii, or U.S. territories). Library open to the public.

▶**NONGOVERNMENTAL**

Intermodal Assn. of North America, *11785 Beltsville Dr., #1100, Calverton, MD 20705-4049; (301) 982-3400. Fax, (301) 982-4815. Joanne F. (Joni) Casey, President, ext. 349.*
General email, info@intermodal.org

Web, www.intermodal.org and Twitter, @Intermodal

Membership: railroads, stacktrain operators, water carriers, motor carriers, marketing companies, and suppliers to the intermodal industry. Promotes intermodal transportation of freight. Monitors legislation and regulations.

International Brotherhood of Teamsters, *25 Louisiana Ave. N.W., 20001; (202) 624-6800. Fax, (202) 624-6918. James P. Hoffa, General President. Press, (202) 624-6911.*
General email, communications@teamster.org

Web, https://teamster.org, Twitter, @Teamsters, Facebook, www.facebook.com/teamsters and YouTube, www.youtube.com/TeamsterPower

Membership: workers in the transportation and construction industries, factories, offices, hospitals, warehouses, and other workplaces. Helps members negotiate pay, benefits, and better working conditions; conducts training programs and workshops. Monitors legislation and regulations.

National Assn. of Chemical Distributors (NACD), *4201 Wilson Blvd., #0515, Arlington, VA 22203; (703) 527-6223. Fax, (703) 527-7747. Eric R. Byer, President.*
General email, nacdpublicaffairs@nacd.com

Web, www.nacd.com and Twitter, @NACD_RD

Membership: firms involved in purchasing, processing, blending, storing, transporting, and marketing of chemical products. Provides members with information on such topics as training, safe handling and transport of chemicals, liability insurance, and environmental issues. Manages the NACD Chemical Educational Foundation. Monitors legislation and regulations.

National Customs Brokers and Forwarders Assn. of America, *8601 Georgia Ave., Suite 612, Silver Spring, MD 20910; (202) 466-0222. Jan Fields, President; Federico (Kiko) Zuniga, Executive Director.*
General email, membership@ncbfaa.org

Web, www.ncbfaa.org

Membership: customs brokers and freight forwarders in the United States. Fosters information exchange within the industry. Monitors legislation and regulations.

National Industrial Transportation League, *10816 Town Center Blvd., #516, Dunkirk, MD 20754-2708; (703) 524-5011. Fax, (703) 506-3266. Nancy O'Liddy, Executive Director.*

Federal Aviation Administration

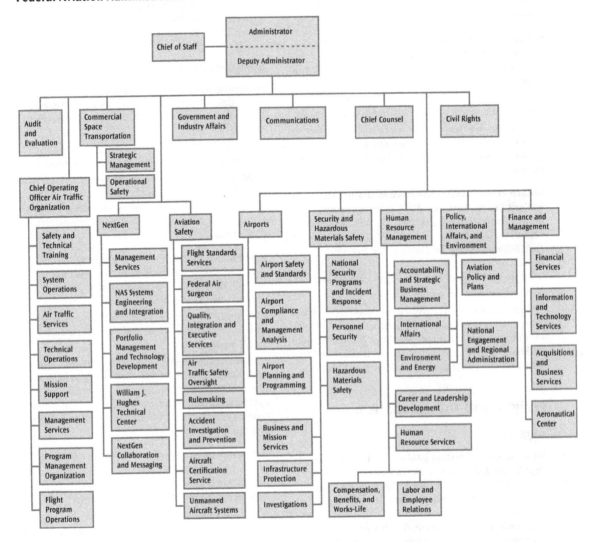

General email, info@nitl.org

Web, www.nitl.org, Twitter, @NITL and Facebook, www.facebook.com/National-Industrial-Transportation-League-143870279404142

Membership: air, water, and surface shippers and receivers, including industries, corporations, chambers of commerce, and trade associations. Monitors legislation and regulations.

AIR TRANSPORTATION

General

▶AGENCIES

Bureau of Economic and Business Affairs (EB) *(State Dept.), Transportation Affairs (TRA), Aviation Negotiations (AN),* 2201 C St. N.W., #3425, 20520-3425;

(202) 647-5865. Fax, (202) 647-9143. Aaron P. Forsberg, Director, (202) 647-9797.
General email, EEB-A-TRA-AN-DL@state.gov

Web, www.state.gov/about-us-division-for-transportation-affairs

Manages bilateral aviation relationships; works with the Transportation Dept. and private sector to negotiate bilateral agreements to support and improve commercial aviation.

Civil Air Patrol National Capital Wing, *200 McChord St. S.W., #111, Joint Base Anacostia-Bolling, 20032; (202) 767-4405. Col. David E. Sterling, Wing Commander.*
General email, cc@natcapwing.org

Web, www.natcapwg.cap.gov

Official civilian auxiliary of the U.S. Air Force. Primary function is to conduct search-and-rescue missions for the Air Force. Maintains an aerospace education program for adults and a cadet program for junior and senior high school students. (Headquarters at Maxwell Air Force Base, Ala.)

Civil Division *(Justice Dept.), Torts Branch, Aviation, Space, and Admiralty Litigation,* 175 N St N.E., 8th Floor, 20002 (mailing address: P.O. Box 14271, Washington, DC 20044-4271); (202) 616-4100. Fax, (202) 616-4002. Barry Benson, Director.
Web, www.justice.gov/aviation-space-admirality-litigation-section

Represents the federal government in civil suits arising from aviation and admiralty incidents and accidents. In aviation, handles tort litigation for the government's activities in the operation of the air traffic control system, regulation of air commerce, weather services, aeronautical charting, and operation of its own civil and military aircraft. In space, responsible for litigation and claims arising from the Space Shuttle *Columbia* and the *Challenger* disasters. In admiralty, defends the government's placement and maintenance of maritime navigational aids, its nautical charting and dredging activities, and its operation and maintenance of U.S. and contract-operated vessels. Brings cases for government cargo damage, pollution cleanups, and damage to U.S. locks, dams, and navaids.

Federal Aviation Administration (FAA) *(Transportation Dept.),* 800 Independence Ave. S.W., 20591; (202) 267-3111. Fax, (202) 267-7887. Steve Dickson, Administrator. Press, (202) 267-3883. Toll-free, (866) 835-5322.
Web, www.faa.gov, Twitter, @FAANews and Facebook, www.facebook.com/FAA

Regulates air commerce to improve aviation safety; promotes development of a national system of airports; develops and operates a common system of air traffic control and air navigation for both civilian and military aircraft; prepares the annual National Aviation System Plan.

Federal Aviation Administration (FAA) *(Transportation Dept.), Commercial Space Transportation (AST),* 800 Independence Ave. S.W., #331, AST-1, 20591; (202) 267-7793. Fax, (202) 267-5450. Kelvin B. Coleman, Associate Administrator.
Web, www.faa.gov/about/office_org/headquarters_offices/ast

Promotes and facilitates the operation of commercial expendable space launch vehicles by the private sector; licenses and regulates these activities.

Federal Aviation Administration (FAA) *(Transportation Dept.), NextGen,* 800 Independence Ave. S.W., 20591; (202) 267-7111. Fax, (202) 267-5621. Paul Fontaine, Assistant Administrator (Acting).
General email, nextgen@faa.gov
Web, www.faa.gov/about/office_org/headquarters_offices/ang

Plans and develops the Next Generation Air Transportation System infrastructure, which integrates technologies including satellite navigation and advanced digital communications, to reduce air transportation delays, save fuel, and lower carbon emissions.

Federal Aviation Administration (FAA) *(Transportation Dept.), NextGen, Systems Engineering and Integration,* 1250 Maryland Ave. S.W., 3rd Floor, 20024; (202) 267-6559. Fax, (202) 385-7105. Greg Burke, Director.
Web, www.faa.gov/about/office_org/headquarters_offices/ang/offices

Designs and maintains the National Airspace System (NAS) Enterprise Architecture and provides systems engineering and safety expertise to bridge the gap between today's NAS and the Next Generation Air Transportation System (NextGen).

Federal Aviation Administration (FAA) *(Transportation Dept.), Policy, International Affairs, and Environment (APL), Environment and Energy Research and Development,* 800 Independence Ave. S.W., #900W, 20591; (202) 267-3576. Fax, (202) 267-5594. Julie Marks, Deputy Director; Kevin Welsh, Executive Director.
Web, www.faa.gov/about/office_org/headquarters_offices/apl/research

Responsible for environmental affairs and energy conservation for aviation, including implementation and administration of various aviation-related environmental acts. Seeks to improve energy efficiency while reducing noise and emission impacts.

Federal Aviation Administration (FAA) *(Transportation Dept.), Policy, International Affairs, and Environment (APL), International Affairs,* 600 Independence Ave. S.W., #6E1500, API-1, 20591; (202) 267-1000. Fax, (202) 267-7198. Lirio Liu, Executive Director.
Web, www.faa.gov/about/office_org/headquarters_offices/apl/international_affairs

Coordinates all activities of the FAA that involve foreign relations; acts as liaison with the State Dept. and other agencies concerning international aviation; provides other countries with technical assistance on civil aviation problems; formulates international civil aviation policy for the United States.

International Trade Administration (ITA) *(Commerce Dept.), Industry and Analysis (I&A), Manufacturing (OM), Transportation and Machinery (OTM),* 1401 Constitution Ave. N.W., Room 22021, 20230-0001; (202) 482-1474. Fax, (202) 482-0674. Scott Kennedy, Director.
Web, http://legacy.trade.gov/about-us/office-transportation-and-machinery

Promotes the export of U.S. aerospace, automotive, and machinery products; compiles and analyzes industry data; seeks to secure a favorable position for the U.S. aerospace, auto, and machinery industries in global markets through policy and trade agreements.

National Aeronautics and Space Administration (NASA), Aeronautics Research Mission Directorate (ARMD), 300 E St. S.W., 20546; (202) 358-2587. Robert A. (Bob) Pearce, Associate Administrator.
Web, www.nasa.gov/aeroresearch and Twitter, @NASAAero

Conducts research in aerodynamics, materials, structures, avionics, propulsion, high-performance computing, human factors, aviation safety, and space transportation in support of national space and aeronautical research and technology goals. Manages the following NASA research centers: Ames (Moffett Field, Calif.), Dryden (Edwards, Calif.), Langley (Hampton, Va.), and Glenn (Cleveland, Ohio).

National Air and Space Museum *(Smithsonian Institution)*, 655 Jefferson Dr. S.W., 20560 (mailing address: 6th St. and Independence Ave. S.W., Washington, DC 20560); (202) 633-2214. Chris Browne, Director (Acting), (202) 633-2350. Archives, (703) 572-4045. Library, (703) 572-4175. Tours, (202) 633-2563.
General email, NASMVisitorServices@si.edu
Web, www.airandspace.si.edu, Twitter, @airandspace, Facebook, www.facebook.com/airandspace and YouTube, www.youtube.com/user/airandspace

Maintains exhibits and collections on aeronautics, pioneers of flight, and early aircraft through modern air technology. Library open to the public by appointment.

National Air and Space Museum *(Smithsonian Institution)*, Steven F. Udvar-Hazy Center, 14390 Air and Space Museum Pkwy., Chantilly, VA 20151; (703) 572-4118. Chris Browne, Director (Acting), (202) 633-2350. Library, (703) 572-4175. Public Affairs, (202) 633-1000.
General email, info@si.edu
Librarian email, AskaLibrarian@si.edu, Web, www.airandspace.si.edu/visit/udvar-hazy-center, Twitter, @airandspace and Facebook, www.facebook.com/airandspace

Displays and preserves a collection of historical aviation and space artifacts, including the B-29 Superfortress Enola Gay, the Lockheed SR-71 Blackbird, the prototype of the Boeing 707, the space shuttle Discovery, and a Concorde. Provides a center for research into the history, science, and technology of aviation and space flight. Open to the public daily 10:00 a.m.–5:30 p.m., except December 25.

National Mediation Board, 1301 K St. N.W., #250E, 20005-7011; (202) 692-5000. Fax, (202) 692-5082. Gerald W. Fauth III, Chair. Information, (202) 692-5050. TTY, (202) 692-5001.
General email, infoline@nmb.gov
Web, www.nmb.gov

Mediates labor disputes in the airline industry; determines and certifies labor representatives for the industry.

National Oceanic and Atmospheric Administration (NOAA) *(Commerce Dept.)*, Marine and Aviation Operations (OMAO), 8403 Colesville Rd., #500, Silver Spring, MD 20910-3282; (301) 713-1045. Fax, (301) 713-1541. Rear Adm. Michael J. Silah, Director, (301) 713-7600. Press, (301) 713-7671.
Web, www.omao.noaa.gov

Operates NOAA's aircraft for hurricane reconnaissance and research, marine mammal and fisheries assessment, and coastal mapping.

Office of the Assistant Secretary of Research and Technology *(Transportation Dept.)*, Bureau of Transportation Statistics, Airline Information, 1200 New Jersey Ave. S.E., #E-34, RTS-42, 20590; (202) 366-4373. Fax, (202) 366-3383. William Chadwick, Director.
General email, oai-support@bts.gov
Web, www.bts.gov/topics/airlines-and-airports-0

Develops, interprets, and enforces accounting and reporting regulations for all areas of the aviation industry; issues air carrier reporting instructions, waivers, and due-date extensions.

Transportation Dept. (DOT), *Aviation Analysis,* 1200 New Jersey Ave. S.E., #W86-481, 20590; (202) 366-5903. Fax, (202) 366-7638. Todd M. Homan, Director. Press, (202) 366-4570. TTY, (800) 877-8339.
Web, www.transportation.gov/policy/aviation-policy/office-aviation-analysis

Analyzes essential air service needs of communities; directs subsidy policy and programs; guarantees air service to small communities; conducts research for the department on airline mergers, international route awards, and employee protection programs; administers the air carrier fitness provisions of the Federal Aviation Act; registers domestic air carriers; enforces charter regulations for tour operators.

Transportation Dept. (DOT), *Aviation and International Affairs,* 1200 New Jersey Ave. S.E., #W88-322, 20590; (202) 366-8822. Carol A. (Annie) Petsonk, Principal Deputy Assistant Secretary. Press, (202) 366-4570. TTY, (800) 877-8339.
Web, www.transportation.gov/policy/assistant-secretary-aviation-international-affairs

Develops and implements public policy related to the airline industry and international civil aviation. Administers laws and regulations over a range of aviation trade issues, including U.S. and foreign carrier economic authority to engage in air transportation, small community transportation, the establishment of mail rates within Alaska and in the international market, and access at U.S. airports.

Transportation Dept. (DOT), *Aviation Consumer Protection,* 1200 New Jersey Ave. S.E., 20590; (202) 366-2220. Blaine A. Workie, Assistant General Counsel. Air travelers with disabilities hotline, (800) 778-4838. TTY, (202) 366-0511.
Web, www.transportation.gov/airconsumer

Addresses complaints about airline service and consumer-protection matters. Conducts investigations, provides assistance, and reviews regulations affecting air carriers.

Transportation Dept. (DOT), *International Aviation,* 1200 New Jersey Ave. S.E., #W86-316, 20590; (202) 366-2423. Fax, (202) 366-3694. Benjamin (Ben) Taylor, Director, (202) 366-1213.
Web, www.transportation.gov/policy/aviation-policy/office-international-aviation

Responsible for international aviation regulation and negotiations, including fares, tariffs, and foreign licenses; represents the United States at international aviation meetings.

▶CONGRESS

For a listing of relevant congressional committees and sub-committees, please see page 762 or the Appendix.

▶NONGOVERNMENTAL

Aeronautical Repair Station Assn. ARSA, 121 N. Henry St., Alexandria, VA 22314-2903; (703) 739-9543. Sarah MacLeod, Executive Director, ext. 114.
General email, arsa@arsa.org
Web, https://arsa.org and Twitter, @ARSAWorks

Membership: repair stations that have Federal Aviation Administration certificates or comparable non-U.S. certification; associate members are suppliers and distributors of components and parts. Works to improve relations between repair stations and manufacturers. Interests include establishing uniformity in the application, interpretation, and enforcement of FAA regulations. Monitors legislation and regulations.

Aerospace Industries Assn. (AIA), 1000 Wilson Blvd., #1700, Arlington, VA 22209-3928; (703) 358-1000. Eric K. Fanning, President. Press, (703) 358-1078.
General email, aia@aia-aerospace.org
Web, www.aia-aerospace.org, Twitter, @aiaspeaks and Facebook, www.facebook.com/AIA.Aerospace

Represents manufacturers of commercial, military, and business aircraft; helicopters; aircraft engines; missiles; spacecraft; and related components and equipment. Interests include international standards and trade.

Air Line Pilots Assn., International, 7950 Jones Branch Dr., #400S, McLean, VA 22102; (703) 689-2270. Capt. Joe DePete, President. Press, (703) 481-4440. Toll-free, (888) 359-2572.
General email, communications@alpa.org
Web, www.alpa.org, Twitter, @wearealpa, Facebook, www.facebook.com/WeAreAlpa and Blog, www.alpa.org/news-and-events/Blog

Membership: airline pilots in the United States and Canada. Promotes air travel safety; assists investigations of aviation accidents. Publishes the Air Line Pilot Magazine. Monitors legislation and regulations. (Affiliated with the AFL-CIO and the Canadian Labour Conference.)

Aircraft Owners and Pilots Assn. (AOPA), Legislative Affairs, 421 Aviation Way, Frederick, MD 21701; (301) 695-2000. Fax, (301) 695-2375. Mark Baker, President; James (Jim) Coon, Senior Vice President, Government Affairs. Toll-free, (800) 872-2672.
Web, www.aopa.org, Twitter, @AOPA and Facebook, www.facebook.com/AOPApilots

Membership: owners and pilots of general aviation aircraft. Washington office monitors legislation and regulations. Headquarters office provides members with a variety of aviation-related services; issues airport directory and handbook for pilots; sponsors the Air Safety Foundation. (Headquarters in Frederick, Md.)

Airlines for America (A4A), 1275 Pennsylvania Ave. N.W., #1300, 20004; (202) 626-4000. Nicholas E. Calio, President. General email, a4a@airlines.org
Web, www.airlines.org, Twitter, @airlinesdotorg, Facebook, www.facebook.com/AirlinesForAmerica and YouTube, www.youtube.com/user/AirlinesforAmerica

Membership: U.S. scheduled air carriers. Promotes aviation safety and security; and the facilitation of air transportation for passengers and cargo. Collects data on trends in airline operations. Acts as advocate for fair taxation and regulations that encourage global competition. Monitors legislation and regulations.

American Institute of Aeronautics and Astronautics (AIAA), 12700 Sunrise Valley Dr., #200, Reston, VA 20191-5807; (703) 264-7500. Daniel L. (Dan) Dumbacher, Executive Director. Toll-free, (800) 639-2422.
General email, custserv@aiaa.org
Web, www.aiaa.org, Twitter, @aiaa and Facebook, www.facebook.com/AIAAFan

Membership: engineers, scientists, students, and corporations in the aerospace field. Holds workshops on aerospace technical issues for congressional subcommittees; sponsors international conferences. Offers computerized database through its Technical Information Service.

Assn. of Flight Attendants–CWA, 501 3rd St. N.W., 20001-2797; (202) 434-1300. Fax, (202) 434-1319. Sara Nelson, President. Press, (202) 550-5520. Toll-free, (844) 232-2228.
General email, info@afacwa.org
Web, www.afacwa.org, Twitter, @afa_cwa and Facebook, www.facebook.com/afacwa

Membership: approximately 50,000 flight attendants. Helps members negotiate pay, benefits, and better working conditions; conducts training programs and workshops. Monitors legislation and regulations. (Affiliated with the AFL-CIO.)

Cargo Airline Assn., 1620 L St. N.W., #610, 20036-2438; (202) 293-1030. Fax, (202) 293-4377. Stephen A. (Steve) Alterman, President.
General email, info@cargoair.org
Web, www.cargoair.org and Twitter, @Cargo_Airlines

Membership: cargo airlines and other firms interested in the development and promotion of air freight.

Coalition of Airline Pilots Assns. (CAPA), 444 N. Capitol St. N.W., #528, 20001; (202) 624-3535. Fax, (202) 624-3536. Larry Rooney, President. Press, (202) 624-3538.
General email, info@capapilots.org
Web, www.capapilots.org, Twitter, @CAPApilots and Facebook, www.facebook.com/CAPApilots

Trade association representing more than 30,000 professional pilots at 14 airlines. Addresses safety, security, legislative, and regulatory issues affecting flight deck crew members, as well as domestic and international policy issues regarding aviation safety and security.

General Aviation Manufacturers Assn. (GAMA), *1400 K St. N.W., #801, 20005-2485; (202) 393-1500. Fax, (202) 842-4063. Peter J. (Pete) Bunce, President.*
General email, info@gama.aero

Web, http://gama.aero, Twitter, @GAManufacturers and Facebook, www.facebook.com/General.Aviation .Manufacturers.Association

Membership: manufacturers of business, commuter, and personal aircraft and manufacturers of engines, avionics, and related equipment. Monitors legislation and regulations; sponsors safety and public information programs.

Helicopter Assn. International, *1920 Ballenger Ave., 4th Floor, Alexandria, VA 22314-2898; (703) 683-4646. Fax, (703) 683-4745. James A. Viola, President.*
General email, rotor@rotor.org

Web, www.rotor.org, Twitter, @HeliAssoc and Facebook, www.facebook.com/HelicopterAssoc

Membership: owners, manufacturers, pilots, and operator-owners and service suppliers of helicopters and affiliated companies in the civil helicopter industry. Provides information on use and operation of helicopters; offers business management and aviation safety courses; sponsors annual industry exposition. Monitors legislation and regulations.

National Aeronautic Assn., *Reagan Washington National Airport, Hangar 7, #226, 20001-6015; (703) 416-4888. Fax, (703) 416-4877. Greg Principato, President.*
General email, naa@naa.aero

Web, www.naa.aero, Twitter, @NatlAero and Facebook, www.facebook.com/NationalAeronauticAssociation

Membership: persons interested in development of general and sporting aviation, including skydiving, commercial and military aircraft, and spaceflight. Oversees and approves official U.S. aircraft, aeronautics, and space records. Serves as U.S. representative to the International Aeronautical Federation in Lausanne, Switzerland.

National Agricultural Aviation Assn., *1440 Duke St., Alexandria, VA 22314; (202) 546-5722. Fax, (202) 546-5726. Andrew D. Moore, Chief Executive Officer.*
General email, information@agaviation.org

Web, www.agaviation.org, Twitter, @AgAviationNAAA and Facebook, www.facebook.com/NationalAgricultural AviationAssociation

Membership: agricultural pilots; operating companies that seed, fertilize, and spray land by air; and allied industries. Monitors legislation and regulations. (Affiliated with National Agricultural Aviation Research and Education Foundation.)

National Air Carrier Assn., *1735 N. Lynne St., #105, Arlington, VA 22209-3928; (703) 358-8060. George D. Novak, President, (703) 358-8065.*
General email, admin@naca.aero

Web, www.naca.aero and Facebook, www.facebook.com/ National-Air-Carrier-Association-191452260962499

Membership: U.S. air carriers certified for nonscheduled and scheduled operations for passengers and cargo

in the United States and abroad, including the US military, the travelling public and businesses. Monitors legislation and regulations.

National Air Transportation Assn., *818 Connecticut Ave. N.W., #900, 20006; (202) 774-1535. Fax, (202) 452-0837. Timothy R. Obitts, President. Toll-free, (800) 808-6282.*
Web, www.nata.aero, Twitter, @NATAareo, Facebook, www.facebook.com/nataaero and Email, info@nata.aero

Membership: companies that provide on-demand air charter, flight training, maintenance and repair, avionics, and other services. Manages an education foundation; compiles statistics; provides business assistance programs. Monitors legislation and regulations. (Affiliated with the National Air Transportation Foundation.)

National Assn. of State Aviation Officials, *1390 Chain Bridge Rd., #A106, McLean, VA 22101; (202) 868-6755. Gregory Pecoraro, Chief Executive Officer, (202) 925-1337.*
General email, info@nasao.org

Web, www.nasao.org, Twitter, @NASAOofficial, Library, www.nasao.org/resources and State Aviation System Plan Library, www.nasao.org/page/state-aviation-system-plan-library

Membership: state and territorial aeronautics agencies that deal with aviation issues, including regulation. Seeks uniform aviation laws; manages an aviation research and education foundation. Online library is accessible to nonmembers.

National Business Aviation Assn. (NBAA), *1200 G St. N.W., #1100, 20005; (202) 783-9000. Fax, (202) 540-9249. Ed Bolen, President. Toll-free, (800) 394-6222.*
General email, info@nbaa.org

Web, www.nbaa.org and Twitter, @NBAA

Membership: companies owning and operating aircraft for business use, suppliers, and maintenance and air fleet service companies. Conducts seminars and workshops in business aviation management. Sponsors annual civilian aviation exposition. Monitors legislation and regulations.

Regional Airline Assn., *1201 15th St. N.W., #430, 20005; (202) 367-1170. Fax, (202) 367-2170. Faye Malarkey Black, President.*
General email, raa@raa.org

Web, www.raa.org, Twitter, @RAAtweets and Facebook, www.facebook.com/RegionalAirlineAssociation

Membership: regional airlines that provide passenger, scheduled cargo, and mail service. Issues an annual report on the industry and hosts an annual convention. Monitors legislation and regulation.

RTCA Inc., *1150 18th St. N.W., #910, 20036; (202) 833-9339. Fax, (202) 833-9434. Terry McVenes, President.*
General email, info@rtca.org

Web, www.rtca.org and Twitter, @RTCAInc

Membership: federal agencies, aviation organizations, and commercial firms interested in aeronautical systems. Develops and publishes standards for aviation, including minimum operational performance standards for equipment; conducts research, makes recommendations to FAA, and issues reports on the field of aviation electronics and telecommunications.

Vertical Flight Society *(American Helicopter Society [AHS International]), (Vertical Lift Consortium [VLC]),* 2700 Prosperity Ave., #275, Fairfax, VA 22031; (703) 684-6777. Fax, (703) 739-9279. Michael Hirschberg, Executive Director, ext. 111. Toll-free, (855) 247-4685.
General email, staff@vtol.org
Web, http://vtol.org, Twitter, @VTOLsociety and Facebook, www.facebook.com/VTOLSociety

Membership: individuals and organizations interested in vertical flight. Acts as an information clearinghouse for technical data on helicopter design improvement, aerodynamics, and safety. Awards the Vertical Flight Foundation Scholarship to college students interested in helicopter technology. (Formerly the American Helicopter Society.)

Airports

▶AGENCIES

Animal and Plant Health Inspection Service (APHIS) *(Agriculture Dept.), Wildlife Services (WS),* 1400 Independence Ave. S.W., #1624 -S, 20250-3402; (202) 799-7095. Fax, (202) 690-0053. Janet L. Bucknall, Deputy Administrator. Toll-free, (866) 487-3297.
Web, www.aphis.usda.gov/wildlife_damage

Works to minimize damage caused by wildlife to human health and safety. Interests include aviation safety; works with airport managers to reduce the risk of bird strikes. Oversees the National Wildlife Research Center in Ft. Collins, Colo.

Federal Aviation Administration (FAA) *(Transportation Dept.), Airport Planning and Environmental Division (APP),* 800 Independence Ave. S.W., #619, APP-400, 20591-0001; (202) 267-3263. Fax, (202) 267-5383.
Robert Craven, Manager.
Web, www.faa.gov/about/office_org/headquarters_offices/arp/offices/app/app400

Leads the FAA's strategic policy and planning efforts to provide a safe, efficient, and sustainable national airport system, coordinates the agency's reauthorization before Congress, and is responsible for national aviation policies and strategies in the environment and energy arenas, including aviation activity forecasts, economic analyses, aircraft noise and emissions research and policy, environmental policy, and aviation insurance.

Federal Aviation Administration (FAA) *(Transportation Dept.), Airports (ARP),* 800 Independence Ave. S.W., #600E, ARP-1, 20591; (202) 267-9590. Fax, (202) 267-5301.
Shannetta Griffin, Associate Administrator.
Web, www.faa.gov/about/office_org/headquarters_offices/arp

Makes grants for development and improvement of publicly operated and owned airports and some privately owned airports; inspects and certifies safety design

standards for airports; administers the congressional Airport Improvement Program and Passenger Facility Charges Program; ensures that airports receiving federal funding comply with federal regulations. Questions about local airports are usually referred to a local FAA field office.

Maryland Aviation Administration, *Terminal Bldg.,* P.O. Box 8766, 3rd Floor, BWI Airport, MD 21240-0766; (410) 859-7111. Wayne S. Pennell, Chief Operating Officer, (410) 859-7335. Toll-free, (800) 435-9294. Press, (410) 859-7027. TTY, (410) 859-7227. Military Flights, (410) 918-6900.
General email, maa@mdot.state.md.us
Web, www.marylandaviation.com and www.bwiairport.com

Responsible for aviation operations, planning, instruction, and safety in Maryland; operates Baltimore/Washington International Thurgood Marshall Airport (BWI) and Martin State Airport.

Metropolitan Washington Airports Authority, *2733 Crystal Dr., Arlington, VA 22202 (mailing address: 1 Aviation Circle, Washington, DC 20001-6000); (703) 417-8600. John E. Potter, President. Press, (703) 417-8370.*
Web, www.mwaa.com and Twitter, @MWAAHQ

Independent interstate agency created by Virginia and the District of Columbia with the consent of Congress; operates Washington Dulles International Airport and Ronald Reagan Washington National Airport.

▶NONGOVERNMENTAL

Airports Council International (ACI), *North America (ACI-NA),* 1615 L St. N.W., #300, 20036; (202) 293-8500. Kevin M. Burke, President.
General email, memberservices@airportscouncil.org
Web, www.airportscouncil.org, Twitter, @airportscouncil and Facebook, www.facebook.com/airportscouncil

Membership: authorities, boards, commissions, and municipal departments operating public airports. Represents local, regional, and state governing bodies that own and operate commercial airports in the United States and Canada. Serves as liaison with government agencies and other aviation organizations; works to improve passenger and freight facilitation; acts as clearinghouse on engineering and operational aspects of airport development. Monitors legislation and regulations.

American Assn. of Airport Executives, *Barclay Bldg., 601 Madison St., Alexandria, VA 22314; (703) 824-0504. Fax, (703) 820-1395. Todd Hauptli, President, (703) 578-2514.*
Web, www.aaae.org, Twitter, @aaaedelivers and Facebook, www.facebook.com/AAAEDelivers

Membership: airport managers, superintendents, consultants, government officials, authorities and commissioners, and others interested in the construction, management, and operation of airports. Conducts examination for and awards the professional designation of Accredited Airport Executive.

Aviation Safety and Security

▶ AGENCIES

Federal Aviation Administration (FAA) *(Transportation Dept.), Accident Investigation and Prevention (AVP),* 800 Independence Ave. S.W., #840, AVP-1, 20591; (202) 267-9612. Fax, (202) 267-3265. Steven Gottlieb, Director.
Web, www.faa.gov/about/office_org/headquarters_offices/avs/offices/avp

Investigates aviation accidents and incidents to detect unsafe conditions and trends in the national airspace system and to coordinate corrective action.

Federal Aviation Administration (FAA) *(Transportation Dept.), Air Traffic Organization (AJO),* 800 Independence Ave. S.W., #1018A, AJA-O, 20591; (202) 267-7224. Fax, (202) 267-5085. Teri L. Bristol, Chief Operating Officer.
Web, www.faa.gov/about/office_org/headquarters_offices/ato

Operates the national air traffic control system; employs air traffic controllers at airport towers, terminal radar approach controls, en route air traffic control centers, and flight service stations in Alaska; maintains the William J. Hughes Technical Center for aviation research, testing, and evaluation.

Federal Aviation Administration (FAA) *(Transportation Dept.), Air Traffic Organization (AJO), Air Traffic Services,* 800 Independence Ave. S.W., #FOB 10-B, #3E1500, 20591; (202) 267-0634. Fax, (202) 493-4306. Jeffrey O. Vincent, Vice President.
Web, www.faa.gov/about/office_org/headquarters_offices/ato/service_units/air_traffic_services

Provides safe, secure, and efficient management for the National Airspace System and international airspace assigned to U.S. control. Responsible for Airport Traffic Control Towers (federal and contract), Terminal Radar Approach facilities, Air Route Traffic Control Centers, and Combined Center Radar Approach Control facilities to guide aircraft through their various phases of flight.

Federal Aviation Administration (FAA) *(Transportation Dept.), Air Traffic Organization (AJO), Technical Operations,* 800 Independence Ave. S.W., #700E-10A, 20591; (202) 267-3366. Fax, (202) 267-6060. Jeffrey (Jeff) Planty, Vice President.
Web, www.faa.gov/about/office_org/headquarters_offices/ato/service_units/techops

Conducts research and development programs aimed at providing procedures, facilities, and devices needed for a safe and efficient system of air navigation and air traffic control.

Federal Aviation Administration (FAA) *(Transportation Dept.), Air Traffic Safety Oversight Service (AOV),* 800 Independence Ave. S.W., 20591; (202) 267-5205. Michael J. O'Donnell, Executive Director.
Web, www.faa.gov/about/office_org/headquarters_offices/avs/offices/aov

Establishes safety standards and provides independent oversight of the Air Traffic Organization.

Federal Aviation Administration (FAA) *(Transportation Dept.), Aviation Safety (AVS), Aerospace Medicine,* 800 Independence Ave. S.W., #800W, AAM-1, 20591; (202) 267-3535. Fax, (202) 267-5399. Susan Northrup, Federal Air Surgeon.
Web, www.faa.gov/about/office_org/headquarters_offices/avs/offices/aam

Responsible for the medical activities and policies of the FAA; designates, through regional offices, aviation medical examiners who conduct periodic medical examinations of all air personnel; regulates and oversees drug and alcohol testing programs for pilots, air traffic controllers, and others who hold safety-sensitive positions; maintains a Civil Aerospace Medical Institute in Oklahoma City.

Federal Aviation Administration (FAA) *(Transportation Dept.), Aviation Safety (AVS), Aircraft Certification Service,* 800 Independence Ave. S.W., #800E, AIR-1, 20591-0004; (202) 267-8235. Fax, (202) 267-5364. Earl Lawrence, Director.
Web, www.faa.gov/about/office_org/headquarters_offices/avs/offices/air

Certifies all aircraft for airworthiness; approves designs and specifications for new aircraft, aircraft engines, propellers, and appliances; supervises aircraft manufacturing and testing. Directs a fuels program and an international division.

Federal Aviation Administration (FAA) *(Transportation Dept.), Aviation Safety (AVS), Flight Standards Service,* 800 Independence Ave. S.W., #821, AFS-1, 20591; (202) 267-8237. Fax, (202) 267-5230. Robert Carty, Executive Director (Acting). Press, (202) 267-3883.
Web, www.faa.gov/about/office_org/headquarters_offices/avs/offices/afx

Sets certification standards for air carriers, commercial operators, air agencies, and air personnel (except air traffic control tower operators); directs and executes certification and inspection of flight procedures, operating methods, air personnel qualification and proficiency, and maintenance aspects of airworthiness programs; manages the registry of civil aircraft and all official air personnel records; supports law enforcement agencies responsible for drug interdiction.

Federal Aviation Administration (FAA) *(Transportation Dept.), Security and Hazardous Materials Safety (ASH),* 800 Independence Ave. S.W., #300E, 20591; (202) 267-7211. Fax, (202) 267-8496. Claudio Manno, Associate Administrator.
Web, www.faa.gov/about/office_org/headquarters_offices/ash

Seeks to ensure air transportation safety by preventing hazardous materials accidents aboard aircraft and protecting FAA employees and facilities from criminal and terrorist acts.

Federal Communications Commission (FCC), *Enforcement Bureau (EB),* 45 L St. N.E., 20554; (202) 418-7450. Fax, (202) 418-2810. Loyaan Egal, Chief (Acting). Press, (202) 418-0500. Toll-free, (888) 225-5322.
Web, www.fcc.gov/enforcement

National Transportation Safety Board

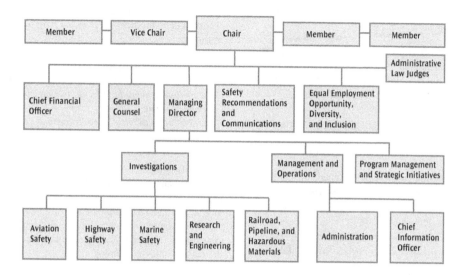

Provides technical services to aid the Federal Aviation Administration in locating aircraft in distress; provides interference resolution for air traffic control radio frequencies.

National Transportation Safety Board (NTSB), *Aviation Safety (AS), 490 L'Enfant Plaza East S.W., #5400, 20594-0001; (202) 314-6000. Tim LeBaron, Director.*
Web, www.ntsb.gov/about/organization/AS/Pages/office_as.aspx

Responsible for management, policies, and programs in aviation safety of civil domestic air carrier, commuter, and air taxi aviation accident investigations, in-flight collisions and nonfatal general aviation accidents, and certain public-use aircraft carriers. Manages programs on special investigations, safety issues, and safety objectives. Acts as U.S. representative in international investigations.

Transportation Security Administration (TSA)
(Homeland Security Dept.), TSA-1, 601 S. 12th St., 7th Floor, Arlington, VA 20598-6001; (571) 227-1398. David P. Pekoske, Administrator. Press, (571) 227-2829. TSA Contact Center, (866) 289-9673.
General email, TSA-ContactCenter@tsa.dhs.gov
Web, www.tsa.gov and Twitter, @TSA

Protects the nation's transportation system. Performs and oversees airport security, including passenger and baggage screeners, airport federal security directors, and air marshals. Questions and concerns regarding travel can be submitted toll-free to the TSA Contact Center.

Transportation Security Administration (TSA)
(Homeland Security Dept.), Office of Law Enforcement, Federal Air Marshal Service, TSA-18, 601 S. 12th St., Arlington, VA 20598-6018; (703) 487-3400. Fax, (703) 487-3405. Michael A. Ondocin, Executive Assistant Administrator.
Web, www.tsa.gov

Protects air security in the United States. Promotes public confidence in the U.S. civil aviation system. Deploys marshals on flights around the world to detect and deter hostile acts targeting U.S. air carriers, airports, passengers, and crews.

▶ **NONGOVERNMENTAL**

Aerospace Medical Assn., *320 S. Henry St., Alexandria, VA 22314-3579; (703) 739-2240. Fax, (703) 739-9652. James R. DeVoll, President; Jeffrey C. Sventek, Executive Director.*
General email, inquiries@asma.org
Web, www.asma.org, Twitter, @Aero_Med and Facebook, www.facebook.com/AerospaceMedicalAssociation

Membership: physicians, flight surgeons, aviation medical examiners, flight nurses, scientists, technicians, and specialists in clinical, operational, and research fields of aerospace medicine. It is organized exclusively for charitable, educational, and scientific purposes. Promotes programs to improve aerospace medicine, human performance and to help maintain safety in aviation by examining and monitoring the health of aviation personnel; members may consult in aircraft investigation and cockpit design. Publishes the AMHP journal and several other informational papers.

Air Traffic Control Assn. (ACTA), *225 Reinekers Lane, #400, Alexandria, VA 22314; (703) 299-2430. Brian R. Bruckbauer, President, ext. 307.*
General email, info@atca.org
Web, www.atca.org, Twitter, @ATCA_now and Facebook, www.facebook.com/AirTraffic ControlAssociation

Membership: air traffic controllers, flight service station specialists, pilots, aviation engineers and manufacturers, and others interested in air traffic control systems. Provides a mentorship program. Compiles and publishes information and data concerning air traffic control; provides information to members, Congress, and federal agencies. Provides scholarships to aviation students and children of air traffic controllers.

American Assn. of Airport Executives, *Barclay Bldg., 601 Madison St., Alexandria, VA 22314; (703) 824-0504. Fax, (703) 820-1395. Todd Hauptli, President, (703) 578-2514. Web, www.aaae.org, Twitter, @aaaedelivers and Facebook, www.facebook.com/AAAEDelivers*

Maintains the Transportation Security Clearinghouse, which matches fingerprints and other personal information from airport and airline employees against FBI databases.

Flight Safety Foundation, *701 N. Fairfax St., #250, Alexandria, VA 22314-2058; (703) 739-6700. Fax, (703) 739-6708. Hassan Shahidi, President. Press, ext. 116. General email, info@flightsafety.org*

Web, www.flightsafety.org, Twitter, @flightsafety and Facebook, www.facebook.com/FlightSafetyFoundation

Membership: aerospace manufacturers, domestic and foreign airlines, energy and insurance companies, educational institutions, and organizations and corporations interested in flight safety. Develops safety standards, provides independent technical assistance, resolves community issues. Sponsors seminars, publishes literature, and conducts studies and safety audits on air safety for governments and industries. Administers award programs that recognize achievements in air safety.

International Society of Air Safety Investigators (ISASI), *107 E. Holly Ave., #11, Sterling, VA 20164-5405; (703) 430-9668. Fax, (703) 430-4970. Steve Demko, U.S. Society President. General email, isasi@erols.com*

Web, https://isasi.org

Membership: specialists who investigate and seek to define the causes of aircraft accidents. Encourages improvement of air safety and investigative procedures through information exchange and educational seminars.

National Academies of Sciences, Engineering, and Medicine (NASEM), *Human-Systems Integration Board, Keck Center, 500 5th St. N.W., 11th Floor, 20001; (202) 334-2326. Fax, (202) 334-2210. Mary Ellen O'Connell, Director, (202) 334-2607. General email, bohsi@nas.edu*

Web, www.nationalacademies.org/bohsi/board-on-human-systems-integration

Conducts studies on human factors and human-systems integration. Research includes air traffic control.

National Air Traffic Controllers Assn., *1325 Massachusetts Ave. N.W., 20005; (202) 628-5451. Fax, (202) 380-9118. Rich Santa, President; Marguerite L. Graf, General Counsel. Toll-free, (800) 266-0895. General email, media@natca.org*

Web, www.natca.org, Twitter, @NATCA and Facebook, www.facebook.com/NATCAFamily

Membership: air traffic controllers engineers, and other aviation safety-related professionals. improve working conditions, and encourage procurement of more modern, reliable equipment. Concerned with airport safety worldwide.

Professional Aviation Safety Specialists, *1200 G St. N.W., #750, 20005; (202) 293-7277. Fax, (202) 293-7727. Dave Spero, President; Jana Denning, Director of Government Affairs. General email, nationaloffice@passmember.net*

Web, https://passnational.org, Twitter, @PASSNational and Facebook, www.facebook.com/PASSNational

Membership: FAA and DoD employees who install, maintain, support, and certify air traffic control and national defense equipment, inspect and oversee the commercial and general aviation industries, develop flight procedures, and perform quality analyses of complex aviation systems used in air traffic control and national defense in the United States and abroad.

MARITIME TRANSPORTATION

General

▶**AGENCIES**

Army Corps of Engineers *(Defense Dept.), 441 G St. N.W., #3K05, 20314-1000; (202) 761-0011. Lt. Gen. Scott A. Spellman (USA), Chief of Engineers. General email, hq-publicaffairs@usace.army.mil*

Web, www.usace.army.mil, Twitter, @USACEHQ and Facebook, www.facebook.com/USACEHQ

Provides local governments with navigation, waterway dredging, flood control, disaster relief, and hydroelectric power services.

Civil Division *(Justice Dept.), Torts Branch, Aviation, Space, and Admiralty Litigation, 175 N St N.E., 8th Floor, 20002 (mailing address: P.O. Box 14271, Washington, DC 20044-4271); (202) 616-4100. Fax, (202) 616-4002. Barry Benson, Director. Web, www.justice.gov/aviation-space-admirality-litigation-section*

Represents the federal government in civil suits concerning the maritime industry, including ships, shipping, and merchant marine personnel. Handles civil cases arising from admiralty incidents and accidents, including oil spills.

Federal Maritime Commission (FMC), *800 N. Capitol St. N.W., 20573-0001; (202) 523-5725. Daniel B. Maffei, Chair, (202) 523-5911. TTY, (800) 877-8339. General email, inquiries@fmc.gov*

Web, www.fmc.gov, Twitter, @FMC_gov and Library, Libraryinquiries@fmc.gov

Regulates the foreign ocean shipping of the United States; enforces maritime shipping laws and regulations regarding rates and charges, freight forwarding, passengers, and port authorities. Library open to the public (Monday–Friday, 8:00 a.m.–4:30 p.m.).

Federal Maritime Commission (FMC), *Certification and Licensing,* 800 N. Capitol St. N.W., #970, 20573-0001; (202) 523-5787. Fax, (202) 566-0011. Cindy Hennigan, Director.
General email, blc@fmc.gov
Web, www.fmc.gov/about-the-fmc/bureaus-offices/bureau-of-certification-and-licensing

Responsible for the Passenger Vessel Certification and Ocean Transportation Intermediary programs. Licenses ocean freight forwarders and nonvessel-operating common carriers. Issues certificates of financial responsibility to ensure that cruise lines refund fares and meet their liability in case of death, injury, or nonperformance.

Federal Maritime Commission (FMC), *Trade Analysis,* 800 N. Capitol St. N.W., #940, 20573-0001; (202) 523-5796. Fax, (202) 523-5867. Kristen Monaco, Director.
Library, (202) 523-5762.
General email, tradeanalysis@fmc.gov
Web, www.fmc.gov/about-the-fmc/bureaus-offices/bureau-of-trade-analysis

Reviews agreement and monitors the concerted activities of ocean common carriers and marine terminal operators under the standards of the Shipping Acot of 1984. Reviews and analyzes service contracts, monitors rates of government-owned controlled carriers, reviews carrier-published tariff systems under the accessibility and accuracy standards, and responds to inquiries or issues that arise concerning service contracts or tariffs. Conducts competition and market analysis to detect activity that is substantially anticompetitive.

Maritime Administration (MARAD) *(Transportation Dept.),* West Bldg., 1200 New Jersey Ave. S.E., 20590; (202) 366-4000. Fax, (202) 366-3890. Lucinda Lessley (USN, Ret.), Administrator (Acting). Press, (202) 366-5807.
Web, www.maritime.dot.gov, Facebook, www.facebook.com/DOTMARAD and Press, maradpressoffice@dot.gov

Conducts research on shipbuilding and operations; provides financing guarantees and a tax-deferred fund for shipbuilding; promotes the maritime industry; operates the U.S. Merchant Marine Academy in Kings Point, New York.

Maritime Administration (MARAD) *(Transportation Dept.),* *Business and Finance Development,* West Bldg., 1200 New Jersey Ave. S.E., MAR-750, 20590; (202) 366-5737. David Heller, Associate Administrator.
General email, marinefinancing@dot.gov
Web, www.maritime.dot.gov

Works with shipyards, ship owners, operations and labor to aid growth of modern shipyards. Functions include financial approval, marine financing, cargo preference and domestic trade, workforce development, and shipyard and marine engineering.

Maritime Administration (MARAD) *(Transportation Dept.),* *Cargo and Commercial Sealift,* West Bldg., 1200 New Jersey Ave. S.E., MAR-640, MS 2, 20590; (202)

366-4610. Fax, (202) 366-5522. Anthony Fisher, Director, (202) 366-7045.
General email, cargo.marad@dot.gov
Web, www.maritime.dot.gov/ports/cargo-preference/cargo-preference

Enforces cargo preference laws and regulations. Promotes and monitors the use of U.S. flag vessels in the movement of cargo on international waters.

Maritime Administration (MARAD) *(Transportation Dept.),* *Education, Maritime Training, and Careers,* West Bldg., 1200 New Jersey Ave. S.E., MAR-650, W23-314, 20590; (202) 493-0029. Sashi Kumar, Director, (202) 366-5469.
General email, careersafloat@dot.gov
Web, www.maritime.dot.gov/education

Administers programs for the U.S. Merchant Marine Academy and State Academies. Promotes maritime workforce development.

Maritime Administration (MARAD) *(Transportation Dept.),* *Federal Ship Financing Program (Title XI),* West Bldg., 1200 New Jersey Ave. S.E., 2nd Floor, 20590; (202) 366-5737. David Gilmore, Director of Title XI; David M. Heller, Director of Finance.
General email, marinefinancing@dot.gov
Web, www.maritime.dot.gov/grants/title-xi/federal-ship-financing-program-title-xi

Provides ship financing guarantees for ship construction and shipyard modernization; administers the Capital Construction Fund Program.

Maritime Administration (MARAD) *(Transportation Dept.),* *International Activities,* West Bldg., 1200 New Jersey Ave. S.E., W28-312, 20590; (202) 366-5493. Lonnie T. Kishiyama, Director.
Web, https://cms.marad.dot.gov/economic-security/office-international-activities

Formulates the agency's position on international issues affecting the U.S. maritime industry with the goal of reducing or eliminating international barriers to trade and improving market access.

Maritime Administration (MARAD) *(Transportation Dept.),* *Policy and Plans,* West Bldg., 1200 New Jersey Ave. S.E., MAR-232, 20590; (202) 366-4000. Fax, (202) 366-3890. Douglas (Doug) McDonald, Director, (202) 366-2145.
Web, www.maritime.dot.gov/about-us/foia/office-policy-and-plans

Supports the agency's policy development process with research, analysis, and documentation. Assesses the effects of legislative and regulatory proposals on maritime programs and maritime industries. Investigates the effects of national and global events on maritime policy and operations.

National Oceanic and Atmospheric Administration (NOAA) *(Commerce Dept.),* *Marine and Aviation Operations (OMAO),* 8403 Colesville Rd., #500, Silver Spring, MD 20910-3282; (301) 713-1045. Fax, (301) 713-1541. Rear Adm. Michael J. Silah, Director, (301) 713-7600. Press, (301) 713-7671.
Web, www.omao.noaa.gov

Operates NOAA's fleet of ships for fisheries research, nautical charting, and ocean and climate studies.

U.S. Coast Guard (USCG) *(Homeland Security Dept.),* *2703 Martin Luther King Jr. Ave. S.E., MS 7000, 20593-7000; (202) 372-4000. Fax, (202) 372-8302.* *Adm. Karl L. Schultz, Commandant. Public Affairs, (202) 372-4600.* *Web, www.uscg.mil, Twitter, @USCG, Facebook, www .facebook.com/UScoastguard and YouTube, www.youtube .com/USCGImagery*

Carries out search-and-rescue missions in and around navigable waters and on the high seas; enforces federal laws on the high seas and navigable waters of the United States and its possessions; conducts marine environmental protection programs; administers boating safety programs; inspects and regulates construction, safety, and equipment of merchant marine vessels; establishes and maintains a system of navigation aids; carries out domestic icebreaking activities; maintains a state of military readiness to assist the Navy in time of war or when directed by the president.

U.S. Coast Guard (USCG) *(Homeland Security Dept.),* *Design and Engineering Standards (CG-ENG), 2703 Martin Luther King Jr. Ave. S.E., MS 7509, 20593-7509; (202) 372-1352. Capt. Benjamin Hawkins, Chief.* *Web, www.dco.uscg.mil/CG-ENG*

Develops and maintains engineering standards for the building of ships, aircraft, shore infrastructure, and Coast Guard facilities. Supports maritime safety, security, mobility, national defense, and protection of natural resources.

U.S. Coast Guard (USCG) *(Homeland Security Dept.),* *Response Policy (CG-5R), 2703 Martin Luther Jr. Ave. S.W., MS 7318, 20593-7318; (202) 372-2011. (202) 372-2014. Rear Adm. Douglas Fears, Assistant Commandant.* *Web, www.dco.uscg.mil/Our-Organization/Assistant-Commandant-for-Response-Policy-CG-5R*

Regulates waterways under U.S. jurisdiction.

▶ **CONGRESS**

For a listing of relevant congressional committees and subcommittees, please see page 762 or the Appendix.

▶ **NONGOVERNMENTAL**

American Maritime Congress, *444 N. Capitol St. N.W., #800, 20001-1570; (202) 347-8020. Fax, (202) 347-1550. James E. (Jim) Caponiti, President.* *General email, info@americanmaritime.org* *Web, http://americanmaritime.org*

Organization of U.S.-flag carriers engaged in oceanborne transportation. Conducts research, education, and advocacy on behalf of the U.S.-flag merchant marine.

Chamber of Shipping of America, *1730 Rhode Island Ave. N.W., #702, 20036-4517; (202) 775-4399. Fax, (202) 659-3795. Kathy J. Metcalf, President.* *Web, www.knowships.org and Twitter, @CSAKnowships*

Represents U.S.-based companies that own, operate, or charter oceangoing tankers, container ships, and other merchant vessels engaged in domestic and international trade and companies that maintain a commercial interest in the operation of such oceangoing vessels.

Marine Engineers' Beneficial Assn. (MEBA), *444 N. Capitol St. N.W., #800, 20001-1570; (202) 638-5355. Fax, (202) 638-5369. Adam Vokac, President.* *General email, mebahq@mebaunion.org* *Web, www.mebaunion.org, Facebook, www.facebook.com/ meba1875/?fref=nf and Twitter, @meba1875*

Maritime labor union. Represents engineers and deck officers, domestically and internationally. Monitors legislation and regulation.

Maritime Institute for Research and Industrial Development, *1025 Connecticut Ave. N.W., #507, 20036-5412; (202) 463-6505. Fax, (202) 223-9093. C. James (Jim) Patti, President, ext. 2.* *Web, www.miraid.org*

Membership: U.S. flagship operators. Promotes the development of the U.S. merchant marine. Interests include the use of private commercial merchant vessels by the Defense Dept., enforcement of cargo preference (Jones Act) laws for U.S. flagships, and maintenance of cabotage laws. Monitors regulations and legislation.

National Academies of Sciences, Engineering, and Medicine (NASEM), *Marine Board, Keck Center, 500 5th St. N.W., 20001; (202) 334-2167. Martha Grabowski, Chair.* *General email, sbrotemarkle@nas.edu* *Web, www.trb.org/MarineBoard/MarineBoard.aspx*

Supports research and provides information relating to new technologies, laws and regulations, economics, the environment, and other issues affecting the marine transportation system, port operations, coastal engineering, and marine governance.

National Marine Manufacturers Assn., *Government Relations, 650 Massachusetts Ave. N.W., #520, 20001; (202) 737-9750. Fax, (202) 628-4716. Frank K. Hugelmeyer, President; Tillie Fowler, Vice President for Government Relations.* *Web, www.nmma.org/government and Twitter, @therealNMMA*

Membership: recreational marine equipment manufacturers. Promotes boating safety and the development of boating facilities. Monitors legislation and regulations. (Headquarters in Chicago, Ill.)

Shipbuilders Council of America, *20 F St. N.W., #500, 20001; (202) 737-3234. Fax, (202) 737-0264. Matthew (Matt) Paxton, President.* *Web, https://shipbuildersusa.org, Twitter, @ShipbuildersUSA and Facebook, www.facebook.com/ ShipbuildersUSA*

Membership: U.S. shipyards that repair and build commercial ships and naval and other government vessels;

and allied industries and associations. Monitors legislation and regulations.

Transportation Institute, *5201 Capital Gateway Dr., Camp Springs, MD 20746-4211; James L. Henry, President. Phone, in Maryland, (301) 423-3335. Phone, in DC, (202) 347-2590.*

General email, info@trans-inst.org

Web, https://transportationinstitute.org, Twitter, @Trans_ Inst and Facebook, www.facebook.com/transportation .institute

Membership: U.S.-flag maritime shipping companies. Conducts research on freight regulation and rates, government subsidies and assistance, domestic and international maritime matters, maritime safety, ports, Saint Lawrence Seaway, shipbuilding, and regulation of shipping.

World Shipping Council, *1156 15th St. N.W., #300, 20005; (202) 589-1230. Fax, (202) 589-1231. John W. Butler, President.*

General email, info@worldshipping.org

Web, www.worldshipping.org

Membership association representing the liner shipping industry. Works with policymakers and other industry groups interested in international transportation issues, including maritime security, regulatory policy, tax issues, safety, the environment, harbor dredging, and trade infrastructure. Monitors legislation and regulations.

Maritime Safety

▶AGENCIES

Maritime Administration (MARAD) *(Transportation Dept.), Environment, West Bldg., 1200 New Jersey Ave. S.E., W28-342, 20590; (202) 366-1931. Michael Carter, Associate Administrator.*

Web, www.maritime.dot.gov/ports/office-environment/ office-environment

Focuses on environmental stewardship, maritime safety, and maritime security; maritime research and development; and maritime international and domestic rules, regulations, and standards. Provides environmental support for America's Marine Highway Program and ensures compliance with the National Environmental Policy Act. Advises Maritime Administrator on domestic and international environmental policies that affect maritime transportation.

Maritime Administration (MARAD) *(Transportation Dept.), Environment and Compliance, Security Office, West Bldg., 1200 New Jersey Ave. S.E., W28-340, 20590; (202) 366-9363. Cameron T. Naron, Director, (202) 366-1883.*

General email, maradsecurity@dot.gov

Web, www.maritime.dot.gov/ports/office-security/office-maritime-security

Promotes security throughout the maritime transportation system through maritime information security support, maritime warnings, and advisories for American vessels by using information technology.

Maritime Administration (MARAD) *(Transportation Dept.), Sealift Operations and Emergency Preparedness, West Bldg., 1200 New Jersey Ave. S.E., W23-302, 20590; (202) 366-1031. Fax, (202) 366-8215. Capt. Douglas M. Harrington, Deputy Associate Administrator for Federal Sealift. Federal Sealift, (202) 366-1875.*

Web, www.maritime.dot.gov/ports/strong-ports/ emergency-and-preparedness-response

Plans for the transition of merchant shipping from peacetime to wartime operations under the direction of the National Shipping Authority. Participates in interagency planning and policy development for maritime security-related directives. Coordinates port personnel and the military for deployments through the commercial strategic seaports. Represents the United States at the NATO Planning Board for Ocean Shipping. (The National Shipping Authority is a stand-by organization that is activated upon the declaration of a war or other national emergency.)

Maritime Administration (MARAD) *(Transportation Dept.), Ship Operations, West Bldg., 1200 New Jersey Ave. S.E., MAR-610, MS 2, W25-336, 20590; (202) 366-1875. Kevin M. Tokarski, Associate Administrator for Strategic Sealift.*

Web, www.maritime.dot.gov/strategic-sealift/office-ship-operations/office-ship-operations

Maintains the National Defense Reserve Fleet, a fleet of older vessels traded in by U.S. flag operators that are called into operation during emergencies; manages and administers the National Defense Reserve Fleet, a fleet of ships available for operation within four to 20 days, to meet the nation's sealift readiness requirements.

Maritime Administration (MARAD) *(Transportation Dept.), Strategic Sealift, West Bldg., 1200 New Jersey Ave. S.E., Mar-600, MS 1, W25-330, 20590; (202) 366-5400. (202) 366-1875. Fax, (202) 366-5904. Kevin M. Tokarski, Associate Administrator.*

Web, www.maritime.dot.gov/national-security/strategic-sealift/strategic-sealift

Administers strategic sealift programs for the Maritime Administration and ensures that merchant shipping is available in times of war or national emergency.

National Oceanic and Atmospheric Administration (NOAA) *(Commerce Dept.), National Ocean Service (NOS), Coast Survey, Silver Spring Metro Center 3, 1315 East-West Hwy., #6147, Silver Spring, MD 20910-3282; (301) 713-2770. Fax, (301) 713-4019. Rear Adm. Ben Evans, Director. Toll-free, (888) 990-6622.*

Web, www.nauticalcharts.noaa.gov and Twitter, @NOAAcharts

Directs programs and conducts research to support fundamental scientific and engineering activities and resource development for safe navigation of the nation's waterways and territorial seas. Prints on demand and distributes nautical charts.

National Transportation Safety Board (NTSB), *Marine Safety,* *490 L'Enfant Plaza East S.W., #6300, 20594-0001; (202) 314-6000. Morgan Turrell, Director.*
Web, www.ntsb.gov/about/organization/MS/Pages/office_ms.aspx

Investigates selected marine transportation accidents, including major marine accidents on or under navigable waters, internal waters, and territorial sea of the United States and U.S. flagged vessels worldwide, as well as any accidents that involve U.S. Coast Guard operations or functions. Determines the facts upon which the board establishes probable cause; makes recommendations on matters pertaining to marine transportation safety and accident prevention.

Occupational Safety and Health Administration (OSHA) *(Labor Dept.), Maritime Enforcement, 200 Constitution Ave. N.W., #N3610, 20210-0001; (202) 693-2399. Fax, (202) 693-2369. Eric Kampert, Director, ext. 32130.*
Web, www.osha.gov/contactus/byoffice/ome

Administers occupational safety and health enforcement program for the maritime industries. Provides comprehensive program guidelines, policies, procedures, technical assistance, and information dissemination.

U.S. Coast Guard (USCG) *(Homeland Security Dept.), Auxiliary and Boating Safety, 2703 Martin Luther King Jr. Ave. S.E., MS 7509, 20593; (202) 372-1507. (202) 372-1062. Commodore Alex Malewski, Commodore; Jeff Decker, Regulations Manager.*
General email, CGAUX@uscg.mil
Web, www.uscg.mil/Our-Organization/Auxiliary and www.uscgboating.org

Tracks and analyzes boating accidents; writes and enforces safety regulations for recreational boats and associated equipment; sets boater education standards; coordinates public awareness and information programs; awards grants to states and nongovernmental organizations to improve safety.

U.S. Coast Guard (USCG) *(Homeland Security Dept.), Deputy for Operations Policy and Capabilities, 2703 Martin Luther King Jr. Ave. S.E., MS 7318, 20593-7318; (202) 372-2000. Rear Adm. Pat DeQuattro, Deputy.*
Web, www.dco.uscg.mil/Our-Organization/Deputy-for-Operations-Policy-and-Capabilities-DCO-D

Establishes and enforces regulations for port safety; environmental protection; vessel safety, inspection, design, documentation, and investigation; licensing of merchant vessel personnel; and shipment of hazardous materials.

U.S. Coast Guard (USCG) *(Homeland Security Dept.), Design and Engineering Standards (CG-ENG), 2703 Martin Luther King Jr. Ave. S.E., MS 7509, 20593-7509; (202) 372-1352. Capt. Benjamin Hawkins, Chief.*
Web, www.dco.uscg.mil/CG-ENG

Develops standards; responsible for general vessel arrangements, naval architecture, vessel design and construction, and transport of bulk dangerous cargoes. Supports national advisory committees and national professional organizations to achieve industry standards.

U.S. Coast Guard (USCG) *(Homeland Security Dept.), Investigations and Casualty Analysis, 2702 Martin Luther King Jr. Ave. S.E., MS 7501, 20593-7501; (202) 372-1029. Capt. Jason Neubauer, Chief.*
Web, www.dco.uscg.mil/Our-Organization/Assistant-Commandant-for-Prevention-Policy-CG-5P/Inspections-Compliance-CG-5PC-/cginv

Handles disciplinary proceedings for merchant marine personnel. Compiles and analyzes records of accidents involving commercial vessels that result in loss of life, serious injury, or substantial damage. Focuses on marine safety and environmental protection through marine inspection activities, including investigation of spills and drug and alcohol testing.

U.S. Coast Guard (USCG) *(Homeland Security Dept.), Marine Safety Center, 2703 Martin Luther King Jr. Ave. S.E., MS 7430, 20593; (202) 795-6729. Capt. Robert C. Compher, Commanding Officer.*
General email, msc@uscg.mil
Web, www.uscg.mil/hq/msc

Reviews and approves commercial vessel plans and specifications to ensure technical compliance with federal safety and pollution abatement standards.

▶ **NONGOVERNMENTAL**

Cruise Lines International Assn., *1201 F St. N.W., #250, 20004; (202) 759-9370. Fax, (202) 759-9344. Kelly Craighead, President.*
General email, info@cruising.org
Web, www.cruising.org, Twitter, @CLIAGlobal, Facebook, www.facebook.com/CLIAGlobal and YouTube, www.youtube.com/cliaglobal

Membership: more than 50 cruise lines as well as other cruise industry professionals. Advises domestic and international regulatory organizations on shipping policy. Works with U.S. and international agencies to promote safety, public health, security, medical facilities, environmental awareness, and passenger protection. Monitors legislation and regulations.

National Maritime Safety Assn., *1420 New York Ave. N.W., 22102; 571-4000-1835. Lauren Brand, Executive Director.*
General email, mto@nmsa.us
Web, www.nmsa.us

Represents the marine cargo handling industry in safety and health matters arising under various statutes, including the Occupational Safety and Health Act. Serves as a clearinghouse on information to help reduce injuries and illnesses in the marine cargo handling workplace. Monitors legislation and regulations.

Ports and Waterways

▶ **AGENCIES**

Army Corps of Engineers *(Defense Dept.), Civil Works, 441 G St. N.W., 20314-1000; (202) 761-0011.*

Alvin (Al) Lee, Director; Maj.
Gen. William H. (Butch) Graham, Deputy Commanding
General for Civil and Emergency Operations.
Web, www.usace.army.mil/Missions/Civil-Works and
General email, hq-publicaffairs@usace.army.mil

Coordinates field offices that oversee harbors, dams, levees, waterways, locks, reservoirs, and other construction projects designed to facilitate transportation, flood control, and environmental restoration projects. Major projects include the Mississippi, Missouri, and Ohio Rivers; Bay Delta in California; the Great Lakes; the Chesapeake Bay; the Everglades in Florida; and the Gulf of Mexico.

Federal Maritime Commission (FMC), *Agreements, 800*
N. Capitol St. N.W., #940, 20573-0001; (202) 523-5793.
Jason Guthrie, Director.
General email, tradeanalysis@fmc.gov

Web, www.fmc.gov/about-the-tmc/bureaus-offices/
agreements

Analyzes agreements between terminal operators and shipping companies for docking facilities and agreements among ocean common carriers.

Maritime Administration (MARAD) *(Transportation*
Dept.), Port Infrastructure Development, West Bldg.,
1200 New Jersey Ave. S.E., MAR-510, W21-308, 20590;
(202) 366-5076. Fax, (202) 366-6988. Robert Bouchard,
Director.
Web, www.maritime.dot.gov/ports/office-port-infrastructure-
development/office-port-infrastructure-development

Provides coordination and management of port infrastructure projects; provides leadership in national congestion mitigation efforts that involve waterway and port issues; promotes the development and improved utilization of ports and port facilities, including intermodal connections, terminals, and distribution networks; and provides technical information and advice to other agencies and organizations concerned with intermodal development. Information and advice include the analysis of intermodal economics, the development of applicable information systems, investigation of institutional and regulatory impediments, and the application of appropriate transportation management systems.

Saint Lawrence Seaway Development Corp.
(Transportation Dept.), 1200 New Jersey Ave. S.E., #E311,
20590; (202) 366-0091. Fax, (202) 366-7147.
Craig H. Middlebrook, Deputy Administrator.
Toll-free, (800) 785-2779.
General email, gls@dot.gov

Web, www.seaway.dot.gov and Twitter, @seawayusdot

Operates and maintains the Saint Lawrence Seaway within U.S. territorial limits; conducts development programs and coordinates activities with its Canadian counterpart.

Tennessee Valley Authority, *Government Affairs, 1*
Massachusetts Ave. N.W., #300, 20444; (202) 898-2999.
Jeffrey J. (Jeff) Lyash, President.
General email, tvainfo@tva.gov

Web, www.tva.gov, Twitter, @TVAnews and Facebook,
www.facebook.com/TVA

Coordinates resource conservation, development, and land-use programs in the Tennessee River Valley. Operates the river control system; projects include flood control, navigation development, and multiple-use reservoirs.

U.S. Coast Guard (USCG) *(Homeland Security Dept.), 2703*
Martin Luther King Jr. Ave. S.E., MS 7000, 20593-7000;
(202) 372-4000. Fax, (202) 372-8302. Adm. Karl L. Schultz,
Commandant. Public Affairs, (202) 372-4600.
Web, www.uscg.mil, Twitter, @USCG, Facebook, www
.facebook.com/UScoastguard and YouTube, www.youtube
.com/USCGImagery

Enforces rules and regulations governing the safety and security of ports and anchorages and the movement of vessels in U.S. waters. Supervises cargo transfer operations, storage, and stowage; conducts harbor patrols and waterfront facility inspections; establishes security zones and monitors vessel movement.

▶ NONGOVERNMENTAL

American Assn. of Port Authorities (AAPA), *1201*
Maryland Ave. S.W., 20024; (703) 684-5700. Fax, (703)
684-6321. Chris Connor, President.
General email, info@aapa-ports.org

Web, www.aapa-ports.org, Twitter, @AAPA_Seaports and
Facebook, www.facebook.com/seaportsdeliverprosperity

Membership: public port authorities, maritime industry partners, and service providers in the Western Hemisphere. Provides technical and economic information on port finance, environmental issues, construction, operation, and security.

American Waterways Operators, *801 N. Quincy St., #500,*
Arlington, VA 22203-1708; (703) 841-9300. Fax, (703)
841-0389. Jennifer A. Carpenter, President.
Web, www.americanwaterways.com and Twitter,
@AWOadvocacy

Membership: operators of barges, tugboats, and towboats on navigable coastal and inland waterways. Acts as liaison with Congress, the U.S. Coast Guard, the Army Corps of Engineers, and other federal agencies. Establishes safety standards and conducts training for efficient, environmentally responsible transportation. Monitors legislation and regulations.

International Longshore and Warehouse Union (ILWU),
Washington Office, 1025 Connecticut Ave. N.W., #507,
20036; (202) 463-6265. Fax, (202) 467-4875. Vacant,
Legislative Director.
General email, washdc@ilwu.org

Web, www.ilwu.org

Membership: longshore and warehouse personnel. Helps members negotiate pay, benefits, and better working conditions; conducts training programs and workshops. Monitors legislation and regulations. (Headquarters in San Francisco, Calif.)

International Longshoremen's Assn., *Washington Office,*
1101 17th St. N.W., #400, 20036-4704; (202) 955-6304.
Fax, (202) 955-6048. John Bowers Jr., Political Director.

General email, iladc@aol.com

Web, www.ilaunion.org

Membership: approximately 65,000 longshore personnel. Helps members negotiate pay, benefits, and better working conditions; conducts training programs and workshops. Monitors legislation and regulations. (Headquarters in New Jersey; affiliated with the AFL-CIO.)

National Academies of Sciences, Engineering, and Medicine (NASEM), *Marine Board, Keck Center, 500 5th St. N.W., 20001; (202) 334-2167. Martha Grabowski, Chair.*

General email, sbrotemarkle@nas.edu

Web, www.trb.org/MarineBoard/MarineBoard.aspx

Supports research and provides information relating to new technologies, laws and regulations, economics, the environment, and other issues affecting the marine transportation system, port operations, coastal engineering, and marine governance.

National Assn. of Waterfront Employers, *211 N. Union St., #124, Alexandria, VA 22314; (571) 400-1835. Lauren K. Brand, President.*

General email, Vrodrigues@nawe.us

Web, www.nawe.us and Twitter, @NAWE_US

Membership: private sector stevedore companies and marine terminal operators, their subsidiaries, and other waterfront-related employers. Legislative interests include trade, shipping, antitrust issues, insurance, port security, and user-fee issues. Monitors legislation and regulations.

National Waterways Conference, *1100 N. Glebe Rd., #1010, Arlington, VA 22201; (703) 224-8007. Fax, (866) 371-1390. Julie Ufner, President.*

Web, www.waterways.org

Membership: petroleum, coal, chemical, electric power, building materials, iron and steel, and grain companies; port authorities; water carriers; and others interested or involved in waterways. Sponsors educational programs on waterways. Monitors legislation and regulations.

Passenger Vessel Assn., *103 Oronoco St., #200, Alexandria, VA 22314; (703) 518-5005. Fax, (703) 518-5151. John R. Groundwater, Executive Director, ext. 22; Edmund Welch, Legislative Director, ext. 27.*

General email, pvainfo@passengervessel.com

Web, www.passengervessel.com and Facebook, www.facebook.com/PassengerVesselAssociation

Membership: owners, operators, and suppliers for U.S. and Canadian passenger vessels and international vessel companies. Interests include insurance, safety and security, and U.S. congressional impact on dinner and excursion boats, car and passenger ferries, overnight cruise ships, and riverboat casinos. Monitors legislation and regulations.

Transportation Institute, *5201 Capital Gateway Dr., Camp Springs, MD 20746-4211; James L. Henry, President. Phone, in Maryland, (301) 423-3335. Phone, in DC, (202) 347-2590.*

General email, info@trans-inst.org

Web, https://transportationinstitute.org, Twitter, @Trans_Inst and Facebook, www.facebook.com/transportation.institute

Membership: U.S.-flag maritime shipping companies. Conducts research on freight regulation and rates, government subsidies and assistance, domestic and international maritime matters, maritime safety, ports, Saint Lawrence Seaway, shipbuilding, and regulation of shipping.

Waterways Council, Inc., *499 S. Capitol St. S.W., #401, 20003; (202) 765-2166. Fax, (202) 765-2167. Debra Calhoun, Senior Vice President, (202) 765-2153.*

Web, www.waterwayscouncil.org, Twitter, @WaterwaysCouncil and Press, dcalhoun@waterwayscouncil.org

Membership: port authorities, waterways carriers, shippers, shipping associations, and waterways advocacy groups. Acts as advocate for a modern and well-maintained system of inland waterways and port infrastructure. Monitors legislation and regulations.

MOTOR VEHICLES

General

▶AGENCIES

Federal Motor Carrier Safety Administration *(Transportation Dept.), Bus and Truck Standards and Operations, 1200 New Jersey Ave. S.E., #N64-330, 20590; (202) 366-5370. Chuck Horan, Director.*

General email, FMCSA-Host@dot.gov

Web, www.fmcsa.dot.gov/safety/data-and-statistics/commercial-motor-vehicle-facts

Regulates motor vehicle size and weight on federally aided highways; conducts studies on issues relating to motor carrier transportation; promotes uniformity in state and federal motor carrier laws and regulations.

▶CONGRESS

For a listing of relevant congressional committees and subcommittees, please see page 762 or the Appendix.

▶NONGOVERNMENTAL

American Assn. of Motor Vehicle Administrators (AAMVA), *4401 Wilson Blvd., #700, Arlington, VA 22203-1753; (703) 522-4200. Anne S. Ferro, President. Press, (703) 908-2955.*

General email, inquiries@aamva.org

Web, www.aamva.org, Twitter, @AAMVAConnection and Facebook, www.facebook.com/AAMVA

Membership: officials responsible for administering and enforcing motor vehicle and traffic laws in the United States and Canada. Promotes uniform laws and regulations for vehicle registration, driver's licenses, and motor carrier services.

American Automobile Assn. (AAA), *Public and Government Affairs,* *1405 G. St. N.W., 20005; (410) 616-1938. Fax, (202) 393-5423. Ragina Ali, Manager of Public Affairs, (443) 465-5020.*
Web, www.aaa.com/public-affairs, Twitter, @AAADCNews and Facebook, www.facebook.com/ AAAMidAtlanticNews

Membership: state and local automobile associations. Conducts public outreach and offers publications through the AAA Foundation for Traffic Safety. Interests include all aspects of highway transportation, travel and tourism, safety, drunk driving, and legislation that affects motorists. Monitors legislation and regulations.

American Bus Assn., *111 K St. N.E., 9th Floor, 20002; (202) 842-1645. Fax, (202) 842-0850. Peter J. Pantuso, President, (202) 218-7229. Press, (202) 218-7220. Toll-free, (800) 283-2877.*
General email, abainfo@buses.org
Web, www.buses.org, Twitter, @AmericanBusAssn and Facebook, www.facebook.com/AmericanBusAssociation

Membership: privately owned intercity bus companies, state associations, travel/tourism businesses, bus manufacturers, and those interested in the bus industry. Monitors legislation and regulations.

American Trucking Assns., *950 N. Glebe Rd., #210, Arlington, VA 22203-4181 (mailing address: Washington Office, 430 1st St. S.E., #100, Washington, DC 20003); (703) 838-1700. Fax, (703) 838-1936. Chris Spear, President. Legislative Affairs, (202) 544-6245. Press, (703) 838-1873.*
General email, media@trucking.org
Web, www.trucking.org and Twitter, @TRUCKINGdotORG

Membership: state trucking associations, individual trucking and motor carrier organizations, and related supply companies. Maintains departments on industrial relations, law, management systems, research, safety, traffic, state laws, taxation, communications, legislation, economics, and engineering.

Highway Loss Data Institute, *4121 Wilson Blvd., 6th Floor, Arlington, VA 22203; (703) 247-1500. David Harkey, President.*
Web, www.iihs.org and Twitter, @IIHS_autosafety

Research organization that gathers, processes, and publishes data on the ways in which insurance losses vary among different kinds of vehicles. (Affiliated with Insurance Institute for Highway Safety.)

International Parking and Mobility Institute (IPMI), *1330 Braddock Pl., #350, Alexandria, VA 22314 (mailing address: P.O. Box, 3787 Fredericksburg, VA 22402); (571) 699-3011. Fax, (703) 566-2267. Shawn D. Conrad, Chief Executive Officer. Toll free, (866) 476-4669.*
General email, info@parking-mobility.org
Web, www.parking-mobility.org

Membership: owners, operators, designers, and builders of parking lots and structures; city managers, government agencies, healthcare centers, universities, airports, convention centers. Provides leadership to professionals in the parking, transportation, and mobility industries. Supports the industry and membership through professional development programs, research and data collection, advocacy, and outreach.

Motorcycle Industry Council, *Government Relations, 1235 S. Clark St., #600, Arlington, VA 22202; (703) 416-0444. Fax, (703) 416-2269. Scott Schloegel, Senior Vice President, ext. 3202.*
Web, www.mic.org

Membership: manufacturers and distributors of motorcycles, mopeds, and related parts, accessories, and equipment. Monitors legislation and regulations. (Headquarters in Irvine, Calif.)

Motorcycle Riders Foundation, *2221 S. Clark St., Arlington, VA 22202 (mailing address: P.O. Box 250 Highland, IL 62249); (202) 546-0983. Mark Buckner, Executive Director.*
General email, mrfoffice@mrf.org
Web, www.mrf.org and Facebook, www.facebook.com/ bikers.rights/timeline

Membership: lobby and advocacy group that supports motorcyclist rights. Sponsors seminars for activists. Interests include motorcycle safety, training, and licensing. Monitors legislation and regulations.

National Institute for Automotive Service Excellence, *1503 Edwards Ferry Rd. N.E., #401, Leesburg, VA 20176; (703) 669-6600. Fax, (703) 669-6122. Marke Polke, President. Toll-free, (800) 390-6789.*
General email, contactus@ase.com
Web, www.ase.com, Twitter, @ASEtests and Facebook, www.facebook.com/ASEtests

Administers program for testing and certifying automotive technicians; researches methods for improving technician training.

National Motor Freight Traffic Assn., *1001 N. Fairfax St., #600, Alexandria, VA 22314-1798; (703) 838-1810. Fax, (703) 683-6296. Paul Dugent, Executive Director. Toll-free, (866) 411-6632.*
General email, customerservice@nmfta.org
Web, www.nmfta.org

Membership: motor carriers of general goods in interstate and intrastate commerce. Publishes *National Motor Freight Classification.*

National Parking Assn., *1112 16th St. N.W., #840, 20036-4880; (202) 296-4336. Fax, (202) 296-3102. Christine Banning, President, (202) 470-6299. Toll-free, (800) 647-7275.*
General email, info@weareparking.org
Web, www.weareparking.org and Twitter, @weareparking

Membership: parking garage operators, parking consultants, universities, municipalities, medical centers, and vendors. Offers information and research services; sponsors seminars and educational programs on garage design and equipment. Monitors legislation and regulations.

National Private Truck Council, *950 N. Glebe Rd., #530, Arlington, VA 22203-4183; (703) 683-1300. Gary F. Petty, President, (703) 838-8876.*
General email, info@nptc.org
Web, www.nptc.org and Twitter, @NPTC1939

Membership: manufacturers, retailers, distributors, wholesalers, and suppliers that operate their own private truck fleets in conjunction with their nontransportation businesses. Interests include standards, best practices, benchmarking, federal regulatory compliance, peer-to-peer networking, and business economics. Supports economic deregulation of the trucking industry and uniformity in state taxation of the industry. NPTC Institute supports continuing education and certification programs.

National Tank Truck Carriers (NTTC), *950 N. Glebe Rd., #520, Arlington, VA 22203-4183; (703) 838-1960. Ryan Streblow, Chief Executive Officer.*
Web, www.tanktruck.org and General email, info@tanktruck.org

Focuses on issues of the tank truck industry and represents the industry before Congress and federal agencies.

NATSO, Inc., *1300 Braddock Pl., #501, Alexandria, VA 22314; (703) 549-2100. Lisa J. Mullings, President.*
General email, editor@natso.com
Web, www.natso.com, Twitter, @NATSO_Inc and Facebook, www.facebook.com/NATSOInc

Membership: travel plaza and truck stop operators and suppliers to the truck stop industry. Provides credit information and educational training programs. Monitors legislation and regulations. Operates the NATSO Foundation, which promotes highway safety.

NGVAmerica (Natural Gas Vehicles for America), *400 N. Capitol St. N.W., #450, 20001; (202) 824-7360. Daniel Gage, President.*
General email, pkerkhoven@ngvamerica.org
Web, www.ngvamerica.org, Twitter, @NGVamerican, Facebook, www.facebook.com/NGVAmerica and YouTube, www.youtube.com/user/NGVAmerica

Membership: natural gas distributors and producers; automobile and engine manufacturers; natural gas vehicle product and service suppliers; research and development organizations; environmental groups; and state and local government agencies. Advocates installation of natural gas and biomethane fuel stations and development of industry standards. Helps market new products and equipment related to compressed natural gas (CNG), liquefied natural gas (LNG), and biomethane-powered vehicles.

Truckload Carriers Assn., *555 E. Braddock Rd., Alexandria, VA 22314; (703) 838-1950. Fax, (202) 217-3877. John Lyboldt, President.*

General email, tca@truckload.org
Web, www.truckload.org, Twitter, @TCANews and Facebook, www.facebook.com/TruckloadCarriers Association

Membership: truckload carriers and industry suppliers. Provides information and educational programs to members. Represents intercity common and contract trucking companies before Congress, federal agencies, courts, and the media.

Union of Concerned Scientists, *Clean Transportation Program, 1825 K St. N.W., 20006-1232; (202) 223-6133. Michelle Robinson, Director.*
General email, ucs@ucsusa.org
Web, www.ucsusa.org/transportation, Twitter, @ucsusa, Facebook, www.facebook.com/unionofconcernedscientists and YouTube, www.youtube.com/user/ConcernedScientists

Develops and promotes strategies to reduce U.S. consumption of oil, including increasing fuel efficiency of cars and trucks, as well as promoting advanced vehicle technology, including battery-electric, hybrid-electric, and fuel-cell vehicles, and next-generation biofuels. (Headquarters in Cambridge, Mass.)

Highways

▶ **AGENCIES**

Federal Highway Administration (FHWA)
(Transportation Dept.), 1200 New Jersey Ave. S.E., #E87-314, 20590-0001; (202) 366-2240. Stephanie Pollack, Administrator (Acting); Thomas D. Everett, Executive Director, (202) 366-2242. Press and Public Affairs, (202) 366-6046.
Web, www.fhwa.dot.gov, Twitter, @USDOTFHWA and Facebook, www.facebook.com/FederalHighwayAdmin

Administers federal-aid highway programs with money from the Highway Trust Fund; works to improve highway and motor vehicle safety; coordinates research and development programs on highway and traffic safety, construction costs, and the environmental impact of highway transportation; administers regional and territorial highway building programs and the highway beautification program.

Federal Highway Administration (FHWA)
(Transportation Dept.), Infrastructure, 1200 New Jersey Ave. S.E., #E75-312, 20590; (202) 366-0371. Fax, (202) 493-0099. Hari Kalla, Associate Administrator, (202) 366-0370.
Web, www.fhwa.dot.gov/infrastructure

Provides guidance and oversight for planning, design, construction, and maintenance operations relating to federal aid, direct federal construction, and other highway programs; establishes design guidelines and specifications for highways built with federal funds.

Federal Highway Administration (FHWA)
(Transportation Dept.), National Highway Institute, 2600 Park Tower Dr., #500, Merrifield, VA 22180; (703) 235-0500. Fax, (703) 235-0593. Michael Davies, Director. Toll-free, (877) 558-6873.

General email, NHICustomerService@dot.gov

Web, www.nhi.fhwa.dot.gov, Twitter, @USDOTFHWA and Facebook, www.facebook.com/FederalHighwayAdmin

Develops and administers, in cooperation with state highway departments, technical training programs for agency, state, and local highway department employees.

Federal Highway Administration (FHWA)

(Transportation Dept.), Operations, 1200 New Jersey Ave. S.E., #E86-205, 20590-0001; (202) 366-9210. Fax, (202) 366-3225. Martin Knopp, Associate Administrator, (202) 366-9210. Press, (202) 366-4650.
Web, www.ops.fhwa.dot.gov

Fosters the efficient management and operation of the highway system. Responsible for congestion management, pricing, ITS deployment, traffic operations, emergency management, and freight management. Includes offices of Transportation Management, Freight Management and Operations, and Transportation Operations.

Federal Highway Administration (FHWA)

(Transportation Dept.), Planning, Environment, and Realty, 1200 New Jersey Ave. S.E., #E76-306, 20590; (202) 366-0116. Fax, (202) 366-3713. Gloria M. Shepherd, Associate Administrator, (202) 366-0581.
Web, www.fhwa.dot.gov/real_estate

Works with developers and municipalities to ensure conformity with the National Environmental Policy Act (NEPA) project development process.

Federal Highway Administration (FHWA)

(Transportation Dept.), Policy and Governmental Affairs, 1200 New Jersey Ave. S.E., 8th Floor, 20590-0001; (202) 366-5085. Fax, (202) 366-3590.
Randall Keith Benjamin, Associate Administrator.
Web, www.fhwa.dot.gov/policy

Develops policy and administers the Federal Highway Administration's international programs. Conducts policy studies and analyzes legislation; makes recommendations; compiles and reviews highway-related data. Represents the administration at international conferences; administers foreign-assistance programs.

Federal Highway Administration (FHWA) (Transportation Dept.), Research, Development, and Technology, 6300 Georgetown Pike, #T306, McLean, VA 22101-2296; (202) 493-3999. Fax, (202) 493-3170. Kelly Regal, Associate Administrator. Library, (202) 493-3058.

General email, TFHRC.webmaster@dot.gov

Web, www.fhwa.dot.gov/research and Library, fhwalibrary@dot.gov

Conducts highway research and development programs; studies safety, location, design, construction, operation, and maintenance of highways; cooperates with state and local highway departments in utilizing results of research. Library access via public library exchange.

U.S. Coast Guard (USCG) (Homeland Security Dept.), 2703 Martin Luther King Jr. Ave. S.E., MS 7000, 20593-7000; (202) 372-4000. Fax, (202) 372-8302. Adm. Karl L. Schultz, Commandant. Public Affairs, (202) 372-4600.

Web, www.uscg.mil, Twitter, @USCG, Facebook, www.facebook.com/UScoastguard and YouTube, www.youtube.com/USCGImagery

Regulates the construction, maintenance, and operation of bridges across U.S. navigable waters.

▶NONGOVERNMENTAL

American Assn. of State Highway and Transportation Officials (AASHTO), 555 12th St. N.W., #1000, 20004; (202) 624-5800. Fax, (202) 624-5806. Jim Tymon, Executive Director, (202) 624-5811.

General email, info@aashto.org

Web, www.transportation.org, Twitter, @aashtospeaks and Facebook, www.facebook.com/AASHTOspeaks

Membership: the highway and transportation departments of the 50 states, the District of Columbia, Puerto Rico, and affiliated agencies, including the U.S. Dept. of Transportation as a nonvoting ex officio member. Maintains committees on all modes of transportation and departmental affairs. Offers technology assistance, web seminars, and publications.

American Highway Users Alliance, 1920 L St. N.W., #525, 20036; (202) 857-1200. Fax, (202) 857-1220. Laura C. Perrotta, Chief Executive Officer.

General email, info@highways.org

Web, www.highways.org, Twitter, @highwayusers and Facebook, www.facebook.com/highwayusers

Membership: companies and associations representing major industry and highway user groups. Develops information, analyzes public policy, and advocates legislation to improve roadway safety and efficiency and to increase the mobility of the American public. (Affiliated with the Roadway Safety Foundation.)

American Road and Transportation Builders Assn. (ARTBA), 250 E St. S.W., #900, 20024; (202) 289-4434. Fax, (202) 289-4435. David (Dave) Bauer, President.

Web, www.artba.org, Twitter, @ARTBA and Facebook, www.facebook.com/ARTBAssociation

Membership: highway and transportation contractors; federal, state, and local engineers and officials; construction equipment manufacturers and distributors; and others interested in the transportation construction industry. Serves as liaison with government; provides information on highway engineering and construction developments.

Assn. for Safe International Road Travel (ASIRT), 11769 Gainsborough Rd., Potomac, MD 20854; (240) 249-0100. Fax, (301) 329-8487. Cathy Silberman, Executive Director.

General email, asirt@asirt.org

Web, www.asirt.org, Facebook, www.facebook.com/ASIRT.org and Twitter, @saferoadtravel

Promotes road safety through education and advocacy with governments in the United States and abroad. Serves as information resource for governments, study abroad programs, travel organizations, nongovernmental organizations, and individual travelers.

Intelligent Transportation Society of America, *1100 New Jersey Ave. S.E., #850, 20003; (202) 484-4847. Laura Chace, President.*
General email, info@itsa.org
Web, www.itsa.org and Twitter, @ITS_America

Advocates application of electronic, computer, and communications technology to make surface transportation more efficient and to improve safety, security, and environmental sustainability. Coordinates research, development, and implementation of intelligent transportation systems by government, academia, and industry.

International Bridge, Tunnel, and Turnpike Assn., *2021 L St. N.W., #100, 20036-3725; (202) 659-4620. Fax, (202) 659-0500. Patrick D. Jones, Executive Director, ext. 21.*
General email, ibtta@ibtta.org
Web, www.ibtta.org, Twitter, @IBTTA, Facebook, www .facebook.com/IBTTA and YouTube, www.youtube.com/ user/IBTTA

Membership: public and private operators of toll facilities and associated industries. Conducts research; compiles statistics.

International Road Federation (IRF), *Madison Place, 500 Montgomery St., 5th Floor, Alexandria, VA 22314; (703) 535-1001. Fax, (703) 535-1007. C. Patrick Sankey, President.*
General email, info@IRF.global
Web, www.irf.global, Twitter, @IRFhq and Facebook, www.facebook.com/IRFhq

Membership: contractors, consultants, equipment manufacturers, researchers, and others involved in the road building industry. Administers fellowship program that allows foreign engineering students to study at U.S. graduate schools. Maintains interest in roads and highways worldwide.

The Road Information Program (TRIP), *1101 Connecticut Ave. N.W., #450, 20036; (202) 466-6706. David Kearby, Executive Director.*
Web, https://tripnet.org, Twitter, @TRIP_Inc, Facebook, www.facebook.com/TRIPtransportationresearch and YouTube, www.youtube.com/user/1971trip

Organization of transportation specialists; conducts research on economic and technical transportation issues; promotes consumer awareness of the condition of the national road and bridge system.

Manufacturing and Sales

▶**AGENCIES**

Energy Efficiency and Renewable Energy (EERE) *(Energy Dept.), Vehicle Technologies (VTO), 1000 Independence Ave. S.W., #5G030, 20585; (202) 586-8055. Fax, (202) 586-7409. David Howell, Deputy Director.*
Web, www.energy.gov/eere/vehicles/vehicle-technologies-office

Works with the motor vehicle industry to develop technologies for improved vehicle fuel efficiency and cleaner fuels.

International Trade Administration (ITA) *(Commerce Dept.), Industry and Analysis (I&A), Manufacturing (OM), Transportation and Machinery (OTM), 1401 Constitution Ave. N.W., Room 22021, 20230-0001; (202) 482-1474. Fax, (202) 482-0674. Scott Kennedy, Director.*
Web, http://legacy.trade.gov/about-us/office-transportation-and-machinery

Promotes the export of U.S. aerospace, automotive, and machinery products; compiles and analyzes industry data; seeks to secure a favorable position for the U.S. aerospace, auto, and machinery industries in global markets through policy and trade agreements.

▶**NONGOVERNMENTAL**

Alliance for Automotive Innovation, *1050 K St. N.W., #650, 20001; (202) 326-5500. John Bozzella, President.*
General email, info@autosinnovate.org
Web, www.autosinnovate.org, Twitter, @auto_alliance and Facebook, www.facebook.com/autosinnovate

Trade association of major automakers. Provides advocacy on automotive issues focusing primarily on environment, energy, and safety. Seeks to harmonize global automotive standards. (Auto Alliance merged with Global Automakers.)

Alliance for Automotive Innovation, *1050 K St. N.W., #650, 20001; (202) 326-5500. John Bozzella, President; Jared Eichhorn, Director of Federal Affairs.*
General email, info@autosinnovate.org
Web, www.autosinnovate.org, Twitter, @autosinnovate, Facebook, www.facebook.com/autosinnovate and YouTube, www.youtube.com/channel/ UCeI7h7s1ZUVzFodhbDBo9Pw

Membership: automobile and light truck manufacturers, original equipment suppliers, technology and other automotive-related companies, and trade associations. Monitors legislation and regulations.

American Automotive Leasing Assn., *600 Pennsylvania Ave. S.E., 20003 (mailing address: 600 Pennsylvania Ave. S.E., Box 15303, Washington, DC 20003); (202) 531-1398. Mike Joyce, Executive Director.*
Web, http://aalafleet.com

Membership: automotive commercial fleet leasing and management companies. Monitors legislation and regulations.

American International Automobile Dealers Assn., *500 Montgomery St., #800, Alexandria, VA 22314; (703) 519-7800. Fax, (703) 519-7810. Cody Lusk, President, ext. 1. Toll-free, (800) 462-4232.*
General email, goaiada@aiada.org
Web, www.aiada.org, Twitter, @AIADA_News, Facebook, www.facebook.com/AIADA.News, President's Twitter, @AIADA_Prez and YouTube, www.youtube.com/user/ aiadaorg2011

Promotes a favorable market for international nameplate automobiles in the United States through education of policymakers and the general public. Monitors legislation and regulations concerning tariffs, quotas, taxes, fuel economy, and clean air initiatives.

Auto Care Assn., *7101 Wisconsin Ave., #1300, Bethesda, MD 20814-3415; (301) 654-6664. Bill Hanvey, President. General email, info@autocare.org*

Web, (240) 333-1077, Twitter, @AutoCareOrg and Facebook, www.facebook.com/autocareorg

Membership: domestic and international manufacturers, manufacturers' representatives, retailers, and distributors in the automotive aftermarket industry, which involves service of a vehicle after it leaves the dealership. Offers educational programs, conducts research, and provides members with technical and international trade services; acts as liaison with government; sponsors annual marketing conference and trade shows. (Formerly Automotive Aftermarket Industry Assn.)

Automotive Parts Remanufacturers Assn., *1602 Belle View Blvd., #3097, Alexandria, VA 22307; (703) 968-2772. Joe Kripli, President. General email, info@apra.org*

Web, www.apra.org, Twitter, @buyreman and Facebook, www.facebook.com/apra

Membership: rebuilders and remanufacturers of automotive parts. Conducts educational programs on transmission, brake, clutch, water pump, air conditioning, electrical parts, heavy-duty brake, and carburetor rebuilding.

Automotive Recyclers Assn. (ARA), *9113 Church St., Manassas, VA 20110-5456; (571) 208-0428. Sandy Blalock, Executive Director, ext. 3. General email, staff@a-r-a.org*

Web, www.a-r-a.org, Twitter, @Automotiverecyclersassociation and Facebook, www.facebook.com/Automotiverecyclersassociation

Membership: retail and wholesale firms involved in the dismantling and sale of used motor vehicle parts. Works to increase the efficiency of businesses in the automotive recycling industry. Cooperates with public and private agencies to encourage further automotive recycling efforts.

Autos Drive America, *801 Pennsylvania Ave. N.W., #620, 20004; (202) 650-5555. Jennifer Safavian, President. General email, info@autosdriveamerica.org*

Web, www.autosdriveamerica.org, Twitter, @AutosDrvAmerica and Facebook, www.facebook.com/AutosDriveAmerica

Membership: international automakers with U.S. operations. Monitors legislation and regulations.

Coalition for Auto Repair Equality, *105 Oronoco St., #115, Alexandria, VA 22314-2015; (703) 519-7555. Fax, (703) 519-7747. Sandy Bass-Cors, Executive Director. Toll-free, (800) 229-5380. General email, care@careauto.org*

Web, http://careauto.org

Works to promote greater competition in the automotive aftermarket repair industry in order to protect consumers. Monitors state and federal legislation that impacts motorists and the automotive aftermarket repair industry.

Electric Drive Transportation Assn. (EDTA), *1250 Eye St. N.W., #902, 20005; (202) 408-0774. Fax, (202) 408-7610. Genevieve Cullen, President. Press, ext. 312. General email, info@electricdrive.org*

Web, https://electricdrive.org

Membership: automotive and other equipment manufacturers, utilities, technology developers, component suppliers, and government agencies. Conducts public policy advocacy, education, industry networking, and international conferences in the areas of battery, hybrid, and fuel cell electric drive technologies and infrastructures.

Japan Automobile Manufacturers Assn. (JAMA), Washington Office, *888 17th St. N.W., #609, 20006; (202) 296-8537. Fax, (202) 872-1212. Manuel Manriquez, USA General Director. Press, (202) 803-6828. General email, info@jama.org*

Web, www.jama.org and Twitter, @JapanAutosUSA

Membership: Japanese motor vehicle manufacturers. Interests include energy, market, trade, and environmental issues. (Headquarters in Tokyo, Japan.)

Manufacturers of Emission Controls Assn., *2101 Wilson Blvd., #530, Arlington, VA 22201; (202) 296-4797. Rasto Brezny, Executive Director. General email, asantos@meca.org*

Web, www.meca.org and Twitter, @MECAforCleanAir

Membership: manufacturers of motor vehicle emission control equipment, both mobile and stationary sources. Provides information on emission technology and industry capabilities. Studies the economic and public health impacts of the industry. Monitors regulations and international activities.

National Automobile Dealers Assn. (NADA), *8484 Westpark Dr., #500, Tysons, VA 22102; (703) 821-7000. Mike Stanton, President. Toll-free, (800) 557-6232. General email, NADAinfo@nada.org*

Web, www.nada.org, Twitter, @NADAUpdate and Facebook, www.facebook.com/NADAUpdate

Membership: domestic and imported franchised new car and truck dealers. Publishes the *National Automobile Dealers Used Car Guide (Blue Book).*

Recreation Vehicle Dealers Assn. of North America (RVDA), *3930 University Dr., Fairfax, VA 22030-2515; (703) 591-7130. Fax, (703) 591-0734. Phil Ingrassia, President. General email, info@rvda.org*

Web, www.rvda.org, Twitter, @RVLearningCtr and Facebook, www.facebook.com/rvlearningcenter

Membership: recreation vehicle dealers. Interests include government regulation of safety, trade, warranty, and franchising; provides members with educational services, certification programs, and conventions; works to

788 • CHAPTER 18 / TRANSPORTATION

improve service standards for consumers. Monitors legislation and regulations.

Recreation Vehicle Industry Assn. (RVIA), *1899 Preston White Dr., Reston, VA 20191-4363; (703) 620-6003. Fax, (703) 620-5071. Craig Kirby, President, ext. 335. Web, www.rvia.org, Twitter, @RV_Industry and Facebook, www.facebook.com/RVIndustryAssoc*

Membership: manufacturers of recreation vehicles and their suppliers. Compiles shipment statistics and other technical data; provides consumers and the media with information on the industry. Assists members' compliance with American National Standards Institute requirements for recreation vehicles. Monitors legislation and regulations.

Tire Industry Assn., *1532 Pointer Ridge Pl., Suite G, Bowie, MD 20716-1883; (301) 430-7280. Fax, (301) 430-7283. Richard (Dick) Gust, Chief Executive Officer; Mason Hess, President. Toll-free, (800) 876-8372. General email, info@tireindustry.org*

Web, www.tireindustry.org, Twitter, @thetireindustry and Facebook, www.facebook.com/tireindustry

Membership: all segments of the tire industry, including those that manufacture, repair, recycle, sell, service, or use new or retreaded tires and also suppliers that furnish equipment or services to the industry. Interests include environmental and small-business issues. Monitors legislation and regulations.

Truck Renting and Leasing Assn., *675 N. Washington St., #410, Alexandria, VA 22314-1939; (703) 299-9120. Jake Jacoby, President. Web, www.trala.org, Twitter, @TRALAorg and Facebook, www.facebook.com/TRALAorg*

Membership: vehicle renting and leasing companies and suppliers to the industry. Acts as liaison with state and federal legislative bodies and regulatory agencies. Interests include truck security and safety, tort reform, operating taxes and registration fees, insurance, and environmental issues. Monitors state and federal legislation and regulations.

Truck Trailer Manufacturers Assn. (TTMA), *7001 Heritage Village Plaza, #220, Gainesville, VA 20155; (703) 549-3010. Jeff Sims, President. Web, www.ttmanet.org*

Membership: trailer manufacturing and supply companies. Serves as liaison between its members and government agencies. Publishes technical and industry news reports.

United Auto Workers (UAW), *Washington Office, 1757 N St. N.W., 20036; (202) 828-8500. Josh Nassar, Legislative Director. Web, www.uaw.org, Twitter, @uaw, Facebook, www.facebook.com/uaw.union and YouTube, www.youtube.com/channel/UCtyZlveXsB4K3bLrWjMAv3g*

Membership: approximately 400,000 active and 600,000 retired North American workers in aerospace, automotive, defense, manufacturing, steel, technical, and other industries. Assists members with contract negotiations and grievances; conducts training programs and workshops. Monitors legislation and regulations. (Headquarters in Detroit, Mich.)

Traffic Safety

▶ **AGENCIES**

Federal Motor Carrier Safety Administration (Transportation Dept.), *1200 New Jersey Ave. S.E., #W60-300, 20590; (202) 366-4000. Fax, (844) 397-9350. Jack Van Steenbury, Executive Director. Consumer complaints, (888) 368-7238. Toll-free hotline, (888) 327-4236. Toll-free information, (800) 832-5660. TTY, (800) 877-8339. Web, www.fmcsa.dot.gov, Twitter, @FMCSA and Facebook, www.facebook.com/FMCSA*

Partners with federal, state, and local enforcement agencies, the motor carrier industry, safety groups, and organized labor in efforts to reduce bus- and truck-related crashes.

Federal Motor Carrier Safety Administration (Transportation Dept.), Bus and Truck Standards and Operations, *1200 New Jersey Ave. S.E., #N64-330, 20590; (202) 366-5370. Chuck Horan, Director. General email, FMCSA-Host@dot.gov*

Web, www.fmcsa.dot.gov/safety/data-and-statistics/commercial-motor-vehicle-facts

Interprets and disseminates national safety regulations regarding commercial drivers' qualifications, maximum hours of service, accident reporting, and transportation of hazardous materials. Sets minimum levels of financial liability for trucks and buses. Responsible for Commercial Driver's License Information Program.

National Highway Traffic Safety Administration (NHTSA) (Transportation Dept.), *West Bldg., 1200 New Jersey Ave. S.E., #42300, 20590; (202) 366-4000. Fax, (202) 366-2106. Steve Cliff, Administrator (Acting). Press, (202) 366-9550. Toll-free 24-hour hotline, (888) 327-4236. TTY, (800) 424-9153. General email, nuts.actingadministrator@nhtsa.gov*

Web, www.nhtsa.gov, Consumer safety information, www.safercar.gov, Twitter, @NHTSAgov and Facebook, www.facebook.com/NHTSA

Implements motor vehicle safety programs; issues federal motor vehicle safety standards; conducts testing programs to determine compliance with these standards; rates vehicles under the 5-star government rating program for crashworthiness and antirollover stability; maintains the website www.safercar.gov, a consumer auto safety information site; funds local and state motor vehicle and driver safety programs; conducts research on motor vehicle safety and equipment, and human factors relating to auto and traffic safety. The Auto Safety Hotline and the website provide safety information and handle consumer problems and complaints involving safety-related defects and noncompliance matters.

National Highway Traffic Safety Administration (NHTSA) *(Transportation Dept.), National Driver Register,* 1200 New Jersey Ave. S.E., #W55-123, 20590-0001; (202) 366-4800. Fax, (202) 366-2746. *Frank Subalusky, Chief. Toll-free, (888) 851-0436. Web, https://one.nhtsa.gov/Data/National-Driver-Register-(NDR)*

Maintains and operates the National Driver Register, a program in which states exchange information on motor vehicle driving records to ensure that drivers with suspended licenses in one state cannot obtain licenses in any other state.

National Transportation Safety Board (NTSB), *490 L'Enfant Plaza East S.W., 20594-2000; (202) 314-6000. Hon. Jennifer Homendy, Chair; Dana Schulze, Managing Director. Press, (202) 314-6100. 24-Hour Accident Response, (844) 373-9922. Web, www.ntsb.gov, Twitter, @NTSB, Facebook, www .facebook.com/NTSBgov and YouTube, www.youtube.com/ user/NTSBgov*

Promotes transportation safety through independent investigations of accidents and other safety problems. Makes recommendations for safety improvement. Operates three regional offices.

National Transportation Safety Board (NTSB), *Highway Safety, 490 L'Enfant Plaza East S.W., 20594-0001; (202) 314-6000. Robert Molloy, Director. Web, www.ntsb.gov/about/organization/HS/Pages/office_ hs.aspx*

In cooperation with states, investigates selected highway transportation accidents to compile the facts upon which the board determines probable cause; works to prevent similar recurrences; makes recommendations on matters pertaining to highway safety and accident prevention.

▶ NONGOVERNMENTAL

AAA Foundation for Traffic Safety, *607 14th St. N.W., #201, 20005; (202) 638-5944. Fax, (202) 638-5943. C.Y. David Chang, Executive Director. General email, info@aaafoundation.org Web, https://aaafoundation.org*

Sponsors "human factor" research on traffic safety issues, including bicycle, pedestrian, and road safety; researches driver behavior and performance, emerging technologies, roadway systems, and drivers and road users; supplies traffic safety educational materials to elementary and secondary schools, commercial driving schools, law enforcement agencies, motor vehicle administrations, and programs for older drivers.

Advocates for Highway and Auto Safety, *750 1st St. N.E., #1130, 20002-8007; (202) 408-1711. Fax, (202) 408-1699. Cathy Chase, President. General email, advocates@saferoads.org Web, https://saferoads.org and Twitter, @SafeRoadsNow*

Coalition of insurers, law enforcement, public health and consumer experts. Acts as advocate for public policy

designed to reduce deaths, injuries, and economic costs associated with motor vehicle crashes and fraud and theft involving motor vehicles. Interests include safety belts and child safety seats, drunk driving abuse, motorcycle helmets, vehicle crashworthiness, and speed limits. Monitors legislation and regulations.

American Highway Users Alliance, *1920 L St. N.W., #525, 20036; (202) 857-1200. Fax, (202) 857-1220. Laura C. Perrotta, Chief Executive Officer. General email, info@highways.org Web, www.highways.org, Twitter, @highwayusers and Facebook, www.facebook.com/highwayusers*

Membership: companies and associations representing major industry and highway user groups. Develops information, analyzes public policy, and advocates legislation to improve roadway safety and efficiency and to increase the mobility of the American public. (Affiliated with the Roadway Safety Foundation.)

American Trucking Assns., *Policy and Regulatory Affairs, 950 N. Glebe Rd., #210, Arlington, VA 22203; (202) 478-6861. Fax, (202) 675-6568. Dean E. Kaplan, Chair; Kathleen Gamble, Director of Political Affairs, (202) 478-6861. Press, (703) 838-1996. Web, www.trucking.org*

Membership: state trucking associations, individual trucking and motor carrier organizations, and related supply companies. Provides information on safety for the trucking industry. Monitors legislation and regulations.

Center for Auto Safety, *4400 Jenifer St. N.W., #331, 20015-2113; (202) 328-7700. Michael Brooks, Executive Director (Acting). General email, contact@autosafety.org Web, www.autosafety.org, Twitter, @Ctr4AutoSafety and Facebook, www.facebook.com/CenterForAutoSafety*

Public interest organization that receives written consumer complaints against auto manufacturers; monitors federal agencies responsible for regulating and enforcing auto and highway safety rules.

Commercial Vehicle Safety Alliance (CVSA), *6303 Ivy Lane, #310, Greenbelt, MD 20770-6319; (301) 830-6143. Collin B. Mooney, Executive Director, (301) 830-6149. General email, cvsahq@cvsa.org Web, http://cvsa.org, Twitter, @CVSA and Facebook, www .facebook.com/CommercialVehicleSafetyAlliance*

Membership: local, state, provincial, territorial, and federal motor carrier safety officials and industry representatives from the United States, Canada, and Mexico. Promotes improved methods of highway and terminal inspection of commercial vehicles, drivers, and cargo; and uniformity and reciprocity of inspection criteria and enforcement across jurisdictions.

Governors Highway Safety Assn., *660 N. Capitol St. N.W., #220, 20001-1642; (202) 789-0942. Jonathan Adkins, Executive Director, (202) 789-0943.*

General email, headquarters@ghsa.org

Web, www.ghsa.org, Twitter, @GHSAHQ and Facebook, www.facebook.com/GHSAhq

Membership: state officials who manage highway safety programs. Interprets technical data concerning highway safety. Represents the states in policy debates on national highway safety issues.

Institute of Transportation Engineers (ITE), 1627 Eye St. N.W., #550, 20006; (202) 785-0060. Fax, (202) 785-0609. Jeffrey F. Paniati, Executive Director, ext. 131.

General email, ite_staff@ite.org

Web, www.ite.org and Twitter, @ITEhq

Membership: international professional transportation engineers. Interests include safe and efficient surface transportation; provides professional and scientific information on transportation standards and recommended practices.

Insurance Institute for Highway Safety, 4121 Wilson Blvd., 6th Floor, Arlington, VA 22203; (703) 247-1500. Fax, (703) 247-1568. David Harkey, President. Vehicle Research Center, (434) 985-4600.

Web, www.iihs.org, Twitter, @IIHS_autosafety and Facebook, www.facebook.com/iihs.org

Membership: property and casualty insurance associations and individual insurance companies. Conducts research and provides data on highway safety; seeks ways to reduce losses from vehicle crashes. (Operates with Highway Loss Data Institute and the Vehicle Research Center.)

Mothers Against Drunk Driving (MADD), *Government Affairs,* 1200 18th St. N.W., #700, 20036; (202) 688-1193. Stephanie Manning, Chief Government Affairs Officer; Ellen Willmott, Executive Officer. 24-hour helpline, 877-MADD-HELP. Toll-free, (877) 275-6233.

General email, policy@madd.org

Web, www.madd.org, Facebook, www.facebook.com/MADD.Official and Twitter, @MADDOnline

Advocacy group that seeks to stop drunk driving and prevent underage drinking. Monitors legislation and regulations. (Headquarters in Irving, Tex.)

Network of Employers for Traffic Safety (NETS), 344 Maple Ave. West, #357, Vienna, VA 22180-5162; (703) 755-5350. Susan Gillies, Executive Director.

Web, www.trafficsafety.org, Twitter, @NETS_RoadSafety and Facebook, www.facebook.com/NETSRoadSafety

Dedicated to reducing the human and economic cost associated with automobile and highway crashes. Helps employers develop and implement workplace traffic and highway safety programs. Provides technical assistance.

Roadway Safety Foundation, 1920 L St. N.W., #525, 20036; (202) 857-1228. Fax, (202) 857-1220. Gregory M. Cohen, Executive Director.

Web, www.roadwaysafety.org and Twitter, @RoadwaySafetyFn

Conducts highway safety programs to reduce automobile-related crashes and deaths. (Affiliated with American Highway Users Alliance.)

U.S. Tire Manufacturers Assn., 1400 K St. N.W., #900, 20005; (202) 682-4800. Anne Forristall Luke, Chief Executive Officer.

General email, info@ustires.org

Web, www.ustires.org, Twitter, @USTires, Facebook, www.facebook.com/USTireAssoc and YouTube, www.youtube.com/USTireManufacturersAssociation

Membership: American tire manufacturers. Provides consumers with information on tire care and safety. Develops safety standards for passenger, light truck, and commercial truck tires. Monitors legislation and regulations. (Formerly Rubber Manufacturers Assn.)

United Motorcoach Assn. (UMA), 113 S. West St., 4th Floor, Alexandria, VA 22314-2824; (703) 838-2929. Fax, (703) 838-2950. Scott Michael, Chief Executive Officer. Toll-free, (800) 424-8262.

General email, info@uma.org

Web, www.uma.org, Twitter, @UMADrives and Facebook, www.facebook.com/unitedmotorcoachassociation

Membership: professional bus and motorcoach companies and suppliers and manufacturers in the industry. Provides information, offers technical assistance, conducts research, and monitors legislation. Interests include insurance, safety programs, and credit.

RAIL TRANSPORTATION

General

▶AGENCIES

Federal Railroad Administration (*Transportation Dept.***),** 1200 New Jersey Ave. S.E., 3rd Floor, 20590; (202) 493-6014. Fax, (202) 493-6481. Amit Bose, Administrator. Public Affairs, (202) 493-6024.

General email, frapa@dot.gov

Web, www.fra.dot.gov, Twitter, @USDOTFRA and Facebook, www.facebook.com/USDOTFRA

Develops national rail policies; enforces rail safety laws; administers financial assistance programs available to states and the rail industry; conducts research and development on improved rail safety. Operates eight regional offices.

Federal Railroad Administration (*Transportation Dept.***), Public Engagement,** West Bldg., 1200 New Jersey Ave. S.E., MS 10, 20590; (202) 493-6014. Fax, (202) 493-6481. Tim Barkley, Director, (202) 493-1305.

General email, frapa@dot.gov

Web, https://railroads.dot.gov/office-administrator/office-public-engagement/office-public-engagement

Plans, coordinates, and administers activities related to railroad economics, finance, traffic and network analysis, labor management, and transportation planning, as well as intermodal, environmental, emergency response, and international programs.

Federal Railroad Administration (*Transportation Dept.***), Railroad Policy and Development,** 1200

New Jersey Ave. S.E., 3rd Floor, 20590; (202) 493-6381. Fax, (202) 493-6330. Paul Nissenbaum, Associate Administrator.

General email, OfficeofRPD@dot.gov

Web, www.fra.dot.gov/about-fra/program-offices/office-railroad-policy-development

Administers federal assistance programs for national, regional, and local rail services, including freight service assistance, service continuation, and passenger service. Conducts research on and development of new rail technologies.

Federal Railroad Administration *(Transportation Dept.), Railroad Safety, 1200 New Jersey Ave. S.E., 3rd Floor, 20590; (202) 493-6014. Fax, (202) 493-6216. Karl Alexy, Associate Administrator.*

General email, rrswebinquiries@dot.gov

Web, https://railroads.dot.gov/railroad-safety

Administers and enforces federal laws and regulations that promote railroad safety, including track maintenance, inspection and equipment standards, operating practices, and transportation of explosives and other hazardous materials. Conducts inspections and reports on railroad equipment facilities and accidents. All safety and/or security issues, such as bomb threats or biochemical threats, are managed by security specialists.

National Mediation Board, *1301 K St. N.W., #250E, 20005-7011; (202) 692-5000. Fax, (202) 692-5082. Gerald W. Fauth III, Chair. Information, (202) 692-5050. TTY, (202) 692-5001.*

General email, infoline@nmb.gov

Web, www.nmb.gov

Mediates labor disputes in the railroad industry; determines and certifies labor representatives for the industry.

National Railroad Passenger Corp. (Amtrak), *1 Massachusetts Ave. N.W., 20001; (202) 906-3000. Stephen J. Gardner, President. Emergency, (800) 331-0008. Press, (202) 906-3860. Reservations, (800) 872-7245. TTY, (800) 523-6590.*

Web, www.amtrak.com, Twitter, @amtrak and Facebook, www.facebook.com/Amtrak

Quasipublic corporation created by the Rail Passenger Service Act of 1970 to improve and develop intercity passenger rail service.

Surface Transportation Board (STB), *395 E St. S.W., #1220, 20423-0001; (202) 245-0245. Martin J. Oberman, Chair. Library, (202) 245-0288. Press, (202) 245-0238/ 1760. TTY, (800) 877-8339.*

Web, www.stb.gov and Email, rcpa@stb.gov

Has jurisdiction over railroad rate, practice, and service issues and rail restructuring transactions, including mergers, line sales, line construction, and line abandonments. The STB also has jurisdiction over certain passenger rail matters, the intercity bus industry, non-energy pipelines, household goods carriers' tariffs, and rate regulation of non-contiguous domestic water transportation (marine freight shipping involving the mainland United

States, Hawaii, Alaska, Puerto Rico, and other U.S. territories and possessions). Library open to the public.

Surface Transportation Board (STB), *Public Assistance, Governmental Affairs, and Compliance, 395 E St. S.W., #1202, 20423-0001; (202) 245-0238. Michael Higgins, Director (Acting). Toll-free, (866) 254-1792. TTY, (800) 877-8339.*

General email, rcpa@stb.gov

Web, www.stb.gov/about-stb/offices/opagac

Informs members of Congress, executive agencies, state and local governments, news media, stakeholders, and other interested persons to provide information and informal guidance as to the STB's procedures, regulations, and actions. Administers the Rail Customer and Public Assistance Program.

U.S. Coast Guard (USCG) *(Homeland Security Dept.), 2703 Martin Luther King Jr. Ave. S.E., MS 7000, 20593-7000; (202) 372-4000. Fax, (202) 372-8302. Adm. Karl L. Schultz, Commandant. Public Affairs, (202) 372-4600.*

Web, www.uscg.mil, Twitter, @USCG, Facebook, www.facebook.com/UScoastguard and YouTube, www.youtube.com/USCGImagery

Regulates the construction, maintenance, and operation of bridges across U.S. navigable waters, including railway bridges.

▶CONGRESS

For a listing of relevant congressional committees and subcommittees, please see page 762 or the Appendix.

▶NONGOVERNMENTAL

American Short Line and Regional Railroad Assn. (ASLRRA), *50 F St. N.W., #500, 20001-1564; (202) 628-4500. Fax, (202) 567-2823. Chuck Baker, President.*

General email, aslrra@aslrra.org

Web, www.aslrra.org, Twitter, @ASLRRA and Facebook, www.facebook.com/aslrra

Membership: independently owned short line and regional railroad systems as well as companies that supply goods and services to short line railroads. Assists members with technical and legal questions; compiles information on laws, regulations, safety, and other matters affecting the industry.

Assn. of American Railroads, *425 3rd St. S.W., #1000, 20024; (202) 639-2100. Fax, (202) 639-2886. Ian Jefferies, President. Press, (202) 639-2345.*

General email, info@aar.org

Web, www.aar.org, Twitter, @AAR_FreightRail and Facebook, www.facebook.com/FreightRail

Membership: major freight railroads in the United States, Canada, and Mexico, as well as Amtrak. Provides information on freight railroad operations, safety and maintenance, economics and finance, management, and law and legislation; conducts research; issues statistical reports.

Brotherhood of Maintenance of Way Employees, *International Brotherhood of Teamsters, National Legislation Department,* 25 Louisiana Ave. N.W., 7th Floor, 20001; (202) 508-6445. Fax, (202) 508-6450. *Jeffery R. Joines, Director of Government Affairs, (202) 508-6446.*
General email, bmwe-dc@bmwewash.org
Web, www.bmwe.org, Twitter, @BMWEDIBT and *Facebook, www.facebook.com/SMWEDIBT*

Membership: rail industry workers and others. Assists members with contract negotiation and grievances; conducts training programs and workshops. Monitors legislation and regulations. (Headquarters in Novi, Mich.)

International Assn. of Machinists and Aerospace Workers, *Transportation Communications Union,* 3 *Research Pl., Rockville, MD 20850-3279; (301) 948-4910. Arthur P. Maratea, National President.*
Web, www.goiam.org/territories/tcu-union

Membership: approximately 46,000 railway workers. Assists members with contract negotiation and grievances; conducts training programs and workshops. Monitors legislation and regulations. (Affiliated with the AFL-CIO and Canadian Labour Congress.)

International Brotherhood of Electrical Workers (IBEW), 900 7th St. N.W., 20001; (202) 833-7000. Fax, (202) 728-7676. *Lonnie R. Stephenson, International President.*
General email, webmaster@ibew.org
Web, http://ibew.org

Membership: workers in utilities, construction, telecommunications, broadcasting, manufacturing, railroads, and government. Helps members negotiate pay, benefits, and better working conditions; conducts training programs and workshops. Monitors legislation and regulations. (Affiliated with the AFL-CIO.)

National Railroad Construction and Maintenance Assn., 80 M St. S.E., 20003; (202) 975-0365. *Ashley Wieland, President.*
General email, info@nrcma.org
Web, www.nrcma.org

Membership: railroad suppliers and contractors. Supports government funding for rail and transit systems. Holds conferences on industry practices, safety, and policy issues.

National Railway Labor Conference, 251 S. 18th St., #750, Arlington, VA 22202; (571) 336-7600. *Brendan M. Branon, Chair.*
Web, www.nrlc.ws

Assists member railroad lines with labor matters; negotiates with railroad labor representatives.

Rail Passengers Assn., 1200 G St. N.W., #240, 20005; (202) 408-8362. Fax, (202) 408-8287. *Jim Mathews, Chief Executive Officer.*
General email, narp@narprail.org
Web, https://railpassengers.org, Twitter, @RailPassengers and *Facebook, www.facebook.com/narprail*

Education and advocacy organization. Works to expand and improve U.S. intercity and commuter rail passenger service, increase federal funds for mass transit, and address environmental concerns pertaining to mass transit. Works with Amtrak on scheduling, new services, and fares. (Formerly the National Assn. of Railroad Passengers.)

Railway Supply Institute (RSI), 2001 K St. N.W., 3rd Floor North, 20006; (202) 367-1126. Fax, (202) 367-2210. *Patty Long, President, ext. 102.*
General email, info@rsiweb.org
Web, www.rsiweb.org and *Twitter, @Railway_Supply*

Membership: railroad and rail rapid transit suppliers. Conducts research on safety and new technology; monitors legislation.

Sheet Metal, Air, Rail, and Transportation Workers (SMART), 1750 New York Ave. N.W., 6th Floor, 20006; (202) 662-0800. *Joseph Sellers Jr., General President. Toll-free, (800) 457-7694.*
General email, info@smart-union.org
Web, https://smart-union.org and *Twitter, @smartunionworks*

Membership: U.S., Puerto Rican, and Canadian workers in the building and construction trades, manufacturing, and the railroad and shipyard industries. Assists members with contract negotiation and grievances; conducts training programs and workshops. Monitors legislation and regulations. (Affiliated with the Sheet Metal and Air Conditioning Contractors' Assn., the AFL-CIO, and the Canadian Labour Congress.)

TRANSIT SYSTEMS

General

▶**AGENCIES**

Federal Transit Administration *(Transportation Dept.),* 1200 New Jersey Ave. S.E., #E56-311, 20590; (202) 366-4043. Fax, (202) 366-3200. *Nuria Fernandez, Deputy Administrator, (202) 366-4040; Matthew Welbes, Executive Director. Information and press, (202) 366-4043. TTY, (800) 877-8339. TTY Voice, (866) 377-8642.*
Web, www.transit.dot.gov, Twitter, @FTA_DOT and *Facebook, www.facebook.com/FTADOT*

Responsible for developing improved public transportation facilities, equipment, techniques, and methods; assists state and local governments in financing public transportation systems; oversees the safety of U.S. public transit.

Federal Transit Administration *(Transportation Dept.), Budget and Policy,* 1200 New Jersey Ave. S.E., #E52-326, 20590; (202) 366-4050. Fax, (202) 366-7116. *Theresa Kohler, Associate Administrator. Press, (202) 366-4043.*
Web, www.transit.dot.gov/funding/budget-performance

Develops budgets, programs, legislative proposals, and policies for the federal transit program; evaluates program proposals and their potential impact on local communities; coordinates private sector initiatives of the agency.

Federal Transit Administration *(Transportation Dept.), Program Management, 1200 New Jersey Ave. S.E., 4th Floor, 20590; (202) 366-2053. Fax, (202) 366-7951. Bruce Robinson, Associate Administrator. Information and Press, (202) 366-4043.*
Web, www.transit.dot.gov/funding/grants/grant-programs

Administers capital planning and operating assistance grants and loan activities; monitors transit projects in such areas as environmental impact, special provisions for the elderly and people with disabilities, efficiency, and investment.

Federal Transit Administration *(Transportation Dept.), Research, Demonstration, and Innovation, 1200 New Jersey Ave. S.E., #E43-431, 20590; (202) 366-4052. Fax, (202) 366-3765. Karina Ricks, Associate Administrator. Information and Press, (202) 366-4043.*
Web, www.transit.dot.gov/research-innovation

Provides industry and state and local governments with contracts, cooperative agreements, and grants for testing, developing, and demonstrating methods of improved mass transportation service and technology.

Maryland Transit Administration, *6 St. Paul St., Baltimore, MD 21202-1614; (410) 539-5000. Holly Arnold, Administrator. Information, (866) 743-3682. MobilityLink (Paratransit), (410) 764-8181. TTY, (410) 539-3497. Press, (410) 767-3936.*
Web, www.mta.maryland.gov, Twitter, @mtamaryland, Facebook, www.facebook.com/mtamaryland and YouTube, www.youtube.com/user/TheMTAMaryland

Responsible for mass transit programs in Maryland; provides MARC commuter rail service for Baltimore, Washington, and suburbs in Maryland and West Virginia.

Surface Transportation Board (STB), *395 E St. S.W., #1220, 20423-0001; (202) 245-0245. Martin J. Oberman, Chair. Library, (202) 245-0288. Press, (202) 245-0238/ 1760. TTY, (800) 877-8339.*
Web, www.stb.gov and Email, rcpa@stb.gov

Has jurisdiction over railroad rate, practice, and service issues and rail restructuring transactions, including mergers, line sales, line construction, and line abandonments. The STB also has jurisdiction over certain passenger rail matters, the intercity bus industry, non-energy pipelines, household goods carriers' tariffs, and rate regulation of non-contiguous domestic water transportation (marine freight shipping involving the mainland United States, Hawaii, Alaska, Puerto Rico, and other U.S. territories and possessions). Library open to the public.

Virginia Railway Express (VRE), *1500 King St., #202, Alexandria, VA 22314; (703) 684-1001. Fax, (703) 684-1313. Rich Dalton, Chief Executive Officer. Press, (703) 838-5416. Toll-free, (800) 743-3873. TTY, (703) 684-0551.*

General email, gotrains@vre.org
Web, www.vre.org, Twitter, @VaRailXpress and Facebook, www.facebook.com/RideVRE

Regional transportation partnership that provides commuter rail service from Fredericksburg and Manassas, VA, to Washington, DC.

Washington Metropolitan Area Transit Authority (Metro), *600 5th St. N.W., 20001; (202) 962-1234. Paul J. Wiedefeld, General Manager. Information, (202) 637-7000. Lost and found, (202) 962-1195. Metro access (for those with disabilities), (800) 523-7009. Press, (202) 962-1051. TTY (Administration), (202) 962-1000. TTY (Metro access), (301) 588-7535.*
Web, www.wmata.com, Twitter, @wmata and Inspector General email, hotline@wmataoig.gov

Provides bus and rail transit service to Washington, D.C., and neighboring Maryland and Virginia communities; assesses and plans for transportation needs. Provides fare, schedule, and route information; promotes accessibility for persons with disabilities and the elderly.

►CONGRESS

For a listing of relevant congressional committees and subcommittees, please see page 762 or the Appendix.

►NONGOVERNMENTAL

Amalgamated Transit Union (ATU), *10000 New Hampshire Ave., Silver Spring, MD 20903; (301) 431-7100. Fax, (301) 431-7117. John A. Costa, International President. Toll-free, (888) 240-1196.*
Web, www.atu.org, Twitter, @ATUComm, Facebook, www .facebook.com/ATUInternational and Twitter, @atucomms

Membership: transit workers in the United States and Canada, including bus, van, ambulance, subway, and light rail operators; clerks, baggage handlers, and maintenance employees in urban transit, over-the-road, and school bus industries; and municipal workers. Assists members with contract negotiations and grievances; conducts training programs and seminars. Monitors legislation and regulations. (Affiliated with the AFL-CIO.)

American Bus Assn., *111 K St. N.E., 9th Floor, 20002; (202) 842-1645. Fax, (202) 842-0850. Peter J. Pantuso, President, (202) 218-7229. Press, (202) 218-7220. Toll-free, (800) 283-2877.*
General email, abainfo@buses.org
Web, www.buses.org, Twitter, @AmericanBusAssn and Facebook, www.facebook.com/AmericanBusAssociation

Membership: privately owned intercity bus companies, state associations, travel/tourism businesses, bus manufacturers, and those interested in the bus industry. Monitors legislation and regulations.

American Public Transportation Assn. (APTA), *1300 Eye St. N.W., #1200 East, 20005; (202) 496-4800. Fax, (202) 496-4324. Paul P. Skoutelas, President, (202) 496-4889. Press, (202) 496-4816.*

General email, apta@apta.com

Web, www.apta.com, Twitter, @APTA_Info and Facebook, www.facebook.com/AmericanPublicTransportation Association

Membership: public organizations engaged in bus, paratransit, light rail, commuter rail, subways, waterborne passenger services, and high-speed rail, as well as large and small companies that plan, design, construct, finance, supply, and operate bus and rail services worldwide. Compiles data on the industry; promotes research. Monitors legislation and regulations.

Assn. of Metropolitan Planning Organizations, *444 N. Capitol St. N.W., #532, 20001; (202) 624-3680. Fax, (202) 624-3685. Bill Keyrouze, Executive Director. General email, ampo@ampo.org*

Web, www.ampo.org, Twitter, @ASSOC_MPOS and Facebook, www.facebook.com/AssocMPOs

Membership: more than 385 metropolitan councils of elected officials and transportation professionals responsible for planning local transportation systems. Provides a forum for professional and organizational development; sponsors conferences and training programs.

Community Transportation Assn. of America, *1341 G St. N.W., #210, 20005; (800) 891-0590. Fax, (202) 737-9197. Scott Bogren, Executive Director, (202) 247-1921.*

Web, http://ctaa.org, Twitter, @OfficialCTAA and Facebook, www.facebook.com/OfficialCTAA

Works to improve mobility for the elderly, the poor, and persons with disabilities; concerns include rural, small-city, and specialized transportation.

National Academies of Sciences, Engineering, and Medicine (NASEM), *Infrastructure and the Constructed Environment Board, Keck Center, 500 5th St. N.W., #WS938, 20001; (202) 334-3505. Fax, (202) 334-3718. Cameron Oskvig, Director; Thomas Bostick, Chair.*

General email, bice@nas.edu

Web, www.nationalacademies.org/bice/board-on-infrastructure-and-the-constructed-environment

Advises the government, the private sector, and the public on technology, science, and public policy related to the design, construction, operations, maintenance, security, and evaluation of buildings, facilities, and infrastructure systems; the relationship between the constructed and natural environments and their interaction with human activities; the effects of natural and man-made hazards on constructed facilities and infrastructure; and the interdependencies of infrastructure systems, including power, water, transportation, telecommunications, wastewater, and buildings.

Rail Passengers Assn., *1200 G St. N.W., #240, 20005; (202) 408-8362. Fax, (202) 408-8287. Jim Mathews, Chief Executive Officer. General email, narp@narprail.org*

Web, https://railpassengers.org, Twitter, @RailPassengers and Facebook, www.facebook.com/narprail

Education and advocacy organization. Works to expand and improve U.S. intercity and commuter rail passenger service, increase federal funds for mass transit, and address environmental concerns pertaining to mass transit. Works with Amtrak on scheduling, new services, and fares. (Formerly the National Assn. of Railroad Passengers.)

United Motorcoach Assn. (UMA), *113 S. West St., 4th Floor, Alexandria, VA 22314-2824; (703) 838-2929. Fax, (703) 838-2950. Scott Michael, Chief Executive Officer. Toll-free, (800) 424-8262. General email, info@uma.org*

Web, www.uma.org, Twitter, @UMADrives and Facebook, www.facebook.com/unitedmotorcoachassociation

Membership: professional bus and motorcoach companies and suppliers and manufacturers in the industry. Provides information, offers technical assistance, conducts research, and monitors legislation. Interests include insurance, safety programs, and credit.

19

U.S. Congress and Politics

ACCESS TO CONGRESSIONAL INFORMATION

Basic Resources

►AGENCIES

Library of Congress, *Law Library,* James Madison Memorial Bldg., 101 Independence Ave. S.E., #LM 242, 20540-3129; (202) 707-5079/80. Fax, (202) 707-1820. Aslihan Bulut, Law Librarian.
Web, www.loc.gov/law, Twitter, @LawLibCongress and Facebook, www.facebook.com/lawlibraryofcongress

Provides research assistance, reference services on U.S. federal and state legal issues to the public; foreign and comparative legal information services; provides print and electronic resources, including Guide to Law Online and legal research guides. Timed entry pass for visitors required, details at loc.gov/visit. Appointments recommended for researchers.

National Archives and Records Administration (NARA), *Center for Legislative Archives,* 700 Pennsylvania Ave. N.W., #8E, 20408; (202) 357-5350. Fax, (202) 357-5911. Richard H. Hunt, Director, (202) 357-5376.
General email, legislative.archives@nara.gov
Web, www.archives.gov/legislative and Twitter, @CongressArchive

Collects and maintains records of congressional committees and legislative files from 1789 to the present. Publishes inventories and guides to these records.

National Archives and Records Administration (NARA), *Federal Register (OFR),* 7 G St. N.W., #A-734, 20401 (mailing address: NF, 8601 Adelphi Rd., College Park, MD 20740-6001); (202) 741-6000. Fax, (202) 741-6012. Oliver A. Potts, Director, (202) 741-6100.
TTY, (202) 741-6086.
General email, fedreg.info@nara.gov
Web, www.archives.gov/federal-register, Twitter, @FedRegister and Legal Email, fedreg.legal@nara.gov

Assigns public law numbers to enacted legislation, executive orders, and proclamations. Responds to inquiries on public law numbers. Assists inquirers in finding presidential signing or veto messages in the *Daily Compilation of Presidential Documents* and the *Public Papers of the Presidents.* Compiles slip laws and annual United States Statutes at Large; compiles indexes for finding statutory provisions. Operates Public Law Electronic Notification System (PENS), which provides information by email on new legislation. Coordinates the functions of the Electoral College and the constitutional amendment process. Publications available from the U.S. Government Printing Office.

►CONGRESS

For a listing of relevant congressional committees and subcommittees, please see page 797 or the Appendix.

Clerk of the U.S. House of Representatives, H154 CAP, 20515-6601; (202) 225-7000. Cheryl L. Johnson, Clerk. Press, (202) 225-1908.
General email, info.clerkweb@mail.house.gov
Web, http://clerk.house.gov

Maintains and distributes House bills, reports, public laws, and documents to members' offices, committee staffs, and the general public. Provides daily schedules, when the House is in session, on website. Provides legislative history of all measures reported by House and Senate committees. Provides additional materials in the *Congressional Record* (also available from the Contact Center, Government Printing Office, Washington, DC, [202] 512-1800 or in electronic format at www.gpoaccess.gov). Provides video coverage of House floor proceedings through http://houselive.gov.

Senate Executive Clerk, S138 CAP, 20510; (202) 224-4341. Rachel Creviston, Executive Clerk.

Maintains and distributes copies of treaties submitted to the Senate for ratification; provides information on submitted treaties and nominations. (Shares distribution responsibility with Senate Printing and Document Services, [202] 224-7701.)

Senate Historical Office, 201 SHOB, 20510; (202) 224-6900. Betty K. Koed, Historian.
General email, historian@sec.senate.gov
Web, www.senate.gov/artandhistory/history/common/generic/Senate_Historical_Office.htm and Twitter, @SenateHistory

Serves as an information clearinghouse on Senate history, traditions, and members. Collects, organizes, and distributes to the public unpublished Senate documents; collects and preserves photographs and pictures related to Senate history; conducts an oral history program; advises senators and Senate committees on the disposition of their noncurrent papers and records. Produces publications on the history of the Senate.

Senate Office of Conservation and Preservation, B15 SROB, 20510; (202) 224-7106. Leona Faust, Librarian.

Develops and coordinates programs related to the conservation and preservation of Senate records and materials for the secretary of the Senate.

Senate Printing and Document Services, B04 SHOB, 20510-7106; (202) 224-7701. Fax, (202) 228-2815. Laura Rush, Director.
General email, orders@sec.senate.gov
Web, www.senate.gov/legislative/common/generic/Doc_Room.htm

Maintains and distributes Senate bills, reports, public laws, and documents. To obtain material send a self-addressed mailing label or fax with request. Documents and information may be accessed on the website.

U.S. House of Representatives, *Legislative Resource Center,* B81 CHOB, 20515-6612; (202) 226-5200. Ronald (Dale) Thomas, Chief.

U.S. CONGRESS AND POLITICS RESOURCES IN CONGRESS

For a complete listing of congressional committees, including their full contact information, leadership, membership, and jurisdictions, please refer to the Appendix on pages 840–963.

HOUSE:

House Administration Committee, (202) 225-2061.
Web, cha.house.gov
House Appropriations Committee, (202) 225-2771.
Web, appropriations.house.gov
    Subcommittee on Financial Services and General
       Government, (202) 225-7245.
    Subcommittee on Legislative Branch,
       (202) 226-7252.
House Budget Committee, (202) 226-7200.
Web, budget.house.gov
House Ethics Committee, (202) 225-7103.
Web, ethics.house.gov
House Judiciary Committee,
   (202) 225-3951.
Web, judiciary.house.gov
    Subcommittee on the Constitution,
       Civil Rights, and Civil Liberties,
       (202) 225-3951.
House Oversight and Reform Committee,
   (202) 225-5051.
Web, oversight.house.gov
    Subcommittee on Government Operations,
       (202) 225-5051.
House Rules Committee, (202) 225-9091.
Web, rules.house.gov
    Subcommittee on Expedited Procedures,
       (202) 225-9091.
    Subcommittee on Legislative and Budget Process,
       (202) 225-9091.
    Subcommittee on Rules and Organization of the
       House, (202) 225-9091.
House Transportation and Infrastructure
   Committee, (202) 225-4472.
Web, transportation.house.gov
    Subcommittee on Economic
       Development, Public Buildings,
       and Emergency Management,
       (202) 225-3014.

JOINT:

Joint Committee on Printing, (202) 225-2061.
Web, cha.house.gov/jointcommittees/joint-committee-
   on-printing
Joint Committee on the Library of Congress,
   (202) 225-2061.
Web, cha.house.gov/jointcommittees/joint-committee-
   library

SENATE:

Senate Appropriations Committee, (202) 224-7363.
Web, appropriations.senate.gov
    Subcommittee on Financial Services and General
       Government, (202) 224-7363.
    Subcommittee on Legislative Branch,
       (202) 224-7363.
Senate Budget Committee, (202) 224-0642.
Web, budget.senate.gov
Senate Finance Committee, (202) 224-4515.
Web, finance.senate.gov
    Subcommittee on Fiscal Responsibility and
       Economic Growth, (202) 224-4515.
Senate Homeland Security and Governmental Affairs
   Committee, (202) 224-2627.
Web, hsgac.senate.gov
    Subcommittee on Emerging Threats and
       Spending Oversight, (202) 224-2254.
    Permanent Subcommittee on Investigations,
       (202) 224-3721.
    Subcommittee on Government Operations and
       Border Management, (202) 224-4551.
Senate Judiciary Committee, (202) 224-7703.
Web, judiciary.senate.gov
    Subcommittee on the Constitution, (202) 224-6361.
Senate Rules and Administration Committee,
   (202) 224-6352.
Web, rules.senate.gov
Senate Select Committee on Ethics, (202) 224-2981.
Web, ethics.senate.gov

General email, info.clerkweb@mail.house.gov
Web, https://clerk.house.gov/About#LRCDetails

Provides legislative information, records and registration, historical information, and library services to the House and the public. Reading room contains computer terminals where collections may be viewed or printed out. Print publications include a biographical directory, a guide to research collections of former House members, and books on African Americans and women who have served in Congress. Collections include House and Senate journals (1st Congress to present); *Congressional Record* and its predecessors (1st Congress to present);

House reports, documents, bills, resolutions, and hearings; Senate reports and documents; U.S. statutes, treaties, the *Federal Register*, U.S. codes, and numerous other documents. (See website or call for a complete list of collections.)

U.S. House of Representatives, *Office of History, Art, and Archives,* B53 CHOB, 20515; (202) 226-1300. Fax, (202) 226-4635. Farar P. Elliott, Chief. Legislative Archives, (202) 357-5350. Toll-free, (866) 272-6272.
General art email, art@mail.house.gov

General archives email, archives@mail.house.gov

Web, http://history.house.gov, Twitter, @USHouseHistory and YouTube, www.youtube.com/USHouseHistory

Works with the Office of the Historian to provide access to published documents and historical records of the House. Advises members on the disposition of their records and papers; maintains information on manuscript collections of former members; maintains biographical files on former members; houses photographs and artifacts of former members. Produces publications on Congress and its members.

U.S. House of Representatives, *Office of the Historian,* B53 CHOB, 20515; (202) 226-1300. Matthew A. Wasniewski, House Historian. Legislative Archives, (202) 357-5350.
General email, history@mail.house.gov

Web, http://history.house.gov and Twitter, @ushousehistory

Works with the Office of Art and Archives to provide access to published documents and historical records of the House. Conducts historical research. Advises members on the disposition of their records and papers; maintains information on manuscript collections of former members; maintains biographical files on former members. Produces publications on Congress and its members.

▶ NEWS SERVICES

CQ Press, 2600 Virginia Ave. N.W., #600, 20037; (202) 729-1800. Fax, (202) 729-1940. Blaise R. Simqu, Chief Executive Officer. Toll-free, (800) 818-7243.
General email, orders@sagepub.com

Web, https://us.sagepub.com/en-us/nam/cqpress, Twitter, @SAGECQPolitics and Facebook, www.facebook.com/SAGEPublishing

Publishes books, directories, periodicals, and online products on U.S. government, history, and politics. Products include *U.S. Political Stats, CQ Press Encyclopedia of American Government,* and *CQ Researcher.* (An imprint of SAGE Publishing; Headquarters in Thousand Oaks, Calif.)

Washington Post, 1301 K St. N.W., 20071; (202) 334-6000. Frederick J. (Fred) Ryan Jr., Publisher; Sally Buzbee, Executive Editor. Toll-free, (800) 627-1150.
Web, www.washingtonpost.com and Twitter, @washingtonpost

Provides news and analysis of congressional activities.

▶ NONGOVERNMENTAL

White House Correspondents' Assn., 600 New Hampshire Ave. N.W., #800, 20037; (202) 499-4187. Fax, (202) 266-7454. Steven Portnoy, President; Steven Thomma, Executive Director.
General email, director@whca.press

Web, www.whca.press and Twitter, @whca

Membership: reporters with permanent White House press credentials. Acts as a liaison between reporters and White House staff. Sponsors annual WHCA Journalism Awards and Scholarships fund-raising dinner.

▶ CONGRESS

For a listing of relevant congressional committees and sub-committees, please see page 797 or the Appendix.

Congressional Record

The *Congressional Record,* published daily when Congress is in session, is a printed account of proceedings on the floor of the House and Senate. A Daily Digest section summarizes the day's action on the floor and in committees and lists committee meetings scheduled for the following day. An index is published biweekly and at the close of sessions of Congress. Since January 1995, House members have not been allowed to edit their remarks before they appear in the *Record,* but senators retain this privilege. Material not spoken on the floor may be inserted through unanimous consent to revise or extend a speech and is published in a distinctive typeface. Grammatical, typographical, and technical corrections are also permitted.

▶ CONGRESS

For a listing of relevant congressional committees and sub-committees, please see page 797 or the Appendix.

Government Publishing Office (GPO), *Main Bookstore,* 732 N. Capitol St. N.W., 20401; (202) 512-1800. Lisa Williams, Director, (202) 512-1065. Bookstore, (202) 512-0132. Toll-free, (866) 512-1800.
General email, ContactCenter@gpo.gov

Web, http://bookstore.gpo.gov

Sells copies of and subscriptions to the *Congressional Record.* Expert help from government information librarians is available at http://govtinfo.org. Orders may be placed on the website. The *Congressional Record* from 1994 to the present is available online at www.fdsys.gov. The actual brick and mortar sore is permantly closed.

Library of Congress, *Law Library,* James Madison Memorial Bldg., 101 Independence Ave. S.E., #LM 242, 20540-3129; (202) 707-5079/80. Fax, (202) 707-1820. Aslihan Bulut, Law Librarian.
Web, www.loc.gov/law, Twitter, @LawLibCongress and Facebook, www.facebook.com/lawlibraryofcongress

Copies of the *Congressional Record* are available for reading. Terminals in the reading room provide access to a computer system containing bill digests from the 93rd Congress to date. The *Congressional Record* can also be accessed online at www.congress.gov. Timed entry pass for visitors required, details at loc.gov/visit. Appointments recommended for researchers.

▶ NONGOVERNMENTAL

Martin Luther King Jr. Memorial Library, 901 G St. N.W., 20001-4599; (202) 727-0321. Maryann James-Daley, Director.
General email, firstfloormlk.dcpl@dc.gov

Web, www.dclibrary.org/mlk

Maintains collection of the *Congressional Record* from 1879 to the present, available in various formats (bound volumes, microfilm, microfiche, and electronic).

Schedules, Status of Legislation

Information can also be obtained from the *Congressional Record* (Daily Digest) and from individual congressional committees (see 117th Congress, p. 839).

▶**CONGRESS**

For a listing of relevant congressional committees and subcommittees, please see page 797 or the Appendix.

Clerk of the U.S. House of Representatives, *H154 CAP, 20515-6601; (202) 225-7000. Cheryl L. Johnson, Clerk. Press, (202) 225-1908.*
General email, info.clerkweb@mail.house.gov
Web, http://clerk.house.gov

Maintains and distributes House bills, reports, public laws, and documents to members' offices, committee staffs, and the general public. Provides daily schedules, when the House is in session, on website. Provides legislative history of all measures reported by House and Senate committees. Provides additional materials in the *Congressional Record* (also available from the Contact Center, Government Printing Office, Washington, DC, [202] 512-1800 or in electronic format at www.gpoaccess.gov). Provides video coverage of House floor proceedings through http://houselive.gov.

House Democratic Cloakroom, *H222 CAP, 20515; (202) 225-7330. Fax, (202) 226-5659. Robert (Bob) Fischer, Manager. House floor action, (202) 225-7400. Legislative program, (202) 225-1600.*
Web, https://democraticcloakroom.house.gov and Twitter, @DemCloakroom

Provides information about House floor proceedings.

House Republican Cloakroom, *H223 CAP, 20515; (202) 225-7350. Fax, (202) 225-8247. Sarah Coyle, Cloakroom Director.*
Web, http://repcloakroom.house.gov and Twitter, @RepCloakroom

Provides information about House floor proceedings.

Senate Democratic Cloakroom, *S226 CAP, 20510; (202) 224-6191. Gary Myrick, Secretary. Senate floor action, (202) 224-8541.*
Web, www.democrats.senate.gov/floor and Twitter, @SenateDems

Provides information about Senate floor proceedings.

Senate Republican Cloakroom, *S225 CAP, 20510; (202) 224-4691. Fax, (202) 224-2860. Robert M. Duncan, Secretary. Senate floor action, (202) 224-8601.*
Twitter, @SenateCloakroom

Provides information about Senate floor proceedings.

U.S. House of Representatives, *Legislative Resource Center, B81 CHOB, 20515-6612; (202) 226-5200. Ronald (Dale) Thomas, Chief.*
General email, info.clerkweb@mail.house.gov
Web, http://clerk.house.gov/about/view/LRCDetailss

Records, stores, and provides legislative status information on all bills and resolutions pending in Congress.

▶**NEWS SERVICES**

Associated Press, *Washington Bureau, 1100 13th St. N.W., #500, 20005-4076; (202) 641-9000. Fax, (202) 263-8800. Anna Johnson, Bureau Chief.*
General email, info@ap.org
Web, www.ap.org, Twitter, @AP, Facebook, www.facebook.com/APNews and YouTube, www.youtube.com/ap

Publishes daybook that lists congressional committee meetings and hearings and their location and subject matter. Fee for services. (Headquarters in New York.)

CQ Roll Call, *FiscalNote, 1201 Pennsylvania Ave. N.W., 6th Floor, 20004; (202) 650-6500. Josh Resnik, Publisher; Tim Hwang, Chief Executive Officer. Toll-free, (800) 432-2250.*
Web, https://info.cq.com and Twitter, @CQnow

Provides nonpartisan online congressional news and analysis, including legislative summaries, votes, testimony, and archival and reference materials. Provides hearing and markup schedules, including time and location, meeting agendas, and full witness listings. Fee for services. (Merger of *Congressional Quarterly*, Roll Call, and Capitol Advantage; subsidiary of the Economist Group.)

United Press International (UPI), *1133 19th St. N.W., 20036; (202) 898-8000. Nicholas Chiaia, President; Michael J. Marshall, Editor-In-Chief (Emeritus).*
Web, www.upi.com, Twitter, @UPI and Facebook, www.facebook.com/UPI

Wire service that lists congressional committee meetings and hearings, locations, and subject matter. Fee for services.

CAMPAIGNS AND ELECTIONS

General

▶**AGENCIES**

Criminal Division *(Justice Dept.),* **Public Integrity (PIN),** *1301 New York Ave. N.W., 10th Floor, 20005; (202) 514-1412. Fax, (202) 514-3003. Corey R. Amundson, Chief.*
Web, www.justice.gov/criminal/pin

Supervises enforcement of federal criminal laws related to campaigns and elections. Oversees investigation of deprivation of voting rights; intimidation and coercion of voters; denial or promise of federal employment or other benefits; illegal political contributions, expenditures, and solicitations; and all other election violations referred to the division.

Federal Election Commission

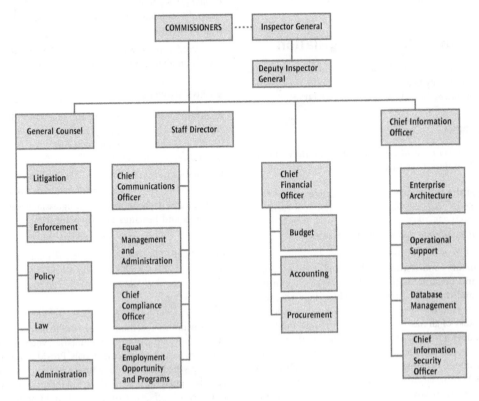

---- Denotes independent operation within the agency

Election Assistance Commission, *633 3rd St. N.W., #200, 20001 (mailing address: 200 Massachusetts Ave. N.W., #700, Washington, DC 20001); (301) 563-3919. Fax, (301) 734-3108. Mark Robbins, Executive Director (Acting). Toll-free, (866) 747-1471.*
Web, www.eac.gov, Facebook, www.facebook.com/eacgov1 and Twitter, @EACgov

Serves as national information clearinghouse on the administration of federal elections. Responsible for adopting voting system guidelines. Tests and certifies voting system hardware and software. Studies election technology and voting accessibility. Reports data from the states for each federal election and maintains the National Mail Voter registration form.

Federal Communications Commission (FCC), *Media Bureau (MB), Policy Division, 45 L St. N.E., 20554; (202) 418-2120. Fax, (202) 418-1069. Maria Mullarkey, Chief, (202) 418-1067.*
Web, www.fcc.gov/media/policy/policy-division

Handles complaints and inquiries concerning the equal time rule, which requires equal broadcast opportunities for all legally qualified candidates for the same office, and other political broadcast, cable, and satellite rules. Interprets and enforces related Communications Act provisions, including the requirement for sponsorship identification of all paid political broadcast, cable, and satellite announcements and the requirement for broadcasters to furnish federal candidates with reasonable access to broadcast time for political advertising. Administers Equal Employment Opportunity (EEO) matters.

Federal Election Commission (FEC), *1050 1st St. N.E., 20463; (202) 694-1100. Shana M. Broussard, Commissioner. Press, (202) 694-1220. Information, (202) 694-1100. Public records, (202) 694-1130. Toll-free, (800) 424-9530. TTY, (202) 219-3336.*
General email, info@fec.gov
Web, www.fec.gov and Twitter, @FEC

Formulates, administers, and enforces policy with respect to the Federal Election Campaign Act of 1971 as amended, including campaign finance disclosure requirements, contribution and expenditure limitations, and public financing of presidential nominating campaigns. Receives campaign finance reports; makes rules and regulations; conducts audits and investigations. Makes copies of campaign finance reports available for inspection.

Federal Election Commission (FEC), *Campaign Financial Data, 1050 1st St. N.E., 20463; John Quinlan, Chief Financial Officer. Public Records Office, (202) 694-1120. Press, (202) 694-1220. Toll-free, (800) 424-9530, ext. 2.*

General email, pubrec@fec.gov

Web, www.fec.gov/data

Makes available for public inspection and copying the detailed campaign finance reports on contributions and expenditures filed by candidates for federal office, their supporting political committees, and individuals and committees making expenditures on behalf of a candidate. Maintains copies of all reports and statements filed since 1972.

►CONGRESS

For a listing of relevant congressional committees and subcommittees, please see page 797 or the Appendix.

House Communications Standards Commission, 1307 LHOB, 20515-6328; (202) 225-9337. Fax, (202) 225-7664. Rep. Mary Gay Scanlon, Chair; Rep. Kat Cammack, Ranking Member.
Web, https://cha.house.gov/about-commission

Issues regulations governing mass mailings by members' offices. Receives complaints, conducts investigations, and issues decisions on disputes arising from the alleged abuse of franked mail by House members.

U.S. House of Representatives, *Legislative Resource Center, Records and Registration,* 135 CHOB, 20515-6612; (202) 226-5200. Steve Pingeton, Manager.
Web, http://clerk.house.gov/about/viewLRCDetails and Email, info.clerkweb@mail.house.gov

Receives personal financial disclosure reports for members of the House, candidates for the House, and certain employees. Open for public inspection.

►NONGOVERNMENTAL

American Assn. of Political Consultants, 1775 Tysons Blvd., 5th Floor, McLean, VA 22102; (703) 245-8020. Fax, (703) 995-0628. Alana Joyce, Executive Director, (703) 245-8021.
General email, info@theaapc.org
Web, www.theaapc.org, Twitter, @theaapc and Facebook, www.facebook.com/AAPCFans

Membership: political consultants, media specialists, campaign managers, corporate public affairs officers, pollsters, public officials, academicians, fundraisers, lobbyists, college students, and congressional staffers. Focuses on ethics of the profession; provides members with opportunities to meet industry leaders and learn new techniques and emerging technologies.

American Bar Assn. (ABA), *Standing Committee on Election Law,* 1050 Connecticut Ave. N.W., #400, 20036; (202) 662-1694. Amy Horton-Newell, Director of Center for Public Interest Law, (202) 662-1693.
General email, election@americanbar.org
Web, www.americanbar.org/groups/public_services/election_law.html

Studies ways to improve the U.S. election and campaign process.

The Campaign Legal Center, 1101 14th St. N.W., #400, 20005; (202) 736-2200. Fax, (202) 736-2222. Trevor Potter, President.
General email, info@campaignlegalcenter.org
Web, https://campaignlegal.org, Twitter, @CampaignLegal and Facebook, www.facebook.com/CampaignLegalCenter

Works to improve the U.S. democratic process across all levels of government through public education, litigation, policy analysis and debate, participation in regulatory proceedings, and drafting prodemocracy laws and policies and advocating their adoption.

Commission on Presidential Debates, 1200 New Hampshire Ave. N.W., #445, 20036 (mailing address: P.O Box 58247, Washington, DC 20037); (202) 872-1020. Janet H. Brown, Executive Director.
Web, http://debates.org, Twitter, @debates and Press, media@debates.org

Independent nonpartisan organization established to sponsor general election presidential and vice presidential debates and to undertake educational and research activities related to the debates.

Common Cause, 805 15th St. N.W., #800, 20005; (202) 833-1200. Karen Hobert Flynn, President. Press, (202) 736-5712.
General email, CauseNet@commoncause.org
Web, www.commoncause.org, Twitter, @CommonCause and Facebook, www.facebook.com/CommonCause

Nonpartisan national citizens' lobby on behalf of open, honest, and accountable government. Through 400,000 members and supporters, works in Washington and state capitals in support of limits on contributions and spending, high ethical standards in government, voting rights, media reform, and economic justice.

CQ Political MoneyLine, 1201 Pennsylvania Ave. N.W., #600, 20004; (202) 793-5300. Kent Cooper, Editor; Tony Raymond, Editor.
Web, www.politicalmoneyline.com

Monitors and reports on money as it is used in campaigns, political action committees, 527s, political parties, and by lobbyists. (Affiliated with Fiscal Note.)

Electionline.org, 2630 Adams Mill Rd. N.W., #208, 20009; (202) 588-7332. Mindy Moretti, Editor-In-Chief.
General email, mmoretti@electionline.org
Web, https://electionline.org and Twitter, @electiononline

Online resource providing news and analysis on election reform. (Receives support from Hewlett Fund and Democracy Fund.)

OpenSecrets.org / Center for Responsive Politics, 1300 L St. N.W., #200, 20005; (202) 857-0044. Fax, (202) 857-7809. Sheila Krumholz, Executive Director. Press, (202) 354-0111.
General email, info@crp.org; press@crp.org
Web, www.opensecrets.org and Twitter, @opensecretsdc

Conducts research on the effects on federal campaign finance and lobbying in connection with congressional and presidential elections and public policy.

Election Statistics and Apportionment

▶AGENCIES

Census Bureau *(Commerce Dept.), Census Redistricting Data, 4600 Silver Hill Rd., #4H057, Suitland, MD 20746 (mailing address: 4600 Silver Hill Rd., #4H057, Washington, DC 20233-0100); (301) 763-4039. Fax, (301) 763-4348. James C. A. Whitehorne, Chief, (301) 763-9051.*
General email, RDO@census.gov

Web, www.census.gov/rdo

Provides state legislatures with population figures for use in legislative redistricting.

Census Bureau *(Commerce Dept.), Customer Liaison and Marketing Services, 4600 Silver Hill Rd., #8H180, 20233 (mailing address: Customer Service, Bureau of the Census, MS 0801, Washington, DC 20233-0500); (301) 763-0228. Misty L. Reed, Chief. Press, (301) 763-3030.*
Web, www.census.gov

Main contact for information about the Census Bureau's products and services. Census data and maps on counties, municipalities, and other small areas are available on the website and in libraries.

Census Bureau *(Commerce Dept.), Population, 4600 Silver Hill Rd., #6H174, Suitland, MD 20746 (mailing address: 4600 Silver Hill Rd., #6H174, Washington, DC 20233-8800); (301) 763-2071. Karen Battle, Chief.*
General email, pop@census.gov

Web, www.census.gov/programs-surveys/popproj.html

Computes every ten years the population figures that determine the number of representatives each state may have in the House of Representatives.

▶CONGRESS

For a listing of relevant congressional committees and subcommittees, please see page 797 or the Appendix.

Clerk of the U.S. House of Representatives, *H154 CAP, 20515-6601; (202) 225-7000. Cheryl L. Johnson, Clerk. Press, (202) 225-1908.*
General email, info.clerkweb@mail.house.gov

Web, http://clerk.house.gov

Publishes biennial compilation of statistics on congressional and presidential elections.

▶NONGOVERNMENTAL

Common Cause, *State Organization, 805 15th St. N.W., #800, 20005; (202) 833-1200. Pam Wilmot, Vice President*

for State Operations, (617) 426-9600. Press, (202) 736-5712.
Web, www.commoncause.org

Nonpartisan citizens' lobby on behalf of open, honest, and accountable government. Offices in Washington, DC, and 35 states. Supports independent redistricting commissions to draw congressional and state legislative districts. Works for laws strengthening voting rights and modern voting equipment.

Voting, Political Participation

▶NONGOVERNMENTAL

America Votes, *1155 Connecticut Ave. N.W., #600, 20036; (202) 962-7240. Fax, (202) 962-7241. Sara Schreiber, Executive Director.*
General email, info@americavotes.org

Web, www.americavotes.org, Twitter, @AmericaVotes, Facebook, www.facebook.com/AmericaVotesOrg and Press, press@americavotes.org

Coalition that seeks to increase voter registration, education, and participation in electoral politics.

Arab American Institute, *1600 K St. N.W., #601, 20006; (202) 429-9210. Fax, (202) 429-9214. James J. Zogby, President.*
General email, communications@aaiusa.org

Web, www.aaiusa.org and Twitter, @AAIUSA

Fosters civic and political empowerment of Americans of Arab descent through research, policy formation, and political activism.

Center for Economic and Policy Research (CEPR), *1611 Connecticut Ave. N.W., #400, 20009; (202) 293-5380. Eileen Applebaum, Co-Director, ext. 116; Mark Weisbrot, Co-Director.*
General email, info@cepr.net

Web, http://cepr.net, Twitter, @ceprdc and Facebook, www.facebook.com/ceprDC

Researches economic and social issues and the impact of related public policies. Presents findings to the public with the goal of better preparing citizens to choose among various policy options. Promotes democratic debate and voter education. Areas of interest include health care, trade, financial reform, Social Security, taxes, housing, and the labor market.

Clare Booth Luce Center for Conservative Women, *112 Elden St., Suite P, Herndon, VA 20170; (703) 318-0730. Fax, (703) 318-8867. Michelle Easton, President.*
General email, info@cblwomen.org

Web, http://cblpi.org, Twitter, @CBLwomen and Facebook, www.facebook.com/CenterforConservativeWomen

Seeks to prepare women for effective leadership and to promote conservative values. Offers mentoring, internship, and networking opportunities. (Formerly the Clare Booth Luce Policy Institute.)

Coalition of Black Trade Unionists, *1155 Connecticut Ave. N.W., #500, 20036 (mailing address: P.O. Box 66268,*

Resources for Political Participation

NATIONWIDE CAMPAIGNS

Democratic Congressional Campaign Committee,
(202) 863-1500; www.dccc.org

Democratic Governors Assn., (202) 772-5600;
www.democraticgovernors.org

Democratic National Committee (DNC), (202) 863-8000;
www.democrats.org

Democratic Senatorial Campaign Committee,
(202) 224-2447; www.dscc.org

FairVote, (301) 270-4616; www.fairvote.org

Fieldworks, (202) 667-4400; www.fieldworks.com

Green Party of the United States, (202) 319-7191;
www.gp.org

League of Women Voters (LWV), (202) 429-1965;
www.lwv.org

Libertarian Party, (202) 333-0008; www.lp.org

National Republican Congressional Committee,
(202) 479-7000; www.nrcc.org

National Republican Senatorial Committee,
(202) 675-6000; www.nrsc.org

Project Mobilize, www.mobilize.org

Republican Governors Assn., (202) 662-4140; www.rga.org

Republican National Committee (RNC), (202) 863-8500;
www.gop.com

Rock the Vote, (202) 719-9910; www.rockthevote.org

IN MARYLAND, VIRGINIA, AND WASHINGTON, D.C.

DC Vote, (202) 462-6000; www.dcvote.org

District of Columbia Board of Elections, (202) 727-2525;
www.dcboe.org

Maryland State Board of Elections, (800) 222-8683 or
(410) 269-2840; TTY,(800) 735-2258;
www.elections.state.md.us

Virginia Dept. of Elections, (804) 864-8901;
www.elections.virginia.gov

Volunteer on Election Day in Maryland, (800) 222-8683 or
(410) 269-2840; www.elections.state.md.us/get_involved

Washington, DC 20035); (202) 778-3318. Fax, (202) 419-1486. Terrence L. (Terry) Melvin, President.
General email, cbtu@cbtu.org

Web, https://cbtu.nationbuilder.com

Monitors legislation affecting African American and other minority trade unionists. Focuses on equal employment opportunity, unemployment, and voter education and registration.

Democracy 21, *2000 Massachusetts Ave. N.W., 20036; (202) 355-9600. Fax, (202) 355-9606. Fred Wertheimer, President.*
General email, info@Democracy21.org

Web, https://democracy21.org, Twitter, @FredWertheimer and Facebook, www.facebook.com/Democracy21News

Focuses on using the communications revolution to strengthen democracy and on eliminating the influence of big money in American politics.

FairVote, *6930 Carroll Ave., #240, Takoma Park, MD 20912; (301) 270-4616. Robert Richie, President.*
General email, hello@fairvote.org

Web, www.fairvote.org, Twitter, @fairvote and Facebook, www.facebook.com/FairVoteReform

Studies how voting systems affect participation, representation, and governance both domestically and internationally. Advocates electoral reform, ranks choice voting, and multimember districts at the local, state, and national levels. (Formerly the Center for Voting and Democracy.)

Internet Education Foundation, *1440 G St. N.W., 20005 (mailing address: 655 15th NW, Suite 800,*

Washington DC 20005); (202) 638-4370. Tim Lordan, Executive Director.

Web, www.neted.org and Twitter, @NetEdFound

Sponsors educational initiatives promoting the Internet as a valuable medium for democratic participation, communications, and commerce. Funds the Congressional Internet Caucus Advisory Committee, which works to inform Congress of important Internet-related policy issues. Monitors legislation and regulations.

Joint Center for Political and Economic Studies, *633 Pennsylvania Ave. N.W., 20004; (202) 789-3500. Fax, (202) 789-6390. Spencer Overton, President.*
General email, info@jointcenter.org

Web, www.jointcenter.org, Twitter, @JointCenter, Facebook, www.facebook.com/JointCenter1970 and YouTube, www.youtube.com/channel/UCp9whNSjW mlqW8v4K1-tyvA

Documents and analyzes the political and economic status of African Americans, focusing on political participation, economic advancement, and health policy. Disseminates information through forums and conferences.

Labor Council for Latin American Advancement, *815 16th St. N.W., 3rd Floor, 20006; (202) 508-6919. Fax, (202) 508-6922. Karla Pineda, Deputy Director.*
General email, headquarters@lclaa.org

Web, www.lclaa.org, Twitter, @LCLAA and Facebook, www.facebook.com/LCLAA

Membership: Latino/a trade unionists throughout U.S. and Puerto Rico. Encourages equal employment opportunity, voter registration, and participation in the political process. (Affiliated with the AFL-CIO and the Change to Win Federation.)

League of Women Voters (LWV), *1233 20th St. N.W., #5000, 20036-4508; (202) 429-1965. Virginia Kase Solomon, Chief Executive Officer.*
General email, lwv@lwv.org
Web, www.lwv.org, Twitter, @LWV and Facebook, www .facebook.com/leagueofwomenvoters

Membership: women and men interested in nonpartisan political action and study. Works to increase participation in government; provides information on voter registration and balloting. Interests include social policy, natural resources, international relations, and representative government.

National Assn. of Latino Elected and Appointed Officials Educational Fund, *Washington Office, 600 Pennsylvania Ave. S.E., #480, 20003; (202) 546-2536. Fax, (202) 546-4121. Arturo Vargas, Executive Director; Rosalind Gold, Chief Public Policy Officer.*
Web, www.naleo.org, Twitter, @NALEO and Twitter, @ArturoNALEO

Research and advocacy group that provides civic affairs information and assistance on legislation affecting Latinos. Encourages Latino participation in local, state, and national politics. Interests include health care and social, economic, and educational issues. (Headquarters in Los Angeles, Calif.)

National Black Caucus of Local Elected Officials (NBC/ LEO), *National League of Cities, 660 N. Capitol St. N.W., 20001; (202) 626-3000. Leon Andrews, Director for Race, Equity, and Leadership, (202) 626-3039. Toll-free, (877) 827-2385.*
General email, constituencygroups@nlc.org
Web, www.nlc.org/initiative/national-black-caucus-of- local-elected-officials-nbc-leo

Membership: Black elected officials at the local level and other interested individuals. Seeks to increase Black participation on the National League of Cities' steering and policy committees. Informs members on issues, and plans strategies for achieving objectives through legislation and direct action. Interests include cultural diversity, local government and community participation, housing, economics, job training, the family, and human rights. Affiliated with the National League of Cities.

National Black Caucus of State Legislators, *444 N. Capitol St. N.W., #622, 20001; (202) 624-5457. Fax, (202) 508-3826. Paula Hoisington, Executive Director. Web, https://nbcsl.org and Facebook, www.facebook.com/ nbcslnews*

Membership: Black state legislators. Promotes effective leadership among Black state legislators through education, research, and training; serves as an information network and clearinghouse for members.

National Coalition on Black Civic Participation, *1666 K St. N.W., 4th Floor, #440, 20006; (202) 659-4929. Fax, (202) 659-5025. Melanie L. Campbell, President.*

General email, ncbcp@ncbcp.org
Web, www.ncbcp.org, Twitter, @NCBCP and Facebook, www.facebook.com/NCBCP

Seeks to increase Black voter civic participation to eliminate barriers to political participation for Black Americans. Sponsors a variety of voter education, registration, and get-out-the-vote and protect-the-vote activities, including Operation Big Vote, Black Youth Vote, Black Women's Roundtable, the Information Resource Center, Civic Engagement, Voices of the Electorate, and the Unity Black Voter Empowerment Campaign. Monitors legislation and regulations.

National Congress of Black Women, *1250 4th St. N.W., #WG-1, 20024; (202) 678-6788. E. Faye Williams, Co-President; Lynn Dymally, Co-President.*
Web, www.nationalcongressbw.org

Nonpartisan political organization that encourages Black American women to participate in the political process. Advocates nonpartisan voter registration and encourages Black American women to engage in other political activities. Develops positions and participates in platform development and strategies that address the needs of communities at every level of government.

National Women's Political Caucus, *1001 Connecticut Ave. N.W., #630, 20036 (mailing address: P.O. Box 65010, Washington, DC 20035); (202) 785-1100. Kate McDonald, Program Director.*
General email, info@nwpc.org
Web, www.nwpc.org, Twitter, @NWPCNational and Facebook, www.facebook.com/NWPC.fb

Membership. Advocacy group that seeks greater involvement of women in politics. Seeks to identify, recruit, and train women for elective and appointive political office, regardless of party affiliation; serves as an information clearinghouse on women in politics, particularly during election campaigns; publishes directory of women holding federal and state offices.

Pew Research Center, *U.S. Politics and Policy Project, 1615 L St. N.W., #800, 20036; (202) 419-4300. Fax, (202) 419-8562. Carroll Doherty, Director, (202) 419-4363.*
Web, www.people-press.org and Director, Twitter, @CarrollDoherty

Studies attitudes toward politics and public policy issues as well as the changing U.S. electorate through public opinion research. Conducts national surveys measuring public attentiveness to major news stories; charts trends in values and political and social attitudes. Makes survey results available online, free of charge.

Republican National Committee (RNC), *Political Director, 310 1st St. S.E., 20003; (202) 863-8500. Fax, (202) 863-8820. Ronna McDaniel, Chair; Thomas O. Hicks Jr., Co-Chair.*
General email, ecampaign@gop.com
Web, www.gop.com

Responsible for electoral activities at the federal, state, and local levels; operates party constituency outreach programs; coordinates voter registration.

Voter Participation Center, *1707 L St. N.W., #950, 20036; (202) 659-9570. Fax, (202) 659-9585. Tom Lopach, President. Toll-free, (877) 255-6750.*
General email, info@voterparticipation.org
Web, www.voterparticipation.org and Twitter, @VoterCenter

Nonpartisan organization that seeks to increase voter participation, especially of unmarried women (single, widowed, divorced, or separated), people of color, and 18-to-29-year-old citizens. (Formerly Women's Voices, Women Vote.)

Women & Politics Institute *(American University), 4400 Massachusetts Ave. N.W., Kerwin Hall, #109E, 20016; (202) 885-2903. Fax, (202) 885-2967. Betsy Fischer Martin, Executive Director, (202) 885-6149.*
General email, wpi@american.edu
Web, www.american.edu/spa/wpi and Twitter, @AU_WPI

Research center that encourages women to participate in politics and addresses women's issues. Administers graduate and undergraduate certificates to academics studying women, policy, and political leadership. Assists women in securing employment in the political sphere through leadership training programs.

Younger Women's Task Force, *1310 L St. N.W., #1000, 20005; (202) 785-7700. Fax, (202) 872-1425.*
Gloria Blackwell, Chief Executive Officer. Toll-free, (800) 326-2289. TTY, (202) 785-7777.
General email, ywtf@aauw.org
Web, www.aauw.org/membership/ywtf, Twitter, @AAUW and Facebook, www.facebook.com/AAUW.National

Grassroots organization that encourages young women to engage in political activism on issues directly affecting them. Provides leadership training and a local and national network for peer mentoring. (Sponsored by the American Assn. of University Women.)

CAPITOL

Capitol switchboard, (202) 224-3121, and Federal Relay Service (TTY), (800) 877-8339. See also 117th Congress (p. 839) for each member's office.

General

▶CONGRESS

Architect of the Capitol, *SB15 CAP, 20515; (202) 228-1793. Fax, (202) 228-1893. J. Brett Blanton III, Architect. Flag Office, (202) 228-4239.*
Web, www.aoc.gov and Twitter, @uscapitol

Maintains the Capitol and its grounds, the House and Senate office buildings, Capitol power plant, Robert A.

Taft Memorial, Thurgood Marshall Federal Judiciary Building, Capitol Police headquarters, and buildings and grounds of the Supreme Court and the Library of Congress; operates the Capitol Visitor Center and the Botanic Garden and Senate restaurants. Acquires property and plans and constructs buildings for Congress, the Supreme Court, and the Library of Congress. Assists the Congress in deciding which artwork, historical objects, and exhibits are to be accepted for display in the Capitol and is responsible for their care and repair, as well as the maintenance and restoration of murals and architectural elements throughout the Capitol campus. Arranges inaugural ceremonies and other ceremonies held in the buildings or on the grounds. Flag office flies American flags over the Capitol at legislators' request.

Senate Commission on Art, *S411 CAP, 20510; (202) 224-2955. Melinda Smith, Curator of the Senate.*
General email, curator@sec.senate.gov
Web, www.senate.gov/art-artifacts/art-artifacts.htm

Accepts artwork and historical objects for display in Senate office buildings and the Senate wing of the Capitol. Maintains and exhibits Senate collections (paintings, sculptures, furniture, and manuscripts); oversees and maintains old Senate and Supreme Court chambers.

Superintendent of the House Office Buildings, *Architect of the Capitol (AOC), 2046 RHOB, 20515; (202) 225-4141. Stephanie Jones, Superintendent, (202) 224-3141.*
Web, www.aoc.gov/about-us/organizational-structure/office-chief-operations/house-office-buildings-jurisdiction, Twitter, @uscapitol, Facebook, www.facebook.com/ArchitectoftheCapitol and YouTube, www.youtube.com/user/AOCgov

Oversees construction, maintenance, and operation of House office buildings; assigns office space to House members under rules of procedure established by the Speaker's office and the House Office Building Commission.

Superintendent of the Senate Office Buildings, *Architect of the Capitol (AOC), G245 SDOB, 20510; (202) 224-3141. Stephanie Jones, Superintendent, (202) 224-3141.*
Web, www.aoc.gov/about-us/organizational-structure/office-chief-operations/senate-office-buildings-jurisdiction, Twitter, @uscapitol, Facebook, www.facebook.com/ArchitectoftheCapitol and YouTube, www.youtube.com/user/AOCgov

Oversees construction, maintenance, and operation of Senate office buildings.

U.S. Botanic Garden, *100 Maryland Ave. S.W., 20001 (mailing address: 245 1st St. S.W., Washington, DC 20024); (202) 225-8333. Saharah Moon Chapotin, Executive Director, (202) 225-1110. Horticulture hotline, (202) 226-4785. Press, (202) 226-4145. Program registration information, (202) 225-1116. Special events, (202) 226-7674. Tour line, (202) 226-2055.*

General email, usbg@aoc.gov

Web, www.usbg.gov and Facebook, www.facebook.com/USBotanicGarden

Collects, cultivates, and grows various plants for public display and study.

U.S. Capitol Police, 119 D St. N.E., 20510; (202) 224-5151. J. Thomas Manger, Chief. Public information, (202) 224-1677. Toll-free, (877) 872-7111.
General email, P10@uscp.gov

Web, www.uscp.gov

Responsible for security for the Capitol, House and Senate office buildings, and Botanic Garden; approves demonstration permits.

▶ **NONGOVERNMENTAL**

U.S. Capitol Historical Society, 200 Maryland Ave. N.E., 20002; (202) 543-8919. Jane L. Campbell, President, ext. 12. Toll-free, (800) 887-9318.
Web, https://uschs.org, Twitter, @CapitolHistory and Facebook, www.facebook.com/USCapHis

Membership: members of Congress, individuals, and organizations interested in the preservation of the history and traditions of the U.S. Capitol. Conducts historical research; offers tours, lectures, workshops, and films; holds events involving members of Congress; publishes an annual historical calendar.

Tours and Events

▶ **CONGRESS**

The House and Senate public galleries are open when Congress is in session. The House galleries are also open when the House is not in session. Free gallery passes are available from any congressional office.

Architect of the Capitol, *Congressional Accessibility Services,* Crypt of The Capitol, 20510; (202) 224-4048. Fax, (202) 228-4679. David Hauck, Director. Service Center, (202) 228-8800. TTY, (202) 224-4049.
Web, www.aoc.gov/accessibility-services

Office works to make the Capitol and its grounds and buildings accessible to members of Congress, staff, and the public.

Sergeant at Arms and Doorkeeper of the U.S. Senate, S151 CAP, 20510-7200; (202) 224-2341. Karen Gibson, Sergeant at Arms and Doorkeeper.
Web, www.senate.gov/reference/office/sergeant_at_arms.htm and Twitter, @Senatesaa

Enforces rules and regulations of the Senate public gallery. Responsible for security of the Capitol and Senate buildings. Approves visiting band performances on the Senate steps. (To arrange for performances, contact your senator.)

Sergeant at Arms of the U.S. House of Representatives, H124 CAP, 20515-6611; (202) 225-2456. Fax, (202) 225-3233. William J. Walker, Sergeant at Arms.
General email, saamail@mail.house.gov

Web, www.house.gov/the-house-explained/officers-and-organizations/sergeant-at-arms

Enforces rules and regulations of the House public gallery. Responsible for the security of the Capitol and House buildings. Approves visiting band performances on the House steps. (To arrange for performances, contact your representative.)

U.S. Capitol Visitor Center, The Capitol, 20510; (202) 226-8000. Beth Plemmons, Chief Executive Officer for Visitor Services. Press, (202) 593-1829. Press, (202) 593-0099. Visitor information, (202) 225-6827.
Web, http://visitthecapitol.gov, Twitter, @visitthecapitol, Facebook, www.facebook.com/USCapitol and YouTube, www.youtube.com/visitthecapitol

Offers the general public free guided tours of the interior of the U.S. Capitol. Provides accommodations for visitors with special needs.

▶ **NONGOVERNMENTAL**

U.S. Capitol Historical Society, 200 Maryland Ave. N.E., 20002; (202) 543-8919. Jane L. Campbell, President, ext. 12. Toll-free, (800) 887-9318.
Web, https://uschs.org, Twitter, @CapitolHistory and Facebook, www.facebook.com/USCapHis

Offers tours, lectures, films, publications, and merchandise; maintains information centers in the Capitol.

CONGRESS AT WORK

See 116th Congress (p. 839) for members' offices and committee assignments and for rosters of congressional committees and subcommittees.

General

▶ **CONGRESS**

For a listing of relevant congressional committees and subcommittees, please see page 797 or the Appendix.

House Recording Studio, 2010 RHOB, 20515; (202) 225-3941. Fax, (202) 225-0707. Mike Allen, Director.
Web, https://cao.house.gov/about/business-units

Assists House members in making tape recordings. Provides daily gavel-to-gavel television coverage of House floor proceedings.

Interparliamentary Affairs, HC4 CAP, 20515; (202) 225-0600. Kate Knudson, Director.
Web, https://speaker.gov

Assists the House Speaker with international travel and the reception of foreign legislators.

Interparliamentary Services, *808 SHOB, 20510; (202) 224-3047. Sally Walsh, Director.*

Provides support to senators participating in interparliamentary conferences and other international travel. Responsible for financial, administrative, and protocol functions.

Office of Photography, *U.S. House of Representatives, B302 RHOB, 20515; (202) 225-2840. Fax, (202) 225-5896. Jeffrey S. (Jeff) Blakley, Director of Digital Media Services. Chief Administration Office, (202) 226-6660.*
Web, cao.house.gov

Provides House members with photographic assistance.

Parliamentarian of the U.S. House of Representatives, *H209 CAP, 20515; (202) 225-7373. Jason Smith, Parliamentarian.*
Web, www.house.gov/the-house-explained/officers-and-organizations/parliamentarian-of-the-house

Advises presiding officers on parliamentary procedures and committee jurisdiction over legislation; prepares and maintains a compilation of the precedents of the House.

Parliamentarian of the U.S. Senate, *S133 CAP, 20510; (202) 224-6128. Elizabeth C. MacDonough, Parliamentarian.*

Advises presiding officers on parliamentary procedures and committee jurisdiction over legislation; prepares and maintains a compilation of the precedents of the Senate.

Senate Democratic Policy and Communications Center, *S318 CAP, 20510; (202) 224-3232. Sen. Debbie Stabenow, Chair; Sen. Joe Manchin, Vice Chair.*
Web, www.democrats.senate.gov/dpcc

Offers radio, television, and Internet services to Senate Democrats and their staffs to more effectively disseminate information to constituents at home.

Sergeant at Arms and Doorkeeper of the U.S. Senate, *Senate Photo Studio, G85 SDOB, 20510; (202) 224-6000. Vacant, Manager.*

Provides Senate members with photographic assistance.

Sergeant at Arms of the U.S. House of Representatives, *Emergency Management Division, 192 FHOB, 20515-6462; (202) 226-0950. Fax, (202) 226-6598. Bob Dohr, Sergeant at Arms Chief Operating Officer.*

Liaises between the House and the Homeland Security Dept., the U.S. Capitol Police, and other responders in the coordination of response to emergency situations.

Leadership

▶HOUSE

See House Leadership and Partisan Committees (p. 864–865).

House Democratic Caucus, *B245 LHOB, 20515; (202) 225-1400. Rep. Hakeem Jeffries, Chair; Rep. Pete Aguilar, Vice Chair.*

General email, democratic.caucus@mail.house.gov
Web, www.dems.gov and Twitter, @HouseDemocrats

Membership: House Democrats. Selects Democratic leadership; formulates party rules and floor strategy; considers caucus members' recommendations on major issues; votes on the Democratic Steering and Policy Committee's recommendations for Democratic committee assignments.

House Democratic Steering and Policy Committee, *233 CHOB, 20515-6527; (202) 225-0100. Fax, (202) 225-4188. Rep. Eric Swalwell, Co-Chair; Rep. Barbara Lee, Co-Chair.*

Makes recommendations to the Democratic leadership on party policy and priorities and participates in decision making with the leadership.

House Republican Conference, *2211 RHOB, 20515; (202) 225-4611. Rep. Elise Stefanik, Chair; Rep. Mike Johnson, Vice Chair.*
Web, www.gop.gov, Twitter, @HouseGOP and Facebook, www.facebook.com/HouseRepublicans

Membership: House Republicans. Selects Republican leadership; formulates party rules and floor strategy, and considers party positions on major legislation; votes on the Republican Committee on Committees' recommendations for House committee chairs and Republican committee assignments; publishes Weekly Floor Briefing and Daily Floor Briefing, which analyze pending legislation.

House Republican Policy Committee, *170 CHOB, 20515-6549; (202) 225-4921. Fax, (202) 225-2082. Rep. Gary Palmer, Chair; Cari Fike, Executive Director. General email, policycommittee@mail.house.gov*
Web, http://republicanpolicy.house.gov, Twitter, @GOPpolicy and Facebook, www.facebook.com/RepublicanPolicyCommittee

Studies legislation and makes recommendations on House Republican policies and positions on proposed legislation.

Majority Leader of the U.S. House of Representatives, *1705 LHOB, 20515; (202) 225-3130. Fax, (202) 225-4300. Rep. Steny Hoyer, Majority Leader.*
Web, www.majorityleader.gov, Twitter, @LeaderHoyer and Facebook, www.facebook.com/LeaderHoyer

Serves as chief strategist and floor spokesperson for the majority party in the House.

Majority Whip of the U.S. House of Representatives, *H329 CAP, 20515; (202) 226-3210. Fax, (202) 225-9253. Rep. James E. Clyburn, Majority Whip.*
Web, http://majoritywhip.house.gov, Twitter, @WhipClyburn and Facebook, www.facebook.com/WhipClyburn/?ref=bookmarks

Serves as assistant majority leader in the House; helps marshal majority forces in support of party strategy.

Minority Leader of the U.S. House of Representatives, *H204 CAP, 20515-6537; (202) 225-4000. Rep. Kevin McCarthy, Minority Leader.*

Web, www.republicanleader.gov and *Twitter, @GOPLeader*

Serves as chief strategist and floor spokesperson for the minority party in the House.

Minority Whip of the U.S. House of Representatives,
1705 LHOB, 20515; (202) 225-3015. Rep. Steve Scalise, Minority Whip.
Web, www.republicanwhip.gov, Twitter, @SteveScalise and *Facebook, www.facebook.com/RepSteveScalise*

Serves as assistant minority leader in the House; helps marshal minority forces in support of party strategy.

Speaker of the U.S. House of Representatives, *Speaker's Office, 1236 LHOB, 20515; (202) 225-4965.*
Rep. Nancy Pelosi, Speaker.
Web, www.speaker.gov, Twitter, @SpeakerPelosi and *Facebook, www.facebook.com/NancyPelosi*

Presides over the House while in session; preserves decorum and order; announces vote results; recognizes members for debate and introduction of bills, amendments, and motions; refers bills and resolutions to committees; decides points of order; appoints House members to conference committees; votes at own discretion.

►SENATE

See Senate Leadership and Partisan Committees (p. 942).

Democratic Policy and Communication Center, *419 SHOB, #731, 20510; (202) 224-3232. Fax, (202) 228-3432. Sen. Debbie Stabenow, Chair, (202) 224-4822.*
Web, www.democrats.senate.gov/dpcc

Studies and makes recommendations to the Democratic leadership on legislation for consideration by the Senate; prepares policy papers and develops Democratic policy initiatives.

Democratic Steering and Outreach Committee, *712 SHOB, 20510; (202) 224-9048. Sen. Amy Klobuchar, Chair. General email, steering@dsoc.senate.gov*
Web, www.democrats.senate.gov/dsoc

Makes Democratic committee assignments subject to approval by the Senate Democratic Conference. Develops and maintains relationships with leaders and organizations outside of Congress.

Majority Leader of the U.S. Senate, *322 SROB, 20510-1702; (202) 224-6542. Fax, (202) 228-3027.*
Sen. Charles E. (Chuck) Schumer, Majority Leader.
Web, www.schumer.senate.gov, Twitter, @SenSchumer and *Facebook, www.facebook.com/senschumer*

Serves as chief strategist and floor spokesperson for the majority party in the Senate.

Majority Whip of the U.S. Senate, *711 HSB, 20510; (202) 224-2152. Fax, (202) 228-0400.*
Sen. Richard J. (Dick) Durbin, Majority Whip.
Web, www.durbin.senate.gov, Twitter, @SenatorDurbin and *Facebook, www.facebook.com/SenatorDurbin*

Serves as majority assistant leader in the Senate; helps marshal majority forces in support of party strategy.

Minority Leader of the U.S. Senate, *317 SROB, 20510; (202) 224-2541. Fax, (202) 244-2499.*
Sen. Mitch McConnell, Minority Leader.
Web, www.mcconnell.senate.gov/public, Twitter, @McConnellPress and *Facebook, www.facebook.com/mitchmcconnell*

Serves as chief strategist and floor spokesperson for the minority party in the Senate.

Minority Whip of the U.S. Senate, *SD 511, 20510; (202) 224-2321. Fax, (202) 228-5429. Sen. John Thune, Minority Whip. Toll-free, (866) 850-3855.*
Web, www.thune.senate.gov/public, Twitter, @SenJohnThune and *Facebook, www.facebook.com/SenJohnThune*

Serves as assistant minority leader in the Senate; helps marshal minority forces in support of party strategy.

President Pro Tempore of the U.S. Senate, *437 RSOB, 20510-4402; (202) 224-4242. Fax, (202) 229-3479.*
Sen. Patrick Leahy, President Pro Tempore.
Web, www.leahy.senate.gov and *Facebook, www.facebook.com/SenatorPatrickLeahy*

Presides over the Senate in the absence of the vice president.

Senate Democratic Conference, *S309 CAP, 20510; (202) 224-3735. Sen. Charles E. Schumer, Chair;*
Sen. Elizabeth Warren, Vice Chair; Sen. Mark R. Warner, Vice Chair; Sen. Tammy Baldwin, Secretary.
Web, www.democrats.senate.gov and *Twitter, @SenateDems*

Membership: Democratic senators. Selects Democratic leadership; formulates party rules and floor strategy and considers party positions on major legislation; votes on the Democratic Steering Committee's recommendations for Democratic committee assignments.

Senate Republican Conference, *405 SHOB, 20510; (202) 224-2764. Fax, (202) 228-4276. Sen. John Barrasso, Chair;*
Sen. Joni Ernst, Vice Chair.
Web, www.republican.senate.gov and *Twitter, @SenateGOP*

Membership: Republican senators. Serves as caucus and central coordinating body of the party. Organizes and elects Senate Republican leadership; votes on Republican Committee on Committees' recommendations for Senate committee chairs and Republican committee assignments. Staff provides various support and media services for Republican members.

Senate Republican Policy Committee, *347 SROB, 20510; (202) 224-2946. Fax, (202) 228-2628. Sen. Roy Blunt, Chair; Stacy McBride, Director.*
General email, SenateRPC_@RPC.Senate.gov
Web, www.rpc.senate.gov and *Twitter, @SenateRPC*

Studies and makes recommendations to the Republican leader on the priorities and scheduling of legislation on the Senate floor; prepares policy papers and develops Republican policy initiatives.

Vice President of the United States, *President of the Senate*, The White House, 20500; (202) 224-2424. Kamala Harris, President of the Senate.

General email, vice.president@whitehouse.gov

Web, www.whitehouse.gov/administration/vice-president-pence and Twitter, @VP

Presides over the Senate while in session; preserves decorum and order; announces vote results; recognizes members for debate and introduction of bills, amendments, and motions; decides points of order; votes only in the case of a tie. (President pro tempore of the Senate presides in the absence of the vice president.)

Officers

▶ HOUSE

Chaplain of the U.S. House of Representatives, HB25 CAP, 20515-6655; (202) 225-2509. Fax, (202) 226-4928. Margaret Grun Kibben (USN, Ret.), Chaplain.

General email, chaplainoffice@mail.house.gov

Web, http://chaplain.house.gov

Opens each day's House session with a prayer and offers other religious services and study groups to House members, their families, and staffs. (Prayer sometimes offered by visiting chaplain.)

Chief Administrative Officer of the U.S. House of Representatives, HB26 CAP, 20515; (202) 226-6660. Catherine Szpindor, Chief Administrative Officer. Press, (202) 226-1041.

Web, https://cao.house.gov, Twitter, @CAOHouse and Facebook, www.facebook.com/caohouseofreps

Responsible for House member and staff payrolls; computer system; internal mail, office furnishings and supplies; telecommunications; tour guides; nonlegislative functions of the House printing services, recording studio, and records office; and other administrative areas.

Clerk of the U.S. House of Representatives, H154 CAP, 20515-6601; (202) 225-7000. Cheryl L. Johnson, Clerk. Press, (202) 225-1908.

General email, info.clerkweb@mail.house.gov

Web, http://clerk.house.gov

Responsible for direction of duties of House employees; receives lobby registrations and reports of campaign expenditures and receipts of House candidates; disburses funds appropriated for House expenditures; responsible for other activities necessary for the continuing operation of the House.

General Counsel of the U.S. House of Representatives, 5140 OHOB, 20515-6532; (202) 225-9700. Douglas N. Letter, General Counsel.

Web, https://ogc.house.gov

Provides legal advice and assistance to Members, committees, officers and employees of the House, without regard to political affiliation, on matters related to their official duties. It also represents the House itself in litigation, both as a party and as amicus curiae in cases in which the House has an institutional interest.

House Legislative Counsel, H2-337 FHOB, 20515-6721; (202) 225-6060. Fax, (202) 225-3437. Ernest Wade Ballou Jr., Legislative Counsel.

General email, legcoun@mail.house.gov

Web, https://legcounsel.house.gov

Assists House members and committees in drafting legislation.

Inspector General of the U.S. House of Representatives, 386 FHOB, 20515-9990; (202) 226-1250. Fax, (202) 225-4240. Michael Ptasienski, Inspector General. Hotline, (202) 593-0068.

General email, HouseIG@mail.house.gov

Web, www.house.gov/the-house-explained/officers-and-organizations/inspector-general

Conducts periodic audit advisory and investigative services of the financial, administrative, and technology-based operations of the House and joint entities.

Sergeant at Arms of the U.S. House of Representatives, H124 CAP, 20515-6611; (202) 225-2456. Fax, (202) 225-3233. William J. Walker, Sergeant at Arms.

General email, saamail@mail.house.gov

Web, www.house.gov/the-house-explained/officers-and-organizations/sergeant-at-arms

Maintains order on the House floor; executes orders from the Speaker of the House. Serves on the Capitol Police Board and Capitol Guide Board; oversees Capitol security (with Senate Sergeant at Arms) and protocol.

Speaker of the U.S. House of Representatives, *Floor Assistant*, 1236 LHOB, 20515; (202) 225-4965. Keith Stern, Director of Floor Operations; Emma Kaplan, Floor Advisor.

Assists the majority leadership and members on legislative matters.

▶ SENATE

Chaplain of the U.S. Senate, S332 CAP, 20510-7002; (202) 224-2510. Fax, (202) 224-9686. Barry C. Black, Chaplain.

Web, www.senate.gov/reference/office/chaplain.htm

Opens each day's Senate session with a prayer and offers other religious services to Senate members, their families, and staffs. (Prayer sometimes offered by visiting chaplain.)

Legislative Counsel of the Senate, 668 SDOB, 20510-7250; (202) 224-6461. Fax, (202) 224-0567. Elizabeth Aldridge King, Deputy Legislative Counsel.

General email, receptionist@slc.senate.gov

Web, www.slc.senate.gov

Assists Senate members, committees, and staff in drafting legislation.

Majority Secretary of the U.S. Senate, *S337 CAP, 20510-7024; (202) 224-3121. Gary Myrick, Secretary.*
Web, www.senate.gov/senators/leadership.htm

Assists the majority leader and majority party in the Senate.

Minority Secretary of the U.S. Senate, *S309 CAP, 20510-7014; (202) 224-3121. Robert M. Duncan, Secretary.*
Web, www.senate.gov/senators/leadership.htm

Assists the minority leader and the minority party in the Senate.

Secretary of the U.S. Senate, *S312 CAP, 20510; (202) 224-3622. Sonceria Ann Berry, Secretary of the Senate.*
Web, www.senate.gov/reference/office/secretary_of_senate.htm

Chief legislative, financial, and administrative officer of the Senate. Responsible for direction of duties of Senate employees and administration of oaths; receives lobby registrations and reports of campaign expenditures and receipts of Senate candidates; responsible for other day-to-day Senate activities.

Senate Legal Counsel, *642 SHOB, 20510-7250; (202) 224-4435. Fax, (202) 224-3391. Patricia Mack Bryan, Legal Counsel.*
General email, mailbox@legal.senate.gov

Advises Senate members and committees on legal matters.

Sergeant at Arms and Doorkeeper of the U.S. Senate, *S151 CAP, 20510-7200; (202) 224-2341. Karen Gibson, Sergeant at Arms and Doorkeeper.*
Web, www.senate.gov/reference/office/sergeant_at_arms.htm and Twitter, @Senatesaa

Oversees the Senate wing of the Capitol; doormen; Senate pages; and telecommunication, photographic, supply, and janitorial services. Maintains order on the Senate floor and galleries; oversees Capitol security (with House Sergeant at Arms); sits on the Capitol Police Board and Capitol Guide Board.

Pay and Perquisites

▶**CONGRESS**

For a listing of relevant congressional committees and subcommittees, please see page 797 or the Appendix.

Attending Physician of Congress, *H166 CAP, 20515-8907; (202) 225-5421. Dr. Brian Monahan, Attending Physician.*

Provides members with primary care, first aid, emergency care, and environmental/occupational health services; provides House and Senate employees, visiting dignitaries, and tourists with first-aid and emergency care.

Clerk of the U.S. House of Representatives, *H154 CAP, 20515-6601; (202) 225-7000. Cheryl L. Johnson, Clerk. Press, (202) 225-1908.*

General email, info.clerkweb@mail.house.gov
Web, http://clerk.house.gov

Prepares and submits quarterly reports covering the receipts and expenditures of the House, including disbursements by each committee and each member's office and staff. Reports available from the Legislative Resource Center.

House Communications Standards Commission, *1307 LHOB, 20515-6328; (202) 225-9337. Fax, (202) 225-7664. Rep. Mary Gay Scanlon, Chair; Rep. Kat Cammack, Ranking Member.*
Web, https://cha.house.gov/about-commission

Oversight of the use of franked mail by House members.

Secretary of the U.S. Senate, *S312 CAP, 20510; (202) 224-3622. Sonceria Ann Berry, Secretary of the Senate.*
Web, www.senate.gov/reference/office/secretary_of_senate.htm

Prepares and submits semiannual reports covering the receipts and expenditures of the Senate, including data on each committee and each member's office and staff. Reports available from the Government Printing Office.

▶**NONGOVERNMENTAL**

National Taxpayers Union, *Communications, 122 C St. N.W., #650, 20001; (703) 683-5700. Kevin Glass, Vice President of Communications.*
General email, ntu@ntu.org

Web, www.ntu.org, Twitter, @NTU and Facebook, www.facebook.com/NationalTaxpayersUnion

Citizens' interest group that publishes reports on congressional pay and perquisites, including pensions and the franking privilege.

Standards of Conduct

▶**AGENCIES**

Criminal Division *(Justice Dept.),* **Public Integrity (PIN),** *1301 New York Ave. N.W., 10th Floor, 20005; (202) 514-1412. Fax, (202) 514-3003. Corey R. Amundson, Chief.*
Web, www.justice.gov/criminal/pin

Conducts investigations of wrongdoing in selected cases that involve alleged corruption of public office or violations of election law by public officials, including members of Congress.

▶**CONGRESS**

For a listing of relevant congressional committees and subcommittees, please see page 797 or the Appendix.

Secretary of the U.S. Senate, *Public Records, Ethics, 232 SHOB, 20510-7116; (202) 224-0758. Dana K. McCallum, Superintendent of Public Records.*
General email, lobby@sec.senate.gov
Web, www.senate.gov/legislative/opr.htm

Receives and maintains the financial disclosure records of Senate members, officers, employees, candidates, and legislative organizations. Receives reports from committee chairs on foreign travel by senators and staff. Records open for public inspection, 9:00 a.m.–5:30 p.m.

U.S. House of Representatives, *Legislative Resource Center, Records and Registration,* *135 CHOB, 20515-6612; (202) 226-5200. Steve Pingeton, Manager.*
Web, http://clerk.house.gov/about/viewLRCDetails and *Email, info.clerkweb@mail.house.gov*

Receives and maintains the financial disclosure records of House members, officers, employees, candidates, and certain legislative organizations. Receives reports from committee chairs on foreign travel by members and staff. Records open for public inspection.

U.S. House of Representatives, *Office of Congressional Ethics,* *425 3rd St. S.W., #1110, 20024 (mailing address: P.O. Box 895, Washington, DC 20515-0895); (202) 225-9739. Fax, (202) 226-0997. Mike Barnes, Chair; Omar Ashmawy, Staff Director and Chief Counsel.*
General email, oce@mail.house.gov
Web, https://oce.house.gov, Twitter, @CongressEthics and *Facebook, www.facebook.com/OfficeofCongressionalEthics*

Independent nonpartisan body charged with reviewing allegations of misconduct against members, officers, and staff of the House of Representatives; refers matters to the House Committee on Ethics.

CONGRESSIONAL SUPPORT GROUPS

General

► **CONGRESS**

For a listing of relevant congressional committees and sub-committees, please see page 797 or the Appendix.

Congressional Budget Office, *FHOB, 2nd and D Sts. S.W., 4th Floor, 20515-6925; (202) 226-2700.*
Phillip Swagel, Director. Legislative Affairs, (202) 226-2837. Press, (202) 226-2602.
General email, communications@cbo.gov
Web, www.cbo.gov, Twitter, @USCBO and *YouTube, www.youtube.com/uscbo*

Nonpartisan office that provides the House and Senate with analyses needed for economic and budget decisions, and with the information and estimates required for the congressional budget process.

Congressional Budget Office, *Health, Retirement, and Long-Term Analysis, FHOB, 2nd and D Sts. S.W., 4th Floor, 20515-6925; (202) 226-2676. Carrie H. Collon, Director.*
Web, www.cbo.gov, Twitter, @USCBO and *YouTube, www.youtube.com/uscbo*

Analyzes federal programs and policies concerning health care and retirement, including Medicare, Medicaid, subsidies to be provided through health insurance exchanges, and Social Security. Responsible for long-term budget protection and analyses of long-term effects of proposed legislation. Prepares reports to Congress.

Government Accountability Office (GAO), *441 G St. N.W., 20548; (202) 512-5500. Fax, (202) 512-5507. Gene L. Dodaro, Comptroller General. Congressional Relations, (202) 512-4400. Information, (202) 512-3000. Publications and documents, (202) 512-6000.*
General email, contact@gao.gov
Web, www.gao.gov, Twitter, @USGAO and *Facebook, www.facebook.com/usgao*

Independent, nonpartisan agency in the legislative branch. Serves as the investigating agency for Congress; carries out legal, accounting, auditing, and claims settlement functions; makes recommendations for more effective government operations; makes reports available to Congress and the public.

Government Accountability Office (GAO), *Applied Research and Methods (ARM), 441 G St. N.W., #6H19, 20548; (202) 512-2700. Lawrence Evans Jr., Managing Director, (202) 512-8678.*
Web, www.gao.gov/about/careers/our-teams

Provides technical and specialist expertise to support GAO teams, including specialized reviews and guidance on methodological issues; conducts studies on questions of interest to Congress that require specialized analysis.

Government Accountability Office (GAO), *Defense Capabilities and Management (DCM), 441 G St. N.W., 20548; (202) 512-2775. Elizabeth Field, Director.*
Web, www.gao.gov/about/careers/our-teams

Provides analyses, recommendations, and policy options to Congress in areas of defense, including planning and force structure, readiness and training, war-fighter support, emerging threats, irregular warfare, homeland defense, strategic human-capital management, logistics, infrastructure, business operations, and budgeting.

Government Accountability Office (GAO), *Education, Workforce, and Income Security (EWIS), 441 G St. N.W., 20548; (202) 512-7215. Jacqueline Nowicki, Director.*
Web, www.gao.gov/about/careers/our-teams

Assists Congress in analyzing the efficiency and effectiveness of federal agency programs that foster the development, education, and skill attainment of children and adults; provide benefits and protections for workers, families, veterans, and those with disabilities; and ensure an adequate and secure retirement for an aging population.

Government Accountability Office (GAO), *Financial Management and Assurance (FMA), 441 G St. N.W., 20548; (202) 512-9377. Cheryl Clark, Director.*
Web, www.gao.gov/about/careers/our-teams

Helps Congress implement the 1990 Chief Financial Officers Act, the 1994 Government Management Reform

Act, the 1996 Federal Financial Management Improvement Act, and other crosscutting financial management legislation.

Government Accountability Office (GAO), *Financial Markets and Community Investment (FMCI),* *441 G St. N.W., 20548; (202) 512-8678. Daniel Garcia-Diaz, Managing Director, (202) 512-4802.*
Web, www.gao.gov/about/careers/our-teams

Supports congressional efforts to ensure that U.S. financial markets function smoothly and effectively, identifies fraud and abuse, and promotes sound, sustainable community investment by assessing the effectiveness of federal initiatives aimed at small businesses, state and local governments, and communities.

Government Accountability Office (GAO), *Forensic Audits and Investigative Service (FAIS),* *441 G St. N.W., #4T21, 20548; (202) 512-6722. Johana R. Ayers, Managing Director, (202) 512-5741. FraudNet, (800) 424-5454.*
Web, www.gao.gov/about/careers/our-teams

Provides Congress with forensic audits, investigations of fraud, waste, abuse, and security and vulnerability assessments; manages FraudNet.

Government Accountability Office (GAO), *Health Care (HC),* *441 G St. N.W., #5A21, 20548; (202) 512-7114. Alyssa Hundrup, Director.*
Web, www.gao.gov/about/careers/our-teams

Provides analyses, recommendations, and policy options to Congress and the executive branch for all federal government health programs, including those administered by the Defense (TRICARE), Health and Human Services, and Veterans Affairs Depts.

Government Accountability Office (GAO), *Homeland Security and Justice (HSJ),* *441 G St. N.W., #6H19, 20548; (202) 512-8777. Gretta L. Goodwin, Director.*
Web, www.gao.gov/about/careers/our-teams

Audits, analyzes, and evaluates for Congress federal administration of homeland security and justice areas and national preparedness programs and activities.

Government Accountability Office (GAO), *Information Technology and Cybersecurity (ITC),* *441 G St. N.W., #4T21, 20548; (202) 512-4456. Carol C. Harris, Director.*
Web, www.gao.gov/about/careers/our-teams

Audits, analyzes, and evaluates for Congress federal information management and information security programs to improve performance and reduce costs.

Government Accountability Office (GAO), *International Affairs and Trade (IAT),* *441 G St. N.W., 20548; (202) 512-2964. Chelsa L. Kenney, Director.*
Web, www.gao.gov/about/careers/our-teams

Audits, analyzes, and evaluates international programs and trade; evaluates economic, political, and security problems worldwide. In addition to federal departments, oversight work includes U.S. Agency for International Development, Office of the U.S. Trade Representative, Broadcasting Board of Governors, North Atlantic Treaty Organization, World Bank, International Monetary Fund, and United Nations.

Government Accountability Office (GAO), *Natural Resources and Environment (NRE),* *441 G St. N.W., 20548; (202) 512-3841. Frank Rusco, Director.*
Web, www.gao.gov/about/careers/our-teams

Audits, analyzes, and evaluates for Congress federal agriculture, food safety, and energy programs; provides guidance on issues including efforts to ensure a reliable and environmentally sound energy supply, land and water resources management, protection of the environment, hazardous and nuclear wastes threat reduction, food safety, and investment in science.

Government Accountability Office (GAO), *Physical Infrastructure (PI),* *441 G St. N.W., #2063, 20548 (mailing address: 441 G St. N.W., #2T23B, Washington, DC 20548); (202) 512-2834. Andrew Von Ah, Director.*
Web, www.gao.gov/about/careers/our-teams

Provides guidance to Congress on the efficiency, safety, and security of the nation's infrastructure, including transportation systems, telecommunications networks, oil and gas pipelines, and federal facilities owned, funded, and operated by both the public and private sectors.

House Legislative Counsel, *H2-337 FHOB, 20515-6721; (202) 225-6060. Fax, (202) 225-3437. Ernest Wade Ballou Jr., Legislative Counsel.*
General email, legcoun@mail.house.gov
Web, https://legcounsel.house.gov

Assists House members and committees in drafting legislation.

Law Revision Counsel, *H2-308 FHOB, 20515-6711; (202) 226-2411. Ralph V. Seep, Law Revision Counsel.*
General email, uscode@mail.house.gov
Web, http://uscode.house.gov and Twitter, @uscode

Develops and updates an official classification of U.S. laws. Codifies, cites, and publishes the U.S. Code.

Library of Congress, *Congressional Research Service, James Madison Memorial Bldg., 101 Independence Ave. S.E., #LM 203, 20540; (202) 707-5700. Mary B. Mazanec, Director.*
Web, www.loc.gov/crsinfo

Provides confidential policy and legal research and analysis exclusively to committees and members of the House and Senate, regardless of party affiliation. Using multiple disciplines and research methodologies, assists at every stage of the legislative process, from early considerations that precede bill drafting, through committee hearings and floor debate, to the oversight of enacted laws and various agency activities.

Senate Legal Counsel, *642 SHOB, 20510-7250; (202) 224-4435. Fax, (202) 224-3391. Patricia Mack Bryan, Legal Counsel.*
General email, mailbox@legal.senate.gov

Advises Senate members and committees on legal matters.

U.S. House of Representatives

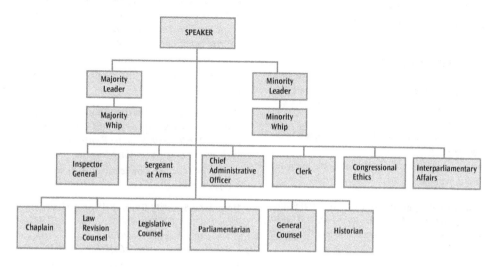

Liaison Offices

►CONGRESS

For a listing of relevant congressional committees and subcommittees, please see page 797 or the Appendix.

Agriculture Dept. (USDA), *Congressional Relations (OCR),* 1400 Independence Ave. S.W., #219-A, 20250; (202) 720-7095. Fax, (202) 720-8077. Anne Knapke, Deputy Assistant Secretary.
General email, ocr@usda.gov

Web, www.usda.gov/our-agency/staff-offices/office-congressional-relations-ocr

Advises Congress on agriculture, nutrition, and forestry legislation and budget proposals.

Agriculture Dept. (USDA), *Rural Development, External Affairs (OEA),* 1400 Independence Ave. S.W., MS 0705, 20250-0705; Marie Wheat, Director. Congressional inquiries, (202) 720-9928.
Web, www.rd.usda.gov/about-rd/offices/office-of-external-affairs and Press Email, RD.Press@usda.gov

Advises Congress on legislation and policy related to housing, lending, and rural development; coordinates agency testimony before congressional hearings.

Alcohol and Tobacco Tax and Trade Bureau (TTB) *(Treasury Dept.),* *Congressional and Public Affairs,* 1310 G St. N.W., Box 12, 20005; (202) 453-2180. Fax, (202) 453-2912. Tom Hogue, Congressional Liaison.
Web, www.ttb.gov/offices/media

Plans, develops, and implements communication regarding TTB affairs. Provides analyses and advice regarding public perception of new or revised bureau initiatives.

Animal and Plant Health Inspection Service (APHIS) *(Agriculture Dept.),* *Legislative and Public Affairs,* South Bldg., 1400 Independence Ave. S.W., #1147, 20250;

(301) 955-1203. Bethany Jones, Deputy Administrator, (202) 799-7030. Public Affairs, (301) 851-4100.
Web, www.aphis.usda.gov/aphis/banner/contactus/sa_aphis_contacts/contact_lpa

Advises Congress on legislation related to agriculture, food, natural resources, and wildlife.

Census Bureau *(Commerce Dept.),* *Congressional and Intergovernmental Affairs,* 4600 Silver Hill Rd., #8H166, Suitland, MD 20746; (301) 763-4516. Fax, (301) 763-3780. Angel Colon Rivera, Chief, (301) 763-4256.
General email, cao@census.gov

Web, www.census.gov/about/cong-gov-affairs.html

Advises Congress on census policies and programs; provides Census data to Congress.

Commerce Dept., *Legislative and Intergovernmental Affairs,* 1401 Constitution Ave. N.W., 20230; (202) 482-3663. Fax, (202) 482-4420. Chris Day, Deputy Assistant Secretary.
Web, www.commerce.gov/bureaus-and-offices/os/legislative-and-intergovernmental-affairs

Advises Congress on legislation related to job creation, economic growth, sustainable development, and improved standards of living.

Drug Enforcement Administration (DEA) *(Justice Dept.),* *Congressional Affairs,* 700 Army Navy Dr., Arlington, VA 22202; (202) 307-7423. Jason Thurman, Chief.
General email, Congressional.Inquiries@usdoj.gov

Web, www.dea.gov/contact/cpa

Point of contact for members of Congress about controlled substances laws and regulations of the United States.

Education Dept., *Legislative and Congressional Affairs (OLCA),* Lyndon B. Johnson Bldg., 400 Maryland Ave. S.W., #6W315, 20202-3500; (202) 401-0020. Fax, (202) 401-1438. Gwen Graham, Assistant Secretary.

General email, olca@ed.gov

Web, www2.ed.gov/about/offices/list/olca

Advises Congress on policy and legislation related to education.

Energy Dept. (DOE), *Congressional and Intergovernmental Affairs,* 1000 Independence Ave. S.W., #7B138, 20585; (202) 586-5450. Fax, (202) 586-4891. Ali Nouri, Assistant Secretary. Toll-free, (800) 342-5363. General email, robert.tuttle@hq.doe.gov

Web, www.energy.gov/congressional/office-congressional-and-intergovernmental-affairs

Advises Congress on energy-related policies, programs, and initiatives.

Equal Employment Opportunity Commission (EEOC), *Legislative Affairs,* 131 M St. N.E., Room 6NE25J, 20507; (202) 663-4191. Fax, (202) 663-4912. Patricia Crawford, Director.

General email, legis@eeoc.gov

Web, www.eeoc.gov/legislative-affairs

Advises Congress on policy and legislation related to equal employment and discrimination in the workplace; coordinates department testimony before congressional hearings.

European Parliament Liaison Office, 2175 K St. N.W., #600, 20037; (202) 862-4734. Joseph Dunne, Director, (202) 862-4731.

General email, epwashington@ep.europa.eu

Web, www.europarl.europa.eu/us and Twitter, @EPWashingtonDC

Acts as the contact point between the European Parliament and the U.S. Congress. Seeks to intensify working relations between the European Parliament and the U.S. Congress at all levels, particularly between corresponding committees of jurisdiction, and between European Parliament lawmakers and U.S. regulators. Represents the Parliament's viewpoint to the U.S. administration and Congress. Principal issues addressed are human rights, the threat of terrorism, economic growth, and environmental protection.

Federal Bureau of Investigation (FBI) *(Justice Dept.),* **Congressional Affairs,** 935 Pennsylvania Ave. N.W., #7240, 20535; (202) 324-5051. Fax, (202) 324-6490. Jill C. Tyson, Assistant Director.

General email, oca@fbi.gov

Web, www.fbi.gov

Advises Congress about FBI activities.

Food and Nutrition Service *(Agriculture Dept.),* **Communications Officer,** 3101 Park Center Dr., #926, Alexandria, VA 22302; (703) 305-2281. Fax, (703) 305-2312. Brooke Hardison, Director (Acting).

Web, www.fns.usda.gov

Advises Congress on policy and legislation related to food and nutrition programs; coordinates department testimony before congressional hearings.

Government Accountability Office (GAO), *Congressional Relations (CR),* 441 G St. N.W., Room 7125, 20548; 202-512-4400. Fax, (202) 512-4641. A. Nicole Clowers, Managing Director, (202) 512-5837.

General email, spel@gao.gov

Web, www.gao.gov/about/careers/our-teams

Point of contact within the GAO for contacts with Congress.

Health and Human Services Dept. (HHS), *Legislation,* 200 Independence Ave. S.W., 20201; (202) 690-7627. Fax, (202) 690-7380. Melanie Egorin, Assistant Secretary. Web, www.hhs.gov/about/agencies/asl

Advises Congress on legislation related to health and human services.

Homeland Security Dept. (DHS), *Legislative Affairs,* MS 0020, 20528; (202) 447-5890. Fax, (202) 447-5437. Alicia Lugo, Assistant Secretary.

General email, CongresstoDHS@hq.dhs.gov

Web, www.dhs.gov/about-office-legislative-affairs

Advises Congress about national threat and hazard response as well as safe and secure borders.

Housing and Urban Development Dept. (HUD), *Congressional and Intergovernmental Relations,* 451 7th St. S.W., Room 10120, 20410; (202) 708-0005. Fax, (202) 708-3794. Sarah Brundage, General Deputy Assistant Secretary.

Web, www.hud.gov/program_offices/gov_relations/dircir

Advises Congress on policy and legislation related to housing and urban development.

Interior Dept. (DOI), *Congressional and Legislative Affairs,* 1849 C St. N.W., MS 6038-MIB, 20240; (202) 208-7693. Fax, (202) 208-7619. Andrew (Drew) Wallace, Director.

Web, www.doi.gov/ocl

Advises Congress on policy and legislation related to natural resources and tribal communities; coordinates department testimony before congressional hearings.

International Trade Administration (ITA) *(Commerce Dept.),* **Legislative and Intergovernmental Affairs (OLIA),** 1401 Constitution Ave. N.W., Room 3424, 20230; (202) 482-2867. Fax, (202) 482-0900. Livia Shmavonian, Director.

General email, ITALegislativeAffairs@trade.gov

Web, www.trade.gov

Advises Congress on legislation and policies related to international trade matters and export opportunities.

Justice Dept. (DOJ), *Legislative Affairs,* 950 Pennsylvania Ave. N.W., #1137, 20530-0001; (202) 514-2141. Peter S. Hyun, Assistant Attorney General (Acting). Public Liaison, (202) 514-3465.

Web, www.justice.gov/ola

Advises Congress on Justice Dept. initiatives; coordinates department testimony before congressional hearings; participates in the Senate confirmation process for federal judges and Justice Dept. nominees.

U.S. Senate

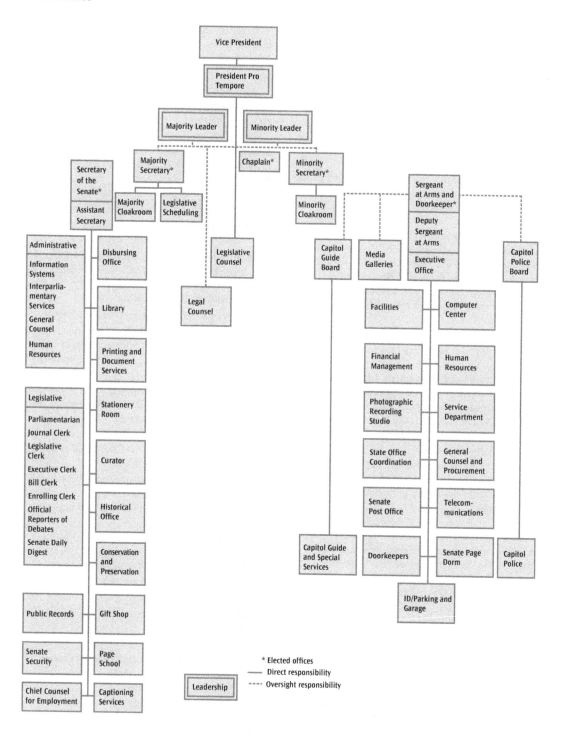

Labor Dept. (DOL), *Congressional and Intergovernmental Affairs,* 200 Constitution Ave. N.W., #S-2220, 20210; (202) 693-4600. Fax, (202) 693-4642. *Vacant, Assistant Secretary.*
Web, www.dol.gov/agencies/ocia

Advises Congress on policy and legislation related to federal labor matters.

National Institute of Standards and Technology (NIST) *(Commerce Dept.), Congressional and Legislative Affairs,* 100 Bureau Dr., MS 1051, Gaithersburg, MD 20899-1002; (301) 975-5675. Fax, (301) 926-2569. *Jim Schufreider, Director.*
General email, kandy.hauk@nist.gov
Web, www.nist.gov/director/congressional-and-legislative-affairs

Advises Congress on policy related to technology, measurements, and standards; coordinates agency testimony before congressional hearings.

National Marine Manufacturers Assn., *Government Relations,* 650 Massachusetts Ave. N.W., #520, 20001; (202) 737-9750. Fax, (202) 628-4716. *Frank K. Hugelmeyer, President; Tillie Fowler, Vice President for Government Relations.*
Web, www.nmma.org/government and Twitter, @therealNMMA

Advises Congress on matters related to boating safety and the development of boating facilities.

National Oceanic and Atmospheric Administration (NOAA) *(Commerce Dept.), Legislative and Intergovernmental Affairs,* 1401 Constitution Ave. N.W., #62004, 20230; (202) 482-4981. *Makedo Okolo, Director; Chris Hayes, Legislative Affairs Specialist.*
Web, www.legislative.noaa.gov

Advises Congress on legislation and policy related to climate change, marine commerce, and ocean and coastal resources; coordinates agency testimony before congressional hearings.

Office of Personnel Management (OPM), *Congressional, Legislative, and Intergovernmental Affairs,* 1900 E St. N.W., #6316G, 20415 (mailing address: Constituent Services, B332 RHOB, Washington, DC 20515); (202) 606-1300. Fax, (202) 606-1344. *Alethea Predeoux, Director. Constituent services, (202) 225-4955.*
Web, www.opm.gov/about-us/our-people-organization/congressional-legislative-intergovernmental-affairs

Advises Congress on federal civil service matters, especially those pertaining to federal employment, retirement, and health benefits programs.

Pension Benefit Guaranty Corp., *Communications and Legislative Affairs Department (COLAD),* 1200 K St. N.W., 20005-4026; (202) 229-4343. Fax, (202) 299-4224. *Michael Rucki, Director (Acting).*
General email, congressionals@pbgc.gov
Web, www.pbgc.gov/about/pg/pbgc-legislative-affairs.html

Advises Congress on policy and legislation related to pension benefits and private-sector retirement benefit plans.

Postal Regulatory Commission, *Public Affairs and Government Relations (PAGR),* 901 New York Ave. N.W., #200, 20268; (202) 789-6800. Fax, (202) 789-6891. *Jennifer Alvarez-Warburton, Director.*
General email, prc-pagr@prc.gov
Web, www.prc.gov/offices/pagr

Advises Congress on policy related to the Postal Service; coordinates commission testimony before congressional hearings.

Securities and Exchange Commission (SEC), *Investor Advocate,* 100 F St. N.E., 20549; (202) 551-3302. *Rick A. Fleming, Director.*
General email, InvestorAdvocate@sec.gov
Web, www.sec.gov/page/investor-advocate-landing-page

Submits reports to Congress concerning SEC activities.

Transportation Dept. (DOT), *Government Affairs,* 1200 New Jersey Ave. S.E., 20590; (202) 366-4573. *Mohsin Syed, Principal Deputy Assistant Secretary.*
General email, OSTGovAffairs@dot.gov
Web, www.transportation.gov/government-affairs

Advises Congress on policy and legislation related to transportation and transportation systems; coordinates department testimony before congressional hearings.

Treasury Dept., *Legislative Affairs,* 1500 Pennsylvania Ave. N.W., #3134, 20220; (202) 622-1900. Fax, (202) 622-0534. *Jonathan Davidson, Assistant Secretary.*
General email, LegAffairs@treasury.gov
Web, www.treasury.gov/about/organizational-structure/offices/Pages/Legislative-Affairs.aspx

Advises Congress on legislation and policies related to economics, finance, and financial security; coordinates department testimony before congressional hearings.

U.S. Commission on Civil Rights, *Public Affairs and Congressional Affairs,* 1331 Pennsylvania Ave. N.W., #1150, 20425; (202) 376-8359. *Saki Martin, Director.*
General email, publicaffairs@usccr.gov
Web, www.usccr.gov

Advises Congress on legisation and policy related to civil rights issues.

U.S.–China Economic and Security Review Commission, 444 N. Capitol St. N.W., #602, 20001; (202) 624-1407. *Daniel Peck, Executive Director.*
General email, contact@uscc.gov
Web, www.uscc.gov and Twitter, @USCC_GOV

Investigates the national security implications of the bilateral trade and economic relationship between China and the United States. Makes recommendations to Congress based on its findings.

►HOUSE

Air Force Legislative Liaison, *B322 RHOB, 20515-0001;*
(202) 685-4531. Fax, (202) 685-2592. Maj.
Gen. Christopher E. Finerty, Director.
General email, usaf.pentagon.saf-ll.list.rss-saf-llh-distro-list@mail.mil

Provides House members with services and information on all matters related to the U.S. Air Force.

Army Liaison, *2024 RHOB, 20515; (202) 685-2676.*
Fax, (202) 256-2674. Col. Richard (Rick) Zampelli, Chief.
Web, www.army.mil

Provides House members with services and information on all matters related to the U.S. Army.

Navy–Marine Corps Liaison, *B324 RHOB, 20515;*
Capt. Eddie Cossman (USN), Navy Director;
Col. Maura Hennigan (USMC), Marine Corps Director.
Navy, (202) 225-7126. Marine Corps, (202) 225-7124 or
(202) 226-7801.
General email (Navy), navyhouseliaison@navy.mil
Web (Marines), www.hqmc.marines.mil/Agencies/Office-of-Legislative-Affairs/US-House-of-Representatives-Liaison

Provides House members with services and information on all matters related to the U.S. Navy and the U.S. Marine Corps.

State Dept., *Capitol Hill House Liaison, 2028 RHOB,*
20515; (202) 226-4642. Kem C. Anderson, Director
(Acting).
Web, www.state.gov/capitol-hill-liaison-office

Advises House members on foreign policy and legislation; provides services related to consular affairs and travel by members of Congress.

U.S. Coast Guard House Liaison, *2022 RHOB, 20515;*
(202) 225-4775. Cmdr. Dorothy Hernaez, Chief.
General email, house@uscg.mil

Provides House members with services and information on all matters related to the U.S. Coast Guard.

Veterans Affairs Dept. (VA), *Congressional and*
Legislative Affairs, 810 Vermont Ave., #500, 20420; (202)
461-6490. Fax, (202) 273-9988. David Ballenger, Director,
(202) 461-6464. House Liaison, (202) 225-2280. Senate
Liaison, (202) 224-5351.
General email, ocla-cls@va.gov
Web, www.va.gov/oca/index.asp

Provides House members with services and information on all matters related to veterans' benefits and services.

White House Legislative Affairs, *House of*
Representatives, White House, 1600 Pennsylvania Ave.
N.W., 20502; (202) 456-1421. Shuwanza Goff, Deputy
Director, House Liaison. White House Switchboard, (202)
456-1414.
Web, www.whitehouse.gov, Press, press@who.eop.gov,
Twitter, @WhiteHouse, Facebook, www.facebook.com/
WhiteHouse and YouTube, www.youtube.com/user/
Whitehouse

Serves as a liaison between the president and the House of Representatives.

►SENATE

Air Force Legislative Liaison (SAF/LL), *182 SROB, 20510;*
(202) 685-2573. Maj. Gen. Christopher E. Finerty, Director.
General email, usaf.pentagon.saf-ll.list.rss-saf-lls-distro-list@mail.mil

Provides senators with services and information on all matters related to the U.S. Air Force.

Army Liaison, *183 SROB, 20510; (202) 224-2881.*
Fax, (703) 693-4574. Col. Scott Wilkinson (USA), Chief.

Provides senators with services and information on all matters related to the U.S. Army.

Navy–Marine Corps Liaison, *182 SROB, 20510;*
Capt. Chase D. Patrick (USN), Navy Director;
Col. Matthew T. Good (USMC), Marine Corps Director.
Navy, (202) 685-6003. Marine Corps, (202) 685-6009 or
(202) 685-0096.
Web (Marine), www.hqmc.marines.mil/Agencies/Office-of-Legislative-Affairs/US-Senate-Liaison

Provides senators with services and information on all matters related to the U.S. Navy and the U.S. Marine Corps.

State Dept., *Capitol Hill Senate Liaison, 189 SROB,*
20002; (202) 228-1602. Leaksmy Norin, Director (Acting).
Web, www.state.gov/capitol-hill-liaison-office

Advises Senate members on foreign policy and legislation; provides services related to consular affairs and travel by members of Congress.

U.S. Coast Guard Senate Liaison, *183 SROB, 20510; (202)*
224-2913. Cmdr. Glenn Goetchius, Chief.
General email, senate@uscg.mil

Provides senators with services and information on all matters related to the U.S. Coast Guard.

White House Legislative Affairs, *White House, 1600*
Pennsylvania Ave. N.W., 20502; (202) 456-3760.
Reema Dodin, Deputy Director, Senate Liaison. White
House Switchboard, (202) 456-1414.
Web, www.whitehouse.gov and Press, press@who.eop.gov

Serves as a liaison between the Senate and the president.

Libraries

►CONGRESS

For a listing of relevant congressional committees and subcommittees, please see page 797 or the Appendix.

Library of Congress, *Congressional Research Service,*
James Madison Memorial Bldg., 101 Independence Ave.
S.E., #LM 203, 20540; (202) 707-5700. Mary B. Mazanec,
Director.
Web, www.loc.gov/crsinfo

Provides members of Congress and committees with research and reference assistance.

Library of Congress, *Federal Research Division,* John Adams Bldg., 101 Independence Ave. S.E., #LA 5281, 20540-4840; (202) 707-3900. Fax, (202) 707-3920. Anna (Annie) Rorem, Chief, (202) 707-3920.
General email, frds@loc.gov

Web, www.loc.gov/rr/frd

Provides research, analysis, and translation services to federal agencies, the D.C. government (excluding congress), and authorized federal contractors.

Library of Congress, *Law Library,* James Madison Memorial Bldg., 101 Independence Ave. S.E., #LM 242, 20540-3129; (202) 707-5079/80. Fax, (202) 707-1820. Aslihan Bulut, Law Librarian.
Web, www.loc.gov/law, Twitter, @LawLibCongress and Facebook, www.facebook.com/lawlibraryofcongress

Provides Congress and the Supreme Court with access to current legal research materials. Timed entry pass for visitors required, details at loc.gov/visit. Appointments recommended for researchers.

Library of the Senate, B15 SROB, 20510; (202) 224-7106. Fax, (202) 224-0879. Leona Faust, Librarian; Hannah Moyer, Catalogue Supervisor.
Web, www.senate.gov and www.senate.gov/reference/reference_home.htm

Maintains special collection for Senate private use of primary source legislative materials, including reports, hearing transcripts, prints, documents, and debate proceedings. (Not open to the public.)

U.S. House of Representatives, *Legislative Resource Center, Library Services,* 135 CHOB, 20515-6612; (202) 225-9000. Rae Ellen Best, House Librarian, (202) 225-6957.
General email, library@mail.house.gov

Web, http://library.clerk.house.gov

Serves as the statutory and official depository of House reports, hearings, prints, and documents for the clerk of the House. Includes the divisions of Library Services, Public Information, Records and Registration, and the House Document Room.

Pages

▶CONGRESS

For a listing of relevant congressional committees and subcommittees, please see page 797 or the Appendix.

Senate Page School, U.S. Senate, 20510-7248; (202) 224-3927. Joshua Dorsey, Principal.
Web, www.senate.gov/reference/reference_index_subjects/Pages_vrd.htm

Provides education for pages of the Senate.

Sergeant at Arms and Doorkeeper of the U.S. Senate, *Senate Page Program,* Webster Hall, #11, 20510; (202) 228-1291. Elizabeth Roach, Director.

Oversees and enforces rules and regulations concerning Senate pages after they have been appointed.

Staff

▶CONGRESS

Human Resources, *House Vacancy Announcement and Placement Service,* H2-102 FHOB, 20515-6201; (202) 226-5836. John Salamone, Chief Human Resources Officer. TTY, (202) 225-1904.
Web, www.house.gov/employment/positions-with-members-and-committees

Assists House members and committees fill staff vacancies by posting job vacancies and maintaining a résumé bank of candidates seeking employment.

Senate Placement Office, 142 SHOB, 20510; (202) 224-9167. Brian Bean, Manager. TTY, (202) 224-4215.
General email, placementofficeinfo@saa.senate.gov

Web, www.senate.gov/visiting/common/generic/placement_office.htm

Provides members, committees, and administrative offices of the Senate with placement and referral services. Compiles Senate Employment Bulletin, an online listing of available jobs.

▶NONGOVERNMENTAL

Congressional Management Foundation, 216 7th St. S.E., 2nd Floor, 20003; (202) 546-0100. Bradford (Brad) Fitch, President, (202) 716-7036.
General email, cmf@congressfoundation.org

Web, www.congressfoundation.org, Twitter, @CongressFdn and Facebook, www.facebook.com/CongressFoundation

Nonpartisan organization that provides members of Congress and their staffs with management information and services through seminars, consultation, research, and publications.

Federal Bar Assn., 1220 N. Fillmore St., #444, Arlington, VA 22201; (571) 481-9100. Fax, (571) 481-9090. Stacy King, Executive Director.
General email, fba@fedbar.org

Web, www.fedbar.org, Twitter, @federalbar and Facebook, www.facebook.com/FederalBar

Organization of bar members who are present or former staff members of the House, Senate, Library of Congress, Supreme Court, Government Accountability Office, or Government Printing Office, or attorneys in legislative practice before federal courts or agencies.

POLITICAL ADVOCACY

General

▶CONGRESS

For a listing of relevant congressional committees and subcommittees, please see page 797 or the Appendix.

Ratings of Members of Congress

The following organizations either publish voting records on selected issues or regularly rate members of Congress.

AFL-CIO, 815 Black Lives Matter Plz. N.W., 20005; (202) 637-5018; www.aflcio.org

American Conservative Union, 1199 N. Fairfax St., #500, Alexandria, VA 22314; (202) 347-9388; Fax,(202) 347-9389; www.conservative.org

American Farm Bureau Federation, 600 Maryland Ave. S.W., #1000W, 20024; (202) 406-3600; www.fb.org

Americans for Democratic Action, 1629 K St. N.W., #300, 20006; (202) 600-7762; Fax,(202) 204-8637; www.adaction.org

Americans for Tax Reform, 722 12th St. N.W., #400, 20005; (202) 785-0266; Fax,(202) 785-0261; www.atr.org

Citizens Against Government Waste, 1100 Connecticut Ave. N.W., #650, 20036; (202) 467-5300; Fax,(202) 467-4253; www.cagw.org

Citizens for Responsibility and Ethics in Washington, 1101 K St. N.W., #201, 20005; (202) 408-5565; Email, info@citizensforethics.org; www.citizensforethics.org

The Club for Growth, 2001 L St. N.W., #600, 20036; (202) 955-5500; www.clubforgrowth.org

Drum Major Institute for Public Policy, 885 Second Ave., 47th Floor, New York, NY 10017; (212) 909-9589; Fax,(212) 909-9489; www.drummajorinst.org

Human Rights Campaign, 1640 Rhode Island Ave. N.W., 20036-3278; (800) 777-4723 or (202) 628-4160; Fax,(202) 347-5323; TTY,(202) 216-1572; www.hrc.org

Leadership Conference on Civil Rights, 1620 L St. N.W., #1100, 20036; (202) 466-3311; www.civilrights.org

League of Conservation Voters, 740 15th St. N.W., #700, 20005; (202) 785-8683; Fax,(202) 835-0491; www.lcv.org

NAACP (National Assn. for the Advancement of Colored People), 1156 15th St. N.W., #915, 20005; (202) 463-2940 or (877) 622-2798; Fax,(202) 463-2953; www.naacp.org

NARAL Pro-Choice America, 1725 Eye St. N.W., #900, 20006; (202) 973-3000; Fax,(202) 973-3096; www.prochoiceamerica.org

National Assn. of Social Workers, 750 1st St. N.E., #800, 20002; (202) 408-8600 or (800) 742-4089; www.socialworkers.org

National Education Assn., 1201 16th St. N.W., 20036-3290; (202) 833-4000; Fax,(202) 822-7974; www.nea.org

National Federation of Independent Business, 555 12th St. N.W., #1001, 20004; (202) 554-9000 or (800) 274-6342; www.nfib.com

National Right to Life Committee, 512 10th St. N.W., 20004; (202) 626-8800; www.nrlc.org

National Taxpayers Union, 122 C St. N.W., #650, 20001; (703) 683-5700; Email, ntu@ntu.org; www.ntu.org

Population Connection, 2120 L St. N.W., #500, 20037; (202) 332-2200 or (800) 767-1956; Fax,(202) 332-2302; Email, info@populationconnection.org; www.populationconnection.org

Public Citizen, Congress Watch, 1600 20th St. N.W., 20009; (202) 546-4996 or (202) 588-1000; www.citizen.org

U.S. Chamber of Commerce, Congressional Affairs, 1615 H St. N.W., 20062-2000; (202) 659-6000; www.uschamber.com

U.S. Student Assn., 1211 Connecticut Ave. N.W., 20036; (202) 640-6570; www.usstudents.org

---

U.S. House of Representatives, *Legislative Resource Center, Records and Registration, 135 CHOB, 20515-6612; (202) 226-5200. Steve Pingeton, Manager. Web, http://clerk.house.gov/about/viewLRCDetails and Email, info.clerkweb@mail.house.gov*

Receives and maintains lobby registrations and quarterly financial reports of lobbyists. Administers the statutes of the Federal Regulation of Lobbying Act of 1995 and counsels lobbyists. Receives and maintains agency filings made under the requirements of Section 319 of the Interior Dept. and Related Agencies Appropriations Act for fiscal 1990 (known as the Byrd Amendment). Open for public inspection.

▶NONGOVERNMENTAL

Bipartisan Policy Center, *1225 Eye St. N.W., #1000, 20005-5977; (202) 204-2400. Jason S. Grumet, President. General email, bipartisaninfo@bipartisanpolicy.org Web, https://bipartisanpolicy.org, Twitter, @BPC_ Bipartisan, Facebook, www.facebook.com/*

BipartisanPolicyCenter and Twitter, President, @JasonGrumet

Think tank advocating bipartisanship policymaking. Interests include health, energy, national and homeland security, the economy, housing, immigration, infrastructure, and governance. Monitors legislation and regulations.

The Brookings Institution, *1775 Massachusetts Ave. N.W., 20036; (202) 797-6000. Fax, (202) 797-6004. John R. Allen, President. Press, (202) 797-6197. Research Library and Archives, (202) 797-6240. General email, communications@brookings.edu*

Web, www.brookings.edu, Twitter, @Brookingsinst and Facebook, www.facebook.com/brookings

Public policy research organization that seeks to improve the performance of American institutions, the effectiveness of government programs, and the quality of public policy through research, analysis and policy recommendations. Sponsors lectures, debates, fellowship programs and policy forums.

Capital Research Center, *1513 16th St. N.W., 20036; (202) 483-6900. Fax, (202) 478-1855. Scott Walter, President.*
General email, contact@capitalresearch.org
Web, https://capitalresearch.org, Twitter, @capitalresearch and Facebook, www.facebook.com/capitalresearchcenter

Conservative think tank that researches funding sources, especially foundations, charities, and other non-profits, of public interest and advocacy groups. Analyzes the impact these groups have on public policy. Publishes findings in newsletters and reports.

Charles F. Kettering Foundation, *Washington Office, 444 N. Capitol St. N.W., #434, 20001-1512; (202) 393-4478. David Mathews, President.*
Web, www.kettering.org, Twitter, @KetteringFdn and Facebook, www.facebook.com/KetteringFoundation

Works to understand democracy and its processes and improve the domestic policymaking process through citizen deliberation. Supports international programs focusing on unofficial, citizen-to-citizen diplomacy. Encourages greater citizen involvement in formation of public policy. Interests include public education and at-risk youths. (Headquarters in Dayton, Ohio.)

Citizens United, *1006 Pennsylvania Ave. S.E., 20003-2142; (202) 547-5420. Fax, (202) 547-5421. David N. Bossie, President.*
General email, info@citizensunited.org
Web, http://citizensunited.org, Twitter, @Citizens_United and Facebook, www.facebook.com/CitizensUnitedDC

Acts as advocate for key elements of the conservative legislative and policy agenda.

Eisenhower Institute, *818 Connecticut Ave. N.W., #400, 20006 (mailing address: 200 Massachusetts Ave. N.W., #700, Washington, DC 20001); (202) 628-4444. Fax, (202) 628-4445. Susan Eisenhower, Chair Emerita; Lauren Cole, Program Manager, Washington Office.*
General email, ei@gettysburg.edu
Web, www.eisenhowerinstitute.org and Twitter, @eighbc

Nonpartisan research and educational organization modeled on President Dwight D. Eisenhower's legacy of public policy formation and leadership, stressing pursuit of facts, respectful dialogue, and a focus on the future. (Affiliated with Gettysburg College in Gettysburg, Pa.)

National Institute for Lobbying and Ethics, *10340 Democracy Lane, #300, Fairfax, VA 22030; (703) 383-1330. Tommy Goodwin, President.*
General email, paul@lobbyinginstitute.com
Web, www.lobbyinginstitute.com, Twitter, @LobbyInstitute and Facebook, www.facebook.com/Lobbyinginstitute

Membership: professional lobbyists and other professional public relations staff. Works to improve the technical skills, ethics, and public image of lobbyists. Monitors lobby legislation and conducts education programs on public issues, lobbying techniques, and other related issues.

Public Citizen, *1600 20th St. N.W., 20009; (202) 588-1000. Fax, (202) 588-7798. Robert Weissman, President.*
General email, pcmail@citizen.org
Web, www.citizen.org, Twitter, @Public_Citizen and Facebook, www.facebook.com/publiccitizen

Public interest consumer advocacy organization comprising the following programs: Congress Watch, Health Research Group, Energy Program, Litigation Group, Global Trade Watch, Democracy is for People Project, and Commercial Alert Program.

Women & Politics Institute *(American University), 4400 Massachusetts Ave. N.W., Kerwin Hall, #109E, 20016; (202) 885-2903. Fax, (202) 885-2967. Betsy Fischer Martin, Executive Director, (202) 885-6149.*
General email, wpi@american.edu
Web, www.american.edu/spa/wpi and Twitter, @AU_WPI

Research center that encourages women to participate in politics and addresses women's issues. Administers graduate and undergraduate certificates to academics studying women, policy, and political leadership. Assists women in securing employment in the political sphere through leadership training programs.

Ethnic Group Advocacy

▶**NONGOVERNMENTAL**

American–Arab Anti-Discrimination Committee (ADC), *1705 DeSales St. N.W., #500, 20036; (202) 244-2990. Fax, (202) 333-6470. Samer E. Khalaf, President.*
Web, www.adc.org and Twitter, @adctweets

Nonpartisan and nonsectarian organization that promotes Arab cultural heritage to the public and policymakers. Sponsors student internships to Washington, DC.

Arab American Institute, *1600 K St. N.W., #601, 20006; (202) 429-9210. Fax, (202) 429-9214. James J. Zogby, President.*
General email, communications@aaiusa.org
Web, www.aaiusa.org and Twitter, @AAIUSA

Fosters civic and political empowerment of Americans of Arab descent through research, policy formation, and political activism.

Armenian National Committee of America, *1711 N St. N.W., 20036; (202) 775-1918. Fax, (202) 223-7964. Aram Hamparian, Executive Director.*
General email, anca@anca.org
Web, www.anca.org and Twitter, @ANCA_DC

Armenian American grassroots political organization. Works to advance concerns of the Armenian American community. Interests include strengthening U.S.–Armenian relations.

Asian Americans Advancing Justice (AAJC), *1620 L St. N.W., #1050, 20036; (202) 296-2300. Fax, (202) 296-2318. Michelle Boykins, Senior Director of Strategic Communications, ext. 0144.*
General email, information@advancingequality.org
Web, www.advancingjustice-aajc.org and Twitter, @AAAJ_AAJC

Works to advance the human and civil rights of Asian Americans and other minority groups through advocacy, public policy, public education, and litigation. Promotes civic engagement at the local, regional, and national levels. Interests include affirmative action, hate crimes, media diversity, census, broadband and telecommunications, youth advocacy, immigrant rights, language access, and voting rights.

B'nai B'rith International, *1120 20th St. N.W., #300N, 20036; (202) 857-6600. Daniel S. Mariaschin, Chief Executive Officer. Press, (202) 857-6699. Toll-free, (888) 388-4224.*
General email, info@bnaibrith.org
Web, www.bnaibrith.org, Twitter, @BnaiBrith and Facebook, www.facebook.com/bnaibrithinternational

Advocates policies in support of Jews and the State of Israel.

Congressional Black Caucus Foundation, *1720 Massachusetts Ave. N.W., 20036-1903; (202) 263-2800. Paul E. Dumars Jr., Co-President Acting; Donna Fsher-Lewis, Co-President Acting.*
General email, info@cbcfinc.org
Web, www.cbcfinc.org, Twitter, @CBCFInc, Facebook, www.facebook.com/CBCFinc and YouTube, www.youtube.com/user/CBCFINC

Conducts research and offers programs on public policy issues with the aim of improving the socioeconomic circumstances of African Americans and other underserved populations. Holds issue forums and leadership seminars. Provides elected officials, organizations, and researchers with statistical, demographic, public policy, and political information.

Japanese American Citizens League, *Washington Office, 1629 K St. N.W., #400, 20006; (202) 223-1240. David Inoue, Executive Director.*
General email, dc@jacl.org
Web, www.jacl.org and Twitter, @JACL_National

Monitors legislative and regulatory activities affecting the rights of Japanese Americans. Supports civil rights of all Americans, with a focus on Asian and Asian Pacific Americans. (Headquarters in San Francisco, Calif.)

Labor Council for Latin American Advancement, *815 16th St. N.W., 3rd Floor, 20006; (202) 508-6919. Fax, (202) 508-6922. Karla Pineda, Deputy Director.*
General email, headquarters@lclaa.org
Web, www.lclaa.org, Twitter, @LCLAA and Facebook, www.facebook.com/LCLAA

Membership: Latino/a trade unionists throughout U.S. and Puerto Rico. Encourages equal employment opportunity, voter registration, and participation in the political process. (Affiliated with the AFL-CIO and the Change to Win Federation.)

League of United Latin American Citizens, *1133 19th St. N.W., #1000, 20036; (202) 833-6130. Fax, (202) 833-6135. Sindy M. Benavides, Chief Executive Officer, ext. 108. Toll-free, (877) 585-2201.*
General email, info@lulac.org
Web, https://lulac.org, Twitter, @LULAC and Facebook, www.facebook.com/lulac.national.dc

Seeks full social, political, economic, and educational rights for Hispanics in the United States. Programs include housing projects for the poor, employment and training for youth and women, and political advocacy on issues affecting Hispanics, including immigration. Affiliated with National Educational Service Centers (LNESCs), which award scholarships. Holds exposition open to the public.

Mexican American Legal Defense and Educational Fund (MALDEF), *National Public Policy, 1016 16th St. N.W., #100, 20036; (202) 293-2828. Andrea Senteno, Regional Counsel for Legislative and Regulatory Affairs.*
General email, info@maldef.org
Web, www.maldef.org/public-policy, Twitter, @MALDEF, Facebook, www.facebook.com/MALDEF and YouTube, www.youtube.com/user/maldef

Works with Congress and the White House to promote legislative advocacy for minority groups. Interests include equal employment, voting rights, bilingual education, immigration, and discrimination. Monitors legislation and regulations. (Headquarters in Los Angeles, Calif.)

National Assn. of Latino Elected and Appointed Officials Educational Fund, *Washington Office, 600 Pennsylvania Ave. S.E., #480, 20003; (202) 546-2536. Fax, (202) 546-4121. Arturo Vargas, Executive Director; Rosalind Gold, Chief Public Policy Officer.*
Web, www.naleo.org, Twitter, @NALEO and Twitter, @ArturoNALEO

Research and advocacy group that provides civic affairs information and assistance on legislation affecting Latinos. Encourages Latino participation in local, state, and national politics. Interests include health care and social, economic, and educational issues. (Headquarters in Los Angeles, Calif.)

National Conference of Puerto Rican Women, *1220 L St. N.W., #100-177, 20005; Vilma Colom, National President; Milagros V. McGuire, President of the Washington, DC, Chapter.*
General email, v_colom@yahoo.com
Web, www.nacoprw.org

Nonprofit, nonpartisan organization promoting the participation of Puerto Rican and other Hispanic women in their economic, social, and political life. Provides training, mentorship, and leadership development at local and national levels through workshops and institutes; provides scholarships to Hispanic individuals.

National Congress of American Indians, *Embassy of Tribal Nations, 1516 P St. N.W., 20005; (202) 466-7767. Fax, (202) 466-7797. Fawn Sharp, President.*
Web, www.ncai.org, Twitter, @NCAI1944 and Facebook, www.facebook.com/NCAI1944

Membership: American Indian and Alaska Native tribal governments and individuals. Provides information and serves as general advocate for tribes. Monitors legislative and regulatory activities affecting Native American affairs.

National Italian American Foundation, *1860 19th St. N.W., 20009; (202) 387-0600. Fax, (202) 387-0800. Jerry Jones, Chief Administration Officer, (202) 939-3102.*
General email, information@niaf.org
Web, www.niaf.org

Represents the interests of Italian Americans before Congress.

OCA: Asian Pacific American Advocates, *900 19th St. N.W. 6th Floor, 20006; (202) 223-5500. Fax, (202) 296-0540. Thu Nguyen, Executive Director, ext. 5.*
General email, oca@ocanational.org
Web, www.ocanational.org, Twitter, @OCANational and Facebook, www.facebook.com/ocanational

Advocacy group seeking to advance the social, political, and economic well-being of Asian Pacific Americans in the United States through education, racial equity and inclusion, civic engagement and census, and workforce development.

Orthodox Union, *Advocacy Center, 820 1st St. N.E., #730, 20002; (202) 513-6484. Nathan J. Diament, Executive Director, ext. 4.*
General email, ouainfo@ou.org
Web, www.ou.org/public_affairs, Twitter, @OUAdvocacy and Facebook, www.facebook.com/OUAdvocacy

Works to protect Orthodox Jewish interests and freedoms through dissemination of policy briefings to government officials. Encourages Jewish law and a traditional perspective on public policy issues. Coordinates grassroots activities. (Headquarters in New York.)

Republican Jewish Coalition, *50 F St. N.W., #100, 20001; (202) 638-6688. Fax, (202) 638-6694. Norm M. Coleman, National Chair; Matthew Brooks, Executive Director.*
General email, rjc@rjchq.org
Web, www.rjchq.org and Twitter, @RJC

Legislative interest group that works to build support among Republican Party decision makers on issues of concern to the Jewish community; studies domestic and foreign policy issues affecting the Jewish community;

supports a strong relationship between the United States and Israel. Monitors legislation and regulations.

Southeast Asia Resource Action Center (SEARAC), *1628 16th St. N.W., 3rd Floor, 20009; (202) 601-2960. Quyen Dinh, Executive Director.*
General email, searac@searac.org
Web, www.searac.org, Twitter, @SEARAC, Facebook, www.facebook.com/searac and YouTube, www.youtube.com/channel/UCu24IlraDLG8FMeZglaYeNQ/featured

Works to advance Cambodian, Hmong, Laotian, and Vietnamese refugee rights through leadership and advocacy training. Collects and analyzes data on Southeast Asian Americans; publishes reports.

Political Action Committees and 527s

The following are some key political action committees (PACs) based in Washington.

▶AGRICULTURE AND FOOD

Agricultural Retailers Assn. PAC, *4201 Wilson Blvd., #700, Arlington, VA 22203; (202) 457-0825. Fax, (202) 463-0474. Hunter Carpenter, Senior Director, Public Policy, (202) 595-1705.*
General email, info@aradc.org
Web, www.aradc.org/arapac and Twitter, @AgRetailers

American Beverage Assn. PAC, *1275 Pennsylvania Ave. N.W., #1100, 20004; (202) 463-6732. Fax, (202) 463-8277. Barbara Hiden, Director of Federal Affairs.*
General email, info@americanbeverage.org
Web, www.americanbeverage.org/initiatives-advocacy, Twitter, @AmeriBev and Facebook, www.facebook.com/AmeriBev

American Sugarbeet Growers Assn. PAC, *1155 15th St. N.W., #1100, 20005; (202) 833-2398. Fax, (240) 235-4291. Zachary Clark, Director of Government Affairs.*
General email, info@americansugarbeet.org
Web, www.americansugarbeet.org

Beer Institute PAC, *440 1st St. N.W., #350, 20001; (202) 737-2337. Fax, (202) 737-7004. Alex Davidson, Director of Public Affairs. Toll-Free, (800) 379-2739.*
Web, www.beerinstitute.org and Twitter, @beerinstitute

CandyPAC, *1101 30th St N.W., #200, 20007; Kelly O'Donnell, Director, (202) 534-1440. Finance, (202) 534-1483.*
General email, info@CandyUSA.com
Web, www.candyusa.com/advocacy/candypac, Twitter, @CandyUSA and Facebook, www.facebook.com/NationalConfectionersAssociation

(Affiliated with the National Confectioners Assn.)

Crop Insurance and Reinsurance Bureau PAC, *50 F St. N.W., #450, 20001; (202) 544-0067. Tara Smith, Deputy Executive Vice President.*
Web, www.cropinsurance.org/cirb-pac

International Dairy Foods Assn., Ice Cream, Milk, and Cheese PAC, *1250 H St. N.W., #900, 20005; (202) 737-4332. Fax, (202) 331-7820. Colin Newman, Director of Political Affairs and Strategic Programs.*
General email, pac@idfa.org
Web, www.idfa.org/dairycounts/pac, Twitter, @dairyidfa and Facebook, www.facebook.com/dairyIDFA

National Cattleman's Beef Assn. PAC, *1275 Pennsylvania Ave. N.W., #801, 20004; (202) 347-0228. Fax, (202) 638-0607. Colin Woodall, Chief Executive Officer; Ethan Lane, Vice President of Governmental Affairs.*
Web, www.ncba.org/policy/political-action-committee, Twitter, @BeefUSA and Facebook, www.facebook.com/BeefUSA

National Corn Growers Assn. PAC, *20 F St. N.W., #900, 20001; (202) 628-7001. Fax, (202) 628-1933. Anne Thompson, Director of PAC and Political Strategy.*
General email, corninfo@ncga.com
Web, www.ncga.com

National Council of Farmer Cooperatives CO-OP/PAC, *50 F St. N.W., #900, 20001; (202) 879-0826. Mary Nowak, Director, Government Affairs.*
General email, kbillings@ncfc.org
Web, www.ncfc.org

National Potato Council PAC, *50 F St. N.W., #900, 20001; (202) 682-9456. Fax, (202) 682-0333. Kam Quarles, Chief Executive Officer.*
General email, info@nationalpotatocouncil.org
Web, www.nationalpotatocouncil.org and Twitter, @ThisSpudsforYou

North American Meat Institute PAC, *1150 Connecticut Ave. N.W., #1200, 20036; (202) 587-4200. Nathan Fretz, Vice President, Legislative Affairs, (202) 587-4224.*
Web, www.meatinstitute.org, Twitter, @MeatInstitute and Facebook, www.facebook.com/AmericanMeatInstitute

The Farm Credit Council PAC, *50 F St. N.W., #900, 20001; (202) 626-8710. Fax, (202) 626-8718. Ophelie Maurice, PAC Manager, (202) 879-0849.*
General email, ask@farmcredit.org
Web, https://farmcredit.com/farm-credit-council and Twitter, @farmcredit

Wine & Spirits Wholesalers of America PAC, *805 15th St. N.W., #1120, 20005; (202) 371-9792. Fax, (202) 789-2405. Dawson Hobbs, Executive Vice President of Government Affairs.*
General email, info@wswa.org
Web, www.wswa.org/issues/wswa-pac and Facebook, www.facebook.com/wswa

▶ BUSINESS AND ECONOMICS

American Bankers Assn. BankPAC, *1120 Connecticut Ave. N.W., 20036; (202) 663-5000. Rob Engstrom, Chief Political Strategist.*
General email, abapac@aba.com
Web, www.aba.com/advocacy/political-engagement, Twitter, @ABABankers and Facebook, www.facebook.com/AmericanBankersAssociation

American Council of Life Insurers PAC, *101 Constitution Ave. N.W., #700, 20001-2133; (202) 624-2000. Leah Walters, Senior Vice President of State Relations.*
General email, pac@acli.com
Web, www.acli.com, Twitter, @ACLINews and Facebook, www.facebook.com/ACLINews

American Hotel and Lodging Assn., Hotel PAC, *1250 Eye St. N.W., #110, 20005; (202) 289-3156. Fax, (202) 289-3199. Brian Crawford, Executive Vice President of Government Affairs.*
General email, gov.affairs@ahla.com
Web, www.ahla.com/hotelpac

Credit Union Legislative Action Council, *99 M St. S.E., #300, 20003; (202) 638-5777. Hannah Truslow, Director of Political Fundraising Development, (202) 508-3633. Toll-free, (800) 356-9655.*
General email, hello@cuna.coop
Web, www.cuna.org/culac and Twitter, @CUNA

Cruise Lines International Assn. PAC, *1201 F St. N.W., #250, 20004; (202) 759-9326. Christina Perez, Government Affairs Manager.*
General email, info@cruising.org
Web, https://cruising.org/about-the-industry/policy-priorities/advocacy/clia-pac and Twitter, @CLIAGlobal

Hardwood Federation PAC, *1101 K St. N.W., #700, 20005; (202) 463-5186. Bryan Brendle, Policy and PAC Director.*
General email, hardwood.federation@hardwoodfederation.com
Web, www.hardwoodfederation.com

Independent Community Bankers of America PAC, *1615 L St. N.W., #900, 20036; (202) 659-8111. Mary Randolph Gannon, Vice President. Toll-free, (866) 843-4222.*
General email, icbpac@icba.org
Web, www.icba.org/advocacy, Twitter, @ICBA and Facebook, www.facebook.com/icbaorg

Independent Insurance Agents and Brokers of America Political Action Committee (InsurPac), *20 F St. N.W., #610, 20001; (202) 863-7000. Fax, (202) 863-7015. Nathan Riedel, Treasurer.*

General email, InsurPac@iiaba.net

Web, www.independentagent.com/governmentaffairs/insurPac/default.aspx

Insurance and Financial Advisors PAC, 2901 Telestar Court, Falls Church, VA 22042-1205; (703) 770-8100. Fax, (703) 770-8224. Stephanie Sheridan, Political Director, (703) 770-8156.
Toll-free, (877) 866-2432.
General email, info@naifa.org

Web, https://leaders.naifa.org/about-ifapac, Twitter, @NAIFA and YouTube, www.youtube.com/user/naifavideo

Investment Company Institute PAC, 1401 H St. N.W., #1200, 20005; (202) 326-5800. Don Auerbach, Chief Operating Officer. Press, (202) 371-5413.
Web, www.ici.org, Twitter, @ICI and Facebook, www.facebook.com/ici.org

Mortgage Bankers Assn. PAC (MORPAC), 1919 M St. N.W., 5th Floor, 20036; (202) 557-2777. Fax, (202) 621-1577. Jeff Taylor, Chair. Toll-Free, (800) 793-6222.
General email, morpac@mba.org

Web, www.mba.org/get-involved/mbas-political-action-committee

The National Assn. of Business Political Action Committees, 700 Pennsylvania Ave. S.E., 2nd Floor, 20003; (202) 341-3780. Micaela Isler, Executive Director.
General email, nabpac@nabpac.org

Web, www.nabpac.org and Twitter, @nabpc

National Assn. of Real Estate Investment Trusts, Inc. PAC, 1875 Eye St. N.W., #500, 20006; (202) 739-9436. Steven Lowery, Director.
General email, reitpac@nareit.com

Web, https://reitpac.org

National Beer Wholesalers Assn. PAC, 1101 King St., #600, Alexandria, VA 22314-2944; (703) 683-4300.
Fax, (703) 683-8965. Linda Auglis, Senior Director.
General email, info@nbwa.org

Web, www.nbwa.org

National Federation of Independent Business, Federal PAC, 555 12th St., #1001, 20004; (202) 554-9000.
Sharon Sussin, National Political Director. Toll-free, (800) 274-6342.
Web, www.nfib.com/advocacy, Twitter, @NFIB, Facebook, www.facebook.com/NFIB and YouTube, www.youtube.com/user/NFIBSmallBusiness

Supports candidates in both federal and state elections who support small business.

National Multifamily Housing Council PAC, 1775 Eye St. N.W., #1100, 20006; (202) 974-2300. Fax, (202) 775-0112. Lisa Costello, Vice President for Political Affairs, (202) 974-2325.
Web, www.nmhc.org, Twitter, @ApartmentWire and Facebook, www.facebook.com/nmhc.org

Restaurant PAC of the National Restaurant Assn., 2055 L St. N.W., #700, 20036; (202) 331-5900. Sean Kennedy, Vice President, Public Affairs. Toll-free, (800) 424-5156.
General email, advocacy@restaurant.org

Web, https://restaurant.org/advocacy/get-involved/restaurant-pac, Twitter, @RestaurantsAct and Facebook, www.facebook.com/RestaurantsAct

Securities Industry and Financial Markets Assn. PAC, 1099 New York Ave. N.W., 6th Floor, 20005; (202) 962-7325. Lauren Alejandro, Political Affairs Associate.
General email, inquiry@sifma.org

Web, www.sifma.org/resources/general/pac

Service Employees International Union Committee on Political Education (SEIU COPE), 1800 Massachusetts Ave. N.W., 20036; (202) 730-7112. Mary Kay Henry, President; Gerry Hudson, Secretary-Treasurer. Toll-free, (800) 424-8592.
Web, www.seiu.org, Twitter, @SEIU and Facebook, www.facebook.com/SEIU

▶ **CIVIL RIGHTS**

American Assn. for Justice PAC, 777 6th St. N.W., #200, 20001; (202) 684-9591. Fax, (202) 338-8709.
Kathleen Nastri, President. Toll-free, (800) 424-2725.
General email, aajpac@justice.org

Web, www.justice.org/advocacy/aaj-pac

(Formerly the Assn. of Trial Lawyers of America.)

Committee for Hispanic Causes CHC, BOLD PAC, P.O. Box 75357, 20013 (mailing address: P.O. Box 33079, Washington, DC 20033); (202) 849-8743. Diane Evans, Treasurer; Rep. Ruben Gallego, Chair.
Web, www.boldpac.com, Twitter, @BOLDPAC, Facebook, www.facebook.com/boldpac and Press, press@chcboldpac.com

(Affiliated with the Committee for Hispanic Caucus.)

Human Rights Campaign PAC (HRC), 1640 Rhode Island Ave. N.W., 20036; (202) 216-1545.
Fax, (202) 347-5323. Mike Mings, Director.
TTY, (202) 216-1572.
General email, hrc@hrc.org

Web, www.hrc.org and Twitter, @HRC

Supports pro-equality candidates for state and federal office who favor lesbian, gay, bisexual, and transgender equality.

JStreetPAC, P.O. Box 66703 Washington, DC 20035; (202) 596-5207. Danny Yu, Vice President of Finance. Press, (202) 670-5397.
General email, info@jstreet.org

Web, https://jstreet.org, Twitter, @jstreetdotorg, Facebook, www.facebook.com/jstreetdotorg and YouTube, www.youtube.com/jstreetdotorg

Focuses on pro-Israel and propeace American relationships and supports candidates in favor of a diplomacy-first approach to advancing U.S. interests in the Middle East and promoting peace and security for Israel.

LGBTQ Victory Fund Federal PAC, 1225 Eye St. N.W., #525, 20005; (202) 842-8679. Fax, (202) 289-3863. Ruban J. Gonzales, Executive Director.
General email, communications@victoryfund.org
Web, www.victoryfund.org and Twitter, @VictoryFund

NARAL Pro-Choice America PAC, 1725 Eye St. N.W., #900, 20006; (202) 973-3000. Fax, (202) 973-3096. Steven Kravitz, Chief Financial Officer.
General email, PACSupport@prochoiceamerica.org
Web, www.prochoiceamerica.org and Twitter, @NARAL

National Assn. of Social Workers Political Action for Candidate Election, 750 1st St. N.E., #700, 20002-4241; (202) 408-8600. Sarah Butts, Director of Public Policy.
Web, www.socialworkers.org/advocacy/political-action-for-candidate-election-pace, Twitter, @nasw and Facebook, www.facebook.com/socialworkers

National Rifle Assn. of America–Political Victory Fund, 11250 Waples Mill Rd., Fairfax, VA 22030; (703) 267-1157. Robert Owens, Treasurer.
Web, www.nrapvf.org, Twitter, @NRAPVF and Facebook, www.facebook.com/NationalRifleAssociation

Women's Campaign Fund, 718 7th St. N.W., 2nd Floor, 20001; (202) 796-8259. Jennifer Atikinson, President; Georgia Berner, Chair (Acting).
General email, info@wcfonline.org
Web, www.wcfonline.org, Twitter, @WCFonline and Facebook, www.facebook.com/WCFonline

A national nonpartisan organization dedicated to dramatically increasing the number of women in elected office.

▶ COMMUNICATIONS AND MEDIA

BSA—The Software Alliance PAC, 20 F St. N.W., #800, 20001; (202) 872-5500. Fax, (202) 872-5501. Joe DeSalvio, Chief Financial Officer.
General email, info@bsa.org
Web, www.bsa.org and Twitter, @BSAnews

Consumer Technology Assn. PAC, 1919 S. Eads St., Arlington, VA 22202; (703) 907-7600. Tiffany Moore, Senior Vice President of Political and Industry Affairs. Toll-free, (866) 858-1555.
General email, CTA@CTA.tech
Web, https://cta.tech/Policy/CTAPAC.aspx, Twitter, @CTATech and Facebook, www.facebook.com/ConsumerTechnologyAssociation

Dell Technologies PAC, 440 First St. N.W., #820, 20001; (202) 770-5275. Christopher Alsup, Government Affairs Director.
General email, PAC@Dell.com
Web, WWW.dell.com/learn/is/en/iscorp1/corp-comm/public-policy

(Dell corporate headquarters is in Red Rock, TX.)

National Assn. of Broadcasters Political Action Committee, 1 M St. S.E., 20003 (mailing address: NABPAC c/o Alyssa Niemiec, 1 M. St. S.E., Washington, DC 20003); (202) 429-5314. Jennifer Fleming, Director.
General email, PAC@nab.org
Web, www.nabpac.com

Membership. Supports candidates for political office who champion broadcast issues.

National Cable and Telecommunications Assn. PAC, 25 Massachusetts Ave. N.W., #100, 20001; (202) 222-2300. Michael Powell, Chief Executive Officer.
General email, info@ncta.com
Web, www.ncta.com, Twitter, @NCTAitv, Facebook, www.facebook.com/NCTAitv and Press, mediaoutreach@ncta.com

PrintPAC, 1325 G St. N.W., #500, 20005; (202) 627-6924. Lisbeth Lyons, Vice President of Government and Political Affairs, ext. 504.
General email, llyons@printing.org
Web, www.printpaconline.org

Affiliated with the PRINTING United Alliance, focused on issues affecting printing and graphic communications companies. (Headquarters in Wexford, Penn.)

Verizon Communications Inc., PAC, 1300 Eye St. N.W., #500 East, 20005; (202) 515-2557. Taylor Craig, Treasurer.
General email, taylor.k.craig@verizon.com
Web, https://vz.epacweb.com

▶ DEFENSE

Council for a Livable World, 820 1st St. N.E., #LL-180, 20002; (202) 543-4100. John Tierney, Executive Director, ext. 2108.
General email, advocacy@clw.org
Web, https://livableworld.org, Twitter, @Livableworld and YouTube, www.youtube.com/channel/UC2zgzMV7CjH_4ZV9/Uyj-yhA/featured

Supports congressional candidates who advocate arms control and progressive national security policy.

▶ ENERGY AND NATURAL RESOURCES

Action Committee for Rural Electrification (ACRE), 4301 Wilson Blvd., Arlington, VA 22203-1860; (703) 907-5500. Gabe Snow, Director, (703) 907-5799.
Web, www.electric.coop/acre

(Affiliated with the National Rural Electric Cooperative Assn.)

American Clean Power Assn. PAC, *1501 M St. N.W., #900, 20005-1700; (202) 383-2500. Fax, (202) 293-2505. Nina Brundage, Government and Public Affairs Coordinator.*
General email, Grassroots@cleanpower.org
Web, www.cleanpower.org

American Forest and Paper Assn. PAC, *1101 K St. N.W., #700, 20005; (202) 463-2755. Katherine Widman, Manager.*
General email, comm@afandpa.org
Web, www.afandpa.org/advocacy/af-pa-pac

American Gas Assn. PAC (GASPAC), *400 N. Capitol St. N.W., #450, 20001-1535; (202) 824-7231. Katie Tomarchio, Senior Manager of Political Programs, (202) 824-7231.*
Web, www.aga.org/about/advocacy/gaspac, Twitter, @aga_naturalgas and Facebook, www.facebook.com/naturalgas

Friends of the Earth PAC, *1101 15th St. N.W., 11th Floor, 20005; (202) 783-7400. Fax, (202) 783-0444. Erich Pica, President, (202) 222-0714. Press, 202 222-0709.*
Web, www.foeaction.org, Twitter, @foeaction and Press, adukule@foe.org

International Paper PAC, *1101 Pennsylvania Ave. N.W., #200, 20004; (202) 628-1223. Chris Keuleman, Vice President for Global Government Relations; Meaghan Killion Joyce, Political Affairs Manager, (202) 628-1321.*
General email, government.relations@ipaper.com
Web, www.internationalpaper.com, Twitter, @IntlPaperCo and Facebook, www.facebook.com/InternationalPaper

National Alliance of Forest Owners PAC, *122 C St. N.W., #630, 20001; (202) 747-0759. Fax, (202) 824-0770. William (Chip) Murray, Vice President for Policy and General Counsel, (202) 747-0742.*
General email, info@nafoalliance.org
Web, www.nafoalliance.org

National Mining Assn., MINEPAC and COALPAC, *101 Constituion Ave. N.W., #500 East, 20001; (202) 463-2600, ext. 66526. Fax, (202) 463-2666. Ryan Jackson, Vice President of Government Affairs.*
Web, www.nma.org

Solar Energy Industries Assn. PAC, *1425 K St. N.W., #1000, 20005; (202) 682-0556. Erin Duncan, Vice President for Congressional Affairs.*
General email, info@seia.org
Web, www.seia.org/seia-solarpac

Sustainable Energy and Environment Coalition PAC, *2463 RHOB, 20515; (202) 226-5034. David Schutt, Executive Director, (202) 564-6885.*

General email, info@seecpac.org
Web, http://seecpac.org, Twitter, @SEEC, Facebook, www.facebook.com/SustainableEnergyandEnvironmentCoalition and House of Representatives Sustainable Energy & Environment Coalition, https://seec-tonko.house.gov

▶ HEALTH

America's Essential Hospitals PAC, *401 Ninth St. N.W., #900, 20004; (202) 585-0100. Jason Pray, Vice President of Legislative Affairs. Press, (202) 585-0102.*
General email, GOV.admin@essentialhospitals.org
Web, www.essentialhospitals.org/essential-hospitals-pac

American Assn. of Orthopaedic Surgeons, *Orthopaedic PAC, 317 Massachusetts Ave. N.E., 1st Floor, 20002; (202) 546-4430. Fax, (202) 546-5051. Brittany Starr, Senior Director of Political Affairs.*
General email, dc@aaos.org
Web, www.aaos.org/advocacy/pac, Twitter, @AAOSAdvocacy and Facebook, www.facebook.com/AAOS1
(Headquarters in Rosemont, IL.)

American College of Obstetricians and Gynecologists PAC, *409 12th St. S.W., 20024-2188 (mailing address: P.O. Box 96920, Washington, DC 20090-9998); (202) 863-2509. Fax, (202) 488-3985. Megan Reenock, Political Strategist, (202) 863-2513.*
General email, govtrel@acog.org
Web, www.obgynpac.org and Twitter, @ACOGAction

American College of Radiology Assn. PAC (RADPAC), *505 9th St. N.W., #910, 20004; Fax, (703) 262-9312. Ted Burnes, Senior Director. Toll-free, (800) 227-5463, ext. 4949.*
Web, www.radpac.org and Twitter, @RADPAC

American Health Care Assn. PAC (AHCA-PAC), *1201 L St. N.W., 20005-4015; (202) 842-4444. Fax, (202) 842-3860. Jennifer Knorr Hahs, Senior Director of Political Affairs, (202) 898-2844.*
General email, PAC@ahca.org
Web, www.ahcancal.org

American Hospital Assn. PAC, *Two City Center, 800 10th St. N.W., #400, 20001-4956; (202) 638-1100. Stacey Hughes, Executive Vice President of Government Relations and Public Policy, (202) 626-2358. Help line, (800) 424-4301.*
Web, www.aha.org, Twitter, @AHAhospitals and Facebook, www.facebook.com/ahahospitals

American Medical Assn. Political Action Committee (AMPAC), *25 Massachusetts Ave. N.W., #600, 20001; (202) 789-7400. Fax, (202) 789-7469. Kevin L. Walker, Vice President of Political Affairs.*
Web, www.ampaconline.org

American Osteopathic Information Assn. PAC, *1090 Vermont Ave. N.W., #500, 20005; (202) 414-0152. Fax, (800) 962-9008. Sean Neal, Director. Toll-free, (800) 962-9008.*
General email, opac@osteotech.org
Web, www.osteopathicpac.org and Twitter, @AOAforDOs

American Psychiatric Assn. PAC, *800 Maine Ave. S.W., #900, 20024; (703) 907-7300. Kevin Madden, Chief Financial Officer.*
General email, advocacy@psych.org
Web, www.psychiatry.org/psychiatrists/advocacy

American Veterinary Medical Assn. PAC, *1910 Sunderland Pl. N.W., 20036-1642; (800) 321-1473. Fax, (202) 223-4877. Dr. Kent McClure, Chief Governmental Relations Officer.*
General email, avmapac@avma.org
Web, www.avma.org/Advocacy/AVMAPAC/Pages/default .aspx

(Headquarters in Schaunburg, Ill.)

Humana Inc. PAC, *975 F St. N.W., #550, 20004; (202) 467-8682. Jay Anmol Khosla, Treasurer.*
General email, humanapac@humana.com
Web, www.humana.com/about/public-policy/political-activity-contributions and Twitter, @Humana

National Active and Retired Federal Employees PAC (NARFE), *606 N. Washington St., Alexandria, VA 22314; (703) 838-7780. Fax, (703) 838-7785. John Hatton, Vice President of Policy and Programs.*
General email, advocacy@narfe.org
Web, www.narfe.org/advocacy/narfe-pac and Twitter, @narfehq

National Committee to Preserve Social Security and Medicare PAC, *111 K St. N.E., #700, 20002; (202) 216-0420. Fax, (202) 216-0446. Dan Adcock, Director of Government Relations and Policy. Press, (202) 216-8378.*
Web, www.ncpssm.org/pac, Twitter, @NCPSSM and Facebook, www.facebook.com/NationalCommittee

Natural Products Assn. PAC, *440 1st St. N.W., #520, 20001; (202) 223-0101. Fax, (202) 223-0250. Daniel Fabricant, President, (202) 204-4721.*
General email, PAC@NPAnational.org
Web, www.npanational.org/advocacy/pac, Twitter, @NPANational and Facebook, www.facebook.com/ NaturalProductsAssociation

Physical Therapy Political Action Committee (PT-PAC), *3030 Potomac Ave., #100, Alexandria, VA 22305; (703) 684-2782. Fax, (703) 684-7343. Michael Matlack, Director of Congressional Affairs, (703) 706-3163. Toll-free, (800) 999-2782.*
General email, ptpac@apta.org
Web, www.ptpac.org, Twitter, @PTPAC and Facebook, www.facebook.com/Physical-Therapy-Political-Action-Committee-172139499510838

Planned Parenthood Action Fund, *1110 Vermont Ave. N.W., #300, 20005; (202) 973-4800. Fax, (202) 296-3242. Jennie Rosenthal, Action Fund Chair. Toll-free, (800) 430-4907.*
General email, actionfund@ppfa.org
Web, www.plannedparenthoodaction.org, Twitter, @PPAct and Facebook, www.facebook.com/PlannedParenthood Action

Nonpartisan organization that supports candidates who advocate for reproductive health care, including sex education, health care reform for women, birth control, and legal abortion access in the United States.

Population Connection Action Fund PAC, *2120 L St. N.W., #500, 20037; (202) 332-2200. Fax, (202) 332-2302. Brian Dixon, Senior Vice President for Media and Government Relations, (202) 974-7744. Toll-free, (800) 767-1956.*
General email, info@popconnectaction.org
Web, www.populationconnectionaction.org, Twitter, @popconnect and Facebook, www.facebook.com/ PopConnectAction

Interests include U.S. foreign aid for international family planning, affordable contraceptives access, and population growth education. Endorses candidates who support everyone's right to control their own reproductive destinies.

Seniors Housing Political Action Committee, *5225 Wisconsin Ave. N.W., #502, 20015; (202) 237-0900. Fax, (202) 237-1616. Jeanne McGlynn Delgado, Vice President of Government Affairs, ext. 2.*
Web, www.ashaliving.org/advocacy/sh-pac-asha-govt-affairs-team

▶ LABOR

Active Ballot Club (ABC) *(United Food and Commercial Workers International Union, AFL-CIO), 1775 K St. N.W., 20006; (202) 223-3111. Fax, (202) 728-1830. Shaun Barclay, Secretary-Treasurer.*
Web, www.ufcwaction.org/abc, Twitter, @UFCW and Facebook, www.facebook.com/ufcwinternational

Acts as advocate for higher wages and paid sick leave, and works toward achieving economic stabilty for workers.

Air Line Pilots Assn. ALPA-PAC, *7950 Jones Branch Dr., #400S, McLean, VA 22102; (703) 689-2270. Capt. Joseph A. Genovese, Jr., Treasurer. Toll-free, (888) 359-2572.*
General email, communications@alpa.org
Web, www.alpa.org/advocacy/alpa-pac

Aluminum Assn. PAC, *1400 Crystal Dr., #430, Arlington, VA 22202; (703) 358-2960. Francesca Licari, Senior External Affairs Specialist, (703) 358-2990.*
General email, info@aluminum.org
Web, www.aluminum.org/aluminum-pac and Twitter, @AluminumNews

Amalgamated Transit Union—COPE (Committee on Political Education), *10000 New Hampshire Ave., Silver Spring, MD 20903; (301) 431-7100. Fax, (301) 431-7117. Kenneth R. (Ken) Kirk, International Secretary-Treasurer. Toll- Free, (888) 240-1196.*
Web, www.atu.org/action/atu-cope, Facebook, www.facebook.com/ATUInternational and Twitter, @ATUComm

American Federation of State, County and Municipal Employees (AFSCME), *1625 L St. N.W., 20036-5687; (202) 429-1000. Fax, (202) 429-1293. Lee A. Saunders, President. Press, (202) 429-1145. TTY, (202) 659-0446.*
Web, www.afscme.org, Twitter, @AFSCME and Facebook, www.facebook.com/AFSCME
    (Affliated with the AFL-CIO.)

American Federation of Teachers (AFT), *Political Dept., 555 New Jersey Ave. N.W., 20001; (202) 879-4400. John Ost, Director. Press, (202) 374-6103.*
Web, www.aft.org/position/federal-legislation-and-advocacy, Facebook, www.facebook.com/AFTUnion and Advocacy, highered@aft.org
    (Affiliated with the AFL-CIO.)

American Road and Transportation Builders Assn. PAC, *250 E St. S.W., #900, 20024; (202) 289-4434. Fax, (202) 289-4435. Nick Goldstein, Assistant General Counsel, (202) 683-1005.*
General email, ngoldstein@artba.org
Web, www.artba.org/government-affairs/political-action-committee and Twitter, @ARTBA

Associated Builders and Contractors PAC, *440 1st St. N.W., #200, 20001; (202) 595-1505. Kristen Swearingen, Treasurer.*
General email, gotquestions@abc.org
Web, www.abc.org, Twitter, @ABCNational and Facebook, www.facebook.com/ABCNational

Carpenters Legislative Improvement Committee, *United Brotherhood of Carpenters and Joiners of America, 101 Constitution Ave. N.W., 10th Floor, 20001; (202) 546-6206. Thomas J. Flynn, General Secretary Treasurer.*
General email, webmaster@carpenters.org
Web, www.carpenters.org, Twitter, @UBCJA_Official and Facebook, www.facebook.com/CarpentersUnited

Committee on Letter Carriers Political Education *(National Assn. of Letter Carriers), 100 Indiana Ave. N.W., 20001-2144; (202) 393-4695. Fredric V. Rolando, President. Press, (202) 662-2850.*
General email, nalcinf@nalc.org
Web, www.nalc.org, Twitter, @NALC_National and Facebook, www.facebook.com/nalc.national
    (Affiliated with the AFL-CIO.)

Committee on Political Action of the American Postal Workers Union, *1300 L St. N.W., 20005; (202) 842-4200. Judy Beard, Legislative and Political Director, (202) 842-4211.*

Web, www.apwu.org, Twitter, @apwunational and Facebook, www.facebook.com/APWUnational

CWA-COPE Political Contributions Committee *(Communications Workers of America), 501 3rd St. N.W., 20001-2797; (202) 434-1100. Sara Steffens, Secretary Treasurer.*
Web, www.cwa-union.org, Twitter, @cwaunion and Facebook, www.facebook.com/CWAUnion
    (Affiliated with the AFL-CIO.)

International Assn. of Fire Fighters PAC, *1750 New York Ave. N.W., #300, 20006-5395; (202) 737-8484. Fax, (202) 737-8418. Shannon Meissner, Director of Governmental Affairs.*
General email, btimmins@IAFF.org
Web, www.iaff.org/firepac

International Assn. of Sheet Metal, Air, Rail, and Transportation Workers, Political Action League, *1750 New York Ave. N.W., 6th Floor, 20006-5386; (202) 662-0800. Fax, (202) 662-0880. Gregory K. (Greg) Hynes, National Legislative Director. Toll-free, (800) 457-7694.*
General email, info@smart-union.org
Web, https://smart-union.org and Twitter, @smartunionworks

International Brotherhood of Electrical Workers PAC, *900 7th St. N.W., 20001; (202) 833-7000. Fax, (202) 728-7676. Kenneth Cooper, International Secretary-Treasurer; Austin Keyser, Director of Political and Legislative Affairs, (202) 728-6046. Press, (202) 728-6014.*
General email, Political@ibew.org
Web, www.ibew.org/Political and Twitter, @IBEW

International Brotherhood of Teamsters, *Political and Legislative Action, 25 Louisiana Ave. N.W., 20001; (202) 624-6993. Fax, (202) 624-6992. Ken Hall, General Secretary–Treasurer.*
General email, drive@teamster.org
Web, https://teamster.org/political-legislative-action

International Union of Operating Engineers, *Legislative and Political Affairs, 1125 17th St. N.W., 20036; (202) 429-9100, ext. 2682. Fax, (202) 778-2688. James M. Sweeney, General Secretary-Treasurer.*
Web, www.iuoe.org/about-iuoe/iuoe-legislative-and-political-affairs

Ironworkers Political Action League, *1750 New York Ave. N.W., #400, 20006; (202) 383-4800. Fax, (202) 638-4856. Ross Templeton, Political and Legislative Director, (202) 340-6502.*
General email, ipal@iwintl.org
Web, www.ironworkers.org, Twitter, @TheIronworkers and Facebook, www.facebook.com/impactironworkers

Laborers' Political League of Laborers' International Union of North America, *905 16th St. N.W., 20006-1765; (202) 737-8320. Fax, (202) 942-2307. Armand E. Sabitoni,*

General Secretary-Treasurer, (401) 751-8010;
David Mallino, Legislative Director, (202) 942-2273.
General email, legislative@liuna.org

Web, www.liuna.org

**Machinists Non-Partisan Political League
(International Assn. of Machinists and Aerospace
Workers, AFL-CIO),** 9000 Machinists Pl., Upper
Marlboro, MD 20772-2687; (301) 967-4575. Fax, (301)
967-4595. Hasan Solomon, Legislative Director;
Dora Cerventes, General Secretary–Treasurer. Press, (301)
967-4520.
General email, info@iamwaw.org

Web, www.goiam.org/mnpl

Membership: represents the IAM in Washington.
Seeks to secure economic justice, security in the workplace
and equality for every member. Helps elect candidates
who supportIAM vlaues.

National Air Traffic Controllers Assn. PAC, 1325
Massachusetts Ave. N.W., 20005; (202) 628-5451.
Fax, (202) 380-9118. Matthew Carter, PAC and Political
Representative. Toll free, (800) 266-0895.
Web, www.natca.org, Twitter, @NATCA, Facebook, www
.facebook.com/NATCAfamily and YouTube, www
.youtube.com/user/NATCANationalOffice

National Assn. of Home Builders, BUILD PAC, 1201
15th St. N.W., 20005-2800; (202) 266-8114. Kate Crowley,
Manager, (202) 266-8110.
Web, www.nahb.org/buildpac

**National Education Assn. Fund for Children and
Public Education,** 1201 16th St. N.W., #510, 20036-
3290; (202) 833-4000. Mary Kusler, Director. Press,
(202) 822-7823.
General email, neafund@nea.org

Web, www.neafund.org

**National Lumber and Building Material Dealers
Assn. PAC,** 2001 K St. N.W., 3rd Floor N, 20006; (202)
367-1169. Kevin McKenney, Director of Government
Affairs.
General email, MemberSupport@dealer.org

Web, www.dealer.org/?page=PoliticalAction and Twitter,
@NLBMDA

National Roofing Contractors Assn. PAC, 324 4th St. N.E.,
20002; (202) 546-7584. Fax, (202) 546-9289. Teri Dorn,
Director of Political Affairs. Toll-free, (800) 338-5765.
General email, info@nrca.net

Web, www.nrca.net/roofing/ROOFPAC and Twitter,
@NRCAnews

National Stone, Sand, and Gravel Assn., ROCK PAC, 66
Canal Center Plaza, #300, Alexandria, VA 22314; (703)
525-8788. Michael W. Johnson, President. Toll-free, (800)
342-1415.
Web, www.nssga.org/advocacy/rockpac and Facebook,
www.facebook.com/nssga

Professional Aviation Safety Specialists AFL-CIO PAC,
1200 G St. N.W., #750, 20005; (202) 293-7277. Fax, (202)
293-7727. Jena Denning, Legislative Affairs Director.
Web, https://passnational.org and Twitter, @passnational

United Mine Workers of America, Coal Miners PAC,
18354 Quantico Gateway Dr., #200, Triangle, VA 22172;
(703) 291-2400. Brian Swanson, Secretary-Treasurer.
General email, info@umwa.org

Web, www.umwa.org and Twitter, @mineworkers

United Mine Workers of America, Power PAC, 18354
Quantico Gateway Dr., #200, Triangle, VA 22172-1779;
(703) 291-2400. Brian Swanson, Secretary-Treasurer.
General email, info@umwa.org

Web, www.umwa.org/policy-politics/what-is-compac

▶ **NONCONNECTED**

314 Action Fund PAC, P.O. Box 14560, 20044; (202)
350-1325. Joshua Morrow, Executive Director;
Shaughnessy Naughton, President.
General email, info@314action.org

Web, https://314action.org, Twitter, @314action, Facebook,
www.facebook.com/314Action and Press, press@314action
.org

Supports candidates who advocate for innovation
in Science, Technology, Engineering, and Mathematics
(STEM) education.

America Votes, 1155 Connecticut Ave. N.W., #600, 20036;
(202) 962-7240. Fax, (202) 962-7241. Sara Schreiber,
Executive Director.
General email, info@americavotes.org

Web, www.americavotes.org, Twitter, @AmericaVotes,
Facebook, www.facebook.com/AmericaVotesOrg and Press,
press@americavotes.org

Seeks to mobilize Americans to register and vote
around critical issues.

Automotive Free International Trade (AFIT-PAC), 1625
Prince St., #225, Alexandria, VA 22314-2889; (703)
684-8880. Mary Hanagan, Executive Director.
General email, information@afitpac.com

Web, www.afitpac.com

Black America's PAC, 1325 G St. N.W., #500, 20005; (202)
552-7422. Fax, (202) 552-7421. Alvin Williams, President.
Web, www.bampac.org and Twitter, @BAM_PAC

Supports conservative candidates of all parties.

Club for Growth, 2001 L St. N.W., #600, 20036; (202) 955-
5500. Fax, (202) 955-9466. David McIntosh, President.
Toll-free, (855) 432-0899.
General email, press@clubforgrowth.org

Web, www.clubforgrowth.org, Twitter, @Club4Growth and
Facebook, www.facebook.com/ClubforGrowth

Promotes mainly Republican candidates with conservative economic policies and voting records. Interests
include limited government, low taxes, estate tax repeal,

social security reform, free trade, tax code reform, school choice, and deregulation.

EMILY's List, *1800 M St. N.W., #375N, 20036 (mailing address: P.O. Box 96612, Washington, DC 20077); (202) 326-1400. Fax, (202) 326-1415. Emily Cain, Executive Director. Toll-free, 800-68-EMILY.*
Web, https://emilyslist.org and Twitter, @emilyslist

Raises money and helps to support prochoice Democratic women candidates for political office.

Gay & Lesbian Victory Leadership Institute, *Victory Fund, 1225 Eye St. N.W., #525, 20005; (202) 842-8679. Fax, (202) 289-3863. Josh Roth, Victory Cabinet Manager.*
Web, www.victoryinstitute.org/about, www.victoryfund .org, Facebook, www.facebook.com/victoryfund and Twitter, @VictoryFund

Giffords PAC, *P.O. Box 51196, 20091; (571) 295-7807. Robin Lloyd, Managing Director.*
General email, info@giffords.org
Web, http://giffords.org and Twitter, @GiffordsCourage

Supports candidates seeking to reduce gun violence.

GOPAC, *1201 Wilson Blvd., #2110, Arlington, VA 22209; (703) 566-0376. Jessica Curtis, Executive Director.*
General email, contact@gopac.org
Web, www.gopac.org and Twitter, @GOPAC

Recruits and trains conservative Republican candidates for local and state office.

KPMG PAC, *1801 K St. N.W., #12000, 20006 (mailing address: P.O. Box 18254, Washington, DC 20036-9998); (202) 533-3000. Fax, (202) 533-8500. Stephen E. Allis, Principal for Government Affairs, (202) 533-3126.*
Web, www.kpmg.us, Twitter, @KPMG_US, Facebook, www.facebook.com/KPMGUS and YouTube, www .youtube.com/user/KPMGMediaChannel

Global network of LLP firms providing audit, tax, and advisory services to businesses.

LPAC, *2120 L St. N.W., #850, 20037; (202) 629-0298. Lisa Turner, Executive Director.*
General email, info@teamlpac.com
Web, www.teamlpac.com, Twitter, @TeamLPAC and Facebook, www.facebook.com/teamlpac

Supports political candidates who champion LGBTQ rights, women's equality, and social justice.

New Democrat Coalition PAC, *1410 LHOB, 20515; Brad Schneider, Action Fund Chair.*
Web, http://newdemactionfund.com, Twitter, @VoteNewDems and Facebook, www.facebook.com/ NewDemActionFund

Supports election and reelection of Democrats to the House of Representatives.

PricewaterhouseCoopers PAC, *600 13th St. N.W., #600, 20005; (202) 414-1000. Fax, (202) 414-1301. Roslyn (Roz) Brooks, Public Policy Leader.*
Web, http://pwc.com and Twitter, @PWC_LLP

Value in Electing Women PAC, *228 S. Washington St., #115, Alexandria, VA 22314; (703) 801-3465. Julie Conway, Executive Director.*
General email, julie@viewpac.org
Web, www.viewpac.org and Twitter, @VIEWPAC

Focuses on supporting female Republican congressional candidates.

The Washington PAC, *444 N. Capitol St. N.W., #203, 20001; (202) 347-6613. Fax, (202) 393-7006. Morris J. Amitay, Treasurer.*
General email, MJA@WashingtonPAC.com
Web, www.washingtonpac.com

Promotes pro-Israel policies.

Women Under Forty PAC, *P.O. Box 66594, 20035-6594; (626) 688-4834. Atalie Ebersole, Treasurer.*
General email, ADMIN@wufpac.org
Web, www.wufpac.org and Twitter, @wufpac

Supports young female congressional candidates.

▶TRANSPORTATION

NADA PAC (National Automobile Dealers Assn.), *8484 Westpark Dr., #500, Tysons Corner, VA 22102; (202) 627-6750. Jonathan Collegio, Senior Vice President of Public Affairs. Legislative Office, (202) 547-5500. Toll-free, (800) 557-6232.*
General email, nadapac@nada.org
Web, www.nada.org/NADAPAC, Twitter, @NADAUpdate and Facebook, www.facebook.com/NADAUpdate

Super Political Action Committees

Independent expenditure-only committees, commonly known as SuperPACs, are organizations registered with the Federal Election Commission that may raise unlimited funds from individuals, corporations, businesses, and others to advocate for or against specific candidates for public office. Direct contributions to candidates' campaigns are prohibited.

▶NONCONNECTED

America Votes Action Fund, *1155 Connecticut Ave. N.W., #600, 20036; (202) 962-7240. Susan Finkle Sourlis, Chief Financial Officer.*
General email, actionfund@americavotes.org
Web, https://americavotes.org/america-votes-action-fund, Twitter, @AmericaVotes and Facebook, www.facebook .com/AmericaVotesOrg

Works with over 400 state and national partner organizations to advance progressive policies, win elections, and protect every American's right to vote.

American Crossroads, *P.O. Box 34413, 20043; (202) 559-6428. Steven Law, President.*

General email, info@americancrossroads.org

Web, www.americancrossroads.org, Twitter, @AmericanXRoads and Facebook, www.facebook.com/AmericanCrossroads

Promotes Republican candidates who support strong defense, free enterprise, and limited government. Targets voters through television ads, mailings, and phone campaigns.

American Dental Assn. PAC, 1111 14th St. N.W., #1100, 20005; (202) 898-2424. Sarah Milligan, Director of Political Affairs.
General email, adpac@ada.org

Web, www.ada.org/advocacy/advocacy-about-adpac

Nonpartisan organization that promotes congressional candidates who advocate for dentists, oral health, and oral health's connection to overall health. Provides educational resources to dentists interested in seeking public office at local, state, or national levels.

Congressional Leadership Fund, 1747 Pennsylvania Ave. N.W., 5th Floor, 20006; (202) 908-2299.
Daniel (Dan) Conston, President, (202) 559-6420.
General email, contact@congressionalleadershipfund.org

Web, www.congressionalleadershipfund.org, Twitter, @CLFSuperPAC and Facebook, www.facebook.com/CongressionalLeadershipFund

Supports a Republican majority in the House of Representatives.

FreedomWorks for America, 111 K St. N.E., 6th Floor, 20002; (202) 783-3870. Noah Wall, Executive Vice President.
Twitter, @FWForAmerica and Web, https://freedomworksforamerica.org

Promotes conservative grassroots candidates who advocate lower taxes and smaller government.

House Majority PAC, 700 13th St. N.W., #800, 20005; (202) 849-6052. Abby Curran Horrell, Executive Director.
General email, info@thehousemajoritypac.com

Web, www.thehousemajoritypac.com, Twitter, @HouseMaj PAC and Facebook, www.facebook.com/HouseMajorityPAC

Supports Democratic candidates for the House of Representatives.

League of Conservation Voters Action Fund, 740 15th St. N.W., 7th Floor, 20005; (202) 785-8683. Fax, (202) 835-0491. Sara Chieffo, Vice President for Government Affairs.
General email, feedback@lcv.org

Web, www.lcv.org, Twitter, @LCVoters and Facebook, www.facebook.com/LCVoters

Supports candidates who implement environmental laws and policies.

National Realtors Assn. Political Action Committee, 500 New Jersey Ave. N.W., 20001-2020; (202) 383-1000. Shannon McGahn, Chief Advocacy Officer, (202) 383-1045.
Toll-free, (800) 874-6500.
Web, www.nar.realtor/topics/rpac

Nonpartisan organization that promotes federal, state, and local candidates who advocate for private property rights and free enterprise. (Headquarters in Chicago, IL.)

Priorities USA Action, 1030 15th St. N.W., 20005; Alexis Antonino, Fundraising Manager.
General email, info@priorities.org

Web, https://priorities.org, Twitter, @prioritiesUSA, Facebook, www.facebook.com/PrioritiesUSA and Press, press@priorities.org

Votercentric progressive advocacy organization and service center for the grassroots progressive movement.

Republican Main Street Partnership PAC, 410 1st St. S.E., #200, 20003 (mailing address: 1300 Pennsylvania Ave. N.W., Box 190, Washington, DC 20004); (202) 812-3806. Sarah Chamberlain, President.
Web, https://republicanmainstreet.org, Twitter, @rmsppac and Facebook, www.facebook.com/mainstreetpac

Represents and supports Republican candidates who work across party lines.

Women Speak Out PAC, 2800 Shirlington Rd., #1200, Arlington, VA 22206; (202) 223-8073. Emily Buchanan, Executive Vice President.
Web, www.sba-list.org/women-speak-out-pac, Twitter, @SBAList and Facebook, www.facebook.com/SusanBAnthonyList

Supports congressional candidates opposed to abortion.

Women Vote!—EMILY's List, P.O. Box 96612, 20077; (202) 326-1400. Laphonza Butler, President. Toll-free, (800) 683-6459.
General email, press@emilyslist.org

Web, http://emilyslist.org/pages/entry/women-vote, Twitter, @emilyslist, Facebook, www.facebook.com/emilyslist and YouTube, www.youtube.com/user/emilyslist

Seeks to influence women to vote for prochoice Democratic women candidates and other Democratic candidates. Targets candidates opposed to these positions.

Working America, 815 16th St. N.W., 20006; (202) 637-5137. Matt Morrison, Executive Director.
General email, info@workingamerica.org

Web, www.workingamerica.org, Twitter, @WorkingAmerica and Facebook, www.facebook.com/WorkingAmerica

Works to elect progressive candidates and pass legislation to improve the lives of working families.

Working for Us PAC, 888 16th St. N.W., #650, 20006; (202) 499-7420. Steve Rosenthal, President.
General email, info@workingforuspac.org

Web, www.workingforuspac.org

Promotes candidates focused on job creation, health care reform, and expanding public services. Campaigns against candidates opposed to these principles. (Affiliated with The Organizing Group.)

Political Interest Groups

▶**NONGOVERNMENTAL**

American Conservative Union (ACU), *1199 N. Fairfax St., #500, Alexandria, VA 22314; (202) 347-9388. Fax, (202) 347-9389. Matt Schlapp, Chairman.*
General email, contact@conservative.org
Web, http://conservative.org, Twitter, @ACUConservative and Facebook, www.facebook.com/ACUConservative

Legislative interest organization that focuses on defense, foreign policy, economics, the national budget, taxes, and legal and social issues. Monitors legislation and regulations.

American Family Voices, *1250 Eye St. N.W., #330, 20005; (202) 393-4352. Michael Lux, President; Lauren Windsor, Executive Director.*
General email, admin@americanfamilyvoices.org
Web, http://americanfamilyvoices.org, Twitter, @AFVhq and Facebook, www.facebook.com/AmericanFamilyVoices

Acts as advocate on behalf of middle-class and low-income families dealing with economic, health care, and consumer issues. Fosters organizations, including civil rights, environmental, women's rights, consumer advocacy and health care with initiatives and research.

American Opportunity, *901 N. Washington St., #206, Alexandria, VA 22314 (mailing address: P.O. Box 320037, Alexandria, VA 22320); (703) 837-0030.*
Amb. Jim Gilmore, President.
General email, contact@americanopportunity.org
Web, www.americanopportunity.org, Twitter, @ameriopp and Facebook, www.facebook.com/americanopportunity.org

Conservative political think tank that promotes traditional values. Primary interests are economic and foreign policy. (Formerly the Free Congress Research and Education Foundation [FCF].)

Americans for Democratic Action, *1629 K St. N.W., #300, 20006; (202) 600-7762. Fax, (202) 204-8637. Don Kusler, National Director.*
General email, info@adaction.org
Web, www.adaction.org, Twitter, @ADAction and Facebook, www.facebook.com/adactionfan

Legislative interest organization that seeks to strengthen civil, constitutional, women's, family, workers', and human rights, and promotes grassroots activism. Interests include education, health care, immigration, peace, tax reform, and voter access.

Americans for Prosperity Foundation, *1310 N. Courthouse Rd., #700, Arlington, VA 22201; (703) 224-3200. Fax, (703) 224-3201. Emily Seidel, Chief Executive Officer. Press, (703) 224-3177.*
Web, www.americansforprosperity.org and Twitter, @AFPhq

Grassroots organization that seeks to educate citizens about economic policy and encourage their participation in the public policy process. Supports limited government and free markets on the local, state, and federal levels.

Specific interests include Social Security, trade, and taxes. Monitors legislation and regulations.

Cato Institute, *1000 Massachusetts Ave. N.W., 20001-5403; (202) 842-0200. Peter Goettler, President. Press, (202) 842-5200.*
General email, pr@cato.org
Web, www.cato.org, Twitter, @CatoInstitute and Facebook, www.facebook.com/CatoInstitute

Public policy research organization that advocates limited government and individual liberty. Interests include privatization and deregulation, low and simple taxes, and reduced government spending. Encourages voluntary solutions to social and economic problems.

Center for American Progress, *1333 H St. N.W., 10th Floor, 20005; (202) 682-1611. Fax, (202) 682-1867. Patrick Gaspard, President.*
General email, progress@americanprogress.org
Web, www.americanprogress.org, Twitter, @amprog, Facebook, www.facebook.com/americanprogress and Twitter, President, @patrickgaspard

Nonpartisan research and educational institute that strives to ensure opportunity for all Americans. Advocates policies to create sustained economic growth and new opportunities. Supports fiscal discipline, shared prosperity, and investments in people through education, health care, and workforce training.

Center for Public Justice, *312 Massachusetts Ave. N.E., 20002 (mailing address: P.O. Box 48368, Washington, DC 20002-0368); (202) 695-2667. Stephanie Summers, Chief Executive Officer.*
General email, inquiries@cpjustice.org
Web, www.cpjustice.org, Twitter, @cpjustice and YouTube, www.youtube.com/user/CPJusticeDC

Christian think tank advocating biblical-based solutions to policymakers. Interests include education reform, foreign affairs, welfare policy, and religious freedom.

Christian Coalition of America, *P.O. Box 37030, 20013-7030; (202) 479-6900. Roberta Combs, President.*
General email, info@cc.org
Web, http://cc.org, Twitter, @ccoalition and Facebook, www.facebook.com/ChristianCoalition

Membership: individuals who support traditional, conservative Christian values. Represents members' views to all levels of government and to the media.

Christian Science Committee on Publication, *Federal Office, 603 2nd St. N.E., 20002; (202) 296-2190. Tessa E. B. Frost, Director of Federal Government Affairs.*
General email, federal@christianscience.com
Web, www.christianscience.com/member-resources/committee-on-publication and Facebook, www.facebook.com/worldwidechristianscience

Works with Congress and regulatory agencies to ensure that the interests of Christian Science are not adversely affected by law or regulations.

Common Cause, *805 15th St. N.W., #800, 20005; (202) 833-1200. Karen Hobert Flynn, President. Press, (202) 736-5712.*
General email, CauseNet@commoncause.org
Web, www.commoncause.org, Twitter, @CommonCause and Facebook, www.facebook.com/CommonCause

Nonpartisan citizens' lobby that works for reform in federal and state government and politics. Advocates national and state limits on political spending, small donor-based public financing of election campaigns, high ethical standards and tough ethics enforcement for public officials, strong voting rights laws and modern voting equipment, and free exchange of ideas online.

Concerned Women for America, *1000 N. Payne St., Alexandria, VA 22314 (mailing address: P.O. Box 34300, Washington, DC 20043); (202) 488-7000.*
Penny Young Nance, Chief Executive Officer.
General email, comms@cwfa.org
Web, https://concernedwomen.org, Twitter, @CWforA, Facebook, www.facebook.com/ ConcernedWomenforAmerica and YouTube, www .youtube.com/user/concernedwomen

Public policy organization that seeks to protect the rights of the family and preserve Judeo-Christian values. Monitors legislation affecting family and religious issues.

The Conservative Caucus (TCC), *332 W. Lee Hwy., #221, Warrenton, VA 20816 (mailing address: P.O. Box 1890, Merrifield, VA 22116); (540) 219-4536. Peter J. Thomas, Chair.*
General email, info@conservativeusa.org
Web, www.conservativeusa.org, Twitter, @Conserv.Caucus and Facebook, www.facebook.com/ConservativeCaucus

Legislative interest organization that promotes grass-roots activity on issues such as national defense and economic and tax policy. The Conservative Caucus Research, Analysis, and Education Foundation studies public issues including Central American affairs, defense policy, and federal funding of political advocacy groups.

Family Research Council, *801 G St. N.W., 20001-3729; Tony Perkins, President. Toll-free, (800) 225-4008.*
Web, www.frc.org, Twitter, @FRCdc and Facebook, www .facebook.com/familyresearchcouncil

Legislative interest organization that analyzes issues affecting the family, faith and freedom and seeks to ensure that the interests of the family are considered in the for-mulation of public policy.

Feminist Majority, *1600 Wilson Blvd., #801, Arlington, VA 22209-2505; (703) 522-2214. Fax, (703) 522-2219. Eleanor Smeal, President.*
General email, feedback@feminist.org
Web, www.feministmajority.org, Twitter, @femmajority, Facebook, www.facebook.com/FeministMajority and Press, erin@feministmajority.org

Legislative interest group that seeks to increase the number of Women/ Feminists running for public office across the state, natin and the world. Promotes non-discrimination on the basis of sex, race, sexual orientation, socio-economic status, religion, ethnicity, age, marital status, nation of origin, size or disability.

FreedomWorks, *111 K St. N.E., #600, 20002; (202) 783-3870. Adam Brandon, President. Toll-free, (888) 564-6273.*
Web, www.freedomworks.org, Twitter, @FreedomWorks and Facebook, www.facebook.com/FreedomWorks

Recruits, educates, trains, and mobilizes volunteer acti-vists to promote lower taxes, less government, and greater economic freedom. Maintains scorecards on members of the Senate and House based on adherence to Freedom-Works positions.

Friends Committee on National Legislation (FCNL), *245 2nd St. N.E., 20002-5795; (202) 547-6000. Fax, (202) 547-6019. Bridget Moix, General Secretary. Toll-free, (800) 630-1330.*
General email, fcnl@fcnl.org
Web, www.fcnl.org, Twitter, @FCNL and Facebook, www .facebook.com/quakerlobby

Advocates economic justice, world disarmament, international cooperation, and religious rights. Acts as advocate on behalf of Native Americans in such areas as treaty rights, self-determination, and U.S. trust responsi-bilities. Conducts research and educational activities through the FCNL Education Fund. Opposes the death penalty. Monitors national legislation and policy. (Affili-ated with the Religious Society of Friends [Quakers].)

Frontiers of Freedom, *4094 Majestic Blvd., #380, Fairfax, VA 22033; (703) 246-0110. Fax, (703) 246-0129. George C. Landrith, President.*
General email, info@ff.org
Web, www.ff.org, Twitter, @FoF_Liberty and Facebook, www.facebook.com/FrontiersofFreedom

Seeks to increase personal freedom through a reduction in the size of government. Interests include property rights, regulatory and tax reform, global warming, national missile defense, Internet regulation, school vouchers, and Second Amendment rights. Monitors legislation and regulations.

The Heritage Foundation, *214 Massachusetts Ave. N.E., 20002-4999; (202) 546-4400. Kevin Roberts, President. Press, (202) 675-1761.*
General email, info@heritage.org
Web, www.heritage.org, Twitter, @heritage and Facebook, www.facebook.com/heritagefoundation

Conservative public policy research organization that conducts research and analysis and sponsors lectures, debates, and policy forums advocating individual free-dom, limited government, the free market system, and a strong national defense.

Institute on Religion and Democracy, *1023 15th St. N.W., #200, 20005-2601; (202) 682-4131. Mark Tooley, President.*
General email, info@theird.org
Web, https://theird.org, Twitter, @theIRD and Facebook, www.facebook.com/TheIRD

Interdenominational bipartisan organization that supports democratic and constitutional forms of government consistent with the values of Christianity. Serves as a resource center to promote Christian perspectives on U.S. national and foreign policy questions. Interests include international conflicts, religious liberties, and the promotion of democratic forms of government in the United States and worldwide.

Log Cabin Republicans, *1220 L St. N.W., #100-407, 20005; (202) 760-3250. Charles T. Moran, President.*
General email, info@logcabin.org

Web, www.logcabin.org, Facebook, www.facebook.com/ logcabingop and Twitter, @LogCabinGOP

Membership: lesbian, gay, bisexual, transgender, and allied Republicans. Educates conservative politicians and voters on LGBT issues; disseminates information; conducts seminars for members. Promotes conservative values among members of the gay community. Raises campaign funds. Monitors legislation and regulations.

National Center for Public Policy Research, *Project 21, 20 F St. N.W., #700, 20001; (202) 507-6398, ext. 11. Stacy Washington, Co-Chair; Horace Cooper, Co-Chair.*
General email, info@nationalcenter.org

Web, www.nationalcenter.org/project-21, Twitter, @Project 21News and Facebook, www.facebook.com/Project21News

Promotes public policies to counter the disenfranchisement of Black Americans. Interests include affirmative action and reparations.

National Organization for Marriage, *17 D St. S.E., #1, 20003; (888) 894-3604. Brian S. Brown, President.*
General email, contact@nationformarriage.org

Web, www.nationformarriage.org, Twitter, @NOMupdate and Facebook, www.facebook.com/NationForMarriage

Supports marriage-related initiatives at state and local levels, with an emphais on the Northeast and West Coast. Opposes same-sex marriage. Monitors legislation.

National Organization for Women (NOW), *1100 H St. N.W., #300, 20005; (202) 628-8669. Christian F. Nunes, President.*
General email, info@now.org

Web, https://now.org and Twitter, @NationalNOW

Membership: women and men interested in feminist civil rights. Acts through demonstrations, court cases, and legislative efforts to improve the status of all women. Interests include increasing the number of women in elected and appointed office, improving women's economic status and health coverage, ending violence against women, preserving abortion rights, and abolishing discrimination based on gender, race, age, and sexual orientation.

National Taxpayers Union, *Communications, 122 C St. N.W., #650, 20001; (703) 683-5700. Kevin Glass, Vice President of Communications.*
General email, ntu@ntu.org

Web, www.ntu.org, Twitter, @NTU and Facebook, www .facebook.com/NationalTaxpayersUnion

Citizens' interest group that promotes tax and spending reduction at all levels of government. Supports constitutional amendments to balance the federal budget and limit taxes.

NDN (New Democrat Network), *800 Maine Ave. S.W., #200, 20024; (202) 544-9200. Simon Rosenberg, President.*
General email, info@ndn.org

Web, www.ndn.org, Twitter, @NDN_NPI and President's Blog, www.ndn.org/blogs/simon-rosenberg

Studies progressive politics as it relates to the rise in conservatism, changing voter trends, and new media strategies for campaigns.

NETWORK (National Lobby For Catholic Social Justice), *820 1st St. N.E., #350, 20002; (202) 347-9797. Mary Novak, Executive Director.*
General email, info@networklobby.org

Web, www.networklobby.org, Twitter, @NETWORKLobby, Facebook, www.facebook.com/NetworkLobby and YouTube, www.youtube.com/user/NetworkLobbies

Catholic social justice lobby that coordinates political activity and promotes economic and social justice. Monitors legislation and regulations.

New America Foundation, *740 15th St. N.W., #900, 20005; (202) 986-2700. Anne-Marie Slaughter, Chief Executive Officer.*
Web, www.newamerica.org, Twitter, @NewAmerica and Facebook, www.facebook.com/NewAmerica

Public policy institute that seeks to bring innovative policy ideas to the fore and nurture the next generation of public policy intellectuals. Sponsors research, writing, conferences, and events. Funds studies of government programs. Seeks to stimulate more informed reporting and analyses of government activities.

No Labels, *1130 Connecticut Ave. N.W., #325, 20036; (202) 588-1990. Nancy Jacobson, Chief Executive Officer.*
General email, info@nolabels.org

Web, www.nolabels.org, Twitter, @NoLabelsOrg, Facebook, www.facebook.com/NoLabels and YouTube, www.youtube .com/user/nolabelsorg

Promotes a bipartisan approach to improving issues such as unemployment, social security and Medicare, the federal budget, and securing energy.

People for the American Way (PFAW), *1101 15th St. N.W., #600, 20005-5002; (202) 467-4999. Fax, (202) 293-2672. Ben Jealous, President. Toll-free, (800) 326-7329.*
General email, pfaw@pfaw.org

Web, www.pfaw.org, Twitter, @peoplefor, Facebook, www .facebook.com/peoplefor and Press, media@pfaw.org

Nonprofit organization that promotes public policies that reflect the values of freedom, fairness, and equal opportunity; acts as advocate for constitutional protections and civil rights, and for strong democratic institutions, including a federal judiciary that upholds individual rights. Conducts leadership development programs for college students, Black religious leaders, and young elected officials.

Public Affairs Council, 2121 K St. N.W., #900, 20037; (202) 787-5950. Fax, (202) 787-5942. Douglas G. Pinkham, President, (202) 787-5964.
General email, pac@pac.org
Web, https://pac.org, Twitter, @PACouncil and Facebook, www.facebook.com/PublicAffairsCouncil

Membership: public affairs professionals. Informs and counsels members on public affairs programs. Sponsors conferences on election issues, government relations, and political trends. Sponsors the Foundation for Public Affairs.

Public Citizen, *Congress Watch,* 215 Pennsylvania Ave. S.E., 20003; (202) 546-4996. Lisa Gilbert, Vice President of Legislative Affairs.
General email, action@citizen.org
Web, www.citizen.org/topic/making-government-work

Citizens' interest group engaged in public education, research, media outreach, and citizen activism. Interests include campaign finance reform, consumer protection, financial services, public health and safety, government reform, trade, and the environment.

Rainbow PUSH Coalition, *Public Policy Institute, Government Relations and Telecommunications Project,* 727 15th St. N.W., #1200, 20005; (301) 256-8587. Fax, (202) 393-1495. Stephen L. Smith Sr., President. Press, (773) 373-3366.
General email, info@rainbowpush.org
Web, www.rainbowpush.org, Twitter, @RPCoalition and Facebook, www.facebook.com/Rainbow.PUSH

Independent civil rights organization concerned with foreign policy and public policy toward political, economic, and social justice for women, workers, and minorities. Interests include poverty and hunger, peace and justice, gun violence, corporate diversity, and voter registration. (Headquarters in Chicago, Ill.)

Taxpayers for Common Sense, 651 Pennsylvania Ave. S.E., 20003; (202) 546-8500. Steve Ellis, President. Press, (202) 546-8500, ext. 106.
General email, info@taxpayer.net
Web, www.taxpayer.net

Nonpartisan organization that works with Congress, the media, and grassroots organizations to reduce government waste and increase accountability for federal expenditures. Disseminates research results to the public via media and Web outreach.

Third Way, 1025 Connecticut Ave. N.W., #400, 20036; (202) 384-1700. Fax, (202) 775-0430. Jonathan Cowan, President; Brenda Bethea, Chief Operating Officer.
General email, contact@thirdway.org
Web, www.thirdway.org, Twitter, @ThirdWayTweet, Facebook, www.facebook.com/ThirdWayThinkTank and YouTube, www.youtube.com/user/ThirdWayVideo

Think tank that works with moderate and progressive legislators to develop modern solutions to economic, cultural, and national security issues. Conducts studies and polls; develops policy papers and strategy documents.

U.S. Chamber of Commerce, *Political Affairs and Federation Relations,* 1615 H St. N.W., 20062-2000; (202) 463-5560. Sara Armstrong, Vice President.
General email, chambers@uschamber.com
Web, www.uschamber.com/political-affairs-and-federation-relations

Federation that works to enact pro-business legislation; tracks election law legislation; coordinates the chamber's candidate endorsement program and its grassroots lobbying activities.

Urban Institute, 500 L'Enfant Plaza S.W., 20024; (202) 833-7200. Sarah Rosen Wartell, President. Public Affairs, (202) 261-5709.
General email, media@urban.org; externalaffairs@urban.org
Web, www.urban.org, Twitter, @urbaninstitute and Facebook, www.facebook.com/urbaninstitute

Nonpartisan research and education organization. Investigates U.S. social and economic problems; encourages discussion on solving society's problems, improving and implementing government decisions, and increasing citizens' awareness of public choices.

Veterans of Foreign Wars of the United States, *National Legislative Service,* 200 Maryland Ave. N.E., 20002-5724; (202) 543-2239. Fax, (202) 543-2746. Carlos Fuentes, Director.
Web, www.vfw.org/VFW-in-DC/National-Legislative-Service

Represents members before Congress and participates in congressional hearings, with a focus on health and quality of life issues. Manages the VFW Action Corps grassroots organization. Monitors legislation and regulations.

Washington Government Relations Group, 1325 G St. N.W., #500, 20005; (202) 449-7651. Fax, (202) 449-7701. Danielle McBeth, President.
General email, info@wgrginc.org
Web, www.wgrginc.org

Works to enrich the careers and leadership abilities of African American government relations professionals working in business, financial institutions, law firms, trade associations, and nonprofit organizations. Increases dialogue between members and senior-level policymakers to produce public policy solutions.

Women Legislators' Lobby (WiLL), *Policy and Programs,* 810 7th St. N.E., 20002; (202) 459-4769. Nancy Parrish, Executive Director; Samantha Blake, Program Manager.
General email, peace@wand.org
Web, www.wand.org/will, Twitter, @WomensAction and Facebook, www.facebook.com/WomensAction

Bipartisan group of women state legislators. Sponsors conferences, training workshops, issue briefings, and seminars; provides information and action alerts on ways federal policies affect states. Interests include federal budget priorities, national security, and arms control. Monitors related legislation and regulations. (Affiliated with

Women's Action for New Directions. National office in Cambridge, Mass.)

Women's Action for New Directions (WAND),
Washington Office, 810 7th St. N.E., 20002; (202) 459-4769. Fax, (202) 544-7612. Nancy Parrish, Executive Director.
General email, peace@wand.org

Web, www.wand.org and Twitter, @WomensAction

Seeks to empower women to act politically to reduce violence and militarism and redirect excessive military resources toward unmet human and environmental needs. Monitors legislation on federal budget priorities. (Headquarters in Arlington, Mass.)

Women's Congressional Policy Institute, *409 12th St. S.W., #702, 20024; (202) 554-2323.*
Cynthia A. (Cindy) Hall, President.
General email, webmaster@WCPInst.org

Web, www.wcpinst.org and Twitter, @WCPInst

Nonpartisan organization that provides legislative analysis and information services on congressional actions affecting women and their families. Works with congressional women's caucus leaders at federal, state, and local levels, as well as other groups, to provide information pertaining to women's issues. Sponsors Congressional Fellowships on Women and Public Policy for graduate students who are placed in congressional offices from January through August to work on policy issues affecting women.

POLITICAL PARTY ORGANIZATIONS

Democratic

▶ **NONGOVERNMENTAL**

Democratic Congressional Campaign Committee, *430 S. Capitol St. S.E., 20003-4024; (202) 863-1500.*
Rep. Sean Patrick Maloney, Chair.
General email, dccc@dccc.org

Web, https://dccc.org, Twitter, @dccc.org and Facebook, www.facebook.com/electdemocrats

Provides Democratic House candidates with financial and other campaign services.

Democratic Governors Assn., *1225 Eye St. N.W., #1100, 20005; (202) 772-5600. Fax, (202) 772-5602.*
Gov. Ron Cooper, Chair; Noam Lee, Executive Director.
General email, dga@dga.net

Web, https://democraticgovernors.org, Twitter, @DemGovs and Press, press@dga.net

Serves as a liaison between governors' offices and Democratic Party organizations; assists Democratic gubernatorial candidates.

Democratic National Committee (DNC), *430 S. Capitol St. S.E., 20003; (202) 863-8000. Jaime Harrison, Chair.*

General email, info@democrats.org

Web, https://democrats.org, Twitter, @TheDemocrats and Facebook, www.facebook.com/groups/DemocraticNational Community

Formulates and promotes Democratic Party policies and positions; assists Democratic candidates for state and national office; organizes national political activities; works with state and local officials and organizations.

Democratic National Committee (DNC), *Assn. of State Democratic Chairs (ASDC), 430 S. Capitol St. S.E., 20003; (202) 863-8000. Ken Martin, President. Press, (202) 863-8148.*
General email, info@democrats.org

Web, https://democrats.org/who-we-are/state-parties

Acts as a liaison between state parties and the DNC; works to strengthen state parties for national, state, and local elections; conducts fund-raising activities for state parties.

Democratic National Committee (DNC),
Communications, 430 S. Capitol St. S.E., 20003; (202) 863-8148. Adrienne Watson, Director.
General email, DNCPress@dnc.org

Web, https://democrats.org and Twitter, @TheDemocrats

Assists federal, state, and local Democratic candidates and officials in delivering a coordinated message on current issues; works to improve and expand relations with the press and to increase the visibility of Democratic officials and the Democratic Party.

Democratic National Committee (DNC), *Finance, 430 S. Capitol St. S.E., 20003; (202) 863-8000.*
Christopher Korge, Chair.
General email, info@democrats.org

Web, https://democrats.org

Responsible for developing the Democratic Party's financial base. Coordinates fund-raising efforts for and gives financial support to Democratic candidates in national, state, and local campaigns.

Democratic National Committee (DNC), *Research, 430 S. Capitol St. S.E., 20003; (202) 863-8000. Vacant, Director. Press, (202) 863-8148.*
General email, info@democrats.org

Web, https://democrats.org

Provides Democratic elected officials, candidates, state party organizations, and the general public with information on Democratic Party policy and programs.

Democratic Senatorial Campaign Committee, *120 Maryland Ave. N.E., 20002-5610; (202) 224-2447. Fax, (202) 969-0354. Sen. Gary Peters, Chair; Christie Roberts, Executive Director.*
General email, info@dscc.org

Web, www.dscc.org, Twitter, @dscc, Facebook, www.facebook.com/dscc and YouTube, www.youtube.com/user/dscclive

Provides Democratic senatorial candidates with financial, research, and consulting services.

Woman's National Democratic Club, *Committee on Public Policy,* 1526 New Hampshire Ave. N.W., 20036; (202) 232-7363. Karen Pataky, Director for Public Policy.
General email, info@democraticwoman.org
Web, www.democraticwoman.org and Twitter, @WNDC_1922

Studies issues and presents views to congressional committees, the Democratic Party Platform Committee, Democratic leadership groups, elected officials, and other interested groups.

Republican

▶**NONGOVERNMENTAL**

College Republican National Committee, 1750 Pennsylvania Ave. N.W., #27920, 20038; (202) 608-1411. Fax, (202) 608-1429. Courtney Hope Britt, National Chair; Ben Rajadurai, Executive Director. Toll-free, (888) 765-3564.
General email, team@crnc.org
Web, www.crnc.org, Twitter, @CRNC and Facebook, www.facebook.com/collegerepublicans

Membership: Republican college students. Promotes grassroots support for the Republican Party and provides campaign assistance.

National Federation of Republican Women, 124 N. Alfred St., Alexandria, VA 22314; (703) 548-9688. Eileen Sobjack, President.
General email, mail@nfrw.org
Web, www.nfrw.org, Twitter, @NFRW, Facebook, www.facebook.com/Nationalfederationofrepublicanwomen and YouTube, www.youtube.com/user/NFRW1

Organizes volunteers for support of Republican candidates for national, state, and local offices; encourages candidacy of Republican women; sponsors campaign management schools. Recruits Republican women candidates for office.

National Republican Congressional Committee, 320 1st St. S.E., 20003-1838; (202) 479-7000. Fax, (202) 863-0693. Rep. Tom Emmer, Chair; John Billings, Executive Director. Press, (202) 479-7070. Toll-free, (888) 606-1023.
General email, website@nrcc.org
Web, www.nrcc.org

Provides Republican House candidates with campaign assistance, including financial, public relations, media, and direct mail services.

National Republican Senatorial Committee (NRSC), 425 2nd St. N.E., 20002-4914; (202) 675-6000. Sen. Rick Scott, Chair; Jackie Schutz Zeckman, Executive Director.
General email, info@nrsc.org
Web, www.nrsc.org

Provides Republican senatorial candidates with financial and public relations services.

Republican Governors Assn., 1747 Pennsylvania Ave. N.W., #250, 20006; (202) 662-4140. Gov. Doug Ducey, Chair; Dave Rexrode, Executive Director.
General email, info@rga.org
Web, www.rga.org, Twitter, @GOPGovs and Facebook, www.facebook.com/GOPgovs

Serves as a liaison between governors' offices and Republican Party organizations; assists Republican candidates for governor.

Republican Main Street Partnership, 410 1st St. S.E., #200, 20003; (202) 812-3806. Sarah Chamberlain, President.
Web, https://republicanmainstreet.org, Twitter, @MainStreetGOP and Facebook, www.facebook.com/MainStreetGOP

Membership: centrist Republican Party members of Congress. Develops and promotes moderate Republican policies.

Republican National Committee (RNC), 310 1st St. S.E., 20003; (202) 863-8500. Fax, (202) 863-8820. Ronna McDaniel, Chair; Thomas Hicks Jr., Co-Chair.
General email, ecampaign@gop.com
Web, https://gop.com, Twitter, @GOP and Facebook, www.facebook.com/GOP

Develops and promotes Republican Party policies and positions; assists Republican candidates for state and national office; sponsors workshops to recruit Republican candidates and provide instruction in campaign techniques; organizes national political activities; works with state and local officials and organizations.

Republican National Committee (RNC), *Communications,* 310 1st St. S.E., 20003; (202) 863-8500. Fax, (202) 863-8820. Michael Ahrens, Director.
General email, RNCpress@gop.com
Web, https://gop.com/news

Assists federal, state, and local Republican candidates and officials in delivering a coordinated message on current issues; works to improve and expand relations with the press and to increase the visibility of Republican officials and the Republican message.

Republican National Committee (RNC), *Counsel,* 310 1st St. S.E., 20003; (202) 863-8500. Fax, (202) 863-8820. Kyle Hupfer, General Counsel.
General email, counsel@gop.com
Web, www.gop.com

Responsible for legal affairs of the RNC, including equal time and fairness cases before the Federal Communications Commission. Advises the RNC and state parties on redistricting and campaign finance law compliance.

Republican National Committee (RNC), *Finance,* 310 1st St. S.E., 20003; (202) 863-8500. Fax, (202) 863-8820. Ron Kaufman, Treasurer.
General email, finance@gop.com
Web, https://gop.com

Responsible for developing the Republican Party's financial base. Coordinates fund-raising efforts for and gives financial support to Republican candidates in national, state, and local campaigns.

Ripon Society, *1155 15th St. N.W., #550, 20005; (202) 216-1008. James K. (Jim) Conzelman, Chief Executive Officer. General email, info@riponsociety.org*

Web, https://riponsociety.org and Twitter, @RiponSociety

Membership: moderate Republicans. Works for the adoption of moderate policies within the Republican party.

Other Political Parties

▶**NONGOVERNMENTAL**

Green Party of the United States, *P.O. Box 75075, 20013; (202) 319-7191. Michael O'Neil, Communications Manager, (202) 804-2758.*

General email, office@gp.org

Web, www.gp.org, Twitter, @GreenPartyUS and Facebook, www.facebook.com/GreenPartyUS

Committed to environmentalism, nonviolence, social justice, and grassroots organizing.

Libertarian Party, *1444 Duke St., Alexandria, VA 22314-3403; (202) 333-0008. Tyler Harris, Executive Director. Press, (202) 333-0008, ext. 222. Toll-free, (800) 353-2887. General email, info@lp.org*

Web, www.lp.org, Twitter, @LPNational and Facebook, www.facebook.com/libertarians

Nationally organized political party. Seeks to bring libertarian ideas into the national political debate. Believes in the primacy of the individual over government; supports property rights, free trade, and eventual elimination of taxes.

117th Congress

Delegations to the 117th Congress

Following are the senators and representatives of state delegations for the 117th Congress. This information is current as of May 12, 2022. Senators are presented first and listed according to seniority. Representatives follow, listed by district. Freshman members appear in italics and "AL" indicates at-large members. # indicates new senators who served in the House of Representatives in the 116th Congress. $ indicates any members of the House of Representatives who were elected on November 3, 2020, both to finish the 116th Congress and for a full term in the 117th Congress; they are italicized with the true freshman members.

ALABAMA

Richard C. Shelby (R)
Tommy Tuberville (R)
  1. *Jerry L. Carl (R)*
  2. *Barry Moore (R)*
  3. Mike Rogers (R)
  4. Robert B. Aderholt (R)
  5. Mo Brooks (R)
  6. Gary J. Palmer (R)
  7. Terri A. Sewell (D)

ALASKA

Lisa Murkowski (R)
Dan Sullivan (R)
Vacant

AMERICAN SAMOA (NON-VOTING DELEGATE)

AL Aumua Amata Coleman
  Radewagen (R)

ARIZONA

Mark Kelly (D)
Kyrsten Sinema (D)
  1. Tom O'Halleran (D)
  2. Ann Kirkpatrick (D)
  3. Raúl Grijalva (D)
  4. Paul A. Gosar (R)
  5. Andy Biggs (R)
  6. David Schweikert (R)
  7. Rubén Gallego (D)
  8. Debbie Lesko (R)
  9. Greg Stanton (D)

ARKANSAS

John Boozman (R)
Tom Cotton (R)
  1. Eric A. (Rick) Crawford (R)
  2. J. French Hill (R)
  3. Steve Womack (R)
  4. Bruce Westerman (R)

CALIFORNIA

Dianne Feinstein (D)
Alex Padilla (D)
  1. Doug LaMalfa (R)
  2. Jared Huffman (D)
  3. John Garamendi (D)
  4. Tom McClintock (R)
  5. Mike Thompson (D)
  6. Doris O. Matsui (D)
  7. Ami Bera (D)
  8. *Jay Obernolte (R)*
  9. Jerry McNerney (D)
  10. Josh Harder (R)
  11. Mark DeSaulnier (D)
  12. Nancy Pelosi (D)
  13. Barbara Lee (D)
  14. Jackie Speier (D)
  15. Eric Swalwell (D)
  16. Jim Costa (D)
  17. Ro Khanna (D)
  18. Anna G. Eshoo (D)
  19. Zoe Lofgren (D)
  20. Jimmy Panetta (D)
  21. *David G. Valadao (R)*
  22. Vacant
  23. Kevin McCarthy (R)
  24. Salud O. Carbajal (D)
  25. Mike Garcia (R)
  26. Julia Brownley (D)
  27. Judy Chu (D)
  28. Adam B. Schiff (D)
  29. Tony Cárdenas (D)
  30. Brad Sherman (D)
  31. Pete Aguilar (D)
  32. Grace F. Napolitano (D)
  33. Ted Lieu (D)
  34. Jimmy Gomez (D)
  35. Norma J. Torres (D)
  36. Raul Ruiz (D)
  37. Karen Bass (D)
  38. Linda T. Sánchez (D)
  39. *Young Kim (R)*
  40. Lucille Roybal-Allard (D)
  41. Mark Takano (D)
  42. Ken Calvert (R)
  43. Maxine Waters (D)
  44. Nanette Diaz Barragán (D)
  45. Katie Porter (D)
  46. J. Luis Correa (D)
  47. Alan S. Lowenthal (D)
  48. *Michelle Steel (R)*
  49. Mike Levin (D)
  50. *Darrel Issa (R)*
  51. Juan Vargas (D)
  52. Scott H. Peters (D)
  53. *Sara Jacobs (D)*

COLORADO

Michael F. Bennet (D)
John W. Hickenlooper (D)
  1. Diana DeGette (D)
  2. Joe Neguse (D)
  3. *Lauren Boebert (R)*
  4. Ken Buck (R)
  5. Doug Lamborn (R)
  6. Jason Crow (D)
  7. Ed Perlmutter (D)

CONNECTICUT

Richard Blumenthal (D)
Chris Murphy (D)
  1. John B. Larson (D)
  2. Joe Courtney (D)
  3. Rosa L. DeLauro (D)
  4. Jim Himes (D)
  5. Jahana Hayes (D)

DELAWARE

Thomas R. Carper (D)
Christopher A. Coons (D)
AL Lisa Blunt Rochester (D)

DISTRICT OF COLUMBIA (NON-VOTING DELEGATE)

AL Eleanor Holmes Norton (D)

FLORIDA

Rick Scott (R)
Marco Rubio (R)
1. Matt Gaetz (R)
2. Neal P. Dunn (R)
3. *Kat Cammack (R)*
4. John H. Rutherford (R)
5. Al Lawson (D)
6. Michael Waltz (R)
7. Stephanie N. Murphy (D)
8. Bill Posey (R)
9. Darren Soto (D)
10. Val Butler Demings (D)
11. Daniel Webster (R)
12. Gus M. Bilirakis (R)
13. Charlie Crist (D)
14. Kathy Castor (D)
15. *C. Scott Franklin (R)*
16. Vern Buchanan (R)
17. W. Gregory Steube (R)
18. Brian J. Mast (R)
19. *Byron Donalds (R)*
20. *Sheila Cherfilus-McCormick (D)*
21. Lois Frankel (D)
22. Theodore E. Deutch (D)
23. Debbie Wasserman Schultz (D)
24. Frederica S. Wilson (D)
25. Mario Diaz-Balart (R)
26. *Carlos A. Gimenez (R)*
27. *Maria Elvira Salazar (R)*

GEORGIA

Jon Ossoff (D)
Raphael Warnock (D)
1. Earl L. (Buddy) Carter (R)
2. Sanford D. Bishop Jr. (D)
3. A. Drew Ferguson IV (R)
4. Henry C. (Hank) Johnson Jr. (D)
5. *Nikema Williams (D)*
6. Lucy McBath (D)
7. *Carolyn Bourdeaux (D)*
8. Austin Scott (R)
9. *Andrew S. Clyde (R)*
10. Jody B. Hice (R)
11. Barry Loudermilk (R)
12. Rick W. Allen (R)
13. David Scott (D)
14. *Marjorie Taylor Greene (R)*

GUAM (NON-VOTING DELEGATE)

AL Michael San Nicolas (D)

HAWAII

Brian Schatz (D)
Mazie K. Hirono (D)
1. Ed Case (D)
2. *Kaialiʻi Kahele (D)*

IDAHO

Mike Crapo (R)
James E. Risch (R)
1. Russ Fulcher (R)
2. Michael K. Simpson (R)

ILLINOIS

Richard J. Durbin (D)
Tammy Duckworth (D)
1. Bobby L. Rush (D)
2. Robin L. Kelly (D)
3. *Marie Newman (D)*
4. Jesús G. (Chuy) García (D)
5. Mike Quigley (D)
6. Sean Casten (D)
7. Danny K. Davis (D)
8. Raja Krishnamoorthi (D)
9. Janice D. Schakowsky (D)
10. Bradley Scott Schneider (D)
11. Bill Foster (D)
12. Mike Bost (R)
13. Rodney Davis (R)
14. Lauren Underwood (D)
15. *Mary E. Miller (R)*
16. Adam Kinzinger (R)
17. Cheri Bustos (D)
18. Darin LaHood (R)

INDIANA

Todd Young (R)
Mike Braun (R)
1. *Frank J. Mrvan (D)*
2. Jackie Walorski (R)
3. Jim Banks (R)
4. James R. Baird (R)
5. *Victoria Spartz (R)*
6. Greg Pence (R)
7. André Carson (D)
8. Larry Bucshon (R)
9. Trey Hollingsworth (R)

IOWA

Chuck Grassley (R)
Joni Ernst (R)
1. *Ashley Hinson (R)*
2. *Mariannette Miller-Meeks (R)*
3. Cynthia Axne (D)
4. *Randy Feenstra (R)*

KANSAS

Roger Marshall (R)#
Jerry Moran (R)
1. *Tracey Mann (R)*
2. *Jake LaTurner (R)*
3. Sharice Davids (D)
4. Ron Estes (R)

KENTUCKY

Mitch McConnell (R)
Rand Paul (R)
1. James Comer (R)
2. Brett Guthrie (R)
3. John A. Yarmuth (D)
4. Thomas Massie (R)
5. Harold Rogers (R)
6. Andy Barr (R)

LOUISIANA

John Kennedy (R)
Bill Cassidy (R)
1. Steve Scalise (R)
2. *Troy Carter (D)*
3. Clay Higgins (R)
4. Mike Johnson (R)
5. *Julia Letlow (R)*
6. Garret Graves (R)

MAINE

Susan M. Collins (R)
Angus S. King Jr. (I)
1. Chellie Pingree (D)
2. Jared F. Golden (D)

MARYLAND

Chris Van Hollen (D)
Benjamin L. Cardin (D)
1. Andy Harris (R)
2. C. A. Dutch Ruppersberger (D)
3. John P. Sarbanes (D)
4. Anthony G. Brown (D)
5. Steny H. Hoyer (D)
6. David Trone (D)
7. Kweisi Mfume (D)
8. Jamie Raskin (D)

MASSACHUSETTS

Elizabeth Warren (D)
Edward J. Markey (D)
1. Richard E. Neal (D)
2. James P. McGovern (D)
3. Lori Trahan (D)
4. *Jake Auchincloss (D)*
5. Katherine M. Clark (D)

6. Seth Moulton (D)
7. Ayanna Pressley (D)
8. Stephen F. Lynch (D)
9. William R. Keating (D)

MICHIGAN

Debbie Stabenow (D)
Gary C. Peters (D)
1. Jack Bergman (R)
2. Bill Huizenga (R)
3. *Peter Meijer (R)*
4. John R. Moolenaar (R)
5. Daniel T. Kildee (D)
6. Fred Upton (R)
7. Tim Walberg (R)
8. Elissa Slotkin (D)
9. Andy Levin (D)
10. *Lisa C. McClain (R)*
11. Haley M. Stevens (D)
12. Debbie Dingell (D)
13. Rashida Tlaib (D)
14. Brenda L. Lawrence (D)

MINNESOTA

Amy Klobuchar (D)
Tina Smith (D)
1. Vacant
2. Angie Craig (D)
3. Dean Phillips (D)
4. Betty McCollum (D)
5. Ilhan Omar (D)
6. Tom Emmer (R)
7. *Michelle Fischbach (R)*
8. Pete Stauber (R)

MISSISSIPPI

Roger F. Wicker (R)
Cindy Hyde-Smith (R)
1. Trent Kelly (R)
2. Bennie G. Thompson (D)
3. Michael Guest (R)
4. Steven M. Palazzo (R)

MISSOURI

Roy Blunt (R)
Josh Hawley (R)
1. *Cori Bush (D)*
2. Ann Wagner (R)
3. Blaine Luetkemeyer (R)
4. Vicky Hartzler (R)
5. Emanuel Cleaver (D)
6. Sam Graves (R)
7. Billy Long (R)
8. Jason Smith (R)

MONTANA

Jon Tester (D)
Steve Daines (R)
AL *Matthew M. Rosendale Sr. (R)*

NEBRASKA

Deb Fischer (R)
Ben Sasse (R)
1. Vacant
2. Don Bacon (R)
3. Adrian Smith (R)

NEVADA

Catherine Cortez Masto (D)
Jacky Rosen (D)
1. Dina Titus (D)
2. Mark E. Amodei (R)
3. Susie Lee (D)
4. Steven Horsford (D)

NEW HAMPSHIRE

Jeanne Shaheen (D)
Margaret Wood Hassan (D)
1. Chris Pappas (D)
2. Ann M. Kuster (D)

NEW JERSEY

Robert Menendez (D)
Cory A. Booker (D)
1. Donald Norcross (D)
2. Jefferson Van Drew (D)
3. Andy Kim (D)
4. Christopher H. Smith (R)
5. Josh Gottheimer (D)
6. Frank Pallone Jr. (D)
7. Tom Malinowski (D)
8. Albio Sires (D)
9. Bill Pascrell Jr. (D)
10. Donald M. Payne Jr. (D)
11. Mikie Sherrill (D)
12. Bonnie Watson Coleman (D)

NEW MEXICO

Martin Heinrich (D)
Ben Ray Luján (D)#
1. *Melanie A. Stansbury (D)*
2. *Yvette Herrell (R)*
3. *Teresa Leger Fernandez (D)*

NEW YORK

Charles E. Schumer (D)
Kirsten E. Gillibrand (D)
1. Lee M. Zeldin (R)
2. *Andrew R. Garbarino (R)*

3. Thomas R. Suozzi (D)
4. Kathleen M. Rice (D)
5. Gregory W. Meeks (D)
6. Grace Meng (D)
7. Nydia M. Velázquez (D)
8. Hakeem S. Jeffries (D)
9. Yvette D. Clarke (D)
10. Jerrold Nadler (D)
11. *Nicole Malliotakis (R)*
12. Carolyn B. Maloney (D)
13. Adriano Espaillat (D)
14. Alexandria
   Ocasio-Cortez (D)
15. *Ritchie Torres (D)*
16. *Jamaal Bowman (D)*
17. *Mondaire Jones (D)*
18. Sean Patrick
   Maloney (D)
19. Antonio Delgado (D)
20. Paul Tonko (D)
21. Elise M. Stefanik (R)
22. *Claudia Tenney (R)*
23. Tom Reed (R)
24. John Katko (R)
25. Joseph D. Morelle (D)
26. Brian Higgins (D)
27. *Chris Jacobs (R)*

NORTH CAROLINA

Richard Burr (R)
Thom Tillis (R)
1. G. K. Butterfield (D)
2. *Deborah K. Ross (D)*
3. Gregory F. Murphy (R)
4. David E. Price (D)
5. Virginia Foxx (R)
6. *Kathy E. Manning (D)*
7. David Rouzer (R)
8. Richard Hudson (R)
9. Dan Bishop (R)
10. Patrick T. McHenry (R)
11. *Madison Cawthorn (R)*
12. Alma S. Adams (D)
13. Ted Budd (R)

NORTH DAKOTA

John Hoeven (R)
Kevin Cramer (R)
AL Kelly Armstrong (R)

NORTHERN MARIANA ISLANDS (NON-VOTING DELEGATE)

AL Gregorio Kilili Camacho
Sablan (D)

OHIO

Sherrod Brown (D)
Rob Portman (R)
1. Steve Chabot (R)
2. Brad R. Wenstrup (R)
3. Joyce Beatty (D)
4. Jim Jordan (R)
5. Robert E. Latta (R)
6. Bill Johnson (R)
7. Bob Gibbs (R)
8. Warren Davidson (R)
9. Marcy Kaptur (D)
10. Michael R. Turner (R)
11. *Shontel M. Brown (D)*
12. Troy Balderson (R)
13. Tim Ryan (D)
14. David P. Joyce (R)
15. *Mike Carey (R)*
16. Anthony Gonzalez (R)

OKLAHOMA

James M. Inhofe (R)
James Lankford (R)
1. Kevin Hern (R)
2. Markwayne Mullin (R)
3. Frank D. Lucas (R)
4. Tom Cole (R)
5. *Stephanie I. Bice (R)*

OREGON

Ron Wyden (D)
Jeff Merkley (D)
1. Suzanne Bonamici (D)
2. *Cliff Bentz (R)*
3. Earl Blumenauer (D)
4. Peter A. DeFazio (D)
5. Kurt Schrader (D)

PENNSYLVANIA

Robert P. Casey Jr. (D)
Patrick J. Toomey (R)
1. Brian K. Fitzpatrick (R)
2. Brendan F. Boyle (D)
3. Dwight Evans (D)
4. Madeleine Dean (D)
5. Mary Gay Scanlon (D)
6. Chrissy Houlahan (D)
7. Susan Wild (D)
8. Matt Cartwright (D)
9. Daniel Meuser (R)
10. Scott Perry (R)
11. Lloyd Smucker (R)
12. Fred Keller (R)
13. John Joyce (R)
14. Guy Reschenthaler (R)
15. Glenn Thompson (R)
16. Mike Kelly (R)
17. Conor Lamb (D)
18. Mike F. Doyle (D)

PUERTO RICO (NON-VOTING DELEGATE)

AL Jenniffer González-Colón (R)

RHODE ISLAND

Jack Reed (D)
Sheldon Whitehouse (D)
1. David N. Cicilline (D)
2. James R. Langevin (D)

SOUTH CAROLINA

Lindsey Graham (R)
Tim Scott (R)
1. *Nancy Mace (R)*
2. Joe Wilson (R)
3. Jeff Duncan (R)
4. William R. Timmons IV (R)
5. Ralph Norman (R)
6. James E. Clyburn (D)
7. Tom Rice (R)

SOUTH DAKOTA

John Thune (R)
Mike Rounds (R)
AL Dusty Johnson (R)

TENNESSEE

Bill Hagerty (R)
Marsha Blackburn (R)
1. *Diana Harshbarger (R)*
2. Tim Burchett (R)
3. Charles J. (Chuck) Fleischmann (R)
4. Scott DesJarlais (R)
5. Jim Cooper (D)
6. John W. Rose (R)
7. Mark E. Green (R)
8. David Kustoff (R)
9. Steve Cohen (D)

TEXAS

John Cornyn (R)
Ted Cruz (R)
1. Louie Gohmert (R)
2. Dan Crenshaw (R)
3. Van Taylor (R)
4. *Pat Fallon (R)*
5. Lance Gooden (R)
6. *Jake Ellzey (R)*
7. Lizzie Fletcher (D)
8. Kevin Brady (R)
9. Al Green (D)
10. Michael T. McCaul (R)
11. *August Pfluger (R)*
12. Kay Granger (R)
13. *Ronny Jackson (R)*
14. Randy K. Weber Sr. (R)
15. Vicente Gonzalez (D)
16. Veronica Escobar (D)
17. *Pete Sessions (R)*
18. Sheila Jackson Lee (D)
19. Jodey C. Arrington (R)
20. Joaquin Castro (D)
21. Chip Roy (R)
22. *Troy E. Nehls (R)*
23. *Tony Gonzales (R)*
24. *Beth Van Duyne (R)*
25. Roger Williams (R)
26. Michael C. Burgess (R)
27. Michael Cloud (R)
28. Henry Cuellar (D)
29. Sylvia R. Garcia (D)
30. Eddie Bernice Johnson (D)
31. John R. Carter (R)
32. Colin Z. Allred (D)
33. Marc A. Veasey (D)
34. Vacant
35. Lloyd Doggett (D)
36. Brian Babin (R)

UTAH

Mike Lee (R)
Mitt Romney (R)
1. *Blake D. Moore (R)*
2. Chris Stewart (R)
3. John R. Curtis (R)
4. *Burgess Owens (R)*

VERMONT

Patrick J. Leahy (D)
Bernard Sanders (I)
AL Peter Welch (D)

VIRGIN ISLANDS (NON-VOTING DELEGATE)

AL Stacey E. Plaskett (D)

VIRGINIA

Mark R. Warner (D)
Tim Kaine (D)
1. Robert J. Wittman (R)
2. Elaine G. Luria (D)
3. Robert C. (Bobby) Scott (D)
4. A. Donald McEachin (D)
5. *Bob Good (R)*
6. Ben Cline (R)

7. Abigail Davis Spanberger (D)
8. Donald S. Beyer Jr. (D)
9. H. Morgan Griffith (R)
10. Jennifer Wexton (D)
11. Gerald E. Connolly (D)

WASHINGTON

Patty Murray (D)
Maria Cantwell (D)
1. Suzan K. DelBene (D)
2. Rick Larsen (D)
3. Jaime Herrera Beutler (R)
4. Dan Newhouse (R)
5. Cathy McMorris
   Rodgers (R)
6. Derek Kilmer (D)
7. Pramila Jayapal (D)
8. Kim Schrier (D)
9. Adam Smith (D)
10. *Marilyn Strickland (D)*

WEST VIRGINIA

Joe Manchin III (D)
Shelley Moore Capito (R)
1. David B. McKinley (R)
2. Alexander X. Mooney (R)
3. Carol D. Miller (R)

WISCONSIN

Ron Johnson (R)
Tammy Baldwin (D)
1. Bryan Steil (R)
2. Mark Pocan (D)
3. Ron Kind (D)
4. Gwen Moore (D)
5. *Scott Fitzgerald (R)*
6. Glenn Grothman (R)
7. Thomas P. Tiffany (R)
8. Mike Gallagher (R)

WYOMING

John Barrasso (R)
Cynthia M. Lummis (R)
AL Liz Cheney (R)

House Committees

The standing and select committees of the U.S. House of Representatives follow. Each listing includes the room number, office building, zip code, telephone and fax numbers, website, minority website if available, key majority and minority staff members, jurisdiction for each full committee, and party ratio. Subcommittees are listed under the full committees. Members are listed in order of seniority on the committee or subcommittee. Many committees and subcommittees may be contacted via web-based email forms found on their websites.

Democrats, the current majority, are shown in roman type; Republicans, in the minority, appear in italic. The top name in the italicized list is the Ranking Minority Member. Vacancy indicates that a committee or subcommittee seat had not been filled as of May 12, 2022. The partisan committees of the House are listed on pages 864–865. The area code for all phone and fax numbers is (202). A phone number and/or office number next to either the Majority or Minority Staff Director indicates a change from the full committee's office number and/or phone number. If no numbers are listed, the individual's office number and phone number are the same as for the full committee.

AGRICULTURE

Office: 1301 LHOB 20515-6001
Phone: 225-2171 **Fax:** 225-8510
Web: agriculture.house.gov
Minority Web: republicans-agriculture.house.gov
Majority Staff Director: Anne Simmons
Minority Staff Director: Parish Braden, 225-0317, 1010 LHOB
Jurisdiction: (1) adulteration of seeds, insect pests, and protection of birds and animals in forest reserves; (2) agriculture generally; (3) agricultural and industrial chemistry; (4) agricultural colleges and experiment stations; (5) agricultural economics and research; (6) agricultural education extension services; (7) agricultural production and marketing, and stabilization of prices of agricultural products and commodities (not including distribution outside of the United States); (8) animal industry and diseases of animals; (9) commodity exchanges; (10) crop insurance and soil conservation; (11) dairy industry; (12) entomology and plant quarantine; (13) extension of farm credit and farm security; (14) inspection of livestock, poultry, meat products, and seafood and seafood products; (15) forestry in general, and forest reserves other than those created from the public domain; (16) human nutrition and home economics; (17) plant industry, soils, and agricultural engineering; (18) rural electrification; (19) rural development; (20) water conservation related to activities of the Department of Agriculture.
Party Ratio: D 27-R 23

David Scott, Ga., Chair	*Glenn Thompson, Pa.*
Jim Costa, Calif.	*Austin Scott, Ga.*
James P. McGovern, Mass.	*Eric A. (Rick) Crawford,*
Alma S. Adams, N.C.	*Ark.*
Abigail Davis Spanberger, Va.	*Scott DesJarlais, Tenn.*
	Vicky Hartzler, Mo.
Jahana Hayes, Conn.	*Doug LaMalfa, Calif.*
Antonio Delgado, N.Y.	*Rodney Davis, Ill.*
Shontel M. Brown, Ohio	*Rick W. Allen, Ga.*
Bobby L. Rush, Ill.	*David Rouzer, N.C.*
Chellie Pingree, Maine	*Trent Kelly, Miss.*

Gregorio Kilili Camacho Sablan, N. Mariana Is.	*Don Bacon, Neb.*
Ann M. Kuster, N.H.	*Dusty Johnson, S.D.*
Cheri Bustos, Ill.	*James R. Baird, Ind.*
Sean Patrick Maloney, N.Y.	*Chris Jacobs, N.Y.*
	Troy Balderson, Ohio
Stacey E. Plaskett, V.I.	*Michael Cloud, Tex.*
Tom O'Halleran, Ariz.	*Tracey Mann, Kans.*
Salud O. Carbajal, Calif.	*Randy Feenstra, Iowa*
Ro Khanna, Calif.	*Mary E. Miller, Ill.*
Al Lawson, Fla.	*Barry Moore, Ala.*
J. Luis Correa, Calif.	*Kat Cammack, Fla.*
Angie Craig, Minn.	*Michelle Fischbach, Minn.*
Josh Harder, Calif.	*Julia Letlow, La.*
Cynthia Axne, Iowa	
Kim Schrier, Wash.	
Jimmy Panetta, Calif.	
Sanford D. Bishop Jr., Ga.	

Subcommittees

Biotechnology, Horticulture, and Research
Office: 1301 LHOB 20515   **Phone:** 225-2171
Stacey E. Plaskett (Chair), Antonio Delgado, Shontell M. Brown, Kim Schrier, Jimmy Panetta, Chellie Pingree, Sean Patrick Maloney, Salud O. Carbajal, Al Lawson, Josh Harder, J. Luis Correa, David Scott (ex officio)
James R. Baird (Ranking Minority Member), Austin Scott, Eric A. (Rick) Crawford, Rodney Davis, Don Bacon, Chris Jacobs, Troy Balderson, Michelle Fischbach, Julia Letlow, Glenn Thompson (ex officio)

Commodity Exchanges, Energy, and Credit
Office: 1301 LHOB 20515   **Phone:** 225-2171
Antonio Delgado (Chair), Sean Patrick Maloney, Stacey E. Plaskett, Ro Khanna, Cynthia Axne, Bobby L. Rush, Angie Craig, Ann M. Kuster, Cheri Bustos, David Scott (ex officio)
Michelle Fischbach (Ranking Minority Member), Austin Scott, Doug LaMalfa, Rodney Davis, Chris Jacobs, Troy Balderson, Michael Cloud, Randy Feenstra, Kat Cammack, Glenn Thompson (ex officio)

AGRICULTURE (continued)

Conservation and Forestry
Office: 1301 LHOB 20515 **Phone:** 225-2171

Abigail Davis Spanberger (Chair), Chellie Pingree, Ann M. Kuster, Tom O'Halleran, Jimmy Panetta, J. Luis Correa, Kim Schrier, David Scott (ex officio)

Doug LaMalfa (Ranking Minority Member), Scott DesJarlais, Rick W. Allen, Trent Kelly, Dusty Johnson, Mary E. Miller, Barry Moore, Glenn Thompson (ex officio)

General Farm Commodities and Risk Management
Office: 1301 LHOB 20515 **Phone:** 225-2171

Cheri Bustos (Chair), Angie Craig, Salud O. Carbajal, Tom O'Halleran, Al Lawson, Sanford D. Bishop Jr., David Scott (ex officio)

Austin Scott (Ranking Minority Member), Eric A. (Rick) Crawford, Rick W. Allen, David Rouzer, Tracey Mann, Mary E. Miller, Glenn Thompson (ex officio)

Livestock and Foreign Agriculture
Office: 1301 LHOB 20515 **Phone:** 225-2171

Jim Costa (Chair), Abigail Davis Spanberger, Jahana Hayes, J. Luis Correa, Josh Harder, Ro Khanna, Cynthia Axne, Bobby L. Rush, Stacey E. Plaskett, Angie Craig, Sanford D. Bishop Jr., David Scott (ex officio)

Dusty Johnson (Ranking Minority Member), Scott DesJarlais, Vicky Hartzler, Trent Kelly, Don Bacon, James R. Baird, Tracey Mann, Randy Feenstra, Barry Moore, Glenn Thompson (ex officio)

Nutrition, Oversight, and Department Operations
Office: 1301 LHOB 20515 **Phone:** 225-2171

Jahana Hayes (Chair), James P. McGovern, Alma S. Adams, Shontel M. Brown, Bobby L. Rush, Gregorio Kilili Camacho Sablan, Salud O. Carbajal, Al Lawson, Ann M. Kuster, Jimmy Panetta, David Scott (ex officio)

Don Bacon (Ranking Minority Member), Eric A. (Rick) Crawford, Scott DesJarlais, Vicky Hartzler, James R. Baird, Chris Jacobs, Michael Cloud, Kat Cammack, Julia Letlow, Glenn Thompson (ex officio)

APPROPRIATIONS

Office: H-307 CAP 20515-6015
Phone: 225-2771 **Fax:** 226-0383
Web: appropriations.house.gov
Minority Web: republicans-appropriations.house.gov
Majority Staff Director: Robin Juliano
Minority Staff Director: Anne Marie Chotvacs, 225-3481, 1036 LHOB
Jurisdiction: (1) appropriation of the revenue for the support of the government; (2) rescissions of appropriations contained in appropriations Acts; (3) transfers of unexpected balances; (4) bills and joint resolutions reported by other committees that provide new entitlement authority as defined in Section 3(9) of the Congressional Budget Act of 1974 and referred to the committee under Clause 4(a)(2).
Party Ratio: D 33-R 25

Rosa L. DeLauro, Conn., Chair
Marcy Kaptur, Ohio
David E. Price, N.C.
Lucille Roybal-Allard, Calif.
Sanford D. Bishop Jr., Ga.
Barbara Lee, Calif.
Betty McCollum, Minn.
Tim Ryan, Ohio
C. A. Dutch Ruppersberger, Md.
Debbie Wasserman Schultz, Fla.
Henry Cuellar, Tex.
Chellie Pingree, Maine
Mike Quigley, Ill.
Derek Kilmer, Wash.
Matt Cartwright, Pa.
Grace Meng, N.Y.
Mark Pocan, Wisc.
Katherine M. Clark, Mass.
Pete Aguilar, Calif.
Lois Frankel, Fla.
Cheri Bustos, Ill.
Bonnie Watson Coleman, N.J.
Brenda L. Lawrence, Mich.
Norma J. Torres, Calif.
Charlie Crist, Fla.
Ann Kirkpatrick, Ariz.
Ed Case, Hawaii
Adriano Espaillat, N.Y.
Josh Harder, Calif.
Jennifer Wexton, Va.
David Trone, Md.
Lauren Underwood, Ill.
Susie Lee, Nev.

Kay Granger, Tex.
Harold Rogers, Ky.
Robert B. Aderholt, Ala.
Michael K. Simpson, Idaho
John R. Carter, Tex.
Ken Calvert, Calif.
Tom Cole, Okla.
Mario Diaz-Balart, Fla.
Steve Womack, Ark.
Charles J. (Chuck) Fleischmann, Tenn.
Jaime Herrera Beutler, Wash.
David P. Joyce, Ohio
Andy Harris, Md.
Mark E. Amodei, Nev.
Chris Stewart, Utah
Steven M. Palazzo, Miss.
David G. Valadao, Calif.
Dan Newhouse, Wash.
John R. Moolenaar, Mich.
John H. Rutherford, Fla.
Ben Cline, Va.
Guy Reschenthaler, Pa.
Mike Garcia, Calif.
Ashley Hinson, Iowa
Tony Gonzales, Tex.

Subcommittees

Agriculture, Rural Development, Food and Drug Administration, and Related Agencies
Office: 2362A RHOB 20515 **Phone:** 225-2638

Sanford Bishop Jr. (Chair), Chellie Pingree, Mark Pocan, Lauren Underwood, Barbara Lee, Betty McCollum, Debbie Wasserman Schultz, Henry Cuellar, Grace Meng

Andy Harris (Ranking Minority Member), Robert B. Aderholt, David G. Valadao, John R. Moolenaar, Dan Newhouse

Commerce, Justice, Science, and Related Agencies
Office: H-310 CAP 20515 **Phone:** 225-3351

Matt Cartwright (Chair), Grace Meng, Charlie Crist, Ed Case, C. A. Dutch Ruppersberger, Brenda L. Lawrence, David Trone

Robert B. Aderholt (Ranking Minority Member), Steven M. Palazzo, Ben Cline, Mike Garcia

Defense
Office: H-405 CAP 20515 **Phone:** 225-2847

Betty McCollum (Chair), Tim Ryan, C. A. Dutch Ruppersberger, Marcy Kaptur, Henry Cuellar, Derek Kilmer, Pete Aguilar, Cheri Bustos, Charlie Crist, Ann Kirkpatrick

Ken Calvert (Ranking Minority Member), Harold Rogers, Tom Cole, Steve Womack, Robert B. Aderholt, John R. Carter, Mario Diaz-Balart

Energy and Water Development, and Related Agencies
Office: 2362B RHOB 20515   **Phone:** 225-3421

Marcy Kaptur (Chair), Debbie Wasserman Schultz, Ann Kirkpatrick, Susie Lee, Tim Ryan, Derek Kilmer, Lois Frankel, Cheri Bustos, Bonnie Watson Coleman

Michael K. Simpson (Ranking Minority Member), Ken Calvert, Charles J. (Chuck) Fleischmann, Dan Newhouse, Jaime Herrera Beutler, Guy Reschenthaler

Financial Services and General Government
Office: 2000 RHOB 20515   **Phone:** 225-7245

Mike Quigley (Chair), Matt Cartwright, Sanford D. Bishop Jr., Mark Pocan, Brenda L. Lawrence, Norma J. Torres, Ann Kirkpatrick

Steve Womack (Ranking Minority Member), Mark E. Amodei, Chris Stewart, David P. Joyce

Homeland Security
Office: 2006 RHOB 20515   **Phone:** 225-5834

Lucille Roybal-Allard (Chair), Henry Cuellar, Lauren Underwood, David E. Price, C. A. Dutch Ruppersberger, Mike Quigley, Pete Aguilar

Charles J. (Chuck) Fleischmann (Ranking Minority Member), Steven M. Palazzo, John H. Rutherford, Ashley Hinson

Interior, Environment, and Related Agencies
Office: 2007 RHOB 20515   **Phone:** 225-3081

Chellie Pingree (Chair), Betty McCollum, Derek Kilmer, Josh Harder, Susie Lee, Marcy Kaptur, Matt Cartwright

David P. Joyce (Ranking Minority Member), Michael K. Simpson, Chris Stewart, Mark E. Amodei

Labor, Health and Human Services, Education, and Related Agencies
Office: 2358B RHOB 20515   **Phone:** 225-3508

Rosa L. DeLauro (Chair), Lucille Roybal-Allard, Barbara Lee, Mark Pocan, Katherine M. Clark, Lois Frankel, Cheri Bustos, Bonnie Watson Coleman, Brenda L. Lawrence, Josh Harder

Tom Cole (Ranking Minority Member), Andy Harris, Charles J. (Chuck) Fleischmann, Jaime Herrera Beutler, John R. Moolenaar, Ben Cline

Legislative Branch
Office: H-306 CAP 20515   **Phone:** 226-7252

Tim Ryan (Chair), Katherine M. Clark, Ed Case, Adriano Espaillat, Jennifer Wexton

Jaime Herrera Beutler (Ranking Minority Member), Mark E. Amodei, Dan Newhouse

Military Construction, Veterans Affairs, and Related Agencies
Office: HT-2 CAP 20515   **Phone:** 225-3047

Debbie Wasserman Schultz (Chair), Sanford D. Bishop Jr., Ed Case, Chellie Pingree, Charlie Crist, David Trone, Susie Lee

John R. Carter (Ranking Minority Member), David G. Valadao, John H. Rutherford, Tony Gonzales

State, Foreign Operations, and Related Programs
Office: HT-2 CAP 20515   **Phone:** 225-2041

Barbara Lee (Chair), Grace Meng, David E. Price, Lois Frankel, Norma J. Torres, Adriano Espaillat, Jennifer Wexton

Harold Rogers (Ranking Minority Member), Mario Diaz-Balart, Guy Reschenthaler

Transportation, Housing and Urban Development, and Related Agencies
Office: 2358A RHOB 20515   **Phone:** 225-2141

David E. Price (Chair), Mike Quigley, Katherine M. Clark, Bonnie Watson Coleman, Norma J. Torres, Pete Aguilar, Adriano Espaillat, Jennifer Wexton, David Trone

Mario Diaz-Balart (Ranking Minority Member), Steve Womack, John H. Rutherford, Mike Garcia, Ashley Hinson, Tony Gonzales

ARMED SERVICES

Office: 2216 RHOB 20515-6035
Phone: 225-4151   **Fax:** 225-9077
Web: armedservices.house.gov
Minority Web: republicans-armedservices.house.gov
Majority Deputy Staff Director: Brian Garrett
Minority Staff Director: Chris Vieson
Jurisdiction: (1) ammunition depots, forts, arsenals, Army, Navy and Air Force reservations and establishments; (2) common defense generally; (3) conservation, development, and use of naval petroleum reserves and oil shale reserves; (4) the Department of Defense generally, including the Departments of the Army, Navy, and Air Force generally; (5) interoceanic canals generally, including measures relating to the maintenance, operation, and administration of interoceanic canals; (6) Merchant Marine Academy and State Merchant Marine Academies; (7) military applications of nuclear energy; (8) tactical intelligence and intelligence-related activities of the Department of Defense; (9) national security aspects of the merchant marine, including financial assistance for the construction and operation of vessels, the maintenance of the U.S. shipbuilding and ship repair industrial base, cabotage (trade or transport in coastal waters or air space, or between two points within a country), cargo preference, and merchant marine officers and seamen as these matters relate to the national security; (10) pay, promotion, retirement, and other benefits and privileges of members of the armed services; (11) scientific research and development in support of the armed services; (12) selective service; (13) size and composition of the Army, Navy, Marine Corps, and Air Force; (14) soldiers' and sailors' homes; (15) strategic and critical materials necessary for the common defense; (16) cemeteries administered by the Department of Defense.

ARMED SERVICES (continued)

Party Ratio: D 30-R 28

Adam Smith, Wash., Chair	Mike Rogers, Ala.
James R. Langevin, R.I.	Joe Wilson, S.C.
Rick Larsen, Wash.	Michael R. Turner, Ohio
Jim Cooper, Tenn.	Doug Lamborn, Colo.
Joe Courtney, Conn.	Robert J. Wittman, Va.
John Garamendi, Calif.	Vicky Hartzler, Mo.
Jackie Speier, Calif.	Austin Scott, Ga.
Donald Norcross, N.J.	Mo Brooks, Ala.
Rubén Gallego, Ariz.	Sam Graves, Mo.
Seth Moulton, Mass.	Elise M. Stefanik, N.Y.
Salud O. Carbajal, Calif.	Scott DesJarlais, Tenn.
Anthony G. Brown, Md.	Trent Kelly, Miss.
Ro Khanna, Calif.	Mike Gallagher, Wisc.
William R. Keating, Mass.	Matt Gaetz, Fla.
Andy Kim, N.J.	Don Bacon, Neb.
Chrissy Houlahan, Pa.	Jim Banks, Ind.
Jason Crow, Colo.	Liz Cheney, Wyo.
Elissa Slotkin, Mich.	Jack Bergman, Mich.
Mikie Sherrill, N.J.	Michael Waltz, Fla.
Veronica Escobar, Tex.	Mike Johnson, La.
Jared F. Golden, Maine	Mark E. Green, Tenn.
Elaine G. Luria, Va.	Stephanie I. Bice, Okla.
Joseph D. Morelle	C. Scott Franklin, Fla.
Sara Jacobs, Calif.	Lisa C. McClain, Mich.
Kaiali'i Kahele, Hawaii	Ronny Jackson, Tex.
Marilyn Strickland, Wash.	Jerry L. Carl, Ala.
Marc A. Veasey, Tex.	Blake D. Moore, Utah
Jimmy Panetta, Calif.	Pat Fallon, Tex.
Stephanie N. Murphy, Fla.	
Steven Horsford, Nev.	

Subcommittees

Cyber, Innovative Technologies, and Information Systems
Office: 2216 RHOB 20515 **Phone:** 225-4151

James R. Langevin (Chair), Rick Larsen, Seth Moulton, Ro Khanna, William R. Keating, Andy Kim, Chrissy Houlahan, Jason Crow, Elissa Slotkin, Veronica Escobar, Joseph D. Morelle, Adam Smith (ex officio)

Elise M. Stefanik (Ranking Minority Member), Mo Brooks, Matt Gaetz, Mike Johnson, Stephanie I. Bice, C. Scott Franklin, Blake D. Moore, Pat Fallon, Mike Rogers (ex officio)

Intelligence and Special Operations
Office: 2216 RHOB 20515 **Phone:** 225-4151

Rubén Gallego (Chair), Rick Larsen, Jim Cooper, William R. Keating, Mikie Sherrill, Jimmy Panetta, Stephanie N. Murphy, Adam Smith (ex officio)

Trent Kelly (Ranking Minority Member), Doug Lamborn, Austin Scott, Sam Graves, Don Bacon, Liz Cheney, C. Scott Franklin, Mike Rogers (ex officio)

Military Personnel
Office: 2216 RHOB 20515 **Phone:** 225-4151

Jackie Speier (Chair), Andy Kim, Chrissy Houlahan, Veronica Escobar, Sara Jacobs, Marilyn Strickland, Mark A. Veasey, Adam Smith (ex officio)

Mike Gallagher (Ranking Minority Member), Stephanie I. Bice, Lisa C. McClain, Ronny Jackson, Jerry L. Carl, Pat Fallon, Mike Rogers (ex officio)

Readiness
Office: 2216 RHOB 20515 **Phone:** 225-4151

John Garamendi (Chair), Joe Courtney, Jackie Speier, Jason Crow, Elissa Slotkin, Jared F. Golden, Elaine G. Luria, Kaiali'i Kahele, Marilyn Strickland, Adam Smith (ex officio)

Michael Waltz (Ranking Minority Member), Joe Wilson, Austin Scott, Jack Bergman, Mike Johnson, Mark E. Green, Lisa C. McClain, Blake D. Moore, Mike Rogers (ex officio)

Seapower and Projection Forces
Office: 2216 RHOB 20515 **Phone:** 225-4151

Joe Courtney (Chair), James R. Langevin, Jim Cooper, Donald Norcross, Anthony G. Brown, Jared F. Golden, Elaine G. Luria, Sara Jacobs, Adam Smith (ex officio)

Robert J. Wittman (Ranking Minority Member), Vicky Hartzler, Sam Graves, Trent Kelly, Mike Gallagher, Jim Banks, Jack Bergman, Jerry L. Carl, Mike Rogers (ex officio)

Strategic Forces
Office: 2216 RHOB 20515 **Phone:** 225-4151

Jim Cooper (Chair), James R. Langevin, John Garamendi, Seth Moulton, Salud O. Carbajal, Ro Khanna, Joseph D. Morelle, Jimmy Panetta, Steven Horsford, Adam Smith (ex officio)

Doug Lamborn (Ranking Minority Member), Joe Wilson, Michael R. Turner, Mo Brooks, Elise M. Stefanik, Scott DesJarlais, Liz Cheney, Michael Waltz, Mike Rogers (ex officio)

Tactical Air and Land Forces
Office: 2216 RHOB 20515 **Phone:** 225-4151

Donald Norcross (Chair), Rubén Gallego, Salud O. Carbajal, Anthony G. Brown, Mikie Sherrill, Kaiali'i Kahele, Marc A. Veasey, Stephanie N. Murphy, Steven Horsford, Adam Smith (ex officio)

Vicky Hartzler (Ranking Minority Member), Michael R. Turner, Robert J. Wittman, Scott DesJarlais, Matt Gaetz, Don Bacon, Mark E. Green, Ronny Jackson, Mike Rogers (ex officio)

BUDGET

Office: 204-E CHOB 20515-6065
Phone: 226-7200 **Fax:** 225-9905
Web: budget.house.gov
Minority Web: republicans-budget.house.gov
Majority Staff Director: Diana Meredith
Minority Staff Director: Mark Roman, 226-7270, 507 CHOB
Jurisdiction: (1) concurrent resolutions on the budget (as defined in section 3(4) of the Congressional Budget

Act of 1974), other matters required to be referred to the committee under Titles III and IV of that act, and other measures setting forth appropriate levels of budget totals for the government; (2) budget process generally; (3) establishment, extension, and enforcement of special controls over the federal budget, including the budgetary treatment of off-budget federal agencies and measures providing exemption from reduction under any order issued under part C of the Balanced Budget and Emergency Deficit Control Act of 1985; (4) study on a continuing basis the effect on budget outlays of relevant existing and proposed legislation and report the results of such studies to the House on a recurring basis; (5)(a) review on a continuing basis the conduct by the Congressional Budget Office of its functions and duties; (b) hold hearings and receive testimony from members, senators, delegates, the resident commissioner, and such appropriate representatives of federal departments and agencies, the general public, and national organizations as it considers desirable in developing concurrent resolutions on the budget for each fiscal year; (c) make all reports required of it by the Congressional Budget Act of 1974; (d) study on a continuing basis those provisions of law that exempt federal agencies or any of their activities or outlays from inclusion in the budget of the government, and report to the House from time to time its recommendations for terminating or modifying such provisions; (e) study on a continuing basis proposals designed to improve and facilitate the congressional budget process, and report to the House from time to time the results of such studies, together with its recommendations; (f) request and evaluate continuing studies of tax expenditures, devise methods of coordinating tax expenditures, policies, and programs with direct budget outlays, and report the results of such studies to the House on a recurring basis.

Party Ratio: D 21-R 16

John A. Yarmuth, Ky., Chair	*Jason Smith, Mo.*
Hakeem S. Jeffries, N.Y.	*Trent Kelly, Miss.*
Brian Higgins, N.Y.	*Tom McClintock, Calif.*
Brendan F. Boyle, Pa.	*Glenn Grothman, Wisc.*
Lloyd Doggett, Tex.	*Lloyd Smucker, Pa.*
David E. Price, N.C.	*Chris Jacobs, N.Y.*
Janice D. Schakowsky, Ill.	*Michael C. Burgess, Tex.*
Daniel T. Kildee, Mich.	*Earl L. (Buddy) Carter, Ga.*
Joseph D. Morelle, N.Y.	*Ben Cline, Va.*
Steven Horsford, Nev.	*Lauren Boebert, Colo.*
Barbara Lee, Calif.	*Byron Donalds, Fla.*
Judy Chu, Calif.	*Randy Feenstra, Iowa*
Stacey E. Plaskett, V.I.	*Bob Good, Va.*
Jennifer Wexton, Va.	*Ashley Hinson, Iowa*
Robert C. (Bobby) Scott, Va.	*Jay Obernolte, Calif.*
Sheila Jackson Lee, Tex.	*Mike Carey, Ohio*
Jim Cooper, Tenn.	
Albio Sires, N.J.	
Scott H. Peters, Calif.	
Seth Moulton, Mass.	
Pramila Jayapal, Wash.	

EDUCATION AND LABOR

Office: 2176 RHOB 20515-6100
Phone: 225-3725 **Fax:** 225-2350
Web: edlabor.house.gov
Minority Web: republicans-edlabor.house.gov
Majority Staff Director: Véronique Pluviose
Minority Staff Director: Cyrus Artz, 225-4527, 2101 RHOB

Jurisdiction: (1) elementary and secondary education initiatives, including the No Child Left Behind Act, school choice for low-income families, special education (the Individuals with Disabilities Education Act), teacher quality and teacher training, scientifically based reading instruction, and vocational and technical education; (2) higher education programs, including the Higher Education Act, which supports college access for low- and middle-income students and helps families pay for college; (3) early childhood care and preschool education programs, including Head Start; (4) school lunch and child nutrition programs; (5) financial oversight of the U.S. Department of Education; (6) programs and services for the care and treatment of at-risk youth, child abuse prevention, and child adoption; (7) educational research and improvement; (8) adult education; and (9) antipoverty programs, including the Community Services Block Grant Act and the Low Income Home Energy Assistance Program (LIHEAP); (10) pension and retirement security for U.S. workers; (11) access to quality health care for working families and other employee benefits; (12) job training, adult education, and workforce development initiatives, including those under the Workforce Innovation and Opportunity Act (WIA), to help local communities train and retrain workers; (13) protecting the right to organize and collectively bargain; (14) worker health and safety, including occupational safety and health; (15) equal employment opportunity and civil rights in employment; (16) wages and hours of labor, including the Fair Labor Standards Act; (17) expanding sick, family, and medical leave; (18) all matters dealing with relationships between employers and employees.

Party Ratio: D 30-R 23

Robert C. (Bobby) Scott, Va., Chair	*Joe Wilson, S.C.*
Raúl Grijalva, Ariz.	*Glenn Thompson, Pa.*
Joe Courtney, Conn.	*Tim Walberg, Mich.*
Gregorio Kilili Camacho Sablan, N. Mariana Is.	*Glenn Grothman, Wisc.*
Frederica S. Wilson, Fla.	*Elise M. Stefanik, N.Y.*
Suzanne Bonamici, Ore.	*Rick W. Allen, Ga.*
Mark Takano, Calif.	*Jim Banks, Ind.*
Alma S. Adams, N.C.	*James Comer, Ky.*
Mark DeSaulnier, Calif.	*Russ Fulcher, Idaho*
Donald Norcross, N.J.	*Fred Keller, Pa.*
Pramila Jayapal, Wash.	*Mariannette Miller-Meeks, Iowa*
Joseph D. Morelle, N.Y.	*Burgess Owens, Utah*
Susan Wild, Pa.	*Bob Good, Va.*
Lucy McBath, Ga.	*Lisa C. McClain, Mich.*
Jahana Hayes, Conn.	*Diana Harshbarger, Tenn.*
Andy Levin, Mich.	*Mary E. Miller, Ill.*
Ilhan Omar, Minn.	*Victoria Spartz, Ind.*
	Scott Fitzgerald, Wisc.

EDUCATION AND LABOR (continued)

Haley M. Stevens, Mich.
Teresa Leger Fernandez, N.M.
Mondaire Jones, N.Y.
Kathy E. Manning, N.C.
Frank J. Mrvan, Ind.
Jamaal Bowman, N.Y.
Mark Pocan, Wisc.
Joaquin Castro, Tex.
Mikie Sherrill, N.J.
John A. Yarmuth, Ky.
Adriano Espaillat, N.Y.
Kweisi Mfume, Md.
Sheila Cherfilus-McCormick, Fla.
Virginia Foxx, N.C.

Madison Cawthorn, N.C.
Michelle Steel, Calif.
Julia Letlow, La.
Chris Jacobs, N.Y.

Subcommittees

Civil Rights and Human Services
Office: 2176 RHOB 20515 **Phone:** 225-3725
Suzanne Bonamici (Chair), Alma S. Adams, Jahana Hayes, Teresa Leger Fernandez, Frank J. Mrvan, Jamaal Bowman, Kweisi Mfume
Russ Fulcher (Ranking Minority Member), Glenn Thompson, Lisa C. McClain, Victoria Spartz, Scott Fitzgerald

Early Childhood, Elementary, and Secondary Education
Office: 2176 RHOB 20515 **Phone:** 225-3725
Gregorio Kilili Camacho Sablan (Chair), Jahana Hayes, Raúl Grijalva, Frederica S. Wilson, Mark DeSaulnier, Joseph D. Morelle, Lucy McBath, Andy Levin, Kathy E. Manning, Jamaal Bowman, Sheila Cherfillus-McCormick, Robert C. (Bobby) Scott
Burgess Owens (Ranking Minority Member), Glenn Grothman, Rick W. Allen, Fred Keller, Mary E. Miller, Madison Cawthorn, Michelle Steel, Julia Letlow

Health, Employment, Labor, and Pensions
Office: 2176 RHOB 20515 **Phone:** 225-3725
Mark DeSaulnier (Chair), Joe Courtney, Donald Norcross, Joseph D. Morelle, Susan Wild, Lucy McBath, Andy Levin, Haley M. Stevens, Frank J. Mrvan
Rick W. Allen (Ranking Minority Member), Joe Wilson, Tim Walberg, Jim Banks, Diana Harshbarger, Mary E. Miller, Scott Fitzgerald

Higher Education and Workforce Investment
Office: 2176 RHOB 20515 **Phone:** 225-3725
Frederica S. Wilson (Chair), Mark Takano, Pramila Jayapal, Ilhan Omar, Teresa Leger Fernandez, Mondaire Jones, Kathy E. Manning, Jamaal Bowman, Mark Pocan, Joaquin Castro, Mikie Sherrill, Adriano Espaillat, Raúl Grijalva, Joe Courtney, Suzanne Bonamici
Mariannette Miller-Meeks (Ranking Minority Member), Glenn Grothman, Elise M. Stefanik, Jim Banks, James Comer, Russ Fulcher, Bob Good, Lisa C. McClain, Diana Harshbarger, Victoria Spartz, Julia Letlow

Workforce Protections
Office: 2176 RHOB 20515 **Phone:** 225-3725
Alma S. Adams (Chair), Mark Takano, Donald Norcross, Pramila Jayapal, Ilhan Omar, Haley M. Stevens, Mondaire Jones, Sheila Cherfilis-McCormick, Robert C. (Bobby) Scott
Fred Keller (Ranking Minority Member), Elise M. Stefanik, Mariannette Miller-Meeks, Burgess Owens, Bob Good, Madison Cawthorn, Michelle Steel

ENERGY AND COMMERCE

Office: 2125 RHOB 20515-6115
Phone: 225-2927 **Fax:** 225-5735
Web: energycommerce.house.gov
Minority Web: republicans-energycommerce.house.gov
Majority Staff Director: Tiffany Guarascio
Minority Staff Director: Nate Hodson, 225-3641, 2322 RHOB
Jurisdiction: (1) biomedical research and development; (2) consumer affairs and consumer protection; (3) health and health facilities (except health care supported by payroll deductions); (4) interstate energy compacts; (5) interstate and foreign commerce generally; (6) exploration, production, storage, supply, marketing, pricing, and regulation of energy resources, including all fossil fuels, solar energy, and other unconventional or renewable energy resources; (7) conservation of energy resources; (8) energy information generally; (9) the generation and marketing of power (except by federally chartered or federal regional power marketing authorities); the reliability and interstate transmission of, and ratemaking for, all power, and siting of generation facilities, except the installation of interconnections between government water power projects; (10) general management of the Dept. of Energy and management and all functions of the Federal Energy Regulatory Commission; (11) national energy policy generally; (12) public health and quarantine; (13) regulation of the domestic nuclear energy industry, including regulation of research and development reactors and nuclear regulatory research; (14) regulation of interstate and foreign communications; (15) travel and tourism. The committee shall have the same jurisdiction with respect to regulation of nuclear facilities and of use of nuclear energy as it has with respect to regulation of nonnuclear facilities and of use of nonnuclear energy.
Party Ratio: D 32-R 26

Frank Pallone Jr., N.J., Chair
Bobby L. Rush, Ill.
Anna G. Eshoo, Calif.
Diana DeGette, Colo.
Mike F. Doyle, Pa.
Janice D. Schakowsky, Ill.
G. K. Butterfield, N.C.
Doris O. Matsui, Calif.
Kathy Castor, Fla.
John P. Sarbanes, Md.
Jerry McNerney, Calif.

Cathy McMorris Rodgers, Wash.
Fred Upton, Mich.
Michael C. Burgess, Tex.
Steve Scalise, La.
Robert E. Latta, Ohio
Brett Guthrie, Ky.
David B. McKinley, W.Va.
Adam Kinzinger, Ill.
H. Morgan Griffith, Va.
Gus M. Bilirakis, Fla.
Bill Johnson, Ohio

Peter Welch, Vt.
Paul Tonko, N.Y.
Yvette D. Clarke, N.Y.
Kurt Schrader, Ore.
Tony Cárdenas, Calif.
Raul Ruiz, Calif.
Scott H. Peters, Calif.
Debbie Dingell, Mich.
Marc A. Veasey, Tex.
Ann M. Kuster, N.H.
Robin L. Kelly, Ill.
Nanette Diaz Barragán,
  Calif.
A. Donald McEachin, Va.
Lisa Blunt Rochester, Del.
Darren Soto, Fla.
Tom O'Halleran, Ariz.
Kathleen M. Rice, N.Y.
Angie Craig, Minn.
Kim Schrier, Wash.
Lori Trahan, Mass.
Lizzie Fletcher, Tex.

Billy Long, Mo.
Larry Bucshon, Ind.
Markwayne Mullin, Okla.
Richard Hudson, N.C.
Tim Walberg, Mich.
Earl L. (Buddy) Carter, Ga.
Jeff Duncan, S.C.
Gary J. Palmer, Ala.
Neal P. Dunn, Fla.
John R. Curtis, Utah
Debbie Lesko, Ariz.
Greg Pence, Ind.
Dan Crenshaw, Tex.
John Joyce, Pa.
Kelly Armstrong, N.D.

Subcommittees

Communications and Technology
Office: 2125 RHOB 20515   **Phone:** 225-2927
Mike F. Doyle (Chair), Jerry McNerney, Yvette D. Clarke, Marc A. Veasey, A. Donald McEachin, Darren Soto, Tom O'Halleran, Kathleen M. Rice, Anna G. Eshoo, G. K. Butterfield, Doris O. Matsui, Peter Welch, Kurt Schrader, Tony Cárdenas, Robin L. Kelly, Angie Craig, Lizzie Fletcher, Frank Pallone Jr. (ex officio)
Robert E. Latta (Ranking Minority Member), Steve Scalise, Brett Guthrie, Adam Kinzinger, Gus M. Bilirakis, Bill Johnson, Billy Long, Richard Hudson, Markwayne Mullin, Tim Walberg, Earl L. (Buddy) Carter, Jeff Duncan, John R. Curtis, Cathy McMorris Rodgers (ex officio)

Consumer Protection and Commerce
Office: 2125 RHOB 20515   **Phone:** 225-2927
Janice D. Schakowsky (Chair), Bobby L. Rush, Kathy Castor, Lori Trahan, Jerry McNerney, Yvette D. Clarke, Tony Cárdenas, Debbie Dingell, Robin L. Kelly, Darren Soto, Kathleen M. Rice, Angie Craig, Lizzie Fletcher, Frank Pallone Jr. (ex officio)
Gus M. Bilirakis (Ranking Minority Member), Fred Upton, Robert E. Latta, Brett Guthrie, Larry Bucshon, Neal P. Dunn, Greg Pence, Debbie Lesko, Kelly Armstrong, Cathy McMorris Rodgers (ex officio)

Energy
Office: 2125 RHOB 20515   **Phone:** 225-2927
Bobby L. Rush (Chair), Scott H. Peters, Mike F. Doyle, Jerry McNerney, Paul Tonko, Marc A. Veasey, Kim Schrier, Diana DeGette, G. K. Butterfield, Doris O. Matsui, Kathy Castor, Peter Welch, Kurt Schrader, Ann M. Kuster, Nanette Diaz Barragán, A. Donald McEachin, Lisa Blunt Rochester, Tom O'Halleran, Frank Pallone Jr. (ex officio)
Fred Upton (Ranking Minority Member), Michael C. Burgess, Robert E. Latta, David B. McKinley, Adam Kinzinger, H. Morgan Griffith, Bill Johnson, Larry Bucshon,

Tim Walberg, Jeff Duncan, Gary J. Palmer, Debbie Lesko, Greg Pence, Kelly Armstrong, Cathy McMorris Rodgers (ex officio)

Environment and Climate Change
Office: 2125 RHOB 20515   **Phone:** 225-2927
Paul Tonko (Chair), Diana DeGette, Janice D. Schakowsky, John P. Sarbanes, Yvette D. Clarke, Raul Ruiz, Scott H. Peters, Debbie Dingell, Nanette Diaz Barragán, A. Donald McEachin, Lisa Blunt Rochester, Darren Soto, Tom O'Halleran, Frank Pallone Jr. (ex officio)
David B. McKinley (Ranking Minority Member), Bill Johnson, Markwayne Mullin, Richard Hudson, Earl L. (Buddy) Carter, Jeff Duncan, Gary J. Palmer, John R. Curtis, Dan Crenshaw, Cathy McMorris Rodgers (ex officio)

Health
Office: 2125 RHOB 20515   **Phone:** 225-2927
Anna G. Eshoo (Chair), G. K. Butterfield, Doris O. Matsui, Kathy Castor, John P. Sarbanes, Peter Welch, Kurt Schrader, Tony Cárdenas, Raul Ruiz, Debbie Dingell, Ann M. Kuster, Robin L. Kelly, Nanette Diaz Barragán, Lisa Blunt Rochester, Angie Craig, Kim Schrier, Lori Trahan, Lizzie Fletcher, Frank Pallone Jr. (ex officio)
Brett Guthrie (Ranking Minority Member), Fred Upton, Michael C. Burgess, H. Morgan Griffith, Gus M. Bilirakis, Billy Long, Larry Bucshon, Markwayne Mullin, Richard Hudson, Earl L. (Buddy) Carter, Neal P. Dunn, John R. Curtis, Dan Crenshaw, John Joyce, Cathy McMorris Rodgers (ex officio)

Oversight and Investigations
Office: 2125 RHOB 20515   **Phone:** 225-2927
Diana DeGette (Chair), Ann M. Kuster, Kathleen M. Rice, Janice D. Schakowsky, Paul Tonko, Raul Ruiz, Scott H. Peters, Kim Schrier, Lori Trahan, Tom O'Halleran, Frank Pallone Jr. (ex officio)
H. Morgan Griffith (Ranking Minority Member), Michael C. Burgess, David B. McKinley, Billy Long, Neal P. Dunn, John Joyce, Gary J. Palmer, Cathy McMorris Rodgers (ex officio)

ETHICS

Office: 1015 LHOB 20515-6328
Phone: 225-7103   **Fax:** 225-7392
Web: ethics.house.gov
Staff Director and Chief Counsel: Tom Rust
Counsel to the Chair: David Arrojo
Jurisdiction: (1) recommend administrative actions to establish or enforce standards of official conduct; (2) investigate alleged violations of the Code of Official Conduct or of any applicable rules, laws, or regulations governing the performance of official duties or the discharge of official responsibilities. Such investigations must be made in accordance with committee rules; (3) report to appropriate federal or state authorities substantial evidence of a violation of any law applicable to the performance of official duties that may have been disclosed in a committee investigation. Such reports must be approved by the House or by an affirmative vote of two-thirds of the committee;

ETHICS (continued)

(4) render advisory opinions regarding the propriety of any current or proposed conduct of a member, officer, or employee, and issue general guidance on such matters as necessary; (5) consider requests for written waivers of the gift rule (clause 5 of House Rule XXV).
Party Ratio: D 5-R 5

Theodore E. Deutch, Fla.,
  Chair
Susan Wild, Pa.
Dean Phillips, Minn.
Veronica Escobar, Tex.
Mondaire Jones, N.Y.

Jackie Walorski, Ind.
Michael Guest, Miss.
David P. Joyce, Ohio
John H. Rutherford, Fla.
Kelly Armstrong, N.D.

FINANCIAL SERVICES

Office: 2129 RHOB 20515-6050
Phone: 225-4247 **Fax:** 225-6952
Web: financialservices.house.gov
Minority Web: republicans-financialservices.house.gov
Majority Staff Director: Charla Ouertatani
Minority Staff Director: Matt Hoffman, 225-7502, 4340 OHOB
Jurisdiction: (1) banks and banking, including deposit insurance and federal monetary policy; (2) economic stabilization, defense production, renegotiation, and control of the price of commodities, rents, and services; (3) financial aid to commerce and industry (other than transportation); (4) insurance generally; (5) international finance; (6) international financial and monetary organizations; (7) money and credit, including currency and the issuance of notes and redemption thereof; gold and silver, including the coinage thereof; valuation and revaluation of the dollar; (8) public and private housing; (9) securities and exchanges; (10) urban development.
Party Ratio: D 30-R 24

Maxine Waters, Calif.,
  Chair
Carolyn B. Maloney, N.Y.
Nydia M. Velázquez, N.Y.
Brad Sherman, Calif.
Gregory W. Meeks, N.Y.
David Scott, Ga.
Al Green, Tex.
Emanuel Cleaver, Mo.
Ed Perlmutter, Colo.
Jim Himes, Conn.
Bill Foster, Ill.
Joyce Beatty, Ohio
Juan Vargas, Calif.
Josh Gottheimer, N.J.
Vicente Gonzalez, Tex.
Al Lawson, Fla.
Michael San Nicolas,
  Guam.
Cynthia Axne, Iowa
Sean Casten, Ill.
Ayanna Pressley, Mass.

Patrick T. McHenry, N.C.
Frank D. Lucas, Okla.
Pete Sessions, Tex.
Bill Posey, Fla.
Blaine Luetkemeyer, Mo.
Bill Huizenga, Mich.
Ann Wagner, Mo.
Andy Barr, Ky.
Roger Williams, Tex.
J. French Hill, Ark.
Tom Emmer, Minn.
Lee M. Zeldin, N.Y.
Barry Loudermilk, Ga.
Alexander X. Mooney,
  W.Va.
Warren Davidson, Ohio
Ted Budd, N.C.
David Kustoff, Tenn.
Trey Hollingsworth, Ind.
Anthony Gonzalez, Ohio
John W. Rose, Tenn.
Bryan Steil, Wisc.

Ritchie Torres, N.Y.
Stephen F. Lynch, Mass.
Alma S. Adams, N.C.
Rashida Tlaib, Mich.
Madeleine Dean, Pa.
Alexandria Ocasio-Cortez,
  N.Y.
Jesús G. (Chuy) García, Ill.
Sylvia R. Garcia, Tex.
Nikema Williams, Ga.
Jake Auchincloss, Mass.

Lance Gooden, Tex.
William R. Timmons
  IV, S.C.
Van Taylor, Tex.

Subcommittees

Consumer Protection and Financial Institutions
Office: 2129 RHOB 20515 **Phone:** 225-4247
  Ed Perlmutter (Chair), Gregory W. Meeks, David Scott, Nydia M. Velázquez, Brad Sherman, Al Green, Bill Foster, Juan Vargas, Al Lawson, Michael San Nicolas, Sean Casten, Ayanna Pressley, Ritchie Torres
  Blaine Luetkemeyer (Ranking Minority Member), Frank D. Lucas, Bill Posey, Andy Barr, Roger Williams, Barry Loudermilk, Ted Budd, David Kustoff, John W. Rose, William R. Timmons IV

Diversity and Inclusion
Office: 2129 RHOB 20515 **Phone:** 225-4247
  Joyce Beatty (Chair), Ayanna Pressley, Stephen F. Lynch, Rashida Tlaib, Madeleine Dean, Sylvia R. Garcia, Nikema Williams, Jake Auchincloss
  Ann Wagner (Ranking Minority Member), Frank D. Lucas, Ted Budd, Anthony Gonzalez, John W. Rose, Lance Gooden, William R. Timmons IV

Housing, Community Development, and Insurance
Office: 2129 RHOB 20515 **Phone:** 225-4247
  Emanuel Cleaver (Chair), Nydia M. Velázquez, Brad Sherman, Joyce Beatty, Al Green, Vicente Gonzalez, Carolyn B. Maloney, Juan Vargas, Al Lawson, Cynthia Axne, Ritchie Torres
  J. French Hill (Ranking Minority Member), Lance Gooden, Bill Posey, Bill Huizenga, Lee M. Zeldin, Trey Hollingsworth, Bryan Steil, John W. Rose, Van Taylor

Investor Protection, Entrepreneurship, and Capital Markets
Office: 2129 RHOB 20515 **Phone:** 225-4247
  Brad Sherman (Chair), Carolyn B. Maloney, David Scott, Jim Himes, Bill Foster, Gregory W. Meeks, Juan Vargas, Josh Gottheimer, Vicente Gonzalez, Michael San Nicolas, Cynthia Axne, Sean Casten, Emanuel Cleaver
  Bill Huizenga (Ranking Minority Member), Ann Wagner, J. French Hill, Tom Emmer, Alexander X. Mooney, Warren Davidson, Trey Hollingsworth, Anthony Gonzalez, Bryan Steil, Van Taylor

National Security, International Development, and Monetary Policy
Office: 2129 RHOB 20515 **Phone:** 225-4247
  Jim Himes (Chair), Josh Gottheimer, Michael San Nicolas, Ritchie Torres, Stephen F. Lynch, Madeleine Dean, Alexandria Ocasio-Cortez, Jesús G. (Chuy) García, Jake Auchincloss

Andy Barr *(Ranking Minority Member)*, Pete Sessions, Lee M. Zeldin, Roger Williams, Warren Davidson, Anthony Gonzalez, J. French Hill

Oversight and Investigations
Office: 2129 RHOB 20515 **Phone:** 225-4247

Al Green (Chair), Emanuel Cleaver, Alma S. Adams, Rashida Tlaib, Jesús G. (Chuy) García, Sylvia R. Garcia, Nikema Williams

Tom Emmer *(Ranking Minority Member)*, Barry Loudermilk, Alexander X. Mooney, David Kustoff, William R. Timmons IV

FOREIGN AFFAIRS

Office: 2170 RHOB 20515-6050
Phone: 225-5021 **Fax:** 225-5393
Web: foreignaffairs.house.gov
Minority Web: republicans-foreignaffairs.house.gov
Majority Staff Director: Sophia Lafargue
Minority Staff Director: Brendan Shields, 226-8467, 2120 RHOB
Jurisdiction: (1) foreign assistance (including development assistance, Millennium Challenge Corporation, the Millennium Challenge Account, HIV/AIDS in foreign countries, security assistance, and Public Law 480 programs abroad); (2) national security developments affecting foreign policy; (3) strategic planning and agreements; (4) war powers, treaties, executive agreements, and the deployment and use of U.S. Armed Forces; (5) peacekeeping, peace enforcement, and enforcement of United Nations or other international sanctions; (6) arms control and disarmament issues; (7) the International Development Finance Corporation, the U.S. Agency for International Development; (8) activities and policies of the State, Commerce and Defense Departments and other agencies related to the Arms Export Control Act and the Foreign Assistance Act, including export and licensing policy for munitions items and technology and dual-use equipment and technology; (9) international law; (10) promotion of democracy; (11) international law enforcement issues, including narcotics control programs and activities; (12) international cyber issues; (13) U.S. Agency for Global Media; (14) embassy security; (15) international broadcasting; (16) public diplomacy, including international communication, information policy, international education, and exchange programs; (17) the Peace Corps, the American Red Cross. The full Committee will have jurisdiction over legislation with respect to the administration of the Export Administration Act, including the export and licensing of dual-use equipment and technology and other matters related to international economic policy and trade not otherwise assigned to a subcommittee, and with respect to the United Nations, its affiliated agencies, and other international organizations, including assessed and voluntary contributions to such organizations. The full-Committee may conduct oversight and investigations with respect to any matter within the jurisdiction of the Committee as defined in the Rules of the House of Representatives.
Party Ratio: D 27-R 23

Gregory W. Meeks, N.Y., Chair
Brad Sherman, Calif.
Albio Sires, N.J.
Gerald E. Connolly, Va.
Theodore E. Deutch, Fla.
Karen Bass, Calif.
William R. Keating, Mass.
David N. Cicilline, R.I.
Ami Bera, Calif.
Joaquin Castro, Tex.
Dina Titus, Nev.
Ted Lieu, Calif.
Susan Wild, Pa.
Dean Phillips, Minn.
Ilhan Omar, Minn.
Colin Z. Allred, Tex.
Andy Levin, Mich.
Abigail Davis Spanberger, Va.
Chrissy Houlahan, Pa.
Tom Malinowski, N.J.
Andy Kim, N.J.
Sara Jacobs, Calif.
Kathy E. Manning, N.C.
Jim Costa, Calif.
Juan Vargas, Calif.
Vicente Gonzalez, Tex.
Bradley Scott Schneider, Ill.

Michael T. McCaul, Tex.
Christopher H. Smith, N.J.
Steve Chabot, Ohio
Joe Wilson, S.C.
Scott Perry, Pa.
Darrell Issa, Calif.
Adam Kinzinger, Ill.
Lee M. Zeldin, N.Y.
Ann Wagner, Mo.
Brian J. Mast, Fla.
Brian K. Fitzpatrick, Pa.
Ken Buck, Colo.
Tim Burchett, Tenn.
Mark E. Green, Tenn.
Andy Barr, Ky.
W. Gregory Steube, Fla.
Daniel Meuser, Pa.
Claudia Tenney, N.Y.
August Pfluger, Tex.
Peter Meijer, Mich.
Nicole Malliotakis, N.Y.
Ronny Jackson, Tex.
Young Kim, Calif.
Maria Elvira Salazar, Fla.

Subcommittees

Africa, Global Health, and Global Human Rights
Office: 2170 RHOB 20515 **Phone:** 225-5021

Karen Bass (Chair), Dean Phillips, Ilhan Omar, Ami Bera, Susan Wild, Tom Malinowski, Sara Jacobs, David N. Cicilline

Christopher H. Smith *(Ranking Minority Member)*, Darrell Issa, W. Gregory Steube, Daniel Meuser, Young Kim, Ronny Jackson

Asia, the Pacific, Central Asia, and Nonproliferation
Office: 2170 RHOB 20515 **Phone:** 226-6434

Ami Bera (Chair), Brad Sherman, Dina Titus, Andy Levin, Chrissy Houlahan, Andy Kim, Gerald E. Connolly, Ted Lieu, Abigail Davis Spanberger, Kathy E. Manning

Steve Chabot *(Ranking Minority Member)*, Scott Perry, Ann Wagner, Ken Buck, Tim Burchett, Mark E. Green, Andy Barr, Young Kim

Europe, Energy, the Environment, and Cyber
Office: 2170 RHOB 20515 **Phone:** 225-5021

William R. Keating (Chair), Susan Wild, Abigail Davis Spanberger, Albio Sires, Theodore E. Deutch, David N. Cicilline, Dina Titus, Dean Phillips, Jim Costa, Vicente Gonzalez, Bradley Scott Schneider

Brian K. Fitzpatrick *(Ranking Minority Member)*, Ann Wagner, Adam Kinzinger, Brian J. Mast, Daniel Meuser, Claudia Tenney, August Pfluger, Nicole Malliotakis, Peter Meijer

FOREIGN AFFAIRS (continued)

Middle East, North Africa, and Global Counterterrorism

Office: 2170 RHOB 20515   **Phone:** 226-7812

Theodore E. Deutch (Chair), Gerald E. Connolly, David N. Cicilline, Ted Lieu, Colin Z. Allred, Tom Malinowski, Kathy E. Manning, William R. Keating, Brad Sherman, Juan Vargas, Bradley Scott Schneider

Joe Wilson (Ranking Minority Member), Scott Perry, Adam Kinzinger, Lee M. Zeldin, Brian J. Mast, Tim Burchett, W. Gregory Steube, Ronny Jackson, Maria Elvira Salazar

International Development, International Organizations, and Global Corporate Social Impact

Office: 2170 RHOB 20515   **Phone:** 225-5021

Joaquin Castro (Chair), Sara Jacobs, Brad Sherman, Ilhan Omar, Chrissy Houlahan, Andy Kim

Nicole Malliotakis (Ranking Minority Member), Darrell Issa, Lee M. Zeldin, Claudia Tenney

Western Hemisphere, Civilian Security, Migration, and International Economic Policy

Office: 2170 RHOB 20515   **Phone:** 225-3345

Albio Sires (Chair), Joaquin Castro, Andy Levin, Vicente Gonzalez, Juan Vargas

Mark E. Green (Ranking Minority Member), August Pfluger, Maria Elvira Salazar

HOMELAND SECURITY

Office: H2-176 FHOB 20515-6480
Phone: 226-2616   **Fax:** 447-5437
Web: homeland.house.gov
Minority Web: republicans-homeland.house.gov
Majority Staff Director: Hope Goins
Minority Staff Director: Daniel Kroese, 226-2616, 176 FHOB
Jurisdiction: (1) overall homeland security policy; (2) organization and administration of the Department of Homeland Security; (3) functions of the Department of Homeland Security relating to the following: (a) border and port security (except immigration policy and nonborder enforcement); (b) customs (except customs revenue); (c) integration, analysis, and dissemination of homeland security information; (d) domestic preparedness for and collective response to terrorism; (e) research and development; (f) transportation security.
Party Ratio: D 19-R 16

Bennie G. Thompson, Miss., Chair	*John Katko, N.Y.*
Sheila Jackson Lee, Tex.	*Michael T. McCaul, Tex.*
James R. Langevin, R.I.	*Clay Higgins, La.*
Donald M. Payne Jr., N.J.	*Michael Guest, Miss.*
J. Luis Correa, Calif.	*Dan Bishop, N.C.*
Elissa Slotkin, Mich.	*Jefferson Van Drew, N.J.*
Emanuel Cleaver, Miss.	*Ralph Norman, S.C.*
Al Green, Tex.	*Mariannette Miller-Meeks, Iowa*
Yvette D. Clarke, N.Y.	*Diana Harshbarger, Tenn.*
Eric Swalwell, Calif.	*Andrew S. Clyde, Ga.*
Dina Titus, Nev.	*Carlos A. Gimenez, Fla.*
Bonnie Watson Coleman, N.J.	*Jake LaTurner, Kans.*
Kathleen M. Rice, N.Y.	*Peter Meijer, Mich.*
Val Butler Demings, Fla.	*Kat Cammack, Fla.*
Nanette Diaz Barragán, Calif.	*August Pfluger, Tex.*
Josh Gottheimer, N.J.	*Andrew R. Garbarino, N.Y.*
Elaine G. Luria, Va.	
Tom Malinowski, N.J.	
Ritchie Torres, N.Y.	

Subcommittees

Border Security, Facilitation, and Operations

Office: H2-176 FHOB 20515   **Phone:** 226-2616

Nanette Diaz Barragán (Chair), J. Luis Correa, Emanuel Cleaver, Al Green, Yvette D. Clarke, Bennie G. Thompson (ex officio)

Clay Higgins (Ranking Minority Member), Michael Guest, Dan Bishop, Andrew S. Clyde, John Katko (ex officio)

Cybersecurity, Infrastructure Protection, and Innovation

Office: H2-176 FHOB 20515   **Phone:** 226-2616

Yvette D. Clarke (Chair), Sheila Jackson Lee, James R. Langevin, Elissa Slotkin, Kathleen M. Rice, Ritchie Torres, Bennie G. Thompson (ex officio)

Andrew R. Garbarino (Ranking Minority Member), Ralph Norman, Diana Harshbarger, Andrew S. Clyde, Jake LaTurner, John Katko (ex officio)

Emergency Preparedness, Response, and Recovery

Office: H2-176 FHOB 20515   **Phone:** 226-2616

Val Butler Demings (Chair), Sheila Jackson Lee, Donald M. Payne Jr., Al Green, Bonnie Watson Coleman, Bennie G. Thompson (ex officio)

Kat Cammack (Ranking Minority Member), Clay Higgins, Mariannette Miller-Meeks, Andrew R. Garbarino, John Katko (ex officio)

Intelligence and Counterterrorism

Office: H2-176 FHOB 20515   **Phone:** 226-2616

Elissa Slotkin (Chair), Sheila Jackson Lee, James R. Langevin, Eric Swalwell, Josh Gottheimer, Tom Malinowski, Bennie G. Thompson (ex officio)

August Pfluger (Ranking Minority Member), Michael Guest, Jefferson Van Drew, Jake LaTurner, Peter Meijer, John Katko (ex officio)

Oversight, Management, and Accountability

Office: H2-176 FHOB 20515   **Phone:** 226-2616

J. Luis Correa (Chair), Donald M. Payne Jr., Dina Titus, Ritchie Torres, Bennie G. Thompson (ex officio)

Peter Meijer (Ranking Minority Member), Dan Bishop, Diana Harshbarger, John Katko (ex officio)

Transportation and Maritime Security

Office: H2-176 FHOB 20515   **Phone:** 226-2616

Bonnie Watson Coleman (Chair), Donald M. Payne Jr., Dina Titus, Josh Gottheimer, Elaine G. Luria, Bennie G. Thompson (ex officio)

Carlos A. Gimenez (Ranking Minority Member), Jefferson Van Drew, Ralph Norman, Mariannette Miller-Meeks, John Katko (ex officio)

HOUSE ADMINISTRATION

Office: 1309 LHOB 20515-6157
Phone: 225-2061   **Fax:** 226-2774
Web: cha.house.gov
Minority Web: republicans-cha.house.gov
Majority Staff Director: Jamie Fleet
Minority Staff Director: Tim Monahan, 225-8281, 1216 LHOB

Jurisdiction: (1) appropriations from accounts for committee salaries and expenses (except for the Committee on Appropriations), House Information Resources; and allowance and expenses of members, delegates, the resident commissioner, officers, and administrative offices of the House; (2) auditing and settling of all accounts described in (1), above; (3) employment of persons by the House, including staff for members, delegates, the resident commissioner, and committees; and reporters of debates, subject to rule VI; (4) except as provided in clause 1(q)(11), matters relating to the Library of Congress, including management thereof, statuary and pictures, acceptance or purchase of works of art for the U.S. Capitol, the U.S. Botanic Garden, and purchase of books and manuscripts; (5) the Smithsonian Institution and the incorporation of similar institutions (except as provided in paragraph (q)(11)); (6) expenditure of accounts described in (1), above; (7) Franking Commission; (8) printing and correction of the Congressional Record; (9) accounts of the House generally; (10) assignment of office space for members, delegates, the resident commissioner, and committees; (11) disposition of useless executive papers; (12) election of the president, vice president, and members of the House of Representatives, senators, delegates, or the resident commissioner; corrupt practices, contested elections, credentials and qualifications, and federal elections generally; (13) services to the House, including the House Restaurant, parking facilities and administration of the House Office Buildings and of the House wing of the U.S. Capitol; (14) travel of members of the House of Representatives, delegates, and the resident commissioner; (15) raising, reporting, and use of campaign contributions for candidates for office of representative in the House of Representatives, delegate to the House of Representatives, and of resident commissioner; (16) compensation, retirement and other benefits of the members, delegates, the resident commissioner, officers, and employees of the Congress.
Party Ratio: D 6-R 3

Zoe Lofgren, Calif., Chair	*Rodney Davis, Ill.*
Jamie Raskin, Md.	*Barry Loudermilk, Ga.*
G. K. Butterfield, N.C.	*Bryan Steil, Wisc.*
Pete Aguilar, Calif.	
Mary Gay Scanlon, Pa.	
Teresa Leger Fernandez, N.M.	

Subcommittee

Elections
Office: 1309 LHOB 20515   **Phone:** 225-2061
   G. K. Butterfield (Chair), Pete Aguilar, Teresa Leger Fernandez
   Bryan Steil (Ranking Minority Member)

JUDICIARY

Office: 2138 RHOB 20515-6216
Phone: 225-3951   **Fax:** 225-7680
Web: judiciary.house.gov
Minority Web: republicans-judiciary.house.gov
Majority Chief of Staff: Amy Rutkin
Minority Staff Director: Christopher Hixon, 225-6906, 2142 RHOB

Jurisdiction: (1) judiciary and judicial proceedings, civil and criminal; (2) administrative practice and procedure; (3) apportionment of representatives; (4) bankruptcy, mutiny, espionage, and counterfeiting; (5) civil liberties; (6) constitutional amendments; (7) criminal law enforcement; (8) federal courts and judges, and local courts in the territories and possessions; (9) immigration policy and nonborder enforcement; (10) interstate compacts generally; (11) claims against the United States; (12) members of Congress, attendance of members, delegates, and the resident commissioner; and their acceptance of incompatible offices; (13) national penitentiaries; (14) patents, the Patent and Trademark Office, copyrights, and trademarks; (15) presidential succession; (16) protection of trade and commerce against unlawful restraints and monopolies; (17) revision and codification of the Statutes of the United States; (18) state and territorial boundary lines; (19) subversive activities affecting the internal security of the United States.
Party Ratio: D 25-R 19

Jerrold Nadler, N.Y., Chair	*Jim Jordan, Ohio*
Zoe Lofgren, Calif.	*Steve Chabot, Ohio*
Sheila Jackson Lee, Tex.	*Louie Gohmert, Tex.*
Steve Cohen, Tenn.	*Ken Buck, Colo.*
Henry C. (Hank) Johnson Jr., Ga.	*Matt Gaetz, Fla.*
Theodore E. Deutch, Fla.	*Mike Johnson, La.*
Karen Bass, Calif.	*Andy Biggs, Ariz.*
Hakeem S. Jeffries, N.Y.	*Tom McClintock, Calif.*
David N. Cicilline, R.I.	*W. Gregory Steube, Fla.*
Eric Swalwell, Calif.	*Thomas P. Tiffany, Wisc.*
Ted Lieu, Calif.	*Darrell Issa, Calif.*
Jamie Raskin, Md.	*Thomas Massie, Ky.*
Pramila Jayapal, Wash.	*Chip Roy, Tex.*
Val Butler Demings, Fla.	*Dan Bishop, N.C.*
J. Luis Correa, Calif.	*Michelle Fischbach, Minn.*
Mary Gay Scanlon, Pa.	*Victoria Spartz, Ind.*
Sylvia R. Garcia, Tex.	*Scott Fitzgerald, Wisc.*
Joe Neguse, Colo.	*Cliff Bentz, Ore.*
Lucy McBath, Ga.	*Burgess Owens, Utah*
Greg Stanton, Ariz.	
Madeleine Dean, Pa	
Veronica Escobar, Tex.	
Mondaire Jones, N.Y.	
Deborah K. Ross, N.C.	
Cori Bush, Mo.	

Subcommittees

Antitrust, Commercial, and Administrative Law
Office: 6240 OHOB 20024   **Phone:** 226-7680

JUDICIARY (continued)

David N. Cicilline (Chair), Joe Neguse, Eric Swalwell, Mondaire Jones, Theodore E. Deutch, Hakeem S. Jeffries, Jamie Raskin, Pramila Jayapal, Val Butler Demings, Mary Gay Scanlon, Lucy McBath, Madeleine Dean, Henry C. (Hank) Johnson Jr.

Ken Buck (Ranking Minority Member), Darrell Issa, Matt Gaetz, Mike Johnson, W. Gregory Steube, Dan Bishop, Michelle Fischbach, Victoria Spartz, Scott Fitzgerald, Cliff Bentz, Burgess Owens

Constitution, Civil Rights, and Civil Liberties
Office: 2138 RHOB 20515   **Phone:** 225-3951

Steve Cohen (Chair), Jamie Raskin, Deborah K. Ross, Henry C. (Hank) Johnson, Sylvia R. Garcia, Cori Bush, Sheila Jackson Lee

Mike Johnson (Ranking Minority Member), Tom McClintock, Chip Roy, Michelle Fischbach, Burgess Owens

Courts, Intellectual Property, and the Internet
Office: 6240 OHOB 20515-6216   **Phone:** 225-5741

Henry C. (Hank) Johnson (Chair), Theodore E. Deutch, Hakeem S. Jeffries, Ted Lieu, Greg Stanton, Zoe Lofgren, Steve Cohen, Karen Bass, Eric Swalwell, Mondaire Jones, Deborah K. Ross, Joe Neguse

Darrell Issa (Ranking Minority Member), Steve Chabot, Louie Gohmert, Matt Gaetz, Mike Johnson, Thomas P. Tiffany, Thomas Massie, Dan Bishop, Michelle Fischbach, Scott Fitzgerald, Cliff Bentz

Crime, Terrorism, and Homeland Security
Office: 6240 OHOB 20515   **Phone:** 225-5727

Sheila Jackson Lee (Chair), Karen Bass, Val Butler Demings, Lucy McBath, Madeleine Dean, Mary Gay Scanlon, Cori Bush, David N. Cicilline, Ted Lieu, J. Luis Correa, Veronica Escobar, Steve Cohen

Andy Biggs (Ranking Minority Member), Steve Chabot, Louie Gohmert, W. Gregory Steube, Thomas P. Tiffany, Thomas Massie, Victoria Spartz, Scott Fitzgerald, Burgess Owens

Immigration and Citizenship
Office: 6320 OHOB 20515   **Phone:** 225-3926

Zoe Lofgren (Chair), Pramila Jayapal, J. Luis Correa, Sylvia R. Garcia, Veronica Escobar, Sheila Jackson Lee, Joe Neguse, Mary Gay Scanlon

Tom McClintock (Ranking Minority Member), Ken Buck, Andy Biggs, Thomas P. Tiffany, Chip Roy, Victoria Spartz

NATURAL RESOURCES

Office: 1324 LHOB 20515-6201
Phone: 225-6065   **Fax:** 225-5929
Web: naturalresources.house.gov
Minority Web: republicans-naturalresources.house.gov
Majority Staff Director: David Watkins
Minority Staff Director: Vivian Moeglein, 225-2761, 1329 LHOB
Jurisdiction: (1) fisheries and wildlife, including research, restoration, refuges, and conservation; (2) forest reserves and national parks created from the public domain; (3) forfeiture of land grants and alien ownership, including alien ownership of mineral lands; (4) Geological Survey; (5) international fishing agreements; (6) interstate compacts relating to apportionment of waters for irrigation purposes; (7) irrigation and reclamation, including water supply for reclamation projects and easements of public lands for irrigation projects; and acquisition of private lands when necessary to complete irrigation projects; (8) Native Americans generally, including the care and allotment of Native American lands and general and special measures relating to claims that are paid out of Native American funds; (9) insular possessions of the United States generally (except those affecting the revenue and appropriations); (10) military parks and battlefields, national cemeteries administered by the secretary of the interior, parks within the District of Columbia, and the erection of monuments to the memory of individuals; (11) mineral land laws and claims and entries thereunder; (12) mineral resources of public lands; (13) mining interests generally; (14) mining schools and experimental stations; (15) marine affairs, including coastal zone management (except for measures relating to oil and other pollution of navigable waters); (16) oceanography; (17) petroleum conservation on public lands and conservation of the radium supply in the United States; (18) preservation of prehistoric ruins and objects of interest on the public domain; (19) public lands generally, including entry, easements, and grazing thereon; (20) relations of the United States with Native Americans and Native American tribes; (21) Trans-Alaska Oil Pipeline (except ratemaking).

Party Ratio: D 26-R 21

Raúl Grijalva, Ariz., Chair	Bruce Westerman, Ark.
Grace F. Napolitano, Calif.	Louie Gohmert, Tex.
Jim Costa, Calif.	Doug Lamborn, Colo.
Gregorio Kilili Camacho Sablan, N. Mariana Is.	Robert J. Wittman, Va.
	Daniel Webster, Fla.
Jared Huffman, Calif.	Tom McClintock, Calif.
Alan S. Lowenthal, Calif.	Garret Graves, La.
Rubén Gallego, Ariz.	Jody B. Hice, Ga.
Joe Neguse, Colo.	Aumua Amata Coleman Radewagen, Am. Samoa
Mike Levin, Calif.	
Katie Porter, Calif.	Daniel Webster, Fla.
Teresa Leger Fernandez, N.M.	Jenniffer González-Colón, P.R.
Melanie A. Stansbury, N.M.	
Nydia M. Velázquez, N.Y.	Russ Fulcher, Idaho
Diana DeGette, Colo.	Pete Stauber, Minn.
Julia Brownley, Calif.	Thomas P. Tiffany, Wisc.
Debbie Dingell, Mich.	Jerry L. Carl, Ala.
A. Donald McEachin, Va.	Matthew M. Rosendale Sr., Mont.
Darren Soto, Fla.	
Michael San Nicolas, Guam	Blake D. Moore, Utah
Jesús G. (Chuy) García, Ill.	Yvette Herrell, N.M.
Ed Case, Hawaii	Lauren Boebert, Colo.
Betty McCollum, Minn.	Jay Obernolte, Calif.
Steve Cohen, Tenn.	Cliff Bentz, Ore.
Paul Tonko, N.Y.	
Rashida Tlaib, Mich.	
Doris O. Matsui, Calif.	
Lori Trahan, Mass.	

Subcommittees

Energy and Mineral Resources
Office: 1522 LHOB 20515   **Phone:** 225-9297

Alan S. Lowenthal (Chair), A. Donald McEachin, Mike Levin, Katie Porter, Diana DeGette, Betty McCollum, Jared Huffman, Debbie Dingell

Pete Stauber (Ranking Minority Member), Yvette Herrell, Doug Lamborn, Paul A. Gosar, Garret Graves, Thomas P. Tiffany

Indigenous Peoples of the United States
Office: 1331 LHOB 20515   **Phone:** 226-9725

Teresa Leger Fernandez (Chair), Rubén Gallego, Darren Soto, Betty McCollum, Michael San Nicolas, Ed Case, Alan S. Lowenthal, Jesús G. (Chuy) García, Melanie A. Stansbury

Vacant (Ranking Minority Member), Jay Obernolte, Aumua Amata Coleman Radewagen, Jerry L. Carl, Matthew M. Rosendale Sr., Lauren Boebert, Cliff Bentz

National Parks, Forests, and Public Lands
Office: 1328 LHOB 20515   **Phone:** 226-7736

Joe Neguse (Chair), Gregorio Kilili Camacho Sablan, Diana DeGette, Paul Tonko, Rashida Tlaib, Lori Trahan, Rubén Gallego, Teresa Leger Fernandez, Debbie Dingell, Ed Case, Michael San Nicolas, Katie Porter

Russ Fulcher (Ranking Minority Member), Thomas P. Tiffany, Louie Gohmert, Tom McClintock, Doug Lamborn, Matthew M. Rosendale Sr., Jody B. Hice, Blake D. Moore, Yvette Herrell, Jay Obernolte

Oversight and Investigations
Office: H2-186 OHOB 20515   **Phone:** 225-7107

Katie Porter (Chair), Nydia M. Velázquez, Jesús G. (Chuy) García, Steve Cohen, Jared Huffman

Paul A. Gosar (Ranking Minority Member), Blake D. Moore, Louie Gohmert, Jody B. Hice

Water, Oceans, and Wildlife
Office: 1332 LHOB 20515   **Phone:** 225-8331

Jared Huffman (Chair), Grace F. Napolitano, Jim Costa, Mike Levin, Julia Brownley, Debbie Dingell, Ed Case, Alan S. Lowenthal, Steve Cohen, Darren Soto, Nydia M. Velázquez, Melanie A. Stansbury

Cliff Bentz (Ranking Minority Member), Jerry L. Carl, Robert J. Wittman, Tom McClintock, Garret Graves, Aumua Amata Coleman Radewagen, Daniel Webster, Russ Fulcher, Jenniffer González-Colón, Lauren Boebert

OVERSIGHT AND REFORM

Office: 2157 RHOB 20515-6143
Phone: 225-5051   **Fax:** 225-4784
Web: oversight.house.gov
Minority Web: republicans-oversight.house.gov
Majority Staff Director: Russell Anello
Minority Staff Director: Mark Marin, 225-5074, 2105 RHOB
Jurisdiction: (1) federal civil service, including intergovernmental personnel; and the status of officers and employees of the United States, including their compensation, classification, and retirement; (2) municipal affairs of the District of Columbia in general (other than appropriations);

(3) federal paperwork reduction; (4) government management and accounting measures generally; (5) holidays and celebrations; (6) overall economy, efficiency, and management of government operations and activities, including federal procurement; (7) national archives; (8) population and demography generally, including the Census; (9) Postal Service generally, including transportation of the mails; (10) public information and records; (11) relationship of the federal government to the states and municipalities generally; (12) reorganizations in the executive branch of the government.
Party Ratio: D 25-R 20

Carolyn B. Maloney, N.Y., Chair	James Comer, Ky.
	Jim Jordan, Ohio
Eleanor Holmes Norton, D.C.	Paul A. Gosar, Ariz.
Stephen F. Lynch, Mass.	Virginia Foxx, N.C.
Jim Cooper, Tenn.	Jody B. Hice, Ga.
Gerald E. Connolly, Va.	Glenn Grothman, Wisc.
Raja Krishnamoorthi, Ill.	Michael Cloud, Tex.
Jamie Raskin, Md.	Bob Gibbs, Ohio
Ro Khanna, Calif.	Clay Higgins, La.
Kweisi Mfume, Md.	Ralph Norman, S.C.
Alexandria Ocasio-Cortez, N.Y.	Fred Keller, Pa.
	Pete Sessions, Tex.
Rashida Tlaib, Mich.	Andy Biggs, Ariz.
Katie Porter, Calif.	Byron Donalds, Fla.
Cori Bush, Mo.	Nancy Mace, S.C.
Shontel M. Brown, Ohio	Yvette Herrell, N.M.
Danny K. Davis, Ill.	Jake LaTurner, Kans.
Debbie Wasserman Schultz, Fla.	Pat Fallon, Tex.
Peter Welch, Vt.	Andrew S. Clyde, Ga.
Henry C. (Hank) Johnson Jr., Ga.	C. Scott Franklin, Fla.
John P. Sarbanes, Md.	
Jackie Speier, Calif.	
Robin L. Kelly, Ill.	
Brenda L. Lawrence, Mich.	
Mark DeSaulnier, Calif.	
Jimmy Gomez, Calif.	
Ayanna Pressley, Mass.	

Subcommittees

Civil Rights and Civil Liberties
Office: 2157 RHOB 20515   **Phone:** 225-5051

Jamie Raskin (Chair), Kweisi Mfume, Debbie Wasserman Schultz, Robin L. Kelly, Ayanna Pressley, Eleanor Holmes Norton, Alexandria Ocasio-Cortez, Rashida Tlaib, Danny K. Davis

Nancy Mace (Ranking Minority Member), Jim Jordan, Clay Higgins, Pete Sessions, Andy Biggs, C. Scott Franklin, Byron Donalds

Economic and Consumer Policy
Office: 2157 RHOB 20515   **Phone:** 225-5051

Raja Krishnamoorthi (Chair), Katie Porter, Cori Bush, Jackie Speier, Henry C. (Hank) Johnson Jr., Mark DeSaulnier, Ayanna Pressley, Shontel M. Brown

Michael Cloud (Ranking Minority Member), Fred Keller, C. Scott Franklin, Andrew S. Clyde, Byron Donalds

OVERSIGHT AND REFORM (continued)

Environment
Office: 2157 RHOB 20515   **Phone:** 225-5051

Ro Khanna (Chair), Jim Cooper, Alexandria Ocasio-Cortez, Rashida Tlaib, Jimmy Gomez, Raja Krishnamoorthi, Cori Bush
Ralph Norman (Ranking Minority Member), Bob Gibbs, Pat Fallon, Yvette Herrell

Government Operations
Office: 2157 RHOB 20515   **Phone:** 225-5051

Gerald E. Connolly (Chair), Eleanor Holmes Norton, Danny K. Davis, John P. Sarbanes, Brenda L. Lawrence, Stephen F. Lynch, Jamie Raskin, Ro Khanna, Katie Porter, Shontel M. Brown
Jody B. Hice (Ranking Minority Member), Fred Keller, Andrew S. Clyde, Andy Biggs, Nancy Mace, Jake LaTurner, Yvette Herrell

National Security
Office: 2157 RHOB 20515   **Phone:** 225-5051

Stephen F. Lynch (Chair), Peter Welch, Henry C. (Hank) Johnson, Mark DeSaulnier, Kweisi Mfume, Debbie Wasserman Schultz, Jackie Speier
Glenn Grothman (Ranking Minority Member), Virginia Foxx, Bob Gibbs, Clay Higgins

Select Subcommittee on the Coronavirus Crisis
Office: 2157 RHOB 20515   **Phone:** 225-4400

James E. Clyburn (Chair), Maxine Waters, Carolyn B. Maloney, Nydia M. Velázquez, Bill Foster, Jamie Raskin, Raja Krishnamoorthi
Steve Scalise (Ranking Minority Member), Jim Jordan, Mark E. Green, Nicole Malliotakis, Marionette Miller-Meeks

RULES

Office: H-312 CAP 20515-6269
Phone: 225-9091   **Fax:** 226-9191
Web: rules.house.gov
Minority Web: republicans-rules.house.gov
Majority Staff Director: Don Sisson
Minority Staff Director: Kelly Dixon, 225-9191, H-152 CAP
Jurisdiction: (1) the rules and joint rules (other than rules or joint rules relating to the Code of Official Conduct), and order of business of the House; (2) recesses and final adjournments of Congress.
Party Ratio: D 9-R 4

James P. McGovern, Mass., Chair	*Tom Cole, Okla.*
Norma J. Torres, Calif.	*Michael C. Burgess, Tex.*
Ed Perlmutter, Colo.	*Guy Reschenthaler, Pa.*
Jamie Raskin, Md.	*Michelle Fischbach, Minn.*
Mary Gay Scanlon, Pa.	
Joseph D. Morelle, N.Y.	
Mark DeSaulnier, Calif.	
Deborah K. Ross, N.C.	
Joe Neguse, Colo.	

Subcommittees

Expedited Procedures
Office: H-312 CAP 20515   **Phone:** 225-9091

Jamie Raskin (Chair), Deborah K. Ross, Norma J. Torres, Mark DeSaulnier, James P. McGovern
Michelle Fischbach (Ranking Minority Member), Tom Cole

Legislative and Budget Process
Office: H-312 CAP 20515   **Phone:** 225-9091

Joseph D. Morelle (Chair), Mary Gay Scanlon, Deborah K. Ross, Joe Neguse, James P. McGovern
Michael C. Burgess (Ranking Minority Member), Tom Cole

Rules and Organization of the House
Office: H-312 CAP 20515   **Phone:** 225-9091

Norma J. Torres (Chair), Ed Perlmutter, Mary Gay Scanlon, Joe Neguse, James P. McGovern
Guy Reschenthaler (Ranking Minority Member), Tom Cole

SCIENCE, SPACE, AND TECHNOLOGY

Office: 2321 RHOB 20515-6301
Phone: 225-6375   **Fax:** 225-3895
Web: science.house.gov
Minority Web: republicans-science.house.gov
Majority Staff Director: Richard Obermann
Minority Staff Director: Josh Mathis, 225-6371, 2321 RHOB
Jurisdiction: (1) all energy research, development, and demonstration, and projects therefor, and all federally owned or operated nonmilitary energy laboratories; (2) astronautical research and development, including resources, personnel, equipment, and facilities; civil aviation research and development; (3) environmental research and development; (4) marine research; commercial application of energy technology; (5) National Institute of Standards and Technology, standardization of weights and measures and the metric system; (6) National Aeronautics and Space Administration; (7) National Science Foundation; (8) National Weather Service; (9) outer space, including exploration and control thereof; (10) science scholarships; scientific research, development, and demonstration, and projects therefor; (11) the committee shall review and study on a continuing basis laws, programs, and government activities relating to nonmilitary research and development.
Party Ratio: D 22-R 19

Eddie Bernice Johnson, Tex., Chair	*Frank D. Lucas, Okla.*
Zoe Lofgren, Calif.	*Mo Brooks, Ala.*
Suzanne Bonamici, Ore.	*Bill Posey, Fla.*
Ami Bera, Calif.	*Randy K. Weber Sr., Tex.*
Haley M. Stevens, Mich.	*Brian Babin, Tex.*
Mikie Sherrill, N.J.	*Anthony Gonzalez, Ohio*
Jamaal Bowman, N.Y.	*Michael Waltz, Fla.*
Brad Sherman, Calif.	*James R. Baird, Ind.*
Ed Perlmutter, Colo.	*Daniel Webster, Fla.*
Jerry McNerney, Calif.	*Mike Garcia, Calif.*
	Stephanie I. Bice, Okla.

Paul Tonko, N.Y.
Bill Foster, Ill.
Donald Norcross, N.J.
Donald S. Beyer Jr., Va.
Charlie Crist, Fla.
Sean Casten, Ill.
Conor Lamb, Pa.
Deborah K. Ross, N.C.
Gwen Moore, Wisc.
Daniel T. Kildee, Mich,
Susan Wild, Pa.
Lizzie Fletcher, Tex.
Melanie A. Stansbury, N.M.

Young Kim, Calif.
Randy Feenstra, Iowa
Jake LaTurner, Kans.
Carlos A. Gimenez, Fla.
Jay Obernolte, Calif.
Peter Meijer, Mich.
Jake Ellzey, Tex.
Mike Carey, Ohio

Subcommittees

Energy
Office: 2321 RHOB 20515   **Phone:** 225-6375
Suzanne Bonamici (Chair), Haley M. Stevens, Melanie A. Stansbury, Jerry McNerney, Donald Norcross, Sean Casten, Conor Lamb, Deborah K. Ross,
Randy K. Weber Sr. (Ranking Minority Member), James R. Baird, Mike Garcia, Michael Waltz, Carlos A. Gimenez, Peter Meijer, Jay Obernolte

Environment
Office: 2321 RHOB 20515   **Phone:** 225-6375
Mikie Sherrill (Chair), Suzanne Bonamici, Daniel T. Kildee, Lizzie Fletcher, Charlie Crist, Sean Casten
Stephanie I. Bice (Ranking Minority Member), Anthony Gonzalez, Randy Feenstra, Carlos A. Gimenez

Investigations and Oversight
Office: 2321 RHOB 20515   **Phone:** 225-6375
Bill Foster (Chair), Ed Perlmutter, Ami Bera, Gwen Moore, Sean Casten
Jay Obernolte (Ranking Minority Member), Stephanie I. Bice, Mike Carey

Research and Technology
Office: 2321 RHOB 20515   **Phone:** 225-6375
Haley M. Stevens (Chair), Melanie A. Stansbury, Paul Tonko, Gwen Moore, Susan Wild, Bill Foster, Conor Lamb, Deborah K. Ross
Randy Feenstra (Ranking Minority Member), Anthony Gonzalez, James R. Baird, Jake LaTurner, Peter Meijer, Jake Ellzey

Space and Aeronautics
Office: 2321 RHOB 20515   **Phone:** 225-6375
Donald S. Beyer Jr. (Chair), Zoe Lofgren, Ami Bera, Brad Sherman, Ed Perlmutter, Charlie Crist, Donald Norcross
Brian Babin (Ranking Minority Member), Mo Brooks, Bill Posey, Daniel Webster, Young Kim

SMALL BUSINESS

Office: 2361 RHOB 20515-6315
Phone: 225-4038   **Fax:** 225-7209
Web: smallbusiness.house.gov
Minority Web: republicans-smallbusiness.house.gov
Majority Staff Director: Melissa Jung

Minority Staff Director: David Planning, 225-5821, 2069 RHOB
Jurisdiction: (1) Assistance to and protection of small business, including financial aid, regulatory flexibility, and paperwork reduction; (2) participation of small-business enterprises in federal procurement and government contracts; (3) the Committee on Small Business shall study and investigate on a continuing basis the problems of all types of small business.
Party Ratio: D 15-R 11

Nydia M. Velázquez, N.Y., Chair
Jared F. Golden, Maine
Jason Crow, Colo.
Sharice Davids, Kans.
Kweisi Mfume, Md
Dean Phillips, Minn.
Marie Newman, Ill.
Carolyn Bourdeaux, Ga.
Troy Carter, La.
Judy Chu, Calif.
Dwight Evans, Pa.
Antonio Delgado, N.Y.
Chrissy Houlahan, Pa.
Andy Kim, N.J.
Angie Craig, Minn.

Blaine Luetkemeyer, Mo.
Roger Williams, Tex.
Pete Stauber, Minn.
Daniel Meuser, Pa.
Claudia Tenney, N.Y.
Andrew R. Garbarino, N.Y.
Young Kim, Calif.
Beth Van Duyne, Tex.
Byron Donalds, Fla.
Maria Elvira Salazar, Fla.
Scott Fitzgerald, Wisc.

Subcommittees

Contracting and Infrastructure
Office: 2361 RHOB 20515   **Phone:** 225-4038
Kweisi Mfume (Chair), Jared F. Golden, Andy Kim, Marie Newman, Troy Carter
Maria Elvira Salazar (Ranking Minority Member), Pete Stauber, Daniel Meuser, Scott Fitzgerald

Economic Growth, Tax, and Capital Access
Office: 2361 RHOB 20515   **Phone:** 225-4038
Sharice Davids (Chair), Marie Newman, Judy Chu, Dwight Evans, Andy Kim, Carolyn Bourdeaux
Daniel Meuser (Ranking Minority Member), Andrew R. Garbarino, Young Kim, Beth Van Duyne, Byron Donalds

Innovation, Entrepreneurship, and Workforce Development
Office: 2361 RHOB 20515   **Phone:** 225-4038
Jason Crow (Chair), Carolyn Bourdeaux, Chrissy Houlahan, Sharice Davids, Dean Phillips, Marie Newman
Young Kim (Ranking Minority Member), Roger Williams, Claudia Tenney, Andrew R. Garbarino, Maria Elvira Salazar

Oversight, Investigations, and Regulations
Office: 2361 RHOB 20515   **Phone:** 225-4038
Dean Phillips (Chair), Angie Craig, Kweisi Mfume, Judy Chu, Dwight Evans, Sharice Davids
Beth Van Duyne (Ranking Minority Member), Daniel Meuser, Byron Donalds, Scott Fitzgerald

Underserved, Agricultural, and Rural Business Development
Office: 2361 RHOB 20515   **Phone:** 225-4038

SMALL BUSINESS (continued)

Jared F. Golden (Chair), Antonio Delgado, Troy Carter
*Claudia Tenney (Ranking Minority Member), Pete
Stauber, Roger Williams, Maria Elvira Salazar*

TRANSPORTATION AND INFRASTRUCTURE

Office: 2165 RHOB 20515-6256
Phone: 225-4472
Web: transportation.house.gov
Minority Web: republicans-transportation.house.gov
Majority Staff Director: Katherine Dedrick
Minority Staff Director: Paul Sass, 225-9446, 2164 RHOB
Jurisdiction: (1) transportation, including civil aviation,
railroads, water transportation, transportation safety (except
automobile safety and transportation security functions of
the Dept. of Homeland Security), transportation infrastructure, transportation labor, and railroad retirement and
unemployment (except revenue measures related thereto);
(2) Commercial space transportation; (3) Coast Guard,
including lifesaving service, lighthouses, lightships, ocean
derelicts, and the Coast Guard Academy; (4) federal management of emergencies and natural disasters; (5) flood
control and improvement of rivers and harbors; (6) inland
waterways; (7) inspection of merchant marine vessels,
lights and signals, lifesaving equipment, and fire protection
on such vessels; (8) navigation and laws relating thereto,
including pilotage; (9) registering and licensing of vessels
and small boats; (10) rules and international arrangements
to prevent collisions at sea; (11) the Capitol Building, the
Senate and House Office Buildings; (12) constructions or
maintenance of roads and post roads (other than appropriations therefor); (13) construction or reconstruction,
maintenance, and care of buildings and grounds of the
Botanic Garden, the Library of Congress, and the Smithsonian Institution; (14) merchant marine (except for national
security aspects thereof); (15) purchase of sites and construction of post offices, customhouses, federal courthouses, and government buildings within the District of
Columbia; (16) oil and other pollution of navigable waters,
including inland, coastal, and ocean waters; (17) marine
affairs, including coastal zone management, as they relate
to oil and other pollution of navigable waters; (18) public
buildings and occupied or improved grounds of the United
States generally; (19) public works for the benefit of navigation, including bridges and dams (other than international
bridges and dams); (20) related transportation regulatory
agencies (except the Transportation Security Administration); (21) roads and the safety thereof; (22) water power.
Party Ratio: D 37-R 31

Peter A. DeFazio, Ore., Chair	*Sam Graves, Mo.*
Eleanor Holmes Norton, D.C.	*Eric A. (Rick) Crawford, Ark.*
Eddie Bernice Johnson, Tex.	*Bob Gibbs, Ohio*
Rick Larsen, Wash.	*Daniel Webster, Fla.*
Grace F. Napolitano, Calif.	*Thomas Massie, Ky.*
Steve Cohen, Tenn.	*Scott Perry, Pa.*
	Rodney Davis, Ill.

Albio Sires, N.J.	*John Katko, N.Y.*
John Garamendi, Calif.	*Brian Babin, Tex.*
Henry C. (Hank) Johnson Jr., Ga.	*Garret Graves, La.*
André Carson, Ind.	*David Rouzer, N.C.*
Dina Titus, Nev.	*Mike Bost, Ill.*
Sean Patrick Maloney, N.Y.	*Randy K. Weber Sr., Tex.*
Jared Huffman, Calif.	*Doug LaMalfa, Calif.*
Julia Brownley, Calif.	*Bruce Westerman, Ark.*
Frederica S. Wilson, Fla.	*Brian J. Mast, Fla.*
Donald M. Payne Jr., N.J.	*Mike Gallagher, Wisc.*
Alan S. Lowenthal, Calif.	*Brian K. Fitzpatrick, Pa.*
Mark DeSaulnier, Calif.	*Jenniffer González-Colón, P.R.*
Stephen F. Lynch, Mass.	*Troy Balderson, Ohio*
Salud O. Carbajal, Calif.	*Pete Stauber, Minn.*
Anthony G. Brown, Md.	*Tim Burchett, Tenn.*
Tom Malinowski, N.J.	*Dusty Johnson, S.D.*
Greg Stanton, Ariz.	*Jefferson Van Drew, N.J.*
Colin Z. Allred, Tex.	*Michael Guest, Miss.*
Sharice Davids, Kans.	*Troy E. Nehls, Tex.*
Jesús G. (Chuy) García, Ill.	*Nancy Mace, S.C.*
Antonio Delgado, N.Y.	*Nicole Malliotakis, N.Y.*
Chris Pappas, N.H.	*Beth Van Duyne, Tex.*
Conor Lamb, Pa.	*Carlos A. Gimenez, Fla.*
Seth Moulton, Mass.	*Michelle Steel, Calif.*
Jake Auchincloss, Mass.	
Carolyn Bourdeaux, Ga.	
Kaiali'i Kahele, Hawaii	
Marilyn Strickland, Wash.	
Nikema Williams, Ga.	
Marie Newman, Ill.	
Troy Carter, La.	

Subcommittees

Aviation
Office: 2251 RHOB 20515   **Phone:** 226-3220
Rick Larsen (Chair), Steve Cohen, André Carson,
Sharice Davids, Kaiali'i Kahele, Nikema Williams, Henry
C. (Hank) Johnson Jr., Dina Titus, Sean Patrick Maloney,
Julia Brownley, Donald M. Payne Jr., Mark DeSaulnier,
Stephen F. Lynch, Anthony G. Brown, Greg Stanton, Colin
Z. Allred, Conor Lamb, Eleanor Holmes Norton, Eddie
Bernice Johnson, John Garamendi, Peter A. DeFazio
(ex officio)
*Garret Graves (Ranking Minority Member), Thomas
Massie, Scott Perry, John Katko, Brian J. Mast, Mike
Gallagher, Brian K. Fitzpatrick, Troy Balderson, Pete
Stauber, Tim Burchett, Jefferson Van Drew, Troy E. Nehls,
Nancy Mace, Beth Van Duyne, Carlos A. Gimenez, Michelle
Steel, Sam Graves (ex officio)*

Coast Guard and Maritime Transportation
Office: 507 FHOB 20515   **Phone:** 226-3552
Salud O. Carbajal (Chair), Rick Larsen, Jake
Auchincloss, Sean Patrick Maloney, Alan S. Lowenthal,
Anthony G. Brown, Chris Pappas, Peter A. DeFazio
(ex officio)
*Bob Gibbs (Ranking Minority Member), Randy K.
Weber Sr., Mike Gallagher, Jefferson Van Drew, Nicole
Malliotakis, Sam Graves (ex officio)*

Economic Development, Public Buildings, and Emergency Management
Office: 586 FHOB 20515 **Phone:** 225-3014

Dina Titus (Chair), Eleanor Holmes Norton, Sharice Davids, Chris Pappas, Grace F. Napolitano, John Garamendi, Troy Carter, Peter A. DeFazio (ex officio)

Daniel Webster (Ranking Minority Member), Thomas Massie, Jenniffer González-Colón, Michael Guest, Beth Van Duyne, Carlos A. Gimenez, Sam Graves (ex officio)

Highways and Transit
Office: 2251 RHOB 20515 **Phone:** 225-6715

Eleanor Holmes Norton (Chair), Eddie Bernice Johnson, Albio Sires, John Garamendi, Henry C. (Hank) Johnson Jr., Sean Patrick Maloney, Julia Brownley, Frederica S. Wilson, Alan S. Lowenthal, Mark DeSaulnier, Stephen F. Lynch, Anthony G. Brown, Greg Stanton, Colin Z. Allred, Jesús G. (Chuy) García, Antonio Delgado, Chris Pappas, Conor Lamb, Jake Auchincloss, Carolyn Bourdeaux, Marilyn Strickland, Grace F. Napolitano, Jared Huffman, Salud O. Carbajal, Sharice Davids, Seth Moulton, Kaiali'i Kahele, Nikema Williams, Marie Newman, Steve Cohen, Peter A. DeFazio (ex officio)

Rodney Davis (Ranking Minority Member), Eric A. (Rick) Crawford, Bob Gibbs, Thomas Massie, Scott Perry, John Katko, Brian Babin, David Rouzer, Mike Bost, Doug LaMalfa, Bruce Westerman, Mike Gallagher, Brian K. Fitzpatrick, Jenniffer González-Colón, Troy Balderson, Pete Stauber, Tim Burchett, Dusty Johnson, Michael Guest, Troy E. Nehls, Nancy Mace, Nicole Malliotakis, Beth Van Duyne, Carlos A. Gimenez, Michelle Steel, Sam Graves (ex officio)

Railroads, Pipelines, and Hazardous Materials
Office: 2029 RHOB 20515 **Phone:** 226-0727

Donald M. Payne Jr. (Chair), Tom Malinowski, Seth Moulton, Marie Newman, Steve Cohen, Albio Sires, André Carson, Frederica S. Wilson, Jesús G. (Chuy) García, Marilyn Strickland, Grace F. Napolitano, Henry C. (Hank) Johnson Jr., Dina Titus, Jared Huffman, Stephen F. Lynch, Jake Auchincloss, Troy Carter. Peter A. DeFazio (ex officio)

Eric A. (Rick) Crawford (Ranking Minority Member), Scott Perry, Rodney Davis, Mike Bost, Randy K. Weber Sr., Doug LaMalfa, Bruce Westerman, Brian K. Fitzpatrick, Troy Balderson, Pete Stauber, Tim Burchett, Dusty Johnson, Troy E. Nehls, Michelle Steel, Sam Graves (ex officio)

Water Resources and Environment
Office: 585 FHOB 20515 **Phone:** 225-4360

Grace F. Napolitano (Chair), Jared Huffman, Eddie Bernice Johnson, John Garamendi, Alan S. Lowenthal, Tom Malinowski, Antonio Delgado, Chris Pappas, Carolyn Bourdeaux, Frederica S. Wilson, Salud O. Carbajal, Greg Stanton, Eleanor Holmes Norton, Steve Cohen, Peter A. DeFazio (ex officio)

David Rouzer (Ranking Minority Member), Daniel Webster, John Katko, Brian Babin, Garret Graves, Mike Bost, Randy K. Weber Sr., Doug LaMalfa, Bruce Westerman, Brian J. Mast, Jenniffer González-Colón, Nancy Mace, Sam Graves (ex officio)

VETERANS' AFFAIRS
Office: 364 CHOB 20515-6335
Phone: 225-9756 **Fax:** 225-2034
Web: veterans.house.gov
Minority Web: republicans-veterans.house.gov
Majority Staff Director: Matt Reel
Minority Staff Director: Maria Triplaar, 225-9756, 3460 OHOB
Jurisdiction: (1) veterans' measures generally; (2) pensions of all the wars of the United States, general and special; (3) life insurance issued by the government on account of service in the Armed Forces; (4) compensation, vocational rehabilitation, and education of veterans; (5) veterans' hospitals, medical care, and treatment of veterans; (6) Soldiers' and Sailors' Civil Relief; (7) readjustment of servicemen to civilian life; (8) national cemeteries.
Party Ratio: D 17-R 13

Mark Takano, Calif., Chair	*Mike Bost, Ill.*
Julia Brownley, Calif.	*Aumua Amata Coleman*
Conor Lamb, Pa.	*Radewagen, Am. Samoa*
Mike Levin, Calif.	*Jack Bergman, Mich.*
Chris Pappas, N.H.	*Jim Banks, Ind.*
Elaine G. Luria, Va.	*Chip Roy, Tex.*
Frank J. Mrvan, Ind.	*Tracey Mann, Kans.*
Sheila Cherfilus-	*Barry Moore, Ala.*
McCormick, Fla.	*Nancy Mace, S.C.*
Gregorio Kilili Camacho	*Madison Cawthorn, N.C.*
Sablan, N. Mariana Is.	*Troy E. Nehls, Tex.*
Lauren Underwood, Ill.	*Matthew M. Rosendale Sr.,*
Colin Z. Allred, Tex.	*Mont.*
Lois Frankel, Fla.	*Mariannette Miller-Meeks,*
Elissa Slotkin, Mich.	*Iowa*
David Trone, Md.	*Jake Ellzey, Tex.*
Marcy Kaptur, Ohio	
Raul Ruiz, Calif.	
Rubén Gallego, Ariz.	

Subcommittees

Disability Assistance and Memorial Affairs
Office: 364 CHOB 20515 **Phone:** 225-9756

Elaine G. Luria (Chair), Elissa Slotkin, Marcy Kaptur, Raul Ruiz, David Trone

Troy E. Nehls (Ranking Minority Member), Barry Moore, Mariannette Miller-Meeks, Jake Ellzey

Economic Opportunity
Office: 364 CHOB 20515 **Phone:** 226-9756

Mike Levin (Chair), Chris Pappas, Sheila Cherfilus-McCormick, David Trone, Rubén Gallego

Barry Moore (Ranking Minority Member), Tracey Mann, Nancy Mace, Madison Cawthorn

Health
Office: 364 CHOB 20515 **Phone:** 225-9756

Julia Brownley (Chair), Frank J. Mrvan, Conor Lamb, Mike Levin, Gregorio Kilili Camacho Sablan, Lauren Underwood, Colin Z. Allred, Lois Frankel

Jack Bergman (Ranking Minority Member), Aumua Amata Coleman Radewagen, Chip Roy, Matthew M. Rosendale Sr., Mariannette Miller-Meeks, Jake Ellzey

VETERANS' AFFAIRS (continued)

Oversight and Investigations
Office: 364 CHOB 20515 **Phone:** 225-9756
Chris Pappas (Chair), Conor Lamb, Elaine G. Luria, Lauren Underwood
Tracey Mann (Ranking Minority Member), Aumua Amata Coleman Radewagen, Jack Bergman

Technology Modernization
Office: 364 CHOB 20515 **Phone:** 225-9756
Frank J. Mrvan (Chair), Mark Takano, Sheila Cherfilus-McCormick
Matthew M. Rosendale Sr. (Ranking Minority Member), Jim Banks

WAYS AND MEANS

Office: 1102 LHOB 20515
Phone: 225-3625 **Fax:** 225-5680
Web: waysandmeans.house.gov
Minority Web: gop-waysandmeans.house.gov
Majority Staff Director: Brandon Casey
Minority Staff Director: Gary Andres, 225-4021, 1139 LHOB
Jurisdiction: (1) customs revenue, collection districts, and ports of entry and delivery; (2) reciprocal trade agreements; (3) revenue measures generally; (4) revenue measures relating to insular possessions; (5) bonded debt of the United States, subject to the last sentence of clause 4(f). Clause 4(f) requires the Committee on Ways and Means to include in its annual report to the Committee on the Budget a specific recommendation, made after holding public hearings, as to the appropriate level of the public debt that should be set forth in the concurrent resolution on the budget; (6) deposit of public monies; (7) transportation of dutiable goods; (8) tax-exempt foundations and charitable trusts; (9) National Social Security (except health care and facilities programs that are supported from general revenues as opposed to payroll deductions and except work incentive programs).
Party Ratio: D 25-R 18

Richard E. Neal, Mass., Chair	*Kevin Brady, Tex.*
Lloyd Doggett, Tex.	*Vern Buchanan, Fla.*
Mike Thompson, Calif.	*Adrian Smith, Neb.*
John B. Larson, Conn.	*Tom Reed, N.Y.*
Earl Blumenauer, Ore.	*Mike Kelly, Pa.*
Ron Kind, Wisc.	*Jason Smith, Mo.*
Bill Pascrell Jr., N.J.	*Tom Rice, S.C.*
Danny K. Davis, Ill.	*David Schweikert, Ariz.*
Linda T. Sánchez, Calif.	*Jackie Walorski, Ind.*
Brian Higgins, N.Y.	*Darin LaHood, Ill.*
Terri A. Sewell, Ala.	*Brad R. Wenstrup, Ohio*
Suzan K. DelBene, Wash.	*Jodey C. Arrington, Tex.*
Judy Chu, Calif.	*A. Drew Ferguson IV, Ga.*
Gwen Moore, Wisc.	*Ron Estes, Kans.*
Daniel T. Kildee, Mich.	*Lloyd Smucker, Pa.*
Brendan F. Boyle, Pa.	*Kevin Hern, Okla.*
Donald S. Beyer Jr., Va.	*Carol D. Miller, W.Va.*
	Gregory F. Murphy, N.C.

Dwight Evans, Pa.
Bradley Scott Schneider, Ill.
Thomas R. Suozzi, N.Y.
Jimmy Panetta, Calif.
Stephanie N. Murphy, Fla.
Jimmy Gomez, Calif.
Steven Horsford, Nev.
Stacey E. Plaskett, V.I.

Subcommittees

Health
Office: 1102 LHOB 20515 **Phone:** 225-3625
Lloyd Doggett (Chair), Mike Thompson, Ron Kind, Earl Blumenauer, Brian Higgins, Terri A. Sewell, Judy Chu, Dwight Evans, Bradley Scott Schneider, Jimmy Gomez, Steven Horsford
Vern Buchanan (Ranking Minority Member), Adrian Smith, Tom Reed, Mike Kelly, Jason Smith, David Schweikert, Brad R. Wenstrup, Gregory F. Murphy

Oversight
Office: 1102 LHOB 20515 **Phone:** 225-3625
Bill Pascrell Jr. (Chair), Thomas R. Suozzi, Judy Chu, Bradley Scott Schneider, Stacey E. Plaskett, Lloyd Doggett, Dwight Evans, Steven Horsford
Tom Rice (Ranking Minority Member), Jackie Walorski, Gregory F. Murphy, A. Drew Ferguson IV, Carol D. Miller

Select Revenue Measures
Office: 1102 LHOB 20515 **Phone:** 225-3625
Mike Thompson (Chair), Lloyd Doggett, John B. Larson, Linda T. Sánchez, Suzan K. DelBene, Gwen Moore, Brendan F. Boyle, Thomas R. Suozzi, Stacey E. Plaskett, Terri A. Sewell
Mike Kelly (Ranking Minority Member), Tom Rice, David Schweikert, Darin LaHood, Jodey C. Arrington, A. Drew Ferguson IV, Kevin Hern, Ron Estes

Social Security
Office: 1102 LHOB 20515 **Phone:** 225-3625
John B. Larson (Chair), Bill Pascrell Jr., Linda T. Sánchez, Daniel T. Kildee, Brendan F. Boyle, Bradley Scott Schneider, Brian Higgins
Tom Reed (Ranking Minority Member), Kevin Hern, Tom Rice, Jodey C. Arrington, Ron Estes

Trade
Office: 1102 LHOB 20515 **Phone:** 225-6649
Earl Blumenauer (Chair), Bill Pascrell Jr., Ron Kind, Danny K. Davis, Brian Higgins, Daniel T. Kildee, Jimmy Panetta, Stephanie N. Murphy, Terri A. Sewell, Suzan K. DelBene, Donald S. Beyer Jr.
Adrian Smith (Ranking Minority Member), Vern Buchanan, Darin LaHood, Jodey C. Arrington, A. Drew Ferguson IV, Ron Estes, Carol D. Miller, Lloyd Smucker

Worker and Family Support
Office: 1102 LHOB 20515 **Phone:** 225-3625
Danny K. Davis (Chair), Terri A. Sewell, Judy Chu, Gwen Moore, Dwight Evans, Stephanie N. Murphy, Jimmy Gomez
Jackie Walorski (Ranking Minority Member), Brad R. Wenstrup, Carol D. Miller, Lloyd Smucker, Kevin Hern

PERMANENT SELECT INTELLIGENCE

Office: HVC-304 CAP 20515-6415
Phone: 225-7690   **Fax:** 226-5068
Web: intelligence.house.gov
Minority Web: republicans-intelligence.house.gov
Majority Staff Director: Jeffrey Lowenstein
Minority Staff Director: George Pappas, 225-4121
Jurisdiction: There shall be referred to the select committee proposed legislation, messages, petitions, memorials and other matters relating to the following: (1) the Central Intelligence Agency, the Director of National Intelligence and the National Intelligence Program as defined in section 3(6) of the National Security Act of 1947; (2) intelligence and intelligence-related activities of all other departments and agencies of the government, including the tactical intelligence and intelligence-related activities of the Department of Defense; (3) the organization or reorganization of the government to the extent that the organization or reorganization relates to a function or activity involving intelligence or intelligence-related activities; (4) authorizations for appropriations, both direct and indirect, for the following: (a) the Central Intelligence Agency, the Director of National Intelligence, and the National Intelligence Program as defined in section 3(6) of the National Security Act of 1947; (b) intelligence and intelligence-related activities of all other departments and agencies of the government, including the tactical intelligence and intelligence-related activities of the Department of Defense; (c) a department, agency, subdivision, or program that is a successor to an agency or program named to or referred to in (a) or (b).
Party Ratio: D 13-R 10

Adam B. Schiff, Calif., Chair	Michael R. Turner, Ohio
Jim Himes, Conn.	Brad R. Wenstrup, Ohio
André Carson, Ind.	Chris Stewart, Utah
Jackie Speier, Calif.	Eric A. (Rick) Crawford, Ark.
Mike Quigley, Ill.	Elise M. Stefanik, N.Y.
Eric Swalwell, Calif.	Markwayne Mullin, Okla.
Joaquin Castro, Tex.	Trent Kelly, Miss.
Peter Welch, Vt.	Darin LaHood, Ill.
Sean Patrick Maloney, N.Y.	Brian K. Fitzpatrick, Pa.
Val Butler Demings, Fla.	Mike Gallagher, Wisc.
Raja Krishnamoorthi, Ill.	
Jim Cooper, Tenn.	
Jason Crow, Colo.	

Subcommittees

Counterterrorism, Counterintelligence, and Counterproliferation
Office: HVC-304 CAP 20515   **Phone:** 225-7690
André Carson (Chair), Jackie Speier, Mike Quigley, Joaquin Castro, Peter Welch, Sean Patrick Maloney
Eric A. (Rick) Crawford (Ranking Minority Member), Brad R. Wenstrup, Chris Stewart, Elise Stefanik, Darin LaHood

Defense Intelligence and Warfighter Support
Office: HVC-304 CAP 20515   **Phone:** 225-7690

Terri A. Sewell (Chair), Jim Himes, Peter Welch, Sean Patrick Maloney, Val Butler Demings
Brad R. Wenstrup (Ranking Minority Member), Eric A. (Rick) Crawford, Markwayne Mullin, Trent Kelly, Brian K. Fitzpatrick

Intelligence Modernization and Readiness
Office: HVC-304 CAP 20515   **Phone:** 225-7690
Eric Swalwell (Chair), Terri A. Sewell, Jackie Speier, Joaquin Castro, Val Demings, Raja Krishnamoorthi
Markwayne Mullin (Ranking Minority Member), Trent Kelly, Darin LaHood, Brian K. Fitzpatrick, Mike Gallagher

Strategic Technologies and Advanced Research
Office: HVC-304 CAP 20515   **Phone:** 225-7690
Jim Himes (Chair), André Carson, Mike Quigley, Denny Heck, Eric Swalwell, Raja Krishnamoorthi
Chris Stewart (Ranking Minority Member), Michael Turner, Elise Stefanik, Markwayne Mullin, Mike Gallagher,

SELECT COMMITTEE ON THE CLIMATE CRISIS

Office: H2-359 FHOB 20515
Phone: 225-1106
Web: climatecrisis.house.gov
Minority Web: republicans-climatecrisis.house.gov
Majority Staff Director: Ana Unruh Cohen
Minority Staff Director: Vacant, 225-1107, H2-361
Jurisdiction: The sole authority of the Select Committee shall be to investigate, study, make findings, and develop recommendations on policies, strategies, and innovations to achieve substantial and permanent reductions in pollution and other activities that contribute to the climate crisis, which will honor our responsibility to be good stewards of the planet for future generations. The Select Committee may, at its discretion, hold public hearings in connection with any aspect of its investigative functions.
Party Ratio: D 9-R 7

Kathy Castor, Fla., Chair	Garret Graves, La.
Suzanne Bonamici, Ore.	Gary J. Palmer, Ala.
Julia Brownley, Calif.	Earl L. (Buddy) Carter, Ga.
Jared Huffman, Calif.	Carol D. Miller, W.Va.
A. Donald McEachin, Va.	Kelly Armstrong, N.D.
Mike Levin, Calif.	Dan Crenshaw, Tex.
Sean Casten, Ill.	Anthony Gonzalez, Ohio
Joe Neguse, Colo.	
Veronica Escobar, Tex.	

SELECT COMMITTEE ON THE MODERNIZATION OF CONGRESS

Office: 164 CHOB 20515
Phone: 225-1530   **Fax:** 225-1580
Web: modernizecongress.house.gov
Majority Staff Director: Yuri Beckelman
Minority Staff Director: Derek Harley
Jurisdiction: The sole authority shall be to investigate, study, make findings, hold public hearings, and develop recommendations on modernizing Congress. This includes

recommendations on (1) procedures, including the schedule and calendar; (2) policies to develop the next generation of leaders; (3) staff recruitment, diversity, retention, compensation, and benefits; (4) administrative efficiencies, including purchasing, travel, outside services, and shared administrative staff; (5) technology and innovation.

Party Ratio: D 6-R 6

Derek Kilmer, Wash., Chair	*William R. Timmons IV, S.C.*
	Rodney Davis, Ill.
Emanuel Cleaver, Miss.	*Robert E. Latta, Ohio*
Zoe Lofgren, Calif.	*Guy Reschenthaler, Pa.*
Ed Perlmutter, Colo.	*Beth Van Duyne, Tex.*
Dean Phillips, Minn.	*David P. Joyce, Ohio*
Nikema Williams, Ga.	

SELECT COMMITTEE TO INVESTIGATE THE JANUARY 6TH ATTACK ON THE U.S. CAPITOL

Office: LHOB
Phone: 225-7800
Web: january6th.house.gov
Staff Director: David Buckley
Jurisdiction: Consistent with the functions described in section 4, the purposes of the Select Committee are the following: (1) to investigate and report upon the facts, circumstances, and causes relating to the January 6, 2021, domestic terrorist attack upon the United States Capitol Complex (hereafter referred to as the "domestic terrorist attack on the Capitol") and relating to the interference with the peaceful transfer of power, including facts and causes relating to the preparedness and response of the United States Capitol Police and other federal, state, and local law enforcement agencies in the National Capital Region and other instrumentalities of government, as well as the influencing factors that fomented such an attack on American representative democracy while engaged in a constitutional process; (2) to examine and evaluate evidence developed by relevant federal, state, and local governmental agencies regarding the facts and circumstances surrounding the domestic terrorist attack on the Capitol and targeted violence and domestic terrorism relevant to such terrorist attack; (3) to build upon the investigations of other entities and avoid unnecessary duplication of efforts by reviewing the investigations, findings, conclusions, and recommendations of other executive branch, congressional, or independent bipartisan or nonpartisan commission investigations into the domestic terrorist attack on the Capitol, including investigations into influencing factors related to such attack.

Party Ratio: D 7-R 2

Bennie G. Thompson, Miss., Chair	*Liz Cheney, Wyo.*
	Adam Kinzinger, Ill.
Zoe Lofgren, Calif.	
Elaine G. Luria, Va.	
Adam B. Schiff, Calif.	
Pete Aguilar, Calif.	
Stephanie N. Murphy, Fla.	
Jamie Raskin, Md.	

HOUSE LEADERSHIP AND PARTISAN COMMITTEES

DEMOCRATIC LEADERS

Speaker of the House: Nancy Pelosi, Calif.
Majority Leader: Steny H. Hoyer, Md.
Majority Whip: James E. Clyburn, S.C.
Assistant Speaker: Katherine M. Clark, Mass.

DEMOCRATIC PARTISAN COMMITTEES

Democratic Congressional Campaign Committee
Office: 430 S. Capitol St. S.E. 20003-4024
Phone: 863-1500
Web: www.dccc.org
Email: dccc@dccc.org
Sean Patrick Maloney, N.Y., Chair

Other Leadership (in alphabetical order)
Tim Persico, Executive Director
Jackie Forte-Mackay, Chief Financial Officer
Alex Smith, Chief of Staff
Chris Hayden, Communications Director
Rep. Don Beyer, Finance Chair
Reps. Steven Horsford and Jennifer Wexton, Frontline Co-Chairs
Rep. Marc Veasey, Recruitment Co-Chairs
Rep. Barbara Lee, Winning with Women of Color Chair

Democratic Caucus
Office: B245 LHOB 20515
Phone: 225-1400   **Fax:** 226-4412
Web: www.dems.gov
Hakeem S. Jeffries, N.Y., Chair
Pete Aguilar, Calif., Vice Chair

REPUBLICAN LEADERS

Minority Leader: Kevin McCarthy, Calif.
Minority Whip: Steve Scalise, La.
Republican Conference Chairman: Elise M. Stefanik, N.Y.

REPUBLICAN PARTISAN COMMITTEES

National Republican Congressional Committee
Office: 425 2nd St. N.E., Washington, D.C. 20002
Phone: 675-6000   **Fax:** 484-2543
Web: www.nrcc.org
Tom Emmer, Minn., Chair

Other Leadership (in alphabetical order)
Katy Williams, Chief Financial Officer
Michael McAdams, Communications Director
John Billings, Executive Director
Rep. Darin LaHood, Finance Chair
Rep. John Katko, Member Services Chair
Rep. Anthony Gonzalez, Outreach Chair
Rep. Richard Hudson, Patriot Chair

Justin Richards, Political Director
Rep. Carol D. Miller, Recruitment Chair
Rep. Mario Diaz-Balart, Redistricting Chair
Matt Wall, Research Director

Republican Conference
Office: 1420 LHOB 20515
Phone: 225-5107   **Fax:** 226-0154
Web: www.gop.gov
Elise Stefanik, N.Y., Chair
Jason Smith, Mo., Secretary

Republican Policy Committee
Office: 207 CHOB 20515
Phone: 225-4921   **Fax:** 225-2082
Web: republicanpolicy.house.gov
Gary J. Palmer, Ala., Chair

Republican Steering Committee
Office: 2468 RHOB 20515
Phone: 225-2915   **Fax:** 225-2908
Web: gop.gov/steering-committee
Kevin McCarthy, Calif., Minority Leader

House Members' Offices

Listed below are House members and their party, state, and district affiliation, followed by the address and telephone number for their Washington office. The area code for all Washington, DC, numbers is (202). The top administrative aide, website, Facebook page, and Twitter account for each member are also provided, when available. Most members may be contacted via the web-based email forms found on their websites. These are followed by the address, telephone and fax numbers, and name of a key aide in the member's district office(s), where available. Each listing concludes with the representative's committee assignments. For partisan committee assignments, see pages 864–865.

As of May 12, 2022, there were 221 Democrats, 209 Republicans, 0 Independents, 5 vacancies, and 6 nonvoting members in the House of Representatives.

Adams, Alma S., D-N.C. (12)

Capitol Hill Office: 2436 RHOB 20515-3312; 225-1510; Fax: 225-1512; *Chief of Staff:* John Christie
Web: adams.house.gov
Facebook: www.facebook.com/CongresswomanAdams
Twitter: @RepAdams
YouTube: www.youtube.com/channel/UCPI9ao1Cr1nxEUD2r-usRjQ
Instagram: @repadams
District Office: 801 E. Morehead St., #150, Charlotte, NC 28202; 704-344-9950; Fax: 704-344-9971; *District Director:* Phanalphie Rhue
Committee Assignments: Agriculture; Education and Labor; Financial Services

Aderholt, Robert B., R-Ala. (4)

Capitol Hill Office: 266 CHOB 20515; 225-4876; Fax: 225-5587; *Chief of Staff:* Kerry Knott
Web: aderholt.house.gov
Facebook: www.facebook.com/RobertAderholt
Twitter: @Robert_Aderholt
YouTube: www.youtube.com/RobertAderholt
Instagram: @robert_aderholt
District Offices: 205 4th Ave. N.E., #104, Cullman, AL 35055-1965; 256-734-6043; *Director of Constituent Services:* Jennifer Taylor
Federal Bldg., 600 Broad St., #107, Gadsden, AL 35901-3745; 256-546-0201; *Field Rep.:* Pam Abernathy
Carl Elliott Federal Bldg., 1710 Alabama Ave., #247, Jasper, AL 35501-5400; 205-221-2310; *District Field Director:* Paul Housel
1011 George Wallace Blvd., #146, Tuscumbia, AL 35674; 256-381-3450; *Field Rep.:* Kreg Kennedy
Committee Assignments: Appropriations; Commission on Security and Cooperation in Europe

Aguilar, Pete, D-Calif. (31)

Capitol Hill Office: 109 CHOB 20515; 225-3201; Fax: 226-6962; *Chief of Staff:* Boris Medzhibovsky
Web: aguilar.house.gov
Facebook: www.facebook.com/reppeteaguilar
Twitter: @RepPeteAguilar
YouTube: www.youtube.com/channel/UCxwbFLOlKDsXrwizV5jah7g
Instagram: @rep.peteaguilar
District Office: 685 E. Carnegie Dr., #100, San Bernardino, CA 92408; 909-890-4445; Fax: 909-890-9643; *District Director:* Teresa Valdez
Committee Assignments: Appropriations; House Administration

Allen, Rick W., R-Ga. (12)

Capitol Hill Office: 570 CHOB 20515; 225-2823; Fax: 225-3377; *Chief of Staff:* Lauren Hodge
Web: allen.house.gov
Facebook: www.facebook.com/CongressmanRickAllen
Twitter: @RepRickAllen
YouTube: www.youtube.com/channel/UCZPoYXHFDAV17BGLMzGAmpg
Instagram: @rep_rickallen
District Offices: 2743 Perimeter Pkwy., Bldg. 200, #105, Augusta, GA 30909; 706-228-1980; Fax: 706-228-1954; *District Director:* Brinsley Thigpen
100 S. Church St., Dublin, GA 31021; 478-272-4030; Fax: 478-277-0113; *District Director:* Brinsley Thigpen
50 E. Main St., Statesboro, GA 30458; 912-243-9452; Fax: 912-243-9453; *District Director:* Brinsley Thigpen
107 Old Airport Rd., Suite A, Vidalia, GA 430474; 912-403-3311; Fax: 912-403-3317; *District Director:* Brinsley Thigpen
Committee Assignments: Agriculture; Education and Labor

Allred, Colin Z., D-Tex. (32)

Capitol Hill Office: 114 CHOB 20515-3515; 225-2231; *Chief of Staff:* Paige Hutchinson
Web: allred.house.gov
Facebook: www.facebook.com/RepColinAllred
Twitter: @RepColinAllred
YouTube: www.youtube.com/channel/UCm3l7ZntoH0EI2vIsvxeVqg
Instagram: @repcolinallred
District Office: 100 N. Central Expressway, #602, Richardson, TX 75080; 972-972-7949; Fax: 888-671-0539; *District Director:* Judith Tankel
Committee Assignments: Foreign Affairs; Transportation and Infrastructure; Veterans' Affairs

Amodei, Mark E., R-Nev. (2)

Capitol Hill Office: 104 CHOB 20515; 225-6155;
Fax: 225-5679; *Chief of Staff:* Molly Lowe
Web: amodei.house.gov
Facebook: www.facebook.com/MarkAmodeiNV2
Twitter: @MarkAmodeiNV2
YouTube: .www.youtube.com/MarkAmodeiNV2
Instagram: @markamodeinv2
District Office: 5310 Kietzke Lane, #103, Reno, NV 89511;
775-686-5760; Fax: 775-686-5711; *District Director:*
Stacy Parobek
Committee Assignment: Appropriations

Armstrong, Kelly, R-N.D. (At Large)

Capitol Hill Office: 1740 LHOB 20515; 225-2611;
Fax: 226-3410; *Chief of Staff:* Roz Leighton
Web: armstrong.house.gov
Facebook: www.facebook.com/RepArmstrongND
Twitter: @RepArmstrongND
YouTube: www.youtube.com/channel/UClBpZFDXVlzJY-
AcG8fXRxw
Instagram: @reparmstrongnd
District Offices: U.S. Federal Bldg., 220 E. Rosser Ave.,
#228, Bismarck, ND 58501; 701-354-6700; *District
Director:* Mary Christy
3217 Fiechtner Dr., Suite B, Fargo, ND 58103; 701-353-
6665; Fax: (844) 315-6438; *District Director:* Mary
Christy
Committee Assignment: Energy and Commerce

Arrington, Jodey C., R-Tex. (19)

Capitol Hill Office: 1107 LHOB 20515; 225-4005;
Fax: 225-9615; *Chief of Staff:* Elle Ciapciak
Web: arrington.house.gov
Facebook: www.facebook.com/JodeyArringtonTX19
Twitter: @RepArrington
YouTube: www.youtube.com/channel/
UCzNP7vqSUoqWdPJX3UGco3w
Instagram: @repjodeyarrington
District Offices: 500 Chestnut St., #819, Abilene, TX
79602; 325-675-9779; Fax: 325-675-5038; *District
Director:* Kaley Mathis
1312 Texas Ave., #219, Lubbock, TX 79401; 806-763-1611;
Fax: 806-767-9168; *District Director:* Lindley Herring
Committee Assignments: Joint Economic; Ways and Means

Auchincloss, Jake, D-Mass. (4)

Capitol Hill Office: 1524 LHOB 20515; 225-5931;
Fax: 225-0182; *Chief of Staff:* Tim Hysom
Web: auchincloss.house.gov
Facebook: www.facebook.com/RepAuchincloss
Twitter: @RepAuchincloss
YouTube: www.youtube.com/channel/
UCLTp0xAT0gBrF8WReNliMwA
Instagram: @repauchincloss
District Offices: 8 N. Main St., #200, Attleboro, MA 02703;
508-431-1110; *District Rep.:* Krista Woods
29 Crafts St., #375, Newton, MA 02458; 617-332-3333;
District Director: Dana Hanson

Committee Assignments: Financial Services;
Transportation and Infrastructure

Axne, Cynthia, D-Iowa (3)

Capitol Hill Office: 1034 LHOB 20515-3515; 225-5476;
Fax: 225-3301; *Chief of Staff:* Joseph Diver
Web: axne.house.gov
Facebook: www.facebook.com/RepCindyAxne
Twitter: @RepCindyAxne
Instagram: @repcindyaxne
District Offices: 501 5th Ave., Council Bluffs, IA 51503;
712-890-3117; *District Director:* Kaitryn Patchett
208 West Taylor, Creston, IA 50801; 641-278-1828;
District Director: Kaitryn Patchett
400 East Court Ave., #346, Des Moines, IA 50309; 515-400-
8180; *District Director:* Kaitryn Patchett; *Field Rep.:*
Tyler Alessio
Committee Assignments: Agriculture; Financial Services

Babin, Brian, R-Tex. (36)

Capitol Hill Office: 2236 RHOB 20515-4336; 225-1555;
Fax: 226-0396; *Chief of Staff:* Steve Janushkowsky
Web: babin.house.gov
Facebook: www.facebook.com/RepBrianBabin
Twitter: @RepBrianBabin
YouTube: www.youtube.com/c/briancbabin
Instagram: @rep.brianbabin
District Offices: 203 Ivy Ave., #600, Deer Park, TX 77536;
832-780-0966; Fax: 832-780-0964; *District Director:*
Kelly Waterman
812 N. 16th St., Orange, TX 77630-5803; 409-883-8075;
Fax: 409-886-9918; *Senior Regional Director:* Lanie
Brown
Tyler County Courthouse, 100 W. Bluff Dr., Woodville, TX
75979; 409-331-8066; *Senior Regional Director:* Rachel
Iglesias
Liberty Satellite Office: Dayton Police Station, 2004 N.
Cleveland St., Dayton, TX 77536; 832-780-0966
Committee Assignments: Science, Space, and Technology;
Transportation and Infrastructure

Bacon, Don, R-Neb. (2)

Capitol Hill Office: 1024 LHOB 20515; 225-4155; *Chief of
Staff:* Mark Dreiling
Web: bacon.house.gov
Facebook: www.facebook.com/RepDonBacon
Twitter: @RepDonBacon
YouTube: www.youtube.com/c/RepDonBacon
Instagram: @repdonbacon
District Office: 13906 Gold Circle, #101, Omaha, NE
68144; 402-938-0300; Fax: 402-763-4947 *District
Director:* James Wright
Committee Assignments: Agriculture; Armed Services

Baird, James R., R-Ind. (4)

Capitol Hill Office: 1314 LHOB 20515; 225-5037;
Fax: 226-0544; *Chief of Staff:* Quincy Cunningham
Web: baird.house.gov
Facebook: www.facebook.com/RepJimBaird

Twitter: @RepJimBaird
YouTube: www.youtube.com/RepJimBaird
District Office: 355 S. Washington St., #210, Danville, IN 46122; 317-563-5567; *District Director:* Quincy Cunningham
Committee Assignments: Agriculture; Science, Space, and Technology

Balderson, Troy, R-Ohio (12)

Capitol Hill Office: 2429 RHOB 20515; 225-5355; *Chief of Staff:* Laura Engquist
Web: balderson.house.gov
Facebook: www.facebook.com/RepTroyBalderson
Twitter: @RepBalderson
YouTube: www.youtube.com/RepBalderson
District Office: 250 E. Wilson Bridge Rd., #100, Worthington, OH 43085; 614-523-2555; *District Director:* David Cordonnier
Committee Assignments: Agriculture; Transportation and Infrastructure

Banks, Jim, R-Ind. (3)

Capitol Hill Office: 1713 LHOB 20515; 225-4436; *Chief of Staff:* David Keller
Web: banks.house.gov
Facebook: www.facebook.com/RepJimBanks
Twitter: @RepJimBanks
YouTube: www.youtube.com/RepJimBanks
Instagram: @repjimbanks
District Office: 1300 S. Harrison St., Fort Wayne, IN 46802; 260-702-4750; *District Director:* Tanner Spencer
Committee Assignments: Armed Services; Education and Labor; Veterans' Affairs

Barr, Andy, R-Ky. (6)

Capitol Hill Office: 2430 RHOB 20515; 225-4706; Fax: 225-2122; *Chief of Staff:* Mary Rosado
Web: barr.house.gov
Facebook: www.facebook.com/RepAndyBarr
Twitter: @RepAndyBarr
YouTube: www.youtube.com/RepAndyBarr
Instagram: @repandybarr
District Office: 2709 Old Rosebud Rd., #100, Lexington, KY 40509; 859-219-1366; Fax: 859-219-3437
Committee Assignments: Financial Services; Foreign Affairs

Barragán, Nanette Diaz, D-Calif. (44)

Capitol Hill Office: 2246 RHOB 20515; 225-8220; Fax: 226-7290; *Chief of Staff:* Liam Forsythe
Web: barragan.house.gov
Facebook: www.facebook.com/CongresswomanBarragan
Twitter: @RepBarragan
YouTube: www.youtube.com/channel/ UC7pIAtcJoXFH8i_yodrholA
Instagram: @repbarragan
District Offices: 701 E. Carson St., Carson, CA 90745; 310-831-1799; Fax: 844-273-0996; *Field Rep.:* Patricia Camacho

205 S. Willowbrook Ave., Compton, CA 90220; 310-831-1799; *Field Rep.:* Norchelle Brown
302 W. 5th St., #201, San Pedro, CA 90731; 310-831-1799 (by appointment only); *Field Rep.:* Francisco Lopez
8650 California Ave., South Gate, CA 90280; 310-831-1799 (by appointment only); *Field Rep.:* Patricia Camacho
Committee Assignments: Energy and Commerce; Homeland Security

Bass, Karen, D-Calif. (37)

Capitol Hill Office: 2021 RHOB 20515; 225-7084; Fax: 225-2422; *Chief of Staff:* Darryn Harris
Web: bass.house.gov
Facebook: www.facebook.com/RepKarenBass
Twitter: @RepKarenBass
YouTube: www.youtube.com/RepKarenBass
Instagram: @repkarenbass
District Office: 4929 Wilshire Blvd., #650, Los Angeles, CA 90010-3820; 323-965-1422; Fax: 323-965-1113; *District Director:* Jacqueline Hamilton
Committee Assignments: Foreign Affairs; Judiciary

Beatty, Joyce, D-Ohio (3)

Capitol Hill Office: 2303 RHOB 20515; 225-4324; Fax: 225-1984; *Chief of Staff:* Todd Valentine
Web: beatty.house.gov
Facebook: www.facebook.com/RepJoyceBeatty
Twitter: @RepBeatty
YouTube: www.youtube.com/repbeatty
Instagram: @repbeatty
District Office: 471 E. Broad St., #1100, Columbus, OH 43215; 614-220-0003; Fax: 614-220-5640; *District Director:* Terri Ifeduba
Committee Assignments: Financial Services; Joint Economic

Bentz, Cliff, R-Oregon (2)

Capitol Hill Office: 1239 LHOB 20515; 225-6730; Fax: 225-5774; *Chief of Staff:* Nick Strader
Web: bentz.house.gov
Facebook: www.facebook.com/RepBentz
Twitter: @RepBentz
YouTube: www.youtube.com/channel/ UCLojpc_2T_36kci7PLnuCqA
Instagram: @repbentz
District Office: 14 N. Central Ave., #112, Medford, OR 97501; 541-776-4646; Fax: 541-779-0204 *Caseworker:* Rina Wonsyld; *Field Reps.:* Joey Minear, Margie Anderson, Wyndess James
2430 4th Ave. S.W., #2, Ontario, OR 97914; 541-709-2040; *Caseworker:* Paulette Pyle; *Field Rep.:* Sage Delong
Committee Assignments: Judiciary; Natural Resources

Bera, Ami, D-Calif. (7)

Capitol Hill Office: 172 CHOB 20515; 225-5716; Fax: 226-1298; *Chief of Staff:* Chad Obermiller
Web: bera.house.gov
Facebook: www.facebook.com/RepAmiBera

Twitter: @RepBera
YouTube: www.youtube.com/repamibera
Instagram: @repbera
District Office: 8950 Cal Center Dr., Bldg. 3, #100, Sacramento, CA 95826; 916-635-0505; Fax: 916-635-0514; *District Director:* Matthew Ceccato
Committee Assignments: Foreign Affairs; Science, Space, and Technology

Bergman, Jack, R-Mich. (1)

Capitol Hill Office: 566 CHOB 20515; 225-4735; Fax: 225-4710; *Chief of Staff:* Tony Lis
Web: bergman.house.gov
Facebook: www.facebook.com/RepJackBergman
Twitter: @RepJackBergman
YouTube: www.youtube.com/channel/UCEGDaO6kZAVxnf77jOkVbnw
Instagram: @repjackbergman
District Offices: 125 G. Ave., #B119, Gwinn, MI 49841; 906-273-2227; *District Director:* Melanie Collinsworth
7676W County Rd. 442, Suite B, Manistique, MI 49854; 906-286-4191
1396 Douglas Dr., #22B, Traverse City, MI 49696; 231-944-7633; Fax: 231-421-8643
Committee Assignments: Armed Services; Veterans' Affairs

Beyer, Donald S., Jr., D-Va. (8)

Capitol Hill Office: 1119 LHOB 20515; 225-4376; Fax: 225-0017; *Chief of Staff:* Zach Cafritz
Web: beyer.house.gov
Facebook: www.facebook.com/RepDonBeyer
Twitter: @RepDonBeyer
YouTube: www.youtube.com/repdonbeyer
Instagram: @repdonbeyer
District Office: 1901 N. Moore St., #1108, Arlington, VA 22209; 703-658-5403; Fax: 703-658-5408; *District Director:* Noah Simon
Committee Assignments: Joint Economic, Chair; Science, Space, and Technology; Ways and Means

Bice, Stephanie I., R-Okla. (5)

Capitol Hill Office: 1223 LHOB 20515; 225-2132; *Chief of Staff:* Amy Albro
Web: bice.house.gov
Facebook: www.facebook.com/RepStephanieBice
Twitter: @RepBice
Instagram: @repstephaniebice
District Office: 500 N. Broadway, #250, Oklahoma City, OK 73102; 405-300-6890; Fax: 855-235-5024; *District Director:* Matt Bluebaugh
Committee Assignments: Armed Services; Science, Space, and Technology

Biggs, Andy, R-Ariz. (5)

Capitol Hill Office: 171 CHOB 20515; 225-2635; Fax: 226-4368; *Chief of Staff:* Kate LaBorde
Web: biggs.house.gov
Facebook: www.facebook.com/RepAndyBiggs

Twitter: @RepAndyBiggsAZ
YouTube: www.youtube.com/channel/UCqSq9kWOxk9yNTeILBCVC1w
Instagram: @repandybiggs
District Office: 2509 S. Power Rd., #204, Superstition Plaza, Mesa, AZ 85209; 480-699-8239; *District Director:* David Romney
Committee Assignments: Judiciary; Oversight and Reform

Bilirakis, Gus M., R-Fla. (12)

Capitol Hill Office: 2354 RHOB 20515; 225-5755; Fax: 225-4085; *Chief of Staff:* Elizabeth Hittos
Web: bilirakis.house.gov
Facebook: www.facebook.com/GusBilirakis
Twitter: @RepGusBilirakis
YouTube: www.youtube.com/RepGusBilirakis
Instagram: @gusbilirakis
District Offices: 8731 Citizens Dr., #135, New Port Richey, FL 34654; 727-232-2921; Fax: 727-232-2923; *Deputy Chief of Staff:* Dan Paasch
Bilirakis Bldg., #38, St. Petersburg College Campus, Tarpon Springs, FL 34689; 727-232-2921 (*This office cannot accept mail.*)
Committee Assignment: Energy and Commerce

Bishop, Dan, R-N.C. (9)

Capitol Hill Office: 1207 LHOB 20515; 225-1976; *Chief of Staff:* James Hampson
Web: danbishop.house.gov
Facebook: www.facebook.com/repdanbishop
Twitter: @RepDanBishop
YouTube: www.youtube.com/channel/UCJhya4oOvU8d5SPadsEcBlQ
Instagram: @repdanbishop
District Offices: 300 N. Main St., Monroe, NC 28112; 704-218-5300; Fax: 844-273-1255550 N. Chestnut St., #152, Lumberton, NC 28358; 910-671-3000, ext. 7111
Committee Assignments: Homeland Security; Judiciary

Bishop, Sanford D., Jr., D-Ga. (2)

Capitol Hill Office: 2407 RHOB 20515-1002; 225-3631; Fax: 225-2203; *Chief of Staff:* Kenneth Cutts
Web: bishop.house.gov
Facebook: www.facebook.com/sanfordbishop
Twitter: @SanfordBishop
YouTube: www.youtube.com/RepSanfordBishop
Instagram: @repsanfordbishop
District Offices: 323 Pine Ave., #400, Albany, GA 31701; 229-439-8067; Fax: 229-436-2099
18 9th St., #201, Columbus, GA 31901-2778; 706-320-9477; Fax: 706-320-9479
300 Mulberry St., #502, Macon, GA 31201; 478-803-2631; Fax: 478-803-2637
Committee Assignment: Appropriations

Blumenauer, Earl, D-Ore. (3)

Capitol Hill Office: 1111 LHOB 20515; 225-4811; Fax: 225-8941; *Chief of Staff:* Willie Smith

Web: blumenauer.house.gov
Facebook: www.facebook.com/blumenauer
Twitter: @repblumenauer
YouTube: www.youtube.com/RepBlumenauer
Instagram: @repblumenauer
District Office: 911 11th Ave. N.E., #200, Portland, OR 97232; 503-231-2300; Fax: 503-230-5413; *District Director:* Jason Little
Committee Assignment: Ways and Means

Blunt Rochester, Lisa, D-Del. (At Large)

Capitol Hill Office: 1724 LHOB 20515; 225-4165; *Chief of Staff:* Jacqueline Sanchez
Web: bluntrochester.house.gov
Facebook: www.facebook.com/RepLBR
Twitter: @RepLBR
Instagram: @replbr
District Offices: 1105 N. Market St., #400, Wilmington, DE 19801; 302-830-233028 The Circle, #2, Georgetown, DE 19947; 302-858-4773
Committee Assignment: Energy and Commerce

Boebert, Lauren, R-Colo. (3)

Capitol Hill Office: 1609 LHOB 20515; 225-4761; *Chief of Staff:* Jeff Small
Web: boebert.house.gov
Facebook: www.facebook.com/RepBoebert
Twitter: @RepBoebert
YouTube: www.youtube.com/RepBoebert
Instagram: @repboebert
District Offices: 835 E. 2nd Ave., #204, Durango, CO 81301; 970-317-6130
743 Horizon Court, #112, Grand Junction, CO 81506; 970-208-0460
503 N. Main St., #426, Pueblo, CO 81003; 719-696-6970
Committee Assignments: Budget; Natural Resources

Bonamici, Suzanne, D-Ore. (1)

Capitol Hill Office: 2231 RHOB 20515; 225-0855; Fax: 225-9497; *Chief of Staff:* Rachael Bornstein
Web: bonamici.house.gov
Facebook: www.facebook.com/CongresswomanBonamici
Twitter: @RepBonamici
YouTube: www.youtube.com/RepSuzanneBonamici
Instagram: @repbonamici
District Office: 12725 Millikan Way S.W., #220, Beaverton, OR 97005; 503-469-6010; Fax: 503-469-6018; *District Director:* Sarah Baessler
Committee Assignments: Education and Labor; Science, Space, and Technology; Select on the Climate Crisis

Bost, Mike, R-Ill. (12)

Capitol Hill Office: 1211 LHOB 20515; 225-5661; Fax: 225-0285; *Chief of Staff:* Matt McCullough
Web: bost.house.gov
Facebook: www.facebook.com/RepBost
Twitter: @RepBost
YouTube: www.youtube.com/channel/ UCxgLCZzKuY7g_8-Iu1PSlPQ

District Offices: Hunter Bldg., 300 E. Main St., #4, Carbondale, IL 62901; 618-457-5787; Fax: 618-457-2990; *District Director:* Katie Main
302 W. State St., O'Fallon, IL 62269; 618-622-0766; Fax: 618-622-0774
Satellite Offices: City Hall, 2000 Edison Ave., Granite City, IL 62040; 618-622-0766
City Hall, 101 E. 3rd St., Alton, IL 62002; 618-622-0766
200 Potomac Blvd., Mt. Vernon, IL 62864; 618-457-5787
Committee Assignments: Transportation and Infrastructure; Veterans' Affairs

Bourdeaux, Carolyn, D-Ga. (7)

Capitol Hill Office: 1319 LHOB 20515; 225-4272; Fax: 225-4696; *Chief of Staff:* **Estefania Rodriguez**
Web: bourdeaux.house.gov
Facebook: www.facebook.com/RepBourdeaux
Twitter: @RepBourdeaux
YouTube: www.youtube.com/channel/ UCH4cTCZ6uOxU-x8muAoKgkQ
District Office: 75 Langley Dr., Lawrenceville, GA 30046; 770-232-3005; Fax: 883-213-3492; *District Director:* Thomaesa Bailey
Committee Assignments: Small Business; Transportation and Infrastructure

Bowman, Jamaal, D-N.Y. (16)

Capitol Hill Office: 1605 LHOB 20515; 225-2464; Fax: 225-5513; *Chief of Staff:* Sarah Iddrissu
Web: bowman.house.gov
Facebook: www.facebook.com/CongressmanBowman
YouTube: www.youtube.com/channel/UCkvPTT-ZWkzm8j95kIwz0ag
Twitter: @repbowman
Instagram: @congressmanbowman
District Offices: 177 Dreiser Loop, Room 3, Bronx, NY 10457; 718-530-7710; *District Director:* Ashley Torres
6 Gramatan Ave., #205, Mt. Vernon, NY 10550; 914-371-9220
Committee Assignments: Education and Labor; Science, Space, and Technology

Boyle, Brendan F., D-Pa. (2)

Capitol Hill Office: 1133 LHOB 20515-3813; 225-6111; Fax: 226-0611; *Chief of Staff:* Tim Barnes
Web: boyle.house.gov
Facebook: www.facebook.com/CongressmanBoyle
Twitter: @CongBoyle
YouTube: www.youtube.com/channel/ UCMP_Anj7lz4eZuSh8GwFqQQ
Instagram: @congressmanboyle
District Offices: 8572 Bustleton Ave., Philadelphia, PA 19152; 215-335-3355; Fax: 215-856-3734; *District Chief of Staff:* Scott Heppard
One & Olney Shopping Center, 5675 N. Front St., #180, Philadelphia, PA 19120; 267-335-5643; Fax: 267-437-3886
2630 Memphis St., Philadelphia, PA, 19125; 215-426-4616; Fax: 215-426-7741

1318 W. Girard Ave., Philadelphia, PA 19123; 215-982-1156; Fax: 267-639-9944

4667 Paul St., Philadelphia, PA 19124; 215-744-7901

Committee Assignments: Budget; Ways and Means

Brady, Kevin, R-Tex. (8)

Capitol Hill Office: 1011 LHOB 20515; 225-4901; Fax: 225-5524; *Chief of Staff:* David Davis

Web: kevinbrady.house.gov

Facebook: www.facebook.com/kevinbrady

Twitter: @RepKevinBrady

YouTube: www.youtube.com/KBrady8

Instagram: @repkevinbrady

District Offices: 200 River Point Dr., #304, Conroe, TX 77304-2817; 936-441-5700; Fax: 936-441-5757; *Deputy District Director:* Vita Swarers

Committee Assignment: Ways and Means

Brooks, Mo, R-Ala. (5)

Capitol Hill Office: 2185 RHOB 20515; 225-4801; *Chief of Staff:* Mark Pettitt

Web: brooks.house.gov

Facebook: www.facebook.com/RepMoBrooks

Twitter: @RepMoBrooks

YouTube: www.youtube.com/RepMoBrooks

District Offices: 302 Lee St., Room 86, Decatur, AL 35601-1926; 256-355-9400; Fax: 256-355-9406 *District Director:* Tiffany Noel

102 S. Court St., #310, Florence, AL 35630; 256-718-5155; Fax: 256-718-5156

2101 W. Clinton Ave., #302, Huntsville, AL 35805-3109; 256-551-0190; Fax: 256-551-0194

Committee Assignments: Armed Services; Science, Space, and Technology

Brown, Anthony G., D-Md. (4)

Capitol Hill Office: 1323 LHOB 20515; 225-8699; *Chief of Staff:* Matthew Verghese

Web: anthonybrown.house.gov

Facebook: www.facebook.com/RepAnthonyBrown

Twitter: @RepAnthonyBrown

YouTube: www.youtube.com/RepAnthonyBrown

Instagram: @repanthonybrown

District Offices: 9701 Apollo Dr., #103, Largo, MD 20774; 301-458-2600; *District Director:* Nichelle Schoultz

2666 Riva Rd., #120, Annapolis, MD 21401; 410-266-3249

Committee Assignments: Armed Services; Transportation and Infrastructure

Brown, Shontel M., D-Ohio (11)

Capitol Hill Office: 2344 RHOB 20515; 225-7032; *Chief of Staff:* Veleter Mazyck

Web: shontelbrown.house.gov

Facebook: www.facebook.com/RepShontelBrown

Twitter: @RepShontelBrown

Instagram: @repshontel

District Offices: 4834 Richmond Rd., #150, Warrensville Heights, OH 44128; 216-522-4900; *District Director:* Kimberly Edwards

1225 Lawton St., #3200, Akron, OH 44320; 330-835-4758

Committee Assignments: Agriculture; Oversight and Reform

Brownley, Julia, D-Calif. (26)

Capitol Hill Office: 2262 RHOB 20515; 225-5811; Fax: 225-1100; *Chief of Staff:* Lenny Young

Web: juliabrownley.house.gov

Facebook: www.facebook.com/RepBrownley

Twitter: @RepBrownley

YouTube: www.youtube.com/RepBrownley

Instagram: @repbrownley

District Offices: 201 E. 4th St., #209B, Oxnard, CA 93030; 805-379-1779; Fax: 805-379-1799

223 E. Thousand Oaks Blvd., #220, Thousand Oaks, CA 91360; 805-379-1779; Fax: 805-379-1799; *District Director:* Megan Bland; *Caseworker:* Sandra Bravo

Committee Assignments: Select on the Climate Crisis; Transportation and Infrastructure; Veterans' Affairs

Buchanan, Vern, R-Fla. (16)

Capitol Hill Office: 2110 RHOB 20515; 225-5015; Fax: 226-0828; *Chief of Staff:* Dave Karvelas

Web: buchanan.house.gov

Facebook: www.facebook.com/CongressmanBuchanan

Twitter: @VernBuchanan

YouTube: www.youtube.com/VernBuchanan

Instagram: @repvern

District Offices: 1051 Manatee Ave. West, #305, Bradenton, FL 34205-4954; 941-747-9081; Fax: 941-748-1564

111 S. Orange Ave., Floor 2R, #202W, Sarasota, FL 34236-5806; 941-951-6643; Fax: 941-951-2972; *District Director:* Sally Shely

Committee Assignment: Ways and Means

Buck, Ken, R-Colo. (4)

Capitol Hill Office: 2455 RHOB 20515-0604; 225-4676; *Chief of Staff:* James Braid

Web: buck.house.gov

Facebook: www.facebook.com/repkenbuck

Twitter: @RepKenBuck

YouTube: www.youtube.com/repkenbuck

Instagram: @repkenbuck

District Offices: 900 Castleton Rd., #112, Castle Rock, CO 80109; 720-639-9165; Fax: 720-639-9134; *District Director:* Monica Daniels-Mika

5626 19th St., Suite A, Greeley, CO 80634; 970-702-2136; Fax: 970-702-2951

Committee Assignments: Foreign Affairs; Judiciary

Bucshon, Larry, R-Ind. (8)

Capitol Hill Office: 2313 RHOB 20515; 225-4636; Fax: 225-3284; *Chief of Staff:* Kyle Jackson

Web: bucshon.house.gov

Facebook: www.facebook.com/RepLarryBucshon

Twitter: @RepLarryBucshon

YouTube: www.youtube.com/RepLarryBucshon

Instagram: @replarrybucshon

District Offices: 20 3rd St. N.W., #1230, Evansville, IN 47708; 812-465-6484; Fax: 812-422-4761; *District Director:* Brenda Goff

901 Wabash Ave., #140, Terre Haute, IN 47807-3232; 812-232-0523; Fax: 812-232-0526

Committee Assignment: Energy and Commerce

Budd, Ted, R-N.C. (13)

Capitol Hill Office: 103 CHOB 20515; 225-4531; *Chief of Staff:* Chad Yelinski

Web: budd.house.gov

Facebook: www.facebook.com/RepTedBudd

Twitter: @RepTedBudd

YouTube: www.youtube.com/channel/ UCMXx2hJZYOMXHTyvQPDJV0Q

Instagram: @reptedbudd

District Offices: 128 Peachtree Lane, Suite A, Advance, NC 27006; 336-998-1313; *District Director:* Kyle Bridges

222 Sunset Ave., #101, Asheboro, NC 27203; 336-610-3300

219 W Elm St., P.O. Box #812, Graham NC 27253; 336-639-7323

Committee Assignment: Financial Services

Burchett, Tim, R-Tenn. (2)

Capitol Hill Office: 1122 LHOB 20515-3515; 225-5435; Fax: 225-6440; *Chief of Staff:* Michael Grider

Web: burchett.house.gov

Facebook: www.facebook.com/RepTimBurchett

Twitter: @RepTimBurchett

YouTube: www.youtube.com/channel/ UCK8lhcSRMq63lrR-WRLiSlQ

Instagram: @reptimburchett

District Offices: 800 Market St., #110, Knoxville, TN 37902; 865-523-3772; Fax: 865-544-0728; *District Director:* Jennifer Linginfelter

331 Court St., Maryville, TN 37804; 865-984-5464

Committee Assignments: Foreign Affairs; Transportation and Infrastructure

Burgess, Michael C., R-Tex. (26)

Capitol Hill Office: 2161 RHOB 20515; 225-7772; Fax: 225-2919; *Chief of Staff:* James Decker

Web: burgess.house.gov

Facebook: www.facebook.com/michaelcburgess

Twitter: @michaelcburgess

YouTube: www.youtube.com/MichaelCBurgessMD

Instagram: @repmichaelburgess

District Office: 2000 S. Stemmons Fwy., #200, Lake Dallas, TX 75065; 940-497-5031; Fax: 940-497-5067; *District Director:* Erik With

Committee Assignments: Budget; Energy and Commerce; Rules

Bush, Cori, D-Mo. (1)

Capitol Hill Office: 563 CHOB 20515; 225-2406; Fax: 226-3717; *Chief of Staff:* Abbas Alawieh

Web: bush.house.gov

Facebook: facebook.com/RepCori

Twitter: @RepCori

Instagram: @repcori

District Office: 6724-A Page Ave., St. Louis, MO 63133; 314-955-9980; *District Director:* Rachell Nord

Committee Assignments: Judiciary; Oversight and Reform

Bustos, Cheri, D-Ill. (17)

Capitol Hill Office: 1233 LHOB 20515; 225-5905; *Chief of Staff:* Trevor Reuschel

Web: bustos.house.gov

Facebook: www.facebook.com/RepCheri

Twitter: @RepCheri

YouTube: www.youtube.com/RepCheri

Instagram: @repcheri

District Offices: 820 Adams St. S.W., Peoria, IL 61602; 309-966-1813; *District Director:* Lucie VanHecke

119 N. Church St., #101, Rockford, IL 61101; 815-968-8011

2401 4th Ave., Rock Island, IL 61201; 309-786-3406; Fax: 309-786-3720

Committee Assignments: Agriculture; Appropriations

Butterfield, G. K., D-N.C. (1)

Capitol Hill Office: 2080 RHOB 20515-3301; 225-3101; *Chief of Staff:* Kyle Parker

Web: butterfield.house.gov

Facebook: www.facebook.com/congressmangkbutterfield

Twitter: @GKButterfield

YouTube: www.youtube.com/user/GKBNC01

Instagram: @gkbutterfield

District Office: 216 Nash St. N.E., Suite B, Wilson, NC 27893-3802; 252-237-9816; Fax: 252-291-0356

Committee Assignments: Energy and Commerce; House Administration; Joint Library

Calvert, Ken, R-Calif. (42)

Capitol Hill Office: 2205 RHOB 20515; 225-1986; Fax: 225-2004; *Chief of Staff:* Rebecca Keightley

Web: calvert.house.gov

Facebook: www.facebook.com/RepKenCalvert

Twitter: @KenCalvert

YouTube: www.youtube.com/RepKenCalvert

Instagram: @repkencalvert

District Office: 400 S. Vicentia Ave., #125, Corona, CA 92882; 951-277-0042; Fax: 951-277-0420; *District Director:* Jolyn Murphy

Committee Assignment: Appropriations

Cammack, Kat, R-Fla. (3)

Capitol Hill Office: 1626 LHOB 20515; 225-5744; Fax: 225-3973; *Chief of Staff:* Larry Calhoun

Web: cammack.house.gov

Facebook: www.facebook.com/RepKatCammack

Twitter: @RepKatCammack

YouTube: www.youtube.com/channel/ UCZOEe8oq1LrZCgHf1A_mwSg

Instagram: @repkatcammack

District Offices: 5550 111th Blvd. N.W., Gainesville, FL 32653; 352-505-0838; Fax: 855-299-1664; *District Director:* Jessica Norfleet

35-1 Knight Boxx Rd., Orange Park, FL 32065; 904-276-9626; Fax: 904-276-9336

Committee Assignments: Agriculture; Homeland Security

Carbajal, Salud O., D-Calif. (24)

Capitol Hill Office: 2331 RHOB 20515; 225-3601; Fax: 225-5632; *Chief of Staff:* Jeremy Tittle
Web: carbajal.house.gov
Facebook: www.facebook.com/repsaludcarbajal
Twitter: @RepCarbajal
YouTube: www.youtube.com/repcarbajal
Instagram: @repcarbajal
District Offices: 360 S. Hope Ave., #C301, Santa Barbara, CA 93105; 805-730-1710; *District Director:* Erica Reyes
1411 Marsh St., #205, San Luis Obispo, CA 93401; 805-546-8348; Fax: 805-439-3574
1619 S. Thornburg St., Santa Maria, CA 93458; 805-730-1710; Fax: 805-439-3574
Committee Assignments: Agriculture; Armed Services; Transportation and Infrastructure

Cárdenas, Tony, D-Calif. (29)

Capitol Hill Office: 2438 RHOB 20515; 225-6131; Fax: 225-0819; *Chief of Staff:* Ahmed El Sayed
Web: cardenas.house.gov
Facebook: www.facebook.com/CongressmanCardenas
Twitter: @RepCardenas
YouTube: www.youtube.com/repcardenas
Instagram: @repcardenas
District Office: 9612 Van Nuys Blvd., #201, Panorama City, CA 91402; 818- 221-3718; Fax: 818- 221-3809; *District Director:* Gabriela Marquez
Committee Assignment: Energy and Commerce

Carey, Mike, R-Ohio (15)

Capitol Hill Office: 2234 RHOB 20515; 225-2015; *Chief of Staff:* Dave DiStefano
Web: carey.house.gov
Facebook: www.facebook.com/RepMikeCarey
Twitter: @RepMikeCarey
District Offices: 492 City Park Ave., Columbus, OH 43215; 614-927-6902; *District Director:* Minyet Palich
69 N. South St., Wilmington, OH 45177
104 E. Main St., Lancaster, OH 43130
Committee Assignment: Budget; Science, Space, and Technology

Carl, Jerry L., R-Ala. (1)

Capitol Hill Office: 1330 LHOB 20515; 225-4931; Fax: 225-0562; *Chief of Staff:* Chad Carlough
Web: carl.house.gov
Facebook: www.facebook.com/RepJerryCarl
Twitter: @RepJerryCarl
YouTube: www.youtube.com/channel/UCrBJ1EYmmeioxI0ns31kR1Q
Instagram: @repjerrycarl
District Offices: 502 West Lee Ave., Summerdale, AL 36580; 251-677-6630

41 West I-65 Service Rd., #305, Mobile, AL 36608; 251-283-6280
Committee Assignments: Armed Services; Natural Resources

Carson, André, D-Ind. (7)

Capitol Hill Office: 2135 RHOB 20515-1407; 225-4011; Fax: 225-5633; *Chief of Staff:* Kimberly Rudolph
Web: carson.house.gov
Facebook: www.facebook.com/CongressmanAndreCarson
Twitter: @RepAndreCarson
YouTube: www.youtube.com/RepAndreCarson
Instagram: @repandrecarson
District Office: 300 E. Fall Creek Pkwy. N. Dr., #300, Indianapolis, IN 46205; 317-283-6516; Fax: 317-283-6567; *District Director:* Megan Sims
Committee Assignment: Permanent Select Intelligence

Carter, Earl L. (Buddy), R-Ga. (1)

Capitol Hill Office: 2432 RHOB 20515-1001; 225-5831; Fax: 226-2269; *Chief of Staff:* Chris Crawford
Web: buddycarter.house.gov
Facebook: www.facebook.com/CongressmanBuddyCarter
Twitter: @RepBuddyCarter
YouTube: www.youtube.com/congressmanbuddycarter
Instagram: @repbuddycarter
District Offices: 777 Gloucester St., #410, Brunswick, GA 31520; 912-265-9010; Fax: 912-265-9013; *District Director:* Brooke Childers
6602 Abercorn St., #105B, Savannah, GA 31405; 912-352-0101; Fax: 912-352-0105; *District Director:* Brooke Childers
Committee Assignments: Budget; Energy and Commerce

Carter, John R., R-Tex. (31)

Capitol Hill Office: 2208 RHOB 20515-4331; 225-3864; *Chief of Staff:* Jonas Miller
Web: carter.house.gov
Facebook: www.facebook.com/judgecarter
Twitter: @JudgeCarter
YouTube: www.youtube.com/RepJohnCarter
Instagram: @judgecarter
District Offices: 1717 N. Interstate Highway 35, #303, Round Rock, TX 78664; 512-246-1600; *Deputy Chief of Staff:* August Alvarado
6544B S. General Bruce Dr., Temple, TX 76502; 254-933-1392
Committee Assignment: Appropriations

Carter, Troy, D-La. (2)

Capitol Hill Office: 506 CHOB 20515; 225-6636; *Chief of Staff:* James Bernhard
Web: troycarter.house.gov
Facebook: www.facebook.com/RepTroyCarter
Twitter: @RepTroyCarter
YouTube: www.youtube.com/channel/UC547LNCEvhr2WtH-YhdEuWA
Instagram: @RepTroyCarter

District Offices: 650 Poydras St., #2435, New Orleans, LA 70130; 504-288-3777; *Director of District Offices:* Demetric Mercadel

3401 General DeGaulle Dr., #100, New Orleans, LA 70114; 504-381-3970

Gretna Courthouse, 200 Derbigny St., #3200, Gretna, LA 70053; 504-381-3999

Satellite Offices: Southern University at New Orleans, 6803 Press Dr., #166, New Orleans, LA 70126

River Parishes Community College, 181 Regala Park Rd., Reserve, LA 70084

T. H. Harris Hall, 801 Harding Blvd., Baton Rouge, LA 70807

Committee Assignments: Small Business; Transportation and Infrastructure

Cartwright, Matt, D-Pa. (8)

Capitol Hill Office: 2102 RHOB 20515; 225-5546; Fax: 226-0996; *Chief of Staff:* Hunter Ridgway

Web: cartwright.house.gov

Facebook: www.facebook.com/CongressmanMattCartwright

Twitter: @RepCartwright

YouTube: www.youtube.com/channel/UCnAOvexSGLBnYidaFzguhTQ

Instagram: @repmattcartwright

District Office: 226 Wyoming Ave., Scranton, PA 18503; 570-341-1050; Fax: 570-341-1055; *District Director:* John P. Blake

Satellite Offices: 20 N. Pennsylvania Ave., #213, Wilkes-Barre, PA 18711; 570-371-0317

1 S. Church St., #100, Hazleton, PA 18201; 570-751-0050

2959 Route 611, #105, Tannersville, PA 18372; 570-355-1818

8 Silk Mill Dr., #213, Hawley, PA 18428; 570-576-8005

Committee Assignment: Appropriations

Case, Ed, D-Hawaii (1)

Capitol Hill Office: 2210 RHOB 20515-3515; 225-2726; Fax: 225-0688; *Chief of Staff:* Tim Nelson

Web: case.house.gov

Facebook: www.facebook.com/RepEdCase

Twitter: @RepEdCase

YouTube: www.youtube.com/RepEdCase

Instagram: @repedcase

District Office: 1003 Bishop St., #1110, Honolulu, HI 96813; 808-650-6688; *District Director:* Jacqueline Conant

Committee Assignments: Appropriations; Natural Resources

Casten, Sean, D-Ill. (6)

Capitol Hill Office: 2440 RHOB 20515-3515; 225-4561; *Chief of Staff:* Chloe Hunt

Web: casten.house.gov

Facebook: www.facebook.com/RepSeanCasten

Twitter: @RepCasten

YouTube: www.youtube.com/channel/UCWP-bfgwv5j4PeqYsm2n7Zg

Instagram: @repseancasten

District Office: 800 Roosevelt Rd., Bldg. C, #210, Glen Ellyn, IL 60137; 630-520-9450; *District Director:* Laura Schock

Satellite Office: 200 S. Hough St., Barrington, IL 60010

Committee Assignments: Financial Services; Science, Space, and Technology; Select on the Climate Crisis

Castor, Kathy, D-Fla. (14)

Capitol Hill Office: 2052 RHOB 20515-0911; 225-3376; Fax: 225-5652; *Chief of Staff:* Lara Hopkins

Web: castor.house.gov

Facebook: www.facebook.com/USRepKathyCastor

Twitter: @USRepKCastor

YouTube: www.youtube.com/RepKathyCastor

Instagram: @usrepkathycastor

District Office: 4144 N. Armenia Ave., #300, Tampa, FL 33607-6435; 813-871-2817; Fax: 813-871-2864; *District Director:* Marcia Mejia

Committee Assignments: Energy and Commerce; Select on the Climate Crisis

Castro, Joaquin, D-Tex. (20)

Capitol Hill Office: 2241 RHOB 20515; 225-3236; Fax: 225-1915; *Chief of Staff:* Danny Meza

Web: castro.house.gov

Facebook: www.facebook.com/JoaquinCastroTX

Twitter: @JoaquinCastrotx

YouTube: www.youtube.com/user/JoaquinCastroTX

Instagram: @joaquincastrotx

District Office: 727 E. Cesar E. Chavez Blvd., #B-128, San Antonio, TX 78206; 210-348-8216; Fax: 210-979-0737; *Constituent Services Director:* Rose Ann Maldonado

Committee Assignments: Education and Labor; Foreign Affairs; Permanent Select Intelligence

Cawthorn, Madison, R-N.C. (11)

Capitol Hill Office: 102 CHOB 20515; 225-6401; *Chief of Staff:* Blake Harp

Web: cawthorn.house.gov

Facebook: www.facebook.com/RepCawthorn

Twitter: @RepCawthorn

District Offices: 113 Green Mountain Dr., Burnsville, NC 28714; 828-808-2148; *District Director:* Hal Weatherman

5 W. Main St., #330, Franklin, NC 28734; 828-452-6022

200 N. Grove St., #121, Hendersonville, NC 28792; 828-435-7310

285 N. Main St., Room 1300, Waynesville, NC 28786; 828-452-6022

Committee Assignments: Education and Labor; Veterans' Affairs

Chabot, Steve, R-Ohio (1)

Capitol Hill Office: 2408 RHOB 20515; 225-2216; Fax: 225-3012; *Chief of Staff:* Jonathan Lowe

Web: chabot.house.gov

Facebook: www.facebook.com/RepSteveChabot

Twitter: @RepSteveChabot

YouTube: www.youtube.com/CongressmanSteveChabot
Instagram: @repstevechabot
District Offices: 441 Vine St., #3003, Cincinnati, OH 45202-3003; 513-684-2723; Fax: 513-421-8722; *District Director:* Joe Abner

11 S. Broadway, Lebanon, OH 45036; 513-421-8704; Fax: 513-421-8722
Committee Assignments: Foreign Affairs; Judiciary

Cheney, Liz, R-Wyo. (At Large)

Capitol Hill Office: 416 CHOB 20515; 225-2311; Fax: 225-3057; *Chief of Staff:* Kara Ahern
Web: cheney.house.gov
Facebook: www.facebook.com/replizcheney
Twitter: @RepLizCheney
YouTube: www.youtube.com/channel/UCvL57Zp99QdDllF-KGziUAA
Instagram: @replizcheney
District Offices: 100 E. B St., Room 4003, P.O. Box 44003, Casper, WY 82602; 307-261-6595; Fax: 307-261-6597; *State/District Director:* Tammy Hooper

2120 Capitol Ave., #8005, Cheyenne, WY 82001; 307-772-2595; Fax: 307-772-2597

222 S. Gillette Ave., #600, Gillette, WY 82716; 307-414-1677; Fax: 307-261-6597

325 West Main St., Unit B, Riverton, WY 82501; 307-463-0482
Committee Assignment: Armed Services

Cherfilus-McCormick, Sheila, D-Fla. (20)

Capitol Hill Office: 2365 RHOB 20515-0532; 225-1313; *Chief of Staff:* Michael McQuerry
Web: cherfilus-mccormick.house.gov
Facebook: www.facebook.com/congresswomanSCM
Twitter: @CongresswomanSC
District Offices: 5701 88th Ave. N.W., #200, Tamarac, FL 33321; 954-733-2800; *District Director:* Charlotte Wright

5725 Corporate Way, #208, West Palm Beach, FL 33407; 561-461-6767
Committee Assignments: Education and Labor; Veterans' Affairs

Chu, Judy, D-Calif. (27)

Capitol Hill Office: 2423 RHOB 20515-0532; 225-5464; Fax: 225-5467; *Chief of Staff:* Sonali Desai
Web: chu.house.gov
Facebook: www.facebook.com/RepJudyChu
Twitter: @RepJudyChu
YouTube: www.youtube.com/RepJudyChu
Instagram: @repjudychu
District Offices: 527 S. Lake Ave., #250, Pasadena, CA 91101; 626-304-0110; Fax: 626-304-0132; *District Director:* Enrique Robles

415 W. Foothill Blvd., #122, Claremont, CA 91711; 909-625-5394; Fax: 909-399-0198 (open Tuesday and Thursday)
Committee Assignments: Budget; Small Business; Ways and Means

Cicilline, David N., D-R.I. (1)

Capitol Hill Office: 2233 RHOB 20515-3901; 225-4911; Fax: 225-3290; *Chief of Staff:* Peter Karafotas
Web: cicilline.house.gov
Facebook: www.facebook.com/CongressmanDavidCicilline
Twitter: @RepCicilline
YouTube: www.youtube.com/RepDavidCicilline
Instagram: @repdavidcicilline
District Office: 1070 Main St., #300, Pawtucket, RI 02860-2134; 401-729-5600; Fax: 401-729-5608; *District Director:* Christopher Bizzacco
Committee Assignments: Foreign Affairs; Judiciary

Clark, Katherine M., D-Mass. (5)

Capitol Hill Office: 2448 RHOB 20515-2107; 225-2836; Fax: 226-0092; *Chief of Staff:* Brooke Scannell
Web: katherineclark.house.gov
Facebook: www.facebook.com/RepKClark
Twitter: @RepKClark
YouTube: www.youtube.com/channel/UCgaI52w7QKI8LtkSeCCmSuw
Instagram: @repkclark
District Office: 157 Pleasant St., #4, Malden, MA 02148; 617-354-0292; Fax: 617-354-1456 (open Monday through Friday, 9 a.m.–5:30 p.m.); *District Director:* Kelsey Perkins
Satellite Office: 116 Concord St., #1, Framingham, MA 01702; 508-319-9757 (by appointment only); *District Director:* Kelsey Perkins
Committee Assignment: Appropriations

Clarke, Yvette D., D-N.Y. (9)

Capitol Hill Office: 2058 RHOB 20515; 225-6231; Fax: 226-0112; *Chief of Staff:* LaDavia Drane
Web: clarke.house.gov
Facebook: www.facebook.com/repyvetteclarke
Twitter: @RepYvetteClarke
YouTube: www.youtube.com/channel/UCuz1ofl3ZqdkjRahPzTKGDQ
Instagram: @repyvetteclarke
District Office: 222 Lenox Rd., #1 & 2, Brooklyn, NY 11226-3302; 718-287-1142; Fax: 718-287-1223; *District Director:* Anita Taylor
Committee Assignments: Energy and Commerce; Homeland Security

Cleaver, Emanuel, D-Mo. (5)

Capitol Hill Office: 2335 RHOB 20515; 225-4535; Fax: 225-4403; *Chief of Staff:* Jennifer Shapiro
Web: cleaver.house.gov
Facebook: www.facebook.com/emanuelcleaverii
Twitter: @repcleaver
YouTube: www.youtube.com/repcleaver
Instagram: @repcleaver
District Offices: 411 W. Maple Ave., Suite F, Independence, MO 64050-2815; 816-833-4545; Fax: 816-833-2991; *District Director:* Whitney Frost

4001 Dr. Martin Luther King, Jr. Blvd., #210, Kansas City, MO 64130; 816-842-4545; Fax: 816-833-2991

1923 Main St., Higginsville, MO 64037; 660-584-7373; Fax: 660-584-7227

Committee Assignments: Financial Services; Homeland Security; Select on the Modernization of Congress

Cline, Ben, R-Va. (6)

Capitol Hill Office: 2443 RHOB 20515; 225-5431; Fax: 540-857-2675; *Chief of Staff:* Matt Miller

Web: cline.house.gov

Facebook: www.facebook.com/RepBenCline

Twitter: @RepBenCline

Instagram: @repbencline

District Offices: 70 N. Mason St., #110, Harrisonburg, VA 22802; 540-432-2391; Fax: 540-857-2675; *District Director:* Debbie Garrett

916 Main St., #300, Lynchburg, VA 24504; 434-845-8306; Fax: 540-857-2675

10 Franklin Rd. S.E., #510, Roanoke, VA 24011; 540-857-2672; Fax: 540-857-2675

117 S. Lewis St., #215, Staunton, VA 24401; 540-885-3861; Fax: 540-857-2675

Committee Assignments: Appropriations; Budget

Cloud, Michael, R-Tex. (27)

Capitol Hill Office: 512 CHOB 20515; 225-7742; Fax: 226-1134; *Chief of Staff:* Adam Magary

Web: cloud.house.gov

Facebook: www.facebook.com/RepCloudTX

Twitter: @RepCloudTX

YouTube: www.youtube.com/channel/UCv_kM3OZukHS0rjWpw_JMWg

Instagram: @repcloudtx

District Offices: 555 N. Carancahua St., Tower II, #980, Corpus Christi, TX, 78401; 361-884-2222; *District Director:* Mark Longoria

111 N. Glass St., #102, Victoria, TX 77901; 361-894-6446; Fax: 361-884-2223

Committee Assignments: Agriculture; Oversight and Reform

Clyburn, James E., D-S.C. (6)

Capitol Hill Office: 274 CHOB 20515; 225-3315; Fax: 225-2313; *Chief of Staff:* Yelberton R. Watkins

Web: clyburn.house.gov

Facebook: www.facebook.com/WhipClyburn

Twitter: @WhipClyburn

YouTube: www.youtube.com/repjamesclyburn

Instagram: @whipclyburn

District Offices: 1225 Lady St., #200, Columbia, SC 29201-3210; 803-799-1100; Fax: 803-799-9060; *District Director:* Robert Nance

130 W. Main St., Kingstree, SC 29556; 843-355-1211; Fax: 843-355-1232

176 Municipal Way, Santee, SC 29142; 803-854-4700; Fax: 803-854-4900

129 South Harvin St., Sumter, SC 29150; 803-883-5020 (open 2nd and 4th Mondays, 10 a.m.–4 p.m.)

Majority Whip

Clyde, Andrew S., R-Ga. (9)

Capitol Hill Office: 521 CHOB 20515; 225-9893; Fax: 226-1224; *Chief of Staff:* Nicholas Brown

Web: clyde.house.gov

Facebook: www.facebook.com/RepresentativeClyde

Twitter: @Rep_Clyde

YouTube: www.youtube.com/channel/UC-o-UOnLuu8pZxZpShG4s7A

Instagram: @repclyde

District Office: 210 Washington St. N.W., #202, Gainesville, GA 30501; 470-768-6520; *District Director:* Joel Katz

Committee Assignments: Homeland Security; Oversight and Reform

Cohen, Steve, D-Tenn. (9)

Capitol Hill Office: 2104 RHOB 20515; 225-3265; Fax: 225-5663; *Chief of Staff:* Marilyn Dillihay

Web: cohen.house.gov

Facebook: www.facebook.com/CongressmanSteveCohen

Twitter: @RepCohen

YouTube: www.youtube.com/RepCohen

Instagram: @repcohen

District Office: The Odell Horton Federal Bldg., 167 N. Main St., #369, Memphis, TN 38103-1822; 901-544-4131; Fax: 901-544-4329; *District Director:* Marzie Thomas

Committee Assignments: Judiciary; Natural Resources; Transportation and Infrastructure

Cole, Tom, R-Okla. (4)

Capitol Hill Office: 2207 RHOB 20515-3604; 225-6165; Fax: 225-3512; *Chief of Staff:* Joshua Grogis

Web: cole.house.gov

Facebook: www.facebook.com/TomColeOK04

Twitter: @TomColeOK04

YouTube: www.youtube.com/TomColeOK04

Instagram: @tomcoleok04

District Offices: 100 E. 13th St., #213, Ada, OK 74820-6548; 580-436-5375; Fax: 580-436-5451; *District Director:* Will McPherson

711 D Ave. S.W., #201, Lawton, OK 73501-4561; 580-357-2131; Fax: 580-357-7477

2424 Springer Dr., #201, Norman, OK 73069-3965; 405-329-6500; Fax: 405-321-7369

Committee Assignments: Appropriations; Rules

Comer, James, R-Ky. (1)

Capitol Hill Office: 2410 RHOB 20515; 225-3115; *Chief of Staff:* Caroline Cash

Web: comer.house.gov

Facebook: www.facebook.com/CongressmanComer

Twitter: @RepJamesComer

YouTube: www.youtube.com/channel/UCPhXjG2P5iCxFOhVCPsHU6Q

Instagram: @congressmancomer

District Offices: 300 S. 3rd St., Paducah, KY 42003; 270-408-1865; *District Director:* Sandy Simpson

200 N. Main St., Suite F, Tompkinsville, KY 42167; 270-487-9509 or 800-328-5629; *District Director:* Sandy Simpson

67 N. Main St., Madisonville, KY 42431; 270-487-9509 (by appointment only)

Committee Assignments: Education and Labor; Oversight and Reform

Connolly, Gerald E., D-Va. (11)

Capitol Hill Office: 2238 RHOB 20515-4611; 225-1492; *Chief of Staff:* Jamie Smith

Web: connolly.house.gov

Facebook: www.facebook.com/CongressmanGerryConnolly

Twitter: @GerryConnolly

YouTube: www.youtube.com/RepConnolly

Instagram: @repgerryconnolly

District Offices: 4115 Annandale Rd., #103, Annandale, VA 22003-2500; 703-256-3071; Fax: 703-354-1284; *District Director:* Marlon Dubuisson

2241-D Tacketts Mill Dr., Woodbridge, VA 22192-5307; 571-408-4407; Fax: 571-408-4708

Committee Assignments: Foreign Affairs; Oversight and Reform

Cooper, Jim, D-Tenn. (5)

Capitol Hill Office: 1536 LHOB 20515-4205; 225-4311; Fax: 226-1035; *Chief of Staff:* Jason Lumia

Web: cooper.house.gov

Facebook: www.facebook.com/JimCooper

Twitter: @repjimcooper

YouTube: www.youtube.com/RepJimCooper

Instagram: @repjimcooper

District Office: 605 Church St., Nashville, TN 37219-2314; 615-736-5295; Fax: 615-736-7479; *District Director:* Cheryl Mayes

Committee Assignments: Armed Services; Budget; Oversight and Reform; Permanent Select Intelligence

Correa, J. Luis, D-Calif. (46)

Capitol Hill Office: 2301 RHOB 20515; 225-2965; *Chief of Staff:* Laurie Saroff

Web: correa.house.gov

Facebook: www.facebook.com/RepLouCorrea

Twitter: @RepLouCorrea

YouTube: www.youtube.com/channel/UCIKJJp4QJIDjnjodc23qKkw

Instagram: @reploucorrea

District Office: Rancho Santiago Community College Bldg., 2323 N. Broadway, #319, Santa Ana, CA 92706; 714-559-6190

Committee Assignments: Agriculture; Homeland Security; Judiciary

Costa, Jim, D-Calif. (16)

Capitol Hill Office: 2081 RHOB 20515-0520; 225-3341; *Chief of Staff:* Juan Lopez

Web: costa.house.gov

Facebook: www.facebook.com/RepJimCosta

Twitter: @RepJimCosta

YouTube: youtube.com/RepJimCostaCA20

Instagram: @repjimcosta

District Offices: 855 M St., #940, Fresno, CA 93721-2757; 559-495-1620; *District Director:* Kathy Mahan

415A West 18th St., P.O. Box 591, Merced, CA 95341; 209-384-1620

Committee Assignments: Agriculture; Foreign Affairs; Natural Resources

Courtney, Joe, D-Conn. (2)

Capitol Hill Office: 2449 RHOB 20515; 225-2076; Fax: 225-4977; *Chief of Staff:* Neil McKiernan

Web: courtney.house.gov

Facebook: www.facebook.com/joecourtney

Twitter: @RepJoeCourtney

YouTube: www.youtube.com/RepCourtney

Instagram: @repjoecourtney

District Offices: 77 Hazard Ave., Unit J, Enfield, CT 06082-3890; 860-741-6011; Fax: 860-741-6036; *District Director:* Ayanti Grant

55 Main St., #250, Norwich, CT 06360; 860-886-0139; Fax: 860-886-2974

Committee Assignments: Armed Services; Education and Labor

Craig, Angie, D-Minn. (2)

Capitol Hill Office: 2442 RHOB 20515; 225-2271; *Chief of Staff:* Nick Coe

Web: craig.house.gov

Facebook: www.facebook.com/RepAngieCraig

Twitter: @RepAngieCraig

YouTube: www.youtube.com/channel/UC-WrWEiOLVjUjUGGpfFp1sA

Instagram: @repangiecraig

District Office: 12940 S. Harriet Ave., #238, Burnsville, MN 55337; 651-846-2120; *District Director:* Liz Young

Committee Assignments: Agriculture; Energy and Commerce; Small Business

Crawford, Eric A. (Rick), R-Ark. (1)

Capitol Hill Office: 2422 RHOB 20515; 225-4076; Fax: 225-5602; Text: 870-292-6747; *Chief of Staff:* Jonah Shumate

Web: crawford.house.gov

Facebook: www.facebook.com/RepRickCrawford

Twitter: @RepRickCrawford

YouTube: www.youtube.com/RepRickCrawford

Instagram: @reprickcrawford

District Offices: 112 S. 1st St., Cabot, AR 72023-3007; 501-843-3043; Fax: 501-843-4955; *Field Rep.:* Jay Sherrod

2400 Highland Dr., #300, Jonesboro, AR 72401-6229; 870-203-0540; Fax: 870-203-0542; *District Director:* Sherrie Mitchell

1001 Hwy. 62 East, #9, Mountain Home, AR 72653; 870-424-2075; Fax: 870-424-3149; *District Director:* Stetson Painter

101 E. Waterman St., Dumas, AR 71639; 870-377-5571; *Field Rep.:* Hunter Selvey

Committee Assignments: Agriculture; Transportation and Infrastructure; Permanent Select Intelligence

Crenshaw, Dan, R-Tex. (2)

Capitol Hill Office: 413 CHOB 20515-3515; 225-6565; *Chief of Staff:* Justin Discigil
Web: crenshaw.house.gov
Facebook: www.facebook.com/RepDanCrenshaw
Twitter: @RepDanCrenshaw
YouTube: www.youtube.com/channel/
   UC2XDiCjAHtJqnSEzrHAY5IQ
Instagram: @dancrenshawtx
District Offices: 1849 Kingwood Dr., #100, Kingwood, TX 77339; 713-860-1330; *District Director:* Kaaren Cambio
9720 Cypresswood Dr., #206, Houston, TX 77070; 281-640-7720
Committee Assignments: Energy and Commerce; Select on the Climate Crisis

Crist, Charlie, D-Fla. (13)

Capitol Hill Office: 215 CHOB 20515; 225-5961; Fax: 225-9764; *Chief of Staff:* Austin Durrer
Web: crist.house.gov
Facebook: www.facebook.com/RepCharlieCrist
Twitter: @RepCharlieCrist
YouTube: www.youtube.com/RepCharlieCrist
Instagram: @repcharliecrist
District Office: 696 1st Ave. North, #203, St. Petersburg, FL 33701; 727-318-6770; Fax: 727-623-0619; *District Director:* Steven Cary
Satellite Offices: 1300 22nd St. South, #316, St. Petersburg, FL 33712; 727-318-6770
9200 113th St. North, #310, Seminole, FL 33772; 727-318-6770
Committee Assignments: Appropriations; Science, Space, and Technology

Crow, Jason, D-Colo. (6)

Capitol Hill Office: 1229 LHOB 20515-3515; 225-7882; *Chief of Staff:* Macey Matthews
Web: crow.house.gov
Facebook: www.facebook.com/RepJasonCrow
Twitter: @RepJasonCrow
Instagram: @repjasoncrow
District Office: 3300 S. Parker Rd., #100, Aurora, CO 80014; 720-748-7514; *District Director:* Maytham Al Shadood
Committee Assignments: Armed Services; Small Business; Permanent Select Intelligence

Cuellar, Henry, D-Tex. (28)

Capitol Hill Office: 2372 RHOB 20515; 225-1640; Fax: 225-1641; *Chief of Staff:* Jacob Hochberg
Web: cuellar.house.gov
Facebook: www.facebook.com/repcuellar
Twitter: @RepCuellar
YouTube: www.youtube.com/henrycuellar
Instagram: @repcuellar

District Offices: 602 E. Calton Rd., #2, Laredo, TX 78041-3693; 956-725-0639; Fax: 956-725-2647
117 E. Tom Landry St., Mission, TX 78572-4160; 956-424-3942; Fax: 956-424-3936
615 E. Houston St., #563, San Antonio, TX 78205-2048; 210-271-2851; Fax: 210-277-6671
Committee Assignment: Appropriations

Curtis, John R., R-Utah (3)

Capitol Hill Office: 2400 RHOB 20515; 225-7751; Fax: 225-5629; *Chief of Staff:* Corey Norman
Web: curtis.house.gov
Facebook: www.facebook.com/RepJohnCurtis
Twitter: @RepJohnCurtis
YouTube: www.youtube.com/channel/UChAQ4MD-HigmGnImSoAKBVA
Instagram: @repjohncurtis
District Office: 3549 N. University Ave., #275, Provo, UT 84604; 801-922-5400; Fax: 385-295-1007; *District Director:* Lorie Fowlke
Committee Assignment: Energy and Commerce

Davids, Sharice, D-Kans. (3)

Capitol Hill Office: 1541 LHOB 20515-3515; 225-2865; Fax: 225-2807; *Chief of Staff:* Allison Sulier
Web: davids.house.gov
Facebook: www.facebook.com/RepDavids
Twitter: @RepDavids
YouTube: www.youtube.com/channel/
   UCNUfpXQeUVdh6oKWVmq3xxQ
Instagram: @repdavids
District Offices: 753 State Ave., #460, Kansas City, KS 66101; 913-766-3993; *District Director:* Danielle Robinson
9200 Indian Creek Pkwy, #562, Overland Park, KS 66210
Committee Assignments: Joint Economic; Small Business; Transportation and Infrastructure

Davidson, Warren, R-Ohio (8)

Capitol Hill Office: 2113 RHOB 20515; 225-6205; *Chief of Staff:* Adam Hewitt
Web: davidson.house.gov
Facebook: www.facebook.com/
   CongressmanWarrenDavidson
Twitter: @WarrenDavidson
YouTube: www.youtube.com/channel/
   UCMzuyZWzk44YRNesFzPTeUw
Instagram: @instawarrendavidson
District Offices: 20 Dotcom Dr., Troy, OH 45373; 937-339-1524; *District Director:* Ben Thaeler
8857 Cincinnati-Dayton Rd., #102, West Chester, OH 45069; 513-779-5400
Satellite Office: 76 E. High St., 3rd Floor, Springfield, OH 45502; 937-322-1120
Committee Assignment: Financial Services

Davis, Danny K., D-Ill. (7)

Capitol Hill Office: 2159 RHOB 20515-1307; 225-5006; Fax: 225-5641; *Chief of Staff:* Tumia Romero

Web: davis.house.gov
Facebook: www.facebook.com/OfficialRepDannyDavis
Twitter: @RepDannyDavis
YouTube: www.youtube.com/channel/
UCj7w8NnoxbCuB1VYKjjod_g
Instagram: @repdannydavis
District Office: 2815 W. 5th Ave., Chicago, IL 60612-2040;
773-533-7520; Fax: 844-274-0426; *District Director:*
Cherita Logan
Committee Assignments: Oversight and Reform; Ways
and Means

Davis, Rodney, R-Ill. (13)

Capitol Hill Office: 2079 RHOB 20515; 225-2371;
Fax: 226-0791; *Chief of Staff:* Bret Manley
Web: rodneydavis.house.gov
Facebook: www.facebook.com/RepRodneyDavis
Twitter: @RodneyDavis
YouTube: www.youtube.com/RepRodneyDavis
Instagram: @reprodneydavis
District Offices: 2004 Fox Dr., Suite D, Champaign, IL
61820; 217-403-4690; Fax: 217-403-4691; *District
Director:* Helen Albert
243 S. Water St., #100, Decatur, IL 62523; 217-791-6224;
Fax: 217-791-6168
1012 Plummer Dr., #205, Edwardsville, IL 62025; 618-205-
8660
108 W. Market St., Taylorville, IL 62568; 217-824-5117;
Fax: 217-824-5121
Satellite Offices: 104 W. North St., Normal, IL 61761;
309-252-8834 (by appointment only)
Committee Assignments: Agriculture; House
Administration; Joint Library; Joint Printing;
Transportation and Infrastructure; Select on the
Modernization of Congress

Dean, Madeleine, D-Pa. (4)

Capitol Hill Office: 120 CHOB 20515-3515; 225-4731;
Chief of Staff: Koh Chiba
Web: dean.house.gov
Facebook: www.facebook.com/RepMadeleineDean
Twitter: @RepDean
YouTube: www.youtube.com/channel/
UCHj4veUyhPzzOW-Jvn7MqUg
Instagram: @repmadeleinedean
District Offices: 115 E. Glenside Ave., #1, Glenside, PA
19038; 215-884-4300; Fax: 215-884-3640; *District
Director:* Kathleen Joyce
101 E. Main St., Suite A, Norristown, PA 19401; 610-382-
1250; Fax: 610-275-1759
Committee Assignments: Financial Services; Judiciary

DeFazio, Peter A., D-Ore. (4)

Capitol Hill Office: 2134 RHOB 20515-3704; 225-6416;
Chief of Staff: Kris Pratt
Web: defazio.house.gov
Facebook: www.facebook.com/RepPeterDeFazio
Twitter: @RepPeterDeFazio
YouTube: www.youtube.com/PeterDeFazio

Instagram: @defazio4oregon
District Offices: 405 E. 8th Ave., #2030, Eugene, OR
97401-2706; 541-465-6732 or 800-944-9603; Fax: 541-
465-6458; *District Director:* Dan Whelan
612 Jackson St. S.E., #9, Roseburg, OR 97470-4956; 541-
440-3523; Fax: 541-465-6458
125 Central Ave., #350, Coos Bay, OR 97420; 541-269-
2609; Fax: 541-465-6458
Committee Assignment: Transportation and Infrastructure

DeGette, Diana, D-Colo. (1)

Capitol Hill Office: 2111 RHOB 20515; 225-4431;
Fax: 225-5657; *Chief of Staff:* Joeana Middleton
Web: degette.house.gov
Facebook: www.facebook.com/DianaDeGette
Twitter: @RepDianaDeGette
YouTube: www.youtube.com/RepDianaDeGette
Instagram: @repdianadegette
District Office: 600 Grant St., #202, Denver, CO 80203-
3525; 303-844-4988; Fax: 303-844-4996
Committee Assignments: Energy and Commerce; Natural
Resources

DeLauro, Rosa L., D-Conn. (3)

Capitol Hill Office: 2413 RHOB 20515-0703; 225-3661;
Fax: 225-4890; *Chief of Staff:* Rebecca Salay
Web: delauro.house.gov
Facebook: www.facebook.com/
CongresswomanRosaDeLauro
Twitter: @rosadelauro
YouTube: www.youtube.com/RosaDeLauro
Instagram: @reprosadelauro
District Office: 59 Elm St., New Haven, CT 06510; 203-
562-3718; Fax: 203-772-2260; *District Director:*
Jennifer Lamb
Committee Assignment: Appropriations, Chair

DelBene, Suzan K., D-Wash. (1)

Capitol Hill Office: 2330 RHOB 20515; 225-6311;
Fax: 226-1606; *Chief of Staff:* Aaron Schmidt
Web: delbene.house.gov
Facebook: www.facebook.com/RepDelBene
Twitter: @RepDelBene
YouTube: www.youtube.com/channel/
UCd00b7TpKDZIr-Ujhaktvjg
Instagram: @repdelbene
District Offices: 450 Central Way, #3100, Kirkland, WA
98033; 425-485-0085; Fax: 425-485-0083; *District
Director:* Kelly Marquardt
204 W. Montgomery St., Mount Vernon, WA 98273; 360-
416-7879; Fax: 425-485-0083
Committee Assignment: Ways and Means

Delgado, Antonio, D-N.Y. (19)

Capitol Hill Office: 1007 LHOB 20515; 225-5614; *Chief of
Staff:* Jessie Andrews
Web: delgado.house.gov
Facebook: www.facebook.com/RepAntonioDelgado
Twitter: @repdelgado

Instagram: @repantoniodelgado
District Offices: 111 Main St., Delhi, NY 13753; 607-376-0090; *District Director:* Amanda De Santis
256 Clinton Ave., Kingston, NY 12401; 845-443-2930
189 Main St., #500, Oneonta, NY 13820; 607-376-0091
Satellite Offices: 59 N. Main St., #301, Liberty, NY 12754; 845-295-6020
420 Warren St., Hudson, NY 12534; 518-267-4123
Committee Assignments: Agriculture; Small Business; Transportation and Infrastructure

Demings, Val Butler, D-Fla. (10)

Capitol Hill Office: 217 CHOB 20515; 225-2176; Fax: 226-6559; *Chief of Staff:* Wendy Anderson
Web: demings.house.gov
Facebook: www.facebook.com/RepValDemings
Twitter: @RepValDemings
YouTube: www.youtube.com/channel/UCkcshqwFNJG6XeduOforhig
Instagram: @repvaldemings
District Office: 2295 S. Hiawassee Rd., #301, Orlando, FL 32835; 321-388-9808; Fax: 202-226-6559; *District Director:* Sonja White
Committee Assignments: Homeland Security; Judiciary; Permanent Select Intelligence

DeSaulnier, Mark, D-Calif. (11)

Capitol Hill Office: 503 CHOB 20515-0511; 225-2095; Fax: 225-5609; *Chief of Staff:* Betsy Arnold Marr
Web: desaulnier.house.gov
Facebook: www.facebook.com/RepMarkDeSaulnier
Twitter: @RepDeSaulnier
Instagram: @repdesaulnier
District Offices: 440 Civic Center Plaza, 2nd Floor, Richmond, CA 94804; 510-620-1000; Fax: 510-620-1005; *District Director:* Lupe Schoenberger
3100 Oak Rd., #110, Walnut Creek, CA 94597; 925-933-2660; Fax: 925-933-2677
Committee Assignments: Education and Labor; Oversight and Reform; Rules; Transportation and Infrastructure

DesJarlais, Scott, R-Tenn. (4)

Capitol Hill Office: 2304 RHOB 20515; 225-6831; Fax: 226-5172; *Chief of Staff:* Richard Vaughn
Web: desjarlais.house.gov
Facebook: www.facebook.com/ScottDesJarlaisTN04
Twitter: @DesJarlaisTN04
YouTube: www.youtube.com/ScottDesJarlaisTN04
Instagram: @desjarlaistn04
District Offices: 808 S. Garden St., 2nd Floor, Columbia, TN 38401; 931-381-9920; Fax: 931-381-9945; *Constituent Services Coord.:* Becky Moon
305 W. Main St., Murfreesboro, TN 37130; 615-896-1986; Fax: 615-896-8218
Satellite Offices: 301 Keith St. S.W., #212, Cleveland, TN 37311; 423-472-7500; Fax: 423-472-7800
Federal Bldg., 200 S. Jefferson St., #311, Winchester, TN 37398; 931-962-3180; Fax: 931-962-3435
Committee Assignments: Agriculture; Armed Services

Deutch, Theodore E., D-Fla. (22)

Capitol Hill Office: 2323 RHOB 20515-0919; 225-3001; Fax: 225-5974; *Chief of Staff:* Joshua Rogin
Web: teddeutch.house.gov
Facebook: www.facebook.com/CongressmanTedDeutch
Twitter: @RepTedDeutch
YouTube: www.youtube.com/CongressmanTedDeutch
Instagram: @repteddeutch
District Offices: 7900 Glades Rd., #250, Boca Raton, FL 33434; 561-470-5440; Fax: 561-470-5446; *District Director:* Wendi Lipsich
Margate City Hall, 5790 Margate Blvd., Margate, FL 33063-3614; 954-972-6454; Fax: 954-974-3191; *Deputy District Director:* Theresa Brier
9500 W. Sample Rd., #201, Coral Springs, FL 33065; 954-255-8336
111 E. Las Olas Blvd., #424, Fort Lauderdale, FL 33301; 954-255-8336
Committee Assignments: Ethics, Chair; Foreign Affairs; Judiciary

Diaz-Balart, Mario, R-Fla. (25)

Capitol Hill Office: 374 CHOB 20515; 225-4211; Fax: 225-8576; *Chief of Staff:* Cesar A. Gonzalez
Web: mariodiazbalart.house.gov
Facebook: www.facebook.com/mdiazbalart
Twitter: @MarioDB
YouTube: www.youtube.com/MarioDiazBalart
Instagram: @repmariodb
District Offices: 8669 36th St. N.W., #100, Doral, FL 33166-6640; 305-470-8555; Fax: 305-470-8575; *Deputy Chief of Staff:* Miguel A. Otero
4715 Golden Gate Pkwy., #1, Naples, FL 34116; 239-348-1620; Fax: 239-348-3569; *District Director:* Enrique Padron
Committee Assignment: Appropriations

Dingell, Debbie, D-Mich. (12)

Capitol Hill Office: 116 CHOB 20515-2212; 225-4071; Fax: 226-0371; *Chief of Staff:* Greg Sunstrum
Web: debbiedingell.house.gov
Facebook: www.facebook.com/RepDebbieDingell
Twitter: @RepDebDingell
YouTube: www.youtube.com/channel/UCnoP3KLT-HOvzDfC1-I-9lQ
Instagram: @repdingell
District Office: 301 W. Michigan Ave., #400, Ypsilanti, MI 48197; 734-481-1100; *District Director:* Kelly Tabay
Committee Assignments: Energy and Commerce; Natural Resources

Doggett, Lloyd, D-Tex. (35)

Capitol Hill Office: 2307 RHOB 20515-4325; 225-4865; Fax: 225-3073; *Chief of Staff:* Michael J. Mucchetti
Web: doggett.house.gov
Facebook: www.facebook.com/RepLloydDoggett
Twitter: @RepLloydDoggett
YouTube: www.youtube.com/doggett
Instagram: @replloyddoggett

District Office: Federal Bldg., 300 E. 8th St., #763, Austin, TX 78701-3224; 512-916-5921; Fax: 512-916-5108; *District Director:* Jocelyn Tau

Committee Assignments: Budget; Joint Taxation; Ways and Means

Donalds, Byron, R-Fla. (19)

Capitol Hill Office: 523 CHOB 20515; 225-2536; *Chief of Staff:* Tyler Haymore

Web: donalds.house.gov

Facebook: www.facebook.com/RepDonaldsPress

Twitter: @RepDonaldsPress

YouTube: www.youtube.com/channel/ UCJy0W7sksMz37IYY27tAZNQ

Instagram: @repdonaldspress

District Offices: 1039 9th Ave. S.E., #308, Cape Coral, FL 33990; 239-599-6033; *District Director:* Jesse Purdon

3299 Tamiami Trail East, #105, Naples, FL 34112; 239-252-6225

Committee Assignments: Budget; Oversight and Reform; Small Business

Doyle, Mike F., D-Pa. (18)

Capitol Hill Office: 270 CHOB 20515; 225-2135; Fax: 225-3084; *Chief of Staff:* David G. Lucas

Web: doyle.house.gov

Facebook: www.facebook.com/usrepmikedoyle

Twitter: @USRepMikeDoyle

YouTube: www.youtube.com/CongressmanDoyle

Instagram: @usrepmikedoyle

District Offices: 4705 Library Rd., Bethel Park, PA 15102; 412-283-4451; Fax: 412-283-4465; *District Director:* Paul D'Alesandro

627 Lysle Blvd., McKeesport, PA 15132; 412-664-4049; Fax: 412-664-4053

2700 Monroeville Blvd., Monroeville, PA 15146; 412-856-3375

2637 E. Carson St., Pittsburgh, PA 15203-5109; 412-390-1499; Fax: 412-390-2118

Committee Assignment: Energy and Commerce

Duncan, Jeff, R-S.C. (3)

Capitol Hill Office: 2229 RHOB 20515-4003; 225-5301; Fax: 225-3216; *Chief of Staff:* Allen Klump

Web: jeffduncan.house.gov

Facebook: www.facebook.com/RepJeffDuncan

Twitter: @RepJeffDuncan

YouTube: www.youtube.com/CongJeffDuncan

Instagram: @repjeffduncan

District Offices: 303 W. Beltline Blvd., Anderson, SC 29625-1505; 864-224-7401; Fax: 864-225-7049; *District Director:* Rick Adkins

100 Plaza Circle, #A1, Clinton, SC 29325; 864-681-1028; Fax: 864-681-1030

Committee Assignment: Energy and Commerce

Dunn, Neal P., R-Fla. (2)

Capitol Hill Office: 316 CHOB 20515; 225-5235; Fax: 225-5615; *Chief of Staff:* Michael Lowry

Web: dunn.house.gov

Facebook: www.facebook.com/DrNealDunnFL2

Twitter: @DrNealDunnFL2

YouTube: www.youtube.com/channel/UCRTGfrYP-RuDzJ2KGok7TRA

District Offices: 840 W. 11th St., #2250, Panama City, FL 32401; 850-785-0812; Fax: 850-763-3764; *District Director:* Will Kendrick

300 S. Adams St., Tallahassee, FL 32301; 850-891-8610; Fax: 850-891-8620

Committee Assignment: Energy and Commerce

Ellzey, Jake, R-Tex. (6)

Capitol Hill Office: 1725 LHOB 20515; 225-2002; *Chief of Staff:* Robert Carretta

Web: ellzey.house.gov

Facebook: www.facebook.com/RepJakeEllzey

Twitter: @repellzey

District Offices: 2340 Interstate 20 W., #224, Arlington, TX 76017; 817-775-0370; *District Director:* Julie Loose

122 N. Beaton St., Corsicana, TX 75110; 903-602-7860

2001 Bates Dr., #120, Waxahachie, TX 75167; 469-550-71650

Committee Assignment: Science, Space, and Technology; Veterans' Affairs

Emmer, Tom, R-Minn. (6)

Capitol Hill Office: 315 CHOB 20515-2306; 225-2331; Fax: 225-6475; *Chief of Staff:* Christopher Maneval

Web: emmer.house.gov

Facebook: www.facebook.com/reptomemmer

Twitter: @reptomemmer

YouTube: www.youtube.com/RepTomEmmer

Instagram: @reptomemmer

District Office: 9201 Quaday Ave. N.E., #206, Otsego, MN 55330; 763-241-6848; Fax: 763-241-7955; *District Director:* Stacy Morse

Committee Assignment: Financial Services

Escobar, Veronica, D-Tex. (16)

Capitol Hill Office: 1505 LHOB 20515-3515; 225-4831; *Chief of Staff:* Eduardo Lerma

Web: escobar.house.gov

Facebook: www.facebook.com/RepEscobar

Twitter: @RepEscobar

YouTube: www.youtube.com/channel/ UC46TX2P8K0CA_4gZv8_R2Og

Instagram: @veronicaescobartx

District Office: Wells Fargo Plaza, 221 N. Kansas St., #1500, El Paso, TX 79901; 915-541-1400; Fax: 915-541-1407; *District Director:* Emily Loya

Committee Assignments: Armed Services; Ethics; Judiciary; Select on the Climate Crisis

Eshoo, Anna G., D-Calif. (18)

Capitol Hill Office: 272 CHOB 20515; 225-8104; Fax: 225-8890; *Chief of Staff:* Matthew McMurray

Web: eshoo.house.gov

Facebook: www.facebook.com/RepAnnaEshoo

Twitter: @RepAnnaEshoo
YouTube: www.youtube.com/RepAnnaEshoo
Instagram: @repannaeshoo
District Office: 698 Emerson St., Palo Alto, CA 94301-1609; 650-323-2984 or 408-245-2339 or 831-335-2020; Fax: 650-323-3498; *District Chief of Staff:* Karen Chapman
Committee Assignment: Energy and Commerce

Espaillat, Adriano, D-N.Y. (13)

Capitol Hill Office: 2332 RHOB 20515; 225-4365; Fax: 226-9731; *Chief of Staff:* Aneiry Batista
Web: espaillat.house.gov
Facebook: www.facebook.com/RepEspaillat
Twitter: @RepEspaillat
YouTube: www.youtube.com/channel/UCi0niBYFhEY70Dz8InbX5OQ
Instagram: @repadrianoespaillat
District Offices: 3107 Kingsbridge Ave., Bronx, NY 10463; 646-740-3632; *District Director:* Cynthia Rodriguez
Harlem State Office Bldg., 163 W. 125th St., #508, New York, NY 10027; 212-663-3900
720 W. 181st St., #2, New York, NY 10033; 212-497-5959
Committee Assignments: Appropriations; Education and Labor

Estes, Ron, R-Kans. (4)

Capitol Hill Office: 2411 RHOB 20515; 225-6216; *Chief of Staff:* Josh Bell
Web: estes.house.gov
Facebook: www.facebook.com/RepRonEstes
Twitter: @RepRonEstes
YouTube: www.youtube.com/c/repronestes
Instagram: @repronestes
District Office: 7701 E. Kellogg Dr., #510, Wichita, KS 67207; 316-262-8992; *District Director:* Debbie Luper
Committee Assignments: Joint Economic; Ways and Means

Evans, Dwight, D-Pa. (3)

Capitol Hill Office: 1105 LHOB 20515; 225-4001; Fax: 225-5392; *Chief of Staff:* Anuj Gupta
Web: evans.house.gov
Facebook: www.facebook.com/RepDwightEvans
Twitter: @RepDwightEvans
Instagram: @repdwightevans
District Office: 7174 Ogontz Ave., Philadelphia, PA 19138; 215-276-0340; Fax: 215-276-2939; *District Director:* Felicia Parker-Cox
Committee Assignments: Small Business; Ways and Means

Fallon, Pat, R-Tex. (4)

Capitol Hill Office: 1118 LHOB 20515; 225-6673; *Chief of Staff:* Shannan Sorrell
Web: fallon.house.gov
Facebook: www.facebook.com/RepPatFallon
Twitter: @RepPatFallon

YouTube: www.youtube.com/channel/UC8t0pnbwG7N5z2xHRuFePsA
Instagram: @reppatfallon
District Offices: 6531 Horizon Rd., Suite A, Rockwall, TX 75032; 972-771-0100; Fax: 972-771-1222; *District Director:* Virginia Hannan
100 W. Houston St., #14, Sherman, TX 75090; 903-820-5170
2500 N. Robison Rd., #190, Texarkana, TX 75599; 903-716-7500
Committee Assignments: Armed Services; Oversight and Reform

Feenstra, Randy, R-Iowa (4)

Capitol Hill Office: 1440 LHOB 20515; 225-4426; Fax: 225-3193; *Chief of Staff:* Matt Leopold
Web: feenstra.house.gov
Facebook: www.facebook.com/RepFeenstra
Twitter: @repfeenstra
YouTube: www.youtube.com/channel/UCX_QgPNI9VoyFXrXe7SdLvA
Instagram: @repfeenstra
District Offices: 723 Central Ave., Fort Dodge, IA 50501; 515-302-7060; *District Director:* Emily Schwickerath
320 6th St., Room 112, Sioux City, IA 51101; 712-224-4692
Committee Assignments: Agriculture; Budget; Science, Space, and Technology

Ferguson, A. Drew, IV, R-Ga. (3)

Capitol Hill Office: 1032 LHOB 20515; 225-5901; Fax: 225-2515; *Chief of Staff:* David Sours
Web: ferguson.house.gov
Facebook: www.facebook.com/RepDrewFerguson
Twitter: @RepDrewFerguson
YouTube: www.youtube.com/channel/UCuK7_j2sREWi_7wBAN477bg
Instagram: @repdrewferguson
District Office: 1601 E. Hwy. 34, Suite B, Newnan, GA 30265; 770-683-2033; Fax: 770-683-2042; *District Director:* Andy Bush
Committee Assignment: Ways and Means

Fischbach, Michelle, R-Minn. (7)

Capitol Hill Office: 1237 LHOB 20515; 225-2165; Fax: 225-1593; *Chief of Staff:* David Fitzsimmons
Web: fischbach.house.gov
Facebook: www.facebook.com/RepFischbach
Twitter: @RepFischbach
YouTube: www.youtube.com/repfischbach
Instagram: @repfischbach
District Offices: 2513 8th St. South, Moorhead, MN 56560; 218-422-2090; *District Director:* Ben Anderson
2211 1st St. South, #190, Willmar, MN 56201; 320-403-6100
Committee Assignments: Agriculture; Judiciary; Rules

Fitzgerald, Scott, R-Wisc. (5)

Capitol Hill Office: 1507 LHOB 20515; 225-5101; *Chief of Staff:* Ryan McCormack

Web: fitzgerald.house.gov
Facebook: www.facebook.com/
CongressmanScottFitzgerald
Twitter: @RepFitzgerald
District Office: 120 Bishops Way, #154, Brookfield, WI
53005; 262-784-1111
Committee Assignments: Education and Labor; Judiciary;
Small Business

Fitzpatrick, Brian K., R-Pa. (1)

Capitol Hill Office: 271 CHOB 20515; 225-4276; Fax: 225-
9511; Chief of Staff: Joseph Knowles
Web: fitzpatrick.house.gov
Facebook: www.facebook.com/RepBrianFitz
Twitter: @RepBrianFitz
YouTube: www.youtube.com/channel/
UCYMNcgHss4_Q5JY2vSvMpgw
Instagram: @repbrianfitz
District Office: 1717 Langhorne Newtown Rd., #225,
Langhorne, PA 19047; 215-579-8102; Fax: 215-579-
8109; District Director: Kyle Melander
Committee Assignments: Foreign Affairs; Transportation
and Infrastructure; Permanent Select Intelligence

Fleischmann, Charles J. (Chuck), R-Tenn. (3)

Capitol Hill Office: 462 CHOB 20515; 225-3271; Fax: 225-
3494; Chief of Staff: Jim Hippe
Web: fleischmann.house.gov
Facebook: www.facebook.com/repchuck
Twitter: @RepChuck
YouTube: www.youtube.com/RepChuck
Instagram: @repchuck
District Offices: 6 E. Madison Ave., Athens, TN 37303;
423-745-4671; Fax: 423-745-6025; District Director:
Steve Howell
900 Georgia Ave., #126, Chattanooga, TN 37402-2282;
423-756-2342; Fax: 423-756-6613
200 Administration Rd., #100, Oak Ridge, TN 37830-8823;
865-576-1976; Fax: 865-576-3221
Committee Assignment: Appropriations

Fletcher, Lizzie, D-Tex. (7)

Capitol Hill Office: 119 CHOB 20515; 225-2571; Fax: 225-
4381; Chief of Staff: Sarah Kaplan Feinmann
Web: fletcher.house.gov
Facebook: www.facebook.com/RepFletcher
Twitter: @RepFletcher
YouTube: www.youtube.com/channel/
UCIWDLoDPvawP118TNWi-9rg
Instagram: @repfletcher
District Office: 5599 San Felipe Rd., #950, Houston, TX
77056; 713-353-8680; Fax: 713-353-8677
Committee Assignments: Energy and Commerce; Science,
Space, and Technology

Foster, Bill, D-Ill. (11)

Capitol Hill Office: 2366 RHOB 20515; 225-3515;
Fax: 225-9420; Chief of Staff: Samantha Warren
Web: foster.house.gov

Facebook: www.facebook.com/CongressmanBillFoster
Twitter: @RepBillFoster
YouTube: www.youtube.com/RepBillFoster
Instagram: @repbillfoster
District Offices: 2711 E. New York St., #204, Aurora, IL
60502; 630-585-7672; District Director: Hilary Denk
815 N. Larkin Ave., #206, Joliet, IL 60435; 815-280-5876
Committee Assignments: Financial Services; Science,
Space, and Technology, Select on Coronavirus Crisis

Foxx, Virginia, R-N.C. (5)

Capitol Hill Office: 2462 RHOB 20515; 225-2071;
Fax: 225-2995; Chief of Staff: Carson Middleton
Web: foxx.house.gov
Facebook: www.facebook.com/RepVirginiaFoxx
Twitter: @virginiafoxx
YouTube: www.youtube.com/RepVirginiaFoxx
Instagram: @repvirginiafoxx
District Offices: 400 Shadowline Dr., #205, Boone, NC
28607-4291; 828-265-0240; Fax: 828-265-0390; District
Director: Audrey Bishop
1303 Dallas Cherryville Hwy., #182, Dallas, NC 28034;
336-778-0211; Fax: 336-778-2290
Committee Assignments: Education and Labor; Oversight
and Reform

Frankel, Lois, D-Fla. (21)

Capitol Hill Office: 2305 RHOB 20515; 225-9890;
Fax: 225-1224; Chief of Staff: Joshua D. Cohen
Web: frankel.house.gov
Facebook: www.facebook.com/RepLoisFrankel
Twitter: @RepLoisFrankel
YouTube: www.youtube.com/RepLoisFrankel
Instagram: @reploisfrankel
District Office: 2500 N. Military Trail, #490, Boca Raton,
FL 33431; 561-998-9045; Fax: 561-998-9048; District
Director: Felicia Goldstein
Committee Assignments: Appropriations; Veterans'
Affairs

Franklin, C. Scott, R-Fla. (15)

Capitol Hill Office: 1517 LHOB 20515; 225-1252;
Fax: 226-0585; Chief of Staff: Melissa Kelly
Web: franklin.house.gov
Facebook: www.facebook.com/RepFranklin
Twitter: @RepFranklin
YouTube: www.youtube.com/channel/repfranklin
Instagram: @repfranklin
District Office: 124 S. Florida Ave., #304, Lakeland, FL
33801; 863-644-8215; Fax: 863-337-4104; District
Director: Alice Hunt
Committee Assignments: Armed Services; Oversight and
Reform

Fulcher, Russ, R-Idaho (1)

Capitol Hill Office: 1520 LHOB 20515-3515; 225-6611
Web: fulcher.house.gov
Facebook: www.facebook.com/RepRussFulcher
Twitter: @RepRussFulcher

YouTube: www.youtube.com/channel/
UCx2AS0O5frzPB8D6TqJ3Mqg
Instagram: @reprussfulcher
District Offices: 33 E. Broadway Ave., #251, Meridian, ID
83642; 208-888-3188; Fax: 208-888-0894; *District
Director:* Mike Cunnington
313 D St., #107, Lewiston, Idaho 83501; 208-743-1388
1250 West Ironwood Dr., #200, Coeur d'Alene, ID 83814;
208-667-0127; Fax: 208-667-0310
Committee Assignments: Education and Labor; Natural
Resources

Gaetz, Matt, R-Fla. (1)

Capitol Hill Office: 1721 LHOB 20515; *Chief of Staff:*
Jillian Lane-Wyant
Web: gaetz.house.gov
Facebook: www.facebook.com/CongressmanMattGaetz
Twitter: @RepMattGaetz
YouTube: www.youtube.com/channel/
UClqXcJew_A3s8qiX-T4a9CA
Instagram: @repmattgaetz
District Office: 226 S. Palafox Pl., 6th Floor, Pensacola, FL
32502; 850-479-1183; *District Director:* Dawn
McArdle
Satellite Office: 1170 Martin Luther King Jr. Blvd., Bldg. 4,
Room 454, Fort Walton Beach, FL 32547; 850-479-
1183
Committee Assignments: Armed Services; Judiciary

Gallagher, Mike, R-Wisc. (8)

Capitol Hill Office: 1230 LHOB 20515; 225-5665; *Chief of
Staff:* Taylor Andreae
Web: gallagher.house.gov
Facebook: www.facebook.com/RepMikeGallagher
Twitter: @RepGallagher
YouTube: www.youtube.com/channel/UCwaErp8t28d-
dVBio7Ii4Ig
Instagram: @repgallagher
District Office: 1702 Scheuring Rd., Suite B, De Pere,
WI 54115; 920-301-4500; *District Director:* David
Brooker
Committee Assignments: Armed Services; Permanent
Select Intelligence; Transportation and Infrastructure

Gallego, Rubén, D-Ariz. (7)

Capitol Hill Office: 1131 LHOB 20515-0307; 225-4065;
Chief of Staff: Grisella M. Martinez
Web: rubengallego.house.gov
Facebook: www.facebook.com/RepRubenGallego
Twitter: @RepRubenGallego
YouTube: www.youtube.com/channel/
UCru0REdL016INldtvq6gaLA
Instagram: @reprubengallego
District Office: 1601 N. 7th St., #310, Phoenix, AZ 85006;
602-256-0551; Fax: 602-257-9103; *District Director:*
Monica Sandschafer
Committee Assignments: Armed Services; Natural
Resources

Garamendi, John, D-Calif. (3)

Capitol Hill Office: 2368 RHOB 20515; 225-1880;
Fax: 225-5914; *Chief of Staff:* Bradley Bottoms
Web: garamendi.house.gov
Facebook: www.facebook.com/repgaramendi
Twitter: @RepGaramendi
YouTube: www.youtube.com/garamendiCA10
Instagram: @repgaramendi
District Offices: 412 G. St., Davis, CA 95616; 530-753-
5301; Fax: 530-753-5614; *District Director:* Debbi
Gibbs
1261 Travis Blvd., #180, Fairfield, CA 94533-6293; 707-
438-1822; Fax: 707-438-0523 (open Monday,
9 a.m.–5 p.m., Tuesday 9 a.m.–3 p.m., and Thursday
9 a.m.–3 p.m.)
Committee Assignments: Armed Services; Transportation
and Infrastructure

Garbarino, Andrew R., R-N.Y. (2)

Capitol Hill Office: 1516 LHOB 20515; 225-7896;
Fax: 226-2279; *Chief of Staff:* Deena Tauster
Web: garbarino.house.gov
Facebook: www.facebook.com/RepAndrewGarbarino
Twitter: @RepGarbarino
YouTube: www.youtube.com/channel/
UCX2bIeS3GwszQNxqPOGmtmw/videos
Instagram: @repandrewgarbarino
District Office: 1003 Park Blvd., Massapequa Park, NY
11762; 516-541-4225; Fax: 516-541-6602; *District
Director:* Donna Boyle
Committee Assignments: Homeland Security; Small
Business

García, Jesús G. (Chuy), D-Ill. (4)

Capitol Hill Office: 1519 LHOB 20515-3515; 225-8203;
Chief of Staff: Don Andres
Web: chuygarcia.house.gov
Facebook: www.facebook.com/RepChuyGarcia
Twitter: @RepChuyGarcia
YouTube: www.youtube.com/RepChuyGarcia
Instagram: @repchuygarcia
District Offices: 5624 W. Diversey Ave., Chicago, IL
60639; 773-342-0774; *District Director:* Patty Garcia
4376 S. Archer Ave., Chicago, IL 60632; 773-475-0833
Committee Assignments: Financial Services; Natural
Resources; Transportation and Infrastructure

Garcia, Mike, R-Calif. (25)

Capitol Hill Office: 1535 LHOB 20515; 225-1956;
Fax: 833-284-9085; *Chief of Staff:* Alan Tennille
Web: mikegarcia.house.gov
Facebook: www.facebook.com/RepMikeGarcia
Twitter: @RepMikeGarcia
YouTube: www.youtube.com/channel/
UCbDGRCQFM8Q7Z5jcclbCz4w
Instagram: @repmikegarcia
District Offices: 1008 W. Ave. M14, Suite E, Palmdale, CA
93551; 661-839-0532; *District Director:* Charles
Navarro

23734 Valencia Blvd., #301, Santa Clarita, CA 91355; 661-568-48551445 E. Los Angeles Ave., #206, Simi Valley, CA 93065; 805-760-9090

Committee Assignments: Appropriations; Science, Space, and Technology

Garcia, Sylvia R., D-Tex. (29)

Capitol Hill Office: 1620 LHOB 20515-3515; 225-1688; Fax: 225-9903; *Chief of Staff:* John Gorczynski
Web: sylviagarcia.house.gov
Facebook: www.facebook.com/RepSylviaGarcia
Twitter: @RepSylviaGarcia
YouTube: www.youtube.com/channel/UCkDqAfUk6rg2namKW5dtQYA
Instagram: @repsylviagarcia
District Office: 11811 E. Freeway, #430, Houston, TX 77029; 832-325-3150; *District Director:* Chris McCarthy

Committee Assignments: Financial Services; Judiciary

Gibbs, Bob, R-Ohio (7)

Capitol Hill Office: 2217 RHOB 20515-3518; 225-6265; Fax: 225-3394; *Chief of Staff:* Hillary Gross
Web: gibbs.house.gov
Facebook: www.facebook.com/RepBobGibbs
Twitter: @repbobgibbs
YouTube: www.youtube.com/RepBobGibbs
Instagram: @repbobgibbs
District Offices: 110 Cottage St., Ashland, OH 44805; 419-207-0650; Fax: 419-207-0655
110 Central Plaza South, Canton, OH 44702; 330-737-1631

Committee Assignments: Oversight and Reform; Transportation and Infrastructure

Gimenez, Carlos A., R-Fla. (26)

Capitol Hill Office: 419 CHOB 20515; 225-2778; *Chief of Staff:* Alex Ferro
Web: gimenez.house.gov
Facebook: www.facebook.com/RepCarlosGimenez
Twitter: @RepCarlos
Instagram: @repcarlosfl
District Office: 1100 Simonton St., Room 1-213, Key West, FL 33040; 305-292-4485; *District Director:* Christina Elias
404 Palm Dr., Florida City, FL 33034; 305-222-0160
14221 120th St. S.W., #115, Miami, FL 33186; 305-222-0160

Committee Assignments: Homeland Security; Science, Space, and Technology; Transportation and Infrastructure

Gohmert, Louie, R-Tex. (1)

Capitol Hill Office: 2269 RHOB 20515-4301; 225-3035; Fax: 226-1230; *Chief of Staff:* Connie Hair
Web: gohmert.house.gov
Facebook: www.facebook.com/RepLouieGohmert
Twitter: @replouiegohmert
YouTube: www.youtube.com/GohmertTX01
Instagram: @replouiegohmert

District Offices: 101 E. Methvin St., #302, Longview, TX 75601-7277; 903-236-8597; Fax: 903-561-7110; *District Director:* Jonna Boersma
300 E. Shepherd Ave., #210, Lufkin, TX 75901-3252; 936-632-3180; Fax: 903-561-7110
102 W. Houston St., Marshall, TX 75670-4038; 903-938-8386; Fax: 903-561-7110
101 W. Main St., #160, Nacogdoches, TX 75961-4830; 936-715-9514; Fax: 903-561-7110
1121 ESE Loop 323, #206, Tyler, TX 75701-9637; 903-561-6349; Fax: 903-561-7110

Committee Assignments: Judiciary; Natural Resources

Golden, Jared F., D-Maine (2)

Capitol Hill Office: 1222 LHOB 20515-3515; 225-6306; Fax: 225-2943; *Chief of Staff:* Aisha Woodward
Web: golden.house.gov
Facebook: www.facebook.com/RepGolden
Twitter: @RepGolden
District Offices: 6 State St., #101, Bangor, ME 04401; 207-249-7400; Fax: 844-269-7569; *District Director:* Barbara Hayslett
7 Hatch Dr., #230, Caribou, ME 04736; 207-492-6009; Fax: 207-493-4436
179 Lisbon St., Lewiston, ME 04240; 207-241-6767; Fax: 207-241-6770

Committee Assignments: Armed Services; Small Business

Gomez, Jimmy, D-Calif. (34)

Capitol Hill Office: 1530 LHOB 20515-0531; 225-6235; Fax: 225-2202 *Chief of Staff:* Bertha Alisa Guerrero
Web: gomez.house.gov
Facebook: www.facebook.com/RepJimmyGomez
Twitter: @RepJimmyGomez
YouTube: www.youtube.com/channel/UCOmm091WM6D01xTdzsWNvbQ
Instagram: @repjimmygomez
District Office: 350 S. Bixel St., #120, Los Angeles, CA 90017; 213-481-1425; Fax: 213-481-1427; *District Director:* Melissa Vargas

Committee Assignments: Oversight and Reform; Ways and Means

Gonzales, Tony, R-Tex. (23)

Capitol Hill Office: 1009 LHOB 20515; 225-4511; Fax: 225-2237; *Chief of Staff:* Luisa del Rosal
Web: gonzales.house.gov
Facebook: www.facebook.com/RepTonyGonzales
Twitter: @RepTonyGonzales
YouTube: www.youtube.com/channel/UCig5n4Otr-enqpM8OSJ8FGA
Instagram: @reptonygonzales
District Offices: 712 E. Gibbs St., #101, Del Rio, TX 78840; 830-308-6200; *District Director:* Jalen Falcon
103 West Callaghan St., Fort Stockton, TX 79735; 432-299-6200
6333 De Zavala Rd., #A216, San Antonio, TX 78249; 210-806-9920; Fax: 210-927-4903

124 Horizon Blvd., Socorro, TX 79927; 915-990-1500 (by appointment only)

2401 Garner Field Rd., Bldg. Q, Uvalde, TX 78801; 830-333-7410 (by appointment only)

Committee Assignment: Appropriations

Gonzalez, Anthony, R-Ohio (16)

Capitol Hill Office: 2458 RHOB 20515; 225-3876; Fax: 225-3059; *Deputy Chief of Staff:* Stephen Hostelley

Web: anthonygonzalez.house.gov

Facebook: www.facebook.com/RepAGonzalez

Twitter: @RepAGonzalez

YouTube: www.youtube.com/channel/UC1GnxY58Cx2F47ULByqT0oA

Instagram: @repagonzalez

District Offices: 4150 Belden Village St., #607, Canton, OH 44718; 330-599-7037; Fax: 440-268-8150; *District Director:* Heidi Matthews

13477 Prospect Rd., #212, Strongsville, OH 44149; 440-783-3696; Fax: 440-268-8150

Committee Assignments: Financial Services; Science, Space, and Technology

Gonzalez, Vicente, D-Tex. (15)

Capitol Hill Office: 113 CHOB 20515; 225-2531; Fax: 225-5688; *Chief of Staff:* Louise Bentsen

Web: gonzalez.house.gov

Facebook: www.facebook.com/USCongressmanVicenteGonzalez

Twitter: @RepGonzalez

YouTube: www.youtube.com/channel/UC5H6oYLKQ_xIXO5CG7fh4hw

Instagram: @repvicentegonzalez

District Offices: 1305 W. Hackberry Ave., McAllen, TX 78501; 956-682-5545; Fax: 956-682-0141; *District Director:* Stephanie Toscano

620 W. Adams, Falfurrias, TX 78355; 361-209-3027 (open Tuesday, 9 a.m.–12 p.m. and 1 p.m.–5 p.m.)

971 W. Court St., Seguin, TX 78155; 830-217-02601 (open 8 a.m.–12 p.m.)

Satellite Offices: 404 S. Mier St., San Diego, TX 78384; 888-217-0261 (open Monday, 9 a.m.–12 p.m. and 1 p.m.–5 p.m.)

131 W. Main St., Benavides, TX 78341; 888-217-0261 (open Wednesday, 9 a.m.–12 p.m. and 1 p.m.–5 p.m.)

Committee Assignments: Financial Services; Foreign Affairs

González-Colón, Jenniffer, R-P.R. (At Large)

Capitol Hill Office: 2338 RHOB 20515; 225-2615; Fax: 225-2154; *Chief of Staff:* Gabriella Boffelli

Web: gonzalez-colon.house.gov

Facebook: www.facebook.com/RepJenniffer

Twitter: @RepJenniffer

YouTube: www.youtube.com/channel/UCZj99h3-GNKjGGeyp7AJeXw

Instagram: @repjenniffer

District Office: P.O. Box 9023958, San Juan, PR 00902-3958; 787-723-6333; Fax: 787-729-6824 or 787-729-7738

Committee Assignments: Natural Resources; Transportation and Infrastructure, Science, Space, and Technology

Good, Bob, R-Va. (5)

Capitol Hill Office: 1213 LHOB 20515; 225-4711; Fax: 225-5681; *Chief of Staff:* Mark Kelly

Web: good.house.gov

Facebook: www.facebook.com/RepBobGood

Twitter: @RepBobGood

YouTube: www.youtube.com/channel/UCGgzX8qiWHfZfbfqfMsJGAg

District Office: 20436 Lynchburg Hwy, Suite F, Lynchburg, VA 24502; 434-791-2596; *District Director:* Sandy Adams

Committee Assignments: Budget; Education and Labor

Gooden, Lance, R-Tex. (5)

Capitol Hill Office: 1722 LHOB 20515-3515; 225-3484; Fax: 202-225-2464; *Chief of Staff:* Mehgan Perez-Acosta

Web: gooden.house.gov

Facebook: www.facebook.com/lancegoodenfortexas

Twitter: @LanceGooden

YouTube: www.youtube.com/channel/UCaEs0pYlL_1cLlPBHfl0RIg

Instagram: @lancegooden

District Office: 220 Burnett Trail, Canton, TX 75103; 903-502-5300; Fax: 903-502-5303; *District Director:* Jennifer Alden

Committee Assignment: Financial Services

Gosar, Paul A., R-Ariz. (4)

Capitol Hill Office: 2057 RHOB 20515-0301; 225-2315; Fax: 226-9739; *Chief of Staff:* Tom Van Flein

Web: gosar.house.gov

Facebook: www.facebook.com/repgosar

Twitter: @RepGosar

YouTube: www.youtube.com/repgosar

Instagram: @repgosar

District Offices: 122 N. Cortez St., #104, Prescott, AZ 86301; 928-445-1683; Fax: 928-445-3414; *District Director:* Penny Pew

6499 S. Kings Ranch Rd., #4, Gold Canyon, AZ 85118; 480-882-2697; Fax: 480-882-2698

No committee assignments

Gottheimer, Josh, D-N.J. (5)

Capitol Hill Office: 203 CHOB 20515; 225-4465; Fax: 225-9048; *Deputy Chief of Staff:* Cheryl Krouse

Web: gottheimer.house.gov

Facebook: www.facebook.com/RepJoshG

Twitter: @RepJoshG

YouTube: www.youtube.com/channel/UCNc_9pTqsP0J3tqNlelh7mA

Instagram: @repjoshg

District Offices: 65 Harristown Rd., #104, Glen Rock, NJ 07452; 201-389-1100

93 Spring St., #408, Newton, NJ 07860; 973-940-1117 (open Monday, Wednesday, Friday, 9 a.m.–5 p.m.)

Satellite Offices: 60 Margaret King Ave., Ringwood, NJ 07456; 973-814-4076 (open Thursday, 1 p.m.–4:30 p.m.)

100 Belvidere Ave., Washington, NJ 07882; 973-814-4076 (open Thursday 9 a.m.–1 p.m.)

21 Church St., Vernon Township, NJ 07462; 973-814-4076 (open Tuesday 9 a.m.–1 p.m.)

65 Central Ave., Hackensack, NJ 07601; 973-814-4076 (open Wednesday 12 p.m.–4 p.m.)

Committee Assignments: Financial Services; Homeland Security

Granger, Kay, R-Tex. (12)

Capitol Hill Office: 1026 LHOB 20515; 225-5071; Fax: 225-5683; *Chief of Staff:* Cole Rojewski
Web: kaygranger.house.gov
Facebook: www.facebook.com/RepKayGranger
Twitter: @RepKayGranger
YouTube: www.youtube.com/RepKayGranger
Instagram: @repkaygranger
District Office: 1701 River Run Rd., #407, Fort Worth, TX 76107-6548; 817-338-0909; Fax: 817-335-5852; *District Director:* Charlie Cripliver
Committee Assignment: Appropriations

Graves, Garret, R-La. (6)

Capitol Hill Office: 2402 RHOB 20515; 225-3901; Fax: 225-7313; *Chief of Staff:* Paul Sawyer
Web: garretgraves.house.gov
Facebook: www.facebook.com/CongressmanGarretGraves
Twitter: @RepGarretGraves
YouTube: www.youtube.com/channel/UCQLg9GGwTDluEFJtXf8seTA
Instagram: @instagravesla
District Offices: 2351 Energy Dr., #1200, Baton Rouge, LA 70808; 225-442-1731; Fax: 225-442-1736

Ascencion Parish Government Bldg., 615 E. Worthy St., Gonzales, LA 70737; 225-450-1672

Livingston Parish Government Bldg., 29261 Frost Rd., 2nd Floor, Livingston, LA 70754; 225-686-4413; Fax: 225-442-1736

908 E. 1st St., NSU Campus, Candies Hall, #405, Thibodaux, LA 70301; 985-448-4103; Fax: 225-442-1736

Committee Assignments: Natural Resources; Transportation and Infrastructure

Graves, Sam, R-Mo. (6)

Capitol Hill Office: 1135 LHOB 20515-2506; 225-7041; Fax: 225-8221; *Chief of Staff:* Nancy Peele
Web: graves.house.gov
Facebook: www.facebook.com/RepSamGraves
Twitter: @RepSamGraves
YouTube: www.youtube.com/channel/UCdg2ybvoHsSW6t7iJnKHlNg
Instagram: @repsamgraves
District Offices: 12200 N. Ambassador Dr., #234, Kansas City, MO 64163; 816-792-3976; Fax: 816-792-0694; *District Director:* Buffy Smith

411 Jules St., #111, St. Joseph, MO 64501-2275; 816-749-0800; Fax: 816-749-0801

6079 County Rd. 425, PO Box 364, Hannibal, MO 63401; 573-221-3400

Committee Assignments: Armed Services; Transportation and Infrastructure

Green, Al, D-Tex. (9)

Capitol Hill Office: 2347 RHOB 20515-4309; 225-7508; Fax: 225-2947; *Chief of Staff:* Jacqueline Ellis
Web: algreen.house.gov
Facebook: www.facebook.com/repalgreen
Twitter: @RepAlGreen
YouTube: www.youtube.com/RepAlGreen
Instagram: @repalgreen
District Office: 3003 S. Loop West, #460, Houston, TX 77054-1301; 713-383-9234; Fax: 713-383-9202
Committee Assignments: Financial Services; Homeland Security

Green, Mark E., R-Tenn. (7)

Capitol Hill Office: 2446 RHOB 20515-3515; 225-2811; Fax: 225-3004; *Chief of Staff:* Stephen Siao
Web: markgreen.house.gov
Facebook: www.facebook.com/RepMarkGreenTN
Twitter: @RepMarkGreen
YouTube: www.youtube.com/channel/UC5kpqepPIdUNaMtfGb-7MwA
Instagram: @repmarkgreen
District Offices: 128 N. 2nd St., #104 Clarksville, TN 37040; 931-266-4483; Fax: 202-225-3004; *District Director:* Steve Allbrooks

305 Public Square, #212, Franklin, TN 37064; 629-223-6050; Fax: 202-225-3004

Committee Assignments: Armed Services; Foreign Affairs; Select on Coronavirus Crisis

Greene, Marjorie Taylor, R-Ga. (14)

Capitol Hill Office: 1023 LHOB 20515; 225-5211; *Chief of Staff:* Ed Buckham
Web: greene.house.gov
Facebook: www.facebook.com/RepMTGreene
Twitter: @RepMTG
YouTube: www.youtube.com/c/RepMTG
Instagram: @repmtg
District Office: P.O. Box 1527, Rome, GA 30162; 706-290-1776 or 706-226-5320; *District Director:* Travis Loudermilk
No committee assignments

Griffith, H. Morgan, R-Va. (9)

Capitol Hill Office: 2202 RHOB 20515-4609; 225-3861; Fax: 225-0076; *Chief of Staff:* Kelly Lungren
Web: morgangriffith.house.gov
Facebook: www.facebook.com/RepMorganGriffith

Twitter: @RepMGriffith
YouTube: www.youtube.com/RepMorganGriffith
Instagram: @hmorgangriffith
District Offices: 323 W. Main St., Abingdon, VA 24210-2605; 276-525-1405; Fax: 276-525-1444; *District Director:* Josh Hess
17 W. Main St., Christiansburg, VA 24073-3055; 540-381-5671; Fax: 540-381-5675
Committee Assignment: Energy and Commerce

Grijalva, Raúl, D-Ariz. (3)

Capitol Hill Office: 1511 LHOB 20515-0307; 225-2435; Fax: 225-1541; *Chief of Staff:* Amy Emerick Clerkin
Web: grijalva.house.gov
Facebook: www.facebook.com/Rep.Grijalva
Twitter: @RepRaulGrijalva
YouTube: www.youtube.com/RaulGrijalvaAZ07
Instagram: @repraulgrijalva
District Offices: 1412 N. Central Ave., Suite B, Avondale, AZ 85323; 623-536-3388; Fax: 623-535-7479; *District Director:* Rubén Reyes
146 N. State Ave., P.O. Box 4105, Somerton, AZ 85350; 928-343-7933; Fax: 928-343-7949
El Pueblo Community Center, 101 W. Irvington Rd, Bldg. 4 and 5, Tucson, AZ 85714; 520-622-6788; Fax: 520-622-0198; *District Director:* Rubén Reyes
Committee Assignments: Education and Labor; Natural Resources, Chair

Grothman, Glenn, R-Wisc. (6)

Capitol Hill Office: 1427 LHOB 20515-4906; 225-2476; Fax: 225-2356; *Chief of Staff:* Alan Ott
Web: grothman.house.gov
Facebook: www.facebook.com/RepGrothman
Twitter: @RepGrothman
YouTube: www.youtube.com/channel/Ucui4k83Cot4aeVW_8T33fgg
Instagram: @repglenngrothman
District Office: 24 W. Pioneer Rd., Fond du Lac, WI 54935; 920-907-0624; Fax: 920-907-0763
Committee Assignments: Budget; Education and Labor; Oversight and Reform

Guest, Michael, R-Miss. (3)

Capitol Hill Office: 418 CHOB 20515-3515; 225-5031; Fax: 225-5797; *Chief of Staff:* Jordan Downs
Web: guest.house.gov
Facebook: www.facebook.com/RepMichaelGuest
Twitter: @RepMichaelGuest
Instagram: @repmichaelguest
District Offices: 308B E. Government St., Brandon, MS 39042; 769-241-6120; *District Director:* Brady Stewart
2214 5th St., #2170, Meridian, MS 39301; 601-693-6681
600 Russell St., #160, Starkville, MS 39759; 662-324-0007; *Deputy District Director:* Kyle Jordan
Satellite Office: 230 S. Whitworth Ave., Brookhaven, MS 39601; 601-823-3400

Committee Assignments: Ethics; Homeland Security; Transportation and Infrastructure

Guthrie, Brett, R-Ky. (2)

Capitol Hill Office: 2434 RHOB 20515-1702; 225-3501; Fax: 226-2019; *Chief of Staff:* Sophie Khanahmadi
Web: guthrie.house.gov
Facebook: www.facebook.com/CongressmanGuthrie
Twitter: @RepGuthrie
YouTube: www.youtube.com/BrettGuthrie
Instagram: @repguthrie
District Office: 996 Wilkinson Trace, Suite B2, Bowling Green, KY 42103; 270-842-9896; Fax: 270-842-9081; *District Director:* Mark Lord
Satellite Offices: 411 W. Lincoln Trail Blvd., Radcliff, KY 40160
2200 Airport Rd., Owensboro, KY 42301
Committee Assignment: Energy and Commerce

Harder, Josh, D-Calif. (10)

Capitol Hill Office: 209 CHOB 20515-3515; 225-4540; Fax: 225-3402; *Chief of Staff:* Rachael Goldenberg
Web: harder.house.gov
Facebook: www.facebook.com/RepJoshHarder
Twitter: @RepJoshHarder
YouTube: www.youtube.com/channel/UC-bcHaK1t-JycGTyUX3tkgw
Instagram: @repjoshharder
District Office: 4701 Sisk Rd., #202, Modesto, CA 95356; 209-579-5458; Fax: 209-702-6569; *District Director:* Rhodesia Ranson
Committee Assignments: Agriculture; Appropriations

Harris, Andy, R-Md. (1)

Capitol Hill Office: 2334 RHOB 20515; 225-5311; Fax: 225-0254; *Chief of Staff:* Bryan Shuy
Web: harris.house.gov
Facebook: www.facebook.com/AndyHarrisMD
Twitter: @RepAndyHarrisMD
YouTube: www.youtube.com/RepAndyHarris
Instagram: @rep.harris
District Offices: 15 E. Churchville Rd., #102B, Bel Air, MD 21014-3837; 410-588-5670
100 Olde Point Village, #101, Chester, MD 21619; 410-643-5425; Fax: 410-643-5429
100 E. Main St., #702, Salisbury, MD 21801; 443-944-8624; *Director of Legislative and Consituent Services:* Bunky Luffman
Committee Assignment: Appropriations

Harshbarger, Diana, R-Tenn. (1)

Capitol Hill Office: 167 CHOB 20515; 225-6356; Fax: 225-5714; *Chief of Staff:* Zac Rutherford
Web: harshbarger.house.gov
Facebook: www.facebook.com/RepDianaHarshbarger
Twitter: @RepHarshbarger
YouTube: www.youtube.com/channel/UCEJr4KThWA5WBmFzIkz10JA

District Office: 205 Revere St., Kingsport, TN 37660; 423-398-5186; Fax: 423-398-5312; *District Director:* Daryl Brady

1501 E. Morris Blvd., #12, Morristown, TN 37813, 423-254-1400; Fax: 423-254-1403

Committee Assignments: Education and Labor; Homeland Security

Hartzler, Vicky, R-Mo. (4)

Capitol Hill Office: 2235 RHOB 20515-2504; 225-2876; Fax: 225-0148; *Chief of Staff:* Chris Connelly

Web: hartzler.house.gov

Facebook: www.facebook.com/VickyForCongress

Twitter: @RepHartzler

YouTube: www.youtube.com/RepVickyHartzler

Instagram: @rephartzler

District Offices: 2415 Carter Lane, #4, Columbia, MO 65201; 573-442-9311; Fax: 573-442-9309; *District Director:* Drew Cannon

1917 N. Commercial St., Harrisonville, MO 64701-1252; 816-884-3411

Cowan Civic Center, 500 E. Elm St., Lebanon, MO 65536-3029; 417-532-5582

Committee Assignments: Agriculture; Armed Services

Hayes, Jahana, D-Conn. (5)

Capitol Hill Office: 1415 LHOB 20515-3515; 225-4476; *Chief of Staff:* Alex Ginis

Web: hayes.house.gov

Facebook: www.facebook.com/RepJahanaHayes

Twitter: @RepJahanaHayes

YouTube: www.youtube.com/RepJahanaHayes

Instagram: @repjahanahayes

District Office: 108 Bank St., 2nd Floor, Waterbury, CT 06702; 860-223-8412; *District Director:* Jennine Lupo

Committee Assignments: Agriculture; Education and Labor

Hern, Kevin, R-Okla. (1)

Capitol Hill Office: 1019 LHOB 20515-3515; 225-2211; Fax: 225-9187; *Chief of Staff:* Cameron Foster

Web: hern.house.gov

Facebook: www.facebook.com/repkevinhern

Twitter: @repkevinhern

YouTube: www.youtube.com/channel/UC9XRRGCgGOEtEOwUAo1rYZg

Instagram: @repkevinhern

District Office: 2448 E. 81st St., #5150, Tulsa, OK 74137; 918-935-3222; Fax: 202-225-9187; *District Director:* Robert Aery

Committee Assignment: Ways and Means

Herrell, Yvette, R-N.M. (2)

Capitol Hill Office: 1305 LHOB 20515; 225-2365; Fax: 225-9599; *Chief of Staff:* Michael Horanburg

Web: herrell.house.gov

Facebook: www.facebook.com/RepHerrell

Twitter: @RepHerrell

YouTube: www.youtube.com/channel/UCuGL0nSO2RZvbJWyHLdyTPQ

Instagram: @repherrell

District Offices: 4440 Sonoma Ranch Blvd., Suite B, Las Cruces, NM 88011; 575-323-6390; *District Director:* Barbara Romero

400 N. Pennsylvania Ave., #1080, Roswell, NM 88201; 575-578-6290

Committee Assignments: Natural Resources; Oversight and Reform

Herrera Beutler, Jaime, R-Wash. (3)

Capitol Hill Office: 2352 RHOB 20515-4703; 225-3536; Fax: 225-3478; *Deputy Chief of Staff:* Jordan Evich

Web: herrerabeutler.house.gov

Facebook: www.facebook.com/herrerabeutler

Twitter: @HerreraBeutler

YouTube: www.youtube.com/RepHerreraBeutler

Instagram: @herrerabeutler

District Office: O. O. Howard's House (Officer's Row), 750 Anderson St., Suite B, Vancouver, WA 98661-3853; 360-695-6292; Fax: 360-695-6197; *District Director:* Pam Peiper

Committee Assignments: Appropriations; Joint Economic

Hice, Jody B., R-Ga. (10)

Capitol Hill Office: 404 CHOB 20515; 225-4101; Fax: 226-0776; *Chief of Staff:* Tim Reitz

Web: hice.house.gov

Facebook: www.facebook.com/CongressmanJodyHice

Twitter: @CongressmanHice

YouTube: www.youtube.com/channel/UCzUMsS8DusN2QLpgweFthgQ

Instagram: @rep_hice

District Offices: 1020 Park Dr., Suite B, Greensboro, GA 30642; 762-445-1776; Fax: 770-266-6751; *District Director:* Jessica Hayes

100 Court St., Monroe, GA 30655; 770-207-1776; Fax: 770-266-6751

Satellite Office: City-County Administration Bldg., 210 Railroad St., Room 2401, Thomson, GA 30824 (by appointment only)

Committee Assignments: Natural Resources; Oversight and Reform

Higgins, Brian, D-N.Y. (26)

Capitol Hill Office: 2459 RHOB 20515-3227; 225-3306; Fax: 226-0347; *Chief of Staff:* Matthew Fery

Web: higgins.house.gov

Facebook: www.facebook.com/RepBrianHiggins

Twitter: @RepBrianHiggins

YouTube: www.youtube.com/CongressmanHiggins

Instagram: @repbrianhiggins

District Offices: 726 Exchange St., #601, Buffalo, NY 14210-1484; 716-852-3501; Fax: 716-852-3929; *District Director:* Megan Corbett

800 Main St., #3C, Niagara Falls, NY 14301; 716-282-1274; Fax: 716-282-2479

Committee Assignments: Budget; Ways and Means

Higgins, Clay, R-La. (3)

Capitol Hill Office: 572 CHOB 20515; 225-2031; Fax: 225-5724; *Chief of Staff:* Kathee Facchiano
Web: clayhiggins.house.gov
Facebook: www.facebook.com/CongressmanClayHiggins
Twitter: @RepClayHiggins
YouTube: www.youtube.com/c/CongressmanClayHiggins
Instagram: @repclayhiggins
District Office: Chase Bldg., 600 Jefferson St., #808, Lafayette, LA 70501; 337-703-6105; *District Director:* John Chautin
Committee Assignments: Homeland Security; Oversight and Reform

Hill, J. French, R-Ark. (2)

Capitol Hill Office: 1533 LHOB 20515-0402; 225-2506; Fax: 225-5903; *Chief of Staff:* Brooke Bennett
Web: hill.house.gov
Facebook: www.facebook.com/RepFrenchHill
Twitter: @RepFrenchHill
YouTube: www.youtube.com/repfrenchhill
Instagram: @repfrenchhill
District Offices: 1105 Deer St., #12, Conway, AR 72032; 501-358-3481; Fax: 501-358-3494; *District Director:* Anushree Jumde
1501 N. University Ave., #630, Little Rock, AR 72207; 501-324-5941; Fax: 501-324-6029
Committee Assignment: Financial Services

Himes, Jim, D-Conn. (4)

Capitol Hill Office: 2137 RHOB 20515-0704; 225-5541; Fax: 225-9629; *Chief of Staff:* Mark Snyder
Web: himes.house.gov
Facebook: www.facebook.com/RepJimHimes
Twitter: @jahimes
YouTube: www.youtube.com/congressmanhimes
Instagram: @repjimhimes
District Offices: 350 Fairfield Ave., #603, Bridgeport, CT 06604-4808; 203-333-6600 or 866-453-0028; Fax: 203-333-6655; *District Director:* Jimmy Tickey
888 Washington Blvd., 10th Floor, Stamford, CT 06901-2902; 203-353-9400; Fax: 203-323-1793; *Constituent Services Rep.:* Gloria DePina
Committee Assignments: Financial Services; Permanent Select Intelligence

Hinson, Ashley, R-Iowa (1)

Capitol Hill Office: 1429 LHOB 20515; 225-2911; *Chief of Staff:* Jimmy Peacock
Web: hinson.house.gov
Facebook: www.facebook.com/RepAshleyHinson
Twitter: @RepAshleyHinson
Instagram: @repashleyhinson
YouTube: www.youtube.com/channel/UCjB2zmmY92PtuUbRq-HusqA
District Offices: 118 3rd Ave. S.E., #206, Cedar Rapids, IA 52401; 319-364-2288; *District Director:* Sam Pritchard
1050 Main St., Dubuque, IA 52001; 563-557-7789
521A Lafayette St., Waterloo, IA 50703; 319-266-6925
Committee Assignments: Appropriations; Budget

Hollingsworth, Trey, R-Ind. (9)

Capitol Hill Office: 1641 LHOB 20515; 225-5315; *Chief of Staff:* Blaine Kistler
Web: hollingsworth.house.gov
Facebook: www.facebook.com/RepTrey
Twitter: @RepTrey
YouTube: www.youtube.com/channel/UCTgS8a_zLg8HpUnk5WXY5ag
Instagram: @rep_trey
District Offices: 100 E. Jefferson St., Franklin, IN 46131; 317-851-8710; *Legislative Director:* Maddie Mitchell
321 Quartermaster Court, Jeffersonville, IN 47130; 812-288-3999
Committee Assignment: Financial Services

Horsford, Steven, D-Nev. (4)

Capitol Hill Office: 562 CHOB 20515; 225-9894; Fax: 225-9783; *Chief of Staff:* Asha Jones
Web: horsford.house.gov
Facebook: www.facebook.com/RepHorsford
Twitter: @RepHorsford
YouTube: www.youtube.com/RepHorsford
Instagram: @rephorsford
District Office: 2250 N. Las Vegas Blvd., #500, North Las Vegas, NV 89030; 702-963-9360; *District Director:* Divya Narala
Committee Assignments: Armed Services; Budget; Ways and Means

Houlahan, Chrissy, D-Pa. (6)

Capitol Hill Office: 1218 LHOB 20515-3515; 225-4315; *Chief of Staff:* Michelle Dorothy
Web: houlahan.house.gov
Facebook: www.facebook.com/RepChrissyHoulahan
Twitter: @rephoulahan
YouTube: www.youtube.com/channel/UCGydnnhsUZqFBscmcWcT-zQ
Instagram: @repchrissyhoulahan
District Offices: 815 Washington St., #2-48, Reading, PA 19601; 610-295-0815; *District Director:* Sue Walker
709 E. Gay St., #4, West Chester, PA 19380; 610-883-5050
Committee Assignments: Armed Services; Foreign Affairs; Small Business

Hoyer, Steny H., D-Md. (5)

Capitol Hill Office: 1705 LHOB 20515; 225-4131; Fax: 225-4300; *Chief of Staff:* Jim Notter
Majority Leader Office: H-107 The Capitol, 20515; 202-225-3130
Web: hoyer.house.gov
Facebook: www.facebook.com/LeaderHoyer
Twitter: @LeaderHoyer
YouTube: www.youtube.com/LeaderHoyer
Instagram: @leaderhoyer
District Offices: U.S. District Courthouse, 6500 Cherrywood Lane, #310, Greenbelt, MD 20770-1287; 301-474-0119; Fax: 301-474-4697; *District Director:* Terrance Taylor

4475 Regency Pl., #203, White Plains, MD 20695; 301-843-1577; Fax: 301-843-1331
Majority Leader

Hudson, Richard, R-N.C. (8)

Capitol Hill Office: 2112 RHOB 20515; 225-3715; Fax: 225-4036; *Chief of Staff:* Billy Constangy
Web: hudson.house.gov
Facebook: www.facebook.com/RepRichHudson
Twitter: @RepRichHudson
YouTube: www.youtube.com/reprichhudson
Instagram: @reprichhudson
District Offices: 325 McGill Ave. N.W., #500, Concord, NC 28027-6194; 704-786-1612; Fax: 704-782-1004; *District Director:* Georgia Lozier
225 Green St., #202, Fayetteville, NC 28301; 910-997-2070; Fax: 910-817-7202
Committee Assignment: Energy and Commerce

Huffman, Jared, D-Calif. (2)

Capitol Hill Office: 1527 LHOB 20515; 225-5161; Fax: 225-5163; *Chief of Staff:* Jennifer Goedke
Web: huffman.house.gov
Facebook: www.facebook.com/RepHuffman
Twitter: @RepHuffman
YouTube: www.youtube.com/RepHuffman
Instagram: @rephuffman
District Offices: 317 3rd St., #1, Eureka, CA 95501; 707-407-3585; Fax: 707-407-3559; *District Director:* Jenny Callaway
430 N. Franklin St., P.O. Box 2208, Fort Bragg, CA 95437; 707-962-0933; Fax: 707-962-0905
206 G St., #3, Petaluma, CA 94952; 707-981-8967
999 5th Ave., #290, San Rafael, CA 94901; 415-258-9657; Fax: 415-258-9913
200 S. School St., Ukiah, CA 95482; 707-671-7449; Fax: 707-962-0905
Committee Assignments: Natural Resources; Transportation and Infrastructure; Select on the Climate Crisis

Huizenga, Bill, R-Mich. (2)

Capitol Hill Office: 2232 RHOB 20515-2202; 225-4401; Fax: 226-0779; *Chief of Staff:* Jon DeWitte
Web: huizenga.house.gov
Facebook: www.facebook.com/rephuizenga
Twitter: @RepHuizenga
YouTube: www.youtube.com/RepHuizenga
Instagram: @rephuizenga
District Offices: 1 S. Harbor Ave., #6B, Grand Haven, MI 49417; 616-414-5516; Fax: 616-570-0934; *District Director:* Todd Whiteman
4555 Wilson Ave. S.W., #3, Grandville, MI 49418; 616-570-0917; Fax: 616-570-0934
Committee Assignment: Financial Services

Issa, Darrell, R-Calif. (50)

Capitol Hill Office: 2300 RHOB 20515; 225-5672; *Chief of Staff:* Veronica Wong
Web: issa.house.gov

Facebook: www.facebook.com/CongressmanDarrellIssa
Twitter: @RepDarrellIssa
Instagram: @repdarrellissa
YouTube: www.youtube.com/user/RepDarrellIssa?app=desktop
District Offices: 570 Rancheros Dr., #250, San Marcos, CA 92069; 760-304-7575; *District Director:* John Franklin
41000 Main St., Temecula, CA 92590; 760-304-7575
Committee Assignments: Foreign Affairs; Judiciary

Jackson, Ronny, R-Tex. (13)

Capitol Hill Office: 118 CHOB 20515; 225-3706; Fax: 225-3486; *Chief of Staff:* Jeff Billman
Web: jackson.house.gov
Facebook: www.facebook.com/RepRonnyJackson
Twitter: @RepRonnyJackson
YouTube: www.youtube.com/channel/UCXhohNmrQ0R-c-5Nv2VfD9g
Instagram: @repronnyjackson
District Offices: 620 S. Taylor St., #200, Amarillo, TX 79101; 806-641-5600; Fax: 806-375-5152; *District Director:* Jake LaGrone
2525 Kell Blvd., #406, Wichita Falls, TX 76308; 940-285-8000
Committee Assignments: Armed Services; Foreign Affairs

Jackson Lee, Sheila, D-Tex. (18)

Capitol Hill Office: 2426 RHOB 20515-4318; 225-3816; Fax: 225-3317; *Chief of Staff (Acting):* Lillie Coney
Web: jacksonlee.house.gov
Facebook: www.facebook.com/CongresswomanSheilaJacksonLee
Twitter: @JacksonLeeTX18
YouTube: www.youtube.com/RepJacksonLee
Instagram: @repjacksonlee
District Offices: 1919 Smith St., #1180, Houston, TX 77002-8098; 713-655-0050; Fax: 713-655-1612; *District Director:* Yuroba Harris
6719 W. Montgomery Rd., #204, Houston, TX 77091-3105; 713-691-4882
420 W. 19th St., Houston, TX 77008-3914; 713-861-4070
4300 Lyons Ave., Houston, TX 77020; 713-227-7740
Committee Assignments: Budget; Homeland Security; Judiciary

Jacobs, Chris, R-N.Y. (27)

Capitol Hill Office: 214 CHOB 20515; 225-5265; Fax: 225-5910; *Chief of Staff:* Kyle Kizzier
Web: jacobs.house.gov
Facebook: www.facebook.com/RepChrisJacobs
Twitter: @RepJacobs
District Offices: 128 Main St., Geneseo, NY 14454; 585-519-4002; *District Director:* George McNerney
8203 Main St., #2, Williamsville, NY 14221; 716-634-2324
Committee Assignments: Agriculture; Budget; Education and Labor

Jacobs, Sara, D-Calif. (53)

Capitol Hill Office: 1232 LHOB 20515; 225-2040;
Fax: 225-2948; *Chief of Staff:* Amy Kuhn
Web: sarajacobs.house.gov
Facebook: www.facebook.com/RepSaraJacobs
Twitter: @RepSaraJacobs
YouTube: www.youtube.com/channel/
UCogCgQqMdYS75RiZaeaxm8w
Instagram: @repsarajacobs
District Office: 2700 Adams Ave., #102, San Diego, CA
92116; 619-280-5353; *District Director:* Paola Guzman
Committee Assignments: Armed Services; Foreign
Affairs; Select on Economic Disparity and Fairness in
Growth; Democratic Steering and Policy

Jayapal, Pramila, D-Wash. (7)

Capitol Hill Office: 2346 RHOB 20515; 225-3106;
Fax: 225-6197; *Chief of Staff:* Lilah Pomerance
Web: jayapal.house.gov
Facebook: www.facebook.com/RepJayapal
Twitter: @RepJayapal
YouTube: www.youtube.com/repjayapal
Instagram: @repjayapal
District Office: 1904 3rd Ave., #510, Seattle, WA 98101;
206-674-0040; Fax: 206-623-0256; *District Director:*
Rachel Berkson
Committee Assignments: Budget; Education and Labor;
Judiciary

Jeffries, Hakeem S., D-N.Y. (8)

Capitol Hill Office: 2433 RHOB 20515; 225-5936;
Fax: 225-1018; *Chief of Staff:* Tasia Jackson
Web: jeffries.house.gov
Facebook: www.facebook.com/RepJeffries
Twitter: @RepJeffries
YouTube: www.youtube.com/repjeffries
Instagram: @repjeffries
District Offices: 445 Neptune Ave., 1st Floor, #2C,
Brooklyn, NY 11224; 718-373-0033; Fax: 718-373-
1333; *District Director:* Maron Alemu
55 Hanson Pl., #603, Brooklyn, NY 11217; 718-237-2211;
Fax: 718-237-2273
Committee Assignments: Budget; Judiciary

Johnson, Bill, R-Ohio (6)

Capitol Hill Office: 2336 RHOB 20515; 225-5705;
Fax: 225-5907; *Chief of Staff:* Mike Smullen
Web: billjohnson.house.gov
Facebook: www.facebook.com/RepBillJohnson
Twitter: @RepBillJohnson
YouTube: www.youtube.com/RepBillJohnson
Instagram: @repbilljohnson
District Offices: 116 Southgate Pkwy., Cambridge, OH
43725; 740-432-2366; Fax: 740-432-2587; *District
Director:* Sarah Keeler
202 Park Ave., Suite C, Ironton, OH 45638-1595; 740-534-
9431; Fax: 740-534-9482
246 Front St., Marietta, OH 45750-2908; 740-376-0868;
Fax: 740-376-0886

192 E. State St., Salem, OH 44460-2843; 330-337-6951;
Fax: 330-337-7125
Committee Assignment: Energy and Commerce

Johnson, Dusty, R-S.D. (At Large)

Capitol Hill Office: 1714 LHOB 20515; 225-2801;
Fax: 225-5823; *Chief of Staff:* Andrew Christianson
Web: dustyjohnson.house.gov
Facebook: www.facebook.com/RepDustyJohnson
Twitter: @RepDustyJohnson
YouTube: www.youtube.com/channel/
UCDeVV7OXKf1lkhZGVo995Tw
Instagram: @repdustyjohnson
District Offices: 304 6th Ave. S.E., Aberdeen, SD 57401;
605-622-1060; *District Director:* Andrea Rose-Prehn
2525 W. Main St., #310, Rapid City, SD 57702; 605-646-
6454; Fax: 605-791-4679
230 S. Phillips Ave., #307, Sioux Falls, SD 57104; 605-275-
2868; Fax: 202-275-2875; *District Director:* Andrea
Rose-Prehn
Committee Assignments: Agriculture; Transportation
and Infrastructure

Johnson, Eddie Bernice, D-Tex. (30)

Capitol Hill Office: 2306 RHOB 20515; 225-8885;
Fax: 226-1477; *Chief of Staff:* Murat T. Gokcigdem
Web: ebjohnson.house.gov
Facebook: www.facebook.com/CongresswomanEBJtx30
Twitter: @RepEBJ
YouTube: www.youtube.com/RepEddieBJohnson
Instagram: @repebj
District Office: 1825 Market Center Blvd., #440, Dallas,
TX 75207; 214-922-8885; Fax: 214-922-7028; *District
Director:* Renee Edwards
Committee Assignments: Science, Space, and Technology,
Chair; Transportation and Infrastructure

Johnson, Henry C. (Hank), Jr., D-Ga. (4)

Capitol Hill Office: 2240 RHOB 20515; 225-1605;
Fax: 226-0691; *Chief of Staff:* Scott Goldstein
Web: hankjohnson.house.gov
Facebook: www.facebook.com/RepHankJohnson
Twitter: @RepHankJohnson
YouTube: www.youtube.com/RepHankJohnson
Instagram: @rephankjohnson
District Office: 5240 Snapfinger Park Dr., #140, Decatur,
GA 30035; 770-987-2291; Fax: 770-987-8721; *District
Director:* Kathy Register
Committee Assignments: Judiciary; Oversight and
Reform; Transportation and Infrastructure

Johnson, Mike, R-La. (4)

Capitol Hill Office: 568 CHOB 20515; 225-2777; Fax: 225-
8039; *Chief of Staff:* Hayden Haynes
Web: mikejohnson.house.gov
Facebook: www.facebook.com/RepMikeJohnson
Twitter: @RepMikeJohnson
YouTube: www.youtube.com/channel/
UCzqBEpeIaDEfvAtsA53Fx2Q

Instagram: @repmikejohnson
District Offices: 2250 Hospital Dr., #248, Bossier City, LA 71111; 318-840-0309; Fax: 318-584-7294; *District Director:* Chip Layton
3329 University Pkwy., Bldg. 552, Room 24, Leesville, LA 71446; 337-423-4232
Satellite Office: 444 Caspari Dr., South Hall, Room 224, Natchitoches, LA 71497; 318-951-4316
Committee Assignments: Judiciary; Natural Resources

Jones, Mondaire, D-N.Y. (17)

Capitol Hill Office: 1017 LHOB 20515; 225-6506; Fax: 225-0546; *Chief of Staff:* Zach Fisch
Web: jones.house.gov
Facebook: www.facebook.com/repmondaire
Twitter: @RepMondaire
YouTube: www.youtube.com/c/RepMondaire
Instagram: @repmondaire
District Offices: 222 Mamaroneck Ave., #312, White Plains, NY 10605; 914-323-5550; *District Director:* Joan Grangenois-Thomas
20 S. Main St., New City, NY 10956; 845-826-8090
Committee Assignments: Education and Labor; Ethics; Judiciary

Jordan, Jim, R-Ohio (4)

Capitol Hill Office: 2056 RHOB 20515; 225-2676; Fax: 226-0577; *Chief of Staff:* Kevin Eichinger
Web: jordan.house.gov
Facebook: www.facebook.com/repjimjordan
Twitter: @Jim_Jordan
YouTube: www.youtube.com/RepJimJordan
Instagram: @jim.jordan.official
District Offices: 3121 W. Elm Plaza, Lima, OH 45805-2516; 419-999-6455; Fax: 419-999-4238; *District Director:* Cameron Warner
13B E. Main St., Norwalk, OH 44857; 419-663-1426; Fax: 419-668-3015
Satellite Office: 500 S. Sandusky Ave., Bucyrus, OH 44820; 419-663-1426 (open Tuesday and Thursday, 8 a.m.–4:30 p.m.)
Committee Assignments: Judiciary; Oversight and Reform

Joyce, David P., R-Ohio (14)

Capitol Hill Office: 2065 RHOB 20515; 225-5731; Fax: 225-3307; *Chief of Staff:* Anna Romeo
Web: joyce.house.gov
Facebook: www.facebook.com/RepDaveJoyce
Twitter: @RepDaveJoyce
YouTube: www.youtube.com/RepDaveJoyce
Instagram: @repdavejoyce
District Offices: 8500 Station St., #390, Mentor, OH 44060; 440-352-3939 or 800-447-0529; Fax: 440-266-9004; *District Director:* Maureen Jeffery
10075 Ravenna Rd., Twinsburg, OH 44087; 330-357-4139; Fax: 330-425-7071
Committee Assignments: Appropriations; Ethics; Select on the Modernization of Congress

Joyce, John, R-Pa. (13)

Capitol Hill Office: 1221 LHOB 20515-3515; 225-2431; Fax: 225-2486; *Chief of Staff:* Dante Cutrona
Web: johnjoyce.house.gov
Facebook: www.facebook.com/RepJohnJoyce
Twitter: @RepJohnJoyce
YouTube: www.youtube.com/channel/UC6F6PTH33VO_wfqfvNjyuiw
Instagram: @johnjoycepa13
District Offices: 5414 6th Ave., Altoona, PA 16602; 814-656-6081
100 Lincoln Way East, Suite B, Chambersburg, PA 17201; 717-753-6344
451 Stoystown Rd., #102, Somerset, PA 15501; 814-485-6020
Satellite Office: 282 W. King St., Abbottstown, PA 17301; 717-357-6320
Committee Assignment: Energy and Commerce

Kahele, Kaiali'i, D-Hawaii (2)

Capitol Hill Office: 1205 LHOB 20515; 225-4906; Fax: 225-4987; *Chief of Staff:* Christine Wagner
Web: kahele.house.gov
Facebook: www.facebook.com/RepKahele
Twitter: @RepKahele
YouTube: www.youtube.com/RepKahele
Instagram: @repkahele
District Office: 99 Aupuni St., #118, Hilo, HI 96720; 808-746-6220
Committee Assignments: Armed Services; Transportation and Infrastructure

Kaptur, Marcy, D-Ohio (9)

Capitol Hill Office: 2186 RHOB 20515; 225-4146; Fax: 225-7711; *Chief of Staff:* Steve Katich
Web: kaptur.house.gov
Facebook: www.facebook.com/RepMarcyKaptur
Twitter: @RepMarcyKaptur
YouTube: www.youtube.com/USRepMarcyKaptur
Instagram: @repmarcykaptur
District Offices: 1 Maritime Plaza, #600, Toledo, OH 43604; 419-259-7500; Fax: 419-255-9623
200 W. Erie Ave., #310, Lorain, OH 44052; 440-288-1500; Fax: 419-255-9623
17021 Lorain Ave., Cleveland, OH 44111; 216-767-5933; Fax: 419-255-9623
Committee Assignments: Appropriations; Veterans' Affairs; Select on Economic Disparity and Fairness in Growth

Katko, John, R-N.Y. (24)

Capitol Hill Office: 2428 RHOB 20515; 225-3701; Fax: 225-4042; *Chief of Staff:* Erin Elliot
Web: katko.house.gov
Facebook: www.facebook.com/RepJohnKatko
Twitter: @RepJohnKatko
YouTube: www.youtube.com/channel/UCNRwSHofKKvDKpL92lZIBiw
Instagram: @repjohnkatko

District Offices: 71 Genesee St., Auburn, NY 13021; 315-253-4068; Fax: 315-253-2435; *District Director:* Thomas Haag

440 S. Warren St., 7th Floor, #711, Syracuse, NY 13202; 315-423-5657; Fax: 315-423-5604

7376 State Route 31, Lyons, NY 14489; 315-253-4068 (by appointment only)

13 W. Oneida St., 2nd Floor, Oswego, NY 13126; 315-423-5657 (by appointment only)

Committee Assignments: Homeland Security; Transportation and Infrastructure

Keating, William R., D-Mass. (9)

Capitol Hill Office: 2351 RHOB 20515; 225-3111; Fax: 225-5658; *Chief of Staff:* Garrett Donovan

Web: keating.house.gov

Facebook: www.facebook.com/USRepKeating

Twitter: @USRepKeating

YouTube: www.youtube.com/RepBillKeating

District Offices: 259 Stevens St., Suite E, Hyannis, MA 02601-5134; 508-771-6868; Fax: 508-790-1959; *District Director:* Michael Jackman

128 Union St., #103, New Bedford, MA 02740; 508-999-6462; Fax: 508-999-6468

50 Resnik Rd., #103, Plymouth, MA 02360; 508-746-9000; Fax: 508-732-0072

Committee Assignments: Armed Services; Foreign Affairs

Keller, Fred, R-Pa. (12)

Capitol Hill Office: 1717 LHOB 20515; 225-3731; Fax: 225-9594; *Chief of Staff:* Jon Anzur

Web: keller.house.gov

Facebook: www.facebook.com/CongressmanFredKeller

Twitter: @RepFredKeller

YouTube: www.youtube.com/channel/UC_IluBx9m7HWoNhEYSoPQNQ

Instagram: @repfredkeller

District Offices: 713 Bridge St., Room 29, Selinsgrove, PA 17870; 570-374-9469; Fax: 570-374-9589; *District Director:* Ann Kaufman

181 W. Tioga St., #2, Tunkhannock, PA 18657; 570-996-6550; Fax: 570-996-6554

1020 Commerce Park Dr., #1A, Williamsport, PA 17701-5434; 570-322-3961; Fax: 570-322-3965; *District Director:* Ann Kaufman

Committee Assignments: Education and Labor; Oversight and Reform

Kelly, Mike, R-Pa. (16)

Capitol Hill Office: 1707 LHOB 20515; 225-5406; Fax: 225-3103; *Chief of Staff:* Tim Butler

Web: kelly.house.gov

Facebook: www.facebook.com/MikeKellyPA

Twitter: @MikeKellyPA

YouTube: www.youtube.com/RepMikeKelly

District Offices: 245 Pittsburgh Rd., #300, Butler, PA 16001; 724-282-2557; Fax: 724-282-3682; *Constituent Services Director:* Stephanie Stevenson

208 E. Bayfront Pkwy., #102, Erie, PA 16507-2405; 814-454-8190; Fax: 814-454-8197

33 Chestnut Ave., Sharon, PA 16146; 724-342-7170; Fax: 724-342-7242

Committee Assignment: Ways and Means

Kelly, Robin L., D-Ill. (2)

Capitol Hill Office: 2416 RHOB 20515; 225-0773; Fax: 225-4583; *Chief of Staff:* Mia Keeys

Web: robinkelly.house.gov

Facebook: www.facebook.com/reprobinkelly

Twitter: @RepRobinKelly

YouTube: www.youtube.com/channel/UCLhcNPX2nNQLNzwKW0nEykg

Instagram: @reprobinkelly

District Offices: 600 Holiday Plaza Dr., #505, Matteson, IL 60443; 708-679-0078; Fax: 708-679-0216; *District Director:* Tony Presta

1000 E. 111th St., Chicago, IL 60628; 773-321-2001

Committee Assignments: Energy and Commerce; Oversight and Reform

Kelly, Trent, R-Miss. (1)

Capitol Hill Office: 2243 RHOB 20515; 225-4306; Fax: 225-3549; *Chief of Staff:* Paul Howell

Web: trentkelly.house.gov

Facebook: www.facebook.com/RepTrentKelly

Twitter: @RepTrentKelly

YouTube: www.youtube.com/channel/UCtDrz-8tdg4ZgOAQHToSWaQ

Instagram: @reptrentkelly

District Offices: 318 N. 7th St., Suite D, Columbus, MS 39701; 662-327-0748; Fax: 662-328-5982; *District Director:* Darren Herring

2565 Caffey St., #200, P.O. Box 218, Hernando, MS 38632; 662-449-3090; Fax: 662-449-4836

431 W. Main St., Tupelo, MS 38804; 662-841-8808; Fax: 662-841-8845

855 S. Dunn St., Eupora, MS 39744; 662-687-1545; Fax: 662-258-7240

4135 County Rd., #200, Corinth, MS 38844; 662-687-1525; Fax: 662-841-8845

107 Courthouse Square, Oxford, MS 38655; 662-687-1540; Fax: 662-328-5982

Committee Assignments: Agriculture; Armed Services; Budget

Khanna, Ro, D-Calif. (17)

Capitol Hill Office: 306 CHOB 20515; 225-2631; Fax: 225-2699; *Chief of Staff:* Geo Saba

Web: khanna.house.gov

Facebook: www.facebook.com/RepRoKhanna

Twitter: @RepRoKhanna

YouTube: www.youtube.com/channel/UCr4KOYv1o1oEQhy1jhhm3pQ

Instagram: @reprokhanna

District Office: 3150 De La Cruz Blvd., #240, Santa Clara, CA 95054; 408-436-2720; Fax: 408-436-2721; *District Director:* Tom Pyke

Committee Assignments: Agriculture; Armed Services; Oversight and Reform

Kildee, Daniel T., D-Mich. (5)

Capitol Hill Office: 200 CHOB 20515; 225-3611; Fax: 225-6393; *Chief of Staff:* Mitchell Rivard
Web: dankildee.house.gov
Facebook: www.facebook.com/RepDanKildee
Twitter: @RepDanKildee
YouTube: www.youtube.com/RepDanKildee
Instagram: @repdankildee
District Office: 601 S. Saginaw St., #403, Flint, MI 48502; 810-238-8627; Fax: 810-238-8658; *District Director:* Chris Flores
Committee Assignments: Budget; Science, Space, and Technology; Ways and Means

Kilmer, Derek, D-Wash. (6)

Capitol Hill Office: 2059 RHOB 20515; 225-5916; Fax: 226-3575; *Chief of Staff:* Rachel Kelly
Web: kilmer.house.gov
Facebook: www.facebook.com/derek.kilmer
Twitter: @RepDerekKilmer
YouTube: www.youtube.com/RepDerekKilmer
Instagram: @repderekkilmer
District Offices: 345 6th St., #500, Bremerton, WA 98337; 360-373-9725; *District Director:* Andrea Roper
950 Pacific Ave., #1230, Tacoma, WA 98402; 253-272-3515
Satellite Office: 332 E. 5th St., Port Angeles, WA 98362; 360-797-3623
Committee Assignments: Appropriations; Select on the Modernization of Congress, Chair

Kim, Andy, D-N.J. (3)

Capitol Hill Office: 2444 RHOB 20515; 225-4765; Fax: 225-0778; *Chief of Staff:* Amy Pfeiffer
Web: kim.house.gov
Facebook: www.facebook.com/RepAndyKimNJ
Twitter: @RepAndyKimNJ
YouTube: www. youtube.com/channel/UCn_FREkpMfHfTU-bSwcM0sw
Instagram: @repandykimnj
District Offices: 429 John F. Kennedy Way, Box 9, Willingboro, NJ 08046; 856-703-2700; Fax: 856-369-8988; *District Director:* Ben Giovine
33 Washington St., P.O. Box 728, Toms River, NJ 08754; 732-504-0490; Fax: 732-714-4244
Committee Assignments: Armed Services; Foreign Affairs; Small Business

Kim, Young, R-Calif. (39)

Capitol Hill Office: 1306 LHOB 20515; 225-4111; *Chief of Staff:* Patrick Mocete
Web: youngkim.house.gov
Facebook: www.facebook.com/RepYoungKim
Twitter: @RepYoungKim
Instagram: @repyoungkim

YouTube: youtube.com/channel/UCy-O5SyyNvoOAZ1ex9z1EXw
District Offices: 701 W. Kimberly Ave., #245, Placentia, CA 92870; 714-984-2440; *District Director:* Linette Choi
1320 Valley Vista Dr., #205, Diamond Bar, CA 91765; 714-984-2440 (open 9 a.m.–5 p.m., Wednesdays and Fridays)
Committee Assignments: Foreign Affairs; Science, Space, and Technology; Small Business

Kind, Ron, D-Wisc. (3)

Capitol Hill Office: 1502 LHOB 20515; 225-5506; Fax: 225-5739; *Chief of Staff:* Alex Eveland
Web: kind.house.gov
Facebook: www.facebook.com/repronkind
Twitter: @RepRonKind
YouTube: www.youtube.com/RepRonKind
Instagram: @repronkind
District Offices: 316 N. Barstow St., Suite C, Eau Claire, WI 54703; 715-831-9214; Fax: 715-831-9272; *District Director:* Karrie Jackelen
205 5th Ave. South, #400, La Crosse, WI 54601; 608-782-2558; Fax: 608-782-4588; *District Director:* Karrie Jackelen
Committee Assignment: Ways and Means

Kinzinger, Adam, R-Ill. (16)

Capitol Hill Office: 2245 RHOB 20515-1311; 225-3635; Fax: 225-3521; *Deputy Chief of Staff:* Maura Gillespie
Web: kinzinger.house.gov
Facebook: www.facebook.com/RepKinzinger
Twitter: @RepKinzinger
YouTube: www.youtube.com/RepAdamKinzinger
District Offices: 628 Columbus St., #507, Ottawa, IL 61350; 815-431-9271; Fax: 815-431-9383; *District Director:* Bonnie Walsh
342 W. Walnut, Watseka, IL 60970; 815-432-0580 (by appointment only); *Deputy District Director:* Patrick Doggett
725 N. Lyford Rd., #3, Rockford, IL 61107; 815-708-8032 (by appointment only)
Committee Assignments: Energy and Commerce; Foreign Affairs; Select to Investigate the January 6th Attack on the U.S. Capitol

Kirkpatrick, Ann, D-Ariz. (2)

Capitol Hill Office: 309 CHOB 20515-3515; 225-2542; *Chief of Staff:* Abigail O'Brien
Web: kirkpatrick.house.gov
Facebook: www.facebook.com/RepKirkpatrick
Twitter: @RepKirkpatrick
Instagram: @repannkirkpatrick
District Offices: 77 Calle Portal, #B160, Sierra Vista, AZ 85635; 520-459-3115; *District Director:* Billy Kovacs
1636 N. Swan Rd., #200, Tucson, AZ 85712; 520-881-3588
Committee Assignments: Appropriations

Krishnamoorthi, Raja, D-Ill. (8)

Capitol Hill Office: 115 CHOB 20515; 225-3711; Fax: 225-7830; *Chief of Staff:* Brian Kaissi
Web: krishnamoorthi.house.gov
Facebook: www.facebook.com/CongressmanRaja
Twitter: @CongressmanRaja
YouTube: www.youtube.com/CongressmanRaja
Instagram: @congressmanraja
District Office: 1701 E. Woodfield Rd., #704, Schaumburg, IL 60173; 847-413-1959; Fax: 847-413-1965; *District Director:* Sabey Abraham
Committee Assignments: Oversight and Reform; Permanent Select Intelligence Select on Coronavirus Crisis

Kuster, Ann M., D-N.H. (2)

Capitol Hill Office: 320 CHOB 20515; 225-5206; Fax: 225-2946; *Chief of Staff:* Pat Devney
Web: kuster.house.gov
Facebook: www.facebook.com/CongresswomanAnnieKuster
Twitter: @RepAnnieKuster
YouTube: www.youtube.com/RepKuster
Instagram: @repanniekuster
District Offices: 18 N. Main St., 4th Floor, Concord, NH 03301; 603-226-1002; Fax: 603-226-1010; *District Director:* Nick Brown
184 Main St., #222, Nashua, NH 03060; 603-595-2006; Fax: 603-595-2016
33 Main St., #202, Littleton, NH 03561; 603-444-7700; *Constituent Services Rep.:* Brian Bresnahan
Committee Assignments: Agriculture; Energy and Commerce

Kustoff, David, R-Tenn. (8)

Capitol Hill Office: 560 CHOB 20515; 225-4714; *Chief of Staff:* Justin Melvin
Web: kustoff.house.gov
Facebook: www.facebook.com/RepDavidKustoff
Twitter: @RepDavidKustoff
YouTube: www.youtube.com/channel/UCK6U4plOKKMrCjv_h59spGQ
Instagram: @repdavidkustoff
District Offices: 242 S. Lindell St., Martin, TN 38237; 731-412-1043
5900 Poplar Ave., #202, Memphis, TN 38119; 901-682-4422; Fax: 901-682-8973
117 N. Liberty St., Jackson, TN 38301; 731-423-4848; Fax: 731-427-1537
425 W. Court St., Dyersburg, TN 38024; 731-412-1037
Committee Assignment: Financial Services

LaHood, Darin, R-Ill. (18)

Capitol Hill Office: 1424 LHOB 20515-1318; 225-6201; Fax: 225-9249; *Chief of Staff:* Steven Pfrang
Web: lahood.house.gov
Facebook: www.facebook.com/replahood
Twitter: @RepLaHood

YouTube: www.youtube.com/channel/UCVRbtFwaBGcixZIkygtalRw
Instagram: @replahood
District Offices: 3004 G.E. Rd., #1B, Bloomington, IL 61704; 309-205-9556 (open Tuesday and Thursday)
201 W. Morgan St., Jacksonville, IL 62650; 217-245-1431; Fax: 217-243-6852
100 Monroe St. N.E., Room 100, Peoria, IL 61602-1047; 309-671-7027; Fax: 309-671-7309; *District Director:* Brad Stotler
235 S. 6th St., Springfield, IL 62701; 217-670-1653; Fax: 217-670-1806
Committee Assignments: Permanent Select Intelligence; Ways and Means

LaMalfa, Doug, R-Calif. (1)

Capitol Hill Office: 408 CHOB 20515; 225-3076; Fax: 226-0852; *Chief of Staff:* Mark Spannagel
Web: lamalfa.house.gov
Facebook: www.facebook.com/RepLaMalfa
Twitter: @RepLaMalfa
YouTube: www.youtube.com/RepLaMalfa
Instagram: @repdouglamalfa
District Offices: 2399 Rickenbacker Way, Auburn, CA 95602; 530-878-5035; Fax: 530-878-5037; *Senior District Rep.:* Lisa Mara
120 Independence Circle, Suite B, Chico, CA 95973; 530-343-1000
2885 Churn Creek Rd., Suite C, Redding, CA 96002; 530-223-5898; Fax: 530-223-5897; *District Rep.:* Brenda Haynes
Committee Assignments: Agriculture; Transportation and Infrastructure

Lamb, Conor, D-Pa. (17)

Capitol Hill Office: 1224 LHOB 20515; 225-2301; Fax: 225-1844; *Chief of Staff:* Craig Kwiecinski
Web: lamb.house.gov
Facebook: www.facebook.com/RepConorLamb
Twitter: @RepConorLamb
YouTube: www.youtube.com/channel/UC7hX59n_ixS1Bz3f8Je02yA
District Offices: 3468 Brodhead Rd., Monaca, PA 15061; 724-206-4860
11 Duff Rd., Pittsburgh, PA 15235; 412-871-2060
504 Washington Rd., Pittsburgh, PA 15228-2817; 412-344-5583; Fax: 412-429-5092; *District Director:* D. J. Ryan
Committee Assignments: Science, Space, and Technology; Transportation and Infrastructure; Veterans' Affairs

Lamborn, Doug, R-Colo. (5)

Capitol Hill Office: 2371 RHOB 20515; 225-4422; Fax: 226-2638; *Chief of Staff:* James Thomas
Web: lamborn.house.gov
Facebook: www.facebook.com/CongressmanDougLamborn
Twitter: @RepDLamborn
YouTube: www.youtube.com/CongressmanLamborn
Instagram: @douglamborn

District Office: 1125 Kelly Johnson Blvd., #330, Colorado Springs, CO 80920-3965; 719-520-0055; Fax: 719-520-0840

Committee Assignments: Armed Services; Natural Resources

Langevin, James R., D-R.I. (2)

Capitol Hill Office: 2077 RHOB 20515; 225-2735; Fax: 225-5976; *Chief of Staff:* Kathryn Mitchell Thomas

Web: langevin.house.gov

Facebook: www.facebook.com/CongressmanJimLangevin

Twitter: @JimLangevin

YouTube: www.youtube.com/jimlangevin

Instagram: @repjimlangevin

District Office: 300 Centerville Rd., #200 South, Warwick, RI 02886-0200; 401-732-9400; Fax: 401-737-2982; *Deputy District Director:* Julio Paz

Committee Assignments: Armed Services; Homeland Security

Larsen, Rick, D-Wash. (2)

Capitol Hill Office: 2163 RHOB 20515; 225-2605; Fax: 225-4420; *Chief of Staff:* Terra Sabag

Web: larsen.house.gov

Facebook: www.facebook.com/RepRickLarsen

Twitter: @RepRickLarsen

YouTube: www.youtube.com/CongressmanLarsen

Instagram: @repricklarsen

District Offices: Wall Street Bldg., 2930 Wetmore Ave., #9F, Everett, WA 98201-4070; 425-252-3188; Fax: 833-696-6499; *District Director:* Ryan Casey

119 N. Commercial St., #275, Bellingham, WA 98225-4452; 360-733-4500; *Community Liaison:* Laura Gelwicks

Committee Assignments: Armed Services; Transportation and Infrastructure

Larson, John B., D-Conn. (1)

Capitol Hill Office: 1501 LHOB 20515-0701; 225-2265; Fax: 225-1031; *Chief of Staff:* Scott Stephanou

Web: larson.house.gov

Facebook: www.facebook.com/RepJohnLarson

Twitter: @RepJohnLarson

YouTube: www.youtube.com/RepJohnLarson

Instagram: @repjohnblarson

District Office: 221 Main St., 2nd Floor, Hartford, CT 06106-1890; 860-278-8888; Fax: 860-278-2111; *District Director:* Maureen Moriarty

Committee Assignment: Ways and Means

Latta, Robert E., R-Ohio (5)

Capitol Hill Office: 2467 RHOB 20515; 225-6405; Fax: 225-1985; *Chief of Staff:* Drew Griffin

Web: latta.house.gov

Facebook: www.facebook.com/boblatta

Twitter: @boblatta

YouTube: www.youtube.com/CongressmanBobLatta

Instagram: @boblatta

District Offices: 1045 N. Main St., #6, Bowling Green, OH 43402-1361; 419-354-8700; Fax: 800-278-8203; *District Director:* David Wirt

101 Clinton St., #1200, Defiance, OH 43512-2165; 419-782-1996; Fax: 800-278-8203

318 Dorney Plaza, #302, Findlay, OH 45840; 419-422-7791; Fax: 800-278-8203; *District Rep.:* Brian Bauman

Committee Assignments: Energy and Commerce; Select on the Modernization of Congress

LaTurner, Jake, R-Kans. (2)

Capitol Hill Office: 1630 LHOB 20515; 225-6601; *Chief of Staff:* Braden Dreiling

Web: laturner.house.gov

Facebook: www.facebook.com/CongressmanJakeLaTurner

Twitter: @RepLaTurner

YouTube: www.youtube.com/c/RepLaTurner

District Offices: 402 N. Broadway St., Suite B, Pittsburg, KS 66762; 620-308-7450; *District Director:* Jake Conard

3550 5th St. S.W., Topeka, KS 66606; 785-205-5253

Committee Assignments: Homeland Security; Oversight and Reform; Science, Space, and Technology

Lawrence, Brenda L., D-Mich. (14)

Capitol Hill Office: 2463 RHOB 20515-2214; 225-5802; Fax: 226-2356; *Chief of Staff:* Curtis Doster Jr.

Web: lawrence.house.gov

Facebook: www.facebook.com/Rep.BLawrence

Twitter: @RepLawrence

YouTube: www.youtube.com/channel/UCf0USy9GNigkB8O9sS1dodw

Instagram: @repbrendalawrence

District Office: 400 Monroe St., #420, Detroit, MI 48033; 313-880-2400

26080 Berg Rd., Southfield, MI 48033; 248-356-2052; Fax: 248-356-4532; *District Director:* Jacqueline Elliot

Committee Assignments: Appropriations; Oversight and Reform

Lawson, Al, D-Fla. (5)

Capitol Hill Office: 2437 RHOB 20515; 225-0123; Fax: 225-2256; *Chief of Staff:* Tola Thompson

Web: lawson.house.gov

Facebook: www.facebook.com/RepAlLawsonJr

Twitter: @RepAlLawsonJr

Instagram: @repallawsonjr

District Offices: 117 W. Duval St., #240, Jacksonville FL 32202; 904-354-1652; Fax: 904-379-0309; *District Director:* Kortney Wesley

435 N. Macomb St., Tallahassee, FL 32301; 850-558-9450; Fax: 850-577-0633; *District Director:* Theresa Frederick

Committee Assignments: Agriculture; Financial Services

Lee, Barbara, D-Calif. (13)

Capitol Hill Office: 2470 RHOB 20515-0509; 225-2661; Fax: 225-9817; *Chief of Staff:* Julie Nickson

Web: lee.house.gov

Facebook: www.facebook.com/RepBarbaraLee
Twitter: @RepBarbaraLee
YouTube: www.youtube.com/RepLee
Instagram: @repbarbaralee
District Office: 1 Kaiser Plaza, #1010, Oakland, CA 94612; 510-763-0370; Fax: 510-763-6538; *District Director:* Anne Taylor
Committee Assignments: Appropriations; Budget

Lee, Susie, D-Nev. (3)

Capitol Hill Office: 365 CHOB 20515; 225-3252; Fax: 225-2185; *Chief of Staff:* Brandon Cox
Web: susielee.house.gov
Facebook: www.facebook.com/RepSusieLee
Twitter: @RepSusieLee
YouTube: www.youtube.com/channel/UCjb-fEQUxeagMKN1rZQm-FA
Instagram: @repsusielee
District Office: 8872 S. Eastern Ave., #210 & 220, Las Vegas, NV 89123; 702-963-9336; *District Director:* Alejandro Rodriguez
Committee Assignment: Appropriations

Leger Fernandez, Teresa, D-N.M. (3)

Capitol Hill Office: 1432 LHOB 20515; 225-6190; *Chief of Staff:* Nathan Schelble
Web: fernandez.house.gov
Facebook: www.facebook.com/RepTeresaLF
Twitter: @RepTeresaLF
Instagram: @replegerfernandez
District Office: 120 S. Federal Pl., #110B, Santa Fe, NM 87501; 505-428-4680; *District Director:* Xochitl Campos Biggs
1103 National Ave., #101, Las Vegas, NM 87701; 505-570-7558
3001 Civic Center Circlr N.E., Rio Rancho, NM 87144; 505-415-7810
Committee Assignments: Education and Labor; House Administration; Natural Resources

Lesko, Debbie, R-Ariz. (8)

Capitol Hill Office: 1214 LHOB 20515-0308; 225-4576; *Chief of Staff:* Rachel Harris
Web: lesko.house.gov
Facebook: www.facebook.com/RepDebbieLesko
Twitter: @RepDLesko
YouTube: www.youtube.com/channel/UCc6-ceGpb-VbP1rmmvYUCWQ
Instagram: @replesko
District Office: 12515 W. Bell Rd., #104, Surprise, AZ 85378; 623-776-7911; Fax: 623-776-7832; *District Director:* Keith M. Forte
Committee Assignment: Energy and Commerce

Letlow, Julia, R-La. (5)

Capitol Hill Office: 1408 LHOB 20515; 225-8490; Fax: 225-5639; *Chief of Staff:* Andrew Bautsch
Web: letlow.house.gov
Facebook: www.facebook.com/repjulialetlow

Twitter: @RepJuliaLetlow
Instagram: @repjulialetlow
District Offices: 4124 Jackson St., Alexandria, LA 71301; 318-319-6465
109 E. Oak St., Amite, LA 70422; 985-284-8490
1900 N. 18th St., #501, Monroe, LA 71201; 318-570-6440; *District Director:* Emma Herrock
Committee Assignments: Agriculture; Education and Labor

Levin, Andy, D-Mich. (9)

Capitol Hill Office: 312 CHOB 20515-2209; 225-4961; Fax: 226-1033; *Chief of Staff:* Ven Neralla
Web: andylevin.house.gov
Facebook: www.facebook.com/RepAndyLevin
Twitter: @RepAndyLevin
Instagram: @repandylevin
District Office: 30500 Van Dyke Ave., #306, Warren, MI 48093; 586-498-7122; *District Director:* Walt Herzig
Committee Assignments: Education and Labor; Foreign Affairs

Levin, Mike, D-Calif (49)

Capitol Hill Office: 1030 LHOB 20515-0549; 225-3906; *Chief of Staff:* Jonathan Gilbert
Web: mikelevin.house.gov
Facebook: www.facebook.com/RepMikeLevin
Twitter: @RepMikeLevin
YouTube: www.youtube.com/channel/UCYFDRohyZgoPy5rXOaVZO-A
Instagram: @RepMikeLevin
District Offices: 33282 Golden Lantern, #102, Dana Point, CA 92629; 949-281-2449; *District Director:* Kyle Krahel-Frolander
2204 El Camino Real, #314, Oceanside, CA 92054; 760-599-5000
Committee Assignments: Natural Resources; Veterans' Affairs; Select on the Climate Crisis

Lieu, Ted, D-Calif. (33)

Capitol Hill Office: 403 CHOB 20515; 225-3976; Fax: 225-4099; *Chief of Staff:* Marc Cevasco
Web: lieu.house.gov
Facebook: www.facebook.com/RepTedLieu
Twitter: @RepTedLieu
YouTube: www.youtube.com/RepTedLieu
Instagram: @reptedlieu
District Office: 1645 Corinth Ave., #101, Los Angeles, CA 90025; 323-651-1040; Fax: 323-655-0502; *District Director:* Nicolas Rodriquez
Satellite Office: 1600 Rosecrans Ave., 4th Floor, Manhattan Beach, CA 90266; 310-321-7664; Fax: 323-655-0502 (by appointment only); *District Director:* Nicolas Rodriquez
Committee Assignments: Foreign Affairs; Judiciary

Lofgren, Zoe, D-Calif. (19)

Capitol Hill Office: 1401 LHOB 20515; 225-3072; Fax: 225-3336; *Chief of Staff:* Stacey Leavandosky

Web: lofgren.house.gov
Facebook: www.facebook.com/zoelofgren
Twitter: @RepZoeLofgren
YouTube: www.youtube.com/RepZoeLofgren
District Office: 635 N. 1st St., Suite B, San Jose, CA 95112; 408-271-8700; Fax: 408-271-8714
Committee Assignments: House Administration, Chair; Judiciary; Science, Space, and Technology

Long, Billy, R-Mo. (7)

Capitol Hill Office: 2454 RHOB 20515; 225-6536; Fax: 225-5604; *Chief of Staff:* Joe Lillis
Web: long.house.gov
Facebook: www.facebook.com/Rep.Billy.Long
Twitter: @UsRepLong
YouTube: www.youtube.com/MOdistrict7
District Offices: 2727 E. 32nd St., #2, Joplin, MO 64804-3155; 417-781-1041; Fax: 417-781-2832; *District Director:* Michael Ussery
3232 E. Ridgeview St., Springfield, MO 65804-4076; 417-889-1800; Fax: 417-889-4915
Committee Assignment: Energy and Commerce

Loudermilk, Barry, R-Ga. (11)

Capitol Hill Office: 2133 RHOB 20515-1011; 225-2931; Fax: 225-2944; *Chief of Staff:* Rob Adkerson
Web: loudermilk.house.gov
Facebook: www.facebook.com/RepLoudermilk
Twitter: @RepLoudermilk
YouTube: www.youtube.com/channel/UC2Kfw8fjca8k3w3KpzL5tNg
Instagram: @reploudermilk
District Offices: 600 Galleria Pkwy. S.E., #120, Atlanta, GA 30339; 770-429-1776; Fax: 678-556-5184; *District Director:* Wayne Dodd
135 W. Cherokee Ave., #122, Cartersville, GA 30120; 770-429-1776
9898 Hwy. 92, #100, Woodstock, GA 30188; 770-429-1776; Fax: 770-517-7427
Committee Assignments: Financial Services; House Administration

Lowenthal, Alan S., D-Calif. (47)

Capitol Hill Office: 108 CHOB 20515; 225-7924; Fax: 225-7926; *Chief of Staff:* Chris Gorud
Web: lowenthal.house.gov
Facebook: www.facebook.com/RepLowenthal
Twitter: @RepLowenthal
YouTube: www.youtube.com/RepLowenthal
Instagram: @replowenthal
District Offices: Gov. G. Deukmejian Courthouse, 275 Magnolia Ave., #1955, Long Beach, CA 90802; 562-436-3828; Fax: 562-437-6434; *Deputy District Director:* Irantzu Pajudas
12912 Brookhurst St., #360, Garden Grove, CA 92840; 714-243-4088; Fax: 562-437-6434
Committee Assignments: Natural Resources; Transportation and Infrastructure

Lucas, Frank D., R-Okla. (3)

Capitol Hill Office: 2405 RHOB 20515-3603; 225-5565; Fax: 225-8698; *Chief of Staff:* Stacey Glasscock
Web: lucas.house.gov
Facebook: www.facebook.com/RepFrankLucas
Twitter: @RepFrankLucas
YouTube: www.youtube.com/RepFrankLucas
Instagram: @repfranklucas
District Office: 10952 Expressway N.W., Suite B, Yukon, OK 73099-8214; 405-373-1958; Fax: 405-373-2046; *District Director:* Grace Enmeier
Committee Assignments: Financial Services; Science, Space, and Technology

Luetkemeyer, Blaine, R-Mo. (3)

Capitol Hill Office: 2230 RHOB 20515; 225-2956; Fax: 225-5712; *Chief of Staff:* Chad Ramey
Web: luetkemeyer.house.gov
Facebook: www.facebook.com/BlaineLuetkemeyer
Twitter: @RepBlaine
YouTube: www.youtube.com/BLuetkemeyer
Instagram: @repblaine
District Offices: 2117 Missouri Blvd., Jefferson City, MO 65109; 573-635-7232; Fax: 573-635-8347; *Legislative Director:* Meghan Schmidtlein
516 Jefferson St., Washington, MO 63090-2706; 636-239-2276
113 E. Pearce Blvd., Wentzville, MO 63385; 636-327-7055
Committee Assignments: Financial Services; Small Business

Luria, Elaine G., D-Va. (2)

Capitol Hill Office: 412 CHOB 20515-4602; 225-4215; Fax: 225-4218; *Chief of Staff:* Shira Siegel
Web: luria.house.gov
Facebook: www.facebook.com/RepElaineLuria
Twitter: @RepElaineLuria
District Offices: 283 Constitution Dr., One Columbus Center, #900, Virginia Beach, VA 23462; 757-364-7650; Fax: 757-687-8298; *District Director:* Karen Thomas
25020 Shore Pkwy., #1B, Onley, VA 23418; 757-364-7631 (by appointment only)
105 Professional Pkwy., #1512, Yorktown, VA 23693; 757-364-7634 (by appointment only)
Committee Assignments: Armed Services; Homeland Security; Select to Investigate the January 6th Attack on the U.S. Capitol; Veterans' Affairs

Lynch, Stephen F., D-Mass. (8)

Capitol Hill Office: 2109 RHOB 20515; 225-8273; Fax: 225-3984; *Chief of Staff:* Kevin Ryan
Web: lynch.house.gov
Facebook: www.facebook.com/repstephenlynch
Twitter: @RepStephenLynch
YouTube: www.youtube.com/RepLynch
Instagram: @repstephenlynch
District Offices: One Harbor St., #101, Boston, MA 02210-2433; 617-428-2000; Fax: 617-428-2011; *District Director:* Nick Zaferakis

37 Belmont St., 2nd Floor, #3, Brockton, MA 02301; 508-586-5555; Fax: 508-580-4692

1245 Hancock St., #41, Quincy, MA 02169; 617-657-6305; Fax: 617-773-0995

Committee Assignments: Financial Services; Oversight and Reform; Transportation and Infrastructure

Mace, Nancy, R-S.C. (1)

Capitol Hill Office: 212 CHOB 20515; 225-3176; *Chief of Staff:* Dan Hanlon

Web: mace.house.gov

Facebook: www.facebook.com/RepNancyMace

Twitter: @RepNancyMace

Instagram: @repnancymace

District Office: 710 Boundary St., Beaufort, SC 29902; 843-521-2530; *District Director:* Matthew Nichols

2000 Sam Rittenberg Blvd., #3002, Charleston, SC 29407; 843-352-7572

Committee Assignment: Oversight and Reform; Transportation and Infrastructure; Veterans' Affairs

Malinowski, Tom, D-N.J. (7)

Capitol Hill Office: 1318 LHOB 20515-3007; 225-5361; *Chief of Staff:* Colston Reid

Web: malinowski.house.gov

Facebook: www.facebook.com/RepTomMalinowski

Twitter: @RepMalinowski

YouTube: www.youtube.com/channel/ UCPBK9PROw46Gv1CPrdNwJnQ

Instagram: @reptommalinowski

District Office: 75-77 N. Bridge St., Somerville, NJ 08876; 908-547-3307; Fax: 844-272-0103; *District Director:* Mitchelle Drulis

Committee Assignments: Foreign Affairs; Homeland Security; Transportation and Infrastructure

Malliotakis, Nicole, R-N.Y. (11)

Capitol Hill Office: 417 CHOB 20515; 225-3371; *Chief of Staff:* Alex Bolton

Web: malliotakis.house.gov

Facebook: www.facebook.com/RepMalliotakis

Twitter: @RepMalliotakis

District Offices: 7716 3rd Ave., Brooklyn, NY 11209; 718-306-1620; *District Director:* Sherry Diamond

1911 Richmond Ave., #100, Staten Island, NY 10314; 718-568-2870

Committee Assignments: Foreign Affairs; Select on Coronavirus Crisis; Transportation and Infrastructure

Maloney, Carolyn B., D-N.Y. (12)

Capitol Hill Office: 2308 RHOB 20515-001; 225-7944; Fax: 225-4709; *Chief of Staff:* Emily Crerand

Web: maloney.house.gov

Facebook: www.facebook.com/RepCarolynMaloney

Twitter: @RepMaloney

YouTube: www.youtube.com/carolynbmaloney

Instagram: @repmaloney

District Offices: 31-19 Newtown Ave., Astoria, NY 11102-1391; 718-932-1804; Fax: 212-860-0704

1651 3rd Ave., #311, New York, NY 10128-3679; 212-860-0606; Fax: 212-860-0704; *District Chief of Staff:* Shelby Garner

Committee Assignments: Financial Services; Oversight and Reform, Chair

Maloney, Sean Patrick, D-N.Y. (18)

Capitol Hill Office: 464 CHOB 20515; 225-5441; Fax: 225-3289; *Chief of Staff:* Matthew McMally

Web: seanmaloney.house.gov

Facebook: www.facebook.com/repseanmaloney

Twitter: @RepSeanMaloney

YouTube: www.youtube.com/channel/UCNiVzzf4Vz-vCMPBcnjGuXQ

Instagram: @repseanpatrickmaloney

District Office: 123 Grand St., 2nd Floor, Newburgh, NY 12550; 845-561-1259; Fax: 845-561-2890; *District Director:* Ernest Klepeis

Committee Assignments: Agriculture; Transportation and Infrastructure; Permanent Select Intelligence

Mann, Tracey, R-Kans. (1)

Capitol Hill Office: 522 CHOB 20515; 225-2715; *Chief of Staff:* Brandon Harder

Web: mann.house.gov

Facebook: www.facebook.com/RepTraceyMann

Twitter: @RepMann

Instagram: @reptraceymann

YouTube: www.youtube.com/channel/ UCGYSHqv8uxVdej-GDuvXCbw

District Office: 100 Military Ave., #203, Dodge City, KS 67801; 620-682-7340; *District Director:* Martha Mendoza

121 S. 4th St., #205, Manhattan, KS 66502; 785-370-7277

Committee Assignments: Agriculture; Veterans' Affairs

Manning, Kathy E., D-N.C. (6)

Capitol Hill Office: 415 CHOB 20515; 225-3065; Fax: 225-8611; *Chief of Staff:* Sarah Curtis

Web: manning.house.gov

Facebook: www.facebook.com/RepKathyManning

Twitter: @RepKManning

YouTube: www.youtube.com/channel/ UClIRFkqQFR0_YHDbOzTG6VQ

Instagram: @repkathymanning

District Office: 100 S. Elm St., #301, Greensboro, NC 27401; 336-333-5005

Committee Assignments: Education and Labor; Foreign Affairs

Massie, Thomas, R-Ky. (4)

Capitol Hill Office: 2453 RHOB 20515; 225-3465; Fax: 225-0003; *Chief of Staff:* Matt Gurtler

Web: massie.house.gov

Facebook: www.facebook.com/RepThomasMassie

Twitter: @RepThomasMassie

YouTube: www.youtube.com/RepThomasMassie

Instagram: @repthomasmassie

District Offices: 1700 Greenup Ave., #505, Ashland, KY 41101; 606-324-9898; *District Director:* Chris McCane

541 Buttermilk Pike, #208, Crescent Springs, KY 41017-3924; 859-426-0080; Fax: 859-426-0061

110 W. Jefferson St., #100, LaGrange, KY 40031; 502-265-9119; Fax: 502-265-9126; *Western District Field Rep.:* Stacey Rockaway

Committee Assignments: Judiciary; Transportation and Infrastructure

Mast, Brian J., R-Fla. (18)

Capitol Hill Office: 2182 RHOB 20515; 225-3026; Fax: 225-8398; *Chief of Staff:* James Langenderfer

Web: mast.house.gov

Facebook: www.facebook.com/RepBrianMast

Twitter: @RepBrianMast

YouTube: www.youtube.com/RepBrianMast

Instagram: @repbrianmast

District Offices: 121 Port St. Lucie Blvd. S.W., Port St. Lucie, FL 34984; 772-336-2877; *District Director:* Jordan Sejour

171 Flager Ave. S.W., Stuart, FL 34994; 772-403-0900

601 Heritage Dr., #144, Jupiter, FL 33458; 561-530-7778

100 N. U.S. Hwy. 1, #217, Fort Pierce, FL 34950

Committee Assignments: Foreign Affairs; Transportation and Infrastructure

Matsui, Doris O., D-Calif. (6)

Capitol Hill Office: 2311 RHOB 20515-0506; 225-7163; Fax: 225-0566; *Chief of Staff:* Jeremy Marcus

Web: matsui.house.gov

Facebook: www.facebook.com/doris.matsui

Twitter: @DorisMatsui

YouTube: www.youtube.com/channel/ UCSqqxVkvskHq3cY2MCbTZsw

Instagram: @repdorismatsui

District Office: 501 Eye St., #12-600, Sacramento, CA 95814-4778; 916-498-5600; Fax: 916-444-6117; *District Director:* Glenda Corcoran

Committee Assignment: Energy and Commerce

McBath, Lucy, D-Ga. (6)

Capitol Hill Office: 1513 LHOB 20515-3515; 225-4501; Fax: 225-4656; *Chief of Staff:* Rebecca Walldorff

Web: mcbath.house.gov

Facebook: www.facebook.com/replucymcbath

Twitter: @RepLucyMcBath

YouTube: www.youtube.com/channel/ UCMuL4H2opqYnxnxRGVhimxw

Instagram: @replucymcbath

District Office: 5775 Glenridge Dr., Bldg. B, #380, Atlanta, GA 30328; 470-773-6330; *District Director:* Chris Speed

Committee Assignments: Education and Labor; Judiciary

McCarthy, Kevin, R-Calif. (23)

Capitol Hill Office: 2468 RHOB 20515; 225-2915; Fax: 225-2908; *Chief of Staff:* Dan Meyer

Web: kevinmccarthy.house.gov

Facebook: www.facebook.com/RepKevinMcCarthy

Twitter: @GOPLeader

YouTube: www.youtube.com/RepKevinMcCarthy

Instagram: @repkevinmccarthy

District Office: 4100 Empire Dr., #150, Bakersfield, CA 93309-0409; 661-327-3611; Fax: 661-637-0867; *District Director:* Robin Lake-Foster

Minority Leader

McCaul, Michael T., R-Tex. (10)

Capitol Hill Office: 2001 RHOB 20515-4310; 225-2401; Fax: 225-5955; *Chief of Staff:* Chris Del Becarro

Web: mccaul.house.gov

Facebook: www.facebook.com/michaeltmccaul

Twitter: @RepMcCaul

YouTube: www.youtube.com/MichaelTMcCaul

Instagram: @congressman_mccaul

District Offices: 3301 Northland Dr., #212, Austin, TX 78731; 512-473-2357; Fax: 512-473-0514 (by appointment only); *District Director:* Andrew Ross

Satellite Offices: 1526 Katy Gap Road, #803. Katy, TX 77494; 281-505-6130 (by appointment only)

401 S. Austin St., Brenham, TX 77833-5800; 979-830-8497; Fax: 979-830-1984 (by appointment only)

Committee Assignments: Foreign Affairs; Homeland Security

McClain, Lisa C., R-Mich. (10)

Capitol Hill Office: 218 CHOB 20515; 225-2106; Fax: 226-1169; *Chief of Staff:* Nick Hawatmeh

Web: mcclain.house.gov

Facebook: www.facebook.com/RepLisaMcClain

Twitter: @RepLisaMcClain

YouTube: www.youtube.com/c/replisamcclain

Instagram: @replisamcclain

District Office: 6303 26 Mile Rd., #110, Washington, MI 48094; 586-697-9300; *District Director:* Kathy Vertin

Committee Assignments: Armed Services; Education and Labor

McClintock, Tom, R-Calif. (4)

Capitol Hill Office: 2312 RHOB 20515-0504; 225-2511; Fax: 225-5444; *Chief of Staff:* Chris Tudor

Web: mcclintock.house.gov

Facebook: www.facebook.com/RepMcClintock

Twitter: @RepMcClintock

YouTube: www.youtube.com/McClintockCA04

Instagram: @repmcclintock

District Office: 2200A Douglas Blvd., #240, Roseville, CA 95661; 916-786-5560; Fax: 916-786-6364; *District Director:* Rocky Deal

Committee Assignments: Budget; Judiciary; Natural Resources

McCollum, Betty, D-Minn. (4)

Capitol Hill Office: 2256 RHOB 20515-2304; 225-6631; Fax: 225-1968; *Chief of Staff:* Bill Harper

Web: mccollum.house.gov

Facebook: www.facebook.com/repbettymccollum

Twitter: @BettyMcCollum04
YouTube: www.youtube.com/BMcCollum04
Instagram: @repbettymccollum
District Office: 661 LaSalle St., #110, St. Paul, MN 55114; 651-224-9191; Fax: 651-224-3056; *District Director:* Joshua Straka
Committee Assignments: Appropriations; Natural Resources

McEachin, A. Donald, D-Va. (4)

Capitol Hill Office: 314 CHOB 20515; 225-6365; Fax: 226-1170; *Chief of Staff:* Tara Rountree
Web: mceachin.house.gov
Facebook: www.facebook.com/RepMcEachin
Twitter: @RepMcEachin
YouTube: www.youtube.com/channel/UCMoPYHuZ3fZho0ZixZCfiFg
Instagram: @repmceachin
District Offices: 110 N. Robinson St., #403, Richmond, VA 23220; 804-486-1840; Fax: 804-269-4139; *District Director:* Charity Howell
131 N. Saratoga St., Suite B, Suffolk, VA 23434; 757-942-6050
Committee Assignments: Energy and Commerce; Natural Resources; Select on the Climate Crisis

McGovern, James P., D-Mass. (2)

Capitol Hill Office: 370 CHOB 20515-2103; 225-6101; Fax: 225-5759; *Chief of Staff:* Jennifer Chandler
Web: mcgovern.house.gov
Facebook: www.facebook.com/RepJimMcGovern
Twitter: @RepMcGovern
YouTube: www.youtube.com/RepJimMcGovern
Instagram: @repmcgovern
District Offices: 24 Church St., Room 27, Leominster, MA 01453; 978-466-3552; Fax: 978-466-3973; *District Rep.:* Eladia Romero
94 Pleasant St., Northampton, MA 01060; 413-341-8700; Fax: 413-584-1216
12 E. Worcester St., #1, Worcester, MA 01604; 508-831-7356; Fax: 508-754-0982; *District Director:* John Niedzielski
Committee Assignments: Agriculture; Rules, Chair

McHenry, Patrick T., R-N.C. (10)

Capitol Hill Office: 2004 RHOB 20515; 225-2576; Fax: 225-0316; *Chief of Staff:* Jeff Butler
Web: mchenry.house.gov
Facebook: www.facebook.com/CongressmanMcHenry
Twitter: @PatrickMcHenry
YouTube: www.youtube.com/CongressmanMcHenry
Instagram: @reppatrickmchenry
District Office: 1990 Main Ave. S.E., P.O. Box 1830, Hickory, NC 28603; 828-327-6100; Fax: 828-327-8311; *District Director:* Brett Keeter
Satellite Office: Iredell County Government Center South, 610 E. Center Ave., 2nd Floor, Mooresville, NC 28115; 800-477-2576 (open Tuesday, 8:30 a.m.–5 p.m. and Thursday 12 p.m.–5 p.m. and by appointment)

Rural Hall Town Hall, 423 Bethania-Rural Hall Rd., #6, Rural Hall, NC 27045; 800-477-2576 (open Monday 10 a.m.–3 p.m. and by appointment)
Committee Assignment: Financial Services

McKinley, David B., R-W.Va. (1)

Capitol Hill Office: 2239 RHOB 20515; 225-4172; Fax: 225-7564; *Chief of Staff:* Mike Hamilton
Web: mckinley.house.gov
Facebook: www.facebook.com/RepMcKinley
Twitter: @RepMcKinley
YouTube: www.youtube.com/RepDavidMcKinley
District Offices: 709 Beechurst Ave., #29, Morgantown, WV 26505-4689; 304-284-8506; Fax: 304-284-8505; *Field Rep.:* Wendy Madden
408 Market St., Parkersburg, WV 26101; 304-422-5972; Fax: 304-422-5974
Horne Bldg., 1100 Main St., #101, Wheeling, WV 26003; 304-232-3801; Fax: 304-232-3813; *District Director:* Libby Reasbeck
Committee Assignment: Energy and Commerce

McMorris Rodgers, Cathy, R-Wash. (5)

Capitol Hill Office: 1035 LHOB 20515; 225-2006; Fax: 225-3392; *Chief of Staff:* Jared Powell
Web: mcmorris.house.gov
Facebook: www.facebook.com/mcmorrisrodgers
Twitter: @cathymcmorris
YouTube: www.youtube.com/McMorrisRodgers
Instagram: @cathymcmorris
District Offices: 555 S. Main St., Suite C, Colville, WA 99114-2503; 509-684-3481; Fax: 509-684-3482; *Deputy District Director:* Andrew Engell
10 N. Post St., #625, Spokane, WA 99201-0706; 509-353-2374; Fax: 509-234-0445; *District Director:* Patrick Bell
26 E. Main St., #2, Walla Walla, WA 99362-1925; 509-529-9358; Fax: 509-529-9379; *District Rep.:* Victor Valerio
Committee Assignment: Energy and Commerce

McNerney, Jerry, D-Calif. (9)

Capitol Hill Office: 2265 RHOB 20515-0511; 225-1947; Fax: 225-4060; *Chief of Staff:* Nicole Damasco
Web: mcnerney.house.gov
Facebook: www.facebook.com/jerrymcnerney
Twitter: @RepMcNerney
YouTube: www.youtube.com/RepJerryMcNerney
District Offices: Antioch Community Center, 4703 Lone Tree Way, Antioch, CA 94531; 925-754-0716; Fax: 925-754-0728; *District Director:* Erich Pfuehler
2222 Grand Canal Blvd., #7, Stockton, CA 95207-6671; 209-476-8552; Fax: 925-754-0728
Committee Assignments: Energy and Commerce; Science, Space, and Technology

Meeks, Gregory W., D-N.Y. (5)

Capitol Hill Office: 2310 RHOB 20515; 225-3461; Fax: 226-4169; *Chief of Staff:* Sophia Lafargue
Web: meeks.house.gov
Facebook: www.facebook.com/RepGregoryMeeks

Twitter: @RepGregoryMeeks
YouTube: www.youtube.com/repgregorymeeks
Instagram: @repgregorymeeks
District Offices: 67-12 Rockaway Beach Blvd., Arverne, NY 11692; 347-230-4032; Fax: 347-230-4045; *District Director:* Robert Simmons
153-01 Jamaica Ave., 2nd Floor, Jamaica, NY 11432; 718-725-6000; Fax: 718-725-9868
Committee Assignment: Financial Services; Foreign Affairs, Chair

Meijer, Peter, R-Mich. (3)

Capitol Hill Office: 1508 LHOB 20515; 225-3831; Fax: 225-5144; *Chief of Staff:* Ken Monahan
Web: meijer.house.gov
Facebook: www.facebook.com/RepPeterMeijer
Twitter: @RepMeijer
YouTube: www.youtube.com/channel/UCBTV_BJELjR7_7zQnTrAIww
Instagram: @repmeijer
District Office: 110 Michigan St. N.W., #460, Grand Rapids, MI 49503; 616-451-8383; Fax: 616-454-5630; *District Director:* Rick Treur
Committee Assignments: Foreign Affairs; Homeland Security; Science, Space, and Technology

Meng, Grace, D-N.Y. (6)

Capitol Hill Office: 2209 RHOB 20515; 225-2601; Fax: 225-1589; *Chief of Staff:* Maeve Healy
Web: meng.house.gov
Facebook: www.facebook.com/repgracemeng
Twitter: @RepGraceMeng
YouTube: www.youtube.com/channel/UCHg516zJKbIBtXFAJ0nu3XQ
District Offices: 40-13 159th St., Suite A, Flushing, NY 11358; 718-358-6364; Fax: 718-445-7868; *District Director:* Tayler Jackson
118-35 Queens Blvd., 17th Floor, Forest Hills, NY 11375 (by appointment only); *District Director:* Anthony Lemma
Committee Assignment: Appropriations

Meuser, Daniel, R-Pa. (9)

Capitol Hill Office: 414 CHOB 20515-3809; 225-6511; *Chief of Staff:* Tyler Menzler
Web: meuser.house.gov
Facebook: www.facebook.com/RepMeuser
Twitter: @RepMeuser
YouTube: www.youtube.com/channel/UCFBiWT7JNlSyUNuxYqjdUtA
Instagram: @repmeuser
District Offices: 1044 E. Main St., Palmyra, PA 17078; 717-473-5375
121 Progress Ave., #110, Losch Plaza, Pottsville, PA 17901; 570-871-6370; *Deputy District Director:* Tom Gerhard
Reading Regional Airport, 2501 Bernville Rd., Reading, PA 19605; 610-568-9959
Committee Assignments: Foreign Affairs; Small Business

Mfume, Kweisi, D-Md. (7)

Capitol Hill Office: 2263 RHOB 20515; 225-4741; Fax: 202-225-3178; *Chief of Staff:* Eric Bryant
Web: mfume.house.gov
Facebook: www.facebook.com/RepKweisiMfume
Twitter: @RepKweisiMfume
YouTube: www.youtube.com/channel/UCbE6PJy-4U0DxosEW2TBQRA/videos?view=0&sort=p
Instagram: @repkweisimfume
District Offices: 1010 Park Ave., #105, Baltimore, MD 21201; 410-685-9199; *District Director:* Anthony Jones
754 Frederick Rd., Catonsville, MD 21228; 410-818-2120
8267 Main St., Room 102, Ellicot City, MD 21043; 443-364-5413
Committee Assignments: Education and Labor; Oversight and Reform; Small Business

Miller, Carol D., R-W.Va. (3)

Capitol Hill Office: 465 CHOB 20515-4803; 225-3452; *Deputy Chief of Staff:* Lauren Billman
Web: miller.house.gov
Facebook: www.facebook.com/RepCarolMiller
Twitter: @RepCarolMiller
YouTube: www.youtube.com/channel/UCw2oLPoyGX-cLILniYOqLWA
Instagram: @repcarolmiller
District Offices: 307 Prince St., Beckley, WV 25801; 304-250-6177; Fax: 304-250-6179; *District Director:* Darian David
2699 Park Ave., #220, Huntington, WV 25704, 304-522-2201; Fax: 304-529-5716
Committee Assignments: Select on the Climate Crisis; Ways and Means

Miller, Mary E., R-Ill. (15)

Capitol Hill Office: 1529 LHOB 20515; 225-5271; Fax: 225-5880; *Chief of Staff:* Ben Demarzo
Web: marymiller.house.gov
Facebook: www.facebook.com/RepMaryMiller
Twitter: @RepMaryMiller
Instagram: @repmarymiller
District Offices: 201 N. Vermilion St., #325, Danville, IL 61832; 217-703-6100; *District Director:* Jim Runyon
101 N. 4th St., #302, Effingham, IL 62401; 217-240-3155
100 E. Locust St., Harrisburg, IL 62946
Committee Assignments: Agriculture; Education and Labor

Miller-Meeks, Mariannette, R-Iowa (2)

Capitol Hill Office: 1716 LHOB 20515; 225-6576; *Chief of Staff:* Tracie Gibler
Web: millermeeks.house.gov
Facebook: www.facebook.com/MillerMeeksIA
Twitter: @MillerMeeks
District Office: 202 W. 2nd St., #705, Davenport, IA 52801; 563-232-0930; *District Director:* Aaron McKay
105 E. 3rd St., #201A & #201B, Ottumwa, IA 52501; 641-244-7020

Committee Assignments: Education and Labor; Homeland Security; Veterans' Affairs; Select on Coronavirus Crisis

Moolenaar, John R., R-Mich. (4)

Capitol Hill Office: 117 CHOB 20515-2204; 225-3561; Fax: 225-9679; *Chief of Staff:* Lindsay Ryan
Web: moolenaar.house.gov
Facebook: www.facebook.com/RepMoolenaar
Twitter: @RepMoolenaar
YouTube: www.youtube.com/channel/ UCnMvVN4a8roZu4crE0UW2DA
Instagram: @repmoolenaar
District Office: 200 E. Main St., #230, Midland, MI 48640; 989-631-2552; Fax: 989-631-6271; *District Chief of Staff:* Ashton Bortz
Satellite Office: 201 N. Mitchell St., #L4, Cadillac, MI 49601; 231-942-5070; Fax: 231-876-9505 (open Monday, Tuesday, and Thursday, 9 a.m.–4 p.m.)
Committee Assignment: Appropriations

Mooney, Alexander X., R-W.Va. (2)

Capitol Hill Office: 2228 RHOB 20515-4802; 225-2711; Fax: 225-7856; *Chief of Staff:* Michael Hough
Web: mooney.house.gov
Facebook: www.facebook.com/CongressmanAlexMooney
Twitter: @RepAlexMooney
YouTube: www.youtube.com/channel/ UCw9CGkF4Re3areluI43TGyA
Instagram: @repalexmooney
District Offices: 405 Capitol St., #306, Charleston, WV 25301; 304-925-5964; Fax: 304-926-8912; *District Director:* Chad Story
300 Foxcroft Ave., #101, Martinsburg, WV 25401; 304-264-8810; Fax: 304-264-8815
Committee Assignment: Financial Services

Moore, Barry, R-Ala. (2)

Capitol Hill Office: 1504 LHOB 20515; 225-2901; *Deputy Chief of Staff:* Shana Teehan
Web: barrymoore.house.gov
Facebook: www.facebook.com/RepBarryMoore
Twitter: @RepBarryMoore
Instagram: @repbarrymoore
District Offices: 505 E. 3 Notch St., #322, Andalusia, AL 36420; 334-428-1129; Fax: 334-222-3342
217 Graceland Dr., Dothan, AL 36305; 334-547-6630; *District Director:* Paul Diaz
408 S. Main St., #200, Wetumpka, AL 36092; 334-478-6330; *Field Rep.:* Mason Bunn
Committee Assignments: Agriculture; Veterans' Affairs

Moore, Blake D., R-Utah (1)

Capitol Hill Office: 1320 LHOB 20515; 225-0453; Fax: 225-5857; *Chief of Staff:* Rachel Wagley
Web: blakemoore.house.gov
Facebook: www.facebook.com/RepBlakeMoore
Twitter: @RepBlakeMoore

District Office: 324 25th St., Ogden, UT 84401; 801-625-0107; 385-405-2155; *District Director:* Peter Jenks
Committee Assignments: Armed Services; Natural Resources

Moore, Gwen, D-Wisc. (4)

Capitol Hill Office: 2252 RHOB 20515; 225-4572; Fax: 225-8135; *Chief of Staff:* Sean Gard
Web: gwenmoore.house.gov
Facebook: www.facebook.com/GwenSMoore
Twitter: @RepGwenMoore
YouTube: www.youtube.com/RepGwenMoore
Instagram: @repgwenmoore
District Office: 250 E. Wisconsin Ave., #950, Milwaukee, WI 53202-5818; 414-297-1140; Fax: 414-297-1086; *District Director:* Shirley Ellis
Committee Assignments: Science, Space, and Technology; Select on Economic Disparity and Fairness and Growth; Ways and Means

Morelle, Joseph D., D-N.Y. (25)

Capitol Hill Office: 1317 LHOB 20515-3515; 225-3615; *Chief of Staff:* Abbie Sorrendino
Web: morelle.house.gov
Facebook: www.facebook.com/RepJoeMorelle
Twitter: @RepJoeMorelle
YouTube: www.youtube.com/channel/UCgqBoBJGq-CR3lD2GVABcPA
District Office: 3120 Federal Bldg., 100 State St., Rochester, NY 14614; 585-232-4850; Fax: 585-232-1954; *District Director:* Kaleigh Benedict
Committee Assignments: Armed Services; Budget; Education and Labor; Rules

Moulton, Seth, D-Mass. (6)

Capitol Hill Office: 1127 LHOB 20515-2106; 225-8020; Fax: 225-5915; *Chief of Staff:* Alexis Prieur L'Heureux
Web: moulton.house.gov
Facebook: www.facebook.com/RepMoulton
Twitter: @teammoulton
YouTube: www.youtube.com/channel/ UC5w5qn7nj5Ljy69LTV7a_fQ
Instagram: @repmoulton
District Office: 21 Front St., Salem, MA 01970; 978-531-1669; Fax: 978-224-2270; *District Director:* Rick Jakious
Committee Assignments: Armed Services; Budget; Transportation and Infrastructure

Mrvan, Frank J., D-Ind. (1)

Capitol Hill Office: 1607 LHOB 20515; 225-2461; Fax: 225-2493; *Chief of Staff:* Mark Lopez
Web: mrvan.house.gov
Facebook: www.facebook.com/RepMrvan
Twitter: @RepMrvan
YouTube: www.youtube.com/channel/UCol0RuYLQXE-DAZkzJ7tDnQ
Instagram: @repmrvan

District Office: 7895 Broadway, Suite A, Merrillville, IN 46410; 219-795-1844; Fax: 219-795-1850

Committee Assignments: Education and Labor; Veterans' Affairs

Mullin, Markwayne, R-Okla. (2)

Capitol Hill Office: 2421 RHOB 20515; 225-2701; Fax: 225-3038; *Chief of Staff:* Ben Cantrell

Web: mullin.house.gov

Facebook: www.facebook.com/RepMullin

Twitter: @RepMullin

YouTube: www.youtube.com/channel/UCLQlm-cbGbJj9baZC6oFsag

Instagram: @markwaynemullin

District Offices: 1 E. Choctaw Ave., #175, McAlester, OK 74501; 918-423-5951; Fax: 918-423-1940; *District Director:* Caleb Cochran

223 W. Patti Page Blvd., Claremore, OK 74017; 918-283-6262; Fax: 918-923-6451

Committee Assignments: Energy and Commerce; Permanent Select Intelligence

Murphy, Gregory F., R-N.C. (3)

Capitol Hill Office: 313 CHOB 20515; 225-3415; *Chief of Staff:* Dave Natonski

Web: gregmurphy.house.gov

Facebook: www.facebook.com/RepGregMurphy

Twitter: @RepGregMurphy

YouTube: www.youtube.com/channel/UCxtUE8bDXDTghP2uDEXpwgQ

Instagram: @repgregmurphy

District Offices: 1105 Corporate Dr., Suite C, Greenville, NC 27858; 252-931-1003; Fax: 252-931-1002; *District Director:* Lindy Robinson

101 W. King St., Suite F, Edenton, NC 27932; 252-368-8866

234 Corridor Blvd N.W., Jacksonville, NC 28540; 910-937-6929

2402 Dr. M. L. K. Jr. Blvd., New Bern, NC 28562; 252-636-6612

Committee Assignments: Education and Labor; Veterans' Affairs; Ways and Means

Murphy, Stephanie N., D-Fla. (7)

Capitol Hill Office: 1710 LHOB 20515; 225-4035; Fax: 226-0821; *Chief of Staff:* John Laufer

Web: stephaniemurphy.house.gov

Facebook: www.facebook.com/RepStephMurphy

Twitter: @RepStephMurphy

YouTube: www.youtube.com/channel/UCmd4mo5owVTGetYcPmkcI1g

Instagram: @repstephmurphy

District Offices: 225 E. Robinson St., #525, Orlando, FL 32801; 888-205-5421; *District Director:* Lauren Allen

110 W. 1st St., #210, Sanford, FL 32771; 888-205-5421

Committee Assignments: Armed Services; Ways and Means; Select to Investigate the January 6th Attack on the U.S. Capitol

Nadler, Jerrold, D-N.Y. (10)

Capitol Hill Office: 2132 RHOB 20515; 225-5635; Fax: 225-6923; *Washington Director:* Amy Rutkin

Web: nadler.house.gov

Facebook: www.facebook.com/CongressmanNadler

Twitter: @RepJerryNadler

YouTube: www.youtube.com/CongressmanNadler

Instagram: @repjerrynadler

District Offices: 6605 Fort Hamilton Pkwy., Brooklyn, NY 11219; 718-373-3198; Fax: 718-996-0039

201 Varick St., #669, New York, NY 10014-7069; 212-367-7350; Fax: 212-367-7356; *District Director:* Robert Gottheim

Committee Assignment: Judiciary, Chair

Napolitano, Grace F., D-Calif. (32)

Capitol Hill Office: 1610 LHOB 20515-0538; 225-5256; Fax: 225-0027; *Chief of Staff:* Joe Sheehy

Web: napolitano.house.gov

Facebook: www.facebook.com/RepGraceNapolitano

Twitter: @gracenapolitano

YouTube: www.youtube.com/RepGraceNapolitano

Instagram: @repgracenapolitano

District Office: 4401 Santa Anita Ave., #201, El Monte, CA 91731; 626-350-0150; Fax: 626-350-0450; *District Director:* Perla Hernandez Trumkul

Committee Assignments: Natural Resources; Transportation and Infrastructure

Neal, Richard E., D-Mass. (1)

Capitol Hill Office: 372 CHOB 20515-2101; 225-5601; Fax: 225-8112; *Chief of Staff:* Lizzy O'Hara

Web: neal.house.gov

Facebook: www.facebook.com/reprichardneal

Twitter: @RepRichardNeal

YouTube: www.youtube.com/RepRichardENeal

District Offices: 78 Center St., Pittsfield, MA 01201; 413-442-0946; Fax: 413-443-2792; *District Director:* Bill Powers

300 State St., #200, Springfield, MA 01105-1711; 413-785-0325; Fax: 413-747-0604

Committee Assignments: Joint Taxation, Chair; Ways and Means, Chair

Neguse, Joe, D-Colo. (2)

Capitol Hill Office: 1419 LHOB 20515; 225-2161; *Chief of Staff:* Jennifer Ven der Heide

Web: neguse.house.gov

Facebook: www.facebook.com/RepJoeNeguse

Twitter: @RepJoeNeguse

YouTube: www.youtube.com/channel/UCukNKhsFrzM-LFtp43XPQtg

Instagram: @repjoeneguse

District Offices: 2503 Walnut St., #300, Boulder, CO 80302; 303-335-1045; Fax: 979-632-5198; *District Director:* Sally Anderson

1220 S. College Ave., #100A, Fort Collins, CO 80524; 970-372-3971; Fax: 979-632-5198

Committee Assignments: Judiciary; Natural Resources; Rules; Select on the Climate Crisis

Nehls, Troy E., R-Tex. (22)

Capitol Hill Office: 1104 LHOB 20515; 225-5951; Fax: 225-5241; *Chief of Staff:* Robert Schroeder
Web: nehls.house.gov
Facebook: www.facebook.com/RepTroyNehls
Twitter: @RepTroyNehls
YouTube: www.youtube.com/channel/UCf4v1ZzngfbZ-Ow9EiagaOA
District Office: 1117 FM 359 Rd., #210, Richmond, TX 77406; 346-762-6600; *District Director:* Mary Davis
Committee Assignments: Transportation and Infrastructure; Veterans' Affairs

Newhouse, Dan, R-Wash. (4)

Capitol Hill Office: 504 CHOB 20515; 225-5816; Fax: 225-3251; *Chief of Staff:* Jess Carter
Web: newhouse.house.gov
Facebook: www.facebook.com/RepNewhouse
Twitter: @RepNewhouse
YouTube: www.youtube.com/channel/UCllbsv_aoIaPS6W3aSonZlw
Instagram: @repnewhouse
District Offices: P.O. Box 135, Grand Coulee, WA 99133; 509-433-7760; *District Rep.:* Rachel McClure
3100 George Washington Way, #130, Richland, WA 99354; 509-713-7374; Fax: 509-713-7377; *District Director:* Jamie Daniels
402 E. Yakima Ave., #1000, Yakima, WA 98901; 509-452-3243; Fax: 509-452-3438; *District Rep.:* Vicki Holleman-Perez
Committee Assignment: Appropriations

Newman, Marie, D-Ill. (3)

Capitol Hill Office: 1022 LHOB 20515; 225-5701; *Chief of Staff:* Ben Hardin
Web: newman.house.gov
Facebook: www.facebook.com/RepMarieNewman
Twitter: @RepMarieNewman
Instagram: @repmarienewman
District Office: 6245 S. Archer Ave., Chicago, IL 60638; 773-948-6223; Fax: 773-767-9395
7902 S. Oketo Ave., Bridgeview, IL 60455; 708-821-1141 (open Tuesdays, 10 a.m.–2 p.m.)
Committee Assignments: Small Business; Transportation and Infrastructure

Norcross, Donald, D-N.J. (1)

Capitol Hill Office: 2427 RHOB 20515-3001; 225-6501; Fax: 225-6583; *Chief of Staff:* Mary Cruz
Web: norcross.house.gov
Facebook: www.facebook.com/DonaldNorcrossNJ
Twitter: @DonaldNorcross
YouTube: www.youtube.com/channel/UC7kXK_PyDiOT8YrdP0jYZHw/feed
Instagram: @donald_norcross

District Offices: 200 Federal St., 5th Floor, Camden, NJ 08103; 856-427-7000; Fax: 856-427-7000
10 Melrose Ave., #210, Cherry Hill, NJ 08003; 856-427-7000; Fax: 856-427-7000
Committee Assignments: Armed Services; Education and Labor; Science, Space, and Technology

Norman, Ralph, R-S.C. (5)

Capitol Hill Office: 569 CHOB 20515; 225-5501; Fax: 225-0464; *Chief of Staff:* Mark Piland
Web: norman.house.gov
Facebook: www.facebook.com/RepRalphNorman
Twitter: @RepRalphNorman
YouTube: www.youtube.com/channel/UCVVIZjUpGRB1pgQGDBVBU8Q
Instagram: @repralphnorman
District Office: 454 S. Anderson Rd., #302B, Rock Hill, SC 29730; 803-327-1114; Fax: 803-327-4330
Committee Assignments: Homeland Security; Oversight and Reform

Norton, Eleanor Holmes, D-D.C. (At Large)

Capitol Hill Office: 2136 RHOB 20515-5101; 225-8050; Fax: 225-3002; *Chief of Staff:* Raven Reeder
Web: norton.house.gov
Facebook: www.facebook.com/CongresswomanNorton
Twitter: @EleanorNorton
YouTube: www.youtube.com/EleanorHNorton
Instagram: @congresswomannorton
District Offices: 1300 Pennsylvania Ave. N.W., #M1000, Washington, DC 20004; 202-408-9041; Fax: 202-408-9048; *District Director:* Karen Owens
2235 Shannon Pl. S.E., #2032A, Washington, DC 20020-7005; 202-678-8900; Fax: 202-408-8844
Committee Assignments: Oversight and Reform; Transportation and Infrastructure

O'Halleran, Tom, D-Ariz. (1)

Capitol Hill Office: 318 CHOB 20515; 225-3361; Fax: 225-3462; *Chief of Staff:* Sally Adams
Web: ohalleran.house.gov
Facebook: www.facebook.com/repohalleran
Twitter: @RepOHalleran
YouTube: www.youtube.com/repohalleran
Instagram: @repohalleran
District Office: 200 W. Magee Rd., #140, Oro Valley, AZ 85704; 520-316-0838; Fax: 855-313-7205
405 N. Beaver St., #6, Flagstaff, AZ 86001; 928-286-5338; Fax: 928-779-6310; *District Director:* Keith Brekhus
Committee Assignments: Agriculture; Energy and Commerce

Obernolte, Jay, R-Calif. (8)

Capitol Hill Office: 1029 LHOB 20515; 225-5861; *Chief of Staff:* Lorissa Bounds
Web: obernolte.house.gov
Facebook: www.facebook.com/jayobernolte
Twitter: @JayObernolte
YouTube: www.youtube.com/c/jayobernolte

Instagram: @jayobernolte
District Office: 9700 7th Ave., #201, Hesperia, CA 92345; 760-247-1815; *Deputy Chief of Staff:* Ross Sevy
Committee Assignments: Budget; Natural Resources; Science, Space, and Technology

Ocasio-Cortez, Alexandria, D-N.Y. (14)

Capitol Hill Office: 216 CHOB 20515; 225-3965; *Chief of Staff:* Geraldo Bonilla-Chavez
Web: ocasio-cortez.house.gov
Facebook: www.facebook.com/repAOC
Twitter: @RepAOC
YouTube: www.youtube.com/channel/UC6XBnYptBnproA__ydn-b0A
Instagram: @repaoc
District Offices: 74-09 37th Ave., #305, Jackson Heights, NY 11372; 718-662-5970; *District Director:* Maribel Hernandez-Rivera
Assembly Members Reyes' Office, 1973 Westchester Ave., The Bronx, NY 10462; 718-662-5970 (open Monday, Tuesday, Thursday, and Friday, 9 a.m.–5 p.m.)
Committee Assignments: Financial Services; Oversight and Reform

Omar, Ilhan, D-Minn. (5)

Capitol Hill Office: 1730 LHOB 20515; 225-4755; Fax: 216-522-4908; *Chief of Staff:* Connor McNutt
Web: omar.house.gov
Facebook: www.facebook.com/RepIlhan
Twitter: @repilhan
YouTube: www.youtube.com/channel/UC4meVUkgJUxyHE5CifWAumQ
Instagram: @repilhan
District Office: 404 3rd Ave. North, #203, Minneapolis, MN 55401; 612-333-1272
Committee Assignments: Education and Labor; Foreign Affairs

Owens, Burgess, R-Utah (4)

Capitol Hill Office: 1039 LHOB 20515; 225-3011; *Chief of Staff:* Keelie Broom
Web: owens.house.gov
Facebook: www.facebook.com/CongressmanBurgessOwens
Twitter: @RepBurgessOwens
YouTube: www.youtube.com/channel/UCxeB7xjbLDJM9Yw6brXsX6Q
Instagram: @repburgessowens
District Office: 9067 S. 1300 West, #101, West Jordan, UT, 84088; 801-999-9801; *District Director:* Nathaniel Johnson
Committee Assignments: Education and Labor; Judiciary

Palazzo, Steven M., R-Miss. (4)

Capitol Hill Office: 2349 RHOB 20515-2404; 225-5772; Fax: 225-7074; *Chief of Staff:* Patrick Large
Web: palazzo.house.gov
Facebook: www.facebook.com/stevenpalazzo
Twitter: @CongPalazzo
YouTube: www.youtube.com/CongressmanPalazzo

Instagram: @congressmanpalazzo
District Offices: 84 48th St., Gulfport, MS 39507; 228-864-7670; Fax: 228-864-3099; *District Director:* Michele Gargiulo
641 Main St., #142, Hattiesburg, MS 39401-3478; 601-582-3246; Fax: 601-582-3452
3118 Pascagoula St., #181, Pascagoula, MS 39567-4215; 228-202-8104; Fax: 228-202-8105 (by appointment only)
Committee Assignment: Appropriations

Pallone, Frank, Jr., D-N.J. (6)

Capitol Hill Office: 2107 RHOB 20515-3006; 225-4671; Fax: 225-9665; *Chief of Staff:* Liam Fitzsimmons
Web: pallone.house.gov
Facebook: www.facebook.com/RepFrankPallone
Twitter: @FrankPallone
YouTube: www.youtube.com/RepFrankPallone
Instagram: @repfrankpallone
District Offices: 504 Broadway, Long Branch, NJ 07740-5951; 732-571-1140; Fax: 732-870-3890; *District Director:* Matthew Montekio
67/69 Church St., New Brunswick, NJ 08901; 732-249-8892; Fax: 732-249-1335; *Constituent Services Director:* Alexandra Maldonado
Committee Assignment: Energy and Commerce, Chair

Palmer, Gary J., R-Ala. (6)

Capitol Hill Office: 170 CHOB 20515; 225-4921; Fax: 225-2082; *Chief of Staff:* William Smith
Web: palmer.house.gov
Facebook: www.facebook.com/CongressmanGaryPalmer
Twitter: @USRepGaryPalmer
YouTube: www.youtube.com/channel/UCYZfP-cNIvlJY3AcAc9OPpQ
Instagram: @repgarypalmer
District Offices: 3535 Grandview Pkwy., #525, Birmingham, AL 35243; 205-968-1290; Fax: 205-968-1294; *District Director:* Ethan Vice
Clanton City Hall, N. 505 2nd Ave., Clanton, AL 35045
Blount County Courthouse, E. 220 2nd Ave., Oneonta, AL 35121
Committee Assignment: Energy and Commerce

Panetta, Jimmy, D-Calif. (20)

Capitol Hill Office: 406 CHOB 20515; 225-2861; Fax: 225-6791; *Chief of Staff:* Pete Spiro
Web: panetta.house.gov
Facebook: www.facebook.com/RepJimmyPanetta
Twitter: @RepJimmyPanetta
YouTube: www.youtube.com/channel/UCmw-aERG51C96edMDPN7fXQ
Instagram: @repjimmypanetta
District Offices: 142 W. Alisal St., Room E116, Salinas, CA 93901; 831-424-2229; Fax: 831-429-1458; *District Director:* Susie Brusa
701 Ocean St., Room 318C, Santa Cruz, CA 95060; 831-429-1976; Fax: 831-429-1458; *Congressional Aide:* Emmanuel Garcia, Ana Calero
Committee Assignments: Agriculture; Armed Services; Ways and Means

Pappas, Chris, D-N.H. (1)

Capitol Hill Office: 323 CHOB 20515-3515; 225-5456; *Chief of Staff:* Steve Carlson
Web: pappas.house.gov
Facebook: www.facebook.com/RepChrisPappas
Twitter: @RepChrisPappas
YouTube: www.youtube.com/channel/ UCMKDg_1K7cjBKbHGgq1YKkg
Instagram: @repchrispappas
District Offices: 660 Central Ave., #101, Dover, NH 03820; 603-285-4300; Fax: 603-343-1326; *Constituent Services Director:* Patrick Carroll
889 Elm St., Manchester, NH 03101; 603-935-6710; *District Director:* Kari Thurman
Committee Assignments: Transportation and Infrastructure; Veterans' Affairs

Pascrell, Bill, Jr., D-N.J. (9)

Capitol Hill Office: 2409 RHOB 20515-3008; 225-5751; Fax: 225-5782; *Chief of Staff:* Benjamin Rich
Web: pascrell.house.gov
Facebook: www.facebook.com/pascrell
Twitter: @BillPascrell
YouTube: www.youtube.com/RepPascrell
Instagram: @billpascrell
District Offices: 200 Federal Plaza, #500, Paterson, NJ 07505-1999; 973-523-5152; Fax: 973-523-0637; *District Director:* Ritzy Moralez-Diaz
330 Passaic St., 1st Floor, Passaic, NJ 07055-5815; 973-472-4510; (open Monday and Wednesday, 9 a.m.–5 p.m.); *Field Rep.:* Celia Anderson
Satellite Offices: 367 Valley Brook Ave., Lyndhurst, NJ 07071; 201-935-2248 (open Monday and Wednesday, 9 a.m.–5 p.m.); *Field Rep.:* Leonardo Fuentes
2-10 N. Van Brunt St., Englewood, NJ 07631; 201-935-2248 (open Tuesday and Thursday, 9 a.m.–5 p.m.)
Committee Assignment: Ways and Means

Payne, Donald M., Jr., D-N.J. (10)

Capitol Hill Office: 106 CHOB 20515; 225-3436; Fax: 225-4160; *Chief of Staff:* LaVerne Alexander
Web: payne.house.gov
Facebook: www.facebook.com/DonaldPayneJr
Twitter: @RepDonaldPayne
YouTube: www.youtube.com/channel/ UCTG_SeYsOgbngjv1Donyu0w
Instagram: @repdonaldpaynejr
District Offices: 253 Martin Luther King Dr., Jersey City, NJ 07305; 201-369-0392; Fax: 201-369-0395; *Constituent Service Coord.:* Elizabeth Lorenzo
60 Nelson Pl., 14th Floor, Newark, NJ 07102; 973-645-3213; Fax: 973-645-5902; *District Director:* Michael Gray
1455 Liberty Ave., Hillside, NJ 07205; 862-229-2994; Fax: 862-225-2941
Committee Assignments: Homeland Security; Transportation and Infrastructure

Pelosi, Nancy, D-Calif. (12)

Capitol Hill Office: 1236 LHOB 20515-0512; 225-4965; Fax: 225-8259; *Chief of Staff:* Terri McCullough
Web: pelosi.house.gov
Facebook: www.facebook.com/NancyPelosi
Twitter: @SpeakerPelosi
YouTube: www.youtube.com/nancypelosi
Instagram: @speakerpelosi
District Office: 90 7th St., #2-800, San Francisco, CA 94103-6723; 415-556-4862; Fax: 415-861-1670; *District Chief of Staff:* Dan Bernal
Speaker of the House

Pence, Greg, R-Ind. (6)

Capitol Hill Office: 211 CHOB 20515; 225-3021; *Chief of Staff:* Kyle Robertson
Web: pence.house.gov
Facebook: www.facebook.com/RepGregPence
Twitter: @RepGregPence
YouTube: www.youtube.com/channel/ UCL2cxXwzTek7uXLOdwbJ3Ag
Instagram: @repgregpence
District Offices: 529 Washington St., Columbus, IN 47201; 812-799-5230; Fax: 844-313-1563 *District Director:* Liz Dessauer
18 E. Main St., #210, Greenfield, IN 46140; 812-799-5233
50 N. 5th St., 2nd Floor, Richmond, IN 47374; 765-660-1083
Committee Assignment: Energy and Commerce

Perlmutter, Ed, D-Colo. (7)

Capitol Hill Office: 1226 LHOB 20515; 225-2645; Fax: 225-5278; *Chief of Staff:* Danielle Radovich-Piper
Web: perlmutter.house.gov
Facebook: www.facebook.com/RepPerlmutter
Twitter: @RepPerlmutter
YouTube: www.youtube.com/RepPerlmutter
District Office: 12600 W. Colfax Ave., #B-400, Lakewood, CO 80215-3779; 303-274-7944; Fax: 303-274-6455
Committee Assignments: Financial Services; Rules; Science, Space, and Technology; Select on the Modernization of Congress

Perry, Scott, R-Pa. (10)

Capitol Hill Office: 2160 RHOB 20515; 225-5836; Fax: 226-1000; *Chief of Staff:* Lauren Muglia
Web: perry.house.gov
Facebook: www.facebook.com/repscottperry
Twitter: @RepScottPerry
YouTube: www.youtube.com/RepScottPerry
Instagram: @repscottperry
District Offices: 800 Corporate Circle, #202, Harrisburg, PA 17110; 717-603-4980; *District Director:* Jay Ostrich
730 N. Front St., Wormleysburg, PA 17043; 717-635-9504; Fax: 717-635-9861
2501 Catherine St., #11, York, PA 17408; 717-893-7868
Committee Assignments: Foreign Affairs; Transportation and Infrastructure

Peters, Scott H., D-Calif. (52)

Capitol Hill Office: 1201 LHOB 20515-0550; 225-0508;
  Chief of Staff: Mary Anne Pintar
Web: scottpeters.house.gov
Facebook: www.facebook.com/RepScottPeters
Twitter: @RepScottPeters
YouTube: www.youtube.com/repscottpeters
Instagram: @repscottpeters
District Office: 4350 Executive Dr., #105, San Diego, CA
  92121; 858-455-5550; *District Director:* Jason
  Bercovitch
Committee Assignments: Budget; Energy and Commerce;
  Joint Economic

Pfluger, August, R-Tex. (11)

Capitol Hill Office: 1531 LHOB 20515; 225-3605; *Chief of
  Staff:* John Byers
Web: pfluger.house.gov
Facebook: www.facebook.com/RepAugustPfluger
Twitter: @RepPfluger
YouTube: www.youtube.com/channel/
  UC8bJT16wpa7co50ELvpMTTg
Instagram: @repaugustpfluger
District Offices: 501 Center Ave., Brownwood, TX 76801;
  325-646-1950; *Regional Director:* Hilary Stegemoller
132 Houston St., Granbury, TX 76048; 682-936-2577
104 W. Sandstone St., Llano, TX; 325-247-2826
6 Desta Drive, #2000, Midland, TX 79705; 432-687-2390;
  Regional Director: Corbette Padilla
119 W. 4th St., #215, Odessa, TX 79761; 432-331-9667
33 E. Twohig Ave., #307, San Angelo, TX 76903; 325-659-
  4010
Committee Assignments: Foreign Affairs; Homeland
  Security

Phillips, Dean, D-Minn. (3)

Capitol Hill Office: 2452 RHOB 20515-3515; 225-2871;
  Fax: 225-6351; *Chief of Staff:* Tim Bertocci
Web: phillips.house.gov
Facebook: www.facebook.com/RepDeanPhillips
Twitter: @RepDeanPhillips
YouTube: www.youtube.com/channel/
  UCQ7y_sateDGmnnw1NVuaTvA
Instagram: @repdeanphillips
District Office: 13911 Ridgedale Dr., #200, Minnetonka,
  MN 55305; 952-656-5176; *District Director:* Emma
  Youngquist
Committee Assignments: Ethics; Foreign Affairs; Select
  on the Modernization of Congress; Small Business

Pingree, Chellie, D-Maine (1)

Capitol Hill Office: 2162 RHOB 20515-1901; 225-6116;
  Fax: 225-5590; *Chief of Staff:* Jesse Connolly
Web: pingree.house.gov
Facebook: www.facebook.com/ChelliePingree
Twitter: @chelliepingree
YouTube: www.youtube.com/CongresswomanPingree
Instagram: @chelliepingree

District Offices: 2 Portland Fish Pier, #304, Portland, ME
  04101; 207-774-5019; Fax: 207-871-0720; *Director of
  Communications:* Victoria Bonney
1 Silver St., Waterville, ME 04901; 207-873-5713; Fax: 207-
  873-5717
Committee Assignments: Agriculture; Appropriations

Plaskett, Stacey E., D-Virgin Islands. (At Large)

Capitol Hill Office: 2404 RHOB 20515; 225-1790;
  Fax: 225-5517; *Chief of Staff:* Angeline Muckle-Jabbar
Web: plaskett.house.gov
Facebook: www.facebook.com/repstaceyplaskett
Twitter: @StaceyPlaskett
YouTube: www.youtube.com/channel/
  UC3V7biFZHDFHDFZy6cCSZUA
Instagram: @stacey_plaskett
District Offices: 60 King St., Frederiksted, VI 00840; 340-
  778-5900; Fax: 340-778-5111
9100 Havensight, Port of Sale Mall, #22, St. Thomas,
  VI 00802; 340-774-4408; Fax: 340-774-8033;
  District Director: Cletis Clendinen
Committee Assignments: Agriculture; Budget; Ways and
  Means

Pocan, Mark, D-Wisc. (2)

Capitol Hill Office: 1727 LHOB 20515; 225-2906;
  Fax: 225-6942; *Chief of Staff:* Glenn Wavrunek
Web: pocan.house.gov
Facebook: www.facebook.com/repmarkpocan
Twitter: @repmarkpocan
YouTube: www.youtube.com/repmarkpocan
Instagram: @repmarkpocan
District Office: 10 E. Doty St., #405, Madison, WI 53703-
  5103; 608-258-9800; Fax: 608-258-0377; *District
  Director:* Dane Varese
Committee Assignments: Appropriations; Education and
  Labor; Joint Economic

Porter, Katie, D-Calif. (45)

Capitol Hill Office: 1117 LHOB 20515-3515; 225-5611;
  Chief of Staff: Nora Walsh-DeVries
Web: porter.house.gov
Facebook: www.facebook.com/repkatieporter
Twitter: @RepKatiePorter
YouTube: www.youtube.com/channel/
  UCRdB2ce4DloCSyuPbWfOZyw
Instagram: @repkatieporter
District Office: 2151 Michelson Dr., #195, Irvine, CA
  92612; 949-668-6600; *District Director:* Cory Mendoza
Committee Assignments: Natural Resources; Oversight
  and Reform

Posey, Bill, R-Fla. (8)

Capitol Hill Office: 2150 RHOB 20515; 225-3671;
  Fax: 225-3516; *Chief of Staff:* Stuart Burns
Web: posey.house.gov
Facebook: www.facebook.com/Congressman-Bill-Posey-
  101464786703
Twitter: @congbillposey

YouTube: www.youtube.com/CongressmanPosey
District Office: 2725 Judge Fran Jamieson Way, Bldg. C, Melbourne, FL 32940-6605; 321-632-1776; Fax: 321-639-8595; *District Scheduler / District Director:* Patrick Gavin
Satellite Offices: Vero Beach Office; 772-226-1701 (by appointment only)
Titusville Office; 321-383-6090 (by appointment only)
Committee Assignments: Financial Services; Science, Space, and Technology

Pressley, Ayanna, D-Mass. (7)

Capitol Hill Office: 1108 LHOB 20515-3515; 225-5111; Fax: 225-9322; *Chief of Staff:* Sarah Groh
Web: pressley.house.gov
Facebook: www.facebook.com/RepAyannaPressley
Twitter: @RepPressley
YouTube: www.youtube.com/channel/UCkhjut8oXdxN7HGg5eRT9Fw
Instagram: @repayannapressley
District Office: 1295 River St., Hyde Park, MA 02136; 617-850-0040; Fax: 202-225-9322; *District Director:* Eric White
Committee Assignments: Financial Services; Oversight and Reform

Price, David E., D-N.C. (4)

Capitol Hill Office: 2108 RHOB 20515; 225-1784; Fax: 225-2014; *Chief of Staff:* Justin Wein
Web: price.house.gov
Facebook: www.facebook.com/RepDavidEPrice
Twitter: @RepDavidEPrice
YouTube: www.youtube.com/RepDavidPrice
Instagram: @repdavideprice
District Office: 2605 Meridian Pkwy., #110, Durham, NC 27713; 919-967-7924; Fax: 919-859-5998; *District Liason:* Tracy Lovett
Committee Assignments: Appropriations; Budget

Quigley, Mike, D-Ill. (5)

Capitol Hill Office: 2078 RHOB 20515; 225-4061; Fax: 225-5603; *Chief of Staff:* Allison Jarus
Web: quigley.house.gov
Facebook: www.facebook.com/repmikequigley
Twitter: @RepMikeQuigley
YouTube: www.youtube.com/RepMikeQuigley
Instagram: @repmikequigley
District Offices: 3223 N. Sheffield Ave., Chicago, IL 60657; 773-267-5926; *District Director:* Erica Reardon
4345 N. Milwaukee Ave., Chicago, IL 60641; 773-267-5926; Fax: 773-267-6583
Committee Assignments: Appropriations; Permanent Select Intelligence

Radewagen, Aumua Amata Coleman, R-Am. Samoa (At Large)

Capitol Hill Office: 1339 LHOB 20515; 225-8577; Fax: 225-8757; *Chief of Staff:* Leafaina O. Yahn
Web: radewagen.house.gov

Facebook: www.facebook.com/aumuaamata
Twitter: @RepAmata
YouTube: www.youtube.com/channel/UCGdrLQbt1PYDTPsampx4t1A
Instagram: @repamata
District Office: 1 Fagatogo Sq., P.O. Box 5859, Pago Pago, AS 96799; 684-633-3601; Fax: 684-633-3607; *District Director:* Pulu Ae Ae
Committee Assignments: Natural Resources; Small Business; Veterans' Affairs

Raskin, Jamie, D-Md. (8)

Capitol Hill Office: 2242 RHOB 20515; 225-5341; *Chief of Staff:* Julie Tagen
Web: raskin.house.gov
Facebook: www.facebook.com/RepRaskin
Twitter: @RepRaskin
YouTube: www.youtube.com/RepRaskin
Instagram: @repraskin
District Office: 51 Monroe St., #503, Rockville, MD 20850; 301-354-1000; *District Director:* Kathleen Connor
Committee Assignments: House Administration; Judiciary; Oversight and Reform; Rules; Select on Coronavirus Crisis; Select to Investigate the January 6th Attack on the U.S. Capitol

Reed, Tom, R-N.Y. (23)

Capitol Hill Office: 1203 LHOB 20515; 225-3161; Fax: 226-6599; *Chief of Staff:* Joe Rizzo
Web: reed.house.gov
Facebook: www.facebook.com/RepTomReed
Twitter: @tomreedNY23
YouTube: www.youtube.com/user/CongressmanTomReed
Instagram: @reptomreed
District Offices: 89 W. Market St., Corning, NY 14830; 607-654-7566; Fax: 607-654-7568; *District Director:* Alison Hunt
433 Exchange St., Geneva, NY 14456; 315-759-5229; Fax: 315-325-4045; *Regional Director:* Taryn Windheim
2 E. 2nd St., #208, Jamestown, NY 14701; 716-708-6369; Fax: 716-708-6058; *Caseworker / Field Rep.:* Katrina Fuller
1 Bluebird Square, Olean, NY 14760-2500; 716-379-8434; Fax: 716-806-1069; *Constituent Services Specialist:* Lee James
Committee Assignment: Ways and Means

Reschenthaler, Guy, R-Pa. (14)

Capitol Hill Office: 409 CHOB 20515-3515; 225-2065; *Chief of Staff:* Aaron Bonnaure
Web: reschenthaler.house.gov
Facebook: www.facebook.com/GReschenthaler
Twitter: @GReschenthaler
YouTube: www.youtube.com/c/RepGuyReschenthaler
Instagram: @guyreschenthaler
District Offices: 700 Pellis Rd., #1, Greensburg, PA 15601; 724-219-4200; *District Director:* Nate Nevala
14 S. Main St., Washington, PA 15301; 724-206-4800
Committee Assignments: Appropriations; Rules

Rice, Kathleen M., D-N.Y. (4)

Capitol Hill Office: 2435 RHOB 20515-3204; 225-5516; Fax: 225-5758; *Chief of Staff:* Liz Amster
Web: kathleenrice.house.gov
Facebook: www.facebook.com/RepKathleenRice
Twitter: @RepKathleenRice
YouTube: www.youtube.com/channel/ UCLYLmjrGtzzCFXMWPBxHAug
Instagram: @repkathleenrice
District Office: 229 7th St., #300, Garden City, NY 11530; 516-739-3008; Fax: 516-739-2973; *District Director:* Cheryl Rice
Committee Assignments: Energy and Commerce; Homeland Security

Rice, Tom, R-S.C. (7)

Capitol Hill Office: 460 CHOB 20515; 225-9895; Fax: 225-9690; *Chief of Staff:* Jennifer Watson
Web: rice.house.gov
Facebook: facebook.com/reptomrice
Twitter: @RepTomRice
YouTube: www.youtube.com/RepTomRice
Instagram: @reptomrice
District Offices: 1831 W. Evans St., #300, Florence, SC 29501; 843-679-9781; Fax: 843-679-9783
2411 N. Oak St., #405, Myrtle Beach, SC 29577; 843-445-6459; Fax: 843-445-6418; *District Director:* Rodney Berry
Committee Assignment: Ways and Means

Rogers, Harold, R-Ky. (5)

Capitol Hill Office: 2406 RHOB 20515; 225-4601; Fax: 225-0940; *Chief of Staff:* Jake Johnsen
Web: halrogers.house.gov
Facebook: www.facebook.com/CongressmanHalRogers
Twitter: @RepHalRogers
YouTube: www.youtube.com/RepHalRogers
Instagram: @rephalrogers
District Offices: 48 S. KY Hwy. 15, Hazard, KY 41701; 606-439-0794; Fax: 606-439-4647; *Field Rep.:* Andrea Begley
110 Resource Court, Suite A, Prestonsburg, KY 41653-7851; 606-886-0844; Fax: 606-889-0371; *Field Rep.:* Adam Rice
551 Clifty St., Somerset, KY 42503; 800-632-8588; Fax: 606-678-4856; *District Director:* Karen Kelly
Committee Assignment: Appropriations

Rogers, Mike, R-Ala. (3)

Capitol Hill Office: 2469 RHOB 20515; 225-3261; Fax: 226-8485; *Chief of Staff:* Chris Brinson
Web: mikerogers.house.gov
Facebook: www.facebook.com/ CongressmanMikeDRogers
Twitter: @RepMikeRogersAL
YouTube: www.youtube.com/MikeRogersAL03
Instagram: @repmikerogersal
District Offices: G. W. Andrews Federal Bldg., 701 Ave. A, #300, Opelika, AL 36801; 334-745-6221; Fax: 334-742-0109; *District Director:* Sheri Rollins

149 E. Hamric Dr., Suite D, Oxford, AL 36203; 256-236-5655; Fax: 256-237-9203
Committee Assignment: Armed Services

Rose, John W., R-Tenn. (6)

Capitol Hill Office: 1124 LHOB 20515-3515; 225-4231; Fax: 202-225-6887; *Chief of Staff:* Van Hilleary
Web: johnrose.house.gov
Facebook: www.facebook.com/repjohnrose
Twitter: @RepJohnRose
District Offices: 321 E. Spring St., #301, Cookeville, TN 38501; 931-854-9430; Fax: 615-206-8980; *District Director:* Rebecca Foster
355 N. Belvedere Dr., #308, Gallatin, TN 37066; 615-206-8204; Fax: 615-206-8980; *Deputy District Director:* Ray Render
Committee Assignment: Financial Services

Rosendale, Matthew M. Sr., R-Mont. (At Large)

Capitol Hill Office: 1037 LHOB 20515; 225-3211; *Deputy Chief of Staff:* Sean Brislin
Web: rosendale.house.gov
Facebook: www.facebook.com/RepRosendale
Twitter: @RepRosendale
Instagram: @reprosendale
District Offices: 3300 N. 2nd Ave., #7 and #8, Billings, MT 59101; 406-413-6720
410 Central Ave., #407, Great Falls, MT 59404; 406-770-6260
7 W. 6th Ave., #3B, Helena, MT 59601; 406-502-1435: *District Director:* Marissa Stockton
Committee Assignments: Natural Resources; Veterans' Affairs

Ross, Deborah K., D-N.C. (2)

Capitol Hill Office: 1208 LHOB 20515; 225-3032; Fax: 225-0181; *Chief of Staff:* Matt Lee
Web: ross.house.gov
Facebook: www.facebook.com/RepDeborahRoss
Twitter: @RepDeborahRoss
Instagram: @repdeborahross
District Office: 300 Fayetteville St., P.O. Box 1548, Raleigh NC 27602; 919-334-0840; *District Director:* Caroline Spencer
Committee Assignments: Judiciary; Rules; Science, Space, and Technology

Rouzer, David, R-N.C. (7)

Capitol Hill Office: 2333 RHOB 20515; 225-2731; Fax: 225-5773; *Chief of Staff:* Anna McCormack
Web: rouzer.house.gov
Facebook: www.facebook.com/RepRouzer
Twitter: @RepDavidRouzer
YouTube: www.youtube.com/channel/ UCBvOxpqoGi1HlHjX9v_gHZw
Instagram: @repdavidrouzer
District Offices: 310 Government Center Dr., #1, Bolivia, NC 28422; 910-253-6111; Fax: 910-253-6114; *District Director:* Chance Lambeth

4001 US Hwy. 301 South, #106, Four Oaks, NC 27524; 919-938-3040; Fax: 919-938-3540; *Deputy District Director:* Lisa Littler

201 N. Front St., #502, Wilmington, NC 28401; 910-395-0202; Fax: 910-395-0209

Committee Assignments: Agriculture; Transportation and Infrastructure

Roy, Chip, R-Tex. (21)

Capitol Hill Office: 1005 LHOB 20515-3515; 225-4236; Fax: 225-8628; *Chief of Staff:* Jason Rogers
Web: roy.house.gov
Facebook: www.facebook.com/ChipRoyforCongress
Twitter: @RepChipRoy
YouTube: www.youtube.com/channel/UCu6wgN7DvYxUMnywD3XE3TQ
District Offices: 5900 Southwest Pkwy., Bldg 2, #201A, Austin, TX 78735; 512-871-5959; (open Monday–Thursday, 9 a.m.–12 p.m.)
125 Lehmann Dr., #201, Kerrville, TX 78028; 830-896-0154; (Monday–Thursday, 8 a.m.–12 p.m.)
1100 N.E. Loop 410, #640, San Antonio, TX 78209; 210-821-5024; Fax: 210-821-5947; *District Director:* John Fletcher
Committee Assignments: Judiciary; Veterans' Affairs

Roybal-Allard, Lucille, D-Calif. (40)

Capitol Hill Office: 2083 RHOB 20515; 225-1766; Fax: 226-0350; *Chief of Staff:* Victor Castillo
Web: roybal-allard.house.gov
Facebook: www.facebook.com/RepRoybalAllard
Twitter: @RepRoybalAllard
YouTube: www.youtube.com/RepRoybalAllard
Instagram: @reproybalallard
District Office: 500 Citadel Dr., #320, Commerce, CA 90040; 323-721-8790; Fax: 323-721-8789; *District Director:* Cynthia Morales
Committee Assignment: Appropriations

Ruiz, Raul, D-Calif. (36)

Capitol Hill Office: 2342 RHOB 20515; 225-5330; Fax: 225-1238; *Chief of Staff:* Tim Del Monico
Web: ruiz.house.gov
Facebook: www.facebook.com/RepRaulRuizMD
Twitter: @RepRaulRuizMD
YouTube: www.youtube.com/RepRaulRuiz
Instagram: @repraulruizmd
District Offices: 445 E. Florida Ave., 2nd Floor, Hemet, CA 92543; 951-765-2304; Fax: 951-765-3784
43875 Washington St., Suite F, Palm Desert, CA 92211; 760-424-8888; Fax: 760-424-8993; *District Director:* Hernan Quintas
Committee Assignments: Energy and Commerce; Veterans' Affairs

Ruppersberger, C. A. Dutch, D-Md. (2)

Capitol Hill Office: 2206 RHOB 20515-2002; 225-3061; Fax: 225-3094; *Chief of Staff:* Tara Oursler
Web: ruppersberger.house.gov

Facebook: www.facebook.com/RepDutchRuppersberger
Twitter: @Call_Me_Dutch
YouTube: www.youtube.com/Ruppersberger
Instagram: @dutchruppersberger
District Office: The Atrium, 375 W. Padonia Rd., #200, Timonium, MD 21093-2130; 410-628-2701; Fax: 410-628-2708; *District Director:* Cori Duggins; *Constituent Liaison:* Lynn Yates
Committee Assignment: Appropriations

Rush, Bobby L., D-Ill. (1)

Capitol Hill Office: 2188 RHOB 20515-1301; 225-4372; Fax: 226-0333; *Chief of Staff:* Nishith Pandya
Web: rush.house.gov
Facebook: www.facebook.com/congressmanbobbyrush
Twitter: @RepBobbyRush
YouTube: www.youtube.com/CongressmanRush
Instagram: @repbobbyrush
District Office: 11750 S. Western Ave., Chicago, IL 60643-4732; 773-779-2400; Fax: 773-779-2401; *District Director:* Mary Datcher
Committee Assignments: Agriculture; Energy and Commerce

Rutherford, John H., R-Fla. (4)

Capitol Hill Office: 1711 LHOB 20515; 225-2501; *Chief of Staff:* Jenifer Nawrocki Bradley
Web: rutherford.house.gov
Facebook: www.facebook.com/RepRutherfordFL
Twitter: @RepRutherfordFL
Instagram: @reprutherfordfl
District Office: 4130 Salisbury Rd., #2500, Jacksonville, FL 32216; 904-831-5205; *District Director:* Chris Miller
Satellite Office: Nassau County; 904-831-5205 (by appointment only)
Committee Assignment: Appropriations

Ryan, Tim, D-Ohio (13)

Capitol Hill Office: 1126 LHOB 20515-3517; 225-5261; Fax: 225-3719; *Chief of Staff:* Ron Grimes
Web: timryan.house.gov
Facebook: www.facebook.com/Congressman-Tim-Ryan-121560497865
Twitter: @RepTimRyan
YouTube: www.youtube.com/TimRyanVision
Instagram: @reptimryan
District Offices: 1030 Tallmadge Ave., Akron, OH 44310; 330-630-7311; Fax: 330-630-7314; *Constituent Liaison:* Jason Miller
197 W. Market St., Warren, OH 44481-1024; 330-373-0074; Fax: 330-373-0098; *District Director:* Rick Leonard
241 W. Federal St., Youngstown, OH 44503-1207; 330-740-0193; Fax: 330-740-0182; *Senior Advisor:* Pat Lowry
Committee Assignments: Appropriations; Joint Library

Sablan, Gregorio Kilili Camacho, D-N. Mariana Is. (At Large)

Capitol Hill Office: 2267 RHOB 20515; 225-2646; Fax: 226-4249; *Chief of Staff:* Robert J. Schwalbach

Web: sablan.house.gov
Facebook: www.facebook.com/congressmansablan
Twitter: @Kilili_Sablan
YouTube: www.youtube.com/CongressmanSablan
Instagram: @kilili_sablan
District Offices: P.O. Box 1361, Rota, MP 96951; 670-532-2647; Fax: 670-532-2649; *Staff Asst.:* Harry Masga
P.O. Box 504879, Saipan, MP 96950; 670-323-2647/8; Fax: 670-323-2649; *District Director:* Paula Bermudes-Castro
P.O. Box 520394, Tinian, MP 96952; 670-433-2647; Fax: 670-433-2648
Committee Assignments: Agriculture; Education and Labor; Natural Resources; Veterans' Affairs

Salazar, Maria Elvira, R-Fla. (27)

Capitol Hill Office: 1616 LHOB 20515; 225-3931; *Chief of Staff:* Tom Moran
Web: salazar.house.gov
Facebook: www.facebook.com/CongresswomanMariaElviraSalazar
Twitter: @RepMariaSalazar
District Office: 3951 7th St. N.W., Bay F, Miami, FL 33126; 305-668-2285; *Deputy District Director:* Dagoberto Restrepo
Committee Assignments: Foreign Affairs; Small Business

San Nicolas, Michael, D-Guam (At Large)

Capitol Hill Office: 1632 LHOB 20515; 225-1188; Fax: 226-4249; *Chief of Staff:* Jennifer Winn
Web: sannicolas.house.gov
Facebook: www.facebook.com/CongressmanMichaelF.Q.SanNicolas
Twitter: @GuamCongressman
YouTube: www.youtube.com/channel/UCVroMJWH3jsh4shPSlp24sw
Instagram: @michael.fq.san.nicolas
District Office: 330 Hernan Cortez Ave., #300, Hagåtña, GU 96910; 671-475-6453
Committee Assignments: Financial Services; Natural Resources

Sánchez, Linda T., D-Calif. (38)

Capitol Hill Office: 2329 RHOB 20515-0539; 225-6676; Fax: 226-1012; *Chief of Staff:* Ricky Le
Web: lindasanchez.house.gov
Facebook: www.facebook.com/RepLindaSanchez
Twitter: @RepLindaSanchez
YouTube: www.youtube.com/LindaTSanchez
Instagram: @replindasanchez
District Office: 12440 E. Imperial Hwy., #140, Norwalk, CA 90650; 562-860-5050; Fax: 562-924-2914; *District Director:* Griselda Ortiz
Committee Assignment: Ways and Means, Democratic Steering and Policy

Sarbanes, John P., D-Md. (3)

Capitol Hill Office: 2370 RHOB 20515-2003; 225-4016; Fax: 225-9219; *Chief of Staff:* Dvora Lovinger

Web: sarbanes.house.gov
Facebook: www.facebook.com/RepSarbanes
Twitter: @RepSarbanes
YouTube: www.youtube.com/RepJohnSarbanes
District Office: 600 Baltimore Ave., #303, Towson, MD 21204-4022; 410-832-8890; Fax: 410-832-8898; *Constituent Services Director:* Fred Hassell
Satellite Offices: 44 Calvert St., #349, Annapolis, MD 21401-1930; 410-295-1679; Fax: 410-295-1682 (open Tuesday, 11 a.m.–1 p.m. or by appointment); *Community Relations Specialist:* Vicki Garcia
14906 Old Columbia Pike, Burtonsville, MD 20866; 301-421-4078 (open Thursday, 11 a.m.–1 p.m. or by appointment)
Committee Assignments: Energy and Commerce; Oversight and Reform

Scalise, Steve, R-La. (1)

Capitol Hill Office: 2049 RHOB 20515; 225-3015; Fax: 226-0386; *Chief of Staff:* Megan Bel Miller
Web: scalise.house.gov
Facebook: www.facebook.com/RepSteveScalise
Twitter: @SteveScalise
YouTube: www.youtube.com/RepSteveScalise
Instagram: @stevescalise
District Offices: 1514 Martens Dr., #10, Hammond, LA 70401; 985-340-2185; Fax: 985-340-3122
8026 Main St., #700, Houma, LA 70360; 985-879-2300; Fax: 985-879-2306; *Field Rep.:* Ramona Williamson
21454 Koop Dr., #2C, Mandeville, LA 70471; 985-893-9064; Fax: 985-893-9707; *Field Rep.:* Danielle Evans
111 Veterans Memorial Blvd., #803, Metairie, LA 70005; 504-837-1259; Fax: 504-837-4239
Committee Assignment: Energy and Commerce, Select on Coronavirus Crisis
Minority Whip

Scanlon, Mary Gay, D-Pa. (5)

Capitol Hill Office: 1227 LHOB 20515-3515; 225-2011; Fax: 226-0280; *Chief of Staff:* Roddy Flynn
Web: scanlon.house.gov
Facebook: www.facebook.com/RepMGS
Twitter: @RepMGS
Instagram: @repmgs
District Office: 2501 Seaport Dr., #BH230, Chester, PA 19013; 610-626-2020; *District Director:* Heather Boyd
Committee Assignments: House Administration; Judiciary; Rules

Schakowsky, Janice D., D-Ill. (9)

Capitol Hill Office: 2367 RHOB 20515-1309; 225-2111; Fax: 226-6890; *Chief of Staff:* Syd Terry
Web: schakowsky.house.gov
Facebook: www.facebook.com/janschakowsky
Twitter: @janschakowsky
YouTube: www.youtube.com/RepSchakowsky
Instagram: @janschakowsky

District Offices: 5533 N. Broadway St., #2, Chicago, IL 60640-1405; 773-506-7100; Fax: 773-506-9202; *District Director:* Leslie Combs

1852 Johns Dr., Glenview, IL 60025; 847-328-3409; Fax: 847-328-3425

Committee Assignments: Budget; Democratic Steering and Policy, Energy and Commerce

Schiff, Adam B., D-Calif. (28)

Capitol Hill Office: 2309 RHOB 20515; 225-4176; Fax: 225-5828; *Chief of Staff:* Patrick Boland
Web: schiff.house.gov
Facebook: www.facebook.com/RepAdamSchiff
Twitter: @RepAdamSchiff
YouTube: www.youtube.com/RepAdamSchiff
Instagram: @repadamschiff
District Office: 245 E. Olive Ave., #200, Burbank, CA 91502; 818-450-2900; Fax: 818-450-2928; *District Director:* Ann Peifer
Satellite Office: 5500 Hollywood Blvd., #416, Los Angeles, CA 90028; 323-315-5555 (by appointment only)
Committee Assignment: Permanent Select Intelligence, Chair; Select to Investigate the January 6th Attack on the U.S. Capitol

Schneider, Bradley Scott, D-Ill. (10)

Capitol Hill Office: 300 CHOB 20515; 225-4835; Fax: 225-0837; *Chief of Staff:* Casey O'Shea
Web: schneider.house.gov
Facebook: www.facebook.com/CongressmanBradSchneider
Twitter: @RepSchneider
YouTube: www.youtube.com/RepBradSchneider
Instagram: @repschneider
District Office: 111 Barclay Blvd., #200, Lincolnshire, IL 60069; 847-383-4870; Fax: 847-793-0677; *District Director:* Greg Claus
Committee Assignments: Foreign Affairs; Ways and Means

Schrader, Kurt, D-Ore. (5)

Capitol Hill Office: 2431 RHOB 20515; 225-5711; Fax: 225-5699; *Chief of Staff:* Chris Huckleberry
Web: schrader.house.gov
Facebook: www.facebook.com/repschrader
Twitter: @RepSchrader
YouTube: www.youtube.com/RepKurtSchrader
District Offices: 621 High St., Oregon City, OR 97045-2240; 503-557-1324; Fax: 503-557-1981; *District Director:* Suzanne Kunse
530 Center St. N.E., #415, Salem, OR 97301; 503-588-9100; Fax: 503-588-5517; *Caseworker:* Mary Ann Smith
Committee Assignment: Energy and Commerce

Schrier, Kim, D-Wash. (8)

Capitol Hill Office: 1123 LHOB 20515-3515; 225-7761; Fax: 225-4272; *Chief of Staff:* Erin O'Quinn
Web: schrier.house.gov
Facebook: www.facebook.com/RepKimSchrier
Twitter: @RepKimSchrier
Instagram: @repkimschrier
District Offices: 1445 Mall St. N.W., #4, Issaquah, WA 98027; 425-657-1001; *District Director:* Louise O'Rourke
301 Yakima St., #329, Wenatchee, WA 98801; 509-850-5340; *District Rep.:* Kelli Scott
Committee Assignments: Agriculture; Energy and Commerce

Schweikert, David, R-Ariz. (6)

Capitol Hill Office: 304 CHOB 20515; 225-2190; Fax: 225-0096; *Chief of Staff:* Kevin Knight
Web: schweikert.house.gov
Facebook: www.facebook.com/repdavidschweikert
Twitter: @RepDavid
YouTube: www.youtube.com/user/RepDavidSchweikert
Instagram: @repdavid
District Office: 14500 N. Northsight Blvd., #221, Scottsdale, AZ 85260; 480-946-2411; Fax: 480-946-2446; *District Director:* Ernestina Borquez-Smith
Committee Assignments: Joint Economic; Ways and Means

Scott, Austin, R-Ga. (8)

Capitol Hill Office: 2417 RHOB 20515-1008; 225-6531; Fax: 225-3013; *Chief of Staff:* Jason Lawrence
Web: austinscott.house.gov
Facebook: www.facebook.com/RepAustinScott
Twitter: @AustinScottGA08
YouTube: www.youtube.com/RepAustinScott
District Offices: 127-B N. Central Ave., Tifton, GA 31794-4087; 229-396-5175; Fax: 229-396-5179; *Outreach Coordinator:* Alice Johnson
120 Byrd Way, #100, Warner Robins, GA 31088; 478-971-1776; Fax: 478-971-1778
Committee Assignments: Agriculture; Armed Services

Scott, David, D-Ga. (13)

Capitol Hill Office: 468 CHOB 20515; 225-2939; Fax: 225-4628; *Chief of Staff:* Catherine Kuerbitz
Web: davidscott.house.gov
Facebook: www.facebook.com/RepDavidScott
Twitter: @repdavidscott
YouTube: www.youtube.com/RepDavidScott
Instagram: @repdavidscott
District Offices: 173 N. Main St., Jonesboro, GA 30236-3567; 770-210-5073; Fax: 770-210-5673; *District Director:* Dylan Nurse
888 Concord Rd., #100, Smyrna, GA 30080-4202; 770-432-5405; Fax: 770-432-5813; *Deputy District Director:* Isaac Dodoo
Committee Assignments: Agriculture, Chair; Financial Services

Scott, Robert C. (Bobby), D-Va. (3)

Capitol Hill Office: 2328 RHOB 20515; 225-8351; Fax: 225-8354; *Chief of Staff:* David Dailey
Web: bobbyscott.house.gov

Facebook: www.facebook.com/RepBobbyScott
Twitter: @BobbyScott
YouTube: www.youtube.com/RepBobbyScott
Instagram: @repbobbyscott
District Office: 2600 Washington Ave., #1010, Newport News, VA 23607-4333; 757-380-1000; Fax: 757-928-6694; *District Director:* Gisele Russell
Committee Assignments: Budget; Education and Labor, Chair

Sessions, Pete, R-Tex. (17)

Capitol Hill Office: 2204 RHOB 20515; 225-6105; *Chief of Staff:* Luis Vega
Web: sessions.house.gov
Facebook: www.facebook.com/petesessions
Twitter: @PeteSessions
YouTube: www.youtube.com/user/PeteSessions
Instagram: @congressmanpetesessions
District Offices: 2700 Earl Rudder Fwy., South Hwy. 6, #4500, College Station, TX 77845-2804; 979-431-6340; *District Director:* Scott Bland
400 Austin Ave., #302, Waco, TX 76701-2139; 254-633-4500; Fax: 254-300-5736
Committee Assignments: Financial Services, Oversight and Reform

Sewell, Terri A., D-Ala. (7)

Capitol Hill Office: 2201 RHOB 20515; 225-2665; Fax: 226-9567; *Chief of Staff:* Hillary Beard
Web: sewell.house.gov
Facebook: www.facebook.com/RepSewell
Twitter: @RepTerriSewell
YouTube: www.youtube.com/RepSewell
Instagram: @repterriasewell
District Offices: Two 20th St. North, #1130, Birmingham, AL 35203-4014; 205-254-1960; Fax: 205-254-1974
2501 7th St., #300, Tuscaloosa, AL 35401; 205-752-5380; Fax: 205-752-5899
101 S. Lawrence St., Courthouse Annex 3, Montgomery, AL 36104; 334-262-1919; Fax: 334-262-1921; *District Director:* Melinda Williams
Federal Bldg., 908 Alabama Ave., #112, Selma, AL 36701-4660; 334-877-4414; Fax: 334-877-4489
Committee Assignment: Ways and Means

Sherman, Brad, D-Calif. (30)

Capitol Hill Office: 2181 RHOB 20515; 225-5911; Fax: 225-5879; *Chief of Staff:* Don MacDonald
Web: sherman.house.gov
Facebook: www.facebook.com/ CongressmanBradSherman
Twitter: @BradSherman
Instagram: @congressmansherman
Youtube: www.youtube.com/user/ShermanCA27
District Office: 5000 Van Nuys Blvd., #420, Sherman Oaks, CA 91403; 818-501-9200; Fax: 818-501-1554; *District Director:* Scott Abrams
Committee Assignments: Financial Services; Foreign Affairs; Science, Space, and Technology

Sherrill, Mikie, D-N.J. (11)

Capitol Hill Office: 1414 LHOB 20515-3515; 225-5034; Fax: 225-3186; *Chief of Staff:* Jean Roehrenbeck
Web: sherrill.house.gov
Facebook: www.facebook.com/RepMikieSherrill
Twitter: @RepSherrill
Instagram: @repsherrill
District Office: 8 Wood Hollow Rd., #203, Parsippany, NJ 07054; 973-526-5668; Fax: 833-709-2034; *District Director:* Kellie Doucette
Committee Assignments: Armed Services; Education and Labor; Science, Space, and Technology

Simpson, Michael K., R-Idaho (2)

Capitol Hill Office: 2084 RHOB 20515; 225-5531; Fax: 225-8216; *Chief of Staff:* Lindsay J. Slater
Web: simpson.house.gov
Facebook: www.facebook.com/Mike-Simpson-96007744606
Twitter: @CongMikeSimpson
YouTube: www.youtube.com/CongMikeSimpson
District Offices: 802 W. Bannock St., #600, Boise, ID 83702-5843; 208-334-1953; Fax: 208-334-9533; *District Director / Communications Director:* Nikki Wallace
1075 S. Utah Ave. West, #240, Idaho Falls, ID 83402-3600; 208-523-6701; Fax: 208-523-2384
650 Addison Ave. West, #1078, Twin Falls, ID 83301-3392; 208-734-7219; Fax: 208-734-7244; *Community Development Coord.:* Linda Culver
Committee Assignment: Appropriations

Sires, Albio, D-N.J. (8)

Capitol Hill Office: 2268 RHOB 20515-3013; 225-7919; Fax: 226-0792; *Chief of Staff:* Gene Martorony
Web: sires.house.gov
Facebook: www.facebook.com/RepAlbioSires
Twitter: @RepSires
YouTube: www.youtube.com/RepSiresNJ13
Instagram: @repsires
District Offices: 800 Anna St., Elizabeth, NJ 07201; 908-820-0692; Fax: 908-820-0694; *Deputy Chief of Staff:* Ada Morell
257 Cornelison Ave., #4408, Jersey City, NJ 07302; 201-309-0301; Fax: 201-309-0384; *Communications Director:* Erica Daughtrey
5500 Palisade Ave., Suite A, West New York, NJ 07093-2124; 201-558-0800; Fax: 201-617-2809; *District Director:* Richard Turner
Committee Assignments: Budget; Foreign Affairs; Transportation and Infrastructure

Slotkin, Elissa, D-Mich. (8)

Capitol Hill Office: 1210 LHOB 20515-3515; 225-4872; Fax: 225-5820; *Chief of Staff:* Matt Hennessey
Web: slotkin.house.gov
Facebook: www.facebook.com/RepElissaSlotkin
Twitter: @RepSlotkin
YouTube: www.youtube.com/channel/ UCavPE_osOr5wM3QYUzfs95A

Instagram: @repslotkin
District Office: 1100 W. Saginaw St., #3A, Lansing, MI 48915; 517-993-0510; Fax: 844-239-4485; *District Director:* Alexa Stanard
Committee Assignments: Armed Services; Homeland Security; Veterans' Affairs

Smith, Adam, D-Wash. (9)

Capitol Hill Office: 2264 RHOB 20515-4709; 225-8901; Fax: 225-5893; *Chief of Staff:* Shana M. Chandler
Web: adamsmith.house.gov
Facebook: www.facebook.com/RepAdamSmith
Twitter: @RepAdamSmith
YouTube: www.youtube.com/Congressmanadamsmith
Instagram: @repadamsmith
District Office: 101 Evergreen Bldg., 15 S. Grady Way, Renton, WA 98057; 425-793-5180; Fax: 425-793-5181; *District Director:* Sarah Servin
Committee Assignment: Armed Services, Chair

Smith, Adrian, R-Neb. (3)

Capitol Hill Office: 502 CHOB 20515; 225-6435; Fax: 225-0207; *Chief of Staff:* Monica Didiuk
Web: adriansmith.house.gov
Facebook: www.facebook.com/AdrianSmithNE
Twitter: @RepAdrianSmith
YouTube: www.youtube.com/RepAdrianSmith
Instagram: @repadriansmith
District Offices: 1811 W. 2nd St., #275, Grand Island, NE 68803; 308-384-3900; Fax: 308-384-3902; *District Director:* Jena Hoehne; *Constituent Services Director:* Alex Straatmann
416 Valley View Dr., #600, Scottsbluff, NE 69361-1486; 308-633-6333; Fax: 308-633-6335; *Office Coord.:* Lenora Brotzman
Committee Assignment: Ways and Means

Smith, Christopher H., R-N.J. (4)

Capitol Hill Office: 2373 RHOB 20515-3004; 225-3765; Fax: 225-7768; *Chief of Staff:* Mary McDermott Noonan
Web: chrissmith.house.gov
Facebook: www.facebook.com/RepChrisSmith
Twitter: @RepChrisSmith
YouTube: www.youtube.com/USRepChrisSmith
Instagram: @repchrissmith
District Offices: 112 Village Center Dr., 2nd Floor, Freehold, NJ 07728; 732-780-3035; Fax: 732-780-3079; *Deputy Chief of Staff:* Jo Schloeder
4573 S. Broad St., Hamilton, NJ 08620; 609-585-7878; Fax: 609-585-9155; *District Director:* Jeff Sagnip Hollendonner
Committee Assignment: Foreign Affairs

Smith, Jason, R-Mo. (8)

Capitol Hill Office: 2418 RHOB 20515-2508; 225-4404; Fax: 226-0326; *Chief of Staff:* Matt Meyer
Web: jasonsmith.house.gov
Facebook: www.facebook.com/repjasonsmith
Twitter: @RepJasonSmith

YouTube: www.youtube.com/RepJasonSmith
Instagram: @repjasonsmith
District Offices: 830 S. Bishop Ave., Suite A, Rolla, MO 65401-4340; 573-364-2455; Fax: 573-364-1053
2502 Tanner Dr., #205, Cape Girardeau, MO 63703; 573-335-0101; Fax: 573-335-1931; *Constituent Services Specialist:* Debbie Colyott
22 E. Columbia St., P.O. Box 1165, Farmington, MO 63640; 573-756-9755; Fax: 573-756-9762; *District Office Manager:* Donna Hickman
35 Court Square, #300, West Plains, MO 65775; 417-255-1515; Fax: 417-255-2009
2725 N. Westwood Blvd., #5A, P.O. Box 4707, Poplar Bluff, MO 63901; 573-609-2996
Committee Assignments: Budget; Ways and Means

Smucker, Lloyd, R-Pa. (11)

Capitol Hill Office: 302 CHOB 20515; 225-2411; Fax: 225-2013; *Chief of Staff:* Kate Bonner
Web: smucker.house.gov
Facebook: www.facebook.com/RepSmucker
Twitter: @RepSmucker
YouTube: www.youtube.com/channel/UCs5iMvWy-oTHyf5HuwB7FCg
Instagram: @rep.smucker
District Offices: 51 S. Duke St., #201, Lancaster, PA 17602; 717-393-0667; Fax: 717-393-0924; *District Director:* Zachary Peirson
118 Carlisle St., Hanover, PA 17331; 717-969-6132
100 Redco Ave., Red Lion, PA 17356; 717-969-6133
Committee Assignments: Budget; Ways and Means

Soto, Darren, D-Fla. (9)

Capitol Hill Office: 2353 RHOB 20515; 225-9889; Fax: 225-9742; *Chief of Staff:* Liana Guerra
Web: soto.house.gov
Facebook: www.facebook.com/RepDarrenSoto
Twitter: @RepDarrenSoto
YouTube: www.youtube.com/repdarrensoto
Instagram: @repdarrensoto
District Office: 804 Bryan St., Kissimmee, FL 34741; 407-452-1171 **Satellite Offices:** 620 E. Main St., Haines City, FL 33844; 407-452-1171
451 3rd St. N.W., Winter Haven, FL 33881; 407-452-1171; *Field Rep.:* Leah West
201 West Central Ave., Lake Wales, FL 33853; *Field Rep.:* Darren Vierday
Committee Assignments: Energy and Commerce; Natural Resources

Spanberger, Abigail Davis, D-Va. (7)

Capitol Hill Office: 1431 LHOB 20515; 225-2815; Fax: 225-0011; *Chief of Staff:* Bonnie Krenz
Web: spanberger.house.gov
Facebook: www.facebook.com/RepSpanberger
Twitter: @RepSpanberger
YouTube: www.youtube.com/channel/UC66jKgZXnDVGUrOnwHjpvNg
Instagram: @repspanberger

District Offices: 4201 Dominion Blvd., #110, Glen Allen, VA 23060; 804-401-4110; *District Director:* Kristi Black

9104 Courthouse Rd., #249, Spotsylvania, VA 22553; 540-321-6130

Committee Assignments: Agriculture; Foreign Affairs

Spartz, Victoria, R-Ind. (5)

Capitol Hill Office: 1523 LHOB 20515; 225-2276; *Chief of Staff:* Renee Hudson

Web: spartz.house.gov

Facebook: www.facebook.com/RepSpartz

Twitter: @RepSpartz

Instagram: @repvictoriaspartz

District Office: 1119 Meridian St., #200, Anderson, IN 46016; 765-639-0671

216 W. Main St., Carmel, IN 46032, 317-848-0201

Committee Assignments: Education and Labor; Judiciary

Speier, Jackie, D-Calif. (14)

Capitol Hill Office: 2465 RHOB 20515; 225-3531; Fax: 226-4183; *Chief of Staff:* Yana Mayayeva

Web: speier.house.gov

Facebook: www.facebook.com/JackieSpeier

Twitter: @RepSpeier

YouTube: www.youtube.com/JackieSpeierCA12

Instagram: @jackiespeier

District Office: 155 Bovet Rd., #780, San Mateo, CA 94402; 650-342-0300; Fax: 650-375-8270; *District Director:* Brian Perkins

Committee Assignments: Armed Services; Oversight and Reform; Permanent Select Intelligence

Stansbury, Melanie A., D-N.M. (1)

Capitol Hill Office: 1421 LHOB 20515; 225-6316; *Chief of Staff:* Scott Forrester

Web: stansbury.house.gov

Facebook: facebook.com/RepStansbury

Twitter: @rep_stansbury

YouTube: www.youtube.com/channel/ UCcAQlm2gRM2NjRUpzc4kBNw

Instagram: @repstansbury

District Office: 300 Central Ave. S.W., #1300 East, Albuquerque, NM 87102; 505-346-6781; *District Director:* Sofia Sanchez

Committee Assignments: Natural Resources; Science, Space, and Technology

Stanton, Greg, D-Ariz. (9)

Capitol Hill Office: 207 CHOB 20515-3515; 225-9888; *Chief of Staff:* Seth Scott

Web: stanton.house.gov

Facebook: www.facebook.com/RepGregStanton

Twitter: @RepGregStanton

YouTube: www.youtube.com/c/repgregstanton

Instagram: @repgregstanton

District Office: 2944 N. 44th St., #150, Phoenix, AZ 85018; 602-956-2463

Committee Assignments: Judiciary; Transportation and Infrastructure

Stauber, Pete, R-Minn. (8)

Capitol Hill Office: 461 CHOB 20515-3515; 225-6211; Fax: 225-0699; *Chief of Staff:* Desiree Koetzle

Web: stauber.house.gov

Facebook: www.facebook.com/RepPeteStauber

Twitter: @RepPeteStauber

Instagram: @reppetestauber

District Offices: Brainerd City Hall, 501 Laurel St., Brainerd, MN 56401; 218-355-0862; *Field Rep.:* Louis Crombie

Cambridge City Hall, 300 3rd Ave. N.E., Cambridge, MN 55008; 763-310-6208; *Field Rep.:* Jack Friebe

Chisholm City Hall, 316 W. Lake St., Room 7, Chisholm, MN 55719; 218-355-0240

5094 Miller Trunk Hwy., #900, Hermantown, MN 55811; 218-481-6396; *District Director:* Isaac Schultz

Committee Assignments: Natural Resources; Small Business; Transportation and Infrastructure

Steel, Michelle, R-Calif. (48)

Capitol Hill Office: 1113 LHOB 20515; 225-2415; *Chief of Staff:* Arie Dana

Web: steel.house.gov

Facebook: www.facebook.com/RepSteel

Twitter: @RepSteel

Instagram: @repsteel

District Office: 17011 Beach Blvd., #570, Huntington Beach, CA 92647; 714-960-6483; *District Director:* Stephanie Hu

Committee Assignments: Education and Labor; Transportation and Infrastructure

Stefanik, Elise M., R-N.Y. (21)

Capitol Hill Office: 2211 RHOB 20515; 225-4611; Fax: 226-0621; *Chief of Staff:* Patrick Hester

Web: stefanik.house.gov

Facebook: www.facebook.com/RepEliseStefanik

Twitter: @RepStefanik

YouTube: www.youtube.com/channel/ UCHvf42C8Vw6QnjwO2L2ukKA

Instagram: @elisestefanik

District Offices: 5 Warren St., #4, Glens Falls, NY 12801; 518-743-0964; Fax: 518-743-1391

137 Margaret St., #100, Plattsburgh, NY 12901; 518-561-2324; Fax: 518-561-2408; *District Director:* Jonathan Carman

88 Public Square, Suite A, Watertown, NY 13601; 315-782-3150; Fax: 315-782-1291; *Regional Director:* Mary Jo Richards

Committee Assignments: Armed Services; Education and Labor; Permanent Select Intelligence

Steil, Bryan, R-Wisc. (1)

Capitol Hill Office: 1526 LHOB 20515-3515; 225-3031; *Chief of Staff:* Ryan Carney

Web: steil.house.gov

Facebook: www.facebook.com/RepBryanSteil

Twitter: @RepBryanSteil

YouTube: www.youtube.com/repbryansteil

Instagram: @repbryansteil
District Offices: 20 S. Main St., #10, Janesville, WI 53545; 608-752-4050 (by appointment only); *District Chief of Staff:* Rich Zipperer
Somers Village/Town Hall, 7511 12th St., Somers, WI 53171; 262-654-1901 (by appointment only)
Racine County Courthouse, 730 Wisconsin Ave., Room 101, Racine, WI 53403; 262-637-0510 (by appointment only)
Committee Assignments: Financial Services; House Administration; Select on Economic Disparity and Fairness in Growth

Steube, W. Gregory, R-Fla. (17)

Capitol Hill Office: 2457 RHOB 20515; 225-5792; Fax: 225-3132; *Chief of Staff:* Alex Blair
Web: steube.house.gov
Facebook: www.facebook.com/RepGregSteube
Twitter: @RepGregSteube
YouTube: www.youtube.com/channel/ UCuhN60FDf0YWlSqJitl2pvg
Instagram: @repgregsteube
District Offices: 1069 U.S. 27 North, Room 116, Lake Placid, FL 33852; 941-499-3214; Fax: 941-575-9103 (by appointment only); *Field Rep.:* Katherine Marks
226 Taylor St., #230, Punta Gorda, FL 33950; 941-499-3214; Fax: 941-575-9103; *District Director:* Sydney Gruters
871 Venetia Bay Blvd., #112, Venice, FL 34285; 941-499-3214; Fax: 941-575-9103
Committee Assignments: Foreign Affairs; Judiciary

Stevens, Haley M., D-Mich. (11)

Capitol Hill Office: 1510 LHOB 20515; 225-8171; Fax: 225-2267; *Chief of Staff:* Justin German
Web: stevens.house.gov
Facebook: www.facebook.com/RepHaleyStevens
Twitter: @RepHaleyStevens
Instagram: @rephaleystevens
District Office: 37695 Pembroke Ave., Livonia, MI 48152; 734-853-3040; Fax: 833-298-8467; *District Director:* Colleen Pobur
Committee Assignments: Education and Labor; Science, Space, and Technology

Stewart, Chris, R-Utah (2)

Capitol Hill Office: 166 CHOB 20515; 225-9730; Fax: 225-9627; *Chief of Staff:* Clay White
Web: stewart.house.gov
Facebook: www.facebook.com/RepChrisStewart
Twitter: @RepChrisStewart
YouTube: www.youtube.com/RepChrisStewart
Instagram: @repchrisstewart
District Offices: 585 W. 500 South, #230, Bountiful, UT 84010; 801-364-5550; Fax: 801-364-5551
253 W. St. George Blvd., #100, St. George, UT 84770; 435-627-1500; Fax: 435-627-1911; *District Director:* Dell Smith
Committee Assignments: Appropriations; Permanent Select Intelligence

Strickland, Marilyn, D-Wash. (10)

Capitol Hill Office: 1004 LHOB 20515; 225-9740; *Chief of Staff:* Andrew Noh
Web: strickland.house.gov
Facebook: www.facebook.com/RepStricklandWA
Twitter: @RepStricklandWA
Instagram: @repstricklandwa
District Offices: Lacey City Hall, 420 College St. S.E., #3000, Lacey, WA 98503; 360-459-8514; Fax: 360-459-8581; *District Director:* Liz Larter
6000 Main St. S.W., #3B, Lakewood, WA 98499
Committee Assignments: Armed Services; Transportation and Infrastructure

Suozzi, Thomas, D-N.Y. (3)

Capitol Hill Office: 407 CHOB 20515; 225-3335; Fax: 225-4669; *Chief of Staff:* Mike Florio
Web: suozzi.house.gov
Facebook: www.facebook.com/RepTomSuozzi
Twitter: @RepTomSuozzi
YouTube: www.youtube.com/channel/ UCHjLmETJ7qXtciV7dlAzzgQ
Instagram: @reptomsuozzi
District Offices: 478A Park Ave., Huntington, NY 11743; 631-923-4100; Fax: 631-923-3660; *District Director:* Cindy Rogers
242-09 Northern Blvd., Douglaston, NY 11363; 718-631-0400 (open Monday, Tuesday, and Thursday, 9 a.m.–5:30 p.m. or by appointment); *District Director:* Cindy Rogers
Committee Assignment: Ways and Means

Swalwell, Eric, D-Calif. (15)

Capitol Hill Office: 174 CHOB 20515; 225-5065; Fax: 226-3805; *Chief of Staff:* Yardena Wolf
Web: swalwell.house.gov
Facebook: www.facebook.com/CongressmanEricSwalwell
Twitter: @RepSwalwell
YouTube: www.youtube.com/ericswalwell
Instagram: @repswalwell
District Office: 20990 Redwood Rd., Castro Valley, CA 94546; 510-370-3322; *District Director:* Mallory DeLauro
Committee Assignments: Homeland Security; Judiciary; Permanent Select Intelligence

Takano, Mark, D-Calif. (41)

Capitol Hill Office: 420 CHOB 20515; 225-2305; Fax: 225-7018; *Chief of Staff:* Kirk McPike
Web: takano.house.gov
Facebook: www.facebook.com/RepMarkTakano
Twitter: @RepMarkTakano
YouTube: www.youtube.com/RepMarkTakano
Instagram: @repmarktakano
District Office: 3403 10th St., #610, Riverside, CA 92501; 951-222-0203; Fax: 951-222-0217; *District Director:* Desiree Wroten
Committee Assignments: Education and Labor; Veterans' Affairs, Chair

Taylor, Van, R-Tex. (3)

Capitol Hill Office: 1404 LHOB 20515-3515; 225-4201; Fax: 225-1485; *Chief of Staff:* Lonnie Dietz
Web: vantaylor.house.gov
Facebook: www.facebook.com/RepVanTaylor
Twitter: @RepVanTaylor
Instagram: @repvantaylor
District Office: 5600 Tennyson Pkwy., #275, Plano, TX 75024; 972-202-4150; *District Director:* Sable Coleman-Jones
Committee Assignment: Financial Services

Tenney, Claudia, R-N.Y. (22)

Capitol Hill Office: 1410 LHOB 20515; 225-3665; *Chief of Staff:* Nick Stewart
Web: tenney.house.gov
Facebook: www.facebook.com/RepClaudiaTenney
Twitter: @RepTenney
Instagram: @repclaudiatenney
District Offices: 49 Court St., #210, Binghamton, NY 13901; 607-242-0200; *Director of Constituent Services:* D. Jason Phelps
430 Court St., #102, Utica, NY 13502; 315-732-0713
Committee Assignments: Foreign Affairs; Small Business

Thompson, Bennie G., D-Miss. (2)

Capitol Hill Office: 2466 RHOB 20515-2402; 225-5876; Fax: 225-5898; *Chief of Staff:* Timla Washington
Web: benniethompson.house.gov
Facebook: www.facebook.com/CongressmanBennieGThompson
Twitter: @BennieGThompson
YouTube: www.youtube.com/RepBennieThompson
Instagram: @benniegthompson
District Offices: 107 W. Madison St., P. O. Box 610, Bolton, MS 39041; 601-866-9003; Fax: 601-866-9036; *Legislative Director:* Claytrice Henderson; *Field Rep.:* Brenda Funches
910 Courthouse Lane, Greenville, MS 38701-3764; 662-335-9003; Fax: 662-334-1304
728 Main St., Suite A, Greenwood, MS 38930; 662-455-9003; Fax: 662-453-0118
3607 Medgar Evers Blvd., Jackson, MS 39213-6364; 601-946-9003; Fax: 601-982-5337; *Senior Caseworker:* Steve Gavin
263 E. Main St., P.O. Box 356, Marks, MS 38646; 662-326-9003; *Caseworker / Field Rep.:* Sandra Jamison
106 Green Ave., #106, P.O. Box 679, Mound Bayou, MS 38762-9594; 662-741-9003; Fax: 662-741-9002
Committee Assignment: Homeland Security, Chair

Thompson, Glenn, R-Pa. (15)

Capitol Hill Office: 400 CHOB 20515-3805; 225-5121; Fax: 225-5796; *Chief of Staff:* Matthew Brennan
Web: thompson.house.gov
Facebook: www.facebook.com/CongressmanGT
Twitter: @CongressmanGT
YouTube: www.youtube.com/CongressmanGT
Instagram: @congressman_gt

District Offices: 3555 Benner Pike, #101, Bellefonte, PA 16823-8474; 814-353-0215; Fax: 814-353-0218; *Office Manager / Caseworker:* Andrea Dubbs
107 S. Center St., Ebensburg, PA 15931; 814-419-8583; Fax: 814-846-5124; *Field Rep.:* Brian Subich
217 Elm St., Suite B, Oil City, PA 16301; 814-670-0432; Fax: 814-670-0868; *District Director:* Brad Moore
Committee Assignments: Agriculture; Education and Labor

Thompson, Mike, D-Calif. (5)

Capitol Hill Office: 268 CHOB 20515-0501; 225-3311; Fax: 225-4335; *Chief of Staff:* Melanie Rhinehart Van Tassell
Web: mikethompson.house.gov
Facebook: www.facebook.com/RepMikeThompson
Twitter: @RepThompson
YouTube: www.youtube.com/CongressmanMThompson
Instagram: @repmikethompson
District Offices: 2721 Napa Valley Corporate Dr., Napa, CA 94558; 707-226-9898; Fax: 707-251-9800; *Deputy Chief of Staff:* Brad Onorato
2300 County Center Dr., #A100, Santa Rosa, CA 95403; 707-542-7182; Fax: 707-542-2745; *Senior Field Rep.:* Rebecca Hermosillo
420 Virginia St., #1C, Vallejo, CA 94590; 707-645-1888; Fax: 707-645-1870; *District Rep.:* Mel Orpilla
Committee Assignments: Ways and Means

Tiffany, Thomas P., R-Wisc. (7)

Capitol Hill Office: 1719 LHOB 20515; 225-3365; *Chief of Staff:* Jason Bauknecht
Web: tiffany.house.gov
Facebook: www.facebook.com/RepTiffany
Twitter: @RepTiffany
YouTube: www.youtube.com/channel/UCFBzqWrIhFKGiXI6D2YHeeg
Instagram: @reptiffany
District Office: 2620 Stewart Ave., #312, Wausau, WI 54401; 715-298-9344; *District Director:* Jon Lanctin
Committee Assignments: Judiciary; Natural Resources

Timmons, William R. IV, R-S.C. (4)

Capitol Hill Office: 267 CHOB 20515; 225-6030; *Chief of Staff:* Moutray McLaren
Web: timmons.house.gov
Facebook: www.facebook.com/RepTimmons
Twitter: @reptimmons
Instagram: @reptimmons
District Office: 114 Trade St., Greer, SC 29651; 864-241-0175; *District Director:* Seth Blanton
Committee Assignments: Financial Services; Republican Steering, Select on the Modernization of Congress

Titus, Dina, D-Nev. (1)

Capitol Hill Office: 2464 RHOB 20515; 225-5965; Fax: 225-3119; *Chief of Staff:* Jay Gertsema
Web: titus.house.gov
Facebook: www.facebook.com/CongresswomanTitus

Twitter: @repdinatitus
YouTube: www.youtube.com/CongresswomanTitus
Instagram: @dinatitusnv
District Office: 495 S. Main St., 3rd Floor, Las Vegas, NV 89101; 702-220-9823; Fax: 702-220-9841; *District Director:* Ana Quintanilla
Committee Assignments: Foreign Affairs; Homeland Security; Transportation and Infrastructure

Tlaib, Rashida, D-Mich. (13)

Capitol Hill Office: 1628 LHOB 20515-3515; 225-5126; Fax: 225-9985; *Chief of Staff:* Larissa Richardson
Web: tlaib.house.gov
Facebook: www.facebook.com/RepRashida
Twitter: @RepRashida
YouTube: www.youtube.com/channel/ UCl5GK07sD5TZIhKcsDNSExA
Instagram: @reprashida
District Offices: 7700 2nd Ave., 4th Floor, Detroit, MI 48202; 313-463-6220
4401 Conner St., Detroit, MI 48215; 313-463-6220
26215 Trowbridge St., Inkster, MI 48141; 313-463-6220
10600 W. Jefferson Ave., Room 207, River Rouge, MI 48218
Committee Assignments: Financial Services; Oversight and Reform

Tonko, Paul D., D-N.Y. (20)

Capitol Hill Office: 2369 RHOB 20515; 225-5076; Fax: 225-5077; *Chief of Staff:* Jeff Morgan
Web: tonko.house.gov
Facebook: www.facebook.com/reppaultonko
Twitter: @RepPaulTonko
YouTube: www.youtube.com/reppaultonko
Instagram: @reppaultonko
District Offices: 19 Dove St., #302, Albany, NY 12210; 518-465-0700; Fax: 518-427-5107; *District Director:* Colleen Williams
61 Church St., Room 309, Amsterdam, NY 12010-4424; 518-843-3400; Fax: 518-843-8874; *Constituent Services Rep.:* Kelly Quist-Demars
105 Jay St., Room 16, Schenectady, NY 12305-1970; 518-374-4547; Fax: 518-374-7908; *Senior Constituent Rep.:* Cora Schroeter
Committee Assignments: Energy and Commerce; Natural Resources; Science, Space, and Technology

Torres, Norma J., D-Calif. (35)

Capitol Hill Office: 2227 RHOB 20515; 225-6161; Fax: 225-8671; *Chief of Staff:* Matt Alpert
Web: torres.house.gov
Facebook: www.facebook.com/RepNormaTorres
Twitter: @NormaJTorres
YouTube: www.youtube.com/channel/UCvWY4qKP6– o3pIJY7hhKDg
Instagram: @repnormatorres
District Office: 3200 Inland Empire Blvd., #200B, Ontario, CA 91764; 909-481-6474; Fax: 909-941-1362; *District Director:* Marisol Guerra
Committee Assignments: Appropriations; Rules

Torres, Ritchie, D-N.Y. (15)

Capitol Hill Office: 317 CHOB 20515; 225-4361; Fax: 225-6001; *Chief of Staff:* Angel Vazquez
Web: ritchietorres.house.gov
Facebook: www.facebook.com/RepRitchie
Twitter: @RepRitchie
Instagram: @RepRitchie
District Office: 1231 Lafayette Ave., #L630, Bronx, NY 10474; 718-503-9610; Fax: 718-620-0658; *District Director:* Nanette Alvarado
Committee Assignments: Financial Services; Homeland Security

Trahan, Lori, D-Mass. (3)

Capitol Hill Office: 2439 RHOB 20515; 225-3411; *Chief of Staff:* Mark McDevitt
Web: trahan.house.gov
Facebook: www.facebook.com/RepLoriTrahan
Twitter: @RepLoriTrahan
Instagram: @reploritrahan
District Offices: 126 John St., #12, Lowell, MA 01852; 978-459-0101; Fax: 978-459-1907; *District Director:* Emily Byrne
Committee Assignments: Energy and Commerce; Natural Resources

Trone, David, D-Md. (6)

Capitol Hill Office: 1110 LHOB 20515; 225-2721; *Chief of Staff:* Lane Lofton
Web: trone.house.gov
Facebook: www.facebook.com/repdavidtrone
Twitter: @RepDavidTrone
YouTube: www.youtube.com/channel/ UCkhS5ZuWjqe3YC2xWnXaK5w
Instagram: @repdavidtrone
District Offices: One Washington Center, 9801 Washingtonian Blvd., #330, Gaithersburg, MD 20878; 301-926-0300; *District Director:* Sonny Holding
217 Glenn St., #500, Cumberland, MD 21502; 240-382-6464; *Director of Constituent Services:* Taylor Donoghue
1850 Dual Highway, #101, Hagerstown, MD 21740; 240-382-6464
10 Hillcrest Dr., #28, Frederick, MD 21703; 240-803-6119
Committee Assignments: Appropriations; Joint Economic; Veterans' Affairs

Turner, Michael R., R-Ohio (10)

Capitol Hill Office: 2082 RHOB 20515-3503; 225-6465; Fax: 225-6754; *Chief of Staff:* Adam Howard
Web: turner.house.gov
Facebook: www.facebook.com/RepMikeTurner
Twitter: @RepMikeTurner
YouTube: www.youtube.com/channel/ UCxbpjLbEoYvOIfuRmfR7CWQ
Instagram: @repmiketurner
District Office: 120 W. 3rd St., #305, Dayton, OH 45402-1819; 937-225-2843; Fax: 937-225-2752; *District Director:* Frank DeBrosse
Committee Assignments: Armed Services; Permanent Select Intelligence

Underwood, Lauren, D-Ill. (14)

Capitol Hill Office: 1130 LHOB 20515-3515; 225-2976; Fax: 225-0697; *Chief of Staff:* Andrea R. Harris
Web: underwood.house.gov
Facebook: www.facebook.com/repunderwood
Twitter: @RepUnderwood
YouTube: www.youtube.com/channel/UC48cu-KUdMVWRCx7ValQySQ?view_as=subscriber
Instagram: @repunderwood
District Offices: 333 Commerce Dr., #700, Crystal Lake, IL 60014; 630-549-2190
490 E. Roosevelt Rd., #202, West Chicago, IL 60185; 630-549-2190; Fax: 630-584-2746; *District Director:* Michelle Thimios
Committee Assignments: Appropriations; Veterans' Affairs

Upton, Fred, R-Mich. (6)

Capitol Hill Office: 2183 RHOB 20515-2206; 225-3761; Fax: 225-4986; *Chief of Staff:* Joan Hillebrands
Web: upton.house.gov
Facebook: www.facebook.com/RepFredUpton
Twitter: @RepFredUpton
YouTube: www.youtube.com/RepFredUpton
Instagram: @repfredupton
District Offices: 350 E. Michigan Ave., #130, Kalamazoo, MI 49007; 269-385-0039; Fax: 269-385-2888
720 Main St., St. Joseph, MI 49085-2182; 269-982-1986; Fax: 269-982-0237; *District Director:* Mike Ryan
Committee Assignment: Energy and Commerce

Valadao, David G., R-Calif. (21)

Capitol Hill Office: 1728 LHOB 20515; 225-4695; *Chief of Staff:* Andrew Renteria
Web: valadao.house.gov
Facebook: www.facebook.com/CongressmanDavidValadao
Twitter: @RepDavidValadao
District Offices: 2700 M St., #250B, Bakersfield, CA 93301; 661-864-7736; Fax: 833-284-9090; *District Director:* Wes Anderson
107 S. Douty St., Hanford, CA 93230; 559-460-6070; Fax: 559-584-3564
Committee Assignment: Appropriations

Van Drew, Jefferson, R-N.J. (2)

Capitol Hill Office: 2447 RHOB 20515; 225-6572; Fax: 225-3318; *Chief of Staff:* Allison Murphy
Web: vandrew.house.gov
Facebook: www.facebook.com/CongressmanJVD
Twitter: @congressman_JVD
YouTube: www.youtube.com/channel/UCc5AGO_bQLeiv313Bbr35fg?view_as=subscriber
Instagram: @jeffvandrew
District Office: 5914 Main St., #103, Mays Landing, NJ 08330; 609-625-5008; Fax: 609-625-5071; *District Director:* Christopher Chin
Committee Assignments: Homeland Security; Transportation and Infrastructure

Van Duyne, Beth, R-Tex. (24)

Capitol Hill Office: 1337 LHOB 20515; 225-6605; 225-0074; *Chief of Staff:* Jacob Olson
Web: vanduyne.house.gov
Facebook: www.facebook.com/RepBethVanDuyne
Twitter: @RepBethVanDuyne
YouTube: www.youtube.com/channel/UC891KwZoimDB36IzK1or_VA
Instagram: @repbethvanduyne
District Office: 3100 Olympus Blvd., #440, Dallas, TX 75019; 972-966-5500; *District Director:* Kristen Doe
Committee Assignments: Small Business; Select on the Modernization of Congress; Transportation and Infrastructure

Vargas, Juan, D-Calif. (51)

Capitol Hill Office: 2244 RHOB 20515; 225-8045; Fax: 225-2772; *Chief of Staff:* Larry Cohen
Web: vargas.house.gov
Facebook: www.facebook.com/RepJuanVargas
Twitter: @RepJuanVargas
YouTube: www.youtube.com/RepJuanVargas
Instagram: @repjuanvargas
District Offices: 333 F St., Suite A, Chula Vista, CA 91910-2624; 619-422-5963; Fax: 619-422-7290; *District Director:* Janine Bryant
380 N. 8th St., #14, El Centro, CA 92243; 760-312-9900; Fax: 760-312-9664
Committee Assignments: Financial Services; Foreign Affairs

Veasey, Marc A., D-Tex. (33)

Capitol Hill Office: 2348 RHOB 20515; 225-9897; Fax: 225-9702; *Chief of Staff:* Nicole Varner
Web: veasey.house.gov
Facebook: www.facebook.com/CongressmanMarcVeasey
Twitter: @RepVeasey
YouTube: www.youtube.com/marcveasey
Instagram: @repveasey
District Offices: JP Morgan Chase Bldg., 1881 Sylvan Ave., #108, Dallas, TX 75208; 214-741-1387; Fax: 214-741-2026
6707 Brentwood Stair Rd., #200, Fort Worth, TX 76112; 817-920-9086; Fax: 817-920-9324
Committee Assignments: Armed Services; Energy and Commerce

Velázquez, Nydia M., D-N.Y. (7)

Capitol Hill Office: 2302 RHOB 20515-3212; 225-2361; Fax: 226-0327; *Chief of Staff:* Melissa Jung
Web: velazquez.house.gov
Facebook: www.facebook.com/RepNydiaVelazquez
Twitter: @NydiaVelazquez
YouTube: www.youtube.com/nydiavelazquez
Instagram: @rep_velazquez
District Offices: 266 Broadway, #201, Brooklyn, NY 11211-6215; 718-599-3658; Fax: 718-599-4537; *District Director:* Daniel Wiley

500 Pearl St., #973, New York, NY 10007; 212-619-2606; Fax: 212-619-4969

Committee Assignments: Small Business, Chair; Financial Services; Natural Resources

Wagner, Ann, R-Mo. (2)

Capitol Hill Office: 2350 RHOB 20515; 225-1621; Fax: 225-2563; *Chief of Staff:* Charlie Keller

Web: wagner.house.gov

Facebook: www.facebook.com/RepAnnWagner

Twitter: @RepAnnWagner

YouTube: www.youtube.com/channel/UCy2v2DXXvQnbRc8Zx77Dnsg

Instagram: @repannwagner

District Office: 301 Sovereign Court, #201, Ballwin, MO 63011-4442; 636-779-5449; Fax: 636-779-5457; *District Director:* Miriam Stonebraker

Committee Assignments: Financial Services; Foreign Affairs

Walberg, Tim, R-Mich. (7)

Capitol Hill Office: 2266 RHOB 20515; 225-6276; Fax: 225-6281; *Chief of Staff:* R. J. Laukitis

Web: walberg.house.gov

Facebook: www.facebook.com/RepWalberg

Twitter: @RepWalberg

YouTube: www.youtube.com/RepWalberg

Instagram: @repwalberg

District Office: 401 W. Michigan Ave., Jackson, MI 49201; 517-780-9075; Fax: 517-780-9081; *District Director:* Stephen Rajzer

Committee Assignments: Education and Labor; Energy and Commerce

Walorski, Jackie, R-Ind. (2)

Capitol Hill Office: 466 CHOB 20515; 225-3915; Fax: 225-6798; *Chief of Staff:* Tim Cummings

Web: walorski.house.gov

Facebook: www.facebook.com/RepJackieWalorski

Twitter: @RepWalorski

YouTube: www.youtube.com/repwalorski

Instagram: @jackiewalorski

District Office: 2410 Grape Rd., #2A, Mishawaka, IN 46545; 574-204-2645; Fax: 574-217-8735; *District Director:* Zachary Potts

Satellite Office: 709 Main St., Rochester, IN 46975; 574-223-4373; Fax: 574-217-8735 (open Tuesday and Thursday, 8 a.m.–5 p.m.)

Committee Assignments: Ethics; Ways and Means

Waltz, Michael, R-Fla. (6)

Capitol Hill Office: 213 CHOB 20515-3515; 225-2706; *Chief of Staff:* Micah Ketchel

Web: waltz.house.gov

Facebook: www.facebook.com/repmichaelwaltz

Twitter: @RepWaltzPress

YouTube: www.youtube.com/RepMichaelWaltz

Instagram: @repmichaelwaltz

District Offices: 120 S. Florida Ave., #324, Deland, FL 32720; 386-279-0707; Fax: 386-279-0874; *District Director:* Ernie Audino

31 Lupi Ct., #130, Palm Coast, FL 32137; 386-302-0442; Fax: 386-283-5164

1000 City Center Circle, 2nd Floor, Port Orange, FL 32129; 386-238-9711; Fax: 386-238-9714

Committee Assignments: Armed Services; Science, Space, and Technology

Wasserman Schultz, Debbie, D-Fla. (23)

Capitol Hill Office: 1114 LHOB 20515; 225-7931; Fax: 226-2052; *Chief of Staff:* Tracie Pough

Web: wassermanschultz.house.gov

Facebook: www.facebook.com/RepDWS

Twitter: @RepDWStweets

YouTube: www.youtube.com/RepWassermanSchultz

Instagram: @repdws

District Offices: 19200 W. Country Club Dr., Aventura, FL 33180-2403; 305-936-5724; Fax: 305-932-9664 (by appointment only); *Deputy District Director:* Laurie Flink

777 Sawgrass Corporate Pkwy., Sunrise, FL 33325; 954-845-1179; Fax: 954-845-0396; *District Director:* Raul Martinez

Committee Assignments: Appropriations; Oversight and Reform

Waters, Maxine, D-Calif. (43)

Capitol Hill Office: 2221 RHOB 20515-0535; 225-2201; Fax: 225-7854; *Chief of Staff:* Mikael Moore

Web: waters.house.gov

Facebook: www.facebook.com/MaxineWaters

Twitter: @RepMaxineWaters

YouTube: www.youtube.com/MaxineWaters

Instagram: @repmaxinewaters

District Office: 2851 W. 120th St., Suite H, Hawthorne, CA 90250; 323-757-8900; Fax: 323-757-9506; *District Director:* Blanca Jimenez

Committee Assignment: Financial Services, Chair, Select on Coronavirus Crisis

Watson Coleman, Bonnie, D-N.J. (12)

Capitol Hill Office: 168 CHOB 20515; 225-5801; Fax: 225-6025; *Chief of Staff:* James Gee

Web: watsoncoleman.house.gov

Facebook: www.facebook.com/RepBonnie

Twitter: @RepBonnie

YouTube: www.youtube.com/channel/UCrxEaX0VKZKwg3930du2D5A

Instagram: @repbonnie

District Office: 850 Bear Tavern Rd., #201, Ewing, NJ 08628; 609-883-0026; Fax: 609-883-2093; *District Director:* Kari Osmond

Committee Assignments: Appropriations; Homeland Security

Weber, Randy K., Sr., R-Tex. (14)

Capitol Hill Office: 107 CHOB 20515; 225-2831; Fax: 225-0271; *Chief of Staff:* Jeanette Whitener
Web: weber.house.gov
Facebook: www.facebook.com/TXRandy14
Twitter: @TXRandy14
YouTube: www.youtube.com/TXRandy14
Instagram: @txrandy14
District Offices: 350 Pine St., #730, Beaumont, TX 77701; 409-835-0108; Fax: 409-835-0578; *District Director:* Jared Bargas
122 West Way, #301, Lake Jackson, TX 77566-5245; 979-285-0231; Fax: 979-285-0271
303 E. Main St., #250, League City, TX 77573; 979-285-0231; Fax:979-285-0271
Committee Assignments: Science, Space, and Technology; Transportation and Infrastructure

Webster, Daniel, R-Fla. (11)

Capitol Hill Office: 2184 RHOB 20515; 225-1002; Fax: 226-6559; *Chief of Staff:* Jaryn Emhof
Web: webster.house.gov
Facebook: www.facebook.com/RepWebster
Twitter: @RepWebster
YouTube: www.youtube.com/repdanwebster
District Office: 318 S. 2nd St., Suite A, Leesburg, FL 34748; 352-241-9220; Fax: 352-241-9181; *District Director:* Christa Pearson
Satellite Offices: 8015 E. County Rd. 466, Suite B, The Villages, FL 32162; 352-383-3552 (open Monday, 9 a.m.–5 p.m. or by appointment only)
212 W. Main St., #208A, Inverness, FL 34451; 352-241-9204; Fax: 352-241-9220 (open Monday, 9 a.m.–5 p.m. or by appointment only)
15 N. Main St., Suite B, Brooksville, FL 34601; 352-241-9230; Fax: 352-241-9220 (open Monday, 9 a.m.–5 p.m. or by appointment only)
Committee Assignments: Natural Resources; Science, Space, and Technology; Transportation and Infrastructure

Welch, Peter, D-Vt. (At Large)

Capitol Hill Office: 2187 RHOB 20515; 225-4115; Fax: 225-6790; *Chief of Staff:* Patrick Satalin
Web: welch.house.gov
Facebook: www.facebook.com/PeterWelch
Twitter: @PeterWelch
YouTube: www.youtube.com/RepPeterWelch
Instagram: @reppeterwelch
District Office: 128 Lakeside Ave., #235, Burlington, VT 05401; 802-652-2450; Fax: 802-652-2497
Committee Assignments: Energy and Commerce; Oversight and Reform; Permanent Select Intelligence

Wenstrup, Brad R., R-Ohio (2)

Capitol Hill Office: 2419 RHOB 20515; 225-3164; Fax: 225-1992; *Chief of Staff:* Greg Brooks
Web: wenstrup.house.gov
Facebook: www.facebook.com/RepBradWenstrup
Twitter: @RepBradWenstrup
YouTube: www.youtube.com/repbradwenstrup
Instagram: @repbradwenstrup
District Offices: 7954 Beechmont Ave., #200, Cincinnati, OH 45255; 513-474-7777; Fax: 513-605-1377; *District Director / Deputy Chief of Staff:* Alex Scharfetter
170 N. Main St., Peebles, OH 45660; 513-605-1380; Fax: 937-798-4024; *Regional Director:* Teresa Lewis
Committee Assignments: Ways and Means; Permanent Select Intelligence

Westerman, Bruce, R-Ark. (4)

Capitol Hill Office: 202 CHOB 20515; 225-3772; Fax: 225-1314; *Chief of Staff:* Sarah Slocum Collins
Web: westerman.house.gov
Facebook: www.facebook.com/RepWesterman
Twitter: @RepWesterman
YouTube: www.youtube.com/channel/UCNshPbmupCwP5a7Hi79jETQ
Instagram: @repwesterman
District Offices: 101 N. Washington Ave., #406, El Dorado, AR 71730; 870-864-8946; Fax: 870-864-8958; *District Director:* Jason D. McGehee
101 Reserve St., #200, Hot Springs, AR 71901; 501-609-9796; Fax: 501-609-9887
211 W. Commercial St., Ozark, AR 72949; 479-667-0075; Fax: 501-609-9887
100 E. 8th Ave., Room 2521, Pine Bluff, AR 71601; 870-536-8178; Fax: 870-536-8364
Committee Assignments: Natural Resources; Transportation and Infrastructure

Wexton, Jennifer, D-Va. (10)

Capitol Hill Office: 1217 LHOB 20515-3515; 225-5136; Fax: 225-0437; *Chief of Staff:* Abby Carter
Web: wexton.house.gov
Facebook: www.facebook.com/CongresswomanWexton
Twitter: @RepWexton
Instagram: @repwexton
District Offices: 21351 Gentry Dr., #140, Sterling, VA 20166; 703-234-3800; *District Director:* Erica Campeau
100 N. Loudoun St., #120, Winchester, VA 22601; 703-236-1300
Committee Assignments: Appropriations; Budget

Wild, Susan, D-Pa. (7)

Capitol Hill Office: 1027 LHOB 20515; 225-6411; *Chief of Staff:* Jed Ober
Web: wild.house.gov
Facebook: www.facebook.com/repsusanwild
Twitter: @RepSusanWild
YouTube: www.youtube.com/channel/UCRuQG9Cp1Oi7FxSYRHlvAgw
Instagram: @repsusanwild
District Offices: 504 Hamilton St., #3804, Allentown, PA 18101; 484-781-6000; Fax: 877-347-4103; *District Director:* Megan Beste

400 Northampton St., #503, Easton, PA 18042; 610-333-1170; Fax: 877-561-7520

637 Main St., #316, Stroudsburg, PA 18360; 570-807-0333 (open Thursday and Friday, 10 a.m.–6 p.m.)

Committee Assignments: Education and Labor; Ethics; Foreign Affairs; Science, Space, and Technology

Williams, Nikema, D-Ga. (5)

Capitol Hill Office: 1406 LHOB 20515; 225-3801; *Chief of Staff:* Melanee Farrah
Web: nikemawilliams.house.gov
Facebook: www.facebook.com/RepNikemaWilliams
Twitter: @RepNikema
Instagram: @RepNikema
District Office: 100 Peachtree St. N.W., #1920, Atlanta, GA 30303; 404-659-0116; *District Director:* Aaron Johnson
Committee Assignments: Financial Services; Transportation and Infrastructure; Select on the Modernization of Congress

Williams, Roger, R-Tex. (25)

Capitol Hill Office: 1708 LHOB 20515; 225-9896; Fax: 225-9692; *Chief of Staff:* John Etue
Web: williams.house.gov
Facebook: www.facebook.com/RepRogerWilliams
Twitter: @RepRWilliams
YouTube: www.youtube.com/channel/UCBtfmMMQarjtLB9U_pWMOhw
District Offices: 5806 Mesa Dr., #390, Austin, TX 78731; 512-473-8910; Fax: 202-225-9692; *District Director:* Robyn Hess
115 S. Main St., #206, Cleburne, TX 76033; 817-774-2575; Fax: 202-225-9692
District Director: Robyn Hess
Committee Assignments: Financial Services; Small Business

Wilson, Frederica S., D-Fla. (24)

Capitol Hill Office: 2445 RHOB 20515; 225-4506; Fax: 226-0777; *Chief of Staff:* Jean Roseme
Web: wilson.house.gov
Facebook: www.facebook.com/RepWilson
Twitter: @RepWilson
YouTube: www.youtube.com/RepFredericaWilson
Instagram: @repwilson
District Offices: 18425 2nd Ave. N.W., #355, Miami Gardens, FL 33169-4534; 305-690-5905; Fax: 305-690-5951; *District Chief of Staff:* Alexis Snyder
West Park City Hall, 1965 S. State Rd. 7, West Park, FL 33023; 954-989-2688 (open Thursday, 9 a.m.–5 p.m.)
Old Library, 2600 Hollywood Blvd., 1st Floor, Hollywood, FL 33020; 954-921-3682 (open 2nd and 4th Thursday, 9 a.m.–5 p.m.); *District Director:* Joyce Postell
Committee Assignments: Education and Labor; Transportation and Infrastructure

Wilson, Joe, R-S.C. (2)

Capitol Hill Office: 1436 LHOB 20515; 225-2452; Fax: 225-2455; *Chief of Staff:* Jonathan Day
Web: joewilson.house.gov
Facebook: www.facebook.com/JoeWilson
Twitter: @RepJoeWilson
YouTube: www.youtube.com/RepJoeWilson
Instagram: @repjoewilson
District Offices: 1930 University Pkwy., #1600, Aiken, SC 29801; 803-642-6416; Fax: 803-642-6418
1700 Sunset Blvd. (U.S. 378), #1, West Columbia, SC 29169; 803-939-0041; Fax: 803-939-0078; *District Director:* Alex Morris
Committee Assignments: Armed Services; Education and Labor; Foreign Affairs

Wittman, Robert J., R-Va. (1)

Capitol Hill Office: 2055 RHOB 20515; 225-4261; Fax: 225-4382; *Chief of Staff:* Carolyn King
Web: wittman.house.gov
Facebook: www.facebook.com/RepRobWittman
Twitter: @RobWittman
YouTube: www.youtube.com/RobWittman
Instagram: @reprobwittman
District Offices: 95 Dunn Dr., #201, Stafford, VA 22556; 540-659-2734; Fax: 540-659-2737
508 Church Lane, P.O. Box 3106, Tappahannock, VA 22560; 804-443-0668; Fax: 804-443-0671
6501 Mechanicsville Turnpike, #102, Mechanicsville, VA 23111; 804-730-6595; Fax: 804-730-6597; *District Director:* Joe Schumacher
Committee Assignments: Armed Services; Natural Resources

Womack, Steve, R-Ark. (3)

Capitol Hill Office: 2412 RHOB 20515; 225-4301; Fax: 225-5713; *Chief of Staff:* Beau T. Walker
Web: womack.house.gov
Facebook: www.facebook.com/RepSteveWomack
Twitter: @rep_stevewomack
YouTube: www.youtube.com/CongressmanWomack
Instagram: @rep_stevewomack
District Offices: 6101 Phoenix Ave., #4, Fort Smith, AR 72903; 479-424-1146; Fax: 479-464-0063
400 N. Main St., #3, Harrison, AR 72601-3508; 870-741-6900; Fax: 479-464-0063
3333 Pinnacle Hills Pkwy., #120, Rogers, AR 72758-9100; 479-464-0446; Fax: 479-464-0063
Committee Assignment: Appropriations

Yarmuth, John A., D-Ky. (3)

Capitol Hill Office: 402 CHOB 20515; 225-5401; Fax: 225-5776; *Chief of Staff:* Julie Carr
Web: yarmuth.house.gov
Facebook: www.facebook.com/RepJohnYarmuth
Twitter: @RepJohnYarmuth
YouTube: www.youtube.com/RepJohnYarmuth

District Offices: Romano L. Mazzoli Federal Bldg., 600 Martin Luther King Jr. Pl., #216, Louisville, KY 40202; 502-582-5129; Fax: 502-582-5897; *District Director:* Dana Mayton

Southwest Government Center, 7219 Dixie Hwy., #216, Louisville, KY 40258-3756; 502-933-5863; Fax: 502-935-6934

Committee Assignments: Budget, Chair

Zeldin, Lee M., R-N.Y. (1)

Capitol Hill Office: 2441 RHOB 20515-3201; 225-3826; Fax: 225-3143; *Chief of Staff:* Eric Amidon

Web: zeldin.house.gov

Facebook: www.facebook.com/RepLeeZeldin

Twitter: @RepLeeZeldin

YouTube: www.youtube.com/repleezeldin

Instagram: @repleezeldin

District Office: 31 Oak St., #20, Patchogue, NY 11772; 631-289-1097; Fax: 866-404-6613; *District Director:* Mark Woolley

Satellite Office: 30 W. Main St., #201, Riverhead, NY 11901; 631-209-4235 (open Tuesday, Wednesday, and Thursday, 10 a.m.–2 p.m. by appointment only)

Committee Assignments: Financial Services; Foreign Affairs

Vacant, Alaska (At Large)

Capitol Hill Office: 2314 RHOB 20515-0201; 225-5765; Fax: 225-0425

District Offices: 471 W. 36th Ave., #201, Anchorage, AK 99503-5920; 907-271-5978; Fax: 907-271-5950; *State Director:* Daniel George

Key Bank Bldg., 100 Cushman St., #307, Fairbanks, AK 99701; 907-456-0210; Fax: 907-456-0279

Vacant, Calif. (22)

Capitol Hill Office: 1013 LHOB 20515-0521; 225-2523; Fax: 225-3404

District Offices: 264 Clovis Ave., #206, Clovis, CA 93612-1115; 559-323-5235; Fax: 559-323-5528; *Field Rep.:* Mark Blackney

113 N. Church St., #208, Visalia, CA 93291-6300; 559-733-3861; Fax: 559-733-3865; *District Director:* Crystal Ragan

Vacant, Minn. (1)

Capitol Hill Office: 1433 LHOB 20515-3515; 225-2472

District Offices: 11 Civic Center Plaza, #301, Mankato, MN 56001; 507-323-6090; *District Director:* Carol Stevenson

1530 Greenview Dr. S.W., #207, Rochester, MN 55902; 507-323-6090

Vacant, Neb. (1)

Capitol Hill Office: 1514 LHOB 20515-2701; 225-4806; Fax: 225-5686

District Office: 301 S. 13th St., #100, Lincoln, NE 68508-2532; 402-438-1598; Fax: 844-272-6454; *District Director:* Marie Woodhead

Vacant, Tex. (34)

Capitol Hill Office: 307 CHOB 20515; 225-9901; Fax: 225-9770

District Offices: 500 E. Main St., Alice, TX 78332; 361-230-9776

800 N. Expressway 77-83, #9, Brownsville, TX 78521; 956-544-8352; Fax: 956-280-5114; *District Director:* Marisela Cardenas Cortez

1390 W. Expressway 83, San Benito, TX 78586; 956-276-4497; Fax: 956-276-4603

301 W. Railroad, Weslaco, TX 78596; 956-520-8273; Fax: 956-520-8277; *Caseworker:* Anissa Guajardo

Joint Committees of Congress

The joint committees of Congress follow. Each listing includes room number, office building, zip code, telephone number, website, key staffers, committee jurisdiction, and membership (in order of seniority) for each committee. Members are drawn from the Senate and House and from both parties. This information is current as of May 12, 2022.

House and Senate Democrats, the current majority in that chamber, are shown in roman type; Republicans, in the minority, appear in italic. When a senator serves as chair, the vice chair usually is a representative, and vice versa. The location of the chair usually rotates from one chamber to the other at the beginning of each Congress. The area code for all phone and fax numbers is (202). A phone number and/or office number next to either the majority or minority staff director indicates a change from the full committee's office number and/or phone number. If no numbers are listed, the individual's office number and phone number are the same as for the full committee.

JOINT ECONOMIC COMMITTEE

Office: G-01 SDOB 20510-6075
Phone: 224-5171;   **Fax:** 224-0240
Web: www.jec.senate.gov
Minority Web: www.jec.senate.gov/public/index.cfm/republicans
Majority Staff Director: Scott Winship
Minority Staff Director: Harry Gural
Jurisdiction: (1) make a continuing study of matters relating to the Economic Report of the President; (2) study means of coordinating programs in order to further the policy of this act; and (3) as a guide to the several committees of the Congress dealing with legislation relating to the Economic Report, not later than March 1 of each year (beginning with the year 1947) to file a report with the Senate and the House of Representatives containing its findings and recommendations with respect to each of the main recommendations made by the president in the Economic Report, and from time to time to make other reports and recommendations to the Senate and the House of Representatives as it deems advisable.
Party Ratio: D 11-R 9

Senate Members

Martin Heinrich, N.M., Vice Chair	*Mike Lee, Utah*
	Tom Cotton, Ark.
Amy Klobuchar, Minn.	*Rob Portman, Ohio*
Margaret Wood Hassan, N.H.	*Bill Cassidy, La.*
Raphael Warnock, Ga.	*Ted Cruz, Tex.*
Mark Kelly, Ariz.	

House Members

Don Beyer, Va., Chair	*David Schweikert, Ariz.*
David Trone, Md.	*Jaime Herrera Beutler, Wash.*
Joyce Beatty, Ohio.	
Mark Pocan, Wisc.	*Jodey C. Arrington, Tex.*
Scott H. Peters, Calif.	*Ron Estes, Kans.*
Sharice Davids, Kans.	

JOINT COMMITTEE ON THE LIBRARY

Office: 1309 LHOB 20515-6157
Phone: 225-2061   **Fax:** 226-2774
Web: cha.house.gov/jointcommittees/joint-committee-library

Majority Staff Director: Khalil Abboud
Minority Staff Director: Jen Doulby; 1309 LHOB 20515-6157; 225-8281
Jurisdiction: considers proposals concerning the management and expansion of the Library of Congress, the development and maintenance of the National Sanctuary Hall Collection and the U.S. Botanic Garden, the receipt of gifts for the benefit of the library, and certain matters relating to placing of statues and other works of art in the U.S. Capitol.
Party Ratio: R 5-D 4

Senate Members

Amy Klobuchar, Minn.	*Roy Blunt, Mo., Chair*
Patrick J. Leahy, Vt.	*Richard C. Shelby, Ala.*

House Members

Zoe Lofgren, Calif., Vice Chair	*Rodney Davis, Ill.*
	Barry Loudermilk, Ga.
Tim Ryan, Ohio	
G. K. Butterfield, N.C.	

JOINT COMMITTEE ON PRINTING

Office: 1309 LHOB 20515
Phone: 225-2061   **Fax:** 226-2774
Web: cha.house.gov/jointcommittees/joint-committee-on-printing
Majority Professional Staff Member: Khalil Abboud
Minority Professional Staff Member: Jen Doulby; 1309 LHOB; 225-8281
Jurisdiction: oversight of (1) the functions of the Government Printing Office and general printing procedures of the federal government; and (2) compliance by federal entities with Title 44 of the U.S. Code, and the Government Printing and Binding Regulations.
Party Ratio: R 3-D 4

Senate Members

Amy Klobuchar, Minn.	*Roy Blunt, Mo., Vice Chair*
Tom Udall, N.M.	*Pat Roberts, Kans.*
	Roger F. Wicker, Miss.

House Members

Zoe Lofgren, Calif., Chair	*Rodney Davis, Ill.*
Jamie Raskin, Md.	*Barry Loudermilk, Ga.*
Susan Davis, Ca.	

Gwen Moore, Wisc.   *Richard Hudson, N.C.*
Marc Veasey, Tex.

JOINT COMMITTEE ON TAXATION

Office: 502 FHOB 20515-6453
Phone: 225-3621   **Fax:** 225-0832
Web: www.jct.gov
Email: JCTInfo@jct.gov
Chief of Staff: Thomas A. Barthold; 225-3621
Deputy Chief of Staff: Robert P. Harvey; 226-7575
Jurisdiction: involved with every aspect of the tax legislative process, including: (1) assisting congressional tax-writing committees and members of Congress with development and analysis of legislative proposals; (2) preparing official revenue estimates of all tax legislation considered by the Congress; (3) drafting legislative histories for tax-related bills; (4) investigating various aspects of the federal tax system.
Party Ratio: D 6-R 4

Senate Members

Ron Wyden, Ore., Vice Chair   *Mike Crapo, Idaho*
Debbie Stabenow, Mich.   *Chuck Grassley, Iowa*
Maria Cantwell, Wash.

House Members

Richard Neal, Mass., Chair   *Kevin Brady, Tex.*
Lloyd Doggett, Tex.   *Vern Buchanan, Fla.*
Mike Thompson, Calif.

COMMISSION ON SECURITY AND COOPERATION IN EUROPE (HELSINKI COMMISSION)

Office: 234 FHOB 20515-6460
Phone: 225-1901   **Fax:** 226-4199
Web: www.csce.gov
Email: info@csce.gov
Chief of Staff: Kyle Parker
Jurisdiction: The commission is authorized and directed to monitor the acts of the signatories that reflect compliance with or violation of the articles of the Final Act of the Conference on Security and Cooperation in Europe, with particular regard to the provisions relating to human rights and cooperation in humanitarian fields. The commission is further authorized and directed to monitor and encourage the development of programs and activities of the U.S. government and private organizations with a view toward taking advantage of the provisions of the Final Act to expand East-West economic cooperation and a greater interchange of people and ideas between East and West.
Party Ratio: R 9-D 8

Senate Members

Benjamin L. Cardin, Md.,   *Roger Wicker, Miss.*
  Chair   *John Boozman, Ark.*
Richard Blumenthal, Conn.   *Marco Rubio, Fla.*
Jeanne Shaheen, N.H.   *Thom Tillis, N.C.*
Tina Smith, Minn.
Sheldon Whitehouse, R.I.

House Members

Steve Cohen, Tenn.,   *Joe Wilson, S.C.*
  Co-Chair   *Robert B. Aderholt, Ala.*
Emmanuel Cleaver, Mo.   *Brian Fitzpatrick, Pa.*

CONGRESSIONAL-EXECUTIVE COMMISSION ON CHINA

Office: 243 FHOB 20515-0001
Phone: 226-3766   **Fax:** 226-3804
Web: www.cecc.gov
Email: infocecc@mail.house.gov
CECC Political Prisoner Database: www.cecc.gov/resources/political-prisoner-database
International Human Rights Materials: www.cecc.gov/resources/international-human-rights-materials
Staff Director: Matt Squeri, 226-3821
Deputy Staff Director: Todd Stein, 226-3798
Jurisdiction: The commission shall: (a) monitor the acts of the People's Republic of China that reflect compliance with or violation of human rights, in particular, those contained in the International Covenant on Civil and Political Rights and in the Universal Declaration of Human Rights; (b) compile and maintain lists of persons believed to be imprisoned, detained, or placed under house arrest, tortured, or otherwise persecuted by the government of the People's Republic of China due to their pursuit of the rights described in subsection (a), and exercise appropriate discretion, including concerns regarding the safety and security of, and benefit to, the persons who may be included on the lists and their families; (c) monitor the development of the rule of law in the People's Republic of China; (d) monitor and encourage the development of programs and activities of the U.S. government and private organizations with a view toward increasing the interchange of people and ideas between the United States and the People's Republic of China and expanding cooperation in areas; (e) seek out and maintain contacts with nongovernmental organizations, including receiving reports and updates from such organizations and evaluating such reports; (f) cooperate with the Special Coordinator for Tibetan Issues in the Department of State; (g) issue an annual report to the president and the Congress setting forth the findings of the commission during the preceding 12-month period, in carrying out subsections (a) through (c); (h) include specific information in the report as to the nature and implementation of laws or policies concerning the rights set forth; (i) hold hearings on the contents of the report; (j) submit to the president and the Congress reports that supplement the annual reports, as appropriate.
Party Ratio: D 8-R 8

Senate Members

Jeff Merkley, Ore., Chair   *Marco Rubio, Fla.,*
Dianne Feinstein, Calif.   * Co-Chair*
Gary Peters, Mich.   *James Lankford, Okla.*
Angus King, Maine (I)   *Tom Cotton, Ark.*
    Steve Daines, Mont.

House Members

James McGovern, Mass.,   *Christopher H. Smith, N.J.*
  Co-Chair   *Brian Mast, Fla.*
Thomas Suozzi, N.Y.   *Vicky Hartzler, Mo.*
Tom Malinowski, N.J.   *Michelle Steel, Ca.*
Rachida Tlaib, Mich.
Jennifer Wexton, Va.

Senate Committees

The standing and select committees of the U.S. Senate follow. This information is current as of May 12, 2022. Each listing includes room number, office building, zip code, telephone and fax numbers, website, minority website if available, key majority and minority staff members, jurisdiction for the full committee, and party ratio. Subcommittees are listed under the full committees. Members are listed in order of seniority on the committee or subcommittee. Many committees and subcommittees may be contacted via web-based email forms found on their websites. A phone number and/or office number next to either the majority or minority staff director indicates a change from the full committee's office number and/or phone number. If no numbers are listed, the individual's office number and phone number are the same as for the full committee.

Democrats, the current majority, are shown in roman type; Republicans, in the minority, appear in italic. The top name in the italicized list is the Ranking Minority Member. Bernard Sanders, I-Vt., and Angus S. King Jr., I-Maine, caucus with the Democrats and accrue committee seniority with Democrats; thus, they are counted with the Democrats in the party ratio, although (I) appears after their names. The partisan committees of the Senate are listed on page 941. The area code for all phone and fax numbers is (202).

AGRICULTURE, NUTRITION, AND FORESTRY

Office: 328A SROB 20510-6000
Phone: 224-2035   **Fax:** 228-2125
Web: www.agriculture.senate.gov
Minority Web: www.agriculture.senate.gov/newsroom/
  minority-news
Majority Staff Director: Joe Shultz
Minority Staff Director: Fitzhugh Elder IV
Jurisdiction: (1) agricultural economics and research; (2) agricultural extension services and experiment stations; (3) agricultural production, marketing, and stabilization of prices; (4) agriculture and agricultural commodities; (5) animal industry and diseases; (6) crop insurance and soil conservation; (7) farm credit and farm security; (8) food from fresh waters; (9) food stamp programs; (10) forestry and forest reserves and wilderness areas other than those created from the public domain; (11) home economics; (12) human nutrition; (13) inspection of livestock, meat, and agricultural products; (14) pests and pesticides; (15) plant industry, soils, and agricultural engineering; (16) rural development, rural electrification, and watersheds; (17) school nutrition programs. The committee shall also study and review, on a comprehensive basis, matters relating to food, nutrition, and hunger, both in the United States and in foreign countries, and rural affairs, and report thereon from time to time.
Party Ratio: D 11-R 11

Debbie Stabenow, Mich.	*John Boozman, Ark.*
Patrick J. Leahy, Vt.	*Mitch McConnell, Ky.*
Sherrod Brown, Ohio	*John Hoeven, N.D.*
Amy Klobuchar, Minn.	*Joni Ernst, Iowa*
Michael F. Bennet, Colo.	*Cindy Hyde-Smith, Miss.*
Kirsten E. Gillibrand, N.Y.	*Roger Marshall. Kans.*
Tina Smith, Minn.	*Tommy Tuberville, Ala.*
Richard J. Durbin, Ill.	*Chuck Grassley, Iowa*
Cory A. Booker, N.J.	*John Thune, S.D.*
Ben Ray Luján, N.M.	*Deb Fischer, Neb.*
Raphael Warnock, Ga.	*Mike Braun, Ind.*

Subcommittees

Commodities, Risk Management, and Trade
Office: 328A SROB 20510   **Phone:** 224-2035
   Raphael Warnock (Chair), Sherrod Brown, Richard J. Durbin, Tina Smith, Kirsten E. Gillibrand, Ben Ray Luján
   John Hoeven (Ranking Minority Member), Mitch McConnell, Cindy Hyde-Smith, Tommy Tuberville, Chuck Grassley, John Thune

Conservation, Climate, Forestry, and Natural Resources
Office: 328A SROB 20510   **Phone:** 224-2035
   Michael F. Bennet (Chair), Patrick J. Leahy, Cory A. Booker, Ben Ray Luján, Sherrod Brown, Amy Klobuchar
   Roger Marshall (Ranking Minority Member), John Hoeven, Cindy Hyde-Smith, Tommy Tuberville, John Thune, Mike Braun

Food and Nutrition, Specialty Crops, Organics, and Research
Office: 328A SROB 20510   **Phone:** 224-2035
   Cory A. Booker (Chair), Patrick J. Leahy, Amy Klobuchar, Kirsten E. Gillibrand, Raphael Warnock, Michael F. Bennet
   Mike Braun (Ranking Minority Member), Mitch McConnell, John Hoeven, Joni Ernst, Roger Marshall, Deb Fischer

Livestock, Dairy, Poultry, Local Food Systems, and Food Safety
Office: 328A SROB 20510   **Phone:** 224-2035
   Kirsten E. Gillibrand (Chair), Patrick J. Leahy, Tina Smith, Richard J. Durbin, Cory A. Booker, Raphael Warnock
   Cindy Hyde-Smith (Ranking Minority Member), Joni Ernst, Roger Marshall, Chuck Grassley, Deb Fischer, John Thune

Rural Development and Energy
Office: 328A SROB 20510 **Phone:** 224-2035
Tina Smith (Chair), Amy Klobuchar, Ben Ray Luján, Sherrod Brown, Michael F. Bennet, Richard Durbin
Joni Ernst (Ranking Minority Member), Mitch McConnell, Tommy Tuberville, Chuck Grassley, Deb Fischer, Mike Braun

APPROPRIATIONS

Office: S-128 CAP 20510-6025
Phone: 224-7363 **Fax:** 224-2100
Web: www.appropriations.senate.gov
Minority Web: www.appropriations.senate.gov/news/ minority
Majority Staff Director: Charles Kieffer
Minority Staff Director: William D. Duhnke III
Jurisdiction: (1) appropriation of the revenue for the support of the government, except as provided in subparagraph (e); (2) rescission of appropriations contained in appropriation Acts (referred to in section 105 of title 1, United States Code); (3) the amount of new spending authority described in section 401(c)(2) (A) and (B) of the Congressional Budget and Impoundment Control Act of 1974 that is to be effective for a fiscal year; (4) new spending authority described in section 401(c)(2) (C) of the Congressional Budget and Impoundment Control Act of 1974 provided in bills and resolutions referred to the committee under section 401(b)(2) of that act.
Party Ratio: D 15-R 15

Patrick J. Leahy, Vt., Chair	*Richard Shelby, Ala.*
Patty Murray, Wash.	*Mitch McConnell, Ky.*
Dianne Feinstein, Calif.	*Susan M. Collins, Maine*
Richard J. Durbin, Ill.	*Lisa Murkowski, Alaska*
Jack Reed, R.I.	*Lindsey Graham, S.C.*
Jon Tester, Mont.	*Roy Blunt, Mo.*
Jeanne Shaheen, N.H.	*Jerry Moran, Kans.*
Jeff Merkley, Ore.	*John Hoeven, N.D.*
Christopher Coons, Del.	*John Boozman, Ark.*
Brian Schatz, Hawaii	*Shelley Moore Capito, W.Va.*
Tammy Baldwin, Wisc.	*John Kennedy, La.*
Chris Murphy, Conn.	*Cindy Hyde-Smith, Miss.*
Joe Manchin III, W.Va.	*Mike Braun, Ind.*
Chris Van Hollen, Md.	*Bill Hagerty, Tenn.*
Martin Heinrich, N.M.	*Marco Rubio, Fla.*

Subcommittees

Agriculture, Rural Development, Food and Drug Administration, and Related Agencies
Office: S-128 CAP 20510 **Phone:** 224-7363
Tammy Baldwin (Chair), Jeff Merkley, Dianne Feinstein, John Tester, Patrick J. Leahy, Brian Schatz, Martin Heinrich
John Hoeven (Ranking Minority Member), Mitch McConnell, Susan M. Collins, Roy Blunt, Jerry Moran, Cindy Hyde-Smith, Mike Braun

Commerce, Justice, Science, and Related Agencies
Office: S-128 CAP 20510 **Phone:** 224-7363

Jeanne Shaheen (Chair), Patrick J. Leahy, Dianne Feinstein, Jack Reed, Christopher Coons, Brian Schatz, Joe Manchin III, Chris Van Hollen, Jeff Merkley
Jerry Moran (Ranking Minority Member), Lisa Murkowski, Susan M. Collins, Lindsey Graham, John Boozman, Shelley Moore Capito, John Kennedy, Bill Hagerty, Mike Braun

Defense
Office: S-128 CAP 20510 **Phone:** 224-7363
John Tester (Chair), Richard Durbin, Patrick J. Leahy, Dianne Feinstein, Patty Murray, Jack Reed, Brian Schatz, Tammy Baldwin, Jeanne Shaheen
Richard Shelby (Ranking Minority Member), Mitch McConnell, Susan M. Collins, Lisa Murkowski, Lindsey Graham, Roy Blunt, Jerry Moran, John Hoeven, John Boozman

Energy and Water Development
Office: S-128 CAP 20510 **Phone:** 224-7363
Dianne Feinstein (Chair), Patty Murray, Jon Tester, Richard J. Durbin, Jeanne Shaheen, Jeff Merkley, Christopher Coons, Tammy Baldwin, Martin Heinrich
John Kennedy (Ranking Minority Member), Mitch McConnell, Richard Shelby, Susan M. Collins, Lisa Murkowski, Lindsey Graham, John Hoeven, Cindy Hyde-Smith, Bill Hagerty

Financial Services and General Government
Office: S-128 CAP 20510 **Phone:** 224-7363
Chris Van Hollen (Chair), Christopher Coons, Richard J. Durbin, Joe Manchin III
Cindy Hyde-Smith (Ranking Minority Member), Jerry Moran, John Boozman, John Kennedy

Homeland Security
Office: S-128 CAP 20510 **Phone:** 224-7363
Chris Murphy (Chair), John Tester, Jeanne Shaheen, Patrick J. Leahy, Patty Murray, Tammy Baldwin
Shelley Moore Capito (Ranking Minority Member), Richard Shelby, Lisa Murkowski, John Hoeven, John Kennedy, Cindy Hyde-Smith

Interior, Environment, and Related Agencies
Office: S-128 CAP 20510 **Phone:** 224-7363
Jeff Merkley (Chair), Dianne Feinstein, Patrick J. Leahy, Jack Reed, Jon Tester, Chris Van Hollen, Martin Heinrich
Lisa Murkowski (Ranking Minority Member), Roy Blunt, Mitch McConnell, Shelley Moore Capito, Cindy Hyde-Smith, Bill Hagerty, Marco Rubio

Labor, Health and Human Services, Education, and Related Agencies
Office: S-128 CAP 20510 **Phone:** 224-7363
Patty Murray (Chair), Richard J. Durbin, Jack Reed, Jeanne Shaheen, Jeff Merkley, Brian Schatz, Tammy Baldwin, Chris Murphy, Joe Manchin III
Roy Blunt (Ranking Minority Member), Richard Shelby, Lindsey Graham, Jerry Moran, Shelley Moore Capito, John Kennedy, Cindy Hyde-Smith, Mike Braun, Marco Rubio

Legislative Branch
Office: S-128 CAP 20510 **Phone:** 224-7363

APPROPRIATIONS (continued)

Jack Reed (Chair), Chris Murphy, Martin Heinrich
*Mike Braun (Ranking Minority Member), Richard
Shelby, Marco Rubio*

Military Construction, Veterans Affairs, and Related Agencies
Office: S-128 CAP 20510 **Phone:** 224-7363
Martin Heinrich (Chair), Brian Schatz, Jon Tester,
Patty Murray, Jack Reed, Tammy Baldwin, Christopher
Coons, Joe Manchin III
*John Boozman (Ranking Minority Member),
Mitch McConnell, Lisa Murkowski, John Hoeven, Susan M.
Collins, Shelley Moore Capito, Marco Rubio, Bill Hagerty*

State, Foreign Operations, and Related Programs
Office: S-128 CAP 20510 **Phone:** 224-7363
Christopher Coons (Chair), Patrick J. Leahy, Richard J.
Durbin, Jeanne Shaheen, Jeff Merkley, Chris Murphy,
Chris Van Hollen
*Lindsey Graham (Ranking Minority Member), Mitch
McConnell, Roy Blunt, John Boozman, Jerry Moran, Marco
Rubio, Bill Hagerty*

Transportation, Housing and Urban Development, and Related Agencies
Office: S-128 CAP 20510 **Phone:** 224-7363
Brian Schatz (Chair), Jack Reed, Patty Murray, Richard
J. Durbin, Dianne Feinstein, Christopher Coons, Chris
Murphy, Joe Manchin III, Chris Van Hollen
*Susan M. Collins (Ranking Minority Member),
Richard Shelby, Roy Blunt, John Boozman, Shelley Moore
Capito, Lindsey Graham, John Hoeven, John Kennedy,
Mike Braun*

ARMED SERVICES

Office: 228 SROB 20510-6050
Phone: 224-3871 **Fax:** 228-0037
Web: www.armed-services.senate.gov
Majority Staff Director: Elizabeth L. King
Minority Staff Director: John Wason
Jurisdiction: (1) aeronautical and space activities peculiar
to or primarily associated with the development of weapons systems or military operations; (2) common defense;
(3) Department of Defense, the Department of the Army,
the Department of the Navy, and the Department of the
Air Force, generally; (4) maintenance and operation of
the Panama Canal, including administration, sanitation,
and government of the Canal Zone; (5) military research
and development; (6) national security aspects of nuclear
energy; (7) naval petroleum reserves, except those in
Alaska; (8) pay, promotion, retirement, and other benefits
and privileges of members of the Armed Forces, including
overseas education of civilian and military dependents;
(9) selective service system; (10) strategic and critical materials necessary for the common defense. The committee
shall also study and review, on a comprehensive basis, matters relating to the common defense policy of the United
States.
Party Ratio: D 13-R 13

Jack Reed, R.I., Chair	*James M. Inhofe, Okla.*
Jeanne Shaheen, N.H.	*Roger F. Wicker, Miss.*
Kirsten E. Gillibrand, N.Y.	*Deb Fischer, Neb.*
Richard Blumenthal, Conn.	*Tom Cotton, Ark.*
Mazie K. Hirono, Hawaii	*Mike Rounds, S.D.*
Tim Kaine, Va.	*Joni Ernst, Iowa*
Angus S. King Jr., Maine (I)	*Thom Tillis, N.C.*
Elizabeth Warren, Mass.	*Dan Sullivan, Alaska*
Gary C. Peters, Mich.	*Kevin Cramer, N.D.*
Joe Manchin III, W.Va.	*Rick Scott, Fla.*
Tammy Duckworth, Ill.	*Marsha Blackburn, Tenn.*
Jacky Rosen, Nev.	*Josh Hawley, Mo.*
Mark Kelly, Ariz.	*Tommy Tuberville, Ala.*

Subcommittees

Airland
Office: 228 SROB 20510 **Phone:** 224-3871
Tammy Duckworth (Chair), Angus S. King Jr., Gary C.
Peters, Joe Manchin III, Jacky Rosen, Mark Kelly, Jack
Reed (ex officio)
*Tom Cotton (Ranking Minority Member), Roger F.
Wicker, Thom Tillis, Dan Sullivan, Rick Scott, Josh Hawley,
James M. Inhofe (ex officio)*

Cybersecurity
Office: 228 SROB 20510 **Phone:** 224-3871
Joe Manchin III (Chair), Kristen E. Gillibrand, Richard
Blumenthal, Jacky Rosen, Jack Reed (ex officio)
*Mike Rounds (Ranking Minority Member), Roger F.
Wicker, Joni Ernst, Marsha Blackburn, James M. Inhofe
(ex officio)*

Emerging Threats and Capabilities
Office: 228 SROB 20510 **Phone:** 224-3871
Mark Kelly (Chair), Jeanne Shaheen, Kirsten E.
Gillibrand, Tim Kaine, Elizabeth Warren, Gary C. Peters,
Jack Reed (ex officio)
*Joni Ernst (Ranking Minority Member), Deb Fischer,
Kevin Cramer, Rick Scott, Marsha Blackburn, Tommy
Tuberville, James M. Inhofe (ex officio)*

Personnel
Office: 228 SROB 20510 **Phone:** 224-3871
Kirsten E. Gillibrand (Chair), Mazie K. Hirono,
Elizabeth Warren, Jack Reed (ex officio)
*Thom Tillis (Ranking Minority Member), Josh Hawley,
Tommy Tuberville, James M. Inhofe (ex officio)*

Readiness and Management Support
Office: 228 SROB 20510 **Phone:** 224-3871
Tim Kaine (Chair), Jeanne Shaheen, Richard
Blumenthal, Mazie K. Hirono, Tammy Duckworth, Jack
Reed (ex officio)
*Dan Sullivan (Ranking Minority Member), Deb Fischer,
Mike Rounds, Joni Ernst, Marsha Blackburn, James M.
Inhofe (ex officio)*

SeaPower
Office: 228 SROB 20510 **Phone:** 224-3871
Mazie K. Hirono (Chair), Jeanne Shaheen, Richard
Blumenthal, Tim Kaine, Angus S. King Jr., Gary C. Peters,
Jack Reed (ex officio)

Kevin Cramer (Ranking Minority Member), Roger F. Wicker, Tom Cotton, Thom Tillis, Rick Scott, Josh Hawley, James M. Inhofe (ex officio)

Strategic Forces
Office: 228 SROB 20510   **Phone:** 224-3871
Angus S. King Jr. (Chair), Elizabeth Warren, Joe Manchin III, Tammy Duckworth, Jack Rosen, Mark Kelly, Jack Reed (ex officio)
Deb Fischer (Ranking Minority Member), Tom Cotton, Mike Rounds, Dan Sullivan, Kevin Cramer, Tommy Tuberville, James M. Inhofe (ex officio)

BANKING, HOUSING, AND URBAN AFFAIRS

Office: 534 SDOB 20510-6075
Phone: 224-7391   **Fax:** 224-5137
Web: www.banking.senate.gov
Minority Web: www.banking.senate.gov/newsroom/ minority-press-releases
Majority Staff Director: Laura Swanson
Minority Staff Director: Brad Grantz
Jurisdiction: (1) banks, banking, and financial institutions; (2) control of prices of commodities, rents, and services; (3) deposit insurance; (4) economic stabilization and defense production; (5) export and foreign trade promotion; (6) export controls; (7) federal monetary policy, including Federal Reserve System; (8) financial aid to commerce and industry; (9) issuance and redemption of notes; (10) money and credit, including currency and coinage; (11) nursing home construction; (12) public and private housing (including veterans' housing) (13) renegotiation of government contracts; (14) urban development and urban mass transit. The committee shall also study and review, on a comprehensive basis, matters relating to international economic policy as it affects U.S. monetary affairs, credit, and financial institutions; economic growth, urban affairs, and credit, and report thereon from time to time.
Party Ratio: D 12-R 12

Sherrod Brown, Ohio, Chair	Patrick J. Toomey, Pa.
Jack Reed, R.I.	Richard C. Shelby, Ala.
Robert Menendez, N.J.	Mark Crapo, Idaho
Jon Tester, Mont.	Tim Scott, S.C.
Mark R. Warner, Va.	Mike Rounds, S.D.
Elizabeth Warren, Mass.	Thom Tillis, N.C.
Chris Van Hollen, Md.	John Kennedy, La.
Catherine Cortez Masto, Nev.	Bill Hagerty, Tenn.
Tina Smith, Minn.	Cynthia M. Lummis, Wyo.
Kyrsten Sinema, Ariz.	Jerry Moran, Kans.
Jon Ossoff, Ga.	Kevin Cramer, N.D.
Raphael Warnock, Ga.	Steve Daines, Mont.

Subcommittees

Economic Policy
Office: 534 SDOB 20510   **Phone:** 224-7391
Elizabeth Warren (Chair), Jack Reed, Tina Smith, Chris Van Hollen, Jon Ossoff

John Kennedy (Ranking Minority Member), Tom Scott, Kevin Cramer, Thom Tillis, Steve Daines

Financial Institutions and Consumer Protection
Office: 534 SDOB 20510   **Phone:** 224-7391
Raphael Warnock (Chair), Robert Menendez, Catherine Cortez Masto, Jon Tester, Chris Van Hollen, Mark R. Warner, Kyrsten Sinema, Elizabeth Warren,
Thom Tillis (Ranking Minority Member), Richard C. Shelby, Cynthia M. Lummis, Tim Scott, Jerry Moran, Mike Rounds, Kevin Cramer, Bill Hagerty

Housing, Transportation, and Community Development
Office: 534 SDOB 20510   **Phone:** 224-7391
Tina Smith (Chair), Jack Reed, Chris Van Hollen, Robert Menendez, Jon Ossoff, Jon Tester, Raphael Warnock, Catherine Cortez Masto
Mike Rounds (Ranking Minority Member), Richard C. Shelby, Jerry Moran, Mike Crapo, Kevin Cramer, Bill Hagerty, Steve Daines, Cynthia M. Lummis

National Security and International Trade and Finance
Office: 534 SDOB 20510   **Phone:** 224-7391
Mark R. Warner (Chair), Jon Tester, Jon Ossoff, Kyrsten Sinema
Bill Hagerty (Ranking Minority Member), Mike Crapo, Steve Daines, John Kennedy

Securities, Insurance, and Investment
Office: 534 SDOB 20510   **Phone:** 224-7391
Robert Menendez (Chair), Jack Reed, Tina Smith, Mark R. Warner, Kyrsten Sinema, Elizabeth Warren, Raphael Warnock, Catherine Cortez Masto
Tim Scott (Ranking Minority Member), Richard C. Shelby, John Kennedy, Mike Crapo, Cynthia M. Lummis, Mike Rounds, Jerry Moran, Thom Tillis

BUDGET

Office: 624 SDOB 20510-6100
Phone: 224-0642   **Fax:** 228-2007
Web: www.budget.senate.gov
Minority Web: www.budget.senate.gov/ranking-member/ newsroom
Majority Staff Director: Warren Gunnels
Minority Staff Director: Nick Meyers
Jurisdiction: (1) all concurrent resolutions on the budget (as defined in Section 3 (a) (4) of the Congressional Budget Act of 1974) and all other matters required to be referred to that committee under Titles III and IV of that act, and messages, petitions, memorials, and other matters relating thereto. (2) The committee shall have the duty (A) to report the matters required to be reported by it under Titles III and IV of the Congressional Budget and Impoundment Control Act of 1974; (B) to make continuing studies of the effect on budget outlays of relevant existing and proposed legislation and to report the results of such studies to the Senate on a recurring basis; (C) to request and evaluate continuing studies of tax expenditures, to devise methods of coordinating tax expenditures, policies, and programs

BUDGET (continued)

with direct budget outlays, and to report the results of such studies to the Senate on a recurring basis; and (D) to review, on a continuing basis, the conduct by the Congressional Budget Office of its functions and duties.

Party Ratio: D 11-R 11

Bernard Sanders, Vt. (I), Chair
Patty Murray, Wash.
Ron Wyden, Ore.
Debbie Stabenow, Mich.
Sheldon Whitehouse, R.I.
Mark R. Warner, Va.
Jeff Merkley, Ore.
Tim Kaine, Va.
Chris Van Hollen, Md.
Ben Ray Luján, N.M.
Alex Padilla, Calif.

Lindsey Graham, S.C.
Chuck Grassley, Iowa
Mike Crapo, Idaho
Patrick J. Toomey, Pa.
Ron Johnson, Wisc.
Mike Braun, Ind.
Rick Scott, Fla.
Ben Sasse, Neb.
Mitt Romney, Utah
John Kennedy, La.
Kevin Cramer, N.D.

COMMERCE, SCIENCE, AND TRANSPORTATION

Office: 254 SROB 20510-6125
Phone: 224-0411   **Fax:** 228-0327
Web: www.commerce.senate.gov
Minority Web: www.commerce.senate.gov/minority
Majority Staff Director: Lila Helms
Minority Staff Director: John Keast
Jurisdiction: (1) Coast Guard; (2) coastal zone management; (3) communications; (4) highway safety; (5) inland waterways, except construction; (6) interstate commerce; (7) marine and ocean navigation, safety, and transportation, including navigational aspects of deepwater ports; (8) marine fisheries; (9) merchant marine and navigation; (10) nonmilitary aeronautical and space sciences; (11) oceans, weather, and atmospheric activities; (12) Panama Canal and interoceanic canals generally, except as provided in subparagraph (c); (13) regulation of consumer products and services, including testing related to toxic substances, other than pesticides, and except for credit, financial services, and housing; (14) regulation of interstate common carriers, including railroads, buses, trucks, vessels, pipelines, and civil aviation; (15) science, engineering, and technology research, development, and policy; (16) sports; (17) standards and measurement; (18) transportation; (19) transportation and commerce aspects of Outer Continental Shelf lands. The committee shall also study and review, on a comprehensive basis, all matters relating to science and technology, oceans policy, transportation, communications, and consumer affairs, and report thereon from time to time.

Party Ratio: D 14-R 14

Maria Cantwell, Wash., Chair
Amy Klobuchar, Minn.
Richard Blumenthal, Conn.
Brian Schatz, Hawaii
Edward J. Markey, Mass.

Roger F. Wicker, Miss.
John Thune, S.D.
Roy Blunt, Mo.
Ted Cruz, Tex.
Deb Fischer, Neb.
Jerry Moran, Kans.

Gary C. Peters, Mich.
Tammy Baldwin, Wisc.
Tammy Duckworth, Ill.
Jon Tester, Mont.
Kyrsten Sinema, Ariz.
Jacky Rosen, Nev.
Ben Ray Luján, N.M.
John W. Hickenlooper, Colo.
Raphael Warnock, Ga.

Dan Sullivan, Alaska
Marsha Blackburn, Tenn.
Todd Young, Ind.
Mike Lee, Utah
Ron Johnson, Wisc.
Shelley Moore Capito, W.Va.
Rick Scott, Fla.
Cynthia M. Lummis, Wyo.

Subcommittees

Aviation Safety, Operations, and Innovation
Office: 512 SDOB 20510   **Phone:** 224-0411
Kyrsten Sinema (Chair), Tammy Duckworth, Jon Tester, Jacky Rosen, John W. Hickenlooper, Raphael Warnock
Ted Cruz (Ranking Minority Member), John Thune, Roy Blunt, Jerry Moran, Mike Lee, Shelley Moore Capito

Communications, Media, and Broadband
Office: 512 SDOB 20510   **Phone:** 224-0411
Ben Ray Luján (Chair), Amy Klobuchar, Richard Blumenthal, Brian Schatz, Edward J. Markey, Gary C. Peters, Tammy Baldwin, Tammy Duckworth, Jon Tester, Kyrsten Sinema, Jacky Rosen, John W. Hickenlooper, Raphael Warnock
John Thune (Ranking Minority Member), Roy Blunt, Ted Cruz, Deb Fischer, Jerry Moran, Dan Sullivan, Marsha Blackburn, Todd Young, Mike Lee, Ron Johnson, Shelley Moore Capito, Rick Scott, Cynthia M. Lummis

Consumer Protection, Product Safety, and Data Security
Office: 512 SDOB 20510   **Phone:** 224-0411
Richard Blumenthal (Chair), Amy Klobuchar, Brian Schatz, Edward J. Markey, Tammy Baldwin, Ben Ray Luján
Marsha Blackburn (Ranking Minority Member), John Thune, Roy Blunt, Jerry Moran, Todd Young, Mike Lee

Oceans, Fisheries, Climate Change and Manufacturing
Office: 512 SDOB 20510   **Phone:** 224-0411
Tammy Baldwin (Chair), Richard Blumenthal, Brian Schatz, Edward J. Markey, Gary C. Peters, Ben Ray Luján
Dan Sullivan (Ranking Minority Member), Ted Cruz, Deb Fischer, Marsha Blackburn, Todd Young, Ron Johnson

Space and Science
Office: 512 SDOB 20510   **Phone:** 224-0411
John W. Hickenlooper (Chair), Richard Blumenthal, Edward J. Markey, Gary C. Peters, Kyrsten Sinema, Ben Ray Luján, Raphael Warnock
Cynthia M. Lummis (Ranking Minority Member), Ted Cruz, Deb Fischer, Jerry Moran, Todd Young, Mike Lee, Rick Scott

Surface Transportation, Maritime, Freight, and Ports
Office: 512 SDOB 20510   **Phone:** 224-0411
Gary C. Peters (Chair), Amy Klobuchar, Richard Blumenthal, Brian Schatz, Edward J. Markey, Tammy Baldwin, Tammy Duckworth, Jon Tester, Raphael Warnock

Deb Fischer (Ranking Minority Member), John Thune, Roy Blunt, Dan Sullivan, Todd Young, Ron Johnson, Shelley Moore Capito, Rick Scott, Cynthia M. Lummis

Tourism, Trade, and Export Promotion
Office: 512 SDOB 20510 **Phone:** 224-0411

Jacky Rosen (Chair), Amy Klobuchar, Tammy Duckworth, Jon Tester, Kyrsten Sinema, Raphael Warnock

Rick Scott (Ranking Minority Member), Dan Sullivan, Marsha Blackburn, Ron Johnson, Shelley Moore Capito, Cynthia M. Lummis

ENERGY AND NATURAL RESOURCES

Office: 304 SDOB 20510-6150
Phone: 224-4971 **Fax:** 224-6163
Web: www.energy.senate.gov
Minority Web: www.energy.senate.gov/republican-news
Majority Staff Director: Renae Black
Minority Staff Director: Richard M. Russel
Jurisdiction: (1) coal production, distribution, and utilization; (2) energy policy; (3) energy regulation and energy conservation; (4) energy-related aspects of deepwater ports; (5) energy research and development; (6) extraction of minerals from oceans and Outer Continental Shelf lands; (7) hydroelectric power, irrigation, and reclamation; (8) mining education and research; (9) mining, mineral lands, mining claims, and mineral conservation; (10) national parks, recreation areas, wilderness areas, wild and scenic rivers, historic sites, military parks and battlefields, and on the public domain, preservation of prehistoric ruins and objects of interest; (11) naval petroleum reserves in Alaska; (12) nonmilitary development of nuclear energy; (13) oil and gas production and distribution; (14) public lands and forests, including farming and grazing thereon, and mineral extraction therefrom; (15) solar energy systems; (16) territorial possessions of the United States, including trusteeships; international energy affairs and emergency preparedness; nuclear waste policy; privatization of federal assets; Trans-Alaska Pipeline System and other oil or gas pipeline transportation systems within Alaska; Alaska Native Claims Settlement Act of 1971; Alaska National Interest Lands Conservation Act of 1980; Antarctic research and energy development; Arctic research and energy development; Native Hawaiian matters. The Committee shall also study and review, on a comprehensive basis, matters relating to energy and resources development.
Party Ratio: D 10-R 10

Joe Manchin III, W.Va.	*John Barrasso, Wyo.*
Ron Wyden, Ore.	*James E. Risch, Idaho*
Maria Cantwell, Wash.	*Mike Lee, Utah*
Bernard Sanders, Vt. (I)	*Steve Daines, Mont.*
Martin Heinrich, N.M.	*Lisa Murkowski, Alaska*
Mazie K. Hirono, Hawaii	*John Hoeven, N.D.*
Angus S. King Jr., Maine (I)	*James Lankford, Okla.*
Catherine Cortez Masto, Nev.	*Bill Cassidy, La.*
Mark Kelly, Ariz.	*Cindy Hyde-Smith, Miss.*
John W. Hickenlooper, Colo.	*Roger Marshall, Kans.*

Subcommittees

Energy
Office: 304 SDOB 20510 **Phone:** 224-4971

Mazie K. Hirono (Chair), Ron Wyden, Bernard Sanders, Martin Heinrich, Angus S. King Jr., Catherine Cortez Masto, John W. Hickenlooper, Joe Manchin III (ex officio)

John Hoeven (Ranking Minority Member), James E. Risch, Lisa Murkowski, James Lankford, Bill Cassidy, Cindy Hyde-Smith, Roger Marshall, John Barrasso (ex officio)

National Parks
Office: 304 SDOB 20510 **Phone:** 224-4971

Angus S. King Jr. (Chair), Bernard Sanders, Martin Heinrich, Mazie K. Hirono, Mark Kelly, Joe Manchin III (ex officio)

Steve Daines (Ranking Minority Member), Mike Lee, Lisa Murkowski, John Hoeven, James Lankford, John Barrasso (ex officio)

Public Lands, Forests, and Mining
Office: 304 SDOB 20510 **Phone:** 224-4971

Catherine Cortez Masto (Chair), Ron Wyden, Martin Heinrich, Mazie K. Hirono, Angus S. King Jr., Mark Kelly, John W. Hickenlooper, Joe Manchin III (ex officio)

Mike Lee (Ranking Minority Member), James E. Risch, Steve Daines, Lisa Murkowski, James Lankford, Bill Cassidy, Cindy Hyde-Smith, John Barrasso (ex officio)

Water and Power
Office: 304 SDOB 20510 **Phone:** 224-4971

Ron Wyden (Chair), Bernard Sanders, Catherine Cortez Masto, Mark Kelly, John W. Hickenlooper, Joe Manchin III (ex officio)

Cindy Hyde-Smith (Ranking Minority Member), James E. Risch, Mike Lee, John Hoeven, Roger Marshall, John Barrasso (ex officio)

ENVIRONMENT AND PUBLIC WORKS

Office: 410 SDOB 20510-6175
Phone: 224-8832 **Fax:** 224-5167
Web: www.epw.senate.gov
Minority Web: www.epw.senate.gov/public/index.cfm/minority
Majority Staff Director: Mary Frances Repko
Minority Staff Director: Richard Russell; 456 SDOB; 224-6176
Jurisdiction: (1) air pollution; (2) construction and maintenance of highways; (3) environmental aspects of Outer Continental Shelf lands; (4) environmental effects of toxic substances, other than pesticides; (5) environmental policy; (6) environmental research and development; (7) fisheries and wildlife; (8) flood control and improvements of rivers and harbors, including environmental aspects of deepwater ports; (9) noise pollution; (10) nonmilitary environmental regulation and control of nuclear energy; (11) ocean dumping; (12) public buildings and improved grounds of the United States generally, including federal buildings in the District of Columbia; (13) public works, bridges, and dams; (14) regional economic development; (15) solid waste disposal and recycling; (16) water

ENVIRONMENT AND PUBLIC
WORKS (continued)

pollution; (17) water resources. The committee shall also study and review, on a comprehensive basis, matters relating to environmental protection and resource utilization and conservation. The committee shall also study and review, on a comprehensive basis, matters relating to environmental protection and resource utilization and conservation, and report thereon from time to time.

Party Ratio: D 10-R 10

Thomas R. Carper, Del., Chair	Shelley Moore Capito, W.Va.
Benjamin L. Cardin, Md.	James M. Inhofe, Okla.
Bernard Sanders, Vt. (I)	Kevin Cramer, N.D.
Sheldon Whitehouse, R.I.	Cynthia M. Lummis, Wyo.
Jeff Merkley, Ore.	Richard Shelby, Ala.
Edward J. Markey, Mass.	John Boozman, Ark.
Tammy Duckworth, Ill.	Roger F. Wicker, Miss.
Debbie Stabenow, Mich.	Dan Sullivan, Alaska
Mark Kelly, Ariz.	Joni Ernst, Iowa
Alex Padilla, Calif.	Lindsey Graham, S.C.

Subcommittees

Chemical Safety, Waste Management, Environmental Justice, and Regulatory Oversight
Office: 410 SDOB 20510   **Phone:** 224-8832
Jeff Merkley (Chair), Bernard Sanders, Edward J. Markey, Mark Kelly, Alex Padilla, Thomas R. Carper (ex officio)
Roger F. Wicker (Ranking Minority Member), Richard Shelby, Dan Sullivan, Joni Ernst, Lindsey Graham, Shelley Moore Capito (ex officio)

Clean Air, Climate, and Nuclear Safety
Office: 410 SDOB 20510   **Phone:** 224-8832
Edward J. Markey (Chair), Benjamin L. Cardin, Bernard Sanders, Sheldon Whitehouse, Jeff Merkley, Tammy Duckworth, Debbie Stabenow, Alex Padilla, Thomas R. Carper (ex officio)
James M. Inhofe (Ranking Minority Member), Kevin Cramer, Cynthia M. Lummis, Richard Shelby, John Boozman, Roger F. Wicker, Joni Ernst, Lindsey Graham, Shelley Moore Capito (ex officio)

Fisheries, Water, and Wildlife
Office: 410 SDOB 20510   **Phone:** 224-8832
Tammy Duckworth (Chair), Benjamin L. Cardin, Sheldon Whitehouse, Edward J. Markey, Debbie Stabenow, Mark Kelly, Thomas R. Carper (ex officio)
Cynthia M. Lummis (Ranking Minority Member), James M. Inhofe, Kevin Cramer, John Boozman, Dan Sullivan, Joni Ernst, Shelley Moore Capito (ex officio)

Transportation and Infrastructure
Office: 410 SDOB 20510   **Phone:** 224-8832
Benjamin L. Cardin (Chair), Bernard Sanders, Sheldon Whitehouse, Jeff Merkley, Tammy Duckworth, Debbie Stabenow, Mark Kelly, Alex Padilla, Thomas R. Carper (ex officio)

Kevin Cramer (Ranking Minority Member), James M. Inhofe, Cynthia M. Lummis, Richard Shelby, John Boozman, Roger F. Wicker, Dan Sullivan, Lindsey Graham, Shelley Moore Capito (ex officio)

FINANCE

Office: 219 SDOB 20510-6200
Phone: 224-4515 **Fax:** 228-0554
Web: www.finance.senate.gov
Minority Web: www.finance.senate.gov/ranking-members-news
Majority Staff Director: Joshua Sheinkman
Minority Staff Director: Gregg Richard
Jurisdiction: (1) bonded debt of the United States, except as provided in the Congressional Budget Act of 1974; (2) customs, collection districts, and ports of entry and delivery; (3) deposit of public moneys; (4) general revenue sharing; (5) health programs under the Social Security Act and health programs financed by a specific tax or trust fund; (6) national social security; (7) reciprocal trade agreements; (8) revenue measures generally, except as provided in the Congressional Budget Act of 1974; (9) revenue measures relating to the insular possessions; (10) tariffs and import quotas, and matters related thereto; (11) transportation of dutiable goods.

Party Ratio: D 14-R 14

Ron Wyden, Ore., Chair	Mike Crapo, Idaho
Debbie Stabenow, Mich.	Chuck Grassley, Iowa
Maria Cantwell, Wash.	John Cornyn, Tex.
Robert Menendez, N.J.	John Thune, S.D.
Thomas R. Carper, Del.	Richard Burr, N.C.
Benjamin L. Cardin, Md.	Rob Portman, Ohio
Sherrod Brown, Ohio	Patrick J. Toomey, Pa.
Michael F. Bennet, Colo.	Tim Scott, S.C.
Robert P. Casey Jr., Pa.	Bill Cassidy, La.
Mark R. Warner, Va.	James Lankford, Okla.
Sheldon Whitehouse, R.I.	Steve Daines, Mont.
Margaret Wood Hassan, N.H.	Todd Young, Ind.
	Ben Sasse, Neb.
Catherine Cortez Masto, Nev.	John Barrasso, Wyo.
Elizabeth Warren, Mass.	

Subcommittees

Energy, Natural Resources, and Infrastructure
Office: 219 SDOB 20510   **Phone:** 224-4515
Michael F. Bennet (Chair), Thomas R. Carper, Mark R. Warner, Sheldon Whitehouse, Margaret Wood Hassan
James Lankford (Ranking Minority Member), John Cornyn, Tim Scott, John Barrasso, Steve Daines

Fiscal Responsibility and Economic Growth
Office: 219 SDOB 20510   **Phone:** 224-4515
Elizabeth Warren (Chair), Ron Wyden
Bill Cassidy (Ranking Minority Member), Richard Burr

Health Care
Office: 219 SDOB 20510   **Phone:** 224-4515

Debbie Stabenow (Chair), Robert Menendez, Thomas R. Carper, Benjamin L. Cardin, Robert P. Casey, Mark R. Warner, Sheldon Whitehouse, Catherine Cortez Masto, Margaret Wood Hassan, Elizabeth Warren

Steve Daines (Ranking Minority Member), Chuck Grassley, John Thune, Richard Burr, Patrick J. Toomey, Tim Scott, Bill Cassidy, James Lankford, Todd Young, John Barrasso

International Trade, Customs, and Global Competitiveness

Office: 219 SDOB 20510   **Phone:** 224-4515

Thomas R. Carper (Chair), Ron Wyden, Debbie Stabenow, Robert Menendez, Benjamin L. Cardin, Sherrod Brown, Michael F. Bennet, Robert P. Casey, Mark R. Warner, Catherine Cortez Masto

John Cornyn (Ranking Minority Member), Chuck Grassley, John Thune, Rob Portman, Patrick J. Toomey, Tim Scott, Steve Daines, Todd Young, Ben Sasse, John Barrasso

Social Security, Pensions, and Family Policy

Office: 219 SDOB 20510   **Phone:** 224-4515

Sherrod Brown (Chair), Ron Wyden, Michael F. Bennet, Robert P. Casey Jr., Margaret Wood Hassan

Todd Young (Ranking Minority Member), Rob Portman, Bill Cassidy, James Lankford, Ben Sasse

Taxation and IRS Oversight

Office: 219 SDOB 20510   **Phone:** 224-4515

Mark R. Warner (Chair), Robert Menendez, Thomas R. Carper, Benjamin L. Cardin, Michael F. Bennet, Sheldon Whitehouse

John Thune (Ranking Minority Member), Mike Crapo, John Cornyn, Richard Burr, Rob Portman, Patrick J. Toomey, James Lankford

FOREIGN RELATIONS

Office: 423 SDOB 20510-6225
Phone: 224-4651   **Fax:** 224-0836
Web: www.foreign.senate.gov
Minority Web: www.foreign.senate.gov/press/ranking
Majority Staff Director: Damian Murphy
Minority Staff Director: Chris Socha; Fax: 228-3612
Jurisdiction: (1) acquisition of land and buildings for embassies and legations in foreign countries; (2) boundaries of the United States; (3) diplomatic service; (4) foreign economic, military, technical, and humanitarian assistance; (5) foreign loans; (6) international activities of the American National Red Cross, and the International Committee of the Red Cross; (7) international aspects of nuclear energy, including nuclear transfer policy; (8) international conferences and congresses; (9) international law as it relates to foreign policy; (10) International Monetary Fund and other international organizations established primarily for international monetary purposes (except that, at the request of the Committee on Banking, Housing, and Urban Affairs, any proposed legislation relating to such subjects reported by the Committee on Foreign Relations shall be referred to the Committee on Banking, Housing, and Urban Affairs); (11) intervention abroad and declarations of war;

(12) measures to foster commercial intercourse with foreign nations and to safeguard U.S. business interests abroad; (13) national security and international aspects of trusteeships of the United States; (14) ocean and international environmental and scientific affairs as they relate to foreign policy; (15) protection of U.S. citizens abroad and expatriation; (16) relations of the United States with foreign nations generally; (17) treaties and executive agreements, except reciprocal trade agreements; (18) the United Nations and its affiliated organizations; (19) World Bank group, the regional development banks, and other international organizations established primarily for development assistance purposes. The committee shall also study and review, on a comprehensive basis, matters relating to national security policy, foreign policy, and international economic policy as they relate to the foreign policy of the United States, and matters relating to food, hunger, and nutrition in foreign countries.
Party Ratio: D 11-R 11

Robert Menendez, N.J., Chair	James E. Risch, Idaho
Benjamin L. Cardin, Md.	Marco Rubio, Fla.
Jeanne Shaheen, N.H.	Ron Johnson, Wisc.
Christopher Coons, Del.	Mitt Romney, Utah
Chris Murphy, Conn.	Rob Portman, Ohio
Tim Kaine, Va.	Rand Paul, Ky.
Edward J. Markey, Mass.	Todd Young, Ind.
Jeff Merkley, Ore.	John Barrasso, Wyo.
Cory A. Booker, N.J.	Ted Cruz, Tex.
Brian Schatz, Hawaii	Mike Rounds, S.D.
Chris Van Hollen, Md.	Bill Hagerty, Tenn.

Subcommittees

Africa and Global Health Policy

Office: 423 SDOB 20510   **Phone:** 224-4651

Chris Van Hollen (Chair), Cory A. Booker, Tim Kaine, Jeff Merkley, Christopher Coons

Mike Rounds (Ranking Minority Member), Marco Rubio, Todd Young, John Barrasso, Rand Paul

East Asia, the Pacific, and International Cybersecurity Policy

Office: 423 SDOB 20510   **Phone:** 224-4651

Edward J. Markey (Chair), Christopher Coons, Chris Murphy, Brian Schatz, Jeff Merkley

Mitt Romney (Ranking Minority Member), Ted Cruz, Ron Johnson, Mike Rounds, Bill Hagerty

Europe and Regional Security Cooperation

Office: 423 SDOB 20510   **Phone:** 224-4651

Jeanne Shaheen (Chair), Benjamin L. Cardin, Christopher Murphy, Chris Van Hollen, Christopher Coons

Ron Johnson (Ranking Minority Member), John Barrasso, Mitt Romney, Rob Portman, Todd Young

Multilateral International Development, Multilateral Institutions, and International Economic, Energy, and Environmental Policy

Office: 423 SDOB 20510   **Phone:** 224-4651

FOREIGN RELATIONS (continued)

Christopher Coons (Chair), Brian Schatz, Cory A. Booker, Benjamin L. Cardin, Jeanne Shaheen

Rob Portman (Ranking Minority Member), Todd Young, Rand Paul, John Barrasso, Mike Rounds

Near East, South Asia, Central Asia, and Counterterrorism

Office: 423 SDOB 20510 **Phone:** 224-4651

Christopher Murphy (Chair), Jeanne Shaheen, Edward J. Markey, Cory A. Booker, Chris Van Hollen

Todd Young (Ranking Minority Member), Rand Paul, Ted Cruz, Mitt Romney, Bill Hagerty

State Department and USAID Management, International Operations, and Bilateral International Development

Office: 423 SDOB 20510 **Phone:** 224-4651

Benjamin L. Cardin (Chair), Time Kaine, Brian Schatz, Chris Murphy, Edward J. Markey

Bill Hagerty (Ranking Minority Member), Rand Paul, Ted Cruz, Ron Johnson, Marco Rubio

Western Hemisphere, Transnational Crime, Civilian Security, Democracy, Human Rights, and Global Women's Issues

Office: 423 SDOB 20510 **Phone:** 224-4651

Tim Kaine (Chair), Jeff Merkley, Benjamin L. Cardin, Jeanne Shaheen, Edward J. Markey

Marco Rubio (Ranking Minority Member), Rob Portman, John Barrasso, Bill Hagerty, Ted Cruz

HEALTH, EDUCATION, LABOR, AND PENSIONS

Office: 428 SDOB 20510-6300
Phone: 224-5375 **Fax:** 228-5044
Web: www.help.senate.gov
Minority Web: www.help.senate.gov/ranking/newsroom
Majority Staff Director: Evan Schatz
Minority Staff Director: David Cleary
Jurisdiction: (1) measures relating to education, labor, health, and public welfare; (2) aging; (3) agricultural colleges; (4) arts and humanities; (5) biomedical research and development; (6) child labor; (7) convict labor and the entry of goods made by convicts into interstate commerce; (8) domestic activities of the American National Red Cross; (9) equal employment opportunity; (10) Gallaudet University (Washington, DC), Howard University (Washington, DC), and St. Elizabeth's Hospital (Washington, DC); (11) individuals with disabilities; (12) labor standards and labor statistics; (13) mediation and arbitration of labor disputes; (14) occupational safety and health, including the welfare of miners; (15) private pension plans; (16) public health; (17) railway labor and retirement; (18) regulation of foreign laborers; (19) student loans; (20) wages and hours of labor. The committee shall also study and review, on a comprehensive basis, matters relating to health, education and training, and public welfare, and report thereon from time to time.
Party Ratio: D 11-R 11

Patty Murray, Wash., Chair
Bernard Sanders, Vt. (I)
Robert P. Casey Jr., Pa.
Tammy Baldwin, Wisc.
Chris Murphy, Conn.
Tim Kaine, Va.
Margaret Wood Hassan, N.H.
Tina Smith. Minn.
Jacky Rosen, Nev.
Ben Ray Luján, N.M.
John W. Hickenlooper, Colo.

Richard Burr, NC.
Rand Paul, Ky.
Susan M. Collins, Maine
Bill Cassidy, La.
Lisa Murkowski, Alaska
Mike Braun, Ind.
Roger Marshall, Kans.
Tim Scott, S.C.
Mitt Romney, Utah
Tommy Tuberville, Ala.
Jerry Moran, Kans.

Subcommittees

Children and Families

Office: 428 SDOB 20510 **Phone:** 224-5375

Robert P. Casey Jr. (Chair), Bernard Sanders, Chris Murphy, Tim Kaine, Margaret Wood Hassan, Tina Smith, John W. Hickenlooper, Patty Murray

Bill Cassidy (Ranking Minority Member), Mitt Romney, Susan M. Collins, Lisa Murkowski, Jerry Moran, Roger Marshall, Tommy Tuberville, Richard Burr

Employment and Workplace Safety

Office: 428 SDOB 20510 **Phone:** 224-5375

John W. Hickenlooper (Chair), Tammy Baldwin, Tina Smith, Jacky Rosen, Ben Ray Luján, Patty Murray

Mike Braun (Ranking Minority Member), Tommy Tuberville, Rand Paul, Tim Scott, Mitt Romney, Richard Burr

Primary Health and Retirement Security

Office: 428 SDOB 20510 **Phone:** 224-5375

Bernard Sanders (Chair), Robert P. Casey Jr., Tammy Baldwin, Chris Murphy, Tim Kaine, Margaret Wood Hassan, Jacky Rosen, Ben Ray Luján, Patty Murray

Susan M. Collins (Ranking Minority Member), Rand Paul, Lisa Murkowski, Roger Marshall, Tim Scott, Jerry Moran, Bill Cassidy, Mike Braun, Richard Burr

HOMELAND SECURITY AND GOVERNMENTAL AFFAIRS

Office: 340 SDOB 20510-6250
Phone: 224-2627 **Fax:** 224-9603
Web: www.hsgac.senate.gov
Minority Web: www.hsgac.senate.gov/media/minority-media
Majority Staff Director: David Weinberg
Minority Staff Director: Pam Thiessen
Jurisdiction: (1) Department of Homeland Security, except matters relating to the Coast Guard, the Transportation Security Administration, the Federal Law Enforcement Training Center, or the Secret Service; and the U.S. Citizenship and Immigration Service; or the immigration functions of the U.S. Customs and Border Protection or the U.S. Immigration and Custom Enforcement or the Directorate of Border and Transportation Security; and the following functions performed by any employee of the Department of Homeland Security: any customs revenue

function, including any function provided for in Section 415 of the Homeland Security Act of 2002; any commercial function or commercial operation of the Bureau of Customs and Border Protection or Bureau of Immigration and Customs Enforcement, including matters relating to trade facilitation and trade regulation; or any other function related to the above items that was exercised by the U.S. Customs Service on the day before the effective date of the Homeland Security Act of 2002; (2) archives of the United States; (3) budget and accounting measures, other than appropriations, except as provided in the Congressional Budget Act of 1974; (4) census and collection of statistics, including economic and social statistics; (5) congressional organization, except for any part of the matter that amends the rules or orders of the Senate; (6) federal civil service; (7) government information; (8) intergovernmental relations; (9) municipal affairs of the District of Columbia, except appropriations therefor; (10) organization and management of United States nuclear export policy; (11) organization and reorganization of the executive branch of the government; (12) U.S. Postal Service; (13) status of officers and employees of the United States, including their classification, compensation, and benefits. The committee shall have the duty of (A) receiving and examining reports of the comptroller general of the United States and of submitting such recommendations to the Senate as it deems necessary or desirable in connection with the subject matter of such reports; (B) studying the efficiency, economy, and effectiveness of all agencies and departments of the government; (C) evaluating the effects of laws enacted to reorganize the legislative and executive branches of the government; and (D) studying the intergovernmental relationships between the United States and the states and municipalities, and between the United States and international organizations of which the United States is a member.
Party Ratio: D 7-R 7

Gary C. Peters, Mich., Chair	*Rob Portman, Ohio*
Thomas R. Carper, Del.	*Ron Johnson, Wisc.,*
Margaret Wood Hassan, N.H.	*Rand Paul, Ky.*
	James Lankford, Okla.
Kyrsten Sinema, Ariz.	*Mitt Romney, Utah*
Jacky Rosen, Nev.	*Rick Scott, Fla.*
Alex Padilla, Calif.	*Josh Hawley, Mo.*
Jon Ossoff, Ga.	

Subcommittees

Emerging Threats and Spending Oversight
Office: SD-342 SDOB 20510   **Phone:** 224-2254
Jon Ossoff (Chair), Thomas R. Carper, Margaret Wood Hassan, Alex Padilla
Ron Johnson (Ranking Minority Member), Rand Paul, James Lankford, Rick Scott

Government Operations and Border Management
Office: SD-342 SDOB 20510   **Phone:** 224-4551
Kyrsten Sinema (Chair), Thomas R. Carper, Alex Padilla, Jon Ossoff
James Lankford (Ranking Minority Member), Ron Johnson, Mitt Romney, Josh Hawley

Permanent Investigations
Office: SD-342 SDOB 20510   **Phone:** 224-3721
Thomas R. Carper (Chair), Margaret Wood Hassan, Jacky Rosen
Rob Portman (Ranking Minority Member), Rand Paul, James Lankford, Mitt Romney, Josh Hawley

INDIAN AFFAIRS

Office: 838 SHOB 20510-6450
Phone: 224-2251   **Fax:** 224-5429
Web: www.indian.senate.gov
Majority Staff Director: Jennifer Romero
Minority Staff Director: Lucy Murfitt
Jurisdiction: (1) all proposed legislation, messages, petitions, memorials, and other matters relating to Indian affairs shall be referred to the committee; (2) study any and all matters pertaining to problems and opportunities of Indians, including but not limited to, Indian land management and trust responsibilities, Indian education, health, special services, and loan programs, the National Indian Gaming Regulatory Act of 1988, the National Indian Gaming Commission, and Indian claims against the United States; (3) the select committee shall from time to time report to the Senate, by bill or otherwise, its recommendations with respect to matters referred to the select committee or otherwise within its jurisdiction.
Party Ratio: D 6-R 6

Brian Schatz, Hawaii, Chair	*Lisa Murkowski, Alaska*
Maria Cantwell, Wash.	*John Hoeven, N.D.*
Jon Tester, Mont.	*James Lankford, Okla.*
Catherine Cortez Masto, Nev.	*Steve Daines, Mont.*
	Mike Rounds, S.D.
Tina Smith, Minn.	*Jerry Moran, Kans.*
Ben Ray Luján, N.M.	

JUDICIARY

Office: 224 SDOB 20510-6275
Phone: 224-7703   **Fax:** 224-9102
Web: www.judiciary.senate.gov
Minority Web: http://judiciary.senate.gov/press/minority-press
Majority Staff Director: Joe Zogby
Minority Staff Director: Kolen Davis; 224-5225
Jurisdiction: (1) apportionment of representatives; (2) bankruptcy, mutiny, espionage, and counterfeiting; (3) civil liberties; (4) constitutional amendments; (5) federal courts and judges; (6) government information; (7) holidays and celebrations; (8) immigration and naturalization; (9) interstate compacts generally; (10) judicial proceedings, civil and criminal, generally; (11) local courts in U.S. territories and possessions; (12) measures relating to claims against the United States; (13) national penitentiaries; (14) Patent Office; (15) patents, copyrights, and trademarks; (16) protection of trade and commerce against unlawful restraints and monopolies; (17) revision and codification of the statutes of the United States; (18) state and territorial boundary lines.
Party Ratio: D 11-R 11

JUDICIARY (continued)

Richard J. Durbin, Ill., Chair	*Chuck Grassley, Iowa*
Patrick J. Leahy, Vt.	*Lindsey Graham, S.C.*
Dianne Feinstein, Calif.	*John Cornyn, Tex.*
Sheldon Whitehouse, R.I.	*Mike Lee, Utah*
Amy Klobuchar, Minn.	*Ted Cruz, Tex.*
Christopher Coons, Del.	*Ben Sasse, Neb.*
Richard Blumenthal, Conn.	*Josh Hawley, Mo.*
Mazie K. Hirono, Hawaii	*Tom Cotton, Ark.*
Cory A. Booker, N.J.	*John Kennedy, La.*
Alex Padilla, Calif.	*Thom Tillis, N.C.*
Jon Ossoff, Ga.	*Marsha Blackburn, Tenn.*

Subcommittees

Competition Policy, Antitrust, and Consumer Rights
Office: 224 SDOB 20510 **Phone:** 224-3244

Amy Klobuchar (Chair), Patrick J. Leahy, Richard Blumenthal, Cory A. Booker, Jon Ossoff

Mike Lee (Ranking Minority Member), Josh Hawley, Tom Cotton, Thom Tillis, Marsha Blackburn

Criminal Justice and Counterterrorism
Office: 224 SDOB 20510 **Phone:** 224- 2921

Cory A. Booker (Chair), Patrick J. Leahy, Dianne Feinstein, Sheldon Whitehouse, Amy Klobuchar, Alex Padilla, Jon Ossoff

Tom Cotton (Ranking Minority Member), Lindsey Graham, John Cornyn, Mike Lee, Ted Cruz, Josh Hawley, John Kennedy

Federal Courts, Oversight, Agency Action, and Federal Rights
Office: 224 SDOB 20510 **Phone:** 224-2823

Sheldon Whitehouse (Chair), Patrick J. Leahy, Mazie K. Hirono, Cory A. Booker, Alex Padilla, Jon Ossoff

John Kennedy (Ranking Minority Member), Lindsey Graham, Mike Lee, Ted Cruz, Ben Sasse, Thom Tillis

Human Rights and the Law
Office: 224 SDOB 20510 **Phone:** 224-7703

Dianne Feinstein (Chair), Christopher Coons, Richard Blumenthal

Josh Hawley (Ranking Minority Member), Ben Sasse, John Kennedy

Immigration, Citizenship, and Border Safety
Office: 224 SDOB 20510 **Phone:** 224-6991

Alex Padilla (Chair), Dianne Feinstein, Amy Klobuchar, Christopher Coons, Richard Blumenthal, Mazie K. Hirono, Cory A. Booker

John Cornyn (Ranking Minority Member), Lindsey Graham, Ted Cruz, Tom Cotton, John Kennedy, Thom Tillis, Marsha Blackburn

Intellectual Property
Office: 224 SDOB 20510 **Phone:** 224-5042

Patrick J, Leahy (Chair), Christopher Coons, Mazie K. Hirono, Alex Padilla

Thom Tillis (Ranking Minority Member), John Cornyn, Tom Cotton, Marsha Blackburn

Privacy, Technology, and the Law
Office: 224 SDOB 20510 **Phone:** 224-7703

Christopher Coons (Chair), Sheldon Whitehouse, Amy Klobuchar, Mazie K. Hirono, Jon Ossoff

Ben Sasse (Ranking Minority Member), Lindsey Graham, Josh Hawley, John Kennedy, Marsha Blackburn

The Constitution
Office: 224 SDOB 20510 **Phone:** 224-6361

Richard Blumenthal (Chair) Dianne Feinstein, Sheldon Whitehouse, Jon Ossoff

Ted Cruz (Ranking Minority Member), John Cornyn, Mike Lee, Ben Sasse

RULES AND ADMINISTRATION

Office: 305 SROB 20510-6325
Phone: 224-6352 **Fax:** 224-1912
Web: www.rules.senate.gov
Minority Web: www.rules.senate.gov/news/minority-news
Majority Staff Director: Elizabeth Peluso
Minority Staff Director: Rachelle Schroeder
Jurisdiction: (1) administration of the Senate office buildings and the Senate wing of the U.S. Capitol, including the assignment of office space; (2) congressional organization relative to rules and procedures, and Senate rules and regulations, including Senate floor rules and Senate gallery rules; (3) corrupt practices; (4) credentials and qualifications of members of the Senate, contested elections, and acceptance of incompatible offices; (5) federal elections generally, including the election of the president, vice president, and members of the Congress; (6) Government Printing Office, and the printing and correction of the *Congressional Record*, as well as those matters provided for under Rule XI; (7) meetings of the Congress and attendance of members; (8) payment of money out of the contingent fund of the Senate or creating a charge upon the same (except that any resolution relating to substantive matter within the jurisdiction of any other standing committee of the Senate shall be first referred to such committee); (9) presidential succession; (10) purchase of books and manuscripts and erection of monuments to the memory of individuals; (11) Senate Library and statuary, art, and pictures in the U.S. and Senate office buildings; (12) services to the Senate, including the Senate restaurant; (13) U.S. Capitol and congressional office buildings, the Library of Congress, the Smithsonian Institution (and the incorporation of similar institutions), and the U.S. Botanic Garden. The committee shall also (A) make a continuing study of the organization and operation of the Congress of the United States and shall recommend improvements in such organization and operation with a view toward strengthening the Congress, simplifying its operations, improving its relationships with other branches of the U.S. government, and enabling it better to meet its responsibilities under the constitution of the United States; (B) identify any court proceeding or action which, in the opinion of the committee, is of vital interest to the Congress as a constitutionally established institution of the

federal government and call such proceeding or action to the attention of the Senate; (C) develop, implement, and update as necessary a strategic planning process and a strategic plan for the functional and technical infrastructure support of the Senate and provide oversight over plans developed by Senate officers and others in accordance with the strategic planning process.

Party Ratio: D 9-R 9

Amy Klobuchar, Minn., Chair	*Roy Blunt, Mo.*
Dianne Feinstein, Calif.	*Mitch McConnell, Ky.*
Charles E. Schumer, N.Y.	*Richard Shelby, Ala.*
Mark R. Warner, Va.	*Ted Cruz, Tex.*
Patrick J. Leahy, Vt.	*Shelley Moore Capito, W.Va.*
Angus S. King Jr., Maine (I)	*Roger F. Wicker, Miss.*
Jeff Merkley, Ore.	*Deb Fischer, Neb.*
Alex Padilla, Calif.	*Cindy Hyde-Smith, Miss.*
Jon Ossoff, Ga.	*Bill Hagerty, Tenn.*

SMALL BUSINESS AND ENTREPRENEURSHIP

Office: 428A SROB 20515-6350
Phone: 224-5175   **Fax:** 224-5619
Web: www.sbc.senate.gov
Minority Web: www.sbc.senate.gov/public/index.cfm/RankingMember
Majority Staff Director: Sean Moore
Minority Staff Director: Meredith West
Jurisdiction: (1) all proposed legislation, messages, petitions, memorials and other matters relating to the Small Business Administration; (2) any proposed legislation reported by the Committee on Small Business and Entrepreneurship that relates to matters other than the functions of the Small Business Administration shall, at the request of the chair of any standing committee having jurisdiction over the subject matter extraneous to the functions of the Small Business Administration, be considered and reported by such standing committee prior to its consideration by the Senate; and likewise measures reported by other committees directly relating to the Small Business Administration shall, at the request of the chair of the Committee on Small Business and Entrepreneurship, be referred to the Committee on Small Business and Entrepreneurship for its consideration of any portions of the measure dealing with the Small Business Administration, and be reported by this committee prior to its consideration by the Senate; (3) study and survey by means of research and investigation all problems of small business enterprises.

Party Ratio: D 10-R 10

Benjamin L. Cardin, Md., Chair	*Rand Paul, Ky.*
Maria Cantwell, Wash.	*Marco Rubio, Fla.*
Jeanne Shaheen, N.H.	*James E. Risch, Idaho*
Edward J. Markey, Mass.	*Tim Scott, S.C.*
Cory A. Booker, N.J.	*Joni Ernst, Iowa*
Christopher Coons, Del.	*James M. Inhofe, Okla.*
Mazie K. Hirono, Hawaii	*Todd Young, Ind.*
Tammy Duckworth, Ill.	*John Kennedy, La.*
	Josh Hawley, Mo.

Jacky Rosen, Nev.	*Roger Marshall, Kans.*
John W. Hickenlooper, Colo.	

VETERANS' AFFAIRS

Office: 412 SROB 20510-6050
Phone: 224-9126   **Fax:** 224-8908
Web: www.veterans.senate.gov
Minority Web: www.veterans.senate.gov/newsroom/minority-news
Majority Staff Director: Tony McClain
Minority Staff Director: Jon Towers
Jurisdiction: (1) compensation of veterans; (2) life insurance issued by the government on account of service in the Armed Forces; (3) national cemeteries; (4) pensions of all the wars of the United States; (5) readjustment of service personnel to civil life; (6) soldiers' and sailors' civil relief, including oversight of and appropriate modifications to the Soldiers' and Sailors' Civil Relief Act of 1940; (7) veterans' hospitals, medical care and treatment of veterans; (8) veterans' measures generally; (9) vocational rehabilitation and education of veterans.

Party Ratio: D 9-R 9

Jon Tester, Mont., Chair	*Jerry Moran, Kans.*
Patty Murray, Wash.	*John Boozman, Ark.*
Bernard Sanders, Vt. (I)	*Bill Cassidy, La.*
Sherrod Brown, Ohio	*Mike Rounds, S.D.*
Richard Blumenthal, Conn.	*Thom Tillis, N.C.*
Mazie K. Hirono, Hawaii	*Dan Sullivan, Alaska*
Joe Manchin III, W.Va.	*Marsha Blackburn, Tenn.*
Kyrsten Sinema, Ariz.	*Kevin Cramer, N.D.*
Margaret Wood Hassan, N.H.	*Tommy Tuberville, Ala.*

SELECT ETHICS

Office: 220 SHOB 20510-6425
Phone: 224-2981   **Fax:** 224-7416
Web: www.ethics.senate.gov
Staff Director: Shannon H. Kopplin
Jurisdiction: (1) receive and investigate allegations of improper conduct that may reflect upon the Senate, violations of law, violations of the Senate Code of Official Conduct, and violations of rules and regulations of the Senate; (2) recommend disciplinary action; (3) recommend additional Senate rules or regulations to ensure proper standards of conduct; (4) report violations of any law to the proper federal and state authorities; (5) sets out ten standards of conduct that should be adhered to by all government employees, including office holders; (6) investigate unauthorized disclosures of intelligence information by a member, officer, or employee of the Senate and to report to the Senate on any substantial allegation; (7) provide guidance and promulgate rules regarding the frank and may investigate complaints involving a violation of the Franking statute; (8) responsible for Financial Disclosure Statements (Title I) and for Outside Employment (Title V) with respect to members, officers, and employees of the Senate; (9) administer the provisions of the Foreign Gifts and Decorations Act with respect members, officers, and

SELECT ETHICS (continued)

employees of the U.S. Senate; (10) as the "supervising ethics office" for the Senate, the committee is responsible for the statutory prohibitions against members, officers, and employees of the Senate giving gifts to an official superior or receiving gifts from employees with a lower salary level, or soliciting or receiving gifts.

Party Ratio: D 3-R 3

Christopher Coons, Del., Chair	James Lankford, Okla.
	James E. Risch, Idaho
Brian Schatz, Hawaii	Deb Fischer, Neb.
Jeanne Shaheen, N.H.	

SELECT INTELLIGENCE

Office: 211 SHOB 20510-6475
Phone: 224-1700   **Fax:** 224-1772
Web: www.intelligence.senate.gov
Majority Staff Director: Christopher A. Joyner
Minority Staff Director: Michael Casey
Jurisdiction: (1) oversee and make continuing studies of the intelligence activities and programs of the U.S. government, including, but not limited to, the Central Intelligence Agency Act of 1949, Classified Information Procedures Act of 1980, classified national security information, foreign intelligence electronic surveillance, Foreign Intelligence Surveillance Act of 1978, National Security Act of 1947, National Security Agency Act of 1959, national security information, President's Foreign Intelligence Advisory Board (Executive Office of the President), Provide Appropriate Tools Required to Intercept and Obstruct Terrorism (PATRIOT) Act of 2001, security requirements for government employment; (2) submit to the Senate appropriate proposals for legislation; (3) report to the Senate concerning such intelligence activities and programs; (4) provide vigilant legislative oversight over the intelligence activities of the United States to assure that such activities are in conformity with the Constitution and laws of the United States.

Party Ratio: D 10-R 10

Mark R. Warner, Va., Chair	Marco Rubio, Va.
Dianne Feinstein, Calif.	Richard Burr, N.C., Chair
Ron Wyden, Ore.	James E. Risch, Idaho
Martin Heinrich, N.M.	Susan M. Collins, Maine
Angus S. King Jr., Maine (I)	Roy Blunt, Mo.
Michael F. Bennet, Colo.	Tom Cotton, Ark.
Robert P. Casey Jr., Pa.	John Cornyn, Tex.
Kirsten E. Gillibrand, N.Y.	Ben Sasse, Neb.
Charles E. Schumer (ex officio)	Mitch McConnell Ky. (ex officio)
Jack Reed R.I. (ex officio)	James M. Inhofe, Okla. (ex officio)

SPECIAL AGING

Office: G-41 SDOB 20510-6050
Phone: 224-5364

Web: www.aging.senate.gov
Minority Web: www.aging.senate.gov/press-room/minority
Majority Staff Director: Stacy Sanders
Minority Staff Director: Neri Martinez; 628 SHOB; 224-0185
Jurisdiction: (1) conduct a continuing study of any and all matters pertaining to problems and opportunities of older people, including, but not limited to, problems and opportunities of maintaining health, of assuring adequate income, of finding employment, of engaging in productive and rewarding activity, of securing proper housing, and when necessary, of obtaining care or assistance. No proposed legislation shall be referred to such committee, and such committee shall not have power to report by bill, or otherwise have legislative jurisdiction. (2) The special committee shall, from time to time (but not less often than once each year), report to the Senate the results of the study conducted pursuant to paragraph (1), together with such recommendation as it considers appropriate.

Party Ratio: D 7-R 7

Robert P. Casey Jr., Pa., Chair	Tim Scott, S.C.
	Susan M. Collins, Maine
Kirsten E. Gillibrand, N.Y.	Richard Burr, N.C.
Richard Blumenthal, Conn.	Marco Rubio, Fla.
Elizabeth Warren, Mass.	Mike Braun, Ind.
Jacky Rosen, Nev.	Rick Scott, Fla.
Mark Kelly, Ariz.	Mike Lee, Utah
Raphael Warnock, Ga.	

INTERNATIONAL NARCOTICS CONTROL CAUCUS

Office: 517 SHOB 20510
Phone: 224-9032
Web: www.drugcaucus.senate.gov
Purpose: The Senate Caucus on International Narcotics Control was created to "monitor and encourage U.S. government and private programs seeking to expand international cooperation against drug abuse and narcotics trafficking" and to "monitor and promote international compliance with narcotics control treaties." As a formal organization of the U.S. Senate, the caucus has the status of a standing committee. The caucus exercises oversight on a wide range of issues, including international counternarcotics assistance and domestic drug prevention and treatment programs. The caucus has held numerous hearings over the years and has issued a number of reports on U.S. narcotics control policy.

Party Ratio: D 3-R 4

Sheldon Whitehouse, Calif., Chair	Chuck Grassley, Iowa., Chair
Richard Blumenthal, Conn.	John Cornyn. Tex.
Margaret Wood Hassan, N.H.	James E. Risch, Idaho
Ben Ray Luján, N.M.	

SENATE LEADERSHIP AND PARTISAN COMMITTEES

DEMOCRATIC LEADERS

Majority Floor Leader: Charles E. Schumer, N.Y.
Majority Whip: Richard J. Durbin, Ill.

DEMOCRATIC PARTISAN COMMITTEES

Democratic Policy and Communications Committee
Office: S-318 CAP 20510
Phone: 224-3232
Web: www.democrats.senate.gov/dpcc
Debbie Stabenow, Mich., Chair
Joe Manchin III, W.Va., Vice Chair
Cory A. Booker, N.J., Vice Chair

Democratic Steering and Outreach Committee
Office: 712 SHOB 20002
Phone: 224-9048   **Fax:** 224-5476
Web: www.dsoc.senate.gov
Email: steering@dsoc.senate.gov
Amy Klobuchar, Minn., Chair
Jeanne Shaheen, N.H., Vice Chair

Democratic Senatorial Campaign Committee
Office: 120 Maryland Ave. N.E. 20002-5610
Phone: 224-2447   **Fax:** 969-0354
Web: www.dscc.org
Email: info@dscc.org

Gary C. Peters, Mich., Chair
Scott Fairchild, Executive Director

REPUBLICAN LEADERS

Minority Floor Leader: *Mitch McConnell, Ky.*
Minority Whip: *John Thune, S.D.*

REPUBLICAN PARTISAN COMMITTEES

National Republican Senatorial Committee
Office: 425 2nd St. N.E. 20002-4914
Phone: 675-6000   **Fax:** 675-4730
Web: www.nrsc.org
Rick Scott, Fla., Chair
Jackie Schutz Zeckman, Executive Director

Republican Conference
Office: 405 SHOB 20510-7060
Phone: 224-2764   **Fax:** 228-4276
Web: www.republican.senate.gov
John Barrasso, Wyo., Chair
Joni Ernst, Iowa, Vice Chair

Republican Policy Committee
Office: 347 SROB 20510-7064
Phone: 224-2946   **Fax:** 228-2628
Web: www.rpc.senate.gov
Email: SenateRPC_@RPC.Senate.gov
Roy Blunt, Mo., Chair

Senate Members' Offices

The following list gives Senate members and their party and state affiliation, followed by the address and telephone and fax numbers for their Washington office. The area code for all Washington, DC, numbers is (202). A top administrative aide, a website, and social media for each senator are also provided, when available. Most members may be contacted via the web-based email forms found on their websites. These are followed by the address, telephone and fax numbers, and name of a key aide for the senator's district office(s). Each listing concludes with the senator's committee assignments. For partisan committee assignments, see page 941.

As of May 12, 2022, there were 50 Republicans, 48 Democrats, 0 vacancies, and 2 Independents who caucus with the Democrats in the Senate.

Baldwin, Tammy, D-Wisc.

Capitol Hill Office: 709 SHOB 20510-0001; 224-5653; Fax: 224-9787; *Chief of Staff:* Ken Reidy
Web: www.baldwin.senate.gov
Facebook: www.facebook.com/senatortammybaldwin
Twitter: @SenatorBaldwin
Instagram: @senatorbaldwin
YouTube: www.youtube.com/senatortammybaldwin
District Offices: 500 S. Barstow St., #LL2, Eau Claire, WI 54701-3608; 715-832-8424; *Field Rep.:* Kelly Westlund
210 S. 7th St., #3, La Crosse, WI 54601-4059; 608-796-0045; Fax: 608-796-0089; *Regional Rep.:* Gregg Wavrunek
30 W. Mifflin St., #700, Madison, WI 53703-2568; 608-264-5338; Fax: 608-264-5473; *State Director:* Janet Piraino
633 W. Wisconsin Ave., #1300, Milwaukee, WI 53203-2205; 414-297-4451; Fax: 414-297-4455; *Office Director:* Tiffany Henry
1039 W. Mason St., #119, Green Bay, WI 54303-1842; 920-498-2668; Fax: 920-498-2701; *Regional Rep:* Jennifer Garner
Committee Assignments: Appropriations; Commerce, Science, and Transportation; Health, Education, Labor, and Pensions

Barrasso, John, R-Wyo.

Capitol Hill Office: 307 SDOB 20510-5005; 224-6441; Fax: 224-1724; *Chief of Staff:* J. Dan Kunsman
Web: www.barrasso.senate.gov
Facebook: www.facebook.com/johnbarrasso
Twitter: @SenJohnBarrasso
Instagram: @senjohnbarrasso
YouTube: www.youtube.com/barrassowyo
District Offices: 100 E. B St., #2004, Casper, WY 82601-7021; 307-261-6413; Fax: 307-265-6706; *Field Rep.:* Ashlee Taylor
2120 Capitol Ave., #2013, Cheyenne, WY 82001-3631; 307-772-2451; Fax: 307-638-3512; *Field Rep:* Laura Curran
324 E. Washington Ave., Riverton, WY 82501-4342; 307-856-6642; Fax: 307-856-5901; *Field Rep.:* Pam Buline
1575 Dewar Dr., #218, Rock Springs, WY 82901-5972; 307-362-5012; Fax: 307-362-5129; *Field Rep.:* Sierra Brown

51 Coffeen Ave., #202, Sheridan, WY 82801-4802; 307-672-6456; Fax: 307-672-5227; *Field Rep.:* Christy McKenzie
Committee Assignments: Energy and Natural Resources; Finance; Foreign Relations

Bennet, Michael F., D-Colo.

Capitol Hill Office: 261 SROB 20510-0608; 224-5852; Fax: 228-5097; *Chief of Staff:* Jonathan Davidson
Web: www.bennet.senate.gov
Facebook: www.facebook.com/senbennetco
Twitter: @SenatorBennet
Instagram: @senatorbennet
YouTube: www.youtube.com/SenatorBennet
District Offices: 609 Main St., #110, Alamosa, CO 81101-2557; 719-587-0096; Fax: 719-587-0098; *Regional Rep.:* Erin Minks
409 N. Tejon St., #107, Colorado Springs, CO 80903-1163; 719-328-1100; Fax: 719-328-1129; *Regional Director:* Annie Oatman-Gardner
1244 Speer Blvd., Denver, CO 80204-3518; 303-455-7600; Fax: 720-904-7151; *State Director:* Amy Friedman
1309 E. 3rd Ave., #101, Durango, CO 81301-6310; 970-259-1710; Fax: 970-259-9789; *Regional Director:* John Whitney
1200 S. College Ave., #211, Fort Collins, CO 80524-3746; 970-224-2200; Fax: 970-224-2205; *Regional Director:* James Thompson
129 W. B St., Pueblo, CO 81003-3400; 719-542-7550; Fax: 719-542-7555; *Regional Director:* Jacqueline Armendariz
225 N. 5th St., #511, Grand Junction, CO 81501-2656; 970-241-6631; Fax: 970-241-8313; *Constituent Advocate:* Alyssa Logan
Committee Assignments: Agriculture, Nutrition, and Forestry; Finance; Select Intelligence

Blackburn, Marsha, R-Tenn.

Capitol Hill Office: 357 SDOB 20510-5005; 224-3344; Fax: 228-0566; *Chief of Staff:* Chuck Flint
Web: www.blackburn.senate.gov
Facebook: www.facebook.com/marshablackburn
Twitter: @MarshaBlackburn

Instagram: @marshablackburn
YouTube: www.youtube.com/channel/
  UCK_JQCLG1Zzea10S9oHAIOA
District Offices: 800 Market St., #121, Knoxville, TN
  37902-2349; 865-540-3781; Fax: 865-540-7952; *Lead
  Constituent Services Director:* Chelsea Ivens;
  Constituent Services Rep.: Heather Hatcher
109 S. Highland Ave., #218, Jackson, TN 38301-2042; 731-
  660-3971; Fax: 731-660-3978; *State Constituent
  Services Coordinator:* Dana Magneson
1105 E. Jackson Blvd., #4, Jonesborough, TN 37659-4998;
  423-753-4009; Fax: 423-788-0250; *Constituent Services
  Rep.:* Kim Cordell
10 W. Martin Luther King Blvd., 6th Floor, Chattanooga,
  TN 37402-1836; 423-541-2939; Fax: 423-541-2944;
  Office Administrator, Constituent Services Rep.: Kelly
  Puckett
100 Peabody Pl., #1125, Memphis, TN 38103-3676; 901-
  527-9199; Fax: 901-527-9515; *Constituent Services
  Rep.:* Jeri Wheeler
3322 W. End Ave., #610, Nashville, TN 37203-1031, 629-
  800-6600; Fax: 615)-298-2148; *Caseworker:* Elizabeth
  Kelly
Committee Assignments: Armed Services, Commerce,
  Science, and Transportation; Judiciary; Veterans' Affairs

Blumenthal, Richard, D-Conn.

Capitol Hill Office: 706 SHOB 20510-0704; 224-2823;
  Fax: 224-9673; *Chief of Staff:* Joel Kelsey
Web: www.blumenthal.senate.gov
Facebook: www.facebook.com/SenBlumenthal
Twitter: @SenBlumenthal
Instagram: @senblumenthal
YouTube: www.youtube.com/senatorblumenthal
District Offices: 90 State House Square, 10th Floor,
  Hartford, CT 06103-3702; 860-258-6940; Fax: 860-258-
  6958; *State Director:* Rich Kehoe
915 Lafayette Blvd., #304, Bridgeport, CT 06604-4706; 203-
  330-0598; Fax: 203-330-0608; *State Director:* Rich
  Kehoe
Committee Assignments: Armed Services; Commerce,
  Science, and Transportation; Judiciary; Special Aging;
  Veterans' Affairs

Blunt, Roy, R-Mo.

Capitol Hill Office: 260 SROB 20510-2508; 224-5721;
  Chief of Staff: Stacy McBride
Web: www.blunt.senate.gov
Facebook: www.facebook.com/SenatorBlunt
Twitter: @RoyBlunt
Instagram: @royblunt
YouTube: www.youtube.com/SenatorBlunt
District Offices: 338 Broadway, #303, Cape Girardeau, MO
  63701-7355; 573-334-7044; *Office Director:* Madison
  Baker
111 S. 10th St., #23.305, St. Louis, MO 63102-1130; 314-
  725-4484; *Office Director:* Mary Beth Luna Wolf
1123 Wilkes Blvd., #320, Columbia, MO 65201-7931; 573-
  442-8151; *Deputy Chief of Staff:* Derek Coats

1000 Walnut St., #1560, Kansas City, MO 64106-2105;
  816-471-7141; *State Director:* Matt Haase
2740B E. Sunshine St., Springfield, MO 65804-2016;
  417-877-7814; *District Office Director:* Sonya
  Anderson
Committee Assignments: Appropriations; Commerce,
  Science, and Transportation; Rules and
  Administration; Select Intelligence

Booker, Cory A., D-N.J.

Capitol Hill Office: 717 SHOB 20510-0001; 224-3224;
  Fax: 224-8378; *Chief of Staff:* Matt Klapper
Web: www.booker.senate.gov
Facebook: www.facebook.com/SenatorCoryBooker
Twitter: @SenBooker
Instagram: @corybooker
YouTube: www.youtube.com/sencorybooker
District Offices: One Port Center, 2 Riverside Dr., #505,
  Camden, NJ 08103-1019; 856-338-8922; Fax: 856-338-
  8936; *South Jersey Director:* Bill Moen
1 Gateway Center, 23rd Floor, Newark, NJ 07102-5323;
  973-639-8700; Fax: 202-224-5702; *State Director:*
  Hanna Mori
Committee Assignments: Agriculture, Nutrition, and
  Forestry; Foreign Relations; Judiciary; Small Business
  and Entrepreneurship

Boozman, John, R-Ark.

Capitol Hill Office: 141 SHOB 20510-0406; 224-4843;
  Chief of Staff: Toni-Marie Higgins
Web: www.boozman.senate.gov
Facebook: www.facebook.com/JohnBoozman
Twitter: @JohnBoozman
Instagram: @johnboozman
YouTube: www.youtube.com/BoozmanPressOffice
District Offices: 106 W. Main St., #104, El Dorado, AR
  71730-5634; 870-863-4641; Fax: 870-863-4105;
  Constituent Services Rep.: Chase Emerson
1120 Garrison Ave., #2B, Fort Smith, AR 72901-2617; 479-
  573-0189; Fax: 479-573-0553; *Constituent Services
  Director:* Kathy Watson
300 S. Church St., #400, Jonesboro, AR 72401-2911; 870-
  268-6925; Fax: 870-268-6887; *Caseworker:* Amanda
  Blaylock
1401 W. Capitol Ave., #155, Little Rock, AR 72201-2942;
  501-372-7153; Fax: 501-372-7163; *Grants Coord.:*
  Jimmy Harris
213 W. Monroe Ave., Suite N, Lowell, AR 72745-9451;
  479-725-0400; Fax: 479-725-0408; *State Director:*
  Stacey McClure
1001 Hwy. 62 East, #11, Mountain Home, AR 72653-3215;
  870-424-0129; Fax: 870-424-0141; *Caseworker:* Sherry
  Slippo
620 E. 22nd St., #204, Stuttgart, AR 72160-9007; 870-672-
  6941; Fax: 870-672-6962; *Field Rep.:* Ty Davis
Committee Assignments: Agriculture, Nutrition, and
  Forestry; Appropriations; Commission on Security and
  Cooperation in Europe; Environment and Public
  Works; Veterans' Affairs

Braun, Mike, R-Ind.

Capitol Hill Office: 404 SROB 20510-0001; 224-4814;
  Chief of Staff: Joshua Kelley
Web: www.braun.senate.gov
Facebook: www.facebook.com/SenatorBraun
Twitter: @SenatorBraun
Instagram: @senatorbraun
YouTube: www.youtube.com/channel/
  UCQ02jR4CJErAbv3522PJffA
District Offices: 115 N. Pennsylvania St., Indianapolis, IN
  46204-2410; 317-822-8240; Fax: 317-822-8353; *State
  Director:* Jason Johnson
203 E. Berry St., #702B, Fort Wayne, IN 46802-2724; 260-
  427-2164; Fax: 260-427-2167; *Regional Director:* Mary
  Martin; *Field Rep.:* Jon Kenworthy
5400 Federal Plaza, #3200, Hammond IN 46320-1855;
  219-937-9650; Fax: 219-937-9665; *Regional Director:*
  Anthony Ferraro
205 W. Colfax Ave., South Bend, IN 46601-1606; 574-288-
  6302; Fax: 574-288-6450; *Field Rep.:* Jackie Dermody
Committee Assignments: Agriculture, Nutrition, and
  Forestry; Appropriations; Budget; Health, Education,
  Labor, and Pensions; Special Aging

Brown, Sherrod, D-Ohio

Capitol Hill Office: 503 SHOB 20510-3505; 224-2315;
  Fax: 228-6321; *Chief of Staff:* Sarah Benzing
Web: www.brown.senate.gov
Facebook: www.facebook.com/SenSherrodBrown
Twitter: @SenSherrodBrown
Instagram: @sensherrodbrown
YouTube: www.youtube.com/SherrodBrownOhio
District Offices: 425 Walnut St., #2310, Cincinnati, OH
  45202-3915; 513-684-1021; Fax: 513-684-1029;
  Southwest Regional Director: Alea Brown
801 W. Superior Ave., #1400, Cleveland, OH 44113-1857;
  216-522-7272; Fax: 216-522-2239; *State Director:* John
  Ryan
200 N. High St., Room 614, Columbus, OH 43215-2408;
  614-469-2083; Fax: 614-469-2171; *Central Ohio
  Regional Director:* Joe Gilligan
200 W. Erie Ave., #312, Lorain, OH 44052-1600; 440-242-
  4100; Fax: 440-242-4108; *Constituent Advocates:*
  Marilee Marks and Paulanne Oaks
Committee Assignments: Agriculture, Nutrition, and
  Forestry; Banking, Housing, and Urban Affairs, Chair;
  Finance; Veterans' Affairs

Burr, Richard, R-N.C.

Capitol Hill Office: 217 SROB 20510-3308; 224-3154;
  Fax: 228-2981; *Chief of Staff:* Natasha Hickman
Web: www.burr.senate.gov
Facebook: www.facebook.com/SenatorRichardBurr
Twitter: @SenatorBurr
Instagram: @senatorburr
YouTube: www.youtube.com/SenatorRichardBurr
District Offices: Federal Bldg., 151 Patton Ave., #204,
  Asheville, NC 28801-2689; 828-350-2437; *State
  Director:* Dean Myers

100 Coast Line St., Room 210, Rocky Mount, NC
  27804-5849; 252-977-9522; *Field Rep.:* Betty Jo
  Shepheard
201 N. Front St., #809, Wilmington, NC 28401-5089;
  910-251-1058; *Constituent Advocate:* Brandon
  Hawkins
2000 W. 1st St., #508, Winston-Salem, NC 27104-4225;
  336-631-5125; *State Director:* Dean Myers
Committee Assignments: Finance; Health, Education,
  Labor, and Pensions; Select Intelligence; Special Aging

Cantwell, Maria, D-Wash.

Capitol Hill Office: 511 SHOB 20510-4705; 224-3441;
  Fax: 228-0514; *Chief of Staff:* Jami Burtess
Web: www.cantwell.senate.gov
Facebook: www.facebook.com/senatorcantwell
Twitter: @SenatorCantwell
Instagram: @senatormariacantwell
YouTube: www.youtube.com/SenatorCantwell
District Offices: 2930 Wetmore Ave., #9B, Everett, WA
  98201-4044; 425-303-0114; Fax: 425-303-8351;
  Northwest Outreach Director: Cameron Caldwell
825 Jadwin Ave., #206, Richland, WA 99352-3562; 509-
  946-8106; Fax: 509-946-6937; *Central Washington
  Director:* Richard Evans
915 2nd Ave., #3206, Seattle, WA 98174-1011; 206-220-
  6400; Fax: 206-220-6404; *State Director:* Tommy
  Bauer
920 W. Riverside Ave., #697, Spokane, WA 99201-1008;
  509-353-2507; Fax: 509-353-2547; *Case Worker:*
  Katelyn Larson
950 Pacific Ave., #615, Tacoma, WA 98402-4431; 253-572-
  2281; Fax: 253-572-5879; *Olympic Peninsula and
  Pierce County Director:* Casey Duss
1313 Officers Row, Vancouver, WA 98661-3856; 360-696-
  7838; Fax: 360-696-7844; *Southwest Washington
  Outreach Director:* Sarah Kohout
Committee Assignments: Commerce, Science, and
  Transportation, Chair; Energy and Natural Resources;
  Finance; Indian Affairs; Joint Taxation; Small Business
  and Entrepreneurship

Capito, Shelley Moore, R-W.Va.

Capitol Hill Office: 172 SROB 20510-0001; 224-6472;
  Fax: 224-7665; *Chief of Staff:* Joel Brubaker
Web: www.capito.senate.gov
Facebook: www.facebook.com/senshelley
Twitter: @SenCapito
Instagram: @sencapito
YouTube: www.youtube.com/channel/
  UCbiXdR4XQ3vD9Xp5lfR9QXw
District Offices: 500 Virginia St. East, #950, Charleston,
  WV 25301-4108; 304-347-5372; Fax: 304-347-5371;
  State Director: Mary Elisabeth Eckerson
300 Foxcroft Ave., #202A, Martinsburg, WV 25401-5341;
  304-262-9285; Fax: 304-262-9288; *Field Rep.:* Chris
  Strovel
48 Donley St., #504, Morgantown, WV 26501; 304-292-
  2310; *Field Rep.:* Jessicah Cross

Committee Assignments: Appropriations; Commerce, Science, and Transportation; Environment and Public Works; Rules and Administration

Cardin, Benjamin L., D-Md.

Capitol Hill Office: 509 SHOB 20510-2004; 224-4524; *Chief of Staff:* Christopher W. Lynch
Web: www.cardin.senate.gov
Facebook: www.facebook.com/senatorbencardin
Twitter: @SenatorCardin
Instagram: @senatorcardin
YouTube: www.youtube.com/SenatorCardin
District Offices: 100 S. Charles St., Tower 1, #1710, Baltimore, MD 21201-2788; 410-962-4436; *State Director:* Carleton Atkinson
10201 Martin Luther King Jr. Hwy., #210, Bowie, MD 20720-4000; 301-860-0414; Fax: 301-860-0416; *State Director:* Carelton Atkinson
13 Canal St., Room 305, Cumberland, MD 21502-3054; 301-777-2957; Fax: 301-777-2959; *State Director:* Carleton Atkinson
451 Hungerford Dr., #230, Rockville, MD 20850-4187; 301-762-2974; Fax: 301-762-2976; *Field Rep.:* Ken Reichard
212 W. Main St., #301C, Salisbury, MD 21801-4920; 410-546-4250; Fax: 410-546-4252; *Field Rep.:* Kim Kratovil
Committee Assignments: Commission on Security and Cooperation in Europe, Chair; Environment and Public Works, Chair; Finance; Foreign Relations, Chair; Small Business and Entrepreneurship, Chair

Carper, Thomas R., D-Del.

Capitol Hill Office: 513 SHOB 20510-0803; 224-2441; Fax: 228-2190; *Chief of Staff:* Emily Spain
Web: www.carper.senate.gov
Facebook: www.facebook.com/tomcarper
Twitter: @SenatorCarper
Instagram: @senatorcarper
YouTube: www.youtube.com/user/SenatorCarper
District Offices: 555 E. Loockerman St., #300, Dover, DE 19901-3298; 302-674-3308; Fax: 302-674-5464; *State Director:* Asi Ofosu
12 The Circle, Georgetown, DE 19947-1501; 302-856-7690; Fax: 302-856-3001; *Sussex County Regional Director:* Karen McGrath
301 N. Walnut St., #102L-1, Wilmington, DE 19801-3974; 302-573-6291; Fax: 302-573-6434; *New Castle County Regional Director:* Bonnie Wu
Committee Assignments: Environment and Public Works, Chair; Finance; Homeland Security and Governmental Affairs

Casey, Robert P. Jr., D-Pa.

Capitol Hill Office: 393 SROB 20510-3805; 224-6324; Fax: 228-0604; *Chief of Staff:* Kristen Gentile
Web: www.casey.senate.gov
Facebook: www.facebook.com/SenatorBobCasey
Twitter: @SenBobCasey
Instagram: @senbobcasey
YouTube: www.youtube.com/SenatorBobCasey

District Offices: 840 Hamilton St., #301, Allentown, PA 18101-2456; 610-782-9470; Fax: 610-782-9474; *Regional Manager:* Amy Cozze
817 E. Bishop St., Suite C, Bellefonte, PA 16823-2321; 814-357-0314; Fax: 814-357-0318; *Regional Manager:* Elizabeth Kisheaugh
17 S. Park Row, #B-150, Erie, PA 16501-1162; 814-874-5080; Fax: 814-874-5084; *Regional Manager:* Kyle Hannon
200 N. 3rd St., #14A, Harrisburg, PA 17101-2105; 717-231-7540; Fax: 717-231-7542; *Director of Constituent Services:* Lindsay Martin
2000 Market St., #610, Philadelphia, PA 19103-3209; 215-405-9660; Fax: 215-405-9669; *Southeastern Regional Director:* Tia Watson
310 Grant St., #2415, Pittsburgh, PA 15219-2249; 412-803-7370; Fax: 412-803-7379; *Southwestern Regional Director:* Marlon Ferguson
417 Lackawanna Ave., #303, Scranton, PA 18503-2013; 570-941-0930; Fax: 570-941-0937; *Executive Assistant:* Leah Mercik
Committee Assignments: Finance; Health, Education, Labor, and Pensions; Select Intelligence; Special Aging, Chair

Cassidy, Bill, R-La.

Capitol Hill Office: 520 SHOB 20510-1804; 224-5824; Fax: 224-6161; *Chief of Staff:* James Quinn
Web: www.cassidy.senate.gov
Facebook: www.facebook.com/senbillcassidy
Twitter: @SenBillCassidy
Instagram: @bill_cassidy
YouTube: www.youtube.com/channel/UCCEyGhUzxgkxFzWCY-rxz8g
District Offices: 3600 Jackson St., #115A, Alexandria, LA 71303; 318-448-7176; Fax: 318-448-5175; *State Director:* Brian McNabb
450 Laurel St., #1400, Baton Rouge, LA 70801; 225-929-7711; Fax: 225-383-3768; *State Director:* Brian McNabb
101 La Rue France, #505, Lafayette, LA 70508-3132; 337-261-1400; Fax: 337-261-1490; *Southwestern Regional Director:* Lauren Casanova
3421 N. Causeway Blvd., #204, Metairie, LA 70002-3731; 504-838-0130; Fax: 504-838-0133; *Southeastern Regional Director:* Rachel Perez
1651 Louisville Ave., #123, Monroe, LA 71201; 318-324-2111; Fax: 318-324-2197; *Regional Director:* Angie Robert
6425 Youree Dr., #415, Shreveport, LA 71105-4675; 318-798-3215; Fax: 318-798-6959; *Regional Director:* Stephanie McKenzie
Committee Assignments: Energy and Natural Resources; Finance; Health, Education, Labor, and Pension; Joint Economic; Veterans' Affairs

Collins, Susan M., R-Maine

Capitol Hill Office: 413 SDOB 20510-1904; 224-2523; Fax: 224-2693; *Chief of Staff:* Steve Abbott
Web: www.collins.senate.gov
Facebook: www.facebook.com/susancollins

Twitter: @SenatorCollins
Instagram: @sensusancollins
YouTube: www.youtube.com/SenatorSusanCollins
District Offices: 68 Sewall St., Room 507, Augusta, ME 04330-6354; 207-622-8414; Fax: 207-622-5884; *State Office Rep.:* Mark Winter
202 Harlow St., Room 20100, Bangor, ME 04401-4975; 207-945-0417; Fax: 207-990-4604; *State Office Rep.:* Carol Woodcock
160 Main St., Biddeford, ME 04005-2580; 207-283-1101; Fax: 207-283-4054; *State Office Rep.:* Alexandria Pelczar
25 Sweden St., Suite A, Caribou, ME 04736-2149; 207-493-7873; Fax: 207-493-7810; *State Office Rep.:* Trisha House
55 Lisbon St., Lewiston, ME 04240-7117; 207-784-6969; Fax: 207-782-6475; *State Office Rep.:* Carlene Tremblay
One Canal Plaza, #802, Portland, ME 04101-4083; 207-780-3575; Fax: 207-828-0380; *State Office Rep.:* Peter Morin
Committee Assignments: Appropriations; Health, Education, Labor, and Pensions; Select Intelligence; Special Aging

Coons, Christopher, D-Del.

Capitol Hill Office: 218 SROB 20510-0805; 224-5042; Fax: 228-3075; *Chief of Staff:* Jonathan Stahler
Web: www.coons.senate.gov
Facebook: www.facebook.com/senatorchriscoons
Twitter: @ChrisCoons
Instagram: @senatorchriscoons
YouTube: www.youtube.com/senatorchriscoons
District Offices: 555 E. Loockerman St., #330, Dover, DE 19901-3298; 302-736-5601; Fax: 302-736-5609; *Kent/ Sussex Coord.:* Kate Rohrer
1105 N. Market St., #100, Wilmington, DE 19801-1233; 302-573-6345; Fax: 302-573-6351; *State Director:* Jim Paoli
Committee Assignments: Appropriations; Foreign Relations; Judiciary; Small Business and Entrepreneurship; Select Ethics, Chair

Cornyn, John, R-Tex.

Capitol Hill Office: 517 SHOB 20510-4305; 224-2934; Fax: 228-1930; *Chief of Staff:* Beth Jafari
Web: www.cornyn.senate.gov
Facebook: www.facebook.com/SenJohnCornyn
Twitter: @JohnCornyn
Instagram: @johncornyn
YouTube: www.youtube.com/SenJohnCornyn
District Offices: Chase Tower, 221 W. 6th St., #1530, Austin, TX 78701-3403; 512-469-6034; Fax: 512-469-6020; *State Field Director:* David James
5001 Spring Valley Rd., #1125E, Dallas, TX 75244-3916; 972-239-1310; Fax: 972-239-2110; *Regional Director:* Collin McLochlin
222 E. Van Buren. Ave., #404, Harlingen, TX 78550-6804; 956-423-0162; Fax: 956-423-0193; *Regional Director:* Ana Garcia

5300 Memorial Dr., #980, Houston, TX 77007-8274; 713-572-3337; Fax: 713-572-3777; *Regional Director:* Jay Guerrero
Wells Fargo Center, 1500 Broadway, #1230, Lubbock, TX 79401-3114; 806-472-7533; Fax: 806-472-7536; *Regional Director:* Joel Riedel
600 Navarro St., #210, San Antonio, TX 78205-2455; 210-224-7485; Fax: 210-224-8569; *Regional Director:* Jonathan Huhn
100 E. Ferguson St., #1004, Tyler, TX 75702-5706; 903-593-0902; Fax: 903-593-0920; *Regional Director:* Kathey Comer
Committee Assignments: Finance; Judiciary; Select Intelligence; International Narcotics Control Caucus

Cortez Masto, Catherine, D-Nev.

Capitol Hill Office: 313 SHOB 20510-0001; 224-3542; *Chief of Staff:* Scott Fairchild
Web: www.cortezmasto.senate.gov
Facebook: www.facebook.com/SenatorCortezMasto
Twitter: @SenCortezMasto
Instagram: @sencortezmasto
YouTube: www.youtube.com/channel/ UCip_83SiKUqwnUT57VOXrCg
District Offices: 333 S. Las Vegas Blvd., #8016, Las Vegas, NV 89101-7075; 702-388-5020; Fax: 702-388-5030; *State Director:* Zach Varagova
Courthouse and Federal Bldg., 400 S. Virginia St., #902, Reno, NV 89501-2109; 775-686-5750; Fax: 775-686-5757; *Regional Reps.:* Bill Chan, Nohely Mariscal, and Kurt Englehart
Committee Assignments: Banking, Housing, and Urban Affairs; Energy and Natural Resources; Finance; Indian Affairs

Cotton, Tom, R-Ark.

Capitol Hill Office: 326 SROB 20510-0001; 224-2353; *Chief of Staff:* Doug Coutts
Web: www.cotton.senate.gov
Facebook: www.facebook.com/SenatorTomCotton
Twitter: @SenTomCotton
Instagram: @tomcottonar
YouTube: www.youtube.com/c/sentomcotton
District Offices: 1401 W. Capitol Ave., #235, Little Rock, AR 72201-2928; 501-223-9081; Fax: 501-244-9633; *State Director:* Vanessa Moody
3333 S. Pinnacle Hills Pkwy., #425, Rogers, AR 72758-9087; 479-751-0879; Fax: 479-464-0648; *State Director:* Vanessa Moody
106 W. Main St., #410, El Dorado, AR 71730-5637; 870-864-8582; Fax: 870-864-8571; *State Director:* Vanessa Moody
300 S. Church, #338, Jonesboro, AR 72401-2911; 870-933-6223; Fax: 870-933-6596; *Projects Director:* Jeff Morris
Committee Assignments: Armed Services; Congressional-Executive Commission on China; Joint Economic; Judiciary; Select Intelligence

Cramer, Kevin, R-N.D.

Capitol Hill Office: 330 SHOB 20510-2605; 224-2043; *Chief of Staff:* Mark Gruman
Web: www.cramer.senate.gov
Facebook: www.facebook.com/SenatorKevinCramer
Twitter: @SenKevinCramer
Instagram: @senatorkevincramer
YouTube: www.youtube.com/c/Senkevincramer
District Offices: 306 Federal Bldg., 657 N. 2nd Ave., Fargo, ND 58102-4727; 701-232-5094; *State Director:* Lisa Gibbens; *Southeast Regional Rep.:* Michael Kelsch
105 Federal Bldg., 100 1st St. S.W., Minot, ND 58701; 701-837-6141; *Northwest Regional Rep., Policy Advisor:* Kaitlyn Weidert
328 Federal Bldg., 220 E. Rosser Ave., Bismarck, ND 58501; 701-699-7020; *Southwest Regional Rep.:* Rick Collin
114 Federal Bldg., 102 N. 4th St., Grand Forks, ND 58203; 701-699-7030; *Northeast Regional Rep.:* Randy Richards
125 Main St., #217, Williston, ND 58801; 701-441-7230; *Senior Policy Advisor:* Chris Marohl
Committee Assignments: Armed Services; Banking, Housing, and Urban Affairs; Budget; Environment and Public Works; Veterans' Affairs

Crapo, Mike, R-Idaho

Capitol Hill Office: 239 SDOB 20510-1205; 224-6142; Fax: 228-1375; *Chief of Staff:* Susan Wheeler
Web: www.crapo.senate.gov
Facebook: www.facebook.com/mikecrapo
Twitter: @MikeCrapo
Instagram: @mikecrapo
YouTube: www.youtube.com/senatorcrapo
District Offices: 251 E. Front St., #205, Boise, ID 83702-7312; 208-334-1776; Fax: 208-334-9044; *Regional Chief of Staff:* John Hoehne
610 Hubbard St., #209, Coeur d'Alene, ID 83814-2287; 208-664-5490; Fax: 208-664-0889; *Regional Director:* Karen Roetter
410 Memorial Dr., #204, Idaho Falls, ID 83402-3600; 208-522-9779; Fax: 208-529-8367; *Regional Director:* Kathryn Hitch
313 D St., #105, Lewiston, ID 83501-1894; 208-743-1492; Fax: 208-743-6484; *State Director:* Tony Snodderly
275 S. 5th Ave., #100, Pocatello, ID 83201; 208-236-6775; Fax: 208-236-6935; *Regional Director:* Farhana Hibbert
202 Falls Ave., #2, Twin Falls, ID 83301-3372; 208-734-2515; Fax: 208-733-0414; *Regional Director:* Samantha Marshall
Committee Assignments: Banking, Housing, and Urban Affairs; Budget; Finance; Joint Taxation

Cruz, Ted, R-Tex.

Capitol Hill Office: 127A SROB 20510; 224-5922; *Chief of Staff:* Steve Chartan
Web: www.cruz.senate.gov
Facebook: www.facebook.com/SenatorTedCruz
Twitter: @SenTedCruz
Instagram: @sentedcruz
YouTube: www.youtube.com/SenTedCruz

District Offices: 300 E. 8th St., #961, Austin, TX 78701-3226; 512-916-5834; Fax: 512-916-5839; *State Director:* Carl Mica
Lee Park Tower II, 3626 N. Hall St., #410, Dallas, TX 75219; 214-599-8749; *Regional Director:* Christine Babcock
Mikey Leland Federal Bldg., 1919 Smith St., #9047, Houston, TX 77002; 713-718-3057; *Regional Director:* Jason Fuller
9901 IH-10W, #950, San Antonio, TX 78230; 210-340-2885; *Regional Director:* Javier Salinas
305 S. Broadway, #501, Tyler, TX 75702; 903-593-5130; *Regional Director:* Jason Wright
200 S. 10th St., #1603, McAllen, TX 78501; 956-686-7339; Fax: 956-618-3692; *Regional Director:* Casandra Meade
Committee Assignments: Commerce, Science, and Transportation; Foreign Relations; Joint Economic; Judiciary; Rules and Administration

Daines, Steve, R-Mont.

Capitol Hill Office: 320 SHOB 20510-2605; 224-2651; Fax: 228-1236; *Chief of Staff:* Jason Thielman
Web: www.daines.senate.gov
Facebook: www.facebook.com/SteveDainesMT
Twitter: @SteveDaines
Instagram: @stevedaines
YouTube: www.youtube.com/SteveDainesMT
District Offices: 218 E. Front St., #103, Missoula, MT 59802; 406-549-8198; Fax: 406-549-0905; *Regional Director:* Danielle Tribble
13 S. Willson Ave., #8, Bozeman, MT 59715; 406-587-3446; Fax: 406-587-3951; *State Director:* Liz Dellwo
222 N. 32nd St., #100, Billings, MT 59101; 406-245-6822; Fax: 406-702-1182; *Field Rep.:* Tory Kolkhorst
104 N. 4th St., #302, Great Falls, MT 59401; 406-453-0148; *Field Rep.:* Robert Bruskotter
30 W. 14th St., #206, Helena, MT 59601; 406-443-3189; *Field Rep.:* Cindy Perdue-Dolan
KM Bldg., 40 E. 2nd St., #211, Kalispell, MT 59901; 406-257-3765; *Reginal Director:* Ron Catlett
Central Plaza Bldg., 609 S. Central Ave., #4, Sidney, MT 59270; 406-482-9010; *Field Rep.:* Charlene Reddig
Committee Assignments: Banking, Housing, and Urban Affairs; Congressional-Executive Commission on China; Energy and Natural Resources; Finance; Indian Affairs

Duckworth, Tammy, D-Ill.

Capitol Hill Office: 524 SHOB 20510; 224-2854; Fax: 228-4611; *Chief of Staff:* Kalina Thompson
Web: www.duckworth.senate.gov
Facebook: www.facebook.com/SenDuckworth
Twitter: @SenDuckworth
Instagram: @senduckworth
YouTube: www.youtube.com/SenDuckworth
District Offices: 230 S. Dearborn St., #3900, Chicago, IL 60604; 312-886-3506; Fax: 312-583-0374; *State Director:* Laron Harris

441 E. Willow St., Carbondale, IL 62901; 618-677-7000; Fax: 618-351-1551; *Southern Community Outreach Coords.:* Jim Kirkpatrick and Katie Keller

8 S. Old State Capitol Plaza, Springfield, IL 62701; 217-528-6124; Fax: 217-528-7043; *Down State Director:* Randy Sikowski

23 Public Square, #460, Belleville, IL 62220; 618-722-7070; Fax: 618-235-4011; *Community Outreach Coords.:* Robin Cromer and Chad Phillips

1823 2nd Ave., #2, Rock Island, IL 61201; 309-606-7060; Fax: 309-786-1799; *Community Outreach Coords.:* Maggie Pappas

Committee Assignments: Armed Services; Commerce, Science, and Transportation; Environment and Public Works; Small Business and Entrepreneurship

Durbin, Richard J., D-Ill.

Capitol Hill Office: 711 SHOB 20510-1304; 224-2152; Fax: 228-0400; *Chief of Staff:* Patrick J. Souders

Web: www.durbin.senate.gov

Facebook: www.facebook.com/SenatorDurbin

Twitter: @SenatorDurbin

Instagram: @durbincampaign

YouTube: www.youtube.com/SenatorDurbin

District Offices: 250 W. Cherry St., #115-D, Carbondale, IL 62901-2856; 618-351-1122; Fax: 618-351-1124; *Staff Asst.:* Vacant

230 S. Dearborn St., #3892, Chicago, IL 60604-1505; 312-353-4952; Fax: 312-353-0150; *Office Manager:* Celeste Gabinski

1504 3rd Ave., #227, Rock Island, IL 61201-8612; 309-786-5173; Fax: 309-786-5404; *Western Illinois Outreach Coord.:* Awisi Quartey

525 S. 8th St., Springfield, IL 62703-1606; 217-492-4062; Fax: 217-492-4382; *State Director:* Bill Houlihan

Committee Assignments: Agriculture, Nutrition, and Forestry; Appropriations; Judiciary, Chair

Majority Whip

Ernst, Joni, R-Iowa

Capitol Hill Office: 730 SHOB 20510-1502; 224-3254; Fax: 224-9369; *Chief of Staff:* Lisa Goeas

Web: www.ernst.senate.gov

Facebook: www.facebook.com/senjoniernst

Twitter: @SenJoniErnst

Instagram: @senjoniernst

YouTube: www.youtube.com/channel/UCLwrmtF_84FIcK3TyMs4MIw

District Offices: 733 Federal Bldg., 210 Walnut St., Des Moines, IA 50309; 515-284-4574; Fax: 515-284-4937; *State Director:* Clarke Scanlon

111 7th Ave. S.E., #480, Cedar Rapids, IA 52401-2101; 319-365-4504; Fax: 319-365-4683; *Field Rep.:* Brittney Carroll

201 W. 2nd St., #806, Davenport, IA 52801; 563-322-0677; Fax: 563-322-0854; *Regional Director:* Joe Krenzelok

194 Federal Bldg., 320 6th St., Sioux City, IA 51101; 712-252-1550; Fax: 712-252-1638; *Regional Director:* Kolby DeWitt

2146 27th Ave. #500, Council Bluffs, IA 51501; 712-352-1167; Fax: 712-352-0087; *Constituent Service Director:* Emily McKern

Committee Assignments: Agriculture, Nutrition, and Forestry; Armed Services; Environment and Public Works; Small Business and Entrepreneurship

Feinstein, Dianne, D-Calif.

Capitol Hill Office: 331 SHOB 20510-0504; 224-3841; Fax: 228-3954; *Chief of Staff:* David Grannis

Web: www.feinstein.senate.gov

Facebook: www.facebook.com/SenatorFeinstein

Twitter: @SenFeinstein

YouTube: www.youtube.com/SenatorFeinstein

District Offices: 2500 Tulare St., #4290, Fresno, CA 93721; 559-485-7430; Fax: 559-485-9689; *District Director:* Shelly Abajian

11111 Santa Monica Blvd., #915, Los Angeles, CA 90025-3343; 310-914-7300; Fax: 310-914-7318; *Deputy State Director:* Peter Muller

880 Front St., #4236, San Diego, CA 92101; 619-231-9712; Fax: 619-231-1108; *District Director:* Bill Kratz

One Post St., #2450, San Francisco, CA 94104-5240; 415-393-0707; Fax: 415-393-0710; *State Director:* Jim Lazarus

Committee Assignments: Appropriations; Congressional-Executive Commission on China; International Narcotics Control Caucus; Judiciary; Rules and Administration; Select Intelligence

Fischer, Deb, R-Neb.

Capitol Hill Office: 454 SROB 20510; 224-6551; Fax: 228-1325; *Chief of Staff:* Joe Hack

Web: www.fischer.senate.gov

Facebook: www.facebook.com/senatordebfischer

Twitter: @SenatorFischer

Instagram: @senatorfischer

YouTube: www.youtube.com/SenatorDebFischer

District Offices: 1248 O St., #1111, Lincoln, NE 68508; 402-441-4600; Fax: 402-476-8753; *State Director:* Holly Baker

11819 Miracle Hills Dr., #205, Omaha, NE 68154; 402-391-3411; Fax: 402-391-4725; *State Director:* Holly Baker

20 W. 23rd St., Kearney, NE 68847; 308-234-2361; Fax: 308-234-3684; *Constituent Services Director:* Josh Jelden

120 E. 16th St., #203, Scottsbluff, NE 69361; 308-630-2329; Fax: 308-630-2321; *Constituent Services Director:* Brandy McCaslin

Committee Assignments: Agriculture, Nutrition, and Forestry; Armed Services; Commerce, Science, and Transportation; Rules and Administration; Select Ethics

Gillibrand, Kirsten E., D-N.Y.

Capitol Hill Office: 478 SROB 20510-3205; 224-4451; Fax: 228-4977; *Chief of Staff:* Jess Fassler

Web: www.gillibrand.senate.gov

Facebook: www.facebook.com/SenKirstenGillibrand

Twitter: @gillibrandny

Instagram: @kirstengillibrand

YouTube: www.youtube.com/KirstenEGillibrand
District Offices: Leo W. O'Brien Federal Office Bldg., 11A Clinton Ave., Room 821, Albany, NY 12207-2202; 518-431-0120; Fax: 518-431-0128; *Regional Director:* Florencia Feleder

Larkin at Exchange, 726 Exchange St., #511, Buffalo, NY 14210-1485; 716-854-9725; Fax: 716-854-9731; *Regional Director:* Courtney Ball

P.O. Box 273, Lowville, NY 13367; 315-376-6118; Fax: 315-376-6118; *Regional Director:* Lisa Hofslich

155 N. Pinelawn Rd., #250, Melville, NY 11747-3247; 631-249-2825; Fax: 631-249-2847; *Regional Director:* Michael Scheid

780 3rd Ave., #2601, New York, NY 10017-2177; 212-688-6262; Fax: 866-824-6340; *State Director:* Emily Arsenault

Kenneth B. Keating Federal Office Bldg., 100 State St., Room 4195, Rochester, NY 14614-1318; 585-263-6250; Fax: 585-263-6247; *Deputy State Director:* Jarred Jones

James M. Hanley Federal Bldg., 100 S. Clinton St., Room 1470, P.O. Box 7378, Syracuse, NY 13261; 315-448-0470; Fax: 315-448-0476; *Regional Director:* Jamie Suess

Committee Assignments: Agriculture, Nutrition, and Forestry; Armed Services; Special Intelligence; Special Aging

Graham, Lindsey, R-S.C.

Capitol Hill Office: 290 SROB 20510-4003; 224-5972; Fax: 224-3808; *Chief of Staff:* Richard S. Perry
Web: www.lgraham.senate.gov
Facebook: www.facebook.com/LindseyGrahamSC
Twitter: @LindseyGrahamSC
Instagram: @lindseygrahamsc
YouTube: www.youtube.com/channel/UClLGZMA5Ei2Z8fR1PLEx6yQ
District Offices: 2142 Boyce St., #404, Columbia, SC 29201-2718; 803-933-0112; Fax: 803-933-0957; *Upstate Regional Director:* Angie Omer

McMillan Federal Bldg., 401 W. Evans St., #111, Florence, SC 29501-3460; 843-669-1505; Fax: 843-669-9015; *Pee Dee Regional Director:* Celia Urquhart

130 S. Main St., 7th Floor, Greenville, SC 29601-4870; 864-250-1417; Fax: 864-250-4322; *State Director:* Van Cato

530 Johnnie Dodds Blvd., #202, Mt. Pleasant, SC 29464-3029; 843-849-3887; Fax: 843-971-3669; *Low Country Regional Director:* Dan Head

124 Exchange St., Suite A, Pendleton, SC 29670-1312; 864-646-4090; Fax: 864-646-8609; *Regional Director:* Angie Omer

235 E. Main St., #100, Rock Hill, SC 29730-4891; 803-366-2828; Fax: 803-366-5353; *Piedmont Regional Director:* Teresa Thomas

Committee Assignments: Appropriations; Budget; Environment and Public Works; Judiciary

Grassley, Chuck, R-Iowa

Capitol Hill Office: 135 SHOB 20510-1501; 224-3744; Fax: 224-6020; *Chief of Staff:* Aaron Cummings

Web: www.grassley.senate.gov
Facebook: www.facebook.com/grassley
Twitter: @chuckgrassley
Instagram: @senatorchuckgrassley
YouTube: www.youtube.com/SenChuckGrassley
District Offices: 111 7th Ave. S.E., P.O. Box 13, #6800, Cedar Rapids, IA 52401; 319-363-6832; Fax: 319-363-7179; *Regional Director:* Rochelle Fuller

2146 27th Ave., #550, Council Bluffs, IA 51501; 712-322-7103; Fax: 712-322-7196; *Regional Director; Constituent Services Specialist:* Donna Barry

201 W. 2nd St., #720, Davenport, IA 52801-1419; 563-322-4331; Fax: 563-322-8552; *Regional Director:* Penny Vacek

721 Federal Bldg., 210 Walnut St., Des Moines, IA 50309-2140; 515-288-1145; Fax: 515-288-5097; *State Director:* Carol Olson

120 Federal Bldg., 320 6th St., Sioux City, IA 51101-1244; 712-233-1860; Fax: 712-233-1634; *Regional Director:* Jacob Bossman

210 Waterloo Bldg., 531 Commercial St., Waterloo, IA 50701-5497; 319-232-6657; Fax: 319-232-9965; *Regional Director:* Matt Rector

Committee Assignments: Agriculture, Nutrition, and Forestry; Budget; Finance; International Narcotics Control Caucus; Joint Taxation; Judiciary

Hagerty, Bill, R-Tenn.

Capitol Hill Office: 248 SROB 20002; 224-4944; Fax: 228-3398; *Chief of Staff:* Adam Telle
Web: www.hagerty.senate.gov
Facebook: www.facebook.com/SenatorBillHagerty
Twitter: @SenatorHagerty
Instagram: @senatorhagerty
YouTube: www.youtube.com/channel/UCqLlLx05ScUwxVHvevyaDFg
District Offices: 2525 Hwy. 75, #101, Blountville, TN 37617-6366; 423-325-6240; Fax: 423-325-6236; *Field Rep.:* Nick Castle

900 Georgia Ave., #260, Chattanooga, TN 37402-2240; 423-752-5337; Fax: 423-752-2504; *Field Rep.:* Laken Shattuck

Ed Jones Federal Bldg., 109 S. Highland Ave., #216, Jackson, TN 38301; 901-544-4224; *Field Rep.:* Matt Varino

Howard H. Baker Jr. U.S. Courthouse, 800 Market St., #112, Knoxville, TN 37902-2303; 865-545-4253; Fax: 865-545-4252; *Field Rep.:* Riley Lovingood

Clifford Davis-Odell Horton Federal Bldg., 167 N. Main St., #1068, Memphis, TN 38103-1858; 901-544-4224; *Field Rep.:* Chris Connolly

3322 W. End Ave., #120, Nashville, TN 37203-6821; 615-736-5129; Fax: 615-269-4803; *Field Rep.:* Stan Settles

L. Clure Morton Federal Bldg., 9 E. Broad St., 3rd Floor, Cookeville, TN 38503; 931-981-4874; *Field Rep.:* Tanner Cox

Committee Assignments: Appropriations; Banking, Housing, and Urban Affairs; Foreign Relations; Rules and Administration

Hassan, Margaret Wood, D-N.H.

Capitol Hill Office: 324 SHOB 20510; 224-3324; Fax: 228-0581; *Chief of Staff:* Marc Goldberg
Web: www.hassan.senate.gov
Facebook: www.facebook.com/SenatorHassan
Twitter: @SenatorHassan
Instagram: @senatorhassan
YouTube: www.youtube.com/SenatorHassan
District Offices: 1589 Elm St., 3rd Floor, Manchester, NH 03101; 603-622-2204; Fax: 603-433-4447; *State Director:* Jennifer Kuzma
143 Main St., #520, Nashua, NH 03060; 603-880-3314; *Special Assistant for Policy and Projects:* Justin Troiano
14 Manchester Square, #140, Portsmouth, NH 03801; 603-433-4445; Fax: 603-433-4447; *Director of Constituent Services:* Elyse Britton
Berlin City Hall, Lower Level, 168 Main St., Berlin, NH 03570; 603-752-6190; *Special Assistant for the North Country:* Ben Belanger
James C. Cleveland Federal Bldg., 53 Pleasant St., Concord, NH 03301; 603-622-2204; *Senior Advisor:* Pam Walsh
Committee Assignments: Finance; Health, Education, Labor, and Pensions; Homeland Security and Governmental Affairs; Joint Economic; Veterans' Affairs

Hawley, Josh, R-Mo.

Capitol Hill Office: 115 SROB 20510; 224-6154; Fax: 228-0526; *Chief of Staff:* Kyle Plotkin
Web: www.hawley.senate.gov
Facebook: www.facebook.com/SenatorHawley
Twitter: @SenHawleyPress
Instagram: @senatorhawley
YouTube: www.youtube.com/channel/UCMzt8xq6qQ3XQ_DlNfJx0-w
District Offices: 555 Independence St., #1600, Cape Girardeau, MO 63703; 573-334-5995; Fax: 573-334-5947; *District Director:* Matt Bain
1123 Wilkes Blvd., #220, Columbia, MO 65201; 573-554-1919; Fax: 573-256-1805; *State Director:* Daniel Hartman
400 E. 9th St., #9350, Kansas City, MO 64106; 816-960-4694; Fax: 816-472-6812; *District Director:* Elizabeth Johnson
901 E. St. Louis St., #1604, Springfield, MO 65806; 417-869-4433; Fax: 417-869-4411; *District Director:* Clayton Campbell
111 S. 10th St., #23.360, St. Louis, MO 63102; 314-354-7060; Fax: 1 314-436-8534; *Field Rep.:* Ben Gruender
Committee Assignments: Armed Services; Homeland Security and Governmental Affairs; Judiciary; Small Business and Entrepreneurship

Heinrich, Martin, D-N.M.

Capitol Hill Office: 303 SHOB 20510; 224-5521; Fax: 228-2841; *Chief of Staff:* Rebecca Avitia
Web: www.heinrich.senate.gov
Facebook: www.facebook.com/MartinHeinrich
Twitter: @MartinHeinrich
Instagram: @senatormartinheinrich
YouTube: www.youtube.com/SenMartinHeinrich
District Offices: 400 Gold Ave. S.W., #1080, Albuquerque, NM 87102; 505-346-6601; Fax: 505-346-6780; *Constituent Services Director:* Miguel Negrete
7450 E. Main St., Suite A, Farmington, NM 87402; 505-325-5030; Fax: 505-325-6035; *Field Rep. / Constituent Services Rep.:* Jim Dumont
201 N. Church St., #305, Las Cruces, NM 88001; 575-523-6561; Fax: 575-523-6584; *Field Rep:* Ashley Beyer
200 E. 4th St., #300, Roswell, NM 88201; 575-622-7113; Fax: 575-622-3538; *Constituent Services Rep.:* Iris Karges
123 E. Marcy St., #103, Santa Fe, NM 87501; 505-988-6647; Fax: 505-992-8435; *Field Rep.:* Patricia Dominguez
Committee Assignments: Appropriations; Armed Services; Energy and Natural Resources; Joint Economic; Select Intelligence

Hickenlooper, John W., D-Colo.

Capitol Hill Office: SR-B85 SROB 20510-0608; 224-5941; Fax: 224-6524; *Chief of Staff:* Kirtan Mehta
Web: www.hickenlooper.senate.gov
Facebook: www.facebook.com/SenatorHick
Twitter: @SenatorHick
Instagram: @senatorhick
YouTube: www.youtube.com/channel/UCU6pcq-AZA9wnmIPBj6ePwQ
District Offices: 102 S. Tejon St., #930, Colorado Springs, CO 80903; 719-632-6706
Byron Rodgers Federal Bldg., 1961 Stout St., #12-300, Denver, CO 80294; 303-244-1628; *State Director:* Shad Murib
2001 S. Shields St., Bldg. H, #104, Fort Collins, CO 80526; 970-484-3502; *Eastern Plains Regional Director:* Kari Linker
801 8th St., #140A, Greeley, CO 80631; 970-352-5546
Wayne Aspinall Federal Bldg., 400 Rood Ave., #220, Grand Junction, CO 81501; 970-822-4530; *Western Regional Director:* Sarah McCarthy
503 N. Main St., #426, Pueblo, CO 81003; 719-543-1324; *State Director:* Shab Murib
329 S. Camino del Rio, Suite Eye, Durango, CO 81303; 970-259-1231; *State Director:* Shad Murib
Committee Assignments: Commerce, Science, and Transportation; Energy and Natural Resources; Health, Education, Labor, and Pensions; Small Business and Entrepreneurship

Hirono, Mazie K., D-Hawaii

Capitol Hill Office: 109 SHOB 20510; 224-6361; Fax: 224-2126; *Chief of Staff:* Alan Yamamoto
Web: www.hirono.senate.gov
Facebook: www.facebook.com/senatorhirono
Twitter: @maziehirono
Instagram: @maziehirono
YouTube: www.youtube.com/CongresswomanHirono
District Office: 300 Ala Moana Blvd., Room 3-106, Honolulu, HI 96850; 808-522-8970; Fax: 808-545-4683; *Deputy Chief of Staff:* Kehau Yap

Committee Assignments: Armed Services; Energy and Natural Resources; Judiciary; Small Business and Entrepreneurship; Veterans' Affairs

Hoeven, John, R-N.D.

Capitol Hill Office: 338 SROB 20510-3406; 224-2551; *Chief of Staff:* Tony Everhard
Web: www.hoeven.senate.gov
Facebook: www.facebook.com/SenatorJohnHoeven
Twitter: @SenJohnHoeven
Instagram: @senjohnhoeven
YouTube: www.youtube.com/SenatorJohnHoevenND
District Offices: U.S. Federal Bldg., 220 E. Rosser Ave., Room 312, Bismarck, ND 58501-3869; 701-250-4618; Fax: 701-250-4484; *Regional Director:* Vacant; *Field Rep.:* Andrew Malloy
123 N. Broadway, #201, Fargo, ND 58103; 701-239-5389; Fax: 202-228-5112; *State Director:* Jessica Lee
Federal Bldg., 102 N. 4th St., Room 108, Grand Forks, ND 58203-3738; 701-746-8972; Fax: 701-746-5613; *Field Rep.:* Tom Brusegaard
100 1st St. S.W., #107, Minot, ND 58701; 701-838-1361; Fax: 701-838-1381; *Regional Director:* Sally Johnson
204 N. Main St., #561, Watford City, ND 58854; 701-609-2727; *Western Director:* Shari Duck
Committee Assignments: Agriculture, Nutrition, and Forestry; Appropriations; Energy and Natural Resources; Indian Affairs

Hyde-Smith, Cindy, R-Miss.

Capitol Hill Office: 702 SROB 20510-2405; 224-5054; Fax: 224-5321; *Chief of Staff:* Doug Davis
Web: www.hydesmith.senate.gov
Facebook: www.facebook.com/SenatorCindyHydeSmith
Twitter: @SenHydeSmith
Instagram: @sencindyhydesmith
YouTube: www.youtube.com/channel/UCJHxkJhGST0NTlkzJHWV03Q
District Offices: 2012 15th St., #451, Gulfport, MS 39501-2036; 228-867-9710; Fax: 228-867-9789; *Southern District Director:* Myrtis Franke
190 E. Capitol St., #550, Jackson, MS 39201-2137; 601-965-4459; Fax: 601-965-4919; *State Director:* Umesh Sanjanwala; *Central District Director:* JoAnn Clark
911 Jackson Ave., Room 249, Oxford, MS 38655-3652; 662-236-1018; Fax: 662-236-7618; *Northern District Director:* Mindy Maxwell
Committee Assignments: Agriculture, Nutrition, and Forestry; Appropriations; Energy and Natural Resources; Rules and Administration

Inhofe, James M., R-Okla.

Capitol Hill Office: 205 SROB 20510-3603; 224-4721; Fax: 228-0380; *Chief of Staff:* Luke Holland
Web: www.inhofe.senate.gov
Facebook: www.facebook.com/jiminhofe
Twitter: @JimInhofe
Instagram: @jiminhofe

YouTube: www.youtube.com/channel/UCk3W3ilX8vGG-300qzNpG7w
District Offices: 302 N. Independence St., #104, Enid, OK 73701-4025; 580-234-5105; Fax: 580-234-5094; *Field Rep.:* Ryan Sproul
3817 Expressway N.W., #780, Oklahoma City, OK 73112; 405-208-8841; Fax: 405-604-0917; *Central and Southwest Regional Rep.:* Bryson Panas
1924 S. Utica Ave., #530, Tulsa, OK 74104; 918-748-5111; Fax: 918-748-5119; *Northeast Regional Rep.:* Jared Ward
Committee Assignments: Armed Services; Environment and Public Works; Select Intelligence; Small Business and Entrepreneurship

Johnson, Ron, R-Wisc.

Capitol Hill Office: 328 SHOB 20510-4905; 224-5323; Fax: 228-6965; *Chief of Staff:* Sean Riley
Web: www.ronjohnson.senate.gov
Facebook: www.facebook.com/senronjohnson
Twitter: @SenRonJohnson
Instagram: @senronjohnson
YouTube: www.youtube.com/SenatorRonJohnson
District Offices: 517 E. Wisconsin Ave., #408, Milwaukee, WI 53202-4510; 414-276-7282; Fax: 414-276-7284; *Regional Director:* Ginger Kollmansberger
219 Washington Ave., #100, Oshkosh, WI 54901; 920-230-7250; Fax: 920-230-7262; *State Director:* Julie Leschke
5315 Wall St., #110, Madison, WI 53718; 608-240-9629; Fax: 608-240-9646
Committee Assignments: Budget; Commerce, Science, and Transportation; Foreign Relations; Homeland Security and Governmental Affairs

Kaine, Tim, D-Va.

Capitol Hill Office: 231 SROB 20510; 224-4024; Fax: 228-6363; *Chief of Staff:* Mike Henry
Web: www.kaine.senate.gov
Facebook: www.facebook.com/SenatorKaine
Twitter: @timkaine
Instagram: @timkaine
YouTube: www.youtube.com/SenatorTimKaine
District Offices: 121 Russell Road, #2, Abingdon, VA 24210; 276-525-4790; Fax: 276- 525-4792; *Regional Director:* Laura Blevins
919 E. Main St., #970, Richmond, VA 23219; 804-771-2221; Fax: 804-771-8313; *State Director:* Keren Dongo
222 Central Park Ave., #120, Virginia Beach, VA 23462; 757-518-1674; Fax: 757-518-1679; *Regional Director:* Diane Kaufman
816 William St., Suite B, Fredericksburg, VA 22401; 540-369-7667; Fax: 540-310-0049; *Regional Director:* Gauston Araoz-Riveros
611 S. Jefferson St., #5B, Roanoke, VA 24011; 540-682-5693; Fax: 540-682-5697; *Regional Director:* Elda Stanco
9408 Grant Ave., #202, Manassas, VA 20110; 703-361-3192; Fax: 703-361-3198; *Regional Director:* Rachel Reieach

Committee Assignments: Armed Services; Budget; Foreign Relations; Health, Education, Labor, and Pensions

Kelly, Mark, D-Ariz.

Capitol Hill Office: 516 SDOB 20515; 224-2235; *Chief of Staff:* Jen Cox
Web: www.kelly.senate.gov
Facebook: www.facebook.com/SenMarkKelly
Twitter: @SenMarkKelly
Instagram: @senmarkkelly
YouTube: www.youtube.com/SenMarkKelly
District Offices: 2201 E. Camelback Rd., #115, Phoenix, AZ 85016; 602-671-7901; *Operations Director:* Gina Fong
407 W. Congress St., #103, Tucson, AZ 85701; 520-475-5177; *Director of Constituent Services:* Travonne Smith
107 N. Cortez St., #101, Prescott, AZ 86301; 928-420-7732; *Northern Arizona Director:* Coral Evans
Committee Assignments: Armed Services; Energy and Natural Resources; Environment and Public Works; Joint Economic; Special Aging

Kennedy, John, R-La.

Capitol Hill Office: 416 SROB 20510; 224-4623; *Chief of Staff:* David Stokes
Web: www.kennedy.senate.gov
Facebook: www.facebook.com/SenatorJohnKennedy
Twitter: @SenJohnKennedy
Instagram: @senjohnkennedy
YouTube: www.youtube.com/channel/ UCDgjkA5Y_npoxeUiSW18JZQ
District Offices: 315 S. College Rd., #140, Lafayette, LA 70503; 337-269-5980; *State Director:* Michael Wong
1651 Louisville Ave., #148, Monroe, LA 71201; 318-361-1489; *Regional Rep.:* Hannah Livingston
6501 Coliseum Blvd., #700A, Alexandria, LA 71303; 318-445-2892; *Regional Rep.:* Hannah Livingston
7932 Wrenwood Blvd., Suite A & B, Baton Rouge, LA 70809; 225-926-8033; *State Director:* Michael Wong
401 Market St., #1050, Shreveport, LA 71101; 318-670-5192; *Regional Director:* John Barr
500 Poydras St., #364, New Orleans, LA 70113; 504-581-6190; *State Director:* Michael Wong
21490 Koop Dr., Bldg. A, Mandeville, LA 70471; 985-809-8153; *Regional Rep.:* Ross White
814 West McNeese St., #213, Lake Charles, LA 70605; 337-573-6800 *Regional Rep.:* Emily Stine
8026 Main St., #700, Houma, LA 70360; 985-851-0956 *Regional Rep.:* Ross White
Committee Assignments: Appropriations; Banking, Housing, and Urban Affairs; Budget; Judiciary; Small Business and Entrepreneurship

King, Angus S. Jr., I-Maine

Capitol Hill Office: 133 SHOB 20510; 224-5344; Fax: 224-1946; *Chief of Staff:* Kathleen Connery Dawe
Web: www.king.senate.gov
Facebook: www.facebook.com/SenatorAngusSKingJr
Twitter: @SenAngusKing
Instagram: @anguskingmaine
YouTube: www.youtube.com/senatorangusking
District Offices: E.S. Muskie Federal Bldg., #412 Augusta, ME 04330; 207-622-8292; *Regional Rep.:* Scott Wilkinson
202 Harlow St., #20350, Bangor, ME 04401; 207-945-8000; *Regional Rep.:* Edie Smith
167 Academy St., Suite A, Presque Isle, ME 04769; 207-764-5124; *Regional Rep.:* Sharon Campbell
227 Main St., Biddeford, ME 04005; 207-352-5216; *Regional Rep.:* Gail Kezer
1 Pleasant St., #4W, Portland, ME 04101; 207-245-1565; *Regional Rep.:* Gail Kezer
Committee Assignments: Armed Services; Congressional-Executive Commission on China; Energy and Natural Resources; Rules and Administration; Select Intelligence

Klobuchar, Amy, D-Minn.

Capitol Hill Office: 425 SDOB 20510-2307; 224-3244; Fax: 228-2186; *Chief of Staff:* Doug Calidas
Web: www.klobuchar.senate.gov
Facebook: www.facebook.com/amyklobuchar
Twitter: @SenAmyKlobuchar
Instagram: @senamyklobuchar and @amyklobuchar
YouTube: www.youtube.com/channel/ UCZZ4_LJnkeGnbiqQPKYDTaA
District Offices: 1200 S. Washington Ave., Room 250, Minneapolis, MN 55415-1588; 612-727-5220; Fax: 202-224-1792; *State Director:* Vacant
121 S. 4th St., Moorhead, MN 56560-2613; 218-287-2219; Fax: 202-224-1792; *Regional Outreach Director:* Andy Martin
1130 1/2 7th St. N.W., Room 212, Rochester, MN 55901-2995; 507-288-5321; Fax: 202-224-1792; *Regional Outreach Director:* Chuck Ackman
Olcott Plaza, Room 105, 820 N. 9th St., Virginia, MN 55792-2300; 218-741-9690; Fax: 202-224-1792; *Regional Outreach Director:* Ida Rukavina
Committee Assignments: Agriculture, Nutrition, and Forestry; Commerce, Science, and Transportation; Joint Economic; Joint Library; Joint Printing; Judiciary; Rules and Administration, Chair; Democratic Steering and Outreach, Chair

Lankford, James, R-Okla.

Capitol Hill Office: 316 SHOB 20510-3604; 224-5754 *Chief of Staff:* Michelle Altman
Web: www.lankford.senate.gov
Facebook: www.facebook.com/SenatorLankford
Twitter: @SenatorLankford
Instagram: @senatorlankford
YouTube: www.youtube.com/channel/ UCz8T6sK5fEycyWmVz6Vpe5Q
District Offices: 1015 N. Broadway Ave., #310, Oklahoma City, OK 73102; 405-231-4941; *Scheduler:* Vacant

401 S. Boston Ave., #2150, Tulsa, OK 74103; 918-581-7651; *Constituent Services Director:* Emily Burner

Committee Assignments: Congressional-Executive Commission on China; Energy and Natural Resources; Finance; Homeland Security and Governmental Affairs; Indian Affairs; Select Ethics

Leahy, Patrick J., D-Vt.

Capitol Hill Office: 437 SROB 20510-4502; 224-4242; Fax: 224-3479; *Chief of Staff:* John P. Dowd
Web: www.leahy.senate.gov
Facebook: www.facebook.com/SenatorPatrickLeahy
Twitter: @SenatorLeahy
Instagram: @senatorleahy
YouTube: www.youtube.com/SenatorPatrickLeahy
District Offices: 199 Main St., 4th Floor, Burlington, VT 05401; 802-863-2525; Fax: 802-658-1009; *State Director:* John Tracy
87 State St., Room 338, Montpelier, VT 05602-9505; 802-229-0569; Fax: 802-229-1915; *Field Reps:* Charles Martin and Pollaidh Major
Committee Assignments: Agriculture, Nutrition, and Forestry; Appropriations, Chair; Joint Library; Judiciary; Rules and Administration

Lee, Mike, R-Utah

Capitol Hill Office: 363 SROB 20510-4404; 224-5444; Fax: 228-1168; *Chief of Staff:* Allyson Bell
Web: www.lee.senate.gov
Facebook: www.facebook.com/senatormikelee
Twitter: @SenMikeLee
Instagram: @senmikelee
YouTube: www.youtube.com/senatormikelee
District Offices: Wallace F. Bennett Federal Bldg., 125 S. State St., #4225, Salt Lake City, UT 84138-1188; 801-524-5933; Fax: 801-524-5730; *State Director:* Rob Axson
196 E. Tabernacle St., #21, St. George, UT 84770-3474; 435-628-5514; *Southern Utah Director:* Heath Hansen
James V. Hansen Federal Bldg., 324 25th St., #1410, Ogden, UT 84401; 801-392-9633; Fax: 801-392-9630; *Northern Utah Director:* Nathan Jackson
Committee Assignments: Commerce, Science, and Transportation; Energy and Natural Resources; Judiciary; Joint Economic; Special Aging

Lummis, Cynthia M., R-Wyo.

Capitol Hill Office: SROB124 SDOB 20510; 224-3424; Fax: 228-0359; *Chief of Staff:* Kristin Walker
Web: www.lummis.senate.gov
Facebook: www.facebook.com/sencynthialummis
Twitter: @SenLummis
Instagram: @sencynthialummis
YouTube: www.youtube.com/channel/UCHUgylNGQo407Ij02pvb-UQ
District Offices: Dick Cheney Federal Bldg., 100 E. B St., #3201, P.O. Box 33201, Casper, WY 82602; 307-261-6572; *Field Rep.:* Jackie King

Federal Center, 2120 Capitol Ave., #2007, Cheyenne, WY 82001-3631; 307-772-2477; Fax: 307-772-2480; *Field Reps.:* Brendan Ames and Martha Wilson
1285 Sheridan Ave., #215, Cody, WY 82414-3653; 307-527-9444; Fax: 307-527-9476; *State Director:* Jennifer Fernandez
80 1st St., #1630, Afton, WY 83110; 307-248-1736; Fax:
120 N. 4th St., Suite B, Sundance, WY 82729; 307-283-3461
Committee Assignments: Banking, Housing, and Urban Affairs; Commerce, Science, and Transportation; Environment and Public Works

Luján, Ben Ray, D-N.M.

Capitol Hill Office: 498 SROD 20510; 224-6621; 202-224-3370; *Chief of Staff:* Carlos Sanchez
Web: www.lujan.senate.gov
Facebook: www.facebook.com/SenatorLujan
Twitter: @SenatorLujan
Instagram: @senatorlujan
YouTube: www.youtube.com/c/SenatorLuj%C3%A1n/featured
District Offices: 201 N. Church St., #201B, Las Cruces, NM 88001; 575-526-5475; Fax: 575-523-6589
120 S. Federal Pl., #302, Santa Fe, NM 87501; 505-988-6511; Fax: 833-702-2621
1103 National Ave., #210, Las Vegas, NM 87701
100 S. Ave. A, #113, Portales, NM 88130; 575-252-6188; Fax: 833-702-2620
Committee Assignments: Agriculture, Nutrition, and Forestry; Budget; Commerce, Science, and Transportation; Health, Education, Labor, and Pension; Indian Affairs; International Narcotics Drug Control Caucus

Manchin, Joe III, D-W.Va.

Capitol Hill Office: 306 SHOB 20510-4803; 224-3954; Fax: 228-0002; *Chief of Staff:* Lance West
Web: www.manchin.senate.gov
Facebook: www.facebook.com/JoeManchinIII
Twitter: @Sen_JoeManchin
Instagram: @joemanchin
YouTube: www.youtube.com/SenatorJoeManchin
District Offices: 900 Pennsylvania Ave., #629, Charleston, WV 25302; 304-342-5855; Fax: 304-343-7144; *State Director:* Mara Boggs
261 Aikens Center, #305, Martinsburg, WV 25404-6203; 304-264-4626; Fax: 304-262-3039; *State Director:* Mara Boggs
230 Adams St., Fairmont, WV 26554; 304-368-0567; Fax: 304-368-0198; *State Director:* Mara Boggs
Committee Assignments: Appropriations; Armed Services; Energy and Natural Resources, Chair; Veterans' Affairs

Markey, Edward J., D-Mass.

Capitol Hill Office: 255 SDOB 20510; 224-2742; *Chief of Staff:* John E. Walsh
Web: www.markey.senate.gov
Facebook: www.facebook.com/EdJMarkey

Twitter: @SenMarkey
Instagram: @senmarkeymemes
YouTube: www.youtube.com/repmarkey
District Offices: 975 JFK Federal Bldg., 15 New Sudbury St., Boston, MA 02203; 617-565-8519; Fax: 616-570-9081; *State Director:* Jim Cantwell

1550 Main St., 4th Floor, Springfield, MA 01103; 413-785-4610; *Regional Director:* Jossie Valentin

Committee Assignments: Commerce, Science, and Transportation; Environment and Public Works; Foreign Relations; Small Business and Entrepreneurship

Marshall, Roger, R-Kans.

Capitol Hill Office: 479A SROB 20510-1605; 224-4774; Fax: 224-3514; *Chief of Staff:* Brent Robertson
Web: www.marshall.senate.gov
Facebook: www.facebook.com/RogerMarshallMD
Twitter: @RogerMarshallMD
Instagram: @senrogermarshall
YouTube: www.youtube.com/channel/UCR3nOFMqBB-kRpKFwgapMaQ
District Offices: 921 Lareu St., Suite C., Garden City, KS 67846; 620-765-7800

7011 W. 121st St., #100, Overland Park, KS 66209; 913-879-7070

402B N. Broadway, Pittsburg, KS 66762; 620-404-7016

204 S. Santa Fe Ave., #1, Salina, KS 67401; 785-829-9000

800 Jackson St. S.W., #600, Topeka, KS 66612; 785-414-7501

100 S. Market St., #102, Wichita, KS 67202; 316-803-6120

Committee Assignments: Agriculture, Nutrition, and Forestry; Energy and Natural Resources; Health, Education, Labor, and Pensions; Small Business and Entrepreneurship

McConnell, Mitch, R-Ky.

Capitol Hill Office: 317 SROB 20510-1702; 224-2541; Fax: 224-2499; *Chief of Staff:* Terry Carmack
Web: www.mcconnell.senate.gov
Facebook: www.facebook.com/mitchmcconnell
Twitter: @McConnellPress and @LeaderMcConnell
Instagram: @mcconnellpress and @leadermcconnell
YouTube: www.youtube.com/RepublicanLeader
District Offices: Federal Bldg., 241 E. Main St., Room 102, Bowling Green, KY 42101-2175; 270-781-1673; Fax: 270-782-1884; *Field Rep.:* Timothy Gilliam

1885 Dixie Hwy., #345, Fort Wright, KY 41011; 859-578-0188; Fax: 859-578-0488; *Field Rep.:* Megan Bankemper; *Field Assistant:* Kim Kraft

771 Corporate Dr., #108, Lexington, KY 40503-5439; 859-224-8286; *Field Rep.:* Stephanie Nelson

300 S. Main St., #310, London, KY 40741; 606-864-2026; Fax: 606-864-2035; *Field Rep.:* Donna Baker-McClure

601 W. Broadway, Room 630, Louisville, KY 40202-2228; 502-582-6304; Fax: 502-582-5326; *State Director:* Robbin Taylor

100 Fountain Ave., #300, Paducah, KY 42001; 270-442-4554; Fax: 270-443-3102; *Field Rep.:* Morgan Alvey

Committee Assignments: Agriculture, Nutrition, and Forestry; Appropriations; Rules and Administration; Select Intelligence
Minority Leader

Menendez, Robert, D-N.J.

Capitol Hill Office: 528 SHOB 20510; 224-4744; Fax: 228-2197; *Chief of Staff:* Jason Tuber
Web: www.menendez.senate.gov
Facebook: www.facebook.com/senatormenendez
Twitter: @SenatorMenendez
Instagram: @senatormenendez
YouTube: www.youtube.com/SenatorMenendezNJ
District Offices: 208 White Horse Pike, #18, Barrington, NJ 08007-1322; 856-757-5353; Fax: 856-546-1526; *State Director:* Raphael Chavez Fernandez

210 Hudson St., Harborside 3, #1000 Jersey City, NJ 07311; 973-645-3030; Fax: 201-434-9272; *State Director:* Raphael Chavez Fernandez

Committee Assignments: Banking, Housing, and Urban Affairs; Finance; Foreign Relations, Chair

Merkley, Jeff, D-Ore.

Capitol Hill Office: 531 SHOB 20510-3705; 224-3753; Fax: 228-3997; *Chief of Staff:* Michael S. Zamore
Web: www.merkley.senate.gov
Facebook: www.facebook.com/jeffmerkley
Twitter: @SenJeffMerkley
Instagram: @senjeffmerkley
YouTube: www.youtube.com/SenatorJeffMerkley
District Offices: 131 N.W. Hawthorne Ave., #208, Bend, OR 97703; 541-318-1298; Fax: 541-318-1396; *Field Rep.:* B. J. Westlund

405 E. 8th Ave., #2010, Eugene, OR 97401-2730; 541-465-6750; *Field Rep.:* Courtney Flathers

10 S. Bartlett St., #201, Medford, OR 97501-7204; 541-608-9102; *Field Rep.:* Eahna Black

1705 Main St., #504, Baker City, OR 97814; 541-278-1129; Fax: 541-278-4109; *Field Rep.:* Jessica Keys

121 Salmon St. S.W., #1400, Portland, OR 97204-2948; 503-326-3386; Fax: 503-326-2900; *State Director:* Jessica Stevens

500 Liberty St. S.E., #320, Salem, OR 97301; 503-362-8102; *Field Rep.:* Stacey Jochimsen

Committee Assignments: Appropriations; Budget; Congressional-Executive Commission on China, Chair; Environment and Public Works; Foreign Relations; Rules and Administration

Moran, Jerry, R-Kans.

Capitol Hill Office: 521 SDOB 20510-1606; 224-6521; Fax: 228-6966; *Chief of Staff:* James Kelly
Web: www.moran.senate.gov
Facebook: www.facebook.com/jerrymoran
Twitter: @JerryMoran
YouTube: www.youtube.com/SenatorJerryMoran
District Offices: 1200 Main St., #402, P.O. Box 249, Hays, KS 67601-3649; 785-628-6401; Fax: 785-628-3791; *Constituent Services Director:* Chelsey Ladd

1880 Kimball Ave., #270, Manhattan, KS 66502; 785-539-8973; Fax: 785-587-0789; *District Rep.:* Kristin Little

23600 College Blvd., #201, P.O. Box 1154, Olathe, KS 66061-8709; 913-393-0711; Fax: 913-768-1366; *State Director:* Alex Richard

306 N. Broadway St., #125, P.O. Box 1372, Pittsburg, KS 66762-4836; 620-232-2286; Fax: 620-232-2284; *District Rep.:* Pam Henderson

100 N. Broadway, #210, Wichita, KS 67202; 316-269-9257; Fax: 316-269-9259; *Deputy State Director:* Mike Zamrzla

1511 E. Fulton Terrace, #1511-2, Garden City, KS 67846; 620-260-3025; *State Director:* Hunter Carson

Committee Assignments: Appropriations; Banking, Housing, and Urban Affairs; Commerce, Science, and Transportation; Health, Education, Labor, and Pensions; Indian Affairs; Veterans' Affairs

Murkowski, Lisa, R-Alaska

Capitol Hill Office: 522 SHOB 20510; 224-6665; Fax: 224-5301; *Chief of Staff:* Kate Williams-Sterne
Web: www.murkowski.senate.gov
Facebook: www.facebook.com/SenLisaMurkowski
Twitter: @lisamurkowski
Instagram: @senlisamurkowski
YouTube: www.youtube.com/senatormurkowski
District Offices: 510 L St., #600, Anchorage, AK 99501; 907-271-3735; Fax: 877-857-0322; *Special Asst.: Cordelia Kellie* Kimbrell

Courthouse Square, 250 Cushman Ave., #2D, Fairbanks, AK 99701; 907-456-0233; Fax: 877-857-0322; *Special Asst.:* Trina Bailey

800 Glacier Ave., #101, Juneau, AK 99801; 907-586-7277; Fax: 877-857-0322; *Delegation Rep.:* Dana Herndon

44539 Sterling Hwy., #203, Soldotna, AK 99669; 907-262-4220; Fax: 877-857-0322; *Special Asst.:* Jane Conway

1900 First Ave., #225, Ketchikan, AK 99901; 907-225-6880; Fax: 877-857-0322; *Delegation Rep.:* Chere Klein

851 E. Westpoint Dr., #307, Wasilla, AK 99654-7183; 907-376-7665; Fax: 877-857-0322; *Special Asst.:* Gerri Sumpter

Committee Assignments: Appropriations; Energy and Natural Resources; Health, Education, Labor, and Pensions; Indian Affairs

Murphy, Chris, D-Conn.

Capitol Hill Office: 136 SHOB 20510; 224-4041; Fax: 224-9750; *Chief of Staff:* Allison Herwitt
Web: www.murphy.senate.gov
Facebook: www.facebook.com/senchrismurphy
Twitter: @SenMurphyOffice and @ChrisMurphyCT
Instagram: @senchrismurphy
YouTube: www.youtube.com/SenChrisMurphy
District Office: Colt Gateway, 120 Huyshope Ave., #401, Hartford, CT 06106; 860-549-8463; Fax: 860-524-5091; *State Director:* Kenny Curran
Committee Assignments: Appropriations; Foreign Relations; Health, Education, Labor, and Pensions

Murray, Patty, D-Wash.

Capitol Hill Office: 154 SROB 20510; 224-2621; Fax: 224-0238; *Chief of Staff:* Mindi Linquist
Web: www.murray.senate.gov
Facebook: www.facebook.com/pattymurray
Twitter: @PattyMurray
Instagram: @senpattymurray
YouTube: www.youtube.com/user/SenatorPattyMurray
District Offices: 2930 Wetmore Ave., #9D, Everett, WA 98201; 425-259-6515; Fax: 425-259-7152; *Regional Director:* Ann Larson

2988 Jackson Federal Bldg., 915 2nd Ave., Seattle, WA 98174-1003; 206-553-5545; Fax: 206-553-0891; *State Director:* Shawn Bills

10 N. Post St., #600, Spokane, WA 99201-0712; 509-624-9515; Fax: 509-624-9561; *Eastern Washington Director:* John Culton

950 Pacific Ave., #650, Tacoma, WA 98402; 253-572-3636; Fax: 253-572-9488; *South Sound Director:* Christine Nahn

The Marshall House, 1323 Officers Row, Vancouver, WA 98661-3856; 360-696-7797; Fax: 360-696-7798; *Southwest Washington Regional Director:* Bryan Stebbins

402 E. Yakima Ave., #420, Yakima, WA 98901; 509-453-7462; Fax: 509-453-7731; *Central Washington Director:* Raquel Crowley

Committee Assignments: Appropriations; Budget; Health, Education, Labor, and Pensions, Chair; Veterans' Affairs

Ossoff, Jon, D-Ga.

Capitol Hill Office: 455 SROB 20510; 224-3521; Fax: 224-2575; *Chief of Staff:* Reynaldo Benitez
Web: www.ossoff.senate.gov
Facebook: www.facebook.com/jonossoff
Twitter: @SenOssoff
Instagram: @jonossoff
YouTube: www.youtube.com/channel/ UCVCG2sRHEP6VW2Ao9LEcDPw
District Office: 3280 Peachtree Rd. N.E., #2640, Atlanta, GA 30305; 470-786-7800; Fax: 404-949-0912; *State Director:* Chandra Harris
Committee Assignments: Banking, Housing, and Urban Affairs; Homeland Security and Governmental Affairs; Judiciary; Rules and Administration

Padilla, Alex, D-Calif.

Capitol Hill Office: 112 SHOB 20510; 224-3553; Fax: 224-2200; *Chief of Staff:* David Montes
Web: www.padilla.senate.gov
Facebook: www.facebook.com/SenAlexPadilla
Twitter: @SenAlexPadilla
Instagram: @senalexpadilla
YouTube: www.youtube.com/channel/ UCKFOqsstH07VwhY7S5CfhNg
District Offices: 2500 Tulare St., #5290, Fresno, CA 93721; 559-497-5109; Fax: 202-228-3864; *State Director:* James Schwab

501 Eye St., #7-800, Sacramento, CA 95814; 916-448-2787; Fax: 202-228-3865; *State Director:* James Schwab

255 E. Temple St., #1860, Los Angeles, CA 90064; 310-231-4494; Fax: 202-224-0357; *Deputy State Director:* Daniel Chen

333 Bush St., #3225, San Francisco, CA 94104; 415-981-9369; Fax: 202-224-0454; *District Director:* Adam Mehis

600 B St., #2240, San Diego, CA 92101; 619-239-3884; Fax: 202-228-3863; *Field Rep.:* Artemis Hodoyan

Committee Assignments: Budget; Environment and Public Works; Homeland Security and Governmental Affairs; Judiciary; Rules and Administration

Paul, Rand, R-Ky.

Capitol Hill Office: 167 SROB 20510; 224-4343; *Chief of Staff:* William Henderson
Web: www.paul.senate.gov
Facebook: www.facebook.com/SenatorRandPaul
Twitter: @RandPaul
Instagram: @senatorrandpaul
YouTube: www.youtube.com/SenatorRandPaulKY
District Office: 1029 State St., Bowling Green, KY 42101-2652; 270-782-8303; *Constituent Services Director:* Bobette Franklin
Committee Assignments: Foreign Relations; Health, Education, Labor, and Pensions; Homeland Security and Governmental Affairs; Small Business and Entrepreneurship

Peters, Gary C., D-Mich.

Capitol Hill Office: 724 SHOB 20510; 224-6221; Fax: 224-7387; *Chief of Staff:* Caitlyn Stephenson
Web: www.peters.senate.gov
Facebook: www.facebook.com/SenGaryPeters
Twitter: @SenGaryPeters
Instagram: @sengarypeters
YouTube: www.youtube.com/channel/UC7LYNbnKSK2VZqQ98YROWHQ
District Offices: Patrick V. McNamara Federal Bldg., 477 Michigan Ave., #1837, Detroit, MI 48226; 313-226-6020; *Scheduler:* Angeli Chawla

124 W. Allegan St., #1400, Lansing, MI 48933; 517-377-1508; *State Director:* Elise Lancaster

Gerald R. Ford Federal Bldg., 110 Michigan Ave. N.W., #720, Grand Rapids, MI 49503; 616-233-9150; *Regional Director:* Peter Dickow

857 W. Washington St., #308, Marquette, MI 49855; 906-226-4554; *State Director:* Elise Lancaster

407 6th St., Suite C, Rochester, MI 48307; 248-608-8040; *Regional Director:* James Jackson

515 N. Washington Ave., #401, Saginaw, MI 48607; 989-754-0112; *Regional Director:* Kevin Hrit

818 Red Dr., #40, Traverse City, MI 49684; 231-947-7773; *Regional Director:* Eric Keller

Committee Assignments: Armed Services; Commerce, Science, and Transportation; Homeland Security and Governmental Affairs, Chair

Portman, Rob, R-Ohio

Capitol Hill Office: 448 SROB 20510; 224-3353; *Chief of Staff:* Kevin Smith
Web: www.portman.senate.gov
Facebook: www.facebook.com/senrobportman
Twitter: @senrobportman
Instagram: @senrobportman
YouTube: www.youtube.com/user/SenRobPortman
District Offices: 312 Walnut St., #3425, Cincinnati, OH 45202; 513-684-3265; *Southwest Ohio District Director:* Nan Cahall

1240 E. 9th St., #3061, Cleveland, OH 44199-2001; 216-522-7095; Fax: 216-522-7097; *Northeast Ohio District Director:* Caryn Candisky

37 W. Broad St., #300, Columbus, OH 43215; 614-469-6774; Fax: 614-469-7419; *State Director:* Kevin Hoggatt

420 Madison Ave., #1210, Toledo, OH 43604-1221; 419-259-3895; Fax: 419-259-3899; *Northwest District Director:* Cayla Shreffler

Committee Assignments: Finance; Foreign Relations; Homeland Security and Governmental Affairs; Joint Economic

Reed, Jack D., D-R.I.

Capitol Hill Office: 728 SHOB 20510-3903; 224-4642; Fax: 224-4680; *Chief of Staff:* Neil D. Campbell
Web: www.reed.senate.gov
Facebook: www.facebook.com/SenJackReed
Twitter: @SenJackReed
YouTube: www.youtube.com/senatorreed
District Offices: 1000 Chapel View Blvd., #290, Cranston, RI 02920-5602; 401-943-3100; Fax: 401-464-6837; *State Chief of Staff:* Christopher Albert

U.S. District Courthouse, One Exchange Terrace, #408, Providence, RI 02903-1744; 401-528-5200; Fax: 202-224-4680; *State Chief of Staff:* Christopher Albert

Committee Assignments: Appropriations; Armed Services, Chair; Banking, Housing, and Urban Affairs; Select Intelligence

Risch, James E., R-Idaho

Capitol Hill Office: 483 SROB 20510-1206; 224-2752; Fax: 224-2573; *Chief of Staff:* Ryan White
Web: www.risch.senate.gov
Facebook: www.facebook.com/SenatorJimRisch
Twitter: @SenatorRisch
YouTube: www.youtube.com/SenatorJamesRisch
District Offices: 350 N. 9th St., #302, Boise, ID 83702-5409; 208-342-7985; Fax: 208-343-2458; *State Director:* Rachel Burkett

Harbor Plaza, 610 Hubbard St., #213, Coeur d'Alene, ID 83814-2288; 208-667-6130; Fax: 208-765-1743; *Regional Director:* Stefany Bales

901 Pier View Dr., #202A, Idaho Falls, ID 83402-5070; 208-523-5541; Fax: 208-523-9373; *Regional Director:* Amy Taylor

313 D St., #106, Lewiston, ID 83501-1894; 208-743-0792; Fax: 208-746-7275; *Regional Director:* Mike Hanna

275 S. 5th Ave., #290, Pocatello, ID 83201-6410; 208-236-6817; Fax: 208-236-6820; *Regional Director:* Renee Richardson

1411 Falls Ave. East, #201, Twin Falls, ID 83301-3455; 208-734-6780; Fax: 208-734-3905; *Idaho Deputy Chief of Staff:* Mike Mathews

Committee Assignments: Energy and Natural Resources; Foreign Relations; International Narcotics Control Caucus; Select Ethics; Select Intelligence; Small Business and Entrepreneurship

Romney, Mitt, R-Utah

Capitol Hill Office: 354 SROB 20510; 224-5251; Fax: 228-0836; *Chief of Staff:* Liz Johnson

Web: www.romney.senate.gov

Facebook: www.facebook.com/senatorromney

Twitter: @SenatorRomney

Instagram: @senatorromney

YouTube: www.youtube.com/channel/UCEnG85eZBypPpcmbKUJNdng

District Offices: James V. Hansen Federal Bldg., 324 25th St., #1018, Ogden, UT 84401; 385-264-7885; *State Director:* Adam Gardiner

125 S. State St., #8402, Salt Lake City, UT 84138; 801-524-4380; *State Director:* Adam Gardiner

648 N. 900 E., #8, Spanish Fork, UT 84660; 801-515-7230; *State Director:* Adam Gardiner

196 E. Tabernacle St., #14, St. George, UT 84770; 435-522-7100; *State Director:* Adam Gardiner

Committee Assignments: Budget; Foreign Relations; Health, Education, Labor, and Pensions; Homeland Security and Governmental Affairs

Rosen, Jacky, D-Nev.

Capitol Hill Office: 713 SHOB 20510; 224-6244; *Chief of Staff:* Dara Cohen

Web: www.rosen.senate.gov

Facebook: www.facebook.com/SenJackyRosen

Twitter: @SenJackyRosen

Instagram: @senjackyrosen

District Offices: 333 S. Las Vegas Blvd., #8203, Las Vegas, NV 89101; 702-388-0205; *State Director:* Nelson Araujo

Bruce Thompson Federal Bldg., 400 S. Virginia St., #738, Reno, NV 89501; 775-337-0110; *Northern Nevada Director:* Emily Lanee-Rose

Committee Assignments: Armed Services; Commerce, Science, Transportation; Health, Education, Labor, and Pensions; Homeland Security and Governmental Affairs; Small Business and Entrepreneurship; Special Aging

Rounds, Mike, R-S.D.

Capitol Hill Office: 716 SHOB 20510-4104; 224-5842; Fax: 224-7482; *Chief of Staff:* Rob Skjonsberg

Web: www.rounds.senate.gov

Facebook: www.facebook.com/SenatorMikeRounds

Twitter: @SenatorRounds

Instagram: @senatorrounds

YouTube: www.youtube.com/channel/UC-pvzimyBdpdkcIfsicrfrQ

District Offices: 603 Omaha St., #100, Rapid City, SD 57701; 605-343-5035; Fax: 605-343-5348; *West River Director:* Adam Kaemingk

320 N. Main Ave., Suite A, Sioux Falls, SD 57104; 605-336-0486; Fax: 605-336-6624; *East River Director:* Tyler Tordsen

514 S. Main St., #100, Aberdeen, SD 57401; 605-225-0366; *Senior Field Manager:* Jennifer Hieb

111 W. Capitol Ave., #210, P.O. Box 309, Pierre, SD 57501; 605-224-1450; Fax: 605-224-1379; *Central South Dakota Director:* Kim Olson

Committee Assignments: Armed Services; Banking, Housing, and Urban Affairs; Foreign Relations; Indian Affairs; Veterans' Affairs

Rubio, Marco, R-Fla.

Capitol Hill Office: 284 SROB 20510; 224-3041; Fax: 228-0285; *Chief of Staff:* Mike Needham

Web: www.rubio.senate.gov

Facebook: www.facebook.com/SenatorMarcoRubio

Twitter: @SenRubioPress

Instagram: @senatormarcorubio

YouTube: www.youtube.com/SenatorMarcoRubio

District Offices: 300 N. Hogan, #8-111, Jacksonville, FL 32202; 904-354-4300; *Regional Director:* Ashley Cook

201 S. Orange Ave., #350, Orlando, FL 32801-3499; 407-254-2573; Fax: 844-762-1556; *Regional Director:* Thomas Self

1 N. Palafox St., #159, Pensacola, FL 32502-5658; 850-433-2603; *Regional Director:* Marybeth Barrows

402 S. Monroe St., #2105E, Tallahassee, FL 32399-6526; 850-599-9100; *Regional Director:* Joshua Gabel

501 E. Polk St., #601, Tampa, FL 33602; 813-947-6288; *Regional Director:* Taylor Sanchez

4580 PGA Blvd., #201, Palm Beach Gardens, FL 33418; 561-775-3360; *Regional Director:* Greg Langowski

7400 87th Ave. S.W., #270, Miami, FL 33173; 305-596-4224; Fax: 305-596-4345; *Regional Director:* Lea Padron

2120 Main St., Room 200, Fort Myers, FL 33901; 239-318-6464; *Regional Director:* London Rotundo

Committee Assignments: Appropriations; Commission on Security and Cooperation in Europe; Congressional-Executive Commission on China, Co-Chair; Foreign Relations; Select Intelligence; Small Business and Entrepreneurship; Special Aging

Sanders, Bernard, I-Vt.

Capitol Hill Office: 332 SDOB 20510-4504; 224-5141; Fax: 228-0776; *Chief of Staff:* Mike Casca

Web: www.sanders.senate.gov

Facebook: www.facebook.com/senatorsanders

Twitter: @SenSanders

Instagram: @berniesanders

YouTube: www.youtube.com/user/SenatorSanders

District Offices: 1 Church St., 3rd Floor, Burlington, VT 05401-4451; 802-862-0697; Fax: 802-860-6370; *State Director:* Kathryn Van Haste

481 Summer St., #107, P.O. Box 4084, St. Johnsbury, VT 05819; 802-332-6186; Fax: 802-860-6370; *Outreach Director:* Beth Stern

Committee Assignments: Budget, Chair; Energy and Natural Resources; Environment and Public Works; Health, Education, Labor, and Pensions; Veterans' Affairs

Sasse, Ben, R-Neb.

Capitol Hill Office: 139 SROB 20510-2707; 224-4224; *Chief of Staff:* Ray Sass

Web: www.sasse.senate.gov

Facebook: www.facebook.com/SenatorSasse

Twitter: @SenSasse

Instagram: @senatorsasse

YouTube: www.youtube.com/channel/ UCYaNGwcM2Dl5yDcDqS6xV2g

District Offices: 115 Railway St., #C102, Scottsbluff, NE 69361; 308-632-6032; *Director of Constituent Services:* Cassie Nichols

4111 4th Ave., #26, Kearney, NE 68845; 308-233-3677; *State Director:* Vacant

1128 Lincoln Mall, #305, Lincoln, NE 68508; 402-476-1400; *State Director:* Vacant

304 N. 168th Circle, #213, Omaha, NE 68118; 402-550-8040; *Director of Military and Veterans Affairs:* Jim Kuester

Committee Assignments: Budget; Finance; Judiciary; Select Intelligence

Schatz, Brian, D-Hawaii

Capitol Hill Office: 722 SHOB 20510; 224-3934; Fax: 228-1153; *Chief of Staff:* Eric Einhorn

Web: www.schatz.senate.gov

Facebook: www.facebook.com/SenBrianSchatz

Twitter: @SenBrianSchatz

Instagram: @senbrianschatz

YouTube: www.youtube.com/senbrianschatz

District Office: 300 Ala Moana Blvd., Room 7-212, Honolulu, HI 96850; 808-523-2061; Fax: 808-228-1153; *Deputy Chief of Staff:* Malia Paul

Committee Assignments: Appropriations; Commerce, Science, and Transportation; Foreign Relations; Indian Affairs, Chair; Select Ethics

Schumer, Charles E., D-N.Y.

Capitol Hill Office: 322 SHOB 20510; 224-6542; Fax: 228-3027; *Chief of Staff:* Mike Lynch

Web: www.schumer.senate.gov

Facebook: www.facebook.com/senschumer

Twitter: @SenSchumer

Instagram: @senschumer

YouTube: www.youtube.com/user/SenatorSchumer

District Offices: Leo O'Brien Bldg., Room 827, Albany, NY 12207; 518-431-4070; Fax: 518-431-4076; *Regional Director:* Steve Mann

15 Henry St., Room 100 A-F, Binghamton, NY 13901; 607-772-6792; Fax: 607-772-8124; *Regional Rep.:* Amanda Spellicy

130 S. Elmwood Ave., #660, Buffalo, NY 14202-2371; 716-846-4111; Fax: 716-846-4113; *Regional Rep.:* Jordan Nicholson

145 Pine Lawn Rd., #300, Melville, NY 11747; 631-753-0978; Fax: 631-391-9068; *Regional Rep.:* Gary Armwood

780 3rd Ave., #2301, New York, NY 10017; 212-486-4430; Fax: 202-228-2838; *State Director:* Martin Brennan

One Park Pl., #100, Peekskill, NY 10566; 914-734-1532; Fax: 914-734-1673; *Regional Rep.:* Lori Nguyen

100 State St., Room 3040, Rochester, NY 14614; 585-263-5866; Fax: 585-263-3173; *Regional Rep.:* Christopher Zeltmann

100 S. Clinton St., Room 841, Syracuse, NY 13261-7318; 315-423-5471; Fax: 315-423-5185; *Regional Rep.:* Joe Nehme

Committee Assignments: Rules and Administration; Select Intelligence

Majority Leader

Scott, Rick, R-Fla.

Capitol Hill Office: 502 SHOB 20510; 224-5274; *Chief of Staff:* Craig Carbone

Web: www.rickscott.senate.gov

Facebook: www.facebook.com/RickScottSenOffice

Twitter: @SenRickScott

Instagram: @flsenrickscott

YouTube: www.youtube.com/channel/UC-Y9pFmW4PYGZHkC8lcqSkQ

District Offices: 111 N. Adams St., #208, Tallahassee FL 32301; 850-942-8415; *Northwest Florida Regional Director:* Sierra Anderson; *State Director:* John Tupps; *Director of Constituent Services:* Lisa Meyer

901 Ponce de Leon Blvd., #505, Miami, FL 33134; 786-501-7141; *Constituent Services Rep.:* Jaime Flores

3299 Tamiami Trail East, Bldg. F, #106, Naples, FL 34112; 239-231-7890; *Southwest Florida Regional Director:* Leah Valenti

225 E. Robinson St., #410, Orlando, FL 32801; 407-872-7161; *Central Florida District Director:* Barry Cotton

801 N. Florida Ave., #421, Tampa FL 33602; 813-225-7040

415 Clematis St., #201, West Palm Beach, FL 33401; 561-514-0189

1 Courthouse Square, #300, Kissimmee, FL 34741; 407-586-7879

211 Palafox Pl., #420, Pensacola, FL 32502; 850-760-5151

400 W. Bay St., #289, Jacksonville, FL 32202; 904-479-7227

Committee Assignments: Armed Services; Budget; Commerce, Science, and Transportation; Homeland Security and Governmental Affairs; Special Aging

Scott, Tim, R-S.C.

Capitol Hill Office: 104 SHOB 20510-4004; 224-6121; Fax: 228-5143; *Chief of Staff:* Jennifer DeCasper

Web: www.scott.senate.gov

Facebook: www.facebook.com/SenatorTimScott

Twitter: @SenatorTimScott

Instagram: @senatortimscott

YouTube: www.youtube.com/SenatorTimScott
District Offices: 1901 Main St., #1425, Columbia, SC 29201; 803-771-6112; Fax: 855-802-9355; *State Director:* Alyssa Richardson
104 S. Main St., #803, Greenville, SC 29601; 864-233-5366; Fax: 855-802-9355; *Constituent Services Directors:* Deb Blickenstaff and Josiah Odio
2500 City Hall Lane, 3rd Floor, North Charleston, SC 29406; 843-727-4525; Fax: 855-802-9355; *Executive Director:* Joe McKeown
Committee Assignments: Banking, Housing, and Urban Affairs; Finance; Health, Education, Labor, and Pensions; Small Business and Entrepreneurship; Special Aging

Shaheen, Jeanne, D-N.H.

Capitol Hill Office: 506 SHOB 20510-2906; 224-2841; Fax: 228-3194; *Chief of Staff:* Chad Kreikemeier
Web: www.shaheen.senate.gov
Facebook: www.facebook.com/SenatorShaheen
Twitter: @SenatorShaheen
Instagram: @senatorshaheen
YouTube: www.youtube.com/SenatorShaheen
District Offices: 961 Main St., Berlin, NH 03570-3031; 603-752-6300; Fax: 603-752-6305; *Special Asst. for Constituent Services/Policy Projects:* Chuck Henderson
50 Opera House Square, Claremont, NH 03743-5407; 603-542-4872; Fax: 603-542-6582; *Special Asst. for Constituent Services/Outreach:* Bethany Yurek
340 Central Ave., #205, Dover, NH 03820-3770; 603-750-3004; *Constituent Services Director:* Cara Wry
2 Wall St., #220, Manchester, NH 03101-1261; 603-647-7500; Fax: 603-647-9352; *State Director:* Sarah Holmes
60 Main St., #217, Nashua, NH 03060-2720; 603-883-0196; *Special Asst. for Constituent Services/Outreach:* Letizia Ortiz
12 Gilbo Ave., Suite C, Keene, NH 03431; 603-358-6604; *Special Asst. for Constituent Services/Outreach:* Pam Slack
Committee Assignments: Appropriations; Armed Services; Foreign Relations; Commission on Security and Cooperation in Europe; Select Ethics; Small Business and Entrepreneurship

Shelby, Richard, R-Ala.

Capitol Hill Office: 304 SROB 20510; 224-5744; *Chief of Staff:* Dayne Cutrell
Web: www.shelby.senate.gov
Facebook: www.facebook.com/RichardShelby
Twitter: @SenShelby
Instagram: @senatorshelby
YouTube: www.youtube.com/SenatorRichardShelby
District Offices: 321 Federal Bldg., 1800 N. 5th Ave., Birmingham, AL 35203-2113; 205-731-1384; *District Rep.:* Christian Sanford
1000 Glenn Hearn Blvd., #20127, Huntsville, AL 35824; 256-772-0460; *District Rep.:* Shanderla McMillian

115 St. Joseph St., Room 520, Mobile, AL 36602-3606; 251-694-4164; *District Rep.:* Tera Johnson
FMJ Federal Courthouse, 15 Lee St., #208, Montgomery, AL 36104-4054; 334-223-7303; *District Rep.:* Susannah Cleveland
2005 University Blvd., #2100, Tuscaloosa, AL 35401; 205-759-5047; *State Director:* Pam Blackwell
Committee Assignments: Appropriations; Banking, Housing, and Urban Affairs; Environment and Public Works; Joint Library; Rules and Administration

Sinema, Kyrsten, D-Ariz.

Capitol Hill Office: 317 SHOB 20510; 224-4521; Fax: 228-0461; *Chief of Staff:* Meg Joseph
Web: www.sinema.senate.gov
Facebook: www.facebook.com/senatorsinema
Twitter: @SenatorSinema
Instagram: @senatorsinema
YouTube: www.youtube.com/c/SenatorSinema
District Offices: 3333 E. Camelback Rd., #200, Phoenix, AZ 85016; 602-598-7327; *State Director:* Michelle Davidson
20 E. Ochoa St., Tucson, AZ 85701; 520-639-7080; *State Director:* Michelle Davidson
Committee Assignments: Banking, Housing, and Urban Affairs; Commerce, Science, and Transportation; Homeland Security and Governmental Affairs; Veteran's Affairs

Smith, Tina, D-Minn.

Capitol Hill Office: 720 SHOB 20510; 224-5641; Fax: 224-0044; *Chief of Staff:* Jeff Lomonaco
Web: www.smith.senate.gov
Facebook: www.facebook.com/USSenTinaSmith
Twitter: @SenTinaSmith
Instagram: @tinasmithmn
YouTube: www.youtube.com/channel/UCj04_g59Ja7T6jRfgQg9yfQ
District Offices: 819 Center Ave., #2A, Moorhead, MN 56560; 218-284-8721; Fax: 218-284-8722; *Outreach Director:* Carson Oullette
515 W. 1st St., #104, Duluth, MN 55802; 218-722-2390; Fax: 218-722-4131; *Outreach Director:* Hannah Alstead
60 Plato Blvd. East, #220, Saint Paul, MN 55107; 651-221-1016; Fax: 651-221-1078; *State Director:* Sara Silvernail
1202-1/2 7th St. N.W., #213, Rochester, MN 55901; 507-288-2003; Fax: 507-288-2217; *Outreach Director:* Bree Maki
Committee Assignments: Agriculture, Nutrition, and Forestry; Banking, Housing, Urban Affairs; Commission on Security and Cooperation in Europe; Health, Education, Labor, and Pensions; Indian Affairs

Stabenow, Debbie, D-Mich.

Capitol Hill Office: 731 SHOB 20510-2204; 224-4822; Fax: 888-406-3330; *Chief of Staff:* Matt VanKuiken
Web: www.stabenow.senate.gov
Facebook: www.facebook.com/senatorstabenow

Twitter: @SenStabenow
Instagram: @senatordebbiestabenow
YouTube: www.youtube.com/SenatorStabenow
District Offices: 719 Griswold St., #700, Detroit, MI 48226; 313-961-4330; Fax: 888-406-3330; *Regional Manager:* Terry Campbell

221 W. Lake Lansing Rd., #100, East Lansing, MI 48823-8661; 517-203-1760; Fax: 888-406-3330; *Scheduler:* Ellen Rodman

432 N. Saginaw St., #301, Flint, MI 48502; 810-720-4172; Fax: 888-406-3330; *Regional Manager:* Dondre Young

3280 E. Beltline Court N.E., #400, Grand Rapids, MI 49525; 616-975-0052; Fax: 888-406-3330; *Regional Manager:* Mary Judnich

1901 W. Ridge, #7, Marquette, MI 49855-3198; 906-228-8756; Fax: 888-406-3330; *Regional Manager:* Jay Gage

3335 S. Airport Rd. West, #6B, Traverse City, MI 49684-7928; 231-929-1031; Fax: 888-406-3330; *Regional Manager:* Melissa Fruge

Committee Assignments: Agriculture, Nutrition, and Forestry, Chair; Budget; Environment and Public Works; Finance; Joint Taxation

Sullivan, Dan, R-Alaska

Capitol Hill Office: 302 SHOB 20510; 224-3004; Fax: 224-6501; *Chief of Staff:* Larry Burton
Web: www.sullivan.senate.gov
Facebook: www.facebook.com/SenDanSullivan
Twitter: @SenDanSullivan
Instagram: @sen_dansullivan
YouTube: www.youtube.com/channel/UC7tXCm8gKlAhTFo2kuf5ylw
District Offices: Federal Bldg. 101, 12th Ave., #328, Fairbanks, AK 99701; 907-456-0261; Fax: 907-451-7290; *Regional Director:* Greg Bringhurst

44539 Sterling Hwy., #204, Soldotna, AK 99669; 907-262-4040; Fax: 907-262-4224; *Field Director:* Elaina Spraker

1900 1st Ave., #225, Ketchikan, AK 99901; 907-225-6880; Fax: 907-225-0390; *Field Rep.:* Chere Klein

510 L St., #750, Anchorage, AK 99501; 907-271-5915; Fax: 907-258-9305; *State Director:* Kate Wolgemuth

800 Glacier Ave., #101, Juneau, AK 99801; 907-586-7277; Fax: 907-586-7201; *Field Rep.:* Dana Herndon

851 E. Westpoint Dr., #309, Wasilla, AK 99654; 907-357-9956; Fax: 907-357-9964; *State Director:* Kate Wolgemuth

Committee Assignments: Armed Services; Commerce, Science, and Transportation; Environment and Public Works; Veterans' Affairs

Tester, Jon, D-Mont.

Capitol Hill Office: 311 SHOB 20510; 224-2644; Fax: 224-8594; *Chief of Staff:* Dylan Laslovich
Web: www.tester.senate.gov
Facebook: www.facebook.com/senatortester
Twitter: @SenatorTester
Instagram: @senatorjontester
YouTube: www.youtube.com/SenatorJonTester

District Offices: Judge Jameson Federal Bldg., 2900 N. 4th Ave., #201, Billings, MT 59101; 406-252-0550; Fax: 406-252-7768; *Regional Director:* Molly Bell

Avant Courier Bldg., 1 E. Main St., #202, Bozeman, MT 59715-6248; 406-586-4450; Fax: 406-586-7647; *Regional Director:* Jenna Rose

Silver Bow Center, 125 W. Granite St., #200, Butte, MT 59701-9215; 406-723-3277; Fax: 406-782-4717; *State Scheduler:* Amanda Casey; *Regional Director:* Erik Nylund

119 N. 1st Ave., #102, Great Falls, MT 59401-2568; 406-452-9585; Fax: 406-452-9586; *Regional Director:* Cheryl Ulmer

208 N. Montana Ave., #104, Helena, MT 59601-3837; 406-449-5401; Fax: 406-449-5462; *Veteran Liaison:* Bruce Knutson

8 E. 3rd St., Kalispell, MT 59901-4588; 406-257-3360; Fax: 406-257-3974; *Regional Director:* Chad Campbell

130 W. Front St., Missoula, MT 59802; 406-728-3003; Fax: 406-728-2193; *State Director:* Pam Haxby-Cote

Committee Assignments: Appropriations; Banking, Housing, and Urban Affairs; Commerce, Science, and Transportation; Indian Affairs; Veterans' Affairs, Chair

Thune, John, R-S.D.

Capitol Hill Office: 511 SDOB 20510-4105; 224-2321; Fax: 228-5429; *Chief of Staff:* Ryan P. Nelson
Web: www.thune.senate.gov
Facebook: www.facebook.com/senjohnthune
Twitter: @SenJohnThune
Instagram: @senjohnthune
YouTube: www.youtube.com/JohnThune
District Offices: 320 S. 1st St., #101, Aberdeen, SD 57401; 605-225-8823; Fax: 605-225-8468; *Northeast Regional Director:* Judy Vrchota

246 Founders Park Dr., #102, Rapid City, SD 57701; 605-348-7551; Fax: 605-348-7208; *West River Regional Director:* Mark Haugen

5015 S. Bur Oak, Sioux Falls, SD 57108; 605-334-9596; Fax: 605-334-2591; *Chief of Staff and State Director:* Ryan P. Nelson

Committee Assignments: Agriculture, Nutrition, and Forestry; Commerce, Science, and Transportation; Finance
Minority Whip

Tillis, Thom, R-N.C.

Capitol Hill Office: 113 SDOB 20510-3309; 224-6342; Fax: 228-2563; *Chief of Staff:* Ted Lehman
Web: www.tillis.senate.gov
Facebook: www.facebook.com/SenatorThomTillis
Twitter: @SenThomTillis
Instagram: @senthomtillis
YouTube: www.youtube.com/channel/UCUD9VGV4SSGWjGdbn37Ea2w
District Offices: 10150 Mallard Creek Rd., #508, Charlotte, NC 28262; 704-509-9087; Fax: 704-509-9162; *State Director:* Kim Candey Barnes

1694 E. Arlington Blvd., Suite B, Greenville, NC 27858; 252-329-0371; Fax: 252-329-0290; *Regional Rep.:* Trey Lewis

1840 Eastchester Dr., #200, High Point, NC 27265; 336-885-0685; Fax: 336-885-0692; *Regional Director of Constituent Advocacy:* Recca Briles

310 New Bern Ave., #122, Raleigh, NC 27601; 919-856-4630; Fax: 919-856-4053; *Regional Rep.:* Joey Nelson

1 Historic Courthouse Square, #112, Hendersonville, NC 28792; 828-693-8750; Fax: 828-693-9724; *District Director:* Jordan Barnes

Committee Assignments: Armed Services; Banking, Housing, and Urban Affairs; Commission on Security and Cooperation in Europe; Judiciary; Veterans' Affairs

Toomey, Patrick J., R-Pa.

Capitol Hill Office: 455 SDOB 20510-3806; 224-4254; Fax: 228-0284; *Chief of Staff:* Dan Brandt

Web: www.toomey.senate.gov

Facebook: www.facebook.com/senatortoomey

Twitter: @SenToomey

Instagram: @senpattoomey

YouTube: www.youtube.com/sentoomey

District Offices: 1150 S. Cedar Crest Blvd., #101, Allentown, PA 18103; 610-434-1444; Fax: 202-228-2727; *Deputy State Director:* Sue Zimskind: *Regional Manager:* Marta Gabriel

U.S. Federal Bldg., 17 S. Park Row, #B-120, Erie, PA 16501-1156; 814-453-3010; Fax: 814-455-9925; *Western Pennsylvania Director:* Sheila Sterrett

320 Market St., #475E, Harrisburg, PA 17101; 717-782-3951; Fax: 717-782-4920; *State Director:* Bob DeSousa; *Regional Manager:* Larissa Bailey

Richland Square III, 1397 Eisenhower Blvd., #302, Johnstown, PA 15904-3267; 814-266-5970; Fax: 814-266-5973; *Regional Manager:* John Frick

U.S. Custom House, 200 Chestnut St., #600, Philadelphia, PA 19106; 215-241-1090; Fax: 202-224-4442; *Eastern Pennsylvania Director:* Brian Langan; *Regional Manager:* Kate Schramm

310 Grant St., #1440, Pittsburgh, PA 15219; 412-803-3501; Fax: 412-803-3504; *Regional Manager:* Colton Fedell

7 N. Wilkes-Barre Blvd., #406, Wilkes-Barre, PA 18702; 570-820-4088; Fax: 570-820-6442; *Regional Manager:* Frank Mazza

Committee Assignments: Banking, Housing, and Urban Affairs; Budget; Finance

Tuberville, Tommy, R-Ala.

Capitol Hill Office: 142 SROB 20510; 224-4124; *Chief of Staff:* Stephen Boyd

Web: www.tuberville.senate.gov

Facebook: www.facebook.com/SenatorTuberville

Twitter: @SenTuberville

Instagram: @sentuberville

YouTube: www.youtube.com/channel/UCbvKb-ZcNkzQ7LEJsxdpqzA

District Offices: 100 W. Troy St., Dothan, AL 36303; 334-547-7441; *Regional Director:* John Ferguson

3000 Riverchase Galleria, #915, Birmingham, AL 35244; 205-760-7307; *Constituent Services Rep.:* Deanna Frankowski

2101 Clinton Ave. N.W., Huntsville, #300, AL 35805; 256-692-7500; *Caseworker:* June Reedes-Weir

BB&T Center, 41 W. I-65 Service Rd. North, #2300A, Mobile, AL 36608; 251-308-7233; *Regional Director:* Andrew Hinkebein

Frank M. Johnson Jr. Annex, 1 Church St., #500B, Montgomery, AL 36014; 334-523-7424; *Regional Director:* Cindy Tate

Committee Assignments: Agriculture, Nutrition, and Forestry; Armed Services; Health, Education, Labor, and Pensions; Veterans' Affairs

Van Hollen, Chris, D-Md.

Capitol Hill Office: 110 SHOB 20510; 224-4654; Fax: 228-0629; *Chief of Staff:* Tricia Russell

Web: www.vanhollen.senate.gov

Facebook: www.facebook.com/chrisvanhollen

Twitter: @ChrisVanHollen

Instagram: @chrisvanhollen

YouTube: www.youtube.com/RepChrisVanHollen

District Offices: 60 West St., #107, Annapolis, MD 21401; 410-263-1325; *Regional Director:* Jaelon Moaney

1900 N. Howard St., #100, Baltimore, MD 21218; 667-212-4610; *State Staffer:* Shannon Sneed

204 Cedar St., #200C, Cambridge, MD 21613; 410-221-2074; *Eastern Shore Regional Director:* Melissa Kelly

1101 Mercantile Lane, #210, Largo, MD 20774; 301-322-6560; *State Staffer:* Latriece Pleasant

111 Rockville Pike, #960, Rockville, MD 20850; 301-545-1500; Fax: 301-545-1512; *State Director:* Joan Kleinman

Satellite Office: 32 W. Washington St., #203, Hagerstown, MD 21740; 301-797-2826; *Western Maryland Regional Director:* Nan Mann

Committee Assignments: Appropriations; Banking, Housing, and Urban Affairs; Budget; Foreign Relations

Warner, Mark R., D-Va.

Capitol Hill Office: 703 SHOB 20510-4606; *Chief of Staff:* Elizabeth Falcone

Web: www.warner.senate.gov

Facebook: www.facebook.com/MarkRWarner

Twitter: @MarkWarner

Instagram: @senatorwarner

YouTube: www.youtube.com/SenatorMarkWarner

District Offices: 180 W. Main St., Room 235, Abingdon, VA 24210-2844; 276-628-8158; Fax: 276-628-1036; *Regional Director:* Shane Clem

101 W. Main St., #7771, Norfolk, VA 23510-1690; 757-441-3079; Fax: 757-441-6250; *Regional Director:* Drew Lumpkin

919 E. Main St., #630, Richmond, VA 23219-4600; 804-775-2314; Fax: 804-775-2319; *State Director:* Lou Kadiri

120 Luck Ave. S.W., Roanoke, VA 24011; 540-857-2676; Fax: 540-857-2800; *Casework Director:* Chris Monioudis

8000 Towers Crescent Dr., #200, Vienna, VA 22182; 703-442-0670; Fax: 703-442-0408; *Regional Director:* Bo Machayo

Committee Assignments: Banking, Housing, and Urban Affairs; Budget; Finance; Rules and Administration; Select Intelligence, Chair

Warnock, Raphael, D-Ga.

Capitol Hill Office: 455 SROB 20510; 224-3521; Fax: 228-1031; *Chief of Staff:* Mark Libell
Web: warnockforgeorgia.com
Facebook: www.facebook.com/SenatorWarnock
Twitter: @SenatorWarnock
Instagram: @raphaelwarnock
YouTube: www.youtube.com/channel/UCEARDmtU8htGQ_hqviHGrVA
District Office: 3280 Peachtree Rd. N.E., #2640, Atlanta, GA 30305; 404-865-0087; Fax: 404-949-0912
Committee Assignments: Agriculture, Nutrition, and Forestry; Banking, Housing, and Urban Affairs; Commerce, Science, and Transportation; Joint Economic; Special Aging

Warren, Elizabeth, D-Mass.

Capitol Hill Office: 309 SHOB 20510; 224-4543; Fax: 228-2072; *Chief of Staff:* Jon Donenberg
Web: www.warren.senate.gov
Facebook: www.facebook.com/senatorelizabethwarren
Twitter: @SenWarren
Instagram: @senwarren
YouTube: www.youtube.com/senelizabethwarren
District Offices: 2400 JFK Federal Bldg., 15 New Sudbury St., Boston, MA 02203; 617-565-3170; Fax: 617-227-1875; *State Director:* Nikko Mendoza
1550 Main St., #406, Springfield, MA 01103; 413-788-2690; *Deputy State Director:* Everett Handford
Committee Assignments: Armed Services; Banking, Housing, and Urban Affairs; Finance; Special Aging

Whitehouse, Sheldon, D-R.I.

Capitol Hill Office: 530 SHOB 20510; 224-2921; Fax: 228-6362; *Chief of Staff:* Monalisa Dugue
Web: www.whitehouse.senate.gov
Facebook: www.facebook.com/SenatorWhitehouse
Twitter: @SenWhitehouse
Instagram: @senwhitehouse
YouTube: www.youtube.com/SenatorWhitehouse
District Office: 170 Westminster St., #200, Providence, RI 02903; 401-453-5294; Fax: 401-453-5085; *State Director:* George Carvalho
Committee Assignments: Budget; Commission on Security and Cooperation in Europe; Environment and Public Works; Finance; Judiciary; International Narcotics Control Caucus

Wicker, Roger F., R-Miss.

Capitol Hill Office: 555 SDOB 20510-2404; 224-6253; Fax: 224-9993; *Chief of Staff:* Michelle Barlow Richardson
Web: www.wicker.senate.gov
Facebook: www.facebook.com/senatorwicker
Twitter: @SenatorWicker
Instagram: @senatorwicker
YouTube: www.youtube.com/SenatorWicker
District Offices: 2909 13th St., 3rd Floor, #303, Gulfport, MS 39501; 228-871-7017; Fax: 228-871-7196; *Field Rep.:* Chris Vignes
321 Losher St., P.O. Box 385, Hernando, MS 38632-2124; 662-429-1002; Fax: 662-429-6002; *Constituent Liaisons:* Kim Chamberlin and Ladonna Worthing
U.S. Federal Courthouse, 501 E. Court St., #3-500, Jackson, MS 39201; 601-965-4644; Fax: 601-965-4007; *State Director:* Ryan Annison
330 W. Jefferson St., Suite B, Tupelo, MS 38804; P.O. Box 3777, Tupelo, MS 38803; 662-844-5010; Fax: 662-844-5030; *Constituent Liaison:* Lisa Johnson
Committee Assignments: Armed Services; Commerce, Science, and Transportation, Commission on Security and Cooperation in Europe, Co-Chair; Environment and Public Works; Joint Printing; Rules and Administration

Wyden, Ron, D-Ore.

Capitol Hill Office: 221 SDOB 20510; 224-5244; Fax: 228-2717; *Chief of Staff:* Jeff Michels
Web: www.wyden.senate.gov
Facebook: www.facebook.com/senatorronwyden
Twitter: @WydenPress and @RonWyden
Instagram: @ronwyden
YouTube: www.youtube.com/SenRonWyden
District Offices: The Jamison Bldg., 131 Hawthorne Ave. N.W., #107, Bend, OR 97701; 541-330-9142; Fax: 541-330-6266; *Field Rep.:* Jacob Egler
405 E. 8th Ave., #2020, Eugene, OR 97401; 541-431-0229; Fax: 541-431-0610; *Field Rep.:* Molley McCarthy
SAC Annex Bldg., 105 Fir St., #201, La Grande, OR 97850-2661; 541-962-7691; Fax: 541-963-0885; *Field Rep.:* Kathleen Cathey
Federal Courthouse, 310 W. 6th St., Room 118, Medford, OR 97501-2700; 541-858-5122; Fax: 541-858-5126; *Field Rep.:* Molley McCarthy
911 11th Ave. N.E., #630, Portland, OR 97232; 503-326-7525; Fax: 503-326-7528; *State Director:* Lisa Rockower
707 13th St. S.E., #285, Salem, OR 97301; 503-589-4555; Fax: 503-589-4749; *Field Rep.:* Fritz Graham
Committee Assignments: Budget; Energy and Natural Resources; Finance, Chair; Joint Taxation; Select Intelligence

Young, Todd, R-Ind.

Capitol Hill Office: 185 SDOB 20510; 224-5623; *Chief of Staff:* John Connell
Web: www.young.senate.gov
Facebook: www.facebook.com/SenatorToddYoung
Twitter: @SenToddYoung
Instagram: @sentoddyoung
YouTube: www.youtube.com/channel/UC0vPqS6JHqPoptRGdyja9Lw
District Offices: 251 N. Illinois St., #120, Indianapolis, IN 46204; 317-226-6700; *State Director:* Andrew Kossack

3602 Northgate Court, #15, New Albany, IN 47150; 812-542-4820; *District Rep.:* Melissa Acton
101 Martin Luther King Jr. Blvd., #110, Evansville, IN 47708; 317-226-6700; *Regional Director:* Ashley Davis
1300 S. Harrison St., #3161, Fort Wayne, IN 46802; 317-226-6700; *Regional Director:* Justin Busch
212 East Lincoln Way, #205A, Valparaiso, IN 46383; 219-747-7780; *State Director:* Andrew Kossack
Committee Assignments: Commerce, Science, and Transportation; Finance; Foreign Relations; Small Business and Entrepreneurship

Ready Reference

Directory of Government Information on the Internet

Listed below are websites that lead to executive, legislative, and judicial information on the Internet. These links were active as of May 12, 2022. Government information can also be explored online through the www.usa.gov, which is the U.S. government's official Internet portal to Web pages for federal and state governments, the District of Columbia, and U.S. territories.

EXECUTIVE BRANCH

The White House

Main: www.whitehouse.gov
Twitter: @WhiteHouse
Facebook: www.facebook.com/WhiteHouse
YouTube: www.youtube.com/user/whitehouse
Instagram: @whitehouse
News: www.whitehouse.gov/briefing-room
President's Bio: www.whitehouse.gov/administration/president-biden
Vice President's Bio: www.whitehouse.gov/administration/vice-president-harris
First Lady's Bio: www.whitehouse.gov/administration/dr-jill-biden
Contacting the White House: www.whitehouse.gov/contact

Agriculture Dept.

Main: www.usda.gov
Twitter: @USDA
Facebook: www.facebook.com/USDA
YouTube: www.youtube.com/user/usda
Instagram: @usdagov
About the Agriculture Dept.: www.usda.gov/our-agency/about-usda
News: www.usda.gov/media
Secretary's Bio: www.usda.gov/our-agency/about-usda/our-secretary
Employee Directory: https://offices.sc.egov.usda.gov/employeeDirectory/app
Link to Regional Offices: https://offices.sc.egov.usda.gov/locator/app
Department Budget: www.usda.gov/our-agency/about-usda/budget
Blog: www.usda.gov/media/blog

Commerce Dept.

Main: www.commerce.gov
Twitter: @CommerceGov
Facebook: www.facebook.com/Commercegov
YouTube: www.youtube.com/user/CommerceNews
Instagram: @commercegov
About the Commerce Dept.: www.commerce.gov/about
News: www.commerce.gov/news
Secretary's Bio: www.commerce.gov/about/leadership/gina-m-raimondo
Employee Directory: https://staff.commerce.gov
Links to State and Regional Offices:
  Census Bureau: www.census.gov/regions
  Commerce Dept.: www.commerce.gov/locations
  Economic Development Administration: www.eda.gov/contact
Department Budget: www.commerce.gov/about/budget-and-performance
Blog: www.commerce.gov/news/blog

Defense Dept.

Main: www.defense.gov
Twitter: @DeptofDefense
Facebook: www.facebook.com/DeptofDefense
YouTube: www.youtube.com/deptofdefense
Instagram: @deptofdefense
About the Defense Dept.: www.defense.gov/about
News: www.defense.gov/newsroom
Secretary's Bio: www.defense.gov/Our-Story/Meet-the-Team/Secretary-of-Defense
Directory of Senior Defense Officials: www.defense.gov/About/Biographies
Department Budget: https://comptroller.defense.gov/Budget-Materials
Live Blog: www.defense.gov/News/Live-Events/#/?currentVideo=28698

Education Dept.

Main: www.ed.gov
Twitter: @usedgov
Facebook: www.facebook.com/ED.gov
YouTube: www.youtube.com/usedgov
Instagram: @usedgov
About the Education Dept.: www2.ed.gov/about/landing.jhtml
News: www2.ed.gov/news/landing.jhtml
Secretary's Bio: www2.ed.gov/news/staff/bios/cardona.html?src=hp
Employee Directory: www2.ed.gov/about/contacts/gen/index.html
State Contacts and Information: www2.ed.gov/about/contacts/state/index.html

Government Hotlines

DEPARTMENTS

Agriculture,

Fraud, waste, abuse, and mismanagement hotline (Office of Inspector General), (800) 424-9121); TTY, (202) 690-1202

Information hotline, (202) 720-2791

Commerce,

Export enforcement hotline, (800) 424-2980

Fraud, waste, abuse, and mismanagement hotline (Office of Inspector General), (800) 424-5197

Trade Information Center, (800) 872-8723

Defense,

Army Department's Casualty and Mortuary Affairs Information Center, (800) 626-3317

Fraud, waste, abuse, and mismanagement hotline (Office of Inspector General), (800) 424-9098

Military OneSource, (800) 342-9647

Education,

Fraud, waste, abuse, and mismanagement hotline (Office of Inspector General), (800) 647-8733

Student federal financial aid information, (800) 433-3243

Civil Rights Hotline, (800) 421-3481

Educational Resources Information Center, (800) 538-3742

Energy,

Fraud, waste, abuse, and mismanagement hotline (Office of Inspector General), (800) 541-1625

Health and Human Services,

Child Welfare Information Gateway, (800) 394-3366

Fraud, misconduct, and criminal activity hotline (Office of Inspector General), (800) 447-8477

Center for Disease Control information hotline, (800) 232-4636

Center for Disease Control information hotline TTY, (888) 232-6348

Medicare hotline, (800) 633-4227

National Cancer Institute cancer information service, (800) 422-6237

National Runaway Safeline, (800) 786-2929

Homeland Security,

Federal Emergency Management Agency disaster assistance, (800) 621-3362

Fraud, waste, abuse, and mismanagement hotline (Office of Inspector General), (800) 323-8603

(Office of the Inspector General) TTY, (844) 889-4357

Investigations tip line, (866) 347-2423

National Emergency Training Center, (800) 238-3358

National Response Center, (202) 267-2675

Detainee hotline, (855) 448-6903

Detention reporting and information line, (888) 351-4024

Housing and Urban Development,

Housing discrimination hotline, (800) 669-9777

Public and Indian Housing Information Resource Center, (800) 955-2232

Fraud, waste, abuse, and mismanagement hotline (Office of Inspector General), (800) 347-3735

Community Connections/Federal Surplus Properties hotline, (800) 927-7588

Housing Counseling Agency Locator, (800) 569-4287

Justice,

Americans with Disabilities Act information, (800) 514-0301

Arson hotline, (888) 283-3473

Bomb information hotline (Bureau of Alcohol, Tobacco, Firearms, and Explosives), (888) 283-2662

Fraud, waste, abuse, or mismanagement hotline (Office of Inspector General), (800) 869-4499

ATF San Francisco Field Division hotline, (800) 283-4867

National Criminal Justice Reference Service, (800) 851-3420

National Institute for Corrections Information Center, (800) 877-1461

Stolen firearms program, (888) 930-9275

Worker hotline, Immigrant and Employee Rights Section, Civil Rights Division, (800) 255-7688

Transportation,

Federal Aviation Administration hotline, (800) 255-1111

Federal Aviation Administration public information hotline, (866) 835-5322

Vehicle safety hotline, (800) 424-9393

Treasury,

Comptroller of the Currency customer assistance hotline, (800) 613-6743

Fraud, waste, mismanagement, and abuse hotline (IRS Office of Inspector General), (800) 366-4484

Identity Theft hotline, (800) 908-4490

Tax forms, tax refund information, and general information, (800) 829-3676

Tax refund status, (800) 829-1954

Taxpayer Advocate Service, (877) 777-4778

Taxpayer assistance, (800) 829-1040

Veterans Affairs,

Veterans Crisis Line, (800) 273-8255, ext. 1; TTY, dial 711 then(800) 273-8255

Benefits assistance service hotline, (800) 827-1000

Debt Management Center, (800) 827-0648

Fraud, waste, abuse, and mismanagement hotline (Office of Inspector General), (800) 488-8244

Insurance policy information, (800) 669-8477

AGENCIES

Consumer Product Safety Commission,

Product safety information, (800) 638-2772

Environmental Protection Agency,

Asbestos hotline, (800) 368-5888

National Lead Information Center and Federal Lead-Based Paint Program hotline, (800) 424-5323

National Pesticides Information Center, (800) 858-7378

National radon hotline, (800) 767-7236

Safe drinking water information hotline, (800) 426-4791

Fraud, waste, abuse, and mismanagement hotline (Office of Inspector General), (888) 546-8740

Emergency Planning and Community Right-to-Know Act (EPCRA), Risk Management Plan Rule (RMP), and Oil Information Center hotline, (800) 424-9346

Export-Import Bank,

Export finance hotline, (800) 565-3946 or (202) 565-3946

Federal Deposit Insurance Corp.,

Banking complaints and inquiries, (877) 275-3342

Federal Election Commission,

Federal Election Commission information hotline, (202) 694-1100

General Services Administration,

Federal government information, (800) 333-4636

Office of Special Counsel,

Prohibited personnel practices information, (202) 804-7000

Hatch Act Unit, (800) 854-2824

Uninformed Services Employment and Reemplyment Rights Act, (202) 804-7022

Small Business Administration,

Fraud, waste, abuse, and mismanagement hotline (Office of Inspector General), (800) 767-0385

Small business assistance, (800) 827-5722

Social Security Administration,

Fraud hotline, (800) 269-0271

Social Security (including Medicare) information, (800) 772-1213

Department Budget: www2.ed.gov/about/overview/
budget/index.html
Blog: https://blog.ed.gov

Energy Dept.

Main: www.energy.gov
Twitter: @ENERGY
Facebook: www.facebook.com/energygov
YouTube: www.youtube.com/user/USdepartmentofenergy
Instagram: @energy
About the Energy Dept.: www.energy.gov/about-us
News: www.energy.gov/newsroom
Secretary's Bio: www.energy.gov/contributors/jennifer-m-
granholm
Employee Directory: www.energy.gov/about-us/staff-and-
contractors
Link to Regional Offices: www.energy.gov/contact-us/
mailing-addresses-and-information-numbers-
operations-field-and-site-offices
Department Budget: www.energy.gov/budget-
performance

Health and Human Services Dept.

Main: www.hhs.gov
Twitter: @HHSGov
Facebook: www.facebook.com/HHS
YouTube: www.youtube.com/user/USGOVHHS
Instagram: @hhsgov
About the Health and Human Services Dept.: www.hhs
.gov/about
News: www.hhs.gov/about/news/index.html
Secretary's Bio: www.hhs.gov/about/leadership/secretary/
alex-m-azar/index.html
Employee Directory: www.hhs.gov/ohrp/about-ohrp/
staff/index.html
Link to Regional Offices: www.hhs.gov/about/agencies/
regional-offices
Department Budget: www.hhs.gov/budget

Homeland Security Dept.

Main: www.dhs.gov
Twitter: @DHSgov
Facebook: www.facebook.com/homelandsecurity
YouTube: www.youtube.com/ushomelandsecurity
Instagram: @dhsgov
About the Homeland Security Dept.: www.dhs.gov/
about-dhs
News: www.dhs.gov/news
Secretary's Bio: www.dhs.gov/secretary
Leadership Directory: www.dhs.gov/leadership
Links to Regional Offices:
  Federal Emergency Management Agency:
    www.fema.gov
  U.S. Citizenship and Immigration Services:
    www.uscis.gov
  U.S. Secret Service: www.secretservice.gov/field_
    offices.shtml
Department Budget: www.dhs.gov/dhs-budget
Blog: www.dhs.gov/news-releases/blog

Housing and Urban Development Dept.

Main: www.hud.gov
Twitter: @HUDgov
Facebook: www.facebook.com/HUD
YouTube: www.youtube.com/hudchannel
Instagram: @hudgov
About the Housing and Urban Development Dept.:
www.hud.gov/about
News: www.hud.gov/press
Interactive Self-Assessment Tool: www.makinghome
affordable.gov
Secretary's Bio: www.hud.gov/about/leadership/marcia_
fudge
Employee Directory: https://peoplesearch.hud.gov/po/i/
netlocator
Link to Regional Offices: https://portal.hud.gov/
hudportal/HUD?src=/states
Department Budget: www.hud.gov/program_offices/cfo/
budget

Interior Dept.

Main: www.doi.gov
Twitter: @Interior
Facebook: www.facebook.com/USInterior
YouTube: www.youtube.com/USInterior
Instagram: @usinterior
About the Interior Dept.: www.doi.gov/about
News: www.doi.gov/news
Secretary's Bio: www.doi.gov/secretary-deb-haaland
Employee Directory: www.doi.gov/employees
Links to Regional Offices:
  Bureau of Indian Affairs: www.bia.gov
  Bureau of Land Management: www.blm.gov
  Bureau of Ocean Energy Management: www.boem.gov
  Bureau of Reclamation: www.usbr.gov
  National Park Service: www.nps.gov
  Office of Surface Mining: www.osmre.gov
  U.S. Fish and Wildlife Service: www.fws.gov
  U.S. Geological Survey: www.usgs.gov
Department Budget: www.doi.gov/budget

Justice Dept.

Main: www.justice.gov
Twitter: @TheJusticeDept
Facebook: www.facebook.com/DOJ
YouTube: www.youtube.com/thejusticedepartment
Instagram: @thejusticedept
About the Justice Dept.: www.justice.gov/about
News: www.justice.gov/briefing-room
Attorney General's Bio: www.justice.gov/ag/staff-profile/
meet-attorney-general
Links to Regional Offices:
  Drug Enforcement Administration: www.dea.gov/
    who-we-are/contact-us
  Federal Bureau of Investigation: www.fbi.gov/
    contact-us/contact-us
  Federal Bureau of Prisons: www.bop.gov/contact
Department Budget: www.justice.gov/doj/fy-2021-
budget-and-performance-summary

Labor Dept.

Main: www.dol.gov
Twitter: @USDOL
Facebook: www.facebook.com/departmentoflabor
YouTube: www.youtube.com/usdepartmentoflabor
Instagram: @usdol
About the Labor Dept.: www.dol.gov/general/aboutdol
News: www.dol.gov/newsroom
Secretary's Bio: www.dol.gov/agencies/osec
Employee Directory: www.dol.gov/general/contact/
contact-phonekeypersonnel
Links to Regional Offices:
Bureau of Labor Statistics: www.bls.gov/bls/
regnhome.htm
Employment and Training Administration: https://
wdr.doleta.gov/contacts
Occupational Safety and Health Administration:
www.osha.gov/dcsp/osp/index.html
Department Budget: www.dol.gov/general/budget

State Dept.

Main: www.state.gov
Twitter: @StateDept
Facebook: www.facebook.com/statedept
YouTube: www.youtube.com/statevideo
Instagram: @statedept
About the State Dept.: www.state.gov/about
News: www.state.gov/press-releases
Secretary's Bio: www.state.gov/biographies/antony-j-
blinken
Employee Directory: www.state.gov/telephone-directory
Link to Regional Offices: www.state.gov/regional-offices
Passport Services: https://iafdb.travel.state.gov
Department Budget: www.state.gov/plans-performance-
budget
Blog: https://blogs.state.gov

Transportation Dept.

Main: www.transportation.gov
Twitter: @USDOT
Facebook: www.facebook.com/USDOT
YouTube: www.youtube.com/user/usdotgov
Instagram: @usdot
About the Transportation Dept.: www.transportation
.gov/about
News: www.transportation.gov/press-releases
Secretary's Bio: www.transportation.gov/meet-secretary/
secretary-pete-buttigieg
Links to Regional Offices:
Federal Aviation Administration: www.faa.gov/about/
office_org
Federal Highway Administration: www.fhwa.dot.gov/
about/field.cfm
Federal Railroad Administration: www.fra.dot.gov/
Page/P0001
Federal Transit Administration: www.transit.dot.gov/
about/regional-offices/regional-offices
Maritime Administration: www.marad.dot.gov

National Highway Traffic Safety Administration:
www.nhtsa.gov
Department Budget: www.transportation.gov/budget

Treasury Dept.

Main: www.treasury.gov
Twitter: @USTreasury
Facebook: www.facebook.com/USTreasuryDept
YouTube: www.youtube.com/channel/UCt2FDbyyFrn_
lw1gWwuBfgQ
Instagram: @treasurydept
About the Treasury Dept.: https://home.treasury.gov/
about/general-information/role-of-the-treasury
News: https://home.treasury.gov/news/press-releases
Interactive Self-Assessment Tool: www.makinghome
affordable.gov
Secretary's Bio: https://home.treasury.gov/about/general-
information/officials/janet-yellen
Directory of Treasury Officials: https://home.treasury
.gov/about/general-information/organizational-chart
Links to Regional Offices:
Comptroller of the Currency: www.occ.gov/
index.html
Financial Management Service: www.fiscal
.treasury.gov
Internal Revenue Service: www.irs.gov/uac/Contact-
Your-Local-IRS-Office-1
Veterans Benefits Administration: https://benefits
.va.gov/benefits/offices.asp
Department Budget: www.treasury.gov/about/budget-
performance

Veterans Affairs Dept.

Main: www.va.gov
Twitter: @DeptVetAffairs
Facebook: www.facebook.com/VeteransAffairs
YouTube: www.youtube.com/deptvetaffairs
Instagram: @deptvetaffairs
About the Veterans Affairs Dept.: www.va.gov/about_va
News: www.va.gov/opa/pressrel
Secretary's Bio: www.va.gov/opa/bios/secva.asp
Link to Regional Offices: www.va.gov/directory/guide/
division.asp?dnum=3&isFlash=0
Department Budget: www.va.gov/budget/products.asp
Blog: www.blogs.va.gov/VAntage

LEGISLATIVE BRANCH

Congress

Main: www.congress.gov
Twitter: @congressdotgov
U.S. Constitution: www.archives.gov/founding-docs
Legislative Process: https://rules.house.gov
How Laws Are Made: www.congress.gov/resources/
display/content/How+Our+Laws+Are+Made+-+Learn
+About+the+Legislative+Process
Biographical Directory of the U.S. Congress: http://
bioguide.congress.gov/biosearch/biosearch.asp

Government of the United States

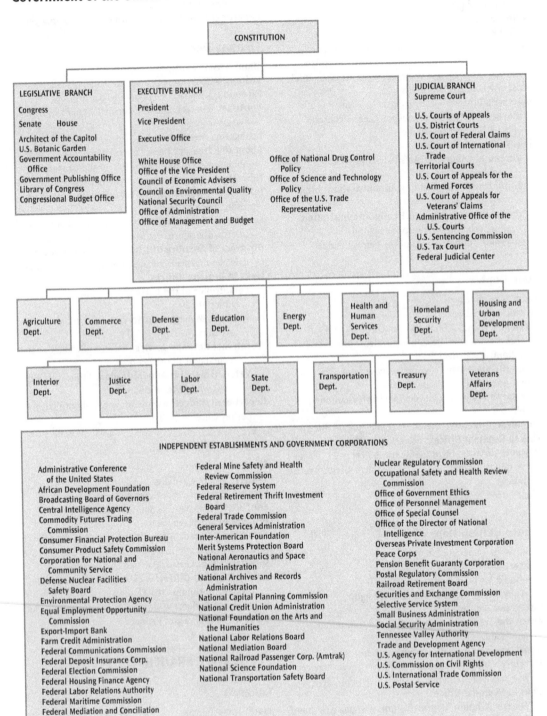

CONSTITUTION

LEGISLATIVE BRANCH

Congress

Senate   House

Architect of the Capitol
U.S. Botanic Garden
Government Accountability
Office
Government Publishing Office
Library of Congress
Congressional Budget Office

EXECUTIVE BRANCH

President

Vice President

Executive Office

White House Office
Office of the Vice President
Council of Economic Advisers
Council on Environmental Quality
National Security Council
Office of Administration
Office of Management and Budget

Office of National Drug Control
Policy
Office of Science and Technology
Policy
Office of the U.S. Trade
Representative

JUDICIAL BRANCH
Supreme Court

U.S. Courts of Appeals
U.S. District Courts
U.S. Court of Federal Claims
U.S. Court of International
Trade
Territorial Courts
U.S. Court of Appeals for the
Armed Forces
U.S. Court of Appeals for
Veterans' Claims
Administrative Office of the
U.S. Courts
U.S. Sentencing Commission
U.S. Tax Court
Federal Judicial Center

Agriculture Dept.

Commerce Dept.

Defense Dept.

Education Dept.

Energy Dept.

Health and Human Services Dept.

Homeland Security Dept.

Housing and Urban Development Dept.

Interior Dept.

Justice Dept.

Labor Dept.

State Dept.

Transportation Dept.

Treasury Dept.

Veterans Affairs Dept.

INDEPENDENT ESTABLISHMENTS AND GOVERNMENT CORPORATIONS

Administrative Conference
of the United States
African Development Foundation
Broadcasting Board of Governors
Central Intelligence Agency
Commodity Futures Trading
Commission
Consumer Financial Protection Bureau
Consumer Product Safety Commission
Corporation for National and
Community Service
Defense Nuclear Facilities
Safety Board
Environmental Protection Agency
Equal Employment Opportunity
Commission
Export-Import Bank
Farm Credit Administration
Federal Communications Commission
Federal Deposit Insurance Corp.
Federal Election Commission
Federal Housing Finance Agency
Federal Labor Relations Authority
Federal Maritime Commission
Federal Mediation and Conciliation
Service

Federal Mine Safety and Health
Review Commission
Federal Reserve System
Federal Retirement Thrift Investment
Board
Federal Trade Commission
General Services Administration
Inter-American Foundation
Merit Systems Protection Board
National Aeronautics and Space
Administration
National Archives and Records
Administration
National Capital Planning Commission
National Credit Union Administration
National Foundation on the Arts and
the Humanities
National Labor Relations Board
National Mediation Board
National Railroad Passenger Corp. (Amtrak)
National Science Foundation
National Transportation Safety Board

Nuclear Regulatory Commission
Occupational Safety and Health Review
Commission
Office of Government Ethics
Office of Personnel Management
Office of Special Counsel
Office of the Director of National
Intelligence
Overseas Private Investment Corporation
Peace Corps
Pension Benefit Guaranty Corporation
Postal Regulatory Commission
Railroad Retirement Board
Securities and Exchange Commission
Selective Service System
Small Business Administration
Social Security Administration
Tennessee Valley Authority
Trade and Development Agency
U.S. Agency for International Development
U.S. Commission on Civil Rights
U.S. International Trade Commission
U.S. Postal Service

Election Statistics (1920–present): https://history.house
.gov/Institution/Election-Statistics
Video: www.congress.gov/video
Blog: https://blogs.loc.gov/law

House

Main: www.house.gov
Twitter: @HouseDemocrats; @HouseGOP
Facebook: www.facebook.com/HouseDemocrats;
www.facebook.com/HouseRepublicans
YouTube: www.youtube.com/channel/
UCxhAOE8DbC8iVNhAgQw5eNg; www.youtube.com/
user/HouseConference
Instagram: @housedemocrats; @housegop
Schedule: www.house.gov/legislative
Daily Business: http://clerk.house.gov/floorsummary/
floor.aspx
Committees: https://clerk.house.gov/committee_info/
scsoal.pdf
Committee Hearing Schedules: https://docs.house.gov/
Committee/Committees.aspx
Link to Roll Call Votes: https://clerk.house.gov/legislative/
legvotes.aspx
Leadership: www.house.gov/leadership
Media Galleries: https://live.house.gov

Senate

Main: www.senate.gov
Twitter: @SenateFloor
Annual Calendar: www.senate.gov/legislative/calendars.htm
Daily Calendar: www.senate.gov/legislative/LIS/executive_
calendar/xcalv.pdf
Committees: www.senate.gov/pagelayout/committees/d_
three_sections_with_teasers/committees_home.htm
Committee Hearing Schedules: www.senate.gov/
pagelayout/committees/b_three_sections_with_
teasers/committee_hearings.htm
Link to Roll Call Votes: www.senate.gov/pagelayout/
legislative/a_three_sections_with_teasers/votes.htm
Leadership: www.senate.gov/pagelayout/senators/a_
three_sections_with_teasers/leadership.htm
Media Galleries: www.senate.gov/galleries
Executive Nominations: www.senate.gov/pagelayout/
legislative/a_three_sections_with_teasers/nominations
.htm

Government Accountability Office

Main: www.gao.gov
Twitter: @USGAO
Facebook: www.facebook.com/usgao
YouTube: www.youtube.com/user/usgao
Instagram: @usgao
About the Government Accountability Office:
www.gao.gov/about/what-gao-does
Comptroller General's Bio: www.gao.gov/about/
comptroller-general/biography
Employee Directory: www.gao.gov/about/contact-us/
find-an-expert
GAO Reports: www.gao.gov/docsearch/repandtest.html
Media: www.gao.gov/about/press-center/media-kit

Government Publishing Office

Main: www.gpo.gov
Twitter: @USGPO
Facebook: www.facebook.com/USGPO
YouTube: www.youtube.com/user/gpoprinter
Instagram: @usgpo
About the Government Printing Office: www.gpo.gov/
who-we-are/our-agency/mission-vision-and-goals
News: www.gpo.gov/who-we-are/news-media/news-and-
press-releases

Library of Congress

Main: www.loc.gov
Twitter: @librarycongress
Facebook: www.facebook.com/libraryofcongress
YouTube: www.youtube.com/libraryofcongress
Instagram: @librarycongress
About the Library of Congress: www.loc.gov/about
Employee Directory: www.loc.gov/flicc/Staff/staff2new
.html
Online Catalog: https://catalog.loc.gov
Copyright Office: www.copyright.gov

JUDICIAL BRANCH

The Supreme Court

Main: www.supremecourt.gov
Twitter: @USSupremeCourt
About the Supreme Court: www.supremecourt.gov/
about/about.aspx
News: www.supremecourt.gov/opinions/slipopinions.aspx
Media: www.supremecourt.gov/publicinfo/publicinfo.aspx
Biographies of the Justices: www.supremecourt.gov/
about/biographies.aspx
Supreme Court Docket: www.supremecourt.gov/docket/
docket.aspx
Visiting the Supreme Court: www.supremecourt.gov/
visiting/visiting.aspx

Federal Judicial Center

Main: www.fjc.gov
History: www.fjc.gov/history/home.nsf
About the Federal Judicial Center: www.fjc.gov/about
Directors: www.fjc.gov/about/board-members

U.S. Federal Courts

Main: www.uscourts.gov
Twitter: @uscourts
YouTube: www.youtube.com/user/uscourts
About the U.S. Federal Courts: www.uscourts.gov/about-
federal-courts
News: www.uscourts.gov/judiciary-news
Biographical Directory of Federal Judges: www.uscourts
.gov/judges-judgeships
Publications: www.uscourts.gov/statistics-reports/
publications

Governors and Other State Officials

Political affiliations, when available, are indicated by (D) for Democrat, (R) for Republican, and (I) for Independent. For key officials of the District of Columbia and other Washington-area localities, see page 357. This information is current as of May 12, 2022.

Alabama   Web, www.alabama.gov

Gov. Kay Ivey (R), State Capitol, 600 Dexter Ave., #S-104, Montgomery 36130; (334) 242-7100; Fax, (334) 353-0004; Web, www.governor.alabama.gov; Facebook, www.facebook.com/KayIveyAL; Twitter, @GovernorKayIvey; YouTube, www.youtube.com/governorkayivey; Instagram, @governorkayivey

Lt. Gov. Will Ainsworth (R), 11 S. Union St., #S-725, Montgomery 36130; (334) 261-9590; Fax, (334) 242-4661; Web, https://ltgov.alabama.gov; Facebook, www.facebook.com/willainsworthAL; Twitter, @willainsworthAL; YouTube, www.youtube.com/channel/UCrvoSgvzkz391Urps8T1PYw; Instagram, @willainsworthal

Secy. of State John H. Merrill (R), State Capitol, 600 Dexter Ave., #S-105, Montgomery 36130, P.O. Box 5616, Montgomery 36103-5616; (334) 242-7200; Fax, (334) 242-2444; Web, www.sos.alabama.gov; Facebook, www.facebook.com/alasecretaryofstate; Twitter, @alasecofstate; YouTube, www.youtube.com/user/alasecretaryofstate

Atty. Gen. Steve Marshall (R), Alabama State House, 501 Washington Ave., Montgomery 36104; P.O. Box 300152, Montgomery 36130; (334) 242-7300; Fax, (334) 242-4891; Web, www.alabamaag.gov; Facebook, www.facebook.com/AGSteveMarshall; Twitter, @AGSteveMarshall; YouTube, Instagram, @agstevemarshall www.youtube.com/channel/UCFyHKAq0vREr7_rsUzHMDng; Instagram, @agstevemarshall

Treasurer Young Boozer (R), State Capitol, 600 Dexter Ave., #S-106, Montgomery 36104; (334) 242-7500; Email, alatreas@treasury.alabama.gov; Web, www.treasury.alabama.gov

Washington, DC, Representative: Casey Rogers, External Affairs Director; 600 Dexter Ave., Montgomery 36130; (334) 353-1188

Alaska   Web, http://alaska.gov

Gov. Michael J. (Mike) Dunleavy (R), State Capitol, 120 4th St., 3rd Floor, P.O. Box 110001, Juneau 99811-0001; (907) 465-3500; Web, www.gov.alaska.gov; Facebook, www.facebook.com/GovDunleavy; Twitter, @GovDunleavy; YouTube, www.youtube.com/channel/UCV-aZVxBDQ-SZU6KPSzG4Pg; Instagram, @govdunleavy

Lt. Gov. Kevin Meyer (R), State Capitol, 120 4th St., 3rd Floor, P.O. Box 1100015, Juneau 99811-0001; (907) 465-3520; Web, www.ltgov.alaska.gov; Facebook, www.facebook.com/LtGovMeyer; Twitter, @ltgovmeyer; Instagram, @ltgovmeyer

(No office of Secretary of State)

Atty. Gen. Tregarrick R. (Treg) Taylor (R), 1031 W. 4th Ave., #200, Anchorage 99501-1994; (907) 269-5100; Fax, (907) 276-3697; Email, attorney.general@alaska.gov; Web, www.law.alaska.gov

(No office of Treasurer)

Washington, DC, Representative: Tyson Gallagher, Deputy Chief of Staff, State Capitol, 120 4th St., P.O. Box 110001, Juneau, 99811; (907) 465-3500

Arizona   Web, http://az.gov

Gov. Doug Ducey (R), State Capitol, 1700 W. Washington St., 9th Floor, Phoenix 85007-2808; (602) 542-4331; Fax, (602) 542-7601; Email: engage@az.gov; Web, www.azgovernor.gov; Facebook, www.facebook.com/dougducey; Twitter, @DougDucey; YouTube, www.youtube.com/channel/UCi_TVbfG4I5SK6Ghj YEfyVQ; Instagram, @dougducey

(No office of Lieutenant Governor)

Secy. of State Katie Hobbs (R), State Capitol, 1700 W. Washington St., 7th Floor, Phoenix 85007-2808; (602) 542-4285; Fax, (602) 542-1575; Web, www.azsos.gov; Facebook, www.facebook.com/SecretaryHobbs; Twitter, @SecretaryHobbs; Instagram, @azsecretartyhobbs

Atty. Gen. Mark Brnovich (R), 2005 N. Central Ave., Phoenix 85004-2926; (602) 542-5025; Fax, (602) 542-4085; Web, www.azag.gov; Facebook, www.facebook.com/GeneralBrnovich; Twitter, @GeneralBrnovich; YouTube, www.youtube.com/user/ArizonaAGO; Instagram, @generalbrnovich

Treasurer Kimberly Yee (R), State Capitol, 1700 W. Washington St., #102, Phoenix 85007-2808; (602) 542-7800; Fax, (602) 542-7176; Web, www.aztreasury.gov; Facebook, www.facebook.com/votekimberlyyee; Twitter, @KimberlyYeeAZ

Washington, DC, Representative: Juan Ciscomani, Senior Advisor; State Capitol, 1700 W. Washington St., Phoenix 85007; (520) 628-6580

Arkansas   Web, www.arkansas.gov

Gov. Asa Hutchinson (R), State Capitol, 500 Woodlane St., #250, Little Rock 72201-1061; (501) 682-2345; Fax, (501) 682-1382; TTY, (501) 682-7515; Web, www.governor.arkansas.gov; Facebook, www.facebook.com/asaforarkansas; Twitter, @AsaHutchinson;

YouTube, www.youtube.com/channel/UCLJcNdgp2
PMEmiqJEoYzqwQ?_ga=2.179473956.1425565623
.1548966350-1965876865.1548966350; Instagram,
@govasahutchinson

Lt. Gov. Tim Griffin (R), State Capitol, 500 Woodlane St.,
#270, Little Rock 72201-1061; (501) 682-2144;
Fax, (501) 682-2894; Email, lg.staff@arkansas.gov;
Web, www.ltgovernor.arkansas.gov; Facebook,
www.facebook.com/LtGovTimGriffin; Twitter,
@LtGovTimGriffin; YouTube, www.youtube.com/user/
RepTimGriffin; Instagram, @ltgovtimgriffin

Secy. of State John Thurston (R), State Capitol, 500
Woodlane St., #256, Little Rock 72201-1094; (501) 682-
1010; Fax, (501) 682-3510; Email, arsos@sos.arkansas
.gov; Web, www.sos.arkansas.gov; Facebook,
www.facebook.com/ARSecofState; Twitter,
@ARSecofState; YouTube, www.youtube.com/user/
ArkansasSOS; Instagram, @sosjohnthurston

Atty. Gen. Leslie C. Rutledge (R), Tower Bldg., 323 Center
St., #200, Little Rock 72201-2610; (501) 682-2007;
Fax, (501) 683-2520; Email, oag@arkansasag.gov; Web,
www.arkansasag.gov; Facebook, www.facebook.com/
AGLeslieRutledge; Twitter, @AGRutledge; YouTube,
www.youtube.com/channel/UCHM7qdWTTF4aFybe
C0qdtaA; Instagram, @agleslierutledge

Treasurer Dennis Milligan (R), State Capitol, 500
Woodlane, #220, Little Rock 72201-1061; (501) 682-
5888; Fax, (501) 682-9692; Email, info@artreasury.gov;
Web, www.artreasury.gov; Facebook, www.facebook
.com/ARTreasurer; Twitter, @ARTreasurer; YouTube,
www.youtube.com/channel/UClewKMfQ55s3ASY
skxsPWTw

In Washington, DC: Kendall Marr, Director; 444
N. Capitol St. N.W., #365, 20001; (202) 434-4842

California   Web, www.ca.gov

Gov. Gavin Newsom (D), State Capitol, 1303 10th St.,
#1173, Sacramento 95814; (916) 445-2841; Fax, (916)
558-3160; TTY (916) 464-1580; Web, www.gov.ca.gov;
Facebook, www.facebook.com/CAgovernor and www
.facebook.com/GavinNewsom; Twitter, @CAgovernor
and @GavinNewsom; YouTube, www.youtube.com/
channel/UCrHSYLKqmLunBzlSfunGDSA; Instagram,
@cagovernor and @gavinnewsom

Lt. Gov. Eleni Kounalakis (D), 1021 O St., #8730,
Sacramento, CA 95814; (916) 445-8994; Fax, (916)
323-4998; Web, www.ltg.ca.gov; Facebook, www.face
book.com/EleniKounalakis; Twitter, @CALtGovernor
and @EleniForCA; Instagram, @eleniforca

Secy. of State Shirley N. Weber (D), 1500 11th St., #630,
Sacramento 95814; (916) 653-6814; Fax, (916) 653-
4795; Web, www.sos.ca.gov; Facebook, www.facebook
.com/CaliforniaSOS; Twitter, @CASOSvote; YouTube,
www.youtube.com/user/CaliforniaSOS Instagram,
@californiasos_

Atty. Gen. Rob Bonta (D), 1300 Eye St., Sacramento 95814-
2919; P.O. Box 944255, Sacramento 94244-2550; (916)
445-9555; Fax, (916) 323-5341, Toll-free, (800) 952-
5225; TTY, (800) 735-2929; TTY Spanish, (800) 855-
3000; Email, piu@boj.ca.gov; Web, www.oag.ca.gov;

Facebook, www.facebook.com/AGRobBonta; Twitter,
@AGRobBonta; YouTube, www.youtube.com/user/
caoag; Instagram, @agrobbonta

Treasurer Fiona Ma (D), 915 Capitol Mall, #110, C-15,
Sacramento 95814; P.O. Box 942809, Sacramento
94209-0001; (916) 653-2995; Fax, (916) 653-3125;
Web, www.treasurer.ca.gov; Facebook, www.facebook
.com/CaliforniaSTO; Twitter, @CalTreasurer;
YouTube, www.youtube.com/channel/UCQ_HING
lTvFvznebJmnrVUw

In Washington, DC: Katie Mathews, Senior Advisor for
Federal Affairs; 444 N. Capitol St. N.W., #134, 20001;
(202) 624-5275; Fax, (202) 624-5280 or (202) 624-5275

Colorado   Web, www.colorado.gov

Gov. Jared Polis (D), State Capital, 200 E. Colfax Ave.,
Room 136, Denver 80203; (303) 866-2471;
Fax, (303) 866-2003; Email, Governorpolis@state.co.us;
Web, www.colorado.gov/governor; Facebook,
www.facebook.com/jaredpolis; Twitter, @GovofCO;
YouTube, www.youtube.com/channel/UCy9OxTXx
C5bYP4hVXqZrlCQ; Instagram, @govofcol

Lt. Gov. Dianne Primavera (D), State Capital, 200
E. Colfax Ave., Room 130, Denver 80203; (303) 866-
4075; Web, www.colorado.gov/ltgovernor; Facebook,
www.facebook.com/LtGovofCO; Twitter,
@LtGovofCO; Instagram, @ltgovofco

Secy. of State Jena Griswold (D), 1700 Broadway, #550,
Denver 80290; (303) 894-2200; Fax, (303) 869-4860;
Web, www.sos.state.co.us; Facebook, www.facebook
.com/coloradoSoS; Twitter, @COSecofState and
@JenaGriswold; Instagram, @cosecofstate

Atty. Gen. Phil Weiser (D), Ralph L. Carr Judicial Bldg.,
1300 Broadway, 10th Floor, Denver 80203; (720) 508-
6000; Fax, (720) 508-6030; Email, attorney.general@
coag.gov; Web, www.coag.gov; Facebook, www.face
book.com/ColoradoAttorneyGeneral; Twitter,
@COAttnyGeneral

Treasurer Dave Young (D), State Capitol, 200 E. Colfax
Ave., #140, Denver 80203-1722; (303) 866-2441; Fax,
(303) 866-2123; Email, treasurer.young@state.co.us;
Web, www.colorado.gov/treasury; Twitter, @Colo
Treasurer and @DaveYoungCO

Washington, DC, Representative: Mara Sheldon, Senior
Policy Advisor; 136 State Capitol, Denver 80203;
(303) 866-2471

Connecticut   Web, www.portal.ct.gov

Gov. Ned Lamont (D), State Capitol, 210 Capitol Ave.,
Hartford 06106; (860) 566-4840; Fax, (860) 524-7396;
TTY, (860) 524-7397; Email, governor.lamont@ct.gov;
Web, www.governor.ct.gov; Facebook, www.facebook
.com/GovNedLamont; Twitter, @GovNedLamont;
YouTube, www.youtube.com/GovNedLamont;
Instagram, @govnedlamont

Lt. Gov. Susan Bysiewicz (D), State Capitol, 210 Capitol
Ave., #304, Hartford 06106; (860) 524-7384;
Fax, (860) 524-7304; TTY, (860) 524-7397;
Web, https://portal.ct.gov/office-of-the-lt-governor;

Email, LtGovernor.Bysiewicz@ct.gov; Facebook, www.facebook.com/LGSusanB; Twitter, @LGSusanB; Instagram, @lgsunsanb

Secy. of State Denise Merrill (D), 165 Capitol Ave., P.O. Box 150470, Hartford 06106; (860) 509-6200; Fax, (860) 509-6209; Email, exec.sots@ct.gov; Web, https://portal.ct.gov/sots; Facebook, www.facebook.com/SOTSMerrill; Twitter, @SOTSMerrill; Instagram, @sotsmerrill

Atty. Gen. William Tong (D), 165 Capitol Ave., Hartford 06106; (860) 808-5318; Fax, (860) 808-5387; Email, attorney.general@ct.gov; Web, https://portal.ct.gov/AG; Facebook, www.facebook.com/CTAttorneyGeneral; Twitter, @AGWilliamTong; YouTube, www.youtube.com/user/WilliamTongCT; Instagram, @williamtongct

Treasurer Shawn T. Wooden (D), 165 Capitol Ave., 2nd Floor, Hartford 06106-1773; (860) 702-3000; Toll-free, (800) 618-3404; Email, state.treasurer@ct.gov; Web, www.ott.ct.gov; Facebook, www.facebook.com/treasurerwooden; Twitter, @TreasurerWooden and @ShawnTWooden; Instagram, @cttreasurerwooden

In Washington, DC: Dan DeSimone, Director; 444 N. Capitol St. N.W., #317, 20001; (202) 403-8654

Delaware   Web, http://delaware.gov

Gov. John Carney (D), 150 S. Martin Luther King Jr. Blvd., Dover 19901; (302) 744-4101; Fax, (302) 577-3210; Web, www.governor.delaware.gov; Facebook, www.facebook.com/JohnCarneyDE; Twitter, @JohnCarneyDE; YouTube, www.youtube.com/channel/UCiD8skExycIfB_Vfh_INHxQ; Instagram, @johncarneyde

Lt. Gov. Bethany Hall-Long (D), 150 S. Martin Luther King Jr. Blvd., 3rd Floor, Dover 19901; (302) 744-4333; Fax, (302) 577-8787; Web, www.ltgov.delaware.gov; Facebook, www.facebook.com/LtGovernorDE; Twitter, @bethanyhalllong; Instagram, @ltgovernorde

Secy. of State Jeffrey W. Bullock (D), Townsend Bldg., 401 Federal St., Dover 19901; (302) 739-4111; Fax, (302) 739-3811; Web, www.sos.delaware.gov; Facebook, www.facebook.com/DEStateDept; Twitter, @DEStateDept; Instagram, @DEStateDept

Atty. Gen. Kathy Jennings (D), Carvel State Bldg., 820 N. French St., Wilmington 19801; (302) 577-8400; Fax, (302) 577-6630; TTY, (302) 577-5783; Email, attorney.general@delaware.gov; Web, www.attorneygeneral.delaware.gov; Facebook, www.facebook.com/DE.AttorneyGeneral; Twitter, @DE_DOJ and @KathyJenningsDE; YouTube, www.youtube.com/user/DelawareDOJ; Instagram, @de_doj

Treasurer Colleen Davis (D), 820 Silver Lake Blvd., #100, Dover 19904; (302) 672-6700; Fax, (302) 739-2274; Email, statetreasurer@delaware.gov; Web, treasurer.delaware.gov; Facebook, www.facebook.com/TreasurerDavis; Twitter, @TreasurerDavis; Instagram, @treasurerdavis

In Washington, DC: Shelia Grant, Deputy Chief of Staff, 444 N. Capitol St. N.W., #542, 20001; (302) 744-4101

Florida   Web, www.flgov.com

Gov. Ron DeSantis (R), The Capitol, 400 S. Monroe St., Tallahassee 32399-0001; (850) 488-7146; Fax, (850) 488-4042; TTY, (850) 922-7795; Email, Governor Ron.Desantis@eog.myflorida.com; Web, www.flgov.com; Facebook, www.facebook.com/GovRonDeSantis and www.facebook.com/RonDeSantisFlorida; Twitter, @GovRonDeSantis and @RonDeSantisFL; Instagram, @flgovrondesantis

Lt. Gov. Jeanette Nuñez (R), The Capitol, 400 S. Monroe St., PL-05, Tallahassee 32399-0001; (850) 717-9331; Email, LtGovernorJeanette.Nunez@eog.myflorida.com; Web, www.flgov.com/lieutenant-governor-jeanette-nunez; Facebook, www.facebook.com/LtGovNunez; Twitter, @LtGovNunez

Secy. of State Laurel M. Lee (R), R. A. Gray Bldg., 500 S. Bronough, Tallahassee 32399-0250; (850) 245-6500; Fax, (850) 245-6125; TTY, (850) 245-6096; Email, SecretaryofState@DOS.MyFlorida.com; Web, www.dos.myflorida.com; Twitter, @FLSecofState

Atty. Gen. Ashley Moody (R), The Capitol, 400 S. Monroe St., PL-01, Tallahassee 32399-1050; (850) 414-3300; Toll-free, (866) 966-7226; Fax, (850) 410-1630; Web, www.myfloridalegal.com; Facebook, www.facebook.com/AshleyMoodyFL; Twitter, @AGAshleyMoody and @AshleyMoodyFL; Instagram, @ashleymoodyfl

Chief Financial Officer Jimmy Patronis (R), 200 E. Gaines St., Tallahassee 32399-0301; (877) 693-5236; Fax, (850) 413-4993; Out of state, (850) 413-3089; Web, www.myfloridacfo.com; Facebook, www.facebook.com/FLDFS; Twitter, @FLSFS; Instagram, @jpatronis

In Washington, DC: Katherine Anne Russo, Washington Representative; 444 N. Capitol St. N.W., #349, 20001; (202) 624-5885

Georgia   Web, www.georgia.gov

Gov. Brian P. Kemp (R), State Capitol, 206 Washington St., #203, Atlanta 30334; (404) 656-1776; Fax, (404) 657-7332; Web, www.gov.georgia.gov; Facebook, www.facebook.com/GovKemp; Twitter, @GovKemp; YouTube, www.youtube.com/channel/UC0aZKC0fKwXt3Q8OB_t5gBA; Instagram, @govkemp

Lt. Gov. Geoff Duncan (R), 240 State Capitol, Atlanta 30334; (404) 656-5030; Email, Geoff.Duncan@ltgov.ga.gov; Web, www.ltgov.georgia.gov; Facebook, www.facebook.com/LGGeoffDuncan; Twitter, @GeoffDuncanGA; Instagram, @lt.governorduncan

Secy. of State Brad Raffensperger (R), 214 State Capitol, Atlanta 30334; (404) 656-2881; Fax, (404) 656-0513; Email, soscontact@sos.ga.gov; Web, www.sos.ga.gov; Facebook, www.facebook.com/GASecretaryofState; Twitter, @GaSecofState; Instagram, @gasecofstate

Atty. Gen. Chris Carr (R), 40 Capitol Square S.W., Atlanta 30334; (404) 458-3600; Fax, (404) 657-8733; Email, AGCarr@law.ga.gov; Web, www.law.ga.gov; Facebook, www.facebook.com/GeorgiaAttorneyGeneral; Twitter, @Georgia_AG

Treasurer Steve McCoy (R), 200 Piedmont Ave., West Tower, #1204, Atlanta 30334; (404) 656-2168; Fax, (404) 656-9048; Email, ostweb@treasury.ga.gov; Web, www.ost.georgia.gov

Washington, DC, Representative: Ben Ayres, Washington Representative; 203 State Capitol, Atlanta 30334; (404) 656-1776

Hawaii   Web, www.hawaii.gov

Gov. David Ige (D), State Capitol, 415 S. Beretania St., Honolulu 96813; (808) 586-0034; Fax, (808) 586-0006; Web, www.governor.hawaii.gov; Facebook, www.facebook.com/GovernorDavidIge; Twitter, @GovHawaii; YouTube, www.youtube.com/c/GovernorDavidIge

Lt. Gov. Josh Green (D), State Capitol, 415 S. Beretania St., Honolulu 96813; (808) 586-0255; Fax, (808) 586-0006; Email, josh.green@hawaii.gov; Web, www.ltgov.hawaii.gov; Facebook, www.facebook.com/LtGovJoshGreen; Twitter, @LtGovJoshGreen; Instagram, @ltgovjoshgreen

(No office of Secretary of State)

Atty. Gen. Holly T. Shikada (D), 425 Queen St., Honolulu 96813; (808) 586-1500; Fax, (808) 586-1239; Email, hawaiiag@hawaii.gov: Web, www.ag.hawaii.gov

Director of Finance Craig K. Hirai (D), P.O. Box 150, Honolulu 96810; (808) 586-1518; Fax, (808) 586-1976; Email, budgetandfinance@hawaii.gov; Web, www.budget.hawaii.gov

Washington, DC, Representative: Sabrina Nasir, Special Assistant; State Capitol, Honolulu 96813; (808) 586-0034

Idaho   Web, www.idaho.gov

Gov. Brad Little (R), State Capitol, 700 W. Jefferson St., West Wing., 2nd Floor, Boise 83720-0034; (208) 334-2100; Fax, (208) 854-3036; Email, governor@gov.idaho.gov; Web, www.gov.idaho.gov; Facebook, www.facebook.com/governorbradlittle; Twitter, @GovernorLittle; YouTube, www.youtube.com/channel/UCMziHVW4DJOWKzt-fqqD5fA; Instagram, @governorbradlittle

Lt. Gov. Janice McGeachin (R), State Capitol, 700 W. Jefferson St., #225, Boise 83720-0057; (208) 334-2200; Fax, (208) 334-3259; Web, lgo.idaho.gov; Facebook, www.facebook.com/IdahoLtGov; Twitter, @JaniceMcGeachin

Secy. of State Lawerence Denney (R), State Capitol, 700 W. Jefferson, #E205, P.O. Box 83720, Boise 83720-0080; (208) 334-2300; Fax, (208) 334-2282; Email, sosinfo@sos.idaho.gov; Web, www.sos.idaho.gov; Facebook, www.facebook.com/IDSecOfState; Twitter, @IDsecofState; YouTube, www.youtube.com/channel/UCWIW8GT6nrLXD3Ptb28cYpg/videos

Atty. Gen. Lawrence G. Wasden (R), State Capitol, 700 W. Jefferson St., #210, P.O. Box 83720, Boise 83720-0010, (208) 334-2400; Fax, (208) 854-8071; Email, AGWasden@ag.idaho.gov; Web, www.ag.idaho.gov; Facebook, www.facebook.com/lawrence.wasden.9; Twitter, @lawrencewasden

Treasurer Julie A. Ellsworth (R), State Capitol, 700 W. Jefferson St., #E110, P.O. Box 83720, Boise 83720-0091; (208) 334-3200; Fax, (208) 332-2959; Web, sto.idaho.gov; Facebook, www.facebook.com/IdahoStateTreasurer

Washington, DC, Representative: Bobbi-Jo Meulem, Director; 700 W. Jefferson St., 2nd Floor, Boise 83720; (208) 334-2100

Illinois   Web, www.illinois.gov

Gov. J. B. Pritzker (D), Capitol Bldg., 207 State House, Springfield 62706; (217) 782-6830; Fax, (217) 524-4049; Web, www.illinois.gov/gov and www.jbpritzker.com; Facebook, www.facebook.com/GovPritzker; Twitter, @GovPritzker; YouTube, www.youtube.com/channel/UCI8FbW3Sm5y_3eP2g8kyXHg; Instagram, @govpritzker

Lt. Gov. Juliana Stratton (D), Capitol Bldg., 214 State House, Springfield 62706; (217) 558-3085; Fax, (217) 558-3094; TTY, (866) 383-1866; Email, LtGovStratton@illinois.gov; Web, www.illinois.gov/ltg; Facebook, www.facebook.com/ltgovstratton; Twitter, @LtGovStratton; Instagram, @ltgovstratton

Secy. of State Jesse White (D), Capitol Bldg., 213 State Capitol, Springfield 62756; (217) 785-3000; Fax, (217) 524-0251; Toll-free (in-state only), 800-252-8980; Web, www.cyberdriveillinois.com; Facebook, www.facebook.com/JesseWhiteSOS; Twitter, @ILSecOfState; YouTube, www.youtube.com/user/ILSECSTATE; Instagram, @ilsecofstate

Atty. Gen. Kwame Raoul (D), 500 S. 2nd St., Springfield 62704-1771; (217) 782-1090; TTY, (877) 844-5461; Web, www.illinoisattorneygeneral.gov; Facebook, www.facebook.com/kwame.raoul.illinois; Twitter, @KwameRaoul

Treasurer Michael W. Frerichs (D), Capitol Bldg., 219 State House, Springfield 62706-1000; (866) 458-7327; Fax, (217) 785-2777; TTY, (866) 877-6013; Web, www.illinoistreasurer.gov; Facebook, www.facebook.com/TreasurerMichaelFrerichs; Twitter, @ILTreasurer; YouTube, YouTube.com/channel/UCqZXaLI5po2MJSTAgoxA6rw; Instagram, @iltreasurer

In Washington, DC: Sam LaPaille, First Assistant Deputy Chief of Staff for Federal Affairs; 444 N. Capitol St. N.W., #400, 20001; (202) 624-7760; Fax, (202) 724-0689

Indiana   Web, www.in.gov

Gov. Eric J. Holcomb (R), State House, 200 W. Washington St., #206, Indianapolis 46204; (317) 232-4567; Fax, (317) 232-3443; Web, www.in.gov/gov; Facebook, www.facebook.com/GovHolcomb and www.facebook.com/HolcombForIndiana; Twitter, @GovHolcomb; YouTube, www.youtube.com/channel/UCmcggUX5rA1za_ya16joSKA; Instagram, @govholcomb

Lt. Gov. Suzanne Crouch (R), State House, 200 W. Washington St., #333, Indianapolis 46204-2790; (317) 232-4545; Fax, (317) 232-4788; Web, www.in.gov/lg; Facebook, www.facebook.com/LGSuzanneCrouch;

Twitter, @LGSuzanneCrouch; Instagram, @lgsuzannecrouch

Secy. of State Holli Sullivan (R), State House, 200 W. Washington St., #201, Indianapolis 46204-2790; (317) 232-6531; Fax, (317) 233-3283; Email, constituent@sos.IN.gov; Web, www.in.gov/sos; Facebook, www.facebook.com/OfficialSOSIN; Twitter, @OfficialSOSIN; Instagram, @officialsosin

Atty. Gen. Theodore E. (Todd) Rokita (R), Indiana Government Center South, 302 W. Washington St., 5th Floor, Indianapolis 46204-2770; (317) 232-6201; Fax, (317) 232-7979; Web, www.in.gov/attorneygeneral; Facebook, www.facebook.com/agToddRokita; Twitter, @AGToddRokita; Instagram, @toddrokita

Treasurer Kelly Mitchell (R), 242 State House, 200 W. Washington St., Indianapolis 46204; (317) 232-6386; Fax, (317) 233-1780; Email, tosstaff@tos.in.gov; Web, www.in.gov/tos; Facebook, www.facebook.com/TOSMitchell; Twitter, @tos_mitchell

In Washington, DC: Debbie Hohlt, Director; 1455 Pennsylvania Ave. N.W., #1140, 20004; (202) 445-8999; Fax, (202) 833-1587

Iowa   Web, www.iowa.gov

Gov. Kim Reynolds (R), State Capitol, 1007 E. Grand Ave., Des Moines 50319-0001; (515) 281-5211; Fax, (515) 725-3527; Web, www.governor.iowa.gov; Facebook, www.facebook.com/IAGovernor; Twitter, @IAGovernor; YouTube, www.youtube.com/channel/UCmISFMoFOM6fo6PeXdHxGDg; Instagram, @kimreynoldsia

Lt. Gov. Adam Gregg (R), State Capitol, 1007 E. Grand Ave., Des Moines 50319; (515) 281-5211; Fax, (515) 725-3527; Facebook, www.facebook.com/IaLtGov; Twitter, @IALtGov

Secy. of State Paul D. Pate (R), Lucas Bldg., 321 E. 12th St., 1st Floor, Des Moines 50319; (515) 281-5204; Fax, (515) 242-5952; Email, sos@sos.iowa.gov; Web, sos.iowa.gov; Facebook, www.facebook.com/IASecretaryofState; Twitter, @IowaSOS; YouTube, www.youtube.com/channel/UCIeockCHC47J2xvZDfgTmew; Instagram, @iowasecretaryofstatepaulpate

Atty. Gen. Tom Miller (D), Hoover State Office Bldg., 1305 E. Walnut St., Des Moines 50319; (515) 281-5164; Fax, (515) 281-4209; Email, webteam@ag.iowa.gov; Web, www.iowaattorneygeneral.gov; Facebook, www.facebook.com/AGIowa; Twitter, @AGIowa; YouTube, www.youtube.com/user/AGIowa

Treasurer Michael L. Fitzgerald (D), Capitol Bldg., 1007 E. Grand Ave., Des Moines 50319; (515) 281-5368; Fax, (515) 281-7562; Email, treasurer@tos.iowa.gov; Web, www.iowatreasurer.gov; Facebook, www.facebook.com/IowaTreasurer; Twitter, @IowaTreasurer; YouTube, www.youtube.com/user/statetreasurerofiowa

In Washington, DC: Meaghan O'Brien, Director of State-Federal Relations; 400 N. Capitol St. N.W., #359, 20001; (202) 624-5479

Kansas   Web, www.kansas.gov

Gov. Laura Kelly (D), Capitol, 300 10th Ave. S.W., #241S, Topeka 66612-1590; (785) 368-8500; Toll-free, (877) 579-6757; Web, https://governor.kansas.gov; Facebook, www.facebook.com/GovLauraKelly; Twitter, @GovLauraKelly; YouTube, www.youtube.com/channel/UChH3fB2PkiJjZlo55c9UH2Q; Instagram, @govlaurakelly

Lt. Gov. David Toland (D), Capitol, 300 10th Ave. S.W., #241S, Topeka 66612-1590; (785) 368-8500; Email, press@ks.gov; Web, https://governor.kansas.gov/about-the-office/lt-governor; Facebook, www.facebook.com/LtGovDavidToland; Twitter, @LtGovToland

Secy. of State Scott Schwab (R), Memorial Hall, 120 10th Ave. S.W., 1st Floor, Topeka 66612-1594; (785) 296-4575; Fax, (785) 296-4570; Email, kssos@ks.gov; Web, sos.kansas.gov; Facebook, www.facebook.com/KansasSecretaryofState; Twitter, @KansasSOS, YouTube, www.youtube.com/channel/UCtLiDyLmzO9qpEyqFwpB2UA?view_as=subscriber

Atty. Gen. Derek Schmidt (R), Memorial Hall, 120 10th Ave. S.W., 2nd Floor, Topeka 66612-1597; (785) 296-2215; Fax, (785) 296-6296; Toll-free, (888) 428-8436; Web, www.ag.ks.gov; Facebook, www.facebook.com/OAGKansas and www.facebook.com/DerekSchmidtKS; Twitter, @KSAGOffice; YouTube, www.youtube.com/user/AGKansas

Treasurer Lynn Rogers (D), Landon State Office Bldg., 900 Jackson St. S.W., #201, Topeka 66612-1235; (785) 296-3171; Fax, (785) 296-7950; Web, www.kansasstatetreasurer.com; Facebook, www.facebook.com/KansasTreasurer; Twitter, @KansasTreasurer; Instagram, @treasurerrogers

Washington, DC, Representative: Adam Nordstrom, Washington Representative; 300 10th St. S.W., Topeka 66612; (202) 258-2084; Fax, (202) 638-1045

Kentucky   Web, www.kentucky.gov

Gov. Andy Beshear (D), State Capitol, 700 Capitol Ave., #100, Frankfort 40601; (502) 564-2611; Fax, (502) 564-2517; TTY, (502) 564-9551; Web, www.governor.ky.gov; Facebook, www.facebook.com/GovAndyBeshear; Twitter, @GovAndyBeshear; YouTube, www.youtube.com/GovAndyBeshear; Instagram, @govandybeshear

Lt. Gov. Jacqueline Coleman (D), State Capitol, 700 Capitol Ave., Frankfort 40601; (502) 564-2611; Fax, (502) 564-2849; Web, www.ltgovernor.ky.gov; Facebook, www.facebook.com/LtGovColeman; Twitter, @LtGovColeman; Instagram, @ltgovcoleman

Secy. of State Michael G. Adams (D), State Capitol, 700 Capitol Ave., #152, Frankfort 40601-3493; (502) 564-3490; Fax, (502) 564-5687; Web, www.sos.ky.gov; Facebook, www.facebook.com/KYSecofState; Twitter, @KYSecState; YouTube, www.youtube.com/channel/UCKgvInkMePrHnyu928k77bw

Atty. Gen. Daniel Cameron (D), State Capitol, 700 Capitol Ave., #118, Frankfort 40601-3449; (502) 696-5300; Fax, (502) 564-2894; Web, www.ag.ky.gov; Facebook, www.facebook.com/kyoag; Twitter, @kyoag

YouTube, www.youtube.com/channel/UC1X2uUpQrq6EQjPf-PK57YA; Instagram; @danieljaycameron

Treasurer Allison Ball (R), 1050 U.S. Hwy 127 South, #100, Frankfort 40601; (502) 564-4722; Fax, (502) 564-6545; Email, treasury.web@ky.gov; Web, www.treasury.ky.gov/Pages/index.aspx; Facebook, www.facebook.com/treasurerball; Twitter, @KYTreasurer

In Washington, DC: Coulter Minix, Director; 444 N. Capitol St. N.W., #380; (202) 220-1350

Louisiana Web, www.louisiana.gov

Gov. John B. Edwards (D), State Capitol, 900 N. 3rd St., 4th Floor, Baton Rouge 70802-9004; P.O. Box 94004, Baton Rouge 70804-9004; (225) 342-7015; Fax, (225) 342-7099; Toll-free, (866) 366-1121; Web, www.gov.louisiana.gov; Facebook, www.facebook.com/LouisianaGov; Twitter, @LouisianaGov; YouTube, www.youtube.com/c/LouisianaGovJohnBelEdwards/featured; Instagram, @louisiana_gov

Lt. Gov. Billy Nungesser (R), Capitol Annex, Bldg. 1051 N. 3rd St., Baton Rouge 70802; P.O. Box 44243, Baton Rouge, 70804-4242; (225) 342-7009; Fax, (225) 342-1949; Email, ltgov@crt.la.gov; Web, www.crt.state.la.us/lt-governor; Facebook, www.facebook.com/LouisianaLtGov; Twitter, @LouisianaLtGov and @BillyNungesser; Instagram, @louisianaltgov

Secy. of State R. Kyle Ardoin (R), 8585 Archives Ave., Baton Rouge 70809; P.O. Box 94125, Baton Rouge 70804-9125; (225) 922-2880; Fax, (225) 922-2003; Email, admin@sos.louisiana.gov; Web, www.sos.la.gov; Facebook, www.facebook.com/Louisianasos; Twitter, @Louisiana_sos; YouTube, www.youtube.com/user/SofState; Instagram, @Louisianasos

Atty. Gen. Jeff Landry (R), 1885 N. 3rd St., Baton Rouge 70802; P.O. Box 94005, Baton Rouge 70804; (225) 326-6079; Fax, (225) 326-6793; Email, ConstituentServices@ag.louisiana.gov; Web, www.ag.state.la.us; Facebook, www.facebook.com/AGJeffLandry; Twitter, @AGJeffLandry; Instagram, @agjefflandry

Treasurer John M. Schroder (R), State Capitol, 900 N. 3rd St., 3rd Floor, Baton Rouge 70802; Mailing address, P.O. Box 44154, Baton Rouge 70804; (225) 342-0010; Fax, (225) 342-0046; Web, www.treasury.la.gov; Facebook, www.facebook.com/LouisianaTreasury; Twitter, @LATreasury; YouTube, www.youtube.com/user/latreasurydotcom; Instagram, @latreasury

Washington, DC, Representative: Alicia Williams, Senior Special Assistant; P.O. Box 94004, Baton Rouge 70804-9004; 225-342-7015

Maine Web, www.maine.gov

Gov. Janet T. Mills (D), 1 State House Station, Augusta 04333-0001; (207) 287-3531; Fax, (207) 287-1034; Toll-free, (855) 721-5203; TTY, (207) 287-6548; Email, governor@maine.gov; Web, www.maine.gov/governor/mills; Facebook, www.facebook.com/GovernorJanetMills; Twitter, @GovJanetMills; YouTube, www.youtube.com/channel/UCiagiuAdRdU2EhWfYddxgAg; Instagram, @governorjanetmills

(No office of Lieutenant Governor)

Secy. of State Shenna Bellows (D), Nash School Bldg., 103 Sewall St., 2nd Floor, Augusta 04333; Mailing address, 148 State House Station, Augusta 04333-0148; (207) 626-8400; Fax, (207) 287-8598; Email, sos.office@maine.gov; Web, www.maine.gov/sos; Facebook, www.facebook.com/MaineSOS; Twitter, @MESecOfState; YouTube, www.youtube.com/channel/UCnZ7LSdDcYOIbCQgSeAwisQ; Instagram, @shennabellows

Atty. Gen. Aaron Frey (D), 6 State House Station, Augusta 04333; Mailing address, 6 State House Station, Augusta 04333-0006; (207) 626-8800; TTY, (207) 626-8865; Web, www.maine.gov/ag; Facebook, www.facebook.com/Maine-Office-of-the-Attorney-General-394265750747931

Treasurer Henry Beck (D), Burton M. Cross Bldg., 3rd Floor, 111 Sewall St., Augusta 04333; Mailing address, 39 State House Station, Augusta 04333-0039; (207) 624-7477; Fax, (207) 287-2367; Email, state.treasurer@maine.gov; Web, www.maine.gov/treasurer; Facebook, www.facebook.com/MaineOST; Twitter, @HenryBeckMaine

Washington, DC, Representative: Beth Beausang, Senior Policy Advisor; 1 State House Station, Augusta 04333; (207) 287-3531

Maryland Web, www.maryland.gov

Gov. Larry Hogan (R), State House, 100 State Circle, Annapolis 21401-1925; (410) 974-3901; Fax, (410) 974-3275; Toll-free, (800) 811-8336; Web, www.governor.maryland.gov; Facebook, www.facebook.com/GovLarryHogan and www.facebook.com/larryhoganmd; Twitter, @GovLarryHogan and @LarryHogan; YouTube, www.youtube.com/channel/UCbheDE_LMwHyl3VShzU73wA; Instagram, @govlarryhogan

Lt. Gov. Boyd K. Rutherford (R), State House, 100 State Circle, Annapolis 21401-1925; (410) 974-3901; Fax, 410-974-5882; Toll free, 1-800-811-8336; Web, www.governor.maryland.gov/ltgovernor; Facebook, www.facebook.com/BoydKRutherford; Twitter, @BoydKRutherford; Instagram, @boydkrutherford

Secy. of State John C. Wobensmith (R), Fred L. Wineland Bldg., 16 Francis St., Annapolis 21401; (410) 974-5521; Fax, (410) 974-5190; Email, dlmdsos_sos@Maryland.gov; Web, https://sos.maryland.gov/Pages/default.aspx; Facebook, www.facebook.com/mdsecretaryofstate; Twitter, @SOSMaryland; Instagram, @md_sos

Atty. Gen. Brian E. Frosh (R), 200 St. Paul Pl., Baltimore 21202; (410) 576-6300; Toll-free, (888) 743-0023; TTY, (410) 576-6372; Email, oag@oag.state.md.us; Web, www.oag.state.md.us; Facebook, www.facebook.com/MarylandAttorneyGeneral; Twitter, @BrianFrosh; YouTube, www.youtube.com/channel/UCo_Cs5Hn4r5rdArhSPz6XIQ

Treasurer Dereck E. Davis (D), Goldstein Treasury Bldg., 80 Calvert St., Annapolis 21401; (410) 260-7160; Fax, (410) 974-3530; Toll-free, (800) 974-0468; Email, treasurer@treasurer.state.md.us; Web, www.treasury.state.md.us

In Washington, DC: Ariel Judah, Director, Federal Relations; 444 N. Capitol St. N.W., #311, 20001; 202-624-1432

Massachusetts   Web, www.mass.gov

Gov. Charlie Baker (R), State House, 24 Beacon St., Room 280, Boston 02133; (617) 725-4005; Fax, (617) 727-9725; Toll-free (in-state only), (888) 870-7770; TTY, (617) 727-3666; Web, www.mass.gov/governor; Facebook, www.facebook.com/CharlieBakerMA; Twitter, @MassGovernor; YouTube, www.youtube .com/user/MassGovernor; Instagram, @massgovernor

Lt. Gov. Karyn Polito (R), State House, 24 Beacon St., Room 360, Boston 02133; (617) 725-4005; Fax, (617) 727-9725; Web, www.mass.gov/person/karyn-polito-lieutenant-governor; Facebook, www.facebook.com/karynpolitoMA; Twitter, @MassLtGov; Instagram, @massltgov

Secy. of the Commonwealth William Francis Galvin (D), State House, 24 Beacon St., Room 340, Boston 02133; (617) 727-7030; Fax, (617) 742-4528; Toll-free (in-state only), (800) 392-6090; TTY, (617) 878-3889; Email, cis@sec.state.ma.us; Web, www.sec.state.ma.us; Twitter, @SecretaryOfMass

Atty. Gen. Maura Healey (D), McCormack Bldg., 1 Ashburton Pl., 20th Floor, Boston 02108-1518; (617) 727-2200; TTY, (617) 727-4765; Email, ago@state.ma .us; Web, www.mass.gov/orgs/office-of-attorney-general-maura-healey; Facebook, www.facebook.com/MassAttorneyGeneral; Twitter, @MassAGO; YouTube, www.youtube.com/user/MassAttorneyGeneral; Instagram, @mass_ago

Treasurer Deborah B. Goldberg (D), State House, 24 Beacon St., Room 227, Boston 02133; (617) 367-6900; Fax, (617) 248-0372; Web, www.mass.gov/treasury; Facebook, www.facebook.com/masstreasury; Twitter, @MassTreasury; Instagram, @mass_treasury

In Washington, DC: Kevin McColaugh, Director; 444 N. Capitol St. N.W., #315, 20001; (202) 624-3616

Michigan   Web, www.michigan.gov

Gov. Gretchen Whitmer (D), Romney Bldg., 111 S. Capitol Ave., P.O. Box 30013, Lansing 48909; (517) 373-3400; Fax, (517) 335-6863; Web, www.michigan.gov/whitmer; Facebook, www.facebook.com/GovGretchenWhitmer; Twitter, @GovWhitmer; YouTube, www.youtube.com/channel/UCTMbahTiYg0uyEkQVMZFByQ; Instagram, @gewhitmer

Lt. Gov. Garlin Gilchrist II (D), Romney Bldg., 111 S. Capitol Ave., 5th Floor, P.O. Box 30013, Lansing 48909; (517) 373-6800; Fax, (517) 241-3956; Text, (313) 488-5270; Web, www.michigan.gov/whitmer/0,9309,7-387-90502—,00.html; Facebook, www.facebook.com/garlingilchristMI; Twitter, @LtGovGilchrist and @garlin; Instagram, @ltgovgilchrist and @garlinii

Secy. of State Jocelyn Benson (D), 430 W. Allegan St., 1st Floor, Lansing 48918-9900; (808) 767-6424; Fax, (517) 373-0727; Toll-free, (888) 767-6424; Email, sos-news@michigan.gov; Web, www.michigan.gov/sos;

Facebook, www.facebook.com/MichiganSoS; Twitter, @MichSos; YouTube, www.youtube.com/user/MichSoSOffice; Instagram, @michigansos

Atty. Gen. Dana Nessel (D), G. Mennen Williams Bldg., 525 W. Ottawa St., 7th Floor, P.O. Box 30212, Lansing 48909; (517) 335-7622; Fax, (517) 335-7644; Email, miag@michigan.gov; Web, www.michigan.gov/agFacebook, www.facebook.com/MIAttorneyGeneral; Twitter, @MIAttyGen; Instagram, @miattygen

Treasurer Rachael Eubanks (D), 430 W. Allegan St., Lansing 48922; (517) 335-7508; Fax, (517) 373-4968; Email, MIStateTreasurer@michigan.gov; Web, www .michigan.gov/treasury; Twitter, @MITreasEubanks

In Washington, DC: Patty Readinger, Director; 444 N. Capitol St. N.W., #411, 20001; (202) 624-3588

Minnesota   Web, www.mn.gov

Gov. Tim Walz (D), State Capitol, 75 Rev. Dr. Martin Luther King Jr. Blvd., Room 130, St. Paul 55155; (651) 201-3400; Fax, (651) 797-1850; Toll-free, (800) 657-3717; Web, www.mn.gov/governor; Facebook, www .facebook.com/GovTimWalz; Twitter, @GovTimWalz; YouTube, www.youtube.com/channel/UC7CPBsekv_4u34kIVqaVtDA; Instagram, @mngovernor

Lt. Gov. Peggy Flanagan (D), State Capitol, 75 Rev. Dr. Martin Luther King Jr. Blvd., St. Paul 55155; (651) 201-3400; Fax, (651) 797-1850; Web, www.mn.gov/governor; Facebook, www.facebook.com/LtGovFlanagan; Twitter, @LtGovFlanagan

Secy. of State Steve Simon (D), 180 State Office Bldg., 100 Rev. Dr. Martin Luther King Jr. Blvd., St. Paul 55155; (651) 201-1324; Fax, (651) 296-9073; Toll-free, (877) 551-6767; Email, secretary.state@state.mn.us; Web, www.sos.state.mn.us; Facebook, www.facebook.com/MNSteveSimon; Twitter, @MNSteveSimon; Instagram, @mnstevesimon

Atty. Gen. Keith Ellison (D), 445 Minnesota St., #1400, St. Paul 55101-2131; (651) 296-3353; Toll-free, (800) 657-3787; TTY, (800) 366-4812; Web, www.ag.state.mn.us; Facebook, www.facebook.com/AGEllison; Twitter, @AGEllison; YouTube, www.youtube.com/channel/UC24VphM2BVBQYrN2oTjjHUQ/videos

Commissioner of Minnesota Alice Roberts-Davis, 50 Sherburne Ave., #200, St. Paul 55155; (651) 201-2601; Fax, (651) 296-8685; TTY, (800) 627-3529; Email, Alice.Roberts-Davis@state.mn.us; Web, www.mn.gov/mmb; Facebook, www.facebook.com/MinnesotaManagementandBudget; Twitter, @MMBCommunicates; YouTube, www.youtube.com/user/adminMinnesota

Washington, DC, Representative: Sasha Bergman, Director; State Capitol, 75 Rev. Dr. Martin Luther King Jr. Blvd., Room 130, St. Paul, 55155; (651) 201-3400

Mississippi   Web, www.ms.gov

Gov. Tate Reeves (R), Sillers Bldg., 550 High St., 19th Floor, Jackson, 39201; Mailing address, P.O. Box 139, Jackson 39205; (601) 359-3150; Fax, (601) 359-3741; Toll-free, (877) 405-0733; Email, governor@governor .state.ms.us; Web, https://governorreeves.ms.gov;

Facebook, www.facebook.com/tatereeves; Twitter, @tatereeves; Instagram, @tatereeves

Lt. Gov. Delbert Hosemann (R), New Capitol Bldg., #315, 400 High St., P.O. Box 1018, Jackson 39215-1018; (601) 359-3200; Fax, (601) 359-4054; Email, ltgov@ senate.ms.gov; Web, https://ltgovhosemann.ms.gov; Facebook, www.facebook.com/DelbertHosemann; Twitter, @DelbertHosemann; Instagram, @delberthosemann

Secy. of State Michael Watson (R), 401 Mississippi St., Jackson 39201, (601) 359-1350; Fax, (601) 359-1499; Email, businesssserices@sos.ms.gov; Web, www.sos.ms .gov; Facebook, www.facebook.com/ MississippiSecretaryofState; Twitter, @MississippiSOS

Atty. Gen. Lynn Fitch (R), Walter Sillers Bldg., 550 High St., #1200, Jackson 39201; Mailing address, P.O. Box 220, Jackson 39205; (601) 359-3680; Fax, (601) 359-3796; Email, lynn.fitch@ago.ms.gov; Web, www.ago.state.ms.us; Facebook; www.facebook .com/lynnfitchag; Twitter, @LynnFitchAG; YouTube; www.youtube.com/channel/UCQrSWmj7K84XHM ifSUo4Lmg; Instagram, @lynnfitchag

Treasurer David McRae (R), Woolfolk Bldg., 501 N. West St., #1101, Jackson 39201, P.O. Box 138, Jackson 39205-0138; (601) 359-3600; Fax, (601) 359-2001; Email, david.mcrae@treasury.ms.gov; Web, www.treasury.ms.gov; Facebook, www.facebook.com/ DavidMcRae.org; Twitter, @DavidMcRaeMS

Washington, DC, Representative: Parker Briden, Chief of Staff; P.O. Box 139, Jackson 39205; (601) 359-3150

Missouri   Web, www.mo.gov

Gov. Michael L. Parson (R), State Capitol, #216, Jefferson City 65101; P.O. Box 720, Jefferson City 65102; (573) 751-3222; Fax; (573) 751-1495; Web, www.governor .mo.gov; Facebook, www.facebook.com/GovMike Parson; Twitter, @GovParsonMO; Instagram; @govparsonmo

Lt. Gov. Mike Kehoe (R), State Capitol, #224, Jefferson City 65101; (573) 751-4727; Fax, (573) 751-9422; Email, ltgovinfo@ltgov.mo.gov; Web, ltgov.mo.gov; Facebook, www.facebook.com/MoLtGovMikeKehoe; Twitter, @LtGovMikeKehoe; YouTube, www.youtube.com/ channel/UCJOGHtAcur4-GTnxJaopCRQ/featured

Secy. of State John R. Ashcroft (R), 600 W. Main St., Jefferson City 65101; (573) 751-4936; Fax, (573) 751-2490; Email, sosmain@sos.mo.gov; Web, www.sos.mo .gov; Facebook, www.facebook.com/MissouriSOS; Twitter, @MissouriSOS; YouTube, www.youtube.com/ channel/UClKeWmPRNu2cpGoMotOGzgw; Instagram, @missourisos

Atty. Gen. Eric Schmitt (R), Supreme Court Bldg., 207 W. High St., P.O. Box 899, Jefferson City 65102; (573) 751-3321; Fax, (573) 751-5818; Web, www.ago.mo.gov; Facebook, www.facebook.com/AttorneyGeneral Schmitt; Twitter, @AGEricSchmitt; YouTube, www .youtube.com/user/moagoffice; Instagram, @agericschmitt

Treasurer Scott Fitzpatrick (R), P.O. Box 210, Jefferson City 65102, (573) 751-8533; Fax, (573) 751-9443;

Email, info@treasurer.mo.gov; Web, www.treasurer .mo.gov; Facebook, www.facebook.com/MOTreasurer; Twitter, @MOTreasurer; Instagram, @motreasurer

Washington, DC, Representative: Johnathan Shiflett, Policy Assistant; State Capitol, #216, P.O. Box 720, Jefferson City, 65102; (573) 751-3222

Montana   Web, http://mt.gov

Gov. Greg Gianforte (R), State Capitol, #204, P.O. Box 200801, Helena 59620-0801; (406) 444-3111; Fax, (406) 444-5529; Toll free, 855-318-1330; Web, https://governor.mt.gov; Facebook, www.facebook .com/GovGianforte; Twitter, @GovGianforte; Instagram, @govgianforte

Lt. Gov. Kristen Juras (R), State Capitol, #207, P.O. Box 200801, Helena 59620-1901; (406) 444-3111; Fax, (406) 444-5529; Web, https://governor.mt.gov/about

Secy. of State Christi Jacobsen (R), State Capitol Bldg., 1301 6th Ave., #260, Helena 59601; Mailing address, P.O. Box 202801, Helena, 59620-2801; (406) 444-2034, Fax, (406) 444-3976; TTY, (406) 444-9068; Email, cjacobson@mt.gov; Web, www.sosmt.gov; Facebook, www.facebook.com/MTSecofState; Twitter, @MTSecofState; YouTube, www.youtube.com/ channel/UC7TbG2FKOTAFN26652tZl1g

Atty. Gen. Austin Knudsen (R), Justice Bldg., 215 N. Sanders St., 3rd Floor, P.O. Box 201401, Helena 59620-1401; (406) 444-2026; Fax, (406) 444-3549; Email, contactdoj@mt.gov; Web, www.dojmt.gov/ agooffice; Facebook, www.facebook.com/AGAustin Knudsen; Twitter, @MTAGKnudsen; YouTube, www.youtube.com/user/montanadoj/featured

Director of Dept. of Administration Misty A. Giles, 125 N. Roberts St., P.O. Box 200101, Helena 59620-0101; (406) 444-2032; Fax (406) 444-6194; Email, doadirector@mt.gov; Web, https://doa.mt.gov; Facebook, www.facebook.com/mtdoa; Twitter, @MTDeptofAdmin

Washington, DC, Representative: Christine Heggem, Chief of Staff; State Capitol, #204, P.O. Box 200801, Helena 59620-0801; (406) 444-3111

Nebraska   Web, www.nebraska.gov

Gov. Pete Ricketts (R), State Capitol, 1445 K St., #2316, P.O. Box 94848, Lincoln 68509-4848; (402) 471-2244; Fax, (402) 471-6031; Web, www.governor.nebraska.gov; Facebook, www.facebook.com/GovernorPeteRicketts; Twitter, @GovRicketts; YouTube, www.youtube.com/ channel/UCcsDw3_CGhTVcVtxoGKRkjlQ; Instagram, @govricketts

Lt. Gov. Mike Foley (R), State Capitol, #2315, P.O. Box 94863, Lincoln 68509-4863; (402) 471-2256; Fax, (402) 471-6031; Web, www.ltgov.nebraska.gov

Secy. of State Robert B. Evnen (R), State Capitol, 1445 K St., #2300, Lincoln; P.O. Box 94608, Lincoln 68509-4608; (402) 471-2554; Fax, (402) 471-3237; Email, sos.info@nebraska.gov; Web, www.sos.ne.gov; Facebook, www.facebook.com/Nebraska-Secretary-of-State-368792313908501; Twitter, @NEvnen

Atty. Gen. Doug Peterson (R), 2115 State Capitol, P.O. Box 98920, Lincoln 68509; (402) 471-2683; Fax, (402) 471-3297; Email, ago.info.help@nebraska .gov; Web, www.ago.nebraska.gov; Facebook, www .facebook.com/AGDougPeterson; Twitter, @AGDougPeterson; Instagram @agdougpeterson

Treasurer John Murante (R), State Capitol, 3rd Floor, P.O. Box 94788, Lincoln 68509-4788; (402) 471-2455; Fax, (402) 471-4390 and (402) 471-0816; Web, www .treasurer.nebraska.gov; Facebook, www.facebook.com/ NebraskaTreasurer; Twitter, @NeTreasurer; YouTube, www.youtube.com/user/nstovideos

Washington, DC, Representative: Lauren Kintner, Policy Director and General Counsel; P.O. Box 94848, Lincoln, 68509-4848; (402) 471-2244

Nevada   Web, www.nv.gov

Gov. Steve Sisolak (D), State Capitol, 101 N. Carson St., Carson City 89701; (775) 684-5670; Fax, (775) 684-5683; Web, https://gov.nv.gov; Facebook; www.face book.com/GovSisolak; Twitter, @GovSisolak or @SteveSisolak; Instagram, @stevesisolak

Lt. Gov. Kate Marshall (D), State Capitol, 101 N. Carson St., #2, Carson City 89701; (775) 684-7111; Fax, (775) 684-7110; Email, Ltgov@ltgov.nv.gov; Web, https:// ltgov.nv.gov; Facebook, www.facebook.com/ KateMarshallNV; Twitter, @KateMarshallNV

Secy. of State Barbara Cegavske (R), State Capitol, 101 N. Carson St., #3, Carson City 89701-4786; (775) 684-5708; Fax, (775) 684-5725; Email, sosmail@sos.nv.gov; Web, www.nvsos.gov; Facebook, www.facebook.com/ NVSOS; Twitter, @NVSOS; YouTube, www.youtube .com/channel/UCz4Pzy6O6WaR_akAdUl2UwQ

Atty. Gen. Aaron Ford (D), 100 N. Carson St., Carson City 89701-4717; (775) 400-0340; Fax, (775) 684-1108; Email, aginfo@ag.nv.gov; Web, ag.nv.gov; Facebook, www.facebook.com/NVAttorneyGeneral; Twitter, @NevadaAG; YouTube, www.youtube.com/user/ NevadaAG

Treasurer Zach Conine (D), State Capitol, 101 N. Carson St., #4, Carson City 89701-4786; (775) 684-5600; Fax, (775) 684-5781; Web, www.nevadatreasurer.gov; Facebook, www.facebook.com/nevadastatetreasurer; Twitter, @NVTreasurer; YouTube, www.youtube.com/ channel/UCHUGwNz8nDGey5ZGoggVVxA; Instagram, @nevadastatetreasurer

Washington, DC, Representative: DuAne Young, Policy Director; State Capitol, 101 N. Carson St., Carson City 89701; (775) 684-5670

New Hampshire   Web, www.nh.gov

Gov. Chris Sununu (R), State House, 107 N. Main St., Concord 03301; (603) 271-2121; Fax, (603) 271-7680; Web, www.governor.nh.gov; Facebook, www.facebook .com/GovernorChrisSununu; Twitter, @GovChris Sununu; YouTube, www.youtube.com/channel/ UC5miBoplJbVV0Zt7NXNYWhQ

(No office of Lieutenant Governor)

Secy. of State David M. Scanlan (R), State House, 107 N. Main St., #204, Concord 03301; (603) 271-3242; Fax, (603) 271-6316; Email, Administration@sos.nh .gov; Web, https://sos.nh.gov; Facebook, www.face book.com/SOS.NH.Gov; Twitter, @NHSecretary

Atty. Gen. John Formella (R), 33 Capitol St., Concord 03301; (603) 271-3658; Fax, (603) 271-2110; TTY, (800) 735-2964; Email, attorneygeneral@doj.nh .gov; Web, www.doj.nh.gov

Treasurer Monica Mezzapelle (D), State House Annex, 25 Capitol St., #121, Concord 03301; (603) 271-2621; Fax, (603) 271-3922; Email, monica.mezzapelle@ treasury.gov; Web, www.nh.gov/treasury

Washington, DC, Representative: Paul Collins, Senior Advisor; State House, 107 N. Main St., Concord 03301; (603) 271-2121

New Jersey   Web, www.newjersey.gov

Gov. Phil Murphy (D), State House, 125 W. State St., P.O. Box 001, Trenton 08625; (609) 292-6000; Fax, (609) 292-3454; Web, www.state.nj.us/governor; Facebook, www.facebook.com/governorphilmurphy; YouTube, www.youtube.com/njgovernorsoffice; Twitter, @GovMurphy; Instagram, @govmurphy

Lt. Gov. Sheila Oliver (D), 225 W. State St., P.O. Box 300, Trenton 08625; (609) 292-6000; Fax, (609) 777-1764; Web, www.nj.gov/governor/admin/lt; Facebook, www.facebook.com/LtGovOliver; Twitter, @LtGov Oliver; Instagram, @ltgovoliver

Secy. of State Tahesha Way (D), 20 W. State St., 4th Floor, P.O. Box 300, Trenton 08625; (609) 777-2581; Email, feedback.sos@sos.nj.gov; Web, www.state.nj.us/state; Facebook, www.facebook.com/NJStateDept and www .facebook.com/SecretaryWay; Twitter, @NJStateDept and @SecretaryWay, YouTube, www.youtube.com/ channel/UCpra_Xk_0KhMXhiJwCc6hzw

Atty. Gen. Matthew J. Platkin (Acting) (D), 25 Market St., 8th Floor, West Wing, P.O. Box 080, Trenton 08625-0080; (609) 292-4925; Fax, (609) 292-3508; Email, citizens.services@njoag.gov; Web, www.njoag.gov; Facebook, www.facebook.com/NewJerseyOAG, Twitter, @NewJerseyOAG; YouTube, www.youtube .com/NewJerseyOAG; Instagram, @newjerseyoag

Treasurer Elizabeth Muoio (D), State House, 225 W. State St., P.O. Box 002, Trenton 08625; (609) 292-6748; Web, www.state.nj.us/treasury; Facebook, www .facebook.com/njtreasury; Twitter, @NJTreasury; YouTube, www.youtube.com/channel/UC9-K4K8yi-7kWZmPSKBYMjg

In Washington, DC: Alexandria Hermann, Director; 444 N. Capitol St. N.W., #201, 20001; (202) 638-0631; Fax, (202) 638-2296

New Mexico   Web, www.newmexico.gov

Gov. Michelle Lujan Grisham (D), State Capitol, 490 Old Santa Fe Trail, #400, Santa Fe 87501; (505) 476-2200; Fax, (505) 476-2226; Web, www.governor.state.nm.us; Facebook, www.facebook.com/GovMLG; Twitter, @GovMLG; Instagram, @govmlg

Lt. Gov. Howie C. Morales (D), State Capitol, 490 Old Santa Fe Trail, #417, Santa Fe 87501; (505) 476-2250; Fax, (505) 476-2257; Web, www.ltgov.state.nm.us; Facebook, www.facebook.com/LtGovMorales; Twitter, @LtGovMorales; Instagram, @lt.gov .howiermorales

Secy. of State Maggie Toulouse Oliver (D), State Capitol, North Annex, 325 Don Gaspar Ave., #300, Santa Fe 87501; (505) 827-3600; Fax, (505) 827-3611; Toll-free, (800) 477-3632; Web, www.sos.state.nm.us; Facebook, www.facebook.com/NMSecofState; Twitter, @NMSecOfState

Atty. Gen. Hector Balderas (D), Villagra Bldg., 408 Galisteo St., Santa Fe 87501; (505) 490-4060; Fax, (505) 490-4883; Toll free, 844-255-9210; Web, www.nmag.gov; Facebook, www.facebook.com/ NMAttorneyGeneral; Twitter, @NewMexicoOAG; Instagram, @nmagofficial

Treasurer Tim Eichenberg (D), 2055 S. Pacheco St., #100 & 200, Santa Fe 87505-5135; Mailing address, P.O. Box 5135, Santa Fe 87502-5135; (505) 955-1131; Fax, (505) 955-1195; Web, www.nmsto.gov; Facebook, www.facebook.com/NMStateTreasurer; Twitter, @NM_Treasurer

In Washington, DC: Courtney Kerster, State-Federal Representative; 444 N. Capitol St. N.W., #411, 20001; (505) 624-3667

New York   Web, www.ny.gov

Gov. Kathy Hochul (D), State Capitol, Albany 12224; (518) 474-8390; Fax, (518) 474-1513; Web, www.governor.ny .gov; Facebook, www.facebook.com/GovKathyHochul; Twitter, @GovKathyHochul; YouTube, www.youtube .com/channel/UCQJp4eSJgbFroNySGthEiqA; Instagram, @govkathyhochul

Lt. Gov. (Vacant)

Secy. of State Robert J. Rodriguez (D), 1 Commerce Plaza, 99 Washington Ave., Albany 12231-0001; (518) 473-3355; Fax, (518) 474-6572; Web, www.dos .ny.gov; Facebook, www.facebook.com/NewYork DepartmentOfState; Twitter, @NYSDOS; YouTube, www.youtube.com/user/nysdosvideos; Instagram, @nysdos

Atty. Gen. Letitia James (D), State Capitol, Albany 12224-0341; (518) 776-2000; Toll-free, (800) 771-7755; Web, www.ag.ny.gov; Facebook, www.facebook.com/ newyorkstateag; Twitter, @NewYorkStateAG; YouTube, www.youtube.com/c/NewYorkStateAG/ featured; Instagram, @newyorkstateag

Commissioner (Acting) Amanda Hiller (D), 110 State St., 2nd Floor, P.O. Box 22119, Albany 12201-2119; (518) 474-4250; Fax, (518) 402-4118; Web, www.tax.ny.gov; Facebook, www.facebook.com/NYSTaxDept; Twitter, @NYSTaxDept; YouTube, www.youtube.com/user/ NYSTaxDepartment

In Washington, DC: Kylah Hynes, Director for Federal Policy; 444 N. Capitol St. N.W., #301, 20001; (202) 434-7100; Fax, (202) 434-7110

North Carolina   Web, www.nc.gov

Gov. Roy Cooper (D), State Capitol, Raleigh 27699; Mailing address, 20301 Mail Service Center, Raleigh 27699; (919) 814-2000; Fax, (919) 733-2120; Web, www .governor.nc.gov; Facebook, www.facebook.com/ NCgovernor; Twitter, @NC_Governor; Instagram, @nc_governor

Lt. Gov. Mark Robinson (R), 310 N. Blount St., Raleigh 27601; Mailing address, 20401 Mail Service Center, Raleigh 27699-0401; (919) 814-3680; Fax, (919) 733-6595; Web, www.ltgov.nc.gov; Facebook, www .facebook.com/mark.k.robinson.lt.gov

Secy. of State Elaine F. Marshall (D), 2 S. Salisbury St., Raleigh, 27601; Mailing address, P.O. Box 29622, Raleigh 27626-0622; (919) 814-5400; Fax, (919) 814-5397; Web, www.sosnc.gov; Facebook, www.facebook .com/NCSecState; Twitter, @NCSecState; YouTube, www.youtube.com/c/NCSecState/featured

Atty. Gen. Josh Stein (D), 114 W. Edenton St., Raleigh 27603; Mailing address, 9001 Mail Service Center, Raleigh 27699-9001; (919) 716-6400; Fax, (919) 716-6750; Web, www.ncdoj.gov; Facebook, www.face book.com/NCDOJ; Twitter, @NCAGO; YouTube, www.youtube.com/user/NCAGO/featured

Treasurer Dale R. Folwell (R), 3200 Atlantic Ave., Raleigh 27604-1385; (919) 814-4000; Web, www.nctreasurer .com; Facebook, www.facebook.com/NCDST; Twitter, @NCTreasurer; YouTube, www.youtube.com/c/ NCDST/featured

In Washington, DC: Jim McCleskey, Washington Representative; 444 N. Capitol St. N.W., #332, 20001; (202) 624-5833

North Dakota   Web, www.nd.gov

Gov. Doug Burgum (R), State Capitol, 600 E. Boulevard Ave., Bismarck 58505-0100; (701) 328-2200; Web, www.governor.nd.gov; Facebook, www.facebook.com/ GovernorDougBurgum; Twitter, @DougBurgum

Lt. Gov. Brent Sanford (R), State Capitol, 600 E. Boulevard Ave., Dept. 101, Bismarck 58505; (701) 328-2200; Web, www.governor.nd.gov/lieutenant-governor-brent-sanford; Facebook, www.facebook.com/ NDLtGovBrentSanford; Twitter, @BrentSanfordND

Secy. of State Al Jaeger (R), State Capitol, 600 E. Boulevard Ave., Dept. 108, Bismarck 58505; (701) 328-2900; Fax, (701) 328-2992; Toll-free, (800) 352-0867; TTY, (800) 366-6888; Email, sos@nd.gov; Web, www.sos.nd.gov; Facebook, www.facebook.com/ NDSOS

Atty. Gen. Wayne Stenehjem (R), State Capitol, 600 E. Boulevard Ave., Dept. 125, Bismarck 58505; (701) 328-2210; Fax, (701) 328-2226; TTY, (800) 366-6888; Email, ndag@nd.gov; Web, attorneygeneral.nd.gov; Facebook, www.facebook.com/StenehjemforAG

Treasurer Thomas Beadle (R), State Capitol, 600 E. Boulevard Ave., 3rd Floor, Dept. 120, Bismarck 58505; (701) 328-2643; Fax, (701) 328-3002; Email, treasurer@nd.gov; Web, www.nd.gov/treasurer Facebook, www.facebook.com/ThomasBeadleND;

Twitter, @ThomasBeadle; YouTube, www.youtube
.com/channel/UCWLq7og6Hgt4QxfD4A19N7w;
Instagram, @thomasbeadlend

Washington, DC, Representative: Jace Beehler, Chief of
Staff; State Capitol, 600 E. Boulevard Ave., Dept. 101,
Bismarck 58505; (701) 328-2200

Ohio   Web, www.ohio.gov

Gov. Mike DeWine (R), Riffe Center, 77 S. High St.,
30th Floor, Columbus 43215-6117; (614) 466-6117;
Fax, (614) 466-9354; Web, www.governor.ohio.gov;
Facebook, www.facebook.com/GovMikeDeWine;
Twitter, @GovMikeDeWine; YouTube, www.youtube
.com/channel/UCRi1V4HUWRyCLEWJ5yNCclg/
videos; Instagram, @govmikedewine

Lt. Gov. Jon Husted (R), Riffe Center, 77 S. High St.,
30th Floor, Columbus 43215-6117; (614) 466-3555;
Fax, (614) 644-9345; Web, https://governor.ohio.gov/
wps/portal/gov/governor/administration/lt-governor;
Facebook, www.facebook.com/LtGovHusted; Twitter,
@LtGovHusted; Instagram, @ltgovhusted

Secy. of State Frank LaRose (R), 22 N. 4th St., Columbus
43215; (614) 466-2655; TTY, (614) 466-0562; Email;
secretarylarose@ohiosos.gov; Web, www.sos.state.oh
.us; Facebook, www.facebook.com/franklarose; Twitter,
@FrankLaRose; Instagram, @franklarose

Atty. Gen. Dave Yost (R), 30 E. Broad St., 14th Floor,
Columbus 43215-3428; (614) 466-4320; Help line,
(614) 466-4986; Toll free, 800-282-0515; Web, www
.ohioattorneygeneral.gov; Facebook, www.facebook
.com/OhioAttorneyGeneral; Twitter, @OhioAG;
YouTube, www.youtube.com/user/OhioAttorney
General; Instagram, @ohioattorneygeneral

Treasurer Robert Sprague (R), 30 E. Broad St., 9th Floor,
Columbus 43215; (614) 466-2160; Fax, (614) 644-7313;
TTY, (800) 228-1102; Email, treasurer@tos.ohio.gov;
Web, www.tos.ohio.gov; Facebook, www.facebook.com/
OhioTreasurer; Twitter, @Ohiotreasurer; YouTube,
www.youtube.com/channel/UC9yf2BtwBDaL4vOeq
HL1aqg; Instagram, @ohiotreasurer

In Washington, DC: Nikki Guilford, Director;
444 N. Capitol St. N.W., #542, 20001; (202) 624-8458

Oklahoma   Web, www.ok.gov

Gov. J. Kevin Stitt (R), State Capitol, 2300 N. Lincoln Blvd.,
#212, Oklahoma City 73105; (405) 521-2342;
Web, www.ok.gov/governor; Facebook, www.facebook
.com/GovStitt; Twitter, @GovStitt; YouTube, www
.youtube.com/channel/UCyE0TZqyRF9AAd6PGz
fcfJA; Instagram, @kevinstittgov

Lt. Gov. Matt Pinnell (R), State Capitol, 2300 N. Lincoln
Blvd., #117, Oklahoma City 73105; (405) 521-2161;
Fax, (405) 522-8694; Web, www.ok.gov/ltgovernor;
Facebook, www.facebook.com/LtGovPinnell and
www.facebook.com/MattPinnellOK; Twitter,
@LtGovPinnell; YouTube, www.youtube.com/
channel/UC80ydjsy-9flQFc4X_vOBog; Instagram,
@ltgovpinnell

Secy. of Brian Bingman (R), State Capitol, 2300 N. Lincoln
Blvd., #122, Oklahoma City 73105; (405) 521-3912;
Email, support@sos.ok.gov; Web, www.sos.ok.gov

Atty. Gen. Mike Hunter (R), 313 21st St. N.E., Oklahoma
City 73105; (405) 521-3921; Fax, (405) 521-6246;
Email, questions@oag.ok.gov; Web, www.ok.gov/oag;
Facebook, www.facebook.com/AttorneyGeneral
MikeHunter; Twitter, @Okla_OAG

Treasurer Randy McDaniel (R), State Capitol, 2300
N. Lincoln Blvd., #217, Oklahoma City 73105; (405)
521-3191; Web, www.ok.gov/treasurer; Facebook,
www.facebook.com/TreasurerMcDaniel; Twitter,
@OKTreasurer

Washington, DC, Representative: Christina Gungoll
Lepore, Washington Representative; State Capitol,
2300 Lincoln Blvd., #212, Oklahoma City 73105;
(405) 521-2161

Oregon   Web, www.oregon.gov

Gov. Kate Brown (D), 900 Court St. N.E., #254, Salem
97301-4047; (503) 378-4582; Fax, (503) 378-6827;
Web, www.governor.oregon.gov; Facebook, www
.facebook.com/OregonGovernor; Twitter, @Oregon
GovBrown; YouTube, www.youtube.com/channel/
UCIvf0TD6Lo0L6_lQEBhGYkQ; Instagram,
@oregongovbrown

(No office of Lieutenant Governor)

Secy. of State Shemia Fagan (D), 900 Court St. N.E.,
#136, Salem 97301-0722; (503) 986-1523; Fax, (503)
986-1616; Email, oregon.sos@oregon.gov; Web,
sos.oregon.gov; Facebook, www.facebook.com/
OregonSecState; Twitter, @OregonSoS; Instagram
@oregonsos

Atty. Gen. Ellen F. Rosenblum (D), 158 12th St. N.E.,
Salem 97301; Mailing address, 1162 Court St. N.E.,
Salem 97301-4096; (503) 378-4400; Fax, (503) 378-
4017; Web, www.doj.state.or.us; Facebook, www
.facebook.com/EllenforOregon; Twitter, @ORDOJ

Treasurer Tobias Read (D), 900 Court St. N.E., #159 Salem
97301-4043; (503) 378-4329; Fax, (503) 373-7051;
Email, oregon.treasurer@state.or.us; Web, www
.Oregon.gov/treasury; Facebook, www.facebook.com/
oregonstatetreasury; Twitter, @OregonTreasury and
@TreasurerRead

In Washington, DC: Annie McColaugh, Director; 444
N. Capitol St., #134, 20001; (202) 508-3847

Pennsylvania   Web, www.pa.gov

Gov. Tom Wolf (D), 508 Capitol Bldg., 501 N. 3rd St.,
Harrisburg 17120; (717) 787-2500; Fax, (717) 772-
8284; Web, www.governor.pa.gov; Facebook, www
.facebook.com/GovernorWolf; Twitter, @Governor
TomWolf; YouTube, www.youtube.com/channel/
UC8cXXCdLzcYoYGa_BqaPsgA; Instagram,
@governotomwolf

Lt. Gov. John Fetterman (D), 200 Capitol Bldg., 501
N. 3rd St., Harrisburg 17120-0002; (717) 787-3300;
Fax, (717) 783-0150; Email, LGoffice@pa.gov;
Web, www.ltgov.pa.gov/Pages/Home.aspx;

Facebook, www.facebook.com/LGFetterman and www.facebook.com/JohnFettermanPA; Twitter, @FettermanLt

Secy. of the Commonwealth (Acting) Leigh Chapman (D), 302 North Office Bldg., 401 N. St., Harrisburg 17120; (717) 787-6458; Fax, (717) 787-1734; Web, www.dos .pa.gov/about-us/pages/secretary-of-the-common wealth.aspx; Facebook, www.facebook.com/ PADepartmentofState; Twitter, @PAStateSec

Atty. Gen. Josh Shapiro (D), 11 N. 3rd St., 16th Floor, Strawberry Square, Harrisburg 17120; (717) 787-3391; Fax, (717) 787-8242; Email, info@attorneygeneral.gov; Web, www.attorneygeneral.gov; Facebook, www .facebook.com/PaAttorneyGen; Twitter, @PAAttorney Gen; YouTube, www.youtube.com/channel/ UC13KvRB_Bca8NbMtkLCaRQg; Instagram, @paattorneygen

Treasurer Stacy Garrity (R), 129 Finance Bldg., Harrisburg 17120; (717) 787-2465; Fax, (717) 783-9760; Web, www.patreasury.gov; Facebook, www.facebook.com/ PATreasurer and www.facebook.com/PATreasurer Garrity; Twitter, @PATreasurer; YouTube, www .youtube.com/c/PATreasuryDepartment; Instagram, @patreasury

Washington, DC, Representative: Jack Groarke, Deputy Chief of Staff for Federal Affairs; Main Capitol Bldg., Harrisburg, 17120; (717) 787-2500

Rhode Island   Web, www.ri.gov

Gov. Daniel J. McKee (D), State House, 82 Smith St., Providence 02903-1196; (401) 222-2080; Fax (401) 222-8096; Email, governor@governor.ri.gov; Web, www.governor.ri.gov; Facebook, www.face book.com/GovDanMckee; Twitter, @GovDanMcKee; YouTube, www.youtube.com/channel/UCkq G0V5x74Oqj1ZtpPJBAAQ; Instagram, @govdanmckee

Lt. Gov. Sabina Matos (D) State House, 82 Smith St., #116, Providence, RI 02903; (401) 222-2371; Web, ltgov.ri .gov; Facebook, www.facebook.com/LGSabinaMatos; Twitter, @LGSabinaMatos

Secy. of State Nellie M. Gorbea (D), State House, 82 Smith St., Room 218, Providence 02903-1120; (401) 222-2357; Fax, (401) 222-1356; TTY, (711)-222-2357; Email, secretarygorbea@sos.ri.gov; Web, www.sos.ri.gov; Facebook, www.facebook.com/ RISecState; Twitter, @RISecState

Atty. Gen. Peter F. Neronha (D), 150 S. Main St., Providence 02903-2856; (401) 274-4400; Fax, (401) 222-1302; Web, www.riag.ri.gov; Twitter, @AGNeronha; YouTube, www.youtube.com/user/ RIAttorneyGeneral/featured

Treasurer Seth Magaziner (D), State House, 82 Smith St., Room 102, Providence 02903; (401) 222-2397; Fax, (401) 222-6140; Web, www.treasury.ri.gov; Twitter, @RITreasury

Washington, DC, Representative: Brenna McCabe, Senior Advisor; State House, 82 Smith St., Providence 02903; (401) 222-2080

South Carolina   Web, www.sc.gov

Gov. Henry McMaster (R), State House, 1100 Gervais St., Columbia 29201; (803) 734-2100; Fax, (803) 734-5167; Email, henry.henrymcmaster.com; Web, www .governor.sc.gov; Facebook, www.facebook.com/ HenryMcMaster; Twitter, @henrymcmaster; YouTube, www.youtube.com/channel/UCto7jOZMBE8CmIXs Walhhsg; Instagram, @govhenrymcmaster

Lt. Gov. Pamela Evette (R), State House, 1100 Gervais St., Columbia 29202; (803) 734-2100; Fax, (803) 734-5167; Email, LtGovernor@scstatehouse.gov or pamela@pamelaevette.com; Web, www.ltgov.sc.gov; Facebook, www.facebook.com/pamelaevettesc; Twitter, @PamelaEvette; Instagram, @PamelaEvette

Secy. of State Mark Hammond (R), 1205 Pendleton St., #525, Columbia 29201; (803) 734-2170; Fax, (803) 734-1661; Web, www.sos.sc.gov; Facebook, www.facebook .com/SecretaryofStateMarkHammond

Atty. Gen. Alan Wilson (R), Rembert Dennis Bldg., 1000 Assembly St., Room 519, Columbia 29201; P.O. Box 11549, Columbia 29211; (803) 734-3970; Fax, (803) 253-6283; Web, www.scag.gov; Facebook, www.facebook.com/AGAlanWilson; Twitter, @SCAttyGenOffice and @AGAlanWilson; YouTube, www.youtube.com/user/AlanWilsonAG

Treasurer Curtis M. Loftis Jr. (R), Wade Hampton Bldg., 1200 Senate St., #214, Columbia 29201; (803) 734-2101; Email, communications@sto.sc.gov; Web, www .treasurer.sc.gov; Facebook, www.facebook.com/ SCStateTreasurer; Twitter, @TreasurerLoftis; YouTube, www.youtube.com/user/treasurerloftis; Instagram, @scstatetreasurer

In Washington, DC: Jordan Marsh, Director; 444 N. Capitol St. N.W., #549, 20001; (803) 509-0581

South Dakota   Web, sd.gov

Gov. Kristi Noem (R), State Capitol, 500 E. Capitol Ave., Pierre 57501; (605) 773-3212; Fax, (605) 773-4711; Web, www.sd.gov/governor; Facebook, www.facebook .com/govnoem; YouTube, www.youtube.com/channel/ UC0X6uYDWpzNse7cLn3xqGRA; Twitter, @govkristinoem; Instagram, @govkristinoem

Lt. Gov. Larry Rhoden (R), State Capitol, 500 E. Capitol Ave., Pierre 57501-5070; (605) 773-3212; Fax, (605) 773-4711; Web, https://governor.sd.gov/governor/lt-governor.aspx; Facebook, www.facebook.com/ lgrhoden; Twitter, @lgrhoden

Secy. of State Steve Barnett (R), State Capitol, 500 E. Capitol Ave., #204, Pierre 57501-5070; (605) 773-3537; Fax, (605) 773-6580; Email, sdsos@state.sd.us; Web, www.sdsos.gov; Facebook, www.facebook.com/ sodaksos; Twitter, @sodaksos

Atty. Gen. Jason R. Ravnsborg (R), 1302 E. Hwy. 14, #1, Pierre 57501-8501; (605) 773-3215; Fax, (605) 773-4106; TTY, (605) 773-6585; Web, www.atg.sd.gov; Facebook, www.facebook.com/SDATG; Twitter, @SDAttorneyGen; YouTube, www.youtube.com/user/ SDAttorneyGeneral; Instagram, @agjasonravnsborg

Treasurer Josh Haeder (R), State Capitol, 500 E. Capitol Ave., #212, Pierre 57501-5070; (605) 773-3378; Fax, (605) 773-3115; Web, www.sdtreasurer.gov; Facebook, www.facebook.com/SDTreasurer; YouTube, www.youtube.com/channel/UCSRdWqPAn-BRKuRlHYuCZag

Washington, DC, Representative: Brad Otten, Policy Advisor; State Capitol, 500 E. Capitol Ave., Pierre 57501; (605) 773-5522

Tennessee   Web, www.tn.gov

Gov. Bill Lee (R), State Capitol, 600 Dr. Martin L. King Jr. Blvd., 1st Floor, Nashville 37243-0001; (615) 741-2001; Fax, (615) 532-9711; Web, www.tn.gov/governor; Facebook, www.facebook.com/GovBillLee; Twitter, @GovBillLee; YouTube, www.youtube.com/c/govbilllee; Instagram, @govbilllee

Lt. Gov. Randy McNally (R), Cordell Hull Bldg., 425 5th Ave. North, #700, Nashville 37243-0202; (615) 741-6806; Fax, (615) 253-0197; Email, lt.gov.randy .mcnally@capitol.tn.gov; Web, www.capitol.tn.gov/senate/speaker.html; Facebook, www.facebook.com/ltgovmcnally; Twitter, @ltgovmcnally; Instagram, @ltgovmcnally

Secy. of State Tre Hargett (R), State Capitol, 600 Dr. Martin L. King Jr. Blvd., Nashville 37243-1102; (615) 741-2819; Fax, (615) 741-5962; Email, tre.hargett@tn .gov; Web, sos.tn.gov; Facebook, www.facebook.com/TennesseeSecretaryofState; Twitter, @sectrehargett; YouTube, www.youtube.com/c/sectrehargett; Instagram, @tnsecofstate

Atty. Gen. Herbert H. Slattery III (R), Cordell Hull Bldg., 425 5th Ave. North, Nashville 37243-0485; P.O. Box 20207, Nashville 37202-0207; (615) 741-3491; Fax, (615) 741-2009; Web, www.tn.gov/attorney general.html; Facebook, www.facebook.com/tnattygen; Twitter, @TNattygen

Treasurer David H. Lillard Jr. (R), State Capitol, 600 Martin L. King Jr. Blvd., 1st Floor, Nashville 37243-0225; (615) 741-2956; Web, treasury.tn.gov; Facebook, www.facebook.com/TNTreasury; Twitter, @TNTreasuryDept; YouTube, www.youtube.com/user/TNTreasury

Washington, DC, Representative: Eric Mayo, Legislative Liaison; State Capitol, 600 Dr. Martin L. King Jr. Blvd., Nashville, 37243-0001, (615) 741-2001

Texas   Web, www.texas.gov

Gov. Greg Abbott (R), State Insurance Bldg., 1100 San Jacinto Blvd., #151B, Austin 78701; P.O. Box 12428, Austin 78711-2428; (512) 463-2000; Fax, (512) 463-1849; Web, https://gov.texas.gov; Facebook, www .facebook.com/TexasGovernor; Twitter, @GovAbbott; YouTube, www.youtube.com/channel/UCqTttg2CGGqDmMYR1S0q5Hw; Instagram, @govabbott

Lt. Gov. Dan Patrick (R), Capitol Station, P.O. Box 12068, Austin 78711-2068; (512) 463-0001; Fax, (512) 463-0677; Email, LTGConstituent.Affairs@ltgov.texas.gov; Web, www.ltgov.state.tx.us; Facebook, www.facebook .com/ltgovtx; Twitter, @LTGovTX; Instagram, @ltgovtx

Secy. of State John B. Scott (R), 1100 Congress Capitol Bldg., #1E.8, Austin 78701; P.O. Box 12887, Austin 78711-2887; (512) 475-2761; Fax, (512) 463-5569; Email, webmaster@sos.texas.gov; Web, www.sos.state .tx.us; Facebook, www.facebook.com/txsecretary; Twitter, @TXsecofstate; YouTube, www.youtube.com/channel/UC7NJ9yjB4K-1MOMFzH6hAbQ/videos; Instagram, @texassecretary

Atty. Gen. Ken Paxton (R), 300 W. 15th St., 8th Floor, Austin 78701; P.O. Box 12548, Austin 78711; (512) 463-2100; Fax, (512) 475-2994; Toll free, (800) 735-2989; Web, www.texasattorneygeneral.gov; Facebook, www.facebook.com/TexasAttorneyGeneral; Twitter, @TXAG; YouTube, www.youtube.com/user/TexasAttorneyGeneral; Instagram, @texasattorneygeneral

Comptroller Glenn Hegar (R), Lyndon B. Johnson Bldg., 111 E. 17th St., Austin 78774; P.O. Box 13528 Capitol Station, Austin 78711-3528; (512) 463-8617; Fax, (512) 463-4902; Toll free, (800) 531-5441; Email, glennhegar@cpa.texas.gov; Web, www .comptroller.texas.gov; Facebook, www.facebook.com/txcomptroller; Twitter, @txcomptroller and @Glenn_Hegar; YouTube, www.youtube.com/user/txcomptroller

In Washington, DC: Wes Hambrick, Director; 660 Pennsylvania Ave. S.E., #203, 20003; 202-638-3927

Utah   Web, www.utah.gov

Gov. Spencer J. Cox (R), State Capitol, 350 N. State St., #200, P.O. Box 142220, Salt Lake City 84114-2220; (801) 538-1000; Fax, (801) 538-1528; Toll-free, (800) 705-2464; Web, https://governor.utah.gov; Facebook, www.facebook.com/govcox; Twitter, @GovCox; YouTube, www.youtube.com/govcox; Instagram, @govcox

Lt. Gov. Deidre M. Henderson (R), State Capitol, 350 N. State St., #220, P.O. Box 142325, Salt Lake City 84114-2325; (801) 538-1041; Fax, (801) 538-1133; Web, https://ltgovernor.utah.gov; Facebook, www .facebook.com/deidrehendersonutah; Twitter, @lghendersonutah

(No office of Secretary of State)

Atty. Gen. Sean D. Reyes (R), State Capitol, 350 N. State St., #230, P.O. Box 142320, Salt Lake City 84114-2320; (801) 366-0260; Fax, (801) 538-1121; Toll free, (800) 244-4636; Email, uag@agutah.gov; Web, attorney general.utah.gov; Facebook, www.facebook.com/UtahAttorneyGeneral; Twitter, @UtahAG; YouTube, www.youtube.com/user/UtahAGoffice

Treasurer Marlo M. Oaks (R), State Capitol, 350 N. State St., #180, P.O. Box 142315, Salt Lake City 84114-2315; (801) 538-1042; TTY, (801) 538-1042; Fax, (801) 538-1465; Email, sto@utah.gov; Web, https://treasurer.utah .gov; Facebook, www.facebook.com/UtahTreasurer; Twitter, @UtahTreasurer; YouTube, www.youtube .com/channel/UCojqcgfn1qiNtPQTdqWG89w; Instagram, @utahtreasurer

In Washington, DC: Gordon Larsen, Senior Advisor; 444 N. Capitol St. N.W., #549, Washington, 20001; (202) 403-8616

Vermont   Web, www.vermont.gov

Gov. Phil Scott (R), Pavilion Office Bldg., 109 State St., Montpelier 05609-0101; (802) 828-3333; Fax, (802) 828-3339; TTY, (800) 649-6825; Web, www.governor .vermont.gov; Facebook, www.facebook.com/ GovPhilScott; Twitter, @GovPhilScott; Instagram, @philscottvt

Lt. Gov. Molly Gray (D), 115 State St., Montpelier 05633- 5401; (802) 828-2226; Fax, (802) 828-3198; Web, www .ltgov.vermont.gov; Facebook, www.facebook.com/ mollyforvermont; Twitter, @LtGovGray; Instagram, @mollyforvermont

Secy. of State Jim Condos (D), 128 State St., Montpelier 05633-1101; Information, (802) 828-2148; Fax, (802) 828-2496; Email, jim.condos@sec.state.vt.us or sos .secretarystatevt@vermont.gov; Web, https://sos .vermont.gov; Facebook, www.facebook.com/ SecretaryOfStateJimCondos; Twitter, @VermontSOS; YouTube, www.youtube.com/channel/ UCdy2e0EwW59oMye-Odnh3rQ

Atty. Gen. TJ Donovan (D), Pavilion Office Bldg., 109 State St., Montpelier 05609-1001; (802) 828-3171; Fax, (802) 828-3187; Email, ago.info@vermont.gov; Web, www .ago.vermont.gov; Facebook, www.facebook.com/ attorneygeneraldonovan; Twitter, @VTAttorneyGen

Treasurer Elizabeth (Beth) Pearce (D), Pavilion Office Bldg., 109 State St., 4th Floor, Montpelier 05609-6200; (802) 828-2301; Fax, (802) 828-2772; TTY, (800) 253- 0191; Toll-free, (800) 642-3191; Email, Treasurers .Office@vermont.gov; Web, www.vermonttreasurer .gov; Facebook, www.facebook.com/Beth-Pearce- 343317092414108; Twitter, @TreasurerPearce

Washington, DC, Representative: Jason Gibbes, Chief of Staff; Pavilion Office Bldg.,109 State St., Montpelier 05609, (802) 828-3333

Virginia   Web, www.virginia.gov

Gov. Glenn Youngkin (R), Patrick Henry Bldg., 1111 E. Broad St., Richmond 23219; Mailing address, P.O. Box 1475, Richmond 23218; (804) 786-2211; Fax, (804) 371-6351; TTY, (800) 828-1120; Web, www.governor .virginia.gov; Facebook, www.facebook.com/ GovernorVA; Instagram, @glennyoungkin.

Lt. Gov. Winsome Earle-Sears (R), Oliver Hill Bldg., 102 Governor St., Richmond 23219; Mailing address, P.O. Box 1195, Richmond 23218; (804) 786-2078; Fax, (804) 786-7514; Email, ltgov@ltgov.virginia.gov; Web, www .ltgov.virginia.gov; Facebook, www.facebook.com/ WinsomeESears; Twitter, @WinsomeSears; Instagram, @winsomesears

Secy. of the Commonwealth Kay Coles James (R), Patrick Henry Bldg., 1111 E. Broad St., 4th Floor, Richmond 23219; Mailing address, P.O. Box 1475, Richmond 23218; (804) 786-2441; Fax, (804) 371-0017; Email, soc@governor.virginia.gov; Web, www.commonwealth .virginia.gov; Facebook, www.facebook.com/ SecOfCommonwealth

Atty. Gen. Jason S. Miyares (R), 202 N. 9th St., Richmond 23219; (804) 786-2071; Email, contact@Virginia.gov;

Web, www.oag.state.va.us; Facebook, www.facebook .com/jasonmiyaresforvirginia; Twitter, @JasonMiyaresVA; YouTube, www.youtube.com/ channel/UCuVXO0SWjSLu8z4bD2E-RNQ; Instagram, @jasonmiyares

Treasurer Manju Ganeriwala (D), James Monroe Bldg., 101 N. 14th St., 3rd Floor, Richmond 23219; Mailing address, P.O. Box 1819, Richmond 23218; (804) 225- 2142; Fax, (804) 225-3187; Web, www.trs.virginia.gov

In Washington, DC: Ali Ahmad, Policy Director; State Capitol, 3rd Floor, Richmond 23219, (804) 786-2211

Washington   Web, www.access.wa.gov

Gov. Jay Inslee (D), Legislative Bldg., 416 Sid Snyder Ave. S.W., 2nd Floor, P.O. Box 40002, Olympia 98504-0002; (360) 902-4111; Fax, (360) 753-4110; TTY (WA only), (800) 833-6388; Web, www.governor.wa.gov; Facebook, www.facebook.com/WaStateGov; Twitter, @GovInslee; Instagram, @govinslee

Lt. Gov. Denny Heck (D), 220 Legislative Bldg., 416 Sid Snyder Ave. S.W., 2nd Floor, Olympia 98504; P.O. Box 40400, Olympia 98504-0400; (360) 786-7700; Fax, (360) 786-7749; Email, ltgov@ltgov.wa.gov; Web, www.ltgov.wa.gov; Twitter, @LtGovDennyHeck

Secy. of State Steve Hobbs (D), Legislative Bldg., 416 Sid Snyder Ave. S.W., 2nd Floor, P.O. Box 98504 Olympia 98504-0220; (360) 902-4151; Fax, (360) 586-5629; Email, secretaryofstate@sos.wa.gov; Web, www.sos.wa .gov; Facebook, www.facebook.com/ WaSecretaryOfState; Twitter, @secstatewa; YouTube, www.youtube.com/user/secstatewa; Instagram, @secstatewa

Atty. Gen. Bob Ferguson (D), 1125 Washington St. S.E., P.O. Box 40100, Olympia 98504-0100; (360) 753-6200; Fax, (360) 664-0228; Toll free (in-state only), (800) 551-4636; TTY, (800) 833-6388; Web, www.atg.wa.gov; Facebook, www.facebook.com/ WAStateAttorneyGeneral; Twitter, @AGOWA; YouTube, www.youtube.com/user/WashingtonAGO; Instagram, @agbobferguson

Treasurer Mike Pellicciotti (D), Legislative Bldg., 416 Sid Synder Ave. S.W., Room 230, P.O. Box 40200, Olympia 98504; (360) 902-9001; Fax, (360) 902-9037; TTY, (360) 902-8963; Web, www.tre.wa.gov; Facebook, www .facebook.com/WaTreasurer; Twitter, @WaTreasurer; Instagram, @treasurermike

Washington, DC, Representative: Morgan Wilson, Director; 444 N. Capitol St. N.W., #372, 20001; (202) 624-3546

West Virginia   Web, www.wv.gov

Gov. Jim Justice (D), State Capitol, 1900 Kanawha Blvd. East, Charleston 25305-0370; (304) 558-2000; Toll-free, (888) 438-2731; Web, www.governor.wv.gov; Facebook, www.facebook.com/WVGovernor; Twitter, @WVGovernor; YouTube, www.youtube.com/ channel/UCnjhqLLesIzuw2V2i-Mg0ww; Instagram, @govjustice

Senate Pres. Craig Blair (R), State Capitol, 1900 Kanawha Blvd. East, Bldg. 1, Room 229M, Charleston 25305-0770; (304) 357-7801; Fax, (304) 357-7839; Email, craig.blair@wvsenate.gov; Web, www.wvlegislature.gov/Senate1/president.cfm; Facebook, www.facebook.com/wvlegislature; Twitter, @wvlegislature

Secy. of State Mac Warner (R), State Capitol, 1900 Kanawha Blvd. East, Charleston 25305; (304) 558-6000; Fax, (304) 558-0900; Email, mwarner@wvsos.gov; Web, www.sos.wv.gov; Facebook, www.facebook.com/wvsos; Twitter, @wvsosoffice; YouTube, www.youtube.com/c/wvsos/featured

Atty. Gen. Patrick Morrisey (R), State Capitol, 1900 Kanawha Blvd. East, Bldg. 1, Room E-26, Charleston 25305; (304) 558-2021; Fax, (304) 558-0140; Web, www.ago.wv.gov; Facebook, www.facebook.com/agwestv; Twitter, @WestVirginiaAG

Treasurer Riley Moore (R), State Capitol, 1900 Kanawha Blvd. East, Bldg. 1, Room E-145, Charleston 25305; (304) 558-5000; Toll-free, (800) 422-7498; TTY, (304) 340-1598; Email, wvtreasury@wvsto.gov; Web, www.wvsto.gov; Facebook, www.facebook.com/WVTreasury; Twitter, @WVTreasury; YouTube, www.youtube.com/user/WVTreasury

Washington, DC, Representative: Rebecca Blaine, Director; State Capitol, 1900 Kanawha Blvd. East, Charleston, 25305; 304-558-2000

Wisconsin   Web, www.wisconsin.gov

Gov. Tony Evers (D), 115 E. Capitol, P.O. Box 7863, Madison 53702-7863; (608) 266-1212; Fax, (608) 267-8983; TTY, (608) 267-6790; Email, EversInfo@wisconsin.gov; Web, www.evers.wi.gov/Pages/Home.aspx; Facebook, www.facebook.com/GovernorTonyEvers; Twitter, @GovEvers; YouTube, www.youtube.com/channel/UCDsNE8BVaxWtvDrz61mIGBA; Instagram, @tony4wi

Lt. Gov. Mandela Barnes (D), 115 E. Capitol, Madison 53702; Mailing address, P.O. Box 2043, Madison 53702; (608) 266-3516; Fax, (608) 267-3571; Email, ltgovernor@wisconsin.gov; Web, www.ltgov.wisconsin.gov; Facebook, www.facebook.com/LGMandela Barnes; Twitter, @LGMandelaBarnes; Instagram, @lgmandelabarnes

Secy. of State Douglas La Follette (D), State Capitol, P.O. Box 7848, Madison 53707-7848; (608) 266-8888; Fax, (608) 266-3159; Email, statesec@wi.gov; Web, https://sos.wi.gov; Facebook, www.facebook.com/sosdoug; Twitter, @DougLaFollette

Atty. Gen. Josh Kaul (D), 17 W. Main St., Madison 53702; Mailing address, P.O. Box 7857, Madison 53707-7857; (608) 266-1221; Fax, (608) 267-2779; Web, www.doj.state.wi.us; Facebook, www.facebook.com/Wisconsin AttorneyGeneral; Twitter, @WisDOJ; YouTube, www.youtube.com/user/WisconsinDOJ; Instagram, @wisdoj

Treasurer Sarah Godlewski (D), B38 W. State Capitol, Madison 53703; Mailing address, P.O. Box 7871, Madison 53707; (608) 266-1714 or (608) 266-1095; Web, https://statetreasurer.wi.gov/Pages/Home.aspx; Email, treasurer@wisconsin.gov;

Facebook, www.facebook.com/witreasurer; Twitter, @WITreasurer; Instagram, @sarah.godlewski

Washington, DC, Representative: Noah Robert, State Federal Director; 115 E. State Capitol, Madison 53707; (608) 266-1212

Wyoming   Web, www.wyo.gov

Gov. Mark Gordon (R), State Capitol, 200 W. 24th St., Cheyenne 82002; (307) 777-7434; Fax, (307) 632-3909; Web, www.governor.wyo.gov; Facebook, www.facebook.com/governormarkgordon; Twitter, @GovernorGordon; Instagram, @governormarkgordon

(No office of Lieutenant Governor)

Secy. of State Edward A. Buchanan (R), Herschler Bldg., 122 W. 25th St., #100 and #101, Cheyenne 82002-0020; (307) 777-7378; Fax, (307) 777-6217; Web, https://sos.wyo.gov; Email, SecOfState@wyo.gov; Facebook, www.facebook.com/wyosos; Twitter, @WyomingSOS

Atty. Gen Bridget Hill (R), 109 State Capitol Bldg., Cheyenne 82002; (307) 777-7841; Fax, (307) 777-6869; TTY, (307) 777-5351; Web, ag.wyo.gov; Email, ag.webmaster@wyo.gov

Treasurer Curtis E. Meier Jr. (R), Herschler Bldg. E., 122 W. 25th St., #E330, Cheyenne 82002; (307) 777-7408; Fax, (307) 777-5411; Web, treasurer.state.wy.us; Email, treasurer@wyo.gov; Facebook, www.facebook.com/wyomingtreas

Washington, DC, Representative: Rob Creager, Policy Advisor; State Capitol, #124, Cheyenne 82002; (307) 777-7434

U.S. TERRITORIES

American Samoa   Web, www.americansamoa.gov

Gov. H. C. Lemanu Peleti Mauga (I), P. Lutali Executive Office Bldg., Pago Pago, American Samoa 96799; (011) 684-633-4116; Fax, (011) 684-633-2269; Email, lemanu.mauga@go.as.gov; Facebook, www.facebook.com/amsamgov

Lt. Gov. H. C. Talauega E. V. Ale (I), P. Lutali Executive Office Bldg., Pago Pago, American Samoa 96799; (011) 684-633-4116; Fax, (011) 684-633-2269

Washington, DC, Representative: Tuimavave Laupola, Chief of Staff; Executive Office Bldg., 3rd Floor, Pago Pago, AS 96799; 011-684-633-4116, ext. 233

Guam   Web, www.guam.gov

Gov. Lourdes A. (Lou) Leon Guerrero (R), Ricardo J. Bordallo Complex, 513 W. Marine Corps Dr., Hagåtña, Guam 96910; (671) 472-8931-6, (671) 472-8936; Fax, (671) 472-4826; Web, https://governor.guam.gov

Lt. Gov. Joshua F. Tenorio (R), Ricardo J. Bordallo Complex, 513 W. Marine Corps Dr., Hagåtña, Guam 96910; P.O. BOX 2950, Hagåtña, Guam 96932; (671) 472-8931-6, (671) 472-8936; Fax, (671) 477-2007; Twitter, @ltgovguam

In Washington, DC: Madeleine Bordallo, Washington Representative; 444 N. Capitol St. N.W., #399, 20001; (202) 508-3836

Northern Mariana Islands   Web, gov.mp

Gov. Ralph Torres (R), Memorial Bldg., Capitol Hill, Caller Box 10007, Saipan, MP 96950; (670) 237-2200; Web, https://governor.gov.mp/governor-bio-ralph-dlg-torres; Facebook, www.facebook.com/GovernorCNMI; Twitter, @ltcnmi; Instagram, @governorcnmi

Lt. Gov. Arnold I. Palacios (R), Memorial Bldg., Capitol Hill, Caller Box 10007, Saipan, MP 96950; (670) 237-2200; Web, https://governor.gov.mp/lt-governor-bio-arnold-i-palacios

Washington, DC, Representative: Jason Osborne, Washington Representative; Caller Box 10007, Saipan, 96950; (670) 664-2280

Puerto Rico   Web, www2.pr.gov

Gov. Pedro Pierluisi (New Progressive Party), 63 Calle Fortaleza, San Juan, 00901, P.O. Box 9020082, San Juan, PR 00902-0082; (787) 721-2400; Fax (787) 723-3287; Facebook, www.facebook.com/pedropierluisi; Twitter, @GovPierluisi; Instagram, @pierluisipnp

Secretary of State Omar J. Marrero (New Progressive Party), FV8M+352 Calle San José, San Juan, PR 00901; (787) 722-2121; Fax, (787) 725-7303; Web, estado.pr.gov/es

In Washington, DC: Lorraine Carrasco, Government Affairs Director; 1100 17th St. N.W., #800, 20036; (202) 778-0710

Virgin Islands   Web, www.vi.gov.

Gov. Albert Bryan Jr., St. Thomas, 5047 (21-22) Kongens Gade, St. Thomas, 00802 or St. Croix, 1105 King St. Christensted, 00820; (340) 774-0001 or (340) 773-1404; Web, www.vi.gov/governor-bryan; Email, albert.bryan@go.vi.gov; Facebook, www.facebook.com/GovernmentHouseUSVI; Twitter, @govbryan; Instagram, @govhouseusvi

Lt. Gov. Tregenza Roach, 5049 Kongens Gade, St. Thomas, VI 00802; (340) 774-2991; Fax, (340) 774-2991; Web, ltg.gov.vi; Facebook, www.facebook.com/Office-of-the-Lieutenant-Governor-US-Virgin-Islands-1465335007120296

In Washington, DC: Teri Helenese, U.S. Virgin Islands Director, State-Federal Relations and Washington Representative; 444 N. Capitol St. N.W., #394, 20001; (340) 774-0001

Foreign Embassies, U.S. Ambassadors, and Country Desk Offices

Following are key foreign diplomats in the United States, U.S. ambassadors or ranking diplomatic officials abroad, and country offices of the State Dept. that follow political, cultural, and economic developments. Also included are the African Union Commission and European Union. This information is current as of May 12, 2022.

For information on investing or doing business abroad, contact the Commerce Dept.'s Trade Information Center at (800) USA-TRAD(E) (800-872-8723) or visit www.export.gov. The Office of the United States Trade Representative also offers trade information by region at www.ustr.gov/countries-regions.

Afghanistan   Web, www.embassyofafghanistan.org

Ambassador: Hamdullah Mohib
Chancery: 2341 Wyoming Ave. N.W. 20008; (202) 483-6410; Fax, (202) 483-6488; Email, info@afghan embassy.us
Social Media: Facebook, www.facebook.com/embassyof afghanistan; Twitter, @Embassy_of_AFG; YouTube, www.youtube.com/channel/UCS8XU0p8jsDMQQzJz UcWuGg; Instagram, @afghanistanembassydc
U.S. Ambassador in Kabul: Ian McCary (Chargé d'Affaires)
State Dept. Country Office: (202) 647-1312

African Union Commission

Web, https://au.int/en/washingtonmission

Chair: H. E. Moussa Faki Mahamat
Ambassador: Dr. Arikana Chihombori-Quao
Chancery: 1640 Wisconsin Ave. N.W., #7001, 20007; (202) 342-1100; Fax, (202) 342-1114; Email, au-washington@ africa-union.org
Social Media: Facebook, www.facebook.com/ AfricanUnionCommission; Twitter, @_AfricanUnion; YouTube, www.youtube.com/user/AUCommission
U.S. Ambassador in Addis Ababa, Ethiopia: Jessica E. Lapenn
State Dept. Country Office: (202) 736-4814

Albania   Web, www.ambasadat.gov.al/usa/en

Ambassador: Floreta Faber
Chancery: 2100 S St. N.W. 20008; (202) 223-4942; Fax, (202) 628-7342; Email, embassy. washington@mfa.gov.al
Social Media: Facebook, www.facebook.com/albanian embassyusa; Twitter, @FloretaFaber, @AlEmbassyUSA
U.S. Ambassador in Tirana: Yuri Kim
State Dept. Country Office: (202) 647-1739

Algeria   Web, www.algerianembassy.org

Ambassador: Ahmed Boutache
Chancery: 2118 Kalorama Rd. N.W. 20008; (202) 265-2800; Fax, (202) 986-5906; Email, mail@algerian embassy.org

U.S. Ambassador in Algiers: Gautam Rana (Chargé d'Affaires)
State Dept. Country Office: (202) 647-4371

Andorra

Web, www.exteriors.ad/en/embassies-of-andorra/ andorra-usa-embassy

Ambassador: Elisenda Vives Balmaña
Chancery: 2 United Nations Plaza, 27th Floor, New York, NY 10017; (212) 750-8064; Fax, (212) 750-6630; Email, contact@andorraun.org
U.S. Ambassador: Conrad Tribble (Chargé d'Affaires)
State Dept. Country Office: (202) 647-2632

Angola   Web, www.angola.org

Ambassador: Joaquim do Espirito Santo
Chancery: 2100-2108 16th St. N.W. 20009; (202) 785-1156; Fax, (202) 822-9049
Social Media: Facebook, www.facebook.com/ embaixadadeangolawashington; Instagram, @angolaintheus; Twitter, @EmbassyAngolaUS
U.S. Ambassador in Luanda: Nina Maria Fite
State Dept. Country Office: (202) 647-9858

Antigua and Barbuda

Ambassador: Sir Ronald Sanders
Chancery: 3234 Prospect St. N.W. 20007; (202) 362-5122; Fax, (202) 362-5225; Email, embantbar@aol.com
U.S. Ambassador: Linda S. Taglialatela (resident in Bridgetown, Barbados)
State Dept. Country Office: (202) 647-4384

Aruba   (See The Netherlands)

Argentina   Web, https://eeeuu.cancilleria.gob.ar/en

Ambassador: Jorge Argüello
Chancery: 1600 New Hampshire Ave. N.W. 20009; (202) 238-6400; Fax, (202) 332-3171; Email, eeeuu@mrecic.gov.ar
Social Media: Facebook, www.facebook.com/ARGinUSA; Instagram, @arginusa; Twitter, @ARGinUSA;

YouTube, www.youtube.com/user/MRECICARG;
Instagram, @arginusa

U.S. Ambassador in Buenos Aires: Marc Stanley (Chargé
d'Affaires)

State Dept. Country Office: (202) 647-4994

Armenia   Web, http://usa.mfa.am/en

Ambassador: Varuzhan Nersesyan

Chancery: 2225 R St. N.W. 20008; (202) 319-1976;
Fax, (202) 319-2982; Email, armembassyusa@mfa.am

U.S. Ambassador in Yerevan: Lynne M. Tracy

State Dept. Country Office: (202) 647-6576

Australia   Web, www.usa.embassy.gov.au

Ambassador: Arthur Sinodinos

Chancery: 1145 17th St. N.W., #GP410, 20036;
(202) 797-3000; Fax, (202) 797-3168

Social Media: Facebook, www.facebook.com/
AusInTheUS; Twitter, @AusintheUS; Youtube,
www.youtube.com/channel/UCEoD8gsW65cF78Cx
5NSXd6Q; Instagram, @ausintheus

U.S. Ambassador in Canberra: Michael Goldman (Chargé
d'Affaires)

State Dept. Country Office: (202) 736-4229

Austria   Web, www.austria.org

Ambassador: Martin Weiss

Chancery: 3524 International Court N.W. 20008;
(202) 895-6700; Fax, (202) 895-6750; Email, inbox@
austria.org

Social Media: Facebook, www.facebook.com/austrian
embassy; Twitter, @AustriainUSA; Instagram,
@austriainusa

U.S. Ambassador in Vienna: Victoria Reggie Kennedy

State Dept. Country Office: (202) 647-4782

Azerbaijan   Web, washington.mfa.gov.az/en

Ambassador: Khazar Ibrahim

Chancery: 2741 34th St. N.W. 20008; (202) 337-3500;
Fax, (202) 337-5911; Email, azerbaijan@azembassy.us

Social Media: Facebook, www.facebook.com/azembassy
.us; Twitter, @azembassyus; Instagram, @azembassyus

U.S. Ambassador in Baku: Earle D. Litzenberger

State Dept. Country Office: (202) 647-9677

Bahamas   Web, www.bahamasembdc.org

Ambassador: Sidney S. Collie

Chancery: 2220 Massachusetts Ave. N.W. 20008;
(202) 319-2660; Fax, (202) 319-2668; Email, embassy@
bahamasembdc.org

Social Media: Facebook, www.facebook.com/Embassy-of-
the-Commonwealth-of-The-Bahamas-Washington-
DC-260374077395076; Twitter, @bahamasembassy

U.S. Ambassador in Nassau: Usha E. Pitts (Chargé
d'Affaires)

State Dept. Country Office: (202) 647-4757

Bahrain

Web, www.mofa.gov.bh/washington/Home.aspx

Ambassador: Shaikh Abdullah bin Rashid bin Abdullah Al
Khalifa

Chancery: 3502 International Dr. N.W. 20008; (202) 342-
1111; Fax, (202) 362-2192; Email, ambsecretary@
bahrainembassy.org

Social Media: Twitter, @bahdiplomatic; YouTube,
www.youtube.com/user/bahrainvideo; Instagram,
@bahdiplomatic

U.S. Ambassador in Manama: Steven C. Bondy

State Dept. Country Office: (202) 647-6562

Bangladesh   Web, www.bdembassyusa.org

Ambassador: M Shahidu Islam

Chancery: 3510 International Dr. N.W. 20008; (202) 244-
0183; Fax, (202) 244-7830; Email, mission.washington@
mofa.gov.bd

Social Media: Facebook, www.facebook.com/Bangladesh
EmbassyUSA; YouTube, www.youtube.com/playlist?
list=PLby_EWM1TmhnIL4ilf_RqZAjLa1WR5TSW

U.S. Ambassador in Dhaka: Peter Haas

State Dept. Country Office: (202) 647-2472

Barbados   Web, www.foreign.gov.bb

Ambassador: Noel Anderson Lynch

Chancery: 2144 Wyoming Ave. N.W. 20008; (202) 939-
9200; Fax, (202) 332-7467; Email, washington@foreign
.gov.bb

Social Media: Facebook, www.facebook.com/
BarbadosEmbassy

U.S. Ambassador in Bridgetown: Linda S. Taglialatela

State Dept. Country Office: (202) 647-4384

Belarus   Web, www.usa.mfa.gov.by

Ambassador: Dmitry Basik (Chargé d'Affaires)

Chancery: 1619 New Hampshire Ave. N.W. 20009; (202)
986-1606; Fax, (202) 986-1805; Email, usa@mfa.gov.by

U.S. Ambassador in Minsk: Julie D. Fisher

State Dept. Country Office: (202) 736-4443

Belgium

Web, https://unitedstates.diplomatie.belgium.be/en

Ambassador: Jean-Arthur Régibeau

Chancery: 1430 K St. N.W., #101, 20005; (202) 333-6900;
Fax, (202) 333-4960; Email, washington@diplobel.fed.be

Social Media: Facebook, www.facebook.com/
BelgiumintheUSA; Twitter, @BelgiumintheUSA;
Instagram, @belgium_unitedstates

U.S. Ambassador in Brussels: Nicholas Berliner (Chargé
d'Affaires)

State Dept. Country Office: (202) 647-5674

Belize   Web, www.belizeembassyusa.mfa.gov.bz

Ambassador: Daniel Gutierez

Chancery: 2535 Massachusetts Ave. N.W. 20008; (202)
332-9636; Fax, (202) 332-6888; Email, reception
.usa@mfa.gov.bz

Social Media: Facebook, www.facebook.com/embassy
.belize.94; Twitter, @MFABelize
U.S. Ambassador in Belmopan: Keith R. Gilges (Chargé
d'Affaires)
State Dept. Country Office: (202) 647-3519

Benin   Web, www.beninembassy.us

Ambassador: M. Jean-Claude
Chancery: 2124 Kalorama Rd. N.W. 20008; (202) 232-6656;
Fax, (202) 265-1996; Email, info@beninembassy.us
U.S. Ambassador in Cotonou: Karen Gustafson de Andrade
State Dept. Country Office: (202) 647-0033

Bhutan

The United States and Bhutan do not maintain formal
diplomatic relations. Informal contact is made between
the U.S. embassy and the Bhutanese embassy in New
Delhi, India.
State Dept. Country Office: (202) 647-2941

Bolivia   Web, www.boliviawdc.org

Chief of Mission: Freddy Bersatti (Chargé d'Affaires)
Chancery: 1825 Connecticut Ave. N.W., #200C, 20008;
(202) 232-4827; Fax, (202) 232-8017; Email,
colivianwdc@boliviawdc.com
U.S. Ambassador in La Paz: Charisse Phillips (Chargé
d'Affaires)
State Dept. Country Office: (202) 647-0464

Bosnia and Herzegovina   Web, www.bhembassy.org

Ambassador: Bojan Vujic
Chancery: 2109 E St. N.W. 20037; (202) 337-1500;
Fax, (202) 337-1502; Email, info@bhembassy.org
Social Media: Facebook, www.facebook.com/BHembassy
.WashingtonDC
U.S. Ambassador in Sarajevo: Michael J. Murphy
State Dept. Country Office: (202) 647-4775

Botswana   Web, www.botswanaembassy.org

Ambassador: David John Newman
Chancery: 1531-1533 New Hampshire Ave. N.W. 20036;
(202) 244-4990; Fax, (202) 244-4164; Email, info@
botswanaembassy.org
U.S. Ambassador in Gaborone: Craig L. Cloud
State Dept. Country Office: (202) 647-9856

Brazil   Web, http://washington.itamaraty.gov.br/en-us

Ambassador: Nestor Forster Jr.
(Chargé d'Affaires)
Chancery: 3006 Massachusetts Ave. N.W. 20008; (202)
238-2700; Fax, (202) 238-2827; Email, pd.washington@
itamaraty.gov.br
Social Media: Facebook, www.facebook.com/
BrazilianEmbassy; Twitter, @BrazilinUSA; YouTube,
www.youtube.com/user/EmbassyofBrazilDC;
Instagram, @brazilinusa
U.S. Ambassador in Brasilia: Douglass Koneff
State Dept. Country Office: (202) 647-1382

Brunei   Web, www.bruneiembassy.org

Ambassador: Dato Paduka Serbini Ali
Chancery: 3520 International Court N.W. 20008; (202)
237-1838; Fax, (202) 885-0560; Email, info@
bruneiembassy.org
Social Media: Facebook, www.facebook.com/people/
Embassy-Brunei-Darussalam/100007977555585
U.S. Ambassador in Bandar Seri Begawan: Emily M.
Fleckner (Chargé d'Affaires)
State Dept. Country Office: (202) 647-7292

Bulgaria   Web, www.bulgaria-embassy.org

Ambassador: Tihomir Stoytchev
Chancery: 1621 22nd St. N.W. 20008, Dimitar Peshev
Plaza; (202) 387-0174; Fax, (202) 234-7973; Email,
office@bulgaria-embassy.org
Social Media: Facebook, www.facebook.com/Bulgarian-
Embassy-in-Washington-DC-156060414441918
U.S. Ambassador in Sofia: Herro Mustafa
State Dept. Country Office: (202) 647-3238

Burkina Faso   Web, www.burkina-usa.org

Ambassador: Seydou Sinka
Chancery: 2340 Massachusetts Ave. N.W. 20008; (202) 332-
5577; Fax, (202) 667-1882; Email, ambawdc@verizon.net
Social Media: Facebook, www.facebook.com/BURKINA-
EMBASSY-IN-WASHINGTON-DC-
193137697424729
U.S. Ambassador in Ouagadougou: Sandra E. Clark
State Dept. Country Office: (202) 647-1540

Burma   (See Myanmar)

Burundi   Web, www.burundiembassydc-usa.org

Ambassador: Gaudence Sindayigaya
Chancery: 2233 Wisconsin Ave. N.W., #408, 20007;
(202) 342-2574; Fax, (202) 342-2578; Email,
burundiembusadc@gmail.com
U.S. Ambassador in Bujumbura: Melanie Harris Higgins
State Dept. Country Office: (202) 647-4965

Cambodia   Web, www.embassyofcambodiadc.org

Ambassador: Keo Chhea
Chancery: 4530 16th St. N.W. 20011; (202) 726-7742;
Fax, (202) 726-8381; Email, camemb.usa@mfa.gov.kh
Social Media: Facebook, www.facebook.com/
CambodiaEmbUS; Twitter, @camemb.usa@mfa.gov.kh
U.S. Ambassador in Phnom Penh: W. Patrick Murphy
State Dept. Country Office: (202) 647-0036

Cameroon   Web, www.cameroonembassyusa.org

Ambassador: Henri Etoundi Essomba
Chancery: 2349 Massachusetts Ave. N.W. 20008;
(202) 265-8790; Fax, (202) 387-3826; Email,
cs@cameroonembassyusa.org
U.S. Ambassador in Yaounde: Christopher John Lamora
State Dept. Country Office: (202) 647-4514

Canada

Web, https://international.gc.ca/world-monde/
country-pays/united_states-etats_unis/washington
.aspx?

Ambassador: Kristen Hillman
Chancery: 501 Pennsylvania Ave. N.W. 20001;
(202) 647-2170; Fax, (202) 682-7726; Email, wshdc
.infocentre@international.gc.ca
Social Media: Twitter, @CanEmbUSA
U.S. Ambassador in Ottawa: David L. Cohen
State Dept. Country Office: (202) 647-2170

Cape Verde   Web, https://cf.usembassy.gov

Ambassador: Carlos Wahnon Veiga
Chancery: 3415 Massachusetts Ave. N.W. 20007;
(202) 965-6820; Fax, (202) 965-1207; Email, admin@
caboverdeus.net
Social Media: Facebook, www.facebook.com/
EmbaixadaCaboVerdeWashingtonDC; YouTube,
www.youtube.com/user/embcvusa
U.S. Ambassador in Praia: John J. Daigle
State Dept. Country Office: (202) 647-1540

Central African Republic

Web, www.usrcawashington.org

Ambassador: Martial Ndoubou
Chancery: 2704 Ontario Rd. N.W. 20009; (202) 483-7800;
Email, centrafricwashington@yahoo.com
U.S. Ambassador in Bangui: Patricia Mahoney
State Dept. Country Office: (202) 647-4966

Chad   Web, https://chadembassy.us

Ambassador: Ngote Gali Koutou
Chancery: 2401 Massachusetts Ave. N.W. 20008; (202)
652-1312; Fax, (202) 758-0431; Email, info@
chadembassy.us
U.S. Ambassador in N'Djamena: Ellen Thorburn (Chargé
d'Affaires)
State Dept. Country Office: (202) 647-4514

Chile   Web, http://chile.gob.cl/estados-unidos/en

Ambassador: Oscar Alfonso Silva Navarro
Chancery: 1732 Massachusetts Ave. N.W. 20036; (202)
785-1746; Fax, (202) 887-5579; Email, echile.eeuu@
minrel.gov.cl
U.S. Ambassador in Santiago: Richard H. Glenn (Chargé
d'Affaires)
State Dept. Country Office: (202) 647-2296

China   Web, www.china-embassy.org/eng

Ambassador: Cui Weidong
Chancery: 3505 International Pl. N.W. 20008; (202) 495-
2266; Fax, (202) 495-2138; Email, chinaembpress_
us@mfa.gov.cn
U.S. Ambassador in Beijing: R. Nicholas Burns
State Dept. Country Office: (202) 647-9141

Colombia   Web, www.colombiaemb.org

Ambassador: Francisco Santos Calderón
Chancery: 1724 Massachusetts Ave. N.W. 20036; (202)
387-8338; Fax, (202) 232-8643; Email, Ewashington@
cancilleria.gov.co
Social Media: Facebook, www.facebook.com/
ColombiaEmbassyUS; Twitter, @colombiaembUSA;
Instagram, @colombiaembassyus; Youtube,
www.youtube.com/channel/UCiNNZFdxCpMVa
TurnZx-TIA
U.S. Ambassador in Bogotá: Philip Goldberg
State Dept. Country Office: (202) 647-3142

Comoros   Web, www.un.int/comoros

Ambassador: Issimail Chanfi (in New York)
Chancery: 866 UN Plaza, #495, New York, NY 10017;
(212)-750-1637; Fax, (212) 750-1657; Email,
comoros@un.int
U.S. Ambassador in Comoros: Amy J. Hyatt
State Dept. Country Office: (202) 647-8284

Congo, Democratic Republic of the (DRC)

Web, www.ambardcusa.org

Ambassador: François Nkuna Balumuene
Chancery: 1100 Connecticut Ave. N.W., #725, 20036;
(202) 234-7690; Fax, (202) 234-2609; Email,
ambassade@ambardcusa.org
Social Media: Twitter, @DrcNotes
U.S. Ambassador in Kinshasa: Mike Hammer
State Dept. Country Office: (202) 647-2216

Congo, Republic of the

Web, www.ambacongo-us.org

Ambassador: Serge Mombouli
Chancery: 1720 16th St. N.W. 20009; (202) 726-5500;
Fax, (202) 726-1860; Email, info@ambacongo-us.org
Social Media: Facebook, www.facebook.com/
AmbaCongoUs; Twitter, @AmbaCongoUs
U.S. Ambassador in Brazzaville: Eugene Young
State Dept. Country Office: (202) 647-4896

Costa Rica   Web, www.costarica-embassy.org

Ambassador: Fernando Llorca Castro
Chancery: 2114 S St. N.W. 20008; (202) 499-2980;
Fax, (202) 265-4795; Email, embcr-us@rree.go.cr
Social Media: Facebook, www.facebook.com/
EmbajadadeCostaRicaenlosEEUU
U.S. Ambassador in San Jose: Cynthia Telles
State Dept. Country Office: (202) 647-3518

Côte d'Ivoire   Web, https://ambaciusa.org

Ambassador: Haidara Mamadou
Chancery: 2424 Massachusetts Ave. N.W. 20008; (202)
797-0300; Fax, (202) 204-3967; Email,
info@ambaciusa.org
U.S. Ambassador in Abidjan: Richard Bell
State Dept. Country Office: (202) 647-3407

Croatia   Web, us.mvep.hr

Ambassador: Pjer Šimunović

Chancery: 2343 Massachusetts Ave. N.W. 20008; (202) 492-4733; Fax, (202) 588-8936; Email, Washington@mvep.hr

Social Media: Facebook, www.facebook.com/croembdc; Twitter, @MVEP_hr; YouTube, www.youtube.com/user/MVEPRH

U.S. Ambassador in Zagreb: Victoria J. Taylor (Chargé d'Affaires)

State Dept. Country Office: (202) 647-4297

Cuba   Web, misiones.cubaminrex.cu/en/usa

Ambassador: José Ramón Cabañas Sr.

Chancery: 2630 16th St. N.W. 20009; (202) 797-8518, ext. 20; Fax, (202) 797-8521; Email, recepcion@sicuw.org

Social Media: Facebook, www.facebook.com/EmbaCubaUS; Twitter, @EmbaCubaUS; Instagram, @embacubaus

U.S. Ambassador in Havana: Timothy Zúñiga-Brown (Chargé d'Affaires)

State Dept. Country Office: (202) 453-8439

Curacao   (See also The Netherlands)

Consul General: Margy Bond

State Dept. Country Office: (202) 647-5279

Cyprus   Web, www.cyprusembassy.net

Ambassador: Leonidas Pantelides

Chancery: 2211 R St. N.W. 20008; (202) 462-5772; Fax, (202) 483-6710; Email, info@cyprusembassy.net

Social Media: Facebook, www.facebook.com/CyprusinUSA/?rf=161477227251673; Twitter, @CyprusinUSA

U.S. Ambassador in Nicosia: Judith Gail Garber

State Dept. Country Office: (202) 647-6976

Czech Republic   Web, www.mzv.cz/washington

Ambassador: Hynek Kmnonicek

Chancery: 3900 Spring of Freedom St. N.W. 20008; (202) 274-9100; Fax, (202) 966-8540; Email, Washington@embassy.mzv.cz

Social Media: Facebook, www.facebook.com/Czechembassydc; Twitter, @CzechEmbassyDC; Instagram, @CzechEmbassyDC

U.S. Ambassador in Prague: Jennifer Bachus (Chargé d'Affaires)

State Dept. Country Office: (202) 647-4811

Denmark   Web, www.usa.um.dk

Ambassador: Lone Dencker Wisborg

Chancery: 3200 Whitehaven St. N.W. 20008; (202) 234-4300; Fax, (202) 328-1470; Email, wasamb@um.dk

Social Media: Facebook, www.facebook.com/DenmarkinUSA; Twitter, @DenmarkinUSA; Instagram, @denmarkinusa

U.S. Ambassador in Copenhagen: Stuart A. Dwyer (Chargé d'Affaires)

State Dept. Country Office: (202) 647-8178

Djibouti   Web, www.djiboutiembassyus.org

Ambassador: Mohamed Siad Doualeh

Chancery: 1156 15th St. N.W., #515, 20005; (202) 331-0270

Social Media: Twitter, @AmbDoualeh

U.S. Ambassador in Djibouti: Jonathan Pratt

State Dept. Country Office: (202) 647-5922

Dominica   Web, www.dominicaembassy.com

Ambassador: Judith Anne Rolle (Chargé d'Affaires)

Chancery: 3216 New Mexico Ave. N.W. 20016; (202) 364-6781; Fax, (202) 364-6791; Email, embdomdc@aol.com

U.S. Ambassador: Vince Henderson

State Dept. Country Office: (202) 647-4384

Dominican Republic   Web, drembassyusa.org

Ambassador: José Tomás Pérez

Chancery: 1715 22nd St. N.W. 20008; (202) 332-6280; Fax, (202) 265-8057; Email, embassydominicanrepublic@gmail.com

Social Media: Facebook, www.facebook.com/DominicanEmbassy; Twitter, @DREmbassy

U.S. Ambassador in Santo Domingo: Robert W. Thomas (Chargé d'Affaires)

State Dept. Country Office: (202) 647-4757

East Timor   (See Timor-Leste)

Ecuador   Web, www.ecuador.org

Ambassador: Francisco Carrión Mena

Chancery: 2535 15th St. N.W. 20009; (202) 234-7200; Fax, (202) 234-7166; Email, embassy@ecuador.org

Social Media: Facebook, www.facebook.com/EmbajadaEcuadorEnEstadosUnidos; Twitter, @EmbajadaEcuUSA; Instagram, @embajadaecuusa

U.S. Ambassador in Quito: Michael J. Fitzpatrick

State Dept. Country Office: (202) 647-1720

Egypt   Web, www.egyptembassy.net

Ambassador: Yasser Reda

Chancery: 3521 International Court N.W. 20008; (202) 895-5400; Fax, (202) 244-5131; Email, consolate@egyptembassy.net

Social Media: Facebook, www.facebook.com/EgyptEmbassyUSA; Twitter, @EgyptEmbassyUSA; Instagram, @egpytembassyusa

U.S. Ambassador in Cairo: Jonathan R. Cohen

State Dept. Country Office: (202) 647-2261

El Salvador

Ambassador: Agustín Vasquez Gomez

Chancery: 1400 16th St. N.W., #100, 20036; (202) 595-7500; Fax, (202) 232-3763; Email, correo@elsalvador.org

Social Media: Facebook, www.facebook.com/EmbajadaSVEUA; Twitter, @EESAenEEUU; YouTube, www.youtube.com/user/embelsalvadorusa

U.S. Ambassador in San Salvador: William H. Duncan
State Dept. Country Office: (202) 647-3505

Equatorial Guinea   Web, www.egembassydc.com

Ambassador: Miguel Ntutumu Evuna Andeme
Chancery: 2020 16th St. N.W. 20009; (202) 518-5700;
Fax, (202) 518-5252; Email, info@egembassydc.com
Social Media: Facebook, www.facebook.com/
egembassydc; Twitter, @EGEmbassyDC; YouTube,
www.youtube.com/channel/UC1zn99_azfsWRfAue-
uvr5Q
U.S. Ambassador in Malabo: Gregory R. Morrison
(Chargé d'Affaires)
State Dept. Country Office: (202) 647-7494

Eritrea   Web, us.embassyeritrea.org

Ambassador: Sophia Tsefamariam Yohannes
Chancery: 1708 New Hampshire Ave. N.W. 20009; (202)
319-1991; Fax, (202) 319-1304; Email,
embassyeritrea@embassyeritrea.org
U.S. Ambassador in Asmara: Steven C. Walker (Chargé
d'Affaires)
State Dept. Country Office: (202) 647-5922

Estonia   Web, https://washington.mfa.ee

Ambassador: Kirstjan Prikk
Chancery: 1990 K St. N.W., #430, 20008; (202) 588-0101;
Fax, (202) 588-0108; Email, Embassy.
Washington@mfa.ee
Social Media: Facebook, www.facebook.com/estemb.
washington; Twitter, @Estonia_in_US
U.S. Ambassador in Tallinn: Brian R. Roraff (Chargé
d'Affaires)
State Dept. Country Office: (202) 647-8179

Eswatini

Ambassador: Njabuliso Gwebu
Chancery: 1712 New Hampshire Ave. N.W. 20009; (202)
234-5002; Fax, (202) 234-8254; Email,
info@swazilandembassyus.com or
embassy@swaziland-usa.com
U.S. Ambassador in Mbabane: Jeanne M. Maloney
State Dept. Country Office: (202) 647-8252

Ethiopia   Web, www.ethiopianembassy.org

Ambassador: Fitsum Arega
Chancery: 3506 International Dr. N.W. 20008; (202) 364-
1200; Fax, (202) 587-0195; Email,
ethiopia@ethiopianembassy.org
Social Media: Facebook, www.facebook.com/ethembassy;
Twitter, @ethembassyUS; YouTube, www.youtube.
com/user/ethembassy
U.S. Ambassador in Addis Ababa: Tracey Ann Jacobson
State Dept. Country Office: (202) 647-1597

European Union   Web, www.eeasneuropa.eu

Ambassador: Stavros Lambrinidis

Chancery: 2175 K. St., 20037; (202) 862-9500; Fax, (202)
429-1766; Email, delegation-usa-info@eeas.europa.eu
Social Media: Facebook, www.facebook.com/EUintheUS;
Twitter, @EUintheUS; YouTube, www.youtube.com/
user/EUintheUS; Instagram, @euintheus
U.S. Ambassador to the EU: Mark Gitenstein
State Dept. Country Office: (202) 647-3474

Fiji   Web, www.fijiembassydc.com

Ambassador: Naivakarurubalavu Solo Mara
Chancery: 1707 L. St. N.W., #200, 20036; (202) 466-8320;
Fax, (202) 466-8325; Email, info@fijiembassydc.com
Social Media: Facebook, www.facebook.com/
FijiEmbassyUS; Twitter, @FijiEmbassyUS
U.S. Ambassador in Suva: Tony Greubel (Chargé
d'Affaires)
State Dept. Country Office: (202) 647-2349

Finland   Web, www.finland.org

Ambassador: H. E. Mikko Hautala
Chancery: 3301 Massachusetts Ave. N.W. 20008; (202)
298-5800; Fax, (202) 298-6030; Email, sanomat
.was@formin.fi
Social Media: Facebook, www.facebook.com/Finn
EmbassyDC; Twitter, @FinlandinUSA; YouTube,
www.youtube.com/user/FinlandintheUS; Instagram,
@FinlandinUSA
U.S. Ambassador in Helsinki: Ian Campbell (Chargé
d'Affaires)
State Dept. Country Office: (202) 736-7443

France   Web, www.franceintheus.org

Ambassador: Philippe Etienne
Chancery: 4101 Reservoir Rd. N.W. 20007; (202) 944-
6000; Fax, (202) 944-6166; Email, info@ambafrance-
us.org
Social Media: Facebook, www.facebook.com/FranceIn
TheUs; Twitter, @franceintheus; YouTube, www
.youtube.com/user/franceintheus; Instagram,
@franceintheus
U.S. Ambassador in Paris: Denise Campbell Bauer
State Dept. Country Office: (202) 647-6557

Gabon   Web, www.gabonembassyusa.org

Ambassador: Michael Moussa-Adamo
Chancery: 2034 20th St. N.W. 20009; (202) 797-1000;
Fax, (202) 332-0668; Email, info@gabonembassy.org
Social Media: Facebook, www.facebook.com/
gabon.embassy.1; Twitter, @GabonEmbassyDC
U.S. Ambassador in Libreville: Samuel R. Watson
(Chargé d'Affaires)
State Dept. Country Office: (202) 647-4896

The Gambia   Web, www.gambiaembassydc.us

Ambassador: Dawda D. Fadera
Chancery: 5630 16th St. N.W. 20011; (202) 785-1399;
Fax, (202) 342-0240; Email, info@gambiaembassy.us

Social Media: Facebook, www.facebook.com/gambia embassydc; Twitter, @dcgambiaembassy; YouTube, www.youtube.com/channel/UCsBa3CkuMgBxn6dtpuZOFKg
U.S. Ambassador in Banjul: Sharon L. Cromer
State Dept. Country Office: (202) 647-2791

Georgia   Web, http://georgiaembassyusa.org

Ambassador: David Bakradze
Chancery: 1824 R St. N.W. 20009; (202) 387-2390; Fax, (202) 387-0864; Email, embgeo.usa@mfa.gov.ge
Social Media: Facebook, www.facebook.com/EmbGeoinUS; Twitter, @GeorgianEmbassy; YouTube, www.youtube.com/channel/UChYbhobpduBOwjmhF5OW8ng; Instagram, @georgiainusa
U.S. Ambassador in Tbilisi: Kelly Degnan
State Dept. Country Office: (202) 647-6048

Germany   Web, www.germany.info

Ambassador: Emily Haber
Chancery: 4645 Reservoir Rd. N.W. 20007; (202) 298-4261; Fax, (202) 298-4249
Social Media: Facebook, www.facebook.com/GermanyinUSA; Twitter, @GermanyinUSA; Instagram, @germanyinusa
U.S. Ambassador in Berlin: Woodward Price (Chargé d'Affaires)
State Dept. Country Office: (202) 647-4555

Ghana   Web, www.ghanaembassydc.org

Ambassador: Alima Mahama
Chancery: 3512 International Dr. N.W. 20008; (202) 686-4520; Fax, (202) 686-4527; Email, info@ghanaembassydc.org
Social Media: Facebook, www.facebook.com/EmbassyofGhanaUSA; Twitter, @GhanaEmbassy_DC; Instagram, @embassyofghanausa
U.S. Ambassador in Accra: Stephanie S. Sullivan
State Dept. Country Office: (202) 647-0033

Greece   Web, www.mfa.gr/washington

Ambassador: Alexandra Papadopoulou
Chancery: 2217 Massachusetts Ave. N.W. 20008; (202) 939-1300; Fax, (202) 939-1324; Email, gremb.was@mfa.gr
Social Media: Facebook, www.facebook.com/GreeceInWashington; Twitter, @GreeceinUSA; YouTube, www.youtube.com/user/GreeceInWashington
U.S. Ambassador in Athens: Geoffrey R. Pyatt
State Dept. Country Office: (202) 735-4013

Greenland   (See Denmark)

Grenada   Web, www.grenadaembassyusa.org

Ambassador: Yolande Y. Smith
Chancery: 1701 New Hampshire Ave. N.W. 20009-2501; (202) 265-2561; Fax, (202) 265-2468; Email, embassy@grenadaembassyusa.org
Social Media: Facebook, www.facebook.com/GrenadaUSA; YouTube, www.youtube.com/channel/UC_CaY4EmicO-8eTMYyZb8kg
U.S. Ambassador in Grenada: Linda Swartz Taglialatela
State Dept. Country Office: (202) 647-4384

Guatemala

Ambassador: Gladys Ruiz Sanchez
Chancery: 2220 R St. N.W. 20008; (202) 745-4953; Fax, (202) 745-1908; Email, info@guatemala-embassy.org
Social Media: Facebook, www.facebook.com/pages/Embassy-of-Guatemala-in-Washington-DC/218824864824114; Twitter, @EmbaGuateUSA; YouTube, www.youtube.com/channel/UCVXhb1KKTBbI2SCs6CpzOoQ
U.S. Ambassador in Guatemala City: William W. Popp
State Dept. Country Office: (202) 647-1510

Guinea, Republic of

Web, http://guineaembassyusa.org/en/welcome-to-the-embassy-of-guinea-washington-usa

Ambassador: Kerfalla Yansané
Chancery: 2112 Leroy Pl. N.W. 20008; (202) 986-4300; Fax, (202) 986-3800; Email, acamara@guineaembassyusa.com
Social Media: Facebook, www.facebook.com/Embassy-of-Guinea-in-the-US-1430331940403860
U.S. Ambassador in Conakry: Troy D. Fitrell
State Dept. Country Office: (202) 647-7494

Guinea-Bissau

There have been several attempts to establish diplomatic relations in recent years.
Contact: P.O. Box 33813, 20033; (301) 947-3958
U.S. Ambassador: Tulinabo Salama Mushingi; resident in Dakar, Senegal; covers matters pertaining to Guinea-Bissau
State Dept. Country Office: (202) 647-4567

Guyana   Web, www.guyanaembassyusa.org

Ambassador: Riyad Insanally
Chancery: 2490 Tracy Pl. N.W. 20008; (202) 265-6900; Fax, (202) 232-1297; Email, guyanaembassydc@verizon.net
U.S Ambassador in Georgetown: Sarah-Ann Lynch
State Dept. Country Office: (202) 736-4628

Haiti   Web, www.haiti.org

Ambassador: Bocchit Edmond
Chancery: 2311 Massachusetts Ave. N.W. 20008; (202) 332-4090; Fax, (202) 745-7215; Email, amb.washington@diplomatie.ht

Social Media: Facebook, www.facebook.com/
EmbassyofHaiti; Twitter, @EmbassyOfHaiti;
Instagram, @embassyofhaiti.usa
U.S. Ambassador in Port-au-Prince: Kenneth H. Merten
(Chargé d'Affaires)
State Dept. Country Office: (202) 453-9909

The Holy See   Web, www.nuntiususa.org
Apostolic Nuncio: Christophe Pierre
Office: 3339 Massachusetts Ave. N.W. 20008; (202) 333-
7121; Fax, (202) 337-4036; Email, nuntiususa@
nuntiususa.org
U.S. Ambassador in Rome: Joe Donnelly
State Dept. Country Office: (202) 647-5659

Honduras   Web, www.hondurasemb.org
Ambassador: Luis Suazo
Chancery: 1220 19th St. N.W., #320, 20036; (202) 966-
7702; Fax, (202) 966-9751; Email, embassy@
hondurasemb.org
Social Media: Facebook, www.facebook.com/Embajada-
de-Honduras-en-los-Estados-Unidos-de-América-
188645814515193; Twitter, @EmbHondurasUSA
U.S. Ambassador in Tegucigalpa: Laura Farnsworth
Dogu
State Dept. Country Office: (202) 647-3519

Hong Kong   (See China)
State Dept. Country Office: (202) 647-6300

Hungary   Web, www.washington.kormany.hu
Ambassador: László Szabó
Chancery: 3910 Shoemaker St. N.W. 20008; (202) 362-
6730; Fax, (202) 966-8135; Email, informacio.was@
mfa.gov.hu
Social Media: Facebook, www.facebook.com/Embassy-of-
Hungary-in-Washington-DC-102507676462147;
Twitter, @HungaryinUSA
U.S. Ambassador in Budapest: Marc Dillard (Chargé
d'Affaires)
State Dept. Country Office: (202) 647-0425

Iceland   Web, www.iceland.is/iceland-abroad/us/wdc
Ambassador: Bergdís Ellertsdóttir
Chancery: House of Sweden, 2900 K St. N.W., #509,
20007-1704, (202) 265-6653; Fax, (202) 265-6656;
Email, washington@mfa.is
Social Media: Facebook, www.facebook.com/IcelandinUS;
Twitter, @IcelandInUS
U.S. Ambassador in Reykjavík: Jeffrey Ross Gunter
State Dept. Country Office: (202) 647-8431

India   Web, www.indianembassy.org
Ambassador: Taranjit Singh Sandhu
Chancery: 2107 Massachusetts Ave. N.W. 20008; (202)
939-7000; Fax, (202) 265-4351
Social Media: Facebook, www.facebook.com/
IndiaInUSA; Twitter, @IndianEmbassyUS;

Instagram, @indianembassyus; YouTube, www
.youtube.com/user/indiausrelations
U.S. Ambassador in New Delhi: Patricia A. Lacina
(Chargé d'Affaires)
State Dept. Country Office: (202) 647-1112

Indonesia   Web, www.embassyofindonesia.org
Ambassador: Rosan Roeslani
Chancery: 2020 Massachusetts Ave. N.W. 20036; (202)
775-5200; Fax, (202) 775-5365
Social Media: Facebook, www.facebook.com/
IndonesiainDC; Twitter, @IndonesiainDC; Instagram,
@indonesiaindc; YouTube, www.youtube.com/
IndonesiainDC
U.S. Ambassador in Jakarta: J Sung Kim
State Dept. Country Office: (202) 647-7292

Iran   Web, www.daftar.org
The United States severed diplomatic relations with Iran in
April 1980. Iran's interests in the United States are
represented by the Pakistani embassy.
Iranian Interests Section: 1250 23rd St. N.W., #200,
20037; (202) 965-4990; Fax, (202) 965-4990; Email,
info@daftar.org
U.S. interests in Iran are represented by the Swiss embassy
in Tehran.
State Dept. Country Office: (202) 647-2577

Iraq   Web, www.iraqiembassy.us
Ambassador: Fareed Yasseen
Chancery: 3421 Massachusetts Ave. N.W. 20007; (202)
742-1600; Fax, (202) 333-1129 **Consulate:** 1801 P St.
N.W. 20036; (202) 483-7500; Fax, (202) 462-8815
Social Media: Facebook, www.facebook.com/
IraqiEmbassyUSA; Twitter, @IraqiEmbassyUSA
U.S. Ambassador to Baghdad: Matthew Tueller
State Dept. Country Office: (202) 647-6351

Ireland   Web, www.embassyofireland.org
Ambassador: Daniel Mulhall
Chancery: 2234 Massachusetts Ave. N.W. 20008; (202)
462-3939; Fax, (202) 232-5993
Social Media: Facebook, www.facebook.com/
embassyofirelandusa; Twitter, @IrelandEmbUSA
U.S. Ambassador in Dublin: Claire Cronin
State Dept. Country Office: (202) 647-5262

Israel   Web, www.israelemb.org
Ambassador: Ron Dermer
Chancery: 3514 International Dr. N.W. 20008; (202) 364-
5500; Fax, (202) 364-5610; Email, info@washington
.mfa.gov.il
Social Media: Facebook, www.facebook.com/IsraelinUSA;
Twitter, @IsraelinUSA; Instagram, @israelinusa
U.S. Ambassador in Tel Aviv: Thomas R. Nides
State Dept. Country Office: (202) 647-3672

Italy Web, www.ambwashingtondc.esteri.it

Ambassador: Mariangela Zappla
Chancery: 3000 Whitehaven St. N.W. 20008; (202) 612-4400; Fax, (202) 518-2154; Email, amb.washington@cert.esteri.it
Social Media: Facebook, www.facebook.com/ItalyInUs.org; Twitter, @ItalyinUS; Instagram, @italyinus; YouTube, www.youtube.com/user/italianembassy
U.S. Ambassador in Rome: Thomas Smitham (Chargé d'Affaires)
State Dept. Country Office: (202) 647-4395

Jamaica Web, www.embassyofjamaica.org

Ambassador: Audrey Patrice Marks
Chancery: 1520 New Hampshire Ave. N.W. 20036; (202) 452-0660; Fax, (202) 452-0036; Email, firstsec@jamaicaembassy.org
U.S. Ambassador in Kingston: John McIntyre (Chargé d'Affaires)
State Dept. Country Office: (202) 736-4322

Japan Web, www.us.emb-japan.go.jp

Ambassador: Koji Tomita
Chancery: 2520 Massachusetts Ave. N.W. 20008; (202) 238-6700; Fax, (202) 328-2187
Social Media: Facebook, www.facebook.com/JapanEmbDC; Twitter, @JapanEmbDC
U.S. Ambassador in Tokyo: Rahm Emanuel
State Dept. Country Office: (202) 647-3152

Jordan Web, www.jordanembassyus.org

Ambassador: Dina Kawar
Chancery: 3504 International Dr. N.W. 20008; (202) 966-2664; Fax, (202) 966-3110; Email, hkjconsular@jordanembassyus.org
Social Media: Facebook, www.facebook.com/JoEmbassyUS; Twitter, @JoEmbassyUS; Instagram, @JoEmbassyUS
U.S. Ambassador in Amman: Henry T. Wooster
State Dept. Country Office: (202) 736-7044

Kazakhstan Web, www.kazakhembus.com

Ambassador: Erzhan Kazykhanov
Chancery: 1401 16th St. N.W. 20036; (202) 232-5488; Fax, (202) 232-5845; Email, washingto@mfa.kz
Social Media: Facebook, www.facebook.com/KazakhEmbassyDC; Twitter, @KazakhEmbassy; Instagram, @kz_in_usa; YouTube, www.youtube.com/user/kazembus
U.S. Ambassador in Astana: Yerzhan Ashikbayev
State Dept. Country Office: (202) 647-6859

Kenya Web, www.kenyaembassydc.org

Ambassador: Lazarus Omabai Amayo
Chancery: 2249 R St. N.W. 20008; (202) 387-6101; Fax, (202) 462-3829; Email, information@kenyaembassy.com
Social Media: Facebook, www.facebook.com/kenyaembassyusa; Twitter, @KenyaembassyDC
U.S. Ambassador in Nairobi: Eric Kneedler (Chargé d'Affaires)
State Dept. Country Office: (202) 647-8295

Kiribati

Kiribati maintains a Permanent Mission to the United Nations.
His Excellency: Teburoro Tito
UN Chancery: 685 3rd Ave., #1109, New York, NY 10017; (212) 867-3310; Email, Kimission.newyork@mfa.gov.ki
U.S. Ambassador: Tony Greubel (Chargé d'Affaires) (resident in Suva, Fiji)
State Dept. Country Office: (202) 647-2349

Korea, Democratic People's Republic of (North)

North Korea maintains a Permanent Mission to the United Nations.
UN Chancery: 515 E. 72nd St., #38F, New York, NY 10021; (212) 772-0712; Fax, (212) 772-0735
The United States does not maintain diplomatic relations with North Korea. The Swedish Embassy in Pyongyang represents the United States as a consular protecting power.
State Dept. Country Office: (202) 647-2316

Korea, Republic of (South) Web, usa.mofa.go.kr

Ambassador: Lee Soo-Hyuk
Chancery: 2450 Massachusetts Ave. N.W. 20008; (202) 939-5600; Fax, (202) 797-0595; Email, consular.usa@mofa.go.kr
Social Media: Facebook, www.facebook.com/mofakr.eng; Twitter, @MOFAkr_eng
U.S. Ambassador in Seoul: Christopher Del Corso (Chargé d'Affaires)
State Dept. Country Office: (202) 647-7717

Kosovo Web, www.ambasada-ks.net/us

Ambassador: Vlora Çitaku
Chancery: 2175 K St. N.W., #300, 20037; (202) 380-3581; Fax, (202) 380-3628; Email, consulategeneral.ny@rks-gov.net
Social Media: Facebook, www.facebook.com/MFAKosovo; Twitter, @MFAKOSOVO; YouTube, www.youtube.com/channel/UCp_iicCGZGGs8fgmc1hMUYg
U.S. Ambassador in Pristina: Jeffrey M. Hovenier
State Dept. Country Office: (202) 647-4290

Kuwait Web, www.kuwaitembassy.us

Ambassador: Salem Abdullah Al-Jaber Al-Sabah
Chancery: 2940 Tilden St. N.W. 20008; (202) 966-0702; Fax, (202) 364-2868; Email, @consulate@kuwaitembassy.us
Social Media: Facebook, www.facebook.com/MOFAKuwait; Twitter, @Kuwait_DC; Instagram, @mofakuwait

U.S. Ambassador in Kuwait City: Alina L. Romanowski
State Dept. Country Office: (202) 647-9005

Kyrgyzstan, Republic of Kyrgyz

Web, www.mfa.gov.kg/en/embassies/embassy?id=63

Ambassador: Otunbaev Bolot Isakovich
Chancery: 2360 Massachusetts Ave. N.W. 20008; (202) 449-9822; Fax, (202) 449-8275; Email, kgconsul@ kgembassy.org
Social Media: Facebook, www.facebook.com/kgembassy usa; Twitter, @kgembassy; Instagram, @kgembassy
U.S. Ambassador in Bishkek: Sonata Coulter (Chargé d'Affaires)
State Dept. Country Office: (202) 647-9119

Laos   Web, www.laoembassy.com

Ambassador: Khamphan Anlavan
Chancery: 2222 S St. N.W. 20008; (202) 328-9148; Fax, (202) 332-4923; Email, embasslao@gmail.com
U.S. Ambassador in Vientiane: Peter M. Haymond
State Dept. Country Office: (202) 647-0036

Latvia   Web, www.mfa.gov.lv/en/usa

Ambassador: Māris Selga
Chancery: 2306 Massachusetts Ave. N.W. 20008; (202) 328-2840; Fax, (202) 328-2860; Email, embassy. usa@mfa.gov.lv
Social Media: Facebook, www.facebook.com/ EmbassyofLatviainUS; Twitter, @Latvia_USA; Instagram, @latviainusa
U.S. Ambassador in Riga: John L. Carwile
State Dept. Country Office: (202) 647-6582

Lebanon   Web, www.lebanonembassyus.org

Ambassador: Gabriel Issa
Chancery: 2560 28th St. N.W. 20008; (202) 939-6300; Fax, (202) 939-6324; Email, info@lebanonembassyus .org
Social Media: Facebook, www.facebook/lebanon embassyus; Twitter, @LebEmbassyUS; Instagram, @lebanonembassyus
U.S. Ambassador in Beirut: Dorothy Shea
State Dept. Country Office: (202) 647-1030

Lesotho, Kingdom of

Web, www.lesothoemb-usa.gov.ls

Ambassador: Sankatana Gabriel Maja
Chancery: 2511 Massachusetts Ave. N.W. 20008; (202) 797-5533; Fax, (202) 234-6815; Email, lesothoembassy@verizon.net
U.S. Ambassador in Maseru: Rebecca E. Gonzales
State Dept. Country Office: (202) 647-9850

Liberia   Web, www.liberianembassyus.org

Ambassador: George S. W. Patten
Chancery: 5201 16th St. N.W. 20011; (202) 723-0437; Fax, (202) 723-0436

U.S. Ambassador in Monrovia: Michael A. McCarthy
State Dept. Country Office: (202) 647-4567

Libya   Web, www.embassyoflibyadc.org

Chargé d'Affaires: Wafa Bughaighis
Chancery: 1460 Dahlia St. N.W. 20012; (202) 944-9601; Fax, (202) 944-9606
Social Media: Twitter, @LibyaEmbassyDC
The U.S. Embassy in Tripoli, Libya, closed on July 26, 2014. Ambassador and diplomatic personnel work from the U.S. Embassy in Tunis, Tunisia.
U.S. Ambassador to Tripoli: Richard B. Norland
State Dept. Country Office: (202) 647-2581

Liechtenstein   Web, www.liechtensteinusa.org

Ambassador: Kurt Jäger
Chancery: 2900 K St. N.W., #602B, 20007; (202) 331-0590; Fax, (202) 331-3221; Email, info@embassyli.org
Social Media: Facebook, www.facebook.com/Embassy-of-Liechtenstein-Washington-DC-263046272021; Twitter, @EmbassyLI
U.S. Ambassador: Eva Weigold Schultz (Chargé d'Affaires) (resident in Bern, Switzerland)
State Dept. Country Office: (202) 647-1457

Lithuania   Web, www.usa.mfa.lt

Ambassador: Rolandas Kriščiūnas
Chancery: 2622 16th St. N.W. 20009; (202) 234-5860; Fax, (202) 328-0466; Email, amb.us@urm.lt or info@usa.mfa.lt
Social Media: Facebook, www.facebook.com/LTinUSA; Twitter, @LTembassyUS; Instagram, @LTinUSA; YouTube, www.youtube.com/channel/UCudmgIwSw_ z-v5CMfhyWZ8A/featured
U.S. Ambassador in Vilnius: Robert S. Gilchrist
State Dept. Country Office: (202) 647-8378

Luxembourg   Web, washington.mae.lu

Ambassador: Gaston Stronck
Chancery: 2200 Massachusetts Ave. N.W. 20008; (202) 265-4171; Fax, (202) 328-8270; Email, luxembassy .was@mae.etat.lu
U.S. Ambassador in Luxembourg: James R. Evans
State Dept. Country Office: (202) 647-5674

Macau   (See also China)

State Dept. Country Office: (202) 647-6300

Madagascar   Web, www.us-madagascar-embassy.org

Ambassador: Amielle Pelenne Niriniavisoa Marceda (Chargé d'Affaires)
Chancery: 2374 Massachusetts Ave. N.W. 20008; (202) 265-5525; Email, contact@us-madagascar-embassy.org
Social Media: Facebook, www.facebook.com/Madagascar .embassy.us; Twitter, @MadagascarembDC
U.S. Ambassador in Antananarivo: Michael P. Pelletier
State Dept. Country Office: (202) 647-8284

Malawi   Web, www.malawiembassy-dc.org

Ambassador: Edward Yakobe Sawerengera
Chancery: 2408 Massachusetts Ave. N.W. 20008;
    (202) 721-0270; Fax, (202) 721-0288
Social Media: Facebook, www.facebook.com/Embassy-of-
    the-Republic-of-Malawi-Washington-DC-
    321451241277730
U.S. Ambassador in Lilongwe: Robert K. Scott
State Dept. Country Office: (202) 647-9856

Malaysia

    Web, www.kln.gov.my/web/usa_washington

Ambassador: Dato' Azmil Mohd. Zabidi
Chancery: 3516 International Court N.W. 20008;
    (202) 572-9700; Fax, (202) 572-9882; Email,
    mwwashington@kln.gov.my
U.S. Ambassador in Kuala Lumpur: Brian McFeeter
State Dept. Country Office: (202) 647-2931

Maldives   Web, www.maldivesmission.com

Ambassador: Thilmeeza Hussain (in New York)
Chancery: 801 2nd Ave., #202E, New York, NY 10017;
    (212) 599-6194; Fax, (212) 661-6405; Email, info@
    maldivesmission.com
Social Media: Twitter, @MVPMNY
U.S. Ambassador: Alaina B. Teplitz (resident in Colombo,
    Sri Lanka)
State Dept. Country Office: (202) 647-1078

Mali   Web, www.maliembassy.us

Ambassador: Mahamadou Nimaga
Chancery: 2130 R St. N.W. 20008; (202) 332-2249;
    Fax, (202) 332-6603; Email,
    administration@maliembassy.us
Social Media: Facebook, www.facebook.com/
    MaliEmbassyUSA; Twitter, @MaliEmbassyUSA
U.S. Ambassador in Bamako: Dennis B. Hankins
State Dept. Country Office: (202) 647-1596

Malta

    Web, https://foreignaffairs.gov.mt/en/Embassies/
    Me_United_States

Ambassador: Keith Azzopardi
Chancery: 2017 Connecticut Ave. N.W. 20008; (202) 462-
    3611; Fax, (202) 387-5470; Email, maltaembassy
    .washington@gov.mt
U.S. Ambassador in Valletta: Gwendolyn Green (Chargé
    d'Affaires)
State Dept. Country Office: (202) 647-2632

Marshall Islands   Web, www.rmiembassyus.org

Ambassador: Gerald M. Zackios
Chancery: 2433 Massachusetts Ave. N.W. 20008; (202)
    234-5414; Fax, (202) 232-3236; Email, info@
    rmiembassyus.org
Social Media: Facebook, www.facebook.com/
    rmiembassyus

U.S. Ambassador in Majuro: Roxanne Cabral
State Dept. Country Office: (202) 647-5156

Mauritania

Ambassador: Mohamedoun Daddah
Chancery: 2129 Leroy Pl. N.W. 20008; (202) 232-5700;
    Fax, (202) 319-2623
U.S. Ambassador in Nouakchott: Michael Dodman
State Dept. Country Office: (202) 647-2637

Mauritius

Ambassador: Vikash Neethalia (Chargé d'Affaires)
Chancery: 1709 N St. N.W. 20036; (202) 244-1491;
    Fax, (202) 966-0983; Email, mauritius.
    embassy@verizon.net or washingtonemb@govmu.org
U.S Ambassador in Port Louis: Judes E. DeBaere (Chargé
    d'Affaires)
State Dept. Country Office: (202) 647-8284

Mexico

    Web, https://embamex.sre.gob.mx/eua/index.php/en/
    home

Ambassador: Martha Bárcena Coqui
Chancery: 1911 Pennsylvania Ave. N.W. 20006; (202) 728-
    1600; Fax, (202) 728-1698; Email, mexembusa@
    sre.gob.mx
Social Media: Facebook, www.facebook.com/
    EmbamexEUA; Twitter, @EmbamexEUA; YouTube,
    www.youtube.com/user/EUAEmbamex; Instagram,
    @embamexeua
U.S. Ambassador in Mexico City: John S. Creamer
    (Chargé d'Affaires)
State Dept. Country Office: (202) 647-8766

Micronesia   Web, www.fsmembassydc.org

Ambassador: Akillino H. Susaia
Chancery: 1725 N St. N.W. 20036; (202) 223-4383;
    Fax, (202) 223-4391
U.S. Ambassador in Kolonia: Carmen G. Cantor
State Dept. Country Office: (202) 647-5156

Moldova   Web, www.mfa.gov.md/en

Ambassador: Eugen Caras
Chancery: 2101 S St. N.W. 20008; (202) 667-1130;
    Fax, (202) 667-2624; Email, washington@mfa.gov.md
Social Media: Facebook, www.facebook.com/
    MoldovainUS; Twitter, @MoldovaEmbUS
U.S. Ambassador in Chisinau: Dereck J. Hogan
State Dept. Country Office: (202) 647-4331

Monaco   Web, www.monacodc.org

Ambassador: Maguy Maccario Doyle
Chancery: 888 17th St. N.W., #500, 20006; (202) 234-1530;
    Fax, (202) 244-7656; Email, info@monacodc.org
Social Media: Facebook; www.facebook.com/
    EmbassyofMonacoDC; Twitter, @MonacoEmbassyDC

U.S. Ambassador: Brian Aggeler (Chargé d'Affaires) (resident in Paris, France)
State Dept. Country Office: (202) 647-3072

Mongolia   Web, www.mongolianembassy.us

Ambassador: Bugaa Altangerel
Chancery: 2833 M St. N.W. 20007; (202) 333-7117; Fax, (202) 298-9227; Email, washington@mfa.gov.mn
Social Media: Facebook, www.facebook.com/ MongoliaDC; Twitter, @MGLEmbassy_USA
U.S. Ambassador in Ulaanbaatar: Michael S. Klecheski
State Dept. Country Office: (202) 647-6789

Montenegro

Ambassador: Nebojša Kaluđerović
Chancery: 1610 New Hampshire Ave. N.W. 20009; (202) 234-6108; Fax, (202) 234-6109; Email, usa@ mfa.gov.me
U.S. Ambassador in Podgorica: Judy Rising Reinke
State Dept. Country Office: (202) 647-7660

Morocco   Web, www.embassyofmorocco.us

Ambassador: Lalla Joumala Alaoui
Chancery: 3508 International Dr. N.W., 20008; (202) 462-7979; Fax, (202) 462-7643; Email, washingtonemb morocco@maec.gov.ma
Social Media: Twitter, @Morocco_usa
U.S. Ambassador in Rabat: David Greene (Chargé d'Affaires)
State Dept. Country Office: (202) 647-1724

Mozambique   Web, https://usa.embamoc.gov.mz

Ambassador: Carlos Dos Santos
Chancery: 1525 New Hampshire Ave. N.W. 20036; (202) 293-7147; Fax, (202) 835-0245; Email, embamoc@ aol.com
U.S. Ambassador in Maputo: Dennis W. Hearne
State Dept. Country Office: (202) 647-8252

Myanmar (Burma)

Web, www.mewashingtondc.org

Ambassador: Aung Lynn
Chancery: 2300 S St. N.W. 20008; (202) 332-3344; Fax, (202) 332-4351; Email, pyi.thayar@verizon.net or washington-embassy@mofa.gov.mm
Social Media: Facebook, www.facebook.com/ MyanmarEmbassyWashingtonDC
U.S. Ambassador in Rangoon: Thomas L. Vajda
State Dept. Country Office: (202) 647-0056

Namibia   Web, www.namibiaembassyusa.org

Ambassador: Monica N. Nashandi
Chancery: 1605 New Hampshire Ave. N.W. 20009; (202) 986-0540; Fax, (202) 986-0443; Email, info@ namibiaembassyusa.org
Social Media: Facebook, www.facebook.com/namibia embassyusa

U.S. Ambassador in Windhoek: Lisa Johnson
State Dept. Country Office: (202) 647-9858

Nauru   Web, www.un.int/nauru

Ambassador: Marlene I. Moses (in New York)
Chancery: 801 2nd Ave., 3rd Floor, New York, NY 10017; (212) 937-0074; Fax, (212) 937-0079; Email, nauru@ onecommonwealth.org
U.S. Ambassador: Tony Greubel (Chargé d'Affaires) (resident in Suva, Fiji)
State Dept. Country Office: (202) 647-2349

Nepal   Web, us.nepalembassy.gov.np

Ambassador: Dr. Arjun Kumar Karki
Chancery: 2730 34th Pl. N.W. 20007; (202) 667-4550; Fax, (202) 667-5534; Email, eonwashington@mofa .gov.np
Social Media: Facebook, www.facebook.com/ nepalembassyUSA; Twitter, @nepalembassyusa
U.S. Ambassador in Kathmandu: Randy Berry
State Dept. Country Office: (202) 647-2941

The Netherlands   Web, http://nlintheusa.com

Ambassador: André Haspels
Chancery: 4200 Linnean Ave. N.W. 20008; (202) 244-5300; Fax, (202) 362-3430; Email, was-ppc@ minbuza.nl
Social Media: Facebook, www.facebook.com/ NLintheUSA; Twitter, @NLintheUSA; YouTube, www.youtube.com/c/NLintheUSA
U.S. Ambassador at The Hague: Marja Verloop (Chargé d'Affaires)
State Dept. Country Office: (202) 647-6555

New Zealand

Web, www.mfat.govt.nz/en/countries-and-regions/ north-america/united-states-of-america/new-zealand-embassy-washington

Ambassador: Rosemary Banks
Chancery: 37 Observatory Circle N.W. 20008; (202) 328-4800; Fax, (202) 667-5227; Email, wshinfo@mfat .govt.nz
Social Media: Facebook, www.facebook.com/ NZEmbassyUS; Twitter, @NZEmbassyUS
U.S. Ambassador in Wellington: Kevin Covert (Chargé d'Affaires)
State Dept. Country Office: (202) 736-4712

Nicaragua   Web, www.consuladodenicaragua.com

Ambassador: Francisco Obadiah Campbell Hooker
Chancery: 1627 New Hampshire Ave. N.W. 20009; (202) 939-6570; Fax, (202) 939-6545; Email, mperalta@ cancilleria.gob.ni
U.S. Ambassador in Managua: Kevin K. Sullivan
State Dept. Country Office: (202) 647-4161

Niger   Web, www.embassyofniger.org

Ambassador: Abdallah Wafy
Chancery: 2204 R St. N.W. 20008; (202) 483-4224; Fax, (202) 483-3169; Email, communication@embassyofniger.org
U.S. Ambassador in Niamey: Eric P. Whitaker
State Dept. Country Office: (202) 647-2637

Nigeria   Web, www.nigeriaembassyusa.org

Ambassador: Sylvanus Adiewere Nsofor
Chancery: 3519 International Court N.W. 20008; (202) 800-7201; Email, info@nigeriaembassyusa.org
U.S. Ambassador in Abuja: Mary Beth Leonard
State Dept. Country Office: (202) 647-3469

North Macedonia

Web, www.mfa.gov.mk/washington

Ambassador: Vilma Petkovska (Chargé d'Affaires)
Chancery: 2129 Wyoming Ave. N.W. 20008; (202) 667-0501; Email, washington@mfa.gov.mk
U.S. Ambassador in Skopje: Kate Marie Byrnes
State Dept. Country Office: (202) 647-3747

Norway   Web, www.norway.no/en/usa

Ambassador: Kåre R. Aas
Chancery: 2900 K St. N.W., #500, 20007; (202) 333-6000; Fax, (202) 469-3990; Email, emb.washington@mfa.no
Social Media: Facebook, www.facebook.com/NorwegianEmbassyinWashington; Twitter, @NorwayUS; Instagram, @norwayinus
U.S. Ambassador in Oslo: Richard Riley (Chargé d'Affaires)
State Dept. Country Office: (202) 647-8431

Oman   Web, www.omani.info

Ambassador: Hunaina Al-Mughairy
Chancery: 2535 Belmont Rd. N.W. 20008; (202) 387-1980; Fax, (202) 745-4933; Email, inquiries@mofa.gov.om
U.S. Ambassador in Muscat: Leslie M. Tsou
State Dept. Country Office: (202) 647-8821

Pakistan   Web, www.embassyofpakistanusa.org

Ambassador: Asad Majeed Khan
Chancery: 3517 International Court N.W. 20008; (202) 243-6500; Fax, (202) 686-1534; Email, consularsection@embassyofpakistanusa.org
Social Media: Facebook, www.facebook.com/PakistaninUS; Twitter, @PakinUSA; YouTube, www.youtube.com/user/pakistanembassy
U.S. Ambassador in Islamabad: Angela Aggeler (Chargé d'Affaires)
State Dept. Country Office: (202) 647-9434

Palau   Web, www.palauembassy.org

Ambassador: Hersey Kyota
Chancery: 1701 Pennsylvania Ave. N.W., #200, 20006; (202) 349-8598; Email, info@palauembassy.org

Social Media: Facebook, www.facebook.com/PalauEmbassyDC
U.S. Ambassador in Koror: John Hennessey-Niland
State Dept. Country Office: (202) 647-5156

Palestine Liberation Organization

On September 10, 2018, the U.S. government ordered the PLO mission to the United States to close.
On October 18, 2018, the U.S. government merged its diplomatic mission serving Palestinians with the U.S. embassy in Israel.

Panama   Web, www.embassyofpanama.org

Ambassador: Juan De Dianous
Chancery: 2862 McGill Terrace N.W. 20008; (202) 483-1407; Fax, (202) 483-8413; Email, info@embassyofpanama.org
Social Media: Facebook, www.facebook.com/EmbassyofPanama; Twitter, @EmbPanamaUSA; Instagram, @embpanamausa
U.S. Ambassador in Panama City: Stewart Tuttle (Chargé d'Affaires)
State Dept. Country Office: (202) 647-4992

Papua New Guinea   Web, www.pngembassy.org

Ambassador: Rupa Abraham Mulina
Chancery: 1825 K St. N.W., #1010, 20006; (202) 745-3680; Fax, (202) 745-3679; Email, info@pngembassy.org
U.S. Ambassador in Port Moresby: Erin E. McKee
State Dept. Country Office: (202) 736-4745

Paraguay   Web, www.mre.gov.py/embaparusa

Ambassador: Manuel María Cáceres
Chancery: 2209 Massachusetts Ave. N.W. 20008; (202) 483-6960; Fax, (202) 234-4508; Email, gabineteembaparusa@mre.gov.py
Social Media: Facebook, www.facebook.com/Embajada-del-Paraguay-en-los-Estados-Unidos-1601585323408266
U.S. Ambassador in Asunción: Joseph Salazar (Chargé d'Affaires)
State Dept. Country Office: (202) 647-1551

Peru   Web, www.embassyofperu.org

Ambassador: Hugo de Zela
Chancery: 1700 Massachusetts Ave. N.W. 20036; (202) 833-9860; Fax, (202) 659-8124; Email, digitaldiplomacy@embassyofperu.us
Social Media: Facebook, www.facebook.com/EmbassyPeruInTheUSA; Twitter, @PeruInTheUSA; YouTube, www.youtube.com/user/TheEmbassyofPeru; Instagram, @peruintheusa
U.S. Ambassador in Lima: Lisa Kenna
State Dept. Country Office: (202) 647-2807

Philippines   Web, https://philippineembassy-dc.org

Ambassador: Jose Manuel del Gallego Romualdez

Chancery: Bataan St., 1600 Massachusetts Ave. N.W. 20036; (202) 467-9300; Fax, (202) 467-9417; Email, ambassador@phembassy-us.org
Social Media: Facebook, www.facebook.com/PHinUSA/app/?sk=app_190322544333196; Twitter, @philippinesusa; YouTube, www.youtube.com/user/philippineembassyusa; Instagram, @philippinesusa
U.S. Ambassador in Manila: John C. Law (Chargé d'Affaires)
State Dept. Country Office: (202) 647-2927

Poland   Web, http://washington.mfa.gov.pl/en
Ambassador: Piotr Wilczek
Chancery: 2640 16th St. N.W. 20009; (202) 499-1700; Fax, (202) 328-6271; Email, washington.amb@msz.gov.pl
Social Media: Facebook, www.facebook.com/EmbassyofPolandWashingtonDC; Twitter, @PolishEmbassyUS; Instagram, @PolishEmbassyUS; YouTube, www.youtube.com/user/PolishEmbassyDC
U.S. Ambassador in Warsaw: B. Bix Aliu (Chargé d'Affaires)
State Dept. Country Office: (202) 647-0460

Portugal
Web, www.washingtondc.embaixadaportugal.mne.pt
Ambassador: Domingos Fezas Vital
Chancery: 2012 Massachusetts Ave. N.W. 20036; (202) 350-5400; Fax, (202) 462-3726; Email, info@embassyportugal-us.org
Social Media: Facebook, www.facebook.com/PortugalintheUS
U.S. Ambassador in Lisbon: Kristin M. Kane (Chargé d'Affaires)
State Dept. Country Office: (202) 647-2632

Qatar   Web, http://washington.embassy.qa/en
Ambassador: Sheikh Meshal Bin Hamad Al-Thani
Chancery: 2555 M St. N.W. 20037; (202) 274-1600; Fax, (202) 237-0061; Email, info.dc@mofa.gov.qa
Social Media: Twitter, @QatarEmbassyUSA; Instagram, @qatarembassyusa
U.S. Ambassador in Doha: Greta C. Holtz (Chargé d'Affaires)
State Dept. Country Office: (202) 647-2129

Romania   Web, http://washington.mae.ro/en
Ambassador: George Cristian Maior
Chancery: 1607 23rd St. N.W. 20008; (202) 332-4829; (202) 332-4846; Fax, (202) 232-4748 Email, washington@mae.ro
Social Media: Facebook, www.facebook.com/romanian.embassy.us; Instagram, @romania.in.us
U.S. Ambassador in Bucharest: David Muniz (Chargé d'Affaires)
State Dept. Country Office: (202) 736-7152

Russia   Web, https://washington.mid.ru/en
Ambassador: Anatoly I. Antonov
Chancery: 2650 Wisconsin Ave. N.W. 20007; (202) 298-5700; Fax, (202) 298-5735; Email, rusembusa@mid.ru
Social Media: Facebook, www.facebook.com/RusEmbUSA; Instagram, @rusembusa; Twitter, @RusEmbUSA
U.S. Ambassador in Moscow: John J. Sullivan
State Dept. Country Office: (202) 647-9806

Rwanda   Web, www.rwandaembassy.org
Ambassador: Mathilde Mukantabana
Chancery: 1714 New Hampshire Ave. N.W., 20009; (202) 232-2882; Fax, (202) 232-4544; Email, info@rwandaembassy.org
Social Media: Twitter, @RwandaInUSA; Instagram, @rwandainusa
U.S. Ambassador in Kigali: Peter H. Vrooman
State Dept. Country Office: (202) 647-4965

Saint Kitts and Nevis
Web, www.oas.org/en/member_states/member_state.asp?sCode=STK
Ambassador: Dr. Everson Hull
Chancery: 1627 K St. N.W. 20006; (202) 686-2636; Fax, (202) 686-5740; Email, stkittsnevis@embskn.com
U.S. Ambassador: Linda S. Taglialatela (resident in Bridgetown, Barbados)
State Dept. Country Office: (202) 647-4384

Saint Lucia   Web, www.embassyofstlucia.org
Ambassador: Anton Edmunds
Chancery: 1629 K St. N.W., #1250, 20006; (202) 364-6792 or (571) 527-1375; Fax, (202) 364-6723 or (571) 384-7930; Email, embassydc@gosl.gov.lc
Social Media: Facebook, www.facebook.com/embassyofsaintlucia
U.S. Ambassador: Linda S. Taglialatela (resident in Bridgetown, Barbados)
State Dept. Country Office: (202) 647-4384

Saint Vincent and the Grenadines
Web, www.embsvg.com
Ambassador: Lou-Anne Gaylene Gilchrist
Chancery: 1627 K St. N.W., #1202, 20006; (202) 364-6730; Email, mail@embsvg.com
U.S. Ambassador: Linda S. Taglialatela (resident in Bridgetown, Barbados)
State Dept. Country Office: (202) 647-4384

Samoa
Web, www.un.int/samoa/samoa/embassy-independent-state-samoa-united-states-america
Samoa maintains a Permanent Mission to the United Nations.
Ambassador: Aliioaiga Feturi Elisaia (in New York)

UN Chancery: 685 3rd Ave., #1102, New York, NY 10017; (212) 599-6196; Fax, (212) 599-0797; Email, samoa@un.int
U.S. Ambassador to Apia: Scott Brown
State Dept. Country Office: (202) 736-4745

San Marino

Ambassador: Paolo Rondelli
Chancery: 1711 N St. N.W., 2nd Floor 20036; (202) 223-2418; Email, smrassistant@gmail.com
San Marino is also represented by Consul General Abigail (Abby) Rupp.
U.S. Ambassador (Virtual Embassy): Thomas Smitham (Chargé d'Affaires)
State Dept. Country Office: (202) 647-3072

São Tomé and Príncipe

Ambassador: Ovidio Manuel Barbosa Pequeno
Chancery: 1211 Connecticut Ave. N.W., #300, 20036; (202) 775-2075, 2075; Fax, (202) 775-2077; Email, embstpusa@verizon.net
U.S. Ambassador: Samuel R. Watson (Chargé d'Affaires)
State Dept. Country Office: (202) 647-4896

Saudi Arabia   Web, www.saudiembassy.net

Ambassador: Princess Reema Bin Abdulaziz Al Saud
Chancery: 601 New Hampshire Ave. N.W. 20037; (202) 342-3800; Fax, (202) 944-5983
Social Media: Twitter, @SaudiEmbassyUSA; YouTube, www.youtube.com/user/saudiembassyusa
U.S. Ambassador in Riyadh: Martina Strong (Chargé d'Affaires)
State Dept. Country Office: (202) 647-7550

Senegal   Web, www.ambasenegal-us.org

Ambassador: Mansour Elimane Kane
Chancery: 2215 M St. N.W. 20037; (202) 234-0540; Fax, (202) 629-2961; Email, contact@ambasenegal-us.org
U.S. Ambassador in Dakar: Tulinabo Salama Mushingi
State Dept. Country Office: (202) 647-6046

Serbia   Web, www.serbiaembusa.org

Ambassador: Marko Djuric
Chancery: 2233 Wisconsin Ave. N.W., #410, 20007; (202) 332-0333; Fax, (202) 332-3933; Email, info@serbiaembusa.org
Social Media: Facebook, www.facebook.com/SerbiaEmbWashin; Twitter, @SRBinUS
U.S. Ambassador in Belgrade: Anthony F. Godfrey
State Dept. Country Office: (202) 647-0310

Seychelles

Web, www.mfa.gov.sc/static.php?filter=11&content_id=24
Ambassador: Ronny Jumeau (in New York)

Chancery: 685 3rd Ave., 11th Floor, #1107, New York, NY 10017; (212) 687-9766, Fax, (212) 972-1786; Email, Seychelles@un.int
U.S. Ambassador: Judes E. DeBaere (Chargé d'Affaires)
State Dept. Country Office: (202) 647-8284

Sierra Leone   Web, www.embassyofsierraleone.net

Ambassador: Sidique Abou-Bakarr Wai
Chancery: 1701 19th St. N.W. 20009-1605; (202) 939-9261; Fax, (202) 483-1798; Email, info@embassyofsierraleone.net
Social Media: Facebook, www.facebook.com/sierraleoneembassy; Twitter, @slembassy_usa
U.S. Ambassador in Freetown: David Reimer
State Dept. Country Office: (202) 647-4567

Singapore   Web, www.mfa.gov.sg/washington

Ambassador: Ashok Kumar Mirpuri
Chancery: 3501 International Pl. N.W. 20008; (202) 537-3100; Fax, (202) 537-0876; Email, singemb_was@mfa.sg
Social Media: Facebook, www.facebook.com/SingaporeEmbassyDC; Twitter, @SingaporeEmbDC
U.S. Ambassador in Singapore: Rafik Mansour (Chargé d'Affaires)
State Dept. Country Office: (202) 647-7292

Slovakia   Web, www.mzv.sk/washington

Ambassador: Radovan Javorcik
Chancery: 3523 International Ct. N.W. 20008; (202) 237-1054; Fax, (202) 237-6438; Email, emb.washington@mzv.sk
Social Media: Facebook, www.facebook.com/SlovakEmbassyUS?fref=pb&hc_location=profile_browser; Twitter, @SlovakEmbassyUS; YouTube, www.youtube.com/user/mzvsr
U.S. Ambassador in Bratislava: Bridget A. Brink
State Dept. Country Office: (202) 647-3191

Slovenia   Web, http://washington.embassy.si

Ambassador: *Tone Kajzer*
Chancery: 2410 California St. N.W. 20008; (202) 386-6601; Fax, (202) 386-6633; Email, sloembassy.washington@gov.si
Social Media: Facebook, www.facebook.com/SLOembassyUSA; Twitter, @SLOinUSA
U.S. Ambassador in Ljubljana: Susan K. Falatko (Chargé d'Affaires)
State Dept. Country Office: (202) 647-4782

Solomon Islands   Web, www.mfaet.gov.sb

Ambassador: Robert Sisilo (in New York)
Chancery: 800 2nd Ave., #400L, New York, NY 10017; (212) 599-6192; Fax, (212) 661-8925; Email, simun@solomons.com
U.S. Ambassador: Erin E. McKee (resident in Port Moresby, Papua New Guinea)
State Dept. Country Office: (202) 736-4745

Somalia   Web, www.somaliembassydc.net

Ambassador: Ahmed Isse Awad
Chancery: 1705 DeSales St. N.W., #300, 20036-4421;
(202) 296-0570; Fax, (202) 833-1523; Email, info@
somaliembassydc.net
Social Media: Twitter, @SomaliEmbDC
The Washington embassy ceased operations May 1991.
The U.S. embassy in Mogadishu is unstaffed. Diplomatic relations are handled out of the U.S. Embassy in
Nairobi, Kenya.
U.S. Ambassador in Mogadishu: Donald Y. Yamamoto
State Dept. Country Office: (202) 647-8284

South Africa   Web, www.saembassy.org

Ambassador: Nomaindiya Cathleen Mfeketo
Chancery: 3051 Massachusetts Ave. N.W. 20008; (202)
232-4400; Fax, (202) 265-1607; Email, crossleyl@
dirco.gov.za
Social Media: Facebook, www.facebook.com/RSAinUSA;
Twitter, @RSAinDC; Instagram, @rsainusa
U.S. Ambassador in Pretoria: John Groarke (Chargé
d'Affaires)
State Dept. Country Office: (202) 647-9862

South Sudan   Web, www.southsudanembassyusa.org

Ambassador: Phillip Jada Natana
Chancery: 1015 31st St. N.W., #300, 20007; (202) 600-238;
Fax, (202) 644-9910; Email, info.ssdembassy@gmail
.com
U.S. Ambassador in Juba: Jon F. Danilowicz (Chargé
d'Affaires)
State Dept. Country Office: (202) 647-7491

Spain

Web, www.exteriores.gob.es/Embajadas/
WASHINGTON

Ambassador: Santiago Cabanas Ansorena
Chancery: 2375 Pennsylvania Ave. N.W. 20037; (202) 452-
0100; Fax, (202) 833-5670; Email, emb.washington@
maec.es
Social Media: Facebook, www.facebook.com/
SpainInTheUSA; Twitter, @SpainInTheUSA;
YouTube, www.youtube.com/channel/UCNHaRlVcSv
DhoGIaZY8Wz0A; Instagram, @spainintheusa
U.S. Ambassador in Madrid: Conrad Tribble (Chargé
d'Affaires)
State Dept. Country Office: (202) 647-3063

Sri Lanka   Web, www.slembassyusa.org

Ambassador: Ravinatha Aryasinha
Chancery: 3025 Whitehaven St. N.W. 20008; (202) 483-
4025; Fax, (202) 232-7181; Email, slembassy@
slembassyusa.org
Social Media: Facebook, www.facebook.com/
slembassyusa; Twitter, @EmbassyofSL
U.S. Ambassador in Colombo: Alaina B. Teplitz
State Dept. Country Office: (202) 647-7483

Sudan   Web, www.sudanembassy.org

Ambassador: Mohamed Abbas
Chancery: 2210 Massachusetts Ave. N.W. 20008; (202)
338-8565; Fax, (202) 667-2406; Email, consular@
sudanembassy.org
U.S. Ambassador in Khartoum: Brian Shukan (Chargé
d'Affaires)
State Dept. Country Office: (202) 647-9778

Suriname   Web, www.surinameembassy.org

Ambassador: Niermala Badrising
Chancery: 4201 Connecticut Ave. N.W., #400, 20008;
(202) 629-4302; Fax, (202) 629-4769; Email, amb.vs@
foreignaffairs.gov.sr
U.S. Ambassador in Paramaribo: Karen L. Williams
State Dept. Country Office: (202) 647-4628

Sweden

Web, www.swedenabroad.se/en/embassies/usa-
washington

Ambassador: Karin Olofsdotter
Chancery: 2900 K St. N.W. 20007; (202) 467-2600;
Fax, (202) 467-2699; Email, ambassaden.washington@
gov.se
Social Media: Facebook, www.facebook.com/
swedeninusa; Twitter, @SwedeninUSA; Instagram,
@swedeninusa
U.S. Ambassador in Stockholm: Pamela M. Tremont
(Chargé d'Affaires)
State Dept. Country Office: (202) 647-9980

Switzerland   Web, www.eda.admin.ch/washington

Ambassador: Jacques Pitteloud
Chancery: 2201 Wisconsin Ave. N.W., #300, 20007-4105;
(202) 745-7900; Fax, (202) 387-2564; Email,
washington@eda.admin.ch
Social Media: Facebook, www.facebook.com/Swiss
EmbassyUSA; Twitter, @SwissEmbassyUSA;
Instagram, @SwissEmbassyUSA; YouTube, www
.youtube.com/user/ThinkSwiss
U.S. Ambassador in Bern: Eva Weigold Schultz (Chargé
d'Affaires)
State Dept. Country Office: (202) 647-1457

Syria

The U.S. Embassy in Damascus suspended operations in
February 2012 and no longer provides routine consular
services. Emergency assistance to U.S. citizens is
available through the U.S. Interests Section of the
Embassy of the Czech Republic in Damascus or the
U.S. Embassy in Amman, Jordan.
Chancery (currently closed): 2215 Wyoming Ave. N.W.
20008; (202) 232-6313; Fax, (202) 234-9548;
Email, info@syrembassy.net
U.S. Special Envoy: Aimee Cutrona (Acting)

Taiwan Web, www.taiwanembassy.org/us_en

Representation is maintained by the Taipei Economic and Cultural Representatives Office in the United States: 4201 Wisconsin Ave. N.W. 20016; (202) 895-1800; Email, usa@mofa.gov.tw

Social Media: Facebook, www.facebook.com/TECRO .USA; Twitter, @TECRO_USA; Instagram, @taiwan_ in_the_us

Representative of the Republic of China (in Taiwan): Stanley Kao

The United States maintains unofficial relations with Taiwan through the American Institute in Taiwan.

American Institute: 1700 N. Moore St., #1700, Arlington, VA 22209-1385; (703) 525-8474; John J. Norris Jr., Director

State Dept. Country Office: (202) 647-7711

Tajikistan Web, https://mfa.tj/en/washington

Ambassador: Farhod Salim

Chancery: 1005 New Hampshire Ave. N.W. 20037; (202) 223-6090; Fax, (202) 223-6091; Email, tajemus@mfa.tj or tajikistan@verizon.net

Social Media: Facebook, www.facebook.com/Tajikistan EmbassyUSA

U.S. Ambassador in Dushanbe: John Mark Pommersheim

State Dept. Country Office: (202) 647-9499

Tanzania Web, www.tanzaniaembassy-us.org

Ambassador: Wilson Mutagaywa Masilingi

Chancery: 1232 22nd St. N.W. 20037; (202) 884-1080; Fax, (202) 797-7408; Email, ubalozi@tanzaniaembassy-us.org

Social Media: Facebook, www.facebook.com/Tanzania EmbassyUS; Twitter, @TZEmbassyUS

U.S. Ambassador in Dar es Salaam: Donald J. Wright

State Dept. Country Office: (202) 647-5924

Thailand Web, www.thaiembdc.org

Ambassador: Thani Thongphakdi

Chancery: 1024 Wisconsin Ave. N.W. 20007; (202) 944-3600; Fax, (202) 944-3611

Social Media: Facebook, www.facebook.com/Thaiembdc; Twitter, @ThaiEmbDC; YouTube, www.youtube.com/channel/UCEo3cdhO2qv6Ql1R7e6qZsQ

U.S. Ambassador in Bangkok: Michael Heath (Chargé d'Affaires)

State Dept. Country Office: (202) 647-3095

Timor-Leste Web, www.timorlesteembassy.org

Ambassador: Domingos Sarmento Alves

Chancery: 4201 Connecticut Ave. N.W., #504, 20008; (202) 966-3202; Fax, (202) 966-3205; Email, info@ timorlesteembassy.org

Social Media: Facebook, www.facebook.com/Embassy-of-Timor-Leste-in-Washington-DC-USA-171109652252; Twitter, @ EmbTlUSA

U.S. Ambassador in Dili: C. Kevin Blackstone

State Dept. Country Office: (202) 647-7292

Togo Web, http://embassyoftogousa.com

Ambassador: Frédéric Edem Hegbe

Chancery: 2208 Massachussetts Ave. N.W. 20008; (202) 234-4212; Fax, (202) 232-3190; Email, embassyoftogo@ hotmail.com

U.S. Ambassador in Lomé: Eric W. Stromayer

State Dept. Country Office: (202) 647-3407

Tonga

Web, http://tongaconsul.com, www.un.int/tonga

Consul General (in California): Sela Tukia

Consulate-General: 1350 Old Bayshore Hwy, #610, Burlingame, CA 94010; (650) 685-1001; Email, consulategeneraloftonga@gmail.com

Tonga maintains a Permanent Mission to the United Nations.

Ambassador to the UN: Mahe 'Uli'uli Sandhurst Tupouniua

UN Chancery: 250 E. 51st St., New York, NY 10022; (917) 369-1025; Fax, (917) 369-1024; Email, tongaun mission@aol.com

U.S. Ambassador: Tony Greubel (Chargé d'Affaires) (resident in Suva, Fiji)

State Dept. Country Office: (202) 647-2349

Trinidad and Tobago

Web, https://foreign.gov.tt/missions-consuls/tt-missions-abroad/diplomatic-missions/embassy-washington-dc-us

Ambassador: Anthony Phillips-Spencer

Chancery: 1708 Massachusetts Ave. N.W. 20036; (202) 467-6490; Fax, (202) 785-3130; Email, embdcinfo@ foreign.gov.tt

U.S. Ambassador in Port-of-Spain: Shante Moore (Chargé d'Affaires)

State Dept. Country Office: (202) 647-4628

Tunisia Web, www.tunisianembassy.org

Ambassador: Fayçal Gouia

Chancery: 1515 Massachusetts Ave. N.W. 20005; (202) 862-1850; Fax, (202) 862-1858; Email, at.washington@ tunisianembassy.org

Social Media: Facebook, www.facebook.com/ TUNISIANEMBASSYUSA; Twitter, @TuniEmbassy

U.S. Ambassador in Tunis: Donald Blome

State Dept. Country Office: (202) 647-4676

Turkey Web, http://vasington.be.mfa.gov.tr

Ambassador: Serdar Kiliç

Chancery: 2525 Massachusetts Ave. N.W. 20008; (202) 612-6701; Fax, (202) 612-6744; Email, embassy .washingtondc@mfa.gov.tr

Social Media: Facebook, www.facebook.com/ turkishembassy; Twitter, @TurkishEmbassy

U.S. Ambassador in Ankara: David M. Satterfield

State Dept. Country Office: (202) 647-1295

Turkmenistan   Web, http://usa.tmembassy.gov.tm

Ambassador: Meret B. Orazov
Chancery: 2207 Massachusetts Ave. N.W. 20008; (202) 588-1500; Email, turkmenembassyus@verizon.net
U.S. Ambassador in Ashgabat: Matthew S. Klimow
State Dept. Country Office: (202) 647-9024

Tuvalu   Web, www.un.int/tuvalu/tuvalu/embassies

Ambassador: Samuelu Laloniu (in New York)
Chancery: 800 E. 2nd Ave., #400B, New York, NY 10017; (212) 490-0534; Fax, (212) 808-4975; Email, Tuvalu.un @gmail.com
U.S. Ambassador: Tony Greubel (Chargé d'Affaires) (resident in Suva, Fiji)
State Dept. Country Office: (202) 647-2349

Uganda   Web, https://washington.mofa.go.ug

Ambassador: Mull Ssebujja Katende
Chancery: 5911 16th St. N.W. 20011; (202) 726-7100; Fax, (202) 726-1727; Email, washington@mofa.go.ug or info@ugandaembassyus.org
Social Media: Facebook, www.facebook.com/Uganda. Washington; Twitter, @UgaEmbaWashDC
U.S. Ambassador in Kampala: Natalie E. Brown
State Dept. Country Office: (202) 647-9742

Ukraine   Web, http://usa.mfa.gov.ua

Ambassador: Volodymyr Yelchenko
Chancery: 3350 M St. N.W. 20007; (202) 349-2963; Fax, (202) 333-0817; Email, emb_us@mfa.gov.ua
Social Media: Facebook, www.facebook.com/ukr.embassy .usa; Twitter, @UKRintheUSA
U.S. Ambassador in Kyiv: Kristina Kvien (Chargé d'Affaires)
State Dept. Country Office: (202) 647-6764

United Arab Emirates

Web, www.uae-embassy.org

Ambassador: Yousef Al Otaiba
Chancery: 3522 International Court N.W., #400, 20008; (202) 243-2400; Fax, (202) 243-2432
Social Media: Facebook, www.facebook.com/ UAEEmbassyUS; Twitter, @UAEEmbassyUS; Instagram, @ uaeembassyus; YouTube, www.youtube .com/channel/UCAtFXa5-B8SP7zdBMqipEnQ
U.S. Ambassador in Abu Dhabi: Sean Murphy (Chargé d'Affaires)
State Dept. Country Office: (202) 647-4709

United Kingdom

Web, www.gov.uk/government/world/organisations/ british-embassy-washington

Ambassador: Karen Pierce
Chancery: 3100 Massachusetts Ave. N.W. 20008; (202) 588-6500; Fax, (202) 588-7870; Email, britishembassy enquiries@gmail.com

Social Media: Facebook, www.facebook.com/ukinusa; Twitter, @UKinUSA; Instagram, @ukinusa
U.S. Ambassador in London: Yael Lempert (Chargé d'Affaires)
State Dept. Country Office: (202) 647-2441

United Nations   Web, https://unicwash.org

Secretary-General: António Guterres
Information Center: 1775 K St. N.W., #500, 20006; (202) 331-8670; Fax, (202) 331-9191; Email, unicdc@unic.org
Social Media: Facebook, www.facebook.com/ UNWashington; Twitter, @unicdc; YouTube, www .youtube.com/user/UNWashington; Instagram, @unicdc
U.S. Ambassador: Linda Thomas-Greenfield
State Dept. Country Office: (202) 736-7555

Uruguay

Ambassador: Andrés Durán
Chancery: 1913 Eye St. N.W. 20006; (202) 331-1313; Fax, (202) 331-8142; Email, urueeuu@mrree.gub.uy
Social Media: Twitter, @UruguayinUSA
U.S. Ambassador in Montevideo: Jennifer Savage (Chargé d'Affaires)
State Dept. Country Office: (202) 647-0653

Uzbekistan   Web, www.uzbekistan.org

Ambassador: Javlon Vakhabov
Chancery: 1746 Massachusetts Ave. N.W. 20036; (202) 887-5300; Fax, (202) 293-6804; Email, info.washington @mfa.uz
Social Media: Facebook, www.facebook.com/ UZEmbassyDC; Twitter, @UZEmbassyDC
U.S. Ambassador in Tashkent: Daniel N. Rosenblum
State Dept. Country Office: (202) 647-6765

Vanuatu   Web, www.un.int/vanuatu

Vanuatu maintains a Permanent Mission to the United Nations.
Ambassador to the UN: Odo Tevi
UN Chancery: 800 E. 2nd Ave., #400B, New York, NY 10017; (212) 661-4303; Email, vanunmis@aol.com
U.S. Ambassador: Erin E. McKee (resident in Port Moresby, Papua New Guinea)
State Dept. Country Office: (202) 736-4745

Vatican City   (See The Holy See)

Venezuela   Web, eeuu.embajada.gob.ve

Chargé d'Affaires: Carlos Vecchio
Chancery: 1099 30th St. N.W. 20007; (202) 342-2214; Fax, (202) 342-6820; Email, despacho.embveus@ mppre.gob.ve
U.S. Ambassador in Caracas: James Story
State Dept. Country Office: (202) 647-4984

Vietnam   Web, http://vietnamembassy-usa.org

Ambassador: Ha Kim Ngoc
Chancery: 1233 20th St. N.W., #400, 20036; (202) 861-0737; Fax, (202) 861-0917; Email, vanphong@vietnamembassy.us
U.S. Ambassador in Hanoi: Dan Kritenbrink
State Dept. Country Office: (202) 647-4023

Western Samoa   (See Samoa)

Yemen   Web, www.yemenembassy.org

Ambassador: Ahmed Awad Binmubarak
Chancery: 2319 Wyoming Ave. N.W. 20008; (202) 965-4760; Fax, (202) 337-2017; Email, information@yemenembassy.org
Social Media: Facebook, www.facebook.com/Yemenembassy.DC; Twitter, @YemenEmbassy_DC
U.S. Ambassador in Sana'a: Christopher P. Henzel
State Dept. Country Office: (202) 647-6558

Zambia   Web, www.zambiaembassy.org

Ambassador: Lazarous Kapambwe
Chancery: 2200 R St. N.W. 20008; (202) 234-4111; Fax, (202) 332-0826; Email, info@zambiaembassy.org
Social Media: Facebook, www.facebook.com/EmbassyOfTheRepublicOfZambia
U.S. Ambassador in Lusaka: David J. Young (Chargé d'Affaires)
State Dept. Country Office: (202) 647-9850

Zimbabwe   Web, www.zimembassydc.org

Ambassador: Sarah Bhoroma
Chancery: 1608 New Hampshire Ave. N.W. 20009; (202) 332-7100; Fax, (202) 483-9326; Email, zimembassydc@gmail.com
U.S. Ambassador in Harare: Brian A. Nichols
State Dept. Country Office: (202) 647-9852

Freedom of Information Act

Access to government information remains a key issue in Washington. In 1966, Congress passed legislation to broaden access: the Freedom of Information Act, or FOIA (PL 89-487; codified in 1967 by PL 90-23). Amendments to expand access even further were passed into law over President Gerald Ford's veto in 1974 (PL 93-502).

Several organizations in Washington specialize in access to government information. See the "Freedom of Information" section in the Communications and the Media chapter for details (p. 112). The Justice Department electronically publishes a clearinghouse of FOIA information at www.justice.gov/oip/foia-resources.

1966 Act

The 1966 Act requires executive branch agencies and independent commissions of the federal government to make records, reports, policy statements, and staff manuals available to citizens who request them, unless the materials fall into one of nine exempted categories:

- secret national security or foreign policy information

- internal personnel practices

- information exempted by law (e.g., income tax returns)

- trade secrets, other confidential commercial or financial information

- inter-agency or intra-agency memos

- personal information, personnel, or medical files

- law enforcement investigatory information

- information related to reports on financial institutions

- geological and geophysical information

1974 Amendments

Further clarification of the rights of citizens to gain access to government information came in late 1974, when Congress enacted legislation to remove some of the obstacles that the bureaucracy had erected since 1966. Included in the amendments are provisions that:

- Require federal agencies to publish their indexes of final opinions on settlements of internal cases, policy statements, and administrative staff manuals. If, under special circumstances, the indexes are not published, they are to be furnished to any person requesting them for the cost of duplication. The 1966 law simply required agencies to make such indexes available for public inspection and copying.

- Require agencies to release unlisted documents to someone requesting them with a reasonable description (a change designed to ensure that an agency could not refuse to provide material simply because the applicant could not give its precise title).

- Direct each agency to publish a uniform set of fees for providing documents at the cost of finding and copying them. The amendment allows waiver or reduction of those fees when in the public interest.

- Set time limits for agency responses to requests: ten working days for an initial request; twenty working days for an appeal from an initial refusal to produce documents; a possible ten-working-day extension that can be granted only once in a single case.

- Set a thirty-day time limit for an agency response to a complaint filed in court under the act; provide that the courts give such cases priority attention at the appeal, as well as the trial, level.

- Empower federal district courts to order agencies to produce withheld documents and to examine the contested materials privately *(in camera)* to determine if they are properly exempted.

- Require annual agency reports to Congress, including a list of all agency decisions to withhold information requested under the act; the reasons; the appeals; the results; all relevant rules; the fee schedule; and the names of officials responsible for each denial of information.

- Allow courts to order the government to pay attorneys' fees and court costs for persons winning suits against them under the act.

- Authorize a court to find that an agency employee has acted capriciously or arbitrarily in withholding information; stipulate that disciplinary action is determined by Civil Service Commission proceedings.

- Amend and clarify the wording of the national defense and national security exemption to make clear that it applies only to *properly* classified information.

- Amend the wording of the law enforcement exemption to allow withholding of information that, if disclosed, would interfere with enforcement proceedings, deprive someone of a fair trial or hearing, invade personal privacy in an unwarranted way, disclose the identity of a confidential source, disclose investigative techniques, or endanger law enforcement personnel; protect from disclosure all information from a confidential source obtained by a criminal law enforcement agency or a lawful national security investigation.

- Provide that separable nonexempt portions of requested material be released after deletion of the exempt portions.

- Require an annual report from the attorney general to Congress.

1976 Government in the Sunshine Act

Passed in 1976 to bolster the FOIA, the Government in the Sunshine Act was designed to further government transparency. As such, the following amendments were made to Exemption 3 of the FOIA:

- Information pertaining to national defense,

- Related exclusively to internal personnel rules and practices,

- Related to accusation of a crime,

- Related to information where disclosure would constitute a breach of privacy,

- Related to investigatory records where the information would harm the proceedings,

- Related to information that would lead to financial speculation or endanger the stability of any financial institution, and

- Related to the agency's participation in legal proceedings.

1984 Amendments

In 1984, Congress enacted legislation that clarified the requirements of the Central Intelligence Agency (CIA) to respond to citizen requests for information. Included in the amendments are provisions that:

- Authorize the CIA to close from FOIA review certain operational files that contain information on the identities of sources and methods. The measure removed the requirement that officials search the files for material that might be subject to disclosure.

- Reverse a ruling by the Justice Department and the Office of Management and Budget that invoked the Privacy Act to deny individuals FOIA access to information about themselves in CIA records. HR 5164 required the CIA to search files in response to FOIA requests by individuals for information about themselves.

- Require the CIA to respond to FOIA requests for information regarding covert actions or suspected CIA improprieties.

All agencies of the executive branch have issued regulations to implement the Freedom of Information Act. To locate a specific agency's regulations, consult the general index of the *Code of Federal Regulations* under "Information availability" or search in www.USA.gov, "FOIA Regulations."

Electronic Freedom of Information Act of 1996

In 1996, Congress enacted legislation clarifying that electronic documents are subject to the same FOIA disclosure rules as are printed documents. The 1996 law also requires federal agencies to make records available to the public in various electronic formats, such as email, compact disc, and files accessible via the Internet. An additional measure seeks to improve the government's response time on FOIA requests by requiring agencies to report annually on the number of pending requests and how long it will take to respond.

Homeland Security Act of 2002

In 2002, Congress passed legislation that established the Homeland Security Department and exempted from FOIA disclosure rules certain information about national defense systems. Included in the act are provisions that:

- Grant broad exemption from FOIA requirements to information that private companies share with the government about vulnerabilities in the nation's critical infrastructure.

- Exempt from FOIA rules and other federal and state disclosure requirements any information about the critical infrastructure that is submitted voluntarily to a covered federal agency to ensure the security of this infrastructure and protected systems; require accompanying statement that such information is being submitted voluntarily in expectation of nondisclosure protection.

- Require the secretary of homeland security to establish procedures for federal agencies to follow in receiving, caring for, and storing critical infrastructure information that has been submitted voluntarily; provide criminal penalties for the unauthorized disclosure of such information.

Executive Order 13392: Improving Agency Disclosure of Information

On December 14, 2005, President George W. Bush issued Executive Order 13392: Improving Agency Disclosure of Information. The order sought to streamline the effectiveness of government agencies in responding to FOIA requests and to reduce backlogs of FOIA requests. The order did not expand the information available under FOIA. The executive order provided:

- A chief FOIA officer (at the assistant secretary or equivalent level) of each government agency to monitor FOIA compliance throughout the agency. The chief FOIA officer must inform agency heads and the attorney general of the agency's FOIA compliance performance.

• A FOIA Requester Service Center that would serve as the first point of contact for a person seeking information concerning the status of a FOIA request and appropriate information about the agency's FOIA response.

• FOIA public liaisons, supervisory officials who would facilitate further action if a requester had concerns regarding how an initial request was handled by the center staff.

• Requirement that the chief FOIA officer review and evaluate the agency's implementation and administration of FOIA pursuant to the executive order. The agency head was mandated to report the findings to the attorney general and to the director of the Office of Management and Budget. The report also must be published on the agency's Web site or in the *Federal Register*. Initial reports were submitted in June 2006, with follow-up plans included in each agency's annual FOIA reports for fiscal years 2006 and 2007 and continuing thereafter.

• The attorney general shall review the agency-specific plans and submit to the president a report on government-wide FOIA implementation. The initial report was submitted in October 2006. The Justice Department publishes annual reports of federal agency compliance on its Web site.

Open Government Act of 2007

On December 31, 2007, President George W. Bush signed the "Openness Promotes Effectiveness in Our National (OPEN) Government Act of 2007." The OPEN Government Act amends the Freedom of Information Act (FOIA) by:

• defining "a representative of the news media";

• directing that required attorney fees be paid from an agency's appropriation rather than from the U.S. Treasury's Claims and Judgment Fund;

• prohibiting an agency from assessing search and duplication fees if it fails to comply with FOIA deadlines; and establishing an Office of Government Information Services within the National Archives and Records Administration to review agency compliance with FOIA.

Executive Order 13526: Classified National Security Information

On December 29, 2009, President Barack Obama issued an Executive Order on Classified National Security Information. The Executive Order contains two parts:

• The government may classify certain types of information pertaining to the national security interests of the United States, even after a FOIA request has been submitted. It may do so if officials believe that keeping the information secret is necessary for National Security.

• Additionally, the order sets a timeline for automatic declassification of old information that has not been specifically tagged as needing to remain secret.

H.R. 4173: The Dodd–Frank Wall Street Reform and Consumer Protection Act

H.R. 4173 was passed in both the House and Senate and signed by President Barack Obama on July 21, 2010. The law has specific implications for the FOIA, and they are as follows:

• Section 9291 of the statute shields the Securities and Exchange Commission (SEC) from FOIA requests, because of the worry that FOIA requests could potentially hinder SEC investigations.

S. 3717, a Bill to Amend the Securities Exchange Act of 1934, the Investment Company Act of 1940, and the Investment Advisers Act of 1940 to Provide for Certain Disclosures under Section 552 of Title 5, United States Code (Commonly Referred to as the Freedom of Information Act), and for Other Purposes

This legislation passed both the House and Senate in late September 2010, and it was signed by President Obama on October 5, 2010. The law's FOIA applications are as follows:

• The provision in S. 3717 essentially rolls back the shielding of the SEC from FOIA requests, as previously mandated by Section 9291 of H.R. 4173.

FOIA Oversight and Implementation Act of 2014 (the FOIA Act)

A bill was introduced by the House on March 15, 2013, to amend the Freedom of Information Act to make it easier to request and receive information. This bill passed the House unanimously on February 25, 2014. Under the amendment, the Office of Management and Budget would be required to operate a free website where users could submit requests for records and receive information on the status of said request. The bill would also:

- Require agencies to determine whether the release of agency records would contribute significantly to public understanding of the operations or activities of government

- Require agencies to document additional search or duplication fees

- Require agencies to submit annual FOIA reports to the director of the Office of Government Information Services, in addition to the attorney general

- Expand the duties of the chief FOIA officer of each agency to require an annual compliance review of FOIA requirements

- Establish the Chief FOIA Officers Council to develop recommendations for increasing compliance with FOIA requirements

- Require each agency to update its FOIA regulations within 180 days of the enactment of this act

- Require the inspector general of each federal agency to:
    ♦ Periodically review compliance with FOIA disclosure requirements, including the timely processing of requests, assessment of fees and fee waivers, and the use of disclosure exemptions; and

    ♦ Make recommendations to the head of an agency, including recommendations for disciplinary action. Make the improper withholding of information under FOIA a basis for disciplinary action.

FOIA Improvement Act of 2014

A bill was introduced by the Senate on June 24, 2014, to improve the Freedom of Information Act. This bill passed the Senate unanimously on December 8, 2014. However, it was not brought to a vote by the House despite its resemblance to the FOIA Act. The legislation would:

- Require agencies to electronically make available disclosed agency records to the public

- Reduce the ability of an agency to charge fees for a request if the agency does not meet the FOIA deadline

- Limit the terms by which an agency can determine records exempt from FOIA

- Put a time limit of twenty-five years on Exemption 5 (b5)

- Expand the duties of the chief FOIA officer of each agency to require an annual compliance review of FOIA requirements

- Expand the duties of the chief FOIA officer of each agency to require an annual compliance review of FOIA requirements

- Establish the Chief FOIA Officers Council to develop recommendations for increasing compliance with FOIA requirements

- Require each agency to update its FOIA regulations within 180 days of the enactment of this Act

- Require the inspector general of each federal agency to:
    ♦ Periodically review compliance with FOIA disclosure requirements, including the timely processing of requests, assessment of fees and fee waivers, and the use of disclosure exemptions; and

    ♦ Make recommendations to the head of an agency, including recommendations for disciplinary action. Make the improper withholding of information under FOIA a basis for disciplinary action.

Justice Dept. "Proactive Disclosure Pilot" of 2015

On July 4, 2015, the Justice Dept. announced a new pilot program at seven agencies designed to test the feasibility of posting online FOIA responses so that they are available to the individual requester as well as the general public. Agencies involved in the pilot program are the Millennium Challenge Corporation, the Office of the Director of National Intelligence, the Environmental Protection Agency, and sections of the Defense, Homeland Security and Justice Depts., the National Archives and Records Administration, and the Office of Information Policy. The purpose of the pilot is to determine the policy implementation costs, the effect on staff, and the effect on government stakeholders, as well as the justifications for exceptions.

FOIA Improvement Act of 2016

The act, passed by the House and unanimously by the Senate on June 13, 2016, was signed into law on June 30, 2016. Issues addressed in the act include:

- Requirement for agencies to make available for public inspection in an electronic format records that have been requested three or more times

- Requirement for agencies to establish a minimum of 90 days to file an administrative appeal

- Codification of the "foreseeable harm" standard in that agencies
    ♦ shall withhold information only if the agency reasonably foresees that disclosure would harm an interest protected by an exemption, or if disclosure is prohibited by law

    ♦ shall consider whether partial disclosure of information is possible whenever the agency determines that a full disclosure of a requested record is not possible

    ♦ shall take reasonable steps necessary to segregate and release nonexempt information

• Amendment to Exception 5 stating that the deliberative process privilege will not apply to records created 25 years or more before the date on which the records were requested

• Notification of the requester, upon extension of a deadline beyond ten days, of right to seek dispute resolution services

• Creation of a new FOIA Council supported by GSA, which will consult on a regular basis with requesters

• Addition of the following elements to agency Annual FOIA Reports:

♦ The number of times the agency denied a request for records under subsection (c)

♦ The number of records made available for public inspection in an electronic format under subsection (a)(2)

Justice Dept. "Proactive Disclosure Pilot" Assessment of 2016

Throughout the 2015 Pilot, the Office of Information Policy maintained a collection of data including communications between the involved agencies and OIP, as well as feedback from the public. This information and the findings from its analysis were presented on the DOJ website on June 30, 2016.

Privacy Legislation

Privacy Act

To protect citizens from invasions of privacy by the federal government, Congress passed the Privacy Act of 1974 (PL 93-579). The act permitted individuals for the first time to inspect information about themselves contained in federal agency files and to challenge, correct, or amend the material. The major provisions of the act:

• Permit an individual to have access to personal information in federal agency files and to correct or amend that information.

• Prevent an agency maintaining a file on an individual from making it available to another agency without the individual's consent.

• Require federal agencies to keep records that are necessary, lawful, accurate, and current, and to disclose the existence of all databanks and files containing information on individuals.

• Bar the transfer of personal information to other federal agencies for nonroutine use without the individual's prior consent or written request.

• Require agencies to keep accurate accountings of transfers of records and make them available to the individual.

• Prohibit agencies from keeping records on an individual's exercise of First Amendment rights unless the records are authorized by statute, approved by the individual, or within the scope of an official law enforcement activity.

• Permit an individual to seek injunctive relief to correct or amend a record maintained by an agency and permit the individual to recover actual damages when an agency acts in a negligent manner that is "willful or intentional."

• Exempt from disclosure records maintained by the Central Intelligence Agency; records maintained by law enforcement agencies; Secret Service records; statistical information; names of persons providing material used for determining the qualification of an individual for federal government service; federal testing material; and National Archives historical records.

• Provide that an officer or employee of an agency who violates provisions of the act be fined no more than $5,000.

• Prohibit an agency from selling or renting an individual's name or address for mailing list use.

• Require agencies to submit to Congress and to the Office of Management and Budget any plan to establish or alter records. Virtually all agencies of the executive branch have issued regulations to implement the Privacy Act.

• Protections exclude foreigners living in the United States as enacted by President Donald Trump in section 14 of the "Enhancing Public Safety" executive order.

To locate a specific agency's regulations, consult the general index of the Code of Federal Regulations under "Privacy Act" or search in www.USA.gov, "Privacy Act."

USA Patriot Act

Following the terrorist attacks of September 11, 2001, Congress passed the USA PATRIOT Act (Uniting and Strengthening America by Providing Appropriate Tools Required to Intercept and Obstruct Terrorism; PL 107-56). Included in the USA PATRIOT Act are provisions that:

• Amend the federal criminal code to authorize the interception of wire, oral, and electronic communications to produce evidence of chemical weapons, terrorism, and computer fraud and abuse.

• Amend the Foreign Intelligence Surveillance Act of 1978 (FISA) to require an application for an electronic surveillance order or search warrant certifying that a significant purpose (formerly, the sole or main purpose) of the surveillance is to obtain foreign intelligence information. The administration of President George W. Bush aggressively defended its use of wiretaps approved by the Foreign Intelligence Surveillance Court, which handles intelligence requests involving suspected spies, terrorists, and foreign agents. Established under FISA, this court operates secretly within the Justice Department.

USA Patriot Improvement and Reauthorization Act of 2005 and USA Patriot Act Additional Reauthorizing Amendments Act of 2006

Some provisions of the USA PATRIOT Act were set to expire at the end of 2005. After a lengthy battle, Congress voted to reauthorize the act with some of the more controversial provisions intact, including the FISA amendments and the electronic wiretap provisions. Civil libertarians were concerned with issues regarding four provisions: sections 206 (roving wiretaps), 213 (delayed notice warrants), 215 (business records), and 505 (national security letters).

The Senate addressed some of these concerns in a separate bill, S. 2271, USA PATRIOT Act Additional Reauthorizing Amendments Act of 2006.

On March 9, 2006, the President George W. Bush signed into law the USA PATRIOT Improvement and Reauthorization Act of 2005 as well as the USA PATRIOT Act Additional Reauthorizing Amendments Act of 2006.

The reauthorized USA PATRIOT Act allows for greater congressional oversight and judicial review of section 215 orders, section 206 roving wiretaps, and national security letters. In addition, the act included requirements for high-level approval for section 215 FISA orders for library, bookstore, firearm sale, medical, tax return, and educational records. The act also provided for greater judicial review for delayed notice ("sneak and peek") search warrants. Fourteen of sixteen USA PATRIOT Act provisions were made permanent, and a new sunset date of December 31, 2009, was enacted for sections 206 and 215.

On February 27, 2010, President Barack Obama signed a one-year extension of sections 206 and 215 of the USA PATRIOT Act.

On May 26, 2011, President Barack Obama signed three expiring provisions of the USA PATRIOT Act into law for four more years. These expiring provisions included sections 215, 206, and 6001.

Homeland Security Act of 2002

The Homeland Security Act of 2002 was also passed in the aftermath of the September 11, 2001, terrorist attacks. It contains provisions that:

- Establish the Homeland Security Department.

- Exempt from criminal penalties any disclosure made by an electronic communication service to a federal, state, or local government. In making the disclosure, the service must believe that an emergency involving risk of death or serious physical injury requires disclosure without delay. Any government agency receiving such disclosure must report it to the attorney general.

- Direct the secretary of homeland security to appoint a senior department official to take primary responsibility for information privacy policy.

Protect America Act and Subsequent Follow-Up Legislation

On August 5, 2007, President George W. Bush signed the Protect America Act, which amended the Foreign Intelligence Surveillance Act of 1978 (FISA), declaring that nothing under its definition of "electronic surveillance" shall be construed to encompass surveillance directed at a person reasonably believed to be located outside the United States. Prior to this act, no court permission was obtained for surveillance of parties located outside the United States, though a warrant was required for electronic surveillance of targets within the United States. The Protect America Act allowed the attorney teneral or the director of national intelligence to direct a third party (i.e., telecommunications provider) to assist with intelligence gathering about individuals located outside the United States and shields such parties from liability without a warrant from the FISA Court. The act did provide FISA Court oversight via requiring the attorney general to submit to the FISA Court the procedures by which the government determines that such acquisitions do not constitute electronic surveillance. The attorney general was required to report to the congressional intelligence and judiciary committees semiannually concerning acquisitions made during the previous six-month period.

The Protect America Act was designed as a temporary act to allow intelligence policy officials six months to establish a permanent law. The act expired 180 days later in January; it was briefly reauthorized and expired in February 2008. The Senate passed the FISA Amendments Act of 2007 (S. 2248) in February, which would make many of the provisions of the Protect America Act permanent. However, House leadership objected to many of the provisions. Instead, the House supported its version, the Respected Electronic Surveillance That is Overseen, Reviewed and Effective (RESTORE) Act (H. 3773). This act authorizes the attorney general and the director of national intelligence to conduct electronic surveillance of persons outside the United States in order to acquire foreign intelligence, but places limitations, including the following: The methods must be conducted in a manner consistent with the Fourth Amendment to the U.S. Constitution. The act prohibits targeting of persons reasonably believed to be in the United States (with exceptions). As amended, the bill allowed for limited retroactive immunity for telecommunications service providers. It provided for greater court oversight for targeting procedures, minimization procedures, and guidelines for obtaining warrants. The act expired December 31, 2009, when certain provisions of the PATRIOT Act expired.

Cybersecurity and Infrastructure Security Agency Act of 2018

Signed by President Donald Trump on November 20, 2018, this bill is an amendment to the Homeland Security Act of 2002. It:

- Establishes the Cybersecurity and Infrastructure Security Agency (CISA), a new agency within the Department of Homeland Security tasked with protecting the United States against cyber threats.

- Replaces the National Protection and Programs Directorate (NPPD) with the CISA.

- Creates the position of director of national cybersecurity and infrastructure security to oversee this agency.

2014–2019 Supreme Court Cases Affecting Privacy

Fernandez v. California
Holding: The Court's decision in *Georgia v. Randolph*, holding that the consent of one occupant is insufficient to authorize police to search a premises if another occupant is present and objects to the search, does not apply when an occupant provides consent well after the objecting occupant has been removed from the premises.

Judgment: Affirmed, 6–3, in an opinion by Justice Alito on February 25, 2014. Justice Scalia and Justice Thomas filed concurring opinions. Justice Ginsburg filed a dissenting opinion in which Justice Sotomayor and Justice Kagan joined.

Navarette v. California
Issue: Whether the Fourth Amendment requires an officer who receives an anonymous tip regarding a drunken or reckless driver to corroborate dangerous driving before stopping the vehicle.

Judgment: Affirmed, 5–4, in an opinion by Justice Thomas on April 22, 2014. Justice Scalia filed a dissenting opinion, in which Justice Ginsburg, Justice Sotomayor, and Justice Kagan joined.

Riley v. California
Issue: Whether evidence admitted at petitioner's trial was obtained in a search of petitioner's cellphone that violated petitioner's Fourth Amendment rights. (Riley's petition had posed a general question about whether the Fourth Amendment allowed police without a warrant to search "the digital contents of an individual's cellphone seized from the person at the time of arrest." In granting review, the Court said it would only rule on this issue: "Whether evidence admitted at [his] trial was obtained in a search of [his] cellphone that violated [his] Fourth Amendment rights.")

Judgment: Reversed and remanded, 9–0, in an opinion by Chief Justice Roberts on June 25, 2014. Justice Alito filed an opinion concurring in part and concurring in the judgment.

United States v. Wurie
Issue: Whether the Fourth Amendment permits the police, without obtaining a warrant, to review the call log of a cellphone found on a person who has been lawfully arrested.

Judgment: Affirmed, 9–0, in an opinion by Chief Justice Roberts on June 25, 2014. Justice Alito filed an opinion concurring in part and concurring in the judgment.

Birchfield v. North Dakota
Issue: A state statute may not criminalize the refusal to submit to a blood test in the absence of a warrant because, while the Fourth Amendment allows for warrantless breath tests incident to an arrest for drunk driving, warrantless blood tests incident to an arrest violate the Fourth Amendment.

Judgment: Affirmed 5–3, in an opinion by Justice Alito, on June 23, 2016. Justice Sotomayor concurred in part and dissented in part, and was joined by Justice Ginsburg.

Justice Thomas filed an opinion concurring in the judgment in part and dissenting in part.

Grady v. North Carolina
Issue: Whether or not a search resulting from participation in a North Carolina monitoring program requiring the petitioner to wear a bracelet tracking his whereabouts was reasonable under the Fourth Amendment.

Judgment: Granted, the judgment of the Supreme Court of North Carolina vacated, and the case remanded for further proceedings not inconsistent with this opinion.

Delaware Strong Families v. Matthew Denn
Issue: Whether a state's interest in increasing information concerning those who support the candidates permits it to condition a charity's publication of a nonpartisan voter education guide, which lists all candidates equally and makes no endorsements, upon the immediate and public disclosure of the names and addresses of individuals making unrelated donations over the previous four years.

Judgment: Denied certiorari, 8–1, in an opinion by Justice Thomas on June 28, 2016. The decision upheld Delaware's disclosure of "third-party advertisements."

Carpenter v. United States
Issue: Whether the government is violating the Fourth Amendment by accessing individual's historical cellphone location records via third-party communication providers without a warrant.

Judgment: Affirmed, 5–4, in an opinion by Justice Roberts on June 22, 2018. Justices Kennedy, Thomas, Alito, and Gorsuch all filed dissenting opinions on the ruling.

Michell v. Wisconsin
Issue: Whether a statute that authorizes a blood draw from an unconscious motorist provides an exception to the Fourth Amendment warrant requirement.

Judgment: Affirmed, 5–4, in an opinion by Justice Alito on June 27, 2019. Justices Sotomayor and Gorsuch filed dissenting opinions on the ruling.

State Laws Regarding Privacy Legislation Passed Since 2017

Nevada Privacy of Information Collected on the Internet from Consumers Act of 2017
Approved by Governor Brian Sandoval on June 12, 2017, this act relates to internet privacy, requiring the operator of an of an Internet website or an online service that collects certain information from the residents of Nevada to provide notice of provisions relating to the privacy of the information collected by the operator. This law went into effect on October 1, 2017. On May 29, 2019, Governor Steve Sisolak approved an amendment to this act with SB 220, which prohibits an operator of an Internet website or online service that collects certain information from consumers in Nevada from making any sale of certain information about a consumer unless so directed by the consumer. This amendment went into effect on October 1, 2019.

Alabama Data Breach Notification Act of 2018
On March 28, 2018, Governor Kay Ivey signed the Alabama Data Breach Notification Act into law, making

Alabama the last state to pass legislature requiring data breach notifications. This law, which went into effect on June 1, 2018, mandates that "covered entities" and "third-party agents" must inform individuals of security breaches concerning their personal information.

Colorado Protections for Consumer Data Privacy Law
The Colorado Protections for Consumer Data Privacy Law, signed on May 29, 2018, went into effect on September 1, 2018. This new law specifies what constitutes Personal Identifiable Information (PII) and tasks personal data companies to create security protocols to protect the PII of their customers. It also gives companies up to 30 days to notify individuals about breaches of security that concern their personal information.

South Carolina Insurance Data Security Act
The South Carolina Insurance Data Security Act was signed by Governor Henry McMaster on May 14, 2018, making it the first state law concerning cybersecurity of insurance information. Having gone into effect on January 1, 2019, the law gives anyone licensed by the South Carolina Department of Insurance to draft a security program.

Vermont's Act 171 of 2018
Approved by Governor Phil Scott on May 22, 2018, Act 171 is the first state law to impose regulations on data brokers who are selling or purchasing personal information. Data brokers are now required to annually register with Vermont's Secretary of State and abide by new security requirements when dealing with personal information. The law went into effect on January 1, 2019.

California Consumer Privacy Act
On June 28, 2018, Governor Jerry Brown signed the California Consumer Privacy Act, designed to protect the personal information of consumers. The four basic rights afforded to citizens under this act are (1) the right to understand what information a business has gathered, (2) the right to prevent businesses from selling their information, (3) the right to demand that their information be deleted by businesses, and (4) the right to guarantee that their services are not impacted by a decision to not share their personal information. Introduced on January 3, 2018, by State Senator Robert Hertzberg and State Assembly Member Ed Chau, the new law took effect at the beginning of 2020.

Ohio Data Protection Act
On August 3, 2018, Governor John Kasich signed the Data Protect Act, making Ohio the first state to incentivize businesses to implement cybersecurity programs by providing safe harbor to businesses that do so. This act went into effect November 2, 2018.

Utah's Electronic Information or Data Privacy Act
This act was signed by Governor Gary Herbert on March 27, 2019, making Utah the first state to pass legislation that requires law enforcement to obtain a search warrant for electronic information or data held by a third party. Effective on May 14, 2019, this act also requires the notification of the owner of the data by law enforcement and that data records taken by law enforcement in violation of this act will be subject to rules governing exclusion of evidence when it is taken in violation of the Fourth Amendment.

Arkansas's Personal Information Protection Act
On April 15, 2019, Governor Asa Hutchinson signed House Bill 1943 into law amending the Personal Information Protection act. This amendment expanded the definition of personal information to include biometric data. The act also strengthens the breach of security legislation by requiring security breaches to be reported within forty-five days of discovery and the retention of a copy of the written determination of a breach of the security of a system for five years from the date of the breach. Effective July 23, 2019.

Maine's Act to Protect the Privacy of Online Customer Information of 2019
Approved by Governor Janet Mills on June 6, 2019, the Act to Protect the Privacy of Online Customer Information prevents internet providers from selling or distributing customer's personal information, search history, or demographic data without the customer's consent. The act went into effect on July 1, 2020.

Texas Privacy Protection Act
On June 14, 2019, Governor Greg Abbott signed the Privacy Protection Act, which amends the states breach notification requirements and creates the Texas Privacy Protection Advisory Council to study privacy and protection laws around the world and report its recommendations for statutory changes to the Texas legislature on September 1, 2019. The breach notification changes took effect on January 1, 2020.

Vermont's Security Breach Notice Act
On March 5, 2020, Governor Phil Scott signed the bill into law, which includes an expansion of the definition of Personally Identifiable Information, an alternate notification process for login credentials, and a change to security breach notice requirements. This act, effective July 1, 2020, has the shortest deadline for providing preliminary notice of a security breach to the state's attorney general in the United States.

California Privacy Rights Act of 2020
On November 3, 2020, the majority of voters approved the California Privacy Rights Act, which expands upon the California Consumer Privacy Act. Taking effect on January 1, 2023, this act permits consumers to (1) prevent businesses from sharing personal information; (2) correct inaccurate personal information; and (3) limit businesses' use of "sensitive personal information"—including precise geolocation; race; ethnicity; religion; genetic data; private communications; sexual orientation; and specified health information.

Virginia Consumer Data Protection Act of 2021
Approved by Governor Ralph Northam on March 2, 2021, the Virginia Consumer Data Protection Act outlines responsibilities and privacy protection standards for data controllers and processors. The act grants consumers the right to access, correct, delete, obtain a copy of personal data, and to opt out of the processing of personal data for the purposes of targeted advertising. The act will take effect January 1, 2023.

Name Index

Goule, Chandler, 17
Graber, Rachel, 576, 587
Grabowski, Martha, 778, 782
Graf, Marguerite L., 776
Graham, Fritz, 962
Graham, Gwen, 175, 813
Graham, Lindsey (R–S.C.), 843, 929, 930, 932, 934, 938, 949
Graham, Michael (Mike), 420
Graham, William H. (Butch), 781
Grancorvitz, Teresa, 343
Grande, Donna, 393
Grande, Lise, 495
Grandi, Flippo, 487
Grangenois-Thomas, Joan, 893
Granger, Kay (R–Texas), 843, 846, 887
Granholm, Jennifer M., 256, 335
Grannis, David, 948
Grant, Ayanti, 877
Grant, Jodi, 201
Grant, Natalie, 736
Grant, Robin, 381
Grantz, Brad, 931
Grassley, Chuck (R–Iowa), 841, 927, 928, 929, 932, 934, 935, 938, 940, 949
Grau, John, 78, 267, 455
Graves, Alexis, 115
Graves, Fatima Goss, 210, 240, 566
Graves, Garret (R–La.), 841, 856, 857, 860, 861, 863, 887
Graves, Sam (R–Mo.), 842, 848, 860, 861, 887
Gravitz, Alisa, 287
Grawe, William R., 312
Gray, Catherine, 87, 383
Gray, Jason, 108
Gray, Lisa A., 236
Gray, Michael, 908
Gray, Tanguler, 735
Grealy, Mary R., 368
Greaves, Holly, 72
Green, Al (D–Texas), 843, 852, 853, 854, 887
Green, David, 536
Green, Dionna, 405
Green, Eric D., 425
Green, Geoffrey, 553
Green, Jonathan M., 697
Green, Kimberly A., 214
Green, Mark, 179
Green, Mark E. (R–Tenn.), 843, 848, 853, 854, 858, 887
Green, Mark L., 718
Greenan, Barbara, 421
Greenberg, Aaron, 189, 492
Greenberg, Jay, 574
Greenberg, Kenneth, 626
Greenberg, Sally, 57, 571
Greenblatt, Jonathan, 565
Greenblatt, Mark Lee, 346
Greenburg, Amy, 27
Greene, Marjorie Taylor (R–Ga.), 841, 887
Greene, Mary, 377
Greene, Robert L., 64, 95
Greenfield, Briann, 149
Greenwell, Amanda Hallberg, 113
Greer, Chris, 267
Gregg, John Paul (Paul), 496, 499, 503, 508
Gregory, Karen V., 340
Greisman, Lois C., 54, 87
Grenchik, Tom, 570
Gressett, Don, 518

Grevatt, Peter, 312, 328
Gribben, Timothy E. (Tim), 44, 45, 62
Grider, Michael, 872
Griffin, Drew, 897
Griffin, James, 404
Griffin, Norma L., 151
Griffin, Robyne, 115
Griffin, Shannetta, 773
Griffis, Sharon, 88
Griffith, Andrew, 275
Griffith, Cara, 51
Griffith, H. Morgan (R–Va.), 844, 850, 851, 887
Griffith, John, 503
Grijalva, Raúl (D–Ariz.), 840, 849, 850, 856, 888
Grimes, Anne, 489
Grimes, Ron, 912
Grimm, Christi, 346
Grimm, Rick, 353, 360
Grinnan, Suzanne E., 87
Grishaw, Letitia J., 301, 579
Grocki, Steven J., 575
Grogis, Joshua, 876
Groh, Sarah, 910
Grosh, Lisa J., 499, 502, 570
Gross, Hillary, 885
Gross, Laura, 648
Grossman, Elizabeth, 227
Grossman, James (Jim), 150
Grothman, Glenn (R–Wisc.), 844, 849, 850, 857, 858, 888
Groundwater, John R., 173, 782
Gruber, Elliot, 141, 355
Gruber, Theresa L., 758
Grubert, Emily, 270
Gruenberg, Martin J., 65
Gruender, Ben, 950
Gruman, Mark, 947
Grumbles, Ben, 286
Grumet, Jason S., 819
Grundler, Chris, 303
Gruters, Sydney, 918
Gryde, Brandon, 129
Guajardo, Anissa, 925
Guarascio, Tiffany, 850
Guardia, Luis, 26, 734
Guenther, John, 340
Guenther, Karen, 609
Guerra, Liana, 916
Guerra, Marisol, 920
Guerrero, Bertha Alisa, 885
Guerrero, Jay, 946
Guerrero, Julian, Jr., 200, 208
Guerrero, Roberto, 680
Guerttin, Nikolas H., Jr., 683
Guest, Michael (R–Miss.), 842, 852, 854, 860, 861, 888
Guest, Sara, 236
Guidroz, Walter Scott, 268
Guilford, Eugene (Gene), Jr., 307
Guillete, Adam, 101
Gum Hamisevicz, Virgina, 79
Gunn, Susan, 169
Gunnarson, Jason, 603
Gunnels, Warren, 931
Gunning, Paul M., 289, 303
Guo, Ruihong, 20
Gupta, Anuj, 882
Gupta, Rahul, 578
Gupta, Roland, 435
Gural, Harry, 926
Gurley, Susan K., 439
Gurtler, Matt, 900

Gusack, Jamie, 540
Gust, Richard (Dick), 788
Gustafson, Peggy E., 346
Guthrie, Brett (R–Ky.), 841, 850, 851, 888
Guthrie, Jason, 781
Guthrie, Luke, 143, 618
Guthrie, William F., 691
Guttman, Maureen, 264, 458
Guyton, Helen Gerostathos, 115
Guz, Justin, 115
Guzman, Isabella Casillas, 37, 93, 335
Guzman, Paola, 892
Gwinn, Maureen, 302
Gwyn, Brigitte Schmidt, 126

Haag, Thomas, 894
Haaland, Deb, 325
Haaland, Debra A., 335
Haaland, Debra Anne (Deb), 283, 313, 321
Haapala, Ken, 291
Haase, Matt, 943
Haass, Richard N., 481
Haberstroh, Michael J., 347
Hack, Joe, 948
Hacker, Kevin M., 249
Hackley, Angela Jones, 213, 234, 740, 757
Hackney, Sarah, 6, 314, 451
Haddad, Mary, 398
Haertel, Paul H., 574
Haffajee, Rececca, 365, 731
Hagen, James, 347
Hagerty, Bill (R–Tenn.), 843, 929, 930, 931, 935, 936, 939, 949
Haglund, Sean, 662
Hagood, Laura Brower, 157
Hague, Doug, 459
Hahs, Jennifer Knorr, 826
Haines, Avril, 671, 676
Haines, John W., 323, 709, 711
Hair, Connie, 885
Halamandaris, Kathleen, 160
Haldar, Swarnali, 108
Hall, Charles J., 32, 518
Hall, Cynthia A. (Cindy), 836
Hall, Debra A., 343
Hall, Ken, 828
Hall, Kym, 123, 156
Hall, Robert, 273, 277
Hall, Tracie, 114, 117, 188, 571
Hall-Rivera, Jaelith, 315
Halliday, Toby J., 473
Halligan, Matthew, 620
Hallman, Timothy J., 718
Halpern, Hugh N., 110
Hamer, Hubert, 7, 48
Hamernik, Deb, 24
Hamill, Gary, 703
Hamilton, Jacqueline, 868
Hamilton, Lasharn, 350
Hamilton, Lindsay, 113
Hamilton, Mike, 902
Hamlette, Martin, 395
Hamm, Susan, 280
Hammer, Thomas A., 17
Hamna, Michael Wahid, 495
Hamod, David, 539
Hamparian, Aram, 541, 820
Hampshire, Robert C., 761
Hampson, Gabrielle, 341, 484
Hampson, James, 869
Hampton, Stephanie, 699
Hamre, John J., 481, 638
Hanagan, Mary, 829

Swinnen, Johan, 31
Swisher, Kent, 34
Swonger, Chris, 596
Swonger, Chris R., 27
Syed, Mohsin, 816
Sylvina, Teresa, 296
Synder, Barbara R., 193
Szpindor, Catherine, 809

Tabak, Lawrence A., 366, 411
Tabarrok, Alexander, 42
Tabay, Kelly, 880
Tagen, Julie, 910
Tai, Katherine, 335, 513
Takano, Mark (D–Calif.), 840, 849, 850, 861, 862, 918
Talaga, Emily, 99
Talebian, Bobak, 115
Talebian, Bobak (Bobby), 112
Talken-Spaulding, Jennifer, 722
Talley, Trigg, 289
Talton, Benjamin, 154
Talucci, Vincent (Vince), 589
Tamarkin, Tanya A., 197, 456
Tankel, Judith, 866
Tarbert, Heath P., 12, 73
Tarlov, Yvette, 103, 552
Tarr, Richard, 182, 245
Tasharski, Dale, 510
Tasharski, Dale N., 511
Tate, Cindy, 961
Tate, Karen, 175, 184
Tate, Vincent, 611
Tau, Jocelyn, 881
Taubenblatt, Joel, 107
Taugher, Ryan, 644
Tauriainen, Ryan, 204
Tauster, Deena, 884
Taylor, Adam R., 171
Taylor, Anita, 875
Taylor, Anne, 898
Taylor, Ashlee, 942
Taylor, Benjamin (Ben), 499, 770
Taylor, Beth, 628
Taylor, Crispin, 703
Taylor, Dianne E., 448
Taylor, Elizabeth G., 398, 597
Taylor, H. Art, 159
Taylor, Houston, 333
Taylor, James E., 643
Taylor, James G., VI, 425
Taylor, Jeff, 824
Taylor, Jennifer, 866
Taylor, Johnny C., Jr., 242
Taylor, Katie, 535
Taylor, Linda S., 383
Taylor, Robbin, 954
Taylor, Terrance, 890
Taylor, Tiffany J., 350
Taylor, Van (R–Texas), 843, 852, 919
Tayman, William P., Jr., 342
Taymans, Susan, 423
Teehan, Shana, 904
Teferra, Tsehaye, 95, 497
Tegeler, Philip, 560, 734
Teitelbaum, Alison Shafer, 394
Tejada, Matthew, 302
Telle, Adam, 949
Templeton, Ross, 828
Tenaglia, John M., 350, 683
Tenney, Claudia (R–N.Y.), 842, 853, 854, 859, 860, 919
Tennille, Alan, 884
Terman, Jennie, 129

Terrell, Louisa, 334
Terry, David, 261
Terry, Sharon, 368, 425, 701
Terry, Syd, 913
Tersine, Anthony G., Jr., 338, 422
Tester, John, 929
Tester, Jon (D–Mont.), 842, 929, 930, 931, 932, 933, 937, 939, 960
Tevlin, Stacey, 48
Textoris, Steven D., 320
Thaeler, Ben, 878
Therit, Tracey, 340
Thevenot, Laura, 419
Thibodeaux, Todd, 684, 714
Thielman, Jason, 947
Thiessen, Pam, 936
Thigpen, Brinsley, 866
Thigpen, Jeremy, 271
Thimios, Michelle, 921
Thomas, Christopher E., 654, 694
Thomas, Clarence, 570
Thomas, Dana, 604, 608
Thomas, Deborah, 111, 149
Thomas, Frederick L., 589
Thomas, James, 896
Thomas, Jody, 356, 360
Thomas, Karen, 899
Thomas, Kathryn Mitchell, 897
Thomas, Kenneth J. (Ken), 350
Thomas, Marzie, 876
Thomas, Peter J., 481, 639, 833
Thomas, Peter O., 298
Thomas, Robert D., 461
Thomas, Ronald (Dale), 112, 796, 799
Thomas, Susan E., 236
Thomas, Teresa, 949
Thomas, Tyshawn, 340
Thomas-Greenfield, Linda, 335
Thomison, Penny, 236
Thomma, Steven, 122, 798
Thompson, Amy C., 113
Thompson, Anne, 823
Thompson, Anthony C., 12, 73
Thompson, Bennie G. (D–Miss.), 842, 854, 864, 919
Thompson, Charles W. (Chuck), Jr., 358
Thompson, Chet, 74, 270
Thompson, Dorothy (Nan), 151
Thompson, Glenn (R–Pa.), 843, 845, 846, 849, 850, 919
Thompson, Heather Dawn, 2
Thompson, James, 942
Thompson, Jamie, 684
Thompson, Kalina, 947
Thompson, Mike (D–Calif.), 840, 862, 919, 927
Thompson, Randi E., 741
Thompson, Regina, 585
Thompson, Sandra, 471
Thompson, Sandra L., 66, 470, 471
Thompson, Tola, 897
Thornburgh, Robert, 469
Thornton, Christopher P., 133
Thorp, Frank IV, 619
Thorton, Thomas, 288
Thrall, Laura, 432, 749
Thrasher, John J., 351
Threatt, Martha, 113
Thueson, Patrick, 740
Thummlapally, Vinai, 513
Thune, John (R–S.D.), 808, 843, 928, 932, 933, 934, 935, 941, 960
Thurman, Jason, 813
Thurman, Kari, 908

Thurmond, Bryan, 200, 756
Tice, Thomas F., 16
Tickey, Jimmy, 890
Ticknor, Scott B., 36, 508
Tiefenthaler, Jill, 218
Tierney, John, 646, 648, 825
Tiffany, Thomas P. (R–Wisc.), 844, 855, 856, 857, 919
Tiglao, Lourdes, 622, 625
Tilden, Jay, 647
Tillis, Thom (R–N.C.), 842, 927, 930, 931, 938, 939, 960
Timmaraju, Mini, 569
Timmons, Jay, 76
Timmons, William R., IV, (R–S.C.), 843, 852, 853, 864, 919
Tin, Annie, 122
Tipton, Sean B., 423
Tischler, Michael Allan, 723
Titcombe, Angie, 340
Tittle, Jeremy, 873
Titus, Dina (D–Nev.), 842, 853, 854, 860, 861, 919
Tlaib, Rashida (D–Mich.), 842, 852, 853, 856, 857, 858, 920, 927
Tobey, William H., 275, 308, 380
Tobias, Carol, 569
Tobias, Janine, 321
Todd, Gregory N., 601
Todd, Jennifer, 132, 181, 199
Todd, Tracy A., 738
Toder, Eric, 52
Tokarski, Kevin M., 665, 779
Tolar, Christopher, 616
Toloui, Ramin, 508
Tolpegin, Tanya, 379
Toma, Robin S., 506
Tomarchio, Katie, 826
Tomasini, Annie, 334
Tomb, Diane, 468
Tomney, Christopher, 662
Tompkins, Stephanie, 653
Toney, Lisa Richards, 131
Tonko, Paul (D–N.Y.), 842, 851, 856, 857, 859
Tonko, Paul D. (D–N.Y.), 920
Tooley, Mark, 168, 833
Toombs, Dionne, 24
Toombs, Dionne F., 2
Toomey, Patrick J. (R–Pa.), 843, 931, 932, 934, 935, 961
Tordsen, Tyler, 957
Toregas, Costis, 117
Tornow, Joanne, 699
Torres Small, Xochitl, 449
Torres, Ashley, 870
Torres, Norma J. (D–Calif.), 840, 846, 847, 858, 920
Torres, Rachel, 234
Torres, Ritchie (D–N.Y.), 842, 852, 854, 920
Torrey, Mike, 4, 81
Toscano, Richard, 236
Toscano, Stephanie, 886
Toth, Chris, 592
Toulou, Tracy, 563
Touton, M. Camille Camlimlim, 317, 324, 326
Towe, Raymond P., 230
Tower, Sonia, 113
Towers, Jon, 939
Town, Maria, 747
Tozzi, James J. (Jim), 331
Tracton, Michael K., 521

Organization Index

Subject Index

NOTE: Entries in **CAPITALS** are chapters.